A HISTORY OF CHESS

ANCIENT IVORY CHESSMAN IN THE BIBLIOTHÈQUE NATIONALE, PARIS.

A HISTORY OF CHESS

BY

H. J. R. MURRAY

OXFORD
AT THE CLARENDON PRESS

OXFORD
UNIVERSITY PRESS

Great Clarendon Street, Oxford OX2 6DP

Oxford University Press is a department of the University of Oxford.
It furthers the University's objective of excellence in research, scholarship,
and education by publishing worldwide in

Oxford New York

Auckland Bangkok Buenos Aires Cape Town Chennai
Dar es Salaam Delhi Hong Kong Istanbul Karachi Kolkata
Kuala Lumpur Madrid Melbourne Mexico City Mumbai Nairobi
São Paulo Shanghai Singapore Taipei Tokyo Toronto

and an associated company in Berlin

Oxford is a registered trade mark of Oxford University Press
in the UK and in certain other countries

Published in the United States
by Oxford University Press Inc., New York

Special edition for Oxbow Books, Oxford
(and their American partner Powell's Books, Chicago)

British Library Cataloguing in Publication Data
Data available

ISBN 0-19-827403-3

1 3 5 7 9 10 8 6 4 2

Printed in Creat Britain
on acid-free paper by
Biddles Ltd.,
Guildford and King's Lynn

PREFACE

The aim of this work is threefold: to present as complete a record as is possible of the varieties of chess which exist or have existed in different parts of the world; to investigate the ultimate origin of these games and the circumstances of the invention of chess; and to trace the development of the modern European game from the first appearance of its ancestor, the Indian *chaturanga*, in the beginning of the seventh century of our era. The subject accordingly falls naturally into two parts: the history and record of the Asiatic varieties of chess, and the history of chess in Europe with its influence on European life and literature.

Many books have been written upon the history of chess, but none covers exactly the same field as this work. The English writers, Hyde (1694) and Forbes (1860), in the main confine their attention to Oriental chess; the great German writer, Von der Lasa (1897), treats almost exclusively of the European game. Van der Linde alone deals with both Oriental and European chess in approximately equal detail, but it is in three distinct works (1874–81).

In his great work, the *Geschichte und Litteratur des Schachspiels* (1874), v. d. Linde was able to incorporate the results of Professor A. Weber's examination of the early references to chess in Sanskrit literature, and to show that Forbes's *History* was both inaccurate and misleading. Since the publication of the *Geschichte*, however, there have been many additions to our knowledge of special features of chess history. The earliest of these were incorporated in v. d. Linde's last work, the *Quellenstudien* (1881), but the later additions can only be found in isolated papers, such as those of Mr. H. F. W. Holt (Chinese chess), Herr A. v. Oefele (Malay chess), Professor A. A. Macdonell (early Indian chess), M. E. V. Savenkof (Siberian and Russian chess), Herr F. Strohmeyer (chess in mediaeval French literature), and Mr. W. H. Wilkinson (Chinese and Corean chess). It was with the idea of making all this information easily accessible to English readers that I formed the plan of writing the present work more than thirteen years ago.

To all these writers, and many others whose names will be found in the list of works consulted, I am greatly indebted, and in particular to Hyde, to v. d. Lasa (whose kindly encouragement to me in 1897 to proceed with work on the history of chess I recall with pleasure), and to v. d. Linde. But the greater part of the book is based upon my own work at original sources, especially at unpublished Arabic and early European manuscripts on chess. It was my good fortune, at an early stage of my work, to enlist the interest of Mr. John G. White, of Cleveland, Ohio, U.S.A., the owner of the largest chess library in the world. Mr. White's generous and unfailing courtesy in placing his library freely at the service of any student of chess has been acknowledged over and over again. To me he has given not only this, but far greater help. He has repeatedly obtained copies of manuscripts which it was important that I should see, but which were inaccessible to me, and has placed these copies unreservedly at my service. Whatever in the way of completeness I have been able to achieve is entirely due to Mr. White's help. Without that help, the book would never have been written. I must also record my indebtedness to Mr. J. W. Rimington Wilson, of Bromhead Hall, Yorkshire, who has lent me many rare books and manuscripts from the chess library which was collected by his father, the late Mr. F. W. Rimington Wilson; to Mr. J. A. Leon, who lent me the valuable sixteenth-century problem manuscript in his possession; to Mr. Bernard Quaritch, who allowed me to examine the Fountaine MS. when it passed through his hands in 1902; and to Mr. H. Guppy, of the John Rylands Library, Manchester, who made special arrangements in 1903, by which I was enabled to consult two important Arabic manuscripts at that time in the possession of the late Mrs. Rylands.

But apart from this assistance in making the original sources available, the very width of the distribution of chess and the many languages in which the literature of the game is written, would have made my task an impossible one if I had not received the help of many scholars. Among these are my father, Sir James A. H. Murray, who has not only helped me with advice of the greatest value, but has introduced me to many scholars whom otherwise I should have scarcely ventured to approach; Dr. A. C. Haddon, F.R.S.; Professor E. J. Rapson, and Dr. W. H. D. Rouse, who have helped me with Sanskrit references; Mr. S. F. Blumhardt, who translated a small Hindustani work on chess for me; Mr. E. J. Colston, I.C.S., to whom I owe the first complete account of Burmese chess; Professor D. S. Margoliouth, to whom I have taken all my difficulties in reading my Arabic sources; Bodley's

Librarian, Mr. Falconer Madan, who has dated many manuscripts for me; my sister, Miss Murray, of the Royal Holloway College, who has helped me with Icelandic references; Mr. W. W. Skeat, who has helped me in connexion with Malay chess; Mr. I. Abrahams, whom I have consulted about Jewish allusions; Mr. B. G. Laws, who has helped me to establish the European source of the problems in modern Indian text-books of chess; and Mr. Charles Platt, of Harrow, who has allowed me to include illustrations of Oriental chessmen from his unique collection. To all these and others I express my most grateful thanks for their help. Unhappily, my thanks can no longer reach the late Professor W. R. Morfill, who gave me most valuable assistance with Russian and Czech, and the late Mr. J. T. Platts and Lieut.-Col. Sherlock, who gave me similar help with Persian and Hindustani.

In conclusion, I should like to express my personal gratification that this book is appearing from the same University Press which, more than two hundred years ago, published the pioneer work on its subject, Thomas Hyde's *Mandragorias seu Historia Shahiludii.*

H. J. R. MURRAY.

CAMBRIDGE, 1913.

ERRATA

Page 67, line 9, *for* pp. 88, 89, *read* p. 89 and plate facing p. 86.
Page 184, line 2 up, *for* caliphal-Muqtadir *read* caliph al-Muqtadir.
Page 218, line 18, *for* al-Bīrūnī *read* al-Bērūnī.
Page 235, line 14, *for* khurūg *read* khurūj.
Page 237, dia. 4, *for* 9 moves *read* 19 moves.
Page 337, line 13, *for* AH 95 *read* AH 94.
Page 383, line 6, *for* 1849 *read* 1649.
Page 445, line 33, *for* thisgame *read* this game.
Page 459, line 12, *for* Marocco *read* Morocco.

CONTENTS

PART I. CHESS IN ASIA

CHAPTER I. INTRODUCTORY

PAGE

European chess of Indian ancestry.—Asiatic games of similar ancestry.—Classification of Board-games.—Indian Board-games.—The Ashṭāpada.—Speculations on the nature of the original Indian chess.—Previous theories as to the ancestry of the game 25

CHAPTER II. CHESS IN INDIA. I

The earliest references in Subandhu, Bāṇa, &c.—The chess-tours in Rudraṭa.—Position in India c. 1000.—Some Arabic references.—Later Indian references.—Nīlakaṇṭ·ha 51

CHAPTER III. CHESS IN INDIA. II

The Four-handed Dice-game.—The account in Raghunandana.—The method of play.—The modern four-handed game 68

Appendix. Attempts to reconstruct the four-handed game 76

CHAPTER IV. CHESS IN INDIA. III

The modern games.—Three main varieties of chess played.—Summary of the nomenclatures.—The crosswise arrangement of the Kings.—Hindustani chess.—Parsi chess.—Standard of play.—Specimen games.—Native chessmen.—The problem 78

Appendix. A selection of problems from Indian sources 92

CHAPTER V. CHESS IN THE MALAY LANDS

Introductory.—Spread in Malay lands.—Early references.—The chessboard.—Nomenclature.—Moves of the pieces.—Rules.—Illustrative games.—Malay chessmen.—Concluding observations 95

CHAPTER VI. CHESS IN FURTHER INDIA

Introductory remarks.—I. Burmese chess.—Name of the game.—The chessboard.—The chessmen.—Nomenclature.—Initial arrangement.—Rules.—II. Siamese chess.—Name of the game.—The chessboard.—The chessmen.—Nomenclature.—Initial arrangement.—Rules.—Specimen game.—III. Annamese chess . . . 108

CHAPTER VII. CHESS IN CHINA, COREA, AND JAPAN

The inter-relationships and ancestry of these games.—I. Chinese chess.—The name.—Early references.—The modern game.—The board.—Nomenclature.—Rules.—Openings.—End-games and problems.—Specimen games.—The games *ta-ma* and *kyu-kung*.—Derivative games.—II. Corean chess.—Board.—Nomenclature.—Rules.—Specimen game.—III. Japanese chess.—The name.—History.—Literature.—Board.—Nomenclature.—Rules.—Specimen game.—Derivative games.—Problems 119

CHAPTER VIII. CHESS IN PERSIA UNDER THE SĀSĀNIANS

PAGE

Literary references.—The *Kārnāmak*.—The *Chatrang-nāmak*.—Probable introduction under Nūshīrwān.—The story in the *Shāhnāma* 149

Appendix. Some notes on the Persian nomenclature 158

CHAPTER IX. CHESS IN THE EASTERN EMPIRE

Chess not a classical game.—The name *zatrikion*.—First references in Arabic works.—References in late Greek literature.—Ecclesiastical censures—Chess in the Turkish rule, and in modern Greece 161

CHAPTER X. THE ARABIC AND PERSIAN LITERATURE OF CHESS

The chess works mentioned in the *Fihrist*, and other bibliographies.—MSS. used for the present work.—Other MSS. in European libraries.—Poems and impromptus on chess, &c. 169

CHAPTER XI. CHESS UNDER ISLAM

Its Persian ancestry.—The date of introduction.—The legal status of chess.—Early Muhammadan chess-players.—The game during the Umayyad and ʿAbbāsid caliphates.—Aṣ-Ṣūlī.—Later references.—Aṣ-Ṣafadī.—Chess at the court of Tīmūr.—Chess in Damascus in the sixteenth century 186

CHAPTER XII. THE INVENTION OF CHESS IN MUSLIM LEGEND

A variety of stories.—The oldest versions associated with India.—The connexion with nard.—The earlier legends from the chess MSS., al-Yaʿqūbī, al-Masʿūdī, and Firdawsī.—The dramatis personae.—The story of the reward for the invention.—The Geometrical progression in literature.—Later stories introducing Adam, the sons of Noah, &c., and Aristotle 207

CHAPTER XIII. THE GAME OF SHAṬRANJ: ITS THEORY AND PRACTICE. I

The chessboard.—The names of the chessmen in Muslim lands.—Symbolism of the game.—Forms of the chessmen.—The arrangement of the men for play.—The moves of the chessmen and technical terms.—Relative values of the pieces.—Aim and method of play.—Notation.—Concordant and discordant men.—Classification of players.—Gradations of odds.—Etiquette of play 220

CHAPTER XIV. THE GAME OF SHAṬRANJ: ITS THEORY AND PRACTICE. II

The divisions of the game.—The Opening.—The 'akhrājāt or taʿbīyāt.—Al-ʿAdlī and aṣ-Ṣūlī.—The work of al-Lajlāj.—Later treatment of the Openings.—Mid-game tactics 234

Appendix. Al-Lajlāj's analysis of the Mujannaḥ, Mashā'īkhī, Saif, and Sayyāl Openings 247

CHAPTER XV. THE GAME OF SHAṬRANJ: ITS THEORY AND PRACTICE. III

PAGE

The End-game.—Chess Endings in Muslim literature.—Summarized conclusions on the more elementary Endings.—The manṣūbāt: their classes and characteristics.—The history of the collections.—The manṣūbāt material; diagrams and solutions.—The Knight's Tour and other Exercises with the chessmen 266

CHAPTER XVI. GAMES DERIVED FROM MUSLIM AND INDIAN CHESS

I. Arabic games.—Oblong chess.—Decimal chess.—Chess as-suʿdīya.—Round chess.—Astronomical chess.—Limb chess.—II. Persian games.—Citadel chess.—Great chess.—Other modern forms.—III. Indian games.—IV. Early Spanish games 339

CHAPTER XVII. THE MODERN GAMES OF ISLAM

The origin and history of the changes in the game.—The modern game of Persia, Turkey, and the lands bordering the Mediterranean.—Rūmī chess, or the Muslim game of India.—Abyssinian chess 352

CHAPTER XVIII. CHESS IN CENTRAL AND NORTHERN ASIA, AND IN RUSSIA

Unclassified varieties.—Paucity of information.—Nomenclature.—References to chess as played by the Tibetans, Mongols, and other Siberian races.—Probable origin of this game.—Chess in Turkestan, Armenia, and Georgia.—The older chess of Russia.—Its ancestry.—Nomenclature.—History.—Pieces.—Possible traces of Asiatic influence farther West.—Ströbeck.—Conclusion 366

PART II. CHESS IN EUROPE

CHAPTER I. CHESS IN WESTERN CHRISTENDOM: ITS ORIGIN AND BEGINNINGS

The ancestry of the game.—The evidence of nomenclature, and the light it throws upon the date of the introduction of chess into Christian Europe.—The European names for chess.—Where was the European game first played?—Mythical stories.—Earliest certain references to chess or chessmen of contemporary date . 394

Appendix. Original texts 413

CHAPTER II. CHESS IN THE MIDDLE AGES

The mediaeval period and its chess literature.—Earliest contemporary references in the different European countries.—The European nomenclature composite.—The game the typical chamber-recreation of the nobility.—A branch of a noble's education.—Played by the ladies.—Reasons for the popularity of chess with the leisured classes.—Chess played by the members of a noble's household.—By the burgesses of the towns.—Frowned on by the Universities.—Does not reach the lowest ranks of society.—The altered position of chess in modern days . . 417

Appendices. I. Chess in Iceland, &c.—II. Chess among the Jews.—III. Some inventories of chess. 443

CHAPTER III. THE MEDIAEVAL GAME

PAGE

Earliest rules.—The chequered board.—Attempts at improvement.—Assizes.—Rules in Spain.—In Lombardy.—In Germany.—In France and England.—In Iceland.—Notation.—Science of play.—Openings.—Odds.—Other arrangements.—The Courier game 452

Appendices. I. The Alfonso MS. of 1283.—II. Description of the Lombard Assize in MS. Paris, Fr. 1173 (PP.).—III. Extracts from Egenolff's Frankfort edition of Mennel's *Schachzabel*, 1536.—IV. Description of a chess notation in MS. Paris, Fr. 1173 (PP.).—V. From MS. Vatican, Lat. 1960, f. 28 . . . 485

CHAPTER IV. THE EARLY DIDACTIC LITERATURE

Introductory remarks. The Einsiedeln and Winchester Poems.—Alexander Neckam, *De scaccis*.—Cod. Benedictbeuren.—The Elegy (*Qui cupit*).—The Deventer Poem.—*It pedes*, and the Corpus Poem.—The Reims Poem.—The *Vetula*.—The Cracow Poem.—The Hebrew poem of Abraham b. Ezra, and other Hebrew works 496

Appendix. Original texts 511

CHAPTER V. THE MORALITIES

Introductory remarks.—The *Innocent Morality*.—John of Waleys (Gallensis) and Alexander of Hales.—Later references to this work.—The *Liber de moribus hominum et officiis nobilium* of Jacobus de Cessolis.—Translations and imitations.—Galwan de Levanto.—The chess chapters in the *Gesta Romanorum*.—Ingold's *Guldin Spil*.—*Les Eschez amoureux*.—Other moralizing works 529

Appendix. Original texts 559

CHAPTER VI. THE MEDIAEVAL PROBLEM. I

Introductory.—The function of the problem in mediaeval European chess.—The problem of Muslim origin.—Its European names.—The European MSS.—Their historical development.—The Alfonso MS. and its European problems. The Archinto MS.—The Anglo-Norman or English group of MSS.—The two British Museum MSS.—The Porter and Ashmole MSS.—The Dresden MS. 564

Appendix. Merels and allied games 613

CHAPTER VII. THE MEDIAEVAL PROBLEM. II

The great collections.—The MSS. of the *Bonus Socius* work classified.—The authorship and date of the work.—Contents.—Additional material in the MSS. of the Picard group.—The MSS. of the *Civis Bononiae* work.—Authorship and date.—Classification of the MSS.—General remarks on the mediaeval problem.—Contents of the *Civis Bononiae* work.—Additional material from single MSS. 618

Appendices. I. The Latin Preface to the *Bonus Socius* work.—II. The introductions to the French translations of the *Bonus Socius* work.—III. Introduction to MS. Florence, Bibl. Nat. XIX. 7. 37 (F).—IV. Some notes on the sections on Tables and Merels in the *Bonus Socius* and *Civis Bononiae* works . 700

CHAPTER VIII. THE MEDIAEVAL PROBLEM. III

Unclassified and later works.—The Munich MS.—MS. Wolfenbüttel 17.30. Aug. 4.—Köbel's *Schachtzabel Spiel*.—Janot's *Sensuit Jeux Partis des Eschez*.—MS. Florence XIX, 11. 87.—The Sorbonne MS.—The Casanatense MS.—Mediaeval problems in the early works of modern chess 704

CHAPTER IX. CHESS IN MEDIAEVAL LITERATURE

PAGE

Longer chess incidents in the *Chansons de geste*.—The magic chess of the Arthurian romances.—Chess in the *Beast romances*.—Allegories based on chess.—Other comparisons and metaphors 736

CHAPTER X. CHESSBOARDS AND CHESSMEN

Mediaeval boards.—Combined boards for chess and other games.—Carved chessmen.—The 'Charlemagne chessmen'.—The Lewis chessmen.—Conventional chessmen.—The Ager and Osnabrück pieces.—The 'St. Louis chessmen'.—Chessmen in MSS. and printed books.—Chess in cookery.—Chess in heraldry . . 756

CHAPTER XI. THE BEGINNINGS OF MODERN CHESS

Time and place of first appearance.—Early literature of the modern game.—*Le Jeu des Eschés de la dame, moralisé.*'—The Catalan *Scachs d'amor*.—The Göttingen MS.—Lucena.—Damiano.—Vida and Caldogno.—Egenolff.—Early problems of the modern game 776

Appendices. I. Extract from Lucena. II. Extract from Egenolff 808

CHAPTER XII. FROM LOPEZ TO GRECO

The great chess activity of Southern Europe during the second half of the sixteenth century.—Ruy Lopez.—Leonardo and Paolo Boi.—Polerio.—Salvio and Carrera.—Greco.—The introduction of castling and other changes in the game.—The problem 811

CHAPTER XIII. FROM GRECO TO STAMMA

Chess in Italy, 1630–1730.—In France and England, 1550–1700.—Asperling.—Cunningham.—Caze.—The Coffee-houses.—Bertin.—Stamma.—Hoyle.—Chess in Germany, 1500–1790.—In Sweden, Denmark, &c.—In Iceland.—Four-handed chess 837

CHAPTER XIV. PHILIDOR AND THE MODENESE MASTERS

Philidor, his chess career and system of play.—Del Rio, Lolli and Ponziani.—The Italian school of play.—The modern problem.—The Parisian Amateurs.—Deschapelles.—Sarratt and his services to English chess.—Allgaier.—The Automaton Chess-player 861

CHAPTER XV. THE NINETEENTH CENTURY

Lewis.—De la Bourdonnais and MacDonnell.—The Berlin Pleiades.—Staunton and Saint-Amant.—The chess magazine and newspaper column.—The 1851 Tournament.—Anderssen and Morphy.—Steinitz and the Modern School 878

LIST OF ILLUSTRATIONS

		PAGE
Ancient Ivory Chessman in the Bibliothèque nationale, Paris		*Frontispiece*
The Algebraical Notation		20
Board from Thebes, Egypt (Abbot Collection, Louvre)		30
Board of Queen Hatasu, British Museum		30
Board from Enkomi, Cyprus		31
Board for Pachīsī and Chaupur		38
Gavalata Board (Culin, *C. & P. C.*, 851)		38
Ashta Kashte Board (Falk., 265)		38
Board, Dice and Men used in Saturankam (*chaturanga*). (Parker, 695)		39
Sīga Board (Parker, 607)		39
The Bharhut Board		40
The Markings on modern Indian Chessboards		41
Divinatory Diagram, Tibet		43
Knight's, Rook's, and Elephant's Tours (Rudraṭa)		54
Elephant's Tour		55
Four-handed Chess. After al-Bērūnī		58
The Elephant's Move in early Indian chess		59
Knight's Tour (Nīlakaṇṭ·ha)		65
Four-handed Chess. After Raghunandana		69
The modern Indian Chess		80
Indian Chessmen (Hyde, ii. 123)	*to face*	86
The Bambra-ka-thūl (Brāhmānābād) Chessmen		88
Indian Chessmen. Eighteenth Century. From Mr. Platt's Collection	*to face*	88
Indian Chessmen from Surat (Hyde)		89
Some modern Indian Chessmen		90
Modern Indian Chessmen. Platt Collection	*to face*	90
Modern Indian Problems		92–3
Malay Chessboards. Skeat Collection, Cambridge		97
Malay Chessboard (Malacca and mainland)		97
Malay Chessboard (Sumatra)		97
Malay Chessmen (Selangor). Skeat Collection	*to face*	105
Malay Chessmen		106
The Markings on Burmese Chessboards, and Burmese arrangements of the Chessmen		110
Burmese Chessmen. Pitt-Rivers Collection, Oxford	*to face*	111
Initial arrangement of the *Nès* (Pawns)		111
Burmese arrangement of the Chessmen. From Bastian		112
Siamese Chessmen. From the *Schachzeitung*		114
The Siamese arrangement of the Chessmen		115
The Chinese and Japanese names for chess		121
Himly's Reconstruction of early Chinese Chess		124
Chinese Chess (Culin)		125
Bronze Chessmen in the British Museum		126
Multiple Checks in Chinese Chess		128

	PAGE
Chinese Chess Problems	129
Game of the Three Kingdoms	133
Chessmen carved in China for the European Game. From Mr. Platt's Collection *to face*	134
Corean Chessboard. After Culin	135
The Japanese Chessboard	141
Japanese Chessman	142
The different scripts for *Kin*	142
Japanese Chess Problems	148
Rook from Egypt. British Museum	224
Older Muslim arrangement of the Chessmen	224
The Muslim taʿbīyāt from al-ʿAdlī and aṣ-Ṣūlī	237–8
Taʿbīyāt from MS. BM	241–2
Taʿbīyāt from MS. RAS	243
Taʿbīyāt from MS. F	243
Taʿbīyāt from MS. Gotha	244
The Mujannaḥ Opening. The position after the twelfth move	248
Drawn position	267
The Muslim Problems	282–306
Muslim Knight's Tours	335–6
Muslim Exercises	337–8
Al-ʿAdlī's Calculating-board	338
Round or Byzantine Chess	342
Indian Problem of Decimal Chess	346
The Game of the Four Seasons, Alf.	349
The Game of Los Escaques, Alf.	350
Turkish Chessmen. From Hyde	354
Numbering of squares attributed to Muḥammad Saʿīd	355
Problems of modern Turkish Chess. From MS. Ber.	357
Modern Muslim (Egyptian) Chessmen. Platt Collection *to face*	361
Kurdish Chessmen. From Culin	361
Turkish Chessmen. After Falkener	361
Abyssinian Chessmen of Welled Selasse	363
Abyssinian Chessmen	363
Soyot Chessmen. After Savenkof	371
Yakutat Chessmen (Alaska). After Culin	375
Russian *Slon* and *Lodya*. After Savenkof	387
Russian *Lodya* from the Platt Collection. Modern	388
Russian Chessmen. Platt Collection *to face*	388
Otto IV, Margrave of Brandenburg (1266–1308), playing Chess. (Book of Manesse, Paris MS., old 7266) *to face*	394
The board for *tablut*	445
Diagram illustrating mediaeval notation	457
Game position from the Munich MS. of *Carmina Burana*	473
Game position from MS. Alf.	473
Short Assize. From MS. Dresden O/59	476
Short Assize. From MS. Paris f. fr. 143	476
Le guy de ly enginous e ly coueytous	477
The Courier game. After Selenus	483
The Chessplayers. By Lucas von Leyden *to face*	484
Köbel's chess notation	490
The chess notation of MS. Paris f. fr. 1173	495

		PAGE
Miniature from MS. Lat. 4660, Munich (*Carmina Burana*)	*to face*	503
Death gives checkmate to a King	*to face*	536
From Caxton's *Game and Playe of the Chesse*		542
From Caxton's *Game and Playe of the Chesse*		543
From the *Libro di giuocho di scacchi*. Florence, 1493		547
Mediaeval European Problems from MS. Alf.		571–3
,, ,, ,, MS. Arch.		575–9
,, ,, ,, MS. Cott.		583–8
,, ,, ,, MS. K..		589–600
,, ,, ,, MS. Port.		602–5
,, ,, ,, MS. Ash.		606–7
,, ,, ,, MS. D.		609–12
Boards for Nine Holes		614
Boards for the Smaller Merels		614
Boards for the Larger Merels		615
Alquerque de Doze		615
Board for Fox and geese		617
Mediaeval European Problems from *Bonus Socius*		629
,, ,, ,, the Picard BS. MSS.		632–6
,, ,, ,, *Civis Bononiae*		654–77
,, ,, ,, other CB. MSS.		694–6
Rook and Pawn, from MS. WA		704
Arms of Rochlitz (Massmann)		705
Rooks from Randle Holme		705
Mediaeval European Problems from Köbel		706
,, ,, ,, MS. Picc.		709–15
,, ,, ,, MS. S		720–5
,, ,, ,, MS. C		727–31
,, ,, ,, Lucena		734
,, ,, ,, MS. WD		735
Inlaid board for Merels and Chess	*to face*	757
The Charlemagne Chessmen. Bibl. nat., Paris	*to face*	758
King. Lewis chessmen in British Museum		760
Queens. Lewis chessmen, and from co. Meath		760
Bishops, Knights, and Rooks. Lewis chessmen		761
Chess Bishops. German, early 13th century		762
The Charlemagne chessmen. Bibl. nat., Paris	*to face*	762
Pawns. Lewis chessmen		763
Knight (Kunstkammer, Berlin)		763
The Ager chessmen: King, Queen		764
Damaged German chess King. British Museum	*to face*	764
The Ager chessmen: Bishop, Knight		765
The Ager chessmen: Pawn, Rook, plain pieces		766
The Charlemagne chessmen. The Dom, Osnabrück	*to face*	766
Knight and King, Brit. Mus.; Rook, Bargello Mus.; Bishops, Helpstone, Beverley, and Northampton Castle		767
The St. Louis chessmen. Cluny Museum		767
Chessmen in the Cluny Museum		768
Figures of Chessmen from Problem MSS.		769
Types of Fifteenth-Century Chessmen		770
Chessmen from Damiano, Egenolff		770
Chessmen from Egenolff, Köbel, Gracco, MS. WD, Selenus, *Studies of Chess*		771

	PAGE
Rooks and other Chess Charges from Randle Holme	772
French Chessmen, Eighteenth Century	772
Knight, English pattern	773
Staunton Chessmen	773
Chess-rook in Heraldry	774
Early Modern Problems from MS. Gött.	794-5
,, ,, ,, Lucena	797-8
,, ,, ,, Damiano	799-800
,, ,, ,, MS. WD	801
,, ,, ,, MSS. Leon and It.	803-5
,, ,, ,, MS. C	807
,, ,, ,, Gracco	836
Marinelli's Three-handed Chess	838
Game position from Allgaier (Holm)	853
Position to illustrate Icelandic mates	858
The Automaton Chessplayer . *to face*	876

(The plates facing pages 88, 134, and 388 appeared originally in the *Field*, and are reproduced here by kind permission of the Proprietors. The plates facing pages 90 and 361 are from photographs taken specially for this work by my brother, Mr. E. T. Ruthven Murray.)

NOTE ON THE TRANSLITERATION OF SANSKRIT, PERSIAN, AND ARABIC WORDS

I HAVE departed in some particulars from the system almost unanimously adopted by Sanskrit and Arabic scholars, with a view to avoiding symbols which would probably confuse the ordinary reader. All these Oriental words will be pronounced with reasonable accuracy if the consonants are given their ordinary English pronunciation, and if the vowels are pronounced as in Italian. The following digraphs represent single sounds :—*ch*, *dh*, *gh*, *kh*, *sh* and *th*.

ch is to be pronounced as in church.

dh in Arabic words as *th* in this, or as *z*.

gh is a guttural, heavier than the Scotch *ch* in loch.

kh is to be pronounced as the Scotch *ch* in loch.

When these combinations are not digraphs, a · is placed between the two letters, as in rat·ha (to be pronounced *răt-ha*, not *rath-a*) and Is·haq (to be pronounced *Is-haq*, not *Ish-aq*). In Arabic words ' is used for the hamza (produced by a compression of the upper part of the windpipe, and practically the French *h aspirée*), ' for the guttural 'ain (produced in Arabic by a more violent compression of the windpipe, and voiced, but in Egypt and Persia practically equivalent to the hamza), and *q* for the deeper *k* which approximates to *g* as in gay.

Certain consonants are written with diacritical marks in order to enable the Arabic scholar to restore the written word.[1]

The vowels *e* and *o* in Skr. words are always long.

[1] The Arabic alphabet is transliterated thus :— ' b t th j ḥ kh d dh r z s sh ṣ ḍ ṭ ẓ ' gh f q k l m n h w y ; the vowels *fat·ha* by a, *kasra* by i, and *ḍamma* by u.

EXPLANATION OF THE CHESS NOTATION USED IN THIS WORK

It has been necessary to adopt some simple method of describing the squares of the board and of recording the moves of a game which could be used uniformly for all the varieties of chess included in this work. Since the ordinary English descriptive notation does not lend itself to such adaptation, I have adopted the literal or algebraical notation which is used in all German chess books. The diagram will make clear the method of this notation, and it can obviously be extended without difficulty to a board of any size. In the cases of the Chinese and Corean games, in which the pieces are placed on the intersections of the lines dividing the board and not on the squares, a similar notation is adopted, but now the successive vertical lines are designated by letters and the horizontal lines by numerals.

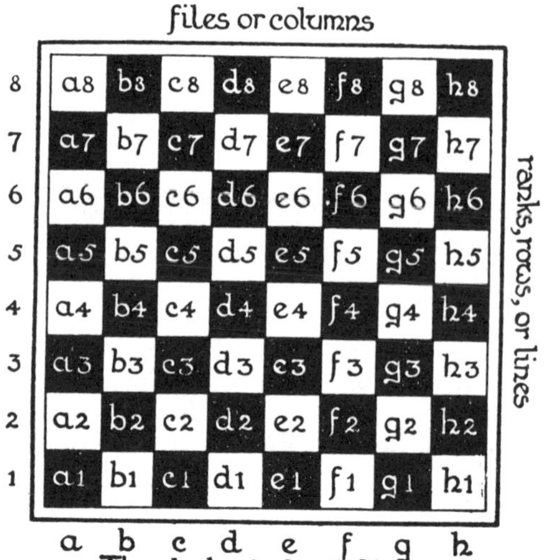

The algebraical notation.

In describing a move, the symbol of the piece that is moved is given first. If it merely move to another square, the description of this square follows the symbol immediately. Thus

Kte2 means Knight moves to the square e2.

If there is any ambiguity, the description of the square from which the piece moves is placed in brackets immediately after the symbol of the piece, or the file upon which it stands is prefixed. Thus

Kt(e2)c4 means the Kt on e2 moves to c4.

aRe1 means the R on the a-file moves to e1.

If the piece make a capture, the description of the square to which the piece moves is omitted, and in its place × or *takes* R, Kt, &c. is written. Thus

Kt × R means Knight takes Rook.

Here again ambiguity is avoided (*a*) by adding the description of the square from which the piece moves in brackets, as above; (*b*) by adding to the symbol of the captured piece the description of the square on which it stands; (*c*) by adding both descriptions; or, in the case of Pawns (*d*) prefixing to one or other, or both of the Pawns, the file upon which it stands. Thus

Kt(e2) × Kt; or Kt × Kt(c4); or Kt(e2) × Kt(c4); or aP × P; or P × dP; or cP × dP; all of which will be intelligible from what has been said before. The briefest method naturally has the preference.

If a piece gives check, this is expressed by placing + or *ch* after the description of the move, with the special forms

dbl+ or + +, *double check*; + d (also *dis ch*), *discovered check*; + r, *checkrook*, a check forking King and Rook; m., mate.

Other symbols are 0–0, *castles on King's wing*; 0–0–0, *castles on Queen's wing*; ~, *moves (the exact move not being specified)*; =, *even game*; !, *good move*; ?, *bad or inferior move.*

CONTRACTIONS

a.	In dates, *ante.*
AF.	Anglo-French.
Ar.	Arabic.
B.	Bishop or corresponding piece.
B.	In dates, *born.*
b.	In Muslim names *ibn* (son of).
Bl.	Black.
c.	Century.
c.	In dates, *circa.*
Cat.	Catalan.
ch.	Check.
Chin.	Chinese.
Cor.	Corean.
Croat.	Croatian.
Cz.	Czech.
D.	In dates, *died.*
Dan.	Danish.
Du.	Dutch.
Eng.	English.
Fr.	French.
G.	In quotations from MF. books, taken from Godefroi.
Ger.	German.
Gr.	Greek.
HG.	High German.
Hun.	Hungarian.
Ic.	Icelandic.
It.	Italian.
Jap.	Japanese.
K.	King or corresponding piece.
K.	In Ar. titles of books, *Kitāb.*
L.	Latin.
LG.	Low German.
m.	Mate, Checkmate.
M.	Middle, in ME., Middle English ; MF. Middle French ; MHG. Middle High German, &c.
N.	Modern, in NDu. Modern Dutch, &c.
O.	Old, in OF., Old French ; OHG., Old High German, &c.
P.	Pawn or corresponding piece.
Per.	Persian.
Pg.	Portuguese.
Pol.	Polish.
Prov.	Provençal.
Q.	Queen or corresponding piece.
R.	Rook or corresponding piece.
Roum.	Roumanian.
Rus.	Russian.
Sc.	Scotch.
Serv.	Servian.
Skr.	Sanskrit.
Sp.	Spanish.
St.	In quotations from MF. books, taken from Strohmeyer.
Sw.	Swedish.
Tib.	Tibetan.
Turk.	Turkish.
Wh.	White.

CONTRACTED TITLES OF MAGAZINES AND PERIODICALS

BCM. British Chess Magazine, Leeds, 1881 onwards. *Reference* to (year), (p.).

CPC. Chess Player's Chronicle, London, 1841-52. New series, 1853-6. Third series. 1859-62. *Reference* to (year), (p.).

CPM. Chess Player's Magazine, London, 1863-4. New series, 1865-7. *Reference* to (year), (p.).

JRAS. Journal of the Royal Asiatic Society, London. *Reference* to (year), (vol.), (p.).

Monatsb. Monatsbericht der Königlichen Akademie der Wissenschaften zu Berlin, Berlin. *Reference* to (year), (p.).

Sch. Schachzeitung, Berlin, 1846-53. Leipzig, 1859 onwards. *Reference* to (year), (p.).

ZDMG. Zeitschrift der Deutschen Morgenländischen Gesellschaft, Leipzig, 1846 onwards. *Reference* to (year), (vol.), (p.).

In accordance with the usual custom, Muslim dates are given according to both Muhammadan and Christian chronology, e. g. 740 (A.H.)/1340 (A.D.).

BOOKS AND ARTICLES CONSULTED FOR THE HISTORY OF CHESS

I. GENERAL

Branch, W. S., *A Sketch of Chess History*, in *BCM*, 1899–1900. Brunet y Bellet, J., *El Ajedrez*, Barcelona, 1890. Culin, S., *Chess and Playing-Cards*, Washington, 1898 (Reference: Culin, *C. & P. C.*). Falkener, E., *Games Ancient and Oriental*, London, 1892 (Reference: Falk.). Forbes, D., *History of Chess*, London, 1860 (Reference: Forbes). Hyde, T., *Mandragorias seu Historia Shahiludii*, Oxford, 1694 (Reference to *Syntagma Dissertationum*, ed. G. Sharpe, Oxford, 1767, as Hyde, II). Van der Linde, A., *Geschichte und Litteratur des Schachspiels*, Berlin, 1874–5 (Reference: v. d. Linde). *Das erste Jahrtausend des Schachspiels*, Berlin, 1880 (Reference: *JT.*). *Quellenstudien zur Geschichte des Schachspiels*, Berlin, 1881 (Reference: *Qst.*). Von der Lasa, *Zur Geschichte und Literatur des Schachspiels*, Leipzig, 1897 (Reference: v. d. Lasa).

II. INDIAN CHESS

Cox, Capt. Hiram, *On the Burmha Game of Chess, compared with the Indian, Chinese, and Persian Game of the same Denomination* (1799), in *Asiatic Researches*, London, 1803, vii. 486–511. Fiske, D. W., *The Early History of Chess*, in the *Nation*, New York, Aug. 16, 1900, 132–4 (Reference: *N. Y. Nation*, Aug. 16, 1900). Jacobi, H., *Ueber zwei ältere Erwähnungen des Schachspiels in der Sanskrit-Litteratur*, in *ZDMG.*, 1896, l. 227–33. Jones, Sir William, *On the Indian Game of Chess*, in *Asiatic Researches*, London, 1790, ii. 159–65. Macdonell, A. A., *The Origin and Early History of Chess*, in *JRAS.*, Jan. 1898, xxx. 117–41 (Reference: Macdonell, *JRAS.*). Murray, H. J. R., *Modern Discoveries in Chess History*, in *BCM.*, 1900, 425–35. Parker, H., *Ancient Ceylon*, London, 1909, 586. 605–7. Singha, G. B. L., in *Chess Amateur*, Stroud, 1909. Thomas, F. W., *The Indian Game of Chess*, in *ZDMG.*, 1898, lii. 271–2; and 1899, liii. 364. Tiruvengaḍāchārya Shāstrī (Trevangadacharya Shastree), *Essays on Chess Adapted to the European mode of play*, Bombay, 1814 (Reference: Tiruv.). Von der Lasa, in *Chess Monthly*, London, 1883–4, iv. 266. Weber, A., *Einige Daten über das Schachspiel nach indischen Quellen*, in *Monatsb.*, 1872, 59–89. *Nachträge zu der Abhandlung über das indische Schachspiel*, in *Monatsb.*, 1872, 562–8. *Neue Nachträge*, in *Monatsb.*, 1873, 705–35. *Stenzler's Lösung des Rösselsprunges*, in *Monatsb.*, 1874, 21–6. Windisch, E., *Zu 'The Indian Game of Chess,'* in *ZDMG.*, 1898, lii. 512.

Chess in India, in *CPM.*, 1865, i. 330; 1866, ii. 34, 100. *Chess Play among the Natives of India*, in *CPC.*, 1843, iv. 149.

Native works. (1) *Hindustani.* Lala Raja Babu Sahib, *Mo'allim ul Shaṭranj*, Delhi, 1901. Syamakiṣora, *Risāla i Shaṭranj*, Benares, 1885. Dalchand Bulandshahri, *Kawā'id i tash o shaṭranj*, Saharampur, 1887. Durgāprasāda, *Risāla i shaṭranj*, Delhi, 1890. (2) *Hindi.* Ambikādatta Vyāsa, *Chaturanga chaturi*, Benares, 1884. (3) *Bengali.* Brahmanānda Chaṭṭopādhyāya, *Akshabala-charita*, Calcutta, 1856. (4) *Marathi.* Mangesa Rāmakrishna Telanga, *Buddhibalāchā khela*, Bombay, 1893. Vinayaka Rajarama Tope, *Buddhibalakrīda*, Poona, 1893.

III. MALAY CHESS

Blagden, C. O., in *JRAS.*, 1898, xxx. 376. Brooke, Raja, of Sarawak, *Journal*; quoted in *CPC.*, 1849, ix. 246, and in Forbes, 271–5. Claine, J., *Chess in Sumatra*, in *BCM.*, 1891, 467. Crawfurd, J., *History of the Indian Archipelago*, Edinburgh, 1820, i. 112; quoted in Forbes, 266–71. Elcum, J. B., *Malay Chess*, in *Singapore Free Press*, c. 1900. Marsden, Dr. W., *History of Sumatra*, London, third edition, 1811, 273; quoted in Forbes, 262–3. Raffles, Sir T. Stamford, *History of Java*, London, 1817; quoted in Forbes, 263–5. Robinson, H. O., *Malay Chess*, in *Cheltenham Examiner*, July 27, 1904. Skeat, W. W., *Malay Magic*, London, 1900, 485–6. Von Oefele, A., *Das Schachspiel der Bataker*, Leipzig, 1904 (cf. *Deutsches Wochenschach*, Berlin, Oct. 8, 1905, xxi. 365). Wilkinson, R. J., *Papers on Malay Subjects, Life and Customs*, Part iii, Kuala Lumpur, 1910, 56–7 and Appendix x. 91–4 (Robinson's paper). Zimmermann, Dr. W. F. A., *Der Vulkanismus auf Java*, Berlin, 1861, 291.

IV. CHESS IN FURTHER INDIA

Bastian, Dr. A., *Schach in Birma*, in *Illustrirte Zeitung*, Leipzig, July 4, 1863. *Schach in Siam*, in *Illustrirte Zeitung*, Leipzig, April 16, 1864. Bowring, Sir J., *Kingdom and People of Siam*, London, 1857. Himly, K., *Das siamesische Schachspiel*, in *Illustrirte Zeitung*, Leipzig, Oct. 11, 1879; whence in *Sch.*, 1880, 321–4. La Loubère, *Du Royaume de Siam*, Paris, 1691, ii. 97. Low, Capt. J., *On Siamese Literature*, in *Asiatic Researches*, London, 1836, xx. ii, 374. Moura, *Royaume du Cambodge*. Scott, Sir J. G. (Shway Yoe), *The Burman*, London, 1882 (Reference: Shway Yoe). Scott-O'Connor, V. C., *The Silken East*, London, 1904, i. 186. Symes, *Account of an Embassy to the Kingdom of Ava*, London, 1800, 466–7.

V. CHINESE, COREAN, AND JAPANESE CHESS

Ball, J. D., *Things Chinese*, London, 1904, 132–6. Barrow, J., *Voyage en Chine, traduit de J. Castro*, Paris, 1805, i. 266. Chamberlain, B. H., *Things Japanese*, London, 1898. Chō Yō, *Japanese Chess*, Chicago, 1905. Culin, S., *Korean Games*, Philadelphia, 1895, 82–99. Himly, K., *Das Schachspiel der Chinesen*, in *ZDMG.*, 1870, xxiv. 172. *Streifzüge in das Gebiet der Geschichte des Schachspiels*, in *ZDMG.*, 1872, xxvi. 121. *Das japanische Schachspiel*, in *ZDMG.*, 1879, xxxiii. 672. *Anmerkungen in Beziehung auf das Schach und andere Brettspiele*, in *ZDMG.*, 1887, xli. 461. *Morgenländisch oder abendländisch?* in *ZDMG.*, 1889, xliii. and 1890, xliv. *The Chinese Game of Chess*, in *Journal of the North China Branch of the Royal Asiatic Society* for 1869–70, Shanghai, 105–21. *Die Abtheilung der Spiele im Spiegel der Mandschu-Sprache*, in *T'oung Pao*, 1895–8. Hollingworth, H. G., *A Short Sketch of Chinese Chess*, in *Journal of the N. China Branch of the R. A. S.*, Shanghai, 1866, 107–12. Holmboe, C. A., *Det chinesiske Skakspil*, Christiania, 1871 (an off-print from *Vidensk. Selsk. Forhandlinger*, 1870). Holt, H. F. W., *Notes on the Chinese Game of Chess*, in *JRAS.*, 1885, xvii. 352–65). Holtz, V., *Japanisches Schachspiel*, in *Mittheilungen der deutschen Gesellschaft für Natur- und Völkerkunde Ostasiens*, Leipzig, I, v. 10. Irwin, Eyles, *Account of the Chinese Game of Chess*, in *Transactions of the Royal Irish Academy*, Dublin, 1793, v. 53–63. Junghaus, *Ostasiatische Brettspiele*, in *Velhagen und Klasing's Monatshefte*, Feb. 1905, xix. 677–87. Menar, K. R., *Stein der Weisen*, 1902, xv. 143–4. Perry, M. C., *Narrative of the Expedition to Japan*, Washington, 1856, 464–6 (incorporating D. S. Green's *The Japanese Game of Sho-ho-ye, corresponding to our Game of Chess*, in the *Japan Expedition Express*, Sept. 7, 1854). Purchas, Rev. S., *Hakluytus Posthumus, or Purchas his Pilgrimes*, London, 1625–6. Samedo, *Relatione della grande Monarchia della China*, Madrid, 1642. Schlegel, G., *Chinesische Bräuche und Spiele in Europa*, Breslau, 1869. Trigauthius, N., *De Christiana expeditione apud Sinas*, Aug. Vind., 1615 (quoted in Selenus, 37). Vaughan, J. D., *Manners and Customs of the Chinese of the Straits Settlements*, Singapore, 1881, 48–9. Volpicello, Z., *Chinese Chess*, in *Journal of the N. China Branch of the R. A. S.*, Shanghai, xxiii. Von Möllendorff, O., *Schachspiel der Chinesen*, in *Mittheilungen der deutschen Gesellschaft für Natur- und Völkerkunde Ostasiens*, Leipzig, 1876, XI, ii. Wilkinson, W. H., *Manual of Chinese Chess*, Shanghai, 1893. *Chess in Korea*, in *Pall Mall Budget*, Dec. 27, 1894 (also in *Korean Repository*). Williams, S. W., *The Middle Kingdom*, London, 1883, i. 827–9.

The Chess World, 1868, 79–84, and the *Chinese Repository*, ix. 160, contain accounts of Japanese chess.

VI. PERSIAN AND MUSLIM CHESS

Bland N., *Persian Chess* in *JRAS.*, London, 1850, xiii. 27 (and also separately published). Browne, W. G., *Travels in Africa, Egypt, and Syria*, London, 1799. Gildemeister, J., *Geschichte und Litteratur des Schachspiels von v. d. Linde*, in *ZDMG.*, 1874, xxviii, 682–98. Grimm, V., *Letters* in *CPC.*, 1851 (whence in Forbes, 243), and *Sch.*, 1865, 361–4. Höst, G., *Efterretninger om Marokos og Fes*, Copenhagen, 1779, 105–6. Jirjis Filuthā'ūs, *Al-bākūra-al-manīra fī la'ba ash-shaṭranj ash-shahīra*, Cairo, 1892. Meakin, D., *The Moors*, London, 1902, 124. Murray, H. J. R., *Ta'biyat and other Battle-Arrays*, in *BCM.*, 1900, 169–76. *The oldest recorded Games of Chess*, in *BCM.*, 1903, 441–9. Nöldeke, *Persische Studien, II*, in *Sitzungsberichte der k. Akademie der Wissenschaften in Wien, phil.-hist. Classe*, Vienna, 1892, CXXVI., xii. Piacenza, F., *I Campeggiamenti degli Scacchi*, Turin, 1683. Plowden, W. C., *Travels in Abyssinia*, edited by T. C. Plowden, London, 1868, 149. Stamma, P., *Noble Game of Chess*, London, 1745. Valentia, Lord, *Travels*, London, 1809, iii. 57 (quoted in Forbes, 240–2).

Das dreyseitige Schachbrett, Regensburg, 1765, 31. *Persian Chess*, in *CPC.*, 1846, 211, 252, 276. *Revista Scacchistica Italiana*, 1903 (Algerian chess). *BCM.*, 1894, 10 (Turkish Chess).

VII. CHESS IN NORTHERN AND CENTRAL ASIA

Amelung, F., *Zur Geschichte des Schachspiels in Russland*, in *Baltische Schachblätter*, 1898, 139. Craufurd, *Sketches relating to the Hindoos*, London, 1792, ii. Cochrane, J. D., *Narrative of a Pedestrian Journey through Russia and Siberian Tartary*, London, 1824, i. 319. Culin, S., *Games of the N. American Indians*, Washington, 1907, 793. Gilmour, Rev. J., *Among the Mongols*, London, 292. Gonyaief, in *Shakhmatni Listok*, 1879. Huc and Gabet, *Travels*, London, third edition, 1856, xx. Jaenisch, *Linguistique de l'échiquier russe*, in *Palamède*, 1842, ii. 163-5. Murray, H. J. R., *Chess in Central and Northern Asia*, in *BCM.*, 1904, 182-4. *On the History of Chess in the Russian Empire*, in *BCM.*, 1907, 1-5, 49-53. Pallas, P. S., *Sammlungen hist. Nachrichten über die mongolischen Völkerschaften*, St. Petersburg, 1776, i. 157. Savenkof, E. V., *K voprosu op evolutsiē shakhmatnoî egry*, Moscow, 1905. Sorokin, S. A., in *Shakhmatnoy Obosrenie*, Moscow, 1892, 222, 307, 342.

VIII. EUROPEAN CHESS

Abrahams, I., *Jewish Life in the Middle Ages*, London, 1896, xxii. 388-98. Allen, G., *Life of Philidor*, Philadelphia, 1863. Allen, Lake, *Chess in Europe during the 13th Century*, in *New Monthly Magazine*, London, 1822, iv. 319, 417; v. 125, 315. Barrington, Hon. Daines, *An Historical Disquisition of the Game of Chess*, in *Archaeologia*, London, 1787, ix. 14-38. Basterot, Le Comte de, *Traité élémentaire du Jeu des Échecs*, Paris, second edition, 1863. Bilguer, P. R. v., *Handbuch des Schachspiels*, seventh edition, Leipzig, 1884.[1] Carrera, P., *Giuoco degli Scacchi*, Militello, 1617. Cook, W., *The Evolution of the Chess Openings*, Bristol, 1906. Dalton, O. M., *Catalogue of Ivory Carvings . . . in the British Museum*, London, 1909. Douce, F., *European Names of the Chess-men*, in *Archaeologia*, London, 1794, xi. 397-410. Eiserhardt, E., *Die mittelalterliche Schachterminologie des Deutschen*, Freiburg i. B. (1912). Fiske, D. W., *Book of the First American Chess Congress*, New York, 1859 (History of Chess in America). *Chess in Iceland*, Florence, 1905. Gay, J., *Bibliographie anecdotique du Jeu des Échecs*, Paris, 1864. *Íslenzkar Gátur*, iv, Kaupmannahöfn, 1892. Lambe, R., *History of Chess*, London, 1764. Leon, J. A., *Old Masters of Modern Chess*, in *BCM.*, 1894, 393, 429; 1895, 1, 109, 149, 245, 453, 501; 1896, 1, 297. Lewis, W., *Letters on Chess from C. F. Vogt, translated by U. Ewell*, London, 1848. Madden, Sir F., *Historical Remarks on the ancient Chess-men discovered in the Isle of Lewis*, in *Archaeologia*, London, 1832, xxiv. 203-91. Massmann, H. F., *Geschichte des mittelalterlichen Schachspiels*, Quedlinburg, 1839. Paluzíe y Lucena, J., *Manual de Ajedrez*, Parte Sexta, Barcelona, 1912. Ponziani, *Il giuoco incomparabile degli Scacchi*, Modena, seconda edizione, 1782. Salvio, A., *Il Puttino*, Naples, 1634. Strohmeyer, F., *Das Schachspiel im Altfranzösischen*, in *Abhandlungen Herrn Prof. Dr. A. Tobler*, Halle, 1895 (Reference: St.). Selenus, Gustavus, *Das Schach- oder König-Spiel*, Leipzig, 1616. Twiss, R., *Chess*, London, 1787-9 (Reference: Twiss). *Miscellanies*, London, 1805, ii. Van der Linde, A., *Das Schachspiel des XVI. Jahrhunderts*, Berlin, 1874 (Reference: v. d. Linde, 16. Jrh.). *Het Schaakspel in Nederland*, Utrecht, 1875. *Leerboek van het Schaakspel*, Utrecht, 1876. Von der Lasa, *Bemerkungen über das mittelalterliche Schach*, in *Der akademische Schachklub München, Festschrift*, München, 1896. Vetter, F., *Das Schachzabelbuch Kunrats v. Ammenhausen*, Frauenfeld, 1892 (incorporating, xxiii-l, W. Wackernagel's *Das Schachspiel im Mittelalter* (in *Abhandlungen, Leipzig*, 1872, 107), and 803-18, v. d. Lasa's *Bemerkungen über das mittelalterliche Schachspiel*—a different article from that mentioned above).

[1] The eighth edition, the issue of which only began after the completion of the printing of the first part of the present work, contains a section upon the history of chess which deserves to be consulted, though it is a matter for regret that it includes (pp. 35-8) a speculation as to the early state of chess which is unsupported by any historical evidence and out of harmony with the known facts of the development of the game.

PART I. CHESS IN ASIA

CHAPTER I

INTRODUCTORY

European chess of Indian ancestry.—Asiatic games of similar ancestry.—Classification of Board-games.—Indian Board-games.—The Ashṭāpada.—Speculations on the nature of the original Indian chess.—Previous theories as to the ancestry of the game.

HISTORICALLY chess must be classed as a game of war. Two players direct a conflict between two armies of equal strength upon a field of battle, circumscribed in extent, and offering no advantage of ground to either side. The players have no assistance other than that afforded by their own reasoning faculties, and the victory usually falls to the one whose strategical imagination is the greater, whose direction of his forces is the more skilful, whose ability to foresee positions is the more developed.

To-day, chess as we know it is played by every Western people, and in every land to which Western civilization or colonization has extended. The game possesses a literature which in contents probably exceeds that of all other games combined.[1] Its idioms and technicalities have passed into the ordinary language of everyday life.[2] The principles and possibilities of the game have been studied for four centuries, and the serious student of chess starts now with the advantage of a rich inheritance of recorded wisdom and experience. Master-play reaches a high standard, and has rightly earned a reputation for difficulty. This reputation has often been extended to the game itself, and has deterred many from learning it. Moreover, Western civilization has evolved other games, and teems with other interests for leisure moments, so that chess to-day can only be regarded as the game of the minority of the Western world. In the Middle Ages chess was far more widely played, and the precedence among indoor games that is still accorded

[1] V. d. Linde's *Das erste Jahrtausend der Schachlitteratur* (Berlin, 1881) gives a handlist of 3,462 works on chess and draughts. The total number of books on chess, chess magazines, and newspapers devoting space regularly to the game probably exceeds 5,000 at the present time.

[2] In English alone I need only instance the words *check*, *cheque*, with all its meanings and derivatives, *Exchequer*, *jeopardy*, the phrase *a pawn in the game*. *Mattus*, the Latin adjective 'mated', has given rise to adjectives in most European languages in the sense of 'dull', 'stupid'.

by courtesy to it is a survival from the period when chess was the most popular game of the leisured classes of Europe.

The ancestry of this European chess can easily be established. A number of the mediaeval European chess terms can be traced back by way of Arabic to Middle Persian. Thus we have

Eur. *ferz*	= Ar. *firz, firzān*	= Per. *farzīn.*
Eur. *alfil*	= Ar. *(al) fīl*	= Per. *pīl.*
Eur. *roc*	= Ar. *rukhkh*[3]	= Per. *rukh.*
Eur. *scac, check!*	= Ar. *shāh*	= Per. *shāh.*
Eur. *mat, mate!*	= Ar. *māt*	= Per. *māt.*

The name of the game in most of the European languages, e.g. Eng. *chess*, Fr. *échecs*, It. *scacchi*, can be traced back, through the Latin plural *scaci* (*scachi*, *scacci*, meaning chessmen), to the Arabic and Persian name of the chess King, *shāh.*

The names of the other chessmen—King and Pawn (L. *pedo*, a foot-soldier), everywhere; Horse, in Southern Europe—reproduce the meaning of the names of the corresponding men in the Arabic and Persian games.

The names of the game of chess in modern Spanish or Castilian (*ajedrez*) and Portuguese (*xadrez*) not only confirm this evidence, but supplement it by taking the pedigree a step farther back. For these two forms appear in older Castilian as *acedrex*, and this word is simply the Arabic *ash-shaṭranj*, *the shaṭranj*, in a European dress. *Shaṭranj*, again, is only an Arabicized form of the Middle Persian *chatrang*, and this Persian word is an adaptation of the Sanskrit *chaturanga.* All these terms are in their respective languages the ordinary names for the game of chess.

The names of the chessmen in Persian and Sanskrit are synonymous. In each game there was a King, a Counsellor, two Elephants, two Horse, two Chariots, and eight Foot-soldiers.

This philological evidence derives some support from the documentary evidence. The earliest works which make mention of chess date from about the beginning of the 7th century A.D., and are associated with N.W. India, Persia, and Islam. It is difficult to assign exact dates, but the oldest of a number of nearly contemporary references is generally assumed to be a mention of chess in a Middle Persian romance—the *Kārnāmak*—which is ascribed with some hesitation to the reign of Khusraw II Parwīz, the Sāsānian king of Persia, 590–628 A.D. The others belong to N.W. India.

It is interesting to note that early Persian and Arabic tradition is unanimous in ascribing the game of chess to India. The details naturally vary in different works, and the names in the tradition are manifestly apocryphal.

[3] The doubling of the final consonant in Arabic is due to the Grammarians who, by this device, made the necessary triliteral root from the biliteral Persian word, and so gave it an Arabic appearance. In the sequel I shall write simply *rukh* for both Persian and Arabic forms, unless there is any special reason for calling attention to the strict Arabic form.

Chess is usually associated with the decimal numerals as an Indian invention, and its introduction into Persia is persistently connected with the introduction of the book *Kalīla wa Dimna* (the *Fables of Pilpay*) in the reign of the Sāsānian monarch Khusraw I Nūshīrwān, 531–78 A.D., and European scholars of Sanskrit and Persian generally accept the traditional date of the introduction of this book as established. The so-called Arabic numerals are well known to be really Indian.

Finally, a comparison of the arrangement and method of the European game of the 11th to 13th centuries A.D. with the Indian game as existing to-day and as described in the earlier records supports the same conclusion. In both games the major pieces occupy opposite edges of the board of 8 × 8 squares, and the Foot-soldiers are arranged on the row in front of the major pieces. The corner squares (a1, a8, h1, h8) are occupied by the *Chariot* with identical move in most of the games;[4] the next squares (b1, b8, g1, g8) by the *Horse* with the well-known move of the Knight; the third squares from the corners (c1, c8, f1, f8) by the *Elephant*;[5] and the two central squares (e1, e8, d1, d8) by the *King* and *Counsellor* respectively with moves that were for long the same in India, Persia, Islam, and Europe.[6] The move of the *Foot-soldiers*, arranged on the 2nd and 7th rows, was also for long the same in the chess of all these countries.

We must accordingly conclude that our European chess is a direct descendant of an Indian game played in the 7th century with substantially the same arrangement and method as in Europe five centuries later, the game having been adopted first by the Persians, then handed on by the Persians to the Muslim world, and finally borrowed from Islam by Christian Europe.

Games of a similar nature exist to-day in other parts of Asia than India. The Burmese *sittuyin*, the Siamese *makruk*, the Annamese *chhôeu trâng*, the Malay *chātor*, the Tibetan *chandaraki*, the Mongol *shatara*, the Chinese *siang k'i*, the Corean *tjyang keui*, and the Japanese *sho-gi*, are all war-games exhibiting the same great diversity of piece which is the most distinctive feature of chess.

There is naturally far less direct evidence respecting the ancestry of these games than in the case of European chess, but there can be no doubt that all these games are equally descended from the same original Indian game. The names *sittuyin* (Burmese), *chhôeu trâng* (Annamese), and *chandaraki* (Tibetan) certainly, and the names *chātor* (Malay) and *shatara* (Mongol) probably, reproduce the Sanskrit *chaturanga*. The names of some of the

4 In some Indian descriptions the Chariot is replaced by a Boat; in others the Elephant and Chariot have changed places; in the modern Indian games the Chariot is often replaced by an Elephant, and the original Elephant by a Camel. The argument from this piece is therefore less decisive than that from the invariable position and move of the Horse.

5 Early Indian records show that the move of this piece was not fixed to the extent that the moves of the other pieces were. Hence we find considerable variety in the Asiatic games.

6 In the European and earlier Muslim games, the Kings stood on the same file: in most modern Asiatic varieties, the Kings each stand on the same file as the opposing Counsellor (Queen).

pieces in the Malay, the Burmese, and probably the Siamese games, have been borrowed from the Sanskrit.

If we examine the nomenclature of these games we also find the same meanings recurring throughout. Thus we have—

Sanskrit .	king . .	counsellor .	elephant .	horse .	chariot .	foot-soldier
Malay . .	,, . .	,, .	,, .	,, .	,, .	,,
Javan . .	,, . .	lord . . .	counsellor .	,, .	boat . .	,,
Tibetan . .	,, . .	tiger . . .	camel . .	,, .	chariot . .	child
Mongol . .	prince .	dog . . .	,, . . also elephant	,, .	,, .	,,
Burmese .	king . .	general . .	elephant .	,, .	,, .	foot-soldier
Siamese . .	lord . .	minister .	? nobleman	,, .	boat . .	shell
Chinese . .	general .	counsellor .	elephant .	,, .	chariot .	foot-soldier
Corean . .	,, .	,, .	,, .	,, .	,, .	,,
Japanese .	,, .	——	——	,, .	,, .	,,

The Malay, Tibetan, and Mongol games are played on a board of 8 × 8 squares, and the initial arrangement of the pieces corresponds closely to the Indian game. The three games of Further India are played on a board of the same size, but the arrangement of the pieces differs from that of the Indian game. The moves of the chessmen are consistent with an Indian ancestry.

The relationship of the Chinese, Corean, and Japanese games is not so obvious. The first two are played on the lines, and not on the squares, of a board of 8 × 8 squares with a space between the 4th and 5th rows which virtually makes the board one of 8 × 9 squares; the third is played on the squares of a board of 9 × 9 squares. There is, however, no doubt that both the Corean and the Japanese games are derivatives of an older form of the Chinese game. Chinese works refer to the introduction of modifications in their game after 1279. These games introduce new pieces, but the salient fact remains that the Chariot with the move of the Rook (modified in Japan) occupies the corner squares (a1, &c.), and the Horse with the characteristic move of the Knight (slightly modified) occupies the adjoining squares (b1, &c.). This coincidence is too striking to be dismissed as merely accidental. Moreover, it is well known that other Chinese games are of Indian origin.

We may contrast the position of these games in Asia with that of chess in Europe. If we except Japan, there are only the beginnings of a literature. Each generation accordingly has to start again from the commencement and to evolve its own science of the game. The standard of play remains of necessity low, and there is nothing to deter any one from learning to play. The game has few rivals with which it must compete for popular favour, and it has had no difficulty in most places [7] in retaining the first place. Thus the majority of Asiatics are chess-players, and chess may without exaggeration be described as the national game of Asia.

It is in the wider sense, in which I have just used the word, that I propose to use *chess* in this book. I include under it all the games which I trace back

[7] In China, Corea, and Japan, the educated classes prefer *wei k'i* to chess.

to the Indian *chaturanga*, and all the freak modifications that have been attempted from time to time. The first part of this history is devoted to a record of the Asiatic varieties of chess, and the evidence rapidly summarized above will be developed at greater length in the sequel. The broad lines of the diffusion of chess from India are fairly clear. Its earliest advance was probably westwards to Persia; the eastward advance appears to have been rather later, and at least three lines of advance may be traced. One route took the game by Kashmīr to China, Corea, and Japan. A second, possibly the same route by which Buddhism travelled, took chess to Further India. At a later date chess spread from the S.E. coast of India to the Malays. The route by which the game reached Tibet and the Northern tribes of Asia is still doubtful. Persia had meanwhile passed on chess to the Eastern Roman Empire, and, as a result of the Muhammadan conquest of Persia, Islam learnt the game. Henceforward the Muslims became the great pioneers of chess, carrying their game as far west as Spain, and east to India where they imposed the Arabic nomenclature on the Northern and Central Provinces of the Peninsula. Christian Europe had begun to learn chess from the Moors as early as 1000 A.D. From the Mediterranean shores it spread northwards over France and Germany to Britain, to the Scandinavian lands, and Iceland.

In its outward furniture chess is only one of many games which require a specially arranged surface for play. Games of this type are conveniently grouped under the generic name of *Board-games*, Ger. *Brettspiele*, although, as Groos [8] has pointed out, the name is not a very fortunate one, since the surface of play is not always a board. Board-games are not only of very wide distribution to-day, but are also of great antiquity. They are by no means confined to the more civilized races: with the exception of the native tribes of Australia and New Guinea, practically every known people has its game or games of this type. It has also been remarked that the difficulty of a board-game is no criterion of the development of the race playing it, for some of the most involved and complicated varieties known are played by tribes that stand lowest in the scale of civilization. Board-games were played by the early inhabitants of Egypt; boards and pieces have been found in tombs even as old as the pre-dynastic period (*a.* 4000 B.C.),[9] they are depicted in paintings in tombs of the Fifth Dynasty (3600–3400 B.C.),[10] and the masons who built the temple at Kurna (1400–1333 B.C.) cut boards on slabs

[8] See Prof. Baldwin's English translation, *The Play of Man*, London, 1901, 190.

[9] A clay gaming board, 7 in. by 2½, with three rows of six squares and eleven conical men varying in height from ⅓ in. to 1 in., from a pre-dynastic tomb at El-Mahasna, eight miles north of Abydos, was shown at the annual exhibition of the Egypt Exploration Fund, King's College, London, July 1909. From other objects in the tomb, it is supposed to have been the burial-place of a medicine-man or magician.

[10] Since these paintings are invariably in profile, they give no information as to the shape of the board. Their importance consists in the fact that none of them shows any differentiation of type of man (apart from what was necessary to discriminate between the two sides playing). The great majority of the boards found in Egyptian tombs fall into two types, which are both shown in my illustration of the board from the Abbot collection. It was usual to arrange the two boards on the upper and lower surfaces of a box containing a drawer for the pieces. The board on the under-surface of the Abbot board-box nearly always exhibits

which were afterwards built into the roof of the temple.[11] Boards, apparently for games, have been found in prehistoric ruins in Palestine.[12] Board-games are mentioned in the earliest Buddhist literature of India,[13] and in early Chinese works.[14] They were played in classical times in Greece and Rome,[15] by the Celts in Ireland and Wales before the Norman Conquest of England, by the Norse vikings before they began to harry the coasts of England

symbols on five outside squares (see the drawing of Queen Hatasu's board), four of which stand for numerals, while the hieroglyphic *nefer* on the fifth square from the end probably marks the termination of the numbered squares. The fragment of another board in the British Museum, which also belonged to Queen Hatasu, with squares of blue porcelain separated by strips of ivory, which Falkener (*Games A. and O.*, plate facing 46) supposed was part of a board of 144 squares, appears to have been for the 3 by 10 board. The pieces found

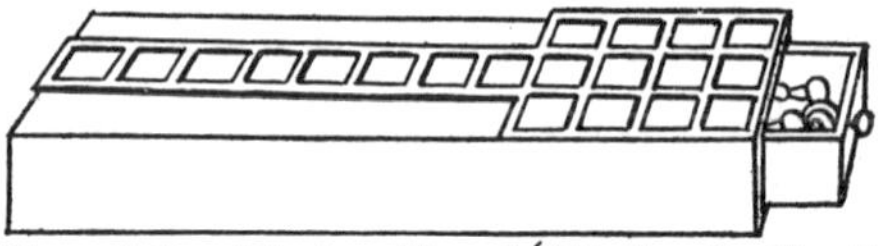

Board from Thebes, Egypt (Abbot collection—Louvre)

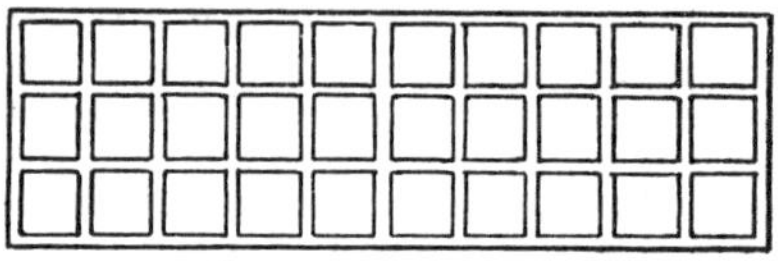

Game on reverse

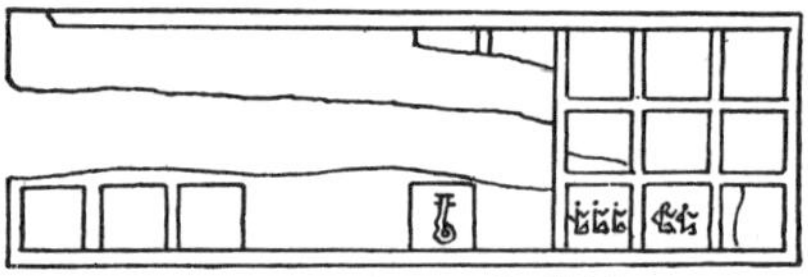

Board of Q. Hatasu. Brit. Museum.

with these two types of board belong to three types; (*a*) conical men of the shape now used in *Halma*, but formerly used for merels, draughts, and as chess-pawns; (*b*) flat reel-shaped pieces; (*c*) pieces with carved heads, generally of the lion. It is probable that there was no discrimination of piece in either game, and that these types are merely conventional shapes adopted to distinguish opposing sides. That the games were dice-games is shown by the fact that astragals or oblong dice (marked 1–4) usually accompany the games. Cf. Falkener, op. cit. (whose conclusions are of doubtful validity), and W. L. Nash, in *Proc. Soc. Bibl. Arch.*, 1902, 341–8.

[11] See H. Parker, *Ancient Ceylon*, London, 1909, 578 and 644. Both the Three and the Nine men's merels boards occur. A board in the Egyptian Rooms at the British Museum, from the time of the Ptolemies, No. 14315, of 3 by 3 squares, now arranged with nine stones on the squares, probably belongs to a variety of the Three men's merels.

[12] Three fragments of limestone boards, apparently of 12 by 12 squares, were found at Tell Zakariya (*Palestine Explor. Fund*, Quarterly Statement, April 1899, 99), and a limestone board of 16 by 11 squares was found at Gezer (op. cit., July 1904, 215). In all four cases, the dividing lines are drawn very irregularly.

[13] See below, p. 34.

[14] See below, pp. 122 and 132.

[15] We know very little that is certain about the classical Greek and Roman board-games. A list of the chief authorities will be found below, page 161, note 1. Among recent discoveries of antiquities which have been held to be intended for game-boards are—

(*a*) An extremely elaborate board found at Knossos (*Annual of Br. Sch. at Athens*, 1900–1, vii. 77–82 and plate). The board, which is quite unlike any other known game-board in arrangement, has only 14 squares, and no men were discovered with it.

(*b*) A board identical in arrangement with one of the Egyptian game-boards, found at

and France,[16] and by the native tribes of America before the time of Columbus.[17]

All known board-games, greatly as they vary in arrangement and method of play, appear to fall into one or other of three well-defined groups:

(1) *Race games*, in which the men are moved along a definite track. The typical European example is the game of *Backgammon* (*tables*, *nard*).

(2) *Hunt* or *Siege games*, in which one side endeavours to block or confine the adversary. The typical European example is the game of *Fox and Geese*.

(3) *War games*, in which the capture of prisoners plays a considerable part. The typical European example is the game of *Chess*.

This classification is convenient, but it must not be pushed too far. In particular, it must not be assumed without further inquiry that it involves any necessary connexion between the individual games of different groups, or even of a single group. However tempting it may be to assume a common ancestry for board-games, it is clear from a closer examination of the various methods of play that the majority have arisen independently, and that only in the case of a small minority in any class is there any evidence of a common origin. The sameness of type which is the foundation of the above classification is at most due to the fact that the games are 'based upon certain fundamental conceptions of the universe' (Culin, *Korean Games*), but more probably, in my opinion, to the universality of the activities which the games symbolize.[18] Identity of origin can only be established by the evidence of

Enkomi, Cyprus (*Journal Hellenic Studies*, London, 1896, xvi. 288; and A. S. Murray, *Excavations in Cyprus*, 12, and Fig. 19).

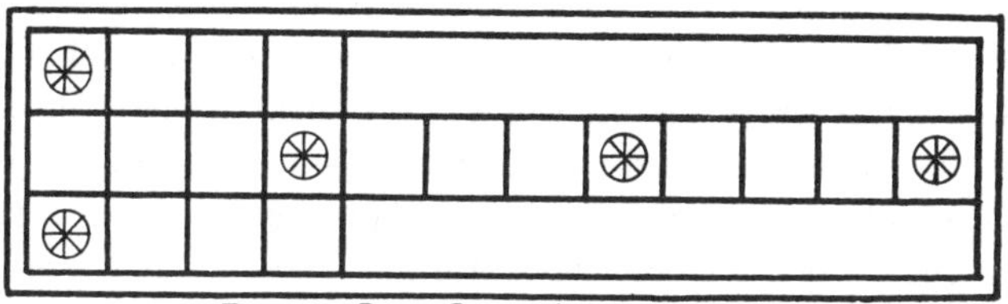

Board from Enkomi, Cyprus

(*c*) A board of 8 by 6 squares, on which 12 men are lying in confusion, forms part of a terra-cotta group found at Athens. It is figured in Richter, *Die Spiele der Griechen u. Römer*, Leipzig, 1887.

(*d*) A board of 4 by 4 squares is carved on a gem of uncertain date, which is figured in the *Bullet. Archeol. di Napoli*, Tav. viii. 5, and in Falkener, op. cit., 82.

(*e*) Several boards, rudely cut in stone, have been found in Roman stations in Northumberland. Three boards, of 9×9, 8×7, and 8×8 unchequered squares, are in the Museum at Chesters, the first two being from Cilurnum. A similar board, 8×7, and fragments of two others, were found at Corstopitum (Corbridge) in 1911.

[16] For the Welsh games, see p. 746. For the Irish *fidchell*, see p. 746. The romances of the Cuchulain cycle also mention board-games called *brandub*, *cennchaem Conchobair* and *buanfach*. Nothing is known as to the nature of any of these. For the Norse game of *hnefatafl*, see p. 445. Part of a board for the Nine men's merels was found in the Gokstad ship (figured in Du Chaillu, *Viking Age*).

[17] E.g. the Mexican game of *Patolli* (Culin, *C. & P. C.*, 854) which is diagrammed in a 16th c. Spanish-Mexican MS. See the following note.

[18] Thus the arguments that American civilization is of Asiatic ancestry (E. B. Tylor, *Journal. Anthrop. Inst.*, 1878, viii; and *Intern. Archiv für Ethnographie*, 1896), or conversely that Asiatic civilization is of American ancestry (Culin, in *Harper's Monthly*, Mar. 1903), which are based upon the superficial resemblance of the Mexican *patolli* with the Indian *pachīsī*, appear to rest upon a very insecure foundation. Both games are race games in which the track

reliable historical documents, by the linguistic evidence derived from the nomenclature of the games, or by the fact that these show so great an identity of feature that the chances of independent invention are mathematically infinitesimal.

The existing games which I include under the name of chess form one of the few groups of games whose common ancestry can be established in this way. It will obviously be far more difficult to carry the pedigree farther back, and to discover the origin or relationships of the parent Indian *chaturanga*, a game already in existence in the 7th century of our era, in still older games. We shall first have to ascertain what board-games were in existence in India at that remote period, and to attempt to elucidate their nature.

Unfortunately, the general characteristics of early Indian literature are not very favourable for such an inquiry. The earlier Sanskrit literature of the Vedic age, and also of the later centuries when the Brāhmanas and Sutras came into existence, was religious in tone and almost entirely poetical in form, and references to games must be exceptional. The later Sanskrit literature gradually extended its field to include secular subjects in general, but as it widened its field the defects of its literary style became more pronounced, and the conceits of the poetry and the extraordinarily condensed character of the prose deprive the allusions of definiteness, and leave too much to depend on the view of the commentator or the personal fancy of the translator. Our knowledge of the older Indian games is thus very vague, and based only upon the comparison of passages, all more or less obscure.

But we do know that board-games were in existence in N.W. India and the Ganges valley considerably before the commencement of the Christian era. We know this from the occurrence in Sanskrit works of words which are used as the names of boards or surfaces upon which games were played. The commonest of these words is *phalaka*, but this is simply a generic term for a game-board and conveys no information as regards shape, size, or arrangement. There are next the terms used in connexion with the simplest forms of dice-play, in which everything turns upon the result of throwing the dice and nothing in the nature of a game with pieces is required. Obviously, all that is necessary in this case is a level surface upon which the dice may fall, and Lüders (*Das Würfelspiel im alten Indien*, Berlin, 1907, 11–15) has shown that *adhidevana* (used in the *Atharva Veda*, and usually translated dice-board) meant simply a smooth flat surface excavated in the ground for this purpose. Of more importance for our present purpose is

runs round a figure in the shape of the cross, and in both games certain squares are cross-cut, i. e. have the diagonals inserted. In the Indian game (as in Asiatic games generally) these cross-cut squares are squares of *safety*, and a man who is posted upon these squares cannot be captured by the adversary. In all the existing American games of the race type (and therefore probably in *Patolli* also) the cross-cut squares are squares of *danger*, and the player tries to avoid them. As stated below, the use of cross-cut squares is a natural improvement on the simpler forms of race-game, and it is probable that games of this type sprang up independently all over the world. Culin has collected a good deal of evidence to show that many games of this type are survivals of magical processes (cf. *C. & P. C.*, 679; and *Korean Games*).

a group of terms which are restricted to boards of definite shape and arrangement. There are two words of this kind: *ashṭāpada*, meaning a square board of 64 squares, 8 rows of 8 squares, and *dasapada*, meaning a similar board of 100 squares, 10 rows of 10 squares. These boards were employed for a more complicated form of game in which the use of the dice was combined with a game upon a board (Lüders, op. cit., 65). Both terms appear to have been used also for the games played upon these boards.

The *ashṭāpada* would seem accordingly to have been identical in shape with our chessboard or draughtboard, and so it is often translated, though the rendering is to be deprecated as suggesting to the ordinary reader that the board was used for a rudimentary form of one of these games. For draughts there is no evidence at all, for chess none before the 7th c. A. D. Still, the coincidence is so striking that it is worth while to try to discover what the *ashṭāpada* game really was, in order to see whether it has not some connexion with the rise of chess.

The meaning of the word is established by Patañjali in his great commentary on the grammar of Pāṇini, the *Mahābhāshya*, which, according to Macdonell (*Skr. Lit.*, 431), was written between the latter half of the 2nd c. B. C. and the beginning of the Christian era. It is here[19] defined as 'a board in which each line has 8 squares'. In the absence of any reference to any alternate colouring or chequering of the squares, we may assume that it was unchequered, like all other native Asiatic game-boards. Two early comparisons suggest that the *ashṭāpada* was a familiar object. In the first book of the *Rāmāyaṇa*,[20] according to Jacobi added after the 2nd c. B. C., the city of Ayodhyā (Oudh) is spoken of as 'charming by reason of pictures consisting of *ashṭāpada* squares, as it were painted'. The regular plan of the city is probably intended, and the passage may be compared with later ones from Muslim historians. Thus Ḥamza al-Iṣfahānī (*c.* 300/912), writing of the building of Jundī Shāpūr by the Sāsānian king Shāhpūr (240–270 A.D.), says: 'the plan of this city was after the fashion of a chessboard; it was intersected by 8 times 8 streets,' to which a later Persian historian adds the pertinent comment, 'the figure was after this fashion, but chess had not yet been invented at that time.' The later geographer Mustawfī (740/1340)[21] has a similar statement about the plan of Nīshāpūr in Khurāsān: 'In the days of the Chosroes, as it was reported, the old town of Naysābūr had been originally laid out on the plan of a chessboard with 8 squares to each side.' There is also a passage in a Northern Buddhist work, cited by Burnouf in his *Lotus de la bonne loi*, Paris, 1852–4, 383, in which the world is described as 'the earth on which *ashṭāpadas* were fastened with cords of gold'—probably alluding to the division by roads, seas, and mountains, or to the succession of field, forest, and desert.[22]

19 *Mahābhāshya*, ed. Kielhorn, iii. 362–3. Weber, *Ind. Stud.*, xiii. 473.
20 *Rāmāyaṇa*, I. v. 12. Weber, *Monatsb.*, 1873, 710, n. 1.
21 Quoted in Le Strange, *Lands of the Eastern Caliphate*, Cambridge, 1895, 386.
22 The word *ashṭāpada* is also included in the *Amarakoṣa*, II. x. 46, an early vocabulary which Macdonell (*Skr. Lit.*, 433) says was 'not improbably composed about 500 A. D.'

Of more importance is a passage in the Pali[23] *Brahma-jāla Sutta*, or *Dialogues of the Buddha*,[24] according to Rhys Davids one of the earliest of Buddhist documents, purporting to record the actual words of Gotama himself, and dating back to the 5th c. B.C. The Buddha is contrasting the conversation and thoughts of the unconverted man with those of the disciple:

It (sect. 7, p. 3) is in respect only of trifling things, of matters of little value, of mere morality, that an unconverted man when praising the Tathāgata, would speak. And what are such trifling, minor details of mere morality that he would praise?

He then proceeds to enumerate all the many trifles which occupy the thoughts of the unconverted man, and finally comes to games, and gives us a most interesting and valuable list of games—quite the oldest known—which from its interest I quote entire:

Or (sect. 14, p. 9) he might say, 'Whereas some recluses and Brahmans while living on food provided by the faithful continue addicted to games and recreations; i.e. to say—

1. Games on boards with boards with 8 or 10 rows of squares.
2. The same games played by imagining such boards in the air (Pāli, *ākāsaṃ*).
3. Keeping going over diagrams drawn on the ground, so that one steps only where one ought to go.
4. Either removing the pieces or men from a heap with one's nail, or putting them in a heap, in each case without shaking it. He who shakes the heap loses.
5. Throwing dice (Pāli, *khalikā*).
6. Hitting a short stick with a long one.
7. Dipping the hand with the fingers stretched out in lac, or red dye, or flour water, and striking the wet hand on the ground, or on a wall, calling out 'What shall it be?' and showing the form required—elephants, horses, &c.
8. Games with balls (Pāli, *akkhaṃ*).
9. Blowing through toy pipes made of leaves.
10. Ploughing with toy ploughs.
11. Turning somersaults.
12. Playing with toy windmills made of palm leaves.
13. Playing with toy measures made of palm leaves.
14, 15. Playing with toy carts, or toy bows.
16. Guessing at letters traced in the air, or on a playfellow's back.
17. Guessing the playfellow's thoughts.
18. Mimicking of deformities.

Gotama the recluse holds aloof from such games and recreations.'

This passage is quoted at length in many other early Buddhist works, e.g. in *Vinaya*, ii. 10, and iii. 180. The translation naturally depends considerably on early native commentaries, and it must be remembered that the earliest commentators are considerably later than the original; indeed they only appeared when changes in the spoken language made the written work archaic and unintelligible to the ordinary reader. The commentator was often in a worse position than the modern scholar for interpreting the text,

[23] By Pali we understand the colloquial language of N.W. India in Buddha's time, c. 500 B.C., which is for this reason now the sacred language of Buddhism. It is a derivative of Sanskrit.

[24] Edited by Rhys Davids in the series *Sacred Books of the Buddhists*, London, 1899, i. Rhys Davids had previously edited it in the series *Sacred Books of the East*, Oxford, 1881, xi.

and we often find his explanation absurd or impossible. We are accordingly compelled to accept the above translation with some reserve.[25]

We are only concerned now with the first two of the games named. These are the *ashṭāpada*—here in its Pali form *aṭṭhapada*—and the *dasapada*. One of the two commentators used by Rhys Davids, the Sinhalese Sanna, who belongs to the 10th c. A.D. or even later, says that each of these games was played with dice and pieces (*poru*, from *purisa* = men), such as Kings and so on.[26] His evidence is far too late to be of any value as to the nature of the games in question, but is important as showing that these boards were still used for dice games in his day in Ceylon. Yet, if the second sentence is accurately translated, the games must have been of a character which permitted 'blindfold' play without the use of material boards.

The game on the *ashṭāpada* also falls into condemnation in an early Brahman work, the *Sutrakrilānga*.[27] The devout Brahman, we are told,

> should not learn to play *ashṭāpada*, he should not speak anything forbidden by the law, a wise man should abstain from fights and quarrels.

A more illuminating reference is to be found in the *Harivaṃsa*, or *Family of Vishṇu*, a supplementary book to the *Mahābhārata*, and generally recognized as a later addition. Macdonell (*Skr. Lit.*, 287) has, however, shown that the *Mahābhārata*, including the *Harivaṃsa*, must have attained to its present form by at least 500 A.D. The passage[28] recounts a meeting for dice-play between Rūkmin and Balarāma. The former had the reputation of being an expert at dice, the latter was fond of it, but not very skilled in play. Enormous stakes were laid, and Rūkmin won thrice in succession. Finally, sorely provoked by Rūkmin's expressions of triumph, Balarāma exclaimed, 'Prince, I wager the vast sum of 100,000 millions, do you accept it? Let us throw the black and red dice on this splendid ashṭāpada.' Rūkmin made no reply, but threw and lost. Then only did Rūkmin reply, 'I refuse the wager.'

[25] Rhys Davids has also made some alterations in the above translation from that which he gave in his previous edition in the *Sacred Books of the East*, xi. *Brahmajālasutta*, sect. 14. *Culavagga*, I. xiii. 2, p. 193. There he translates No. 2 (*ākāsaṃ*) by 'tossing up'; No. 6, 'trapping'; No. 8, 'tossing balls'; and No. 16, 'shooting marbles from the fingers'. The word *akkha* (= Skr. *aksha*) used in No. 8 usually means a die for gaming, but both commentators give the explanation which Rhys Davids has followed. Macdonell (*JRAS.*, 121) seems to have confused Nos. 5 and 8, since he says that the Pali word rendered dicing (i. e. No. 5) is *akkha*. See for his argument, note 41 below.

[26] Rhys Davids in his note on No. 1 says, 'Chess played originally on a board of 8 times 10 squares was afterwards played on one of 8 times 8 squares. Our text cannot be taken as evidence of real chess in the 5th c. B.C., but it certainly refers to games from which it and draughts must have developed.' He would seem to have obtained his primitive chessboard of 8 by 10 squares from this passage; I know of nothing else that could have suggested it. It will be evident that there is no evidence for it in Indian literature. I develop in the text a different view of these board-games to what he takes.

[27] Edited by Jacobi in the *Sacred Books of the East*, xlv, *Jaina Sūtras*, Oxford, 1895, 303. Although Jacobi uses the word *chess* to translate *ashṭāpada*, his note on the passage makes it clear that he regarded the game of the text as something different, as he refers to the later *Haravijaya* of Ratnākara as containing the earliest mention of chess known to him.

[28] Cf. Langlois' French version, *Harivansa*, London, 1834, i. 502. Also Weber, *Monatsb.*, 1872, 563 seq. Langlois had first (*Mon. lit. de l'Inde*, Paris, 1827, 137–46) rendered *ashṭāpada* by *chess*, but in his later version he substituted 'une espèce de Tric-trac'. See v. d. Linde, i. 15.

Neither this, nor Rūkmin's continued references to his victory, upset Balarāma's self-control, but when a voice from the skies awarded the victory to him on the ground that 'silence gives consent', Balarāma's long-restrained wrath blazed forth, and seizing the large golden ashṭāpada, he struck Rūkmin to the ground. A second blow broke the teeth of the King of Kalinga. Then, tearing up one of the golden pillars of the hall, Balarāma strode forth, wielding it as a club.[29]

We may probably find in this story a reason for the condemnation which Buddhist and Brahman alike pronounce upon the game ashṭāpada. Neither religion countenanced dicing, but neither has been able at any time to suppress it in India. Too great stress has been placed upon the efficacy of legislation, such as is to be found in the *Code of Manu*, against the use of the dice.[30] It is abundantly evident from the whole extent of Sanskrit literature that gambling with dice has been at all times the chief recreation in India. One of the very few secular poems in the *Rigveda*, occurring in the very oldest part of the collection, which can hardly be put later than 1000 B.C., contains the lament of a gambler who is unable to tear himself away from the dice, although he is fully conscious of the ruin he is bringing upon himself and his home. Lüders (op. cit.) has collected a large number of instances from the epic literature which show the extent of the passion for dicing in post-vedic times. In the *Mahābhārata*, Nala and Yudhishthira are represented as gambling away their very kingdoms in dice-play.[31] The Arabic historian al-Maṣ'ūdī, writing about 950 A.D., draws a lurid picture of what was currently believed

[29] The same incident is told more briefly in the *Vishnu Purāna*, v. 28 (tr. Wilson, ed. FitzEdward Hall, London, 1870, v. 84–6); and also in the *Bhāgavata Purāna* (tr. Burnouf, Paris, 1840–7).

[30] *Ordinances of Manu* (tr. A. C. Burnell, ed. E. W. Hopkins, London, 1891). See ii. 179, iv. 74, viii. 159, and in particular ix. 221–7, where the vices of gambling (defined as that play which is performed by means of things without life) and prize-fighting are denounced as open robbery, and the King is urged to suppress both, and to punish offenders by maiming and banishment. The *Code of Manu*, according to Macdonell (*Skr. Lit.*, 428), 'probably assumed its present state not much later than 200 A.D.' There is good reason, however, to believe that the section ix. 221–7 is not so old, but was 'inserted long after the epic was completed' (Hopkins, ad loc.). In later times the vice of gambling was turned to account, and royal gambling houses were established, where play was legalized (cf. *Nārada*, a code of laws probably compiled *c.* 500 A.D., xvi). The definition of gambling is wide enough to include all games, whether of chance or pure skill.

[31] Careless translators have represented the game as chess. Another passage in the *Mahābhārata* is thus Englished by Protap Chandra Roy (*Mahābhārata*, Calcutta, 1886, iii. 2 = Virāta Parva. 1): 'Hear what I shall do on appearing before King Virāta. Presenting myself as a Brahmana, Kanka by name, skilled in dice and fond of play, I shall become a courtier of that high-souled king. And moving on boards beautiful pawns made of ivory, of blue and yellow and red and white hue, by means of black and red dice, I shall entertain the king.' The same passage was translated by E. W. Hopkins (*Journal Amer. Or. Soc.*, Newhaven, 1889, xiii. 123): 'I shall become a dice-mad, play-loving courtier, and with the bejewelled holders fling out the charming beryl, gold, and ivory dice, dotted black and red.' On reference to the original Sanskrit, it is perfectly clear that there is no term that necessitates chess. The word used for *board* is the perfectly general term *phalaka*.

The use of dice of different colours was usual in the epic period. In the *Harivaṃsa* game, red and black dice were used, and the final throw is described by the term *chāturakhsha* (explained by Nīlakaṇṭ·ha, probably wrongly, as *chāturaṅkankite 'kshe*). In the instance from the *Bālabhārata* about to be cited, the two dice are red and black respectively. Lüders (op. cit., 66) thinks that Bhartrihari's comparison of the two dice to day and night in the verse quoted below (p. 52, n. 2) was suggested by the use of red and black dice. In all these games, the dice will certainly have been of the oblong variety, Skr. *pasaka*.

in his day of the gambling propensities of the Indians. He is writing of the uses of ivory, and continues:[32]

> But by far the most frequent use of ivory is for the manufacture of men for chess and nard. Several of the chessmen are figures of men or animals, a span high and big, or even more. During the game a man stands by, specially to carry the men from one square to the other. When the Indians play at chess or nard, they wager stuffs or precious stones. But it sometimes happens that a player, after losing all his possessions, will wager one of his limbs. For this they set beside the players a small copper vessel over a wood fire, in which is boiled a reddish ointment peculiar to the country, which has the property of healing wounds and stanching the flow of blood. If the man who wagered one of his fingers loses, he cuts off the finger with a dagger, and then plunges his hand in the ointment and cauterizes the wound. Then he returns to the game. If the luck is against him he sacrifices another finger, and sometimes a man who continues to lose will cut off in succession all his fingers, his hand, his fore-arm, his elbow, and other parts of his body. After each amputation he cauterizes the wound with the ointment, which is a curious mixture of ingredients and drugs peculiar to India, of extraordinary effectiveness. The custom of which I have spoken is a notorious fact.

At the present day games of chance are among the most popular of Indian games, and are associated with religious festivals, especially with those in which it is necessary to keep watch the whole night through.[33]

The *ashṭāpada* is also mentioned in an account of a game between Sakuni and Yudhishthira in Amarachandra's *Bālabhārata* (II. v. 10 ff). In this game two dice (respectively red and black) are used, and each player has an ashṭāpada upon which he throws his die.[34] The game was played with pieces (*sāri*), of which half were red and the other half were black. These are moved in obedience to the throws of the dice; the 'clatter' which they make when placed upon the new position is mentioned, and the *sāri* are compared to monarchs, since like these they are set up, moved, taken captive, and released.

It seems clear that we have to do here with a game of the *race-game* class. We may find some confirmation for this conclusion from the comparative study of other Asiatic board-games in which dice are used to define the movements of the men. In India itself there exist a number of examples of games of this class, of which the best known are the games *pachīsī* and *chaupur*, which are played upon a four-armed board.

Games of this type appear to have been practised over the greater part of the world from the earliest times. A wide selection of examples is to be found in Mr. Stewart Culin's books on games.[35] The underlying principle is practically the same in all. The board is arranged so that the divisions or *points* constitute a track along which the men (in Asia commonly called *horses*

[32] See Barbier de Meynard's French version of the *Murūj adh-dhahab*, *Les Prairies d'or*, Paris, 1864, III. xxxiii. 9.

[33] Cf. Weber, *Monatsb.*, 1872, 62. Falkener (258 ff.), quoting from the *Calcutta Review* for 1851, gives a lively picture of the passions aroused by the game of *pachīsī*.

[34] This is a surprising use of the *ashṭāpada*, but Lüders (op. cit., 67) says that the Sanskrit can only mean this. The remainder of the passage, however, clearly requires a board on which the *sāri* move.

[35] Specially in his *Games with Dice*, Philadelphia, 1889; his *Chinese Games with Dice and Dominoes*, Washington, 1889; and his *Chess and Playing Cards*, Washington, 1898.

or *dogs*) are moved in obedience to the throws of the dice or equivalent implements (e.g. staves, shells, seeds, teetotums). The players, who may be two or more in number, are each given a certain number of men whom they have to enter on, move through, and remove from the board in a prescribed manner. Any player can remove, with certain limitations, an opponent's man from the board by playing one of his own men to the point occupied by the former, and the man so removed has to commence again from the beginning. The player who first succeeds in removing all his men from the board after completing his appointed track, wins the game.

Probably the oldest and simplest Asiatic game of this type is the game for two players which we call *backgammon*. It is now played with little

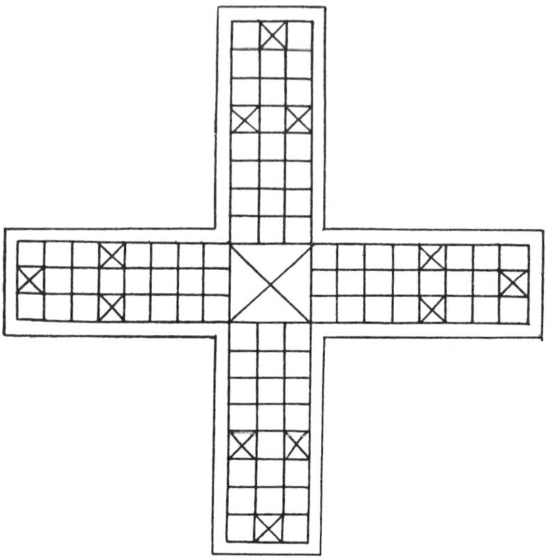

Board for Pachīsī and Chaupur.[38]

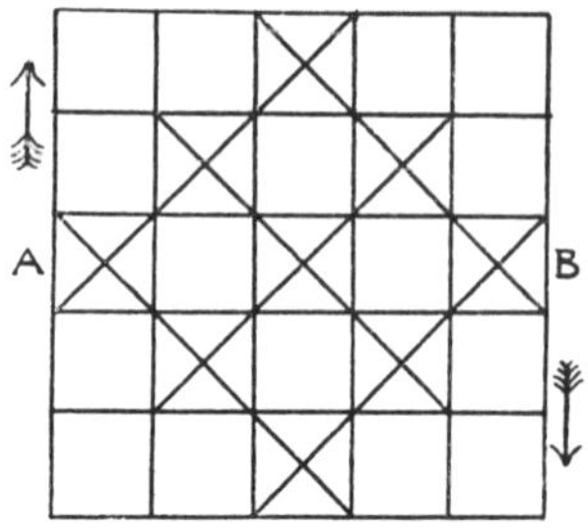

Gavalata Board (Culin, *C. & P. C.*, 851).

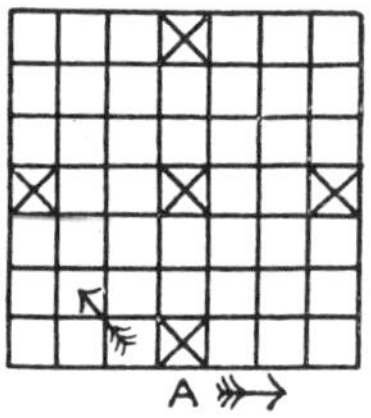

Ashta Kashte Board (Falk., 265).

variety over all Southern Asia, from Syria to Japan. Chinese records mention its introduction from India with the name *t'shu p'u* (= Skr. *chatush-pada*, mod. Indian *chaupur*) as early as 220–65 A.D. Weber[36] has collected a number of references to games of this character from early Indian literature, the earliest being from the *Mahābhāshya*, in a passage in which Patañjali discusses Pāṇini's explanation of the word *ayānayīna*,[37] in which the termination *-ina* has the force of 'to move to'.

It was possibly the desire to frame a game for four players on similar lines

[36] *Ind. Stud.*, xiii. 472–3; and *Monatsb.*, 1872, 564–6.

[37] '*Ayānayīna*: to move to the *ayānaya*. But we do not know what is *aya*, and what is *anaya*. The *aya* moves to the right, the *anaya* to the left. If the squares (*pada*) of the men (*sāri*) going to the right and left are not held by the enemy, it is *ayānaya*. The man which is to move to the *ayānaya* is called *ayānayīna*.' The term *ayānaya* (lit. luck and unluck) was mistaken by both Weber and Macdonell for the name of a game (see Luders, op. cit., 67).

[38] The main difference between these two games consists in the fact that pachīsī is played with cowries instead of dice, and chaupur is played with the oblong dice. The name pachīsī, *twenty-five*, is taken from the value of the highest throw of the cowries (all six cowries mouth downwards). The position of the cross-cut squares differs in different boards; see Hyde, ii. 264, and Culin, *C. & P. C.*, 852–6.

which led to the invention of the four-armed and square boards of which we have several Indian examples. All these boards exhibit a further modification in the special markings that are placed on particular squares. The device is not peculiar to Indian games: it represents an obvious way of adding additional interest to the game which occurred independently to players in many regions. A man which is played to one of these *cross-cut squares* is treated differently from one played to an unmarked point. It may secure the option of a shorter route home, as in the Corean *nyout*. It may secure immunity from capture so long as it occupies that point, as in these Indian games, and indeed in the majority of Asiatic race-games. It may be penalized by being compelled to return to the starting-point again, as in the American games of

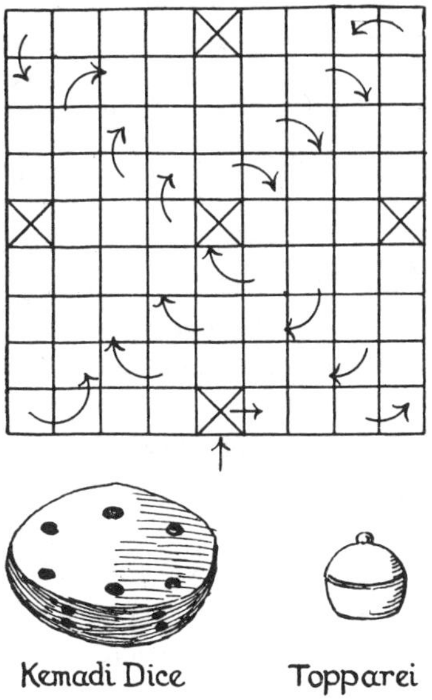

Board, Dice, and Men used in Saturankam (*chaturanga*), (Parker, 695).

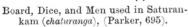

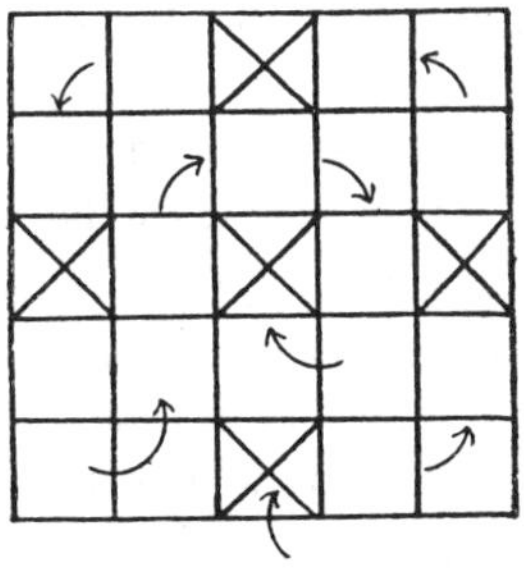

Sīga Board (Parker, 607). The arrows show the direction of the moves. [The same game is in the Museum für Völkerkunde, Berlin, I. c. 5708 a, as *Saduraṅgam.*]

this class. It may be subjected to other penalties, or be given other privileges, as in the various race or promotion games which are invented annually in Europe, America, and elsewhere.

Although specially arranged for four players, these games can easily be adapted to use by two players only, and the Indian games of which I give diagrams are often so used. The Ceylon game *Gavalata* is played by two or four players. When two play, the men enter at A and B respectively, when four, the centre point on each side is the point of entry for one of the players. Each player has one or two cowries instead of men, and four or five cowries are used instead of dice. The men move in the direction of the arrows, and the object is to traverse all the squares to the centre. A player returns an adversary to the starting-point when he plays one of his men to the same point occupied by the adversary, unless it stands on a cross-cut square, or castle. *Sīga,* which Mr. Parker (*Ancient Ceylon,* London, 1909, 607) describes as played in Colombo, is the same game, but men similar to the one shown in the diagram of *saturankam* are used when a proper board (generally of cloth) is employed. Often, however, the game is played upon a board marked for the occasion on the ground, and then the players make use of sticks of distinctive colour or length which they set upright in the square occupied. *Saturankam* and *Ashta kashte* are similar games on boards of 81 and 49 squares respectively. A similar game is probably depicted in the gambling scene Chitupada Sila on the coping of the Stupa of Bharhut, a Buddhist monument illustrative of Buddhist legend and history which is now considered to belong to the 4th c. A. D. Here we have four men squatting in pairs on opposite sides of a board of 6 × 6 squares. Beside the board lie 7 square pieces, 6 in a group and one nearer the board and in front of one of the players. They appear to be rudely engraved with dissimilar patterns, and have been variously identified as dice (or similar implements) or coins. The board is scratched on the ground and shows no cross-cut squares, but a short stick has been set up on one of the squares which—from the analogy of *Sīga*—probably represents a man in course of play.

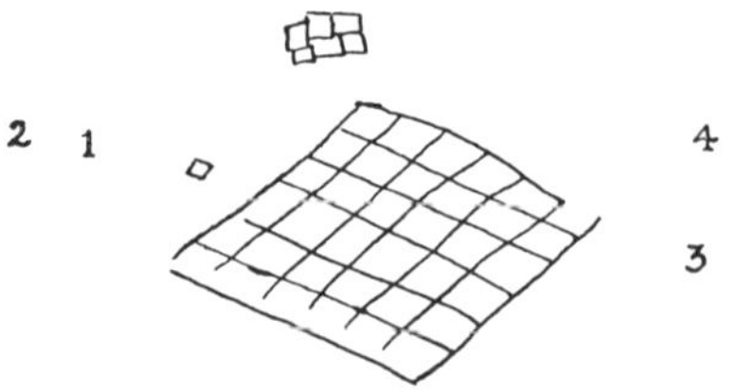

The Bharhut Board.[39] The numbers show the positions of the players.

The existing board-games of this special type in Southern India and Ceylon are all played on boards with an odd number of squares, so that there is a single central square which serves as point of exit for all four players alike. In *Pachīsī* on the other hand, each player has his own point of exit, and there seems no reason why a similar arrangement should not have been tried upon a square board. In this case the square would obviously be one with an even number of points, and the four central points would serve as the four points of exit for the four players.

It is to this more complicated type of race-game that I assign the early Indian game on the ashṭāpada board. I find support for my belief in a peculiarity of the modern Indian chessboard which has no importance for chess and has never been explained in a satisfactory manner. On all native chessboards which I have seen, certain squares are cross-cut precisely as in the games of *Pachīsī* and *Gavalata.* Native books from the time of Nīlakaṇṭ·ha (17th c.) onwards carefully preserve the marked squares, but attempt no explanation of them. They have even survived the chequering of the board. In their complete form the boards contain no less than 16 cross-cut squares—a1, a4, a5, a8, d1, d4, d5, d8, e1, e4, e5, e8, h1, h4, h5, h8. Other boards omit some of these markings, but do not substitute other cross-cut squares for them.

39 A. Cunningham, *Stupa of Bharhut,* 1879, Plate xlv. (Brunet y Bellet, *Ajedrez,* 404, gives a drawing of a carving at Orissa as showing a game. I cannot see that a game is intended at all.)

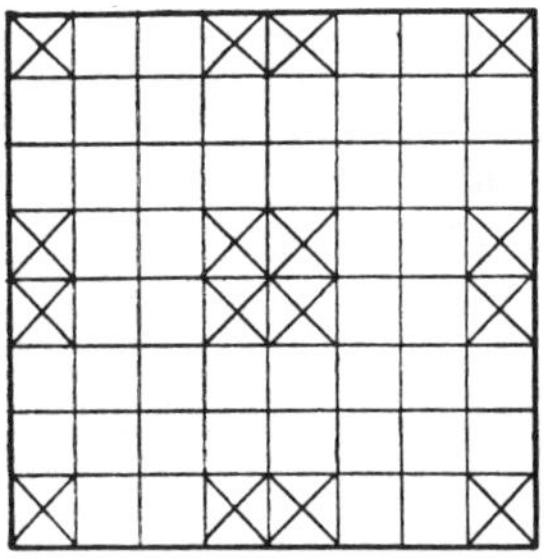

A

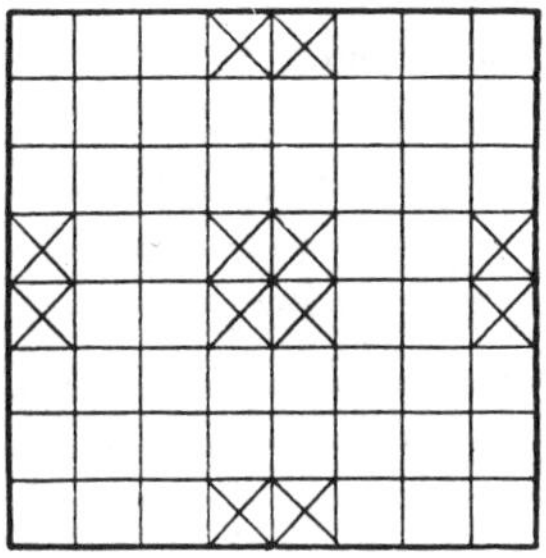

B

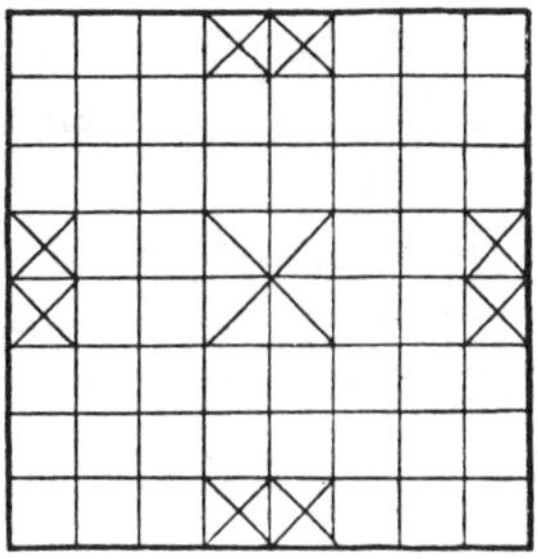

C

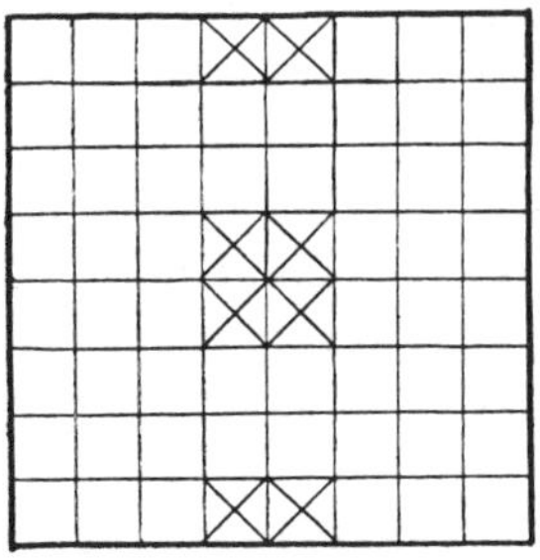

D

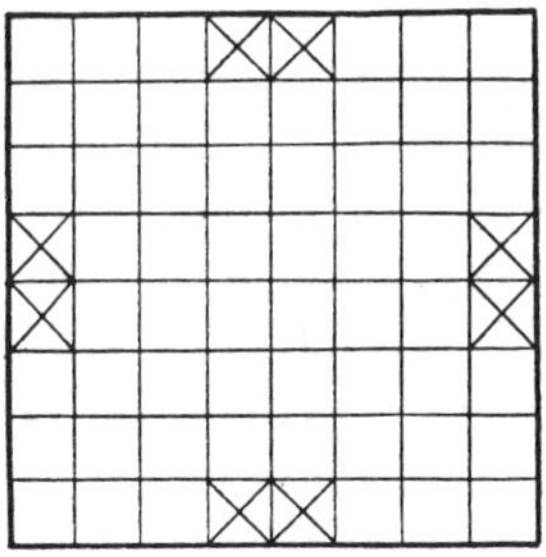

E

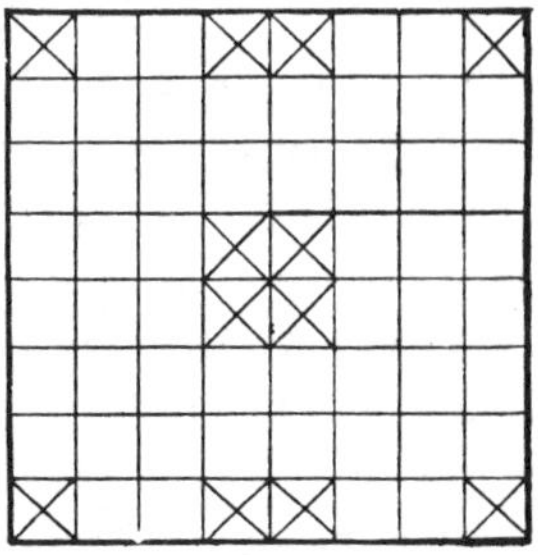

F

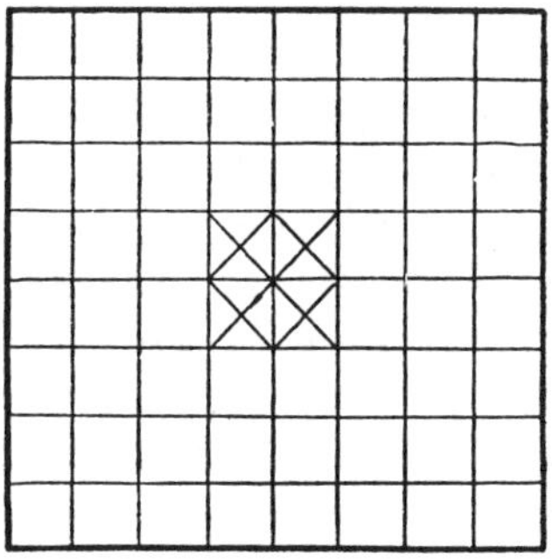

G

THE MARKINGS ON MODERN INDIAN CHESSBOARDS.

A. Hyde, ii. 74; Nīlakaṇṭ·ha; Brit. Mus.; Platt Collection.
B. Weber (v. d. Linde, i. 124, *Bombay*); *Poona*; Platt Collection.
C. Chequered board in Platt Collection.
D. Weber (v. d. Linde, i. 124, *Tanjore*).
E. *Delhi*.
F and G. *Patiala*.

In the chequered boards the markings on the four central squares are not completed.

This peculiarity is not confined to the Indian chessboard. There are markings on the Burmese, Malay, Chinese, and Corean boards, but these do not correspond to the Indian markings, and in some cases are now associated with special features of play. The older Muslim literature of chess makes no reference to the existence of marked squares, but Mr. Falkener possessed a modern Turkish chess cloth in which the squares a4, a5, d1, d8, e1, e8, h4, h5 are marked in one way and d4, d5, e4, e5 in another and more elaborate way.[40]

The explanation of these cross-cut squares is, I believe, to be found in the fact that the Indian chessboard is simply the old ashṭāpada board, and preserves its original features, although their purpose has long been forgotten. The *ashṭāpada* game was, I believe, very similar to the modern *gavalata*. If two players played, each entered his men at opposite sides of the board; if four, then at each edge. The track ran round the outer edge, then round the inner blocks of 36 and 16 squares, and finished in the centre of the board. The cross-cut squares were citadels, or squares on which a man was immune from capture. As will be seen in the following chapter, this hypothesis provides a simple explanation for the curious fact that the Ceylon game of this type is now called *saturankam*, i.e. chaturanga.

The game of chess was invented when some Hindu devised a game of war, and, finding the ashṭāpada board convenient for his purpose, adopted it as his field of battle.[41] The fact that he gave his game a new name, *chaturanga*, shows that his game had no connexion with the game of whose board he availed himself. The meaning of this name is perfectly plain. It is an adjective, compounded from the two words *chatur*, four, and *anga*, member, limb, with the literal meaning *having four limbs*, *four-membered*, *quadripartite*. In this original sense it appears in the *Rigvēda* (X. xcii. 11), in reference to the four-limbed human body, and in the *Satapātha Brahmaṇa* (XII. iii. 2. 2). It also occurs repeatedly in the *Mahābhārata* (which existed in its present form by 500 A.D.), in *Rāmāyaṇa* (which goes back in its oldest form to the 5th c. B.C.), in Kāmandaki's *Nītisāra* (dating from the beginning of the Christian era), and in the *Atharva Veda-Parisiṣṭas* (which are not earlier than 250 A.D.), either in agreement with the word *bala*, army, or used absolutely as a feminine or neuter substantive, in the sense of *army composed of four members*, and *army* generally. It is clear that the word *chaturanga* became the regular epic name for the army at an early date in Sanskrit. Weber states

[40] See Falkener, plate facing 198.

[41] This is the view put forward by E. B. Tylor in his *Anthropology*, London, 1892, 307. Prof. Macdonell (*JRAS.*, 121) argues differently. He thinks it incredible that the ordinary and primitive game of dice should have required a board of sixty-four squares, and from the existence of the term *adhidevana*, and the mention of dicing in addition to ashṭāpada in the *Brahmajālasutta*, he argues that the ashṭāpada game must have been something different, and therefore that 'it is highly improbable that the ashṭāpada was used for anything but some primitive form of chess, played with or without the aid of dice, sometime before the beginning of our era'. F. W. Thomas (*ZDMG.*, liii. 365) goes further, and attributes to Macdonell the assertion that the Indian backgammon was *never* played upon the ashṭāpada.

that the use of the word, as also of the variant *chaturañgin*, is not only common in Sanskrit, but also in Pali.

What was meant by the four members of the Indian army is perfectly plain from the repeated connexion of the word *chaturanga* with chariots, elephants, cavalry, and infantry. In *Rāmāyana* (I. lxxiv. 4), in *Mahābhārata* (III. 1504. 4), and in *Amarakoṣa* (III. 8. 21), the army is expressly called *hasty-ashwa-rat·ha-padātam,* the total or aggregate of elephants, horses, chariots, and foot-soldiers. Macdonell (op. cit., 118) notes that this was the regular

Prof. Macdonell overlooks that (*a*) there is no necessity for a board at all in the ordinary game of dice: the board-game of the race type is something very different; (*b*) there is no necessity to suppose that the early Indians only possessed one form of race-game. Lüders (op. cit., 67) regards the ashṭāpada game as a variant, and possibly the original of our backgammon, and finds Macdonell's view extremely improbable.

An interesting use of an 8×8 board for what appears to be a Buddhist promotion-game has been discovered by Culin (*C. & P. C.*, 821) in a diagram which Schlagintwert (*Buddhism in Thibet*) gives from a great roll of divinatory diagrams. In this board the 2nd, 4th, 6th, and 8th rows are occupied by figures of religious emblems. The figure on a8 also covers a7

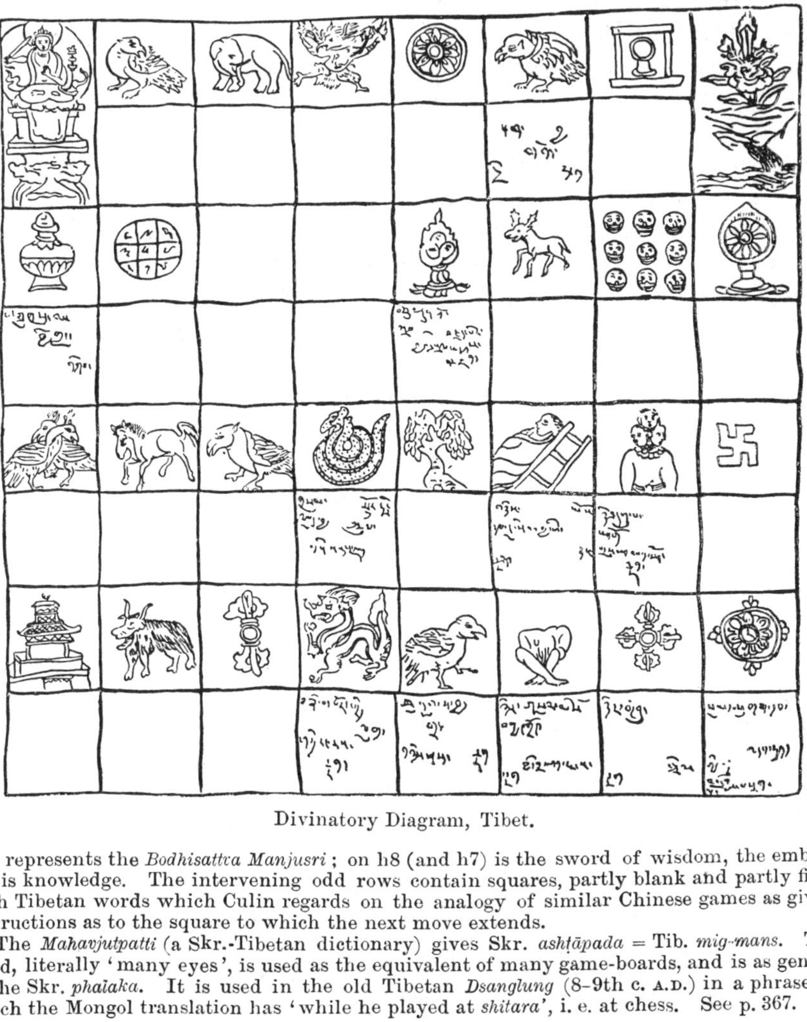

Divinatory Diagram, Tibet.

and represents the *Bodhisattva Manjusri*; on h8 (and h7) is the sword of wisdom, the emblem of his knowledge. The intervening odd rows contain squares, partly blank and partly filled with Tibetan words which Culin regards on the analogy of similar Chinese games as giving instructions as to the square to which the next move extends.

The *Mahavjutpatti* (a Skr.-Tibetan dictionary) gives Skr. *ashṭāpada* = Tib. *mig-mans*. This word, literally 'many eyes', is used as the equivalent of many game-boards, and is as general as the Skr. *phalaka*. It is used in the old Tibetan *Dsanglung* (8–9th c. A.D.) in a phrase for which the Mongol translation has 'while he played at *shitara*', i. e. at chess. See p. 367.

composition of the complete Indian army at least as early as the 4th c. B.C., for the Greek accounts of the invasion of N.W. India by Alexander, in 326 B.C., state that the army of Pauras consisted of 30,000 infantry, 4,000 cavalry, 200 elephants, and 300 chariots. The Greek historian Megasthenes, who spent some time at the court of Pāṭaliputra (Patna) about 300 B.C., when speaking of the military administration of the Indian state, says that there were six departments responsible for the management of the elephants, cavalry, chariots, infantry, baggage, and boats.[42] The *Code of Manu* (vii. 185) also speaks of an army of six parts, to which the scholiast Kullūka Bhaṭṭa (16th–17th c.) adds that the six parts are *hasty-ashwa-rat'ha-padāti-senapāti-karmakara*, or elephants, horses, chariots, foot-soldiers, general, and camp-followers, i. e. the regular army with its commander and that motley following that always attends an Indian army on its march, and yet adds no fighting-strength to it on the day of battle.[43] The *Nītisāra* of Kāmandaki, 'a work of policy dating probably from the early centuries of our era' (Macdonell, *JRAS.*, 118), contains an important and instructive chapter (ch. xix) of 62 slokas, which specially treats of the *chaturangabala*, or army. The chapter states that the army is composed of elephants, chariots, horse, and infantry; it discusses the ground most suitable for the evolutions of each of these members; it estimates a horseman as equal to three foot-soldiers, and the elephant and chariot as each equal to five horsemen. It suggests several arrangements as suitable for use in war, e.g., infantry, horse, chariots, elephants; elephants, horse, chariots, infantry; the horse in the centre, the chariots next, and the elephants on the wings.[44]

We are, therefore, entitled to conclude that the fourfold division of the Indian army into chariots, cavalry, elephants, and infantry, was a fact well recognized already before the commencement of our era.[45]

The same four elements—chariots, horse, elephants, foot-soldiers—appear as four out of the six different types of force in the board-game *chaturanga*. The remaining types prefigure individuals, not types of military force. The presence of the King needs no justification. The addition of the Minister or Vizier is in complete agreement with Oriental custom, and the *Code of Manu* (vii. 65) lays stress upon the dependence of the army on him. The

[42] Megasthenes' statement that there were six departments responsible for the Indian army has led to some misconception. It has led some chess writers who had no special knowledge of Sanskrit to explain the *chatur* of chaturanga as referring to four *players*. Similar misconceptions are to be met with in modern Urdū works; thus Durgāprasāda (*Risāla i shaṭranj*, Benares, 1885) explains the *chatur* as meaning four kinds of piece subordinate to the King and Vizier, or four different kinds of move.

[43] An earlier commentator, Medhātithi (*c.* 1000), replaces the *general* by *treasure*. According to Monier Williams, *Indian Wisdom* (London, 2nd ed., 1875, 264), the word *chaturanga* itself occurs in the *Code of Manu* in the sense of army.

[44] Weber, *Monatsb.*, 1873, 703; and v. d. Linde, i. 76.

[45] Forbes (11) asserts that the four members were anciently horse, elephants, infantry, and *boats*. There is, however, no trace of any evidence in Sanskrit literature to support this statement, and he can only have obtained it from the fact that the four-handed chess described in the *Tithyāditattvam* substitutes the boat for the chariot, and his belief that this account went back to the *Bhavishya Purāṇa*. But even if it did, it would not establish his contention, for the references to the army in the *Mahābhārata* and *Rāmāyana* are older than any *Purāṇa*, and these have the chariot already.

self-consistency of the nomenclature and the exactness with which it reproduces the composition of the Indian army afford the strongest grounds for regarding chess as a conscious and deliberate attempt to represent Indian warfare in a game. That chess is a war-game is a commonplace of Indian, Muslim, and Chinese writers.

But the parallelism does not end with the name of the game and the chessmen. It extends to the termination of the play. The immediate object of warfare is the overthrow of the enemy, and in early times this object was secured with equal certainty either by the capture or death of the opposing monarch, or by the annihilation of his army. These are exactly reproduced by the two methods of winning in early chess—the checkmate and the baring of the opponent's King.

It would be unreasonable to assume that the attempt to carry out the idea of arranging a war-game between Indian armies upon the ashṭāpada was immediately successful in producing the game as it appears in the oldest records, or even a workable game. But the comparative evidence of the Indian and non-Indian forms of chess shows that the period of experiment was practically past before the game had spread from its earliest centre, and that the moves, method of play, and rules were broadly settled as we know them in the oldest records. Still, one or two of the points of difficulty in the development of the game must be briefly considered.

1. *The number of players.* I have already suggested that the use of square boards for race-games may have resulted from the desire to give the track a fourfold symmetry which would allow of four players playing at one time. We have, however, seen that the ashṭāpada was frequently used by two players only, so that we cannot assume that a square board necessarily suggested a game for four players. Moreover, the race-game and the war-game are not really similar. The former is a one-dimensional game, since it only requires a track; the latter is a two-dimensional game and needs a surface.

We shall see that by the year 1000 there were Indian varieties of chess in existence both for two and for four players. In each variety the four elements of the *chaturaṅgabala* are completely represented. In the two-handed game the King and his Minister are added, in the four-handed game the King only. The advocate for the priority of the four-handed chess might argue that its representation presents a closer parallel to the Indian army than does the chess for two players. He could also point to the fact that Indian policy has always had an eye on a warfare in which four kings were concerned, to wit, the aggressor, his foe, the neutral, and the one called the 'middlemost'.[46] But I do not think that either argument carries much weight. I have already expressed the opinion that the presence of the Minister in a war-game can be justified from Sanskrit discussions of his functions. And this philosophical view of warfare as involving four Kings can only be looked upon as a generalization, for it is obvious that the aggressor and his foe would be quite capable of conducting a war without the intervention of the

[46] Cf. Jacobi, *ZDMG.*, l. 233, who cites Kāmandaki (vii. 20), and Macdonell (*JRAS.*, 140).

other two monarchs. So far as Indian evidence goes, I do not think that it is decisive for or against the priority of either form of chess, though the probabilities are stronger for the priority of the two-handed game. On the other hand the comparative evidence of the non-Indian games tells strongly in favour of the original game of chaturanga having been for two players. This conclusion seems to me also the more natural one. The development of a four-handed game may have been helped by considerations like the above: the analogy of the development of four-handed race-games from the simpler two-handed variety supplies a more probable reason for its appearance.

2. *The arrangement of the forces.* Kāmandaki's treatise shows us that the Indians paid considerable attention to the theoretical arrangement of an Indian army on the battle-field. The problem how best to arrange the elements on the ashṭāpada was a far simpler one, since all disturbing factors were eliminated. The advantages of a symmetrical arrangement must have been obvious from the first, and we may explain the duplication of the chariot, horse, and elephant, and the eight foot-soldiers in this way. The larger number of the last named is explained by the fact that the infantry is numerically the largest part of the army. The positions of the King and his Minister on the two central squares of the first row, and of the Foot-soldiers on the eight squares of the second row, follow so naturally that I think they must have been so from the commencement. But there is no obvious reason why the remaining pieces should be arranged in any particular way, and the existing arrangement, a1 Chariot, b1 Horse, c1 Elephant, was probably only arrived at after experiment. The position of the Horse (b1, g1) is so invariable in all forms of chess, that it must have been fixed very early. As regards the other pieces, the earlier Indian references show that there was uncertainty until comparatively late in India, and now the Chariot, now the Elephant appears on the corner squares. The comparative evidence of the non-Indian forms of chess points, however, to the arrangement a1, Chariot; b1, Horse; c1, Elephant; d1 and e1, King and Minister; f1, Elephant; g1, Horse; h1, Chariot, as having been the more usual Indian one.

3. *The powers of move.* We have seen from Kāmandaki that the four elements of the Indian army were of very different values. If war was to be represented by a game, it was necessary to discover some means of reproducing this difference of value. This was cleverly achieved by the original idea of giving different moves to the chessmen, so that the freedom or range of the move should suggest roughly the actual method of movement of the original element in war. The general identity of move in the earlier forms of chess the world over shows the skill with which the idea was carried out: the variation in move of the Elephant recorded in early Indian chess, and exhibited to-day in existing Asiatic forms of chess, may be taken as showing that the final result was only obtained after experiment.

4. *The method of play.* All race-games are dice-games, and it is probable that all board-games were in the first instance played by means of dice or other implements of similar import. There is no reason, as far as I can see,

why we should make an exception to this in the case of chess. Previous writers have approached the question with *a priori* arguments. V. d. Linde (i. 79–80) lays stress on the incompatibility of dice and chess, and considers it a dualism that could not be original. V. d. Lasa (1) thought that the greatest probability was in favour of the original game having been a pure game of combination. Macdonell (*JRAS.*, 140) is disposed to take the view that there was a dice-age in the development of chess, as offering a more natural development than that which the opposite view offers. The evidence of the earlier Indian references to chess is purely negative. Dice are nowhere mentioned, but nowhere of necessity excluded from use. It is only at a comparatively late date that we begin to hear of varieties of chess in which the moves were given by the throws of the dice. The four-handed game was a dice-game in its earlier history. The Muslims played their oblong chess on a board of 4 × 16 squares with the help of dice. Even in Europe varieties of dice-chess were not unknown in the 13th c., though it is probable that some of these were of European invention.

But the later Indian references to the two-handed chess, and the comparative evidence of the non-Indian games show that at quite an early period the possibility of playing chess without dice had been discovered, and the resulting improvement of the game had been recognized. The excellence of the game because it depended upon the intellect alone is already praised in the Middle Persian *Chatrang-nāmak*.

With the adoption of a rule of procedure by alternate turns of a single move each, a rule that does not always obtain in Indian dice-games, the game was complete so far as concerns essentials, and players had a workable game of war. Whether its invention may be ascribed to the Buddhist disapproval of bloodshed, which suggested to some enthusiast the possibility of replacing actual warfare by a game, it is impossible to say. It is at least suggestive that we shall find the game first mentioned in India in connexion with a stronghold of Buddhism, and that other early references will be associated with Buddhist regions.

The date when it occurred to some Indian to represent the chaturanga and its evolutions in a game cannot be fixed, though naturally it cannot be earlier than the organization of the army on which it is based. Chess was certainly in existence in the 7th century A.D., and it had already at that time penetrated to Persia. The evidence upon which the same has been asserted of China is unsatisfactory. The silence of Greek writers as to its existence, although after the time of Alexander the Greeks enjoyed an uninterrupted intercourse with India for two centuries, has been claimed by v. d. Linde (i. 78) as evidence for the non-existence of both the game of chess and also the ashṭāpada at that time, and although his conclusion has been disproved as far as the ashṭāpada is concerned, it is probably correct as regards chess. Writers who romance of 'five thousand years ago' and the like are indulging in mere speculation; the real position has been well put by Prof. D. W. Fiske:

'*Before the seventh century of our era, the existence of chess in any land is not demonstrable by a single shred of contemporary or trustworthy documentary evidence. . . . Down to that date it is all impenetrable darkness.'* [47]

The foundations of the modern investigations of early Indian literature for references to chess were laid by Prof. Albrecht Weber (B. 1821, D. 1901) in a series of papers read before the Berlin Royal Academy of Science in 1872–4. Before his attention was directed to the question by v. d. Linde, the only Sanskrit passage known to relate to chess was one which was first given in translation by Sir William Jones (B. 1746, D. 1794) in his essay *On the Indian Game of Chess* (*Asiatic Researches*, London, 1790, ii. 159–65). This gave a description of a four-handed dice-chess, and according to his informant, the Brahman Rādhakant, the Sanskrit text was an extract from the *Bhavishya Purāṇa*. Sir William Jones himself regarded this game as a modification of the primitive two-handed non-dice chess.[48] The exaggerated views current in the early part of the 19th century with regard to the antiquity of Sanskrit literature necessarily led to similar views regarding the age of this four-handed game, and Captain Hiram Cox propounded a new view in his paper *On the Burmha Game of Chess* (*Asiatic Researches*, London, 1801, vii. 486–511) by claiming that this four-handed game was the rudimental game of chess, and that the two-handed game was a modification of it. In the hands of Prof. Duncan Forbes (B. 1798, D. 1868) [49] this opinion was further developed into a complete theory of the development of chess. Briefly stated, the Cox-Forbes theory is this: A primitive four-handed dice-chess was practised in India about 5,000 years ago. As a result of the action of certain rules, or from the difficulty of always securing a full quota of players, the game gradually became a two-handed game. At a later time the civil and religious ordinances against the use of dice led to the abandonment of the dice-character of the game; and finally, by a rearrangement of the pieces, the game of chess as known to the Persians and Muslims came into existence.

In its inception this theory depended solely upon the supposed priority of the evidence for the existence of the four-handed game, and when Weber showed the unsatisfactory nature of the evidence in support of the statement that the Indian text was derived from a *Purāṇa*, scholars abandoned the theory altogether. In any case the 5,000 years of Forbes would have to be reduced greatly in view of the fact that modern scholarship does not place the *Purāṇa* earlier than 500–550 B.C.

We possess three texts of the passage in question,[50] which, however, all appear to go back to the same source, the *Tithyāditattvam* (*Tithitattva*) of Raghunandana, a writer of the late 15th or early 16th century. All are written

[47] *The Nation*, New York, June 7, 1900, p. 436.

[48] He states in this essay 'that this game is mentioned in the oldest law-books—(Where? It is not mentioned in the *Code of Manu*)—and that it was invented by the wife of Rāvan, King of Lankā, in order to amuse him with an image of war, while his metropolis was closely besieged by Rāma, in the second age of the world'.

[49] In a series of articles, *Some Observations on the Origin of Chess*, in the *Illustrated London News*, July 8, 1854—May 12, 1855, which were reprinted as *Observations on the Origin and Progress of Chess*, London, 1855, and as the *History of Chess*, London, 1860.

[50] Viz. the Saharampur edition of Raghunandana's work, *The Institutes of the Hindoo Religion* by Rughoo Nundun, i. 88–9; a Berlin MS. of the same work (Skr. MS. 1177, Chambers, 629,

in the Bengali dialect of Sanskrit in which the remainder of this legal work is composed. Weber claimed that there was nothing to show that the account is not an integral part of Raghunandana's own book. On the other hand, as will be evident from an examination of the translation which I give in Chapter III, the text of the passage is defective towards the close, and the verses appear to be disarranged. This looks as if Raghunandana had used an earlier source, though since the three existing texts all show the same lacuna and preserve the same order, we are probably right in regarding the *Tithitattva* as the immediate source of our knowledge of the passage. For the view that the ultimate source is a *Purāṇa*, we have only the bare word of the Brahman Rādhakant.

When Weber wrote his papers, the *Bhavishya Purāṇa* was not accessible to European scholars. Several MSS. are now known to exist in India, and the work has been printed at Bombay (2 vols., 1897), but this edition is of no value for purposes of exact scholarship, as the editors have made extensive additions on their own responsibility. More useful are two MSS. now in the Bodleian Library, Oxford, of which Aufrecht has given good analyses in his *Catalogue of the Sanskrit MSS.* in that library. He makes no mention of any chess passage, and there is no connexion in which it might conceivably occur. Weber had already stated that later works based upon the *Bhavishya Purāṇa*, as the *Bhavishyottara Purāṇa*, contain no chess passage. And the silence of all other Sanskrit works before 600 A.D. makes Rādhakant's assertion improbable in the highest degree.

Another theory of the ancestry of chess has been put forward by Mr. Culin in his *Chess and Playing Cards* (Washington, 1898). He sees in our present games the survivals of magical processes adopted in order to classify according to the four directions objects and events which did not of themselves reveal their proper classification. Dice or some similar agent represent one of the implements of magic employed for the purpose. According to his theory, chess is a game derived from a game of the race type, and the steps of the ascent are (1) two-handed chess; (2) four-handed dice chess (chaturājī); (3) Pachīsī, a four-handed race-game; (4) a two-handed race-game. It is therefore a development of the Cox-Forbes theory, which aims at carrying the pedigree still farther back. Culin's argument is thus stated (op. cit., 858):

> The relation of the game of Chaturanga (i. e. the four-handed dice-chess) to the game of Pachisi is very evident. The board is the square of the arm of the Pachisi cross, and even the castles of the latter appear to be perpetuated in the camps, similarly marked with diagonals on the Chinese chessboard. The arrangement of the men at the corners of the board survives in the Burmese game of chess. The four-sided die is similar to that used in Chausar (i. e. Chaupur). The pieces or men are of the same colours as in Pachisi, and consist of the four sets of men or pawns of the Pachisi game, with the addition of the four distinctive chess pieces, the origin and significance of which remain to be accounted for. By analogy, it may be

ff. 107b to 109b; and the great Sanskrit lexicon of Rādhākānta Deva (not to be confused with Sir William Jones's friend), the *Sabdakalpadruma*, Calcutta, 1743 = A.D. 1821, s. v. *chaturanga*. Apparently from Forbes and Weber's silence this work does not give the source of its quotation.

assumed that the board, if not indeed all boards upon which games are played, stands for the world and its four quarters (or the year and its four seasons), and that the game was itself divinatory.

After stating that students of the history of chess do not now generally accept the Cox-Forbes theory, Mr. Culin continues:

> Apart from this discussion, the relation of chess to an earlier dice-game, such as Pachisi, appears to be evident. The comparative study of games leads to the belief that practically all games as Chess, played upon boards, were preceded by games in which the pieces were animated by dice, cowries or knuckle-bones, or by staves, as in the Korean Nyout, the Egyptian Tab, and many aboriginal American games.

All students of the history of games owe very much to Mr. Culin for his careful investigations into the nature, implements, and rules of existing games. His suggestion that race-games may have originated in magical processes deserves consideration,[51] and there is much to be said for his view that dice-games preceded games of pure combination. But neither hypothesis has as yet been established as fact, and the further step in his argument which deals with the connexion of the war-game chess and the race-game pachīsī is a very weak one. It has yet to be established that pachīsī or chaupur is older than chess.[52] Mr. Culin's argument depends too much upon resemblances which are only superficial, or can be explained equally satisfactorily in other ways. It shows signs of insufficient acquaintance with the known facts of chess history.

The theory that chess is a development of an earlier race-game involves the hypothesis that some reformer changed the whole nomenclature in order to make it self-consistent as a war-game, and secured the agreement of all his contemporaries. I find this hypothesis incredible.

[51] There is also a good deal of evidence pointing to the merels board having been originally a diagram with a magical significance (see Parker, *Anc. Ceylon*, 577–80).

[52] The earliest representation of chaupur is apparently the carving of Sīva and Pārvatī playing the game in the Brahmanical cave temples at Elura. Burgess and Ferguson (*Reports Archaeol. Survey of India*, 1884, iv) place the date of these temples between 579 and 725 A.D.

CHAPTER II

CHESS IN INDIA. I

The earliest references in Subandhu, Bāṇa, &c.—The chess-tours in Rudraṭa.—Position in India *c.* 1000.—Some Arabic references.—Later Indian references.—Nīlakaṇṭ·ha.

ALLUSIONS to chess begin to appear in Sanskrit literature with the seventh century of our era, and a number of passages from works of that period have been discovered which have been held by Sanskrit scholars to contain references to chess. They vary considerably in value, and only one or two are sufficiently definite to convey any information as to the character of the game mentioned. In others, the only foundation for the belief that chess is intended is the use of the term ashṭāpada. Since this may equally well mean the older dice-game on the ashṭāpada board, these allusions cannot be conclusively attributed to the younger game of chess.[1]

The earliest of these references occurs in Subandhu's *Vāsavadattā* (ed. Hall, 284), a prose romance, written according to Macdonell (*Skr. Lit.*, 232) 'quite at the beginning of the seventh century', which tells the popular story of Vāsavadattā, the Princess of Ujjayinī, and Udayana, King of Vatsa. In this work Subandhu thus describes the rainy season:

> The time of the rains played its game with frogs for chessmen (*nayadyūtair*), which, yellow and green in colour, as if mottled with lac, leapt up on the black field (or garden-bed) squares (*koshṭhikā*).

The reference to chess in this passage appears to me to be quite satisfactory, although neither the name of the game nor the chessboard is mentioned. Had the race-game been intended, the men would almost certainly have been called *sāri*: the term *nayadyūtair*, which Thomas translates chessmen, is explained by the commentator as referring to chaturanga, and the comparison of the frogs hopping from plot to plot to the lac-stained chessmen moving from square to square is not inappropriate. From the mention of two colours only we may perhaps infer that Subandhu was thinking of a two-handed form of chess. Quite as interesting is the use of the word *koshṭ·hikā*, a cognate of *koshṭ·hāgāra*, for square. This word, meaning literally *store-house* or *granary*, is generally used in the sense of *house*, and thus presents a complete parallel to the Arabic *bait*, house, and the Italian *casa* (French *case*), house, which are both used in chess in the technical sense of *square of the board*. It has sometimes been suggested that the Sanskrit term was used as a result of the well-known Arabic legend of the reward bestowed upon the inventor of chess,

[1] Compare E. Windisch, *ZDMG.*, lii. 512.

a calculation which is so thoroughly Indian in character that it may be supposed to be much older that the earliest record of it now existing. It is more likely, I think, that the name *koshṭhikā* suggested the calculation of the sum of the grains of wheat than that the calculation suggested the name for the square of the board.

F. W. Thomas was the first to call attention to this passage in the *ZDMG.* (lii. 271). In a later note (ibid., liii. 364) he called attention to the use of the word *varshākāla*, 'time of the rains', or 'the rains as Kāla', and endeavoured to establish the reference to Kāla as a technicality of the game. As his argument is based upon the assumption that the Indian chessboard was already chequered in Subandhu's time, it loses any weight it might otherwise have had. The chessboard has only begun to be chequered in Asia in our own time as the result of European influences. If the reference to Kāla has anything behind it, it is probably nothing more than the old and widely spread commonplace that fate plays its game with men for pieces.[2]

Slightly later than Subandhu is Bāṇa, who lived in the early part of the seventh century. Several possible references to chess have been discovered in his works by Macdonell and Thomas. Macdonell first called attention in the *Athenaeum* (July 24, 1897) to a passage in the *Harshacharita*, 'the earliest attempt at historical romance in Indian literature', in which Bāṇa gives an account of Srīharsha (Harshavardhana), the famous King of Kānyakubja,[3] and supreme ruler of Northern India from 606 to 648 A.D., under whose patronage the work was produced. The passage contains a number of puns, and among others Bāṇa in describing the peace and good order of the realm remarks (Bombay edn., p. 86, l. 11; Kashmir edn., p. 182, l. 1) that

> under this monarch (Srīharsha) . . . only bees (*shatpada*) quarrel in collecting dews (dues); the only feet cut off are those in metre: only *ashṭāpadas* teach the positions of the *chaturanga*.[4]

This reference seems to me particularly clear, and the rhetorical figure (*parisankhyā*) employed is admirably illustrated by the play on the two meanings of the word *chaturanga*. The mention of the name of the game, *chaturanga*, makes it plain that in this passage the word *ashṭāpada* is used in its original sense of a game-board, and not as the name of a game.

[2] A commonplace by no means confined to chess. Bhartrihari (D. 651), in his *Vairāgya-śataka* or *Century of Renunciation* (39), referring to a game of the race type, says: 'Where in some houses was many a one there afterwards stands one, Where again one, there subsequently are many, and then too at the last not even one, Even so throwing day and night like two dice Kāla with Kālī plays, a skilful gamester with the living for pieces.' Similar parallels are to be found in other literatures. Cf. Thomas, in *ZDMG.*, liii. 364; and v. d. Linde, i. 43, for other instances.

Lüders (op. cit., 40–3 and 52–4) has shown that *kālī* is used in the poems in the *Rigveda* and *Atharvaveda* as the name of one of the '*ayas*': but there is apparently no reference to the *ayas* here.

[3] Modern Kanauj, now a ruined city on the banks of the Ganges, about 100 miles due East from Agra. At this time it was a large and prosperous city, and a centre of Buddhist influence. Hiouen Thsang, a Chinese Buddhist traveller who also visited Srīharsha's court, saw there a tooth of the Buddha. Under the Persian name Kanūj, the town is associated by Firdawsī in the *Shāhnāma* with the introduction of chess into Persia under Khusraw I Nushirwan, 531–79 A.D.

[4] See the English translation by Cowell and Thomas, p. 65.

Thomas (*ZDMG.*, lii. 272) has pointed to another passage of a highly figurative character in the same work. In this Bāṇa (Bombay edn., p. 10, ll. 10–12; Kashmir edn., p. 20, ll. 5–8; Eng. trans., p. 6) describes an angry sage as

contracting a frown which, as if the presence of Kāla had been obtained, darkened the *ashṭāpada* of his forehead, and was the crocodile ornament which bedecks the wives of Yama.

The scholiast explains *ashṭāpada* as *chaturangaphalaka*, i.e. the chessboard, but there is nothing in the passage itself to require chess. The simile would be suggested by the resemblance between the deep furrows on the brow of the angry sage, and the dividing lines of the game-board. Thomas suggested an explanation depending on the 'mottled squares of the chessboard': this is of course an anachronism.

Two passages also from Bāṇa's *Kādambarī* have been cited as possibly containing references to chess. In Redding's English version they are thus translated:

dice and chessmen (*sāryaksheshu*) alone left empty squares (p. 6),

and

Chandrapida went away at her departure followed by maidens sent for his amusement by the poetess at Kādambarī's bidding, players on lute and pipe, singers, skilful dice and draught (*ashṭāpada*) players, practised painters and reciters of graceful verses (p. 152).

I do not think that we can accept either of these allusions as relating to chess. The use of the word *sāri* in the earlier passage makes it practically certain that a race-game of the pachīsī type is intended. In the second there is nothing to exclude the possibility that the older *ashṭāpada* game was intended.

Much more certain are the two references from Kashmirian poets of the ninth century which Jacobi gave in the *ZDMG.* in 1896 (l. 227 ff.). The earlier of these occurs in the *Haravijaya* or *Victory of Siva* (xii. 9), an extensive mahākāvya or artificial epic, by Ratnākara, a poet who mentions Bālabrihaspati or Chippata-Jayāpīda, King of Kashmīr, 837–47, as his patron, and whom a later writer, Kalhaṇa (*Rājataraṅginī*, v. 34), states to have been celebrated under Avantivarman, 857–84. The chess passage is worded with the double meaning that was so favourite a device of the later Sanskrit poets. The poet is speaking of Aṭṭahāsa, one of Siva's attendants, and if we read the passage one way it describes him as one

who continually turned the enemy in spite of the latter's four-square force, of his abundance of foot-soldiers, horses, chariots, and elephants, and of his skilled operations with peace (*sandhi*) and war (*vigraha*), into one whom defeat never left (*anashṭa-āpadam*).

When read another way it may be translated—

who turned not into a chessboard (*an-ashṭāpadam*) the enemy who had a four-square (*chaturasra*) form, who abounded in foot-soldiers (*patti*), horses (*ashwa*), chariots (*rat'ha*), and elephants (*dvipa*), and who had the form (*vigraha*) of combination (*sandhi*),

i. e. according to Jacobi (op. cit., 228) and Macdonell (*JRAS.*, 123), of two halves folding together, with reference to the symmetry of the arrangement. There can be no doubt from the mention of the four members along with the *ashṭāpada* that chess is intended, notwithstanding the non-use of the word *chaturanga*. The commentator, Alaka, son of Rājanaka Jayānaka, who probably lived in the 12th c., so understood it, for he explains *ashṭāpada* as *chaturaṅgaphalaka*.

The second passage is from the *Kāvyālaṅkāra*, a work by a slightly later writer, Rudraṭa, who is ascribed to the reign of Saṅkaravarman, 884–903 (adhyaya 6). He is enumerating different kinds of stanzas, composed to imitate the forms of various objects, and speaks (v. 2) of verses which have the shapes of

> wheel, sword, club, bow, spear, trident, and plough, which are to be read according to the chess-board squares (*chaturangapīt·ha*) of the chariot (*rat·ha*), horse (*turaga*), elephant (*gaja*), &c.

1	30	9	20	3	24	11	26
16	19	2	29	10	27	4	23
31	8	17	14	21	6	25	12
18	15	32	7	28	13	22	5

1. Knight's Tour (Rudraṭa).

1	2	3	4	5	6	7	8
16	15	14	13	12	11	10	9
17	18	19	20	21	22	23	24
32	31	30	29	28	27	26	25

2. Rook's Tour (Rudraṭa).

1	3	5	7	9	11	13	15
2	4	6	8	10	12	14	16
17	19	21	23	25	27	29	31
18	20	22	24	26	28	30	32

3. Elephant's Tour (Rudraṭa).

The commentator Nami, who dates his work 1125 Vikr. = 1069 A.D., and who lived in Guzerat, explains *chaturaṅgapiṭha* as *chaturaṅgaphalaka*, and adds the comment 'known to players', and *etc.* as *nara*, by which we are to understand the foot-soldier (*patti*).[5]

Rudraṭa next goes on to give examples of these metrical puzzles, and Jacobi discusses the three chess-puzzles at considerable length. The principle of construction is as follows: certain syllables are placed in the various squares of a half chessboard in such a way that whether the syllables be read straight on as if there were no chessboard, or be read in accordance with the moves of a particular piece the same verse is obtained. The ability to frame such puzzles argues considerable acquaintance with the moves of the chess-pieces, and the metrical conditions of the puzzle add largely to the difficulty of construction.

There is no difficulty in the cases of the *rathapadapātha* (chariot or rook tour) and the *turagapadapātha* (Knight's tour). With the help of the commentator the solutions are easily ascertained. The move of the *Turaga* or Horse is identical with the existing move of the Knight. The *Rat·ha*'s move also is consistent with the existing move of the Rook. Both tours are so constructed that they can easily be extended to cover the whole board. Jacobi (op. cit., 229) notes that the Knight's tour appears to have been very

[5] This last is absurd, for a Pawn's tour is an impossibility. Perhaps a King's tour was intended.

popular, since the commentator Nami gives a sloka which names the squares of the chessboard by *akshara ka* to *sa*.

The *gajapadapātha*, or Elephant's tour, presents considerable difficulty. In the first place a complete tour is impossible of construction with the move ordinarily associated with the Elephant (Bishop) in early chess. We have accordingly to do here with an unusual move. If we examine the commentator's solution, exhibited in diagram 3 above, we see that it consists of two halves, each occupying two lines of the board, that the two halves are precisely the same, and that they are connected by a move from h7 to a6, right across the board. Jacobi treated the diagram as containing two separate solutions, each being an Elephant's tour upon two lines of the board, and ignored the abnormal leap that apparently connects them as inconsistent with any move ever used in any ordinary game of chess. He then shows that the moves in these two tours are consistent with a fivefold move which al-Bērūnī records as in use in the Punjab in his time, which is still the Elephant's move in Burmese and Siamese chess, and which occurs in Japanese chess as the move of the differently named piece which occupies the same initial position as the Elephant in most varieties of chess. This move was one to the four diagonally adjacent squares and to the square immediately in front; see diagram 3 on p. 59. Jacobi's explanation is, however, met by the obvious objection that such a move can easily be extended to cover the half board without the necessity to use an abnormal leap, and it is necessary to explain why it happened that Rudraṭa did not complete his tour in an orderly way when apparently possible, before we can accept the explanation. The fivefold move only admits one possible chess solution which is distinct from a Rook's tour, viz. that of the diagram on this page, where the lower rows repeat the tour of the upper rows in the reverse direction. Rudraṭa's problem, however, is not solely or even in the first case a chess one, but is governed by difficult metrical conditions—the syllables must give the same reading whether read as written or read in accordance with the chess rules. A brief examination of the diagram on this page shows that the tour there described allows the use of only two different syllables in the third and fourth lines; thus *aababba, abbbabaa*. The composer has to replace *a* and *b* by two syllables which will afford an approach to a meaning when arranged according to this sequence. Such a task approaches sufficiently near to impossibility to justify the abandonment of the chess condition in part; the composer has carried out a task of quite sufficient difficulty in providing two different metrical solutions for the tour over the two lines.[6]

1	3	5	7	9	11	13	15
2	4	6	8	10	12	14	16
31	29	27	25	23	21	19	17
32	30	28	26	24	22	20	18

Elephant's Tour

A still later allusion to chess occurs, as Weber pointed out,[7] in Halāyudha's

6 See Jacobi (op. cit.). Rudraṭa's tour would also be satisfied by the move of either King or Queen in modern European chess, but in neither case would the metrical conditions have presented any serious difficulty. Obviously it would only have been necessary to repeat the two lower lines of the Rook's tour.

7 Weber, *Ind. Stud.*, viii. 193, 202, 230; and *Monatsb.*, 1872, 60.

commentary on Piṅgala's *Chandaḥsutra*, which belongs to the end of the tenth century. Halāyudha is discussing the form of certain metres, and incidentally instructs the reader to

> draw a table of 64 squares (*koshṭhāgara*) as in the game of *chaturanga*.

These passages include all the known references to chess in Indian literature prior to the year 1000. We cannot claim that they establish much beyond the existence of the game, or that we have travelled far from the 'impenetrable darkness' of the earlier period. We can, perhaps, form some opinion of the spread and popularity of the game in India from these allusions. We find chess specially connected with the North-West of India, and the upper basin of the Ganges; we find it sufficiently well known in the 7th c. in this region for it to furnish comparisons to the poets and romancers of the time, and so well known in Kashmīr in the 9th c. that not only did poets employ similes derived from its special features, but that the ingenious also devised complicated and difficult puzzles which depended for their solution upon a practical knowledge of chess. The commentator on these puzzles shows that in the 11th c. the game was known in Guzerat, so that by that time we can safely assert that a knowledge of the game was common to all Northern India. The same century may have seen chess practised in the Deccan, if Dr. Bühler's statement that the Mānasollāsa of the Ṣālukya (Solanki) Prince Someṣvara mentions chess among his recreations can be proved to be accurately translated.[8] It is not clear whether chess had reached the South of the peninsula in the year 900, for the Arabic traveller, Abū Zaid as-Sīrāfī,[9] when describing the gambling habits of the inhabitants of the coast opposite Ceylon, only alludes to nard and cock-fighting among their recreations. If, however, the date assigned to the Sinhalese commentator to the *Brahma-jāla Sutta* is correct, chess cannot have been much later in reaching the South of India and Ceylon.

The oldest foreign references to the practice of chess in India occur in Arabic works. Two of these are of great importance, for in place of the usual Arabic legends of the invention of chess which will be discussed in a later chapter, they give us more or less detailed accounts of the game as it was played in India at the time these works were compiled.

The earlier of these is a short note which probably formed part of the lost chess work of the Arabic master al-ʿAdlī, who was at the height of his fame about 840 A.D. The note is preserved in two later MSS. based in part upon al-ʿAdlī's work, of which I have made great use in my chapters on the Muslim chess. In AH (f 24a = C f 33a) the note concludes the section on derivative games which is introduced by the rubric 'Al-ʿAdlī has said', which throughout the MS. precedes extracts from this writer. In H (f 20)[10] the

[8] Dr. G. Bühler, Allahabad, Mar. 26, 1874; in *Monatsb.*, 1875, 280–3.

[9] Quoted by Renaud, *Relation des Voyages*; see *Qst.*, 259, n. 1.

[10] See below, ch. x, for fuller particulars about these MSS. Both AH and H are compilations from the works of al-ʿAdlī and aṣ-Ṣūlī, but each is completely independent of the other.

note is given in a much condensed form, but again concludes the same section from al-'Adlī's book. The passage in AH runs as follows:

And this form is the form of chess which the Persians took from the Indians, and which we took from the Persians. The Persians altered some of the rules, as is agreed. It is universally acknowledged that three things were produced from India, in which no other country anticipated it, and the like of which existed nowhere else: the book *Kalīla wa Dimna*, the nine cyphers with which one can count to infinity, and chess. The Indian claim to Astrology and Medicine is disputed by the Persians and Greeks.

Of the Indian rules of chess, one is observed by the people of Ḥijāz, and is called by them the *Medinese Victory*. If there be with the Kings two pieces, and the King can take a piece, then which ever first takes, so that the other is left with nothing, wins: for the other side will have been left at a particular time destitute of comrades. This is an Indian rule according to which the people of Medina play.

Another Indian rule is that when the King cannot find a square into which to move, and the other King has nothing wherewith to checkmate him, the first has won. But this is not a Persian rule.[11]

Another Indian rule is that the Elephant is placed in the corner, and omits one square in a straight line to jump into the second in a straight line. And this it does in all the squares of the board. Each Elephant has 16 squares, and the company of Elephants can get into all the squares without collision. But in the form of chess which we have taken from the Persians, and which is played now, the Elephants have only half the board, and each Elephant has 8 squares. The number of squares has been reduced because they go slantwise.

An Indian was asked why they put the Elephant in the corner, and replied that the Commander of an army in which there are elephants must, owing to his importance, be given the place of commander of either the right or left wing. The Persians, however, think that he should be put next the King, being required for pursuit or flight. The Rooks, he said, are horses in . . . (a lacuna, after which the writer goes on to praise the horse and falcon, and discusses the relative precedence of the kings of Babylon, India, China). . . . The value of the Indian Elephant is the same as that of the Firzān (counsellor, the mediaeval Queen).

The second account is to be found in al-Bērūnī's *India*. The author, Abū'r-Raiḥān Muḥammad b. Aḥmad al-Bērūnī, was born at Khiva in Khwārizm in 362/973 and lived in Hyrcania on the Southern shores of the Caspian. He died at Ghazna 440/1048. He travelled into India but penetrated no farther than the Punjab, and, besides other works of a historical and chronological character, he wrote *c.* 421/1030 an account of the religion, philosophy, literature, chronology, astronomy, customary laws, and astrology of India. His work is an extremely valuable record by a keen inquirer, but unfortunately he appears to have brought away a rather hazy impression of that variety of chess which was peculiar to India. In this, however, he is no worse than the vast majority of observers even in modern times. He says:[12]

In playing chess they move the Elephant straight on, not to the other sides, one square at a time like the Pawn, and also to the four corners like the Firzān. They say

[11] In H the passage runs thus: 'It is related that it is a rule of the Indian chess that when the two Kings have a piece each in similar positions it is drawn, but if the opponent's King can be bared (Ar. *munfarid*), it is a win. Another rule is that when the King cannot find a square to move into, and the other has nothing wherewith to checkmate him, the confined one wins provided he has nothing else that he can move. This is a rule according to the people of India, but not according to the Persians.'

[12] *Alberuni's India*, ed. by E. Sachau, Arabic text, 1887; English translation, 1888. The chess passage occurs on i. 183–5 of the latter, and follows a reference to nard, in which we

that these five squares—i. e. the one straight forward, and the others at the corners—are the places occupied by the trunk and the four feet of the Elephant.

They play chess, four persons at a time, with a pair of dice. Their arrangement of the figures on the chessboard is the following:

As this kind of chess is not known to us, I shall explain what I know of it. The four persons playing together sit so as to form a square round a chessboard, and throw the two dice in rotation. Of the numbers of the dice the 5 and 6 are not required. Accordingly, if the dice show 5 or 6, the player takes 1 instead of 5, and 4 instead of 6, because the figures of these two numerals are drawn in the following manner—

5			6
1	2	3	4

so as to exhibit a certain likeness of form to the 4 and the 1 in the Indian cyphers.

The name of *King* applies here to the *Firzān* (Minister).

Each number of the dice causes a move of one of the figures. The *One* moves either the *Pawn* or the *King*. Their moves are the same as in the common chess. The King may be taken, but is not required to leave his place.

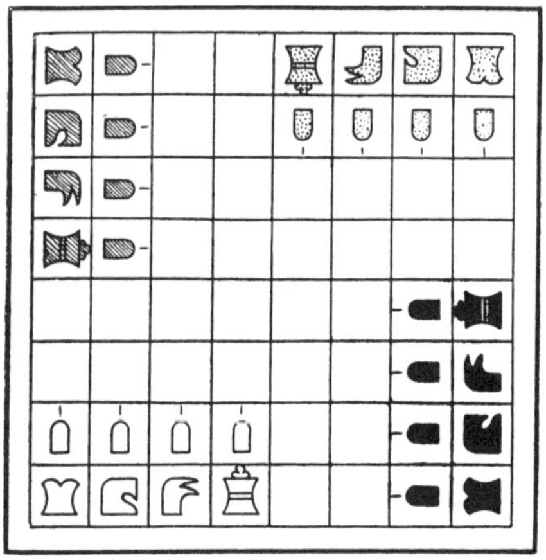

Four-handed chess. After al-Bērūnī.

The *Two* moves the *Rook*. It moves to the third square in the diagonal direction, as the Elephant moves in our chess.

The *Three* moves the *Horse*. Its move is the generally known one to the third square in the oblique direction.

The *Four* moves the *Elephant*. It moves in a straight line, as the Rook does in our chess, unless it be prevented from moving on. If this be the case, as sometimes happens, one of the dice removes the obstacle, and enables it to move on. Its smallest move is one square, its greatest 15 squares, because the dice sometimes show two fours, or two sixes, or a four and a six. In consequence of one of those numbers, the Elephant moves along the whole side on the margin of the chessboard; in consequence of the other number it moves along the other side on the margin of the chessboard, in case there be no impediment in the way. In consequence of these two numbers the Elephant in the course of his move occupies the two ends of the diagonal.

The pieces have certain values, according to which the player gets his share of the stakes; for the pieces are taken and pass into the hands of the player. The value of the King is 5, that of the Elephant 4, of the Horse 3, of the Rook 2, and of the Pawn 1. He who takes a King gets 5, for two Kings he gets 10, for three Kings 15, if the winner is no longer in possession of his own King. But if he has still his own King, and takes all three Kings, he gets 54—a number which represents a progression based on general consent, and not on an algebraic principle.

In the main this is a description of the four-handed dice-chess to which I devote the next chapter. Falkener (139–42) thought that al-Bērūnī only

are told that when two players sat down to nard, a third threw the dice for them. The chess passage had been previously extracted, and v. d. Linde printed it in *Qst.*, 256–9, with a translation by Gildemeister. I have made some slight alterations in Sachau's version in the light of Gildemeister's, and have excided an 'also' which both insert in the first sentence of the second paragraph. The diagram in Sachau's edition has been reversed by mistake in printing.

refers to this game, and that he never saw the two-handed game in India. But Falkener treats al-Bērūnī in a very cavalier manner, going so far as to declare that he can have been no chess-player. On the other hand Sachau, Gildemeister, v. d. Linde, and v. d. Lasa all agree in thinking that al-Bērūnī did see both games in India, and the last two writers think that it is possible to infer from his describing the four-handed game in terms of the ordinary chess, that he regarded the former game as a modification of the latter. This seems to be going too far: al-Bērūnī, writing for Arabic readers, would naturally explain the Indian game by comparing it with the Muslim game that his readers knew. But I think it is quite clear that al-Bērūnī did see the two-handed game in India, firstly from the fact that he gives two descriptions of the Elephant's move; secondly from the curious clause that the name of the King applies also to the Firzān. Four-handed chess is still played in India, and it is usual to use the ordinary set of chessman for the purpose. The two allies share out the men of one colour, and one uses the 'Queen' as

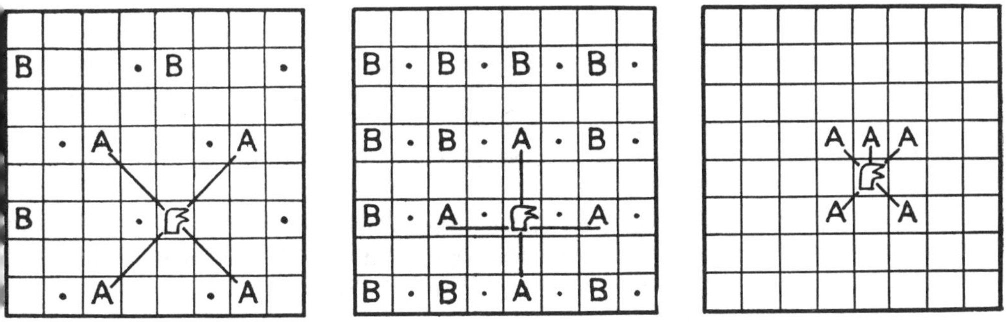

1. Indian Four-handed chess. 2. Indian (al-'Adlī). 3. Indian (al-Bērūnī).

The Elephant's Move in early Indian chess.[13]

a King. I believe that the clause refers to this custom, and that it accordingly presumes the existence of ordinary chessmen and consequently a knowledge of the two-handed game.

The fivefold move of the Elephant has been felt to be a difficulty. Falkener suggested that al-Bērūnī must have obtained it from Japanese chess! But there was no necessity to go so far afield. The move exists in the Burmese and Siamese games, and Rudraṭa's tour raises the presumption that it existed in the Punjab or at least in Kashmīr before al-Bērūnī's visit. Moreover, the al-'Adlī account shows that the move of the Elephant was not fixed in India. We have records of no less than three moves of this piece having been tried in India, and with the discovery of this uncertainty the difficulty that has been felt ought to disappear.

These three moves are exhibited in the diagrams on this page. The first, a diagonal leap, became the widest spread, and it is probable that it is the

[13] A = squares to which the Elephant can move from his present position. B = other squares accessible to him in course of play. The dot shows the squares accessible to the player's other Elephant.

oldest move. It is the only one which passed westwards, and it exists in Chinese chess also. It became again at a later date the ordinary Indian move. Al-Bērūnī records it as existing in the four-handed game, though in connexion with the Rook. The appearance of the other two moves may have been due to a feeling that the original move was not in harmony with the value of the elephants in war. In actual life they were highly esteemed as one of the most potent divisions of the army; on the chessboard it must have soon become evident that the Elephant was the weakest of the major pieces. The obvious remedy for this want of verisimilitude was to increase the power of move of the chess-piece. Al-ʿAdlī records one such attempt. The power is evidently increased, twice as many squares are now accessible to each Elephant, and one or other of the four Elephants on the board can now reach each of the 64 squares; the power is now estimated to be equal to that of the Firzān (counsellor). The attempt which al-Bērūnī records appears to be a later one, and it has proved more enduring. It has the advantage of fitting in with the peculiarly Indian idea that the elephant is a five-limbed animal, which has resulted commonly in the description of the trunk as a hand. The move also gives the piece a higher value which has been estimated as rather more than that of a Knight. This move appears to have been in the main associated with Buddhist centres, and its disappearance from India may be connected with the overthrow of Buddhism there.

Al-ʿAdlī's statement that in India the Elephants occupied the corner squares is the earliest reference to the uncertainty in the position of this piece, to which I have already referred. From a comparison of the existing information the following points become clear.

(1) In the four-handed game the piece with the Rook's move stood next the King, and the piece with the Elephant's move stood in the corner. The piece next the King retained the name of Elephant.

(2) Two authorities (al-ʿAdlī and the late Vaidyanātha, see later) transfer this arrangement of the moves to the ordinary chess, so that the piece with the Rook's move stood next the King, and the piece with the Elephant's move stood in the corner. In these cases the names were also interchanged, and the Elephant stood on a1, &c.

(3) By the 17th c. generally the piece with the Rook's move had been definitely fixed on the corner squares, but changes were introduced in the nomenclature. To-day three main divisions may be made. The original nomenclature, Chariot a1, Horse b1, Elephant c1, is the usual nomenclature in Northern India and in the Maldive Islands. The inverted nomenclature, Elephant a1, Horse b1, Chariot c1, is the rule in the extreme South of India among the Tamils, Telugus, and Kannadis. A new nomenclature, Elephant a1, Horse b1, Camel c1, is widely spread. It has been noted as far North as Delhi, and is the rule over the greater part of Central India and the Deccan.

From al-ʿAdlī we learn that the Indian rules varied in two particulars from those of Baghdad. One of these variations relates to *Stalemate*, a situation without parallel in war, which is a consequence of the limited area of the board, and the method of play by alternate moves. The rules regarding Stalemate have varied all through the history of the game, and this old Indian rule by which the victory is given to the player whose King is stalemated, illogical as it is, reappeared in England from 1600 to about 1800. In India the rule has long been replaced by other conventions.[14]

The other relates to the ending which, following the usage of early English chess, I call *Bare King*. In early chess the player who was robbed of all his men lost the game. Occasionally it happened that at the close of a game both sides were reduced to the King and a single piece, while the player whose turn it was to move could take the enemy's last piece, leaving his own piece *en prise*. Indian—and Medinese—players counted this a win to the first player on the ground that the opponent was first bared. Persian, and Arabic players generally, reckoned such an ending as drawn.

Chess must have received a great stimulus in India as a result both of the Muhammadan invasion and conquest of North-Western India, begun before 750 and completed by 1100, and of the settlement in South-West India of Persian (Parsi) refugees in search of an asylum where they could still practise their Zoroastrian religion. But while the Parsis appear to have adopted the native Indian method of play, the Muslim conquerors brought with them their own game, and have retained it ever since almost entirely free from Indian influence. It is probably due to this Muslim conquest that the references to the ordinary two-handed chess that I have been able to collect for the 11th to 18th centuries are drawn entirely from Central and Southern India.

It is a very remarkable fact that in these Southern works, chess, the two-handed game of pure combination, is no longer called *chaturanga*, but has received a new name. The exact form of this name varies from one authority to another, but in every case the word is a compound of the Skr. *buddhi*, intellect, and all the forms may be translated by the one English name, *the Intellectual Game*.[15] But it is perhaps even more remarkable that the name *chaturanga* appears side by side with the new name of chess as the name of a dice-game. It has generally been assumed that this was a two-handed dice-chess, but this does not seem to have been the case. All the evidence goes to show that this dice-chaturanga was a game closely allied to the original ashṭāpada game, if not that game itself.

I imagine that the explanation of this strange transference of name is as follows. The invention of chess did not interfere with the popularity of the ashṭāpada game, and for a long time the games existed side by side, the race-game preserving its old name, and chess being known as chaturanga. Gradually the term 'ashṭāpada' passed out of use: we have already seen how commentators of the older literature found it necessary to explain ashṭāpada by *chaturangaphalaka*, chessboard. At the same time the original meaning

[14] Cf. my paper *Stalemate*, *BCM.*, 193, 281–9.

[15] I have noted in the older literature the forms *buddhidyuta* and *krīdā buddhibalāṣrita*; and in modern Marathi works the forms *buddhibalakrīḍa* and *buddibalāchā*.

of 'chaturanga' was forgotten and the word was known in colloquial language merely as the name of a game, the game played on the *chaturangaphalaka.* The time then came when—possibly only in Southern India, far from the original home of chess—'chaturanga' was used indifferently for both games played on the chessboard. With the necessity for discrimination between two games so different in character, the name 'chaturanga' became confined to the more popular game, which happened to be the race-game, and a new name had to be found for the less popular game, chess. A name was chosen which admirably described the distinctive feature of chess, its freedom from the sway of chance, and its presentation of a struggle between two minds for the mastery. To-day chess is practically unknown to the natives of Ceylon, but the race-game on the board of 9 × 9 squares is known in Ceylon and Southern India as *Saturankam* or *Chaturanga*.[16]

This Southern Indian use of *chaturanga* as the name of a race-game provides a satisfactory explanation of certain statements by commentators which have hitherto puzzled chess-writers. Thus Govardhana (12th c.) in his *Saptasatī* mentions a poor woman who lives and dies, tormented by the fire of separation, and revives again at a kind look from the eye of the villain (lit. *player*, but the word had obtained the derived sense of *villain* from the unfair play that the gambler so often employed) like a *sāri*. The commentator Ananta (1702 without era, therefore either 1646 or 1780) adds, 'i.e. like a chaturanga-man (*chaturaṅgagūṭikā*, lit. chess-horse), which, as often as it dies, i.e. is placed out of the game, is always again restored by the fall of the dice.' Similarly, the undated commentator to Dhanapāla's *Rishabhapañchāsikā* (*c.* 970 A.D.) explains the obscure passage—'The living beings become like *sāri* on the board (*phalaka*) of life, although torn from the senses (i.e. set in motion by the dice) if they espy you (the point of the board) not sharing in imprisonment, murder and death'—as referring to *chaturanga*. For Dr. Klapp's consequent mistake, see *ZDMG.*, xxxiii. 465, and *Qst.*, 5. The chaturanga of both these scholiasts is, I feel certain, the race-game, not chess.[17]

[16] Parker, op. cit., 586 and 605–7. A drawing of the board and implements of play in *Saturankam* was given on p. 39. The full account of the method of play which is given by Mr. Parker may be summarized thus: Two curious hollow brass four-sided dice (marked 1, 3, 6, 4) called *Kemadi* (Skr. *kshema*, prosperity + *dita*, pp. of $\sqrt{da}$, to give) are used. They are rolled between the palms and then along the table. Each player has two men called *topparei*; if two play, the men are coloured red and black. The middle squares of opposite edges are points of entry (*kaṭṭi*), the central square the point of exit (*tāchi*); the plain squares are termed *kōḍu* in Tamil, *gaeta* in Sinhalese. Each player begins by placing his men in his *kaṭṭi*. They throw the dice in succession; the total of the two throws may be divided in any way to secure suitable moves of the two men, or may be used to move one only. Doublets secure a second throw. A player must move if he can. The cross-cut squares are points of safety; but either player can 'chop' an opponent's man on a plain square by playing to the same square, or to a square beyond. A *chopped* man is removed from the board and can only be entered by a throw of 1 + 1 which enters it on the *kaṭṭi*. In order to enter the *tāchi*, the player must throw the exact number required. It is best to bring up both men together, for the total throw can still be divided at choice. If 1 only be required the player must throw 1 + 1 before he can go out, even though he have only one man to play out; similarly double 3 and double 4 must be thrown to issue from a point 3 or 4 respectively from the *tāchi*. Saduraṅgam, a similar game on a board of 5 by 5 squares, is in the Museum für Völkerkunde, Berlin, as played by both Hindus and Muhammadans (see diagram, p. 39).

[17] Nīlakaṇṭha also refers to this game in his note on the *Harivaṃsa*, quoted on p. 36, n. 31.

The same game is obviously intended in the passage quoted by Weber[18] from a MS. of 1475 Samvat (= 1419 A.D.) of the *Siṅhāsanavātriṅṣika,* in which a gambler discourses at length to King Vikramāditya on the different games that he knows and their special excellencies, among them being *chaturaṃga.*

Chess and this race-game chaturanga appear in sharp contrast in the *Pañchadandachattraprabandha,* a Jaina version of the tales of King Vikramāditya,[19] which contains many Persian words and is not older than the 15th c. In the story the King is set the task of defeating the daughter of a wise woman thrice at play. The King offers her the choice of games, and like Yvorin's daughter in *Huon of Bordeaux,* she prefers not to risk her reputation upon the chances of the dice.

The king said: 'What game will you play?' She answered, 'What are the other games worth, *rāmdhika, nāla, chashi, lahalyā, chaturaṃga-ṣāri, paṣika,* &c.? We will play the intellectual game (*buddhidyuta*).' 'As you wish', said the king. The king ordered a board (*phalaka*) to be brought; the game was arranged on both sides: Prince (*nṛipa*), Counsellor (*mantri*), Elephants (*hasty*), Horse (*aṣva*), Infantry (*padāty*), and Forerunner (*agresara*). They began step by step to play the moves (?). The king decided naturally upon an involved game, and he began to play with the help of his invisible āgnika.[20]

The list of the pieces leaves no doubt as to the identity of *buddhidyuta* with chess. All the original members of the chaturanga are here except the Chariot, whose place is taken by the Forerunner (*agresara*). Weber (op. cit.) and Gildemeister (*Schaakwerld,* 1875, 330) see in the use of this term one of the Persicisms so frequent in the work, and recall the occasional use of the Per. *mubariz,* champion, as an epithet of the Rook in the *Shāhnāma.* But there is no evidence that the Persians ever gave the piece any name except *Rukh,* and this explanation has nothing to recommend it. I think we must regard it as entirely Indian. There has always been a greater variety in the names of the pieces in Indian chess than in the game elsewhere.

We have a very important section on chess at the end of the fifth book (the *Nītimayūkha*) of Bhaṭṭa Nīlakaṇṭ·ha's great encyclopaedia of ritual, law, and politics, the *Bhagavantabhāskara.* This work was written about 1600 or 1700 at the command of Bhagavantadeva, son of Jayasiṅha. The fifth book treats of monarchs, their anointing and consecrating, the whole course of the royal method of life, and the instruments by which the king governs. One of these is the army (*bala*), and in this connexion Nīlakaṇṭ·ha permits himself a digression in which he speaks of the game which depends not on mere material force but on mental powers.[21]

1. After the discussion of the foregoing subject, viz. the deportment of kings, which is most important for princes, Nīlakaṇṭ·ha, the son of Ṣaṃkara, describes the intellectual game (*krīḍā buddhibalāṣritā*).

18 *Ind. Stud.,* iv. 419; cf. *Qst.,* 4.

19 Ed. by Weber, *Märchen von König Vikramāditya,* Berlin, 1877, 13.

20 The dice-game is also mentioned on p. 38 (ed. cit.). He said: 'I am a player ruined by *chaturaṃga,* who dwell in the mountain region, and have lost my wife at play. I will give you up to the Bhilla in the great wood and release my wife.'

21 Weber, *Monatsb.,* 1873, 705–35. Sanskrit text and German translation.

2. We draw eastwards 9 lines and also northwards 9 similar lines upon a piece of cloth, or on a board or on the ground. Thus we obtain the board of 64 squares (*catuḥshashṭipadā*).

3. We mark the corner squares with geese-feet, also the two middle squares in the same lines, also in the centre we mark 4 squares, and we arrange the warring forces of the two armies on the board.

4. On the two centre squares of the last 8 squares stand the King (*rājā*) and Counsellor (*mantrī*), by them the Camels (*ushṭra*), then the two Horses (*vāha*), then the two Elephants (*dantī*). In the next row are placed the 8 Pawns (*patti*). The host on the other side is arranged similarly, and both are ready for battle.

5. The King moves straight and aslant to 8 squares; the Counsellor aslant only; the Camel (*karabha*) moves similarly but it passes over a square in the middle like a chain; the Horse (*vājī*) passes over a square different from the square lying in the straight line into 8 aslant squares. The Elephant (*kuñjarā*) moves straight out to all squares in its file. The Pawn goes straight forwards.

6. It takes always moving obliquely. When it arrives at the last square, it becomes a Counsellor when it is returned thence to the square it occupied previously. If it arrive at the end on a goose-foot it becomes a Counsellor at once, and not only after the return to the former square. Thus the rule is correctly taught according to the regulation.

6*. Dividing itself by non-repetition, and variety, the game is doubly desired. There is a division for the square, and what is placed upon it, and through this the first is doubly desired. (Text corrupt, and meaning doubtful.)

7. Hereupon the two Pawns (*padati*) which stand before the two Counsellors (*sachivā*), and along after them the two Counsellors themselves are to be moved two squares distant. Also another piece which goes one square distant is advanced at the same time by others.

8. A piece standing in the way does not hinder the Horse (*haya*) and Camel (*ushṭra*) from going and coming. The Horse and the rest hinder the Elephant (*gaja*) if they stand before it.

9. The two Pawns (*patti*) which are placed next the back corners of the Counsellor are firm, so also are the two which go in the chain behind the Camel.

10. This army placed in double array which accomplishes the slaughter of the enemy according to the usual arrangement is called *durokhaṣa*.

11. If the Elephant (*dvipa*) is placed in the centre opposite to the opposing King after the removal of his own, it is called *kātīṣa*.

12. No piece should be placed without protection, and it is desirable to protect by a weaker piece. It is not proper to protect another piece rather than the King. The slaying of the King is yet considered proper.

13. Imprisonment is counted as a defeat of the King. If the King is left entirely alone it is reckoned a half-victory, if he is checked 64 times in succession he is also held to be defeated.

14. When a King is imprisoned without standing in check, and no other of his pieces can move, he may slay the piece of the enemy in his vicinity which imprisons him.

15. If a piece remains over in the army of the imprisoned King, the player of it counts up the counter-marks (?); then he adds 2 for himself and doubles the sum. (Meaning not clear.)

16. When he has finished, he numbers the marks, if there are 64 against him, he loses. If he has as many he is equally defeated, if he has more the result is reversed.

Immediately following this text are three Knight's tours, the solutions of which are concealed by syllables written on the chessboard, which, when read in the correct order of the tour, yield a connected text. These tours are not only re-entrant, but also to a certain extent symmetrical, and the verses are all based on the same tour, starting from different squares.[22] The text begins :—

Draw a diagram of 64 squares, write the syllables *siṃ na hi* beginning in the S.W. (top right-hand) corner, and also in the N.E. (bottom left-hand) corner. Afterwards move the Horse by reading these syllables, *ṣri siṃ, hana,* &c.

The solution to the first diagram, ascribed to a king of Sinhaladvīpa (Ceylon), is—

There was a rich host of wise men under king Ṣrī Siṇhaṇa. They knew how to move the Horse into every square, a move at a time.

The second diagram is ascribed to Nīlakaṇṭ·ha's father, Ṣamkara.

Ṣamkara moved the Horse from his square by 63 leaps in the incomparable palace of Prince Rāmeṣa surnamed Nārāyaṇa.

The third diagram is solved by a poem, which concludes :—

Thus again Nīlakaṇṭ·ha moved his Horse from here.

It is accordingly Nīlakaṇṭ·ha's own.

2	XIX	6	15	XXXII	25	28	23
7	14	1	XVIII	5	22	XI	26
XX	3	8	XXXI	16	27	24	29
9	XXX	13	4	XVII	X	21	XII
12	XXI	10	17	IV	XIII	30	IX
XXIX	XXIV	XXVII	XVI	31	VIII	III	20
XXVI	11	XXII	V	18	I	XIV	VII
XXIII	XXVIII	XXV	32	XV	VI	19	II

Knight's Tour (Nīlakaṇṭ·ha).

It has generally been assumed that Nīlakaṇṭ·ha describes a game that has been largely influenced by Persian usages. This view depends mainly upon Weber's clever conjecture that the two technical terms *durokhaṣa* and *kātīṣa* were Sanskrit transliterations of Persian terms — *du-roka-shāh* (two Rooks-King, i. e. the game in which these pieces have their usual positions) and *kaṭ-i-shāh* (the migration of the King, i. e. the game of transposed King and Rook). This, however, is entirely a matter of nomenclature, and I can detect no other evidence of Persian influence. The method of play is unlike that of the Persian *Shaṭranj*, and the rules are throughout essentially Indian. We may account for the two Persian technicalities by ascribing their introduction to Parsi players.

Nīlakaṇṭ·ha's account of chess is on the whole clear and intelligible ; the few obscurities only concern minor points, such as the method of calculating the result in the case of stalemate. The instructions for describing the chessboard are very interesting ; the scratching of the diagram on the ground is contemplated, and the marked squares are carefully defined. Apparently the arrangement of the chessmen is the normal one, and the two Kings are placed upon the same file (see § 11). The want of fixity in the names of the pieces is typically Indian. The name of each piece is constant, but four different names are used for the Elephant, three for the Horse, and two each for the

22 The first two tours were resolved by Weber, *Monatsb.*, 1873, the third by Stenzler (ibid., 1874, 21-6). The three tours are really identical, the second starting at 19 and ending at 18, third starting at 2 and ending at 1. The same tour occurs in the Persian MS. *Sardārnāma* (Oxf. 189).

Camel, Counsellor, and Pawn. I infer from this that Nīlakaṇṭ·ha was accustomed to play with carved pieces which reproduced the actual figures of men and animals. The two players (7) commence the game by each making a double move: Pd4 and Qd3, Pd5 and Qd6. Some players moved a third man on this move, apparently a second Pawn. The initial double step (9) is only allowed to the Pawns on the a, d, and h files; the other Pawns can move only one square at a time. Promotion (6) is connected with the marked squares; the Pawn 'queens' at once on the marked squares a8, d8, e8, h8; but elsewhere it has to make some further move—apparently to the square it had occupied the previous move, but the text is not sufficiently explicit. Checkmate and Perpetual check are wins, Bare King a half win. A King in a position of stalemate is allowed to remove the piece which confines him: the final result of this position apparently varies with circumstances.

Nīlakaṇṭ·ha's rules are important as the earliest statement of the rules of the native chess of Southern India. In some points his rules approximate to rules observed in Malay chess; in others they show a remarkable similarity with the rules associated with the German village of Ströbeck. In common with existing forms of Indian chess (specially the form I call *Parsi chess*) are the restrictions on the double step of the Pawn, and the abnormal method of playing the first move. In contrast are the rules of Pawn promotion.

Slightly later than Nīlakaṇṭ·ha is a work by Vaidyanātha Pāyaguṇḍa, who lived in the first half of the 18th century or later. This work has for title *Chaturaṅgavinoda*, The Game of Chess, but only the last chapter of 44½ slokas treats of the game. The text of the unique MS.[23] is hopelessly corrupt, and Weber could only give a few extracts. It deals with the ordinary two-handed game without dice. Beyond this we only know—

> The Chariots (*ratha, syandana*) occupy the corners, next to them are the Horses (*turaja*), then the Elephants (*dvīpa, nāgendra, nāga*), and in the centre are the King (*rājā, nripa*) and his Counsellor (*mantri*). The 8 Foot-soldiers (*padāti*) stand in front. . . .
> The Chariot leaps diagonally into the third field. . . .
> The Horse goes (?) to the corners of a square standing on 4 squares. . . .
> The Elephant goes in the 4 streets. . . .
> The Counsellor goes one or two or all squares diagonally. . . .
> The King goes to all the squares round about. . . .
> The Pawn goes one field forwards, and takes to both sides. . . .

The special points about this description are: (1) the name *chaturanga* is still used for the ordinary two-handed chess, (2) the original names of the pieces remain, (3) the Chariot and Elephant have interchanged moves, precisely as al-Bērūnī describes in the case of the four-handed game, and (4) the Counsellor's move is approximating to the modern move of the Queen: it is apparently identical with our Bishop's move.

I have now come to modern days, when Europeans were again coming

[23] In private hands in Gujarat. Cf. G. Bühler, *Catalogue of MSS. from Gujarat*, ii. 84. The MS. consists of 59 leaves of 18 lines. The final section was seen by Weber in transcript. See *Monatsb.*, 1874, 24-6.

into direct contact with India. We possess no satisfactory accounts of Indian chess in the descriptions of the early voyages to the East. A few sets of native chess were brought home, and Hyde obtained some from Sheldon and describes them in his *Mandragorias*.[24] Forbes (162–3 and 249–51) quotes from two English volumes of memoirs of the close of the 18th cent. some references to games between Europeans and natives, but the information is too unscientific to be of much value.

[24] Hyde, ii. 123–4. See also Lambe, *Hist. Chess*, London, 1764, 26–32. Hyde's drawings are reproduced below, pp. 88, 89.

CHAPTER III

CHESS IN INDIA. II

The Four-handed Dice-game.—The account in Raghunandana.—The method of play.—The modern four-handed game.

In the present chapter I propose to deal with the history and practice of the four-handed chess of which I have already given an early account from al-Bērūnī's *India*. Considerable reference has been made already to this game in the concluding pages of Chapter I, in connexion with the Cox-Forbes theory of the ancestry of chess, in which it plays an important part. Present opinion, on the other hand, regards the four-handed game as only one of the many modifications of the two-handed chess which have appeared from time to time in Asia. From this point of view, one of the most remarkable features of this variety of chess is its unusual vitality. Al-Bērūnī wrote his description of the game *c.* 1030. The Bengali account which Forbes used is contained in a work written somewhere about 1500. The game—reformed by the abandonment of the dice—is still played in India to-day. Modifications of chess have not as a rule exhibited such powers of life. Special circumstances may give them a certain vogue for a time, but with the removal of these influences the game has generally fallen into complete disuse.

The only clear ancient reference to the present variety that I know in Indian literature occurs in Kalhaṇa's *Rājataraṅgiṇī*, a metrical chronicle of the Kings of Kashmīr, which M. A. Stein, the English translator, dates 1148–9 A.D. The passage[1] runs:—

> The king, though he had taken two kings (*Loṭhana* and *Vigraharāja*), was helpless and perplexed about the attack on the remaining one, just as a player of chess (who has taken two Kings and is perplexed about taking the third).
>
> He had no hidden plan (of game) to give up for its sake (his figures). Yet he did not pay any regard to his antagonists who were taking his horsemen, peons and the rest.

This seems to be a quite satisfactory reference to the highest form of victory possible in this game—*chaturājī*.

We are fortunate in possessing two descriptions of this four-handed game which Sir William Jones and later writers have designated *chaturājī*.[2] The earlier of these—al-Bērūnī's—has been already cited; the later—Raghunan-

[1] Kalhaṇa's *Rājataraṅgiṇī*, tr. M. A. Stein, Westminster, 1900, ii. 234, Bk. viii. v. 2969–70.

[2] Although in the first place probably due to a misconception as to the meaning of the first sloka, the name is convenient, and has been used by Macdonell and others to designate this variety of chess.

dana's—was given in translation by both Sir W. Jones and Forbes. Van der Linde gave in the *Geschichte* (I, *Beil.*, 3–13) the Bengali text and a German version, which Weber had prepared at his suggestion from the three known texts of the ṣlokas in the *Tithitattva*.[3] Weber's German version has served as the basis of the following translation :—

Yudhisthira having heard of the game of *chaturanga* applied to Vyasa for instructions concerning it.

Yudhisthira said—

1. Explain, O supereminent in virtue, the game on the eight times eight board. Tell me, O my master, how the *Chaturājī* may be played.

Vyasa said—

2. On a board of eight squares place the red forces in front, the green to the right, the yellow at the back, and the black to the left.

3. To the left of the King (*rāja*), O Prince, place the Elephant (*gaja*), then the Horse (*aṣwa*), then the Boat (*naukā*), and then four Pawns (*vaṭi*) in front.

4. Opposite place the Boat in the corner, O son of Kunti; the Horse in the second square, the Elephant in the third.

5. And the King in the fourth. In front of each place a Pawn (*vaṭikā*). On throwing 5, play Pawn or King; if 4, the Elephant (*kuñjara*).

6. If 3, the Horse; if 2, then, O Prince, the Boat must move. The King moves one square in every direction.

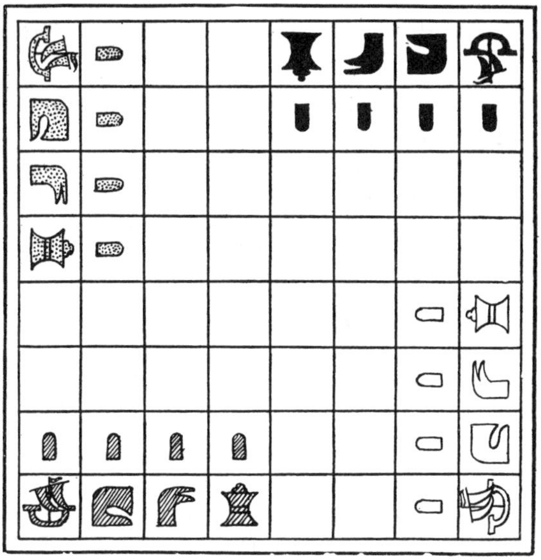

Four-handed chess. After Raghunandana.

7. The Pawn moves the same, only forwards, and takes what happens to be in either angle in advance; the Elephant moves at pleasure in the four cardinal directions.

8. The Horse (*turaṃga*) moves aslant, crossing three squares at a time; the Boat moves aslant two squares at a time, O Yudhisthira.

9. *Sinhāsana*, *Chaturājī*, *Nṛipākṛishṭa*, *Shaṭpada*, *Kākakāshṭha*, *Vṛihannaukā*, *Naukākṛishṭaprachāraka*.

10. The Pawn and Boat take whether they can be taken or not, O Yudhisthira; the King, Elephant, and Horse (*hayaṣ*) take, but avoid being taken themselves.

11. The player should guard his forces with all possible care; the King, O Prince, is the most important of all.

12. The most important may be lost if the weaker are not protected, O son of Kunti. As the King's chief piece is the Elephant, all others must be sacrificed to save it.

13. To enable the King to obtain *Sinhāsana* or *Chaturājī* all other pieces—even the Elephant—should be sacrificed.

[3] See p. 48, n. 50.

I. SINHĀSANA (A throne).

14. If a King enters the square of another King, O Yudhisthira, he is said to have gained a *Sinhāsana.*

15. If he takes the King when he gains *Sinhāsana,* he gains a double stake; otherwise it is a single one.

16. If the King, O Prince, mounts his ally's throne, he gains a *Sinhāsana,* and takes over the command of both armies.

17. If a King, seeking a *Sinhāsana,* moves six squares away, he is exposed to danger although he still seems well protected.

II. CHATURĀJĪ (The four Kings).

18. If you still keep your own King, and take the other Kings, you obtain *Chaturājī.*

19. If your own King slays the others in obtaining *Chaturājī,* you gain a double stake; otherwise it is a single one.

20. If the King slays the other Kings on their own squares, his stakes are fourfold.

21. If, at the same time, *Sinhāsana* and *Chaturājī* are both possible, the latter deserves the preference.

III. NṚIPĀKṚISHṬA (Exchange of Kings).

22. If you have two Kings in your hand, and your own King is still there, the King who is taken by the enemy is taken back again.

23. If you have not the two Kings in your hand although the enemy has the other, the King must kill a King at his own risk.

24. If a King marches out through the *nṛipākṛishṭa,* he must be killed for death or life. There is no rescue afterwards.

IV. SHAṬPADA (The move of six squares).

25. If a Pawn reaches the edge excepting in the corner and the King's square, he assumes the power of the square, and this procedure is called the *Shaṭpada.*

26. If *Chaturājī* and *Shaṭpada* are both obtainable, O Prince, *Chaturājī* naturally has the preference.

27. If the Pawn's *Shaṭpada* is marked with King or Elephant (*hasti*), it cannot assume it.

28. If the Pawn stands through ten (? i.e. for many moves) on the seventh square, the weak forces opposite can be slain at pleasure.

29. O son of Kunti, if the player has three Pawns left, according to Gotama, he cannot take *Shaṭpada.*

30. If, on the contrary, he has beside the Boat only one Pawn, it is called *gāḍhā,* and no square matters to him.

V. KĀKAKĀSHṬHA (A draw).

31. If there are no forces left upon the board it is called *Kākakāshṭha.* So say all the Rākshasas. It is a drawn game.

32. If there be a fifth King created by the *Shaṭpada* of a Pawn, and he is taken, it is a misfortune. He will then slay as he moves the moveable forces. (Meaning doubtful.)

33. If this happens a second time the victor slays the hostile forces.

34. If, O Prince, *Kākakāshṭha* and *Sinhāsana* happen together, the latter preponderates, and no account is taken of the other.

VI. VṚIHANNAUKĀ (The Boat's triumph).

35. If a square is occupied, and on the four squares behind it the four Boats are collected, he who causes this to happen by his Boat obtains all four ships.

36. The gaining of the four Boats is called *Vṛihannaukā.*

VII. NAUKĀKṚISHṬA (The exchange of Boats).

(There is a gap here.)

. . . Never place an Elephant opposite another Elephant.

37. That would be very dangerous. If, however, there is no other square, then, O Prince, Gotama says the Elephant (*hasti*) may be placed opposite the Elephant.

38. If you can take two Elephants (*gaja*), slay that to the left.

This description is rather fuller than that given by al-Bērūnī, but in the main the two accounts appear to be consistent with one another. It is, however, defective towards the end; and the rules that define the circumstances under which the exchange of Boats was permitted are wanting. The last 2½ ṣlokas seem to be out of place, and Weber moved them to the close of the opening portion, following ṣloka 11, while Falkener has attempted a more extensive rearrangement of the poem.[4]

So far as the names, positions, and moves of the pieces, and the interpretation of the throws of the dice go, the two accounts are in agreement, except that the Bengali text substitutes a Boat for the Rook or Chariot, and al-Bērūnī contemplates the use of a cubical die in the place of the oblong die of the poem.[5] The cubical die is, however, only a substitute for the oblong die, since the other throws (the 1 and 6) are made equivalent to two of the throws of the oblong die. The change, of course, disturbs the chances of the game (if a dice-game throughout) by leading to a more frequent use of the King, Pawn and Elephant, with a consequent shortening of the game.

It is probable that the replacement of the Rook or Chariot by the Boat was confined to Bengal, where the same change has been made in the nomenclature of the two-handed game. It is most probably the result of an attempt to discover a meaning for the Muslim chess term *rukh*, which had been introduced into Northern India in consequence of the Muhammadan conquest. The original meaning of the word *rukh* was not generally known either by the Persian or by the Arabic grammarians, and many popular etymologies were current among them. The Hindu in Bengal associated it with the Sanskrit *roka*, a boat or ship, and carved the chess-piece accordingly. Once carved so, it is easy to see how, with the loose nomenclature used in our Indian authorities, it became usual to employ the more ordinary term, *nauka*, for the boat in Bengali.

It will be seen in the sequel that the Boat has replaced the Rook in Russian, Siamese, Annamese, and Javan, probably in most of these cases independently. If this explanation of the origin of this term in Bengali is correct, it is another argument for the late date of the passage in the

4 Falkener's order (pp. 125–8) is ṣlokas 1–8, 10–12, 36b–38, 9, 14–20, 13, 21–25, 27–30, 26, 35, 36, 31–34. His translation, in which he had the assistance of Prof. Bendall, has been of some service in the preparation of my rendering.

5 Long dice—generally of hard wood, two inches or so in length—are still common in India, and are used in the game of chaupur. The general arrangement of the pips is 1 + 6, 2 + 5. Such a die, now called pāsā, was found with the chessmen at Bambra-ka-thūl by Mr. Bellasis (see p. 89). The chaturājī die would presumably have had faces 2 + 5, 3 + 4. I do not know of the existence of any dice with this arrangement in any European collection.

Tithitattva, since it puts the appearance of the Boat at a date subsequent to the Muslim invasion of India.

It is a peculiarity of the game that the King is not obliged to move when attacked, and that the King is liable to capture precisely in the same way that every other piece is liable in the ordinary game. Indeed, the whole game seems to have had for its aim the capture of as many prisoners as possible. Al-Bērūnī tells us that every piece had its definite value, and the division of the stakes was governed by the number and value of the pieces taken. The value of the Pawn is 1, of the Rook (Boat) 2, of the Horse 3, of the Elephant 4, of the King 5. If a player preserved his own King and captured the other three, he obtained 54. Al-Bērūnī was unable to explain the reason for this number and regarded it as a mere convention of the game. But it is the exact value of the other three armies when calculated in accordance with his figures, and thus represents the highest score possible, and it may have been obtained in that way. It then agrees with the poem, where this mode of winning is given as the most profitable. The poem only deals with the stakes realized by the capture of the Kings or the taking of their thrones. The victory appears to be estimated in a different way from that described by al-Bērūnī.

The scale in the poem may be summarized thus :—

NAME.	FORM OF VICTORY.	PRIZE.
Chaturājī .	A King captures 3 Kings on their original squares . . .	Fourfold stake.
	A King captures 3 Kings not all on their original squares	Double stake.
	A player captures 3 Kings not necessarily by his King .	Single stake.
Sinhāsana .	A King captures a King on its original square	Double stake.
	A King occupies the original square of any other King .	Single stake.

The game is played by four players allied in pairs. In the poem red and yellow are allies, green and black. The nature of the alliance does not clearly transpire: it can hardly have been very cordial and sincere, when it was equally profitable to capture the ally's King or an enemy's King, and a necessity for the gain of the most profitable victory. The poem adds a further inducement to treachery in the privilege that the seizure of the throne of the ally's King involved the elimination of the ally, and secured the sole conduct of the two armies.

We do not know for certain how the move circulated. The analogy of other four-handed Indian games, Pachīsī, Chaupur, &c., would require the move to go round in a counter-clockwise direction. From the advice in ṣloka 38 to take the Elephant on the left in preference to that on the right, Forbes argued that the move went in the opposite direction, and *prima facie* his argument seems sound.

When we come to the actual method of play, further difficulties appear. Both accounts speak of the use of dice to determine which of the various men are to be played, but neither account is sufficiently explicit, and while al-Bērūnī speaks of a pair of dice, the poem does not seem to contemplate the use of more than a single die. Nor is it stated anywhere with absolute clearness that the die or dice are to be employed throughout the game, though I think that the continuous use of the dice is implied from al-Bērūnī's curious disquisition on the Elephant's move, and I see nothing in the poem inconsistent with the use of a pair of dice. Neither source again has anything to say as to what was done in cases in which the dice gave impossible moves. At the outset no Elephant can move. With two dice such as al-Bērūnī prescribes, the chances are 2 to 19 on the throws 4, 4 or 6, 6, which can only be met by a move of the Elephant, and 11 to 10 on one of the dice giving a 4 or a 6; with a single die the chances are 1 to 3. Did the player lose his turn, or could he throw again? And when the game had been some time in progress, many throws must have been quite impossible to use. A player loses his Horse, for instance, and the throw of 3 is useless. Did the game as it went on resolve itself more and more into a long and wearisome succession of shakes of the dice-box with moves upon the board at greater and greater intervals, and, if so, what were the elements of vitality that kept the dice-game alive for at least 500 years?

To these questions there is no certain answer possible. The various solutions that have been suggested will be briefly discussed in the Appendix to this chapter. It is not a difficult matter to construct a playable game of chance out of what we know by framing a code of laws to meet all the cases which the two accounts leave uncertain. But it would be a hard matter to prove that any such conjecture had accurately reproduced the original game; while the existing four-handed Indian game affords but little help, for the game is no longer played with dice, and it is to the use of the dice that all the uncertainty is due.

The rules of pawn-promotion (the *shaṭpada*) are rather vague. It is clear that the Pawn could only be promoted at the edge opposite to that from which it started to move, for otherwise there would be no reason for the exact term *shaṭpada* (*six* steps). Promotion is not allowed on the squares originally occupied by King or Elephant (27); these are two of the marginal *marked squares*, and in the ordinary game promotion is facilitated, not prohibited, on these squares. No Pawn can be promoted until a Pawn has been lost (29), and probably also, though not explicitly stated, until the master-piece of the file has been lost. Probably in such a case it is debarred from moving to the 8th rank. Promotion is to the rank of the master-piece of the file (25). But when a player has lost all his superior men save his Boat and one Pawn he may promote this Pawn on any square of the opposite edge to the rank of any piece, King included (30, 32).

The four-handed game would appear to have been played chiefly in Bengal, the North-West Provinces, and the Punjab. Sir William Jones's authority, the Brāhman Rādhakant, told him 'that the Brahmans of Gaur or Bengal were once celebrated for superior skill in the game, and that his father, together with his spiritual preceptor Jagannāth, now living at Tribeni, had instructed two young Brāhmans in all the rules of it, and had them sent to Jayanagar at the request of the late Raja, who had liberally rewarded them.'[6]

According to Raghunandana the four-handed dice-game was chiefly played on festivals like that of the full moon, when it is occasionally incumbent upon the worshippers to keep watch throughout the night. He states that on these occasions it was customary to relieve the tedium of the night with games of dice, and specially with chaturājī. I know of no living authority who has seen this game so played. None of the modern Indian chess-books which I have consulted mention the game as a living variety of chess, and the two which make any reference to it at all have obtained their knowledge of it from European works, and only include it for its historical interest. The Hindu Ram Chandra Pradan, in reply to questions from v. d. Linde in 1874 (v. d. Linde, i. 79), had never heard of this dice-game and declined to believe in its possibility.

On the other hand, a four-handed game of chess played without dice is still played in India. Ram Chandra Pradan told v. d. Linde that he had often seen this non-dice form played. The opposite players were partners, and chessmen of only two colours were used. It has been seen more recently in the Punjab at Naushahra, near Peshawar. Mr. J. Cresswell, who has recorded the fact,[7] was shown the game at the conclusion of an ordinary game of chess which he had been watching. Three of the players were Muhammadans, the fourth a Hindu. They used the ordinary chessmen, dividing each colour between the allied players, and using the *Farzīns* (*Counsellors*, '*Queens*') to supply the places of the two extra Kings required. The partners sat opposite one another, the game was played without dice, and there was no wager on the result, nor any value attached to the prisoners taken. He was informed that the game terminated

(1) when one side succeeded in capturing both of the opposing Kings;

(2) when one side succeeded in capturing all the opponent's men excepting the Kings;

(3) when all four Kings were left bare; in which case the game was drawn.

On this occasion there was no exchange of captured Kings, no attempt to capture the partner's King, and no promotion of Pawns was necessary. In the Autumn of 1909 I met a young Punjabi from Lahore who was in this country for purposes of education. He told me that *shaṭranj* was played in Lahore either as a two-handed or as a four-handed game; the two-handed game was the more usual.

Although these modern authorities speak of the use of the ordinary chessmen of the two-handed game being used, special sets for the four-handed game are not unknown. Mr. Falkener possessed a fine set in two colours,

[6] Or is not Rādhakant here referring to the ordinary two-handed game? It is not quite clear to me from Sir W. Jones's paper that the four-handed game is intended.

[7] See *BCM.*, 1900, 6. The particulars in the text were sent me by Mr. Cresswell, in reply to a series of questions.

in which the Rooks are Boats, and has given a photograph of it in his *Games, &c.* (facing 119).

The modifications in the method of play which Mr. Cresswell describes appear to be natural ones after the removal of the dice and the abandonment of the method of scoring based upon the numerical values attached to the pieces taken. The game has gained in strategy, and the alliance between the partners is now straightforward. There is no longer any point in capturing the partner's King, and each side can devote its entire energies to the task of winning without fear of treachery. Rules for Pawn-promotion probably exist, but from the nature of the game they can only seldom come into operation.

This is the game which in the Cox-Forbes theory is the primitive chess. Forbes discovered the seed from which our chess was to spring in the privilege that a player who gained his partner's throne henceforward secured the sole conduct of the two armies. He considered that this manœuvre was an object of prime importance, and that it would often happen 'that after some 20 or 30 moves, the contest remained to be concluded between two players only'. Moreover, he finds the use of the dice not only alien to the spirit of the game, but forbidden by the rigid law and religion of the Hindus. It is a small step to imagine that *two* players often sat down to chaturājī, and played it from the start without using dice at all. To unite the allied armies of red and yellow along one edge, to move the allied armies of black and green from their respective sides to the other edge, to replace two of the Kings by Viziers, are changes which appeared to Forbes with the advantage of the knowledge of the two-handed game, simple, obvious, and natural.

I feel bound to differ. Quite apart from the historical difficulties narrated in Chapter I, which appear to me to be insuperable, the transformation so glibly described seems to me unnatural, unlikely, and incredible. The value of the manœuvre by which the third and fourth players are eliminated seems exaggerated so long as the moves are dictated by dice, and the possibility of its successful accomplishment is much smaller than Forbes imagined. It will take a King seven moves at least to reach his partner's throne, and he must move right down the front of the two opposing armies, exposed the whole way to attack and possible capture. The probability of seven fives turning up in the first 20 or 30 throws is extremely small. Again, undue weight is laid upon the religious and legal ordinances against the use of dice. Nothing is more certain than the continuous existence of gambling in India from the earliest times, and the two divinities, Siva and Parvati, are often depicted playing a dice-game. The theory of the final transformation I leave, as I believe it condemns itself.

APPENDIX

ATTEMPTS TO RECONSTRUCT THE FOUR-HANDED GAME

Of the two old descriptions of the game, that of al-Bērūnī contains most information as to the practical play, the Bengali poem being mainly concerned with advice to the player as to the considerations which should guide him in making captures or exchanges, and with a description of the different values of the various forms of victory. The rules governing the division of the stakes need not detain us now, except in so far as they suggest aims to be kept in view through the game, since they do not affect the broad question as to how the game was played. Both authorities agree in the initial positions of the forces, and in the moves of the pieces and the interpretation of the throws of the dice.

5 (including 1) K or P moves.
4 (including 6) Elephant (with move of our R) moves.
3 Horse (with move of our Kt) moves.
2 Boat or Rook (with move of Elephant in diagram no. 1, p. 59) moves.

Turning to al-Bērūnī's account, we notice that he speaks of the use of two dice, though he does not explain how they were to be used. It only appears incidentally from his note on the Rook's move that the dice are to be thrown simultaneously, although this would of course be the natural conclusion one would draw in any case. Nor is the method of interpretation of the throws at all clear. There would seem to be five possible ways of using the throws. These are: (1) The sum total of the pips might be taken and interpreted as laid down above. But this does not harmonize with the account of the Rook's move, and of the 21 (or, supposing the two dice are distinguishable the one from the other, 36) combinations possible, 12 (21) give totals of 7 and upwards, and are unintelligible. (2) One die gives the piece to be moved, the other prescribes its move. But this again does not harmonize with the Rook's move, and, besides, both King and Horse have more than six moves open to them in some positions, and the cubical die could not distinguish between more than six. (3) A combination of (1) and (2), which would involve the difficulties of both at the least. (4) Only one of the throws is to be used at the option of the player. This would reduce the number of unintelligible throws, and allow for the exercise of a certain amount of discretion. But again the Rook's move is a difficulty, unless there is a special privilege attached to the throw of doublets. If so, 5 . 1 and 6 . 4, as meaning 5 . 5 and 4 . 4 respectively, would have to be counted as doublets. If both dice could give moves in such cases, this hypothesis satisfies the account of the Rook's maximum move. (5) Both throws are used, and the players may, if the dice both give intelligible moves, play two moves simultaneously. This also satisfies the Rook's move. The solution appears to me to rest between (4) and (5), and the latter of these is the less complicated in working.

The analogy of *Pachīsī* may help to solve some points. In this game a player has considerable liberty with regard to his use of his throws. In the first place he continues to throw and play until he throws one of the three lowest throws of the eight possible. There is accordingly nothing un-Indian about the simultaneous play of two or more moves, and the orderly succession of alternate moves is not an absolute necessity. In the second place, a player may decline to take his throw when it is his turn, or even if he throw, he may decline to play the throw if he would spoil his position by so doing.

Of previous writers, only Forbes and Falkener have attempted to lay down rules for the game, though v. d. Linde experimented with the game, and published the results in the *Schachzeitung* (1874, 33). Forbes, who only contemplated the use of the single die, suggested that a player forfeited his move when the die gave an unintelligible throw, and cited the analogy of English backgammon. This receives some support from the rules of the Arabic dice oblong chess (see Ch. XVI). Falkener considered that the die was only used to determine the first move, and was discarded afterwards, because 'the game is too ingenious to be subject to a chance which would render inoperative the most brilliant conceptions, and by which the worst player, having luck on his side, might defeat the most skilful'. And he surmounted the difficulty of an unintelligible throw occurring at the start, e.g. a 4, by supposing that there are only four openings, and that 'the throws of the die on starting meant one of the principal pieces *or* its pawn, and this seems supported by the Rajah and its Pawn being mentioned together for the first throw, verse 5 (of the poem).' But an examination of the ṣloka, upon which he relies, does not support his interpretation. The throw of 5 moves a King or *a*—not *his*—Pawn. There are also not four, but nine possible opening moves (one of each Pawn, one of the B, two of the Kt, and two of the K), and his argument about the ingenious nature of the game ignores the root-idea of dice-games. It is precisely the possibility that he deprecates that is the fascination in the use of the dice.

I have satisfied myself by trial that a playable game is possible, using two dice throughout, on the basis of allowing either both throws to be used, or only one, at choice. But these are not the only ways of constructing playable games from the material supplied by al-Bērūnī and the Bengali poem.

CHAPTER IV

CHESS IN INDIA. III

The modern games.—Three main varieties of chess played.—Summary of the nomenclatures.—The crosswise arrangement of the Kings.—Hindustani chess.—Parsi chess.—Standard of play.—Specimen games.—Native chessmen.—The problem.

Chess is played at the present time over the whole of India and the adjacent islands. There is, however, no absolute uniformity of rule as in Europe, and native writers tell of three main types of play as existing in the peninsula, to which they give the names of the *Hindustani*, the *Parsi*, and the *Rūmī* chess. Of these the first two appear to be the modern descendants of the original Indian chess, while the third may be traced back to the Muslim game which has been introduced by the Muslim conquerors of Northern India. The rules of this Rūmī chess have been fixed for the last hundred years, and the game seems able to resist the influence of the European moves and rules of play. Neither the Hindustani (North Indian) nor the Parsi (South Indian) game exhibits the same fixity of rule; it is not always easy to classify the type of game described by European observers; both games are very susceptible to the influence of the European chess, and there are also everywhere local peculiarities of rule. The characteristic feature of both games consists in the rules of Pawn promotion. Native observers say that these games are gradually losing ground, and there can be little doubt that in the long run both forms will be replaced by the European chess.

Although it is convenient to collect together in the present chapter the nomenclature of all types of Indian chess, I only propose to deal here with the Hindustani and Parsi games—those which I regard as the modern representatives of the older Indian chess. The Rūmī game will be described later in Ch. XVII, with the other modern forms of the Muslim chess with which it is intimately connected.

Naturally in a land that contains so many different languages as India, the names of the chessmen vary from place to place with language or dialect. The game itself is called *shiṭranj* (*shaṭranj*) in the Muhammadan regions: in the Deccan and Southern India the name, as already stated, is a compound of the word *buddhi*, intellect. The information that I have been able to collect as to the names of the chessmen is exhibited in the following table. For purposes of comparison I include the earlier nomenclature from the passages quoted in the two preceding chapters.

Reference	K	Q	B	Kt	R	P
Primitive chess (*conjectural*)	*rāja*	*mantri*	*hasty*[1]	*ashwa*	*rāṭ-ha*[2]	*padāti*
Ratnākara, c. 850	—	—	dvipa[1]	ashwa	ratha[2]	patti
Rudraṭa, c. 875	—	—	gaja[1]	turaga	ratha[2]	
Pañchadandrachattra-prabandha, c. 1450.	nṛipā	mantri	hasty[1]	ashwa	agresara[4]	padāty
Raghunandana, c. 1500 . .	rāja nripa	—	gaja[1] kuñjara[1] hasty[1]	ashwa turaṃga hayaṣ	nauka[5]	vati vatikā
Nīlakaṇṭ·ha, 1600–1700 . .	rāja	mantri sacivā	ushṭra[3] karabha[3]	vāha vājī haja	danti[1] kuñjarā[1] gaja[1] dvipa[1]	patti padāti
Vaidyānatha, c. 1725. . .	rāja nripa	mantri	dvīpa[1] nāgendra[1] nāga[1]	turaja	raṭha[2] syandana[2]	padāti
Muslim (Hyde), 17th c.[7] .	shāh	wazir	fīl[1]	suara	rukh[2]	piyada
Parsi (Hyde), 17th c. . .	shāh	ferz	hatehi[1]	cahura	ruch[2]	chajer
MOGHUL & Persian, Delhi, 1890[8].	shāh	wazīr farzīn	fīl[1]	asp	rukh[2]	piyāda
Hindi, Delhi, 1890[8] . .	shāh	wazir mantri	unt[3]	ghora	hat-hi[1]	paida paidal
Bengali, Calcutta, 1857[9]	rāja	mantri	gaja[1]	ghora	nauka[5]	piyāda
Bengali, Burdwan, 1909[9a]	raja	mantri daba	gaj[1] pil[1]	ghora aswa	nauka[5]	boray
Hindustani, Benares, 1885.[10]	shāh padshāh	wazir farzīn	fīl[1]	asp ghora	rukh[2] ratha[2] kashti	piyada paidal
ditto, Saharampur, 1887[11]	shāh badshāh	farzīn	fīl[1]	asp	rukh[2]	piyāda
Hindi, Benares, 1884[12] .	padshāh	wazir	pīl[1]	ghora	rukh[2]	piyada
Hindi (Gillay), 1901[13] .	rajah	wazir	voutay[2] ratha[2]	kutherai ashwa	array[1] athi[1]	·pathay
PARSI. Bombay (Himley)	pāssā	wazir	ōt[3]	ghora	hatthi[1] qal'e[6]	pāda
Maldive Is. (Culin) . .	padshah	wazir	fīl[1]	asp ghora	rukh[2] burj[6]	piyada
Bombay (Weber), 1874 .	rāja	mantri	ushthra[3]	ashwa	hasti[1]	padati
MARATHI. Poona, 1893[14]	rāja	wazir	unt[3]	ghora	hat-thi[1]	piyada
Bombay, 1893[15] . . .	rāja	wazir	unt[3]	ghora	hattī[1]	piyada
KANNADI (Gillay), 1901[13]	dorai	munthri prathani	voutai[2] theru[2]	kutherai ashwa	array[1]	pathay
TAMIL / TELUGU (Gillay), 1901[13]	dorai	munthri	voutai[2] ther[2]	kutherai ashwa	array[1]	algo sepoy

[1] Meaning Elephant.

[2] Meaning Chariot. In this connexion the following note, contributed by the Sanskrit scholar H. T. Colebrooke to Hiram Cox's paper *On the Burmha Game of Chess*, is of importance. It exactly describes the position with regard to the replacements of the Rook in India.

'Another sort of Chaturanga, the same with the Persian and the Hindustāni chess, is played by two persons, and without dice. In Bengal, a boat is one of the pieces at this game likewise; but in some parts of India a camel takes the place of the bishop, and an elephant that of the rook; while the Hindus of the Peninsula (I mean those of the Carnátaca above the Gháts) preserve, as I am informed, the chariot among the pieces of the game. I found also in an ancient Treatise of Law, the elephant, horse, and chariot, mentioned as pieces of the game of *Chaturanga*. The substitution of a camel or of a boat, for the chariot, is probably an innovation.'

[3] Meaning Camel.

[4] Meaning Forerunner or Scout.

[5] Meaning Boat or Ship.

[6] Meaning Castle. Of very doubtful authority, and in any case conscious translations from English or French.

[7] Hyde, ii. 87; from Garcias ab Orte as used by the Moors in India.

[8] From Durgāprasāda and Lala Raja Babu.

[9] From Sri Brahmanānda.

[9a] From Mr. G. B. L. Singha (*Chess Amateur*, 1909, 294).

[10] From Syamakiṣora. Parker (*Ancient Ceylon*, 586) gives the colloquial pronunciation in Upper India as shatrĕñ; K. shāh; Q. farthīr; B. fīl; Kt. ghōdā; R. rūkh; P. piyātha or paithal; the accent on shatreñ being on the last syllable, and the final *n* being nasalized. In farthīr, piyātha, and paithal the *th* is pronounced as in *then*.

[11] From Dalchand Bulandshahri.

[12] From Ambikādatta Vyāsa.

[13] Communicated by Mr. K. A. Gillay of Dusserah, in the Deccan.

[14] From Vinayaka Rajarama Tope.

[15] From Mangesa Rāmakrishna Telanga.

The initial arrangement of the men in the Hindustani and Parsi games is exhibited in the accompanying figure. The only difference between this arrangement and the European one consists in the relative positions of the Kings and Ministers (Counsellors, Viziers—our Queens). In the European game both Kings stand on the same file and the white Queen stands on her King's left and the black Queen on her King's right. In the Indian games each Minister stands on the King's *left,* and as a result each Minister faces his opponent's King.[16] This method of arranging the pieces, conveniently termed *crosswise,* is now the rule in all games of chess upon the board of 64 squares that are played in Southern Asia, with the exceptions of Burmese and Rūmī chess. In Turkish chess, Egyptian chess, and these Indian games the Minister stands on the King's *left*: in Persian chess and the Malay games, on the King's *right.* This diversity of plan makes impossible the explanation favoured sometimes that the crosswise arrangement had its origin in considerations of court etiquette which forbad the Minister to stand on a particular side of his sovereign. The most probable explanation is that it is a result of the unchequered nature of the Oriental chessboard, which prevented the growth of conventions which could be defined by reference to the colour of particular squares, as is the case in modern European chess. In their fullest form granting the right of beginning the game to the player of a particular colour, these conventions are quite recent in origin, and are merely matters of convenience to secure uniformity and even conditions of play; they are not essential to chess, and have no real importance for the theory of the game. If the need were felt for similar conventions for the arrangement of the chessmen upon an unchequered board, it is obvious that the arrangement can only be defined in terms of the relative positions of King and Minister, and the crosswise arrangement gives no real or imagined advantage to either side. But the change seems to have been made without remark, and, so far as the evidence goes, it appears to be of quite recent introduction. It was not the rule in Nīlakaṇṭha's account of the Indian chess, and the Persian MS. Y,[17] copied in Delhi in 1612, still shows the European opposite arrangement. The earliest reference that I know to the crosswise arrangement in any country is contained in the passage from Hamilton's *Egyptiaca* (London, 1809) which is quoted later (p. 357).

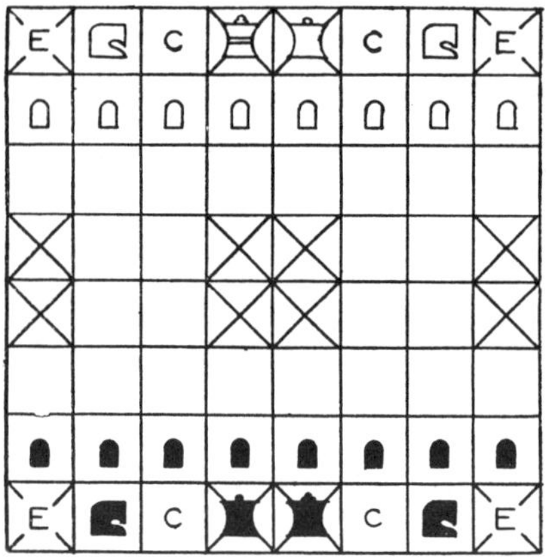

The Modern Indian Chess.
C = Camel ; E = Elephant.

[16] One authority only, Mr. G. B. L. Singha of Ukhara, near Bardhwan in Lower Bengal, puts the Minister on the King's *right.* His account of chess (*Chess Amateur,* 1900, iii. 294, 327, 357 ; iv. 6, 70) differs from all other accounts in many particulars.

[17] See below, p. 179, for particulars about this MS.

In *Hindustani chess* the ordinary moves of the pieces are identical with those of the European pieces occupying the equivalent initial positions. The Rook (elephant, chariot, boat) moves as our Rook, the Horse as our Knight, the Elephant (camel) as our Bishop, and the Vizier (minister) as our Queen. The King (raja, padshah) moves to any of the squares contiguous to the one he is occupying, and in addition he is permitted once in the game, whether he has already moved or not, to leap as a Knight, but this privilege is lost if he be checked before he has availed himself of it. The Pawns move straight forward one square at a time only, and capture in the same way that is the rule in the European game. Singha in his account (which in many ways describes a game that seems more like the *Parsi chess*) adds the information that the King cannot capture on his leap, nor exercise it to cross a square which is commanded by a hostile piece.

A Pawn which arrives at the 8th row receives promotion to the rank of the master-piece of the file, i.e. a Pawn reaching a8 (a1) or h8 (h1) becomes a Rook, reaching b8 (b1) or g8 (g1) a Horse (Kt), reaching c8 (c1) or f8 (f1) an Elephant (B), and reaching d8 (d1) or e8 (e1) a Vizier (Q). The possibilities of promotion are further complicated by the rule that no Pawn may be promoted until the player has lost a piece of the rank that the Pawn must adopt on reaching the eighth row. Before a Pawn can be promoted to an Elephant (B), that particular Elephant which could reach the 'queening' square must have been lost. A player may not have on the board more pieces of any kind than he had at the commencement of the game. Accordingly, we have a further rule that no Pawn on the 7th row can be advanced to the 8th, until its immediate promotion is legally possible. Thus a player with an advanced Pawn on d7 cannot play Pd8 so long as he has a Vizier on the board: if he wishes to 'queen' this Pawn, he must first sacrifice the existing Vizier. During this pause the advanced Pawn enjoys no immunity from capture: it can be taken like any other piece.[18]

The game is played from the commencement by alternate moves, precisely as is the case in the European game.[19]

18 According to Singha every Pawn except the KtP can on obtaining promotion immediately make a move with its new power and even capture an opposing piece, provided (1) it does not give check (*kisti*) on the promotion square, (2) the promotion square is not commanded by an opposing piece. If the KtP is a *sāra* piece (i. e. the only piece left to the player), it can also make this privilege move under the same limitations. He gives the following examples of the move and its limitations:

(1) White, Kf2, Pg3, Ph7; Black, Rc8, Kd7. White plays Ph8 = R, but cannot on this move take the black R 'because the black R commands the 8th row'.

(2) White, Kh2, Pg3, h7; Black, Kd7, Rc6. If Black plays Rh6+, White has a valid reply in Ph8 = R and takes R.

(3) White, Kh2, Pg2, h7; Black, Kd8, Pc7, Rb6. If Black now plays Rh6+, White cannot reply as in the preceding, since Ph8 = R is check.

(4) White, Kh8, Pg7; Black, Kd7, Pb6, Qd1. Black plays Qh5+, and White can play Pg8 = Kt and Kth6 because it is a *sāra* piece.

(5) White Kh8, Pg7; Black, Ke7, Pb6, Qd1. Black plays Qh5+. White cannot now play as in (4), for Pg8 = Kt is check.

This privilege is unknown to all my native authorities for the Hindustani chess, and looks to me to be derived from an indistinct recollection of a special feature of the Parsi chess. The indistinctness of the recollection has made the privilege the exact opposite of what obtains in the Parsi game.

19 Here again Singha is at variance with all other authorities. He says that the game

Three conclusions of a game are recognized—

checkmate, which is identical with the European checkmate: the Urdu term is *māt*.

burd, or half-win, when a player succeeds in capturing all his opponent's superior pieces, whether he leave him any Pawns or not.[20]

bāzī qā'īm, or draw, when both players are left with a single piece. Singha terms this termination *chaturbolla*.

Stalemate is not recognized, and a player is not permitted to make a move which stalemates his opponent.[21] Perpetual check is recognized as a drawn game, but the game must not be abandoned, so says Durgāprasāda, until check has been given 70 times in succession!

The following specimen of Hindustani chess is taken from the Benares work of Syamakiṣora. The Kings are to be placed upon e1 and d8:

White	Black	White	Black	White	Black	White	Black
1 Pe3	Pb6	19 Q × Kt[22]	Q × R	37 Ra8 +	Ke7	55 P × P	Bb4
2 Ktf3	Bb7	20 Ra1	Qb5	38 R × R	B × B	56 Ph6	Bc5
3 Pg3	Pc6	21 Bf1	Qh5	39 R × P	B × Kt	57 Kd2	Bd4
4 Bg2	Pd6	22 Bg2	Pe5	40 K × B	Qd3 +	58 P × B +	K × P
5 Pd3	Pc5	23 Qa3	Kte4	41 Q × Q	P × Q	59 Ph7	Pe3 +
6 Ke2	Pe6	24 Q × P +	Kc7	42 R × P	Ke6	60 Ke1	Kc3
7 Rf1	Kd7	25 Ra6	Pd5	43 Ke1	Pe4	61 Rd6	Pd2 +
8 Kg1	Ktc6	26 Q × P +	Kd7	44 Pc4	Ba5 +	62 Ke2	Kc2
9 Pb3	Rc8	27 Ra7	Rc7	45 Kd1	Pf6	63 Rd3	Kb2
10 Bb2	Kb8	28 Kt × Kt	P × Kt	46 Pc6	Kd6	64 Ph8 = R	Kc2
11 Pa3	Be7	29 Ktd2	Qd1 +	47 Rb7	K × P	65 Ra8	Kb2
12 Pc3	Ktf6	30 Ktf1	Qd5	48 Rb5	Bc3	66 Ra8–a3	Kc2
13 bKtd2	Kta5	31 Ra5	Rc5	49 Ph3	Kd6	67 Rd3–c3 +	Kb2
14 Pb4	P × P	32 P × R	Bd8	50 Ph4	Ke6	68 Ra3–b3 +	Ka2
15 aP × P	Ktc6	33 Qb5 +	Bc6	51 Ph5	Pf5	69 Rb4	Ka1
16 Ra4	Kte5	34 Ra7 +	Bc7	52 Rb6 +	Ke5	70 Ra3m.	
17 Qa1	Kt × P	35 Bh3 +	Kd8	53 Rg6	Pf4		
18 Qa3	Kt × B	36 Qa6	Bd7	54 Pg4	P × P		

The *Parsi chess* differs considerably from the game that I have just described. The moves of the superior pieces are the same, except that the King is allowed to make his single leap as a Knight out of check, and can even capture a hostile piece by it.[23] But the Pawns' moves are quite different.

is commenced by each player in succession making two moves in one turn. This again resembles the Parsi rules. He gives a number of examples of opening play, e. g. (Kings on d1 and e8): I. 1 Pd3 and Pc3, Pe6 and Pd6; 2 Ktd2, Pg6; 3 Pg3, Bg7; 4 Bg2, Ke7; 5 Pe3, Ktf6; 6 gKtf3, Rf8; 7 Rf1, Kg8; 8 Ke2, Pe5; 9 Kg1, &c. II. The Opening *Gangebandi*. 1 Pd4, Pd5; 2 Pe3, Pc6; 3 Pc3, Ktd7; 4 Pf3, Pe6; 5 Pe4, Be7; 6 Bd3, gKtf6; 7 Be3, Qc7; 8 Ktd2, Pb6; &c.

[20] Singha makes no mention of this ending. Since he gives the term *Fakir* as meaning a solitary King, and also gives endings in which one player has no superior piece left, it is clear that it was disregarded in the variety which he describes.

[21] Singha says there is no stalemate 'because it is a draw'. I do not understand what he means. Parker (op. cit.) gives the term *Burad*, i. e. burd, as equivalent to stalemate. In this he is certainly wrong. He gives the other technicalities *kisht*, check; *shāh kō kisht*, check to the King; *Farthī ko kisht*, check to the Queen; *marnā*, to take, lit. kill; *ghar*, or *khāna*, a square of the board, lit. house; *chalnā*, to move.

[22] Or 19 R × aP, Ktc4; 20 Kt × Kt, R × Kt; 21 Qa1, Qc6.

[23] So Lala Raja Babu, and the writer in *CPC.*, 1843, 149–52. Tiruvengadāchārya and Gillay, however, state that the King cannot exercise his power of leaping as a Knight after he has once been checked, and that he cannot take a piece on the leap. This makes the rule identical with the Hindustani rule given above. Another European observer, *CPM.*, 1866, 34,

Each of the four Pawns which stand in front of the King, Vizier, and Rooks, i.e. on the a, d, e, and h files, is allowed the full European initial move, so long as the master-piece of the file, which stands behind the Pawn it is desired to play, has not been moved. The other four Pawns, as in the Hindustani game, can only move one square at a time.[24]

There is also some variation with respect to Pawn-promotion. It is not clear from my authorities that the restriction to promotion of a BP, which I have recorded in the case of the Hindustani game, obtains in the Parsi game. On the other hand, the Pawn which is promoted on the Knights' files is specially privileged. When the player moves the Pawn from the 7th sq. to the 8th, and promotes it to the rank of Horse (Kt), he can, if he choose, on the same move, make a further Knight's move with the newly promoted piece.[25] There are also some local peculiarities with regard to the Pawn promoted on its King's file. According to one European writer (*CPM.*, 1866, 35), the Deccan player was at liberty in this case to select the rank of any piece that he had already lost for the promotion-value of this Pawn. Another observer (*CPC.*, 1843, 150) extends this privilege to a Pawn queening on the Vizier's file also. Tiruveṇgaḍāchārya and Gillay, both native authorities, give the rule as I give it for Hindustani chess.

At the commencement of the game, the player who has the move begins by playing a certain number of moves in succession. In so doing he is not allowed to cross into the opponent's half of the board. The native chess-books generally speak of 4 or 8 moves being played in this way,[26] but they give examples of arrangements which they recommend for use which require from 4 to 9 moves. Mr. Gillay told me that 4 moves were usually played in Northern, and 3 in Southern India, 'as the player wishes to bring the King in a good position'. Lala Raja Babu says that in Parsi chess the players commence by playing 4 simultaneous moves. When the first player has made the number of moves that had been agreed upon, or which suited his plans, the second player proceeds to make an equal number of moves with the same restriction that he must keep to his own half of the board. At the conclusion of this rearrangement of the forces the game continues by alternate moves, precisely as in European chess. The earliest trace of this custom is to be seen in the chess passage which I have quoted from Nīlakaṇṭ·ha. The native player Tiruveṇgaḍāchārya Shastrī defends the

says of the Deccan, 'Some of the native players, through their intercourse with Europeans, have introduced the practice of castling. Hence I have seen them practise castling in a great variety of strange fashions, and I once observed a player move his King to Bishop's 2nd sq., then leap the R to K sq. over the heads of B and Kt, and finally place his K in the corner, all these evolutions being considered as one move'.

24 All authorities agree that the manœuvre P takes P in passing is quite unknown. The opportunity for it could hardly occur.

25 In some parts of S. India, this additional leap is compulsory. Tiruv. says: 'If the P be on the Kt's file, the Kt, immediately on being made, takes one move in addition to the last move of the P, unless some other piece command the square to which the P was advancing.' Mr. Gillay also makes the leap compulsory, but adds, 'if the opponent's K is distant a Kt's move from the promotion square the P cannot be promoted or advanced from Kt7.'

26 Tiruv. says '4 or 8 moves, as may be determined'. The two European authorities do not mention this peculiarity.

custom in his *Essays on Chess* (xiv), as allowing 'of a general disposition and all the pieces being brought out before any exchange takes place, without giving to either player any decided advantage', a consummation which he considered would be more likely than the European method of play 'to bring forward the learner', and 'to produce the greatest number of good players': an opinion which has certainly not been borne out in the experience of the 19th c.

The following combinations of opening moves are given in the native chess-books which I have used. The order of the moves is naturally immaterial. The Kings stand on e1 and d8.

A. *In four moves.* I.—Pd4, Pe4, Pc3, Pf3. II.—Pe4, Pd3, Pf3, Be3. III.—Pe4, Pd4, Ktc3, Ktf3. IV.—Pe4, Pd4, Ktc3, Be3. V.—Pd3, Bf4, Pe3, Be2. VI.—Pe4, Pd4, Be3, Bd3. VII.—Pd4, Ph4, Bf4, Ktf3. VIII.—Pd4, Pc3, Pg3, Ktd2. IX.—Pe4, Pd4, Pc3, Be3. X.—Pe3, Pd3, Pc3, Pf3. XI.—Pb3, Pg3, Bb2, Bg2.

B. *In six moves.* XII.—Pe4, Pd4, Be3, Bd3, Ktc3, Ktf3. XIII.—Pd3, Pc3, Pb3, Pa3, Ktf3, bKtd2.

C. *In seven moves.* XIV.—Pe3, Pd3, Pg3, Bg2, Ktf3, Kc2, Re1.

D. *In eight moves.* XV.—Pe4, Pd4, Be3, Bd3, Pc3, Pf3, Kte2, Ktd2. XVI.—Pd4, Bf4, Ph4, Pa3, Pc3, Pc4, Ktc3, Ktf3. XVII.—Pe4, Pd4, Be3, Bd3, Ktf3, Ktc3, Ke2, Re1. XVIII.—Pe4, Pd4, Be3, Be2, Ktc3, Ktf3, Ph3, Kf1.

E. *In nine moves.* XIX.—Pe4, Pd4, Be3, Bd3, Ktc3, Ktf3, Pg3, Kg2, Re1.

There are different methods of concluding the game. While the ultimate object—the mate of the opponent's King[27]—is the same as in European chess, the Parsi and Southern Indian chessplayer is more fastidious than the modern European as to the method by which he gives mate. The European esteems all his pieces alike for the purpose. The Indian thinks differently. In his opinion the highest achievement and the most brilliant conclusion is the mate with a Pawn,[28] and he will steer his way past opportunities for brilliant sacrifice and past obvious mates on the move, if he thinks that he can, at the end of a long and wearisome manœuvre, give checkmate with a Pawn.

Stalemate is not recognized. 'Stalemate is not known in the Hindoostannee game,' says Tiruveṇgaḍāchārya; 'if one party get into that position the adversary must make room for him to move. In some part of India he that is put into this predicament has a right to remove from the board any one of the Adversary's pieces he may choose.' Perpetual check is also forbidden: the attacking player must vary his procedure.

If a player lose all his superior pieces, whether he has Pawns remaining or not, the game is said to be *būrd* or *būrj* and is reckoned as drawn. Tiruveṇgaḍāchārya gives it as a win to which very little credit is attached, and adds that in many

[27] Marathi *shāh māt, māt*; according to Gillay, *kattoo* or *mathoo*.

[28] Marathi *shāh piyādī*; according to Tiruv. *piedmat*; Gillay, *pathay mathoo*. There was also a stage in the development of the European chess problem when the Pawn mate was highly esteemed.

parts it is only counted a draw. Mr. Gillay says that it is called *panchamobara būrj* if the superior force has four pieces besides the King when the game is abandoned as *būrj*. Another observer in the Deccan (*CPM.*, 1866, 34) says: 'If at the end of the game, either player is left with only one piece, with or without Pawns, the game is drawn; or, if only Pawns are left, the game is drawn. This rule, however, admits of various modifications. In some cases, if one piece only is left, it becomes endowed with new powers and renders it difficult for the adversary to escape. But this, I assume, is rather a mode of giving odds than a distinct variety of the game.' Something like this has been recorded of one form of Malay chess.

The following specimens of play with the Parsi rules are taken from the two Marathi chess-books which have been used as authorities for this form of chess. The Kings are to be placed on e1 and d8:

I

	White	Black
1	Pe4	Pd5
	Pd4	Pc6
	Pf3	Pe6
	Pc3	Bd6
2	Bg5 +	Pf6
3	Bh4	Bd7
4	Bd3	Kte7
5	Kte2	Kc7
6	Ktd2	Rf8
7	Rc1	Pg6
8	Kc2	Pg5
9	Bf2	Pc5
10	Kb1	cP × P
11	P × P + d	bKtc6
12	Qa4	Rc8
13	Pe5	P × P
14	P × P	B × P
15	Qa5 +	Kb8
16	Qa3	Ktf5
17	R × Kt	R × R
18	Q × P +	Kc8
19	Ktb3	Qd8 ?
20	Kta5	Rc7 ?
21	Qa8m.	

II

	White	Black
1	Pe4	Pe5
	Pd4	Pf6
	Pc3	Kte7
	Be3	Pb6
2	Bd3	Bb7
3	Ktd2	Qg6
4	Kf1	Ph6
5	Kte2	Ktd5
6	Qc2	Kt × B +
7	P × Kt	Bd6
8	Pd5	Qg5
9	Ktc4	Bc5
10	Qc1	Rf8
11	Pb3	Pb5
12	Pb4	Bb6
13	Kt × B	cP × Kt
14	B × P	Pf5
15	Kg1	P × P
16	Bc4	Rf3
17	Ph3	R × eP
18	Kh2	Pd6
19	Rf1	Ktd7
20	Pa4	Ktf6
21	Qd1	Ke7
22	Bb3	Rf8
23	Pc4	Kc8
24	Pa5	Qh4
25	Pg3	Ktg4 +
26	Kg2	Rf2 +
27	R × R	Kt × R
28	K × Kt	Rf3 +
29	Kg2	Qg5
30	P × P	P × P
31	Rc1	Rd3
32	Qf1	R × B
33	Qf8 +	Kd7
34	Rf1	Rf3
35	R × R	P × R +
36	Q × P	Bc8
37	Ph4	Qg6
38	Pg4	Ph5
39	Kg3	Kc7
40	Pg5	Bg4
41	Qe3	Qc2
42	Ktc3	Qf5
43	Kta4	Kd7
44	Kt × P +	Ke8
45	Pc5	Pe4
46	Qf4	Qe5
47	Q × Q +	P × Q
48	Ktc4	Ke7
49	Kt × P	Pe3
50	Ktc4	Pe2
51	Kf2	Kd8
52	Pb5	Kc7
53	Pd6 +	Kb7
54	Pc6 +	Kc8
55	Pb6	Kd8
56	Pb7	Ke8
57	Pb8 = Kt & leaps to a6	Kf7
58	Ktc5	Kg6
59	Kte4	Bd7
60	K × P	B × P
61	Ke3	Kf5
62	Ktc5	Kg4
63	Kte5 +	K × P
64	Kt × B *Būrj*.	

III

	White	Black
1	Pe3	Pb6
	Pd3	Pg6
	Pf3	Bb7
	Pc3	Bg7
2	Pb3	Pe5
3	Pg3	Pf6
4	Bg2	Pd5
5	Pc4	Pd4
6	Pe4	Ktc6
7	Kf2	Ph5
8	Kte2	Ph4
9	Ktd2	Ktb4
10	Re1	Pf5
11	eP × P	gP × P
12	gP × P	R × P
13	Kg1	Kt × Pd3
14	Rf1	Bh6
15	Qc2	Be3 +
16	Kh1	Ktf2 +
17	Kg1	Ktg4 + d
18	Kh1	Kt × P
19	Re1	Kt × fP + d
20	Bh3	Qh5
21	Kt × Kt	R × B +
22	Kg2	R × Kt [29]
23	Bb2	Qg5 +
24	Kh2	Rf2 +
25	Kh3	Qh5 +
26	Kg3	Pf4 +
27	Kt × P	P × Ktm.

IV

	White	Black
1	Pe4	Pe6
	Pd4	Pf6
	Be3	Pg6
	Bd3	Ph6
	Ktf3	Ktc6
	Ktc3	gKte2
2	Kd2	Ph5
3	Rc1	Pg5
4	Kb1	Bh6
5	Qe2	Ktg6
6	Pg3	Pd6
7	hRe1	Rg8
8	Qd2	Ktb4
9	Pa3	Ktc6
10	Pd5	cKte5
11	Kt × Kt	Kt × Kt
12	Be2	Ph4
13	Pg4	Qf7

[29] Black ignores the mate by 22.., Q × Kt, because he intends to mate with a Pawn.

White	Black	White	Black	White	Black	White	Black
14 P × P	B × P	28 R × B(e7)	Qf8	42 Qc7 +	Kb5	56 Qb7	Be6
15 Pf3	Ktc4	29 R × P +[30]	Kb8	43 Qc5 +	Ka4	57 Ph5	Bd5
16 B × Kt	B × B	30 Kte7	Bc4	44 Bd8	Bb3	58 Qb6	Bc4
17 cRd1	Bf8	31 R × R +	Q × R	45 Pc3	Pa5	59 Ph6	Ba2
18 Kta4	Ba7 +	32 Rc8 +	Q × R	46 Q × gP	Pb6	60 Ph7	Bb3
19 Ka1	Bc4	33 Kt × Q	K × Kt	47 B × P	Bd5	61 Ph8 = R	Bc4
20 Qc3	Be7	34 Q × P	Kc7	48 Qd2	Bg8	62 Rb8	Bb3
21 Ph3	Bb5	35 Qg7 +	Kd8	49 Bf2	Bd5	63 Qd6	Ba2
22 Ktc5	Kc8	36 Qf6 +	Kc7	50 B × P	Bc4	64 Rb6	Bb3
23 Ktb3	Rd8	37 Bb6 +	Kb8	51 Be7	Bb3	65 Qd4 +	Bc4
24 Ktd4	Pa6	38 Qd6 +	Kc8	52 Ph4	Bc2	66 Qd7 +	Bb5
25 Ktf5	Pd5	39 Qf8 +[31]	Kd7	53 Pg5	Bb3	67 Ka2	B × Q
26 Bf2	Bc6	40 Q × R	Bd5	54 Pf4	Bc2	68 Pb3m.	
27 P × P	B × dP	41 Qd8 +	Kc6	55 Qd5	Bb3		

In addition to the ordinary chess, and the games upon larger boards, or with other than the usual pieces, which I shall discuss in a later chapter, there appears to be a variety played in parts of Western India in which the usual arrangement of the men and the ordinary rules are observed with the single exception that no piece can be taken so long as it is supported by some other man.[32]

When we compare the rules of these two modern India games with the little information that we possess with reference to the older game of India, or even with the transitional forms described by Nīlakaṇṭ·ha and Vaidyanātha, it becomes clear that contact with European players has already made profound changes in the native chess. Thus, the European modifications in the rules of certain pieces, introduced in Europe just before 1500, have been adopted in Indian chess since Nīlakaṇṭ·ha's day, and the older moves of Elephant or Camel (our Bishop) and Minister or Vizier have completely disappeared. The existing move of the King in India is based upon the rule current in Europe in the later Middle Ages. The Pawn's move in Parsi chess exhibits a limitation to the general use of the double step which for long was in existence in German chess. Even the rules of Pawn promotion—to-day the most typical feature in the Indian games—would seem to have their origin in a peculiarity of English chess about 1600. In the older Indian chess, just as in the Muslim chess and the older European chess, the only promotion possible was to the rank of the Vizier (Firzān, Queen). In English chess *c.* 1600 a player was allowed to promote to the rank of any piece which had been already lost. Indian players have developed this in characteristic fashion, making the tactics of the End-game very different from those in our chess. The same European inspiration can be seen in other aspects of Indian chess of which I have still to speak. All the native text-books which I have seen betray very considerable signs of the use of European books, and must be used with much caution. Most of them teach the European rules

[30] 29 Q × P would be mate.

[31] He naturally avoids 39 Qc7 m.

[32] See *CPM.*, 1866, 36.

Indian Chessmen
Hyde, ii. 123

as well as the native ones: one book, that of Lala Raja Babu, has incorporated an English work on the End-game[33] making the necessary changes in it to make it applicable to the Hindustani chess.

From the evidence of European chessplayers the general standard of play in India is not high. This is not surprising, since all the conditions that make for the development of great skill are wanting. The science of chess has never been developed, and the literature of the game is still elementary in character. Chess clubs are few in number, and for the most part exist for the practice of the European game. Only a few names have stood out as of importance in the history of chess. I may mention Tiruveṇgaḍāchārya Shastrī of Tirputty near Madras, who made a reputation in Bombay among the small European chess circle, to whom he was familiarly known as *the Brahmin.* He was the author of a Sanskrit poem,[34] which he afterwards translated into English under the title of *Essays on Chess*, Bombay, 1814, in which he attempted to adapt the native chess to the European and gives the earliest collection of Indian problems of non-Muslim workmanship that we possess. The compromise which he attempted between the two games naturally reduces the value of his work from the historical point of view. Ghulam Kassim, a Madras player, made his mark in the European game. He took part in the correspondence match between Madras and Hyderabad in 1829, and in collaboration with James Cochrane published an *Analysis of the Muzio Gambit*, Madras, 1829.

Indian chessmen, like those of all countries except China and Japan, may be grouped into two classes. We find sets in which the pieces are actual carvings, reproducing in miniature the animals and men whose names they bear, and other sets in which the pieces have conventional shapes which are easier and cheaper to produce and must therefore have always been the material employed by the ordinary chessplayer. Of the more elaborate type there are many examples in European museums and in private collections. To these al-Maṣʿūdī undoubtedly referred in the passage on the uses of ivory which I have already quoted, though I know of no pieces approaching the bulk of which he speaks, unless the so-called Charlemagne King in the Bibliothèque Nationale, Paris, is of Indian workmanship. Indian it undoubtedly is in treatment, but it bears an Arabic inscription on its base which purports to give the carver's name.[35]

[33] Freeborough's *Chess Endings*, London, 1891.

[34] Entitled *Vilas muni munjuri.* The Diamond Flower-bed of Amusement. The Sanskrit poem has never been seen, and some authorities have questioned its existence.

[35] This piece has no connexion with the other chessmen which are now preserved in the same case, and are popularly associated with it. This piece is 16 cm. in height, and bears on the base the Kufic inscription 'min 'amal Yūsuf al-Bāhilī', 'of Yūsuf al-Bāhilī's making'. The carving represents a raja riding in his howdah on an elephant, the base of the piece being surrounded by horsemen in order to give greater stability to the piece (a common device in early European chessmen). V. d. Linde (i. 34), who opposed the chess character of the carving, dated it *c.* 1560, and believed that the piece was only brought to France after the commencement of European settlements in India.

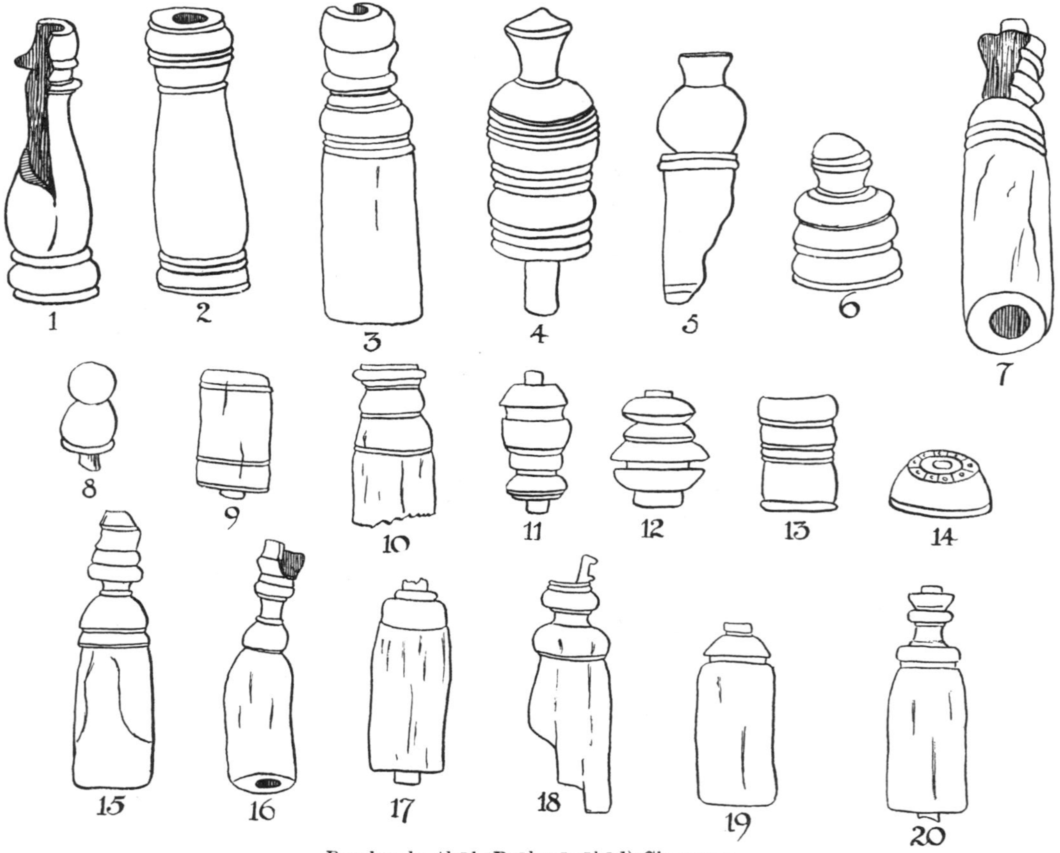

Bambra-ka-thūl (Brāhmānābād) Chessmen.

Indian Chessmen, Eighteenth Century
From Mr. Platt's Collection

Hyde (1767, ii. 123) gives some illustrations of a fine set of this character which Sir D. Sheldon had brought back from Bombay, which I reproduce. He says that both Persians (by whom he means Parsis) and Moghuls used men of this type.

More modern pieces of this type are often treated on freer lines. It would seem to have been a favourite device of workers in ivory at the end of the 18th century to make the chessmen symbolize the struggle between the East India Company and the native states. Thus a set in the Gotha Museum has on one side two elephants with palanquins (K and Q), two rhinoceroses (B), two horsemen (Kt), two towers bearing small figures with flags (R), and eight soldiers in European uniform. The other side replaces the rhinoceroses by buffaloes, the horsemen by men on camels, and the infantry by eight native soldiers carrying what appear to be folded umbrellas. The presence of the castle for the Rooks is a plain proof of European influences at work. I reproduce a similar set from Mr. Platt's collection of chessmen.

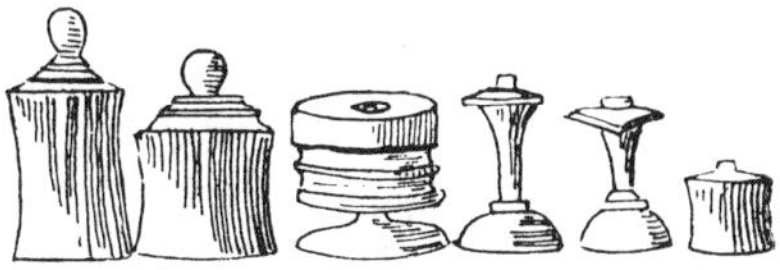

Scachi Indici plani Lignei.

Scachi Indici plani Eburnei solidi.

Scachi Indici plani Eburnei cavi.

Indian Chessmen from Surat (Hyde).

The references to chess in the earlier Indian literature seem to me from their want of fixity of nomenclature to suggest that carved pieces of this first type were in the writers' minds; but at the present time the conventional type of chessman is by far the more usual. The conventional Indian chessmen are very similar to the ordinary Muslim pieces, and it is quite possible that the Indian type has been developed from, or influenced by, the Muslim pattern. The chief difference is to be found in connexion with the Rook. In the Sunnite Muslim sets this is a tall piece with a very distinct type of head; in Indian sets the Rook is now often a low piece with a flat top which at times is almost like the modern European draughtsman. It is thus of a shape very similar to the Siamese and Malayan Rooks. The change in shape would appear to be of recent date, since the Indian conventional chessmen which Hyde obtained from Surat have much taller and bolder heads.

The only ancient chessmen of conventional shape which have been discovered in India were found in 1855 or 1856 by Mr. A. F. Bellasis in the course of some excavations upon the site of a ruined city at Bambra-ka-thūl, 47 miles N.E. of Haidārābād, the present capital of the lower Sind. The city, which had unmistakably been destroyed by an earthquake, was at first identified with the Hindu city Brāhmanābād, which was already in ruins in the time of al-Baladhūrī (D. 279/892–3). It is now recognized to be the Muslim town of Manṣūra, which replaced Brāhmanābād in the latter half of the 8th c. and was still in existence in the time of al-Bērūnī (1030), although there is reason to believe that the earthquake had happened a little before his time.[36] The chessmen accordingly belong to the early 11th c., and are Muslim rather than native Indian. They are now in the British Museum along with a long die (2 + 5, 1 + 6), a cubic die (1 + 6, 2 + 5, 3 + 4), the fragments of a small box or coffer which was formerly assumed to be the fragments of an inlaid chequered chessboard, and a few other objects obtained at the same time. The chessmen are of ivory, black and white, but are now in a very decayed state, and the ivory has degenerated into a condition not unlike that of lime or chalk. There are now 37 pieces or fragments of pieces. None can be identified with any approach to certainty. Since the various fragments either end in pegs or contain holes of the same size

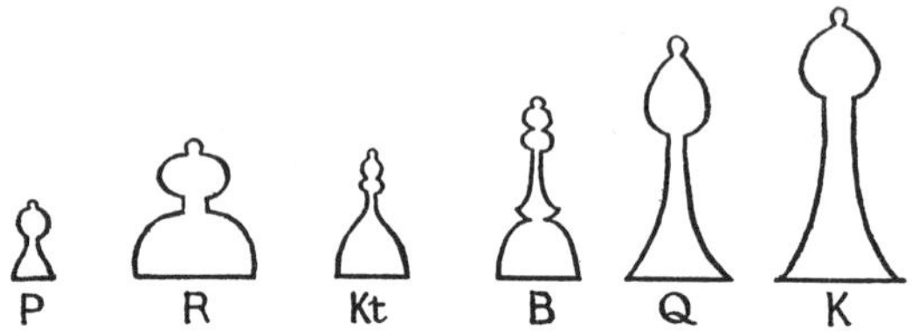

From Lala Raja Babu's work.

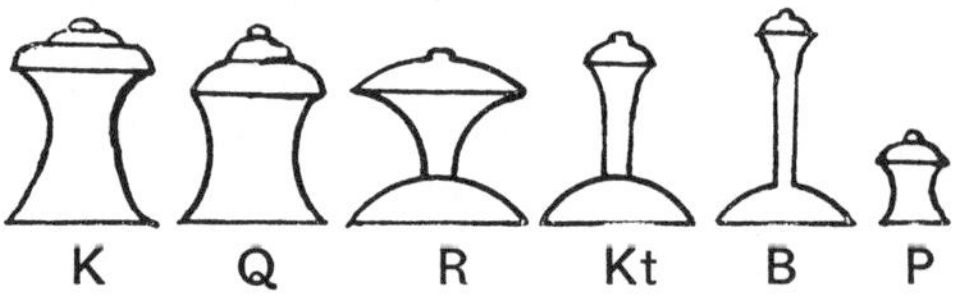

From Vinayaka Rajarama Tope's work.

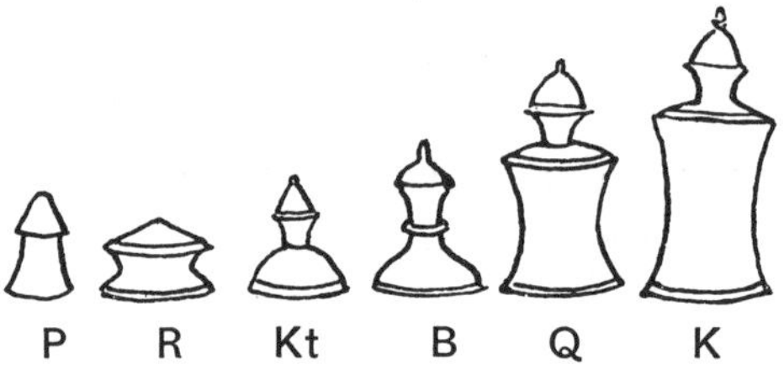

Some Modern Indian Chessmen.

as the pegs, I imagine that they were carved in sections and pieced together; this seems more likely than the view that the men were pegged for use on a board with holes.

The chessmen which Hyde possessed were coloured red and green, and these are still the usual colours at the present day; less frequently we meet with sets with red and black, or with white and black chessmen.

These conventional sets must not be confused with the curious elaborate sets carved in India for the European market, in which the English chessmen

36 Brāhmānābād (Cunningham, *Anc. Geog. India*, ii. *The Buddhist Period*, 1871, 267-77) is the modern Dilura, $1\frac{1}{2}$ miles distant. The coins found at Bambra-ka-thūl were Muhammadan, chiefly of Manṣūr b. Jumhūr (744–9) and of ʿOmar b. Abdallāh, a contemporary of al-Masʿūdī (930). Since Maḥmūd of Ghaznī left the town on one side on his Indian

Modern Indian Chessmen
Platt Collection

Face page 90]

are treated on Indian lines. The characteristic feature of these curios is the development of the Bishop's mitre, though the representation of the Rook as a Castle betrays the foreign source of inspiration. Often beautiful works of art and wonderful examples of the native skill in carving, these sets have but little importance for the history of the game: too elaborate for ordinary play, they are the result of the requirements of the European collector of curios.

The study of chess endings and problems (Urdū *naqsh*) would seem to have been a late development in non-Muhammadan India. It is somewhat singular that whereas the Muslim players had achieved much success in this branch of chess before the end of the 10th c., it was not until after Hindu players had come into contact with the European game that we find any trace of Hindu problems. The Indian Muslim players were familiar with the traditional Muslim material, and we possess Persian problem MSS. which were copied in India. I am not sure that we possess any problems by players of the Hindustani game which are uncoloured by European ideas. The only native problems which are composed on other lines belong to the Parsi chess. The earliest of these are contained in the already mentioned work of Tiruveṇgaḍāchārya Shastrī (1814). Of the 96 positions in his *Essays on Chess*, 32 are composed 'agreeably to the European mode of Play', and are indeed in part drawn from European works. The remaining 64 are said to be composed under the Indian rules.[37] Many of these are repeated in Mangesa's collection of 81 Pawn mates. Another Marathi work (Vinayaka) gives a still larger collection, classified under the heads: Mates with a piece, Pawn mates, Self mates, *Būrj* positions, Draws by perpetual check or stalemate, Mates under European rules. Most of the other native chess-books I have seen give collections of problems which have been taken from European books and newspapers.

An examination of the accessible problems shows that the Pawn mate is held in the highest esteem. Excepting that the position must be possible in that it conforms to the rules of the game in the pieces employed, and in the necessity of leaving the losing player sufficient force to avoid the ending *būrj*, there seem to be no canons of taste governing the composition of the native problem. The recognition of the higher standard of the modern European problem has probably arrested the development of the native art, which came into existence too late to strive successfully against its Western rival. A selection of Indian problems is given in the appendix to this chapter.

expedition, it is inferred that the earthquake had already happened: had the town been of its former importance Maḥmūd would hardly have passed it by. For an account of the excavations, see A. F. Bellasis, *An Account of the Ancient and Ruined City of Brahminabad*, Bombay, 1856; *Illustr. London News*, Feb. 21 and 28, 1857. See Elliott, *Hist. India*, 1867, i. 369 seq. and Thomas, *Prinsep's Essays on Indian Antiquities*, 1858, ii. 119.

37 It is possible that the Persian MS. *Sārdārnāma* (Oxf.) which is some 16 years older than the *Essays on Chess*, contains some Indian work among its problems of the Rūmī game. Since the bulk of the problems belong to the traditional Muslim material, I have included the work among my authorities of Muslim chess. It contains, however, some problems of the European chess, in the main modernized settings of older Muslim positions. In a few I can detect, I think, a different style of work, which may possibly be Parsi.

APPENDIX

A SELECTION OF PROBLEMS FROM INDIAN SOURCES

I have restricted my selection to problems that occur in the work of Tiruveṇgaḍāchārya (referred to as 'T'), and in the two Marathi works of Vinayaka Rajarama Tope ('V'), and Mangesa Rāmakrishna Telanga ('M'), since all the other works that I have used have obtained some at least of their problems from European sources. I have already given some indication of the contents of these three books. Of my selection, the first four are mates with a piece, a variety that is only found treated on Indian lines in V; Nos. 5 to 14 are mates with a Pawn, the ordinary type of problem composed in India; Nos. 15 to 17 are *būrj* endings, and the last problem is a self mate.

The problems in V are re-numbered in each class. By 'a' I mean the *būrj* positions, by 'b' the mates with a piece, by 'c' the non-Indian positions[1], by 'd' the Pawn-mates, and by 'e' the other drawn positions.

The Indian rule prohibiting the winner from taking the last piece of his opponent naturally renders possible new lines of defence. The loser has the chance of drawing by *būrj* by compelling the capture of his last piece. Accordingly we find that there is a strong tendency to reduce the number of pieces on the losing side, and most of the problems in M which are peculiar to that work leave Black with King and a single piece.

The solutions which follow are those that are given in the works from which the problems are taken. I have not attempted to prove them the only, or the shortest, solutions.

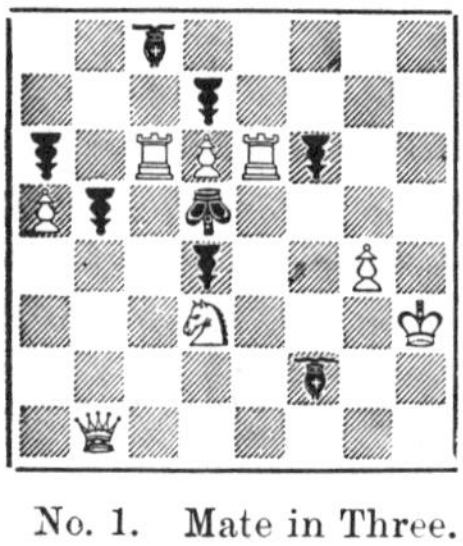

No. 1. Mate in Three.

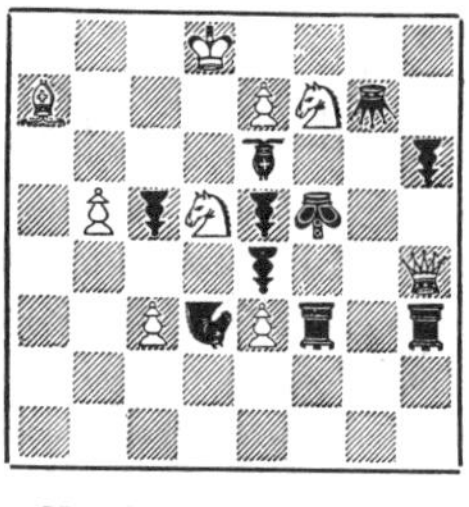

No. 2. Mate in Four.

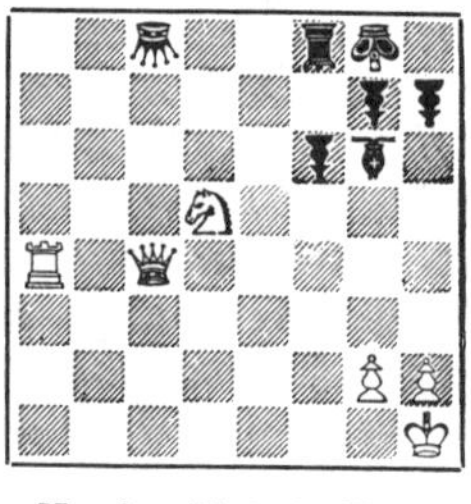

No. 3. Mate in Four.

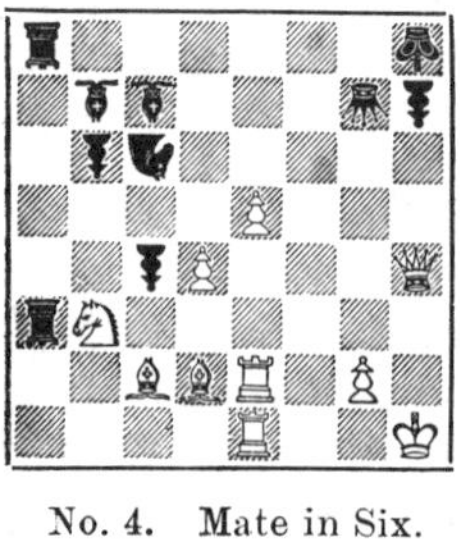

No. 4. Mate in Six.

No. 5. Mate with Pawn in Three.

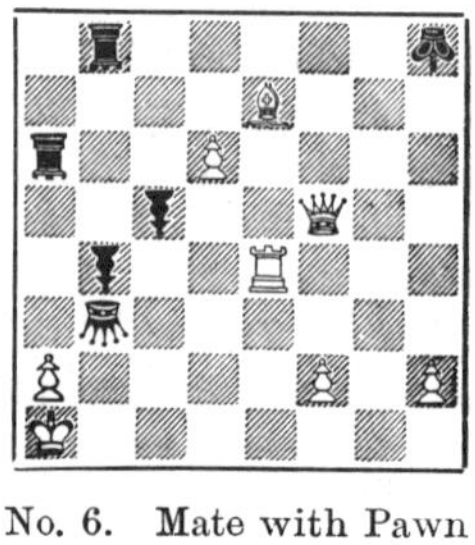

No. 6. Mate with Pawn in Four [or Black mates with Pawn in Five].

[1] Many of these exhibit solitary Ks: e. g. the first is White, Ka8, Qa1, Bf8, h7, Pd2, g5; Black Kd5. Mate in two (1 Qb1, Kc4; 2 Qd3 m.).

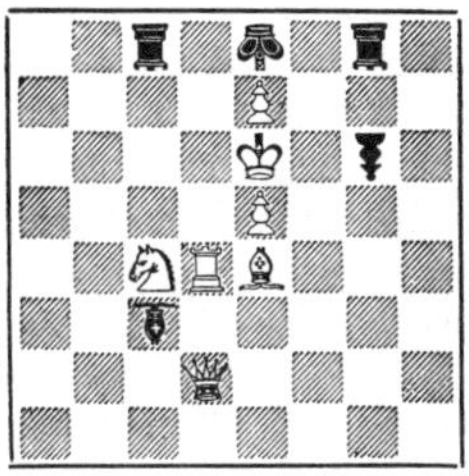

No. 7. Mate with Pawn in Five.

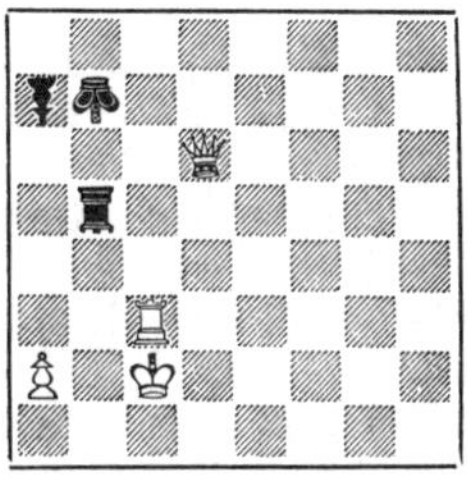

No. 8. Mate with Pawn in Six.

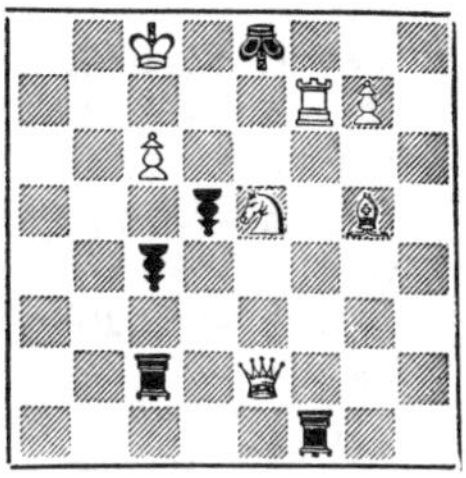

No. 9. Mate with Pawn in Six.

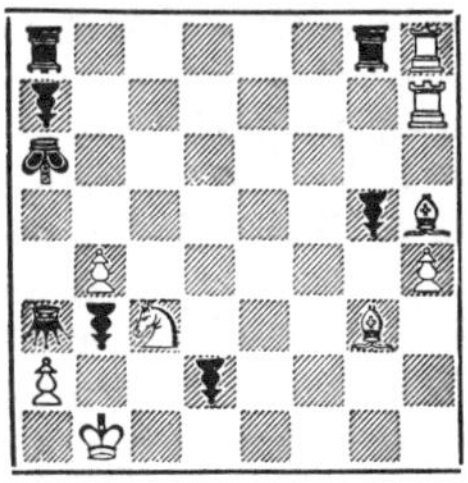

No. 10. Mate with Pawn in Seven.

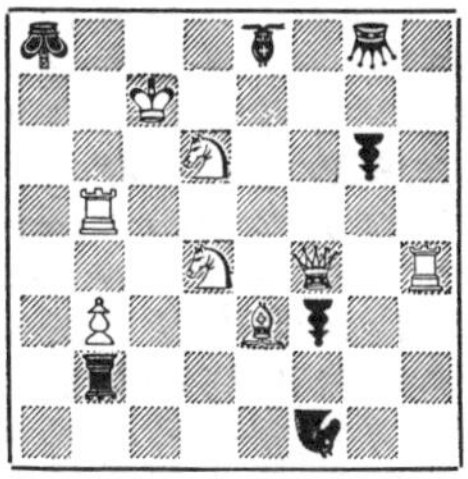

No. 11. Mate with Pawn in Eight.

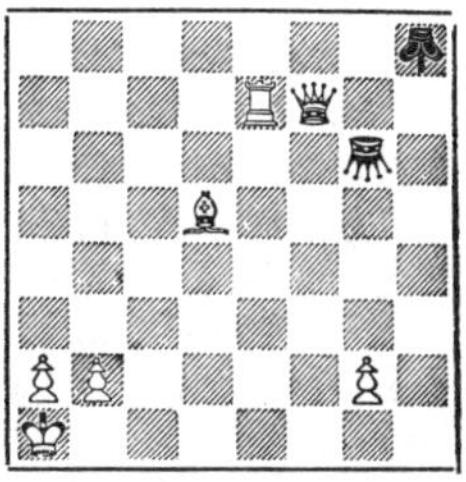

No. 12. Mate with Pawn in Nine.

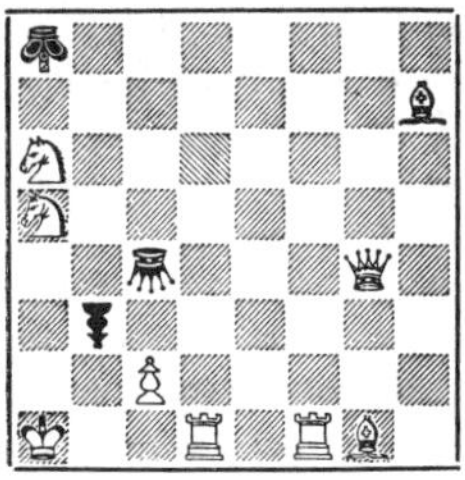

No. 13. Mate with Pawn in Ten.

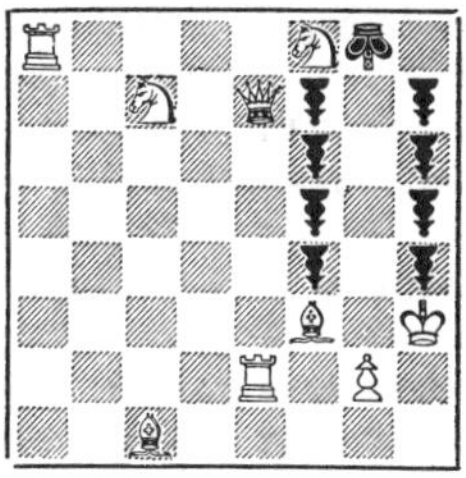

No. 14. Mate with Pawn in Fourteen.

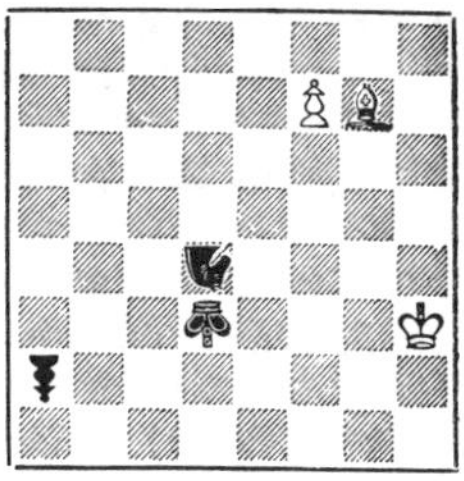

No. 15. Drawn.

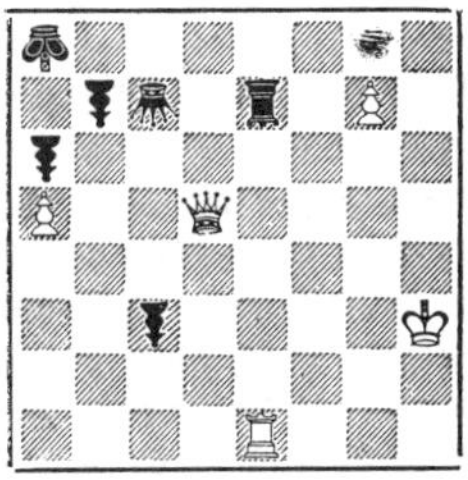

No. 16. Drawn.

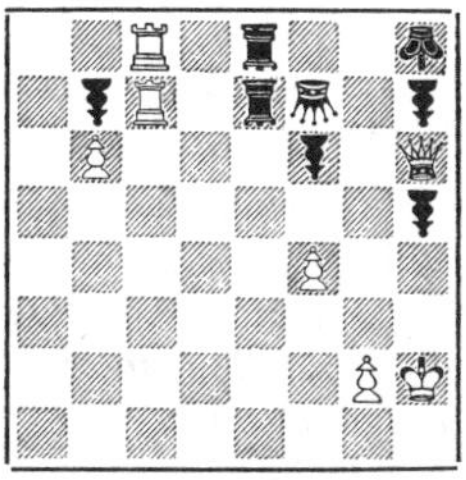

No. 17. Drawn.

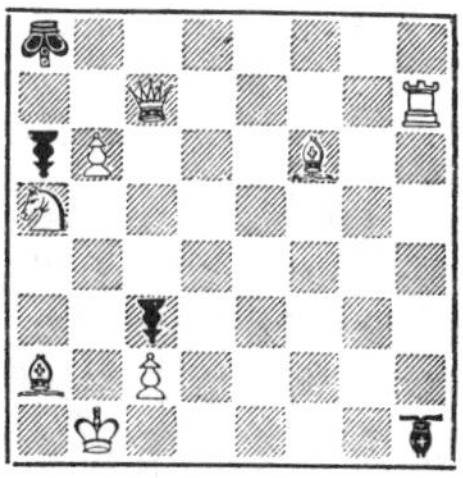

No. 18. Self Mate in Six [or Mate with Pawn in Four.]

Solutions:

No. 1.—V b66. 1 Qa1, Be3; 2 Qa2+, K×R; 3 Qg2 mate.

No. 2.—V b74. 1 Q×P+, K×Q; 2 Ktd6+, K×Kt; 3 Pe4+, K×Kt; 4 Bb8 mate.

No. 3.—V b77. 1 Kte7+, Kh8; 2 Qg8+, R×Q; 3 Kt×B+, P×Kt; 4 Rh4 mate.

No. 4.—V b26. 1 Bg5, Bd8; 2 Bf6, B×B; 3 P×B, Qf7; 4 Re8+, R×R; 5 R×R+, Q×R; 6 Q×P mate.

No. 5.—T 35; M 6; V d65. 1 Rb8+, R×R; 2 Qb7+, R×Q; 3 P×R mate.

No. 6.—V d89. White: 1 Rh4+, Kg7; 2 Qg4+, Kf7; 3 Rh7+, Ke8; 4 Pd7 mate. Black: 1 Qd1+, Kb2; 2 R×P+, K×R; 3 Qc2+, Ka1; 4 Qc1+, Ka2; 5 Pb3 mate.

No. 7.—V d52. 1 Rd8+, R×R; 2 Qd7+, R×Q; 3 Ktd6+, R×Kt; 4 P×R, ~; 5 Pd7 mate.

No. 8.—T 48; M 32; V d57 and 87. 1 Qc6+, Kb8; 2 Qe8+, Kb7; 3 Qc8+, Kb6; 4 Rc6+, Ka5; 5 Ra6+, Kb4; 6 Pa3 mate.

No. 9.—T 49; M 33; V d58. 1 Rf8+, R×R; 2 Qh5+, Rf7; 3 Qg6, ~; 4 Qe6+, Re7; 5 Qd7+, R×Q; 6 P×R mate.

No. 10.—V d45. 1 Be2+, Kb6; 2 Bf2+, Kc6; 3 Bf3+, Kd6; 4 Bg3+, Ke6; 5 Bg4+, Kf6; 6 Kte4+, Kg6; 7 Ph5 mate.

No. 11.—T 65; M 56. 1 Rb8+, Ka7; 2 Ktc8+, Ka3; 3 Rb6+, Ka5; 4 Ktc6+, B×Kt; 5 Bd2+, Kt×B; 6 Q×Kt+, R×Q; 7 Ra4+, B×R; 8 Pb4 mate.

No. 12.—M 64. 1 Re8+, Qg8; 2 Qf6+, Kh7; 3 Be4+, Qg6; 4 Qf7+, Kh6; 5 Rh8+, Qh7; 6 Qf6+, Kh5; 7 Bf5, Q×R; 8 Qg6+, Kh4; 9 Pg3 mate.

No. 13.—V d17. 1 Rd8+, Qc8; 2 P×P, Q×R; 3 Be4+, Qd5; 4 Pb4, Q×B; 5 Rf8+, Qe8; 6 Pb5, Q×R; 7 Qg2+, Qf3; 8 Qg8+, Qf8; 9 Pb6, Q×Q; 10 Pb7 mate.

No. 14.—V d69. 1 Ktd7+d, Kg7; 2 Rf8, Kg6; 3 Kte6, P×Kt; 4 Qf7+, Kg5; 5 Kte5, P×Kt; 6 Be4, P×B; 7 Be3, P×B; 8 Qe7, Kg6; 9 Kh2, Ph3; 10 Pg3, Ph4; 11 Pg4, Ph5; 12 Pg5, Ph6; 13 Qf6+, Kh7; 14 Pg6 mate.

No. 15.—V a16. 1 B×Kt, K×B; 2 Pf8 = B, Pa1 = R; 3 Bg7+, K~; 4 B×R.

No. 16—V a22. 1 Qg8+, Ka7; 2 R×R, Q×R; 3 Qa8+, K×Q; 4 Pg8 = Kt and takes Q.

Nos. 15 and 16 illustrate the peculiarities of Pawn-promotion. In another position, V a17 (White: Kg2, Re3, Ktd7, Pb6, g6, h5; Black, Kg8, Rd8, Pd6, g7, h6), the promoted KtP does not make the additional leap after promotion because b8 is commanded by the R. (See p. 83, n. 25.) Solution: 1 Pb7, Pd5; 2 Pb8 = Kt, Pd4; 3 Ktc6, Ra8; 4 Rb3, Rc8; 5 Rb8.

No. 17.—V a24. 1 R×R(e8), Q×R; 2 Q×P(f6)+, Kg8; 3 R×R, Q×R; 4 Q×Q.

No. 18. T 94. Self mate by 1 Bd5+, B×B; 2 Rh8+, Bg8; 3 Ktb3, Pa5; 4 Bg5, Pa4; 5 Kta1, Pa3; 6 Bc1, Pa2 mate. Mate in four by 1 Bd5+, B×B; 2 Rh8+, Bg8; 3 Ktc6, Pa5; 4 Pb7 mate.

[Note.—The earlier volumes of the *CPC.* contain several problems which were sent to Staunton by subscribers in India. Some of these positions are the work of native players and are similar in style to the Pawn mates quoted above. Others were the work of English composers. The most famous of these positions is the so-called *Indian problem* which was published in February 1845 (*CPC.*, vi. 54.—White: Ka1, Rd1, Bg2, h6, Pa2, b3, f2, g4; Black: Ke4, Ktf3, Pb5, b6, e5. Mate in four; 1 Bc1; 2 Rd2; 3 K~; 4 Rd4 mate), and is now recognized to be the creation of the Rev. Henry A. Loveday (cf. Kohtz u. Kockelkorn, *Das indische Problem*, Potsdam, 1903), and therefore of European, not Indian workmanship.]

CHAPTER V

CHESS IN THE MALAY LANDS

Introductory.—Spread in Malay lands.—Early references.—The chessboard.—Nomenclature.—Moves of the pieces.—Rules.—Illustrative games.—Malay chessmen.—Concluding observations.

ALTHOUGH chess is known and played in every Asiatic country to the east of India, the forms of the game that are played by the different peoples present at first sight as wide differences as are found anywhere in chess. On closer investigation, however, it is possible to discover certain common features in some types which enable us to classify these games in three groups, corresponding to the known ethnological families and religions of Eastern Asia. To one group, comprising the chess of Burma, Siam, and Annam, three countries linked by that form of Buddhism which is conveniently called Southern, I devote Chapter VI; to a second group, comprising the chess of China, Corea, and Japan, I devote Chapter VII; while in the present chapter I shall deal with the varieties of chess current among the Malays, which are united by the phenomenon of a nomenclature which has been drawn from many sources, and by a type of move which is closely akin to that of modern European chess.

To-day, chess is very widely played by the Malay races, and ranks as one of their most popular games.[1] On the mainland we possess records of its practice in the British Straits Settlements (Malacca), in the Protected States (Selangor), at Kelantan, and at Johore. We also possess good descriptions of the game as played in Sumatra, in Java, and in Borneo. Von Oefele, who has made a most patient and valuable study of the game as played in Sumatra by the Orang-Batak,[2] records that practically every male Batak has some knowledge of chess, while nearly every village meeting-hut has a chessboard carved upon its wooden floor. So violent are the passions aroused at times by the game, which is always played for a stake, that the headman of the village has occasionally had to forbid the practice of the game for a season.[2a]

[1] Other Malay board-games are *main chongkak* (African *manqala*), *main dam* (draughts or checkers), *main rimau* or *machan* (the tiger game, a game of the hunt or siege type), *main tabal* (backgammon, played in two ways), and *apit-sodok*. See Skeat, *Malay Magic*, 486–7; Culin, *C. & P. C.*, 849, 861, 872, 875; and *Mancala, the National Game of Africa*, Washington, 1896, 600; and Wilkinson, *Papers on Malay Subjects*, Kuala Lumpur, 1910, 56–7, 91–4.

[2] The Bataks form the greater part of the population of the mountainous region to the south of Acheh. In appearance they are taller and darker than the true Malay. They still practise cannibalism to some extent. The game is restricted to the male sex entirely.

[2a] Chess appears to be unknown to the natives both in Madagascar and, what is more surprising, in the Philippines.

We know very little of the history of chess in these lands. The few Europeans who have made any study of the early history of the Archipelago speak of four successive waves of foreign culture and religion, all of which have in turn left a notable impress upon the customs of these islands. Somewhere about the 7th c. A.D. the Hindu religion established itself in Sumatra and Java, to be followed by Buddhism, and rather later—from the 13th to the 15th c.—by Muhammadanism. From the beginning of the 16th c. the coastal regions have been in continual contact with Europeans, first with the Portuguese, afterwards with the Dutch, and at a later date still with the English. Malay chess reflects all these invasions, since it shows unmistakable traces of Indian and of Arabic, and also of European influence.

The game is certainly older than any European influences, for on the arrival of the first Portuguese expedition off Malacca in 1509 its commander, Diego Lopez, was playing chess when a Javan from the mainland came on board. The native recognized the game at once, and had some conversation with Lopez on the forms of chessmen used by his countrymen.[3]

There is also a reference to the game in the *Sĕjarah Malayu*, a native history dating from the early 17th century, ch. xviii, in connexion with a visit to Malacca by a certain Tan Bahra, of Pasei in Sumatra.[4] The passage goes on to say—

> Now this Tan Bahra was a very skilful chessplayer, and one that was unequalled at the game in that age, and he played at chess with the men of Malacca . . . and beat them all: but Tan Pakarma, son of the Bandahara Paduka Raja, was able to make some resistance . . . and if Tan Bahra threw away a pawn at the corner, then he was beaten by Tan Pakarma.

Broadly speaking, all forms of Malay chess are played in the same way, the differences only appearing in the refinements of the game. It will therefore be simpler to treat of the game as one, and to deal with the variations of rule or practice as they arise. Even in Java, where for some unexplained reason the otherwise universal Malay nomenclature is replaced by another, the game remains practically the same as in the other parts of the Malay world.

The game of chess has two names in Malay. The commoner name is *main chātor*,[5] in which *main* is the Malay word for game, and *chātor* can hardly be anything but a broken-down form of the Skr. *chaturanga*. This name is the only one recorded for Borneo, Java, and the Batak race. It is given as the ordinary name by all my authorities except Dr. Marsden,[6] who both in his *History of Sumatra* (ed. 1811, 273) and in his *Malayan Dictionary* (Part ii, Eng. and Malayan, s.v. *chess*) only gives the name as *main gājah*, i.e. the game of the elephant. This name has been recorded as used on the mainland both by Robinson and by v. Oefele, who gives it in the form

[3] De Barros, *Asia*, Lisbon, 1778, iv. 412. Quoted by v. d. Linde, *Leerboek van het Schaakspel*, Utrecht, 1876, 22 n. 1.

[4] Quoted by C. O. Blagden, *JRAS.*, xxx. 376.

[5] Also written *chātūr*, which is a more regular transliteration of the written name.

[6] Marsden was a very sound writer, and for Englishmen will always be the pioneer of Malay studies. Cf. Blagden, Introduction to Skeat's *Malay Magic* (xiv).

permainan gājah. This form may be due to the influence of the name of another favourite game, the *main rimau*, or 'game of the tiger',[7] though it is not easy to see why the Elephant should have been selected for mention, rather than the Horse or any other piece. The hypothesis that it may be due to Chinese influence—which is based upon the presence of Chinese settlers on the sea coast of the Peninsula, and all the islands, and upon the fact that one possible meaning of the Chinese name of chess, *siang k‘i*, is 'the game of the

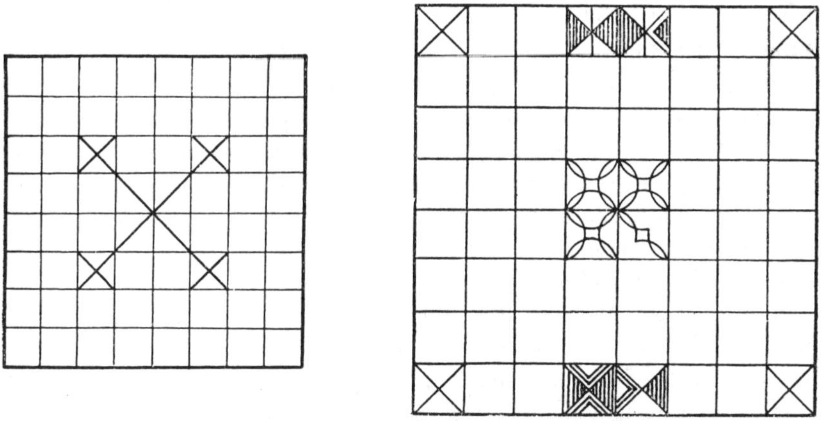

Malay Chessboards. Skeat Collection, Museum of Archaeology and Ethnology, Cambridge.

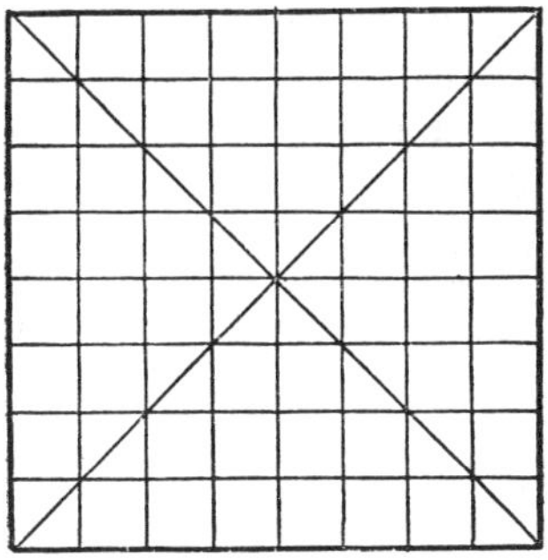

Malay Chessboard.
(Malacca and mainland.)

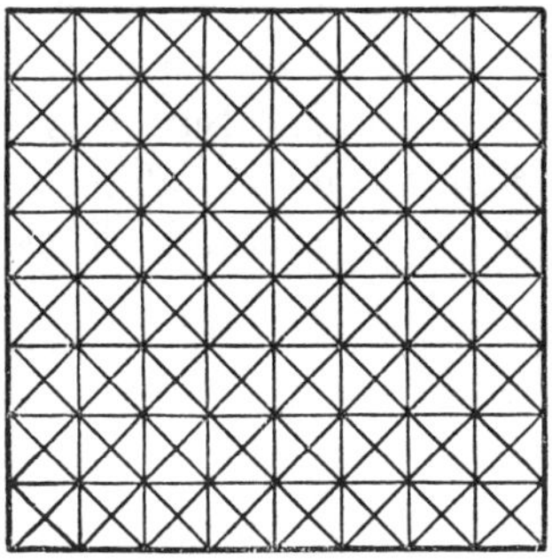

Malay Chessboard.
(Sumatra.)

Elephant'—must be rejected, because in all other cases of cultural borrowings, the Malays have adopted, and not translated, the Chinese name. Moreover, it is not easy to see why the Chinese chess, which does not appear to the casual observer to have any connexion with the Malay game, should have been able to exert an influence which was at once so strong that it led to the introduction of a new name for the game, and so weak that it left the actual method of play absolutely untouched.

[7] Culin, *C. & P. C.*, 875, calls this *dam harimau*, 'tiger game'. Skeat, op. cit., 487, gives the alternative name *main rimau kambing*, 'tiger and goat game'.

The Malay chessboard (*lōh chātor* or *pāpan chātor*[8]) is unchequered, but exhibits special markings which are characteristic of all Oriental boards. These vary so much in the few Malay boards which I have seen that it is clear that no traditional arrangement survives, and I think it probable that they have often become merely decorative. Some of the arrangements are very like those of neighbouring countries; thus one of the boards in the Skeat collection at Cambridge has a traditional Indian marking while the other resembles one of the Burmese markings. The ordinary board of the mainland is said by Mr. Robinson to have only the main diagonals marked—again a Burmese marking—and these diagonals are connected now with the rules of Pawn-promotion, and have probably suggested them. In Sumatra the board has a far more intricate appearance, since the complete network of diagonals of all the 64 small squares of the board is inserted. V. Oefele explains their presence as arising from the method of constructing the board. In order to obtain the correct proportions, he says, the Batak player first draws the outer square, then he inserts the diagonals to obtain the centre of the board and draws parallels to the sides through this point. By repeating this method he obtains accurately the quarter board and the eighth, and so obtains his 64 squares all of a size. Finally, to preserve the symmetry, he adds the missing diagonals, and the complicated figure is complete. This explanation does not seem to me to be satisfactory: while it certainly gives a convenient way of producing the final Sumatran figure, it is by no means the most natural way to draw a board of 8 by 8 squares.

The board is often made of wood, with the lines incised. This may be done upon a board of the floor of the hut, and a board for permanent use may be so secured. But it is also often scratched in the ground for an alfresco game when a movable board is not at hand.

The two nomenclatures may usefully be contrasted thus:

Equivalent	K	Q	B	Kt	R	P	check	mate
Malay[9] . .	rāja	mantri	gājah	kūda	tēr chemōr	bīdaq	sah	mat
Javan . . .	ratu	pateh	mantri	jaran	prahu	bidaq		

Of the ordinary Malay names, *rāja* (=king), *mantri* (=counsellor, minister), and *gājah* (= elephant) are all Sanskrit words, and we have already seen that they are or have been in regular chess use in India. *Kūda* (=horse), *tēr* (=chariot), and *chemōr* (=chariot) are Tamil and Telugu, languages spoken on the south-east coast of India, in the vicinity of Madras. The use of *chemōr*

[8] *Lōh* is the Arabic *lūḥ*, a board, writing-tablet, or plank. *Pāpan* is the ordinary Malay word for board, plank, and is in common use for a game-board. Cf. *pāpan dam* (draught-board) in de Hollander's *Handleiding tot de kennis der Maleische Taal* (Leyden, 1856).

[9] As usual, the transliteration varies in different authorities. Culin (*C. & P. C.*, 861) has *muntrie*, *gejah*, and *teh*. Clifford and Swettenham, *Dict. of the Malay Lang.* (Taiping, Perak, 1894–7, s.v. *chātor*) give *mĕntrī* and *tēr* or *tor*. Robinson (in Wilkinson, R. J., *Papers on Malay Subjects*, 1910, App. x) and v. Oefele have *tīr* or *tōr*. The Javan terms are given by Raffles and Zimmermann, the latter writing *djaran*, *pati*, *prahoë*, and *baidah*.

in chess in India has not yet been verified, but *tēr* is used as the name of the Rook in Tamil, and *ghora*, the original Indian form of *kūda*, is widely used as the name of the Knight. *Chemōr* (*chemūr*) is given as in colloquial Malay use only by Blagden (*JRAS.*, 1898, xxx. 376). *Bīdaq* and the two technical terms *sah* and *mat* have been taken from the Arabic game. Marsden (op. cit.) gives the alternative terms *māti* (Malay, = dead) and *tammat* (Arabic, = finished) as also in use.

Of the Javan names, *mantri* is Sanskrit. So also is probably *pateh* (Skr. *pati* = lord or master). *Ratu* (= king), *jaran* (= horse), and *prahu* (= boat) are all Malay. From this it would seem that the Javan nomenclature preserves an older usage. On the other hand the disappearance of the Elephant and its replacement by two Counsellors is obviously the result of intercourse with the Dutch, with whom the corresponding piece has been long called by the name of Counsellor.[10] It is more difficult to account for the replacement of the Chariot by the Boat. The same change has been made in the chess of the neighbouring lands of Siam and Annam, and also in the game as played in Bengal, where, however, it cannot be shown to be older than 1500. But Siam has exerted hardly any influence upon Malayan customs, and it is difficult to believe that Bengal can have had an influence sufficiently strong to affect the Javan nomenclature. I think it more likely that the change was made independently. The Chariot or Cart is of little use in a land of jungles, and it may very well have been replaced in chess by the Boat as representing the more usual means of transport.

Collectively the chessmen are called *būwah chātor*, i.e. the pieces (lit. fruit) of the chess.[11]

At the commencement of the game the chessmen are arranged as in the Indian game (diagram, p. 80) with the one exception that the relative positions of the Rāja and Mantri are reversed. In the Javan game, if MacGleans (*Sch.*, 1867, 226) is correct, the Indian arrangement is followed. The Mantri is stationed at the right-hand of the Rāja. The arrangement is consequently crosswise. The powers of move of the pieces hardly differ at all from those which existed in European chess in the middle of the 16th century. The Mantri, Gājah, Kūda, and Tēr have exactly the same moves as their respective equivalents, the Queen, Bishop, Knight, and Rook, in modern European chess. The ordinary move of the Rāja is identical with the ordinary move of the King to any adjacent square. In addition he possesses certain powers of leaping into a square two squares distant. This liberty is not uniform throughout the Malay lands. In Borneo, according to Raja Brooke of Sarawak,

> The King, when checked for the first time, has the right of making the Knight's move, or to move two squares. After this sally, he is reduced to the same powers as a European King. The first move (in which he can of course take), on being checked, alters the game considerably, as one great object then becomes to prevent the check of your own King early in the game, and to gain a check of your

[10] Du. *raadsheer*; earlier *raad* (15th c. *raet*).

[11] Similarly the draughtsmen are named *būwah dam* (de Hollander, op. cit.) and the *chongkak* men are called *būwah gorek* (Skeat, op. cit., 486), these last being actual seeds.

adversary . . . for it will be evident if the King be once checked, he is deprived of one great advantage which your adversary still holds. Castling is not allowed except in two moves, the first being the Castle's move up to the King, and on the King receiving a check, he can exercise his right of jumping to the inside of the Castle.[12]

In Java, according to Sir T. Stamford Raffles,

The King, if he has not been checked, may move two squares the first time, either as a Knight or otherwise. . . . The King cannot castle after having been checked. Castling is performed by two moves; the Castle must first be brought up to the King; after which the King may pass over the Castle at any future move, provided he shall not have been checked, or that no piece has occupied the square he would move into.[13]

According to Mr. H. O. Robinson,

Castling is effected in various ways in different parts of the Malay Peninsula and Straits Settlements; the recognized method in Selangor is to move two squares whether a piece intervenes or not,[14] but not in conjunction with one of the Rooks. This is permitted even if the King is in check. The King may, also, before he is checked or moved from his own square, once move or take like a Knight. In Clifford and Swettenham's Malay Dictionary it is stated that the King may, also, if he has not moved or been checked, move once over two vacant squares[15]; this privilege move is unknown to the Selangor Malays.

Finally v. Oefele says that in Batak chess the King may, for his first move, move from e1 to any of e2, e3, d1, d2, d3, c1, c2, f1, f2, f3, g1, g2—12 squares in all. Five of these are in virtue of its ordinary power of move, and 7 are to a second square. There are also two other squares, viz. c3 and g3, which are also only distant two squares, but no mention is made of them, and we must conclude therefore that the old leap of the Elephant in Arabic chess is prohibited. The leap may be made to remedy the first check, but at no subsequent turn of play, even if the first check is remedied by the interposition of a man or by the capture of the checking piece.

The use of the term 'castling' is of course inaccurate, since the manœuvre intended takes two moves. The leap naturally follows the Rook's move, since the latter piece has no power of jumping. The manœuvre is quite well known, and occurs nine times in the nine games from native play that v. Oefele gives; on two of these occasions the King leaps out of check. In another game he makes the Knight's leap in order to capture a Pawn.

[12] I imagine the Raja was deceived by the fact that players generally postponed the leap to the latest moment, and that as a matter of fact there was no real obligation to defer it so long, but that the leap could be made any move, up to and including that following the first offer of check.

[13] Zimmermann (epitomized in *Qst.*, 263) merely says: 'Castling occupies two moves; the Rook must move first, and the King at a later move; if the King be in danger, he may leap over a piece.'

[14] This is not quite consistent with the prohibition of the leap 'over two vacant squares' mentioned later in the description, since the leap to complete the so-called castling is obviously not a Knight's leap. But see the following note.

[15] This description occurs, s.v. *chator*, and runs: 'In the Malay game the king, if he has not been checked, can be castled, but over one space only, not over two, as in the English game. (What does this mean?) The king may, also, before he is checked or moved from his own square, move once, like a knight, either to left or right, and he may also, if he has not moved or been checked, move once over two vacant squares instead of one. (Why vacant?)' A very inexact account, which is probably intended for the practice of Perak.

The differences in practice are accordingly in connexion with two points: (1) whether the Rāja can or cannot make the leap when checked for the first time; and (2) to which of all the squares two steps distant the leap can be made. The rules given by the older observers are not sufficiently explicit here.

Every Bīdaq or Pawn is permitted the double-step for its first move, precisely as in European chess. Variety of practice appears to occur in connexion with taking in passing. Raja Brooke (Borneo) says:

A Pawn, moved out, cannot pass an adversary's Pawn; his first move being restricted to one square in this case.

Sir T. Stamford Raffles (Java), on the contrary, allows the Pawn 'passar battaglia';

The Pawn may move two squares the first move, even though it should pass the check of an adversary's Pawn.[16]

Robinson and v. Oefele give the rule thus: A Pawn can only take another Pawn in passing when its own advance is blocked by another Pawn; e.g. with white Pawns on g2 and h3 and a black Pawn on h4, if White plays Pg4, Black may reply P × P *in passing*[17]; if however there were no Pawn on h3, Black could not take the Pawn on g4 in passing, because he is not now blocked. This is a refinement which a casual observer would miss, and it is quite possible that it is the rule in Borneo and Java, and that the apparent discrepancy does not really exist.[18] Robinson notes a further peculiarity in Pawn-play among the Selangor Malays. If White has a Pawn on h2, and Black a Pawn on g3, White being to play, he cannot play Ph3 or Ph4, but must play P × P, i.e. if he move the h-Pawn. If however White had also a Pawn on f2, he may now play either of the Pawns to its 3rd or take the Black Pawn, but he may not play either Pawn to its 4th.

V. Oefele states that the Bataks allow the King's Pawn to defer its double step until its second move, e.g. 1 Pd3; 2 (or later) P(d3) d5; in such a case it is liable to be captured in passing on its second move, with similar conditions to those already given.

Pawn-promotion is quite different from the European practice. Generally a Pawn is promoted immediately on reaching the 8th rank only on the corner squares. Elsewhere it has to make some further move or moves. Raja Brooke says 'two extra moves' and illustrates the rule in the case of a Pawn played to c8; it is promoted by 1 Pb8, 2 Pa8; or 1 Pb8, 2 c7 or a7; or 1 d8,

[16] Zimmermann has the extraordinary rule, a Pawn may move two steps for its first move, and if a Pawn confronts it, it may leap over it.

[17] Robinson says, 'P × P *en passant* or captures the P on h3 (R3) as he pleases, but must always move diagonally.' I fail to understand the last, since Black cannot possibly take the hP with his hP and yet move diagonally.

[18] The risk of misapprehension is well shown by v. Oefele's work. It is obvious to any one who reads his careful record of Batak chess that he spared no pains to make it as accurate as possible. Yet, in a subsequent letter in *Deutsches Wochenschach* (Oct. 8, 1905, p. 365), he has to admit that he had failed to understand the rules on this one point, and he gives the rule that I give in the text as the result of further inquiry made on a visit to the Karobataks, a Batak tribe which has been visited by hardly any Europeans.

2 e8 or e7. He explains that 'this is a delay rather than a prevention, as from the number of squares which may be taken, it is extremely difficult to guard them all'. Sir T. Raffles, on the other hand, says that the Pawn after reaching its 8th rank on any file excepting the Rook's files 'must retrograde three moves before it can become a Queen'. This in Zimmermann's somewhat loose description becomes: 'the 3 joy-leaps (Freudensprünge) of Ströbeck are necessary before queening a Pawn.' Robinson's full account will again help to clear up these discrepancies. He says:

When a Pawn has reached the eighth square on the Rook's file it queens at once; the player has also the option of selecting any other piece. If on reaching R7 a piece on Kt square is *en prise* and captured on the next move, the Pawn must move back one square diagonally before queening. On reaching the eighth rank of the Knight's file it has to move back one square diagonally, either to the right or left, before queening; on the Bishop's file two squares, and on the King's or Queen's file three squares.

I think it is obvious from this that the two diagonal lines that are drawn on the chessboard of the Peninsula are associated with this rule of promotion. The diagonals pass through the Rook's squares, and promotion takes place at once, the Kt square is distant one square diagonally, and an additional diagonal move is necessary before promotion takes place. The B square is distant two, and the K and Q squares are distant three squares, and in these cases two and three diagonal moves are respectively necessary.

V. Oefele's rules of Pawn-promotion are different again. Some of the Bataks do not know any rule, and when a Pawn has reached its eighth rank it turns about and retraces its way square by square across the board still moving and capturing as a Pawn, and it has the possibility of marching up and down the board an unlimited number of times.[19] Generally the Batak players require an additional diagonal move to be made before promotion is possible. The two concluding steps—that from the 7th to the 8th rank, and the diagonal step—may both be made in the same turn of play, a double move called *gelong*, which is subject to the opponent's right to take the Pawn *in passing* on the 8th rank. A Pawn may make a capture on the second move of the *gelong*. The *gelong* may not be played if the Pawn give check by the first part of the move. For example: White P on e7, Black R on f7. White can play P–e8–f7 taking the R, all in one move. If, however, the Black K be on d7 he can only play Pe8, check! Similarly, if it is possible to take a piece on the 8th rank, this capture is obligatory when the Pawn is moved, and the *gelong* is forbidden. In these two cases a second move is necessary to secure the right to promotion. Apparently the promotion is still incomplete and the Rāja must next make a move.[20] The promoted Pawn is now permitted to move in accordance with its new dignity, but it is still debarred from making a capture until its second move. It is not stated

[19] V. Oefele notes that the few Bataks who play in this way are a poorer race, the result of a strong admixture of Malay blood.

[20] V. Oefele says, *der oberste Kriegsherr*, by which I take it he can only mean the Rāja. Unfortunately, the complicated manœuvre is not exemplified in any of his illustrative games.

whether the Pawn is immune from capture during these operations. When finally promoted it can take the rank of any piece.[21]

This is a very long and complicated process, and very different from the rule as given by Robinson. It will be remembered that the Batak board is also covered with an elaborate network of lines which would not suggest a rule for promotion in the same way as the board of the mainland.

It is usual on the mainland to warn a player that his Mantri is under attack. Blagden gives *mor* as the call for this purpose. Robinson gives *dōman* as used at Selangor when the capture is threatened by another Mantri, and *mā* as used when any other piece makes the threat.

The term for discovered check is *aras*.[22] This is derived from the Arabic *iʿra* (Per. *ʿirā*, Hindustani *ʿarop*) which is regularly used in this sense in the earlier writers. Robinson gives *aras sah* as meaning double check and *aras mā* as a check which forks the Mantri. V. Oefele notes that the Bataks make a distinction between *sah*, direct check, and *aras*, discovered check. If the latter is irremediable—i. e. in European parlance is mate—the Batak calls the game drawn (*sri*): e.g. White, Kg1, Qh6, Kth7; Black, Kh8; the move Kt(h7)f6 is *aras* and the game is drawn. This leads to a still greater anomaly, a piece which is covering a check is deemed to have no power of giving check to the opposing King: e.g. White, Kg5, Bg4; Black, Ke2, Rf3, Pd3; White can calmly play Kf4 and draw the game.

Stalemate, called *metuh* (v. Oefele), or *mūttu* (Robinson), is reckoned as a draw.

There appear to be no special rules respecting *Bare King* in the Batak game. Sir T. Raffles says for Java:

> A piece or Pawn must remain on the board till the last; if the King is left alone it is considered as stalemate, and he wins.

The allusion is probably to the English rule of stalemate at the beginning of the 19th century, in which the King who was put into the position of stalemate was counted as having won the game. MacGleans (*Sch.* 1867, 227) says of Java, however, that Bare King is a drawn ending. At Selangor the rule is different again; Mr. Robinson says:

> Towards the end of a game care must be exercised in not capturing all the opponent's pieces, for if the King be left solus the game is practically drawn, as he may move just as he pleases, like a King, Queen, Bishop, Knight, Rook or Pawn! He is then termed Rāja Lela with powers to *bermaharaja lela*, i. e. to play the Maharaja Lela.[23] . . .

[21] Promotion to the rank of any piece is also the rule in Borneo. The evidence for Java is not clear. Sir T. Raffles merely says that there is no limit to the number of Queens possible at one time in the game. This suggests that promotion is limited to the rank of Mantri.

[22] Wilkinson in his *Malay Dictionary* appears to have misunderstood this term, for he defines *aras* thus: 'Arabic, an expression in Chess, "Guard your Queen", "The Queen is *en prise*", only used, however, when the Queen is threatened by a Knight.' The comparative evidence of Arabic, Persian, and Urdu chess-books supports Robinson and v. Oefele.

[23] 'The only person who in former days was not in the least affected by the royal taboos which protected the regalia from the common touch was the (now I believe extinct) official who held the post of Court Physician (*Maharaja Lela*). He, and he alone, might go freely in the royal apartments wherever he chose, and the immunity and freedom which he enjoyed

The fact that the game is generally played for a stake naturally leads to the game at odds being often played. V. Oefele notes that the usual odds given by a strong player is to undertake to mate the opponent on one of the four central squares (d4, e4, d5, e5). This is called *Tepong*.

The crosswise arrangement of the Rājas, combined with the modern powers of move, has led to the prevalence of the wing attack in the actual game. Raja Brooke remarks that the ordinary method of opening the game in Borneo was to advance the QRP, the QKtP and QBP and to manœuvre the Q behind them. This is well illustrated in the nine games which v. Oefele gives from Batak play. After recording some games played by natives in his neighbourhood, he arranged a match between the best of the local players, by name Singambati, and Sibayak, whom popular opinion declared to be one of the best living Batak players. Sibayak had no difficulty in beating his opponent by 4–0. From his experience of native play, v. Oefele states that there are certain regular lines of opening play which are popular among players. The better players observe the rule that a piece once touched must be played.[24] The study of the simpler endings is also attempted with some system.

I select three games from v. Oefele's work as illustrating well the main features of Batak play. In all of them I give the move to White, and the Kings are to be placed upon d1 and e8.

No. 1

Loetong v Singambati

	White	Black
1	Pd3	Pa6
2	Pg4	Pd5
3	Bg2	B × P
4	Ktc3	Pc6
5	Pf4	Bf5
6	Qf2 [25]	Ktf6
7	Ktf3	bKtd7
8	Ph3	Qc7
9	Ktd4	Bg6
10	Pf5	Bh5
11	Rf1	Rc8[26]
12	Bf4	Pe5 [27]
13	Bg3	Qb6
14	Ktf3	B × Kt
15	B × B	Bc5
16	Pe3 ?	Pd4
17	Kta4	Qb4
18	Kt × B	Q × Kt
19	P × P	Q × P
20	Re1	Qd6
21	Rc1	Rf8
22	Kb1	Kg8
23	Ph4	Pb5
24	Ph5	Pa5
25	Qh2	f Re8
26	Ph6	Pg6
27	P × P	f P × P
28	cRd1	Ktd5
29	B × Kt	P × B
30	Pd4	Qc7
31	P × P	Qc4
32	Pe6	Ktc5
33	Pb3	Qg4
34	R × P ?	Kte4
35	Re5	Q × B
36	Q × Q	Kt × Q
37	R(e1)e3	Ktf5
38	Rf3	Kt × P
39	Rf1	Pa4
40	f Re1	P × P
41	aP × P	Ktf 5
42	R(e1)e4	Ktd6
43	Rb4	Rc3
44	Rd4	Ktf 5
45	Rb4	Kte3
46	R × P	Kt × P
47	Kb2	cRc8
48	Pe7	Ktd4
49	bRd5	Ktc6
50	Re6	R × P
51	dRd6	eRc7
52	Re1	Kta5
53	eRd1	Rb7
54	R(d6)d3	Ktc4 +
55	Kbl	cRb8
56	Kc2	Kta5
	Resigns.	

No. 2

Siabas v Singambati

	White	Black
1	Pd3	Pa6
2	Pg4	Pb5
3	Bg2	Pd5
4	Ph3	Pc5
5	Pf4	Bb7
6	Qf2	Qc7 [28]

in this respect passed into a proverb, the expression "to act the Court Physician" (*buat Maharaja Lela*) being used to describe an altogether unwarrantable familiarity or impertinence.' Skeat, op. cit., 39.

[24] This rule is obviously necessary whenever the game is played for a stake, if it is desired to obviate a fruitful cause of dispute. V. Oefele notes that one player washed his face before playing, in order that he might see more clearly.

[25] This is the general position of the Q in the opening.

[26] V. Oefele says that the play up to this point frequently recurs in Batak play, and that it may accordingly be regarded as one of their regular openings. In the match-games between Sibayak and Singambati a more cautious and less stereotyped method of opening was adopted.

[27] The Bataks use the term *chawang* (= fork) for this 'forking' of two pieces.

[28] The Black development up to move 6 is traditional (cf. Raja Brooke, cited above), and is called *Prung gunung* (= crag war), since the opening is much played by the mountain tribes.

MALAY CHESSMEN (SELANGOR)
From the Skeat Collection in the Museum of Archaeology and Ethnology, Cambridge

White	Black	White	Black	White	Black	White	Black
7 Ktc3	Pd4	No. 3		16 Pa4	Ktg6	34 K × R	Rc1 +
8 Ktd5	B × Kt	Sibayak v Singam-		17 Ph4	Kte5	35 Kb2	Rc5
9 B × B	Ra7	bati[29]		18 Pf3	Ba6	36 Rd3	Kf8
10 Pf5	Ktf6	1 Pd3	Pe6	19 Kth3	Ktg6	37 Rc3	Ke7
11 Bf4	Pe5	2 Bf4	Bd6	20 Ktf2	Qc3	38 Kc2	Pf6
12 B × P +	K × B	3 Bg3	Kte7	21 Q × Q	P × Q	39 Kd3	Ph6
13 Bg5	Ktd5	4 Pe4	Pb5	22 Bf1	B × B	40 Rc4	Kd7
14 Qf3	Qd6	5 B × B	P × B	23 cR × R	Kte5	41 Pb4	P × P
15 Rc1	Kte3 +	6 Ktc3	Pa6	24 Ktd3	Kt × Kt	42 R × P	Rc7 ?
16 Kb1	Pc4	7 Pd5[30]	Rf8	25 P × Kt	Kg8 ?	43 Pa5	Ra7
17 B × Kt	P × B	8 Pg4	Bb7	26 Kc2	fRe8	44 Rb5	Kc7
18 Q × P	Rc7	9 Bg2	Qc7	27 P × P	dP × P	45 Kc4	Pg5
19 Ktf3	Pc3	10 Rc1	Pb4	28 Pd4	Pe5	46 Ph5	Rb7
20 Kte5 +	Kg8	11 Kta4	Pa5	29 Pd5	Rc5	47 R × R	K × R
21 Pd4 !	P × P ?	12 Pb3	Kta6	30 Rd1	eRc8	48 Kb5	Kb8
22 Qb3 +	Rf7	13 Kb1	Rc1	31 hRe1	Rb8	49 Kb6	Ka8
23 Q × R mate.		14 Qd2	Ktc5	32 Re3	Rc7	50 Kc6	Resigns.
		15 Kt × Kt	Q × Kt	33 R × P	R × R +		

There is no systematic study of the problem in Malay chess, but v. Oefele notes that a position is occasionally arranged on the board and a wager laid upon its solution. One such position that he had seen is the well-known European problem, White, Ke5, Re1; Black, Ke8, in which White gives mate on the third move.[31]

The chessmen in use on the mainland are generally clumsily carved from soft wood, with no distinction of colour, the one side being only distinguished from the other by a daub of lime or paint. Mr. Skeat tells me that the Pawns are often made afresh on each occasion of play. Ivory sets for royal use, and other sets of harder wood are not unknown. I give illustrations of some of the chessmen in the Skeat Ethnological Collection, and of some other sets as well. The more highly finished chessmen approximate in pattern to the modern Muslim pieces used in India. Since the Malays of the Peninsula are Sunnite Muhammadans of the Shafiʿite school, the use of carved pieces, images of the actual forms represented, is forbidden by their religion.

In Sumatra, it is usual to make fresh chessmen on each occasion of playing. This only occupies about 10 minutes. A piece of bamboo or the midrib of a palm leaf is obtained and the pieces are quickly cut after a conventional pattern. The two sides are distinguished by slight variations in the shape. The pattern does not look to me to be derived from the Muslim type of the mainland. Most noteworthy is the fact that the Mantri is made the tallest of the pieces. The Kūda, with head cut aslope, may be a recollection of an early type of European Knight which is still occasionally repeated in English sets, and the Tĕr with its cleft in the top recalls the old shape of the European Rook.

The country whence the Malays obtained their chess has been represented

[29] From the match of four games.

[30] For the deferred double step, see p. 101 above.

[31] Solved by 1 Ke6, ⌐ ; 2 Rc1 or g1 according to Black's play, Ke8 ; 3 R mates.

by different writers as Arabia, Persia, and India.[32] The philological evidence derived from the nomenclature is only satisfied by the hypothesis of an Indian

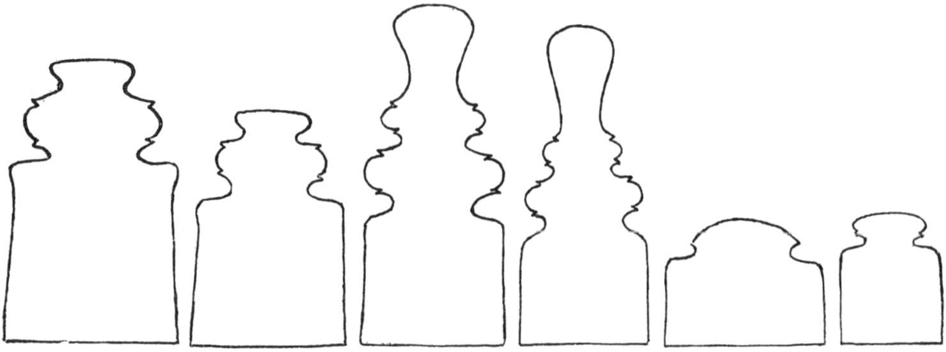

Rāja. Mantri. Gājah. Kūda. Tēr. Bīdaq.

I. A set of hard wood in the possession of Mr. Robinson.

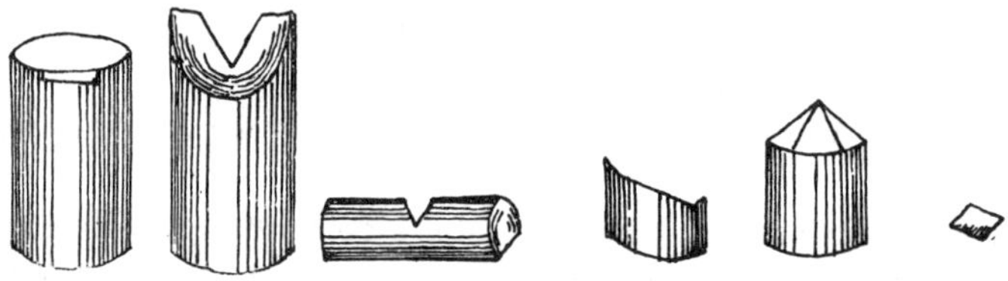

Rāja. Mantri. Tēr. Kūda. Gājah Bīdaq.

II. From v. Oefele.

Rāja. Mantri. Tēr. Kūda. Gājah. Bīdaq.

III. From Mr. Claine's paper, *BCM.* 1891.

MALAY CHESSMEN.

ancestry, with later modifications as a result of the knowledge of Arabic which resulted from the introduction of the Muslim religion from Southern India. It is not improbable that the Tamil and Telugu terms were also introduced with Muhammadanism.

The evidence of the practical game points to Southern Europe[33], and

[32] Arabia is the opinion to which Clifford and Swettenham incline. There is, of course, strong Arabic influence in the nomenclature, but the presence of Skr. terms, and the name of the game, *chātor*, seem fatal to the claim. Persia (i. e. probably the Parsis in S. India) was suggested by Crawfurd (*Hist. Ind. Arch.*, Edinburgh, 1820, i. 112), the intermediaries being the Telingas, and the date of the introduction comparatively recent. Forbes supported the view that I have taken in the text (263, 265, 275). He argued for a greater antiquity than I think probable, from the presence of the Prahu in the Javan game. This piece he associated with the Boat in the four-handed Bengali game.

[33] Thus the rule that the Rāja loses its power of leaping after the first check, even though it remains unmoved, existed in the chess of certain parts of Italy, and possibly elsewhere in Southern Europe, in 1600 and later.

suggests that extensive modifications have been made in rule and move as a result of the intercourse with Portuguese and Dutch since 1500. The existing variations all appear to me consistent with the view that the European practice of the middle and later half of the 16th century remodelled the native game. The differences are superimposed, not fundamental. They occur just in those points in which uncertainty exists to-day among beginners, or in circles out of touch with the literature of the modern game. At the same time the use of the unchequered board, and the whole question of Pawn-promotion, is still pure Asiatic. To the objection that the European powers of move had already taken root in India, and that there is the simpler possibility that the change came via India, the Pawn's move seems a sufficient answer. Had the change come from Southern India, we should have found the double step restricted to particular Pawns, or hedged about with conditions: we should probably also have found restrictions placed upon the free promotion to the rank of any piece.

CHAPTER VI

CHESS IN FURTHER INDIA

Introductory remarks.—I. Burmese chess.—Name of the game.—The chessboard.—The chessmen.—Nomenclature.—Initial arrangement.—Rules.—II. Siamese chess.—Name of the game.—The chessboard.—The chessmen.—Nomenclature.—Initial arrangement.—Rules.—Specimen game.—III. Annamese chess.

MODERN European observers have recorded the practice of chess in each of the three great political divisions of Further India (Indo-China). Their accounts show that each of these countries has its own peculiar variety of chess, while the Chinese game has been introduced by the numerous Chinese settlers, and is widely played in Siam and Annam.

At first sight the native Burmese and Siamese games, of which alone we have sufficiently detailed information as to the method of play, look very diverse. Closer investigation, however, results in the discovery of certain features which link the two games together. These are—(*a*) the fivefold move of the Elephant, which al-Bērūnī recorded as existing in India in his day, occurs in each game; (*b*) both games begin from a different arrangement of the chessmen from that followed elsewhere: in Burmese there is no prescribed arrangement for the pieces, but only for the Pawns; in Siamese chess a definite initial arrangement exists; (*c*) the rules of Pawn-promotion are unusual.

I have already shown that the Burmese and Annamese names for their forms of chess both go back ultimately to the Skr. *chaturanga*, and thus point to the Indian ancestry of both games. Although the Siamese name for chess is of different origin, the names of the pieces show a closer connexion between Siamese and Annamese chess than between either of these games and Burmese chess. We know too little of the history of these nationalities to be very certain as to the history of their games, but it seems most probable that chess, which has always been in attendance on great missionary movements, reached Further India with Buddhism, and spread over the peninsula with that religion. It has been commonly held that Buddhism reached Burma from Ceylon and that its further spread was by way of the river basins. The introduction is placed in the 5th c. A.D., and the diffusion from the Irawadi basin to Arakan first, and later to Kambaya, Pegu, and Siam, where Buddhism was introduced in the 7th c. There is, however, good reason to believe that the overthrow of Buddhism in Northern India resulted in migrations into Burma from the Ganges basin direct, and that Buddhism spread down, as well as up, the river valleys. Chess may well have reached Burma by land.

Chess is undoubtedly of high antiquity in Burma, but no tradition of its history has been recorded.[1]

I. Burma.

The earliest accounts of Burmese chess are contained in Symes's *Account of an Embassy to the Kingdom of Ava* (in 1795), London, 1800, 466–7, and in Captain Hiram Cox's paper *On the Burmha Game of Chess compared with the Indian, Chinese, and Persian Games of the same Denomination*, which was written in 1799 and was published, after the author's death, in *Asiatic Researches*, Calcutta, 1801, vii. 488–511. Captain Cox had obtained his knowledge of Burmese chess during his residence at the court of Amarapura. Of more recent date are the accounts of Dr. Adolf Bastian (*Leipziger Illustr. Zeit.*, July 4, 1863) and of Sir J. G. Scott, who devotes a whole chapter of his work on Burma to Burmese chess.[2] The following account is based upon information given me by Mr. E. Colston, I.C.S., who, a chess-player himself in England, had learnt and played the native game in Burma. The accuracy of the details has been established by reference to native players.

The Burmese name for their chess is *sittuyin*, pronounced in Arakanese *sitturin*.[3] The game is also called colloquially *sitbuyin* (Arakanese, *sitburin*). In both these forms *sit* is the Burmese word for army, and is probably the direct Burmese descendant of the Skr. *chaturanga*.[4] *Sittuyin* may be translated 'representation of the army'. *Sitbuyin* is identical in form with the Burmese military term for 'generalissimo', 'commander-in-chief', but Mr. Colston and the Burmans whom I have consulted do not recognize any connexion between the two words.

The Burmese chessboard (*sittuyin-kon*; *kya-kwet*=a square of the chessboard or any similar board) is unchequered.[5] It is usually very large, and is raised above the ground for the convenience of the players who, following the ordinary Burmese custom, squat upon the ground. The chess-table, for so it becomes, is supplied with a drawer to hold the chessmen when not in use, and often a supply of lime, areca nuts, and betel ready for the player to chew during play. Like the Indian and Malay boards, the surface exhibits

1 The story which a Rangoon player told Sir J. G. Scott (Shway Yoe), that chess was invented 'by an ancient Talaing queen, who was passing fond of her lord, and to keep him by her and out of war invented chess' (Shway Yoe, *The Burman, His Life and Notions*, London, 1882, ii. 70), can hardly be dignified by the name of tradition.

2 The *Burman*, already quoted above. Other writers have followed one or other of these authorities, often misunderstanding them. Falkener's account (177–190) is quite worthless, and his second variety, in which he allows a Pawn to receive the rank of the Rook on promotion, is a game of his own invention. It is unknown in Burma.

3 I follow the official transliteration. Symes's spelling, *chedreen*, and Cox's, *chit-tha-reen*, are attempts to reproduce the Burmese word by ear. Himly's forms (*chatturan, chachturan, tsitturan*; *tsat-bhuran, tsil-boyen*) are due to obsolete methods of transliteration.

4 The word has lost all trace of its original meaning of four-membered. Judson (*Dict. Burmese Lang.*) quotes the phrase *sit inga le ba*, 'an army composed of four parts'.

5 Mr. Colston has seen boards that have been chequered for purposes of decoration.

other marks than the lines which divide the squares from each other. These marks vary on different boards, and may even be entirely absent, but the player must always supply them mentally. They govern the whole question of Pawn-promotion.

These markings are something like those recorded in the Malay boards from the mainland, where again, though in a different way, they are associated with Pawn-promotion. On the other hand, they widely differ from the markings of the Indian boards. The most persistent marks on the Indian board are connected with the central squares on opposite edges and

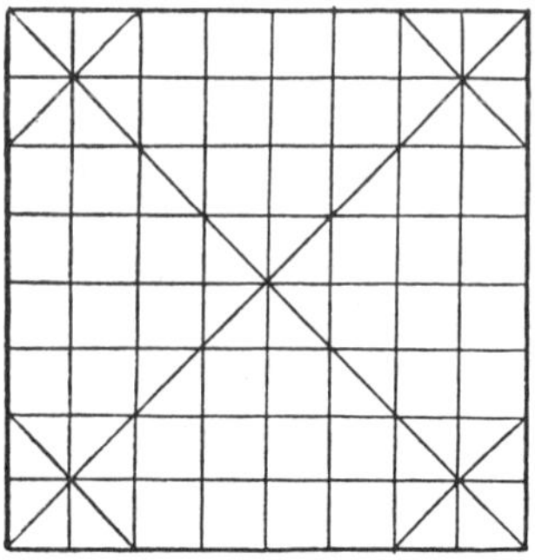

The ordinary Burmese Board (Bassein, &c.).

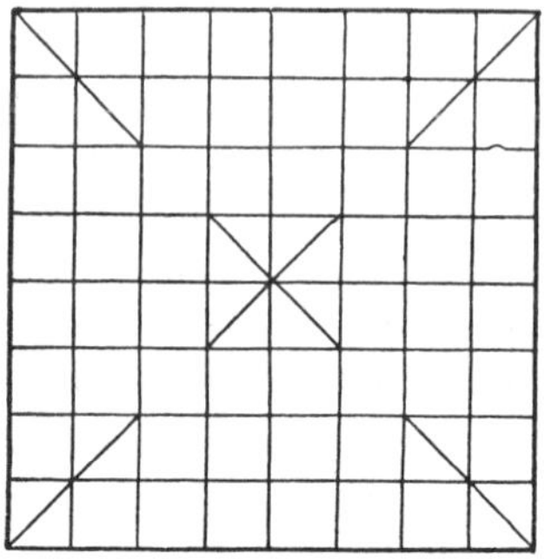

From a Board belonging to Mr. A. J. Neilson, Glasgow.

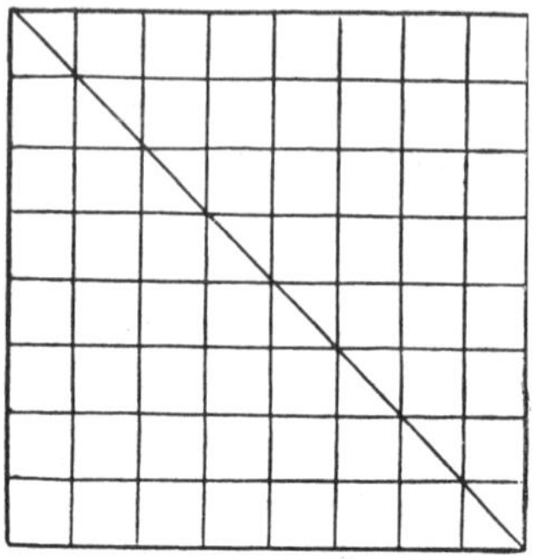

Falkener.

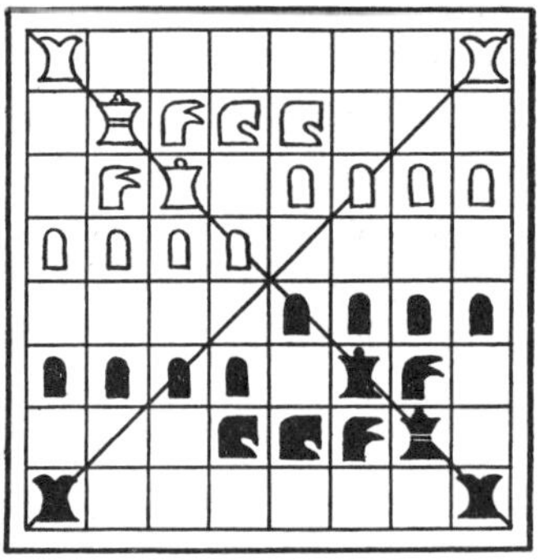

Shway Yoe.

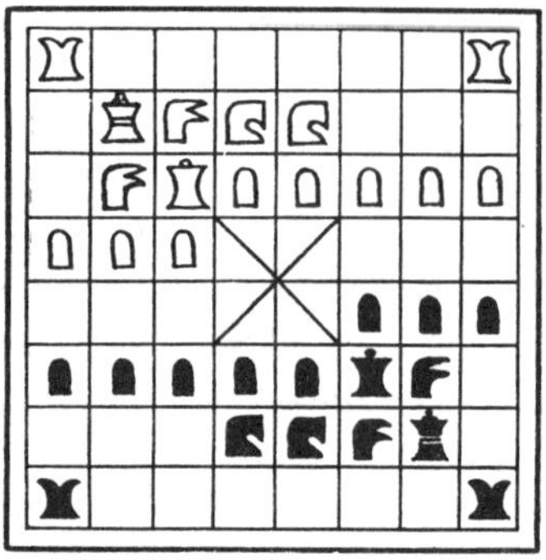

Capt. Cox.

The markings on Burmese Chessboards, and Burmese arrangements of the Chessmen.

the four squares in the middle of the board. The marks on the Burmese board deal rather with the board as a whole than with particular squares on it. I am at a loss to explain them, for the anomalous rules of Pawn-promotion must, I think, be due to the marks, and not the marks to the rules: indeed, I see no other way of accounting for the appearance of the rules than to suppose that they were suggested by the markings. None of my Burman informants could give any explanation of them. They thought that the markings were only added 'for ornament'.

Burmese chessmen are always actual figures, though the carving of them is

BURMESE CHESSMEN
Pitt-Rivers Collection, Oxford

[Face page 111

very rude and tends to become conventional. They are nearly always made of wood and stained red and black.[6] The red Pawns are carved as men, the black as monkeys, in reference to the battle in the *Rāmāyana* between Rāma and the monkeys. Ivory sets are very rare; none of the Burmans whom I consulted had ever seen any ivory sets in use. There are ivory sets, however, at South Kensington and in the Pitt-Rivers Museum, Oxford; of the latter set I give a picture. The ivory sets are coloured white and red.

The names and powers of the Burmese chessmen are given in the following table:

No.	Burmese Name.[7]	Translation.	Power of Move.	Equivalent.
1	mín-gyi	Great King	One step in every direction	K
2	sit-kè (sit-bo)	Lieutenant-General	One step in the four diagonal directions	Q
3–4	sin	Elephant	One step in five directions, viz. the four diagonal directions and vertically forwards only	B
5–6	myin	Horse	The Knight's leap	Kt
7–8	yattah	Chariot	The Rook's move	R
9–16	nè		One step vertically forwards, capturing as in European chess	P

All the major pieces capture as they move.[8] The title *sit-kè* was formerly employed for civil as well as military officers of subordinate rank. *Yattah* (in Arakanese *ratta*) is simply the Skr. *rat·ha*.

At the commencement of the game the sixteen *Nès* or Pawns are placed upon the board in the position shown in the accompanying diagram. This arrangement of the *Nès* is never varied. The game now commences with alternate moves, and each player in turn places one of his major pieces on the board on any vacant square in his own half of the board. As a rule the players begin by placing their *Mín-gyis* (K) on g2 and b7; their *Myins* (Kts) are placed so as to support one another, one *Sin* (B) is placed next the *Mín-gyi* (K), and the *Yattahs* (R) are placed on files which are comparatively empty of pieces in order that they may break through

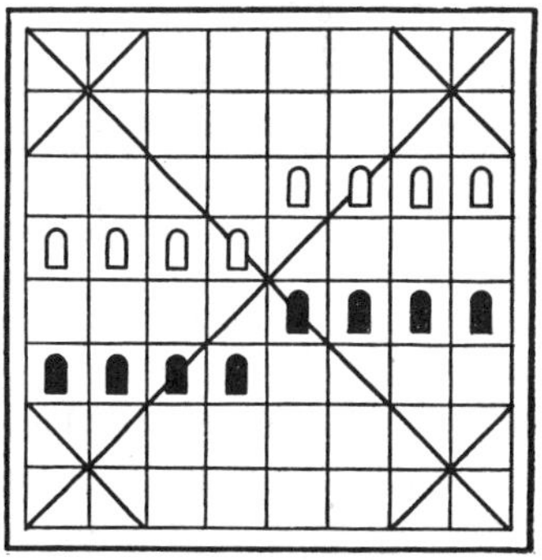

Initial arrangement of the *Nès* (Pawns).

[6] Mr. Colston has only seen black and red chessmen. Other authorities speak of red and green chessmen; possibly the green are only black men which have worn badly. There are pictures of native boards and chessmen in Falkener, facing 177, and in Culin, *C. & P. C.*, plate 32, facing 859.

[7] I follow the official transliteration. Earlier writers have followed different methods or have attempted to take the names down orally. Thus Symes has *meem* (K), *chekey* (Q), *mene* (Kt), *yettay* (R), *maundelay* (P). Cox has *ming* (K), *chekoy* (Q), *chein* (R), *mhee* (Kt), *rut·ha* (R), *yein* (P); Bastian *seekay* (Q), *yetta* (R); Shway Yoe, *si'ke* (Q), *yittah* (R).

[8] Cox limited the *sin's* power of capture to the diagonal directions. Later authorities know nothing of any limitation of move, and Mr. Colston and my Burman informants agree that Cox is wrong here.

as soon as possible. If a player think it expedient to place one of his major pieces upon a square already occupied by one of his *Nès* (P), he is at liberty to do so and to place the *Nè* elsewhere behind the row of *Nès*. In the position given by Bastian, Black has evidently done this, placing his *Sit-kè* on h4 and the *Nè* from h4 on e3.

When all the pieces are disposed on the board, the players are still at liberty in the following moves to continue to rearrange their pieces by abnormal moves, removing one piece in each turn of play. With the advance of the first *Nè* (P), this liberty ceases, and the game continues by alternate legal moves of the chessmen.

Most Burmans have a favourite disposition for their pieces, though obviously a good deal ought to depend upon the arrangement adopted by the opponent. Previous observers have recorded the favourite arrangements of their native informants. Earlier chess writers (cf. Forbes, 261) have associated these varying arrangements with the Arabic taʿbīyāt, or the Indian custom of opening the game with a number of simultaneous moves. It is obvious from Mr. Colston's full description of the whole manœuvre that we have something utterly different here. I imagine that the Burmese initial play has developed out of an older arrangement of the board of which the Siamese arrangement is perhaps a survival. Both Symes and Cox would seem to point to an earlier condition of things. According to the former, each player arranges his men on three lines by which eight squares are left unoccupied. This would exactly fit the Siamese arrangement as given below. A young Burman from Moulmein drew the Siamese arrangement and gave the Siamese rules when I asked him to describe the chess that he played at home.[9] The arrangement which Cox gave (see p. 110) shows an intermediate position of the Pawns between the Siamese and the modern Burmese.

Burmese arrangement of the Chessmen. From Bastian.

Any *Nè* (P) that is played to a marked square can be promoted to the rank of *Sit-kè* (Q), provided that the player has no other *Sit-kè* on the board at the moment. In promoting the *Nè* the player is at liberty to place the *Sit-kè* (which replaces the *Nè*) upon the square occupied by the promoted *Nè*, or upon any adjacent square which is not commanded by an opponent's piece. If a player whose turn it is to play has a *Nè* standing on a marked square, and no *Sit-kè* on the board, he can, if he likes, simply promote the *Nè* without moving at all. In certain positions, when a player cannot make a move without disadvantage, this may become a valuable privilege. Obviously the *Nès* most favourably situated for promotion are those on the player's right wing. It is in consequence of this, and the difficulty of promoting a Pawn on the other wing, that Cox and Shway Yoe would limit promotion to the

[9] But other Burmans to whom I showed this arrangement refused to recognize it as Burmese. I believe there is a considerable Siamese colony in Moulmein, and perhaps Maung Kin only gave me the Siamese arrangement and rules of Pawn-promotion.

Pawns on the right wing, which alone could advance to the sinister diagonal (a1 to h8) on which promotion is most easily secured.[10]

The most useful piece with which to give mate is the *Sin* (B); Burmese players accordingly do not like to exchange their *Sins*. For 'check' they say *kwĕ* (Cox, *kwai*), and for check-rook, a move forking King and Rook, *kwadot*. There is no term for mate; the winner generally says *Neinbe*, 'I have won'; the loser, *Shonbe*, 'I have lost'.

Stalemate is not known in Burmese chess; a player is not allowed to place his opponent in a stalemate position. He must give the *Mín-gyi* room to play.

At the conclusion of a game it is usual for the winner to give the loser a dab on the cheek with the soft powdered lime that Burmans always carry with them in order to prepare the betel for chewing. In this way the score of a succession of games at a sitting may be kept. Some players give a dab for every check in the game. Chess is mainly played by elderly Burmans, and, according to Mr. Colston, is of all Burmese games the freest from betting. Shway Yoe, on the other hand, says that there is always heavy betting on the games, and that during matches between the more famous players the excitement becomes so intense that it is not uncommon for the spectators (who advise the players freely) to come to actual blows.[11]

The Burmans have paid no attention to the composition or study of chess problems.

II. Siam.

La Loubère, the envoy-extraordinary of Louis XIV of France to the court of Siam in 1687–8, tells, in the account of Siam which he published on his return to Europe,[12] that the Siamese 'jouent aux échecs à nôtre manière, et à la manière chinoise'. This information agrees with that given by travellers in the present century, and explains the apparent discrepancies that exist between other descriptions of Siamese chess. An admirable account of the games of Siam (first written in 1829) was contributed in 1836 to *Asiatic Researches* (XX, part ii, pp. 374 seq.) by Capt. James Low, M.R.A.S.C., and Falkener supplements this by giving reliable native information which he obtained from Prince Dewawongse, the Siamese Minister of Foreign Affairs, through the assistance of Mr. E. B. Gould, our consul at Bangkok in 1889.[13]

[10] Cox allowed promotion to 5, Shway Yoe to 4 *Nès* only. The latter gives the rule about the position of the new *Sit-kè* thus: 'When, however, the Pawn replaces the dead leader (Q), he is not allowed to remain on the square where he gained the distinction. He must be placed on one of the eight surrounding checks at the player's option, and therefore often falls a victim to his new-gained eminence.' Falkener has misunderstood this passage completely. Mr. Colston and my Burman informants agree that Shway Yoe's statement is incomplete, and give the rule as stated in the text.

[11] Cf. Shway Yoe, op. cit., and V. C. Scott O'Connor, *The Silken East*, London, 1904, i. 186.

[12] M. de la Loubère, *Du Royaume de Siam*, Paris, 1691, i. 191. Sir John Bowring, *Kingdom and People of Siam*, London, 1857, i. 151–2, apparently used La Loubère as his authority for Siamese chess and merely describes the Chinese game.

[13] Other information is to be found in the *Leipzig. Illustr. Zeit.*, April 16, 1864 (by Dr. A. Bastian), which was summarized by v. d. Linde, i. 84; in the *Leipzig. Illustr. Zeit.*, Oct. 11, 1879 (which served as the basis for an article in the *Sch.*, 1880, 321); and in the *BCM*, 1893, 382, quoting from the *New York Tribune*. The German accounts describe the native game, but the

As the Chinese chess of Siam does not appear to differ materially in move or rule from that of China itself, I propose in the present chapter to confine my attention to the native variety alone.

It is not possible to discover any trace of Indian ancestry in the nomenclature of Siamese chess. This is the more remarkable, for the word *chaturanga* has actually been adopted in Siamese in the sense of army.[14] The game bears the name of *mak-rūk*, a word of which both origin and signification have been forgotten. It cannot be explained by reference to any existing Siamese root, and is therefore in all probability a loan-word adopted from some neighbouring language.[15] Loan-words in Siamese often undergo such radical changes that the original word is completely disguised; the language, being originally monosyllabic, although it now shows a large admixture of Burmese and

Siamese Chessmen. From the *Schachzeitung*.

Burmese Pali, has a tendency to reduce all foreign words to a monosyllabic form.

The Siamese chessboard is unchequered, and, so far as information goes, exhibits none of the additional lines that are to be found on the Indian and other boards of the far East.

The Siamese chessmen are fashioned after a conventional pattern, approximating somewhat to European and somewhat to Indian models. For the Pawns it is usual to use cowrie shells, placing them with the aperture downwards. On promotion the player merely turns the shell over so that now the aperture is uppermost. Instead of shells the glass counters used in the Chinese game of *wei-k'i* are often used.

BCM. describes Chinese chess, and apparently the use of dice is contemplated, for the note concludes: 'As a rule the powers of the pieces are more circumscribed than those in our game, and the moves to some extent are regulated by the throw of the dice, but the end is the same—checkmate to the King.'

[14] See Pallegoix, *Siamese Vocab.*, 87, '*Chatu rong*, quatuor agmina exercitus cum suis quatuor ducibus.'

[15] The first element, *mak*, appears in the names of other games. Low mentions *mak-yep*, a board-game played with 14 counters on a board of 16 squares; *mak khom*, the game of *manqala*; and *maak-yek*, played on the chessboard between two sides of 16 men which are arranged on the 1st and 3rd (6th and 8th) rows of the board. The men move on the squares in all directions without limit to the number crossed (? i. e. move like the Rook), and the aim is to place a man between two opponents, when he captures both. In another variety one man opposes 16, and moves in any direction, not diagonally, and takes by leaping over an opponent into a blank square beyond. (Similar games exist in Japan, see p. 147.) It looks, accordingly, as if *mak* meant board-game or something similar, especially as the names of the other games commence with *len* (=play), e. g. *len doat*; *len cũa kin ngoa* (the tiger game); *len choa*; *len saké* (backgammon).

The names and power of move of the Siamese pieces are exhibited in the following table:

No.	Siamese Name.	Translation.	Power of Move.	Equivalent.
1	khūn	Lord	One step in every direction. For its first move the Knight's leap also	K
2	met	Minister (*Low*)	One step in the four diagonal directions. For its first move a double step (e1–e3 only)	Q
3, 4	khōn	Nobleman (post, supporter, *Low*)	One step in five directions, the four diagonal directions and vertically forwards only	B
5, 6	mā	Horse	The Knight's leap	Kt
7, 8	rüa	Boat	The Rook's move	R
9–16	bia	Cowrie shell	One step vertically forwards. It captures as the European P does	P

The meanings of the Siamese names are not altogether certain. *Khūn* is the ordinary word for nobleman, but the King's name may be a contraction for *khūn luang*, meaning king. *Met* in Siamese means a small seed or trifle, but the name is not very appropriate, and it has been suggested that *met* may be really Skr. *mantri*. The chief objection to this conjecture is the absence of any other trace of Skr. nomenclature. According to Mr. Gould *khōn* has no meaning at all. Falkener's conjecture that *khōn* = Burmese *chein* (Cox), *sin* (Shway Yoe), is too far-fetched. *Mā* is Chinese for horse. *Bia* means a cowrie shell and is due to the common use of these as Pawns.

The *Boat* also appears among the chessmen in the Annamese game, and we have already met with it in the modern chess of Bengal, and in the Javan game. I have already expressed the opinion that these coincidences are accidental. Siam and Annam are both countries in which the principal means of communication is by water, and the presence of the *Boat* in chess may reflect this fact.

The Siamese arrangement of the Chessmen.

The initial arrangement of the game is invariable and yet not that of Indian chess. The Kings are placed crosswise, each *met* (Q) being on the King's *right*. The eight Pawns on each side are all advanced to the third rank. We have already seen that there is some evidence for the existence of this or a similar arrangement in Burmese chess.

The same arrangement of the Pawns upon the third line is found in the Japanese game. The resemblance is probably accidental, although there are other features of Siamese chess which approximate curiously to features of the Japanese game. The fivefold move of the *Khōn* (B) appears in Japanese chess as the move of the *Gin*, which also is posted on the third square from the corner (c1, &c.). Still more curious is the fact that in both games the row upon which promotion takes place is the third from the opponent's edge of the board—in Siamese chess the player's sixth row, upon which the opponent's Pawns were originally posted. But the resemblance is probably accidental and extends no further, for, while in Japanese chess pieces and Pawns alike obtain promotion, in the Siamese game promotion is confined to the Pawns. A Pawn reaching the sixth row becomes at once a *Met* (Q), whether the player's original *Met* be on the board or not. There is no limit to the number of *Mets* that a player may have at any one time.[16]

Capt. Low gives the following rules in connexion with the ending (op. cit., 378):

> The following are established rules. If a King is left alone to contend, his aim is to get so placed as to prevent being checkmated within a certain number of moves. In the first place, however, the number of pieces actually on the board is deducted from the prescribed number of moves in each case. Thus, if the King has opposed to him a King and two Castles, the number of pieces on the board (4) is deducted from the prescribed number 8. If the adversary has only a Castle, the prescribed number is 16. If he has two Bishops, it is 22. If with one, 44. If with three Knights, 33. If with one Knight, 66. If with a mét, it is a drawn game. If with a Queen or mét and two Pawns, 88 moves; with a Queen, Bishop, Knight, and Castle, 16 moves are prescribed.[17]

This is a curious attempt to overcome the slowness of the game: of all varieties of chess that I have studied, the Burmese and Siamese are the most tedious and prolonged.

Stalemate is a drawn game.

The differences between Siamese and Burmese chess have the effect of making the former game at once older and more modern in type. The existence of an initial arrangement of the men in Siamese chess, and the absence of any limitations to Pawn-promotion, belong to an older type of game than the Burmese, while the crosswise arrangement, and the larger powers of move of King and *Met* are more modern in type than anything in the existing Burmese game.

The following specimen of Siamese chess was supplied by Prince Dewawongse to Mr. Gould and is taken from Falkener. The white men were played by Chong Kwa and Coy consulting, the black by Nai Chang. All three were reputed to be good players.

White	Black	White	Black	White	Black	White	Black
1 Pe4	Pe5	9 Bc2	Kf7	17 Bc2	aRc8	24 Ktd2	Qd6
2 Pf4	Bf7	10 aRf1	Bc6	18 Pg4	Pg5	25 Bf3	cRf8
3 Ktf3	Be6	11 Pa4	bKtd7	19 P × gP	P × gP	26 Ph5	Kd8
4 bKtd2	Pf5	12 Pb4	Qc7	20 Ph4	Pd5	27 Pg5	Bf5
5 Qf2	Ktf6	13 Bb3	Ke2	21 Kt × gP	P × P	28 Pg6 = Q	Pe4
6 Qe3	Bc7	14 fRg1	Pb5	22 Kt(d2)	Kt × Kt	29 Q × B	R × R
7 Bf2	Rg8	15 Pa5	P × eP	× eP		30 R × R	P × B =
8 Ke2	Pc5	16 dP × P	Pc4	23 Kt × Kt	B(c6)d5		Q +

[16] Low adds: 'The pawns on reaching an adversary's line become pieces of higher value without reference to the number of these which may have been taken from their side.' I suppose this is intended for the rule of the text, but if so it is expressed with extraordinary looseness.

[17] Low gives the score of a game in 85 moves which was eventually abandoned as drawn because 'the King had got to his own country within 16 moves'—a reference to the rules for shortening the ending of the game. The game begins 1 Pe4, Pd5; 2 Qf2, Qc7; 3 Qe3, Pc5; 4 Kte2, Ktd7; 5 Ktf4, Bf7; 6 P × dP, Pe5; 7 Ktg2, Qd6; but owing to errors in the score, and the looseness of the method of describing the moves, the game is unintelligible.

White	Black	White	Black	White	Black	White	Black
31 Kt × Q	R × Q	52 Bf5	Re1	73 Rf7	Rf1 +	94 Bc6	Rh7
32 Ph6 = Q	Kc7	53 Rg6 +	Kb7	74 Kg5 ?	Kte4 +	95 Qc7	Ka7
33 Qg5	Be4	54 Rd6	Bc6	75 B × Kt	R × R	96 Ktf5	Rh3
34 Ktd4	Re5	55 Be4	Kc7	76 Ktf5	Ke6	97 Kd7	Rh8
35 Q(g5)f4	Re7	56 Rh6	Kb7	77 Qe5	Rh7	98 Qb6 +	Ka8
36 Rg6	Bd5	57 Kf4	Rg1	78 Ktd4 +	Kd7	99 Kte7	Rf8
37 Ktf5	Re6	58 Ktf5	Rf1 +	79 Kte2	Rh3	100 Qc5	Ka7
38 Rg7	Kd8	59 Ke3	Kc7	80 Qd4	Kd6	101 Kc7	Rb8
39 Kd2	Rf6	60 Ktg3	Rf6	81 Bd5 +	Kd7	102 Qb6 +	Ka8
40 Ktg3	Rh6	61 Rh7	Kd8	82 Ktf4	Rh8	103 Ktd5	Re8
41 Bd1	Re6	62 Qe5	Re6	83 Ktg6	Rh1	104 Kd7 ?[18]	Rg8
42 Be2	Be4	63 Kf4	Kc8	84 Kth4	Ke7	105 Ktc7 +	Kb8
43 Qd4	Kc8	64 Ktf5	Kd8	85 Ktg6 +	Kd7	106 Kt × P +	Ka8
44 Rg5	Kc7	65 Ktd4	Rg6	86 Kte5 +	Kc7	107 Ktc7 +	Kb8
45 Q(f4)e5	Bd5	66 Kf5	Rg3	87 Kf6	Rh6 +	108 Ktd5	Rg6
46 Q × Q +	K × Q	67 Kt×B+	Kc8	88 Ke7	Rh7 +	109 Pa6 = Q	Rg7 +
47 Be3	Kc6	68 Qd4	Rg1	89 Ktf7	Rg7	110 Kte7	R × Kt +
48 Rg7	Rf6	69 Bd5	Rf1 +	90 Qc5	Rh7	111 K × R	Kc8
49 Ke2	Re6	70 Kg5	Rg1 +	91 Qb6 +	Kb7	112 Bc7 mate.	
50 Kf3	Rf6 +	71 Kf4	Ktf6	92 Ke6	Rh3		
51 Bf4	Re6	72 Kte7 +	Kd7	93 Ktd6 +	Ka8		

The Siamese have paid no attention to the End-game or the chess problem.

III. Annam.

Our information as to Annamese chess is very slight, but sufficient to show that, like the Siamese, the Annamese play chess in two ways, one resembling Indian chess, the other identical with Chinese chess. The latter is called *cờ tu'ong* (*kö tüöng*), which is the Annamese form of the Chinese *siang k'i*. Himly notes that the names of the chessmen—called *kon kö* = Chinese *k'i tzĕ*—follow the Chinese with the exception of the horse, which is called *ngüa* instead of *ma*.[19]

Strangely enough, the native game has preserved a name which is derived from the Sanskrit *chaturanga*, though a popular etymology has done its best to disguise the word. Aymonier, in his *Dictionnaire khmêr*, p. 181, s.v. *trang*, has *chhŏeu trăng*[20] (for *chadorang*) chess; where *chhŏeu* is the native word for *wood*, and the perversion of the word is undoubtedly due to the attempt to explain the chess as wooden something, an attempt suggested by the wooden pieces for play. Aymonier gives also *léng chhŏeu trang* = to play chess; *kedâ* (= board) *chhŏeu trang* = chessboard; *kâun* (= son) *chhŏeu trang* = chess-man.[21]

18 Overlooking 104 Bb7 mate.

19 Himly, in *ZDMG.*, xli. 466, and in *T'oung Pao*, May 1897, viii. 158. He also gives *kö vay* = Ch. *wei k'i*; *kö tien* = Ch. *sien k'i*; *kö song luo* = Ch. *shwan lu k'i* (allied to Eng. back-gammon); *dañ kö* = to play chess; *ban kö* = Ch. *k'i phan*, Eng. chessboard.

20 Himly, op. cit., has *chhötrang*.

21 I quote from Himly, *ZDMG.*, xliii. 415. *Leng* (= to play) is found in Janneau's *Manuel pratique de la langue cambodgienne*, p. 107, in connexion with a number of games of Chinese origin. The Siamese form is *len*. *Leňg biér* (Aymonier writes *bié* = cowrie shell, domino, obviously the same with the Siamese *bia* = cowrie shell, mussel, pawn) = to play at dominoes. Moura explains the Siamese *leň bia* as a dice game.

Moura, in his *Royaume du Cămlodge* (i. 391), says of Cambodia :

Almost all classes play chess. As is to be seen, this game is one which is spread over the whole world; it is well known in Europe, and is played in India, Tibet, Mongolia, Indo-China, Annam and China. The Cambodian board resembles ours; it is divided into 64 squares. Each player has 8 pieces, and 8 pawns. The pieces are one King (*sdach*), one Queen, two Knights, two Generals in the place of Castles, and lastly two Boats instead of two Bishops. The 8 other men are simply Pawns which the Khmer designate Fishes (*trey*, less commonly *mîchha* = Skr. *matsya*). The game consists in each player trying to prevent his opponent from giving him 'check', and it is played almost as in Europe.

It is unfortunate that Moura has given so brief and unsatisfying an account. The game is evidently closely akin to that of Siam. Presumably Moura has confused the pieces, and the *Boat* should replace the Rook, not the Bishop.

The pieces probably resemble the Siamese, for among a number of other stories [22] we read in the *Riddles of Thménh Chei* how once Thménh Chei was bidden by his royal master to follow him into a certain forest with a horse, and not being able to find one in the flesh, he appeared with a Horse from the chessboard in his hand, a misinterpretation of the king's command such as might have been anticipated from the famous jester of Indo-China.

[22] Aymonier, *Textes khmêrs*, pp. 20-30 (Himly).

CHAPTER VII

CHESS IN CHINA, COREA, AND JAPAN

The inter-relationships and ancestry of these games.—I. Chinese chess.—The name.—Early references.—The modern game.—The board.—Nomenclature.—Rules.—Openings.—End-games and problems.—Specimen games.—The games *ta-ma* and *kyu-kung*.—Derivative games.—II. Corean chess.—Board.—Nomenclature.—Rules.—Specimen game.—III. Japanese chess.—The name.—History.—Literature.—Board.—Nomenclature.—Rules.—Specimen game.—Derivative games.—Problems.

The development of chess in the far Orient—in China, Corea, and Japan—presents one of the most puzzling chapters in the history of the game. The existing forms of chess are farthest removed from the primeval Indian game, and it is difficult at first sight to believe that a common origin is possible. In Chinese and Corean chess we see the pieces moving, not on the squares, but on the lines of the chessboard. In Japanese chess, not only Pawns but also pieces obtain promotion, while a player is at liberty to place the men he has taken from his adversary again upon the board and to add them to his own army. And yet there is no uncertainty as to the immediate parentage of the Japanese chess. Japanese authorities are unanimous in ascribing their game to China, in complete accord with all that we know of the lines of development of Japanese religion, culture, and literature. The game also itself approximates somewhat to the earlier type of Chinese chess played under the T'ang and Sung dynasties (A.D. 618–1279). We must regard Japanese chess as a modification of the older Chinese chess in one direction, the modern Chinese chess (and the Corean game, which closely resembles it) as a modification in another.

The Indian ancestry of the Chinese game is supported partly by internal evidence based upon the identity of certain essential features in the two games,[1] and partly upon what is known of the indebtedness of China to India in religion, culture, and, above all, in games.

In both Chinese and early Indian chess we find that the pieces from angle to middle of the back line are named

Chariot, Horse, Elephant,[2] Counsellor,

[1] V. d. Linde's suggestion that the Chinese name of the game, *siang k'i*, might be a corruption of the Skr. *chaturanga* is justly condemned by Himly.

[2] As Himly has pointed out, chess must have been invented in a country in which elephants formed a usual and necessary branch of the army. India, of course, satisfies this condition. But so also, apparently, does China. Macdonell (*JRAS.*, 131 n.) quotes Prof. Douglas as stating 'that elephants were numerous in China in the old days, and that the commentator Tso (who lived within a century after Confucius) says they were employed in battle between the states of Wu and Ts'u (512 B.C.)'.

and that these pieces possess essentially similar moves.[3] The Indian Raja has been replaced by a less exalted general, but there would appear to have been weighty reasons for the change.[4] The identity of position and close resemblance of move are too remarkable to be explained as merely due to chance.

From very early times an important trade route has existed from North-west India by Kashmīr, Leh, the Karakoram Pass, Yarkhand, to the basin of the Hoang Ho and the fertile plains of Northern China.[5] By this route Buddhism penetrated to China, together with much else of Indian culture. It was for long the principal road from West to East. And by this route other Indian games reached China, of which tables or backgammon is one of the most interesting, because it long retained a name revealing its Indian origin. This name, *t'shu-p'u*, is a Chinese transliteration of the Indian *chaupur* (= Skr. *chatush-padam*). Chinese works mention its introduction as having taken place as early as A.D. 220–265, and the game had reached Japan before the end of the seventh century.[6]

At one time there was supposed to be actual historical evidence for the introduction of chess from India in the reign of Wu-Ti (A.D. 560–578).[7] As will be seen below, this belief arose from a confusion between chess and another game.[8]

3 The moves in the Chinese game are more restricted than those in the Indian game. At first sight, following the analogy of the Western development of chess, this suggests that the Chinese chess may preserve an older type of the game than we find even in the oldest Indian accounts, and even supports the view that chess is really of Chinese invention. But further investigation shows that the whole tendency of the Chinese game has been in the direction of restriction of power or liberty, and hence I conclude that the restriction of move which we note in the case of these pieces is a Chinese modification of the Indian game.

4 Thus Ssŭ-ma Kuang, in his *T'ung kien nun* (A.D. 1084), tells that the Emperor Wên-Ti (of the Sui dynasty, A.D. 589–605) once visited an inn where foreigners resorted, and found a game of *t'shu-p'u* in progress, in which one of the men was called *I pai ti* (white emperor). He was so enraged at the want of reverence for his august title that this showed, that he put all the inmates to death. This game cannot have been the Indian *chaupur*, as we know it, for that game shows no differentiation of man.

5 This caravan route keeps to the north of the tableland of Tibet, a fact which explains the entire difference of the Tibetan chess from the Chinese game.

6 The Chinese references to this game were collected by Himly. The *Hun Tsun Sü* (of the Sung period, 960–1279) says that *t'shu-p'u* was invented in Western India, and spread to China in the time of the Wei dynasty (A.D. 220–265), where it attained its greatest vogue between 479 and 1000. It adds the information that the game had four other names in succession, *uu-sho* (spear-seizing), *thshan-han* (long row), *po-lo-sai-hi*, and *shwan-liu* (double sixes), its present name. The *Ki Tsuan Yüan Hai* says that the *shwan-liu* came from India, and is called *po-lo sai* in the *Nie-pan-kin* (i.e. the *Nirvāna-sutra*, translated by the Yüe-chi or Indo-Scythian monk, Chĭ-Chang, in the latter half of the second century A.D.). The *Pŏ-Wŭh-Chĕ* (a later reconstruction of a lost work of the third century) says that Lao-Tzû (end of 6th c. B.C.) invented *t'shu-p'u* when he went to Central Asia. This would associate it with the introduction of Buddhism. In Japan it is called *sunoroko* or *sugoroku* (= *shwan-liu*), and was prohibited by the Emperor Jito (A.D. 690–7). (At the present time the game is obsolescent in Japan, and is only played by a club of thirty or forty members, which was formed to resuscitate the game. The name *sugoroku* is ordinarily used to designate the children's games of the race-type.) The identity of *t'shu-p'u* with *tables* seems to be established by a passage in the *T'ang Kwo Shĭ Pu*, which states that the game is played with fifteen black and fifteen yellow men on opposite sides, and two dice.

7 This was first announced by Freret, in a paper which he read before Louis XV, at a meeting of the French Academy in 1719 (*Hist. de l'Académie*, Paris, v. 252). He gave as his authority the *Haï-pien*, a dictionary no longer in existence, though often cited in the *Siang-haï*, the great dictionary of the Manchu dynasty.

8 There remains the possibility that China obtained its knowledge of chess from Persia, and not from India direct. There was early political intercourse between China and Persia; thus the *Chou-Shu* mentions the arrival of an embassy from Po-sze (Persia) in A.D. 563, and another from An-si (Parthia) in A.D. 567, both during the reign of Wu-Ti. There are

I. China.

Chess appears always to have borne the name of *Siang k'i* [9] in China. The meaning of this name has been much discussed. *K'i* is the usual term for a board-game, as in *wei k'i*, the game of enclosing (the national game of China), *sam k'i*, the 'three' game, merels. Holt (*JRAS.*, xvii. 352 seq.) points out that the ideogram *k'i* in *siang k'i* differs from that in *wei k'i*. In the former it is built up from the radicle *muh*, wood; in the latter from the radicle *shih*, stone.

The meaning of *siang* is more difficult to determine. This word has several meanings in Chinese. Originally meaning *elephant*, it has also the derived senses of (1) ivory, (2) celestial figure, (3) figure, or image. The *Hang Fei tze* (3rd c. B.C.) justifies the last meaning on the ground that it is possible to represent a living elephant by the ivory of a dead one. *Siang k'i* may accordingly mean (*a*) the Elephant Game (as Himly advocated), (*b*) the Ivory Game (*c*) the Astronomical Game, or (*d*) the Figure Game (as

The Chinese name.

The Japanese name.

v. d. Linde and Holt advocate). Japanese chess affords no help in deciding between these, for the Japanese have replaced *siang* by *tseung* (general), both words being pronounced *sho* in Japanese, though written with different ideograms.

Although at first sight the meaning *Figure Game* looks the least likely of the four possibilities, the game now being played without figures or pieces but with inscribed draughtsmen only, it is yet probably the correct rendering. Some of the older references to the Chinese game, which will be quoted later, show that the game of *siang k'i* must formerly have been played with figures, just as was the case in India and Persia, since the whole point of the references

coincidences in the use of a chessboard of 10 by 10 squares in both China and Persia in early times, and in the mention of a river in Firdawsī's description of the appearance of this board in the *Shāhnāma*. Chinese chess again (but not Corean, nor Japanese chess) retains the move of the Elephant which existed in Persian chess. On the whole, however, the difficulties of the history on the assumption of a Persian parentage are greater than on that of a direct Indian parentage.

Forbes's conclusion (262) that 'Chinese chess is merely a variation or modification of the Burmese game' is opposed to the known facts as to the early trade and culture routes between India and China.

[9] The Chinese name is variously rendered, though the form *siang k'i* is the commonest. Eyles Irwin (1793) and the Japanese writer Chō-Yō give *chong-ki(e)*; Hiram Cox, *choke-choo-hong-ki*, the play of the science of war (*choo-hong = siang*); Culin gives *tséung k'i*; Holt, *seang chi*. The word *siang k'i* is given in the *Shwo-wên*, a dictionary dating from c. A.D. 100 (Himly, *T'oung Pao*, viii, May 1897, p. 172). In the same article, Himly gives the Manchu name as *gang ju*, and adds that the chessboard is called *k'i p'an* in Chinese, and *tonikō* in Manchu.

depends on the use of actual figures for the chessmen. In the substitution of conventional forms for carved images of the men or objects named, Chinese chess has only followed the ordinary line of development, it only differs in carrying the use of conventional forms a step farther by using the simplest of types. The name of *Figure Game* would reflect one of the most striking peculiarities of chess ; our own name *chess* means nothing more.

But *Siang-k'i* can also mean the Astronomical Game, and in early times it was the name of an astronomical game. This makes it necessary to examine early references to the game *Siang-k'i* with great care, in order to discriminate between this game and chess.

The Astronomical Game is attributed to the Tatar Emperor Wu-Ti (of N. Chou dynasty, A.D. 560–578). Thus the *San-t'sai-t'u-hwei*,[10] an encyclopaedia dating from the commencement of the Manchu dynasty (1616–1912), quoting from the *T'ai-ping-yü-lan*, a work that was revised in A.D. 984, says :

> The *sian-hi* was discovered by Chou-Wu-Ti ; the pieces, whose moves are given in the manual composed by his office-bearer Wang-Pao, were called after the sun, the moon, the planets, and the star-houses (*sin-t'shên*). This does not agree with the present time.

The *Chou Shu*, the official history of the Chou dynasty, states that the Emperor Wu-Ti wrote a book on this game which he expounded to a meeting of 100 literati in 569, and that the famous scribe Wang-Pao added annotations to the imperial work. The *Sui Shu*, the history (compiled in the first half of the 7th c.) of the Sui dynasty (581–619), enumerates several editions of this book.[11] Finally we have an indication that there were other games with the name *siang-k'i*, from the title *San-kü-siang-king* (Manual of the *three siang-k'is*) given to Wu-Ti's book in the 32nd book of the history of the T'ang dynasty [12] (618–907).

Wu-Ti adopted the name of Chou from the older dynasty of that name (1135–256 B.C.). It happens that the first emperor of the older house was named Wu-Wang (1135–1115 B.C.), and this has led to confusion. First Wu-Ti's *siang-k'i* is identified as chess, next Wu-Ti is interchanged with Wu-Wang, and in this way the origin of the usual statements claiming a high antiquity for Chinese chess is obtained.[13] The more reliable Chinese historians

[10] *Qst.*, 272, from the Japanese version, *San sai dzu e* (A.D. 1712), which is partly a translation of the Chinese work, partly a commentary on it, and partly a new work.

[11] Namely (1) *Siang king*, the Emperor's work ; (2) *Wang Pao chu*, Wang Pao's commentary ; (3) *Wang Yu chu* ; (4) *Ho T'o Chu* with *Siang-king-fa-hien-i*, Ho T'o's commentary, with the explanation of the meaning of *siang k'i*.

[12] In the biography of Lü-Ts'ai. The Emperor T'ai-Tsung (627–650) was puzzled by the phrase *t'ai-tze-si-ma* ('the crown-prince washes the horses' : 'to wash the dominoes' means 'to shuffle them' in modern Chinese ; *ma* or 'horse' is used for the pieces in a game. The phrase probably meant 'the crown-prince shuffles the men'). He consulted Yün Kung, who had known the phrase as a young man but had forgotten it, and then Lü-Ts'ai. The latter, after a night's consideration, explained the point, and recovered the method of play of the astronomical game and the actual position.

[13] Eyles Irwin gave an extract from the Concum or Chinese Annals which attributes the invention of chess to the Mandarin Hansing (Han-Hsin, D. B.C. 196) during an expedition into the Shensi country in the reign of Hung Cochu (Han Kao-Tsu, B.C. 206–194), King of Kiangnan (Ch'ang-ngan), 379 years after Confucius (D. B.C. 479). The Concum is probably the *Kang kien*,

notice this and warn their readers of the confusion. Thus the *Ko chĭ king Yüan*, 'the Mirror of Investigations into the Origin of Things,' quoting from the *Shi-Wu-chi-yüan* the passage, 'Yung Mong Chou said to Mêng Chʻang-chün (D. B.C. 279): Sir, when you have leisure, play *siang-kʻi*,' adds the pertinent question, 'But was *siang-kʻi* known at the time of the Warring Kingdoms (B.C. 484–221)?' and the encyclopaedia *Tʻai Ping Yü Lan* discusses the point at great length:

The *Wu-tsa-tsu* says the tradition that *sian-hi* was invented by Wu Wang at the time of the war of the Chou is contrary to fact. The chariot was still esteemed in warfare at the time of the Warring Kingdoms. The ability of the soldiers to cross the boundary, and to advance, but not to retreat, signifies that the boat must be sunk, and the axe broken. Although opportunities and chances are somewhat restricted in *Wei-kʻi*, there are countless opportunities for the practice of strategy in attack, in defence, and in alliance.

This passage is very obscure, but it appears to argue that chess represents a type of warfare that was inconsistent with its existence as early as the third c. B.C.

The earliest certain reference to Chinese chess occurs in the *Hüan Kwai Lu*, 'Book of Marvels',[14] a work dating from the close of the 8th c. The passage, which is also quoted in the *Ko chĭ king Yüan*, runs as follows:

In the first year of the period of Pao Ying (A.D. 762), Tsêng-Shun of Ju-Nan heard one night the sound of a military drum in the Lady Lü's house. A man in full armour announced the news from the General of the golden elephant (*kin siang tsiang kun*) about the battle with the thieves of Tien-No. Shun kindled a light in order to see better, and after midnight a mouse-hole in the east wall changed into a city gate. Two armies stood opposite one another. When he had arranged the army, the general (*shwai*) entered and said: 'The celestial horse (*tʻien ma*) springs aslant over three, the commanders (*shang-tsiang*) go sidewards and attack on all four sides, the baggage-waggons (*tzĕ chö*) go straight forwards and never backwards, the six men (*liu kia*) in armour go in file but not backwards.' Then the drum sounded and from either army a horse moved out three steps aslant. Again the drum sounded and on either side a foot-soldier moved sidewards one step. Once again the drum was sounded, the waggons moved forwards, and in an instant

an abridgement of the *Tung chien kang mu*, 'the General History of China,' which was compiled 1130–1200. Himly (*Tʻoung Pao*, viii. 179) says that the passage is not to be found in his copy of the *Kang kien*, and Holt (op. cit., 358 seq.) says that, while the parent work has plenty to say about Han-Hsin's expedition, it nowhere connects him with chess. Holt quotes three passages from this work in which *kʻi* is used for a game, and equates this game with chess. They are: (1) B.C. 154; Liu Hsien was playing at court with a prince when a dispute arose with reference to a doubtful move, and the prince killed him with a blow from the game-board. (2) A.D. 263; Yüan Tsi was playing when news of his mother's death was brought to him. He finished the game. (3) A.D. 960: Tʻai Tsu, the founder of the Sung dynasty, staked at play, and lost, a certain temple in the province of Honan.

He also cites (1) from *Mun Yü*, the Dialogues of Confucius (Kʻung Fu-Tzŭ, 551–479 B.C.), xxii, a passage in which the master deprecates idleness, and continues, 'Is there not at least chess-playing?' (*yih*, the older word, now replaced by *kʻi*); and (2) from Mencius (Mêng Kʻo, 372–289 B.C.), xxx, a passage in which chess-playing (*yih*) is held to be unfilial.

There is nothing in any of these five passages to show what form of game was intended; *kʻi* is quite indefinite, and there is nothing to justify so exact a rendering as is implied by the use of the word 'chess'. Even if it be conceded that *siang kʻi* is meant, it has still to be established that at each of these dates *siang kʻi* meant chess only.

[14] Written, according to the *Kʻiu tʻang shu*, the History of the Tʻang Dynasty (written *a.* 907 and printed *a.* 1088), by Niu Sêng-ju (D. A.D. 847), in ten books. The reference implies that *siang kʻi* was even then a well-known game.

the shot from the cannon (*p'ao*) fell in confusion. He made a hole through the east wall, and found a set of *siang k'i* in an old tomb, with waggons (*kü*) and horses in rank and file.

The *Ko chĭ king Yüan* quotes from the *Chao Wu Kin Sü*, a work of the Sung writer, Chao Wu King (flourished between 970 and 1127). After explaining chess as a representation of warfare, Chao goes on to say that he had seen people playing *siang k'i* in his boyhood, and that at a later time he had made a new game by dividing the board lengthways and across, so that he made 19 lines[15] out of the original 11, and by increasing the number of the men from 32 to 98. This game, however, did not come into general use.

The *Hu Ying Lin Pi T'sung* gives a valuable commentary on these two passages. This again is also quoted in the *Ko chĭ king Yüan*:

The story of Tsêng-Shun in the *Hüan Kwai Lu* serves as evidence for the kind of chess in use among the contemporaries of the T'ang dynasty (618–907). The Horse went aslant three lines, and the Soldier (*tsu*)[16] went one line sidewards, just as they do now, but the Chariot went straight forwards and could not retire, which is like the present soldier, and I conclude that the remaining moves do not entirely agree. Chao's Sü says that the chess of the Sung dynasty (960–1279) had 11 lines lengthways and sideways. Now there are 10 lines lengthways and 9 sideways, which again is very different from that time. The *Shĭ Wu Ki Yüan* of the Sung period quotes the story of Tsêng-Shun to show that the chess there mentioned was identical with the game of the Sung dynasty, which proves that chess was played in the same way under the T'angs and the Sungs, whereas our chess probably agrees with neither.

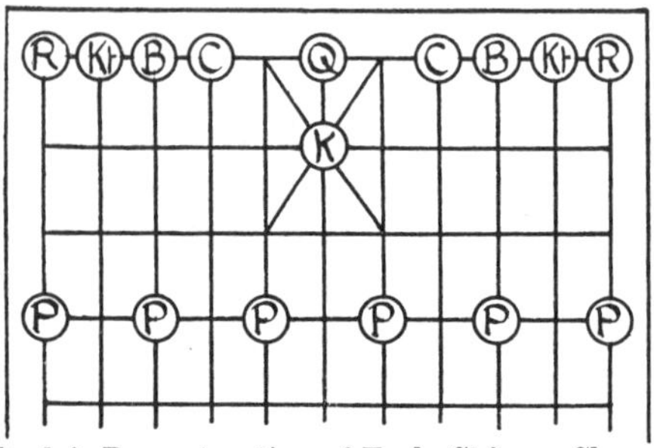

Himly's Reconstruction of Early Chinese Chess.
R = *Kü*. Kt = *ma*. B = *kin siang*. C = *p'ao*.
Q = *tsiang kin* or *swai*. K = *shang tsiang*. P = *kia*.

And finally the *T'ai Ping Yü Lan*, which has been quoted already, says:

In the work *Siang-hi-t'u-fa* (= method of playing chess with examples) of Ssŭ-ma Wêng Kung of the Sung period occur the figures (*siang*) of generals (*tsiang*), councillors (*shĭ* = litterati, bodyguard), foot-soldiers (*pu-tsu*), chariots (*kü*), horses (*ma*), and cannon (*nu p'ao*), which are in use at the present time.

The Elephant (*siang*) is here omitted, probably (as Himly suggests) from an error of a copyist who supposed the repetition of the word *siang* to be an error.

From these passages we can draw a certain amount of information as to the practice of Chinese chess prior to the close of the 13th c. The game was a figure game in fact as well as in name. The whole point of Tsêng-Shun's dream consists in this, and the use of the word *siang* by Ssŭ-ma Wêng Kung implies the same thing. It was played on a board of 100 squares or 121 points. There is no clear statement as to whether the game was played

15 *Wei-k'i*, of course, is played upon a board of 19 × 19 squares.
16 The term *tsu* is not used in the *Hüan Kwai Lu*.

on the squares or on the points, but the fact that there were only 6 Pawns points to the latter as alone affording a symmetrical arrangement. The total number of men on the two sides was 32, and the names of the men were identical with the existing men in the present game. Assuming that the arrangement of the men was symmetrical at the outset, the 16 men on each side would be composed of 6 Pawns, 2 Chariots, 2 Horses, 2 Elephants, and 2 Cannon, General, and Counsellor. Himly's[17] reconstruction of the array is shown in the diagram on page 124. The information as to the moves of the men is incomplete, but points to moves intermediate between the existing Chinese and Japanese games. The General and Horse appear to possess the Chinese moves, the Pawn and Chariot the Japanese moves. We have no information as to the other pieces.

If Himly's reconstruction is correct, the game shows a remarkable approximation to the Arabic and Persian decimal chess.[18]

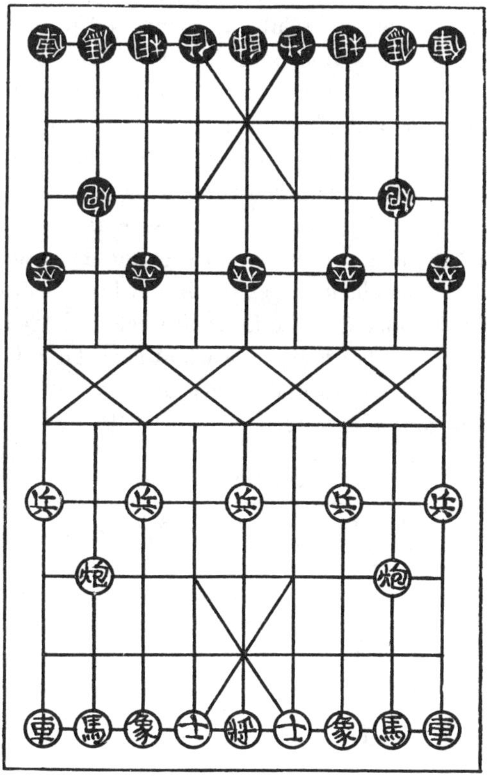

Chinese Chess (Culin).

For the modern Chinese game which is played in China proper, in Annam, in Siam, and possibly also in parts of the Malay Archipelago, we are fortunate in possessing an abundance of reliable evidence. The first knowledge of the game was brought—together with actual game-sets—to Europe by the early Jesuit missionaries in the latter part of the 16th c. Since then there have been a number of records,[19] the most valuable being the *Manual of Chinese Chess* (Shanghai, 1893), which Mr. W. H. Wilkinson, a most careful observer and student of Oriental games, based upon *The Secrets of the Orange Grove*, a Chinese work dating from 1632, and still a standard book on the game.

The Chinese chessboard consists of two halves of 8 × 4 squares which are

[17] *T'oung Pao*, viii. 169.

[18] The Cannon's move might have been developed from some variety of move of the *dabbāba* in one of the derived Muslim games, e.g. the vertical move to a third square, which included a power of leaping. See below, p. 344.

[19] See the list at the commencement of the book. Cf. also v. d. Linde's books (he had the assistance of Prof. J. J. Hoffmann, of Leyden, for Chinese and Japanese chess) and Culin's *Korean Games* and *Chess and Playing Cards*.

separated by a space, the width of one square, and generally left blank, which is variously called *kyai-ho* (=boundary river), *hwang-ho* (=yellow river), and *t'ien-ho* (=celestial river, the Milky Way), and commonly by English writers the 'river'. As for all practical purposes the river is merely an additional row of squares, the board is practically one of 8 × 9 squares. Four squares in the centre of the two opposite ends of the board, viz. two on the outer row and the two on the second row immediately before them, are considered as forming special areas, and the diagonals of these areas are drawn for the purpose of defining them, and the resulting square of nine points is called *kyu-kung* or the 'nine castle'. Western writers have wavered between the terms 'palace' (Culin), 'camp' (Wilkinson), and 'fort' (Cox). The squares are not coloured, and the board is generally made of paper and destroyed at the end of the game. The pieces are placed upon the intersections of the lines instead of on the squares as in most varieties of chess, so that the board becomes one of 9 × 10, or 90 stations. The chessmen consist of circular disks of wood, ivory, or other convenient material, all alike in pattern, size, and colour. The names of the several pieces are inscribed upon the upper face of the disk, in two colours generally described as red and black, but in ivory sets the black is really blue, while in wooden sets yellow replaces red, and brown black. The favourite colour is red, the choice of which abandons the right to play first: 'he who takes the red does not take the first move.'

The names and power of move of the Chinese pieces [20] are exhibited in the following table:

No.	Names of Chessmen.[21]				Power of Move.	Position.	Equivalent.
	Chinese Ideogram.	Canton dialect.	Mandarin dialect.	Translation.			
			I. Pieces confined to the Nine-Castle.				
1	將	tséung	tsiang	General	One step vertically or horizontally	e1	K
	師	sut[22]	shwai	Governor		e10	
2, 3	士	sz'	shĭ	Counsellor	One step diagonally	d1, f1 (d10, f10)	Q

[20] Prof. Rapson calls my attention to the fact that there are three bronze Chinese chessmen among the Central Asiatic antiquities in the Coin Room of the British Museum. These

Bronze Chessmen in the British Museum.

form part of a collection of miscellaneous antiquities made by Mr. G. Macartney, the Special Assistant for Chinese Affairs to the Resident in Kashgar. He was told that all came from

No	Names of Chessmen.[21] Chinese Ideogram.	Canton dialect.	Mandarin dialect.	Translation.	Power of Move.	Position.	Equivalent.
	II. Pieces confined to their own Half of the Board.						
4, 5	象	tséung	siang	Elephant	Diagonally to the next point but one; the intervening point must be unoccupied[23]	c1, g1	B
	相	séung[22]	siang	Assistant		c10, g10	
	III. Pieces free to Move over the whole Board.						
6, 7	馬	ma	ma	Horse	A move compounded of a step vertically or horizontally followed by a step diagonally; the intervening point must be unoccupied	b1, h1 (b10, h10)	Kt
8, 9	車	kii	ch‘e	Chariot	Any distance vertically or horizontally	a1, i1 (a10, i10)	R
10,11	炮	p‘ao	pa‘o	Cannon or Catapult	The same; but it can only *capture* if some other piece (called the 'screen') intervenes	b3, h3 (b8, h8)	C
12-16	兵	ping[22]	ping	Foot-soldier	One step vertically forwards; when across the river, one step vertically forwards or laterally. There is no promotion	a4, c4, e4, g4, i4 (a7, c7, e7, g7, i7)	P
	卒	tsut	ts-uh	,,			

Every piece takes as it moves with the exception of the Cannon. It may

the Takla Makan Desert (near Khotan). These men were at first mistaken for modern coins or tokens, but Dr. S. W. Bushell pointed out that they were respectively the chessmen called *pao, ping*, and *shih*. (A. F. Rudolf Hoernlé, C.I.E., *Report on the British Collection of Antiquities from Central Asia*, Part I (Extra No. of the *JAS.* of Bengal for 1899), Calcutta, 1, 1899, p. 22, and Plate ii, No. 25; and ibid. Part II (*JAS.* of Bengal, vol. lxx, Part i, Extra No., No. 1 of 1901, Supplement to Pt. I, p. 6).) The pieces are quite modern, and it is doubtful whether they ever saw the Takla Makan Desert. They weigh 80·5, 108·5, and 89·5 gr., and are 0·83 in. in diameter.

The *San t‘sai t‘u hwei* gives the present valuation of the pieces thus: K = 20, R = 10, C = 7, Kt = 6, B = 4, Q = 3, P = 2. Total of all the 16 men = 90.

21 There is considerable variation in the transliteration of the Chinese names. The text follows Himly. Hyde has K, çiang and çai; Q, sú; B, siang and siang; Kt, mà or bà; R, cū or che; C, păó; P, ping and çŏ. Irwin: K, chong; Q, sou; B, tchong; Kt, mai; R, tche; C, pao; P, ping; of which Cox corrected K, choohong; Q, soo; C, paoo. Hollingworth has K, tseang and sae; Q, sze; B, sëang; Kt, ma; R, keu; C, p‘aou; P, ts‘uh and ping. Culin has K, tséung; Q, sz‘; B, tséung; Kt, má; R, ch‘é; C, p‘áu; P, ping and tsut. Holt has K, tseang and shuai; Q, sze; B, seang; Kt, ma; R, chē; C, p‘ao; P, ping or ts'uh. V. Möllendorff gives the Pekin names as K, chiang; Q, shîh; B, hsiang; Kt, ma; R, chii; C, p‘ao (= jumper); P, ping. He adds the technical terms, hsiangchi = chess; tê = take; chih = eat, take; ta = shoot, take (said of the cannon); têng = trample on, take (of the horse); chü = remove (in literary use); ta-chiang = I hit the general, check; ssè-liao = dead, mate; shu-liao = slain, mate; sheng = to win; ying-liao = won; chieh-‘ho = the 'river'. Himly (*T‘oung Pao*, viii. 162) notes the term zhön- (= human beings) as used for the chessmen in general.

22 *Shwai, siang* (assistant), *tsut*, are used for the red men, i.e. the second side: *tsiang, siang, ping*, for the black men.

23 So say most authorities very distinctly. Himly, however, quotes (*T‘oung Pao*, viii. 165) the *T‘ao-lio yüan ki pai kie ki-p‘u* as stating that the Elephant can leap, but the Horse not.

perhaps make the power of this piece clearer if its power at the commencement of the game be examined. The Cannon on b3 can move without taking as far as b7 forwards, b2 backwards, as far as g3 and a3 laterally, just as if it were a Rook or Chariot. It can also capture the Kt on b10 which is 'screened' by the Cannon on b8. The capture is effected by removing the Kt on b10, and placing the Cannon on that square. Any piece, red or black, can act as 'screen'.

A General is in check (*siang*), (1) when it is under attack by any piece, and could—but for its immunity from capture—have been taken on the following move if nothing were done to remove the attack; (2) when the two Generals face one another upon the same file with no intervening men. When

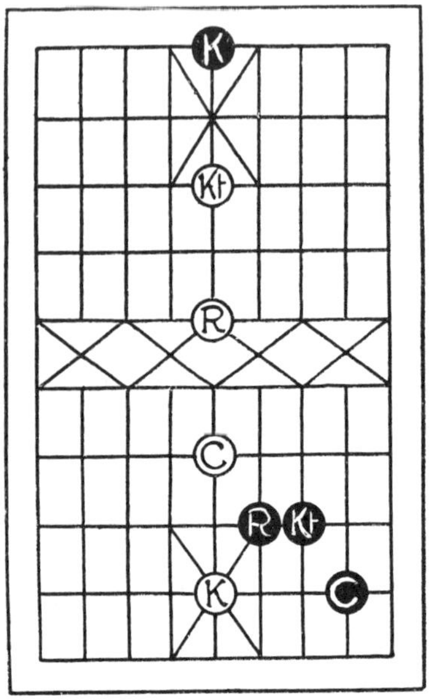

Either player can give triple check. Red by Kt c9 or g9, Black by Rf2.

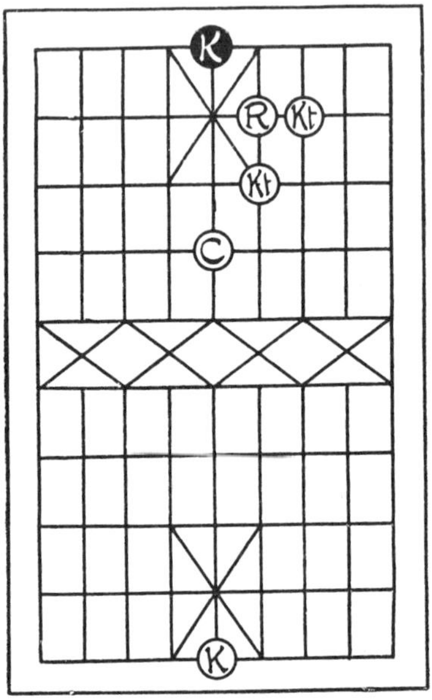

Red gives quadruple check by Re9.

Multiple Checks in Chinese Chess.

check is given (1) the attacking piece must be taken, or (2) the General must move out of check, or (3) the check must be covered. If none of these can be done, the General is defeated, *szĕ* (=dead) or *tsao liao* (=in Pekin, destroyed) being the technical term. A check can always be covered, in the case of the Kt by interposing a piece at the 'angle' of its move; in the case of the Cannon either by interposing a second piece or by removing the 'screen' behind which the Cannon is attacking. The greater possibilities permitted by the variety of checks that can be covered or discovered lead to such complicated checks as triple and quadruple check.

The game is won either by checkmate or by stalemate. A player must not give perpetual check; in such a case he must vary his move.

At the present time the knowledge of chess is very widely spread through China, but the game is hardly held in the same esteem as in Europe. The more educated classes prefer *Wei-k'i,* which is considered to be a far more difficult game, and skill at *Wei-k'i* is highly appreciated and adds greatly to the reputation of its possessor. But chess is the game of the masses, and is used more as a means of passing away the time than as a serious mental exercise. A small stake is generally played for, the Chinese being a born gambler.[24] At several points of the walls of Pekin inscribed chessboards may be found on the top of the ramparts, which have been carved by the soldiers

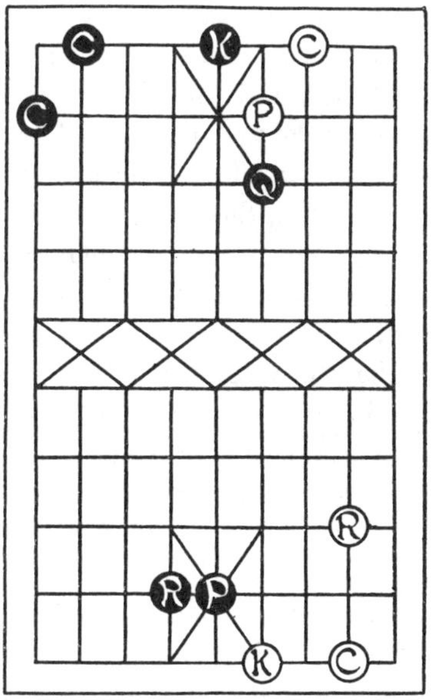

Red mates in 5.

1 Rh3–e3 + / Ke10–d10
2 Re3–e10 + + / Kd10–d9
3 Ch1–h9 + / Qf8–e9
4 Re10–d10 / K × R
5 Pf9–f10m.

[Black mates in 3.]

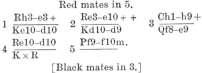

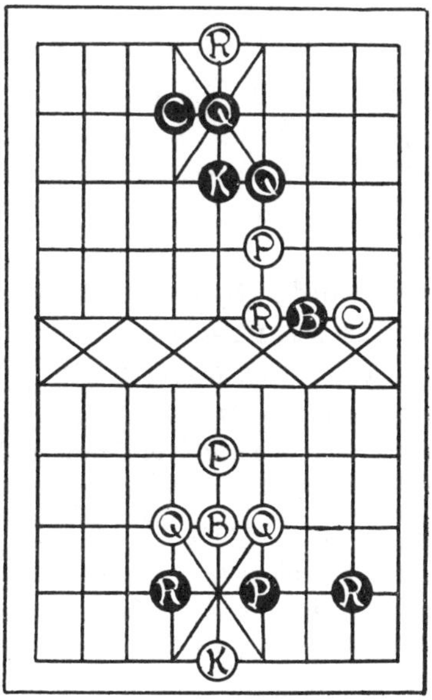

Red wins in 7.

1 Pf7–e7 + / Ke8–d8
2 Rf6 × Q + / Q × R
3 Re10–e8 + / B × R
4 Pe7–d7 + / Cd9 × P
5 Ch6–d6 + / Cd7–e7
6 Cd6 × Rd2 + / Ce7–d7
7 Cd2 × Rh2.

[Black mates on the move.]

Chinese Chess Problems.

who guarded the walls.[25] Idlers and even beggars may be seen playing chess in the streets of any Chinese town, and the average standard of play remains low. The practical game is less popular than the study of problems, and while works on the latter abound, only a few treatises appear to be in existence which deal with the openings, or the game as a whole. A knowledge of chess problems is a valuable source of income to a gambler. The majority

[24] So Chō-Yō and other recent writers. Hyde, following his native authority Shin Fo Sung, says that chess is rarely played for a stake.
[25] Himly, in *ZDMG.*, xxiv. 175.

of these are constructed so that the one player is apparently on the point of being mated, but can, with the move, by a long series of checks obtain the victory.[26] 'There are few towns in China', writes Mr. Wilkinson, 'where the professional player is not prepared to set up an end game on the board, give you choice of men, and beat you for a wager.'[27] On the preceding page I give two problems as specimens of the Chinese art.

Nevertheless the Chinese have in the past paid some attention to the theory of the Openings, though it is perhaps significant of the want of popularity of the game among the more educated classes that Mr. Wilkinson found that a book published nearly 300 years ago was still the standard Chinese work on the Openings. Before the appearance of the *Manual of Chinese Chess* only the barest indications as to the best or most usual methods of play had reached Europe.[28] We now possess a collection of 33 games and 291 variations, arranged under the headings of (1) games won by the first player, (2) games won by the second player. Of these games and variations, which are nearly all played to a decisive issue, the first player wins 211, the second 102, while 11 are left doubtful. It would appear from this that the first player has a very decided advantage, but an examination of the games weakens this conclusion largely, for—like Greco—the author often allows a weak move on the part of the second player for the sake of a brilliant or interesting mate. One of the most striking points of the games in the *Manual* is their brevity; no game runs to 40 and very few to 30 moves; the majority terminate between the 13th and the 20th move. This is largely due to the openness of the position, arising from the absence of Pawns on four files, and the limitations attached to the *nine-castle*. The player always knows where his opponent's King is to be found, and frames his attack on the centre from the first move. With a knowledge of the simpler mating positions stored in his memory, it is his endeavour to reproduce one of these in the game, and this idea dominates his play throughout. As most of these mating nets require a Cannon on the centre file, the opening move C h3–e3 has become the normal line of play. The science of Pawn-play does not exist, the battle is mainly one of the three superior pieces (R, C, and Kt). Compared with the European game, the Rook is far more powerful, the Knight less so.

I add a brief summary of the chief Openings from the *Manual*. The various names employed are due to Mr. Wilkinson. The distinctive moves in the different openings are printed in italics.

[26] The problems are often given fanciful names from the supposed resemblance of the concluding position. V. d. Linde (*Qst.*, 274) gives one called 'The flying wild geese' (Position—Black: Kd1, B a3 and g1, R g5 and i3, C g6 and g7, P a5 e9 and h8. Red: Kd10. Rd8, Cc10, P c5 d3, e2). The game is drawn after 28 moves, the concluding position being—Black: Ke1, B c5 and g5, P d9 and f9. Red: Ke8, Ce4, P d2 and f2. This position is said to depict three flying wild geese.

[27] V. Möllendorff notes that the *beating* may be a *physical* one if you are so unfortunate as to mate the professional player. The latter generally has a body of friends near for the purpose of creating a disturbance if he is getting the worse of the game.

[28] These were mainly to be drawn from specimen games. Of these Hollingworth gave two, and v. d. Linde gave one in the *Qst.* (275), from a native book with the title *T'ao-lio-yüan-chi*, dated 1801. These games are all longer than those in the *Manual*.

A. Regular Opening: Left Cannon Defence.

	1	2	3	4	5	
	Ch3–e3 / Ch8–e8	Kth1–g3 / Kth10–g8	Ri1–i2 / Ri10–h10	Ri2–d2[29] / —		
The Preparation			— / *Cb8–d8*	Ri2–d2 / Qd10–e9	Cb3–b7 / —	
					Pa4–a5 / —	
The Masked Cannon					Ce3–e2 / —	
				— / Qf10–e9	Pa4–a5 / —	
The Seventh File Cannon			— / *Ktb10–a8*	Ri2–d2 / *Cb8–c8*		
			Ri1–h1 / Ri10–i9	Rh1–h7 / Ri9–d9	Rh7 × Pg7[30] / Rd9–d2	
			— / *Ktb10–c8*			Two Knights' Defence

B. Regular Opening: Right Cannon Defence.

	1	2	3	4	
	— / Cb8–e8	Kth1–g3 / Kth10–i8	Ri1–h1 / Ri10–h10	Ktb1–a3 / Ktb10–c8	Giuoco Piano[31]
		— / Ktb10–c8	Ri1–h1 / Ch8–g8		
		— / Kth10–g8	Ri1–h1 / Ktb10–c8		Two Knights' Defence

C. The Knight's Defence.

1	2
— / Kth10–g8	Kth1–g8 / Ktb10–a8
	— / Bg10–i8
	— / Ri10–h10 !

D. Irregular Defences.

1	2	
— / Ktb10–c8	Kth1–g3 / Kth10–g8 or i8	Two Knights' Irregular Defence
Bc10–e8 / —		Bishop's Defence

E. Irregular Openings.

1	
Kth1–g3 / —	Knight's Opening
Bg1–e3 / —	Bishop's Opening

29 Five replies: 4.., Kt b10–c8 and 4.., R h10–h6, regular; 4.., Q d8–e9, hazardous; and 4... Kt b10–a8, and 4.., Qf10–e9, irregular.

30 6 Kt b1–c3. This represents the best line of play for both sides in this opening.

31 This represents the best line of play in this defence.

Attention has also been paid to the End-game. The resulting decisions are for the most part so obvious as to stand in need of no demonstration. There would seem to be nothing corresponding to the fine End-game play which is possible in European chess. The simpler endings are (1) K and R wins against K by mate; (2) K and 2 Kts win against K by mate; (3) K and Kt win against K; (4) K and P not on base line win against K, both by stalemate; (5) K and C against K, (6) K and Bs against K, (7) K and Qs against K, (8) K and P on base line against K are all drawn games. If more pieces are present the play is more complicated, and the *Manual* contains several positions from the 46 discussed in the Chinese work.

The following games are taken from the *Manual*:

I. Left Cannon Defence, Irregular. (*Manual*, pp. 15, 16.)

Black	Red	Black	Red	Black	Red	Black	Red
1 hCe3	hCe8	6 Pa5	Rh4 [33]	11 C × C	R × C [35]	16 C × Q	Q × C
2 Ktg3	Ktg8	7 Kta3	R × gP	12 Rf9	C × P +	17 Kd1	R × Kt [36]
3 Ri2	Rh10	8 Ra2	Cb6 [34]	13 dQe2	Cg4	18 fR × Q +	Kt × R
4 Rd2	fQe9	9 Rf2	Cg6	14 Qf3	C × B +	19 Rd10 mate.[37]	
5 Rd9	Kta8 [32]	10 Ktb5	C × Kt	15 Q(f1)e2	R(g3)g5 ?		

II. Left Cannon Defence, X. (*Manual*, pp. 26, 27.)

Black	Red	Black	Red	Black	Red	Black	Red
1 hCe3	hCe8	4 Rh7	Rd9	7 Cb5	Kta8 [39]	10 R × Kt	C × R
2 Ktg3	Ktg8	5 R × gP	Rd2	8 Ra3 [40]	bCd8	11 Mate in 2	
3 Rh1	Ri9	6 Ktc3 [38]	Rc2	9 Cg5	Cd3 ? [41]		

We have seen that the existing Chinese chessboard is different from that which was used under the T'ang and Sung dynasties (618–1279). The present board would, however, appear to have been already in existence at that time, but to have been used for a distinct game called *ta-ma*, or 'take horses', i. e. 'game-men', which seems to have been a dice-game allied to the 'game of goose'. Himly [42] has given a full description of the modifications introduced in the board for this game, which chiefly consist in names for special points, more or less geographical in character, and in the marking of stations for the game on the lines connecting these points. The game was

[32] Better is 5 . . , Ktc8.

[33] Better is 6 . . , Rh2 or h6.

[34] Continuing his counter-attack. Otherwise 8 . . , Cd8 or Rf4 to meet the threatened 9 aRd2, f2 or h2.

[35] 11 . . , C × P + loses every way.

[36] Fatal. His only move is 17 . . , Rd5; 18 R × R, Be8.

[37] A brilliant termination, helped by weak play on Red's part. 13 . . , Rb10; 14 Ktd6, Ce6: 15 Kte8, Rb1; 16 Kd1, Rg4 threatening 17 . . , R × cP is better.

[38] Wilkinson notes that the *Manual* gives no correct reply to this move. He suggests 6 . . , Pc6 preparatory to bringing out the right-hand Kt.

[39] If 7 . . , R × Kt; 8 Cc5 with the better game.

[40] Or 8 Kt(g3)e2, bCc8; 9 Cg5, Kti9; 10Ch3 !, Ra9 or Ch8. [If Rd2; 11 Mate in 4.]

[41] A weak move for the sake of a pretty mate.

[42] In *ZDMG.*, xli. 470–3. Himly used the Chinese *San-t'sai-t'u-hwei* (the Japanese recension omits the passage). The game is mentioned in the *T'ang kwo shi pu*, which was composed according to some authorities by Li Chao, who lived in the T'ang times (618–907). The book was printed in the Ming period (1368–1644).

played with six men called *ma* or horses, and five dice, coloured black and white, which from the explanations of the throws have obviously taken the place of some simpler agent. The throws generally move the men forwards, but some throws move them backwards. The additional marked squares, eleven in number, were separated by eight points, apparently distinct from the points of the chessboard, and were in the main obstacles to advance.

The *nine-castle* appeared on the *ta-ma* board, though it is not clear that it served any purpose in the game. It is therefore very improbable that the use for *ta-ma* was original; the board may very well be anterior both to *ta-ma*

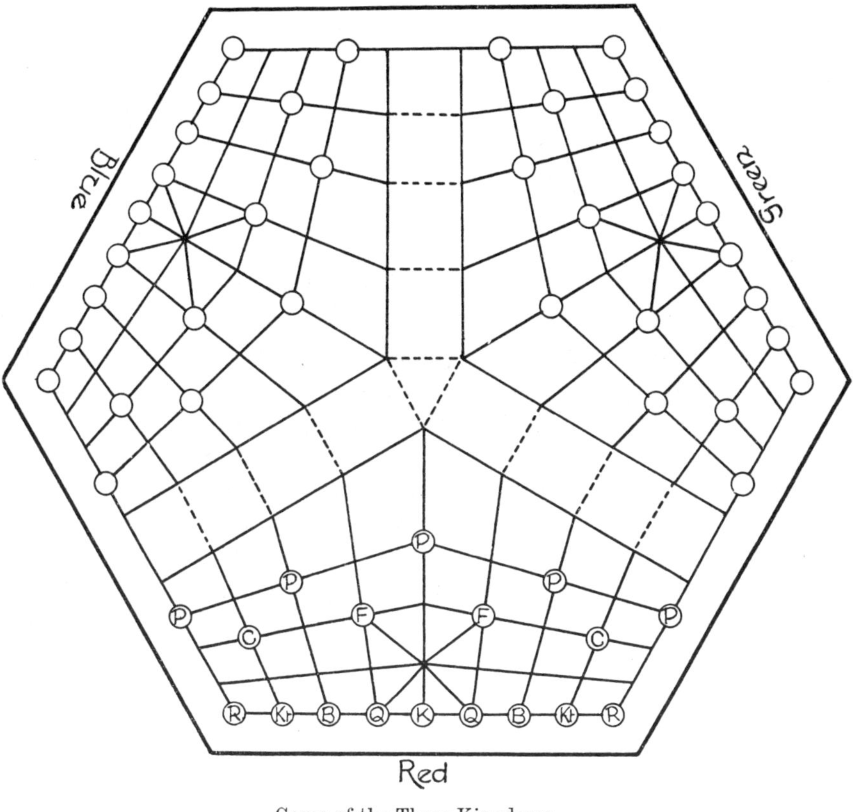

Game of the Three Kingdoms.

and to chess: if the name of 'Milky Way' for the River is original, the origin of the board may be found in Wu-Ti's astronomical game of *siang-k'i*. The board must have been very ill-adapted for *ta-ma*.

The *Nine-castle* takes its name from a board of nine points used for a game essentially identical with the *three men's merels,* which has existed in China from at least the time of the Liang dynasty (A.D. 502–57). The *Swei shu* (first half of the 7th c.) gives the names of twenty books on this game.

There are also enlarged games of chess in China. One of these is the *San-kwo-k'i,* or Game of the Three Kingdoms, which is described by v. Möllendorf. It is supposed to illustrate the war of the Three Kingdoms, *Wei* (blue), *Shu* (red), and *Wu* (green), A.D. 221–64. I give a diagram of the board; it will be noticed that the lines are not straight throughout, and that each kingdom faces the other two. The pieces consist of the usual 16 with, in addition, 2 new pieces [F] in each of the three armies. These are called: Red, *Chuo* (fire); Blue, *Ch'i* (banner); Green, *Feng* (wind). Their move is an extended Kt's leap, viz. two steps vertically or horizontally and then one diagonally. The game is said to be very complicated and difficult, but is not considered as interesting as the ordinary chess. When one of the Generals, who are named *Wei*, *Shu*, and *Wu* after the names of the three kingdoms, is mated, the player who has mated him removes the King from the board and adds the remainder of his army to his own.

It is probable that some of the enlarged Japanese chess-games enumerated below were originally of Chinese invention. V. Möllendorf cites the following names of pieces in a derived game from a Chinese romance:—*Kin-siang tsiang-kiun* (General of the golden elephant), *kin-tsiang* (gold-general), *yu-tsiang* (jewel-general), *yin-tsiang* (silver-general), *kio-tsiang* (horn-general), *t'ien-ma* (celestial horse), *pu-ping* (foot-soldier).[43]

During the last hundred years a considerable trade has developed between China and Europe in elaborately carved ivory chess sets. These are something quite different from the inscribed counters which are the sole type of man used in the native game, and are obviously not intended for use in the native chess, since the set consists of King, Queen, two Priests or Mandarins, two Horsemen, two Castles, and eight Soldiers on each side. It is evident that these sets, which commonly represent Chinese on the one side and Mongols on the other, are only the result of an attempt to treat the European chessmen from a Chinese point of view. Interesting and charming as these 'Chinese chess-pieces' are as specimens of elaborate and dainty workmanship, they are of no value for the history of chess. They merely illustrate that popularity of chess in Europe which has created a market for curious and recherché implements of play.

II. Corea.

Corean chess, *Tjyang Keui*, on the whole approximates to the Chinese game and its nomenclature is identical, allowing for the slight variations in pronunciation which have arisen in the course of time. Nothing is known as to the period when the game was introduced into Corea, but the small variations in the existing game would not require any long time for their development. Nor is it known whether there have not been, as in China itself, earlier types that have been superseded by the present game, though the wide difference between Chinese and Japanese chess suggests that this is probable. The present game cannot have been the origin of the present Japanese chess. Our entire information as to Corean chess is

[43] There are also in China chess card-games. See *Qst.*, 276 note.

Chessmen carved in China for the European Game

From Mr. Platt's Collection

Face page 134]

due to Mr. W. H. Wilkinson, who contributed the section on chess in Culin's *Korean Games*,[44] and this section is the source of the present account.

The design of the chessboard is practically the same as that of the Chinese game; the *river*, however, is ignored, and the files are carried across it, making the board one of 8×9 squares. The board is rather wider than it is long, the width of the squares being increased to facilitate the moves on the base lines. The men are generally octagonal in shape, and differ slightly in size according to their value, the General being larger and the Counsellors and Foot-soldiers smaller than the other men. The men are inscribed with their names, the sides being distinguished by the colour of the ideogram; one side is generally red and the other green.

The following table gives the names, powers, and initial places of the

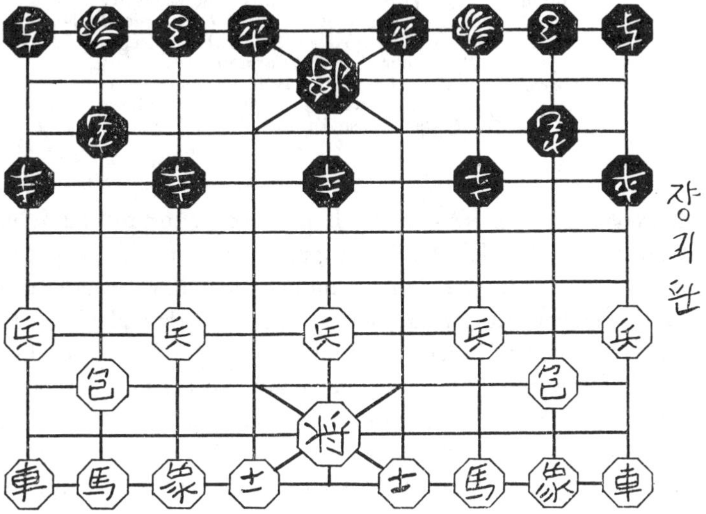

Corean Chessboard. After Culin.

chessmen. It will be noted that the Generals occupy a more advanced post than in Chinese chess. There is, moreover, considerable latitude with regard to the initial places of the Elephants and Horses, the player being allowed to arrange them as he pleases on the squares b1, c1 (b10, c10), and g1, h1 (g10, h10), so long as there are Elephant and Horse on each wing.

No.	Corean name.	Translation.	Power of Move.	Position.	Equivalent.
		I. PIECES CONFINED TO THE NINE-CASTLE.			
1	tyang (or more generally koung)	General	One step along any marked line	e2, e9	K
2, 3	să	Counsellor	The same	d1, f1 d10, f10	Q

[44] No. LXXIV. Tjyang-Keui Chess. Mr. Wilkinson had previously written on 'Chess in Korea' in the *Pall Mall Budget*, Dec. 27, 1894, and in the *Korean Repository*. Cf. Culin, *C. & P. C.*, 866.

No.	Corean name.	Translation.	Power of Move.	Position.	Equivalent.
			II. Pieces free to move over the whole Board.		
4, 5	syang	Elephant	A move compounded of a step vertically or horizontally followed by two steps diagonally, all the intervening points being unoccupied	see above	B
6, 7	ma	Horse	A move compounded of a step vertically or horizontally followed by a step diagonally, the intervening point being unoccupied	see above	Kt
8, 9	tcha	Chariot	Any distance vertically or horizontally with no power of leaping: within the nine-castle along any marked line	a1, i1 a10, i10	R
10, 11	hpo	Cannon	Any distance vertically or horizontally combined with a leap over a piece called the 'screen', which must be other than the Cannon	b3, h3 b8, h8	C
12–16	pyeng or tjol	Foot-soldier	One step vertically forwards or laterally: within the nine-castle along any marked line	a4, c4, e4, g4, i4 a7, c7, e7, g7, i7	P

The diagonals of the *nine-castle* fill a more important place in Corean than in Chinese chess. In the latter game they merely help to visualize the extent of the *nine-castle*; in the former they have caused considerable changes in the movements of the pieces. It is a principle in Corean chess that every piece which is capable of playing along a line into the adjacent point can within the *nine-castle* play along any marked line. We accordingly find that both General and Counsellor possess the same power of move, a power that varies from point to point. Thus from d1 either can move to d2, e1, e2, since there are marked lines connecting these three points to d1; it is only from e2 that they can move in all eight directions, for that is the only point in the castle from which eight lines are actually drawn. Both Chariot and Foot-soldier possess similar powers in the *nine-castle*.[45]

As in Chinese chess, two Generals are not allowed to be upon the same file unless there are intervening pieces. Corean chess, however, extends certain privileges to the weaker side. If one player has an overpowering advantage, the weaker player is permitted to give check to his opponent by playing his General on to the file commanded by the latter's General. By so doing the player is considered to confess his inferiority, and he is not allowed to do more than draw.[46] A game is considered drawn if the mating

[45] Thus Rd3 commands e2, f1, in addition to the points commanded as a result of his ordinary powers. It must be noticed that this enlarged power does not extend to broken or crooked lines, e.g. Rd3 does not command e1 or f2, nor is such a move as Ra3 to f1 (via b3, c3, d3, e2) possible.

[46] Thus in the position— Green: Ke1, Rg1, Pg4
Red: Kf9, Pc4 and f4
Red playing, draws thus: 1 Ke9 +, Kd1 or f1; 2 K + &c.
It is essential that the player be actually numerically weaker; if he be only positionally weaker, he is not allowed the privilege. Thus in the position given in the following paragraph of the text, in which Red threatens mate by Pe2 mate, if Green is to play he may not play Kf1 +, for he is numerically stronger.

piece is only defended by the General.[47] A 'bare' General is not obliged to move at all. In this case the player simply turns his General over when it is his turn to play.[48]

The Cannon requires a *screen* if he is to move at all. In this he differs from the Chinese Cannon. Thus in the position—

Green : Ke1, Ra7, Ca6, Ktc7, Pc6.
Red : Kf10, Qe10, Ktc3, Be9, Pd3 ;

the Cannon has two screens, viz. Ra7 and Pc6. He may accordingly move forwards to any of a8, a9, or a10—from the last of these he gives check, the red Qe10 providing the necessary screen; or horizontally to any of d6, e6, f6, g6, h6, or i6; these are his only moves that are possible. One Cannon can neither use another Cannon as a screen, nor capture another Cannon; but it is permissible to cover check by a Cannon by interposing a Cannon.

All other pieces capture as they move.

The technical term for 'check' is *tjyang*, for 'mate' *tyousa*.

The game accordingly differs from Chinese chess in a good many points: in the absence of the *river*, in the initial position of the General, in the liberty to place the Elephant and Horse differently, in the moves of the Elephant, Cannon, and Foot-soldier, in the greater freedom of move in the *nine-castle*, and in the privileges accorded to the weaker player. Mr. Wilkinson notes that there appear to be no native works on the game, and no collections of problems. 'Chess is regarded as a somewhat frivolous pastime, suitable for young persons and rustics. The educated Korean, deeply imbued as he is with Chinese sympathies, affects to prefer Patok,' i.e. *Wei-k'i*.

It is usual to concede the first move to the weaker player, which shows that the opener is considered to have some advantage. As a general rule, the game is commenced by Pb4 or Ph4, or Kt⌒ in order to facilitate the early play of the Cannon.

The following example of Corean chess is taken from Culin; for the sake of uniformity the notation has been altered. The Elephants (B) are to be placed upon c1, h1, b10, g10.

Red	Green	Red	Green	Red	Green	Red	Green
1 aPb4	iPh7	9 fQe2	Rf6	17 Cg2	Pc5[54]	25 R × Kt	Qd9
2 Ktf3[49]	Ktd8	10 iPh4	Pa6	18 cP × P	hCh8	26 Rb8	Cc9
3 hBe3	bCe8	11 Rd5	Pb6	19 Cg10 +	fQg9	27 Rb10 +	Qd10
4 Ktc3[50]	ePf7[51]	12 bCd3	Ra1	20 Ri10	Kth10	28 aBc7 +	Ke9[55]
5 Kte5[52]	gBe7[53]	13 cBa4	C × hP	21 R × Kt	eB × gC	29 gR × Q	K × R
6 gPf4	hKtf9	14 Ri9	Cc8	22 R × B+	Qf10	30 R × Q mate	
7 Ke1	bBd7	15 dCg3	bPc6	23 Kt × B	cP × Kt		
8 Ra5	Ri6	16 Cg9 +	Ke10	24 R × P	cC × Kt		

[47] Thus in the position—Green : Ke1, Ra9, Ba10 ;
Red : Kf10, Ktc3, Pd2,
in which Red would play Pe2 mate, Green only draws by Re9 +.

[48] Thus from actual play—Green : Kd2.
Red : Ke9, Qd9, Ktc3 and d4, Pe3.
Green plays. 1 K turns, Kte6 ; 2 Kd1, Ktf4 ; 3 Kd2, Pe2 mate.

[49] To form a screen for the Cannon.

[50] To defend P on e4.

[51] Bringing the Cannon to bear on B on e3.

[52] The Green Cannon now bears on the P.

[53] Threatening P on g4.

[54] Better is 17 . . , cPd6.

[55] The only move.

III. Japan.

The Japanese game of chess is called *Shō-gi* (*Shō-ngi*). So far as the pronunciation goes this may represent either the Chinese *siang-kʻi* or *tsiang-kʻi*, but the ideogram for the latter form is used, giving the word the meaning of 'the Generals' game.' In all probability this is due to folk-etymology. The Japanese chessboard is occupied by Generals of many types—Jewelled Generals, Golden Generals, Silver Generals—and the majority of the pieces obtain in the course of a game promotion to the rank of General. And to explain the name as meaning the Generals' game would appear far more appropriate than to call it the Figure game or the Elephants' game, when the game shows no Elephants and the men are all alike five-edged tablets, plain save for the written name each one bears. Not only is there no evidence to show that the Japanese ever used carved figures in their chess, although their skill as carvers of ivory has long been famous, but the very peculiarities of Japanese chess would preclude the possibility of any other type of piece than the simple variety of 'draughtsmen' now in use. For promotions from one rank to another are very frequent in the game, and—a stronger argument still for the draughtsman type of chessman—a piece may change sides often in the course of the game.

Our knowledge of the history of chess in Japan is confined to a few notices in different Japanese works[56] which were translated for the *Quellenstudien* by Professor Hoffmann of Leyden. In the main these notices are identical, and probably go back to the *San sai dzu e*, Simayosi Anko's Japanese translation and revision of the Chinese encyclopaedia *San-tʻsai-tʻu-hwei*, which was completed in 1712. None of these works give any information as to the date of the introduction of chess into Japan beyond the statement that the word *shōgi* is not to be found in the *Wa-mei-seu*, the dictionary of the older Japanese language, the compiler of which died about A.D. 986. It seems a reasonable inference from this that chess had not reached Japan in the 10th cent. The introduction, however, has been associated with the name of Kobodaisi, the introducer of the reformed Buddhism in the first decade of that century, but I cannot discover upon what authority.[57]

The ordinary route followed by Chinese culture on its road to Japan lies through Corea. We may probably assume that this was also the route followed by chess, though there is no evidence that would directly support this hypothesis. Japanese chess has no affinities with the present Corean game. Some resemblances between the Japanese and the Siamese games have been put forward as suggesting another route, but these seem too slight to bear the weight of a theory that finds no support from history. Other influences than Chinese have undoubtedly been at work, and have transformed the game from a representation of warfare to a game in which it is difficult to find a repre-

[56] Viz. Simayosi Anko's *Wo kan san-sai dzu e* (1713), Ran-zai Yama-saki Uyemon's *Fak buts-zen* (1768), Taka Asiya's *To-kwai sets-yu fyak-ka tsu* (1801 and 1819), *Man dai sets yu*, and Ta-ura Dai-an's *Dai-fuku sets-yu* (1863). See *Qst.*, 271-84, and *JT.*, Nos. 1313-18.

[57] So Himly, *ZDMG.*, xxvii. 126, without source.

sentation of anything;[58] but these influences have possibly been religious in character, reflecting the known theoretical objections of Buddhism to war and slaughter. The rapid promotion which can be attained by all the minor pieces reminds one of other Buddhist games of the 'promotion' type in which the counter, as it moves round the appointed course in obedience to the throws of the dice, passes through a succession of incarnations until it reaches the Buddhaship which is its goal.

The Japanese authorities are unanimous in ascribing the origin of their chess to China, while they admit the wide differences that now exist between the two games. Unfortunately they have nothing to say as to the origin or cause of these changes in the Japanese chess, but this is not surprising, as the present game was fully developed before the earliest accounts of it were written. The encyclopaedias also treat the game almost entirely from the practical side, and after a few references to the Ohashi family they pass on to a discussion of the names and powers of the pieces in the various varieties of chess that have been played in recent times. To these I return later.

The present game was certainly played before the close of the 16th century, for it was under the Mikado Go-yo-zei, who ruled from 1587 to 1611, that the first and most noted of all the Ohashi family flourished. This player, Ohashi-Sokei, ranks in tradition as the greatest master of Japanese chess, and his chess works are still sold as standard books on the game. His renown was more useful to him than is generally the case with chess champions, for he was appointed by the Mikado chief chess-player of the empire, a dignity that was made hereditary in his family. The Japanese Government in old days would seem to have been excellent patrons of *shōgi*, for the *Fak-buts-zen* (1768) says that at the time of its compilation the Government allowed the best player of each generation to build a house called *Shōgi-tokōro*, 'chess-place', where the principles of the game were taught, and the player received an official salary for his services. And in 1860 there were seven State teachers of chess in Yeddo alone.[59]

Government patronage also extended to the holding of an annual tournament for chess. According to a notice in the *Japanese Mail*, quoted in the *Times*, April 16, 1890, the palmy days of *shōgi* were during the long peace which Japan enjoyed under the rule of the Shōguns.

'Once every year, on the 17th day of the 11th month, the masters of the game met in Yedo, and fought a grand tourney[60] in an appointed place within the precincts of

[58] Chō-Yō, however, insists on the parallelism with warfare all through his *Japanese Chess* (1905).

[59] Not only chess but *ī-go* (Chinese *wei k'i*) also came under Government patronage. *Wei-k'i*, according to Japanese authorities, was introduced by the priest Kibi, who spent twenty years in China, and brought the game back to Japan with him in A.D. 735. The encyclopaedias give a long list of famous players, from I-un Ronin, who lived under the Emperor Go Tsutsi mikado, 1465–1500, downwards. Ohashi Sokei's contemporaries were Hon In Bō, called the *ī-go* sage, who established a special *ī-go* school (called *Ten-ka no go-shō* = Imperial Ī-go place) in the monastery of Ziyak-kwu, and Nikkai Hōin of Jakkoz. Hon In Bō received an official salary for his skill, and this appears to have been the general custom. (Culin, *Korean Games*, 90.)

[60] From the Japanese terms for a tourney, *makenuké jumban*, *totüri makenuké jumban*, *torinoké jumban*, I infer that these tournaments were arranged on the 'knock-out' principle. Indeed,

the palace. Judges, umpires, strict rules, and all things necessary to the combat were provided, and after the fight was over the ranks of the various combatants were officially fixed. The number of ranks was seven in all, the seventh being the highest.[61] Rarely did any player attain the distinction of reaching this, but the sixth generally had one or two representatives. There appears to have been a certain element of heredity in the game as played in Japan, for certain families took the lead for many generations, and the contests between these champions were a salient feature of every tourney. To this time-honoured custom, as to many another of even greater merit, the Revolution of 1867 put a stop. A long era of neglect ensued for chess-players, but it did not fall into disuse because Court patronage was wanting. Its votaries still studied their gambits and elaborated their variations, and now once more the science promises to resume its place of importance. In October last (1889), a grand meeting of all the important chess-players in Japan was organized in Tokio. Over 200 players assembled, all boasting greater or less degrees of skill, from the first up to the sixth. Count Todo, the former Daimio of Tsu, who has the honour of belonging to the sixth rank, is among the chief promoters of the revival. Another meeting took place on the 18th of January (1890), when a ceremonial in honour of the revival of chess was performed.'[62]

It is not unknown for Japanese to play *shōgi* blindfold (Jap. *mekakushi shōngi* or *mekura shōbu* = blindfold chess).

There is a very considerable Japanese literature on the game, and many of the Ohashi family have distinguished themselves as chess authors. Thus among the standard authorities are works by Ohashi Sokei, the founder of the house, by his son Ohashi Soko, who is generally named with his father as a great master, by Saindaime Ohashi Soyo, and Ohashi Soyei, by Goidame Ohashi Sokei (1810), by Ohashi Eshun, by the brothers Ohashi Soyei and Ohashi Riyo Yei (1839), the grandsons of the fourth Ohashi (Ohashi Soyei). Among other writers on the game may be mentioned Tukuzhima Zhunki, Ito Sokan (1694), Ito Kanju (1821), Ito Sokan (1849), Ito Soin, Ito Kanju (1858), S. Hamashuna (1891), S. Hasegawa (1892), S. Yamashima (1821), and Kuwabara Kunchu. The chess works of these writers comprise treatises on the practical game, on games at odds, on End-games, chess studies, and collections of problems. The advanced character of some may be judged from the fact, stated in the *Japanese Mail*, that 'one leading work contains problems, the solution of which is said to make the player worthy to be placed in the sixth rank'.

Chess is very widely practised in Japan at the present time, but its popularity is greatest amongst the middle and lower classes: with the upper and the educated classes it comes only second, *wei-k'i* (*ī-go*) being 'the classical or, rather, aristo-plutocratic game' of Japan.

Shōgi[63] or *Seo Shōgi* (small *shōgi*—to distinguish it from the enlarged varieties) is played upon a board (*shōgi-ban*) of 9 × 9, or 81 squares. Unlike the other games of this group it is played upon the squares, not on the inter-

otherwise, with the numbers given above, it is difficult to see how a tournament could have been conducted.

[61] According to Chō-Yō there are now nine ranks, the ninth (called *kū-dan*) being the highest, and the first (called *sho-dan*) being the lowest.

[62] Quoted by Falkener, 166 ff.

[63] For a list of authorities on Japanese chess, see the beginning of the book.

sections of the lines. The technical term for the squares, *ma,* means spaces, intervals, or eyes, and the last meaning can be paralleled from other Asiatic languages.[64] There is no *river* on the Japanese board, and no *nine-castle.* Nor is there any trace of these characteristic Chinese additions ever having existed in Japanese chess, nor of the game ever having been a line-game. The board is in general a small four-legged table, with a drawer for holding the chessmen, and the players squat on the ground on either side of it; but, as in China, paper diagrams are also in common use. The board is not exactly square, as the squares are slightly elongated to facilitate the play with the long-shaped chessmen.[65] At the four corners of the central block of nine squares there are small marks, either small circles or crosses upon the intersection of the lines, which are intended to mark off the three rows at each end

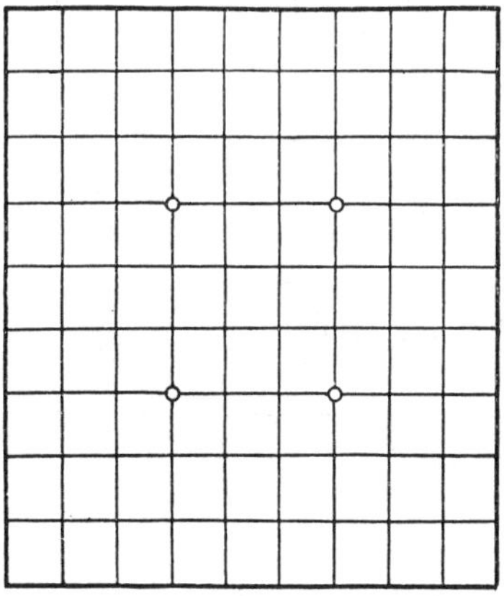

The Japanese Chessboard.

of the board. It is on these three rows that a player arranges his men at the commencement of the game, and they are called his dominion or territory (Jap. *ryōbun*). They have additional importance, since a piece may receive its legal promotion as soon as it is played into the opponent's territory.

The chessmen are five-sided or punt-shaped pieces of wood or ivory which lie flat upon the board. They are made rather thicker at the base than at the vertex, and differ slightly though not materially in size, the *Kyōsha* and *Fu* being rather narrower than the other pieces. Each man bears on the one face its ordinary name, and on the opposite face its promotion name. This is, in the case of the majority of the pieces, *Kin* or *Kin-shō*, but it is rendered possible to tell the original value, without it being necessary to turn the man over, by the use of certain variations in the manner of writing the word *kin.*

[64] *Ma* is also used for the points of the backgammon board. In Tibetan and other Central Asian languages, the squares of the chessboard are also called 'eyes'. Other Japanese terms for features of the chessboard are: *taté*, a file of the board (*akitōshi*, *sukitōshi*, *tsukitōshi*, open file); *yoko*, rank or line of the board; *izuwari*, the squares e1, e9, on which the *Ō-shō* stand; *setsuin* (closet), a corner square; *miyako* (capital), the central square of the board (e5); *nanamé* or *sujikai*, a diagonal of the board.

[65] The native books give the relative dimensions as length 1·2, breadth 1·1 feet. Falkener possessed a table $5\frac{3}{4} \times 6\frac{1}{2}$ in., and a paper board $10\frac{1}{4} \times 12\frac{1}{4}$ in.

This is a matter of some moment when there is a choice of captures possible. There is no distinction between the pieces on the two sides, but each player places his men with the vertex towards his opponent, and the direction in which the point projects alone determines to whom any particular piece

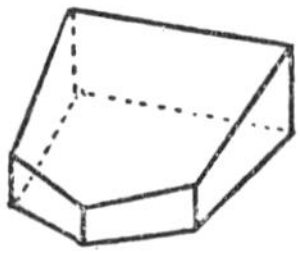

Japanese chessman

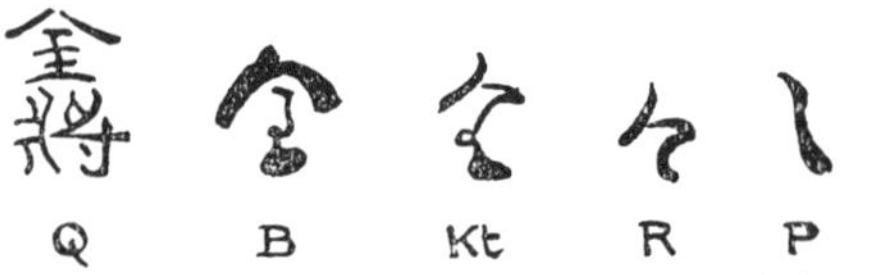

The different scripts for Kin

belongs. When a player promotes one of his men he merely turns it over so as to show its new rank.

The pieces are called *ma uma*, or more commonly *koma*, meaning a colt or small horse. It is possible that the form *koma* contains the word *go*, = Chinese *k'i*, game;[66] it is by no means uncommon to find the men used in a game called 'horses'. Each player has twenty *koma* at the commencement of the ordinary game. Their names, powers of move, and promotion values are exhibited in the following table. All the pieces take as they move.

No.	Japanese[67] Name.	Translation.	Power of Move.	Position.	Promotion.	Equivalent.
1	Ō-shō	Jewelled General	One step in every direction	e1; e9	—	K
2, 3	Kin-shō	Gold General	One step in six directions, viz. the four horizontal and vertical directions, and the two diagonal directions in advance	d1, f1; d9, f9	—	Q
4, 5	Gin-shō	Silver General	One step in five directions, viz. the four diagonal directions, and vertically forwards only	c1, g1; c9, g9	Kin-shō [B*]	B
6, 7	Kei-ma	Honourable, or laurel horse	The Knight's leap, but only in the two most forward directions	b1, h1; b9, h9	Kin-shō [Kt*]	Kt
8, 9	Kyōsha or Yarī	Fragrant Chariot or Spearman	Any distance vertically forwards only	a1, i1; a9, i9	Kin-shō [R*]	R
10	Hisha	Flying Chariot	Any distance vertically or horizontally	h2; b8	Ryō-wō	C
11	Kaku-ko or Kakkō	'Angle-going'	Any distance diagonally	b2; h8	Ryō-ma	D
12-20	Fū-hyō or Hō-hei	Foot-soldier	One step vertically forwards	a–i 3; a–i 7	Kin-shō [P*]	P
[	Ryō-wō	Dragon King	Move of Ō-shō + Hisha			C*]
[	Ryō-ma	Dragon Horse	Move of Ō-shō + Kakko			D*]

[66] This is Himly's suggestion, *ZDMG.*, xxxiii.

[67] The transliteration varies with the different sources. The text follows Culin (except kako-ko) and Chō-Yō (except ryū-ō and ryū-ma). Hoffmann (*Qst.*, 281) has K, wau-siyau;

Players generally say *Ō*, *Kin*, and *Gin* for *Ō-shō*, *Kin-shō*, and *Gin-shō*. The *Fu-hyo* is usually called *Fu* or *Hyo*, and the *Keima* is often simply *Kei*. In the problem works the opponent's King is called *Gyok-ō-shō* or simply *Gyok-ō*, i. e. the Usurper General.

The relative values (*kurai*, rank) of the *koma* are thus estimated by Chō-Yō: Q=9 (9·8 %), B=7 (7·6 %), Kt=4 (4·3 %), R=3 (3·2 %), C=D=18 (19·5 %), P=1 (1·1 %). This estimate is probably only a rough one, since it assigns the same value to both *Hisha* and *Kakko*, pieces with the moves of our Rook and Bishop respectively; the experience of the European game would suggest that there must be a considerable difference of force between these pieces.

As soon as a *Gin*, *Keima*, *Kyōsha*, *Fu*, *Hisha* or *Kakkō* is played to a square within the opponent's territory, it may at once be promoted to its promotion rank; in the first four cases this is that of *Kin*, in the last two cases this is respectively *Ryō-wō* and *Ryō-ma*. This promotion is made in the same move with the move to the qualifying square. A player may, however, postpone the promotion to a later move if this suits his plans better. The ordinary term for the operation is *naru* (to turn), or more fully, *kin-ni* (*ryō-wa-ni*, &c.) *naru* (becomes a *Kin*, &c.). Other terms are *natta* (turned), *naraseru* (to cause to turn over), *kaeru* (to turn over), *hikkurikaeru* (to turn upside down), or if the promotion is made by capturing an opposing piece, *torité naru* (take and turn). It is not always advantageous to exercise the right of promoting a piece. The *Keima*, notwithstanding its limited move, is often more useful as a *Keima* than as a *Kin*, for as a *Keima* it can leap over occupied squares and its check cannot be covered.

The greatest peculiarity of *shōgi* arises from the power that a player possesses through the possibility of the replacement of prisoners (*toriko*) on the board.[68] Since a player generally keeps his prisoners in his hand this possibility is called *tengoma* (*tegoma*) or *mochingoma* (*mochigoma*) (man in hand). Instead of moving one of his men on the board, a player may, at any time when it is his turn to play, enter one of his prisoners on any unoccupied square and so add it to his effective forces. This manœuvre makes a capture doubly valuable; there is not only the negative value arising from the loss of the piece, but the positive value arising from its possible replacement on the board. This power, however, is subject to certain limitations and a convention. The limitations are—

Q, kin-siyau; B, gin-siyau; Kt, kema; R, kiyau-siya; C, hi-siya; D, kaku-giyau; P, ho-hei; C*, riu-wau; D*, riu-ma. Himly (*ZDMG.*, xxxiii. 672) agrees with Chō-Yō except R, kōsha or yarī (this latter term is nowhere mentioned by Chō-Yō) and P, ho-hei, which again is not given by Chō-Yō. Chamberlain and Culin (*Korean Games*, 90) give as the popular forms K, o; Q, kin; B, gin; Kt, keima; R, yari; C, hisha; D, kaku; P, fu; ryō-wō, and ryō-ma. *BCM.*, 1896, pp. 200–2, agrees with Chamberlain excepting K, ou; Kt, keima uma. V. d. Linde (ii. 136) and *BCM.*, 1899, p. 447, give K, yok sho; Q, kin sho; B, yin sho; Kt, kema; R, kioshia (koshia); C, hyshia; D, kakusho; P, hohei. Falkener (157) has K, o *or* sho; Q, kin; B. ghin; Kt, ka ma; R, yari *or* kioshia; C, hisha (promotion, nari hisha); D, kaku (promotion, nari kaku); P, fu *or* hio. *Nari hisha* and *nari kaku* are palpably erroneous.

[68] The Japanese terms are *toru*, *ikedoru*, *toriko-ni-suru* (to capture); *tokkaeru* or *torikaeru* (to exchange); *tokushite torikaeru* (to win the exchange); *sonshite torikaeru* (to lose the exchange); *ryotenbin* (to fork).

(1) A second *Fu* may not be entered on any file upon which the player already has an unpromoted *Fu*. Doubled *Fus* (*nifu*) are not tolerated in *shōgi*, and if a player, either by inadvertence or intention, should place a second *Fu* in this way his opponent simply removes it from the board (Jap. *nameru*, *nametoru*, *suitori*, *tadatoru*, or *tadatori*, to huff), and plays his own move, precisely as a player at draughts plays 'the huff'.

(2) A *Fu* or *Hisha* may not be entered upon the opponent's back line, nor a *Keima* on his second or back line: this is because these pieces would then be unable to move and could not be promoted.

(3) A re-entered piece only possesses its original value, even if it be entered within the opponent's territory. In the latter case it qualifies for promotion after making one move.

The convention is that it is bad form to re-enter a piece where it does not actively assist in attacking the opponent; a *machingoma* or waiting game is, according to Chō-Yō, considered cowardly.

This peculiarity of the game differentiates Japanese chess from all other varieties, and renders it difficult for a European to appreciate the science of *shōgi*. A Japanese generally holds his prisoners in his hand, but must show them at any time when requested. The usual phrase is *té-ni-wa* (*O-té-ni-wa* or *té-ni*), meaning 'In your hand?'

Check in Japanese is *ō-té*, i. e. Jewel's move. Double check is *ryō-ōté* or *niju-ōté*; discovered check, *akiōté*; the dangerous divergent checks which attack simultaneously the *Hisha* or *Kakko* are *hishaté-ōté* or *hishatori-ōté* and *kakuté-ōté* or *kakutori-ōté*. Checkmate is *tsumi*, *tsumu*, or *tsunda*, all meaning 'fixed'. Mate on the K square is *izuwari zeme*; mate in the corner, *setsuin zeme*; mate on the midmost square of the board (e5), *miyako zeme*. To checkmate is *tsumeru* (to fix). Stalemate is not permitted, and it is considered bad form to mate with a *Fu*.

The move is generally determined by throwing up a *Fu*, when the opponent cries '*Fu*' or '*Kin*', and wins when his cry falls uppermost. In a sequence of games the winner begins in the following game. In the tournaments the match appears to be for the best of three games. The rule of 'Touch and move' is disregarded by ordinary players, who say '*matta*', '*matta-naraz*', or '*matté*' ('wait, please wait') when they wish to take back a move, but experts hold to the strict rule with the penalty of moving the *Ō-shō* for its breach. A player who wishes to put a piece straight says '*gomen* (or *shikkei*) *naoshite*' ('pardon me, I adjust').

The works which I have used give very little information about the Openings in *shōgi*. Chō-Yō says that all openings (*uchidashi*) of repute have distinctive names and are classified as regular (*teishiki*) or irregular (*futeishiki*). He gives the following: (1) The *Kakuté* method (Pc3), (2) The *Nakabisha* method (beginning 1 Pe4 and 2 Ce2), (3) The *Hishaté* method (beginning Ph4), (4) an attacking opening (1 Bc2; 2 Pc4; 3 Bc3; 4 Pb4; 5 Pb5; 6 Bb4), (5) a defensive one (1 Qc2; 2 Bd2; 3 Qg2; 4 Bf2; 5 Kf3).

There is an elaborate gradation of odds (*orosu, otosu*), the scale being as follows: (1) aP or iP, (2) bP, (3) aP + iP, (4) R, (5) both R, (6) R + Kt on same wing, (7) both R + Kt, (8) both R + both Kt, (9) the same + a,b,h,iP, (10) C or D, (11) C + D, (12) the same + both R, (13) as 12 + both Kt, (14) all the pieces except K, Q, and B.

An expert playing against a novice will remove all his own men excepting the *Ō* from the board, and undertake to win with the move if he be allowed to retain three *Fus* in his hand. He commences by placing a *Fu* in front of the novice's *Kakko*, winning it the following move. This chess joke is called *Fu-san-mai*.

The following specimen game is taken from Himly's paper in the *ZDMG*., xxxiii. 672 seq.[69]

White	Black	White	Black	White	Black	White	Black
1 Pc4	Pg6	13 D*i8	D on e6	25 Kth8,*	B × Kt*	37 C*f8 +	P on c8
2 Pb4	Ph6	14 C × P	B × Kt	26 Q × B	bC × Q	38 D*d4	Kt × P +
3 D × D	B × D	15 Ch9,* +	Kf8	27 D* × C	Q on h7	39 B × Kt	Q × hR
4 Ph4	Ktg7	16 R on h1	P on h3	28 C on g9 +	Kt on f9	40 D* × bP	Q × iR
5 Pi4	Pi6	17 Bg2	Kt on g5	29 D*g8	Kd8	41 Kt on c7	Ch1,*
6 Kti3	Pi5	18 Kt on i6	Pf6	30 C × Kt,*	Kc8	42 Kt × Kt,* +	K × Kt*
7 Ph5	iP × P	19 P on h7	Pb6	31 D*f7	Qd8	43 Pc7,*	R on b8
8 Ch3	Kt × P	20 Ph8,*	Q × P*	32 B on d9 +	Kb7	44 P* × R +	K × P*
9 Kt × Kt	Bg9	21 D* × Q	D × C*	33 D*d5 +	Pc6	45 R on b7 +	Ka8
10 D on g7 +	Qf8	22 D* × D	C on h6	34 C* × fP	Qc7	46 D on b9, *tsunda*.	
11 D × R,*	Qg8	23 Q on f7 +	Ke9	35 Pc5	Kb8		
12 Ktg7	Bh8	24 Qg8	Ph2,*	36 P × P	Qd6		

In addition to the ordinary chess, Japanese works make mention of five other varieties of chess, *tsiu shōgi* (=intermediate chess), played on a board of 12 × 12 squares with 46 men a side;[70] *dai shōgi* (=great chess), on a board of 15 × 15 squares with 65 men a side; *maka dai-dai shōgi*, on the same 15 × 15 board with 96 men a side; *dai-dai shōgi*, on a board of 17 × 17 squares; and *dai-shōgi*, on a board of 25 × 25 squares with 177 men a side. No further particulars appear to be known of the last four of these, but the *tsiu shōgi* would seem to have been still played in the 18th century. The names of the different chessmen are an interesting illustration of the thoroughness with which the war-character of chess has been eliminated in Japan, and the powers of move exhibit the care with which the various possibilities of move have been investigated.

The names, powers, and positions of the pieces of *tsiu shōgi* are exhibited in the following table.

69 In this game and in the problem solutions on pp. 147–8, I describe the replacement of a prisoner on the board thus: D (C, &c.) on g7, &c.; and the promotion of a piece by an asterisk preceded by a comma, e.g. Ch9,* means 'Hisha plays to h9 and becomes a Ryō-wō' (C*).

70 Since Himly (*T'oung Pao*, viii. 170) quotes from the Chinese *San t'sai t'u hwei* a mention of a *chung siang k'i*, which is the Chinese equivalent of the Japanese *tsiu shōgi*, with ninety-two pieces in all, it is possible that this game was originally borrowed from China.

No.	Japanese Name.	Translation.	Power of Move.	Position (one side only).	Promotion.
1	ō-shō	as	in Shōgi	f1	—
2	siu zo	Drunk Elephant	One step in all directions except vertically backwards	g1	tai-se
3, 4	kin-shō	as	in Shōgi	e1, hi	hisha
5, 6	gin-shō	as	in Shōgi	d1, i1	shu-go
7, 8	dou-sho Ch. thung tsiang	Copper General	One step vertically or diagonally forwards	e1, j1	woo-go
9, 10	mau-hau Ch. möng pao	Horrible Panther	One step diagonally, and vertically forwards and backwards	b1, k1	kakkō
11, 12	kyōsha	as	in Shōgi	a1, l1	hakku
13	ki-rin Ch. ki-lin	Unicorn	One step diagonally, or a leap into the second square vertically and horizontally	f2	sisi
14, 15	hoo-woo Ch. fong huang	Phoenix	One step vertically and horizontally, or a leap into the second square diagonally	g2, d5	hon-woo
16, 17	mau-ko Ch. möng hu	Blind Tiger	One step in all directions, except vertically forwards	e2, h2	fi-roku
18, 19	kakkō	as	in Shōgi	c2, j2	ryō-ma
20, 21	fan-sha Ch. fan chö	Retreating Chariot	Any distance vertically forwards or backwards	a2, l2	kei-gei
22	sisi Ch. shi-tze	Lion	A leap to second field in all eight direct directions [71]	f3	—
23	hon-woo Ch. pon wang	Fleeing King	= fan-sha	g3	—
24, 25	ryō-wō	as	in Shōgi	e3, h3	fi-ziu
26, 27	ryō-ma Ch. lung-ma	as	in Shōgi	d3, i3	kaku-yu
28, 29	hisha	as	in Shōgi	c3, j3	ryō-wō
30, 31	shu-go Ch. shu-hing	Straight-goer	Any distance vertically forwards or backwards, or one step horizontally	b3, k3	fi giu
32, 33	woo-go Ch. höng-hing	Sideways-goer	Any distance horizontally or one step vertically	a3, l3	hon-tsio
34–45	hōhei	as	in Shōgi	a–l 4	?
46	tsiu-yin Ch. chung-zhön	Adjutant	One step vertically forwards and backwards	i5	siu-yo
		Pieces	after Promotion.		
	tai-se	Crown-prince	= ō-shō		
	hakku	White Horse	Any distance vertically forwards and backwards, and diagonally forwards only		
	fi-roku	Flying Stag	Any distance vertically forwards and backwards ; one step in all other directions		
	kei-gei	Whale	Any distance vertically forwards and backwards, and diagonally backwards only		
	fi-ziu	Flying Eagle	Any distance in all directions except diagonally forwards; a leap to second square diagonally forwards		
	kaku-yu	Horned Falcon	Any distance in all directions except vertically forwards and backwards; a leap to second square vertically forwards		
	fi-giu	Flying Ox	= kakkō		
	hon-tsio	Flying Pig	Any distance in all directions except vertically forwards and backwards		

The ordinary chessboard of 81 squares is used for two other games, each of which is named a variety of chess. In *Tobi-shōgi* (jumping chess), each player arranges his eighteen men, now considered to be all of equal value, upon the first and second rows. Each man can move straight forward or laterally, and captures as in the English game of draughts. In *Hasami-shōgi* (intercepting chess) each player arranges his nine *Fus* upon his back row. Each man can move any distance forwards or laterally. When two men occupy the two squares adjacent to that occupied by an opposing man, in either a horizontal or a vertical direction, the opposing man is captured.

Two other games with the chessmen are only played by children. Neither requires the board. In the first, *Furi-shōgi* (shaking chess), the chessmen are used as dice. If the chessman falls face upwards it counts 1, if face downwards, 0; if it stands on its end, 10, and if it stands on its side, 5. In the other, *Uke-shōgi* (receiving chess), the chessmen are used as dominoes. A certain number are dealt out, and the first player challenges his opponent to pair a named piece in his hand. If he succeeds, the move passes to the opponent; if he fails, the first player throws out this piece, and challenges with a second piece, and so on. The player who first succeeds in getting rid of his hand wins.[72]

Mention has already been made of the extensive problem literature of Japanese chess. Very few examples of Japanese chess problems have been printed in Europe, and the following selection would seem to show that the problem art is at a much more rudimentary stage than is the case in Europe. The liberal use which is made of the *mochingoma* powers removes much of the difficulty of construction. In none of the problems (Jap. *mondai*) is the winner's King on the board, which means that the resources of the defence are materially circumscribed. As a whole, the problems show little sign of any appreciation of economy of force as a beauty of construction. The solutions show a long succession of checks, and European players will probably consider them to be on a lower plane than the Muslim problems which I give in Chapter XV, many of which were composed in Baghdād a thousand years ago.

(Problems 1–5 are taken from Chō-Yō's *Japanese Chess*, to which reference has already been made. No. 6 was given by v. d. Linde in his *Leerboek*, Utrecht, 1876, 299.)

Solutions.

1.—1 Cd9,* +, K × C*; 2 D × Kt*,* +, K × D*; 3 De6 +, B × D; 4 Kt on d6 +, Kc9; 5 Ktb7 +, Kb9; 6 Ktc7 m.

2.—1 R × P + d, P* × D; 2 Ce5 +, K × C; 3 Ktf3 +, Ke6; 4 Df5 +, K × D; 5 Ci5,* +, Ke6; 6 C*e5 +, Kf7; 7 Ktg5 +, Kg8; 8 C* × B +, B × C*; 9 B on g7 +, K × P*; 10 P on f8 +, Kg9; 11 Rh8, *m.

3.—1 Qb3 +, K × Q; 2 Bc4 +, Ka3; 3 C*b4 +, R × C*; 4 Kt on b1 +, R × Kt,*; 5 P on a2 +, Kb4; 6 Cb2 +, R* × C; 7 P on b3 +, R* × P; 8 Bc5 +, Kb5; 9 Qb6 m.

[71] The Lion possessed additional powers. These are by no means clear, but apparently he could devour any piece on an adjacent square. If the Lions on both sides came together, other things could happen, but the text is unintelligible. See *Qst.*, 283 and note.

[72] From information given me by Professor Tsuboi, a well-known Japanese ethnologist.

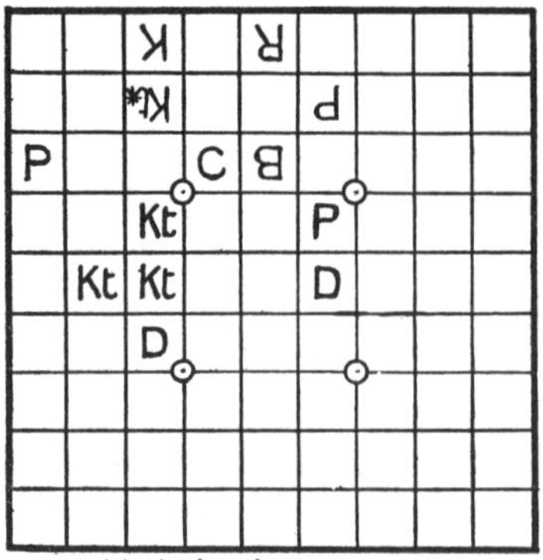

No.1 In six moves

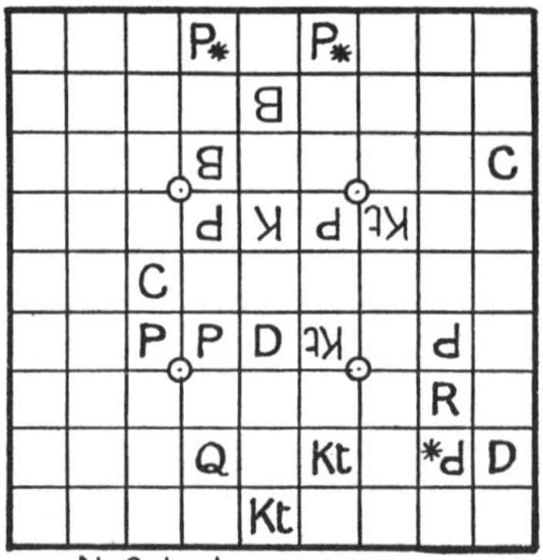

No.2. In eleven moves

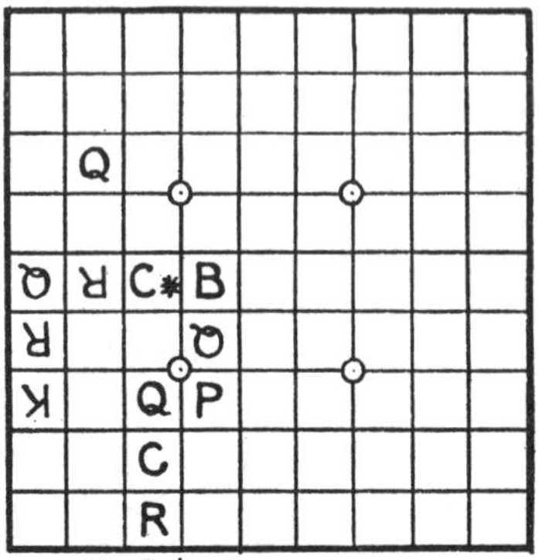

No.3. In nine moves
Black has in hand Kt and two Pawns

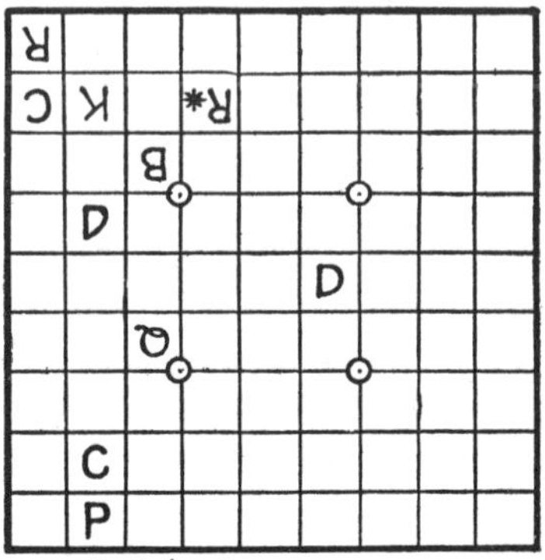

No.4. In nine moves
Black has in hand Q and five Pawns

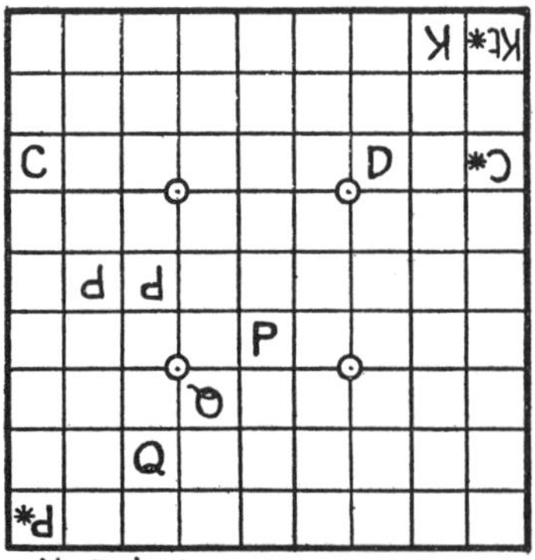

No.5. In twenty-one moves
Black has in hand Q and three Kts

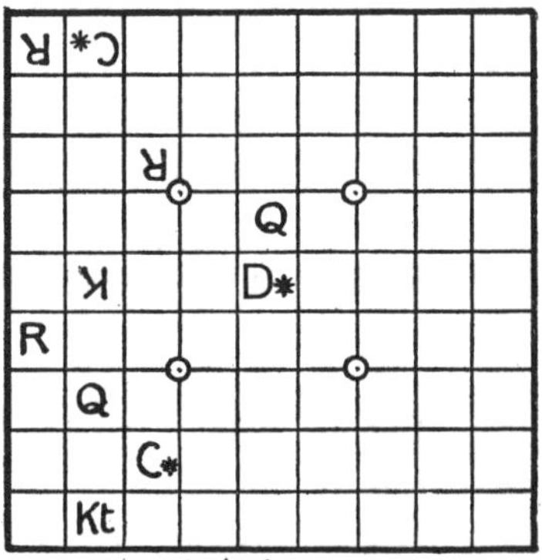

No.6. In two moves

4.—1 Q on c8+, R*×Q; 2 Da7,*+, K×D*; 3 P on a6+, K×P; 4 D×R*,*+, C×D*; 5 P on a5+, K×P; 6 P on a4+, K×P; 7 P on a3+, K×P; 8 P on a2+, Ka4; 9 R on a3 m.

5.—1 D×Kt*,*+, Kg9; 2 Kt on h7+, C*×Kt; 3 D*h9+, Kf9; 4 Kt on g7+, C*×Kt; 5 D*g9+, Ke9; 6 Kt on f7+, C*×Kt; 7 D*f9+, Kd9; 8 Kt on e7+, C*×Kt; 9 D*e9+, Kc9; 10 Ca9,*+, Kc8; 11 Q on c6+, C*×Q; 12 C*d9+, Kb7; 13 D*×C*,+, K×D*; 14 C on c8+, Kb5; 15 C*d5+, Ka4; 16 Ca8,*,+, Kb4; 17 C*a3+, K×C*; 18 C*×Q+, Kb4; 19 C*a3+, Kc4; 20 Q on d4+, K×Q; 21 C*d3 m.

6.—1 Kta3+, Kb6; 2 D*×R m.

CHAPTER VIII

CHESS IN PERSIA UNDER THE SĀSĀNIANS

Literary references.—The *Kārnāmak*.—The *Chatrang-nāmak*.—Probable introduction under Nūshīrwān.—The story in the *Shāhnāma*.

When Ardawān saw Artakhshīr, he rejoiced and esteemed him highly. He commanded him to accompany his sons and knights to the chase and to the games of ball. Artakhshīr did this, and by God's help he became doughtier and more skilled than them all in ball-play, in horsemanship, in chess (*chatrang*), in hunting, and in other accomplishments.

So runs the earliest reference to chess in all literature, occurring in the *Kārnāmak-i-Artakhshatr-i-Pāpakān*, a middle-Persian or Pahlawī romance which is based upon the career of Ardashīr (Artaxerxes), the son of Pāpak, the founder of the Sāsānian dynasty, who ruled over Persia A.D. 226–41. This interesting romance is largely mixed with legend and fable, and the mention of chess establishes nothing more than the fact that chess was known and esteemed at the time of its compilation. This date, however, can only be fixed approximately. Nöldeke[1] states frankly that there is no linguistic evidence available to fix the real date of any particular work. In the case of the *Kārnāmak* the external evidence is also very slender. There is a doubtful indirect reference to it in a 7th cent. work, another in a work of 815 or 816, while the first direct mention occurs in al-Maṣ'ūdī in 943–4. On the other hand, the references of the Greek historian Agathias (A.D. 580) to written Persian chronicles of their kings in his accounts of Sāsān, Pāpak, and Ardashīr show that works of the class of the *Kārnāmak* were already in existence in his time. Nöldeke's final conclusion is that there is much in favour of ascribing it to the last period of the Sāsānian rule—possibly to the reign of Khusraw II Parwīz (A.D. 590–628). With this verdict competent authorities have generally agreed; Prof. Browne, in his luminous *Literary History of Persia*, London, 1902, p. 122, sums up the general opinion thus—'The *Kārnāmak* was probably composed about 600 A.D.,' and Jacobi, calling attention to the form *chatrang*, accepts the same date when he says that this reference is *at most* 50 years older than the earliest mention of chess in Indian literature. But even if it prove to be later than the references in Subandhu and Bāṇa, it cannot be denied that the present mention would still imply the greater antiquity of the game. For not only does it imply that the game was fairly generally known in Persia, but also that popular opinion had seized on chess as a characteristically national game in which it was fitting that the

[1] Who edited the *Kārnāmak* with a German translation in 1878: *Gesch. des Artachšīr-i-Pâpakân aus dem Pehlewi übersetzt* (*Bezzenberger's Beiträge*, iv), Göttingen, 1878.

national hero should be skilled. Such opinions do not grow in a day, and a considerable period of time must be postulated for their growth in an age of slow and imperfect methods of communication. Even in mediaeval Europe it took chess more than a century to achieve a like result. And beyond this there is the further interval required for the passage from India to Persia, and the previous life in India itself.

The *Kārnāmak* reference has also a philological value. Scholars have long perceived that the Arabic *shaṭranj* and the Greek *ζατρίκιον* both point to an older Persian *chatrang* as an intermediate step from the Sanskrit *chaturanga*. With the discovery of the present passage philological theory has been replaced by historic fact.

Another non-religious Pahlawī romance—considered to be of later date than the *Kārnāmak*, though still older than the *Shāhnāma*, and ascribed by Nöldeke with some hesitation to the first centuries of Islam (say 650–850)[2]—treats much more fully of chess under the same form *chatrang*. This is the *Chatrang-nāmak*, also called the *Mātīgān-i-chatrang*, a short work which treats of the introduction of chess into Persia, and of the invention of nard, in the time of Khusraw I Anūshak-rūbāno (Nūshīrwān, 531–578).

Although it would have been very easy to over-estimate the importance of this little work, this has not happened. It obviously stands in some sort of relationship to the poetical version of the same story in the *Shāhnāma*, and the extreme caution of Nöldeke's references[3] has led v. d. Lasa and other chess historians to put it aside as of no independent value. To Persian scholars its sole interest has consisted in its relationship to the *Shāhnāma*, and in the problems to which this question gives rise. But quite apart from any questions as to the literary or historical value of the *Chatrang-nāmak*, the romance has a certain importance as being the first work that we possess which throws any light upon the nature or nomenclature of chess. Nowhere else can we ascertain the names of the chessmen in Persia before it was swallowed up in Islam, nowhere else can we learn for certain that the Persian *chatrang* was a two-handed game of skill.

Nöldeke's conjectural date receives some confirmation from the use of the word *chatrang* rather than *shaṭranj*. In modern Persian the latter Arabic form has completely displaced the older *chatrang*: so early as Firdawsī (A.D. 1000) this had taken place. Indeed the change must have been still earlier and have been complete within 200 years of the conquest, for not only do we find no trace of the remembrance of the older form in any of the Arabic grammarians, themselves largely of Persian blood, but we should hardly have

[2] Nöldeke, *Sitzungsberichte der K. Akademie der Wissenschaften in Wien, phil.-hist. Classe*, Vienna, 1892, vol. cxxvi, Abh. xii. *Persische Studien*, ii, pp. 20–6, sums up the question of date thus (p. 26)—'Das kleine Buch ist jedenfalls älter als der Schâhnâme. Sehr wahrscheinlich ist es, dass es auch schon früher als Ja'qûbî's Werk geschrieben ist. Auf der andern Seite ist es gewiss ziehmlich viel später als die Zeit, worin es seine Geschichte versetzt. Vermuthlich gehört es den ersten Jahrhunderten des Islâms an.'

[3] Thus (op. cit. p. 20), he says: 'Eine kleine Erzählung . . . die, so gering ihr Werth in historischer wie in ästhetischer Hinsicht ist, doch darum unser Interesse beansprucht, weil sie in naher Beziehung zu einem Abschnitt des Schâhnâme steht.'

found so careful a historian as al-Yaʿqūbī (end 9th cent.) explaining *shaṭranj* as derived from the Persian '*hashat-ranj*' (eight-sided) if any recollection of its real origin had survived to his day.

The *Chatrang-nāmak* is one of the works contained in the oldest MS. of Pahlawī works (J2) of 1323.[4] The following version is based in the main on Salemann's German translation.

THE HISTORY OF CHATRANG.

1. In the name of God! It is related that in the reign of Khusraw-i-Anūshakrūbān, Dēwasārm, the great ruler of India, devised the chatrang with 16 emerald and 16 ruby-red men in order to test the wisdom of the men of Īrān, and also from motives of personal interest. With the game of chess he sent 1,200 camels laden with gold, silver, jewels, pearls and raiment, and 90 elephants, of all of which an inventory was made, and he sent Takhtarītus, who was the most famous of the Indians, in charge of them. Moreover, he had written the following in a letter: 'Since you bear the name of Shāhānshāh (King of Kings) and are king over all us kings, it is meet that your wise men should be wiser than ours: if now you cannot discover the interpretation of the chatrang, pay us tribute and revenue.

2. The Shāhānshāh asked for 3 days' time, but there was none of the wise men of Īrān who could discover the interpretation of the chatrang.

3. On the third day Wajūrgmitr of the house of Būkhtak rose and said, 'Live for ever! I have not revealed the interpretation of the chatrang until this day, in order that you and every dweller in Īrān may know that I am the wisest of all the people of Īrān. I shall easily discover the interpretation of the chatrang, and take tribute and revenue from Dēwasārm. And I will make yet another thing and send it to Dēwasārm, which he will not discover, and we shall take double tribute and revenue from him. And from that day none shall doubt that you are worthy to be Shāhānshāh, and that your wise men are wiser than those of Dēwasārm.'

4. Then said Shāhānshāh: 'O Wajūrgmitr, hail to our Takhtarītus!', and he commanded that 12,000 dirhems should be given to Wajūrgmitr.

5. On the next day Wajūrgmitr called Takhtarītus before him and said: 'Dēwasārm has fashioned this chatrang after the likeness of a battle, and in its likeness are two supreme rulers after the likeness of Kings (*shāh*), with the essentials of Rooks (*rukh*) to right and to left, with a Counsellor (*farzīn*) in the likeness of a commander of the champions, with the Elephant (*pīl*) in the likeness of a commander of the rearguard, with the Horse (*asp*) in the likeness of the commander of the cavalry, with the Foot-soldier (*piyādak*) in the likeness of so many infantry in the vanguard of the battle.' Thereupon Takhtarītus arranged the chatrang, and played with Wajūrgmitr. Wajūrgmitr won 12 games against Takhtarītus, and there was great joy throughout the whole land.

6. Then Takhtarītus stood up and said: 'Live for ever! God has bestowed upon you such glory and majesty and power and victory. Verily you are lord of Īrān and An-īrān.

7. Several wise men of India devised this chatrang with much toil and labour,

[4] It was first published in a native Indian magazine in 1854, next by Peshutan Dastur Behramji Sanjana, *Ganjeshayágán*, *Andarze Atrepát Máráspandán*, *Mádegáne chatrang*, and *Andarze Khusroe Kavátán*, Bombay, 1885, with Gujarati and English translations. This edition is based on four modern MSS., not all independent. The English version is by no means literal, and is in places obviously inaccurate. C. Salemann published in 1887 (*Mélanges asiatiques tirés du Bull. de l'Acad. Imp. de St.-Pétersbourg*, IX. iii. 220–30 = *Mittelpersische Studien* in the *Bull. de l'Acad. Imp. de St.-Pétersbourg* for 1887, pp. 417 seq.) a brilliant attempt to recover the actual pronunciation of the Pahlawī text. E. W. West, *Note on the Catrang-nāmak* (*JRAS.*, xxx. 389), gave the complete text of sect. 5 from MS. J 2, the Bombay MSS. being defective here. Cf. also Nöldeke, *Sitzungsber. der Wiener Akad.*, 1892, pp. 20–6; and *Grundriss der iranischen Philologie*, ii. 145; and E. W. West in ibid., 119, § 103. Cf. also Macdonell, *JRAS.*, 128.

The MS. employs the Huzvārish terms *malkā* for *shah* and *sūsyā* for *asp*. Salemann transcribes *shāh, frazīn, asp, piyādah*.

and sent it hither and (?) arranged it. There was none who could expound it, but Wajūrgmitr by his innate wisdom has interpreted it with ease and speed and has added many riches to the Shāhānshāh's treasury.'

8. On the next day the Shāhānshāh called Wajūrgmitr before him and said to him: 'My Wajūrgmitr, what is that thing of which you said, "I will make it and send it to Dēwasārm"?'

9. Wajūrgmitr replied: 'Of all the rulers of this millennium has Artakhshīr been the most active and the wisest, and I erect a game Nēw-Artakhshīr[5] after the name of Artakhshīr. I fashion the board of Nēw-Artakhshīr in the likeness of the land of Spandārmadh, and I fashion 30 men in the likeness of the 30 days and nights; I fashion 15 white in the likeness of day and 15 black in the likeness of night; I fashion the movement of each after the likeness of the movement of the constellations, and in the likeness of the revolution of the firmament.'

10. (*The explanation of the spots on the faces of the dice*) 'I fashion "one" in movement in this likeness because Hurmazd is one, and he has created all that is good.

11. "Two" I fashion in the likeness of heaven and earth.

12. "Three" I fashion in this likeness because good thoughts treat of words, works, and thoughts.

13. "Four" I fashion in this likeness because there are 4 temperaments of which man is formed, and because the points of the world are 4, East, West, South, and North.

14. "Five" I fashion in this likeness because there are 5 lights, the sun, the moon, the stars, fire, and the light which comes from heaven, and because the divisions of day and night are 5.

15. "Six" I fashion in this likeness because the creation of the world was in the 6 times of the Gahanbār.

16. The arrangement of Nēw-Artakhshīr upon the board, I fashion in this likeness because Hurmazd the lord placed the things which he had created upon the world.

17. The movement of the men in this direction and in that I fashion in this likeness because man's energy in this world is linked with the heavenly bodies; and the 7 stars move in 12 fixed circles, and fall when it is time for one to defeat and remove another, just as men in this world defeat and remove one another.

18. When (?) all are removed ... it resembles man because men must all depart from the world, and when they are again arranged, it resembles man because at the resurrection all men are made alive again.'

19. When the Shāhānshāh heard this oration he was filled with joy and commanded (his servants to provide) 12,000 Arab steeds all adorned with gold and pearls, and 12,000 young men, the most distinguished in Īrān; and 12,000 coats of mail with 8 ...; and 12,000 belts with 7 clasps; and everything else that is necessary to equip 12,000 men and horses in the most worthy fashion. And he placed Wajūrgmitr of the house of Būkhtak over them as leader at an auspicious season, and he arrived in India in good health by God's help.

20. When Dēwasārm, the great ruler of India, saw him in this manner he asked Wajūrgmitr of the house of Būkhtak for 40 days' time, but there was none of the wise men of India who could discover the interpretation of the game of Nēw-Artakhshīr; and Wajūrgmitr received from Dēwasārm twice the tribute and revenue; and he returned in good health and with great ceremony to Īrān.

21. The solution of the interpretation of the chatrang is this, that in it the understanding in particular is recognized as the essential weapon by virtue of which, as certain wise men have said, 'the victory is obtained by intellect'. The principle of play in chatrang is to watch and strive to maintain one's own pieces, to take great pains as regards the being able to carry off the opponent's pieces, and in the desire of being able to carry off the opponent's pieces not to play an unfair game. The player

[5] Bomb. has *Vinearthsadar*. Nöldeke (op. cit., 21) has *Nēw Artakhshēr*. Salemann has *Nēw Ardashīr*. For a discussion of the form, which is also found in Arabic as *Nardshīr*, see Hyde, ii. 232, and Nöldeke, op. cit., 25 ff.

must always guard that one piece which is most convenient for the (?) move, and take care to (?) move in a fair way so that he may stand blameless in the matter of good manners.

It is obvious that we have here a literary work, not a simple record of historical fact. The intention of the narrative lies upon the surface, the exalting of the wisdom and fame of the Persian race at the expense of a neighbouring people. The *Shāhnāma* shows many similar examples of this form of patriotic writing. The colour and treatment of the stories are entirely literary, but behind all these embellishments there is always to be found a basis of fact from which the narrative has been developed. In the present case the basis of the story is the historical fact that the game of chess was introduced into Persia from India, coupled with the popular tradition that this event had taken place in the reign of Nūshīrwān.

The literary construction of the *Chatrang-nāmak* is crude and conventional. The parallelism of the incidents, the embassies, their riddles, the attempts at solution, the amazing success of the one party and utter failure of the other, all betray the want of experience and skill of the early explorers in the field of fiction. The plot of the story by which rival monarchs stake tribute or lands upon the solution of a puzzle or riddle recurs very frequently in rudimentary forms of literature.[6]

In opposition to the Indian invention of chess is placed the Persian invention of *nard* (tables or backgammon); surely a very unsatisfactory contrast from the patriotic Persian point of view, for the invention of chess seems in every way the more wonderful achievement. But the romance shows no sign of any suspicion of this, and the writer would appear to have judged of *nard* by the elaborate symbolism of the game which occupies so considerable a portion of his work. We cannot give him credit for the invention of the interpretation: it is almost a commonplace among Arabic writers; and Nöldeke has suggested that it may everywhere go back to a Neo-Platonic or or Neo-Pythagorean Greek source. It is, however, possible that the writer's choice of *nard* for the Persian reply to the Indian invention of chess, may be due to the admiration that he felt for this symbolic explanation of the game. In any case the choice was unfortunate. The history of *nard* has still to be written, but its antiquity is undoubtedly very great. Chinese works record its introduction from India into China in the 3rd c., A.D. As will be seen in the following chapter, there is good reason to believe that the game was known to the Greeks in the 6th c., A.D., by the name of *tabla* or *taula*. The older Arabic historians attribute its invention to India, and associate it with the mythical kings whom they allot to that peninsula. At the same time other Arabic works show a persistent attempt to connect the invention of *nard* with Ardashīr, the first of the Sāsānians, and the hero of the *Kārnāmak*. I think that this was due to the popular attempts to explain the alternative Arabic name of *nardshīr*,[7] though it also requires a greater antiquity than the

[6] Cf. Benfey, *Kleine Schriften*, ii. 165, 178 ff. [7] See above, and the references in note 5.

Chatrang-nāmak allows. It seems clear that we can attach no weight to this portion of the story. The embassy to India is pure invention.

Nor can we attach any more weight to the story of the embassy from India which brought chess to Persia. The wisdom of Buzūrjmihr has at all times been extolled to Persian literature, but in this story it transcends belief. To discover the moves of the chessmen and the rules of play from a study of the board and pieces is to do something miraculous. Moreover, it is impossible to identify the Indian characters with any contemporaries of Nūshīrwān. Like all Arabic writers before al-Bērūnī, our author appears to have thought of India as a political entity similar to Sāsānian Persia. He shows no intimate knowledge of Indian history, for although he has given his Indian king a Sanskrit name (*Dēwasārm* answers to *Devasharman*[8]), it is difficult to see whence he obtained it. Nöldeke hazards the conjecture that it may be really identical with the name *Dabshalim*, the king in the *Kalīla wa Dimna*, and that the legendary *Shahrām* or *Shihrām* of another chess story may be a further perversion or misreading of the same name. The deficiencies of the Pahlawī script made misreadings of unfamiliar words that could not be guessed from the context extraordinarily easy. The name *Takhtarītus*[9] also presents difficulties. Nöldeke suggests that the first element is the Per. *takht*, chessboard; West sees in it a compound term *takht-rad*, priestly counsellor of the throne, which he supposes may be a Mid. Per. rendering of some Sanskrit title or name. This much alone seems certain : the name is not Sanskrit.

We therefore come back to the simpler tradition that lies behind the *Chatrang-nāmak*, that chess was introduced into Persia in the reign of Nūshīrwān. The same tradition is to be found in al-Maṣʿūdī's *Murūj adh-dhahab* (A. D. 947). In his account of the reign of Nūshīrwān he says:

> He had sent from India the book *Kalīla wa Dimna*, the game of chess, and a black dye called *hindī*, which dyes the hair to its roots a brilliant and permanent black.[10]

That is to say, the initiative in the introduction of chess was taken by Nūshīrwān, as was the case also in the translations of Greek and Sanskrit classics which were made in his reign. This reference in al-Maṣʿūdī appears to me to be quite distinct in origin from the *Chatrang-nāmak*, especially as it shows no attempt to magnify the reputation of the Persians, and as al-Maṣʿūdī adopts elsewhere a different opinion of the invention of *nard*.[11] It will be noted that al-Maṣʿūdī connects the introduction of chess with the arrival in Persia of the collection of Indian fables called *Kalīla wa Dimna*.[12] Most Persian

[8] The Pahlawī reading is not certain. Nöldeke once writes (?) *Spēsharm*. Salemann writes *Dēwsarm*; the Bombay edition *Dēwasārm* and *Dēwsarām*. According to Leumann, Skr. names in *-sharman* are Brahman, but they would scarcely be used by the Kshatriya or royal caste. See Nöldeke, op. cit., 24.

[9] The form is again not absolutely certain. Nöldeke gives *Tākhtalītus*, *Tātarītus*, *Tālalītus* as all possible readings.

[10] In Barbier de Meynard's French edition, ii. 203.

[11] Nöldeke's attitude is non-committal. 'This may be derived from our history (the *Chatrang-nāmak*), but it may also be a good historical note, and also, if it be incorrect, it may correspond with the statement of another older source : in both cases it is possible that our history has been manufactured from this statement' (op. cit., 221).

[12] This book, the Skr. *Pañchatantra*, is better known to Europeans by its name of *The Fables of Pilpay*, *Pilpay* being a corruption of *Bidpai*, the Arabic rendering of the Skr. *vidyāpati*, chief

scholars accept the evidence for the transmission of this work to Persia in the time of Nūshīrwān as satisfactory when stripped of the absurd embellishments and details that are added to the story in the *Shāhnāma*.

The only difficulty that I can see in accepting this traditional date of the introduction of chess as historical is the shortness of time which it leaves for the general adoption of chess in Persia. Within 120 years the game has attained the reputation which is evidenced by the reference in the *Kārnāmak*, and the fixity of nomenclature which the Arabic nomenclature requires. But no other Persian king is associated with the introduction in any known Arabic work. Ardashīr, son of Pāpak, is the Sāsānian most likely to be made the hero of a fictitious story, but he is only named in connexion with the discovery of nard. Shahrām (Shihrām), the king in the story of *The Doubling of the Squares*, is an Indian monarch. The phenomenon of the rapid spread of chess, however, can be paralleled by diffusions equally rapid at later points of the history of the game, and is indeed one of the most characteristic features of that history. If chess reached the royal Persian court first, and became the fashion there, its spread first to the upper classes and then to the lower orders may easily have taken place in the course of three generations.

The story of the *Chatrang-nāmak* appears again, but in a rather different form, in the national epic of Persia, the *Shāhnāma* of Abū'l-Qāsim Manṣūr Firdawsī (begun by Daqīqī, 975; finished 1011).[13] It is not certain whether Firdawsī had the earlier version before him. Wherever it has been possible to check the *Shāhnāma* by the older legends—as in the case of the *Kārnāmak* and the *Yātkār-i-Zarīrān*—the general fidelity of the later poet to ancient legend, even in matters of minute detail, has been established. In the present legend there are fundamental differences between the two versions, extending to the whole second part of the story. Nard, with the elaborate account of its symbolism, has gone entirely, and in its place Firdawsī describes another game of uncertain origin and arrangement.

The whole setting of the story in the *Shāhnāma* is different, and the story is told with greater literary skill. In one point alone does Firdawsī adopt a more sober colouring. He replaces the jewelled chessmen of the older writer by pieces of ivory and teak. The colours of the older work would seem, though, to be the more accurate historically. Red and green have apparently always been the favourite colours for the pieces in India, if not in Persia. Ath-Tha'ālibī, in his *Ghurar akhbār mulūk āl-Furs* (1017–21),[14]

pundit. *Kalīla* (Skr. *Karaṭaka*) and *Dimna* (Skr. *Damanaka*) are the names of the two jackals that appear in the tales. The Syriac translation (*c.* 570) and the Arabic translation by b. al-Muqaffa' (*c.* 750) were made from the Pahlawī version. The Arabic version is the immediate source of the mediaeval European versions. Cf. Macdonell, *JRAS.*, 130.

[13] This work is based upon the earlier records of the Sāsānian monarchy, the collection of which was commenced by Nūshīrwān. The intervening works—the Greek *History of Persia* by Sergius, First Interpreter at Nūshīrwān's court; Dānishwar's *Khudhāy-nāmak* (100 years later); b. al-Muqaffa''s Arabic translation, the *Siyar mulūk al-'ajam*; and the Zoroastrian work of 957–8—are all lost.

[14] Ed. Zotenberg, with French trans., Paris, 1900, 700. This work is largely based upon the *Shāhnāma*, and contains (ed. cit., 622) a much condensed version of the two chess stories that are contained in the Persian poem.

in his description of the marvellous treasures of Khusraw II Parwīz (590–628) says:

He had also the game of chess, of which the pieces were made of red rubies and of emeralds, and the game of nard made of coral and of turquoise,—

a treasure which in later historians [15] was magnified until the chessmen were made of single rubies and single emeralds, and their value had grown until the smallest of the pieces was estimated at 3,000 golden dīnārs. Can it be that the story of the embassy from India arose from the existence of this chess set?

Firdawsī commences his story [16] with a description of the magnificence of Nūshīrwān's court, to which one day an ambassador from the Raja of India came, bringing many noble presents from Kanūj. Macdonell points out that the mention of this town as the home of the Indian monarch is very happy, since Kanūj (= Skr. *Kānyakubya*) is the very place where Bāṇa represents chess as being known not long after Nūshīrwān's time.[17]

When he had displayed the treasures, the Indian envoy presented a richly illuminated letter from the Raja to Nūshīrwān and a chessboard constructed with such skill that it had cost a fortune, and proceeded to deliver the following message:

O king, may you live as long as the heavens endure! Command your wise men to examine this chessboard, and to deliberate together in every way in order that they may discover the rules of this noble game, and recognize the several pieces by their names. Bid them try to discover the moves of the Foot-soldiers (*piyāda*), the Elephants (*pīl*), and the other members of the army, viz. the Chariots (*rukh*), the Horses (*asp*), the Counsellor (*farzīn*), the King (*shāh*), and how to place them on their squares. If they can discover the rules of this beautiful game, they will excel all the wise men of the world, and we will willingly remit to this court the tribute and dues which the king demands of us, but if the wise men of Īrān are unable to solve the riddle, they ought to desist from demanding tribute from us, for they will not be our equals in wisdom; nay, rather, you ought to pay tribute to us, for wisdom is more excellent than everything else of which man may boast himself.

The message ended, the chessmen were presented and placed on the board. One side was of polished ivory, the other of teak. In reply to some questions from the king, the ambassador said that the game was a representation of war, and that in the game would be found the course, the plans, and all the apparatus of a battle. Nūshīrwān then asked and was granted a space of seven days for the investigation. For several days the wise men of Persia tried in vain to discover the game, but in vain. At last Buzūrjmihr, who

[15] Hyde (ii. 82) quotes the account from the Persian historian Majdī, and the further information from *Al-mustaṭraf*, an anthology of the first half of the 15th century: 'It is reported that some of the Persian kings had a game of chess of red ruby, and that the value of the smallest piece (*qiṭ'a*) was 3,000 dinars.' Forbes (194) estimates from this the value of the whole set at a quarter of a million sterling.

[16] I have used the French version in *Le Livre des Rois par Abou'l Kasim Firdousi*, publié, traduit et commenté par M. Jules Mohl, Paris, 1838–78, vi. 384–400, verses 2697–2888.

[17] It must be remembered, however, that Kānyakubya was a large and famous city of India, and if Firdawsī wished to add local colour to the story, it would be only natural that he should use the name of what was probably one of the best-known cities of India.

had hitherto stood aloof, approached his king, and promised to solve the riddle which had proved too much for all the other wise men of the nation. He took the chess home to his house, and after a day and a night's experimentation, he unravelled the whole game.

At his request the Indian ambassador was summoned, and made to recount again the terms of the challenge. Then Buzūrjmihr produced the chessmen, and proceeded to arrange the forces.

> He placed the king in the centre, and on his right and left the ranks of the army, the brave foot-soldiers in the van, the prudent vizier beside the king to advise him in the battle, next to king and vizier were the elephants both observing the battle, then the horses ridden by two expert riders, lastly at the two extremities were the rukhs, both rivals, and ready for the battle on the right and on the left.

The Indian was overwhelmed at the discovery, and his admiration for the wisdom and penetration of Buzūrjmihr passed all bounds. He returned to India, and Buzūrjmihr was covered with honour by his grateful monarch.

But Buzūrjmihr was planning further triumphs for Persia. He withdrew himself and pondered deeply until by his unaided genius he invented nard. The game is thus described:

> He made two dice of ivory, with figures the colour of ebony. He then arranged an army similar to that of chess, he placed the two sides in order of battle and distributed the troops, ready for battle and for the assault of the town, among eight houses. The field was black, the battle-field square, and there were two powerful kings of good disposition who should both move, without ever receiving injury. Each had at his side an army in its arrangements, collected at the head of the field, and ready for the fray. The two kings advanced upon the field of battle, their troops moved on all sides around them, each endeavouring to outgo the other, now they fought on the heights, now on the plains; when two on one side had surprised a man by himself, he was lost to his side, and the two armies remained thus face to face until it was seen who was beaten.

Nūshīrwān was of course delighted at this fresh proof of his minister's wisdom and ingenuity, and he sent him on an embassy to India to confound the wise men at the Raja's court with the game of nard. As in the older story the Indians fail ignominiously, and Buzūrjmihr returned in triumph to receive fresh honours at the hand of his grateful king.[18]

In giving Firdawsī's story at this time, I have rather anticipated the history of chess in the East, although in a way the real connexion is better preserved thus. For Firdawsī voiced again the aspirations of the Persians, and the *Shāhnāma* is the first great work in which Persian again came to the front after a period of eclipse. The eclipse, however, was only apparent, and extended to little beyond the language. As has so often happened in history, the race that was vanquished on the battlefield became the victor in the years of peace that ensued. The view of those who consider that the two or three centuries which immediately succeeded the Muslim conquest of Persia were intellectually barren, is quite erroneous. On the contrary,

[18] A second story (*The History of Talkhand and the Discovery of the Game of Chess*) follows this narrative in the *Shāhnāma*. I shall deal with this in Ch. XII, in connexion with the Oriental legends of the invention of chess.

it was 'a period of immense and unique interest, of fusion between the old and the new, of transformation of forms and transmigration of ideas, but in no wise of stagnation or death'. Old ideas and philosophies had to be restated in terms better fitting the changed conditions, and in every branch of learning there was a process of moulding and fusion in full swing; even the faith of Islam took on a new spirit, 'ce sont eux (les Persans) et non les Arabes, qui ont donné de la fermeté et de la force à l'islamisme,' writes Dozy.[19] And in the intellectual sphere the debt is still more remarkable; we should leave every branch of Arabic science poor indeed if we removed the work of Persian writers. The whole organization of the state was Persian, and, although at first it was the Arabs who composed the invincible armies that conquered Syria, Egypt, and Persia, by the end of the Umayyad period the Persians had regained the military supremacy, and it was Persian armies that placed the 'Abbāsids on the throne. In so doing the Persians had a full revenge for their overthrow at the hands of the early Caliphs. Not without reason does al-Bērūnī[20] boast that the 'Abbāsids were a Khurāsānī, an Eastern, dynasty, for at their court Persian influences and ideas were supreme, attaining their zenith under al-Ḥādī, Hārūn ar-Rashīd, and al-Ma'mūn. The history of Muslim chess will be largely a history of Persian players, the development, a history of Persian ideas.

The importance of the pre-Islamic existence of chess in Persia can hardly be over-estimated, for it has left an impress upon the game that has proved greater and more lasting than that of any other period of its history. In that time Persia gave the game a fixity of arrangement, a method of play, and a nomenclature that have attended the game everywhere in its Western career. By a singular freak of fate the very name of the game in every country of Western Europe, except Spain and Portugal, has become a witness for the passage of chess through Persia. When the chess-player cries 'check', and probably also when he cries 'mate', he bears his unconscious testimony to the same fact. It is not too much to say that European chess owes more to its Persian predecessor chatrang than to its more remote and shadowy ancestor, the Indian chaturanga.[21]

APPENDIX

SOME NOTES ON THE PERSIAN NOMENCLATURE

I have already above (p. 150) dealt with the older name of chess in Persia, and shown the importance of the two recorded uses of it. *Chatrang* is very close in form to the Sanskrit *chaturanga*, and its existence is a valuable link in the chain of chess history.

[19] See Victor Chauvin's French translation, *Essai sur l'Histoire de l'Islamisme*, Leyden-Paris, 1879, 156.

[20] In his *Al-āthār al-bāqiya* (Chronology of Ancient Nations), translated by Sachau, London, 1879, 197.

[21] For the modern game of Persia, see Ch. XVII below. The Parsi chess of S.W. India has no connexion with the game of Persia, see Ch. IV above.

The names of the pieces are given in the *Chatrang-nāmak* and in the *Shāhnāma*. They are *shāh* (king), *farzīn* (wise man, counsellor), *pīl* (elephant), *asp* (horse), *rukh* (chariot), and *piyādah* (foot-soldier). In the *Shāhnāma* the word *mubāriz* (champion) is occasionally used to describe the *rukh*.

Shāh is the Middle and Modern Persian form of the Old Per. *khsháyathiya*, which is found on the cuneiform inscriptions on the rock-face of the cliffs at Behistūn. In Pahlawī writing the Huzvārish form *malka* was used in its place. It has always been the royal title of the Persian monarch. When the Shāh in chess was attacked by any other piece it was usual to call attention to the fact by saying *Shāh*, it being incumbent upon the player whose Shāh was attacked to move it or otherwise to remedy the check. This usage passed into Arabic, and was adopted in European chess, although with the change in name of the piece it ceased to have any obvious meaning. Indeed in Med. Lat. the word *scac* in this sense was simply treated as an interjection. When the Shāh was left in check without resource, *māt* or *shāh māt* was said. *Māt* is a Persian adjective meaning 'at a loss', 'helpless', 'defeated', and is a contracted form of the adjective *mand*, *manad*, *manīd* (RAS[2] uses regularly *shāh manad* and *manad* for *shāh māt* and *māt*), which is derived from the verb *mandan*, *manīdan*, 'to remain'.[1]

When a check 'forked' another piece, it was usual to name this second piece also, thus *shāh rukh* meant a check that also attacked a Rook. In Muslim chess this was a check that would generally decide the game, since the Rook excelled the other pieces so much in value.

Farzīn (later in Ar. as *firzān*, *firz*, and *firza*) is connected with the adjective *farzāna*, 'wise', 'learned', and means literally 'a wise man', 'a counsellor'. It has no connexion with *wazīr*, 'vizier', and a wise man is not necessarily a vizier. That the piece was at a later time associated with the vizier of the Persian kings and 'Abbāsid caliphs was due to its position on the chessboard at the side of the king.

Pīl, later Arabicized as *fīl*, means elephant. It is not, however, a native Persian word, nor is it Skr. Gildemeister suggests that the Persians may have obtained the word from a language that was spoken by some tribe situated between Persia and India. The elephant was not a native Persian animal.

Asp is the ordinary Persian word for horse.

Rukh is less simple. The European dictionary statements that the word means 'an elephant bearing a tower on its back', or 'a camel', are based upon guesses suggested by the modern carved Parsi pieces, and have no Persian authority whatever behind them. The guess of Herbelot that *rukh* meant 'hero' in Middle Persian has been shown to depend upon the use of the word *rukh* in the chapter-heading of the legend of the Eleven Champions, which has been added by some later copyists of the *Shāhnāma*. It is true that Firdawsī does describe the Rukh as a champion or hero, reflecting the rôle that the chariot rider has always played in the Indian epics, just as in Homer. But it is necessary to show that Firdawsī or other early Persian writers used *rukh* where one would naturally expect *mubāriz* (hero), and this has not been done.

[1] See Hyde, ii. 133, who quotes a number of Persian dictionaries for the form *manid*; a note by Mirza Kasim Beg in the *Journal Asiatique*, 1851, ii. 585; Gildemeister in *ZDMG.*, xxviii. 696; and Dozy's *Supplément aux dictionnaires arabes*, Leyden, 1878. The old view of the pre-scientific philologists that *māt* was the Ar. verb *māta*, 'to die'—a view which began to be current at an early period in the life of Muslim chess—has been abandoned by modern scholars.

[2] See p. 177.

The word has two other well-established senses in Persian, (1) the cheek, and (2) the fabulous bird, familiar to readers of the Arabian Nights. Its derivation in both these senses is unknown.[3]

There can be no doubt that the chess-term *Rukh* meant simply chariot. The regular practice in the westward march of chess has been this: the term the meaning of which was well known to all who used it was translated into the new language and thus was replaced by a native and intelligible word; the term the meaning of which had ceased to be familiar to those who were using it in the land whence chess was travelling was adopted unchanged or in a native dress. *Rat·ha* can never have been unintelligible in Sanskrit chess circles, and the analogy of the rule followed in the case of every other of the chessmen requires that the Persians translated *rat·ha* also by some Persian word meaning chariot. Although *rukh* has never been the ordinary word in use for chariot in Persian, there is some evidence to show that it did bear that meaning both in Persian and Arabic. In Vullers' *Persian Lexicon*, Bonn, 1855–64, s.v. *shaṭranj* (chess), p. 410, a native Persian dictionary is quoted as giving *ʿaraba* as an alternative name for the *rukh*. *ʿAraba* is the ordinary Arabic word for chariot, which, like so many other Arabic words, has been adopted as Persian. This makes the authority somewhat late, and accordingly evidences the persistence of this knowledge of the real meaning of *rukh* in Persia. The knowledge was, of course, by no means general. For Arabic we have two valuable entries in early Arabic-Latin glossaries, the knowledge of which we owe to Dozy. The earlier of these is the *Leyden Glossarium* MS. 231 from the *Leg. Scaliger*, the MS. of which is dated 12th c. by palaeographists. Here we have *currus*, rukhkh;[2] *quadriga* rukhkh dhū arbaʿa 'aflāk (rook of four wheels); and *auriga*, rukhkh, thumma ṣāniʿ ar-rukhkh (rook, then chariot-maker). In the other glossary, the *Vocabulista*, a Florence MS. of which has been edited by Schiaparelli (Florence, 1871) we have, p. 106, *rukhkh*, currus; and, p. 329, *currus*, ʿajala,—rukhkh, to which a marginal gloss adds *roc de scas*. It seems quite clear from these two entries in Spanish glossaries that the word *rukhkh* was in common use among the Moors in Spain in the sense of chariot. There is also the evidence of the chess-pieces in the Bibl. Nat. at Paris, which are popularly known as Charlemagne's chessmen, in which the Rook is carved as a two-wheeled chariot with a single man in it. Also a 15–16 c. Hebrew MS. (Vatican, 171, f 2), which contains a poem on chess (v. d. Linde, i. 180, text, 189), substitutes the chariot for the rook. There is a possible reference in a Latin poem on chess (MS. Einsidlensis, 365) which is probably older than 1100 (ll. 141–2):

> Extremos retinet fines inuectus uterque
> Bigis seu rochus, marchio siue magis.

Piyādah, older *payādah*, which was Arabicized as *baidaq*, is a derivative of the Persian *pai*, 'a foot', and means a foot-soldier.

[3] See Hyde (ii. 109 ff.) and Bland (64) for the native attempts to explain the name of the chessman as derived from a fabulous Indian monster which preyed upon elephants and rhinoceroses.

CHAPTER IX

CHESS IN THE EASTERN EMPIRE

Chess not a classical game.—The name *zatrikion*.—First references in Arabic works.—References in late Greek literature.—Ecclesiastical censures.—Chess in the Turkish rule, and in modern Greece.

It was a common belief among mediaeval writers that chess was a game, if not of Trojan, at least of Greek invention, and that various references to the practice of games among the Greeks and Romans in classical times related to chess. In the light of the facts of the history of the spread of chess which have been narrated in the preceding chapters, this view can no longer be seriously maintained. Quite apart from the fatal anachronisms involved in the claim, it can be shown to be improbable, if not impossible, on *a priori* grounds, from an examination of the character of the references and allusions to board-games in classical Greek. When these references are carefully examined, it is found that they reveal not the slightest trace of any allusion to any characteristic at all similar to the essential characteristics of chess—pregnant in possibilities of allusion, simile, or metaphor as these have proved in every chess-playing country. It is inconceivable that such a silence could have existed throughout Greek and Latin literature had any of the classical games shown those peculiarities of piece, form, and move which are the special property of chess. Nor, again, would it have been necessary, as v. d. Lasa has acutely pointed out, for the Byzantines to have introduced a new name for chess if the *petteia*, or *the game of the sacred way*, or any other of the classical games had been chess. Slight and conjectural as is our knowledge of these games, whether requiring the agency of dice or not, this much at least is certain: none of them was chess and none of them was like chess.[1] Games of skill some of them certainly were, but all lacked the vitality that chess has always shown, and it is clear that they had dropped into desuetude by the sixth century of our era, for long before that date commentators were revealing, by their curious and inconclusive attempts to explain the classical allusions to the *petteia* and other games, their complete ignorance on the subject.

With the games of the Byzantine period (A.D. 365–1450) we are not much better off for information. Our knowledge is small and goes but little

[1] The nature of the classical games was first discussed by the European scholars named in the text as responsible for the little we know as to the Byzantine games. In modern times they have been discussed by H. Coleridge, whose paper forms one of the appendices to Forbes' History, by v. d. Lasa, in a series of essays in the *Schachzeitung* (1863, pp. 161, 193, 225, and 257); by the Rev. W. Wayte, in Smith's *Dict. Gk. and Roman Antiquities*, London, 1891; by Saglio and Darembourg, *Dict. des Antiquités*, Paris, 1804; by L. Becq de Fouquières, *Les jeux des anciens*, Paris, 1869; by Dr. W. Richter, *Die Spiele der Griechen u. Römer*, Leipzig, 1887; by Marquardt, *Privatleben der Römer*, 2nd ed., Leipzig, 1886; by Falkener, whose reconstructions of these games I am unable to accept; and by Professor Lanciani (*Gambling and Cheating in Ancient Rome*, *N. Amer. Review*, July 1892).

beyond the names of a few of the games that were current. Our want of knowledge may, it is true, be due in part to the uninviting nature of the later Greek literature. The number of scholars who have ventured upon that dreary and unprofitable field is very small, and we are practically indebted for what little we know of the Byzantine games to the first zeal of the scholars of the Renascence; no later writer has added anything of material value to the information first arranged by the four scholars of the 17th c., Jules-César Boulenger, Johannes Meursius, Daniel Souterus, and Andrew Senftleben, the salient facts of which may be seen most conveniently in the pages of Gronovius or the lexicons of Ducange.[2]

That chess should be found among the games of the later half of the Byzantine period is not surprising. On the contrary, when the political intercourse which subsisted between the Eastern Empire and the later Sāsānian monarchy and the ʿAbbāsid caliphate is remembered, together with the general adoption of Persian customs and luxuries at the court of Constantinople, it would be strange indeed if a knowledge of chess had not penetrated to the Imperial court.

The earliest references to Eastern games in Byzantine Greek are probably those relating to *tabla,* in later Gk. *tavla,* which was probably identical with the Persian and Arabic *nard* or *nardshīr*. Etymologically the word *tabla* is merely an adaptation of the L. *tabula,* table, which was already used by Juvenal in the sense of gaming-table, and at a later time appears to have become the ordinary name for the *ludus duodecim scriptorum* of the classical period.[3] If this game was ever played in the Eastern Empire, it was soon supplanted by the Persian nard, a game of the same class, and the name of *tabla* was transferred to this latter game.[4] It is this game *tabla* which is mentioned in some epigrams of Agathias the scholastic of Myrine in Asia, who flourished A.D. 527–67; the longest of these (*Anthol. Pal.*, IX. 482) describes an extraordinary position in the game which had occurred to the Emperor Zeno (A.D. 475–81). The position has been recovered independently by M. Becq de Fouquières and by Prof. Jackson of Cambridge, and their reconstruction shows that the game was identical with the Persian nard. Hyde (ii. 255–6) quotes notes on the Gk. *tabla* from Cedrenus, Suidas, and Isaac Porphyrogenitus which contain the germ of the astronomical explanation of nard which we have met already in the *Chatrang-nāmak*. It is noteworthy that this Greek name for *nard* has replaced the older name in Syria, Turkey, and generally along the S. coast of Asia, where the game on the backgammon board is now commonly called *tawūla*.

Chess makes its appearance in Byzantine Greek under the name ζατρίκιον,

[2] Boulenger, *De ludis privatis ac domesticis veterum*, 1627; Meursius, *De ludis*, 1622; Souterus, *Palamedes*, 1622; Senftleben, *De Alea veterum*, 1667; Gronovius, *Thesaurus Graecarum antiquitatum*, vii. 1697.

[3] More than a hundred game-boards with 3 by 12 squares have been discovered in Rome alone in recent years (see Lanciani, *N. Amer. Review*, July 1892). The Latin game was also called *alea* in late Latin (cf. Bp. Isidore's *Origines*, XVIII, lx–lxviii).

[4] This transference of meaning does not seem to have extended to the L. singular *tabula*, for when nard reached the Western Empire, it received the name *ludus tabularum* or *tabulae* (pl.) from the draughtsmen (*tabulae*) with which it was played.

zatrikion. This word is unknown in classical Greek, and is incapable of explanation from native roots. As Hyde and Forbes have shown, the word is 'simply a barbaric or foreign word with a Hellenic termination'. It can be shown that this form answers exactly to the Middle Persian *chatrang*, when allowance is made for the different range of the Greek and Persian alphabets. 'The Greek alphabet', writes Forbes, 'had no letter or combination of letters capable of expressing the sound of the Persian *ch*-, and as the nearest approximation they employed for that purpose the letter ζ, *z*.' For similar reasons they had to transliterate the Semitic *sh*-, by σ, *s*, or by σι, *si*-. The nearest Greek approximation to Per. *chatrang* would be ζατράγκ or ζατρέγκ, and this, on Greek analogies, gave ζατρίκιον, the form actually found. (An *n* sound in such a position was often transposed or altogether suppressed.) *Shaṭranj*, the Arabic and modern Persian name of chess, would have given *satrantz*. Ducas has σαντρὰτζ (with *n* transposed).

The form *zatrikion* accordingly becomes of importance in connexion with the date of the introduction of chess into the Byzantine Empire. The presumption is that the knowledge of the game was obtained at a time when the Persians still used the older form *chatrang*, and not from the later Persians, the Arabs, or the Syrians, all of whom had substituted the form *shaṭranj* for it. Forbes (190–5) assumed that this required the introduction to be anterior to the Muhammadan conquest of Persia, i.e. before the middle of the 7th cent., and fixed upon the exile of Khusraw (II) Parwīz as the date which with 'strong possibility' saw the introduction of chess into Eastern Europe. That would place it in the first quarter of the 7th century.

Forbes, however, assumed that the influx of Arabic words and forms into Persian was an immediate result of the Islamic conquest, A.D. 638–51. Such was certainly not the case. *Chatrang* may have easily remained in use for another 200 years, the earliest evidence for its disappearance belongs to the 3rd century of Islam (A.D. 830–930). All we can assert is that the philological evidence points to the introduction of the word *zatrikion* not later than the 9th century A.D., while it does not at all necessarily follow that the practice of the game began so early: the knowledge of the existence of a thing may precede its use by a considerable interval of time. It is quite possible that the word *zatrikion* came into Greek first in accounts of travel in Persia, or in descriptions of Persian life.

Sound as these conclusions undoubtedly are, they cannot be substantiated by contemporary Greek records, and not one of the earlier uses of the word *zatrikion* can be dated with any approach to exactness. The earliest evidence exists only in Arabic works, and establishes a knowledge of chess and its technicalities at Byzantium by the year A.D. 800. In the *K. akhbār ar-rusul wal-mulūk* of the historian aṭ-Ṭabarī (B. 224/838, D. 310/923)[5] we read:

It is related that when Niqfūr (Gk. *Nicephorus*) was king, and the Byzantines

[5] Ed. Goege, 1881, ii. 695. From aṭ-Ṭabarī the story is copied almost verbatim by the historian b. al-Athīr (B. 555/1160, D. 630/1234) in his *K. al-kāmil fī't-ta'rīkh* (ed. Tornberg, vi. 126) and thence by Abū'l-Fidā' (Abulfeda) (B. 672/1273, D. 732/1331) in his *Mukhtaṣar ta'rīkh al-bashar* (ed. Reinske, 1789–94, ii. 44), whence the incident is generally quoted. The late date of

had assembled in allegiance to him, he wrote to ar-Rashīd: 'From Niqfūr, King of Byzantium, to Hārūn, King of the Arabs, now the Empress to whom I have succeeded estimated you as of the rank of the Rook, and estimated herself as of the rank of the Pawn, and paid a tribute to you, which you rightly should have paid to her. But this was because of a woman's weakness and folly. When therefore you have read my letter, return the tribute that has been previously paid to you, and come yourself with what you have to repay. If not, the sword is between us and you.' It is reported that when ar-Rashīd read this letter, his wrath was kindled . . . and he called for an ink-pot and wrote on the back of the letter: 'In the name of God! the compassionate and merciful! From Hārūn, Commander of the Faithful, to Niqfūr the dog of Byzantium. I have read your letter, son of an infidel woman. The answer is what you will see, not what you will hear.' And he struck his camp that day, and marched until he encamped at the gates of Hiraqla (Gk. *Heracleia*, 65 m. N.W. of Tarsus).

The ruthless conduct of this invasion soon compelled Nicephorus to consent to continue the tribute that his predecessor Irene had paid. The incident is told under the year A.H. 187 (=A.D. 802), in which Nicephorus became Emperor.

The rather later geographer and historian al-Masʿūdī (D. 345–6/956) refers to the Greeks in connexion with chess in two places in his *Murūj adh-dhahab*. At the close of his account of the invention of chess in India in the reign of the mythical King Balhait, he says:

The Greeks (*al-Yūnānīyan*) and Byzantines (*ar-Rūm*) and other peoples have special theories and methods about this game, as we may see in the works of chess-players from the most ancient down to al-ʿAdlī and aṣ-Ṣūlī.

And much to the same effect at the conclusion of a digression on the modifications of chess (among which is 'the round board attributed to the Byzantines') he remarks:

The Indians and others, the Greeks, Persians, and Byzantines who play at chess have given accounts of the manner and fashion of the pieces in chess, its arrangements, its beginnings, the various motives underlying it, its peculiarities, and the classifications of the *qawāʾim* and *mufridāt*, and the classes of the noteworthy *manṣūbāt*.[6]

Greek literature and tradition are alike silent as to the existence or otherwise of these works and theories, and when we turn to the Arabic chess MSS. which are based upon the works of al-ʿAdlī and aṣ-Ṣūlī, we find the only references to Greek chess relate to the philosophers Hippocrates and Galen, and to Aristotle. Hippocrates and Galen apparently found in chess a potent antidote to diarrhoea and erysipelas, and prescribed it with success, while Aristotle figures among the many hypothetical inventors of chess. Another story tells how Galen once met a friend whom he had not seen for some time, and learnt that he had been into the country to see a farm which he had purchased with the result of his gains at chess, whereupon the physician exclaimed with what sounds like a strong flavour of irony, 'What a fine thing chess is, and how profitable!' Pure fiction, the whole of it, of course.

Abū'l-Fidā', coupled with the omission of the correspondence in the anonymous *K. al-ʿuyūn* (12-13th c.), led Gildemeister and v. d. Linde to doubt its authenticity. Finding it in aṭ-Ṭabarī, almost a contemporary writer, I can no longer discredit the story.

6 For the meaning of these technicalities see pp. 228–9 below.

Most of the MSS. agree with al-Maṣʿūdī in giving some account of round chess under the title of *ash-shaṭranj ar-rūmīya*, or Byzantine chess, while they lay stress upon the fact that it is only a modification of the ordinary or Indian chess.[7] It is difficult to understand its designation unless there were some historic justification for it.

It would appear that the earliest use of the word *zatrikion* occurs in works treating of the interpretation of dreams. This is a Science which was apparently first exploited by the Greeks,[8] but soon passed to Persian and Arabic writers. The Muhammadan *tābiʿ* Muḥammad b. Sīrīn (B. 33/653–4, D. 110/729), of Persian parentage, was skilled in this lore, and became the first of a long line of Oriental writers on the subject. One of these Arabic works was retranslated into Greek, and thence into Latin by Leo Tuscus in 1160. A later Latin version is due to the German traveller John Leunclavius (B. 1533, D. 1593), who ascribed the Greek work to Apomazares, in whose name we may recognize the Arabic oneirocritic Abū Maʿshar (D. 272/885). Nicholas Rigault (B. 1577, D. 1654) printed the Greek text in 1603 with Leunclavius's translation, and ascribed it to Achmet fil. Seirem. This is generally understood to mean Muḥammad b. Sīrīn, though on the strength of the Greek version Achmes appears in some lists of Greek authors as flourishing, now as early as A.D. 750, now as late as A.D. 950! Since the work contains the interpretation of a dream that happened to al-Maʾmūn, who reigned A.D. 813–833, it cannot be b. Sīrīn's work, and Bland has shown[9] that there are grounds for believing that it is of Christian authorship. The Greek can hardly be earlier than the 10th century. Chapter 241 treats 'Of *zatrikion*. From the Persians and Egyptians'.[10]

If any one dreams that he plays chess (*zatrikizo*, vb.) with a man he knows, they will quarrel over money affairs, &c.

If a king or grandee or general dreams that he plays chess, he will think of the place for joining battle with the enemy, &c.

If he dreams that he takes many pieces in the game,[11] he will take many of the enemy, &c.

If a king or grandee or general dreams that he has lost or broken or been deprived of his *zatrikion*, he will lose his army, &c.

Besides this passage, Ducange quotes two other references in MSS. accessible in his time, one attributed—but certainly wrongly—to Astrampsychus, in which twice occur the words 'chess and tables',[12] the other from an anonymous MS. on Persia, *De arte Persica*, 'slaves and games of *bolgon* and chess and love of women.' Neither of these passages can be dated, and

[7] For a description of this game see p. 342 below.

[8] The earliest oneirocritic is said to have been Artemidorus, a Greek writer of the 2nd c., A.D. A later writer was Astrampsychus, who flourished 'possibly as late as 350 A.D.'.

[9] On the Muhammadan Science of Tabir (*JRAS.*, xvi, pp. 118–71). Cf. also Steinschneider, *Ibn Schahin und Ibn Sirin, zur Lit. der Oneirokritik* (*ZDMG.*, xxii. 227 ff.) and *Das Traumbuch Daniel's und die oneirokritische Lit. des Mittelalters* (Serapeum, 1863, No. 13 and 14); and v. d. Linde, ii. 306.

[10] Ἐκ τῶν Περσῶν καὶ Αἰγυπτίων περὶ ζατρικίου.

[11] ὅτι παίζων ἔλαβε πλείονας τῶν τοῦ παιγνίου προσώπων.

[12] Astrampsychus ἐν τῷ Πυθαγ. λαξοντ. MS. Ἔχει κοινωνίαν πρὸς γυναῖκα καὶ παῖδας ἀγγυνείους πρὸς εὐνούχους, καὶ παιγνία, καὶ ζατρίκια καὶ ταυλία. Idem καὶ ζατρίκια καὶ ταυλία.

the present location of the MSS. is unknown to me. The only point of importance about either appears to be that chess is associated with other notorious features of Persian luxury. It has probably never been in worse company.

A fourth instance occurs in a scholiast's commentary on Theocritus, *Idyll*, vi. 18,[13] where there is an allusion to the Greek game of *petteia*—'he moves away the pebble from the line.' This, the commentator explains, 'is a figurative expression borrowed from the phraseology of those who play at the game commonly called *zatrikion*'—an absurdity that provoked Dr. Hyde's scornful comment, 'quantum hallucinatus est Scholiastes!' Here again we have no clue to the date of the writer.[14]

It is not until we come to the 12th century that we have an instance of *zatrikion* to which we can assign a definite date. In the twelfth book of the *Alexiad* of the Princess Anna Comnena (D. 1148), a laudatory biography of her father, the Emperor Alexis Comnena (D. 1118), we read in an account of the Emperor's recreations:

> He had certain familiar friends with whom he played chess, a game that was discovered in the luxury of the Assyrians, and was brought to us.[15]

Here again chess is associated with Oriental luxury. Assyria, of course, was no longer a kingdom in Anna Comnena's day, and her use of the name probably only refers to the traditional splendour of the earlier Oriental empires.

The Emperor Alexis's fondness for chess may have been the cause of raising a powerful and bitter hostility to the game. It is at least singular to find that the first ecclesiastical denunciation of chess on the part of the Eastern Church was voiced by John Zonares, who, after filling the post of commander of the Emperor's bodyguard, retired as a monk to the Monastery of Mt. Athos and died there in 1118. It was during his retirement that he wrote his commentary on the canons of the Eastern Church.

That the early mediaeval Church viewed the use of dice with strong disfavour is evident from the attempts that were made to suppress it by legislation. The early list of rules known as the Apostolic Canons[16] requires both clergy and laity to give up the use of dice.

> 42. A Bishop, Priest, or Deacon addicted to dice (Gk. κύβοι, Lat. *alea*) shall either give them up, or be deposed.
>
> 43. A Sub-deacon, Reader, or Singer doing the same shall either give them up, or be deposed. So also the laity.

These rules were adopted by the Trullan Synod (Third Council of Con-

[13] Quoted in Gaisford's *Ed. Poetae Minores Graeci*, Oxford, 1816, ii. 107.

[14] A fifth mention is quoted by Hyde from a late glossary. It explains *zatrikion* as meaning 'the stocks'. Since ζατρεῖον has the latter meaning and is omitted in the Glossary, it is evident that we have the result of some scribe's blunder, who has made one entry out of two.

[15] Εἶχε τῶν συγγενέων τινὰς παίζων τὸ ζατρίκιον· παιδιὰ δὲ τοῦτο ἐκ τῆς τῶν Ἀσσυρίων τρυφῆς ἐξευρημένον καὶ εἰς ἡμᾶς ἐκεῖθεν ἐληλυθός.

[16] An uncritical compilation from the decrees of local Eastern Synods, first made *c.* 500, and extended from fifty to eighty-five rules by John Scholasticus, *c.* 560. The Western Church has never acknowledged the genuineness of either collection.

stantinople) in 680,[17] and have since then formed part of the Nomo-canon of the Eastern Church. It was natural that, in the course of time, the attempt should be made to explain the prohibition of *kuboi* or *alea* by defining exactly the games which were to be included under these terms. This attempt was not confined to the Eastern Church: the later Latin use of *alea* as the name of a game helped to confuse the lawyers of the Western Church, and we shall find Cardinal Damiani arguing in a letter of 1061 that the prohibition of *alea* extended to chess. The Western Church took this view for a considerable time.

Zonares makes the following note on the 42nd rule of the Apostolic Canons:

> Because there are some of the Bishops and clergy who depart from virtue and play chess (*zatrikion*) or dice or drink to excess, the Rule commands that such shall cease to do so or be excluded; and if a Bishop or elder or deacon or subdeacon or reader or singer do not cease so to do, he shall be cast out: and if laymen be given to chess-playing and drunkenness they shall be excluded. . . .

We shall see later that this extension of the term *kuboi* was for long adopted by the Russian Church, and we may probably account in part for the paucity of references to chess in the Eastern Empire as being due to the intolerance of the Church.

The beginning of the 13th century saw the Latin or Western Emperors established in Constantinople, who must have known chess in Western Europe before they laid hands on the Empire of the East. The result of this may be detected in the latest reference to *Zatrikion* in Byzantine Greek. The history of Ducas, written about 1400, nearly at the close of the Eastern Empire, contains an account of the incidents which led to the naming of Tīmūr's son Shāhrukh from a technicality of chess. In this passage Ducas adds the information that the Persians call *zatrikion santratz* (σαντρὰτζ), and the Latins call it *scacum* (σκάκον). Later on he uses σκάκον for a chessman and σκάκου παιγνίον for the game of chess, which are evidently adaptations from the Latin *scacus*, a chessman, and *scacorum ludus*, the game of chess. Shāhrukh is transliterated *Siachrouch* (σιαχρούχ), with the information that the Latins call it σκάκω ζόγκω, a curious misrendering of *scac-roc*. It seems clear to me that Ducas knew more of the Latin than of the Greek chess.

There is one branch of the later Greek literature, fairly circumscribed in extent, which might possibly give us some reference to chess earlier in date than any I have cited. The mathematical problem known as 'the doubling of the squares of the chessboard' may have been known to the later Greek mathematicians, as we find it included in the oldest Western mediaeval MSS. on mathematics. The Greek MSS. have not so far been examined for this purpose.

With the fall of Constantinople (1453) and the last outposts of independent Christianity in Asia Minor (1461), the last vestiges of the Byzantine

[17] Canon 50: 'No one at all, whether clergy or lay, is to play with dice (*alea*) from this time forward.' Cf. also the Code of Justinian (I. vi. 17), in which the clergy are forbidden *ad tabulas ludere* (Novelles, *tablizare*).

Empire passed away, and the Greeks became a subject race and largely adopted the language of their conquerors. The game of *zatrikion*, whatever special points and rules it may have possessed, must be held to have become obsolete, and its very name soon passed into oblivion. Whatever chess was played would assuredly be the Turkish chess of the ruling race. A curious confirmation of this at the very end of the Turkish dominion over Greece itself is to be found in the name, 'the Greek Defence', which Allgaier, following the usage of Viennese chess-players, gave to the Fianchetto defences, which are still to-day a striking characteristic of the native Turkish chess. This result was probably assisted both by the small degree of popularity that chess would seem to have secured among the Greeks,[18] and by the ecclesiastical opposition to its practice.

With *zatrikion* forgotten, it is only natural to discover the use of a new name more closely representing the Turkish *shaṭranj*. The poverty of the Greek alphabet necessitated changes in the form of this word when the attempt was made to reproduce it in a Greek dress. The semitic *sh* was variously replaced by *s* or *si*, the *j* by *tz* or *z*. *Shaṭranj* accordingly gives rise regularly to *santratz*, as in Ducas, or *santraz*, the form which Hyde gives as in use in his time.[19] Modern dictionaries give *santratsi* as in vulgar use, and add still another form, *Satrengion* (*Σατρένγιον*, *σατρέγγιον*), which is a modern adaptation from the Egyptian dialect of Arabic.[20]

Turkish chess has met the same fate in Greece that befell zatrikion, and the modern Greek has turned to the West for his knowledge of chess, and the name of the game, *skaki* (*σκάκι*), and the translations from the French which do duty for the names of the chessmen, betray at once the origin of the modern Greek chess of our day. The attempt to revive the word *zatrikion*, as seen in the title of the only Greek work on the game, the *Encheiridion Zatrikion* of Leo Olivier (Athens, 1894), is due to the workings of national aspirations.

[18] The want of popularity is illustrated by the fact that the Greek version of the mediaeval romance *Floire and Blanchefleur* substitutes *tavla* for the chess of the original, thus reversing the usual custom of translators.

[19] Hyde (ii. 43) adds that the word *santraz* had a secondary meaning derived from the difficulty of the game, and quotes a couple of phrases as given him by a Greek divine.

[20] V. d. Linde (ii. 137 and 191) gives the following terms on the authority of the Greek librarian Demetrius Patsopoulus: Chess, *σκάκι*; King, *βασιλεύς*; Queen, *βασίλισσα*; Bishop, *στρατηγετικός* or *τρέλλος*; Knight, *ἵππος*; Rook, *πύργος*; Pawn, *στρατιώτης*. Olivier has: King, *βασιλεύς*; Queen, *κυρία*; Bishop, *τρέλλος*; Knight, *ἱππεύς*; Rook, *πύργος*; Pawn, *στρατιώτης*; chessboard, *ἀβάκιον*; chessmen, *τεμάχιον*; to castle, *μετατίθεσθαι*; check, *ἔφοδος*; mate, *νεκρός*; checkmate, *ἔφοδος-νεκρός*; stalemate, *ἀκίνητος*. In N. Contopoulos, *Lexicon Eng.-Gk.*, Athens, 1904, besides other terms (e.g. stalemate, *στασιμότης τοῦ βασιλέως*) which can hardly be in ordinary use, I find: Chess, *σκάκι*, *ζατρίκι*, *σαντράντσι*; castling, *ῥοκάρισμα*; square of the board, *σαντράτσι*; chessman, *πιόνι*, *πεδόνι*; chess-player, *σκακιστής*. The *Gk.-Eng.* volume only contains the terms *ζατρίκιον*, *ζατρικιστής*, *σαντράτσι*. *Pedoni* is obviously derived from the Italian *pedona*, and shows that the possibility of the maritime Greeks having acquired a knowledge of chess in the course of Italian trade must not be forgotten.

CHAPTER X

THE ARABIC AND PERSIAN LITERATURE OF CHESS

The chess works mentioned in the *Fihrist*, and other bibliographies.—MSS. used for the present work.—Other MSS. in European libraries.—Poems and impromptus on chess, &c.

THE beginnings of the vast literature of chess are to be found in the Golden Age of Arabic, the first two centuries of the ʿAbbāsid caliphate, that short period during which alone Islam has shown any powers of original thought and discovery. In b. Isḥāq an-Nadīm's great bibliographical work, the *K. al-fihrist,* compiled 377/988, we find a section devoted to the authors of books on chess.

These are the chess-players who wrote books on chess.

AL-ʿADLĪ. His name is (left blank). He wrote *Kitāb ash-shaṭranj* (Book of the chess). He also wrote *Kitāb an-nard* (Book of the nard).

AR-RĀZĪ. His name is (left blank). He was of equal strength with al-ʿAdlī. They used to play together before Mutawakkil (Caliph, 233/847 – 248/862). The book *Laṭīf fī'sh-shaṭranj* (Elegance in chess) is by him.

AṢ-ṢULĪ. Abū-Bakr Muḥammad b. Yaḥyā, who has been mentioned already. He wrote *Kitāb ash-shaṭranj*, the first work, and *Kitāb ash-shaṭranj*, the second work.

AL-LAJLĀJ. Abū'l-Faraj Muḥammad b. ʿObaidallāh. I have seen him. He went to Shīrāz to the king ʿAḍudaddaula (ruled 338/949 – 366/976), and died there in the year 360/970 and a few. He was excellent at the game, and among the books on it *Kitāb manṣūbāt ash-shaṭranj* (Book of chess-positions or problems) belongs to him.

B. ALIQLĪDISĪ. Abū Isḥāq Ibrāhīm b. Muḥammad Ṣāliḥ. He is reckoned among the brilliant players, and wrote the *Kitāb majmuʿ fī manṣūbāt ash-shaṭranj* (Collection of chess problems).

The other much later great Arabic bibliography, the *Kashf aẓ-ẓunūn fī asāmī'l-kutub wal funūn* of Ḥājjī Khalīfa (D. 1068/1658) has a shorter catalogue of chess books.

10224. *Kitāb ash-shaṭranj* by the authors Abū'l-ʿAbbās Aḥmad b. Muḥammad as-Sarakhsī, the physician, who died in the year 286/899; Yaḥyā b. Muḥammad aṣ-Ṣūlī; and a later author who wrote in Persian and boasts not without arrogance that he was the best player of that game in our own time in the whole world. He drew the figure of the chessboard and sketched the pieces and enumerated the authors who had previously written on this game.

As-Sarakhsī[1] ranks as the most important of the pupils of the Arabic philosopher al-Kindī, who lived in Baṣra and Baghdād in the caliphates of

[1] The epithet *as-Sarakhsī* means the inhabitant of Sarakhs in Khurāsān. 'Sarakhs lies on the direct road from Tūs to Great Marv, and on the right or Eastern bank of the Mashhad river, which is now known as the Tajand.' G. Le Strange, *Lands of Eastern Caliphate*, Cambridge, 1905, 395.

al-Ma'mūn and al-Muʿtaṣim. He himself held a position at the court of al-Muʿtaḍid, but fell into disfavour by revealing a secret which this caliph had entrusted to him, and was thrown into prison and executed, 286/899. An-Nadīm, however, makes no mention of a chess work in his list of as-Sarakhsī's writings,[2] nor does al-Qiftī (568/1172 – 646/1248); a later biographer of as-Sarakhsī, b. Abī Uṣaibiʿa (B. 600/1203, D. 668/1270), on the other hand, who wrote on the lives of the Arabic physicians, mentions it under the title *K. fī'sh-shaṭranj al-ʿālīya* (Book of the higher chess) in his *K. ʿuyūn al-anbā' fī ṭabaqāt al-aṭibbā'*.

An-Nadīm left a blank in the place of al-ʿAdlī's personal name, thereby implying that he was unable to discover it. In some modern works, e. g. in the catalogue of the Library of the Sultan ʿAbd-al-Ḥamīd Khān, however, his name is given as Abū'l-ʿAbbās Aḥmad al-ʿAdlī, thus making his personal name identical with that of as-Sarakhsī. I have been unable to discover the authority for the modern statement, and am inclined to think that it has arisen from the assumption that al-ʿAdlī and as-Sarakhsī were one and the same person. This assumption would certainly account for the omission of al-ʿAdlī's work in Ḥājjī Khalīfa's bibliography, but it introduces chronological difficulties. We know from aṣ-Ṣūlī that al-ʿAdlī had stood alone in the first class of chess-players for some considerable time when he was defeated by ar-Rāzī in a match which we know from an-Nadīm was played in the presence of the caliph Mutawakkil (A. D. 847–862). After his death ar-Rāzī in his turn stood alone in the first class for some time, and was dead before aṣ-Ṣūlī came to the front under al-Muktafī (A.D. 902–8). It seems reasonable to infer that al-ʿAdlī was past his prime at the time of his defeat, and that he probably did not survive it many years. As-Sarakhsī, on the other hand, must have been still a young man in Mutawakkil's time, since his master al-Kindī flourished A. D. 813–842, and he himself only met with his death so late as A. D. 899. Moreover, the MS. RAS gives al-ʿAdlī the local epithet of ar-Rūmī, which implies that he was a native of some town in the lands of the old Byzantine Empire. Had he come from Sarakhs, al-Khurāsānī would have been the more appropriate designation. On the other hand, if, as seems most likely, the two men were really distinct, the silence of all the Muslim chess writers concerning as-Sarakhsī is somewhat remarkable.

Of the other authors named above, ar-Rāzī[3] has been identified with the celebrated physician Muḥammad b. Zakarīyā ar-Rāzī, the 'Rhasis' of mediaeval science, who died 311/923 or 318/932. This identification is palpably false. The chess-player belonged to an earlier generation and was dead before A. D. 900. Of aṣ-Ṣūlī and al-Lajlāj I shall have more to say in the following chapters; b. Aliqlīdisī is not otherwise known, but Ḥājjī

[2] This is not necessarily conclusive against its existence, for an-Nadīm partly classifies Arabic books by their subject-matter, and devotes a separate entry to chess. Aṣ-Ṣūlī's other works, for instance, appear under a separate entry. A single book on chess might easily have been overlooked.

[3] The epithet *ar-Rāzī* means the inhabitant of Rai (Ray, ar-Rayy, Gr. Rhages), an important city of Persia, close to the modern Tihrān (Teheran), which b. Ḥauqal (367/977) described as 'except for Baghdād the finest city of the whole East' (Le Strange, op. cit., 214).

Khalīfa's anonymous and bombastic Persian MS. appears to be the one I refer to below as *RAS*.

B. ʿArabshāh, the biographer of the great Tīmūr, in his digression upon the chess-players of the Court incidentally refers to another work by a contemporary of Tīmūr (D. 1405).

ʿAlā'addīn Tabrīzī, commonly called ʿAlī ash-Shaṭranjī, has composed a treatise on the game of chess and its situations.

Finally Ahlwardt, in his *Catalogue of the Arabic MSS. of the Royal Library at Berlin*, gives without stating the source of his information the following list of chess works at the conclusion of his description of the chess treatises in the library.

Kitāb shaṭranj by Aḥmad b. Muḥammad as-Sarakhsī (D. 287/899). *'Istawʿa'n-nahj fī taḥrīm al-laʿb bi'sh-shaṭranj*, by Muḥammad b. ʿAli b. Muḥammad al-Hadhāmī b. an-Najār (D. 723/1323). *Īqāẓ an-nāṣib fīma fī'sh-shaṭranj min al-manāṣib*, by ʿAlī b. Muḥammad al-Mauṣilī b. ad-Duraihim (D. 762/1361).

I now come to the Arabic and Persian works of which I have been able to make use for this book.

There is much similarity about the MSS. which deal with the practical game, and it will be more convenient to summarize their contents in a table and so to avoid considerable repetition. There is usually an introductory section dealing with the legendary accounts of the invention of chess, and the evidence for the lawfulness of chess-playing for Muslims. Chapters dealing with the classification of players, with the relative value of the pieces, with the symbolism of the game, with the decisions as to the result in the simpler Endings of the game, with notation, and the derived chess-games generally follow. There are also chapters dealing with the normal positions for Opening play (the taʿbīyāt), and the body of the work is devoted to a collection of manṣūbāt or problems. Less frequently we find an anthology of chess poems as a crown to the book. These MSS., it will be obvious, deal with nearly every aspect of chess.

1. AH = *MS. ʿAbd-al-Ḥamīd I, Constantinople, no.* 560.
2. C = *MS. Khedivial Lib., Cairo, Muṣṭafa Pasha, no.* 8201.

These are two MSS. of the same Arabic work, the *Kitāb ash-shaṭranj mimma'l-lafahu'l-ʿAdlī waṣ-Ṣūlī wa ghair-huma*, 'Book of the chess; extracts from the works of al-ʿAdlī, aṣ-Ṣūlī and others.'

AH is one of the Arabic MSS. the knowledge of whose existence we owe to Dr. Paul Schroeder. It is no. xviii of v. d. Linde's list (*Qst.*, 331 seq.). It is a beautifully executed paper MS. of 142 leaves, 27.8 cm. by 21.2, written in a careful nashkī hand by Abū Isḥāq Ibrāhīm b. al-Mubārak b. ʿAlī al-Mudhahhab al Baghdādī, 535/1140, as we learn from a note on f. 54 b. Both the main title-page and the subsidiary one on f. 55 a are richly coloured, the titles being in the kufic character upon a blue ground.

C is no. viii of v. d. Linde's list (*Qst.*, 21). It consists of 157 leaves, 26 cm. by 18. From the richly illuminated title-page, now unfortunately much faded, it is evident that this MS. formerly belonged to a Sultan of Egypt, whom a former librarian, Dr. W. Spitta, identified from considerations of handwriting and ornamentation with Qāitbāi (A.D. 1468–96). He dated the MS. itself *c.* 770/1370.

Neither MS. gives any information as to the name of the writer who put together this compilation. A later note on a blank page at the commencement of AH attributes the work to al-Lajlāj, but the fact that this MS. includes a short treatise on chess principles, naming al-Lajlāj as its author, makes it very improbable that this player was the author of the whole work. In the official catalogue of MSS. in Constantinople libraries it is described as '560. *Risāla fi'sh-shaṭranj*, one volume in Arabic, by Abū'l-ʿAbbās Aḥmad al-ʿAdlī'—an entry due to the occurrence of al-ʿAdlī's name in the title of the MS.

Neither MS. is complete. There are gaps in AH between ff. 75 and 76 (the latter leaf beginning in the middle of a problem solution), and 139 and 140 (the poem on the former leaf is incomplete). Ff. 121–123 should be placed between ff. 129 and 130, and f. 21 between ff. 22 and 23. The disarrangement of the entries on ff. 25–29 goes back to a MS. lying behind AH.[4] C is a copy of AH, or of a MS. derived from AH.[5] It is not so extensive, the text on ff. 133 b–142 b of AH being missing. There are also gaps between ff. 5 and 6, 17 and 18, and 23 and 24. The leaves from f. 34 onwards are now in great confusion; none, however, is missing, and they can be arranged in their original order with the help of AH.

The introduction to AH and C shows that aṣ-Ṣūlī's book was largely a critique on al-ʿAdlī's. It runs as follows:

> In the name of God, the compassionate and merciful! There is no prosperity except through God! Al-ʿAdlī gives several accounts of the invention of chess, which Abū-Bakr aṣ-Ṣūlī criticizes. We narrate some of what al-ʿAdlī relates, with aṣ-Ṣūlī's criticisms thereon, and also the problems which al-ʿAdlī placed in his book, with aṣ-Ṣūlī's criticisms and appreciations. We have also added some problems from aṣ-Ṣūlī's book, and some from other authors, together with the traditions which aṣ-Ṣūlī collected on the lawfulness of chess-playing.

The compiler accordingly claims to treat his authorities with some discrimination, and generally makes it clear from whom he is quoting. Extracts from previous writers are commenced by the words *qāla'l-ʿAdlī* or *'ṣ-Ṣūlī*, as the case may be, and are generally in the first person.

The earlier chapters in AH are unusually full and informing. There is also near the end (AH, ff. 133 b – 135 a; not in C) an important *tadhkira* or treatise on chess principles by al-Lajlāj, of which I give the substance in Ch. XIV. The extensive contents of this MS. make it one of our best authorities for Muslim chess.

[4] For a fuller discussion of the question of the original order of the contents of AH, see pp. 236 and 273.

[5] As is shown by the fact that the hiatus between ff. 75 and 76 in AH occurs in the middle of the first line of f. 143 a in C. The writer of C cannot have noticed that there was a gap in the MS.

3. BM = *MS. British Museum, Arab. Add.* 7515 (*Rich*).

This is a quarto MS. on vellum of 132 leaves, which was completed 16 Jumādā II, 655/1257. It formed part of the library that Claudius J. Rich (B. 1787, D. 1820) collected while Resident at Baghdād in the service of the East India Company, and was bought by the Museum Trustees from his widow.

Forbes (74) represented this MS. as a copy of a work written between 1150 and 1250. The arrangement of the MS. does not bear out this view. It has all the appearance of a work planned upon a larger scale than was carried out, the gaps in which the writer filled in later without regard to their surroundings. There are leaves missing between ff. 7 and 8, 16 and 17, 27 and 28, 34 and 35.

There is nothing in the MS. to show the name of its author, but he has made liberal use of al-ʿAdlī's work, and quotes from al-Lajlāj with approval. Aṣ-Ṣūlī is on the whole ignored; the few extracts from his work, e.g. from his preface on f. 8 b, are unacknowledged. The text to fourteen of the problems is identical with that in AH, and it is possible that the aṣ-Ṣulī extracts may have been taken at second hand from a compilation like AH. The MS. is dedicated to a Prince whose name has been erased. Forbes identified him from the special titles and epithets used with one of the Ayyūbid dynasty who ruled over Egypt, A.D. 1193–1250, but I cannot reconcile what is left of the name of the Prince in the MS. with the name of any member of this house, and Cureton (*Cat. Arab. MSS. in the Brit. Mus.*, ii. 351, No. 784) does not pretend to identify either the Prince or his dynasty. From the compiler's knowledge of al-Lajlāj's work, I should be inclined to believe that the MS. was compiled farther East than Egypt, and possibly in Persia.

The most noteworthy feature of the contents is the brief chapter on the Openings of the writer's time, f. 11 a. I quote this original contribution to the history of the taʿbīyāt in Chapter XIV.

The front page, f. 1 a, contains a number of entries in later hands. These consist of (*a*) a title, *Kitāb ash-shaṭranj al-Baṣrī*, 'al-Baṣrī's chess book', which is a manifest error due to the fact that a quotation from al-Ḥasan al-Baṣrī (D. 110/728) stands at the top of f. 2 b: (*b*) a title *Kitāb fī'sh-shaṭranj wa manṣūbāt-hi wa mulaḥ-hi*, 'Book of chess, its problems and subtleties': (*c*) a note in an 18th-century hand giving the differences of move between the chess of the MS. and the chess of the writer's day, which I quote below, p. 354: (*d*) a note in a 15th-century hand giving the sum of the doubling of the squares of the chessboard: and (*e*) a calculation of the same total in Turkish.

4. L = *MS. Asʿad Efendī, Constantinople, No.* 1858.

A MS. of 81 worm-eaten leaves, which was discovered by Schroeder (*Qst.*, No. XVII, pp. 382–9). The binding bears the title *Risāla al-Lajlāj fī bayān laʿb ash-shaṭranj* ('Al-Lajlāj's treatise on the demonstration of the game of chess'), and the title-page that of *Kitāb ash-shaṭranj taʾalīf Abī'l-Muẓaffar b. Saʿīd 'urifa bi'l-Lajlāj*, 'Book of the chess, composed by Abū'l-Muẓaffar b. Sa'īd who is known as al-Lajlāj' (i.e. the stammerer). The MS. is undated, but may be as much as three centuries older than an entry on the title-page chronicling the fact that the Sultan Bāyazīd Khān gave the book to his chief butler, Yūsuf b. 'Abdallāh, the first day of Shawwāl, 893/1487.

The MS. is a treatise on the practical game, and contains a full analysis of certain of the more popular openings, with the view of establishing the superiority of the Mujannaḥ Opening. It is in consequence a work of prime importance for the history of the practical game: it is the only work on the subject prior to those of the first analysts of the modern European game, and, being the work of a master of the first rank, who expresses his own indebtedness to his own master, aṣ-Ṣūlī, the greatest of all the Muhammadan masters, we may safely regard it as recording the highest point of development reached in the whole history of the older chess. The MS. is incomplete at the end, where it breaks off to give a problem which al-Lajlāj had mentioned—though not in the present work—under the name ad-dūlābīya (the water-wheel). Leaf 9 is out of place, it should come between ff. 37 and 38.

5. AE = *MS. As'ad Efendī, Constantinople, No.* 2866.

An undated, anonymous Persian MS. of 609 pages, with the title *Kitāb ash-shaṭranj*, which is No. XXI of v. d. Linde's list (*Qst.*, 333). V. d. Linde gives no account of the MS., but merely quotes the opinion of Aḥmad Ḥamdī Efendī, a Turkish scholar who examined it for Schroeder, that it was a work of 'no value'. This hasty judgement cannot be accepted. The MS. proves on examination to be a compilation treating of all branches of chess. The writer, however, has carefully excluded all reference to his sources, and only names 'Adlī and Lajlāj Shaṭranjī as supporting certain verdicts in the End-game. After a lengthy preface on the creation, of which the noblest work was man, and on man's glory, to wit his intellect, of which chess and nard are the most striking fruits, the work continues with a close and complete translation of al-Lajlāj's Arabic work which we possess in L. The leaves are in some confusion, but the text affords a valuable means of testing the accuracy of L, especially as AE contains 60 diagrams showing the position at various points of the analysis. It also supplies the conclusion which is missing in L.

The second section of the MS. consists of a long list of decisions on the Endings. The third section is an extremely valuable collection of 194 problems, with which I deal in Chapter XV.

6. V = *MS. Vefa ('Atīq Efendī), Eyyub, No.* 2234.

A paper MS. of 77 leaves, 24 cm. by 19, one of those discovered by Dr. Schroeder, and No. XIX of v. d. Linde's list (*Qst.*, 390–6). Schroeder, gave as its title *Manṣūbāt li Abī Zakarīyā Yahyā b. Ibrāhīm al-Ḥakīm*, but the official catalogue gives no author's name, and I think that Schroeder has in transcribing his notes confused this MS. with MS. Abd-al-Ḥamīd, No. 561 (see below). The opening leaves of the MS. are lost, and the MS. itself as a result throws no light upon the question of authorship. It was copied 21 Ramaḍān 618/1221 by Muḥammad b. Hawā b. ʿOthmān, the mueddib, as appears from the conclusion on f. 77 b.

In addition to the loss of leaves at the commencement of the MS., there is a gap between ff. 14 and 15 (f. 14 ends with the chapter-heading, 'Chapter of the 'ibdīyāt which the different classes of chess-players have chosen,' and 15 begins in the middle of a problem solution). The text of this MS. is in the main identical with that of AH, without retaining the order of that MS., and the seven pages of poems (ff. 60–62 a) all occur in AH.[6]

7. H = *MS. John Rylands Library, Manchester, Arab.* 59.

8. Z = *MS. Abd-al-Ḥamīd I, Constantinople, No.* 561.

These are two MSS. of the same Arabic work, the *Nuzhat al-arbāb al-ʿaqūl fī'sh-shaṭranj al-manqūl* ('The delight of the intelligent, a description of chess'), by Abū Zakarīyā Yaḥyā b. Ibrāhīm al-Ḥakīm. The author flourished in the middle of the fourteenth century. He quotes from the great dictionary of his contemporary al-Fīrūzābādī (D. 817/1414, aged 85), the *al-Qāmūs* (H, f. 4 a), and there is a quotation from al-Ḥakīm's book in b. Abī Ḥajala's work, which will be described next. Neither MS. is dated, but H is ascribed to the latter half of the fifteenth century. Z is a modern MS., written perhaps towards the end of the eighteenth century.

H consists of 57 paper leaves, 175 mm. by 130. This MS. and the companion chess MS. in the Rylands Library (Man., see below) were brought to England from Damascus in the eighteenth century, and formed part of the collection of J. G. Richards, until in 1806 they passed into the possession of John Fiott, of St. John's College, Cambridge, who subsequently took the name of Lee on inheriting property from his mother's family.[7] Nathaniel Bland borrowed them from Dr. Lee for use in the preparation of his paper on *Persian Chess* (London, 1850), but failed to return them, and subsequently efforts to recover them which were made at the instance of Prof. Duncan Forbes between 1855 and 1860 proved fruitless. Bland's Oriental library was sold *en bloc* in 1866 to the Earl of Crawford and Balcarres, and the 'Lee MSS.' passed into the Haigh Hall Library, and were duly entered in the printed Hand-list to the Oriental MSS. of that library. In 1906 Lord Crawford's Oriental MSS. were purchased by Mrs. Rylands, who subsequently

[6] The analysis of this MS. in *Qst.* is not very accurate. The first three pages repeat some of the traditions about early Muslim chess-players, concluding with a list of their names. At the foot of 2 a begins an extract from al-ʿAdlī's work, giving his three stories of the invention of chess. The astrological tables mentioned in *Qst.* are merely diagrams to illustrate the symbolism of nard.

[7] He held a Travelling Fellowship from Cambridge, and was in the East 1807–10, where he made a valuable collection of Arabic and Persian MSS. On his return he practised at the Bar, and proceeded to the degree of LL.D. in 1816. He was elected F.R.S. in 1831. In 1827 he inherited Hartwell House, Bucks., where he died, Feb. 25, 1866.

placed them in the noble library which she had founded in memory of her husband.

Z is a paper MS. of 56 leaves, 143 mm. by 70. It has no title, and the entry in the official catalogue ('561. *Risāla fi'sh-shaṭranj*, one volume in Arabic, by Yaḥyā b. Muḥammad aṣ-Ṣūlī') is unwarranted by anything in the MS., which names al-Ḥakīm as its author in the opening sentence.

Al-Ḥakīm's work is based upon the works of al-ʿAdlī and aṣ-Ṣūlī, and carefully discriminates between the problem material which was taken from each of these lost works. The introduction contains a large number of stories relating to chess which are not given in any of the older MSS., and the conclusion contains a number of chess-poems, together with sections on the game at odds, and on the technical terms used in chess, and some notes on a group of famous players of the end of the 12th c.

The two MSS. are in the main identical in contents, with some variation in the order of the problems which is sufficient to show that Z is not a transcript from H. Z also omits one of the Knight's tours included in H.

9. Man. = *MS. John Rylands Library, Manchester, Arab.* 93.

A MS. of 89 quarto leaves, 174 mm. by 130, copied 850/1446, bearing the title *Kitāb 'anmūdhaj al-qitāl fi laʿb ash-shaṭranj* ('Book of the examples of warfare in the game of chess'), by Shihābaddīn Abū'l-ʿAbbās Aḥmad b. Yaḥyā b. Abī Ḥajala at-Tilimsānī alḤ-anbalī (B. 725/1325, D. of the plague, 776/1375).

This work is written in eight chapters with introduction and conclusion. Each chapter concludes with five diagrams, (1) an Opening, (2) and (3) two won problems, (4) and (5) two drawn problems. The introduction deals with the stories of early Muslim players, the question whether chess was *makrūh* or *ḥarām* (see Ch. XI), under what conditions Muslims might play the game, and the correct spelling of the word *shaṭranj*. Ch. i (f. 14 b) treats of the invention of chess; ch. ii (f. 26 a) of the classes of players, the values of the pieces, and the symbolism of the game: ch. iii (f. 31 a) contains a long extract from aṣ-Ṣūlī giving maxims and advice for chess-players, to which b. Abi Ḥajala added a critical commentary. Aṣ-Ṣūlī's advice is very similar to that contained in the treatise by al-Lajlāj which is contained in AH. Ch. v (f. 41 b) deals with the temperaments of chess-players: ch. vi (f. 46 b) contains quotations in praise and dispraise of chess, among others one on f. 47 b is said to be taken from the *K. al-manṣūbāt* of Abū Zakarīyā Yaḥyā b. Ibrāhīm al-Ḥakīm, the author of the MSS. H and Z. Ch. vii (f. 54 a) treats of the varieties of chess and exercises or puzzles (see Ch. XV below); ch. viii (f. 76 b) is a poetical miscellany of extracts relating to chess; and the conclusion (f. 81 a) is a *maqāma shaṭranjīya*, a prose essay in the elaborate style set by al-Ḥarīrī (D. 515 or 516/1122), and dedicated to the Sultan al-Malik aṣ-Ṣāliḥ of Mārdīn.

One of the most valuable features in this MS. is the information which it supplies as to the nature of the traditional diagrams of normal positions in the Openings.

10. Al. = *The chess chapters in al-Amulī's encyclopaedia.*

The encyclopaedic Persian *Nafā'is al-funūn fī ʿarā'is al-ʿuyūn* ('Treasury of the Sciences') of Muḥammad b. Maḥmūd al-Āmulī (D. 753/1352) concludes with three chapters on chess. MSS. of this work are common in European libraries, though the chess chapters, as the last in the work, are often copied perfunctorily, and, if the MS. be defective or unfinished, they generally suffer. I have used eight MSS., four in the Bodleian, two in the British Museum, one in the India Office Library, and one in the Imperial Library, Vienna. None gives the diagrams complete.

The first chapter is introductory, dealing with the Indian invention of the game; the second chapter deals with the derived games of chess; the third with problems; and the work concludes with 'some amusing and sensible remarks respecting the morals and social observances or amenities of the Royal Game'.

11. RAS = *MS. Royal Asiatic Society, Persian, No.* 211.

A MS. of 64 quarto leaves, 9¾ in. by 7 in., written in nashkī hand. The MS. is imperfect at the end, and the leaves are in some confusion. It was presented to the Society by David Price, and was formerly catalogued as No. 260.

This appears to be Ḥājjī Khalīfa's third chess work; since it is mainly devoted to the praise of ʿAlī ash-Shaṭranjī, the great player at Tīmūr's court, it has been suggested that this player may be the author of the MS., in which case it may be the work mentioned by b. ʿArabshāh.

Ff. 1 b–32 a are occupied by diagrams, one a page, with actual players depicted to the right and left of the board, which is placed with the files vertical (in my extracts from this MS. I regard the *h*-line as being at the foot of the page). The whole is illuminated, but the pieces are merely indicated by their names in red and black ink. At the head of the page is the heading of the problem, with the name of the player to whom the author has ascribed it. This MS. differs from all other older Muslim MSS. in giving no solutions to the problems.

The remainder of the MS., according to Forbes, can be rearranged to give (1) a single leaf forming a portion of the preface, in which the writer boastfully records his own achievements at chess, (2) 12½ leaves on the beneficial effects of chess, (3) 7½ leaves with a diagram on the Complete chess (Tīmūr's chess), for which see Chapter XVI below, (4) 7½ leaves on the invention of the ordinary chess in India, (5) 3½ leaves containing sections on the relative values of the chess-pieces, on the gradation of odds, and on End-game decisions. See Bland (1–17) for a fuller account of the MS.

The MS. is probably of the 16th century.

12. F = *MS. Nūri Osmānīye, Stambul, No.* 4073.
13. Q = *MS. Munich*, 250. 25 *Quatr.*

These are two MSS. of the *Shaṭranj nāma-i kabīr* of the noted Turkish poet Firdawsī at-Ṭahīhal, the author of the immense *Sulaiman nāma*, a poem which, according to the present work (F, f. 7 b), filled 366 volumes, and contained 1,838 chapters and 890,000 verses. The chess work was compiled at Balakasri in Liva Karasi for the Sultan Bāyazīd II (A. D. 1481–1512), after the completion of the vast epic.

F is a MS. of 94 leaves, which was discovered by Dr. Schroeder, and is No. XXII of v. d. Linde's list (*Qst.*, 398 seq.). It was completed 907/1503 (f. 94 a). Q, a MS. of 87 leaves, 251 mm. by 180, also belongs to the sixteenth century, and was in Egypt from 1553 until the Napoleonic invasion. This MS. has several leaves missing. There are gaps between ff. 29 and 30, 41 and 42, 60 and 61, 62 and 63, 69 and 70, 73 and 74, 77 and 78, and the concluding leaves are missing.

Firdawsī arranged his work in eight chapters, in agreement with the eight squares on the edge of the chessboard. To these must be added a lengthy introduction treating of the history of the composition of the book, and a shorter conclusion. Chapter i treats of the invention of chess and legends associating the prophet Idrīs, Jimjīd, and Solomon with chess; chapter ii deals with the mastership of Lajlāj, later named in full as Abū'l-Faraj b. al-Muẓaffar b. Sa'īd; chapter iii treats of the match which Lajlāj played with Buzūrjmihr in the presence of Nūshīrwān; chapter iv gives the rules and maxims as laid down by the prophet Idrīs; chapter v tells the story of the tribute of the grains of corn which Lajlāj demanded from Nūshīrwān, and adds chess legends of Iskander (Alexander the Great) and other rulers; chapter vi gives the ta'bīyāt, and chapter vii the manṣūbāt; chapter viii discusses the legality of chess-playing. Almost every chapter concludes with a poem, and every problem with a couplet.

Firdawsī's work is in the main a compilation from other works. He specially notes (F, f. 11 a) his indebtedness to the *Shāhnāma* of his great namesake, to the *'Ajā'ib makhlūqāt* (probably by aṣ-Ṣafadī, 896/1490), to the *Qābūs-nāma* (written A. D. 1082–3 by 'Unsuru'l-Ma'ālī Kaykā'ūs, Prince of Ṭabaristān), to the *Gharā'ib mawjūdāt*, and to the *Ikhwān aṣ-ṣafā*.

14. R = *MS. Rustem Pasha, Constantinople, No.* 375.

A paper MS. of 90 leaves, 21 cm. by 15.2, which forms part of a MS. of miscellaneous contents which was written by Aḥmad b. Aḥmad al-Muhtār al-Ḥanafī al-Miṣrī at Balat, Stambul, in 983/1575. It contains nothing but problems, one to the page, with solutions.

15. S = *MS. Bodleian Lib., Oxford, Arab. Pocock* 16.

A small parchment MS., completed 979/1579, containing three treatises by Muḥammad b. Aḥmad b. Muḥammad b. Jamāladdīn b. Sukaikir ad-Dimashqī, preacher of the mosque al-ʿĀdilīya at Halab (Aleppo, in Syria) (D. 987/1579). The first two treatises are theological; the third, which extends from f. 22 a to f. 39 b, treats of chess under the title *Nafḥāt kimā'īm al-ward fī tafḍīl ash-shaṭranj ʿalā'n-nard* ('The fragrance of the rose: on the superiority of chess over nard'). The MS. was once in the possession of Dr. Hyde, who made large use of it for his *Mandragorias*.

The MS. discusses the lawfulness of chess-playing, summarizing for the purpose aṣ-Ṣūlī's collection of traditions, but while giving the usual legends as to the invention of chess—in his day there were people who thought that aṣ-Ṣūlī had invented chess—b. Sukaikir adds some interesting particulars as to notable feats at chess, some of which had taken place in his presence. He only gives 10 problems, omitting the solutions, but indicating the number of moves to be taken. He gives a number of impromptu verses on chess.

16. Y = *MS. Brit. Mus., Add.* 16856.

A Persian MS. of 62 leaves, 10 ins. by 6, written in a neat nestalik hand, with ʿUnwān and gold-ruled borders, dated 1021/1612, from the library of Col. Wm. Yule. It is a Persian translation by Muḥammad b. Ḥusām ad-Daula of the Arabic work *K. al-munjiḥ fī ʿilm ash-shaṭranj* ('A book to lead to success in the knowledge of chess') by Muḥammad b. ʿOmar Kajīnā, a work stated in the preface to be the most useful treatise on chess. As there was, however, only one copy of it in the land, and that an incorrect one, it appeared desirable to make an abridged version of it in Persian, and the author performed that task at the order of a sovereign whose titles and epithets are given at length, but whose proper name does not appear.[8]

It is divided into fourteen chapters, but the copy, although showing no sign of loss since it left the writer's hand, is not complete; only three lines of chapter ix are given, and the termination of chapter xi and the whole of chapters xii and xiii are missing.

The chapters deal, i, with stories of early Muslim players; ii, with the question of the lawfulness of chess-playing; iii, with the advantages of chess; iv, with the invention of chess; v, with technicalities of the game; vi, with the etiquette of play; vii, with maxims for players; viii, with the End-game decisions; ix, with the taʿbīyāt; x, with conditional problems; xi, with problems in general; and xiv, with blindfold chess.

With this work I complete the list of the Oriental MSS. of the older chess which I have made the basis of my chapters on the practical game and the Muslim manṣūbāt. In the case of BM, H, Man., RAS, S, and Y, I have been able to refer to the original MSS. themselves. For the opportunity of consulting the other MSS. I am indebted to the generosity of Mr. J. G. White. He has placed at my service his photographic copies of AH, V, Z, RAS, Q, and R, and modern transcripts of AH, C, BM, AE, V, and F.

I now give a tabular summary of the contents of these MSS.

[8] So Rieu (*Pers. MSS. in Brit. Mus.*, ii. 490 a), correcting Bland (18–25) and Forbes (76).

CONTENTS OF THE MSS. DESCRIBED ABOVE.

Name of MS.	AH	C	BM	AE	V	H	Z	Man.	Al.	RAS	F	Q	R	S	Y
Date of MS.	1140	c. 1370	1257	...	1221	15 c.	18 c.	1446	...	16 c.	1503	c. 1550	1575	1571	1612
Date given on f.	54 b	...	132 a	...	77 a	...	...	87 a	...	...	94 a	...	...	39 b	63 b
Number of leaves	142	157	132	609 pp.	77	57	56	89	...	64	94	87	90	18	63
Lines to the page	19	15	16-17	13	17-18	17-20	17	15	...	15	17	17	...	23	10
Preface or Introduction	1 b, 4 b	1 b	1 b, 8 b	p. 1	...	2 b	1 b	3 b	ch. 1	61 a	7 b	3 b	...	22 b	...
Invention of the game	1 b	1 b	4 a	...	2 a	4 b	3 b	14 b	,,	45 b	11 b 25 a	...	...	24 a, 37 a	13 b
Greek philosophers and chess	4 a	5 b	127 a	..	...	6 b	6 b	42 b	...	...	...	...	...	...	...
Traditions as to the legality of chess	7 a	8 b	1 b	...	1a	6 b	6 b	6 b, 70 a	...	...	85 b	78 b	...	26 a, 28 b	7 a
General principles of play	13 a, 133 b	18 a	6 b	...	...	16 b	18 b	31 a	ch. 3	...	20 b	22 b	...	...	22 a
The game at odds	...	...	...	...	...	50 b	50 b	...	...	54 a	...	...	...	...	...
Arrangement of the board	19 b	27 b	6 b	...	12 b	...	...	27 b	...	...	85 b	78 b	...	...	...
Classes of chess-players	14 a	19 a	8 b	...	13 b	16 b	19 a	26 a	...	...	...	...	...	...	...
Value of the pieces	14 b	20 b	10 a	p. 242	14 a	18 a	20 b	27 a	...	57 b	...	...	...	...	...
End-game decisions	15 a	21 b	9 a	p. 242	9 a	18 a	21 a	...	...	33 b	...	...	...	...	31 a
Al-ʿAdlī's calculating board	20 a	28 b	127 a	...	7 a	...	...	...	...	...	...	...	...	...	...
Derived Games	21 a	30 b	127 b	...	7 b	19 a	23 a	54 a	ch. 2	46 a	...	...	...	...	...
Note on Indian chess	24 a	33 a	...	...	...	20 a	23 b	...	...	...	...	...	...	...	...
The Openings	24 b	34 a, 60 a	11 a, 42 a	pp. 5–233	14 b	20 b	24 a	passim	...	2 a	31 a	32 a	...	...	33 b
Number of diagrams	8	8	11	60	...	3	3	9	...	2	6	6	...	...	...
The Problems	29 b–133 a	36 a–156 b	13 a–127 a	pp. 251–609	15 a–77 a	21 a–38 b	24 b 37 b	passim	ch. 3	3 a–33 a	36 a–85 a	37 a–78 b	1 a–89 a	34 b–37 a	36 a
Number of diagrams	183	181	200	194	108	67	67	33	24	60	78	71	84	10	52
Knight's Tours	74 a–75 b, 142 b	47 b–48 b, 141 b–142 a	...	...	67 b	39 a	37 b	56 b	...	...	...	...	...	...	...
Other Puzzles	...	...	128 a–129 b	...	...	...	...	55 a	...	...	...	...	...	...	...
Poems, &c.	135 b	...	7 b	...	59 a–62 a	39 a	38 a	56 b	...	...	...	...	...	...	...
Invention of Nard	1 b	1 b	5 a, b	...	2 a	4 b	4 a	16 a	...	...	...	...	...	25 a	...

[The reference to AE is to the pagination of Mr. White's copy.]

In addition to these MSS. I have, for the purposes of the problem, made use of a number of other MSS. which are based upon Muslim chess works. These are—

17. Alf. = *the Spanish MS. known as the Alfonso MS.*

(This MS., written in 1283, is described below in connexion with the European game, in the early history of which it is an important authority. Since, however, 89 of its 103 problems are of unmistakable Muslim origin, I have included them in my collection in Chapter XV. The derived games of this MS. will also be found in Chapter XVI.)

18. Oxf. = *MS. Bodleian Lib., Oxford, Pers. e.* 10.

A modern Persian MS. of 112 leaves, 7⅛ by 5½ ins., with the title *Sardārnāma*, by Shīr Muḥammad-khān (takhalluṣ, Īmām), who wrote it, 1211–2/1796–8 for a great lover of chess-playing, Ḥusainaddīn-khān Bahādur. who was in the service of the Nizām of Dakhan (Deccan), Niẓām 'Alī-khān Bahādur Niẓām-al-mulk Āṣafjāh II (1175/1762 – 1217/1802). In 1810 the MS. was in the possession of Henry George Keene. The Bodleian bought it at Sotheby's sale, Aug. 25, 1884.

The work is modern and central-Indian, and must accordingly be used with caution. It is largely based on earlier books, and much of the problem material is old: it is mainly in this connexion that I have used the MS.

It consists of an introduction and six chapters called ma'rakāt or 'arenas for combat'. M. i, f. 7 b, contains 99 problems of Rūmī, i. e. Turkish (or old) chess. M. ii, f. 58 b, contains 60 problems of Ferinɡhī, i. e. European chess. M. iii, f. 88 b, 8 problems ending in *burd*, therefore probably Indian chess. M. iv, f. 92 b, 4 drawn games. M. v, f. 94 b, 12 problems of decimal chess. M. vi, f. 102 a, contains the Complete chess (12 × 12), with explanatory text, a Knight's tour, and the key to the notation. This last is interesting, as it is a form of the algebraical notation that I have adopted in this work.

19. Ber. = *MS. Royal Lib., Berlin, Landberg, No.* 806.

A Turkish MS. of about 150 leaves, 205 by 133 mm., of which only 2 b–34 a and 51 b–97 b are filled. It was written about 1210/1795 and is in two hands, the one filling the earlier part with 128 chess problems, the other the later part with 182 dāma (Turkish draughts) problems. There are no solutions, but the number of moves is usually stated, and occasionally there are hints to the solution. The chess problems are nearly all of modern chess, and many are repeated. Their interest is, as a result, in connexion with the Turkish chess of the present day.

20. RW = *MS. in possession of Mr. Rimington Wilson.*

A small collection of 29 problems with a Knight's tour, translated by Mr. George Swinton for George Walker from a modern Persian (? Indian) original. It is of little value, but was the source of a couple of papers by George Walker in the *CPC.*, 1844, 180; and 1845, 240.

In addition to the above MSS. I have been able to consult a number of smaller treatises dealing with particular aspects of chess, generally the question of the lawfulness of chess-playing for strict Muslims, or the legend of the discovery of the game by Ṣiṣṣa b. Dāhir, and the calculation of his reward—the sum of the doubling of the squares.

Of the former[9] are:

MS. Berlin, Wetzstein, II, 1739, ff. 57 b–68 a, the *An-nāṣīha lil-ḥurr wal-ʿabd bijtināb ash-shaṭranj wan-nard* of ʿAbdarraḥmān b. Khalīl al-Qābūnī al-Adhraʿī Zainaddīn (D. 869/1464).

MS. Berlin, Sprenger, 850, f. 93 b, an extract from the *Al-ḥāwī* of the Qāḍī Abū'l-Ḥasan ʿAlī b. Muḥammad b. Habīb al-Māwardī (D. 450/1058).

Of the latter are:

MS. Bodl. Oxford, Arab. 182.

MS. Berlin, Wetzstein, II, 1149, f. 69 b (copied *c.* 1150/1737).

MS. Berlin, Wetzstein, II, 1127, f. 78 a (copied 996/1588).

MS. Berlin, Orient Qu., 583, f. 24 b (copied 1077/1667).

MS. Gotha, Arab. 919, Pertsch; three short treatises.

I have also seen:

MS. Khusrū Pasha, 758, Eyyub; a Turkish tract with title *Risāla fī'sh-shaṭranj*.

MS. Bāyazīd, Walī-addīn, 1796, Constantinople; the Persian *Risāla fī dar asrār saṭranj* of Sheikh ʿAlā'addaula; which treats of the parallel between chess and war.

MS. Gotha, Turc. 18, Pertsch (1033 Moeller), f. 95 a, which gives two diagrams of taʿbīyāt.

MS. Berlin, Orient, 4°, 124, ff. 92 b, 93 a; which contains two problem diagrams (Ar. 83 and 214), one of which is attributed to the Sultan Tīmūr.

There are only two existing Muslim chess MSS., the existence of which has been recorded, which I have failed to see. These are:

K. ash-shaṭranj ta'līf al-imām al-ʿālim lisān al-adab waj al-ʿarab Sadraddīn Abū'l-Ḥasan ʿAlī . . ., a copy of which (*Qst.*, 333, No. XX) was formerly in the possession of Münif Pasha. Its present location is unknown to me.

MS. 12, 23476, Phillips Library, Cheltenham, Arabic, of the 18th century.

There is a number of Arabic poems on the game of chess, some being the composition of well-known poets. Two longer ones, the *Urjūza shiʿrīya* of Abū Yaʿla Muḥammad b. al-Habbārīya (D. 504/1100),[10] and the *Urjūza fī'sh-shaṭranj* of Aḥmad Bek al-Kaiwānī (D. 1173/1760),[11] have been often copied. According to Bland, the Brit. Mus. MS. of the *Diwān* of at-Tilimsānī

[9] Cf. MS. ʿĀshir Efendī 1154, Constantinople; the Arabic *K. fī taḥqīq laʿb ash-shaṭranj*.

[10] See Brockelmann, *Gesch. d. arab. Litt.*, Berlin, 1902, i. 253. V. d. Linde (ii. 256) is wrong in identifying him with Muḥammad b. Sharīf al-Qīrwānī, from whom Hyde quoted an allusion to chess, which is repeated in H, f. 50 a, and in Man., f. 77 b.

[11] See Brockelmann, op. cit., ii. 282. I know the poem from the two Berlin MSS.—Wetzstein, II, 1218, f. 82 b, and II, 140, f. 130 b.

ash-Shābb aẓ-Ẓarīf (D. 688/1289) contains a poem of 80 lines on chess. Among the poems contained in the MSS. which I have used, I have noted poems by three poets whose poems were edited by the chess master aṣ-Ṣūlī, viz. Abū Nuwās (D. 190/806), the greatest poet of his period—H, ff. 40 b, 41 a, 42 b (= V, 60 a); b. ar-Rūmī (D. 283/896)—H, f. 40 a; and b. al Muʿtazz D. 296/908)—V, f. 60 a, which is translated below; and by Abū Firās (D. 357/968)—V, f. 61 a; ar-Ramādī (D. 403/1012), an Arabic poet of Spain—H, ff. 41 a, 41 b; and b. Wakīʿ (D. 393/1003), an Egyptian poet—H, f. 42 b.[12]

Chess also proved a very fruitful source of similes, metaphors, and word-plays for both Arabic[13] and Persian poets. The twofold meaning of the Persian word *rukh*, the 'rook in chess', and the 'cheek', suggested a host of conceits and brought chess into the love poem.[14] Occasionally the reference takes on a darker colour, as in the well-known quatrain from Fitzgerald's translation of the *Rubaiyāt* of ʿOmar Khayyām (D. 517/1123):

'Tis all a Chequer-board of Nights and Days
Where Destiny with Men for Pieces plays;
Hither and thither moves, and mates, and slays
And one by one back in the Closet lays.

[12] I omit from this list the poems which supply the keys to the Knight's Tours in AH and V, because their subject-matter is not chess. The construction of these poems, of course, exhibits an acquaintance with the game of no slight extent.

[13] References in Arabic poetry are very common, the favourite points being the strength of the Rook in attack and the promotion of the Pawn. Man., ff. 76 b–78 b, gives many instances, some of which are given by Hyde from other sources: e. g. from b. Qalāqis (B. 532/1138, D. 567/1171)—

There is a poor man whose walk results in the great noble submitting himself to him: viz. the motion queens the Pawn so that the *fīl* yields to it in value in the game;

and from Abū'l-Faḍl at-Tamīmī—

. . . just as the Rook's Pawn when it moves forth in the game becomes most easily a *firzān*.

See also the similar allusion in the verse quoted from al-Farazdaq in the following chapter, which has a special importance as the earliest known mention of chess in Arabic literature.

[14] Al-Mutanabbī (D. 354/965) says in one of his poems (ed. with al-ʿOkbarī's commentary, Cairo, 1287, 137)—

Other hearts than mine are a mark for the fair,
Other fingers than mine are bearers of Rooks.

Bland (40 seq.) supplies a number of instances from Persian poets; viz. from Kamāl:

Kamāl upon thy lip staked all his soul and lost;
Play not against an adversary with two Rukhs (cheeks);

from Bisātī:

For one moment draw the rein of friendship with the hand of mercy,
That Bisātī may lay his Rukh (cheek) before the horse of his king;

from Kamāl of Khojend:

When my beloved learnt the chess-play of cruelty,
In the very beginning of the game her sweet cheek (rukh) took my heart captive;

and again:

That cheek (rukh) of hers would win from all the fair ones of the world at the chess-play of beauty
Though each one of them should have a rukh (cheek) of ivory.

Some of these plays on chess are so elaborate as to be almost unintelligible. Thus we read in a memoir of the poet Abū'l-Faraj-i-Rūnī (D. *post* 492/1099) by Awhadī—

The Līlāj (Mod. Pers. form of the name al-Lajlāj) of his genius, when it played the nard of knowledge, gave the three-stroke move to the coursers of the hippodrome in the board of power, and when he manœuvred the two-knight game in the exercise of imagination on the chessboard of composition would give two rooks and a ferz to the Shāhāfīl of intelligence.

For other instances see Bland's paper.

though the thought here is of course far older, and the setting more modern, than 'Omar.[15]

The importance of these allusions for chess is to be found in the evidence they furnish for the extraordinary popularity of the game among the Muslims all through history, despite the suspicion with which Muhammadan jurists have always regarded it.

Of rather a different character are the impromptus which are made during the progress of the game, a characteristic feature of the play, and indeed of all social life in the time of the 'Abbāsid caliphs. Of these al-Maṣ'ūdī writes:[16]

Chess-players employ different kinds of pleasantry and jests designed to astound. Many maintain that these incite people to play, and add to the flow of resource and accurate deliberation.[17] They have been compared to the short improvised verses which warriors employ when encountering the enemy, or which camel-drivers compose during the slow movements of the camels, or the drawers of water during the raising of the bucket. They are just as much part of the apparatus of the player, as the song and improvised verse is of the warrior. Many verses describing this have been composed; e.g. the following by a player:

Hotter than the glow of charcoal glows the player's timely jest,
Think how many a weaker player it has helped against the best!

In the following passage the game is described with a rare felicity of expression:[18]

The square plain with its red surface is placed between two friends of known friendship.
They recall the memories of war in an image of war, but without bloodshed.
This attacks, that defends, and the struggle between them never languishes.
Observe with what strategy the horsemen run upon the two armies, without trumpets or flags.

Out of many poems in the same style, which are remarkable for their elegance and the neatness of the descriptions which they give, we quote this by Abū'l-Ḥasan b. Abū'l-Baghal al-Kātib, who not only distinguished himself as a scribe and agent of government, but was also renowned for his clever and polished play[19]:—

[15] Cf. also the lines written by the Persian poet 'Unsurī (D. 1040-50) on his patron, Maḥmūd of Ghaznī:

The monarch played chess with a thousand kings for the kingdom,
And to each king he gave checkmate in a different way;

and from the *Mufarrih al-Qulūb*:—

The addition of royalty to other monarchs than him
Is like the name of king bestowed on a few wooden chessmen.

The poet Anwarī of Khāwarān in Khurāsān (D. *c.* 582/1186) boasts in his poems of his skill in calligraphy, chess, and nard. His poems have been edited by Valentin Zhukořski, St. Petersburg, 1883.

[16] Ed. Barbier de Meynard, viii. 315 seq.

[17] B. Sukaikir, ff. 31 a–34 b, quotes a number of these impromptus, with the circumstances which gave rise to them.

[18] The authorship of these lines is disputed. In the Bulaq edition of al-Maṣ'ūdī they are ascribed to the caliph al-Ma'mūn, and the historians b. Badrūn (558/1163 – 580/1184) and as-Suyūṭī (B. 849/1445, D. 911/1505) give the same authorship. The Paris edition of al-Maṣ'ūdī and ar-Rāghib (D. 502/1108) give no author's name. The *Al-mustaṭraf* of al-Abshīhī (D. *c.* 850/1446) says that some writers have ascribed it to al-Ma'mūn, others to 'Alī b. al-Jahm, a poet who accompanied al-Ma'mūn on his expedition from Khurāsān to Baghdād, 204/819. In the chess MSS. the poem is ascribed to b. al-Jahm in V, f. 596, and to the caliph in H, f. 40 b.

[19] This poem is quoted in the chess MSS.; in BM, f. 8 a, and H, f. 40 a (the latter quoting from al-Maṣ'ūdī) as by Abū'l-Baghal, the vizier of the caliphal-Muqtadir (*Fihrist*, i. 137), but in V, f. 63 a, as by ar-Rūmī.

The skilled player places his pieces in such a way as to discover consequences that the ignorant man never sees.
He foresees the surprises of the future with the assurance of the wise man in face of foolish banalities;
And thus he serves the Sultan's interests, by showing how to foresee disaster,
Since the strategy of the chessboard for an experienced man is equal to that of the battle-field.

Ath-Thaʿālibī (D. 429/1038) included in his *K. al-laṭā'if waẓ-ẓarā'if fī madḥ al-ashyā' waaḍdādhā* a short section containing a selection of passages in praise and dispraise of chess.[20] This section is repeated in his *K. yawāqīt al-mawāqīt fī madḥ ash-shai' wadhammihi*, from which Bland made some quotations, one of which—the verses of b. Muʿtazz, that unfortunate son of a chess-playing caliph—has been repeated frequently in books on chess:

O thou whose cynic sneers express
The censure of our favourite chess,
Know that its skill is science' self,
Its play distraction from distress.
It soothes the anxious lover's care,
It weans the drunkard from excess;
It counsels warriors in their art,
When dangers threat, and perils press;
And yields us, when we need them most,
Companions in our loneliness.

It concludes with a number of witticisms borrowed from the language of chess: thus the sight of a beautiful girl duly chaperoned provoked the comment, 'There goes a *firzān-band*'; a man of little stature might be termed a *Pawn* (see p. 196); the activity of a prominent person in his town was referred to by the remark, 'There is a Rook on the board;' and the assertiveness of an upstart was silenced by the inquiry, 'Hullo, Pawn, when did you queen?'

[20] The section is quoted in Man., f. 49 a.

CHAPTER XI

CHESS UNDER ISLAM

Its Persian ancestry.—The date of introduction.—The legal status of chess.—Early Muhammadan chess-players.—The game during the Umayyad and ʿAbbāsid caliphates.—Aṣ-Ṣūlī.—Later references.—Aṣ-Ṣafadī.—Chess at the court of Tīmūr.—Chess in Damascus in the sixteenth century.

THAT Islam derived its knowledge of chess from Persia cannot be disputed for a moment. The Arabic historians who make any reference to the matter, however much they may differ as to the ultimate origin of the game, agree in stating categorically and as an undisputed fact, 'We learnt chess from the Persians.' Of greater weight is the philological evidence derived from the Arabic nomenclature of chess. The Persian consonant *ch* has never existed in Arabic, and had to be represented in Arabic by *sh* or *ṣ*. Examples of both will be found below, p. 217, n. 20. The Arabic letter *j* (= Hebrew *gimel*), which perhaps still retained the original sound of the 'hard' *g* under the early caliphate, was used to represent the 'hard' Persian *g*. The Arabic *j* is still pronounced as 'hard' *g* in Egypt; elsewhere it is pronounced as the English (or even French) *j*. *Shaṭranj*,[1] the Arabic name of chess, is accordingly the regular Arabicized form of the Persian *chatrang*. With one exception, the Persian names of the chess-pieces are retained in Arabic, and *shāh*, *firzān*, *fīl*, *rukhkh*, and *baidaq* or *baidhaq* (pron. *baizaq*) are the regular Arabicized forms of the Persian *shāh*, *farzīn*, *pīl*, *rukh*, and *payādah*. The 'horse' alone received a native name, t e Persian *asp* being translated by the Arabic *faras*.

[1] Under the influence of the Arabic grammarians, who objected to the form *shaṭranj* as unsupported by the analogy of any other Arabic word, the form *shiṭranj* has become the more usual in modern times. Man., ff. 12a–14b, quotes several passages from the earlier grammarians upon this question of the correct form. Thus b. as-Sikkīt (D. 243/857) gives *shaṭranj* in his *Iṣlāh al-manṭiq*. B. Jinnī (D. 392/1002) and al-Baṭalyūsī (D. 521/1127) give *shiṭranj* as the correct form, while al-Ḥarīrī (D. 515-6/1122) adds that the popular pronunciation was *shaṭranj*. Al-Jawālīqī (D. 539/1145), in giving *shaṭranj* as a Persian word Arabicized, adds that some people say *shiṭranj*.

At a later time, when the origin of the word was completely forgotten, other alterations in spelling appear, which were probably suggested by some of the strange etymologies that were being invented. This led to the discussion whether the initial consonant ought to be *sh* or *s*. Jamāladdīn b. Malik is quoted as having used *s* or *sh*, *a* or *i*, indiscriminately. Aṣ-Ṣafadī (D. 764/1363), who discusses the point in his *Sharḥ Lāmīyat al-ʿAjam*, professed to prefer the spelling with the *s* (*sīn*) as harmonizing with the derivation from the Ar. *saṭr*, a line, but he also gives other derivations, the Ar. *shaṭr*, half, or the Per. *shash rang*, six colours or species. This last is on the lines of the older view that *shaṭranj* was from the Per. *hashat rang*, eight species, which is given by al-ʿAdlī (c. 850 A.D.; cf. AH, f. 2a), and by al-Yaʿqūbī (a little later, c. 875 A.D.; cf. p. 209). Later writers have written the word with the ordinary *t* in place of the emphatic *ṭ*, and with the emphatic *ṣ* (*ṣad*) for the *s* (*sin*) or *sh* (*shin*) (*ṣaṭranj*, *ṣdtranj*, *ṣa ṣatranj*), to suit the fanciful derivations from Per. *ṣad rang* or *ṣad ranj*, 100 artifices, or 100 sorrows (others have *shāh rang* or *ranj*, kingly artifices or sorrows; the Turkish writer, Ecter Kara Hisārī, has *shud ranj*, dispelling sorrow). Sir J. W. Redhouse, *Turk. and Eng. Lexicon*, Constantinople, 1890, gives *ṣanṭranj* as a vulgar name for chess, and *shaṭranj* as the literary name. Hyde, who devotes some pages to the question, records from a Persian dictionary a form *saharīj*, explained as *ṣatranj*. Hyde himself accepted the derivation from Per. *satrang*, the mandrake plant, the root of which resembles the human figure, and he thence derived his fanciful title of *Mandragorias* for his work on chess. Cf. Hyde, ii. 47-51; v. d. Linde, i. 131; and Bland, 20.

Nor can there be much doubt that the introduction of chess was a result of the conquest of Persia which took place between the years A.D. 638 and 651, in the caliphate of ʿOmar b. al-Khaṭṭāb, the second of the four orthodox caliphs, and thus some years after the death of Muḥammad himself (A.D. 632). Most probably the prophet had never heard of the existence of chess, since the Muhammadan jurists have been unable to settle the question of the legality of chess-playing by any direct decision of Muḥammad as recorded in the *Qur'ān*, or in authentic tradition. Such at any rate was the opinion of the earlier lawyers.

This question of the legal position of chess-playing exercised the early Muslim lawyers not a little. The whole possibility of a Muslim chess depended upon the decision that was reached. Muslim law is far wider in scope than anything that the Western world has ever known. As D. B. Macdonald puts it in his *Development of Muslim Theology, Jurisprudence, and Constitutional Theory* (London, 1903, p. 66), 'Muslim law in the most absolute sense fits the old definition, and is the science of all things, human and divine. It tells us what we must render to Caesar and what to God, what to ourselves, and what to our fellows. The bounds of the Platonic definition of rendering to each man his due it utterly shatters. While Muslim theology defines everything that a man shall *believe* of things in heaven and in earth and beneath the earth—and this is no flat rhetoric—Muslim law prescribes everything that a man shall *do* to God, to his neighbour, and to himself. It takes all duty for its portion and defines all actions in terms of duty.' Nor was this any empty claim. A Muslim's citizenship depends upon his character, as judged by his conformity to the letter of the law, and it is only the evidence of a man of 'blameless life' that possesses any validity in a court of law. If the practice of chess was established to be illegal, no true Muslim could be a chess-player. It became, therefore, a matter of importance to ascertain the legal position of chess and chess-playing.

It was not, however, until the second century of Islam that any serious attempt was made to systematize and codify Muslim law. Prior to this lawyers had been mainly opportunists, though the seeds of the broad separation of Muhammadans into Sunnites—those who accepted the caliphate *de facto*—and Shiʿites—those who upheld the right of the descendants of ʿAlī and his wife Fāṭima, the Prophet's daughter, were already there. But in the second and third centuries Sunnite law was systematized by a number of schools or sects, of which four stand out above the others. These are the Ḥanīfite, the Mālikite, the Shāfiʿite, and the Ḥanbalite schools, so called from their respective founders, Abū Ḥanīfa (D. 150/767), Mālik b. Anas (D. 179/795), ash-Shāfiʿī (D. 204/820), and Aḥmad b. Ḥanbal (D. 241/855). To one or other of these sects practically every Sunnite Muslim belongs to-day, and in broad outline Shiʿite law is not very dissimilar.

Muslim law divides all actions into five classes—(1) necessary actions (*farḍ, wājib*), the omission of which is punished, and the performance of which is rewarded; (2) recommended actions (*mandūb, mustaḥabb*), the omission of which entails no penalty, but the performance of which is rewarded; (3) permitted actions (*jā'iz, mubaḥ*) which are indifferent legally; (4) disliked actions (*makrūh*) which are disapproved but not under penalty; and (5) forbidden actions (*ḥarām*), the performance of which is punished by law.[2] The criteria for the proper classification of actions have varied somewhat from time to time, and with different schools, but all agree that the final criterion is the *Qur'ān*, and that next in importance comes the evidence of a clear and authentic tradition of Muḥammad or of the earliest age.[3]

Chess is mentioned nowhere by name in the *Qur'ān*, but, adopting the principle of analogy (*qiyās*) by which the doubt could be resolved by a decision on some similar case, appeal was made to *Sura* V. 92, a chapter that belongs to the Medina or last period of Muḥammad's life. In this verse we read—

> O true believers, surely wine and lots (*maisīr*) and images (*'anṣāb*) and divining-arrows (*'azlām*)[4] are an abomination of the works of Satan, therefore avoid ye them that ye may prosper.

It is by extending the condemnation of lots—*maisīr*—and images *'anṣāb*—that the attempt has been made to condemn chess and chess-playing. There is fair agreement among the commentators that *maisīr* was intended to include every game which is subject to hazard or chance, or which is played for money or a stake. It is on this verse that the prohibition of nard (tables, backgammon),[5] and the later-discovered games of cards is based. There is, however, a tradition which is preserved by al-Baihaqī (D. 458/1066) that the caliph ʿAlī once described chess as the Persian *maisīr*, though the genuineness of the tradition is disputed by other writers—b. Sukaikir, for instance. The noted Ḥanbalite b. Taimīya (D. 728/1328) makes the sensible distinction that in chess it is only the playing for money that is *maisīr*, and quotes the opinion of Mālik b. Anas that the stake made chess a far worse game than nard. The Sunnite Muslim sees a prohibition of carved chess-pieces which actually reproduce the King, Elephants, Horses, &c., in the prohibition of images.[6] Persian commentators, however, have explained the term as referring to idols,[7] and the Shiʿite and Moghul chess-players have no objection to using real carved chessmen. The Sunnite player, on the contrary, will only use pieces of a conventional type in which it is impossible to see any resemblance to any living creature.

In the second place, the lawyers turned to the traditions (*ḥadith*) of

[2] Cf. Macdonald, op. cit., 73.

[3] The other criteria are: (1) the agreement (*ijmā'*) of the companions of the prophet, extended later to the agreement of the jurists of any particular time; (2) analogy (*qiyās*), by which a decision on one question was invoked to settle another which was more or less analogous; (3) equity or common sense, variously disguised as opinion (*rā'ī*), preference (*istiḥsan*), used by Abū Ḥanīfa, public advantage (*istiṣlaḥ*), used by Mālik; and (4) local usage (*'urf*).

[4] This covers an early form of divination in which Culin (*C. & P.*, 679, 685, &c.) sees the progenitor of dice.

[5] Some Shāfiʿites claimed that it was only the stake that made nard illegal, and that nard without a stake was permissible (*jā'iz*). This was not the view of ash-Shāfiʿī himself, who agreed with the other imams in declaring it forbidden (*ḥarām*) whether played for a stake or not.

[6] Cf. the ʿAlī tradition, quoted below.

[7] Cf. Hyde, ii. 24.

Muḥammad and his immediate companions, in order to deduce what their practice in the matter of games was. And here at the outset lay the difficulty of settling the genuineness or otherwise of the tradition. Islam was flooded with traditions by the end of the second century,[8] and the vast majority of these were forgeries. Only the crudest tests could be applied in an age that had no appreciation of the science of historical criticism. But crude as the tests were, they disposed of ninety-nine per cent of the traditions.[9] And in the winnowed material three traditions survived which dealt with Muḥammad's attitude towards recreations. One of these emphasizes his hatred of games of chance, another shows his approval of martial exercises with lance or bow, and the third preserves a statement that a believer should restrict his amusements to his horse, his bow, and his wife or wives.

These traditions form the basis of the discussion as to the status of chess in the works of the founders of the four great schools. Abū Ḥanīfa reduces the question to a dilemma: either the game is played for a stake, or for amusement. In the first case it is forbidden by the *Qur'ān*, in the second it is not one of the three forms of recreation allowed by Muḥammad. Chess, nard, and fourteen [10] are all clearly illegal. There is, however, a difference of degree. Chess is only disapproved (*makrūh*), not forbidden (*ḥarām*), as is nard. It is a sin that leads into error, and Abū Ḥanīfa did not himself refuse to greet a chess-player when at his game. The Ḥanīfite code was the official ʿAbbāsid canon, but later lawyers had to exercise considerable casuistry to reconcile their law with the wishes of the caliphs.[11]

Mālik b. Anas and b. Ḥanbal took a more hostile view. In the *K. al-muwaṭṭa'*, of Mālik's Spanish pupil Yaḥyā b. Yaḥyā (D. 234/848) there is added to the citation of the tradition in which Muḥammad interdicts games of chance the following reminiscence of his master's hatred of chess:

> I heard Mālik say that there was nothing good about chess. He pronounced it *ḥarām*. I heard him denounce chess-playing and other vanities as *ḥarām*, quoting *Sura* X. 33, 'When the truth has been scorned, what is left except error.'

Indeed Mālik held that chess was far worse than nard, since the game exercised a far greater fascination over its players. The Ḥanbalite school were equally opposed to chess, but they took the more natural view that nard was still worse.

[8] B. Abī Awja (ex. 155/771) confessed that he had put into circulation 400 false traditions. Another noted forger of traditions was Kaʿb (see p. 219).

[9] The *K. al-jāmiʿ aṣ-ṣaḥīḥ* contains 7,000 sound traditions as a result of the examination of 600,000.

[10] To these games later writers, e.g. ar-Rāfiʿī (quoted by al-Qābūnī (D. 869/1464) in his *An-naṣīḥa lil-ḥurr wal-ʿabd bijtināb ash-shaṭranj wan-nard*), add *qirq*, i.e. merels. *Fourteen* was a game played with small stones on a wooden board which had three rows of holes (al-Qābūnī).

[11] We possess the *K. al-jāmiʿ aṣ-ṣaghīr* of Abū Ḥanīfa's pupils ash-Shaibānī (D. 189/804) and Abū Yūsuf (D. 182/795). The latter is the qāḍī who in the *Arabian Nights* is represented as the companion of Harūn ar-Rashīd on many of his nocturnal adventures. A later Ḥanīfite work, the *K. hidāyat al-mubtadī* by al-Marghīnānī (D. 593/1197), which has been translated into English by C. Hamilton (1791, 2nd ed. 1870), discusses the point whether it is right to disturb a chess-player in his game to bid him the usual greeting *salāmu ʿalaika*. Abū Ḥanīfa said the interruption was permissible, but his two pupils ash-Shaibānī and Abū Yūsuf dissented from him.

Ash-Shāfiʿī enunciated a more liberal view. He found Abū Ḥanīfa's dilemma defective, since he claimed that chess is an image of war, and it is possible to play chess not for a stake, not for pure recreation, but as a mental exercise for the solution of military tactics. When played for this last purpose, he denied that the player was doing anything illegal. According to al-Māwardī (D. 450/1058) he regarded chess as *makrūh*, not because it leads into error—that ash-Shāfiʿī denied—but as a sin of recreation. And provided the player took care that his fondness for chess did not cause him to break any other rule of life, he saw no harm in playing. Ash-Shāfiʿī, indeed, played chess himself, defending his practice by the example of many of the companions and tābiʿs. The chess-players naturally attached great importance to the example of these early players, to whom all the legal schools looked back with reverence, and all the MSS. contain in more or less detail the traditions that enshrine the record of this or that tābiʿ's approval or practice of chess. The great master and historian aṣ-Ṣūlī gave these traditions in text (*matn*) and chain of authority (*'isnād*), and the MSS. AH and C have preserved his work for us. I shall make use of his traditions in this chapter. They contain the germs of the conditions which ash-Shāfiʿī finally laid down as defining the lawfulness of play. These were four in number, the game must not be played for a stake, and no money must be paid in connexion with the game, the game must in no way be allowed to interfere with the regular performance of prayer or other religious duty, the player must refrain from angry and improper language, and the game must not be played in the street or other public place. It is obvious that these conditions are not compelled by any inherent quality in chess, but are due to the weakness and depravity of human nature. This is b. Sukaikir's contention, that there is nothing wrong in the game itself, but only in the circumstances of play. He claims, therefore, that common-sense ought to justify the game, while he reluctantly admits that the general consensus of legal opinion is hostile.[12]

If we omit a very doubtful tradition that ascribes the story given below in connexion with the caliph ʿAlī to the first caliph Abū-Bakr (D. 13/634), the first traditions that connect a caliph with the game relate to ʿOmar b. al-Khaṭṭāb, the father-in-law of Muḥammad (D. 23/643). A widely recorded tradition tells how he was once asked as to the legal status of chess. 'What is chess?' asked the caliph. He was told that there was once a queen whose son was slain in battle. His comrades hesitated to tell her the news, and when she asked how the battle had gone, they invented chess and showed it to her. By means of the explanation they conveyed the news of the prince's death.[13] ʿOmar listened to the tale, and then replied: 'There is nothing wrong in it; it has to do with war.' The fact that ʿOmar once greeted Hilāl b.

12 This appeal to common-sense naturally did not commend itself to the lawyers. Thus az-Zarqānī (D. 1122/1710) insists that the only way in which chess-players could silence their opponents was by establishing tradition on their side. He thought this still possible, as he was not satisfied with the opposing traditions.

13 This is probably the earliest trace of one of the favourite legends of the invention of chess. See p. 212.

Khasīb, a maula (dependent, client) of Sulaiman b. Yashār (D. 107/725), the great tābiʿ of Medina,[14] while he was engaged in chess is handed down in a tradition with particularly good *'isnad*.[15]

The caliph ʿAlī b. Abū Tālib (D. 40/660), the son-in-law of Muḥammad, is connected with the following story, the genuine nature of which was allowed by the traditionists:

> ʿAlī once chanced to pass by some people who were playing at chess, and asked them, 'What images are these upon which you are gazing so intently?', for they were quite new to him, having only lately been introduced from Persia, and the Pawns were soldiers, and the Elephants and Horses were so depicted according to the custom of the Persians.

It is inferred from this that ʿAlī only objected to the carved chessmen and not to the game itself, and it is in deference to this that the Sunnite Muslims use men of a conventional pattern.

Al-Māwardī (D. 450/1058) quotes traditions that connect several of the 'Companions' (*aṣḥāb*) with chess. Abū Huraira (D. 57/676–7),[16] ʿAbdallāh b. ʿAbbās, and ʿAbdallāh b. Zubair are stated to have been seen to play chess, while al-Ḥusain (sl. 68/610), the ill-fated son of the caliph ʿAlī, is recorded to have played with his children, and also to have watched a game and to have prompted the players.

The traditions regarding the tābiʿs are equally trivial in detail, and their main interest consists in the evidence they afford for the practice of chess in the first centuries of Islam. Since some of these early players are said to have played the game blindfold, it is reasonable to conclude that the standard of play must have been fairly high. The cosmopolitan nature of Islam is well illustrated by the nationalities of these chess-players.

The list includes the names of Saʿīd b. al-Musayyib[17] (D. 91/709–10), of Medina, an Arab, who played in public and declared the game permissible provided there was no stake; ʿAlī b. al-Ḥusain Zain al-ʿābidīn (D. 94/712–3), one of the Imāms of the Shiʿites, whose father was, as already mentioned, a chess-player, and whose mother according to legend was Shahr-bānū, the daughter of Yazdigird III, the last of the Sāsānian kings of Persia; Saʿīd b. Jubair (ex. 95/714), a negro, who excelled in blindfold play; Ibrāhīm b. Ṭalha b. ʿObaidallāh (D. 98/717), the son of one of Muḥammad's earliest converts, who had been seen to play chess in public in Medina; al-Qāsim

[14] According to al-Qābūnī, Sulaiman himself disapproved of chess.

[15] It is, however, handed down in another form which says that it was either the caliph or ʿAmr b. al-ʿĀsī (D. 45/665), the great Muslim general and conqueror of Egypt, who greeted the chess-players. ʿAmr is associated by the late historian as-Suyūṭī (D. 911/1505) with the introduction of chess from Persia in a passage in his *K. al-wasā'il ilā ma'rifat al-awā'il* (ed. Gosche, Halle, 1867, p. 24), which apparently goes back ultimately to Mālik b. Anas:

> 'The first to introduce writing, chess, and nard was ʿAmr b. al-ʿĀsī, he learnt them in al-Hira.'

I cannot accept this statement; it is certainly inaccurate as regards writing, and ʿAmr's earlier biographer, an-Nawāwī (D. 676/1278), says nothing about it.

[16] Al-Qābūnī, however, claims that Abū Huraira was an opponent of chess, and quotes a tradition that he once refused to greet some people who were playing 'with 'azlām, chess, and nard'.

[17] Al-Qābūnī, however, quotes a tradition that contains his opinion that chess was a vanity.

b. Muḥammad[18] (D. 101/719–20), by his father a grandson of the caliph Abū-Bakr, and by his mother of Yazdigird, who once rebuked some chess-players for using figures (*sūrun*) for pieces (*dawābb*); ash-Shaʿbī (D. 108/722–3), of Persian descent, who played chess and nard for a stake and forgot the hour of prayer, and played in the street, covering his head so that he should not be known; ʿIkrima (D. 107/725–6), a Berber; Muḥammad b. Sīrīn (D. 110/728–29), a Persian, who was famous for his interpretation of dreams, and could also play chess blindfold; al-Ḥasan al-Baṣrī (B. 110/728), who saw no harm in chess provided there was no stake and no neglect of the times of prayer; ʿAṭāʿa (D. 115/733–4), a deformed mulatto; az-Zuhrī (D. 124/742), the great lawyer of the Umayyad period; Muḥammad al-Munkadir (D. 131/748–9); Rabīʿa ar-Rai (D. 136/753–4), of Persian descent; Hishām b. ʿUrwa (D. 146/763–4), another blindfold player, whose three granddaughters Safī'a, Aʿīsha, and ʿUbaida also all appear as chess-players; al-Aʿamash (D. 148/765), a Persian; and Abū ʿAun (D. 151/768), another Persian. Although Mālik b. Anas was so opposed to chess, he numbered among his friends a chess-player, al-Mughīra b. ʿAbdarraḥmān, and his own son Yaḥyā b. Mālik b. Anas, who was a lawyer in Medina, played chess in his home. Finally, the great lawyer, ash-Shāfiʿī, is credited with skill in blindfold play.

Probably the most interesting in these names is that of Saʿīd b. Jubair. According to b. Taimīya (Man., f. 10 b), he gave the following curious reason for his playing chess. He had reason to believe that al-Ḥajjāj desired to appoint him *qāḍī*, and, fearing that the patronage of this noted man would be detrimental to his piety, he took up chess in order to disqualify himself for the post. Chess-playing he regarded as the less of the two evils, and since acts are to be judged by the intention, even a more heinous sin would have been permissible in his necessity. He was only forty-nine when the same al-Ḥajjāj put him to death for taking part in a revolt against ʿAbdalmalik b. Marwān. His murderer is said to have dreamt that God would kill him once for every man he had killed in his ruthless career, but seventy times for the death of Saʿīd b. Jubair. Other traditions in AH tell us that Saʿīd had played chess all his life, that he played with equal ease whether he saw the board or not, and that his method of playing blindfold was to turn his back on the board; then he would ask the slave who attended him what his opponent had moved, next he bade the slave 'move such and such a man'. His name is the earliest one that is associated with play without the use of a material board, but he may have had many followers among the Muslim players. Other references to players who could play blindfold are given later in this chapter, and a Muslim whose name is given as Buzecca or Borzaga is mentioned as the first exponent of the art of blindfold play in Europe. This player visited Florence in 1265.[19]

[18] Al-Qābūnī quotes a tradition to the effect that he said that chess and nard were *maisīr*, because they take possession of the mind just as wine does the body.

[19] In Giovanni Villani, *Tratto dell' Origine di Firenze*, Venice, 1537, VII. xii, whence in Selenus, *Das Schach- oder König-Spiel*, Leipzig, 1616.

The earliest of the Umayyad caliphs who is associated with chess is ʿAbdalmalik b. Marwān (D. 86/705). An earlier caliph, Yazīd I b. Muʿāwiya (D. 64/683), the hated murderer of the Imām Ḥusain b. ʿAlī, is stated by b. Khallikān to have been a nard-player, and accordingly a man whom it was legally permissible to curse. There are three stories of ʿAbdalmalik in H (ff. 8 a, 11 a, and 14 b). They merely exhibit the caliph as a chess-player, but one brings in the noted poet al-Akhṭal (D. 92/710), and another tells how ash-Shaʿbī, whom we have already heard of as an inveterate chess-player, once asked the caliph if he was not ashamed of playing. The caliph answered by some questions. Was the game *ḥarām*? or *maisīr* or *'anṣāb*? Since ash-Shaʿbī could only answer all these in the negative, the caliph continued to play. AH, f. 12 b, has a curious story, which the later *K. al-ʿuyūn*, a generally trustworthy history of the 5th or 6th c. of Islam (say A.D. 1150–1250, ed. de Goeje in *Fragmenta Hist. Arab.*, Lugd. Bat., 1871, p. 102), repeats in connexion with ʿAbdalmalik's younger son, the caliph Hishām (D. 125/742), while MS. Brit. Mus. Add. 7320, f. 42 b, which has been identified by H. F. Amedroz as the work of b. al-Jauzī (' An unidentified MS. by ibn al-Jauzī', *JRAS.*, Jan. 1907, see p. 865), attributes it to the elder son, the caliph Walīd I b. ʿAbdalmalik (D. 96/714). The caliph was once engaged in playing chess when a visitor,[20] a Syrian, was announced. The caliph ordered a slave to cover over the chessboard, and the visitor was allowed to enter. The caliph then proceeded to examine his guest in order to find out how far he was instructed in the Muslim religion, and, discovering that he was quite unlearned, he bade the slave uncover the board, and resumed his game, for 'there is nothing forbidden to the uneducated'. This story is gravely told by aṣ-Ṣūlī as evidence for the legality of chess-playing. Its unsatisfactory nature and the fact that it is cited and not suppressed in the chess MSS. is in favour of its genuineness.

The chess MS. Y and some later (for the more part Indian) chess works give a story of ʿAbdalmalik's son and successor Walīd I (D. 96/714). He was once playing chess with a courtier who purposely played negligently to avoid beating the caliph. On discovering this the latter took umbrage, and broke his flatterer's head with a blow with his *firzān*, saying, ' Woe be to you! are you playing chess, and in your senses?' The silence of earlier works tells against this story.

A thoroughly satisfactory reference of about this time is to be found in a passage in one of the poems of the noted poet al-Farazdaq (D. *c.* 110/728). This is the more important since there is an allusion to a technicality of chess which would not have been appropriate unless the game were fairly generally

[20] According to b. al-Jauzī (D. 597/1200), Walīd was playing with ʿAbdallāh b. Muʿāwiya b. ʿAbdallāh b. Jaʿfar b. Abī Ṭālib, and the visitor was a member of the Thaqīf tribe on the way to fight the unbeliever. According to the *K. al-ʿuyūn* Hishām's visitor was his maternal uncle, a badawīn of the Makhzūm tribe.

AH gives a second 'isnad for this story, in which it is attributed to a still later caliph, Walīd II b. Yazīd (D. 126/743).

Gildemeister, to whom we owe many of the earlier references in Arabic historical works, was the first to call attention to the passage in the *K. al-ʿuyūn*. See *Qst.*, 6–12.

known. It must take time for a peculiarity of a game to become sufficiently known to take its place in literary idiom. The couplet in question runs:

And, as for us, if Tamīn reckons his ancestors in the rank of the forelocks of the noblest victors of the race-course, I keep you from your inheritance and from the royal crown so that, hindered by my arm, you remain a Pawn (*baidaq*) among the Pawns (*bayādiq*).

—an allusion to the promotion of the Pawn when it reaches the end of the board.[21] So it is interpreted by al-Jawālīqī (D. 539/1145) in *K. al-mu'arrab*, a work on Arabic loan-words which has been edited by Sachau, Leipzig, 1867, where the verse is quoted. Al-Jawālīqī states, rather loosely, that the Pawn which advances to the limit of the board 'obtains the weapons of the King'.

Another contemporary poet, al-Aḥwaṣ (D. 110/728), is connected with chess in a passage in the *K. al-aghānī* of Abū'l-Faraj (compiled A.D. 918–67) (ed. Bulaq, 1285, iv. 51). A certain 'Abdalḥakam b. 'Amr b. 'Abdallāh b. Ṣafwān al-Hujamī possessed a house in Mecca where he kept sets of chess, nard, and merels,[22] and books on all the sciences. The walls were provided with pegs, so that every one who entered could hang up his cloak. He was then expected to take a book, or to choose a game and to play with some other guest. Once 'Abdalḥakam came across a stranger in the Ka'ba to whom he took a fancy. He brought him home with him, and after hanging up their cloaks he took down the chess and challenged him to a game. Just then the singer al-Abjar entered, and greeted the unknown with, 'Hullo, heretic!' and to 'Abdalḥakam's astonishment presented him as the Medinese poet al-Aḥwaṣ. This incident must have taken place after al-Aḥwaṣ's return from banishment in 101/719.

Ar-Rāghib (D. 502/1108) in his *K. muḥāḍarāt al-udabā'*[23] relates that the Persian Abū Muslim (D. 137/754–5) once quoted a verse of one of the older poets in a new sense when he was checkmated in a game of chess.

We may safely assert that chess had already become a popular game throughout Islam, from Spain to the banks of the Indus, before the commencement of the 'Abbāsid caliphate.

The only chess story that brings in the name of the second caliph of the new dynasty, al-Manṣūr (D. 158/775), that I have come across, occurs in the chess MS. H (f. 10 b). The vizier of this caliph, Abū Ayyūb al-Muriyānī (D. 154/771), had a friend who was a skilled chess-player. The MS. quotes a witty couplet which the latter wrote to the vizier, inviting him to a game of chess.

Al-Mahdī (D. 169/785), the third of the 'Abbāsid caliphs, the son of al-Manṣūr and father of Hārūn ar-Rashīd, looked—at least officially—with disfavour upon chess. A letter of his, written in 169/780 to the people of

[21] The verse occurs almost at the end of the Oxford MS. of the *Naqā'id Jarīr wal Farazdaq* (Bodl. I. 1224). The chess allusion is perfectly certain, for *baidaq* has no other meaning than that of the chess-piece.

[22] Ar. *ash-shaṭranjāt*, *an-nardāt*, and *qirqāt*; all plurals.

[23] Ar-Rāghib says elsewhere in the same work that the Medinese refused to give their daughters in marriage to chess-players, since chess already usurped the position of a wife. Cf. *Qst.*, 7.

Mecca, is given in Arabic text in Wüstenfeld's *Die Chroniken der Stadt Mekka* (Leipzig, 1861 ff., iv. 168). In this the following passage occurs:

Facts about you have been reported to the Commander of the Faithful which he has heard with regret and which he condemns and abominates. He desires you to abandon these things, and directs you to do away with them, and to cleanse the Sanctuary of God from them. To these things belong . . . . the assembly of fools for nard, dicing, archery, chess, and all vanities that lead astray and from the remembrance of God, which interfere with the fulfilment of your duty to Him, and the performance of prayers in His mosques.

Notwithstanding this, chess must have been played at al-Mahdī's court, for we know from the *K. al-aghānī* (ed. cit., xix. 69) that the poet Abū Ḥafṣ ʿOmar b. ʿAbdalʿazīz, of Persian ancestry, was educated there, and that he obtained his surname of *ash-Shaṭranjī*, the chess-player, from his fondness for and skill in chess. After al-Mahdī's death he remained in the service of the caliph's daughter ʿUlayya, who is remembered for her love of music. Abū Ḥafṣ also played chess blindfold.[24]

Although the MS. V (f. 24 a) attributes a problem (No. 181 below) to al-Mahdī, with the unusual information that the position was not derived from an actual game, it does not follow that the ascription has any historical weight. The MSS. show an ever-growing tendency to assign the authorship of approved problems to noted characters, and their statements need to be treated with much caution.[25] In the present instance the ascription is in conflict with the evidence of the historian Muḥammad b. ʿAlī al-Miṣrī, as recorded in al-Masʿūdī's *Murūj adh-dhahab* (ed. cit., viii. 295):

Ar-Rashīd was the first caliph to establish the game of *assauljān* (a Per. ball-game like polo) in the field, the use of the bow, and practice with the lance, with the ball, and rackets; he recompensed those who distinguished themselves in the different exercises, and people followed his example. He was also the first of the ʿAbbāsid caliphs to play chess and nard. He favoured good players and granted them pensions.

I have already quoted the letters that passed between Hārūn ar-Rashīd (170/786 – 193/809) and Nicephorus in 802. This is the only allusion to chess in Arabic historical works in which Hārūn is concerned. The occasional chess passages in that well-known compilation from early and late sources, the *Alf laila walaila*, 'the Thousand and one Nights,'[26] are naturally of an unhistorical character, and can only be accepted for the Mamlūk period during which the collection of tales took its present shape in Egypt. The chess MS. H is the only one of those that I have used which contains much to connect Hārūn with chess, and none of its seven stories[27] has any real importance, apart from the impromptu verses to which they gave occasion.

24 Gildemeister (*ZDMG.*, xxviii. 682–98) adds a reference to a poem of Aṣmaʿī (D. 216/831) quoted in the *K. badāʾiʿ al-bidāya* of ʿAlī b. Ẓāfir (D. 603/1205–6) (ed. Cairo, 1278, p. 117). Abū Ḥafṣ is also mentioned in b. Khallikān (ed. Slane, Paris, 1843–71, iii. 92.)

25 The MS. V is early (copied 618/1221) and generally reliable; but the same problem occurs in other MSS. without the ascription.

26 Cf. E. W. Lane's translation, ch. xx, note 22.

27 The passages occur on ff. 6 b, 7 a, 9 a, 10 b, 11 a, and 13 b in H. The opinion of b. Māsawaihi as to the appropriateness of chess-playing during illness also occurs in Man. at f. 42 a.

Four stories show the caliph in an inquiring mood. He asked his physician, b. Māsawaihi (D. 243/857), whether chess could be played during illness, and received the answer that it was generally suitable, but that at certain times—all detailed—it was inadvisable to play. Another time, on a wet day, he asked Yahyā b. Aktham the qāḍī (D. 242/847) what could be done on such a day, and received an enigmatical reply, which was interpreted as meaning to drink wine and play chess. On a third occasion he asked b. Māsawaihi what he thought of chess, and was told it was legally permissible; and on a fourth he started a controversy between the great Ḥanīfite, Abū Yūsuf the qāḍī (D. 182/795), and a Mālikite, Yaḥyā b. Bakair, on the same point. At first Abū Yūsuf defended the legality of chess, but when Yaḥyā declared that he had heard Mālik b. Anas forbid chess and reject the evidence of chess-players, he gave up his contention, and agreed that Mālik's opinion settled the matter. Another story tells the history of a slave girl who was famed for her skill at chess. Hārūn bought her for 10,000 dinars and proceeded to try conclusions with her at chess. He lost three games in succession, and when the slave was asked to choose her reward, she begged forgiveness for a certain Aḥmad b. al-Amīn. In these stories the noted poet Abū Nuwās appears as an intimate friend of the caliph. Another of Hārūn's friends bore the name of Muḥammad al-Baid'aq, where the surname is derived from the name of the chess-pawn, and was given because the man was little of stature.[28]

Hārūn's eldest son and successor, al-Amīn (D. 198/813),[29] was also a chess-player. Ar-Rāghib tells an amusing story of this caliph and the musician Isḥāq al-Mauṣilī (D. 235/849–50)[30] in the *K. muḥāḍarāt al-udabā'*, a work of which I have already made use. Al-Amīn and Isḥāq were once playing chess, and the latter had wagered his cloak on the game. The caliph won, but hesitated to take his opponent's cloak, until the happy idea occurred to him to give up his own cloak as a gift. Al-Amīn's fondness for chess led him to indulge in the game at unseasonable times. At the critical point of the siege

[28] Later writers have given chess a far more important place in the history of Hārūn ar-Rashīd. Von Hammer (cf. Bland, 35) quotes a curious wager between the caliph and his wife, Zubaida, as even influencing the succession to the caliphate. Another MS. quoted by Bland (36) associates the fall of the Barmakids with chess.

'Ar-Rashīd was devoted to the game of chess, and he had a sister, called 'Abbāsīya, who played well. Now Ja'far (b. Yaḥyā al-Barmakī, ex. 187/803) used to beat ar-Rashīd at chess, as also did his sister, and it was ar-Rashīd's wish to see which of the two, Ja'far or 'Abbāsīya, would prove the superior in his presence. So he said to Ja'far, "I will give thee 'Abbāsīya in marriage, on condition that thou approach her not except by my command and appointment", and ar-Rashīd sent for the qāḍī and he wrote 'Abbāsīya's marriage contract with Ja'far, and 'Abbāsīya used to sit with Ja'far, whether ar-Rashīd were present or not, and used to play with him.'

Unfortunately Ja'far and his wife forgot Hārūn's condition, and the birth of a child led to Ja'far's disgrace and death. Neither of these stories is authenticated by any historian of repute, and modern scholars generally have rejected them as apocryphal.

[29] Al-Amīn's tutor, al-Kisā'ī, a Persian by descent (D. 189/804–5), is one of the Muslims whom aṣ-Ṣūlī quotes as supporting the lawfulness of chess-playing.

[30] A remark in passing, in the *K. al-aghānī* (v. 92), connects Isḥāq again with chess: 'Isḥāq al-Mauṣilī, the celebrated musician, had seen 'Abdallāh b. Ṭāhir play chess.' A similar note (xv. 11) tells how the poet Abū Shiṣ (D. 196/812) had found the well-known Abū Dulaf (D. 226/840–1) playing chess. The contemporary general, Ṭāhir b. al Ḥusain b. Muṣ'ab (D. 207/822) is associated in AH with the invention of the *shaṭranj ar-rūmīya* (see p. 342).

of Baghdād, when the city was on the verge of capture, the messenger who was sent to the caliph to advise him of his peril found him deep in chess with his favourite Kauthar. 'O Commander of the Faithful,' he exclaimed, 'this is not the time to play, pray arise and attend to matters of more serious moment.' 'Patience, my friend,' coolly replied the caliph, 'I see that in a few moves I shall give Kauthar checkmate." [31]

Al-Ma'mūn (D. 218/833), who succeeded his brother al-Amīn in the caliphate, was equally addicted to chess, though apparently with less success. 'Strange that I who rule the world from the Indus in the East to Andalūs in the West cannot manage 32 chessmen in a space of two cubits by two,' is the remark that aṣ-Ṣafadī records of this caliph. Al-Yazīdī (D. 310/922) is quoted by b. Badrūn and as-Ṣuyūṭī as giving Ma'mūn's opinion that chess was more than a game, and that to play it was an excellent training for the mind. The caliph tried to improve the game by introducing some novelties, which never took root. He also insisted on his opponent playing his best. Thus in the MS. Y we read—

> Al-Ma'mūn was one day playing with a courtier who appeared to be moving negligently in order to allow the caliph to win the game. Al-Ma'mūn perceived it, and in great wrath upset the board, exclaiming, 'You want to treat me as a child, and to practice on my understanding.' He then addressed the onlookers: 'Bear witness to the vow which I now make that I will never play chess with this person again.'

But if al-Ma'mūn himself was only a weak player, he yet liked to have strong players about him. On his expedition from Khurāsān to Baghdād in 204/819 he watched Rabrab,[32] Jābīr al-Kūfī, and 'Abdalghaffār al-Anṣārī play. The presence of the caliph manifestly embarrassed the players. 'Chess and reverence,' observed al-Ma'mūn, 'don't seem to agree. They ought to talk together just as they would do if they were by themselves.' This incident is most interesting, for Jābīr and Rabrab are named in the chess MSS. as belonging to the highest class of players, that of the *'alīyāt* or grandees. These MSS. give some End-game positions that are drawn from actual games between Rabrab and Abū'n-Na'ām, whose name follows that of Rabrab in the list of *'alīyāt*. The names are plainly in chronological order, and this age of al-Ma'mūn must have been a notable one in the history of Muslim chess, since it saw three grandees of chess living at one time.

The next caliph—still another son of Hārūn—al-Mu'taṣim (D. 227/842), possesses a chess reputation that appears to have no real basis.[33] The only

[31] This rests upon the authority of Jirjīs al-Makīn (George Elmacini, D. 672/1273), whose *K. al-majmū' al-mubārak* was edited with Latin translation by the Dutch scholar Erpenius (*Hist. Saracenica*, Lugd. Bat., 1625, see p. 129). Erpenius was evidently ignorant of the Arabic chess terms, and, confusing *shāh* (king) with *shāh* (sheep), which ends in the dotted *ha*, he translated the caliph's reply, 'Taurus sylvestris moriturus apparuit mihi contra Guterum'! See Hyde, ii. 4, and Forbes, 177. Cf. p. 224, n. 7.

[32] The name of this player is doubtful. Ar-Rāghib, who records the incident, writes Zairab; the chess MSS. vary between Zairab, Zabzab, and Rabrab. In using the last form I follow Forbes and v. d. Linde. *RAS.* calls him Rabrab Khatā'ī, i. e. of Chinese Turkestan.

[33] This is due to the ascription of the authorship of two problems (Nos. 91 and 152 below) to this caliph in the late MS. *RAS.* Forbes (p. 83) accepted this as fact, and printed one of them as 'the most ancient problem on record'. Earlier MSS., e. g. AH and V, give the

certain chess fact of al-Muʿtaṣim's caliphate is the appreciation of the function of the *fīl* in chess which I quote in Ch. XIII, which was pronounced by his famous vizier Muḥammad b. az-Zayyāt (ex. 233/847).

During the rule of al-Wāthiq (D. 227/842) and al-Mutawakkil (D. 232/847) [34] the great master al-ʿAdlī ranked alone in the highest class of players. It was only towards the end of his life that a rival appeared to dispute his position in the person of ar-Rāzī. The match took place in the presence of al-Mutawakkil, and, by defeating his older opponent, ar-Rāzī was successful in establishing his claim to be ranked among the *ʿalīyāt.* Both players were chess authors, but while we possess large portions of al-ʿAdlī's work in the various MSS., all that has survived of ar-Rāzī's work is a few opinions on the End-game, a few aphorisms, and a couple of problems. Notwithstanding this neglect, aṣ-Ṣūlī considered that ar-Rāzī was the greatest of his predecessors. Of al-ʿAdlī he had a poorer opinion, and much of his own chess work took the form of a criticism of al-ʿAdlī's book.

Aṭ-Ṭabarī (D. 310/923) in his *K. akhbār ar-rusul wal-mulūk* (ed. Goege, 1881, iii. 1671) [35] describes how the caliph al-Muʿtazz (D. 255/869) received the news of his predecessor and rival al-Mustaʿīn's defeat and death in 252/866. The caliph was seated at chess when a messenger arrived bringing the head of al-Mustaʿīn. Al-Muʿtazz paid no attention to the news until he had finished his game.[36]

An incident that al-Masʿūdī (op. cit., viii. 13) tells of Aḥmad b. Mudabbir, collector of taxes in Palestine under al-Muhtadī (255–6/869–70) shows that wealthy people kept good chess-players in their households. A certain b. Darraj intruded into b. Mudabbir's house on one occasion and was discovered among the company. His host addressed him thus—

> A parasite may be pardoned his intrusion upon other people's society whereby he disturbs the charm of their intimacy and discovers their secrets, but only on the condition that he is endowed with certain talents, as a knowledge of chess or nard, or the ability to play the lute or guitar (*tonbūr*).

The stranger replied that he excelled in all these accomplishments, so b. Mudabbir ordered one of his pages to play the intruder at chess. The latter asked what reward he would get if he proved successful. He was promised 1,000 dirhems if he proved himself superior to all the company in his accomplishments. The money was brought and placed on the table, since

problems without naming any composer, and it is quite clear from an examination of the names in *RAS.* that the addition of the names of authors is an embellishment that must not be taken seriously (see below, p. 272). Some later writers, relying on Forbes, have claimed that al-Muʿtaṣim was the originator of the chess-problem.

Al-Muʿtaṣim was surnamed the Octonary caliph, and Arabic works give several reasons for the name. In quoting these, Forbes (179) adds some others drawn from chess, which do not appear to be based upon any Arabic source.

[34] A metaphorical expression drawn from chess that the philosopher Ibrāhīm b. Nazzām (D. 230/845) employed is recorded by ath-Thaʿālibī (D. 429/1038) in his *Aḥāsin kalim an-nabī* (*Talibii Syntagma dictorum* . . . , ed. Valeton, Lugd. Bat. 1844, 73):—'I moved a Rook from my mind against him,' i. e. 'I attacked him with a powerful argument.'

[35] From whence it was copied by b. al-Athīr (D. 630/1234). Since Gildemeister only knew the latter authority in 1874, he did not attach much importance to the story. Aṭ-Ṭabarī, of course, was alive at the time the incident occurred.

[36] I have already quoted the chess-poem of this caliph's son, b. Muʿtazz, p. 185.

the parasite said its presence would stimulate him to his best efforts. He won the game of chess and was about to take the money, when the doorkeeper, who saw a danger of punishment for his carelessness in allowing the stranger to enter, intervened, and said that he was sure another of the pages could beat the stranger at chess. This page was summoned and the stranger was beaten. He claimed a game at nard, first winning and then being beaten by a better player, and so the contest went on, the porter endeavouring to escape the consequences of his carelessness and the stranger to escape the thrashing he deserved for his impertinence.

Al-Muʿtaḍid, caliph 279/892–289/902, was also a chess-player. Al-Maṣʿūdī mentions (op. cit., viii. 271) that his vizier Qāsim b. ʿObaidallāh once heard him quote a verse from b. Bassām during a game.

It was under the following caliph, al-Muktafī (289/902–295/908), that the historian Abū-Bakr Muḥammad b. Yaḥyā aṣ-Ṣūlī [37] first came into note as a chess-player of consummate skill. Ar-Rāzī was already dead, and no one had taken his place, when a certain al-Māwardī made his appearance at court and announced that his skill exceeded all that ar-Rāzī had ever possessed (H, f. 13 a). The caliph took al-Māwardī into favour, and when aṣ-Ṣūlī's extraordinary talent at chess was reported to the caliph, he was not disposed to believe it. A match was arranged between the two players and took place in the caliph's presence. Al-Muktafī was so led away by his partiality for his favourite that he openly encouraged him during the game. At first this embarrassed and confused aṣ-Ṣūlī, but he soon recovered his nerve, and finally defeated his adversary so completely that no one could doubt but that aṣ-Ṣūlī was by far the better player. When the caliph was thus convinced, he lost all his partiality for al-Māwardī, and said to him, 'Your rose-water (*māward*) has turned to urine!'

The new grandee of chess was descended from Ṣul-takīn, a Turkish prince of Jurjān, whose ancestral home was situated at the south-east corner of the Caspian Sea, on the banks of the River Atrek. Yazīd b. Al-Muhallab converted the warrior during the conquest of Khurāsān. His grandson married a sister of the poet al-Ahnaf, and a son of this marriage, Ibrāhīm b. al-ʿAbbās aṣ-Ṣūlī (D. 243/857), was known as a poet of some ability. Ibrāhīm's nephew was the chess-player, who also proved himself a ready versifier and was moreover a convivial and entertaining companion. It was to the latter qualities that he owed his position at court under al-Muktafī and his successors, al-Muqtadir [38] (D. 320/932) and ar-Rāḍī (D. 329/940). To this last caliph we owe a happy reference to aṣ-Ṣūlī's play. In his youth the chess-player had acted as his tutor, and a warm friendship seems to have arisen as a result. Al-Maṣʿūdī, who himself was intimate with aṣ-Ṣūlī and owed to him much of

[37] Also called an-Nadīm (the courtier) and ash-Shaṭranjī. The name aṣ-Ṣūlī is derived from Ṣūl, the domain in Jurjān whence the family descended. Aṣ-Ṣūlī's life is given in b. Khallikān (ed. cit., iii. 71), and the incidents in the text are all included.

[38] I have already quoted (p. 184) some lines from al-Maṣʿūdī, which were written by this caliph's vizier, b. Abū'l-Baghal (D. 321/932-3). May not aṣ-Ṣūlī be referred to in them?

his information about the later caliphs, says (ed. cit., viii. 311 : also b. Khallikān ; and H, f. 13 b, where it is attributed in error to al-Muktafī) :

It is related that ar-Rāḍī-billāh was once walking in his country seat at Thurayya, and called attention to a lovely garden, replete with lawns and flowers. He asked his courtiers if they had ever seen anything more beautiful. The courtiers immediately began to dilate on the wonders of the garden, to extol its beauty, and to place it above all the wonders of the world. 'Stop,' cried the caliph, 'Aṣ-Ṣūlī's skill at chess charms me more than these flowers, and more than all that you have mentioned.'

After ar-Rāḍī's death, aṣ-Ṣūlī found himself out of favour, and an incautious statement that revealed his leanings towards the party of the 'Alids (later the Shi'ites) was so resented that he had to flee from Baghdād and go into hiding at Baṣra. Here he died in very reduced circumstances in 335/946.[39]

Aṣ-Ṣūlī's reputation in chess remained unchallenged in Arabic circles for more than 600 years. To his successors he represented all that was possible in chess, much as Philidor stood for the unattainable ideal to the early nineteenth century. His biographer, b. Khallikān says :

He stood alone in chess in his own time, for there was no one in that age who was his equal in skill. His play has passed into a proverb, and when men speak of any one who is remarkable for the excellence of his play, they say, 'He plays chess like aṣ-Ṣūlī.'

Many Muslim players supposed from this proverb that aṣ-Ṣūlī was the actual discoverer or inventor of chess, and aṣ-Ṣafadī, b. Khallikān, and b. Sukaikir all point out the erroneousness of this belief.

We possess in the MSS. which have come down to us sufficient of aṣ-Ṣūlī's work to form an opinion of the chess-activity of this master. We see him criticizing his predecessors not unkindly but with the touch of superior knowledge. We have his favourite openings, founded no longer on mere caprice but on definite principles. We have End-games which happened to him in play over the board and in blindfold play, with an occasional anecdote that shows how much the master's play excelled that of his opponent. We see him as the first player to try to discover the science of the game or to enunciate the underlying principles of play. We may even possess some snatches of actual games in the analysis in the chess treatise contained in MSS. L and AE, the work of his grateful and able pupil al-Lajlāj.

This player, whose name is given by an-Nadīm in the *Fihrist* as Abū'l-Faraj Muḥammad b. 'Obaidallāh, and in the MSS. as Abū'l-Faraj al-Muẓaffar b. Sa'īd, probably owed his surname of al-Lajlāj (the stammerer) to a physical defect. The only fact that we know of his life is that recorded by an-Nadīm, who had seen him in Baghdād. In 360/970 he settled in Shīrāz at the court

[39] His literary works include a history of the Arabic poets, monographs on several of the more noted poets, a history of the viziers, an uncompleted history of the 'Abbāsid house, and an anthology of the poems written by the descendants of the caliph 'Alī b. Abī Ṭālib. Several of these works are extant in European or Constantinople libraries. See Brockelmann, *Gesch. d. arab. Litt.*, Weimar, 1898, i. 143.

of the Būyid ʿAḍudaddaula, where he died not long after. Both master and pupil are commemorated in a punning line in an elaborate essay in praise and dispraise of chess by Muḥammad b. Sharaf al-Qīrwānī, which is quoted by Hyde (ii. 57) from aṣ-Ṣafadī's *Sharḥ Lāmīyat al-ʿAjam.*

Like aṣ-Ṣūlī, al-Lajlāj has been remembered as a great chess master, but while aṣ-Ṣūlī's reputation has been in the main preserved in Syria and Egypt, al-Lajlāj's memory has only survived among the Persians, the Turks, and the Moghul Hindus. To these peoples he has become the great historic figure in chess, and all the myths of the game have been attached to his name. As Lajāj, or more commonly Līlāj, he is the inventor of chess: he appears in the story of the Indian embassy to Nūshīrwān as the Indian ambassador; the fabulous Ṣaṣṣa b. Dāhir is represented as his father; and the Persian and Turk have forgotten aṣ-Ṣūlī entirely.[40]

After the time of these great players there is a gap in the succession of references to chess at the court of Baghdād.[41] The light of the Eastern caliphate was flickering out, and the centre of Muslim life was moving elsewhere. A few references may be quoted from other parts of Islam that show the wide spread of chess.

ʿOmāra b. ʿAlī Najmaddīn al-Yamanī (D. 569/1175) in his *Ta'rīkh al-Yaman* (*Yaman . . . by Najm ad-din ʿOmarah al Hakami*, ed. H. C. Kay, London, 1892, pp. 88–92) gives a long account[42] of the events leading up to Jayyash's successful revolt at Zabīd in Southern Arabia in 482/1089. Jayyash had returned to Zabīd from India, and was living there in the disguise of an Indian faqir. He made use of his skill at chess to ingratiate himself with the vizier ʿAlī b. al-Kumm. To do this he took up his position each day at the bench at the outer gate of the vizier's house.

Husayn, son of ʿAly the Kummite, the poet, came forth on a certain day. He was at that time the most skilful chess-player of all the inhabitants of Zabīd. 'Indian,' he asked me, 'art thou a good chess-player?' I answered that I was. We played, and I beat him at the game, whereupon he barely restrained himself from violence against me. He went to his father and told him that he had been beaten at chess. His father replied that there had never been a person at Zabīd who could overcome him, excepting only Jayyash, the son of Najah, and he, he continued, has died in India. ʿAly, the father of Husayn, then came forth to me. He was an exceedingly skilful player and we played together. I was unwilling to defeat him, and the match ended in a drawn game.

[40] Cf. Hyde, ii. 57, who quotes from Turkish dictionaries. Cf. also the MS. F (see p. 178). The Urdu work of Durgāprasāda makes Lajlāj Rūmī the son of Sīsa, and credits him with the invention of the Rūmī manner of playing chess.

I have already quoted a Persian reference to Līlāj (p. 183). Bland also quotes (p. 44) from Ṭāhir of Nasrābād, the author of some memoirs on the poets who lived in the reign of Shāh ʿAbbās, that one of these poets, ʿAzīm or Nāzim of Yazd, used to boast of his skill at chess, saying that he could have given even Lajlāj a Knight and have beaten him. Ṭāhir, however, goes on to say that he himself, notwithstanding his own want of skill, had beaten the braggart several times.

[41] Gildemeister calls attention to chess verses by poets of this period, viz. by b. Kushājim (D. c. 350/961), quoted in ad-Damīrī's *Ḥayāt al-ḥayawān*; and by Sari ar-Raffah (D. 360–70/961–72) in ar-Rāghib's *K. muḥāḍarāt al-udabā'*.

[42] More briefly in b. Khaldūn (D. 808/1406), where the incidents are ascribed to Jayyash's vizier, Khalf b. Abū Ṭāhir.

From this time Jayyash played frequently with the vizier, until he incautiously betrayed his identity by an involuntary exclamation after a game in which he had allowed Ḥusain to beat him for reasons of policy.

In Egypt the mad Fāṭimid ruler al-Ḥākim biamrillāh prohibited chess in the year 1005, and ordered all the sets of chess to be burnt. The order did not extend to the magnificent sets of chess in the palace treasury, for in a description of the treasures of a later ruler, al-Mustanṣir billāh (1036–94), al-Maqrīzī (D. 1441) mentions 'chess and draught (read nard) boards of silk, embroidered in gold, with pawns (read men) of gold, silver, ivory, and ebony'. Much of this treasure had belonged to the 'Abbāsid caliphs before the Fāṭimids acquired it.[43]

I have already quoted from the Persian writer al-Bērūnī. His patron, the Ziyārid Qābūs b. Washmgīr (976–1012) of Tabaristān,[44] refers to chess in a poem in which he recounts his favourite occupations:

The things of this world from end to end are the goal of desire and greed,
And I set before this heart of mine the things which I most do need,
But a score of things I have chosen out of the world's unnumbered throng,
That in quest of these I my soul may please and speed my life along.
Verse and song, and minstrelsy, and wine full flavoured, and sweet,
Backgammon, and chess, and the hunting-ground, and the falcon and cheetah fleet;
Field, and ball, and audience-hall, and battle, and banquet rare,
Horse, and arms, and a generous hand, and praise of my lord and prayer.

B. al-Athīr (Cairo ed., ix. 128) tells a story of the famous Maḥmūd of Ghaznī, which shows him as a chess-player.[45] In the spring of 420/1029 he seized Rai and dethroned Majdaddaula. He summoned the latter before him, and the following colloquy took place:

'Hast thou not read the *Shāhnāma* and aṭ-Ṭabarī's history (i.e. Persian and Arabic history)?'

'Yes.'

'Your conduct is not as of one who has read them. Do you play chess?'

'Yes.'

'Did you ever see a Shāh approach a Shāh?'

'No.'

'Then what induced you to surrender yourself to one who is stronger than yourself?'

Thereupon Maḥmūd exiled him to Khurāsān.[46]

[43] Quoted from Quatremère's *Hist. des Sultans Mamelouks*, Paris, 1837–45, by S. Lane Poole in his *Hist. Egypt in the Middle Ages*, London, 1901, p. 147. For al-Ḥākim see the same work, p. 126, and v. d. Linde, i. 29.

[44] The translation is taken from Browne's *Lit. Hist. Persia*, London, 1902, 471.

[45] Browne, *Lit. Hist. Persia*, London, 1906, ii. 160.

[46] A verse from Sa'dī's *Gulistān* (1258) must be quoted, since the blundering mistranslation of Olearius (*Persianisches Rosenthal*, Hamburg, 1660, 247) has led to error in the past (cf. v. d. Linde, i. 114 n.; *Qst.*, 262; and *Handbuch*, 1874, 24). The verse really says, 'Marvellous! the ivory Foot-soldier who has traversed the squares of the chessboard becomes a Firzān, but the pilgrim who has crossed deserts in his pilgrimage on foot is worse off at the end.' Olearius made of this, 'I am surprised that the ivory Elephant at chess can so traverse the board that he betters himself, and can gain the rank of the Queen'; to which he adds the explanation that when the Queen has been lost, an Elephant that takes five of the principal pieces is promoted to the rank of Queen. It is difficult to imagine whence Olearius got this idea. Amelung's suggestion that it is drawn from draughts, which v. d. Linde (*Qst.*, 262) found satisfactory, seems to me to be no explanation at all, since it does not account for the mention of the number five.

References to chess in Muhammadan Spain have, perhaps, a greater interest for us. I have already mentioned a chess poem by the Spanish poet ar-Ramādī as being quoted in the MS. H. There are one or two references belonging to the eleventh century. B. Hayyān (D. 469/1075), one of the best historians of Spain, records that the vizier Abū Jaʿfar Aḥmad b. al-ʿAbbās of Almeria (D. 1038) was a keen chess-player. B. Ammār is said by al-Marrākoshī (writing 621/1224) to have played chess with the Christian King Alfonso VI of Castile, *c.* 1078. The poet b. al-Labbān ad-Dānī (*c.* 485/1092) wrote:

In the hand of fate we resemble the chess, and the *shāh* is often defeated by the *baidaq*.

There is a reference to chess in al-Maqqarī's (D. 1041/1632) *Nafḥ aṭ-ṭīb* (ed. Dozy, &c., Leyden, 1855–61, i. 480) in connexion with the biography of the qāḍī Abū-Bakr b. al-ʿArabī (D. 543/1148); and b. Abī Uṣaibiʿa (D. 668/1270) in his *K. ʿuyūn al anbā'*, in his biography of b. Zuhr al-Ḥafīd of Seville (D. 596/1200), of Jewish descent, describes him as a good chess-player, who used to spend many an hour at chess with a friend of the tribe of al-Yanaqī.[47]

Towards the end of MS. H (f. 51 a) we have a note from Abū'l-ʿAbbās b. Juraij (B. 533/1139, D. 630/1232) that gives some information as to the chief players of his day in Spain. It will be seen that the blindfold game had many exponents.

Abū'l-ʿAbbās b. Juraij said: I was contemporary with aṣ-Ṣaqālī (*the Sicilian*), al-Yahūdī (*the Jew*), and b. an-Nuʿmān, all of whom played blindfold: he goes on to say that Abū-Bakr b. Zuhair was equal to b. an-Nuʿmān. He says that Abū-Bakr b. Zuhair told him as follows: 'There were assembled at one time in my house in Seville the following experts, aṣ-Ṣaqālī, his father, as-Sijilmāsī, aṭ-Ṭarābulusī, b. an-Nuʿmān, and az-Zaʿfarān.' Abū'l-ʿAbbās said: now in our time Muḥammad al-Ghamārī (?), Abū'l-Ḥusain b. ash-Shāṭibī, b. ʿUlāhim al-Mukānisī, and Abū Muḥammad ʿAbdalkarīm, an eminent man of Fez, formed one class, and b. Abī Jaʿfar al-Mursī (*the Murcian*), b. al-Qaiṭūn, and b. Ayyūb and b. Abī'ẓ-Ẓafar b. Mardanīsh (?) formed another.

We have an interesting collection of players here from Sicily, Fez, Sijilmāsa, Tripoli, Murcia, and Seville. It evidences the spread of the game of chess in Muhammadan lands.

Both Fouché of Chartres[48] and William of Malmesbury,[49] in their accounts of the siege of Antioch (1097–8) during the First Crusade, tell how Peter the Hermit found the Turkish general Karbuga at chess when he was sent to treat with him at a critical point of the siege.

[47] Quoted in Pascal de Gayangos' *Hist. Moh. Dynasties in Spain by al-Makkari*, London, 1840–3, i. App.

Some modern writers (e. g. J. Mason, *Social Chess*, London, 1900, p. 7) have asserted that the immense library of Ḥākim II of Cordova (961–76) contained Arabic MSS. on chess. This is quite possible, but there is no evidence that it actually was so. The statement has apparently arisen from a misrendering of a sentence in v. d. Linde (i. 136): 'If therefore original Arabic chess MSS. did actually exist in Ḥākim's time, his library would have certainly been the cause of their introduction into Spain.' In 1874, v. d. Linde did not believe in the existence of Arabic MSS. of the tenth century.

[48] In *Gesta Peregr. Francorum*, c. xiv:—'Quod statim Corbagath intimauit (Amirdalis): Quid scaccis ludis? En Franci ueniunt.'

[49] Rolls Ed., ii. 419. 'Non erat Corbaguath eius facilitatis ut legatum dignaretur responso; sed scacchis ludens et dentibus infrendens inanem dimisit: hoc tantum dicto iam conclamatam esse Francorum superbiam.'

Aṣ-Ṣafadī (D. 764/1363), in his *Sharḥ Lāmīyat al-ʿAjam*, to which I have already referred, gives some interesting particulars as to chess in his day.

I once saw a soldier named ʿAlā'addīn in Egypt who was blind, and yet he used to play chess with the nobles and to beat them utterly. I say moreover that nothing pleased me more than the way in which he sat with us and talked and recited poetry, and narrated strange histories, showing that he was taking part in what we were doing. He would withdraw, and when he returned he had forgotten nothing that he had been doing. This is certainly surprising. The man was very famous in Cairo, and there were very few chess-players who did not know him.

At another time, in 731/1331, I saw in Damascus a man named an-Niẓām al-ʿAjamī, who played chess blindfold before Shamsaddīn. The first time that I saw him playing chess, he was playing with the shaikh Amīnaddīn Sulaimān, chief of the physicians, and he defeated him blindfold. We indeed knew nothing until he gave him checkmate with a Fīl, and we did not see that it was mate until he turned to us and said, 'It is checkmate.' I have also been told that he sometimes played two games at once blindfold. The sahib al-Maula Badraddīn Ḥasan b. ʿAlī al-Ghazzī told me that he had seen him play two games blindfold and one over the board at the same time, winning all three. He also vouches for this: Shamsaddīn once called to him in the middle of a game, 'Enumerate your pieces (*qiṭʿa*), and your opponent's,' and he rehearsed them in order at once, just as if he saw them before him.[50]

Chess again appears under royal patronage at the court of the great Moghul emperor Tīmūr (B. 1336, D. 1405). His historian b. ʿArabshāh (D. 854/1450) makes several references to chess in his *ʿAjā'ib al-maqdūr fī nawā'ib Tīmūr*.[51]

Tīmūr ordered a city to be built on the farther bank of the Jaxartes, with a bridge of boats across the river, and he called it *Shāhrukhīya*.[52] It was built in a spacious position. The reason why he gave this name of *Shāh Rukh*[53] to his son, and also to this city was as follows. He had already given orders for the building of this city on the river's bank, and he was engaged in playing chess with one of his courtiers as was his wont: one of his concubines was also with child. He had just given *shāh-rukh* (check-rook) by which his adversary was crippled and weakened, and while his adversary was in this helpless position, two messengers arrived. One announced the birth of a son, and the other the completion of the city, and therefore he called both by this name[54] (i. 218).

Tīmūr was devoted to the game of chess because he whetted his intellect by it, but his mind was too exalted to play at the small chess (*ash-shaṭranj aṣ-ṣaghīr*), and therefore he only played at the great chess (*ash-shaṭranj al-kabīr*), of which the

[50] These anecdotes are quoted by b. Sukaikir, and thence by Hyde, ii. 10.

[51] I have used S. H. Manger's ed., *Ahmedis Arabsiadis Vitae et rerum gestarum Timuri historia*. Leovardiae, 1767–72. There is a metaphorical use of *baidaq ash-shāh* (King's Pawn) on i. 48.

[52] The only city of this name that Lestrange (*Lands of the Eastern Caliphate*, Cambridge, 1905, p. 482) mentions, stood on the site of the older Banākath, just below the junction of the Sir Daria (Jaxartes) and the Angran. Banākath (Banākit, Per. Fanākant) had been the second largest town of the Shāsh district. 'The town stood on the right bank of the Jaxartes where the Khurāsān road coming up from Samarkand crossed the river going to Shāsh, and it continued to be a place of great importance till the 7th (13th) century, when it was laid in ruins by Changīz Khan. More than a century later, in 818 (1415), Fanākant was rebuilt by order of Shāh Rukh, the grandson of Tīmūr, and then received the name of Shāhrukhīyah, under which it is frequently mentioned by ʿAlī of Yazd.' I think that this must be the town meant by b. ʿArabshāh, despite the discrepancy in the explanation of its name.

[53] Several of the Moghul Princes bore this name in consequence of this example.

[54] Forbes gives Shāh Rukh's birthday as Aug. 20, 1377. The Greek historian, Ducas, gives quite a different account of the origin of Shāh Rukh's name. He says :

'Tīmūr and his son were playing chess at the moment when Bāyazīd was brought captive into their tent. The son gave the check *shāh rukh* to his father at that instant, and Tīmūr ever after gave the former that name.' (Cf. p. 167.)

board is 10 squares by 11, and there are 2 *jamals*, 2 *zurafas*, 2 *ṭali'as*, 2 *dabbābas*, a *wazīr*, &c. A diagram of it is attached. The small chess is a mere nothing in comparison with the great chess [55] (ii. 798).

Among chess-players (in Tīmūr's reign) were Muḥammad b. 'Aqīl al-Khaimī and Zain al-Yazdī, &c., but the most skilled at that game was 'Alā'addīn at-Tabrīzī, the lawyer and traditionist, who used to give Zain al-Yazdī the odds of a Baidaq and beat him, and b. 'Aqīl the odds of a Faras and beat him. Tīmūr himself, who subdued all the regions of the East and the West and had given mate to every sultan and king, both on the battle-field and in the game, used to say to him, 'You have no rival in the kingdom of chess, just as I have none in government; there is no one to be found who can perform such wonders as I and you, my lord 'Alī, each in his own sphere.' He has composed a treatise on the game of chess and its situations. There was no one who could divine his intention in the game before he moved. He was a Shāfi'ite. . . . He told me that he had once seen in a dream 'Alī, the Commander of the Faithful, and had received from him a set of chess in a bag, and no mortal had beaten him since then.[56] It was noteworthy about his play that he never spent time in thought but the instant his opponent made his move after long and tedious thought, 'Alī played without delay or reflection. He often played blindfold against two opponents, and showed by his play what his strength would have been over the board. With the Amir (Tīmūr) he used to play at the great chess. I have seen at his house the round chess (*shaṭranj muddawara*) and the oblong chess (*shaṭranj ṭawīla*). The great chess has in it the additional pieces that I have already mentioned. Its rules are best learnt by practice; a description would not have much value (ii. 872).

We have sundry references to this great master under the name of Khwāja 'Alī Shaṭranjī in Persian literature,[57] while the MS. RAS gives no less than 21 positions from his games. When this circumstance is considered in connexion with the preface to this work, it certainly lends colour to the view that the MS. is the work which b. 'Arabshāh tells us 'Alī himself wrote. The passage runs—

I have passed my life since the age of 15 years among all the masters of chess living in my time; and since that period till now, when I have arrived at middle age, I have travelled through 'Irāq-'Arabī, and 'Irāq-'ajamī, and Khurāsān, and the regions of Māwarā'n-nahr (Transoxiana), and I have there met with many a master in this art, and I have played with all of them, and through the favour of him who is Adorable and Most High I have come off victorious.

Likewise, in playing blindfold, I have overcome most opponents, nor had they the power to cope with me. I have frequently played with one opponent over the board, and at the same time I have carried on four different games with as many adversaries without seeing the board, whilst I conversed freely with my friends all along, and through the Divine favour I conquered them all. Also in the great chess I have invented sundry positions, as well as several openings, which no one else ever imagined or contrived.

[55] Descriptions of this and the other modifications of chess mentioned will be found below, Ch. XVI.

[56] 'Alī Shaṭranjī was not the only dreamer. AH and Y tell of a man (in AH, Abū'l-Mulaiḥ; in Y, Sharr b. Sā'd) who had a son who was passionately fond of chess. The father forbade him, but in vain. Then the father dreamt that he met the Prophet of God himself and complained to him, 'O Prophet of God! I have a son who is passionately addicted to chess, and I have forbidden it, and he will not cease playing.' Muḥammad replied: 'There is no harm in it.'

For references to chess in Oriental works on the interpretation of dreams, see Bland, 38.

[57] Awhadī wrote his life. Bland, 42, quotes a highly figurative passage from this biography. 'When he moved his Rook (face) in the arena (board) of imagination, he gave the odds of two *faras* and *fīl* to the *Shāhs* of rhetoric; the problem-players (*manṣūbah-bāz*) of fancy fell mated in the *fīl-band* of confusion from his *piyāda*.'

There are a great number of ingenious positions that have occurred to me in the course of my experience, in the common game, as practised at the present day; and many positions given as won by the older masters I have either proved to be drawn, or I have corrected them so that they now stand for what they were intended to be. I have also improved and rendered more complete all the rare and cunning stratagems hitherto recorded or invented by the first masters of chess. In short, I have here laid before the reader all that I have myself discovered from experience as well as whatever I found to be rare and excellent in the labours of my predecessors.

Chess remained one of the favourite recreations at the courts of Tīmūr's descendants, and the *Baber Autobiography* (tr. Leyden and Erskine, London and Edinburgh, 1826, pp. 187–195), names several courtiers at the court of Ḥusain Mirza, King of Khurāsān (D. 1506), as inveterate chess-players. Among these were Zūlnūn Arghūn, Ḥassan ʿAlī Jelāir, Mīr Murtāz, and the poet Bināi of Heri.

My last authority for the unreformed Muhammadan chess is b. Sukaikir, the author of one of the MSS. which I have described in Chapter X. By birth a Damascene, he travelled through Syria, and visited Constantinople before filling the post of Preacher of the Mosque al-ʿĀdilīya at Ḥalab (Aleppo), where he died 987/1579. In his chess work he mentions some experiences of his own. In 964 or 5/*c.* 1557 he saw a blind player at Damascus, who had played in the presence of the Sultan Sulaimān in Stambul. During the game the Sultan removed one of his men. The blind man quickly detected the fact, remarking that if the Sultan had done it there was nothing to be done but to play his best, but if any one else had done it he would appeal to the Sultan. In 967–8/1559 one of the best players in Damascus was a certain az-Zain al-Mathakaʿa. Once when he was on the point of mating an Egyptian, to whom he had given the odds of the *firzān*, a ragged Persian who was watching the game interposed and showed the Egyptian the move to thwart the attack. Az-Zain was naturally angry, and his anger was not appeased by the Persian telling him not to lose his temper because he did not know how to play. However, he agreed to play the beggar, who began by deliberately sacrificing *faras*, *fīl*, and three *baidaqs* without any equivalent. Then he asked az-Zain to name the piece with which he would choose to be mated. Az-Zain chose a *baidaq*, and the Persian gave him mate with a *baidaq*. Az-Zain, recognizing the Persian's skill, took him into his service. The Persian would never play except at the odds of the 'marked piece'. In 970/1562 he saw a Greek, Yūsuf Chelebī, at Trablis (Tripoli in Syria). This man used men of a larger pattern, and played blindfolded by touch. Finally he saw a blindfold player in Constantinople in 975/1567, who played often in his presence with uniform success. Like an-Niẓām al-ʿAjamī, he could at any time describe the position of every man on the board. The MS. Y narrates that there have been players who could play four or five games simultaneously blindfold, and goes on to say:

I have seen it written in a book, that a certain person played in this manner at ten boards at once, and gained all the games, and even corrected his adversaries when a mistake was made (Bland, 24).

CHAPTER XII

THE INVENTION OF CHESS IN MUSLIM LEGEND.

A variety of stories.—The oldest versions associated with India.—The connexion with nard.—The earlier legends from the chess MSS., al-Yaʿqūbī, al-Masʿūdī and Firdawsī.—The dramatis personae.—The story of the reward for the invention.—The Geometrical progression in literature.—Later stories introducing Adam, the sons of Noah, &c., and Aristotle.

THE main facts of the earlier history of chess were well recognized by the older Muslim historians and chess-writers. They admit without reservation that the ordinary chess on the board of 64 squares was originally an Indian game which had reached them through the medium of Persia. But they were not content to leave the history in so bare a dress, and they endeavoured to take it farther back, to find a motive for the invention of the game, and to explain the manner of its discovery. Only in all this they had no historical foundations upon which to build other than the obvious relationship in arrangement, plan, and nomenclature that existed between the game of chess and the army and the tactics of war. This left an excellent opportunity for the literary artist, and he did not hesitate to adorn the story with details derived from his own imagination. Thus there appeared in quite early Muslim times a number of stories, more or less plausible, to account for the invention of chess, and the compilers of works on chess, from al-ʿAdlī down, were diligent in collecting these from the sources at their service. Even writers of repute like al-Yaʿqūbī (*c.* 297/907) and al-Masʿūdī found a place for them in the pages of their historical works, while Firdawsī gave literary shape to one of the most widely known in the *Shāhnāma*. We find single legends repeatedly also in MSS. of miscellaneous contents in Arabic, Persian, and Turkish.

When we survey the material[1] at our disposal we find that the legends fall into three groups: those which are connected with India, those which associate the game with characters drawn from Scripture history, and those which bring in noted names from Greek philosophy. These two last groups are of later date, and have none of the detail that accompanies the stories of the first group, and it is not difficult to see a motive for the departure from the earlier association with India.

The legends of the earlier group are all, openly or tacitly, concerned with an Indian king or with the wise men of India. The connexion, however, is

[1] Viz. in AH, C, and V, 3 legends which go back ultimately to al-ʿAdlī's work; in BM, 1; in H, 8; in Man., 5; in RAS, 3; in Al, 1; in S, 4; in Y, 3; in al-Yaʿqūbī, 2; in al-Masʿūdī, 1; in b. Khallikān, 2; in the *Shāhnāma*, 1; and some 7 or 8 in isolated MSS. mentioned in Ch. X.

quite general, in that a special kingdom or district of India is seldom specified. The earlier Muslim writers appear to have formed their conception of a country on the model of the Eastern Roman Empire, or of the Sāsānian Empire which their forefathers had overturned.[2] India was to them a single kingdom, and it was long before they discovered that India was a geographical, not a political entity. Only a few of the legends give names to the king or sage of whom they treat, and still fewer attempt to fix the date at which the events they are recording took place. The ordinary story is quite indeterminate as to locality, *dramatis personae*, and date.

Several legends, however, connect the invention of chess in some way or other with the game of *nard* (*tables*, *backgammon*). We have already met with one instance of this association of games in the story of the introduction of chess into Persia in the time of Nūshīrwān. This linking of two games that to us seem so dissimilar—chess, a game in which chance plays the smallest of parts, and nard, a game in which chance plays the dominant part—appears somewhat singular, yet no association of games has been so persistent or has endured so long. It was not only prominent in Muslim lands, where it runs all through the legal discussion, the literature, and the traditions, but even in Christian Europe chess and tables appear in constant juxtaposition. The player of chess appears almost everywhere in the literature of the Middle Ages as a player of tables also, and the larger European problem MSS. treat of chess, tables, and merels. In these collections, however, the essential distinction between chess and tables is minimized, since in most of the problems on tables the constraint of the dice has been replaced by the liberty to select the throw desired, but this is, so far as the evidence goes, a purely European innovation. In Muslim literature it is upon the essential difference between chess as the game of skill and nard as the game of chance that stress is everywhere laid. The player's complete liberty to select the move he wished to make in chess is contrasted with the player's subjugation to the dominion of blind chance in nard. Throughout the legends with which I am about to deal, nard appears as the older and chess as the younger game; this is the reverse of what we find in the Nūshīrwān story as told in the *Chatrang-nāmak* and in the *Shāhnāma*. There, it will be remembered, the invention of nard is Buzūrjmihr's reply to the Indian challenge to discover the nature of chess.

One of the older legends which occurs in AH (f. 1 b), C (f. 1 b), and V (f. 2 a), with the omission of all proper names, as an extract from the work of al-ʿAdlī, and in almost identical words, with the addition of the proper names, in the *Ta'rīkh* of al-Yaʿqūbī (ed. Houtsma, Lugd. Bat., 1883, i. 99–102), brings the two games together. In this legend, an Indian monarch named Hashrān

[2] Cf. AH, f. 24 b :—'The noblest of the kings is the king of horsemen who is the King of Babylon, called *Shāhānshāh* (King of kings) next comes the king of elephants who is the King of India; next the King of China who is the king of infantry. But this is not the view taken by the author of the *Ā'īn*, who says "there are only four Kings" and omits the King of India, because the Indians are governed by provincial rulers whom he does not number among the kings. When he says "there are four kings" he means the Kings of Babylon, the Turks, Byzantium, and China.'

is represented as appealing to an Indian sage, Qaflān by name, to devise a game that should symbolize man's dependence upon destiny and fate, and depict the way in which these forces work by means of man's environment. The philosopher accordingly invented the game of nard, and explained to the king that the board stood for the year. It had 24 points ('houses') in all, because there are 24 hours to the day. It was arranged in two halves, each with 12 points to symbolize the 12 months of the year, or the 12 signs of the Zodiac. The number of men ('dogs') was 30, because there are 30 days to the month. The two dice[3] stood for day and night. The faces were arranged with the 6 opposite to the 1, the 5 opposite to the 2, and the 4 opposite to the 3, so that the total of the dots on each pair of opposite faces should be 7, to bring in the number of days of the week and the 7 luminaries of the heavens.[4] The players threw one of the dice in order to determine the order of play, and the one who secured the higher throw commenced, and moved his men in obedience to the throws given by the two dice. In this way man's dependence upon fate for good or evil fortune was made evident. Hashrān was delighted with the game and introduced it in India, where it became extremely popular.

At a later date there arose a king, Balhait by name, who was advised by a Brahman that this game was contrary to the precepts of his religion. The king accordingly planned to replace nard by a new game, that should demonstrate the value of such qualities as prudence, diligence, thrift, and knowledge, and in this way oppose the fatalist teaching of nard. His Brahman friend undertook the task, and invented chess, explaining its name of *shaṭranj* by the Persian *hashat-ranj*, in which *hashat* means eight and *ranj* means side.[5] The board was 8 by 8 squares, and there were 16 men (*kalba*, = dogs) on either side, viz. *shāh*, *firz*, 2 *fīls*, 2 *faras*, 2 *rukhs*, and 8 *pawns*. It was made on the model of war, because war is the most effective school for teaching the value of administration, decision, prudence, caution, arrangement, strategy, circumspection, vigour, courage, force, endurance, and bravery. Balhait was charmed with the game, and did his best to induce his subjects to adopt it in the place of nard.

Al-Maṣʿūdī's version of the story is very similar, but there is some variation in the characters of the story. He does not, however, give it as one story, but places the two incidents in what he considered to be their proper chronology. Thus in ch. vii of his *Murūj adh-dhahab* (ed. cit., i. 157), under the reign of al-Bāhbūd, the eldest son of al-Barahman, we read:

It was at this time that nard and its rules were invented. It is symbolical of property, which is not the reward of intelligence or strength in this world, just

[3] Most of the mediaeval European games on the backgammon board required three dice. Apparently from an impromptu quatrain of the Persian poet Azraqī (end of 12th c.; see Browne, *Lit. Hist. Persia*, ii. 39), two dice only were used in the Muhammadan game.

[4] By which are meant the components of the Solar System, as then understood: the Sun and Moon, and the planets Saturn, Jupiter, Mars, Mercury, and Venus.

[5] This shows that neither al-ʿAdlī nor al-Yaʿqūbī knew of the earlier Per. form *chatrang*, nor the Skr. *chaturanga*. It is amusing to see the Brahman represented as going to Persian for a name for his game.

as possessions are not gained by scheming. Others say that Ardashīr b. Bābak discovered and invented this game, which was suggested to him by the contemplation of the changes and caprices of fortune. He made its points 12 after the number of the months, and the men ('dogs') 30, after the number of days in the month. The two dice represent fate and its capricious dealings with men. The player, when the chances are favourable, secures what he wants; but the ready and prudent man cannot succeed in gaining what a happy chance has given to the other. Thus it is that property is due in this world to a fortunate chance.

A little later in the same chapter (ed. cit., i. 159) we read:

The next king (to Dabshalim) was Balhait. At this time chess was invented, which the king preferred to nard, because in this game skill always succeeds against ignorance. He made mathematical calculations on chess, and wrote a book on it called *Taraq jankā*,[6] which has continued popular among the Indians. He often played chess with the wise men of his court, and it was he who represented the pieces by the figures of men and animals, and assigned them grades and ranks. He likened the *Shāh* to the chief ruler, and similarly with the rest of the pieces. He also made of this game a kind of allegory of the heavenly bodies (the 7 planets and the 12 zodiacal signs), and dedicated each piece to a star. The game of chess became a school of government and defence; it was consulted in time of war, when military tactics were about to be employed, to study the more or less rapid movements of troops. The Indians ascribe a mysterious interpretation to the doubling of the squares of the chessboard; they establish a connexion between the First Cause which soars above the spheres and on which everything depends, and the sum of the square of its squares. This number equals 18,446,744,073,709,551,615 . . . The Indians explain by these calculations the march of time and of the ages, the higher influences which govern the world, and the bonds which link them to the human soul. The Greeks (*al-Yūnānīyan*), the Byzantines (*ar-Rūm*), &c. have special theories and methods about this game, as we may see in the works of the chess-players from the most ancient down to aṣ-Ṣūlī and al-ʿAdlī, the two most famous players of our time. Balhait reigned until his death, for 84 or, as other authorities say, 300 years. [His successor was Qūrush.]

The same legend, but told more baldly and with omission of names, occurs in Man., f. 16 b. The root idea of the story is seen in the witty remark which al-Masʿūdī quotes on a later stage of the same book (ed. cit., viii. 320), at the close of some additional remarks on nard.

Lastly, a Muslim philosopher has maintained that the inventor of chess was a muʿtazilite believer in the freedom of the will, while the inventor of nard was a fatalist who wished to show by this game that man can do nothing against fate, and that the true wisdom is to mould one's life in agreement with the decrees of chance.

It is assumed in this legend that nard was a game of Indian invention, and in so far the story is opposed to the other tradition, that nard was the invention of Artakhshīr the son of Bābakān, the first of the Sāsānian kings of Persia (A. D. 226–40), which is quoted at length in BM f. 5 b, in H f. 4 b, and in Man. f. 16 a. The attempt was made by later writers to bring the two legends into harmony by introducing modifications into the chess story. The motive for the discovery of chess is no longer the moral improvement of the

[6] The suggestion that this name is really a corruption of the Skr. *chaturanga* was made so long ago as 1838 by Gildemeister in his *Scriptorum Arabum de Rebus Indicis*, Bonn, 1838, p. 142. The reading *Torok hanká taïdá* which occurs in Sprenger's *El Masʿúdí's 'Meadows of Gold'*, London, 1841, p. 171, is due to a misreading of the Arabic.

Indian nard-players, but becomes the humiliation of the Persians. King Balhait is represented as being so aggrieved at the boastings of the Persians because of their discovery of nard, that he called upon a philosopher of his court, Ṣaṣṣa b. Dāhir, to invent a game that should transcend nard. The game of chess was Ṣaṣṣa's reply. We find this in the chess MSS. H (f. 5 a), and Man. (f. 16 a)—in the latter from b. Taimīya (D. 728/1328).

It is this story which is included in the life of aṣ-Ṣūlī the chess-player in the *K. wafayāt al-aʿyān* of b. Khallikān (D. 681/1282),[7] whence it was taken by aṣ-Ṣafadī (D. 764/1363) in his *Sharḥ Lāmīyat al-ʿAjam*, and by b. Sukaikir (S f. 25 a).

I have met many people who thought that aṣ-Ṣūlī was the inventor of chess. This is a mistake, for chess was invented by Ṣiṣṣa b. Dāhir for King Shihrām. Ardashīr b. Bābak, the founder of the last Persian dynasty, discovered nard, which was hence named *nardashīr*. Balhait was King of India at that time, and Ṣiṣṣa invented chess for him. The wise men of that time held it to be more excellent than nard. It is said that when Ṣiṣṣa had invented chess and produced it to King Shihrām, the latter was filled with amazement and joy. He ordered that it should be preserved in the temples, and held it the best thing that he knew as a training in the art of war, a glory to religion and the world, and the foundation of all justice. He expressed his joyful thanks for the favour which heaven had granted to his reign through such a discovery, and said to Ṣiṣṣa, 'Ask whatever you desire,' &c.

There is an obvious contradiction in this allusion, and both of the later writers endeavoured to remove it. Aṣ-Ṣafadī omits all mention of Shihrām, and names the Indian monarch Balhait throughout. B. Sukaikir, on the contrary, calls the monarch Shihrām and expressly describes him as an Indian king. He adds the note: 'Some say that it was invented for Balhith, e. g. al-Yāfiʿī.'[8]

The analogy existing between chess and war is the motive for four legends which are peculiar to the chess books. In one of these (BM f. 4 a, H f. 6 a, and RAS) the game is invented to find a distraction for a king who was passionately fond of war, but who had overcome all his enemies and was falling ill from ennui at not being able to pursue his favourite occupation. A philosopher produced for him chess, and showed him how he could still conduct forces and devise tactics in this game. The king tried the game, ascertained that the philosopher had spoken truly, and found distraction and health in playing chess. All the MSS. place the scene in India, H has no names for the characters of the story, BM calls the philosopher Ṣuṣa b. Dāhir, while RAS names the king Kaid, and the philosopher Ṣaṣṣa, placing the event shortly after the invasion of Alexander the Great. In this particular version, however, Ṣaṣṣa merely abridges the 'Complete Chess'[9] by reducing the size of the board from 11 by 11 to 8 by 8 squares, and the number of pieces from 56 to 32, because the Indians were incapable of appreciating so com-

[7] Cf. M. G. de Slane's English edition of the *Lives*, London, 1843–71, iii. 71. The Arabic text is partially given by Hyde, ii. 58.

[8] See the Arabic texts in Hyde, ii. 60 and 61.

[9] For a description of this game, see Ch. XVI. The story in RAS is given *in extenso* by Forbes, 60 seq.

plicated a game. The complete chess itself was the invention of a Greek sage, Hermes, and had been introduced into India by Alexander and his soldiers.

In the second of these (AH f. 3 a, C f. 4 a, V f. 5 a, from al-ʿAdlī's work, and in RAS) the game is invented to assist in the military education of a young prince who pleaded that he was incompetent to lead his armies in war owing to his want of experience. The game of chess is alleged to have given the necessary training in tactics to convert him into an efficient commander. In both manuscript accounts the scene is laid in India, but RAS alone attempts to determine the characters of the story. These are stated to have been the young son and successor of Fūr (Pauras, the opponent of Alexander) and his vizier Ṣaṣṣa b. Dāhir. RAS again substitutes the abridgement of a Greek game for the invention of a new one.

The third story again represents chess as invented for the purpose of affording an opportunity for the practice of military tactics, and only differs from the previous legend in the matter of the particular circumstance of the invention. This story occurs in AH f. 3 b (C f. 4 b, V f. 5 b, H f. 6 a, Man. f. 15 b, Y and S) as one of the three versions occurring in al-ʿAdlī's book. Its special interest consists in the fact that the game is represented as invented for a certain king[10] named Shahrām [11] by the Indian sage Ṣaṣṣa b. Dāhir, who gave the game to the king 'with the 14 taʿbīyāt which are depicted in this book'.[12] The story of the reward is attached in AH to this story. B. Khallikān, at the end of his biography of aṣ-Ṣūlī the chess-player, interpolates a reference to this story when he mentions Shihrām as the monarch for whom Ṣiṣṣa b. Dāhar invented chess.

The fourth story is told in Man. f. 15 a, on the authority of b. Makhsharī. It is to the effect that a certain King of India, who was peaceably inclined, procured the invention of chess in order that his fellow-monarchs might settle their disputes over the board without effusion of blood.

I have left to the last what is probably the oldest of all the legends on the subject, dating back to pre-Muhammadan days. I have already called attention to the allusion to it in the tradition connecting the caliph ʿOmar b. al-Khaṭṭāb with chess, which I believe to be a genuine tradition. The legend is neither in al-ʿAdlī (AH) nor in al-Maṣʿūdī, but al-Yaʿqūbī has a version of it which is interesting because of some of the details (ed. cit., i. 102–5).

It is related by some of the wise men of India that when Ḥūsīya, the daughter of Balhait, was Queen, a rebel rose against her. Now she was a prophetess with four children, and she invested her son. And the rebel slew her son. Now the men of her kingdom honoured him, and they guarded against her learning it.

[10] His kingdom is not definitely stated in these MSS., but b. Sukaikir speaks of him as an Indian king. I think it clear that the MSS. intended to lay the scene in India, because the sage is Indian, while Al-ʿAdlī elsewhere (quoted in AH f. 24 a, and H f. 19 a) states that the ordinary chess is ascribed or attributed to India.

[11] So V. The text in AH and C is corrupt at this point, but there is no doubt that this name occurs in the corrupt sentence.

[12] This sentence occurs in AH and the allied MSS. C and V, and also in Man. f. 15 b. It is appropriate to none of these works, and can only mean that al-ʿAdlī gave 14 taʿbīyāt in his work, and pretended that they were as old as chess.

So they went to the philosopher Qaflān who was possessed of knowledge, wisdom, and prudence, and told him of it. He asked for three days and they granted it. He spent the time in thought. Then he called his disciple, 'Summon a carpenter with wood of two colours, white and black.' Then he devised the chessmen and ordered the carpenter to carve them. Next he called to him, 'Bring me tanned leather.' He ordered him to mark 64 squares on it, and he did so. Then he arranged a side, and studied it until he understood and had learnt it. Then he said to his disciple, 'This is war without bloodshed.' So he came to the men of the kingdom and produced it, and when they saw it they knew that no one exceeded him in wisdom. He made his disciple fight, and there befell *shāh māt*, and the Shāh was conquered. Now the Queen was interested in the news about Qaflān, and she visited him and bade him show her his invention. He called his disciple with the chess, and arranged it square by square. They played, and the winner said *shāh māt*. And she remembered and knew what he wished her to know, and she said to Qaflān, 'My son is dead.' He said, 'You have said it.' Then she said to the doorkeeper, 'Let the people enter to comfort me.' And when she had made an end, she summoned Qaflān and said to him, 'Ask what you will.' He said, 'Give me a gift in grains of corn upon the squares of the chessboard. On the first square one grain (on the second two), on the third square double of that on the second, and continue in the same way until the last square.' She said, 'How much is this?' and she ordered the corn to be brought. So they went on until she had exhausted the corn in the country. Then he estimated its value in money, and received that. And when this went on for a long time, he said, 'I have no need of it: a small portion of worldly goods suffices me.' Then she asked him about the number of grains that he had demanded.

Whereupon follows the total of the Geometrical Progression, which I give below.

There is a brief allusion to this story in H f. 6 a, but it is best known through its inclusion in the *Shāhnāma* (ii. 2889–3431; in Mohl's edition, Paris, 1868, vi. 400–444),[13] where Firdawsī names as his immediate authority a certain Shāhūī. As Nöldeke has pointed out,[14] this is probably a misreading of the name Māhūī, Māhūī Chorsēdh, the son of Bahram of Shāpūr, being one of the four Zoroastrian priests to whom Abū Manṣūr al-Maʿmarī entrusted the work of arranging the national annals of Persia in A. D. 957–8. The section now bears the title of 'The history of Gau and Talkhand, with the invention of chess'. The titles of the various sections do not, however, go back to Firdawsī.

The story treats of some incidents in the history of a kingdom in North-West India, which comprised Kashmīr and all the land to the confines of China, with Ṣandalī for capital. A king of this realm, Jamhūr, who excelled Fūr (Pauras) in fame, had died, leaving a widow and an infant son, Gau. He was succeeded by his brother, Mai, who married the widow and, after a short reign, died, leaving an infant son, Talkhand, who was five years younger than his half-brother. During the minority the widow held the regency, the question of the ultimate succession being left in abeyance. Each of the princes considered that his claim was the stronger, and their mother

[13] Whence the brief version in ath-Thaʿālibī's *Ghurar akhbār mulūk al-Furs* (ed. Zotenberg, Paris, 1900, p. 624).

[14] *Grundriss d. iran. Phil.*, ii. 144.

foolishly encouraged each in turn. As the boys grew up, the disputes became more bitter, and Talkhand adopted a most aggressive attitude. Gau, on the other hand, was as conciliatory as possible. Finally, however, Talkhand forced an appeal to the arbitrament of war. Gau gave the strictest instructions to his supporters that Talkhand's life was to be spared. In the first battle Gau was successful, but Talkhand managed to collect his scattered forces, and a second battle took place close to the sea-shore. At the close of the battle, Talkhand was separated from his army and surrounded by the forces of his opponent, but when these came up to him, he was found to be already dead. The tidings plunged his mother into the deepest sorrow, and in her grief she accused Gau of slaying his brother. Gau defended himself, but to no purpose, and finally he offered to destroy himself if he could not demonstrate clearly to her how Talkhand's death really happened. In order to compass this, Gau took counsel with his tutor, and by his advice convened all the wise men of the kingdom and laid the case before them. After a whole night's consideration,

These experienced men ordered ebony to be brought, and two strong men made from it a square board to represent the ditch, the field of battle, and the armies drawn up opposite one another. They marked on this board 100 squares on which the armies and the two kings were to move, and finally they made two armies of teak and ivory, and two kings with heads erect, majestic and crowned. The infantry and cavalry formed the ranks in the battle array. They carved the figures of horses, elephants, viziers, and brave men charging on horseback against the enemy, all just as they went to the battle, some leaping in their haste, others moving calmly.[15] Ready for battle, the *Shāh* (king) stood in the centre; on one side was the *Firzāna* (counsellor), his faithful companion. Next to the *Shāh* on both sides were two *Pīls* (elephants) who raised a dust, dark as indigo, about the throne. Two *Shuturs* (camels) were placed next to the *Pīls*, and two men of pure intention were mounted on them. Next to the *Shuturs* were two *Asps* (horses) with their riders, ready to fight on the day of battle. As warriors the two *Rukhs* at the two ends of the lines of battle raised their empty hands to the lips, as if to drink the foe's heart's blood. In front and rear moved the *Piyāda* (foot-soldiers), who were to come to the assistance of the others in the battle; if any pressed through to the other end of the field of battle, he was placed beside the *Shāh* like the *Firzāna*. The brave *Firzāna* never moved in the battle more than one square from his *Shāh*. The mighty *Pīl* ran through three squares, and observed the whole battle-field, two miles wide. The *Shutur* also ran through three squares, snorting and stamping on the field. The *Asp's* move also extended over three squares, in crossing which one of the squares remained untouched. To all sides ran the vindictive *Rukh*, and he crossed the whole field of battle. Each piece moved in its own area, and made neither less nor more than its appointed move.[16] If any one saw the *Shāh* in the battle, he cried aloud, 'Remove, O Shāh!' and the *Shāh* left his square until he was able to move no longer. The other *Shāh*, the *Asp*, *Rukh*, *Farzīn*, *Pīl*, and *Piyādas* had closed the road to him. When the Shāh had looked about him on all four sides, and with knit brows had seen his army overthrown, and his road barred by the water and the ditch, while the enemy were to left and right, before and behind, he died (was mate) of weariness and thirst.

[15] The text of the following lines, giving the position and moves, varies in different MSS. I have followed Pertsch's translation (v. d. Linde, i. 68-9); Hyde's text and translation (ii. 75-8) vary considerably.

[16] Hyde's text adds two lines here: 'When one man attacked another, each one watches to bring help to his comrade.'

Gau took this game of chess which thus explained the death of Talkhand to his mother. She continued to study it day and night without desiring food, until death released her from her sorrow. And from that time the chessboard has remained in the knowledge of mankind.

It is somewhat remarkable that in this legend Firdawsī has replaced the ordinary chess by a variety requiring an enlarged board, when no motive for the change can be discovered. As will be seen from the account of the derived forms of chess in Chapter XVI, he has not even adopted the standard variety on the 10 by 10 board of the chess books, but describes a form that is not mentioned elsewhere. The legend is repeated in RAS, as from the *Shāhnāma*, but the author of that MS. set out with the deliberate intention of enhancing the age and importance of another modification of chess, the Complete chess that was preferred by his sovereign the Mongol Tīmūr, and he has substituted for Firdawsī's account of the invention a new version which makes Ṣaṣṣa b. Dāhir abridge the Complete chess into a game on the 8 by 8 board. We have already seen that he has dealt similarly with two other older legends.

Gildemeister (cf. *Qst.*, 16) has expressed dissatisfaction with the ordinary texts of the *Shāhnāma* for this story. He points out that there is much variety of text in accessible MSS., and suggests that a scribal error first led to the appearance of the camel in one line which gives the names of the pieces, and that then later scribes restored the self-consistency of Firdawsī's description by altering the dimensions of the board from 8 by 8 to 10 by 10, and introducing the lines relating to the camel's position and move. It is much to be desired that a critical examination of the known MSS. could be made, but the immensity of the task of doing this for the *Shāhnāma* has probably deterred scholars from attempting it. The gain would not be worth the toil, except for points like the present, which do not touch the literary or historical value of the epic.

There is, however, at least one other work which makes the same substitution of the 10 by 10 board for the 8 by 8. This is the short history of ar-Ristāmī (840/1436–7), contained in MS. Gotha Arab. 1738 (old 1419). It mentions the introduction of chess into Persia thus (f. 3 a)—

> After the sage Barzūya had brought the *K. Kalīla wa Dimna* from India with the Complete chess (*ash-shaṭranj at-tamma*), which has 10 by 10 squares, he translated it from Indian into Persian.

To this, however, I attach no importance. I do not know what authorities this late writer followed.

Various attempts have been made to identify the characters whose names recur most frequently in these legends, on the assumption that the names are really Indian in origin. The task is, however, one of great, if not insuperable, difficulty. The history of India, as it appears in the pages of early Muslim writers, is as unreal as their knowledge of the condition of India in their own days. Foreign names were peculiarly liable to misrepresentation when they were put into an Arabic dress. Moreover we are not certain of the forms of the proper names in the legends.[17] The reader will have already noticed how I have used different vowels with different MSS. In the older Arabic MSS. the short vowels are unmarked, and when MSS. began to contain instructions as to the vocalization of the names, it was too late for them to have any historical authority behind, and the directions are based upon the analogy of native Arabic words. How unsafe a guide this analogy could be, we have already seen in the substitution of *shiṭranj* for *shaṭranj*. But there are other elements of uncertainty and error that are more serious still. The accuracy of the consonants in Arabic depends upon the close and accurate copying of the diacritical marks which distinguish many of the letters. Errors were always possible, but they are most dangerous in the case of foreign words, where detection is most difficult. If, again, the word has been derived from Pahlawī MSS., as is not impossible in the case of some of these legends, there is the additional possibility of error due to the deficiencies of the Pahlawī script. Nöldeke[18] sees nothing impossible in tracing Shihrām or Shahrām, al-Ya'qūbī's Hashrān, the Dabshalīm of the Kalīla wa Dimna, and the Dewasarm of the *Chatrang-nāmak* all back to one Pahlawī original. If this be so, how can we feel certain of anything?

Among other suggestions as to the identity of Shahrām are Hyde's (ii. 60), that the name is a scribal error for Baharam or Bahram, a name which occurs frequently among the Sāsānian kings, and also was used in India; and Pertsch's, that Shahrām = Shāh Rāma (v. d. Linde, ii. 441). Sir H. M. Elliott in his *History of India by its own historians* (i. 409–10) suggests that Shahrām was Shahr Irān or Shahriyār (i.e. Kobād Shīrūyah), one of the last of the Sāsānian kings of Persia, who ruled for a few months (A.D. 628–9) during the disturbed period that followed the death of Khusraw II Parwīz. He, however, assumed that b. Khallikān described Shihrām as a Persian king, which is not the case. In any case it is difficult to see why the least important of all the Sāsānians should have been selected to adorn the legend. I return to Elliott's argument below.

Balhait, Balhīt or Balhīth is the other Indian king who is frequently mentioned in the stories. Hyde (ii. 62) says that the form Balhīb also occurs. He suggested that these forms, which in the Arabic only differ in the diacritical dots to the last consonant, are intended to represent the Indian dynasty of the Balabhi or Balhara, who ruled in Guzerat from A.D. 319 to 613. This would make the name a title and not a personal name, and in this way he explains the apparent contradiction in the legend as given by b. Khallikān. This is ingenious, but not convincing, since other Arabic writers frequently use the correct form Balhara. It is, however, the only close resemblance that I can discover. Al-Maṣ'ūdī's succession of Indian kings—Barahman, 366 years; al-Bāhbūd, 100 years; Ramāh, 150 years; Fūr, 140 years (the Pauras or Porus of Alexander's time, B.C. 326); Dabshalim, 120 years; Balhīth, 80

[17] The ordinary forms now used are in the main due to b. Sukaikir (S f. 25b, see Hyde, ii. 59), who prescribes Shihrām and Sissa b. Dāhar.

[18] Nöldeke, *Sitzungsb. d. K. Akad. d. Wissenschaften*, Wien, 1892, cxxvi. 24.

or 300 years; Kūrush, 120 years (who was followed by many Princes down to al-Ballahra, who was al-Masʿūdī's contemporary in A.D. 943)—is of no assistance whatever to the solution of the difficulty.

Although no light has been thrown on the name Qaflān, the more ordinary name given to the inventor himself, viz. Ṣaṣṣa b. Dāhir,[19] appears to be satisfactorily explained. These two names occur in connexion with a Brahman dynasty which ruled in the lower Scinde towards the close of the Umayyad caliphate, when the Muhammadans conquered this part of India. The kings of this family were Khakha, 632–72; Khandar, 672–79; Dāhir, 679–712. Khakha, the founder of the dynasty, appears in Persian histories as Chach the son of Silāīj, and in Arabic histories (aṭ-Ṭabarī, and al-Balādhūrī) as Ṣaṣṣa, while his son Dāhir retains his Indian name. Al-Balādhūrī gives the latter a son Ṣaṣṣa b. Dāhir, but only mentions him incidentally as having fled from the Muslims to a certain fortress. Elliott,[20] who develops the identification, is inclined to see more in it than a coincidence or a conscious appropriation of names. He thinks that the king Khakha or Ṣaṣṣa was the cause of the introduction of chess to the Western world, and associates in the story the nearly contemporary Sāsānian Shahriyār (Shīrūyah). I do not think that this view can be made to harmonize with the history of the game as now known. It puts the introduction into Persia too late for the facts, it ignores the difficulties that Shahrām in the stories is an Indian, not a Persian king, that Ṣaṣṣa is the son, not the father, of Dāhir, that Ṣaṣṣa is a philosopher, not a usurping monarch. I think the truth is to be found in the view that the earliest teller of the legend chose the Indian names that were most familiar to his generation, in order to give verisimilitude to his story. This leaves to Khakha the more modest share in the history of chess of lending his name to the hero of chess-romance.

Bland (62) suggested that Ṣaṣṣa is a corruption of the name Xerxes, and identified him with the philosopher who in European fable is associated with the discovery of chess.[21] I am inclined to agree with his identification, only I think the perversion of name has been in the other direction, and that the European Xerxes is an attempt to explain the Arabic Ṣaṣṣa.

All the MSS., al-Yaʿqūbī, and b. Khallikān add to one or other of their legends a conclusion which tells how the philosopher was rewarded for his invention of chess. When the king invited him to choose his own reward, he is said to have asked for a quantity of corn which was to be placed upon the chessboard in a particular way. The first square was to hold one grain,[22]

[19] The name varies considerably in the MSS. I have used. I have collected the following forms: Ṣaṣṣa b. Dahar or Dāhir (AH, C, H without parentage, Man., Gotha 1738, Bodl. Ar. 182); Ṣiṣṣa b. Dāhir (B. Khallikān, aṣ-Ṣafadī, S); Ṣuṣa b. Dāhir (BM); Ṣahṣaha b. Dāhir (Al, RAS); Ṣaʿṣaʿa b. Dāhir (Gotha 1343, Wetz. ii. 1149); Ḍaḍa b. Tāhir (Khusru 758); Ḍaḍa b. Dāhir (V); Naṣir b. Dāhir (quoted in Hyde, ii. 67); Ṣiṣa (Y); Ṣisa (F).

[20] Op. cit., i. 409–10. Elliott shows that the transliteration of Per. Chach as Ar. Ṣaṣṣa is quite reasonable. To his instances I may add the geographical ones Per. Chāhik = Ar. Ṣāhik; Per. Chaghāniyan = Ar. Ṣaghāniyān. The Per. Chāch (the older name of Tashkand), however, became in Ar. Shāsh. Aṭ-Ṭabarī died 310/923; al-Balādhūrī, 279/892.

[21] In Cessolis' *De moribus hominum et officiis nobilium.*

[22] The calculation is occasionally made in dirhems, in which case Forbes (65, n. 1) says the sum is a cube of gold with an edge six miles long.

the second two, the third four, the fourth eight, and so on, each square containing double the number of grains that were placed upon the preceding square. The quantity of corn asked is, of course, enormous, the number of grains being the sum of a geometrical progression of sixty-four terms, with 1 for the first term and 2 for the common ratio. The total is $2^{64}-1$, or

18,446,744,073,709,551,615 grains,

a quantity which would cover England to a uniform depth of 38·4 feet.[23] It is added that the king did not know which to admire the most, the invention of chess or the ingenuity of the request.

This calculation is undoubtedly of Indian origin, the early Indian mathematicians being notoriously given to long-winded problems of this character. In its earliest form it may be older than chess, and be based upon the *ashṭāpada* board.[24] I have already quoted a passage from al-Maṣʿūdī in which he speaks of the importance which the Indians attached to the sum of the Progression. It would appear to have also been a favourite calculation among the Muslims, though they generally shirked the complete solution by reducing to larger units whenever the figures grew inconveniently large. This also made the immensity of the sum more easy of comprehension. Thus al-Bīrūnī reduces the total to 2,305 mountains 'which is more than the world contains'. He also makes use of the real sum in his *Al-āthār al-bāqiya* (ed. Sachau, Leipzig, 1878, and Eng. tr., London, 1879) to illustrate the different systems of numeration current in his day. At least two Arabic treatises were written on the problem, viz. the *Taḍʿif buyūt ash-shaṭranj* of al-Missisī (9–10th c. A.D.)[25] and the *Taḍʿif ʿadad ruqʿa ash-shaṭranj* of al-Akfānī (D. 749/1348), and several shorter discussions occur in MSS. which I have seen. The MS. Man. gives no less than five methods of treating the problem, one from b. Khallikān (who naïvely states that he did not believe the total could be so great until he met an accountant of Alexandria who showed him the actual calculation), two from ar-Rāghib,[26] the fourth from the *Durrat al-muḍī'a* of Quṭbaddīn Muḥammad b. ʿAbdalqādir, and the fifth from al-Akfānī. MS. Gotha Ar. 1343 has also three calculations, the last of which is interesting since the story is different from the usual one. In this a Sultan who used to challenge all comers at chess, beheading all whom he defeated, after beating ninety-nine opponents met his superior in a dervish. The latter claimed the usual reward—in dirhems.

The calculation reached Europe with the Arabic mathematics, and was discussed by Leonardo Pisano in his *Liber Abbaci*. Other European references to the Progression will be found below in Part II, Chapter IX.

The later Arabic legends which bring chess into association with Bible history need not detain us. They are clearly an attempt to rehabilitate the

[23] Lodge, *Easy Mathematics*, London, 1905, 215; where a modernized version of the story is attempted.

[24] Cf. Macdonell, *JRAS.*, 126–8. He thinks that the Skr. name *koshṭhāgāra* (granary) for the squares of the chessboard may have suggested the problem. Gildemeister differs (*ZDMG.*, xxviii, 682 ff.).

[25] *Fihrist*, p. 281. Cf. Hammer, *Literaturgeschichte*, iv. 366.

[26] In the *Muḥāḍarāt al-udabā'*.

game of chess at a time when the legal schools were looking with disfavour upon it. The earliest record of this type of tradition that I know occurs in the preface to aṣ-Ṣūlī's *K. ash-shaṭranj*. After referring to al-ʿAdlī's statement that chess was invented by Ṣaṣṣa b. Dāhir, aṣ-Ṣūlī goes on to say that this is a fabrication which he had found in many works. For himself he preferred to accept the 'statement based on sound tradition' which he traces back to Kaʿb al-Akhbār, one of the most notorious forgers of traditions that Islam ever knew, that chess was invented by Būshāqūs, Yūshʿa b. Nūn (Joshua) and Kālab b. Yūfannā (Caleb), and that the first who played the game was Qārūn (Korah). Būshāqūs taught the game to the Persians. Later writers are still more daring in their assertions. The MS. H suggests that chess was invented by Adam to console himself for the death of Abel, and numbers Shem, Japhet, and King Solomon among the chess-players.

From the time of al-Ma'mūn onwards, the writings of the more famous Greek philosophers became known to the Muslim world in translation. It was, perhaps, inevitable that the scattered allusions to the Greek board-games which occur in Plato and other writers should be misapplied to chess, but to this we owe the statements in H and later chess books that Aristotle, Galen, and Hippocrates were also chess-players.

CHAPTER XIII

THE GAME OF SHAṬRANJ: ITS THEORY AND PRACTICE. I

The chessboard.—The names of the chessmen in Muslim lands.—Symbolism of the game.—Forms of the chessmen.—The arrangement of the men for play.—The moves of the chessmen, and technical terms.—Relative values of the pieces.—Aim and method of play.—Notation.—Concordant and discordant men.—Classification of players.—Gradations of odds.—Etiquette of play.

THE *shaṭranj* board resembles all native Asiatic boards in being unchequered, but differs from the Indian and other boards in showing no trace of any regular marking of certain squares. The term 'board', however, is somewhat deceptive. The Arabic names,[1] *ruqʿa* (a patch or piece of paper), *sufra* (a table-cloth or napkin), *naṭʿa* (a cloth) and *bisāt* (a carpet), all imply a soft material, and from the earliest days of the Muslim game down, the board has generally been a square piece of cloth or other substance upon which the dividing lines of the squares (Ar. *bait*, house, pl. *buyūt*; Per. *khāna*, pl. *khānahā*; Turk. *au*, pl. *aular*) are worked in another colour. In more elaborate chess-cloths the individual squares may bear a pattern of some simple type, or be merely indicated by the regular recurrence of a conventional design which occupies the centre of the otherwise undivided squares, while these patterns or designs may even, as in the case of the so-called Turkish cloth of which Falkener gives a photograph (196), show a further differentiation on lines analogous to the Indian marked squares. In the desert rougher materials still are employed: Stamma (*Noble Game of Chess*, London, 1745, xii) notes:

> The wild Arabs draw the Squares on the Ground, and pick up Stones of different Shapes and Sizes, which serve them for Pieces.

Boards of more solid materials — it will be remembered that al-Yaʿqūbī describes Qaflān as making his board of leather—and even chequered boards are not entirely unknown, but the chequering is incidental to the ornamentation of the chessboard, and is not essential for its use. With the fondness of the Egyptian, the Turk, and the Persian for inlaid work in wood, it would be strange indeed if so obvious a method of beautifying the board had not suggested itself. The artist, painting a chess scene for some MS., found the same device at hand.[2] But all these are by way of exception only; with

[1] The Per. terms are *pistar*, *takht*; the Turk, *takhtasi*; the Syrian Arabs use the word *tast* (Ar. *dasht*).

[2] Forbes (90) mentions a drawing of a chequered board in MS. 18,804, f. 260, written c. 1700. Bland (46) quotes a couplet from Ghazālī of Meshed which he thought referred to a chequered board. He translates, 'Fortune, to win the ready stake of thy life, Chequered

the limited powers of move of the older Muslim game, the chequered board was less of a convenience than it is in modern days, when more pieces move with larger sweeps.

Other Arabic terms in connexion with the chessboard which I have noted from the older MSS. are *ḥāshyā*, margin (generally of the Rooks' files); *wijh*, *wujh*, *jiha* (pl. *jahāt*), *jānib*, side or wing of the board; *nāḥīa al-firzān*, the Queen's wing; *zāwaya*, *rukn* (R and H only), corner square; *wasṭ ar-ruqʿa*, the four central squares; *sāf* (pl. *sāfāt*), file, as *sāf ar-rikhākh*, the Rooks' file; *ṣaff* (pl. *ṣufūf*), *ṣaffa*, file or row, as in *ṣaff al-awsaṭ*, a central file; *mashya* (rarely), file.

The names of the chessmen (Ar. *dābba*, pl. *dawābb*, beast—used apparently at times in a more restricted sense, e.g. L, 14 b, *firzān wa dawābb*, Queen and Pieces, and f. 65 b, *dawābb kull wa bayādiq*, all the Pieces and Pawns; *qiṭʿa*, piece; *kalb*, pl. *kilāb*, dog; *mithāl*, pl. *'amthila*, *tamāthīl*, figure. Per. *kālā*, pl. *kālāhā*, in RAS only; *muhrah*. Collectively: Ar. *ālāt ash-shaṭranj*) that are used by the Muhammadans of India and Malaya have been already given, but it will be convenient to collect in a table those that are used by other Muslim peoples. To these I add the Abyssinian (Amharic) terms, since the Abyssinian chess is a variety of the Muslim game.

Language.	K.	Q.	B.	Kt.	R.	P.
Arabic. (*MSS.*)	shāh nafs	firzān firz firza	fīl	faras	rukhkh	baidaq baidhaq
(*Colloquial*) .		(wazir)		(begir) (houssān)		baizaq (peda)
Persian . . .	shāh	farzīn	pīl (fīl)	asp (faras)	rukh	piyāda (baizaq)
Turkish . .	shāh	firzān	fīl	āt (faras)	rukh	baizaq
Moorish . .	shāh	lella	fīl	faras	rukhkh	hāri
Abyssinian .	negus	firz	fīl	faras	derr	medak

(NOTE. The ordinary Arabic names are those of the MSS.; the other terms, which I designate as colloquial, are taken from descriptions by Europeans: Hamilton, who gives *houssān* from Egypt, and Grimm, who obtained his terms from Syria.)

The military character of chess was well understood by the earlier Arabic writers on the game. Apart from many allusions in general literature, there are three descriptions in the chess MSS. which I quote because of the light which they throw upon other features of the Muslim game. The first of these is the work of aṣ-Ṣūlī, and is contained in AH (f. 19 b), V (f. 12 b), and Man. (f. 27 b):

The chessmen are classified in this chapter. The *shāh*, it is said, is the king. The *firzān* is the vizier, because he protects and covers the king, and is placed next to him, advancing before him in the battle. Muḥammad b. ʿAbdalmalik az-Zayyāt[3] says, 'How beautiful is the function of the *fīl* in chess! He resembles the secretary who reveals and plans. His use in war is slight except when he does a deed of

in white and black the chessboard of day and night.' The Per. term *shaṭranj* means chess in general, and chessboard is too narrow a translation; and I do not think that the poet had anything more in mind than the colours of the opposing sides.

[3] The unfortunate vizier of al-Muʿtaṣim, executed 233/847.

renown. His is the secretary's cunning, as when he gives *shāh-rukh* or *shāh-faras* or forks two pieces. Or, perhaps in another game when a number of pieces are collected against him, and he draws the game since none of them can attack him. The *firzān* has the same power. In a case like this the *fīl* is better than the *faras*, and when there are several *firzāns* it is even better than a *rukh* when the latter cannot attack it.' The *faras*, it is said, is different: he is a bold horseman, and this is his function in chess. The *rukh*, it is said, is like a commander and a general of an army: like the *faras* he is a horseman, and the command is his. His work is to confine the game, and his strength is manifest when the ninth (read *seventh*) of the game is his.[4] The *baidaqs* (Ar. *bayādiq*), it is said, are like the foot-soldiers who move in advance and hinder the horses (*'afrās*) and rukhs (*rikhākh*); but when the *rukh* gets behind them and attacks them from the rear, he destroys them just as horsemen in war destroy the foot-soldiers.[5]

The second passage occurs in Man. (f. 18 a), in the course of a version of the Ṣaṣṣa legend:

The ḥakīm arranged it thus and it was chess, and he made it in the likeness of a battle between two armies. He made the *nafs* to resemble the king, the *firzān* to resemble the vizier, and the two *rukhs* the commanders of the right and left wings. Next to these he placed the two *faras*, and then the two *fīls*. These are reckoned as the more important members of the army. The *baidaqs* resemble the infantry. He then made each piece's move (*ḥaraka*) proportionate to its strength in the army, and fixed that the victory is gained when the *shāh* is slain, his army still being in existence—this is mate—or when his army is captured.

In the third passage from BM (f. 6 b) a different interpretation is attempted:

The inventor of chess made the board to represent a field of battle upon which two armies are drawn up for the contest, and the six figures, *shāh*, *firzān*, *fīl*, *faras*, *rukh* and *baidaq* represent the six classes upon which war turns and which are essential to it. Of these the first is the king who rules, the second the vizier who leads, the third the commander of the army who arranges, the fourth the cavalry, the fifth the fortresses (*ḥuṣūn*), and the sixth the infantry. He represented the king by the *shāh*, the vizier by the *firzān*, the commander of the army by the *rukh*, the cavalry by the *faras*, the fortresses by the *fīls*, and the infantry by the *baidaqs*. This is the classification of the chessmen (*ālāt ash-shaṭranj*).

The following was his intention in the arrangement. He put the *shāh* in the centre because the king ought to be in the heart of his army. He put the *firzān* next him because the vizier ought to be in the king's vicinity. He put the *fīl* next the *firzān* because the strongest places in the battle array ought to be where king and vizier are. He put the *faras* between *fīl* and *rukh* because cavalry ought to be the defence of the fortresses. He put the *rukh* next the *faras* because the commander ought to be in command of the right and left wings. He put the *baidaqs* in a line in front of these because the infantry is placed in the van in battle. This was his intention in the arrangement of the chessmen.

His intention in the arrangement of the pieces in the game was to liken the game to a struggle and attack. He gave the *baidaq* a move of one square in

[4] All the MSS. read *ninth*, but the two Arabic words are very similar when written, and the error is an easy one to make. Elsewhere in the MSS., players are advised to double their Rooks on their seventh rank, and I imagine that the text originally referred to this.

[5] The text in Man. ends here, but AH continues the extract from aṣ-Ṣūlī with an anecdote in which the master tells how he once mated an opponent by sacrificing *rukh*, *firzān*, and *faras* in order to hem in his opponent's King. From this aṣ-Ṣūlī draws the following lesson: a game of chess 'resembles two armies which defend and attack in a war that is waged between them. Each must attack the king of the opposing army in particular, and aim for him, for the victory is obtained thus.' In conclusion aṣ-Ṣūlī quotes a remark of ar-Rāzī's, to the effect that the most correct procedure in chess was to make a direct attack on the opponent's King, and points to the collection of *manṣūbāt* as illustrating this line of play.

a straight line, because it is not right for the foot-soldier to quit his position in battle, nor to advance except step by step. He made it take obliquely because the injury he inflicts on his enemy in the battle happens unexpectedly. He appointed that he should become a *firzān* when he reached the end of the board, because a man who advances and penetrates to the enemy's camp, and preserves himself from capture or overthrow, deserves the viziership in war. He gave the *faras* a far-reaching move, because the horseman, being mounted, can transport himself to a distance, and can fall back to his camp when he is threatened. He made his move an oblique one in moving forwards and backwards and in capturing, because the horseman of necessity attacks his enemy, lance in hand, and takes him by swift and sudden movements. He gave the *rukh* the move in the four cardinal directions as far as the end of the lines confronting him, which is the most extended move of the pieces, because in war it is the commanders of the right and left wings who harass and burden to their utmost the enemy's weak points which are opposite to them. He made the *shāh's* move a single square in every direction, because the King is not one who should move swiftly. He is free to move at choice either forwards or backwards. The rule for the *firzān* is the same, except that his liberty of move is less than the *shāh's*. When he takes, he takes according to his ward.[6]

The text omits the description of the move of the *fīl*, but I have given it entire as in the MS. because it shows very clearly the extent to which the original parallelism that was intended between chess and war was still recognized by Arabic writers as late as 1250 A. D., notwithstanding the fact that the older Indian explanation had been forgotten. The explanation of the Rook as a commander shows that the original meaning of the name of the chess-piece was not generally known, while the new interpretation of the *fīls* in the BM extract suggests that the use of the elephant in war was also passing from memory. The new interpretation is far-fetched, and yet after all only a foreshadowing of the European substitution of the Castle (at first borne on an elephant's back) for another piece, the meaning of whose name has been entirely forgotten, the Rook.

I have already cited passages to show that the use of pieces (*ṣūra*) which were actual images of the men and animals from which the chessmen took their names was opposed on religious grounds. The legal objection to so elaborate a type of piece was undoubtedly assisted by the economic difficulty that few players would be able to afford such costly implements of play. The invention of a simpler and cheaper type of chessmen was a direct result of the great popularity of chess, and at an early date a definite conventional type of man came into use. The oldest examples are the chessmen from Bambra-ka-thūl in the British Museum (see p. 88), but there are other early Muslim chessmen, mostly from Egypt and probably none as old as 1000 A. D., in the Museum in the case of chessmen in the Mediaeval Room. They may be easily identified, from their resemblance either to the modern Muslim chessmen or to the earlier European conventional pieces. We may

[6] Two translations of this last extract are given in *Qst.*, 30–33, one by Gildemeister, the other by Rieu. Neither of these scholars had any practical knowledge of chess, and both experienced some difficulty with the technical terms, and especially with the word *'uqda*, knot, which I translate *ward* in the last sentence. In the other MSS. I find the verb *'aqada* used repeatedly of two *firzāns* or *firzān* and *baidaq* in the sense of 'unite', 'tie together', 'place so that the two pieces mutually defend one another'. AH f. 16b has *firzān wa baidaq ma'qūd bihi*, Queen and Pawn united with it.

safely conclude that the original Muslim type comprised (*a*) three pieces of different sizes, but all more or less cylindrical in shape, of which the tallest represented the *shāh*, the intermediate one the *firzān*, and the smallest (an exact replica of the *firzān*) the *baidaq*; (*b*) two pieces with long and narrow necks, one with a slightly cleft head for the *fīl*, the other for the *faras*; and (*c*) another piece, rather more massive than the *fīl* or *faras*, with a well-marked top which in early times was flattened on two sides and contained a deep cleft in the centre, which represented the *rukh*.

Rook B.M.
Egypt

The opposing sides were distinguished by the different colours of the two sets of chessmen. In the MSS. these are called red and black (probably because inks of these colours were most easily procurable), and only rarely white and black. The modern sets which I have seen are white and black, white and red, red and green, and red and black.

The arrangement of the pieces at the opening of the game is generally shown in the MSS. as here diagrammed. In only one MS., the late Pers. Y, is the red King placed on e1. At first sight this appears to be out of harmony with the European arrangement. The latter is, however, purely conventional, and depends upon the convention governing the placing of the chequered board and the very modern custom of giving the first move exclusively to White. In earlier times the Black pieces were preferred:—H (f. 51b) says, 'the Black men are for the chief, and the White for the inferior'; and the chess-player generally visualized the board from the Black point of view. The important fact in these MS. diagrams is the unanimity with which they support the European opposition of King to King and Queen to Queen, and oppose the antiquity of the modern Asiatic crosswise arrangement.

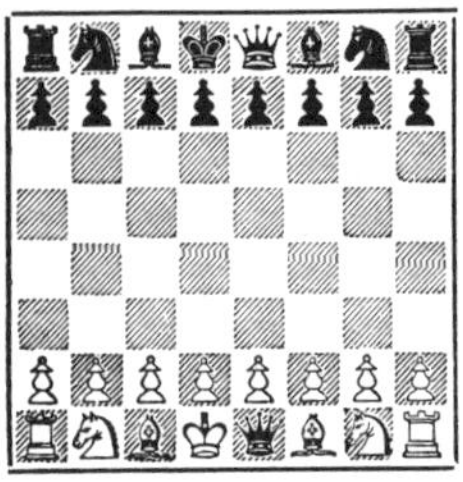

The moves of the pieces were as follows:—

The *Shāh* or *Nafs*, King (K),[7] moved one square at a time into any of the eight or fewer squares surrounding that on which he happened to be standing, the square selected being unoccupied by one of his own pieces or a protected piece of his opponent's, and being out of the range of attack

[7] I have only met with *Nafs* (soul, self, person) in two of the MSS., viz. R, where it is the ordinary term used for the King, and in Man., where it is used twice—once in the passage quoted on p. 222, and again in an extract from aṣ-Ṣūlī (Man., f. 34a), where the King's Fīl (*fīl ash-shāh*) is called *fīl an-nafs*. Stamma (op. cit., x) gives a more modern example of its use. He says, 'A certain King of *Persia*, a splenatic Man, is said to have forbidden the Game, on Account of the Expression *Shâh-mât*; his Successor took off the Prohibition, but ordered that for the future they should on that Occasion say *Nefs-mât*, that is, *The Person is dead*.' Elsewhere, he says that an Oriental, playing with his Sovereign, substitutes *Shāh-em* (O my King!) for *Shāh māt*.

B. al-Labbān (D. 749/1349, quoted in Man. f. 14a) says that the common people often said *shāt* for *shāh*, as if it were written with the dotted *ha*. This spelling is not uncommon in the MSS.

of any hostile piece at the moment of moving. He captured in the same way that he moved. He could not move into check, and whenever he was checked he was obliged to remedy it as in the modern game. If he was unable to do so it was *shāh māt* (Per. *shāh māt*), *māt*, rarely *shāh wa māt*, checkmate, and the game was ended. When a player gave check it was usual for him to warn his opponent of the fact by saying *shāh*, coupling with the name of the King the name of any other piece that was simultaneously attacked, e. g. *shāh war-rukh*, *shāh wa rukh* (Per. *shāh rukh*), a check forking King and Rook; *shāh wal-fīl*, a check forking King and Fīl (L, f. 26 a); *shāh wa firz* (H, f. 37 a), or *shāh wa firzān* (AH, f. 55 b), a check forking King and Firzān; *shāh wa faras* (AH, f. 56 a), a check forking King and Faras; and even *shāh wa baidaq ash-shāh* (L, f. 63 a), a check forking King and King's Pawn. Another technicality in AH (f. 92 b) is *shāh mubaṭṭanān*, an intimate check, used of a check by a Rook on an adjacent square (e. g. Re7 checking Ke8). From this use of the name of the piece is derived the verb *shāha* (imp. *yashīhu*; IV stem, *'ashāha*; VII stem, *inshāha*), to check. At a later date it became usual to say *kisht* (also written *qish*, *qishāh*) and *kisht māt* instead of *shāh* and *shāh māt* when giving check and checkmate, and this is the ordinary expression at the present time in Arabic, Persian, Turkish, and Urdū. The earliest examples I know occur in the Turkish MS. F. For discovered check we have the technicalities in Arabic *shāh fī'l-kashf* (*kashf*, discovery) and *shāh min iʿrā* (*shāh min al-iʿra*), where *iʿrā* (from the root *ʿariya*, to be naked) is a term peculiar to chess, occurring in Persian as *ʿirā*, in Urdū as *ʿarop*, and in Malay as *aras*. The Persian *Madar al-afāzil* (Bland, 49) defines *ʿirā* as 'that piece at chess which is interposed between a King and a Rook to protect', but in the Arabic MSS. it is used rather of the whole position of a file dominated by a Rook, in which the check is for the moment covered by an intervening piece of either colour between the Rook and King. We have accordingly such expressions as 'to move into *iʿrā*' (to play the King on to a file where there is the possibility of a check by discovery by the removal or capture of an intervening piece), 'to expose to *iʿrā*', 'the position in *iʿrā*'. To cover check is in Arabic *satara ash-shāh*; to mate, *māta* (imp. *yamūtu*).

The *Firzān* (pl. *farāzīn*), *firz*, or *firza*, Counsellor (Q),[8] also moved one square at a time, moving diagonally into any one of the four or fewer diagonally adjacent squares to that on which he was posted, the square chosen being unoccupied by a piece of his own side. He captured in the same way that he moved. He could only play to 32 squares, and on a chequered board he would be restricted to squares of one colour. Al-Lajlāj attached great importance to the development of the Firzān in the game, and aimed at securing a clear path (Ar. *sabīl* or *ṭarīq*, pl. *ṭurūq* and *ṭuruqāt*) by which it could be brought into the opponent's half of the board.

The *Fīl* (pl. *fiyala*, *'afyāl*), or Elephant (B), possessed a diagonal move, which consisted of a leap over a diagonally adjacent square, whether occupied or

[8] B. Jinnī (D. 1002, quoted in Man., f. 14 a) says that the common people generally said *firz* or *firza*, comparing this mispronunciation to that of *shāt* for *shāh*.

empty, into the square beyond on the same diagonal. This is commonly, though ambiguously, described as a diagonal leap into the third square; it is a move familiar to English draughts-players as the move of a man in making a single capture without the removal of the man thus captured. The Fīl captured as he moved. Only eight squares of the board were accessible to any Fīl, and no Fīl could ever encounter or attack any other Fīl. The two Fīls were distinguished as *Fīl ash-shāh*, KB, and *Fīl al-firzān*, QB, or as the *right-* and *left-hand Fīl*. The King's Fīl was also called *Fīl al-qā'ima*, *Fīl al-man'a*, the drawing Fīl, or *Fīl an-nafs*, the Naf's Fīl.

The *Faras* (pl. *'afrās*), or Horse (Kt), and the *Rukhkh* (pl. *rikhākh*, mod. *rikhakha*), or Rook (lit. Chariot) (R), possessed precisely the same moves as their European equivalents, Knight and Rook, possess to-day. The squares commanded by one of these pieces were termed in Arabic its *muqāṭa'a*, or province. Other technicalities are *jama'a*, to double, to place both Rooks on the same file; *ar-rukhkh al-a'la*, the front Rook of two on the same file.

The *Baidaq*, *Baidhaq* (pronounced *baizaq*; pl. *bayādiq* or *bayādhiq*), or Pawn (P), moved and captured as the European Pawn does, with the difference that it possessed no power of moving over two squares for its first move. There is consequently no question of one Pawn taking another in passing. On reaching the eighth line it ceased to be a Pawn, and was at once promoted to the rank and took the name of Firzān. No other promotion was possible, and there was no limit to the number of Firzāns that a player might possess at any time of the game. The Arabic verb to promote, 'queen', is *farzana* (V stem *tafarzana*). The Pawns were distinguished by associating with them the name of the piece on whose file they were standing, e.g. *baidaq ash-shāh*, King's Pawn, &c. In addition, the Rook's Pawn was often called *baidaq al-hāshīyā* (*hawāshī*), the marginal Pawn, and the King's or Firzān's Pawn, *baidaq aṣ-ṣadr*, the central Pawn. Fanciful names were attached to the advanced Firzān's Pawn (*baidaq as-saif*, the sword Pawn), and the advanced King's Bishop's Pawn (*baidaq as-sayyāl*, the torrent Pawn) in the analysis of the opening developments. Other terms that I have noted are *baidaq al-firzān al-'aṣlīya*, the original QP of two on that file; and *baidāq al-faras aṣ-ṣadr*, the front KtP of two on that file; and *baidaq firzān al-aswad al-mutaqallab 'an baidaq shāh-hu*, Black's QP that has been changed from KP (by making a capture). Al-Lajlāj attaches great importance in his analysis to the maintaining of an advanced Pawn, and speaks of establishing (Ar. vb. *makuna*, V stem, *tamakkana*) a Pawn, of the establishment (*tamkīn*) of a Pawn, and of an established Pawn (*baidaq tamkīn*), meaning the posting of a Pawn on an advanced square, and its support there so that it was practically untakable except at the cost of superior force.

The Arabic MSS. which I have used supply chess uses of many ordinary words in connexion with the movements and other activities of the chessmen. Some of these may be noted here. To move a piece for the first time is *kharaja* (IV *'akhraja*), to develop. Of ordinary moves the ordinary expression is, 'White comes with his Rook to (*jā'a, bi, 'ila*) such a square': but this is only rarely used of the Fīl or Baidaq. A player pushed (*dafa'a*) a Baidaq (very rarely also a Rukh, Faras, Firzān, or Shāh), and threw (*ramā*, also of Faras and Firzān; *ṭaraḥa*, also of Faras; or *alqaya*) or shifted (*ḥawwala*) a Fīl. He placed (*waḍa'a* or *ja'ala*), played (*la'iba*), went away with (*dhahaba bi*, also of Faras), or advanced (*madda*) a Rukh. The Shāh and Firzān ascended (*ṣa'ada* or *ṭala'a*), descended (*nazala* or *ḥadara*, VII *'inḥadara*), or entered (*dakhala*, IV *'adkhala*) a square. Or the Shāh removed (*ba'uda*), passed (*marra*), walked (*masha*), or limped (*zamala*)—all suggested by his move of a single square. In general use I have noted *ḥaruka* (II *ḥarraka*), *zāla* (II *zauwala*, IV *'azāla*), *naḥa* (II *naḥḥa*, V *tanaḥḥa*), and *naqala*, all meaning move, remove. For the substantive, *move*, there is similar diversity of expression. In addition to the general terms *ḥaraka*, *ḍarb* (pl. *ḍarba*, *ḍurūb*), *mashya* (walk) is used of the Shāh, *taḥrīk* or *ḥurk* of the Firzān, *ṭarḥ* and *nazwān* (leap) of the Fīl, *munzā* of Firzān, Fīl and Faras, *daf'* or *daf'a* of the Baidaq. Adverbs of direction are *mustawīyan*, in a straight line, *farasīyan*, as a Faras, *firzānīyan*, as a Firzān, and *fīlīyan*, as a Fīl. More general terms are *'akhadha*, to take (*'akhadha bāṭilan* or *majjānan*, to take without loss); *dhahaba*, *'aṭā'a* or *hāta*, *bāṭilan*, to sacrifice; *ḍaraba* or *waqa'a 'ala*, to attack; *ḍarb* or *wuqū'*, an attack; *ḥāmala*, to offer to exchange (of Rukh only); *sāma* or *ṣarafa*, to exchange; *waqa'a baina*, to fork; *ḥabasa*, *ḥaṣara*, to shut in or confine; *ḥafiẓa*, *ḥamā*, to defend; *ḥifẓ*, *hamā*, *ḥimā'i*, defence.[9]

Both al-'Adlī and aṣ-Ṣūlī made an attempt in their chess-books to estimate the relative values of the chessmen in the early part of the game. The method adopted was based upon a monetary scale and the *dirhem* was taken as a convenient unit. BM (f. 11 a) gives a brief extract from al-'Adlī's work, and AH (f. 14 b), V (f. 14 a), H (f. 18 a—shortened text), BM (f. 10 a), and Man. (f. 27 a) give aṣ-Ṣūlī's chapter. An independent, but not materially different, estimation is given in AE and RAS. I have adopted the text in Man. as the basis of the following translation.

Values of the chessmen, calculated for their original positions.

Aṣ-Ṣūlī has said: The Shāh is reckoned beyond value because of his superior dignity. The highest in value after the Shāh is the Rukh. Its value is one dirhem. The Faras' value is $\frac{2}{3}$ dirhem. The Firzān's value is $\frac{1}{3}$ dirhem, but some say $\frac{3}{8}$ dirhem. The Fīl's value is $\frac{1}{4}$ dirhem. KP and QP, each $\frac{1}{4}$ dirhem; BP and KtP, each $\frac{1}{6}$ dirhem rising to $\frac{1}{5}$ dirhem; a marginal P $\frac{1}{8}$ dirhem because it can only take on one side. I consider the KKtP better than QBP; aṣ-Ṣūlī has said that this is because this Baidaq is a spy against the return of the opponent's stronger Fīl and Firzān. He gave these values for the commencement of the game; the values of the pieces may increase or diminish afterwards. The better of the Fīls is the *Fīl an-nafs*, which is the *Fīl al-man'a* (the *drawing* Fīl, called by al-Lajlāj, AH f. 133 b, *Fīl al-qā'īma*). It is better than KP, and the other Fīl is better than QP. The two central Baidaqs are better than Firzān and Fīl, and any two Baidaqs are better than the Firzān. Rabrab and Abū'n-Na'ām used to advise the exchange of the Firzān for the two marginal Baidaqs, the exchange of the Fīl for two Baidaqs under all circumstances, and the exchange of the weaker for the better Baidaqs. Do not exchange Fīl and Baidaq for Firzān unless your opponent has gained your Firzān. If your Rukh is confined, try to exchange it for Faras and Firzān, but otherwise not.

[9] A number of Persian terms for *move*, *take*, &c., are given by Bland, 58.

AH goes on to show that these values may be altered completely in the End-game, where even the advantage (Ar. *faḍl*) of a Rukh may be insufficient to convert a draw into a win, e. g. Kt *v.* R is a drawn game, and so is R and Kt *v.* R. Even the Fīl might become of higher value than a Faras (Kt *v* four concordant Qs loses, but B *v.* four concordant Qs draws) or a Rukh (R *v.* four concordant Qs loses, B *v.* the same draws).

The values in RAS are calculated with greater nicety, but the MS. shows a tendency to over-estimate the value of the minor pieces. The MS. gives Q $\frac{1}{2}$ or $\frac{5}{12}$ dirhem; B $\frac{1}{4}$ or $\frac{1}{3}$ dirhem; KP $\frac{1}{4}$ dirhem; QP $\frac{5}{24}$ dirhem; Kt and BP $\frac{1}{6}$ dirhem; and RP $\frac{1}{8}$ dirhem.

Aṣ-Ṣūlī's estimate enables us to form some kind of comparison with the modern game. I adopt as the unit of my scale the value of the RP in the Muslim game, and as the connecting link the value of the Knight, whose move is the same in both games.

Muslim chess.					Modern European chess. (Values taken from the *Handbuch.*)				
	Value.	Total of side.	Percentage of all pieces.	Percentage of each piece.		Value.	Total of side.	Percentage of all pieces.	Percentage of each piece.
Baidaq	1 to 2	$8\frac{2}{3}$	20·5	2·6	Pawn	1·5	12·0	18·2	2·3
Faras	$5\frac{1}{3}$	$10\frac{2}{3}$	25·2	12·6	Knight	5·3	10·6	16·2	8·1
Fīl	2	4	9·5	4·8	Bishop	5·3	10·6	16·2	8·1
Rukh	8	16	37·7	18·9	Rook	8·6	17·2	26·0	13·0
Firzān	3	3	7·1	7·1	Queen	15·5	15·5	23·4	23·4
Total force		$42\frac{1}{3}$	100		Total force		66	100	

The great increase in the powers of the Bishop and Queen in modern chess has naturally resulted in a relative diminution in the value of the other pieces.

The method of play in the older Muslim game was identical with that followed in the modern European game. The players played alternately, each making a single move (*dast*, pl. *dusūt*; *ḍarb*) in his turn of play.[10]

The aim of play was twofold, either to give checkmate to the opponent's King, or to annihilate his army. To this latter form of victory I have given the Middle-English name of *Bare King*, which answers closely to the terms *Shāh munfarid*, isolated King, and *mufrad*, pl. *mufridāt*, isolations, of the Arabic MSS. It was obtained whenever a player captured the whole of his opponent's army, the King excepted, and still retained some of his own men upon the board, or at least one man *out of reach* of the opponent's King. If the solitary King could take his opponent's last remaining man in his move

[10] As will be seen in the next chapter, the evidence that this was so is overwhelming. Forbes (106) imagined that the modern Indian practice of commencing the game by allowing each player in succession to make a number of moves in his turn of play went back to the Muslim game. In this he was misled by the diagrams of the ta'bīyāt in the MSS. he used, which he assumed depicted game positions, whereas they show two unconnected normal positions upon a single diagram. If Forbes's account is compared with Tiruveṇgaḍāchārya's description of the Parsi chess, it will be seen that this latter work is the source of his section upon the Muslim Openings.

following that in which he was bared, the game was considered drawn. We have already seen (p. 57) that in Ḥijāz there was a local variation in the rule regarding Bare King. There a solitary King was defeated the instant that he was bared, whether he could bare his opponent the following move or not. This win was called the *Medinese victory*.[11]

It occasionally happened in the course of the game that a player, whose turn it was to play, found himself unable to move any of his pieces in a legal manner, and yet at the instant his King was not in check. This Ending, to which we give the name of *stalemate* (Ar. *zā'īd*, rarely *mazīd*, from the verb *zāda*, imp. *yazīdu*; or *zā'īda* to stale, deprive of the power of moving, very rarely used of any other piece than the Shāh), was decisive in Muslim chess. The player who found himself in this predicament was held to have lost the game.[12]

A game to which for any reason a decisive result could not be obtained was said to come to a stand (Ar. *qā'īm*, *'iqāma*, *qayām*; pl. *qawā'īm*, *qā'īma*, *'iqāmāt*—all derived from *qāma*, to stand; cf. mod. *qūwima*, to be drawn), or to be inaccessible (*mana'a*: a later term, not used in AH, frequent in H), i. e. to be drawn. This might happen from equality of force (e. g. R *v.* R); insufficiency of force (e. g. R *v.* Kt); inability to force exchanges (e. g. Qs and Bs moving on squares which on a chequered board would all be of one colour *v.* Qs and Bs moving on squares of the other colour); perpetual check; or repetition of move. The problems will contain examples of all these forms of drawn game.[13]

The chess MSS. employ two different methods of describing the squares of the board, which we may conveniently distinguish as the *descriptive* and the *literal*, or as it is often called, the *algebraic notations*. The former is by far the commoner, and is indeed employed in all the MSS. except Oxf. in the problem solutions.

In the *descriptive notation* the board is regarded as belonging half to one player and half to the other, and the two halves are called Red's and Black's accordingly. In each of these halves the squares are defined in terms (1) of

[11] This local rule may be illustrated thus: Red Kd6, Rh3; Black Kc8, Ra8. If Red play 1 Rh8+, Kb7; 2 R×R would win in Ḥijāz: elsewhere Black was allowed to play now K×R and draw. If the Kings had been on e6 and d8, 1 Rh8, Kc7; 2 R×R would have won everywhere.

[12] The rule is established from the solutions to certain Muslim problems (Nos. 225, 226, 371 below). Forbes, while correctly stating the result, so hedges it round with conditions that its occurrence would have become almost impossible. He has made the mistake of transferring the highly artificial rules of the later modification of chess, the *shaṭranj kāmil* (Tīmūr's chess), to the ordinary game. The rules of Bare King and Stalemate as given in the text survived until Stamma's time, for (op. cit., xi) he gives them thus:

'He that gives a *Stale-mat* wins the Game, contrary to the Rule observed in England; . . .

'If one *King* be stripp'd of all his Pieces, and the other have either Piece or *Pawn* left, the later wins the Game, tho' he should not have wherewithal to give *Mat*, as a *Bishop*, or a *Knight*, &c.'

[13] From the Arabic *qā'īm* (also used in Persian, see the extracts from Persian dictionaries in Bland, 55) is derived the Per. *shāh qām* (formed on the analogy of *shāh māt*), the game is drawn, lit. the King has arisen. This term evidently puzzled the lexicographers—who were not always expert chess-players—and we find a number of absurd explanations in native dictionaries. Bland (53) quotes the *Bahāri 'Ajam*, which makes it equivalent to 'the King moves', and explains that harmless action as 'the extreme degree of defeat', and the *Burhāni Qāṭī*, which explains it as equivalent to perpetual check. A different explanation is attempted in RAS in connexion with the *shaṭranj kāmil*. Bland and Forbes understood this to mean stalemate, but the MS. says it is a check ' when the King is separated from his men'.

the side, e.g. left-hand or right-hand, less frequently King's and Firzān's; (2) of the master-piece of the file; (3) of its distance from the edge where the player sits. Thus, assuming that Red sits at the foot, Black at the upper edge of the diagram, g4 is *Red's right-hand Faras' fourth square,* and g5 is *Black's left-hand Faras' fourth square.* Very occasionally the notation was extended right across the board, and we have g7 termed *Red's right-hand Faras' seventh square.* A little ambiguity is introduced as a result of the want of fixity in the initial positions of King and Firzān. In the analysis in L, where the original position of the Kings is known absolutely, the notation is consistent throughout, but in the problem solutions where it is impossible to say for certain where the King stood originally, now the *e*-file and now the *d*-file is called the King's. In many problem positions, the Firzān's file can be determined on the assumption that the Firzāns in the diagram are the original Firzāns of the game, and in these cases the solutions almost invariably name the central files accordingly. The important fact is that the notation in the vast majority of the solutions assumes the normal arrangement of the opposing Kings. In a few solutions (not more than five in all) the notation is confused, and squares on both central files are described as on the King's file. I have only found one solution in which the notation is consistent with a crosswise arrangement of the Kings.

This notation does not possess the merit of brevity, but its clearness has given it a long and fruitful life, and with but slight modification it is still the most popular notation in Europe outside of Germany and Switzerland, and in America at the present time. Al-ʿAdlī strongly advised players to commit it to memory, and it forms the foundation upon which Y built its hints upon playing chess blindfold.

In the algebraic notation each square is denoted by two letters, the first of which is common to all squares of the same file, the second to all squares of the same row. It is very similar to the notation which I employ in this book. Thus the successive files which I call *a*, *b*, &c. are termed in AH, where this notation is employed in connexion with the Knight's Tours, *t*, *sh*, *r*, *f*, *m*, *l*, *k*, *y*, with the numerical meanings of 400, 300, 200, 100, 40, 30, 20, 10. In Oxf., where this notation is used in all the problem solutions, the letters *f* (80), ʿ (70), *s* (60), *n* (50) are substituted for the older letters of the files *a*–*d*. Both MSS. use for the rows 1, 2, to 8, the letters *a*, *b*, *j*, *d*, *h*, *w*, *z*, *ḥ*, with the numerical meanings 1, 2, 3, 4, 5, 6, 7, 8. Thus e5 is *r h* in AH or *s h* in Oxf., e3 is *m j*, f6 is *l w*, &c. This notation was also introduced into Europe—first at an early date, and again, in an improved form, by Philip Stamma of Aleppo in 1737. With small alterations it has become the normal notation of German chess-players.

F (Q) and R alone, of all the MSS. which I have consulted, make no use of a regular notation, but describe the moves by reference to other pieces on the board, e.g. 'moves next to the Firz,' or by such adverbs as 'up', 'down', 'aslant', 'straight'.

The unchequered state of the Muslim board made it a matter of some difficulty to see whether two Firzāns on the same side could defend, or whether two Firzāns of different sides could attack one another. This was a matter of very considerable importance in the Ending, and might mean all the difference between a won and a drawn game. The older masters (see BM, f. 10 b) gave cumbrous rules by which a player could ascertain whether a Pawn promoted on a certain square would move on the same 32 squares as another Firzān. Firzāns and Fīls which moved on *different* sets of squares (different coloured squares on a chequered board) were said to be discordant (Ar. *khālif, mukhtalif, takhāluf, mukhālif,* contrary, different), while those which moved on the same set of squares (squares of the same colour on a chequered board) were called concordant (Ar. *talāqī, mutlaqī, mutalliq,* that which meets, or less frequently *muwāfiq,* concordant). The existence of these terms is clear evidence for the uncoloured nature of the Muslim chessboard.

Most of the MSS. attempt a classification of chess-players in regard to their skill in play. The different classifications do not entirely agree, and the discussion would seem from the first to have been more academic than practical. Probably at no time did a position in any but the highest class carry any great weight in popular estimation. Apparently al-ʿAdlī was the first to treat of the classes of chess-players, but we only know of his proposals from a brief reference which aṣ-Ṣūlī added at the end of his own chapter on the question.

Al-ʿAdlī recognized five classes of players. The highest contained the *ʿālīyāt* or grandees. The second class, the *mutaqāribāt* or proximes, received the odds of the Firzān from the *ʿālīya.* The third class received the Rook—'which is silly,' comments aṣ-Ṣūlī. We know nothing of the remaining classes.

Aṣ-Ṣūlī also recognized five classes, and gives the name of *ʿālīya* to the highest. There have never been more than three at any time or place in this class. He names Jābir, Rabrab, Abū'n-Naʿām al-ʿAdlī and ar-Rāzī as having been of the first class. The later MS., BM, substitutes al-ʿArī for ar-Rāzī (a clerical error, I believe) and adds the names of two Baghdād players, b. Dandān, and al-ʿQunāf, who must accordingly have flourished between 950 and 1250. The later MSS. merely repeat aṣ-Ṣūlī's information, and strangely enough none adds aṣ-Ṣūlī's own name, or that of al-Lajlāj, both of whom were certainly of the highest skill. Aṣ-Ṣūlī goes on to say that Rabrab and ar-Rāzī were the greatest of these masters, that al-ʿAdlī had for a while stood alone in the class until ar-Rāzī challenged him and proved his mastership, that ar-Rāzī also stood alone in the class for a time and died before another grandee appeared. The second class, the *mutaqāribāt* or proximes, contains players who win from two to four games in ten when playing with a grandee, and who receive odds from him, the best, QKtP or RP, the weakest, KP or QP. The grandee is credited with the ability to calculate ten (AH says twenty—an error, surely) moves ahead, the proxime sees far less. The test of a player's class is his success with a player of known class when playing without odds. If he wins regularly seven or more games in ten, he belongs to a higher class; if fewer, not. The third class receive the odds of the Firzān from the *'ālīya*, the fourth class the Faras, the fifth class the Rook. If a player requires greater odds his skill is accounted nothing; as a player he is beneath contempt. Al-'Adlī once said, 'You do not give the odds of the Faras to a player who can plan *shāh wa rukh* or *shāh-māt*.' Elsewhere in the preface of his book, aṣ-Ṣūlī specially instances skill in solving manṣūbāt (problems), knowledge of the Endings and End-game decisions, and knowledge of the ta'bīyāt, and when to abandon or modify them in play, as distinguishing marks of the *'ālīya*.

The later MSS., H and Man., recognize six classes, introducing one between the third and fourth of aṣ-Ṣūlī's list, who receive odds from the *'ālīya* greater than the Firzān but less than the Faras.

Closely connected with the classification of players is that of the proper gradation of odds (Ar. *ḥaṭṭ*). The only discussion of this occurs in RAS, and Forbes (99) abridges the passage thus:

> Having now explained the moves of the pieces and their exchangeable value, I shall proceed, O Reader! to inform you of the different degrees of odds established by the masters of old. A true Chess-player ought to play with all sorts of people, and in order to do so, he must make himself acquainted with his adversary's strength, in order to determine what odds he may give or accept. A man who is unacquainted with the rules for giving or receiving odds is not worthy of the name of Chess-player. It is only by equalizing the strength of the combatants that both of them may reap amusement and edification; for what interest could a first-rate player, such as 'Adali (i.e. al-'Adlī), or Ṣūlī, or 'Alī Shaṭranjī, find in playing even with a man to whom they could each give the Knight or the Rook?
>
> The smallest degree of odds, then, is to allow the adversary the first move. The second degree is to give him the Half-Pawn, which consists in taking either Knight's Pawn off his own file and placing it on the Rook's third square. The third species of odds is the giving the Rook's Pawn; the fourth, that of the Knight; the fifth, that of the Bishop; the sixth, that of the Queen. The seventh degree of odds is to give the adversary the King's Pawn, which is the best on the board. The eighth species of odds is the King's Bishop. The ninth is the Queen's Bishop. The tenth degree of odds is the Queen. The eleventh, the Queen and a Pawn; or what is equivalent, a Knight; for though the Queen and Pawn be slightly inferior to the Knight at the beginning, yet you must take into account the probability of the Pawn becoming a second Queen. The twelfth species of odds is the Knight and Pawn. The thirteenth, the Rook. To give any odds beyond the Rook can apply only to women, children, and tyros. For instance, a man to whom even a first-class player can afford to give the odds of a Rook and a Knight has no claim to be ranked among Chess-players. In fact, the two Rooks in Chess are like the two hands in the human body, and the two Knights are, as it were, the feet. Now, that man has very little to boast of on the score of manhood and valour who tells you that he has given a sound thrashing to another man who had only one hand and one foot.

There is an interesting passage in H, ff. 50 b–51 a, in the middle of an anthology of poems relating to chess, which shows that it was thought useful to discuss the proper line of play to adopt when giving odds. The passage is not very clear, but it deals with the opening play when the odds of the Rook are given in return for a Pawn, the odds of Faras for Pawn, of Faras, of Firzān, and of a Pawn. In the first case, when the Rook is given for a Pawn, two lines of play are given, but it is not stated which Rook and which Pawn are to be removed from the board. As is often the case in Arabic analysis, the play on one side only is given; it can be taken as suggesting the lines upon which the player should attempt to model his development. The two lines of play are as follows: I. (1) Pe3; (2) Kte2; (3) Pg3; (4) Pg4; (5) Ktf4; (6) Ktg2; (7) Pf3; (8) Pf4; (9) Qe2; (10) Qf3; (11) Ph3; (12) Pd3; (13) Pd4; if the opponent now moves P(c6)c5, do not take the Pawn, but play (14) Pc3; if he takes the d-Pawn, play (15) eP × P; (16) Bd3; (17) Pf5. If he takes this Pawn, then retake by g-Pawn. II. (1) Pc3; (2) Pc4; (3) Pd3; (4) Ktc3; (5) Pb3; (6) Pd4; (7) Qc2; (8) Pe3; (9) Kd2; (10) Pa3; (11) Pa4; (12) Ba3; (13) Bd3.

The same line of play is recommended when giving the Faras for a Pawn, but is not advisable in the case of the odds of the Faras alone. The play when giving the Firzān is discussed in a single sentence, too corrupt to be intelligible. When giving a Pawn, the following plan of development is given as best: (1) Pd3; (2) Pd4; (3) Pc3; (4) Pf3; (5) Kth3; (6) Ktf2; (7) Qc2; (8) Qd3; (9) Pg3; (10) Ph3; (11) Ph4.[14] If, however, the opponent play first,

move the Pawns in a body, and do not let him outstrip them. Then bring your Kt to e2. If he moves against your d-P, do not take him until he takes. If you take first, it is to his advantage and spoils your game. If he takes, it is not advisable to take with c-P.

The discussion is interesting, as showing that chess analysis was carried on in Muslim circles to a greater extent than had generally been supposed was the case.

The later MSS., and especially Y,[15] attach considerable importance to the etiquette of play. Thus when two players sit down to their game, the lower in rank is to spread out the board, and to shake the pieces from the bag in which they are kept. He is next to wait until his superior has made his choice of colour, and in arranging his men he is to take care not to place his King and Firzān until his opponent has placed his; he is then to place his King opposite to the other King. If the players are of equal rank, the first to seize the men chooses the positions of the Kings. The stronger player should offer fair odds. Ordinary rules of good manners should be observed; onlookers should keep silence and refrain from remarks on the state of the game or from advice to the players. An inferior should not wilfully play to lose.

It is quite evident from the stories of the early Muslim players that much of this etiquette did not obtain in their time. Traditions respecting Saʿīd b. al-Musayyib, al-Ḥasan al-Baṣrī, ash-Shaʿbī, and Muḥammad b. Sīrīn relate how these tābiʿs used to advise players as to their moves while watching the game.

14 I have corrected the order of the moves. In the MS. move 4 follows move 8. And it is not stated that the Pawns moved on the 9th and following moves are on the King's wing.

15 Durgāprasāda, in his Urdū *Risāla i shaṭranj* (Delhi, 1890), ch. vii, has a somewhat similar discussion. He recommends the rule of 'touch and move' as a counsel of perfection, and deprecates slowness of play.

CHAPTER XIV

THE GAME OF SHAṬRANJ: ITS THEORY AND PRACTICE. II

The divisions of the game.—The Opening.—The 'akhrājāt or ta'bīyāt.—Al-'Adlī and aṣ-Ṣūlī.—The work of al-Lajlāj.—Later treatment of the Openings.—Mid-game tactics.

THE Muslim chess-masters[1] divided a game of chess into the same three parts into which we divide it at the present day. There is the Opening (Ar. *'awā'il ad-dusūt*), during which the players develop their pieces from their original squares to others where they occupy positions more suitable for attack or defence. This period lasts so long as both players' plans are governed solely by the principles of development, and ceases directly one player passes to active attack upon his opponent. Then the Mid-game (Ar. *awsāṭ ad-dusūt*) commences, during which the forces are at close quarters, and the actual battle is in progress. Strategy is the ruling principle here. Finally, when the forces are so reduced in number that the right line of play for either side has become capable of mathematical demonstration, we have the End-game (Ar. *akhir ad-dusūt*). In the modern game analysis is both possible and necessary in the Ending, and also in the Opening, where the best way of posting the chessmen so that each can exercise its powers of attack or defence to the greatest extent, can be reduced more or less to general principles. In the Muhammadan game the analysis of the End-game was equally possible, but for the Opening, the necessity for investigation and the cogency of general principles were less obvious than is the case in modern chess. In the older game the powers of move of the majority of the chessmen were disproportionate to the size of the chessboard, and it took several moves before the pieces could be said to be in contact. Hence the exact order of the initial moves of a game appeared a matter of but little importance, and a player could generally rely upon a dozen moves or so of comparative immunity from attack, and upon securing after that number of moves the position that he desired.

The result of this was that in popular estimation the final position of the Opening was the important one to memorize: instead of learning a succession of moves, the player learnt a position and endeavoured to reproduce it in the opening moves of the game, making the necessary moves in the order which occurred to him as most suitable at the moment. Hence in almost all the

[1] For instance aṣ-Ṣūlī, quoted in Man., ff. 31 a seq., and al-Lajlāj in his *tadhkira*, given in AH, f. 133 b. These two treatises are very similar, and they are summarized below, pp. 245 ff.

older Muslim chess-works which have come down to us, in the place of an orderly treatment of opening play on lines analogous to those with which the modern player is familiar, we find nothing beyond a collection of type-positions, each with its own distinctive name, which are recommended to the player as models for his imitation. Occasionally brief historical notes are added. Diagrams of these type-positions were a regular feature of the chess-works from the time of al-ʿAdlī down to the 17th c.[2]

These positions were popularly called *taʿbīya* (pl. *taʿbīyāt* or *taʿābī*), a derived infinitive passive from the root *ʿabā*, to array an army, which may be translated 'battle array'. This was not the only name; aṣ-Ṣūlī generally used the term *bad'*, *badā'* (pl. *ibdīyāt*, *bādī*, or *'abdā*), which answers to our word 'opening', and al-Lajlāj preferred *'akhrāj* (pl. *'akhrājāt*), 'development'. Other terms are *fat·ḥ*, opening, and *kharj* (pl. *kharjāt*), *khurūg*, development.

In order to economize space, the majority of the MSS. place two developments upon each diagram, one appearing as the red pieces, the other as the black.[3] The explanatory text relating to the red arrangement is placed at that side of the board upon which the red men are stationed, and is written in red. The text relating to the black men is in black ink and is placed similarly at the black side of the board. This ought to have been perfectly clear, but the explanation was somehow overlooked, and it was long assumed that the diagrams represented positions from games in which the play was supposed to be the best possible for either side. This led to many difficulties; the chief of these being that the number of moves that had been played on the two sides was generally different, so that the diagrams were assumed to be inaccurate, and the attempt was made to rectify them. In Man., however, the different developments are given on half-boards,[4] and the independent nature of each *taʿbīya* is manifest.

The older MSS. profess to give bibliographical details as to the sources whence they obtained the different openings which they diagram. The oldest *taʿbīyāt* are those which I give as Nos. 1–16, which have been obtained from the MSS. AH (C), BM, and Man. Each of these *taʿbīyāt* is stated to be derived from one or other of the great Muslim masters, al-ʿAdlī or aṣ-Ṣūlī. There is, however, considerable discrepancy between the statements as given

[2] They have a certain resemblance to the so-called 'normal positions' which are recognized in some openings in modern chess, e. g. in the Evans Gambit, the Queen's Pawn Game, and the Fianchettos. It is worthy of note that two recent writers, F. K. Young and E. C. Howell, have attempted in their *Minor Tactics of Chess* (London, 1895) to treat the modern game on the lines of the *taʿbīyāt*. Their 'primary bases' are the exact counterpart of the Muhammadan *taʿbīyāt*.

[3] Cf. Forbes, 106 seq., v. d. Linde, i. 101 seq., and *Qst.*, 29, 342, 400–3. I was the first person to announce the entire independence of the associated developments, in a paper on 'The Taʿbīyāt and other Battle-arrays', in the *BCM.*, 1900, 169–176. For this I had no other material than the diagrams and texts quoted in *Qst.*, and I was led astray in some matters of detail. A later paper, 'The oldest recorded Games of Chess,' *BCM.*, 1903, 441–9, written after I had obtained access to the MSS. AH, C, BM, AE, and L, corrected these errors. Since then the recovery of the MS. Man. has completely established the correctness of my conclusions.

[4] With the single exception of the Mujannaḥ and Sayyāl, which are given on f. 85a on one board as in the older MSS. The diagram is accompanied by an appreciation of these openings by Abū Rīāsh.

in the different MSS. Fortunately it is possible by careful comparison to separate the older material that was taken from al-ʿAdlī from the later material from aṣ-Ṣūlī with complete certainty.

From a brief remark in the text of the Ṣaṣṣa legend in AH, C, and V, which was taken from al-ʿAdlī's lost work, we know that this writer included fourteen distinct *taʿbīyāt* in his book.[5] We also know from an extract which I quote below from AH (f. 28 b = C, f. 61 b) that aṣ-Ṣūlī only gave ten Openings in his book, and that some of these were taken by him from al-ʿAdlī's work.

Now AH and C contain sixteen *taʿbīyāt* which they classify thus: eight common to both al-ʿAdlī and aṣ-Ṣūlī, six special to aṣ-Ṣūlī, and two special to al-ʿAdlī. It is clear that we have a discrepancy with the real facts, since this attributes ten to al-ʿAdlī and fourteen to aṣ-Ṣūlī.

In BM we find (on ff. 42 a–43 a) a chapter with this title:—

Chapter of the *taʿābī* which al-ʿAdlī describes. And at the present time these are abandoned, because the modern are better.

Here we have twelve arrays. The MS. accordingly omits two of the al-ʿAdlī Openings.

Man. contains ten *taʿbīyāt*, and its frequent quotations from aṣ-Ṣūlī in the texts associated with the diagrams show that this MS. has used aṣ-Ṣūlī's work as its source.[6]

I arrive at the following conclusions. The following eight openings were included by both al-ʿAdlī and aṣ-Ṣūlī: *watad al-ʿanz*, *ʿajāʾiz*, *mujannaḥ*, *sayyāla*, *mashāʾikhī*, *muʿaqrab* (all of which are stated to be common to both works in AH, are given as in al-ʿAdlī in BM, and as in aṣ-Ṣūlī in Man.), *muraddad* (common to both in AH and Man., omitted in BM), and *ḥiṣa firʿauna* (common to both in Man., omitted in BM, in aṣ-Ṣūlī only in AH: this last is certainly wrong). The following six Openings belong to al-ʿAdlī, and were omitted by aṣ-Ṣūlī: *al-ʾibṭ*, *al-kirmānī* (so AH and BM; neither are in Man.), *saif* (AH in error says common to both writers, BM gives as al-ʿAdlī, Man. omits), *jaish*, *band al-khadam*, and *raqūʾīqī* (in BM as al-ʿAdlī, not in Man., AH says in aṣ-Ṣūlī only—which is certainly wrong). The Openings which are special to aṣ-Ṣūlī are the two, *muwashshaḥ* and *mutalāḥiq* (so AH and Man.; BM omits them).

But this does not exhaust the difficulties of the MSS. The diagrams are very corrupt, and the same arrangement occurs with different names in different MSS. or the same name is given to different arrays. Obviously the whole material was rapidly becoming traditional by the time that the existing MSS. were compiled. It is only by a careful collation, and in some cases

[5] AH, f. 3 b = C, f. 5 a = V, f. 6 a = Man., f. 15 b. 'He (Ṣaṣṣa b. Dāhir) arranged the chess and made for it the 14 taʿbīyāt which we have arranged in this book of ours.' The compiler of AH (C) states that he is quoting from al-ʿAdlī, and a later quotation (AH, f. 5 b) from aṣ-Ṣūlī's preface refers to this particular legend again as being taken from al-ʿAdlī's book.

[6] H gives six *taʿbīyāt* (really five, since one diagram is repeated), and uses both al-ʿAdlī and aṣ-Ṣūlī. Its evidence is of less value here than in connexion with the problems, since it neither names all the arrays, nor states clearly their sources.

a weighing of probabilities that I have been able to sort out the different arrays, and to recover the original positions as given in figures 1–16. In so doing I have relied mainly upon Man., where the *ta'bīyat* are treated separately. I have also found valuable help for the identification of the *mujannaḥ, saif, mashā'īkhī*, and *sayyāla* in the MSS. L and AE. The diagrams are arranged on the assumption that the King stood originally on e1 (see p. 247).[7]

AH 1 (bl.) : C 1 (bl.) : BM 65 (red) : Man. 50.

1. Watad al-'anz [16 moves].

AH 1 (red) : C 1 (red) : Man. 1.

2. Muraddad [19 moves].

AH 4 (bl.) = 5 (bl.) : C 4 (bl.) = 41 (bl.) : Man. 6.

3. Ḥiṣa fir'auna [19 moves].

AH 2 (red) : C 2 (red) : BM 63 (red) : Man. 60 : H 5 (red).

4. 'Ajā'īz [9 moves].

BM 60 (bl.) : Man. 66 (bl.): H 3 (red) = 4 (bl.).

5. Mujannaḥ [12 moves].

AH 3 (red) : C 3 (red) : BM 60 (red) : Man. 66 (red) : H 3 (bl.).

6. Sayyāla [12 moves].

BM 63 (bl.) : Man. 11: H 5 (bl.).

7. Mashā'īkhī [19 moves].

AH 4 (red) ? = 3 (bl.): C 4 (red) ? = 3 (bl.) : BM 61 (red) : Man. 16.

8. Mu'aqrab [19 moves].

AH 2 (bl.) : C 2 (bl.): BM 61 (bl.) : H 4.

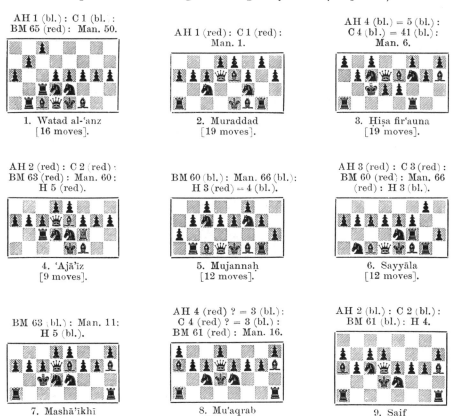

9. Saif [19 moves].

[7] The evidence of the MSS. may be summarized thus :

No. 1. Name attached to diagram in BM and Man. AH and C, which give the *watad al-'anz* and *muraddad* on one diagram, have transposed the names.

No. 2. Name attached to diagram in Man. only. See note to No. 1. The text in AH, which refers to the abnormal position of the Kts, supports the identification.

No. 3. Name attached to diagram in AH (C) once, and Man. AH repeats the position as *mashā'īkhī*.

No. 4. Name attached to diagram in AH (C) once, in BM and in Man. H repeats the diagram as *kirmānī*.

No. 5. Name attached to diagram in BM, Man., RAS, L, and AE. H gives the diagram twice but without name. AH in error gives a different diagram somewhat resembling No. 8.

No. 6. Name attached to diagram in AH, BM, and Man. H gives the diagram without name. L and AE support the identification.

No. 7. Name attached to diagram in BM and Man. H gives the position as *qirb*. AH repeats the diagram of *ḥiṣa fir'auna*. L and AE support the identification.

No. 8. Name attached to diagram in AH, BM, and Man. AH apparently repeats the diagram as *mujannaḥ*.

No. 9. Name attached to diagram in AH (C), and BM. L and AE support the identification.

AH 5 (red) : C 41 (red) : BM 65 (bl.).

10. Band al-khadam [18 moves].

AH 6 (bl.) : C 42 (bl.) : BM 64 (bl.).

11. Jaish [20 moves].

AH 6 (red) : C 42 (red).

12. Raqū'iqī [8 moves].

AH 8 (bl.) : C 44 (bl.) : BM 62 (red) = 64 (red).

13. 'Ibt [8 moves].

AH 8 (red) : C 44 (red) : BM 62 (bl.).

14. Kirmānī [18 moves].

AH 7 (bl.) : C 43 (bl.) : Man. 21.

15. Muwashshaḥ [17 moves].

AH 7 (red) : C 43 (red) : Man. 55.

16. Mutalāḥiq [16 moves].

Since the notes that accompany the diagrams in the older MSS. are not without historical interest I translate them in full, taking the text in AH as the original, and adding in the notes the variations that I find in the other MSS. I have rearranged the text in agreement with the conclusions that I have formed as to the sources of the different *ta'bīyāt*, but I have added numbers to the paragraphs so as to show their order in the MS. AH.

¶ These are the *'ibdīyāt* which al-'Adlī and aṣ-Ṣūlī both gave. (1).

This is called *watad al-'anz* (the goat-peg). (2, rubric).[8]

This is the *muraddad* (moved to and fro). Jābir, and after him Rabrab, used to begin with it. It is a good opening which requires skill, and is a strong defence. It is called *muraddad* from the repeated movement of the two Knights. (3).

These openings are not diagrammed thus because one opposes the other. One should strive in every opening to play according to what is necessary, and to

Nos. 10 and 11. Name attached to diagrams in AH and BM.

No. 12. Name attached to diagram in AH (C) only. BM repeats the position of *al-'ibt* with this name.

Nos. 13 and 14. These positions are associated on the same diagram in AH and BM. I follow AH; BM transposes the names, and repeats the position of 13 as *rafūnaghī*. The respective identifications of these two *ta'bīyāt* are accordingly doubtful.

Nos. 15 and 16. Name attached to diagram in AH and Man.

[8] BM has simply '*watad al-'anz*' : Man. '*ta'bīya watad al-'anz*, described by aṣ-Ṣūlī'.

oppose (a move) by what will make a stand against it: this is only achieved by skill. (4).[9]

The ta'bīya *ḥiṣa fir'auna* (Pharaoh's stones). Abū'l-Bain[10] played it. (14, rubric).

The ta'bīya *al-'ajā'īz* (the old women). 'Uqda used to begin with it. (6).[11]

The ta'bīya *al-mujannaḥ* (the winged, or flanked). Shaqī used to begin with it. (7, rubric).[12]

The ta'bīya *as-sayyāla* (the torrent). Abū Sharara the elder used to begin with it. (8).[13]

¶ Aṣ-Ṣūlī says: None of the openings given by al-'Adlī are better than these two, *al-mujannaḥ* and *as-sayyāla*. (9).

The ta'bīya *al-mashā'īkhī* (the sheikh's opening). Na'īm used to begin with it. (10).[14]

Al-mu'aqrab (the strongly built). Fam al-Ḥūt used to begin with it. (11).[15]

¶ Aṣ-Ṣūlī says: Of these eight openings none are weaker than these two, *mu'aqrab* and *al-mashā'īkhī*, and yet I consider them better than the remaining openings which al-'Adlī gave and which I omit. (12).[16]

¶ These are the openings which al-'Adlī gave, and aṣ-Ṣūlī omitted. (21).

The ta'bīya *as-saif* (the sword). Na'īm al-Khādim used to begin with it. (5, rubric).[17]

The ta'bīya called *band al-khadam* (the slave's banner). (14).

The ta'bīya *jaish* (army), with which people used to begin. (15, rubric).[18]

The ta'bīya *ar-raqū-īqī* (?). Ghudāf used to begin with it. (17).[19]

The ta'bīya *al-'ibt* (the shoulder). Abū Sharara the younger played it. (22).[20]

The ta'bīya *al-Kirmānī* (of Kirmān, a province of Persia). 'Omar b. Ṭā'ūn played it. (23, rubric).

¶ These are the openings which aṣ-Ṣūlī gave, but not al-'Adlī. (13).

This is an opening that I often play. It is called *al-muwashshaḥ* (the richly girdled). (18, rubric).[21]

I chose this opening, and I name it *al-mutalāḥiq* (the conjoined),[22] because the pieces defend one another. (19).

¶ Aṣ-Ṣūlī says: We have mentioned ten openings, and these are sufficient. These openings were invented and described by people in order that the opener should satisfy himself with them, without noticing the play of his opponent: for when the opener makes it his object to produce one of these figures exactly, and neglects his opponent till his plan is in working order, he wins very quickly. However, the game varies, and if in the opening there occur something which gives him an advantage, he can abandon his opening, and make for it. (20).

[9] This is repeated in Man.

[10] Man. (f. 28 b) has Abu 'Aun.

[11] BM has '*Ta'bīya badā' al-'ajā'iz*, of 'Uqda'.

[12] BM has 'The *mujannaḥ* of Shafi'ī, associating this opening with the famous tābi'.

[13] BM has 'The *ta'bīya as-sayyāla* of Abū Sharara the elder'.

[14] BM has 'The *ta'bīya badā' al-mashā'īkhī* of Tamīm'. Man. (f. 39 a) also has Tamīm.

[15] BM has 'The *ta'bīya al-mu'aqrab* of Fam al-Ḥūt'.

[16] Man. (f. 43b), in repeating this note, substitutes 'better' for 'worse', completely altering the meaning, and continues, 'This opening (i.e. the *mu'aqrab*) and the one that stands opposite it are better than the *ta'bīyāt as-saif*, *al-'ajā'iz*, *al-muraddad*, *watad al-'anz*, *mujannaḥ*, and *sayyāla*.' There is obviously a copyist's blunder here, since many passages in the MSS. bear witness to the preference that aṣ-Ṣūlī and al-Lajlāj felt for the *mujannaḥ*.

[17] BM has 'The *ta'bīya as-saif* b. Shadād'.

[18] BM has simply '*Band al-khadam*' and '*Ta'bīya badā' jaish*' against these openings.

[19] BM has '*Ta'bīya ar-rafānaghi* of Ghudāf'. The name of this array is uncertain, owing to the omission of diacritical marks in the MSS. In the text I follow AH and C.

[20] BM has '*Ta'bīya band al-'ibt* of Abū Sharara the younger'.

[21] Man. has, 'Aṣ-Ṣūlī's *ta'bīya*, and he called it *ta'bīya al-muwashshaḥ*. He used to play it often because he preferred it to the *ta'bīyāt* in his book.'

[22] Man. names it *mulāḥiq*, which has the same meaning.

The note following the *muraddad* is a clear warning to the reader that the two openings figured upon one diagram are quite independent of one another.

The names given to these positions look somewhat fanciful. The names *mujannaḥ* and *mutalāḥiq* alone have an obvious propriety. In the one case the game is opened on the wings, and leads to a wing or flank attack; in the other the array is governed by the rather whimsical principle that every piece is to be defended by another. The names of two other arrays are explained incidentally in L and AE. In both these arrays the underlying principle of the attack is the rapid advance of a particular Pawn, in the *saif* the QP, and in the *sayyāla* the KBP. The advanced QP was popularly called the 'sword-Pawn' (*al-baidaq as-saif*), and the advanced KBP the 'torrent-Pawn' (*al-baidaq as-sayyāla*).

It is interesting to see how different Openings were associated with the names of the players who invented them, or made them famous. More interesting, though, is the brief note with which aṣ-Ṣūlī's concluded his chapter on the Openings, since it shows that the ordinary player opened his game in his own way, without troubling about the theories of the expert, and that he presumed upon his immunity from attack during the development-period to concentrate all his attention on his own play, and to ignore his opponent's. Aṣ-Ṣūlī's advice in his concluding sentence to pay attention to the game, because even in the Opening there were opportunities that made it worth a player's while to abandon his original plan and to fasten his attention upon the weakness that he had detected in his opponent's arrangement, is the first sign of an appreciation of the principles underlying development. Aṣ-Ṣūlī does not appear to have carried his discovery any farther. It was left to his pupil al-Lajlāj to demonstrate it and drive the advice home. This he did in his *Risāla fī bayān laʿb ash-shaṭranj* ('Treatise on the demonstration of the game of chess') which we possess in MSS. L and AE. This work should have opened a new era, for al-Lajlāj formed the original and ambitious idea of investigating the Openings, and by pursuing the play into the mid-game he endeavoured to determine the relative values of the principal Openings played in his day. His great discovery was the value of time in chess, and his enthusiastic advocacy of the *mujannaḥ* and *sayyāl* as the best of the Openings is due to the fact that these could both be completed in twelve moves. By opposing the *mujannaḥ* to two of the slower developments, the *saif* and *mashā'īkhī*, he established the truth and importance of his discovery. Elsewhere he showed how it was possible even in the first dozen moves to thwart the opponent's intentions, and prevent the formation of his pet array.

This work is so important for the history of the practical game that I give it in abstract in the Appendix to this chapter. It is the only work on its subject of whose existence we know, prior to the first analysts of the modern game. It is not until we come to the *Libro de la invencion liberal y arte del Juego del Axedrez* of Ruy Lopez (Alcala, 1561) that we meet with a work at all comparable to it. Unfortunately it passed almost unnoticed. As in mediaeval Europe, so in Islam, the literature of chess was almost entirely confined to the problem.

The only sign of the influence of al-Lajlāj's researches in later works is to be found in BM. I have already quoted a passage from this MS. which shows that the traditional Openings were obsolete in the writer's time—say 1250. The MS. contains a new chapter on the Openings, which was evidently intended to give the practice of the chess-players of the day. It is found on ff. 11 a–12 b.

Chapter of the *ta'ābī*; what is agreed about them. Their greatest number is 5.[23]

(1) The first is ascribed to al-Lajlāj, because he chose this *ta'bīya* and said that it is better than the others since the pieces are developed from their squares in 12 moves.[24] He chose to develop the right-hand QR to Kt2, then to KB2, and the left-hand R to KKt sq, next his Q to B2, and to advance his left-hand KtP. He made the game on this wing, because it is better than the other. This is the figure which he has mentioned at its first development. Upon this he founded his game correctly.

(2) This is the Opening of the Ṣūfī 'Omar al-Baghdādī, and of Abū-Bakr al-Mauṣilī ash-Shaṭranjī.[25]

(3) This is another of al-Lajlāj's Openings. In this he does on the Q's wing what in the first Opening he did on the K's wing, in order to establish his Q in QKt5, if he play well.

(4) This is the Opening of the *baidaq as-sayyāl*, according to which he played in every Opening. It is a good Opening, and most people of our time adopt it. This is its figure. It is demolished, as we have said, by Black playing P to R4 (i. e. Ph5).[26]

(5) This Opening is played by most of the moderns. What al-'Adlī says on the Openings is mentioned later, but in our time these are abandoned. No one to my knowledge plays according to them. What the moderns have discovered in the Openings and Problems is better, neater, and easier to understand.

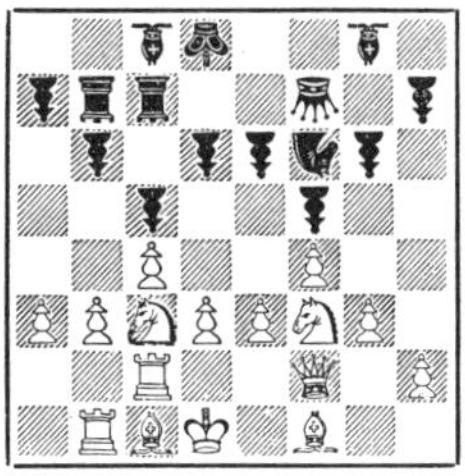

17. BM 1.

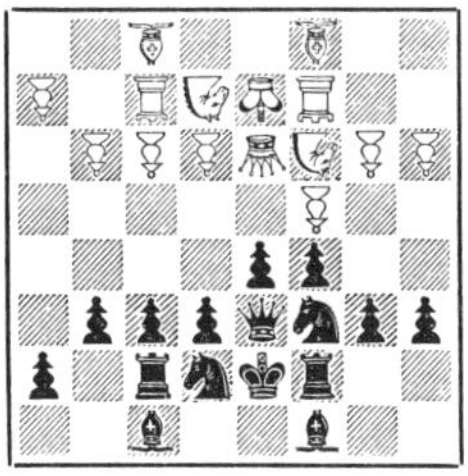

18. BM 2.

19. BM 3.

These BM diagrams (Nos. 17–21) differ from the diagrams in AH which I have been discussing, in that each figure claims to represent a game position,

[23] The diagrams are Nos. 17–21 in this chapter.

[24] Cf. L f. 2 a. 'I begin . . . with the opening called *al-mujannaḥ* . . . because it shows the most adequate and correct developments, because its form is symmetrical, and because all players have expressed their preference for it. Also it is the only one of the openings in which all the pieces are moved in 12 moves.' And f. 2 a. 'In this development there are three manners of play. The first way is to advance the KRP and KKtP; this is best. . . . The third is to advance QRP and QKtP; this is worst.' The whole passage is translated in the Appendix to this chapter.

[25] It is possible that aṣ-Ṣūlī is meant by this second player, but I think it more likely that it refers to a later player nearer the writer's own day.

[26] Compare again L f. 73 a: 'The *sayyāla* is only demolished by the RP which is opposite it.' And again, f. 73 b: 'The game is to Red's advantage when he pushes his left-hand RP (i. e. KRP) to its fourth square, and he develops the remainder of his pieces according to the *mujannaḥ* development.'

and not to give two distinct Openings fortuitously placed upon the same diagram. This is clear from the title to the chapter, but it is by no means so clear from the diagrams themselves. It is of course obvious that they are inaccurately copied. In 17 a black Kt is missing from c6, and Bb8 should be on c8. Each side has played 16 moves. In 18 a red P is missing from e5: each side has played 19 moves. The other three diagrams are less easy of correction. In 19 Red has played 16 and Black 18 moves. In 20 Red has played 20 moves and Black only 15, and the Qs are concordant. In 21, if we replace the missing Kts on e2 and g8, Red has played 14 moves and Black 16.

It is easy to recognize 17 and 19 as positions in the double *Mujannaḥ*. The parallel passages which I quote in the foot-notes from L explain the discrepancies between the figures and the descriptive text. It is clear to me that the writer of the MS. has made unintelligent use of the work of al-Lajlāj.

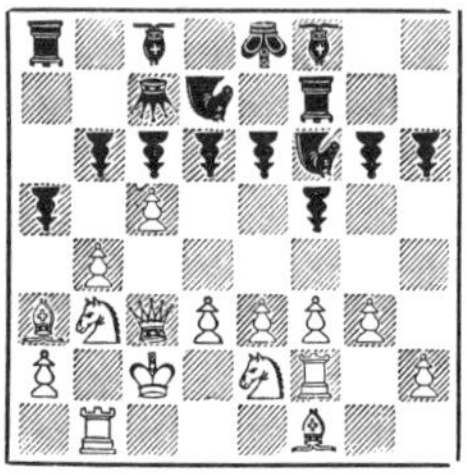

20. BM 4.

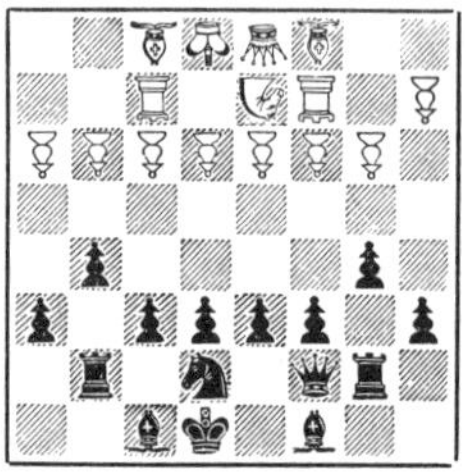

21. BM 5.

Instead of taking the position which al-Lajlāj gave of this Opening at the 12th move, the writer has taken a later position from the first part of the analysis in L.

The second position appears to be a double *Saif*; the fourth, the *Sayyāl*, again shows in its accompanying text evidence of the use of al-Lajlāj's treatise, since the reference to the strength of the move Ph4 in reply to this attack occurs in the beginning of the section on this opening in L.

As promised, the MS. at a later page (f. 42 a) reproduces al-ʿAdlī's *taʿābī*; I have already used this chapter, above.[27]

The day of better things soon passed, and chess writers returned to the older material. Probably this was due in no small degree to the prestige that these Openings enjoyed from their association with the name of aṣ-Ṣūlī, and to the exaggerated respect which the Muslim pays to tradition and authority. We can hardly expect an age that esteemed aṣ-Ṣūlī as the greatest exponent of chess the world had ever seen, to do anything else but treat his recorded

[27] This satisfactorily explains one of the apparent inaccuracies for which v. d. Linde (i. 101) attacked Forbes. Forbes (107) stated quite correctly that BM contains eleven diagrams of *taʿbīyāt*, but omitted to say that they were given in two different chapters in different parts of the MS. Rieu only discovered the earlier chapter when he examined the MS. for v. d. Linde, and the historian, who unfortunately was unable to let escape any opportunity of attacking Forbes, at once assumed that Forbes had never examined the MS. critically.

opinions on the Openings with the utmost deference. And so we find Man. and H repeating the ancient developments.[28]

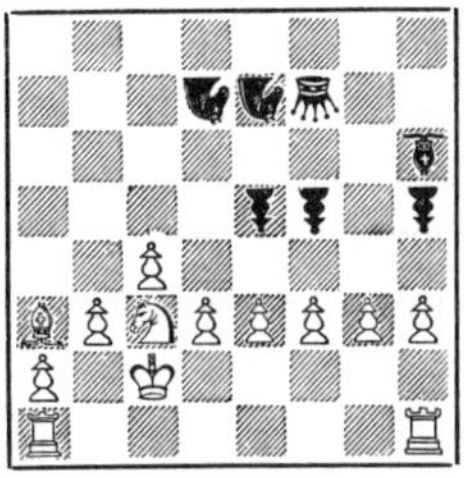

22. RAS 1. Muʻaliq and Halīlī.

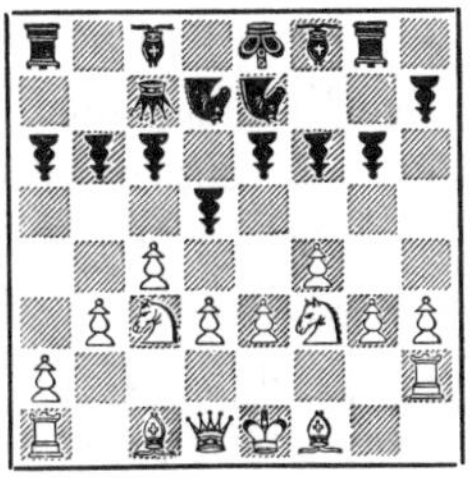

23. RAS 2. Mujannaḥ and Chanāj.

RAS varies to some extent. This MS. only gives two diagrams (see Figs. 22 and 23), each of which contains two Openings as in the older MSS. The first is now so worn as to be almost illegible. There are traces of black men on a6, a8, b6, c6, c7, c8, d6, g6, g8 and of red men on e1, f2. It gave the *Muʻaliq* (Red) and the *Halīlī* (Black). The second gives the *Mujannaḥ* (Red) and the *Chanāj* (Black). It is interesting to find the *Mujannaḥ* retaining its popularity in the chess circle at the court of Tīmūr.

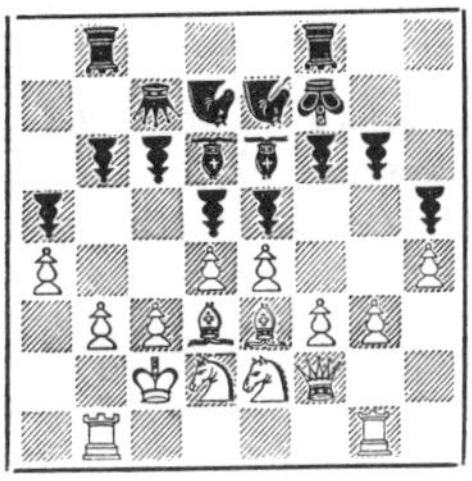

24. F 1. Ṭabarīya.

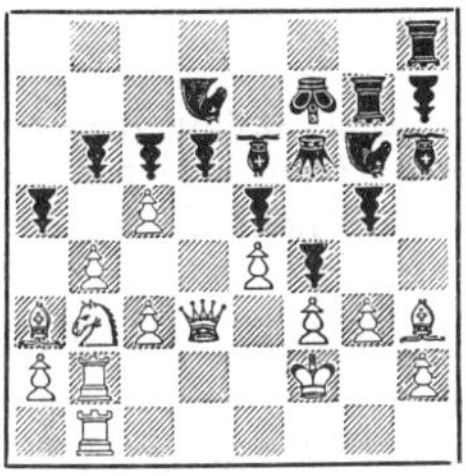

25. F 2. ʻIrāqīya.

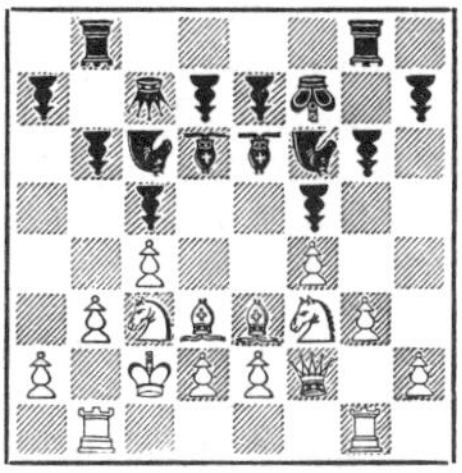

26. F 3. Ḥaṣīn firʻauna.

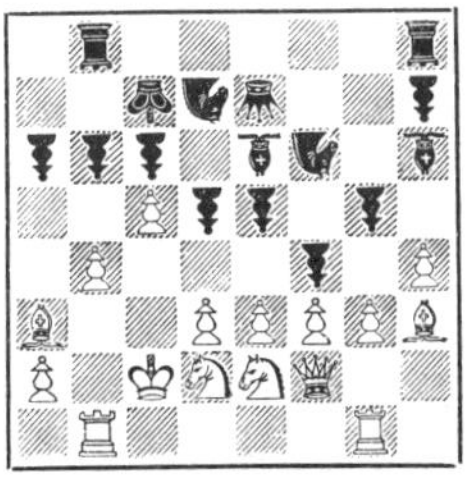

27. F 4. Watad-al-fazz.

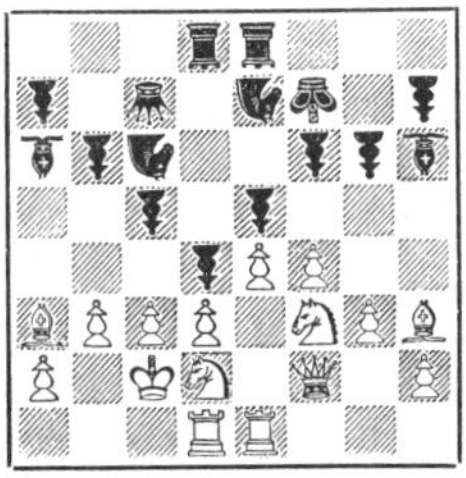

28. F 5. Ṭarḥīya.

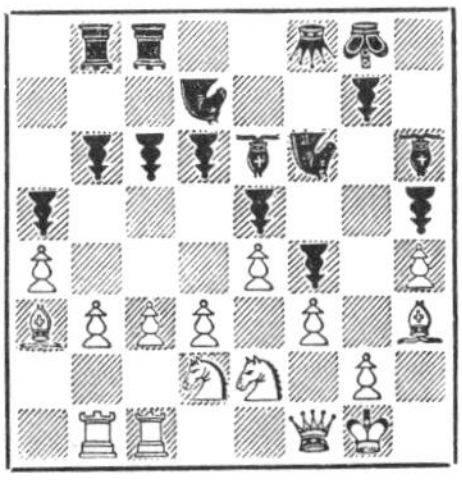

29. F 6. Gharība wa malīḥa.

The Turkish MS. F of 1501 has an interesting chapter on Openings, with six diagrams (see Figs. 24 to 29). It will be seen that some diagrams show a cross-

[28] I have dealt with the material in Man. above. H gives three diagrams as from the works of al-ʻAdlī and aṣ-Ṣūlī (ff. 20 b, 21 a). The first is Red, *Mujannaḥ*; Black, *Sayyāl*. The second is Red, *Saif*; Black, *Mujannaḥ*. The third, which alone has any names, is said to be from aṣ-Ṣūlī and to be *qirl* and *Kirmānī*. As a matter of fact it is Red, *ʻAjā'iz*; Black, *Mashā'īkhī*.

wise arrangement of Kings, which, if really intended, would be the earliest instances of this. Since the later MSS. S and Y still retain the older arrangement, while the Turkish MS. itself makes large use of older material which is clearly based on the 'opposite' arrangement of the Kings, I am inclined to see here some error in the diagrams. Many of them show exactly similar developments on the part of both players, and in these cases the crosswise arrangement may be due to the fact that the names on the upper half of the boards are written upside down. I think the writer did not observe when he reversed his book in order to enter these names that he also ought to 'reflect' the position. I can hardly believe that so great a change as that involved in the crosswise arrangement could have been made in Constantinople without so diligent a writer as b. Sukaikir having referred to the fact in his book (S).

The text of F is as follows:

The first arrangement is called *Ṭabarīya*: it is suitable for beginners. It is said that the people of Ṭabaristān play in this way. Whoever will adopt this opening and practise moving as in this figure will defeat his opponent, who will inevitably succumb.

The second arrangement is called *'Irāqīya*. The players of 'Irāq adopt it. It is very scientific. Whoever will play in this way will defeat his opponent. . . . Victorious day after day, he will at length attain to the skill of Lajlāj at chess.

The third arrangement is called *ḥaṣīn fir'auna* (Pharaoh's fortress). It is so called from its great strength. Some players of 'Irāq and Khurāsān play thus. Whoever, &c.

The fourth arrangement is called *watad al-fazz*, or *gechi gazighi* (goat-peg). It is so called because he who plays it wins with his pawns. They are like a peg in his opponent's clothes, and the opponent is like a man with his hands bound. Whoever, &c.

The fifth arrangement is called *ṭarḥīya* because it is very beautiful and scientific. Whoever, &c.

The sixth arrangement is called *gharība wa malīḥi* (the wonderful and lovely). It is very lovely and scientific. If any one undertakes to play a game in which he will never receive a check and makes a bet to this effect, he ought to play thus, and his opponent will succumb.

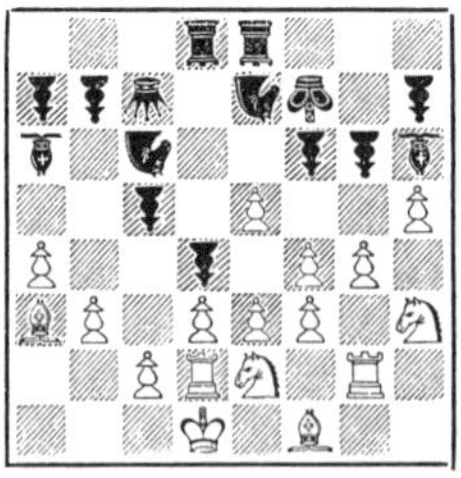

30. MS. Gotha (obviously very corrupt).

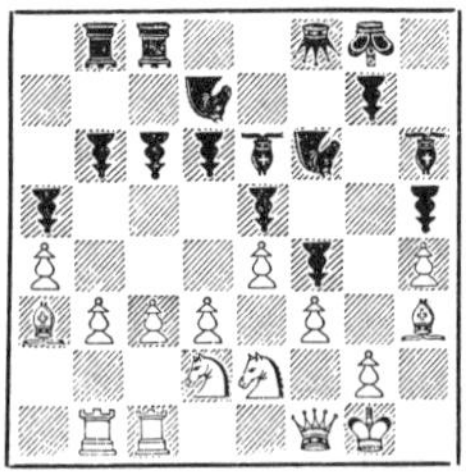

31. MS. Gotha.

A more modern Gotha MS. (Turc. 18, Pertsch, = 1033, Moeller) has two diagrams (Nos. 30 and 31) which are evidently Openings. They bear some resemblance to the Openings in F (cf. F 5 and F 6). A poem of six couplets accompanies the diagrams, of which a metrical version was given in *Serapeum* (Leipzig, 1867), XXVIII. 177–88 (quoted by v. d. Linde, i. 130).

The inevitable tendency of the use of the *taʿbīyāt* by the ordinary player was the neglect of the careful study of the opening moves. A player started with a position in mind and made the necessary moves to produce it on the board. He knew that he would enjoy practical immunity from attack for some dozen or fifteen moves, and he gave no attention to his opponent until his opening position had been secured. His opponent meantime was doing precisely the same. When each had made his *taʿbīya* the game began. Up till that point it did not appear very important whether the orderly succession of alternate moves was observed or not. The important thing was to get through the preparatory tactics as quickly as possible, so that the real tussle might begin. And so hurried, simultaneous, and unconsidered play gradually became the rule for the earlier moves of the game, and the modern Muslim and Abyssinian method of opening came into existence. It is obviously something quite different from the introductory tactics of the Indian game, in which only one player plays at a time, and the number of moves that he may make is strictly settled.

For Mid-game tactics we possess treatises both by aṣ-Ṣūlī and by his pupil al-Lajlāj. The former appears to have formed a part of aṣ-Ṣūlī's lost chess work, whence it is quoted at length in Man.,[29] and in extract in Y. The latter is given at the end of AH (ff. 133 b–135 a). The two works are largely identical, and aṣ-Ṣūlī's may be summarized thus:

The first player should adopt the *Mujannaḥ* array. He should try to be the first to develop his *Fīls*. He should not move his *Shāh* except under compulsion; his original square is his best post. He should not move in a Rook's line of attack (*iʿrā*) unless two or three other pieces intervene. When checked cover with *Firzān* or *Fīl* rather than with a superior piece. If a *Faras* gives check, move a *Fīl's* move distant from him. Beware of an attack on the *Shāh* with two superior pieces. If the opponent's men cramp the *Shāh*, attack his pieces and compel exchanges. Avoid checks. Do not hesitate to sacrifice a man if an advantage is to be gained in that way. In a series of exchanges, take in such an order that a piece is won, i.e. if this is possible. With the better game do not let the opponent draw, with the worse, play for the draw. Look after your own men, and your opponent's also. Examine every move of his. When you see three moves ahead which appear trustworthy, play the first, but before playing the second and third examine them again. If you win a piece, try and win the game as a result. If you lose a piece, do not relax your efforts. There was an Indian player who never lost a Pawn without corresponding advantage for 40 years. When your opponent moves his *Shāh*, move yours, keeping opposite him. When he plays his *Firzān*, play yours. Put your Rooks opposite his in the opening. If he advance a Pawn, advance that one of yours which counters it, e.g. he moves QRP, you do the same; he moves QKtP, you move QBP; he moves QBP, you move QP,[30] &c. In the opening it is best to play with *Firzān*, *Faras*, and Pawns. Try to be the first to enter the adversary's territory, but take care that you are not compelled to return again. The best post for the *Firzān* is Q3; for *Faras*, either the centre of the board or the margin in the opponent's half of the board; for Rook, your opponent's Kt2 or R2 or your own KKt2. The worst square for the Rook is R2 (Lajlāj: Because the *Fīl*

[29] Ch. ii, ff. 31 a–34 b, followed by a criticism of b. Abī Ḥajala on ff. 34 b–39 a, which is of little importance for the practical game.

[30] I imagine the text here is in error, and QKtP should counter QKtP; QBP, QBP; and so on. Such an error in copying might very easily happen.

can attack it. The worst square for the *Faras* after the corner is Kt2. The corner is bad for everything except the Rook). A *Faras* at liberty is worth more than a confined Rook. After opening the game on the wings, open it in the centre. Take care of your central Pawns (Y: Some say they are better than the *Faras*; all agree that they are better than a *Firzān*), they are the best of the Pawns; KP is better than QP, QP than BP, BP than KtP, KtP than RP. Some say that KKtP is the best of all the Pawns except the two central ones, because it is a spy against the return of the adversary's stronger *Fīl* and *Firzān*, so it should be guarded and not thrown away lightly. QRP is better than KRP. Take care of the *Fīl an-Nafs* (Lajlāj: Keep your *Fīl al-qā'ima*; this is the KB). It is better than the *Fīl al-Firzān* (QB), because it is the defensive *Fīl*. Do not sacrifice it, except in a case of necessity or to gain material advantage. Take care of KP. It should not be advanced farther than K3 except to attack the *Firzān*, or to open a cramped game. QP is to be played to Q4 (i. e. d4) as a general rule. If 3 Pawns are in a line, take the middle one (Lajlāj adds: if the capture is made by a Pawn). Shun the game of greed (*tama'*).

To this al-Lajlāj adds but little new. He cites ar-Rāzī as laying down rules when chess-playing is inexpedient, as for instance, when the mind is occupied with other matters, or when taking food. From aṣ-Ṣūlī, to whom he gratefully expresses his indebtedness for his knowledge of chess, he quotes the following advice:

Never snatch at an offered piece until the consequences have been fully weighed. Do not sacrifice a piece unless you see your way clear to regain it shortly, or a certain win. Do not let your *Shāh* be hemmed in. Beware of the move of the *Fīl*. Never play a move without a reason. Do not open your game on the *Firzān's* wing; the general rule is to advance on the *Shāh's* wing. Do not advance P to K4 unless the QP is beside it, or it is necessary to guard one of your pieces, or to drive back one of your opponent's, or your game is blocked and you have no other way of opening it. Do not be in a hurry to play Q to Q3 or B3. Double your Rooks on the 7th row. Do not move Rooks or *Faras* from their squares during the development. You lose two moves if you advance a piece and then have to return it. A strongly posted Rook is worth Rook and *Firzān* at least. When you see a good move for a piece, look out for a better. In making a move do not think about the actual move, but about winning or drawing the game. The right thing to do with your *Fīl* is to sacrifice it for a Pawn. Avoid a divergent check.

Obviously there is much of this good counsel that is equally applicable to the modern European game.

APPENDIX

AL-LAJLĀJ'S ANALYSIS OF THE MUJANNAḤ, MASHĀ'IKHĪ, SAIF, AND SAYYĀL OPENINGS

As has already been stated, this analysis is contained in the *Risāla al-Lajlāj fī bayān la'b ash-shaṭranj* ('Al-Lajlāj's treatise on the demonstration of the game of chess') by Abū al-Muẓaffar b. Sa'īd al-Lajlāj ash-Shaṭranjī, of which we possess an Arabic text in L and a Persian text in AE. I have not attempted to preserve the order of the original work: Arabic chess notation is so diffuse, and the arrangement of the variations so disorderly, that considerations both of space and of convenience have determined me to arrange the analysis on modern lines. By this means I can give it entire, and the reader will find it easy to appreciate the principles of play that the great Muslim master observed. Following modern usage, again I have given the move throughout to Red (White); the occasions in which Black plays first in the MSS. are, however, noted as they occur. In the MSS. the Red K stands on d1, the Black K on d8; here again I have 'reflected' the arrangement, and I record the moves throughout on the assumption that the Kings stand on the *e*-file.[1]

The analysis contains very few notes on the play, other than those necessary to explain the connexion of a variation with the main line of play, but what there are will be found in the notes to my tables. The moves are not numbered, and they follow one another without any attempt at spacing or paragraphing. When a variation is finished, a rubric, 'The game returns to such and such a move,' introduces the new line of play. A new trunk line is introduced with a diagram of the position from which the analysis commences.

The work may be divided into five sections, which deal with (1) the Mujannaḥ when opposed by the Mujannaḥ, which I call for short the Double Mujannaḥ, (2) the uncompleted Mujannaḥ, (3) the Mujannaḥ when opposed by the Mashā'īkhī and alternatively, (4) the Saif, and (5) the Sayyāl. In the case of the Double Mujannaḥ, the play is not given from the first move, since the order of the moves is not material provided the player take care that the opponent cannot prevent him posting his BPs on their fourth squares. The introduction deals with this one point, and the subsequent analyses all start from positions on the 10th to the 15th move. In the majority of the other sections the play is recorded from the first move, though in the Sayyāl games there are often long gaps in the record which can only be filled with the help of the diagram of the position finally secured.

[1] The player who wishes to reproduce the 'atmosphere' of the Muslim board can easily adapt my notation by lettering the files from right to left instead of from left to right.

The introduction to the work runs as follows:—

In the name of God the compassionate and merciful! The sheikh al-Imām Abū'l-Muẓaffar b. Sa'īd, surnamed al-Lajlāj (the stammerer)—May God have mercy upon him!—says: 'Praise be to God the all-good who made the creation, and the blessing of God light upon our Lord Muḥammad, the best of all His followers! There is no might except with God, wherefore we rely on Him, and call upon Him for help!'

I have noticed that while my predecessors have arranged figures which are used in the game of chess, and have diagrammed the recognized Openings, and have taught the moves of the pieces by means of problems, yet no one has attempted to instruct the player who has learnt to identify the Openings from the diagrams in books, in the correct method of play which is appropriate to each Opening. I have accordingly taken the trouble to investigate the Openings with which the game is commenced, and which are adopted by the majority of players in spite of their opposition to correct principles, and to form an opinion as to the excellence, mediocrity, or badness of each game. Some of these games are played to an end, others continue even until the victory or draw follows.

I hope that in the present work I have opened a door to the student through which he may easily attain to this knowledge. The games which I have not explained either because of their length, or because of their great similarity to other games, are commended to the student's attention. In this investigation, I have had no forerunner, not even among the greatest experts, and I have spent long days in the selection of this treasure and the solution of its problems. The numerous instructions which I have received in long talk with and continuous inquiry from Abū-Bakr Muḥammad b. Yaḥyā aṣ-Ṣūlī have put me in a position to compose this book.

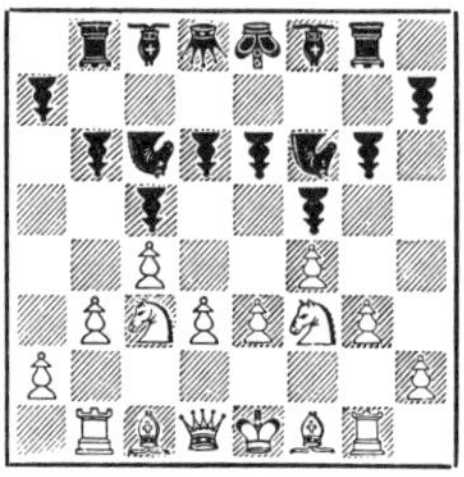

The Mujannaḥ Opening.
The position after
twelfth move.

I begin in God's name with the Opening called AL-MUJANNAḤ and those which resemble it, because it shows the most adequate and correct development, because its form is symmetrical, and because all players have expressed their preference for it. Also it is the only one of the Openings in which all the pieces are moved in twelve moves. This is its diagram as drawn in the books. We shall follow it out from the first move and (?) repeat them until they show sufficiently the way that follows. Then we shall describe the developments which resemble the Mujannaḥ, and conclude with the complete erection of those which do not do so, if God wills.

In this development there are three manners of play. The first way is to advance the KRP and KKtP; this is best. The second way is to advance QP; this is the central attack adopted by many; at the present time this is the usual line of play. The third is to advance QRP and QKtP; this is worst.

We suppose that Red has the first move. The position in the diagram is obtained in twelve moves. Red moves the left-hand BP (1 Pf3); if Black moves any of the following, KP, KBP, KKtP, KRP, Red moves his left-hand BP a second move (2 Pf4). If, however, Black move any of these, QP, QBP, QKtP, or QRP, Red moves his right-hand BP twice. He secures the advantage of the attack on the King's wing because he retains the move in the opening by moving KKtP. The result is, Red fixes the Q's wing by opening on the K's wing, and fixes the game with the Q by leaving QRP in a3. Whatever Black plays on the Q's side is bad for him, and good for Red as we shall make clear.

The discussion returns to the moment when the development has been completed according to the diagram.

That is to say, al-Lajlāj proposes now to continue his analysis from the position after move 12, and to omit the previous moves by which that position is obtained. The crucial point is at the commencement. Red plays 1 Pf3, but he has to watch his opponent to see which wing he is going to open first. If this is the K wing, he can continue 2 Pf4, but if the opponent chooses to commence his Q wing development, Red must continue 2 Pc3 in order that he may not be behindhand on that wing.

The analysis now follows. Those moves which I have supplied by the help of the diagrams only, are throughout printed in italics.

Table 1. The Double Mujannah.

1. *Pf3, Pf6*; 2. *Pf4, Pf5*; 3. *Ktf3, Ktf6*; 4. *Pg3, Pg6*; 5. *Pc3, Pc6*; 6. *Pc4 Pc5*; 7. *Ktc3, Ktc6*; 8. *Pb3, Pb6*; 9. *Pe3, Pe6*; 10. *Pd3, Pd6*; 11. *Rb1, Rb8* 12. *Rg1, Rg8.*

	1.	2.	3.	4.	5.	6.
13	Ph3 / Pa6	/ Rb7				
14	Pa3[1] / Pb5	Rb2 / Ph6	/ bRg7	/ Rf7		
15	P×P ! / P×P	Pg4 / Rf7	bRg2 / Ph6	Rf2 / Ph6		
16	Pb4. / P×P	bRg2 / Rh8	Pg4 / P×P	Pg4 / P×P		
17	P×P / Rg7[2]	Kth2 / Qc7 or Pa6	P×P / Pg5	P×P / Pg5		
18	Rg2 / Rc7	Ph4 / P×P[10]	Pf5 / Pd5 !	Pf5 / P×P[22]		
19	Rc2[3] / Pe5[4]	Kt×P / Kth5[11]	P×eP / P×P	P×P / Ktd7[23]		
20	Pe4 ![5] / P×eP[6]	Qe2 / Kte7	bP×P / B×P	Ktd2 / Kte7		
21	dP×P / P×P	Kth2[12] / any[13]	Ktd5 ![19] / Kt×gP[20]	Bh3 ![24] / Pg4		
22	P×P / Bh6[7]	Qf3 / any	R×Kt / B×R	fRg2 / Ktf6[25]	/ Rh8[30]	/ Ph5
23	Pe5 / P×P	Qg4 / Ktf6	Ktf6 *ch* / Kf7	Kt(d2)e4 / Kt×Kt ![26]	R×P / Kte5	Kt(d2)e4 / Rh8
24	P×P / Kth5	Ph5 / Pg5[14]	Kt×R / Bd6 ![21]	Kt×Kt / Ph5	R(g4)g2 ![31] / Kt×P *ch*	Ktg5 / Rg7[33]
25	Bd3 ?[8] / Ktf4	Pf5 ![15] / Pe5[16]	Kt×P *ch* /	Qe2 / Rh8	Kf1 / Kt×P[32]	Ktf3 / gRg8[34]
26	B×P ![9] / Kt×eP	Kte4 / Kt(f6)g8[17]		Ktg5 / Rf6[27]	B×Kt / R×B	Kth4 / P×B
27	Kt×Kt / Re7	Ktg3 / Rg7		Kte4 / fRh6[28]	Rf2	R×R / Kt×R !
28	Re2 / Kt×R	Qf3 / Pg4		Rf2 / any		Rh1[35]
29	K×Kt / Kt×Kt *ch*	Kte4[18]		Bf1[29]		
30	Be3 !					

Notes to Table 1.

[1] Or 14 Rb2, Pb5; 15 bRf2 or g2 ignoring the counter-attack on the Queen's wing. 15 . ., P×cP; 16 bP×P followed by Q to b3, Ba3, Kta4, winning the cP. 15 . ., Pb4; 16 Kte2 !, Pa5; 17 any on K wing, Pa4; 18 Qc2 !, P×P; 19 Q×P, Ra8 ! but Red can eventually bring his Q to b5. 15 . ., Kta7 to follow with the advance of the aP leaves Red time to continue his own attack on the other wing.

[2] 17 . ., Ph6; 18 Pg4, P×P; 19 P×P, Pg5; 20 P×P, P×P; =.

[3] 19 Pg4, Pe5; 20 P×eP, P×eP; 21 Pd4, Pe4; 22 Ktd2 !, Ph3.

[4] 19 . ., Pd5; 20 Kte2 (a), Bd6; 21 Kt(f3)d4. Kt×bP; 22 R×R, Q×R; 23 Ktc3 to follow with Kt(d4)×bP. The games are even.

(a) 20 Kte5, Kte7; 21 Ba3 to follow with Bc5.

[5] 20 P×P ?, P×P; 21 Pe4, P×P; 22 P×P, Bd6; 23 Ktd5, Kt×Kt; 24 P×Kt, Kt×bP; 25 R×R, Q×R; 26 Kt×P, Kt×P with a P more. If 20 any other, Pe4; 21 Ktd2 (or h2), Pd5 !; 22 Pg4, Pd4; 23 Kta2 ! (a), P×dP; 24 B×P, Bd6 winning the bP.

(a) 23 Kte2, P×eP; 24 B×P, P×dP; 25 B×P, P×gP; 26 P×P, Kt×gP and will win the bP. If 23 Pg5 ?, Kt×bP, winning.

[6] 20 . ., Ktd4; 21 Kt×Kt, P×Kt; 22 Kte2, R×R; 23 Q×R, P×eP; 24 Kt×P !, P×P; 25 Q×P !.

[7] 22 . ., Kth5; 23 Ktd5, with better game.

[8] 25 Ktd5, Rd7; 26 R×Kt, R×Kt. Red has the advantage, since his Ps block the Bl. Q's entry.

[9] 26 Kt×P ?, Kt×B *ch*; 27 K∼, R×Kt, with better game.

[10] 18 . ., any on Q wing; 19 Ph5, Kte7 (a); 20 P×gP, Kt×P(g6); 21 P×fP, Kth4; 22 Rf2, Kt×P; 23 Bh3, Kt∼; 24 Pf5.

(a) 19 . ., Pg4 (b); 20 P×fP, eP×P; 21 P×P, P×P. Or 19 . ., P×hP; 20 P×fP, P×P; 21 Bh3, with better game.

(b) 19 . ., P×gP; 20 P×P, Rg7; 21 Kt×gP, R×P !; 22 Kt×Kt *ch*, R×Kt. Red continues with Bh3, Rf2, Pf5, with better game.

[11] 19 . ., Kt×Kt; 20 R×Kt, Kte7; 21 Ph5, P×hP (a); 22 Rh4, any; 23 R×hP followed by Rh2, Rf2, Bh3, and Pf5. If now Bl. plays Pe4, Red replies R(f2)g2; but if P×P, Red replies R(g1)f1 and B×P, with better game.

(a) If 21 . ., Pg5; 22 P×P.

[12] Or 21 Ktf2, probably not quite so good.

[13] But not 21 . ., Pd5 ?; 22 P×P, P×P; 23 Ktf3, with better game.

[14] 24 . ., P×P; 25 Qf3, Pd5; 26 Pf5 or P×dP !, with better game.

[15] 25 P×gP, P×gP.

[16] 25 . ., P×P; 26 Q×P, sacrificing a P for the better game.

[17] 26 . ., Kt×Kt; 27 Kt×Kt. This assumes 21 Ktf2. See note 12 above.

[18] Following with Q×P, with the superior game.

[19] The sacrifice of the gP is praised as sound.

[20] Or 21 . ., Kt×Kt ?; 22 P×Kt. Or 21 . ., Qe7 or Rg6; 22 Kt×Kt *ch* and 23 Qe2, with a clear road to the centre of the board. Or 21 . ., Ktd7; 22 Qe7, &c.

[21] 24 . ., K×Kt; 25 R×B, and has won a piece.

[22] 18 . ., Pd5; 19 P×eP, B×P; 20 P×P, Kte7; 21 Kte5 !, Kt×gP !; 22 Kt×R, Kt×R; 23 P×B, Kt×Q; 24 Kt×Kt. Or 18 . ., Qe7; 19 Ktd2, R(f7)g7; 20 Qe2, Pd5; 21 P×eP, P×P; 22 bP×P, B×P; 23 Qf3.

[23] 19 . ., Kte7; 20 Pd4, Kt×P (a); 21 Kt×P, Kt×dP or eP (b); 22 Kt×R, K×R; 23 R×Kt *ch*, K×R; 24 R×R, winning.

(a) 20 . ., P×P; 21 Kt×dP.

(b) 21 . ., R×Kt; 22 R×R, P×R; 23 R×Kt, with better game.

[24] 21 Pe4, Ktc6 followed by R(f7)g7, Kf7, and Bl. can establish his Q in d4 or f4, winning.

[25] 22 . ., Kte5; 23 Qe2 (a), Rh8 (b); 24 Rf2 !, P×B; 25 Pf6, Ktc6 !; 26 Kt(d2)e4 or Ktd5. If 25 . ., Ktg8; 26 Ktd5 and if 25 . ., Kt(e7)g6; 26 Pd4. Red has the better game.

(a) 23 Pd4, Ktd3 *ch*; 24 Kf1, Kt×fP (c); 25 B×Kt, R×B *ch*; 26 Ktf3, R×Kt *ch*; 27 Ke2; or 26 Ke2, Kt×B *ch* drawn.

(b) 23 . ., any other; 24 Pd4, P×P; 25 P×P, Ktc6; 26 R×P, with the advantage.

(c) 24 . ., P×P; 25 P×P, Ktf4; 26 R×P, R×R; 27 R×R, Kt×B.

[26] Or 23 . ., P×B; 24 Kt×Kt *ch*, R×Kt; 25 R×R, with the better game.

[27] If 26 . ., P×B; 27 Kt×R. And if 26 . ., Rg7; 27 Ktf3, hRh7; 28 Kth4, P×B; 29 Rg5, Red retains the advantage.

[28] 27 . ., Rf7; 28 Pf6 followed by Rf2 !.

[29] Red will bring K to c3 and play Pd4.

[30] 22 . ., fRg7; 23 Kt(d2)e4 !, Kf7; 24 Pf6, Kt×fP; 25 Rf1, Rg6; 26 gRf2, wins the Kt.

[31] 24 R(g4)g3, Kt×P *ch*; 25 Kf1, Kt×P (a); 26 B×Kt, R×B *ch*; 27 Ke2 ! drawn. Not 27 Ktf3 ?, R×Kt *ch*; 28 Ke2, Kte4, winning.

(a) 25 . ., Kt×B; 26 Qc2 followed by Kf2 or g2, wins the Kt.

[32] 25 . ., Kte5; 26 Qc2 followed by Ke2, Q to d5, and Kt(d2)e4, winning.

[33] 24 . ., Rf6; 25 Kt(c3)e4, fRh6; 26 gRf2, P×B; 27 Kt×hP or Rh1 and R×P(h3). He plays his K to c3 and advances dP.

[34] 25 . ., gRh7; 26 Kth4, P×B; 27 Rg5 followed by Kte4, K to c3, and Pd4; if now Bl. takes dP, Red replies P×dP, and then Be3 to keep the Bl. Q out of the game. Next Rh1 and R×P(h3).

[35] To follow with Qe2 and R×P(h3).

Table 2. The Double Mujannaḥ.

Moves 1 to 12 as in Table 1.

	7.	8.	9.	10.	11.	12.
13	Ph3					
	Ph6					
14	Pg4			*Qc2*	*Ph4*	
	P×P			*Ph5*[11]	*Ph5*	
15	P×P			Pd4	*Rb2*	
	Pg5			P×P	*Rb7*	*Pb5*
16	Pf5[1]	P×P !		P×P	*Re2*	*Re2*
	Pd5 ![2]	P×P		Kte4	*Re7*	*Pa6*
17	P×dP[3]	Pd4 !		Kte2	*gRg2*	*Qc2*
	P×dP	Pd5[4]	Rb7	Pb5	*gRg7*	*Pb4*
18	Pe4	Qc2	Rb2	Qd3[12]	*Qc2*	*Kta4*
	Ph5	Qc7	Rf7	Ktf6	Qc7[18]	Qc7[25]
19	P×hP	P×dP !	Rf2	Ktc3	Pd4	Pd4
	Pg4	eP×P[5]	Pd5	P×P	P×P[19]	Qb6
20	Kth4 or d2	P×P	cP×P[8]	P×P	P×P	Qd3
		P×P	eP×P	R×R	Pe5[20]	Kd7
21		Ba3	Kte5	Kt×R	fP×P	Kd1
		Pd4[6]	Kt×Kt	Ph4	P×P	Kc7
22		P×P[7]	P×Kt	Pg4[13]	P×P ![21]	Kc2
		P×P	Ktd7	Bh6	Ktg4	Kb7
23		Kte2	Kt×P	Pg5[14]	Ktd5	Kb2[26]
		Rb5	R×R	Kth5	Re6 ![22]	
24		Bc1	K×R	Pd5[15]	Ktf4	
		Pd3	Rg7	P×P	Kt(c6)×P ![23]	
25		Q×P	Qe2	P×P	Ktd4 !	
		R×gP	Kt×P	Kte7	eRe7[24]	
26			Ktf6 *ch*	Qc4[16]	Ktd5	
			Kf7	Ba6 ![17]	eRf7	
27			Kte4	Qb5	Ktc6	
			Be6	Kt×dP	Qd6	
28			Qf3	Q×B		
			Qe7	Bf8		
29			Kg3	~		
			Qf6	hKt×fP		
30			Bh3			
			Rh7			
31			Rd1			
			Bh6[9]			
32			Ktf2			
			B×P[10]			
33			Kt×B			
			Kt×Kt			
34			K×Kt			

Notes to Table 2.

[1] Compare Table 1, cols. 3 and 4. The move is bad here, where the Rs are not united.

[2] If 16 . ., Ph5; 17 P × hP, Pg4; 18 Kth4, P × fP; 19 Kt × P, or 18 . ., Pe5; 19 Ktg6, or 18 . ., any other; 19 P × eP.

If 16 . ., Pe5; 17 Ktd2 !, Ph5; 18 P × P, Pg4; 19 Kt(d2)e4.

If 16 . ., P × P; 17 P × P, Kte7; 18 Rb2 ! (*a*), Kt × P; 19 Rf2, Qe7 !; 20 Kt × P, Kt × P; 21 B × Kt, P × Kt; 22 R × gP, R × R !. Otherwise 23 gRf5 and Bg5.

(*a*) 18 Bh3 or Pe4 give a long, but easy game.

[3] If 17 Pd4, P × dP; 18 eP × P, P × fP; 19 P × fP, Pg4, &c.; or 18 cP × P, P × dP; 19 P × dP, Ph5; 20 P × P, Pg4; 21 Kt∼, Kt × P, with better game.

If 17 P × eP, P × P; 18 bP × P, B × P; 19 Ktd5, Kt × gP; 20 R × Kt, B × R; 21 Ktf6 *ch*, Kf2; 22 Kt × R, K × Kt and Bl. has a P more.

If 17 any other, Pd4; 18 P × dP, cP × P; 19 Kte2, Pe5; 20 Ktd2, Pe4; 21 Kt × P, Kt × Kt; 22 P × Kt. Or 21 P × P, and Bl. brings his Q to e5, his Kt(c6) to f7, and R to e7, with a won game.

[4] 17 . ., P × P; 18 P × P followed by Be3.

[5] 19 . ., cP × P; 20 eP × P, P × P; 21 Bd3, Bd6 =.

[6] 21 . ., Pc4; 22 P × P, R × R; 23 Kt × R, P × P; 24 Ktc3 or d2 to follow with Bc1, Q to e4, via d1, e2, f3, abandoning his gP in order to establish his game, and finally he emerges a P ahead, since he can win either cP or gP.

[7] 22 Kta4, Pc4 (*a*); 23 P × dP, Be6; 24 Ktc3, B or Kt × gP. Red will win gP with B and Kt, remaining a P ahead.

(*a*) 22 . ., P × P; 23 B × P and 24 B × P.

[8] 20 Qc2, Qe2; 21 cP × P (*a*), eP × P (*b*); 22 Kte5, P × P; 23 P × P (*c*), Kt × Kt; 24 P × Kt, Ktd2 =. If the Bl. Q was on c7 the game might continue 25 Re2, Re7; 26 Kt × P attacking Q and R and threatening check-rook on f6. Had Red played 19 Re2, Bl. could not have played 22 . ., P × P for 23 Ktb5 wins a P.

(*a*) 21 Qd3, Qd6 =.

(*b*) 21 . ., Kt × P(d5); 22 Kte4, with better game.

(*c*) Or 23 Kt × Kt, P × Kt; 24 Kt × P and 25 Ktb5 and 26 Kt × cP winning a P. But not 23 Kt × R ?, P × Kt; and the Red Kt has no escape.

[9] 31 . ., Rh5; 32 Ktf2 followed by R moves. The Q is established and the Bl. pieces are scattered.

[10] 32 . ., any other; 33 Qe4 to follow with Qf5, and Ktf4. Red might also play Rd5, Pe4 and Pe5. If Bl. then plays Q × P; R × Q fixes the gP, and if Bl. does not take the P, Red's game is still better.

[11] The analysis commences from the position after this 14th move of Bl., which is diagrammed. I have changed the colours of the MS. The column is intended to show the advantage of the development on the K-wing. Bl. adopts it here, and generally secures the better game.

[12] 18 Pd5, Kte7 (*a*); 19 Qd3, Ktf6; 20 P × eP, P × P; 21 Q × P, B × P; 22 Qd3, Bh6 +. Bl. will exchange his B for 2 Ps, and secures the quicker development.

(*a*) 18 . ., P × dP; 19 P × bP, Kt∼; 20 Qd3; Bl. has doubled Ps.

[13] If 22 Kt × P, Kt × P. If 22 P × P, Bh6 and 23 . ., B × P. If 22 Pd5, P × dP.

[14] 23 P × P, eP × P ! (*a*); 24 Pd5, Kte7; 25 Kt × P, B × P. Bl. proposes by Ba6, B × cP, Q to e5 or b6 to establish himself on the Q wing.

(*a*) 23 . ., gP × P; 24 R × R, Kt × R; 25 Pd5, P × P; 26 P × P, Kte7, with better game.

[15] 24 P × B, Kt × P.

[16] 26 Ktc3, Kt × fP; 27 Qc4, Bf8 and the Red dP is fixed.

[17] 26 . ., Bf8; 27 Kf2, Kt × fP; 28 Ke3, Kth5; 29 Ktc3, Pa6 ! to keep the Q from c6; 30 Kt × P with the more open game.

[18] The analysis commences with the position after this move, which is diagrammed.

[19] 19 . ., Pd5 !; 20 Qd3, Qd6 =.

[20] 20 . ., Pd5; 21 Qd3 to follow with Be3, Pc5, Bg5 confining the range of the Bl. Q.

[21] 22 Pd5, Pe4; 23 Ktg5 !, Ktd4; 24 Rd2, Ktf3 *ch*; 25 K∼, Kt × R. If 24 Re3, Ktg4: and if 24 eRf2, Ktg4; 25 Rf4, Bh6, Bl. wins in all.

[22] If 23 . ., eRd7 or f7; Red wins a R by similar play to that suggested for Bl. in note 21. If 23 . ., Kt(c3) × P; 24 Kt × Q *ch*, K∼(*a*); 25 Kt × Kt, Kt × Kt; 26 Kt moves and Red has gained a Q.

(*a*) 24 . ., R × Kt; 25 Kt × Kt, Kt × Kt; 26 R × Kt *ch* with gain of a Q.

[23] 24 . ., Re7; 25 Ktd3 ! and continues by Kd2, Rd1. If Bl. doubles his Rs on the *e*-file, Red plays Pa3, Pb4, Pc5, Qb3, Kc2, and, when possible, Be3 and g5, winning.

[24] 25 . ., Rd6 ?; 26 Ktd5, Pa6 (*a*); 27 Bd3, Rf7; 28 Ktf3, Re6; 29 Ktg5 wins a R.

(*a*) 26 . ., Kd8; 27 Ktb5 wins the aP.

[25] The analysis commences from the position after this move.

[26] The analysis of this game is not worked out. The lines of play recommended for each player are given separately. Red aims at posting his Rs on e1 and d1, his Q on f3, and Kt on g5 before advancing his dP to d5. Bl. aims at doubling his Rs on the *e*-file, at exchanging Ps on d4 and advancing eP.

Table 3. The Double Mujannaḥ.

Moves 1 to 10 as in Tables 1 and 2.

	13.	14.	15.	16.	17.	18.
11	*Rb1* *Rb8*					*Rg1* *Rg8*
12	*Rg1* *Ph6*		*Ph3* *Rg8*			*Ph3* *Rg7*
13	*Ph3* *Ph5*		*Ph4* *Ph6*			*Ph4* *Re7*
14	Rg2 Qc7 [1]	Qc2 Rh7 [6]	Pd4 [15] P×P	Qc2 Rg7		*Qc2* *Ph6*
15	Qc2 Rg8	Pd4 P×P	P×P Kte4	Pd4 P×P		*Kd1* *Qc7* [25]
16	Pd4 P×P [2]	P×P Kte4	Kte2 [16] Pb5	P×P Kte4		Pd4 P×P
17	P×P Kte4	Kte2 [7] Pb5	Qc2 [17] P×P	Kte2 Pb5		P×P Pe5
18	Kte2 [3] Pg5 [4]	Qd3 Ktf6	P×P R×R	Qd3 Ktf6		Pa3 [26] Pe4
19	Qd3 P×P	Ktc3 P×P	Q×R Ba6	Pc5 [18] P×P ! [19]	Pd5 Kte7 [22]	Pd5 P×Kt [27]
20	Pd5 [5] Kte7 !	P×P R×R		P×P Ktd7	P×eP [23] P×P	P×Kt Kte4 [28]
21	P×eP Ktf6	Kt×R Rb7		Be3 ! Qe7 ! [20]	Q×P B×P	Ktd5 [29] Ktf2 *ch*
22	Kt×P Bh6	Ktc3 Ba6 [8]		Bg5 Qf6 [21]	Qd3 Ph5	Kd2 Re2 *ch*
23	Kte2 B×P	Pa3 [9] Rb3			Ktc3 Bh6	
24		Kd2 [10] Rb2 *ch*			Bh3 Ktd5 [24]	
25		Kd1 [11] Rf2				
26		Qe2 B×P				
27		Ke1 Kte4				
28		Ktd2 (or g5) [12] Kt×Kt(c3) [13]				
29		K×R Kt×Q				
30		R~ Kt×B				
31		Kt×B [14] Kt×P				

Notes to Table 3.

[1] The analysis begins with Red's 14th move, and the position is diagrammed after Bl.'s reply.

[2] 16 . . , Pd5 with a difficult game; 17 dP×P (or Qd3), bP×P (*a*); 18 P×P, P×P; 19 Ba3, Qd6; 20 Kta4. If now 20 . . , Ktd7; 21 Pg4. If 20 . . , Rb4; 21 Qd3, Ktb5 and Kta6 = (Red has some advantage in the retention of his eP, and the Bl. Ps are fixed). If 20 . . , Pc4; 21 P×P, P×P; Red has eP *v.* cP. He brings his Q to f3, and plays Pe4, establishing his Q. Or 20 . . , Be6, and Bg4 to prevent this.

(*a*) If 17 . . , dP×P; 18 cP×P, aP×P; 19 P×P, with gain of a Pawn.

[3] 18 Ktd1, Pg5; 19 Qd3, Pg4; 20 Kth4!, Ktf6; 21 Pd5 and 22 Kt×fP, with better game.

[4] 18 . . , Pb5; 19 Qd3, Ktf6; 20 Pc5 (*a*), P×P; 21 P×P, Ktd7; 22 Be3, Qd8 (intending to play to f6); 23 Bg5, Kt×P; 24 Rc1 wins a Kt, or the game by establishing his Q in f3 followed by Bh3 and Ktd2 or d4.

(*a*) 20 Ktc3, P×P; 21 P×P, R×R; 22 Kt×R followed by 23 Be3 and 24 Rb2 establishing his game and winning.

[5] Red has 'greed' in the game when he refrains from playing 20 Q×Kt and pushes on the other Kt. If 20 Q×Kt, P×Q; 21 Ktd2, Pf3 wins a piece.

[6] The analysis commences from this move, the position being diagrammed after Bl.'s 14th move. I have changed the colours.

[7] 17 Kt×Kt, P×Kt; 18 Ktg5, Re7; 19 Pd5 (*a*), P×P; 20 P×P, Ktb5; 21 Qd1, Kt×dP, Bl. has the better game.

(*a*) 19 Kt×P(e4), Kt×dP!.

[8] 22 . . , Rb2; 23 Ph4, Pe5; 24 fP×P (*a*), P×P; 25 P×P, Ktg4; 26 any, Kt×P; 27 Kt×Kt!, Kt×Kt; 28 Qe2, Rc2; 29 Ktd1, R×B winning. Or 28 . . , Bh3 and 29 . . , Bg5 attacking the Q, winning.

(*a*) 24 Pd5?, Pe4; if 25 P×Kt, P×Kt; and if 25 Ktd2 or g5, Ktd4.

[9] If 23 Rg2 to stop the Bl. R from the 2nd line, B×P; 24 Q×B, Rb4! wins Q or P.

[10] 24 Ktd1 or a4, B×P.

[11] If 25 Qc2, B×P; and if 25 Ke1, B×P; 26 Q×B, Rc2 winning the Q.

[12] 28 Kt×Kt, R×Q *ch*; 29~, R×Kt wins.

[13] 28 . . , Kt×dP; 29 Kt (d2 or g4)×Kt (*a*), R×Q *ch*; 30 Kt×R, Ktf3 *ch*; 31 Kf2 (*b*), Kt×R; 32, however Red retakes, Bl. wins one of the Kts and remains with Q and central Ps *v.* Kt. The game will probably end in a draw.

(*a*) 29 Kt(c3)×Kt?, R×Q *ch*; 30 K~, P×Kt.

(*b*) 31 Kd1, B×Kt! and wins R or Kt.

[14] This supposes 28 Ktd2. If Ktg5 had been played then, Red might play 31 Ktf3, Pd5; 32 Ktd2, Kt×P.

[15] The analysis commences with this move, the position after Bl.'s 13th move being diagrammed. I have changed the colours. Most play this way.

[16] 16 Kt×Kt, P×Kt; 17 Ktd2, Kt×P; 18 Kt×P. Bl. has two centre Ps as against two BPs.

[17] 17 P×P, R×P.

[18] With the intention of confining the Bl. Q.

[19] 19 . . , Pd5; 20 Be3, any; 21 Bg5 (still endeavouring to confine the Q), P×B; 22 hP×P and the Q is confined. Red has the better chance of winning.

[20] 21 . . , Ph5; 22 Bg5, Kt×P; 23 Rc1 wins a Kt.

[21] Intending 23 . . , Kf7 with later Ba6, Pe5 (if now P×P, Q×P), with advantage.

[22] 19 . . , P×dP; 20 P×bP (to double the Bl. Ps), R×P; 21 Bh3, Kf7; 22 Ktd4, R~; 23 B×P, P×B; 24 Pa3 to follow with Pb4 and Be3 with the better game, since he has hindered the development of the Bl. Q.

[23] 23 P×bP, Kt(d2)×P.

[24] Each player gives up his B for 2 Ps. Bl. secures dP *v.* bP for the ending, with rather the better game. The game is probably intended to run 25 Kt×Kt, Kt×Kt; 26 Ktd4, B×P; 27 B×P, P×B; 28 Kt×P, Rd2; 29 P×B, Kt×P; 30 Qe4.

[25] The position is diagrammed after this move (with which the analysis commences). I have changed the colours.

[26] Or 18 Rg2. Or 18 dP×P, P×P; 19 P×P, Kt×P securing fP *v.* cP and establishing his Q.

Or 18 fP×P, P×P; 19 Pd5, Ktd8 to follow with Pe4 and Qd6 and e5, and Ktf7 with the better game.

Or 18 Pd5, Ktd8! (*a*); 19 any, Kth5; 20 Kte2 (*b*), Kf7; 21 any, P×P; 22 P×P (*c*), Be6. If 23 P×B, Kt×eP secures two Ps for the B. If 23 P does not ×B, Bg4; 24 Kt(e2)~, Kt×fP wins a P.

(*a*) 18 . . , Kta5; 19 Rb1, Ba6; 20 Pb4, Ktb7; 21 Qb3 to follow with Q via a4 and b5 to c6+.

(*b*) 20 P×P, P×P; 21 Pg4, Ktf6!; 22 P×P =.

(*c*) 22 Kt×P, Kt×Kt; 23 P×Kt, Re4.

[27] 19 . . , Ktd8; 20 Ktd4 to follow with Be3, Pa4, Kd2, Ktd1, Bg5. If now P×B; hP×P and Red secures the better game. If Bl. does not accept the B, Red continues Kte3, Bh3, and sacrifices his B for 2 Ps, and has again the better game.

[28] 20 . . , Ktg4; 21 Ktd5?, Re2. If 22 Kt×Q *ch*, K~; 23 Kt×R?, Ktf2 mate.

[29] 21 Kt×Kt, P×Kt. If 21 any other, the games are even, except that Bl.'s fP is better posted than Red's cP.

Table 4. On Opening the Game with the Mujannaḥ on the King's Wing, without completing the Development.

1. Pf3, Pf6 ; 2. Pf4, Pf5 ; 3. Ktf3, Ktf6 ; 4. Pg3, Pg6 ; 5. Rg1, Rg8 ; 6. Ph3, Ph6 ; 7. Pe3,[1] Pe6 ;[2] 8. Pg4, P × P ; 9. P × P, Pg5.

	19.	20.	21.	22.	23.	24.
10	Pf5 ?	P × P				
	Pd6	P × P[5]				
11	P × P[3]	Pd3[6]				
	B × P	Pd6				
12	Kth2	Pe4				
	Kt(b8)d7	Pe5				
13	Qe2	Be3				
	Kte5	Be6				
14	Qf3	Kt × gP				
	Pd5	Ke7			Kd7	
15	Pd3	Pc3			Pc3[20]	
	Ph5[4]	Kt × gP			Kt × gP	
16		Ke2			Ke2	
		Pc6			Qe7	Pc6
17		Pd4			Bh3[21]	Pd4
		Pd5			Qf6	Pd5
18		Pb3			Bf5 *ch*	Pb3
		Pb6[7]			Ke7	Pb6
19		Ktd2			Kth3	Qc2
		Ktd7			Pc6	Qe7
20		Qc2			Pd4	Qd3
		Qc7			Pd5	Qf6
21		Qd3			Qc2	Kth3
		Qd6			P × dP	Bh6
22		Kt(d2)f3			cP × P	Ktd2
		Kt(d7)f6			P × P	Kta6
23		Bh3			Ktf2	Pa3
		Bh6				Ktc7
24		Bf5				Pa4
		Bf4				Kte8
25		aRc1 !				Ktf2
		Pa6	Pc5	aRc8		Ktd6
26		Pc4	P × cP	Pb4		Kt × Kt
		aRc8[8]	P × cP	Pa6[16]		B × Kt *ch*[22]
27		Pc5 !	P × P	Pa3		Kf3
		P × cP[9]	Kt × P	Pa5		Bf4
28		B × P *ch*	Qe4	P × aP		Ktb1
		Ke8[10]	Kt(d5) × B[13]	Pb5 ![17]		[23]
29		P × eP	Bh3	Pa4		
		Kt(g4) × P[11]	Bc4 *ch*	Bc4 *ch*[18]		
30		Kt × B	Kd3 ![14]	Q × B		
		R × R[12]	aRd8[15]	dP × Q[19]		

NOTES TO TABLE 4.

[1] If 7 Pg4, Bl. fixes fP and wins it with his B.
[2] If 7 . . , Pg5 ; 8 Bd3.
[3] 11 Pd3, Pe5 ; 12 Pc3, Kt(b8)d7 ; 13 Kt(b1)d2, Pd5 ; 14 Pe4, Pc6 with better game, since he can continue Bd6 and Bf4 attacking Kt(d2) and so winning eP.
[4] To follow with Ktg6 and h5.
[5] 'In this game is *tam'a* (greed). I have never seen it played. I do not think there is any advantage to either side in it, except as a result of calculation.'
[6] 11 Ktc3, Pd6 ; 12 Qe2, Pe5 ; 13 Qd3, Be6 ; 14 Qe4, B or Kt × P ; 15 Qf5 + attacking B and fixing the Bl. gP.
[7] The two 18th moves are necessary to prevent the checks by the Bs.
[8] 26 . . , P × dP ; 27 Kt × dP. Or 26 . . , P × eP ; 27 Q × P, B × P *ch* ; 28 P × B and 29 Qd5 or Pd5, establishing the Red game.
[9] 27 . . , Qc7 ; 28 P × dP and 29 P × eP with better game.
[10] 28 . . , Q × B ; 29 R × Q with better game.
[11] 29 . . , Q × P ; 30 Kt × B wins the B.
[12] Continued 31 R × R, Kt × Kt ; 32 K × Kt. If 31 . . , Q × B ; 32 Kt × Kt !. If 30 . . , Kt × Kt ; 31 R × R *ch* and 32 K × Kt and 33 K × B with gain of a B.
[13] 28 . . , Kt(d5)f6 ; 29 Bh3 and 30 Qf5 or d5. In the latter case Red plays 31 Pc4.
[14] 30 P × B ?, aRb8 ; 31 Qf5, Rb2 *ch* ; 32 Kd3 and the Kt escapes.
[15] Continued 31 Qf5, Qc7 *dis ch* ; 32 Ke4, and wins the Kt.
[16] 26 . . , Bc4 *ch* ? (this is bad as a general rule) ; 27 Q × B, P × Q (*a*) ; 28 Rg2, any ; 29 cRg1, P × P ; 30 P × P and 31 Pe5 with better game.

(*a*) 27 . . , P × eP ; 28 Kth4. Red doubles his Rs on the *g*-file, then Bh3 fixing the Bl. eP with the superior game.

[17] 28 . . , P × aP ; 29 Rb1, Rb8 ; 30 P × eP, Kt × P(e5) (*a*) ; 31 Bc5 *ch*, Q × B (*b*) ; 32 R × R, Kt × Kt (*c*) ; 33 Rb7 *ch* and 34 K × Kt with gain of a R.

(*a*) If 30 . . , R × R ? ; 31 P × Kt *ch* and 32 R × R. If 30 . . , Q × P ; 31 Bc5 *ch*, Kd6 ; 32 Ktf7 *ch*, K × B or Ke7 ; 33 Kt(f7) × Q =.

(*b*) 31 . . , Kd8 or e8 ; 32 R × R *ch* wins a R.

(*c*) 32 . . , R × R ; 33 Kt × Kt wins a Kt.

[18] If 29 . . , P × aP ; 30 Rb1 as in the previous note.
[19] Continued 31 P × bP, P × bP ; 32 Rb1, Rb8 ; 33 Bc5 *ch*. If now 33 . . , Q × B ; 34 P × P wins a Kt. If 33 . . , Kd8, e8 or c8 ; Red doubles his Rs on the *b*-file, and wins bP and cP, securing B and 3Ps *v.* Q and fixed marginal P, so that if he can queen one of his Ps he will win. If 30 . . , bP × Q ; 31 P × dP and 32 Rb1. If 30 . . , P × eP ; 31 Kth4, P × Q ; 32 Rb1, Rc2 = ; or 32 . . , Rb8 ; 33 Ktg6 *ch* wins R.
[20] 15 Ktd2 or Bh3 ! to follow with Bf5 *ch*.
[21] 17 Pd4, Qf6 ; 18 Kth3, Pc6 ; 19 Pd5 !, P × P ; 20 P × P, Pe4 ! ; 21 Ktd2 winning eP. If 20 . . , Bc8 ; 21 Ktd2 to follow with Q to e4, Pc4, Pb3, guarding dP with the better game.
[22] 26 . . , R × Kt ; 27 R × R.
[23] Bl. has a slight advantage as his development is rather better than Red's.

TABLE 5. MUJANNAḤ-MASHĀ'ĪKHĪ OPENING.

1. *Pf3, Ph6*; 2. *Pf4, Pb6*; 3. *Ktf3, Pf6*; 4. *Pg3, Pe6*; 5. *Pc3, Pd6*; 6. *Pc4, Kte7*; 7. *Ktc3, Ktd7*; 8. *Pb3, Pe5*; 9. *Pe3, Pd5*; 10. *Pd3, Pc6*; 11. *Rb1, Qc7.*

	25.	26.	27.	28.	29.	30.
12	*Rg1* / *Qd6*					*Ph3* / *Qd6*
13	*Pb4* / *Pg6*	Pg4 / Pg6 [6]				*Rh2* / *Pg6*
14	*Ba3* / *Be6* [1]	P × dP / P × dP	Ph3 / Pa6			*Pg4* / *Pa6*
15	P × eP / P × eP	Pf5 / Pg4 [7]	Ba3 / Pg5		— / Be6	*Ba3* / *Be6* [21]
16	Pc5 / Qc7 [2]	Pb4 / Pa6	Pf5 / Pb5		P × dP / P × dP [18]	P × eP / P × eP
17	Pb5 / P × bP [3]	Pb5 / Pa5 [8]	P × dP / P × P		Pf5 / P × P	P × P / P × P
18	Kt × bP [4] / Kd8	Pe4 / Pd4 [9]	Pb4 / — [11]		P × P / Bc8 [19]	Pb4 / Rc8
19	Ktc3 / P × P	Kta4 [10] /	Rg2 / Ktb6		Pb4 / Pb5 [20]	Rc1 / Pb5
20	B × P / Kt × B		Bc5 / Ktc6		Bc5 / Kt(e7)~	Pd4 [22] / Pe4
21	Kt × eP [5] /		Pd4 ! / Pe4 [12]		Kt × dP /	Ktg1 / Ktb6 [23]
22			Ktg1 / Ph5			Bc5 / Ktc6
23			P × P / R × P			Pa3 / Rh7 [24]
24			Pa3 / ~			Kt(g1)e2 / Pg5 !
25			Pa4 / P × P [13]			Rf2 / Rf7
26			Pb5 / Ktb8 ! [14]			R × R / K × R
27			P × P / Kt(b8)d7			Ktg3 / Kg6 [25]
28			Pa7 ! [15] / Ba6 !	— / any other		Rc2 / Rc7 [26]
29			gRb2 / Qc7	gRb2 / Qc7		Kth5 / Rf7
30			gKte2 /	R × Kt / Kt × R [16]		Rb2 / R~ [27]
31				R × Kt / Q × R		Pa4 / P × P [28]
32				Kt × dP / Q × B [17]		Pb5 / P × P [29]

Notes to Table 5.

[1] The analysis commences from the position after this move, which is diagrammed.

[2] 16 .., P×P; 17 P×P, Qc7. Red's game is established.

[3] 17 .., P×cP; 18 P×P, Kt×P; 19 Kt×dP, Qd6 or b6; 20 B×P. If now Bl. take the B, 'there is check-rook on one side or the other'. It is accordingly best not to take the B.

[4] 'It often happens that Bl.'s hP is on h7.' If so Red has a fine position if 18 .., Kd8; 19 Ktg5 !.

[5] Bl.'s dP is fixed.

[6] The position is diagrammed at this point. The analysis commences with Red's 13th move.

[7] 15 .., P×P; 16 P×P, Kt×P; 17 Kt×dP with the better game.

[8] 17 .., P×P; 18 Kt×bP and secures a road for his Q to b5, fixing the dP with the better game.

[9] 18 .., P×P; 19 P×P and plays his Q to d5 or c6.

[10] Intending to play his Q to c6. Accordingly Bl. should play Ba6 in reply to Qb3. If Red take the B, Pb5. Red must move the Kt, and then Pa4 keeps the Q out. Red's best reply to Ba6 is Ktb2, and then Qa4, &c., taking the B and entering his Q in c6 or d5. If Bl. withdraw the B, Red plays Ktc4, Ba3, Rc1, gR to c2, Kt(f3) to h5, K to g3. Bl's play should be on similar lines. Red may with advantage sacrifice Kt for Q in the early play, since he can easily recover the advantage.

[11] The MSS. say 18 .., Pb5, which has already been played.

[12] 21 .., P×P; 22 P×P to follow with 23 Bd3; 24 B×bP, P×B; 25 Kt×bP with two Ps for the B.

[13] 25 .., Kt×aP; 26 Kt×dP. If 25 .., any other; 26 Pa5. In either case Red wins both Bl.'s central Ps.

[14] 26 .., P×P; 27 R×bP, Rb8 or a6; 28 R×Kt, R×R; 29 Kt×dP attacking R(b6) and fP with check-rook. If Bl. had played 24 .., Rh8, the game might now continue 29 .., R∼; 30 Kt×P *ch*, K∼; 31 Kt×eP with good game.

[15] To prevent the R coming to the defence of the Kt(b6).

[16] 30 .., Q×R; 31 Kt×dP, Kd8 (*a*); 32 Kt×Q, Kt×Kt; 33 R×Kt, Rh6; 34 Kte2 and wins eP and fP. Red secures the ending Kt and Q and five Ps *v.* R and wins.

(*a*) If 31 .., Q×B; 32 Ktc7 *ch* and 33 Kt×R. If 31 .., Ba6; 32 R×Q, Kt×R; 33 Ktc7 *ch* and 34 Kt×R.

[17] Continued 33 Kt×fP *ch*, K∼; 34 Kt×R followed by 35 Ktg3, 36 Kt×eP, 37 Kt×gP securing two Kts and three Ps *v.* R and B.

If 32 .., Kf7; 33 Kt×Q, Rb8; 34 P×R, queens, securing two Kts, Q and P *v.* R winning.

[18] 16 .., Kt×dP; 17 Kt×Kt, P×Kt; 18 Pf5.

[19] 18 .., Kt×P; 19 Kt×dP with good game.

[20] 19 .., any other; Red should first defend fP and return Bc1, for if at once 20 Pb5, P×P; 21 R×P, R×B; 22 Kt×dP, Kt×fP; 23 Kt×bP, Kt×eP with better game.

[21] The position after this move is diagrammed, and the analysis begins with Red's 16th move.

[22] Not 20 Bc5 ?, Q×B. The dP must be advanced first.

[23] 21 .., Ktf6; 22 Rf2 with better game.

[24] 23 .., Bc4 (to prevent the Kt coming out from g1); 24 Rb1, Rh7; 25 Pa4, P×P; 26 Pb5 (Ba3 ! threatening to win dP), P×P; 27 R×P, Rb8; 28 KtdP threatening either to win the Kt or by Ktf6 *ch* to win R or eP.

[25] 27 .., Ke8; 28 Kth5 wins a P by threatening check.

[26] The text in L is by no means clear from this point, and AE omits the greater part of the conclusion. If 28 .., Rb8; 29 Kth5 followed by Rf2, and an attack with R and Kt that may end in mate : or 29 Qe2, and 30 Bd3, P×B; 31 Q×P establishing the Q in the centre of the board. This generally happens. The player must play which seems best.

[27] 30 .., Rb7 would defeat the line of play adopted.

[28] 31 .., Kt×aP; 32 Kt×dP wins eP.

[29] Continued 33 R×P, Rb7; 34 Kt×dP (*a*), Qc7 (*b*); 35 Kt×Q, R×Kt; 36 R×Kt and is a Q ahead and will win the isolated eP.

(*a*) 34 Ktf6, K×Kt (or the Kt wins the central Ps); 35 R×Kt, R×R; 36 Kt×dP *ch*, K∼; 37 Kt×R and wins eP.

(*b*) 34 .., Kt×Kt; 35 R×R with better game.

TABLE 6. MASHĀ'ĪKHĪ-MUJANNAḤ.

1. *Ph3*, *Pf6*; 2. *Pg3*, *Pf5*; 3. *Pf3*, *Ktf6*; 4. *Pe3*, *Pg6*: 5. *Pd3*, *Pc6*; 6. *Pc3*, *Pc5*; 7. *Pb3*, *Ktc6*; 8. *Kte2*, *Pb6*; 9. *Ktd2*, *Pe6*; 10. *Pd4*, *Pd6*; 11. *Pe4*, *Rb8*; 12. *Qc2*, *Rg8*.

	31.	32.	33.	34.	35.	36.
13	*Qd3*					
	Pb5	*Pg5*				
14	*Rg1*	*Pa3*				
	Ba6 [1]	*Ph6*				
15	Pe5	*Be3*				
	Ktd7 [2]	*Ba3* [3]				
16	P×dP	P×fP	Pe5		Pd5	Rh2
	P×P	P×fP	Ktd7 [5]	Ktd5	P×dP [8]	P×eP
17	P×P	P×P	P×dP	B×P	P×fP [9]	P×eP
	B×P	bP×P	P×P	P×P [6]		P×P
18		B×P	P×P	B×P [7]		P×P
		P×B	B×P			Rg7
19		Pg4				Rc1
		P×P [4]				Rc8 [10]
20						Pb4
						Pb5
21						Rf2
						Qe7
22						Ktb3
						Bc5
23						Q×B
						P×Q
24						R×P
						Kt×eP
25						Rf3 [11]

NOTES TO TABLE 6.

[1] The analysis begins from Red's 15th move. The position is diagrammed at this point. I have changed the colours of the sides.

[2] 15.., P×eP; 16 P×P and Bl. has doubled Ps, 'which is detestable'.

[3] The analysis begins from Red's 16th move. The position is diagrammed at this point. I have changed the colours of the sides.

[4] Both Qs are established, but Red's game is slightly the better. It should probably end in a draw.

[5] Compare col. 31 and note 2. If 16.., P×eP; 17 P×cP to leave Red with doubled Ps.

[6] 17.., bP×B; 18 P×dP? and Bl. has the better game.

[7] Followed by 19 Pb4 to guard the B when it is returned to c5.

[8] 16.., Kte7; .17 Pf4.

[9] And Bl. has doubled Ps.

[10] 19.., Kd7; 20 Rf2, Rg6; 21 R×Kt(c6), K×R; 22 Pe5 and takes the Kt. Or if 20.., Qe7? Bl.'s game is confused.

[11] Followed by 26 Pb5, winning one of the Kts with the better game. (The MSS. say 25 Rf4, forgetting the Bl. P on g5. Or they may mean 25 Rf3, Pg4; 26 Rf4.)

TABLE 7. THE SAIF.[1]

	37.	38.	39.	40.	41.	42.
1	Pd3 / Pc6				*Pc3* / *Pd6*	
2	Pd4 / Pb6				*Pb3* / *Pd5*	
3	Pc3[2] / Pc5		— / *Pd6*		*Pd3* / *Pc6*	
4	Pe3 / Pe6	Pd5 / Ktf6	*Pc4* / *Pe6*		*Pe3* / *Pc5*	
5	Pf3[3] / Pf6	Pc4 / Pb5	*Pb3* / *Pg6*		*Pg3* / *Pb6*	*Pf3* / *Pe6*
6	Pg3 / Pf5	Pb3[9] / P × P	*Ktc3* / *Pf6*[11]		*Pc4* / *Ktc6*	*Kte2* / *Pf6*
7	Qc2 / Ktf6	P × P / Ba6	Pd5 / Pb5	*Pe3* / *Kte7*	Ktd2[20] / Pd4	*Pf4* / *Pb6*
8	Kte2 / Ktc6	Kta3 or d2 / B × P	Qc2[12] / P × cP[13]	*Pf3* / *Pf5*	Kte2 / Pe6	*Ktd2* / *Ktc6*[27]
9	Pb3 / Pd6	Kt × B / Kt × P[10]	bP × P / Ba6	*Qe2* / *Pc5*	Ktf3 / Pe5	Pc4 / Pd4
10	Pc4 / Pg6		Qd6[14] / B × P	Pd5[16] / P × P	Pg4 / Be6	P × P / P × P
11	Kt(b1)c3[4] / P × P		Q × B / cP × P	P × P / Kta6	Ph3 / Ph6	Pb4[28] / Pe5[29]
12	P × P / Kte7		Q × P ! / P × Q	Pa3[17] / Ktc7	Kth4 / Kt(g8)e7[21]	P × P / P × P
13	Qd3 / Pa6		Kt × P / [15]	Pe4 / P × P	Ktg3 / Pg6	Ktf3 ![30] / any
14	Be3 / Ph6			P × P / Pg5	Qe2 / Pf6	Pb5 / Kt~
15	Ph3 / Ra7			Ph3 / Ktg6	Qf3 / Ph5 !	Kt × eP[31] /
16	Rc1 / Rd7			Ktf3 / Ph6[18]	P × hP / Pg5[22]	
17	Rh2 / Pd5			Be3 / Qe7	Ktg6 ![23] / Kt × Kt[24]	
18	Pc5[5] / P × P[6]			Pe5 / Ktf4[19]	P × Kt / Rg8	
19	P × P[7] / Ktc6[8]				Qe4 / B × P !	
20					Qf5[25] / Ktb4[26]	

NOTES TO TABLE 7.

'The player who adopts the *Saif* can only establish it against the Mujannaḥ if the player who adopts the latter Opening makes a mistake.' (L, f. 65b.)

[1] In cols. 37–40 the attack, and in cols. 41–42 the defence, plays the Saif. In cols. 37–39 Bl. opens with the Mujannaḥ.

[2] Intending to continue with Pc4, Ktc3, Pd5, and to play his Q to keep a P in d5; this advanced QP is called the Saif (sword).

[3] Abandoning the attempt to establish his dP, and adopting another plan of development —the Mashā'īkhī.

[4] Threatening Pd5.

[5] 18 P×P, Kt(f6)×P; 19 Kt×Kt, R×Kt!, and Bl. fixes the Red dP and will eventually win it.

Or 18 any other, P×P; and will still win the dP eventually.

[6] 18 .., Pb5 to follow with Ktc6 fixing the dP.

[7] 19 B×P, Ktc6! fixing dP.

[8] He has united Ps in the centre, and threatens 20 .., Pd4; 21 Kt~, P×B, preparatory to attacking on the K wing. He has fixed dP and so frustrated the root motive of the Saif.

[9] 6 P×P, Kt×dP.

[10] With two Ps for his B.

[11] The analysis starts from this move. The previous moves are described thus: 'Red (I have changed the colours) has moved dP twice, cP twice, bP once and Ktc3. Bl. has moved all his Pawns excepting the two Rooks' Pawns once each.'

[12] Or 8 P×bP, cP×dP. Or 8 P×cP, P×P; 9 P×P, Ba3 winning a P. Or 8 P×eP, P×P; 9 P×P, B×P winning a P.

[13] Or 8 .., Pb5; 9 Kt~, P×P. If, however, the Bl. aP had been on a6, Red by 9 Kta4, cP×P; 10 P×P, P×P; 11 Ktb6!, R~; 12 Kt×P would have isolated the dP and fixed the bP with the better game.

[14] 10 P×eP or cP, B×P and wins the advanced P.

[15] Bl. has demolished the Saif and has the advantage of Q for B.

[16] The analysis starts from Red's 10th move. If he plays any other, then 10 .., P×dP, fixing the Red dP.

[17] 12 Qd3, Ktb4; 13 Pe4, P×P; 14 P×P, Kta6; 15 Qc4 establishing Q in c6.

[18] 16 .., Qe7. If 17 Pe5, Ktf4 wins Q or gP.

[19] Winning Q or gP.

[20] The analysis starts from this move. Red allows Bl. to play Pd4.

[21] 12 .., Ph5; 13 Pg5, Pf6; 14 P×fP, P×fP; 15 Ktg3, Kth6 (threatening 16 .., Kte7 and preventing the entry of the Red Q); 16 Ba3 securing either 2 Ps for his B or his Q's entry.

Or 12 .., Ktf6; 13 Ktg3, B×gP!; 14 P×B, Kt×P; but Red establishes his Q in d5 with the better game.

[22] 16 .., P×hP; and the Red Q is established.

[23] 17 Kt(h4)f5, Kt×Kt; 18 Kt×Kt, Kte7; 19 Qe4, Kt×Kt (*a*); 20 Q×Kt, B×P; 21 bP×B, R×P. Red's game is established.

(*a*) If 19 .., R×P?; 20 Ktg7 check-rook. And if 19 .., Kf7; 20 Ktg3.

[24] 17 .., Rg8; 18 Kt×Kt and can enter his Q in d5 or g6.

[25] More correct than 20 P×B, since it secures the entry of his Q wherever he likes.

[26] Threatening check-rook, and winning the aP. 'The players must now play their moves as seems best to them.'

[27] The analysis starts from this move.

[28] Or 11 Ktf3!, Pe5; 12 P×P, P×P; 13 Pb4 winning the centre Ps as in the col. itself. Then Ktd2, Ktg3, Q to e4 with the superior game.

[29] 11 .., Kt×P!; 12 Kt×P.

[30] Or 13 Pa3 to allow the entry of his Q in the centre of the board.

[31] To follow with Kt×dP. 'In all cases in which one or other player advances his dP to the 5th square, his opponent either wins it or is able to establish his Q in the centre of the board.'

Table 8. The Sayyāl.

	43.	44.	45.	46.	47.	48.
1	Pg3 / Ph6		— / Pg6	— / Pf6		
2	Pg4[1] / Pf6		Pg4 / Pg5	Pg4 / Pg6		
3	Ph3 / Ph5		Pe3 / Pe6	Pe3 / Pf5	— / Pe6	
4	Pg5 / Pf5[2]		Kte2 / Kte7	P×P / P×P	Kte2 / Pd6	
5	Ph4[3] / *Pg6*		Pf3 / Pf6	Kte2 / Pe6	Rg1 / Pc6	
6	*Pf3* / *Rh7*		Pf4 / P×P	Rg1 ! / Kte7 or f6	Pf3 / Pb6	
7	*Pf4* / *Rf7*		Kt×P[3] / *Pa6*[12]	Pf3 / Rg8 !	Pf4 / Pa6	
8	*Pe3* / *Pe6*		*Ph3* / *Ph6*	R×R / *Kt×R*[3]	Pf5 / gP×P[15]	— / Pe5
9	*Pd3* / *Pd6*		*Ph4* / *Pa5*	*Pf4* / *Ktc6*	P×P / P×P[16]	Pd3[19] / Pg5[20]
10	*Pc3* / *Pc6*		*Pd3* / *Pd6*	*Pd3* / *Pd6*	Bh3 / Kte7	*Pe4* / *Pd5*
11	*Pb3* / *Pb6*		*Pd4* / *Pd5*	*Ktd2* / *Kt(c3)e2*	Rf1 / Rg8	*Ktg3* / *Bd6*
12	*Ktd2* / *Ktd7*		*Pc3* / *Pc6*	*Ktf3* / *Ktf6*	Ktg3 / Rg5	*Ph3* / *Qd7*
13	*Bh3* / *Kte7*	*Pc4* / *Kte7*	*Ktd2* / *Ktd7*	*Bh3* / *Bh6*	B×P / Ph6	*Be3* / *Ph6*
14	*Kte2* / *Qc7*	*Pb4* / *Qc7*	*Rg1* / *Rh7*	*Pc3* / *Pc6*	Bh3 / Ktd7	*Pc3* / *Rh7*
15	*Rf1* / *Rb8*	*Rb1* / *Rb8*	*Ktf3* / *Ba6*	*Qc2* / *Qc7*	Pd3 / Pd5	*Pb3* / *Bf8*
16	*Ktg3* / *Pa6*[4]	*Ba3* / *Pd5*[4]	*Ba3* / *Rc8*	*Kd2* / *Kd7*	Pc3 / Qc7	*Ktd2* / *Qd6*
17	Pe4 / P×P[5]	Pc5 / Pb5[8]	*Rc1* / *Rc7*	*Ba3* / *Ba6*	Pb3 / Ra7	*Ktf3* / *Rc7*
18	P×P / Pe5[6]	Pd4 / Ba6	*Rc2* / *Pb6*	*Rg1* / *Rg8*[14]	Pc4[17] / *Bd6*	*Kth5* / *Kf7*
19	Pf5 / P×P	Bc1[9] / Bc4	*Bc1* / *Bc8*		*Ktc3* / *Be6*	*Rb1* / *Ktd7*
20	P×P[7]	Rh2 / Pa6	*Rh2* / *Qe7*		*P×P* / *P×P*	*Rb2* / *Rb8*
21		Ktb3 / Bd6	*Qe2* / *Qd6*		*Pd4* / *Bf1*	*Rc2* / *Kte7*[21]
22		Kta5[10] / ~	*Bd3* / *Kte7*[4]		*Rf2* / *Qd3*	B×P / fP×B[22]
23		Pa3[11]	Kth5 / Kf7 ![13]		*Pb4* / Rc7[18]	Ph4 / Ktf6[23]

Notes to Table 8.

'The Sayyāl is only demolished by the Rook's Pawn which confronts it. This Pawn often demolishes it when the Rook's Pawn is not moved in support. The opener often adopts the Sayyāl. If the second player adopts it, the opener can outstrip him by moving his f-Pawn twice and so preventing the establishment of the Sayyāl. The second player can only establish the Sayyāl with the concurrence of the first player.' (L, f. 73b.)

1 'This Pawn is the root in the Sayyāl, and by it the *f*-Pawn is established in f5.' This latter Pawn is called the Sayyāl (Torrent).

2 4 . . , P×P; 5 Ktf3, Pg6; 6 Kt×gP and fixes hP by 7 Ph4. Red then develops the rest of his pieces as in the Mujannaḥ.

3 The essential point in the opening being obtained, the MSS. omit the following moves and diagram the position at a later stage, from which the analysis begins again. I give the moves that are necessary to secure this position, but my order is of course not essential.

4 The position after this move is diagrammed, and the analysis is resumed.

5 If 17 . . , any other; 18 P×P, eP×P; 19 Ktc4 and 20 Kte3.

6 18 . . , Pd5; 19 Pe5 to confine the Bl. Q, or 19 Pf5 opening his game. If 18 . . , any other; 19 Qe2 to follow with Qf3, Ke2, Ba3, aRe1, Kd1 and Pf5, opening his game.

7 With two united passed Pawns. The Bl. hP is fixed. Red should reply Pf5, when Bl. advances either *d* or *e* P to its fourth square.

8 17 . . , P×P?. Red's game is established.

9 The MSS. give two diagrams [(*a*) and (*b*)] which appear to be intended to illustrate the possibilities of the position for Red.

(*a*) is derived from this position by the Red moves Kt(d2)-f3, Bc1, Pa3, K-d2-c3, Kt-e1-d3, R-h2-a2-a1, Ktf3. In such a position Red's line of play would be 1 Kt(d3)e5, Kt×Kt; 2 Kt×Kt, 3 Bd3, 4, 5 Q-c2-b3, 6 B×bP, R×B; 7 Pa4, Rb8; 8 Qc2 followed by doubling Rs in b1 and b2 and the advance of bP, winning.

(*b*) is derived from this position by the Red moves Kt-b3-a5, Rb2, Kt-d2-c3, Kd2, Qc2, Bd3, hRb1, Bc1, Pa3. In such a position the line recommended for Red is 1 B×bP, P×B; 2 Pa4, 3 P×bP, P×bP; 4 Qb3, 5 Ra1, 6 Ra2, 7 Qa4, P×Q; 8 Pb5, 9 R×aP, winning.

10 For otherwise 22 . . , B×P; 23 P×B would hopelessly block the position. Bl. cannot now do so, for after 22 . . , B×P; 23 R×B, Red can open his game by 24 Bd3, 25 B×P, P×B; 26 Pa4, P×P; 27 R×aP, &c.

11 Bl.'s game is terribly confined. Red's best line of play appears to be K to c3 and R-h2-a2-a1. The position is becoming like one of the two sketched in note 9 above.

12 If 7 . . , Pf5; 8 P×P, Kt×P; 9 Rg1.

13 Continued 24 Pg5, hP×P; 25 P×P, Ktg8 (*a*); 26 Pg6, Re7; 27 Rf2 intending Kth2 and Ktg4 to win the fP. Bl. plays 27 . . , Pe5; 28 Kth4, to follow with Ktf5 and Pg7 winning a piece; or 27 . . , Pc5; 28 Kd2, &c.; or 27 . . , Kth6; 28 Pg7 winning a piece.

(*a*) Or 25 . . , P×P; 26 Kt×P. Or 25 . . , Rh7; 26 Kt×P *ch*, Kt×Kt; 27 P×Kt, R×R; 28 Kt×R, winning Bl. Kt shortly.

14 The position is diagrammed at this point. The games are exactly similar. Red now endeavours to exchange his KB for two Ps.

15 The MS. (here L is defective, and AE is my authority) says that Bl. has 9 continuations, viz.:

(*a*) 8 . . , Kte7; 9 Bh3 to continue with Ktg3, Pd3, Pd4, Qe2, Qf3; or 9 P×eP.

(*b*) 8 . . , Kth6; 9 P×eP (*k*), B×P; 10 Ph3 (*l*), Ktd7; 11 Kf2 (*m*), B×P; 12 P×B, Kte5; 13 Pg5, Kt (h6)g4 *ch* and 14 . . , P×P.

(*k*) 9 Bd3, Ktd7; 10 Pa3, Pc5; 11 Ph3, Pd5; 12 P×P, B×P; 13 Ktf4, B×P; 14 Kt×dP. Or 9 Ktc3 threatening Kte4 and Kt×fP.

(*l*) 10 Pg5, P×P; 11 R×P, Bg4; 12 Kt(e2)~, Qe7 and 13 . . , Qf6 and the R must move.

(*m*) 11 any other, B×P; 12 P×B, Kte5 threatening Ktf6 *ch*, winning gP.

(*c*) 8 . . , Pe5; 9 P×dP. The text is obscure.

(*d*) is col. 47, note 16.

(*e*) 8 . . , Pg5; 9 P×P, B×P. The analysis stops here, though a later position in this variation is diagrammed, which might be reached by 10 Ph3, Ph6; 11 Pd3, Kte7; 12 Pd4, Pd5; 13 Pb3, Rg8; 14 Pb4, Pb5; 15 Bd3, Rg2; 16 Rf1, Rf7; 17 Ktg3, Qc2; 18 Kth5, Ktd7; 19 Ktc3, Qd3; 20 Rb1, Rb8.

(*f*) 8 . . , eP×P; 9 P×P, Pg5; 10 Ktg3 to follow with Kth5, Ph3, Qe2-f3-g4-h5-g6.

(*g*) is col. 48, note 19. (*h*) is col. 47. (*i*) is col. 48.

16 Or 9 . . , Pe5; 10 Ktg3, Ra7; 11 Rg2 and 12 Pe4. This is var. (*d*) of note 15.

17 There is a hiatus in the MS. after this move.

18 The analysis resumes here. The sufficiency of my reconstruction of the missing five moves is established by the diagram of the position in AE after Red's 29th move. Bl. must not play 23 . . , Pb5. The game continues 24 Kd2, Pb5 (*a*); 25 Ba3, Ktb6; 26 Bc5, Ktc6; 27 Pa3, Kf2; 28 Qc2, Bc4; 29 aRf1, Rg6 (*b*); 30 Kth5, Ke8 (*c*); 31 Kt×P *ch*, Kd8; 32 Kt(f6)×P, gRg7 (*d*); 33 R×B *ch*, Kd7; 34 Bf5 *ch*, Ke6; 35 Ktf4 mate.

(*a*) 24 . . , Bc4 ; 25 Pb5, Rg4 ; 26 Qc2, Be6. Or 25 . . , P × bP ; 26 Rb1 followed by R × P.

(*b*) 29 . . , Ktd7 ; 30 Rf5, R × R (if 30 . . , Kt × dP ; 31 P × Kt) ; 31 R × R, Ktb6 ; 32 Kth5.

(*c*) 30 . . , Kg8 ; 31 Kt × P *ch*, Kh8 ; 32 Kt(f6) × P, Kt × Kt ; 33 R × B *ch*, Kg7 ; 34 Kt × Kt.

(*d*) 32 . . , Kt × Kt ; 33 R × B *ch*, Kd7 ; 34 Kt × Kt.

[19] Or 9 Ktg3, Pd5 ; 10 Qe2, Qe7 ; 11 Qf3, Qd6 ; 12 Pb3, Kte7 ; 13 Pb4, Rg8 ; 14 Pc3, Rg7 ; 15 Pc4, Rf7 ; 16 Pd3, Ktd7 ; 17 Ktc3, Rb8 ; 18 Bh3, &c. This is var. (*g*) of note 15.

[20] The MS. now diagrams the position after Bl.'s 20th move, omitting all the moves from Red's 10th. I have, as in other similar cases above, attempted to supply the missing play, although the order of the moves is, of course, only tentative.

[21] The analysis resumes from the position now reached.

[22] Or 22 . . , Ktg8 ; or 22 . . , hP × B ; 23 Ph4, P × hP ; 24 Pg5, P × gP ; 25 Kt × gP.

[23] Continued 24 P × gP, Kt × Kt ; 25 P × Kt, P × gP (*a*) ; 26 Kt × gP *ch*, Kf6 (*b*) ; 27 Kth7 *ch*, Kf7 ; 28 cRg2, P × P ; 29 Rg7 *ch* (*c*), Ke8 ; 30 Ktf6 *ch*, Kd8 ; 31 Rf7, Bh6 ; 32 R(g1)g7 wins.

(*a*) The position is now diagrammed in AE (p. 221), but with the unimportant variation that the Pa2 and Rc2 are placed on a4 and a2 respectively. Neither alteration affects the subsequent play in the least.

(*b*) 26 . . , Ke8 ; 27 Pf6, Ktg1 ; 28 Pf7 *ch* wins.

(*c*) Or 29 P × P ?. Or 29 Pf6, Ktg8 ; 30 Rg7 *ch*, Ke8 ; 31 R × Kt ; 32 Rg5.

A further variation (AE, p. 224) is wrongly diagrammed, and is accordingly unintelligible.

CHAPTER XV

THE GAME OF SHAṬRANJ: ITS THEORY AND PRACTICE. III

The End-game.—Chess Endings in Muslim literature.—Summarized conclusions on the more elementary Endings.—The manṣūbāt; their classes and characteristics.—The history of the collections.—The manṣūbāt material; diagrams and solutions.—The Knight's Tour and other Exercises with the chessmen.

THE End-game is certainly the principal feature in all the early literature of chess, both in Muslim lands and in Europe. With the single exception of the MS. L, all the early works on the practical game, which I have seen, devote the greater part of their pages to collections of diagrams of End-game positions, which vary in extent from ten positions in S to nearly 200 in BM. It is also clear from the titles of the lost MSS. given in the *Fihrist* that these works were arranged upon the same lines. These End-game positions are called in Arabic *manṣūba*, pl. *manṣūbāt* or *manaṣib*, this word being the passive participle of the verb *naṣaba*, 'to erect', 'set up', 'appoint', or 'arrange', and meaning accordingly 'that which has been erected, set up, or arranged', an 'arrangement', 'position', or 'situation'— in modern chess language, a 'problem'.

Nine of the MSS.[1] also contain short sections which contain conclusions or decisions as to the result of certain elementary Endings in which few pieces on either side are engaged. Just as in the case of the sections on the Opening developments, we have no orderly or scientific exploration of the field of End-game play, and no justification of the conclusions given is attempted. These sections present a mere collection of decisions, rulings, or opinions, apparently more or less haphazard in origin, which are repeated with but little variation from one work to another. Nor is the principle of arrangement much more orderly. In the older MSS. there is a rough classification under the four headings, (*a*) Rook *v.* Rook, (*b*) Rook *v.* other pieces than the Rook, (*c*) Faras Endings, and (*d*) Endings with only Firzāns, Fīls and Baidaqs. In the later works the Rook and Faras, and the Firzān and Fīl endings are contrasted. In all the MSS. the decisions follow one another without pause, break, or stop, and nothing is done to facilitate reference. Occasionally the ruling is embellished with an anecdote, as, for instance, when AH (f. 15 b) adds to the decision that R, Q, and discordant B *v.* R is a won game, the story that the Ending once happened to ar-Rāzī when playing against a weaker player, and that the master, after spending the whole day trying to force the win, gave up the attempt in disgust. The MS. goes on to say that the Ending is really won, but that the defence can be maintained for a long while. Occasionally, also when different opinions were held as to the nature of a par-

[1] Viz. AH (C, V), BM, AE, H (Z), RAS, and Y.

ticular Ending, the masters al-'Adlī, ar-Rāzī, aṣ-Ṣūlī, or al-Lajlāj are cited as holding one opinion or the other, or the reader is referred to an illustrative problem in the body of the work. But as a rule the decisions are given without justification, and their brevity suggests strongly that it was intended that the lists should be committed to memory. We know from aṣ-Ṣūlī that the knowledge of these decisions was one of the distinctive marks of the master of the first rank.

These decisions are much complicated by the rigidity and restricted range of move of the Baidaq, Firzān and Fīl. Not one of these pieces by itself could under any circumstances gain or lose a move in a game. Moreover, it was only the Shāh, Rook, and Faras that were able to reach any and every square of the board. The Firzān could only reach thirty-two of the squares, those on a chequered board of the same colour as the square on which it was standing, and the original Firzāns could never come into conflict with one another. Only eight squares were accessible to each Fīl, and no Fīl under any circumstances could attack or defend any other Fīl. Hence it became a matter of great importance to know the nature of the Firzāns or Fīls in an Ending, in order to know whether the Firzāns could capture or defend the other Firzāns or Fīls in the position in question. It might easily happen from this peculiarity of move that a player with a great preponderance of force might be quite impotent for purposes of attack, and that the weaker force would draw the game from this cause. Such a position is diagrammed on this page. Black, despite the fact that he has six Firzāns more than his opponent, is quite unable to touch (Ar. *laqiya*) any of the Red men, and the game is a forced draw.

AH 11 : C 46.
Drawn position.[2]

But even beyond this the decisions often seem strangely at variance with modern experience, even in the cases in which Rook and Faras alone, pieces whose moves have never been changed, are concerned. This, of course, arises from the different rules governing the conclusion of the game which existed in the Muslim shaṭranj. We have only one way in which a game can be won, the Muslim had three. The checkmate of the opponent's King, the annihilation of his army, or the stalemate of his King and men, were all conclusions that carried victory with them. The last is of minor importance because the position of stalemate is of comparatively rare occurrence under any circumstances, but the victory of *Bare King* completely altered the character of End-game play. It must have been the ordinary form of victory, for the smaller range of power of the pieces reduced enormously the possibility of securing checkmate. The only piece that could mate without the assistance of other pieces beyond the Shāh was the Rook; while of two pieces, the mate with Faras and Firzān is comparable as regards difficulty

[2] Quoted by aṣ-Ṣūlī from al-'Adlī with the comment, 'Al-'Adlī said this is drawn, and Allāh only knows what he meant by giving it a diagram.' AH and C in error add the rubric, 'Al-'Adlī said, Red plays and wins.'

with our ending of Knight and Bishop, and Faras and Fīl could only mate in two angles of the board, which involves conditions that could not be compelled. In either case the game would be won far more easily by baring the opponent's King. It must have been an occurrence of every day for a player to be left without mating force. But the rule of *Bare King* presented a complete compensation for all this. The gain of a Pawn in the early part of the game, if maintained through a series of equal exchanges, would in the end lead to the winning of the game through the exhaustion of the opponent's forces. The player had two lines of attack instead of one, as in the modern European game, and, though doubtless this was a disadvantage to the ordinary player, as leading to divided counsels and uncertain plans, yet in the ending it allowed of many victories where in our game there is nothing but a draw.

The game ended in a draw when one player gave perpetual check, or persisted in a repetition of the same moves. Examples of both varieties of drawn games will be found among the manṣūbāt later in the chapter; e. g. of perpetual check, no. 38, of repetition of moves, no. 35. A draw was also the result of equality of position or force, or of inability to secure the ending *Bare King* through the discordance of the pieces or any other reason.

The MS. decisions are summarized in the following tables. I begin with those in which one player has a Rook, then I give those in which the chief force engaged is the Faras, and follow with those in which the Firzān, the Fīl, and the Baidaq respectively are the principal pieces engaged. The decisions merely say if the forces on either side are strong enough to compel a definite result ('win') or not ('draw'). They do not assign the win to either side; it is assumed that the player knows on which side the preponderance of force lies.[3]

R *v.*	
B + 2 tied P . .	= win
2B	= win
2B + P	= draw
Q + tied P . .	= win
Q + B	= draw
2Q	= draw
2cQ + tied P . .	= win
3Q	= draw
3dQ + 2B . . .	= draw
4cQ	= win
4Q (3 + 1) . . .	= draw
4Q (2 + 2) + 2B .	= win
Kt	= draw
Kt + 2cQ + B . .	= draw
Kt + 2dQ + B .	= win (?)
Kt + 2cQ + 2B .	= draw
Kt + 2dQ + 2B .	= win
2Kt + B + 2P .	= draw
2Kt + Q . . .	= draw
2Kt + Q + B . .	= win

R + P *v.*	
2B	= draw

R + B *v.*	
Q + B + P . . .	= [4]
2cQ + B . . .	= draw
4Q	= draw
4Q + B	= draw
Kt + B	= win
Kt + 2B . . .	= draw
2Kt + Q . . .	= win
2Kt + Q + 2B .	= win [5]

R + 2B *v.*	
2cQ	= win
2dQ	= draw
2cQ + B . . .	= draw
Kt + Q . . .	= draw
Kt + Q + 2B . .	= draw
2Kt + Q . . .	= win [5]
R	= draw

R + Q *v.*	
Kt + cQ . . .	= draw
Kt + dQ . . .	= win
Kt + dQ + B . .	= win

R + Q + B *v.*	
Kt + Q + B . .	= win
Kt + cQ + B . .	= draw
Kt + Q + 2B . .	= win
2Kt	= win
2Kt + B . . .	= draw
R	= win [6]
R + B	= draw [7]
R + Q	= draw [8]

[3] When there are several Firzāns in an Ending, I write cQ and dQ for concordant and discordant Firzāns respectively, or add in a bracket the number of Firzāns of each kind. A Pawn united with and defended by a Firzān or Fīl is called a 'tied' Pawn.

[4] A win if the B can be pinned on a square which the Q does not command.

[5] 'A win, but some say a draw.'

[6] 'It is easier when the Q and B are concordant, than when discordant.'

[7] 'An unsound draw.'

[8] 'A draw, but some say a win.'

R + Q + 2B *v.*

Kt + Q + 2B . . = win
R + cB . . . . = win [5]
R + dB . . . . = draw [8]
R + Q . . . . = draw [9]

R + 2Q *v.*

(*a*) Qs conc.[10]

2cQ . . . . = [11]
2Kt + 2B . . . = win
R + cQ . . . . = draw [8]
R + dQ . . . . = win [12]

(*b*) Qs disc.

2Kt + B . . . = win
2Kt + 2B . . . = draw

(*c*) Qs either.

Kt + 2B . . . = win

R + 2Q + B *v.*

2Kt + 2B . . . = win
R . . . . . . = win

R + 2Q + 2B *v.*

R + 2Q . . . . = draw

R + 3cQ *v.*

2Q + B all c . . = win [13]

R + Kt *v.*

R . . . . . . = draw

2R *v.*

4Q . . . . . = draw
4Q + B or 2B . = draw
Kt + 2Q . . . = win
Kt + 2Q + B . . = draw
Kt + 2Q + 2B . = draw
2Kt . . . . . = win
2Kt + B . . . = win
2Kt + 2B . . . = draw [14]
R . . . . . . = win
R + B . . . . = draw
R + 3Q . . . . = draw
R + 4Q (3 + 1) . = draw
R + Kt . . . . = draw
R + Kt + B + 2cQ = draw [8]
R + Kt + B + 2dQ = win
R + Kt + 2B + 2cQ = win

2R + B *v.*

Kt + Q + dB . . = win
Kt + 2Q . . . = win
R + Kt . . . = win
R + Kt + B . . = draw [8]
R + Kt + 2B . . = draw [8]

2R + Q *v.*

R + 2Kt . . . = win

Kt *v.*

B . . . . . . = draw
Q . . . . . . = draw
2cQ + 2B . . . = draw
3cQ . . . . . = draw
3dQ . . . . . = win
3Q + 2B . . . = draw
4cQ . . . . . = win
4Q (2 + 2) . . = draw

Kt + B *v.*

4dQ . . . . . = draw
Kt . . . . . . = draw

Kt + 2B *v.*

2Q + 2B . . . = draw
Kt . . . . . . = draw

Kt + Q *v.*

Q + B . . . . = win [15]
Q + 2B . . . . = draw
2cQ . . . . . = win [16]
2Q (all 3 c) . . = draw

Kt + Q + cB + tied P *v.*

Q + B + tied P . = win [17]

Kt + 2Q *v.*

Kt + 2B . . . = win
Kt + Q . . . . = draw

Kt + 3dQ *v.*

2cQ + cB . . . = draw

2Kt *v.*

Q + 2B . . . . = win
2Q . . . . . . = win
3Q . . . . . . = draw
Kt . . . . . . = win [18]

Q *v.*

P . . . . . . = [19]
B or 2B . . . = draw
Q . . . . . . = [19]

Q + B *v.*

2P . . . . . = draw
B . . . . . . = draw
Q . . . . . . = draw

Q + 2B *v.*

B . . . . . . = win
Q . . . . . . = win

2Q *v.*

P . . . . . . = [19]
2B . . . . . = draw
Q . . . . . . = win
Q + B . . . . = win

2Q + B *v.*

2B . . . . . = win
2Q . . . . . = draw [8]

2Q + 2B *v.*

2B . . . . . = win
2Q . . . . . = win

4Q (3 + 1) *v.*

2cQ . . . . . = draw

4Q (3 + 1) + B or 2B *v.*

2cQ . . . . . = draw

B *v.*

P . . . . . . = draw

B + P *v.*

P . . . . . . = draw
B . . . . . . = draw

2B .

P . . . . . . = win

P *v.*

P . . . . . . = [19]

[5] 'A win, but some say a draw.'
[8] 'A draw, but some say a win.'
[9] 'The draw is easier when the two Qs are discordant.'
[10] According to al-Lajlāj.
[11] Al-'Adlī gave this as a win; ar-Rāzī as a draw.
[12] So aṣ-Ṣūlī; most players considered it as drawn.
[13] The Qs on one side are discordant with those on the other.
[14] Ar-Rāzī gave this as a win; other players as a draw.
[15] If the two Qs are concordant, a draw is more probable.
[16] The Qs on one side are discordant with those on the other. Otherwise this Ending is drawn.
[17] Provided the P on promotion is discordant with the Q.
[18] Al-'Adlī said a draw; both aṣ-Ṣūlī and al-Lajlāj gave it as a win.
[19] The result in these Endings depends entirely upon position.

Many of these decisions, of course, depend upon the possibility or otherwise of securing the ending *Bare King*, but even then much depended upon position, and the collections of manṣūbāt show many examples of special positions in which a game that would ordinarily be drawn could be won, or vice versa. Indeed these End-games, all of which are reproduced below, ought to be studied in connexion with the decisions, and are the raw material from which the analyst might produce a scientific treatment of the End-game in Muslim chess.[20]

I now turn to the collections of manṣūbāt, the gross total of which in the MSS. exceeds 1,600. Many positions are, however, repeated in different MSS., and a careful comparison of the positions, based ultimately upon the MS. solutions, has enabled me to reduce the number of distinct manṣūbāt to some 553. The labour of collation has been no light one, and I do not expect to have avoided a few duplicates (what constitutes a distinct position is often a matter of opinion), but it has given me a clearer idea of the capabilities of the Muslim game, and a high opinion of the skill of the earlier players. I have thought it better to reproduce the whole material rather than to confine myself to a mere selection.

From the very first the manṣūbāt filled the greater part of the Muslim books on chess, and whatever fame may be supposed to attach to the first compiler of a collection of chess problems belongs to the master al-ʿAdlī. In its origin the manṣūbā was nothing more than the termination of an actual game played over the board which was deemed worthy of preservation by the players or their contemporaries, because of the brilliance, the difficulty, or other special feature in the play. Other players were challenged to reproduce the concluding play from the position recorded, or beginners might learn the moves of the pieces by playing the manṣūba with the help of the solution. Both al-ʿAdlī and aṣ-Ṣūlī recommended beginners to use the manṣūbāt in this way.

[20] The following may serve as a rough index to the endings among the mansūbāt reproduced below:—

Rook *v.* Q2P, 239; QB, 185, 244; 3Q, 192; 3QB, 78; Kt, 10, 108, 125, 189, 223; 2KtB, 324; 2KtQ, 196. Rook + Pawn *v.* B3P, 336; 2B, 339; KtB2P, 38; Q2P, 470; QBP, 248; R, 540. Rook + 2 Pawns *v.* BP, 340; 2KtBP, 153; RP, 240. Rook + Bishop *v.* 2QP, 130; Kt, 330; Kt2B, 280; R, 259, 323; R2P, 178. Rook, Bishop + Pawn *v.* KtP, 326; RB, 470. Rook + 2 Bishops *v.* 2Q, 44; R, 542; RB, 63. Cf. 140, 205, 437. Rook + Queen *v* 3Q, 251; KtQ, 190; 2KtB, 203; R, 8, 127, 319, 415. Cf. 36, 65, 144, 338, 444, 541. Rook, Queen + Bishop *v.* RP, 281. Cf. 35. Rook + Knight *v.* R, 13, 68, 116, 317, 319, 414. Cf. 69, 329, 374. Rook, Knight, Bishop *v.* R, 66, 117. Cf. 11, 52, 169, 224, 254, 275, 290, 291, 325, 327, 331, 337. 2 Rooks *v.* RKtQP, 469; RKtQB, 141; 2R, 458. Cf. 42, 53, 88, 195, 204, 341.

Knight *v.* B, 262, 418; Q, 322; Q2B, 188. Cf. 12, 148, 237, 408, 412, 436. Knight + Bishop *v.* B2P, 434. Cf. 321. Knight + 2 Bishops *v.* 2B, 246; QB, 184. Cf. 249. Knight + Queen *v.* 2Q, 279; Kt, 51, 62, 81, 114, 272, 539; KtB, 49. Knight, Queen + Bishop *v.* Kt2P, 151; KtQ, 76, 221. Cf. 135, 238. Knight + 2 Queens *v.* —, cf. 202, 328. Knight + 3 Queens *v.* 3Q, 274. 2 Knights *v.* —, cf. 64.

Queen *v.* 2P, 48, 154, 269; BP, 252; 2B, 320; Q, 1, 112, 122, 277. Cf. 37, 45, 106, 131, 145, 191, 225, 236, 271, 371, 445. Queen + Bishop *v.* 2P, 128, 129; B, 193; Q, 43, 194, 231; Q3P, 276. Cf. 121, 168, 218, 222, 250, 265, 474. Queen + 2 Bishops *v.* —, cf. 9, 47, 75, 182, 235. 2 Queens *v.* P, 247; 2B, 245; 2Q, 335. Cf. 234. 2 Queens + Bishop, &c., *v.* —, cf. 41, 134, 138, 264.

Bishop *v.* P, 39, 273, 372; 2P, 46, 146, 333, 373. Bishop + Pawn *v.* P, 34, 243, 263; B, 228. Cf. 105, 118, 150, 229, 407, 428. 2 Bishops *v.* 2P, 72. Cf. 159, 242, 413.

Pawn *v.* P 186, 187, 278, 316, 332, 334.

These positions from play fall naturally into two fairly well defined classes: those containing few pieces in which the chief feature is the accuracy of the play, and those containing many pieces in which the charm consists in the unexpectedness or brilliance of the mating play. The former—the *End-game*—would appeal to the strong player with analytic tastes: the latter—which I may term the *Problem* (implying a resemblance to the problems of the middle of the nineteenth century, but none with those of the present day)—would always be the popular favourite. But, obvious as this classification is to us, there is no sign in the collections that it was obvious to the earliest masters.

Al-ʿAdlī divided his collection of manṣūbāt into games *maghlūbāt, qawāʾim*, and *maqmūrāt*,[21] or won endings, drawn endings, and undecided games.[22] Aṣ-Ṣūlī apparently attempted no classification at all. His contemporary, the historian al-Masʿūdī, however, in a passage quoted above (p. 164), refers to a classification into *qawāʾim* and *mufridāt* (i. e. isolations—Bare King Endings), as recognized by the players of his time, and at the same time speaks of the 'classes of the noteworthy manṣūbāt', by which, I imagine, he meant the various kinds of mate-positions. Neither the al-ʿAdlī nor the al-Masʿūdī classification recognized another type of game which was already exemplified in the work of the former. It is not until the time of b. Abī Hajala (*c.* 1350) that we find a special name *mikhāriq* given to these games. In the *mikhāriq* there is no question of mate or of the ordinary methods of play, but the exercise is one of a more strictly mathematical character and illustrates the moves of the chessmen. The best known example of the type is the Knight's Tour. To these *Exercises*, I devote a separate section of this chapter.

The ordinary headings to the manṣūbāt in the older MSS. run thus:

Red (Black) wins, and the play is his.
Red (Black) wins, and the play is Black's (Red's).
Drawn, and the play is Red's (Black's).

There is no convention that the winning side should be of a particular colour, nor that the diagram should be arranged so that the winner, or the player of a particular colour, should play from a particular side of the board. Any difficulty as to the direction in which the pieces moved was prevented by the custom of writing the names of the pieces on the diagram so that the player of each colour could read the names of his own men from his own side of the board.

As the titles show, the number of moves in the solution was of no importance. The problem was to win, not to win in any particular number of

[21] The *maqmūrāt* are few in number (five only, viz. 189, 190, 192, 196, 221), and show a few pieces arranged at the opposite edges of the board. Most illustrate Endings as to the result of which players were in doubt, e.g. the Ending R *v.* Kt. In all, apparently, either player might begin, and the ending was played just as an ordinary game. The term *maqmūra* is the participle of the vb. *qamara*, to 'play at a game of chance', to 'gamble'. We might consequently render it 'game of chance', 'wager-game', though more probably the term referred to the uncertainty of the result only. According to V, No. 146 below is not a *maqmūra* position because the correct result of the game is known.

[22] I conclude this from the sequence of the al-ʿAdlī positions in the older MSS.

moves. I have noted in verifying the solutions of the MSS. a few cases in which a shorter line of play is possible than that of the MS. These point to faulty composition or to errors in the diagram, for it was the business of the composer to see that there were no additional solutions,[22a] and a preference for the shortest method of winning arose at an early date. Aṣ-Ṣūlī thought it worth mentioning in the preface to his work on chess, that he had discovered a shorter solution to one of al-ʿAdlī's manṣūbāt, and repeats both solutions in his text on the position—my No. 1. If the number of moves in the solution happened to be noted, each single move of Red and Black was counted as a distinct move, and what we should call a mate in IV was reckoned as a mate in VII. This has remained the rule among extra-Indian Muslims almost to our own time.[23] It is only in the Spanish Alf. and the Indian Oxf. that we meet with the European method of counting the moves of a game. I have also noticed that the MSS. usually ignore in their solutions a sacrifice on the part of the loser which merely delays the mate without adding to the resources of the defence.

The earlier MSS. generally add information as to the work whence they took the problem and the names of the players from whose play the position was derived. I see no reason to doubt the authenticity of these statements when they appear in the titles or solutions of individual manṣūbāt. It is different with the similar ascriptions of authorship in the later MSS. By 1450 or thereabouts, a custom had arisen of attaching to every problem the name of an author—generally some name of mark in Muslim history. These statements are often palpably false, and it is impossible to allow any weight to them. They merely reflect the fashion of the period. In modern times the custom has been carried to more extravagant lengths still, and Oxf. claims to contain problems by Socrates, Galen, Buzūrjmihr, Shāfiʿī, &c. I have not thought it worth while to record all these absurdities, although I have been careful to preserve all the historical details from the older MSS.

In the following collation of the problem material, I have made no attempt to arrange or classify the positions other than by their MS. source. I have first decided upon a grouping of the MSS. based upon their respective dates and historical associations. I have then taken the problems in the order in which they occur in the first of these MSS., continuing with the fresh material that I have found in the successive MSS. according to my grouping. I have adopted this course deliberately after considerable experiment, because I have satisfied myself that any other method would, while inevitably introducing ideas belonging to modern chess, have obscured the historic development of the problem in Muslim chess. It is the obvious duty of a historian to present this development in the clearest light possible. I have attempted no critical collation of the diagrams; I have not hesitated to take my figure

[22a] A noteworthy exception is the problem No. 7 below, to which al-ʿAdlī gave two solutions of equal length.

[23] Thus al-ʿAdlī spoke of his solution of No. 1 below as in 18 moves, where we should say 9, and aṣ-Ṣūlī of his correction as in 8 moves, where we should say 4. The MSS. S and Ber. both reckon the moves in their solutions in this same method.

from a later MS. when the older MS. was at fault; at times I have reconstructed the figure from a comparison of several diagrams, or built it up from the solution alone. I have endeavoured to carry out such restoration in the spirit of Muslim chess, and to confine it within the narrowest limits; and I believe that I have added a note in every case. In identifying duplicate problems and repetitions in other MSS., I have relied in the main upon the solutions of the MSS., and have found no other test approach this in certainty and ease of application. Finally, I have preferred to refer to the problems in each MS. by number rather than by folio or page, although the manṣūbāt are unnumbered in every MS. except S, because the numerical order of the problems in a particular MS. often throws valuable light upon the sources of that collection.

The classical collections of manṣūbāt for all the existing MSS. were those of al-ʿAdlī and aṣ-Ṣūlī. The work of ar-Rāzī, at one time in the possession of aṣ-Ṣūlī, was apparently lost before the manufacture of compilations began. Unfortunately, the other two works are now lost also, and all our knowledge of their contents is derived from the later MSS. which were based upon them. Three works, AH (in a MS. of 1140, and a copy—the MS. C—of *c.* 1370), V (in a MS. of 1221), and H (in a MS. of the 15th c.), claim to have used the original collections, and I regard them accordingly as forming our authorities of the first or oldest group. All the manṣūbāt in these MSS. probably go back to A. D. 1000 at least. The MSS. AH and V stand in close connexion, and the texts of their solutions are throughout nearly identical. H, although a later work and later in terminology and briefer in text, is valuable in that it carefully attaches to each of its problems the source from which it was taken.

AH contains 197 diagrams on the ordinary chessboard, but the first eight (AH 1–AH 8) are taʿbīyāt and have been used in Ch. XIV, while six others (AH 91–4, 196–7) are connected with the Knight's tour. The MS. divides its problems into four sections:[24]

a, beginning on f. 29 b, contains five problems (AH 9–13) from al-ʿAdlī, which aṣ-Ṣūlī criticized adversely in his work;

b, beginning f. 32 b, contains fourteen problems (AH 14–27) from al-ʿAdlī, which aṣ-Ṣūlī praised in his work;

c, beginning f. 41 a, contains a selection of thirty-one problems (AH 28–58) from al-ʿAdlī which were not given by aṣ-Ṣūlī; and

d, beginning f. 55 a, contains a selection of 137 problems and four tours (AH 59–90 and 95–195 problems, 91–4 tours) from aṣ-Ṣūlī, which also contains a few problems from other sources.

It is important to ascertain as far as possible to what extent we may rely upon this classification.[25] If we admit its accuracy as given in the original MS. of the work, of which we possess later copies in AH and C, the possibilities of error in the existing copies are of two kinds. The leaves of AH and C

[24] Three problems occur twice over in AH (viz. AH 15 = 107, 31 = 105, 57 = 80); in the table on p. 274 I have omitted the duplicate entries, and reckon these positions as belonging to the section of the MS. in which they first occur.

[25] The error in the order of the diagrams of the taʿbīyāt, which I have established in Ch. XIV, suggests the possibility of error in the case of the manṣūbāt.

may have become disarranged since they were written, or they may be copies of MSS. the leaves of which were already disarranged, without the later writers observing the fact. Since the earlier Muslim MSS. are not arranged on the plan so generally adopted later of allotting each page to a single problem, it is comparatively easy to ascertain from a careful study of the text whether the leaf-succession is now correct. Thus a comparison of AH and C shows that C is a copy of AH or of a MS. preserving the order of AH, of which the leaves at a later date have been badly disarranged. With the help of AH we can recover the original leaf-order, and in so doing we discover that three leaves in AH (ff. 121–3) have in their turn been disarranged since the MS. was completed. They ought to come between ff. 129 and 130. Where, however, we find a group of problems of which the first begins at the top of the *recto* of a leaf, and the last ends at the foot of a *verso* of a leaf in both AH and C, we cannot be certain from a mere comparison of the two MSS. that the group as a whole has not been displaced. It is necessary now to study the problem-succession in other Muslim MSS. In the main their evidence points to the substantial correctness of the order in AH, and consequently the accuracy of the classification of that MS., with one important exception. The ff. 55 and 56 in AH have been reversed there, and the original order of the pages was 56 b, 56 a, 55 b, and 55 a. This removes problems AH 59–61 from the section containing problems from aṣ-Ṣūlī, &c., to that containing problems from al-ʿAdlī only, and thus removes the only discrepancy between the MSS. AH and H. At the same time all the evidence still leaves possible gaps between ff. 34 and 35, 75 and 76, 88 and 89, and 106 and 107 in AH: i. e. between problems AH 17 and 18, 94 and 95, 120 and 121, and 151 and 152. That there is a real hiatus between AH ff. 75 and 76 is obvious, for the former leaf concludes a selection of Tours and the latter commences with the concluding lines of the solution of a problem (No. 82 below), which we know from L was claimed by al-Lajlāj. The following table, illustrating the recurrence of the AH problems in other MSS., lends support to the view that the last three divisions, which I have indicated as possible, mark real breaks in the AH compilation:—

	Groups in AH.[27]	The number of these problems[26] occurring in							
		AH	BM	AE	V	H	F	Y	Alf.
α {	9–17	9	7 (11)	2	2	6	2 (3)	4	3
	18–61	44	38 (54)	21	17	32 (33)	29 (34)	14 (15)	11 (15)
σ	62–90	28	7	19	14	8	1 (2)	5	9 (12)
β	95–120	24	5 (9)	5	1	3	20 (21)	2	4 (10)
γ	121–151	31	4 (5)	11	28 (29)	1	0	1	5 (6)
δ	152–195	44	19 (21)	16	30	6	0	8	12 (13)

This table shows clearly that the al-ʿAdlī collection was the favourite storehouse from which all later collections have drawn most freely for their

[26] The numbers in brackets give the total number of times that the positions are diagrammed, reckoning all duplicate entries separately.

[27] I have retained the order of the problems in the MS. as now existing, and have made no attempt to restore the original order, so far as numbering the problems is concerned.

problems. It also shows how curiously unevenly the problems in the section in AH which claims to be taken from aṣ-Ṣūlī are distributed in the other MSS. If we accept the statement of AH, we must either suppose that the later MSS. only had access to incomplete copies of aṣ-Ṣūlī's work, or of a compilation such as AH, or that the later selections were made very much at haphazard, the compiler merely copying without discrimination from a few successive pages of an older MS. It would almost seem simpler to adopt the view that AH is a compilation from a wider range of works than its author chose to admit. This view certainly receives support from the details of the table. We see how sparingly the problems in groups σ, β, and γ are represented in BM. Since this MS. is one which shows very few signs of a direct use of aṣ-Ṣūlī's work, this fact acquires a certain significance. AE, on the other hand, is a MS. which—in its earlier part at least—owes much to al-Lajlāj, and therefore indirectly to aṣ-Ṣūlī, and we find that it is rich in the problems in σ. The contrast between V and F is striking. If we exclude the problems which these MSS. have derived from al-ʿAdlī,[28] there is only one problem left which is common to both MSS.[29] The table shows that σ is common to AH, AE, and V; β to AH and F; γ to AH, V, and perhaps AE; and δ to AH, BM, AE, and V; or putting it another way, that σ was not used by BM or F, β not by V or Y, γ not by BM, F, or Y, and δ not by F.[30] It is difficult to believe that all these results are merely coincidences. May we not explain them in part by the hypothesis that σ is the original aṣ-Ṣūlī selection which the compiler of AH made, that β is a selection from the lost work of al-Lajlāj, and that γ and δ are derived from other works now lost which may in part have been based independently upon aṣ-Ṣūlī's works.[31]

There are 109 manṣūbāt in V, the first being preceded by the conclusion of a solution to a problem whose diagram (V 0) is missing because of a hiatus in the MS.[32] There are no duplicate entries. V. d. Linde has pointed out that this MS. is distinguished by the accuracy of its diagrams. This suggests that its source is an earlier compilation from sources used in the preparation of AH. The accuracy, however, does not extend to the order of its problems, and this deprives a few notes to the solutions of their value.[33] Both in V and in the later part of AH there are several notes of a more personal character, which v. d. Linde assumed to be aṣ-Ṣūlī's own. I am not so sure about them. The general rule of the MSS. is to introduce a quotation by the

[28] Viz. eight from group a. [29] Viz. No. 84 (= V 8, F 55) below.

[30] I assume that the exceptions which I have ignored in this summary may have been obtained from compilations only.

[31] A fair case might be made for the view that δ is a misplaced section of the al-ʿAdlī group. On the whole I think it less probable than the view put forward tentatively above.

[32] V 93 is a Knight's tour.

[33] E. g. V 56 (=AH 26, No. 18 below) ends, 'This is the last which we have taken from al-ʿAdlī, and we have given those which we consider to be good. We now commence our problems.' In AH this note follows AH 27, and is prefaced by the words, 'Aṣ-Ṣūlī has said'. V 57 (= AH 27, No. 19 below) begins, 'This happened to al-Mahdādī (name doubtful), and the game is defective. It is not in al-ʿAdlī's book.' AH merely says, 'aṣ-Ṣūlī has said "this happened to al-Hadādī, and the game is defective".' H gives both problems as from al-ʿAdlī. Presumably V used a copy of aṣ-Ṣūlī (? or a MS. based upon it) in which a leaf was inverted. But why should it suppress the acknowledgement of indebtedness to aṣ-Ṣūlī?

words 'Aṣ-Ṣūlī (or al-ʿAdlī) has said'. Where these words are omitted, I think that it is possible that these notes are the addition of the compiler of the collections as we possess them.

There are 16 problems in V which are not in AH. One of these is said to be from al-Lajlāj. The majority of these new problems are End-games; 6 of these 16 also occur in BM, and may go back ultimately to al-ʿAdlī, or possibly the AH source which I have designated δ.

I number 75 diagrams in H, but of these H 1–2 are of modifications of chess, H 3–5 are of taʿbīyāt, and H 73–75 are Knight's tours. All, except H 74, occur in the later MS. of this work, Z, though with some slight variation in the order.[33a] This leaves 67 manṣūbāt, of which 42 (H 6–47) are each said to be taken from al-ʿAdlī, 23 (H 48–70) are similarly ascribed to aṣ-Ṣūlī, and 2 (H 71–2) have no author stated. The MS. supplies 9 new positions.

The manṣūbāt contained in this group of MSS. are singularly rich in End-games, which bear every sign of having occurred in play over the board. Many of the mate-positions are also from actual play, and with one exception (No. 181 below) the compilers of the MSS. appear to have intended that this should be believed of all the problems. Most of the mate-problems belong to one type. The pieces are so posted that the mate is achieved by a succession of checks of greater or less number. The whole difficulty consists in discovering the right succession to adopt, and the difficulty is enhanced more often by increasing the length of the solution than by adding to the number of alternative lines of play. We may briefly describe them as mate-drives, and in their most pleasing form they show the power of a few well-posted pieces. Generally the solution is simply a chase of the King into a mating net that has been prepared in the position diagrammed. A favourite refinement was to employ a single Rook or Knight, or the two Knights alternately, to chase the King into this net, which again was often so arranged that the King had to be driven round the board and back to his first position. The 'water-wheel' problems 82 and 86, below, are good examples of this. The solutions already exhibit a knowledge of many of the devices which have only been enunciated in later times, e.g. the sacrifice of superior force to allow a weaker piece to exert its strength unexpectedly, the skilful use of the cramping power of defensive forces too closely packed together, the waiting move (this but rarely), the unexpected check by discovery and double check. We may also discover certain definite canons of taste to which the problems generally conform. The position must be *possible*, i.e. it must be one which might have occurred in a real game of chess. We must not, however, push this too far. It was only an ar-Rāzī or an aṣ-Ṣūlī who could demonstrate the impossibility of a particular disposition of the Pawns. In practice, *possibility* merely meant that no Bishop could stand upon a square that was inaccessible to him in an ordinary game,

[33a] The problems in H occur in Z in the following order, 1–20, 25–8, 21–4, 33–6, 29–32, 37–8, 43–6, 39–42, 47–75.

but even this limited meaning of the term put the Muslim problem upon a higher plane than was ever reached by the problems composed in Europe in the Middle Ages. There are, however, apart from the positions of the Bishops, many problems which show Pawns on squares that they could never have reached in play, or positions that could only have occurred as the result of palpable connivance on the part of the loser.

The winner's King, again, must be under threat of an obvious and immediate mate. He rarely plays any part, active or passive, in the mate. As a rule he is placed at a remote edge of the board and walled off by a couple of Rooks, or hemmed in by other pieces. The origin of this custom is probably to be found in the endeavour to cut out other first moves than the one intended. Obviously, lines of play commencing with a non-check move were shut out by the device. But positions derived from actual games were freely treated in order to satisfy this artistic taste. Often the treatment is overdone, and destroys the verisimilitude of the arrangement. Generally there is considerable freedom in the treatment of pieces which are not essential for the intended solution, and the different MSS. disagree in their grouping of the non-essential pieces about the winner's King. Economy of force was a principle of composition that was not yet dreamed of, and the presence of inactive and superfluous men was no blemish in Muslim eyes. On the other hand, a study of the mate-problems shows that it was a definite principle of composition that the pieces on the two sides should be as nearly as possible of equal force, and that the winner's advantage should be reduced to nothing more than the possession of the first move. This is so characteristic a feature of the older Muslim work that it becomes one of the most reliable means of separating Muslim from European problems in the European MSS.

There are no conditional problems in these MSS. In a few cases, later MSS. have, in repeating problems, added an apparent condition, 'mate to be given with a particular piece, or upon a particular square', but upon examination these conditions are found to exercise no restraint upon the play, and may be dismissed as nothing more than hints to the solver to help him in his play.

It is the appearance of conditional problems in BM (in a MS. of 1257), AE (MS. undated), Alf. (MS. of 1283), Man. (MS. of 1446), and Al. (written *c.* 1340), combined with the slightly later style of these works, that has led me to make a second group of them. The conditional problem is certainly a later development than the simpler type of End-games and mates which are the rule in the MSS. of which I have been treating. There are only two species of conditional problem in the Muslim MSS.—in the one, mate is to be given by a specified piece; in the other, mate is to be given upon a specified square. It is difficult with these conditions, though not impossible, to keep up the pretence of the position being taken from actual play, and there is a tendency to reduce the number of pieces for the defence. The enchanced difficulty of the task is sufficient justification for the attack's advantage in force.

In the Piece-mate, the favourite pieces selected for the purpose were naturally those of least power, the Bishop and the Pawn, and the Bishop was the favourite. At a later time this preference became still more pronounced in Muslin chess, and extended to the ordinary game also. Some of the allusions to chess which Bland quoted from later Persian poets drew their point from the high repute in which the mate with the Bishop was held, and the late Per. MS. RW speaks of players who were noted for their skill in the 'Bishop's Game', i. e. in ending a game by a mate with a Bishop.

BM contains 214 diagrams (of which nine are blank but have accompanying text, and three are blank without text), and the terminations of two problems, the diagrams of which were on leaves now missing from the MS. These I have included in my numbering. The author intended a classification of his material based upon the character of the diagrams: thus the following chapter-headings are given:

f. 11 a, Chapter of the *taʿābī* (BM 1–5).

f. 13 a, Chapter of the manṣūbāt that are won (*maghlūbāt*) with the King pinned (BM 6–59).

f. 42 a, Chapter of the *taʿābī* which al-ʿAdlī mentioned (BM 60–67, of which BM 66 and 67 are *maqmūrāt*).

f. 44 a, Chapter of the manṣūbāt in which the King is not pinned (BM 68–165; of which 106–129 are drawn games).

f. 103 b, Chapter of the manṣūbāt that are drawn (*qawāʿīm*) and have solutions (BM 166–216; the contents of this section are more miscellaneous than are those of the other sections, e.g. 171, 173, 183–196 are *maghlūbāt* positions, 201–2, 212–16 are *mikhāriq* or modifications of chess).

The MS. contains many duplicates; no fewer than twenty-three positions occur twice, while four appear thrice in it. This, combined with the want of order in the concluding part of the MS., gives it more of the character of a note-book. I imagine that the author made many entries after he had completed his original plan, using the surplus blank pages for the purpose. Like V, the MS. is rich in End-games, and it adds no less than seventy-six positions to our collection.

The author generally adds to the original title the name of the piece which is to be moved first, e. g. 'Black wins, and the play is his with the Knight,' &c. The conditional problems have a longer title, e. g. BM 7, 'Red wins, and the play is his with the King to bring it opposite his Rook, and the condition (Ar. *sharṭ*) is to win it, checkmate on the square on which he is with the Bishop.' There are six problems of this character in the MS. (BM 6, 7, 9—a resetting of AH 100, 50, 51, and 171 = 173).

The MS. is in the main based upon al-ʿAdlī's work. Thus it omits aṣ-Ṣūlī's solutions to Nos. 1 and 10 below.

AE, with 194 problem positions and very full and exhaustive solutions, is probably the most interesting and most important of all the manṣūbāt collections. The problems are arranged without remark, on more extensive lines than elsewhere. AE 1–65 and 176–194 are ordinary mate-problems;

66–96 and 166–175 are End-games (note the stalemate, 166); 97–111 are problems in which A plays but B wins; 112–130 are drawn games; and 131–165 are conditional problems (including 131–143, mates with Bishop, and 144–160, mates upon a particular square). There are no duplicates. No less than 106 of its problems are not to be found in the MS. already examined. On the whole, these new problems strike me as being superior to the AH problems, and therefore as being presumably of later date. The positions Nos. 282–3, 290–1, 296–300, 303, 366, and 384 are especially beautiful. The conditional problems also show an advance upon those in BM.

The relationship of AE to the earlier MSS. is not easy to determine. The MS. supplies no information as to its sources, and suppresses all personal touches, except in its section on the End-game decisions, where it mentions Lajlāj and ʿAdlī as authorities in certain doubtful cases. In proportion to other MSS. it contains fewer problems from al-ʿAdlī's work. The author must, I believe, have been a master of the first rank. Whether that master were al-Lajlāj, the original author of the treatise which forms the earlier portion of AE, or aṣ-Ṣūlī, who, as we know from the *Fihrist*, was the author of two works on chess, we cannot tell. But the collection is worthy of either master.[34]

Alf. is a European collection of problems, the compiler of which has in the main used Arabic sources. Of his 103 problems, 1–72 and 88–103 are so unmistakably Muslim, and so dissimilar to the European type of problem, that I have not hesitated to include them in the present material. The MS. is weak in End-games and contains few drawn games, and some of the positions suggest that the Arabic sources employed were compiled by players of less skill than were the MSS. discussed above; e.g. Alf. 1 (No. 388) is a rendering of No. 82 in which the artistic mate is forgotten. Only twenty of its problems are new.

The fanciful principle of arrangement adopted by the compiler, by which he makes his order depend upon the number of men employed in the position, effectively conceals his indebtedness to the older works. The table on p. 16 shows, however, that all the sources of AH are represented, and specially al-ʿAdlī and δ. As might have been expected from the principle of arrangement adopted, duplicates are fairly common, ten positions occur twice, one thrice, and two four times.

It was b. Abī Ḥajala's plan to end each of the eight chapters in Man. with five diagrams: the first a taʿbīya, the second a game won by Red, the third a game won by Black, the fourth an easy draw, and the fifth a hard draw.

[34] The leaves of the existing copy of the MS. are either disarranged slightly, and possibly incomplete, or it is a mechanical copy of an earlier MS. which was out of order. In the copy which I have used—made for Mr. J. G. White by a Turkish scribe in Constantinople—there are several breaks in the continuity of the text which occur in the middle of the solution to a problem, and in the middle of a line and of a page of the text. The new matter proves nearly always to be the missing termination of a problem whose solution is broken off in this way on another page of the MSS. Thus, the solution to AE 1 is incomplete: the missing termination is 179a, i.e. the apparent termination to the solution of 179. These misplaced conclusions may be identified thus: 15a = end of 42; 18a = end of 15; 21a = end of 18; 145a unidentified; 148a unidentified; 157a = end of 145; 158a = end of 148; 187a = end of 179. The conclusions of 157, 158, and 187 are apparently missing.

Chapter VI, dealing with the modifications of chess and the *mikhāriq*, contains a number of diagrams of these and two other non-chess puzzles (Man. 29–49).[35] At the end of the MS. are three extra diagrams (65 a problem, 66 a taʿbīya, and 67 blank). One problem occurs twice. The 33 manṣūbāt add eight to our collection. Although the MS. quotes aṣ-Ṣūlī largely, it is richer in problems from al-ʿAdlī, twelve being traceable to the latter writer.

The identification of the problems in al-Āmulī (Al.) is by no means easy. Of the eight MSS. which I have compared, none gives the problem-diagrams and text in an orderly way, and most omit to place the chessmen on the diagrams altogether. The diagrams in the India Office MS. are all filled in black ink, and correspond neither to the solutions in the text nor to any other Muslim problems. A study of the text shows that the most complete MSS. contain twenty-four problems, of which, however, 13–18 merely repeat 7–12 and 19 is identical with 1. This leaves seventeen distinct positions, all of which, except Al. 21 (a drawn game), have been identified from the solutions; ten prove to be from al-ʿAdlī, and two are new.

I have made my third group of five works of the 15th–17th centuries, RAS (in a 15th c. MS.), F (written 1501), R (written *c.* 1575), S (written 1571), and Y (in a MS. of 1612). It is in these MSS. that we meet with the first signs of the fanciful ascriptions and problem-legends, of which the Dīlārām story (see the solution to No. 83, below) is the best-known example.

There are sixty-four diagrams in RAS, arranged one a page with overscript, but without solutions. Sixty of these contain manṣūbāt,[36] of which sixteen occur in AH fairly evenly distributed over the five sections into which I divide that MS. Nearly every position is attributed to a player, and the majority to ʿAlī Shaṭranjī, the great player of Tīmūr's day, or to contemporaries of his. Some of the AH positions are thus post-dated. Most of the thirty-five new positions are said to be from actual games in which odds were given, or the winner played blindfold or other games at the same time. In several the winning line of play is by no means obvious.

F, with eighty-four diagrams (F 1–6 are taʿbīyāt), is in the main based upon the older collections: the composite nature of its sources is well shown by the ten duplicate and two triplicate entries. The succession of the problems is often the same as in AH; it owes nothing to H and V; al-ʿAdlī problems (thirty-two) and aṣ-Ṣūlī (twenty, if β be by aṣ-Ṣūlī) are both used largely. Ten problems are new to us. The second MS. of this work (Q) omits, owing to gaps, eight of the problems in F (F 14, 44, 51, 55–6, 78 and 84), and places F 61 between F 39 and 40.

R, with eighty-three diagrams, two of which are unfilled, stands in close

[35] Man. 36–45 relate to aṣ-Ṣafadī's problem of the ship (see Hyde, ii. 23): to arrange 15 Christians and 15 Muslims in a circle so that by counting round and rejecting every *n*th man, all the Christians are rejected. Man. 46–9 illustrate another problem: to arrange 32 men against the sides and in the angles of a square room so that the total counting along each wall is 12, and then to add 4, 8, and 12 men without altering this total of 12 along a wall. The *taʿbīyāt* are Man. 1, 6, 11, 16, 21, 50, 55, 60, and 65; the *mikhāriq*, Man. 28–35.

[36] RAS 1 is blank, 2 and 3 are taʿbīyāt, 61 is a diagram with the 8 Red Pawns on the 2nd and the 8 Black Pawns on the 7th line.

relationship with F, only six problems in that work not occurring in this, while only four positions in R are not contained in F. Two of these are not contained in any of the earlier MSS. The MS. is carelessly compiled; of its eighty-one positions, eleven occur twice, and four three times. The writer repeatedly cuts short a long solution by the words *shāh māt* long before that position is reached. He adds the comment, 'This is marvellous,' to No. 32 (R 55), and gives as the solution 1 Ktc6, Kc7 (there is nothing to prevent Q × Kt spoiling the whole thing); 2 Re7 mate (when the King can escape by Kc6, that square being unoccupied in his arrangement of the position)!

S contains a small collection of ten problems without solutions, and possesses little importance. Only one position is new, and I have failed to discover the author's solution in eighteen moves.

Y, a Persian translation of a lost Arabic work somewhat on the lines of Man., contains fifty-two diagrams (of which 1–3, 6–8, and 52 are blank, and 51 exhibits the ordinary arrangement of the pieces) with one duplicate. It, again, is based on old material; eighteen of its forty-four problems are from al-ʿAdlī, and only six are unknown from older works.

My fourth and last group of MSS. contains two late Persian works, Oxf. (written 1796–8) and RW (in a 19th c. Eng. trans.). Both were composed in India, and are to some extent influenced by non-Muslim ideas.

Oxf. contains 171 diagrams of positions on the ordinary board, which are grouped in four sections or *maʿrakāt*; f. 7 b, manṣūbāt of Rūmī chess (1–99); f. 58 b, manṣūbāt of Feringhī, i.e. European, chess (100–159); f. 88 b, Būrd positions (160–167); f. 92 b, Qā'īm positions (168–171);—a classification coloured in part by Indian ideas. Many of the problems, however, are derived from Muslim MSS., and most are composed in accordance with the Muslim rules of move. Others, and especially the Pawn-mates, have little else in common with the earlier manṣūbāt. On the whole, the seventy-one problems which I have added from this work seem to me of minor interest.

RW is a small collection of twenty-eight problems and a Knight's tour; it is very similar in character to Oxf., and adds eleven problems of the same type.

Skill in the solution of problems has always been highly esteemed in the East, and the Per. terms *manṣūba-dān*, 'one cunning in problems,' and *manṣūba-bāz*, 'a problem-player,' have passed into the ordinary idiom in the sense of a 'far-sighted' or 'resourceful man'.

The solution, that I give to the problems are those of the MSS., except that I have as a rule omitted all forced moves on the part of the defence, and all variations that lead to the win in a less number of moves. I have not examined the solutions more closely than to satisfy myself that they are sound. In a few cases, chiefly in RAS problems, I have given the solutions from Forbes or v. d. Linde, or have supplied them myself. An indication is added in each case.

2.
AH 10 : C 45 : BM 135 : Y 11 : Man. 51 : H 31.

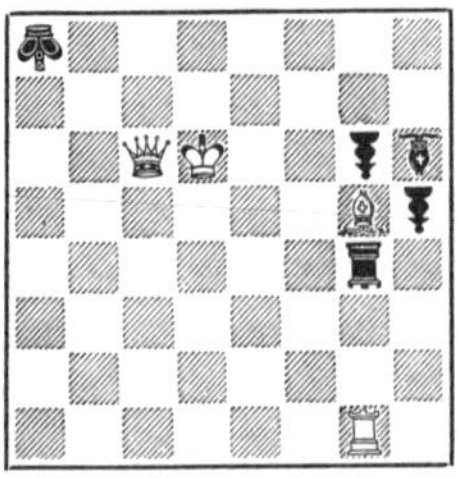

Red plays and wins.

4.
AH 12 : C 48 : BM 85 : F 17 = 76 : H 32 : Alf. 60 : Al. 12 = 18 : R 27 = 35 = 65.

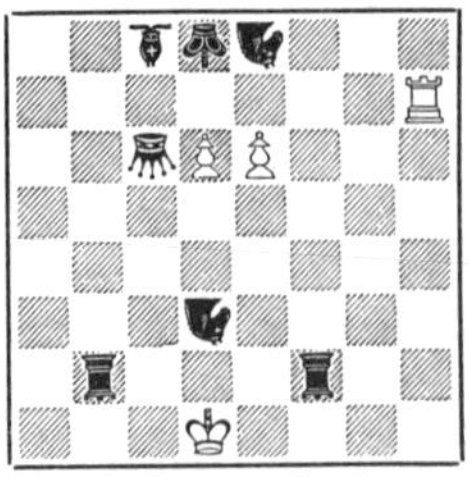

Red plays and wins.

5.
AH 13 : C 49 : BM 57 : S 10 : H 35 : Man. 19 : Oxf. 165.

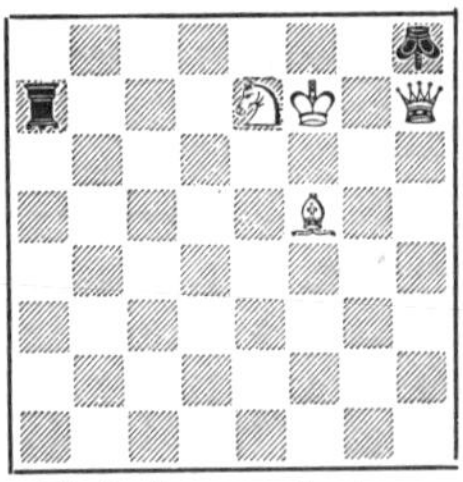

Red plays and wins.

6.
AH 14 : C 50 : BM 20 = 38 : AE 6 : Y 37 : Alf. 35 : H 23 : V 2.

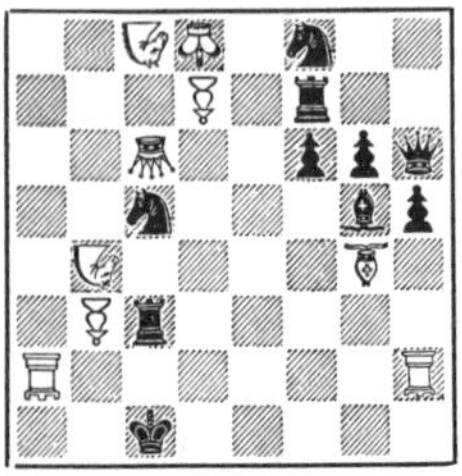

Black plays and wins.

7.
C 182 = 51 : F 62 : AH 107 = 15 : BM 21 = 22 = 39 : Alf. 14 : H 7 : V 3.

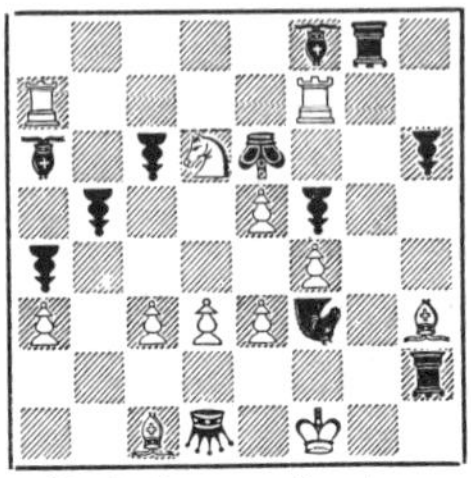

Red plays and wins.

8.
AH 16 : C 5 : Y 42 : AE 73 : BM 138 = H 17.

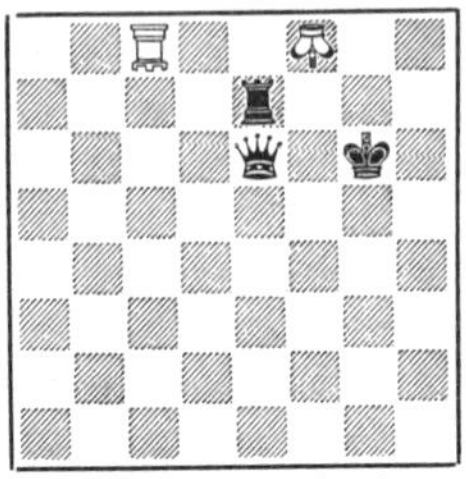

Black plays and wins.

10.
AH 18 : C 120 : Man. 2 : BM 143 : AE 72 : V 0 (end of text only).

Red plays and wins.

11.
AH 19 : C 121 : V 4 : BM 167 : H 43.

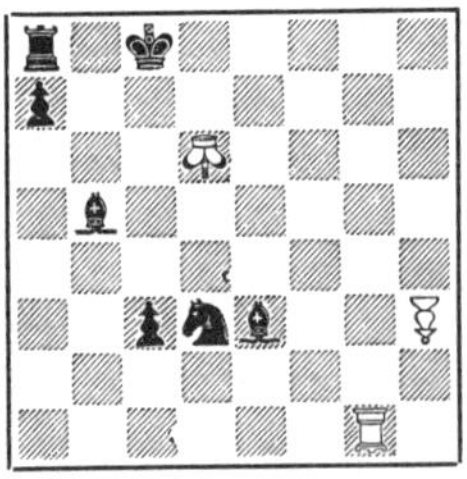

Red plays. Drawn.

12.
AH 20 : C 122 : BM 139 : V 5 : AE 90 : H 24.

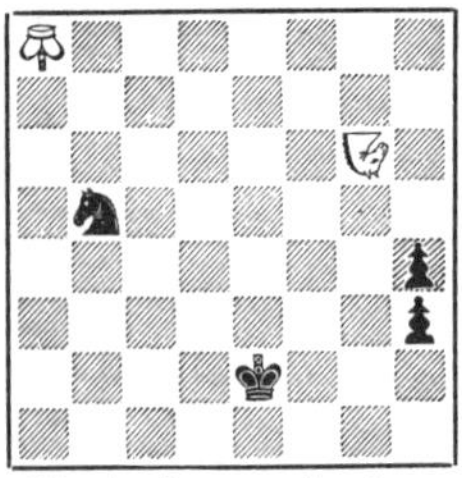

Black plays and wins.

14.
AH 22 : C 8 : F 50 : V 7 : BM 131 : RW 12 : H 12 : R 13.

Black plays and wins.

15.
AH 23 : C 131 : BM 12 : H 6.

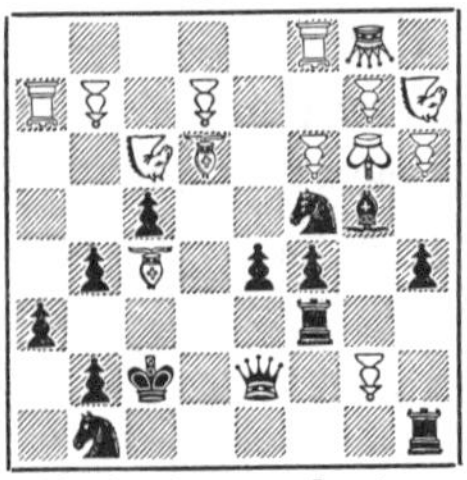

Black plays and wins.

16.
AH 24 : C 132 : BM 27 = 141 : F 29 : Y 29 : V 59 : AE 44 : Alf. 53 : H 34 : R 2.

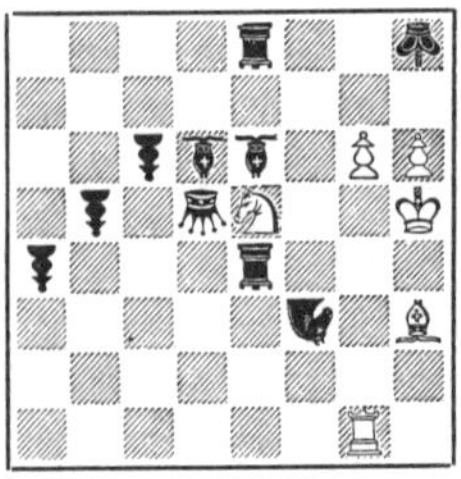

Red plays and wins.

17.
AH 25 : C 133 : F 30 : V 60 : BM 130 = 142 : RAS 56 : H 19 : R 69.

Black plays and wins.

18.
AH 26 : C 134 : BM 23 : F 32 = 51 : Alf. 23 : H 33 : Oxf. 47 : V 56 : R 79.

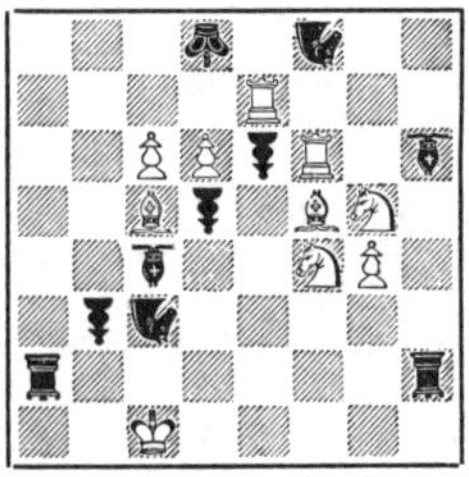

Red plays and wins.

19.
AH 27 : C 135 : BM 18 = 19 = 150 : F 33 = 67 : Alf. 15 : AE 136 : H 10 : V 57 : R 18 = 23 = 29.

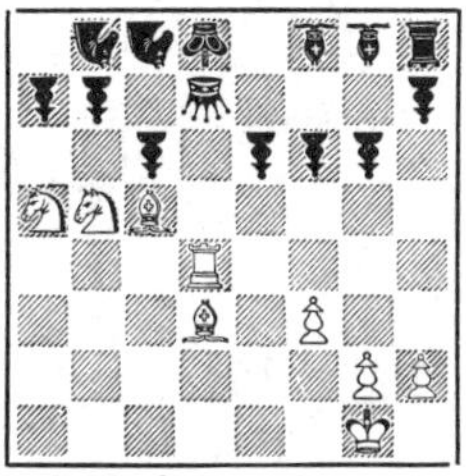

Red plays and wins.

20.
AH 28 : C 136 : BM 25 : F 34 : Alf. 40 = 72 : AE 135 : H 8 : V 107 : R 70.

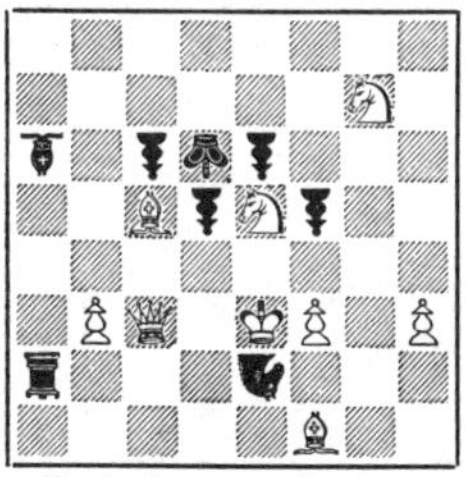

Red plays and wins.

21.
AH 29 : C 9 : BM 16 = 151 : F 35 : AE 63 : H 9 : R 1.

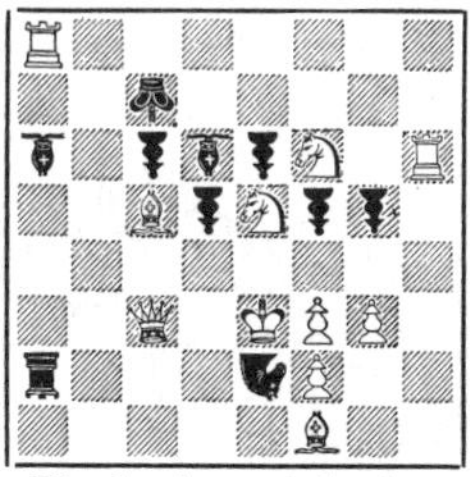

Black plays and wins.

22.
AH 30 : C 123 : BM 133 = 144 : F 36 : Alf. 30 : AE 95 : H 27 : Al. 3 : R 3.

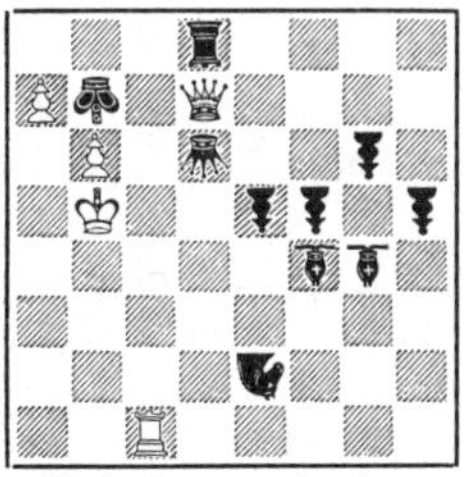

Red plays and wins.

23.
AH 31 = 105 : C 124 = 180 : F 37 : BM 17 = 138 a : Alf. 99 : AE 184 : RW 11 : H 11 : R 7.

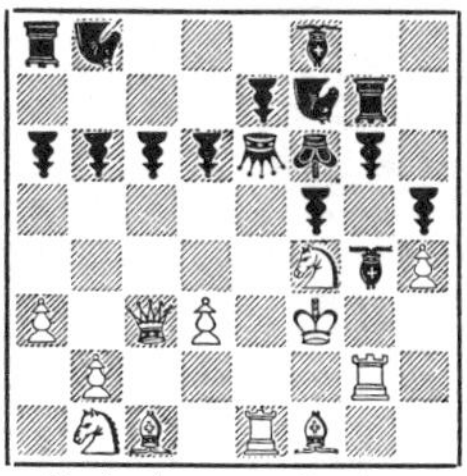

Red plays and wins.

24.
AH 32 : C 125 : BM 56 : Man. 52 : H 36 : Al. 8 = 14 : F 38 : Oxf. 80 : R 16.

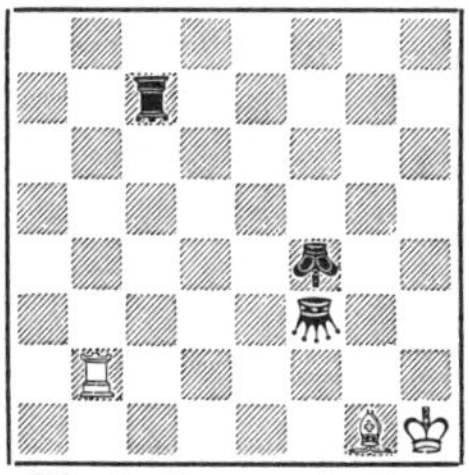

Black plays and wins.

25.
AH 33 : C 126 : F 8 = 39 = 72 : BM 32 = 33 : Y 12 : Al. 1 : H 30 : Oxf. 20 : R 14 = 21 = 61.

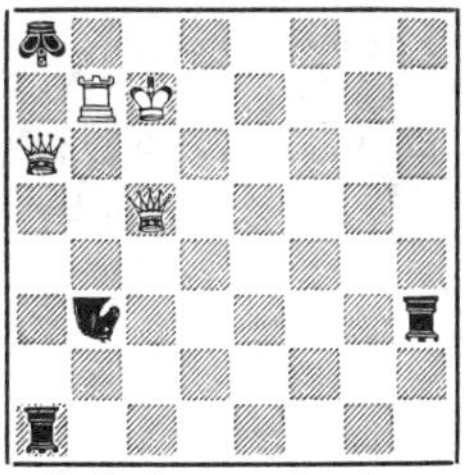

Red plays and wins.

26.
AH 34 : C 127 : F 40 : Y 9 : H 28 : Al. 23 : R 5.

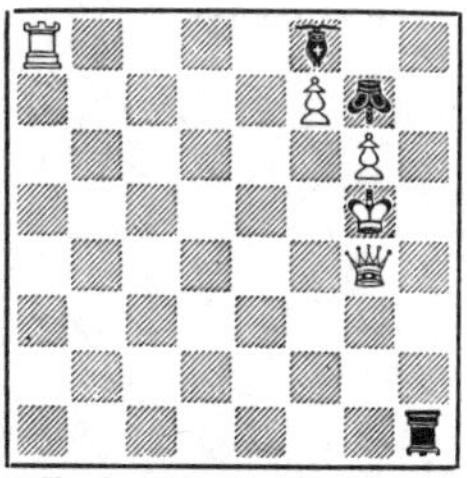

Red plays and wins.

27.
AH 35 : C 128 : BM 40 : Man. 18 : H 25 : F 41 : Al. 10 = 16 ; AE 105.

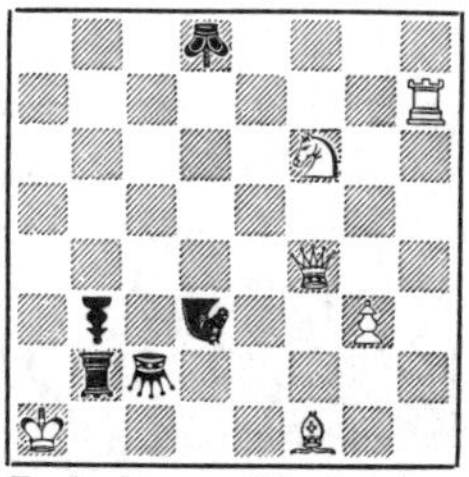

Red plays. Black wins.

28.
AH 36 : C 52 : BM 145 : F 42 : Y 10 : Alf. 41 : AE 37 : Al. 2 : H 38 : R 4.

Black plays and wins.

29.
AH 37 : C 53 : BM 29 : F 43 : Alf. 59 : H 13 : Al. 22 : R 8.

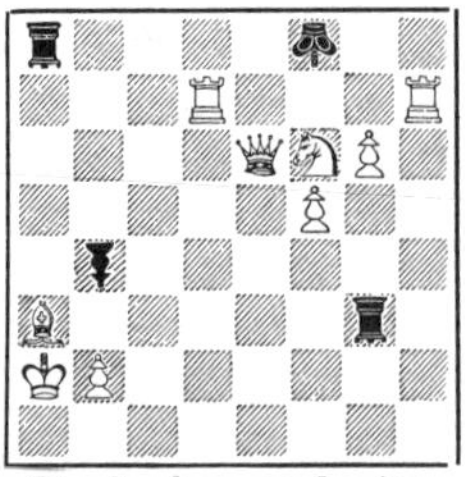

Black plays and wins.

30.
AH 38 : C 129 : BM 28 = 153 : F 45 : Alf. 39 (in II) : AE 30 : Oxf. 11 : H 14 : R 17.

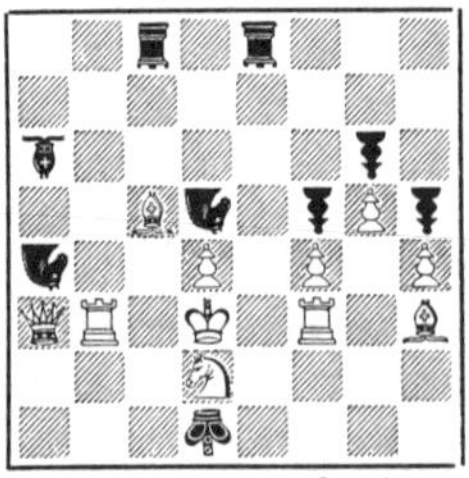

Black plays and wins.

31.
AH 39 : C 130 : F 46 : BM 97 = 152 : R 54.

Black plays. Red wins.

32.
AH 40 : C 56 : BM 30 = 140 : F 47 : R 55.

Red plays and wins.

33.
AH 41 : C 57 : F 48 : Y 13 : BM 197 = 158 : H 18 : Man. 8 : R 15.

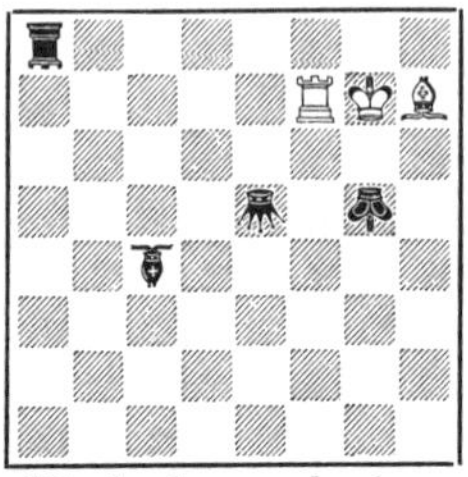

Black plays and wins.

35.
AH 43 : C 55 : BM 107 : F 14 : Y 16 : Oxf. 171 : H 46 : Man. 9 = 64 : AE 125.

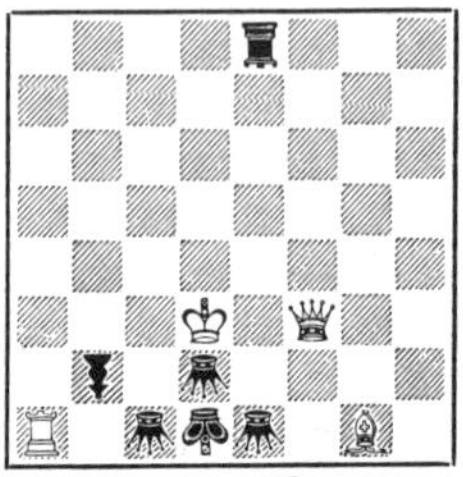

Red plays. Drawn.

42.
AH 50 : C 62 : Y 19 = 30 : AE 126 : BM 166 : Oxf. 169 : H 42 : Man. 24 : V 86.

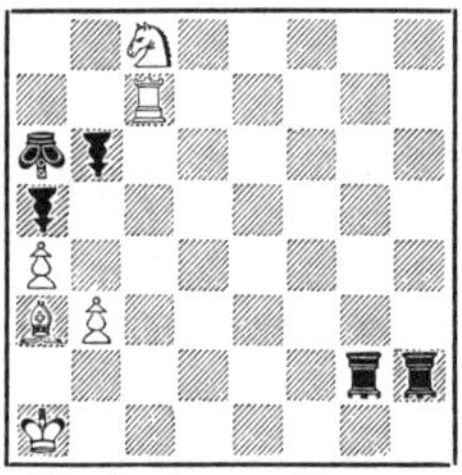

Black plays. Drawn.

49.
AH 57 = 80 : C 143 = 156 : Y 31 : RAS 9 : AE 82.

Red plays and wins.

50.
AH 58 : C 144 : F 57 = 80 : AE 36 : R 31.

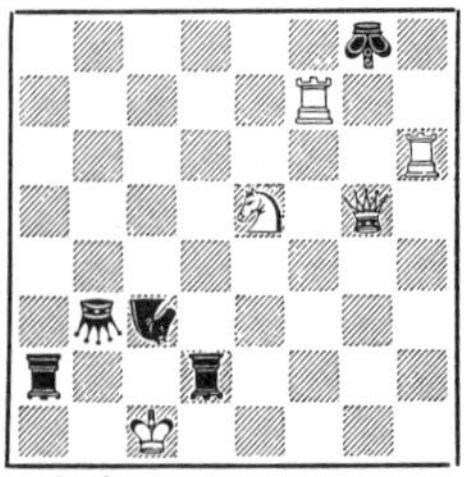

Red plays and wins.

51.
AH 59 : C 10 : BM 147 = 184 : Y 28 : H 26 : AE 84 : Oxf. 166.

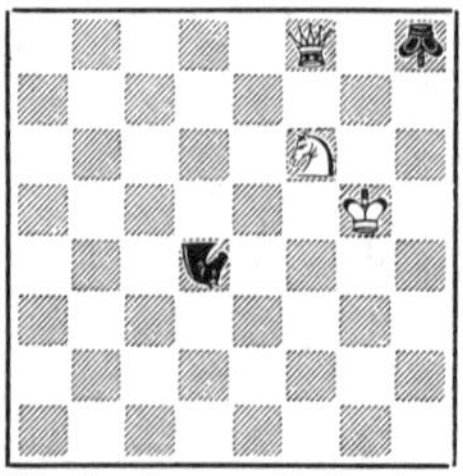

Black plays. Red wins.

52.
AH 60 : C 11 : BM 134 : Y 50 : H 37 : V 54.

Black plays and wins.

53.
AH 61 : C 12 : F 56 : Man. 62 : BM 10 = 194 : H 16 = 55 : V 55 : Alf. 58 = 63 = 64 = 97 : Oxf. 149 : Al. 11 = 17 ; R 52.

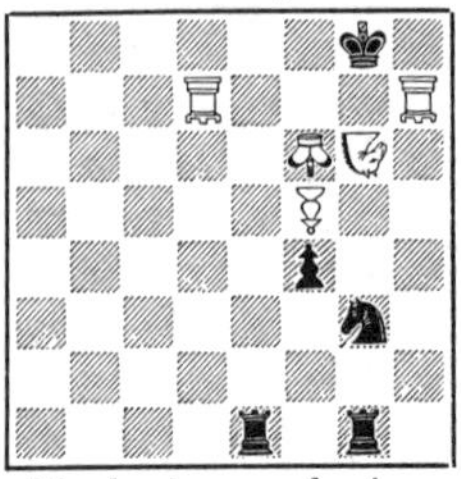

Black plays and wins.

54.
AH 62 : C 13 : AE 2 :
F 78 : H 50 : R 40.

Red plays and wins.

55.
AH 63 : C 14 : AE 5 :
Alf. 37 (in VII) :
BM 41 : H 58.

Black plays and wins.

56.
AE 55 : AH 64 : C 15 :
BM 42 : Alf. 7 : S 6 :
H 64.

Red plays and wins.

57.
AH 65 : C 16 : H 53.

Black plays and wins.

58.
AH 66 : C 17 : AE 56 :
Alf. 8 (in XI).

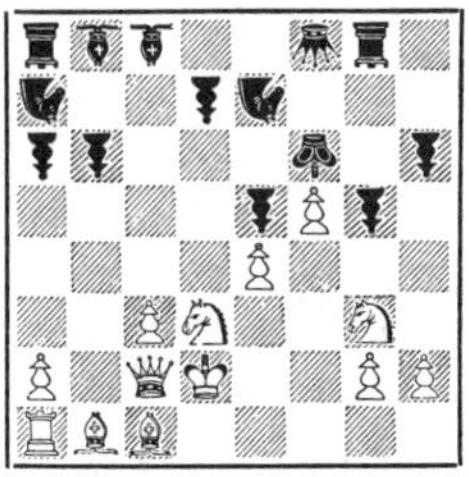

Red plays and wins.

59.
AH 67 : C 18 : BM 45 :
AE 12 : H 52.

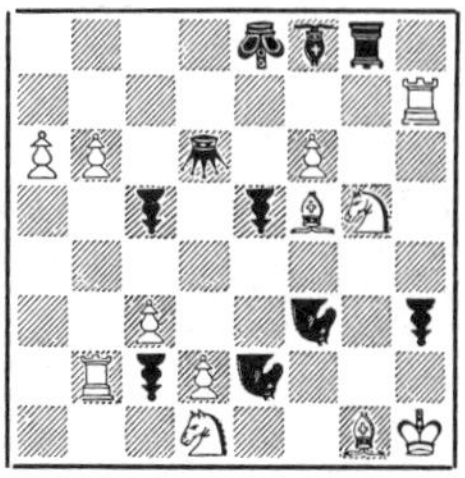

Red plays and wins.

60.
AH 68 : C 19 : BM 46 :
AE 8 : Alf. 12.

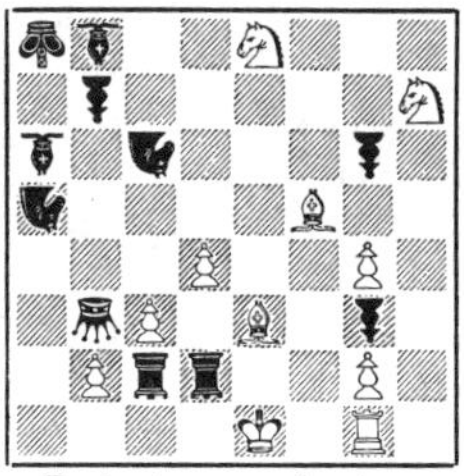

Red plays and wins.

61.
AH 69 : C 145 : S 4.

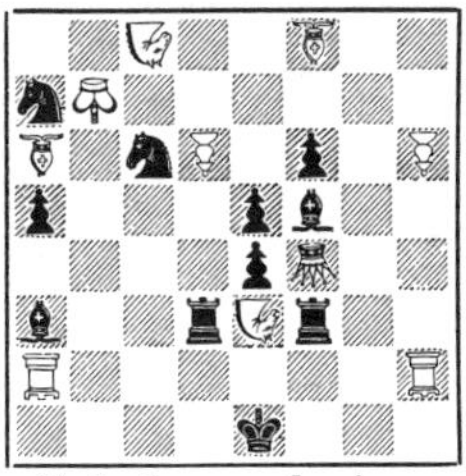

Red plays and wins.

64.
AH 72 : AE 108 : C 148.

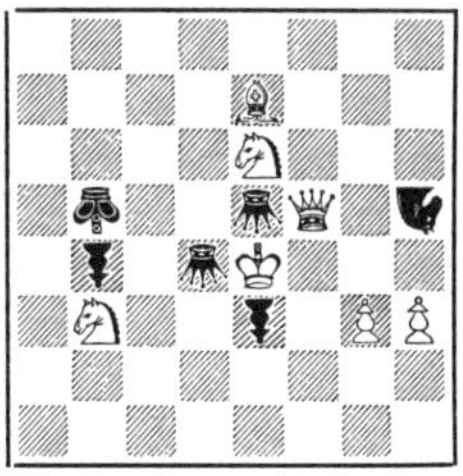

Black plays. Red wins.

65.
AH 73 : C 149 : V 67 :
AE 96 : BM 156.

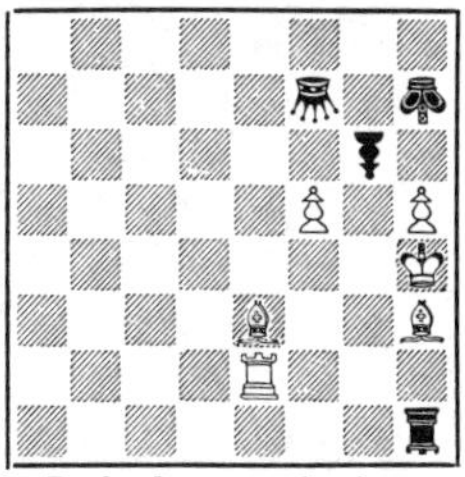

Red plays and wins.

69.
AH 77 : C 153 : Y 25 :
V 97.

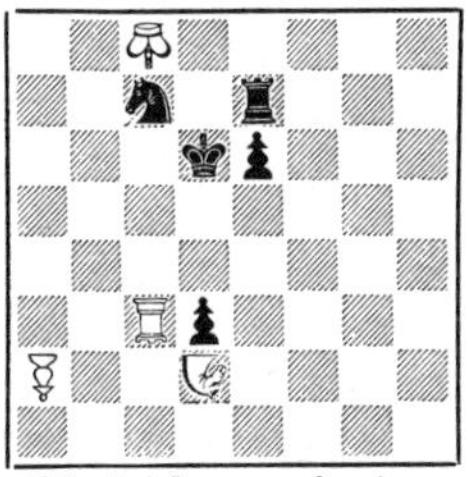

Black plays and wins.

70.
AH 78 : C 154 : Alf. 45
(in VI).

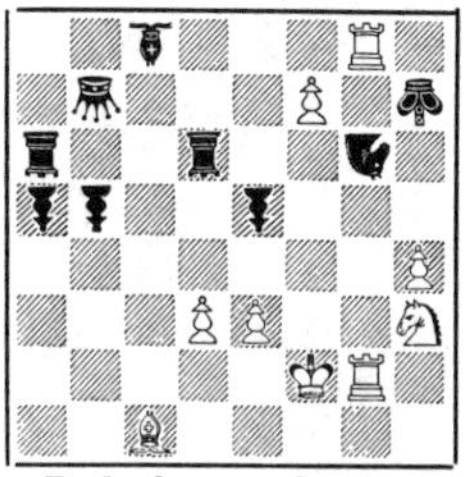

Red plays and wins.

71.
AH 79 : C 155 : V 103 : AE 26.

Black plays and wins.

73.
AH 82 : C 158 : AE 132 : RAS 6 : Y 26 : Alf. 10 = 26 : H 54 : V 25.

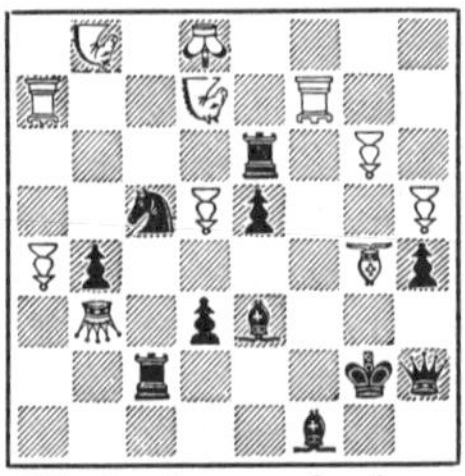

Black plays and wins.

74.
AH 83 : C 159 : AE 35 : Y 32 : Alf. 70 : H 56 : V 26.

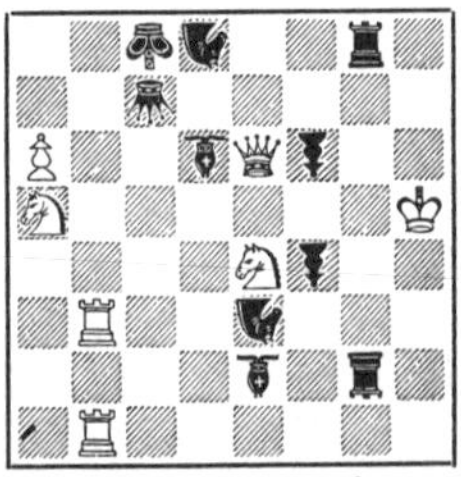

Red plays and wins.

75.
AE 89 : AH 84 : C 160 : V 27 : Y 46.

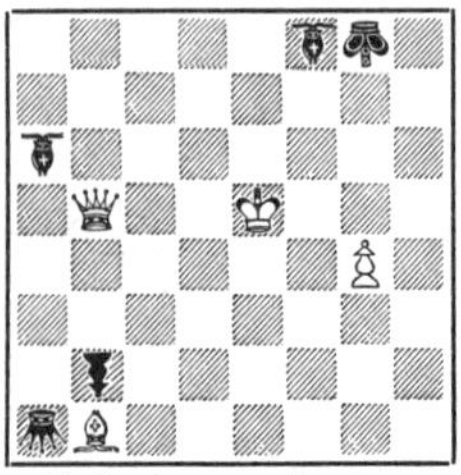

Red plays and wins.

76.
AH 85 : C 161 : AE 172 : Y 38 : V 94.

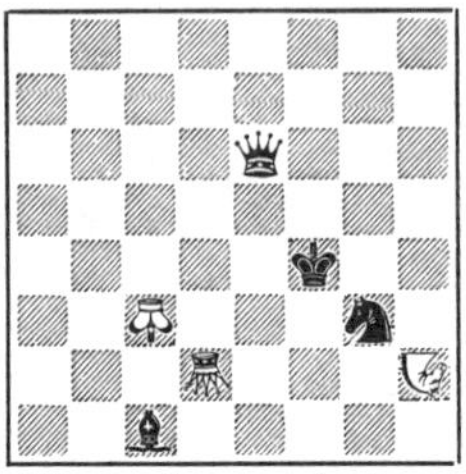

Black plays and wins.

77.
AH 86 : C 162 : Alf. 25 = 27 = 101 : Oxf. 35 : H 61 : V 95 : AE 27.

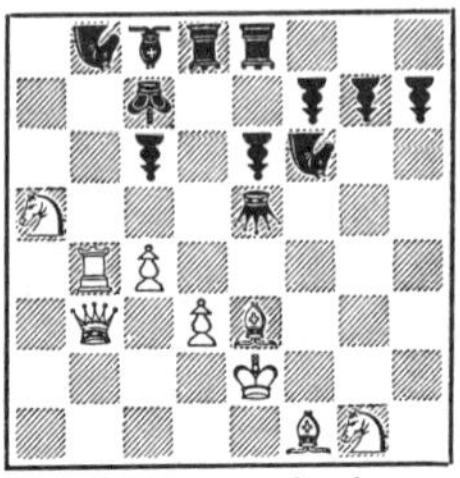

Red plays and wins.

78.
AH 87 : C 163 : Alf. 94.

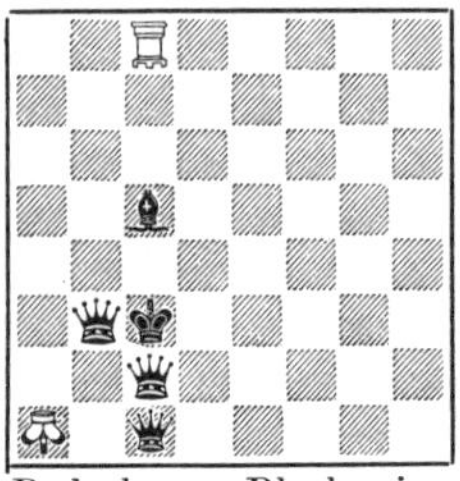

Red plays. Black wins.

79.
AH 88 : C 164.

Black plays and wins.

80.
AH 89 : AE 7 : C 165.

Red plays and wins.

82.
AE 182(corr.): AH 95 and C 170 [text only] : L 33 : BM 52 : Oxf. 1.

Red plays. Mate on e1 in XXXVI.

83.
S 2 : AE 38 (in V): AH 96: C 171 : F 7 : Y 44 : Alf. 54 = 57 = 90 = 100 (in V) : Oxf. 45 : RW 1 (in VII): Man. 57 (in VII) : H 70: R 62.

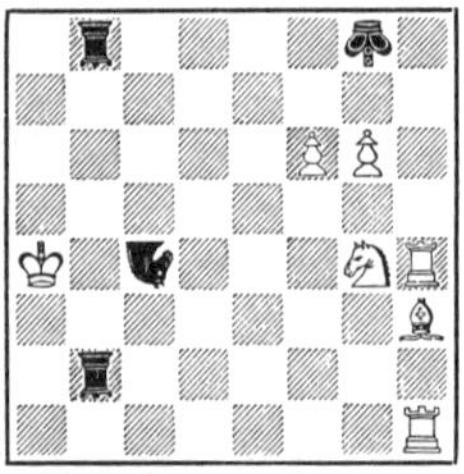

Red plays and wins.

84.
AH 97 : C 172 : F 55 : Alf. 69 = 91 : V 8 : R 20.

Red plays and wins.

85.
AH 98 : C 173 : F 83 : Y 41 : R 76.

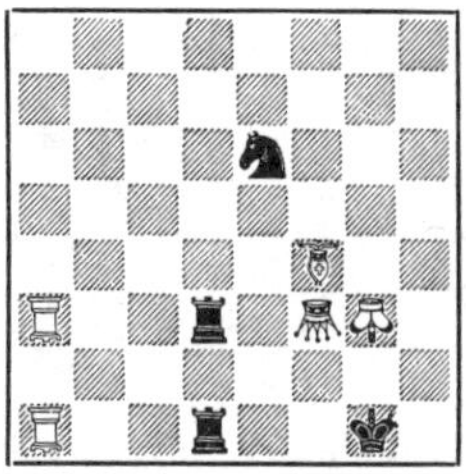

Red plays and wins.

86.
AH 99 : C 174 : BM 8 : S 8 : F 44 : AE 151 : Alf. 38 = 95 : Oxf. 97 : Man. 17 : H 68 : R 6.

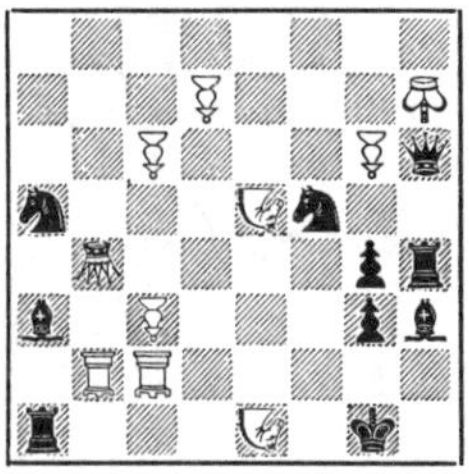

Black plays and wins.

87.
AH 100 : C 175 : BM 9 = 15 : F 82 : Alf. 22 = 89 : R 25.

Black plays and wins.

88.
AH 101 : C 176 (corr.).

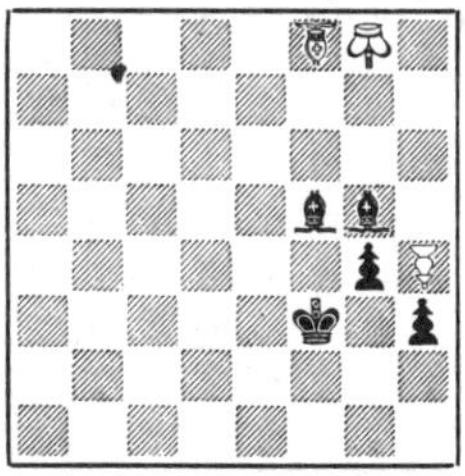

Black plays and wins.

89.
AH 102 : C 177 : F 54 : R 32.

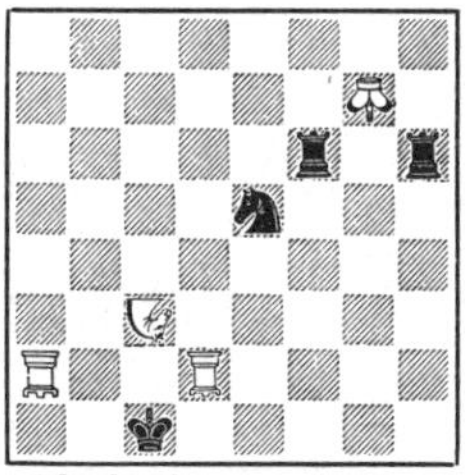

Black plays and wins.

90.
AH 103 : C 178 : F 53 : Oxf. 73 : R 48.

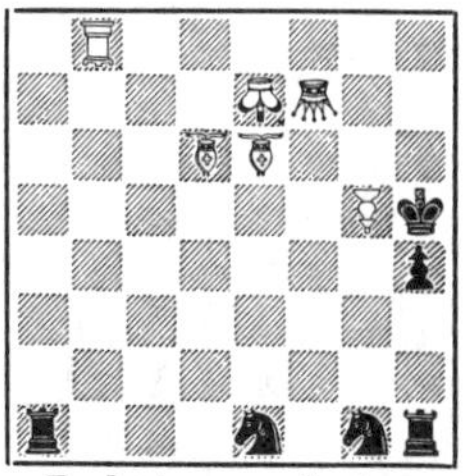

Red plays and wins.

91.
AH 104 : C 179 : F 52 : RAS 57 : S 5 : AE 181 : K 51 = 53.

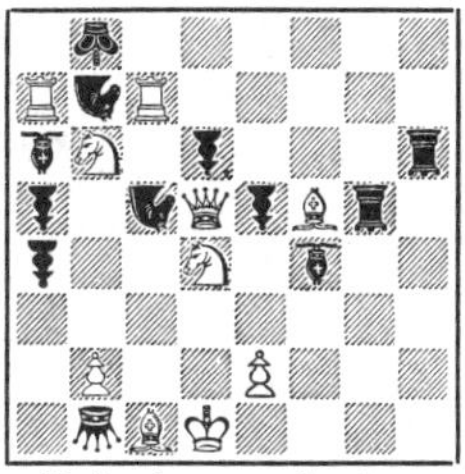

Red plays and wins.

92.
AH 106 : C 181 : BM 132 = 148 = 185 : F 15 = 61 : H 15 : R 10 = 42.

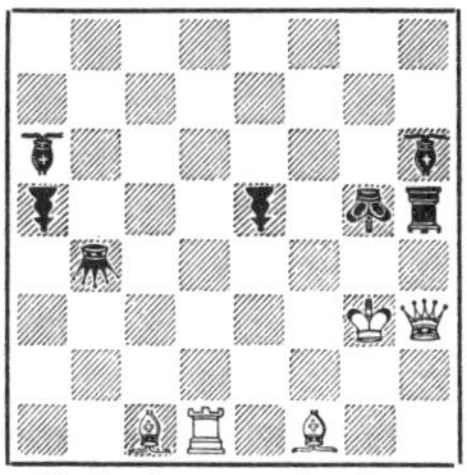

Red plays and wins.

93.
AH 108 (corr.) : C 183 : F 13 : R 9 = 12.

Black plays and wins.

94.
AH 109 : C 184 : F 20 : R 50.

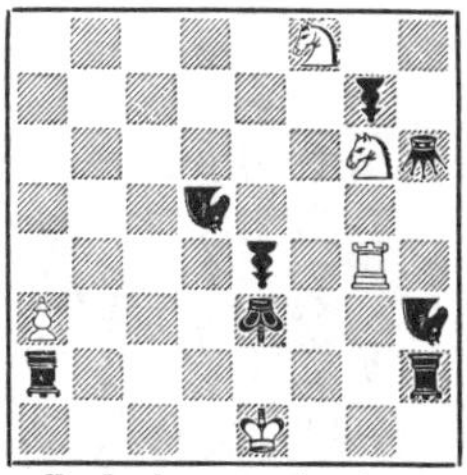

Red plays and wins.

95.
AH 110 : C 185 : F 22 : R 59.

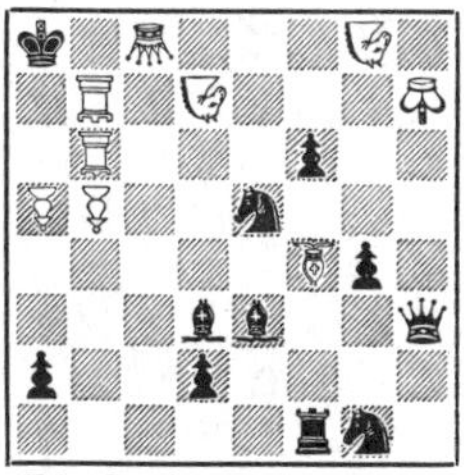

Black plays and wins.

96.
AH 111 : C 186 : F 23.

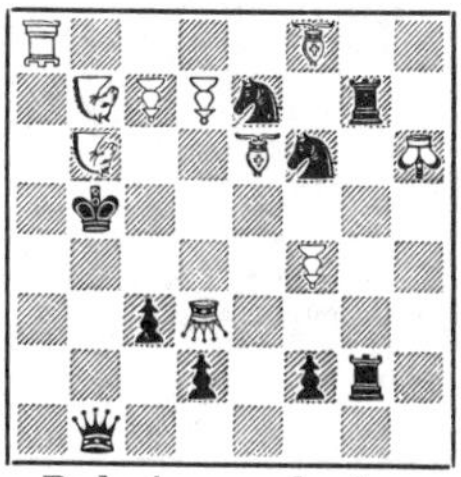

Red plays and wins.

97.
AH 112 : C 187 : F 24 :
R 49.

Red plays and wins.

98.
AH 113 : C 188 : F 25 :
R 67.

Black plays and wins.

99.
AH 114 : C 189 : F 26 :
R 60 = 68.

Red plays and wins.

100.
AH 115 : C 190 : F 27.

Black plays and wins.

101.
AH 116 : C 191 : F 28 :
R 19.

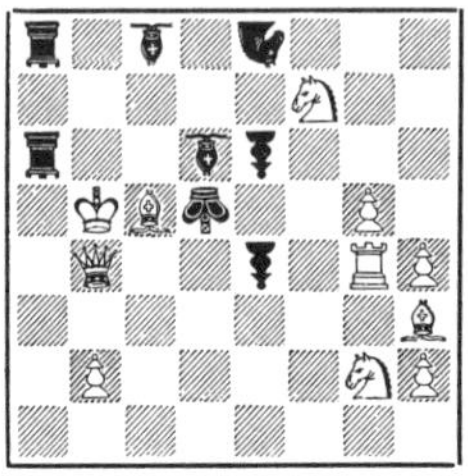

Red plays and wins.

102.
AH 117 : C 192 : F 65 :
R 37.

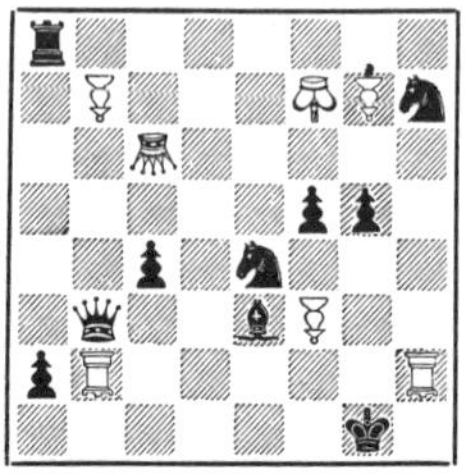

Black plays and wins.

103.
AH 118 : C 193 : F 79 :
R 26.

Red plays and wins.

104.
AH 119 : C 194.

Red plays and wins.

107.
AH 122 : C 108 : RAS 52 :
V 102 : BM 49 (text only).

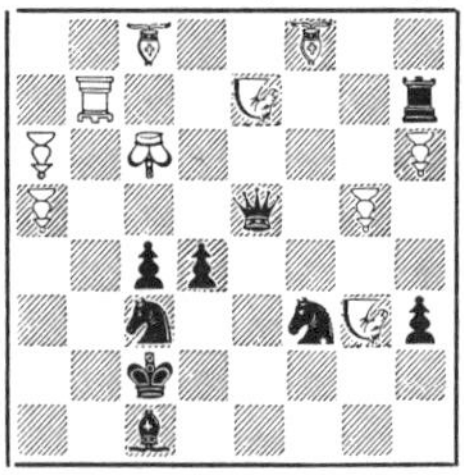

Black plays and wins.

109.
AH 124 : C 110 : V 12.

Black plays and wins.

110.
AH 125 : C 111 : V 13.

Black plays and wins.

111.
AH 126 : V 14 : C 112 :
Alf. 51 (in IV).

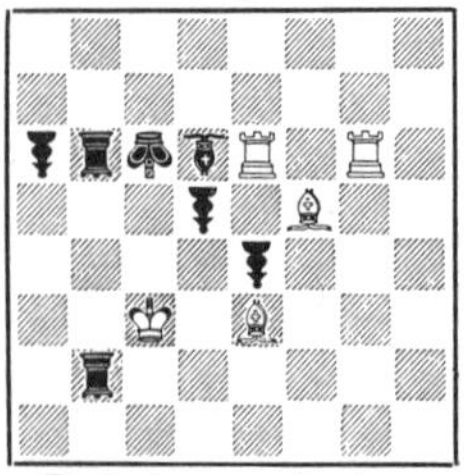

Red plays and wins.

113.
AH 128 : C 114 : V 43 : Alf. 71 (in X) : Oxf. 7 : AE 25.

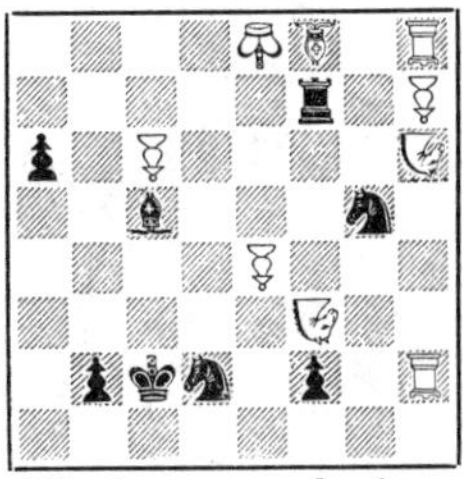

Black plays and wins.

115.
AH 130 : V 19 : C 116 : Alf. 32 (in V) = 102 (in V).

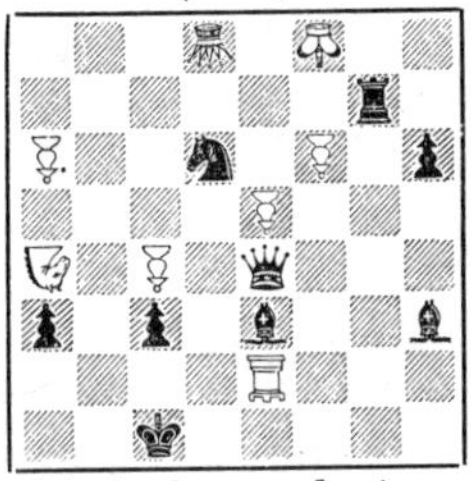

Black plays and wins.

117.
AH 132 : C 118 : AE 99 : V 21.

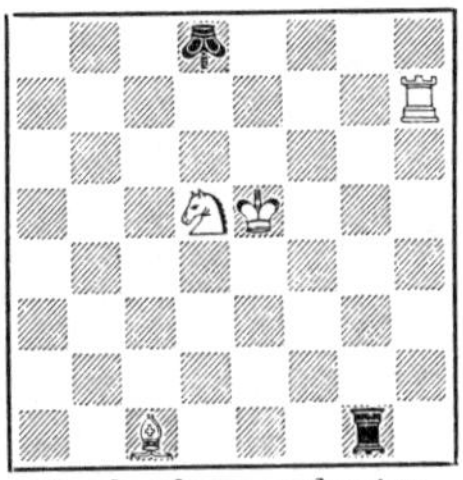

Black plays and wins.

118.
AH 133 : V 22 : C 119 : AE 174 : Y 39.

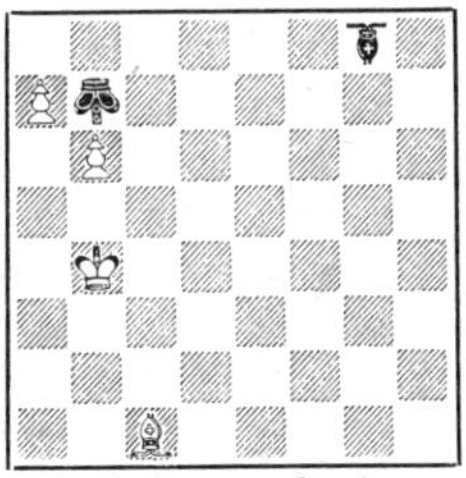

Red plays and wins.

119.
AH 134 : C 23 : V 23.

Black plays and wins.

120.
AH 135 : C 24 : V 66 : Alf. 52 : AE 33.

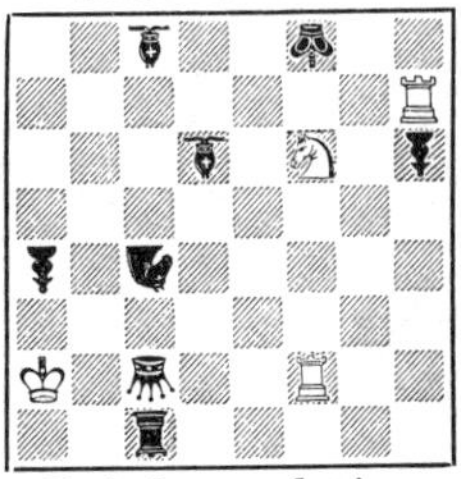

Red plays and wins.

123.
AH 138 : C 27 : AE 28 : V 58.

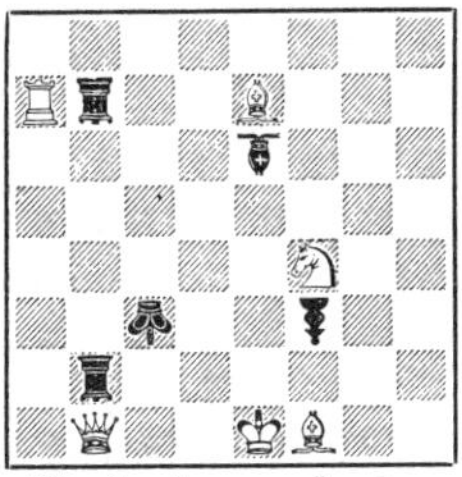

Black plays and wins.

124.
AH 139 : C 28 : V 106 : Alf. 42 : AE 137.

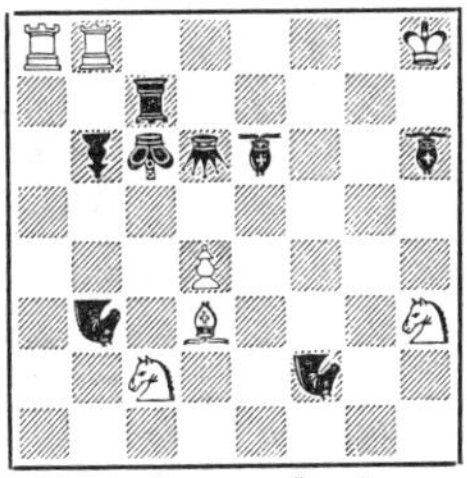

Red plays and wins.

126.
AH 141 : C 30 : V 100.

Black plays and wins.

130.
AH 145 : C 34 : H 66 : V 47.

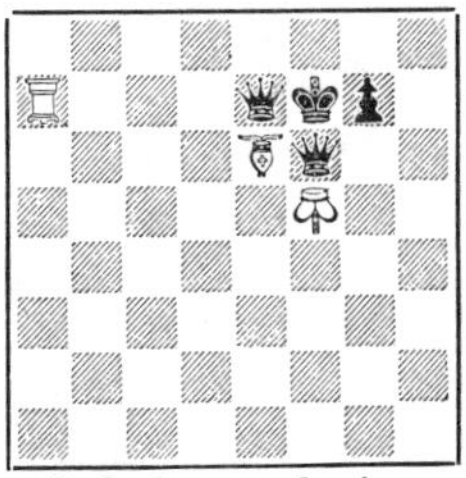

Red plays and wins.

132.
AH 147 : C 36 : BM 68 : AE 101 : V 49.

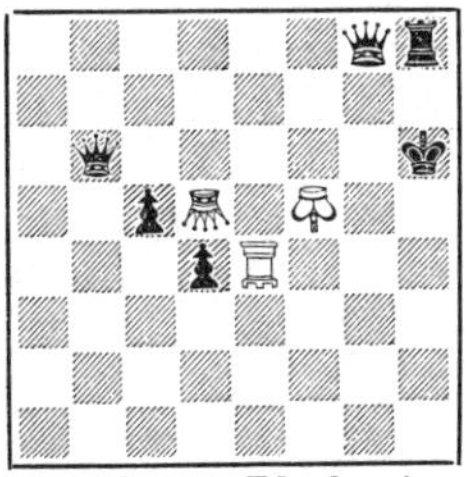

Red plays. Black wins.

133.
AH 148 : C 37 : BM 69 : V 53.

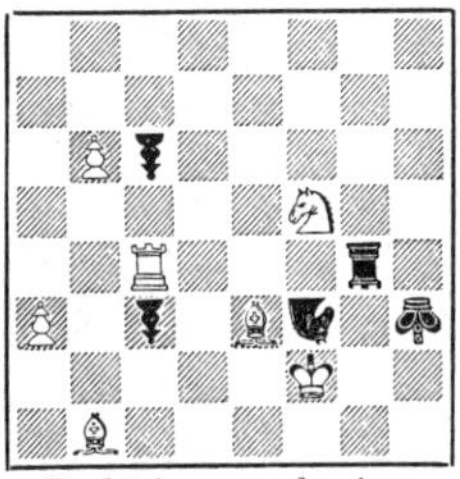

Red plays and wins.

135.
AH 150 : C 39 : AE 173.

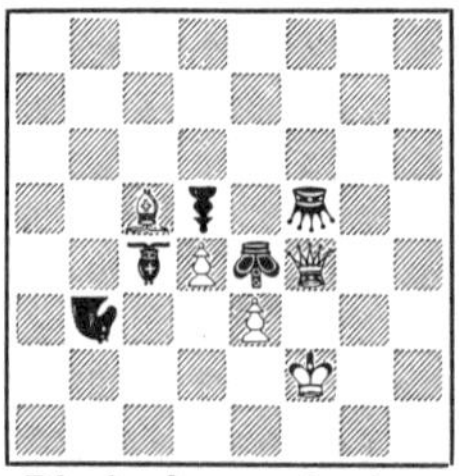

Black plays and wins.

136.
AH 151 : C 40 : V 71 :
Oxf. 54.

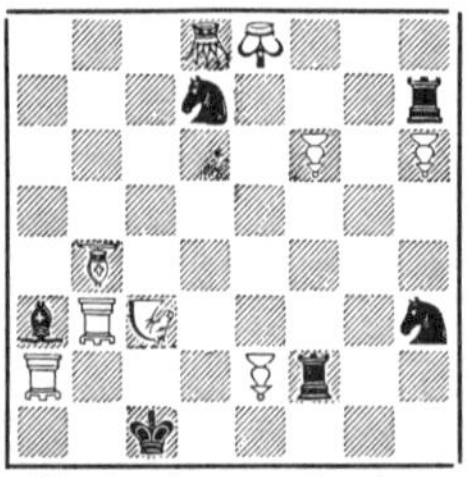

Black plays and wins.

137.
AH 152 : C 65 : BM 53 :
RAS 53 : V 99.

Red plays and wins.

139.
AH 154 : C 67 : BM 71 :
AE 100 : V 62.

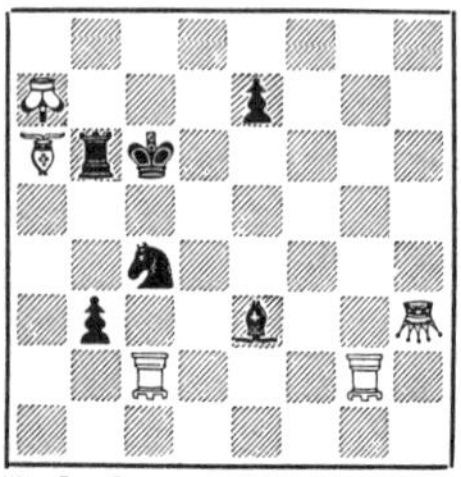

Red plays. Black wins.

140.
AH 155 : C 68 : BM 72 :
V 74.

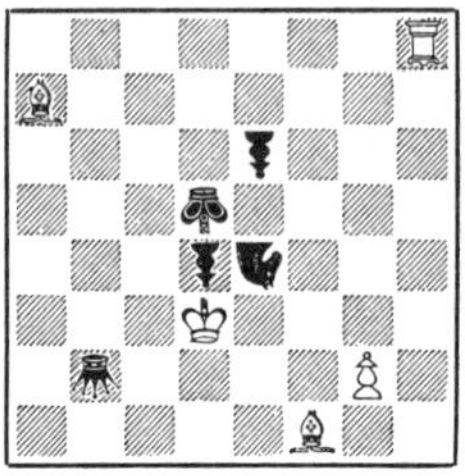

Red plays and wins.

141.
AH 156 : C 69 : V 75.

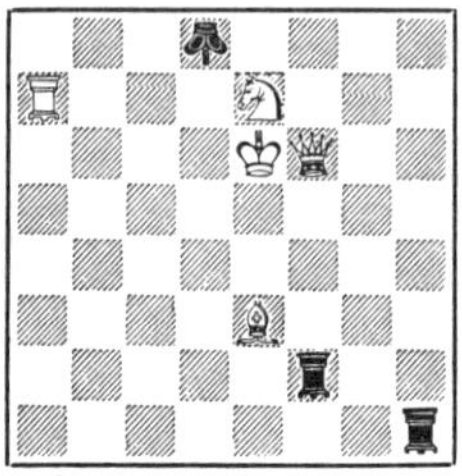

Red plays and wins.

142.
AH 157 : C 70 : BM 73
= 93 : V 28 : RAS 5 :
Alf. 49 (in IV) : AE 94.

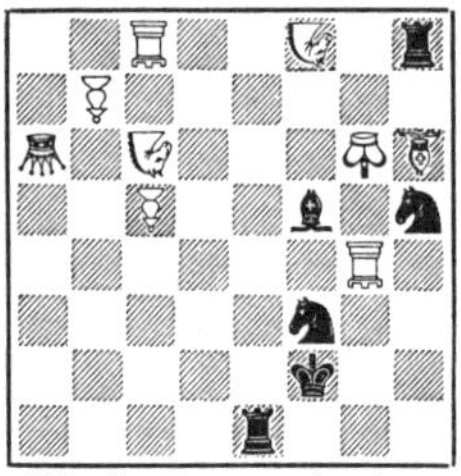

Black plays and wins.

143.
AH 158 : C 71 : BM 74.

Red plays and wins.

144.
AH 159 : C 72 : BM 75 :
H 65.

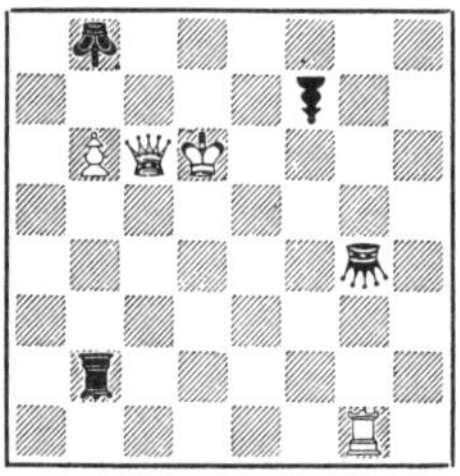

Red plays and wins.

145.
AH 160 : C 73 : BM 76 :
V 1 : AE 175.

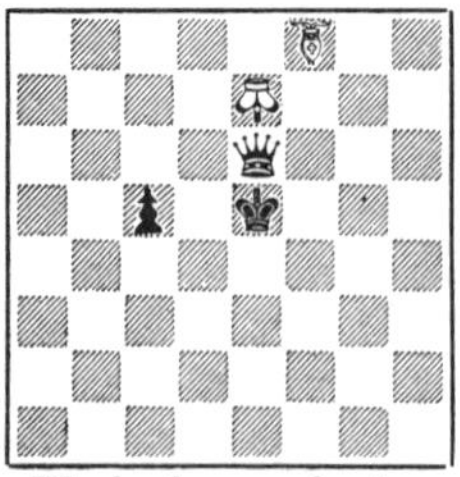

Black plays and wins.

147.
AH 162 : C 75.

Black plays and wins.

148.
AH 163 : C 76.

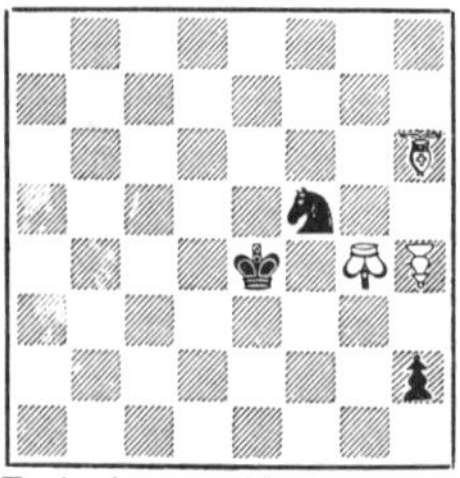

Red plays. Black wins.

149.
AH 164 : C 77 : BM 81 : V 104.

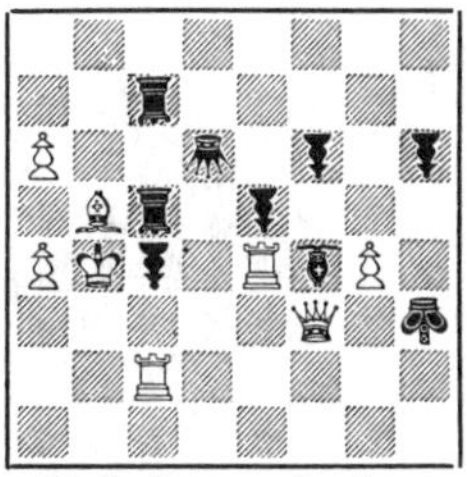

Red plays and wins.

151.
AH 166 : C 79 : BM 78 : V 33.

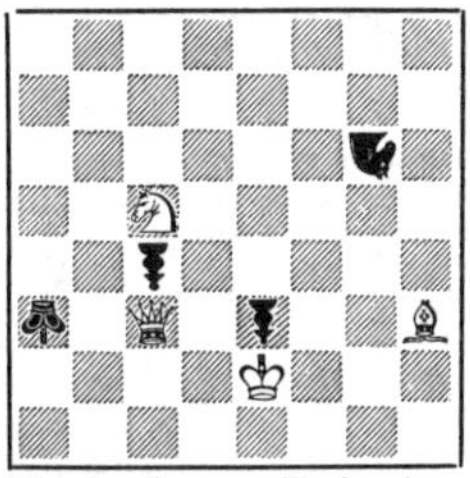

Black plays. Red wins.

152.
AH 167 : C 80 : RAS 27 : V 34.

Red plays and wins.

155.
AH 170 : C 83 : BM 87.

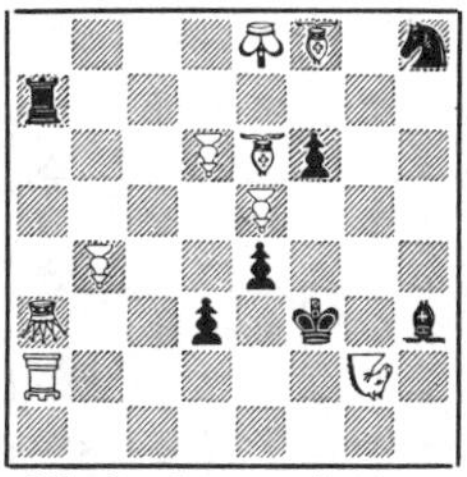

Black plays and wins.

156.
AH 171 : C 84.

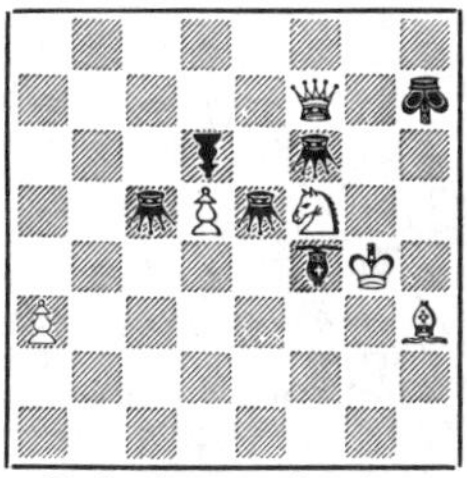

Red plays and wins.

157.
AH 172 : C 97 : Y 48 : Alf. 34 : AE 46 : H 60.

Black plays and wins.

158.
AH 173 : C 98 : BM 43 (text only) : AE 31.

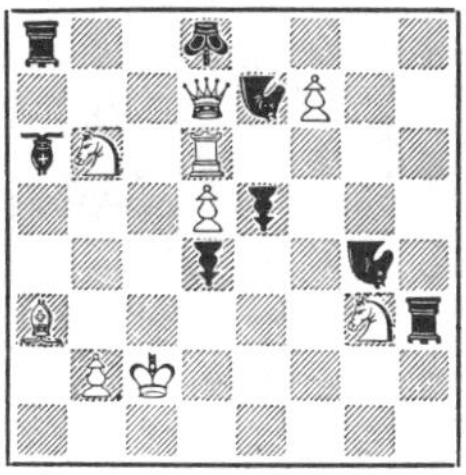

Red plays and wins.

160.
AH 175 : C 100 : BM 44 : Oxf. 64 (in IX) : V 41.

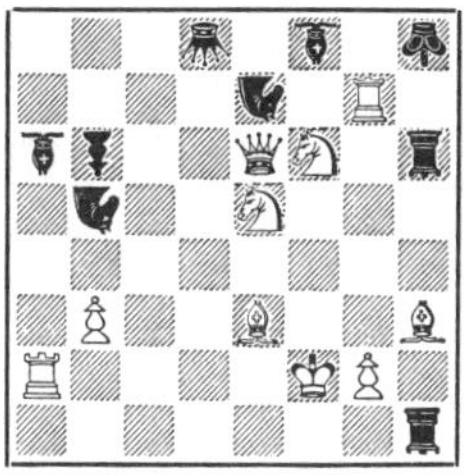

Red plays and wins.

161.
AH 176 : C 101 : Y 24 : RAS 4 : Alf. 24 : Oxf. 139 = 150 : V 15.

Black plays and wins.

162.
AH 177 : C 102 : Alf. 28 (in VI) : Oxf. 89 = 65 : V 17 : AE 51.

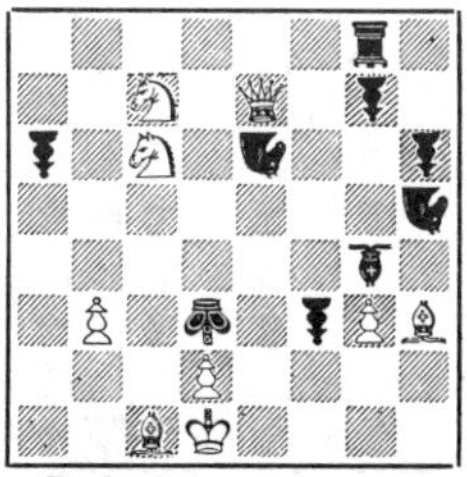

Red plays and wins.

163.
AH 178 : C 85 : RAS 26 : V 37.

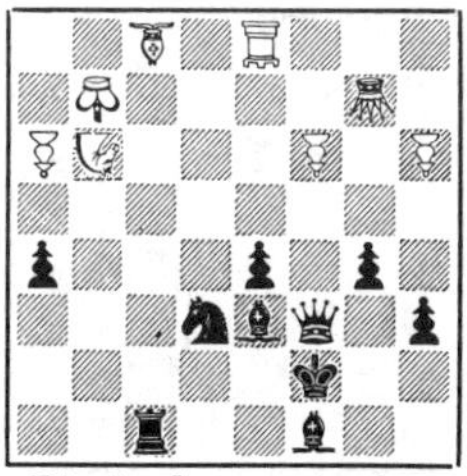

Black plays and wins.

164.
AH 179 : C 86 : S 9 : Alf. 16 = 20 : H 51 : V 38.

Red plays and wins.

165.
AH 180 : RAS 7 : C 87 :
Alf. 11 : AE 185 :
H 49 : V 39.

Red plays and wins.

166.
AH 181 : C 88 : V 40.

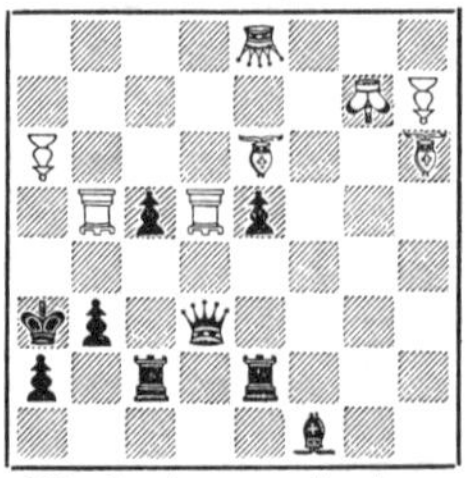

Black plays and wins.

167.
AH 182 : C 89.

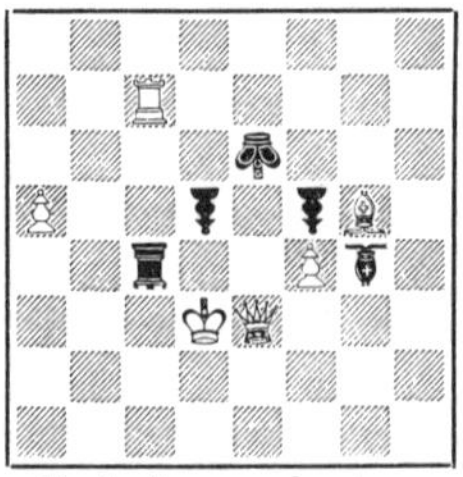

Red plays and wins.

169.
AH 184 : C 91 : BM 82.

Red plays and wins.

170.
AH 185 : C 92 : Alf. 17
(in V).

Red plays and wins.

171.
AH 186 : V 72 : C 93 :
Y 34 : Alf. 13.

Black plays and wins.

172.
AH 187 : C 94 : Y 27 :
Alf. 29 : Oxf. 36 :
V 105 : AE 24.

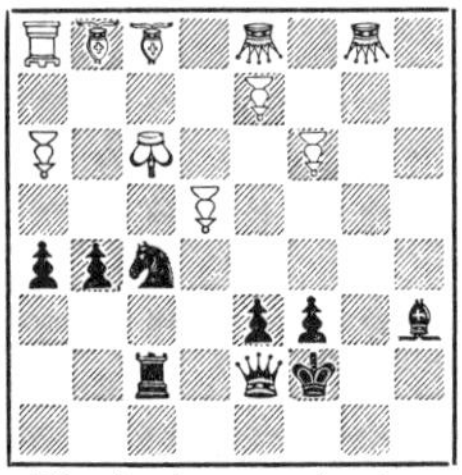

Black plays and wins.

173.
AH 188 : C 95 : BM 54 :
Alf. 4 : AE 187 : S 7 :
H 62 : V 31.

Red plays and wins.

174.
AH 189 : C 96 : BM 35
(text only) : Y 20 :
AE 50 : H 63 : V 32.

Black plays and wins.

175.
V 16 : C 103 : AE 32 :
AH 190.

Black plays and wins.

176.
AH 191 : C 104 : Y 23
(text) : Alf. 50 : Oxf. 38 :
V 18.

Red plays and wins.

177.
AH 192 : C 105 : Alf. 36 :
Oxf. 9 : V 50.

Black plays and wins.

179.
AH 194 : C 106 (title only) : Y 35 : V 29.

Black plays and wins.

180.
AH 195 : AE 76.

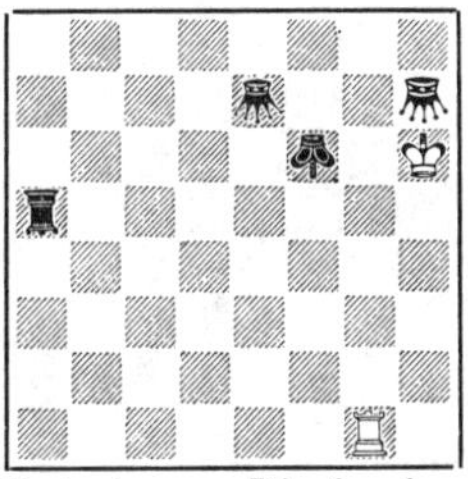

Red plays. Black wins.

181.
AE 180 : V 10 : BM 13 (text only): Alf. 18 (in XX) : H 48 (in XIX).

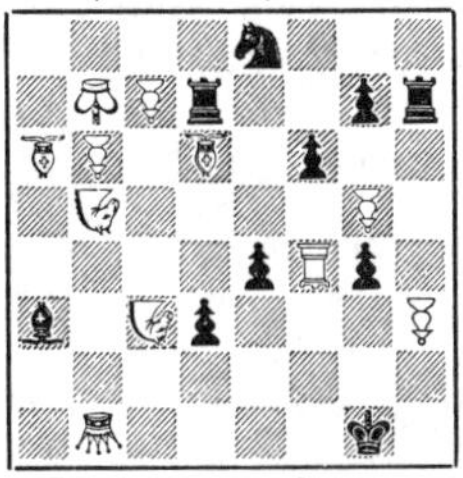

Red plays and wins.

195.
V 96.

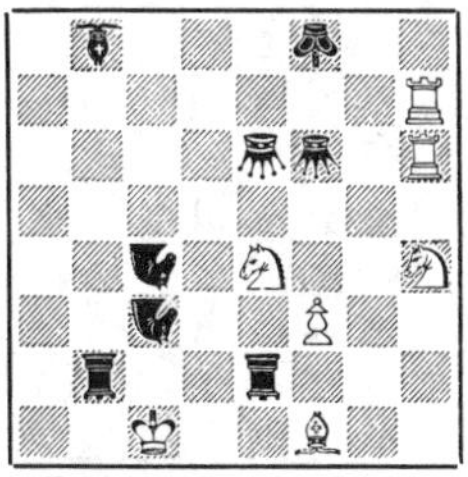

Red plays and wins.

197.
H 20.

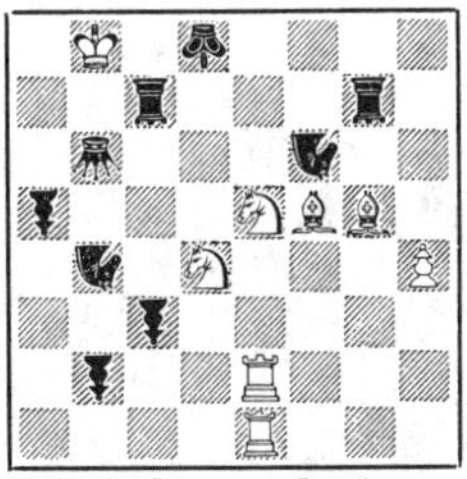

Red plays and wins.

198.
BM 26 : AE 54 : S 3 : H 22.

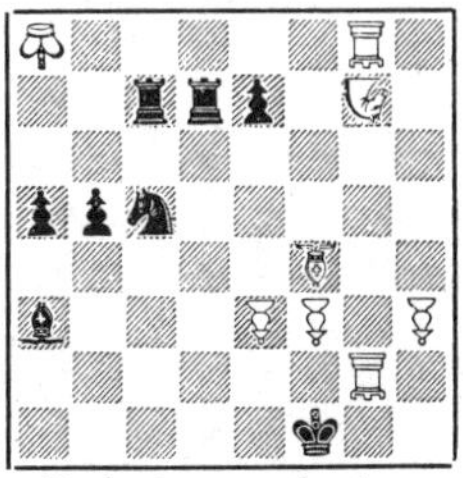

Red plays and wins.

199.
H 29 : Alf. 43.

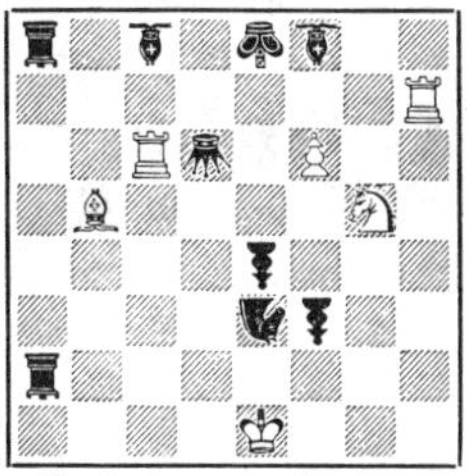

Red plays and wins.

200.
H 57.

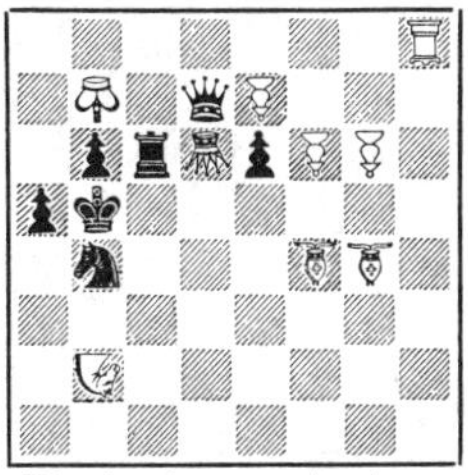

Black plays and wins.

201.
H 59.

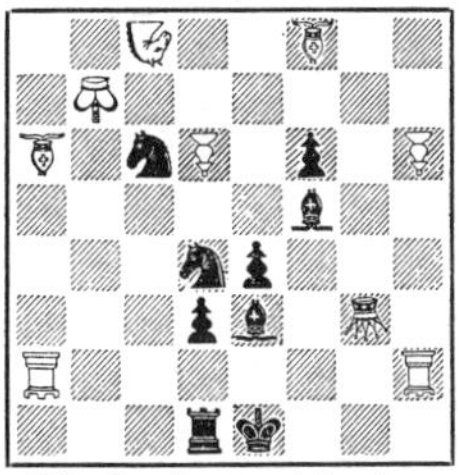

Black plays and wins.

204.
Alf. 55 : H 71 (in II) : Oxf. 58.

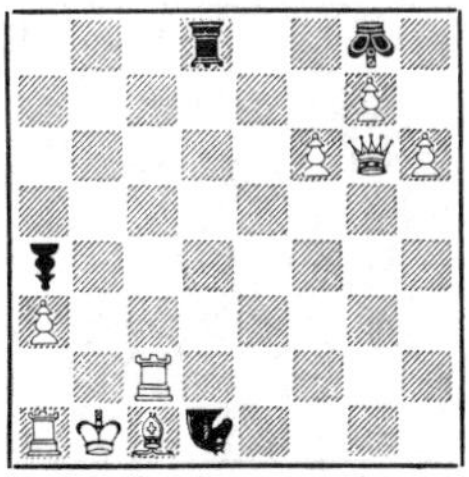

Black plays. Mate in III.

206.
BM 6.

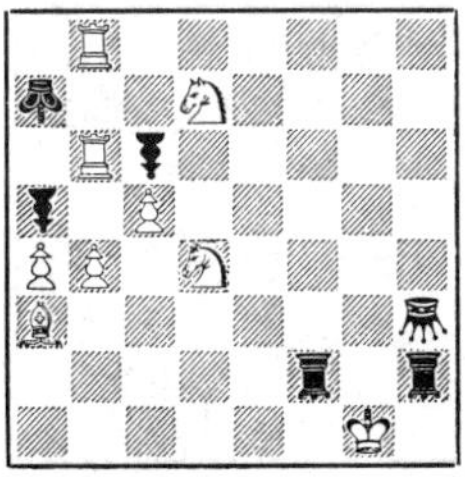

Red plays. Mate with B.

207.
BM 7.

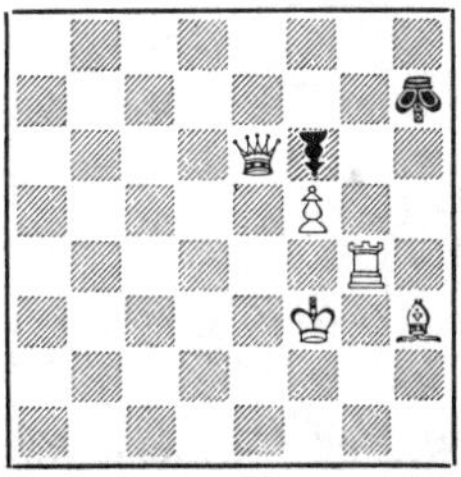

Red plays. Mate on h7 with B.

208.
BM 11 = 188: AE 144 (in VI).

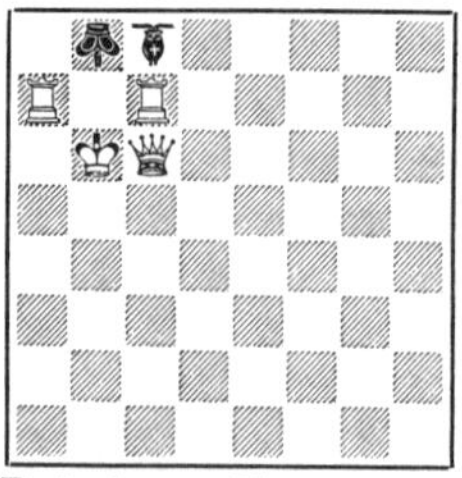

Red plays. Mate on a8.

209.
BM 14 (corr.).

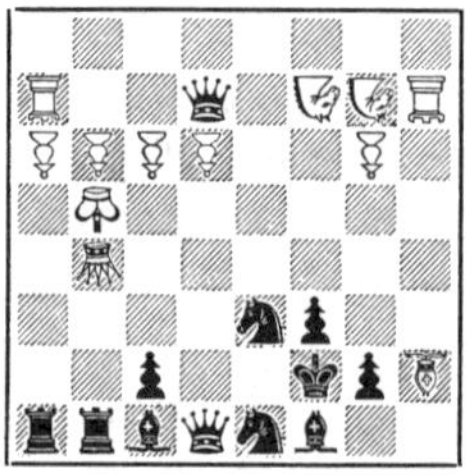

Black plays and wins.

210.
BM 24.

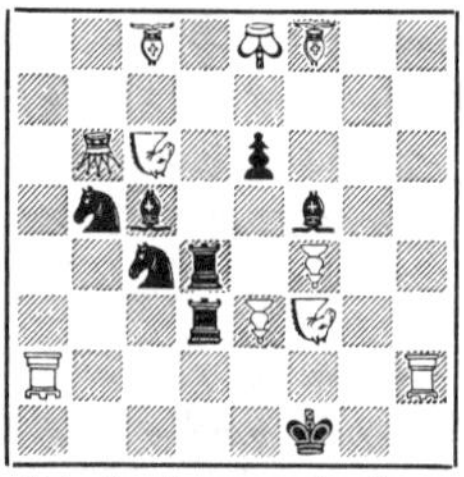

Black plays and wins.

212.
BM 34: AE 48.

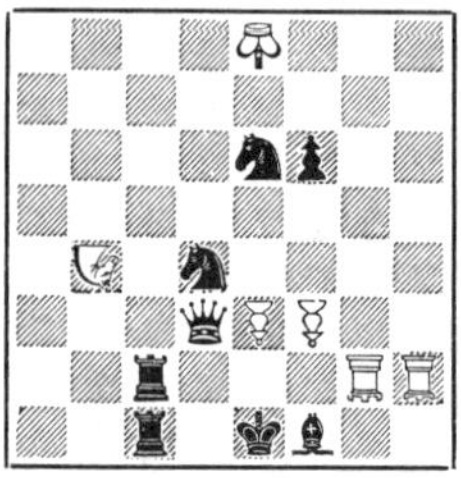

Red plays and wins.

213.
BM 36.

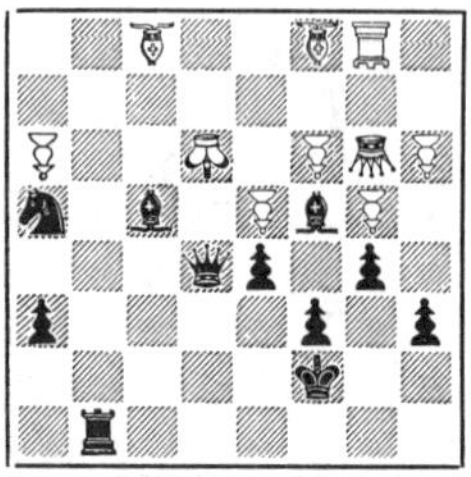

Black plays and wins.

214.
AE 13: RAS 37: Alf. 47 (in XV): BM 37 (in XV).

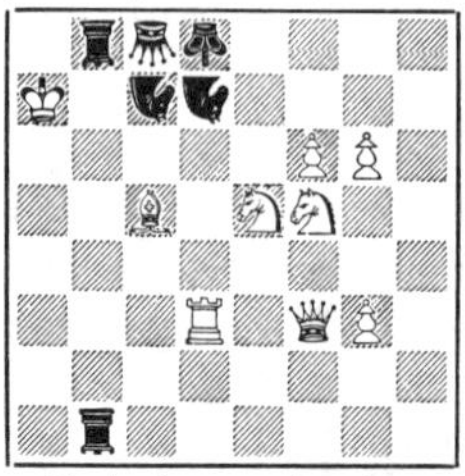

Red plays and wins.

215.
AE 47: BM 48 (text only).

Black plays and wins.

217.
BM 51.

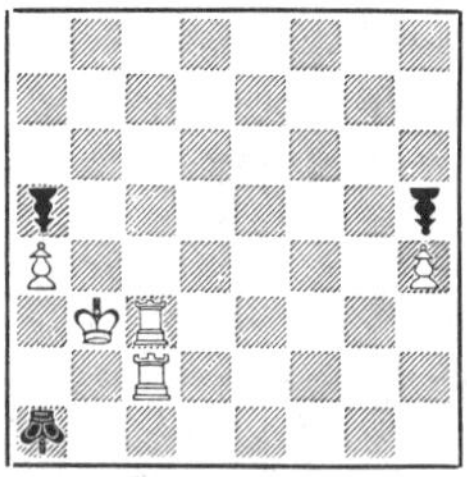

Red plays. Mate with promoted P on a1 or h1.

219.
BM 58: Y 45.

Black plays and wins.

220.
BM 59 (text only): Alf. 88 = 96: RW 9.

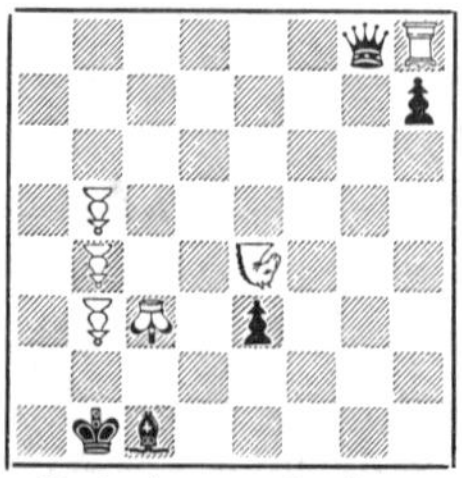

Red plays and wins.

225.
BM 90.

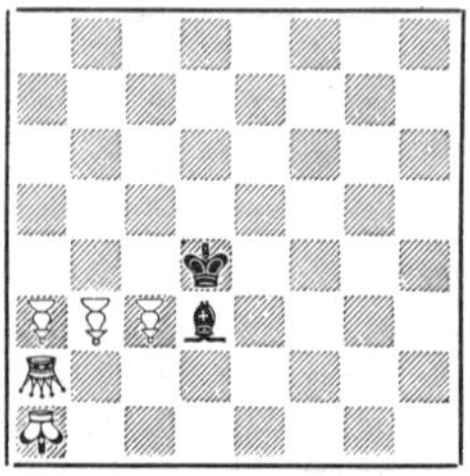

Black plays and wins.

226.
BM 91.

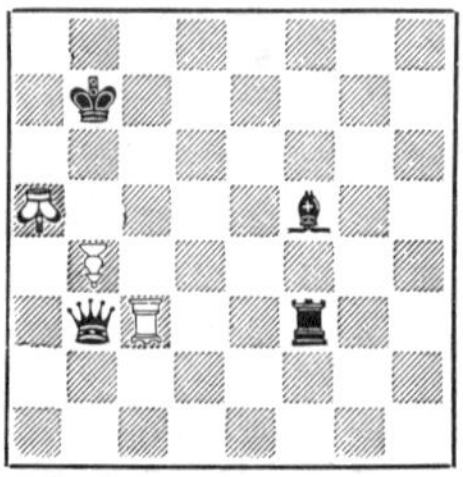

Black plays and wins.

227.
BM 92.

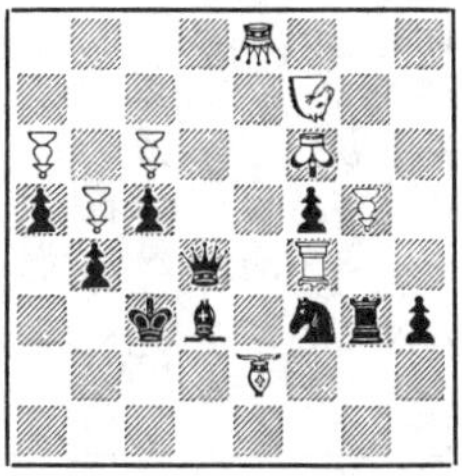

Black plays and wins.

232.
BM 99.

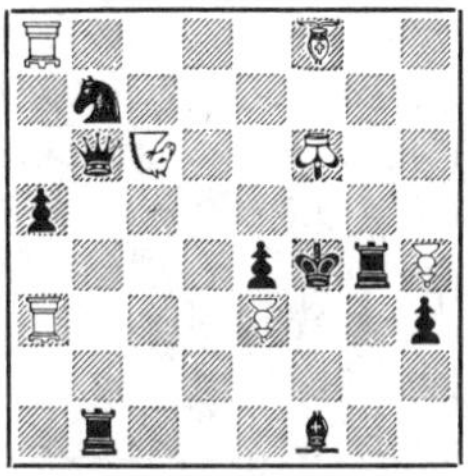

Red plays and wins.

257.
BM 154.

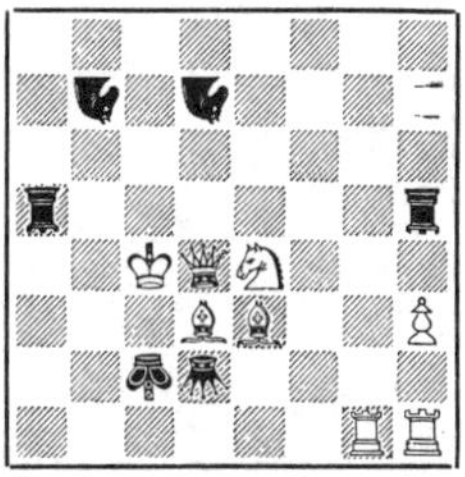

Red plays and wins.

258.
BM 155 (corr.).

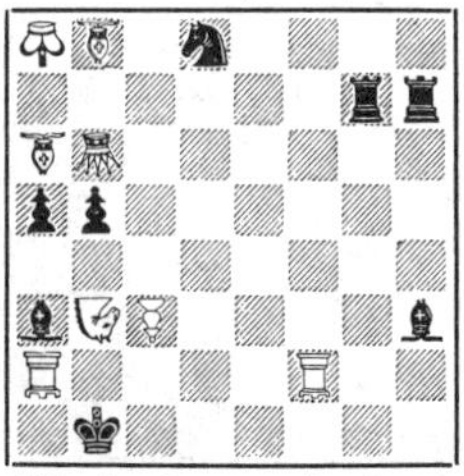

Black plays and wins.

260.
BM 159 = 21 (text): AE 62:
Oxf. 98 (no Bl.).

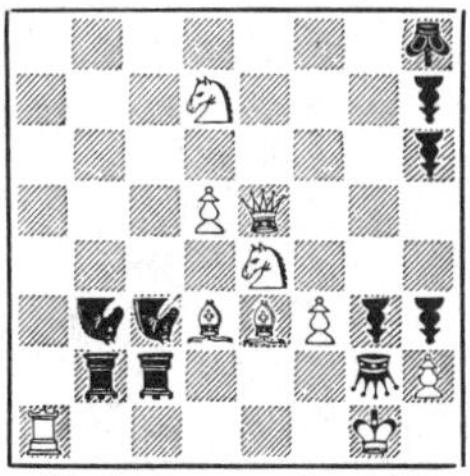

Red plays and wins.

261.
BM 160.

Black plays and wins.

266.
BM 165.

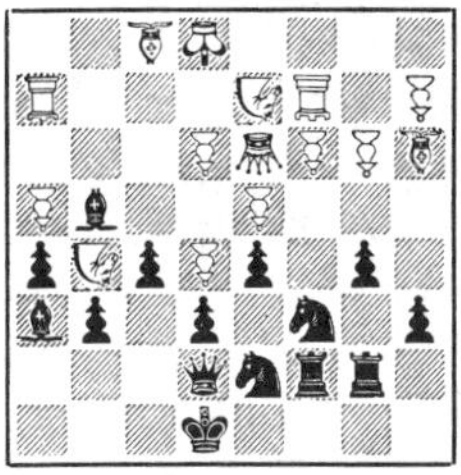

Black plays and wins.

270.
BM 187 (corr.).

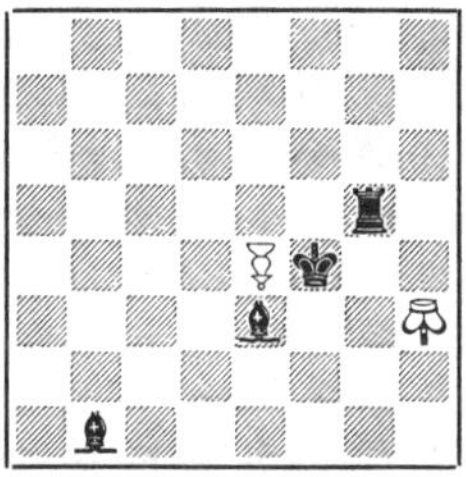

Black plays. Mate with 2 Bs.

282.
AE 1 and 179a.

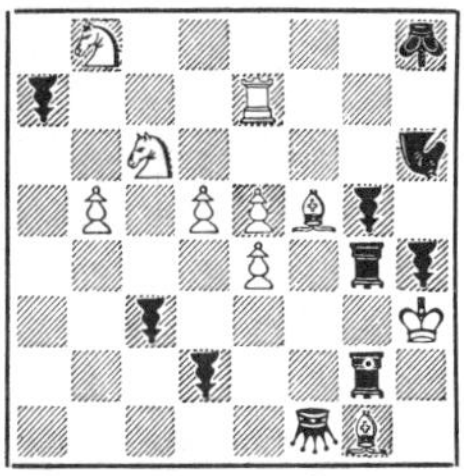

Red plays and wins.

283.
AE 3.

Black plays and wins.

284.
AE 4: Oxf. 140: R 80.

Black plays and wins.

285.
AE 9.

Black plays and wins.

286.
AE 10.

Black plays and wins.

287.
AE 11 : RAS 29.

Red plays and wins.

288.
AE 14.

Black plays and wins.

289.
AE 15 and 18 a.

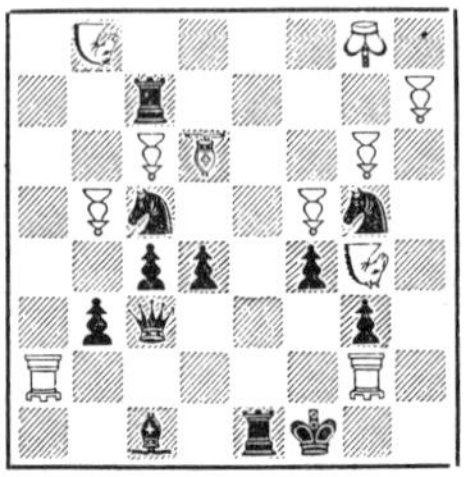

Black plays and wins.

290.
AE 16.

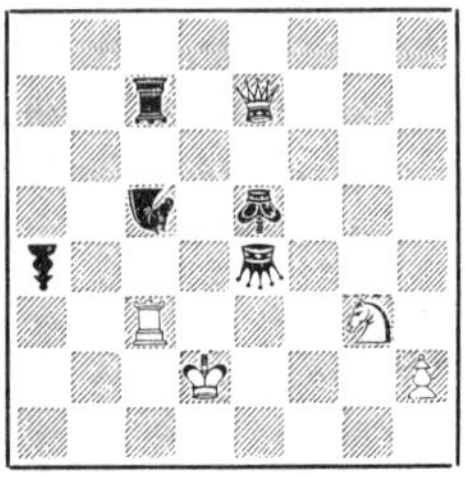

Red plays and wins.

291.
AE 17.

Red plays and wins.

292.
AE 18 and 21 a.

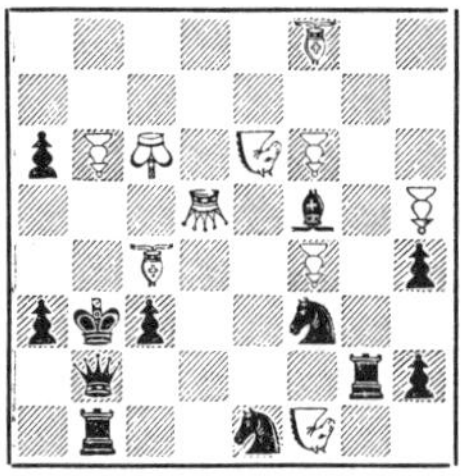

Red plays and wins.

293.
AE 19.

Red plays and wins.

294.
AE 20.

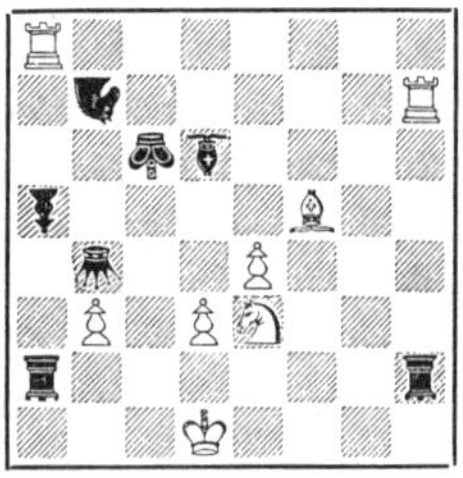

Red plays and wins.

295.
AE 21.

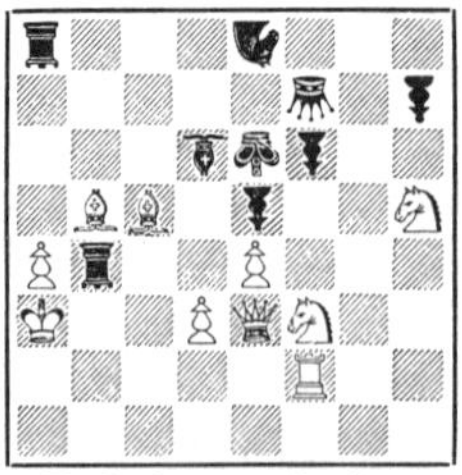

Red plays and wins.

296.
AE 22.

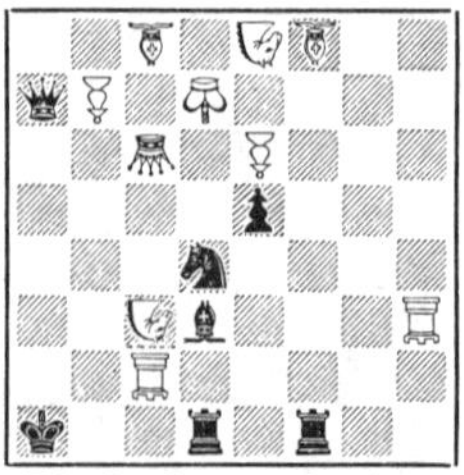

Black plays and wins.

297.
AE 23 : RW 8 : Oxf. 83.

Black plays and wins.

298.
AE 29.

Black plays and wins.

299.
AE 34 : RW 16.

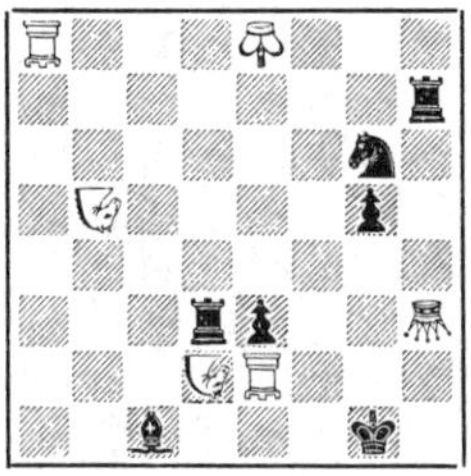

Red plays and wins.

300.
AE 39 : Alf. 65 (in II).
Oxf. 148 = 126 (in IV).

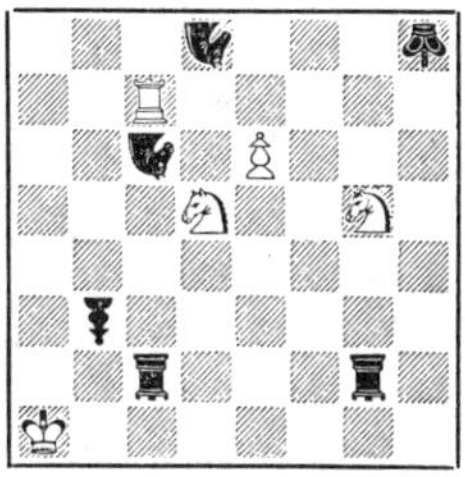

Red plays and wins.

301.
AE 40.

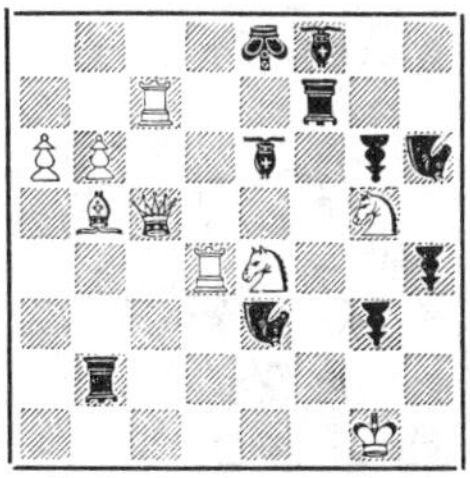

Red plays and wins.

302.
AE 41.

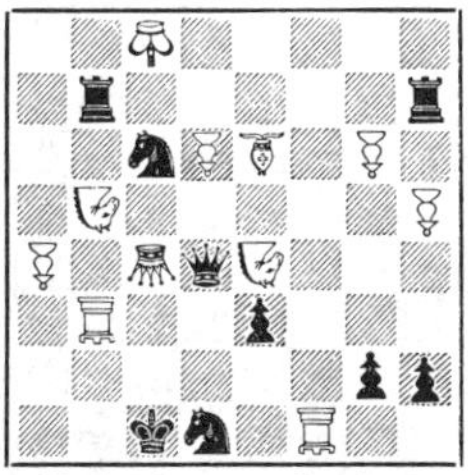

Red plays and wins.

303.
AE 42 and 15 a.

Red plays and wins.

304.
AE 43.

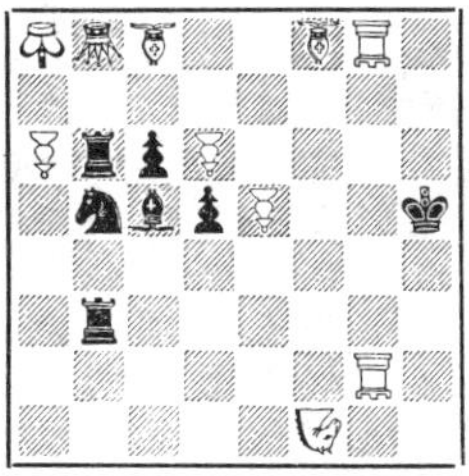

Black plays and wins.

305.
AE 45.

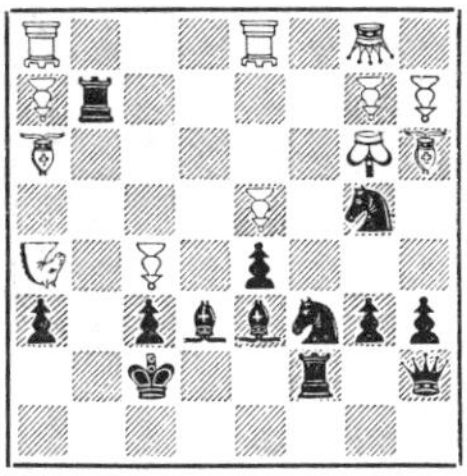

Black plays and wins.

306.
AE 49.

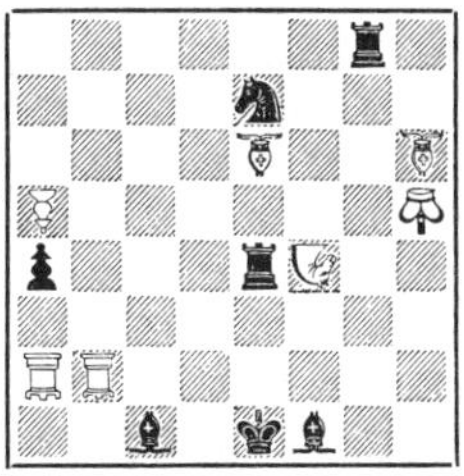

Black plays and wins.

307.
AE 52.

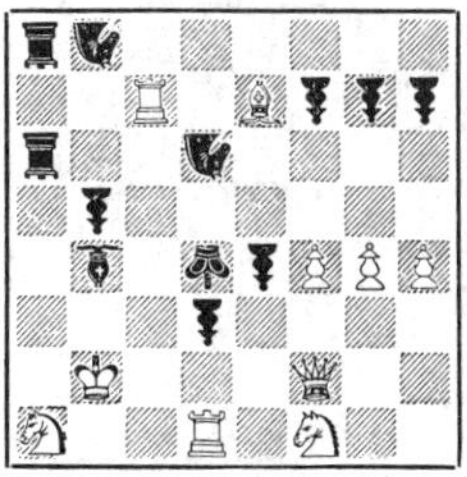

Red plays and wins.

308.
AE 53 : F 10 = 73 :
R 39 = 63.

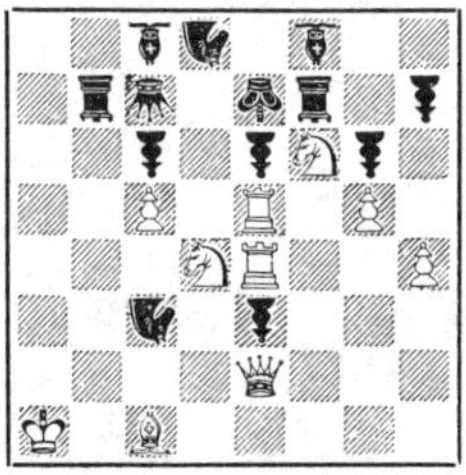

Red plays and wins.

309.
AE 57.

Red plays and wins.

310.
AE 58.

Red plays and wins.

311.
AE 59.

Red plays and wins.

312.
AE 60.

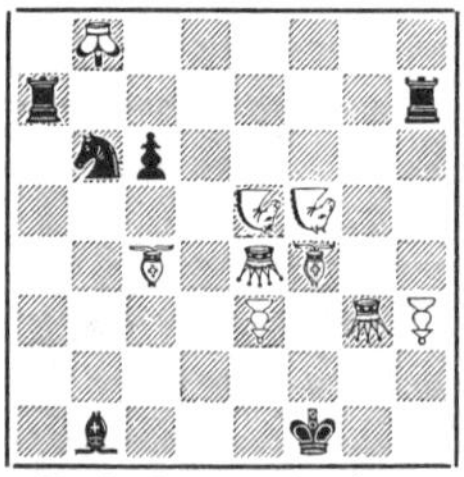

Red plays and wins.

313.
AE. 61.

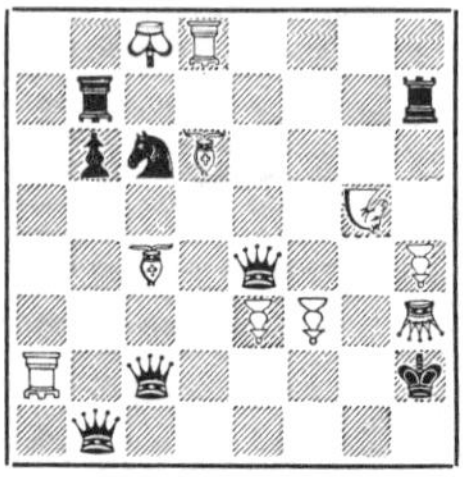

Red plays and wins.

314.
AE 64 (corr.).

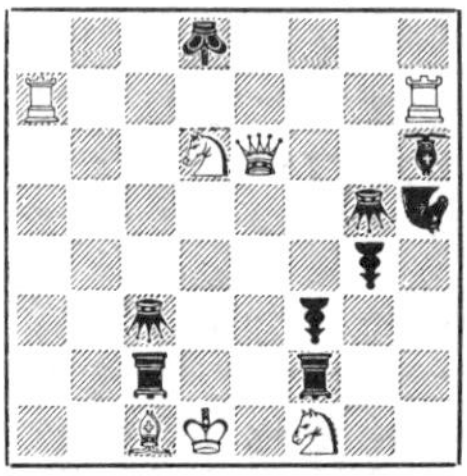

Black plays and wins.

315.
AE 65 : RAS 28.

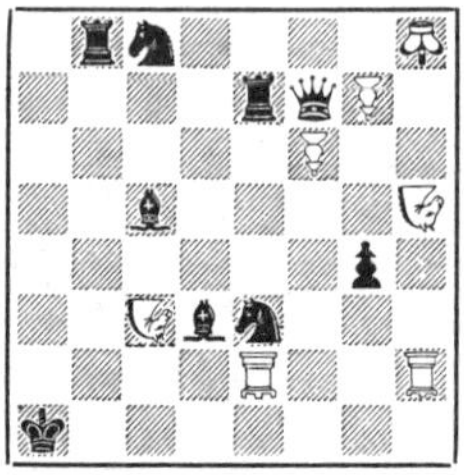

Black plays and wins.

321.
AE 83 : RAS 33.

Red plays and wins.

322.
AE 85.

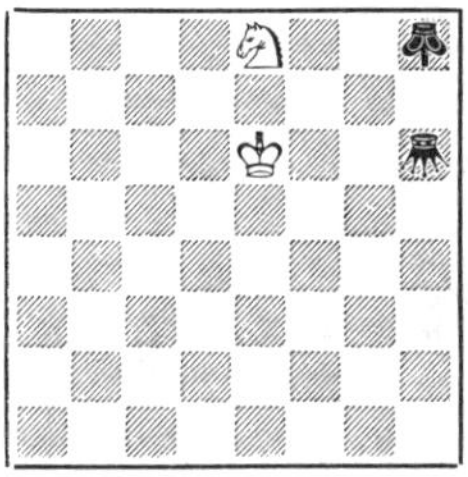

Red plays and wins.

323.
AE 88 : Al. 20 (?).

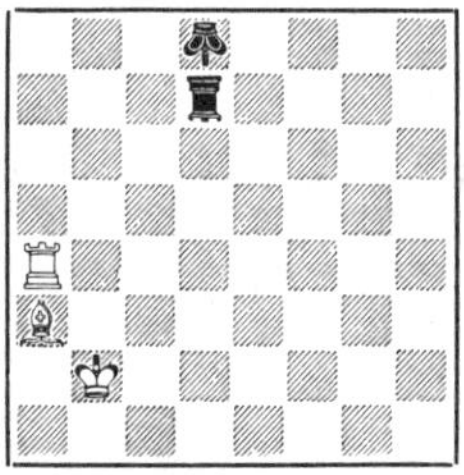

Red plays and wins.

324.
AE 93.

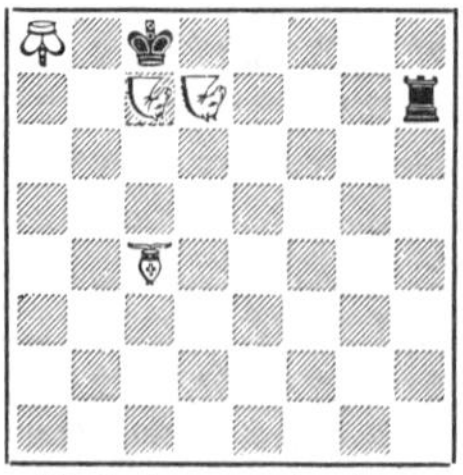

Red plays and wins.

325.
AE 97.

Red plays. Black wins.

326.
AE 102.

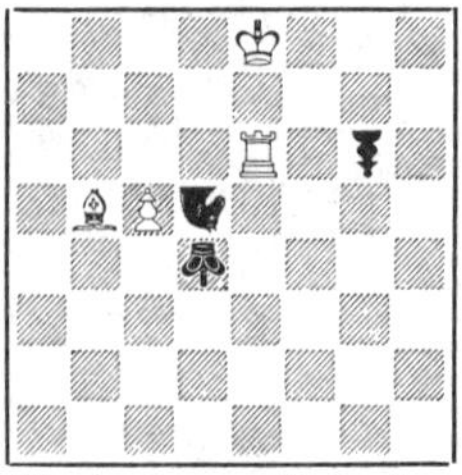

Black plays. Red wins.

327.
AE 103.

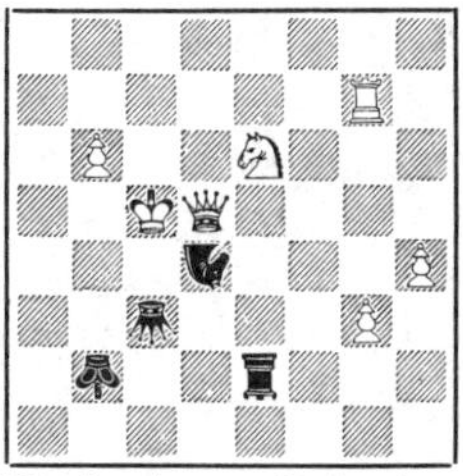

Black plays. Red wins.

328.
AE 104.

Red plays. Black wins.

329.
AE 106.

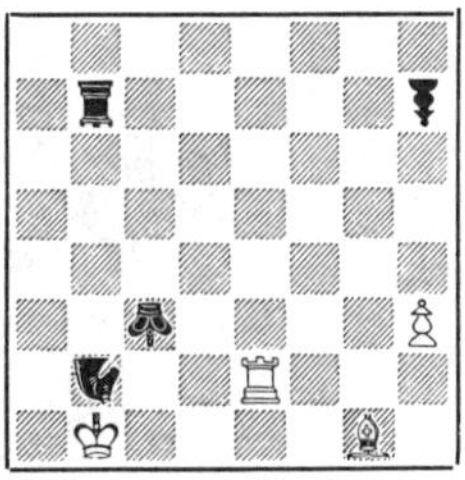

Red plays. Black wins.

330.
AE 109 : Y 49.

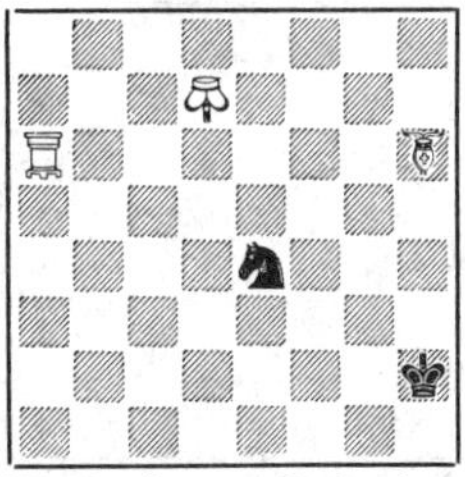

Black plays. Red wins.

331.
AE 110.

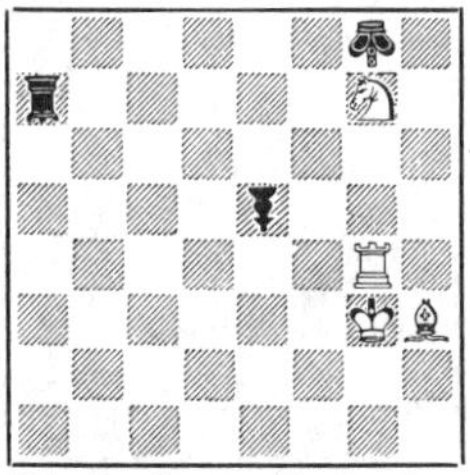

Black plays. Red wins.

336.
AE 122.

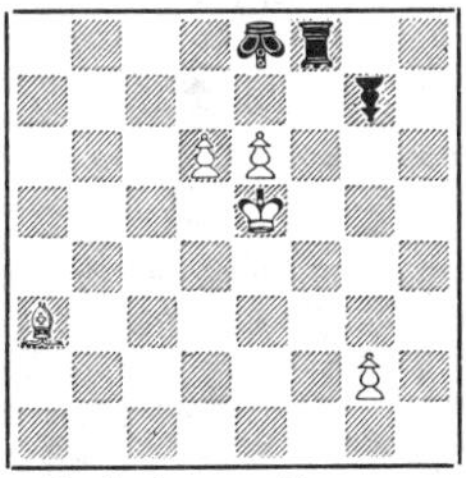

Red plays. Drawn.

337.
AE 123.

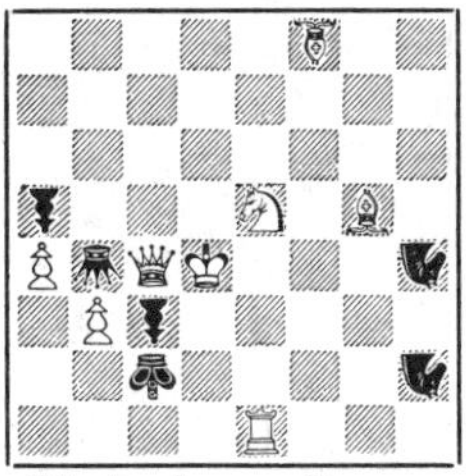

Black plays. Drawn.

338.
AE 124 : Y 33.

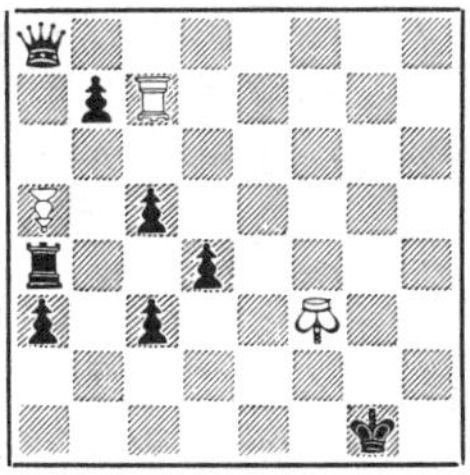

Red plays. Drawn.

339.
AE 127 : Man. 5.

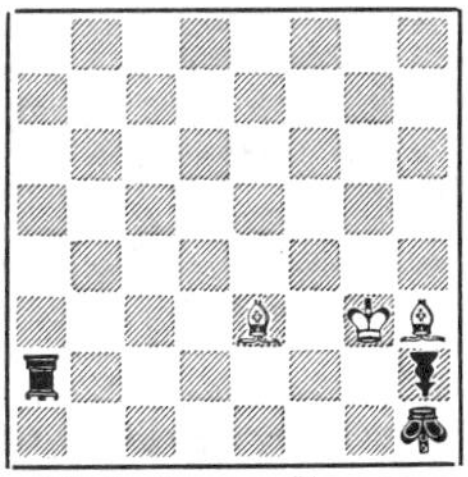

Red plays. Drawn.

340.
AE 128 : Man. 54.

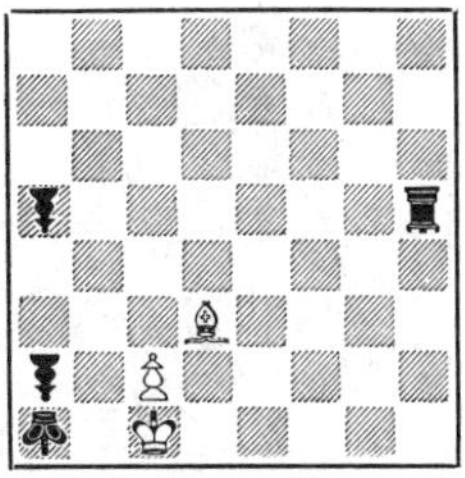

Red plays. Drawn.

341.
AE 130.

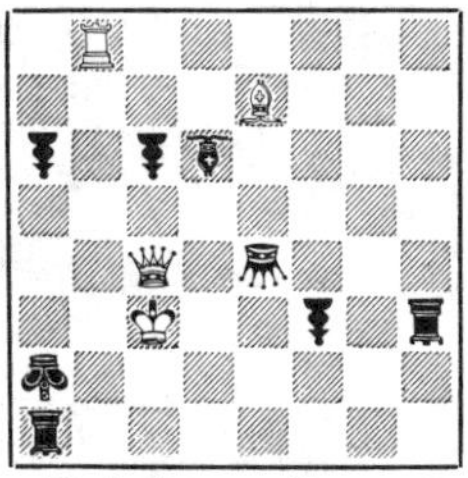

Red plays. Drawn.

342.
AE 131 : Oxf. 57.

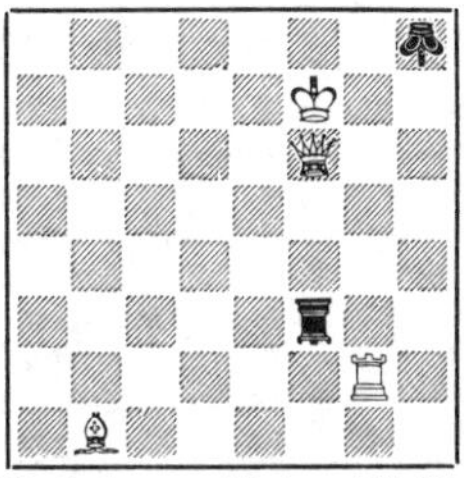

Red plays. Mate with B.

343.
AE 133.

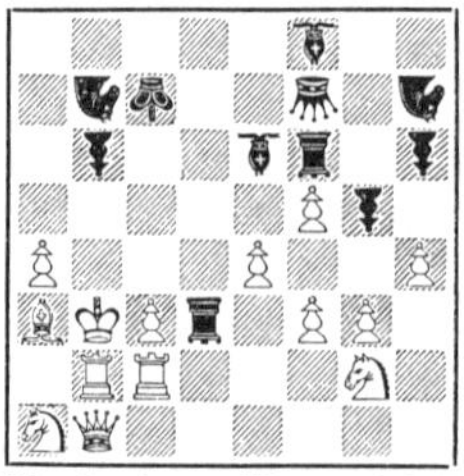

Black plays. Mate with B.

344.
AE 134.

Black plays. Mate with B.

345.
AE 138.

Red plays. Mate with B.

346.
AE 139 (corr.).

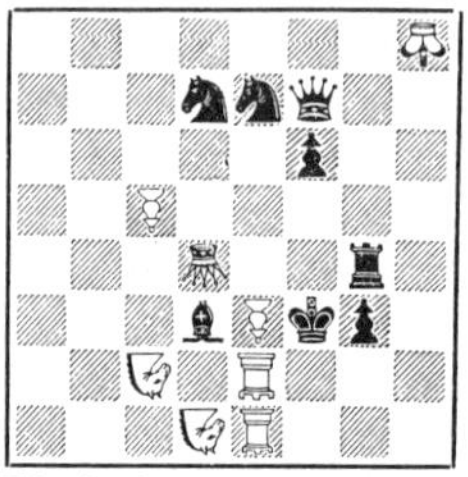

Black plays. Mate with B.

347.
AE 140.

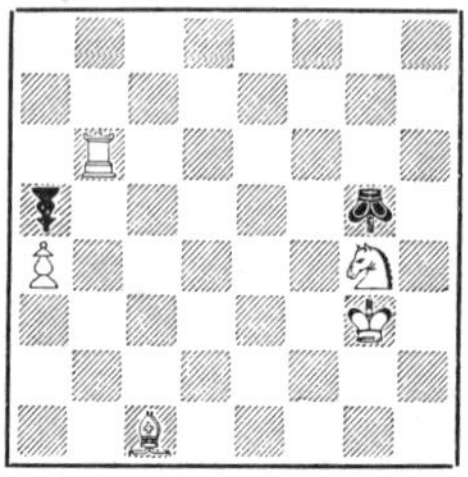

Red plays. Mate with B.

348.
AE 141.

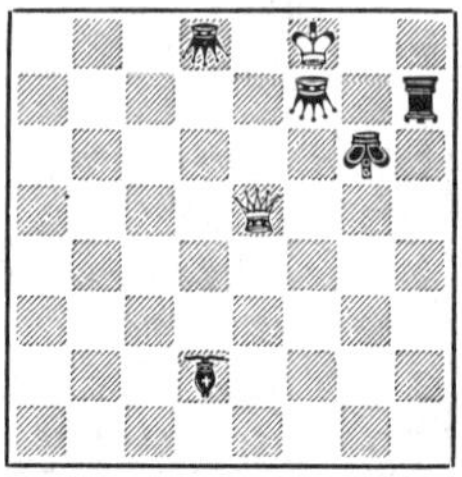

Black plays. Mate with B.

349.
AE 142.

Red plays. Mate with B.

350.
AE 143.

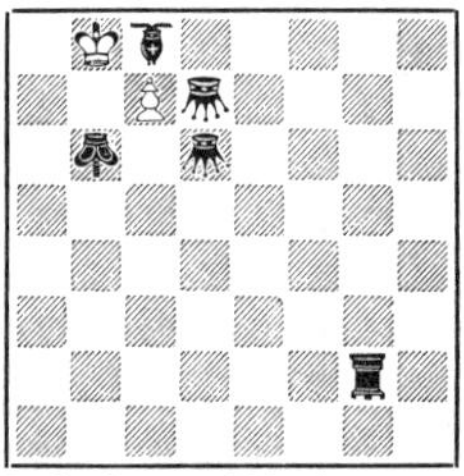

Red plays. Black mates with B.

351.
AE 145 (corr.): RAS 16.

Red plays. Black mates on b2.

352.
AE 146.

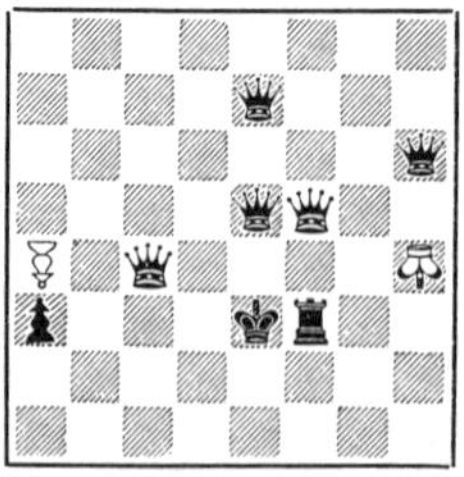

Black plays. Mate on e5.

353.
AE 147.

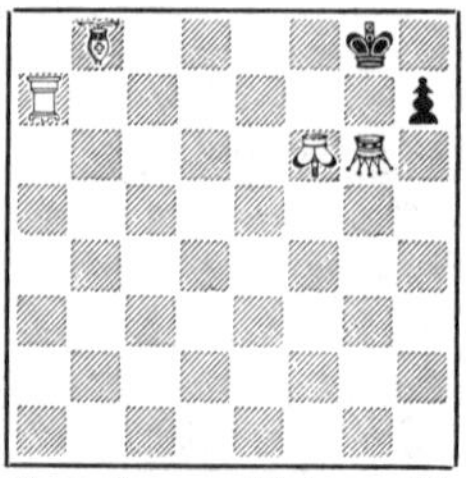

Red plays. Mate on f8.

355.
AE 149.

Red plays. Black mates on d5.

356.
AE 150.

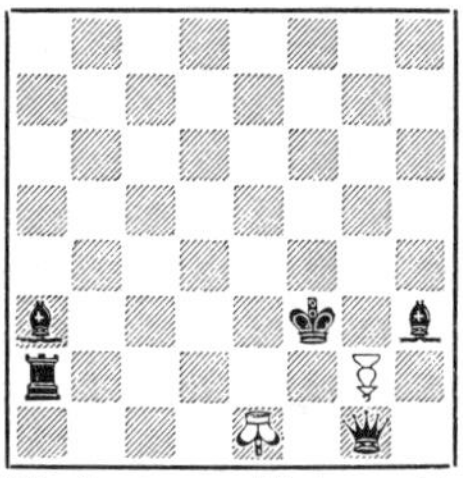

Black plays. Mate on d4.

357.
AE 152 (corr.).

Red plays. Mate on h8.

358.
AE 153 (corr.).

Black plays. Mate on b4.

359.
AE 154 (corr.).

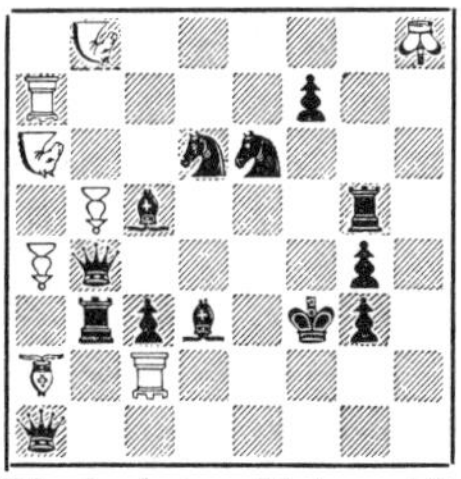

Black plays. Mate on b3.

360.
AE 155 (corr.).

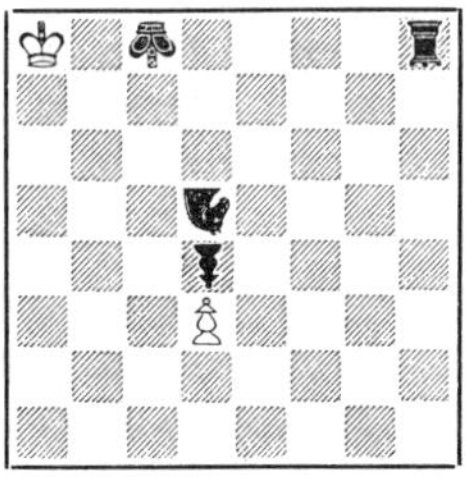

Red plays. Black mates on d4.

361.
AE 156 : Alf. 85.

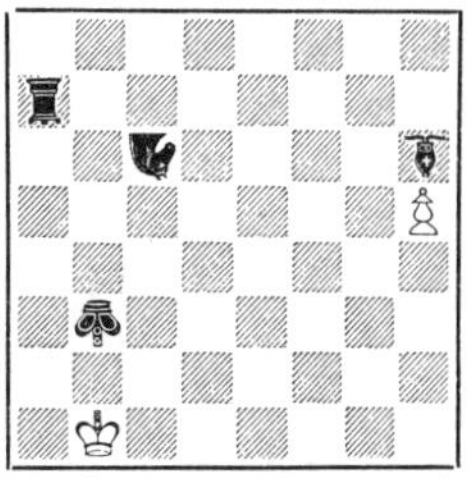

Black plays. Mate on e4.

362.
AE 157.

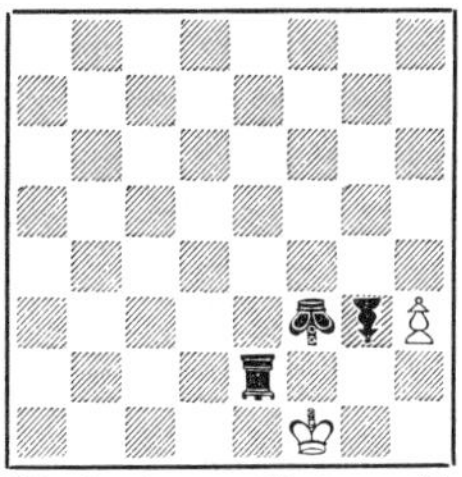

Black plays. Mate on f1.

364.
AE 159.

Black plays. Mate on d4.

365.
AE 160.

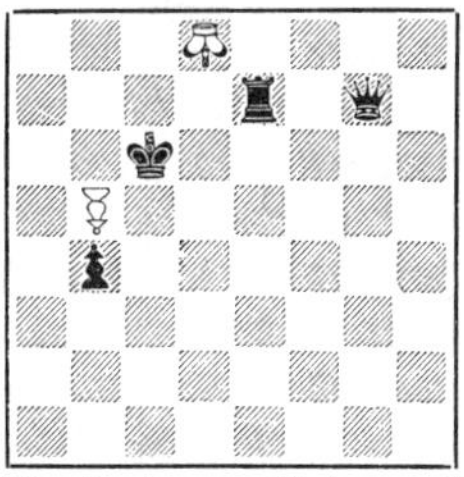

Black plays. Mate on c8 with P.

366.
AE 161.

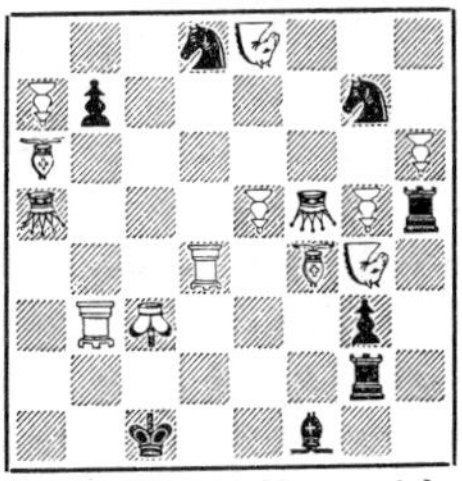

Red plays. Mate with P, or Q, or Kt, or R or B.

367.
AE 162.

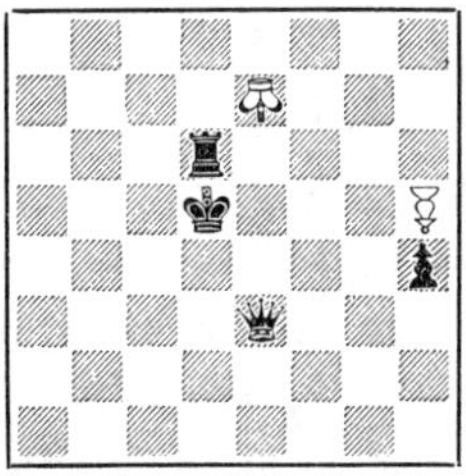

Red plays. Black mates with Q.

368.
AE 163 (corr.).

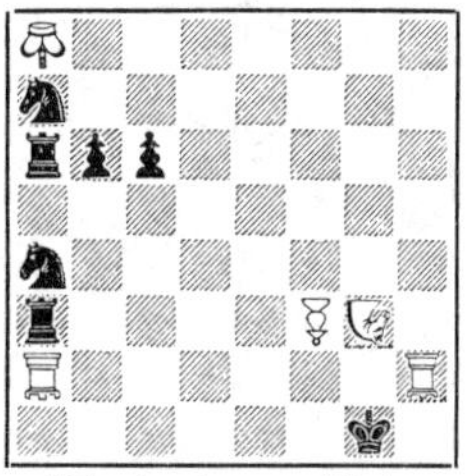

Black plays. Mate with Ps.

369.
AE 164.

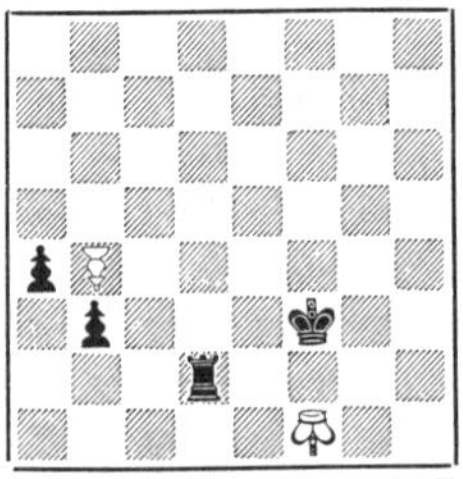

Black plays. Mate with P.

370.
AE 165 (corr.).

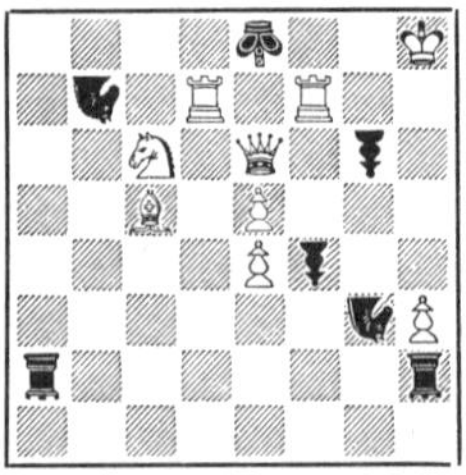

Red plays. Mate with P.

371.
AE 166.

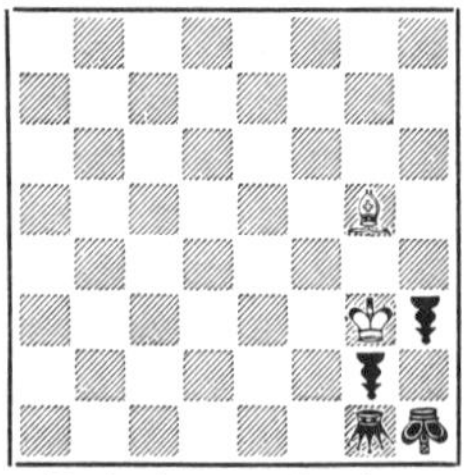

Red plays and wins.

374.
AE 171.

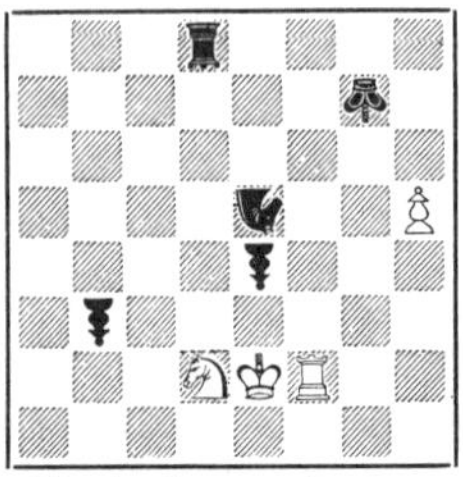

Black plays and wins.

375.
AE 176.

Red plays and wins.

376.
AE 177.

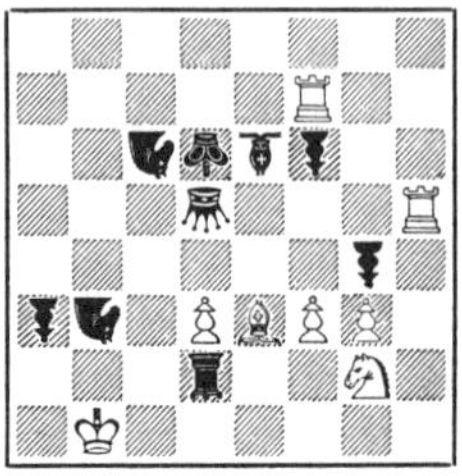

Red plays and wins.

377.
AE 178.

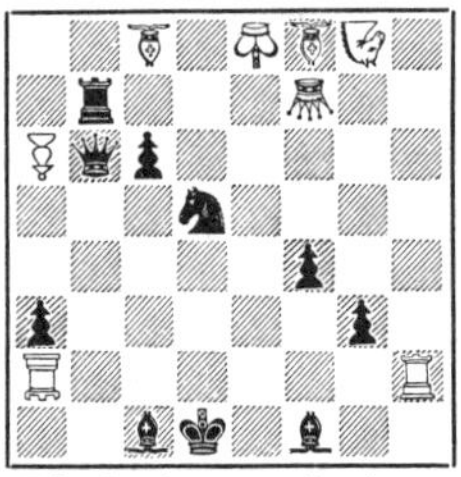

Black plays and wins.

378.
AE 179.

Black plays and wins.

379.
AE 183 : RAS 59.

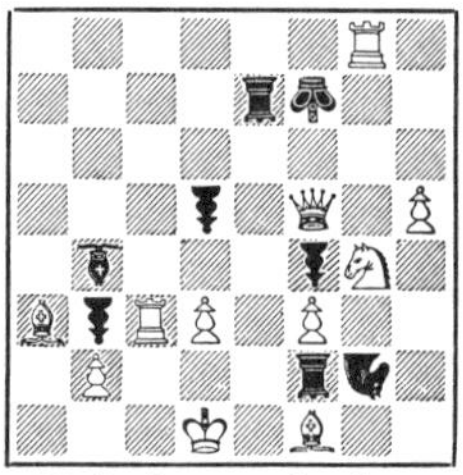

Red plays and wins.

380.
AE 186 : R 72.

Red plays and wins.

381.
AE 188.

Black plays and wins.

382.
AE 189.

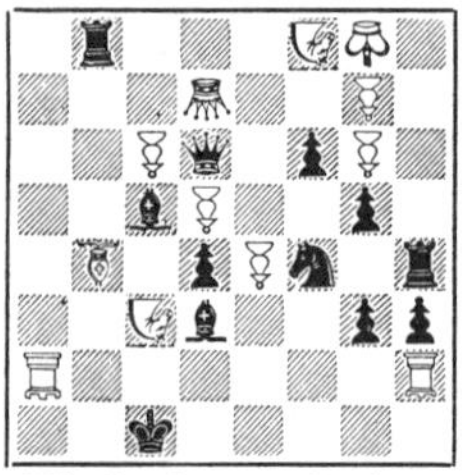

Black plays and wins.

383.
AE 190.

Black plays and wins.

384.
AE 191.

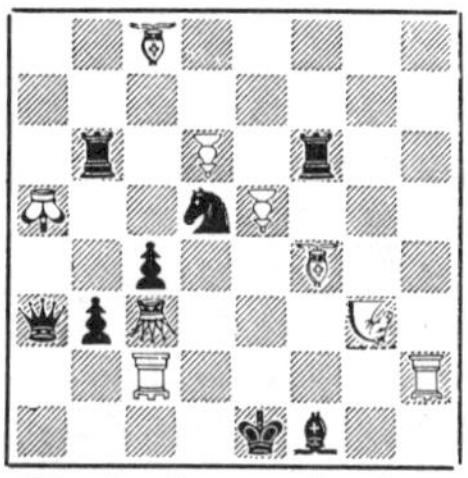

Black plays and wins.

385.
AE 192.

Red plays and wins.

386.
AE 193.

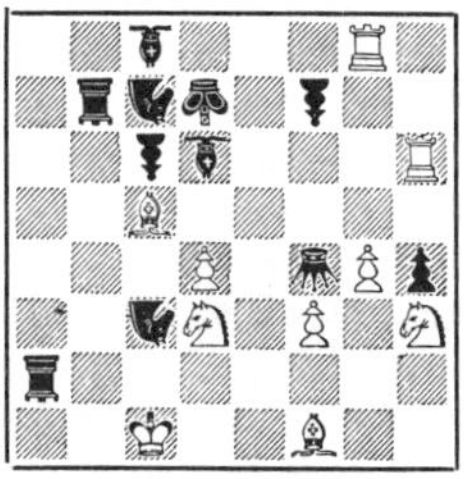

Red plays and wins.

387.
AE 194.

Black plays and wins.

388
Alf. 1.

Red plays. Drawn.

389.
Alf. 2.

Black plays. Drawn.

390.
Alf. 3.

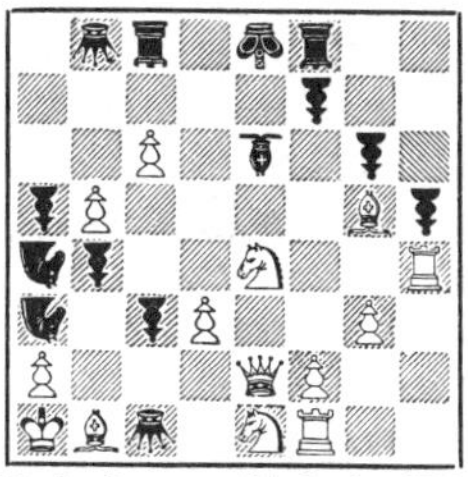

Red plays. Mate in XI.

391.
Alf. 5.

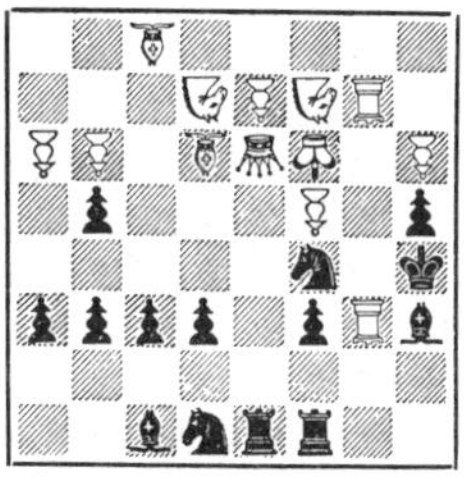

Black plays. Mate in IV on d5.

392.
Alf. 6.

Red plays. Mate in XII.

393.
Alf. 9.

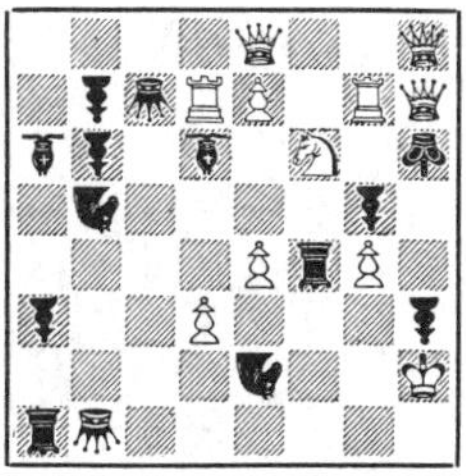

Black play. Mate in XVIII.

394.
Alf. 19.

Red plays. Mate in VI on a4.

395.
Alf. 21.

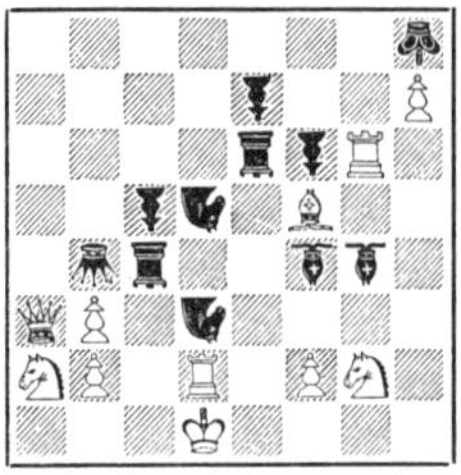

Black plays. Mate in IV on d1.

396.
Alf. 31.

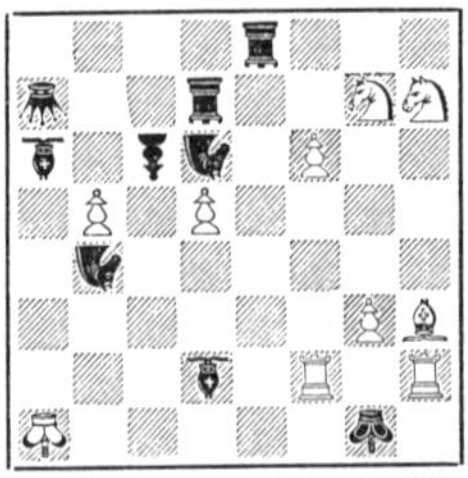

Black plays. Mate in VI.

397.
Alf. 33.

Black plays. Mate in XI.

398.
Alf. 44.

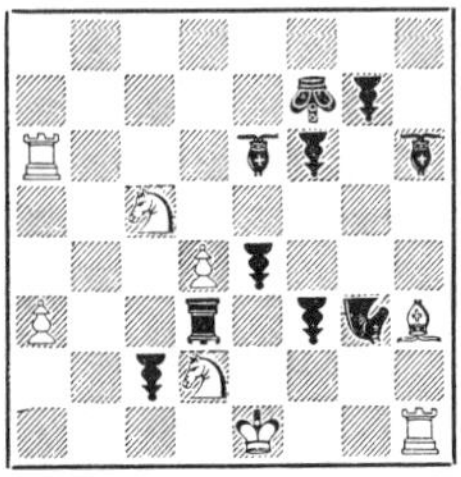

Black plays. Mate in VI.

399.
Alf. 46 = 92.

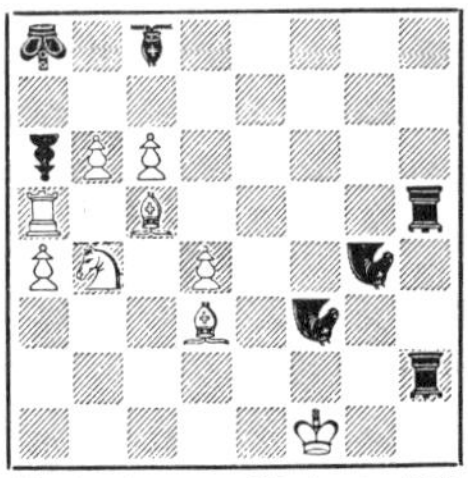

Red plays. Mate in IV.

400.
Alf. 48 : F 9 = 84 :
Man. 56 : RW 13 : Al 24 :
R 28 = 64.

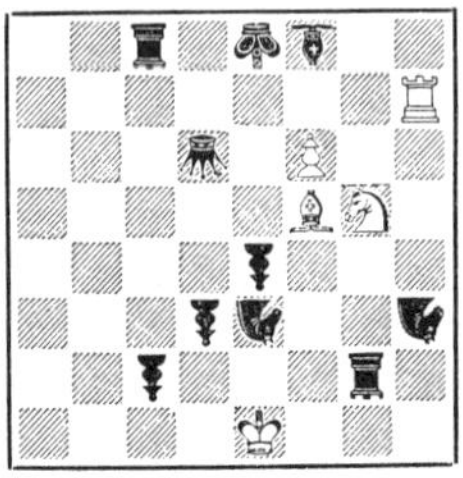

Red plays. Mate in III.

406.
Alf. 98.

Red plays. Mate in V.

409.
Man. 7. Al. 4.

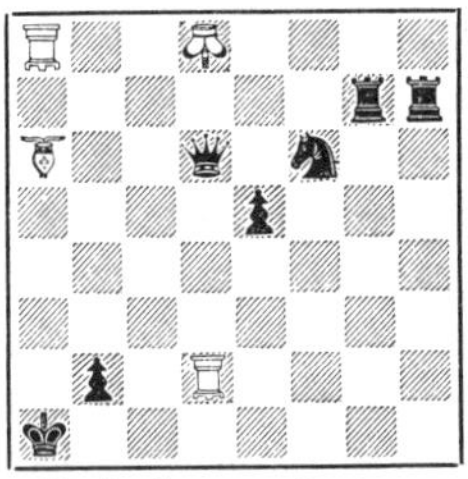

Red plays and wins.

410.
Man. 12.

Red plays. Mate with B.

411.
Man. 13 (corr.).

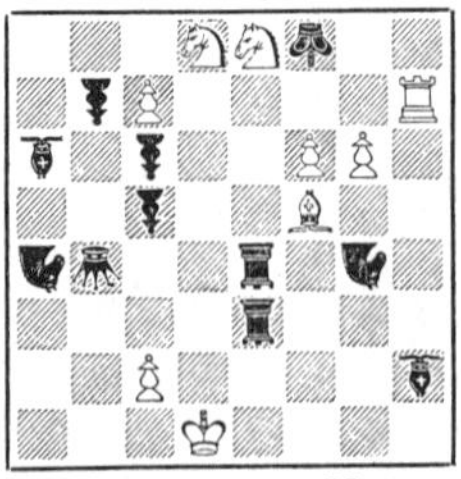

Black plays. Mate with Bs.

416.
Al. 5: RW 4 (corr.).

Black plays and wins.

417.
Al. 6.

Black plays and wins.

459.
F 68 : R 34.

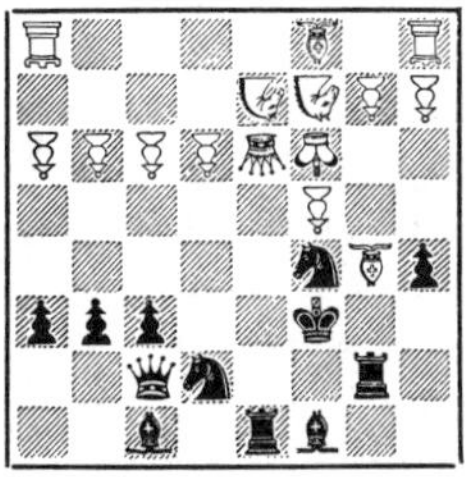

Black plays and wins.

460.
F 69 : R 75.

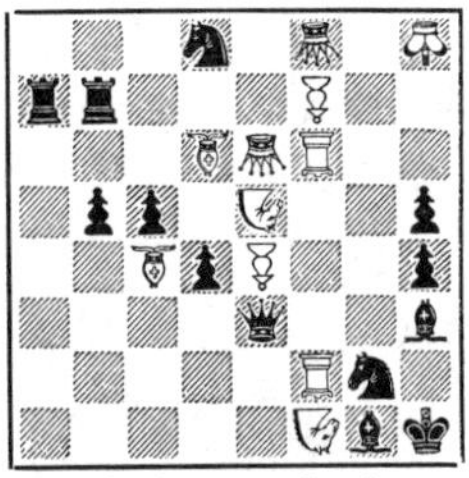

Red plays and wins.

461.
F 70 : R 58 = 44.

Red plays and wins.

462.
F 71 : R 41.

Red plays and wins.

466.
Y 4.

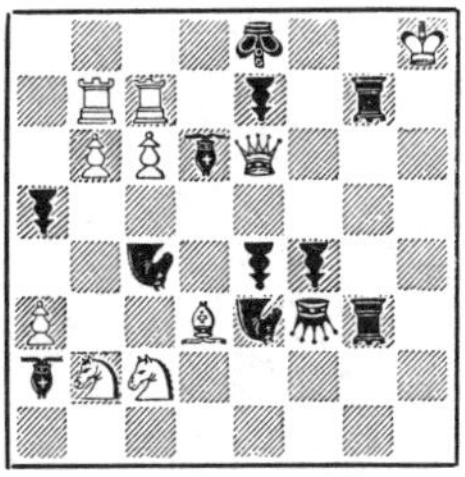

Black plays. Mate with Bs.

468.
Y 21.

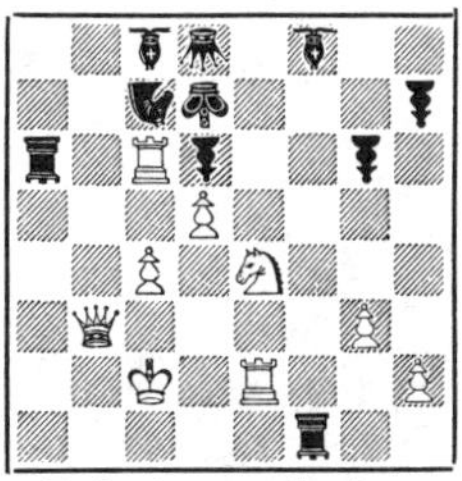

Red plays and wins.

484.
Oxf. 18.

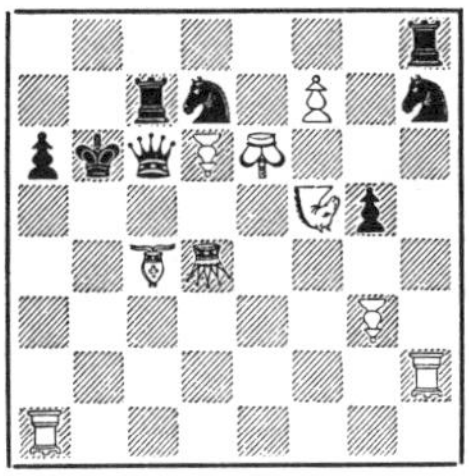

Black plays. Mate with P.

490.
Oxf. 25.

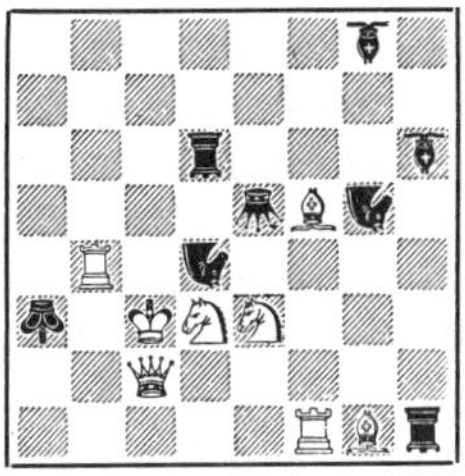

Red plays. Mate in XII with 2 Bs.

493.
RW 23 : Oxf. 28.

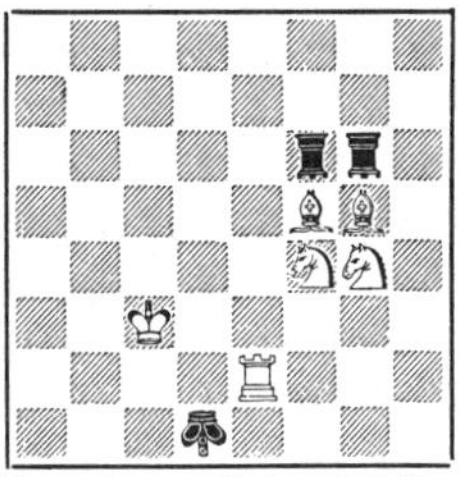

Red plays. Mate with Bs.

502.
Oxf. 40.

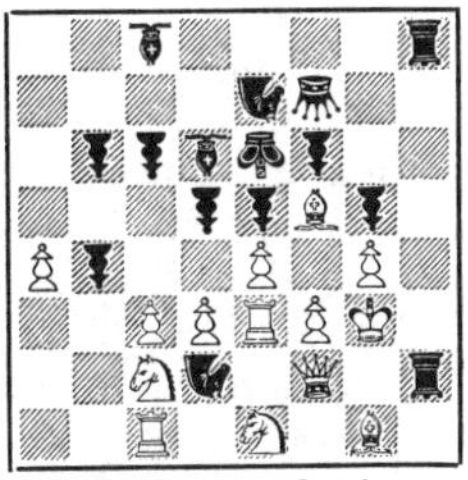

Red plays and wins.

512.
Oxf. 61.

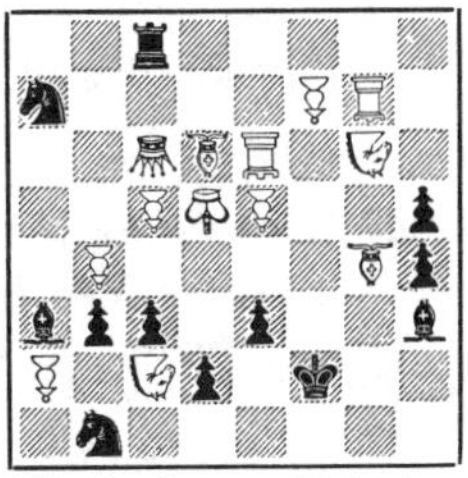

Black plays. Mate in VIII with Bs.

514.
Oxf. 66 (corr.).

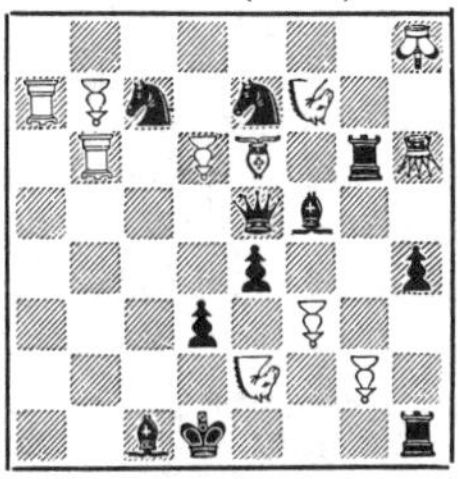

Black plays. Mate in X.

515.
Oxf. 67.

Red plays. Mate in X.

517.
Oxf. 69 = 88.

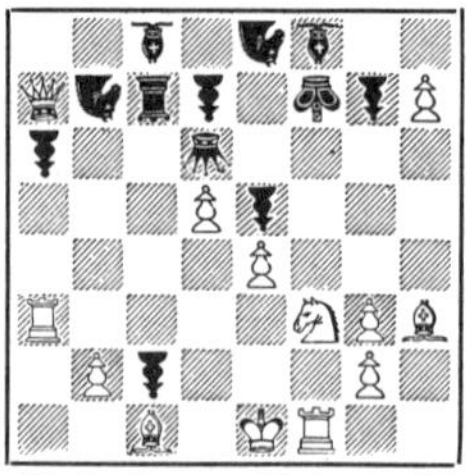

Red plays. Mate in X with 2 Bs.

527.
Oxf. 82.

Black plays. Mate after 5 successive Pawn checks.

530.
Oxf. 91.

Red plays and wins.

543.
RW 5.

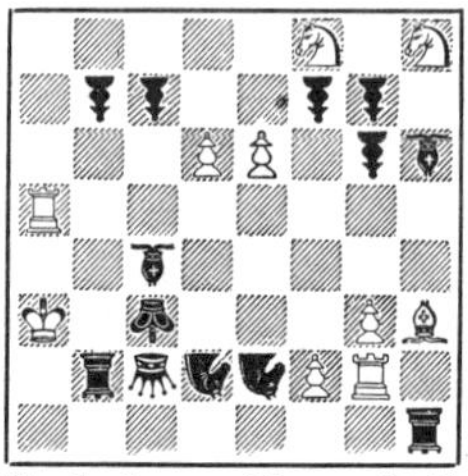

Black plays. Mate with P.

553.
RW 29.

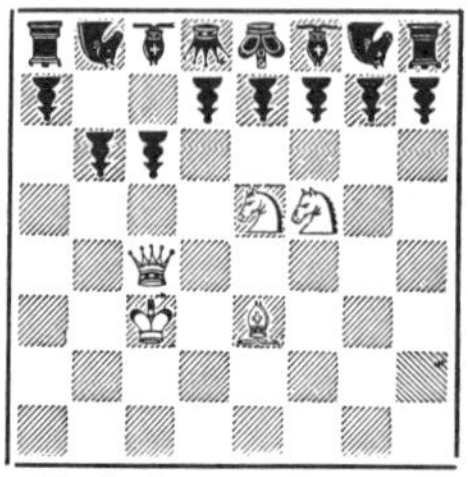

Red plays and wins.

SOLUTIONS TO PROBLEMS AND NOTES

I. Problems from AH.

(1–5 *are described as problems from al-'Adlī's work, which aṣ-Ṣūlī criticized in his book.*)

1. AH 9: C 47: BM 149 = 186: Y 14: Al. 7 = 13. Red, Ke4, Qh8; Bl., Ke7, Qh6. Black plays and wins. Al-'Adlī's solution was 1 Ke6, Kf4; 2 Kf6, Kg4; 3 Kg6, Kh4; 4 Qg5+, Kg4; 5 Qf6, Kf4; 6 Kf7, Kf5; 7 Qe7, Ke5; 8 Kg8, Ke6; 9 Qf8, Kd7 loses (by Bare King). This is said to be in '18' moves. Aṣ-Ṣūlī shortened it to '8' moves by 1 Kf8, Kf5; 2 Kf7, Kg4; 3 Kg8, Kh5; 4 Kh7, K~ and loses by Bare King. BM only gives al-'Adlī's solution; Al. only aṣ-Ṣūlī's. Cf. for the ending Q v. Q, Nos. 112, 132, and 277.

2. 1 Kc7, R×R; 2 Qb7+; 3 Be3 and compels m. with B. Aṣ-Ṣūlī blames al-'Adlī for suppressing the fact that the problem was from the play of Rabrab.

3. AH 11: C 46. See p. 267 above.

4. 1 Rd7+; 2 Pe7 m. Al-'Adlī said that this was from a game in which the odds of R or Kt were given. Apparently his figure was overloaded with men, and the pieces given as odds were on the board (cf. the setting BM 85 which adds Red Ra1 and Pc5 and f5, moves Rh7 to g7, and adds Bl. Bf4, Pc3, g5 and h6). Aṣ-Ṣūlī pointed out the absurdity of this.

5. 'Red plays his Q round until he covers his Kt by it, and then says checkmate with the Kt.' Al-'Adlī says that this was from play. Aṣ-Ṣūlī thought it too elementary to be preserved. Later writers thought differently, and b. Sukaikir recommends it as elegant, and worthy of study. At the end of the solution in AH (f. 32 b) is a note from aṣ-Ṣūlī to the effect that the caliph al-Muktafī had given him some sheets of problems in ar-Rāzī's writing. He says that some of these problems are headed 'Drawn', and are really 'Won', while others said to be 'Won' are really 'Drawn'.

(6–19 *are described as problems from al-ʿAdlī's work, which aṣ-Ṣūlī praised in his book. 'There are not many of them.'*)

6. 1 Kt (f8) e6 +, P × Kt !; 2 Rd7 +, Q × R !; 3 Ktb7 +; 4 Pf7 +; 5 Pg7 +; 6 Rf3 +, Kg8 !; 7 Rf8 +; 8 Rh8 m.

7. Al-ʿAdlī gave two solutions. (*a*) 1 Rf6 +; 2 Pe4 + (MSS. omit P × P; 3 P × P +); 4 Be3 +; 5 Rb7 +; 6 R × P +; 7 Ktb7 m. (*b*) 1 R (f7) e7 +; 2 Pe4 + (MSS. again omit P × P; 3 P × P +); 4 Be3 +; 5 Ktc8 +; 6 R × B +; 7 Ra7 m. Both solutions are given in AH 15 : C 51 : V 3 : BM 22 = 39. H 7 has only the first; AH 107 : C 182 : Alf. 14 only the second.

8. 1 Qd7, Rd8; 2 Kf6, Ra8 or b8; 3 Re6, R~; 4 Rc6, R~; 5 Rc8, R × R; 6 Q × R. Or 1 . ., Ra8 or b8; 2 Kf6, Rd8; 3 Rh7, Kg8; 4 Rg7 +; 5 Re7 wins as before (AE).

9. AH 17 : C 6. Red, Kd4, Qc4, Bd3 and e3, Pb3 and d5; Bl., Kd6, Bf8, Pb4. Black plays; drawn. 1 Bh6; 2 Bf4. Then K to d8 and Bd2 if the K attack the P, or Kc6 if Red play Pd6. Then Bf4, if K × P; B × P +, and K to b8 preventing the red P from queening.

10. The solution of this problem, which is a classical position in the modern treatment of the ending R *v.* Kt,[37] varies in the different MSS. Al-ʿAdlī solved 1 Rh5, Kb8; 2 Kc6, Ktd8 +; 3 Kd7, Ktb7; 4 Rb5; 5 Kc7 wins the Kt. Aṣ-Ṣūlī added 1 Ra1 +, Kb8; 2 Kc6, Ktd8 +; 3 Kd7, Ktb7; 4 Ra3, Ktc5 +; 5 Kc6, Kte6; 6 Ra5, Ktc7 (if Ktd8 +; 7 Kd7, &c.); 7 Re5, Kta6; 8 R + wins. AE (with Rh1 on g6) solves 1 Rg8, Ktd6 +; 2 Kc6, Ktc4; 3 Rd8, Ktb6 (or Kte5 +; 4 Kc5 wins; or Kta5 +; 4 Kc7, Ktb7; 5 Rd7, Ka8; 6 Kb6 wins); 4 Rd4, Ktc8 (or Ka6; 5 Rb4 wins); 5 Ra4 +, Kb8; 6 Rb4 +; 7 Kc7 wins. The position occurred in a game between Rabrab (red) and Nāʿīm al-Khādim, and Rabrab made an exhaustive study of the ending (AH). Cf. for the ending R *v.* Kt, Nos. 108, 125, 189, and 223.

11. 1 Rg8 +; 2 R × R, K × R !; 3 Kc7, Ktf4; 4 Ph2, Ktd5 +; 5 Kc8. Red can easily prevent (*zād*) the Bl. K from moving.

12. 1 Ph5, Ktf4 +; 2 Kf3, Kt × P (h3) (if Kt × P (h5); 3 Ktc7 +; 4 Kte8 wins Kt; if any other, Bl. secures two Qs, winning); 3 Ktc7 +; 4 Kte6, Ktg1 +; 5 Kf2, Kth3 +; 6 Kg2 wins Kt. From a game, Rabrab (Bl.) *v.* Nāʿīm.

13. AH 21 : C 7 : H 21 : V 6 : BM 146 = 183 : AE 70. Red, Kb5, Rd2, Ktc5, Pf7; Bl., Kb8, Rf1. Black plays and Red wins. 1 R × P, Rd8 +; 2 Kc7, Kte6 +; 3 Kb7, Rf8; 4 R~, Rf7 *iʿra*; 5 R × R, Ktd8 + r; 6 K~, Kt × R. Bare King. From a game, Abū'n-Naʿām (Bl.) *v.* Rabrab. Cf. Nos. 68, 116, 317, 318, 414.

14. 1 Rg6, R × R; 2 R × P +; 3 Ra7 +; 4 Rc7 m. From the play of Yūsuf at-Turkī.

15. 1 Ph5 +; 2 Kt × B +; 3 Pf5 +; 4 Kt × B +, Kd4 !; 5 Rd1 +, K × Kt !; 6 Pb3 +; 7 Ktc3 +; 8 Pb5 +; 9 Pb4 +; 10 P × Kt +; 11 Ktd5 +, Ka5 !; 12 Ra3 +; 13 Rb3 +, K × P !; 14 Rc3 +, Kd6 !; 15 Kte7 + d; 16 Ktg6 +; 17 Rc4 +; 18 Rd5 +; 19 Ktf4 +; 20 R × P +; 21 Re7 +; 22 Kte6 m. Al-ʿAdlī gave this as the termination of a game between an-Naṣrānī (Bl.) and b. Hishām. Aṣ-Ṣūlī, quoting from the ar-Rāzī MS. which the caliph al-Muktafī had given him (f. 38 b), says that ar-Rāzī states that he had himself composed this problem from the end of one of his own games. As evidence of this ar-Rāzī pointed to the red Pg2. Obviously it did not belong originally to any of the *f*, *g*, or *h*-files. Nor was it a central P, for ar-Rāzī had taken these in the game. As a matter of fact, it was an embellishment which he had added to the original game-position, and he argued that it was impossible that the ending as diagrammed could have occurred in a real game. But H and BM, which probably preserve al-ʿAdlī's figure, both omit this red P (as also does AH 131), so that ar-Rāzī's claim looks very doubtful.

16. 1 Pg7 +, Kg8 !; 2 Ph7 +; 3 Pg8 = Q +, R or B × Q; 4 Bf5 +; 5 Ktf7 m.

17. 1 Rg2 +, Kf7; 2 Rh7 +; 3 R × R wins. Or 1 . ., Rg7; 2 Rh7; and

[37] See Berger, *Theorie u. Praxis der Endspiele*, Leipzig, 1890, 266–9; Freeborough, *Chess Endings*, London, 1891, 136; and F. Amelung, *Baltische Schachblätter*, Berlin, 1890, vi. 156–61.

3 Ktf6 + winning. From a game of Yūsuf at-Turkī, AH. By Rabrab Khatā'ī, RAS, probably wrongly; by Shāh Muẓaffar, F.

18. 1 R × Kt +; 2 Re8 +; 3 Pd7 +; 4 Kt × P +; 5 Kt × B m. Cf. 28, 210, 416.

19. 1 Kt × P (b7) +; 2 Ktc7 +; 3 R × Q +; 4 Ktd8 +; 5 Kte8 +; 6 Ktf7 +; 7 Ktg7 +; 8 Pg3 +; 9 Bf1 m. 'Aṣ-Ṣūlī says: This happened to al-Hadādī, and the game was defective,' AH. From al-'Adlī, H. 'Not in al-'Adlī's book,' V, which writes the player's name al-Mahdādī.

AH concludes this problem with a note that aṣ-Ṣūlī said that this was the last problem that he had taken from al-'Adlī's book. V has attached this note to the preceding problem, No. 18.

(20–50 *are described as problems from al-'Adlī's work, which aṣ-Ṣūlī omitted from his book.*)

20. 1 Kte8 +, K × B!; 2 Ktd7 +; 3 Ktd6 +; 4 Ktb7 +; 5 Bd3 m.

21. 1 Pf4 +, P × P; 2 P × P +; 3 Ktc1 +; 4 Ktb3 +; 5 Kt × B +; 6 Ktb3 +; 7 Ktc1 +; 8 Pc5 +; 9 Ktb3 +; 10 Ra5 m. This is obviously derived from the preceding position.

22. 1 Rc7 +, Q × R; 2 Qc6 +, Ka8; 3 Ka6, Rb8; 4 Pb7 +; 5 Q × R m.

23. 1 R × Q +; 2 R × P +, R × R; 3 Kt × P +; 4 Pd4 +; 5 Ktf4 +; 6 Ktd2 +; 7 Bd3 +, Ka5; 8 Qb4 +; 9 Pb3 m. Cf. No. 391.

24. 1 Rh7 +, Rh2; 2 Kg3, R × R; 3 Qg2 m. So runs the original solution. If 2 . . , Be3; 3 R × R +; 4 Qg2; 5 Rh1 m.

25. 1 Rb8 +; 2 Ra8 +; 3 Qb7 +; 4 Qb6 m. Oxf. credits this to the Amīr Tīmūr!

26. 1 R × B, K × R; 2 Kf6, Rf1 +; 3 Qf5, Rg1; 4 Pg7 +, R × P; 5 Qg6, R~; 6 Red takes R, Bare K.

27. 1 Rh8 +; 2 Ktd5 +; 3 Ktc3. Ra2 +; 4 Kt × R, Pb2 m.

28. 1 R × Kt +; 2 R × P +, B × R; 3 Pe2 +; 4 Kt × B m.

29. 1 Pb3 +, Kb1; 2 Rg1 +, Bc1; 3 Ra1 +; 4 R × B m.

30. 1 Re3 +, B × R!; 2 Rc3 +; 3 Ktb4 +; 4 Ktb2 m.

31. 1 Qg6 +, Kt × Q; 2 P × Kt +, K × P; 3 R × Kt +, K × R; 4 Kf7, Pg8 = Q +; 5 K × Q, Kg6 and soon m.; or if K does not take Q, Red wins the 2 Bs.

32. 1 Ktf7 +; 2 R × B +; 3 Re8 +; 4 Kte6 m.

33. 1 Qf6 +; 2 Rg8 +, Kf7; 3 Rf8 +, K × R; 4 K × R, Kg8; 5 Kg6, Kh8; 6 Be6 wins.

34. AH 42: C 54: F 49. Red, Ke4, Be3, Ph6; Bl., Ka5, Pb5. Black plays and Red wins. 1 Kb4. Bl. will draw if he succeed in queening the P; Red prevents this, queens his own P and wins.

35. Easy draw. 1 Ra8 and plays the R continually to attack the Bl. R. If 1 . . , R × R; 2 Qe2 m.

36. AH 44: C 60: H 45: BM 106: Man. 10: Y 15: Oxf. 170. Red, Ka1, Qe3, Ktd4, Bc1; Bl., Kc3, Rb2, Qb3, Pa2. Red plays; drawn. 1 Ktb5 +, Kc2; 2 Ktd4 +, K × B; 3 Qd2 +, R × Q!; 4 Kt × Q +; 5 Kt × R, K × Kt; 6 K × P. Drawn.

37. AH 45: C 61: H 39: F 64: AE 120: BM 179: Man. 20: R 73. Red, Kh8, Qh7, Pg7; Bl., Kf6, Be6. Red plays; drawn. 1 Qg8, Kg6; 2 Qf7 +, K × Q; 3 Kh7, &c. AE tries 3 . . , Ke8; 4 Kh6, Ke7; 5 Kg6, Kd8; 6 Kh6, Ke8, &c.

38. AH 46: C 58: F 63: AE 129: Y 17: BM 168 = 198: H 44: R 38. Red, Kb5, Ktb8, Bc1, Pa5 and a7; Bl., Ke5, Ra8, Ph7. Black plays; drawn. 1 Kd6 (or R × P, Ktc6 + r; or R × Kt, P × R = Q), Kb6; 2 Ph6, Kb7; 3 Ph5, K × R; 4 Kc7, Kta6 +; 5 Kc6, Ktb8 +, perpet. check. An interesting ending.

39. AH 47: C 59: AE 119: H 40: F 60: BM 182: R 30. Red, Kc3, Ph6; Bl., Kf6, Bc1. Black plays; drawn. 1 Kc2, Be3; 2 Kd3, Bg1 (or Bc1; 3 Kc2, Ba3; 4 Kb3, Bc5; 5 Kc4, Be3; 6 Kd3; or 5 . . , Be7; 6 Kd5, Kg6; 7 Ke6); 3 Ke2, Kg6; 4 Kf2. (AE.) Cf. for ending B *v.* P, Nos. 273, 372.

40 AH 48: C 137: F 59: BM 169: H 41: R 71. Red, Kg2, Ra1, Qd7 and

e8, Bb1 and c5, Pd6; Bl., Kd8, Re3, Qh8, Pb3. Black plays; drawn. 1 Re2+; 2 Ra2, R×R; 3 P×R; 4 Pa1 = Q.

41. AH 49: C 138: RAS 49: F 58: Y 18: H 47: R 74. Red, Kd4, Qb4, c7 and e5, Bc5, Pa3, a5, d6, f4, g3, and h4; Bl., Kb3, Bc8, Pa6 and g4. Black plays; drawn. 1 Be6; 2 Bc4, &c. By Farazdaq Yūnānī (RAS).

42. 1 Rh1+, Bc1; 2 Rg7, R×R (if R does not take; 3 R opposite R perpetually, draws); 3 R×B+; 4 R×Kt draws.

43. AH 51: C 63: BM 176: V 89: Man. 25. Red, Ka8, Qb7; Bl., Kc7, Qb6, Bc8. Black plays; 'a long draw; there is not a longer; there is no solution,' AH. Man., contradicting AH, says that this is from aṣ-Ṣūlī.

44. AH 52: C 64: BM 116: V 78. Red, Kd5, Rg8, Bd7 and e7; Bl., Kh2, Qf2 and f3. 'A long draw; there is no solution,' AH.

45. AH 53: C 139: BM 124. Red, Kg7, Bf8; Bl., Kg4, Qg6, Pe5 and h5. Drawn; no solution. BM places Pe5 on d4, but then, I think, Bl. can win.

46. AH 54: C 140: V 79: BM 180: AE 115. Red, Ke6, Pc5 and g5; Bl., Kg7, Bf8. Red plays; drawn. 1 Kd7, Kh7; 2 Kd8, Kh8; 3 Kc8, Kg8; 4 Kc7, Kg7; 5 Kd7, Kh7, &c. Or 1 Pc6, Kg8; 2 Kd7, Kh8; 3 Ke6, Kh7; 4 Ke7, Kg8; 5 Pc7, Kg7; 6 Kd7, Kh7; 7 Ke6 draws, or 7 Pc8 = Q, Kh8; 8 K~, Kh7; 9 Ke7, Kg8; 10 Qd7, Kg7; 11 Qe6, Kg8; 12 Qf7+, Kg7; 13 Ke6, Kh7; 14 Kd7, Kh8!; 15 Ke7, Kg7; 16 Qe6, Kg8; 17 Qf7+ draws (AE).

47. AH 55: C 141: BM 114. Red, Kf1, Qf5, Bd3 and e3, Pe5; Bl., Kf7, Bf8. Either plays; drawn.

48. AH 56: C 142: Y 36: V 36. Red, Kf8, Qa1; Bl., Ke6, Pg6 and h6 going to the 8th line. Drawn. Cf. No. 154.

49. 1 K×Q, Ktg7; 2 Kf7, Kth5; 3 Bh3, K~ (or Ktg3; 4 Ktc3, Kth5; 5 Kte2, or 4 . . , Kth1; 5 Kte4. Added from AH 80 and AE); 4 Kg6, Ktg3; 5 Ktc3, Kth1 (or Kc6; 6 Kg5, Kc5; 7 Kg4, Kth1; 8 Kf3, K~; 9 Kg2. Added from AE.); 6 Kte4 (AH 57 and AE). By 'Adlī Rūmī (RAS).

50. 1 Rg6+; 2 Rf8+; 3 Rh6+; 4 Qf6+; 5 R m.

(51–180 *are described as problems from aṣ-Ṣūlī's work, which are not in al-'Adlī. A few are not in aṣ-Ṣūlī.*)

51. 1 Kte6+, Kg6; 2 Kt×Q+, Kf7; 3 Kth7, Kte4 and wins the Kt. In opposition to the heading to this section in AH, H states definitely that this problem is from al-'Adlī. The idea of the problem was a favourite one, and other Muslim settings are: AE 86 (Red, Ke4, Kth4, Qh3; Bl., Kh1, Kte1. Red plays and wins); F81, R57 (Red, Ka8, Ktd8, Qb7; Bl., Kd5, Kta5, Q c6 and f6. Black plays and wins); BM 178 (Red, Kh8, Kth4; Bl., Kd4, Rg7, Kte8. Red plays and wins); Alf. 93 (Red, Kd5, Kta5, Pb6; Bl., Ka8, Ktd8. Red plays and wins). A modern setting is Oxf. 163: Red, Ka8, Ktd8, Bb7; Bl., Kd5, Kta5, Qc6. Black plays and wins.

52. 1 Ktg5+, Kd5!; 2 Rd8+, Kc4!; 3 Rc8+, Kb3; 4 R×Kt, K×R; 5 Kte4+; 6 Kt×R, P×Kt+; 7 K×P wins. From a game al-Khath'amī (Bl.) *v.* ar-Riāḥī, AH, V. From al-'Adlī, H.

53. 1 Kth5+; 2 R×Kt+; 3 Re6 m. 'This happened to Abū'n-Na'ām, and he used to boast of it,' AH. From both al-'Adlī and aṣ-Ṣūlī, H. As already stated on p. 274, I accept the evidence of H as to the origin of this and the two preceding problems in preference to that of AH.

The claim that this position represents the termination of an actual game must be qualified. The position has clearly been edited to satisfy the artistic canons of Muslim chess, for Red's attack is so strong that he must have had a mating attack the preceding move. The problem supplies a good example of this embellishment. It has been a favourite, both in West and East: see Ber. ff. 3a(1), 4a(2), 12a(2), 14a(2), and 18b(1).

54. 1 Kt(e5)f7+; 2 Kte6+; 3 Pg5+; 4 Bd3+; 5 Kte5+, Kh4; 6 Re4+, Kh3 or g3; 7 Re3+, Kg2; 8 R×Q+, K×R; 9 Ktg4+, Kg1!; 10 Rg3+; 11 Rh3+, Kg1; 12 Be3+; 13 Ktf4 m. From aṣ-Ṣūlī, H.

55. 1 Qb7 +; 2 Ktc6 +; 3 Pd6 +; 4 Bb5 +; 5 Pf5 +; 6 Rd2 +; 7 Rc1 +, Kb3!; 8 Ktd4 +, Ka3 (or Kb4; 9 Rb2 +, Ka3; 10 Rb3 +, Ka2; 11 Rc2 +; 12 Ra3 +; 13 Bd3 m.); 9 Bc5 +, Ka4; 10 Ra2 +; 11 Rb2 +, Ka5; 12 Ktc6 +; 13 Bd3 m. From aṣ-Ṣūlī, H.

56. 1 Pb5 +, Kb7 !; 2 Qc6 +; 3 Ktc8 +; 4 Kt × P(b6) + d; 5 Ra8 +; 6 Ra6 +; 7 Ba3 +; 8 Pb3 +; 9 Bf5 +; 10 Bc1 +; 11 Rh3 m. From Aṣ-Ṣūlī, H. The diagram in AH and C is badly disarranged.

57. 1 Rg2 +, Kf7; 2 Rg7 +, Ke6; 3 Ktd4 +; 4 Ktf4 +; 5 P × P +; 6 Kte2 +; 7 Pd4 +; 8 Ktf4 m. From aṣ-Ṣūlī, H.

58. 1 Kth5 +; 2 Kt × P +; 3 Ktf6 +; 4 Ktf7 +; 5 Kte8 +, Kc6; 6 Ktd8 +, Kc5; 7 Be3 +, Kc4; 8 Qb3 +; 9 Ktc7 +; 10 Ktb7 m.

59. 1 Re7 +, Q × R; 2 Pf7 +; 3 Kte6 +; 4 Pb7 +; 5 Pa7 +; 6 Pb8 = Q +; 7 Ktc7 +; 8 Rb5 +; 9 Ktb2 +; 10 Ktc4 +, Ka2 (or Ka4; 11 Ra5 +; 12 Ra3 +; 13 Pd3 m.); 11 Ra5 +; 12 Bd3 +; 13 Ra1 m. From aṣ-Ṣūlī, H.

60. 1 Ktc7 +; 2 Bc5 +; 3 Ktd5 +; 4 Bd7 +, Kc4; 5 Kte3 +; 6 Bb5 +; 7 Ktf6 +; 8 Kt(e3)d5 +; 9 Be3 +, Kh6; 10 Rh1 +; 11 Rh7 +; 12 Ktd7 +, Ke8; 13 Kt(d5)c7 +; 14 Kte6 +; 15 Ktb6 m.

61. 1 Rb3 +, Kc7; 2 Ktb5 +, Kb7; 3 Kt(b5)d4 + d, Kc7; 4 Kte6 +; 5 Ktd8 +, Kc7; 6 Rb7 +; 7 Rd7 +; 8 Pf7 m.

62. AH 70: C **146**: AE 77. Red, Kf7, Ktd5, Qf3; Bl., Kb7, Kth5. Red plays and wins. 1 Kg6, Ktg3; 2 Kte3, Kth1 !; 3 Kf5, Ktf2; 4 Qe2, Kth3; 5 Ktd1, Ktg1; 6 Ktc3, Kth3; 7 Kg4, Ktf2 +; 8 Kg3, Kth1 +; 9 Kg2 wins Kt.

63. AH 71: C 147: V 64. Red, Kh4, Rh3, Bh2; Bl., Ke2, Rb6, B b5 and c1. Black plays and wins. 1 Rh6 +; 2 R × R, K × R; 3 Kf3; 4 Bd3; 5 Be3; 6 Bf1; 7 Kg3 wins the B.

64. 1 Kt × P +; 2 Kt × Q, Kt × Q +; 3 Q × Kt, Kt × Q +; 4 Kt × Kt, K × Kt; 5 Pe2, Ke3; 6 Pe1 = Q, Ke2; 7 Kc4, K × Q; 8 Kc3, Kd1; 9 Kb2, Bc5; 10 Pb3, Ph4; 11 Ka1, Ph5; 12 Pb2, Kc2; 13 Pb1 = Q +, Kc3; and Red, confining the Bl. K in the corner, queens his P and brings it across and mates (AE). AH concludes with the personal note (? by aṣ-Ṣūlī): 'This happened to me when playing a man at odds. Abū'n-Na'ām boasted that he had played a similar game. There is not, however, one in the least like it among the problems of Abū'n-Na'ām.'

65. 1 P × P +, Q × P; 2 P × Q +, K × P; 3 Rg2 +, Kh7; 4 Bg1, Kh6 (position is now AE 96, cf. BM 156); 5 Kg3, Kg6 (or Kh5; 6 Bf1, Kg5 or g6 !; 7 Rh2, R × B +; 8 Kf2, Rg4; 9 Rg2); 6 Kf2 + d, Kh5; 7 Rg5 +, Kh4; 8 Kg2, R × B (h3); 9 Rh5 wins. BM only gives 7 . . , K × R; 8 Kg2; 9 K × R wins.

66. AH **74**: C 150: V 68: AE 98: BM 47. Red, Ka8, Rh8; Bl., Ke4, Rd3, Kta4, Be3. Red plays and Black wins. 1 Rh4 +, Kd5; 2 R × Kt, Kc6; 3 if Kb8, Rd8 + wins; if Ka7, Ra3; 4 R × R, Bc5 + wins R; and if Ra6 +, Kc7; 4 Ra7 +, Kb6 wins.

67. AH 75: C 151: V 65. Red, Ke8, Rh5, Ba6, Pg3; Bl., Kd4, Kte5, Qe7, Pf6 and g7. Red plays and Black wins. 1 R × Kt, K × R; 2 Kf7, Kf5; 3 ~, Pg8 = Q +; if 4 K × Q, Kg6; 5 ~, Pf7 + and m. in two more.

68. AH 76: C 152: Man. 22: AE 67: BM 191: RAS 24: V 70. Red, Kc6, Rb1, Ktd6; Bl., Ka7, Rh6. Red plays and wins. AH solves 1 Rb4, Rg6; 2 Rh4, Re6; 3 Ra4 +, Kb8; 4 Re4, R~; 5 Re7, R~; 6 Re8 +, Ka7; 7 Ktb5 +, Ka6; 8 Ra8 m. AE solves 1 Rg1, Kb8; 2 Rg7, Ka8 (Rh8; 3 Rd7, Rh6; 4 Kb6, Rh8; 5 Re7); 3 Rd7, Rh8; 4 Kb6, Rb8 + (or Kb8; 5 Ktb7; 6 Rd8 +); 5 Ktb7; 6 Rd8 +. By Surkh Shaṭranjī, RAS (absurd).

69. Two solutions: (*a*) 1 Ktd5, R × P; 2 Kc6, Kb8; 3 Rb7 +, Kc8; 4 Ktb6 +; 5 Rb8 +; 6 Ktd5 +. (*b*) 1 Ktb5, R × P +; 2 Kc6, Kd8; 3 Rh7, Ke8 !; 4 Pe7, Rd7; 5 Ktc7 + or Rh8 +.

70. 1 Ph5, if Kth4 or e7; 2 Ktg4 +; 3 Rh8 +; 4 Pf8 = Q +, Kf6 !; 5 Rh6 +, Kf5; 6 Pe4 +; 7 Kth3 m. AH overlooks the defence 1 . . , Rf6 +. Alf. 45 gives the position after move 1, omitting the Bl. Kt.

71. 1 Re8 +; 2 Ktc5 +, Kc6; 3 Re6 +; 4 Ktc7 +; 5 Qb3 m.

72. AH 81: C 157: AE 111: V 24. Red, Kb6 Pa7 and c6; Bl., Ka8, Be6

and h6. Red plays and Black wins. 1 Pc7, Bc8; 2 Kc6, K × P; 3 Kd7, Ba6; 4 Kc6, Bf8; 5 Kd7, Kb7; 6 Kd8, Kc6. Or 1 Ka6, Bc8 +; 2 Kb6, Bf8; 3 Kc7. Or 1 Kc5 or c7, K × P; 2 Kd6, Kb6; 3 Kd5, Kb5; 4 Pc7, Kb6.

73. 1 Ktb7 +; 2 Re8 +; 3 Rc8 +; 4 Bg5 +; 5 Re8 +, Re7; 6 R × R +; 7 Bh3 +; 8 Qg3 m. From aṣ-Ṣūlī, H. By ʿAdlī Rūmī, RAS. By substituting Bl. Q for Pe5, AE 132 makes 7 Bh3 m., and converts the problem into a conditional one, 'mate with B'.

74. 1 Kt × B +; 2 Rb8 +; 3 R (b8)b7 +, Kt × R; 4 R × Kt +, Kd8 (or Kc8; 5 Qd7 +; 6 Ktc6 m.); 5 Ktc6 +; 6 R or Q m. accordingly. From aṣ-Ṣūlī, H.

75. 1 Kf6, Bd6; 2 Qc6, Kf8; 3 Qd7, Kg8; 4 Qe6, Bc4; 5 Qf7 +, Kh7!; 6 Pg5; 7 Bd3; 8 Bf5 +; 9 Pg6; 10 Pg7 m.

76. 1 Kte4 +; 2 Kt × Q, K × Kt; 3 Kg3, Ktf1 +; 4 Kf2, Kth2; 5 Qf5 wins.

77. 1 Rb7 +; 2 Pc5 +; 3 Qc4 +; 4 Ktf3 +; 5 Rb3 +; 6 Kte3 m. From aṣ-Ṣūlī, H.

78. 1 R × B +, Kb4; 2 Rc8, Ka3; 3 Ra8 +, Qa4; 4 Rb8, Qb2 +; 5 R × Q, Q(a4)b3 and wins the R. 'This is ar-Rāzī's; he took it from al-ʿAdlī's manṣūba,' AH. Al-ʿAdlī's problem is No. 26 above.

79. 1 Ktc7 +; 2 Pa6 +, Kc8; 3 Rf8 +, K × Kt; 4 Rh7 +; 5 Rd8 +; 6 Re7 +, Kf5; 7 Rd5 +, Kg4; 8 R × P +; 9 Rf7 +; 10 Re5 +, Kd3; 11 Rd7 + (Bd6; 12 R × B + omitted); 13 Rd4 +; 14 Rb4 m.

80. 1 Ktc6 +; 2 Kte8 +; 3 Rf7 +, Ke6; 4 Re7 +; 5 Ktf6 +, Kc5; 6 Be3 +, Kc4; 7 Re4 +; 8 Rb4 +, Ka2; 9 Rb2 +, Ka1; 10 Rb1 +; 11 Ktb4 +; 12 Ktc2 +, Ka4; 13 Ra1 +; AE continues 14 Ktd4 +; 15 Ra4 m.; AH, 14 Ra3 +; 15 Ra4 +; 16 Rb4 +; 17 Rb2 m.

81. AH 90: C 166: RAS 8: V 73. Red, Ke6, Ktd5, Qd3; Bl., Kc8, Kte8. Red plays and wins. 1 Ke7, Ktg7; 2 Kf6, Kth5 +; 3 Kg6, Ktg3; 4 Ktb6 +, Kb7; 5 Ktc4, Kc6; 6 Kg5, Kth1; 7 Kf4, Ktf2; 8 Ktb2 wins. The solution is a long one in AH. Cf. No. 62 above, which it resembles closely. By Rabrab Khatā'ī, RAS.

82. 1 Kth5 +; 2 Kth4 +; 3 Ktg3 +; 4 Ktg2 +; 5 Ktf1 +; 6 Kte1 +; 7 Ktd2 +; 8 Ktc2 +; 9 Ktb3 +; 10 Ktb4 +; 11 Ktc5 +; 12 Ktc6 +; 13 Ktd7 +; 14 Kt (c6) × Q +; 15 Ktf6 +; 16 Ktg6 +; 17–32 repeat, playing 18 Kt(g6) × R +; 33 Kth5 +; 34 Kth4 +; 35 Ktg3 +; 36 Kt × P m. AH and C have only the end of the text, owing to the lacuna in the MSS. The problem is given at the end of L with the following text: 'This is the manṣūba mentioned by Abū'l-Muẓaffar al-Lajlāj which is known by the name *ad-dūlābīya* (the water-wheel), because the K is driven round three times by the Kts, and is conquered on his own square, and because the player of the Kts can, if he likes, drive him round for ever. This problem is of marvellous skill, and the win is on the original square after seventy-one moves. Wherefore know it. My solution was found carved on a stone of the time of the Greeks, and was then translated into Arabic.' Oxf. has also a mythical composer in the person of the Imām Shāfiʿī. None of the MSS. gives the diagram correctly. Cf. No. 388.

83. 1 Rh8 +; 2 Bf5 + d, Rh2; 3 R × R +; 4 Rh8 +; 5 Pg7 +; 6 Kth6 m. From aṣ-Ṣūlī, H. The problem appears without any story in AH, C, H, AE and Man. In S it is called *manṣūba al-jārīya* (the maiden's problem). In F it is called the problem of Dilārām chengī, and the following story is told, as from al-Lajlāj.[38] Dilārām was the favourite wife of a certain nobleman, who had given her this name because his heart knew no peace without her, the name Dilārām meaning 'heart's ease'. Once he was playing chess with a very strong player, and finally staked Dilārām on the game. The game went badly for him, and he found himself in such a position that his opponent appeared to have a certain mate on the next move. At this moment Dilārām cried out in distress, 'Sacrifice your two Rooks, and not me.' Her lover saw the line of play that she meant, and won the game. With ever-increasing embellishment this story is given in all the later MSS., and reaches its

[38] No importance can be attached to this use of al-Lajlāj's name, for he plays an entirely mythical part in this work.

most ornate form in Durgāprasāda's Urdū work. Here the hero of the game is the Moghul Emperor Shāh Jahān, and his four wives all advise him, but Dilārām alone sees how to save the game. This problem was one of the most popular of all the Muslim problems. It occurs in Ber. in its old-chess form, among problems with the modern moves.[39] In Europe it was the origin of nearly 200 wager-positions in the Middle Ages.

84. 1 Rf7+, Ke8; 2 Ktf6+; 3 Rf8+; 4 Ktd5+, Kb7; 5 Rf7+, Kc8; 6 Rc7+; 7 Rd7+, Ke8; 8 Ktf6+; 9 Rf7 m. From a game of aṣ-Ṣūlī, playing blindfold, AH.

85. 1 Bd2, R × B; 2 Qe2, Rd4!; 3 R × R+, R × R; 4 Q × R wins.

86. 1 Qg7+d; 2 Rh8+; 3 Rf8+; 4 Rf6+; 5 Rd6+; 6 Rd4+; 7 Rf4+; 8 Rf2+; 9 Bf1+; 10 Rf4+; 11 Rd4+; 12 Rd6+; 13 Rf6+; 14 Rf8+; 15 Rh8 m. From aṣ-Ṣūlī, who said that it was composed by Muḥammad b. az-Zayyāt (the vizier of the caliph al-Mu'taṣim),[40] H. The problem *ad-dūlābīya*, Man. (cf. No. 82 above). By Rabrab, S. With the substitution of a Bl. B for Qh6, to adapt it to the modern moves, it occurs in Ber. f. 18 (2), whence it is given in G. Walker's *Philidor*, London, 1832, p. 157.

87. 1 Kt × P+; 2 Bf5+; 3 Rd8+; 4 Rf8+; 5 R × P+; 6 Pe4+; 7 Rd6+; 8 Rd3+; 9 Qb3+; 10 Be3 m.

88. The diagram in the MSS. is quite corrupt, and I have reconstructed it with the help of the solution. 1 Be3; 2 Bd3; 3 Pg5, Kh5; 4 Bb5; 5 Kf4, Bd6+; 6 Ke5, Bb4; 7 Kf6; 8 Kg7; 9 Kh7; 10–12 P to g8 = Q; 13 Qf7; 14 Qg6 m.

89. 1 R(f6)g6+; 2 Rh8+; 3 Rh7+, Kf8; 4 Rf7+; 5 Rg8 m.

90. 1 Rh8+; 2 Rh5+; 3 Kf6; 4 Q or B+; 5 B or Q m.

91. 1 R(a7) × Kt+; 2 Rc8+, Ka7; 3 Ktb5+; 4 Rc6+; 5 Bd7+; 6 Rb6+; 7 Rb5+; 8 Pe3+; 9 Rb3+; 10 Bb5 m. By the caliph al-Mu'taṣim, RAS, an ascription which is too late to carry any weight.

92. 1 Rd6, Bf8; 2 Be3+; 3 Qg4+, Ke4; 4 Qf3+, Kf5 (or K × B; 5 Rd3 m.); 5 Bd3 m. From al-'Adlī, H.

93. 1 Rf8+; 2 Bg5+; 3 Kt × R+; 4 Ktb5+; 5 Ktd7+, Ka5; 6 Ra8+; 7 Qc3+; 8 Kt × Q+; 9 Ra2+; 10 B or R+; 11 Rd2 or Be3 m. accordingly.

94. 1 Rg3+; 2 Kte6+; 3 Kte5+; 4 Rb3+, Ka6; 5 Ktc5+, Ka7; 6 Ktc6+; 7 Rb8 m.

95. 1 Bf5+, Kh6; 2 Pg5+; 3 Qg4+; 4 Kt(g1)f3+; 5 Rg1+; 6 Ktd3+; 7 Re1 m.

96. 1 Ra5+; 2 Bd6+; 3 Ktc5+; 4 Ktc4+; 5 Ktb3+; 6 Ktb2+; 7 Re5+; 8 Kt × P+; 9 Re1+; 10 Ktf3+; 11 Rh1+; 12 R × R m.

97. 1 Bc4+; 2 Ktf3+; 3 Bd6+; 4 Re2 m.

98. 1 Bd3+; 2 Ktf3+; 3 Rd6+; 4 Kte4+; 5 Pa3+, Kb3 (or Ka5; 6 Qb6+; 7 Ktc3+; 8 Kt m.); 6 Kt(f3)d2+, Ka2; 7 Ktc3+; 8 Ktb3 m.

99. 1 Kte5+; 2 Re2+; 3 Ktb6+; 4 Ktc6+d, Kte4; 5 R × Kt+; 6 Ktd5+; 7 Re5+; 8 Kte3+; 9 Ktd4 m.

100. 1 Bh3+; 2 Ktd3+; 3 Rd6+, B × R; 4 R × B+; 5 Rd4+; 6 Rb4+; 7 Kte1+; 8 Rb1+; 9 Ktd4+; 10 Kte3+; 11 Rg1+; 12 Kt m.

101. 1 Kte3+; 2 Qc3+; 3 Bf1+; 4 Rg2+; 5 Kte5+; 6 Rf2+; 7 Ktc4+; 8 Rd2 m. V. d. Linde shortened by 3 Kte5+; 4 Rg2+; 5 Qd2 m. (*Qst.*, 377, no. 103).

102. 1 Pg6+; 2 Bg5+; 3 Ktf8+; 4 Kte6+, Kb6; 5 Pc4+; 6 Ktd6+; 7 Ra4+; 8 Kte4+; 9 Rd4+; 10 Ktc3+; 11 Rd1 m.

103. 1 Ktf2+; 2 Kth3+, Kf1; 3 Pg2+; 4 Ktf3+; 5 Ktf2+; 6 Kte1+, Kc3; 7 Ktd1+; 8 Ktc2+; 9 Re6+; 10 Bh6+; 11 Rg6+, Kh2 (or Kh4; 12 Rg4+; 13 Ktf2+; 14 Pg1 = Q m.); 12 Pg1 = Q+, Kh2; 13 Ktf2+; 14 Rg4 m. The MSS. miss the fact that 8 Ktf3 is mate, and also overlook the shorter solution 1 Pg2+, Kh2; 2 Pg1 = Q+, Kh3; 3 Ktf2; 4 Rg4 m.

[39] A modernized version is Oxf. 152, manṣūba Dilārām. Red, Kb8, Qh1, Rg8, Kte8, Pd6, e5, f4, g5; Bl., Kf1, Ra1 and a4, Ktb4, Ba2 and g1, Pb6, c6, d5, e4, f3, g4. Black mates in V with Kt. 1 Ra8+; 2 Bc4+; 3 Ra8+; 4 Pb7+; 5 Kta6 m.

[40] See p. 198.

104. 1 Pc3+; 2 Ra2+; 3 Rd2+; 4 Rd4+; 5 Ktg3+; 6 Rd6+; 7 Rg6+, Kf8; 8 Bd6+; 9 Rg8 m.

105. AH 120: C 195: BM 80 = 193: AE 79. Red, Kg2, Bf8, Pc5, d6, and e5; Bl., Kc8, Bf5, Pa4, c4, d3, and e4. Black plays and wins in '63' moves. 1 Kd7, Kg3; 2 Ke7, Bh6; 3 K × P, Kf4; 4 Ke6!, Bf8; 5 Kf7, Bh6; 6 Kg6, Bf8; 7 Kg7, Bd6; 8 Kf7, Bb4; 9 Ke6; 10 Kd5; 11–14 P to a8 = Q; 15 Bd7; 16 Bb5; 17–21 Q to f5; 22 Kd6, Bb4+; 23 K × cP, Bd2; 24 Kd5, Bb4; 25 Pc5, Bd2; 26 Kd6, Bb4+; 27 Ke6, Bd2; 28 Kd5, Bb4; 29 Pd4, P × P!; 30 Kc4; 31 Kd3!; 32 K × P and wins the B. From aṣ-Ṣūlī, who gave this as the best play on either side. There is some variation in the order of the moves in the different MSS., but the method is the same in all.

106. AH 121: C 107: V 63. Red, Kb3, Pa6 and b5; Bl., Ka1, Qa5, Pb4, going to b8. Black plays and wins. The solution is only sketched. Black, with care, easily wins the Pawns.

107. 1 Qf6, if Kt(g3)f5; 2 Kte5+, Kb6 (or Kd6; 3 Kte4+, Ke6; 4 Ktc5+); 3 Kta4+, Ka74; R × Kt, Kt × R; 5 Q × Kt, R × Q; 6 Ktc6+r. If 1 . ., Kt(e7)f5; 2 Kte5+, Kb6; 3 Kta4+; 4 Ktc6+; 5 Ktb6+; 6 Ra7 m. By 'Adlī Rūmī, RAS.

108. AH 123: C 109: Man. 23: V 9 = 11. Red, Kb8, Kte6; Bl., Kb6, Rc1. Black plays and wins. 1 Kc6, Ktd8+; 2 Kd7, Ktb7; 3 Ra1, Ktc5+; 4 Kc6, Kte6; 5 Ra5, Ktc7 (or Ktd8+; 6 Kd7, Ktb7; 7 Rb5; 8 Kc7; 9 R × Kt); 6 Re5, Kta6; 7 Re8+; 8 Re7+; 9 Kb6; 10 R wins Kt or mates.

109. 1 Qc3, Rc1 (or R × Q; 2 Rh8+; 3 Ktb5+r); 2 Kc6, Kte5+ (or R × Q+; 3 Kb6, Be6; 4 Rb7+; 5 Ktb5 wins); 3 Kb6, Rb1+; 4 Qb4, R × Q+; 5 P × R wins.

110. The solution to this position is worked out at great length in the MSS. In AH it fills forty-four lines and provides a good example of Muslim End-game analysis. 1 Bf5, Q × R (or *a*, *b*, to *f*); 2 Kt × Q m. (*a*) 1 . ., Q × B; 2 R(e1)e7, Qe6; 3 Kt × Q+, B × Kt (or Kt × Kt; 4 Rd7+; 5 R(f7)e7 m.); 4 Rd7+, Kc8; 5 R × Kt+; 6 Kt × P wins. (*b*) 1 . ., Ph6; 2 Rd7+, Ke8 (or Q × R; 3 Ktf7 m.); 3 Kt × P, Kt × Kt (or Kta6; 4 Re7+; 5 Ktf7+, Q × Kt; 6 Rd7 m.); 4 Kt × Q, Kte7 (or B × Kt; 5 R × Kt m.); 5 Ktc7+r; 6 R × Kt+; 7 Kt × R wins. (*c*) 1 . ., Bd6 or h6; 2 Rd7+, Ke8; 3 R × Kt wins. (*d*) 1 . ., Ba6; 2 Kt × Q+, Kt × Kt; 3 R × Kt, Bh6 (or Bd6; 4 Rd7+; 5 Rh6 wins Kt); 4 Rd7+; 5 R × B wins Kt. (*e*) 1 . ., Kte8; 2 Kt × P, Kt(e8)f6 [41] (or Q × R; 3 Kt × Q m. Or Q × Kt; 3 Rd7 m. Or Ktd6; 3 R × Q, B × R; 4 Kt × B+, Kc8; 5 Rc7+ and m. in two with either Kt); 3 R × Q, B × R; 4 Kt × B+, Kc8; 5 Rc7+; 6 Kte7; 7 Ktc6 m. (*f*) 1 . ., Kta6; 2 Kt × P, B(f8)~ (or Ktb8; 3 R × Q+, B × R; 4 Kt × B+; 5 R m. If 3 any other; 4 Rd7+ forces m. with R or Kt); 3 Rd7+, Ke8; 4 R × Q+, B × R; 5 Re7+, Kf8 (or Kd8; 6 Ktf7+r; 7 Ktd6; 8 R m.); 6 Kt × B+; 7 Ktf6+, Kt × Kt; 8 Rg7 m.

111. 1 R × B+, Kb7; 2 Rg7+, Ka8 (or Kc8; 3 Rg8+; 4 Rd7+; 5 Rg6+; 6 R × R+, K × R; 7 K × R wins); 3 Rg8+, Ka7 (or Rb8; 4 R × P+; 5 R × R+, K × R; 6 K or R × R); 4 Bc5+ (or Rd7+, Rb7; 5 Bc5+; 6 R × R+, K × R; 7 K × R); 5 Rd7+; 6 Rc8+; 7 K × R wins.

112. AH 127: C 113: RAS 38: V 42. Red, Kh8, Qa1; Bl., Kf6, Qc3. Black plays and wins. 1 Kg6, Kg8; 2 Qd2, Kf8; 3 Qc1, Ke7, &c. The text in AH and V ends with the note, 'There is also a problem without solution of Q *v.* Q which is the 10th after this, which resembles this.' See No. 122, which is in the right place in AH, but occurs nowhere in V. By Abū'l-Fatḥ Hindūstānī, RAS.

113. 1 Re7+; 2 Kte6+; 3 Rc7+; 4 Pa7+; 5 Rc8+; 6 Rb8+; 7 Ktc7; 8 Ktc4+; 9 Pb3m.

114. AH 129: C 115: AE 78: V 51. Red, Ke7, Ktg3; Bl., Ke3, Kta7, Qg4. Black plays and wins. AH solves: 1 Ktc6+, Kf8 (or Kd6; 2 Kf3, Ktf1; 3 Kta5, Ktd2+; 4 Ke3, Ktb1; 5 Kd4; 6 Ktc4+ wins Kt); 2 Ktd4, Ke7; 3 Ktf3, Kf6; 4 Ktd2, Kg5; 5 Kf3, Kh4; 6 Ktc4, Ktf1; 7 Kte5, Kt~; 8 Kf4 wins. AE solves: 1 Ktc8, Kf6 (or Ke6; 2 Ktb6, Ktf1+; 3 Ke2, Ktg3+; 4 Kf3, Ktf1; 5 Ktc4 wins); 2 Ktd6, Kg5; 3 Kf3, Ktf1; 4 Kte4+, Kh4; 5 Kf2, Kth2; 6 Qf3 wins.

[41] The stronger defence 2 . ., Kt(h5)f6 is overlooked.

115. 1 Qf3 !, R × B; 2 Bf5, R × P +; 3 Kd2, R × Q; 4 Rf7 +; 5 Ph7 +; 6 R × P, Ktc3 (or Rg3; 7 Rf8 +; 8 Rg8 +; 9 R × R); 7 Rg6, Kte4 +; 8 Ke2 and after Red has exhausted his checks R or Kt mates.

116. AH 131 : C 117 : AE 71 : V 20. Red, Ke4, Rc4, Ktd4; Bl., Kd2, Ra2. Red plays and wins. 1 Ktb3 +, Kd1 (or Ke1; 2 Kf3, Rf2 +; 3 Ke3, Re2 +; 4 Kd3; 5 R +); 2 Rc1 +; 3 Ra1, Rb2; 4 Ra2, R × R; 5 Ktc1 + r wins.

117. 1 R × B, Kd6; 2 Ke8, Ktc7 +; 3 Kf8, Kte6 +; 4 Kg8, Rg7 +; 5 Kh8, Ke7; 6 Rc8, Rg5; 7 Kh7 or Ra8 both lose. AE gives a fuller analysis. 'This is ar-Rāzī's. He took it from al-'Adlī's mansūba,' AH. The problem referred to is No. 13 above.

118. The solution in all MSS. runs 1 Kc5, Ka8; 2 Kc6, Be6; 3 Pb7 +, K × P; 4 Kd6, B~; 5 Kc7; 6–7 B to c5; 8 P m. This does not entirely suit the position diagrammed, which is probably to be solved by Bare King.

119. 1 Qe7 +; 2 Pd7 +; 3 Ktg3, Qe6; 4 Kth5; 5 Ktf6 m.

120. 1 Ktd7 +, Kg8 (or Ke8; 2 Rf8 +, B × R; 3 Ktf6 +; 4 Rd7 m.); 2 Rg2 +, K × R; 3 Ktf6 +; 4 Rg8 m. Cf. 136.

121. AH 136 : C 25 : V 108. Red, Kf2, Qd3, Bf1, P a6, e3 and h2; Bl., Kf7, Bf8, P d6 and e6. Red plays and wins. 1 Kf3, Pd5; 2 Qe4, P × Q; 3 Kg4!, Kg6; 4 Pa7, &c.

122. AH 137 : C 26. Red, Kb3, Qc3; Bl., Ke4, Q omitted in both MSS. Black plays; Red wins. The solution begins:—

'If Red were to play he would win after three moves. Black has nothing except to go to his Firzān's 4th, a Faras-move from the Red Firzān, for every square other than this to which he can move loses. The Red Shāh mounts to his Faras 4th. Black has nothing except his Firzān's 3rd.'

The solution is then dismissed, partly because it is lengthy, and partly because aṣ-Ṣūlī was extremely proud of it. He goes on to say:—

'This is very old, yet neither al-'Adlī nor any one else has said whether it is drawn or can be won. Nor has any one interpreted it, or pointed (diagrammed) it because of its difficulty. There is no one on earth who has solved it unless he was taught it by me. I have never learnt that there was any one before, for if any one had solved it, he would either have written down the solution, or have taught it to some one else. This is the word of aṣ-Ṣūlī.'

123. 1 Pf2 +; 2 Rd2 +; 3 R × Q +; 4 Rd1 +; 5 Bc4 +; 6 Ra1 m.

124. 1 Ktb4 +; 2 Rd8 +; 3 Ktd5 +; 4 Ktg5 +; 5 Rg8 +, B × R; 6 R × B +; 7 Ktf6 +; 8 Ktf3 +; 9 Bf5 m.

125. AH 140 : C 29 : V 98. Red, Ke5, Rd3; Bl., Kc5, Kte2. Red plays and wins. 1 Re3, Ktg1; 2 Kf5; 3 Kg4, Kd4; 4 Kf4; 5 Kg3, Kd4; 6 Kf2 wins the Kt. 'This is ar-Rāzī's,' AH. He specially pointed out that Red must not play Kf4 at once, but only in reply to Kd4 attacking the Kt.

126. 1 Rc7, Kte6 (or Kte8; 2 Re7 +, Be6; 3 Pd4 +; 4 R × Kt, R × R; 5 Ktf6 + r); 2 Pd4 +, Kd5 (or Kt × P; 3 Rc5 + ; 4 K × Kt); 3 Ktf6 +; 4 Rd7 +; 5 Pd5 +; 6 P × Kt.

127. AH 142 : C 31 : AE 75 : V 44. Red, Kb6, Rc5, Qa6; Bl., Kb8, Rh8. Red plays and wins. 1 Qb7, Rh6 +; 2 Rc6, Rh8; 3 Re6, Rg8; 4 Re7, Rg6 + (or ~; 5 Qc6, Kc8; 6 Ra7, Kb8; 7 Rb7 +, if Kc8; 8 Qd7 +; 9 Rb8 +; and if Ka8; 8 Re7; 9 Qd7 wins); 5 Qc6, Rg8; 6 Qd7, Rg6 +; 7 Re6 wins.

128. AH 143 : C 32 : V 45. Red, Kd3, Pc7 and h6; Bl., Kf3, Qf4, Bc8. Black plays and wins. 1 Qe5 !, Kc4; 2 Qd6 !, Kd5; 3 Q × P, Ke5 !; 4 Kg4, Kf6; 5 Kh5, Ph7 (or Kg7; 6 Q~ wins); 6 Qd6, Ph8 = Q; 7 Qe5 +, Kf7; 8 Kg5 wins. Black has to play carefully to avoid a draw.

129. AH 144 : C 33 : V 46. Red, Kd7, Qd8, Be7; Bl., Kb7, P b4 and d3. Red plays and wins. 1 Kd6, Kb6 (or Kc8; 2 Kc5 !, K × Q; 3 Bg5, Kd7; 4 K × P, Ke6; 5 Kc3, Kf5; 6 Be3, Ke4; 7 Bc1 wins); 2 Kd5, Kb5; 3 Kd4, and K × P wins. If Qd8 were on c7 it is drawn thus: 1 Kd6, Pb3; 2 Kc5, K × Q; 3 Kc4, Kd6; 4 Bg5, Pd2; 5 K × P, Ke5; 6 Kc7, Kf4; 7 Be7, Ke3.

130. 1 Bg8, K × B; 2 Kg6, Kh8; 3 Ra8 +, Pg8 = Q; 4 Re8, Qg7; 5 R × Q wins. From aṣ-Ṣūlī, H.

131. AH 146: C 35: V 48: RAS 44. Red, Kb3, Qc1, Pa6 and b5; Bl., Kb7, Bc5, Pa3, b4 and d6. Black plays and wins. 1 K × P, Ka4; 2 Kb6, Qb2; 3 Pd7, Q × P; 4 B × Q, K × P; 5 Bc1, Kc4; 6 Be3, Pb4; 7 Ka5, Kb3; &c. By 'Abdallāh Khwarizmī, RAS (probably falsely). 'A pretty game,' AH.

132. 1 Rh4 +, Kg7; 2 R × R, K × R; 3 Kg6, Qh7 +; 4 Kf7, Qc7; 5–10, Qc6 and d5, Q to g7; 11 Qc6, Qg6 +; 12 K × Q, Kg8 and gets across in time to save and queen the cP.

133. 1 K × Kt, R × R; 2 Bd3, Ra4; 3 Bf1 +; 4 Kth6, Ra8!; 5 Ktg4 +; 6 Kg3, Rg8; 7 Bd3, Pc2; 8 Bf5, Pc1 = Q; 9 B × Q, Kg1; 10 Bd3; 11 Be3 +; 12 Bf5, and Bl. must eventually exchange R for Kt to avoid mate. 'A beautiful game,' AH.

134. AH 149: C 38: BM 69a (text only) = 77. Red, Kd6, Qa1, Pb2; Bl., Kd3, Qd5 and e6, Bb1 and e3. Black plays and wins. He stales the K by means of K, Qs and Be3.

135. Black takes the B and advances the P, winning. If Red had the move, he would draw by 1 B~, or Kg3. AE, as usual, gives full solution.

136. 1 Kt × P +; 2 Ktd7 +, Kg8; 3 Rg2 +; 4 Ktf6 +; 5 Rg8m. Cf. 120.

137. 1 Pd5, Kt × P; 2 Rf7 +; 3 R × P, R × Kt; 4 R × R, R × R; 5 K × R. Or 3 . ., Kte7; 4 Ktd4 +; 5 Kt × R, Kt × R (or R × Kt; 6 Rf7; 7 R × Kt +); 6 B × Kt +; 7 Kt~. Or 3 . ., Rd2; 4 Ktd4 +; 5 Rf7 +, Kd8; 6 Ktc6 +; 7 Re8 m. Or 3 . ., Rc5; 4 Ktc3 +; 5 Kt × Kt, R(c5)c2; 6 Kte3. By Farazdaq Yūnānī, RAS.

138. AH 153: C 66: BM 70: V 69. Red, Kb6, Bf4, Pd6; Bl., Kc4, Qa8 and e6, Bc1, Pe4. Black plays and wins. The solution is only sketched. The K attacks the B until Red K is in g5, Bl. B in h6, and K in h7; he then brings his Qs to f7 and g6, and K via e6, d7 (if necessary), and K × P; next Be3, K to f5, Pe5. If Bl. B is in h6, P~; but if it is in f1, Ke5 and f5. Finally Bl. has to play Bh6, and Pe7 wins.

139. 1 R × Kt + (if 1 B × Kt, Bc5 +; 2 Ka8, Kc7; 3 Rg8, Rb7; 4 Rc8 +, K × R; 5~, R m. If 1 Rg6 +, Kc7; 2 R × R, Bc5 +; 3 Ka8, Kt × R m.), P × R; 2 Rg6 +, Kc7; 3 R × R, Bc5 +; 4 Ka8, K × R; 5 Kb8 (or B × P, Kc7; 6~, Pe8 = Q, &c.), K × B; 6~, Pe8 = Q, &c.

140. 1 Rd8 +, Ktd6!; 2 R × Kt +, K × R; 3 K × P, Pe5 +; 4 Kc4!, Pe4; 5 Bc5!.

141. 1 Rd7 +; 2 Ktd5, Rc2; 3 Ktc7 +, R × Kt; 4 R × R, Kd8; 5 Rc2, Rh7; 6 Bg5, Rh6; 7 Rc3, Rg6; 8 Rh3, Rg8; 9 Kf7, Re8; 10 Rd3 + wins R.

142. 1 Rg8 +, K × B (or Kf7; 2 R × R wins. Or K × Kt; 2 Rh1 +, &c.); 2 Rg5 +, R × R; 3 Kth4 +; 4 Ktf6 +; 5 R m. By Khalīl Miṣrī, RAS.

143. 1 Ktd6!, Ra7; 2 Kt × Kt, R(a7) × Kt (or R(d7) × Kt; 3 Ktb7 +; 4 R × R); 3 R × R, K × R (or R × R?; 4 Ktb7 +; 5 Rd8 +; 6 Ktd6 +; 7 Kte8 + r); 4 Kte8 +; 5 R × R; 6 Kt × fP and wins hP and eP. From a game b. Ḥassān (Abū'l-Ḥasan 'Alī b. Wahshūzān) *v.* Abū'l Mughith (Bl.).

144. 1 R × Q, R × P; 2 Rg8 +; 3 Kc2, Rb4; 4 Rg1, Ra4; 5 Qb5, Ra5; 6 Rg4, Pf6; 7 Ra4, R × R; 8 Q × R, Ka6; 9 Kc6, Ka5; 10 Qb5, Kb4; 11 Qa6, Pf5; 12 Kd5, Pf4; 13 Qb7, Ka5; 14 Qc6, Kb6; 15 Qd7, Pf3; 16 Ke4, Pf2; 17 Kf3, Pf1 = Q; 18 Kf2, Kc7; 19 Qe6, Kd6; 20 Qf5, Ke5; 21 Qg4, Kf4; 22 Qf3; 23 K × Q. Bare King. 'This game is deceptive, but beautiful,' AH. From aṣ-Ṣūlī, H.

145. 1 Kf5, Bh6; 2 Kg6, Bf4!; 3 Qd5, Kd7; 4 Kf5, Bh6; 5 Kg5, Bf8; 6 Kg6, Ke8; 7 Qc6, Ke7; 8 Kg7, Ke8; 9 Kf6, Kd8!; 10 Kf7, Bh6; 13 Kg7, Bf4; 12 Kg6, Kc7; 13 Qb5; 14 Kg5 wins. In correction of al-'Adlī, who gave the game as drawn, AH.

146. AH 161: C 74: BM 79: AE 116. Red, Ka4, Ph3 and h5; Bl., Kc4, Bf8. Black plays and wins (AH), but draws only (AE). AH solves 1 Bh6, Ka4!; 2 Kd5, Kb5; 3 Ke5, Kc4; 4 Ke4, Kc5; 5 Kf5, Kd4; 6 Kf4, Kd5; 7 Kg5, Ke4 (or Ke5; 8 K × P); 8 Kh4!, Kf5; 9 K × P(h5). The solution in AE fills 8 pages. Al-'Adlī gave the position with the B on h3 as drawn (Bl. playing), but gave no solution. 'This is correct,' AH. Al-'Adlī's position is BM 174: V 92.

147. 1 Kt × B, Bd6; 2 Ktf4, B × Kt (or 2 Qc4 +; 3 K × Q, Rg4; 4 Qb4 wins): 3 Pa5 +; 4 Qb4 +; 5 Qc5 +; 6 Ra7 m. (really after Red has sacrificed the R).

148. 1 Bf8!, Ph3; 2 K × P, Kf4; 3 Kg2 (or Kh2, Kt × P; 4 Bh6 +, Kf5; 5 B~,

Ke5; 6 ~, Ktg6. If 4 Bd6 +, Kf3), Kt × P +; 4 Kh3, Ktg6; 5 Bd6 +, Ke5; 6 Bb4, Ktf4 +; 7 K ~, Ktd3; 8 Bd2 loses. 'I have been asked to solve this. The result is clear, though it is obscure in parts,' AH. I have not given all the variations worked out in the MS.

149. 1 Rg2, Bh2 (or Pc3; 2 Pg5, Kh4; 3 P × fP, Pc7; 4 Re1, Rc4 +; 5 Ka5, Bh2; 6 R(e1)g1, Kh5; 7 R × B +; 8 Qg4 +. Or 1 . ., Kh4; 2 Pg5, hP × P; 3 Qg4, Pf5; 4 Re1); 2 Pg5, Pf5 (or hP × P; 3 R(e4)g4, Bf4; 4 R(g4)g3 +, Kh4; 5Qg4); 3 Re1; 4 Rh1; 5 Pg6; 6 R × B m.

150. AH 165: C 78: AE 167. Red, Kb3, Bh6, Pa2 and f4; Bl., Ke7, Bf1, Pe5, g3, and g5. Black plays and wins. 1 Pg4!, Bf8; 2 Pg6!, Bh6; 3 Pg5, Bf8; 4 Pg7, Pa1 = Q; 5 P × B = Q wins.

151. 1 Ktf4 +, K × P; 2 Kt × B, Kte6; 3 Kb3, Qd4; 4 Kc2, Kf3; 5 Kd3, Kg2; 6 Ktf4, Kt × Kt +; 7 Ke4, Qc3; 8 K × Kt loses. Or 4 Pc3, Kf3; 5 Pc2, Kg2; 6 Kc4, K × Kt; 7 Kd5, Qc3; 8 K × Kt, Qb2; 9 Kd5, Kg3; 10 Kd4, Kf2; 11 Kd3, Qc1 wins.

152. 1 Kt × Q, Ba6!; 2 Ktb7, R × Kt; 3 Pa3 +, Ka4; 4 Ra5 +, P × R; 5 Bd3; 6 Ktc5 m. By the caliph al-Muʿtaṣim, RAS, too late to carry any weight.

153. AH 168: C 81: AE 91: BM 86: V 35. Red, Kg1, Ktd7 and e5, Bf1, Pf6; Bl., Kh8, Rg8, Pe4 and g4. Red plays and wins. 1 Ktf8, R × Kt!; 2 Ktg6 +, Kg8; 3 Kt × R, K × Kt; 4 Kf2, Kf7; 5 Ke3, K × P; 6 Kf4. If 6 . ., Ke6; 7 K × eP wins. If 6 . ., Kg6; 7 K × gP wins. If 6 . ., Pg3; 7 Bh3. If 6 . ., Pe3; 7 Bd3, Pe2; 8 K × P wins.

154. AH 169: C 82: V 83. Red, Kg8, Qa1; Bl., Ke6, Pg6 and h6 going to h8. Black plays and wins. The solution requires Kg8 on f8. 1 Kd5, Ke7; 2 Ke5, Kf8; 3 Kd4, Ke7; 4 Kc3, Kf6; 5 Pg7, Kf7; 6 Kc2, Kg6; 7 Pg8 = Q, K × P; 8–13 Q to a2; 14 Kb1; 15 K × Q. Cf. 48 above. The problem is drawn (*a*) if Kg8 is on h8, (*b*) if Qa1 is on a2 (AH gives the solution of this last, on exactly similar lines to the text solution).

155. 1 Ktf7, Kth4 +; 2 Kg3, Ktg6; 3 Bf5, Rc2; 4 Rd7, Bc8!; 5 Ktg5, Kth8 (or Bh6; 6 Pf7 +; 7 Kth7 +; 8 Pf8 = Q +; 9 Rg7 +; 10 Ktf6; 11 R m.); 6 Pf7 +, Kt × P; 7 Kt × Kt wins.

156. 1 Pa4, Qb6; 2–5 K to c4; 6 Kb5, Qc5; 7–10 aP queens; 11 Kc6; 12–20 Qa8 to h5; 21 Q(h5)g6 +; 22 Qe6, Kg8; 23–4 K to e8; 25 Qh7 +, K × Q; 26 Kf7; 27 Kth4; 28 Qf5; 29 Qg6 +, Kh8; 30 Bf5; 31 Qh7; 32 Ktg5 m.

157. 1 Ra5 +; 2 Ra7 +; 3 Ktb5 +, Kb6; 4 Ktd7 +; 5 Ktc7 +; 6 Bc5 m. From aṣ-Ṣūlī, H.

158. 1 Qc6 +; 2 Rd7 +, K × Kt; 3 Rb7 +; 4 Rb5 +; 5 Pb3 +; 6 Ra5 +; 7 Ra4 +; 8 Kte4 +; 9 Rb4 +, Kc7; 10 Rb7 +, Kd8; 11 Rd7 +; 12 Ktd6 +; 13 Rb7 m.

159. AH 174: C 99: V 101. Red, Kf5, Bc4 and d6, Pd4 and h3; Bl., Kd7, Pb5 and c6. Red plays and wins. 1 Ke5, Pb6; 2 Kd5, Pb7; 3 Kc5, Pc7; 4 Ba6, Pb8 = Q; 5 P~!, Qh7; 6 Bc8!, K × B; 7 Kc6 wins.

160. 1 Rg8 +; 2 Ktf7 +; 3 Kte8 +, Kg6; 4 Kte5 +, Kh5; 5 Ktg7 +; 6 Ktf3 +; 7 Qf5 +; 8 Pg3 m.

161. 1 Rg8 +; 2 Pe6 +; 3 Ktd4 +, Kc5; 4 Rc8 +; 5 Rc4 +; 6 Ktb4 +; 7 Rc2 +; 8 Ktd3 m. By Jalāladdīn Nakhjawānī, RAS.

162. 1 Bf1 +; 2 Pd3 +; 3 Bh3 +, Kg5; 4 Be3 +; 5 Kte5 +; 6 Bf5 +; 7 Kt m.

163. I give the text in AH in full:—

Aṣ-Ṣūlī says: 'This happened to me when playing against a man who thought himself a good player. I checked him with the Faras, saying, "You lose your Firzān or your Faras." But he did not see what I meant and did not expose himself to the *iʿra* (check by discovery), or play Shāh to Faras's square, when the Firzān would be taken, nor did he see how the Faras was threatened. So when I said check, he moved his Shāh to Rukh's second. Then I pushed the Baidaq against his Faras, saying, "You lose it." He laughed, saying, "How, by Allah?" and he removed his Faras to the corner. So I developed my Rukh to Faras's square, saying, "Now you lose both Rukh and Faras." But he did not see the continuation and descended with his Rukh to his Shāh's second to avoid checkmate. Then I played my

Faras in his Firzān's second, sacrificing it in order to mate with the Fīl. He played Faras to Faras's third, and I checked with the Fīl. If he goes to the corner, I take Faras with Faras, checking, and then Rukh with Fīl; and if he exposes himself to *i'ra*, I take Rukh with Fīl, keeping the Faras opposite the *i'ra*. He did not see my move sacrificing the Faras.'

That is, 1 Ktc5 +, Ka7; 2 Pa5, Kta8; 3 Rb1, Re7; 4 Ktd7, Ktb6; 5 Bc5 +, Ka8 (or Kb7 or 8; 6 B × R wins); 6 Kt × Kt +; 7 B × R wins.

Despite all this, RAS attributes the problem to 'Othmān Dimashqī.

164. 1 Rd6 +, Ke8; 2 Ktf6 +; 3 Rd8 +; 4 R × R +; 5 Pe5 +; 6 Rg5 +; 7 R × bP +, Kf3; 8 Qg2 +; 9 R × P +; 10 Kte4 +, Kd1; 11 Rd3 +; 12 Rc3 +; 13 Rb1 m.

165. 1 Ra7 +; 2 Ktc7 +; 3 Rh8 +, (Bf8; 4 R × B + omitted) Bc8; 5 Kta6 +; 6 R × B +; 7 Ktc7 +; 8 Bc5 +; 9 R × Q +; 10 Ra8 +, Kb4; 11 Pa3 +, Kb3; 12 Rb8 +, Ktb5; 13 R × Kt +; 14 Rb4 +; 15 Bf1 m. From aṣ-Ṣūlī, H. By Farazdaq Yūnānī, RAS.

166. 1 Qc4, B × Q; 2 P × B, Ra5 +; 3 Kb4, R(d5) × cP; 4 Bd3, R × P; 5 Bb5 wins the R.

167. 1 R × R, P × R +; 2 K × P, Kd7; 3 Kc5, Kc7; 4 Kb5, Kb8; 5 Kb6, Ka8; 6 Pa6, Be2; 7 Pa7, Bg4; 8–12 Q to b8, B to e2; 13–15 K to e5, B to c4; 16 K × P, Kb7; 17 Ke5, Ka8; 18 Pf5, Kb7; 19–21 K to b5, Ba6 and K to b7; 22 Pa8 = Q +, K × Q; 23 K × B, Bare King.

168. AH 183: C 90: Y 40: BM 83: AE 107. Red, Kd4, Pa6 and c6; Bl., Kb4, Qc7, Bc5, Pc4. Red plays and Black wins. 1 Pa5 +, K × P; 2 K × B, Qd6 +; 3 K × P, Kb6; 4 Kd5, Qc5 wins. Or 3 K × Q, Kb6; 4 Kd7 (or Pc5, Kb5), Pc5 wins. By an-Na'ām, who was proud of it, AH.

169. 1 Kt × Q, Ke5!; 2 Qe3, R × Kt +; 3 Qd4 +, K~ (if Kd5; 4 Rc5 m.); 4 R × R wins.

170. 1 Ktg7 +; 2 Rf1 +, Kg8; 3 R × Kt +, K × R; 4 Kt(g7)e6 +, Kg8; 5 Rg2 +, Kf7; 6 Rg7 +; 7 Ktc7 +, Kd8; 8 Kt(c5) e6 +; and m. with Bf5 and Pb7.

171. 1 Pd5 +; 2 Bc5 +, Kf8; 3 Ra8 +, Kte8; 4 R × Kt +, Kg7; 5 Rh7 +; 6 Ktf6 +, Kg7; 7 Rg8 +, K × Kt; 8 Pg5 +; 9 B m.

172. 1 Kta5 +, Kd6; 2 Rc6 +, Ke5; 3 Pf4 +; 4 Qf3 +; 5 Bf1 +; 6 Ktb3 +; 7 Rc1 or Qe2 m.

173. 1 Ktc7 +; 2 Ktd6 +; 3 Pb6 +, P × P; 4 aP × P +; 5 Bf5 +; 6 Bg5 +; 7 Pg7 +; 8 Be3 + d, B × R; 9 R × B +, Kf8; 10 Rg8 +; 11 Bg5 +; 12 Rg6 m. From aṣ-Ṣūlī, H.

174. 1 Kte7 +, K × Kt; 2 Rf7 +; 3 Rf8 +, Kg7; 4 Rg8 +; 5 Pg6 +; 6 Rh8 +; 7 Rh7 +; 8 Pg7 +; 9 Rh8 m. From aṣ-Ṣūlī, H.

175. 1 Pc6 +, Kd6; 2 R(f3)f6 +; 3 Ktf3 +; 4 Rf4 +; 5 Bc5 +, Kf2; 6 Kte1 +, Kg1; 7 Rg4 +; 8 Rf1 +; 9 Rg2 +; 10 Rh1 m.

176. 1 Ktf5 +; 2 Rg7 +; 3 Pg5 +; 4 Re7 +; 5 Kte3 +; 6 Re4 +; 7 B +; 8 Rd4 +, Rd3; 9 R × R +; 10 Rd1 m.

177. 1 Kte6 +, Kf7; 2 Rg7 +, K × Kt; 3 Ktc7 +; 4 Kte8 +; 5 Pd5 +; 6 Ktc7 m.

178. AH 193: C 106: V 52. Red, Kf7, Re8, Pg5 and h6; Bl., Kd4, Rh8, Qf8, Bc5. Black plays and wins. 1 Qg7, R × R (or R~; 2 Q × P, Pg4; 3 Qg5; 4 Be3 wins); 2 Q × R, Kg8; 3 Ke5, K × Q; 4 Kf6, Kh7; 5 Be3, Pg4; 6 Bg1 wins.

179. 1 Qf7; 2 Ph8 = Q +, K × Q; 3 Kf6; 4 Q × P, B × Q (or Kg8; 5 Qf7 +; 6 Bf5; 7 Pg7 m.); 5 Kf7; 6 Bf5; 7 Pg7 m.

180. 1 Rf1 +, Rf5; 2 Rg1, Kf7; 3 Rg7 +, Ke6 (or Ke8; 4 R × Q, Rf7; 5 Rh8 +, Rf8; 6 Rh7, Rg8; 7 Kh5, Rg1; 8 Rh8 +, Qf8 wins); 4 R × Q, Rf7 (or Kf6; 5 Rh8, Rf1 wins); 5 Rh8, Rf8; 6 Rh7, Rg8; 7 Kh5, Rg1 wins.

II. Problems from V.

181. 1 Kte2 +, Kh1; 2 Rf1 +; 3 Rf2 +, K × P; 4 Ktf4 +; 5 Rg2 +; 6 Ktd4 +; 7 Ktc2 +; 8 Kte1 +; 9 Re2 +; 10 Ktf3 +; 11 Rc2 +; 12 Ktd4 +; 13 Pb5 +; 14 Ktc6 +; 15 Rb2 +, Kc5; 16 Kt × P +; 17 Rb5 +; 18 Bc8 +; 19 Kt(d3)e5 +;

20 Be6 +; 21 Ktg6 m. From aṣ-Ṣūlī, H. 'Al-Mahdi (the father of Hārūn ar-Rashīd) made this; it did not occur in a game,' V.

182. V 30. Red, Kf3, Qc3, Bd3 and e3, Pe4; Bl., Ke6, Bd6, Pe5. Either plays. Drawn. No solution. 'This is al-Lajlāj's,' V.

183. V 61: BM 170: Man. 63. Red, Kd6, Rd1, Qe1 and d3; Bl., Ke3, Rc8. Red plays. Drawn. 1 Kd5 or d7, Rc7 or c5, never leaving the *c*-file.

184. V 76: Man. 53. Red, Kg2, Qg3, Bf1; Bl., Ke5, Ktf6, Bd6 and e6. Drawn. No solution. Aṣ-Ṣūlī gave it as a test for a player's fitness to be placed in the class mutaqāriba (the second class), Man., V.

185. V 77: BM 117. Red, Ke6, Ra8; Bl., Ke3, Qf3, Bd3. Drawn. No solution.

186. V 80: AE 114: Man. 4. Red, Ka1, Ph4; Bl., Ka8, Ph5. Drawn.

187. V 81: BM 111: AE 113. Red, Ke1, Pe4; Bl., Ke8, Pe5. Drawn.

188. V 82: BM 177. Red, Kc6, Ktb7; Bl., Kc4, Qb4 and e7, Bb5 and c5. Drawn.

189. V 84. Red, Ke8, Ktb8; Bl., Ke1, Rh1. Drawn.

190. V 85. Red, Ke8, Rh8, Qd8; Bl., Kd1, Qe1, Ktg1. Drawn.

191. V 87: Man. 58. Red, Ke5, Qe6, Pf6; Bl., Kg8, Bh6. Black plays. Drawn. 1 Kh8! 'Aṣ-Ṣūlī says in his book that some people think it can be won,' Man.

192. V 88. Red, Kd8, Qc7, c8 and e8; Bl., Kd1, Rh1. Drawn.

193. V 90. Red, Kd4, Bd3; Bl., Ke6, Qd5, Bd6. Drawn.

194. V 91. Red, Kc2, Qb2; Bl., Ke2, Qd2, Be3. Drawn.

195. 1 R × Q +, Ke8; 2 R × Q +, Kd8; 3 Rh8 +, Kc7; 4 Re7 +, Kc6; 5 Rc8 +, Kb6; 6 R × B +, Kc6; 7 R × R, Kt × R; 8 Kt × Kt, R × R; 9 K × Kt wins.

196. V 109: BM 67. Red, Ke8, Rh8; Bl., Kd1, Ktb1 and g1, Qe1. Drawn.

III. Problems from H.

197. 1 Ktf7 +, R × Kt; 2 Re8 +, Kt × R; 3 Kte6 m. From al-ʿAdlī, H.

198. 1 Rg1 +; 2 Ktf5 + d; 3 Rg1 +; 4 Pf2 +; 5 Ktg3 m. From al-ʿAdlī, H. In S called *al manṣūba al-jārīya* (the maiden's problem) from its close resemblance to the Dilārām problem, No. 83 above.

199. 1 R × B +; 2 Re7 +, Q × R; 3 Pf7 +; 4 Kte6 m. From al-ʿAdlī, H.

200. 1 Rc7 +, Q × R; 2 Pa6 +, Ka8 (or Kb8; 3 Ktc6 +; 4 Pb7 m.); 3 Pb7 +; 4 Ktc6 m. From aṣ-Ṣūlī, H.

201. 1 Rb1 +, Kc7; 2 Kte6 +; 3 Ktd8 +; 4 Rb7 +; 5 Rd7 +; 6 Pf7 m. From aṣ-Ṣūlī, H. But the solution in the MS. forgets the possibility of Red's playing 1 .., Rb2, which spoils the mate entirely. It can be made sound by moving Pd3 to a5, and Rd1 to d3, but this is a more drastic reconstruction than usual. Probably the possibility of interposition was ignored, as is the case in other problems.

202. H 67: Oxf. 168. Red, Ka7, Ktg3, Qb4 and c3, Pb2 going to b8; Bl., Ke5, Ktd4, Qe2. Black plays. Drawn. 1 Kf4, Kth5 +; 2 Kg5, Ktg7; 3 Kg6, Kte8; 4 Ktb5 +, Kb6; 5 Kf7, K × Kt; 6 K × Kt, Kc4; 7 Kf7, Kd4; 8 Qf3 and unites with K, drawing. From aṣ-Ṣūlī, H.

203. H 69: BM 196: AE 92. Red, Ke5, Ktc5 and f6, Be3; Bl., Ke7, Rh6, Qf7. Red plays and wins. 1 Kte6, R × Kt (or Q × Kt; 2 Ktg8 + wins R.); 2 Bg5 +; 3 Ktc5 (or c7) +; 4 K × R wins. From aṣ-Ṣūlī, H.

204. 1 Rb8 +, Ka2; 2 Rb2 +; 3 Ktc3 m.

205. H 72. Red, Kd8, Ra8, Bc8 and f8, Pe5 and f6; Bl., Kf2, Be3 and h3, Pe4, f3 and g3. Drawn. No solution.

IV. Problems from BM.

206. 1 R(b6)b7 +; 2 Pb5 +; 3 Rb6 +; 4 Ra6 +; 5 P × P +; 6 Pb6 +; 7 Ra8 +; 8 Pc6 +; 9 Pb7 +; 10 Ktb5 +; 11 Ktc7 +; 12 Bc5 m. 'This problem is hard.'

207. 1–5 K to f7, K to h8!; 6 Rg8 +; 7 Bf1; 8 Rg7; 9 Rg6; 10–14 K to

f3; 15 Qf7; 16 Rh6+; 17 Rh8, K×P; 18 Re8; 19 Bd3, Pf5; 20 Re6, Pf4; 21 Rg6+, Kh4; 22 Bf1; 23 Rg4; 24 Ke4, Kh5; 25 Kf5, Pf3; 26 Qe8, Pf2; 27 Qf7; 28 Rg5; 29 Rg6; 30 Kf6; 31 Kg5; 32 Rg8+; 33 B~, Pf1=Q; 34 Bf5 m.

208. 'The conditions are that Red mate in the corner, without taking the B or discovering check. This problem is good and clever.' BM. 1 Kc5, Ba6; 2 Kd6, Bc8; 3 Ke7, Ba6; 4 cRb7+, Kc8; 5 Ke8, B~; 6 Rc7+; 7 aRb7+; 8 Rc8 m.

209. 1 R×Q+, K×R; 2 Pc3+, K×P; 3 Ra3+, Kd4; 4 Ra4+, Ke5; 5 Re4+; 6 Ktg4+, Kf5; 7 Bd3+; 8 Be3+, Kh5; 9 Ktf6+; 10 Ktg8+; 11 Rh4+; 12 Pg3+, Kh5; 13 Pg4+; 14 Ktg2+; 15 Bf1 m.

210. 1 Rd8+; 2 R×Kt+; 3 Pe7+; 4 Ktd6+; 5 Kt×B m.

211. BM 31, with blank diagram. Black wins, playing with the P. The solution is 1 P×Q+, B×P; 2 Q×B+, K×Q; 3 Kt to Q3+, K to B3; 4 Kt to middle of the board m.

212. 1 Kt×Q+, B×Kt; 2 Rg1+; 3 R×B+; 4 Rh1 m.

213. 1 Rb6+; 2 Rb7+, Kd6; 3 Rd7+; 4 Re7+; 5 Ktb7+; 6 Ktd8+, Kb6; 7 Rb7+; 8 Ktc6+; 9 Rb4 m.

214. 1 Ktc6+; 2 Ktd6+; 3 Pg7+; 4 Kte7+; 5 Pg8=Q+, Kh6; 6 Ktf7+; 7 Pg4+; 8 Ktf5+; 9 Ktg5+; 10 Rd2+, Kg1; 11 Rg2+, Kf1; 12 Kte3+; 13 Re2 m. By Niẓām Shīrāzī, RAS.

215. 1 Kt×R+, B×Kt; 2 Pe4+, K×P; 3 Ktf5+; 4 Be3+, Kb4; 5 Pa3+; 6 Ktd4+; 7 Qb7+; 8 Kt×R m.

216. BM 50. Red, Kf3, Rg7, Qf1, Bd3; Bl., Kh3, Pf2. Red plays. Mate with B. 'This problem is difficult.' 1 Rg2; 2 Ke4, Kh3; 3 Kf4; 4 Rg3; 5 Rg4; 6 Rh4+. Now drive the K into line 8, then to file *a*, and secure position Red, Kc3, Rb3, Qf1, Bf5; Bl., Ka1, Pf2. Next 1 Rb4; 2 Ra4+; 3 Bd3+; 4 Rb4; 5 Rb5; 6 Re5; 7 Qe2+, Ke1; 8 Qf3; 9 Bf1. Next drive K to a1 with R and Q, the position being Red Kd2, Qb3, Rc2. Now 1 Ra2+; 2 Bd3 m.

217. 'Red may not take either Bl. P.' Red forces the Bl. K to take one of the RP's (in the position Pa4 is the easier). He then compels Bl. to take up the position Ka1, Pa2, his own K being on c2 and Rs on f7 and b4. Now 1 Rg4, P×R; 2 Ph5, Pg3; 3 Ph6, Pg2; 4 Rf1+, P×R=Q; 5 Ph7. Red queens the hP and brings it to b2 mating, playing Kc1 if the Bl. Q checks.

218. BM 55. Red, Kb1, Bc1; Bl., Kc4, Qg4, Bg8, Pb4. Black plays and wins. 1 Kc3, Be3; 2 Qf3, Kc1; 3 Qe2; 4 Pb3; 5 Be6, &c.

219. 1 Rc8+; 2 Pd7+; 3 Ktc6 m.

220. 1 Ktd2+; 2 Pb2+; 3 Pb3+; 4 Kte4; 5 Ra8 m.

221. BM 66. Red, Ke8, Ktg8, Qc8; Bl., Ke1, Ktg1, Qd1, Bf1. Maqmūra position without solution.

222. BM 84. Red, Kf7, Bc8 and f8, Pc5, d6 and e5; Bl., Kc3, Qg7, Ba3, Pb3, c4, d3, and f5. Black plays and wins. 1 Q×B, K×Q; 2 Kd2, Ke7; 3 Ke3, Kf6 (or Kd7; 4 B×P, P×B; 5 Ke4, Kd6; 6 Pf6); 4 Ke4, Ba6; 5 Kd5, K×P; 6 K×P, Pe4; 7 P×P+, K×P; 8 Kc7, Kd4; 9 Kb7, B×P; 10 P×B, K×P; 11 Kc6; 12 B×P wins.

223. BM 88. Red, Ka7, Ktb7; Bl., Kc6, Rh8. Red plays and Black wins. 1 Kta5+, Kb5; 2 Ktb7, Rg8; 3 Ktd6+, Kc6; 4 Ktc4, Rd8; 5 Kta5+(or Ktb6, Rd4; 5 Ktc8, Ra4+; 6 Kb8, Rb4+; 6 K~, Kc7), Kb5; 6 Ktb7, Rd7; 7 Kb8, Kb6 wins.

224. BM 89: AE 170. Red, Ke8, Rf6, Ktc6, Bb8 and c8; Bl., Kh6, Rg4, Ktg6, Bh7. Red plays and wins. 1 Kte5, Rg5; 2 Kt×Kt, R×Kt; 3 Kf7, R×R+; 4 K×R, Kh5; 5 Be6, Kh6; 6 Bd6, Kh5; 7 Bf8, Kh4; 8 Kg6.

225. 1 K×P, Pb2; 2 Kc2, Qb1+; 3 B×Q, Ka2; 4 Bd3, Ka1; 5 Kb3, Pb1 = Q; 6 Bf5, Qa2+; 7 Kc2, Qb1+; 8 Kc3, Ka2!; 9 Bd3, Ka1; 10 Kb3, Qa2+; 11 Kc2, Qb1+; 12 B×Q, Ka2!; 13 Bd3, Ka1; 14 Kb3, Pa2; 15 Kc2 and the Bl. K is stalemate. Cf. No. 371 below.

226. 1 Rd3, Rc5 (or R×R; 2 B×R, stalemate); 2 Bd7, R~; 3 R+; 4 R m.

227. 1 Ph4, Pg4 (or P×P; 2 Rg6+; 3 Ktg1); 2 Ktd2; 3 Qe3 wins R.

228. BM 94. Red, Ke1, Bg4, Pb5; Bl., Ka1, Be3. Red plays and wins. 1 Kd2, B~; 2 Kc2; 3 Pb4; 4 Be6; 5 Bc4; 6 Pb3; 7 Pb2 m.

229. BM 95. Red, Kd6, Bc8; Bl., Kd4, Bc1, Pa7 and b4. Black plays and wins. 1 Pb5, Kc7; 2 Kd5, Kb6; 3 Pa8 = Q, Kc7!; 4 Kc5, Kb8; 5 Kc6, K × Q; 6 Kc7; 7 Be3; 8 Bc5; 9–10 P to b7 m. Cf. No. 228.

230. BM 96. Red, Kh2, Rf4, Pg2 and h4; Bl., Ke2, Rg8, Qf2, Be3. Black plays and wins. 1 Qg3 +, P × Q; 2 Rh8 m. (really only after sacrifice of the Red R).

231. 1 BM 98. Red, Kb1, Qf8; Bl., Kd3, Qb3, Ba3. Black plays and wins. The solution gives the first move to red. 1 Kb2, Kc4; 2 K × B, Qc2; 3 Kb2, Qd3; 4 Kc1, Qe4; 5 Kd2, Kd4, and easily reaches the Red Q first, winning.

232. 1 Bh6 +; 2 Ktd4 +; 3 Ra2 +, Kh1; 4 Ktf3, Rg2; 5 Rg8, R(b1)b2; 6 R(a2) × R; 7 R m. (really only after the sacrifice of the Rb2).

233. BM 100. Red, Ka8, Rb6, Kth1, Qh3, Ph6; Bl., Ke5, Rc3, Ktc6, Qa6, Pa2. Black plays and wins. 1 Rb3, R × R!; 2 P × R and advances this P to b7, mating.

234. BM 101. Red, Kg7, Qf6, Bf8; Bl., Kf5, Qf7 and g6, Pc5 and h7. Black plays and wins. 1 Ph8 = Q +; 2 K × Q, Bh6; 3 Qf5, Kh7; 4 Qg8 +, K × Q; 5 Kg6, Bf4; 6 Kg5, Bd2; 7 Kg4, Kf7; 8 Kf3, Kf6; 9 Ke3, Bb4; 10 Kd3; 11 Kc3 wins B.

235. BM 102. Red, Kg7, Bf8; Bl, Kg5, Qh5, Bb5 and c5, Pf5. Black plays and wins. 1 Pf6 +, Kg8; 2 Bd3, Kf7; 3 Kf5. Black easily queens the P, winning.

236. BM 103. Red, Kg7, Bf8; Bl., Kg5, Qh5, Pa5 and d5. Black plays and wins. 1 Qg6, Bd6; 2 Kf5, Kf8; 3 Ke6; 4 Qf7 wins.

237. BM 104. Red, Ka3, Kta5, Pd4 going to d1; Bl., Kc1, Qb3, Bb1, Pa2 and d3. Red plays and wins. 1 Kt × Q +, P × Kt; 2 K × P, Kd2; 3 Kb2, Ke2; 4 K × B, Kf3; 5 Kc2, Ke4; 6 Kc3; 7 K × P.

238. BM 105. Red, Kd3, Kte4, Qg3, Bf4, Ph7; Bl., Ke5, Kth5, Qb5, Bc5, Pa4. Black plays and wins. 1 Qc4 +, K × Q; 2 K × Kt, K × B; 3 Kt × Q, Bd2; 4 Kd3, &c.

239. BM 108: Al. 19. Red, Kf8, Ra6; Bl., Kf6, Qe6, Pf7 and g3 going to eighth line. Red plays. Drawn. 1 Ra4, Qf5; 2 Ra6 +, Qe6. Drawn by repetition of moves.

240. BM 109: Al. 9 = 15. Red, Kh8, Ra7, Pe5 going to e1; Bl., Kh3, Rh4, Pe4 and h7. Red plays. Drawn. 1 R × P, Kg4!; 2 R × R, K × R.

241. BM 110. Red, Kc5, Rh3, Qb4, Bd6, Pd4; Bl., Kb3, Ktc4, Qc2, Bd3, Pa4. Red plays. Drawn. 1 R~, Bb5; 2 R~, Qd3 (with repetition of moves).

242. BM 112. Red, Ke4, Bc8, Ph4; Bl., Kg6, Bc1 and f1, Pd4, e3, f4, and h3. Black plays and wins. No solution.

243. BM 113. Red, Kh8, Bh6, Ph5; Bl., Kc1, Ph3. Black plays. Drawn. 1 Kd2, Kg7; 2 Ke3, Kg6; 3 Kf2, Kg5; 4 Kg2, Kh4; 5 Kh2, Bf4 +; 6 Kg2, Kg5; 7 Kg3 draws.

244. BM 115. Red, Ke4, Ra2; Bl., Ke2, Qd2, Bf1. No text.

245.[42] BM 119. Red, Kc4, Qd4 and e4; Bl., Kc2, Bb1 and c1. Red plays. Drawn. Solution sketched only. It suggests that the diagram is incomplete, and that a Red Kt has been omitted.

246. BM 120. Red, Kd4, Kte4, Bc4 and f4; Bl., Kc2, Bb1 and c1. Red plays. Drawn. Solution sketched only. The position is contrasted with No. 245.

247. BM 121. Red, Ka1, Qb1 and b2; Bl., Kb3, Ph6 going to h8. Red plays. Drawn. 1 Qa2 +, Kc2; 2 Qb1 +, &c.

248. BM 122. Red, Kc3, Rh1, Pa5; Bl., Ka3, Qb3, Bb5, Pa4. Red plays. Drawn. 1 Ra1 +, Qa2.

249. BM 123. Red, Kg6, Qf6, Bg4 and h6, Ph5; Bl., Ke4, Ktd4, Be3 and h3, Pg2, g3, and h4. Black plays. Drawn.

250. BM 125: Man. 15. Red, Kb1, Ba3; Bl., Kd4, Qd3, Bb4, Pc3. Black plays. Drawn.

[42] BM 118 with blank diagram, has text, 'Red plays. Drawn.' The solution is only sketched, but shows that the game reduced to R *v.* Q and B.

251. BM 126. Red, Kb5, Ra5, Qc5; Bl., Kd2, Qc2, d3 and e2. Black plays. Drawn. 1 Kc3, Qb4 +; 2 Kb2; 3 Qb3; 4 Kc2.

252. BM 127: RAS 23. Red, Kb1, Qh8; Bl., Kd3, Ba3, Pb3. Red plays. Drawn. 1 Kb2, B ~; 2 K × P; 3 Qg7, &c. By Maḥmūd Karmānī, RAS.

253. BM 128. Red, Ke8, Qd7 and f7; Bl., Kf6, Qd6, e7, and f5, Bg5. Black plays. Drawn.

254. BM 129. Red, Ke8, Re2 and f2, Qb3, Pb2 and c3 going to first line. Bl., Kb1, Re6, Kte7 and e5. Black plays. Drawn. 1 Ktd5 + d, Kf8; 2 Rf6 +, R × R; 3 Kt × R, R × Kt; 4 Ktd7 + r.

255. BM 135 (corr.). Red, Ke8, Rg1, Qh5, Bc8, Ph7; Bl., Kf5, Kte7 and g5, Qh8, Pf6, g7, h3 and h4. Red plays and Black wins. 1 Qg6 +, Kt × Q; 2 P × Kt +, K × P; 3 R × Kt +, K × R; 4 Kf7, Pg8 = Q +; 5 K × Q, Kg6 and wins.

256. BM 137. Red, Kc2, Qa1 and d2, Pb2; Bl., Kc4, Rf1, Ba3 and h3. Black plays and wins. 1 Rb1, K × R; 2 Kb3; 3 Bf1; 4 Bd3 m.

257. 1 Rc1 +, Kb2; 2 Qc3 +, Q × Q; 3 Rb1 +, Ka2 (or Ka3; 4 Rb3 +; 5 Kt × Q m.); 4 Kt × Q +; 5 Rb3 m.

258. 1 Ra7 +; 2 R × Q +; 3 Pb6 +; 4 Pb7 +; 5 Bc5 m.

259. BM 157 (corr.). Red, Ke6, Rc1, Bg4; Bl., Kg8, Ra8. Red plays and wins. 1 Kf6, Rf8 + (or Ra6 +; 2 Be6 +; 3 R m.); 2 Kg6, R ~; 3 Rc8 +, R × R; 4 Be6 + r.

260. 1 Ra8 +; 2 Qf6 +, Kg6; 3 Kte5 +, Kh5; 4 Kt × P +; 5 Qg5 +; 6 Ktg6 +; 7 Rh8 m.

261. 1 Re8 +; 2 Ktc5 +, Kc6; 3 Re6 +; 4 Qe4 +; 5 Rc2 m.

262. BM 161: AE 87. Red, Ka8, Bh6; Bl., Ka6, Ktg6. Black plays and wins. 1–4 K to e6, K to e8; 5 Kte7, Kf8 (or Bf1; 6 Ktf5, Kd8; 7 Kf7. Or 5 . . , Kd8; 6 Ktf5); 6 Ktf5, Bf4; 7 Ke5, Bd2; 8 Ktd6, Bb4; 9 Ktc4; 10 Kd5; 11 Kc5. Cf. No. 418 below.

263. BM 162. Red, Kg5, Pf5; Bl., Kh1, Ph2, Bd6. Black plays and wins. The solution does not agree with the diagram. It runs, 1 K makes a Q move; K to B4, K to B3, K makes a Q move attacking the B; 3 B to R3, K to B3; 4 K to B4, K to Kt3; 5 B to Bsq, K to Kt2; 6 B to K3, K to B3; 7 P advances.

264. BM 163. Red, Kd8, Qe4 and f3, Bb4; Bl., Ke6, Qd7 and f7. Red plays and wins. 1 Qd5 +, K × Q; 2 K × Q, Qe6 +; 3 Ke7, &c.

265. BM 164. Red, Kc7, Qa6, Bc8, Pe6; Bl., Kb4, Bf1, Pa5, b5, c5, and e5. Black plays and wins. 1 P × Q, B × P; 2 Kb5, Bc8; 3 Pa6, B × P; 4 K × B, Kc6; 5 Ka5, K × P, &c.

266. 1 Pg5, Bf4; 2 P × P, R × P? (Kt (e7) c6!); 3 Bc5, P × B; 4 Kt × eP, and wins the Bf4.

267. BM 171. Red, Kc8, Bg8; Bl., Kc6, Ktc4, Qe7, Bc5. BM 173 has Bg8 on f8 and Ktc4 on d5. Black mates with B. The two solutions are practically identical in the MS., viz., 1 Kt +, Kb8; 2 Q to c7 +, Ka8; 3 K to c8; 4 Q to a5; 5 Kte8 (BM 173 has e4, probably in error); 6 Ba3; 7 Ktc7 +; 8 Bc5 m. I do not see how in 171 the Bl. K can retain his position on c8, while in 173 1 Ktb6 +; 2 Qd8; 3 Qc7 is mate, and if ever Red plays Ktd6, B × Kt is possible. The solution seems unsound.

268. BM 172. Red, Kb6, Rg4; Bl., Kb8, Rh5, Qb5 and c8. Drawn.

269. BM 175. Red, Ka5, Ph4 and h6 going to h1; Bl., Kc5, Qd4. Black plays; drawn.

270.[43] 1 Rg4; 2 Rg3; 3 Bc5, Kh2; 4 Re3, Kg2; 5 Re2 +, Kf1; 6 Ke3; 7 Rf2; 8 Kf4, Kg1; 9 Kg3, Pe3; 10 Re2, Kf1; 11 Kf3; 12 Bd3; 13 Kg3; 14 Rg2 +; 15 Kh3; 16 Bb1; 17 Rh2 +; 18 Be3 +; 19 Bd3 m.

271. BM 189: AE 81 (after Red's 2nd move). Red, Kf8, Bc8; Bl., Kf6, Qc6, Pf7. Red plays and Black wins. 1 Ba6, Qd5; 2 Bc8, Qe6; 3 Ba6, Ke5 (so AE; BM plays Qf5; 4 Bc8, Qg6; 5 Ba6, Qh7; 6 Bc8, Qg8, &c.); 4 Bc8 (or Ke7, Kd5; 5 Bc8, Pf8 = Q +; 6 K × Q, Qd7; 7 Ba6, Qc6; 8 ~, Qb7), Qd7; 5 Ba6, Ke6;

[43] BM 181 with blank diagram is 'Black plays. Drawn. 1 BP queens, K to P; 2 K to Q3, K to Kt sq; 3 K to B2, Q +; 4 K to Kt2, K to Q2; 5 K to Kt sq. Drawn. Or 1 K to K sq, K to Kt sq; 2 K to Q sq, K to R sq; 3 K to Q2, K to R2; 4 K to K3, K to Kt3. Drawn.'

6 Bc4 +, Kf6; 7 Ba6, Qc6; 8 Bc4, Qb5; 9 Be2, Kf5; 10 K × P, Kf4 and Kf3 wins.

272. BM 190. Red, Ka5, Ktb8; Bl., Kd6, Ktc2, Qd4. Black plays and wins. 1 Kc7, Kta6 +; 2 Kb7, Kb5; 3 Kta3 +, Ka5; 4 Ktc4 +, Kb5; 5 Ktd6 +, Ka5; 6 Qc3, Ktc5 +; 7 Kc6; 8 Ktb7 +; 9 Ktc5 wins. 'This problem is excellent,' BM.

273. BM 192.[44] Red, Kd3, Pg6; Bl., Kf3, Be3. Red plays and Black wins. 1 Kd4, Kf4; 2 Kd3, Bg1; 3 Ke2, Kg3; 4 Kf1, Be3; 5 Ke2, Bc1; 6 Kd1 or d2; Ba3; 7 Kc2, Kf3; 8 Kb3, Bc1; 9 Kc2, Be3; 10 K ~, Bg1; 11 Kd2, Ke4; 12 Ke2, Be3. 'This is difficult,' BM.

274. BM 204.[45] Red, Kh8, Qe7, f6, and g5; Bl., Kte6, Qf7, g6, and h5. Either plays. Drawn. The diagram is defective (it wants Bl. K).

275. BM 205. Red, Ke6, Rb1, Ktb6, Bc4 and h6, Pa6, b5, d5, f5, h4; Bl., Ka3, Kte5 and h5, Qf3, Bc5, Pd4, e3, h3. Black plays; drawn. 1 Ktg7 +, Kd6; 2 Kte8 +, Ke6; 3 Ktg7 +, Kf6; 4 Kth5 +, Ke6, drawn. If 4 . ., Kg5; 5 Be7 +; 6 Qg4 +; 7 P × P m.

276. BM 206 (corr.). Red, Kb2, Qc3, Bc1; Bl., Kc4, Qb3, Pa2, f4 and h2. Black plays; drawn. 1 Pa1 = Q +, Kb1; 2 K × Q, K × Q; 3 Ph1 = Q, Ba3; 4–8 Q(h1)–c2, Bc1; 9 Qc4, Ka2; 10 Q(c2)d3, Ba3; 11 Kc2, Bc5; 12 Qb3 +, Ka1 draws.

277. BM 207. Red, Kf6, Qa1; Bl., Ke3, Qe4, Red plays; drawn. 1 Ke5, Qf3!.

278. BM 208. Red, Ke1, Pe3; Bl., Ke8, Pe6. Black plays; drawn. 'This problem is good.' There is a full analysis in the MS.

279. BM 209. Red, Ke8, Qc8 and d7; Bl., Kd1, Ktb1, Qe1. Red plays; drawn. Red K plays to centre of board with his Qs behind him, and if checked plays to f5 and back to e5 as soon as possible.

280. BM 210. Red, Kd1, Ktb1, Bc1 and f1; Bl., Kd8, Ra8, Bc8. Black plays; drawn. Red posts K in f2, Bs in f1, g1, and Kt in e3. If Bl. had had Bc8 on f8, he would have posted them similarly on the left wing.

281.[46] BM 211. Red, Ke8, Ra8, Qc8; Bl., Ke1, Rh1, Qd1 and e2. Black plays; drawn. No solution.

V. Problems from AE.

282. 1 Rh7 +; 2 Kte7 +; 3 Ktd7 +; 4 Ktf6 +, Kd8; 5 Ktc6 +; 6 Kt × P +, Kb8; 7 Ktc6 +, Kc8; 8 Rh8 +, Kc7; 9 Pd6 +, Kb6; 10 Ktd7 +; 11 Rb8 +, Ka4; 12 Ktc5 +; 13 Rb3 +; 14 Ktb4 +; 15 Ra3 +, Kb2; 16 Ra2 +, Kc1; 17 Ktb3 +, Kd1; 18 Ra1 +; 19 Ktd4 +; 20 Ktd3 +; 21 Ktf3 +; 22 R × Q +; 23 Ktf2 m.

283. 1 Rb1 +; 2 Ktb3 +; 3 Ktd4 +, Kc3; 4 Rb3 +, K × Kt; 5 Kt × P +; 6 Pf6 +, K × P; 7 Rf3 +, Ke7; 8 Rf7 +, Kd8; 9 Rd7 +, Ke8; 10 Kt × P +; 11 Rd8 +; 12 Re8 +; 13 Rf8 +, Ke5; 14 Rf5 +; 15 Ktb5 +; 16 Rf3 +; 17 Rd3 +, Kc2; 18 Ktd4 +; 19 Rb3 +; 20 Ktc2 m.

284. 1 Ra2 +; 2 Ra1 +; 3 Qb2 +; 4 Kt(a4)c3 +; 5 Ktd4 +; 6 Bb4 +; 7 Ktc2 +; 8 Ktd1 +; 9 Kte1 +, Kh3; 10 Ktf2 +; 11 Ktg2 +; 12 Kth3 +; 13 Kth4 +; 14 Ktg5 +; 15 Ktg6 m.

285. 1 Ra2 +, Kb3; 2 Ktc5 +; 3 Ra4 +; 4 Pb6 +; 5 Ba2 + d; 6 Re4 +; 7 Re6 +; 8 Rg6 +; 9 R × Q +; 10 Ktf3 m.

286. 1 Kta4 +, Kc2; 2 Rb2 +; 3 Ktc3 +; 4 Re2 +; 5 Qg2 +; 6 Re1 +; 7 Rf1 +, Kg3; 8 Kte2 +; 9 Rh1 +; 10 Ph6 +; 11 R × Kt +; 12 Kt × P +; 13 Re5 m.

287. 1 Ktb5 +; 2 Rd4 +; 3 Pf4 +; 4 R × Q +; 5 Ktc3 +, Ke1; 6 Rd1 +; 7 Rd2 +; 8 Re2 m. By Khaṭṭab ʿIrāqī, RAS.

288. 1 Rf8 +; 2 Rc8 +, K × Kt; 3 Rc6 +; 4 Bd7 +; 5 Ra6 +; 6 Ra3 +; 7 Kte3 +; 8 Qd2 + d; 9 Ktc2 +; 10 Rc3 m.

[44] BM 195, 199, 200 are blank without text; 201–2 are *mikhāriq*.

[45] BM 203 is text only. 'Black plays. Drawn. 1 R +. Red has only four sqs. safe. viz. R sq, Kt sq, B sq, and B2; if K to one of these, drawn; if K to Q2; 2 Kt to K5 +, K to K2; 3 other Kt +, 4 R m.'

[46] BM 212 is blank (text describes decimal chess), 213 shows the ordinary arrangement of the men, 214–6 are *mikhāriq*.

289. 1 Re8 +; 2 Rg7 +, K × R; 3 Kt(c4)e6 +, Kf6; 4 R × B +; 5 Rf7 +; Ke8; 6 Ktg7 +; 7 Kt(g5)e6 +; 8 Rc7 m.

290. 1 R × Kt +, R × R; 2 Qd6 +, K × Q; 3 Kt × Q +; 4 Kt × R, K × Kt; 5 Kc3, Kb5; 6–11 P to h8 = Q, Kc5 and b5; 12–14 Q to g5; 15 Qf4, Kd5; 16–20 Q to a3, Kc5; 21 Kd3, Kd5; 22 Qb4, Kc6; 23 Kc4, Kb3; 24 Qa3, Ka5; 25 Kc5 wins.

291. 1 Bc4 +, Kf1; 2 Rd1 +, Kg2; 3 Rd2 +, Kh1; 4 R × R +, K × R; 5 Ktf3 +; 6 Ktd4, Ph8 = Q; 7 Bf4; 8 Bd6 wins Kt.

292. 1 Ktc5 +, Kc2; 2 Kte3 +, Kd2; 3 Ktb3 +; 4 Qe4 +; 5 Ktc5 +, Kd4; 6 Kt × B +; 7 Pb5 +; 8 Bd6 +; 9 Ktb3 m.

293. 1 Kta5 +; 2 Pd5 +, P or Kt × P; 3 Ktd4 +; 4 Ba3 m.

294. 1 Rc7 +, K × R; 2 Ktd5 +; 3 Rc8 +; 4 Bd7 +; 5 Ra8 m.

295. 1 Ktg5 +; 2 Rf6 +; 3 Ktg7 m.

296. 1 Rf7 +; 2 Kt × Q +; 3 Rd7 +; 4 Bf5 +; 5 Rd7 m.

297. 1 Rg4 +, R × R; 2 Rf4 +, Kt × R (or R × R; 3 Ktg3 +; 4 Bb5 m.); 3 Ktc3 +; 4 Bb5 m. (RW says from a game Wazīr Miḥmundī *v.* ʿAdlī Shaṭir (Bl.).)

298. 1 Rd1 +; 2 Rg1 +; 3 Rg3 +; 4 Rg4 +, Kd5; 5 Rd4 +; 6 Rd6 +; 7 Rb6 +; 8 Rb8 m.

299. 1 Ktf3 +, Kf1; 2 Qg2 +; 3 Ra2 +, Kd1; 4 Ktc3 +; 5 Rd2 m.

300. 1 Rh7 +; 2 Ktf6 +; 3 Pe7 +; 4 (the position is now that of a favourite European problem, CB 1, &c.) Rf7 +; 5 Kte6 m.

301. 1 Rd8 +; 2 Kt × B +; 3 Ktf6 +; 4 Ktg7 +; 5 Rd7 +; 6 Pb7 +; 7 Rd8 +; 8 R m.

302. 1 R × Kt +, K × R; 2 Rb1 +, Ke2; 3 Bg4 +; 4 Rf1 +; 5 Pd5 +; 6 Rf5 m.

303. 1 Rh2 +; 2 Rg2 +, Kf1; 3 Rf2 +, Ke1; 4 Ktd3 +; 5 Rd2 +; 6 Ra2 +, Rb2; 7 R × R +; 8 Kt(g4)f2 m.

304. 1 R × Q +; 2 Ktc7 + d; 3 Rb7 +; 4 Rd7 +; 5 Re7 +; 6 Pc7 m.

305. 1 Kth4 +; 2 Pg4 +; 3 Ktf3 +; 4 Bf5 +; 5 R × P +, Kf4; 6 Ktd2 +; 7 Rf3 +; 8 Rg2 +; 9 Rf1 m.

306. 1 Re5 +; 2 Ktf5 +; 3 Ktg3 +; 4 Rh5 +; 5 Ktf5 m.

307. 1 Ktb3 +; 2 Kte3 +; 3 Ktd4 +; 4 Ktd5 +; 5 Ph5 +; 6 Pg5 +; 7 Rh1 +, Kg4; 8 Kte3 +; 9 Rh4 +; 10 Rc5 +; 11 Rd5 m.

308. 1 R × P +, B × R; 2 R × B +; 3 Kt × P m.

309. 1 Ktb6 +, Q × Kt; 2 Ra3 +, Kb7; 3 R × Q +; 4 R × B m.

310. 1 Ktb5 +; 2 Kta5 +; 3 Ba3 +; 4 Ktc3 +, K × Kt(c3); 5 Rb3 +; 6 Rd3 m.

311. 1 R(f7)e7 +; 2 Pe4 +; 3 Ba3 +; 4 Ktc8 +, Ka5; 5 R × B +; 6 Ra7 m.

312. 1 Pe2 +, Kg1; 2 Qh2 +, Kf2; 3 Qg1 +; 4 Ktf3 +, Kf2; 5 Pe1 = Q +; 6 Ktg3 m.

313. 1 Bf4 +, Kg1; 2 Rd1 +; 3 Rg2 +, Kf1; 4 Rf2 +; 5 Rf1 +; 6 Qg2 +; 7 Pf2 or Kth3 m. accordingly.

314. 1 R(c2)d2 +, Kt × R; 2 R × Kt +; 3 Pf2 +; 4 Ktg3 +; 5 Pf1 = Q +; 6 Rg2 m.

315. 1 Re8 +; 2 Rh8 +; 3 Kte7 +; 4 Rh8 +; 5 Ktg6 +; 6 Bf5 +; 7 Pg5 +; 8 Be7 +; 9 Ktg4 m. By Farazdaq Yūnānī, RAS.

316. AE 66. Red, Ka8, Pc5; Bl., Kh1, Pc4. Black plays and wins. 1 Kg2, Kb7; 2 Kf3, Kc6 (or Ka6; 3 Ke4, Ka5; 4 Ke5, Ka4; 5 Kd6, Kb4; 6 Kd5); 3 Ke4, Kd6; 4 Kf5, Kc6; 5 Ke5, Kb6.

317. AE 68: RAS 19. Red, Kg8, Ra5; Bl., Kh5, Rd7, Ktb5. Black plays and wins. 1 Kg6, Ra6 + (or Kf8; 2 Rf7 +, Ke8; 3 Ktd6 +; 4 Ktb7 + r); 2 Rd6, Ra8; 3 Ktc7, Rc8; 4 Ra6. By ʿAdlī Rūmī, RAS.

318. AE 69: RAS 51. Red, Ke8, Rh5; Bl., Kd5, Rg7, Kte5. Black plays and wins. 1 Ke6, Kd8; 2 Kd6, Kc8; 3 Rc7 +, Kd8; 4 Ktf7 +; 5 Ke6, Kf8; 6 Kf6, Ke8; 7 Re7 +; 8 Rd7, &c. By Surkh Shaṭranjī, RAS.

319. AE 74. Red, Kc3, Rh8, Qc2; Bl., Kc5, Rc1. Red plays and wins. 1 Rc8 +, Kd6; 2 Rd8 +; 3 Rd1 wins R.

320. AE 80. Red, Kd5, Bd7 and e7; Bl., Kc1, Qb4. Red plays and wins. 1 Kc4, Qa3; 2 Kc3, Qb2 + (or Kb1; 3 Bc5, Qb2 +; 4 Kb3, Q ~; 5 Ba3, Q ~; 6 Bb5); 3 Kb3, Qa1; 4 Bc5, Qb2; 5 Be3 +, Kb1; 6 Bb5, Ka1; 7 Bd3.

321. 1 Kta5, Ktf7; 2 Ktb7, Kf2 (or Kth6+; 3 Ke6, Ke4; 4 Ktd6+, Kf4; 5 Bd3, Kg5; 6 Ktf7+); 3 Kf6, Kth6; 4 Ktd6, Ktg8+; 5 Kf7, Kth6+; 6 Kg7. By Shams Karmānī, RAS.

322. 1 Kf7, Kh7; 2 Ktf6+, Kh8; 3 Kg6, Qg7; 4 Kth5, Qf8; 5 Kf7, &c.

323. 1 Ra8+, Ke7; 2 Ra7, R × R; 3 Bc5+r.

324. 1 Kte6, K × Kt (or R × Kt; 2 Ba6 m. Or R ~; 2 Ktb6 m.); 2 Ktf8+r.

325. 1 Be3 (or Rh2, Rh7), Rd1+; 2 Bg1, Rb1; 3 R~, R × Kt; 4 Rh2, Rb1; 5 R~, Re1; 6 R~, Re8; 7 Be3, R × B wins.

326. 1 Ktc7+; 2 Kt × R, K × Kt; 3 Kc4, Pc6; 4 K × B, Pc7; 5 Kc6, Pc8 = Q; 6 Kc7, Qd7; 7 Pg5, Qe8; 8 Kd8, Qf7; 9 Pg4, Qg6; 10 Pg3, Kf5; 11 Ke7, Kg4; 12 Kf6, Qh5; 13 Pg2, Kg3; 14 Kg5, Qg4; 15 Pg1 = Q, Qh3; 16 K~, Qg2; 17 K~, Qh1 wins.

327. 1 R × Kt, Q × R; 2 Kt × Q+, Kd6; 3 Kt × R, Pg4; 4 Kte8+, Ke7. Or 4 Kb3, Ke7; 5 Kb4, Kf7. Or 4 Kc2, Ph5; 5 Kd3, Ph6.

328. 1 Kt × Q+, Kt × Kt; 2 Q × Kt, Pb8 = Q; 3 Bd6+, Ke5; 4 B × Q, Pa7; 5 K × P, K × Q; 6 Kb6, Kd7; 7 Kb7, Qc4; 8 Kb6, Qd5; 9 Kb7, Qc6+; 10 Kb6, Bc1; 11 Kc5, Kc7; 12 Bd6, Be3+ wins.

329. 1 Rc2+, Kd3; 2 R × Kt, R × R+; 3 K × R, Ke2; 4 Kc3, Kf2; 5 Kd4, K × B; 6 Ph4, Kh2 wins.

330. 1 Ktc5+, Kc6; 2 Kt × R, Bf4+; 3 Kg3, Bd6; 4 K~, Kb6 wins.

331. 1 R × Kt, Kh4; 2 Kf7 (or Pe4, R × P+), R × R+; 3 K × R, Kg5 wins. Cf. No. 240 for a somewhat similar game.

332. AE 112. Red, Kb2, Ph2 (going to h8); Bl., Kb8, Pa5. Red plays; drawn.

333. AE 117. Red, Ke7, Bf8; Bl., Kg7, Pf7 and h5. Black plays; drawn. 1 Kg8 (or Kg6, Ke6; 2 Kg7, Ke7), Bd6; 2 Ph6, Kf6; 3 Pf8 = Q, Bf4; 4 Kh7 or Qg7+ or Ph7 all draw.

334. AE 118. Red, Ka7, Pb7 (going to b1); Bl., Kc7, Ph7. Black plays; drawn. 1 Ph8 = Q, Ka6; 2 Qg7, Pb6; 3 Kc6, Ka5; 4 Qf6, Pb5; 5 Kc5, Ka4; 6 Qe5, Pb4; 7 Kc4, Ka3; 8 Qd4, Pb3; 9 Kc3, Pb2; 10 Kc2, Ka2; 11 Qc3, Pb1 = Q+; 12 Kc1, Kb3.

335. AE 121. Red, Kf8, Qg8 and h8; Bl., Kg6, Qf6 and d7. Red plays; drawn. 1 Qf7+, Kh7; 2 Qg7, Q × Q+ (or Qg5; 3 Qg8+); 3 Ke7, Qc6; 4 Kd6, Qb5; 5 Kc5, Qa4; 6 Kb4 wins Q and draws.

336. 1 Pd7+, Kd8; 2 Kd6, Rf6; 3 Pg3, Pg6; 4 Pg4, Pg5; 5 Bc5, Rh6; 6 Be3, Rg6; 7 B × P, Rf6; 8 Be3, Rg6; 9 Pg5 (Bc5 is a transposition), Rg7; 10 Bc5, Rg6; 11 Be3, Rg7; 12 Bc5, Rg6.

337. 1 Kt(h2)f3+, Kt × Kt; 2 Kt × Kt+, Ke3; 3 Kt × R, Ke2; 4 Ktg2, Kf3; 5 Kth4+, Kg4; 6 Ktg6, Kf5; 7 Kth8, Kf6 wins Kt and draws.

338. 1 Rg7+, Kf1; 2 Rh7, Ke1; 3 Ke3, Kd1; 4 Kd3, Kc1; 5 K × P, Kd1; 6 Kd3, Ke1; 7 Ke3, Kf1; 8 Kf3, &c.

339. 1 Kf3, Ra7; 2 Kg3, Rg7+; 3 Kf2, Rf7+; 4 Kg3, Rf8; 5 Bc5, Kg1; 6 Be3+, Kh1. Drawn. B. abī Hajala describes this problem as difficult. His attention was drawn to it by Shihābaddīn Aḥmad al-Mitarjim, who had won money from an-Niẓām al-ʿAjamī at Damascus for solving it.

340. 1 Pc3, Rh1+; 2 Kc2, Pa4; 3 Bb5, Rh2+; 4 Kc1, Rh5; 5 Bd3. Man. 54 adds Red Kte1, gives Bl. the move and plays 1 . . , Rh1; 2 Pc3, R × Kt, and the position is that of AE 128 after the first move.

341. 1 Qb3+, Kb1; 2 Rh8, R × R; 3 Qc2+, Ka2; 4 Qb3+, Kb1; 5 Qc2+, &c.

342. 1 Rh2+; 2 Qg7+; 3 Bd3; 4 Bf5 m.

343. 1 Kta5+, Kb4; 2 Ktc6+, Kb5; 3 R × P(f5)+, P × R; 4 Rd5+; 5 B m.

344. 1 R × Kt+, Q × R; 2 Rb7+; 3 Kt × P+; 4 R × Q+; 5 Pg7+; 6 Kth6+; 7 Bf5 m.

345. 1 Rh2+; 2 Rg2+; 3 Rg1+; 4 Qf2+; 5 Pg2+; 6 Bf4 m.

346. 1 Rg8+; 2 Ktf8+; 3 Rg6+; 4 Pg4+; 5 Rh6+; 6 Kte6+; 7 Ktg8+; 8 Ktf8+; 9 Ktg6+; 10 Bf5 m.

347. 1 Rf6 ; 2 Kte5 ; 3 Ktd7 ; 4 Ktb6 ; 5 Ktd5 ; 6 Ktc7 ; 7 Kte8 ; 8 Ra6 ; 9 Re6 ; 10 Ktg7 + ; 11 Be3 m.

348. 1 Kf5, Qf4 ; 2 Ke6, Qe5 ; 3 Bb4, Qd6 ; 4 Qe7 +, Q × Q(e7) ; 5 Bd2 ; 6 Bf4 ; 7 B m.

349. 1 Ra2 + ; 2 Ra1 + ; 3 Qb2 + ; 4 Re1 + ; 5 Ktd2 + ; 6 Qc2 + ; 7 Bd3 m.

350. 1 Ka8, Ra2 + ; 2 Kb8, Be6 ; 3 Pc8 = Q, Bc4 ; 4 Qb7, Ra7 ; 5 Qc8 or c6, Qe8 ; 6 Qd7, Qc7 + ; 7 Kc8, B m.

351. 1 Ka2, Pb4 ; 2 Ka1, Pb5 ; 3–5 ~, bP queens ; 6–9 ~, Q to b4 ; 10–16 ~, K to a4 ; 17 Ka2, Qc3 ; 18 Ka1, Ka3 ; 19 P × Q, Kb4 ; 20 Ka2, Pd4 ; 21–4 ~, dP queens ; 25–8 ~, Q to d4 ; 29 Ka1, Bd3 ; 30 Ka2, Qb1 + ; 31 Ka1, Kta5 ; 32 Pc2, Ktb3 + ; 33 Kb2, Qc3 m. By Farazdaq Yūnānī, RAS.

352. 1 Qd5 ; 2 Qg5 ; 3 Rh3 ; 4 Rg3 ; 5 Rg5 m.

353. 1 Rg7 +, Kh8 ; 2 Rf7 ; 3 Rf8 + ; 4 Qf7, Ph8 = Q ; 5 Bd6 m.

354. AE 148 and 158a. Red, Kc5, Rh7, Pg2 (going to g8) ; Bl., Kc8, Pc6. Red plays. Mate on c4. The text is not clear but Red first queens P and secures the position Qc4, R on *e*-file, Bl. Kd8. Now 1 Kd6, Pc5 ; 2 R~ ; 3 Kc6, Kd8 ; 4 Re2 ; 5 Rd2 ; 6 Qb3, Pc4 ; 7 Qc2, Pc3 ; 8 Rd7 ; 9 Rd8 + ; 10 Re8 ; 11 Re7 ; 12 Ra7 + ; 13 Ra8, Kc4 ; 14 Ra4 m.

355. 1 Ka7, Ktb6 ; 2 Ka6, Ktc6 ; 3 Kb5, Kb7 ; 4 Kc5, Ktc4 ; 5 K~, Ktd4 ; 6–13 K to d5, K to d3 ; 14 Kc5, Qd6 + ; 15 Kd5, Qa4 ; 16 Pb3, Qb5 ; 17 Pb2, Qc6 m. (H.J.R.M.)

356. 1 Rc2 ; 2 Rc1 + ; 3 Qf2, Pg1 = Q (or Kd3 ; 4 Qe1, Kd4 ; 5 Rc5 ; Kd3 ; 6 Bf5 + ; 7 Qd2, Pg1 = Q ; 8 Qc3 m.) ; 4 Qe1 + ; 5 Bf1 + ; 6 Rc5, Qf2 ; 7 Qd2, Qe3 ; 8 Qc3 m.

357. 1 Rf8 + ; 2 Rg8 + ; 3 Rg6 + ; 4 Re6 + ; 5 Re4 + ; 6 R × P + ; 7 Rc2 + ; 8 Rc1 + ; 9 Rb1 + ; 10 Rb3 + ; 11 Rd3 + ; 12 Pc6 + d, Qc5 ; 13 R × Q + ; 14 Rd6 + ; 15 Rg6 + ; 16 Rg8 m. MS. has 12 Rd5 + ; 13 R × Q +, &c., but 13 . . , Ke5 is now possible, upsetting the solution.

358. 1 Rb8 +, Ktc8 ; 2 R(c7) × Kt + ; 3 Rc7 + ; 4 Rd8 +, K × Kt ; 5 Rc5 + ; 6 Rf5 + ; 7 Rf3 + ; 8 Kte2 + d ; 9 Qb3 + ; 10 Ktc3 + ; 11 Ra8 + ; 12 Ra2 + ; 13 Kt × R + d, Kb4 ; 14 Ra4 m.

359. 1 Rg8 + ; 2 Ktf8 + ; 3 Pg5 + ; 4 Pg4 + ; 5 Ktf5 + ; 6 Bf1 + ; 7 Rh8 + ; 8 Be3 + ; 9 Ktg3 + ; 10 Rh1 + ; 11 Kte4 + ; 12 Rd1 + ; 13 Ktd6 + ; 14 Rb1 + ; 15 R + R m.

360. 1 Ka7, Kc7 ; 2 Ka6, Ra8 + ; 3 Kb5, Kd6 ; 4 Kc4, Rb8 ; 5 K × P, Rb4 m.

361. 1 Ktd4 ; 2 Ra1 + ; 3 Kc4 ; 4 Ra2 ; 5 Re2 m. Cf. No. 360.

362. 1 Pg2 + ; 2 Re1 + ; 3 Pg1 = Q + ; 4 Qf2 + ; 5 Rg1 ; 6 Rg3 ; 7 Qg1 + ; 8 Rg2 ; 9 Qf2 ; 10 Qg3 ; 11 Rh2 + ; 12 Rh4 ; 13 Qf2 + ; 14 Rh1 m. (H.J.R.M.)

363. AE 158. Red, Kh6, Pf2 ; Bl., Kf6, Rg8, Qf3. Black plays. Mate on f3. 1 Rg5 ; 2 Rg6 ; 3 Qe4, Pf3 ; 4 Qf5, Pf4 ; 5 Rg3 ; 6 Rg4, Kh8 ; 7 Kf7 ; 8 Rg8 ; 9 Rg7 ; 10 Rg6 ; 11–14 K to h6 ; 15 Rg4 ; 16 &c., K to f1 when Red Kh2 ; now (1) Rh4 + ; (2) Rh8 ; (3) Rh3 m.

364. 1 Re1 + ; 2 Ktc3 ; 3 Rd2 + ; 4 Qc2 + ; 5 Ktg1 + ; 6 Qf4 + ; 7 Qc5 m.

365. 1 Qf6 ; 2 Rd7 ; 3 Qe5, Kc8 ; 4 Qd6 ; 5 Rd8 + ; 6 Re8 ; 7 Re1 ; 8 Ra1 + ; 9 Qc7 + ; 10 Ra4, P × R ; 11–13 P to b7 m.

366. 1 Rd1 + ; 2 Rb1 + ; 3 Bc4 + ; 4 Pe5 m. with P. Or 4 R × B +, Rf2 ; 5 Pe5 + ; 6 Kte3 + ; 7 Qg4 m. with Q. Or 7 Pg4 + ; 8 Rh1, Rh2 ; 9 Ktg2 m. with Kt. Or 1 Rb1 + ; 2 Rd1 + ; 3 Bc4 + ; 4 Ra1 + ; 5 R × R m. with R. Or 4 Qb4 + ; 5 Ra1 +, Ra2 ; 6 R × R + ; 7 Ra5 + ; 8 Rc5 + ; 9 Rc7 + ; 10 Ktf6 + ; 11 Bd6 m. with B.

367. 1 . . , Ke8 ; 2 Ke6 ; 3 Rd7, Ke8 ; 4 Qf4 ; 5 Re7 ; 6 Rf7 ; 7 Kf6 ; 8 Qg5 ; 9 Kg6 ; 10 Qf6 ; 11 Qe7 ; 12 Rf1 ; 13 Kh6 ; 14 Rf4 ; 15 Rg4, P × R ; 16 Kg6, Pg3 ; 17–19 P to h7 ; 20–21 Q to g7 m.

368. 1 Ktb5 + d ; 2 Ra8 + ; 3 Ktc5 + d ; 4 P + ; 5 P m.

369. 1 Re2 ; 2 Re1 + ; 3 Rf1 ; 4 Rf2 ; 5 Rg2, Kh3 ; 6 Pa5 ; 7 Rg3 ; 8 Rg4 ; 9 Kf4, Kh5 ; 10 Kf5 ; 11 Rg5 ; 12 Rg6 ; 13 Kf6 ; 14 Pa6 ; 15 Rh6 + ; 16 Rh5 ; 17 Rh7, Kg8 ; 18 Kg6 ; 19 Rg7 ; 20 Rf7 ; 21 Kf6, Ke8 ; 22 Ke6 ; 23 Re7 ;

24 Rd7; 25 Kd6, Kc8; 26 Kc6; 27 Rc7; 28 Kb6; 29 Pa7+; 30 Rc3, P × R; 31 Ka6; 32–35 P to b7 m.

370. 1 Rd8+; 2 Qd7+; 3 Kt × Kt+; 4 Kte6+; 5 Ktg5+; 6 Kth7+; 7 Pe6 m.

371. 1 Be3, Qh2+; 2 Kf2, Qg1+ (or Pg1 = Q+; 3 Kf3, Qg3; 4 K × Q, Qh2+; 5 Kf2 = position after Red's 11th move in main play); 3 B × Q, Kh2; 4 Be3, Kh1; 5 Kg3, Pg1 = Q; 6 Bg5, Qh2+; 7 Kf2, Qg1+; 8 Kf3, Qh2; 9 Be3, Qg1; 10 Kg3, Qh2+; 11 Kf2, Qg1+; 12 B × Q, Kh2 (or Ph2; 13 Be3 stalemate); 13 Be3, Kh1; 14 Kg3, Ph2; 15 Kf2 stalemate. Cf. No. 225 above. These positions are important for the history of stalemate.

372. AE 168. Red, Kc1, Bd6; Bl., Ka1, Pb7. Red plays and wins. 1 Kc2, Ka2; 2 Kc3, Ka3; 3 Kd4, Ka4; 4 Kc4, Ka5; 5 Kc5, Ka6; 6 Kc6, Ka7; 7 Kb5, Ka8 (or Pb8 = Q; 8 Kc6, Ka8; 9 Kb6, Qa7+; 10 Kc7); 8 Ka6, Pb8 = Q; 9 Kb6, Qa7+; 10 Kc7.

373. AE 169; Oxf. 164. Red, Kf5, Pc5 and e5; Bl., Ke7, Bf8. Red plays and wins. 1 Kg6, Kd7; 2 Kf6, Ke8 (or Bh6; 3 Pe6+, Kc6; 4 Kg5, Bf8; 5 Pe7); 3 Pe6, Bh6 (or Kd8; 4 Pe7+); 4 Pe7, Kd7 (or Bf4; 5 Ke6 and cP queens); 5 Kg5.

374. 1 R × Kt+, K × R; 2 Pe3+, K × P; 3 Ktg4+; 4 Kt × R, K × Kt; 5 Kh6 wins.

375. 1 R × Q+; 2 Bg5+, Kd7; 3 Rb7+, Ktc7; 4 Kt × Kt+; 5 Pc5 m.

376. 1 R × Q+; 2 Rd7+; 3 Pf4+; 4 Kth4 m.

377. 1 Re7+, Kt × R; 2 Ktf6+; 3 Pc7 m.

378. 1 Ra8+, Rb8; 2 R × R+; 3 R × B+; 4 Ph5+; 5 Be3+; 6 Rh4+; 7 Rh3+, Kg2; 8 Qf3+; 9 Rh1 m.

379. 1 Kth6+; 2 Rc6, Bd6 (or Ke5; 3 Ktg4+, Kd4; 4 Rc4+; 5 Rd8+; 6 R × R+; 7 R × B m.); 3 Rg6+; 4 Ktg4+, Kd4; 5 Rc4+; 6 R × B m. By Jamāladdīn Shīrāzī, RAS.

380. 1 Rc3+; 2 Pd5+, P × P; 3 P × P+; 4 Bd6+; 5 Rg2+; 6 R × P+; 7 Ktg2 m.

381. 1 R × B+; 2 Rg8+; 3 Bf5+, Ke6; 4 Ktc7+, Kf7; 5 Rg7+; 6 Kte6+; 7 Ktf6 m.

382. 1 Rh8+, K × R; 2 R × Kt+; 3 Bf5+; 4 Pg6+; 5 Rh8+; 6 Rh5+; 7 Qe7 m.

383. 1 Qb7+; 2 Ra7+, K × P; 3 Rb4+; 4 Ktc6+; 5 R or Kt m. accordingly.

384. 1 Qb4+; 2 Rb5+; 3 Kt × Q+; 4 Rf7+; 5 Rb8+; 6 Ktc6+; 7 Ra7 m.

385. 1 Ktc6+; 2 Rh7+ (Ktg7; 3 R × Kt+); 4 Pd5+; 5 Ba3+, Kb4; 6 Qc3+; 7 R × P+; 8 Pb4+; 9 R × B m.

386. 1 R × B+; 2 Rd8+; 3 Kt × Q+; 4 Kth5+; 5 Rg8+, Kh6 (or Kh7; 6 Ktf6+; 7 Pg5 m.); 6 Pg5+; 7 Kt m.

387. 1 Bd3+; 2 R × P+; 3 Re7+; 4 Ktb5+, Kc5; 5 Rc7+; 6 Qc3+, K × P; 7 Ktd4+; 8 Ra7 m.

VI. Problems from Alf.

388. 1 Kt(b6)c4+, Kc1; 2 Ktb3+; 3 Ktb2+; 4 Ktc1+; 5 Ktd1+, Kg3; 6 Kte2+; 7 Ktf2+, Kf5; 8 Ktg3+; 9 Ktg4+; 10 Ktf5+; 11 Ktf6+; 12 Kte7+; 13 Kt(f6)d5+; 14 Ktc6+; 15 Ktb6+; 16 Kta5+. Drawn, by repetition of moves. Cf. No. 82.

389. 1 Rg1+; 2 Rg3+; 3 Re3+; 4 Re1+; 5 Rc1+; 6 Rc3+; 7 Ra3+; 8 Ra5+; 9 Rc5+; 10 Rc7+; 11 Ra7+; 12 Ra5+. Drawn, by repetition of moves.

390. 1 Ktf6+; 2 Rd4+; 3 Rd7+; 4 Rb7+; 5 Kte4+, Kd5; 6 Rd7+; 7 Ktf3+; 8 Rd5+; 9 Ktf6+; 10 Rh1+; 11 Rh2 m.

391. 1 R × Q+; 2 Ktd5+; 3 Pd4+; 4 Kte3 m. Cf. No. 23 above.

392. 1 Pf2+; 2 Kte3+; 3 Pb2+; 4 Pa2+; 5 Pb1 = Q+; 6 Ktc2+; 7 Rb4+; 8 Ktb7+; 9 Ktc5+, Ka7; 10 Ra4+; 11 Ra6+; 12 Pd6 m.

393. 1 Rf2+, K × P; 2 Ktf4+; 3 Rg2+; 4 Ktd4+; 5 Ktc2+; 6 Kte1+;

7 Rc2+; 8 Ktf3+; 9 Rc2+; 10 Ktd4+; 11 Pb5+; 12 Ktc6+; 13 Rb2+, Kc5; 14 Kte6+; 15 Rb5+; 16 Bc8+; 17 Kte5+; 18 Be6 m.

394. 1 Kt×cP+; 2 Ktd6+; 3 Pb5+; 4 Be3+; 5 Ktd5+; 6 Rd4 m.

395. 1 Rc1+; 2 Re1+; 3 Kt×fP+; 4 Kte3 m. The first move is unnecessary.

396. 1 Re1+; 2 Ktc4+, Kc3; 3 Re3+; 4 Ktc2+; 5 Qb6+; 6 Rc7 m.

397. 1 Re1+; 2 Ktf3+, Kd1; 3 Kte3+; 4 Pb2+; 5 Ktd2+; 6 Pb1=Q+, B×Q; 7 Rb2+, K×P; 8 Kt×B+; 9 Ktc3+, Ka5; 10 Ktc4+; 11 Ra2 m.

398. 1 Re3+; 2 Re2+, K×Kt; 3 Rg2+; 4 Rg4+; 5 Pg6+; 6 Rh4 m.

399. 1 R×P+, Kb8; 2 Pc7+; 3 Ra7+; 4 Pa5 m.

400. 1 Re7+, Q×R; 2 Pf7+; 3 Kte6 m. According to F, this was the termination of a game between Maḥmūd Faḍil Pasha, the vizier of Muḥammad II, the conqueror of Constantinople, and an ambassador from the Persian shāh, Ūzūn Ḥasan. The latter had sent the ambassador with a jewelled chessboard and a demand for the surrender of certain lands in Asia Minor, basing his demand upon the envoy's invincible skill at chess. The vizier won the game, and the ambassador was expelled the court in ignominy. In revenge, Ūzūn Ḥasan laid waste the province of Takat. Pure romance this, so far as the present problem is concerned.

401. Alf. 56. Red, Kg8, Rb3 and b8, Ktb7 and e5; Bl., Ka6, Re8 and g3, Ktd8 and e6, Qf8, Pg4. Black plays. Mate in VI on d5. 1 Qg7+d; 2 Rh8+; 3 Rh6+; 4 Rf6+; 5 Rf4+; 6 Rd4 m.

402. Alf. 61 = 66. Red, Kg2, Ra6 and b7, Kte5; Bl., Ke8, Rf3, Qg3, Pf4, g4, and h4 going to 1st line. Black plays. Mate in V. 1 Ph3+, Kg1; 2 Ph2+, Kg2; 3 Rf2+; 4 Rf1+; 5 Rg1 m.

403. Alf. 62. Red, Ka8, Rg2 and h2, Pg3 and h3 (going to 8th line); Bl., Kd1, Rb3 and h8, Ktd6, Bg8. Black plays. Mate in III on a6. 1 Be6+d; 2 Rb7+; 3 Ra8 m.

404. Alf. 67. Red, Kh6, Rh7, Kta4 and c4, Pc6 (going to c8); Bl., Kc8, Rf1 and g2. Red plays. Mate in III. 1 Ktd6+, Kb8; 2 Rb7+; 3 Ktb6 m.

405. Alf. 68. Red, Kf1, Re7 and f8, Ktf5; Bl., Kf3, Ra2 and h2. Red plays. Mate in III. 1 Ktd4+; 2 Rg7+; 3 Rh8 m.

406. 1 Re8+; 2 Rg6+; 3 Kta6+; 4 Rb8+; 5 Ktc6 m.

407. Alf. 103: RW 18. Position in RW: Red, Ke8, Bf5, Pa5, f6, and h6; Bl., Kg8, Pa6. Red plays and mates with P. 1 Pf7+; 2 Pf8=Q; 3 Ke7+; 4 Qg7+; 5 Bd3; 6 Kf6; 7 Ke6; 8 Kf5; 9 Kf6; 10 Bf5+; 11 Ph7 m. The solution in Alf. follows European rules.

VII. Problems from Man.

408. Man. 3. Red, Kg7, Kth6; Bl., Kg5, Ktf4, Pa3 (going to a8). Black plays and wins. 1 Kth5+, Kh7; 2 Ktf6+, Kg7; 3 Kte8+, Kh7; 4 Ktd6, Ktg8; 5 Ktf5, Kh8; 6 Kg6 wins.

409. 1 Bc4+d; 2 Ra1+; 3 Rd1 m.

410. 1 Ra8+, Ra7; 2 R×R+, Ba3; 3 R×B+; 4 Pb2+; 5 Bc4 m.

411. 1 Re1+; 2 R(e4)e2+; 3 Pc4+; 4 Pc5+; 6 Ktb6+; 6 Re6+; 7 R×Kt+; 8 Bc8+; 9 Bf4 m.

412. Man. 14. Red, Kh8, Kte4, Pf5, f6, h7; Bl., Kf8, Pa4 (going to a1), Drawn.

413. Man. 59. Red, Kc2, Bb1 and g1, Pb3; Bl., Ke4, Bf4 and g4, Pa5, b4, and d4. Red plays; drawn. 1 Bd3, Pa4; 2 Bb1!, P×P+; 3 Kd1, Kf3; 4 Ke1, Ke4; 5 Kf2 draws.

414. Man. 61. Red, Ka6, Re1, Ktg4; Bl., Kd7, Rg7. Red plays and wins. 1 Ktf6+, Kc8 or d8; 2 Re8+; 3 Rg8, Rf7; 4 Rg7, R×R; 5 Kte8+r.

415. Man. 65. Red, Kb1, Rf4; Bl., Kc4, Re8, Qd4. No text.

VIII. Problems from Al.

416. 1 R×Kt+; 2 Rd1+; 3 Pe2+; 4 Kt×P m. Cf. No. 18 above.

417.[47] 1 Rh8+, Bf8; 2 Qd7+; 3 R×B+; 4 Kte6 m.

[47] Al. 21 is text only. 'Black plays; drawn.' The solution is 1 K to Bsq or B2, Kt ~; 2 P ~ draws.

IX. Problems from RAS.

(In the MS. diagrams the *h*-file is the 1st line. There are no solutions in the MS.)

418. RAS 10. Red, Kf2, Bg1; Bl., Kd3, Kte5. Black plays and wins. From a blindfold play of 'Alī Shaṭranjī.

419. RAS 11. Red, Kd1, Ktd8, Qd4 and e1, Bd7, Pb7, c5, f2, g3; Bl., Kh8, Rc3, Ktb6, Qb3 and d3, Bg4, Pa6, c4, c6, e6. Black plays and wins. 1 Qe2+; 2 Rd3+; 3 Rd1+; 4 Kta4+; 5 Pa5, Ktf7+; 6 Kg7; 7 Ra1 m. (H.J.R.M.) From a blindfold play of 'Alī Shaṭranjī.

420. RAS 12. Red, Kc3, Rd2, Qc4 and e4, Ba3 and f1; Bl., Kb1, Pa4. Red plays. Mate with a B. 1 Q(e4)d3, Ka1; 2 Rd1+; 3 Bc5; 4 Rd2+, Ka1; 5 Qb3, Kb1 (or Pa2; 6 Kc4; 7 Rd1+; 8 Q(d3)c2; 9 Be3; 10 Rb1, 11 Bc5 m.); 6 Q(d3)c2+, Ka1; 7 Kc4, Kb2; 8 Rd1; 9 Be3 and m. in two more with Bc5. (H.J.R.M.) By Surkh Shaṭranjī.

421. RAS 13. Red, Kb8, Rf1 and f2; Bl., Ke8, Rg7 and h7, Ktc5 and d6, Qc6 and d8, Bc4 and f8. Black plays. Mate with a B. 1 Rb7+; 2 Rb8+; 3 Kta6+; 4 Ra7+; 5 Ktc8+; 6 Ktc7+; 7 Bd6+; 8 B m. (Forbes.)

422. RAS 14. Red, Ke3, Ra1, Ktc2, Bg5, h7, Pa2, b3, c3, d4, e4, f3, g2, h4; Bl., Ke6, Ra8, b7, Ktf7, Qe8, Bc8, f8, Pa7, b6, c6, d6, e5, f6, g6. Red plays and wins. By 'Alī Shaṭranji (giving odds of R).

423. RAS 15. Red, Kh8, Rd6, g3, Kte3, Qc7, Ba6, f8, Pa4 (Black in MS.), b6, c5, f4, g6, h4; Bl., Ke2, Re1, f7, Ktd7, Qd1, Bf1, g5, Pc3, d5, e4, e7, f3, f6, g4, h3. Red plays and wins. 1 Rg2+; 2 Pc4+; 3 Rd2+; 4 Re6+, K×R; 5 Bc8+; 6 Qd6+; 7 Ktg2 m. (Forbes.) By 'Alī Shaṭranjī.

424. RAS 17. Red, Kd1, Re7, f7, Ktf6, Qb6, Pc5, f5; Bl., Kc8, Ra2, e2, Qb5, Ba6, d6, Pa3, b3, e4, h4. Black plays and wins. 1 R(a2)d2+; 2 Pb2+; 3 Rd1+; 4 Pb1=Q+; 5 Rd3 m. (Forbes.) By Farazdaq Yūnānī.

425. RAS 18. Red, Kf7, Rc7, c8, Kte6, e7, Qd6, Bb4, g4, Pa5, b6, c5, d5, e4, f5, g6, h5; Bl., Ke1, Rb2, f2, Ktc2, g3, Qb3, Bc1, h3, Pa4, b5, c3, d4, e3, f4, g5, h4. Red plays and wins. By Mas'ūd. (This looks like an early game position —each has played twenty-nine moves.)

426. RAS 20. Red, Kf3, Re4, h4, Qg2, Ba7, h3, Pb6, f2, h5; Bl., Kf7, Rg4, Qd1, e7, Bc8, d6; Black plays and wins. By 'Alī Shaṭranjī.

427. RAS 21. Red, Kd6, Ra8, e8, Qf7, Be6, h6, Pa6, c6, g7, h7; Bl., Kf2, Rb7, Qc3, Be3, f1, Pa2, b2, e4, f4, g3, h3. Black plays and wins. 1 Pe5+; 2 Rd7+, Kc4; 3 Rd4+; 4 Rb4+; 5 Rb7, Pc5; 6 B×P, Ka4; 7 Qb4; 8 Pb3 m. (Forbes.) By 'Alī Shaṭranjī (giving odds of R).

428. RAS 22. Red, Kd2, Pd5, e4, f7, h5; Bl., Ke5, Bf8, Pd6, h6. Red plays; drawn. By 'Adlī Rūmī.

429. RAS 25. Red, Kf4, Qe1, f2, f3, Bg1; Bl., Kh3, Pg2. Red plays. Mate with B. 1 Kg5; 2 Kh4; 3 Be3, Kh2 (Pg1=Q leads to a similar solution); 4 Qg3+; 5 Kh3; 6 Bg5, Qf2; 7 Qh4; 8 Be3 m. (H.J.R.M. This may involve the capture of the Q on the last move, but I see no other way.) By Maḥmūd Karmānī. Cf. 350.

430. RAS 30. Red, Ke6, Re2, g2, Ktf3, Qh2, Ba6, Pd6; Bl., Kf1, Rf4, f7, Kte4, f2, Bd3, Pd4, e3. Red plays and wins. 1 R(e2)×Kt+; 2 Rg1+; 3 Bc4+; 4 Rg3+; 5 Pd5 m. (Forbes.) By Farazdaq Yūnānī.

431. RAS 31. Red, Kc6, Rf8, Ktb4, c8, Qc7, Pb6, c5, d4, e6, g6; Bl., Ke4, Ra1, e2, Kta3, d2, Qb2, Bd3, g5, Pa4, b3, c4, e5, f4. Red plays and wins. By 'Alī Shaṭranjī (playing blindfold).

432. RAS 32. Red, Ke1, Rd7, Ktf3, Qd6, Be7, h3, Pa3; Bl., Kb8, Ra1, b6, Ktc1, e8, Bg4, Pb7, c3, c6, d5, f5. Red plays and wins. 1 Rd8+; 2 Bc5+; 3 Ra8+; 4 Ktd4+; 5 Ra4+, Kd3; 6 Bf1+; 7 Kte2+d, Rb4; 8 R×R+, Pd4; 9 R×P+; 10 Rf4+; 11 Rf2+, Kh1; 12 Ktg3+; 13 Be3 m. (Forbes.) By Muḥammad Kāzrūnī.

433. RAS 34: Oxf. 10: RW 14. Red, Kd3, Rc4, f2, Kte4, f6, Pa3, b3; Bl., Kd1, Re5, f7, Ktc6, Qd2, Be7, h3. Black plays and wins. 1 Rd5+, Kt×R; 2 Rf3+, R×R; 3 Kte5+; 4 Kt×R+; 5 B m. (Forbes.) By 'Abdallāh Khwārizmī.

434. RAS 35. Red, Kc4, Ktc6, Bd6; Bl., Ka4, Bc5, Pa3, b4. Red plays and wins. By Mas'ūd Shaṭranjī Tabrīzī.

435. RAS 36. Red, Kh8, Ra4, Qb2, c6, Bd6, g4, Pb5, h7; Bl., Rf7, h3, Kth5, b8, Qf4, f8, Bc5, f5, Pa6, c2, d5, e3, f3, g2. The diagram is much blurred; there seem to be Red men (? Kts) at c8 and e8, another Red man (? Q) at d3. The Bl. K is wanting (? Kd1). Red plays and wins. By Muḥammad Kāzrūnī.

436. RAS 39. Red, Kd1, Ktd6, Pe7 (going to e1); Bl., Kb1, Ktf1. Red plays and wins. By Abū'l-Fatḥ Hindūstānī.

437. RAS 40. Red, Ke5, Re1, Be3, h3, Pg3, h4; Bl., Kf7, Qe7, Bf8, g8, Pg6, h5. Black plays; drawn. By 'Alī Shaṭranjī (playing blindfold).

438. RAS 41. Red, Kf5, Rb3, h1, Ktc1, e2, Bf1, Pa2, d3, f3, h2; Bl., Kc8, Rc2, Ktc6, f6, Qe5, Ba6, h6, Pc5, d6, g7, h7. Black plays and wins. By 'Alī Shaṭranjī (playing blindfold and giving odds of R for P).

439. RAS 42. Red, Rh7, Ktb3, g3, Qb6, Pa2, a4, c5, d3, e4; Bl., Ka6, Ktf3, g4, Qf6, Be6, Pa5, b4, c6, d5, g5. Diagram omits Red K. Black plays and wins. From a game 'Alī Shaṭranjī (Bl.) *v.* Tajaddīn.

440. RAS 43. Red, Kd3, Ra1, Ktb1, h1, Qc2, Bf1, Pa2, b3, c5, e3, f3, g3, h4; Bl., Kf7, Re7, Ktb5, e4, Qc7, Pa6, b4, c6, e5, f5, g6, h7. Black plays and wins. By 'Alī Shaṭranjī (giving odds of R).

441. RAS 45. Red, Kd5, Re6, Bc4, Pa6, b5; Bl., Kb2, Rh2, Qe2, Bc1, Pa5. Red plays and wins. By Far'ūn Miṣrī.

442. RAS 46. Red, Kf3, Ra1, g1, Kta2, b1, Qg2, Ba3, f5, Pa5, b3, c5, d3, e4, g3, h3; Bl., Ke7, Rc7, d2, Kta7, Qa6, Be6, f8, Pb5, c6, d4, f7, g5, h5. Black plays and wins. By 'Alī Shaṭranjī (giving odds of Kt for P).

443. RAS 47. Red, Ka4, Rd6, Ktd5, Qg4, Bc4, f4, Pe5, h7; Bl., Kd1, Rb1, b2, Ktb7, e4, Bc1, Pc3, d7, f3, g7. Red plays and wins. By 'Alī Shaṭranjī.

444. RAS 48. Red, Kb7, Rf3, Qg4, Ph3 (going to h1); Bl., Kb5, Rc5, Qb6, Pa5, e3, h2. Red plays; drawn. By Surkh Shaṭranjī.

445. RAS 50. Red, Ka5, Bc4, Pa2, d5, e6, f5; Bl., Kd3, Qe5, Pd4. Red plays; drawn. By Ḥājī Niẓām Shīrāzī.

446. RAS 54. Red, Kb7, Rb2, c8, Pa6, b4, g6, h7; Bl., Kd6, Re4, Kte6, Bc5, d3, Pa5, h6. Black plays and wins. By 'Alī Shaṭranjī.

447. RAS 55. Red, Kf6, Re8, f7, Ktc7, Qb2, Bh6, Pa4, b6, c6, e6, f3, g4; Bl., Kf1, Rd2, e1, Kta2, b1, Qc2, Bc1, Pa3, b5, c3, d3, f2, g3. Red plays and wins. By 'Alī Shaṭranjī.

448. RAS 58. Red, Kb4, Rg7, Ktc4, g4, Qh5, Bc5, f1, Pb5, c3, d2, g2, h4; Bl., Kf5, Rc2, f4, Kta1, d6, Qf7, Bf8, Pe2, e6, h6. Red plays and wins. 1 Kt(c4)e3 +; 2 Pd3 m. By Bahā'addīn Shīrāzī.

449. RAS 60. Red, Ke2, Rh2, Kte3, g3, Pf3, g4; Bl., Kg1, Ra4, e7, Ktg6, Bd6, e6, Pf4, g5. The leaf has been repaired, and the position is uncertain; there appear to be other men. Red plays and wins. By Surkh Shaṭranjī.

450. RAS 62. Red, Kd2, Rc2, Ktb2, b3, Qe1, Bc1, d3, Pd4, f3, g3, h2; Bl., Ke7, Rb1, Ktb6, Qb4, Bd6, g4, Pa5, b7, e2, f4. Black plays and wins. By 'Alī Shaṭranjī (giving odds of Kt).

451. RAS 63. Red, Kd1, Ra1, g1, Ktd2, e1, Bc1, Pa5, b2, c2, f3; Bl., Kf7, Rh2, Ktb6, c5, Qe6, Bd6, g4, Pa7, c6, e7, f6, g5. Black plays and wins. By 'Alī Shatranjī.

452. RAS 64. Red, Kd7, Rb8, c6, Kta4, Qa2, Bc8, f4, Pd6, e5, f6, h4, h6; Bl., Kc2, Re1, g1, Ktc1, d1, Qc3, Be3, f1, Pa5, d5, e4, f3, g3, h3. Red plays and wins. 1 R × Q +; 2 Rb2 +, Kd3; 3 Ktc5 +; 4 Ba6 m. (Forbes.) The end of a game played at the odds of Kt for P.

X. Problems from F.

453. F 11 = 74: R 36 = 46. Red, Kb8, Ktb2, Qg5, Bc8, Pd4, e5, e7, f6; Bl., Kb6, Ra4, Qc6, Bc5, f1, Pf3. Black plays and wins. 1 Ra8 +; 2 Kc7; 3 Qb7 m.

454. F 12 = 75: R 33 = 43 = 66. Red, Kc5, Rh1, Qe6, Bd6, e2, Pf5; Bl., Kc2, Ra6, Ktc6, Qc4, Bf1, Pd3. Black plays and wins. 1 Pd4 +; 2 Ra5; 3 Rc5 m.

455. F 16 = 31 = 77: R 22 = 45. Red, Ke3, Rd4, g3, Bd3, Pe4; Bl., Ke1, Ra2, Qg5, Be6. Black plays and wins. 1 Re2 +; 2 Rf2 +; 3 Qf4 m.

456. F 18 = 19: R 11 = 78: Oxf. 46 = 92 = 145: RW 2. Red, Kd5, Rb5, Bd3, Pc5, d6; Bl., Kd7, Re4, e8, Bc8, Pa7, g6. Red plays and wins. 1 Rb7 +; 2 Rd7 +; 3 Pc6 +; 4 Pc7 +; 5 Bb5 m. By ʻAdlī, RW; by ʻOthmān Dimashqī, Oxf.

457. F 21: R 47. Red, Kh8, Kte5, Bg8, Pg5, h6; Bl., Kf6, Ra7, Qg6, Bf5, Pe6. Red plays; drawn. 1 Ktg4 +.

458. F 66: R 24. Red, Kd8, Ra8, c5; Bl., Kd6, Re2, h2. Red plays; drawn. 1 Rh5, R × R; 2 Ra6 +; 3 Ra5 +; 4 R × R draws.

459. 1 R × Q +, B × R; 2 Kth5 +; 3 Re2 +; 4 Ktf4 +; 5 Be3 +; 6 Bd3 +; 7 Ktc5 m. (3 Ktc5 +; 4 Rd2 +; 5 Be3 +; 6 Bd3 m. saves a move). Cf. No. 23.

460. 1 Ktg3 +; 2 Bf4 +, Q × B; 3 Ktg4 +; 4 Rf3 +; 5 Be2 +; 6 Rf5 +; 7 Qg7 m.

461. 1 R × Kt +, P × R; 2 Rh4 +, Kg5; 3 Rg4 +, Kh6; 4 Kt(e3)f5 +; 5 Rh4 +; 6 Rh6 +; 7 Be3 +, Kf4; 8 Rh4 +; 9 Re4 +; 10 Kth5 +; 11 Rg4 +, Kh7; 12 Ktf6 +; 13 Rh4 +; 14 Rh6 m. (H. J. R. M.). Cf. the following problem.

462. R × Kt +, P × R; 2 Rd4 +, Kg5; 3 Rg4 +; 4 Kt(e3)f5 +; 5 Rh4 +; 6 Rh6 +; Kg5; 7 Be3 +, Kf4; 8 Rh4 +; 9 Re4 m. (v. d. Linde).

XI. Problems from R.

463. R 82 = 84. Red, Ke1, Rh6, b7, Ktc6, Qa4; Bl., Ka6, Rd2, f2, Kte3, h2, Pg3, h4. Red plays and wins. 1 Ktd8 +; 2 Ra6 +; 3 Qb5 +; 4 Ktc6 m. Both diagrams are defective and allow Black pieces to interfere with the intended solution.

464. R 83: Oxf. 96. Red, Kb8, Ra2, g8, Kth2, Qe5, Ba6, d6, Pf6; Bl., Ke1, Ra7, h4, Ktb5, c5, Bh3. Black plays and wins. 1 Rb7 +, Kc8; 2 Rc7 +, Kd8; 3 Kte6 +; 4 Re7 +; 5 Rh7 +, Rg7; 6 R × R +; 7 Kt(b5)c7 m.

XII. Problem from S.

465. S 1. Red, Kf3, Ra2 and b2, Ktf5, g4, Qe3, Bb1, c1, Pe5; Bl., Kc3, Rh1, h8, Ktd7, g8, Qc8, Be6, f8, Pe7, g6, h7. Black plays and mates in XVIII.

XIII. Problems from Y.

466. 1 Rg8 +; 2 R(g3)g7 +; 3 Bf8 +; 4 Rg5 +; 5 Ktg2 +; 6 Rg3 +; 7 Rh8 +; 8 Kte3 + d; 9 Rg2 +; 10 Rh1 +; 11 Kt × Kt +; 12 Kt(c4)e3 +; 13 R × B +; 14 R × Kt +; 15 Ktd4 + d; 16 Ktb5 +; 17 Rb1 +; 18 Ktc3 +; 19 Rb5 +; 20 Bc4 +; 21 Ra5 +; 22 Bd6 +; 23 B m.

467. Y 5: Oxf. 43. Red, Ka1, Rb8; Bl., Ka3, Rd3, g2, Bf5. Black plays and wins (Mate in IV with B, Oxf.). 1 Rd1 +; 2 Rc1; 3 Ra2 +; 4 Bd3 m. By ʻAdlī Rūmī, Oxf. (which omits the Red men). Y adds two useless Bl. Kts on e3, d4.

468. 1 R × P +, Ke7 (or B or R × R; 2 Ktc5 m.).

469. Y 22. Red, Ke7, Rg6, Kte3, Qb6, Pc5 (going to c8); Bl., Ke1, Ra8, h5, Black plays and wins. 1 Re5 +, Re6; 2 Re8 +, K × R; 3 R × R +; 4 R × Kt.

470. Y 43. Red, Kc8, Rg2, Bb8; Bl., Kc6, Rh3, Bc5, Pg3. Red plays; Black wins. 1 Rd2.

471. Y 47. Red, Ka1, Qb8, Pa7 (going to a8), c5; Bl., Kh1, Ra8, Pc6. Red plays; drawn. Cf. No. 38.

XIV. Problems from Oxf.

472. Oxf. 2 = 63. Red, Kf5, Ra6, h2, Ktc6, e5, Be6, f4, Pg6, h5; Bl., Kd1, Re3, g1, Ktc2, g2, Qg7, Bc1, Pb4, f3. Black mates in V with B. 1 Kth4 +; 2 Ktd4 +; 3 Rg5 +; 4 R × Kt +; 5 Be3 m.

473. Oxf. 3. Red, Kh8, Rg3, h1, Ktf3, h2, Qg8, Bc5, h7; Bl., Kh6, Re4, g7, Ktg5, Bb4, g4. Black mates in V with B. 1 Ktf7+; 2 R×B+; 3 Re8+; 4 Be6+; 5 Bd6 m.

474. Oxf. 4. Red, Kf7, Qf6, Bd3, Pg3; Bl., Kh7, Pg4. Red plays and wins. 1 Qe7; 2 Qf8, Kh7; 3 Bf5+, Kh6; 4 Kf6; 5 Kg7; 6 Bd3; 7–10 Q to f4+; 11 Kf7; 12 Bf5; 13 Kf6; 14 Qg5+; 15 Bh3; 16 Kf5; 17 Pg4 m.

475. Oxf. 5. Red, Ka7, Ra2, b2, Ktb7, Qa8, Bf4, Pd5, f6, h6; Bl., Kh1, Rh7, Ktd6, g1, Qh4, Ba3, f5, Pa5, b5, g4, h3. Black mates with B. 1 Bc5+; 2 Rh8+, Kc7; 3 Rc8+; 4 Rc6+; 5 Ktf3+; 6 Re6+; 7 Re3+; 8 Qg3+; 9 Bd3m.

476. Oxf. 6 = 81. Red, Kb5, Ra5, Qc7, Bc5, Pb6, c4; Bl., Kb7, Ra8, h4, Ph5. Red mates in III. 1 R×R, K×R; 2 Ka6; 3 Pb7 m.

477. Oxf. 8. Red, Kc8, Rd3, Ktc7, Qf1, Bg5, h3, Pa2, f3, g2; Bl. Ka5, Rc1, f2, Ktf4, Qd2, Bb4, Pd4, f7, g7. Red mates in VI with Bs. 1 Ra3+; 2 Ra6+; 3 Be7+; 4 Rc6+; 5 Bf5+; 6 Bg5 m. Said to be by Khwāja Ḥāfiẓ Shīrāzī.

478. Oxf. 12 = 86. Red, Ke4, Rg4, Ktc4, h5, Bc5, Pa3, b3, d4, f5; Bl., Kf7, Rb8, h8, Ktb7, c8, Qf6, Bf8, g8, Pa4, b6, d7, e5, h6. Red mates in VIII. 1 Rg7+; Q×R; 2 Kt×P+; 3 Kt×Q+; 4 Ktf7+; 5 Kte8+; 6 Ktd8+; 7 Ktc7+; 8 Pb4 m.

479. Oxf. 13. Red, Kh8, Ph3 (going to h1); Bl., Kg6, Rf2, Qf8, Ph2. Black mates in VII with P. 1 Qg7+; 2 Rg2; 3–7 P to h7 m.

480. Oxf. 14. Red, Kb8, Re2, g2, Ktd6, d8, Qb7, Bh6, Pg4, h2; Bl., Kh1, Ra7, c7, Ktb4, d5, Qe8, Bf5, Pa5, b5. Black plays and wins. 1 R(c7)×Q+, Kt(d6)×R; 2 Ra8+; 3 Ktc7+, Ka7; 4 Pb6+; 5 Kta6+; 6 Qd7 m. This and the following are said to be by Jālīnūs, i. e. Galen!

481. Oxf. 15. Red, Kb2, Rg4, h4, Ktb1, d8, Qd7, Pb3, c3, e2; Bl., Kd5, Rf2, h2, Kta6, c6, Qb5, Bc8, d6, Pb6, c7, e5, f3, h3. Red plays and wins. 1 Pc4+, Kc5; 2 Ktb7+; 3 Pc5+d, Bf4; 4 R×B+, P×R; 5 R×P+, Ktd4; 6 R×Kt+, Qc4; 7 R×Q+; 8 Kta3 m.

482. Oxf. 16 = 146. Red, Kf7, Rd6, g6, Bd7, Pg5; Bl., Kh7, Re1, e8, Bg4, Pg7. Red mates with B. 1 Rh6+; 2 Pg6+; 3 Pg7+; 4 Bf5 m. Said to be by Saqrāt Hakīm, i. e. Socrates!

483. Oxf. 17. Red Ka3, Rc2, f4, Bf5, g5, Pd2; Bl., Ka1, Rc5. Red mates with Bs. 1 Ra2+; 2 Rf1+; 3 Rd1; 4 Bd3+; 5 Be3 m. This and the two following are said to be by Līlāj (the mythical Lajlāj).

484. 1 Kt(h7)f8+; 2 Ktf6+d; 3 Rd7+; 4 Kte6+d, R×R; 5 Rc7+; 6 Ktd7+; 7 Rc8+; 8 Ktc7+; 9 Qb7+; 10 P×R m.

485. Oxf. 19. Red, Kg3, Rd8, g1, Kta2, h4, Qc3, Ba3, h3; Bl., Ke3, Rb5, Ktf4, g4, Qd6, Be2, Pc4, e4, e6, g5. Red mates in V. I do not follow the solution in the MS. There is a solution in III—1 Ktg2+, Kt×Kt (or Kd3; 2 Kte1+; 3 Bc1 m.); 2 Rd1; 3 Bc1 or Qd4 m.

486. Oxf. 21. Red, Ka1, Rf7, g7, Kte5, Qg6; Bl., Kh8, Rb3, d7, Ktc3, d1, Qe6, Ba6, h6. Red mates in III with Kt. 1 Rg8+; 2 Qh7+; 3 Ktg6 m. This and the following are said to be by Amīr Tīmūr!

487. Oxf. 22. Red, Ke6, Ra8, f7, Kte7, f6, Qd6, Bc8, f8, Pa6, c6, e5, f4, g5, h6; Bl., Ke1, Rb6, d7, Kte4, g1, Bc1, f5, Pa5, c3, d3, f3, g2, g4, h5. Black plays and wins. 1 R×Q+; 2 Ktc5+; 3 Pc4+, K×Kt; 4 Ba3+; 5 Kte2+; 6 B m.

488. Oxf. 23. Red, Kc3, Ra8, b8, Ktc2, Bg5; Bl., Ka2, Ra4, g1, Ktb2, g3, Qd1, Pa3. Red mates in VI with B. 1 R×Kt+; 2 R×R+; 3 Kta3+, Ka1; 4 Ktc4+; 5 Ktd2+; 6 Be3 m.

489. Oxf. 24. Red, Ka4, Rg7, Kte3, e5, Ba3, Pb5, d4, e6, f6, h6; Bl., Ke8, Rb8, h8, Ktg4, h4, Qf8, Bc8, d6, Pc4, d5, h5. Red plays and wins. 1 Re7+. Q×R; 2 Pf7+, Kd8; 3 Ktc6+; 4 Kt×P+; 5 Kta5+, Ka8; 6 Ktc7+; 7 Bc5+; 8 Ktd5 m. Said to be by Shāh Jahān.

490. 1 Ktc4+, Ka2; 2 Qb1+; 3 Qa2+d; 4 Ktc1+; 5 Rb1+; 6 Ktd2+; 7 Ktd3+d; 8 Ktb4+; 9 Ktc4+; 10 Ra1+; 11 Bd3+; 12 Be3 m.

491. Oxf. 26. Red, Ka7, Rg1, g3, Ktd5, g5, Ba2, h6, Pd4; Bl., Kf2, Rb3, b8,

Kta6, e8, Ba3, Pc2. Black mates with B. 1 Ra8 + ; 2 Ktc7 + , Kt × Kt ; 3 Kt × Kt + ; 4 Bc5 m.

492. Oxf. 27 = 50 : RW 25. Red, Kf7, Rh1, Qf6, Pb5, h6 (going to h8) ; Bl., Kh8, Kta8, Pb6, h7. Red mates with P. 1 Re1, Ktc7 ; 2 Re8 + , Kt × R ; 3 Qg7 + , Kt × Q ; 4 P × Kt m.

493. 1 Kte3 + ; 2 Ktd3 + ; 3 Re1 + ; 4 Ktb4 + ; 5 Ktc4 + ; 6 Ra1 + ; 7 Bd3 or d7 + ; 8 B m. Cf. No. 490 above.

494. Oxf. 29. Red, Ke5, Rg4, h7, Ktd5, e4, Qa7, h8, Bc5, Pc6, e7, g3, g5 ; Bl., Kf7, Re1, g6, Ktc7, d6, Qd8, g2, g7, Bf4, g8, Pa6, b3, b7. Red plays and wins. 1 R × Q + , R × R ; 2 R × B + , Kg6 ; 3 Rf6 + , Kh5 ; 4 Rh6 + ; 5 Rh4 + ; 6 Rf4 + ; 7 Rf2 + , Kd3 ; 8 Rd2 + ; 9 Rd4 + ; 10 Rb4 + , K × P ; 11 Rb6 + ; 12 R × Kt + , Ke8 ; 13 R × Q + ; 14 Rf8 + ; 15–24 repeat moves 3–12 ; 25 Kt × Kt + ; 26 Rf6 m. Contrast with Nos. 82 and 388 above.

495. Oxf. 30. Red, Kf1, Ktf8, Qf7, g6, Ba3, f5, Pc3, h2 ; Bl., Kg5, Rb2, c2, Kta1, h6, Qd1, Bc4, f4, Pa2, b5, e5, g3, h4. Red mates in VI with B. 1 Kth7 + ; 2 Ph3 + ; 3 Ktg5 + ; 4 Bc5 + ; 5 Kte4 + ; 6 Be3 + ; 7 Bd3 m.

496. Oxf. 31 : RW 15. Red, Kd3, Rc2, c3, Be3, f1 ; Bl., Kd5, Ra4, f4, Bd6, e6. Black plays and wins. 1 R(a4)d4 + ; 2 Bg4 + ; 3 Rd1 + ; 4 R × B + ; 5 Bf4 + ; 6 Rd1 + ; 7 R × R m.

497. Oxf. 32. Red, Kc7, Ph4 ; Bl., Kc2, Rc3, Kte3, Bg5, Pa5, b5, c4, g2, h3. Black mates with Ps. Said to be by Shāh Aʿzam (D. 1707).

498. Oxf. 33. Red, Ka1, Rg5, g7, Ktc7, e7, Qg4, Be3, f5, Ph4 ; Bl., Kh8, Ra7, b4, Ktf6, f7, Qe8, Be6, h6, Pa2, b7, c4, e5, h7. Red mates in V with P. 1 R × P + ; 2 Rg8 + ; 3 Ktg6 + ; 4 Kt × Q + ; 5 Ph5 m.

499. Oxf. 34. Red, Kf4, Rg8, Ktb7, d7, Qc7, Ba6, Pa5, b6, d6, f5, h6 ; Bl., Kf2, Rb2, Ktg1, Qf3, Pa4, b4, c3, d3, g5. Black mates in X with P. 1 Kth3 + ; 2 Re2 + ; 3 Ktf4 + ; 4 Pb5 + ; 5 Kte6 + ; 6 Kt × Q + ; 7 Kt × B + ; 8 Ktc7 + ; 9 Kte6 + ; 10 Pd4 m.

500. Oxf. 37. Red, Ka1, Rg5, Kth4, Bf5, Pa5, f6 ; Bl., Kh8, Rb7, f7, Ktc3, h6, Qc1, Ba6, f8. Red mates in IV with Kt. 1 Ktg6 + ; 2 Kte7 + ; 3 Rg8 + ; 4 Ktg6 m.

501. Oxf. 39 (corr.). Red, Ka4, Rd1, d3, Kte2, Pd6 ; Bl., Kc2, Rg5, Ktd7, Qc6, Be3. Black plays and wins. 1 Ktb6 + ; Kb4 ; 2 Rb5 + ; 3 Ra5 + ; 4 Ra4 m.

502. 1 Ktd4 + ; 2 P × P + ; 3 Pc4 + , Kt × P ; 4 P × Kt + ; 5 Ktd3 m.

503. Oxf. 41. Red, Kh8, Pa5 (going to a1) ; Bl., Kf6, Qe7, Pa4, g5, h5. Black mates with P. 1 Qf8, Kg8 ; 2 Qg7 ; 3 Ph6 ; 4 Ke6 ; 5 Kf5 ; 6 Kf6 ; 7 Pg6, Kg8 ; 8 Ph7 m. Said to be by Sheikh ʿAlī Shaṭranjī (showing that his fame was not confined to his own day).

504. Oxf. 42. Red, Ka1, Ph3 (going to h1) ; Bl., Kh1, Rh2. Black mates with the R's first move. 1 Kg1 ; 2 Kf1 ; 3 Ke1 ; 4 Kd1 ; 5 Kc2 ; 6 Kc3, Kb1 ; 7 Kc4, Kc1 ; 8 Kd3, Kb1 ; 9 Kc3, Ka1 ; 10 Kb3 ; 11 Rh1 m. Called manṣūba mūsūmīya.

505. Oxf. 44 (corr.) : RW 24 (in X). Red, Kb3, Qc3, d2 ; Bl., Ka1, Pa2, b4 (going to 1st line). Red mates in VIII. 1 Qb2 + ; 2 Qa1 ; 3 Kc2, Pb3 + ; 4 Kc1, Pb2 + ; 5 Kc2, Pb1 = Q + ; 6 Kc1 ; 7 Qc3 ; 8 Qb2 m.[48]

506. Oxf. 52 = 93. Red, Kg7, Re2, g5, Ktb2, c3, Qd3, Bf8, g8, Pa6, c6, e6, g6 ; Bl., Kc1, Rf4, h3, Ktc8, Qb8, Ba3, Pb6, d4, e5. Black mates in IX with R. 1 Rf7 + ; 2 Rh7 + ; 3 Re7 + ; 4 Qc7 + ; 5 Re8 + , Kd7 ; 6 Rd8 + ; 7 Bc5 + ; 8 Rd7 + ; 9 Re7 m.

507. Oxf. 53. Red, Ke8, Rh2, Kta3, c4, Qf3, Bf4, Pb7, c3, d2, e7, f6 ; Bl., Kd1, Rh5, Kte6, Qc2, Bg5, h3, Pa4, a5, e5, f5, g3. Black mates with P. 1 Rh8 + , Kd7 ; 2 Rd8 + ; 3 Rc8 + , Kd5 ; 4 Rc5 + ; 5 Qd3 + ; 6 Rd5 + ; 7 Rd4 + ; 8 P + B m.

508. Oxf. 55. Red, Kd3, Ra2, b2, Ktd5, Qe6, Pf5, g4 ; Bl., Ke1, Rc4, f1, Ktd6, Qe5, Bh3. Black plays and wins. 1 Rf3 + , P × R ; 2 Bf1 + ; 3 Re4 + ; 4 Kt m.

509. Oxf. 56. Red, Ke2, Re8, h6, Ktc7, g4, Qg7, Ba6, d6 ; Bl., Kc3, Rc1,

[48] Oxf. 48, 49, 51 are of Feringhi (i. e. modern European) chess.

Ktc6, Qf4, Bb5, e3. Black plays and wins. 1 Ktd4 + ; 2 Rc2 + , Kf1 ; 3 Bd3 + ; 4 Ktf3 + ; 5 Rd2 m. (H.J.R.M.).

510. Oxf. 59. Red, Ka4, Rb8, h2, Ktc1, h5, Qg2, Bh6, Pa3, c6, e7, f3, g3, h3 ; Bl., Kg1, Rb2, f5, Ktd2, f7, Qc5, Bd3, g5, Pb6, d5, e5, Black mates in V with R. 1 Rb4 + ; 2 Ktc4 + ; 3 Ra4 + ; 4 Ra7 + ; 5 Rc7 m.

511. Oxf. 60. Red, Kc3, Ktd5, d7, Bc1, Pa3, e4 ; Bl., Ka4, Rb5, d2, Ktc6, e7, Qe1, Bd6, e6, Pa5. Red mates in IV with B. 1 Kt(d5)b6 + ; 2 Ktc5 + ; 3 Pa4 + ; 4 B m.

512. 1 Pc4 + ; 2 Pd3 + ; 3 Bf1 + ; 4 Ktd2 + ; 5 Bh3 + ; 6 Kte4 + ; 7 B × P + ; 8 Bf5 m. (By 'Othmān Dimashqī).

513. Oxf. 62 (no Bl.): RW 3. Red, Kf2, Rg6, Ktf6, g3, Qf1 ; Bl., Kh4, Rd6, f7, Ktd5, h6, Bf4. Red plays and wins. 1 Ktf5 + , Kt × Kt ; 2 Rg4 + ; 3 Qg2 + ; 4 Rh4 + ; 5 Ktg4 m. (By 'Alī Shaṭranjī, Oxf. ; from a game, Sa'īd Khātib *v.* Aḥmad Baghdādī, RW.)

514. 1 Rg8 + ; 2 Ktg6 + ; 3 Kte8 + ; 4 Ph5 + ; 5 Be3 + ; 6 Ktf6 + ; 7 Rh3 + ; 8 Ktg4 + ; 9 Kth2 + ; 10 R × P m.

515. 1 R × P + ; 2 Pe8 = Q + ; 3 Kte7 + , Kh7 ; 4 Bf5 + ; 5 Pg5 + ; 6 Qg4 + ; 7 Ktg6 + ; 8 Kte4 + ; 9 Ktf4 + ; 10 Ktg3 or Bd3 m. according as Black plays.

516. Oxf. 68. Red, Kd1, Rf1, Ktc6, Qe7, Bc1, h3, Pb3, c4, d2, g3, h4 ; Bl., Kd3, Rg2, g8, Ktc2, e6, Qe4, Bg4, h6, Pa2, f3, g7, h5. Red mates in VII with Kt. 1 R × P + , Q × R ; 2 Bf1 + ; 3 Pd3 + ; 4 Bh3 + ; 5 Kte5 + ; 6 Bf5 + ; 7 Kt m.

517. 1 Kt × P + ; 2 Rf7 + ; 2 R × P + ; 4 Ktc6 + ; 5 Qb8 + ; 6 Rb3 + ; 7 Ba3 + ; 8 Rb4 + ; 9 Bf1 + ; 10 Bc1 m.

518. Oxf. 70. Red, Ke8, Rd7, f7, Kta7, h1, Qe7, g1, Bf8 ; Bl., Ke5, Rb2, d2, Kte1, e6, Qc5, Ba3, Pe2. Black mates with B. 1 Rb8 + , Ktc8 ; 2 R × Kt + , Qd8 ; 3 R × Q + , R × R + ; 4 R × R + ; 5 Qd6 + ; 6 Bc5 m. (H.J.R.M.).

519. Oxf. 71 = 127. Red, Kh8, Pa3 ; Bl., Kh6, Re5, Ktf3, Pa2, e4. Black mates in VI with P. 1 Re7 ; 2 Kth4 ; 3 Ktf5 ; 4 Re8 + ; 5 Ktd6 + ; 6 Pe5 m. (By Ḥājī 'Alī Tirḥazī). Cf. No. 538.

520. Oxf. 72. Red, Kg8, Rb1, b8, Ktb6, e5, Qc3, Bd6, e6 ; Bl., Ka7, Ra2, g5, Ktc6, f5, Qb7, Be7, h3, Pf6, g7. Red mates in VI. 1 Ra8 + ; 2 Ktc8 + ; 3 Bc4 + ; 4 Kt × Kt + ; 5 Ktb6 + ; 6 Qb4 m.

521. Oxf. 74 = 87. Red, Kg4, Rb8, Kta5, c6, Qb1, e6, Bc8, f4, Pd4, d7, g3, h4 ; Bl., Kf1, Rc4, e8, Ktg8, Qh6, Bd3, Pe2. Black mates in V. 1 Ktf6 + ; 2 Kg1, Pg2 ; 3 Bf5 + , Q × B ; 4 Rc3 + ; 5 Re3 m. (By Khalīl Miṣrī.)

522. Oxf. 75. Red, Kg7, Rg6, Qf5, Bc5, Pg3 ; Bl., Kh5, Rg2, Be2, Pf4, h4. Black plays and wins. 1 Qg4 + ; 2 Be7 ; 4 R m.

523. Oxf. 76 = 125. Red, Kg4, Rb2, g6, Ph4, h5 (going to h8) ; Bl., Kh8, Pb3, b4. Red mates in VI with P. 1 Rf2 ; 2 Rf8 + ; 3 R(g6)g8 ; 4 Rh8 + ; 5 Ph6 + ; 6 Ph5 m.

524. Oxf. 77. Red, Ka4, Re2, f2, Ktf4, g4, Qc6, Bh6, Pb3 ; Bl., Kc3, Re4, h1, Ktb4, f5, Qd4, Be3, h3, Pb2, e6. Black mates in VI. 1 Ra1 + ; 2 Ktd6 + ; 3 Qc5 + ; 4 Kta6 + ; Pe7 + ; 6 Bf5 m.

525. Oxf. 78 = 84. Red, Ka8, Rb7, c1, Ktc5, d1, Qd4, Pa7, d5 ; Bl., Ka3, Rc6, Kte8, f7, Qb5, Pb3. Black mates in V with P. 1 Rc8 + ; 2 Ktc7 + ; 3 Ktd6 + ; 4 Kt × P + ; 5 Pb4 m.

526. Oxf. 79. Red, Ka2, Ra1, g5, Ktd8, Bc1, d7, Pb2, c2 ; Bl., Kh8, Rh3, Ktc4, Pa4, b4. Black mates with Kt. 1 Pb3 + , P × P ; 2 P × P + ; 3 Ktd2 m.

527. 1 Qf7, Kd7 ; 2 Re8 ; 3 Ke6 ; 4 Kd6 ; 5 Rd8 ; 6 Qe8 ; 7 Qd7 ; 8 Rc8 ; 9 Kte6 ; 10 Ktc7 ; 11 Ke6 ; 12 Kf5 ; 13 Ra8 + ; 14 Pa6 + ; 15 Pb6 + ; 16 Pc6 + ; 17 Pd6 + ; 18 Pe6 m.

528. Oxf. 85. Red, Ka7, Rg1, g3, Ktd5, g5, Ba2, h6, Pd4 ; Bl., Kf2, Rb3, b8, Kta6, e8, Ba3, Pc2. Either mates with B. Red by 1 Kth3 + ; 2 Bc4 + ; 3 Bf4 m. Black by 1 Ra8 + ; 2 Ktc7 + ; 3 Kt × Kt + ; 4 Bc5 m.

529. Oxf. 90. Red, Kf7, Pb7 ; Bl., Kf2, Re3, Bf1, Pb6. Black mates with B. The solution is only sketched.

530. 1 Ktf7 + , Kg7 ; 2 Kt × gP + d ; 3 R or Kt m. accordingly.

531. Oxf. 94. Red, Kg8, Rb7, h2, Ktf3, h3, Qg3; Bl., Kh6, Re1, Ktb5, Pf4, g4, h4 (going to 8th line). Black mates in V with P. 1 Re8+; 2 Ktd6+; 3 Pg5+; 4 P × Kt+; 5 P × Kt m.

532. Oxf. 95. Red, Ka8, Rf2, g2, Kte5, h4, Qb8, Pa7; Bl., Kh1, Rb5, e7, Ktd4, e6, Qf3, Bc5, d3. Red mates in III. 1 Rh2+; 2 Kt × Q+; 3 Kt × Kt m.

533. Oxf. 99. Red, Kh8, Ra2, Qa1, Pa3, b2, d5, e6, f7; Bl., Kh4, Rg3, Kte5, Qf6, Pc3. Black mates with P.[49]

534. Oxf. 101. Red, Ka8, Pf3, f4 (going to f1); Bl., Ka6, Rc6, Ktf2, Pb5. Black mates on a7 with P. 1 Ka5, Ka7; 2 Kte4, Pf2; 3 Ktd6, Pf1 = Q; 4 Rc7+; 5 Rc8+; 6 Pb6 m. (By Amīr Tīmūr; ? Feringhi chess.)

535. Oxf. 103. Red, Ke8, Pa3, d3 (going to d1); Bl., Kh6, Ra2, g7, Ktd2, Pe6, f6, g6. Black mates with Ps. 1 Kte4, Pd2; 2 Rc2, Pd1 = Q; 3 Ktd6+, Kf8; 4 Rf7+; 5 Rf8+; 6 Pe7+; 7 Pf7+; 8 Pg7 m.

536. Oxf. 121 = 124. Red, Kh6, Re7, Ktc6, Pg6; Bl., Kf8, Ktb7. Red mates in IV with Kt. 1 Pg7+; 2 Kg6, Ktd6; 3 Re8+; 4 Kte7 m.

537. Oxf. 129. Red, Kc6, Rb1, Ktd6; Bl., Ka7, Rh7. Red plays and wins. 1 Ktc8+, Ka8; 2 Ktb6+, Kb8; 3 Ktd7+; 4 R m.

538. Oxf. 154: RW 21 = 28. Red, Kh1, Pa4 (going to a8); Bl., Kh3, Rb2, Ktb4, Pa5, e5. Black mates with P. 1 Re2; 2 Re1+; 3 Ktd3+; 4 Pe4 m. Cf. No. 519.

539. Oxf. 160. Red, Kd2, Ktc1; Bl., Kb2, Kta3, Qe4. Black plays. Būrd.[50] 1 Ktc4+, Kd1; 2 Qf3, Ktd3+; 3 Kc3.

540. Oxf. 161. Red, Kc8, Rd8; Bl., Kc6, Rh1, Pe6 (going to e8). Black plays. Būrd. 1 Pe7, Rg8; 2 Rd1; 3 Rd6; 4 Rf6; 5 Rf8.

541. Oxf. 162. Red, Kf8, Rg7; Bl., Ke5, Rh1, Qe2, Pf7, g6 (going to g8), Black plays. Būrd. 1 Kf6. Cf. No. 26.

542. Oxf. 167. Red, Ka7, Ra6; Bl. Kb3, Rb2, Ba3, b1. Black plays. Būrd. 1 Bc1. (By Ṣūlī Mausilī, i.e. aṣ-Ṣūlī.)

XV. Problems from RW.

543. 1 Ktb1+; 2 Ra2+; 3 Ktd4+; 4 Pb6+; 5 R × R; 6 Qd3+; 7 Ktc2+; 8 Ktd2+; 9 Be2+; 10 Pg5+; 11 Pg4+; 12 Rh5+; 13 R × B+; 14 Kte4+; 15 Ktd4+; 16 Pf6+; 17 Pc6 m. (Played before Shāh Jahān.)

544. RW 6. Red, Ka1, Re1, g5, Ktc5, f4, Bb5, e3, Pd6; Bl., Ke8, Ra8, b4, Ba6, f8, Pf7. Red plays and wins. 1 Re5+; 2 Re8+; 3 Bg5+d; 4 Re8+; 5 Pd7+; 6 Kte6+; 7 Kt × P m.

545. RW 7. Red, Kg2, Ra5, d8, Qa2, Bd7, e7, Pa3, b2, b5, g6; Bl., Ke3, Rh3, Ktd2, e4, Qg4, Pf4, g5. Black mates with P. 1 Pf3+; 2 Pf2+; 3 Pf1 = Q+; 4 Ktf3+; 5 Kt(e4)d2+; 6 Rh2+; 7 Kte4+; 8 Rh4+; 9 Rf4+; 10 Rf6+; 11 Rd6+; 12 Rd4+; 13 Kt(f3)d2+; 14 Rc4+; 15 Ktf2+; 16 Ktd3+; 17 Kt × P+; 18 Ktf3+; 19 Rc1+; 20 Rg1+; 21 Pg4 m.

546. RW 10 (corr.). Red, Kc2, Ra7, c7, Qg4, Bb1, c1, Pb2, c3, e3, h4; Bl., Ke8, Rb6, h8, Ktf3, h7, Qe4, Bf8, Pb4. Black plays and wins. 1 Pb3+; 2 Rd6+, Bd3; 3 R × B+; 4 Rd2+; 5 Rd1+, Kg2; 6 Rg1+; 7 Kt(h7)g5 m.

547. RW 17. Red, Kg7, Re4, f2, Qd5, e6, g2, Bc5, f1, Pe2, g3; Bl., Kg5, Ra8, h8, Ktg6, h6, Bg4, h2, Ph4. Red plays and wins. 1 R × B+, K × R; 2 Qh3+, Kg5; 3 Be3+; 4 Pg4+; 5 Rf5 m.

548. RW 19. Red, Kb3, Rf2, g2, Bf5; Bl., Ka1, Rd1, h4. Red mates with B. 1 Ra2+; 2 R(g2)b2+; 3 Rc2+; 4 R(a2)b2+; 5 Rc1+; 6 Ra2+; 7 Bd3 m.

549. RW 20. Red, Ke1, Rh7, Ktd4, e4, Bg5; Bl., Kf8, Rh2, Ktf6, g8, Qh6, Bf4. Red plays and wins. 1 Kte6+; 2 Kt × Kt+; 3 Re7 m.

550. RW 22. Red, Ke1, Pa4; Bl., Ke3, Rd2, Pa5. Black plays and wins. 1 Rd5; 2 Rg5; 3 Rg1 m. Indian influence cut out the solution 1 Rd4; 2 R × P. Bare King.

[49] Oxf. 100, 102, 104–123, 128, 130–8, 141–4, 147, 151–9 are of Feringhi (i.e. modern European) chess.

[50] i.e. Drawn. See p. 82.

551. RW 26. Red, Kb4, Rb2, Ktd3, Qc2, Pb3 (going to b1); Bl., Ka1, Ktc3. Red plays and wins. 1 Rb1 +; 2 Pb2 +; 3 Qb3 m.

552. RW 27. Red, Kd7, Rc1, Bc8; Bl., Kb8, Pc7. Red plays and wins. 1 Rb1 +; 2 Kc3; 3 Ra1 +; 4 Ra2; 5 Ra8 m. (But why not 1 Kc6 and m. in III more.)

553. This is really a setting of No. 19; but in RW it is called *Dilārām's Legacy*, and a story is attached. An epidemic has devastated the Red forces, and the Red King is reduced to the necessity of approaching the Black King to beg for quarter. The Black King orders his Vizier to bring the Red King to his presence, but the Vizier pleads indisposition, and sends two soldiers (QBP and QKtP) forward one square for the purpose of executing the King's command. The latter, in a fit of passion at his Vizier's disobedience, slays him (remove Bl. Q from the board). This intemperate act shows the Red King that he can expect no clemency, and he resolves upon a desperate attack. At midnight he sends out his trusty horsemen, they surprise the sentries, and the Black King seeks safety in flight (1 Kt × gP +; 2 Kt × fP +). A hot pursuit ensues (3 Kte8 +; 4 Ktd8 +; 5 Ktc7 +; 6 Ktb7 +), in which the Red Vizier joins (7 Qb3 +), and the Red Elephant tramples the Black King to death (8 Bc1 m.).

Mikhāriq.

Finally it is necessary to say something about the quasi-mathematical problems in the Muslim MSS. which are based upon the moves of the chessmen. The most considerable collection of these is to be found in Man., and it is from this MS. that I have taken their Arabic name of *mikhrāq*, pl. *mikhāriq*, lit. 'invention, composition', which we may conveniently render *Exercise*, or *Puzzle*.

The most important of these Exercises is the *Knight's Tour*, the treatment of which in the Arabic MSS. reaches a higher level of achievement than do the examples of later date which I have quoted elsewhere from Indian sources. In its earliest form, both in India and among the Muslims, the Exercise seems to have been confined to the half-board of 4 × 8 squares. A player placed the 32 chessmen on the half-board, and then endeavoured to move one of the Knights from its position by legal moves in such a way that it captured one of the remaining 31 men on each of its first 31 moves, or in other words he endeavoured to visit each of the other 31 squares in 31 moves of the Knight. The next step was to extend the tour to the whole board, either by combining two half-tours (as in the annexed diagram and also in No. 555), or independently (as in 554, 556–7); and the third step was to make the tour re-entrant, i.e. to bring the Knight back to its starting-point on its 64th move (as in 554–6). This is as far as the early Muslim masters went.[51]

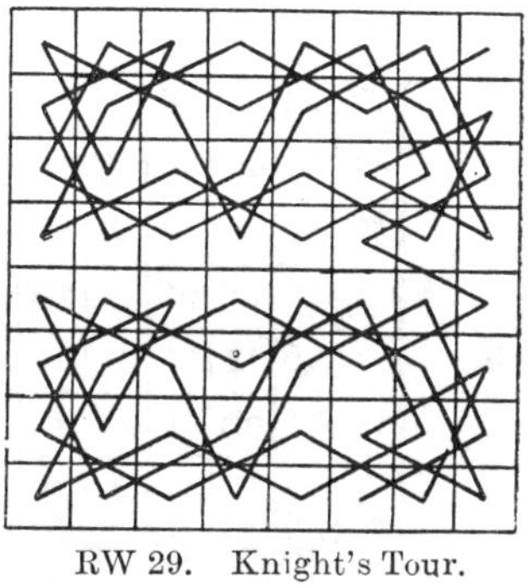

RW 29. Knight's Tour.

[51] Cf. my paper *The Knight's Tour, Ancient and Oriental*, BCM, 1902, 1. RAS in its preface undertakes to show how to describe tours on the whole, half, and quarter board, but the text was on one of the lost leaves The last is an impossibility. Both Oxf. (189) and RW 29) have tours. The former is identical with the tour in Nīlakaṇṭha (see p. 65); the latter is made by the union of two identical half-tours and is non-re-entrant.

554.

AH 91 : C 21 = 167

32	35	30	25	8	5	50	55
29	24	33	36	51	56	7	4
34	31	26	9	6	49	54	57
23	28	37	12	1	52	3	48
38	13	22	27	10	47	58	53
19	16	11	64	61	2	43	46
14	39	18	21	44	41	62	59
17	20	15	40	63	60	45	42

Knight's Tour

555.

AH 92 : C 21 = 168 : V 93

35	40	47	44	61	8	15	12
46	43	36	41	14	11	62	9
39	34	45	48	7	60	13	16
50	55	42	37	22	17	10	63
33	38	49	54	59	6	23	18
56	51	28	31	26	21	64	3
29	32	53	58	5	2	19	24
52	57	30	27	20	25	4	1

Knight's Tour

556.

H 73 = 75

60	11	56	7	54	3	42	1
57	8	59	62	31	64	53	4
12	61	10	55	6	41	2	43
9	58	13	32	63	30	5	52
34	17	36	23	40	27	44	29
37	14	33	20	47	22	51	26
18	35	16	39	24	49	28	45
15	38	19	48	21	46	25	50

Knight's Tour

557.

H 74

34	47	22	11	36	49	24	1
21	10	35	48	23	12	37	50
46	33	64	55	38	25	2	13
9	20	61	58	63	54	51	26
32	45	56	53	60	39	14	3
19	8	59	62	57	52	27	40
44	31	6	17	42	29	4	15
7	18	43	30	5	16	41	28

Knight's Tour by 'Ali C. Mani.

558.

AH 94 : C 22 = 169

49	42	40	51	9	34	36	11
47	52	54	45	39	12	14	33
41	50	48	43	37	10	8	35
55	44	46	53	15	32	38	13
61	22	16	63	5	26	28	7
19	56	58	21	31	64	2	25
17	62	60	23	29	6	4	27
59	20	18	57	3	24	30	1

Knight-Bishop Tour

559.

AH 196

37	14	16	35	33	18	24	31
15	36	34	17	19	32	30	25
13	38	48	11	21	26	28	23
39	12	10	49	27	20	22	29
9	42	40	47	61	50	52	63
43	8	46	41	51	60	62	53
45	6	4	59	57	2	64	55
7	44	58	5	3	56	54	1

Knight-Queen Tour

In AH (and C) we have a further refinement of the Exercise in the form of two tours (558–9) in which the touring piece moves alternately (*a*) as Kt and B, (*b*) as Kt and Q. Both tours are re-entrant, and are capital performances for the 10th century.

The solutions of these tours are given in the MSS. in various ways. Sometimes the successive positions of the Knight are indicated by numbering the squares (AH 91, 95, 197; C 20, 22, 167, 169; H 75 are all solved thus): sometimes the algebraical notation is employed, and the solution is given by the initial letters of the lines of a poem which give the notation of the successive squares touched by the Knight. In AH there are no less than four poems, the first by Ṭahir al-Baṣrī, the second by b. Duraid (D. 321/934), which give the solution of AH 92; and a fifth by ʿAlī b. Abī ʿAbdallāh ash-Shīrāzī solves AH 95.[52] A third method of concealing the solution was to write words upon the squares which, when read in the order of the tour, would produce a poem given in the MS. H 73 and 74 are solved thus.

The remaining mikhāriq follow. Of less interest in themselves, they are of considerable importance historically as illustrating the extent of the indebtedness of the earlier European players to Muslim sources.[53]

560. Man. 31: BM 201. The Kt on g6 undertakes to take the 8 Ps which are arranged on the diagonal a1–h8 in 15 moves. Solution: The Kt moves in succession to h8 ×, f7, e5 ×, d3, b2 ×, d1, c3 ×, e4, f6 ×, h5, g7 ×, f5, d4 ×, c2, a1 ×, capturing the Ps at the moves marked ×.

561. BM 202. The Kt on g3 undertakes to take the 16 Ps which are arranged on the two major diagonals in 30 moves. Solution: The Kt moves in succession to h1 ×, f2, d1, b2 ×, a4, b6, a8 ×, c7, e8, g7 ×, e8 (h5), f6 ×, d5 ×, c3 ×, e4 ×, d6, b7 ×, a5, c6 ×, e5 ×, f7 (g6), h8 ×, g6, f4 (h4), g2 ×, e1 (h4), f3 ×, d4 ×, c2 (b3), a1 ×.

562. To interchange the Black and White Kts in 16 moves without going outside the 9 squares. Solution: Each Kt plays in four moves to the opposite angle, the respective Kts being played in such a way that they avoid blocking one another.

563. *The mikhrāq of the seven Pawns.* To place 7 Ps in the position of the diagram, each P being a Kt's move distant from the one previously placed. To solve it, place the first P on a1 or c1.

562.

Man. 29.

563.

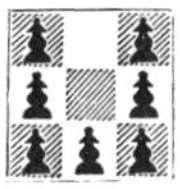

Man. 30.

564. Man. 35. *Aṣ-Ṣūlī's mikhrāq of the Pawns.* The eight Pawns are placed on the first row, and they are then to be moved to the 8th row, each P making 4 Kt's moves. Solution: Ph1–g3–f5–g7–e8, &c.

565. Man. 28: BM 214. Two Rooks are placed one on a1, the other on h8. Neither may cross a line commanded by the other. Whoever begins, loses.

566. BM 215. One player has 16 Ps arranged on the 7th and 8th rows; the other has 2 Rs on a1 and h1. The Ps should win, unless the Rs can get behind them. Even then the game can be drawn if 4 of the Pawns queen.

567. Man. 34. A similar game. One player has 10 Ps arranged on the 2nd row and on c1 and f1; the other has one R on a8. Here again the Pawns should win.

[52] V 93 is solved by Ṭahir al-Baṣrī's poem, which is also given in this MS. C 21 = 168 is intended to be solved thus, but the MS. omits the poems.

[53] Thus 562, 563, 565, and 568, are all repeated in European MSS of the 14th to 16th cc.

568. The *mikhrāq al-'afyāl*, the Exercise of the Bishops. The 4 Bs take all the other pieces, each taking 7 in 10 moves; or 40 moves in all.

568.
BM 216: Man. 33.

A brief note in AH f. 20 a (C f. 28 b: BM f. 127 a: and V) deals with a use of the chessboard as a kind of abacus for purposes of calculation. The note is taken from al-ʿAdlī's work, and the figure is given as one that could be conveniently used in cases in which it was inconvenient to do the calculation mentally or on paper. The calculation was to be carried out by the help of small stones that were heaped up on the squares as necessary. This is a parallel use of the chessboard to that which gave a name to the Exchequer in Norman England.

8	4 mill.	6	6 mill.	4	8 mill.	2	10 mill.
400,000	60	600,000	40	800,000	20	1 mill.	9
600	60,000	400	80,000	200	100,000	90	300,000
6000	4000	8000	2000	10,000	900	30,000	700
40,000	800	20,000	1000	9000	3000	7000	5000
80	200,000	100	90,000	300	70,000	500	50,000
2 mill.	10	900,000	30	700,000	50	500,000	70
1	9 mill.	3	7 mill.	5	5 mill.	7	3 mill.

Al-ʿAdlī's Calculating board.

CHAPTER XVI

GAMES DERIVED FROM MUSLIM AND INDIAN CHESS

I. Arabic games.—Oblong chess.—Decimal chess.—Chess as-suʿdīya.—Round chess.—Astronomical chess.—Limb chess. II. Persian games.—Citadel chess.—Great chess.—Other modern forms. III. Indian games. IV. Early Spanish games.

Most of our Arabic and Persian authorities devote some space to the description of various enlarged or modified varieties of chess. These would seem to have enjoyed a greater popularity in the East than they have ever obtained in Europe. But even there, these 'Bastard games', as v. d. Linde has called them, have seldom possessed the elements of vitality, though the innate conservatism of the Oriental, the want of originality of the later writers on chess, and the caprice of a monarch, may have given them the semblance of a longer life, and as a result they are not without some historical interest.

In dealing with these games I have found it convenient to adopt a method of grouping which is partly based upon historical and partly upon geographical considerations. My first group consists of the games that date back to the palmy days of early Muslim chess. These were so fortunate as to arouse the interest of the historian al-Maṣʿūdī. My second group comprises games of a later type, for which the encyclopaedia of al-Āmulī is our chief authority, together with the later games which have been invented in Muslim lands since his time. My third group contains the Indian varieties, many of which are of quite recent date. And, for convenience of comparison, I have added a fourth group containing the varieties named in the Spanish work of Alfonso the Wise of Castile, which are probably ultimately of Muhammadan, not Christian, origin.

The first group contains six games, of which al-Maṣʿūdī mentions five in his already quoted *Murūj adh-dhahab*.[1] Of some of these we possess fuller descriptions in several of my authorities, and though the texts are often incomplete and generally obscure, we can learn enough to present a fair account of nearly all the games. The six games are Oblong chess, Decimal chess, a variety of the game on the 8-square board called as-suʿdīya,[2] Circular chess, Astronomical chess, and Limb chess. I give a table showing where the accounts are to be found in the various MSS.

[1] Ed. cit., viii. 312–15. Cf. Gildemeister's translation in *Qst.*, 251–5.

[2] The spelling varies. The later MS. Man. writes *aṣ-ṣaʿīdīya* (with initial *ṣad*) with meaning 'belonging to Upper Egypt', 'Egyptian'. In the text I use the vocalized spelling given in the MS. AH.

Name of Game.	Maṣ'ūdī.	AH	C	BM	V	H	Man.	Al-Āmulī.
Oblong chess .	*	22 a	31 b		7 b		54 b	*
Decimal chess .	*	21 b and 23 a	29 b and 31 a	127 b		19 a	54 a	
As-su'dīya . .		22 b	29 b				54 b	
Round chess . .	*	21 a and 22 b	29 a and 30 b		8 a	19 b and 20 a	54 b	*
Astronomical game	*							*
Limb chess . .	*							

I. (1) Oblong chess, called by al-Maṣ'ūdī *al-mustaṭīla*, by b. 'Arabshāh *aṭ-ṭawīla* (long, oblong), by b. Abī Hajala *al-mamdūda* (lengthened), and by al-Āmulī *aṭ-ṭawila* or *al-mamdūda*,[3] was played with the help of the dice on a board of 4 by 16 squares. The pieces employed are those of the ordinary game, and they have the same powers of move. They are arranged across the narrow ends of the board, but the MS. diagrams show considerable variety of arrangement. I have noted the following. The opponent's arrangement is similar, but I give in brackets the position of his King.

(*a*) AH, C. Kc1(c16); Qb1; B a1, d1; Kt b2, c2; R a3, d3; Pawns on lines 5 and 7.

(*b*) V, Man. As in (*a*) except Kc1(b16); Pawns on lines 5 and 6.

(*c*) Al. (India Office). Kb1(b16); Qc1; B a1, d1; Kt b3, c3; R a3, d3; Pawns on lines 2 and 4.

(*d*) Al. (Elliott 274, and Bland). Kc2(c15); Qb2; B a2, d2; Kt b1, c1; R a1, d1; Pawns on lines 3 and 4.

(*e*) Al. (Vienna). Kc1(c16); Qb1; B b3, c3; Kt b2, c2; R a1, d1; Pawns on lines 5 and 6.

(*f*) Al. (Elliott 275, and Bland). As in (*e*) except Kb1(c16); Qc1.

(*g*) Al. (BM 16827, Fr. 175). As in (*e*) except Kc1(b16); Pawns on lines 4 and 5.

The text in AH, C, and V runs as follows:

This is the chess which is lengthened from the Indian chess. It contains 4 rows of 16 squares. It is played with dice used for nard. It is a rule that the arrangement is according to the right hand, with the Fīls in the corners. It is a rule that 6 moves the Shāh, 5 the Firzān, 4 the Fīl, 3 the Faras, 2 the Rukh, and 1 the Baidaq. It is a rule that when check happens to either Shāh, he must play by the die, and cannot play at all until the die gives a 6. By this he rescues his Shāh.[4] The cloth of this chess is made in two pieces, and the stations for nard are made on the back of each piece, so that a player can use it for this chess with the dice, or reverse it and use it for nard, as he likes. The pieces can be used combined or singly.

Since these three MSS. all distinctly state that their account of the derivative games is taken from al-'Adlī, this game was already in existence by A. D. 850, and it presents the earliest recorded instance of the use of dice

[3] V, in error, heads the diagram, 'This is the *shaṭranj al-hindīya*' (Indian chess). In the text, which is identical with AH and C, no distinctive name is used.

[4] There is a hiatus here in AH and C. V has 'and if it does not give one, he must remain for two moves'. The next sentence is corrupt.

to determine the moves of a form of chess. This makes the game one of considerable importance. Apparently it was played with a single die. It is described in al-Āmulī with the same interpretation of the throws. As a game, with or without dice, it is quite playable.

I. (2) Decimal chess, called in the MSS. *at-tāmma* (the complete), was played with the help of additional men upon a board of 10 by 10 squares. We have already seen that such a board was in existence for a game called *dasapada* (ten-square) long before the Christian era. But no allusion to any game on a ten-square board has been reported from the later Skr. literature, and I think it far more likely that we have here an independent Muslim creation than a survival of the use of the early Indian board. The idea of enlarging the eight-square board was evidently a favourite one with Arabic players. Besides the game described in the chess MSS., al-Masʿūdī mentions a variety that had been attempted by a certain al-Khalīl b. Aḥmad, who flourished from 100/718–175/791, and was, although no musician, the author of a work on harmony.

He also found no pleasure in chess until he had increased the number of pieces by a *jamal* (camel). Some of the crowd of chess-players played with it, but afterwards it was laid aside.[5]

Firdawsī also describes another variety, in which the new pieces are Camels (Per. *shutur*), in his account of the invention of chess in the *Shāhnāma*. In this game the Camels were stationed—not at the extremities of the line of pieces, as in b. Aḥmad's game—but between the Faras and Fīl, and their power of move was the complement of that of the Fīl in Muslim chess, to wit, in the four rectilineal directions a leap over one square, whether occupied or not, into the square beyond. It is the move ascribed to the Fīl in Indian chess in the early Arabic account quoted on p. 57.

In the Complete chess of the MSS. the full complement of pieces is obtained by adding two pieces called *Dabbāba* (the military instrument called by the Romans *Vinea*, and in the Middle Ages *Sow*) and two Pawns to the forces on either side. The Dabbābas were placed between the Fīl and the Shāh and between the Fīl and the Firzān. Their move was identical with that of the Shāh, one square in any direction. The 10 Pawns were arranged on the 3rd line. The MSS.[6] say:

There is the *Complete chess*, whose squares are 10 by 10, and it is increased by 4 pieces of one kind, called *dabbāba*. Their places are between the Fīl and Shāh, and between the Firzān and Fīl. Their figure is fashioned square, the head furrowed, and of the same height as the Firzān. Their move is the Shāh's move, only they both take and can be taken. Their value is between that of Rukh and Faras. $\frac{5}{6}$ dirhem. It is a rule that when one of the two Shāhs has won his opponent's square, it is half the *qamar*. Also a Baidaq cannot queen while the Firzān is on the board; if a player queens one, the other takes it. Also the Shāh must play when he has no pieces left. When the game is set up, the pieces are arranged, then a line is left, and the Baidaqs are set up.

[5] Also mentioned in b. Nubāta's Commentary on b. Zaidūn: 'He has placed two Camels at the two sides of the board, wherewith people played for a time long, but this was then abandoned.' B. Nubāta died 768/1366–7.

[6] My translation is derived from a text produced by the collation of the sections in AH, C, BM, H, and Man.

Bland, quoting from RAS, describes the *dabbāba* as 'shaped like an inkstand, six-sided, and on the top it has a knob as an inkstand has'.

The restriction placed upon Pawn-promotion is interesting, since similar restrictions have existed from time to time in the ordinary chess. The half-win is curious, but not described sufficiently explicitly.[7]

I. (3) AH and Man. conclude their account of the Decimal chess by a reference to a variety of chess that was played upon the ordinary 8-square board under the name of *ash-shaṭranj as-suʿdīya* (or *aṣ-ṣaʿīdīya*). Unfortunately description in each MS. is defective, breaking off at the same point. The last quotation continues:

And in like manner the chess *as-suʿdīya* is set up, except that its squares are 8 as in the Indian chess. The rule in *as-suʿdīya* is as aforesaid in that a Baidaq cannot be queened, and when one is queened—[here the MSS. break off].

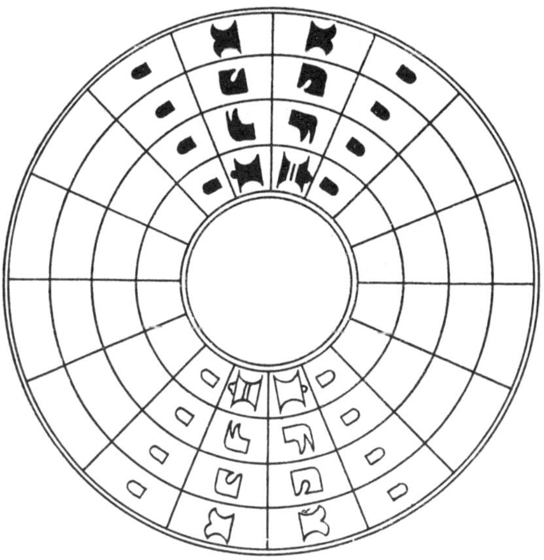

Round or Byzantine chess.

We have therefore (*a*) the Pawns arranged on the 3rd line, (*b*) only one Firzān allowed at a time.

I. (4) Round chess, called in AH, C, V, and Man. *ar-Rūmīya* (Byzantine), and in al-Masʿūdī[8] and Al. *al-mudawara* (circular), was played upon a circular board of 64 squares, arranged in 4 concentric rings of 16 squares. The men of the ordinary chess are employed and the arrangement of the earlier MSS. is shown in the diagram. Most MSS. of Al. reverse the arrangement of the pieces entirely, placing the Shāhs and Firzāns on the outer ring, and also continue the diagonals bounding the quadrants in which the men are placed right across the central space, thus creating four additional squares, which al-Āmulī calls *ḥuṣūn* (sing. *ḥiṣn*), or citadels. If a player can play his Shāh to one of these squares he cannot lose the game. This is an addition entirely in accordance with the taste of al-Āmulī's time. The game is thus described in AH and V:

This is the *Byzantine chess* which Siwār al-Ḥarrānī gave to Dhū'l-Yamīnain Ṭāhir b. al-Ḥusain b. Muṣʿab, when he resided in Mesopotamia.[9] We see that its properties, the number of its squares, and its form resemble the Indian chess, except

[7] ? Half the stakes. The verb *qamara* means to gamble, play for a stake.

[8] 'The round board (*al-āla al-muddawara*), which is ascribed to the Byzantines (*ar-Rūm*).' It is a pity that the MSS. attempt no justification for the name.

[9] Ṭāhir was the general who won the crown for al-Ma'mūn; he was at one time Governor of Mesopotamia. He died 207/822 (B. Khallikān, ed. cit., i. 649).

that the Indian Baidaq can queen because it has a limit, while the Byzantine Baidaq cannot queen because it has no limit. The squares of the Byzantine Rukh exceed those of the Indian Rukh, and the squares of the Indian Faras exceed those of the Byzantine Faras. The Indian game is longer than the Byzantine, and there is no difference between them except that the Indian plan is square and the Byzantine round. The Byzantine Fīls are concordant while the Indian are not. It is agreed that the Byzantine game is more modern than the Indian: the original, as people agree, is the Indian. It is a rule that when 2 Baidaqs of one species[10] meet, the player of the other species takes them for nothing.

The game is quite playable, and an attempt was made to revive it in London, Calcutta, and in Germany in the first half of last century as a result of a reference to it in Twiss's *Chess* (London, 1789, ii. 9).[11] It is mentioned in the AF. MS. Brit. Mus., Cotton, B. ix, f. 9 a, where there is a diagram of the board. The explanatory text has been completely erased.[12]

I. (5) Only al-Maṣʿūdī and al-Āmulī of my Eastern authorities mention the Astronomical game. Unfortunately only two of the Al. MSS. which I have seen attempt to diagram the board, and their figures are incomplete and unintelligible. It is possibly the game of *Escaques,* described below from Alf. Al-Maṣʿūdī's account runs:

Next, the round Astronomical board which is called *al-falakīya* (the celestial). It has 12 squares, corresponding to the number of the constellations of the zodiac, divided into two halves. Seven pieces of different colours move on it, in agreement with the number and colours of the 5 planets and 2 luminaries.

I. (6) Al-Maṣʿūdī is our only authority for Limb chess. He says:

Then there is another board, called that of the limbs (*al-jawārḥīya*), which has been discovered in our time. It contains 7 by 8 squares. There are 12 pieces, on each side 6, and each of the 6 is called after a human limb, i.e. the limbs by which we speak, hear, see, grasp, and move—these are the (five) senses—and the universal sense belonging to the heart.

As al-Maṣʿūdī gives no diagrams we cannot tell how the board was arranged or how the game was played.[13] Probably it never really lived.

I commence my second group with the games described by al-Āmulī in the *Nafā'is al-funūn.* These are five in number, but three of them—Oblong, Round, and Astronomical chess—are practically identical with games which I have already described. The other two are a new variety of Decimal chess, called *Shaṭranj al-ḥuṣūn*, or Citadel chess, and the *Shaṭranj al-kabīr*, or Great chess.

[10] By 'species' we are to understand 'side' or 'colour'. When two Ps had been played right round the ring and blocked one another, the opponent simply removed them.

[11] Lala Raja Babu gives two varieties in his *Mo'allim ul-shaṭranj* (193), of which the first is al-Āmulī's game, and the second only differs in omitting four of the vacant rows between the players, two on each side. The India Office MS. Al. arranges the major pieces on the outer ring, and the Pawns on the next ring, the arrangement of each side being that of the ordinary chess. This is palpably wrong.

[12] V. d. Linde, *Leerboek*, Utrecht, 1876, p. 256, states that the text begins, 'Tabula rotunda greci usi sunt.' When I examined the MS. I could not read even as much as this.

The historian b. 'Arabshāh saw both the Oblong and the Round games at 'Alī Shaṭranjī's house. See p. 205, above.

[13] V. d. Linde (i. 66, 108, and Fig. 113) has fallen into error through relying upon v. Hammer-Purgstall's mistranslation of the passage from al-Maṣʿūdī in his *Literatur-Geschichte der Araber*, iv. 537–8.

II. (7) This game is very carelessly diagrammed in all the MSS. that I have seen, but the board differs from the earlier board by the addition of four extra squares, called citadels (*ḥiṣn*, pl. *ḥuṣūn*), at the four corners of the board. Elliott 274 places these squares in the 1st and 10th rows, outside the Rooks' squares; Elliott 275, Vienna, and B.M. 23555 place them directly behind the Rooks' squares; while Fr. 175, India Office, and B.M. 15827 place them diagonally behind, as if at the angles of a 12 × 12 board. These squares were privileged, in that a player could at any time draw the game if he succeeded in playing his King to one of them—probably, though not always expressly stated, the citadel selected had to be one on the opponent's side of the board. The extra pieces are two Pawns and two Dabbābas on each side. These are placed between Fīl and Shāh and Fīl and Fīrzan, and move 'like the Rukh but obliquely', i. e. like the modern European Bishop. The Pawns are arranged on the 2nd and 9th rows; Elliott 275, Vienna, and B.M. 23555 have the Ks on e1 and e10; B.M. 16827 and Fr. 175 have them on f1 and e10.[14]

II. (8) Great chess, *shaṭranj al-Kabīr*, was played on a board of 11 × 10 squares which had two additional *citadels*, one at the right-hand extremity of the 2nd row of 11 squares, the other at the left-hand extremity of the 9th row. Only Elliott 274 of the Al. MSS. attempts to diagram this game, but RAS gives a full description of it under the name of *shaṭranj kāmil*, perfect or complete chess, and most MSS. of b. ʿArabshāh's *ʿAjā'ib al-maqdūr fī nawā'ib Tīmūr* give diagrams of it as being the favourite chess of Tīmūr himself.

Owing partly to Tīmūr's preference, partly to the lengthy analysis of the peculiarities of the game in RAS, and partly to Forbes's lengthy and laudatory account in his *History of Chess* (138–154), this variety of chess—obsolete in the East since Tīmūr's day—has obtained a notoriety beyond its deserts.

In addition to the pieces of the ordinary chess the game included (1) a *Wazīr* (vizier), made like the Firzān, and moving one square in the four rectilineal directions; (2) two *Dabbābas*, made like a six-sided inkstand with a knob on the top, and moving with a leap into the 3rd square in the four rectilineal directions; (3) two *Ṭalīʿas* (scouts), made like the *Fīl*, but with two faces, and moving like the modern European Bishop except that they could not move one step only; (4) two *Jamals* (camels), made like a camel with head, neck, and hump, but without fore-paws or hind-feet like the other pieces, and moving with a slant leap to the opposite corner of a rectangle 2 × 4; (5) two *Zurāfas* (giraffes), made like the Asp or Faras, but with two faces, and moving with a slant move compounded of a diagonal move of one square, followed by a straight move of three or more squares. If any of the squares it was thus proposed to traverse were occupied, the Zurāfa was debarred from making that move; unlike Asp and Jamal, he had no power of leaping.

[14] The India Office MS. places the Dabbābas on a1 and j1; B.M. 16827 substitutes *Asps* (Per. *asp* = horse) for the Dabbābas, and places them on a1, j1. As usual, the diagrams are corrupt.

Ten of the eleven Pawns were allotted, one to each of the ten types of piece, which not only bore the name of the piece throughout (e. g. in Ar. *baidaq aṭ-ṭalīʿa* or in Per. *piyāda al-farzīn*), but were made to resemble their allotted piece. The eleventh Pawn was made like an ordinary chess-pawn, and was called in Per. *piyāda piyādagan* (Pawn of the Pawns) or *piyāda aṣl* (Original Pawn) and in Ar. *baidaq al-bayādiq*. All the Pawns moved and captured as in the ordinary game, but their promotion was restricted to the rank with which they were associated by name. The Pawns' Pawn was treated in a special way. On reaching the end of the board he remained there as a 'dummy Pawn', immune from capture, until his owner chose to employ him to 'fork' two of the opponent's pieces, or to attack a piece which had no retreat open, when he could place the Pawns' Pawn in the necessary position to make the capture on the following move, and if this square was occupied by any piece whatever of either colour he could remove it and substitute the Pawn. After this the Pawns' Pawn continued to advance normally as a Pawn until he reached the end of the board again. He now became King's Pawn, and was placed upon that Pawn's original square. Finally, on reaching the end of the board for the third time, he became *Shāh maṣnūʿa* (adventitious King) with the King's move. The original KP became *Shāhzāda* (Prince).

I find considerable variation in the arrangement of the board in the different authorities.[15]

(*a*) RAS (1).—Kf2, Qe2, Wg2, B a1 and k1, J c1 and i1, De1 and g1, Zd2 and h2, T c2 and i2, Kt b2 and j2, R a2 and k2, PPa3, DPb3, JPc3, BPd3, QPe3, KPf3, WPg3, ZPh3, TPi3, KtPj3; RPK3. The *Ḥiṣn* adjoins k2.

(*b*) RAS (2).—The same, except Kf1, Qe1, Wg1, D e2 and g2, KPf2.

(*c*) b. ʿArabshāh, 5 MSS.[16]— Kf1, Qe1, Wg1, B a1 and k1, Jc1 and i1, Z e2 and g2, Td2 and h2, D c2 and i2, Kt b2 and j2, R a2 and k2, PPa3, QPb3, WPc3, JPd3, BPe3, KPf2, ZPg3, TPh3, DPi3, KtPj3, RPk3.

The conclusion of the game was hedged in with special rules. *Shāh qām* could not happen so long as the confined King had any of his own pieces remaining in his vicinity; *shāh māt* could not easily be given so long as other pieces were remaining in the army of the attacked King, for he could (once only) change places with another of his pieces[17] when so checked or staled. Finally, if a player could reach the citadel in his opponent's half of the board the game was drawn, unless that square were occupied by the *shāh maṣnūʿa*. Further refinements of vocabulary are to be found in *shāh fāt*, a check remedied by the above manœuvre; *shāh āt*, a check that can be covered; *shāh tāt*, one that cannot be covered; and *shāh qām*, when the King was separated from his men.

[15] The opponent's men are arranged precisely similarly from his point of view, e. g. PPk8, DPj8, &c.

[16] Viz. Oxf. Laud 148 and Digby Or. 16; Gotha, Möller 293 and 455; and the Vienna MS. The diagram in Al. (Elliott 274) is incomplete. It resembles that of ii. 9, below, in that the vacant squares are filled, but I can only read the names of the pieces added on f1 (*Kashshāf*), i1 (*Shutur*, camel), and j1 (*Shīr*, lion).

[17] The piece so sacrificed was called *fidā* (victim). This word is still in use in Turkish chess, in the simple sense of 'sacrifice'. Several problems in Ber. are headed ***rukh fidā***, &c.

This clumsy 'improvement' of the ordinary game is attributed by the author of RAS to a Greek philosopher called Hermes, who was a contemporary of Moses. It was, so he avers, introduced into India at the time of Alexander the Great's invasion, and the ordinary chess was abridged from it by Ṣaṣṣa b. Dāhir, and, according to our romancer, the game was completely spoiled thereby.

II. (9) The copyist of the MS. Brit. Mus. 7322 of b. ʿArabshāh found himself unable to resist the temptation to fill in the vacant squares of the Great chess with new pieces whose names show a departure from the war-derived nomenclature of the original Indian chess. He gives no information as to the moves that his new pieces were to possess. Adopting as the basis of the arrangement of the pieces that of II. 8 (*a*) he has added on b1 and j1 *'Asads* (lions), on d1 and h1 *Thaurs* (bulls), on f1 a *Kashshāf* (sentinel), and has replaced the Wazīr on g2 by a *Lukhm* (crocodile). The Pawns are arranged as in the RAS (1) figure, but the Lion's Pawn is added on c4, the Sentinel's Pawn on f4, and the Bull's Pawn on i4.

II. (10) A more modern *Shaṭranj al-kabīr* (Great chess) is described in a Turkish encyclopaedia, the *ad-durar al-muntakhabāt al-manīhūr fī iṣlāh al-Ghalaṭāt al-mashhūra*, of Amīnallāh Abū'r-Rafīd Muḥammad Ḥafīd, which was lithographed at Constantinople in 1221/1805–6. This game is played on a board of 13 × 13 squares with 26 men on each side. These are the 16 men of the ordinary chess, 5 extra Pawns, a *Great Ferz* (Z), and two *Karkaddan* (rhinoceros, Rh), and two *Āhū* (gazelle, G). The *Great Ferz* has the move of *Zurāfa* in II (8); the Rhinoceros combines the moves of the modern Bishop and Knight; the Gazelle has the move of the *Jamal* in II (8). The Pawns occupy the 4th and 10th lines, and the pieces are arranged thus: R a1 and m1, Kt b1 and l1, B c1 and k1, Rh d1 and j1, G e1 and i1, Zf1, Kg1, and Qh1.

My third group comprises games from Indian sources, and my oldest authority is the MS. Oxf., which I have described in Chapter X. It contains two games.

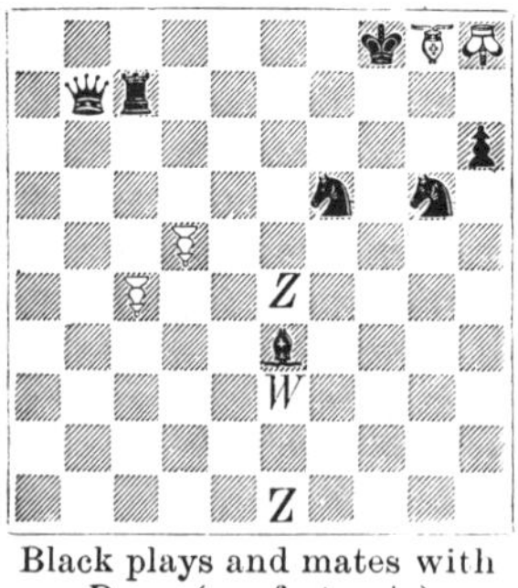

Black plays and mates with Pawn (see foot-note).

III. (11) A modern variety of Decimal chess with 22 men on either side, is described in the fifth maʿraka of this work, ff. 95 a – 101 b. The first six leaves contain twelve problems with solutions,[18] f. 101 a gives the arrangement of the board, 101 b the explanation of the algebraical notation used in the solutions of the problems. The new pieces are a *Wazīr*, with the moves of our Bishop and Knight; a *Zurāfa*, moving as our Queen and our Knight; and two *Dabbābas* moving as our Rook and Knight. The arrangement of the board is: Kf1 (e10); R a1 and j1; Kt b1 and i1; B c1 and h1; Wd1, Ze1,

[18] These are for the most part incorrect. As a specimen I give one from f. 97 a, to which the MS. gives the following solution in seven moves: 1 Rj9 +; 2 Kti8 +; 3 Wd4 +; 4 Be5 +; 5 Zf6 +; 6 Qj9 +; 7 P × Z mate.

Qg1 (d10), D e2 and f2, Ps on a2,, b2, c2, d2, e3, f3, g2, h2, i2, j2. The ordinary chessmen move as in the modern game, except that the Pawns have no initial double step.

III. (12) The same MS. describes a Great chess (*shaṭranj kabīr*) on ff. 102 a seq. It is played on a board of 12 by 12 squares, and there are 32 pieces on either side. The new pieces are those of III (11), two Lions (*shīr*), and other pieces whose names I cannot discover, but which are designated on the diagram by the contractions *M*, *Shḥ*, and *Wkh*. The arrangement of the board is Kg1 (f. 12); R a1, l1; Kt b1, k1; B c1, j1; Lion d1 (i12); We1; Zf1; Shḥ h1 (e12); Wkh i1; Mf2 (g11); Qg2; D f3, g3; P a2, b2, c2, d2, e2, e3, e4, f4, g4, h2, h3, h4, i2, j2, k2, l2.

Three other games are supplied by Lala Raja Babu's *Mo'allim ul shaṭranj*.[19]

III. (13) *Atranj* or *Qaṭranj*, a variety of Decimal chess with 22 pieces a side. Two diagrams are given of this game, one on p. 189 and a corrected one on p. 340. The only difference consists in the names of the pieces. The game closely resembles No. 11 above. The arrangement of the board is *Shāh*, f1 (e10): *Rukh*, a1, j1; *Ghora* (Kt), b1, i1, e3, f3; *Fīl*, c1, h1, with move of our Bishop; *Bukhshī*, paymaster, d1 (g10), with move of modern Bishop + Knight; *Wazīr*, e1 (f10), with move of our Queen; *Shāhzāda*, prince, g1, with move of our Queen + Knight; *Qalmāqīni*, armed female attendant, e2, f2, with move 'one square towards the opponent's King'; *Paidal* (P), a2, b2, c2, d2, g2, h2, i2, j2. The corrected diagram puts the *Wazīr* on d1 (g10); *Shāhzāda* on e1 (f10); *Pādshāh* (K) on f1 (e10); *Kōtwāl*, chief of police, on g1, with the Bukhshī's move; and replaces the *Qalmāqīni* by *Urdabegīni*, armed female attendants.

III. (14) A variety, also on a 12 × 12 board, with 24 pieces on either side. The arrangement of the board is *Rukh* (R), a1, l1; *Ghora* (Kt), b1, k1; *Dahja*, standard, c1, j1, with move of Bishop; *Rat·ha*, chariot, d1, i1, with move of Rook; *Fīl*, e1, h1; *Wazīr*, f1 (g12); *Pādshāh*, K, g1 (f12). The second row is occupied by 12 *Paidal* or Pawns.

III. (15) A third variety, played on a 14 × 14 board, with 28 men on either side, is thus arranged: *Rukh*, a1, n1; *Ghora*, b1, m1; *Dahja*, c1, l1; *Rat·ha*, d1, k1; *Fīl*, e1, j1; *Shāhzāda*, f1 (i14) and *Wazīr*, g1 (h14), both with move of our Queen; *Rāja*, h1 (g14), and *Rānī*, queen, i1 (f14), both with move of our King. The 14 Pawns are placed on the second and thirteenth lines.

Of the making of these games there need be no end, and I have no doubt that many other varieties have been proposed and perhaps played, of which

[19] The work describes other games, e.g. (1, 2) *round chess*, see above; (3) *shaṭranj dīwāna shāh*, in which White with solitary King plays against the whole of the Black forces, with the compensating liberty of moving as any one of the chessmen (Falkener, 217, describes this game under the fanciful name of the *Maharaja and the Sepoys*); (4) the *game of the Pawns*, each player having King and eight Pawns on their original squares; (5) *shaṭranj shīr bakrī*, in which two *shīr* (Lions) on d1, e1 fight against thirty-two *bakrī* (Goats) on the 5th, 6th, 7th, and 8th rows—a game of the *Fox and Geese* type; (6) *chaturājī*, taken from Forbes; (7) *shaṭranj Tīmūrī*, also from Forbes; and (8) *Four-handed chess*, on a cruciform-shaped board, made by adding three rows of eight squares to each edge of the ordinary board. Every Pādshāh stands on his Wazīr's right.

we have been spared the knowledge. Thus in the *Memoirs of the War in Asia from* 1780 *to* 1784 (London, 1789) mention is made of two more complex games of chess which were played in Southern India, in one of which there were 60 men employed. Mr. Platt possesses an incomplete set of chess of Indian workmanship, in which there are additional pieces, although there are only eight Pawns. It may accordingly belong to a game like Lala Raja Babu's *Atranj*.

My fourth group contains the various modifications of chess which are given in the last section of the *Libro del Acedrex* of Alfonso X of Castile (the MS. Alf.).

IV. (16) Decimal chess, *Acedrex de las diez casas*. No account of this game is given in the MS., but it appears from the instructions as to the making of the special dice required for playing it (f. 84 a) that in addition to the ordinary pieces it contained two major pieces, called *Juyz* (Judge), and two additional Pawns. No information is given as to the move of the *Juyz*. The game could be played either without dice, or by the help of dice with seven faces, which were specially designed for this game. In the latter case the throws were interpreted thus: 7, the Rey (K) moves; 6, the Alfferza (Q); 5, the Roque (R); 4, the Cavallo (Kt); 3, the Juyz; 2, the Alffil (B); 1, the Peon (P). The dice were also used for a variety of Tables (*el Iuego de las Tablas del Acedrex de las Diez casas*) on a board of 28 points with 34 men (f. 85 a).

IV. (17) Great chess, *Grande acedrex* (f. 81 a). This game, the invention of which Alfonso attributes to India, was played on a board of 12 × 12 squares.

The pieces, their positions and moves are shown in the following table:

No.	Sp. Name.	English.	Position.	Move.
1	Rey .	King .	f1 (f12)	To any adjacent sq. with a leap to a 3rd sq. (d1, d3, f3, h3, h1 only) for 1st move.
1	Aanca .	Gryphon	g1 (g12)	A move compounded of one step diagonally, followed by any number straight.
2	Unicornio	Unicorn	c1, j1	First move = Kt (but cannot capture), afterwards = modern B.
2	Roque .	Rook .	a1, l1	As our R.
2	Leon .	Lion .	b1, k1	Leap to 4th sq. in straight directions, e. g. from b1 to b4 or e1.
2	Cocatriz .	Crocodile	e1, h1	As our B.
2	Zaraffa .	Giraffe .	d1, i1	Diagonal leap to opposite corner of a rect. 5 by 2. It changed the colour of its sq. each move.
12	Peon .	Pawn .	On 4th (9th) row	As our P, but with no double step. Promotion to master-piece of file; on *f*-file, to Aanca.

The game was played without or with dice. In the latter case dice with eight faces were used, which were specially made for this game. The throws were interpreted thus: 8, Rey moves; 7, Aanca; 6, Roque; 5, Leon; 4, Leon; 3, Cocatriz; 2, Zaraffa; 1, Peon. This interpretation follows what Alfonso considered the order of value of the pieces.

IV. (18) Four-handed chess, *Acedrex de los quatro tiempos* (f. 87 a).

The four players symbolized the struggle between the following groups of four:

Seasons.	Elements.	Colours.	Humours.
Spring	Air	Green	Blood
Summer	Fire	Red	Choler
Autumn	Earth	Black	Melancholy
Winter	Water	White	Phlegm

The ordinary chessboard was used for this game, but the two major diagonals were drawn across the centre group of 16 squares. The reason given for this is that it divided the players, and showed in which directions the Pawns were to be moved. I give a diagram of the arrangement of the board. It will be noted that each player has K, R, Kt, B, and 4 Ps, as in the four-handed Indian dice-chess, but that the arrangement is different. The Pawns play in the directions that they face, along the edges of the board, and on reaching the opposite edge become Alferzas (Qs) at once. Green commences, and the order of play is Green, Red, Black, White. Each player attacks the player who succeeds him, and defends himself from the player who preceded him. There is no alliance between opposite players, but, as they have to a certain extent common interests, it is probable that an informal alliance obtained. When a player was mated he fell out, his conqueror appropriated his surviving men, and the three survivors continued the game. The final survivor won. The game was played for money, and the MS. lays down rules for the payments to be made for captures, checks, and mates, and arranges a pool which goes to the final winner. The game was played without dice, though, as in the case of the ordinary chess, dice might be used. In this case the throws were interpreted: 6, K moves; 5, Q moves; 4, R; 3, Kt; 2, B; 1, P moves. A variety of *Tables*, played on a circular board with 6 points to each quadrant, by 4 players with 12 men apiece, is attached to this chess in the MS.

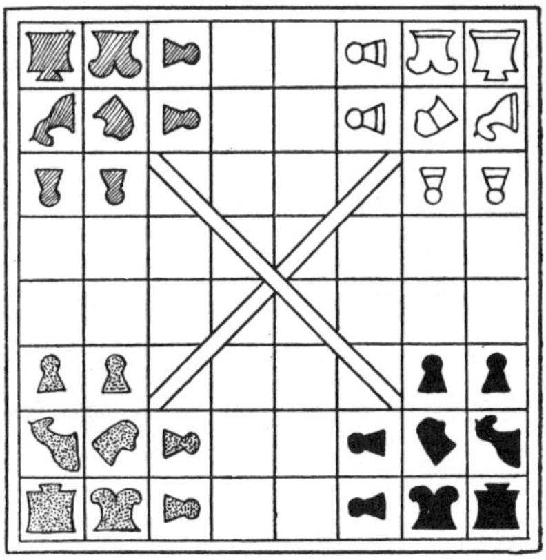

The Game of the Four Seasons, Alf.

IV. (19) *Los Escaques* (f. 95 a). This game is possibly identical with the Astronomical chess named by al-Maṣʿūdī and al-Āmulī. It is singular that Alfonso gives it for name the Castilian form of the Latin *scacci*, which was elsewhere in Western Christendom given to the ordinary chess. The board consists of 7 concentric rings, which are divided into 12 equal parts by radii from the common centre. Each of these 12 'houses' is allotted to one of the constellations of the Zodiac, and each ring is the orbit of a luminary of the Ptolemaic system. The arrangement is as follows, starting from the innermost ring and moving outwards:

No. of ring.	Name.	Sign.	No. of points in each House.	Starting-Point.	Colour.
Innermost	Moon . .	☾	1	Cancer . .	White
2	Mercury .	☿	2	Virgo . .	Parti-coloured
3	Venus . .	♀	3	Taurus. .	Violet
4	Sun . .	☉	4	Leo . .	Yellow
5	Mars . .	♂	5	Scorpio .	Red
6	Jupiter .	♃	6	Sagittarius .	Green
7	Saturn .	♄	7	Aquarius .	Black

The seven players throw a seven-faced die in order to determine the choice of luminary, and the throws are interpreted by columns 2 and 4 above.

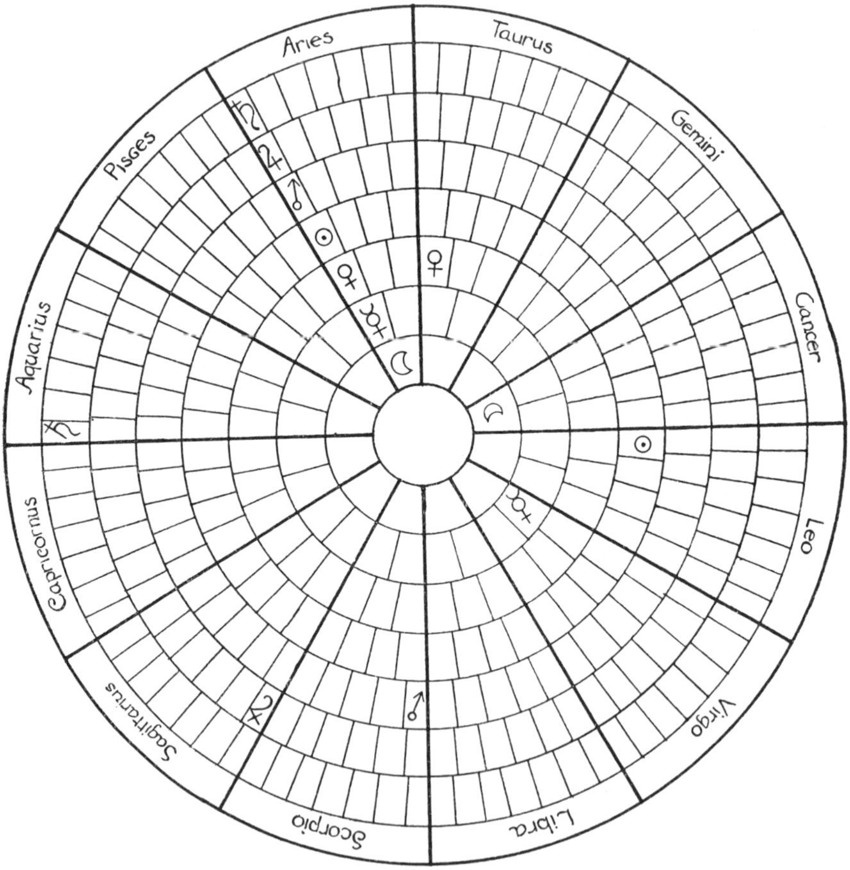

The Game of Los Escaques, Alf.

They then play in turn, throwing the die in order to determine the number of points through which to advance their pieces. Each luminary keeps to its own path, but points are scored whenever a player moves his piece in sextile (i. e. 2 'houses' distant from another piece), when he wins 24 from the other player, or trine (i. e. 4 'houses' distant), when he wins 36. If, however, he play in quadrature (3 'houses' distant) he loses 36, if in opposition (6 'houses' distant) he loses 72, and if in conjunction (the same 'house' with another piece) he loses 12. The game continues as long as the players like to play. As in the case of the other games, there is an allied game of Tables (f. 97 a) upon a circular board divided into 7 sectors with 7 points in each sector. The players have seven men apiece.

None of the astronomical games named in this chapter has any connexion with that described in W. Fulke's *Οὐρανομαχία*, or *Astrologorum ludus*, which was published in London in 1571 and reissued in 1572 and 1575.

CHAPTER XVII

THE MODERN GAMES OF ISLAM

The origin and history of the changes in the game.—The modern game of Persia, Turkey, and the lands bordering the Mediterranean.—Rūmī chess, or the Muslim game of India.—Abyssinian chess.

In the preceding Chapters, from X to XV, I have treated fully of the ordinary eight-square chess as it appears in Muslim authorities, covering a period of about 700 years, from the time of al-ʿAdlī of Baghdād to that of b. Sukaikir of Damascus and Aleppo. None of the works that I have used shows any signs of a loss of popularity, or any traces of a desire for changes in the rules of chess. So far as Muslim evidence goes, Muhammadans were playing at Damascus in 1575 the identical game that al-ʿAdlī had played in 850. The player who desired to experiment enlarged his board and introduced new pieces in his 'greater chess'; he left the ordinary game alone. It is plain that there were no forces making for change from within, and, if changes were to come, the motive forces must be looked for from without.

We may discover them in the chess of Western and Southern Europe, a game that had been received from the Muslim world before the year 1000. European players have never exhibited the reluctance to make changes in the game of chess which was shown by the Muslims. Certainly from 1275, and probably even earlier, players had come to the conclusion that the game could be improved by alterations in the moves of some of the pieces, and the changes culminated before 1500 in the adoption of the moves of the chessmen which we use to-day. The new game, which appeared just before 1500 and was practically complete and adopted generally through Western Europe by 1600, compelled methods of play that emphasized the science of the Opening, and tactics which were hardly needed in the older game. By 1600 the differences were unmistakable; before 1500 a casual observer might be excused for thinking the Muslim and the European games identical.

Political relations between the Muhammadan countries and Western Europe, with the additional difficulties imposed by the existence of the Greek Eastern Empire, can hardly be held to have been favourable for a chess-intercourse between East and West. But there was always a trade with the Levant from the Italian republics, and sooner or later it was inevitable that players of the two games should come in contact with one another. Then it may well have happened that the two games would be compared, that the supposed advantages of each would be canvassed, and that varying opinions would be put to the test of an actual game. Doubtless long before

1600 there would be, from one end of the Mediterranean to the other, a more or less clear knowledge among chess-players of the salient features of the Muslim and European games, and this knowledge would mean the introduction of modifications in the less advanced game. European chess was essentially a reformed variety of Muslim chess, and that it was an improved, not a retrograde, form had been demonstrated by the experience of centuries.

Changes would therefore be expected first in the trade centres, and it would be a mere question of time before they had spread back to the chess circles of the interior. The gradual nature of the process is illustrated by uncertainty of rule or practice, and by the persistence of the unreformed game in distant or inaccessible corners. We have an example of this in Abyssinian chess, which to-day is practically still untouched by the influence of European chess.

The earliest records of changes in Muslim chess occur, as might have been expected, in Italian works. Perhaps the earliest account is that which is given in an Italian MS. work, *Libro che insegna giocar a scachi,* written between 1620 and 1640, and now in Mr. J. G. White's possession. This work contains two references to Turkish chess which are not entirely in harmony. The earlier passage is mainly describing the chess 'al'antiga' of Europe, and the addition 'as can be observed to-day among the Turks' is probably not to be taken too absolutely. There is no attempt made to discriminate in details between the older European and the Turkish game, and the only rule which is definitely described as being observed in Turkish chess is that the Bishop (*delfino*) moves as in old chess. The second passage, f. 101, describes the 'chess *al'antiga* as practised by the Moors and Turks' in the following way:

> It is noted for your greater knowledge that the Bishop leaps from 3 squares to 3 squares, neither more nor less, aslant or cornerwise, and like the Knight it can leap over every piece, whether forwards or backwards, and it captures thus and not otherwise.
>
> The Queen makes its move always on the white squares; it cannot leap more than one square aslant or cornerwise, whether forwards or backwards, excepting the first time that it moves, when it can at once leap 3 squares in all directions, whether aslant or rectangularly, and over every piece, and its power of capture is not otherwise than in one way only, it not being allowed the first move. This is for the white Queen; the black Queen does the same, except that its path is always on a black square.
>
> If the Pawn shall be made Queen on a white square it will always go by the white squares from square to square as the principal Queen goes, and when it is made it can leap the first time the 3 squares as is said above of the Queen. If it be made Queen on a black square it will always go on the black.

We see from this that the 'Queen's leap' had penetrated to some forms of Muslim chess. This addition to the power of the old *Fers* or Queen and to that of the promoted Pawn had already been made in some forms of European chess before 1300, and was adopted generally in the 14th c. By 1500 a different move for the Queen was in use in Spain and in Italy, and the older move was probably obsolete in the Mediterranean lands by 1560.

The suggestion is that this change must have commenced in the Levant before 1500; after that date we should expect to find the modern move of the Queen.

At the end of the same century we have another reference in Francesco Piacenza's *I Campeggiamenti degli Scacchi* (Torino, 1683). Chapter v of this work treats 'Of the customs which the Turks, Moors, and Levantine Jews[1] hold in castling the King, and in their first moves of the Pawns'. Our gossipy author says:

In the city of Livorno in Tuscany there was prisoner a Chiaus or Ambassador from the realm of Egypt who boasted that he was the first chess-player in the world. As I was urged by some of my friends, I went to play with him in the Bagno of that city, and the first day we played 13 parties or games, the first of which the Chiaus won, and the other 12 I won in succession and with such ease that I think I could beat him in my sleep. But in all this I was obliged to condescend to castle my King in the cursed African fashion, which is first to move him one square into the row of Pawns, and then another move, to move the Rook and at the self-same time to place the King on the Rook's square.[2] In this way I continued to play, not only with him, but also with a Jew from Smyrna named Moses, who besides the above custom of castling the King had another beautiful kind of chessboard as is mentioned in the following chapter. . . . The moves of the Pawn which these transmarines make are also different from ours, i.e. the Pawn cannot be played or pushed more than one square at a time. . . .

The following chapter (vi) describes 'The form of the chessboard which is used in the Levant and in Africa', with a figure of an unchequered board. Piacenza greatly overestimated the difficulty of playing on such a board. He goes on to say:

Their pieces are all of a form, so that it is difficult to distinguish between Knight and Bishop or Rook, or Rook and Queen, or Queen and King or Pawns.

Hyde, a contemporary, gives illustrations, which I reproduce, of the chessmen

Turkish chessmen (K, Q, B, Kt, R, P). From Hyde.

in use in Muslim lands in his time. These may help to explain Piacenza's complaint.

An important note on the first leaf of MS. BM explains the difference between the chess of the MS. and that of the writer's day. Sir R. K. Douglas dates the note 'probably 18th c.' It belongs to Baṣra or Baghdād.

This book differs from what we recognize in our time, for the Firzān now unites the power of the Firzān and the 2 Fīls; and one of the Fīls moves diagonally through half the squares of the cloth as it likes when there is no obstacle in its way, and the

[1] The Jews probably often acted as the intermediaries in the diffusion of the European rules Eastwards.

[2] I.e. Black, K on its own sq., d1, KR on a1, c2 blank. Black plays 1 Kc2; 2 Rd1 and Ka1.

other diagonally through the remaining half. The Fīl of this book, however, marches aslant 3 squares setting snares diagonally, neither exceeding nor falling short of this number. The Firzān marches like the Baidaq, except that it goes aslant every way, to the right and left, and so backwards. It does not march in the straight directions. The Shāh's march is greater than the Firzān's, for he moves one square every way in the straight directions, and also shares in the diagonal move of one square in every direction. If we draw a board of 9 lines by 9, there will be 64 squares. Each square is of this type (see Figure): the corners are named by a single letter, and the sides by two, thus A, B, J, and D are corners, and AB is a side. The squares are numbered with the Indian numerals (see Figure).

Baidaq, Shāh, and Rukh go one way in it. The Rukh marches in direction AB as far as 57, and in direction BD as far as 8, as it likes when there is no obstruction. In whatever square it happens to be, it marches in these four directions. There is no limit or end to its march unless there is obstruction. The Baidaq moves similarly from 9 to 17, thence to 25, reckoning square by square, except that it takes aslant, as from 9 to 18 and thence to 27 or 25.

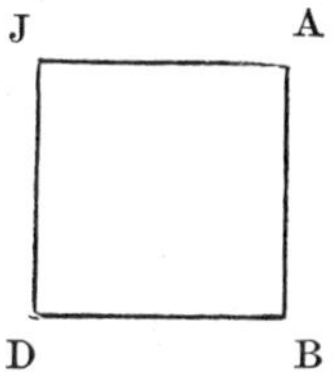

The Shāh steps from 4 to 3, 5, 11, or 13. Similarly from 13 to 5, 12, 14, or 21, straight, and also to 4, 6, 20, or 22. So he moves square by square in eight directions, taking in just the same way.

The move of the Firzān of the book resembles that of the Shāh, except that its move is cornerwise and not straight. Thus from 13, it takes in 4, 6, 20, and 22, and not in 5, 12, 14, or 21.

8	7	6	5	4	3	2	1
16	15	14	13	12	11	10	9
24	23	22	21	20	19	18	17
32	31	30	29	28	27	26	25
40	39	38	37	36	35	34	33
48	47	46	45	44	43	42	41
56	55	54	53	52	51	50	49
64	63	62	61	61	59	58	57

Numbering of squares attributed to Muḥammad Sa'īd.

The right-hand Fīl goes from 6 to 20 or 24, from 20 to 2, 6, 34, or 38, and in no other way.

The left-hand Fīl in 3 goes to 21 or 17, from 21 to 7, 3, 35, or 39.

The conventional Fīl on the right-hand goes from 6 to 41 as it likes, or to 24 as it likes. From 24 it goes to its original position or to 59 as it likes. So it follows the same rule diagonally that the Rukh follows in the straight directions, but the Fīls halve the squares of the cloth between them, while the Rukhs can move independently to every square. The Fīls of the book only go round half the board conjointly and not singly, because the Fīls in 3 and 6 do not complete singly but only conjointly, while the conventional Fīls complete singly and conjointly their own special halves, whereas the Fīls in the book are independent, each with a quarter. The conventional Firz unites the powers of the Rukh, the conventional Fīl, and of one of the Faras.

We have here evidence of a great advance towards the moves of the modern European game, though there is still some uncertainty. In one place the Firzān is said to unite the moves of Firzān (? read Rook) and Fīls, in the other it is given the moves of Rook, Fīl, and Faras. This is a more extensive move than has ever been tried in the ordinary European game, but there is plenty of evidence to show that the Queen was given the Knight's move, in addition to the move that it has in our game, in countries in which the European rules were ousting the original native method of play. Russian chess went through this phase, and the Queen in Georgian chess still possessed this extended move in 1874. For Turkish chess we have the statement from a contemporary source, which Twiss has preserved in his *Miscellanies* (London, 1805, ii.

112–3), in explanation of the success with which the Turkish ambassador played with Philidor in 1795.

> It must be observed that the Turk could only play with his own men, which were very different from those used by us, and difficult to be distinguished, and that the Queen had likewise the move of the Knight, as in *Russia.*

Phillip Stamma, who described himself as a native of Aleppo in Syria, and who was for some time Interpreter of the Oriental Languages to King George II, gives some information about the Syrian game as he knew it, in the Preface to his *Noble Game of Chess* (London, 1745). The Orientals 'don't allow of Castling'; a promoted Pawn can only become a Queen, the player giving stalemate or baring his opponent's King wins the game. The board is commonly an unchequered handkerchief or piece of calico, the dividing lines being in another colour.

The German translation of Marinelli's *Il Giuoco degli Scacchi fra tre* (Napoli, 1722), published under the title of *Das dreyseitige Schachbrett* (Regensburg, 1765), contains a note (pp. 31–6) on chess in Africa. The translator met in Vienna in 1748 a certain Osman Effendi, who was there as an envoy from Tripoli, and played chess with him with very even results. He tells us that the Tripolitans 'castled', played chess for a stake (especially the Jews), could still win by 'baring' the opponent's King, and played on unchequered cloths.

The Dane, Georg Höst, speaking of Morocco, in his *Efterretninger om Marokos og Fes* (Copenhagen, 1779, pp. 105–6), says:

> All games of chance are prohibited in the 2nd and 5th chapters of the Qur'ān; however, they play them in private, and especially the Spanish game al-Hombre. Setrengsgh or chess is alone permitted, and is their chief game. Some are real masters at it. They do not play for money, but whoever loses must allow the other to place a feather or straw in his turban or cap, which rarely irritates them. They call the King *eschech,* the Queen *lella,* the Rook *erroch,* the Knight *elfers,* the Bishop *elfil,* and the soldiers *elhari.* The pieces, however, have no resemblance to any creature but have only certain distinctions and marks of difference on them which foreigners have first to learn to recognize.[3]

To the close of the 18th c. belongs the MS. 'Ber.', which has been briefly described on p. 181. This Turkish MS. gives no definite information as to the rules governing its problems, and only rarely adds any hints for their solution.

[3] We may recognize *ash-shāh, ar-rukh, al-faras,* and *al-fīl* in these forms, which attempt to preserve the pronunciation of the Maghrib dialects. *Lālla, Lāllah, Lāllī* (Dozy, *Suppl. aux dict. arabes,* Leiden, 1878) is the Maghrib name for a lady of the better classes. The use of the word in chess can only be explained as a result of Spanish influences. These are so potent that to-day the Moors of the coast towns of Morocco use European chessmen, notwithstanding the fact that the Knight is thus undoubtedly an image of a horse. Culin (*CPC.*, 862, n. 1) tells of the failure of the U.S. Nat. Museum to obtain native pieces. A recent work on Morocco, D. Meakin's *The Moors,* London, 1902, p. 124, would seem to show that the popularity of chess is on the wane:

'Indoors the Moors have few amusements, chess being indulged in by a small proportion of the better educated only, though draughts are more common, being played in coffee-houses with astonishing rapidity, accompanied by voluble remarks not always complimentary.'

In a footnote Mr. Meakin tells how the qāḍī at Shīrāz had expressed to him his horror at the practice of chess, first alleging that it was a game of chance and accordingly illegal, and when this was disproved, he said it was abhorrent to all Shī'ites because the murderers of al-Ḥasan and al-Ḥusain had played it just before the murders.

It is clear, however, that the bulk of its problems are played with the European moves of the men, although a few favourite problems of the older game—as for instance the *Dilārām position*—have been included, without any reference to the fact that the moves of the pieces are not the same as in the other games. A few problems are resettings of older material, but I have not identified any as occurring among the 100 problems that Phillip Stamma included in his *Essai sur le Jeu d'Échecs* (Paris, 1737). One problem from the MS. is, however, repeated in the *Ghalaṭāt al-mashhūra* (Stambul, 1221/1805–6), a work which I have already cited for a modern form of Great chess. I give four positions from this MS. Generally the number of moves in which the solution

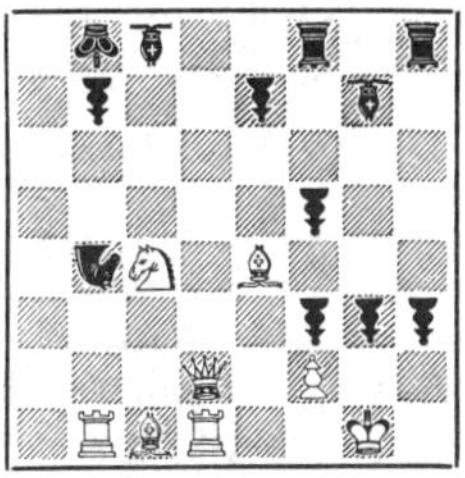

No. 1. f. 2b. 'White begins. Mate 13.'

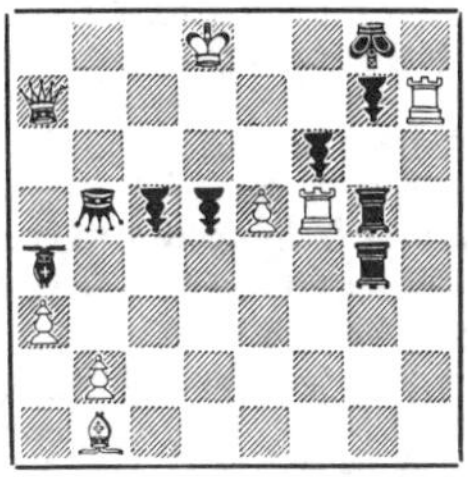

No. 2. f. 11a. 'White begins. Q and R sacrifice. Mate 7.'

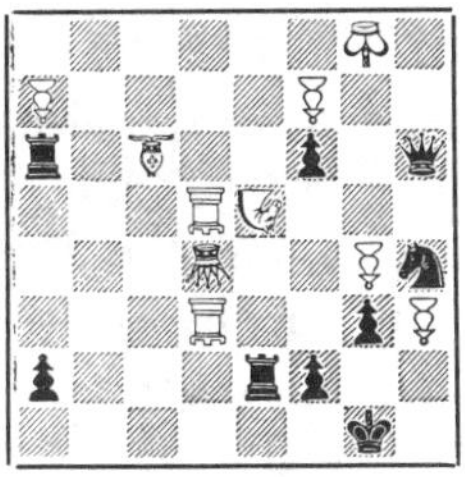

No. 3. f. 26a. 'White begins.'

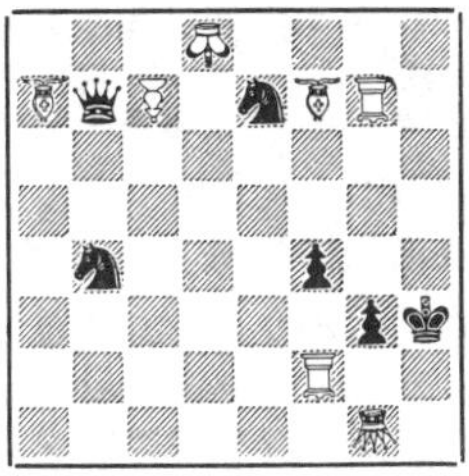

No. 4. f. 34a. 'Black begins.'

Problems of Modern Turkish chess; from MS. Ber.[4]

is intended is given, but the moves of each player are counted separately, what we should call a mate in 5 being described as a mate in 9.

None of these 18th c. references makes any allusion to a crosswise arrangement of the Kings, and Stamma's silence seems to me to be conclusive as to its non-existence in the native circles in Aleppo in his time. There is nothing to show whence the change came, but it now exists throughout Islam, excepting in India, and it is mentioned by all the observers of the 19th c.

[4] Solutions to the four problems from MS. Ber.:

No. 1. Mate in 7 by 1 Qf4 +, Ka8 !; 2 Ra1 +, B × R !; 3 Qb8 +, K × Q; 4 Bf4 +, Be5; 5 B × B +; 6 Ra1 +, Kta6; 7 R × Kt m. The P (e7) cannot interpose on move 1, since there is no 'double step' in Turkish chess.

No. 2. Mate in 4 by 1 Qf7 +, K × Q !; 2 R × P (f6) +, Kg8; 3 Rh8 +, K × R; 4 Rf8 m.

No. 3. Mate in 5 by 1 Rd1 +, Kh2 !; 2 Q × P +, R × Q !; 3 Rh1 +, K × R; 4 Rd1 + d, Kh2; 5 Rh1 m.

No. 4. Mate in 7 by 1 bKtc6 +, Kd7; 2 Qc8 +, Kd6; 3 Qd8 +, Kc5; 4 Qd4 +, Kb5; 5 Qb4 +, Ka6; 6 Qa5 +, Kb7; 7 Q × B m. This problem is also in the *Ghalaṭāt al-mashhūra*, whence in v. d. Linde, i. 132; and in Walker's *Philidor* (1832), p. 156, whence elsewhere.

The earliest of these descriptions occurs in Hamilton's *Egyptiaca* (London, 1809, p. 258):

At chess we were by no means his (Elfi Bey's) equals. He played well, and with great quickness. The board and pieces were but little different from those in use with us. The squares are of one uniform colour divided by broad white lines. The Pawns are not allowed to move two squares the first move, nor are the Queens, who are called Vezirs, opposite to one another. Our Bishop is with them the Elephant. The Castle is called Rukh, which is the name given in Arabia to a fabulous bird of enormous size. The Knight is called Houssān, or the Horse, and the Bishop Fīl, or the Elephant.

Next we have an account of modern Persian chess in the *CPC.*, 1846, 211, 252, 278.[5] It was obtained from a party of young Persian noblemen who were sent to Paris about 1845–6 by Shāh Muḥammad for purposes of education. We may summarize the facts thus:

(1) The King is placed on the 4th square from the left-hand corner, i.e. on d1 and e8. The Queen consequently stands on the King's right.
(2) The Pawns can never move more than one square at a time.
(3) Provided the King has never been checked, he may move once as the Knight, or may castle on his own side, this manœuvre being played thus: K(d1)b1 and R(a1)d1 in one move. A similar manœuvre on the other wing takes three moves (1 R~, 2 Ke2, 3 Kg1, using the Kt's leap).
(4) A plurality of Queens is not admitted.
(5) The player who bares his opponent's King wins the game.

These notes on Persian chess are accompanied by three games that the European informant had played with Riza Khan. They cannot be regarded as really illustrative of Persian chess, but they show that the Persian player had the same predilection for close, and specially for 'fianchetto' Openings that we shall shortly see to be characteristic of Turkish players.

We owe two valuable letters on Syrian chess to Vincenz Grimm, a noted Hungarian chess-player, who was exiled for his share in the revolution of 1848. He settled first in Smyrna, from whence he addressed a letter to the *CPC.* in 1851,[6] and then in Constantinople, from whence he addressed a second to the *Schachzeitung* in 1865. In the latter he says (*Sch.*, 1865; 361–4):

. . . Now as regards the rules in so far as they vary from ours. The Queen stands on the King's left, and consequently opposite to the opponent's King. The Pawn can only go one step, and can only be exchanged on the 8th line for a piece which has already been captured. I have heard different opinions about castling. Most players do not in the least know what it means. Some castle in 2 moves: in the first the King moves 2 or 3 steps towards the Rook, and in the second the Rook leaps over the King. Others take 3 moves; 1 Ke2 or f2; 2 R~; 3 K makes a Kt's move behind the Pawns. All, however, agree that you can only castle during the 'opening'. I could never arrive at a definition telling when the 'opening' ceases, but I imagine it comes to an end whenever a capture is made. All this only became clear to me when I observed that a player always waited then for his

[5] Cf. also Forbes, 247, who quotes the first passage from the *CPC.* This was modified considerably in the later communication.

[6] This letter is given *in extenso* by Forbes, 243 seq. It contains an amusing anecdote of an Aleppo player of the eighteenth century, who played before the Sultan in Constantinople.

opponent's reply. For the first time that I played with an Arab and invited him to commence the game, he made with incredible rapidity 10 or 12 moves one after the other without in the least troubling himself about my play. When I asked in astonishment, 'When does my turn come?' he rejoined in just as much astonishment, 'Why are you not moving?' All this moving amounts to nothing more than an alteration of the initial arrangement, in which it is a matter of no consequence whether the one makes a couple of moves more than the other. I have also noticed that during this preliminary play they never make two moves with the same man (excepting the King in castling) so that the Pawns can never come to close quarters. When each has arranged his army according to the new plan, the real game begins.

For instance one moves Pe3, Pg3, Bg2, Ktf3, Ke2, Re1, Kg1, Pb3, Bb2, Pd3, Kt(b1)d2, Qe2, R(a1)d1. Now he looks to see if his opponent has got so far. If he has not, he waits a little.

Elsewhere, Grimm remarks upon the absence of strong players: he had only encountered two of average strength, the one a young Druse at Damascus, the other a peasant near Aleppo. On the other hand, he thought that the strongest European player could easily lose, provided that he played on the native board, with the native pieces, the native rules, and the native rapidity of play.[7] As elsewhere throughout the East—and in Russia, Grimm adds—the spectators take an active share in a game. He gives the Arabic names of the pieces as K *shāh*, Q *vezir* (= *wazīr*), B *fīl*, Kt *begir* (= horse), R *roch* (= *rukh*), P *peda*.

Grimm's account is corroborated by a brief note which first appeared in the *Chicago Times*, and was copied thence into the *BCM.*, 1894 (p. 10):

In setting the men, K faces Q. Pawns advance one square only. Castling is carried out in two moves (not necessarily consecutive, I think), K first passing to Kt sq.; in so doing either K or R may leap over intervening Bishop, but not over both Q and B on Q's side. The R then moves to K sq., or on Q side to Q sq. The first take is a bar to Castling, as also, of course, is the fact of the K having moved. . . . Favourite Openings would seem to be—move out the centre Pawns, then the two Bs to K3 and Q3, followed by the two Kts to K2 and Q2. Or the Bs may be developed after style of Fianchetto by P–Kt3 both sides, and B–Kt2, both appearing to make the same moves in the former case. The openings are played so rapidly that often the second player appears to have got a move ahead of the first. It is all but impossible to follow them. . . . Alla Franca chess is now played quite as much by educated Turks as the old-fashioned game.

This curious method of introductory play—which is also characteristic of Abyssinian chess—is quite different from the more orderly Openings that are known in the non-Muslim Indian games of chess. I believe that it has arisen from the fact that opening play has always been more or less formal in nature in Muslim chess. The taʿbīyas of the early masters show that there was far greater uniformity in the opening tactics than would be thought possible. The popular openings at any one time were only one or two in number, and there was a conviction that the opening did not matter. Aṣ-Ṣūlī referred to

[7] This rapidity of play was noted in the case of the Cairo players by W. G. Browne, who was there between 1792 and 1798, and who published his *Travels in Africa, Egypt, and Syria* in 1799. See v. d. Linde, ii. 174. At the present day, as I am informed, chess is losing popularity in Egypt, and *manqala* and other simpler board-games are more generally preferred.

this when he complained of the small amount of attention that the ordinary player gave to his opponent's moves. Each player had his own idea of the opening position that he preferred, and each player made for it, regardless of what his opponent was about. It was only when the one took a man that the attention of the other was perforce arrested, and then the real game began. Up to that point careless play led to rapid play, and rapid alternate play would easily degenerate into the simultaneous disorderly hurry for a position which has puzzled observers.

I possess a small Arabic manual on chess, the *Al-bākūra al-manīra fi laʿba ash-shaṭranj ash-shahīra* of Jirjis Fīlūthā'ūs,[8] which was published in Egypt in 1892. While it is partly drawn from French sources, it also gives a specimen of play from the Levant, which is introduced by the brief note—

In the following game from the Levant, the King of either colour is placed on the right hand; in castling the King, the Rook is moved as the players like up to K sq.; the Pawn only goes a square at a time; the King can move once as a Knight.

The game follows. The Kings are placed on e1 and d8.

	White	Black		White	Black		White	Black		White	Black
1	Pg3	Pb6	10	Bb2	Pf6	19	Ktb3	Ph4	28	Q × cP +	Rd7
2	Bg2	Ktc6	11	Pa3	Pg6	20	Pg4	P × P	29	Qc5 +	Ke8
3	Ktf3	Bb7	12	Pa4	Bg7	21	Kt × P	Kt × Kt	30	Q × B +	Rd8
4	Bayyat	Bayyat[9]	13	Pd3	Ph5	22	Q × Kt	Qg6	31	Bc6 +	Kf8
5	Ph3	Pa6	14	Pd4	Pg5	23	Ktc5	Bc8	32	Q × R +	Qe8
6	Kth2	Pd6	15	Pc3	Pf5	24	Kte4	P × Kt	33	Q × Q mate.	
7	Pe3	Pd5	16	Pb4	Kth6	25	Q × eP	Qf7			
8	Qe2	Kta7	17	Pa5	Pb5	26	Qa8 +	Kd7[9a]			
9	Pb3	Ph6	18	Ktd2	Pe6	27	Q × Kt	Ke7			

This work contains a vocabulary of technical terms, among which are *bāt* or *bāṭa*, stalemate, which is given as a draw; *bidl* (or *kassar*, which is more usual now), an exchange of two pieces of equal value: *bayyat* (also *taḥaṣun*), castling in one move; *tafarzana*, to queen a pawn; *tasatara*, to cover an attack; *taqābala*, to take the opposition; *qi'sh-shāh* or *kish*, check, also said to the Queen when attacked; *qa'īm*, a drawn game. Some of these are also found in the older writers; but *bāt*, *bāṭa*, is obviously simply the French *pat*, and the valuation of this ending is borrowed from European chess.

A second game from Algiers was published in the *Rivista Scacchistica Italiana* in 1903, whence it was copied into other papers, as the *Westminster Gazette*. According to the note that accompanied the game, the Kings are placed on e1 and d8; there is no castling, but the King can once make a Knight's move, provided he has neither been checked nor moved; and the player giving stalemate wins the game.

[8] From his name a Greek (George Philotheus). I suspect that Stamma was also a Greek. His name cannot be Arabic. The title of Jirjis' book means 'The brilliant firstfruits of the famous game of chess'.

[9] I.e. castles, White by Kg1 and Re1; Black by Kb8 and Rd8.

[9a] 'King makes a Knight's move.'

MODERN MUSLIM (EGYPTIAN) CHESSMEN
Platt Collection

The game was played between Shaikh ʿAlī and Sidi Zuaui, the former having the white pieces.

White	Black	White	Black	White	Black	White	Black
1 Pg3	Pb6	10 Kd2	Rd8	19 P × P	Kt × P	28 Pf2	Re8
2 Bg2	Ktc6	11 Qf3	Kc8	20 Qf4	B × Kt	29 Rd1	Re7
3 Ktc3	Bb7	12 Re1	Kb8	21 Kt × B	Kt × Kt +	30 R(c3)d3	Pf6
4 Pb3	Ktf6	13 Pb4	Pd5	22 Kc1	Q × Q	31 Rd7	R × R
5 Bb2	Pg7	14 Pa3	Qe7	23 P × Q	Pd4	32 R × R	P × P
6 Pg4	Bg6	15 Kb1	Kt × bP	24 B × B	K × B	33 R × hP	R × P
7 Ph3	Pe6	16 P × Kt	Q × P	25 B × Kt	P × B	34 Rh6	Pa6
8 Pe3	Pd6	17 Kt(g1)e2	Pe5	26 Re3	Rd4	35 R × P	R × P
9 Pd3	Ke7	18 Pg5	Pe4	27 R × P	R × P	36 R × P	Rc3 wins

The chessmen used at the present time by Sunnite Muhammadans do not differ very much from those that were used centuries ago; the only considerable change being in the shape of the Rook, which no longer exhibits the

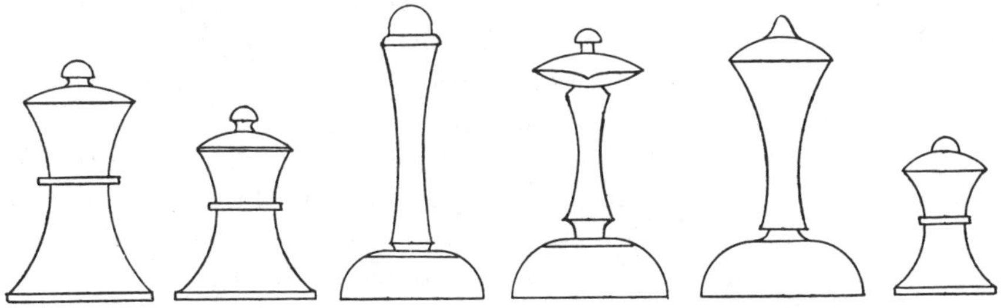

Kurdish chessmen (K, Q, B, Kt, R, P). From Culin.

expanded wings that were distinctive of this piece in the Middle Ages in Europe also. Europeans generally complain of the difficulty in distinguishing between the Fīl and the Faras. The latter piece has the more knob-like head. I give some illustrations of modern chessmen from the Nearer East. Other Muslim sects are not so opposed to using images for their chessmen, and both in Persia and India the wealthier players use sets consisting of beautiful carvings of kings, elephants, horses, &c. But here also the simpler 'mushroom' type of piece is used by the ordinary players.

Turkish chessmen (P, Q, K, B, Kt, R). After Falkener.

In India, Muslim chess was exposed to different influences from those which have remodelled the game on the shores of the Mediterranean. Here it had to contend with a form of chess that was not obviously superior to itself, so that the most powerful force for change was wanting. Religious and social lines of cleavage also tended to reduce the possibility of extensive alteration. The Muslim chess has, as a result, retained a definite form not far removed from that which was played under the ʿAbbāsid caliphate, and Indian writers have given it the name of *Rūmī shaṭranj* to distinguish it from the two native games, *Hindustani chess* and *Parsi chess*, and from *Feringhi chess* (the game of the governing European classes). *Rūmī*, originally the Arabic for Roman, and generally associated with the Eastern Roman or Byzantine

Empire, is now the colloquial term for 'Western Asiatic', and the phrase *Rūmī shaṭranj* has been variously translated Roman, Byzantine, Greek, Grecian, and Turkish chess.

Durgāprasāda's *Risāla i shaṭranj* (Delhi, 1890) attributes the invention of this form of chess to Lajlāj Rūmī, the son of Sīsa, and grandson of Da'īr, thus uniting all the principal characters of the Muhammadan chess legend.

The earliest description of the Rūmī chess that I have found is contained in a brief note which had been pasted in the cover of the Persian MS. 'Oxf.' by a former owner, the Rev. George Keene, in 1810. The first ma'raka or arena of this MS. contains 99 problems, which are of the Rūmī chess. Mr. Keene's note agrees with the later information in Durgāprasāda's book, and with that in Lala Raja Babu's *Mo'allim ul shaṭranj* (Delhi, 1901, p. 187). The board is arranged as in the older Muslim and as in the European chess; that is to say, the crosswise arrangement of the Kings does not extend to Rūmī chess. In this it is unlike all the other varieties of Asiatic chess on the eight-square board with which we have yet met. All the pieces preserve the moves of the older Muslim game as described in Ch. XIII, with two small exceptions. The Queen for its first move can be placed on its third square (Qd3 or Qd6), passing if necessary over the unmoved Pawn on its second square. The Queen's Pawn for its first move can be placed on the Queen's fourth square (Pd4 or Pd5), passing, if necessary, over the Queen on her third square. These two moves must be played as the first and second moves of the game. Thenceforward the Queen can only move one square at a time diagonally, as in the older game. A Pawn on reaching the end of the board becomes a Queen only, and there is no limit to the number of Queens a player can possess at one time.

An older form of the Muslim game is also found in Abyssinia, apparently the only part of that continent outside the Mediterranean countries in which chess is played except by European settlers. Our earliest authority for Abyssinian chess is Mr. Henry Salt (B. 1780, D. 1827), who was acting as Secretary to Lord Valentia during his travels in the East, 1802–6. Abyssinia was then almost an unknown land to Europeans, and in 1805 Lord Valentia sent Mr. Salt thither on a mission to obtain information about the country. He visited Welled Selasse, the Ras of Tigre, and brought away with him Welled's chessmen, and the following note on the game, which was incorporated in Lord Valentia's *Travels* (iii. 57).

On our arrival at Antalow, we found the Ras at breakfast, and were invited to join him. . . . In the evening we went into the hall, and found the Ras at Chess in the midst of his chiefs. The chessmen, which were coarsely made of ivory, are very large and clumsy; when they have occasion to take any one of their adversary's pieces, they strike it with great force and eagerness from its place. I observed that their game differs much from ours. Bishops jump over the heads of Knights, and are only allowed to move three squares. The Pawns move only one step at starting, and get no rank by reaching the end of the board. They play with much noise; every person around, even the slaves, having a voice in the game, and seizing the pieces at pleasure to show any advisable move. We observed, however, that they always managed with great ingenuity to let the Ras win every game.[10]

[10] The *Palamède* for 1838 has a translation of this description, which has been considerably modified by the translator.

The chessmen are now in the British Museum, along with three other isolated pieces which are probably Kings. They are ivory, of undoubted Muslim pattern, massive and plain in design. Originally one side was stained or painted red, but the colour has nearly all worn away, and it is not easy to distinguish between the sides.

A much better account of the Abyssinian game is to be found in W. C. Plowden's *Travels in Abyssinia*, edited after his death from his MS. by T. C.

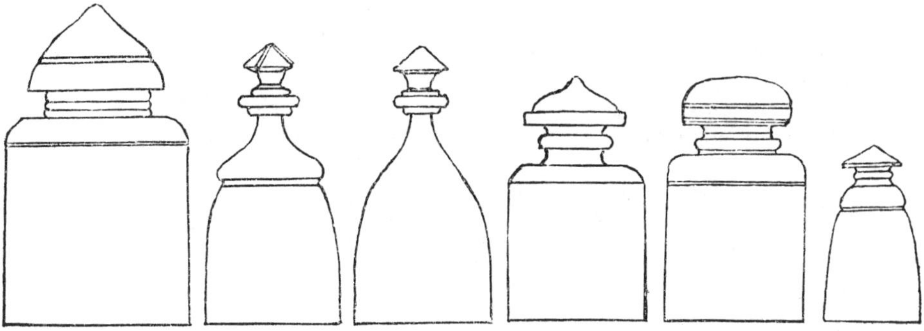

Abyssinian chessmen, of Welled Selasse (K, Kt, B, Q, R, P).

Plowden (London, 1868). Mr. Plowden, who was British Consul in the country, learnt the Abyssinian chess during his travels there in 1843–7, when he played repeatedly with the natives at their own games. This makes his evidence the more valuable. He names chess as one of the subjects of education for a chief in Teegray. The Amharas, on the other hand, are not so devoted to the game. He gives the following account of the Abyssinian game (p. 149):

Abyssinian chessmen.[11]

The game of . . . chess is found also in Ethiopia, and is denominated Sunteridge.[12] . . .

The chessboard consists of the usual number of squares (64), and that in use by Abyssinians is generally a piece of red cloth, the squares marked out by strips of black sewn across at equal distances. The chessmen are made of ivory or hippopotamus, or lighter ones of horn; the former are ponderous and massive, and all simple in their form—the difference being just sufficient to mark the distinction of the pieces, and with no ornament or fancy-work. The number of the pieces corresponds with ours, and the only difference in their arrangement on the board is the placing of the two Kings opposite each other.

[11] The left-hand one is of ivory, the other two are wood, coloured red with white stripes, and the head-piece is white.

[12] Evidently for *shaṭranj*. The names of several of the pieces are obviously Arabic also. Unfortunately the MS. was only legible with difficulty, and the printed work gives *furz* for both *firz* and *faras*. Dillmann, *Lexicon Linguae Aethiopicae* (Leipzig, 1865) has *säntäräj* or *säntäräzh*; Isemberg, *Dict. Amharic Lang.* (London, 1841), *säntärij*; W. C. Harris, *Highlands of Æthiopia* (London, 2 ed., 1844, iii. 170), has *shuntridge*.

The names and powers of the pieces are these: at each extreme, as our 'Rooks', are the *derr*, moving as the Rook precisely; next to them the two Knights, or *furz*, the same as our Knights; next to them are the *pheels*, or Bishop. This piece moves obliquely, like our Bishop, but can only move or cover three squares, including its own; it cannot stop at the Knight's second square, even if vacant; at the same time it can pass over any interposing piece on that square, or any other. The King (*negoose*) and the *furz* occupy the two centre squares, the King the same as with us; but the *furz* has only the very limited powers of moving one square in any direction, taking only obliquely, however. The Pawns (or *medaks*) are the same as ours; in every respect there is no obligation to take.

The game is commenced in a singular manner, and in this consists one of the excellences of a good player, as it frequently decides the fate of the game. Both parties move as many pieces one after the other as they can lay their hands on, and continue to do so till one takes a Pawn, when all proceeds as with us; up to that time the confusion appears great to a stranger, yet each keenly watches the moves of the other, and changes his tactics as he sees occasion, frequently withdrawing the moves he has already made and substituting others, so that he may be in the more favourable position at the moment of the first take, whether by himself or his adversary. The game then proceeds as with us, varied only by the difference, that I have described, in the powers of some of the pieces.

The next peculiarity is the manner of giving checkmate, all not being equally honourable. For instance, a checkmate with the Rooks or the Knights is considered unworthy of the merest tyro—that is, these, though assisting in throwing the net round the enemy, must not deal the fatal stroke. Checkmate with the *furz* is just endurable, and with one Bishop is tolerably good, but with two applauded—that is, so entangling the King that he has but two squares free, which, being commanded by your Bishops, you check with the one, and mate with the other. Mating with one, two, three, or four Pawns, the two latter particularly, is considered the *ne plus ultra* of the game.

Another peculiarity in the game, that renders this selection of your checkmate more meritorious, is that you must not denude the adversary's King of all his capital pieces, and, in fact, it is almost necessary to leave him two; if you reduce him to one, say Bishop or Knight, he commences counting his moves, and you must checkmate him before he has made seven with that piece; and as you cannot take it (there being no mate with the King alone on the board, or with only Pawns), he moves it in a way to obstruct you, and you, consequently, frequently fail from the shortness of time allowed, or are obliged to give an ignominious mate with a castle or knight, which is hailed almost as a triumph by the foe.

Furthermore, if you are a superior player, and wish to make a game of it, you will find it advisable to leave two good pieces to your adversary—say Rook and Bishop, or Rook and Knight—as if you leave him only *furz* and Bishop, for instance, he will probably force you in self-defence to take one of them; and in the other case, having still hopes of winning, he will struggle until you, having arranged your pieces so that you have the mate desired in hand, may take one or not as you find most convenient. A Pawn arriving at the eighth square takes the powers of a *furz*.

It will be seen, I think, that the game under these circumstances is less brilliant and more tedious than ours. There is, however, still ample scope for developing the powers of the players, and showing the differences in their abilities. The great point is in the skilful arrangement of your Pawns at the commencement, and a careful defence of them during the game, as it is generally by their moves that you so hamper the adversary's King as to be enabled to select the ground on which to give him mate. A piece is not considered moved till settled on a square, and your hand withdrawn from it.

I have been unable to discover any evidence for the practice of chess in Equatorial or Southern Africa, or even in Muhammadan Western Africa. In modern times the favourite board-game, called by a variety of names, is the Arabic *manqala*. This is recorded throughout the Guinea coast and the Niger basin, in Uganda, and indeed so widely over the continent that Culin is thoroughly justified in styling it ' the national game of Africa '.[13]

Hyde, however, mentions (ii. 52) that the Hanzoannite envoys, with whom he had conversed, told him that they called chess *Ufūba* in their language, and he includes in the later part of his work (ii. 378) a game which he calls *Ufūba waḥúlana*, which is played with 24 counters—12 a side—on a board of 5 by 5 squares. It is possible, therefore, that the word *ufūba* means simply game-board.

[13] Cf. S. Culin, *Mancala, the National Game of Africa*, Washington, 1896; and Lieut. R. Avelot, *Le Jeu des Godets*, in *Bull. de la Soc. d'Anthropologie de Paris*, 5th series, VII. iv (1906), 267–271, and *Le Ouri*, ibid., IX. i (1908), 9–22.

CHAPTER XVIII

CHESS IN CENTRAL AND NORTHERN ASIA, AND IN RUSSIA

Unclassified varieties.—Paucity of information.—Nomenclature.—References to chess as played by the Tibetans, Mongols, and other Siberian races.—Probable origin of this game.—Chess in Turkestan, Armenia, and Georgia.—The older chess of Russia.—Its ancestry.—Nomenclature.—History.—Pieces.—Possible traces of Asiatic influence farther West.—Ströbeck.—Conclusion.

THE question of the relationships of the forms of chess that have been discussed hitherto has been fairly simple of solution, and I have been able to arrange the games in accordance with what I conceive to have been the historical lines of development. The history of the chess of Western Europe should naturally follow now, since this game is an immediate descendant of the Muslim *shaṭranj*. But this history will run to some considerable length, and it will be more convenient, before turning to European chess, to complete the record of the game in Asia by collecting in this chapter those varieties of Asiatic chess whose place in the pedigree of the game is uncertain. To these I add the older chess of Russia, which is obviously of different parentage from the Western European game.

The Asiatic varieties are those which are played in Tibet, Mongolia, Siberia, Turkestan, and Trans-Caucasia. The uncertainty as to the connexions of these varieties with the chess of the neighbouring nations is very largely due to the scanty nature of our information. We have no records of their history, and know very little that is complete respecting the actual methods of play at the present time. It is only in the last few years that ethnologists have begun seriously to turn their attention to these remote and difficultly accessible regions,[1] and we are as a result—with the one notable exception of M. Savenkof's paper on the *Evolution of Chess*[2]—dependent for our information upon the chance references to chess in works of travel, written by explorers whose interest in the game was never keenly roused. We do know, however, that for the last 100 years at least chess has been played by every race in the North and Centre of Asia, with the exception of the Chukchis and Koriaks who inhabit the extreme N.E. corner of Siberia, and that the present game does not greatly differ from the modern European game with which it has long been in contact, owing to the large and constant influx of settlers and exiles from Russia.

It will be most convenient to begin by giving a table summarizing all the available information for the nomenclature of chess among these races.

[1] Those ethnologists who have worked in Siberia are also at the moment interested more in collecting material for other studies than in tracing the spread of board-games in N. Asia.

[2] E. V. Savenkof, *Kvoprosu op evolutsiē shakhmatnoi egry. Sravnētelno-etnografēcheskiē ocherk.* Ottēsk ēz lxiv kn. Etnografēch. Obozrâniya. Moscow, 1905.

Name of Race.	No.	Name of Game.	King = prince, leader.	Queen.	Bishop = camel.	Knight = horse.	Rook = cart, waggon.	Pawn = child.	Check.	Mate.	Other terms.
TIBETAN . .	1	chandaraki chandraki chadraki	dpon seng-ge [(lion)	stag (tiger)	rnge-mong	rta	shing-rta	bu	kish	ma't	p'a't (stalemate), zandarbegi (to castle)
,, East	(2)	—	(seng-ghe) (lion)	—	(nga-mong)	(ta; in Ladak, sta)	(shing-ta)	(bhu)	—	—	mig-máng (chessboard) [re'u-mig (v. d. Gabelenz, *Schu-king in Mandschuischer Uebersetzung*, Leipzig, 1864), chessboard. migdmangs (Schröter, *Dict. Bhotan Lang.*, Sahavampur, 1826, 275), 'one of the squares of the chessboard'.]
,, West	(3)	—	(seng-ge) (lion)	—	(nga-bong)			(bu)	—	—	
	4	—	—	—	—	—	—	—	chik	mat	
BURIAT . . .	5	shatara	khan noïn	berze	zân (elephant) temen	mörin	tergen	köbun	—	—	kulge (chessboard)
	6	shaturayin chabtaghai	—	—	—	—	—	—	shat sh't	—	
	7	shatara, shiitara	—	—	—	—	—	—	—	—	
KALMUCK, East	8	—	(khagan)	—	—	—	—	(köbegün)	—	—	
,, West	9	shatar	noyou	—	—	mörin	tergen	köbun	—	—	shatariin biche (chessboard)
	10	shatir	khan	ber; sin	temen	—	tergin	kübün	chicha	mat	jit (draw)
Old Mongol	11	—	—	—	(temegen)	—	(terge)	(köbegün)	—	—	shitaraja nagaju (to play chess)
SOYOT . . .	12	shodra chodra	noyion —	bar-merze arzlan-merze	täbä	ot	tärgä	ōl	Kt R Q sha, B too, P sott	—	khaem boshe (draw)
	13	—	noyion	oot (dog)	täbä	at	tärgä)	ōl	—	—	khol (board)
	(14)	koul-shodra	—	(arzlan (lion))	(taima)	(at)	(tairgā)	tolai (hare), thas (goose)	—	—	
OSTIAK . . .	15	—	—	—	—	—	—	—	—	—	
SAMOYEDE . .	16	—	—	—	—	—	—	—	—	—	
YUKAGIRI . .	17	—	—	—	—	—	—	—	—	—	
KAMCHADALE .	18	—	—	—	—	—	—	—	—	—	
TUNGUS . . .	19	sfenj	—	—	—	—	—	—	—	—	
YAKUT . . .	20	—	—	—	—	—	—	—	—	—	
TATAR . . .	21	—	—	—	—	—	—	—	—	—	
KHIRGHIS . .	22	—	—	—	—	—	—	—	—	—	
TURKOMAN . .	23	—	—	—	—	—	—	—	—	—	

I have endeavoured to group them on natural lines, taking first the Tibetans; next the three divisions of the Mongols proper, the Buriats (about Lake Baikal), and the E. and W. Kalmucks (Central Siberia, and the mouth of the Volga); third a group of races who have not been classified, the Uryankhs or Soyots (near the source of the Yenesei), the Ostiaks (in the lower Yenesei basin), the Samoyedes and Yukagiris (along the shores of the Arctic Ocean), and the Kamchadales (in Kamtchatka and the Aleutian Islands); fourth the Manchus of Siberia, viz. the Tunguses (Central Siberia); and lastly the Turki peoples, the Yakuts (Lena basin), the Tatars (Obi basin), the Khirghis (the steppes round the Sea of Aral), and the Turkomans of Turkestan. Where none of the columns is filled, it means that we know nothing except that chess is played by the particular people.

The authorities that I have followed in this table are:

No. 1. M. Padérin in v. d. Linde, ii. 134, 136, 197. M. Padérin was Secretary to the Russian Consulate in Mongolia in 1874. He presumably obtained them from some Buddhist pilgrim who had visited Tibet. It is possible that he merely translated the Mongol names into Tibetan. The terms *p'a't* and *zandarbegi* look very suspicious, and, following v. d. Linde, I give them with considerable hesitation.

Nos. 2 and 3 are added for comparison from H. A. Jaeschke's *Short Practical Grammar of the Tibetan language*, Kye-Lang, 1865. None of them is given as used in chess, excepting *mig-máng*, for which see p. 43, n. 41.

No. 4. Huc and Gabet, cited below.

Nos. 5–9 are given in v. d. Linde, ii. 136, 141. No. 5 contains the terms in use among the Aginsk Buriats. No. 6 was given by Budmajew. No. 7 is from Schmid's *Wörterbuch*. No. 9 is from Prof. Galstunsky.

No. 10. Quoted in Savenkof's paper from Nebolsin's *Sketches of Life among the Kalmucks of the Khoshoÿtof camp* (Lower Volga).

Nos. 12–14 are from Savenkof. No. 12 from E. K. Yakovlef. No. 13 from N. Ph. Katanof. No. 14 from the catalogue of the Minusinsk Museum.

No. 19 was given by M. Peredolsky, cf. *BCM.*, 1904, p. 148.

TIBET. The Tibetan name for chess, *chandaraki*, is evidently derived per metathesin from the Skr. *chaturanga*, and its existence is valuable evidence for the fact that the Tibetans obtained their knowledge of the existence of chess direct from India. At the same time, the present game appears to be identical with that played by the Mongol tribes to the North, who are brought into close relationship with Tibet from their frequent pilgrimages to Lhasa and other Buddhist shrines.

Our oldest and best information as to Tibetan chess is contained in the correspondence of Mr. George Bogle, Jr., of Daldowie, a Scotsman, who was sent by Warren Hastings on a mission to Tibet in 1775. This was included in Craufurd's *Sketches relating to the Hindoos* (London, 1792, II). In a letter from Teshoo Loombo, March 20, 1775, Bogle says:

Among the Tartars, who have come some three, and some four months' journey on pilgrimage to the Lama, I have met with some masterly chess-players. The game is exactly the same as with us, except that the privilege of moving two steps is confined to the first Pawn played by each player; Castling is unknown; and if the King is left alone, it is considered as a drawn game. They generally begin with the Queen's Pawn.[3] They have no idea of our unsociable method of playing. When a Siberian sits down to chess, he gets surrounded by three or four of his countrymen, who lay their heads together and consult with him about the propriety of every move. I had nothing for it but to engage an equal number of Tartars on my side, and so combat them with their own weapons. Some of the Tibetans are also acquainted with chess, which they have learned from the Calmacks, but they are, I think, far inferior to their masters. I met, however, with one man, a General, who, under all the disadvantages of playing with new pieces, fought a tough battle, but he was ordered away upon service the next day, and I had an opportunity of playing only one game with him.

From two other letters we only learn in addition that Bogle's opponents were generally Kalmucks, and that these players knew nothing of stalemate. He found the Kalmucks 'tough hands' to beat.

A second reference occurs in the well-known volume of Travels of the Jesuit Fathers Huc and Gabet (xx. 531, of the third London ed. of 1856):

We enjoyed at Lang-ki-Tsoung a few days of salutary agreeable repose. . . . Prayers, walks, and some games of chess contributed to the delights of those days of leisure. The chessmen which we used had been given to us by the Regent of Lha-Ssa; the pieces were made of ivory, and represented various animals, sculptured with some delicacy. The Chinese, as is known, are passionately fond of chess, but their game is very different from ours. The Tartars and Thibetians are likewise acquainted with chess; and, singularly enough, their chessboard is absolutely the same as our own; their pieces, although differently formed, represent the same value as ours, and follow the same moves; and the rules of the game are precisely the same in every respect. What is still more surprising, these people cry 'chik' when they check a piece, and 'mate' when the game is at an end. These expressions, which are neither Thibetian nor Mongol, are, nevertheless, used by every one, yet no one can explain their origin and true signification. . . . We have seen among the Tartars first-rate players of chess; they play quickly and with less study, it seemed to us, than the Europeans apply, but their moves are not the less correct.

Finally Mr. Rockhill, in his brief account of his travels in Tibet, notes that Tibetan chess is practically identical with the European game.

MONGOL RACES. A reference in Ssanang Ssetsen's *Chungtaiji* (ed. with trans. by I. J. Schmidt as the *Geschichte der Ost-Mongolen*, St. Petersburg, 1829, p. 228) suggests that this race was familiar with chess at the end of the 16th c. A certain Ssetsen Chaghan-Noyan is mentioned quite incidentally to have been playing chess (Mongol *shitaraju nagadchu*) with his mother. Another instance has been quoted above, p. 43, n. 41.

I have collected the following references to chess:—

(1) Prof. P. S. Pallas, in his *Sammlungen hist. Nachrichten über die mongolischen Völkerschaften* (St. Petersburg, 1776, i. 157), says with respect to the games of the Kalmucks[4]:

In winter, chess and cards (*kusö*) are the usual pastimes of the men, who are now

[3] It is definitely stated in one of the other letters that these rules are also those observed by the Tibetan players.

[4] Cf. W. Tooke, *Russia*, London, 1780-3, iv. 39 and 499: 'The Kalmucs likewise play at Chess, Cards, and Toccodillo much as we do.' And in Clarke's *Russia*, 244, 'The Calmuck Tartars play at Chess and Backgammon.'

compelled to be idle. At chess there are many who are very expert, particularly among the priests, and this originally Oriental game is also at home among the Mongols. They observe the most usual rules completely, except that at the beginning of the game they commence by moving three pieces. When we say check they say *shat* or *sh't*, and they call the game *Shaterä*. They say mate as we do. They have also a kind of draughts (*mingma*) in which the men are placed on white squares, and the black are left bare, and besides this they know and play backgammon under the name of *Narr*.

(2) The great English missionary to the Mongols, the Rev. James Gilmour, in his book *Among the Mongols* (London, n.d., p. 292), describes a game of chess that he once saw played in the prison at Kalgan (about 120 m. N.E. from Pekin) with an improvised board and pieces. He mentions pieces called Camels, Mandarin, and Child. It would therefore appear to have been the Mongol game.

(3) Baron A. E. Rosen, in his *Otechest v. Zapeski*, 1876, No. 4, p. 465 (*Shakhm. Listok*, 1879, p. 335 ; *Shakhm. Obosr.*, 1902, p. 4), says that—

A Buriat beat our best players, and told us that this game had been known to him from childhood, and that it had come to them from China. (Savenkof, op. cit., 39.)

(4) A. P. Byelyaef, in his *Bospominaniyakh o perezhitom i pereduman nom s. 1803* ('Memories of Life and Thought since 1803,' *Shakhm. Obosr.*, 1892, p. 378), tells of a similar experience, and concludes:

Speaking generally, the Asiatics played with such skill as to be able to contend with good players.

Nothing is said about any peculiarities of rule or differences from the European game (Savenkof, op. cit., 39).[5]

(5) P. Nebolsin, in his *Ocherki bïta kalmïkov khoshoutovskago ilusa*, Bibl. dlya. cht. 1852, No. 7 ('Sketches of life among the Kalmucks of the Khoshoÿtof camp,' *Shakhm. Obosr.*, 1892, pp. 4 and 410), gives some information regarding the nomenclature which I have used above, and states that the Kalmucks continue the game, even with a single King (Savenkof, op. cit., 41).

THE URYANKHS or SOYOTS. This race is one of the least civilized of all the native tribes of Northern Asia. Their chess would appear to be an offshoot of the Mongol game, since the nomenclature is largely Mongol, *merzé* (dog), *täbä* (camel), *ot* (horse), and *ōl* (child) being the only native terms.

It is to this game that M. Savenkof devotes the first chapter of his paper. He obtained some information when at Minusinsk in the early eighties, and at a later date secured some native chessmen and further information from E. K. Yakovlef, and again in 1889 from Prof. N. Ph. Katanof of Kazan. I take these sources of knowledge in order.

(1) The catalogue of the Minusinsk collection (Trans-Sayan district, Soyots, Dept. VI, 6 ; Games for adults, p. 112) has the following entries:—

I. KOUL-SHODRA (chess); 32 pieces carved in agalmatolite (the work of the Soyot Nomjal, at the source of the Yenisei). Height, 2–5 cm. Pieces: master

[5] This passage was cited in full in a paper by S. A. Sorokin in the *Shakhmatnoy Obosrenie*, Moscow, 1892, p. 378.

(*noyion*), lion (*arslan*), two-humped camel (*taima*), horse (*at*), hare (*tolai*), goose (*khas*), and monument (*tairga*).[6]

II. The same in wood, rougher workmanship.

III. BOUGE-SHODRA (boars' chess). Somewhat resembling the game of *Volki i ovtsy* (wolves and sheep). On one side are 2 boars, on the other 24 calves (*bouza*).

The piece which is described as a monument is probably only an elaborately decorated car. One of M. Savenkof's *tärgä*, of which I give a drawing, might easily be mistaken for some kind of monument if one did not know that its name *tärgä* (*tairga*) means a car or cart. There is no difference of colour or decoration by which the pieces on one side can be distinguished from those on the other, and I suppose that the major pieces could only be distinguished by careful attention to the direction in which they faced on the board. On the other hand, I think that the pawns are represented as hares and geese to separate the two armies.

There are no chessboards in the Museum, but M. Savenkof learnt that the

Soyot chessmen. After Savenkof.

board consisted of 8 by 8 squares, all uncoloured. The pieces are arranged for play as in the European game, but he was unable to obtain any exact information as to the rules or method of play. The game was thought to be very similar to chess as usually played.

At a later date M. Savenkof secured some sets of Soyot chess, of which he gives the engravings which are reproduced here. The *noyion*, or master of the house, is represented sitting and wearing the costume of a wealthy Uryankh, which is not unlike the Chinese dress. The *merzé*, or dog, is an immense mastiff standing on guard. The Camel and Horse are riderless. The Car in one set is a four-wheeled chariot with palanquin, in another is merely indicated by a single wheel. The Pawns are recumbent puppies, but

[6] I am not quite sure of these Museum names, and suspect that in the case of the Camel and Pawns the Soyot names are merely the native words for the figures depicted, and are not necessarily appropriate to chess.

in one set they are half-naked wrestlers, the one side squatting on their heels, the other resting on one knee.

(2) E. K. Yakovlef, who had also travelled beyond Sayan and in Mongolia, supplied the nomenclature[7] that I have given above as No. 12, in the Table on p. 367, from the description of a Soyot lama named Soitjen-kolen, and continued:

Peculiarities in the rules of the game: the board was always so placed that the corner square to the left of each player was black, an entirely superfluous convention in view of the following: the K and Q do not occupy a fixed position[8] but always stand side by side on the middle squares of the border line, yet invariably so that the K stood opposite K, and the Q opposite Q. The positions of the remaining pieces were as usual. The Q moves in a diagonal direction only to the next square. If a P gets to the border line it becomes a *merzê*. Even if the *merzê* is not yet taken the P becomes one only after a move in the diagonal direction on to the next square. Only at the beginning of the game is it possible for a P to miss a square. At the end of the game there must be no P left, otherwise it is *khaem-boshê*,[9] i.e. a drawn game. There is no castling, nor taking a P *en passant*. If the Kt, R, or Q checks, they say *sha*; if the B, *too*; if the P, *sott*. The first move is a matter of reciprocal courtesy.

The pieces are cut with a knife out of wood or soft stone; those belonging to opponents are distinguished not so much by colour as by peculiarities in the carving. The *noyion* is sometimes represented in the likeness of the God-inspired Buddha. The *merzê* or dog lies with paws extended before it. The *täbä* is an unloaded camel. The *ot* is an unsaddled horse. The *tärgä* is a wheel. The *ol* are small puppies.

M. Yakovlef also sent the score of the commencement of a game which he had played with a Soyot named Tardzhi.[10] Games between Europeans and natives are not very valuable, since they cannot present an uncoloured picture of native play. In the present case M. Yakovlef played first, and his play was evidently coloured by preconceived ideas as to what tactics would be most appropriate to the older European game. From a careful examination of Tardzhi's play I conclude that his rules were different from those which M. Yakovlef obtained from Soitjen-kolen. He never moved his Bishop except to the third diagonal square (as in shaṭranj); and he moved his Queen from d8 to e7, and at a later move from e7 to f7. No Pawn was advanced two squares in one move after the first move (Pd4, Pd5). I am inclined to think that Tardzhi's own game was of an older type than Soitjen-kolen's.

M. Yakovlef also notes that the initial consonant of *shodra* is closer in sound to *ch*, and thinks *chodra* a better transcription.

(3) Prof. Katanof obtained his information from a Soyot named Domba,

[7] Of the terms he gives, *noyion* means master, *bar* means tiger, *arzlan* or *arslan* means lion, and *merzé* means dog.

[8] This shows that the use of chequered boards is an innovation that has not yet affected the older method of arrangement.

[9] M. Savenkof gives the last element thus with hesitation. He was not able to decipher the MS. *Boté*; *boyué* or *bolé* are all possible readings.

[10] The score runs: M. Yakovlef *v.* Tardzhi (arrangement as in European chess). 1 Pd4, Pd5; 2 Ktc3, Pc6; 3 Bf4, Pe6; 4 Pe3, Bd6; 5 Bd3, B×B; 6 P×B, Kte7; 7 Pf3, Ktf5; 8 B×Kt, P×B; 9 Kf2, Be6; 10 Kth3, Ktd7; 11 Re1, Ktb6; 12 Ktg5, Kd7; 13 R×B, P×R; 14 Ktf7, Qe7; 15 Kt×R, R×Kt; 16 Qe2, Ktc4; 17 Pb3, Kta5; 18 Kta4, Pb6; 19 Re1, Re8; 20 Pg3, Pg6; 21 Pg4, Ph6; 22 Ph3, Ph5; 23 Kg3, hP×P; 24 fP×P, P×P; 25 P×P, Qf7; 26 Rh1, Ktb7; 27 Qe5, Ktd6; 28 Ktc3. No more was recorded. M. Yakovlef used the modern moves of Q and B, but accepted the restriction of the P's first move.

who lived on the River Elleges. After giving the names of the pieces (see No. 13 in the Table) he continues:

The board is the same as the Russian. Between rows 4 and 5 of the board passes a line, 1 cm. in breadth, marking the boundary between the dominions of the two princes. The moves for all the pieces are the same as the corresponding European ones. The pieces are set out as follows: K e1 and e8; Q d1 and d8; R a1, h1, a8, h8; B c1, f1, c8, f8; Kt b1, g1, b8, g8; Ps along rows 2 and 7.

The board is called *khol*, a Mongol word, and the game itself *chidera*, a Mongol word.

He goes on to argue that the Soyot game is derived from the Mongol, the latter from the Persian.

Here we have a third set of moves which agrees with neither of those given by M. Yakovlef. The game seems to me to be clearly in a plastic condition, and undergoing changes as the result of the contact with Russian chess. Probably other observers would have discovered other varieties of rule showing the same tendency towards the European game.

OTHER SIBERIAN RACES. Here our information is very scanty. I give it for what it is worth.

(1) In Capt. John Dundas Cochrane's (R.N.) *Narrative of a Pedestrian Journey through Russia and Siberian Tartary* (London, 1824, i. 319) we read:

The fair (by the fortress of Ostrovnaya, on the banks of the Aniuy or Anjui, within the Arctic circle, 160–170 E. long.) at length finished. I prepared to depart for Nishney Kolymsk with many thanks to my venerable Yukagir host for all his kindness. I passed the time very agreeably at his house; he was a very good chess-player and was fond of the game. His manner of play added another instance to many I have witnessed, that there is, in various parts of the world, little or no difference anywhere in the moving of the pieces. I have played the game with Yakuti, Tongousi, and Yukagiri; but the Tchuktchi laughed at me for such a childish employment of my time. While upon this subject, I may remark, as a circumstance relative to the game of chess, and which has repeatedly surprised me, that wherever a people recognize and play it, they are infallibly Asiatics. Neither the Tchuktchi nor the Koriaks understand anything of it, but all the Kamtchatdales, and other Asiatics, are familiar with it.

(2) The *BCM.*, April, 1904, translates (via the *Schachrubrik der Bohemia*) a letter in the *St. Petersburger Zeitung*, in which Herr Kupffer says:

Herr Perédolsky, conservator of the University of St. Petersburg, informs me that . . . he was sent in the year 1895 on a special mission to Northern Siberia, and that he devoted many months to ethnological investigations among the Tungusians and the Yakoots. . . . He found that all the tribes (the Samoyedes, the Tungusians, the Yakoots, &c.) are enthusiastic 'board-game' players. The game of draughts is played with the greatest frequency; the game of chess with the greatest enthusiasm. The people make boards for themselves in a very short time. With the help of a hot iron, they burn 32 of the squares black; and they cut pieces, which are somewhat crude, out of bone. The Pawns are rather smaller than the pieces; and it is a noticeable fact that the Pawns and pieces are similar in shape. They are like the latest types of our Rooks. The distinctive marks are as follows: Bishops are cross-hatched with straight lines; Knights with semi-circular and straight strokes; and Rooks with small circles. The King alone is coloured red. A game lasts for hours; often it is not finished till the second day. Hard by sits a crowd of spectators, who stare in silence at the board. When, however, a move is made, if it be unexpected, pretty, or brilliant, and more particularly if it be the sacrifice of a piece, the spectators jump up, shout out loudly, exhibit signs of delight, or dance, or even weep through excitement. A player often thinks for an hour before he makes a move. The finishing of a game is quite a scene of festivity. Excitement often causes the players to raise their stakes, until the loss of the game involves the absolute ruin of the loser. A game, to begin with, is for the reindeers; then for the dogs; for clothes; for a man's whole belongings; and, in the end, even the women are gambled away. Herr Kupffer adds that Herr Perédolsky showed him a board and set of men which had been bought for half a pound of the commonest kind of tobacco-leaf, from a Tungusian of the lower levels between the Yenisei and the Chatanga. The board was of the ordinary size, and made in the way described above; the men were about an inch in height, cross-hatched, with the usual distinguishing marks. The Tungusian name for the game is 'Sfenj'.

(3) A. A. Pavloff, *Zhivopisnoi Rossiē* (Picturesque Russia, 1884, xi. 93), states that in the course of excavations on the site of a ruined city in the Kurgan district, Tobolsk Government (55° 26′ N., 83° E.), some bone articles resembling chessmen were found. The city goes back to the commencement of the Iron Period, and Pavlof attributes the articles to the Mongol rule of the descendants of Tīmūr Leng (Savenkof, op. cit., 35).

(4) The Prussian postmaster Wagner, who was exiled to Siberia, 1759–63, says that when, seven versts from Tobolsk (58° 2′ N., 85° 54′ E.), on the banks of the Irtish, he was stopped by the ice, he stayed at a Tatar camp and played chess with his Tatar host. M. Savenkof, who cites the Russian translation of J. L. Wagner's *Schicksäle*, Berlin, 1789, thinks that possibly draughts is meant, since there was some confusion about 1800 in Russian books between *shakhmati* (chess) and *shashka* (now restricted to draughts).

(5) M. Savenkof states, on the authority of A. N. Maximof, that the inhabitants of the Aleutian Islands play chess. He quotes Benjaminof's *v. Aleutov* ('Among the Aleutian Islanders'), ii. 16, 308.

(6) This branch of chess reached its final limit in Alaska. The U. S. Nat. Museum contains (Cat. No. 16300) a collection of 22 carved wooden chessmen, from 1 to 3 ins. in height, which were obtained from the Yakutat Indians (Koluschan Stock) at Port Mulgrave, Alaska, by Dr. W. H. Dall. They are figured in Stewart Culin's *Games of the North American Indians* (24th Annual Report of the Bureau of American Ethnology, Washington, 1907, p. 793). Mr. Culin includes this game among the games learnt from Europeans, but the shapes of the pieces show no trace of European influence and compel me to place this game beside those treated in the present chapter.

This completes the available evidence. It is obviously too vague and incomplete to serve as the foundation for any but the most tentative of conclusions. It suggests, however, a common origin for the practical game as played at the present time by Tibetan, Mongol, and Soyot, and I think it not improbable that all these Siberian varieties of chess go back to an older Mongol chess which had spread over Northern Asia before the Russian conquest, and which, since that time, has been everywhere modified through its contact with the Russian game during the last 200 years.[11] The different accounts of Soyot chess show these changes in progress at the present day. In less inaccessible regions probably they have been completed for a century at least. The chief value of the pictures of Soyot chess consists in the indications that they give of the earlier rules of Mongol chess.

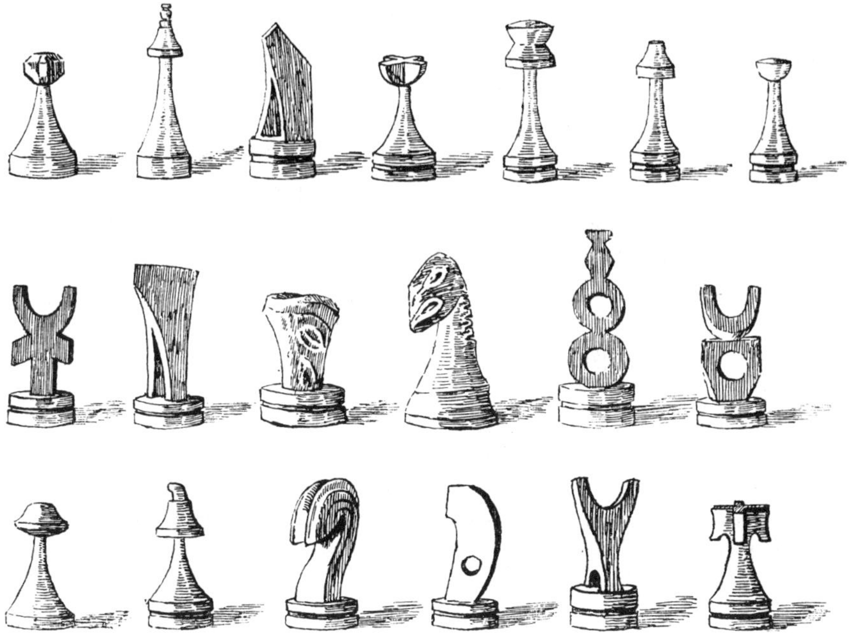

Yakutat chessmen (Alaska). After Culin.

This game would appear to have been one in which—

(1) The ordinary rules of the older varieties of chess were followed: viz. the Pawn only able to move a single step in any turn of play, the King without power of leaping, the Queen confined to a diagonal move to an adjacent square,[12] the Bishop leaping over one square diagonally into the one beyond.[13]

[11] M. Savenkof dissents from the view that the changes that Mongol chess has undergone, and which Soyot chess is undergoing, are the result of the influence of the European game. He condemns it as based upon *a priori* reasoning and as unsupported by ethnological evidence. He says, 'The newest form of chess in Asia is in our opinion to be regarded more correctly as the final evolutionary form which has begun to settle, or in its principal features has already settled in Asia independently,' and declares that ethnography alone can solve the problem of the development of the ancient Indian chaturanga or the Muslim shaṭranj in Asia. This is an extravagant claim to make, and M. Savenkof overlooks the improbability of two independent races developing a game like chess on identical lines. Unless it can be established (which I dispute) that there is for each chessman only one possible development of move from the original move possible, the mathematical probability that Asia and Europe independently hit upon the same improvements in chess is infinitesimal. European chess, with all the prestige that attaches to the game of the ruling and the more civilized people, has been in contact with the native game sufficiently long to account for all the observed changes. We know what has been the result of the influence of the chess of the few thousand European settlers in India in altering the native game; in Siberia the Europeans are as numerous as the Asiatics.

[12] Soitjen-kolen.

[13] This is less certain, but I think it can be inferred from Tardzhi's play.

(2) The ordinary arrangement of the board with King opposite King and Queen opposite Queen was observed. (The board being unchequered, there was no rule necessary to fix the relative positions of King and Queen.)

(3) The game was commenced by each player in order making a definite number of moves in the first turn of play.[14] After the first 'move' the game was continued by each player in succession making single moves in his turn of play. This has crystallized in Tibetan and Soyot chess, and—possibly generally—into a double move of a Pawn being possible and usual for the first move made by each player.[15]

(4) *Bare King* drew only,[16] and stalemate was not permitted.

All this points rather to a game derived directly from India than to a development of the Muslim shaṭranj. We cannot, of course, neglect the more certain evidence which is afforded by the nomenclature of the game in Siberia, when we attempt to ascertain the parentage of this Mongol chess. There would appear to be two parentages possible, the one Persian or Muslim, the other Indian direct.[17] In the first case the game would have travelled N.E. from the province of Sūghd with its twin capitals of Bukhārā and Samarqand—both destroyed in 616/1219 in the first Mongol invasion of Changīz Khān—following the reverse route to that taken by the Mongol hordes in that war. The probable date would be later rather than earlier, say *c.* 1300. In the second case the game would have travelled from India by some route that left the Muslim lands well to the west, by Tibet or Chinese Turkestan.

The evidence of nomenclature is, however, indecisive. While the Tibetan *chandaraki*, *chandraki*, *chadraki* point to the Skr. *chaturanga*, the Mongol *shatara*, *shitara*, *shatir*, *shodra* point to the Arabic and Persian *shaṭranj*. There is no necessity in Mongol to seek for some means of representing the sound of *ch* as there was in Arabic. The fact that the Kalmucks call backgammon *narr* (= Ar. and Per. *nard*) is indirect confirmation for the Muslim ancestry of the name *shatara*.[18] The Tibetan and Mongol terms for check and mate are all of Muslim origin. The Soyot *khaem-boshé* may also contain the Per. *qām* (Ar. *qā'īm*), which has the same meaning of 'drawn game'.

The game, with its prince, dog, camel, horse, car, and children, has lost all signs of that connexion with the army which is so prominent in Indian and Muslim chess. It may instead be accepted as a picture of the nomad life of a Mongol family, but there is no evidence that the native player has ever

[14] See the passage quoted above from Prof. Pallas.

[15] Probably this generally resolves itself into 1 Pd4, Pd5; but none of the authorities restrict the privilege to this P, as is the case in the Rūmī chess of Muhammadan India.

[16] I do not pretend to understand the ending *Khaem-boshé* in the Lama's description.

[17] I reject the possibility of a Chinese ancestry because the Mongol chess is totally unlike the Chinese game; and I reject the other possibility, that the Mongols obtained their chess from Europe, because the nomenclature is incompatible with this view.

[18] On the other hand the Kalmuck *mingma* (draughts) is obviously the Tibetan *migmang* (chessboard), so that there is evidence for the Tibetan origin of one Mongol board-game. If, moreover, M. Savenkof is right in saying that *chodra* represents the Soyot pronunciation more accurately than *shodra*, we cannot exclude the possibility of this word being derived from the Tibetan *chadraki*.

taken this view. Compared with other forms of chess, the names of the pieces present three striking features—the replacement of the Counsellor by an animal, the dog or tiger; the disappearance of the Elephant, and the appearance of the Camel in its place; and the survival of a clear knowledge of the corner piece as a car, wagon, or chariot.

The dog naturally plays an important part in the life of these nomad tribes, but I do not think that we can explain its presence on the chessboard in that way.[19] With v. d. Linde[20] I see here the workings of popular etymology, assisted by the use of actual carvings of real objects for chessmen. The unintelligible foreign name *firz* was, I believe, confused with the two native words *bars*, a tiger, and *merzé*, a dog, which gave the carver of pieces an inspiration for his work. The other Soyot terms—*oot* (dog), *bar-merzé* (tiger-dog), *arzlan-merzé* (lion-dog), *arzlan*, would all follow naturally from the use of carved pieces. Wherever the chessmen are actual figures of animate objects we find a greater variety in the nomenclature of the men. If this view be correct, that there has been a confusion between the Muslim *firz* and native words, we have here another important example of Persian influence in the Mongol game.

If we confine our attention to the ordinary chess, we have no instance of the replacement of the Elephant by the Camel in Persian chess. The change has been made in many forms of chess that have been recorded in India, but in every case the Elephant remains upon the chessboard in the place of the Rook. There is no known instance of any Indian game of chess in which the Camels stand on c1 and f1 (c8 and f8), and at the same time the Chariots stand on the corner squares. I conclude, therefore, that we have here an independent Mongol change, in which the typically Indian beast of burden is replaced by the typical Mongol beast, the two-humped or Bactrian camel, which is a native of Central Asia.

The survival of the Chariot (car or wagon) among the pieces is somewhat remarkable. In later Indian chess it has entirely dropped out of use, except in Southern India. Although it is certain that the Persian *rukh* as a name of a chessman meant chariot, and the use of this word with the same meaning is recorded in dialectal speech both in Persian and Arabic, yet this meaning was largely forgotten by the Muslims,[21] and it is unlikely that the Mongols learnt the true meaning of the name from them.

The evidence accordingly shows that both Persian (or Muslim) and Indian influences have acted upon the Mongol game. I think that the simplest solution of the problem of the parentage of these games is to regard them as Indian varieties which have been profoundly affected, first by Persian and

[19] Nor can I accept the suggestions of M. Savenkof that its presence is due to Shamanist worship of the dog, or to a conscious replacement of the Queen, or (as it would conceivably have been) the wife, by the dog, as a more important member of the nomad household. There can be no question of the 'Queen' in an Asiatic variety of chess.

[20] V. d. Linde, ii. 197; and *Qst.*, 263.

[21] The general use of the conventional mushroom type of piece would certainly help in this.

then, at a much later date, by European influences. I attach considerable importance to the rules of initial play as given by Bogle and Pallas, which I think are probably Indian in origin.

TURKESTAN, &c. We have still less information for the chess of Turkestan [22] and the trans-Caucasian provinces of the Russian Empire than for the games which we have been discussing. It is, however, clear that Muslim chess has had ample opportunities for reaching these peoples. Bukhārā, Marv, and Samarqand were all at one time under the Caliphate, and were governed by Muhammadan rulers from 1300 until the Russian annexation. There is, accordingly, but little occasion for the rise of any different variety from the Persian game. M. Savenkof quotes M. Chernevski (who contributed a paper on chess in Turkestan to the *Shakhmatni Listok* in 1877, pp. 268–70, 'Shakhmati v. Turkestānā') as saying that two varieties of chess are now played in Bukhārā, viz. the European and Persian games. As we have seen in the case of India, the recognition of the differences between two varieties of chess has stopped the tendency to amalgamate the games.

In Armenia chess is called *satranj*, which shows that the game is the Muslim variety, as is also established by the Kurdish chessmen depicted on page 361.

V. d. Linde (ii. 197) gave the following list of names for the pieces in the Georgian game. Although he received them from Prof. Zagareli of St. Petersburg, he was somewhat sceptical as to their genuineness, and in repeating them I cannot guarantee that they are reliable.

K.	Q.	B.	Kt.	R.	P.
mephe	lazieri	rku (? tortoise)	mchedari	etli (wagon)	potki

The German *Handbuch des Schachspiels* (1874) has an incidental note (p. 503) that the 'Queen' in the Georgian game possesses the move of the Knight in addition to that of the European Queen. This suggests that the new move of this piece reached Georgia from Russia or Turkey in the eighteenth century. Jaenisch (*Palamède*, 1842) wrote that there were many first-class players among the Georgians, but that they did *not* castle.

RUSSIA IN EUROPE. Right down to the time of Peter the Great (1689–1725) Russia remained almost completely out of touch with Western Christendom, and all its affinities were with Asia. Neither the Russian name for

[22] Cf. Dr. H. Lansdell's *Russian Central Asia*, London, 1885, ii. 444 n. (a work that contains a valuable bibliography of these countries): 'When not engaged in plundering, they (the Turkomans) are extremely idle, lying about their tents playing chess, at which they are skilful, or gossiping,' for which he gives as his authority a paper by Bn. Benoist-Methin, read before the Paris Geog. Soc. in 1884. M. Savenkof quotes Chernevski (*Shakhm. Obosr.*, 1892, 410), Gonyaief (*Shakhm. Listok*, 1879, 334), Verechagin, and Komarof (*Shakhm. Obosr.*, 1893, 250), who describe the national game of Turkestan as *Turkestanskiya shashki* (? Turkestan draughts). He also gives other references to notes in Russian magazines. In one of these (*Shakhm. Listok*, 1879, 335) is an account of a game played at Khojend on a 'board' traced in the sand, with stones for chessmen.

chess, nor the pieces of the Russian game, show any trace of European origin. We are consequently driven to look for the parentage of Russian chess in the game of some one or other of the non-Christian Asiatic races that are situated on the confines of Russia, or in the game of the Byzantine Empire to which the country owes its Eastern Christianity.

At one time it was supposed[23] that chess was introduced into Russia by the Mongols or Tatars, who overran the country from 1200 to 1400 in a succession of invasions of the most destructive and ruthless character. With the discovery of authentic references to chess in Russian works which date back to a period anterior to the earliest Mongol incursions, this view must be abandoned. It is, however, quite possible, and indeed, I believe, certain, that the chess of these peoples left at a later date an impress upon the Russian game.

Since these earliest references occur exclusively in ecclesiastical literature, M. Sorokin next advocated a Byzantine ancestry through the intermediary of the Eastern Slavonic races, the Serbs and Bulgars. He developed this view in a series of papers in the *Shakhmatnoy Obosrenie* (Moscow, 1892, ii. 222, 307, 344 seq.). It had been suggested previously, but without evidence in support, by the Russian historian, I. E. Sabelin, in his *Home life of the Russian Tsarinas in the 16th and 17th centuries* (Moscow, 1872, 742).

M. Savenkof, however, rejects this view, for reasons which appear to me sufficient. As I have already shown, there is no evidence that *zatrikion* ever was popular among the Byzantine Greeks. From 1100 at the latest, chess was condemned by the Eastern Church, and the early Russian references also are all condemnatory of the game. In these chess is called *shakhmaté*, a name that is simply the Persian or Arabic *shāh māt* (checkmate), and not *zatrikion* or a modification of this word, as we should naturally expect had the game been introduced from Byzantium. I think it more probable that Christianity found chess already popular in Russia, and attempted to stamp it out as a relic of heathenism.

A third route by which chess could have reached Russia is to be found in the trade route from the mouth of the Volga to Baghdād, which was already of importance by 850 A.D. In this commerce the Khuzār hordes which had established themselves upon the steppes of Southern Russia before the 8th c. acted as the intermediary between Muslim and Slav. M. Savenkof gives several references to Arabic geographers to testify to the extent of this trade. The earliest and most interesting occurs in the *K. al-masālik wa'l-mamālik* of b. Khordādhbeh, a work which was written 230–4/844–8. B. Khordādhbeh tells how the Russian merchants brought their wares from the most distant parts of their country to the South, and thence, either by the Black Sea to the cities of Greece, where the Byzantine Emperors exacted the trade duty of $\frac{1}{10}$, or by the Don and Volga valleys to the great Khuzār market of Itil at

[23] By C. F. Jaenisch (*Palamède*, 1842, 163–5 and *CPC.*, 1852, 368–70), whence by Forbes (226–30), by v. d. Lasa in 1854, by v. d. Linde (ii. 192), and by M. K. Gonyaef (*Shakhm. Listok*, 1879).

the mouth of the Volga, where the Khuzār khān received his tax of $\frac{1}{10}$. Thence the merchants sailed along the Caspian to the south-east shore, and finally they carried their wares by camel trains right to Baghdād, where b. Khordādhbeh had himself seen Russian merchants. Additional evidence for this trade is afforded by the numerous finds of Arabic coins which have been made in the Dnieper basin. The bulk of these hoards consists of coins of the 9th and 10th cc., but there are some which contain nothing but coins of the 8th and early 9th cc., which shows that the trade had already commenced before 900 A.D. It probably was ended by the Mongol invasions. While it lasted it is probable that it provided the Muslim world with the Slav slaves that were so common in the 10th and 11th cc.

It is to this route that M. Savenkof attributes the introduction of chess into Russia. In this I think he is probably right. When, however, he goes on to suggest that the introduction may have taken place so early as the 5th or 6th c. A.D. from Sāsānian Persia, I think he is claiming too great an antiquity for Russian chess. We can only say that the game was well enough known by 1150 to have a native name.

We have already seen that the condemnation of dice-play in the Eastern Nomocanon had been extended by John Zonares to include chess. Christianity had been introduced into Russia in 988, over a century before the time of Zonares. Thenceforward there was a large and increasing Greek element resident in Kiev and other towns of Southern Russia, and the higher ranks of the clergy were mainly recruited from Greeks. It was only natural that the Nomocanon and its numerous commentaries should have been introduced into Russia, and the early Russian translations, of which several are known to exist in MS., are now known under the name of the Kormch books. Among other commentaries that of John Zonares also reached Russia in the earlier half of the twelfth century. In the Russian translation of the note to the 42nd Rule of the *Apostolic Canons* which I have quoted in Ch. IX, the Greek word *zatrikion* is replaced by *shakhmaté*.

The influence of this commentary is to be traced in the *Svodni* (Photian) *Kormch*. In this MS. the Greek *kuboi* (dice) is rendered *zerniyu* or *shakhmaté*; while the 50th Rule of the Canons published by the 6th General Council (3rd Council of Constantinople, A.D. 680) is translated:

No clergy nor layman shall play at *zerniyu*,[24] *shakhmaté* and *tablei*.[25]

The *Clementine Kormch* (of the end of the 13th c.) contains also a series of directions or advice on conduct which were to be given to the priest at

[24] *Zerniyu* is obviously connected with the Mod. Gk. *zari*, *azari*, *azarē*, *zargia*, *zaria*, and the Turkish *zār*, all meaning dice. The origin of these terms is unknown. They are probably connected with the Arabic *zār*, which, in the form *az-zār*, with the article prefixed, came into Spain as the name of a popular dice-game, and is the source of our word *hazard*.

[25] *Tablei* is the Gr. *tabla*. The name suggests strongly that this game had been introduced into Russia by the Greeks. It may be claimed also that it indirectly supports the Byzantine parentage of Russian chess. But (1) *tabla* was evidently a very popular game among the Greeks, and the evidence seems to show that chess never attained any great popularity in the Eastern Empire, (2) the fact that tables retained a Greek name while chess had a native name from the first is evidence against a common method of introduction.

ordination. Th. I. Buslaef has edited these under the title of *Svetok zakonynyĭe* ('Book of the Law'). Among these directions we read :

Even if invited, do not attend feasts and banquetings, wear a garment that extends to the ankles, not of many hues nor with worldly adornments, do not read prohibited books, . . . play no games of magic, do not listen to foolish fables, put away from you *leké* and *shakhmaté*.

A later work, the *Pchela* ('Bee'), which exists in a MS. of the 14th c. (§ 17), has the following lament :

Tell me which of you . . . has taken books in his hand and read the writing? If he tries to write, no one can read it. But *tablei* and *shakhi* are found in many of your houses. Books there are none in any of your houses. or only perhaps in a few, &c.

In a similar strain the Metropolitan Daniel, who had been appointed by Vassili III in 1522, deals with games in his charge to the clergy :

Now there are certain of the clergy, elders, deacons, subdeacons, readers, and singers, who amuse themselves by playing on the psaltery and fiddle . . . and also play *zerniyu, shakhmaté*, and *tablisti*, and sing diabolical songs, and indulge in immoderate and continual drinking . . . whereby great harm results to themselves and to others, &c.

About 1550 the Protohierarch Sylvester wrote his *Domostroi* ('Household Government'). In this work (ch. xxiv, On Evil Living) he extends the denunciation of games to the laity :

But the man who does not live according to God and the Christian life, . . . who is a drunkard, . . . who lives a dissolute life, or practises witchcraft and divination, who compounds poisons, who goes hunting with dogs or birds or bears, who practises all kinds of diabolical gratifications, taking pleasure in buffoons and their doings, in dancing . . . and diabolical songs, or plays *zerniyu, shakhmaté* and *tableu*, whether he do it himself or his master or mistress or his children, servants, or peasantry do it and he do not forbid and prevent it . . . verily they shall all dwell in hell together, and shall be accursed on earth.[26]

Finally the opposition of the Church to all games proved strong enough to influence the civil power, and the civil code of Ivan IV, which was issued in 1551 as the *Stoglaf* ('Hundred Chapters'), devoted a section to 'Pastimes of Hellenic devilry' in which chess, dice, tables, are declared illegal, together with dancing, acting, and playing upon certain musical instruments (ch. xcii).

Like all other ordinances against chess in East or West, this law failed in its purpose. Chess was not stamped out: on the contrary, it flourished far more vigorously than in any part of Western Europe. Hardly anything

---

[26] We learn the ecclesiastical punishment that was imposed on chess-players from another MS. of the 16th c., which pretends to be a work of John Chrysostom's. It adds 'cards' to the forbidden games. (*Shakhm. Listok*, 1880, p. 269.) The punishment is as follows : 'If any of the clergy, be he monk, priest, or deacon, play *shakhmaté* he shall be dismissed from his office. If a clerk or layman play, he shall do public penance for two years, and make 200 obeisances each day, because the game is derived from the lawless Chaldeans, the priests of idols, and by means of this game emperors consult with demons concerning victory : it is a temptation of Satan.' Another MS. of the same century contains an edifying story of a man 'who saw no sin in games with chess, or in other games with pieces'. The devil arrived one day to play him at chess. They played all night and the devil won. He dragged the sinner through the roof of the house with such violence that the house was destroyed, and vanished, carrying the sinner away with him.

struck the early travellers and traders more about Russia than the extraordinary prevalence of chess, and the high average of skill shown by the players. Paulus Oderbornius, writing in 1581, says:

Russi seu Moschi, summa solertia, proelia latronum ludunt; ut gemini inter se Reges, Albusque, Nigerque, pro laude oppositi, certent bicoloribus armis. In haec profecto arte, ita excellunt, ut haud sciam, an ulla gens, cum illis, comparari debeat.[27]

And in a similar strain in Turberville's *Account of Russia* (Hakluyt, 1589, p. 412) we read:

The common game is chesse, almost the simplest will
Both give a checke and eke a mate, by practise comes their skill.

This popularity of chess is also exhibited in the many references to chess which are to be found in the traditional ballad literature, the roots of which are to be placed as far back as the 15th century, though the ballads have been repeatedly modernized in the course of oral transmission. In these *bîlini* the boyars and boyarins, the princes, and the merchants all play chess, *shakhmaté*, *shashké-shakhmaté*, *shakhmaté Turetski* (Turkish chess), and although the references are generally incidental and without great detail, they are yet vivid and accurate in move and language.[28]

The Tsars themselves played chess, and Ivan the Terrible was on the point of commencing a game when he was seized with his fatal illness. We possess a graphic description of the scene in the *Diary* which Horsey kept of his visit to Moscow (ed. 1856, p. 201):

Brought forth, setts him downe upon his bead; calls Rodovone Boerken a gentilman whome he favored to bringe the chess board. He setts his men (all savinge the kinge, which by no means he could not make stand in his place with the rest upon the plain board[29]): his chieff favorett and Boris Fedorowich Goddonove and others about him. The Emperor in his lose gown, shirtt and lynen hose, faints and falls backward. Great owtcrie and sturr; one sent for Aqua vita, another to the oppatheke for marigold and rose water, and to call his gostlie father and the phizicions. In the mean he was strangled and stark dead.

Two pages later (p. 203) we read:

The lord Boris Fedorowich (Tsar 1598; D. 1605; of Mongol descent) sent for me at eavening, whom I found playenge at chess with a prince of the bloud, Knez Ivan Glinscoie.

[27] Quoted in Selenus, p. 39. In Tanner's *Legatio Polono-Lithuanica in Moscoviam*, 99, we are told that the Russian merchants were addicted to chess.

[28] Beyond a brief survey of the Russian ballad literature in W. R. Morfill's *Slavonic Literature*, London, 1883, pp. 43 ff., and a longer account in W. Wollner's *Untersuchungen über die Volksepik der Grossrussen*, Leipzig, 1879, there is very little information available for those who are unacquainted with Russian. In the ballad of *Mikhailo Potyk*, the hero plays on three successive occasions with the heathen King of Poland, who, asking him how men in Russia amused themselves, received the reply, 'With chess'; on the first occasion he staked his own head, and after losing twice won the deciding game; next he played for the kingdom of Poland, losing the first two but winning the deciding third game; finally he played for the heathen King's head, again winning the deciding game after losing the first two. In the ballad of *Churilla Plenkovitch* the hero plays with Katharine Mikulishna of Kiev, winning 500, 1,000, and 2,000 roubles in successive games. In the ballad of *Stavr Godinovitch*, the hero's wife plays Prince Vladimir of Kiev and checkmates him thrice in succession. In the ballad of *Sadko the merchant*, we read of a costly chessboard with golden pieces which the hero takes with him to the bottom of Lake Illman. In *Vassili Buslaevitch*, the hero on his return home after a long absence is not recognized by his wife. He reminds her how they used to play together at *Turkish chess*.

[29] i. e. flat or level—not uncoloured—board.

In an inventory of the royal treasures at this period we meet with chess sets of crystal, of amber, of stone, and two of ivory.

Enforcement of the law must have appeared as mere persecution when the Court played openly. The only instances of legal activity that M. Sorokin cites relate to Siberia, sufficiently far away from the inconsistent Tsar. A ukase of the Tsar Alexei, Dec. 13, 1849, recounts the ill deeds of the inhabitants of Tobolsk, among which are playing at *zerniyu*, *karté*, and *shakhmaté*, and decrees that the laity are to obey their spiritual fathers, and that offenders are to be whipped and imprisoned. A decree of a later Tsar in 1686 liberated from confinement to an island a working man named Marchko Khomyakof whose sole crime had been the abuse of a chessman. He had confused his *Tsar* and *Ferz* at a critical point in a game and in his vexation had cursed his Tsar. For this he was brought before the voivode, put to the torture to extract a confession, and sentenced to confinement to an island. This happened at Verkhne-Karaülni on the Yenisei.[30]

Board-games continued very popular at the Russian court throughout the 17th century. I. E. Sabelin gives many references in his *Domashnië byt Russkago naroda v. XVI e XVII vyekakh* ('Domestic Life of the Russian People of the 16th and 17th cc.'). The favourite games of the Tsars were *shakhmaté*, *tableī*, *saki*, and *birki*, and they kept special craftsmen at the Oruzheni Palace who were called *shakhmatniks*, because they were entirely employed in making and repairing the imperial chess sets and other board-games. Game sets were common Easter offerings to the Tsar. Thus, April 23, 1663, seven sets of bone chessmen and two chessboards with carved and gilded edges were presented. In 1675 the Tsar received six sets of ivory chessmen, two larger and two smaller, and sets for *birki*, *saki*, and *tablei* on a tray, while two elaborately executed chessboards, and a board with *saki* on the one side and *birki* on the other were painted by the court ikon painters.[31] The inhabitants of Kholmogory (a town on the Northern Dwina, about 50 miles south of Archangel) were famed for their skill in carving,[32] and in 1669 the Tsar Alexei Mikhailovitch ordered ten sets of chessmen from them.[33]

In 1685 a Muscovite embassy to Louis XIV, consisting of two boyars and a suite of fifty men, visited Paris. A contemporary French account praises their skill at chess, and declared that 'our best players are mere scholars in comparison with them'.[34]

This brings us to the reign of Peter the Great (1689–1725),[35] under

[30] Savenkof, op. cit., 94, from *Russkoe Starenye*, 1892, 456. Also in *Shakhm. Obosr.*, 1901, 62.

[31] F. Amelung (*Balt. Schachbl.*, vi, Berlin, 1898, p. 139 seq.) identifies *saki* with *Hölzchenspiel* (? merels) and *birki* with *Leonorchen*.

[32] The Moscow Museums have no chess sets of this period, but the private museum of P. G. Shchukin contains 'large collections of bone chessmen, the majority being from Kholmogory' (Savenkof, op. cit., 94).

[33] M. Sorokin adds other references. In 1616 a rich purple cloth is given out as a support for the chessboards. Sept. 13, 1680, the Tsar orders the chess and game boards to be sent to him. Ap. 30, 1686, the Tsarina sends for the chessboards in her rooms at the Kremlin.

[34] Quoted in G. Touchard-Lafosse's *Chroniques de l'Œil-de-bœuf*. The misprint of 1635 for 1685 has puzzled the Russian writers.

[35] Peter the Great was, for his time, a good player. Sabelin quotes the following from F. W. v. Bergholz, one of his Gentlemen of the Bedchamber, whose diary appeared in

whom Western European influences—under his successors to be increasingly German—began to be powerful in Russia. The nobles came in this way into contact with Western chess, and it became fashionable to follow the Western rules and to use the Western chessmen.[36] The history, therefore, of the chess of the upper and educated classes since 1700 really belongs to the history of the game in Western Europe. M. Savenkof thinks that the older chess died out entirely soon after 1700 as the result of the persecution of both civil and ecclesiastical authorities.[37] In this view I do not concur. I believe that the older chess has continued right down to our time, and that it is still the game of all the middle and lower classes who have never seen a chess book nor entered a chess club, nor come into contact with the Western game. There are several small indications which seem to me to point in this direction.

There was considerable uncertainty in Russia, from 1770 until 1820 or so, as to what was the right move of the *Ferz*. Mr. Coxe, who was in Russia in 1772, states this clearly in an interesting note on the then popularity of chess, which Twiss has recorded in his *Chess* (i. 26):

> Chess is so common in *Russia*, that during our continuance at *Moscow*, I scarcely entered into any company where parties were not engaged in that diversion; and I very frequently observed in my passage through the streets, the tradesmen and common people playing it before the doors of their shops or houses. The Russians are esteemed great proficients in chess. With them the Queen has, in addition to the other moves, that of the Knight, which, according to Philidor, spoils the game, but which certainly renders it more complicated and difficult, and of course more interesting.

In 1821 I. Butrimof, the author of the first Russian text-book of chess, which was naturally based upon Western European books, protested against

Büschings Magazin, Hamburg, 1767-93: 'Peter came, 18 Mar., 1722, with the Duke of Holstein to Preobrashensk and visited Menshikof in his palace. H.M. the Emperor sat there with an old Russian at chess, which he is said to play excellently, as is the case with a large number of the high Russian officials.' We know from other works that Peter was fond of chess, while on the other hand he rarely played cards. He is said to have known only the one game *Gravias*, which he had learned in Holland.

Elsewhere in his diary v. Bergholz describes the Assemblies that were given in Moscow and St. Petersburg. In both towns it was the rule to provide materials for smoking, and tables for chess. Of Moscow he says, '. . . several game-tables for chess and draughts, but cards are not played in the Assemblies there.' In St. Petersburg, on the other hand, 'the gentlemen . . . smoke tobacco, and play cards and chess.'

F. Amelung, op. cit., viii. 441-4, has collected some later instances of chess in Imperial circles. He shows that Potemkin, the powerful minister of Catherine II (1762-96), was a keen player, who became so engrossed in his game that he forgot the rules of Court etiquette, while Catherine's son and successor, Paul I, during his stay in Paris in 1781-2 paid a visit incognito to the Café de la Régence—then the head-quarters of French chess—and won a wager over the right move in a difficult game that he was watching. His nephew, Prince Eugène of Würtemberg, and Gen. Klinger also played at Catherine's court.

The 19th c., with its international chess life, has seen a succession of brilliant Russian players and writers.

36 A set of silver and partly painted chessmen which belonged to the Romanof Tsars is in the Moscow Museum (Savenkof, 103, n. 1). It is said to date from the 17th c. The 'Bishops' are couriers, running warriors with winged helmets and shoes. The Rooks are elephants, out of all proportion to the other pieces, with single riders.

37 M. Savenkof (op. cit., 98) notes that there are, even at the present day, survivals of this opposition to chess on the part of the civil authorities. The game is not allowed by the police in cafés and restaurants in the capital or towns in which the majority of the population belongs to the orthodox faith. In Riga, Warsaw, and Odessa, where this is not the case, the police permit chess in public.

the popular practice of giving the Ferz the power of three pieces and allowing it to 'gallop like the *Kon*' (horse or Knight). Dahl, the great Swedish lexicographer of Russian, in his *Tolkovie Slovar* includes under *Ferz* the phrase *ferz vsyacheskya*, i. e. all kinds of Ferzes, which again evidences the existence of varying powers of move. Uncertainty like this always points to a recent extension of move from that of the older game (a single diagonal step) to that of the modern game.

The earlier rules of the St. Petersburg Chess Club, which were printed in 1854 (see *Sch.*, 1854, 265–91), point to other variations in practice, since it was found necessary to legislate on such points as castling (§ 24), taking in passing (§ 27), Pawn-promotion (§ 28), and stalemate (§ 30).

It is still usual outside the chess clubs to commence the game by the moving of two or more men in the first turn of play of each player. The prevalence of this custom in 1854 is shown by the fact that the St. Petersburg rules recognize it as allowable with the consent of both players. The condition is imposed that in this initial play neither player may move a man into the opponent's half of the board (§ 4). The reviewer of v. d. Linde's works in the *Stratégie* (May–July, 1880) states that it was still usual then to begin the game in Russia by playing two simultaneous moves. We have seen that this rule has obtained in Mongol and Tibetan chess, while it is one of the most striking peculiarities of the modern Indian (Parsi) game from the time of Nīlakaṇṭ·ha at least. I am inclined to see in it a survival of Mongol influence that has continued since the Mongol period in Russia.

It was at one time (see St. Petersburg rules, § 17) usual for a player to warn his opponent when the Queen was attacked.

In some parts (*Chess Amateur*, Dec. 1907, 70) a curious rule is followed. If a player succeeds in moving his King to the 8th line of the board, he is entitled to replace any Pawn that has previously been taken upon any vacant square on the file upon which his King is now standing.

Most important of all, however, is the evidence of nomenclature. Whatever may have been the fate of the rules of the older game, its nomenclature has undoubtedly survived. The ordinary name for chess throughout its history in Russia has been *shakhmaté*; *shakhmatnoy egry*, meaning 'the game of chess', containing an adjectival form. The form *shakhi*, quoted above from a 14th c. MS., must always have been of rare occurrence. The name *shakhmatí* is obviously derived from the technical term for the conclusion of the game—*shāh māt*, checkmate, Russian *shakh mat*. It is somewhat remarkable that such a name should have come into use. We should naturally have expected to find a derivative of *shaṭranj* had the adoption of the game followed normal lines. It may, however, be paralleled with what has happened over the greater part of Western Europe, where chess has taken a new name with the meaning of 'the game of the chessmen (*scaci*)', that ultimately goes back to the Persian name of the King (*shāh*). Singularly enough, *shahmat* appears as the name for chess in the early Hebrew poem of the Spanish rabbi, Abraham b. Ezra (D. 1167). This must have been quite an independent use of the name, but it is of interest as showing that the concluding shout of victory struck other people as a feature sufficiently characteristic of chess to give the game a name.[38]

From *shakh*, ?king, or *shakhi*, chess, the diminutive *shashka* has been formed. This word is now used as the name for the Russian game of draughts, which is played on the ordinary chessboard. An alternative name which Savenkof gives, *damka*, is obviously of Western origin.

The names of the pieces are as follows:

	K.	Q.	B.	Kt.	R.	P.
1	*Korol* (king)	Korolevna (queen) Bâba (nurse) Krala (queen)	*Slon* (elephant)	*Kon* (horse)	*Lodya*, (boat)	Pieshka (footman)
2	Kniaz (prince) Tsar (emperor)	*Ferz* Koroleva (queen) Dama (lady)				
3			Durak (fool) Ofizer (officer)	Kavaler (horseman)	Tyra Bashnya (castle)	

Our earliest authority is Hyde, who gives the names marked (1). Those marked (3) are taken from the modern chess literature, and show unmistakable signs of their Western origin. The ordinary native terms are given in italics, *Korol* having now replaced the older *Tsar*,[39] which in its turn had taken the place of *Kniaz*. It is possible that the King was originally named *shakh*, but there is no evidence for this.

In chess works, *Ferz* is now a masculine noun, but in dictionaries (e. g. in Dahl), in the few passages in 18th c. works in which the word occurs, and in chess books as late as those of A. D. Petroff (1824 and 1827), it is a feminine noun. The idea that the *Ferz* was a woman is clearly as old as Hyde; and it would seem to have arisen from considerations regarding the symbolism of chess akin to those which made the *Ferz* a Queen in Western Europe, and gave the word a feminine ending (*alfferza* in Spanish, *fercia* in Latin). The return in modern times to what must have been the original gender appears to be due to N. Krukof's translation of La Bourdonnais' *Nouveau Traité du jeu des échecs*, which was published in Moscow, 1839.

The most remarkable of these names is that given to the Rook. *Lodya* (said by Jaenisch to be only in use in literary Russian: *Palamède*, 1842)

[38] An isolated English use occurs in Holyday's *Juvenal* (*a.* 1661), p. 223. 'The name of the game, checkmate, is derived . . . from the Hebrew.'

[39] Tsar (formerly generally written Czar in English) is a Slavonic form of the Latin Caesar, familiar as a title of the later Roman emperors. Korol is derived from the name of Karl the Great (Charlemagne). Jaenisch uses *Tsar* for the chess King.

has the meaning of *ship* or *boat,* and the piece is now generally carved as a frigate or man-of-war flying the Russian flag (the St. Andrew's cross). It is a curious coincidence that the Rook should be replaced by a Boat in lands so far apart and so independent as Russia and Siam, Bengal and Java. M. Savenkof has attempted an ingenious theory to account for the replacement of the chariot, car, or wagon, by the boat in Russia. He says that it is an established fact that so late as the time of the Petty Principalities (i. e. the 16th c.) the boat and sledge were the only means of locomotion on the Russian plains. If this be so, the substitution would have been quite natural.

Other technicalities are *shakh*, check; *shakh mat*, *shakh i mat*, check-mate; *mat*, mate; *pat*, stalemate; *nechyu*, even game; and *rokerovka*, to castle. *Pat* and *rokerovka* are obviously quite modern, and derived from the German.

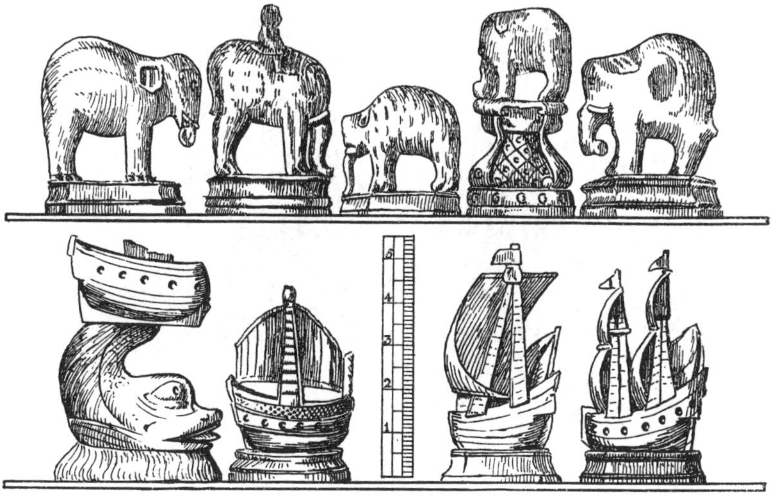

Russian *Slon* and *Lodya*. After Savenkof.

Savenkof quotes several Russian proverbs, which are taken from the game of chess. Thus, in a 16th c. MS. collection of Proverbs occurs, 'He gave check to him, and drove him from the field'; in another of 1749, 'When playing chess one must save his pieces.' Modern proverbs are 'Check and mate and the game is finished'; 'there are many checks (*shakhanie*), but only one mate'; 'to play with a man as a *pieshka*'.

The older nomenclature is consistent with the view that the Russian game is a direct offshoot of the Muslim game of Persia, and shows no trace of Mongol or Greek influence. We see here, as elsewhere, the understood names translated, and the unintelligible name borrowed. In this process there has been no attempt to keep up the war symbolism of chess: it was a feature of the game that would not be very obvious to the foreigner.

All the native sets of chessmen that I have seen are actual figures reproducing the meanings of the pieces. The *Korol* sits upon his throne, the *Ferz* is an armed warrior, the *Slon* and *Kon* are respectively horse and elephant with or without riders, the *Lodya* is a ship, and the *Pieshkas* are smaller warriors of the same pattern as the *Ferz*. I give some illustrations of pieces from Mr. Platt's collection, and reproduce the illustrations which M. Savenkof

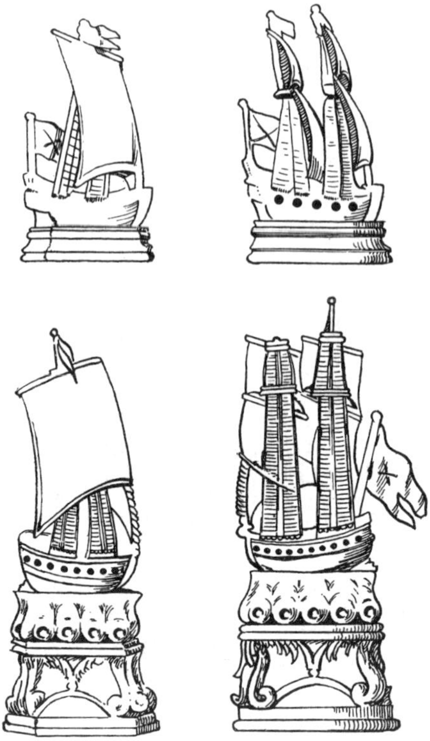

Russian *Lodya* from the Platt collection. Modern.

gives of pieces in his own possession. The first *Lodya*, borne aloft by a sea-monster, is modern; the second, M. Savenkof thinks, may be early 17th c.; the third is not earlier than the 18th c., and the fourth is modern.

Possible Traces of Mongol Chess in Central Europe.

Certain peculiarities of play that began soon after 1600 to appear in chess as played in different regions on the great Central Plain of Europe are identical with some of the special features that exist in Russian chess, or in the Asiatic games described in this chapter. These peculiarities of rule have generally been held to be due to an undercurrent of Mongol or Asiatic influences that was travelling westwards during the Middle Ages.

The most striking of these rules are—

(*a*) The game is commenced by each player in turn making a number of moves—generally two—in his first turn of play.

(*b*) It is usual to warn the opponent, when a move is played that attacks

RUSSIAN CHESSMEN
Platt Collection

his Queen, by saying '*Guard*' or '*Queen*' (England), '*Dame*', '*Gardez*', or '*Gardez la reine*' (Germany and Holland).[40] In its extreme form, the rule decrees that the Queen cannot be captured on the following move if the warning has been omitted.

(*c*) The player whose King is placed in the position of stalemate wins the game.

There is reason to believe that each of these peculiarities of rule has existed in the non-standardized or 'native' chess of Russia. Some of them also exist in Eastern varieties of chess; thus (*a*) occurs in Nīlakaṇṭ·ha's account of Indian chess, in Tibetan and in Mongol chess; (*b*) is observed in Malay chess;[41] while (*c*) was the rule in an early stage of Indian chess (see p. 57).

These peculiarities of rule do not, however, all stand upon the same footing. Rules (*a*) and (*c*) may be of Asiatic origin, but (*b*), in its simplest form merely requiring warning to be given when the adverse Queen is attacked, is certainly European, and a natural result of the great extension of move given to the Queen at the end of the fifteenth century. Thus not only does the Earl of Surrey (executed 1547) show, in a chess poem to be quoted later, that English players in his time said 'Check and guard' when King and Queen were attacked simultaneously, but the Italian lawyer, Thomas Actius, in his *De ludo scacchorum in legali methodo tractatus*, Pisa, 1583, lays it down as a rule of courtesy that a player should warn his opponent of the fact whenever he attacked his Queen with a piece other than the Queen. This custom does not appear to have crystallized into law in Italy, Spain, or France.

These peculiarities of rule appear to have been current chiefly in Germany and Holland. They begin to appear soon after 1600 as distinctive of a method of play alternative to and co-existent with the ordinary European game. The older German writers, Chr. Egenolff (*Des Schachzabels grüntlich bedeutung*, Frankfurt a. M., 1536), and Lucas Wielius (*Schachzabel*, Strassburg, 1606), know nothing of this second variety of chess.

We possess most evidence for the spread of the first peculiarity—the commencement of the game with two or more moves. That this is the case is undoubtedly due to the fact that the rule represents the most conspicuous departure from the ordinary European rules.

The earliest allusion that I have found occurs in the *Traitté de Lausanne* (*Traitté du Ieu royal des Echets*, par B.A.D.R.G.S., Lausanne, n.d., but *c.* 1675), where the author's 20th rule (p. 14) runs:

> Il n'est point permis pour le premier coup que l'on joue de pousser deux pions à la fois.

On the other hand, in a MS. German treatise now in the Hague Library (the *Kurze .... Anweisung und Regeln zum Schach-Spiel* of G. F. D. v. B., 1728;

[40] I know of no evidence for the existence of this custom in France, and the use of French terms for the warning is probably only due to the position that French held in the 18th c. as the language of polite society.

[41] Where, however, it is almost certainly due to Dutch influences.

summarized in *Qst.*, 325–8), permission is given to commence the game by the simultaneous moving of Pe4 and Pd4, if the player so wishes.[42] A four-fold move is given in MS. Gotha, chart. B. 1229 (the *Kurtzer und Deutlicher Unterricht*) of 1740, which pretends to be based on the English work of Capt. Bertin (*The Noble Game of Chess*, London, 1735). After describing the ordinary method of opening play, the MS. (f. 5 a) continues :

> The second manner of opening with the Pawns is simultaneously to advance the two royal and two Rooks' Pawns 2 squares at the start . . . and this is counted as one move, and the enemy has then the same liberty: in this case the other four Pawns can never afterwards in the whole game go more than one step. But the manner previously given is more usual, and they play in that way in England and France, viz. they only start with one Pawn, moving it either one or two steps.[43]

This is a more elaborate move, somewhat akin to that associated with the Ströbeck game described below. The more usual commencement with two simultaneous moves is mentioned by Philidor (*L'Analyze des Échecs*, London, 1749, p. xv) :

> En plusieurs endroits de l'Allemagne on a desfiguré ce jeu . . . premierement on fait joüer deux coups de suite en commençant sa partie.

According to C. W. v. Königstedt (*Kort Afhandlung*, Stockholm, 1784, p. 16) it was usual in his day in Sweden to begin the game with two moves.

Although the practice of commencing the game by moving two Pawns was sternly prohibited in the code of rules which J. Allgaier included in his *Neue theoretisch-practische Anweisung zum Schachspiele* (Wien, 1795–6, 1802, 1811, 1819, 1823), the extent to which the practice still obtained in Germany in the early 19th c. is shown both by the inclusion of a short section in the first edition of the German *Handbuch* (1843, 225), in which, in reply to 1 Pd4 and Pe4, Pe6 and Pd5 is recommended, and by club-rules prohibiting the practice. The section in the *Handbuch* disappeared in later editions, a result, not of the death of the custom, but of the increasing influence of chess clubs and chess books. So late as 1874, however, v. d. Linde could write (i. 316): 'I have not only met with this variety in Germany and Holland very frequently right up to the present time, but it must be regarded still as the ruling variety there, except in the official chess clubs.'[44]

The habit of announcing an attack upon the Queen was general in non-standardized chess circles in Germany and Holland in the middle of the

[42] 'Die zwey Bauren, welche vor dem König und der Königin stehen, kan man : jedoch wilkürlich: auf einmahl und zugleich ziehen, wenn beide noch auf ihren ersten Platz stehen.'

[43] 'Die zweyte Manier des Auszugs mit den Bauern ist, dass man gleich Anfangs mit den 2 Königlichen und 2 Rochen-Bauern auf einmal 2 Schritt hervortritt . . . und dieses wird vor einen Zug gerechnet, und der Feind hat alsdann eben die Freyheit : In diesem Fall aber dürffen die übrigen 4 Bauern im gantzen Spiel niemals mehr als nur 1 Schritt thun. Allein vorhin gemeldte Manier ist gebräuchlicher, wie sie denn auch in England und Frankreich also spielen, nehmlich dass sie nur alle mahl mit einem Bauer heraus gehen, es sey mit 1 oder 2 Schritt.' See *Sch.*, 1872, 273–9.

[44] He describes some of his experiences in his *Schachspiel des XVI. Jahrhunderts*, Berlin, 1874, 7 and 118. One Berlin opponent began 1 Pe4 and Bc4 with the remark, 'Dat jeht ja schneller' ; others began 1 Pe4 and Pd4.

19th c., and even later.[45] It also existed in Iceland and in England, and I have met with elderly players who were aggrieved because I had omitted to cry 'Queen' before capturing their Queen.

The curious rule regarding stalemate first appears in Europe in A. Saul's *Famous Game of Chesse-Play*, London, 1614, where it is justified by the argument that the player who has staled his opponent 'hath disturbed the course of the game, which can only end with the grand Check-mate'. I have already suggested elsewhere[46] that its appearance in England was a result of the flourishing English trade with Russia in Tudor times, and of the extraordinary impression that the prevalence and strength of chess-play in Russia had made upon English merchants. We find the rule repeated by Beale (*Royall Game of Chesse-Play by Biochimo*, London, 1656), by Capt. Bertin (op. cit., 1735), who gives some endings as 'won by the Patt', and by Stamma (*Noble Game of Chess*, London, 1745). It was embodied in the code of laws framed by the Chess Club which from 1774 made Parsloe's, St. James's Street, London, its head-quarters, and is repeated in the laws of English chess in the later editions of Philidor's *Analysis*. J. H. Sarratt, in his *Treatise*, London, 1808, was the first to adopt the French and Italian rule by which stalemate was a drawn game, and, though the minor chess writers, led by Peter Pratt, fought hard for the 'English' rule, the influence of Sarratt, W. Lewis, and the London Chess Club was strong enough to cause the rule to disappear from club-play before 1820. Since then the rule has only lived in traditional handbooks (like those of Hoyle) which were re-issued from year to year without alteration.[47] The rule has also lived in Germany, but has never attracted the attention or gained the importance that it did in England.

All these peculiarities are to be found in a small German handbook that appeared in 1872, O. Klemich's *Das Schach- oder Kriegs- oder Königs-Spiel*, Leipzig, 1872 (cf. *Sch.*, 1873, 79–82). This work describes the unrecognized variety of German chess which the magazines and clubs contemptuously dismiss as the *Korkser* chess. The special features of this game are: (1) it is a matter for mutual agreement whether the Pawns be allowed to make an initial move to the 4th line, (2) a Pawn can only be promoted to the rank of a piece already lost, and if none has been lost the Pawn must remain as a 'dummy' until a piece has been sacrificed, (3) a King loses its right to castle if it has been checked, (4) the player who stalemates his opponent loses the game, (5) an attack on the Queen cannot be made effective unless 'Gardez la reine' has been said, (6) it is 'almost a law' that the game must be begun with two simultaneous moves (said to be usually 1 Pd4 and Pe4 or Ph3; but one illustrative game begins 1 Pd4 and Pc4, Pd4 and P×P, crossing the middle of the board).

[45] V. d. Linde gives an instance from his own experience in his *Schachspiel des XVI. Jahrhunderts*, 119, where a Berlin doctor objected to the capture of his Queen on the ground that v. d. Linde had not said 'Gardez' on the previous move.

[46] In an article 'Stalemate' in *BCM.*, 1903, 281–9.

[47] The rule still appeared in editions after 1857, and I have met with players who argued that the rule was so. V. d. Linde played with an American student at Göttingen in 1861 who still observed the rule (*Leerboek*, p. 274).

Another variety of chess, exhibiting some of the special features just described, has long been associated with the village of Ströbeck near Halberstadt, in the Harz Mountains, which has been noted since the beginning of the 17th c. for the fact that chess has maintained an extraordinary popularity among all classes of its inhabitants. The earliest account of this chess-playing village is given by Gustavus Selenus (i. e. Augustus, Duke of Brunswick-Lüneburg) in his *Schach- oder Königs-Spiel*, Leipzig, 1616. The inhabitants of 'Ströpeke' then played chess in three ways, Courier, Old chess, and 'Welsch' (i. e. foreign, generally Italian) chess. The first of these is a modification of chess played with additional pieces upon a board of 12 by 8 squares. The second is the unreformed mediaeval game as described by Egenolff. The third is the reformed European game, but with certain peculiarities. It was begun with the advance of the *a*-, *d*-, and *h*-Pawns, to their 4th squares and the 'Freudensprung' (joy-leap) of the Queen to her 3rd square. Each player made these four moves in his first turn of play, and the game then continued in the ordinary way by alternate moves of single pieces. This opening was also compulsory in the Courier game. The same opening was found in use by the 19th c. players who made pilgrimages to Ströbeck,[48] attracted by the chess-reputation of the village. There are also other rules of which Selenus omits to give (1) and (4): (1) the board is always placed with a black square to the player's right hand; (2) after the initial move no Pawn can move more than one square at a time; (3) the King can only move to an adjacent square, hence castling is impossible; (4) a Pawn on reaching the 8th row has to make three 'Freudensprünge'[49] to the 6th, 4th, and 2nd rows on the same file before it can receive promotion. It then becomes a Queen only. It can neither take nor leap over a piece during the 'Freudensprünge'. It is immune from capture while on the 8th row, but not during its leaps back to its original square, which need not be in consecutive moves.

The history of the popularity of chess in Ströbeck is very obscure, and none of the many legends that are current appear to have any historical foundation. The game has been regarded as a survival of Asiatic influences that have penetrated through Russia. It is singular that the opening play is identical with the opening that Nīlakaṇṭ·ha gives as usual in India in his day, and the obstacles to Pawn-promotion may be compared with similar features in the Soyot (p. 372) and Malay games.

The reputation of the play of the villagers has always been in excess of the real facts. None of the 19th century visitors found any player of more than medium ability.[50]

The village possesses a board, arranged on the one side for chess and on

[48] Silberschmidt (1825), W. Lewis (1831), Bledow, and Max Lange (1850 and 1853).

[49] Also called *Rücksprünge*, and *Probesprünge* (*Sch.*, 1850, 199).

[50] Several games played against villagers have been printed, e.g. two by Silberschmidt *Die neuentdeckten Geheimnisse*, Brunswick, 1826, whence in *CPC.*, 1846, 178; three by Lewis in his *Fifty Games*, London, 1832; one by Bledow in the 1st ed. of the *Handbuch*, 1843, p. 365; one by Max Lange in his *Sammlung neuer Schach-Partien*, Leipzig, 1857, p. 196.

the other for Courier,[51] which bears an inscription recording the fact that it was given by Frederick William I of Prussia, 13 May, 1651. The pieces which belonged to the board have long been lost. In 1744 Frederick the Great visited the village and played chess with one of the inhabitants. The continuance of the chess-life of the village has been ensured since 1823 by a small endowment, the income of which is to be used to maintain a supply of chessboards to be given as prizes for an annual competition among the children in the village school.[52]

The hypothesis that these German varieties of chess represent the western limit of a migration by way of Central Asia has this in its favour, that it enables us to arrange the story so as to show an orderly and self-consistent development. But, apart from the internal evidence of the rules—and it is easy to exaggerate the importance of this—there is but little other evidence to support it. Liegnitz, in Prussian Silesia, once the frontier town of Poland, was the extreme point on the Great Plain touched by the Mongols themselves (1241), and their invasions, even in Russia itself, were singularly fruitless in influencing language or customs. We are really thrown back upon the argument that the mathematical chances are so great against two peoples developing the same varieties of rule, that the existence of common rules must presuppose a relationship between the games in which they occur.

We may probably rely upon the mathematical argument in all cases in which the number of common features is considerable; the difficulties arise when the number of common features is small. We appear to have at least one case of an independent appearance of the same rule in unconnected games in the restriction of the Pawn's initial double-move to the *a*-, *d*-, *e*-, and *h*-Pawns, which existed in Germany from about 1500 until 1750 at least, and also exists in the modern Parsi chess of Southern India. V. d. Linde at one time was inclined to consider the Ströbeck rules as a fossilized form of this older German rule, though later he adopted the view that the game was a Mongol survival. There is, of course, the possibility that his first view is the true one, and that the method of commencing the game with simultaneous moves is German in origin and that its appearance in the Russian and Mongol games is an introduction from the West. On the whole, however, I am inclined to think that the other view is the more probable, and that these peculiarities of rule are of Eastern origin.

[51] The Courier game (see p. 483) was extinct when Lewis visited Ströbeck in 1831, and the ordinary chess was beginning to replace the special variety in 1883, when the local Schachbund began to take interest in the village and its older games.

[52] There is a considerable literature on Ströbeck. To the list given by v. d. Linde (i. 312-6) may be added *Sch.*, 1873, 370; 1883, 142 and 330; 1885, 171. *BCM.*, Xmas, 1893, 14; 1902, 421 and 472. Also see v. d. Linde's *Leerboek*, 264.

PART II. CHESS IN EUROPE

CHAPTER I

CHESS IN WESTERN CHRISTENDOM: ITS ORIGIN AND BEGINNINGS

The ancestry of the game.—The evidence of nomenclature, and the light it throws upon the date of the introduction of chess into Christian Europe.—The European names for chess.—Where was the European game first played?—Mythical stories.—Earliest certain references to chess or chessmen of contemporary date.

Historically, modern European chess is an advanced variety of Muslim chess, which has been differentiated from the parent game as the result of a long series of improvements in move and rule. When chess entered Western Europe it took its place for the first time in the main stream of civilization. There it became subject to those laws of development and progress which were working in all other branches of human activity. The history of chess in Europe,[1] therefore, is a story of advance in form and rule which has ended in placing the game in its position of pre-eminence among other games of its type.

When, however, chess was first played by Christians in Western Europe it was played with the same rules that were followed throughout the Muhammadan world, and for a period—lasting, perhaps, as late as 1200—there was no serious difference of rule or move from the Indus to the Atlantic and from the Sahara to Iceland. The Muslim game had then the brighter prospects, since it already possessed a literature and its masters had developed a science of play. All that the European player received with chess was the bare rules of play and a number of End-game positions, problems, or exercises with the pieces. The whole development of the game in Europe is European from start to finish. It is interesting to note that the Muslim game stood still the whole time that the European game was advancing, and that all subsequent advance in the Muslim game can be traced to the influence of the Christian chess.

The Muhammadan parentage of European chess is established by the identity of rule exhibited in the earliest European literature of the game, by the Arabic End-games and puzzles in the European problem collections, and by the Arabicisms in the nomenclature of the European game. It is to this

[1] I use 'Europe' in the sequel in the limited sense of Western Christendom, and exclude from it all those countries which, at the particular time of which I happen to be writing, belonged to the Eastern Church or to Islam.

Otto IV, Margrave of Brandenburg (1266–1308), playing Chess
Book of Manesse; Paris MS. old 7266

last evidence, and to the conclusions to which it leads, that I now propose to turn.

Hitherto one of the most striking pieces of evidence for the passage of chess from one people to another has been found in the fact that the name of the game was transmitted together with the game itself. Thus the Sanskrit *chaturanga* became the Persian *chatrang*, and the Persian *chatrang* became both the Greek *zatrikion*[2] and the Arabic *shaṭranj*. It is noteworthy that the same thing did not happen when the Arabic *shaṭranj* became a European game. It is only in the two Iberian dialects which political events have raised into the literary languages of Spanish and Portuguese that we find any trace of the Arabic name of chess. The Spanish *ajedrez* (formerly pronounced ashedrés, now a-khe-dréth) and the Portuguese *xadrez* (pronounced she-drés) are both descended from the Arabic *ash-shaṭranj*, 'the shaṭranj', 'the chess'.[3] Elsewhere in Europe—and even in the Catalan dialect of North-East Spain—chess has received a new name, one, indeed, that still goes back to an Arabic chess-term, but to a word which was never used in Arabic in the sense of 'the game of chess'.[4]

The European borrowings are confined to the use of the Arabic names of three of the pieces of the Muslim game, to the adoption of the name of a fourth piece—the *shāh*—in a novel sense, and to the use of the striking technicalities of play—the warnings *shāh*, *shāh wa rukh*, and *shāh wa māt* or *māt*.

The names of the pieces *firz* (our Queen), *fīl*, with article prefixed *al-fīl* (our Bishop), and *rukh* (our Rook) were retained in the Latinized forms *ferzia*, *alphiles*, and *rochus*. While these transliterations are quite regular, the spelling *rochus* throws valuable light upon the immediate source of European chess. It shows that the word was taken from the Maghrib or Western dialect of Arabic, which was spoken by the Muslim peoples of the Mediterranean shores to the West of Egypt, and especially in Morocco and Moorish Spain. One of the marked peculiarities of this dialect is the pronunciation of the vowel damma, which in Arabia, Egypt and Syria, and among Eastern Muslims generally, is pronounced *u* (*ū* = *oo* in *moon*: *ŭ* = *oo* in *book*). In the Maghrib dialect this vowel is more open, and is pronounced *o* (*ō* as in *note*; *ŏ* as in *not*). The Ar. *rukhkh* accordingly becomes *rokhkh* in Maghrib, a pronunciation that has given the Latin *roc* and *rochus*.

More interesting is the development of the Arabic word *shāh* in Latin, and thence in other European languages. In Arabic this word is used in chess

[2] Whence the Latin 6 zatricium, 7 zatrichium, and the Fr. 9 zatrikiologie, -ique, and the Eng. 9 zatrikiological. (Following the practice of the *New English Dictionary*, I use the numerals 1, 2, 3,...9 to show that the name or form to which they are prefixed occurs in works or records belonging to the 11th, 12th, 13th,...19th centuries respectively.)

[3] I have noted the following forms: Sp. 3 acedrex, alcedrex, 4 axadrezes, 5–9 axedres, 6–9 axedres, 6 axderez, axederez, axedreces, 7 axadres, 9 ajedrez. Pg. 6 axedrez, 7 axadres, achadres, 9 xadrez. The Sp. *ajedrez* and the Pg. *xadrez* are also used in the nautical sense of 'netting' or 'grating'.

[4] That is, in the early period before the European had developed the name of *chess*. Al-Maqqarī (D. 1041/1632) in his *Nafḥ aṭ-ṭīb min ghuṣn al-Andalus* (ed. Dozy, Dugat, Krehl and Wright, Leyden, 1855–61, i. 480), uses *'a'wād ash-shāh* in the sense of 'chessmen' (*'a'wād* = sticks), but it is probable that this isolated instance is taken from the European terminology.

solely as the name of the piece which we name *King*, and although it was used to give the opponent warning of the fact that the player's move had given check to the King, it is easy to see from the expressions *shāh wa rukh* (King and Rook), *shāh wa fīl* (King and Bishop), &c., which were used when the check attacked another piece at the same time, that this warning was simply a repetition of the name of the piece. From it, however, the Arabic players had formed the verbs *shāha*, *'ashāha* and *inshāha*, with the meaning 'to say shāh', 'to check'.

In Latin we find no less than five distinct adaptations of the Arabic *shāh*, viz. (1) the interjection *scac, scacum*; (2) the neuter noun *scacum*, meaning 'a check'; (3) the adjective *scacus*, meaning 'checked'; (4) the verb, *scacare*, 'to check'; and (5) the masculine noun *scacus*, which really reproduces the Arabic noun, but has in Europe undergone an important and unexpected development of meaning.

The form and pronunciation (with hard *c* like *k*, *skak*, &c.) of the Latin words do not appear at first sight to be natural adaptations of the Arabic word, and yet both can be shown to be completely in accordance with Latin usage of the eighth and following centuries. The Semitic sibilant *sh* was unknown to classical Greek and Latin, and in adopting Semitic words it was necessary to replace this sound by that sound or combination of sounds already in these languages which appeared to provide the closest approximation. In Greek the chosen equivalent was *s* or *si*;[5] in Latin, until as late as the 5th c. A.D. *s* was also used. Thus in the Vulgate, the Old Testament names *Shem* and *Sharon* become *Sem* and *Saron*. After the fall of the Roman Empire of the West, the practice in Latin changed, and the combination *sc*, undoubtedly pronounced *sk*, came into use. This was in regular use as early as the 8th c., and examples of its use are not unknown even as late as the 13th and 14th cc., by which time the sound of *sh* had itself become a usual and recognized European sibilant. The Latin written aspirate *h*, again, did not answer to any of the Semitic aspirates, which are all clearly voiced. The various methods of writing the guttural tenuis sound in Latin: *c*, *cc*, *ch*, were all accordingly used to represent the Semitic aspirates. Hence *scac*, *scach*, *scacc*, with or without the terminations *-us*, *-um*, *-āre*, are all of them normal Latin methods of representing the Arabic *shāh*, if the word was introduced not earlier than about the 8th c. A.D.[6]

[5] Cf., for example, Ducas's rendering of *Shāhrukhkh*, Σιαχρούχ, and the Mod. Gk. *σατρέγγιον*, *σατρένγιον*, for *shaṭranj*.

[6] I have noted the following forms (those with *t* are due to misreadings of MS. *c*):

(*a*) the interjection scac, scacum; the noun scacum.

2–5 scach(um, 3–6 scacc(um, 3 scat(um, 4–6 scac(um, scacchum, 4 schachum, schacum, schaccum, 5 scacha, scak, schach, schaek, escaccum, scaccus, statum, 6 schac, scacch. Also 5 scaccatus (gen. -us), scactificacio (= scacum).

(*b*) the adjective scacus.

2– scaccus.

(*c*) the verb scacare.

2–5 scaccare (part. scaccatus in sense of *chequered* only). Also 5 scactificare.

(*d*) the noun scacus, a chessman.

1, 5 schacus, 1 eschacus, 3–5 scaccus, scacus (dat. pl. scacibus). 4–5 scachus, 5 scakus, status, 5–6 scacchus, 6 schaccus; *dim.* 4 scaculus; *collect.* 3–6 familia; 5 schacalia (*Gest. Rom.*).

For the plural forms (*scaci*), see below, note 20.

Moreover, the European words were pronounced *skak*, *-us*, *-um*, *-āre*. This is established (1) by the occurrence of the variant spelling *skakkus* in MSS. of English origin, (2) by the fact that it had in OHG. in the 10th–11th cc. the form *scáh* (pronounced *skākh*), from an earlier OHG. and OLG. *scác*; and (3) by the sound-development undergone in the transition from Latin to the mediaeval and modern Romanic languages. This development is precisely the same as that undergone by classical Latin words with the initial syllable *sca-*.

This last fact is particularly important since it shows that the word *scác* (*-us*, *-um*, &c.) must have been in Latin before the sound laws that modified *sc-* had begun to work. On phonetic grounds it seems certain that *scac*, *-us*, *-um*, were in Latin by the ninth century. The development of these words, the plural form *scaci*, and the verb *scacare* in the Romanic languages has followed regular lines, and the difference of form between *scac*, *scacum*, and *scacus* has naturally disappeared. Thus we have[7]

Latin . .	scac, scacus, scacum	pl. scaci	vb. scacare
Catalan . .	scach	scachs	
Italian . .	scacco	scacchi	(scacchiare)
Provençal .	escac	escas	
Middle French	eschec	esches	eschequier
Modern French	échec	échecs[8]	
Anglo-French .	eschek	esches	eskekier
English . .	check	chess	check

The OHG. *scáh*[9] became *schách* in MHG., and *schach* in NHG., with a number of dialectal and popular perversions such as *schaf*, *schoff*. From an OLG. *scác* or *skák* (not yet recorded) come the LG. dialectal forms *schaek*, *schay*, and *schaig*, and the Middle Dutch *scaec* (= *scác*), Modern Dutch *schaak*; all these forms being in complete harmony with well-known phonetic laws. The Norse forms—the Middle Icelandic *scác*, the Modern Icelandic and Danish *skák*, the Norwegian *skag*, and the Swedish *schak*—are also drawn from the OLG. *scác* or *skák*.

From the MHG. the word passed into Czech and appears in the 15th c. in the form *ssach* (pronounced *shakh*) and in Modern Bohemian and Polish as

---

[7] The forms in the Romanic languages for the noun, interjection and verb are as follows :
(a) *Scac*, *scacum*; *scacus* (a *chessman*). Cat. 5 scach, 9 escach. (Sp. 3–7 xaque, 7 xaques, 9 jaque; Pg. 9 xaque, cheque are probably direct from the Ar.) It. 4– scacco, 5–6 scacho, schacho, schaccho, 5–7 scaco, 6 schacco, chacco, chaccho, ischacho, ischaccho, schaco, ischaco, 6–7 scaccho. Prov. 3 escac, eschah. Fr. 2–7 eschec, 2–5 eschek, 2–4 eschet, 3–4 eschat, eskiek, 4–6 eschiec, eschac, 4–5 escac, scac, 4 eskec, eschecs, 5 escat, scat, escha, schac, eschack, 7– echec. AF. 3–4 eschek. Eng. 4– check, 4–6 chek, checke, 4-5 chekke, 4 cheke, 5 chicke, chec. Sc. 5 chak, chek, check, eschesk (int.).
(b) *Scacare*. Fr. eschequier, eschecquer, eskekier, eschecker. Eng. 4–6 chek(e, 5 chekk, -yn, 5–6 chek, 6–7 checke, 6- check. Sc. 5 chac, 9 chack.
[8] Darmesteter (*Hist. Fr. Gram.*, Eng. tr. by Hartog, London, 1899, 258) states that *échecs* is pronounced *éché*, but adds the note, 'We may remark, however, that the present tendency is to pronounce *échek's* and not *échès*.'
[9] It is a curious coincidence that *scac* took in OHG. a form that was identical with a genuine native Germanic word meaning theft, robbery, pillage. From this Teutonic root we find in MHG. *schách* = robbery; *scháchære* = robber; and *scháchen* = to rob; whence also in early Frankish and Lombard laws are found the Latin words *scachum* = theft, and *schachator* = robber. Cf. also the NHG. *schächer*, and NDu. *schaken*. The same root occurs in the name of the Jura Pass, *Schafmatte* (older *Schachmatte*). It is possible that this coincidence helped the mediaeval Latin scholars towards the identification of chess with the classical *ludus latrunculorum*.

szach (pron. *shakh*) and in Croatian as *šah*. The Lettish *schach* certainly, and the Hungarian *sakk* probably, are also of German parentage.[10]

It is clear from this brief summary of the facts that the form-development of this one word *shāh* in the European languages reveals important information not only as to the time of the coming of chess into Western Europe, but also as to the manner of its diffusion over the continent.

The sense-development of *scacus*, the exact equivalent of the noun *shāh*, is also interesting. It ought to have appeared in Latin in its Arabic meaning of 'the King in the game of chess'. I know of only one instance of its use in this sense, late in date, and suspicious on other grounds.[11] As a matter of fact, the chess King was everywhere given a native name. The ordinary meaning of *scacus* in Latin and in the Romanic languages is that of 'chessman' without restriction to piece or Pawn. Thus in Cessolis we read:

> Sextus scachus ante alphilem hanc formam accepit.[12]

and—

> A ternario autem numero omnis scachus moveri incipit.[13]

There is no Arabic authority for this extension of meaning. In that language there was no regular term for the chessmen in general and we find them called *ash-shaṭranj* (in connexion with the Knight's tour over the whole or the half board) and *ālāt* (implements), or *dawābb* (animals); while *mithal* (image) and *qiṭʿa* (piece) occur more rarely in less technical descriptions. We must, therefore, regard this development in the meaning of *scacus* as a European extension. It is tempting to argue that it shows a want of intimate knowledge of chess since it ignores its most characteristic feature, the difference of piece; and that it is a change of meaning that would be quite intelligible if a knowledge of chessmen had preceded the

10 I have noted the following forms for the interjection: HG. 4 schâch, 5- schach, 5 schacht, schauch, 5–7 schoch. LG. 4 dialects, schag, schaig, schaek, schak, schack; Du. 3–5 scaec, 4 scace, 5–6 schaeck, 8- schaak (pronounced skhāk). Ic. 4 scác, 6- skák. Dan. 7–9 schak, 9 skak. Sw. 8- schack. Cz. šach. Pol. szach. Croat. šah. Hun. sakk.

In German (and Dutch) schachen (schaaken) means 'to play chess'. The Ic. skáka, and Dan. 7 skaaka, 9 skaka, mean 'to give check'.

11 Viz. in a German-Latin Vocabulary of 1482, cited in L. Frisch's *Deutsch-Lateinisches Wörterbuch*: 'Schach, der Ober-Räuber, rex in ludo latrunculorum.' Here is obvious confusion between the two German words *schâch*, assisted considerably by the knowledge that in later Latin *latro* (= soldier) had developed the meaning of thief or freebooter.

12 Ed. Köpke, Brandenburg, 1879, 26.

13 Ibid., 31. Instances could easily be multiplied from the Latin, French, and Italian Problem MSS. Apparently the use of *scacus* and its Romanic forms in the sense of *chessman* was confined to Italian and French. In other languages the terms in use are—

Sp. 3- trebeio, 6 trebejo.

Pg. 9 trebelho.

AF. 3 homs, 4 home. (Whence in Lat. 4–5 homo.)

Eng. (1) sing. 6- chess-man, 7- chessman (rare). (2) pl. 5- men; 5–6 chesemen, chessemen, 6- chessmen, 6-7 chesmen, 6 chestmen, chessemen, 7- chess-men (Sc. 6 chasmen); collect. 4–5 meyne, 4 meine, 5 meny of the cheker, 5 chesse-meyne; 5 esches (once in Lydgate); also 5 chequer (once in Caxton); 7 chesse pin; 7–8 pin.

Ic. 6- skákmaður; pl. 8- skákmenn; 7- menn.

Ger. 4- stein, 5-7 stain, 6 steinn, 9 schachstein: 2-4 gestein, 4 schachzabelgesteine. (Whence in L. 4–5 lapis.)

Du. 4 steen, 6-7 schaek-schijve.

There are also more general terms, viz.: L. 4–6 calculus (It.). Sp. 5- pieza, 6 pieça. Pg. 9 pieza. It. 6- pezzo, 6 pezo, fighura. Fr. 7- pièce. Eng. 6- piece, 6 peece, 7 peice. Ger. schach-figur. Du. 6 schaeksteck, 9 stuk, schaakstuk. Dan. brikke, schak-brikke. Sw. pjes, schack-pjes.

knowledge of chess itself.[14] Unfortunately there is no evidence that this was the case.

By a natural extension of meaning *scacus* acquired the wider sense of 'game-piece' or 'man' in general. It is accordingly used in the *Vetula* (iii. xxxv)[15] for the counters with which the arithmetical game Rythmomachy was played, and in the *Catholicon Anglicum*[16] for the men with which Tables was played. This extended meaning is found in the case of the Middle French *eschec*, and in that of the German *schachzabel*. In the Bavarian Lowlands and in Nürnberg, *schafzagel* now means the game of Merels, Ger. *Mühlenspiel*.[17]

The Italian *scacco*, the Spanish *escaque*, and the English *check* have the further meaning of 'square of the chessboard'.[18] I have not met with any instance of the use of *scacus* in this sense, and I am inclined to believe it due to a mistaken idea of the origin of the Latin name for the chessboard *scaccarium*.

It is this word *scacus* in its meaning of chessman which has given chess its European name. The only classical Roman game of pure skill, the *ludus latrunculorum* (*latronum* or *calculorum*) took its names from the *latrunculi* (*latrones* or *calculi*) with which it was played. It was natural in naming a new game to follow the analogy of the names of older games. *Ludus scacorum*, the game of the chessmen, or more briefly *scaci*, the chessmen, became in this way the Latin names for chess. The same analogy was followed in the case of other new or revived board-games, and in mediaeval Latin we begin to hear of *ludus tabularum* (*tabulae*), the game of the table-men—the Arabic *nard*, and *ludus marellorum* (*marelli*), the game of counters—the Arabic *qirq*,[19] in conjunction with *ludus scacorum*, chess—the Arabic *shaṭranj*. And when at a later time the game of draughts came into existence it also received for its name a similar periphrasis, and was known as *ludus dominarum* (*dominae*) because the draughtsman was, so far as move went, identical with the then-existing chess Queen (*domina*).

[14] Suppose some isolated Indian carvings of chess Rajas had reached Venice in the early days of its Oriental trade (8th c.), and had attracted attention as novelties. The Muhammadan middlemen would naturally call them *shāh*, and the Latin-speaking merchant would reproduce this as *scacus*. There might even be the explanation, 'a piece used in playing a game'. When other chessmen followed, either singly or in complete sets, the name *scacus* would be ready for them. I think it very probable that the lone Indian Shāh (see Frontispiece and p. 87) in the Bibl. Nat. in Paris reached Europe in this way.

[15] 'Numeros hinc inde tabellae/Seu scaci portunt.' And again: 'Ideo quoque Scaci/Pyramidales sunt.'

[16] (1483), London, 1881, p. 376. A Tabylle man; scaccus, calculus. The Spanish *escaques* is used in the Alfonso MS. for an astronomical game which is described, p. 349.

[17] Schmeller, *Bairisches Wörterbuch*, iii. 334.

[18] I have noted the following terms for 'the square of the board': L. 3-6 punctum, 4-5 punctus; 1-5 tabula; 4-5 domus, 4 dommus; 4 campus; casa, cassa; quadrus; locus; 4-6 sedes, 4 seddes; 5 quadra; pirga. It. 4-6 punto; 6- scacco, 6 schacco; 6- casa. Sp. 3 casa; 5- punto; 9 escaque; casella. Pg. 9 quadrado. Fr. 2-5 point, 4 poynt; 7- case; 5 querreure; 6 cellule. Eng. 4 pointe, 5-6 poynt; 6 cheker, 9 chequer (rare); 7-8 house; 8- square. Ger. 3- feld, 4-5 veld, 5 velt. Du. veld. Ic. 7- reitur. Sw. rutor, schackruta, fält. Cz. pole. Pol. kratka. Hun. negyszögor, koczka.

[19] The relationship of these games with the Arabic ones still awaits investigation. There is some reason to believe that both tables and merels were known in classical times to the Romans, and Fiske (*Chess in Iceland*, 1905, 361) has suggested that the East obtained them from the West. It is clear, however, from the Spanish name of merels—*alquerque*—that in Spain, at least, the mediaeval knowledge of merels came from the Arabs.

From the terms *ludus scacorum* or *scaci* are derived the ordinary names of chess in every language of Western Christendom except Spanish, Portuguese, and Welsh, viz. the Italian *scacchi*, the Catalan *escachs*, the French *échecs*, the English *chess*, the German *schachspiel*, the Dutch *schaakspel*, the Danish *schak-spil*, the Icelandic *skaktafl*, the Swedish *schack-spil*, the Lettish *schacha-spehlê*, the Czech *šachy*, the Polish *szachy*, the Croatian *šah*, the Servian *shkak*, the Roumanian *šah* (pl. *šahurĭ*), and the Hungarian *sak(k)játék*.[20] As we have already seen, Spanish and Portuguese have kept the Arabic name, and thereby demonstrated a closer connexion between their chess and the Arabic game than is found elsewhere in Europe: Welsh has drawn its name of *seccyr* from the Latin *scaccarium*.

It is almost a commonplace of modern writers to paraphrase chess and *ludus scacorum* as the 'Royal Game', as though this were the real meaning of the name.[21] It is of course true that the original meaning of the word *shāh* in Persian is 'King', but, so far as the European word 'chess' is concerned we must adopt a more democratic note. There is no allusion to the chess King or any single type of chessman; the name 'chess' includes the whole estate of the chessmen with whom the game is played.

In the later Middle Ages an attempt was made to substitute other names for *ludus scacorum*, which were either based on the supposed history of the game, or satisfied a growing fastidiousness in the use of Latin. Thus we have (3, 5) ludus Ulyxis, (7) ludus Palamedis, (5–7) ludus latrunculorum, (6) latrunculi, (7) lusus latrunculorum, (8) ludus latronum, and (6–8) ludus latruncularius, and the more artificial (7) scacchiamachia and shahiludium or schahi-

[20] I have noted the following forms: L. 1–6 scachi, 1–3 schaci, 2–7 scacci, 2–6 scaci, 4 scaqui (Prov.), cachi (Maussac bequest), 5 schaki, 5–6 scacchi (It.); 1–6 ludus scachorum, 2–7 ludus scaccorum, 2–5 ludus scacchorum, ludus scacorum, 2 ludus skakkorum, 4–8 ludus schachorum, 4–6 ludus schacorum, 4–5 ludus schacchorum (It.), 5 ludus schaccorum, ludus schakorum, 6 ludus shacorum; 5 jocus saccorum (3, 5 scachus, 5 scaccus, 7 scacchus, 5 scaco (It.), 6 scaccia; 6 ludus scachicus; 6–7 ludus scacchiae). Cat. 5 scacs, sachs, schachs, escuachs, 5– escachs, scachs, 5–6 squachs, esquachs, 9 escaques. It. 4– scacchi, 5–7 scachi, 5–7 scaco, 6 schacchi. Prov. 3 escax, escas, escacs, escacx, escaxs, escatz, escadz. Fr. 2–7 eschez, 2–6 esches (eschés, eschès), 2–5 eschas, eschax, 2–4 escies, 2 escays, 3–5 esches, escas, 3–4 eschies, eskies, 3 eskas, escès, eskès, 4–8 echecs, 4–7 eschetz, eschecz, 4–6 eschecs, eschais, 4 eschaz, echez, eschiecz, 5–7 eschets, 5 eschack, ekies, 6 eschatz, 7– échecs, 7 échets. AF. 4 eschekes, 5 shetes. Eng. 4–5, 7 ches, 4–5 chees, 4–7 chesse, 4, 7– chess, 5 esches, schesse, 5–7 chesses, 6 chestes, cheast(e)s, 6–7 chests; 7 chesse play, chesse-play. HG. 1–2 scâhzabel, 2–6 schâchzabel(spil, 2–4 schazabel(spil, 2–3 scâchzabel, scahzabil, 2 schahzâbel, scazzabel, schâchzagelspil, 3–7 schachzabel(spil, 3–4 schâch, schâfzabel, 3 schåchzabel, schâhzabel, schâchzavel, schachtzabel, 4–5 schaffzagel, 4 schachzcabilspil, schachzagel(spil, sachzagelspil, schafzagel, schaffzabul, schafzaln, 5–6 schachzagl, schaffzabelspil, 5 schachzabell, schachzafel, schachczagl, schachzawel(spil, schachtzagel, schachtzabel, schauchzabil, schochzabel(spil, schochtzabil, schafzabel(spil, schaffczabelspil, schaffeczabel, schaffzapelspil, schafzawel, schaffzawelspil, schafzagel, schaffzagel, schaufzawel, schafzagll, schagzagl, 6 schakspil, schachspyl, 7– schachspiel, 7 schacht, schachtspill. LG. 4 schaektafelspil, schachtafelspil, 5 schachttafel, schatabel, schattavel, schattafel, schottafel, schafftafel; 4 scecspel, schakspil, schaekspel, schaeckspoel, schackspel, schakspel. Du. 3–5 scaec, 4–5 scaken, 4 scaeken, scak, 5–7 schaek, 6– schaak, 6 schaek; 3–4 scaecspel, 6–7 schaeckspel, 7–8 schaakspil, 8 schaakspel; 4–5 schaktafel(n, 4 schacktafel. Ic. 3 scáctafl, 4– skáktafl; 7– skák; (9 manntafl, mannskák). Dan. 8– schachspil, 8 shakspil, 8– skakspil, 9 schakspil, skak. Nor. 6 skag-taffl, skagspill. Sw. 5 skaktafuil, skaftauils-lek, 7 skaktafl, skack, skakspil, 8 schakspel, 8– schack, schackspel, schackspil. Cz. 5 ssach, 7 szachy, 9 šachy.

[21] Apparently first used by Lydgate in his *Reson and Sensuallyte* (written *ante* 1412; a translation of *Les eschez amoureux*), 5809, 'that playe most Royal (not in the French original).' It appears also in the title to the French edition of Lopez, *Le Royal Iev des Eschecs*, Paris, 1615, and in Beale's Greco, *The Royall Game of Chesse-play*, London, 1656.

ludium. Hyde's mandragorias is the most remarkable of these ink-horn terms.

Just as *tabula*, the tableman, gave rise to the noun *tabularium*, the board upon which tables is played, so *scacus* gave *scaccarium*, the chessboard, and scaccarium is the parent of the Italian *scacchiere*, the French *échiquier*, and the English *exchequer*, *checker*, and *chequer*.[22] Chess was often called *ludus scaccarii*, and *ludere ad scaccarium* was the usual way of expressing the idea 'to play at chess'. It is in this way that the Welsh *seccyr* came to mean the game itself. To trace the extraordinary development of sense which the derived forms of *scacum* and *scaccarium* exhibit in most of the modern European languages would take me too far afield; probably few people associate the *Exchequer* and a bank *cheque* with the chessboard and the cry of 'Check!'

Of the remaining Arabic technicalities *shah wa rukh* appeared in Latin as *scac-roc*, and at a later date gave a surname to a German family.[23] Only a few of the European languages retained this term.[24] *Shah mat* appeared in Latin as *scac mat*, *scac et mat*, whence in Italian *scacco matto*, the French *échec mat*, the English *checkmate*, the German *schach matt*, &c.,[25] while *mat*

[22] I have noted the forms: L. 2–6 scaccarium, 3–5 scacherium, 4–5 scacarium, schacarium, 5 scacharium, schacerium, schacherium, scakarium, scaccharium, scacerium, schakerium, schatherium, 6 scaccherium, 5 scaccarius. It. 4–7 scachiere, -o, 4 scacchiere, -o, 6 scachiero. Prov. 3 escaquier, esquaquier. Fr. 2–5 eschekier, 2–4 eskiekier, 2–7 eschequier, 2 esckequier, 3 eschaquier, eschaquer, 3-6 eschiquier, 4 eschiekier, escheqir, 5 eskequier, eschaiquier, esquierquier, excequier, esquicquier, esquicquiert, scachier, scacchier, 6 eschicquier, 8- échiquier. AF. 3 eschekker, 4 eschecker, cheker, echecker, eschecher, eschekker. Eng. (*a*) 3–5 chekere, 4–7 cheker, 4–5 chekyr, chekir, checkere, 4 scheker, 5 checure, chekar, chekkir, chekier, chekyre, chekur, chekkare, chakkere (Sc.), 4–6 chekker(e, 4– chequer, 6 checker, chekkar (Sc.), 7 chaker (Sc.), 7– checquer; (*b*) 6 cheker bourde, 7 checker-boord; (*c*) 4 eschekkere, escheqers, escheker, 5 eschekere, estcheker, eschequer. Du. 4 scakier. Whence the L. scaccariatus; Fr. p. part. eschekeré, exchequeré; Eng. vb. 5 chekyr, 6 cheker, 7– checquer, 5– checker, 7– chequer.

I add other European names for the chessboard. The Teutonic languages generally use a cognate of the Eng. *board*.

Eng. 5 chesborde, 6–7 chesse board, 6 chesse bourd(e, chesse boord, chest borde, cheste-borde, cheast bourde, cheste-bourde, 7– chessboard, 7 chest-board, chesse-boord. MHG. 4 (schachzabel, &c.) -bret, -pret, 7– schachbret. MLG. 4 schakesbred. Ger. schachbrett. Du. 3 scaecbert, -bart, 6–7 schaeckberd(t, 9 schaakbord. Ic. 9 skakborð. Dan. schakbræt. Sw. schackbord, schackbräde. Cz. šachovnice. Pol. szachowice. Hun. sak(k)tabla. Serv. shkaknitsa. (More general terms have naturally been used also, e.g. L. 1–6 tabula, 4 scatabula (Cz.), 4–5 tabularium; Cat. tauler; Sp. tablero; Pg. tabolero; It. 6 taulier(o, tauo(g)liero; Fr. 2–7 tablier, 7 damier; Ic. tafl.)

[23] Simon von Schaechroech received a grant of Pledensheim in 1322 from the Emperor Lewis the Bavarian (*Qst.*, 15).

[24] L. 4–5 scac roc, 2–5 scach roch, 5 sac roc, schach roch, schah roch (schaco zocho, Ducas), It. 7 scacco rocco. Fr. scac roc, scat por le roc, eskec au roc, eschac por le roc. Eng. 5 chek rook, chec for the roke. HG. 4–5 schach roch, 7 schoch roch.

[25] L. 2 scacha-mattum, 4–6 scac mat, scac et (cum) mat, 4–5 scachmatt (Ger.), 4 scacco macto (It.), 5 scacum matum, scach math, schach matt (Ger.), scac math, chekmate (Eng.), schaek mate (LG.), scac math, scach mat, schak mat, scaccum mactum, 6 scacch mact, scacch mat, schac mat. It. 6–9 scacco matto, 6 schacho matto, scacho mato. (Sp. 3 xamat, xaque et mate, 9 jaque mate; Pg. 9 xamate, xaque-mate, xaque e mate, cheque mate.) Prov. 3 escat mat, escac mat. Fr. 2–3 eschek et mat, 3–7 eschec et mat, 4–6 eschiec et mat, 4 eschac et macht, eskiek et mat, eschiec mat, scat mat, scat et mat, scac mat, scac et mat, eschec mat, schac mat, 8– échec mat. AF. 3 escheke mat, 4 eschec mat, eschek mat, mat eschek, 5 eschek math. Eng. 4 chekmat, 4–5 chek mate, 5– checkmate, 5 chek maat, 5–6 checmate, 6–8 checkmate, 6 checke-mate, check(e and mate, chekemate, 6–7 check mate, 7 chec-mate, checquemate. Ger. 5 schâchmat, 3 schach und mat, 5 schôchmatt, 6 schachtmatt, 7– schachmatt. LG. 5 schaig mat. Du. 7 schaeck-mate, 9 schaakmat. Ic. skak og mat. Dan. 8 skaak og maat, 9 schak-mat. Sw. 8– schack-matt. Lettish, schach mat. Cz. šachmat. Pol. szachmat. Croatian, šah-mat. Hun. sak(k)matt, (tönk-sakk). Serv. shkak i mat.

appeared in Latin as *mat*, *matum*, and gave rise to a noun *mattum*, 'a mate in chess'; a verb *mattare*, 'to mate'; and an adjective *mattus*, 'mated'.[26] This last soon passed into the idiom of everyday life in a number of transferred senses, all quite obvious as regards origin, but instructive as evidencing the early popularity of chess. Already in a Latin glossary of the 10th c., the *Gloss. Paris*, we find '*mattus*', '*tristis*', and the senses 'overcome', 'vanquished', 'exhausted', 'dead-tired', 'faint' followed at an early date. Most of these meanings are found in all the Romanic and in many of the Teutonic languages.

The evidence derived from the nomenclature of chess points to a knowledge of the game and its technicalities in parts of Christian Europe outside the Iberian peninsula certainly at an earlier date than 1000 A. D., and probably earlier than 900 also. This is an earlier date than either v. d. Linde or v. d. Lasa was ready to allow. But neither of these historians knew of the philological evidence which I have collected, nor was their generation prepared to admit its cogency. The discovery of the laws of sound development, of the relentless certainty of their action, of their relations to time and place defining the duration and extent of their validity, has only been completed within the memory of the present generation. V. d. Linde and v. d. Lasa based their work upon the evidence of written and contemporary documents, and we possess none that mention chess or chessmen whose dates are absolutely certain until the first decades of the 11th c. They laid great stress also upon the striking feature in the history of chess that references to the game appear everywhere but little later than the arrival of the game itself. This attitude represented a great advance upon that of their predecessors, since it meant the replacement of mere guess-work by historic fact, but the argument from the silence of literature must not be pushed too far. It obviously depends upon the nature and extent of the literature of the period. If a biographer omits chess from the recreations of his hero, as Eginhard does in his *Vita Caroli Magni*, or if an old English scribe omits chess from a list of games in a 10th c. Vocabulary, we are entitled to draw conclusions, because, had chess been known to either, it would certainly have been mentioned; but in the case of general literature the chances of the appropriateness of an allusion to the game must be considered. We possess too little of the literature of the 8th–10th cc. to be able to attach much weight to the

[26] *The inter.*: L. 2–6 mat, 2–5 mattum, 4–6 mact(um, 5 math. It. 5– matto, 6 mato. Cat. mat. (Sp., Pg. 3– mate.) Prov. 3 mat. Fr. 3– mat, 3–4 mate, 4–5 mas, 4 math, macht. Eng. 3– mate, 3–5 mat, 3 matt, 4 mete, 4–5 maat, 5 maate, matte, math. Sc. 5 met, mayt(t, 5–7 mait. Ger. 3–6 mat, 7– matt. Du. 3 matt, 4– mat, 4 matte, macht. Ic. 7– mat, 7 matt. Sw. matt. Dan., Lettish, Cz., Pol., Croat., Hun. mat. *The noun*: L. 5 matacio. Fr. 3–4 mateson, 3 matyson, 4 mateysoun, matesoun. Eng. 4 mattyng, 5 matyng. *The verb*: L. 4–6 mat(t)are, mactare. It. 5– mattare, 5 matare, 6 a)mactare. (Sp. matar.) Prov. 3 matar. Fr. 3– mater. Eng. 3– mate, 3–5 mat, 3 maten, 5 maat(e, mat(t)yn. Sc. 6 mayt, mait. Ger. and Du. matten. Ic. mata. Sw. matta. *The adjective*: L. 2–5 mattus, 3–5 matus, 5–6 mactus (sad, tired, foolish). Sp., Pg. mate (dull, faded). It. matto (foolish). Fr. mat (indec. = mated, fem. mate = dull, whence vb. matir). Eng. 7 matte, 9 mat(t (lustreless, whence the vb. mat, to make dull). Ger. matt (dull). Sw. matt (weak). Ic. mat (foolish).

The Latin forms with the *c* are due to confusion with the verb *mactare*, to afflict, punish, kill.

The MHG. 'Matthäi am letzten' (*Abr. a S. Clara*, viii. 77) is a play on the word *matt*.

non-mention of chess. We may state the position quite fairly thus: contemporary documents establish a knowledge of chess in Southern Europe at the beginning of the 11th c., but philological evidence requires that that knowledge must have commenced at least a century earlier.

At one time an earlier date was thought possible, and both Sir Frederic Madden [27] and Professor Forbes [28] advocated the view that chess had reached the Frankish Court before the time of Charles the Great. In support of this hypothesis they submit two possibilities: the Muslim invaders of Aquitaine might have taught it to the Christians in that region before the battle of Tours, or one of the embassies to the early Carlovingians might have brought it from Constantinople. These are pure guesses: the thirty years of Muslim rule in Septimania have left no trace behind in the language or customs of that part of France,[29] the two years' raid that was ended at Tours offered no opportunity for the peaceful spread of a game, and the silence of Eginhard is fatal to the view that Charlemagne was a chessplayer.[30] The chess stories which Forbes drew from the mediaeval cycle of Charlemagne romances naturally belong to the period when these romances were written, and only reflect the position which chess held in the life of the feudal nobility of the 12th and 13th cc. The ascriptions to Charlemagne of chessmen in the museum of the Bibl. Nat., Paris, and in the Dom treasury, Osnabrück, prove on investigation only traceable to the 17th c., and seem to be explained satisfactorily as the expression by an uncritical age of its sense of the antiquity or value of the relics.[31] The only statement connecting chess with the Carlovingian period that *looks* historical is the account of a donation of crystal chessmen to the abbey of Maussac by King Pepin, A. D. 764, on the occasion of the translation thither of the bones of St. Stremon. But the story rests upon a mediaeval Latin work, the *Gesta et Passio S. Austremonii*, of unknown date, which from internal evidence cannot be older than the 13th c. This work is printed in Labbe's *Nov. Bibl. MSS. Lib.* (Paris, 1657), ii. 505,[32] but Labbe states that his text is a composite one from a variety of sources, and only based in part upon an incomplete MS. then belonging to the church of Lerina, Île de Hyères in the Gulf of Lyons. This deprives his text of much of its value. The donation is mentioned in connexion with a description of an ostentation of the relics in 1197. The older life of St. Stremon in Gregory of Tours' *Lib. de Glor. Confess.*, xxx, however, makes no reference to a royal donation. The story accordingly only rests upon a statement of a thirteenth-century writer at the earliest, and can only record a tradition.

[27] In his 'Historical Remarks on the Introduction of the Game of Chess into Europe, and on the ancient Chessmen discovered in the Isle of Lewis', in *Archaeologia*, London, xxiv (1832), 203–91.

[28] Forbes, 199–237.

[29] Reinaud, *Invasions des Sarrasins en France*, 306–7.

[30] Still more absurd is the view of the same writers that chess was taken to Scandinavia by soldiers of the Varangian Guard on their return from Constantinople. It is inconsistent with the whole evidence of the Norse nomenclature.

[31] For a description of these chessmen see Ch. X, below.

[32] Whence it was incorporated in the *Acta Sanctorum Ord. S. Benedict.*, Paris, 1672, iv. 192.

It has no historical value for the time of King Pepin, and the donation of chessmen was probably made at a much later date.[33]

There are other instances of bequests or gifts of chessmen to churches and monasteries. Two will be mentioned directly as being the oldest certain references to chess in European history. A third donation above suspicion is that by Ponce Hugo, Count of Ampurias, to the cathedral of Gerona, in 1309. The contemporary record (quoted in Villanueva, *Viage liter. á las iglesias de España*, xii. 122) describes the gift thus:

> Tabula argenti quae est desuper de iaspi et cristallo incilata et cum perlis parvis ibi incastatis, et cum quatuor leonibus argenti in ea fixis, et cum quatuor pedibus de argento et uno ludo tabularum et altero ludo scacorum de iaspi et cristallo et cum duobus marsupiis fili aurei in quibus dicti ludi tabularum et scacorum reservantur; et cum quadam caxia picta de colore viridi et cum signis regalibus et aquila, in qua dicta tabula cum suis apparatibus reservatur.[34]

An early English donation is of doubtful authenticity. Dugdale quotes it in an account of the destruction of Hyde Abbey, Winchester, in 1144, during the civil war in the reign of Stephen, from a Cotton MS. (Vitell. E. 12, ff. 30 *seq.*), which has since been so damaged by fire as to be unusable. Among the many gifts which King Cnut made to the abbey, most of which perished in 1144, occur—

> vas argenteum ad aquam benedictam cum duobus jocis saccorum a domino rege Knutone donata.[35]

Had this statement been alone, I should have unhesitatingly rejected it as mere tradition. Since, however, two other and unconnected passages (both considerably later than Cnut's time) mention chess in connexion with this king, I am inclined to think that it may be founded on fact.[36]

In the Maussac legend the crystal chessmen are given to the monastery with precious stones and a quantity of gold, the whole to be used in the construction and adornment of a reliquary, in which the saint's bones were to be kept. In this and other cases of gifts of crystal chessmen in the early Middle Ages, I have no doubt that the intention of the gift was to provide a convenient supply of rock-crystal for church-work, such as the embellishment of church vessels, or the enrichment of the binding of the service books. We can see from existing church treasures what a demand there must have been for this mineral. This use of rock-crystal may explain the incompleteness of all the surviving crystal sets of chessmen in ecclesiastical keeping.

We have no means of determining the exact place or places where chess

[33] The Latin text runs:

'A quo loco (Wluico) Pipinus inclytus Rex Francorum . . . postea deportauit (corpus B. Austremonii) Mauziacum. Vbi pro reuerentia B. Martyris plurima reliquit insignia, Scilicet cachos crystallinos & lapides pretiosos, & auri plurimum de quo fieret vas, in quo corpus B. Austremonii honorifice reconderetur.'

The suggestion that *cachos* is a scribal error for *scachos* is apparently due to Ducange. There is no reason to doubt the correctness of this emendation.

[34] This object is no longer at Gerona, but Villanueva found some crystal chessmen at Ager, which were said to have been given by a Count of Urgel. See Ch. X, below.

[35] Dugdale's *Mon.* (1819), ii. 437.

[36] See pp. 419 and 443.

first became a European game. A few small indications that may be gathered from the subsequent spread and development of chess in Europe would seem to point to at least two distinct centres of early activity, the one somewhere in Italy, the other in Spain. The essential condition for the passage of chess from Muslim to Christian was peaceful intercourse in everyday life, in the schools, or in trade. The third condition would be satisfied by any port with an extensive Oriental trade, Venice for instance; the second by any of the numerous Arabic centres of learning to which the European scholars of the period were in the habit of resorting; [37] the first is not so easy to satisfy. Contact between Christian and Muslim there was, from 900 on, along the shore of the Mediterranean from Messina to the Ebro, but it was normally hostile throughout. The Saracens conquered Sicily, 827–78, and simultaneously they occupied the Duchy of Beneventum, captured Baii, burnt Ostia, and threatened Rome itself. Though the energy of Pope Leo IV saved Rome and Naples by the victory of Ostia, 849, he could not put an end to the devastation of the shores of Italy and Provence in a long succession of raids which went on until 972. The expulsion of the Saracens from Southern Italy was only completed just before 1000, while Sicily remained Muslim for another sixty years and more. In Spain alone were there interludes in this long struggle; it is there, accordingly, that one would place the introduction on *a priori* grounds; it is in Spain, also, that we find the earliest certain references to Christian chess.

These references are found in two bequests of chessmen in wills of members of the family of the Counts of Barcelona. The earlier of these bequests occurs in the castrensian will of Ermengaud I, Count of Urgel, which is preserved in the 12th c. cartulary of the church of Seu de Urgel, a town in Catalonia, not far from the small republic of Andorra. The will is dated from Tuxen—the modern Tujent, near Puigcerda in N.E. Spain—28 July, 12 Robert (of France), i.e. 1008, the Spanish Marches forming an integral portion of France until the reign of St. Louis. There is, however, good ground for supposing that the will should really be dated 1010. By a castrensian will is meant one which was drawn up in a less formal way in camp when an impending battle rendered it desirable to execute a will forthwith. Count Ermengaud was engaged in such an expedition in 1010. There were continuous wars between the nobles of the Marches and the Muslims, and although the caliph Ḥākim II (961–76) had reconquered Barcelona, the Christian cause recovered again soon after 1000 through the misfortunes of the next caliph, Hishām II. In 1010 the Christians made a great expedition against the Muslims, only to suffer a crushing defeat not far from Cordova, Sept. 1, 1010. Count Ermengaud took part in this expedition, and was killed in the battle. It would seem more probable that the will was executed on the eve of the march south rather

[37] V. d. Linde (i. 142) suggests that the medical schools of Salerno may have helped the introduction of chess into Europe. This suggestion must, however, be rejected. It is now established that Salerno was quite independent of Arabic influences until *c.* 1080, while for long after those influences were extremely small. 'So far from the rise of the fame of Salerno having been due to Oriental influences, it was those influences which brought about its fall.' See Rashdall's *Universities of Europe in the Middle Ages*, Oxford, 1895, i. 80–5.

than in 1008, otherwise there would have been an opportunity of making a more formal will before the great raid of two years later.

The special bequest may be translated:

I order you, my executors, to give . . . these my chessmen to the convent of St. Giles, for the work of the church.[38]

The meaning of the last phrase, which occurs elsewhere in the will, has been disputed. V. d. Lasa (32), recalling the opera del duomo of some Italian cathedrals (e. g. Siena and Florence), where plans and other materials connected with the fabric are kept, thought it might mean 'for the treasury'. Catalan scholars, on the other hand, insist that by *opera* actual works alone can be meant, and suggest that the chessmen were to be sold and the proceeds devoted to the fabric of the convent church. I think neither explanation is the right one, and regard the solution which I have suggested above in the case of the Maussac donation as the correct one.

The will does not specify where the convent of St. Giles was situated. The Counts of Barcelona, however, were frequent benefactors of the convent of St. Giles at Nîmes in the south of France, not far from Montpellier, and I think it clear that this is the convent intended.

The second bequest occurs in the will of the Countess Ermessind, a daughter of Roger I, Count of Carcassonne, and the widow of Raymond Borel, Count of Barcelona (B. 972, D. 1017), the elder brother of the Count Ermengaud of whose will we have been treating. The Countess survived her husband for more than 40 years, during the greater part of which she continued to take an active share in the government of her son's and grandson's dominions. Her will, dated 6 March, 27 Henry I (of France), i. e. 1058, is now preserved in the original rough draft in the archives of the crown of Aragon.

The MS. presents some curious features. Apparently, the Countess had postponed making her will until too late, and had died before the will was ready for attestation. Her death made it necessary to produce the will in haste, and, five days after the Countess's death, the executors made from memory a hasty transcript of the instructions that had been given them. The MS. consists of four sections of unequal length, with intervening gaps, and contains additions and erasures which are certified by the scribe at the foot of the record. I extract from it the following:

We, William son of Wifred, deacon, and William son of Amat, saw and heard when the Countess Donna Ermessind was sitting on her bed . . . in her house . . . in the county of Ausona . . . and, sitting there held down by illness, she recited her will which she had there with her . . . And she left to the lord the Pope her wooden cup with the gold ornamentation, and to St. Giles of Nîmes her crystal chessmen for the board . . . Donna Ermessind aforesaid chose us as her executors . . . as is written above, in the full possession of her memory, 26 Feb. 1058 . . . and died, 1 Mar. at evening. . . . Written by the hand of William . . . with the over-writing in line 8 (i. e. the words 'for the board'), and the erasures in lines 12, 15, and 17, 6 Mar. 1058.[39]

[38] For text, see Appendix I. In the above paragraphs I have made free use of the admirable discussion of the points involved in v. d. Lasa, 28–32.

[39] For text, see Appendix II. Cf. also v. d. Lasa, 35–40.

Here again there is some obscurity as to the meaning of the terms of the bequest. The phrase *ad tabula⁻*, = *ad tabulam*, added above the line as an afterthought, has puzzled scholars. M. Brunet, who was the first to call attention to these Catalonian wills,[40] translated it 'for the table', implying that the chessmen were to be sold, and the proceeds devoted to the support of the convent table. If this were the intention, surely the word *mensa* would have been used. V. d. Lasa understood it as meaning 'game-board' and as added for the more exact definition of the *eschaci christalini*, and in this I think he is right. The word *tabula*[41] is certainly used in the sense of game-board in other early works to which I shall shortly refer.

The form *eschaci* merits a note in passing. In all the transalpine Romanic languages a prosthetic *a* or *e* was regularly prefixed to certain initial consonantal combinations, of which *sc-* was one. As here, this was often added to the Latin word itself. Some writers have seen in this prosthetic *a* or *e* a remnant of the Arabic article *al* (or before *sh-*, *ash*), as if *ash-shāh* and not *shāh* had been adopted into Latin. This ignores the evidence of the other European forms, which show that the original Latin term must have been *scaci* without any initial vowel, and is an attempt to explain the regular action of a phonetic law which stands in no need of explanation at all.

I have elsewhere (p. 203) mentioned that the Arabic writer al-Marrākoshī (621/1224) describes Alfonso VI of Castile as playing chess with b. Ammār about 1078. Although neither Gildemeister nor v. d. Linde (*Qst.*, 64) attached much weight to this anecdote, there is nothing inherently impossible in it. Alfonso's physician was the Jew Moses Safardi, who became a Christian in 1106 under the name of Petro Alfonsi. The latter includes

40 In *La Stratégie*, 1888. Cf. also his *Ajedrez*, Barcelona, 1890, 272–5.

41 The complete history of the word *tabula* in Latin, and of the forms derived from it in other European languages, has yet to be worked out. For Greek and Arabic see p. 162. In Latin it was used—

(1) for the board of the non-dice ludus latrunculorum. Varro (Berlin, 1826), x. 165: 'ut in tabula solet in qua latrunculis ludunt.'

(2) a board for a dice game, and, by extension, the dice-game itself. This may have been played on the backgammon board.—*Synod of Elvira*, A.D. 306, can. 79: 'De his qui tabulam ludunt: si quis fidelis aleam, id est tabulam, luserit numis, placuit eum abstineri.' Latin version of the *Code of Justinian*, lib. I, tit. vii, cap. 17: 'Interdicimus sanctissimis episcopis et presbyteris . . . aut schematis constitutis ad tabulas ludere, aut aliis ludentibus participes esse, aut inspectores fieri, aut ad quodlibet spectaculum spectandi gratia venire,' &c. (in Julian Antecessor's older version of *c.* 550, the *Novelles*, cxv. 439, this is rendered: 'Neque Episcopus neque presbyter . . . tablizare audeat,' &c.); and Bp. Isidor of Seville's *Origines* (*a.* 636), xviii. 60: 'alea est tabula' (with some information as to the game which is not very illuminating).

In mediaeval Latin I find four game meanings—

(1) A game-board, as in the instances in this chapter.

(2) A dice-game (rare). John of Salisbury (*c.* 1156) includes tabula in a list of ten dice-games in his *Polycraticus seu De nugis curialium*; this may be an echo of Bp. Isidor.

(3) The round 'draughtsman' with which the game of tables was played, the tableman. From this sense the *ludus tabularum* took its name, and not from the fact that the board, the *tabularium*, was often made in two halves hinged together. The latter was a popular belief in England, as is seen by the common name 'a pair of tables'.

(4) A drawn game. This sense is common in the problem MSS. Hence the verb *tabulare*, to draw. Tabula passed into Teutonic at the time of the German Wars, and is, therefore, common to all the Teutonic languages, appearing in OHG. as *zabel* (*Qst.*, 55 quotes two 10th c. glosses: spillone zaples = ludere tabulis; and zabel = alea), in Norse as *tafl* (pronounced tabl), and in OE. as *tæfl*. It also passed into Celtic as *taol*, Breton *taul*, Welsh *tawll* (in *tawll-bwrdd*). For much information as to this word and its derivatives, see Fiske, *Chess in Iceland*, Florence, 1905, passim.

chess in a list of knightly accomplishments in his *Disciplina Clericalis*,[42] and one would expect his patron to be skilled in all the seven that he names. Chess must have been quite familiar to the Christians of the Peninsula before the year 1100.

After the wills of the Spanish marches, the next reference to chess to which we can assign an exact date belongs to central Italy, occurring in a letter to the Pope-elect Alexander II and the Archdeacon Hildebrand (later Pope Gregory VII) in which Petrus Damiani (B. 1007, D. 1072), the Cardinal Bishop of Ostia, requests permission to withdraw to a monastery. The letter itself is undated, but since it addresses the Pope as elected only, and not as enthroned, it must have been written between the election, 1 Oct., 1061, and the enthronement early in 1062. In the course of his letter Damiani writes in strong terms of the sin committed by the clergy who took part in lay sports and amusements.

I restrain my pen, for I blush with shame to add the more disgraceful frivolities, to wit hunting, hawking, and specially the madness of dice or chess, which indisputably altogether exhibit the priest as a mimic actor, but chiefly make his eyes, hands, and tongue, at once a true mime. . . .

Hence, if I relate clearly what happened to me with the venerable Bishop of the city of Florence, I believe it will not be unsuitable for edification. Once when I was his companion on a journey, and had arrived at our lodgings for the night, I withdrew myself to a priest's hut, but he sat down in the spacious house with the crowd of travellers. Next morning, however, it was told me by my groom that the aforesaid Bishop had taken the lead in chess. This word assuredly pricked my heart most sharply like an arrow, and inflicted a wound of displeasure. So, choosing an hour which seemed good to me, I went up to the man and attacked him bitterly, selecting this commencement for my reproof. 'I hold rods', I said, 'in my uplifted hands, and seek to deal blows, if any will submit their backs.' Said he, 'Produce the fault, and I will not refuse the penance.' 'Very good,' I replied; 'and was it your duty at evening to take part in the vanity of chess, and to defile your hand, the offerer of the Lord's body, and your tongue, the mediator between God and His people, by the contamination of an impious sport, especially when canonic authority decrees that Bishops who are dice-players (*aleatores*) are to be deposed? And what does it profit a man whom authority has effectually condemned, even if judgement does not befall him from without?' He, however, made a shield of defence for himself from the difference of the names, and said, '*Scachus* is one thing, *alea* another; that authority therefore forbade dice-play, but by its silence permitted chess.' To which I made answer, 'The decree does not mention *scachus* but includes the class of either game under the name of *alea*. Wherefore, when *alea* is forbidden, and nothing is said expressly of *scachus*, it is established beyond the shadow of doubt that each game is included under the one name, and condemned by the authority of one decision.' Then he, a man of mild disposition and acute intellect, abandoning his contentions, humbly assented, resolved with a sure promise that the fault should

42 'Probitates vero haec sunt: equitare, natare, sagittare, cestibus certare, aucupare, scacis ludere, versificari' (Paris, 1824, p. 42). We may contrast this with a stanza by Earl Rognwald of Orkney, *c.* 1125 (Vigfússen and York Powell, *Corpus Poeticum Borealium*, Oxford, 1883, ii. 276), which has often been translated as referring to chess. The original, however, has merely *tafl*, which is quite general.

Tafl em-ek ærr at efla / íþrottir kann-ek nío; / týni-ek trauðla rúnom: / tíð erom bók ok smíðir: / skríða kann-ek á skíðom; / skyt-ek ok ræk svá-at nýtir; / hvárt-tveggja kann-ek hyggja, / harp-slætt ok brag-þætto.

'I am strong at table-play. I know nine accomplishments. I never mistake a rune. I am used to book-learning and carpentry. I can stride on snow-skates, and I can shoot and row as well as needs be. I understand both harp-playing and poet-craft.'

never be repeated, and asked that a penance should be imposed upon him. I soon decreed for him that he should run carefully through the psalter three times, and wash the feet of twelve poor men, with the payment of as many pieces of money, and their refreshment. . . . But this we have said that it may be known from the correction of another, how shameful, how senseless, nay how disgusting this sport is in a priest.[43]

Damiani does not name the Bishop of Florence, but some later writers[44] have identified him as Gerard, who became Pope Nicholas II in 1058, and was Alexander II's immediate predecessor in the papacy. This would add particular piquancy to the anecdote, but it is a mere guess—and a rather improbable one—at best.

To the modern student, Damiani's whole argument is puzzling. We can understand the ascetic Cardinal's personal dislike of all secular amusements, but he attempts to justify his special objection to chess by arguments which are difficult to follow. He begins by speaking of 'the madness of dice or chess', as if he thought that there were very little difference between the two, and he goes on to argue that the canonic prohibition of dice-games—*alea*—applies to chess also. *Alea* is of course a comprehensive term that includes games of hazard with the dice alone, as well as board-games that are played with the assistance of the dice, but its use always implies the use of the dice. There is only one conclusion possible to explain the discussion, to make the Cardinal's argument worthy of so skilled a dialectician, and to justify the Bishop's speedy submission, and that is that the two disputants knew chess as a game that was often played with the help of the dice. The hypothesis that the Bishop had played for a stake does not help, since Damiani lays stress upon the sin of using hand and tongue in a forbidden game and thereby clearly condemns, not the accessories, but the game itself. But if Damiani and the Bishop of Florence had seen chess played with dice, the whole passage becomes intelligible, and we can justify the position of each disputant. The Bishop thought that if only he played chess without dice, he was keeping within canon law, but Damiani argues, 'No: the game is a dice-game, and to omit the dice is a mere subterfuge or evasion. The canons[45] forbid not merely the dice but the game also.' And the Bishop accepts the contention (which is quite a plausible one for any one who had seen chess generally played with dice, and who knew nothing of the history of chess) and acknowledges his fault.

Nor is this conclusion unreasonable. Although the Muslims do not appear to have used dice in connexion with the ordinary chess, we know that they made use of them in a derivative form of chess in the 9th c., and there is evidence that dice-chess was played in Europe not long after Damiani's time. A German glossary of the 11th–12th c. (*Gloss. Trev.* 9, 10, *Summ. Heinr.* 257) has 'alea, *scāhzabel*', adopting Damiani's position entirely. The same word—*alea*—recurs also in a German Latin poem of 1160, which is quoted below.

[43] For text, see Appendix III.

[44] Apparently Ughelli (*Italia Sacra*, Rome, 1647, iii. 93) was the earliest to do so.

[45] Viz. *Apostolic Canons*, cap. 42 (quoted above, p. 166); *Justinian Code*; and *Synod of Elvira*, cap. 79 (quoted in note 41 above).

But we have other references still more explicit. Alfonso X's MS. *Libro del Acedrex* (1283) explains the popularity of the problem as due to the fatigue that players found in playing the proper game through its great length, and then continues:

For the same reason dice have been brought into chess, so that it can be played more quickly.[46]

and gives instructions for the explanation of the throws of the dice. The *Vetula*, a Latin poem of the 13th c., concludes its account of chess with a condemnation of the use of dice in the game:

But he defiled the game who first played at it with dice, for the chessman will languish unmoved unless the chance of the dice move it: and this has only been done, either because few know how to play slowly, or for hope of gain.[47]

Finally, the 13th c. French romance of *Huon of Bordeaux* contrasts the dice variety with the ordinary game in the story of the hero's game with Ivoryn's daughter:

'Lady', said Huon, 'which game will you play? Will you have it with moves or with dice?' 'Let it be with moves', said the lady with clear voice.[48]

Damiani's passionate denunciation of the clergy for their fondness of chess led the way to a number of ecclesiastical decrees [49] which placed chess on the list of games forbidden to the clergy, secular or monastic, and the knightly orders. Unlike the decrees of the Eastern Church, these Western decrees prescribed no law for the laity, though a narrow-minded ruler might make the attempt,[50] and they are more local than general in scope. They ceased

[46] See for the Spanish text, p. 488.

[47] See for the Latin text, p. 521, and for this passage, p. 508.

[48] Ed. Paris, 1860, lines 7494–6. Quoted below in Ch. IX.

[49] Most synodal decrees contain articles forbidding dice-games, but prohibitions of chess are rarer. I have noted the following:

(*a*) France. (1) Odo Sully, Bishop of Paris (D. 1208), decreed 'Ne (clerici) in suis domibus habeant scaccos, aleas vel decios, omnino prohibetur' (*Praecept. Synodal.*, 29). (2) Provincial Council of Béziers, 8 May, 1255, decreed 'Praeterea prohibemus districtius quod nullus omnino ad taxillos ludat, sive aleis, sive scacis' (J. D. Mansi, Archiep. Lucensis, *Sacrorum Conciliorum nova collectio*, Venice, 1778, xxiii. 882).

(*b*) Germany. (1) Council of Trier, 1310, c. 44, 'Ne monachi ludant cum istis. Item, ludos chorearum, scacorum, anulorum, et globorum monachis interdicimus omnino' (Martene and Durand, *Thesaurus novus anecdotorum*, Paris, 1717, iv. 249). (2) Synod of Würzburg, 1329, 'Ludos alearum, cartarum, schacorum, taxillorum, anulorum, et globorum monachis et monialibus prohibemus districte' (Würdtwein, *Nova Subsid. diplom.*, ii. 272).

(*c*) England. Some writers (e. g. Ashton, *History of Gambling in England*, London, 1898, 14) have discovered a prohibition of chess in the following decree of a Worcester synod in 1240: 'Prohibemus etiam Clericis ne intersint ludis inhonestis vel choreis vel ludant ad aleas vel taxillos, nec sustineant ludos fieri de Rege et Regina, nec arietes levari nec palaestras publicas fieri.' I very much doubt whether chess is meant; the game was sufficiently well known to be mentioned by name, had it really been intended. In 1291 Archbishop Peckham concludes a letter with the recital of 'grave wickedness' in the Priory of Coxford, Norfolk. 'The Prior and Canons, one and all, had been led astray by an evilly-disposed person named Robert de Hunstaneston, who had actually taught them to play chess, which heinous vice was to be banished, even if it came to three days and nights on bread and water' (H. W. Saunders, 'History of Coxford Priory,' in *Proc. Norfolk and Norwich Arch. Soc.*, xvii (1910), 391).

[50] Thus (*a*) St. Louis IX promulgated the decree, Paris, Dec. 1254, in which occurs 'Volumus autem et praecipimus quod baillivi nostri et alii quorumque officium tenentes sub ipsis, necnon et omnes qui vadia nostra recipiunt, abstinere debeant a ludo etiam cum taxillis sive aleis, vel scacis' and 'Praeterea inhibemus districte ut nullus omnino ad taxillos ludat sive aleis, aut scacis' (Martene and Durand, op. cit., i. 437, 439). (*b*) John I of Aragon (1390) is said to have forbidden chess. The *Ordenacions e bans del Comptat de*

before 1400. This result was doubtless due to the intellectual renascence of the 12th c. in Lombardy, which led to the renewal of the study of Roman Law. Damiani's argument came again under review in connexion with the section in the code of Justinian forbidding the clergy to play or even watch the game *tabula*, and the lawyers came to a different conclusion. The glossators agreed that the prohibition of *tabula* did not extend to chess, since chess is played by means of a man's native intelligence, and in no wise depends upon chance.[51] The attempt to extend the prohibition of chess to the various knightly orders, which had begun with St. Bernard of Clairvaux's rule for the Knights Templar,[52] was abandoned by Werner v. Orseln, the Grand Master of the Teutonic Order in the 15th c., on the ground that chess was a proper amusement for a knight. The abandonment of the wider prohibition was a wise move, for it is very evident that the prohibition was already a dead letter. Much of the early European literature of chess was the work of members of the monastic or preaching orders.

At a later date, according to Salvio (*Il Puttino*, Naples, 1634), ecclesiastical lawyers went to the other extreme. Not only was it declared legal to play at chess, but if a clerk quarrelled with his opponent and killed him, it was accounted a casual, and not a deliberate homicide, the reason given being that he was engaged in a lawful occupation. Salvio cites Innocent and il Panormitano *in cap. lator. de homicid.*

Chess was not long in penetrating from Italy to Southern Germany, and we possess two very early references to the game in Latin MSS. from this region which may be even older than 1050, and therefore older than Cardinal Damiani's allusion to the game. One of these, a MS. in the library of the monastery at Einsiedeln in Switzerland, is certainly of the 11th century, and an early copy of it exists, which must have been made *c.* 1100. I propose to discuss this poem in Chapter IV with the other mediaeval poems on chess. The other reference to the game is contained in a fragment of a poem in leonine hexameters, of which thirty-four leaves were recovered at Munich from the binding of a volume that came originally from the monastery of Tegernsee in Upper Bavaria. This poem, now known by the name of *Ruodlieb*, from the fact that it contains an episode which in the Germanic 'Heldensage' occurs to a king of that name, is dated *c.* 1030 by the latest authorities. The MS., believed to be the author's own holograph, is written in an early 11th c. hand, while a scene in the poem, in which two kings hold a conference on a bridge, is believed to contain an allusion to the conference held in 1022 by the Emperor Henry II and King Robert of France

Ampuries contain a decree of the same date, 'Item que tot hom qui juch anagun joch de daus ni de scachs en cose de mangar ni an altres coses de dias exceptal joch de taules que pach x sols com' (Brunet, *Ajedrez*, 226). (*c*) I may add a curious letter from Adam, Abbot of Persigny, to the Countess of Perche, *c.* 1197, which warns her against unprofitable addiction to chess: 'Non interest ludus aleae, non ei est cordi scaccorum otiosa sedulitas, ipsius puritati non congruit scurrilitas histrionum' (Martene and Durand, op. cit., i. 678).

[51] *Cod. Justin.* Lib. I, tit. vi, cap. 17. The gloss is 'Sed quid si ad scacos? respo. forte secus, quia in ingenio naturali consistit, nec committitur viribus fortunae'.

[52] *Exhortatio ad Milites Templi*, cap. iv: 'scacos et aleas detestantur'.

on a bridge over the Maas. '*Ruodlieb* is a purely German poem in Latin garb'; and is probably a monkish translation of one of the numerous epics which were carried from place to place by travelling minstrels. The author's name is unknown; we may presume that he was a monk of Tegernsee, but he shows such intimate knowledge of court life that we may infer that he had spent his youth at the imperial court, and had only retired to the monastery in later life.[53]

Chess is mentioned in the following connexion. Two kings had been at war, and the hero of the poem was sent by the victor with terms of peace. On his return, he was asked how he had spent his time at the other court. He replied that he was entertained at first by the Viceroy, who had treated him well, and had made many attempts to beat him at chess (*ludus scachorum*), but the hero had only lost when he deliberately played to lose. After five days spent in this way, during which the Viceroy tried in vain to discover his errand, he was admitted to the king's presence, gave his message, and was promised his answer on the morrow.

The king, calling for the board (*tabula*), orders a chair to be placed for himself, and orders me to sit on the couch opposite to play with him. This I strongly refuse, saying: 'It is a terrible thing for a poor man to play with a king.' But when I see that I cannot withstand him, I agree to play, intending to be beaten by him. I say: 'What profit is it to poor me to be beaten by a king? But I fear, Sir, that you will soon be wrath with me, if fortune help me to win.' The king laughed and answered jestingly: 'There is no need, my dear man, to be afraid about that; even if I never win, I shall not become more angry. But know clearly that I wish to play with you, for I wish to learn what unknown moves you will make.' Immediately both king and I moved carefully, and, as luck would have it, I won three times, to the great surprise of many of his nobles. He lays down a wager against me, and would not let me lay down anything against him. He gives what he had wagered, so that not one coin remained. Many follow, anxious to avenge him, proposing bets and despising my bets, sure of losing nothing and trusting much to the uncertainty of fortune. They help one another, and do harm by helping too much. They are hindered while they consult variously; through their disputes I win quickly three times, for I would not play any more. They now wished to give me what they had wagered. At first I refused, for I thought it disgraceful to enrich myself at their expense, and to impoverish them. I said: 'I am not accustomed to win anything by play.' They say: 'While you are with us, live as we do; when you get home again, live there as you like.'[54]

In dismissing him, the king said: 'I think that you will always be very fond of this game, by which you have shod your shoes so well.'

Although chess is only named in the earlier portion of this narrative, there is no reason to doubt that it was chess also at which the king played. The whole unity of the story demands as much. The poem throws a most valuable light upon the position that chess already occupied in the life of the nobility. We see also that the stake added to enhance the moment of victory is considered a necessary concomitant by the nobles, although the hero's reluctance to accept the money he has won shows that chess was not

[53] See J. G. Robertson's *History of German Literature*, Edinburgh, 1902, 32-3; v. d. Linde, ii. 142-9 (who argues for a rather later date); and v. d. Lasa, 48-52.

[54] For text, see Appendix IV.

always played for money. May we infer that it was not usual at the German court to play for a stake, but that it was known that the wager was usual in other countries? The whole scene is extraordinarily vivid for so early a writer.

Rather more than a century later, another monk of Tegernsee,[55] by name Metellus, included a reference to chess in his *Quirinalia*, which scholars date c. 1160. The incident is connected with the Charlemagne cycle of romances which had reached Upper Germany by the Low Countries, and describes the tragic death of a young Bavarian noble at the Frankish court of Pepin the Short (752–68). The incident is thus briefly recorded:

> The king's son used to meet him at the game of the *tabula*, till at length the latter being the cleverer obtained the alea more quickly. The vanquished picks a quarrel, deeming himself the stronger in the affection of his father, and, taking aim with a Rook, he dealt him a mortal wound.[56]

The incident, although repeated with other details in later chronicles, has no historic importance, and the characters belong to romance only. The chess interest is also but small. Were it not for the one word *rochus*, there would be nothing in the passage to necessitate chess. The author's acquaintance with chess would seem very slight: *alea*, I suppose, is used to mean 'the game'—if it has any precise meaning other than the suggestion of a gambling atmosphere: *tabula* is again, as in *Ruodlieb*, used in the sense of 'chessboard'.

APPENDIX

ORIGINAL TEXTS

I. Will of Count Ermengaud I of Urgel, 1008 (1010).

From the 12th c. manuscript Cartulary of the Church of Seu de Urgel, whence it was printed in Petro de Marca's *Marca Hispanica*, Paris, 1688, col. 973, App. No. clxii.

In nomine Sanctae & individuae Trinitatis. Ego Ermengaudus gratia Dei Comes & Marchio vobis manumissores meos id est Salla gratia Dei Episcopus & Guillelmus Vicecomes, et Miro de Abilia et Guillelmus de Lavancia, et Raimundo de Petramola et Poncius Abba, et Vivas Sacerdos et Dacho . . . ordino vel hortor vos ut donare faciatis omnem meum avere propter remedium animae meae. In primis ad sanctum Petrum Romae centum uncias de auro, . . . ad sanctae Mariae Sedis Gerundae ad ipsa opera uncias quinque de auro, & ad suos sacerdotes uncias decem de auro, . . . Et ad sancti Aegidii cenobii ipsos meos schacos ad ipsa opera de Ecclesia. . . . Aliud quodcunque invenire potueritis in aliqua re, donare faciatis pro anima mea. Facto isto testamento v Kalendas Augusti anno .xii. regnante

[55] Tegernsee is again met with in connexion with chess as an earlier home of the Low German Problem MS., now in the Munich Library; see Ch. VIII, below.

[56] For text, see Appendix V. The passage and the later Chronicles which repeat the story (viz. a Latin Bavarian Chronicle, and two German Chronicles, all quoted by Gust. Selenus) were claimed by Forbes (201-5) to provide authentic evidence for the existence of chess at the Carlovingian court. The unhistorical nature of the whole narrative was exposed by v. d. Linde (i. 28-30). Forbes accepted the entire Charlemagne romance as literal history, overlooking all the anachronisms involved.

Rotberto Rege. Ermengaudus Comes qui hunc testamentum feci & testes firmare rogavi . . . Signum . . . Bernardus sacerdos qui hunc testamentum scripsi et subscripsi die & anno quo supra.

II. Will of Countess Ermessind of Barcelona, 1058.

From the MS. (Raymond Berenger I, No. 223) in the Archives of the Kingdom of Arragon at Barcelona, whence it was printed in Prospero de Bofarull's *Los Condes de Barcelona vindicados*, 18, vol. ii, p. 55.

Nos Guillermus Guifredi Levita et Guillermus Amati vidimus et audivimus quando domina Ermessindis comitissa sedebat in lecto . . . in domo . . . in comitatu Ausonae . . . et ibi sedens ab egritudine detenta, laudavit suum testamentum, quod secum ibi habebat . . . Imprimis dimissit mihi Guillermo clerico praefato mulam unam. . . . Et dimissit domino Papae suos sciphos ligneos fornatos auro. Et Sancto Egidio Nemausensi suos eschacos christalinos ad tabula¯. Et dimissit Sancto Guirico praefato tantum argenti et auri ex quo possit esse una obtima crux et suum obtimum breviarium dimissit Stae Mariae Gerundae et suos sciphos argenteos quos aput se habebat et ipsos quos habebat in vico unde eam portaremus Gerundam. . . . Praedicta donna Ermessindis elegit nos suos manumissores . . . sicut superius scriptum est in sua plena memoria, IIII kalendas Marcii Anno xxvii Henrici Regis regni . . . et obiit kalendas Marcii vespere facto. . . . Sicut ipsa donna Ermessindis nobis praecepit jam dictis, ita et hic fideliter scriptum est. Postmodum haec ultima voluntas . . . patuit publice secundo nonas Marcii in capitulo Sanctae Mariae Gerundi coram (etc.). Scriptum manu Guillermi . . . cum litteris suprapositis in VIII versu (i.e. ad tabula¯) et rasis in XII et in XV et XVII, secundo nonas Marcii xxvii Henrici Regis.

III. Letter of Cardinal Damiani to Pope Alexander II, 1061.

Contained in all the printed editions of Damiani's epistles (e.g. in Damianus, *Opera Collecta*, Rome, 1606, vol. i, p. 24). Also in Margerinus de la Bigne's *Sacrae Bibliothecae Sanctorum Patrum*, Paris, 1578–9, vol. iii. The text below is from MS. Monte Cassino 358, 359; fol. 180 *b*–181 *a*, of the early 12th cent.

Reprimo calamum: Nam ut turpiores attexantur ineptie pudore suffundor; videlicet, venatus, aucupium, alearum insuper furie, uel scachorum. Que nimirum, de toto quidem sacerdote exhibent mimum sed precipue oculos manus et linguam, quasi unum uerum simul efficiunt: sicque conditos, et qui suauius sapiant, cibos demonum mensis apponunt.

Hic plane, si quod michi de uenerabili Florentine sedis Episcopo contigerit recolo: alienum esse ab edificatione non credo. Dum aliquando sibi essem comes itineris, uespertinum tandem subeuntes hospitium, ego me in presbiteri cellam semoui: is autem in spaciosa domo cum commeantium turba resedit. Mane autem facto a meo michi agasone significatum est, quod predictus Episcopus ludo prefuerit scacchorum. Quod prefecto uerbum uelut sagitta cor meum acutissime pupugit, et indignationis vulnus inflixit. Hora autem, que michi uidebatur electa, conuenio hominem et acriter inuehor, hoc igitur initium sermonis arripiens. Aio: librata manu uirgas exero plagas infligere quero, si sit qui terga subiciat. Et ille: Inferatur, inquit, culpa, non recusabitur penitentia. Rectene, inquam, tuique erat officii uespere in scacchorum uanitate colludere, et manum, Dominici corporis oblatricem, linguam inter Deum et popolum mediatricem sacrilegi ludibrii contaminatione fedare? Praesertim cum canonica decernat auctoritas, ut aleatores Episcopi deponantur? Et quid prodest ei, quem efficaciter auctoritas damnat, etiam si judicium extrinsecus non accedat? Ille autem ex diuersitate nominum defensionis sibi faciens scutum, ait, aliud scachum esse, aliud aleam; aleas ergo auctoritas illa prohibuit, scachos uero tacendo concessit. Ad quod ego: Scachum, inquam, Scriptura non ponit, sed utriusque ludi genus alee nomine comprehendit. Quapropter dum alea prohibetur, et nominatim de scacho nil dicitur, constat procul dubio, utrumque genus uno uocabulo comprehensum, unius sententie auctoritate damnatum. Tunc ille—ut mitis est animi et perspicacis ingenii—redditis rationibus humiliter adquieuit: culpam nullatenus iterandam certa pollicitatione constituit, iniungi sibi penitentiam postulauit. Cui mox precepi, ut ter psalterium meditando percurreret, ac duodecim pauperum pedem sub totidem numismatum erogatione, eorumque recreatione lavaret. Hac scilicet ratione perspecta, ut quoniam hec culpa manibus potissimum et sermone committitur, lauando pauperum pedem, suas potius a culpe contagio manus ablueret, et imprimis alienis ora uestigiis pacem sibi cum Domino, quem per flendos iocos offenderat, reformauit. Hoc autem diximus, ut, quam inhonestum, quam absurdum, quam denique fedum sit in sacerdotem ludibrium ex alterius emendatione noscatur.

IV. Ruodlieb.

A fragment of an early epic poem, which has been edited by F. Seiler, Halle, 1882, from the unique MS. at Munich. Cf. v. d. Lasa in *Sch.*, 1881, 33–41 and 65–72. A German translation of the poem by M. Heyne was published, Leipzig, 1897. Simrock, *Heldenbuch*, Stuttgart, 1871, vi. 10 seq., has incorporated a free and (from the standpoint of chess) inaccurate version in his *Amelungen-Lied.*

Respondit 'Summus mihi clemens fit vicedomnus
Procurans multum, defectum ne paterer quem.
Scachorum ludo temptat me vincere crebro,
Nec potuit, ludo ni sponte dato sibi solo.
Quinque dies sic me non siverat ante venire.
Explorare cupit meus adventus quid eo sit.
Investigare nulla quod dum valet arte,
Post me rex misit, sibi quae dixi satis audit
In cras responso, dixit velut, induciato.
Rex poscens tabulam jubet opponi sibi sellam
Et me contra se jubet in fulchro residere,
Ut secum ludam, quod ego nimium renuebam
Dicens: "terribile miserum conludere rege."
Et dum me vidi sibi non audere reniti,
Ludere laudavi, cupiens ab eo superari.
"Vinci de rege" dicens, "quid obest miserum me?
Sed timeo, domine, quod mox irasceris in me,
Si fortuna juvet, mihi quod victoria constet."—
Rex subridendo, dixit velut atque jocando:
"Non opus est, care, super hac re quid vereare;
Si numquam vincam, commotior haut ego fiam,
Sed quam districte noscas, ludas volo cum me,
Nam quos ignotos facies volo discere tractus."—
Statim rex et ego studiose traximus ambo,[1]
Et sibi gratia sit, mihi ter victoria cessit,
Multis principibus nimis id mirantibus ejus.
Is mihi deponit, sibi me deponere nil vult.
Et dat quae posuit, (pisa quod non) una remansit.

[1] Simrock paraphrases these lines thus:
Ich sprach: 'Mit Königen kämpfen missziemt geringerem Manne.'
Er aber sass und rückte schon beide Bauern voran.
V. d. Lasa (51) rightly describes the licence by which the poet has introduced a peculiarity of 18th c. German chess (see p. 389) as 'unpardonable'. There is no particle of evidence for the custom of commencing with two simultaneous moves in early European chess.

Plures succedunt, hunc ulcisci voluerunt,
Pignora praebentes, mea pignora despicientes,
Perdere nil certi, dubiae fisi bene sorti.
Alterutrumque juvant, nimiumque juvando nocebant.
Praepediebantur, varie dum consiliantur,
Inter litigium cito vincebam quod eorum
Hoc tribus et vicibus, volui nam ludere non plus.
Quae deponebant mihi mox donare volebant.
Primo respueram, vitiosum namque putabam
Sic me ditari, vel eos per me tenuari.
Dixi: "non suevi quicquam ludendo lucrari."
(Dicunt: "inter nos dum sis, tu vive velut nos.)
Donec inter nos sis, fac vel vive velut nos.
Quando domum venias, ibi vivere quis veluti vis."
Cum sat lorifregi, quae porrexere recepi, †
Commoda cum laude mihi fortuna tribuente.'—
Rex ait: 'hunc ludum tibi censeo semper amandum,
Quo sunt sarcita tua tam bene calciamenta;
Nunc grates habeas, causas quod agis bene nostras.'—

† Marginal gloss, *zugilprechoto*.

V. Metellus, Quirinalia, *c.* 1160.

Huic ludo tabulae regis erat filius obvius
Donec doctior hic, obtinuit promptius aleam.
Rixam victus agit, corde patris forte potentior
Et rocho jaculans, mortifere vulnus adegerat.

CHAPTER II

CHESS IN THE MIDDLE AGES

The mediaeval period and its chess literature.—Earliest contemporary references in the different European countries.—The European nomenclature composite.—The game the typical chamber-recreation of the nobility.—A branch of a noble's education.—Played by the ladies.—Reasons for the popularity of chess with the leisured classes.—Chess played by the members of a noble's household.—By the burgesses of the towns.—Frowned on by the Universities.—Does not reach the lowest ranks of society.—The altered position of chess in modern days.

THE history of the development of chess in Europe falls into two well-defined sections, the boundary line between them synchronizing with the conclusion of the Middle Ages and marking the general adoption of the modern moves of the Queen and Bishop. This reform was historically only the culmination of a long series of experiments with the moves of the pieces, carried out during the mediaeval period, but its adoption led at once to such changes in the method of play that the reformed chess was almost a new game. Practically the whole of the science, the literature, and the problem lore of the older game were no longer applicable, and they became obsolete in the course of two or three generations. The completeness of the revolution makes it possible to treat of the unreformed mediaeval game as a whole, and in the next few chapters I propose to confine myself almost entirely to the history of this older chess, its rules, its nomenclature, its literature, and its influence upon the life of the five centuries (*c.* 1000–*c.* 1500) during which it was played in Western Europe.

This game had a very considerable literature, and a great deal more of it has survived to our day than we should have anticipated, when we remember that the game became obsolete soon after the invention of printing.[1]

[1] The most notable losses are (1) the Problem collection of Vicent, 1495. (2) A Catalan poem on chess by Moses Azan, of which a Castilian version of 1350 was once in the Escurial (v. d. Linde, i. 177). (3) A work of the mathematician Luca Paciulo (B. 1445, D. after 1514) (Staigmüller, in *Z. f. Math. u. Physik*, xxiv. 150, quoted in Cantor, *Gesch. d. Math.*, 1892, ii. 282). (4) The *De ludo latrunculorum* of Hierome Cardan (B. 1501, D. 1576), an Italian work beginning 'Non per vitio alcuno', to which he refers in some of his extant works, thus: 'Latrunculis et aleae tam immodice operam dedi ut me dignum repræhensione fore intelligam. Lusi per plures annos utroque modo, sed latrunculis supra xl: alea circa xxv, nec solum tot annis, sed totis diebus turpe dictu. Multa et praeclara quamquam invenerim in libro de latrunculis, quaedam tamen ob occupationes exciderunt: viii aut x quæ numquam licuit recuperare, ea omnino humanam solertiam excedere, et impossibilia inventu esse videbantur. Ob it haec adjeci ut monerem (quod spero venturum) si quando occurrant curiosis, ut coronidem, seu apicem adjiciant.' (These discoveries can hardly have been anything but partita, *problems*; cf. v. d. Lasa, 181-3.) *De Vita Propria* (1575), xix. 'Deditus fui etiam

There are only a few early printed works of which chess is the subject-matter, and the bulk of the early literature is still in manuscript, much of it consisting of very short works, which fill odd pages in MSS. that have been left blank between longer treatises.

We may divide the earlier literature into three distinct groups of works, to each of which I propose to devote special attention in subsequent chapters. These are:

(1) Didactic works, generally in verse, which are intended to teach beginners the moves and the most elementary principles of play, or to give a rapid description of the game; the most important being the chapter *De scaccis* in Alexander Neckam's *De naturis rerum*, and a Latin poem of German authorship in a Cracow library.

(2) Moralizing works, in which chess is made the text for a parable or a homily, or provides the framework for a collection of stories; the most noted work in this class being the *Liber de moribus hominum et officiis nobilium* of the Lombard friar, Jacobus de Cessolis.

(3) Collections of chess problems, of which we possess a number of MSS. of two greater compilations, and several shorter and more or less independent works. Some of these MSS. contain prefatory sections giving valuable information about the game.

It is at first sight remarkable that we have no works similar to our modern books on the Openings, and no collections of games. But it was one of the chief defects of the older game that the general principles of play were so obscure in their action, and that the development of a game was so slow, that the necessity for recording games was hardly evident. Even the Muslim masters, who reached a standard of skill that was never approached in mediaeval Europe, only produced one work of analysis and two discussions on general principles. One of the first results of the great reform in chess at the end of the 15th c. was the discovery that it was necessary to analyse opening play, and worth while to record games. Already before 1500 we possess two works of the reformed chess which attempt to do this.

In the preceding chapter I have used contemporary evidence to establish the knowledge of chess in the Spanish marches of France by the year 1010, in Central Italy by 1061, and in Southern Germany by about 1050. In a similar way it is possible to establish the knowledge of chess in the other countries of Western Europe by the middle of the 13th c. Thus the two *French* historians of the First Crusade, Fouché of Chartres [2] and Robert

immodice ab ipsa adolescentia ludo latrunculorum; quo etiam Francisco Sfortiae Mediolani Principi innotui, & nobilium amicitiam multorum mihi comparavi' (ibid). 'Per idem tempus librum de latrunculorum ludo scripsi, quem anno aetatis xxiii absolvi; magnitudo Justini historici liber, materna scriptus lingua, quod existimarem eos, qui ludis delectantur, minime majore ex parte esse eruditos: divisi autem illum in iv libros. In primo de ludo latrunculorum, in secundo de ludis fritilli, in tertio de ludis: ostendi ludos xl' etc. (*Libellus de libris propriis*, 1543).

In a later bibliography (1554) he says that the first book of 100 leaves treated of chess and games that only require industry. In the third edition of this last work he gives the number of leaves as 150.

[2] Quoted above, p. 203.

de St. Remi, mention chess. The latter, writing of the Crusaders (who were for the most part drawn from France), names chess as one of their relaxations.[3] Both writers date from the commencing years of the 12th c. We possess a Latin poem of *English* authorship—the Winchester Poem—which was written in the first half of the 12th c., while the historian, William of Malmesbury, writing *c.* 1140, also mentions chess.[2] That chess must have been familiar to the Norman kings in the 11th century is clear from the fact that from about 1100 they used the name of the chessboard, L. *scaccarium*, AF. *eschecker*, for the name of the department of state in England and in Normandy which dealt with the collection and administration of the royal revenues. The name of *Exchequer* (an ignorant corruption of the ME. *escheker* caused by mistaking *es-* in this word for the OF. *es-*, L. *ex-*) has survived to the present day in England as the name of the modern descendants of the Norman office; in Normandy the name *Eschequier* was altered to *Parlement* in the reign of Francis I. It is disputed whether this application of the chess term originated in England or in Normandy. According to the *Dial. de Scaccario* of Richard, Bp. of London, 1178, the term *scaccarium* was taken from the table, about 10 ft. by 5 ft., upon which the accounts were worked out by means of a cloth divided into strips about a foot wide, on which counters (*calculi*) representing the moneys were placed and moved. The Bishop says that the table was so named 'quod scaccarii lusilis similem habet formam', but shows that—

> as in chess the battle is fought between Kings, so in this it is chiefly between two that the conflict takes place and the war is waged—the treasurer, namely, and the sheriff who sits there to render account: the others sitting by as judges, to see and to judge (E. F. Henderson, *Select Hist. Doc. Middle Ages*, London, 1905, 23).

It has sometimes been argued on the strength of two 12th c. works, Gaimar's *Lestorie des Engles*, which represents Ordgar as playing chess in the reign of Eadgar (D. 975),[4] and the *Ramsey Chronicle*, which describes King Cnut (D. 1035) as discovered relieving the tedium of the night in playing games of dice or chess,[5] that chess was played in Southern England before the Norman Conquest. Both of these passages are in date too long after the event to possess any serious historical value, and against them we must place the complete silence of all pre-Norman English works, and the omission of chess in the list of games in certain Old English vocabularies of the 10th and

[3] 'Cumque hæc crebro vicissitudinem actitarentur impulsu, præambulus quidam aduenit qui nuncios principis Babyloniæ in crastinum præconebatur aduenire et a Principiis castrorum fiduciam quaerit veniendi secure: Qui libenter annuunt, seque eorum susceptioni sollemniter praemuniunt. Tentoria variis ornamentorum generibus venustantur: terræ infixis sudibus scuta apponuntur, quibus in crastinum *Quintane* ludus, scilicet equestris exerceretur: aleæ, scaci, veloces cursus equorum flexis in frenum gyris non defuerunt, et militares impetus: hastarumque vibrationes in alterutrum ibi celebratæ sunt. In quibus actibus monstrabatur quod nullo pauore trepidabant qui talia operabantur.' ('Hist. Hierosol.,' lib. v, *Gesta dei per Francos*, Hanover, 1611, i. 55.)

[4] Quoted below, p. 432, n. 45.

[5] 'Ipse (Aethericus episcopus) quoque mannum, curiam aditurus, ascendens, ipsumque calcaribus urgens, regem (Canutum) adhuc tesserarum vel scacchorum ludo longioris taedia noctis relevantem invenit.' *Chron. Abbat. Rameseiensis*, clxxxv. (London, 1886), 137. The text of the Chronicle is certainly later than 1160, and probably than 1170. For Cnut and chess see pp. 404 and 443.

11th centuries. Cnut *may* have learnt chess during his pilgrimage to Rome in 1027, but it is very improbable that chess was ordinarily played in England before the Conquest. The word 'chess' and the normal English names of the chessmen are all of Norman-French introduction.[6]

The Norman barons took chess with them to Scotland and Wales. The *Reg. Dunelm.* (13th c.) mentions a carver of chessmen as living at Kirkcudbright, Scotland, *c.* 1150.[7] A Welsh version of one of the Charlemagne romances, dating from 1336, mentions chess,[8] and a 15th c. Irish MS. of the *Second Battle of Moytura* has incorporated in the older text a marginal comment from its parent MS. which identifies an older Irish game with chess.[9]

The game is mentioned in many of the translations of the old French romances which were made in German, Dutch, Danish, Swedish, and Icelandic from the very beginning of the thirteenth century. The Icelandic *St. Olaf's Saga*, a part of the *Heimskringla*, and written *c.* 1230, contains a chess incident.[10] A MS. with chess parallels has been in Reval on the southern shore of the Gulf of Finland, in the Middle Ages in the territory of the Teutonic Order, since 1270, and a Riga merchant of the same period was surnamed *Shakhmat*.[11] In 1335, Robert, King of Hungary, sent John, King of Bohemia, 'tabulae pro scacis' (John de Thwrocz, *Chron. Hungar.*, xcvii), while a 14th c. Czech vocabulary (by Klen Rozhochany, in Hanka's *Zbérka nejdávn. slovn.*, Praze, 1833, 98) gives a list of chess terms with barbarous Latin equivalents: ssach, scacus: kralík, cral, rexus: králevna, rexa: pop, arippus: rytieř, militus: roch, rochus: pěšec, pedes: šachovnice, scatabula.[12]

[6] The other view, voiced by Thrupp (*Anglo-Saxon Home*, 1862, xvi), received apparent support from Hyde's curious title of the early 12th c. *Winchester Poem* (see p. 499). Grein (see Grein-Wülker, *Bibl. der Angelsächsischen Poesie* (1881), i. 333) makes the suggestion that the name of the rune ᛈ, *peorð*, which is associated with play (ᛈ peorð buþ symble pleȝa and hlehter wlancum . . . , ðar wiȝan sittaþ on beorsele bliþe ætsomne), may be connected with the Ic. *peð* = Pawn in chess, but this is philologically impossible, and later scholars reject the suggestion utterly. The only facts which seem to me to promise any serious support to a belief in the existence of a pre-Norman chess in England, are the names for the Bishop in the *Winchester Poem* and in Neckam (see Ch. IV, below), for parallels to which we must go to early Italian and German chess.

[7] 'Quidam de villula (Kirkcudbright) in confinio posita artificiosus minister, sub diurno tempore studiosus advenit, cujus negotiationis opus in pectinibus conformandis, tabulatis et scaccariis, talis, spiniferis et caeteris talibus, de cornuum vel solidiori ossuum materie procreandis et studium intentionis effulsit.' (Cap. lxxxviii.)

[8] *Campeu Charlymaen*, ed. Williams, Welsh MS. Soc., 1878–80, 7. 'Rei onadunt yn gware seccyr, eraill yn gware gwydbwyll' (which the editor translates, 'some of them were playing chequers, others chess'). And again, 8, 'Ac yna y disgynassant yr neuad vrenhinawl yn yr honn yd oed anneiryf lluossogrwyd o wyrdda yn gware seccyr a gwydbwyll' (translated 'and then they descended to the royal hall in which was a countless multitude of good men playing chequers and chess').

[9] In *Revue Celtique*, xii. 78 (cf. Meyer and Nutt, *Voyage of Bran*, ii. 176). 69 As ed atbertsom go rocurt fidhcelda na Temrach dia saigidh-sium annsin, ⁊ gou rug-som a toichell, conad andsin dorigne an Cró Logo. Acht masa i n-uamas an catha Troianna rohairged in fi(d)ceall ni torracht Herinn andsin í, uair is a n-áonaimsir rogniadh cath muigi Tuired ⁊ togail Traoi. (This he (the King) said then, that the chessboards of Tara should be fetched to him (samildánach) and he won all the stakes, so that then he made the *Cró* of Lugh. But if chess was invented at the epoch of the Trojan war it had not reached Ireland then, for the battle of Moytura and the destruction of Troy occurred at the same time.)

[10] See Appendix I to this chapter for Icelandic chess.

[11] F. Amelung, 'Zur Balt. Schachgesch.' in *Balt. Schachbl.*, vi. 132. Amelung thinks that chess reached Livonia from Germany, and that the game was popular there with all classes during the Middle Ages.

[12] For other references to Bohemian chess, see Zíbrt, *Dějiny hry šachové*, Praha, 1888.

All of these references, however, are to chess as something already fairly generally known. No chronicler took the trouble to record the first occasion when he heard of chess or saw it played by a fellow-countryman. When we seek more information as to the details of the advance northwards from the shores of the Mediterranean, we find no direct evidence that can help. It is only from the nomenclature of the game that we can form any conclusions as to the source from which any particular country obtained its knowledge of chess. It is only in terms of centuries that we can date the introduction of chess among any people.

I have already stated that the Arabic names of three of the pieces (*firzān* in its popular form of *firz*, *fīl* in the form *al-fīl* with article prefixed, and *rukh*) were adopted in European chess. This, however, is not a complete statement, and it is necessary to qualify it to some extent. For the European nomenclature is a composite one, and in hardly any of the European languages was it uniform and fixed throughout the mediaeval period. It will be remembered that the early Indian literature shows a great variety of name for the various pieces, though the meaning of the name of each piece is a constant one: a phenomenon which I explained as probably due to the use of actual carvings of men, animals, &c., for the chessmen. In Europe the phenomenon is different, and we find—in two cases at least—a variety of meaning in the different names for the same piece. In this the action of the European player was an exception to the rule generally followed when chess was adopted by a new people, by which the intelligible names were translated and the unintelligible ones were borrowed. This anomaly seems to me to throw light upon the way in which chess reached the different parts of Western Europe.

The Arabic *Shāh* (King—K) became everywhere in Europe the *King*: L. rex, Sp. rey, Pg. rei, Cat., Prov. réy, It. rè, Fr. roi (OF. roy(s, AF. rey(s); Eng. king, Ger. könig (MHG. künic, MLG. kuninc), Du. koning (MDu. coninc), Ic. konungur, Sw. konung or kung, Dan. konge: Lettish karalis, Cz. král, Pol. król, Croat. kralj, Serv. kraly, Hun. király.[12a] This is, of course, a simple translation from the Arabic.

The Arabic *Faras* (Horse—Kt) became the *Horse* in the Peninsula, at a later date but still in the mediaeval period in Italy, and in modern times in some other parts of Europe also: L. equus, Sp. caballo, Pg. and It. cavallo; NDu. pard; NSw. häst, Cz. Pol. koník, Serv. koñ, koñits, Hun. lo.[13] Generally in Europe it became the *Horseman*, who was soon identified with the feudal *Knight* who warred on horseback, and this name was occasionally used in

[12a] L. 1– rex, 4 rexus, (5 regia majestas). Sp. 3– rey. Cat. 4– rey. It. 4– re, 7 rey. Fr. 4–7 roy, 4–5 roys, 4, 7– roi, 4–5 rois. AF. 3 rei(s), 4 rey(s). Eng. 4–6 kyng, 5–6 kynge, 7– king. HG. 3–7 künig, 3–5 künec, küneg, 3–4 künic, 4–5 küng, 4–7 kung, 5 kunig, 6– könig, 7 könnig. LG. 3 kuninc, 4 koninc, konink, kunninc, kuninc, koningk, koningh, konyngh, 5 koning. Du. 3–5 coninc, 5 coninck, 7– koning, 7 koonink (8 wetgever). Ic. 3– konungur, 7–8 kongur. Sw. 4– konung, 7 kong, 9 kung. Cz. 4 cral, kralík, 4– král.

[13] L. 4–6 equus, 4–5 equs, 4 caballus. Sp. 3– cavallo, 3 caballo. Pg. 6– cavallo. It. 6– cavallo, 6 chaualo, chauolo, caualo, chauallo (pl. chauagli). (Fr. 7 cheval). (Eng. 6–7 horse). (Ger. 7 pferd). Du. 8– paard, 9 pard. Sw. 8– häst.

Southern Europe also; L. earlier eques, later miles, MSp. cavallero, Pg. cavalleiro (still in occasional use), Cat. cavaller, MIt. cavaliero, Prov. cavalier, Fr. chevalier, Eng. knight, MHG. ritter, MLG. and MDu. ridder, Ic. riddari, MSw. riddar, MDan. ridder, Cz. rytieř, Hun. huszar.[14] In modern times several countries have followed the lead of Germany in adopting *Jumper* as the name of the piece: NGer., NDan. springer, Sw. springare, Lettish sirdsinsch, Cz. jerdec, Croat. skakač, Hun. ugro.[15]

The Arabic *Baidaq* (Foot-soldier—P) came into Europe as the *Foot-Soldier*; L. pedes, pedo, pedinus, It. pedona, pedina, Sp. peon, Pg. pião, pedes, Cat. peó, Prov. pezon, Fr. pion (OF. paon, AF. poun), Eng. pawn, Welsh paenod, NDu. pion, Serv. peon, Roum. pion, Ic. peð, Cz. pêšec, píšek, Pol. pieszek, Croat. pješak, MHG. and MLG. vende, MDu. vinne, MSw. finna, Hun. gyalog. Occasionally a diminutive form was used, e.g. L. pesculus, OF. paonnet, MHG. vendelîn.[16] In modern times, several countries have followed the lead of Germany in adopting *Peasant* as the name of the piece: NGer. bauer, Sw., Dan. bonde or knegt.[17]

The Arabic *Rukh* (Chariot—R) became everywhere in Europe the *Rook*: L. rochus, It. rocco, Sp., Pg. roque, Cat. roch, OF. roc, ros, ME. rok(e, NE. rook, MHG. roch, MLG. rog, MDu. roch, Ic. hrókur, MSw. rok, MDan. rock, Cz. hroch:[18] a sure sign that the meaning of the Arabic word was generally unknown or forgotten. There are a few indications that another

[14] L. 1–7 eques, 2 caballarius, equester, 2–6 miles, 4 militus, 5 milles (tragilis, 7 capripes, equitatus). Sp. 5 cavaller, 3–7 cavallero. Cat. 4 cavaler, 9 cavaller. It. 4–6 chaualiere, 4–5 caualiero, 4 caualliero, 7 cavagliere (5 equite, 6 milite). Prov. 3 cavalier. Fr. 3–5 chivalier, 3–4 chivaler, -ir, 3 chevalier, 4 cevalier, cavalier, 5 chevaliers. (Du. 8 cavalier.) Eng. 4–5 knyȝt, 5–6 knyght, 5 knyht, knigt, knyht, knihgt, knyhgt, kniht, 5– knight, 6 knighte. Sc. 5 knicht, 6 knycht(e). MHG. 3–4 rîter, 3–7 ritter, 4 ritâr, riter, 7–8 reuter. MLG. 4 ridder, rydder, ritter, -ir. MDu. 3–7 ridder, 8 ruiter. Ic. 3– riddari. Sw. 4 riddar. Cz. 4– rytier.

[15] Ger. 7 sprenger, 8– springer (8 schreiber). Dan. 7– springer. Sw. 7 springare. For the sake of completeness I add the rare Du. 8 agent.

[16] L. 1–7 pedes, 2 pedester, 3–5 pedinus, 4–6 pedo, pedona, 4 pes, 6–7 pedina, 7 pedestis. (Also 3 architenens, 5 popularis, popularium, pesculus, servus, cliens, juvenis, mancipes, 7 peditatus, rusticus). Sp. 3– peon. Pg. 9 pião, peão, pedes. Cat. 5 peo(n), peho(n), paho(n), 9 peó. Prov. 3 pezon(et). It. 4– pedona, 6 pedo, 6– pedina, 7 pedon(e), pedino (5 adolescentulo). Fr. 3 poon, 4–5 paon, 4 peon, pannet, panounet, paounet, paonet, 4–5 paonnet (pl. paonnes), 5 paont, pionnet, pioncel, 5– pion, 6 pennet, 7 pieton (Godefroi adds pehon, pedon, pyon, peon(n)et, poon(n)et, pavonet). AF. 3–4 poun. Eng. 4 poun, 4–5 poune, 5 pown(e, poyn, pone, 5–6 pon, 5– pawn, 5–7 pawne, 6 panny, 6–7 paune. Sc. 5 poun (also 6 yoman (popular), 7 footman). MHG. 7 pion. Du. 8– pion. Ic. 3– peð (pl. peðmaður, peðlingur). Cz. 4– pěšec, pešec, 9 pišek, piony. MHG. 3–7 vende, 3–4 vendelîn, 4–7 fende, 5 vent, vinde, 6 fendlin, 7–8 vendt, 7 vend, fend, fendel, finde, wende, 8 fähnel, fändel, fändlein (also 6 pedina, 7–8 soldat, 7 fussgenger, knabe, 8 fussvolk). MLG. 4 vende, vinne. MDu. 3–5 vinne, 4 vende, vinde, 5 vin (also 5 pedoene, voetghangher, voet-knegt, voetganger, 7 nimph, nymph, 8 soldat). Sw. 4 finna.

[17] NGer. (7 knecht), 6– bauer, 7 bawr, baur, bawer. Du. 8 boer, burger. Sw. 7– bonde, 8 knegt. Dan. 7–8 knegt, 8– bonde. Ic. 9 bonde. Lettish, kahjneeks. Cz. sedlák. Hun. paraszt.

[18] L. 1–6 rochus, 2–5 rocus, 2, 5 roch, 3–6 roccus, roc, 4–6 rocchus, 5 rokus, 6 rocch (also 2 Janus biceps, bifrons rochus; 1 marchio, 5 rector, rectus, praeses, ultor, dux, comes, interrex). Sp. 3–7 roque, 5 roch. Pg. 6 roque. Cat. 4 roch. It. 4–7 rocco (pl. rocchi), 5–6 rocho, 4–6 roccho, roco, rrocho, 7 rocca. Prov. 3 roc(s). Fr. 3–7 roc, 4 rok, roch, 4–5 ros, rocq, 4 roz, 7 roche. Eng. 4–6 rok(e), 4– rook, 5 roc, roche, 5, 7 rocke, 6–7 rock, 7 rooke. Sc. 5 rouk, 6 rowke. MHG. 3–8 roch, 4 roc, rogh, 6 rach, 8 roche. MLG. 4 rog(he), roch, 4–5 rock, 8 rog(ge). MDu. 3–5 roc(k). Ic. 3– hrókur, 7 rogur. Sw. 4 rok. Dan. 7 rock. Cz. 4 roch, 9 hroch. Cf. Welsh, 6 bran Owain ap Urien (= *raven*).

The name *Rook* is obsolete in many European languages. The history of the change of name is given below, Ch. XI, but for convenience of reference I add the form-history of the

name had been attempted in several parts: e.g. Germany, *marchio*, the marquess or lord of the marches; Italy, *rector* or *comes*; England, *biceps Janus*; but none of these seems to have been ever widely used.

The Arabic *Firz*, *Firzān* (wise man, counsellor = Q) has received a variety of names in Europe, but the older sources show only two.

The Arabic name was adopted in Spain, France, and England: Sp. alfferza, Prov. fersa, OF. fierce, fierge, ME. fers, whence the L. ferzia and, in problem collections only, the It. ferce.[19]

The piece was replaced by a *Queen* in Italy, the Germanic and Norse lands: L. regina, It. reina; MHG. künegîn, MLG. koninginne, MDu. coninginne; Ic., Sw. drottning, Dan. dronning; Cz. kralevna.[20] The same name appears as an alternative in French and English, and later in Spanish also: Sp. reyna, OF. royne, reyne; ME. quene. In English there are instances of *queen* (in Latin MSS.) older than any of *fers*.

The fact that *firz* was adopted and not translated in some of the European languages proves that the meaning of the Arabic name was not understood. The Spanish MS. Alf. of 1283 shows that the Spanish player connected the *alfferza* with the standard-bearer, Sp. *alferez* = Ar. *al-faris*, the horseman, from *faras*, a horse: an explanation which confuses *firzān* with *faras*, and suggests that the Western Muslims had forgotten the derivation of the former word.

The name 'Queen' is a characteristically European innovation, suggested probably by the position of the piece upon the board and by the general symmetry of the arrangement of the pieces, which pointed to the pairing of the two central pieces.[21] The name has reacted curiously upon the

modern names here. (*a*) *Elephant*. L. 6 elephas, elephantus turritus, 7 turrigerus bos. Fr. 6 elefans. Eng. 6 elephante, 7 elephant. Ger. 7 elephant, 8 elefant. Sw. 7 elephant. Dan. 7– elephant. Ic. 9 fill. (*b*) *Tower*. L. 7 arx, rupes, turris, turris scaccaria, turriculum. Sp. 9 torre, castello, castillo. Pg. 9 torre, castello. It. 5 (custode della rocha o arce), 7 rocca, tore, 8 rocchiere, 8– torre. Fr. 7 roche, 7– tour. Eng. 6 tower, tower-keeper, 7– castle, 7 fortress. Ger. 7 festung, 7– turm, thurm. Du. 8 kasteel, 8– toren, 8 tooren, 9 fort. Sw. 9 tärn, Dan. 9 taarn. Lettish, tornis. Cz. věž. Pol. wieža. Croat. toranj. Hun. bástya, torony. Serv. toroñ, kula. (*c*) Also L. 6 cyclops, 7 satelles. Eng. 6 judge, 7 duke. Ger. 7 herzog, fähnrich, 8 statthalter, oberster. Du. 7 schildwagter, wachter, 8 richter.

[19] L. 2 ferzia, 3–5 fercia, 4–5 ferz, 4 firgia, 5 forcia, fforcia, fortia, fortis, ferzs, fera, fergia, 6 ferce, ferza; also in MSS. of Fr. origin, 5 fere, fiere; and of Eng. origin, 4–5 ferce, 5 ferze, fierte (certe), fferte, ffers. It. 4 ferça, ferza, ferçe, 6 fercia. Sp. 3 alfferza, 5 alfere(z)za. Prov. 3 fersa. Fr. 3–4 fierce, 4–5 ferge, 4 ferce, fierge, firge, fierche (serge, sergens). AF. 3–4 fierce, ferce. Eng. 4–7 fers, 5–6 ffers, 5 fiers, 6 ferse, fferce, ferce, 7 feers; pl. 4 ferses, 7 feerses. Sc. 5 feir(e)s, fers, feiris.

[20] L. 1– regina, 4 rexa (Cz.). Sp. 5 regina, 7 reyna, 9 reina. Cat. 4 reyna, reina, regina, 9 rainha. Pg. 9 rainha. It. 5–6 regina, 5–7 reina, 6 rejna, rigina. Fr. 4–7 royne, 4, 7 reyne. 4 roine, roiine, 5 roigne. Eng. 4–6 quene, 6 qwene, quyene, 6–7 queene, 7 queen. Sc. 6 quheyne. MHG. 3–4 künigin(ne), 4–7 künigin(n), 4 künneginne, 5 küneginne, küngin, 6– königin, 6–7 köngin, 7 königinne, köningin, könnigin, 7–8 königinn. MLG. 4 koninginne, kunniginne, kuninginne, konynghinne, koninghinne, koningynne. Du. 3–5 coninginne, 5 coningine, coninghin(ne), 7 koninginne, koninghinne, 8 koningen. Ic. 8– drottning, Sw. 4 drotning, 7– drottning. Dan. 7 dronninge, 8– dronning. Cz. 4 królevna, králova, 9 královna. Pol. królowa. Hun. királyné.

[21] Freret (*Origine du jeu des échecs*, read to the French Academy, 24 July, 1719, printed in *Hist. de l'Académie*, V, Paris, 1729, 250–9) tried to explain the change of name by supposing that French players confused the words *fierge* (fers) and *vierge* (L. virgo), and that the latter—possibly by way of 'the Virgin', 'the Queen of Heaven', 'the Queen'—suggested the terrestrial Queen. The historical evidence is strongly opposed to this pretty guess, though the similarity of sound between *fierge* and *vierge* naturally led to comparisons in poems, e. g. in the Fr. translation of the *Vetula*, in Gautier de Coincy, &c.

borrowed name *fers*, and has everywhere altered the gender. All the European names, and even the Sp. *alfferza* in the Alfonso MS. of 1283, are feminine nouns. We have already seen that the same is true of the Russian word *fers*.

At a later date, though still in the mediaeval period, other names came into general use for the chess Queen. I shall return to these later.

Of all the chessmen the Arabic *Fīl, Al-fīl* (elephant, the elephant — B) has acquired the greatest variety of names in the European languages.

On the one hand we have the borrowed name *Aufin*: L. alphiles, alfinus, and a number of other forms, Sp. alffil (later arfil), Cat. orfil, Prov. alfi, OF. aufin, ME. aufin, Welsh elphyn, which appeared in Italian before the 14th c. as alfino, later alfiero, delfino, &c., and in MDu. as alphyn (a single instance in a translation from the French).[22]

On the other hand we have four different names of European origin. The piece is replaced:

(1) By a *Sage* or *old man* in Italy (MS. Arch.), in England in the oldest references, in Germany, the Netherlands, and Sweden: L. curvus, calvus, senex; MHG. alte, MLG. alde, MDu. oude, Sw. ollin.[23]

(2) By a *Bishop* or other ecclesiastic (more frequently in early times determining the shape of the carved piece than its actual name). Instances of carved piece or the use of the name are found in England, France, Germany, Iceland, and Bohemia: L. cornutus, episcopus, ? calvus; MF. cornu; Eng. (since 1500) bishop; Ic. biskup; Cz. póp.[24]

(3) By a *Count* in the oldest German references: L. comes.[25]

(4) By a *Fool*, primarily in France: L. stultus, stolidus; Prov., MF. fol; Ger. narr (late, rare, and under Fr. influence).[26]

Although the MS. Alf. shows that Spanish players knew that *al-fīl* meant the elephant, the knowledge was not general. The elephant was only known to most Europeans through literature, and its use in war was hardly known at all. There could therefore have been no appropriateness in European eyes in placing the elephant among the chessmen, and popular etymology tried hard to discover a plausible meaning for the name *aufin*.

[22] L. 2–5 alphicus, 2, 4 alficus; 3–6 alphinus (dat. pl. -ibus), 4–6 alfinus, 4 alfin, 5 alphinius, alfinis; 4 alfilus, 5–6 alphilus, 5 alphilis, 8 alphillus; 3 alferius; 3 alpheus; 4 arfilus; 5 africus; 5–6 delphinus. Sp. 3 alffil, 5, 9 arfil, 7 arfilo, delfil, 9 alfil. Pg. 9 alfil, alfim, alfir, arfil, arfim. Cat. 4 orfil(l), 9 alfil. It. 4–7 alfino, 6– alfiero, -e, 6 alfier, alfero, allfiero, 7 arfil(l)o, 8 alfido, alifido, 6– delfino, 6 delphino, 7 dolfino. Prov. alfi. Fr. 3–5 alfin, aufin, 4–5 aufins, 4 alfyn, alfine, alphin, aulphin, aufyn, auphin, afin, offin, oufin, 5 auffin, dauffin, delphin, 7 alfir, alfier. Eng. 5–7 alphyn(e), aufin, 5–6 aufyn, 5 alfyne, awfyn, 6 alfyn, affyn, afyn, 7 aphen. Sc. 4–6 alphyne, 4 alphing, 6 alphine, alphoyne. HG. ? altvil. Du. 5 alphyn. (Cf. L. 6 vexilliferus.)

[23] L. 1–4 curvus, 2–4 calvus, 4 chalvus, 2, 5 senex, 5 senator, antiquus, vetus, inveteratus, senilis, 7 (vir consularis). MHG. 3–8 alte, 4–7 alt, 4–6 altin, 5 altt, 7 altherr. MLG. 3–4 alde, 5 olde. MDu. 4–5 oude, 5 oulde, ouwe. MSw. 4 ollin. Hence (Ger. 7 rath, rath-herr, rathmann). Du. 5 raet, raat, raetslude, 8– raadsheer.

[24] L. 3–5 episcopus, 4–5 cornutus, 4 aripus (Cz.), 7 (mystes, censor moris). Pg. 9 bispo, mitra. OF. 3–4 cornu. Eng. 6– bishop, 6 byshop, bishoppe. (Ger. 7 pfaffe, bischoff.) Ic. 7– biskup, 9 byskup. Dan. 7–8 bisp, biscop. Cz. 4 póp. Pol. pop.

[25] L. 1 comes. (Cf. L. 6–7 satelles. It. 5 taciturnulo, secretario.)

[26] L. 3 stolidus, 3–7 stultus, 5 estultus, solidus. Prov. 3 fol. Fr. 3, 6–7 fol, 7– fou. (Ger. 7 narr.) Cz. komík. Hence the mod. Gk. *τρέλλος*.

The attempts naturally led to perversions of the word, and we find *alphiles* reproduced as *alphicus*, a leper, *alpinus*, the Alpine, *africus*, the African, *Alpheus* (a man's name), and in Italian as *alfiere*, the standard-bearer.[27] Gradually *alfinus*, *alphinus*, emerged as the ordinary Latin form of the word, though at a later date *delphinus*, with its associations with the Dauphin of France, who might appropriately be placed next the King and Queen, came into favour in Southern Europe. Other changes of name came about in the sixteenth century after the adoption of the modern game, and have displaced the older names in Germany and other countries of Central and Northern Europe.[28]

We have accordingly two well-marked systems of nomenclature, the one with King, Fers, Aufin, Knight (Horse), Rook, and Pawn; the other with King, Queen, Bishop (Sage, Count, Fool), Knight, Rook (Margrave), and Pawn. If we examine the diffusion of these nomenclatures it becomes evident that the first system, which is founded on the normal laws of translation and adoption, is characteristic of the Spanish chess, and that it has extended thence with but little diminished force into the older French chess and the English game of Norman times. The second system, with its non-Muslim names, is characteristic of the German game, and to a less degree of the oldest Italian and English chess. There is an underlying unity about each set of names: the normal names carry on the Muslim and Indian tradition that chess is a war-game; the moralists discovered a unity in the new European names by regarding chess as a picture in miniature of the European state.

At a later date, though still early in the European life of chess, the two nomenclatures overlapped and became confused. We may explain this as due on the one side to the vogue of the problem, on the other to the diffusion of the moralities. The problem-lore spread over Europe by means of collections of diagrams which, following Arabic usage, bore the written names of the pieces—not emblems of the chessmen, as is usual in our days—and these carried the Arabic derived names into Italy and even into Germany. The scribe, who was not necessarily acquainted with chess, copied the problem diagram mechanically: the chess-player added the solution intelligently and employed the chess names with which he was familiar. Thus the older Latin MSS. show invariably in the diagrams *fers* for the Queen, but the solutions just as regularly use the term *regina*.

I see, therefore, two influences at work, one with its centre in Spain which carried on the Muslim tradition, the other with its centre in Italy. The Muslim tradition spread northwards from Spain through France, and into

[27] A late instance of popular etymology at work is to be found in Minsheu's *Ductor in Linguas*, 2nd ed. 1627, London, s. v. *Bishop*—(†)1499 *a* Bishop *at Chesse play, clouen in the head like a miter.* I. *Alfiere.* I. 2. H. Arfilo, *corrupte à Lat.* Infula, *i. a miter.*

[28] See below, Ch. XI. For convenience of reference I give the form-history of these newer names here: (*a*) *Archer.* L. 6 sagittifer, sagittarius. Fr. 6 archer. Eng. 6–7 archer. Ger. 7–8 schütze, 7 schutze, (armbrust). (Du. 7 schutter.) (*b*) *Runner.* Ger. 8– läufer, 8 laufer, lauffer, läuffer. Du. 9 looper. Dan. 7 löber, 9 løber. Sw. 7 lopare, 8– löpare. Lettish, ihdsineeks. Cz. běhoun. Pol. giermek. Croat. lovac. Hun. futó, futár. (*c*) Other names. Eng. (6 counsell-keeper, secretary—see the It. forms in note 25). Ger. (8 doppelter söldner). Du. (8 zol, administrateur).

England as a result of the Norman Conquest, and into North Germany and Iceland as a result of the spread of the romantic literature and the problem. The European tradition spread northwards from Italy into Southern Germany, and thence into Prussia, Bohemia, and the Norse lands, and possibly touched England before the Norman-French nomenclature had established itself there. As a result of the moralities it again modified the chess terminology in England, and also affected that of France.

When the two streams mingled, and a variety of name became possible or actual for the same piece, the position became one of unstable equilibrium. No one uses with absolute impartiality two names for the same object, and in the course of time one or other name must go. Thus the original chess name *Horse* has again ousted the European *Knight* from Italian chess, and has maintained its position in Spain. On the other hand, the original term *Aufin*—once the ordinary name for the *Bishop* in France and England, and seemingly so well established that it had passed in a derived sense into the ordinary idiom—has been displaced in each of those countries by a new name that is pure European.[29] *Fers*, again, has vanished from Western chess, the name of *Queen* taking its place in England, while a new name, *Lady* (It. donna, Sp., Pg. dama, Fr. dame, Ger., Sw., Dan., Du. dame, Lettish, Cz., Pol., Croat., Serv., Hun., Roum., dama, all going back to the L. domina; Ic. frú), has replaced it elsewhere in Europe.[30] The introduction of this term in the Romanic languages dates back to the mediaeval period, and it had taken the place of the earlier names in French and Italian before the final change in the Queen's move had so altered the power of that piece that there was real justification for a change of name. The origin of this change is obvious enough, and affords an interesting illustration of the moralizing tendencies of the mediaeval European player.

In the Muslim game, the Pawn which reached the 8th line became at once a *Firzān*, whether the original *Firzān* was still upon the board or not. There was no incongruity in this, for there was no limit to the number of viziers that could exist at the same time under the ʿAbbāsid caliphate. The same promotion awaited the Pawn in European chess, but the new European game introduced unforeseen difficulties. Not only had the Pawn to change its sex, a contradiction to which attention was directed by Neckam and others, but by its becoming a Queen when the original Queen was still upon the board the moral sense of some players was outraged. Various attempts were made to get rid of this difficulty. The boldest attempt was the prohibition of promotion so long as the original Queen was untaken. This is

[29] I do not think that the usual hypothesis that the OF. *fol* (NF. *fou*) is a perversion of the Ar. *fīl* as a result of the workings of popular etymology can be accepted. It requires the popular use of *fīl*, and not *al-fīl*, for the name of the piece in France, and not a single instance of this is on record.

[30] The form-history is as follows:—L. 2–5 femina, 5 ffemina, 3–5 regalis femina; 3 virgo, (regia virgo, 5 bellatrix virgo); 5 domina; 6 mulier, (regia conjux); 7 amazon. Sp. 5– dama. Pg. 6– dama. Cat. 6– dama, 6 damma. It. 5–7 dona, 6– donna, 6–7 dama, 6 dame. Fr. 5– dame; 6 amason. Eng. (5 lady, 6–7 dame, 7 amazon). Ger. (4–6 frauw, 7 frow), 8– dame, (8 amazone, feldmarschall). Du. 7– dame, 7 dam, (8 directeur). Ic. 7– fru, (7 gamla). Sw. dame, 9 dam. Dan. 7–8 dame, 9 frue. Cz. 9 dáma. Also Pol. hetman. Hun. vezér.

the rule in the early German chess of the Einsiedeln poem and in the Spanish chess as described in the Alfonso MS., while it recurs at a later date in Catalan, French, and English chess. The restriction, however, still further reduced the brightness of the game, and was opposed to its spirit; it never commanded universal acceptance. Since the Queen was weaker than the Knight or Rook, the idea of allowing the Pawn a wider choice of value upon promotion never occurred to the mediaeval player. More usually, the difficulty arising from the possible plurality of Queens was evaded by an alteration in the nomenclature. Thus at quite an early date we begin to meet with a more general name for the Queen than *Regina*, e. g. *Femina*, *Virgo*, and later *Mulier*. The usual practice, however, was to use a different name for the promoted Pawn from that of the original Queen, and in France and England where there was a possible choice between Reine (Queen) and Fierce (Fers), many players tried to restrict the use of Reine (Queen) to the original Queen, and Fierce (Fers) to the promoted Pawn.[31] In Italy a similar result came about in the course of the 14th–15th cc., the term *Regina* being used for the original Queen, and a new term *Domina* being introduced for the promoted Pawn. This is the case in the majority of the problems added to the *Civis Bononiae* collection in the 15th c. Florence MS. of that work.[32] This use of *Domina* spread to France and England also. The late 15th c. Sorbonne MS. S uses this term on three occasions for a promoted Pawn. The Anglo-French MS. K uses the term *Dame* in the fourth position, *Le guy de dames*, the diagram using *Reyne* in the place of the usual *Ferce*. The English *Corpus Poem* uses *Domina* for the promoted Pawn. The new name, It. *donna*, Sp. *dama*, Fr. *dame*, gained rapidly in popularity, and ere long was used generally

[31] Thus—

(1) The 12th c. *Winchester Poem* (English) uses *Regina* for the ordinary Queen, but says of the promoted Pawn:

Cum pedester usque summam venerit ad tabulam,
Nomen eius tunc mutetur; appelletur *ferzia*;
Eius interim regine gratiam obtineat.

(2) The *Deventer Poem* (of French origin) also uses *Regina* for the original Queen, and says of the Pawn:

Si valet extremum tabule perstringere demum
Tunc augmentatur, tunc *fercia* iure vocatur.

(3) See the extract from the text of the problem 4 in K, an AF. MS. of the early 14th c., which is quoted in Ch. VI, below.

(4) The original (and English) chess chapter in the *Gesta Romanorum* has (MS. Sloane 4029, f. 36 b):

Primus pedinus . . . cum uenerit ad mensam fit *ferzs*;

a passage which is reproduced in a very corrupt form in other MSS. The original Queen is called *Regina*.

[(5) The 14–15th c. *Corpus Poem* (English) uses *Femina* for the original Queen and *Domina* for the promoted Pawn:

Lex sibi iure datur *domine* si fine locatur.]

(6) Caxton makes the following additions to his original in his English version of Cessolis:

'. . tyll he hath ben in the furdest ligne of theschequer / And that he hath taken the nature of the draughtes of the quene / And than he is a fiers / . . . And whan he is thus comen to the place where ye nobles his aduersaries were sette he shall be named white fiers or black fiers / after the poynt that he is in /.'

[32] *Facere dominam* (of the Pawn) occurs 19 times, *facere reginam* twice only; *Domina* is used eight times of a new Queen, *Regina* only once; *Regina* is always used of the Queen in the diagram.

for any Queen, whether obtained by promotion of a Pawn or not, throughout Italy, the Peninsula, and France. In England its use is confined to translations from the French and Italian, and argues an ignorance of chess on the part of the translator. The use of *Dame* in Germany, Holland, and Scandinavia belongs to modern chess only.

Perhaps the most remarkable features in the early history of chess in Europe are the extraordinary rapidity with which the game became well known, and the completeness of its conquest of the leisured classes. We have already seen how few and unimportant are the references to chess in the eleventh century. After 1100 the number of references increases fast: I have collected more than fifty from the twelfth century, mainly from France and England, but a few also from Germany, and I have no doubt that I should have found many more had the earlier Italian and Spanish literature been as accessible as is the French. From thirteenth-century works I have collected well over a hundred allusions to the game which establish its popularity from Italy to Iceland and from Portugal to Livonia. Italy seems to have led the way in the scientific study of the game. In 1266 a great Saracen chess-master named Buzecca (Buchecha, Borzaga) visited Florence and played three of the leading players of the city simultaneously, conducting two of the games blindfold, and playing the third over the board.[33] A century later, a Florentine player named Mangiolino obtained notoriety as a blindfold player.[34] The fame of the players of Lombardy was known throughout Western Europe from the twelfth to the fifteenth centuries. The mediaeval players owed to Lombardy the best of the moralities and the two largest collections of problems.

During the latter part of the Middle Ages, and especially from the thirteenth to the fifteenth century, chess attained to a popularity in Western Europe which has never been excelled, and probably never equalled at any later date. By 1250 the early prejudice of the Church against chess had begun to weaken in view of the royal and noble patronage of the game, and the monastic orders were freely accepting chess as a welcome alleviation of the monotony of convent life, while a knowledge of chess had spread downwards from the inmates of castle and monastery to the wealthier burgesses and merchants of the towns. It was widely played by the Jews in the Ghettoes. It was an essential portion of the equipment of the troubadour or minstrel that he should be a chess-player, and he carried the implements of play with him. Thus, Sir Tristram, travelling disguised as a minstrel,

> His harpe, his croude (i. e. organ) was rike,
> 1227 His tables, his ches he bare.

[33] 'In questi tempi (1266) venne in Firenze un Saracino che havea nome Buchecha, il miglior giuocatore a Scacchi che si trovasse, et in sul palagio del Popolo, dinanzi al Conte Guido Novello, giuocò a un hora a tre Scachieri co' migliori maestri di giuoco di Firenze, giuocando con due a mente e col terzo a veduta, et due vinse e'l terzo fece tavola. La qual cosa fu tenuta gran maraviglia.' Giovanni Villani, *Tratto dell' origine di Firenze*, Venice, 1559, VII. xii. 172.

[34] 'Proximo seculo Mangiolanus item Florentinus adeo in hoc ludo fuerat exercitatus, ut memoriter per alium luderet minime respiciens adversario et vidente diligentius et prudente.' Rafael Volaterranus, *Comment. Urban.* xxix, Basel, 1559, 693.

Chess was, however, in the main a game of the upper classes, and this was recognized so generally that it is mentioned again and again in literature as one of the typical chamber recreations of the feudal nobility. We have already seen how Petro Alfonsi included a knowledge of chess in his list of accomplishments which were characteristic of the nobility as opposed to the clergy. A favourite passage, which is repeated in more or less detail in many of the Charlemagne romances, gives a valuable picture of the daily life of the French noble of the 11th–13th cc.; and chess and tables are given as after-dinner occupations.[35] There are many similar references in other French, English, and German romances. Thus Philippe de Beaumanoir gives the following picture in his *Blonde of Oxford* (written *c.* 1270–83, ed. Paris, 1885):

Après mangier lavent leurs mains,
Puis s'en vont juer, qui ains
Ou en forès ou en rivières,
Ou en deduis d'autres manières.
Jehans au quel que il veut va
Et quant il revint souvent va
Jouer ès chambres la contesse,
O les dames, qui en destrèce
Le tienent d'aprendre franchois
Et il fait en dist com courtois
Quanqu'eles li voelent priier,
Com cil qui bien s'en seut aidier.
De jus de chambres seut assés,
D'eschès, de tables, et de dés,
Dont il sa damoisele esbat,
Souvent li dist eschek et mat.[36]

[35] E. g. in *Fierabras* (written *c.* 1170, ed. Guenard, in *Les anciens poètes de France*, Paris, 1860, p. 88):

Et respont li paiens : 'Tout ce sont pardonné.
Quel gent sont cil de France, di par ta loiauté,
Et comment vivent il çà en vostre regné ?'
—'Par foi', dist li dus Namles, 'quant li rois a digné
Lors va esbanoier pour son cors deporter ;
Et li un escremissent et salent par ces prés :
Li pluisieur vont as tables et as esciés juer.
Au matin oent messe et servent Damedé,
Et font largues aumosnes volentiers et de gré,
Et servent Jhesu Christ par boine volentés ;
Quant vienent en bataille, vassal sont esprouvé.'

[which is amplified in the English *Sir Ferumbras* of *c.* 1380 (ed. E. E. T. S.) :

'Tel me furst by þy lay : wat doþ ȝour men of fraunce ; 2216
Of hure disport & ek hure play : what is ȝour mest vsaunce ?'
'þe manere of hem', þan sayde he : is erly gon to cherche,
& after-ward ech man on his degree : after his stat þay werche.
þo þat lordes buþ of þe lond : in som tyme of the ȝere,
þay takeþ hure facouns faire an hond : & fareþ to ryuere ;
& summe a deer honteþ of hem þar went : & some to fox and hare ;
& to ioustes and tornyment : wel mo þer wendeþ ofte þare.
þo þat willieþ to leue at hame : pleyeþ to þe eschekkere,
& summe of hem to iew-de-dame : and summe to tablere :
Summe þay vseþ a maner of play : to caste wel a spere ;
And somme for to sckyrme asay : with swerd & bokelere.
þys buþ þe games of my contre : þat y þe telle here.'
'ȝea : alle þese buþ noȝt worþ a stre' : þan saide Lucafere.

The passage is omitted in the Celtic version.]

[36] See also *Li Romans de Durmart le Galois* (*a.* 1235, ed. Stengel, Stuttgart, 1873), 368–76, and Chrestien de Troyes' *Erec et Enide* (*c.* 1165, ed. Foerster, Halle, 1909, 348–60).

In *Robert of Gloucester* (1297) we have a similar account of the daily manner of life at the court of King Arthur:

> Sone after þis noble mete. as riȝt was in such tyde.
> þe kniȝtes atyled hom. aboute in eche syde.
> In feldes & in medes. to prouy hor bachelerye.
> Some wiþ launce & some wiþ suerd. wiþoute vileynie.
> Wiþ pleyn de atte tables. oþer atte chekere.
> Wiþ castinge oþer wiþ ssetinge. oþer in some manere.
> & woch so of eny game, adde þe maistrie.[37]

Geoffrey of Monmouth (*c.* 1150) in his account of the festivities at the coronation of Arthur says that 'others spent the remainder of the day in other diversions such as . . . playing at dice and the like'. When later writers amplified his narrative, chess was naturally added. Thus Wace, *Le Romant de Brut* (1155), has—

> Li un dient contes et fables,
> Auquant demandent dez et tables:
> Tex i a joent à hasart,
> Ce est uns geus de male part,
> As eschas joent li plusor,
> Au geu del mat ou au mellor.
> Dui et dui au geu s'acompeignent:
> Li un perdent, li un gaheignent: etc.[38]

And Robert of Brunne (*c.* 1330)—

> Dysours y-nowe tolde þem fables
> & somme pleide wyþ des & tables
> & somme pleide at hazard fast.
> & lore & wonne wiþ chaunce of cast;
> Somme þat wolde nought of þe tabler
> Drowe forthe meyne for þe cheker
> Wyþ draughtes queinte of knight & rok,
> & oþer sleyghtes ilk oþer byswok (i. e. cheated)
> At ilka mattyng þei seide 'chek';
> þat most þer loste sat y þe blek.

But we are not dependent upon the evidence of literature alone for the position of chess as a favourite occupation of the nobility. According to the

[37] Other English parallel passages occur in *Ipomydon* (trans. from the Fr. *c.* 1440, ed. 1810), 2265–8, and in Caxton's *Charles the Grete* (1485, ed. E. E. T. S., 118), which incorporates the passage quoted above from *Fierabras*. Chess is mentioned among other knightly occupations by the German writers, Konrad v. Würzburg (*Der werlte lon*, 28, written *a.* 1287) and Rüdiger v. Hünchkover (*Beliant*, written *c.* 1290).

[38] The remainder of the passage (10843–64) gives a lively picture of play with the dice, which involves the use of many technicalities. Some MSS. have a different reading of lines 10839–40. One has:

> Es esches joent li pluisor
> Ou à la mine ou à greignour.

and another:

> Ou à la mine al gieu majors.

From other passages in OF. literature (see Godefroi, s. v. *mine*), it is clear that *la mine* was some kind of game with the dice; probably *greignour* was a similar game.

The other English version of Layamon (*Brut*, 8133) has simply 'summen pleoden on tauelbrede' (A text, *c.* 1205) or 'some pleiode mid tauel' (B text, *c.* 1275). *Tauel* is the OE. word derived from the L. *tabula*.

Flores Historiarum, a St. Albans work of *c.* 1265 which was once attributed to Matthew of Westminster, Henry I allowed his brother Robert, Duke of Normandy, to play chess during the earlier part of his imprisonment, 1106–34.[39] Rizardus de Camino, an imperial official in Lombardy was murdered in 1312 'dum more nobilium scachis luderet pro solacio'.[40] John I of Aragon ordered the bailiff of Valencia, Oct. 10, 1390, to provide his lodging with a board to play at tables and chess, and the necessary pieces (Brunet y Bellet, *Ajedrez*, 226 n.). The manor of Kingston Russel, co. Dorset, was held by sergeanty of the King 'ad narrandum familiam Schacarii Regis in camera Regis et ponendum in loculo cum Rex ludum suum perfecerit', as appears from an inquisition held 1330 (3 Ed. III) on the death of Nichola de Morteshore, who had held it for term of life from Sir William Russel, the real owner (Blount, *Frag. Antiq.*, ed. S. Beckwith, London, 1815, 98 n.). King James I of Scotland was playing chess when his murderers broke in upon him in 1437.[41] An interesting picture of the games that were played in country houses in the same century is afforded by a letter of Margery Paston, Dec. 24, 148(?)4, to her husband (*Paston Letters*, 1872, iii. 314):

> Plese it you to wete that I sent your eldest sunne to my Lady Morlee to have knolage wat sports wer husyd in her hows in Kyrstemesse next folloyng aftyr the decysse of my Lord, her husbond (in 1476); and sche seyd that ther wer non dysgysyngs, ner harpyng, ner lutyng, ner syngyn, ner non lowde dysports, but pleyng at the tabyllys, and schesse, and cards. Sweche dysports sche gave her folkys leve to play and non odyr.

Chess was equally popular in France, and there are many references to the fondness of members of the House of Valois for the game. Louis, Duke of Orleans (D. 1407), purchased an elaborate board in 1397,[42] and his son, Charles, Duke of Orleans (B. 1391, D. 1465), the poet, was a keen, and in the opinion of his contemporaries, a good player. He retained players at his court of Blois, Guiot Pot, Guillelme de Fontenay, and Gilles des Ourmes. On a journey down the Saône from Macon to Lyon, he played chess, merels, and tables with Jehannet de Sauveuzes. He owned the problem MS., Paris, f. Lat. 10286, and in another MS. from his library is a note commemorating the fact that he won the volume at chess from M. Jean Caillau. In May 1457, he entertained at Blois a Lombard player, Jouvenal Nègre.[43] And he introduced chess into the strange *ballade* in which he mourned the death of

[39] 'Rex autem, memor fraternitatis, eundem comitem Robertum in libera carceris custodia sine ciborum penuria vel luminis beneficio vel preciosarum vestium ornatu, salvo tamen fecit reservari. Liceret etiam ei ad scaccos et aleas ludere' (*Fl. Hist.*, 1890, ii. 39).

[40] *Cortusii Patavini duo . . ., Hist. de Novitatibus Paduae et Lombardiae*, I. xvii, in Muratori, *Rev. Ital. Script.*, xii. 783.

[41] See J. Shirley, *Dethe K. James*, written 1440, ed. 1818, 12; and another account printed in the Appendix to Pinkerton's *Hist. Scotland*, which, according to Mr. Hume Brown, *Hist. Scotland*, 1899, i. 217, is of less credibility.

[42] '5 fév. 1397. Un tablier de bois garni de tables et d'eschez, et deux cannettes de fil d'or de Chipres au prix de 41 sols parisis.' Accounts, quoted in Champollion-Figeac, *Louis et Charles, Ducs d'Orléans*, Paris, 1844, 364, 379, Part iii, 35. (Plates 42 and 48 also illustrate chess.)

[43] Another noted Lombard player, Galeotto Belgioioso, is mentioned in the *Archivo Storico Lombardo*, xiii. 870 n.

his first wife, the widow of our Richard II.[44] His relative, Charles the Bold, Duke of Burgundy (B. 1433, D. 1477), is described by Oliver de la Marche (*Mémoires*, xxii) as the best player of his time.

If, therefore, it was desired to add 'colour' to an incident in a romance, in which a noble was concerned, it was natural to represent the noble as engaged in chess at the particular moment. Thus messengers often surprise him at chess.[45] This often happened in real life. King John was playing chess when the deputies from Rouen arrived in 1213 to implore his help against King Philip Augustus, who was besieging the city. The ill-fated Conradin was playing chess when his approaching execution was announced to him in 1268.

It is but a slight step further to make the chess incident play an important part in the development of the plot of the romance. I shall deal with incidents of this character in a later chapter.

The acquisition of a knowledge of chess and tables formed a considerable part of the somewhat narrow education of a noble's children,[46] and there are

[44] See below, Ch. IX. Compare also for Charles of Orleans and chess, Pierre Champion, *Charles d'Orléans, joueur d'échecs*, Paris, 1908, and Le Comte de Laborde, *Les Ducs de Bourgogne*, Paris, 1852, iii. 383.

[45] I give a few instances:

1. Gaimar (*c.* 1150), in his *Lestorie des Engles* (Rolls Ser.), represents Ordgar, Earl of Devonshire (D. 970), as seated at chess with his daughter Alfthryth, when King Eadgar's messenger arrived to test the truth of the rumours of the latter's beauty:

> Orgar iuout a vn esches, 3655
> Vn giu kil aprist des Daneis;
> Od lui iuout Elstruet la bele,
> Sur ciel nout donc tele damesele.

2. Jehan Bodel (*a.* 1200) makes news of an invasion reach the Saxon King while playing chess, in his *La Chanson des Saxons* (ed. Michel, Paris, 1839, i. 91–2):

> Guiteclins de Sessoigne, qi le Saisne justise,
> Ou palais de Tremoigne demenoit sa justise
> . . . .
> A lui joe as eschas Escorfaus de Lutise;
> Sebile les esgarde qi do jeu est aprise.
> A tant ez I message qi li conte e devise
> Que la granz oz de France en sa terre s'est mise. (St.)

3. In Cuvelhier's *Chronique de Bertrand du Guesclin* (*a.* 1400; ed. Charrère, 1839, i. 82);

> Li ducs fu en son tref, qui au eschès joua 2229
> A Jehan de Chando, qui noblement régna;
> Le conte de Montfort qui le gieu regarda; &c.

4. In *Coer de Lion* (*c.* 1325) we read:

> The messengers them hyed hard,
> Till they came to king Richard. 2170
> They found kyng Richard at play,
> At the chess in his galeye;
> The Earl of Richmond with him playd,
> And Richard won all that he layd.

5. In Marie of France's lay, *Milun* (*c.* 1175), 195–202, two knights are described as being so engrossed in their game that the porters slip unnoticed through the hall (ed. Warnke, Halle, 1900).

[46] 1. The education of Alexander the Great, in the *Romans de Alexandre* (*c.* 1100; Bartsch, *Lang. et Litt. Fr.*, 212, 4):

> Li reis Felips quist a son fil doctors:
> De tote Grece eslist les .vii. mellors;
> Cil li aprenent des esteles les cors,
> Del firmament les soveirains trestors,
> Les vii planetes e les segnes auçors,
> E les vii. arz e toz les granz autors,
> D'eschas, de tables, d'esparvers e d'ostors,
> Parler ot dames corteisament d'amors,
> De jugement surmonter jugeors,
> Bastir agait por prendre robeors. (G.)

several instances in the romances of children playing at chess,[47] and, sad to relate, quarrelling over their game.[48] It was for this reason that Aiol's father advises his son not to play at chess or tables:

As eskiés ne as tables, fieus, ne iués,
Celui tient on à sot, qui plus en set;
Car se li uns les aime, l'autre les het,
Lors commenche grans guerre sans nul catel. (*Aiol*, 165–8, St.)

2. The education of Charlemagne's children, in Philippe Mouskes' *Chronique* (1243, ed. Bruxelles, 1836):

Li rois ama moult ses enfans, 2836
Ausi les petis com les grans.
Ses fius aprist à cevaucier
Et leur armes à manoier,
Selonc la coustume de France,
Et bien porter escut et lance,
Et de boscage et de rivière
Savoir trestoute la manière;
S'aprisent d'esciés et de tables,
Et de siervir à hautes tables,
Et de clergie, pour entendre,
Lor fist mainte manière aprendre.

3. The education of Blancardin, in *Blancardin et l'orgueilleuse d'amour* (Bartsch, op. cit., 570, 5):

Li latimiers par fu tant sages
Que bien l'aprist de tos langages,
D'eskes, des tables et des des,
De tot çou fu bien escoles,
Ne mais li rois ne voloit mie
C'on li moustrast chevalerie. (G.)

4. The education of the Duchess Parise's son Hugh, in *Parise la Duchesse* (13th c. MS.; ed. Guenard et Larchey, Paris, 1860, p. 29):

Quant l'anfes ot .xv. anz et compliz et passez,
Premiers aprist à letres tant qu'il en sot assez,
Puis aprist il as tables et à eschas a joier,
Il n'a ome an cest monde que l'en peüst mater.
Bien sot .i. cheval poindre, et bien esperoner,
Et d'escu et de lance sot moult bien beörder.
Et quant il ot .xv. anz et compliz et passez,
N'ot anfant en la terre de si aut pare(n)té
Qui tant fust an .xv. anz ne creüs n'amendez.

5. The education of Alexius, in *St. Alexius* (MS. Laud 622 of *c.* 1400; ed. E. E. T. S.):

And hou he was to þe Emperowre
Ysent to be man of valoure
And lernen chiualrie
Of huntyng, and of Ryuere,
Of chesseplaieynge and of tablere.
Al nas worþ a flye;
Leuer hym was to conne good
And seruen god wiþ mylde mood,
And his moder Marie.

6. Even in Tudor days Eliot includes chess in the subjects of a liberal education in his *Instruction of a Gentleman* (H. viii, b):

'The games of Chests and Tennisplay, because thone is an ancient pastime, and proffyteth the wyt, the other good for ye exercise of the body, measurably taken are mete to be used.'

[47] In *Boeve de Haumtone* (1200–50) the children

Apres unt l'esches seynes 3036
Et juent entre eus, kar bien sont apris.

And in *Durmart* (ed. cit., 3098–125), two pages play in a lady's boudoir.

Et par devant le lit seoient
Dui jovencel qui là juoient
Sor un eschequier as eschès. (St.)

[48] E.g. in Pierre Regnault's *Chron. Norm.* (Rouen) is an account of a game between Prince Louis (afterwards Louis VI) of France and Henry (Beauclerk) of England:

'Et une fois entre les autres lois le filz du roy philippe joua aux eschez apres disner au dit henri le quel fist mat le dit loys et de grant despit quil eut apella le dit henri filz de

A preference for chess over tables was, on the whole, accepted as a mark of superior wisdom. Strohmeyer quotes two examples of this. In the *Chanson de Roland* (*c.* 1165, ed. Gautier, Tours, 1884) we read:

Sur palies blancs siedent cil chevalier,
As tables juent pur els esbaneier,
E as eschas li plus saive e li vieill.[49]

And in the *Comte de Poitiers* (*a.* 1200, ed. Michel, Paris, 1831, p. 57):

Li un juent à l'escremir
A l'entre deux, por miex ferir:
As tables li conte palès,
Li viel et li sage as escès.

Skill in play was esteemed in a knight as an accomplishment befitting his rank and position, and, while a knowledge of chess is attributed to almost every character of rank in the romances,[50] the heroes are regularly credited with a very high degree of proficiency.[51] Nor was the game confined to the

bastard et lui jeta les eschetz au visage. Henri leva leschicquier et en ferit lois tant quil le fist seigner et leust occis se neust este robert que soutvint . . .'

Unfortunately for the truth of this story, the French prince was only nine years old at the time; Henry was nineteen.

Other children's games ending in quarrels will be found in Ch. IX.

[49] In the German version of Konrad v. Regensburg (*Rolandslied*, *post* 1131), the passage occurs in a description of the things which the ambassadors from the Saracen king of Massilia saw on their arrival at Charlemagne's court. When they reached the Emperor's presence:

Sie vunden then keiser zewâre
obe theme scâhzabele (ed. Bartsch, 681–2).

[50] Instances occur *passim* in the present chapter and in Ch. IX. I may add to these the list of accomplishments with which Wace in his *Roman de Rou* (*c.* 1160, ed. Andresen, i. 103) credits Richard I, Duke of Normandy, 943–96:

Richart sout en danois e en normant parler 1762
L'altrui sout e le suen bien prendre e duner,
Une chartre sout lire e les parz deviser.
Li pere l'out bien fait e duire e doctriner:
D'esches sout e des tables sun cumpaignun mater;
Bien sout paistre un oisel e livrer e porter,
En bois sout cuintement e berser e vener;
As talevas se sout e cuvrir e moller,
Metre pie destre avant e entredous dubler,
Taluns sout remuer e retraire e noxer,
Saillir devers senestre et treget tost geter. (St.)

[51] E. g. Huon of Bordeaux (see Ch. IX); Hugh, son of Parise (see note 46 above); William of Palerne (*Guillaume de Palerne*, *c.* 1205, quoted in *Will. of Palerne*, E. E. T. S., p. 21):

Si set plus desches et de tables,
doiseax, de bois, de chacerie,
que nus qui soit en Lombardie,
nen toute la terre de Rome.

Girard de Roussillon (*Girard de Roussillon*, *a.* 1200):

Descays sab e de taulas, de joxs de detz.

Regnaut (*Fierabras*, ed. Becker, iv):

Regnaut savoit du jeu asses et largement.

Tristan (*Tristan*, quoted from a Brit. Mus. MS. by Massmann; his reference is wrong):

il sceut tant des eschez et des tables que nul ne l'en peult macter.

Doglas, the son of Priam (*Roman de Troie*, ed. cit. 8089–90):

Nus hom ne saveit plus d'eschas.

King Arthur, Guinevere, and Lancelot, in *Lancelot* (ed. 1533, ff. 100–1; St.).

Deduit, the son of Venus, in *Les Eschez amoureux*; I quote from Lydgate's translation *Reson and sensuallyte* (*a.* 1412, ed. E. E. T. S.):

He ys expert; and eke also
At al(le) pleyes delytables:

male sex alone: the noble's daughter learnt chess beside her brother,[52] and grew up every whit as fond of the game as he, and proved in general as good a player as, or even better than, the knights of her acquaintance. Queen Guinevere, la Manekine, Fezonas in the *Vœux du Paon*, Yvorin's daughter in *Huon de Bordeaux*, and the lady in *Les Eschez amoureux* are all described as players of the highest skill.[53] In one version of the *Ballad of Young*

At mereles, dees, and tables
He kan pley(en) passyngly;
But best and most specialy
At the Chesse he dooth excelle
That philomestor[a], sothe to telle,
For to make comparyson,
Ne was nat lyke him of renoun,
That first founde this play notable,
With him to play(e) was not able.
And I dar also specefie
The play he kan of Ryghtmathye[b],
Which dulle wittis doth encombre,
For thys play stant al by noombre,
And hath al his conclusions
Chefly in proporsions
By so sotil ordynaunce,
As hyt ys put in remembraunce
By thise Philosophurs olde.

[Side notes from the MS.:—[a] Iste philosophus secundum quosdam inuenit ludum Scaccorum. [b] Rihtmachia est ludus philosophorum et consistit in arsmetrica et proporcionibus numerorum.]

And finally from a poem of Sir David Lindsay's (1520–40; in Pinkerton's *Scotch Poems*):

Thay past the time with chess & tabill
For he to euery game was abill.
. . . .
He wan the pryse above thame all,
Baith at the buttis and the futeball.
Till every solace he was abill
At cartes, and dyce, at ches, and table.

52 E. g. *Three Kings' Sons* (c. 1500 from the French; ed. E. E. T. S., p. 10):
'And to the sone of the hous taught he such thynges of honour, that folkes meruailed to se hym so wele ensured / And the doughter taught he to syng / to harpe, & to play at the chesse, and al such goodly thynges as bilonge to a gentilwoman of honour.'

53 Guinevere, see note 51 above; Fezonas, see Ch. IX. La Manekine, in Philippe de Beaumanoir's *Roman de la Manekine* (1277; ed. Bannatyne Club, 1840):

Nis li rois durement l'amoit;
Toutes les fois qu'il sejornoit
A Dondeu, ù il ert manans,
Vers la Manequine ert tornans;
A li jouoit courtoisement:
Des eskès savoit ele tant
Que nus mater ne l'en peüst,
Jà tant de ce jeu ne seüst.
Des eskès savoit et des tables,
D'assés d'autres jeus delitables,
Dont ele se jouoit au roy
Sans felonnie et sans desroi.

Yvorin's daughter, in *Huon de Bordeaux* (a. 1200; ed. Guessard et Grandmaison, Paris, 1860, pp. 219–24):

Des eskiés set à moult grande plenté;
Ainc ne le vi de nul home mater.

The Lady in *Les Eschez amoureux* (MS. Dresden O 66, f. 22 b):

Car celle damoiselle auoit
Le nom par tout quelle sauoit
Sj tres bien la maniere & lart
Du Jeu des eschecz quautre part
Ne fust trouuee sa pareille,

which in Lydgate's translation (ed. cit.) becomes:

And this mayde of whiche I telle
Had a name and dyde excelle

Tamlane (*Minstrelsy of Scott. Border*, by Sir W. Scott, ed. London, 1869, p. 476:

> Four and twenty ladies fair
>   Were playing at the chess,
> And out there came the fair Janet,
>   As green as any grass.

—the only instance in our ballad poetry in which chess is mentioned.[54]

Unfortunately man did not always take his defeat well. When Jeanne, the daughter of Baldwin IX, Count of Flanders (married 1211), beat her husband, Ferrand of Portugal, in his wife's right Count of Flanders (B. 1233), at chess, he retaliated with his fists. In revenge, she left him in captivity from 1213 to 1226, refusing to ransom him.[55] Another curious story is told in Walter Map's *De nugis curialium*, IV, XV (Camden Soc., 18). Two Breton nobles had quarrelled, and one had mutilated the other. The King of France patched up the quarrel by marrying the son and daughter of the two contestants. One day the pair were playing chess, when the husband was called away. A knight took his place, and was mated by the lady, who said pointedly, 'Non tibi, sed orbi filio *mat*.' When the husband heard of this, he went straightway and treated his wife's father in the same way that his father had been treated, and returned home with the members of which he had deprived his victim. He called for the chess, and as he won he tumbled them on the board, saying, 'Filiae orbi dico *mat*.'

All encounters between knight and lady were not so tragic; at chess the sexes met on equal terms, and the freedom of intercourse which the game made possible was much valued. It was even permissible to visit a lady in her chamber to play chess with her, or for her amusement. Thus, in *Guy of Warwick*, Mordagowre proposes to Guy to visit a lady in this way to play chess before her, with the treacherous intent of entrapping him there.[56] In *Raoul*

> To pleyen at this noble play,
> She passede alle, yt ys no nay,
> And was expert and knyw ful well
> At the maner euerydell.
> Ther was nat fonde to rekne all.
> That was in craft to hir egall,
> For she surmountede euerychoon.

[54] Unfortunately Sir Walter's text has been so much modernized that the authenticity of any part is doubtful. Other texts of the ballad have *ba'* for *chess*.

[55] See *Chron. Senoniensis Richerii* (Labbe, *Mélanges curieux*, II. 638).

[56] Mordagowre proposes (C text):

> 'Go we now to chaumbur same
> On some maner tô make vs game,
> To the chesses or to the tabels
> Or ellys to speke of fabels
> Before the bedde of þat feyre maye
> For sche the louyth boþe nyght and day.'
> Into hur chaumbur þo þey yode:
> Before hur bedde the mayde stode.
> 'Syr Gye', sche seyde, 'welcome ye be:
> Ys hit yowre wylle to kysse me?'
> Gye hur kyssyd curteslye
> And sythen they spake preuelye.
> Then downe was the chekur leyde
> And before þe maydenys bedde dysplayde.
> Gye was queynte of hys playe
> And wanne þe furste game, wythouten nay,
> And the tother wyth the beste
> And the thrydde, or he wolde reste.

de Cambrai, Beatrix has fallen in love with young Bernier, but he is afflicted with shyness; she invites him, therefore, to play at chess or tables in her room, in order to give him a chance of speech. Lancelot visits Guinevere in her chamber under the pretext of playing chess, and Tristan, Yseult. In these three cases we have examples of the value of chess to the lover. Marie of France, in her lay, *Eliduc*, gives another example in which two lovers come to an agreement while playing chess in the castle hall (ed. Warnke, 1900, 483 ff.). A similar incident occurs in the German romance *Willehalm*. The *Clef d'amors* has much to say about the etiquette of chess from this point of view: especially how the knight is to subordinate his chess to the desire of pleasing the lady, and how the lady will find a knowledge of chess of the greatest value in her courtship.

In establishing the position of chess among the nobility, I have relied in the main upon the evidence which can be drawn from the mediaeval romances. It is perhaps necessary to add a word of caution regarding the value of these works from the historical point of view.[57] They often deal with historical characters, e.g. Alexander the Great, the early Carlovingian monarchs, the Norman dukes, even striking figures of the feudal period. There may be historical foundation for the broad outlines of the story, but this is as far as it is possible to generalize: the historical value of a particular romance is a matter for special research. But it is certain that the colour and atmosphere of the romances is not historical in the sense that the writer has taken it from historical sources, or traditions handed down from the time which he is describing. They are the writer's contribution to the romance, and his inspiration was drawn entirely from the manners and customs of his own day. They are not the result of study of the past. The poet everywhere describes life as it existed about him, and his hearers or readers recognized themselves and their habits in the rich colouring with which the old legend was treated. If we use the romances in this way, they have for the student of feudal manners a real historical value.

The inventories of chessmen, and bequests and purchases of chessmen, contained in Appendix III to this chapter, supply confirmatory evidence for the popularity of chess among the leisured classes.

At first sight this extraordinary popularity of chess with the feudal nobility appears somewhat incredible. We unconsciously contrast the present position of chess; we lay stress upon those characteristics of the game which are most prominent to-day, its difficulty, its seriousness, its weakness on the social side. We do not associate the mental vigour, the concentration of attention, and the powers of calculation, which are essential attributes of the chess-player of the present day, with the mediaeval knight or feudal noble. We are at a loss to discover a reason for the general popularity of the game among a class which was distinguished by physical, rather than intellectual, prowess, and which was more at home on the battle-field or in the chase than in the hall or boudoir.

[57] The caution seems necessary, since Forbes, 201–5 and 216–18, based arguments upon the assumption that the incidents of the Charlemagne romances are historical facts.

The explanation is to be found, partly in the conditions of life of the feudal nobility, and partly in the general demand for new forms of occupation, which was the result of the definite organization of feudalism and the establishment of a stronger central government in most of the countries of Western Europe. The three main features of the life of the noble in the 10th–12th centuries were his isolation, his absence of regular occupation, and the grey monotony of his existence. At home he was cut off by the traditions of his order from any regular society, except that of his own family. He had no political duties, no obligatory duties, no regular duties. It was the duty of his dependents to supply the food and labour that were necessary for the maintenance of his family. The noble recognized no responsibilities. He tried to occupy his days with the pursuit of the chase—an aimless pursuit, because he did not hunt to provide himself with food; with hawking, with martial exercises, with an occasional tournament. When all these palled upon him, he found new interest in life by joining in a Crusade. Ignorant of all instruction, his evenings at home were even more difficult to fill than his days, and the long winter evenings the most difficult of all. It was then that he turned to games, in the hope of finding in them a distraction that would beguile away the tedious hours, and would provide the mental exercise that was necessary to preserve his mind from utter stagnation. Small wonder, too, that the travelling minstrel, with his repertoire of song, romance, and trick, was everywhere certain of a warm welcome.

Moreover, the political activity of the period which saw the final expulsion of the Muslim raiders from Southern France and Italy, which saw the rise of Norman dynasties in England and Sicily, of a Burgundian dynasty in Portugal, a French dynasty in Jerusalem, a German dynasty in the Empire, and above all the establishment of the Capetan house in France, had its counterpart in a new activity in lay society. The growth of the ideas which we connote under the term 'chivalry', the institutions of jousts and tournaments, the beginnings of a wider social intercourse, in which women were to play the leading part, all marked the opening of a new social era. And it was just at this time that chess arrived to satisfy the want for a more strenuous occupation of the mind which should also fit in with the social instinct that was coming into being.

Nor had chess any serious rivals with which to contend at the moment. The earlier Middle Ages had few other indoor games. The board games of the classical periods had been forgotten since the fall of the Empire of the West. By the 12th c. we hear only of *tables*—a group of games played on the backgammon board—and a smaller group of games which the Muslim world included under the one name *qirq*, and the European under that of *merelli* (*ludus merellorum*).[58] In the former group the dice were a necessary concomitant of play: the latter group was of such marked simplicity that

[58] See the Appendix to Ch. VI, below. John of Salisbury gives a list of games in his *Polycraticus* (c. 1156); all involve the use of the dice, and probably most of them needed no other apparatus. He is speaking of the invention of the dice under Attalus Asiaticus in Asia Minor, whence the dice came to Greece, and continues:

'Hinc tessera, calculus, tabula, urio vel dardana pugna, tricolus, senio, monarchus, orbiculi, taliarchus, volpes, quorum artem utilius est dediscere quam docere.'

these games were often dismissed as only suited for children or rustics.[59] Chess was practically the only game known in which there was any real mental exercise possible. It was also recognized as symbolic of warfare, while the pieces could be made emblematic of the various elements of the society of the period. It only needed to become once the fashion to show promise of a long popularity; when ladies also adopted chess as a pastime, this promise became a certainty.

From the nobility the game naturally extended to the other members of the castle household. In *Floire et Blancheflor* the porter or gaoler plays, in *Guy of Warwick* the steward, in *Elie de St. Gille* the grooms, in *Durmart* the sergeants and squires. On the other hand, the fact that a menial knew anything of chess aroused suspicions as to his identity. Huon of Bordeaux, disguised as the varlet to a travelling minstrel, found that his word was doubted when he boasted of his skill at chess; and the Devil is discovered in the guise of a servant, in Gautier de Coincy's *Miracles de la Sainte Vierge* (*c.* 1230, Paris, 1857, 528), through his unusual accomplishments.[60] From the castle the game probably passed to the mercenary military classes and even to the more lawless knights of fortune, among whom we meet with chess-players in *Parise la Duchesse*.

It was one of the results of the inclusion of the burgesses of the towns in the feudal organization of society that a knowledge of chess spread to this class also. To what extent, however, the inhabitants of the towns adopted chess is not certain: Wackernagel concluded that in Germany the game only reached the wealthier classes, while Strohmeyer allowed a more general knowledge for France. I think that the latter conclusion is probably true for England, Spain, and Italy.[61] In many romances, however, the predilection

[59] E. g. the *Vetula*, I. xxxiv (which in the Fr. version has the title, *Ci parle du gieu des Merelles auquel souloient anciennement jouer les pucelles*):

Sunt alii ludi parvi quos scire puellas
Esse decens dixi: sed parva movere pudebat
Nuncque magis, quam tunc, pudet illa minora referre.

[60] His master boasts to a Bishop:

Il est de tout bons menesteriex,
Il set peschier, il set chacier,
Il set trop bien genz solaçier,
Il set chançons, sonnez et fables,
Il set d'eschez, il set des tables,
Il set d'arbalestre et d'airon;
Ainc ne veistes nul garçon
Ne nus varlet de tel affaire.

[61] Thus 14 May, 1335, Alfonso IV of Aragon dealt with the complaint of Jaime de Eritis, a merchant of Pisa, that two Barcelonese captains had robbed him of a cargo of wheat near Cardena, and had also taken 'unum pulcherrimum tauler scacorum munitum ebore.' (Brunet y Bellet, op. cit., 379 n.)

In the *Fabliau du Prestre et d'Alison* (*Recueil génér. des Fabliaux* par Montaiglon et Reynaud ii. 17), a chessboard which is hanging on the wall in a small huckster's house is used as a surface on which to count out money (St.).

A quick-witted clerk, who was struck by the English political crisis of 1289, narrated the events in a mock-parable which shows his knowledge of chess:

. . . Est Adam de Strat^{e} in scaccario per escheke mat,
Sumitur ille rocus nec minor ille locus.

(*State Trials of Ed. I* (Camden Soc., 1906, 93).

Sachetti's story of the curate who rang the church bell to call together his parishioners to verify his victories at chess, and rang it once too often (*Novelle*, clxxxiv, written *c.* 1400), seems to imply wide knowledge of chess in an Italian village.

for chess is represented as one of the things which distinguished the noble from the merchant, and one which the merchant could neither understand nor appreciate—in short, a sign of blue blood.[62] It was probably as much a result of the prestige which chess enjoyed from its association with the leisured classes as of any opinion as to the virtue of the game itself, that chess was so generally excepted from the list of forbidden pastimes in the mediaeval town statutes. Sometimes the condition is added that the stakes are not to exceed a specified amount.[63] Apprentices were bound by their indentures to abstain from chess and tables.[64] Gamesters whose fondness for play led to the neglect of more serious occupations would enter into legal bonds to abstain from games entirely or for a season; chess is sometimes included and sometimes specially excepted.[65]

[62] In *Aiol* (c. 1200; ed. Förster, Heilbronn, 1876–82) the hero stays at Roimorentin in the house of a great usurer named Hunbaut. The latter has married the daughter of a knight who had fallen into his power through inability to repay a loan. Their son, Antelme, takes after his mother's family, and will have nothing to do with his father's business. As his mother boasts to her guest:

Or ai de lui (i. e. Hunbaut) un fil que vous ichi vees.
Nient plus que li escoufles peut l'ostoir resambler
Ne se peut li mieus fiex à son sens atorner.
Mes fiex demande tables et eskies por juer,
Les chiens et les oiseus ne peut il oblier,
De la route as frans homes ne le peut on geter. (St.)

In *Les Enfances Vivien* (*a.* 1200; Gautier, *Épop.* iii. 395) the hero has been adopted by a heathen merchant, who tries to make a merchant of Vivien also. But Vivien always barters the goods entrusted to him for things of no value or for knightly weapons. Once when the merchant talked seriously to him after a more than usually foolish exchange, Vivien interrupted him with, 'Do you know what I should do, if I were you? I would build a castle with a great hall, where I could play chess and tables all day long!'

[63] The game was allowed in Marseilles (*Statuts de Marseilles*, 505: 'ludere ad scacos et ad tabulas'); Bologna (*Statuta Bononiae*, i. 502); Bergamo (*Statuta Bergami*, 337–8); Strassburg (1362 *Stat. Strassb.* in *Zeitschr. f. Gesch. des Oberrheins*, vii. 64: 'wol mag jederman in siner geselleschaft, do er hin höret, wurfzabel und schachzabelspil tûn umbe einen pfenning und nüt höher bi der vorgeschriben pene'); Verona (*Lib. jur. civ. urbis Veronae*, I. i. 141–54 in Carle, iii. 31); Nuremberg (1381–4 *Pflichtbuch*, in Ch. G. v. Murr, *Journal zur Kunstgeschichte*, 1776, ii. 98: 'Auch haben die Burger gesetzt daz niemant dheni Spil niht tun sol wie daz genant ist, ez sey fraw oder man, damit man den pfennigk verlieren oder gewinen mag . . . Awzgenommen rennen mit pferden, schiessen mit Armbrusten, Carten, Schofzagelpretspil (vnd Kugeln, vmb einen pfennink zwen zu vier poten'); Regensburg (1393 in Gemeiner's *Chron.* ii. 188, 301: schafzaln; *Limpurger Chron.*, 50: schachtafel.); Dissenhofen (Pupikofer, *Gesch. d. Turgaus*, i. 214, Beil. 62); Haarlem (1390 *Keuren ende Ordonnantien*: 'Item so en moet men generhande boeverien doen binnen hairlem, al hoe se genoemt is, hoger dan om vier scellingen, op eene boete van een pont, en een duysent steens, wtgescit in dolen te scieten, te scaken ende te caetsen binnen hairlem'); Delft (c. 1425 Soutendam, *Keurboek van Delft*, 78: games of pure chance as dubbelen, potreinen, minquen, quinque, passen are prohibited, but games in which subtlety also comes in are allowed, e. g. scaecken, quaerten, trouven, mit scijven te verkeeren, ticktacken); Bocholt (Wigand, *Archiv f. Gesch. u. Altertumskunde Westfalens*, Lemgo, 1826: 'Allen borgheren, ynwoners, kyndern vnde knapen ys von older ynsettinge des ghemenen rades verboeden, dat nyeman dobbelen, crucemunten of enych spyl spelen sal daer men geld mede wynnen unde verliesen mach vppe ghenen steden of tyden bynnen of buten Bockholt, uetgesagt schaktafeln, werptafeln, bozelen oft dergliken'); Frankfurt (1428: 'doch vszgescheide nczemlich bretspil vnd schaffczabelspiel'); Leiden (inferred from a case of 1469 in *Leidsch Kenningboek*, f. 296, in which the plea was admitted that a stake at chess was recoverable at law, because chess is not an illegal game—'dat scaken geen boeverie'). These instances are drawn from Ducange, *Qst.*, 59–60, and Vetter's *Ammenhausen*, p. xxxiii. Eiserhardt adds other permissions, e. g. St. Gall (14–15 c.), Frankfurt (1428), Munich (1433).

[64] See a form of Indenture for apprenticeship in R. Redman's *Parvus Libellus*, 1527.

[65] In the Avignon Library, MS. 2812, f. 3, is a 'Donation de 3 florins d'or et demi par une mère à son fils, sous certaines conditions, entre autres qu'il ne jouera plus avec des dez, au jeu des échecs, 18 dec. 1374.' (*Cat. Fr. Lib.*, XXVIII. ii. 697.)

A Marseilles lawyer named Laurent Aycardi, 30 Aug., 1381, drew up a deed by which

The Universities as a rule took a sterner line than the towns and forbad all knightly occupations, as jousts, hunting and hawking, and chess and games of chance. An exception was sometimes made in the case of chess and tables on festivals and public holidays, on condition that the stakes were limited to eatables and drinkables.[66]

It is improbable that chess reached at all widely to the lowest orders of society: in general, the conditions of life for the peasant were too severe to allow him time, or to encourage any inclination for such a game as chess. George Owen, however, in his *Description of Pembrokeshire* (1603), says of the parish of Whitchurch that 'in ancient times the meanest and simplest sort of people, yea, the plain ploughmen, were skilful at chess play'. He adds that he had seen many good players there. There are also several references in French and English works which show that chess was often played in taverns, and the sign 'The Chequers' may originally have been adopted to advise customers that chess could be played within.[67] It was in an Italian tavern that Cardinal Damiani found the Bishop of Florence playing chess. The chessboard also appears as a rude implement of gambling in the old English

Jacques Jean was forbidden to play at aloe taxilli, nahipi, scaqui, paletum. (H. René, *Les Cartes à jouer*, Paris, 1906, i. 14.)

In 1461, Peter Kraft, junior, of Ulm, promised his parents to give up cards and all games for a time, schachzagel and archery alone excepted (Eiserhardt, 47).

Jews often made these self-denying ordinances: see p. 446.

[66] See Rashdall, *Universities of Europe*, ii. 669 seq. He gives the following details:

(1) William of Wykeham, in his *Statutes New Coll. Oxf.*, 48, included chess among the noxious, inordinate, and unhonest games which are forbidden to scholars.

(2) At Heidelberg (Hautz, *Heidelberg*, ii. 394), visits to public chess tables were forbidden, especially on legible days.

(3) At Bologna, students were forbidden to enter into or to keep gaming-houses. The prohibition is extended to Doctors also, but an exception is made in favour of playing *ad scacos vel ad tabulas* for recreation.

(4) At Louvaine, in 1476, Charles the Bold, Duke of Brabant (Molanus, ii. 940), forbad the students games with dice or cards (*ludis taxillorum et chartarum*), but allowed honest games like chess (*scacci*) to be played on suitable occasions, but only in private houses and with moderate frequency.

The Statutes of the *Savoy Hospital* (MS. Cott. cv. f. 24) ordained 'quod nullus magister, vicemagister, capellanus perpetuus vel conductilius, aut aliquis alius minister vel servitor hospitalis praedicti pro tempore existens ad talos, cartas, vel aliquos alios jocos illicitos et prohibitos infra hospitale praedictum clam vel palam quoque modo ludet. Poterint enim omni tempore ludere ad scaccos'.

[67] In *Aiol* (ed. cit., 2525–7), the owner of an inn of bad reputation produces his largest chessboard to provide a level surface upon which his guests may throw their dice. (St.)

Wycliffe on two occasions attacks the clergy for frequenting taverns to play games. In his *Office of Curates* (E. E. T. S. 152) he says:

'þei haunten tauernes . . . þei fallen to nyse pleies, at tables, chees and hasard, and beten þe stretes, and sitten at þe tauerne til þei han lost here witt.'

In his *Order of Priesthood* (E. E. T. S., 168):

'Prestis also sclaundren þe peple bi ensaumple of ydelnesse and wauntounnesse: for comynly þei chouchen in softe beddis whanne oþere men risen to here labour . . . and soone anoon to tables and chees and tauerne and betynge of pauement, and þan speken of lecherie.'

[In his *How Antichrist and his Clerks travail to destroy Holy Writ* (E. E. T. S. 259), he says:

'þerfore cristen men schulden . . . not sette here feiþ ne triste in synful prelatis and here cursed clerkis ne in here vnderstondynge of holy writt, for þei ben vnable wiþ þis worldly lif ful of pride, coueitise, glotonye, and ydelnesse, as haukynge and huntynge, and pleiynge at þe chees and tables, and riot and daunsynge, and festis makynge, dronkenesse and lecherie, to perceyue þe treuþe of holy writt and heiȝe preuytees of god.'

Other Early English passages in dispraise of chess are contained in the *Ayenbite of Inwyt* (E. E. T. S. 52) of Dan Michel, 1340, in a list of ways of mis-spending time:

Efterward/ ine zuyche wakinges: me deþ many kueades (sins) ase playe ate ches. oþer at tables. and me zayþ/ manye bisemers (mockings). and folyes. and þus wasteþ/ þe wreche game of quek.[68] In Iceland, where the long winter nights deprived all orders of the possibility of outdoor occupations, it is probable that chess was played far more widely than elsewhere in Europe.

So far as it is possible to judge from the references to chess in the Middle Ages and in the sixteenth century, chess-players were in the main concerned with chess as a game. But before 1300, collections of End-game positions or problems were being made, and whatever the original attitude to these positions may have been, the existence of these collections can only mean that some players were beginning to take interest in the positions as problems. If we can draw any parallel from our own day we must conclude that the player who took interest in the problem would lose interest in the game itself. Still there is nothing to show that the mediaeval problem ever became a serious rival to the practical game, and it was from quite another direction and for other reasons that any change in the popularity of chess came about. It was not only, nor even mainly, dissatisfaction with chess which brought about the decline in favour. The great changes in the circumstances of life, the wider interests and activities open to men of all ranks of society, made games less necessary. Men no longer played games because they knew no other way of filling the hours which were without any settled occupation. They played them as a relief from other occupations, and to attract the ordinary man a game had to be less strenuous, less prolonged, less serious than chess. Playing-cards, which came into general use in the fourteenth century, really satisfied the needs of the time better than chess, tables, or merels. Card-games provided a far simpler means of gambling than any board-game, and they gradually took the place of chess as the favourite game of the leisured classes. The reform in the moves of chess towards the close of the fifteenth century delayed the triumph of cards for a time, but by the end of the eighteenth century cards had displaced chess as the typical game of the nobility, and chess fell finally from the position which it held throughout the Middle Ages.

his time/and his wyttes/and his guodes. and wreþeþ god. and harmeþ his bodi/and more þe saule;

and in the regret of the author of the Northumbrian poem, *Cursor Mundi*:

I ha me liked ai vm-quile 28336
In vnnait wordes, lath and vile,
Til idel gammes, chess and tablis,
Bot or eigning hert and rime and fablis.]

[68] Quek appears in a list of games declared illegal in 1477 (Act 17 Ed. IV, c. 3): 'Diversez novelx ymaginez jeuez appellez Cloishe Kayles half kewle Hondyn & Hondoute & Quekeborde.' Cf. the contemporary passage, quoted in Freeman's *Exeter*, 1887, 161: 'Yong peple . . . within the said cloistre have exercised unlawful games as the toppe, queke, penny prykke.'

More light is thrown upon the nature of this game by the record of a gaming case of 1376, quoted in Riley, *Lond. Mem.*, 1868, 395, and in Ashton, *Hist. Gambling in Engl.*, London, 1898, 14. John atte Hille and his brother William prosecuted Nicholas Prestone, tailor, and John Outlawe, for deceit and falsehood. Outlawe had invited them to win money at tables or chequers, commonly called quek, and they had accompanied him to Preston's house, where they found a pair of tables on the outside of which was painted a chequer board that is called a quek. They first tried tables and then quek, losing regularly until their total losses amounted to 39*s.* 2*d.* They then examined dice and board. All were false. On the board, all the black squares were depressed in three quarters, and on the remaining quarter the white squares were depressed. The board was adjudged to be burnt, and the cheats were sentenced to the pillory.

APPENDICES

I. CHESS IN ICELAND, ETC.

If the record can be accepted as historical, the earliest appearance of chess in the Norse lands is one recorded in Snorri Sturluson's *Ólafs Saga helga*, which was written *c.* 1230. In this work our King Knut is described as playing chess in his Danish capital, Roskilde, on the eve of St. Michael's day, 1027, with Jarl Úlf, who had come to regain the King's favour, forfeited by a recent act of rebellion. In the course of the game Knut left his Knight *en prise* by mistake, and Úlf took it. Knut asked the Jarl to replace the Knight and make another move, or to allow him to recall his previous move. Úlf refused and upset the board. Hot words followed, and the quarrel ended with the murder of Úlf in the choir of the church whither he had fled for sanctuary.[1] Icelandic scholars (e.g. Fiske and Vigfússon) point out the similarity of the details of this story with those of other quarrels at chess in Icelandic literature, and are of opinion that Snorri has modernized the details and substituted chess for the older Norse game of *hnefatafl*. The discovery of two other references to Knut as a chess-player makes it just possible that Snorri's account of the incident is strictly accurate.

According to the *Knýtlinga Saga*, King Sweyn attempted to kill his brother-kings, Knut V and Valdemar, while the latter was playing chess in Roskilde in 1157. Valdemar alone escaped.[2] This incident may be correct in its details, though there is nothing in it that necessarily requires chess. With events of the thirteenth century which are chronicled in contemporary works we are on more certain ground.

The *Árons Saga* mentions incidentally that Snorri Sturluson's nephew Þórður Sighvatsson played chess in Norway in the autumn of 1238 with another Icelander, Hrani Koðránsson ('Þeir Þórðr ok Hrani sátu at skáktafli', *Sturlunga Saga*, 1878, ii. 344).

An incident of 1241–2, strangely similar to the Knut story, is recorded in the *Þorgils Saga skarða*. Snorri's grand-nephew, Þorgils Böðvarsson, a lad of fifteen, a hostage in the hands of Jarl Gizur, was playing chess with Sámur Magnússon, a kinsman of Gizur's, when Sámur wished to take back a move by which he had set a Knight *en prise*. Þorgils refused to allow this, but a bystander interfered with the advice that the Knight should be replaced on its old square 'and don't be brawling at chess'. Þorgils suddenly swept the pieces into the bag and struck Sámur with it, causing his ear to bleed.[3]

The *Guðmundar Saga góða* tells how Bishop Bótólf of Hólar, North Iceland (1237–45), once advised a chess-player in his game, so that he turned a probable

[1] 'En er þeir léku at skáktafli, Knútr konungr ok Úlfr jarl, þá lék konungr fingrbrjót miklinn; þá skækði jarl af honum riddara; konungr bar aptr hans ok segir, at hann skyldi annat leika; jarl reiddisk ok skaut niðr taflborðinu stóð upp ok gekk í brot.' (*Heimskringla*, København, 1896, ii. 370–2.)

[2] For the Icelandic text see *Fornmanna Sögur*, Kaupmannahöfn, 1828, xi. 366–7, quoted in Fiske, 11. A later chess-tragedy in Danish history is the capture of King Eric Plowpenny on Aug. 9, 1250, while playing chess with Henrick Kerkwerder at Slesvig, which was followed shortly after by his execution.

[3] 'Sá atburðr varð, at þá skilði á um tafl, Þorgils Böðvarsson ok Sám Magnússon frænda Gizurar, vildi Sámr bera aptr riddara, er hann hafði telft í uppnám, en Þorgils lét þvi ekki ná. Þá lagði til Markús Marðarson, at aptr skildi bera riddarann, "Ok látið ykkr ekki á skilja um tafl." Þorgils sagðisk ekki fyrir hans orð mundu göra; ok svarfaði taflinu, ok lét í punginn; ok stéð upp; ok laust við eyra Sámi, svá at blæddi,' &c. *Sturlunga Saga*, 1878, ii. 105.

defeat into a victory. The loser—a priest—told the bishop that he would be better employed in preparing his sermon than in thinking about chess (*Biskupa Sögur*, Kaupmannahöfn, 1878, ii. 186; quoted in Fiske, 13).

Chess sets are mentioned in Norwegian deeds of the fourteenth century (Vigfússon cites *Diplom. Norvég.*, Kristiania, 1849–95, ii. 186; I have failed to verify the reference).[4]

Chess is occasionally mentioned in the mythical sagas which date from the latter part of the 13th c. Thus the *Króka-Refs Saga* includes in a list of presents which were sent to Harald harðráði from Greenland a *tanntafl*, i.e. a tooth-board, one carved out of walrus ivory, and the saga-man adds the note, 'It was both a hnefa-board and a chessboard' (Það var bæði hneftafl og skáktafl, *Kroka-Refs Saga*, Köbenhavn, 1883, 23), probably one on either face of the board. Other passages (e.g. from the *Viglundar Saga* and the *Hervarar Saga*) are of interest only from the use of certain technicalities of chess. The game in *Frithiof's Saga*, which modern translators have made chess, is in the original Icelandic *hnefatafl*.[5]

The romantic sagas, translations from the French of the 13th and 14th cc., naturally repeat the chess references of the original works, but, treating the details with much freedom, they add somewhat to our knowledge of Icelandic chess. The player always sits with the board on his knees; no wonder that in moments of passion it was often upset. In the *Bragða-Mágus Saga* we have two long chess incidents, in each of which a match of three games is played, the winner of the third game being the conqueror. King Játmundur or Loðóvíkus of Saxland plays Jarl Hirtungur three games to redeem the articles which he had given in ransom for a captive princess. The Jarl wins all three games; in the first he gives *hróksmát*, mate with a Rook; in the second *peðsmát*, mate with a Pawn; in the third *fretstertumát*, the most disgraceful of all mates. King Loðóvíkus also plays the fifteen-year-old son of Jarl Ámundi, Rögnvald, the king wagering three gold rings against Rögnvald's head. Rögnvald won all three games, the first after three hours' play, the positions being nearly even; the second ended in *hróksmát* after three hours' more play; the third lasted a bare half-hour and ended in *peðsmát*. A quarrel ensued, the king smote Rögnvald in the face with the bag of chessmen so that the blood flowed, and Rögnvald's elder brother Vigvarð killed the king with his battle-axe (see Fiske, 16–23).

Fiske (1–9) argues from the Icelandic chess-terms *hrókur* and *biskup* that the game reached Iceland from England, and was disposed to place the introduction in the second half of the twelfth century, when three noted Icelanders visited Britain. He did not know that cognates of *hrókur* were in regular use in the other Norse languages in the Middle Ages, and that the English chess-term *bishop* is not found before the sixteenth century. The only Icelandic chess-terms which really lend any support to Fiske's contention are the plural nouns *skákmenn* and *menn*, which are used by writers from the sixteenth century onwards. None of the other Norse

[4] For the Icelandic chessmen which were discovered in the island of Lewis in 1831, see Ch. X, below.

[5] Since many of the Icelandic works use the indeterminate word *tafl*, board-game, in the game incidents, it is only natural that many passages have been annexed for chess without clear warrant. Madden quotes several such in his 'Historical Remarks on the ancient Chess-Men discovered in the Isle of Lewis' (*Archaeologia*, xxiv), among them being a group of riddles from the *Hervarar Saga*, with answers explaining them as referring to chess. The answers, however, are a forgery of the eighteenth century, and the original riddles refer to hnefatafl.

languages use the word *men* for the chessmen, and its use is confined to Anglo-French, English, and Icelandic. I do not think that this is sufficient evidence upon which to base an English parentage for Icelandic chess, and moreover, the form *skák* is opposed to such a theory. There seems no valid reason for supposing that chess arrived in Iceland by any different route from that taken by other adoptions of European customs.

[*Hnefatafl.* There has been much speculation in the past as to the nature of this game, and Fiske, after devoting several years to the recovery of the game, gave the problem up as insoluble. The game became obsolete in Iceland soon after the introduction of chess, probably before the end of the thirteenth century.

The only early references which throw any light upon this game are the riddles in the *Hervarar Saga*, and a passage in *Frithiof's Saga*. From the first we learn that the game (like the Welsh *tawlbwrdd*) was played between the sides composed, the one of sixteen 'fair' (white) men, the other of a King (called *hnefa* or *hunn*) and eight 'dark' (black) men. From the second we learn that a 'double attack' was possible.

Game-pieces have been discovered in Scandinavia which probably belong to this game; some of these are plain and hemispherical in shape, others are shaped with a man's head or a dog's head.

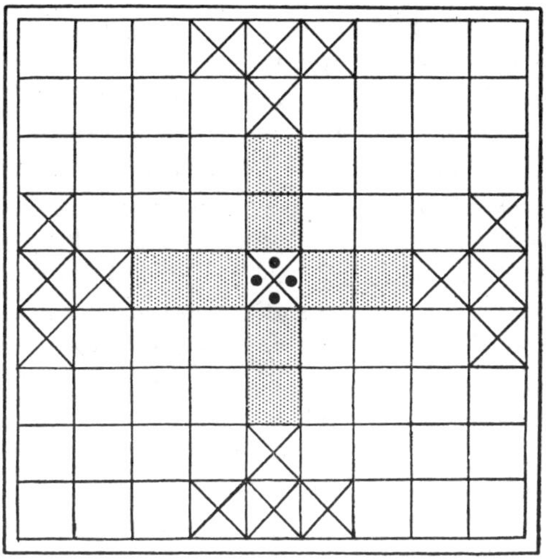

The board for *tablut*.

Now a game satisfying all the requirements of the early Icelandic references was still played in the eighteenth century by the Laplanders in the North of Sweden under the name of *Tablut*, and was seen and described by the botanist Linnaeus in 1732. I think that it is extremely probable that thisgame is identical with the old *hnefatafl.*

Tablut is played on a board of eighty-one squares marked as in the diagram. One side consists of the King, who is stationed on the central square, and eight Swedes, who are placed upon the shaded squares. The other side consists of sixteen Russians, who occupy the crosscut squares. All the pieces have the same move—that of the Rook in chess. Play is by alternate moves, and the one player endeavours to bring his King to the edge of the board while the other tries to confine him so that he has no power of moving. In either case the game comes to an end. The King cannot be taken; any other man is taken when two of the opposing men occupy two squares adjacent to it and in the same straight line with it. No other piece than the King can ever play to the central square. If the King be on d5 and three Russians are on c5, d4 and d6, he is considered to be confined, and the Russians win. If the King be on e5, a Swede on f5, and Russians on d5, e4 and e6, the Russians can capture the Swede by playing a fourth man to g5. Whenever the King has a free road to the edge, the player must give notice to the enemy by saying *raichi*, if there is a choice of two free roads, he says *tuichu*. (See the account in *Lachesis Lapponica*, or a tour in Lapland, edited by J. E. Smith, London, 1811, ii. 55–58.)

It is interesting to note that the method of capture in this game is identical with that in the unknown Latin game *ludus latrunculorum*, in the game which Firdawsī attributes to Buzūrjmihr in the Shāhnāma, the Egyptian *sīga*, and a few other Eastern board-games.]

II. CHESS AMONG THE JEWS

THERE is no evidence to support the view that the Jews obtained a knowledge of chess in any other way than from their Christian neighbours, or that they played an independent part in the development of the game in Europe. 'As a general rule, the Jews established no independent standard of conduct with regard to their amusements. They played the same games as their Christian neighbours, and played them with the same rules and at the same tables' (Abrahams, *Jewish Life in Middle Ages*, London, 1896, 398).

The frequently expressed belief that chess is mentioned in the *Babylonian Talmud* has no basis in fact, and is due to blunders on the part of commentators in explaining the terms *nardshir* and *isqundari* (*Ketuboth*, 61 b). The nature of *nardshir* is established from Arabic works, where it is identified with the game of nard, the mediaeval tables. It is indeed so explained by Nathan b. Yeḥiel (of Rome, 1103) in his *Arukh*: 'nardshir = Ar. an-nard = It. dadi.' The identification with chess goes back to Rashi (Solomon son of Isaac of Troyes, D. 1105), who says 'nardshir = isqaqis' (*'Erubin*, 61 a). The meaning of the term *isqundari* is less certain. Several authorities deny that it means a game at all, explaining it as meaning 'young dogs or puppies'. Others (e.g. the 14th c. Nissim Gerondi, and the *Sefer Khasīdīm*, Bologna, 1538, 400), translate it by 'small pieces of wood for a game', and identify it with a game of the merels type.[1]

Chess very early attained to considerable popularity with the European Jews and, as a result, had to pass through a period of suspicion on the part of the rabbis. Maimonides (1155–1204), who seems to refer to a forced mate, included (*Commentary to the Mishnah, Sanhedrim*, iii. 3) chess (*sartanj*) among the forbidden games when played for money, and declares professional chess-players to be unworthy of credence in the law-courts. Kalonymos b. Kalonymos (in his *Eben Boḥan*, 1322) condemned chess altogether, whether played for a stake or not. These extreme opinions, however, failed to influence the general attitude towards chess, and by the 16th c. the game had become a recognized pastime for men on the Sabbath and on festivals, though as a rule on these occasions the stake was omitted, and special pieces of silver were employed.[2]

In times of trouble the rabbis often prohibited games in general for a season, but chess was often omitted from the ban. Thus in 1416 the Jews of Forli bound themselves not to play dice, cards, or any game of chance for ten years. Exceptions

[1] See Franz Delitzsch, *Ueber das Schach u. die damit verwandten Spiele in den Talmuden*, 1840.

[2] An old responsum in a Bodleian MS. says that isqas (? read isqaqs) was sanctioned by the Spanish rabbis (Dukes, *Ben Chananja*, 1864, 601). Moses Isserls (of Cracow, D. 1573) approved of the game with bones called *ṭshekh* on the Sabbath, so long as it was not played for money. Shilṭe hag-Gibborim on *'Erubin*, 127 b (16th c., Germany), prescribes the use of silver chessmen, but does not absolutely prohibit wooden men.

were made (*a*) in favour of one dice-game whose identity is doubtful, and of chess, provided the stake never exceeded four silver bolognini, (*b*) in favour of cards on fast-days or in time of sickness, provided the stake never exceeded one quattrino. After the plague of Cremona, 1575, the three rabbis declared that 'all games except *isqaqi* were primary evils and the cause of all troubles', and all games, with the single exception of chess when not played for money, were prohibited for a year (Lampronti, *Paḥad Yizḥaq*, Venice, 1789, iii. 54). Similar prohibitions obtained in Venice in 1628, and in Frankfurt after the great fire of 1711. In the latter case none but sick persons might play chess for fourteen years.

Abrahams quotes instances of personal vows to abstain from games for a season, which occur frequently from the beginning of the 15th c. One, of April 1, 1491, undertakes not to play any game except draughts (the translation is doubtful; possibly merels is meant) and chess.

Like all indoor games in the Middle Ages, chess was largely played by Jewish women. Carrera (1617, p. 102) mentions a young Venetian Jewess as a player of great skill.

There are a number of smaller Hebrew works on chess of the 12th to the 16th cc. which are accessible in Hyde and v. d. Linde. The more important of these are made use of in Ch. IV, below.

Chess plays an important part in the final form of the curious mediaeval legend of the Jewish pope Andreas. The pope is described as devoted to chess, and this brought him into contact with many Jewish players, among others with the Rabbi Simeon (Simeon hag-Gadol, a historical character who lived in Mainz at the beginning of the 11th c.), who was esteemed as the first player of his time. The pope defeated the rabbi in play, but the rabbi recognized him as his son Elḥanan through his making a particularly strong move which he had taught the latter in childhood. The oldest form of the legend contains no reference to chess (Steinschneider, in v. d. Linde, i. 187–8).

[There is no distinctive Hebrew name for chess; the Jews generally transliterated the ordinary name in the country where they were writing. Thus we have in Abraham b. Ezra 2 shahmat; in Catalonian works, 2 isqāqīs, isqās, 4 isqas, isqaqs from the Cat. scachs; in Italian works, 4 sqaqi, sqaqire, 4–6 isqaqi, 5 isqāqi 6 hisqāqi, shakh from It. scacchi, scacchiere, and in a Polish work 6 ṭshekh from Pol. szach. The pieces are called: King, 2– melekh; Queen, 2 fers; 6– shegel, malkah (= queen); Bishop, 2– fīl; Knight, 2–7 sūs, 6 farash (= horse); Rook, 2–6 ruḥ, 6 ruq, rūq; alʿanqa (a bird); merkaba (= chariot); migdal (= castle); Pawn, 2– ragal, 6 gibbor. Check is 6 shāh; mate, 2– māt, 6 shāhmāt.]

III. SOME INVENTORIES OF CHESS

I HAVE collected many references to chess-sets in inventories, wills, and accounts of the period from 1100–1600, and I give a selection of these here.

I. SPAIN.

The inventory of King Martin of Aragon, 1410, contains many boards and pieces for chess and tables. Ivory and ebony, or jasper and crystal, appear as the favourite materials from which the more costly sets were carved.

Una bossa morada gran e dues poques morades fetes dagulla en los quals stan daus.—XX Scachs entre vermeys e blaus de diuerses colors de vidre.—XXI Scachs de Crestays = XV Scachs de jaspi = Taules de jaspi de jugar = X Taules de Crestay.—Una pedre de jaspi obruda a manera de Scach ab un cordo negre. —Un tauler gornit dargent ab son stoig de cuyro ab scachs de vori e de banus gornits dargent: son XXXII pesses e XXX tauletes dargent smeltades, III han argent ab stoix dargent e III de crestay.—Unes taules de vori petites en que ha VI pesses ab les cubertes e son conseruades en un stoix de cuyr negre.—Un tauler de taules de gingolers ab joch de scachs de la una part e ab algunes taules debanus e de fust ab son stoix de cuyr.—Un tauler de jugar a taules ab les puntes de jaspi e de nacre ab IV cases que ha pintades de figures e de la altre part ha joch de Scachs ab les cases de nacre e altres de fulla dargent smaltades de blau, e fall hi. Iª, barre dargent.—III bossets de cuyr on ha jochs de scachs e de taules.—Dues taules de jaspi e de crestay e de porfi gornits ab puntes dargent e de la altre part scachs en que ha en les cases diuerses figures domens e de babolyns e la vn conseruat en vn stoix de cuyr cruu negre e laltre en un tros de drap de li ab jochs de taules de jaspi e de crestay.—Una capce plene de Scachs de vori e de banus qui son XXXII.—Un tauler de Scachs e de taules de IIII pesses ab stoix de cuyr e escachs.—Un altro tauler de Scachs petit trencat.—Una bosse de cuyr blanch ab diuersos scachs e taules e altres mesquineses.—Un stoix de cuyr negre on hauia conseruat un tauler de fust ab marquets e lo joch dels scachs ço es lo blanch es de nacre ab taules de vori e negres e los scachs de vori e negres.—Un tauler de scachs de vori e debanus ab I. circuit de ymatges poques dangels de vori e apres ha I. cercle de banus tot pla ab marquets e apart de sota serueix a tauler de taules tot de banus ab semblants cercle e circuit ab I. stoix dell mateix de fust de dues cases en la 1ª de les quals hauia XXXII taules e en laltre XXXII pesses de scachs la meytat de vori el altre meytat de banus lo qual tauler ere reseruat dins vn stoix de fust: a son mollo fet ab sou pany e clau pochs lo cual fo stoiat dins un dels armaris demunt dits.—IV peus qui eren de 1ª taula de tauler de scachs e de taules de jugar los cuals peus hauien cascun son leho qui pesaren encamerats XXIII march et I onze los quals podien pesar nets entorn XII marchs de Barchinona qui a raho de . . . lo march valen . . .—Lo dit tauler de scachs de crestay de fulla dargent e dintre embotil de fust.—1ª tauler de meniar en dues pesses ab armes de Castella, de Portogal e Darago ab un joch de scachs al mig.—1ª capsa de fust cuberta de cuyr de camus ab I cordo de fil groch e morat en que hauia III manechs de vori duas dents de leo dos scachs I de jaspis e altre de calsadonia e vn baricle rodo petit.—Una capsa de fust pintada plana cayrada ab alguns scacs de fust.—I sach de cuyr blanch ab huns scachs e taulas de fust e vna cadena de fust lo qual es conseruat en vn stoig de cuyr lis abte a tenir calzes. (Brunet y Bellet, *Ajedrez,* 217–8.)

The inventory of the Prince of Viana, 1461, contains the following chess entries:

Una bucheta de os lavorado a joch de scachs e taules e dins una avellana ab les taules scachs e daus.—En hun stoig de cuyro negre hun taullel obrat de os pera schachs e taules ab son joch complit dels scachs e de les taules de os.—En altre gran stoig de cuyro negre hun gran taulell ab sos scachs obrat de os te entorn tota la istoria de sant Jordi obrada per personatges.—Hun taulell lavorat de os ab son joch descachs e de taules en ses bosses.

These sets passed into the possession of the royal family of Aragon, and are mentioned in two later inventories with their estimated values in Catalan money, these being respectively £3, £40, £65, and £33. (Bofarull y Mascéro, *Coleccion de Documentos inéditos del archivo de la Corona de Aragon,* Barcelona, 1847–76, xxvi. 135, 136, 159, 199, 200, 220, 259.)

II. France.

Ducange quotes from an inventory of 1320:

Item unum scacarium de jaspide et alia parte de jaspide et calsidonio cum familia, viz. una parte de jaspide et alia parte de cristallo.

Godefroi quotes the following:

1408, 1er sept.–1409, 1er sept. *Compte de la recette générale de Hainault* (*Arch. Nord*): Item au varlet Anthoine de la Fauconerie, pour i. jeu d'esches et de tables qu'il raporte de Paris, ix. s.

1412. *Comptes roy.*, in Laborde, *Émaux*: Un eschiquier de jaspre et de cristal fait aux armes de feu pape Gregoire (Gregory XI, 1370–8, or Gregory XII, 1406–9), et est par dehors de cippres, et y a un marrellier[1] de marqueterie, et est garni d'eschez de mesme, tout en un estui.

1416. Inv. de Jean de Berry, ap. *idem*: Une tres belle table ployant en trois pieces, en laquelle est le marelier, deux jeux de tables, et l'eschiquier, faiz de pourfiz de Romme.—Une table de bois marquetée du jeu des eschas, et de tables et de mareliers et sont les tresteaux tenant a la dicte table.

1429, 7 avril. *Exécut. test. de Jacques Caulier* (*Arch. Tournai*) pour un esquicquiert, ungs taveliers.

In an inventory of the property of Charles the Bold, Duke of Burgundy (1467–77), occur many chess items:

Unes besaces de pluseurs patenostres de toutes sortes, où a dedens des eschetz de cristal.—Ung petit tablier et ung eschiquier d'ivoire, garni de tables, dedens une boursse. Tablier et eschiquier de ciprès de quatre pièces.—Une layecte plaine d'eschetz de cristal.—Ung eschequier d'argent d'un costé et de l'autre costé armoyé des armes de MS., garni d'eschetz de cristal.—Ung eschiquier d'ivoire noir et blanc.—Ung bel eschiquier d'ivoire armoyé des armes de Madame, et de l'autre costé ung tablier, et est en ung estuy.—Ung eschequier d'un costé d'yvoire, entaillé à l'entour bien et gentement, et de l'autre costé tablier. (Laborde, *Les Ducs de Bourgogne*, Paris, 1852, ii. 193–4.)

III. England.

The wardrobe accounts of Edward I for the years 1299–1300 show him in possession of—

Una familia pro scaccario de jaspide et cristallo, in uno coffro.—Una familia de ebore pro ludendo ad scaccarium (*Liber quotid. garderobae a. r. Edw. I*, 28, London, 1787, 350, 351).[2]

An inventory of the effects of Roger de Mortimer at Wigmore Castle and Abbey, 15 Edw. II (1322), contains—

alia coffre continet j. speculum de amallis et j. familiam de ebore pro scaccario,

which was kept in his wife's wardrobe (*Arch. Journal*, xv, 1858, 362).

A similar inventory of the property of Hugh le Despenser in 1397 mentions—

escheqirs faitz de noitz muge d'une part et de la racyne de gyngure d'autre part, ove treis peirs meines de crestall et tables de ivoir, ove la meine de ivoir et d'eban (*Rot. Parl.* 21, *Rd.* II).

[1] The *mareliers* are boards for merels, the *tabliers* for tables.

[2] Edward I, as a young man, had a narrow escape from death while playing chess. The incident is related in Nicholas Trivet's *Annales*, ed. London, 1845, 282: 'Adolescens cum milite quodam in camera testudinata ludo scaccarii occupatus, subito nulla occasione praestita inter ludendum surgens discesserat, lapisque immensae magnitudinis, qui sedentem conquassasset, in eodem loco ceciderit.'

Joan Stevens of Bury (*Bury Wills*, 180) left in her will, 1459, 'vnum par de tablis cum chesemen et tabilmenys.' [3]

In Henry VIII's Wardrobe Accounts (MS. Harl. 1419) are two inventories of the royal possessions. In the first occur—

One boxe blacke w[t] chessemen graven in bone.—One paire of tables of brassell.—One bagge of grene velvett w[t] chessemen and tablemen for the same.—A chesse bourde gilte w[t] a case to the same.—A paire of tables of bone clasped with silver w[t] Tablemen & Chestmen.—A case of black leather conteynynge chestmen & tablemen w[t] a paire of tables.—A paire of tables of bone w[t] tablemen & chestmen.—A chesse bourd with divers kindes of tabulls in yt to playe.—Oon paier of plaieing tables of blacke and white bone with roynt plat & one locke of silver & gilte with a set of chestmen of blacke & white bone to them in a case of blacke leather lined with greane clothe.—A boxe blacke with chessemen graven in bone.—A payre of tables of bone w[t] chestmen belonging to the same.—A payer of chestmen in a case of blacke leather.

The second gives the contents of a closet at Greenwich:

2 payre of playing tables of bone.—A payr of chesmen in a case of blacke lether.—A blake satin bag with chesmen.

The 'pairs of tables' are pretty obviously folding chessboards with chess on the outer sides and backgammon in the inner sides, for each of these boards has men both for chess and for backgammon.

In an inventory of the royal wardrobe of Scotland of 1539 we meet with 'ane pair of tabillis of silver ourgilt with gold indented with jasp & cristallyne with table men & chess men of jasp & cristalline', and in another of 1578 of 'greit chas men of bane'.

In the *Howard Household Books* (1841, 514) occurs the entry, 'Pay(d) to the chesmaker for ij chesplayes, viijd.'

IV. Germany.

The will of Count Siboto of Neuenburg or Falkenstein, *c.* 1180, quoted in *Mon. Boica*, vii. 502, mentions—

unum scahzabel, unum wurfzabel—tria scahzabel, tria wurfzabel—elefantei lapides tam ad wurfzabel quam ad scahzabel pertinentes.

Lapides, Ger. *Steine*, *Gestein*, is a typically German term for game-pieces.

Count William IV of Holland bought at Venice in 1343, when starting on a pilgrimage to the Holy Land, two chessboards for the use of himself and his fellow-travellers:

Item Aernt van Kessel wedergegeven by Ysebouts hant, die hi gegeven hadde bi myns heren bevelen om 2 scaecborde ende sciven (i.e. table-men) ende scaecspel daertoe 48 sc. backat, valent 9d. gr. 7 m.

And again:

Item om 2 tafelbort ende scaecspel ende sciven ende 1 coperen orinael 2 ducaten valent 2 sc. 4½ d. gr. 1 ester. (*Qst.*, 60).

Adolphus, Duke of Gueldres, bought in 1440 from Fyken v. Bourbon a bone set of chessmen for 2 guelders, and a new chessboard with a ring to hang it up by for 28 kronen:

[3] There are other early bequests of chessmen, e.g. one of 1562 (*Lanc. Wills*, 1857, 183), 'A sett of chest men of oliphants teeth.'

een beynen Schaeckspoel voor ii gl. ende een nye Bret myt enen Ryngesken voor xxviii kr. (*Tolnboek v. Lobede*, s. a. 1440; in v. d. Linde, *Het Schaakspel in Nederland*, 71).

In the inventory of the Duke's property in 1447, a more valuable set of chessmen is mentioned:

Item dat schaeckbret mit schaek ende wortafelspiel as half golt ende silver (G. v. Hasselt, *Bydragen voor d'oude geldersche maaltyden*, Arnhem, 1805, 19; in v. d. Linde, *op. cit.*, 71).

In another work (J. v. d. Holt, *Koikenb.*, s. a. 1465; in v. d. Linde, *op. cit.*, 71) the purchase of a bag to hold the board and pieces is recorded. The inventory of Viglius van Zuichem of 1577 also mentions a velvet box for holding the chessmen.

CHAPTER III

THE MEDIAEVAL GAME

Earliest rules.—The chequered board.—Attempts at improvement.—Assizes.—Rules in Spain.—In Lombardy.—In Germany.—In France and England.—In Iceland.—Notation.—Science of play.—Openings.—Odds.—Other arrangements.—The Courier game.

THE earliest European rules are probably those which are given in the earlier poems which are discussed in the next chapter. These poems only deal with the rules in broad outline, but so far as can be seen these are identical with the rules of the contemporary Muslim game. They may be conveniently summarized thus:

Board: unchequered.

Position of the men: Bishops, Knights, Rooks, and Pawns as in modern chess; King and Queen on d1 and e1 (d8 and e8), but no rule as to relative position; the two Kings opposite one another.

Moves: *King*, to any adjacent square, not commanded by a hostile man; *Queen*, to an adjacent diagonal square; *Bishop*, a leap over any adjacent diagonal square into the square beyond in the diagonal; *Knight* and *Rook*, as in modern chess; all these pieces take as they move. *Pawn*, as in modern chess, except that it has no move of two squares for its first move; capture, as in modern chess; promotion, to Queen only.

Termination: a game was won by checkmating the opponent's King, or by robbing him or denuding him of his forces—an ending called *Bare King* in the sequel. There is no certain evidence as to how Stalemate was treated.

At a very early date it became usual in Europe to use a chequered or parti-coloured board. This is no necessity of the game, but, as the *Einsiedeln Poem* (*c.* 1100) remarks, it simplifies the calculation of moves, and is a ready means for preventing the occurrence of false moves. Exactly when or where the change was introduced is not known. The *Einsiedeln Poem* mentions it as an improvement which some players had adopted, as if it were not usual in the writer's own circle. Three of the other poems describe the board as chequered, generally white and red.[1] The Spanish work compiled by Alfonso X of Castile in 1283 (hereafter referred to as Alf.) prescribes the use of a chequered board. The *Innocent Morality* makes a parallel between the alternation of black and white squares and the succession of death and life, blame and favour.

[1] The 12th c. *Elegy* gives the colours as white and red, black, grey or reddish. Later works, e. g, the *Innocent Morality*, Alf., Cessolis, Köbel, generally speak of white and black only.

Once the use of the coloured board became general it was possible to frame rules to govern the position of the board when placed for play. The diagrams in Alf. have invariably a white square to the player's right-hand side, but other problem MSS. and the drawings of games of chess which are to be found in early illuminated MSS. show that there was no uniformity of practice.[2] The modern convention or rule that each player must have a white square at his right-hand corner was certainly not established during the mediaeval period.[3]

The use of the chequered board also made it possible to frame a rule to govern the relative positions of King and Queen. There is nothing in Alf. to show that Spanish players had formulated a law in the 13th c., but the contemporary work of the Lombard *Jac. de Cessolis* by placing the Black King on a white square supports the modern rule of—

Rex ater in albo ; servat regina colorem.[4]

The same arrangement is described in the later *Corpus Poem*.[5]

At an early date European players began to make changes in the powers of move of the chessmen and in the rules of the game. These changes reveal an attitude towards chess which was destined to lead to far-reaching results. The intention behind the early experiments is obvious, because all the alterations of move were directed towards the improvement of one portion of the game. They show that the European player, unlike the Muslim, felt some disappointment with chess. While the game provided him with a valuable means of recreation and an addition to the pleasures of life, it did not afford him all the enjoyment that he anticipated. The game was long in coming to a point, and the tactics of the prolonged opening play were by no means easy to discover. The modern player, with all the

[2] Thus the Problem diagrams in the three illuminated MSS. of the *Bonus Socius* group have the square h1 white on the recto, and black on the verso of each leaf. This is clearly due to the format of these MSS. The diagrams on front and back of each vellum leaf exactly cover one another, and the illuminator found himself obliged to oppose black squares to black owing to the transparency of the leaves. In MS. *Cott.*, where the boards are white and yellow, white and red, and white and black, only four diagrams show h1 white as against fourteen where it is not. The diagrams in the Italian MSS. *Ricc.* and *Gu.* are evenly divided. Of other early chess drawings, that of Otto Margrave of Brandenburg playing chess, which I reproduce from a Paris MS., has h1 black. The miniature in the Munich MS. of the *Carmina Burana* has h1 white. Three miniatures in the Bodleian MS. of the *Vœux du Paon* (MS. Bodl. 264, f. 128) show respectively boards black and red (h1 red), yellow and black (h1 black), and black and white (h1 white). Among early printed books, the Florence edition of the Italian Cessolis, 1483, the two Venice editions of Publicius's *Ars oratoria*, 1482 and 1485, Lucena, and the Köbel and Egenolff editions of Mennel's *Schachzabel*, all have h1 white. Caxton, on the other hand, in the second edition of the *Game and Playe of the Chesse*, *c.* 1480, has two pictures of games ; in one h1 is white, in the other black.

[3] Lucena, after giving the rule *rey blanco en casa negra : y rey negro en casa blanca*, goes on to advise a player who preferred the black men and could not secure them, to give the board a half-turn, and so bring his white King on his Queen's left. Of course, h1 is now black. See the Spanish text, Ch. XI, appendix, below.

[4] Cessolis, ed. Kopke, Brandenburg, 1879, 31, has : 'Cum enim resideat in quarto quadro cum sit ipse niger, habet a dextris in albo militem ; alphilem vero et rochum in nigro.' Cessolis throughout describes the arrangement of the black pieces as viewed from the standpoint of the white player, or as shown in a diagram in which the white are at the lower edge of the board.

I have not found the hexameter line quoted in the text in any earlier work than Beale's *Royall Game of Chesse-Play*, London, 1656.

[5] See lines 6–9 of this poem, p. 519.

advantages of a literature on the analysis and principles of his game, is apt to think that a more serious objection must have arisen from the fact that the inevitable exchanges of the middle game can rarely have left sufficient force for a quick and brilliant conclusion by checkmate. There is not, however, the slightest evidence that the theoretical difficulty of giving mate troubled the mediaeval player, who played perforce by the light of nature: we shall see that the ending of *Bare King* was abandoned at an early date in precisely that part of Europe where the standard of play was reputed to be highest. If the European player found chess 'slow', it was because he had no grasp of chess principles and no plan for the long introductory play before his forces were at close grips with the enemy. The whole policy of alteration of move was directed to the one end—how to quicken the introductory play.

That this disappointment was a real one seems clear from a passage in the MS. Alf., in which the writer speaks of 'the weariness which players experience from the long duration of the game when played right through'. It is from this sense of weariness that he explains the existence of dice-chess, and the popularity of the chess-problem with many players. Two ways of avoiding the tedium of the Muslim game are here indicated, neither of which was widely adopted or found in the long run satisfactory. The use of the dice reduces the necessity for thought and the formation of a plan of campaign, but it destroys the liberty of play which is so closely associated with the differentiation of piece, and ruins the real entity of chess. Besides, there were other games in which the dice worked more smoothly and more appropriately. So far as the evidence goes, whatever popularity the problem enjoyed in Europe among serious chess-players was due, not to the idea that it was a substitute for the real game, but to the belief that the solution of problems was one of the best means of acquiring skill in actual play. The real patron of the problem was the gambler, who found in it rare possibilities of trickery and deceit.

Three other possibilities remained which preserved the essential character of chess and might add brightness to the game. These were the extension of the powers of move, the rearrangement of the pieces, and the enlargement of the board with the introduction of new forces. All of these were tried in the Middle Ages, but the first is the only attempt at improvement which has stood the test of time. The second, in which the pieces were rearranged so as to be more nearly in contact at the commencement of play, might have survived if the reform of the fifteenth century had not come about: with the modern moves of Queen and Bishop it brought the forces too close together, and it dropped into disuse at once. The third possibility proved a failure. Enlarged games of chess have rarely shown any vitality. The eight-square board has been found by experience both large enough and small enough a field for a game which demands the assistance of all the mental powers, and yet is to be a recreation.

I shall first trace as far as possible the history of the development of move prior to the great reform of the 15th c., and afterwards return to the other attempts at improvement.

In the Middle Ages there was no tribunal whose word on the game of chess could be final. All attempts at the improvement of the game were from the necessity of the case individual at the outset, and each had to win its way to universal or national acceptance. Hence the first result of such attempts was a loss of uniformity, and the rise of local rules which differentiated the game of one locality from that of another. It took time for a happy improvement discovered perhaps in Spain to reach Germany, England, or Iceland, and all the modifications did not commend themselves to players in other countries. This led to the growth of what were called *Assizes*, the different codes of rules by which chess was played in different places or at different times. Thus we hear of the *Lombard assize*—the rules of the game as played by the famous players of Lombardy. We also hear in England of the *long* and *short assizes*, of which the former would appear to have been the ordinary mediaeval game, and the latter a game commencing from a different and more advanced arrangement of the pieces. We have a reference to the former in the Scotch version of the Tristram romance, *Sir Tristrem* (*c.* 1320; ed. S.T.S. 1886), in the story of how the Norwegian merchants kidnapped the young Tristram.

¶ Þer com a schip of norway
To sir rohandes hold
Wiþ haukes white and gray
And panes fair y fold.
Tristrem herd it say,
On his playing he wold
Tventi schilling to lay.
Sir rouhand him told
    And tauȝt;
For hauke siluer he ȝold,
Þe fairest men him rauȝt.
¶ A cheker he fond bi a cheire,
He asked who wold play.
Þe mariner spac bonair:
'Child, what wiltow lay?'
'Oȝain an hauke of noble air
Tventi schillinges, to say.
Wheþer so mates oþer fair
Bere hem boþe away.'
    Wiþ wille
Þe mariner swore his fay:
'For soþe ich held þer tille.'
¶ Now boþe her wedde lys,
And play þai bi ginne;
Ysett he haþ þe long asise
And endred beþ þer inne
Þe play biginneþ to arise,
Tristrem deleþ atvinne;
He dede als so þe wise:
He ȝaf has he gan winne
    In raf.
Of playe ar he wald blinne,
Sex haukes he ȝat and ȝaf.
¶ Rohand toke leue to ga,
His sones he cleped oway;
Þe fairest hauke he gan ta
Þat tristrem wan þat day;
Wiþ him he left ma
Pans for to play.
Þe mariner swore also
Þat pans wold he lay
    An stounde.
Tristrem wan þat day
Of him an hundred pounde.[6]

The only other references known to me occur in the AF. Problem MS. Brit. Mus., King's Lib. 13 A. xviii (K) of about the same date. In this MS. are two problems on f. 165 b, the first, No. 25, being said to be of the *court assise*, and the second, No. 26, of the *long assise*. The latter problem (see

[6] The incident is given in other versions of the romance, but without the mention of the long assize.

K 26 on p. 594) shows the ordinary arrangement of the pieces, excepting that the positions of the Knights and Bishops are interchanged (probably unintentionally), but the conditions of play are abnormal, and the title of the problem *Couenant fet ley* shows that these are to limit the operation of the ordinary rules of the assize.

The existence of different national assizes made it necessary to formulate some ruling as to which assize should govern the play when two players accustomed to different methods of play met in contest. The question was discussed by the lawyers in the Lombard Universities, and the commonsense decision was reached that the rules of the country in which the game was being played ought to be observed.[7] Another chess point which interested the lawyers was connected with the End-game. If a player undertook to mate with a Pawn, was he at liberty to queen it? Cynus de Pistoia (1310) decided thus: If the player undertook to mate with a Pawn, not specifying any Pawn in particular, he could not claim to have kept the conditions if he mated with a promoted Pawn, but if he undertook to mate with a particular Pawn, he was at liberty to promote it and mate with it as a Queen.[8] This decision was even invoked later in connexion with the legal case whether a Bishop, promoted to be an Archbishop, was competent to proceed with the trial of a lawsuit commenced before him before his promotion.[9]

In tracing the history of the earlier attempts to improve chess by the introduction of modifications of move, we can use a variety of sources. First in importance must rank the descriptions of the national assize of Spain at the end of the 13th c., which are given by Abraham b. Ezra and in Alf.; of the Lombard assize of about the same date which are given by Cessolis and in the introduction to the problem MS. Paris, F, fr. 1173 (PP); and of the German assize which are given in the *Cracow Poem* and the Köbel and Egenolff editions of Mennel's *Schachzabel*. Next in order come the conclusions which are based upon certain peculiarities of rule special to particular regions, as preserved in the earlier works of the reformed chess, and a few indications drawn from the romance literature. There remain the moralities

[7] Cf. Guido de Baysio's *Rosarium decreti*, dist. viii: 'Ludus ad scachos debet servare consuetudinem loci in quo luditur.'

[8] 'Promittens dare mattum cum pedite certo est curandum an sit factus regina, quia constat de corpore (peditis) et dignitas augmentata non mutat statum priorem. Sed si promisi simpliciter dare mattum cum pedite, non possum dare cum pedite affecto regina, quia artificium confundit officium.'

[9] Cf. John Andreas (D. 1348), Commentary on Duranti's *Speculum juris*, sect. *De judice delegato*: 'Delegata fuit causa episcopo Pragensi. Novissime per dominum Clementem ecclesia illa facta est Archiepiscopalis. Quaeritur an Archiepiscopus procedere possit in causa prius inchoata vel non inchoata. Si nomen Arnesti fuisset expressum, dic intrepide ipsum procedere posse. Certum est istum esse episcopum Pragensem. Non enim per dignitatem archiepiscopalem desinit esse episcopus. Unde et Papa se vocat episcopum. Augmentum igitur honoris et jurisdictionis metropoliticae non tollit primam sed auget. Et interponam ad propositum, per legem illam fuisse judicatum, quod qui in ludo schacorum convenit mattare socium cum pedona victor est, si mattat cum pedona facta regina. Audivi Paduae pronunciatum contrarium per leg. Distinguendo tamen procedit utrumque dictum, et sic Bononiae in scholis disputatum fuit et terminatum: primum scilicet dictum esse verum, quando conventio fuit de aliqua certa pedona, secus si de certa non convenisset, sed in genere de pedona. Jam inducta distinctionem probant et sic soluta est contrarietas.'

and the evidence of the problems, both of which have to be used with caution. The writers of the moralities often attached more importance to their symbolic interpretation than to the accuracy of the chess. The compilers of a problem MS. gathered his material from sources both old and new. The old problems, as we shall see in the case of Alf., were often already archaic: the new were composed with little regard to the strict rules of chess.

These early modifications of move extend to the moves of three pieces only, the Queen, including the Queen created in the course of the game by the promotion of a Pawn, the Pawn, and the King. To each of these pieces for its first time of moving a wider range of move was permitted than it strictly possessed; this being generally a leap into what was called in the Middle Ages a 'third' square, though in modern phraseology we should describe it as a leap to a square two squares distant, since we no longer reckon the square of departure as one of the squares crossed. The diagram will make clear the mediaeval mode of reckoning the distance of squares from any given starting-point, in this case e5.

5	4	4	4	4	4	4	4
5	4	3	3	3	3	3	4
5	4	3	2	2	2	3	4
5	4	3	2	*	2	3	4
5	4	3	2	2	2	3	4
5	4	3	3	3	3	3	4
5	4	4	4	4	4	4	4
5	5	5	5	5	5	5	5

Diagram illustrating the mediaeval method of reckoning the distance of squares from the square e5.

A still more extended leap was allowed to the King in Italian chess. There were also cases in which a player was permitted to make in one single turn of play a combination of moves of more than one piece.

Although the original intention in these changes was nothing more than the acceleration of the opening development, the changes had a more important effect in another part of the game. It was now for the first time possible for the player to gain a move in the End-game. The choice of move permitted in the case of the unmoved Pawn and newly-promoted Queen made it possible to win many Endings which under Muslim rules could only be drawn.

In addition to the introduction of these modifications of move, alterations were frequently made in the rules governing the termination of the game, and in particular the endings of *Bare King* and *Stalemate*.

Spanish Chess.

Our most valuable source is the MS. Alf., of which I have already made considerable use in connexion with the Muslim problems.

This MS. opens with a long description of the game of chess which is out of harmony with the rules followed in its Muslim problems and obviously describes the rules of the game as played in Spain in the writer's time, i. e. about 1280. I print the Spanish text *in extenso* in Appendix I to this chapter, and only give a rapid summary of it here. Where, however, it gives important information about the rules I translate it literally.

The MS. opens with the reasons for its composition, and gives a list of the games to be described. Among these chess takes the precedence as being the most regular and honourable of them all. The chessboard is described, and the rule laid down that—

> Half of the squares must be of one colour, and half of another.

Next follow the names and functions of the chessmen, in the course of which we are told:

> Also it is appointed for the Queen, that when she has been lost, any one of the Pawns that can reach the extreme square on the other side of the board where the major pieces are, is thenceforward a Queen, and can behave itself just as the first Queen, and can move in the same way.

From the following section on the moves of the chessmen I extract:

> The King . . . . cannot go more than one square, straight or aslant. . . .
>
> The Queen goes one square aslant: she is to guard the King[10], is not to leave him, is to cover him from checks and mates when these are said to him, and to go farther afield and help him to win when the game is well opened. Moreover, she can for the first move leap to a third square, either straight or aslant, and even if another piece stands on the intervening square. . . .
>
> The Bishops leap 3 squares diagonally. . . .
>
> The Knights leap 3 squares, counting 2 straight from them, and taking a third aslant in any direction.
>
> The Rooks move straight as far as they can go forwards or backwards or to the right or to the left.
>
> The Pawns do not go more than one square straight forwards. . . . But there are some who are accustomed to play with the Pawns to a third square for the first move. This is until a capture is made, for afterwards they cannot do this.

Next comes a section which describes how the chessmen capture. Of special interest is:

> But the Queen cannot take on its first move when it makes the move to the third square.
>
> The Pawns, however, although they can go to the third square their first move, cannot take on it, but take aslant, advancing one square.

After this section follow others on the relative advantages of the chessmen, upon the range of power of the pieces and the number of squares accessible to each,[11] upon the shapes of the pieces,[12] and in conclusion the writer describes

[10] A playful reference to this occurs in the writings of the Parmese minorite Salimbene (1250–1300). When describing the war in Apulia between the Emperor Henry VI (D. 1197) and his wife Constance, the heiress of Sicily, he remarks:

'Fuit discordia et guerra maxima inter eos, ita ut sapientes et litterati dicerent: isti non sunt vir et mulier bene sibi consentientes, secundum doctrinam Ecclesiastici xxv; jocolatores vero dicebant: si quis modo diceret regi scacchum, regina non defenderet eum.' (Salimbeni, *Mon. hist. ad Provincias Parmensem et Placentinam pertinentia*, Parma, 1857, 175.)

[11] The *alfferzada* is described as a position in which a Queen and two Pawns mutually defend one another, e.g. Pf3, Qg4, Ph5.

The *alffilada* is a similar position in which a Bishop and two Pawns mutually defend one another, e.g. Bb5, Pc4, Pd3. This arrangement often occurs in the problems.

[12] Incidentally, Alf. lays down rules for the interpretation of the throws of the dice in dice-chess: viz. 6, the K moves; 5, the Q; 4, the R; 3, the Kt; 2, the B; and 1, the P.

a variety of chess in which the players were obliged to take whenever they could do so.

We also speak of the game that is called *forced*. Because it must be played by calculation, one must use force in it, for it all goes contrary to the player's will. He loses the greatest piece for a Pawn, and he must do it willingly, or ought not to bring the man to such a square that the other can take it by force. . . . This game is arranged just like the former, and the pieces move and capture in the same way, except for the compulsion. So those wise men who play it must see that they do not place the superior pieces in places where they may have to give them up for the inferior and less valuable ones. And in this consists the whole science and difference of this game. We have called it the *Forced game*, because of this compulsion. Since some relate that the maidens in the land of Ultramar (Morocco) first discovered it, it is called the *Maidens' game* (juego de Doncellas).

This description of chess is far in advance of anything else that we possess prior to the 16th c. It shows three important departures from the Muslim rules: two of these became general throughout Western Europe, but the third was abandoned even in Spain itself. The first innovation is the Queen's leap—a privilege move allowed to the Queen for her first move in the game. Thus the unmoved Q on d1 had the option of moving to c2 and e2 if unoccupied, and of taking an opponent on either of these squares, by virtue of her ordinary move, or of leaping to b1 or b3 or d3 or f3 or f1, if unoccupied, by virtue of this new privilege, whether the intervening square (c1, c2, d2, e1, e2 as the case might be) was occupied or not, but it could not capture an opponent on any of these five squares, nor did it check the hostile King on any of them. Although the text says nothing about the power of a new Queen made by the promotion of a Pawn to make the leap, it is clear from the problems that it was allowed to do so.[13] This would appear to have been the earliest modification of move attempted in Europe.

The second innovation is the introduction of the modern move of the Pawn. The MS. was written at a time when the change was in process of adoption, and there are still restrictions upon the liberty of making the more extended move. Thus it is said that the privilege ceased as soon as either player made a capture. It is important to note that the leap is otherwise free to all Pawns, and not restricted to certain Pawns only, as was the practice in Germany later, and as is the case in certain Asiatic varieties of chess at the present day.

The third innovation is the restriction of the Pawn's right to promotion on reaching the 8th rank. In Muslim chess a similar restriction existed in the chess as-suʿdīya on the eight-square board, and in the older decimal chess.[14] In Europe the same restriction is made in the *Einsiedeln Poem*,[15] and in the recently discovered Catalan poem, *Scachs d'amor*. I have attempted to account for the European restrictions on moral grounds: but these were probably less cogent in early Spanish chess, in which no piece bore the name

[13] E.g. Nos. 47 (= Ar. no. 214, where the position has been Europeanized somewhat, see CB 216), 79, 81, 103 (Ar. no. 407, where the solution is Europeanized, see CB 277).
[14] See p. 342.
[15] See lines 67–70 of this poem, p. 514.

of Queen, and it is possible that the Alfonsine rule arose quite independently of the earlier similar restriction in Southern Germany. V. d. Linde and v. d. Lasa, neither of whom knew of the Catalan poem, refused to accept the statement of the MS., and pointed out that the second problem in the MS. contains 3 white Queens and 6 white Pawns. Evidently two of the Queens must be promoted Pawns,[16] and both historians accordingly dismissed the rule restricting Pawn-promotion as at variance with the practice of the MS. This argument might have weight if we could be sure that the problems were the composition of the author or his Spanish contemporaries, or that any importance was attached in Spain to the possibility [17] of a problem. It is certain, however, that the bulk of the problems, including the one in question, were composed some centuries earlier by Muslim artists and must have been already archaic in Spain, while the non-Arabic additions occur in other MSS. of undisputed European origin. Since the latter MSS. show no trace of any acquaintance with the Spanish MS., it seems probable that King Alfonso obtained his non-Muslim problems from European sources. Nor throughout the whole of the Middle Ages did European composers attach any importance to the possibility of a problem. Two minutes' examination of Alf. 2 is sufficient to establish the impossibility of the position.[18]

The MS. makes no reference to the endings *Bare King* and *Stalemate*, both of which were decisive in Muslim chess. The problems, however, suggest that the former method of winning a game still survived in Spain, for not only are two Arabic problems (Alf. 93 = Ar. no. 51 ; Alf. 94 = Ar. no. 78) in which the game is won by baring the opponent's King included in the collection, which would hardly have happened had the ending *Bare King* not continued decisive,[19] but those European problems which in other collections show a solitary King have been modified by the addition of a blocked Pawn of that King's colour. The only explanation for this is that the addition avoided an undesired solution by *Bare King*.

The Hebrew poem of Abraham b. Ezra, translated in the next chapter, represents a still earlier stage in Spanish chess than is described in Alf., since only one modification of the Muslim rules is recorded. The Queen (Fers) is allowed for the first move a leap to the 'third' square.[20]

At the close of the mediaeval period Lucena (*c.* 1497) describes the rules of the old chess as they existed at the time of the introduction of the modern game. We can supplement his brief reference by means of other works of the

[16] The position is Ar. no. 389.

[17] I. e. the possibility of the position being obtainable in the course of a real game.

[18] White must have made at least four captures to secure his Pawn arrangement, and there are still fourteen Black pieces on the board.

[19] The titles of these problems are (Alf. 93) *Los Blancos iuegan primero e ellos vencen con los sus iuegos mismos*, and (Alf. 94) *Los Prietos iuegan primero, e ellos son vençudos*.

[20] In the Hebrew text of this poem, which Hyde printed (ii. 163–6) from a Bodleian MS. of the 17th c., the lines describing the leap are differently placed, with the result that the leap is transferred to the Pawn, and previous writers have accepted this reading without question, although it gave a result inconsistent with the account of Spanish chess in Alf. On investigation I find that all the other MSS. of the poem have the lines in the order which I have followed above. See p. 509.

following century, notably that of Ruy Lopez (1561). We learn thus that at the close of the 15th century—

(1) The Queen could not capture by her privilege leap.

(2) An advanced Pawn on its 5th rank, which had just been passed by an adversary's Pawn by means of its power of making a double step for its first move, could capture that Pawn the following move in passing, as though the latter had only moved one step.

(3) Neither Lucena nor Lopez knew of any restriction to Pawn promotion. The promoted Pawn became a Queen and could make a privilege leap its next move. Lucena would have liked to allow a leap as a Knight in addition to the older leap.[21]

(4) The King for his first move could leap to any unoccupied third square (e.g. from e1 to any of c1, c2, c3, d3, e3, f3, g3, g2, g1) provided he had never been checked and in leaping did not cross a square commanded by a hostile piece.[22]

(5) Bare King, called *Robado,* was an inferior kind of victory, and only won half the stake. If a player gave mate by capturing the opponent's last piece, it counted as mate and not *robado.*

(6) Stalemate, called *mate ahogado,* was also an inferior kind of victory, and only won half the stake.

If we compare the rules of the Spanish chess of 1490–1500 as given by Lucena with those of 1283 as given in Alf., we see that the game must have undergone a continuous process of development of move during the mediaeval period. It is reasonable to believe that this is also true of the chess of every other country of Western Europe.

Lombard Chess.

The *Liber de moribus hominum et officiis nobilium* of Jacobus de Cessolis belongs to the same half-century as Alf., and gives us a companion picture of the Lombard game. We also possess in the introduction to the Paris MS. PP of the 14th c., which is given in the second Appendix to this chapter, an independent account of this assize. The following changes in the Muslim rules appear:

(1) the King was allowed for his first move a leap to a third or more distant square. In PP this is described loosely:

> And the King leaps one square, or two, or three, or four, the first move, how and in what manner he pleases, but so that he does not go through check.

Cessolis describes the move with more care, naming the exact squares to which the King could leap. The liberty possessed by the K on e1 appears,

[21] For text, see Ch. XI, App., below. [A 16th c. Spanish MS. (Brit. Mus. Add. 28710, f. 360 b) gives this additional leap as a species of odds which might be allowed a weaker player: 'Dama cavallota, es que tambien salta y coge y da Jaque como cavallo y tambien se podria decir esto de otras pieças como arfil y Roque cavalloto, pero no se suele decir sino de la dama y la razon es porque considerando los jugadores, que la dama tenga movimiento de todas las pieças del tablero salvo del cavallo, le dieron tambien ese movimiento diziendo le cavalloto.]

[22] Later Spanish writers allow the leap also after a check, provided the King had not been moved.

therefore, to have been a leap similar to the Queen's leap, to c1 (omitted in text), c3, e3, g3, g1 ; a leap as a Knight, to c2, d3, f3, g2—all these being third squares in the mediaeval sense; and a leap to b1 and b2—these being fourth squares. In no case could the King leap across a square commanded by a hostile piece, or capture by the leap. Later evidence shows that the King could not leap out of check, while the question whether an unmoved King could exercise the privilege after he had been checked and had covered it, was resolved differently in different places.

(2) An unmoved King and Queen could make a joint move for their first move, the whole counting as a single move of the game.

(3) The Queen, and the promoted Pawn, could for their first move make a move into certain third squares, viz. those which could have been reached by two ordinary moves. The intervening square might be occupied by another piece, but the privilege could still be exercised.[23] Neither piece, however, could capture on this move, and a Pawn queening on a square within 'leaping distance' of the opposing King did not give check on that move (e. g. White, Pe7 ; Black, Kc8. 1 Pe8 = Q did not check). Neither of our authorities says this expressly, but it is established by the uniform practice of the problem solutions.

(4) The Pawn had its modern move. Neither work says anything about the right of an advanced Pawn to take *in passing*, but it is clear from later works that no such right was admitted in Italy, and that a Pawn (e. g. on c2) faced by an opponent Pawn (e. g. on d4) could make the double step (Pc4) without fear of capture. This was termed in Italy *passar battaglia.*

(5) A bared King was not defeated through being bared. As PP says—

And one may take all the men so that the King is left all alone, and he must move, move for move, so long as it pleases the other side, and there is no help.

(6) Stalemate was a drawn game. Neither work mentions the ending, but the rule is established by the text of two problems in the Florence CB MS. (F. 306, 313) which is given below, in Ch. VII.

While the Lombard assize was in broad outline followed in Italy, it is clear from the contemporary accounts of the rules observed in different parts of Italy in the 16th and early 17th centuries that there were many local exceptions, especially with reference to the King's leap. The details will be found on a later page,[24] they show that in some places the leap was more extended even than the Lombard leap, in others was limited to the Spanish leap as in Lucena, in others was prohibited entirely. In some places the

[23] PP makes the curious statement: 'And when a Pawn is made Queen, *whether in a corner square or elsewhere,* he leaps three squares the first move . . . or one if it is agreeable to him.'

This suggests a possible origin of the extension of the Queen's leap to the promoted Pawn. The Rook's Pawn is well known to be the easiest of the Pawns to queen, but the new Queen thus obtained in the older chess had only one flight square open to it, and, if attacked on the queening square, would generally be attacked still after making a move. PP seems to suggest that the Queen's privilege leap was first allowed to this Pawn alone, and was extended to the other promoted Pawns at a later date.

[24] See Ch. XII, below.

analogy of the combined move of King and Queen had given rise to a combined move of King and Pawn. This is established by a passage in Damiano's work.[25]

German Chess.

Our accounts of the German assize are later in date than those which I have used for the Spanish and Lombard games: this is the less serious because German chess lagged behind that of the rest of Western Europe in development. Our authorities—the hitherto unused *Cracow Poem* of 1422, and the additions to Mennel's *Schachzabel* made by his republishers, Köbel of Oppenheim (*c.* 1520) and Egenolff of Frankfurt am Main (1536)—are particularly full, the latter in the descriptions of the moves of the pieces, the former in the rules of the game. The *Cracow Poem* shows that there was much uncertainty as to the rules at that time, and endeavours to give the correct code. This makes it of special value from the historical point of view. The material portions of the text will be found on pp. 522–6; that of Egenolff's Mennel is given as the third Appendix to this chapter. German chess shows the following changes from the Muslim rules:

(1) The King has the extended leap of Lombard chess, and possibly one still more extended.

> The King on his first move . . . . may, if he likes, ride three steps from the square of his exit (which is to the fourth square) against his opponent, and take up his position on the same square, or also on the second, or on the third, all according to his pleasure (Egenolff).

According to the *Cracow Poem* (421–9) no combined moves of two pieces (such as that of King and Queen in the Lombard game) were allowed. Köbel and Egenolff, however, allow the combined move of King and Queen, and permit the player when moving his King for the first time to move one of his pawns a step to make room for the King, and at the same time to move the Queen also. They also allow the King to make the leap out of check, but not across a square commanded by a hostile piece. In one place it is stated that—

> if an opponent would hinder him from such a move (to a third square), he may strike him himself and remove him.

In the following paragraph, however, it is expressly stated that no piece, King, Queen, or Pawn, can capture on its first privilege leap. This is also implied in the *Cracow Poem* when it states that none of these pieces could act as a guard to a piece upon a square which it could only reach by means of the leap.

(2) The Queen and promoted Pawn have the power of leaping on their first move that these pieces possessed in the Spanish and Lombard games (Egenolff, and *Cracow Poem*).

[25] Damiano also says the Pawn cannot *passar battaglia* to cover check. See Ch. XII, below.

(3) The Pawn is allowed the initial double step by all three authorities, provided no man has been taken:

You must know that these Pawns, if they wish, for the first move can go straight forward to the first or second square, so long as no man is taken. But when one or more pieces are taken, then no Pawn may go farther than the next square before him, with the exception that the two side Pawns which stand before the Rooks can at any time, for their first move, move to the second square (Egenolff).

The restriction of the double step to four only of the eight Pawns, viz. the KP, QP, and the two RP's, must have been general in Germany. We find it in the earliest German works of the reformed chess, and it survived into the eighteenth century.

(4) Stalemate, according to the *Cracow Poem*, is a drawn game, though some players treated it as equivalent to mate (384–402).

(5) The *Cracow Poem* gives Bare King as a win (475–87), though some players supposed that the player whose King was first bared won the game. An early 13th c. poem of the Minnesinger Reinmar v. Zweter seems to suggest that players in his day ignored this Ending.[26] Köbel and Egenolff have nothing to say about these two Endings.

French and English Chess.

We have no accounts of chess in France and England which we can place beside those which I have used for other national forms of the game. We have to rely upon scattered references in general literature, the earliest accounts of the reformed game, and the doubtfully valid evidence of the problem MSS. and the moralities. From the first we learn that two forms of chess were played in both countries from about 1150 to 1450, known as the long and short assizes, and differing in the opening arrangement and probably in rule also. This makes it the more difficult to interpret the position, for the rules of the short assize do not appear to have differed at all from those of the Muslim game, while those of the long assize or ordinary game underwent much the same development as in other countries. On the whole, there would appear to have been little, if any, difference in rule between the French and English game at any particular moment. The long assize, to which alone I direct attention at this time, occupies a position intermediate between the Spanish and Italian forms, the moves being those of the Spanish, the rules of the Ending those of the Italian game.

The chief features of the development of the mediaeval game in France and England would appear to have been these:

(1) The Queen, whether original or made by the promotion of a Pawn, was in course of time allowed the privilege leap that I have described as allowed in the three assizes already described.

26 Ich hân den künic alleine noch
und weder ritter noch daz roch,
mich stiuret niht sîn alte
noch sîn vende. (In v. d. Hagen's *Minnesinger*, ii. 204 b.)

The leap is made without remark in problems in the Anglo-French group of MSS. in the case of promoted Pawns. There is, however, some evidence that would seem to suggest that restrictions were placed upon the power of the original Queen to make the leap. A curious problem in a late 15th c. Latin MS. of French authorship (Paris, L 24274, f. 73 a = S 57) speaks of a Queen as unable *prelium saltare* on its first move when the square over which it would leap was commanded by an opposing Pawn. This must have been an event of such rare occurrence that it would seem puerile to legislate for it, and I am accordingly inclined to dismiss the rule as one of the trick conditions that the mediaeval problemist so often added to his work. As a rule, however, these conditions are set out at the head of the problem; here they are only to be inferred from the solution to the unsound problem and its sound variation. Apart from this, the problem has a literary interest as containing the oldest known reference to the Italian chess term *passar battaglia*.[27]

(2) The Pawn gained its modern move, and had the power of taking another Pawn *in passing*, precisely as in modern chess.

I infer that this was so from the fact that the rule is given thus in the earlier works of the reformed chess that appeared both in England and France. Greco, who appears to have taken considerable trouble to master the local peculiarities of rule, gives the rule as I have stated it, and in the unpublished MSS. of his games which he made for English players he makes use of the move P × P *in passing*.

(3) The King in course of time came to possess the leap as given by Lucena for Spanish chess, but not the more extended leap of the Lombard assize. The privilege continued so long as the King was unmoved, whether he had been checked or not; it could not be used to make a capture, nor to remedy a check.

Here, again, I depend upon the evidence of the earlier works of the reformed chess. There is, however, some evidence that would seem to suggest that the King's power of move had been reduced instead of being extended in some parts of England and France. Thus the ordinary text of the *Innocent Morality* (of English authorship) only allows the King to move to the four adjacent squares of a different colour, thus making its move the complement of the Queen's ordinary move; and this move is repeated in that chapter of the *Gesta Romanorum* on chess which, based upon the *Innocent Morality*, is peculiar to the English MSS. of that work. I hope to show, however, in Chapter V that the existing text of the *Innocent Morality* has suffered interpolation in the account of the King's move, and that a portion of the text really belongs to the Rook's move. If this portion is removed, the passage gives the King's move as we know it in Muslim chess, in Neckam, and in the European poems.

The same move is given in the fifth book of Rabelais' *Faicts et dicts heroiques du bon Pantagruel* (printed at Lyons in 1564, after the death of the

[27] For problem and text of the solution see Ch. VIII, below.

author)[28] at a time when we know that the ordinary move to any adjacent square and the privilege leap were the rule in France. Any restriction of move is opposed to the whole history of the development of chess in Europe; but while it is easy to account for the misstatements of the moralities, it is more difficult to explain the very definite statement in Rabelais' work. It is very improbable that this writer was only imperfectly acquainted with the rules of chess, and very reluctantly I think that we must accept his restricted move of the King as having existed in the middle of the 16th c. in some isolated French chess circles. In isolated places the rules must have often varied in small points.[29]

(4) In France, at least, the ending *Stalemate* was reckoned as a drawn game.

There are, however, a certain number of problems, specially numerous in MS. Dresden O/59 (= D), in which a player who could not legally move when it was his turn to play simply forfeited his move, while his opponent continued playing successive moves until it suited him to release his opponent's King from the position of stalemate and the ordinary practice of play by alternate moves was resumed.[30] In other cases it is specially stated that the player may not enclose or stale his opponent before mating.[31] The instances seem rather too numerous for us to dismiss this practice as simply a problem convention, and it possibly represents a phase in the treatment of the ending *Stalemate* in France. It is somewhat remarkable that in the case of so many problems in all the European collections it should be expressly stated that play is to be by alternate moves, L. *tractum pro tractu*, Fr. *trait pour trait*.

Soon after 1600 we find that in England the player whose side was placed in the position of stalemate was adjudged to have won the game. The reason given for this in Saul's *Famous game of Chesse-play* (London, 1614) is puerile,[32] and, as I have suggested elsewhere, I think that this was an innovation introduced about 1600, possibly from Russian chess.[33] There is no evidence that the rule went back to the mediaeval game.

[28] 'Les Roys marchent et prennent leurs ennemis de toute façon en carré: et ne passent que de carreau blanc et prochain au jaulne, et au contraire: exceptez qu'à la premiere desmarche, si leur filiere estoit trouvée vuide d'autres officiers, fors les Custodes, ils les peuvent mettre en leur siège, et à costé de luy se retirer' (ch. xxiv).

[29] There was a long discussion on the point in a series of papers, *Chess in Europe during the 13th c.*, which Lake Allen contributed to the *New Monthly Magazine* in 1822. In their preparation he hád the assistance of Sir Frederic Madden. Forbes (109–15) exposed the hollowness of much of the reasoning upon which Allen endeavoured to establish that the restricted move was the rule in European chess at the commencement of the 13th c., but in his turn he mistranslates the passage in the *Innocent Morality*. Allen's statement is repeated in Rowland's *Problem Art*, Dublin, 1887, and is there supported by a problem which is said to be taken from a MS. in the British Museum, in which the King is not allowed to move angularly (White, Rd6, Pc4 and e2; Black, Ke5. Mate in III by 1 Rf6, Ke4; 2 Rf5, Ke3 or d4; 3 Re5 or f4 accordingly, mate). I have examined every known chess MS. in the British Museum for this problem in vain. There is nothing in the least like it in any of the European problem MSS., and I believe that it is a modern forgery on the part of Mr. Rowland's informant on the subject of the mediaeval problems. There are other statements on the mediaeval problem in this work which lend support to my opinion.

[30] See D 24, 50, 53, 55, in Ch. VI, below.

[31] See D 18, 21, 30, 37, 43, 54, 58, 64.

[32] 'He that hath put his adversary's King into a stale, loseth the game, because he hath disturbed the course of the game, which can only end with the grand Check-mate.'

[33] See p. 391, and my article, 'Stalemate', *BCM.*, 1903, 281–9.

(5) The evidence relating to the ending *Bare King* is contradictory, but it is probable that players clung for a long time to the Muslim rule, by which the player baring his opponent's King won the game. Four problems in the MS. D [34] are won by making the King *seul*, and two in K,[35] the text to the problem K 51 beginning

Ceste guy ne enseygne point de mater
Mes enseygne le guy ganyer.

On the other hand, both of these MSS. have a large number of problems in which the King to be mated is already bare, and the solution to another problem common to the two English collections (P 25 = Ash. 20) begins 'Take is auf. & make hym bar' (Ash. 'Take Hys aufyn ande make hym bar'), and then goes on to the mate.

Several references in general literature attach importance to the ending. Thus the English chess chapter in the *Gesta Romanorum* says of the King:

Sed quum non curat de deo nec habet familiam fit sibi chekmat,

which gives colour to the view that in the writer's time the bare King lost the game in England. Too much weight, of course, must not be attached to the evidence of this morality, but the evidence for French chess is considerably stronger. In the metrical version of *Les Eschez amoureux*, the term *ave* is twice employed as a technical term to describe the condition of a King who has been defeated in some other way than by checkmate.[36] The same word is used in Chrestien de Troyes' *Ivain* (written *c.* 1172).[37] The verb *haver* in the *Roman de la Rose* [38] is closely connected, and establishes the chess meaning of

[34] See D 12, 29, 44, 53.

[35] See K 50 (*Mal veysyn*) and 51, in Ch. VI, below.

[36] In *Les Eschez amoureux*, MS. Dresden O/66, f. 23 a,

Mais chascun s'est si bien tenu
Qu'il ny a mat ne ave ëu ;

and f. 26 b,

Ne me chaloit de mat ne d'ave

where the prose version has 'ne luy chaloit mais, s'il estoit matz et desconfitz'.

[37] Ed. W. Foerster, Halle, 1891 :

Se vos volez m'amor avoir
Et de rien nule m'avez chiere,
Pansez de revenir arriere
A tot le mains jusq'a un an
Huit jors aprés la saint Jehan :
Hui an cest jor sont les huitaves.
De m'amor seroiz maz et haves,
Se vos n'estes a icel jor
Ceanz avuec moi a sejor. (2570–78)

So also in two other passages quoted in Godefroi:—Thib. de Marly, *Vers sur la mort*, V (Crapelet):

Qui se paine d' iaus pourcachier
Tant ne aves les ait fais ou mas ;

and J. Bruyant (*Menagier*, ii. 7):

pâle et décharné
have estoit et eschevelée.

Cf. also W. Foerster in *Zeitschrift f. romanische Philologie*, 1881, v. 97, where he establishes the term *hāve* as a *terminus technicus* of chess, and J. Mettlich, *Die Schachpartie in . . .'Les eschez amoureux'*, Münster i. W., 1907, 27.

[38] See below, Ch. IX.

the term. It is the OF. word for *Bare King*; its existence is evidence of the importance attached to the ending, while the fact that it is used in the *Eschez amoureux* and in *Yvain* as an alternative to *mat* shows that it was equally decisive as an ending to the game.

(6) Two problem solutions in the English MS. Ash. point to the existence of some recognized limit to the number of moves in which mate had to be given when one player was left with the decisive advantage of a Rook or more. The first occurs at the end of Ash. 20 (f. 12 b), a conditional mate in the centre of the board 'w^t^in ix drawghtis (moves)', where the compiler adds the sentence, 'He will ande may tell hys ix drawghtis for thow hast a Roke abord.' The second is in the solution of Ash. 36 (f. 20 b), 'Thow shalt mate hym with a Pon at v draughtis yf thow play wel affter thy Roke, and if thou knowe itt not thow shalnot mate hym at ix draughtis ffor he woll tel his draughtis for cause of thi Roke.'

There is nothing to show when these modifications of move and rule reached French or English chess. They appear to have been unknown to Neckam (*c.* 1180), and none of the poems allude to them. The problem MSS. Cott. and K, however, show that the Queen's privilege leap at least was known before 1300. On the other hand, two passages in K suggest that the double step of the Pawn was late in reaching England. In one (K 5, *Le guy de damoyseles*) the Pawn's move is given with no mention of the double step, in the other (K 26, *Couenaunt fet ley*) a problem which in Cott. (Cott. 8, *Couenant lci vint* on f. 6 a) is solved in five moves is lengthened to one in eleven. The solution in K begins, 'Le poun ke est en hp. (i. e. h2) deuz foyz treyera,' which brings it to h4. There is no apparent object in prolonging the solution to eleven moves, and I conclude that the player who altered the problem did not know the double step.[39]

Icelandic Chess.

The most extraordinary alterations in rule were those which were made by the Icelandic players; but it is not certain to what extent these changes belong to old, and to what extent to new chess. These alterations relate to the conclusion of the game only; so far as the evidence goes, the development of move in Iceland followed the same lines as elsewhere in Europe, probably at some interval of time. In the romantic sagas (where the chess details of the French originals are freely treated) stress is laid upon the method of mate. Already in the *Mágus Saga* we meet with special terms, such as *hróksmát* (mate with the Rook), *peðsmát* (mate with the Pawn), *fretstertumát* (according to Olaus Verelius, mate with King's Pawn), which is 'the most disgraceful of all mates', *biskupsmát* (mate with the Bishop). Icelandic chess has a number of these expressions.[40]

[39] See the problems and solutions, pp. 586, 594.
[40] See below, Ch. XIII. The *Mágus Saga* has also *the little taflsmunr* (in some MSS. *the little munr*), apparently meaning Bare King.

The win by Bare King (Ic. *bert*) was never abandoned in Icelandic chess, although it was regarded as a very inferior form of victory. If mate and Bare King happened on the same move it was called 'great Bare King' (*stóra bert*); if the last capture did not give mate, the game ended in 'little bare King' (*litla bert*).

Chess Notation.

At the root of all advance in the science of chess-play lies the necessity of discovering an intelligible system of notation, by means of which the squares of the board may be easily defined and the moves of the pieces recorded. The compilers of the European problem MSS. generally evaded the necessity by the addition of letters, crosses, dots, and other signs upon the squares which they wished to designate. The indolence that lay behind this is characteristic of the mediaeval chess-player. There were, however, other systems of notation, and some of these are recommended in the problem MSS., although not often used. The Spanish MS. Alf., with its strong Arabic colour, uses a descriptive notation, learnt from Muslim players, that is practically identical with the notation used by all English writers of the early 19th c. Thus e4 is 'la quarta casa del Rey blanco', and e5 'la quarta casa del Rey prieto', and so on. The Italian MS. Arch. uses the same notation, but I have only noticed one instance of its use in the other MSS. of the older chess,[41] though it came to the front again when the reformed chess introduced the analysis of the Opening, and it is used in the Göttingen MS., in Lucena, Damiano, &c., for the purpose of recording games, though not in the problem solutions. It thus became the usual notation in Europe until the time of Stamma (1737), and has survived in England, France, and Europe generally outside Germany, until our own day.

A literal or algebraic notation was also used in Europe in the mediaeval period. Like the descriptive notation, its use would appear to have been borrowed from Muslim players. The French MS. PP describes it carefully in the introductory chapter, which I give entire in Appendix IV. The files are named *a*, *b*, to *h*, as in the notation used in this book; but the ranks are lettered from the 8th rank to the 1st (the reverse order to that employed now), the 8th rank having no special letter, and the 7th, 6th, . . . 1st being *k*, *l*, to *q*; thus e4 is *en*, f8 is *f*, and h2 is *hp*. The MS. PP itself nowhere uses the notation; but a former owner of the MS. PL, who probably lived in the 15th c. (possibly Charles, Duke of Orleans), regularly used it in his marginal notes, while the Anglo-French MS. K uses in all its solutions a notation which only differs in that the 8th rank is lettered *i*.[42] The diagrams in this MS. are, for the convenience of the reader, bordered *a* to *h* along the top, and *i* to *q* down the right-hand side. The notation of the MS. K is also used in many MSS. of *Les Eschez amoureux* in the diagrams of the initial position of

[41] Viz. in the MS. F, f. 161 b, where d8 is called *punctus regine nigre* and e8 *punctus regis nigri*.

[42] I give the solution of K 31 in extenso, p. 595, as an example of the use of this notation.

the game therein described, while the prose text makes use of it in its account of the play, justifying the use thus:

> pour ce qu'on puist myeulx entendre et concevoir les traitz et le procès du jeu ymaginé par l'eschequier sensible, nous seignerons les poins de l'eschequier par lettres.[43]

This notation is essentially the same as that which Stamma reintroduced from the East in 1737, which is the original of the normal notation of German chess-players, and of the notation employed in this work.

In the early 16th c., Köbel made use of another literal notation in his chess work, the diagram of which is given in Appendix III, while Italian players began to use a numerical notation, numbering the squares 1, 2, to 64, commencing from h1 to a1, h2 to a2, and so on to a8. Both of these notations are clumsy and awkward to use.[44]

Science of Play.

When we turn to the science and method of play, we find that the mediaeval player possessed very little knowledge of the relative values of the pieces, or of the underlying principles of play. Here he remained far behind the Muslim players of the 10th c. He, of course, recognized that the Rook and Knight were the strongest of the chess forces,[45] and he relied almost entirely upon them when he had brought them into play. But he knew very little of the value of the other pieces. The main use that he made of his Queen was to keep her in close attendance on the King to interpose her when the opponent's Rook checked from the other side of the board. The Muslim masters manœuvred from the first to secure a road for the Queen into the heart of the enemy's position, the European kept her near home.[46] The *Cracow Poem*, which places the Queen quite early on her third square, lays great stress upon the importance of supporting it there, and uses for this purpose the King's Bishop and the Queen's Bishop's Pawn, neither of which should be moved from the original position (see lines 42–4, 56–70, &c.). The Bishop was a sore puzzle to the European player. He evidently found its move a difficult one to remember, and the many references to the Bishop as a 'spy' and a 'thief' bear witness to the frequency with which the more valuable pieces fell victims to its attack. Still, the general opinion of the value of the piece was not a high one, and the word *aufin* passed into ordinary use both in French and in English as a term of contempt or reproach.[47] Only in the two Anglo-

[43] Mettlich, op. cit., p. 9.

[44] Other notations have been proposed from time to time without success, e. g. by Wielius (1606), Wildt (1802, used by Koch), Kieseritzky (1846); see v. d. Linde, ii. 233–41. The Italian numerical notation was used by Selenus (1616), and by a few unimportant writers of later date. Its use has always effectively destroyed any influence the work employing it might otherwise have possessed.

[45] Cf. from Provençal writers: P. Bremond, *Ricas novas*: En la mar,—'mot sai ab cavalier gen jogar et ab roc', and G. Adhemar, *Ben fora*:—'Aissi cum dels escas lo rocs Val mais que l'autre joc no fan.' The term *roc* is used in French literature as a term of praise. See the examples quoted below, Ch. IX.

[46] Several references in literature seem to show an exaggerated opinion of the value of the Queen. See below, Ch. IX.

[47] See the instances quoted below, Ch. IX.

French MSS. Cott. and K do we find a better opinion stated, and this may be merely a result of the great rôle which the Bishop played in the mediaeval problem.[48]

The desirability of employing the King's leap to remove this piece into a position of greater security was early recognized by German and English players, and some attempt was made to discover satisfactory ways of doing this. The manœuvre was termed in England *ward-making*, and in Germany to make a *hut* (*hut*, fem. = guard)[49]; in Latin, *hospitari*. The *Cracow Poem*, Köbel, and Egenolff give between them several examples of *huts* which they recommend, and the latter writers advise the player to make his *hut* early, to make it on the opposite wing to that chosen by the opponent, and to employ few rather than many pieces in making the *hut*.[49] The *huts* accordingly become something very like Openings, and I shall treat them so.

Pawn play, again, was but little understood. For this we have a curious piece of evidence in the Vatican MS. Lat. 1960 (*c.* 1350). Four methods of developing the Pawns are mentioned in the eighth chapter of this short *Tractatus de ludo scachorum*, which I quote in Appendix V, viz. the advance of the Pawns on both wings producing a scissors-shaped arrangement, the advance of a central Pawn supported by the Pawns on either side producing a pyramidal arrangement, an arrangement of the Pawns about the King which the MS. calls circular, and an advance in a straight line. The first two are said to be good for attack, the wing attack against a few, and the central attack against many men, the circular is praised for defence, and the square which also happens in the game is only of moderate value. There is not much to be made out of this.

Some positions in the problem MSS. show that players possessed some idea of the Opposition and of the principle of restraint. Apart from this we have only a few isolated pieces of obvious advice, such as 'avoid a discovered check'[50] and 'beware of check-rook (a check which simultaneously attacked a Rook).' Ingold in his *Guldin Spil* (1432–3; ed. Schröder, Strassburg, 1882, 33) quotes a Latin line which gives a simple rule for avoiding the latter risk:

Disparibus campis numquam schach roch tibi fiet.[51]

We may form some idea of the tactics pursued in the *Opening* from the instructions which on the one hand the *Cracow Poem* and on the other Köbel and Egenolff give for making the *hut*. In each case the treatment is incomplete, since it only considers the moves of one player. It must be

[48] See the extracts from the solutions to the *Guy de alfins* (Cott. 11 and K 6), pp. 587, 590. It is interesting to contrast the high praise accorded to the Bishop in Cott. 11 with the concluding line of the poem *It pedes* in the same MS.

[49] See the quotation from Lydgate's *Troy Book*, p. 501, n. 5. Both the Eng. *ward* and Ger. *hut* are regularly used also to translate the L. *custodia* in the problem MSS. A piece defended by a second piece is said to be in the *ward* or *hut* of the second piece.

[50] Thus Charles of Orleans in one of his *Rondels* (*Poésies*, ed. Champollion-Figeac, 297) says:

Aux eschés s'estes bons joueurs
Gardez l'eschec à descouverte.

[51] Cf. the similar rule (471–5) in the *Cracow Poem*. Cessolis also directs attention to the danger of *check-rook*.

remembered that all these writers use the *German* rules. The *Cracow Poem* gives six Openings, the first general, the other five, called *custodiae*, *urbes*, or *pura* (sing. *pus*), mainly concerned with the defence of the King. I summarize the difficult text thus:

I. (Ke1) 1 Pe4; 2 Pd4; 3 Kte2; 4 Ph4; 5 Pa4; 6 Bh3; 7 Ba3; 8 Pg3; 9 Pf3.

II. (h1 black, Kd1) 1 Pd4; 2 Pe4; 3 Qe3; 4 Pg3; 5 Ph4; 6 Bh3; 7 Rh2; 8 *Kg2*.

III. (h1 black, Kd1) 1 Pd4; 2 Pe4; 3 Qe3; 4 Pb3; 5 Pa4; 6 Ba3; 7 *Kb2*; 8 Ktc3; 9 Ph4; 10 Bh3.

IV. (h1 black, Kd1) 1 Pc4; 2 Pd4; 3 Pa4; 4 Ba3; 5 *Kb3*; 6 Qc3; 7 Bd3; 8 Ktd2.

V. (h1 black, Kd1) 1 Pa4; 2 Ph4; 3 Ra3; 4 Rf3; 5 Ba3; 6 Pc3; 7 Pd3; 8 Ktd2; 9 *Kb1*; 10 Qc1.

VI. (h1 white, Kd1) 1 Pc4; 2 Pb3; 3 Pa4; 4 Ba3; 5 Pd3; 6 *Kc3*; 7 Qc1. Köbel gives the following moves:

1 Pd4, Ktc6; 2 Pc3 (Pe3 is said to be inferior), Pa5; 3 Pa4 (to prevent 3 . ., Pa4.), . . ; 4 Ph4, . . ; 5 Ba3, . . ; 6 Bh3, . . . Now the player is to form his *hut* on the opposite wing to that chosen by his adversary, combining the King's move with the Queen's leap, e. g. 7 Kc2 and Qd3. This is to be followed by the development of the two Kts, and the two Rs are to be brought together behind the unmoved Pawns opposite the opponent's *hut*.

Egenolff adds to this three Openings in each of which the player makes his *hut* early:

I. 1 Pf4; 2 Pf5; 3 Pe4; 4 Pd3; 5 Bh3; 6 B (h3) takes the Pawn or piece which had taken P (f5); 7 Be3; 8 Ph4; 9 Bg5; 10 Kf2 and Qf3 forming the *hut*.

II. The Iron ward (*die eisern hutt*). 1 Ph4; 2 Pe3; 3 Bh3; 4 Ktf3; 5 Kg1 and Qf1.

III. 1 Pd4; 2 Pc3, Kc2, and Qd3, all as one move!

Köbel advised the beginner *always* to begin by moving the Queen's Pawn, and said that it is usual to move it to d4. Otherwise, so he says, there is risk of a mate in 3 or 4 moves, and he quotes a Latin saw in support of his advice:

Ante Reginam debes producere primam.

We may accordingly regard the *Queen's Pawn Opening* as the regular commencement in the older European chess—a conclusion which is supported by the descriptions of games which are to be found in some of the mediaeval romances. Thus the game in *Lancelot* (*c.* 1220) begins—

1 dP ~, dP ~; 2 cP ~, cP ~; 3 Kt ~, Kt ~; 4 Kt ~, Kt ~; 5 R ~, R ~,

while the *Vœux du Paon* gives a long account of a game between Baudrains and the lady Fezonas, in which the latter gives the odds of Knight and move and undertakes to mate in the corner, which begins—

1 dP ∼ , Ktc6 attacking the P; 2 Q ∼ to save the P, B ∼ to win Q or P, or force the Q to retreat.

Both second moves are impossible in a game starting from the ordinary arrangement of the men and played with the mediaeval rules, but probably we must not tie the poet down to the accuracy of his record: his only aim is to create a chess atmosphere for the story.

Two miniatures of early positions of games in progress also support the popularity of the *Queen's Pawn Opening* in the Middle Ages. The first of these is taken from a Munich MS. of Goliard poetry dating from the 12th c., which has been printed under the title of *Carmina Burana* (Second edition, Breslau, 1883). It occurs on f. 91 b, between the two chess poems which I quote in the next chapter. The first player has the black men (the black men were the favourite ones in the Middle Ages, if the player had the choice of men), the board is arranged so that h1 is white, but the Black Queen is on

Game position from the Munich MS. of *Carmina Burana*,

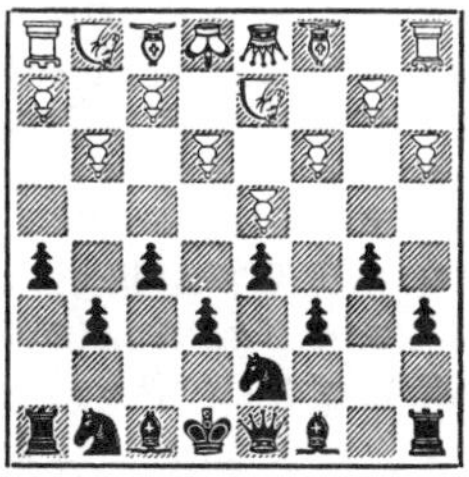

Game position from MS. Alf. f. 5 a. White is about to play.

the white square d1. The first player is drawn in the act of placing his rook on h4. The game may have commenced—

1 Pd4, Pd5; 2 Pe3, Pe6; 3 Pf3, Pf6; 4 Pa4, Pa5; 5 Pb3, Pb6; 6 Ph4, Ba3; 7 Ph5, Ph6; 8 Rh4.

The second miniature illustrates the *Juego forçado* (see p. 459) in the *Alfonso MS.* It is less accurate, for Black has played at least nine moves and White at most seven. V. d. Linde corrected it without remark (*Qst.*, 83) by placing the Pawns on g4, c4, and a7 on g2, c2, and a5 respectively. In the MS. h1 is white, and the Black Queen on e1 is accordingly on a black square. The corrected position may have been obtained by some such succession of moves as—

1 Pe4, Pe5; 2 Pc3, Pf6; 3 Pd3, Pd6; 4 Pa4, Pa5; 5 Pb3, Pb6; 6 Ph3, Ph6; 7 Kte2, Kte7.

Both players have obstructed the egress of their Queen's Bishop; evidently not much importance was attached to its early development.

A miniature of the 15th c., reproduced without stating the MS. source in Champollion-Figeac's *Louis et Charles, Ducs d'Orléans* (Paris, 1844, plate 46), shows a game (h1 white) between a lady and gentleman in which the lady is beginning the game by advancing her KtP.[52]

[52] Miniatures of chess in mediaeval MSS. seldom throw any light on the game. The board is often drawn with too few squares, and as a rule all the white men are placed on black squares and all the black on white squares.

It is possible that some of the earliest analysis of modern chess may be based upon the Openings of the older game. There are indications of this in the play in the Openings 1 Pc4 and 1 Pf4 in the Göttingen MS., and in Lucena. It has sometimes been supposed that the so-called *Damiano Gambit* is a survival of old chess. It may be so as far as 1 Pe4, Pe5; 2 Ktf3, Pf6—quite a good defence in the older game, since 3 Kt × P was utterly pointless.

The romances show that the game at odds was well known. They also show that players took pride in securing certain mating positions, and were ready to handicap themselves by undertaking to give mate with a particular piece or upon a particular square. In the long account of the game in the *Vœux du Paon*, the discussion as to the terms of the game between Baudrains and the lady Fezonas is ended by the lady offering the knight the odds of Rook or Knight and undertaking to say *coi* [53] in the far corner of the board with a Bishop; she also gives him the move, 'for it is far better for her that he should have it.' The mate with a Bishop, with a Pawn, with a Pawn after a check with another Pawn on the preceding move, are all fairly frequent in the problem MSS. In early times the mate in the centre of the board was highly esteemed, especially in France and England.[54] In the banter that went on between Charlot and Bauduinet during their game in *Oger de Danemarche*, Charlot says that he does not think much of a player who can only mate with a Knight or Rook; the player who knows how to drive the King into the *four points* and can then mate him with a Pawn, is the one who deserves praise. By the *four points* are meant the four squares d4, d5, e4, e5, in the centre of the board. To mate in a corner square of the board was another favourite undertaking that is often mentioned in the romances.[55] Four other squares obtained a special name in the mediaeval period from the difficulty of mating a King on them; b2, b7, g2, g7, the four squares a Fers's move from the corner squares, were called *les poyns estraunges* in the AF. MS. K.

Chess was usually played for a stake. Probably there was no game played in the Middle Ages in which it was not the ordinary rule to increase the interest by this simple device of attaching a prize to the victory and a penalty to the defeat. If the stake is a less prominent feature of board-games in modern Europe, it is solely due to the fact that in other games

[53] An alternative term in French for *mate*, of which there are a few instances in literature. It is the L. *quietus*, Eng. *quiet*, *coy*.

[54] See the extracts from the *Rommant de la Rose*, and Chaucer's *Book of the Duchesse*, in Ch. IX, and from the problem MSS. K (where this form of mate is called *le guy cotidian*—the ordinary game), Port. and Ash. in Ch. VI. In *Les Eschez amoureux* (MS. Dresden, f. 27) there is another reference to the *four points*:

Mais celle demoura garnie
De deux rocz et d'aultre mesnie,
Si qu'elle mater me peuist,
En quelque lieu qu'il luy pleuist,—
Es quatre poins, ou aultrement,
A sa voulenté purement.

[55] It ends the games in *Les Eschez amoureux*, in the *Vœux du Paon*, in *Oger de Danemarche*, in *Huon de Bordeaux*, in *Merlin*, in *Lancelot*, and in *Artur* (MS. Richel. 337, f. 218 b: 'Et comencerent le geu trois foiz et materent en l'angle'). The *mate in the corner* became a favourite metaphor with French poets, see Ch. IX, below.

we enjoy more opportunities of wagering money than were open to our ancestors. Chess is often now played without a stake, but in the Middle Ages the absence of a stake usually calls for remark as something unusual.[56] The stake would ordinarily be of money only: thus Henry VII lost on one occasion 56*s.* 8*d.* 'at Tables, Chess, Glassez, &c.'[57] In the romances it is often of a more serious character. In the first problem in MS. Cott., the Knight has wagered his head against the hand of his opponent's daughter in marriage. In Gauvain, on one occasion, the winner is to do what he pleases with the loser, on another, Galheret plays a lady on condition that if he win he obtains possession of her magic castle, and if he lose he becomes her prisoner. The reader will find many other wagers over chess in Chapter IX and elsewhere.

From the custom of playing for a stake arose certain rather obvious parallels, e. g. life is a game of chess between Man and the Devil, the stake being the Man's soul. More important for the development of chess was the fact that the existence of the stake necessitated strict rules of play. The man touched had to be played, and the move made had to stand. The oldest existing codes of rules belong to the early works of the modern game, and deal with precisely those points which the presence of the stake made important: the penalty for false moves, for taking one of one's own men, for playing a pinned piece and uncovering check, &c.

Moreover the conduct of the bystanders had to be regulated. Chess was treated as a social game, and the spectators in feudal days were by no means silent. We have already seen in the chess incident in *Ruodlieb* how the bystanders advised the nobles when they played with the envoy. In *La mort Aymeri de Narbonne* (Paris, 1884, 2204–8), Hernauz prompts his brother with a good move,

As eschés joe Guillaumes au cort nés,
Hernauz et Bueves et danz Garins li ber.
Cil troi se sont encontre lui torné.
Hernauz ses frere lor a un trait mostré
Par quoi li autre furent del jeu maté.

[56] E.g. in *Ruodlieb*, p. 411–13. Deduit in *Les Eschez amoureux* plays the lady without a stake. As Lydgate (*Reson and sensuallyte*, a 1412) translates:

But yt was don of noon hatrede 5853
But of love and frendelyhede
And her hertis to releve;
For noon lyst other for to greve
But, lyke as I haue memoyre,
Oonly for to han victoire
With-oute surplus of wynnyng
Of any other foreyn thing;
For they play for no profyte
But for Ioy and for delyte.

[57] Losses at chess are recorded in the two following passages:

(Anno 1368) Item die mijn here (Jan van Blois) verscakede (i.e. lost at chess) jeghens Cralen den piper, 3 oude scilden (De Lange van Wijngaerden, *De Herren en Stad van der Goude*, i. 577; cf. also 129, 571, 572; quoted by v. d. Linde, *Het Schaakspel in Nederland*, 68).

(Anno 1438) Myns Heeren gen. (the Duke of Gueldres) in syn hant gedaen in gen. zomer to Gelre, doe myn Heere van Moirss daer was, ende syne gen. tegen myn Joncker van Ghemen schaeckten viii. Wilhelmus schilden en daerne to Buren, doe syne gen. laitsten dair waren vi. Ryns gln. per Holthusen in profesto Martini per Luyken ii. Ryns gln. ten R. doe syne gen. tegen Henricus schaeckten (in G. v. Hasselt, *Roozendaal*, Arnhem, 1808, 287; quoted in v. d. Linde, op. cit., 68).

In the *Vœux du Paon*, the bystanders carried on a running stream of banter and advice all through the game. In *Oger*, Bauduinet defends this concomitant of chess as of the essence of the game. This was a tradition of chess which had been handed on by the Muslim players (see p. 184). In opposition to the general rule, Huon of Bordeaux made it a condition in his game that the spectators should keep silence.

That chess in the Middle Ages was a game involving risk of limb and even life will appear in the sequel. Players had yet to learn to win without excess of exultation, and to lose without loss of temper.

The Short Assize. The diagrams which I have used above in discussing the mediaeval 'Openings' all show positions in actual games in progress, the players themselves being depicted in the miniatures. There are, however, two other diagrams which show a different arrangement of the chessmen (but one that can still be obtained from the normal arrangement) without claiming to show positions in games in progress. These occur, the one in the early 15th c. problem MS. D (Dresden O/59), the other in some of the MSS. of both verse and prose versions of *Les Eschez amoureux*, e. g. MS. Venice, MS. Paris Fr. 143, f. 355, and MS. Paris Fr. 1508.

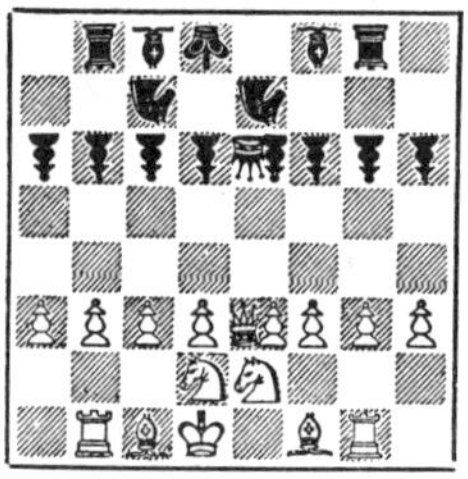

From MS. Dresden O/59, f. 81b.

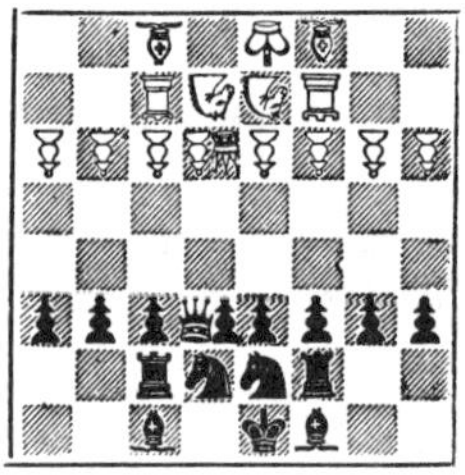

From MS. Paris Fr. 143, f. 355.

In the Dresden MS. the position follows a diagram of the normal arrangement of the chessmen (K d1 and d8) to which the following text is attached:

Cest le premier gieu que xerces le philozophe trouua des eschies. Et peut chascun eschet (i.e. chessman) passer .iii. poins au premier trait. Et puis il ne doit aller fors selonc la nature de son trait seulement.

The second diagram in the MS. has the following text attached:

C'est lautre gieu que le philozophe trouua et en ceste assiete chascun est en garde lun de lautre. lon ne les puet aler prendre en leur siege sans estre pris. Et le mieux est de traire tous iours en garde.

The diagram is somewhat carelessly executed, and I think the Kt(c7) should be on d7 to preserve the symmetry of the arrangement, and to defend the P (f6) since the text makes such a point of the fact that every piece is guarded by another.

The other position shows the initial arrangement of the chessmen for the game between the lady and her suitor, the account of which, occupying some 580 lines of the 30,060 of the poem, has given the romance its title. In the Paris MSS. each square of the unchequered board bears its designation in the notation of the MS. K, and the positions of the chessmen are indicated, not by their proper names but by the qualities of which they are supposed in the poem to be symbolical. The arrangement only differs from that intended in the MS. D in the position of the Rooks.

The extraordinary point about both diagrams is, of course, the position of the Queens, which are placed upon the same square as the Queen's Pawns. The posting of two chessmen upon a single square is so opposed to all the usual rules of chess that v. d. Linde in copying the Dresden MS. rectified the position without remark by advancing the Queen's Pawns each a square to d4 and d5, and the position is so diagrammed by v. d. Lasa in the *Forschungen* (110), while Dr. Sieper (*Les échecs amoureux*, Weimar, 1898), in reproducing the diagram of Paris MS. Fr. 143, omitted the Queens altogether.

It is, however, quite certain that the diagrams are not in error in this point. As will be seen below, the text of the romance *Les Eschez amoureux*, in both the original poem and the prose version, expressly state that the Queen and Pawn occupy a single square, and in the course of the game the lover loses both Queen and Pawn at one stroke.

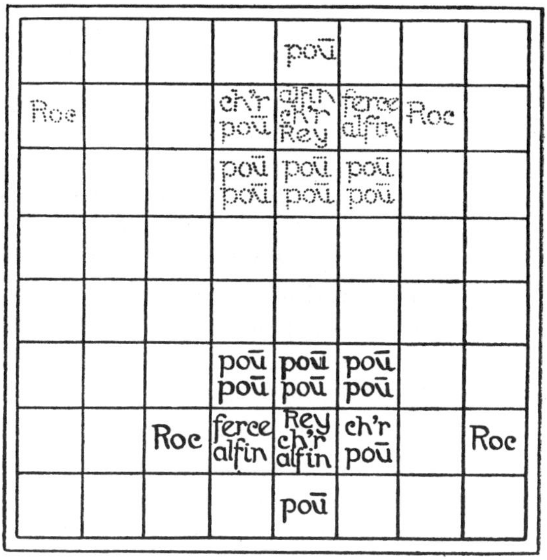

K 25. *Le guy de ly enginous e ly coueytous.*

A similar, but more extravagant position, in which as many as three pieces are placed upon a single square, is contained in the problem MS. K (K. 25, *Le guy de ly enginous e ly coueytous*), where it is said to be of the *short assize*.[58]

As a problem it is a very poor affair; there is no forced mate, but the first player (*ly enginous*) can mate the second (*ly coueytous*) in five moves in one of the *four points* with a Pawn, provided the second player plays to win pieces and not for defence. The MS. gives the solution 1 Kt(f2)e4, ~; 2 Kt × Ps(d6), K × Kt; 3 Bb4 +, Kd5 or e5; 4 Pe4, and 5 P m. It can, of course, be prevented in many ways. The sole importance of the problem lies in the light it throws upon the positions in D, and the MSS. of *Les Eschez amoureux.*

I think that we can fairly conclude that these latter diagrams also belong to the *short assize*, the problem exhibiting an extravagant version of the same assize. The name is derived from the shortening of the opening play which follows from the more advanced arrangement of the pieces, and suggests that the *long assize* was the game from the ordinary arrangement. The special features of the *short assize* would appear to be—

58 See the extract from the AF text, p. 594.

1. The initial arrangement of the chessmen for a game was different from that of the ordinary game of chess. Generally speaking, the chessmen occupied a more advanced position. The Pawns were placed on the third line, the Queen on her third square, and the other pieces were arranged symmetrically on the second and first lines. The arrangement of the two sides corresponded exactly.

2. In the opening arrangement it was permissible to place two pieces upon a single square. Each piece, however, moved separately, and no piece could move to a square already occupied by a piece of the same colour. This is clear from the problem solution.

3. The rules of play were identical with those of the European games before the introduction of any of the modifications of move. The game was won either by checkmating or by baring the opponent's King. The refinements of the ending by which mate was given with a particular piece, or on a particular square, played a prominent part in the games played from this assize.

There would appear to be an allusion to this assize, as contrasted with the ordinary game, in Neckam's chess chapter, in a sentence which has puzzled chess writers considerably. Neckam says:

> The Pawns are placed in one straight line, the rest of the chessmen according to different arrangements being allotted different positions. Yet according to the original invention of the game, the Pawns will be arranged on the second line of the chessboard, the men of higher rank being posted on the first line.[59]

If this be so, this variety of chess must have been played in Paris and England in the latter half of the twelfth century.

I regard this assize as another of the European attempts to improve the game of chess. It certainly adds interest to the game, and it would not be a difficult matter to investigate the possibilities of opening play in the position in the MS. D. I do not think that the assize is based upon anything that existed in the ordinary Muslim chess, although the experiment of placing the Pawns on the third line was attempted in the chess as-suʿdīya. The resemblance of the Dresden arrangement to that of aṣ-Ṣūlī's development *al-mutalāḥiq* is probably only a coincidence, which arose from the fact that both arrangements represent attempts to arrange the chessmen as quickly as possible in such a way that every piece on the board was guarded by another.

The romance *Les Eschez amoureux* describes in considerable detail the course of a game played from its initial arrangement. The description in the poem would have been unintelligible without the diagram, which, however, is not given in all MSS. of the poem, and very difficult to follow without the fuller text of the prose version. The use of the literal notation in the prose work fortunately removes every possibility of doubt as to the course of the game.

59 Wright, the editor of Neckam, supposed that the first sentence referred to the ordinary arrangement of the men, and the second sentence put forward a theory as to the original arrangement of the board, in which the Pawns occupied the back line, and the pieces were placed on the second line. V. d. Lasa (69), characterizing this as an unnatural rendering, argued that both sentences referred to the same arrangement—that of the ordinary game. I formerly held this view also, but the discovery of the evidence now set out has convinced me that Neckam had two assizes in view.

The first nine moves of the game are given exactly as they were played. From this point the course of the game is only sketched roughly, until a position is reached which is described so carefully that it can be set up on the board, and the concluding play from this point in which the lady gives mate in the angle with her Queen, is again given fully. The lady plays first, using what we should consider the Black men. I give the moves in our notation, and the texts of both versions.[60] The chessmen are to be arranged as in the figure on p. 476 from the Paris MS. Fr. 143.

	Moves.	Poem.	Prose version.
	Lady / Suitor		
1	Pb6–b5	Adont commencha la bataille, Qui me mist a desconfiture, S'en orez toute l'auenture. Quant la damoisell entendit Le dieu d'amours plus n'atendit ; Ains ala traire maintenant D'un paonnet trop auenant, ... Ce fu de celluy qui secons, Au lès de sa main destre estoit, Qui la rose en l'escu portoit ...	Le premier trait ... de la damoiselle ... fut d'ung sien paonnet qui estoit le second devers sa dextre main, lequel portoit en son escu l'enseigne d'une rose ... Elle trait donc premierement de *bl* en *bm* ...
1	Pb3–b4	Nientmains quant elle ot tant (v. trait) ainsy, Je tray d'un paonnet aussy Second vers ma senestre main. Ce fu pour traire plus ad plain Et plus droit encontre celly Qui à veir tant m'abelly ...	l'acteur ... trait aussi après, pour deffendre son jeu contre la damoiselle, de son paonnet qui portoit en son escu la clef, ... et fut celuy trait de *bo* en *bn*.
2	Pc6–c5	Adont la belle au doulz viaire, Sans plus attendre a la retraire Pour conforter son premier trait D'un paonnet de doulz attrait, Qui apprès l'autre estoit li tiers ...	Après ce trait aussi secondement la jeune damoiselle, pour conforter son premier trait, de *cl* en *cm* ...
2	Pc3–c4	... Je trais et boute auant Contre son trait comme deuant Vn paonnet : ce fu cely Qui en son escuchon poly Auoit le tigre figuré.	Et celluy après secondement retrait contre celuy aussi, c'est à savoir de *co* en *cn* du paonnet qui le tigre portoit...
3	Pb5 × Pc4	Mais il n'y a pas demouré Longuement, car elle le m'oste En trayant du paon sur coste Dont elle ot trait premierement Et par ce trait meïsmement Peuist ma fierge apprez reprendre S'auis n'euisse du deffendre ...	Le tiers trait de la damoiselle fut en trayant sur coste de Beaulté, c'est assavoir de *bm* en *cn*, et là print elle Doulx Penser ... en menassant la fierge de son adverse partie et le paon qui estoit avec elle.
		Nientmains je ne reculay pas, Ains voiz lors traire et me conforte D'un paonnet qui la clef porte. Si repris tout aussy le sien	Et pour ce retrait il après ce tiercement de *bn* en *cm*, où il reprint Simplesce de Regard en menassant aussi

[60] I give the poem from photographs of the Dresden MS. which Mr. J. G. White placed at my service, and the prose text from Prof. Mettlich's *Die Schachpartie in ... 'Les eschez amoureux'*, Münster i. W., 1907. For further particulars of the allegorical explanation of the chessmen, see Ch. VI below.

Moves.	Poem.	Prose version.
3 Pb4 × Pc5	Qu'elle auoit pris deuant le mien, En trayant par voye samblable Contre sa fierge esmerueillable Et contre le paon joly Qui estoit assis aueuc ly, A la fin que, s'elle prenoit Ma fierge, a quoy elle tendoit, Que je repreïsse la soye . . .	pareillement sa fierge avec le paonnet aussi qui la gardoit, car c'estoit son entencion, sicome il faint, s'elle prendroit sa fierge, qu'il reprendroit aussi après la sienne.
Pc4 × P & Qd3 4	Quant celle me vit ainsy traire Elle n'atendy pas ny (l. une) heure, Ains prist ma fierge sans demeure Et le paonnet ensement Qui fu dez le commencement Assiz en ce meisme lieu . . .	Le quart trait de la damoiselle fut après ce, de *cn* en *do*, où elle print sa fierge de Beaulté et le paon qui estoit avec elle . . .
4 Bf8 × Pd3 (*for it* 4 *Pc5 × P & Qd4* *Pd3 × Rc2*) 5	Or cuiday je pareillement Reprendre sa fierge ensement . . . Mais je m'arrestay vn petit, Se me suy adont perchëus, Que j'auoye esté dechëus, Et que trop euisse mespris Se j'euisse sa fierge pris : Car elle peuist sans mesprendre Vn de mes rocz pour néant prendre . . . Si ques de ce trait me refrains Et pris aussy comme constrains Le gentil paonnet parfait Qui m'auoit tel dompmaige fait De l'auphin qui a destre fu Qui le signe ot du ray de fu . . .	Adonc se trouva decëu l'acteur, sicome il faint, et se advisa que se il prenoit aussi pareillement sa fierge et son paon il perdroit après et pour néant ung de ses rocz . . et pour ce ne la print il pas; ains trait lors de son alphin dextre de *fq* en *do*, si print le paonnet qui luy avoit osté sa fierge dessus dite et son paon . . .
Ktd7 × Pc5 5	La belle de très gent atour Se rauisa d'un aultre tour Dont j'os plus fort temps que deuant; Car elle fist saillir auant Son cheualier a le licorne . . . Briefment la puchelle auenant A la traire plus n'attendy D'un cheualier que je vous dy S'en prist de la première voye Le paonnet dont je deuoye Prendre sa fierge à l'autre trait . . .	Après ce . . . elle fist saillir son chevalier avant qui portoit le unicorne . . . et en print lors le paonnet dont il cuydoit devant prendre sa fierge . . . C'est proprement à dire que Honte print Regard en trayant de *dk* en *cm*.

(The lover is at a loss what to move, and thinks a long time.)

Moves.	Poem.	Prose version.
5 Pg3–g4	Toutesfois pour le jeu parfaire Le dieu qui ne se pot plus taire M'escrie que je me deffende Et que je traye ou je me rende ; Si que je tray vaille que vaille Pour continuer la bataille : Ce fu se sauoir le voules Du paonnet de l'aultre lès Qui auoit le cigne pourtrait — Je ne soz faire meilleur trait	E celluy aussi . . . trait après ce, quant il se ravisa, ung de ses paonnetz devers sa dextre main qui portoit l'enseigne de ung fier cigne . . . et fut ce trait de *go* en *gn* . . .

Moves.	Poem.	Prose version.
6 Ktc5 × Bd3 + r	Adont prist elle mon aulphin Mais encore ot jl aultre fin, Car c'estoit eschec à mon roy Dont je fus mis en tel arroy Que j'en perdis mon rocq senestre . . .	A l'aultre trait après aussi, VIe, la jeune damoiselle trait de son chevalier mesmes, dessusdiz, de *cm* en *do* et la print son alphin . . . Et avec ce dist eschec a son roy . . . car elle en print aussi à l'autre trait son roc senestre pour le chevalier . . .
6 Ke1–f1	Quant j'oz cel eschecz percëu Dont trop me trouuay decëu J'ostay mon roy & en voiz traire, Pour ce qu'il estoit néccessaire Si le fis reculer vers destre Pour mains perilleusement estre.	Adonc l'acteur . . . retrait son roy vers dextre pour fouyr son eschec . . .
7 Rc7 × Rc2	Et celle qui peu me deporte Prent tantost mon rocq si l'emporte . . .	la damoiselle . . . ains print tantost son roc à son VIIe trait . . . en trayant de son roc . . . de *ck* en *cp*.
7 Ktd2–e4	(Omitted.)	Et celluy aussi après pour son roc second conforter retrait aussi après d'ung de ses chevaliers qui portoit le lyon . . . de *dp* en *en*.
8 Ktd3 × Rf2	A enuis l'euist respité, Car ses jeux estoit sans pité : Mais encor pas ne li souffist. Car à l'autre trait qu'elle fist Elle reuint l'aultre happer, Je n'en pos àmains eschapper ; Car il estoit aussy ou point De son cheualier tout apoint.	A l'autre trait aussi, VIIIe, la damoiselle qui n'estoit contente du roc qu'elle avoit pris, reprint son roc qui portoit la coulombe en son escut, . . . et le print de son chevalier . . . en trayant de *do* en *fp*.
8 Kte4 × Ktf2	Sans faille pour mon rocq secont Pris je son cheualier adont Du mien dont deuant trait auoie Pour le mettre hors de sa voie . . . Ainsy perdis je mes deux roz Pour son cheualier que jou roz . . .	Et celluy aussi le reprint, sans demeure, de son chevalier dessusdit en trayant de *en* en *fp* . . .
9 Kte7–d5	[Omitted in Dresden : Venice has— Quant celle qui tant ha de pris Vit que j'os son cheualier pris, Elle fit salir l'autre auant (s. paour) Pour moy plus greuer que deuant . . .]	Quant la damoiselle advisa qu'il avoit prins ainsi son chevalier, elle fist son IXe trait de son aultre senestre chevalier, qui portoit l'enseigne du lièvre . . . et fut ce trait de *ek* en *dm*.
9 Pe3–e4	Lors tray je sans delayement Vn paon que en ordre yert quins, Et vne grant pièce me tins Contre la belle à mon pouoir S'en yert li jeux biaux à veoir.	Et celluy aussi retrait encontre elle d'ung de ses paonnetz qui portoit le liepart . . . et fut celluy trait de *eo* en *en*.

It would be too long, says the romance, to give all the moves of the game. It will be sufficient to give the principal moves only. After many moves had been made, and many pieces taken, the Lady made several moves with her Queen and a Pawn which always followed the Queen to defend it and be defended by it. At which moves the Lover marvelled greatly, and took so much pleasure in them that he forgot all his game. But who could oppose her moves? Not even Philometer, nor Ulysses himself, the first discoverer of chess. The Lady advanced her Queen and Pawns steadily, playing the latter in good order to defend the Queen. The Lover moves now here, now there, as the game required. After a while he moves his Pawn with the mirror (KBP), and, dazzled by the sight of the precious chessmen reflected in the mirror, he exclaimed that he did not mind whether he was mated or made bare (*ave*) by his opponent. At last the game came to this position:

Black: Ke8, Rf1, g2, Qb4, Bc4, Pa5, f6.
White: Ka1, Bc1, Pf5.

The Lady had left him two pieces: *pour ce sont ces deux eschez du moins necessaire au mat faire.* But the Lady remained with so many pieces herself that she could mate him easily on any square that she liked, even in the four points themselves.

The game now concluded:

Poem.

Elle fist son paon saillir
Et sa fierge très avenant
Pour parfaire le remenant.
Quant ordonné les ot à point
Elle dont je ne me plaing point
Du paonnet de bel arroy
Me vint dire eschec à mon roy
Qui s'estoit vers mon aulphin trais
Si qu'il convint, qu'il fust retrais
En l'angle sans plus longue attente,
Et puis de la fierge excellente
A la fin que tout consommât
Elle me dist eschec et mat.

Prose version.

Pour ce fist celle damoiselle de son paonnet dessus dit qu'elle avança deux traitz dont le premier fut de *am* en *an* et le second fut de *an* en *ao* et le tiers après fut de sa fierge de *bn* en *co*. Et pour ce que le Roy qui est ainsi encloz n'a point ou il puist traire si ce n'est de *aq* en *bq* et de *bq* en *aq* retourner, et il convient qu'il traye quant il n'y a aultre eschec qui puist traire, come il est en ce cas: se nous considérons donc bien, il est nécessité que le paonnet dessusdit, au quart trait qu'il fera, le treuve lors en *bq* et qu'il luy dye eschec, en trayant de *ao* en *ap*. Et lors sauldra la fierge qui traira de *co* en *bp*, en luy disant eschec et mat en l'angle.

That is:

$$1\ \frac{\text{Pa4}}{\text{Kb1}},\ 2\ \frac{\text{Pa3}}{\text{Ka1}},\ 3\ \frac{\text{Qc3}}{\text{Kb1}},\ 4\ \frac{\text{Pa2}}{\text{Ka1}},\ 5\ \frac{\text{Qb2}}{\quad}\ \text{mate.}$$

There only remains the record of the attempts during the Middle Ages to improve chess by means of the enlargement of the board. Three such varieties of chess are described in the Spanish MS. Alf., viz. a game on a board of 10 × 10 squares, another on a board of 12 × 12 squares, and a third on the ordinary board which was played by four players. No special stress is laid upon these games in the MS., and I am inclined to think that the compiler of the MS. obtained them from Muslim sources. I have accordingly already described them in connexion with the Oriental modifications of chess.[61] The only other game of the kind which is mentioned in works of the mediaeval period is one which appeared at an early date in Germany and, after an exceptionally long life for an enlarged variety of chess, only became obsolete in the village of Ströbeck, its last home, towards the beginning of the 19th century.

This game, known as the *Courier game*, was played upon a board of 12 × 8 squares between two sides of 24 pieces each, the board being placed with the longer sides adjacent to the players. Each player had the 16 pieces of the ordinary chess, and in addition two Couriers, one Counsellor or Man, one *Schleich*, and four more Pawns. The pieces were arranged as in the diagram.

The pieces borrowed from the ordinary chess possessed the mediaeval powers of move, wit the following modifications: the Queen could for its first

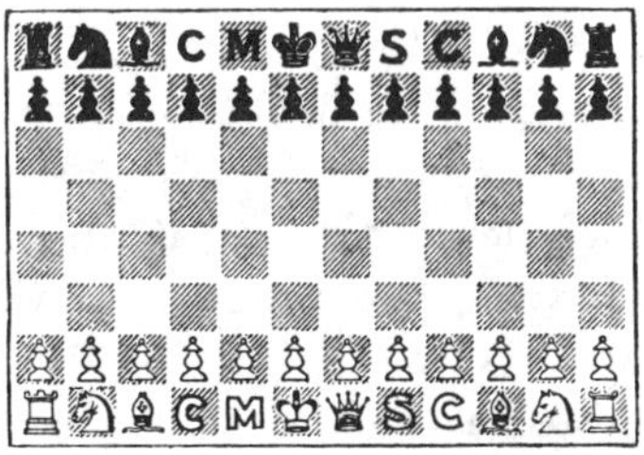

The Courier Game. After Selenus.
(C = Courier ; M = Rath or Mann ; S = Schleich.)

move leap to its third square ; the Rook's and Queen's Pawns only could make the double step for their first move. The King had no power of leaping. The *Courier* moved precisely as our modern Bishop ; the *Schleich* could move to an adjacent square in a vertical or horizontal direction, i. e. to an adjacent square of a different colour to its own square : its move was the complement of that of the Queen in the mediaeval game. The *Man* could move to any adjacent square : its move was identical with that of the King without the limitations to the latter's freedom of move.[62]

It was obligatory to commence playing by advancing the two Rooks' Pawns and the Queen's Pawn two squares each, and moving the Queen to her third square. The opponent did the same, and the subsequent play proceeded by alternate single moves as in the ordinary game of chess.

The game took its name from the Couriers, which were popularly supposed to be the most powerful pieces. This estimation was certainly wrong ; the Rook must have been far stronger.

The game was already in existence in the beginning of the 13th c., and it is mentioned in the *Wigalois* of Wirnt v. Gravenberg (1202–5, ed. Pfeiffer,

[61] See pp. 348–51.

[62] We know nothing of the rules of Pawn-promotion. In the special Ströbeck game, the Pawn had to return to his original square by means of three 'joy-leaps' (see p. 392). It is possible that this rule obtained in the Courier game also.

Leipzig, 1847), a very free translation of the French *Li bel inconnu* of Renaud de Beaujeu. Here it replaces the usual mention of chess:

> dâ lâgen vor der frouwen fier,
> wurfzabel (i.e. tables) unde kurrier
> geworht von helfenbeine;
> mit edelem gesteine
> spilten si, mit holze niht
> als man nu frouwen spilen siht.
> Si heten kurzewile vil
> von maniger hande seite spil
> daz die frowen kunden.

The game is also mentioned in two of the German (Alemanic) metrical versions of Cessolis. Heinrich v. Beringen (early 14th c.) briefly alludes to the introduction of the Couriers as an improvement of chess.[63] Kunrat v. Ammenhausen (1337) tells at considerable length how he had on one occasion seen in Constance a game with 16 more men than were in the 'right chess', each side having a *Trülle* (trull), two *Couriers*, a *Râtgeb* (counsellor), and four *Vendelîn* (Pawns). Excepting on that one occasion, he had never seen the game anywhere in Provence, France, or Kurwalhen.[64]

A painting in the Königliches Museum, Berlin, said to have been painted in 1520 by Lucas von Leyden, shows a game of Courier in progress. The board is chequered so that a1 is black.

Gustavus Selenus devoted a chapter of his *Das Schach- oder König-Spiel* (Leipzig, 1616) to the three games of chess which were played at Ströbeck,

63 hât ieman sîn iht mêr erdâht
dem spil ze bezzerunge,
daz velschet niht mîn zunge.
doch wizzet endelîchen daz,
daz sîn niht mêr von êrsten was.
Die kurrier sider sint erdâht
und in daz spil durch zierde brâht.

64 2623 Ouch wil ich zellen, die ich sach mê,
als ich hab gesprochen ê:
ze ietweder sîte aht steine,
vier grôsse und vier kleine;
die grôssen wil ich nennen,
so mügent ir si erkennen:
es ist ein trülle und zwên currier
und ein râtgeb, das werdent vier.
die son ze ietweder sîte stân
der röcher; ieklicher hân
sol vor im ein vendelîn:
die zellent, sô mügen ir sehzehen sîn
das wirt ietwedrent ahter mê;
die tuont zuo dien, die ich nand ê;
sô wirt ir ûf das bret ze vil.
. . . .
doch ist mir ze guoter mâs erkant
in Provenz und in Frankrich
und in Kurwalhen. doch gesach ich
nie, das dâ mê steine hat,
wan ze Kostenz in der stat,
dâ sach ich eins, kein anders nie
wan das, swar ich reit oder gie.
swas ieman anders hat gesehen,
dem gan ichs wol, wil ers verjehen.

Photograph by Hanfstaengl

The Chessplayers

By Lucas von Leyden. Königl. Museum, Berlin

and gives a valuable account of the Courier game, to which we owe all that is known of the method of play. He names the special pieces in the game *Currier*, *Man(n)* or *Geheimer Raht*, and *Schleich* or *Kurtzweyliger Raht*, L. *morio*; and gives woodcuts of these pieces, the Courier being a man galloping on horseback with a horn to his lips, the Man a long-bearded sage, the *Schleich* a fool with cap and bells.

The village of Ströbeck still possesses a board, on the one side marked with the 8 × 8 board, on the other with the 12 × 8 Courier board, with an inscription narrating that this game of chess and Courier was presented to the village by the Elector-Prince Frederick William of Brandenburg on May 13, 1651.[65] The inscription necessitates a1 in each game being white. The original silver pieces were lent in the 18th c., and never returned; but there is a complete set of wooden men for the game. The use of them had been forgotten when Silberschmidt and Lewis visited Ströbeck in 1825 and 1831 respectively. In more recent days, e. g. in 1883, the game has been occasionally revived as a curiosity.[66]

APPENDIX

I. The Alfonso MS. of 1283.

(2 *b*) . . . E por que el Acedrex es mas assessegado iuego e onrrando que los dados nin las Tablas; fabla en este libro primeramientre del & muestra como ha a seer el tablero fecho. & quantas casas ha en el. & quales son los iuegos & quantos, & como a nombre cada uno dellos & en quales casas an de seer. & como los mueuen iogando con ellos & tomando los unos con los otros & quales meiorias an los unos trebeios sobre los otros. E como han a seer apercebudos los jogadores de saber iogar en guisa que uenzcan: & non sean uençudos. & de como dan xaque al rey, que es el mayor trebeio de todos los otros: que es una manera de affrontar al sennor con derecho & de comol dan mate que es una manera de grant desonrra: assi como sil uenciessen ol matassen. E otros iuegos a y de muchas maneras. Pero todos fueron fechos a semeiança de las cosas que acaecieron segund los tiempos que fueron, o son, o podrien seer, mostrando de como los Reyes en el tiempo delas guerras en que se fazen las huestes, han de guerrear a sus enemigos punnando delos uençer. prendiendolos & matandolos o echandolos de la tierra. E otrossi como en el tiempo delas pazes han de mostrar sus thesoros & sus riquezas & las cosas que tienen nobles & estrannas. & segunt aquesto fizieron iuegos. los unos de .xii. casas. los otros de .x. los otros de ocho. los otros de .vi. & los otros de quatro. & assi fueron descendiendo fasta en una casa: que partieron en ocho partes. E todo esto fizieron por grandes semeianças segunt los saberes antigos: que usauan los sabios. Pero entre todos los otros iuegos escogieron por meior & mas comunal el delas .viii. casas: por que non es tan uagarosa, como el de las diez, o dent arriba. ni otros si tan appresurado: como el delas seys, o dent ayuso. E por endel usan comunalmientre los omnes [3 *a*]

[65] Dass Seren^{ssmus} Churfe. Durchl. Zu Brandenburg und / Fürst zu Halberstadt Herr Herr FRIEDRICH WILHELM etc. DIESES / SCHACH- und CURJER-SpIEL am 13 MAY Ao 1651 dem Fleken Ströpek / aus Sondern Gnaden verehret, und Bey ihrer alten Gerechtigkeit zu schützen / gnädigst zugesagt, solches ist zum ewigen Gedechtniss Hierauf verzeichnet.

[66] See *Sch.*, 1847, 214; 1853, 7; 1861, 223; 1883, 330. Also cf. a short article of mine, 'The Courier Game,' *BCM.*, 1902, 421.

en todas las tierras: mas que los otros iuegos. E la figura del tablero es que a de ser quadrado. & ha de auer ocho carreras: & en cada carrera ocho casas que son por todas sessaenta & quatro casas. E la meytad de las casas an de seer duna color & la meytad de otra: & otrossi los trebeios.

De quantas colores an de seer todos los trebeios del acedrex.

Los trebeios an de seer treynta & dos. E los xvi. duna color: deuen se entablar en las dos carreras primeras del tablero. E los otros dizeseyes dela otra color an de seer entablados dell otro cabo del tablero en essa misma manera: en derecho delos otros. E destos xvi. trebeios los .viii. son menores: que fueron fechos à semeiança del pueblo menudo, que ua en la hueste. E los otros iuegos que son mayores es el uno a semeiante del *Rey*: que es sennor de la hueste. & aquel deue estar en la una de las dos casas de medio. E cabo dell en la otra casa de medio: esta otro trebeio, que es a semeiança del alfferez que tiene la senna de las sennales del Rey. & algunos omnes: à que non saben el nombre. & llamanle: *alfferza*. E estos dos trebeios cada uno iuega por si & non a otro ninguno en todos los .xvi. trebeios: que los semeie. E en las otras dos casas al lado destas: estan otros dos trebeios que se semeian & llaman los *alffiles* en Algarauia que quiere tanto dezir en nuestro lenguaie: como *eleffantes* que solien los Reyes leuar, en las batallas, & cada uno leuaua al menos dos que si ell uno muriesse: quel fincasse ell otro. E en las otras dos casas cabo destas; estan otros dos trebeios que se semeian & llaman los todos comunalmientre *cauallos*. mas los sus nombres derechos son *caualleros*, que son puestos por cabdiellos por mandado del Rey: pora ordenar las azes de la hueste. E en las otras dos casas de cabo: (3*b*) estan otros dos trebeios que se semeian otrossi, e llaman los *Roques*. & son fechos anchos & tendudos que son a semeiança de las azes de los caualleros.

En la primera az estan los iuegos mayores que dixiemos. E en la segunda los peones. E como quier que estos iuegos son nueue quanto en las casas: no son mas de seys segund se doblan. Ca los alffiles & los Cauallos & los Roques que son seys: tornan en tres. & con el Rey & con el alfferza & con los peones que son cada uno por si: fazense seys. E pusieron los assi doblados. por que quando alguno daquellos toman: que finque otro di aquella natura pora dar xaque & mate al Rey: ò pora ampararle. Otrossi pusieron del alfferza que quando se perdiesse: podiendo llegar qualquiere delos peones fasta la casa postremera dell otra parte del Acedrex. onde mueuen los iuegos mayores: dent adelant fuessen alfferzas. & que se pudiessen desponer bien como la primera & andar dessa guisa. E esto es por que suben del estado de los menores al de los mayores.

El Rey pusieron que nol pudiessen tomar. mas quel pudiessen dar xaque por quel pudiessen fazer salir de aquel logar do souiesse: como desonnrado. E sil arenconassen de guisa que no ouiesse casa do yr. pusieronle nombre *xamat* que es tanto como muerto. & esto fizieron por acortar el iuego. Ca se alongarie mucho. si todos los trebeios ouiessen a tomar: fasta que fincassen amos los Reyes solos: o ell uno dellos.

Capitulo dell andamiento de los trebeios del acedrex.

El andar delos iuegos fue puesto otrossi por esta razon que uos diremos: ca assi como el Rey non se deue arrebatar en las batallas mas yr muy a passo & ganando siempre eldos enemigos & punnando como los venzca. assi el *Rey* delos trebeios: no a de andar mas de a una casa en so derecho. o en sosquino, como qui cata a todas partes en derredor dessi metiendo mientes en lo que ha de fazer.

Ell *alferza* anda a una casa en sosquino ; & esto es por aguardar al Rey & non se partir del, & por encobrirle delos xaques & delos mates quando gelos dieren & pora yr adelante ayu dandol a uencer quando fuere el iuego bien parado. Pero bien puede la primera uez saltar a tercera casa o en derecho o en sosquino & aunque este otro trebeio en medio. & esto es a manera de buen cabdiello, que se adelante en los grandes fechos & en las batallas & acorre a todas partes alli o lo an mester. E en este andamiento ayuntasse con los sus peones & bueluesse con ellos assi como si los esforçasse que non se partiessen & estudiessen en uno pora fazer lo meior & en esto aguarda assi, & a ellos teniendo los unos antessi : & parandosse ante los otros. E por ende quando ell alferza esta assi trauada con los peones : llamanle *Alfferzada.*

Los *alffiles* saltan a tres casas en pospunta a semeiança delos eleffantes que trayen entonce los Reyes. que no osaua ninguno parasseles delante & fazien les los que en ellos estauan yr en sosquino a ferir en las azes de sus enemigos de guisa que non se les pudiessen guardar.

Los *Cauallos* saltan a tres casas contando las dos en derecho dessi : & tomando la tercera en sosquino a qual parte quiere. E esto es a semeiança delos buenos cabdiellos, que acabdiellan las azes voluiendo los cauallos a diestro e a siniestro pora aguardar los suyos, & vençer los enemigos.

Los *Roques* iuegan en derecho quanto pueden yr antessi o a caga o a diestro o a siniestro. & esto a semeiança de las azes delos caualleros que uan todauia quanto pueden en derecho o contra qual parte entienden que sera meior. por que mas ayna puedan uencer a aquellos con que lidian :

(4 *a*) Los *Peones* non uan mas de a una casa en su derecho assi como la peonada de la hueste : non pueden andar si no poco por que uan de pie. & lievan a cuestas sus armas & las otras casas que an mester. Pero bien a y algunos que usan a iogar delos peones a tercera casa la primera uez. & esto es fasta que tomen ca depues no lo pueden fazer. E esto es a semeiança que quando el pueblo menudo roban algunas cosas : que las lieuan a cuestas.

Capitulo de qual manera deuen tomar con los juegos del acedrex.

El tomar de los iuegos unos a otros es desta guisa. El Rey toma en todas las casas que diziemos que podie yr : qualquiere trebeio dela otra parte que y este. sino ouiere y otro alguno dela otra parte de aquel trebeio quel ampare. E esso mismo fazen los otros iuegos mayores assi como los alffiles & los cauallos & los Roques. mas ell alfferza non puede tomar la primera uez sisse despusiere yendo a tercera casa. mas depues que fuere despuesta tomara en la segunda casa : en sosquino. segunt es su andamiento.

Los peones otrossi como quier que puedan yr a tercera casa la primera uez si quisieren : non pueden tomar en ella mas tomaran en sosquino yendo adelante a una casa. E esto es a semeiança delos peones que se non pueden ferir estando en derecho ell uno contral otro, aguardandosse : mas fiere all otro que esta en sosquino que se : no aguarda del tanto.

Capitulo delas auantaias de los trebeios dell acedrex.

Las auantaias delos trebeios que an los unos sobre los otros : son grandes. Ca el *Rey* es acotado en guisa que puede tomar a todos & ninguno non puede tomar a el. E esto es a semeiança del Rey que puede fazer iusticia en todos los que merecieren : mas por esso non deue poner la mano ninguno en el : pora prender le ; nin ferir le nin matarle: aunque el fiera o prenda o mate. Mas bien le pueden fazer uerguença en tres maneras: faziendol salir dela casa do esta, o embargandol la casa o quiere entrar: & nol dexar tomar lo que quiere.

Ell *Alfferza* a otrossi grant auantaia: por que guarda mas de cerca al Rey que los otros iuegos & es meior que los alffiles porque a mas casas en que puede andar & tomar que ellos. E otrossi guarda & toma adelante & atras: lo que los peones non pueden fazer como quier que faga alfferzada con ellos: segunt es sobredicho.

Los *Alffiles* an auantaia sobre los peones por que toman mas de luenne & fazen otrossi alfilada desta guisa. Quando ell alffil esta en el tablero, si algun peon esta depos ell a una casa en sosquino segunt su andamiento: guarda el peon al alffil. E si otro peon esta en guarda del primero en la otra casa do ell alffil puede yr: guardal ell alffil. E desta guisa se guardan todos tres uno a otro. & a esto llaman *Alffilada.*

El *cauallo* a mayor auantaia que todos los otros trebeios dell *acedrex*, sino el Roque. ca el que sopiere con el cauallo bien iogar mouiendol de la primera casa dell un canto del tablero: tomara quantos trebeios fueren en todas las casas del tablero que son sessaenta & tres: sin la casa dondel mouiere: que nunqua yerre de tomar segunt su andamiento.

El *Roque* a mayor auantaia que todos los otros trebeios dell acedrex por que puede yr en una uez dell un cabo del tablero fastal otro en su derecho, a qual parte quisiere. si no estuviere en la carrera algun trebeio delos suyos quel embargue o otro ageno que tome por que avera de fincar en la casa daquel que tomo.

Capitulo de como el Rey & todos los otros trebeios del acedrex pueden andar & tomar: los unos en todas las casas del tablero: los otros en dellas.

El *Rey* puede andar & tomar en todas las casas del tablero en .lxiiii. uezes; (4 *b*) & tornarse a su casa.

Ell *alfferza* puede andar en treynta & tres uezes todas las casas del tablero que el la deue andar: & tornarse a su casa. pero nol contando quandol acaece por fuerza de entrar dos uezes en una casa.

Ell *alffil* puede andar & tomar a seys casas del tablero con la suya: & no a mas.

El *peon* puede seer fecho alfferza en .vj. uezes que ande las casas una a una & tornarse a su casa pues que fuere alfferzado en tantas uezes: como la otra alfferza. andando todas las casas del tablero que puede andar: E maguer que dos uezes entre en una casa nolo podiendo escusar: que non sea contada mas de por una.

Ell andar del *Roque* non puede seer contado por que anda luenne & cerca por todo el tablero poro quiere en so derecho a todas partes: segunt su andamiento.

E estos andamientos todos conuienen que los sepan aquellos que bien quisieren iogar ell acedrex, ca menos desto no lo podrien saber. nin entender los iuegos departidos que an sabor de saber los omnes. por ell enoio que an dell alongamiento del mayor iuego quando se faze todo complidamientre, bien como metieron por aquella razon misma los dados en ell acedrex, por quesse iogasse mas ayna.

E pusieron el seys que es la mayor suerte del dado: al Rey que es el mas onrrado iuego del tablero. E el cinco all alfferza. E el quatro al Roque. E el tres al cauallo. E el dos: all alffil. E ell un punto que llaman As: al peon.

E por que los iuegos dell acedrex se departen de muchas maneras maguer que fagan en ellos iuegos departidos: en algunos y a que toman los trebeios todos: & en los otros dellos. Queremos uos aqui fablar primeramientre del iuego que se faze de todos los trebeios complidos & mostrarmos de como es fecho el tablero, & las fayciones delos trebeios. mas las que se fazen meior & mas complidamientre: an de seer fechas desta manera.

El *Rey* deue estar en su siella con su corona en la cabeça & la espada en la mano assi como si iudgasse o mandasse fazer iusticia.

Ell *alfferza* deue seer fecha a manera del alfferez mayor del Rey que lieua la senna delas sennales del Rey quando an a entrar en las batallas.

Los *alffiles* an a seer fechos a manera de eleffantes & castiellos en cima dellos llenos de omnes armados: como si quisiessen lidiar.

Los *cauallos* an de seer fechos a manera de caualleros armados: assi como cabdiellos que son puestos por mandado del rey pora acabdellar las azes.

Los *Roques* deuen seer fechos assi como azes de caualleros armados que estan much espessas teniendosse unos a otros.

Los *Peones* an a seer fechos a manera del pueblo menudo que estan armados & guisados quando quier lidiar. Mas: por que en todas las tierras que iuegan el acedrex serien muy grieues de se fazer tales iuegos como estos: buscaron los omnes manera de como se fiziessen mas ligeramientre, & mas sin costa: pero que se contrassemeien en algun poco a aquestos que diximos. E la figura dellos que es mas usada en todas las tierras e sennaladamientre en Espanna es esta que aqui esta pintada.

(5 *a*) Pves que acabado auemos el iuego mayor del acedrex de como se iuega complidamientre: Queremos dezir de los iuegos departidos que assacaron los omnes. en el que son como cosas nueuas & estrannas de oyr. & por esso se pagan dellas. & otrossi por que se iuegan mas ayna. Ca son iuegos contados. & sabudos. & saben a quantas uegadas depues que iogaren: san dacabar. Pero fablaremos primero delos mayores iuegos departidos que se fazen con todos los trebeios del acedrex: que non cuellen ende ninguno. & depues diremos de como uan minguando fasta los menos que pueden seer. E queremos luego dezir: del iuego que llaman *forçado.* E esto es por que como quier que se iuegue por cuenta: A en el dauer fuerça, por que ua omne contra su uoluntad. perdiendo el meïor trebeio por el peor, & auiendolo a fazer: queriendo o non poniendol en casa que ell otrol aya a tomar por fuerça, segund ell andamiento del trebeio so quel pusiere. E este iuego se entabla bien como el primero & daquella guisa andan los trebeios: & se toman unos a otros. sino que es y la fuerça demas. E por ende an a seer sabidores los quel iogaren, que non pongan los trebeios meiores: en logar que los ayan a dar por los menores e mas uiles. Ca en esto yaze toda la ssabiduria deste iuego, & el departimiento. E por esta fuerça que diximos, le llaman *iuego forçado.*

Mas por que algunos cuentan que las donzellas le fallaron primero en la tierra de Vltra mar: dizen le *iuego de Donzellas.*

II. Description of the Lombard Assize in MS. Paris Fr. 1173 (PP.).

(f. 3 *a*) Pour chou ke tout chil ki che liure v*er*ro*n*t puissent mix *et* plus legiereme*n*t sauoir *et* entendre *com*ment ne en quele maniere ches *par*tures ki en che *pre*sent liure sont contenues sont ordenees *et* selon quele assise eles so*n*t baillies. car assises se diu*er*sefient en pluseurs manieres. si doivent tout sauoir ke eles sont ordenees selonc lassise lombarde. ki est tele ke en che *pre*sent eskiek*er* est contenu.[1] Et deves savoir ke selonc ceste assise li paounet salent au tiert poi*nt*. le *pre*mier trait ke il t*ra*ient ou vn sans pl*us, et* ne pueent *pre*ndre fors ke .i. point *pre*s dans selonc droite prise de paounet. Et saut li rois (f. 3 *b*) vn point o .ij. o .iij. o .iiij. le *pre*mier t*ra*it co*m*ment ne en quele maniere ke il li plaist. mais ke il ne voist par un eskiec. *et* li roiine saut o .i. point o .iij. le *pre*mier t*ra*it *et* li roys *et* li roine juent ensaule le *pre*mier trait se il vuelent o chascuns par lui. Et puet on *pre*ndre toute le gent *et* demeure li rois tous seus et li conuient t*ra*ire trait por t*ra*it tant ke il plaist a se contre partie ne n'i a point daiue[2]. Et quant uns paounes se fait roine soit en langle ou dautre part il saut .iij. poins. le *pre*mier t*ra*it en quel liu ke che soit. o .i. se il li plaist. Et est ceste assise forte *et* soutiue *et* anieuse a bien sauoir, *et* pour chou conuient ke on en ait lusage.

III. Extracts from Egenolff's Frankfort Edition of Mennel's Schachzabel, 1536.

(Title) Des Altenn Ritterlichenn spils des Schachzabels / grüntlich bedeutung vnnd klarer bericht / dasselbig künstlich zuziehenn vnnd spilen. Mit eim newenn zusag ettlicher besonderen meisterstück / nach der Current / welschen art / vñ von Hutten / deszgleichen ettlichenn besondern Regeln des Schachziehens / vormals nie auszgangen (followed by diagram of board with pieces arranged on a and h lines, a1 being white, and 6 lines of verse addressed Zu dem Schachzieher).

(A. ij *b*) Von form vnd gestalt desz Schachzabel brets / vnnd seinen vnderschyden feldern.—Das sachbret helt in jme Fier und sechtzigk vnderscheyd oder veldt / Deren das ein halbtheil schwartz / vnd das ander halbtheil weisz sein sollen / vnnd ist gestalt wie die nachuolgend Figur auszweist. . . .

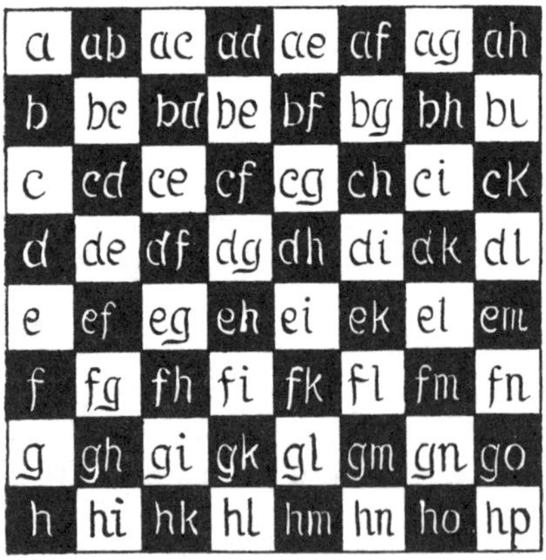

(A. iij) . . . Wie die Bilder odder stein nach rechter ordenung vnnd art disz Spiels inn das schachbret / gestelt werden sollen / Vnnd zum ersten von den Schwartzenn steinen oder Bildern. Der schwartz König sol am erstenn gestelt werden auff das weisz feldt / Vnnd sol neben jme die Künigin stehn auff dem schwartzen feldt / zu der rechten seitten. . . .

(A. iv) Wie einn ieglicher Steinn odder Bilde sein auszgang haben solle / Vnd zu dem ersten von den König.—Der Künig in seinem erstenn auszgang so er zu feldt ziehenn will / mag (ob er will / drey schritte von dem feldt seines auszgangs / das ist auff das vierd feldt) gegen seinenn feindenn reittenn / vnnd auff

[1] The chess diagram on f. 3 *a* shows the ordinary arrangement of the board (h1 white), and the pieces (red Ke1, gold Ke8).

[2] The reading here—quite distinct in the MS.—has led to a deal of trouble and erroneous reasoning. V. d. Linde corrected the word *daiue* into *dame,* and assumed that *dame* meant chessman or game-piece in general. On this he built up an elaborate theory of the origin of the chess name *dame* for the Queen, and also of the origin of the game of draughts. *Aiue* is the ordinary Picard form of the OF. *aïde,* our word *aid,* with the same meaning. The suggestion that *aiue* might be a form of *ave, have* (see p. 467), the OF. chess term for 'bare King', is rejected as impossible by all the Romanic scholars whom I have consulted.

dem selbenn feldt halten bleiben / oder auch auff dem zweitten / odder auff dem dritten / alles nach seinem gefallen vnd gestalt der züge seins widertheils / das er keins schachs besorgenn dürffe. Er mag auch zu dem selben seinen ersten auszgang ein Fendlin so jn hindert / fürsich stossen auff das nechst feldt / vnnd darnach fürter nach seiner ordnung gan. Das ist nach dem erstenn auszgang alweg auff das nechst feldt so vmb jnn ist / jm am meinsten geliebt. Also mag er gerings vmb sich / auff das ander feldt gehn / hinder sich / für sich / vnnd neben sich über ort / auff schwartz vnd weisz felder / alles nach seinem willenn / gefallen / vnd gelegenheit / Vnd mag auch also nemen vnd rauben / doch hab er acht auff die Schach.

Von der Künigin. — EJnn jegliche Küniginn sol durch die felde jrer farb / über ort / vnnd nit anderst spacieren mögenn gehen. Vnd so sie ausz jrem here (das ist vonn jrem standt) zum ersten mal gehn wil / sol sie nit über zwen schritte (das ist über das dritt feldt) sich herfürthun. Darnach sol sie alweg auff das ander feldt ghan. Jst sie weisz / so geht sie über eck auff ein weisz feldt. Jst sie schwartz / so geht sie über eck auff ein schwartz feldt.

Von den Alten. — DJe Altenn gehnd vnnd springenn überzwerch auff das dritt feldt / also. Welcher Alt auff einem weissenn feldt stehet / musz dasselbig nicht verwandelenn / sonnder widderumb auff das dritt weisz (A. iv *b*) weisz (*sic*) feldt geschrenckt über ort schreitten / hindersich / fürsich / nebensich / vnnd mag auch also auff alle ort rauben vñ nemen. Der gestalt sol sich der schwartz Alt auch haltenn.

Von den Rittern.—Die streitbarn Ritter mögenn allwegenn auff das dritt feldt gegen den Feinden springen / also / Welcher auff einem weissen feldt gerüst helt / musz über ort auff ein schwartz feld sprengenn / vnnd sich inn dieselbig ordenung schicken / vnnd welcher auff eim schwartzen feldt helt / über ort auff ein weisz feldt springen. — Hie bei ist zumercken das der Ritter zwen sprüng hat / ein nahern vñ ein fernern / welcher einer so vil gilt als der ander Exempel / der Ritter so auff ag steht / mag auff bf springen / ist ein naher sprung / er mag auch auff ch springen / das ist ein ferner sprung / ist einer als vil als der ander / Deszgleichenn mugen auch die andern für vnnd für durchs gantz spiel auszthun.

Von den Rachen. — Die Rach lauffenn schnell / vnnd widerstreben allen feinden / sie durchreitten alle felder / weisz vnnd schwartz / hinder sich / fürsich / nebensich / auff beiden seitten (aber schlecht / vn nit über ort) wo sie frey feldung vmb sich habenn (das ist / so ferr jnen sunst kein stein im weg steht) vnd was sie ergreiffen / rauben vnd nemen sie auch also.

Von den Fendlin. — Demnach allen obgenanten steiñ odder Bildern / als dem König / der Künigen / Alten / Rittern / vnnd Rachen / Fuszknecht (das seind Fendelin) für gestelt werden / solt du wissen / das dieselben fendelin / so sie zu dem ersten auszgehn wöllen / mögenn auff das erst odder zweit feldt schlecht fürsich gehn / alle die weil noch kein steiñ genommen ist. So aber einer (B. i) odder mehr steinn genommenn seind / so mag als dann kein Fendlin ferrer dann auff das nechst feldt / vor jm / gehn / auszgescheiden die zwey ort fendlin / die vor den Rachen stehnd / mögen zu allen zeitten jres ersten auszgangs gehn auff das zweit feldt / Vnnd mag kein fendlin fürsich / sonder musz alweg über ort nemen odder rauben. Wann auch ein Fendlin vnuerhindert were von seinem gegentheil / so möcht es allweg auff das nechst feldt für vnnd für gehn / als lang bisz es zu dem ende an die spang kompt. So es die erreycht / so hat es erlangt die freiheit der frawen / also / das es darnach widerumb heim gehn mag / als die Künigin über ort / die auch zu dem erstenn auff das dritt feldt / vnnd darnach auff das ander odder zweit feldt / alles nach jrem willenn / schreitenn mag.

Von den Priuilegierten oder gefreitten steinnen. — Also hastu hie nun zumerckenn / das ausz oberzelten steinnen etliche seinn / so sondere freiheyt vnnd recht haben / als erstlich der König / Solcher mag wie oben gemelt / des ersten zugs vff das zweitt oder dritt feldt gehn / so jm geliebt / Jtem ob jn ein fend an solchem seinem auszgang hindern würde / möcht er denselbigen für sich stossenn vnnd jm platz machen. Auch möcht er so es von nöten were / vnnd es sein gelegenheit erfordert / die Künigin im ersten mit sich auszfüren neben seiner seitten als weit als er geht / doch sol er sie auff jrer farb lassen. Deszgleichenn mag die Künigin im ersten gang auch auff das dritt feldt gehn so es jr geliebt / Item die zwen eck fenden mögenn allweg vff das dritt feldt ziehen in jrem ersten auszgang / es seien steinn geraubt odder nit. Aber die übrigenn stein habenn kein freiheit / sonder müssen bei jren ordenlichen rechten bleiben.

Doch so merck hie bei dise gemeine Regel. — (B. i *b*) Demnach der König / Küngin / vnnd die Fendlin vor andern steinen im erstenn auszgang ferrer zu gehn macht haben / Solt du wissen das der selben keins in seinem ersten gefreitten auszgang rauben oder nemen darff / sonder darnach inn den andern zügen / nach dem ersten auszgang / das behalt in gedechnusz.

Noch ein Regel. — So dem König ein Schach gebotten würt / musz er weichen vnd so es sein erster auszgang were möcht er in das dritt feldt (so es die not also erfordert gehn) entweichen / er dorfft aber in solchem seinem auszgang durch kein Schach gehn / das ist / so jm vff dem feldt dardurch er gehn wil / künt ein Schach gebotten werden / darff er durch das selb nit schreitten / sonder müst es sunst vmbgehn.

Vngefarlicher bericht vnd anweisung wie sich ein angehender Leeriung desz Ritterlichen Schachzabelspiel schickenn vnnd lernen solle / dein streit anzuheben / die stein zu ziehen / sein Feinden zubegegnen / widerfechten / abbrechen / nemen / vnd sie fahen solle. — So nun der Schwartz vnnd Weisz König zu streitten vnnd auszzuziehen bereit seind / vnnd einer wider den andern fechtenn wil / als dann sol der / so am erstenn anhebt / seinn vngewapnet fusz volck (das seindt die Fendlin) wider die streitbarenn Ritter / vnnd die starckenn Rach seins gegentheils / in das feldt zuziehen ordnen / sie reitzen / vnnd gegen jnen fechten lassenn / vnnd inn solcher ordnung / wie nachuolgt / sie anschicken.

Zu dem ersten / soltu nach dem Spruch der Alten Schachzieher / alweg den Fendenn vor den Frawenn am erstenn ziehenn / dann so du nit thust / mag dich einn fürsichtiger Schachzieher im dritten oder vierden zug matten / Vnnd wirt dieser Fende gemeinlich den erstenn zug auff das dritt (B. ii *a*) feldt fürsich gezogen / wie auch oben gemelt.

Nach diesem ersten zug hab acht auff deinen feind / vnnd zeücht er zum ersten seiner Ritter einen / so verware du dein vorgezogen ersten Fendenn / mit deinenn andern Fenden / so werden alsz dann bald drey Fenden auff einn ander warten.

Hie merck / das du den selben dein ersten auszgezogen Fendenn / nit mit dem Fenden der vor dem König steht verwaren solt / lasz jn vor dem König stehn / vnnd ziehe ein andern zu hilff dem ersten.

Nach diesem zug sehe dich aber wol für / vnnd ziehe der ort Fenden einen der vor dem Rach steht / Vnnd nach dem selben ziehe den andern Fenden vor dem Rach auch / so dein Feindt dir dasselb feldt nit verstelt / Vnnd mögen die selben ort Fenden auff das drit feldt gehn / es sei geraubt oder nit / wiewol etlich sollichs nit zulassen wöllen.

Darnach ziehe deinen Altenn hinder den Fendenn der bei der Künigin gestanden ist / vor das Rach.

Demselben nach / ziehe den andern Altenn auch auff das feldt darauff er gehört vnnd geht.

Nach dem / mach deinn hut auff welche seit dich dunckt am bestenn / vnnd also / das ie ein stein den andern verwaren möge / Vnnd hab sonderlich acht welch seit deinn widertheil sein hut machen wil / das du dein hut auff die ander seit machest.

So das also auszgericht / als dann ziehe deinn Ritter beide herfür / vnnd lasz sie ein weil allein Ritterlichen fechten / redlich rauben / vnnd was sie ergreiffen mögenn / nemmenn vnnd inn sack stossen.

Auff das sehe dich wol vmb / vnnd wirt es dir müglich / so ziehe die beide Rach zuhauff / hinder die vnuerwartenn Fenden. Dann so dieselbenn Fenden genommen werdenn / odder hinweg gezogenn / so sehenn dein Rach vonn eim ort zu dem anderen / vnnd mögenn leichtlich raubenn vnnd nemen.

Du junger Schachzieher / hab inn deinem ziehenn alweg (B. ii *b*) auffsehens / das du über eck / odder über ort ziehest / also / So deinn gegentheil / sein hut auff der linckenn seittenn / vnnd du deinn hut auff der rechtenn seittenn hast / so ziehe deinn Rach auff der linckenn seittenn herfür / alsz bald es sich schickenn wil / vnnd arbeit für vnnd für / über eck / zu deines gegentheils spitzenn / an dem ende seiner hut / das du daselbst mögst inbrechenn / so magstu desto Ritterlicher gesigenn / vnnd das feldt behalten.

Vnd solt wissen / das nichts grössers in disem Ritterlichen spil ist / dann das du die augen nit in seckel legest. . . .

(E. iii *a*) Von hütten / was die seien / vnnd wie die zumachenn sampt etzlichenn gutten Exempeln.—Ein ieder Schachzieher thut weiszlich vnnd wol wenn er in seinem spilen erstlich den König in ein sicher hut stelt / vnnd demnach mit dem übrigenn zeuge gegen den feinden arbeittet. Nun ist ein hut anders nicht denn dasz der König mit etlichenn gepreüchlichen steinen also versehen vnnd versichert wirt / das er rüig stehen / vnd des Schachbiettens / durch solchen schirm seiner stein / sicher sein möge / welches dann gar ein grosser vortheil vnd behelff in diesem spil ist / Dann so der könig blosz steht / vnd zun (E. iii *b*) seittenn odder sunst mag alweg mit dem Schach reycht werdenn / so wirt er gar leichtlich veldtflüchtig / vnnd musz einn statt nach der andern raumenn / dessenn er dann alles durch die hutten gesichert sein kan.

Die beste hutt ist die / so sich alle stein wol zusamen schliessenn / vnnd ie einer den andern doppel verwart. Auch ist die hutt besser vnnd bestendiger an orten dann mittenn im veldt/vnnd nützer vonn wenigenn steinenn dann von vielenn.

Einn gutt vnd sicher hutt zumachen / so zeug wie volgt. Erstlich deinn könig seer vff hm / so zeug denn Fendenn vor dem Alten vff ek. im zweitten zug vff di. im dritten denselb gen zuhulff den fenden vor dem König vff ei. demnach zeug den Fenden vor der Künigin vff nechst veldt das ist fi. (mit solchen dreien zügen der fenden magstu es ongeferlich haltenn). demnach zeug den einn Altenn vff fn. vnnd so das veldt mit di bezeichent / durch die ersten Fenden geraumpt vnnd gesichert ist / so zeug denn selbigen Altenn vff fn. volgents daselbst drauff / vnd dann den anderen Alten vff fk. den Fenden vff go. zeug vff em / den Alten vff fk. zeug vff dk. demnach zeug den König vff cm. vnd füre die Künigin mit jm ausz vffs dritt veldt vff fl. So nun die steinn also stehnn / so heist es einn hutt / vnnd ist der König vorm Schachen sicher.

Ein ander gute hutt so man die eisern hutt nennet.—So der König vff. hl. steht / so zeug den einen ort Fenden vff e. demnach den fenden vorm König vff hk. das ist sein nechste statt / dein Altenn am König zeug vff f. dein Ritter an selben Alten zeug vff fh. demnach zeug den König vnd füre zusampt mit jme ausz die Künigin in eim zug / also / das der König stehe vff hi. die Künigin vff hk. So (E. iii *a*) ist also die Künigin über eck erstes auszgangs gangenn ins dritt veldt / So nun die stein also stehn / so heist es die eisern hutt vnnd ist einn gute sichere hutt.

Noch einn gute hutt / vnnd die behend zumachen ist.—Der König stehe vff hm. Nun so zieg den Fenden vor der Künigin ausz / vffs dritt veldt / das ist eh. denn so zeug den König ausz vffs gi. so findt er aber ein Fendenn vff dem selben veldt / den mag er (wie oben gelert) im erstenn auszgangk wol fürtschiebenn / vnnd an die statt stehn / Item mit dem könig zieg als bald auch die Künigin ausz in dritt veldt vff fi. also hastu inn zweienn zügenn auch einn gutte hutt.

Sunst sein noch viel gutter hutenn / aber ausz teglichem brauch wirdestu die selbigen wol selber erfaren / vnnd lassen sich auch die hutten (wie sunst disz gantz spiel) besser mit dem augenscheinn lernenn / dann ausz dem vorschreibenn.

Auch soltu es nit verstehn / als ob die züge also eben vff einander gezogenn werdenn mögenn / sonder magstu wol einn andere ordnung darin fürnemenn / vnnd ietzt hie dann dort einen ziehen / so du die stein doch endtlich also ordenst wie ich dir angezeigt hab / vnnd wie sie in der hutt stehn solenn.

Wie sich der gegentheil halten soll.—Der gegentheil so er vermerckt wie seinn widderparth vmbgeht / sol er sich befleissenn desselbigen fürhaben zu brechen / vnnd ime also vnder augen vnnd in wegk zu ziehenn das er die hutt seins willens mit fug nit machen könne / sonder ime in alle weg fürkommen vnnd ablauffenn was er mag / Auch mitler weil sich auch zu einer hutt schickenn / vnnd gleicherweisz seinen König einschantzen vnd versichern.

(E. iii *b*) Etzlich gemeine Regel im Schachziehen.

I.

Wiltu das spil behaltenn /
So ziehe den erstenn vor denn Alten.

II.

Den Fenden vor der frawen klug
Soltu ausz ziehen im ersten zug /
Ante Reginam
Debes producere primam.

III.

Hut gegen hut
Thet selten gut /

IIII.

Vbersehen
Ist geschehen.

V.

Zürnen viel
Verleurt das spiel.

IV. Description of a Chess Notation in MS. Paris Fr. 1173 (PP.).

(f. 4*a*) Pour chou ke plaisans cose *et* delitaule est a tous entendans q*ua*nt une cose est ordenee *et* despondue par vne brief maniere. soutiue *et* sustanssieuse selonc le sage *qui* dist. ke les bries p*ar*oles soutuies rendent lentendeme*n*t del home volentiu a oir *et* a entendre. car mouteplîances de p*ar*oles enge*n*re*n*t anuianche au cuer. Et ie vous ai empris a t*ra*itier du ieu des eskes *com*ment ne en q*ue*le maniere il puet estre abregies par partures *et* coument on fait les assises a se volente selonc ce ki on les veut auoir de pau de t*ra*is o de pluseurs.
(f. 4*b*) car tant est li ieus soutieus *et* biaus ke nus ne porroit croire la g*ra*nt q*ua*ntite des p*ar*tures ke on i porroit trouu*er* ki le soutiuere aroit. Mais tout ne puet mie iestre sent par .i. home si ne les puis toutes sauoir ne monstrer. Mais chou vous en monsterrai ke mes entendeme*n*s en puet comp*re*ndre. par le plus brief *et* le plus araigna*n*t maniere ke ie porrai. Et tout cil ki voelent aucune p*ar*ture reporter par escrit ne pueent mie auoir leskekier appareilliet por lor parture asseoir. Si fu besoins ke aucuns hom sages *et* soutieus trouuast aucune brief maniere de faire co*m*ment li point del eskekier seroient no*m*me. par coi on peust en brief parole une p*ar*ture escrire *et* retenir. Et est la maniere trouee tele co*m*me en cest part a deseure est contenu. Et doiue*n*t tout sauoir ke li p*re*miers poins del eskiekier ki siet deseure en le partie senestre e*st* apieles .a. *et* li autres ap*re*s ensiuans uenans v*er*s le destre partie est apeles .b. *et* ensi tous iors siuans par lordene del abece duskes v dest*re* angle. ki est apieles .h. Et li autres poins ki est desous .a. est compos de .a. et de .k. *et* est apeles .ak. *et* chieus desous .al. *et* ensi tout li autre par lordene del abece. Et tout en autele maniere est il desous .b. *et* desous .c. *et* desous tous les autres. car tous iors est il compos de lune de ces lettres. *et* de .k. v de lettre siuant si *com*me (f. 5*a* last line) vous porres en leschekier ap*er*teme*n*t veoir.

a	b	c	d	e	f	g	h
ak	bk	ck	dk	ek	fk	gk	hk
al	bl	cl	dl	el	fl	gl	hl
am	bm	cm	dm	em	fm	gm	hm
an	bn	cn	dn	en	fn	gn	hn
ao	bo	co	do	eo	fo	go	ho
ap	bp	cp	dp	ep	fp	gp	hp
aq	bq	cq	dq	eq	fq	gq	hq

V. From MS. Vatican. Lat. 1960, f. 28.

VIII. Pars. *Qualiter motus scachorum productionem acierum significat.*

Secundum autem quod scacherium scachis est altrinsecus exornatum variis ludi processus varios modos acies producendi demonstrat. Aliquando enim scachi ex utraque parte scacherii producuntur et fit in processu quasi forficularis figura. Aliquando pedona de medio producitur et ceterae a lateribus subsecuntur et fit pyramidalis figura. Aliquando ordinantur pedites circa regem et fit quasi circularis figura, aliquando omnes equaliter producuntur in bellis. Si contra paucos pugnetur, ad illos capiendos forficulariter procedendum est, si contra multos pyramidaliter, talis enim acies de facili frangi non potest, et hae duae maiorem efficaciam contra hostes; circularis vero pro defensione est utilior. Quadrata vero sicut et in ludo ad modium utilis est.

CHAPTER IV

THE EARLY DIDACTIC LITERATURE.

Introductory remarks.—The Einsiedeln and Winchester Poems.—Alexander Neckam, *De scaccis*.—Cod. Benedictbeuren.—The Elegy (*Qui cupit*).—The Deventer Poem.—*It pedes*, and the Corpus Poem.—The Reims Poem.—The Vetula.—The Cracow Poem.—The Hebrew poem of Abraham b. Ezra, and other Hebrew works.

I PROPOSE in the present chapter to deal with the didactic literature of early European chess, the chess evidence from which has only been summarized in Chapter III. In this literature I include two descriptions of the game which form portions of larger works, and a number of poems dealing exclusively with chess which have the appearance of having been intended for the instruction of beginners, or, perhaps, of being mere school exercises in metrical form. As a rule these poems only deal with the game in broad outline, and omit all reference to the minutiae of rule, the local varieties, or the less striking methods of terminating the game. They are often obscure, and we can only recognize the author's meaning because we know from other sources what he was desirous of saying. The mediaeval writer was expert neither in description nor in definition. With a few exceptions all these works are in Latin.

It is not easy to determine the date or place of origin of these poems. Only one poem has a date attached to it; the poems generally occur in MSS. of composite form containing entries of very different date, and only exceptionally is any date attached to any single section of the manuscript. We are accordingly thrown back upon palaeographical considerations when we attempt to assign a date to any particular part of a MS., and the conclusions that have been drawn in this way have been very startling. Occasionally the history of a MS., but more often the nomenclature of the poem, has enabled me to suggest the probable nationality of the author.

Attention was first directed to the existence of mediaeval poems on chess by Hyde, who included the texts of two of them in his *Mandragorias*, and added the text of the Hebrew poem of Abraham b. Ezra with a valuable Latin translation. Next Massmann printed all the texts known in his time with the various readings found in the different MSS.; then v. d. Linde attempted in the *Quellenstudien* to date the poems from internal evidence; and finally v. d. Lasa devoted a luminous chapter in the *Forschungen* to a criticism of the chess rules as given in the poems. As literature these Latin poems have but little importance or interest. I accordingly only propose to give brief summaries of their contents, and shall only go into detail with reference to points of obscurity or of special chess interest. The original texts, with a list of the accessible MSS. (to the number of which I have been able to make several additions), will be found in the Appendix to this chapter. The following is a list of the works to be discussed in the chapter itself:

Language.	Name of work.	Country of origin.	Date of oldest MS.	Date of work.
Latin	Einsiedeln Poem	S. Germany	11 c.	11 c.
	Winchester Poem	England	1100–50.	Early 12 c.
	Neckam, *De scaccis*	England		*c.* 1180
	Codex Benedictbeuren	S. Germany		? 12 c.
	The Elegy (*Qui cupit*)	?	12 c.	? 12 c.
	Deventer Poem	France	13 c.	? 13 c.
	Fournivall, *Vetula*	France		13 c.
	It pedes	?		? 13 c.
	Corpus Poem	England	15 c.	15 c.
	Reims Poem	France		
	Cracow Poem	Germany	1422	1422
Hebrew	Abraham b. Ezra	Spain	1450	12 c.
	Bonsenior b. Yaḥya	Spain	1450	

The oldest of these works is an elegiac poem of 98 lines, which exists in two MSS. at Einsiedeln in the canton of Schwytz in Switzerland, from whence it is generally known as the *Einsiedeln Poem*. The older MS. occupies both sides of a single leaf, which has been bound up in modern days with other stray leaves in a composite volume (Einsid. 365). It bears the original title *Versus de scachis*. At a date but little later than the date at which it was written this leaf was used in the binding of another MS. (Einsid. 125) in such a way that the back of the leaf containing lines 68–98 was still exposed to view. Some industrious scribe next copied this visible portion into another volume (Einsid. 319), and, possibly not recognizing the subject-matter, he added a new title, *De aleae ratione*.[1] Photographs of both MSS. were submitted by v. d. Linde and v. d. Lasa to a number of German palaeographists, with the result that a variety of dates beginning with 900–50 and ending with the 12th c. were assigned to them. Curiously, all these experts agree in regarding the incomplete copy as being written in the earlier hand. V. d. Linde thought that he could detect signs of the influence of the work of Cessolis, and accordingly placed it in the 13th c. at the earliest. With this conclusion I cannot agree; I see nothing that necessarily compels the knowledge of Cessolis's work, while the whole nomenclature points to a much earlier date. I am convinced that the chess evidence requires that the poem was written before 1100. In this opinion I am confirmed by Mr. Falconer Madan, who kindly examined the photographs for me and dated the complete text 11th c. and the copy *c.* 1100. They are accordingly among the oldest European documents of chess. There is no reason to

[1] Cf., however, the instances quoted on p. 409 of the early use of *alea* in connexion with chess.

suppose that the poem was composed anywhere else than Einsiedeln: the nomenclature agrees with that exhibited in other MSS. of early German chess. The complete MS. is presumably the author's holograph, and therefore complete. V. d. Lasa thought that there was a hiatus after line 66, but the poem, though not very logical or orderly in arrangement, still seems to me to follow a natural line of thought. Nor do I see any grounds for supposing that the order of the lines has been disarranged.

The poem may be summarized thus:

(1–10). If it is lawful to play games, here is one which you will rank first among delightful games. It is free from deceit, no stake is necessary, and it does not require dice.

(11–20). The board contains 8 by 8 squares (*tabulae*), which some players make chequered. The two colours help calculation and make the moves easier to follow.

(21–44). The game is played with 32 men, 16 on either side, one side being white, the other red. Different men have different names and moves. On the first row 8 men are arranged; the King (*rex*) and Queen (*regina*) in the middle; next these their supports, the Counts (*comes*, later *curvus* = the Aged one), are placed to hear with their ears the spoken words of their lords; next the Knights (*eques*); and the Rook (*rochus*), or rather the Margrave (*marchio*) in his two-wheeled chariot, occupies the corner squares. The second row is filled by the Pawns (*pedes*).

(45–54). The game is commenced by moving the Pawns: each moves to the square immediately in front, and takes aslant a piece that confronts it on an adjacent square of the same colour.

(55–61). Any piece that is taken is removed from the board, excepting the King, who never falls.

(62–66). The King moves to any adjacent square, the Queen to a square of the same colour; she cannot change her colour.

(67–70). The Pawn which reaches the eighth rank can move afterwards like the Queen, provided the original Queen is no longer on the board.

(71–76). The Aged one moves aslant to the third square. He cannot change his original colour of square.

(77–82). The Knight moves to the third square of a different colour; he can reach any square of the board.

(83–86). The Rook goes always in a straight path as far as the player chooses.

(87–98). The Knights and Rooks are the chief fighting forces. When they are taken the battle soon dies; they should be carefully guarded. The King is never taken, but when he is surrounded by his enemies the game comes to an end.

The most striking feature of this rather tedious poem is its freedom from Arabic terminology. The words *check* and *mate* are not used, and it is only the name of the game, *scachi*, in the title, and the word *rochus* that show that the writer is dealing with a game that is not of European invention. The nomenclature of the game is drawn from that of the state, and not from that of the army. There is even an attempt to substitute a new name for the Rook, borrowed from the political life of Germany. On the other hand, ll. 41–2, in placing this Margrave in a two-wheeled chariot, seem to show a memory of the original meaning of the term *Rook*. With the exception of the rule respecting Pawn-promotion, the rules are identical with those of Muslim chess; there is no reference to any leap for Queen or King, and ll. 47–8 preclude the possibility of the Pawn's initial double step. The Pawn is promoted to the rank of Queen, but only after the loss of the original

Queen. There is a similar restriction in the Spanish MS. Alf., and I have already attempted to explain the reason for it.

The poem lays great stress upon the fact that chess is not a dice game, and not necessarily played for a stake. (*There are no fraudulent perjuries, you do not injure your body or any of your limbs, you pay nothing, and compel no one to pay, no player will be deceitful. Dice will effect anything by an injurious game, this game avoids all by its straightforwardness.*) This agrees well with the position in Germany in the 11th c., as illustrated by the passage in Ruodlieb. The chequered board was in process of introduction, and the poet shows that he fully realized the advantages of its use.

The next of these Latin poems according to date is a poem of 36 lines from a MS. in the Bodleian Library, Oxford, of the first half of the 12th c., which Hyde printed under the title *De Shahiludio: Poema tempore Saxonum exaratum.* The MS. itself gives no title to the poem, and Hyde's title is certainly misleading as regards date. I prefer to call it the *Winchester Poem*, from the fact that it occurs in a MS. of miscellaneous contents which was written at Winchester.

Here again it is probable that we possess the author's own holograph. In the MS. the poem occupies a blank page between a work against the monks by a certain Serlo, otherwise unidentified, and a poem *Contra simoniacam Romam.*

The contents of this poem follow:

If any one wishes to make a War-game to play at war, let him arrange the men thus upon the plain of *tabulae*. The King (*rex*) first, on his right the Queen (*regina*), next the Bald-head (*calvus*) as a guard. (The King for his first move takes the second square; he cannot go farther.) Next the Horseman (*equestris*), and the two-faced Rook (*bifrons rochus*) is at the end of the line. On the other side of the King are a Cavalier (*caballarius*) and a Rook. The Pawns (*pedes, -itis*) are in front. The Pawns (*pedestris*) commence the battle; they go straight forward, cannot return backward, and they take in a diagonal direction. The Bald-head moves diagonally to the third square; he lies in ambush like a thief. The Knight (*eques*) takes the Knight, the Pawn the Pawn, and the Rook the Rook, but the Bald-heads have a compact never to harm one another; nor can one Queen interfere with another since they are allotted to the Kings as a guard. The Queen rules two squares diagonally in every direction. When the Pawn (*pedestris*) reaches the end line he changes his name and is called Fers (*ferzia*) and is given the Queen's move. The King is invulnerable; when he is attacked, check! (*scachum*) must be said; then he must move to another square, and if there is none possible it is checkmate (*scacha-mattum*).

There is some want of fixity about the names of the pieces, the Knight being named *eques* twice and *equestris* and *caballarius* once each, and the Pawn being *pedestris* thrice and *pedes* twice. I think it is clear that the poet was more familiar with the names of the pieces in some language other than Latin. *Calvus* (Bald-head) for the Bishop recalls the *curvus* of the Einsiedeln Poem and the *alte* of early German chess. We shall see immediately, however, that the idea of this piece as an old man was not confined to Germany, but existed in England also. There may possibly be an allusion to the tonsured clergy in the use of *calvus,* which would make the name a forerunner of the modern

English Bishop. The absence of any reference to the name *aufin* is somewhat remarkable in an English work, for the ordinary English nomenclature of Norman times keeps close to the Arabic. The view of the Bishop as a thief lying in wait to capture an unsuspecting wayfarer is a favourite one in mediaeval works. No special word is used for the chessboard, and there is no description of it, so that we cannot tell whether the chequered board was in use in England in the early part of the 12th c.

The Queen is described as placed on the right-hand side of the King. It is obvious, however, that the poet is only speaking of the arrangement of one side of the board, for later on he expressly says that the Queens cannot attack one another. Unfortunately we do not know whether he is describing the white or the black pieces.

The moves of the chessmen are given very briefly, and the moves of the Knight and Rook are omitted entirely. The account of the Queen's move is very obscure; the words 'let her rule two squares diagonally in every direction' mean, I suppose, the diagonally adjacent squares, *bini* being loosely used for *secundi* and the squares being counted in the mediaeval manner.[2] Otherwise the statement can only refer to the Queen's original position at the edge of the board, when only two squares were open to her. The King's move is brought in very awkwardly in the middle of the account of the arrangement of the pieces. It is thus described: 'Let the King about to go against the King hasten cautiously, seeking in the first place to take possession of the second square, for he refuses the liberty to be led afar.' V. d. Lasa thought that this might be an obscure reference to the King's leap, overlooking the fact that in this case *tertiam*, and not *alteram*, would have been used. The lines clearly limit the King's move to the eight (at most) squares adjacent to the one from which it moves. The Pawn is called *Ferzia* after promotion, and receives the Queen's move: this is a typically English restriction of the name 'Fers'.

The lines dealing with the powers of capture are loosely expressed. Taken literally, they imply that the Knight could only capture a Knight, the Pawn a Pawn, and the Rook a Rook. This is, of course, absurd; the author is contrasting the freedom of those pieces with the restricted powers of the Bishop and Queen. He means to say that the three first pieces could take any piece even of its own rank, but that the two last pieces had a smaller amount of liberty and were unable to take an opponent of their own rank.

We may compare this poem with chapter clxxxiv, *De scaccis*, in the *De Naturis Rerum* of the great English scholar, Alexander Neckam. Neckam, the foster-brother of Richard I, was born at St. Albans, Sept. 1157, and educated at the monastery of his native town. At an early age he was placed in charge of the dependent school at Dunstable, and in 1180 he was in Paris and already famed as a teacher. Within the next ten years he produced a number of works on science, rhetoric, theology, and philosophy, the *De*

[2] As is obviously the case in this poem, from the use of *tertius* in describing the Bishop's move.

Naturis Rerum being one of the most considerable of them. In 1213 he became Abbot of the Augustines at Cirencester, and died in 1217 at Kempsey.

The chess chapter follows one on dice games, which he ascribed to the Trojans. Of chess (*ludus scaccorum*) he says in effect:

Chess was invented by Ulysses. There are different arrangements of the men, but in the original game the Pawns are arranged on the second line and the pieces on the first line of the board. The Pawn (*pedes*) moves straight forward, but takes obliquely. When he reaches the last line, he becomes a Queen (*regina*), changing his sex, and thereafter moves obliquely. The Old man (*senex*), commonly called *Alphicus*, is a spy wearing the form of Nestor. His move is oblique and twice that of the Queen. The Knight (*miles*) unites the moves of the Queen and Pawn, and the resulting move is partly oblique and partly straight. The Rook (*rochus*), symbolizing a lightly equipped soldier, was formerly called *Janus biceps*, and is accordingly made with two heads; he follows a straight path. The King (*rex*) moves both aslant and straight, and can never be taken.

Returning to 'the vanity of chess', Neckam goes on to marvel at the absorption of players in their game, at the importance they attach to the victory, at the readiness with which they renew the game, at the sudden fits of passion to which the players seemed peculiarly prone. Often the game degenerated into a brawl. How many thousands of souls were sent to hell in consequence of that game in which Reginald the son of Eymund, while playing with a noble knight in the palace of Charles the Great, slew his opponent with one of the chessmen!

Neckam begins, accordingly, by ascribing the invention of chess to Ulysses. There would appear to have been at least four views current in the early Middle Ages relative to the origin of chess. Two of these associated the game with the town of Troy, one making it a Trojan invention, the other a Greek one; a third associated the discovery with Attalus Asiaticus, while the fourth placed it in the time of Evil-Merodach, the son of Nebuchadnezzar, and named the philosopher Xerxes or Philometor as the inventor. Neckam's statement is repeated in the *Vetula* discussed below, whence it was taken by the prose commentator on *Les Eschez amoureux*, and the 14th c. Vatican MS. 1960.[3] I have not been able to discover its source. The parallel statement that chess was a Trojan invention obtained its wider currency from its occurrence in the Latin *Historia Troiana* of Guido de Columna, which was written in the 13th c.[4] This work was translated into most of the Western European languages, and we possess two English versions, the more ambitious being the work of that prolific writer John Lydgate, 1412–20.[5] The tradition is not due to Columna, but may be traced back to his ultimate

[3] 'Scacorum ludum ab Vlixe inuentum, ne marcido torperet ocio obsidentibus Troiam Graecis nonnulli autumant.' The MS. then continues, following Cessolis: 'a pluribus uero repertum a Xerse philosopho babilonico captiuitatis tempore imperante Babilonijs Euilmerodach sevo rege.'

[4] Book V, ch. iv (ed. 1486, c2b, col. 1): 'Huius ergo ciuitatis diuersorum ludorum diuersa genera diuersis in ea adinuentionibus statuerunt. Ibi primo adinuenta fuerunt schacorum solacia curiosa. Ibi ludi subito irascibiles alearum, hic repentina damna & lucra momentanea taxillorum.'

[5] Lydgate, *Troy Book* (E. E. T. S., 1906, I. ii. 806–23):

And þer was founde by clerkys ful prudent,
Of þe Ches þe pleye most glorious,
Whiche is so sotyl and so meruelous,
Þat it wer harde þe mater to discryue;
For þouȝe a man stodied al his lyve,

authority, the French *Roman de Troie* of Benoit de Ste More, written *c*. 1165.[6]

The third tradition, which ascribes the invention to Attalus Asiaticus, is familiar to students of Chaucer, who gave it in his *Book of the Duchesse*. Chaucer obtained it from the *Rommant de la Rose*, where Jehan le Meung gives as his authority the *Policraticus* of John of Salisbury. This last work, however, only names (I. v) Attalus as the inventor of certain dice-games, of which the names are given, and chess is not one of them. The reference is to Attalus Philometor, King of Pergamos, who is named in Pliny's *Nat. Hist.*, xviii. 3 and xxviii. 2 (Warton, *Hist. Eng. Poet.*, 1871, iii. 91).

The fourth tradition was adopted by Cessolis, and owes its general acceptance in the Middle Ages to the popularity of the *Liber de moribus hominum et officiis nobilium.*

Neckam's nomenclature is interesting. The Arabic name of the Bishop makes its appearance, though the L. *senex* is given as the more scholarly name. The piece again appears as a spy, lurking for his enemy. There is also, as was the case in the *Winchester Poem*, a very clear reference to the shape of the Rook.

There is no account of the chessboard, and the moves, which are not very clearly explained, show none of the European modifications. There is an interesting story in illustration of the fact that the chess King is free from capture. In a chance skirmish in the vicinity of Gisors, 1110, Louis VI of France was nearly taken prisoner. An English knight laid hands on him, and shouted that the king was taken. 'Ignorant and insolent knight,' exclaimed the king, 'not even in chess can a King be taken.' This story

He schal ay fynde dyuers fantasyes
Of wardys makyng, & newe iuparties (MS. C imparties)
þer is þer-in so gret diuersite.
And it was first founde in þis cite,
Duryng þe sege, liche as seyth Guydo,
But Iacobus de Vitriaco (? error for Cessolis)
Is contrarie of oppynyoun :
For, like as he makyth mencioun,
And affermeth fully in his avys,
How Philometer, a philysofre wys,
Vn-to a kyng, to stynte his cruelte,
Fond first þis pleie & made it in Calde ;
And in-to Grece from þense it was sent.

The second English version is the anonymous poem in alliterative verse, the *Destr. Troy*, written *c.* 1440, 1619–23 :

In þat Cite for sothe, as saith vs the story,
Mony gaumes were begonnen þe grete for to solas.
The chekker was choisly þere chosen þe first,
The draghtes, the dyse, and oþer dregh gaumes
Soche soteltie þai sought to solas hom with.

(To the requirements of this form of verse we owe the inclusion of the game of draughts, this being one of the earliest references to the game.)

[6] Unc el monde n'ot majestire
N'afetement qu'en poïst dire,
Dont len éust deduit ne joie
Que ne trovassent cil de Troie.
Eschès et tables, geus de dez
I fu, iço sachez, trovez,
Et maintes ovres convenables,
Riches, mananz et delitables.

Miniature from MS. Lat. 4660, Munich (*Carmina Burana*)

is repeated in other works, e.g. Mouskes, *Chronique*, and is probably well founded.[7]

Upon the whole, Neckam appears to have thought poorly of chess. He did not understand the fascination that the game exercised over players, and the evil passions that it roused so often in his day. Like Cardinal Damiani, he speaks of 'the vanity of chess' (*vanitas ludi scaccorum*). The allusion to the chess story in the Charlemagne romance of *Renaud de Montaubon* is important: it is one of the earliest references to that romance, and shows that the chess passage belongs to a still older recension of the romance than any we now possess.

There are still two other Latin poems that must be placed in the 12th c., in addition to the Hebrew poem of Abraham b. Ezra, which I shall discuss at the end of this chapter. One of these, *Codex Benedictbeuren*, only consists of four lines and therefore throws no light upon the rules. V. d. Linde printed it as the oldest European chess poem, but I do not think this claim can now be seriously maintained. The text is obviously corrupt: if we substitute *tot cape* for the meaningless *tost capra* in the third line we have a brief but vivid picture of the noise which accompanied a keenly fought game of chess in Southern Germany. The first line is an attempt to include the names of all the chessmen in a single hexameter line. We shall meet with other attempts shortly. Check-rook (*scachroch*) is named as a frequent precursor of the mate (*mat*).

The poem is followed by a miniature showing a game in progress, of which I have already made use because of the light which it throws upon Opening play.

The second poem, which I call the Elegy, from its ordinary title in the MSS., *Elegia de ludo scachorum*, is one of the most widely spread of all these poems. I know of no less than seven different MSS., of dates varying from the 12th to the 16th cc., of which three are in German libraries, two in Italian libraries, one is in France, and one is at Oxford. The last was in pre-Reformation days the property of the Priory at Bridlington, Yorkshire. There is nothing to show in what country this poem of 38 elegiac lines was originally composed.

The poem may be summarized thus:

> If any one desires to learn about the famous game of chess (*egregium scacorum ludum*), let him attend to this poem which I have written on the game. There are eight stations (*loca*) on the board (*tabula*), which are alternately white and red or black or grey or reddish. In the first is placed the Rook (*rochus*), in the second the Knight (*eques*, in the It. MSS. *equus*), third the Aufin (*alficus*, other MSS. *alfinus*, *alfinis*), who is the royal guard, fourth the King (*rex*), fifth the Lady (*femina*), after this the former nobles recur. The Pawn (*pedes*) advances and takes to the right and left; when he reaches the limit of the board he takes the Queen's (*regina*) move, and changing sex wields royal power. The Pawns begin the game. The Rook goes the

[7] A similar allusion occurs in a political poem on the battle of Neville's Cross, 1346, in which David II of Scotland was captured. Wright's *Political Poems and Songs* (Rolls series, London, 1859, p. 46):

Regem Scotorum licuit captum retinere,
Regem scaccorum iura vetant capere.

whole length of the board in any direction he likes, provided he is not obstructed. Any piece can take any other. The Knight runs rapidly and misleads the opponent. The Aufin of the three ways is to be dreaded, with his horned head, for he misleads the opponent. Pawns take pieces and pieces Pawns, and both perish in the mêlée, but the King is not taken; when he loses his wife (*conjunx*) there is nothing of any value left on the board. Often is he mate, and every one shouts Mate! mate! mate! Then, if you like, you can play it over again.

This is the most difficult of all the poems. The confused order of ideas, the repetitions, the omissions, and, above all, the extraordinary importance that is attached to the Queen, have raised doubts as to the accuracy of the text. V. d. Linde (*Qst.*, 91) gave an emended text which had been prepared for v. d. Lasa by Dr. D. Deutsch of Berlin, an authority on mediaeval Latinity. But since 1880 three other MSS. (D, R, and F) have been discovered, and none of these lend the slightest support to Deutsch's emendations.

The poem describes the board as coloured, and places the King's Rook on a white square. We do not know, though, of which side the arrangement is being described. The moves of Rook and Pawn alone are clearly given. The promoted Pawn becomes a Queen (*regina*), the original Queen being called *femina*. The Knight and Bishop, from their oblique moves, are styled deceivers; there appears to be here a reminiscence of some interpretation like those that we shall meet in the Moralities. The lines about the Bishop are obscure, and the MSS. vary considerably in their readings. The correct reading would appear to be—

Alficus trivius cornuta fronte timendus,
Ante retro comites decipit invigiles.

But N has *alficus curuus*, F *alfinis constat*, and D *alficus curnus uelud et fur fronte timendus*. *Trivius* is an adjective derived from the noun *trivium*, a place where three ways meet, and in classical Latin was used as an epithet of those deities whose temples were erected at these places. It is used in two other poems in connexion with the Bishop, and appears to be loosely used with reference to the Bishop's leap into the 'third' square. The reading *curvus* in N has in its favour that Curvus was undoubtedly used as a name for the Bishop in early times.[8] *Cornuta fronte*, of course, alludes to the shape of the chessman.

But undoubtedly the chief difficulty of the poem is the position allotted to the mediaeval chess Queen. Unfortunately the move of this piece is not given; but when speaking of the progress of the game and the diminution of the pieces by capture, the poet continues: 'The King alone remains untaken when his wife is taken away: when his wife is taken away, nothing is of value on the board'; or as four MSS. (A, N, R, and B) have it, 'nothing remains on the board'; while of the Queen obtained by the promotion of a Pawn it is said: 'the man become a woman abides a lord wielding royal power, he governs and reigns, here he takes, there he gives way.' In this last *regiferus* (W *tegiferus*)[9] may contain a recollection of the word *fers*, for

[8] V. d. Lasa (87) rejected *trivius*, and suggested *constans* as probably correct. I cannot agree.

[9] Massmann adopted the emendation *regni ferus*. *Ferus arbiter* is rather strong for the mediaeval Queen, though, as v. d. Lasa points out, not more so than Vida's *crudelis virgo* for the modern Queen.

which *fera* is used in some problem MSS. The writer could hardly have said more had he been writing of the Queen in the reformed game, with her greatly extended power of move. V. d. Lasa leaves the difficulty as insoluble, after pointing out that the repetition in lines 33 and 34 is pointless, and accordingly possibly due to a scribal blunder in some early copy that lies behind the existing texts. I think that it may be due to moralizing influences, to the existence of which I have already called attention. Similar exaggerated valuations of the Queen are not unknown in mediaeval literature: I have collected several examples in Chapter IX below.[10] In most of these cases, however, the poetical justification for the high estimation is more evident.

Another poem of wide distribution is the *Deventer Poem*, which has received this name from the fact that its existence was first made known by Hyde from a MS. said to be of Flemish origin, in the library of Deventer, Holland. Since then it has been found in six other MSS., one in Italy, two in England, two in France, and one (quite late in date) in Germany. It probably dates from the 13th c., and, since the Bishop is called *stultus*, it will be of French origin. It is rather interesting to see that in two MSS. (C and D) the scribe has added a gloss to the name *stultus*—in C, *alfinus*, in D, *li aufins*. The poem consists of 37 leonine hexameters, and presents few difficulties.

The text may be given in brief thus:

If any one wishes to know the beautiful game of chess (*scacorum ludum decorum*), let him learn this poem. The battle takes place upon a square board, chequered with different colours. The two Kings (*rex*) arrange their forces in two lines. In the van are the eight Pawns (*pedes*). Behind are the swift Rooks (*rocus*), the fierce Knights (*eques*) who war unfairly, and the King, Queen (*regina*), and the two bodies of Fools (*stolidus*, in B *solidus*). The old archer (*architenens vetus* = Pawn) begins the battle; he moves aslant to capture, and when he reaches the limit of the board he is promoted and called Fers (*fercia*, B *forcia*). The Knight (*miles*) goes obliquely and changes his colour. The Rook goes straight, awkwardly and swiftly; he can go forwards and backwards. The Fool (*stultus*), a leaper of the three ways, is like a thief and a spy; if he is white to begin with, he can never become red. The royal Fers (*Fercia regalis*, B *forcia*, A *gregalis*) is a leaper of four ways and keeps her colour. The King can move to any of the eight surrounding squares, he must move in reply to checks (*scaccibus*), and if he is unable every one shouts Mate! mate! mate! (*mattum*).

The board (*asser quadratus*) is described as chequered, the individual squares (*tabulae*) being red and white. There is a little uncertainty as to the nomenclature, though the alternatives in the case of Bishop and Knight are synonymous. The mention of the Pawn as an 'old archer' is probably due to poetic licence and borrowed from the military tactics of that day; it is the solitary appearance of the archer until Vida re-introduced the name as a poetical name for the Bishop. The Pawn becomes a Fers on promotion, though this name, apparently, is not restricted to the Promoted Pawn. *Trivius* is again used as an epithet of the Bishop, while *quadrivialis* is used of the Queen. I suppose that this adjective refers to the fact that the Queen could move in four directions as a maximum; it certainly does not imply

[10] See p. 753.

a leap to a 'fourth' square (e.g. from d1 to d5). Its use is, therefore, not strictly parallel to the use of *trivius* for the Bishop.

The pieces are called red and white, not from the colour of the side upon which they belong, but from the colour of the square upon which they happen to be standing; each player has accordingly a red Bishop and a white one. This was a common method of describing the chessmen in the Middle Ages, and is the one used by Cessolis and his translators.

To this century, if not to the twelfth, belongs a short poem beginning *It pedes ad bellum*, which has been found in MSS. in London, Cambridge, Paris, and Berne, while separate lines appear in a Wolfenbüttel MS. of Cessolis as headings to the different chapters of the fourth Book. The poem is written in leonine hexameters, but varies in length in the different MSS. from seven lines to fourteen. Of the seventeen lines which a collation of the MSS. produces, the initial pair are a memory of the lines beginning the Deventer Poem, while the concluding pair (obtained from the English MSS.) clearly come from elsewhere. The first is a hexameter line formed out of the names of the chessmen, different from those in Codex Benedictbeuren and in the *Vetula*, and also different from the popular line of the Vocabularies:

Rex, rocus, alphinus, miles, regina, pedinus.

There is a reference to the second line in Alanus, *De Parabolis*.

The poem deals very briefly and clearly with the moves of the chessmen as existing in Muslim chess. The pieces are called *rex*, *regalis femina*, *alphilus* (*africus*, *alpheus* in other MSS.), *miles*, *rocus*, and *pedes*; the concluding hexameter varying with *regina*, *alphinus*, *roc*, and *pedinus*. Other technicalities are *punctum* for the square of the board, *scaccum*, *scaccare* (vb.), and *matus* (adj.). The word *trivium* is again used in describing the Bishop's move.

The brevity of this poem led to its amplification at the hand of some Englishman, whose version we possess in two closely connected MSS., of which the older is in the library of Corpus Christi College, Cambridge. This, the *Corpus Poem*, consists of thirty-eight hexameter lines with the MS. title *Incipit modus et scientia ludi scaccorum.* The hexameters are partly leonine, and partly rhyme in pairs—a sure indication of the composite nature of the poem.[11]

The contents of this poem follow. The portions borrowed from the preceding poem are printed in italics.

Let those who wish to know the famous game of chess, attend to our lines. The game is played upon a square and chequered board (*tabula*). The magnates are placed on the first line, and the Pawns (*pedes*) on the second. The King (*rex*) and Queen (*regina*) are in the centre, the white King being on a red square, and the red King on a white square; each Queen (*femina*) is on a square of her own colour. Next is the Aufin (*alphicus*), then the Knight (*miles*), and at the end is the Rook (*rochus*). Eight Pawns are associated with the eight nobles. The enemy are arranged similarly, and the game is ready. *The Pawn begins the battle, he advances slowly, cannot retreat, and takes aslant.* When he reaches the end of the board he is

[11] Thus lines 1–13 rhyme in pairs, the companion to the halting third line being missing; then follow 19 leonine lines, and the concluding 6 lines again rhyme in pairs.

given the Lady's (*domina*) move. *The Rook takes far and near when there is no obstruction*, but he has no power in an oblique direction. *The Knight is a strong piece, and leaps aslant, leaving the centre*, and he changes the colour of his square each move. *The Aufin lays snares in the three-ways, leaping diagonally. The Queen* (regalis femina) *has an oblique move* and lays snares in the two-ways. *The King* (regia maiestas) *defends all the adjacent squares.* He cannot be taken, but when attacked, 'Check' (*scak*) must be said. When he has no flight-square, his whole side are vanquished.

The position of the King is carefully described, and agrees with the rule of the modern game: to complete it, all that is wanting is a direction as to the placing of the board. The promoted Pawn is given a special name, but *domina* has replaced the earlier *fercia*.

Another poem of the 13th c. is the *De natura scatorum*, which exists in a single MS. at Reims. In its fourteen lines it deals solely with the original moves of the chessmen, with an obscure reference to check (*cacus*) and checkmate in the concluding four lines.

There is an interesting digression upon games in the *Vetula*, a Latin romance which is now recognized as the work of Richard de Fournivall, chancellor of Amiens in the 13th c., but which was popularly ascribed to Ovid in the Middle Ages, one of whose adventures it purports to tell. According to Jehan Lefevre, procureur en Parlement, who translated the poem into French in the 14th c. (*La Vieille*, ed. Cocheri, Paris, 1861), the poem was discovered in an ivory casket in Ovid's tomb 400 years after his death—an ingenious way of evading the doubt as to its classical origin which its absence in the Latin MSS. of the poet's works might have aroused. The games described in the *Vetula* include tables, chess, merels, and rythmomachy. The chess passage occupies sections 31–33 of Bk. I, and comprises fifty-nine lines in all. In the French version this extends from l. 1417 to l. 1672.

This poem approaches very close to the Moralities, in that it attempts a complete explanation of chess as symbolical of the motions of the heavenly bodies. It may be summarized thus:

There is another game, chess, which Ulysses invented at the siege of Troy to prevent the nobles suffering from ennui in time of truce or sickness. He is much to be praised for it. It was very clever to think out six types of move so that no two games are ever identical. He drew his inspiration from the movements of the planets. There are six chessmen (*scaci*), and three leap into the first field, and three into the second. The King (*rex*), Pawn (*pedes*), and Maid (*virgo*) leap into the first field. The Maid goes aslant, the Pawn in a direct line, and the King combines the two moves. The King and Maid can go forwards and backwards, the Pawn forwards only, except that he takes diagonally forwards. When he reaches the end of the board, he is given the Maid's leap. Into the second field leaps Rook (*roccus*), Aufin (*alphinus*), and Knight (*miles*). The Rook goes in a straight line, and alone has no limit to his leap, but can move for a shorter or a greater distance than to the second square. The Aufin leaps aslant, and the Knight combines both moves. The King is the Sun, the Pawn Saturn, the Knight Mars, the royal Maid (*regia virgo*) Venus, the Aufin, himself a Bishop (*episcopus*), Jupiter; and the wandering Rook the Moon. Mercury is the promoted Pawn. Chess is a noble game so long as it is played in moderation and is not played to amass money. To play with the help of dice is to defile it; the man who first did this either could not appreciate a slow game, or was greedy of gain.

It will be noted that the modern method of numbering the squares is adopted in this poem. Although dating from the 13th c. the description of the moves shows no sign of any acquaintance with any of the European changes, although these must have been already in common use in France. The nomenclature is somewhat unusual; we should not expect to find the Queen called *virgo*, and the recognition of the Aufin as a Bishop is rare in Continental chess. The *Vieille* has *roy*, *fierge* (*La roine que nommons fierge*), *alphin* or *auphin* (*L'auphin portant d'evesque mitre*), *chevalier*, *roc* (*roch*), and *peon* (after promotion *fierge*). A paraphrase of the poem in MS. Paris F. fr. 143 (ff. 3v–4v) has *roy*, *fierge*, *alphir*, *chevalier*, *roc* (pl. *rocz*), and *paonnet* (pl. *paonnez*; after promotion *fierge*).

The recognition of the infinite variety of chess, the condemnation of the use of dice and of the playing for a stake, show that Fournivall was in advance of his time. The original owner of MS. Florence, Nat. Lib. XIX. 7. 37 (F), found this high tone uncongenial, and, in extracting part of the *Vetula* passage, he altered the concluding lines so that his text expressly approves the play for a stake.

The last of the Latin poems describing the mediaeval chess is one of 488 lines in a Cracow MS. (Jagellonne, 1954) which bears the title *De ludis Scaccorum*, and is dated 1422. I have already made considerable use of the contents of this, the *Cracow Poem*, pp. 463–72. The poem is written in execrable Latin—the writer usually substitutes *sunt loquentes* for *loquuntur*—and is very obscure. A very brief summary is all that I can give here. The more interesting portions of the poem itself will be found in the Appendix.

Lines 1–14. The inventor of chess. Some attribute it to the Trojans at the time of the Siege; others to a Greek King; others to the Romans. Ulysses is the real inventor.

Lines 15–25. The pieces.

Lines 26–45. The ordinary method of opening the game.

Lines 46–180. The Wards (I, 53–80; II, 81–108; III, 109–140; IV, 109–140; IV, 141–160; V, 161–180).

Lines 181–383. Rules for mating (K, Q, R *v.* K, 181–191; K, Kt, R *v.* K, Q, 192–203; ?, 204–7; ?, 208–217; K, R, Q *v.* K, Q, 218–231; K, R, B *v.* K, Q, P, 232–240; K, Q, 2R, Kt, B *v.* K, Q, R, B, Kt, 241–250; K, R, B *v.* K, B, 251–266; K, B, Kt, Q *v.* K, B, 267–279; mate with B, 280–300; with two Bishops, 301–383).

Lines 384–488. General rules (Stalemate, 384–403; privilege leaps only allowed before the first capture, 404–420; combined move of King and Queen forbidden, 421-429; the new Queen, 430–437; pinned pieces, 438–470; check-rook, 471–474; Bare King, 475–488).

There is no uniform nomenclature for the chessmen, and a number of terms are used for the Bishop (*senex*, *antiquus*, *vetus*, *inveteratus*), Knight (*miles*, *eques*, *quirites*, *tragilis*), and Pawn (*pesculus*, *cliens*, *servus*, *verna*, *juvenis*). The use of *lapis* for a chessman, of *abscacco* for discovered check, and the names of the Bishop, betray the German origin of the poem.

In the concluding section of the poem the writer gives first the incorrect statement of the rule which some players used, and then the correct rule as fixed by Ulysses. Thus in treating of Bare King (475–488), he says:

When your lord King and also the hostile King at the end of the game have yet one man only, and the King wishes to bare and despoil the other, some say and maintain that he who robs the other last remains the winner. This saying is also seen to be similarly false. But this ought to be said and maintained, that he who robs the other first remains the winner. For the bare King is despoiled of his own strength; also to be bared is like being killed. Every game ought to be mate or bare (*nudatus*). The King who was first robbed or despoiled of his Pawn (slave), that King has truly lost the game.

The section which precedes this passage deals correctly with the question whether a pinned piece lost its power of giving check thereby. This question long troubled German players. V. d. Linde (*16. Jrh.*, 113) refers to a discussion on the point in a German magazine of 1783.

Nearly half the poem is occupied with hints as to how to give mate. This part of the poem is perhaps the most obscure of any, and is of very little importance or interest. It is the earliest European attempt to deal with the End-game, but it deals in the main with those features of it in which mediaeval players were most interested—the mate in general, and the mate with the Bishop in particular.

To the Middle Ages also belong four Hebrew works on chess, three of which are in verse. Of these the most important is a poem of seventy-six lines which Hyde first printed with a Latin translation from a MS. in the Bodleian Library, Oxford (Mich. Add., 67, f. 33 b, of the 16th c.). Since Hyde's death three other MSS. have been noted, the earliest being Brit. Mus. Add. 19668, f. 70 b, which is dated 1450. A collation of the other three MSS. was made by Steinschneider for v. d. Linde, and is included in the *Geschichte*, i. 198.

All four MSS. ascribe the poem to the celebrated Spanish rabbi Abraham b. Ezra (B. at Toledo, 1088; D. ? 1167). Steinschneider (v. d. Linde, i. 159–68) and Egers, who has edited b. Ezra's poetry, argue against this authorship—'with too much emphasis,' says Abrahams (*Jewish Life in Mid. Ages*, London, 1896, 390). From the point of view of chess there is no anachronism involved in accepting the authorship of b. Ezra. The poem describes a condition of the rules which was already obsolescent in Spain when the Alfonso MS. was compiled in 1283. If b. Ezra did not write the poem, it must have been written by a contemporary.

A translation of this poem will be found in the Appendix to this chapter. In this I adopt the order of the lines in the three MSS. which were not known to Hyde. This order differs from that of the poem as printed by Hyde and v. d. Linde; the printed text places my lines 33 and 34 six lines earlier, between lines 26 and 27; that is to say, it transfers the privilege leap on the first time of play from the Queen to the Pawn. I have always felt that Hyde's text introduces a difficulty at this point, for the MS. Alf. implies that the Queen's leap was introduced prior to the Pawn's double step. The discovery that the older MSS. do not uphold the order of the Bodleian MS. removes the inconsistency and brings the rules of the MS. into harmony with those of the Alfonso MS.

In broad outline the poem is similar to the Latin poems which we have been examining. The game is played between pieces of two colours which are symbolized as Ethiopians (Black) and Edomites (Red), and the former commence the game. The moves are those of Muslim chess with the single exception already mentioned; the Queen's privilege leap is permitted.

The text is not always clear, and it is possible that it is corrupt in places. V. d. Lasa found a difficulty in the lines describing the move of the Bishop. The move itself is given with sufficient accuracy, but the poem appears to contrast the value of the Bishop and Queen to the advantage of the former. It is, of course, certain that the Queen was considerably more valuable than the Bishop in the mediaeval game.

Hyde also published a prose Hebrew work on chess which he ascribes to the rabbi Bonsenior b. Yaḥya, who is otherwise unknown. The text had been printed earlier, without the name of any author, in Berachyah han-Naqdan's *Mishle Shuʿalim*, Mantua, 1557/8, f. 86 b. It occurs, however, in MS. Brit. Mus. Add. 19668, f. 73 b (written 1450), as by b. Yaḥya. This treatise is written in elegant prose, but the sense is not easy to unravel. Hyde's text has never been collated with the Brit. Mus. MS., and, in addition, his translation is not always reliable. A summary is all that is possible.

The (White) King stands at the beginning on the fourth square, with the Queen (*shegel*) on his right; each has two Knights (*farash* or *sūs*), two Elephants (*fīl*), and two Rooks (*rūq*) on the flanks. Before them are two others whose station is not hidden, these are heroes (*gibbor*). The King moves one square in all directions, the Elephant aslant to the third square, the Knight one square aslant and then one straight, the Rook straight but with no power of leaping over a man. The King must not be left bare. The Queen for her first move goes two or three squares in each direction, and afterwards one step only aslant. The Black King raises his head on the fourth white square and has his Queen on his left. Otherwise there is no difference between the two sides. Black wins because of the number of his Pawns (*gnebed*), who move straight forwards and take aslant, and on reaching the limit of the board become Queens.

The passage which apparently substitutes two pieces whose moves afterwards are omitted for the White Pawns is clearly quite corrupt. The Pawns are themselves called *gibbor* in other Hebrew chess MSS., and it is probable that they are intended here, and the existing sentence which has puzzled all translators is due to a blundering attempt to correct an unintelligible reading in an earlier MS.

It is clear that the mediaeval game in a stage not much later than that of the preceding poem is intended. The MS. is probably of Spanish origin, where there was in the Middle Ages a noted Jewish family of the name b. Yaḥya.

Steinschneider, in his valuable monograph *Schach bei den Juden* (v.d. Linde, i. 155–202), gives the Hebrew text of two other poems which deal with the mediaeval game. The longer, from a Bodleian MS., consists of thirty-eight lines and is the work of Solomon b. Mazzalṭob of Constantinople (1513–1549). The other, only fourteen lines in length, is derived from a Vatican MS. of the 15th c. Both are imitations of the older poem of Abraham b. Ezra, and add nothing to our knowledge of mediaeval chess.

APPENDIX

ORIGINAL TEXTS

I. Alexander Neckam, de Naturis Rerum, *c.* 1180.

(Ed. T. Wright, in the Rolls Series, 1863.)

Cap. clxxxiv.—*De Scaccis.*

Fateor me plus debere Graecis quam Dardaniis. Unde ex quo de ludo Troum inventioni abnoxio paucis egi, de scaccorum ludo, qui se Ulyxis subtilitati debere fertur a nonnullis, scribere non erit molestum.

Pedites igitur in una linea disponuntur, reliquis secundum varias dispositiones varia loca sortientibus. Secundum primitivam tamen ludi adinventionem pedites in secunda linea scaccarii ordinabuntur, dignioribus personis in prima linea dispositis. Pedes directo tramite incedit, nisi cum iniurias suas in hoste persequitur. Tunc enim gressum obliquat, cum praedo efficitur. Cum vero expleto cursu ultimam tenet lineam reginae dignitatem adipiscitur, sed sexus privilegio destitui videtur. Tiresiatur veniens ad Gades suas noveque fruitur incessu, Iphis alter. Ovidius:—

Sequitur puer (comes) Iphis euntem
Quam solita est maiore gradu.[1]

Angulariter incedit postquam sublimatus est qui in directum tendebat quamdiu privata erat persona.

Senex Nestoris personam gerens explorator est, qui vulgo Alphicus dicitur. Reginae geminat cursum, gressum obliquans, tanquam insidiator.

Miles, illorum militum qui castra sequuntur repraesentans personam, reginae gressum cum incessu peditis unico transitu metitur, partim obliquans cursum, partim directo tramite legens iter.

Rochus expeditissimum militum in re militari repraesentans, qui et ab antiquis Ianus biceps dictus est, unde et duobus capitibus munitur, nunquam cursum obliquare dignatur, semper directum iter observans.

Rex vero nunc pro nutu dignitatis ipsius gressum obliquat, nunc in directum movetur; cujus haec est privelegiata dignitas, ut capi non queat. Unde et rex Francorum Ludovicus Grossus, cum a rege Henrico I. confectus esset, fugae sese committens patrocinio, milite quodam strenuo acerrime fugientem persequente, sed et habenas equi apprehendente et proclamante regem esse captum, 'Fugi' inquit 'indisciplinate miles et proterve; nec etiam regem scaccorum fas est capi'. Et gladium vibrans, ictu fulmineo corpus militis in duas divisit portiones.

[1] Metam. ix. 785.

Sed ad vanitatem ludi scaccorum redeamus, cui tantam diligentiam adhibent ludentes ac si magnum emolumentum ex victoria essent consecuturi. Quid? Immo victori videtur se laurea dignum esse. Confunditur qui ludum amisit ac si magnum discrimen incurrerit. Instauratur iterato ludus, disponuntur acies altrinsecus, exeunt a locis suis pedites, tamquam primitus cum hostibus congressuri. Totum se intra se colligit uterque ludentium, vires ingenii sui uterque ex successu ludi metitur. Et dum ingenii acumen existimatur feliciter exercitari, fatigatum nimis hebetatur. Emergunt repentinae indignationes, et furorem animi indignantis inclusum prodit nunc pallor oris liventis, nunc igneus rubor vultum accendens. Saepe in medium convitia proferuntur, et ludus non in serium negotium nobilitatur, sed in rixam degenerat. O quot millia animarum Orco transmissa sunt occasione illius ludi quo Reginaldus filius Eymundi in calculis ludens militem generosum cum illo ludentem in palatio Karoli magni cum uno scaccorum interemit.

II. The Einsiedeln Poem.

[MSS. (*a*) MS. Einsidlensis, 365; *Versus de Scachis.* (*b*) MS. Einsidlensis, 319; *De aleae ratione.*

(*a*) occupies a single leaf which was formerly a portion of the binding of MS. Einsid. 125, when only the latter part of the poem, ll. 65–98, was visible. (*b*) is an early copy of this visible part. The original leaf was carefully loosened from the binding by Gallus Morell, the Superior of the Monastery, in 1846, and inserted in the composite volume, MS. 365.

The text was printed by Hagen, *Carmina medii aevi maximam partem inedita*, Berne, 1877, pp. 137–141, in the *Nordisk Skaktidende*, Copenhagen, 1877, pp. 77–83, with a Danish translation, and in Vetter's *Das Schachzabelbuch Kunrats v. Ammenhausen*, Frauenfeld, 1892, p. xxxiii, note c. A German version by Hagen is in *Der Bund*, Berne, 21 Oct. 1876, and in the *Sch.*, 1876, p. 335, and an English one by H. Aspinwall-Howe in the *Montreal Gazette*, c. 1890–1. Collated from photographs.]

Versus de Scachis.

Si fas est ludos abiectis ducere curis
  Est aliquis, mentem quo recreare queas.
Quem si scire uelis, huc cordis dirige gressum,
  Inter complacitos hic tibi primus erit.
Non dolus ullus inest, non sunt periuria fraudum,
  Non laceras corpus membra vel ulla tui.
Non soluis quicquam nec quemquam soluere cogis;
  Certator nullus insidiosus erit.
Quicquid damnoso perfecerit alea ludo
  Hic refugit totum simplicitate sui.
Tetragonum primo certaminis æquor habetur
  Multiplicis tabulæ per sua damna ferax.
Quamlibet octonos in partem ducite calles,
  Rursus in oblicum tot memor adde uias.
Mox cernes tabulas æqui discriminis octo,
  Octies ut repleas æquoris omne solum.
Sunt quibus has placuit duplici fucare colore,
  Grata sit ut species et magis apta duplex.

Dum color unus erit, non sic racionis imago
  Discitur: alternus omne rependit iter.
Illic digeritur populus regumque duorum
  Agmina: partitur singula quisque loca.
Quorum quo numerus ludenti rite patescat,
  Post bis quindenos nouerit esse duos.
Non species eadem, nomen non omnibus unum:
  Quam racio uaria, sic neque nomen idem.
Nec color unus erit diuisis partibus æquis:
  Pars hæc si candet, illa rubore nitet.
Non diuersa tamen populorum causa duorum:
  Certamen semper par in utroque manet.
Sufficit unius partis dinoscere causas;
  Ambarum species, cursus et, unus erit.
Ordo quidem primus tabulas diuisus in octo
  Prefati ruris agmina prima tenet,
In quorum medio rex et regina locantur,
  Consimiles specie, non racione tamen.
Post hos acclini comites, hinc inde locati,
  Auribus ut dominum conscia uerba ferat.
Tertius a primis æques est hinc inde, paratus
  Debita transuerso carpere calle loca.
Extremos retinet fines inuectus uterque
  Bigis seu rochus, marchio siue magis.
Hos qui precedit (retinet quis ordo secundus
  Æquoris), effigies omnibus una manet:
Et racione pari pedites armantur in hostem
  Proceduntque prius bella gerenda pati.
Liquerit istorum tabulam dum quisque priorem
  Recte, quæ sequitur, mox erit hospes ea.
Impediat cursum ueniens ex hostibus alter:
  Obuius ipse pedes prœlia prima gerit.
Namdum sic uni ueniens fit proximus alter,
  Dissimiles capiat ut color unus eos,
Figenti fuerit cui primum lata facultas,
  Mittit in obliquum uulnera sæua parem.
Obuius ex reliquis dum sic fit quisque ruina
  Hac preter regem precipitatus erit.
Quilibet hic ruerit, non ultra fugere fas est:
  Tollitur e medio, uulnere dumque cadit.
Solus rex capitur nec ab æquore tollitur ictus,
  Irruit, ut sternat, nec tamen ipse ruit.
Hic quia prima tenens consistit in æquore semper,
  Circa se est cursus quemque tabella sibi.
At uia reginæ facili racione patescit:
  Obliquus cursus huic color unus erit.
Candida si sedes[1] fuerit sibi prima tabella,
  Non color alterius hanc[2] aliquando[3] capit.

Hoc iter est peditis, si quando pergit in hostem,
Ordinis ad finem cumque meare potest.
Nam sic concordant: obliquo tramite, desit
Ut si regina, hic quod et illa queat.
Ast quos uicinos dominis curuosque notaui,
Transuerso cursu sat loca pauca petunt.
Istarum fuerit positus quoquisque [4] colore,
Primo dissimilem non aliquando pete.
Post primam tabulam mox fit sibi [5] tercia [6] sedes,
Qua fit reginæ, dissonus ille uiæ.
Preterea cursus æquites [7] girosque facessunt.
Sunt quibus obliqui multiplicesque gradus:
Dum primam sedem quisquis contempnit eorum,
Discolor a prima tercia [6] carpit eum.[8]
Sic alternatim tenet hunc illumque colorem,
Quęlibet ut cursus esse tabella queat.
At rochus semper procedit tramite recto
Utque datur racio,[9] porrigit ille gradum.
Quattuor in partes gressum distendere fas est
Atque uno cursu tota meare loca.
Hi certamen habent æquitesque [10] per horrida bella,
Ut, si defuerint, prœlia pene cadunt.[11]
In quibus et reliquis extat custodia sollers:
Inconsultus enim prœlia nemo petit.
Cuique datur custos, ne incautum uulnera sternant:
Solus, heu, facile, si petat arua, ruit.
Cum uero cuncti certatim prœlia densant,
Hostis in hostilem fit celer ire necem.
Hanc rex deuitat, hac numquam sternitur ille,
Hoc facto reliquis amplius ipse potest.
Dum tamen hunc hostis cogit protendere gressum,
Si conclusus erit, prœlia tota ruunt.

Various Readings from MS. (*b*): [1] fides. [2] hinc. [3] aliquanda. [4] quo quisque. [5] tibi. [6] tertia. [7] equites. [8] iter. [9] ratio. [10] equitesque. [11] cadant.

III. The Winchester Poem (*Poema temp. Sax.*).

[From MS. Bodl. Oxford, Auct. F. 2. 14, f. 110 *b*, without title. The text was printed by Hyde with the title *De Shahiludio, Poema tempore Saxonum exaratum, Carmine politico seu Pseudo-Trochaico*, in his *Mandragorias*, 1698, 179; whence in Massmann, 125. Collated from a photograph.]

Belli cupit instrumentum. Qui ludendo fingere.
Atque arte perfluosa. Prelium componere.
Duos tabularum reges. Ponat per planiciem.
Rex paratus ad pugnandum. Primum locum teneat.
Eius atque dextrum latus. Regina possideat.
Iuxta illam caluum pone. quasi pro custodia.
Rex iturus contra regem. Pedetemptim properet.

Primitus alteram petens. occupare tabulam.
Procul namque duci eum. Repellit licentiam.
Tunc equestris apponatur. Prope ad certamina.
Bifrons rochus ordinetur. In extrema tabula.
Alter caluus iuxta regem. Parte sit ex altera.
Caballarius itemque. ad propugnandum facilis.
Sic et rochus aduocetur. Ad currendum agilis.
Unusquisque precedentes. Assequantur pedites.
Tunc incipient pedestres. Prelium committere.
Neque uerti retro queant. Sed directe properent.
Quod reppererint incautum. Per transuersum feriant.
Cadit caluus per transuersum. tertiam ad tabulam.
Sedet semper in occulto. Quasi fur ut rapiat.
Sepe namque suo furto. Se parat uictoriam.
Eques equitem. pedestrem. Pedes prendit pariter.
Rochus rochum interimit. Se sequentem iugulans.
Firmum pactum calui tenent. Neque sibi noceant.
Nam regina non ualebit. Impedire alteram.
Sui regi deputata. Velut pro custodia.
Circunquaque per transuersum. Binas regat tabulas.
Cum pedester usque summam. Venerit ad tabulam.
Nomen eius tunc mutetur. Appelletur ferzia.
Eius interim regine. Gratiam obtineat.
Ergo regem non audebit. Vllus posse tangere.
Habet namque potestatem. Cunctos interimere.
Contra ipsum non audebit. Nisi scachum dicere.
Si clametur regi scachum. Vel ab uno pedite.
Declinare statim debet. Proximam ad tabulam.
Si non habet ubi pergat. Scacha mattum audiat.

IV. Codex Benedictbeuren.

[From MS. Munich, L. 4660, f. 91 *b*; of the 13th c. Printed in *Carmina Burana* (ed. Schmeller, Stuttgart, 1847), and in v. d. Linde, ii. 168.]

Roch, pedes, regina, senex, eques, insuper et rex.
Conflictus uocat edictus uox Martis ad ictus.
Uox sonat in Rama: trahe tost capra concine clama
Uictus ab hoste gemat qui dum fit schach roch et hie mat.

V. The Elegy ('Qui cupit').

[The following MSS. are known to me:
B = MS. Munich Monac. Emmeran. K. 6, f. 41; of 12th c.
D = MS. Bodl. Oxford, Digby 53, f. 16 *b*; of end of 12th c.
A = MS. Munich, L. 4660, f. 92; of 13th c.
R = MS. Reims, 1275 (I, 743), p. 430; of 13th c.
N = MS. Naples, Musei Borbonici CCLXI, iv. f. 13; of 14th c.
W = MS. Wolfenbüttel, Aug. 85. 7, f. 18 *b*; end of 15th c.
F = MS. Florence, Laurenziana, P. L. xci. Sup. 28, f. 97; of 15–16 c.

Printed by Massmann, 128; in *Carmina Burana*, 246; in *Qst.*, 91 (a 'restored' text by Deutsch). I have examined D, A, R, and N.]

Elegia de Ludo Scachorum.[a]

Qui cupit egregium scacorum noscere ludum
  Audiat, ut potui carmine composui.
Versibus in paucis dicam sibi prelia litis.
  Quatuor in tabula bis loca sunt uaria;
Albescit primus, rubet atque colore secundus,
  Aut niger aut clacus[b] pingitur aut rubeus.[c]
In primo rochus committere bella minatur,
  Statque secundus eques[d] ludicra iura tenens,
Tertius alficus custos regalis habetur,
  Quartus rex retinet, femina quinta sedet.
Post illos procerum reuocabitur ordo priorum.
  Procedit peditum turba uelox nimium.
Stat pedes, et dextra rapit et de parte sinistra
  Quem sibi diuersum cernit et oppositum;
Et si quando datur tabule sibi tangere summam,
  Regine solitum preripit officium.
Vir factus mulier regiferus[e] arbiter heret,
  Imperat et regnat, hinc capit inde labat.
Bella mouent primi pedites, labuntur et ipsi
  Et reliquis timidam dant moriendo uiam.
Per spacium tabule roco conceditur ire
  In qua parte uelit, si nihil obstiterit.
Maior maiores rapit, et fallendo minores
  Sepius, et minimis fallitur a sociis.
Belliger insignis prudens celer aptus et armis
  Currit eques rapidus,[f] quo patet arte locus;
Decipit insontes socios et fraude carentes
  Terret et insequitur, hinc capit hinc capitur.
Alficus[g] triuius[h] cornuta[k] fronte timendus
  Ante retro comites decipit inuigiles.
A dominis minimi, domini capiuntur ab imis,
  Sic mixti procerum turba perit peditum.
Rex manet incaptus, subtracta coniuge solus,
  Coniuge subtracta, nil[l] ualet[m] in tabula.
Sepius est mattus seruorum turbine septus
  Et mattum suffert si uia nulla patet.[n]
Omnis enim mattum clamat mattum sibi mattum;
  Sic quoque ludatur denuo si placeat.

VARIOUS READINGS. [a] *A, R have no title; D has* De ludo skakkorum; *N* De scacchis libellus. [b] *A* claucus; *D* glaucus; *N* blancus; *R* flaucus. [c] *R, N* uarius. [d] *N* equus. [e] *W* tegiferus. [f] *N* equus rabidus. [g] *R* alphicus; *F* alfinis. [h] *D, N* curuus; *R* trinus; *F* constat. [k] *D* uelud et fur cornuta. [l] *A, N* rex. [m] *A, N, R* manet. [n] *D, N, R end here.*

VI. THE DEVENTER POEM.

[The following MSS. are known to me:

A = MS. Deventer, 1791, last leaf; of *c.* 1400. (37 lines.)
D = MS. Coll. Arms, London, E. D. N. No. 11; of 13th c. (28 lines.)
E = MS. Montpellier, 10, f. 1; dated 24 March 1380. (33 lines.)

B = MS. Bodleian, Oxford, 2067. 46, f. 66; of 15th c. (31 lines.)
O = MS. Orleans, 308 (261), pp. 7–9; of 15th c.
C = MS. Padua; of 15th c. (30 lines.)
F = MS. Berlin, 236; of 18th c.

Printed by Hyde, 1694, 181; by Massmann, 126; by v. d. Linde, Het Schaakspel, 24. I have examined A, D, B, C.]

De Scachis.[a]

Si quis scacorum ludum uult scire decorum[b]
Hoc carmen discat, si docte ludere gliscat.
Asser quadratus, uario colore notatus
Depictusque bene, fit campus litis amene.
Hic fit formosa sine sanguine pugna iocosa.
Ordine duplici[c] bini reges inimici
Agmina componunt. Pedites in fronte reponunt
Principio belli reges sub sorte duelli.
Si quot sint scire cupis, octoque potes reperire.
Roci[d] ueloces stant post, equitesque feroces
Hi stant; utrique gemini bellantur inique.[e]
Rex et regina stolidorum[f] corpora bina
Agmine supremo latitant post hos quoque nemo.[g]
His ita compositis si litem scire uelitis,
Aures aptate quum loquor enucleate.
Architenens uetus[h] miscet certamina letus,
Tendit in obliquum cum fallere uult inimicum.
Si ualet extremum tabule perstringere[k] demum,
Tunc augmentatur, tunc fercia[l] iure uocatur.[e]
Miles it obliquo bello metuendus iniquo;
Si prius albescit, dum prosilit ipse rubescit.
At rochus[m] seuus dextro graditur modo leuus,
Uelox ipse quoque, si uult salit ante retroque.
Stultus saltator triuius, quasi fur speculator,
Si rubet in primo, nunquam candescit in imo.[n]
Fercia[o] regalis[p] saltatrix quadriuialis[q]
Postquam candebit nunquam rubicunda parebit.
Restat oportunus tuto rex tot hostibus unus;
Iste suam gentem regit ut uidet hunc uenientem.[g]
Quatuor et totidem cum uult loca circuit idem.
Hostibus hic obicit scaccibus, post denuo dicit,[r]
Affirmo uere si se nequit inde mouere
Omnis homo mattum clamat mattum sibi mattum.[s]
Reges utrique discurrunt semper ubique,
Et modo dextrorsum modo sursum nuncque deorsum.
Obuius hic scacum geminat scacum sibi scacum;
Si steterit mattum omnes clament sibi mattum.

VARIOUS READINGS. [a] *A, D have no title; B* Ludus scaccorum; *C* Incipit ludus scacorum. [b] *B, C, D place line 5 before line 1.* [c] *A* triplici; *B, D* cum triplici; *C* quadruplici. [d] *D* roxii; *C* prompti. [e] *B omits this line.* [f] *B* solidorum. [g] *C omits this line.* [h] *A, B* cetus; *C* ectus; *D* setus. [k] *B, C* pertingere; *D* contingere. [l] *C* fortia. [m] *C* rectus (*gloss* rochus); *D* roccus; [n] *This and the preceding line follow line 27 in D.* [o] *C* tertia; *B* fforcia. [p] *A* gregalis; *C* regallis (regina). [q] *C* uel quadrivialis; *D* obliqualis. [r] *B, D omit this line.* [s] *B, C, D end here.*

VII. The Hexameter Line.

[In Catholicon Anglicum, 1483, s.v. Roke; MS. Brit. Mus., Harl. 1002, f. 113 (Wright-Wülker, A.-S. and OE. Vocabs., I. xvi); in Waleys' Summ. Coll., I. x. vii (ed. Zell, Cologne); in Hales, Destr. Viciorum, 1497, IV. xxiii; and in MS. Brit. Mus., Sloan 3281, f. 81 *a*.]

Rex, rocus, alphinus, miles, regina, pedinus.

VIII. It Pedes ad Bellum.

[I know the following MSS:

C = MS. Brit. Mus., Cotton Cleop. B. ix. f. 10 *b*; of end of 13th c. (14 lines.)
T = MS. Trin. Coll. Cambridge, O. 2. 45; of 13th c. (14 lines.)
B = MS. Berne, 531, ff. 50 *b* and 197 *a*; of 15th c. (9 lines.)
P = MS. Paris, 1170, of 15th c. (7 lines.)
H = MS. Wolfenbüttel, Weissenb. 89; 15th c. MS. of Cessolis in which 6 lines from this poem are quoted at the commencement of the chapters of Book IV.

The poem is printed in Hagen, *Carm. med. aevi*, Berne, 1877, p. 141, No. lxxxiii; in Vetter, *Schachzabelbuch Kunrats v. Ammenhausen*, 1892, p. xxxiv, note c, and in *Qst.*, 93 and 191. A German translation by Hagen is in his *Räthselpoesie*, Biel, 1869, p. 35, in *Der Bund*, Berne, 21 Oct. 1876, and in the *Sch.* 1876, p. 337.]

Carmina Ludi Scachorum.[a]

Ludum scachorum si tu uis scire decorum,
Hoc carmen lector discas, et ludere gliscas.
It pedes ad bellum prior, incipit ipse duellum,
Pergit in obliquum punctum feriens inimicum.
Alphilus[b] in triuiis[c] parat insidias inimicis,
Pugnat potenter, temptatque ferire latenter.
Miles in aduerso puncto mediante relicto
Prosilit, et fortem prosternit fortior hostem.
Linea si pateat roco[d] capit omne quod obstat.
Pergit in obliquum regalis femina punctum.
Rex loca circa se clipeo defendit et ense.
Si scacces regem, regalem perdere sedem
Cogitur, et totus sit rex de sede remotus.
Dic regi scaccum; si semita non patet illi,
Matus erit factus nusquam latuisse coactus.
Miles et alphinus, rex, roc, regina, pedinus,
Et inter scaccos alphinus inutilis astat.[e]

Various Readings. Lines 1 and 2 occur only in B; they are taken from the *Deventer Poem*. Lines 12 to the end occur only in C and T. B also omits lines 4 and 6, P lines 4 and 8 (for which it substitutes line 6); C and T line 11. H has only lines 3, 5, 7, 9, 10 and 11. [a] *This title is from* B^2, *the other MSS. have none.* [b] *B* affricus; *C* alpheus. [c] *P* ternis. [d] *B, H, P* rochus. [e] Cf. Alanus, *De Parabolis*, 'Sic inter scacchos alphinus inutilis exstat, inter aves bubo.'

IX. The Corpus Poem.

[A composite poem, based apparently on No. VII, in two MSS.:

C = Cod. Corpus, Cambridge, 177, f. 50 *b*, of 15th c.
L = Cod. London, Bibl. Reg., 12 EE. xxi, f. 103, of 15th c.

Extracts from L were given in Allen's paper, 'Chess in Europe during the Middle Ages', in the *New Monthly Magazine*, London, 1822, iv. 319 and 417, and v. 125 and 315.]

Incipit Modus et Scientia Ludi Scaccorum.

Egregium ludum : scaccorum scire uolentes
Intendant nostris : scriptis ut sint sapientes
Luditur iure tabula : quadrataque uariata
Linea prima tenet : magnates nobiliores
Altera iure[1] tenet : pedites quoque debiliores
Rex sedet in medio : cum quo Regina locatur
Albus rex rubro[2] : spatio primum poteatur[3]
Et rubrus[4] niueum : spatium rex iure tenebit
ffemina rubra rubro : candens[5] niueo possidebit[6]
Proximus Alphicus est : illum post huc[7] quoque miles
ffine sedet rochus : qui scit prosternere uiles
Octo nobilibus : octo pedites copulantur
Conueniunt hostes : post hoc et bella parantur
It pedes ad bellum : prior incipit ille duellum
Semper procedit : paulatim nec retrocedit
Uadit in obliquum : cum ledere uult inimicum
Lex sibi iure datur : domine si fine locatur
Rochus quem cernet : prope uel longe ut[8] sternit
Nec[9] est in bello : quisque uelocior illo
Si nihil[10] obstiterit : hostes tunc undique querit
Hic tamen obliquis : parcet cunctis inimicis
Miles ab obliquo : puncto mediante relicto
Prosilit et fortem : prosternit fortior hostem
Cum uenit ad bellum : saltando mutat agellum
Alphicus in triviis (*MSS.* inter imis) : parat insidias inimicis
Saltans incedit : per obliquum sic quoque ledit
Condit in obliquum : regalis femina passum
Semper et in binis[11] : parat insidias inimicis[12]
Regia maiestas : datur ingens atque potestas
Per loca uaria[13] se : clipeo defendit et ense
Ante retroque ferit : hostes et sternere querit
Si seruat legem : non debet tangere regem
Cum quis insidias : regi per uerba minatur
Rex illi cedat : ne deuictus uideatur
Nam dum scak' dicunt : regi si cedere nescit
Mox captiuus erit : et sic crimen sibi crescit
Deuicto rege : pariter socii superantur
Cetera turba iacet : nec habet quo rege rogantur.

VARIOUS READINGS. [1] *C* in. [2] *C* rubeo. [3] *C* potiatur. [4] *C* rubeus. [5] *L* andens. [6] *C* residebit. [7] *C* hunc. [8] *C* cito. [9] *C* non. [10] *C* nichil. [11] *C* bimo. [12] *C*, *L* inimico. [13] *C* certa.

X. DE NATURA SCATORUM.

[MS. Reims, 1275 (I. 743), p. 183. A composite volume from the Abbey of St. Arnoul of Metz. 13th c.]

Nil pedes excedit, numquam redit, anteat, errat
Dum capit, in fine fercia nomen ei.

Seruat in alfino primum natura colorem
Qui torte sequitur per tria puncta uiam.
Saltanti similis oblique miles oberrat
Cui numquam remanet qui fuit ante color.
Rocus agit totum nisi sint obstacula lustro,
Antea, uel retro, uel per utrumque latus.
Paulatim per puncta uagans propriique coloris
Non oblita manet fercia qualis erat.
Non tangit regem. Rex nil transit, uariatur
Quem cacus demat sepe timere facit
Interea predantis spacium si uenerit hostis
Preda fit illius, linea cuius erat.

XI. The Vetula. Bk. I.

[MSS. of this Poem are fairly plentiful; there are two in the Brit. Mus., Harl. 3353 and 5263. The poem was printed, Cologne, *c.* 1470 and 1479; again 1533 (place and printer unknown); Frankfurt, 1610; Wolfenbüttel, 1661 and 1702.]

xxxi. Est alius ludus scacorum, ludus Ulyxis,
Ludus Troiana quem fecit in obsidione
Ne vel tederet proceres in tempore treuge
Vel belli si quis pro vulneribus remaneret
In castris: ludus, qui castris assimilatur
Inventor cuius iure laudandus in illo est.
Sed causam laudis non advertunt, nisi pauci,
Quam subtile fuit, species sex premeditari
Saltus in campis, quos tantum multiplicare
Possemus, quod ab initio nulli duo ludi
Omnino similes fuerint! advertite pauci,
Quod sicut vultus hominum sibi dissimilantur
Hactenus in tantum, quod non fuerint duo, qui non
Distingui possent, cum tantae disparitatis
Causa sit in coelo; (quia coeli nulla figura
Est alii similis, tanta alternatio motus;
Quam septem faciunt, per bis sex signa, planetae!)
Et tamen est numerus finitus motibus ipsis,
Sicut et astrorum domini scripsisse leguntur:
Sic ludus, factus motus coelestis ad instar,
Est ex finitis saltus speciebus in agris,
Infinitata tamen est multiplicatio ludi.
xxxii. Sex species saltus exercent, sex quoque scaci,
Miles et alphinus, roccus, rex, virgo, pedesque;
In campum primum de sex istis saliunt tres,
Rex, pedes, et virgo. Pedes in rectum salit, atque
Virgo per obliquum, Rex saltu gaudet utroque.
Ante retroque tamen tam Rex, quam virgo, moventur,
Ante pedes solum, capiens obliquus in ante,

Cum tamen ad metam stadii percurrerit, ex tunc
Sicut virgo salit. In campum vero secundum
Tres alii saliunt, in rectum roccus, eique
Soli concessum est, ultra citraque salire.
Oblique salit alphinus, sed miles utroque
Saltum componit. Coeli veniamus ad instar.
xxxiii. Campos, signa, modos saliendi, scito planetas;
Rex est Sol, pedes est Saturnus, Mars quoque miles,
Regia virgo Venus, Alphinus episcopus ipse est
Juppiter, et roccus discurrens Luna. Quid ergo
Mercurius? numquam non omnibus omnia? certe
Omnia Mercurius: cuius complexio semper
Est convertibilis ad eum cui iungitur ipse;
Sunt et astrorum domini scripsisse leguntur;
Aut quia Mercurii complexio frigida, sicca,
Sicut Saturni, licet intense minus. Ex quo
Pervenit ad metam pedes, ex hinc Mercurii fit,
Praesertim quia tunc salit ut virgo, Venerisque
Mercuriique locus doctrina quaeritur una.
Et mediis cursus est idem semper eorum;
Sicut et astrorum domini scripsisse leguntur.
Nobilis hic ludus, nulli suspectus, et omni
Personae licitus, moderate dum modo ludat,
Dum modo quaeratur victoria sola per ipsum:
Non lucrum, ne cum praedictis annumeretur.
Cum deciis autem qui primus lusit in illo,
Foedavit ludum, languebit namque satelles
Immotus, nisi sors deciorum moverit ipsum
Nec fuit hoc factum: nisi vel quia non nisi pauci
Ludere noverunt tractim; vel amore lucrandi.

[This passage is extracted in the prefatory matter of MS. Florence, Nat. Lib. xix. 7. 37 (Florence CB), but it is shortened to 24 lines, and the order of these is different. After the introductory six lines, this MS. continues with lines 16–19 of xxxiii, which it utterly perverts thus:

Nobilis hic ludus nulli suspectus, et omni
Persone licitus, moderate dum modo ludat,
Dum non pecunia queratur sola per ipsum
Ne cum predictis decijs anumeretur.

The MS. then continues with the lines of xxxii (omitting l. 6) and concludes with the first line of xxxiii.

The following extracts are from the French translation *La Vieille*:

1. Car six especes de saillir Ne puent les eschecs faillir, Qui sont six, si com vous orrez. En deux pars veoir y pourrez: Roy, roc, chevalier et alphin, Fierge et peon, tendans afin De leur ennemis desconfire.

2. Et quant le peon fait sa trache, Tant qu'il vient au bout de l'estache, Lors de fierge fait tout l'office Et est pareil en exercise.

3. La roine que nommons fierge Tient de Venus qui n'est pas vierge, Aimable est et amoureuse, Debonnaire et non orgueilleuse.

4. L'aulphin, portant d'evesque mitre, De Jupiter ensuist le tiltre, Signifiant religion; Moult bonne est sa conjonction.]

XII. The Cracow Poem.

[MS. Jagellonne Lib., Cracow, 1954, pp. 405–420. A critical edition is promised by Freiherr v. Holzhausen.]

Ad me transire debet qui uult bene scire
Iludum scacorum; cum sit ludus dominorum,
Iludus multorum quoque debet esse iocorum.
Sunt aduersantes plures et commemorantes,
Scacorum factor ludi, seu quis fuit auctor.
Sunt affirmantes quidam, necnon reputantes,
Iludum prot(r)actum presertim tunc fore factum
Quando plebs vrbem perlustrauit Troianam.
Sed quidam fatur prorecto sic meditatur,
Quod Grece ludum rex vnus edidit istum.
Sed sunt ponentes alii simul atque loquentes
Quod pridem Rome ludus factus fuit iste.
Nunc omnes vere debent istud retinere,
Vlixes ludum prudens qui condidit istum.
Ludum querentes scacorum sunt retinentes
Normas presentes, quas scripserunt sapientes,
Cum quibus exorte trahit semper sine sorte,
Iludus scacorum lapidum tractus variorum.
Sunt triginta duo lapides ludo memorato,
Assere ponuntur per quos scacos oriuntur.
Sunt lapides isti sex in specie memorati,
Hii sunt rex, regina, senex, pariter quoque miles,
Pesculus atque rochus, hiis sit ludusque totus.
Nunc sistit fandum necnon vbique palandum,
Qualiter exire debent lapides resilire.
Sit tibi (*MS.* tibus) primus iens regis proprius modo cliens,
Hic tibi saltabit ternum campum properabit;
Necnon exibit properanter tunc simul ibit
Regine ternum seruus digne super aruum.[1]
Post hoc miles iter mox arripiet sibi dexter
Tunc prope reginam, sic deuitesque ruinam.
Post hoc exibitque rochi tunc pesculus ibit,
Huius et illius qui stat ad ternum siue secundum.
Sepe manet ludus ex hoc firmus quoque tutus,
Raro fit peius cum proximus est locus eius.
Antiqui dextri gressus fietque sinistri
Ante rochum super ad campum medium quoque planum,
Et faciet saltum campum tunc immediatum
Militis ipsius cliens dexterque sinister.
Pesculus antiqui dexter simul immediatum
Transiet ad campum, rapiet tunc quoque alienum,
Sed cliens veterem qui stans est ante sinistrum
Propter reginam nullus debet properare,

Idem regine custos quia dicitur esse:
Pesculus oppositi faciet simul hoc senis idem.
Nunc est tractandum, pariter necnon reserandum,
Qualiter in scacis fiunt vrbes tibi petis.
Nunc harum fore sistunt aut quinque figure,
Nam cum regina fiet custodia bina
Ad palmum prima dextrumque secunda sinistrum.
Quod sit primus iuuenis domini regis tibi cliens,
Regine cursum seruus faciet tibi rursum.
Prima custodia. Hii faciunt terminis cito mancipites duo saltum;
Post hoc regina ternum tunc transiet ipsa.
Vt demonstratum prius est et commemoratum
Pesculus antiqui nigri seruus quoque dextri
Albe regine nunc custos dicitur esse,
Atque senex albus fiet custos simul eius.
(Hoc semper tu ne debes sic retinere,
Si tua regina fuerit tunc nobilis alba;
Assere tunc uerso fiet contrarius ordo,
Ipsius niger senis extunc verna sinister;
Atque senex doctor albus fiet tibi semper
Albe regine domine custos tibi nempe.
Aduerso scriptum ludo serues memoratum,
Et cum regina domina fuerit tua nigra,
Albi tunc veteris hic pesculus atque sinistri
Custos regine fiet domine tibi nigre,
Atque senex niger illam temptet tibi semper.
Assere tunc uerso, reliqu(u)m sensum retinebis,
Quod cliens albi seu pesculus inueteratus
Antiqu(u)s niger simul hanc temptetque sinister.)
Exponens iuuenem dextrum stans ante quiritem
Hic faciet saltum campum tunc immediatum.
Pesculus ante rochum ternum capiet sibi campum.
Concipiasque rochum dextrum qui stat tibi palmum,
Hunc iuuenem dexter antiqu(u)s tunc commitetur.
Intra rex vrbem confestim tunc sibi factam,
Rex tunc a scacis locus hic tutus sibi pacis;—
Primaque sic nota tibi sit custodia tota.

[*Four more 'wards' are described with similar prolixity. Then follows:*]

Regule de mattis. De ludis varios scacorum dicere formas
Ast uolo diuersas nunc mattandi dare rationes.
Si quem mattare cupis, non excoriare,
Rex super aduersans quem campum sit tibi pergens,
Ad campum similem proprium sic tu loca regem;
Ponere reginam semper debes prope regem.
Similiterque rochum tunc in fine retinebis;
Linea tunc reliqua prope lamen sit locus eius.
Aduersa regis excessimque uetat idem,

Reginam propriam ponas similiter anteque regem ;
Mattum percipiet confestim rex inimicus.

Regula secunda.

Regula mattalis rursum datur altera talis.
Rex milesque rochus si ludi fine manebunt,
Et rex aduersus reginam si retinebit,
Reginam tollas eius veterem sibi mittas,
Extremum lamen regem tu pelle, repelle,
In riga reliquaque rochum ponas prope lamen.
Quo rex aduersans vadit, penses diligenter.
Ast equitem contra regem ponas memoratum,
Qui regi gressum vetat vlteriorem.
Ast equitem proprium loca semper tu prope regem,
Ante tuum regemque rocho mattum dabis illi.
Tuncque rochum proprium custodit rex herus ipse.

[*Nine more rules of this kind follow. Then we come to the general rules.*]

Ad lamen regem cum sis pellens inimicum,
Atque vias omnes sibi clausisti quoque gressus,
Ast cuius famulans regis gressa similiter eget,
Quidem dicentes sunt prorecto retinentes,
Id quod vere rex mattus dicitur esse
Et quod sit certe sit ludus perditus iste.
Hoc nullus vere dictum debet retinere,
Hoc dictum certe quia falsum dicitur esse
Quod rex sit mattus et ludus commemoratus,
Ex quo rex nullus nec poteris fore mattus
Ludus nec alliquis raro nudus fine factus (*MS.* factis).
Extremo fine, qui dant matti quoque causam
Insuper in campo cum rex stet sine soluto,
Quo rex mattus eget prorecto nec habet illum
Claussus et abstractus fertur ludus memoratus.
Si sic fit tractus idem ludus quoque factus,
Tunc nullum lucrum fertur nec dat quoque dampnum,
Ex quo non mattus rex per scacum nequit captus,
Cum stans sit campo rex idem certe soluto,
Hunc regem mattum per scacos nec fore factum.
Penses quid fatur hec regula que comitatur.
Ad ternum campum lapidis facit ante rapinam
Pesculus egressum necnon primum bene saltum ;
Post illam transire nequit lapidisque rapinam,
Pesculus ad ternum quiuis campum memoratum.
Vlixes fatur pariter quoque nempe probatur,
Ad ternum campum non debet pes(c)ulus
Si costodire uult quem lapidem super illum.
Ad ternum campum lapidis tunc ante receptum,
Rex et regina possunt tibi condere saltum,
Nec rex ullius lapidis poterit (*MS.* -is) fore custos
Ad ternum campum si mallet condere saltum.

Consimili more regina nequit fore custos
Vllius lapidis si ternis idem super aruis,
Ex quo regina uel quiuis pesculus atque rex
Si transire cupit et uult ternum super aruum
Hunc faciunt saltum lapidis tunc ante rapinam.
Vlixes sicut de scaccis asseris ipse
In codice suo manifestum sistit in illo,
Iubentur ludi scacorum qui fore fertur
Ex isto certe tunc infertur manifeste:
Rex et regina nullos debent simul ire,
Sed dominus per se rex gressum debet habere,
Sic ecciam per se domina debet properare.
Sicut in gressu lapidis prius sit memoratum:
Sic bini lapides nequ(e)unt pariter properare.
Nunc de reginis sit tractandum faciendis,
Si noua regina sistit ludo generata,
Saltandi normam retinet simul hanc quoque formam,
Quemquam ad campum ternum tibi condere saltum.
Si lapidis cuius uult et fore debet custos,
Regula tunc talis sit prorecto semperualis,
Ternumque nulla regina potest super aruum
Vllius lapidis transfatum [2] condere saltum.
Si quis in scacco lapidis sit stans atque locatus,
Ante suum regemque scaccis protegit ipsum,
Et scaccum rege lapidis alter prebeat hosti
In gressu lapidis sic in scaco situati
Quod rex aduersansque locatus uel prope sit stans,
Quidem narrantes idem sunt et reputantes
Quot rapere nempe poterit (*MS.* -is) tunc rex inimicus
Hunc lapidem scaccum qui donat memoratum.
Assignant eciam paulisper certe valentem
Quod sic in abscaco lapidis sit stans certe ligatus,
Atque per abscaccum propria sit vi spoliatus,
Vllius lapidis nec sic poterit (*MS.* -is) fore custos.
Illud dicentes omnes sunt arte carentes
Ludi scacorumque tene(n)t dictum puerorum.
Hoc dictum certe verum non cernitur esse,
Quod sic in abscaco lapidis est stans sicque ligatus;
Hoc regis sistit, est non lapidis ratione.
Hoc dictum certe falssum sistit manifeste,
Cum sic in abscacco lapidis sit quis stansque locatus,
Quod tunc vi propria lapidis idem sit sua degens.
Nam si sic sequitur tunc non lapis et . . (*MS.* lp̄) esset.
Hoc pariter ad sensum semper pure fore falssum,
Nam lapis sit vere cum scaccum pertinet ipse
Quem rochus aduersans eius regi fuerit dans.
Si quis vi propria lapidis eget, non lapidem ex(s)tat;

Non debet vere ludo lapis ille manere,
Sed deponendus sit aliunde remouendus,
Cum lapis sit talis quoque dictus raptus ut alter.
Ergo deducendum restat semper retinendum
Vim lapis hic propriamque habet necnon tenet veram
Cum sit in abscaco pro rege suo scāblicus,
Et bene custodit hunc quem rex fortiter odit,
Si sic contingant ut sepius sit manifestum
Quot regi proprio donat prebet quoque scaccum.
  Hostilis miles regis cognoscere debes,
Dissimilem proprium ponas super aruum,
Nam paribus campis semper scacroch fiet tibi campis.
  Quum tuus dominus rex necnon rex inimicus
In ludo fine tantum lapidem tenet vnum,
Necnon nudare rex uult alium spoliare,
Quidem dicentes idem sunt et retinentes,
Extrema reliquum priuans retinet sibi lucrum.
Cernitur hoc dictum similem necnon fore fictum ;
Sed quod deducendum sistit necnon retinendum,
Qui primo reliquum priuat retinet sibi lucrum,
Cum rex nudatus propria sit vi spoliatus,
Item nudatus velud exstat mortificatus.
Mattus uel nudus omnis debet fore ludus:
Seruis priuatus rex primo seu spoliatus
Qui fuerit, vere rex ludum perdidit iste.

Et sic sit finis huius, Deo gracias Amen. Anno Dni. M.CCCC. vicessimo secundo, in feria quinta in Via natalis Xpi. sit finitum libro isti.

[1] *i.e.* campum. [2] *i.e.* transgressum.

XIII. The Hebrew Poem on the Game Shah-mat, attributed to Abraham b. Ezra.

[The following translation is based upon the Latin version in Hyde, 1767, ii. 163–6, and the German translation by Steinschneider (v. d. Linde, i. 164–7). I have also consulted the English translation by Miss Nina Davis (Mrs. Salomon) in her *Songs of Exile*, Philadelphia, 1901, pp. 129–31.]

I sing a song of an arranged battle
Ancient, invented in the days of old,
Arranged by men of prudence and intelligence,
Based upon the eight ranks.
  On each rank are marked
On the table eight divisions.
Moreover, the ranks are four-square and united together,
And there the camps stand close together.
The Kings (*malik*) stand with their camps
For war, and a space is between the two,
And the face of all is ready for fighting.

They move out steadily and quietly,
Yet no swords are drawn in the combat,
Their warfare is a mental work only.
They are to be recognized by signs only, and distinguishing marks
Marked and stamped on their persons.
Whoever observes them in motion,
To him they appear as Edomites and Ethiopians.
The Ethiopians stretch out their hands for the struggle,
And the Edomites move out after them.
The Pawns (*regel*) come first of all
To the battle in a straight march.
The Pawn marches straight forwards,
Yet he turns aside to capture the foe.
He does not turn aside in his march
Nor does he turn his steps backward.
And if he has travelled far from his position,
And advanced to the eighth rank,
He can turn to each side like the Fers
And counts as her in the battle.
The Fers (*fers*) turns her steps
And makes her move to her four squares;
Moreover, if she like, she can at the outset, leap
Three squares distant in each direction.
The Elephant (*fīl*) always steps near to the battle;
He stands at the side like a spy;
His step resembles that of the Fers, but it
Has this advantage, that it is a triple one.
The foot of the Horse (*sūs*) is very light in the battle;
He goes by a crooked path,
His ways are crooked and not straight,
Three houses are his boundaries.
The Rook (*rukh*) goes straight on his way
And in the land according to breadth and length,
He seeks no crooked path,
His path is neither oblique nor crooked.
The King steps in all directions
To all the winds, and helps his dependants.
He takes care of himself when he sits or moves
To the combat and wherever he encamps himself,
So that if the enemy mounts in hostility against him
And threatens him, he flees from his place;
Or if the Rook drives him with fear
And follows him from one room to another,
Then he must flee before him to the sides.
At the sides, however, his hosts collect about him,
And all, the one as well as the other, kill,
And this blots out that with great fury.

But the heroes of either King
Are laid low without effusion of blood.
At times the Ethiopians are the victors,
And the Edomites flee from before them.
At times the Edomites triumph, and the Ethiopians
With their King are overthrown in the battle.
And if by chance the King is caught
And ensnared pitilessly in the net
And there is no way out to save himself, and no refuge
And no escape to a strong city of refuge,
He is doomed and removed by the foe;
There is none to save him, and by death is he mate (*mat*);
And his hosts all die for him
And offer their lives for his.
And their glory is departed, they are annihilated
When they see how their lord is slain.
Yet does the battle begin over again,
And the killed ones once more stand up.

CHAPTER V

THE MORALITIES

Introductory remarks.—The *Innocent Morality*.—John of Waleys (Gallensis) and Alexander of Hales.—Later references to this work.—The *Liber de moribus hominum et officiis nobilium* of Jacobus de Cessolis.—Translations and imitations.—Galwan de Levanto.—The chess chapters in the *Gesta Romanorum*.—Ingold's *Guldin Spil*.—*Les Eschez amoureux*.—Other moralizing works.

It will be a matter for no surprise to any one familiar with the characteristics of the European literature of the Middle Ages to discover that works were written in which attempts were made to give a symbolical or allegorical explanation of the game of chess, or to find parallels between the organization of human life and activities and the different names and powers of the chessmen. For among the most potent and vital forces behind that literature, from at least the 13th century onwards, were instruction, allegory, and satire. When we find Stephen Langton, Archbishop of Canterbury, taking as his text on one occasion a popular ballad of his day—*Main se leva bele Aeliz*—and explaining *bele Aeliz* as typifying the Virgin Mary; when we find the German Oberlin in his *Bihtebuoch* discovering the articles of the Creed symbolized in ecclesiastical vestments, and another German poet, Reinmar v. Zweter (B. *c.* 1200), explaining each different piece of feminine attire as showing a virtue which a good woman ought to possess, it would indeed be surprising if such popular amusements as dice or chess escaped a similar allegorical interpretation. So we find the pips on the die elaborately explained as emblematic of Christianity by Reinmar v. Zweter, the ace standing for the Unity of God, the two for heaven and earth, the three for the Trinity, the four for the Gospels, the five for the five senses, and the six for the Lenten fast, the whole being a cunning invention of Satan to introduce the Christian to the implements of gambling under the guise of symbols of religion.

Quite a number of works were devoted in the Middle Ages to the allegorical explanation of chess, generally on the broad line that the game was emblematic of the social condition of the time. In the Middle Ages these works were widely known by the name of *Moralities*, and modern writers have generally adopted this name. A considerable portion of the chess moralities has but little to do with chess; the writers' interests were always engaged more with the allegory than with the game. Still, they are not without importance in the development of chess in Europe. They exercised a potent influence on the nomenclature of the pieces; they may have carried a knowledge of chess to circles where it had not penetrated before; they may have helped to break down the ecclesiastical prejudice against the game. On the other hand, the chess setting may have directed the attention of chess-players to the moral instruction which was the ultimate purpose of the morality.

I have already had occasion to warn the reader against accepting blindly everything that is said about the moves in the moralities. To the moralist the fable was of far greater importance than the details of the game, and the details had to fit the explanation rather than the reverse.

Apparently, the oldest of the chess moralities is a short Latin treatise which generally bears in the MSS. the title of *Quaedam moralitas de scaccario*, to which is added, in some MSS. only, the further words *per* (or *secundum*) *Innocentium papam* (or *tertium*). We may accordingly conveniently call it the *Innocent Morality*, leaving the question of authorship open.

We may paraphrase this work thus:

The world resembles a chessboard which is chequered white and black, the colours showing the two conditions of life and death, or praise and blame. The chessmen are men of this world who have a common birth, occupy different stations and hold different titles in this life, who contend together, and finally have a common fate which levels all ranks. The King often lies under the other pieces in the bag.

The King's move and powers of capture are in all directions, because the King's will is law (see below).

The Queen's move is aslant only, because women are so greedy that they will take nothing except by rapine and injustice.

The Rook stands for the itinerant justices who travel over the whole realm, and their move is always straight, because the judge must deal justly.

The Knight's move is compounded of a straight move and an oblique one; the former betokens his legal power of collecting rents, &c., the latter his extortions and wrong-doings.

The Aufins are prelates wearing horns (but not like those that Moses had when he descended from Sinai). They move and take obliquely because nearly every bishop misuses his office through cupidity.

The Pawns are poor men. Their move is straight, except when they take anything: so also the poor man does well so long as he keeps from ambition. After the Pawn is promoted he becomes a Fers and moves obliquely, which shows how hard it is for a poor man to deal rightly when he is raised above his proper station.

In this game the Devil says 'Check!' when a man falls into sin; and unless he quickly cover the check by turning to repentance, the Devil says 'Mate!' and carries him off to hell, whence is no escape. For the Devil has as many kinds of temptations to catch different types of men, as the hunter has dogs to catch different types of animals.

The Latin text, based upon a comparison of ten of the eleven MSS. which I have been able to consult and the printed text in the *editio princeps* of John of Waleys' *Summa collationum*, will be found as the first Appendix to this chapter. Even after collation the text is still corrupt in places, and especially so in the passage relating to the King. When this is compared with the passage relating to the Rook it is clear that a whole clause from the latter has been interpolated in the former, with the result that the existing text limits the King's move to one in four directions only (the Rook's shortest move); if, however, the interpolated clause is removed, the passage reads—

In isto autem ludo rex uadit ubique et capit undique semper in signum quod quicquid agit rex iusticia reputatur quia quicquid principi placet legis habet uigorem;

and is now not only self-consistent, but also accurate from the point of view of chess. The explanation of the perversion of the text is fairly obvious. The principle underlying the interpretation of the chess moves is this: a direct or straight move, i. e. one along a row or file of the board, symbolizes a straightforward, just, or equitable action; an indirect, oblique or aslant move, a crooked, unjust, or inequitable action. In the desire to represent the King as the fountain of justice, the King's oblique moves were a difficulty that had to be overcome, and it appeared easier to evade it by suppressing all mention of the oblique moves, and representing the King as only moving in a direct line. Now the justification of the Rook's move applied to the King's also, and the clause was brought into the morality of the King.[1]

It is interesting to note that S, a MS. which varies so much from the other MSS. that I have disregarded it in the reconstruction of the ordinary text, has here quite correctly—

Nota quod rex vndique potest capere quia quod principi placuit iuris habet vigorem, scilicet in presenti.

This MS. throughout defines the move in terms of the power to capture.

The other MSS. show an extraordinary number of small differences of the order of words and of expression. These enable us to group them to a certain extent. Thus H, R, and KG preserve an early text of the morality; K, C, and Ad. contain a text that has been touched up and improved. O pays particular attention to the literary style and grammatical accuracy of the work, while J[1], J[2], Lin., and G add clauses to bring out the allusions more clearly. A still more ambitious working up of the text is to be seen in the *Destructorium vitiorum*, with which I deal below. The authorship of the morality is ascribed in the MSS. to two distinct writers; K, R, O, C, and J[1] attribute it to Pope Innocent III; KG, G, and the *Destructorium vitiorum* to Johannes Gallensis, both writers belonging to the 13th c.; the other MSS. give no authorship.

The former of these writers, Pope Innocent III (Lothario de' conti di Segni, B. *c.* 1163, elected Pope Jan. 8, 1198, D. July 16, 1216), ranks as 'the most proud and powerful of all the Popes', and was the author of a number of sermons which enjoyed marked popularity in the 13th and 14th cc. He was the Pope with whom King John came into conflict.

The latter, John of Waleys, from his surname of Welsh nationality, was a Franciscan friar, and connected with both Oxford (where he was B.D., and in 1260 D.D. and Regent Master of the Franciscan College) and Paris (where he was lecturing on Theology in 1262). At a later date, Oct. 1282, he was sent by Edward I on an embassy to the revolted Welsh, but he was in Paris again in 1283. His great work was the *Communiloquium sive summa collectionum*

[1] See p. 465. A later perversion occurs in S and also the printed text G. Here the account of the move of the promoted Pawn differs from that in the earlier MSS., and it is said—S *statim pertransit duo puncta cum tertio oblique*; G *tunc duo puncta pertransit, tertium obliquat*, using the words of the morality in describing the Knight's move. This is another interpolation which is disastrous to the accuracy of the description from the chess point of view. V. d. Lasa's unsatisfactory attempt (72) to explain the passage in the G text is accordingly unnecessary.

(or *collationum*),[2] and the *Innocent Morality* is to be found in many of the Continental MSS. and in several of the early printed editions of this work in Pars I, dist. x, cap. 7. The *Destructorium vitiorum* quoted it from a MS. in which it occurs in Pars I, dist. ix, cap. 8.

The internal evidence of the morality, however, shows that neither authorship can be accepted in its present form. One of the most striking features of the morality is its frank and outspoken attack upon the dignitaries of the Church. Originally the criticism was confined to bishops only, but in the second recension (K, C, Ad.) Pope, cardinals, and archbishops are added to the list. This attack is out of place, and indeed impossible in the work of a Pope, particularly of one who took the exalted view of the position of the Church that Innocent III took. And the morality is equally out of place in its setting in the *Summa collationum*. It occurs in a chapter that is devoted to the virtues of bishops, and the taxes and dues from which they are exempt by reason of their position. The morality has nothing in common with all this, and is clearly a later interpolation. I think that the evidence of KG goes far to confirm this: it is the only English MS. of the *Summa collationum* which contains the morality, and here it occurs in an appendix to the main work.

There is, nevertheless, much to be said in support of the Waleys authorship. The author was clearly an Englishman, and one familiar with English law terms. The itinerant justice (*iusticiarius perambulans*), tallage (*tallagia*), ferm (*firma*), all point unmistakably to England, and are inconsistent with an Italian origin. The existing Latin MSS. are all of English workmanship, and the chess terms, where not Latin, are Anglo-French: *fers* (*fierce*); *poun* (*pown*); *fierce* for the promoted Pawn; *eschek* (*chek*); while in some MSS. *nek* (neck) for *covered check* is an English chess technicality only. *Familia scaccarii*, for the chessmen, is rare except in Latin works from the north of France and England. The bitter attack upon the bishops only voices what every Englishman in the reign of Henry III knew was true of his country. The visitation of the Papal Legate Otho to Oxford in 1238, which ended in a riot, in which the first blood was drawn by a countryman of Waleys' and which cost the University dear, had happened only a short time before Waleys' day. Otho's taxes, extortions, and greed were notorious. The Franciscans, pledged to poverty, felt no sympathy with the higher clergy, and were as ready as the laity to denounce the greed and injustice of clergy and monks. The morality might very well be an early production of Waleys which was at first kept separate from his *magnum opus*, and only at a later date incorporated in it by a meddlesome scribe, in what appeared to him to be the most appropriate place.

Hyde attempted to reconcile the English origin of the morality with the Innocent authorship by a 'convenient hypothesis' that the work was written by an English monk named Innocent Pape, or Pope, who lived *c.* 1300, and was at a later time confused with an occupant of the papal see. Although this hypothesis has been accepted by Sir Frederic Madden and others, I do

[2] Cf. A. G. Little, *Greyfriars in Oxford*, 144-51.

not think that the guess is even plausible. The MSS. undoubtedly refer to Innocent III in all good faith: in R it occurs in a MS. of the Pope's sermons. But it is not easy to see how the belief in the papal authorship came into existence.

In any case, the morality belongs to the middle of the 13th c., i.e. to Waleys' day. The oldest MS., H, belongs to the first quarter of the following century, but there already appears to be an allusion to it in a MS. in the Reval Gymnasium dating from 1260–70, which was brought back to Reval from France by the Dominican Mauritius of Reval on his return to take up the lectorship in the Dominican convent of his native town. Another possible reference is to be found in Hugo v. Trimberg's *Renner* (*c.* 1300). In neither case is the reference certain. The idea that the bag in which the chessmen lose all rank was analogous to the grave, in which all men are equal, may quite well have occurred independently in different places.

The moralist sees in chess an allegory of human life, and the chessmen stand for the different ranks and occupations of men. Before the commencement of the game, and after its conclusion, the pieces are kept in promiscuous confusion in the bag, where the King lies sometimes above, and sometimes below, the Pawn. The common birth and common death of all mankind is an obvious parallel, and one that was very popular all through the Middle Ages. The chessmen prefigure: the King (*rex*) the king; the Queen (*regina*, popularly called *fers*) women, the Rooks (*roccus*) the judges, the Knights (*miles*) the temporal aristocracy, the Bishops (*alphinus cornutus*) the spiritual hierarchy, and the Pawns (*pedinus*, popularly *poun*) the commonalty. *Check* is identified with temptation, *covered check* with repentance, *mate* with mortal sin from which there is no redemption.

The most interesting passage is that relating to the Aufin, which must have commenced originally *Alphini uero cornuti sunt episcopi non ut Moyses ex colloquio diuino. Cornutus* (OF. *cornu*) appears elsewhere as a name of the piece, and is obviously derived from its mediaeval shape, with two horns projecting upwards or sideways. The allusion to Moses is drawn from the *Vulgate*, where (Exodus xxxiv) it is said of Moses on his descent from Sinai that '*videbant faciem esse cornutam*'—a misrendering of the Hebrew.

The moves are those of the earliest European chess with none of the European modifications. In describing them, the usual mediaeval method of counting the squares is followed. The description of the Knight's move—two squares in a straight line and then one aslant—is accordingly more exact than is often the case. The promoted Pawn becomes a Fers, but has no power of leap on its first move. In G there is evidence of an attempt to bring the chess more up to date, thus *domina* is introduced as an alternative name for the Queen.

The concluding section, in which the Devil is represented as playing chess with man for his soul, is interesting as containing certain technicalities, although its connexion with the previous explanation of the chessmen is of the slightest. Nowhere else, so far as I am aware, do we meet with the AF.

technicality for *covered check* which corresponds to the ME. *neck*. This term is given very variously in the MSS., as *liqueret*, *liueret*, *delineret*.

The knowledge of the morality was not entirely confined to England. The existence of an old French version has been recorded, and there is an Italian translation at the end of a Bodleian MS. of the Italian version of Cessolis which is dated 1458. An Icelandic summary of it, the work of Gottskálk Jónsson of Glaumbæ (D. 1593), is contained in MS. Brit. Mus. Add. 11242, f. 52.[3]

The *Innocent Morality* is also incorporated in a considerably amplified form in the *Destructorium vitiorum*, a compilation from many sources which attained its final form in 1429, and was then attributed to the great Franciscan theologian Alexander of Hales (D. 1245). Whether the work is really based upon any treatise of the *Doctor irrefragabilis* is by no means certain:[4] in any case, the additions of the fifteenth century are so numerous that we must regard the *Destructorium* in its printed text as a German compilation of the early 15th c. The Morality is given here as an extract from the *Summa collationum* of Waleys, but the interpretations are developed at far greater length (thus the Pawn is now 'the poor workman or poor cleric or parish priest'), without, however, adding to our knowledge of the chess moves: only in the concluding section does it add a little to our knowledge of the etiquette of mediaeval chess:

> On this chessboard the Devil plays against a sinner. The Devil cries 'Check!' attacking the sinner with the dart of sin. Unless the latter replies 'Neck!' through penitence, the Devil cries 'Mate!' and hales the sinner off to hell. There are many presumptuous players who lay great stakes and sacrifice many of their men, hoping to mate in the end, and before they are aware, the opponent exclaims 'Checkmate!' and they have lost everything. So also there are men who during life follow the Devil, hoping in the end to cheat him of their souls by the mercy of God, but death surprises them before they expect it, and the Devil says 'Checkmate!' Wherefore play the game of life warily, for your opponent is full of subtilty, and take abundant thought over your moves, for the stake is your soul.

The prominence attached to the stake on the result of the game shows, as we know already from other works, that the game was commonly played in this way. The *Destructorium* does not think the worse of chess on that account, and the game is included in the class of honest games (*genus ludorum socialis honestatis*) so long as the stakes are of moderate amount. The following chapter treats of the game which the writer wished to condemn (*de ludis inhonestis et de his qui consequuntur illos ludos*).

It is interesting to notice the influence which the *Innocent Morality*, or at least the allegory behind it, exerted in mediaeval literature. This was not affected by the greater currency of the chess sermon of Jacobus de Cessolis: indeed, the less ambitious morality was able to exert considerable influence upon the greater work when it was translated into the various European languages. The earliest Continental reference to the allegory of chess as

[3] The text is given in *Íslenzkar gátur*, Copenhagen, 1892, iv. 375.

[4] It is not mentioned in the account of Alexander's life and works in the *Dict. Nat. Biog.*

a picture of human life, which is the motive of the *Innocent Morality*, is to be found in the MS. which Maurice of Reval brought home from France. In this volume are no less than three parables drawn from chess, which I now give in abstract.[5]

Of the World.—The world resembles a game of chess in which the whole *familia* runs aslant to seize some temporal advantage by lies, deceit, and usury. Moreover, so long as the game continues, one is King, another Knight, and so on. One or two appear to rule the whole game, but when it comes to an end, the same thing happens to King and soldier alike and to the least of the *familia*, because they are all thrown together into the bag, and sometimes the King is at the bottom while the least of the *familia* is on top. Thus is the world like a game of chess. As long as the game—i.e. the world—lasts, one is King, another is a soldier, one is great, another is of low rank. But when death comes they are all laid in the same bag, the earth, and the same fate happens to the King as to the soldier. The vassal is in the same position as his lord.

Of belated Penitence.—The man who postpones his repentance until death resembles a chessplayer who, understanding but little of the game, thinks to himself: I will allow my *familia* to be taken, and then at the end I will mate (*mactabo*) my opponent in the corner, while he knows all the time that his opponent is a skilful player. As there the unskilful player, so also the sinner . . . for the master-player is the Devil . . . How can the sinner believe that he will be able to mate him in the corner—i.e. conquer at the end of his life—when the Devil tries the harder?

Of Love to God.—See that you consider carefully to whom you can best give your heart from love. . . . Have you not seen how the chessplayer retains for a long time in his hand the piece he has lifted from the board, considering long where he will place it out of his enemy's reach? Do likewise with your heart, and take care not to place it in a shameful and dangerous place; give it rather to God.

This MS., says Amelung, served for 300 years as a storehouse of apt illustration and parable for the Esthonian clergy. The second and third parallels are new, and strike me as being particularly happy. They exhibit the original author of the collection as a keen observer of the habits of his fellow-men.

The lesson of the chessmen and the bag in which they were kept was often pushed home in the Middle Ages, and even later. We find it in Hugo v. Trimberg's *Renner* (c. 1300),[6] in Hermann v. Fritzlar (1345),[7] in John

[5] See the *Verh. d. Gelehrten estnischen Gesellschaft*, Jurjew, 1897; and *Baltische Schachbl.*, vi. 132 and vii. 276.

[6]
Disiu werlt ist als ein goukeltabel :
wan si hât als ein schâchzabel
künig unde ouch künigîn,
roch, ritter, alten, vendelîn.
des hât got wol sîn goukelspil
mit uns, derz rehte merken wil.
der goukler sprichet 'wider in die taschen!'
sô sprichet got, 'wider in die aschen
von der ir alle sît bekomen,
rîch unde arm, boese mit den fromen!' (248 a).

[Elsewhere in this poem Hugo v. Trimberg compares the passing of the bread to and fro on the table with the movements of the chessmen on the board:

Got, lâ mich nimmer dâ gesitzen,
dâ man mit brôtes snitzen
schâchzabel ziuhet ob den tischen!
möhte ich ein künic dâ erwischen
oder ein roch, sô füere ich wol:
mit venden wird ich dâ selten vol. (65 b).]

[7] 'Ein meister glîchit dise werlt eime schâfzabele; dâ stân ûffe kunige und kuniginnen

Raulin's *Doctrinale mortis* (Paris, 1518, 5 a),[8] in a Fromantient MS. Book of *Apologues* which are attributed to St. Basil,[9] in Elizabethan and early Stuart plays,[10] in *Don Quixote*,[11] and probably elsewhere. A more ambitious development of the idea is exhibited in Sebastian Brant's half-Latin, half-German poem *De periculoso scacorum ludo* (in his *Carmina*, Olpe, 1498), which is quoted by v. d. Linde, i. 151.

It is to this morality, or perhaps to a fuller work that carries out the same interpretation, rather than to the sermon of Cessolis, that Fitzherbert alludes in the prologue to his *Book of Husbandry* (1554), when he divides the chessmen into six classes—King, Queen, Bishops, Knights, Judges, and Yeomen.[12]

Chess naturally suggested many parallels to the preacher,[13] the most obvious being that Death always says 'Checkmate' in the end. Several early paintings and miniatures in manuscripts illustrate this by a game between a monarch and Death. Melanchthon went so far as to describe God as playing chess or cards, with men for pieces or cards, and taking the Pope with Martin

und ritter und knappen und venden; hie mite spilen si. Wanne si mûde gespilet haben, sô werfen si den einen under den anderen in einen sack. Alse tût der tôt: der wirfet iz allez in di erden. Welich der rîche sî ader der arme sî ader der bâbist sî ader der kunic, daz schowet an deme gebeine: der knecht ist dicke uber den herren geleget, sô si ligen in deme beinhûse.' (Pfeiffer's *Deutsche Mystiker*, i. 164.)

[8] 'Accidit eis sicut accidit in familia ludi scaccarii: ludo enim durante rex omnia personagia excellit, ubi perdatur et accipit; sed in fine, cum clauditur in sacculo cum cetera familia, aliquando est profundius in sacco quam ceteri.'

[9] 'Simile est de hiis divitibus quod fit in ludo scacorum qui ponuntur extra sacculum, quidam dicuntur Reges, quidam Milites, quidam Duces, quidam Pedines, et ludunt de talibus qui allum potuerit vincere probus dicitur. Itorum in bursa ponuntur sine ordine collocantur. Sic omnes homines veniunt de uno sacco de utero matris. Postea ludit unus cum alio. Unus aufert alii unum ludum, tandem matat in fine colliguntur et iterum sine ordine in sacco ponuntur. Sic in hoc mundo ludit unus cum alio, unus amittit, alius lucratur, alius matatur . . .' (From the Douce Twiss in the Bodleian.)

[10] Viz. *Jacke Drum's Entertainment*:

> And after death like chesmen having stood
> In play for Bishops some for Knights and Pawnes,
> We all together shall be tumbled up
> Into one bagge.

In Middleton's play, *A Game at Chess*, there are many allusions to the bag which holds the chessmen when not in use, and in the last scene the Black men are one after the other popped into the bag.

[11] 'Como aquella del juego del Axedrez, que mientras dura el juego, cada pieza tiene su particular oficio, y en acabandose el juego, todas se mesclan, juntan, y barajan, y dan con ellas en una bolsa, que es como dar con la vida en la sepultura' (ch. lxiv).

[12] 'But who that redeth in the boke of the moralytes of the chesse, shal therby perceyue, that euerye man, from the hyest degree to the lowest, is set and ordeyned to haue labour and occupation: and that boke is deuyded in vi. degrees, that is to saye, the kynge, the quene, the byshops, the knightes, the iudges, and the yomenne. In the which boke is shewed theyr degrees, theyr auctorytyes, theyr warkes, and theyr occupations, and what they ought to do. And they so doynge, and executynge theyr auctorytyes, warkes, and occupatyons, haue a wonders great study and labour, of the which auctorytyes, occupations, and warkes were at this tyme to longe to wryte. Wherfore I remytte that boke as myn auctour therof: The whiche boke were necessary to be knowen of euery degree, that they myghte doo, and ordre them selfe accordynge to the same. And in so moche the yomen in the sayde moralytes and game of the chesse be set before to labour, defende, and maynteyne all the other people, as husbandes and labourers, therefore I purpose to speake fyrste of husbandrye.'

See also my letter on this passage in the *Athenaeum*, June 22, 1901.

[13] Thus the Franciscan Berthold v. Regensburg (1220–72) said: 'Wanne iu hât unser hêrre gar grôz êre und guot dar umb verlihen, leben, und schône loben, und hât iu anderes niht ze schaffen geben wan daz ir im sinen edelen schatz wol behuetet und bewaret, als verre als er iu bevolhen ist und als iu got dar zuo geordenet hât. Ez sol iuwer schâchzabel sîn und iuwer federspil und iuwer tagalt und iuwer kurze wîle!' (Ed. Kling, 1824, 38.)

DEATH GIVES CHECKMATE TO A KING

Copper-plate engraving by an unknown artist. Bâle, Noppe der unbekannten Meister, K. I. 6. S. 38. No. 32

Luther.[14] Many metaphors borrowed from chess have taken their place in the vocabulary of everyday life. I give some examples of the older metaphors in Chapter IX; perhaps the commonest in modern usage is to represent diplomatists, politicians, or anybody who is pursuing a large plan without revealing his ultimate intentions, as engaged in a game in which the Pawns are the innocent tools with which the plan is carried through.[15]

I now turn to the *Liber de moribus hominum et officiis nobilium* of Jacobus de Cessolis, the most ambitious, and from the literary point of view, the most important of all the chess moralities. There is a very large number of MSS. of this work in existence of the 14th and 15th cc., both in the original Latin and in translation into the spoken languages of the time: indeed it is probable that no other work of mediaeval times was so much copied. Its popularity exceeded that of the *Gesta Romanorum*, and, if we may judge from the number of the existing MSS., must have almost rivalled that of the Bible itself.[16]

The author tells us in the commencing sentences of his work that he was a friar of the Order of Friars Preachers, constituted in 1216, and now commonly known as the Dominicans from the name of their founder, the Spaniard Dominic. Ferron, who translated Cessolis' work into French, calls him *Jaques de Cessoles, maistre en divinité*. These are the only authoritative statements regarding Jacobus de Cessolis that we possess. Trithem (*De scriptoribus ecclesiasticis*, 1536) knows nothing about Jacobus de Cessolis except that he had written *De ludo skacorum* in four books, and a volume of sermons. It has often been stated on the authority of Quétif and Échard, *Scriptt. Ord. Praedicat.*, Paris, 1719, i. 471), that he was a Master of Theology of the convent of the Order in Rheims, who flourished *c.* 1300. This statement is, however, of doubtful validity. Quétif and Échard would seem to have derived it from Lawrence Pignon's chronicle of the Order, which was written in the first half of the 15th c. (MS. Paris, *Fonds de Saint-Victor*, 676, n. 114), where is the entry—

'Frater Johannes de Teriace, de conventu Remensi, fecit Moralitates super ludum Scacchorum';

while there is no mention of Jacobus de Cessolis. It seems evident that the French writers have confused two different authors. Pignon could hardly have confused *Jacobus* de Cessolis with *Johannes* de Teriace,[17] and the title

14 'Wenn ich reich wäre, so wollte ich mir ein gülden Schach und silbernen Kartenspiele werklich lassen zurichten zu einer Erinnerung. Denn Gottes Schach und Karte sind grosse mächtige Fürsten, Könige, Kaiser, da er immer einen durch den andern sticht oder schlägt, das ist aushebt und stürzt. Nun ist Ferdinand die vier Schellen, der Papst die sechs Schellen, der Türke acht Schellen, der Kaiser ist der König im Spiel. Letzlich kommt unser Herr Gott, theilet das Spiel aus, schlägt den Papst mit dem Luther, das ist sein Tauss.' (Quoted in v. d. Linde, i. 153, from Massmann.)

15 Two instances may suffice. Carlyle, *Sartor Resartus*, I. iii: 'While Councillors of State sit plotting, and playing their high chess-game, whereof the pawns are Men.' And A. C. Benson, *Upton Letters*, London, 1905, 125: 'I became aware that I was, for the moment, one of the pawns in his game, to be delicately pushed about where it suited him.'

16 V. d. Linde (i., Beilage, 34, 105–12) gives a list of eighty MSS. of the Latin text alone. This could be easily extended. V. d. Lasa (95) found copies of the Latin text in nearly every Italian library which he visited in search of chess MSS.

17 Teriace, L. *Teoracia* or *Tirascia*, mod. F. *la Tierache*, is a part of the old province of Picardy adjoining Champagne in the Bishopric of Laon. Quétif and Échard were no doubt

Moralitates super ludum scacchorum is one that I have never found used for Cessolis' work. It is probable that Johannes de Teriace's *Moralities* was a much smaller work on the lines of the *Innocent Morality* which has entirely perished. On the strength of their identification Quétif and Échard describe Cessolis as a Frenchman, a native of the village of Cessières in the diocese of Laon, Picardy.

This is certainly a mistake. It is quite clear from the evidence of Cessolis' work that its author was a Lombard. Not only does he describe the rules of the Lombard assize, but there are many expressions and allusions that require a personal acquaintance with Lombardy. Thus in II. iv, the church of St. John the Baptist, Tortona, is described with some exactness; in II. v, there is an attack upon the Lombards which bears signs of intimate knowledge of their faults;[18] in III. iv, a story is told upon the authority of the merchant Obertus Guterinus of Asti, Genoa; in III. vi, is another story from Parma, and an Italian rendering of a proverb;[19] in III. viii, the will of Giovanni de Canazia is quoted in the original Italian;[20] and in IV. i, the measurement of the walls of Babylon is given first in Lombard miles, and then in French leagues.

The MSS. show very considerable variety in the spelling of the name Cessolis. V. d. Linde (i., Beil., 19) says that of the MSS. which he catalogues the Latin MSS. have Cessolis (Sessolis) more than 30 times, Cessulis (Cesulis, Cessullis) about 20 times, Casulis 7 times. The German versions have Cassalis 20 times, the Italian da Cesole, Dacciasole. In addition to these, he notes the spellings Cessoles, Chessolis, Czessalis, Cessalioz, Cassal, Cazzalis, Gazalis, Gaczellis, Cossoles, Cessalis, Cessol, Cesul, Ceusis, Cecilia, Courcelles, Tessolis, Thessalis, Thessalonia, Tessolonia, and Funolis.[21] He decided in favour of Cessoles, and v. d. Lasa adopted this in his *Forschungen* with some reluctance. If we translate the *de* by *of* (Ger. *von*), this is correct; but, retaining the Latin *de*, I prefer to follow Kopke and Vetter and to write de Cessolis.[22]

influenced in identifying Teriace with Cessolis by the coincidence that the village of Cessières is in this district.

[18] 'Sed heu, hodie Lombardos ubique bella premunt, ad quae non arma (seu missilia) ac iacula ferunt, sed proditiones, dolositates, fraudulentiae quotidie succrescunt, hostes proterunt; nulla lex, nulla fidelitas, nulla iuramenta, nulla pacta custodiunt homines, et vassalli contra dominos naturales prodidisse suspirant.'

A Frenchman would surely have attacked his own countrymen, and not the men of another country. Félix Lajard (*Hist. litt. de France*, XXV, Paris, 1869, 9–41) accepts the Lombard nationality of Cessolis.

[19] 'Cortexia de bocha asa vale e pocho costa' (ed. Kopke, 26, n. 36).

[20] 'Questo si lo testamento de Iohanne Cavaza. Chi se per altro lasa, ammazato sia da questa masa' (ed. Kopke, 29).

[21] The names beginning with the letter *t* are due to the similarity of the forms of the letters *c* and *t* in 14th c. MSS. Thus we find the reading *stacarium* for *scacarium*, and throughout the problem MS. M *scat* for *scac*. The form Funolis may be due to a misunderstanding. A copy of Cessolis, formerly in the Phillips Library, Cheltenham, was there catalogued as the work of Vitalis de Fontibus. After the Trustees of that Library had sold it, I had an opportunity of examining the MS., only to find that the statement of the MS. that the *index* to Cessolis' work had been compiled by Vitalis de Fontibus had been misunderstood.

[22] Kopke, in his *Iacobus de Cessolis*, Brandenburg, 1879, a scholarly edition of the Latin text to which I am indebted for much that I say as to the nationality of Cessolis and his authorities: and Vetter, *Das Schachzabelbuch Kunrats von Ammenhausen*, Frauenfeld, 1892, a valuable work which gives the text of Mennel's *Schachzabel* (Constance, 1507), and a

The name is probably derived from the district Cessole in the South of Piedmont, to the north-west of Genoa. A family of the name of Cessole is still existing in Nice, whose members have from time to time held municipal office.[23]

The *Liber de moribus hominum et officiis nobilium* almost certainly belongs to the second half of the 13th c. A superior limit to its date is afforded by the inclusion of a description of a marble gate over a bridge at Capua which was surmounted by a statue of the Emperor Frederick II (D. 1250), which was erected by this emperor about 1240.[24] There is possibly an allusion to the interregnum, 1254–73, in the Empire in a passage (II. ii), in which Cessolis expresses his preference for the hereditary succession, and details some of the obvious drawbacks to an elective monarchy.[25] An inferior limit to the date of the work is obtained from the use made of it in the *Gesta Romanorum* in chapters going back to the first half of the 14th c., by the dates of the German metrical versions of the Pherrer zu dem Hechte (1335) and Kunrat v. Ammenhausen (1337)—both later in date than the German version of Henry v. Beringen—and of the French translation of Jehan Ferron (1347). The oldest dated MS. of the Latin text is apparently MS. Leipzig, Pauline Lib., 42, of 1358. We shall not be far wrong if we date Cessolis' work 1275–1300.

In its origin the book was a sermon, and it was only in deference to the repeated requests of his fellow friars and other friends that Cessolis reduced it to writing. As he states in his introduction:

'Ego frater Jacobus de Cessolis ordinis predicatorum multorum fratrum ordinis nostri et diversorum secularium precibus persuasus dudum munus requisitum negavi ut transscriberem solacii ludum scacorum viz. regiminis morum ac belli humani generis documentum. Sane cum illum ad populum acclamatorie predicassem multisque nobilibus placuisset materia, honori eorum ac dignitati curavi ascribere, monens

collation of the printed text of Cessolis with some Wolfenbüttel MSS. It contains an important introduction (xxiii–l) by Wackernagel (originally published in *Kurz u. Weissenbach's Beiträge zur Gesch. u. Litt.*, Aarau, 1846, i. 28–45) on mediaeval German chess, to which Vetter has added many notes.

Brunet y Bellet (*Ajedrez*, 280–97) makes a futile attempt to claim Cessolis (which he writes Casulis = of Gasull) as a Spaniard.

[23] Casalis, *Dizionario geografico stor.-stat.-commerciale degli stati di S. M. il re di Sardegna*, iv. 437 (quoted by Vetter), says:

'*Cessole* (*Cessolae*), comune nel mand. di Bubbio, prov. dioc. di Acqui, div. di Alessandria. Depende dal senato di Casale . . . giace a' pie di una collina tra Bubbio e Vesme sulla manca sponda del Bormida ; . . . antico castello gia proprio del conte Ospitaliere de Cessole.'

To this Vetter (xl) adds that Cessole was first governed by the Marchesi of Savona, then since 1209 by the republic of Asti; after the fall of the republic by the Marchesi again, and after the death of Emperor Henry VII by Manfred, Marchese of Saluzzo. Its population is about 1200.

Since there was another Cessole in the neighbourhood of Chieri in the old county of Turin, we cannot be certain as to which village gave Cessolis his surname. This second Cessole was destroyed by the counts of Biandrati in 1260 and the population removed to Chieri.

[24] The gate was destroyed in 1577. The mutilated fragment of the Emperor's statue is now in the Capua museum. Cessolis' description is incorporated in the *Gesta Romanorum* (ed. Oesterley, liv, *De regni celesti*).

[25] 'Nam melius est reges habere per successionem primogeniturae quam per electionem vel principum voluntatem. Saepe enim principes diversis causis interventientibus discordis fiunt et dissidentibus voluntatibus necesse est aut electionem tardari, aut propriis utilitatibus intendentes personam regis in electione non meliorem aut digniorem eligere, sed utiliorem propriis commodis affectare.'

The allusion (first pointed out by v. d. Lasa, 98) is by no means established.

eos, ut formas eorum menti inprimerent ut sic bellum ipsum et ludi virtutem possint facilius obtinere cordetenus. Hunc autem libellum de moribus hominum et officiis nobilium sy placet intitulari decrevi. Et ut in eo ordinatius prosequar ante ipsum capitola preposui ut, quod in eo sequitur, plenius elucescat.'

The sermon is divided into four books or tractates, and, as promised in the introduction, the MSS. generally commence with an index to the contents. In Caxton's English translation this is given as follows:

This booke conteyneth .iiii. traytees /
The first traytee is of the Invencion of this playe of the chesse / and conteyneth .iii. chapitres
The first chapitre is under what kynge this play was founden
The .ii. chapitre / who fonde this playe
The .iii. chapitre / treteth of .iii. causes why hit was made and founden
The second traytee treteth of the chesse men / and conteyneth .v. chapitres
The first chapitre treteth of the form of a kynge and of suche thinges as apperteyn to a kynge
The .ii. chapitre treteth of ye quene & her forme and maners
The .iii. chapitre of the forme of the alphins and her offices and maners
The .iiii. chapitre is of the knyght and of his offices
The .v. is of the rooks and of their maners and offices
The thirde traytee is of the offices of the comyn peple And hath .viii. chapitres
The first chapitre is of the labourers & tilinge of the erthe
The .ii. of smythis and other werke[r]s in yron & metall
The .iii. is of drapers and makers of cloth and notaries
The .iiii. is of marchantes and chaungers
The .v. is of phisicyens and cirugiens and apotecaries
The .vi. is of tauerners and hostelers
The .vii. is of ye gardes of the citees & tollers & customers
The .viii. is of ribauldes disepleyars and currours
The .iiii. traytee is of the meuyng and yssue of them And hath .viii. chapitres
The first is of the eschequer
The second of the yssue and progression of the kynge
The thirde of the yssue of the quene
The fourth is of the yssue of the alphyns
The fifth is of the yssue of the knyghtes
The sixty chapitre is of the yssue of the rooks
The seuenth is of the meuynge & yssue of the comyn peple
And the eyght and laste chapitre is of the epilegacion.
And of the recapitulacion of all these forsaid chapitres.[26]

Within these twenty-four chapters Cessolis gathers a whole host of anecdotes and instances drawn from Biblical, ancient, and modern history with much sound and pregnant advice upon the duties of men in their several callings. His immediate source and inspiration was, according to Prof. Köpke, the *Polycraticus seu De nugis curialium et vestigiis philosophorum* of John of Salisbury, Bishop of Chartres, and sometime Secretary to Thomas à Becket during his Archbishopric of Canterbury, who died in 1180. In the latter portion of this work, Salisbury treats of the state and duties of a king, his

[26] I quote from the first edition. In the second the titles of the chapters in the third book are occasionally given differently: e.g. ch. iii: 'Thoffyce of notaries / aduocates, scriueners and drapers and clothmakers'; ch. v: 'The forme of phisiciens leches spycers and appotycaryes'; ch. vi: 'Of tauerners hostelers & vitaillers'; ch. vii: 'Of kepers of townes Receyuers of custum and tollenars'; and ch. viii: 'Of messagers currours Rybauldes and players at the dyse.'

great officials, and knights. The whole style of Cessolis' sermon is modelled upon this part of the *Polycraticus*, and the greater part of the quotations which Cessolis made from classical authors are to be found in the older work.[27] It is not certain whether Cessolis quotes any classical author at first hand. He certainly shows very little knowledge of the great writers of the Augustan period, and the favourite Latin author for quotation is Valerius Maximus, a writer of the post-Augustan or silver period. Of writers of the mediaeval period Cessolis quotes from the *Polycraticus* by name twice, from the Spanish physician Petro Alfonsi (*c.* 1106), from Gaultier de Chatillon (Philip Walter de Castillione), who wrote *c.* 1200 an epic poem on the life of Alexander the Great, and from the Cistercian Helinand, who wrote a Chronicle and other works in the beginning of the 13th century.[28]

It is only in his first and fourth books that Cessolis has much to say of any historical importance about chess. In the one he states his belief as to the origin of the game, in the other he deals with the moves of the chessmen. The two intervening books explain the Pieces and Pawns as symbolical of various orders and ranks of society, and, under the classes thus obtained, Cessolis arranges his anecdotes and illustrations. It is these two books (ii and iii) which made the sermon one of the most favourite works during the Middle Ages, and gave it a vitality that outlasted the variety of chess it describes. That the popularity was not due to the chess which supplied the framework, but to the stories which crowd the canvas, is clear from the way in which the fourth book is treated in many MSS. and in several translations. We repeatedly find it abbreviated, disfigured by serious omissions, omitted entirely, and even replaced by other moralizing works. Had chess been the secret of the popularity of the sermon this would have been impossible.

Cessolis deals very briefly with the history of chess. He attributes the invention to an Eastern philosopher, named by the Chaldeans Xerses or Hyerses and by the Greeks Philometer, who invented it in the reign of Nebuchadnezzar's son and successor, Evil-Merodach, who is presented regularly in mediaeval works as a monster of cruelty.

'Under this kynge than Evilmerodach was this game and playe of the chesse founden / Trewe it is that some men wene / that this playe was founden in the tyme of the bataylles & siege of troye. But that is not soo For this playe cam to the playes of the caldees as dyomedes the greek[29] sayth and reherceth That amonge

[27] W. E. A. Axon, in the introduction to his reprint of Caxton's *Game and playe of the chesse* (London, 1883) gives the *De regimine principum* of Guido de Colonna (D. 1316) as Cessolis' source. This is impossible. Colonna's work at earliest is only contemporary with Cessolis' sermon.

[28] The authors quoted by Cessolis, arranged according to frequency of quotation, are—Valerius Maximus (48); Seneca (13); Cicero, Ovid, Suetonius (through John of Salisbury) (7); Jerome, Helinand (5); Quintilian, Publius Syrus, Augustine (4); Gellius, Orosius, *Proverbia sapientis* (3); Terence, Varro, Sallust, Virgil, Josephus, Claudian, Boethius, Paulus Diaconus, Petro Alfonsi, John of Salisbury, Macrobius, *Catonis disticha* (2); Theophrastus, Socrates (? Aristotle), *Pseudo*-Kallisthenes, Trojus Pompeius, Florus, Tacitus, Ausonius, Tibullus, Martial, Lucan, Diogenes Laertius, Cassiodorus, Juvenal, Quintus Curtius, Horace, Pliny, Julius Valerius (2), *Collationes*, Symmachus, Ambrose, Gualtier de Chatillon, *Catonis breves sententiae*, *Dialogus creaturarum*, Josephus *in libro de causis rerum naturarum* (1).

[29] The name of this philosopher occurs nowhere in classical literature, and it is not known whence Cessolis obtained it.

the philosophrs was the most renomed playe amonge all other playes / And after that / cam this playe in the tyme. of Alixandre the grete in to Egipte And so unto alle the parties toward the south / '

Whence Cessolis obtained this legend is uncertain, but if Lydgate's statement in his *Troy Book* is well founded, it occurs in the chronicle of the earlier writer Jacobus de Vitriaco (D. 1240–4); this, however, is inaccessible to me. Cessolis adds three reasons for the invention: to correct the evil manners of the King, to avoid idleness and sadness, and to satisfy the natural desire for novelty by means of the infinite variety of the play.

From Caxton's *Game and playe of the chesse*.

The different chapters of the second and third books of Cessolis' work, which treat of the allegorical interpretation of the chess forces, begin with descriptions of the manner in which the characters symbolized should be depicted. In many of the MSS. and early printed editions, miniatures are added which carry out the directions of the text. Probably the best known are those in the second edition of Caxton's translation.[30]

In the interpretation, the King (*rex*) and Knight (*miles*) remain typical

[30] These are reproduced in Axon's reprint, and also in Brunet y Bellet's *El Ajedrez*. Massmann gives the figures from a Munich MS. of Cessolis, *Volgarizzamento* (Milan, 1829) those of the Florence 1493 edition of the Italian version; and Schlüter gives those of the Lübeck edition of Stephan's metrical version in his reprint of that poem.

of these ranks; the Queen (*regina*) also is treated as a Queen, though the section deals with women in general. Since the names Aufin (*alphiles*) and Rook (*roccus*) suggested nothing definite, Cessolis found himself free to adopt what explanation he liked. He accordingly identifies the Aufins with judges, and the Rooks with the king's legates or representatives (*vicarii seu legati regis*), depicting the latter as unarmed horsemen. The justification for these interpretations is to be found in the idea that a king's judges or counsellors should be at his elbow, while his deputies govern on his behalf the confines of the realm: ideas clearly suggested by the positions of the Aufins and

From Caxton's *Game and playe of the chesse.*

Rooks on the board. The weakness of this allegory of the nobility is that it is not exhaustive, since it omits entirely the whole order of clergy. This omission is remarkable, and destroys the completeness of the picture. Some translators clearly recognized this, and attempted to complete the picture. Cessolis divided his judges into those for criminal and those for civil cases; Ammenhausen divides them into civil and ecclesiastical judges, and includes the whole of the clergy under the second type.

The most original and remarkable feature of Cessolis' work is his treatment of the Pawns (*populares*). Instead of treating them as one group, representative of the commonalty in mass, as is the general method of the moralities, he differentiates between the eight Pawns, and makes each Pawn typical of some group of allied trades or professions. By this means he is enabled to add definiteness to his picture, and to secure greater orderliness in the arrangement of the matter he had collected in illustration of the activities of the lower orders. Cessolis accordingly classifies his Pawns thus: KRP *agricola*; KKtP *faber*; KBP *notarius, lanificius, carnifex, scriptor*; KP *mercator*; QP *medicus*; QBP *tabernarius, tabularius, hospes*; QKtP *custos civitatis*; QRP *ribaldus, cursor, lusor*. The English equivalents as they appear in Caxton are given in the table of contents quoted above. This fanciful nomenclature, although developed in the book with much care and system, has of course never passed into practical use. Even the few MSS. and other works that attempted to repeat it in the Middle Ages generally failed to do so accurately. Thus MS. Vatican 1960, f. 286 b, has a finely executed chessboard, on which one side is shown pictorially, while the other is shown by the names of the pieces. In this the Pawns[31] are thus described: KRP *albergator qui recipiat uenientes ad eum* (= QBP in Ces.); KKtP *agricola qui fructus ei portat* (= KRP, Ces.); KBP *sartor et islipartus*; KP *mercatores*; QP *medicus*; QBP *notarius propter acta* (= KBP, Ces.); QKtP *faber propter arma et edificia paranda* (= KKtP, Ces.); QRP *officialis ciuitatis cum clauibus mensis et bursa* (= QKtP, Ces.). A similar diagram in the early printed editions (1482 and 1485) of the *De arte memoriae* of Jacobus Publicius has KRP *colonus*; KKtP *faber*; KBP *scriptor*; KP *thesaurarius* (not Ces.); QP *medicus*; QBP *caupo*; QKtP *teolonarius* (not Ces.); QRP *lusor*.[32]

It is only with the fourth book that we come to the practical game, though even here Cessolis still loses no opportunity for moralization. He describes the chessboard as representing the city of Babylon, and lays stress upon four points: the 64 squares agree with the traditional shape of the city, which was four-square and 16 miles each way; the raised edges of the board (*labia tabularii*) figure the walls of the city; the commonalty are arranged before the nobility because the nobles can do nothing without the people, *gloria ergo nobilium ac vita populares sunt*; and lastly, the chessmen when arranged for play occupy just half the board and leave the other half empty, thus providing a kingdom for each monarch and space for play. There is also a somewhat obscure allusion to the vastness of the sum of the geometrical progression—the duplication of the chessboard.

In the succeeding chapters the moves of the pieces are described at considerable length with reference to their original positions, and not in general terms, as is usually the case in mediaeval works. In doing this Cessolis makes use of the fact that the board is coloured, and refers to particular squares in

[31] The major pieces are thus described: KR *Rochus est legatus Regis*; Kt *Miles armis defendit iusticiam* (QKt adds *contra inobedientes*); B *Arfili* (KB *sunt*) *ascessores* (KB adds *quod s. leges consulant*; K and Q *Rex et Regina cum coronis et regiis circonstantiis in catedris amicto sedent in honore*. The board is drawn at right angles to the ordinary position of diagrams: the K is on e1.

[32] Publicius uses an unusual nomenclature for the major pieces; R *interrex*; Kt *eques auratus*; B *vir consularis*; K *rex*; Q *regina*. The Ks are on d1 and d8: h1 is white. Since the printer has made all pieces on the white squares black, and all on the black white, we cannot tell which side was intended to be White.

terms of their colours and their position relative to the original posts of the chessmen; thus e6 is *quadrus albus ante mercatorem*. The initial arrangement of one side only—the Black—is given, and the reader is supposed to view them from the opposite edge of the board, precisely as we view them in a printed diagram to-day. Cessolis accordingly speaks of the squares f8, g8, h8 as being to the right of the King on e8. As he says of the King—

cum enim residet in quarto quadro et cum ipse sit niger, habet in dextris in albo militem, alphilem vero et rochum in nigro.[33]

As is the case in other mediaeval works, a player's pieces are also termed *black* or *white* from the colour of the squares to which they are confined, and quite independently of the colour of the side to which they belong. Black's KB is consequently called his *black* Bishop and his QB his *white* Bishop, because they are confined to the black and to the white squares of the board. A promoted Pawn is similarly called *black* or *white* according as it moves on black or on white squares.

I have already, in my description of the Lombard assize, epitomized the information as to the moves which Cessolis supplies, and it is therefore unnecessary to repeat that information here. It is remarkable that Cessolis nowhere refers to the termination *checkmate* by name: we should hardly have expected the moralizer to have forgone the possibilities suggested by the conclusion of the game. The same thought has evidently occurred to many early scribes who were transcribing the sermon, for many MSS. substitute *scacmat* for the term *scacroc* in the passage at the end of the description of the King's move, without regard to the fact that the alteration makes nonsense of the passage. Nor does Cessolis give us any indication as to the popularity of chess, e.g. whether it was confined to the upper classes only in Lombardy, or to what extent it was played by the middle classes also. We should also have expected some reference to the chess problem, which must have been already known in Lombardy in Cessolis' day.

The *Liber de moribus hominum et officiis nobilium* was translated early and repeatedly into the modern European languages. A list of these versions will show how popular Cessolis' work was.

French Versions.

1. In 1347 (the MSS. give as the date of the commencement of the translation 4 May, 1347) the friar Jehan Ferron, 'de l'ordre des Frères precheurs, de Paris' and chaplain to Bertrand Auberi of Tarascon, translated it into French for his patron, under the title *Le gieu des eschas moralisé*.

2. Almost simultaneously, the friar Jehan de Vignay, 'hospitalier de l'ordre du Hault-Pas (de l'ordre de St. Jacques, MS. Vat.)', translated it as *Le livre*

[33] See v. d. Lasa's note in Vetter, op. cit., cols. 803–22, provoked by the diagram of the arrangement of the pieces which Zimmermann had given in his edition of v. Beringen's metrical version. This puts the board with h1 black, and the Kings on e1 and d8. V. d. Lasa had little difficulty in showing that this arrangement was inconsistent with many passages in Cessolis. Zimmermann had failed to grasp Cessolis' method of describing the position of the pieces.

des eschecs moralisé en françois. Vignay's version is dedicated to John, Duke of Normandy, who succeeded his father Philip VI as King of France, 1350. In some MSS. John's mother, Jane of Burgundy (who died 1349), is associated in the dedication. Vignay's version was printed in folio 1504, and in quarto 1505.

3. Some MSS. of a French translation give the Vignay authorship combined with the Ferron dedication. Without investigation, it is impossible to say whether these MSS. represent a combination of the two texts, or whether they are not simply MSS. of the Ferron text in which the name of Vignay, as the better-known translator, has been substituted for Ferron. On the other hand, MS. Paris, f. fr. 1170, is a deliberate compilation from the two prose French versions.

While there is considerable variety in the earlier portion of the two French versions, they approximate very closely in the latter part of the work. It is generally assumed that Vignay obtained access to Ferron's version after he had commenced his translation, and that he made considerable use of the earlier French work.

4. A metrical French version of 1,200 lines, in which the text is considerably abbreviated and rearranged, was written by Guillaume de Saint André in the 15th century (MS. Paris, f. fr. 14978). It begins:

> Mes si d'esbat te prend tallant,
> Pren ton esbat deuement,
> Mes si a jouer tu vieulx attendre
> C'est des eschecs qui est licite
> Et a touz biens les gens incite, etc.

St. André omits all the stories of his original, places the Fourth Book in front of the Second and Third, and concludes with a moral discourse which the philosopher addressed to Evil-Merodach after the game of chess had moved the latter to repent of his previous evil life. The moves are described in 42 lines (139–80). The King's leap is given, and the double step of the Pawn; the Queen is only given her Muslim move. The pieces are called *roy*, *roigne* or *dame*, *dauffin*, *chevalier*, *roc*, and *paonnet*, *pion*, *paont* or *paon*. The initial letters of the last 22 lines, when read in the reverse order, give the author's name.

Italian Version.

5. *Libro di giuocho di scacchi intitulato de costumi degli huomini et degli officii de nobili*. An anonymous translation of the 14th c., of which there is a great number of MSS. It was printed in Florence 1493, in Venice 1534, and has been reprinted under the title *Volgarizzamento*, Milan, 1829.

Catalan Version.

6. *Lo libre de les costumes dels homens e dels oficis dels nobles sobrel Joch dels Escachs*, existing in MSS. of the 15th c., two of which have been edited; viz. by Brunet y Bellet, Barcelona, 1900, and by de Bofarull, Barcelona, 1902.

Spanish (Castilian) Version.

7. *Dechado de la vida humana moralmento sacado del juego del Axedrez*, tradizido . . . per el licenciado Reyna, vezino della villa de Aranda de duero, Valladolid, 1549, quarto. There are considerable gaps in Book IV, dealing with the moves of the chessmen.

From the *Libro di giuocho di scacchi*, Florence, 1493.

English Versions.

8. *The game and playe of the chesse*, translated from Vignay's French version [34] by William Caxton in 1474, and printed shortly after at Bruges, and again, with the addition of 24 woodcuts, at London, *c.* 1480. It has been reprinted several times in the 19th c., the latest edition being that of W. E. A. Axon, London, 1883.

[34] The statement in Blades' *Biography of Caxton*, London, 1882, that Caxton made use of both French versions, although adopted by others (e. g. Axon, op. cit., and the *Cambridge Hist. Eng. Lit.*), is based upon insufficient evidence, and is almost certainly erroneous. It depends upon the fact that the printed text of Vignay's work accidentally omits the adjective *joli* in his description of Evil-Merodach, whereas both Ferron and Caxton have it. It translates the *lascivus* of Cessolis, and I have found it in MSS. of Vignay's version. There is no reason to disbelieve Caxton's own statement as to his original.

9. *The buke of ye chess*, a metrical Scotch version of 2,122 lines, of the 16th c., which is independent of Caxton's version. It was printed from the unique MS. of John Sloane's writing by the Auchinleck Press, 1818, under the title of *Frondes caducae.*

German Versions.

10. *Das buch menschlicher sitten vnd der ampt der edeln.* A MHG. prose version, of which the MSS. go back to the beginning of the 15th c. (MS. Munich, cod. germ. 49 is dated 1407), which was printed in folio four times before 1500 (viz. Augsburg, 1477, 40 ff., and 1483, 34 ff.; Strassburg, 1483, 39 ff.; and an edition without place or date, but *a.* 1480). In this text there are considerable gaps in the fourth book.

11. A MHG. metrical version of 10,772 lines was written by Heinrich von Beringen in the early part of the 14th c., and has been edited by P. Zimmermann from the unique Stuttgart MS. (written 1438), *Das Schachgedicht Heinrichs v. Beringen*, Litt. Verein in Stuttgart, CLXVI, Tübingen, 1884.

12. A MHG. metrical version of 7,594 lines, written in N.E. Germany by the Pherrer zu dem Hechte, belongs to 1335. It was edited by E. Sievers, *Zeitschr. f. dtsch. Altertum*, Berlin, XVII, New Ser. V, 1874, 162–389, from the London MS. (Add. 19555).

13. The MHG. *Schachzabelbuch* of Kunrat von Ammenhausen, a metrical version in 19,340 lines, completed in 1337. It has been edited by F. Vetter, *Das Schachzabelbuch Kunrats v. Ammenhausen*, Bibl. älterer Schriftwerke d. dtsch. Schweiz, 1892, in a very valuable work which also gives the Latin text and Mennel's later German version.

14. *Van dogheden vnde van guden zeden secht dyt boek wol dat vaken ouer lest de wert ok des schaekspeles klok*, a MLG. metrical version of 5,886 lines by Meister Stephan, written at Dorpat in Esthonia, 1350–75, and printed at Lübeck, *c.* 1489. It has been edited by W. Schlüter, *Meister Stephans Schachbuch*, Verh. d. Gelehrten estnischen Gesellschaft, XI, Dorpat, 1883.

15. Jacob Mennel's *Schachzabel*, Constance, 1507, is an abbreviated version of v. Ammenhausen's poem in 586 lines. I have already made considerable use of the two later editions of this book by Köbel, Oppenheim, *c.* 1520; and by Egenolff, Frankfort, 1536, on account of the new matter which is added.

Dutch Version.

16. A MDu. version of the beginning of the 14th c. or earlier (MS. La Hague, 228, is dated 1402), by Franconis (Vranconis), was printed at Gouda, 1479; Delft, 1483; and Louvain, 1551. In this translation the Fourth Book is omitted entirely.

Swedish Version.

17. *Skaftauils lek*, a metrical version which exists in two MSS. of 1476 and 1492 respectively, and has been edited by Rietz and Sjöberg as a University dissertation, *De ludo scacchorum*, Lund, 1848.

Czech Version.

18. A Czech version exists in a Vienna MS. of the 15th c., which has been edited by F. Menčik, *Knízky o hrě šachové*, Prague, 1879. This work is more of an imitation than a translation. While it follows the order of Cessolis' work, it systematically substitutes Bohemian instances for the classical anecdotes of the latter. It abandons the elaborate interpretation of the Pawns and deals with them as a single class, and it materially shortens the section on the moves of the chessmen. There are some differences also in the moves and rules as given in this Czech work. The Pawn's double step and the King's leap are allowed, though the description of the latter is by no means so exact as in Cessolis. The combined move of King and Queen is given, but I am unable to discover any reference to the Queen's leap, though the fact that the combined move is given shows that this must have existed. Two methods of terminating the game are given as decisive—Checkmate and Bare King. Finally, the Czech work concludes with the parallel between the bag that holds the chessmen and the grave that receives all mankind, which we know from the *Innocent Morality*.

It is interesting to note the number of editions of these translations of Cessolis' work which were printed in the early days of printing. No less than six editions of the Latin text are also known: viz., a folio edition of 40 ff. printed at Utrecht, *c.* 1473; two Milan editions in folio, 1478 and 1497; a Vienna quarto of 1505; and two 15th c. quarto editions, both without place or date.

But little later than the sermon of Jacobus de Cessolis is Galwan de Levanto's *Liber Sancti Passagii Christicolarum contra Saracenos pro recuperatione Terrae Sanctae*, of which an imperfect copy from the Phillips Library is now in the Bibliothèque Nationale, Paris (nouv. acquis. lat. 669). Galwan was a Genoese and physician to Pope Boniface VIII, and in this work, written between 1291 and 1296, he tries to induce Philip IV of France to undertake a new Crusade. The work, which is exceedingly obscure in style, is divided into two tractates of 59 (really 58) and 16 (of which the last 10 are missing) chapters respectively. The first tractate bears the sub-title of *De regimine principum atropologice educto de ludo scachorum*, the second of *De persuasione neophyta Christicolis ad Passagium Sanctum*. Only the first tractate deals with chess, and even here the chess references are but few. In ch. i, the invention of chess is ascribed to a philosopher named Justus for the reformation of a Persian tyrant, Juvenilis. The remainder of the work deals with the qualities of the good king, the duties of his subjects, and the beauty of certain virtues, e. g. justice and mercy. The chessmen give a little order to the work. They are called *rex*, *regina* (= *collateralis regis*), *alferii* (= notaries and chancellors), *milites* (= nobles), *rochi* (who serve to the king as lightning before thunder and to the kingdom as fenced cities), and *pedites* (the commonalty). The work throws very little light upon the rules: Pawns are promoted to the rank of Queen; and the two technicalities, *scaco* and *scaco çuie* or *scaco matho* are the subjects of two chapters. To say 'Check!' is explained as meaning a reminder to the King to cultivate justice; checkmate is the end of all things. The explanation of 'check!' is not very unlike the 'facias michi ius!' of Cessolis. Otherwise there is no evidence that Galwan had any knowledge of his contemporary's more famous work. He shows much less knowledge of chess; thus, in dealing with each piece, he devotes chapters, first to its meaning (*de significatione regis*, &c.), and then to its 'pride and humility' (*de humilitate et superbia regine*, &c.). In these latter chapters he seems to contemplate the possibility of a less important piece arrogating to itself the powers of a more important one by occupying its place. This is all very well for the allegory where, for instance, Galwan wants to show the unfitness of the notary to pose as a noble, but it is only another instance of the way in which the moralist strained the chess to suit his morality.

I have already stated that Cessolis' work is the original of some chapters in the *Gesta Romanorum.* A collation of the contents of the known MSS. of this collection of stories and moralities shows that three chapters relate to chess. In Oesterley's standard edition of the *Gesta Romanorum* (Berlin, 1872) these are numbered clxvi, *De ludo schacorum*; clxxviii, *De omnium divitiarum matre, providentia*; and cclxxv, *De Antonio Imperatore.* The *Gesta Romanorum* has no single motive behind it, and it is only natural that it grew in compass as time went on. Its original sources were in part Oriental, in part classical, in part European. The latest writer from whom parallels were borrowed appears to have been the English Austin friar, Robert Holcot, a victim of the Great Death in 1349. The oldest existing MS. of the *Gesta Romanorum*, MS. Innsbruck Univ. Library, Oenip. lat. 310, which was written in 1342, already contains chapters derived from Holcot's *Moralities.* This MS. is entitled *Gesta Imperatorum*, and contains 220 chapters. One of these is the *De ludo schacorum.* The two remaining chess chapters are not included in this MS.

The existing MSS. of the *Gesta Romanorum* fall into two groups, the one with a smaller number of chapters exists only in MSS. written in England, and is accordingly called the English version; the other, with a larger number of chapters, exists only in Continental MSS., and was apparently compiled in Germany. We may call it the Continental version. The exact relationship of these two versions is matter of dispute. Earlier scholars regarded the English version as the older, and the Continental version as being based upon it. The latest writer on the subject, Mr. J. A. Herbert (*Catalogue of Romances in the Depart. of MSS., Brit. Mus.*, vol. iii, London, 1910, 163–271), takes exactly the opposite view. According to him, the collection was made in Germany not long before 1342, and the English version, all the MSS. of which belong to the 15th century, is derived from it.

It does not appear that any of the writers on the matter have used the evidence which can be drawn from a critical examination of the two chapters *De ludo schacorum* and *De Antonio Imperatore.* The latter chapter only exists in the English version, the former in the Continental version. It is absolutely certain that the English chapter *De Antonio Imperatore* served as the foundation of the Continental chapter *De ludo schacorum.* It has not been possible for me to compare other chapters of the two versions, but the evidence of these two chapters is so striking, that I consider Mr. Herbert's view untenable. The *Gesta Romanorum* was originally commenced in England, and revised and expanded on the Continent. It was first printed in Utrecht, 1473, with 150 chapters, and in Cologne, *c.* 1473, with 151 chapters. Ulrich Zell's Cologne edition, between 1472 and 1475, contained 181 chapters, and is the basis of Oesterley's edition.

If my belief that the English version is the older is correct, the compilation of the *Gesta Romanorum* must have commenced at an earlier date than Mr. Herbert allows, probably in the first third of the 14th century.

I begin accordingly with the chapter *De Antonio Imperatore.* The Continental recension, *De ludo schacorum*, was written before 1342. The third chapter, *De omnium divitiarum matre*, which commonly goes by the name of the *Wall-painting*, seems to have been added later. I have not discovered in what MS. it first occurs.

The Latin text of the chapter *De Antonio Imperatore* is very corrupt in all the MSS. which I have been able to consult, and the early English translation of *c.* 1440 (*Gesta Romanorum*, E. E. T. S., London, 1879, xxi. 70–2) adds other difficulties of its own. The Latin text is given in the Appendix to this chapter; the English version follows:

XXI. *Antonius the Emperoure.*—Antonius was a wys emperour' regnyng in the cite of Rome, the which vsid moche to pley with houndys, and aftir þat pley all þe day after he wolde vse þe chesse. So yn a day, as he pleide at þe chesse & byheld the kyng sette yn the pley, som tyme hy and som tyme lowe, among aufyns and pownys, he thought þerwith þat hit wold be so with him, for he shuld dey, and be hid vndir erth. And þerfore he divided his Reame in thre parties; and he yaf oo part to the kyng of Ierusalem; þe secunde part vnto þe lordis of his Reame or his empire; and the thrid partie vnto the pore people; & yede him self vnto the holy londe, and ther' he endid his lyf in peas.

Moralite.—Seth now, good sirs; this emperour', þat lovith so wele play, may be called eche worldly man þat occupieth him in vanytes of the world'; but he moste take kepe of the pley of the chesse, as did the emperoure. The chekir or þe chesse hath viij. poyntes in each partie. In euery pley beth viij. kyndes of men', *scil.* man, woman', wedewer, wedowis, lewid men', clerkes, riche men, and pouere men'. at this pley pleieth vj. men', the first man', þat goth afore, hath not but oo poynt, but whenne he goth aside, he takith anoþer; so by a pouere man'; he hath not, but when he comyth to þe deth with pacience, þen shall he be a kyng in heuen', with þe kyng of pore men. But if he grucche ayenst his neighbour' of his stat, and be a thef, and ravissh þat wher' he may, þen he is ytake, and put in to the preson' of helle. The secund, *scil.* alphyn', renneth iij. poyntes both vpward and douneward; (he) bytokenyth wise men', the whiche by deceyuable eloquence & takyng of money deceyueth, & so he is made oonly. The iij. *scil.* þe knyȝt, hath iij. poyntes, & goth þerwith; (he) betokenyth gentilmen þat rennyth aboute, & ravisshith, and ioyeth for her kynrede, & for habundaunce of richesse. The fourth *scil.* þe rook, he holdith length & brede, and takyth vp what so is in his way; he betokenyth okerers and false merchaunts, þat rennyth aboute ouer all, for wynnyng & lucre, & rechith not how thei geten', so that thei haue hit. The fifthe is þe quene, that goth fro blak to blak, or fro white to white, and is yset beside þe kyng, and is ytake fro the kyng. This quene bytokenyth virgyns and damesels, þat goth fro chastite to synne, and beth ytake by the devill for glovis or such maner yiftes. The vj. is to whom all owe to obey and mynystre; and he goth forth, and bakward ayen', & in either side, & takith ouer all; so sone discendith in to þe world, and ascendith to god by praiers; But when he takith (no) kepe of god, and hath no meyne, þan is hit to þe man chekmate. And þerfore let vs not charge of oure estates, no more þan is with þe men', when þei be put vp in þe poket; then hit is no charge who be above or who be byneth; and so by the Spirit of loulynesse we may come to þe ioy of heuen'. And þat graunt vs, qui viuit, &c.

The reference to the bag or pocket in which the chessmen are put away, which levels all ranks of piece, may be derived from the *Innocent Morality*, but otherwise the chapter is original and shows no trace of the influence of any other Morality. The Pawn is explained as typical of the poor man, who becomes at the end a king in heaven, but when he turns aside to steal is taken and sent to hell. The Aufins are wise men, the Knights gentlemen of good birth, the Rooks dishonest merchants, the Queens virgins, and the King is apparently a king. The interpretation of the last two pieces is not very clearly worked out.

The moves also are by no means clearly expressed, but they show no sign of any knowledge of any of the European improvements. It is not clear whether the King can move diagonally. The Queen is said to keep to squares of one colour, although the allegory would be better suited by a move from one colour to the other. The description of the Pawn's move has been curtailed in the English version. In the original Latin the text ran—

primus est pedinus qui cum procedit non habet nisi vnum punctum et quum vadit lateraliter ex alia parte capit alium et cum venerit ad mensam fit ferzs,

though the MSS. are very corrupt at this point, Harl. 5259 substituting 'fortis' for 'fers'. On the whole, I think that neither the original author nor his later copyists and translator had much knowledge of chess.

When this chapter reached the Continent, it fell into the hands of some-one who was familiar with Cessolis' chess sermon. This writer proceeded to remodel the chapter with the help of the larger work, and the result is the chapter *De ludo schacorum* of the Continental MSS. of the *Gesta Romanorum*. The attempt to make a harmonious whole out of two Moralities which took such different views as to the interpretation of chess would seem foredoomed to failure; but the failure is made all the more glaring by the carelessness of the compiler, who was clearly incompetent to write anything exact on chess.

When we examine the construction of the new chapter we find that the compiler omits the introductory story of the *De Antonio*, and plunges straight into the Morality. Here he alters the order in which he takes the pieces, and instead of commencing with the Pawn, he takes the Rook first, beginning with a carelessly copied extract from Cessolis. By the time he has completed this, he has forgotten that the *De Antonio* began with the Pawn, and proceeds to copy from that text the concluding sentence describing the Pawn's method of capture and allegorical interpretation. The result is a hopeless muddle.[35] He draws his description of the Aufin's move from Cessolis, and in so doing introduces without explanation the special names of some of the Pawns (e.g. *agricola*) in Cessolis. The allegory is taken from *De Antonio*, but is lengthened considerably. The description of the moves of the Knight and Pawn is taken from Cessolis; the interpretations are quite new, though the conclusion of the section on the Pawn is taken verbatim from Cessolis. The first sentence on the Queen is a quotation from the *De Antonio*, but uses a MS. which, like Harl. 5259 and Linc. L. 12, by the omission of four words has converted the Queen's diagonal move into one in which she changes colour every move. The following sentences are from Cessolis. The explanation is again new, but it concludes with another long extract from Cessolis. The account of the King's move is again taken from Cessolis, but only a portion of the chapter is used, with the result that it is only partially described.[36] The interpretation of this piece is quite new.

The Aufins mean the wise men of this earth, and the three squares of their leap in a forward direction denote their three characteristics, intellect, reason, and fortitude. They ought to direct themselves upwards to God, but they aim downwards through eloquence and dishonesty. The aslant move of three squares in the backward direction then means gluttony, robbery, and pride. Finally, the opposing King, i.e. the devil, takes them, and thrusts them into hell to await the day of judgement. The Knight is the Christian warring against the devil, and defending his King (i.e. his soul) from the tempter. The eight squares which a Knight commands from the centre of the board are the eight beatitudes. The Pawns denote people of every condition and sex, who go straight so long as they follow the advice of their confessors and obey the rules of the Church. The Queen is the soul. The Queen is white and black, white by confession and absolution, black by sin: she should always keep close to the King. The King is Our Lord Jesus Christ, who is King of Kings. For when he moves he is surrounded by the choir of angels, just as the chess King is surrounded by Rook, Aufin, and the other chessmen (*rochum et alphilem aliaque schacalia*). He occupies the place of all in every direction by a straight path (*et locum universorum recto tramite occupat circumquaque*), which can hardly refer to a restriction of the King's move after the quotation from Cessolis with its mention of leaps like those of Rook, Knight, and Bishop.

It is a curious parallel, and not very thoroughly thought out.

The remaining chapter—that of the wall-painting—nowhere mentions chess, but is nevertheless based upon the directions in Bks. II and III of Cessolis' work as to how the various chessmen were to be depicted, and it betrays its chess origin when it describes the positions of the common people.

[35] See the extract in the Appendix to this chapter, p. 562. The right-hand Rook stands on a white square (although later on we are told that the right-hand Knight stands on a white square), and moves always in a straight line whether forwards or backwards and never aslant, and when it goes aslant it takes someone from the other side and becomes a thief. It seems inconceivable that no one discovered the absurdity of all this.

[36] The account only allows the Ke8 to move to c8, d8, f8, g8, and b7. In the last case the Queen may be moved at the same time. What happened after the first move is not stated.

The painting obviously exhibited the chessmen, which were fashioned as imagined by Cessolis, drawn up on the board in readiness for a game of chess.

A certain king, so the chapter begins, wished to know how to govern his kingdom and himself. He summoned the wisest of his subjects, and asked for guidance. We may recognize the monarch as Evil-Merodach, and his adviser as the philosopher Xerses or Philometer. The latter proceeded to paint a picture upon the palace wall, in which he figured all orders of society. The description of the painting, almost in the words of Cessolis, and the interpretation of the various figures follows. So far as the commonalty is concerned, there is but little variation from Cessolis, but the explanation of the nobility shows some interesting differences, and approximates to the explanations given in the *Innocent Morality*. Thus:

The King is the good Christian, by preference a prince or prelate; the Queen is charity. The Knight again is a good Christian, who interprets his faith in a militant spirit. The Assessors, figured as judges on their seats, are prelates and preachers who ought to guard the commands of the Lord, and unfold the Scriptures to the people.[37] The Vicarii, figured as unarmed Knights on horseback, are judges.[38] The last two parallels are those of the *Innocent Morality*, not of Cessolis.

Cessolis' work (probably by way of Ammenhausen's German poem) served also as the source of the description of chess (*schaffzawelspil*) in Meister Ingold's *Guldin Spil*, which was written 1432–3 (cf. Schröder's *Das goldene Spiel* von Meister Ingold, Strassburg, 1892). In this work the Dominican Ingold, whom Schröder identifies with Johannes Ingold, canon of Surburg, who died 1465, treats of the seven deadly sins, illustrating each one with its opposing virtue in connexion with a special game. Thus *chess* illustrates pride and humility; '*bretspiel*', gluttony and temperance; *cards*, unchastity and chastity; '*würfelspiel*', avarice and charity; *harp-playing*, hatred and love; *shooting*, anger and meekness; *dancing*, idleness and devotion.

To chess, Ingold devotes seven sections, one introductory, and the other six dealing with the six types of chessmen, the whole filling more than half of his book. He explains the chessmen (*stain*, *gestain*) thus: the King (*küng*) is reason, the Queen (*küngin*) will, the Bishop (*alte*) memory, the Knight (*riter*) is a warrior, and the Rook (*roch*) is a judge. The Pawns are classified on similar lines to those adopted by Cessolis without being absolutely identical. Ingold's types are (1) *portner*; (2) *arzat* (*jäger*, *pfister*, *koch*, *vischer*, *appeteger*, &c.); (3) *kantzler* (*schreiber*); (4) *peichtiger*; (5) *cappelan* (*almüssner*); (6) *panerher*; (7) *weinschenck* (*keller*, *kredentzer*); (8) *marschalk* (*wagenman*, *läffel*). As a whole, the Pawns betoken the gifts of the Holy Ghost. Finally, Ingold ventures upon a 'spiritual' interpretation: K = Jesus Cristus,

37 'Item assessores scilicet iudices in cathedra: isti sunt prelati et predicatores, qui debent mandata domini custodire, libros, i. e. sacram scripturam aperire populo.'

38 'Item vicarii et unus miles positus in equo, &c. Miles iste est iudex qui debet poni in equo iusticie et clamide misericordie et capucio cum pellibus variis. Per capucium fidem cum multis auctoritatibus sanctorum et exemplis patrum in iudiciis dandis. Virgam extensam scilicet tam pauperi quam diviti.'

Q = Maria, B = patriarchs and prophets, Kt = martyrs, R = the twelve Apostles, and P = men on earth.[39]

In his section on the King, Ingold makes use of the parable of the chess-bag which we know from the *Innocent Morality*. He says:

And therefore is the chessboard (*das spilpret des schachzawel*) black and white, and four-square; and when the board is put away the game is ended, and the men are all put into a bag, and the King lies as often at the bottom as at the top, wherefore the men are then all alike. So it happens with pride. The board is Time, checkered white for daylight and black for night. When Time is put away by Death, the game is at an end, and no one has the advantage over another that any should be preferred, or another less esteemed. No one is King or Knight or Judge or Gentleman: all are equal in the bag of the earth.

The immense success that attended the *Roman de la Rose* in all circles of society resulted in that poem setting the literary fashion for the fourteenth century, and, it must be confessed, in much laborious and often tedious imitation. One of these imitations is the anonymous allegorico-didactic poem *Les Eschez amoureux*, a work of upwards of 30,000 lines, which professes to give the author's adventures in the Garden of Pleasure. The adventures commence with a chess encounter with a lady who was as skilled at chess as she was beautiful. I have already made use of the account of this game because of the valuable light which it throws upon the *Short assize*, and there only remains now to explain the allegory which lies behind the game.

The chessboard was of pure gold and precious stones, the squares being alternately amber and adamant, two substances which attract other bodies, and it exceeded in value the board upon which Sir Lancelot and Queen Guinevere were wont to play. The chessmen were also of priceless value. The lady's men were made of jewels, the Pawns (*paonnet*) emerald, the Queen (*fierge*) ruby, the Knights (*chevalier*) sapphire, the Bishops (*aulphin*) heliotrope, the Rooks (*roc*) topaz, and the King (*roy*) diamond. The author played with pieces of gold. The Kings were knights on horseback and the Queens crowned queens, but all the other chessmen were represented by knights on foot who were only to be distinguished from one another by the badges on their shields. All were emblematic of human qualities as developed in the

[39] The following particulars are of interest from the point of view of chess. The chessboard has 64 squares, generally black and white. The King at his first exit can leap to a '3rd square', the Queen is also allowed the ordinary leap, and the Pawns can play to the fourth line for their first moves. When they reach the end of the board they receive an 'extended' move. The Bishop's leap of three squares means (1) God's honour, (2) the King's honour, (3) his own honour. He keeps to squares of one colour, i.e. he must follow the truth. The Rooks cannot play until a way is opened for them. When on the same colour as the King there is danger of check-rook; a Judge loses his power in the King's palace. Elsewhere Ingold quotes the advice 'disparibus campis numquam schachroch tibi fiet', i.e. check-rook cannot be given if the player is careful to keep King and Rook on squares of different colours. One Knight guards the King's 'hut', and one the Queen's, when posted on c3 and f3. King and Queen should keep at least two Pawns before them, and then the game is well guarded.

Chess was discovered before the siege of Troy by a master named Xerses for the correction of a King whose arrogance and wrong-doing no one else had ventured to rebuke. This is, of course, from Cessolis, but the description of the moves is probably corrected to answer to the German rules. The Lombard peculiarities, the King's extended leap and the combined move of King and Queen, are omitted.

courtois love of early French society. The allegorical meanings are not explained in the text of the poem itself, but are given in marginal notes and a Latin commentary in some of the MSS. (e. g. the Venice MS.), but they appear in the prose version and were known to Lydgate, who translated a small part of the romance into English *a.* 1412. His version ends in the middle of the description of the chessmen, but he was incorporating the explanations in his poem. The allegories and badges will be most conveniently exhibited in a table. They naturally play an important part in the progress of the game, which becomes a parable of the course of love between two lovers. Thus the Lady begins by playing her Beauty, and the Author replies by Regard, i. e. sight. The Lady next supports Beauty by Simplicity, and the Author replies with *Doux penser.* The exchange of Pawns that follows shows that the author has surrendered his freedom in order to pursue the Lady's love. This will perhaps be sufficient to show the lines upon which the poet has worked: it would be tedious to reproduce the whole of his allegory.

THE LADY'S CHESSMEN.

	QRP	QKtP	QBP	QP	KP	KBP	KKtP	KRP
badge	crescent moon	rosebud	lamb	rainbow	ring	serpént	panther	eagle
Poem	Jonesche	Beautes	Simplesche	douls samblant	faiticetes	sens	bontes	noblesche
Latin commentary	iuventus	pulcritudo	simplicitas	dulcis aspectus	(Fr. fetitesse)	providentia	(Fr. bounte)	nobilitas
Lydgate	youth	beauty	symplesse	sueet looks	port & manere	providence	bounty	high noblesse

	QR	QKt	QB	Q	K	KB	KKt	KR
badge	lark	unicorn	pelican	balance	turtle	dove	hare	mermaid
Poem	douls regart	honte	franchise	maniere	li rois amourous en li courages	pites	paour	belacoeil
Lat. com.								
Lydgate								

THE LOVER'S CHESSMEN.

	QRP	QKtP	QBP	QP	KP	KBP	KKtP	KRP
badge	barren tree	key	tiger	blackbird	leopard	mirror	swan	dog
Poem	oyseuse	regars	dous pensers	plaisanche	doubte de falir	souuenir	bieu maintien	bien cele
Lat. com.								
Lydgate								

	QR	QKt	QB	Q	K	KB	KKt	KR
badge	cock	lion	ship	butterfly	peacock	flame	Orpheus with lute	dove
Poem	perseueranche	hardement	espoir	delis	li rois amourous en li courages	desirs	douls parler	patience
Lat. com.								

With the remaining (and greater) portion of the romance in which a system of education is enunciated, we have no concern: the chess interest ceases with the conclusion of the game.

Although Dr. Sieper, the editor of Lydgate's translation, *Reson and Sensuallyte*, is inclined to think that the author of *Les Eschez amoureux* merely incorporated an earlier morality of chess and love, extracts from which form the Latin commentary to which I have referred, I do not find myself able to subscribe to this view. The Latin text incorporates some of the French terms used in the romance, and I think it more probable that it owes its existence to the poem, rather than that the poem had any other forerunner than the *Roman de la Rose*.[40]

These were certainly not the only moralities of chess that were written in Europe during the Middle Ages. Some, like the work of John de Teriache mentioned above, have probably perished entirely; one or two, however, of less interest than those which I have already discussed, are known.

Ch'est li Jus des Esqiés, a poem of 298 lines, written by Engebrans d'Arras towards the end of the 13th c., exists in a Paris MS. (F. fr. 25566, ff. 239 b–241 b), and deals with the game in an obscure moralizing manner. The fate of the chessmen at the end of the game is again mentioned. The King drops to the bottom of the bag because it is the heaviest of the chessmen.

An AF. poem at Oxford (MS. Corpus Christi Coll., 293, f. 142 b), of 48 lines, compares the world to a game of chess:

Il me semble del munde cum del escheker
V sunt reis et aufyns. roks. et cheualers.
De ceo se entrejuent deu et li maufe.
Li neyrs pertenent al diable. li blancs pertenent a deu.

Adam was the king (*reis*) in the first game of chess (*echeker*), and the devil by three false moves confined him in an angle of the board and mated him.[41]

Li diables par iij. faus tres cest reis en angla
E lui dist vn echek et issi le mata.

God then commenced a second game, with the following white men: *Reis*, Jesus Christ; *Reyne*, the Virgin; *Rokis*, the Apostles; *Aufins*, confessors; *Pouns*, men who are caught by the devil with the delight of the flesh, the love of the world, honours, and riches.

Another French poem is the *Comment l'estat du monde puet estre comparu au*

[40] The reader who wants to know more of this romance is referred to the following works: E. Sieper, *Lydgate's Reson and Sensuallyte* (E.E.T.S.), specially vol. ii; E. Sieper, *Les Échecs amoureux*, Weimar, 1898; E. Langlois' review of this work in *Vollmöller's Krit. Jahresbericht ü. d. Fortschritte d. Roman. Phil.*, V. 3; and Sieper's rejoinder in *Engl. Studien*, XXVIII. 310–12; J. Mettlich, *Ein Kapitel ü. Erziehung aus einer altfr. Dichtung d. 14ten Jhts.*, Münster, 1902; J. Mettlich, *Die Schachpartie in Les Eschez amoureux*, Münster, 1907; G. Körting, *Altfr. Uebersetzung d. Remedia Amoris d. Ovid*, Leipzig, 1871; H. P. Junker, *Ueber d. altfr. Epos 'Les Échecs amoureux'*, Frankfurt a. M., 1886.

[41] This is not the only occasion on which we meet with false moves in mediaeval literature. Cf. Chaucer, *Book of the Duchesse*, 617–741, where it is said of false Fortune that 'With hir false draughtes divers / She stal on me, and took my fers.'

Jeu des eschecz, 190 lines, which occurs in a MS. of the poems of Alain Chartier (MS. Paris, Arsenal, 3521, f. 263 b), and may be by that famous poet (*c.* 1410). The parable of the bag plays, as usual, a prominent part in this poem. The only chess passage of any real interest is the following:

Et voit vn bien vng paonnet
Se juer dessoubx ung bonnet,
Qu'il prend vng Roc ou vng aulphin,
Qui bien cuide jouer au fin,
Voire mener jusques en l'angle
Vng Roy sy qu'il n'est tel qui jangle
Et puis que ly Roix est mattez. (lines 69-75.)

The elaboration of moralities founded upon the game of chess did not come to an end, as has often been supposed, with the rise of the reformed chess after 1475. At least one work on familiar lines was written for the new game, *Le jeu des esches de la dame, moralisé*, known to us from the unique MS. in the British Museum (MS. Add. 15820) of the end of the 15th c. Dedicated to a lady of noble birth, the work is written upon the model of the moralities of the older chess. The plan is to describe a game in detail on the lines of *Les Eschez amoureux*, but the allegory is now religious. The board is the world. During play, the King, Queen, and other chessmen stand according to their several degrees. When the game is over, all are tumbled back into the bag, and Pawns may lie above Kings, and Bishops above Rooks. The lady plays a game of chess with the devil, her soul being the stake. The chessmen are K, *roy*, charity; Q, *dame, royne*, humility; KB, *le petit delphin de vostre roy*, honesty; QB, *fol* (the usual term for all Bishops), honesty, knowledge of self; KKt, *chiualier*, true friendship; QKt, truth; KR, *roch*, patience; QR, loyalty; KP, *pion*, love of God; QP, continence; KBP, devotion; KKtP, benevolence; QKtP, constancy; KRP, temperance; QRP, fidelity. The QBP is omitted from the list. Her adversary's chessmen are K, pride; Q, ambition; KB, pleasure: QB, hypocrisy; KKt, discord; QKt, a lie; KR, grumbling; QR, falseness; KP, love of self; QP, curiosity; KBP, inconstancy; QBP, fiction; KKtP, slander; QKtP, perjury; KRP, blasphemy; QRP, treason.[42] In the course of the game, c8 is called *le siege de humilite*, and e7, *le lieu d'amour desordonnée.* Underlying the game is an allegory of temptation.

[42] This symbolism is not kept strictly throughout the game. In the game the rôles of the adversary's QP and QBP are reversed. For the game itself see below, Ch. XI.

APPENDIX. ORIGINAL TEXTS

I. THE INNOCENT MORALITY.

[The following MSS. of the 14th and 15th cc. have been consulted. They are all of English origin.

H = Brit. Mus. Harl. 2253, f. 135 b, written 1307–27, without title or ascription of authorship. I print the text of this, the oldest MS.

R = Bodl. Lib. Oxford, Rawl. A. 423, f. 46 b. A MS. of the sermons of Pope Innocent III, among which the morality occurs with the introduction 'Rex. Rocus. Alphinus. Miles. Regina. pedinus. Loquitur de dilectione et dicitur quod nichil valet diligere secundum libitum huius mundi, quia mundus iste totus, &c.'. This text is very close to H.

C = Corpus Christi Coll., Cambridge, 177, f. 50 b, 15th c., with title 'Sequitur quedam moralitas de scaccario per dominum Innocencium papam' and conclusion 'Explicit moralitas de scaccario secundum dominum Innocencium papam'.

K = Brit. Mus., Kings, 12. E. xxi, f. 103 b, 15th c., with title and conclusion identically as in C, of which MS. this text is a copy.

Ad. = Brit. Mus., Add. 37075, f. 38 a, late 15th c., without title or conclusion. The text resembles that of C and K.

KG = Brit. Mus., Kings, 8. D. x, f. 203 a, 15th c. A MS. of the *Summa Collationum* of Waleys, to which work the morality is added as an appendix with the reference f. 101^{v}. There is no title or conclusion. The text is fairly close to H.

O = Bodl. Lib. Oxford, 52, f. 59 b, written 1410–20, with title 'Moralitas de scaccario secundum dominum Innocentium tercium', and conclusion 'Explicit tractatus de scaccario'. This is the text printed in Prideaux's *Hypomnemata Logica, Rhetorica,* &c., Oxford, 1657, pp. 375–9.

L = Lincoln Coll., Oxford, Lat. 12, f. 220 b, early 15th c., without title or conclusion.

J^1 = St. John's Coll., Oxford, 135, f. 47 b, 15th c., following a MS. of Cessolis, with the title 'Hec moralitas sequens de scachario est domini Pape Innocencij tercij' and conclusion 'Explicit'.

J^2 = St. John's Coll., Oxford, 135 (same MS.), f. 53 b, a second text of the morality without title or conclusion.

S = Sidney Sussex Coll., Cambridge, 85. 4. 23, 14th c., f. 97 b, with the title 'De Scaccario Innocencius 3us'. This MS. differs so widely from the other texts that I have not used it in preparing the following text.

I have also used—

G = the *Communiloquium sive Summa Collationum* of John of Waleys (Johannes Gallensis); the printed editions of U, Zell, Cologne, n. d. (editio princeps) and of Argentinae, 1489, Pars I, dist. x, cap. 7. The morality occurs in some, but not all, of the other printed editions.

If we except KG, I have failed to find the morality in any of the English MSS. of the *Summa Collationum* which I have examined. On the other hand, it occurs in many MSS. of Continental origin; thus 12 MSS. at Munich, all of the 15th c., all contain it, viz. 3054 (f. 164), 3821 (f. 57), 7588 (f. 167), 11427 (f. 341v.), 12281 (f. 237v.), 14054 (f. 78), 14241 (f. 74v.), 14893 (f. 166), 16211 (f. 60v.) 17657 (f. 61), 18430 (f. 174), 22374 (f. 65).

D = the *Destructorium vitiorum*, Nuremberg, 1496, attributed to Alexander of Hales, Pars IV, cap. xxiii, where an extended version of the morality is said to be derived from *Vuallerensis in Summa Collationum*, I. xxxiv. 8. In this work the interpretations are carried to a great length.

An OF. translation was formerly in the possession of Conte Alessandro Mortara (see his *Codici MSS. Canoniciani Italici*, Oxford, 1864, 4).

There is an Italian version (Venetian dialect) in MS. Bodl. Lib., Oxford, Can. It. 4, f. 58 b, where it follows a MS. of the Italian version of Cessolis, and bears the title 'Pappa inocencio iij mette questo exempio supra el dito juego de schacchij: segue El Mondo, &c.', and the conclusion 'Scripto lanno domini nostri ihu. xpi. mcccc lviiij (1459).'

Finally there is an abbreviated Icelandic version, the work of Gottskálk Jónsson of Glaumbæ (D. 1593) in MS. Brit. Mus. Add. 11242, f. 52 *a*.]

I have made no attempt to give a complete collation of all the Latin MSS., and only give a few variant readings which seem to me to be of special chess interest.

Moralitas de Scaccario.

Mundus iste totus quoddam scaccarium est, cuius vnus punctus albus est, alius vero niger, propter duplicem statum vite et mortis, gratie et culpe.

ffamilia autem huius scaccarii sunt homines huius mundi, qui de vno sacculo materno extrahuntur, et collocantur in diuersis locis huius mundi, et singuli habent diuersa nomina. Primus enim rex est, alter regina, tertius rocus, quartus miles, quintus alphinus (J[1], alphilus), sextus pedinus. (J[2], G, Unde versus: Rex, Rocus, Alphinus, Miles, Regina, Pedinus.)

Istius autem ioci conditio talis est, vt vnus alterum capiat; et cum ludum compleuerint, sicut de vno sacculo exierunt, ita iterum reponuntur. Nec est differencia inter regem et peditem (L, pedinum) pauperum, quia simul in vnum diues et pauper.

Et sepe contingit quod quando familia scaccarii reponitur in sacculum, rex inferius collocatur et reponitur; sic fere quique maiores in transitu huius seculi inferius collocantur, scilicet in inferno, sepeliuntur, pauperes in sinum Habrahe deportantur.

In isto autem ludo *rex* vadit vbique (C, K, O, KG, J[1], J[2], G, vadit circumquaque directe) et capit vndique directe in signum quod rex omnia iuste corrigat, et in nullo omissa iusticia obliquari debet. Sed quicquid agit rex, iusticia reputatur, quia quicquid principi placet, legis habet vigorem.

Regina (J[2], G sive *domina*), que dicitur *ferce* (R fierte; C, K, Ad, ffers; KG, le ferce; O, certe; L, J[1], ferce; J[2], fferte; G, ferze), vadit oblique, et capit vndique indirecte, quia cum auarissimum sit genus mulierum, nichil capit nisi mere detur ex gratia nisi rapina et iniusticia.

Rocus est Iusticiarius perambulans totam terram directe in linea in signum quod omnia iuste corrigat, et in nullo omissa iusticia muneribus corruptus obliquari debet. Set modo est quod peruertit iudicium, vt scribitur 'peruertisti iudicium in amaritudinem, et fructum iusticie in absinthium'. (Other MSS. have Sed e contra iam de illis verificatur Amos iii, &c.)

Miles tres punctos pertransit, duos directos (other MSS. than H and R, Miles vero in capiendo duo puncta transit directa, et tertium obliquat), in signum quod milites et terreni domini possunt iuste capere redditus sibi debitos et iustas emendas secundum exigentia delicti, set tercium punctum obliquat cum tallagia et exactiones iniustas extorquent a subditis.

Alphini vero (G, vero cornuti; KG, vero corrupti) sunt episcopi (C, K, Ad begin Alphini vero prelati sunt ecclesie papa et (Ad. only, cardinales) archiepiscopi et episcopi cornuti), non vt Moyses ex colloquio diuino, set potius regio imperio prece vel pretio sublimati et sic promoti. Isti alphini oblique currunt et tres punctos currendo pertranseunt indirecte, quia fere omnes prelati odio, amore, munere, seu fauore, peruertuntur ne delinquentes corrigunt et contra vicia latrent, set potius annuo censu peccata ad firmam tradunt. Sic diabolum ditant, unde qui debuerunt esse viciorum extirpatores, iam per cupiditatem facti sunt viciorum promotores, et diaboli procuratores.

Pedini pauperculi sunt, qui incedendo duos punctos pertranseunt directos, quia dum pauper manet in sua simplicitate et paupertate semper directe viuit, set cum capere vult, obliquat, quia cum cupit aliquid temporale vel honores consequi, semper capiendo cum falsis iuramentis vel adulationibus seu mendaciis, obliquat, donec ad summum gradum scaccarii perueniat, et tunc de *poun* (R, S, poun ; C, pown ; K, powne ; Ad., pedone ; O, pone ; L, J[1], poune ; other MSS. omit) fit *fierce,* et tunc incontinenti capit cum maximo dominio, et tres punctos pertransit (G, D duo puncta pertransit, tertium obliquando) quia, vt dicitur in Alexandro, 'asperius nichil est humili cum surgit in altum.' (C, K, Ad. transpose the two preceding paragraphs.)

In isto autem ludo diabolus dicit *eschek* (so all except KG, chek ; O, cheke ; G, eschack), insultando vel percuciendo aliquem peccati iaculo qui (sit) percussus nisi cicius dicat *liqueret* (R, S, liueret ; C, K, deleueret ; KG, nek ; O, deliueret ; L, nec ; J[2], lyuereth ; G, linqueret), ad penitenciam et cordis compunctioni transeundo, diabolus dicit ei *Mat* (so R, S ; C, K, L, G, math ; Ad., mate ; KG, chekmate ; O, mayte ; J[1], eschek math ; J[2], maat), animam secum ad tartara deducendo, vbi non liberabitur, nec prece, nec pretio, quia in inferno nulla est redemptio. (C, K, Ad., O, L, J[1], G continue: Et sicut venator diuersos habet canes ad diuersas carnes (bestias) capiendas, sic diabolus et mundus diuersa habent peccata quibus diuersemodo homines illaqueant, quia omne quod est in mundo vel est concupiscentia carnis, vel concupiscentia oculorum vel uite superbia.)

[NOTE.—There is very little of interest about the amplified text in the *Destructorium vitiorum* beyond the passage translated above, p. 534, which runs in the original as follows:

In isto scacario diabolus est lusor ab vna parte et homo peccator ab alia parte, cui diabolus dicit *schaek,* percutiendo eum iaculo peccati. Cui nisi peccator citius dicat *neck,* ad penitentiam recurrendo in breue et antequam sciuerit peccator, dicit sibi diabolus *schaekmate* animam suam ad infernum deducendo, a quo non liberabitur prece nec pretio, quia in inferno nulla est redemptio. Sed vt videtur multototiens aliqui presumptuosi ludentes ad scacarium sunt ita audaces in ludo suo quod promittunt ludentes secum lucrari et magnam partem familie sue accipere, sperantes in fine ludi recuperare. Sed contingit quod antequam sciuerint, ex improuiso decipiuntur, et dicitur eis *schaekmate* (elsewhere in text *chekmate*), et sic perdit totum quod in ludo ponitur, et tunc videntes se perdidisse, vellent recuperare ludum quod tamen nolunt cum eis ludentes . . . Ideo consulo quod tempestiue caueatis quo trahatis, quia cum subtili et peruerso luditis, et cogitate, quia non luditis pro nihilo ; sed in ludo vestro posuistis preciosissimum iocale quod habetis, scilicet animas vestras, &c.]

GESTA ROMANORUM. DE ANTONIO IMPERATORE.

[I have used the following MSS. :

H[1] = Brit. Mus., Harl. 2270, cap. xxvii, f. 24b, 15th c.
H[2] = Brit. Mus., Harl. 5259, cap. xxvii, f. 25b, early 15th c.
H[3] = Brit. Mus., Harl. 406, cap. vii, f. 107b, first half of 15th c.
H[4] = Brit. Mus., Harl. 3132, cap. xxv, f. 34, middle 15th c.
H[5] = Brit. Mus., Harl. 7333, cap. xxi, f. 161b, middle 15th c.
S = Brit. Mus., Sloane 4029, cap. xxiv, f. 36b, middle 15th c.
A = Brit. Mus., Add. 33784, cap. xxxv, f. 44b, early 15th c.

L = Lincoln Coll., Oxford, Lat. 12, cap. xxvii, f. 107, beginning 15th c., which also contains the *Innocent Morality*.

(The chapter also occurs in MS. Balliol Coll., Oxford, 320, cap. xxvii, middle 15th c.)

Oesterley, *Gesta Romanorum*, Berlin, 1872, apparently used another MS. for his cap. cclxxv, p. 675. His text is very indifferent, and the transcriber has made mistakes in amplifying the contractions in the MS.

I have made L the basis of the following text. Where I have introduced readings from other MSS., I have put the passage in italics and stated my source.]

Antonius in ciuitate Romana *regnauit prudens valde* (H¹), qui multum cum canibus ludere solebat et post ludum tota die in ludo scaccarii *se* occupabat. Cum semel ludebat et vidit regem ludi in sacculo poni, alium post alium sub alium et supra, intra se cogitabat: cum sic mortuus ero sub *terra* (H¹) absconsus ero. Statim diuisit regnum in tres partes, vnam dedit regi Ierusalem, aliam satrapis imperii, terciam pauperibus, et ad terram sanctam perrexit vbi in pace vitam suam finiuit. *Moralitas.* Karissimi, iste imperator qui ludum diligebat potest dici quilibet mundanus qui in mundi vanitatibus occupatur. Verumptamen debet curam accipere de ludo scaccarii sicut fecerat imperator. Scaccarii habent octo puncta in omni parte. In ludo mundi sunt octo genera hominum, scilicet, vir et mulier, weddes et veweddes, laici et clerici, diuites et pauperes. Ad istud ludum ludunt sex homines. Primus est pedinus qui cum procedit non habet nisi vnum punctum et quando uadit lateraliter ex altera parte capit alium, et cum venerit ad mensam fit *ferzs* (S, H² and L have *fortis*). Sic pauper verus nichill habet, sed cum venerit ad mortem cum paciencia erit rex in celo iuxta regem pauperum, sed si contra Iesu Christum murmurauerit de statu suo et fit fur et rapit quicquid potest, tunc capitur et in carcere inferni tradetur. Secundus alfinus currit tria puncta sursum et deorsum per eloquenciam fraudulenciam et pecuniarii captionem, et sic fit *solus* (H¹, H²) Tercius miles *habet* (H²) tria puncta lateraliter. Significat generosos currentes et capientes et gloriantes in prosapia et diuiciarum affluencia. Quartus est *rocus* (L has *robus*) qui vadit omnibus modis in longum latum et capit quicquid inuenit; et significat vsurarios et mercatores falsos qui discurrunt vbique vt possint lucrari, nec curant quomodo ita quod habent. Quinta est regina que vadit de *nigro in nigrum vel de albo in album* (H¹. L has *de albo in nigrum*), et ponitur iuxta regem, et quando recedit a rege capitur. Ista regina signat puellas virgines que quando vadunt de castitate in peccatum capiuntur a diabolo propter cerotecas et *cinglium* (L has *singilum*) et huius modi. Sextus est rex (S adds *est ouyrhyng mundi et ecclesie*) cui omnes debent obbedire et ministrare, et vadit ante et retro et a latere et capit vbique. Sic illi qui descendunt in mundum et habent familiam et ascendunt ad deum per oracionem. Sed quando non curant de deo nec familiam habent fit sibi check mat. Videamus ergo quod post ludum omnes *ponuntur* in sacculo nec curatur quis erit supra vel in profunditate. Sic de omnibus nobis post ludum istius mundi erit, ergo studeamus vitam corrigere et in bonis operibus permanere quod poterimus ad gloriam eternam peruenire, ad quem nos perducat.

De Ludo Schacorum. Oesterley, Cap. CLXVI.

[I merely quote the introductory paragraph. Passages from Cessolis are in italics.]

Schacarium habet lxiv puncta per viii divisa, scilicet, virum et mulierem, sponsos et sponsas, clericos et laicos, divites et pauperes. Istum ludum sex homines ludunt.

Primus est rochus, et est in duplici genere, scilicet, albus et niger. Dexter est albus (*infra*, alphinus . . . qui est niger ad dexteram regis collocatur, *and* militum, quorum dexter est albus) et sinister niger; huius virtus est, quod *cum omnes schaci fuerint in locis suis situati, tam nobiles quam populares, habent virtualiter certos terminos, ad quos possunt progredi; soli autem rochi, cum sunt inclusi, nullam habent progrediendi virtutem, nisi eis per nobiles aut populares via fuerit expedita, et vadit recto semper tramite et nunquam ad angulum, sive antecedat sive revertatur*, et quando vadit lateraliter, ex altera parte capit alium et fit fur. Carissimi, sic pauper verus nihil habet, nisi unum transitum paupertatis sue, per quam recto tramite incedit ad omnium pauperum dominum Ihesum Christum, et fit regina iuxta regem regum. Sed si murmurans de statu suo lateraliter retrocedat, fit fur et rapit quicquid potest; nec de regine solio curat.

(It is somewhat curious to find in MS. Wolfenbüttel, 39, 7 Aug., art. 19, ff. 495–8, an Italian work on chess, dedicated to Maria Maddalena d' Austria, Granduchessa di Toscania, which is essentially a translation of this chapter of the *Gesta Romanorum*. It belongs to a period when the mediaeval chess was quite obsolete, and yet makes no reference to the difference in the moves described from those of the current chess.)

CHAPTER VI

THE MEDIAEVAL PROBLEM. I

Introductory.—The function of the problem in mediaeval European chess.—The problem of Muslim origin.—Its European names.—The European MSS.—Their historical development.—The Alfonso MS. and its European problems.—The Archinto MS.—The Anglo-Norman or English group of MSS.—The two British Museum MSS.—The Porter and Ashmole MSS.—The Dresden MS.

THE study and composition of game-positions or 'problems' is a branch of chess activity for which the European player was indebted to the Muslim world. Owing to the prominent part which the problem played in the literature of chess in the Middle Ages, and also to the extraordinary development which it underwent in Europe, it will be necessary to devote considerable attention to this side of chess.

We have already seen how important a feature the problems of *manṣūbāt* were in the literature of chess in the Muslim world from the ninth century onwards. With only two exceptions, all the Arabic and Persian MSS. relating to the practice of chess are essentially collections of game-positions. When the European player turned to the Arabic literature of chess with the intention of making it known to his fellow-Christians he was at once brought face to face with this aspect of chess. That a knowledge of the contents of MSS. of this character reached Europe at an early period in the life of European chess is certain. An examination of the problems included in the older European MSS. reveals a very considerable number of positions which actually occur in existing Muslim MSS. and a number of others so similar in appearance that it is impossible to doubt that they are also derived from Arabic sources.

It is certain that the Muslim opinion respecting the manṣūbāt reached Europe with the positions themselves. In the East it has always been recognized that the main utility of the manṣūbāt was as exercises in the moves of the chessmen, and in the art of combination by which the player directs the attack of a number of pieces towards a single point. This was also the common opinion held in Europe, not only by the earlier generation of players, but right down to the closing years of the mediaeval game. In the Archinto MS. the problems are called 'practica', *exercises*. In the *Book of the Duchess* Chaucer makes his hero, defeated at chess by Dame Fortune, exclaim:

> But god wolde I had ones or twyes
> Y-koud and knowe the Ieupardyes
> That coude the Grek Pithagores!
> I shulde have pleyd the bet at ches,
> And kept my fers the bet therby (lines 665–9)—

showing that he regarded the jeopardies or problems simply as a means of acquiring skill in the ordinary game. So again in the introductory verses to the two MSS. Cott. and K, to be described below, the English author recommends the study of problems to his readers as an excellent way to gain skill in chess. In them he will learn the science of the game, the subtle moves, the mates and defences. Having gained this knowledge he will see that any one who has a good knowledge of problems 'will assuredly be able to play more skilfully in all courts'—by which we are to understand the castles of the nobility and not merely the royal courts of France and England.[1] And finally, Köbel justifies the inclusion of some problems in his edition of Mennel's *Schachzabel* by the statement that the player would, by solving them, obtain practice in chess which would facilitate progress in the knowledge of the game.

This is a view of the early unsophisticated mediaeval problem which is entirely correct, but the problem could also be regarded in other ways. We have already seen from the Alfonso MS. that some players seized on the brevity of the problem, as contrasted with the game, as an excellence. The writer of the Picard MS., PP (MS. Paris, f. fr. 1173) expresses the same view when he undertakes to teach his readers 'the fashion of the game, its assizes, and how it can be abbreviated by partures,' i. e. by problems. The definiteness of the problem made it a convenient subject for a wager, and this view of the problem commended it to other players. The most typical line of development followed in the case of the shorter European problems was that which converted the problem into the wager-game. To this aspect of the problem, which is most obvious in the Italian collections, it will be necessary to recur later.

Apart from the evidence afforded by the existence of the problem MSS. themselves, we have very little means of judging of the popularity of the problem with mediaeval players. I have found only two passages in the general literature of the Middle Ages that mention the problem, out of many hundreds that refer to chess. These are the passage from Chaucer which I have quoted above, and one from Lydgate (see p. 501, n. 5) in which he speaks of the great diversity of new problems which is possible. Neither the moralities nor the poems ever refer to the existence of the problem. We cannot, therefore, speak of the mediaeval problem as displacing the ordinary game, or as rivalling it in popularity. It probably only appealed to a minority of chess-players, and reached its greatest popularity towards the end of the mediaeval period, and in Italy.

No existing problem MS. is as old as 1250. The introduction of the problem to European players was, however, probably accomplished at an earlier date than this. All the existing problem MSS. are copies of older MSS., and many are compilations from a number of distinct sources. The *Bonus Socius* compilation was made before 1300.

[1] This is the ordinary meaning of *court* in England in the 13th and 14th cc. See *N. E. D.*, s. v. court i. 2, quoting *Robert of Gloucester*.

It is evident that the knowledge of the manṣūbāt was derived as much from Arabic books on chess as from players. There is consequently no special reason why we should regard Spain as the necessary point of introduction of the chess-problem into Europe. The Arabic literature of science, mathematics, logic, and philosophy reached Europe from many points, and on *prima facie* grounds Italy, Southern France, and even Paris or Oxford are quite as likely places as Spain for the home of the first problemists of Christian Europe. The evidence, however, of the existing MSS. points to Italy and France as the two great centres of problem activity, and since the great collections were compiled in the former country it is possible that the problem made its entry into European chess through the hands of Italian players.

That the study of the problem began early is certain on philological grounds. The European player gave to the manṣūbāt the Latin names of *jocus partitus* or *partitum*, using the participle of the verb *partire* or *partiri*, 'to divide' or 'distribute'.[2] From *jocus partitus* we have the It. *giuoco de partito*, the Sp. *juego de partido*, the Cat. *joch partit*, the Prov. *joc partit*, the F. *jeu parti*, the AF. *giu parti*, and the ME. *jupertie*, our modern word *jeopardy*.[3] From *partitum* are derived the It. *partito*, the Sp. *partido*, the F. *partie*, the last of which has replaced the MF. *parture* (from a L. *partura*, which I have not found in any chess MS.). All these terms have the literal meaning of 'divided play or game', 'even game', but, although originating in connexion with chess and other board-games, at an early date they passed into the ordinary idiom in derived senses. Thus the L., F., and Eng. terms acquired the sense of 'a position in a game, undertaking, &c., in which the chance of winning and losing hang in the balance; an even chance; an undecided state of affairs; uncertainty; chance.' Instances of this sense are common from the middle of the 13th c.,[4] and the meaning of *jeopardy* in modern English is a simple extension of it.

At a still earlier date, by the middle of the 12th c. at latest, the Prov. *joc partit* had acquired a definite technical sense in connexion with the Courts of Love, which had become a prominent feature in the social life of the nobility of Southern France. One of the favourite amusements of these Courts of Love was a form of debate, in which two speakers argued before an umpire a question of casuistry relating to the 'courtois' love, one speaker taking one side and the other adopting perforce the other. These debates were called *jocs partitz*, and when a similar device was introduced into Provençal poetry the poems were called *jocs partitz* also, or *partiments*.

[2] Since it was the general practice in the Middle Ages to translate technical Arabic expressions literally (in the course of which many curious blunders were perpetrated), I was once inclined to explain *jocus partitus* as an attempt to reproduce the Ar. *manṣūba* by an exact equivalent, the verb *partire* being used in Plautus almost in the sense of 'to arrange'. The best authorities think otherwise, and I follow the *N. E. D.* in the text.

[3] The *d* in our modern spelling has nothing to do with the F. vb. *perdre*. It is a phonetic change similar to that which led to the ME. form jubertie. See *N. E. D.*, s. v. jeopardy.

[4] Thus in Bracton (*c.* 1250), IV. i. 32: 'nec potest (ballivus) transigere, nec pascisci, nec jocum partitum facere.' And in Britton (1292), II. xvii. 8: 'mes ne mie en jeupartie de perdre ou de gayner, tut le voillent les parties.' The earliest English instance of a transferred sense is in the 13th c. romance *Siriz* (276, quoted in Wright's *Anecd. Lit.* (1844) 9): 'For I shal don a juperti (i. e. a deed of daring) And a ferli maistri.'

Our knowledge of the European *partita* is gained from a number of collections, of which the existing MSS. date from the last quarter of the 13th to the first quarter of the 17th century. The majority of these MSS. were copied in the course of the hundred years 1340–1450. Two collections—of which one is apparently entirely lost,[5] and the other survives in a single copy [6]—were printed in the early days of printing.

Although between 30 and 40 MSS. dealing entirely or in part with *partita* are known still to exist, these must represent only a portion of the output in the Middle Ages; the problem-lover could not do much without his own collection of *partita*. Every one of the five MSS. named in the inventory of the library of Martin V of Arragon (1395–1410) [7] has disappeared, and the present location of another MS. which a London bookseller offered for four guineas in 1798 [8] is quite unknown. These MSS. will all have been works of considerable size, and less likely to be destroyed or mislaid than the smaller collections, which were all that the ordinary player would be able to afford.

The existing material, however, is sufficient to enable us to trace the development of this literature. In this connexion the relative age of the existing MSS. is of only secondary importance. The modifications of move prior to 1475 or so were too small to affect seriously the utility of any of the problem material, and the older MSS. were repeatedly copied. Even in the cases in which we possess several MSS. of the same collection, it by no means follows that the older MS. is better than the later. The one may only

[5] The *Libre del jochs partits dels schachs en nombre de 100. ordenat é compost per mi Francesch vicent, nat en le ciutat de Segorb é criat é vehi de la insigne é valorosa ciutat de Valencia.* This Catalan work ended *A loor é gloria de nostre Redemtor Jesu-Christ fonc acabat lo dit libre que ha nom libre dels jochs partits dels scachs en la insigne ciutat de Valencia é estampat per mans de Lope de Roca Alemany é Pere trincher librere á xv dias de May, del any MCCCCLXXXXV.* The quarto book was seen by Panzer (1795, iii. 60) in the library of the monastery of Montserrat, but the library was destroyed during the campaigns of 1811 and 1834. Cf. also Fuster, *Bibl. Valenciana*, 1827, i. 40.

[6] The *Sensuit Ieux Partis des eschez*; for which see below, Ch. VIII.

[7] The *Inventory*, made in 1410, is now in the Crown archives of Arragon (Reg. no. 2326). I quote from Brunet y Bellet, *Ajedrez*, 220.

f. 5 b. 34. Un altre libre appellat *Dels jochs de Scachs e de taules* scrit en paper ab posts de fust cubert de cuyrs vermell squinsat ab sos tancadors de cuyro vermell lo qual comença en la primera carta 'Los blanchs juguen primers' e faneix en la derrera carta 'Segons que per tu pots veura'.

f. 6 b. 41. Un altre libre appellat *Jochs de Scachs dapartit* scrit en paper ab cuberta de pergami sanar ab un correix larch de albedina per tancador lo qual comença 'Diu lo libre' e faneix 'explicit liber scacorum'.

f. 12. 84. Un altre libre appellat *Del Joch de Scachs* en cathala scrit en paper ab posts de fust cubert de cuyro vert ab tancadors de perxa de seda verda lo qual comença 'lo blanch' e faneix 'segons que per tu pots veura'.

f. 13 b. 96. Un altre libre appellat *De Scachs* en frances scrit en pergamins ab posts de fust e cuberta de cuyro vermell empremptades ab un tancador de cuyro vermell lo qual comença 'nul altre' e faneix 'Aparon jeu'.

f. 40. 272. Un altre libre appellat *Dels Scachs* en frances scrit en pergamins ab posts de fust cubert de cuyro vermell empremptat ab dos tancadors de cuyro vermell lo qual comença en vermello 'Ci comença' e en lo negre 'A tres noble et accellent princep' e faneix 'Si fanist se liure e sope'.

(King Martin also possessed a copy of the Catalan translation of Cessolis.

f. 9. 58. Un altre libre appellat *Dels Scachs* en cathala scrit en paper ab posts de paper engrutades e cuberta de cuyro vert ab dos tancadors de bagua lo qual comença en vermello 'Comenza lo prolech' e en lo negre 'Amonestat per pregarias' e faneix 'en los segles de los segles amen'.)

[8] In Egerton's *Catalogue*, 1798: *Echecsiana*, 7710. MS. Treatise on Chess in Old French, on vellum, with 210 illuminated schemes of various Games, elegant, in russia leather, £4 4*s*.

reproduce the original work at third or fourth hand, while the later MS. perhaps repeats it at first or second.

The original European MSS. must have been small works and translations entirely from Arabic into Latin. None of these earliest collections have survived, but we can infer their nature from existing MSS. There is nothing to show that any of the larger Arabic works were translated in their entirety.

The next stage in the history begins with the composition of new *partita* by European players themselves. The owner of a MS. of *manṣūbāt* would add these at the end of his MS. Of this stage I believe that we possess two examples.

The older of these collections is contained in the beautiful parchment MS. now in the library of the Monastery of St. Lorenzo del Escorial, near Madrid, which was executed by order of Alfonso (X) the Wise, King of Castile (1251–84), and completed in Span. 1321 = A. D. 1283. This is the work which I have used, both in connexion with the Muslim chess and in Ch. III under the reference Alf.

The Alfonso MS. consists of 98 leaves of 39·5 cm. by 28, in a sheep-skin binding with the title 'Juegos de axedrez, dados y tablas' on its back. Leaves 86, 90, 94, and 98 and the versos of leaves 64 and 80 are entirely blank. It has no title, but the title

> Juegos diuersos de Axedrez, dados, y tablas con sus explicationes, ordenados por mandado del rey don Alonso el sabio

has been added on the fly-leaf, and the head-lines 'Libro del Acedrex', 'Libro de los Dados', 'Libro de las Tablas', and 'Libro del Alquerque' are written across the verso of one leaf and the recto of the next in agreement with the subject-matter of the text below. The MS. is written in two columns in a beautiful hand, with a great number of illuminated initials, both large and small, and is adorned with no fewer than 150 beautifully executed and coloured drawings, ten of them occupying whole pages.[9]

The arrangement of the MS. divides it into seven parts. The first, extending from ff. 1 a to 64 a, is devoted to chess. Ff. 1–5 a, with six miniatures, contain the introductory section, the greater part of which is quoted in the Appendix to Ch. III. Ff. 5 b – 64 a contain a collection of 103 *juegos de partidos*, the diagram of each problem following the solution, and being treated as a miniature, the position being diagrammed on a board placed between two players. The boards are drawn upright, with a complete disregard of perspective, and are placed at right angles to the arrangement ordinarily adopted in chess works. The boards are chequered black and white, and h1 is uniformly white. The pieces are represented pictorially. There are often onlookers in addition to the players.

The second part, extending from f. 65 a to 71 b, treats of games of chance with the dice alone. This section contains twelve miniatures, and describes

[9] A full account of the miniatures, with two coloured reproductions from the section on Tables, will be found in F. Janer's *Museo español de antiguedades*, Madrid, 1874, III, 225–55. There is a briefer account in Brunet y Bellet's *Ajedrez*, 243–68.

twelve different methods of play, viz. *Mayores*, *Triga* (in three varieties), *Azar* (i. e. hazard) *o Reazar*, *Marlota*, *Riffa*, *Par con As*, *Panquist*, *Medio-Azar*, *Azar-pujado*, and *Guirguiesca*. Here again, as throughout the MS., the drawing follows the text to which it belongs.

The third part, ff. 72 a – 80 a, treats of the different games on the backgammon board under the headline 'Libro de las Tablas'. Fifteen games are described, and there are sixteen miniatures in all. The games described are *Las quinze tablas*, *Los doze canes o doze hermanos*, *Doblet*, *Fallas*, *Seys dos e as*, *Emperador*, *Barata*, *El medio imperador*, *Pareja de entrada*, *Cab e equinal*, *Todas tablas* (which is our game of backgammon), *Laquet*, *La buffa cortesa*, *La buffa de baldrac*, *Los Romanos reencontrat*.

The fourth part, ff. 81 a – 85 b, with four full-page miniatures, treats of enlarged games of chess, viz. *Grande acedrex* on a board of 144 squares (see p. 348), and the eight-sided dice used in this game, the seven-sided dice used in a decimal chess, and a variety of tables on a board of 28 points with 17 men a side, in which the same dice were used.

The fifth part, ff. 87 a – 89 b, with two full-page miniatures, contains the game of *Acedrex de los quatro tiempos* (see p. 348), and an allied game of tables, *El mundo*, for four players, which was played on a board of 24 points with 6 men a side.

The sixth part, the Libro del Alquerque, extends from f. 91 a to 93 b, and describes the *Alquerque de doze*, *De cercar la liebre*, a form of 'Fox and geese' on the same board, the *Alquerque de nuevo*, played with and without dice (the larger merels or nine men's morris), and the *Alquerque de tres* (the smaller merels).[10] This section contains five miniatures.

The seventh and last part of the MS., comprising ff. 95 a–97 b, with two full-page miniatures, deals with *Escaques*, an astronomical game (see p. 349), and a similar board of tables on a circular board with 49 points for seven players, each having 7 men.

The text of the MS. concludes on f. 97 a, with a colophon in the same hand as the rest of the MS.:

> Este Libro fue comencado e acabado en la cibdat de Seuilla: por mandado del muy noble Rey don Allfonso fijo del muy noble Rey Don Ferrando & dela Reyna Donna Beatriz Sennor de Castiello & de Leon de Toledo de Gallizia de Seuilla de Cordoua de Mvrcia de Talen de Badaioz e dell Algarue: en treynta & dos annos que el Rey sobredicho regno. En la Era de mill & trezientos e veynt e un Anno.

Era 1321 is the year A. D. 1283.[11]

I now turn to the 103 problems which, according to the statement of the MS. on f. 5 a/1, are arranged by the number of men employed in the setting, those with most men coming first, and the others following regularly in descending order.

[10] For these games, see the Appendix to this chapter.

[11] There is a copy of this MS. in the Library of the Hist. Acad. of Madrid, which was made in 1334. I have used a photographic copy of the Escurial MS., which Mr. J. G. White placed at my service.

The problems of the MS. are reproduced on diagrams in *Qst.*, 72–120. Cf. also v. d. Lasa, 115–20.

This arrangement, however, only extends as far as the 69th problem,[12] by which time we have reached the positions with only 6 men. The next three (70–2) have each 18 men, and the remaining problems follow without any regard to the number of pieces employed, though the number is still stated in the formal title to each problem.

We have, accordingly, an arranged work of 69 problems, followed by an appendix or supplement of 34 additional, but not always new, positions. The collection is a compilation from various sources.[13]

The original collection is unmistakably Muslim. The type of problem agrees in all particulars with the type which we have learnt from the earlier Muslim collections. All but 18 of these 69 positions actually occur in other Muslim MSS. which I have used. Of the supplementary problems, also, nos. 70–2 and 88–103 are exactly similar in type. Nine, indeed, of the 19 had already been included in the main collection, while only one of these new positions is not already known from other Muslim works. Nor has the treatment of these manṣūbāt been modified at all; the winner's King lies under threat of imminent mate; the diagram is as liberally covered with pieces as ever (on the average 18 men go to every one of these 88 problems); the loser is placed under no inferiority in force. I have, as a result, treated this part of the Alfonso MS. as one of my authorities for the Muslim manṣūbāt, and have included the problems in my collection, see pp. 279 ff., and it has, therefore, no further importance for us now.

But included in this supplementary collection is a small group of 14 problems (nos. 73–87, of which 82 and 87 only differ in the colours of the players and 85 is an inferior setting of a Muslim problem) which stands out in sharp contrast to the rest of the MS. The diagrams show no excess of pieces—on the average only 8 men go to each position; and the attack has a strong advantage in material, actual and numerical—on the average it has two men to each one for the defence. Moreover, the conditions of the problems are new. In six it is laid down that mate is to be given in an *exact* number of moves, neither more nor less; in one problem, men are fidated (*atreguado*), and their capture is prohibited; another has no solution, and the proper defence is pointed out. Bishops occupy impossible squares, and promoted Queens leap to a 'third' square without remark. We are in a different world, the creation of the European problemist. Somehow or other, the compiler of Alf. had lighted upon a small collection of problems, the work of a European composer, and he proceeded at once to add it to his collection of manṣūbāt.

The solutions in Alf. of even the shortest problems cover a great amount of space. As an example, I have given the original text of the solution to Alf. 78, mainly because v. d. Linde (*Qst.*, 111) has missed the fact that it is one of the wager-games, or unsound problems, of which so many examples are contained in later MSS.

[12] I assume that Nos. 57 and 58 (which are out of order) have been transposed by accident.

[13] As might have been suspected from the repetitions. 11 positions are given twice each, 1 three times, and 2 four times! (10 = 26; 16 = 20; 22 = 89; 25 = 27 = 101; 32 = 102; 38 = 95; 40 = 72; 46 = 92; 54 = 57 = 90 = 100; 58 = 63 = 64 = 97; 61 = 66; 69 = 91; 82 = 87; 88 = 96).

Almost all of these European positions in Alf. occur, in idea at least, in other European MSS. But even in those cases in which the treatment is the same, the setting is never quite the same in Alf. Alf. never omits the winner's King, as is often done in later MSS. in problems in which this King is not actively concerned in the play, and always precludes the possibility of the ending 'Bare King' by the addition of other forces—generally a blocked Pawn—to the defence.[14] I have already remarked that the ending Bare King (Sp. *robado*) never lost its validity in Spain during the mediaeval period. The MS. shows no keener an appreciation of 'possibility' in a problem than do any of the other mediaeval European MSS. Four diagrams show Bishops on impossible squares.[15] The MS. shows on the whole no marked preference for either White or Black as the attacking colour. In the 88 Muslim problems, White begins 46 times, but in the 15 European problems White only begins 5 times. The European problems in Alf. now follow:

Alf. 73.

Bl. mates in III with Pd4. Soln. 1 Kc3; 2 Ktb2+; Pd3 m.

Alf. 75.

Bl. mates in IV on e4. Soln. 1 Qc4; 2 Rg1; 3 Rg2; 4 Re2 m.

Alf. 74.

(Bl.)

Wh. mates in IV exactly with Pe4. Soln. 1 Ktd3+; 2 P×Kt; 3 R~ or Pe5 accordingly; 4 Pd2 m.

Alf. 76.

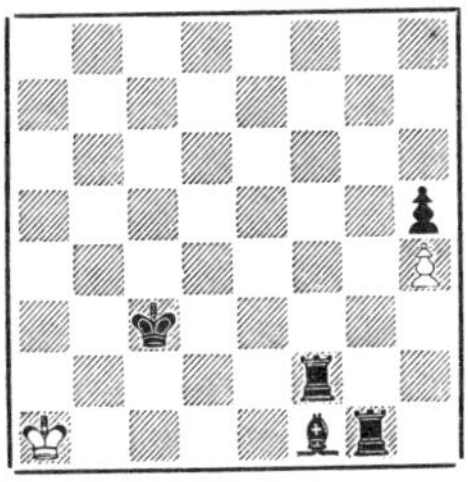

Bl. mates in V exactly on b1 with B. Soln. 1 Rd2; 2 Rd1+; 3 Ra1+; 4 Kb3; 5 Bd3 m.

14 Contrast Alf. 76 with CB 135, or Alf. 81 with CB 162.

15 Viz. Nos. 47, where the European player has added Bishops on a1 and a8 to block shorter solutions (excluded in the Muslim MSS. by making the problem a conditional one), 76, 79, and 86.

Alf. 47 is not the only Muslim problem which has been 'Europeanized'. Alf. 103 (Wh. Kb8, Ph3; Bl. Kd7, Bc5, Pa6, c6, h2; cf. Ar. 407 on p. 327) is solved by means of the Queen's leap, which was unknown in Muslim chess (Soln. 1 Pc7+; 2 Pc8=Q; 3 Qc6; 4 Qb7+; 5 Be7; 6 Kc6; 7 Kd6; 8 Kc5; 9 Kc6; 10 Bc5+; 11 Pa7 m.). Cf. CB 277. In the *B.S.* MS. PL 290 = Fn. 290 the Queen's leap is not used.

Alf. 77.

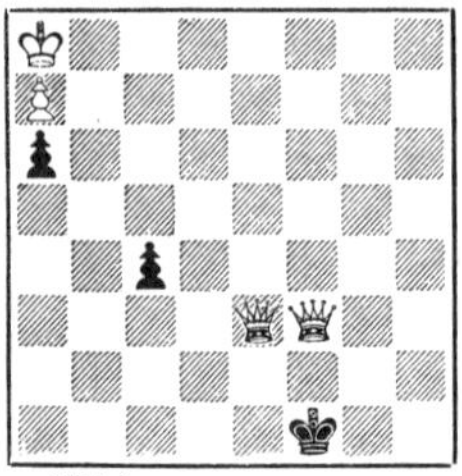

(Bl.)

Wh. mates in VII; the Qs are fidated. Soln. 1 Qf2; 2 Qe1; 3 Qg2; 4 Qf2; 5 Qh3; 6 Qg1; 7 Qg2 m.

Alf. 78. Cf. CB 77.

(Bl.)

(49*b*/1) *Este es otro iuego de partido en que a onze trebeios que son entablados assi como estan en la figura dell entablamiento & an se de iogar desta guisa.*

Los blancos iuegan primero & an de dar mathe al Rey prieto en tres uezes de los sus iuegos mismos ni mas ni menos si los prietos no lo sopieren alongar, & si lo sopieren alongar fincan los blancos por uençudos.—El primer iuego poner el peon blanco en la segunda casa del alffil prieto dando xaque al Rey prieto, & si el Rey prieto entrare en la casa del su alffil es mathe a los tres lanços desta guisa. El segundo iuego poner el alffil blanco en la quarta casa del otro alffil prieto. & el Rey prieto non puede iogar ninguna cosa dessi mismo nin de los Roques, por que non sea mathe al tercero iuego con el peon blanco poniendol en la segunda (49 *b*/2) casa del cauallo prieto o con el cauallo blanco dando xaque & mathe al Rey prieto o darle xaque & mathe con el cauallo blanco.

E por ende es meior pora los prietos quando los blancos dan xaque al Rey prieto con el peon blanco en la segunda casa del alffil prieto, que entre el Rey prieto en la casa del su Roque, & lo meior que pueden iogar los blancos es poner el alffil blanco en la su tercera (read 4ª) casa, & sera el segundo iuego. E pora deffenderse el Rey prieto del mate deue iogar con el su Roque prieto que esta en la segunda casa del Roque blanco poniendolo en la tercera casa del Roque prieto, & tomando el peon blanco que esta en ella. & assi fincan vençudos los blancos: por que non pueden dar mate al Rey blanco en las tres uezes sobre dichas, ca non descubre. E esta es ell arteria deste iuego.

Alf. 79.

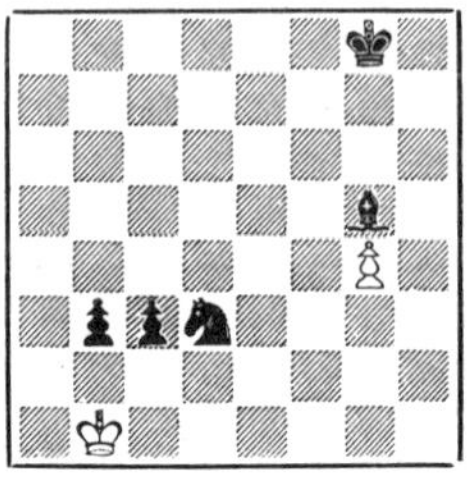

Bl. mates in VIII exactly. Soln. 1 Pc2 +; 2 Pc1 = Q; 3 Qa3; 4 Ktc1; 5 Kta2; 6 Be3; 7 Ktc3; 8 Pb2 m.

Alf. 80.

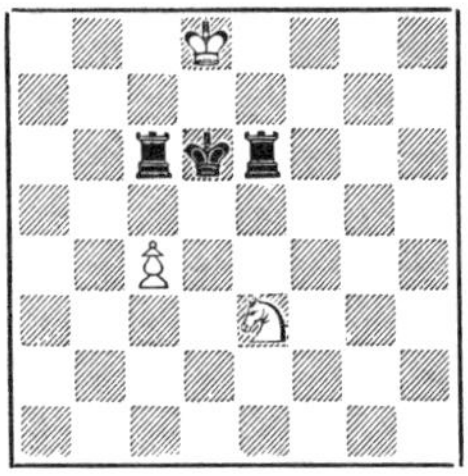

Bl. mates in III exactly. Soln. 1 R × Kt; Pc5 +; 2 Ke6; 3 Rc8 m.

Alf. 81.

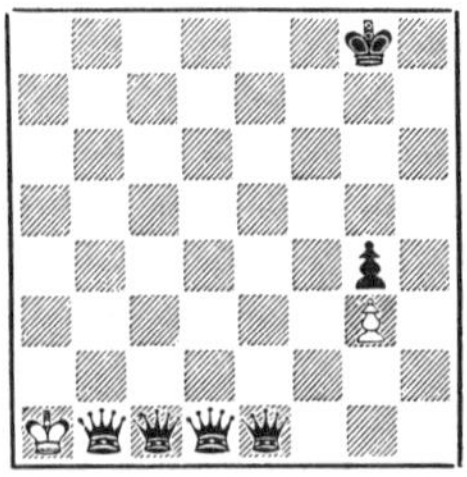

Bl. mates in VII exactly. Soln. 1 Q(b1)b3; 2 Q(e1)d2; 3 Q(c1)a3; 4 Q(d1)d3; 5 Q(d2)c3; 6 Q(d3)c2; 7 Q(a3)b2 m.

Alf. 82 = 87 (col. ch.).

(Bl.)

Bl. mates in III on d2, each Piece playing once. Soln. 1 R × Kt; 2 Kf2; 3 R(f3)d3 m.

Alf. 84.

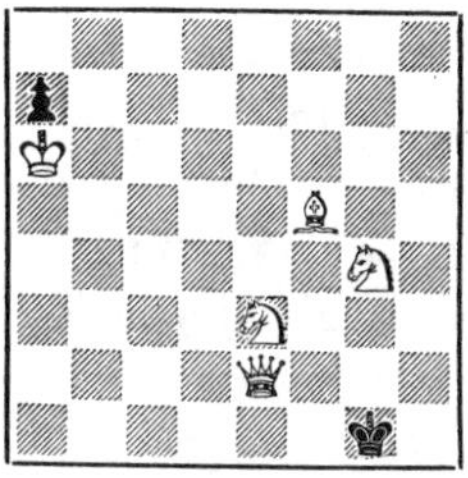

Wh. mates in VI on h1. Soln. 1 Qf1; 2 Bd3; 3 Ktf5; 4 Kth4; 5 Ktf3 +; 6 Ktf2 m.

Alf. 83.

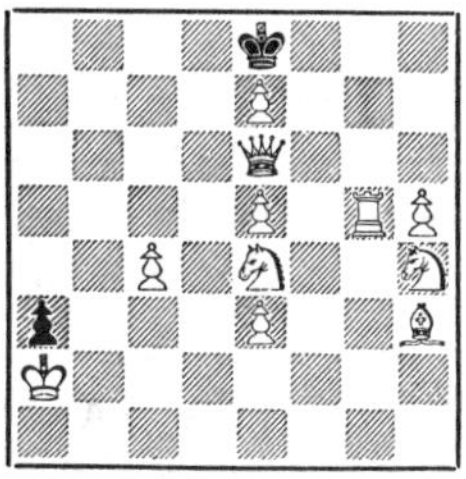

Wh. mates in V on e4. Soln 1 B~; 2 Rg8; 3 Rg7; 4 Rg6; 5 Re6 m.

Alf. 85 : Ar. 361.

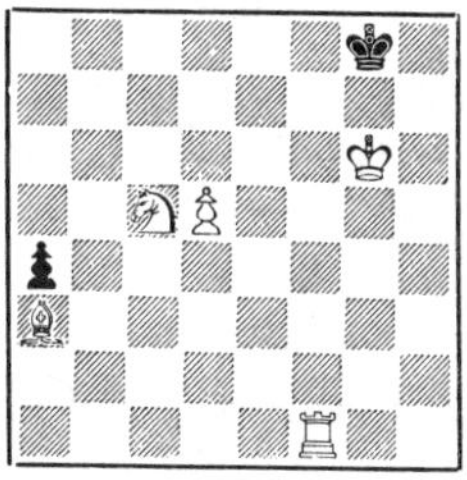

Wh. mates in VII on d5. Soln. 1 Ktd3; 2 Kte5; 3 Rh1; 4 Rh8 +; 5 Kf5; 6 Rh7; 7 Rd7 m.

Alf. 86.

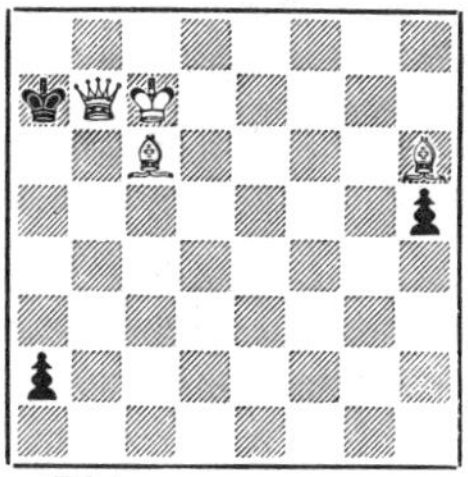

(Bl.)

Wh. mates in XIV or less on a8. Soln. 1 B(c6)~; 2 Bc6; 3 Be4; 4 Bc2; 5 Qc8; 6 Be4, Ka7!; 7 Qd7; 8 Kb6, Kb8!; 9 Bc6; 10 Ba8; 11 Bf8, Kb8!; 12 Bd6 +; 13 Qc6; 14 Qb7 m.

The other example of this stage in the history of the problem literature is afforded by a collection of twenty-nine problems, which occupies ff. 85–92 of a vellum MS. containing a number of Latin tractates written in different 14th c. hands. It follows an incomplete text of Cessolis (here named Jacobus de Cesulis; the text begins f. 73), both texts being written in the same Italian handwriting of about 1370–75. The MS., which for purposes of reference I denote by Arch., was once in the possession of the Counts Archinto, then in the Phillips Library, Cheltenham, and is now in the library of Mr. J. G. White of Cleveland, Ohio, U.S.A.

The problem text bears the title *Incipiunt pratice scachorum artificialiter designate per exempla.* Two problems are diagrammed on each page, one over the other, and the title and conditions are placed over each board. The pieces are denoted by letters,[16] and in seventeen of the problems the letters denoting the pieces playing from the top of the board are inverted—following the rule of the earlier Muslim MSS. The solutions are written in columns on either side of the diagrams.

The MS. opens with ten manṣūbāt, of which the setting is on strictly Muslim lines. All of these are to be found in existing Muslim MSS., and all but one were included among the manṣūbāt in the chess work of the Muslim master al-ʿAdlī. Of the other positions in Arch., four more at least are of Muslim origin, and nine, including four wager-games and a self-mate, are undoubtedly of European composition.

The style of the MS. strikes me as more decidedly Muslim, if that were possible, than Alf. Each problem has two titles, one a rubric and the second in black ink. The rubrics correspond exactly to the titles in the earlier Arabic MSS.: *Niger* (*Rubeus*) *primus uadet* (*aget*) *et uincet hoc modo* is the usual form. The second heading gives the number of moves in the solution, but does not seem quite to take the normal European view. In cases in which one line of play leads to the mate in a less number of moves than the other, both numbers are stated, e.g. *Fit mactum in duobus tractibus ad minus uel .iiij*^{or}. *ad plus.* The headings also to the wager or unsound games are unusual: *Rubeus primus aget et uincet. Fit mactum in tribus cum pedite per unam uiam*: as though the discovery of that way (involving a weak move on the part of the Black) were all that was necessary. The moves are described in the same notation as in Alf. and the Arabic MSS., while the unusual absence of anything approaching a stereotyped vocabulary reminds me strongly of the solutions in the Arabic MS. AH.[17]

The whole work must have been already archaic when the present copy was made. By then, the great collections were already in existence. The MS., however, shows no signs of any knowledge of them, and owes its preservation to the happy chance that it fell into the hands of a scribe who felt that the work of Cessolis was incomplete without something closer to the practical game. These *practica*, 'exercises', were the best illustrations of the game that he had, and he added them with all their old-world vocabulary to his book. The unusual nature of the latter is well shown, both by his key to the diagrams, and by a slip of the pen in the solution to his eleventh *practicum*,

[16] A footnote on f. 73 gives the clue: Rochus—R; Miles (in the text *equus*, *eques*, once *caballus*)—e; Alfilus (in the text, *calvus*)—c; Rex—b; Regina—f; Pedes (in the text often *pes*)—p.

[17] For 'square' we have *cas(s)a*, *sedes*, *dom(m)us*, *locus*, and *tabula*; the squares attacked by a piece are its *feritorium* (exactly the Ar. *muqāṭaʿa* of AH and L): for the vb. 'to take' we have *accipere*, *carpere*, *sum(m)ere*, *capere*; for 'to move' we have *movere*, *removere*, *vadere*, *agere*, *amovere*, *cedere*, *incedere*, *precedere*, *succedere*, *recedere*, *procedere*, *descendere*, *deducere*, *ducere*, *ponere*, *collocare*, *intrare*, *subire*, *appropinquare*, *reuertere*, and *premere* of the Pawn, this last reproducing the Ar. *dafaʿa* (used almost exclusively for the Pawn also). The 'fidated' piece of the later MSS. is called *liber* or *franchus*. A 'solution' is *tabulla*; the later term *glosa* never occurs.

where he substituted the more familiar *alfiuo* for the *caluo* of his text, and adds the note *id est caluuo.* From the occasional forms *chaluus*, *chooperire*, I infer that he belonged to Tuscany.

The problems in this MS. now follow :

Arch. 1 : Ar. 30.[17a]

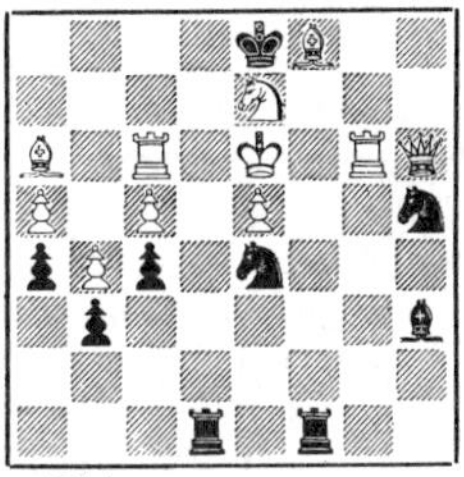

(Bl.)

Niger primus uadet & uincet hoc modo. Fit mactum in duobus tractibus ad minus uel iiii^{or} ad plus. Niger Rocchus de tertia casa regine scachum dicat, quem si cum roccho acceperit. Eques de quarta casa rubei calui pedite accepto mactum inferat. Si uero predictum Rocchum nigrum cum caluo carpserit, alius niger rocchus de tercia cassa calui sibi scacchum dicat quo cum rubeo accepto ineuitabile. niger equs de quarta casa sinistri equitis scacchum dicat quo iterum cum regina accepto alius equus de seconda cassa equitis mactum inferrat.

Arch. 2 : Ar. 18.

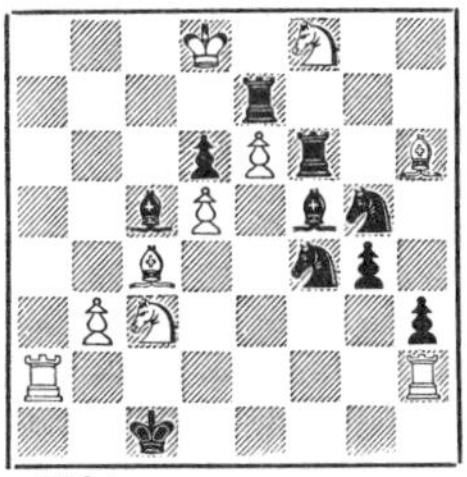

(Bl.)

Niger primus aget & uincet hoc modo. Fit mactum in quinque tractibus nec plus nec minus. Soln. 1 R × Kt + ; 2 Re8 (sedes regine) + ; 3 Pd7 + ; 4 Kt × P + ; 5 Kt × B m.

Arch. 3 = CB 73 = Ar. 53, q.v.

Arch. 4 : Ar. 29.

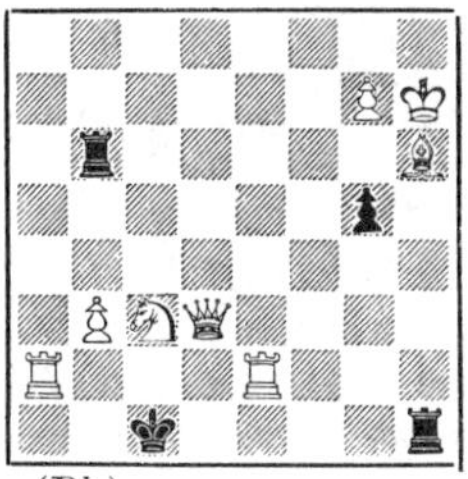

(Bl.)

Niger primus aget & uincet. Fit mactum in duobus ad minus & ex iiii^{or} ad plus. Soln. of MS. 1 Pg6 + , Kg8 ; 2 Rb8 + , Bf8 ; 3 Rh8 + ; 4 R × B m.

Arch. 5 : Ar. 4.

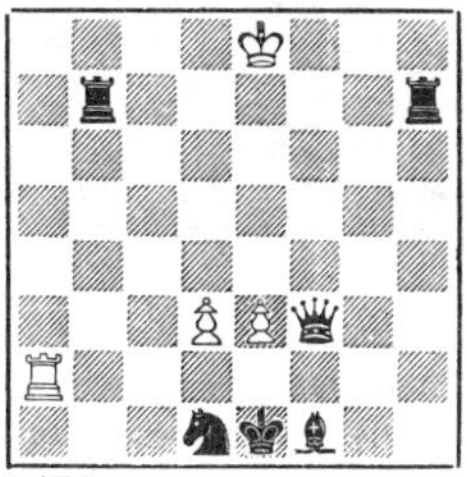

(Bl)

Rubeus primus aget & uincet. Fit mactum in duobus tractibus nec plus nec minus. Soln. 1 Re2 + ; 2 Pd2 m.

Arch. 6 : Ar. 32.

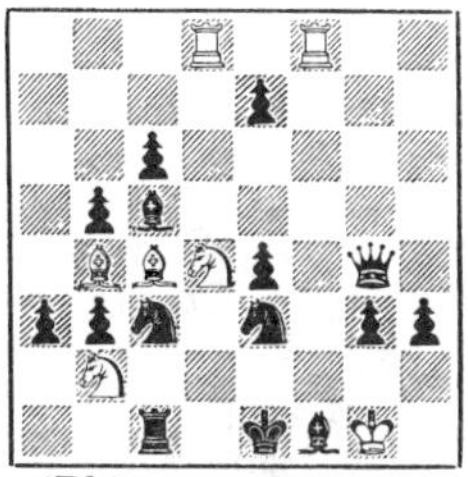

(Bl.)

Rubeus primus aget & uincet. Fit mactum in duobus ad minus et quatuor ad plus. Soln. 1 Ktc2 + , R × Kt ! 2 R × B + ; 3 Rd1 (*casa regine*) + ; 4 Ktd3 m.

[17a] This refers to the collection of Muslim manṣūbāt, pp. 282–338 above.

Arch. 7 : Ar. 400.

(Bl.)

Rubeus primus aget & uincet sic. Fit mactum in tribus tractibus nec plus nec minus. Soln. 1 Rd2 + ; 2 Pc2 + ; 3 Ktd3 (*de tercia domo regis*) m.

Arch. 8 (corr.) : Ar. 5.

(Bl.)

Rubeus primus aget & uincet hoc modo. Fit mactum in diuersis tractibus. Rubeus reginam in tercia domo equitis moueat ac deinde eam paulatim ducendo inde equitem suum & rocchum nigrum in seconda domo regis collocet. Deinde cum equite de tercia sede equitis mactum dicat.

Arch. 9 : Ar. 27.

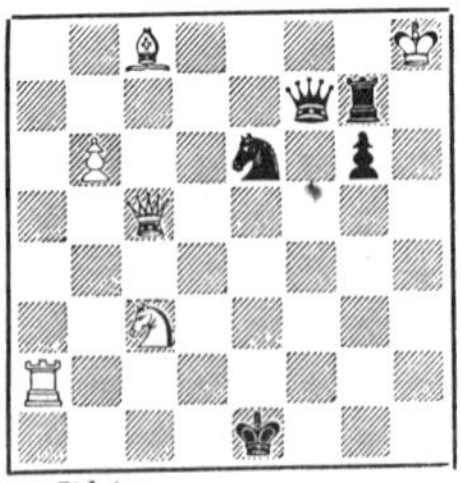

(Bl.)

Rubeus primus aget. Set niger uincet. Fit mactum in quatuor tractibus. Soln. 1 Ra1 + ; 2 Kte4 + ; 3 Ktf6, Rh7 + ; 4 Kt × R, Pg7 m.

Arch. 10 : Ar. 28.

(Bl.)

Rubeus (l. *Niger*) *primo uadit & mactat nigrum* (l. *rubeum*) *in domo ubi est.* Fit mactum in iiii^or tractibus uel in tribus ad minus. Soln. 1 R × Kt + ; 2 R × P + , B × R ! ; 3 Pd7 + ; 4 Kt × B m.

Arch. 11. Cf. Alf. 86.

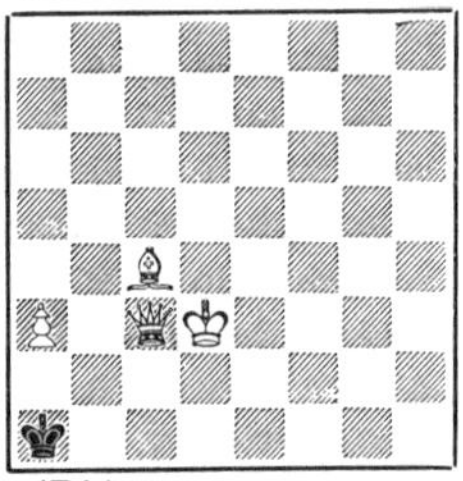

(Bl.)

Rubeus primus aget et uincet hoc modo. Fit mactum in sex tractibus, etc. Rex niger debet mactari in domo equitis sui sinistri infra sextum tractum hoc modo. Regina dicat scachum. ipse autem subeat domum sui militis. deinde submoueat caluum ac deinde ubi caluus fuerat regem ponas. ab hinc in locum ubi prius Regina fuerat Rex descendat. postea cum alfino, id est caluuo, Scachum dicas, et statim cum pedite mactum inferras.

Arch. 12. Cf. Ar. 208.

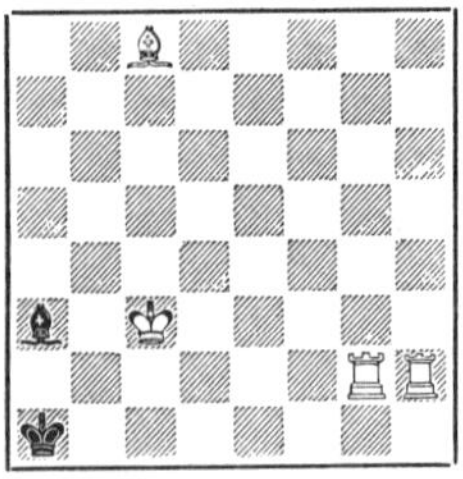

Rubeus uadat & mactet nigros in domo ubi est. Fit mactum in diuersis tractibus. Niger caluus nullatenus capiatur qui et ipse ceteros cum suo rege si potest capiet. Caluus anteferior inmobilis est. hoc autem modo mactari potest. paulatim deducatur Rex usque quo caluus eius ponatur in choopperturam sui regis in domo seconda Rocchi rubei dextri, et sic cum roccho uno et cum rege potest cito quo uellis angullo mactari.

Arch. 13 = CB 53 (Wh. Kd6, Rc5, e5; Bl. Kd8), q.v.

Arch. 14. Cf. CB 12.

Rubeus primus aget & sic uincet. Fit mactum in duobus tractibus. Regina libera ab omnibus sit et vadat in secondam domum equitis dicendo scachum. tunc niger in domum sui equitis uadit. postea regina intret domum rocci per discooperturam rocci rubei mactum dicat.

Arch. 15.

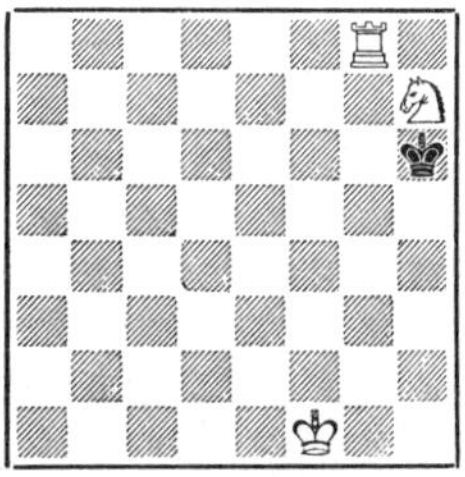

Niger primus uadet & rubeus uincet sic. Fit mactum in diuersis tractibus. Roccus non mouetur nisi semel in ultimo scacco macto. Rex rubeus inmobilis permanet equs semper cursitat per uim donec capiat Regem nigrum ne possit moueri in domo Rocci prima uel seconda; tunc Rocchus mactum inferat.

Arch. 16 (corr.).

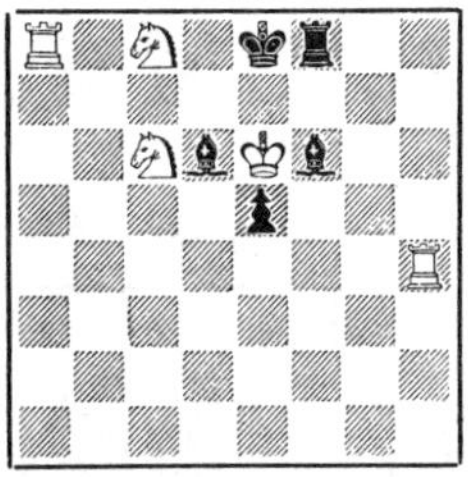

Rubeus primo vadit & uincet hoc modo. Fit mactum in duobus tractibus. Roccus Rubeus qui est in quarta domo sui uadat in quintam domum regis nigri in feritorio calui et peditis. tunc niger ducat quidquid uellit. Equs rubeus qui est in domo calui in tercia domo regis mactum inferrat.

Arch. 17 = CB 185 (Qc4 on c2) = Ar. 19.

Arch. 18.

Rubeus primo vadet et vincet sic. Fit mactum in sex tractibus cum regina sic. Rubei milites precedent semper scaccando sicut dictum est in precedenti tabulla. tunc in sexto tractu Regina rubea mactum dicat atque inferrat.

Arch. 19 = CB 15 (Bl. Kd8, Qd6, e6, Ra3, Ktd2; Wh. Kd4), q.v.

Arch. 20.

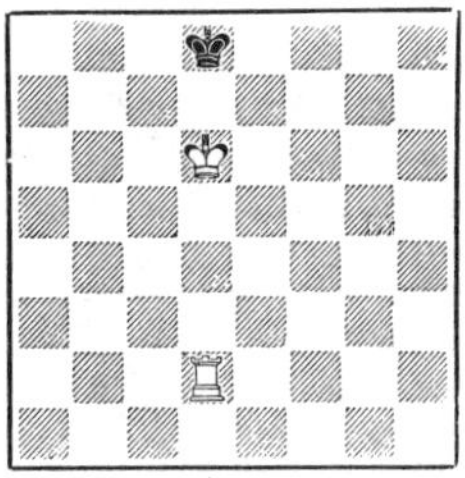

Rubeus uincet et niger primo vadit. Fit mactum in duobus tractibus. Rex niger vadit ad dextram uel sinistram.

tunc rocchus precedit eum in una tabula. postea reuertitur Rex per vim in domum propriam schacum audiens ab ipso Roccho & erit mactum.

Arch. 21.

Rubeus primus aget & vincet niger. Fit mactum in duobus cum pedite per vnam uiam. Rocchus rubeus si ducetur per lineam rectam versus Regem nigrum usque quatuor domus vel quinque uel sex non fiet in duobus tractibus. Si autem per aliam uiam ab dextris uel sinistris fit hoc modo. ducatur Rocchus rubeus et ferat scachum. Chaluus chooperit regem et discoperit Rubeum dicendo scachum. tunc rocchus rubeus per uim cooperit suum Regem. tunc pedes mactum inferrat atque diccat.

Arch. 22 = CB 48 (add Bl. Pa6 and reflect), q.v.

Arch. 23.

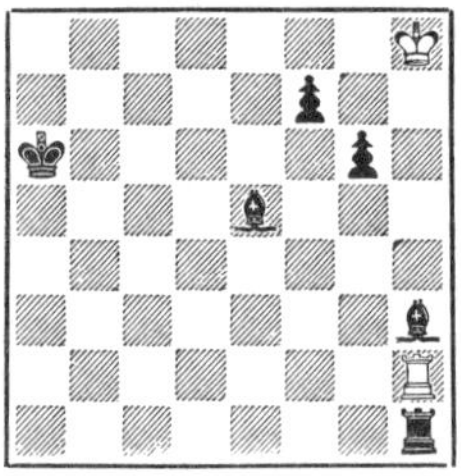

Niger primus vadet & vincet. Fit mactum in duobus tractibus per vnam viam, sed per aliam non. Vincet in duobus tractibus cum pedite qui est in tercia domo militis. si autem Rocchus Rubeus qui est franchus ab omnibus ducetur in terciam domum sue case non fit, qui(a) non discooperiet regem pedes. Caluus uadit in quartam domum calui nigri uel rubei. Rubeus Roccus qui est liber uadat quoconque preter dictam domum. in alio tractu niger cum pedite mactum diccat.

Arch. 24. Cf. CB 248.

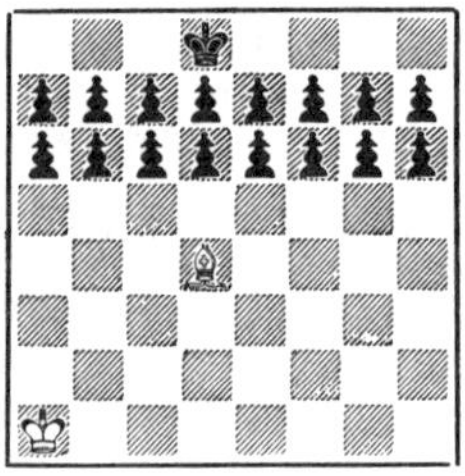

Niger non potest rubeum uincere caluo libero existente. Non potest rubeum mactari caluo libero existente. Cum caluo omnes quos poteris capies. omnes enim pedites regine sunt, et semper in custodiam scachi Regis caluum ducas, in cuius feritorio capiuntur omnes, & ita inuincibilis est.

Arch. 25. Cf. Alf. 74.

Rubeus primus vadit & uincet in 4^{r} *tractibus. & defenditur quod non.* Fit mactum in iiii^{r} tractibus & impeditur solum in vno loco. Equs rubeus dicit scachum in tercia casa Regine, quo accepto cum equo nigro pedes tunc recipit equum nigrum. tunc quo(cun)que uoluerit Rocchus uadat niger. Si uadit in terciam domum alterius rocci non fit in quatuor, et non est alia uia Quia scacum dicit Roccus niger & sic impeditur. Et nota quod mactari debet de pedite qui est iusta Regem. Et nota quod si premitur pedes qui est super regem, tunc ponas Roccum per lineam rectam ad accipiendum peditem cum quo debet mactari. tunc etiam non fit in quatuor.

Arch. 26 = CB 243 (inverted).
(Qui primo vadit perdit. Vnus Roccus non potest transire per feritorium alterius. Caue igitur ne precedas quod si per cuspides tabularii te sequente te capiet.)

Arch. 27.

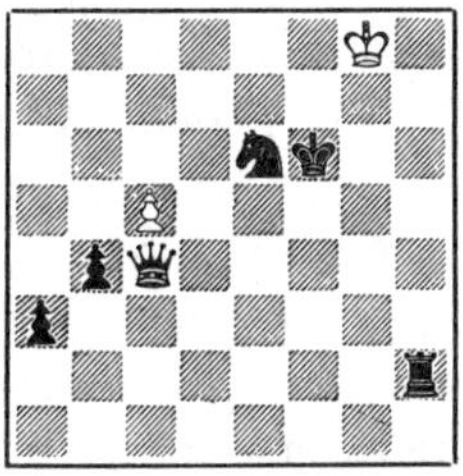

Rubeus primus aget & vincet inuitus. Fit mactum in diuersis tractibus. Regina francie ludens cum milite suo vasallo habebat rubeos et dixit 'ludum amissi' uollens manus in ludo apponere et destruere illum. Milles uero respondit 'non decet me contra dominam meam uictorem insurgere. Vnde expedit quod victrix assurgatis de ludo et cum pedite macteris me'. Ecce rubeus pedes accepit peditem. Regina vadit in terciam domum militis. Iterato pes rubeus alium peditem aufert. tunc Rocchus dicit scacum. Rex rubeus vadit sicut vult. tunc Regina preoccupat peditem ne procedat in locum Rocci nigri et subtiliter tum milite aufertur domus militis nigri. tunc Rex niger intrat domum rocci nigri et posito rocco & oblato cum pedite mactatur equite ingeniosse ludente.

Arch. 28.

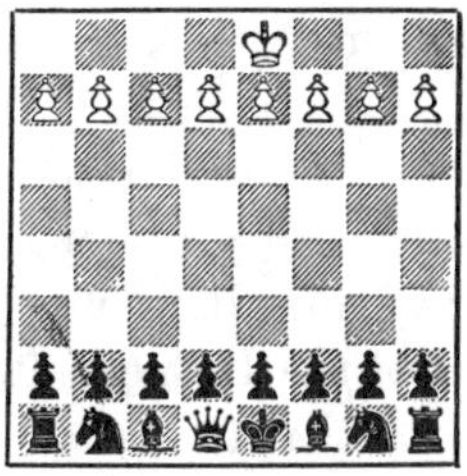

Rubeus primus aget & uincet bis semper eundo. Fit mactum in diuersis tractibus. Pedites regine sunt et semper habent duos tractus et denique victrices remanent cum victoria.

Arch. 29 = CB 249.

(*Rubeus Rex primo poni & nigre vincant semper dando scacum.* Fit mactum in xvi tractibus nec plus nec minus. Non poteris in aliquo loco in tabulario locare regem quod cum sedecim reginis non mactem ipsum. Ponas ergo Reginas tuas per ista quatuor media semper dicendo scacchum regi illius. Explicit vigessimum nonum praticum ludi scacorum.)

Neither Alf. nor Arch. appears to have been known to any of the compilers of the later MSS. Both remain the sole European authorities for a considerable number of their Muslim positions.

The third stage in the history of these collections began when players commenced to compile MSS. from many sources, with the intention of including all the known material. In so doing, the sharp lines of division between Eastern and Western work, to be seen clearly in Alf. and rather less so in Arch., were obliterated altogether, and Muslim and European problems follow one another indiscriminately. At first, no attempt was made to arrange this heterogeneous material.

To this stage belong a group of four MSS. which has been designated *The Anglo-Norman group*, because the two earlier MSS. of the group are written in the English dialect of French, at one time called Norman-French, but now more accurately, Anglo-French. All four MSS. were written in England, and all probably go back to one Latin original. These MSS. are:

Brit. Mus. Cotton Lib., MS. Cleopatra, B. ix . .	= Cott.
,, King's Lib., MS. 13, A. xviii . .	= K.
MS. formerly in the possession of Mr. George Baker, the historian of Northamptonshire (Porter MS.)	= Port.
Bod. Lib. Oxford, MS. Ashmole 344 . . .	= Ash.

A fifth MS., Dresden Lib. 0/59 (= D), has sometimes been associated with this group, but I think that the resemblances are not of sufficient importance to justify this conclusion. It belongs, however, to the present stage in the development of the literature.

The Cotton MS. is a small octavo MS. of 70 parchment leaves, containing a number of miscellaneous treatises which are all written in one hand of the latter part of the 13th c. These include several works on the Calendar, one of which shows that the writer was connected with the Dorsetshire monastery of Abbotsbury, while another (f. 64 b) gives the movable feasts for the years 1273–1380. There is no apparent reason why 1273 should be selected for the commencing year of such a table, unless it were the date of transcription of the table, and we may accordingly place the date of the already-written chess treatises as not later than 1273.

The chess items of the MS. come at the beginning of the book, and occupy ff. 4 a–10 b.[18] On ff. 4 a–8 a, with an unfortunate hiatus between ff. 5 and 6—the result of the loss of some leaves of the MS.—is written, two columns to the page, an AF. collection of problems, the text partly in verse and partly in prose, with 15 diagrams, of which the squares are chequered in different colours, and the pieces are sometimes figured and sometimes denoted by their names being written in black and red ink on the squares occupied.[19] On f. 8 b is a diagram (No. 16) which is partly erased. On f. 9 a is a diagram (No. 17) of the Circular chess of the Muslim MSS., which was once surrounded by text, but this has been erased beyond recovery.[20] On f. 10 a is a diagram (No. 18) illustrating the calculation of the Geometrical Progression (the 'doubling of the squares'),[21] and below it are two diagrams of problems (Nos. 19, 20), placed side by side, with Latin title over and AF. text below. On f. 10 b is the Latin *Cotton Poem*, which I have discussed above, pp. 506 and 518.

The last three items also occur in a vellum MS. of miscellaneous contents in the library of Trinity College, Cambridge (O. 2. 45, ff. 2 b and 3 a), which belongs to the second half of the 13th century, and, from the details of a Calendar which it includes, was written at the Dorsetshire monastery of Cerne Abbey. Folio 2 b contains, without text, diagrams of the boards used for

[18] At the top of f. 3 b the first two lines of the text on the following page are repeated as guide lines (Seignors vn poi m'entendez / Ki les gius de esches amez.).

[19] No. 1, Red men drawn in black, Bl. men written in black, board yellow (h1) and white; 2, names written, board white (h1) and yellow; 3, pieces as in 1, squares red (h1) and white; 4, pieces as in 2, squares as in 3; 5, pieces as in 2, squares as in 1; 6, pieces as in 2, squares black (h1) and white; 7–15, as 5; 16, pieces drawn Ka8, Ra2, b2, Pa6, b5, c4, d3, e2 (erased R on a4, b3). Names written in black: Rei e1, roc g2, h1, al/fin, f1, poū a7, b6, c5, d4, e3, f2, g1 (erased Re h5, roc g8, h8—these three in red); 17, squares black and white, names in black on lowest quadrant only (each square of outer sectors, *poun*; inner, from centre outwards, left, *rei*, *alfin*, *chiualir*, *roc*; right, *fierce*, *alfin*, *chiualir*, *roc*); 19 and 20, men drawn, red and green, squares white (h1) and dark brown. The names of the pieces used are *rei*, *roc*, *cheual*, *cheualer* or *che.*, *alfī*, *alfin* or *alf'*, *fierce* (*reine* in No. 8 only), *poū*, *po* or *poun*.

[20] The beginning of the text given by v. d. Linde (*Leerboek*, 256) is hypothetical, I fear. The passage is quite illegible.

[21] The number on each square is entered in *grana* up to the 17th square, where the total becomes a *scutella*. The total is further reduced on the 24th square to *j summa*, on the 32nd to *j horteum*, on the 40th to *j tertona*, on the 48th to *j comitatus*, and on the 56th to *j regnum*. The 64th square accordingly holds *cclvi regna*.

tables, the nine men's merels, and Alfonso's alquerque de doze. At the top of f. 3 a are the two problems Cott. 19 and 20 side by side (Cott. 20 preceding Cott. 19), with the same Latin text over, and the same AF. text, now almost illegible, below. The board of Cott. 20 is chequered green and white (h1 white), and of Cott. 19, blue and yellow (h1 yellow). The men, drawn conventionally, are yellow and green and red and green respectively. The diagram of Cott. 19 is arranged sideways. The lower half of the leaf is occupied by the text of the *Cotton Poem.* This MS. obviously stands in close relationship with Cott.

The King's Library MS. is a quarto parchment MS. which contains a number of different treatises in different hands of the 13th and 14th cc. The chess work follows a short treatise upon the game of tables (ff. 157 b–160 a),[22] and is entitled *Ici comencent les iupertiez des eschez.* It occupies ff. 161–73 (old foliation 166–9, 190–8, but there is nothing wanting). Both works are in the same hand, of the last quarter of the 13th c., as a short chronicle of England down to the reign of Henry III (1216–72). The chess work is written in Anglo-French (without trace of any English words), and forms a poem of 1,843 lines, divided into an introduction and 55 sections, each numbered with an Arabic numeral. Each section has normally its own title, and concludes with the diagram or diagrams of the positions described in the text. There are 58 of these diagrams, each of which, from the ninth onwards, is girt above and on the right-hand side with a key to the literal notation used in the solutions. The diagrams are unchequered, and the names of the pieces[23] are written on the squares which they occupy.

These two MSS. have a great deal in common. Both begin with the same introductory verses, although—as is generally the case—the text in Cott. is longer than that in K. I have already pointed out that this preface regards the problems simply as exercises in chess, by playing over which a player could improve his knowledge of the game. There is no allusion here to the habit of playing the problem for a stake, but from later passages in both MSS. it is clear that this was the general practice.[24] The author states that he has written his book in response to an oft-repeated request:

> Good brother, you have often requested me to translate according to my ability the *jeopardies* into Romance, and send them to you.

In doing so, however, he begs his friend not to make the book too widely known, and charges him not to lend it even, without first obtaining the writer's permission. His ostensible reason for this is that a thing too well

[22] Printed from a careless transcript in Fiske, *Chess in Iceland*, 161–6.

[23] Viz. *rey* (rarely, towards the end of the MS., *roy*), *roc* (after f. 168 *rok*), *ch'r*, *ferce* or *fierce* (*reyne* in two diagrams, those to 4 and 22), *alfin* (rarely *alfyn*), *poū*.

[24] In the story to Cott. 1, the two players had wagered, the one his daughter's hand, the other his own head. In Cott. 12 the text contains the warning *Kar ki sun auer* (i. e. goods, property) *mettra. Plegge su il perderat. Prenge il defense v matesun. Si le giu sace sun compaignon* (so K 32). K 48 warns the player that the given mate in five moves can be delayed two moves by checks on the part of the loser, so that, if the player undertakes to mate in five moves, *Jeo luy dy verrayment. Ke il perdreyt soun argent.*

known is little esteemed, but it is possible that he wished to avoid the loss of a source of income which he possessed in the knowledge of these positions. Again and again the MS. remarks in connexion with particular problems how few people knew the solution. The important points about this lively preface are the admission that the work is a translation into the vulgar tongue—almost certainly from Latin—and the light it throws upon the rise of the popularity of the problem. When the original preface was written, problems were not widely known, and it was necessary to give reasons to recommend the study of them.

Of the 15 problems in the Cott. work proper, the first 14 occur in K also (but not in the same order), with in many cases similar or (in part) identical introductory texts. The solutions differ in form, since Cott. generally gives them in prose only, and describes the moves in circumlocutory fashion, without using any special notation, while K gives them in verse and employs the special notation described above, p. 469. Only two of the Cott. positions are ordinary mates, and both of these are Muslim; three are conditional problems, of which one is Muslim; four are self-mates; three are exercises (Ar. *mikhāriq*) or puzzles; three are end-games, two of these being concerned with Kings and Pawns only. The erased diagram is probably another self-mate, and the two additional positions on f. 10 a (Nos. 19 and 20) are Muslim mate-problems.

We may classify the positions in K similarly. There are 11 exercises (four Muslim); 3 self-mates; 17 mate-problems (eight at least Muslim); 13 conditional problems (six being to give mate on one of the four central squares of the board—*en my lu del eschecker*; and two to give mate on b7—*le poynt estraunge*; three are Muslim); 2 Bare King endings, both Muslim; and 9 End-games, of which four are concerned with Kings and Pawns only; one at least of these is Muslim. In several positions in both MSS. there is a satisfactory defence, which is explained in the solution; these positions have no connexion with the deliberately falsified wager-games of the later MSS.

In both MSS. (in K with only two exceptions, in Cott. spasmodically) short titles or mottoes are attached to the problems, which aptly hit off some special feature of the position or solution. Both MSS. have a more pronounced literary flavour than is found in the case of any other of the Problem MSS., and do not confine themselves to a dry recital of conditions or solutions. Thus in K 22 the saw *Meut vaut engyn ke force* is illustrated from the capture of Troy and the fate of Samson, and in K 47 the value of the Pawn is compared with the value of a maid to her mistress as seen in the story of Tristram and Ysoude.

Both MSS. show a strong preference for the Black pieces; in only one problem in Cott., and in only five in K, does the player of the Red forces win the game.

The problems in Cott. and K follow. I have made large extracts from the original texts.

MS. COTTON, CLEOPATRA, B. IX (COTT.)

Introductory Lines.

(4 a/1) Seignors, un poi m'entendez,
Ki les gius de esches amez,
E ieo vne partie vus dirray
Solum iceo ke apris en ai,
Les gius partiz numeement
Ke me vnt apris diuerse gent.
De plusiers meistres les ai apris,
Grant veisie iad m'est auis
E mult li purra len amender
Ki à tuz les esches voldra iuer.
Kar ki ke uoldra ententiuement
Des gius aprend*er*e le doct*ri*nement
Des sutils trez, des matesons,
Des defenses cum les aprendrons,
Bien purra ueer e parceueir
Ke gius partiz a g*ra*nt saueir
En tutes curz aseurement
Juer purra plus afeitement.
Mes vne genz sunt ke en despit
Vnt les giuspartiz e prisent petit
Pur ceo q*ue* poi enseiuent ou iuent,
Mes ceo n'est pas a dreit iugement
De despire ceo du*n*t nen seit la u*er*ité,
Kar toust peot estre en curt gabbé,
Kar coment purra len iuger
Dunt il ne se seit riens aider;
Pur ceo ne uist deuant q*u'i*l seit certeins,
Kar s'il fait tenu eit pur vilains.
Beal frere, souent m'auez requis
Ke ieo solum le mien auis
Les guispartiz *tra*nslatasse
En romans e vus les enueasse.
Fet les ai, ore les receuez.
Si dit en ai poi ne me blamez,
Kar mult est grief u*er*rayment
D'aprendre les gius p*ar* enseignement
Ki ne fust assis à l'eschekier
V lom peust les traiz iuger.
ffet est nekedent, ore le receuet
Mun liueret e pas nel peoplez,
(4 a/2) Kar chose ke trop est poplée
Meins volt e miens est amée;
E sens e aueir plus uil ensunt
Kunt co*m*mun est à tut le mond;
Kar si les set sages de Rome
Nen seusent plus ke altre home,
Nient plus ne fust de eus parlé
Ke d'altres ke del siècle sunt alé;
E si li or fut si communs
Cum fer, v acer, v plumbs,
Nient ne fut de greignur chirté
Ke l'autre metal ke ai nomé.
Pur ceo, beal frere, par icele fei
Vus coniur que feistes amei
Ke vust cest liuere pas n'aprester
Si vus congie de mei ne aiez.

Cott. 1 : Ar. 87.

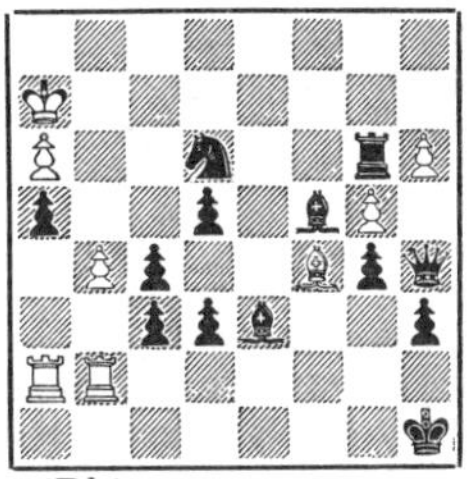

(Bl.)

(4 a/2) Dui baron esteient iadis
ki des esches vrent apris.
A vn ior par atie s'asistrent
As esches giuer e grantment mistrent;
Li vns mist sa teste pur coporer,
L'aultre sa fille s'il net pout mater.
Tant iuerent k'il fust suspris
ke sa teste al giu ont mis.
Mult fut dolent pur mort se tint.
Kant la nouele à la pucele vint
Ke sis amis à mort eit liuerez,
Kant ele l'entent, auale les desgrez
De la chaumbre, en la sale entra,
Vit sun ami suspris, mult li peisa.
G*ra*nt piece estut e estudia
Coment deliuerer le purra,
Puis dit ' m*u*lt est fols e bricun
Ke sa teste met en raancun
As esches si bien ne purueit
Vltre le neofime tret e aparceit
Quele chose aider le porra.'
Plus ne dit, sis peres se coroca
E iura ke mal ot parlée.
La pucele en chaumbre riest alée.
(4 b/1) Le chiualer à ki ile ceo ot dit
Mult estudia e tant puruit
k'il vit la defense e la mateson
Si cum nus ici le aprendrum.
Li reis neir tret premirement
Si nun tost eust sun iugement.
Del vns des alfins eschek dirra,
Mes li vermeil aler porra
En l'angle, mes si il iert alé
Tost serreit del roc maté.
E s'il delez l'angle veit

Li roc sempre li muueraz plait
En sun le bord eschek li dirra
E delez le chiualier le ualera.
Al tierz trait en la garde del chiualier
Li dirra li roc eschek plenir
Si ke li estuuera le chiual*ier* prendre.
Mes al quart tret uoldra descendre
Li roc en la garde de sun poun,
E fra le rei aler uoille il v nun
Entre le poun e le neir alfin
Ki enkui li ert m*ul*t mal veisin.
E al q*ui*nt treit l'encuntera
Li neir poun e munter le fra.
Al sime li suit le roc al dos.
Al setime nel lerra auer repos
Ainz le vet en la garde eschekier
Del Alfin qu'il trait premier.
Al vtime ne se uolt celer,
La fierce le fet al borde aler.
Al neofime vie*n*t auant li cornuz
Si li mostre ses corns aguz.
Si compainz comença la medlée
Icist cornu corne la menée.

[i.e. 1 Bc5+, Kb8; 2 Rg8+; 3 Rc8+; 4 Rc6+; 5 Pd4+; 6 Re6+; 7 Re3+; 8 Qg3+; 9 Be3 m. The diagram allows 5 Re6 m. In K (28) and Ash. (30) the position is given more correctly.]

Cott. 2.

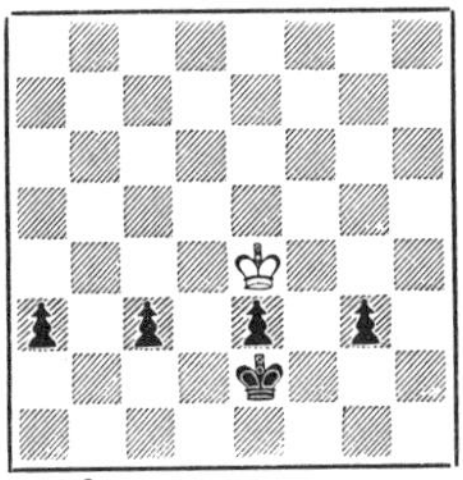

(Bl.)

(4 b/2) Assez iad de ceus giupartiz
ke nule manier par escriz
Ne purreit len les traiz deuiser
Ne la mateson al oil mustrer,
E bien le puet hom a parceuer
Par cest giu ke ieo di veir,
kar si mil homme fussent assis
A cest giu iuer, ceo m'est auis,
Chescun diuersement purreit
Traire solum ceo que li plavreit.
Pur ceo vus pri ne me blame
Si io les treiz n'ai deuisez,
Kar la maniere e la mestrie
Solum ke sai ne celerai mie.
Li reis neir primes traire deit
Mes s'il vn de ses homs perdeit
Li gius serreit del tut finiz.
De il reuoil k'il seit gainez
Quen vne rei leneseit commons
Le rei vermeil od ses pouns
Ne qu'il face ses pouns aescient
Tuz fierces communement.
Kar quant serreint de vne colur
le rei vermeil n'auereit pour.

Cott. 3 (corr.).

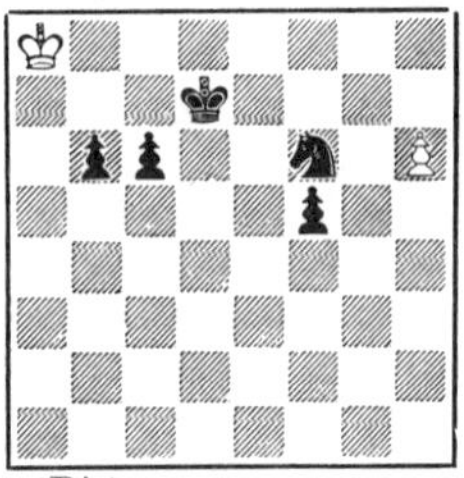

(Bl.)

De vn altre giu reuoil parler
ke pas ne fet à vblier
(5 a/1) ke mult est bons e poi seu,
De tant iest plus chir tenu.
Cist giu resemble nos lettrez,
Nos eueskes e nos abbez,
ke tant riche sunt de g*ra*nt auer
E tant sages de terrien saucr
E à degree e tut aescient.
Lur almes liurent à turment
Si ke li diable uoillent v nun
Les liuerent à perdicion,
Kar il alienent filles e fiz
E lur paienz e lur norriz
E tant se efforcent de els leuer
ke il se liuerent à tormenter.
D'altres mals trop sunt enbui
Kar le conter me semble ennui
Mes de almone v d'altre charité
N'iert ia entrets vn mot soné,
Si de els mes di ieo ne puis mes
Trop les uei porter g*ra*nz fes
Si ke les lais frunt mes errer
Se deus nen peut del amender.
Ausi veit de cest giuparti
Ka force fet sun enemi
Li mater uoille il v nun
Sisi ki ert sa perdicion.

[Pf5 is omitted in the diagram of this self-mate. The solution—in prose—is only sketched. 1 Kth5; 2–4 fP=Q; 5 etc. the other Pawns queen, and the position, Wh. Kh1, Ph3; Bl. Kf2, Ktd4, Qd2, d3, f3, h2, is obtained. Now Qg2, P×Q m.]

Cott. 4.

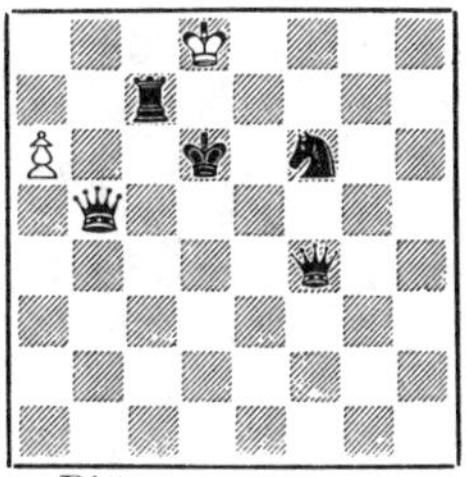

(Bl.)

(5 a/2) Icist gius tret a meismes la fin
ke deuant fist son veisin,
kar il fet son compaynon
Mater sei uoille il v non.
Les treiz ne sunt pas numbré
kar chescun puet mettre diuerseté
En cest giu ad grant mestier
Des sutilz treiz de chiualier,
kar bien est dreit e reison
ke chiualier seit si prodhom,
(5 b/1) E de bien fere tant penez
k'en tutes curz seit honurez.
Numeiment il seruise sun seignur,
Seit mettre sa force e sa vigor,
Chiuals e armes e sun aueir,
E sun cors e sun sauer,
E sei meimes si mestier fust
Aeinz ke si sires hounté eust.
E bien sace cil ke ceo fra
ke grant honor li enuendra.
E cest chiualer fet ensement
Mult peine deseruir a talent.
A mon giu uoil ore repeirer,
E solum min petit poer enseigner
La mestrie de la mateyson
kar les traiz aprendre ne poura.

(Another self-mate with sketched solution.—'Li neir reis trait premirement. & numeiment sa fierce ke esta en la prise del poun vermail e la mettra al tierz trait el point de lez l'angle v il poun tent a aler. Puis ke li pouns ert issi estalé, li rei neir merra le rei vermeil par le bord des qu'en l'angle destre, e de cel angle le merra des k'en l'altre ke est tut aual del eschekier à la destre partie et eit dis dedenz le bord en apris od le roc od le chiualer e od l'autre fierce. amerra le rei vermeil dedenz la foreine ligne desque enz el point ke tierz e del angle v la fierce a tent, e ilokes seit estalé issi ke le neir rei seit en la corniere dedenz la ligne meimes par si ke le chiualier seit al treit d'un alfin del angle v li rei vermeil s'est assis, e le roc seit asis en la garde del chiualier en la secunde ligne. Kant ceo iert fet: si mettra le roc en la prise del poun vermail ki des esches ankes sauera, le derreyn treit iuger porra.' Which may serve as an example of the obscurity of the solutions in this MS.)

Cott. 5.

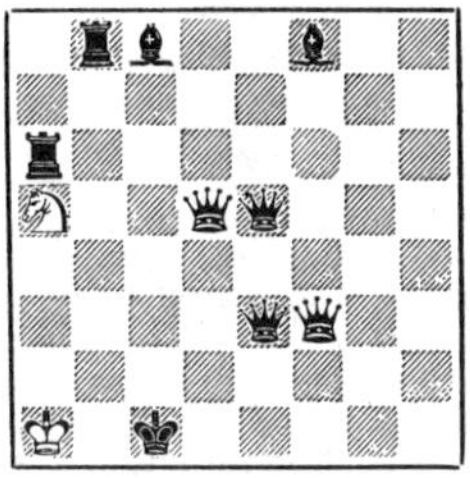

(5 b/2) Icist giu tut ensement. Se fet mater a escient. Cum firent li dui compaignon. Dunt nus dit ici auome. Mes de taunt iad diuersitéz: Ke ci sunt le traiz numbréz. Kar al vintime trait mat serra. Li reis vermail ke bien uerra. Le rei neir trerra primirement. Or entendez si dirrai coment.

[Another self-mate. 1 Rb1 + ; 2 Qc4; 3 Rb2; 4 Kb1; 5 Ka1; 6 Qd3; 7 Qc2; 8 Qb1; 9 Qd2; 10 Qc1; 11 Qd4; 12 Qe3; 13 Qe4; 14 Qf3; 15 Bd6; 16 Be6; 17 Ra2 +; 18 Rb6 +; 19 Qb2 +, Kd3; 20 Rb3 +, Kt × R m.]

Cott. 6.

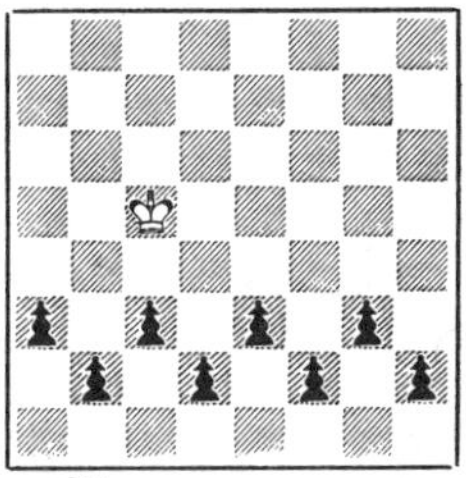

(Bl.)

[The beginning of the text is missing, the conclusion is practically identical with K 5. The Pawns undertake to mate the solitary Red K, who is allowed to move and capture as Q, R, Kt, B, or P.]

Cott. 7.

(6 a/1) Ki peot si prenge cest giu ad non.
Assez m'est auis par reisun,
Kar li bons reis Salomon
Ki tant fut sages e prozhom

Ne poiet par force pas mater,
Nul ke le giu seust iuer
Pur tant lauum mis à conuenir
Ke nus ne pouns a chif venir,

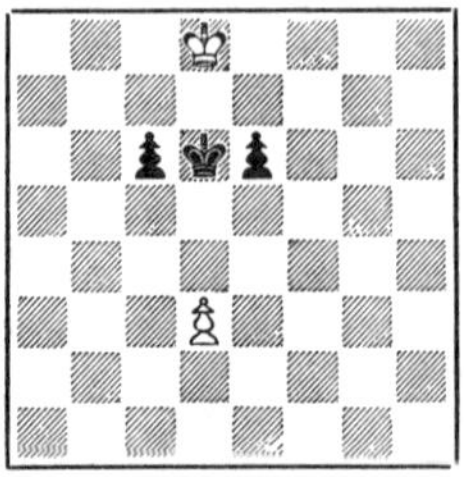

Kar ceo serreit impossibilité
Ke nul à force fust maté.
Pur tant nekedent mult le pris
Ke merueil est bons e sutilz.
E si ne trouerez gueres de gent
Tels treis iuurs entre cent
Ke se sacent del mat defendre
Sil n'aient esté al aprendre.

Li reis reir treit premirement par tel couenant ke le rei vermail ne deit traire sun poun deuant quil seit estalé.

[1 Pe7 +, Kc8; 2 Pe8 = Q, Kb8; 3 Kc5, Kc7; 4 Qd7, Kb8; 5 Kb6; 6 Qc8; 7 Qb7, Pd2; 8 Pc7 m.]

Cott. 8.

(Bl.)

(6 a/2) Cuvenant lei ueint cist giu ad nun. Assez à dreit e à reisun. Kar le couenant ke cist dui rai: vnt establi entre sei. freint la lei del escheker. E fet l'un rei l'autre iugier. Li couenanz dunt vos di. Est si fet e establi. Ke le vermail rei pur (6 b/1) nul estuuer: Si pur eschek nun. ne se deit muuer. Ne nul des seons pur nul destreit: Si il d'altri prendre ne poeit. Li reis neir comence la bataille. E al quint treit sanz nule faille. Le vermail rei veit matant. Entre les suens u se afie tant.

[Wh. only plays if checked or if one of his men is taken. Bl. mates in V. 1 Ra3; 2 Ktg3; 3 Kte4; 4 Re3; 5 Ktf6 duble eschek e issi mat.]

Cott. 9 : Ar. 368.

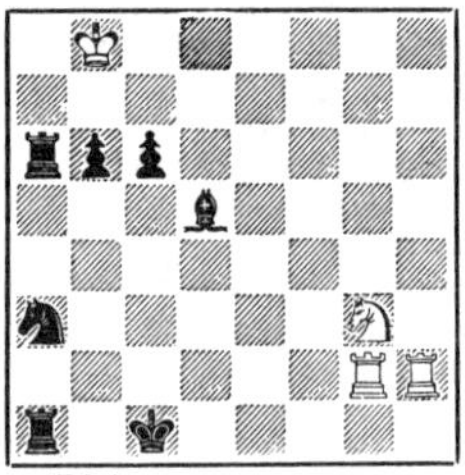

(Bl.)

(6 b/1) Un granz sens nus aprent cest giu. Ke li haute homme mult ad eschiu. Ceo est largement doner. Pur se cherir e honurer. Kar ki ne done chose amée: Ne prendra chose desirée. Le rei neir mult ad bien apris. E retenu sen m'est auis. Kar s'il ne donast largement: Mat serreit estutement. Il deit les treiz comencier: E al quint trait l'altre iugier.

[The Dilārām problem, 1 Ra8 +; 2 Ktb5 +, Kb8; 3 Ra8 +; 4 Pb7 +; 5 Pc7 m.]

Cott. 10.

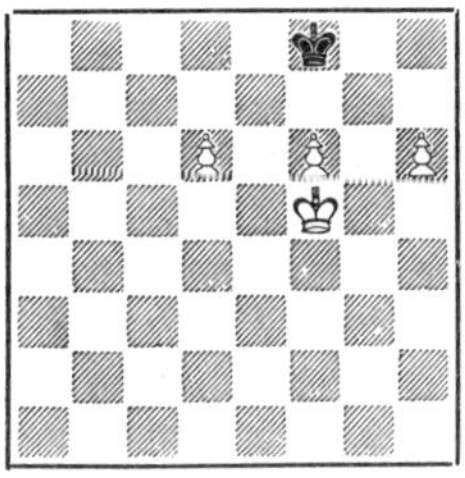

(6 b/2) Cest ad à nun muse uilain. Kar par muser. Cil ki cest gui uoldra iuer: Ja tant ne se sache pener. Kar li gius ne peot estre matéz à force : pur nul ceo sachiez. Ja ne sit il si bon iuur. Encontre un bon defendur. Mes ne trouerez nekedent. Icels iuurs espessement. Si uus sauez le giu iuer. Ke uus ne puisset mater. Le vermail rei primes trarra: Iceo qu'il peot fere: si fra.

[Wh. cannot win against the best play, for his Pawns when queened will all be on black squares. 1 Pd7, Kf7; 2 Pd8 = Q. 'Jeo ne vus puis pas les traiz deuiser de la mateson, ne la defense, kar chescun i purra traire à sun plesir. Mes de ceo uus gardez ke le poun ke est al bord ne face fierce e iames ne uus materaz, se uus iuez sagement. E ne descendet pas il point deuant le poun meien, quant sun rei serra encontre.']

Cott. 11.

(7 a/1) Ore iuent le giu des alfins. Ke n'est pas poure ne frarins. Tut seit iceo qu'il seit cornuz. Ne deit estre pur fol tenuz. Kar mult par ad grant mestier. Li alfins en l'eschekier. E ki des esches se seit aider: Amer le deit e tenir chier. Kar d'une chose puet estre certeins: K'il des gius est bons gardeins. E si puet mult le giu afermer: Si bon iuur l'ad agarder. Feint semblant ad altre part. Feinte chire feint regard. Par unt deceu sunt la gent. Quant ueint plus aseurement. Les traiz ne sunt pas deuiséz. Kar humme bien en doctrinéz. Mielz puet le giu par sei iuer. Ke ieo par enseignement mustrer. De ceo uoil garnier le neir rei: K'il ne lesse passer deuers sei. Sun enemi les traiz des alfins. Kar si il fet. fet en est fins.

Cott. 12 (corr.): Ar. 208.

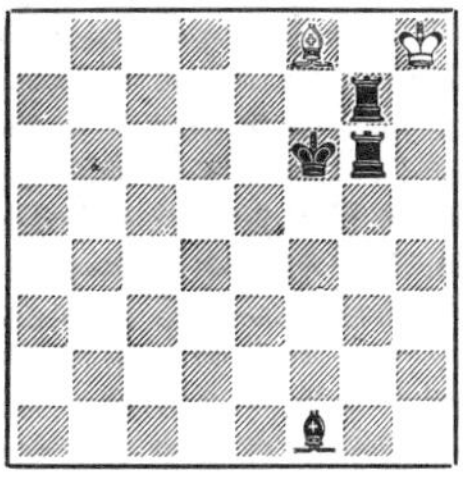

(7 a/2) Icist giu est entre genz usé. Pur tant ne deit estre refusé. Kar matesun bel durement: Jad sutilz traiz ensement. E giu m'est auis fet à loer. V len sage puet trouer. Le neir rei trarra tut premier. E si matera sun aduersier. Al seszime trait. u dedenz. Mes en tiels est icel couenz. Ke le neir alfin ne se mouera. Ne le vermail pars ne serra. En l'angle meimes u il esta. Le rei vermail mater deuera.

[I restore the erased Bl. R on g6. Now 1 Rg8+; 2 R(g6)g7+; 3 Re7, Bd6; 4 Rg6+; 5 Re5+; 6 R(g6)g5, Bb4; 7 Kf5, Bd2; 8 Re4+, Bf4; 9 Rg1; 10 Rh1+, Bh2; 11 Rg4; 12 Rg5; 13 Rg6; 14 Ke6; 15 Kf7; 16 Rh6 m.]

Cott. 13.

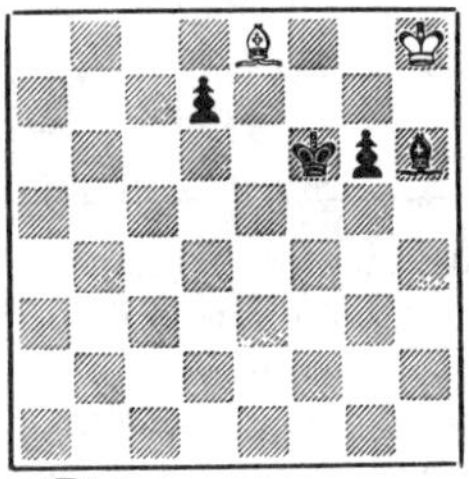

(Bl.)

(7 b/1) Cest giu apel ceo fol sil prent. Asez m'est uis reisnablement. Kar ki sun auer mettra. Plegge su il perderat. Prenge il defense v matesun. Si le giu sace sun compaignon. Si des esches trop ne seit sultiz. E trop ne sace des guipartiz. Li neir rei trarra tut auant. Le vermail matera par couenant. En l'angle sanz traiz numbréz. Kar a force ne puet estre matéz.

[Bl. undertakes to mate on h8. This is evidently impossible, but the MS. takes forty-eight lines of text to demonstrate it.]

Cott. 14. Cf. Ar. 504.

(Bl.)

(7 b/2) Di cest giu uus dirrai mon auis. Solum ceo qu'en ai apris. Li gius est bon e bel assez. E al sezime trait ert matéz. Le vermeil rei tret auant. veinz par estrusse couenant. ke le neir rei le poun prendra. ne fere fierce nel larra.

[Wh. plays and Bl. mates in XVI, without taking the P which may not queen. 1.., Kf1; 2 Kf3, Ke1; 3 Ke3, Kd1; 4 Kd3; 5 Kc4, Kd1; 6 Kb3; 7 Ka2, Kd1; 8 Kb1; 9 Kc1; 10 Kd1; 11 Ke1; 12 Kf2; 13 Kf3+, Kg1; 14 Rc1+; 15 Ra1, Pc2; 16 Rc1, Kh3; 17 Rh1 m.]

Cott. 15.

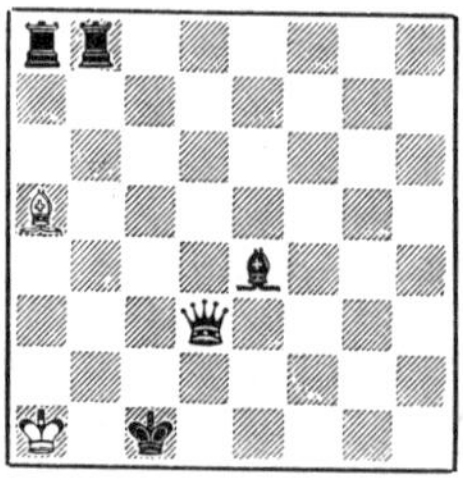

(8 a/1) Cest giuparti n'est pas mult grant
Mes mult est bel e auenant.
Le neir rei de primes dit
Ke sanz menconge e contredit
Le rei vermail le matera
En meimes l'angle ou il esta
Al vnzime trait uoille il v nun
Del Alfin ke tant est prodhom.

[Another self-mate. Soln. 1 Rb1 +; 2 Qc2; 3 Rb2; 4 Kb1; 5 Ka1; 6 Qb1; 7 Ra6; 8 Bc6 +; 9 Rc2; 10 Rb6 +; 11 Re3 +, B × R m.]

At the foot of f. 8 b/1 is a partially erased diagram (Cott. 16): Red, Ka8, Ra2, b2, Pa6, b5, c4, d3, e2; Bl. Ke1, Rg2, h1, Bf1, Pa7, b6, c5, d4, e3, f2, g1. (Erased are Red, Kh5, Rg8, h8; Bl. Ra4, b3.) There is no text.

Cott. 19 : Ar. 83.

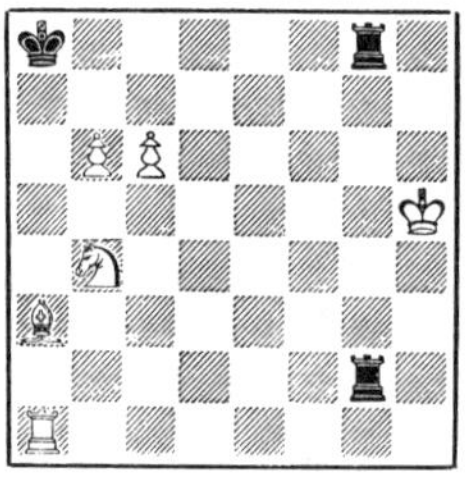

(10 a/1) Quando duos tenet ultima linea regis. Aufin trere pur eschek dire. ki ne done ceo kum eyme. ne prene ke desire. Qui non dat quando amat. non accipit omne quod optat.

[The Dilaram position. 1 Bc5 + d, Ra2; 2 R × R +; 3 Ra8 +; 4 Pb7 +; 5 Kta6 m.]

Cott. 20 : Ar. 214.

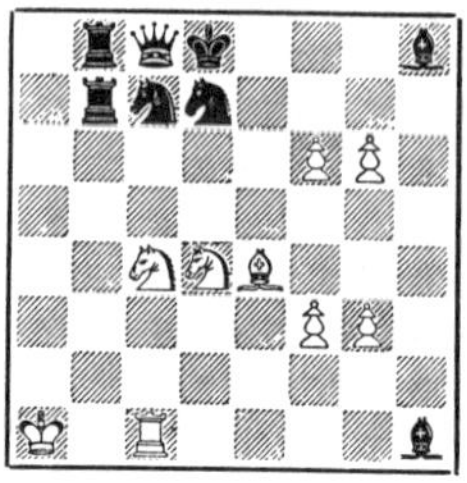

(10 a/2) Quem sequitur fugiens astanti sit color idem.

Cest rei de ça dit al rei de la al quinzime tret le matera en le point ou sun roc esta par la reisun ke de primes treira.

[Soln. 1 Ktc6 +; 2 Ktd6 +; 3 Pg7 +; 4 Kte7 +; 5 Pg8 = Q +; 6 Ktf7 +; 7 Pg4 +; 8 Ktf5 +; 9 Ktg5 +; 10 Rc2 +; 11 Kth3 +; 12 Ktg3 +; 13 Re2 +; 14 Ktf2 +; 15 Rc2 m. The condition mate on c1 cuts out the move 5 Rh2 m.]

These last two positions are also associated in the Persian MS. Berlin Orient. 4°. 124, where they fill two stray leaves (92 b, 93 a).

MS. KING'S, 13, A. XVIII (K)

Introductory Lines.

(The text is an abbreviated version of the introduction to the Cotton MS.)

Ici comencent les iupartiez des eschez.

Seignours, vn poy entendes
Vus ke les gius des eschez ames,
E ieo vn partie vus dirray
Solunc ceo ke apris en ay.
De plusures mestres les ay apris
Graunt ueisdie iad moy est Auys.
Kar ky voudra ententiuement
Des guispartiez aprendre le doctrinement,
Les sutiles trayt & les mateysounes,
Les defenses cum les aprenderounes,
En une cours sisseurement.
Juer porra le plus afeitement.
Mes vus ke ceste liueret en auez
Vus requer ke trop ne le pupliez,

Kar choce qe trop est pupliéz
Meyns vaut & meyns est amée;
E sens & auer plus vil ensount
Kaunt comoun sount A tut le mouns;
Kar si le set sage de Rome
Ne suissent plus ke altre home,

K1

23	26	11	4	49	52	45	40
10	3	22	25	46	41	48	51
27	24	5	12	53	50	39	44
2	9	28	21	42	47	54	59
29	20	13	6	61	58	43	38
8	1	16	19	32	35	60	55
17	30	7	14	57	62	37	34
	15	18	31	36	33	56	63

1. *Guy de Chivaler.*

En ceste giu n'ad poynt de matesoun. Ne tret si de chiualer noun. Ke en vn angle esta. E par touz les poyns de eschecker passera. E vn foytz soulement en checun poyn treyera. E en le angle le tret final auera. E pur leger auer enseignement. Les tres ay ieo escrit en present. Per noumbre ke vus enseygnera. Quel checun tret par ordre serra (27–36).

K 2.

2. *Guy de Chivaler.*

En altre maner le poez juer. Si en la moyté de le eschecker. Seyoiren le homes ie ambe pars assys. E par le chiualer en le angle douz serunt pris. Les pouns blanks prendres primerement. E puys les neyres ensement. Mes ceo fetes à coste treant. Le echecker deuz fethe enuirounent. Puys les alfinz blankes perres. A dunkes les neyrs a puys chiualerez. Puys les rokes e puys les reynes. Puys les reys ke serount dreynes (37–48).

Nient plus ne fut ore de eus parlé
Ke des altres ke del siècle sunt passé;
E si li or fut si comuns
Ou fer ou asser ou plumbs,
Il ne fut de plus chierré
Ke altre metal que ay nomé.

K 3: Ar. 563.

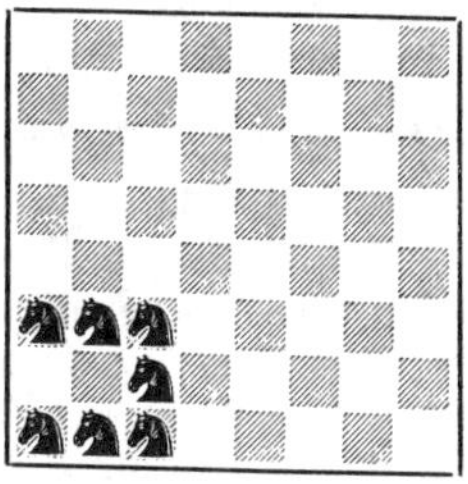

3. *Guy de Chivaler.*

Ceste giu de chiualers si ad noun. E en ceo n'ad poynt de matesoun. Mes en ceo est la mestrye. Ore le entendez cum ieo le vus dye. En la manere cum issy veyes. Set chiualeres vs i mettres. De deyns le neof poyns del echecker. E tous par le tret de vn chiualer. Issi ke les neof poyns ne isses. Mes ke deyns touz iours treyes. A iceo fere primes tochés. Quele poynt ke vus voliés. E de cel poynt à tret de chiualer. Deuez le primer chiualer asseer. Puys del secunte chiualer altre poynt tochaunt. Sil asseez en poynt ke tochastes deuant. E en mesme la manere les altres assees. E iames salier ne porres (49–66).

4. *Le Guy de Dames* (CB 249).

Apres les guys de chiualer. De guy de dames volie parler. E pur ceo ke ou dames est la medlé. Le guy de dames si est nomé. Tiel est de ceo guy le couenaunt. Ke .xvi. fierces auera le vn iuaunt. L'altre soun rey soulement auera. E en quel poynt qe ly plest si saudra. Si noun par force rolle luy seyt. E a dreyn par force mate sereyt. Primes deyt il soun rey asseer. La v il vaudra en le eschecker. E en la manere cum cy veyes. Les fierces si asseyeres. E à checun tret eschec dires. E à dreyn par force li materes. Par vn soul poynt ne remeyndra. V le rey reposa porra. Mes à primes del couenaunt fet seyt. Ke nul fierce pris iseyt (67–86).

K 5.

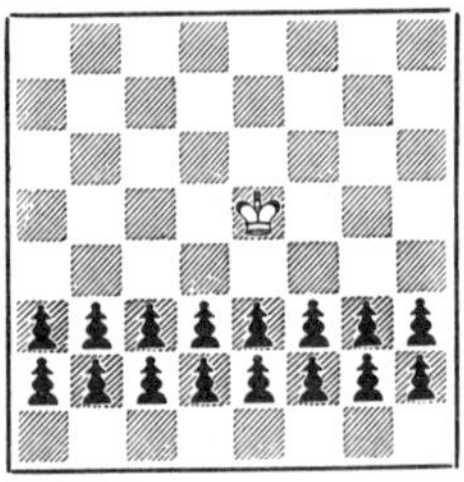

5. *Le Guy de Damoyseles.*

Les damoiseles me ont requis. Ke leur guy ne seyt oblis. E pur l'amour qe a eus ay. Lour guy en ceste escrit mettray. Seygnoures, li poun ceo m'est auys. Signefient meschines de pris. Kar reynes faimes de pounes. E dunkes fierces les appellomes. E pur ceo damoyseles signefiunt. Noun pas garcounes cum les vnes diunt. Kar si li poun males estoyt. Iames femeles ne deuen droyt. De altre part il vount simplement. Cum à meschines bien apent. Dreyt auant e peut pas. De cy la ke fierces les fras. E pur ceo ke ceste guy est ou poun. 'Le guy de damoiseles' appellom. Tiel est de ceste guy le couenaunt. Ke .xvi. pouns auera le vn juant. E mater deyt le vermail rey. Si ly grauntera en countre ley. Ke il soyt reyne Roc chiualer. Aufyn poun kaunt ert mester. E kaunt ke il en sa warde trouera. Si il put prendre si prendra. E tut solonc sa volenté. De trere eyt il la poesté. Mes ke il traye naturelment. Soloum ceo ke checun des guys apent. Mes de vne chose vus ke iues. Purueuz e garniz à primes seyes. Ke si il prent vn soul poun. Le guy est torné à destructioun. Mes ky sey voudra de ceo ganer. E sagement le iu traer. Legerement le put mater. Sanz ceo ke il put arester (87–124).

6. *Le Guy de Alfins* (Cott. 11).

Vn guy des alfins ore vus diray. Si com ieo apris le ay. E de vne choce seyer certeyns. Ke aufin de guy est bon gardeyns. Si bon Juour l'ad agarder. Et pur ceo deyt hom les deuer chier. Le vn roy .iiij. alfins auera : E par force l'altre rey matera. Mes les treyz ne sount pas diuisés. Kar hom q'est bien endoctrinés. Meut pur par sey le guy juer. Ke par enseygnement moustrer (125–36).

7. *Le Guy de Alfins* (CB 281, Ar. 568).

Altre guy dirray meyntenaunt. Des alfins cum l'altre deuaunt. Mes en ceo n'ad poynt de mateysoun. Kar .iiij. reys tout environn. Sege sount de dore pars. Ke mouer ne pount en nule plas. E dor confundu serreyount. Si altre socour ne aueyount. Ces .iiij. alfins sunt soudeours. Ke à eus veniunt pur socours. Le vn alfin va costetunt. Le eschecker tut enuirounant. Cink homes prent si repeyrera. En le lu dount il mua. Les altres alfins ensi frunt. Si ke .iiij. rokes soul remeyndrunt. Puys chescun alfin vn roc prent. Lour soud demaund cum il apent. Les reys à eus responient. Ke ren à eus doner ne volient. Les alfins repeyrount à lour lu primer. Si cey vount eirrer eus conselier. Coment despit les fere pusount. Ke les guerdoner ne voleyount. Chescun alfin va eschec dire. A vn roy pur eus despire. Puys les roys par ire graunt. A tret de ferce vount eus suant. Pur eus venger si il pussount. Mes les alfins ensemble treyount. E altre foyth eschec diunt. De quey les reys plus irrés sunt. Si diunt ke sey voliunt venger. De ces alfins en tote maner. Mes entre eus teles couenanz sount. Ke touz .iiij. reys primes treyerount. Puys touz les .iiij. alfins suant. Vncore il ad altre couenaunt. Ke nul rey Alfin prendreyt. Fors ceo ke a luy eschec diseyt. Ore comence la medlé. Entre les alfins e les reys sené (145–86).

K 8 (the ring is placed on square a5).

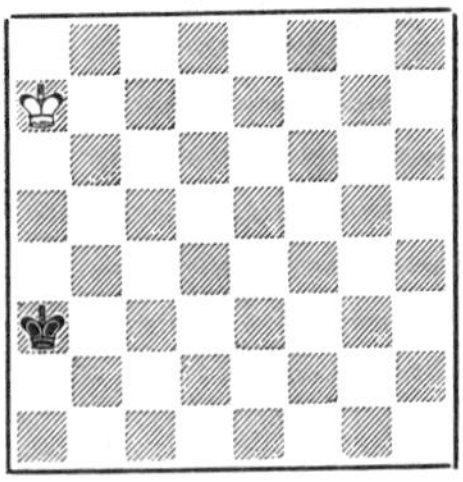

8. *Le Guy de Anel.*

Cest vn guy sutil & beal. Si est appellé guy de anel. Le rey blank mys en le eschecker. Vn anel entre luy & soun aduerser. E à le rey neyr graunté le ad. Si il par force ganier porrad. E si ad mult bele mestrie. De le garder ke ne le perde mie. Mes ke solunc mey le iuera. Plegge suy ke ne le perdera. Car à force ne le punt prendre. S'il iad qe sache defendre (187–98).

9. *Le Guy de Couenaunt* (Cott. 12).

Guy de couenant si ad à noum. Ceste guy cum nous appelloum. E si est entre genz mult vsé. Pur daunt ne deyt estre refusé. Kar trop bele mateysoun iad. E sutiles trayz ke aprendre voudrad. Le neyr rey treyera tout primer. E si matera soun aduerser. A seizime tret v devaunt. Mes entre eus est tiel couenaunt. Ke le neyr alfin ne sey mouera. Ne le vermail pris ne serra. E en l'angle meismes v il esta. Le vermail rey mater deuera. E pur ces couenauns ke nus diroum. Guy de couenaunt le appelloum (214–30).

10. *Guy de Propre Confusioun* (Cott. 3; Pf5 on f4).

Guy de propre confusioun. Ceste guy-partie si ad noun. Pur ceo ke il fet soun aduerser. Voile ou noun ly mater. E mult biel est & poy seuz. Pur ceo est il plus chier deuuz (249–53).

11. *Guy de Propre Confusioun* (Cott. 4: Pa6 on a5, Qb5 on a4, omit Qf4).

Ceste guy trait à mesme la fin. Ke deuant fit le seon veisyn. Kar il fet soun compaignoun. Sey mater volie v nun (289–92).

12. *Guy de Propre Confusioun* (Cott. 5: Qe3, f3 on d4, e4).

Ceste guy est de tiel couenaunt. Cum les deuz altres furunt devaunt. Le rey neyr treyera à primer. E soun compaignoun li fra mater (309–12). . . . Par ces treys guys vus poez sauer. Coment vus fres vostre aduerser. Vus mater volie ou noun. E ceo fut ma entencioun (331–4).

K 13 (corr.).

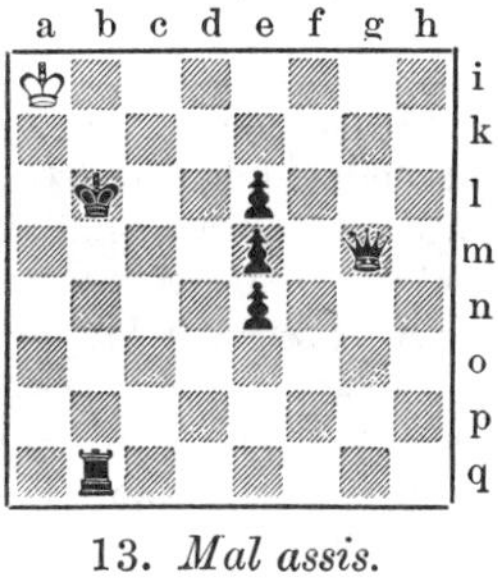

13. *Mal assis.*

Ceste guy si ad noun mal assis. Mes il n'est mye del meyns pris. Le neyr rey primes treyera. E al sine tret si matera. Tut par force soun aduerser. En my lu dreyt del eschecker (335–40). A conditional mate in VII on e5 by 1 Ra1+; 2 Kc6; 3 Rb1; 4 Rb8+; 5 Kc5, 6 Rb7; 7 Re7 m.

K 14.

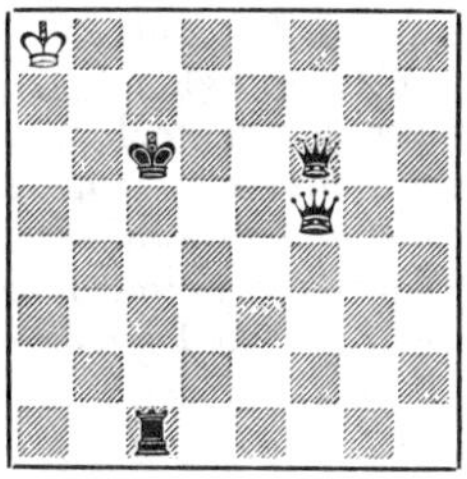

14. *Guy cotidian.*

Ceste guy dunt ore vus diroum. Guy cotidian si appelloum. E pur ceo ke il est si comoun. Guy cotidiane si ad à noun. Kar cely ke setz bien juer. En ceste guy put touz diz entrer. Kar souente fethz il auendra. Ke deuz ferces & vn roc le vn auera. Kaunt le altre nul home ne conyt. Fors soun rey. E si ency seyt. Al setime tret si put mater. Le altre en my lu del eschecker. E si par auenture ensy seyt. Ke alfin ou altre home eyt. Cele home en nul manere ne pues. Auaunt ke vos gentz assys eyes. En la manere cum cy veyes. E dunkes vostre iupartie juez (351–68). Another conditional mate in VIII, not VII, 'in the four points'. 1 Ra1+; 2 Kb6; 3 Ra8+; 4 Rh8; 5 Rh7; 6 Kb5, Kd6 (If Kd4; 7 Rh3; 8 Rd3 m.); 7 Rg7; 8 Rd7 m.

K 15 (1).

And two other diagrams (I. Red, Ka8; Bl. Kc6, Rc1, Ktg5, g6; II. Wh. Ka8; Bl. Kc6, Rc1, e1).

15. *Le Guy cotidian.*

Ces treys Juparties suant. Matunt en la manere cum ceo deuant. Kar à setime tret funt mater. Le rey en my lu del eschecker. E pur dire la verité. Il ne ad nul diuersité. Fors ke altres homes ensount. E altrement en le eschecher esteunt. Kar queles geittz ke sount. Ke ces .iiij. poyntz garder porrunt. En. Em. El. Ek. Cum vus dis ay mat serra. E en mesme la manere cum cy veyez. En poynt devis li mater porrez. Kar il ne ad poynt en le eschecker. Ke en cel ne ly poez mater. Fors cel poynt ke est. Del angle de fierce la tret. E en cel poynt mater vus apprendrum. A procheyn guy ke nus diroum. mes les trayz ne volie escrire. Ne les mettre en ceste liuere. Pur ceo ke checun ke sache juer. Par sey mes es le porra mater. Par si ke de ceus quatre Juparties. Eyt apris les vudyes (383–409). These only differ from the previous game in the method adopted for blocking the *e*-file.

K 16.

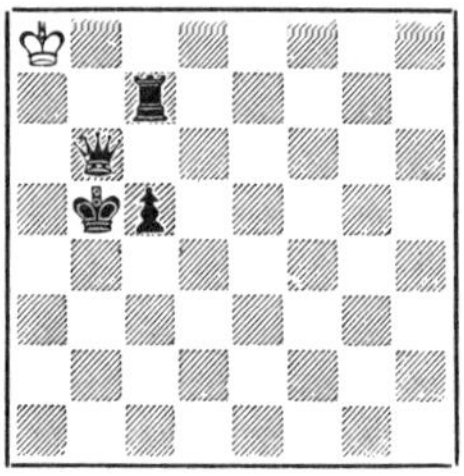

And a second diagram (Wh. Ka8 ; Bl. Kb5, Rc7, Qb6, Bf3).

16. *Le Poynt estraunge.*

Le guy doun me en parleroum. Le poynt estraunge si ad à noum. Car il ne ad poynt en le eschecker. Ke pys est pur leyns mater. Cum cel poynt ke del angle est. De vne fierce le tret. Mes si vn roc & fierce eyez. E altre home ke trere poez. E al roy kaunt en cel poynt est. Eschec dire kant il vus plest. Dunkes vus poez de leger. En cel poynt ly mater. Mes à primes vus purueyez. Ke en la manere cum cy veyez. Ke vos gentz seyunt assis. E dunkes lu materés cum ieo vus diz (409–24). Mate on b7: 1 Rh7; 2 Rh8 + ; 3 Pc6 m.

K 17.

17. *Le Poynt estraunge.*

Vncore ieo voyl plus plener. De mesme ceo Jupartye parler. Kar plus i ad diuersité. Kaunt vus ne auez altre mené. Fors vn roc & deuz chiualeres. Mes ne pur kaunt asset est legers. De ly mater à vostre volunté. En le poynt auaunt nomé. Par sy ke vos genz assiez. En la manere cum cy veyez. E al tierce tret ly poez mater. Ou le roc v ou le chiualer. En le poynt ke assigné est. Ou quele de euz ke vus plest. Mes sachez ke en diuerse maner. Ou le roc vus li poez mater. Mes entre mil à peyne vn serra. Ke ou le chiualer le mater sauera. E pur ceo ke il ne serreyt en vbliaunce. Le mat escrit ay pur remembraunce (435–53). Soln. 1 Rc8 + ; 2 Ktc6 + ; 3 Ktd6 m.

K 18.

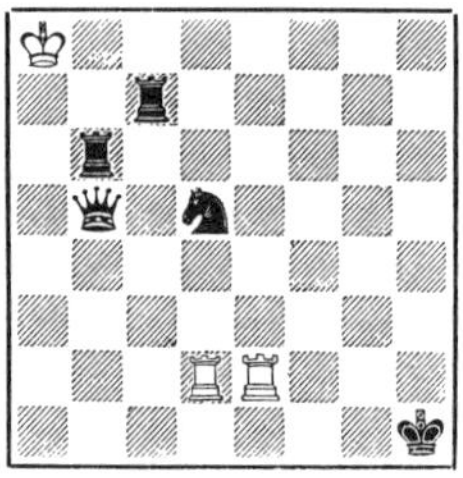

18. *Ky perde sey salue.*

Ky perde sey sauue ce guy ad noun. E si ly ad trop bieal mateysoun. E ja seyt ceo ke il seyt leger. Ne deyt pur ceo estre meyns chier. Car ky voet tuz les gius aprendre. Les legeres lestoet od les forz entendre. Mes il iad vne manere de gent. Ceo ke il seuent ne preysent nient. E si de altre apris ne lour fust. Par sey aprendre falier peust. Le rey neyr primes trere deyt (461–71). Mate in IV: 1 Rc8 + ; 2 Ra6 + ; 3 Qc6 + ; 4 R m. accordingly.

19. *Ky ne doune ceo ke il eyme ne prent ke desire* (Cott. 9).

K 20.

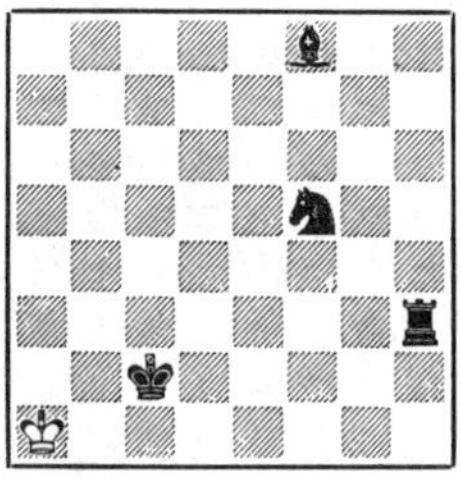

20. *Bien troué.*

Ceste guy si ad noun bien troué. E si est il sutils & de graunt bealté. Kar al sime tret matera soun aduerser. A force en my lu del eschecker. E bien fut troué & bien fust fet. Kar en li n'ad pur veir nul tret. Ke ne porte graund force en sey. En my l'eschecker pur mater le rey. E souent en guy venir put. Kar si vus eyez vn roc & vn chiualer. E vn altre hom ke put garder. Le poynt ke dl. est només. Vostre purpos dunkes auerés (505–18). Mate in VI. 1 Ktd4; 2 Rh1; 3 Ra1+; 4 Kd3; 5 Rb1; 6 Rb5 m.

K 21 (corr.).

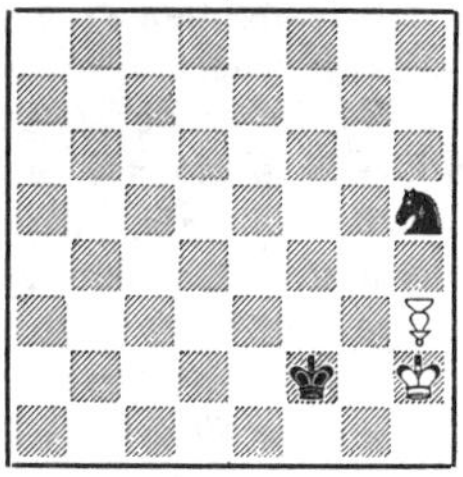

21. *Beal petis.*

Ceste guy si ad noun beal petiz. E nepurkaunt si est bien sutilz. Soulement vn chiualer le neyr auera. E à le quinte tret l'altre matera. E touz le tretz de ceste guy sount de chiualer (527–31). Mate in V. 1 Ktf6; 2 Kte4, Kh2!; 3 Ktd2; 4 Ktf1; 5 Ktg3 m.

K 22.

22. *Meut vaut engyn ke force.*

Seygnours ceste guy est appelléz. Mieut vaut engyn ke force de assez. De quey n'estut mie duter. Kaunt par example le puse puer. Kar Troye fut set aunz assegé. Vnkes par force ne fut ganyé. Mes par engyn fut conquis. Destrut & à cendre mis. De altre part li fort Sampsons. Cum en nos liueres le trouoins. Vnkes par force ne fust conquis. Mes par engyn de femme fut trays. Des saumples seygnours taunt i ad. Ke homme counter ne les porrad. Ensy est de ceste Jupartie. Kar le rey vermal ert mal balye. Si engyn plus ke force ne fu. En poy de houre ert confundu. Le vermail primes trayera. E à secunde tret l'altre matera. Primes eschec ou le roc serra. Issy ke à force ou le alfin prendra. E à le altre tret procheyn suant. Mat serra del poun erraunt (545–68).

23. *Ky est larges est sage* (CB 73; Ar. 53).

Ky est larges est sages ceo guy ad noun. E ensy est appellé de graunt resoun. Kar hom dist ke par largement doner. Pur hom bien soun enemy asorber. Le rey vermail ceo moy est auys. Ke ceste sauoyr si as bien apris. Kar s'il ne vst doné le seon largement. Confundu enfust saunz allegement. Mes par soun doner bien est delitueré. E soun aduersarie sa ad encoumbré. Seygnours pur ceo ieo vus pri pensez. Ke coueytise a queor trop ne eyez. Par auarice est vn pyr meyn. Ke n'est de perdre le pee v le mayn. Kar ky le vn de ceus perdu aueyt. Prodomme apres estre porreyt. Mes ly coueytous prodomme n'ert ja. Kar li plus ke il eyt le plus coueytra (569–81).

K 24.

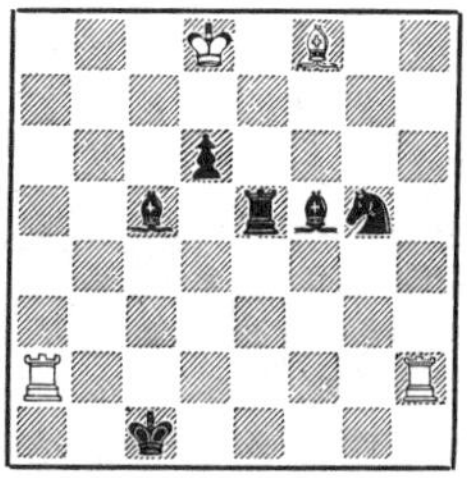

24. *Ky doune ganye.*

Ki doune ganye ceste guy ad noun. E cum ceo deuant ad tiel condicioun. Kar le neyr rey par doner si eschuera. Soun meschief & à tierce tret l'altre matera (593–6). Mate in III. 1 Re8+; 2 Pd7+; 3 Kte6 m.

25. *Le Guy de ly enginous e ly coueytous.*

De engynous & couetous ceo guy si ad noun. Par coueyase noun par force ert le mateysoun. Ensy est en batalie kaunt le deyt cumbater. Souent sount descounfis ky vount entour spolier. Kar lour coueytise est si graunt ke tut sount vuglez. Ke na veyunt lour enemis ke lour venunt de leez. E sachez ke ceste guy est dele court asise. E celi ke tret primer put par coueyase. A le quinte tret soun aduersarie mater. Ou vn poun erraunt en my lu del eschecker (601–10). The solution will be found on p. 477.

K 26.

26. *Couenaunt fet ley.*

Couenaunt fet ley ceo guy si ad noun. E cy est appellé de graunt resoun. Kar vn couenaunt ke deyt estre ley. Si vat establi le deuz reys entre sey. Le couenaunt est tiel ke le vermail rey. Si pur eschec noun ne deyt mouer sey. Ne nul de le seons trere ne deyt. Si noun ke del altre part prendre porreyt. De le long assise ceste guy est. Sy pust estre jué de quel part ke vus plest. Mes en ceste maner cum vus enseygneray. Le neyr rey à vermail la batalie fray. E al vnzime tret l'altre deyt mater. E ky seth le vn guy l'altre puet juer (621–34). Cf. p. 455 and Cott. 8, of which this is a lengthened version in XI.

1 Ph3; 2 Ph4 (le poun ke est en hp deuz foyz treyera); 3 Rh3; 4 Re3; 5 Ktg3; 6 Kte4; 7 Ktd3; 8 Ktf4; 9 Kth5; 10 Kt(h5)f6+, P×Kt; 11 Kt×P m. V. d. Linde (*Qst.*, 208) has misunderstood the conditions; Bl. can only move when checked or to make a capture.

K 27 : Ar. 23.

27. *De pres sen ioyst ky de loyns veyt.*

Ceste guy est appellé de dreyt. De pres sen ioist ke loyns veyt. E moult graunt sens si enseygne. A home ke deyt fere vn graunt oueraygne. Nien purueu deuant estre deyt. S'il volie ke soun purpoys eyt. Le rey vermail ensy ad fet. Ke l'altre matera à neofime tret (649–56). Mate in IX. 1 R×Q+; 2 R×P+; 3 Kt×P+; 4 Pe5+; 5 Ktc5+; 6 Kte7+; 7 Be6, Kh4+; 8 Qg5+; 9 Pg6 m. Or 7 . . . Kh5; 8 Pg6+; 9 Qg5 m.

28. *Meschief fet hom penser* (Cott. 1).

Meschef fet home penser ceo guy ad noun. E n'est meruelie il ad enchesoun. Le neyr rey si il ne vst pensé de bon defensioun. Vnkes ne vst eschapé de mat la confusioun. Mes cy ad il pensé ke la mat eschapera. E à le tret neofime l'altre matera (679–84).

K 29.

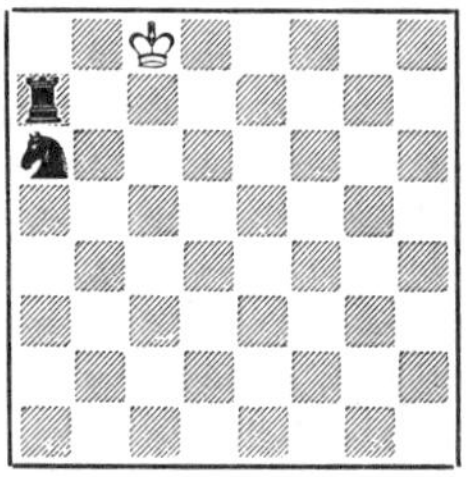

29. *La Chace de Chiualer.*

La chace du chiualer ceo guy sy ad noun. Pur ceo ke nul tret serra si de chiualer noun. E ja ceo ke il ne enseygne poynt de le rey mater. Nepurkaunt bon est de apprendere la chacer. Kar à ceus ke voliunt à les esches juer. En diuerse cas souent lour put valer (695–700). Wh. plays, and Bl. drives the K to h8, and stales him there. 1 Kd8, Ktb8, 2 Kc8, Ktd7; 3 Kd8, Ktb6. Or 2 Ke8 Ktc6, &c.

K 30.

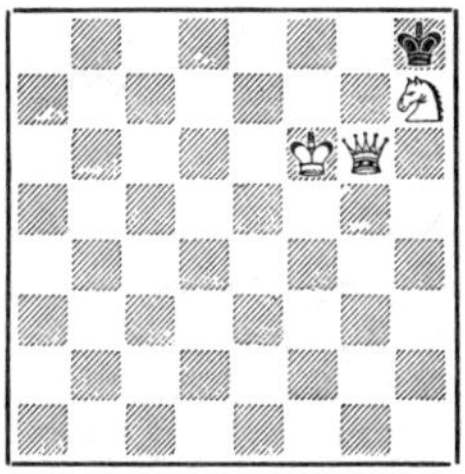

30. *La Chace de Ferce & de Chivaler.*

Vn altre chace vus volie enseygner. De la ferce & de vn chiualer. Kar si vostre ferce trere ne poez. En le angle v le altre rey auez. James par force ne ert maté. A taunt ke en tiel angle seyt chacé. Mes ceo à force estre ne puth. Si vostre aduerser la defense suth. Mes entre cent à peyne vn serra. ke la defense bien sauera (715–24). The Kt and Q cannot mate against the best play, 1 Ktg5; 2 Ktf7; 3 Qh7; 4 Kte5, Kd8! &c.

K 31.

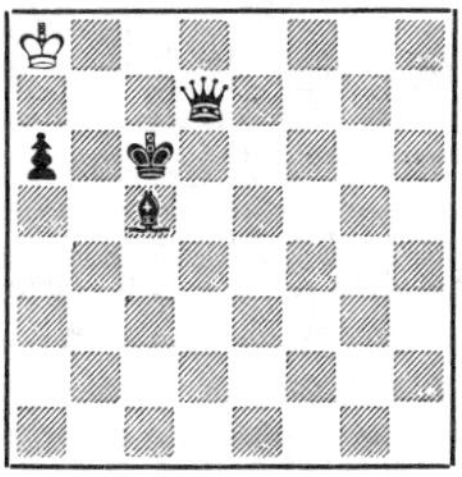

31. *Bien fort.*

Bien fort ceo guy si ad noun. E si ad il mult bieal mateysoun. Ke neyr rey treyera à primer. E à disme tret l'altre deyt mater. En Cj. la fierce primes treyera. Puys le neyr rey en dk. Puys ou le ferce eschec direz. En Eo. le alfin puys treyez. Puys vostre rey treyez en Cl. E puys apres en Dl. En. Cm. ou Rey al tret setime. E puys en Cl. al tret vtime. Le Alfin dunkes eschec dirra. Puys ou le poun mat serra (816–29). This may serve as an example of the literal notation of this MS.

32. *Fol si prent* (Cott. 13).

Fol si prent ceo guy ad noun. E moult estraunge est la mateysoun. E ky soun auer à ceo guy mettra. Plegge su ke il le perdera. Prenge il la defense ou la mateysoun. Si le guy sache soun compaignoun. Si il des esches trop ne seyt sutils. Ou trop resacye de jupartis (830–7).

K 33.

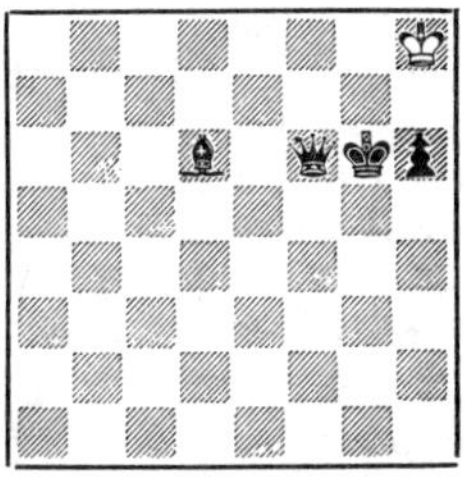

33. *Ly Ennoyous.*

Ceo guy est nomé ly ennoyus. E par dreyt kar mult est contrarious. Kar le neyr rey treyera à primer. E ly altre ad enpris pur mater. A quatorzime tret v deuaunt. E en le angle ceo lour couenaunt (904–9). Mate in XIV on h8. 1 Qg7 +; 2 Kf6; 3 Kf5; 4 Ke6; 5 Kf6; 6 Bf4; 7 Qf8, Kh8; 8 Kf7; 9 Qe7; 10 Kg6; 11 Bd6; 12 Qf8; 13 Ph7 +; 14 Qg7 m.

K 34.

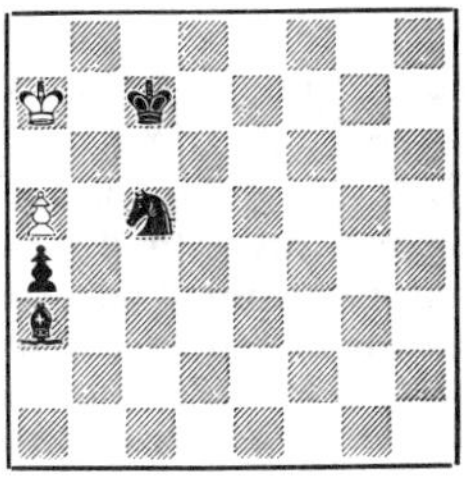

34. *Le Seon sey ennoye.*

Le seon sey ennoye ceo guy ad noun. E si li ad trop bel mateysoun. Kar le rey neyr deyt trere primer. E à sime tret l'altre mater (938–41). Mate in VI. 1 Kd7; 2 K~; 3 Kc7; 4 Ktd7; 5 Bc5 +; 6 Kt m.

K 35.

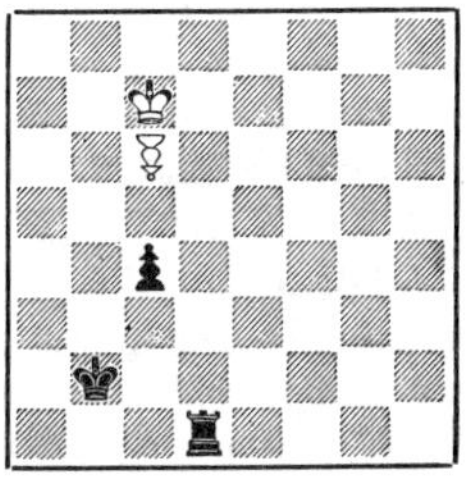

35. *Le Veyt conu.*

De le veil conu ore volie parler. Ke est moult à preyser. Kar il est bonez & beals assez. E en plusurus cours mult amez. E mult i ad iours ke fust troué.

Pur taunt le ay le veil conu nomé. Le neyr rey treyera à primer. E si ad enpris del altre mater. En le poynt v est le vermail poun. Ceo est la mestrie de ceo mateysoun. Le tretz de ceo guy ne volie noumbrer. Pur ceo ke en diuerse manere len le put juer (952–64). Confine the red K to the 8th line by Rg7, then confine it to a8 by Ka6. This compels him *de son poun boter auant*, whereupon 1 Rg1 ; 2 Ra1 + ; 3 Ra2 ; 4 Ra6 m.

K 36 : Ar. 218.

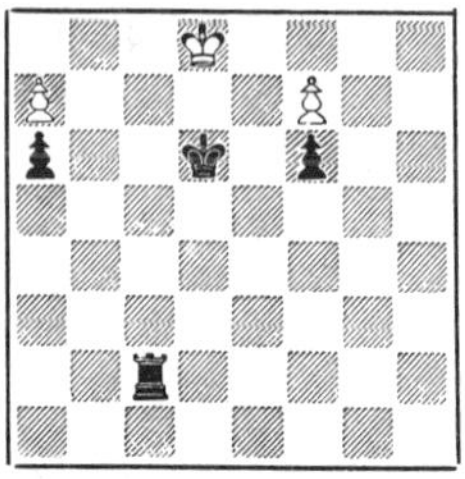

36. *Le Haut Enprise.*

Le haut enprise ceo guy ad noun. Pur ceo ke estraunge est la mateisoun. Kar le neyr rey enpris ad ke le altre matera. En temps kaunt nul Roc ne auera. E bien sauera à les esches juer. Ke le matera saunz enseygner. Le mateysoun ore vus diray. Si cum ieo apris le ay (980–7). To sacrifice R and mate. The K is driven via h8, h1, a1, to a6 and compelled to take the aP; he is then driven back to a1, staled, and compelled to play his aP to a2, Bl. then sacrifices his R on g6, queens the fP and mates with it.

37. *Le Guy de Cundut* (Cott. 14).

Jupartie de cundut ceo guy si ad noun. E si est appellé de graunt resoun. Kar le rey neyr le mat si ad enpris. Par tiel couenaunt ke le poun ne seyt pris. Le rey vermail treyra primer. E pur ceo est il estraunge de le mater (1004–9).

38. *Ky put se prenge* (Cott. 7).

Ky put se prenge ceo Jupartie ad noun. Kar si vus ne poez prendre soun poun. Issy ke treys pouns de diuerse colour eyez. James à force l'altre ne materez. Mes en tiel manere ia ne deuez prendre. Si vostre aduerser le sache defendre. Bon & beal & sutilz si est nekedent. Kar vn bon defendour ne trouerez entre cent. Si soun rey vne foytz treyes malement. Mat ert à force si vus diray coment. Kar si vus poez vne foytz soun rey estaler. Dunkes serreyt leger de ly mater (1026–37).

39. *La Batalie saunz aray* (Cott. 2).

La batalie sanz aray ceo guy si ad noun. Pur ceo ke si despupliéz sunt ly poun. E ne pount estre ferces si noun de vn colour. Pur ceo del mater la mestrie est greuiour. Nepurkaunt à force put estre maté. Mes les tretz coment ne sunt diuisé. Kar si mil homes le deyuent juer. Diuersement checun si porreyt treyer (1070–7).

K 40.

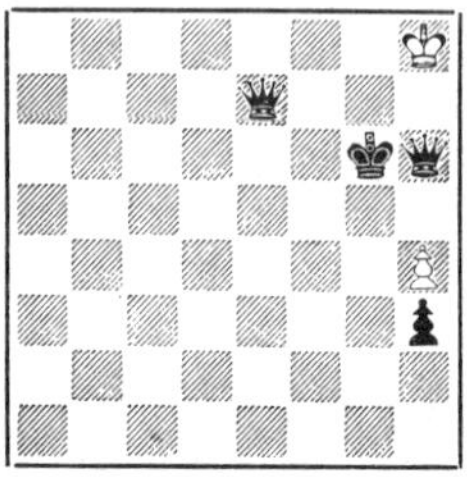

40. *Le Tret emble.*

Le tret emble ceo guy si ad noun. E si est appellé de graunt resoun. Kar si vus ne poez vn tret fenier. James ne le poez à force mater. Le neyr Rey en ceo guy primes treyera. E tiel est lour couenaunt ke le poun ne prendra (1098–1104). Mate in (XXI) without taking Ph4. 1 Qg7 + ; 2 Kf6 ; 3 Q(e7)f8 ; 4 Ke6 ; 5 Kf5 ; 6 Kf6 ; 7 Qe7 ; 8 Qh6, Kh7 ; 9 Qg5, Kh8 ; 10 Kf7 ; 11 Qd8 ; 12 Kg6 ; 13 Qe7 ; 14 Qf4 ; 15 Qg3, Kh8 (15 . . , P × Q ; 16 Ph4 and m. in V more) ; 16 Qf8 ; 17 Qg7 ; 18 Ph4 and m. in III more.

K 41.

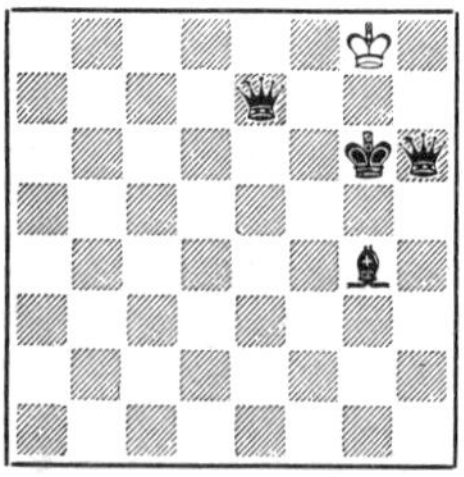

41. *Le Tret emble.*

Ceste guy est de mesme semblaunt. Cum le altre fut deuant. Kar le neyr roy treyera primer. E ou le alfin l'altre deyt mater (1142–5). I solve in IX. 1 Kf6, Kh7; 2 Qg7; 3 Q (g7) f8, Kh8; 4 Kg5; 5 Kh5, Kh8; 6 Kh6; 7 Kg6, &c.

K 42.

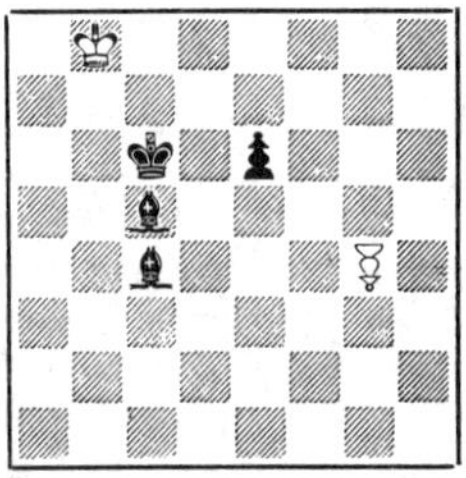

42. *Ly Desperéz.*

Li desperés ceo guy ad noun. E si est vn beal mateisoun. Kar si rey vermail sy haper put. Ke soun poun ferce fut. Bien porreyt dunkes eschaper. Ke soun aduerser ne ly deyt mater. E pur ceo si maté estre deyt. Desturber couent ke ferce ne seyt. Ou si le poun il prendre put. Dunkes le mat asset leger fut. E pur ceo ke estraunge est de fere issy. Ly desperéz ad noun ceste Juparty. Le neyr rey primes treyera (1146–57). Mate in XIII. 1 Pe7, Kc8; 2 Be6 +; 3 B × P; 4 Be6 +; 5 Pe8 = Q; 6 Qd7; 7 Bc4; 8 Kb6; 9 Be7; 10 Kc7; 11 Qc6; 12 Qb7 +; 13 Bc5 m. Or 1 . . , Pg3; 2 Be3, Pg2; 3 Bg1, Kc8.

K 43 : Ar. 352.

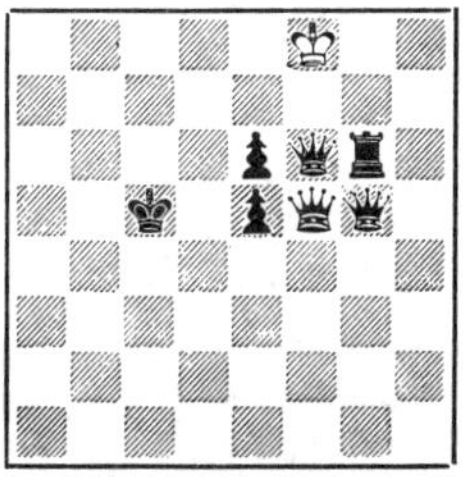

43. *Ly Meruelious.*

Li meruelious ceo guy ad noun. Kar meruelious apert le mateysoun. Le Rey neyr treyera primer. E al quinte tret soun aduerser. Dreyt en my luy del eschecker. En Em. si deyt mater (1180–5). Mate in V on e5. 1 Qe4; 2 Qe7; 3 Rg8; 4 Rg7; 5 Re7 m.

K 44.

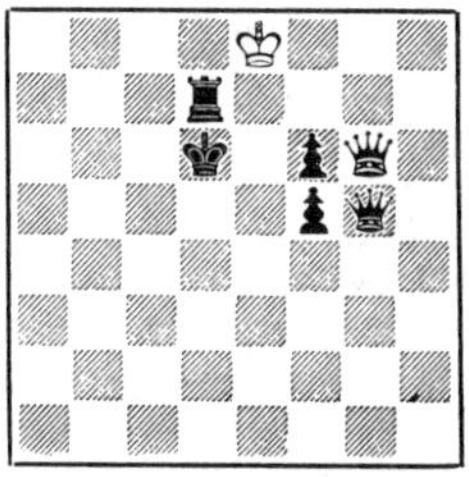

44. *Ly Meruelious.*

Assez sount apurtenaunt. Jceste guy & l'altre deuant. Kar ambedeuz en vn maner. Matount par force lour aduerser. Mes en taunt i ad diuerseté. Ke ceste Roy ad meynz mené. E si ad enpris se mater. A vn tret meyns soun aduerser. Le noyr Rey primes treyera. E al quarte tret l'altre matera. En le poynt fl (i.e. f6) nomé. Ke soun poun ad occupé (1196–1206). Soln. 1 Qf7 +; 2 Rd8 +; 3 Qh6; 4 Rf8 m.

K 45.

45. *De poun ferce home fet.*

Ceste guy apellé est. De poun ferce home fet. Et si apert à primer vuhe. De mult petit value. Nekedent cum m'est avis. Ke est mye de meyndre pris. Kar si touz les pouns ferces facez. Ia par force ne le materez. Ou si le poun ke fierce e fet. Malement de hors seyt tret. Ia par force ne ert maté. E pur ceo est il se graunt bounté. Pur sauer le mateysoun. Ou ces quatre poun. Ke vut enpris de mater. Le Roy vermail sanz altre eyder. Il comenserunt primes à trere. E al xi tret materount lour aduersere (1216–33). Soln. 1 Pd7; 2 Pe7; 3 Pe8 = Q; 4 Qe6; 5–8 Q (e6) to a6; 9 Pd8 = Q; 10 Qc7 +; 11 Qb7 m. If the Red K had been on b8 originally, the mate is in XII, Bl. playing 4 Qf7, &c. —‘ Kaunt fet auez vostre poun ferce. Vus ne la frez en el. *salier*. Mes soulement en fk. le fete *muer*.’

46. *Muse vyleyn* (Cott. 10).

K 47.

47. *Le Guy de Dames & de Damoyceles.*

Vn altre guy Vus enseygneray. Que de dames & de damoyseles apellé ay. E par resoun si est nomé. Kar ensemble sunt la medlé. E si les pounes reynes fusunt. Que les damoyseles signefiunt. Le Roy de euz nul force freyt. Pur quant que vules fere poreyt. Kar touz serreyent de vn colour. E à mater sanz valour. Mes kaunt li counseil est comunes. Des les reynes & de pounnes. Bon espleyt si porrunt fere. E à force mater lour aduersere. Pur ceo deyuent les dames amer. Lour meschines & honurer. · Kar eles sceuent lour mester. Pur succurrer & counselier. Tout seyent eles simple & coye. Entre gentz en sale & voye. En chaumbre sount il engignousez. E en destreste artiliousez. Si ke les dames mult souent. Par lour sen gardunt de dorment. E ky de ceo riens ert dotaunt. Par essample le uoys paruant. Kar Brengueyn la lele meschine. Mult valut a Ysoude la reyne. Qui por lamour de Sire Tristram. Mult suffry peyne dolour & han. E ele souent fust mal baillyé. Si ne fust par Brengueyn eydé. Le rey neyr primes treyera (1344–76). Black plays. 1 Qb7+; 2 Ka6; 3 Pe5, Kb8 (if Kd7; 4 Kb6; 5 Kc6, &c.; and if Kd8; 4 Kb6, Kd7; 5 Pg5; 6 Kc6, &c.); 4 Qe6; 5 Ka7; 6 Kb6; 7 Qf5, Kd7; 8 Pg5; 9 Kc6 and the K is driven to h8 and mated there. If, however, Qf5 were on f4, Bl. cannot mate against *vn bon defendour*.

K 48.

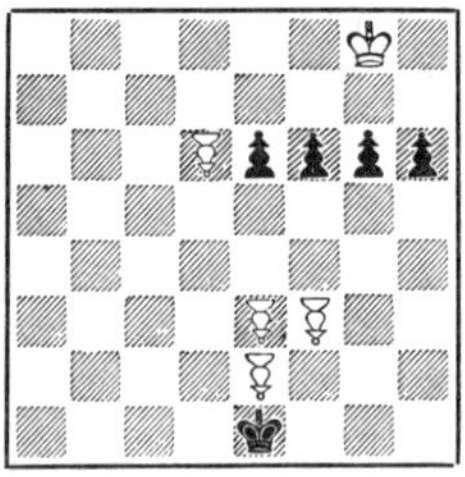

48. *Fol si sey fie.*

Ceste guy seygnours est appelléz. Fol si fie & à dreyt noméz. Kar qui une feyez le veyt iuer. De riens ne guide puys doter. Mais cum il sey plus certains guidra. Plus tost descomfrez sey tendra. Kar soun aduerser sey tourne de altre part. Si luy fet tenir por musard. Ly rey neyr ke est en prisoune. De primes trere ad poeste. Al quinte tret mater l’altre deyt. Ou al quart il meismes mat serreyt. E sachez qe si le rey vermail à primer. ffust assis en le corner. L’altre à force deyt mater. Sanz nul desturber (1426–41). Bl. mates in V. 1 Pe7; 2 Ph7+; 3 Pe8 = Q; 4 Qg8 (en gj. saliera); 5 Pg7 m. White, however, by checks can delay the mate for two moves: hence the name of the game. The text concludes: Sachez ke vn veisdre ilia. De quey meynt hom desceu serra. Si nul i seyt ke enprisa. Ke al quinte tret matera. Kar pur dire la verité. Le mat put estre prolonyé. taunt ke al septime tret. E ceo par deuz eschekkes est. Ke les pounnes vermailes dire pussent De queles les juoures garde ne funt. Pur ieo si nul engagé vst. Ke al quinte tret mater le dust. Jeo luy dy verreyment. Ke il perdreyt soun argent (1450–63).

K 49.

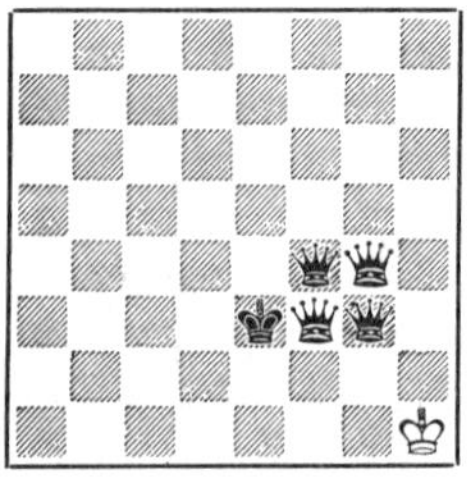

49. (*Without title.*)

Ceste guy est assetz leger. De le roy vermail mater. Nekedent ki le apris ne vst. A quart tret mater falier pust (1464–7). Mate in IV. 1 Qh2; 2 Kf2; 3 Qg2 +; 4 Qg3 m.

K 50 : Ar. 5.

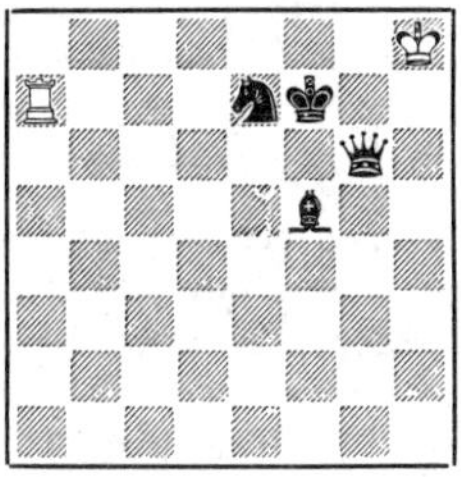

50. *Mal veysyn.*

Ceo guy ad noun mal veysyn. Pleyn est de art & de engyn. Kar le Roy neyr enpris ad. Ke l'altre à force materat. V soun Roc gaynera. E issy le guy perdera (1474–9). A Muslim Bare King End-game. 1–7 Q to d7, R × Q; 8 B × R. Or 7 . . , R on 6th line; 8 Ktg6 +; 9 K × R. If 7 . . , any other; 8 Ktg6 m.

K 51.

51. (*Without title.*)

Ceste guy ne enseygne poynt de mater. Mes enseygne le guy ganyer. Nekedent à primes il apert. Ke ia à force perdu ne ert. Le Roy neyr treyera primer. Si deyt le guy à force ganyer. Al quar tret v deuaunt. E ensy perfournera le couenaunt (1532–9). Another Bare King Ending. 1 Re8 +, Ka7 (if Kc7; 2 Re7; 3 R × R); 2 Re7, R × R; 3 Bc5 eschek rok — E si auez de guy le fyn.

K 52.

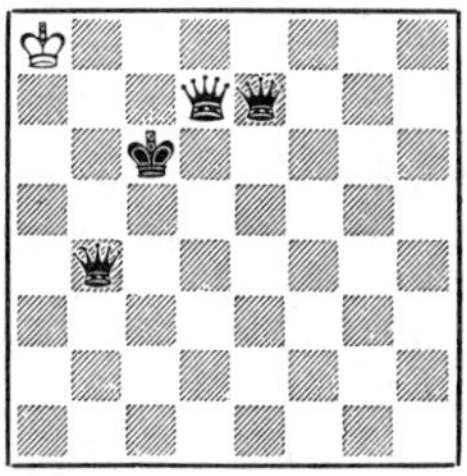

52. *Le Mat de Ferces.*

Le mat de ferces ceo guy ad noun. E si est il mult comoun. Bon & beal est nekedent. Kar en guy vient mult souent. E si est il mult leger. En cel angle le rey mater. V le deuz fierces puissent entrer. Mes en le altre angle bien porreyt falyer. Ki cel guy ne vst apris. Pur ceo ke ay ieo en escript mys (1550–9). Mate in V. 1 Qc8; 2 Qb7; 3 Qd6; 4 Qa5; 5 Qc7 +; 6 Qb6 m.

K 53.

53. *ffour de Guys.*

Ceste guy pur sa sutilité. fflour de guys est appellé. Kar touz les altres ke ay escrit. Vers ceste valiount fors petit. Ne ke plus estraunge est de mater. Pur ceo flour de guys lem fet appeller. Seygnours ke estes des esches apris. Nen est mestrie come m'est auys. De mater vn Roy tut à tours. Ou treys fierces de deuz colours. Come al altre guy vus enseygnay. Pur ceo cest vus apprendray. Ke plus estraunge est de mater. Ke de les autres vn nulier. Kar celi ke ceste guy trouad. Tiel couenaunt fet en ad. Ke le rey neyr deyt estaler. Primes le altre & puys mater. E ke le vermail trere ne estoet. Si par eschek noun fors kaunt il voet (1568–87). Bl. mates with conditions, Wh. need not move unless he is checked, and Bl. may first stale and then mate him. The solution runs 1 Qc6 +, Kb8 or c8 [if Ka8 ?; 2 Qc7; 3–5 Q(e5)–b6; 6 Ka6; 7 Qb7 m.]; 2 Kb6; 3 Qd6, Kc8; 4 Qe6, driving the K to the angle and mating him there. The MS. adds solutions for the following five positions: I. Bl., Kg4, Qf6, e6, e7; Wh., Kg6. II. Bl., Ke5, Qd7, f6, g5; Wh., Kg6. III. Bl., Kb6, Qe6, d6, e5; Wh., Kc8. IV. Bl., Kb6, Qd5, e5, d6; Wh., Ke8. V. Bl., Kc5, Qd6, e5, e4; Wh., Ke6. The text to this highly praised game extends from 1568 to 1803.

K 54 : CB 243 : Ar. 565.

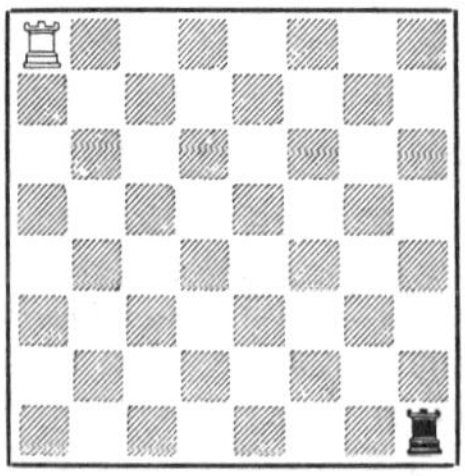

54. *La Batalie de Rokes.*

La batalie de Rokes ceo guy si ad noun. E en ceste guy n'ad nul mateysoun. Nekedent bon est & beal come mey est auys. E estraunge de ganyer & cely ke le n'ad aprys. En les angles trauers les Rokes esterunt. E come vus diray ambedeuz treyerunt. Chescoun de euz le tret de Rok auera. Mes nul de euz la role de altre passera. E kaunt vn de euz ensy est chacé. Ke trere ne put le guy est ganyé. E vus dy de certeyn qe cely perdera. Ke al comencement primes treyera. Par si vus volez le guy ganyer. Le poynt v soun rok estet deuez regarder. Tut à trauers tant ke à vostre role. E la deuez trere pur dire verite. E en cele manere tutdyz treyerez. E le guy à force dunkes ganyerez (1804–21).

K 55.

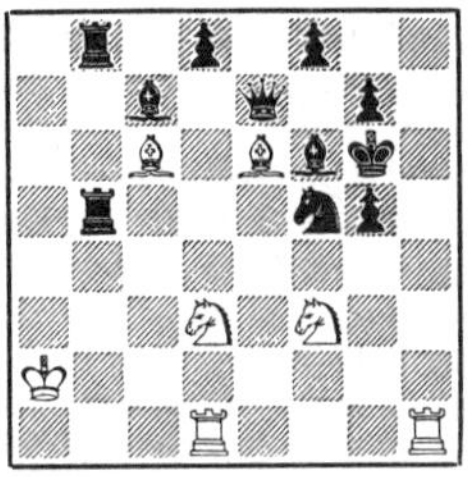

55. *Duble Eschec.*

Dubble eschec ceo guy ad noun. E si ad mult biel mateysoun. E en moutz des guys put valer. A ceus ke voliunt à esches juer. Kar les vnes juoures tele assise vunt. E de ses gentz tiel chastel enfunt. Ke à li dire eschek nul ne poet. Si noun se gentz perdre voet. E ensy fet ad ceo neyr rey. Issy ke de nul eschek donré sey. Nekedent vn dubble eschec ert conclus. & tut le bele guy à force perdus. De tous ses homes ke entour ly a. Oy valierunt kar mat à force serra. Le rey vermail treyera primer. E al quarte tret matera soun aduerser. Kar si rey neir le primer tret vst. A le primer tret l'altre mater dust. Primes ou le alfyn eschec si dira. Altre eschec ou le chivaler que soun poun prendra. La tierce eschec ou le alfyn ke treyera. L'altre chivaler à discouert eschec mat dira (1821–43). Mate in IV by 1 Be4+; 2 Kt×P+; 3 Bg6+; 4 Kte5 m., which, however, does not keep to the assise described in the introductory text.

The other two MSS. of the Anglo-Norman group are written in English, and the text of the solutions of the 28 problems which are common to both MSS. is practically the same in both works.

The older of the two (Port.) occupies 5 leaves of a small quarto paper MS., written soon after 1450, which contains a number of treatises in Latin and English dealing with Fishing, Heraldry, and Hunting. The chess MS. immediately precedes a brief chronicle of England for 1066–1453, apparently written by a man of the name of Porter.[25] Each of the pages in the chess portion of the MS. contains 4 diagrams with accompanying text, making

[25] A marginal note on one page records the fact that Hugh Joly and John Porter were elected Burgesses of Parliament for the city of Worcester, 25 Hen. VI (1446). The MS. belonged in 1610 to Sir Wm. Dethick, Garter. Later it belonged to Bp. Percy of Dromore (D. 1811) by whose daughter, Mrs. Isted of Eton, it was given to Mr. Geo. Baker, the historian of Northamptonshire, whose library was sold in 1842. Its present location is unknown to me.

40 problems in all. These have been copied very negligently; the diagrams are often incorrect, and the solutions to Nos. 7 and 8 have been transposed. In seven of the positions (Nos. 1, 2, 11, 12, 18, 19, 20—all of which are *Exercises*) the men are denoted by numerals,[26] and the text, if any, is in Latin. In the remainder, the text is in English and the names of the pieces are written on the diagrams, and the squares mentioned in the solution bear letters for the purpose of identification. This is the ordinary rule of the mediaeval Problem MSS.

The second MS. (Ash.) is a very small quarto, or short square octavo, composite volume, now consisting of 61 written vellum leaves and 2 fly-leaves. The chess work occupies ff. 3 a–23 a and contains 41 problems, one a page, with the diagram on the inner edge and the solution down the outer margin and at the foot of the page. It is written in a different hand to the Latin treatise on Rythmomachy, which occupies the remainder of the MS., and is dated *c.* 1470 by Mr. F. Madan. From a note on f. 3 a it appears that the MS. belonged in 1529 to Roger Hartwell, son of Thomas Hartwell, *panarius Londinensis*. Hartwell has added brief notes in a very crabbed hand at the foot of most pages, which in the main commemorate his successful solution of the problem above.[27] The MS. itself is far more carefully copied than is Port. Both MSS. are written in a Northern dialect, and there is good reason to believe that an older English text lies behind them, and between them and the Latin text from which Cott. and K are other selections.

Port. 20 gives on a single diagram three Exercises with the Kt: if we reckon these as three distinct problems, the MS. contains 19 positions which are in Cott. or K (11 mates, 2 mates in the 'four points', 6 Exercises), and 23 more, of which 17 are mates, 2 are mates in the 'four points', and 4 are Exercises. Ash. contains 12 positions which are contained in Cott. or K (15 mates, 2 mates in the 'four points', 1 self-mate, 1 Exercise), and 14 positions which are given in Port. (12 mates, 2 mates in the 'four points'). The remaining eight positions are made up of 6 mates and 2 self-mates. Many of the new positions in these MSS. illustrate simple Endings, in which Rooks or Pawns are the only forces.

The problems in Port. and Ash. follow.

The Porter MS.

(Note.—The remaining problems will be found thus. Port. 1 = CB 244; 2 = K 7; 3 = K 23; 7 = Cott. 19; 11 = Cott. 6; 12 = CB 233; 14 = K 18; 15 = K 44; 18 = 11; 19 = K 8; 21 = K 14: 24 = K 15; 29 = Arch. 20; 33 = K 48; 34 = K 45; 36 = K 33; 37 = K 34.

There is no text to Port. 1, 2, 18, 19, 20.

At the end of the solution to Port. 4 is the note: 'The most craft of pleying of Jupertis is for to bring yn odde drauȝtis wᵗ þi kyng'. This note occurs in Ash. at the end of the solution to Ash. 4.)

[26] The key is given in the text to Port. 11: Rex signatur 6. Regina 5. Rok 4. Miles 3. Alfin 2. Pedun 1.

[27] As appears by his frequent *probatum* (a previous owner of Cott. has made a similar entry to many problems in that MS.). Other notes are longer, and appear to contain cross references, or to record his failure to understand the solution of the MS.

Port. 4.

Mate in VI on h4.

Draw þi white aufen & sey chec. þen he goys in to A / chec wt þi roke þen he gois into B / yet chec wt þi roke in þe pown ward þen he goþe into C yet chec in þe pown ward pen he gois into D. Þen chec wt þi pown & mate wt þe oþer pown þer þe cros standith þis is don at 6 drauȝtis.

(Ash. text is: Draw thy blak Aufyn and say chek. Then the blak kyng goth in to A. Siþen chek with thy Roke. Then he goth into B. Yet chek wt thy Roke in thy Pon Ward. Than he goth in to D. Then chek wt thy Pon ande mate hym wt thy other Pon ther þe crosse standeth.

At v draughtis þis Jupertye is plaied. A is on d4, B on e5, C on f4, D on g4, + on h4 in Port. Ash. omits C, and puts D on f4 and + on g4, shortening the solution a move. In the text Port. calls Bc1 *White aufin*, implying that c1 is a white square, and that h1 is black; Ash. calls it *Black aufin*, which makes h1 a white square.)

Port. 5 (corr.): Ar. 300.

At iij (*read* ii) drauȝtis þis is pleyd / þe white men drauȝt furst. chec wt R in knyȝts ward & he take it vp wt þe knyȝt. þen mate wt þi knyȝt in A (g6).

Port. 6 (ext. v. of K 31).

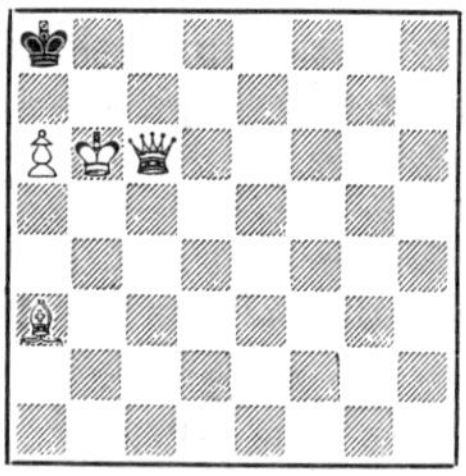

(Soln. from Ash. 6.) The black kyng draw first þen draw þe ffers in to A (d7). Sithen the Aufyn in to B (c5). Ande þen þi king þer þi ffers stode. Sithen thi ffers to bord (*to the margin*). then the king in A. Then chek with the ffers in þi Pon ward then withdraw the aufyn (Port. þen awey wt þi auf.). then set thy king ther þi ffers stode first. then in to C (d6). then in to B. then ayen ther thi ffers stode first. then chek with thy aufyn. Ande þan mate hym with thy Pon.

Port. 8.

The white furst men. þen he sey chec wt þe roke in poun ward. þen he takiþe wt þe knyȝt. þen mate wt þe poun.

Port. 9.

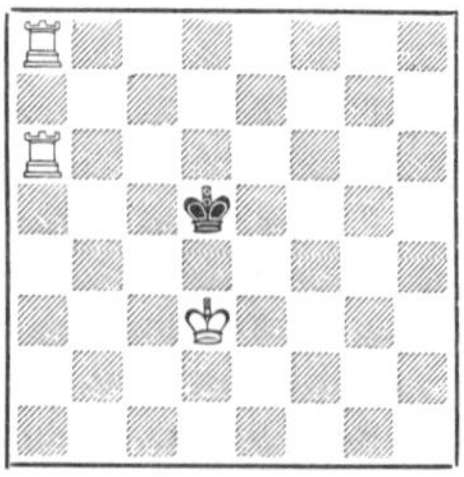

At ij drauȝtis þe pley is don / þe blac kyng drau þe furst. yf he draw in to A (c5) drawe þe rok into B (b8) / yf he draw into C (e5) draw þe same rok into D (f8), & mate at þe next.

Port. 10.

The blac mot be mate in þe corner at v drauȝtis. chec w^{t} þi roke in A (c8) & sithyn w^{t} þe same roke in B (c7). & ryȝt in C (a7). and þen chec w^{t} þi knyȝt in D (c6) & mate w^{t} þi roke in E (b8).

Port. 13.

Draw thi roke & sey checke in B (a1). then þi roke in C (b1). þen mate w^{t} thi ro. at iij drauth in þe poyn þer þe cros stant (e3).

Port. 16.

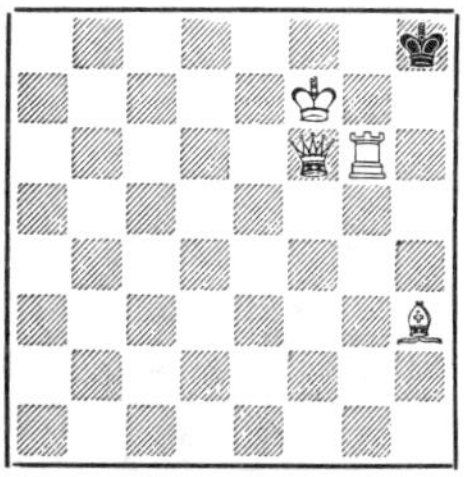

(Soln. from Ash. 14.) No fors who draw^{t} first. ffolow hym tyll thow haue þe blacke kyng at souch plight. Then say chek with thi Roke in A (g8). Sithen chek with thi Roke in the corner. þen chek with thy ffers. Then say chek mate w^{t} þi Aufyn in C (f5) / Thus thow may lese thy Roke and mate hym w^{t} thy Aufyn. ande to conclude is wele plaied.

Port. 17 (corr.).

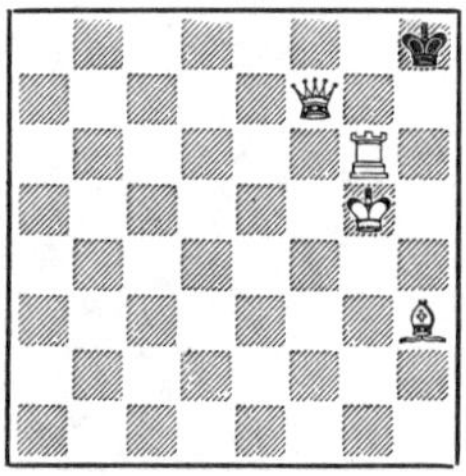

The blac draw furst. þen draw þi kyng in A (h5). chec in fers ward. mate w^{t} þi aufen & yf he be aufyn of diuers colors dryue into þe corner (Ash. other) side & lose þi roke & þen mate hym w^{t} þi aufyn on þe same maner þ^{t} þe Jupertye aboue telliþe & yf þu schalt losse þi ro. or þu mate hym w^{t} þi aufen, þi aufen & þi fers must be of diuers colors or þu cannot mate hym.

Port 20.

Three exercises with the Kt are placed on one diagram. (*a*) Kts on a7, a8, b6, b8, c6, c7, c8 : = K 3. (*b*) Kts on f6, f7, f8, g6, h6, h7, h8, another variety of the same. (*c*) Kts on f1, f3, h1, h3 : = CB 236.

Port. 22 (corr.).

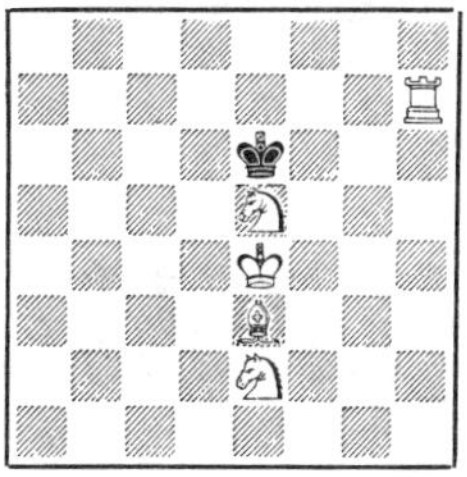

(Soln. from Ash. 17.) At ij drawghtis the black King shalbe mated. The white men draw first. Sett thy lowyst kni. in A (d4) or B (f4). Then goth he in to C (d6) or D (f6). Then say chek mate with thy Roke in F (f6) or G (d6).

Port. 23 (corr.).

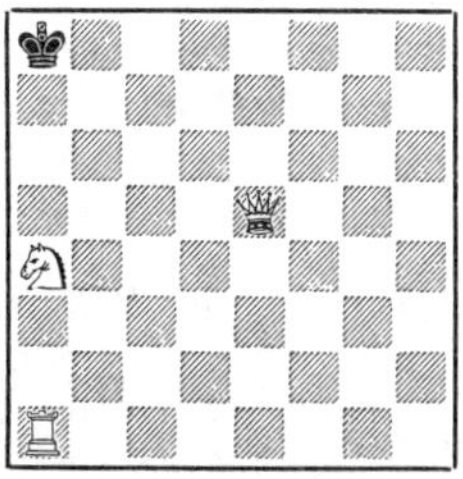

Chec w^{t} k. and drawe into A (c5). þen draw thi fers in B (d6) and mate w^{t} thi roke.

Port. 25 (corr.).

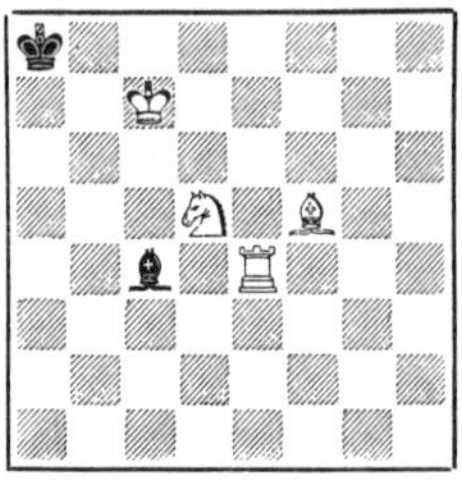

Take is auf. & make hym bar & mate hym after w^tin 9 drauȝtis in j of iiij poyntis (Ash. 20 adds 'with þi Roke'). furst he drauȝt in A (a7). draw þi R in B (e8). þen he goþe into C (a6). þen chec in þe corner þen he goþe into D (b5). draw þi kyng into þi knyȝtis for losing for yf þu stop þi knyȝt (Ash. for lesyng of hym ande let hym stonde still. for if he be mouyd) þu may not mate in 9 drauȝtis in j of 4 poyntis þen he is þer his aufyn stod draw thi roke in E (b8) þen he go into F (d4) þen mate w^t þi roke in G (b4). (Ash. adds, 'He will ande may tell hys ix drawghtis for thow hast a Roke abord.')

The solution runs 1 R × B; 2 Rc6; 3 Re6; 4 Re8; 5 Ra8+; 6 Kd6; 7 Rb8; 8 Rb4 m.

Port. 26.

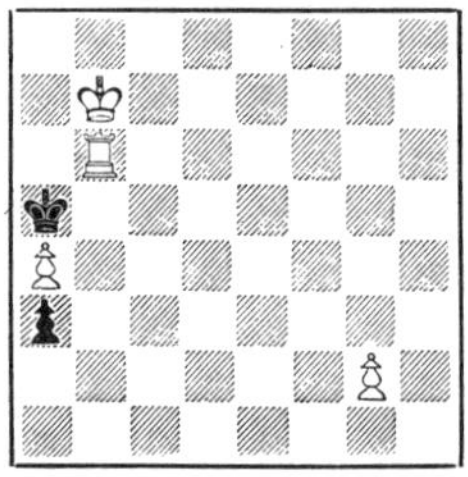

(Soln. from Ash. 21.) This is covenant þ^t the whight king shal lose hys Roke or he mate y^e black king. Suffre hym to take thi pon. Affter þ^t driue hym in to A (a1). Ande stale hym tyll hys Pon come in to B (a2). And when his Pon is in B, loke thy Roke be in C (f2; MS. has f8). þan drawe thy Roke in his pon ward. Than go up w^t thy pon as fast as thou may & make hym a ffers. then draw hym to thi kyng & mate the other kyng in the corner. But þou must be wyse to do. Dryue hym sotelly and war'.

Port. 27.

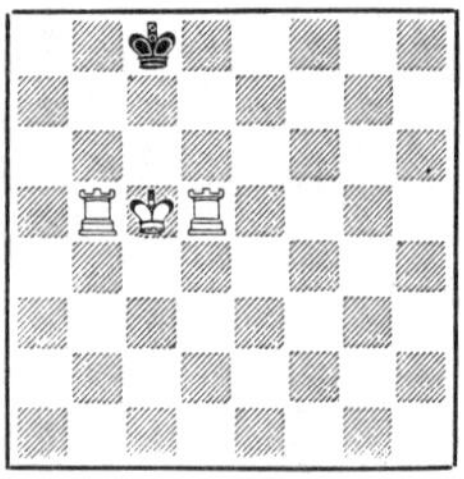

(Soln. from Ash. 22.) Mate hym at iij drawghtis ande euery man a drawght. The black kyng draw^t first. þen draw thy Roke in to A (d1). Sythen thy kyng in to B (d6). ande þen he goith before thy kyng ande mate hym w^t thy other Roke in C (b8). But loke that euery man haue but oon draught for that ys couenant.

Port. 28.

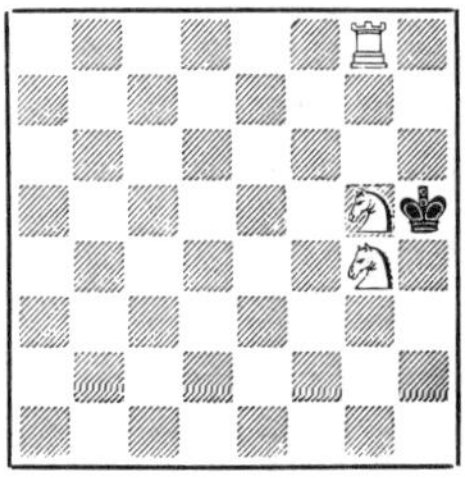

Chec w^t þe rok in A (f6). yf. he go into B (h6) þen mate w^t þi oþer rok (*read* Kt) in C (f7). yf he draw into D (h4) sey chec w^t þi oþer R (*read* Kt) in E (f3). yet w^t þe same in F (g1). yf he go into D. þen mate w^t þi roc in þi knyȝtis ward. yf he go into G (h2) draw þi oþer kyng (*read* Kt) into H (d5). þen into J (f4). þen chec fro H into G (*read* E). þen mate w^t þi roke in F þer þe cros stant (h1).

Port. 30.

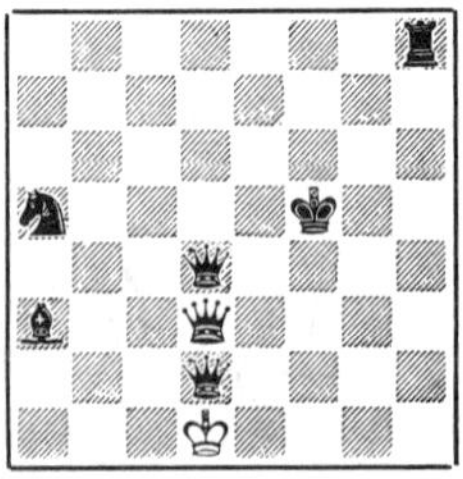

Chec w^t thi roke in A (h1) þen feyn in B (g1). þen in C (g2). then is he mate (only after 4 Rg3; 5 Rd3).

Port. 31.

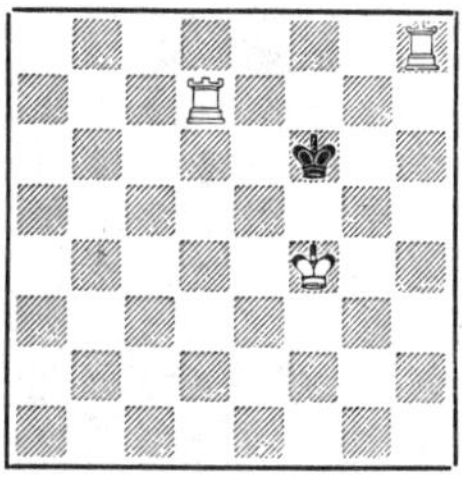

The blacke drauȝt in A (e6). draw þi roke in to B (h7) þen mate in C (h6). yf he draw into þe oþer poynt set þi roke in B & mate sicut prius.

Port. 32 (Wh., Kf7, Ktf5, f6; Bl. Kh8).

The blac kyng may not be mate but by rechilnesse (recklessness) wt ij kny. & a kyng.

Port. 35.

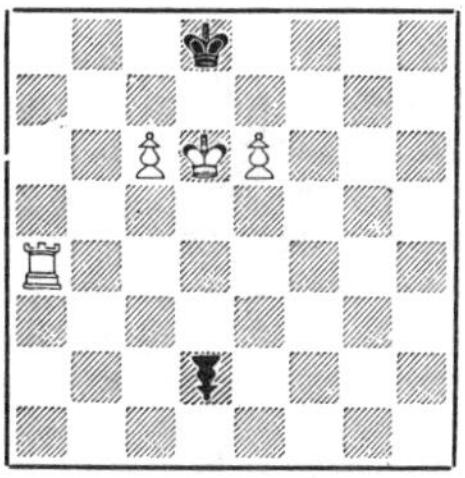

Sey chec wt þi pown in A (c7). yf he drawe byforn thi poun draw thi kyng þer thi poun stod & stale hym. þen make a fers of þi oþer poun & mate wt þe same. yf he draw at þe furst in to B (e8). draw þi roke into C (f4). then make a fers & stale hym. þen mate hym wt þe poun.

Port. 38 (Wh., Kh1, Rb1; Bl., Ka8. A on c2, B c3, C c4, D c5, E c6, F a1).

The whiȝt drauȝt furst but draw into A as fast þu may. þen into B C D E. þen mate wt thi rok in F.

Port. 39 (Wh., Kb6, Rh1; Bl., Ka8. A on a1, B a6, C c6, D a7, E d6, F e6, G f6, H f7, I h6, +h8).

Sey checke wt thi roke in A. þen wt thi roke go into B. þen wt þi kyng in C. þen wt þi R. in D. þen þi kyng in E F G H. þen þi R. ayen in B & þen mate wt þi roke in J. þer þe cros stand. he may be mate long erst but yf he defend the bettur.

Port. 40 (Wh., Ke3, Ra1, h8; Bl., Ke5. A on a6, B d5, C c8, D f5, E g8).

Draw þi roke in A. and yf he go in B draw þi oþer R. into C & mate wt þe same. yf he go furst into D set thi roke in E & mate next.

The Ashmole MS.

[Note.—The common material in Ash. and Port. is exhibited in the following table:

ASH.	PORT.	ASH.	PORT.	ASH.	PORT.	ASH.	PORT.
1–2	= 3–4	10	= 8	24	= 33	27–28	= 36–37
3–4	= 9–10	11–15	= 13–17	25	= 30	29	= 35
5–7	= 5–7	16–23	= 21–28	26	= 34	31	= 38

The remaining positions are: Ash. 9 = K 29; 30 = Cott. 1; 32 = Cott. 3; 33 = K 21; 39 = K 30; 41 = K 49.

In Ash. 2 the White Bishop on c1 is termed 'thy blak Aufyn'; i.e. c1 is a black square, or h1 is white.

Ash. 15 ends with the words, 'This is a faire Jupertie to mate a man in on of the iiij poyntis for it cumyth offt in play'. This sentence is really the title of the following problem (Ash. 16).

Ash. 19 ends, 'The drawghtis arn forgotten in the other Jupertie aboue (i.e. Ash. 16) therfor play the oon be the other'.

Ash. 26 adds the note on the variant position Ka8 on b8: 'And yf his kyng stode at the begynning from the corner, draw thy ffers that thou makist first but a poynte or els he ys not mated at xl draughtis. Ande yf he defende oute he shal neuer be mated etc.'

Ash. 27 adds the note: 'And if it be not couenant to mate hym in the corner thou shalte mate hym wt a pon yf thou play slylye so thou haue the fyrst draught'.]

Ash. 8 (Wh., Kh1, Ra7; Bl., Kh8. A on g2, B f3, C e4, D d5, E c6, F d6, G e6, H f6, I g6).

This is couuenant þt the White king shalbe draw first And his Roke shall never be drawen tyll he say chek mate with his Roke. Draw first thi kyng in A. Sithen in B. and then in C. and in D. then in E. in F. in G. in H. And then in I. And then chek mate with þi Roke. At ix draughtis as couuenant is at the begynnyng. And yf he defend it not welle it may be mated long afor.

Ash. 34.

The white men draw first ande shall mate the blake kyng at iij draughtis. Say chek wt thi Roke in the pon ward & he must nedis take it wt his knyght. Say thou est chek with thi Roke in the same poynte & he must nedis take it with his other knight and lese hym. Then say chek mated in thy pon warde. This is a faier Jupertie for thow leses thy booth Rokes or thou mate hym the blake kyng. (He overlooks 1 Re7 +; 2 Pf7 m.)

Ash. 35.

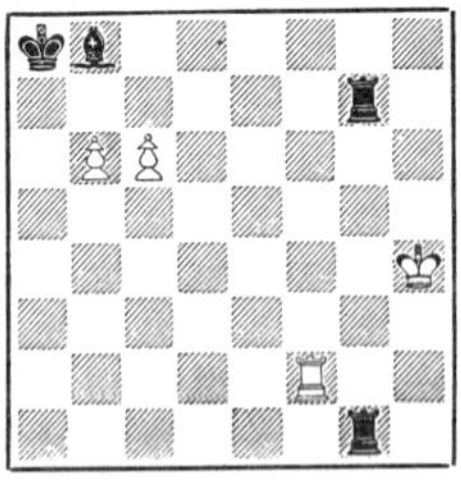

Say chek in A (a2) with thi white roke then he must nedis helde hym with his roke. Then chek mate wt thi pon for he maynot take thy pon with his roke for discouering. Neuerthelesse affter the first chek thow may mate hym ande take vpp his roke. But it is faier to mate hym with a pon.

Ash. 36.

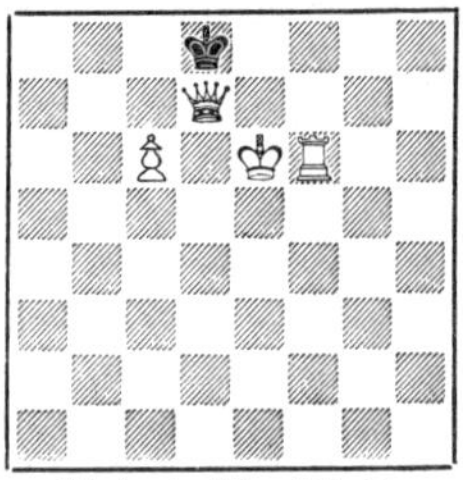

Mate in V with P.

Thow shalt mate hym with a Pon at v drawghtis yf thow play wel affter thy Roke & if thou knowe itt not thow shal not mate hym at ix draughtis ffor he woll tel his draughtis for cause of thi Roke. ffirst draw thi roke in to A (f1). Sithen in to B (b1) than in to C (b2). Than chek in thy pon warde that is in D (b7). & then chek mated wt thi pon in D (*read* E c7). Ande if ye be a great plaier & can well defende your game ye shall neuer mate hym at ix draughtis with thy roke for sothe &c.

Ash. 37.

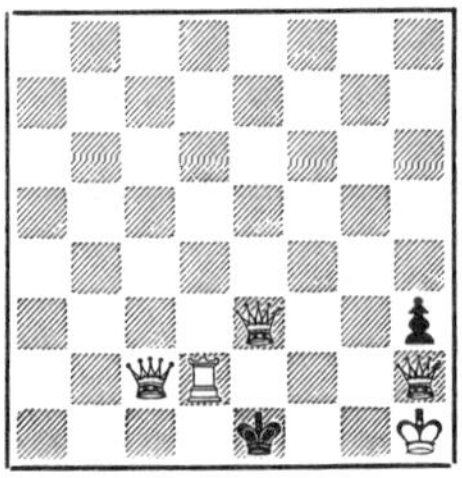

Self-mate.

A Jupertye to do a man mate the. Driue hym to this plyght for it is no maystre. Then shall he draw first. Say thou chek wt thy roke in thy ffers warde aboue. Att next draught after set thy rok in his pon ward. þen sett thi nether ffers fast by thy other fers ande stale hym. Then must he take vp thy Roke wt his Pon & say chek mate & thus shalt þu do a man mate the wheþer he will or nout. But be war' thou stale hym not tyll thy Roke be in his pon ward & þu must stale hym at next draught after thi Roke is set or els thou shuldest lese thy rok for nowght & therto neuer the more mate shulde ther be. Ande the most connyng of playe is gettyng' of odde draughtys.

Ash. 38 (same figure as the preceding: A on d1, B d4, C d3).

Dryue hym to this plight wt thi roke

& ij fers. Ande then if þe draught be hese draw thy fers in A. þen thi roke in B & siþen ther he stode first. Then thi ffers that standeth in A drawe hym ayene there he stode first. Then set thi roke in his Pon warde & if he take it / then art thou mate. Yf he take it not but draw his kyng þen say chek with thi fers. Then drawith he & is stale. Then draw thi fers in to A. & fayn a draught. Then must he nedys take up thy roke & say chek mate to thi kyng with hys Pon.

Ash. 39.

Black play; White mate in XI.

Thus shalt thou bryng in þi odde drawghtis in cas þu be a drawght be-hynde. He draw^{t} first. Draw þu thi knight an aufyns draught fro hym þ^{t} bryngeth þi ffers to thi king. Then draw thi kyng in A (c7). þen draw betwixt both kingis & yet draw thy knight in to B (a5). Then chek with thy knight. Then the next drawght after chek / set thi knyght in C (b4). then set thi fers in D (a6) in the knyghtis ward. Then chek with thi fers in D and at next draught mate w^{t} thi knyght. But this is a Jupertie that may neuer be mated out of thi medyll of the table yf it be well defended of connyng plaier.

(The text is a little obscure, but Wh. has to win a move; Bl. begins; 1 Kb8, Kb6; 2 Ka8, Kc7; 3 Ka7, Qc6; 4 Ka8, Qb5; 5 Ka7, Ktb7, followed by 6 Kta5; 7 Ktc6 +; 8 Ktb4; 9 Qa6; 10 Qb7 +; and 11 Ktc6 m. as in the text.)

Ash. 40 (Wh., Kh6, Rb7; Bl., Kh8. A on a7, B e8, C f7, D f6, E f5, F g8, G g6).

He that hath the white men shall mate the blak king upon a couenant that the roke shal neuer be drawen til he say chek mate. Thou þ^{t} hast the white men draw thy kyng as fast as thow may in to A. & forth in to the lyne ther his kyng goth yn. & forth affter tyll thow art in B. than draw in to C. Then chek discouer in D. Ande if he draw afor thi kyng then chek mate at bord. When þu art in C. and seiest chek discouert yf he go in to the pointe next the corner draw in to oon of the iiij poyntis & then draw tyll his king com before hym than mate a Bord.

The problems of the early collection from which the four Anglo-Norman MSS. are derived are distinguished from those of the later compilations by certain broad characteristics which may be summed up thus. Unusual prominence is attached to the Exercise (the Ar. *mikhrāq*) in which the powers of a single piece are explored. In none of the later MSS. is there so large a proportion of positions of this type. The problems are generally of a very elementary and simple type; those of European composition are more primitive in type than most of the Muslim *manṣūbāt.* The wager-game is almost entirely absent; its only representative is K 48, *Fol si sey fie.* The workmanship is of an early stage of European chess, but it is European, not Muslim. It lays little account by possibility. In Cott. 13, 15, 20, K 16 (2), 25, 33, 42, 55 Bishops are placed upon squares that they could not occupy in a game. It disregards the possibility of *Bare King*, not necessarily because it was no longer of force—K 50 and 51 are examples of wins by *Bare King*—but because the aim of the problem was to give practice in mating combinations.

The MS. Dresden 0/59 (= D), like Arch., contains a collection of problems as a supplement to the work of Cessolis, in this case in the French translation of Jehan de Vignay. The MS.[28] is a folio of 78 leaves written in a hand of the end of the 14th or beginning of the 15th c., with initials in blue and red. The *Moralités du gieu des ésches par Jehan de Vignay* occupies ff. 1–61 a, and is followed by a collection of 69 chess diagrams, of which the first occupies the lower half of f. 61 a and the remainder follow, two to the page, until the foot of f. 78 a. The first two diagrams are diagrams of initial arrangements (see p. 476), and are unnumbered, but the third and following diagrams are numbered 1–67. The boards are chequered yellow and white, h1 being white in 46 and yellow in 23 diagrams. The names of the pieces were first written at the foot of the squares occupied, and generally the names of the pieces playing from the top of the board are inverted. Subsequently the illuminator of the MS. inserted pictorial representations of the pieces, coloured red and black for the *blans* and *jaune* of the text respectively, in some cases so carelessly that they occupy other squares than the ones intended. It is clear that he did not trouble to study the positions critically. It is also doubtful whether the scribe who copied the text knew much about chess, for in the text of D 11 he has written *Sierche* for *Fierche*, while in copying D 66 from a French *Bonus Socius* MS. he has misread the 'le roc a *treues* (roccus est affidatus) du roy noir' of his original, and has reproduced it as the meaningless 'le Roc a iij du Roy noir'. The MS. is in an East-central French dialect.

If we except the three positions D 65–67, which have been obtained from a French text of the *Bonus Socius* work, the text which accompanies the diagrams only gives the conditions of the problems and not the solutions. In a few cases the diagram is placed at right angles to the usual arrangement of the MSS. I have found occasional diagrams oriented thus in all the larger European MSS., and believe that they go back to an earlier MS. in which this arrangement was the rule.

The diagram of D 64 is not completed, and it is impossible to identify the problem intended from the text; the text of D 38 and the first part of that of D 60 do not belong to these positions, but merely reproduce the text of D 39 and 59 respectively.

Excluding D 64–67, we may classify the remaining 63 positions thus: 10 (of which 4 are Muslim) are Exercises; 1 (D 38) is, I think, a self-mate; 26 (of which 8 are Muslim) are ordinary mates; 17 (of which 3 are Muslim) are conditional mates, 2 being mates in the 'four points'; 4 (of which 1 is Muslim) are positions which can be won by 'Bare King'; and 5 (of which 1 is Muslim) are End-game positions, 3 being concerned with Kings and Pawns only.

[28] From the Catalogue of the Dresden Library we learn that the present volume is only the opening portion of a MS. which originally contained over 200 leaves, that it belonged formerly to the Counts De la Marche and Dukes de Nemours, that it has belonged to Anne Henrietta, Duchess de Condé (D. 1723), and Count Brühl (who bought it in 1737). Cf. also R. Wuttke, *Aus Schachhandschriften der kgl. Bibl. zu Dresden*, in *Dresdner Schachbl.*, 1893, No. 2; W. Benary, *Zur Kritik der Schachquellen im Mittelalter*, in *Wochenschach*, 1908, 389, 397, 405, 425. I have used a photographic reproduction of the MS., for which I am indebted to the kindness of Mr. J. G. White.

Four positions show Bishops on impossible squares, viz. D 8, 24, 33, 67. There are several duplicates; thus D 5 = 6; 9 = 26 = 47; 15 = 42; 17 = 63; 18 = 45; 19 = 20 (text wrong) = 40; 22 = 23; 41 = 59; 51 = 60. One of the most remarkable features of the MS. is the number of problems in which a player is allowed to stale his opponent and yet continue playing, Examples are D 15, 24, 42, 50, 53, 55: in the case of the last two, the condition would appear to be unnecessary.

The problems follow:

[NOTE.—The remaining problems in D will be found thus. D 1 = CB 53 (all one to right, the illuminator has forgotten Re6); 2 = CB 52; 4 = CB 236 (Kts on c4, c6, e4, e6); 5 = CB 185; 7 = CB 258 (Wh. Kd3, Pb3, d4, f3, h3; Bl. Kd5; Le roy blanc auesques les iiij paonnes qui se puent faire fierches doiuent mater le roy jaune et il se doit deffendre se il puet); 11 = CB 233; 12 = CB 161 (Qh8 on d8; Rb3 on b4); 13 = CB 230 (Ph5 on h7); 14 = CB 243; 18 = CB 136; 21 = CB 162; 25 = CB 1 (Wh. Kf4, Rh7, Ktf5, e6; Bl. Ke8, Ktd7, c8); 27 = CB 273 (Wh. Kh2; Bl. Ka6, Bc8 immovable); 28 = CB 250 (reflected, B on h6; Bl. play); 29 = CB 257 (diagram half-turned to the right); 31 = CB 251 (Ka8 on d8, Kc6 on e6, Bc5 on d6; mate in XXXIII or less); 32 = CB 105 (Wh. Rb5, d7, Ktb7, d5; Bl. Kc6, Pc5—? to avoid 'Bare King'); 35 Wh. Pd1, d2; Bl. Pe7, e8; Les paons blans vont contre les jaunes mes le plus soubtil joueur vaincra); 36 = CB 280; 37 = CB 198 (Ks on d6 and a8 and diagram inverted); 46 = K5 (Kd5; Pawns on 7th and 8th rows); 48 = CB 216 (fidated Qs—in diagram Ks—for Bs on a1, a8; Pb6, c6 for Qc6; Ktd5 on f5; diagram inverted); 50 = CB 225 (Kf6 on h6, omit Qg8, reflect); 51 = CB 148 (Wh. Kb8, Ra8, Ktb5, Ba6, Pb3, c3; Bl. Ka1, Rf6, g6;—the illuminator has put the Wh. B, Kt, and Ps on a7, b6, b4, c4); 52 = CB 219 (Wh. Kb3, Rb2, d2, Bh3; Bl. Ka1, Bc1); 54 = CB 189 (reflected); 57 (Kta4, 15 Ps on the other squares of the square a1–d1–d4–a4. Le cheualier doit leuer de son droit trait tous les paounes l'un apres l'autre; which is impossible in 15 moves, cf. p. 335); 58 = CB 207 (Wh. Kd3, Rc2; Bl. Kd1); 59 = CB 255 (Wh. Kd6, Rd4, Pa6, h6; Bl. Kd8, Pa7, h7); 60 = CB 148 (Wh. Ka8, Rh1, Ktg4, Bh3, Pf6, g6; Bl. Kh8, Rc4, f2; mate in IV); 61 = CB 277 (transfer to corner a1; the illuminator has put the Wh. Kd2 on d3 in error); 62 is the Knight's tour over the half board without solution; 65 = CB 6 (Kd3 on c3, Pd2 on c2, omit Bd4, 'a' on d2; none of the Wh. pieces are drawn); 66 = CB 9; 67 = CB 8.]

D 3. Wh. Ke6, Pd6, f6; Bl. Kd8. (Cf. CB 140; Cott. 7.) Les blans doiuent mater les jaunes qui se deffendront se il puent. Et le blanc ne pert pas se le jaune est enclos. Et les blans traient les premiers.

D 6: Ar. 19.

Les blans doiuent mater le roy jaune à vi trais. Et si traient les blans trois trais auant qui ne sont comptés que pour vn. (The Wh. K should be on b3.)

D 8.

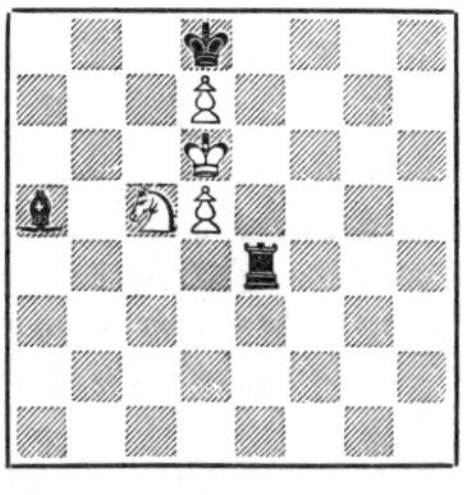

Les blans doiuent mater le roy jaune à iij trais du paounet qui est desriere le roy et si traient li blanc premier. (Cf. CB 64. The D position is solved 1 Kte6+; 2 P×R; 3 Pe7 m.)

D 9.

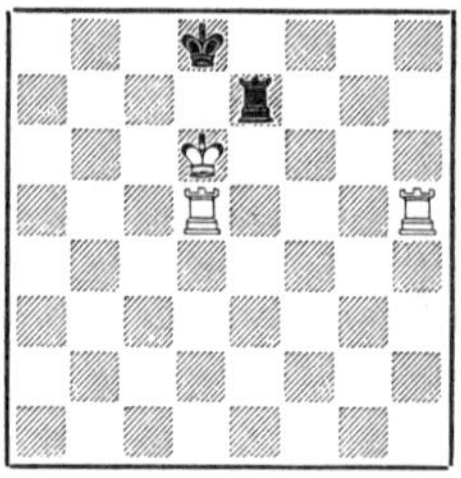

Les blans doiuent mater le roy jaune à iij trais et si traient auant. (3) 1 Rh8 +; 2 Rb5, &c. The idea is CB 58. There are two other settings in D, viz. D 26 (Wh. Kf6, Ra7, f5; Bl. Kf8, Re1), D 47 (Wh. Kb6, Rb1, h1; Bl. Kb8, Rc7).

D 10.

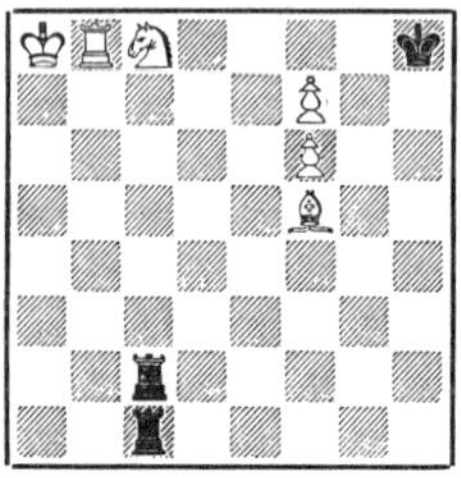

Les blans doiuent mater le roy jaune à ij trais et si traient auant. (1 Kte7 + d; 2 Ktg6 m. solves it.)

D 15. Wh. Kh1, Ra7, Kta6; Bl. Kc8. (Cf. CB 222; K 29). Le blanc doit mater le roy jaune à xvi trais ou à mains. Et le roy (*read* roc) blanc ne se doit mouuoir tant que il die mat. Et le roy jaune le tient enclos i. trait. Le roy (roc) blanc ne se muet et le blanc trait auant. [White can stale the K for one move and then mate him. K 29 is only to stale; CB 222 avoids the stale by adding a Bl. Kt. D 42 (Wh. Ra7, Kta8; Bl. Kc6) is really the same. Les blans doiuent mater le roy jaune et s'il peut il se deffendra et peut faire un trait clos.]

D 16: Ar. 35.

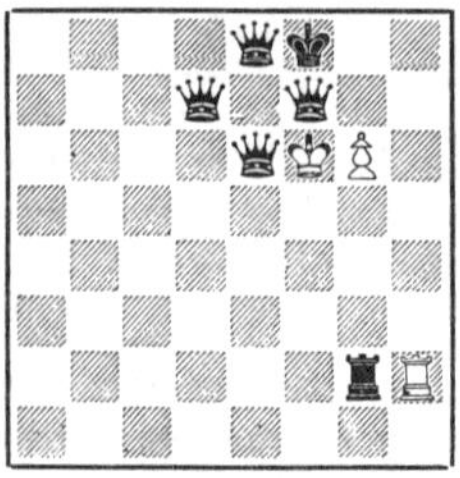

Les blans doiuent mater le jaunes ou faire communal (i.e. draw) et si doiuent traire auant. (An inaccurate rendering of a Muslim ending. 1 Rh8 +; 2 Rh2 and plays opposite the R continually. Cf. Cas. 55.)

D 17.

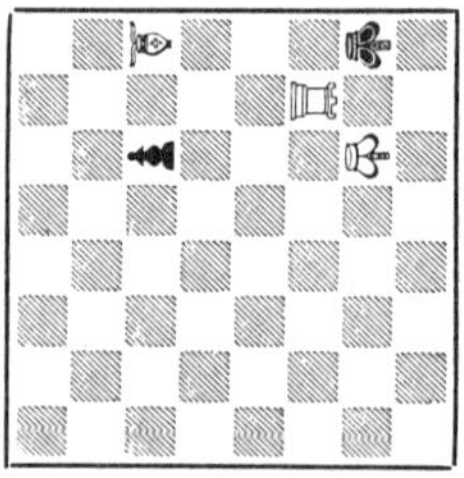

Les blans doiuent mater les jaunes à vj trais de l'auphin et si traient auant et le paon doit aler deuers les roseites (i.e. to a6). (1 Bf6 +; 2 Rg7 and the position is CB 112, mate in IV. D 63—Wh. Kf2, Rb3, Bh6; Bl. Kh2, Pf7—is another setting in V.)

D 19.

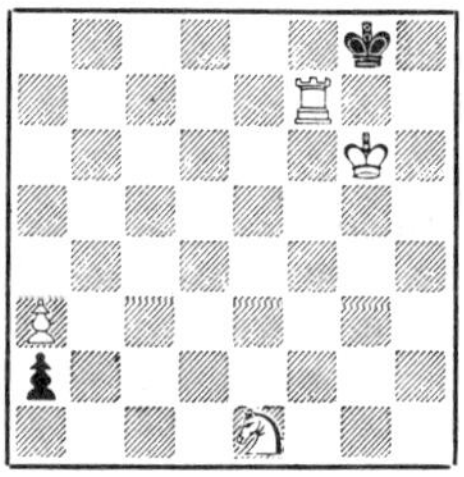

Les blans doiuent mater les jaunes v v (*sic*) point de l'angle deuers les ij paounes à xxv trais ou à mains et si traient auant et le paounet jeune est affié. [An extended version of CB 208. D 20 (Pa3 on a4) is the diagram of a variation, BS 173. That these variations were diagrammed separately is clear from S 1 and 191. D 40 (Wh. Kf6, Rb8, Ktb5, Pa3 (drawn on a4 in error); Bl. Kg8, Pa2) in XIV is the same.]

D 22.

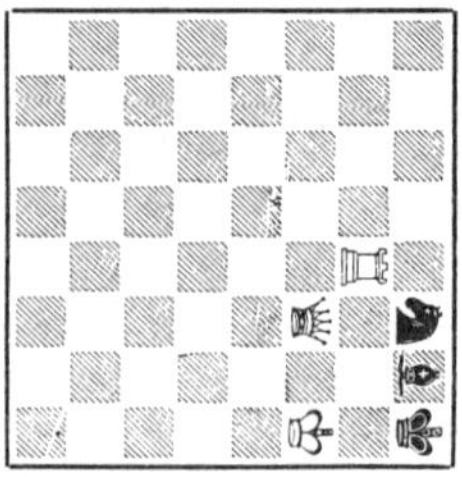

Les blans doiuent mater le roy jaune à ij trais n'à plus n'à mains. Et tous sont affiéz sans prendre et li blanc traient auant. [An earlier setting of CB 9, 10, 12. Cf. Arch. 14. D 23 (Wh. Ke8, Rg6, Qf6; Bl. Kh8, Bh7, Kth6) is another setting.]

D 24 = CB 212 (omitting the Bf1 which is added there to prevent the stale). Les blancs doiuent mater le roy jaune à xv trais ou à mains et si le tient bien enclos et le paonnet jaune est affié.

D 26, see D 9 above.

D 30.

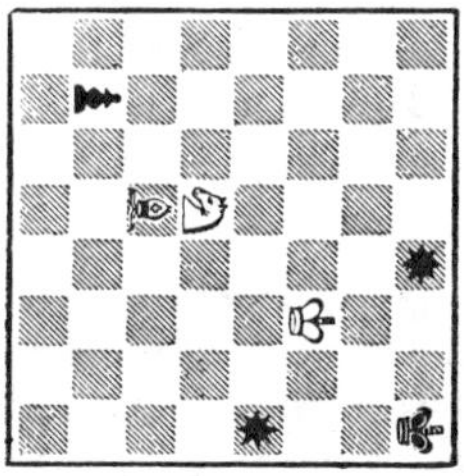

Les blans doiuent mater le roy jaune et se il passe les deulz roseites il la perdu et sans enclorre et blans traient premiers. (1 Be3, Kh2; 2 Ktf4; 3 Kg3; 4 Kth3; 5 Ktf2 m., or 1 . . , Pa7 = Q; 2 Kg3; 3 Ktf4; 4 Kth3; 5 Ktf2 m. If the Q can leap, the second line of play fails for 4 . . , Q × B is possible. Either the Q could not leap when this problem was composed or we must put the P on c7. I see no point in the rosettes.)

D 33.

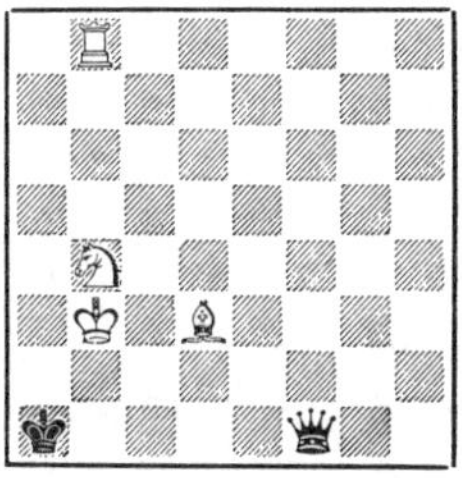

White mates in VI. (Probably intended for a mate in the four points, cf. CB 149, but if so the diagram in which Kb3, Ktb4, and Bd3 are drawn on b4, b5, d4 respectively, is in need of correction.)

D 34.

White mates in V. (1 Pg7 +; 2 Pg6 +; 3 Kf6; 4 Rg1; 5 Rh1 m. Cf. Alf. 88 and 96; D 56 below; CB (F) 331; S 11; WA 7; WD 157. The group b1, b2, c1 should be one line to the left.)

D 38.

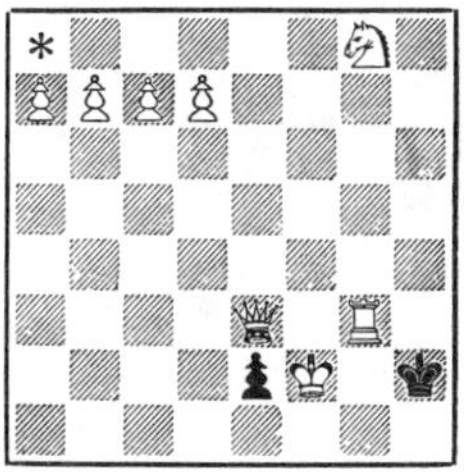

(The MS. repeats the text of D 39. I think the position is intended for the self-mate CB 235.)

D 39 (corr.).

Mate in VI on d4. [Cf. K 20, CB 149, &c. D 49 (Wh. Kb6, Rc5, Ktd5, Bd3; Bl. Ka8; * on e5). Mate in VI, 'v millieu de l'eschequier là ou la roseite est,' is a similar problem.]

D 40, see D 19.

D 41.

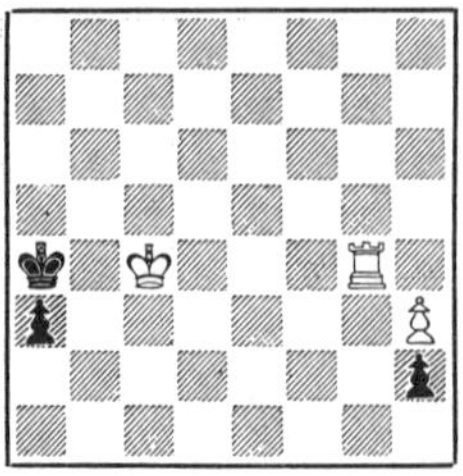

Les blancs doiuent mater les jaunes a xxx trais du paounet blanc et le paounet jaune qui est apres le blanc si est affié et les jaunes traient auant. (Kc4, Rg4 are drawn on c5 and g5 in error. A similar problem to D 59, CB 255.)

D. 42, see D 15.

D 43 (corr.).

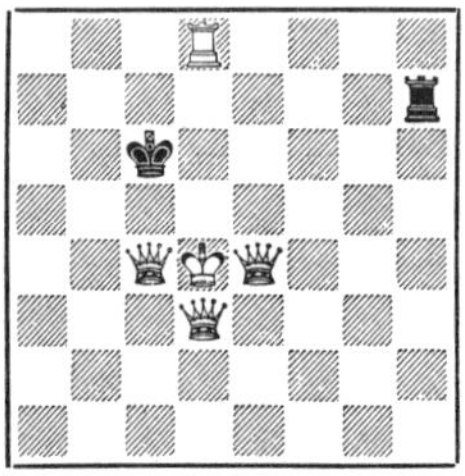

(The MS. has Wh. Kd6, Qb5, d5, d7, Rh5; Bl. Kf5, Rg1.)

Les blans doiuent mater le roy jaune sanz encloire et il se doit deffendre et si traient auant. (Bl. plays. 1 . . , Rd7 +; 2 Qd5 +; 3 R~, R opp. R; 4 R × R, stalemate. So C 112. CB 254 is an improved version.)

D 44. Wh. Kc7, Pg3; Bl. Kg4, Qa8. Qui premier est seul il la perdu. Et se le paounet se fait fierche et fait vn trait, il la gaaignie. (Wh. plays. 1 Pg2, Kg3; 2 Pg1 = Q, Kg2; 3 Qe3, and gets over to the Wh. K, which is then able to win the Bl. Q. Cf. Ar. 39.)

D 45, see D 18; D 47, see D 9.

D 49, see D 39.

D 53 = CB 256 (omitting Ph6).

Les blans doiuent mater les jaunes en vn des poins ou les roseites sont (i.e. a8, b8) et se le roy jaune hist hors de l'un des deulz poins il la gaaigne le blanc ne pert pas sil tient enclos li jaune. Les jaunes traient auant & s'il le doit mater ou faire seul à vj trais. (Another position in which stalemate is ignored. CB as usual prevents the stalemate.)

D 55 = CB 113 (Wh. Kc3, Rb8, Ktd4, Qc2, Pc4; Bl. Kc1, Ra1; in the MS. the Wh. K, Q, and P are in error drawn on c4, c3, c5 respectively). Mate in IV with Pc4, le roy jaune se puet bien tenir enclos. (CB 113, by the addition of a Pawn, obviates the stalemate.)

D 56.

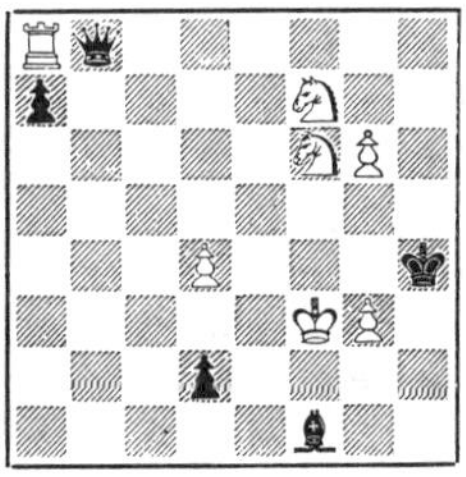

(In the MS. the Wh. Kts in error are drawn on f7, f8.)

Les blans doiuent mater les jaunes à iij trais du roc & ceulz aus roseites (i.e. Bf1, Pd4, Pa7) sont affiés et les blans traient auant. (1 Pg5 +; 2 Pd3; 3 Rh8 m. Cf. D 34, above.)

D 63, see D 17.

D 64. Diagram blank except for Bl. Kb8. Les blans doiuent mater les jaunes à v trais sans enclorre v point ou la Rosete est et les blans traient auant.

We may identify some 25 positions in D as occurring in one or other of the MSS. of the Anglo-Norman group. All but one of these occur also in the *Civis Bononiae* collection. Since both the Anglo-Norman group and D contain a number of positions which are not repeated in the encyclopaedic *Civis Bononiae* work, it follows that the compiler of the last-named has used neither of these earlier collections. I conclude that the material common to the three collections must have been included in other MSS., now lost, which lie behind the *Civis Bononiae* text; that is, that they form part of the common stock of European problems of the earlier period. The only position which is peculiar to the Anglo-Norman group and D is D 46 (Cott. 6, K 5, Port. 5). This is strictly not a problem at all, but a diagram of a derivative form of chess. The greater collections limit themselves to problems and exercises, and their omission of this game accordingly carries little or no weight. I do not think that the evidence is sufficient to assign D to the Anglo-Norman group of problem MSS.

The general style of problem in D strikes me as being more artificial than that of the Anglo-Norman MSS., and as belonging to a lower level of skill. The wager-game is still scarcely represented (though the mate in *n* moves exactly appears), and the problems remain for the most part exercises for the practical game. The disregard, however, of stalemate is a retrograde step which robs the exercise of much of its value for the ordinary game. It points to a generation of players who were removed from the Muslim tradition which was on the whole characteristic of French and English chess.

The MS. is obviously a copy of an earlier work, which from the absence of solutions may have been nothing more than a rough note-book, intended to be the basis of a MS. with solutions complete. Its unfinished character is exhibited in the concluding problems. The transcriber had obtained access to a *Bonus Socius* MS. and had begun to make extracts. After copying two problems with text complete and the diagram of a third, he was interrupted, and the MS. was never completed.

APPENDIX

MERELS AND ALLIED GAMES

The mediaeval board-games of Western Europe included, in addition to chess and tables, a number of games which were known by the name of merels, L. *marelli* ('coins', 'counters' or 'tokens': a diminutive from L. *marrus*), or *ludus marellorum*. In Alf. these games are called *alquerque*, a term adopted from the Arabic, in which *al-qirq* was formerly used in the same sense. Two instances have been quoted already (p. 189, n. 10, and p. 194). The modern Arabic name is *drīs* (Dozy), a Persian term which is apparently often confused with *Edris*, the Ar. name of the patriarch Enoch (Culin, *C. & P. C.*, 857). The word *qirq* is neither Arabic nor Persian, and its origin is not known: it might be simply the L. *circus*, but this word is not known as the name of a board-game.

In modern usage the term *merels* (or 'mill', which has replaced the older term in Germany, Iceland, Italy, and elsewhere) is restricted to those games in which the player's aim is to place three men upon adjacent points of the board in such a way that they form an uninterrupted straight line. The different types of board used would all seem to be based upon the 'guarded cross'; all are of great antiquity, and their diagrams have been found incised on articles from European lake-dwellings and from the oldest strata of ruins on the site of Troy (Parker, *Anc. Ceylon*, 579); they are still used as charms against evil influences in Ceylon (ibid.), and the Arabs of Central Arabia trace the simplest type in the hearth-ashes when making a solemn asseveration (Doughty, *Arabia Deserta*, 1888, i. 267). In the Middle Ages, as may be seen from Alf., other games were included under the name of merels. These games fall into three types, (1) games of the modern merels type, (2) games resembling draughts, (3) games of the fox-and-geese type.

I

A. *Nine Holes.*

Two players have three men apiece, and, playing alternately, they place a man at a time upon any vacant point of the board, with the aim of posting the three in a straight line. When all are placed on the board, a man can be moved to any vacant point.

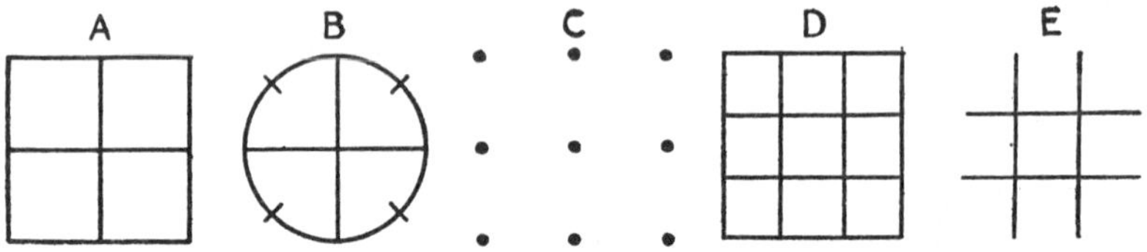

Boards for Nine Holes

In diagrams D and E, the points of the other diagrams are replaced by squares.

Played in England (boards A and C as *Nine Holes*, E as *Noughts and Crosses*: in this last case no movement is possible); Germany (A, *kleines Mühlenspiel*, formerly, according to Hyde, *nulochen*); Holland (C); Sweden (A, D, *liten qvarn*; E, *Tripp, trapp, trull*); by the Arabs (D, *drīs ath-thalātha*); in Japan (A, *San-noku-narabe*); and by the Ainus (A, *Chikkiri*).

Formerly played in Egypt (A is inscribed on the roof slabs of the temple at Kūrna, 14th c. B.C.; a board, D, from Ptolemaic times is in the British Museum (B.M., 14315)).

B. *Three men's morris* (the smaller merels).

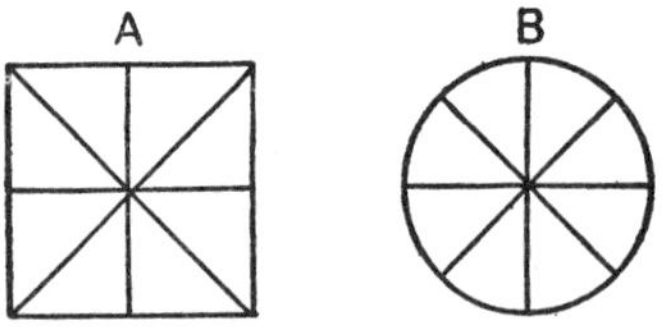

Boards for the Smaller Merels

The same game, but after all the men are placed on the board, a man can only be moved along a marked line to the adjoining point.

Played in England (board A); Spain (A, Castilian, *tres en raya, alquerque*; Catalan, *marro*; the *alquerque de tres* of Alf.); France (A, *merelles*); Italy (A, *mulinello semplice*); Philippines (A, *tapatan*); China (A, *luk tsut k'i*); North American Indians (A, from Spanish settlers). Apparently not played in Germany or the Scandinavian lands.

Formerly played in Ceylon (A), Egypt (A, B are both on the temple roof at Kūrna). Very large diagrams of B occur frequently on the Forum pavement at Rome and Pompeii: their purpose is unknown.

C. *Five (six) men's morris.*

Said to have been played on a board of three similar triangles, one within the other and united by lines joining the corresponding angular points (*Notes and Queries*, 8th Ser., xii. 333), but I know of no certain evidence that this was so.

D. *Nine men's morris* (the larger merels).

Each player has nine men. As often as a player secures three men in a straight line he removes an opponent's man. The game is won when the player is left with only two men, or when he is blocked so that he cannot move. Men move along any marked line to an adjoining vacant point.

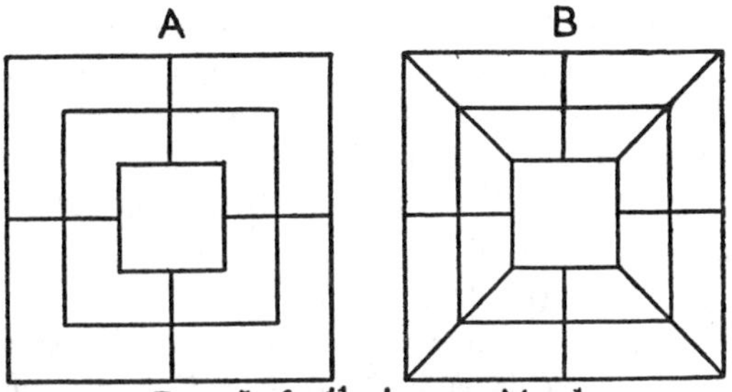

Boards for the Larger Merels

This (board A) is the game of the problem MSS. It was also played by the help of dice in the Middle Ages (Alf., *Vetula*). The board was also completed by the insertion of the diagonals, and the number of men increased to eleven or twelve, for *Eleven* (*Twelve*) *men's morris*.

Played in England (A, nine men; B, eleven or twelve men); United States (B, twelve men); France; Germany; Holland; Scandinavia (A, B, with nine men); Iceland (A, *mylna*); Russia (*melniza*); Italy; Hungary; by the Arabs (A, B, with nine men, *drīs at-tis'a*); in Ceylon (A, *nerenchi*); in Assam, China (B, *sam k'i*); in Corea (B, *kontjil*); and by the N. American Indians (A, B, with nine men, from Spanish settlers).

Formerly played in Egypt (Kūrna); Spain (Alf., *alquerque de nueve*). A fragment of a board from Viking days was found in the Gokstad Ship, and others are cut on the steps of the Acropolis, Athens (*Notes and Queries*, 8th Ser., xii. 173).

II

E. *Alquerque de doze.*

Each player has twelve men, which are arranged for play as shown in the diagram. A man can move along any line to the adjoining vacant point, and captures an opponent by leaping over it into the vacant square beyond it, in the same straight line—the method employed in draughts. Any number of men can be captured in one move (Alf.), and a man which does not capture when it can do so is huffed (Covarruvias, *Tesoro de la lengua castellana*, Madrid, 1611).

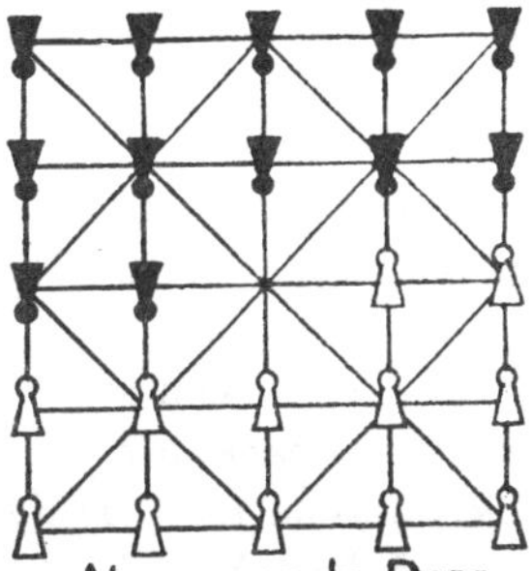
Alquerque de Doze

The game is played in Spain (Castilian *castro* or *alquerque*, Catalan *marro*); in Italy (*marelle*); by the North American Indians in Arizona and New Mexico, who learnt it from the Spaniards.

It was formerly played in France (*Vetula*) as *mereles qui se fait par douze mereles*; and in England (there is a diagram in MS. Trinity College, Cambridge, O. 2 45; and an inscribed board in the cloisters at Norwich Cathedral).

F. *Draughts.*

This game on the chessboard was formerly called *marro de punto* in Catalan and Castilian (Torquemada, 1547, 'El . . . juego de marro de punto o damas'; Montero, 1590, 'Del juego de las damas, volgarmente el marro'; Valls, 1597, 'Del juego de las damas, por otro nombre el marro de pvnta'), and *marella* in Sicily (Carrera, 1617, 35). We may therefore properly include it in the present group of games.[1] The name of *Damas* (L. *ludus dominarum* in MS. Per.), Fr. *dames*, It. *dama*, which took its place, is obviously due to the fact that the ordinary move of the draughtsman in the Western European game was identical with that of the mediaeval Queen in chess, who, as we have already seen, was so frequently called *domina* (dama, dame, donna, &c.) in the 14th and following centuries. There are only two certain references to the game before the 16th c., both occurring in English versions of French romances (*c.* 1380, *Sir Ferumbras*, 2225: 'Summe of hem to iew-de-dame; and summe to tablere'; *c.* 1400, *Destr. Troy*, 1622: 'The draghtes, the dyse, and other dregh (i.e. tedious) gaumes'). In neither case has the French original any mention of draughts. This does not point to any wide popularity of draughts at the time, and it is probable that the game sprang suddenly into favour in the sixteenth century. There was, however, a game in France in the 13th and 14th cc., called *fierges*, i.e. ferses, in which a player might have a King. Thus Philippe Mouskes, praising Philip Augustus of France, says (*Chronique*, 23617–21):

> Cis n'estoit mie rois de gas[2],
> Ne rois de fierges, ne d'escas,
> Ains iert a droit fins rois entirs,
> Rubins, esmeraude, et safirs.

It seems probable that it is of this game that the Arabic writer Abū'l-Faḍl Ja'far b. Shāraf wrote an account. In a list of this writer's works in b. Diḥya's *K. al-muṭrib min ash'ār ahl al maghrib* (quoted, *Qst.*, 411, from a Brit. Mus. MS. of 1251 A.D.) we read: 'His work on games, with the game named *Farīsīa* (which means the player's Queen), wherewith one plays as with chess, which work belongs to the most remarkable productions of that period.' *If* this game were identical with draughts, it would clear up a puzzling line in Chaucer's *Book of the Duchess*, 723, 'Thogh ye had lost the ferses twelve,' which cannot be explained satisfactorily from chess.

There are two theories as to the origin of draughts. The one, proposed by v.d. Linde and strongly supported by Fiske, is that the game is a simplified chess; the other, suggested by Brunet y Bellet and others and developed by Mr. W. S. Branch in a series of articles in the *Pittsburg Leader*, 1911–12, is that the game is a result of the transference of Alfonso's *alquerque de doze* to the chessboard. There are difficulties in either case, and it may be that the truth lies in a combination of the two theories. The board and the idea of promotion seem due to chess, the method of capture, the multiple capture, and the huff, to alquerque. It is important to note that the arrangement and method of move of the older Western European game are different from those of the Turkish (and older German) game, though the Muslim name of the game, *dāma*, is obviously borrowed from the Southern European name.

III

G. *De cercar la liebre* (? mod. *juego de la liebre*).

Twelve (eleven or ten) men arranged from one end of the alquerque de doze board endeavour to hem in a solitary piece (the hare). The men move as in alquerque

[1] Hollybrand, *Treas. Fr. Tong.*, 1580, has 'Le jeu des merelles, the playe of dammes'.
[2] *Gas* occurs repeatedly in connexion with *esches* and *mine* in OF. works as the name of a game. Nothing is known as to its nature.

de doze, and the hare alone has the power to take. This is the game in Alf.; it is still played by North American Indians, who have been taught it by the Spaniards. Some Indian tribes omit the diagonal lines in part or in entirety, while others give the board a circular outline.

A similar game on the same board has been played in the Far East, e.g. in Japan (the older *Juroku musashi*), in Assam (T. C. Hodson, *The Nāga Tribes of Manipur*, London, 1911, 62–3), in Siam (*Sua ghin gnua*), and in Burma (*Lay gwet kyah*). Both the last-named games omit the diagonal lines of the board. The Indian and Malay 'Tiger game' seems to be a development of this simpler game.

In Europe and Samoa, Fox and Geese is now often played on the chessboard between four Geese, with the move of the ordinary draughtsman, and a Fox who moves as the English draughts King.

H. *Fox and Geese.*

The older European game was played with a Fox and thirteen Geese upon a board composed of five smaller merels boards put together to form a cross (the 'solitaire' board). The older game survives in Iceland (where it is called *Refskák*, 'fox-chess'), Hawaii, and among the North American Indians. In Europe, the number of Geese has been increased, first to fifteen, and then to seventeen, and with this number of Geese the game is played in France, Germany, England, and the United States. Edward IV (*Accts. Roy. Household*, 1461–83, in V. B. Redstone, *England during the Wars of the Roses*, Trans. R. Hist. Soc., 1902, 195) purchased 'two foxis and 46 hounds of silver overgilt' to form two sets of 'marelles'. In the sixteenth and seventeenth century, more elaborate boards were employed. Randle Holme speaks of double and triple Fox and Geese, with more men and larger boards.

For further information as to these games the reader is referred to Hyde (ii. 337–52 and 357–65), and especially to Fiske, *Chess in Iceland*, 1905 (97–156).

CHAPTER VII

THE MEDIAEVAL PROBLEM. II

The great collections.—The MSS. of the *Bonus Socius* work classified.—The authorship and date of the work.—Contents.—Additional material in the MSS. of the Picard group.—The MSS. of the *Civis Bononiae* work.—Authorship and date.—Classification of the MSS.—General remarks on the mediaeval problem.—Contents of the *Civis Bononiae* work.—Additional material from single MSS.

We have now arrived at the fourth stage in the history of the European problem MSS., in which the attempt was made to reduce the existing material to order. The method of classification adopted was based upon the number of moves in which the solution of the problem was to be accomplished,[1] a purely mechanical method, which allows the same idea to appear in many different settings.

Two great Latin works on these lines were compiled in Lombardy in the mediaeval period, which are generally known as *Bonus Socius* and *Civis Bononiae*, from the pseudonyms adopted by the compilers in the most important MSS. of the two collections. These works became the favourite mediaeval collections of problems, and were repeatedly copied or translated, the *Bonus Socius* work being current chiefly in France, and the *Civis Bononiae* work in Italy. Both works aimed at being encyclopaedic, and contain *partita*, not only of chess, but also of tables and merels, the other popular board-games of the Middle Ages.[2]

The two collections cover very much the same ground, and often for pages together the same positions follow in the same order in both works. The text of the solutions, however, is different in the two works, except in the section on tables, where the earlier portion of the *Civis Bononiae* text is identical with that of the majority of the *Bonus Socius* MSS. Generally speaking, the text is in each work on uniform lines, and each compiler has been at pains to remove any trace of the source from which he obtained the problems. Apparently, the diagrams of the positions, with all the explanatory letters and symbols by means of which the description of the moves of the solution was simplified, were copied from the older MSS., and the solutions were then written anew by each compiler. In this way the chess name *ferz*, *fercia*, which

[1] This method of classification has been the general principle of arrangement adopted in all European collections right down to the present time.

[2] As noted above (p. 581), the MS. K also contains a treatise on the game of tables, which concludes with some problems (here called *jupertiae*); but this treatise is not so closely connected with the chess work as are the sections on tables and merels in the great collections.

is alone used on the diagrams, is in each work in the text of the solutions replaced by the more literary term *regina*.[3] The only clear evidence of the use of different sources is supplied by the diagrams. While the great majority are oriented in the way universally followed in modern text-books, a small number in each work are at right angles to the ordinary arrangement. These[4] must have been derived from a MS. in which the positions were drawn on the supposition that the players were seated to the right and left of the board. The Persian MS. RAS and the Spanish MS. Alf. are examples of this type of MS., but neither can have been the source used by the compilers of *Bonus Socius* and *Civis Bononiae*.

The number of scholars who have up to the present time attempted a critical study of the chess contents of the two great collections is very small, but all are agreed in regarding the *Bonus Socius* work as the older. The majority of the existing MSS. of this work are earlier in date than any *Civis Bononiae* MS., and they are drawn from a wider extent of Europe. In each section the *Bonus Socius* work is the less extensive. Thus *Bonus Socius* contains 194 problems of chess, from 34 to 48 of tables, and 24 of merels; *Civis Bononiae*, 288 of chess, from 76 to 80 of tables, and 48 of merels. That neither work is a selection from a larger work is evident from the introductions. Each professes to give the whole of the problem-material known to its compiler.

These considerations apart, it is difficult to draw any conclusions from the language of the solutions in the two works or from the diagrams. V. d. Lasa has pointed out that the *Bonus Socius* text is often less clear than that in *Civis Bononiae*, and, on the whole, the style strikes me as being older. In one or two cases (e.g. CB 100 = BS 75) *Civis Bononiae* preserves an older arrangement of the position than *Bonus Socius*, but these cases are too few to justify any conclusion.

The most important MS. of the *Bonus Socius* group is that in the National Library, Florence (MS. Nat. Lib. Florence, Banco dei Rari, B. A. 6, p. 2, No. 1, to which I refer as BS). This is a beautifully executed parchment late 13th c. Latin MS., which contains 1–119 quarto leaves (1*, blank; 1*b, a much faded miniature representing a King and a Moor seated at a blank chessboard, chequered gold and black (a1 black), with two ladies looking on; 1 a, introduction or preface; 1 b–99 a, 194 problems of chess, two diagrams on each recto except 98 a and 99 a, with the solutions on the verso facing; 99 b–112 a, twenty-four problems of merels with solutions similarly arranged, 100 a and 101 a have only one diagram each, the other rectos two diagrams each; 112 b–118 a, eleven problems of tables with solutions similarly arranged,

[3] In one or two cases the *Bonus Socius* MSS. of French origin have substituted *fierge*, *firgia*, for *regina*. Thus Br. 7, PF 6, M 7, all of which are the problem BS 7, have *fierge* in the solution. The other MSS. (W, PL, Fn., PP) have *roine*, *regina*. The other instances occur in PL, Fn., and PP in solutions of non-BS positions.

[4] Viz. CB 6, 146, 158, 182, 183 and the corresponding BS positions BS 13, 116, 125, 152, 153. The following positions are without Pawns, but would show Bishops on possible squares if the players were supposed to be seated on the right and left of the diagram: CB 98, 127, 128, 135, 151, 160, 161, 171, 219. All occur also in BS.

117 a has only one diagram ; 118 b and 119, blank).[5] A note on the inside of the cover (a 16th c. leather binding with brass bosses and clasp), in a hand of the 16th c., shows that the MS. was for long in the possession of the Baldovinetti family :

> Questo libro insegna il modo e le regole di giuocare alli scacchi e merita che ne sia tenuto conto per la sua antichità e per la diligenza con la quale fu scritto, e miniato, e perchè fù acquistato dà nostri antenati, ed è molto tempo che si trova in casa nostra de' Baldovinetti.

It was purchased from the Baldovinetti family by the Grand Duke of Tuscany in 1852. Mr. Magee's guess that the Baldovinetti family inherited it from the Dati family in 1767 is probably unfounded.

The *Bonus Socius* work was undoubtedly translated early into Italian, but no MSS. have survived, and we only know that this was the case from the fact that a couple of leaves from a quarto parchment MS. of the 14th c. were discovered a few years ago in the binding of a later work. The leaves contain the four problems BS 169, 172, 173, 174, one to each page. They are now in the possession of Mr. J. G. White.

A later problem-lover made a fresh Italian version of the MS. BS in the course of the first half of the 16th c. This is the more remarkable because the translator was already familiar with the reformed chess. His version of the BS work is contained in another MS. of the National Library, Florence—MS. XIX. 7. 51 (=It.), which was once in the possession of the Emperor Francis I (1745–65), and later in the Magliabechian Library, Florence. It consists of 211 quarto paper leaves (1 a–25 a, 28 a–29 b, and 149 b, 54 problems of the reformed chess 'a la rabiosa' and a Knight's tour; 51 a–149 a, 197 problems (of which three are duplicates) from the MS. BS; 186 a and b, two exercises (K 3 and CB 249); 25 b–27 b, 30 a–50 b, and 150 a–185 b, blank diagrams for chess; 187 a–198 b, 24 diagrams of problems of merels without solutions, taken from BS; 199 a–203 b, 10 diagrams of problems of tables from BS, of which the last alone, called 'l'abbaco di fuori', has solution; 204 a–210 a, blank; 210 b–211 b and continued on the fly-leaf, notes on card games and the puzzle of the 'Ship'[6]). The writer merely copied the diagrams from BS, and re-wrote the solutions: in a few cases (ff. 146 a, 147 b, 148 b–149 b) he has omitted to add the solutions. The importance of this MS. is in connexion with the modern game.

The *Bonus Socius* work must have reached France early in the 14th c., for we possess no less than seven MSS. of French production, of which the oldest are little, if any, later than the MS. BS itself. None of these MSS. exactly reproduces the

[5] The work *Good Companion* (*Bonus Socius*) of James F. Magee, jr., of Philadelphia, Florence, 1910, contains 38 full-page photographs from the MS., but is otherwise incomplete and gives less help to the student than the extracts in *Qst.*, 127–77.

[6] This puzzle of Muslim origin (see p. 280) occurs in other European MSS. The usual form is to arrange 15 Christians and 15 Moors on board a sinking ship in a circle in such a way that the 15 Moors may be left alive after 15 men have been thrown overboard as the result of counting round and drowning every ninth man. The arrangement was remembered by the hexameter 'Populeam virgam mater regina ferebat', in which the vowels (a = 1, e = 2, i = 3, &c.) give the numbers of Moors and Christians in each successive group (i. e. 4 Moors, 5 Christians, 2 Moors, &c.).

earlier form of the work, and all possess certain features in common, while they fall naturally into two groups containing three and four MSS. respectively, each of which groups exhibits other and marked characteristics of its own.

That group of MSS. which reproduces most closely the text, the diagrams, and the sequence of the Florence MS. BS, consists of three MSS., which are so alike in general workmanship that it is difficult to avoid the conclusion that they are the work of a single scriptorium in N. E. France. In each MS. the diagrams are beautifully executed and coloured. The chessboards are chequered white and black, h1 being white on the recto and black on the verso of each leaf, an arrangement which is due to the fact that the diagrams on front and back of each leaf exactly cover one another, and the semi-transparency of the parchment compelled the illuminator to oppose black squares to black. The chessmen are drawn, reproducing somewhat conventionally the actual forms of the chess pieces; the opposing sides are coloured, and described as gold and red. These three MSS. are:

PL = MS. Nat. Lib., Paris, Lat. 10286. A magnificent folio MS. of the middle of the 14th cent. with Latin text (an occasional lapse into the Picard dialect of French reveals the writer's native tongue), which contains 264 leaves (1 a, blank; 1 b, two miniatures, the one above the other, the upper a battle between two knights, the lower two people playing chess on a board chequered red and blue (h1 blue); 2, blank; 3, the introduction; 4 a–148 b, 290 problems of chess, one a page;[7] 149 a–172 b, 48 problems of tables; 173 a–184 a, 23 problems of merels; 185 a–264 b, Vignay's French version of *Cessolis*). The MS. once belonged to Charles, Duke of Orleans (D. 1467), and an attempt has been made in M. Pierre Champion's *Charles d'Orléans, joueur d'échecs*, Paris, 1908, to prove that the many sidenotes made by a former owner, in which the algebraic notation is regularly employed, are by this prince. The MS. is richly illuminated throughout; in the first initial A of the text three coats of arms are blazoned, the one over the other. The top one is probably the arms of the Emperor, since it contains a black two-headed eagle on a brown ground; the middle one is the ancient arms of France; and the lowest is the arms of England. I imagine that the illuminator selected these as the arms of the three Powers nearest to Picardy.[8]

PP = MS. Nat. Lib. Paris, F. fr. 1173. A similar MS. of the 14th c. with text in the Picard or Walloon dialect of French, which consists of 216 folio leaves (1 a, blank; 1 b, two miniatures, the one over the other, the upper a battle, the lower a siege; 2 a–4 b, the introduction; 5 a–179 a, 348 problems of chess; 179 b, blank; 180 a–203 b, 48 problems of tables; 204 a–216 b, 25 problems of merels; 217 blank). At the foot of f. 216 b is a title in a slightly later hand, 'Chius roumans est des parchons des eschies, des taules, et des merelles a neuf.' At the foot of many leaves (practically

[7] When the solution was too long to be completed in the page, the scribe has completed it at the foot of some neighbouring page where there happened to be room. The same device is followed in PP and Fn.

[8] V. d. Lasa (144) associated the arms with Burgundy (Arles), France and Aquitaine, and so connected the MS. with the South of France.

every fifth leaf) is the MLG. note, 'Ach mocht es sijn,' which appears to be the wail of the weary illuminator. In this MS. the introduction is much longer than in the other *Bonus Socius* MSS. I have already made considerable use of it in dealing with the Lombard Assize and the mediaeval notation (see pp. 461, 469, 495).

Fn. = The Fountaine MS. (so called from its having been from about 1700 to 1902 in the possession of the Fountaine family at Narford Hall, Norfolk; at the sale of the Fountaine library in 1902 the MS. was bought by Mr. Quaritch for £800, and is now in the library of the late Mr. J. Pierpont Morgan of New York). A similar MS. of the 14th c. with text in the Picard dialect of French, which now consists of 216 folio leaves (1 a–145 b, 290 problems of chess;[9] 147 a–168 b, 44 problems of tables; 169 a, blank; 169 b–182 b, 25 problems of merels; 182 b, blank). The MS. has suffered mutilation; the opening leaves have been cut away, as has also a leaf between ff. 146 and 147, which contained the first two problems of tables; in other places illuminated initials have been cut out. The MS. was once in the possession of a French family named Vaubouton.

A small collection of chess problems which occur on ff. 81 a–82 a of the MS Sloan, 3281, in the British Museum (= Sl.), written in the 14th c., is allied to this group of MSS. The chess entry is very carelessly made, the diagrams are imperfectly filled, and the problems follow one another without system, two columns to the page. At the foot of f. 81 a_1 is the Latin line which gives the solution to the problem of the 'Ship', and the favourite hexameter 'Rex, roc, alphinus, miles, regina, pedinus'. The eleven problems are Sl. = BS 12, 2 = BS 16, 3 = BS 1, 4 = BS 54, 5 = BS 45, 6 = BS 108, 7 = BS 118, 8 = BS 29, 9 = BS 9 (the solution is longer, as in all the Picard group), 10 = BS 18, 11 = BS 62.

Although the three MSS. PL, PP, and Fn. contain many more chess problems, they are essentially based upon the BS work. With few exceptions the BS problems follow one another in the same order as in BS, with closely similar text, and occur in blocks together, the additional problems coming in blocks either before or after the BS positions in the same number of moves. We may divide the chess problems thus:

	From BS	Common to all three MSS.	Common to two MSS.			Only in one MS.			Total.
			PL & Fn.	PL & PP	Fn. & PP	PL.	Fn.	PP	
PL	192	89	5	4	—	0	—	—	290
Fn.	191	89	5	—	4	—	1	—	290
PP	193	89	—	4	4	—	—	58	348

(PL omits BS 74, 76: Fn. omits BS 10, 11, 33: PP omits BS 8.)

[9] The problems were originally numbered (Roman numerals) at the foot of the page, but in many cases the numbers have been cut away in binding. In adding the numbering, the scribe has made a mistake somewhere between f. 100 b (where is the number 100) and f. 116 a (where is 271). The intervening numbers have been cut away, but there are no leaves missing. In PL and PP the problems in tables and merels are 'numbered' by the letters of the alphabet.

The new material is for the most part problems in two, three, and four moves, many of which are variations of BS positions, or are based upon the 'Dilārām' idea, but it also includes some longer problems and exercises which are of an older type and in part of Muslim origin. Some of these new positions occur in the *Civis Bononiae* work, but they do not appear to have been obtained from that collection. There are indications which point to their having been obtained from an older French MS. (see especially the solution of PL 271 below. The greater extent of PP is more apparent than real: the compiler has, as a rule, diagrammed separately every variation in BS or the other Picard MSS. which is mentioned in the text of the solutions; if we exclude these artificial additions, we shall reduce the number of positions unique to this MS. to 13 only. I reproduce the additional material of the Picard group of *Bonus Socius* MSS. below.

The second group of *Bonus Socius* MSS. of French workmanship contains four MSS., all in French dialects spoken in Central or Eastern France, and a fifth MS. in Middle Low German. The complete MSS. of this group all omit the last problem (BS 194) in the Florence MS., and add ten chess positions to the 193 positions which they have from the *Bonus Socius* work. Five of these are really duplicates of problems in BS and already in the MSS. of the group, but the text of the solutions differs from the BS text, and the identity of the problems would seem to have escaped notice. These duplicate solutions do not occur in the three MSS. of the Picard group. The other five positions, on the other hand, are included in the Picard MSS. None of the MSS. of this 'Central French' group exhibit the orderly arrangement of the Florence MS. or the Picard group of MSS., and a comparison of the existing order in the different MSS. shows that the disorder must go back to a MS. that lies behind them and between them and the original *Bonus Socius* work, whose order was BS 1–150, 155–170, 151–154, 191, 193, 171–178, 181–190, 192, A, 179–180, B–K, where I have used the letters A–K to denote the ten additional problems.[10] The existing MSS. are still more disarranged than this, but this is due to the accidental displacement of leaves, and in M, the only MS. of the group which does not regularly allot one page to each position, to a deliberate attempt to economize space.

The MSS. which I include in this group are:

W = MS. Wolfenbüttel, Extrav., 118. This is a parchment MS. with French text of the middle of the 14th c., of 133 quarto leaves (1 a, introduction; 1 b–103 b, 205 problems of chess, one a page with solution below—two problems are repeated in error; 104 a–116 a, 25 problems of merels; 116 b, blank; 117 a–133 b, 34 problems of tables, somewhat carelessly copied. The last leaf ends, 'Ci achieue le liure des eschecs et des tables et des merelles').

M = MS. Montpellier, Faculty of Medicine, H. 279 (Fonds de Bouhier, E. 93). This is a 14th c. vellum MS. of 128 quarto leaves (1 a, blank;

[10] These problems are A = PL 286; B = PL 240; C = BS 173v; D = PL 287; E = PL 288; F = BS 174v; G = BS 99v; H = BS 188v; J = BS 183 v; K = PL 279.

1 b, a title, 'Chi commenche le livres des partures des esches et de tables et de merelles et se claime cis livres Bakot et le trouva Nebrou le joiant qui fit premiers en Babylone la tour con claime Babel, ou li langage furent mue par la volente nostre seigneur, qui vit lor outrecuidanche. Et de la fu Bakot aportes a troie la grant. Et de troie en Gresse apres la destruction de troie. Et de gresse vint en franche, et encore i est, dont loue soit Dieu'; 2 a–88 a, 206 numbered problems of chess, one or two to the page, of which three are repeated in error; 89 a–113 b, 48 problems of tables, carelessly copied with many duplicate entries; 114 a–128 a, 28 problems of merels; 128 b, blank). The original first leaf has been cut out. The MS. formerly belonged to Jean Bouhier, Conseiller laic au parlement de Dijon in 1630.

PF = MS. Nat. Lib., Paris, F. fr., 1999. A 15th c. parchment MS., in a Central French dialect, of 135 quarto leaves (1 a, blank; 1 b, a miniature of a pelican nourishing its four young with its own blood, surrounded by the motto, 'Ensy est comant quyl aille haute sens faylle'; 2 a, blank; 2 b, two entries in a later hand, one the title, 'Liuret de diuers Jeux partis du tablier'; 3 a–104 a, 203 problems of chess, the text at the head, the diagram at the foot of each page—six problems are repeated in error; 104 b–105 b, blank; 106 a–117 b, 24 problems of merels; 118 a–134 b, 34 (four duplicates) problems of tables; 135, blank).

Br. = MS. Brussels, 10502. A parchment French MS. of the second half of the 14th c., of 56 quarto leaves (1 a–56 b, 112 problems of chess, one a page, with text below—three are repeated in error). A title on the front cover, 'Liure du jeu des Eschetz'; a note on the back cover, 'E ce sera moy Nassau'; and sundry notes scattered through the MS. (*faulx* on 42 b, 56 b; *parfait*, 24 b; *parfait éprouvé*, 49 a; *parfait et bon*, 54 b), are all in one hand of the 16th c. V. d. Linde (i. 302) thought the owner might be the Count of Nassau, chamberlain of the Archduke Maximilian of Austria in 1485. This MS. contains no problems of tables or of merels.

Lobk. = MS. Lobkowitz Lib., Prague, 497 a. A parchment 14th c. MS., in Low German, of 8 leaves, containing 31 problems of chess (one on f. 1 a, two side by side at the foot of each succeeding leaf, with text below). Formerly in the Blankenheimer Library. It was edited by Kelle in *Haupt's Zeitschrift f. d. Alterthum*, Neue Folge, II. i. 179–89, Berlin, 1867.

To this group probably belonged two of the problem MSS. in the library of Martin V of Arragon (see p. 567).

In all of these French and German translations (with the possible exception of M, where the solution of M 1 has in one place *aussi* instead of *aufin*, plainly a blunder of the scribe, whose ignorance of chess is revealed by his writing *scat* for *scac* throughout) the text is a close and literal translation from the Latin, and not a transcript of an older French MS. This is shown by the different renderings of the L. *fiducia* in the translations of the same BS problem in the various French MSS. by minor differences of expression, and by the blanks which the translators of Fn. and Lobk. have left when they came across unfamiliar Latin terms. In Fn. the scribe has regularly left a space of the number of letters in the unknown Latin word, and occasionally he has inserted the Latin word itself in a minute hand in the space. Since these omissions are nearly always of terms technical to the games they suggest that the scribe was often unfamiliar with chess and tables.

I have so far endeavoured to classify the *Bonus Socius* MSS. by means of the broad characteristics of the chess contents. In the main, the other two sections (tables and merels) support this classification, but there are greater variations, especially in the case of the problems of tables, and these sections have been copied with less care. The two Florence MSS., BS and It., have an entirely different section of tables from that of the other MSS. of the *Bonus Socius* work, and the problems common to the two sections have different texts in the solutions. The *Civis Bononiae* MSS. show that the section as it exists in the 'French' MSS. was certainly known in Italy, for it has served as the foundation of the section on tables in these MSS.

It would, of course, have been possible to base the classification upon other considerations, such as variations in the text or the diagrams. I have not, however, found that the former consideration has been very fruitful. It supports the grouping together of PL, Fn., PP, and Sl. by the longer text of BS 9, which is found in all these MSS., as I have already mentioned. V. d. Lasa (105) based some arguments upon the omission of the concluding words of BS 173 in the corresponding problem in PL (PL 257, where, however, the words are not wanting), but I do not think that we can argue safely from isolated omissions, and v. d. Lasa confessed that they often lead to contradictory results. The diagrams, on the other hand, provide a safer test when care is taken to eliminate accidental differences. The omission of a piece or letter, the posting of single pieces on wrong squares, the raising or lowering of a whole row of pieces, are mistakes which any transcriber might easily make, and a single mistake common to two MSS. may be only due to a coincidence;[11] but when a group of MSS. show many coincidences of this character it is impossible to explain them away as the result of accident, and we can draw conclusions with certainty. And it is a fair inference in all cases in which some MSS. diagram a position correctly and others incorrectly, that the former MSS. are not derived from the latter, for none of the *Bonus Socius* MSS. exhibit any trace of critical examination at the hand of the transcriber.[12]

Examined in this way, the evidence of the diagrams will be found to support entirely the classification of the MSS. which I have already suggested, and, in addition, to show that no existing MS. of the two French groups is a direct or indirect copy of any other existing MS. It shows a closer con-

[11] A curious example of this is to be found in the foliation of BS and the *Civis Bononiae* MS. B. Sig. Fantacci, who made the first transcript of BS, accidentally turned over the two leaves (then unfoliated) 45 and 46, and as a result omitted the positions on BS f. 46 (BS 88 and 90) from his copy. In numbering the leaves of B the leaf 52* was omitted in the same way. This leaf contains the same two positions as BS f. 46!

[12] I have already mentioned the fact that subsequent owners of Br. and PL have made a critical examination of these MSS., but this is quite a different matter.

nexion between PL and Fn. than between either of these MSS. and PP, and between M and Br. on the one hand, and W and PF on the other, than between either of the first pair and either of the second pair of these MSS. of the Central French group. It will be convenient to embody in a table the relationships of the different MSS. so far as I have been able to ascertain them. I add notes which summarize the evidence of the diagrams. The general result of the collation is to establish BS as the most accurate of all the *Bonus Socius* MSS. so far as the chess portion is concerned. Its diagrams are also closest to the original *Civis Bononiae* work.

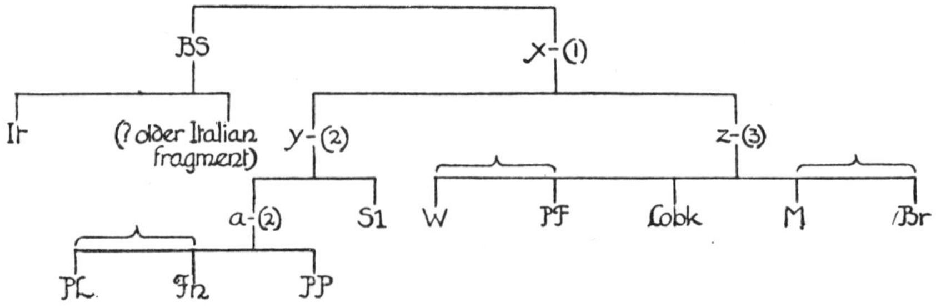

(1) Errors common to *y* and *z* occur in the diagrams of BS 3, 18, 24, 31, 52, 64, 72, 80, 138, 143.

(2) The diagrams of BS 30, 46, 132, 133 group PL, Fn., and PP together. The order of PL and Fn. has more in common than has the order of PL or Fn. and PP.

(3) The diagrams of BS 9, 12, 21, 23, 46, 53, 59, 78, 83, 94, 96, 99, 105, 112, 115, 121, 131, 132, 135, 141, 145, 156, 158, 159, 171 group the MSS. W, PF, M, Br., Lobk. together. The closer relationships between W and PF, and M and Br., are inferred from the order of the problems in these MSS.

The Florence MS. BS commences with an introduction or preface in which the compiler of the collection gives a brief account of the genesis of his work. This introduction also commences the Paris Latin MS. PL, but with an important addition, to which I shall return directly. In translation it is repeated in the French MS. W, while it forms the foundation of a more ambitious introduction in the Picard MS. PP. It probably also originally commenced the MS. Fn., the first leaf of which is now missing. It is important to note that it occurs in MSS. of each of the groups into which the *Bonus Socius* MSS. fall, because this goes far towards establishing the introduction as a part of the original work.

The different texts of this introduction will be found in the Appendix to this chapter. The BS text commences with a reference to the weakness of human memory as a justification for the compilation of a collection of *partita*. The argument is strengthened by numerous references to passages in legal and religious works. It then continues :

'Wherefore I, *Bonus Socius*, consenting to the prayers of my *socii*, have taken pains to collect in this little book the *partita* which I have seen, and which I have by study newly discovered, of the games of chess, dice, and also of merels, in order that by their instruction and practice knowledge may be the more easily obtained of others which can be made.'

It then concludes with a request that his masters (*domini*), *socii*, and friends will pardon and correct all imperfections which they may discover in his book.

The term *socius*, which I have left untranslated, had a definite technical meaning in the Lombard Universities. It was used by the Professors and lecturers to describe their fellow-teachers, as opposed to the students, of the universities. From the use of the term in this preface, and from the many references to legal and other scholastic works, it is generally accepted that the anonymous writer was a member of one of the Lombard Universities.

The pseudonym *Bonus Socius* is not used in the other MSS. which repeat the preface, although *socii* (W *compaignons*) is used in the concluding passage, in which the author craves their indulgence for his mistakes. In its place PL and W have the initials 'N. de N.', and PP amplifies this into 'Nicholes de St. Nicholai, clers', and in a later passage adds *dwelling in Lombardy* ('demourans en lombardie'). A side-note in PL also gives the name as Nicholaus de Nicolai, but I do not know how old this note is.

The earlier writers who discussed the authorship of the *Bonus Socius* work, including v. d. Linde, had no hesitation in accepting the statement of the three MSS. PL, W, and PP. V. d. Lasa, on the other hand, who devotes several pages of the *Forschungen* (135–6, 143–8) to the point, rejects it, but on grounds which seem to me to be insufficient.[13] He attempts to account for the substitution of the initials or name in the MSS. of French origin in some such way as this. The collection was the work of an anonymous writer who used the pseudonym *Bonus Socius*. Soon after the appearance of the work a Picard monk, Nicholas of St. Nicholas, came across the work during a sojourn in a Lombard monastery, and sent home, first the Latin text, and later a new preface (that of PP) in the Picard dialect, in which he represented himself as the author of the work. This new introduction was then prefixed to a Picard translation of the Latin text. At a later date, the transcribers of PL and W heard of this and inserted the initials in their copies of the original introduction, possibly because they were doubtful of the genuineness of the claim. V. d. Lasa does not appear to have come to any conclusions as to the relationships of the *Bonus Socius* MSS.: had he done so, I think that he would have seen that the fact that the initials occur in MSS. of both groups of French MSS. leads to the conclusion that they were already in the parent MS. '*x*' of these groups, while the age of the existing MSS. compels the conclusion that this MS. must have been at least as old as the Florence MS. BS. V. d. Lasa's idea that the scribes who made the MSS. W and PL worked

[13] V. d. Lasa's doubts arose from (*a*) a supposed difference in dialect between the introduction of PP and the remainder of the work; (*b*) a scribal error in PL, 'idcirco ego N. de N. meorum precibus acquiescens', by which the word *sociorum* is omitted; (*c*) his own uncertainty as to the reading 'N. de N.', owing to the form of N used. The reading is, however, quite certain.

critically must, I think, be rejected. The MSS. were copied for, but by no means necessarily by, chess-players.

I can discover no valid reason for rejecting the Nicholas authorship. Like many other young scholars in France and England, he had probably travelled to the Lombard Universities in search of knowledge, and had remained, after completing his studies, to teach other scholars. There may have been reasons for preserving his anonymity in copies of his work circulating in the Universities or in Lombardy. He may, for instance, have felt that his subject was hardly worthy of a University lecturer.[14] But the same reasons would not necessarily prevail outside Lombardy, and in sending copies away, he would feel no difficulty in giving his initials or even his full name. His native place may possibly have been St. Nicholas (in the Middle Ages, St. Nicholai), between Ghent and Antwerp.

In the passage which I have quoted from the preface to BS the author claims to have included *partita* of his own composition. How far this claim is true cannot be determined. It is possible that Nicholas merely added a few variations of existing problems. Certainly, all that is best in his work is either Muslim or occurs in idea at least in older European collections.

The longer introduction to PP gives information first, how, by whom, and where the game of chess was first discovered: and next of the fashion of the game and the assizes, and how it can be shortened by problems (*partures*). The game was invented (so the story runs) at the siege of Troy, by a Trojan knight and his lady. After the fall of the city they brought the game to Lombardy, whence it spread throughout the country, for 'the Lombards are the wisest and most subtle at this game that there are'. The problems in the MS. are said to be composed according to the rules of the Lombard assize.

We have no means of discovering the date of the compilation of the *Bonus Socius* work other than from the dates of the existing MSS. and their relationships. There is nothing in the text that throws the slightest light upon the period at which Nicholas lived, or the date of his writing. I do not think that we need assume any very long period for the missing steps in my pedigree. I think that it is more likely that the work achieved an instant popularity among problem-lovers, and that there was a great multiplication of copies within a short time of the writing of the work. I would ascribe it to the second half of the 13th century.

Since almost all of the chess problems in BS recur in CB, I have not thought it worth while to give the contents of the former MS. separately. The table below will show where the problems will be found in the larger work, which I reproduce in abbreviated form below. Readers who wish to see the problems of the BS work in their original order are referred to *Qst.*,

[14] Richard de Fournivall also half apologizes for writing about the game of merels in the *Vetula* (I. xxxiv):

Sunt alii ludi parvi quos scire puellas
Esse decens dixi: *sed parva movere pudebat*
Nuncque magis, quam tunc, pudet illa minora referre.

127–177, where they will find the problem diagrams and shortened solutions, with one slight error. The copy of the MS. which v. d. Linde used accidentally omitted two positions (BS 89 and 90), and these are omitted in the *Qst.* series. The missing problems will, however, be found in *Qst.*, from other BS MSS., on pp. 178 (no. 6) and 179 (no. 7). In comparing the present work with *Qst.* it will be necessary to remember that my numbering of the BS problems, from BS 91 on, is two higher than that of *Qst.*

BS PROBLEMS IN CB.

(Problems in which CB changes the colours of the sides are marked with a *. Problems in which the CB arrangement is not identically that of BS are given in italics. Full details of all differences will be found with the CB solutions.)

BS	CB	BS	CB	BS	CB	BS	CB	BS	CB	BS	CB	BS	CB
1	32*	28	23	56	85	84	97	112	142	140	171	167	201
2	34	29	22	57	86	85	98	113	143	141	172	168	202
3	*2*	30	21	58	87	86	99	114	144	142	173	169	203
4	4*	31	*20**	59	88	87	101	115	145	143	174	170	204
5	*5**	32	49	60	89	88	102	116	146	144	175	171	205
5 v	45*	33	50	61	56	89	103	117	147	145	176	172	206
6	3	34	51	62	*53*	90	104	118	149	146	177	173	208
7	29	35	52	63	91	91	105	119	*150*	147	178	174	210
8	30	36	61	64	55*	92	106	120	151	148	*186*	175	262
9	*35*	37	60	65	90	93	*107*	121	152	149	*179*	176	213
10	41	38	*65**	66	92	94	*119**	122	153	150	180	177	215
11	–	39	*72*	67	*93*	95	108	123	154	151	181	178	217
12	7*	40	66	68	94	96	109	124	155	152	182	179	216
13	*6*	41	67	69	62	97	*115*	125	156	153	183	180	220
14	9	42	73	70	63	98	*132*	126	157	154	184	181	*219*
15	8	43	71	71	59	99	124	127	158	155	185	182	222
16	11	44	75	72	47	100	125	128	159	156	187	183	223
17	14*	45	*43*	73	44*	101	126	129	160	157	190	184	*253*
18	13*	46	76*	74	112	102	127	130	162	157 v	189	185	247
19	*18**	47	74	75	*100*	103	128	131	*161*	158	191	186	*250*
20	15	48	78	76	113	104	129	132	163	159	192	187	–
21	16	49	77*	77	*116*	105	133	133	164	160	193	188	*225**
22	*17*	50	79	78	120*	106	134	134	165	161	196	189	251
23	28	51	80	79	95	107	135	135	166	162	197	190	255
24	27	52	82	80	121	108	136	136	167	163	–	191	218
25	26	53	81	81	122	109	137	137	168	164	211	192	257
26	25	54	84	82	123	110	*139*	138	169	165	199	193	256
27	24	55	83	83	96	111	138	139	*170*	166	200	194	194

BS 11.

(Bl.)
Mate in II exactly. The R is fidated from K, and Q from all pieces.

BS 163.

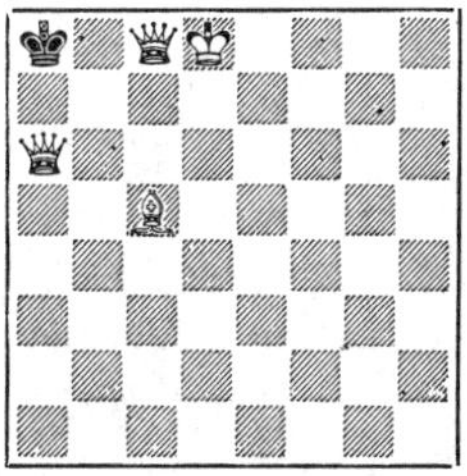

Mate in X with B.
Unsound.

BS 187.

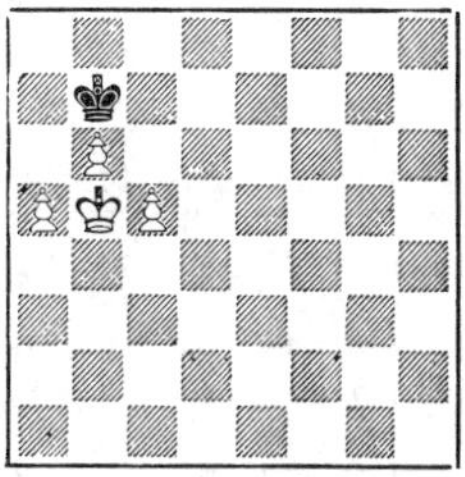

White wins.
The new Qs cannot leap.

Solutions.—BS 11. ‘Albi primo trahunt, et roccus habet fiduciam a rege, et regina ab omnibus, et uolunt mattare nigros ad ii tractum et fieri potest. Trahere roccum ante pedonem non ualet, quia nigri caperent alfinum album, et postea non fieret in secundo tractu, quia roccus non posset dicere mat quia licet sit affidatus a rege, non tamen a milite. Sed tu qui habes albos cape pedonem nigrum de rege tuo, et secundo dabis mat cum regina.’

BS 163. ‘Albi trahunt et dicunt se uelle mattare regem nigrum ad x tractum de alfino. Defende subtiliter, quia non fit ad x sed ad xii si bene defendis. Ipse trahet regem in A (e7), et in B (d7), et in C (c6), postea reginam in B, et aliam reginam iuxta alfinum, et postea retrahet alfinum, et tu uade ubi alfinus percussit, postea in angulum, et defendes. Sed cum rex stat in C et regina in B, si uis quod fiat ad xii, trahe regem in unum punctum (b5) et postea in duo (b6); postea retrahe reginam sinistram et alfinum. Tunc pone regem in D (c7), et reginam in E (c8), et de eadem da scac et mat de alfino.’

BS 187. ‘Albi trahunt et mattabunt regem nigrum, et cum aliquis pedo fiet regina, non saltabit, quia tunc diuersimode posset ludi. Da scac de pedone dextro. Ipse ibit directe superius quia illud est suum melius. Tu facias iiii tractus cum rege tuo secundum alphabetum (A c4, B b4, C b5, D a6); scac de pedone quem primo traxisti. Si uadat in angulum, mattus est, vnde oportebit eum exire. Tu poteris facere reginas de omnibus pedonibus, nec oportet saltare cum aliqua noua regina et uinces eum si scias in omne angulo.’

The following tables show where the problems in BS occur in the other MSS. of the *Bonus Socius* work. I include in the tables the references to the problems which have the *Bonus Socius* text in the Paris MS. S, which is described in the following chapter.

BS	It.	PL	Fn.	PP	W	PF	M	Br.	Lobk.	S
1	101	8	19	21	1	1	1	1	1	95
2	102	9	53	22	2	2	2	2	–	96
3	103	12	20	23	3	3	3	3	–	97
4	104	13	21	24	4	36	4	4	–	93
5	105	15	23	26	5	37	5	5	–	92
6	106	14	22	25	6	6	6	6	–	98
7	107	16	24	27	7	7	7	7	2	99
8	108	17	25	–	8	8	8	8	3	143
9	109	18	26	29	9	9	9	9	–	–
10	110	19	–	31	10	42	10	10	–	169
11	111	20	–	32	11	43	11	11	–	100
12	112	21	27	33	12	12	12	12	–	101
13	113	24	28	34	13	13	13	13	–	170
14	114	25	29	35	14	14	14	14	–	172
15	115	28	30	37	15	16	15	17	–	102
16	116	29	31	38	16	15	16	15	–	103
17	117	32	32	40	17	18	17	19	–	168
18	118	30	33	28	18	17	18	18	–	174
19	119	34	34	41	19	20	19	21	–	105
20	120	35	35	42	20	19 =77	20	20	–	104
21	121	36	36	43	21	22 =23	169	23	–	171
22	122	37	37	44	22	21	170	22	–	173
23	123	38	38	45	23	25	173	25	4	106
24	124	39	39	46	24	24	174	24	5	175
25	125	42	40	47	25	27	143	27	–	177
26	126	43	41	48	26	26	144	26	–	179
27	127	44	42	49	27	29	145	29	–	181
28	128	45	43	51	28	28	146	28	–	130
29	129	50	44	54	29	31	147	31	–	176
30	130	51	45	52	30	30	148	30	–	178
31	131	52	46	55	31	33	149	33	–	132
32	132	74	91	104	32	32	150	32	–	134
33	133	75	–	81	33	34	151	34	–	180
34	134	77	93	79	31	35	152	35	–	182
35	136	76	92	80	35	4	153	37	–	129
36	137	78	94	82	36	5	154	36	–	131
37	138	79	95	83	37	38	155	39	–	183
38	139	81	97	88	38	39	156	38	–	133
39	140	80	96	85	39	40	157	43	–	135
40	141	82	98	87	40	41	158	40	–	188
41	142	83	99	105	41	10	183	41	–	136
42	143	84	100	106	42	11	184	42	–	185
43	144	85	101	107	43	44	185	45	–	189
44	145	86	102	108	44	45	186	44	–	138
45	146	87	103	109	45	46	187	47	–	184
46	147	88	104	111	46	47	188	46	–	186
47	148	89	105	112	47	48	189	49	–	139
48	149	90	106	113	48	49	190	48	–	140
49	150	91	107	114	49	50	191	51	–	124
50	151	92	108	115	50	51	192	63	–	125
51	152	93	109	116	52	53	194	52	–	137
52	153	94	110	117	51	52	193	53	–	141
53	155	95	111	118	53	54	121	55	6	126
54	154	96	112	120	54	55	122	54	7	127
55	156	97	113	119	55	56	123	57	–	128
56	157	98	114	122	56	57	124	56	–	145
57	158	99	115	124	57	58	125	59	–	146
58	159	100	116	121	58	59	126	58	–	–
59	160	101	117	125	59	60	127	61	8	144
60	161	102	118	126	60	61	128	60	9	142
61	162	103	119	123	61	62	129	50	–	187
62	135 =163	104	120	128	62	63	130	62	–	–
63	164	105	121	132	63	80	131	65	–	–
64	165	106	122	127	64	81	132	64	–	–
65	166	107	123	131	65	82	133	67	–	–
66	167	108	124	134	66	83	134 =136	66	–	–

BS	It.	PL	Fn.	PP	W	PF	M	Br.	Lobk.	S
67	168	109	125	133	67	–	135	69	–	–
68	169	110	126	136	68	84	137	68	–	–
						=85				
69	170	111	127	139	69	107	138	71	10	–
								=87		
70	171	112	128	141	70	86	139	70	11	–
71	172	113	129	147	71	87	140	73	12	–
72	173	114	130	149	72	88	141	72	13	–
73	174	115	131	135	73	89	142	75	–	–
								=91		
74	175	–	148	190	74	90	51	74	–	–
								=90		
75	176	169	149	191	75	91	54	77	14	–
76	177	–	150	192	76	92	52	76	15	–
77	178	143	153	193	77	93	55	79	–	–
78	179	144	152	194	78	94	53	78	–	–
79	180	145	151	195	79	95	57	82	–	–
						=96				
80	181	146	154	196	80	–	56	80	–	–
81	182	147	155	197	81	98	59	84	–	–
82	183	148	156	198	82	97	58	81	–	–
83	184	149	157	199	83	–	61	86	16	–
84	185	150	158	200	84	99	60	83	17	–
						=100				
85	186	151	159	201	85	102	62	–	18	–
86	187	152	160	202	87	119	21	–	20	–
87	188	153	161	203	86	101	63	85	19	–
88	189	154	163	204	88	120	22	–	21	–
89	190	155	162	205	89	121	23	–	–	–
90	191	156	164	206	90	122	24	–	–	–
91	193	157	165	207	91	123	25	–	–	–
92	192	158	166	208	92	124	26	–	–	–
93	194	159	167	209	93	125	27	–	–	–
94	195	160	168	210	94	126	28	–	–	–
95	196	161	169	211	95	127	29	–	–	–
96	197	162	170	212	199	64	30	–	–	–
97	199	163	171	213	200	65	31	–	–	–
98	198	179	173	231	201	66	32	–	–	–
99	200	181	176	216	202	67	159	–	–	–
100	201	180	174	233	203	68	160	–	–	–
101	202	182	175	234	204	69	161	–	–	–
						=72				
102	203	183	177	235	205	70	162	–	–	–
103	204	193	186	236	96	71	163	–	–	–
104	205	184	178	237	97	74	164	–	–	–
105	207	185	179	238	98	73	165	–	–	–
106	206	186	180	239	99	–	166	–	–	–
107	208	187	181	240	100	75	167	–	–	–
108	209	188	182	243	101	76	168	–	–	–
109	210	189	183	245	102	79	171	–	–	–
							=195			
110	211	190	184	246	103	78	172	–	–	–
							=196			
111	212	191	185	247	104	–	197	–	–	–
112	213	194	201	249	105	144	198	–	–	–
113	215	195	203	250	106	145	199	–	–	–
114	214	196	202	251	107	146	200	–	–	–
115	216	197	189	252	108	147	201	–	–	–
116	217	198	190	253	109	148	202	–	–	–
117	218	199	191	254	110	149	203	–	–	–
118	219	200	192	255	111	150	204	–	–	–
119	220	201	193	256	112	151	205	–	–	–
120	221	202	194	257	113	152	206	–	–	–
121	222	203	195	258	114	153	175	–	22	–
122	223	204	204	259	115	154	176	–	23	–
123	224	205	196	260	117	156	177	–	–	–
124	225	206	205	261	116	155	178	–	–	–
						=158				
125	226	207	206	262	118	–	179	–	24	–
126	227	208	207	263	119	157	180	–	25	–

BS	It.	PL	Fn.	PP	W	PF	M	Br.	Lobk.	S
127	228	209	208	264	120	128	181	97	26	–
128	229	210	209	265	121	159	182	–	27	–
129	231	211	210	266	122	141	111	99	–	–
130	230	212	213	268	123	129	112	100	–	–
131	232	213	212	269	124	132	113	101	–	–
132	233	214	214	270	125	131	114	98	–	–
					=127					
133	234	215	215	271	126	134	115	103	–	–
					=128					
134	235	216	216	272	129	133	116	102	–	–
135	236	217	217	273	130	136	117	105	28	–
136	237	218	218	274	131	135	118	104	29	–
137	238	219	219	275	132	138	119	107	–	–
138	239	220	220	276	133	137	120	106	–	–
139	240	221	221	277	134	140	64	109	–	–
140	241	222	222	278	135	139	66	108	–	–
141	242	223	223	279	136	142	65	111	–	–
142	243	224	224	280	137	130	67	110	–	–
143	244	225	225	281	138	160	68	–	–	–
144	245	226	226	282	139	143	70	112	–	–
145	246	227	227	283	140	162	69	–	–	–
146	247	228	228	284	141	161	72	–	–	–
147	248	229	229	285	142	164	71	–	–	–
148	249	230	230	286	143	163	73	–	–	–
149	250	231	231	287	144	166	74	–	–	–
150	251	232	232	288	145	165	75	–	–	–
151	252	233	233	289	163	184	92	–	–	–
152	253	234	234	290	162	183	93	–	–	–
153	254	235	235	291	164	186	94	–	–	–
	=256									
154	255	236	236	292	165	185	95	–	–	–
	=257									
155	258	237	237	293	146	168	77	–	–	–
156	259	238	238	294	147	167	76	–	–	–
157	261	239	239	295	148	170	47	–	–	–
158	260	241	240	297	149	169	78	–	–	–
159	262	243	241	298	150	172	48	–	–	–
160	263	242	242	299	151	171	49	–	–	–
161	264	245	244	301	154	176	84	–	–	–
162	265	246	245	302	153	173	83	–	–	–
163	266	247	246	303	152	174	50	–	–	–
164	267	248	247	304	155	175	85	–	–	–
165	268	249	253	305	156	178	86	–	–	–
166	269	250	248	306	157	177	87	–	–	–
167	270	251	249	307	158	180	88	–	–	–
168	271	253	250	308	159	179	89	–	–	–
169	272	252	251	309	160	182	91	–	–	–
170	273	254	252	310	161	181	90	–	–	–
171	274	255	254	311	185	106	98	–	–	–
172	275	256	255	312	186	105	99	–	–	–
173	276	257	256	313	187	108	100	93	–	–
						=195				
174	277	258	257	315	188	109	101	92	–	–
						=196				
175	278	259	258	316	189	110	102	95	–	–
176	279	260	259	317	190	111	103	94	–	–
177	280	261	260	318	191	112	104	–	–	–
178	281	262	261	319	192	–	105	96	–	–
179	282	265	264	322	172	194	36	–	–	–
180	283	266	265	323	173	193	37	–	–	–
181	284	267	266	324	193	114	106	–	–	–
182	285	268	267	325	194	113	107	–	–	–
183	286	269	268	326	195	116	108	–	–	–
184	287	270	269	327	196	115	109	–	–	–
185	288	281	282	329	197	118	110	–	–	–
186	289	273	273	328	198	117	79	–	–	–
187	290	272	272	330	166	187	80	–	–	–
188	291	276	276	333	167	188	81	–	–	–
189	292	284	284	334	169	190	82	–	–	–
190	293	280	280	337	168	189	33	–	–	–

	BS	It.	PL	Fn.	PP	W	PF	M	Br.	Lobk.	S
	191	294	282	281	343	184	103	97	89	–	–
	192	295	278	278	342	170	191 =192	34	–	–	–
	193	296	274	274	331	183	104	96	88	–	–
	194	297	285	285	339	–	–	–	–	–	–
A	–	–	286	286	340	171	–	35	–	–	–
B	–	–	240	–	296	174	196	38	–	30	–
C	–	–	–	–	–	175	–	39	–	31	–
D	–	–	287	287	341	176	198	40	–	–	–
E	–	–	288	288	344	177	197	41	–	–	–
F	–	–	–	–	–	178	200	42	–	–	–
G	–	–	–	–	–	179	199	43	–	–	–
H	–	–	–	–	–	180	202	44	–	–	–
J	–	–	–	–	–	181	201	45	–	–	–
K	–	–	279	279	348	182	203	46	16	–	–

I now proceed to give the additional chess material from the three 'Picard' MSS., PL, Fn., and PP.

PL 1 : Fn. 1 : PP 10.

Mate in II exactly.

PL 2 : Fn. 2 : PP. 11.

Mate in II exactly.
The Bl. R is fidated.

PL 4 : Fn. 4 : PP. 2.

Black mates in II exactly.
The Q is fidated.

PL 6 : Fn. 5 : PP 5.

(Bl.)
Mate in II exactly.
The Bl. R is fidated from the K. Unsound.

PL 7 : Fn. 6 : PP 6.

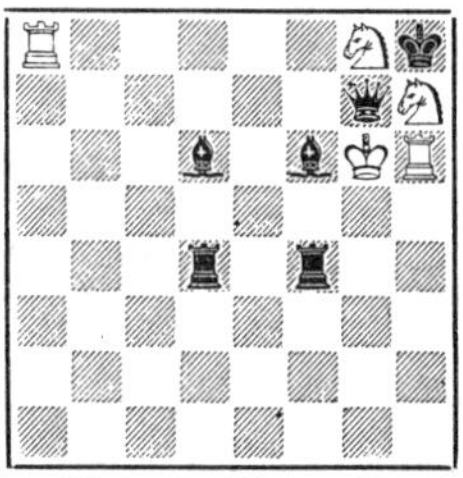

Mate in II exactly.

PL 10 (corr.): Fn. 7 : PP 8, 12.

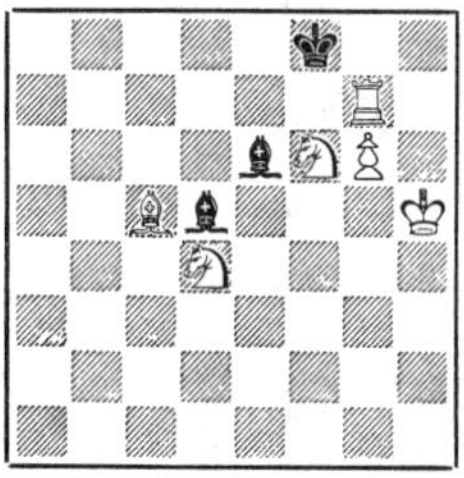

Mate in II exactly.

PL 22 : Fn. 9 : PP 14.

Mate in II exactly.
Rb7 is fidated from K, and Q fidated entirely.

PL 26 : Fn. 11 : PP 4.

Mate in II exactly.

PL 27 : Fn. 12 : PP 7.

(Bl.)

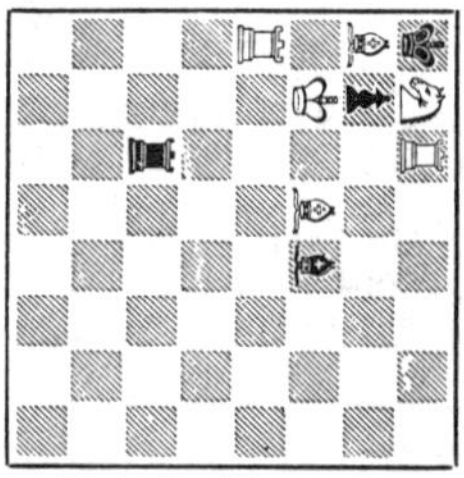

Mate in II exactly.
Unsound.

PL 33 : Fn. 13 : PP 13.

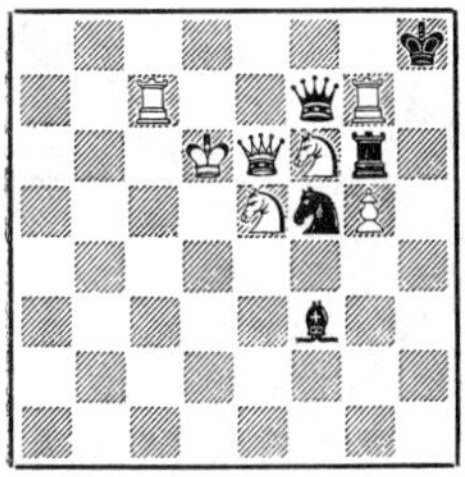

Mate in II exactly.
Unsound.

PL 41 : Fn. 15 : PP 16.

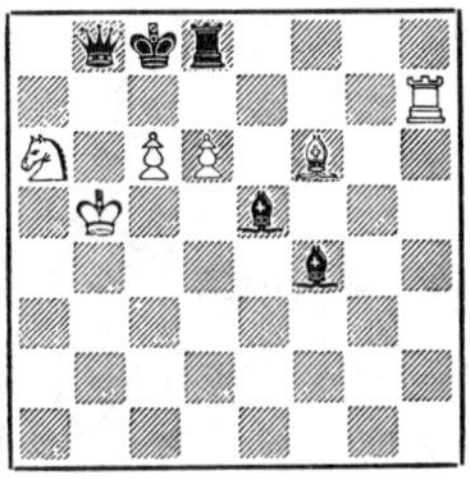

Mate in II exactly.

PL 46 : Fn. 16 : PP 18.

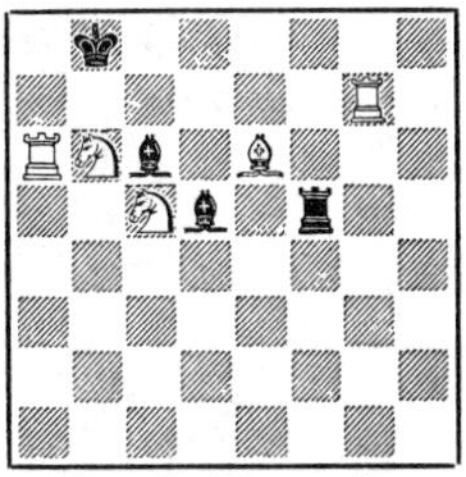

Mate in II exactly.

Pl. 55 : Fn. 49 : PP 56.

Black plays, and White mates in II exactly.
All the men are fidated.
Unsound.

PL 56 : Fn. 51 : PP 60.

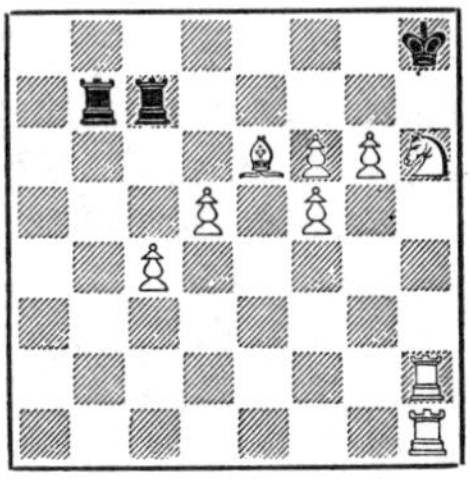

Mate in II exactly.

PL 57 : Fn. 50 : PP 59.

Black plays, and White mates in II exactly.
All the men are fidated.
Unsound.

PL 59 : Fn. 56 : PP. 64.

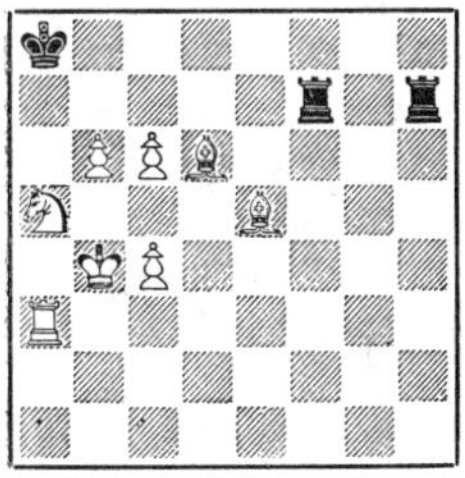

Mate in II exactly.
Unsound.

PL 116 : Fn. 132 : PP 152.

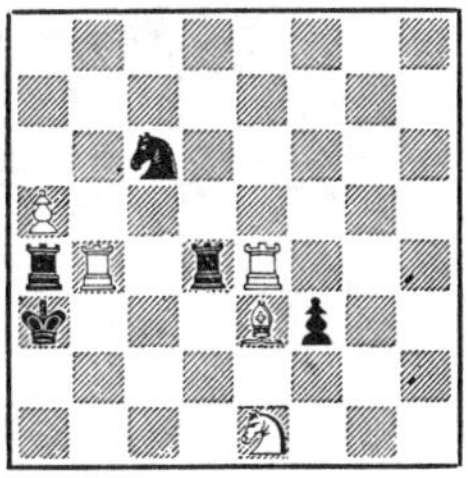

(Bl).
Mate in III exactly.
Unsound.

PL 117 : Fn. 133 : PP 151.

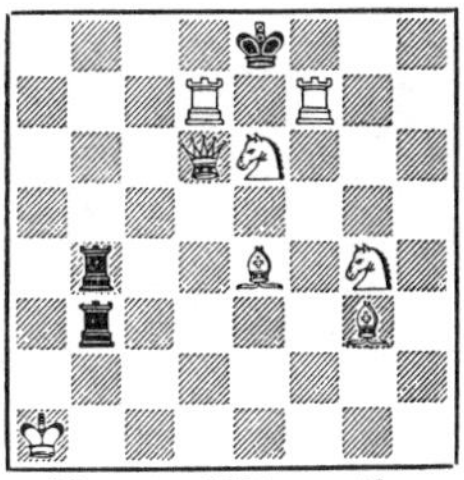

Mate in III exactly.

PL 121 : Fn. 69 : PP 137

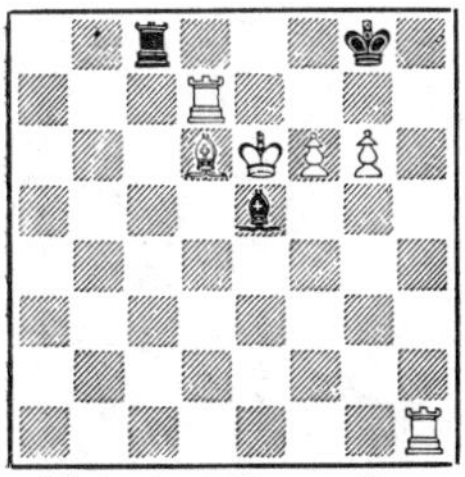

Mate in III exactly.

PL 122 : Fn. 70 : PP 138.

Mate in III exactly.
Rh1 is fidated.

PL 123 : Fn. 71 : PP 140.

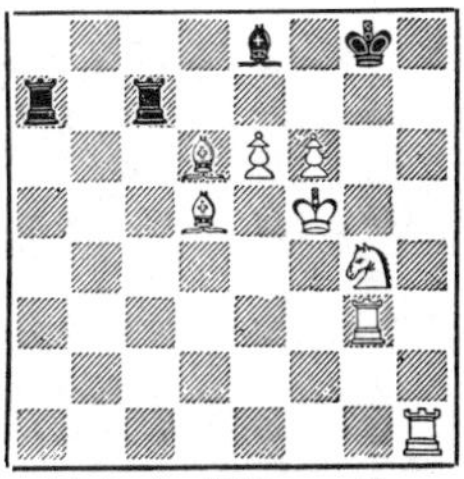

Mate in III exactly.
Unsound.

PL 124 : Fn. 72 : PP 143 : Ar. 409.

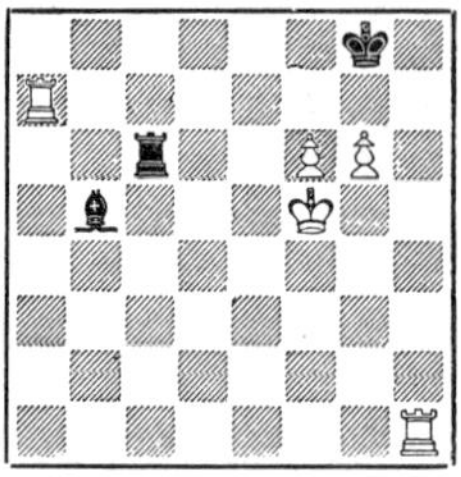

Mate in III exactly.

PL 125 (corr.) : Fn. 73 : PP 144.

Mate in III exactly.
Unsound.

PL 126 : Fn. 74 : PP 146.

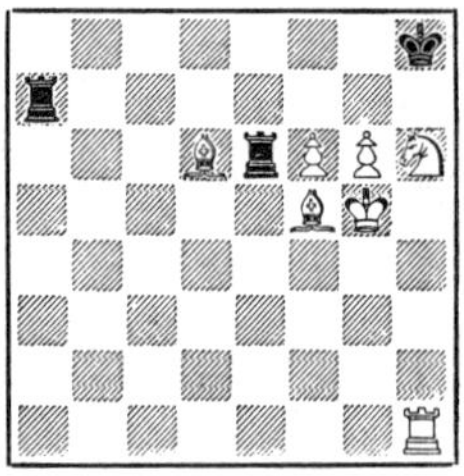

Mate in III exactly.

Pl. 128 : Fn. 76 : PP 154.

Mate in III exactly.
Rd2 is fidated.

PL 129 : Fn. 77 : PP 156.

Mate in III exactly.
Both Rs are fidated.

PL 130 : Fn. 78 : PP 157.

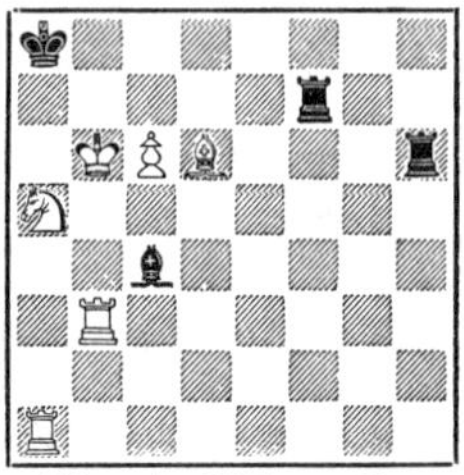

Mate in III exactly.
Unsound.

PL 133 : Fn. 81 : PP 161.

Mate in III exactly.
All the men are fidated.

PL 134 : Fn. 82 : PP 162.

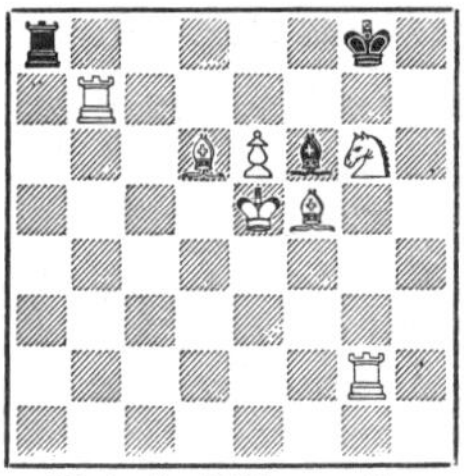

Mate in III exactly.

PL 135 (corr.) : Fn. 83 : PP 163.

Mate in III exactly.

PL 136 : Fn. 85 : PP 165.

Mate in III exactly. Pb7 is immovable, Bb4 may not play first move, and Ra3 may only move to give mate.

PL 138 (corr.) : Fn. 87 : PP 168.

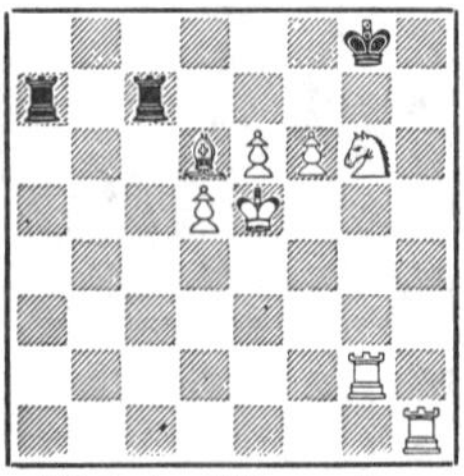

Mate in III exactly.

PL 140 : Fn. 90 : PP 171.

Mate in III exactly.
The Bl. K may not be bared.

PL 142 : Fn. 84 : PP 164.

Mate in III exactly.

PL 172 : Fn. 147.

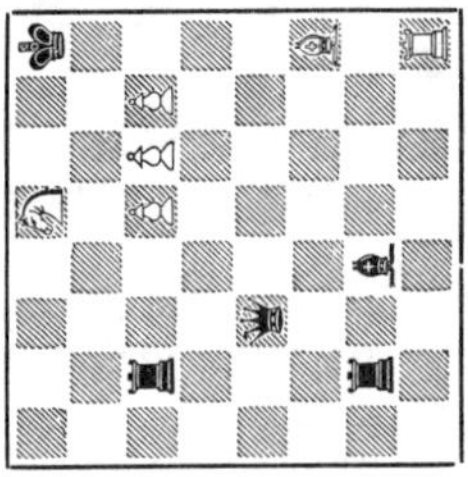

Mate in IV exactly.

PL 173 : Fn. 187 : PP 225.

(Bl.)
Either plays. White mates in V. Unsound.

PL 175 (corr.) : Fn. 197 : PP 226.

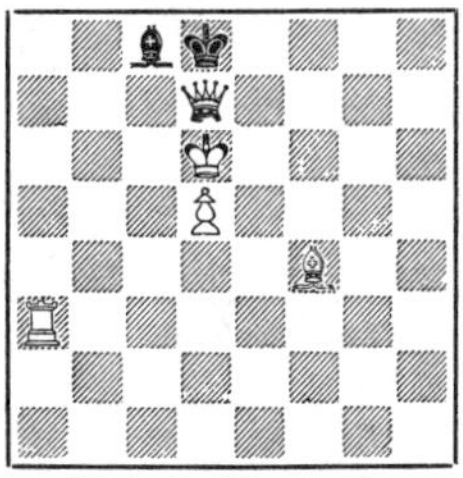

Mate in V exactly.
Bc8 is fidated.

PL 176 : Fn. 198 : PP 227 : Ar. 53.

Mate with Kt in V exactly.

PL 244 : Fn. 243 : PP 300 : Ar. 87.

(Bl.)
Mate with B on f8 in IX exactly.

PL 263 : Fn. 262 : PP 320 : Ar. 86.

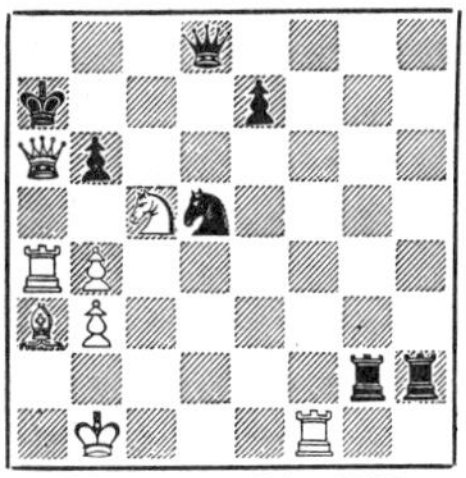

Mate on a7 in XV exactly.

PL 289 : Fn. 289 : PP 345.

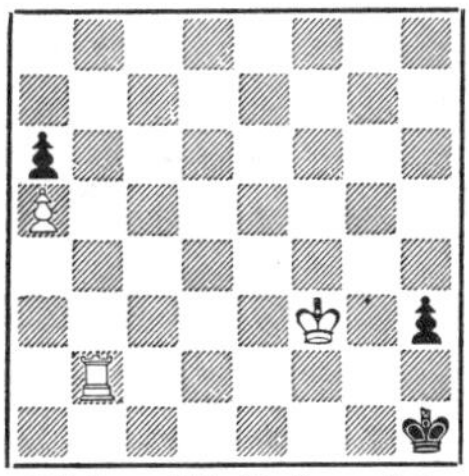

Mate with Pa5 on h1 (in XVII). The Ps are fidated.

Fn. 52.

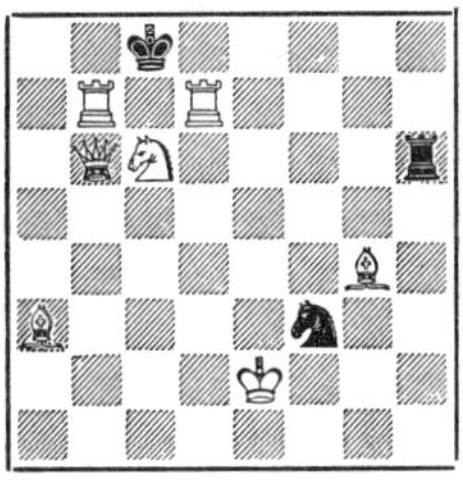

Mate in II exactly.

Fn. 141 : PP 221.

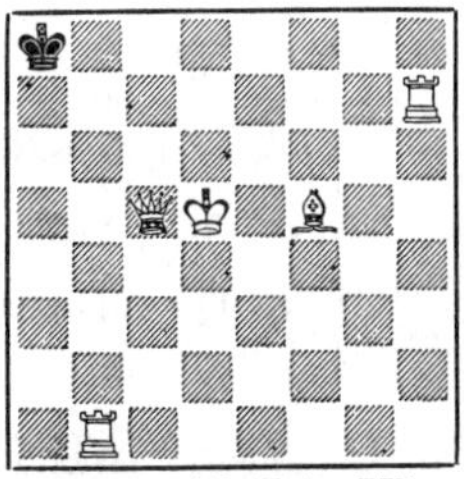

Mate with B in IV exactly.

Fn. 270 : PP 347.

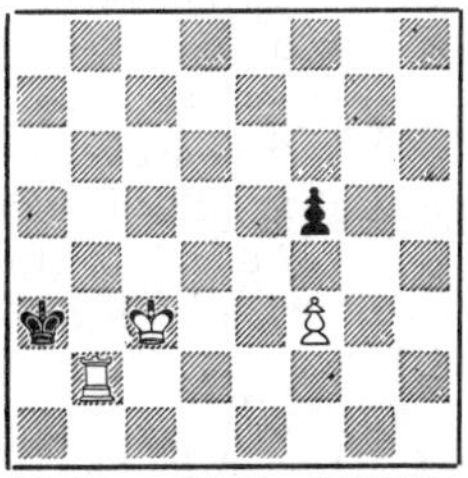

Mate on f5 (in XXIV). The R may only move 7 times.

PP 180 (corr.).

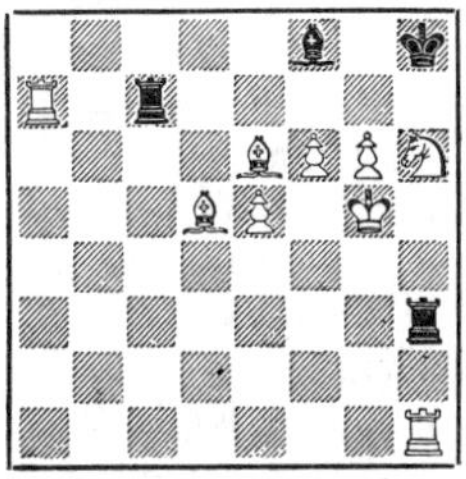

Mate in III exactly.

PP 181.

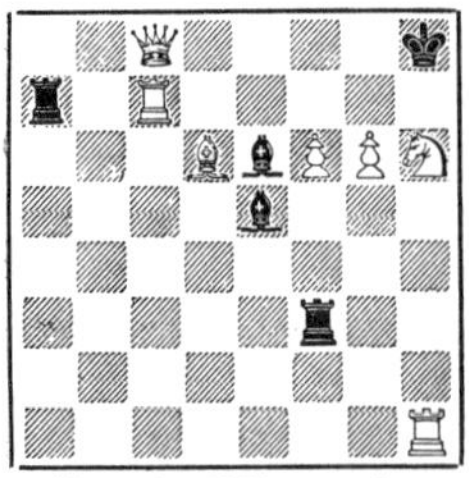

Mate in III exactly.

PP 183.

Mate in III exactly.

PP 184.

Mate in III exactly.

PP 185.

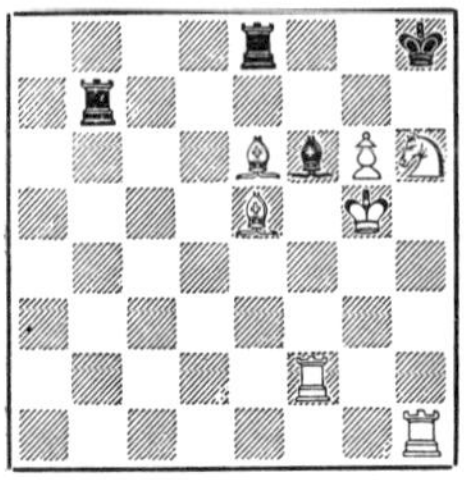

Mate in III exactly.

PP 186.

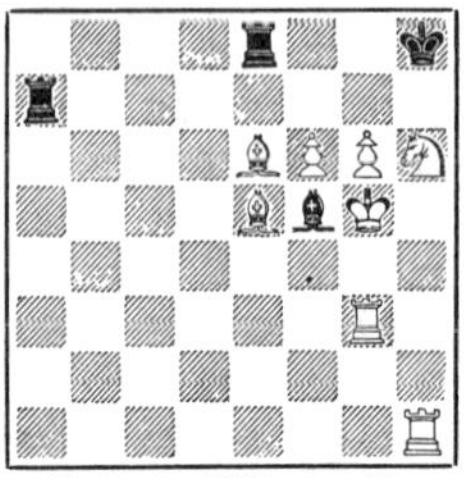

Mate in III exactly.

PP 215.

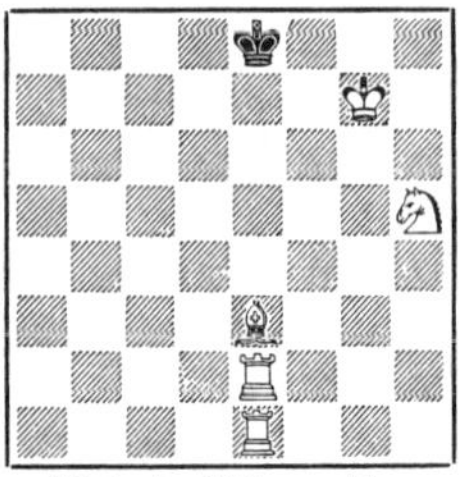

Mate in IV exactly.

PP 230.

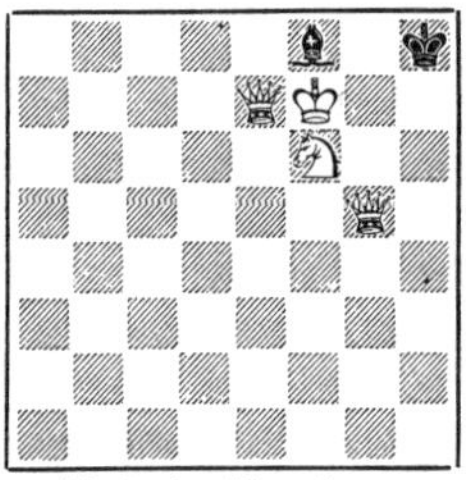

Mate in V or less.
Bf8 is fidated.

(*a*) Problems from PL.

1. 1 Bb7, R × P(a5) + ; 2 Ktf5 + d, Rh7. If 1 Bf7, R × cP. If 1 K~, R~, or Bf3, Rh7. Variation: Kg5 on f5. Sound. 1 Pg7 + , R × P ; 2 Ktf7 m. Or 1 . . ., Kh7 ; 2 Ktf7 m. PL 119 is the same position; mate in III exactly. 1 Ktf5 + d, Rh7 ; 2 Pg7 + , R(a7) × P + ; 3 P × R m. Cf. CB 35.

2. 1 Ktf5 + d, Rh7 ; 2 Pg7 m. Variation: The Kt may not play first move. Unsound. 1 Bf7 or Pf7, Rb2. Otherwise 1 . . ., Rf7 blocks f7. Cf. CB 36.

3 = Fn. 3 = PP 1 is CB 3 var.; position reflected.

4. 1 Rh7 + ; 2 Qg7 m. Cf. CB 9.

5 = Fn. 66 = PP 89. Same position as PL 4. Black mates in III exactly; the Bl. Q is fidated, and the Bl. R is fidated from the K. Unsound. 1 R × R, Ktg6 ; 2 Rf8, Kt × B. If 1 Rg5, Rg7 ; 2 R × R, Be6, &c.

6. 1 any, Pa6 or R~. Variation: Pa7 on a6. Sound. 1 Q × B; 2 Rh7 m. Cf. CB 9.

7. 1 Ktg5 + d, Q × R ; 2 Ktf7 m. Cf. CB 25. Variation: Mate in III exactly. 1 Ktg5 + d ; 2 Kt × B + d ; 3 Ktf7 m.

10. 1 Kh6 ; 2 Kt × B(e6) or Rg8 or Rf7 m. accordingly.

11 = Fn. 8. A variation of PL 10. Add Bl. Ktf3. Mate in II exactly; Wh. R is fidated. 1 Re7 ('only move'), Kt~ ; 2 Pg7 m. Or 1 . . , Bf7 + ; 2 R × B m. 1 Rd7 or c7 will also do, and the fidation of the R seems unnecessary.

22. 1 R × B + ; 2 Ra8 m. Cf. CB 9.

23 = Fn. 10 = PP 3 is really the same as CB 27 (replace Bc3 by two Bl. Ps on d3, e2, and Ph6 by Wh. Kt). PL 120 (same position as PL 23) is a variation in III exactly. Unsound. 1 B × R, B × Kt + ; 2 Kc7, Ra5. If 1 Ktc5 + d, Ba6 + ; 2 Kt × B, Rf8 + .

26. 1 Be6, Bg7 ; 2 Q × B m. Or 1 . . , any other ; 2 Qg7 or Rh7 m. Variations: (1) Be5 fidated. Unsound. 1 Be6, Bg7. (2) Mate in III exactly; Be5 fidated. 1 Be6, B~ ; 2 K~ (not g3), B~ ; 3 Rh7 m. This is PP 91.

27. 1 Ktf6 + d, B × R ; 2 Be6 + d, Bf8. Or 1 . . , P × R = Q ; 2 Be6 + d, Qf8. Variation: Pg7 goes to g8 or is a Q. Sound. 1 Be6 + ; 2 R × P(Q) m. PP 92 is another variation; Q for Pg7. Mate in III exactly. Unsound. 1 Be6 + d, Qf8 ; 2 Ktf6 + d, B × R.

31 = PP 91 is really CB 64 (omit Pg4, colours changed). Mate in III exactly. Unsound. 1 P × B, Rc8 ; 2 B~ + d, Kt × R ; or 2 Rd8 + , Kt × R + . If 1 K × B, Rc8 ; 2 any, Kt × R.

33. 1 R(c7) × Q, R × Kt (or R). If 1 R × R, Bd5 or h5. If 1 Kt × R + , K × R ; 2 R × Q + , K × Kt(g6). Variation: Add Wh. Be4. Sound. 1 Kt × R + , K × R ; 2 R × Q m. Or 1 . . , Q × Kt ; 2 Rg8 m. PP 94 is another variation: Add Wh. Be4. Mate in III exactly. Unsound. 1 R × R, Q × R. If 1 Rg8 + , Q × R. If 1 Kt × Q + , K × R.

40 = Fn. 14 = PP 15. A different arrangement of CB 26 (Qf6 on f7, Ktf4 on c3, add Wh. Bd3. Mate in II exactly. 1 Re6 + , B × R ; 2 Kte4, Bb4, or Bf4 m. Variation: P for Qf7. Unsound. 1 Re6 + , K × R.

41. 1 Rh8, R × R ; 2 Pd7 m. Or 1 . . , B × P ; 2 R × R m. Or 1 . . , Qc7 ; 2 Pd7 m. Variation: Be5 on e6. Unsound. 1 Rh8, Bg8. This is PP 17.

46. 'Aurei primo trahunt, et uolunt matare rubeos ad duos tractus nec plures nec pauciores. Tu qui habes aureos trahe primo roccum tuum in A (a8), et dicas ei scac. Ipse capiet te de suo alphino, et tu dabis ei scac et mat de tuo milite in loco ubi erat roccus. Sed si traheres primo roccum tuum in B (a7), ipse traheret alphinum suum in C (b7), et deffenderetur. . . . Item si tu traheres primo alium roccum in B, ipse traheret roccum suum in D (f7) et deffenderetur. Item potest istud partitum esse trium tractuum (PP 96) et fit taliter. Tu qui habes aureos trahe primo roccum tuum in G (e7). Si trahat roccum suum in D, trahe roccum tuum in A, et postea mat de milite in loco rocci. Item si traheres alphinum tuum in A, uel alibi, ipse traheret roccum suum in B. Item si traheret alphinum suum in E (d7), dicas scac in A, et postea cape alphinum suum et mat.'

47 = Fn. 17 = PP 19. A variation of PL 46 (Wh. P for Ktb6, Bd5 on b5). Mate in II exactly. 1 R(a6)a7, R × Kt ; 2 R(g7)b7 m. Or 1 . . , Bd7 ; 2 Kta6 m. Or 1 . . , any ; 2 R(g7)b7 or Kta6 m. accordingly. Variation: Mate in III exactly; all the Bl. men are fidated. 1 Rc7, R × Kt ; 2 R(a6)a7, B(c6)~ ; 3 R(c7)b7 m. If 1 . . , Rf6 or e5 ; 2 R(a6)a7, R × B ; 3 Kta6 m. This is PP 97.

48 = Fn. 18 = PP 20. A different setting of CB 6 (Wh. Rb3, g7, Kta6, Bc5, d4 ; Bl. Ka8, Ktc8, Bd6, e5). Mate in II exactly. 1 R(g7)b7, B(e5)~ ; 2 Ktc7 m. Or 1 . . , Kt(c8)~ ; 2 Ra7 m. Or 1 B(d6)~ ; 2 Rb8 m. The MS. solution 1 Rd7 is foiled by Bb4.

49 = Fn. 54 = PP 61 is CB 274 (omit Ps e4 and e5 ; add Bl. Bh6 ; reflect), but adds the variation: Remove P. Unsound. 1 any, Bc4. This is PP 62.

52 is BS 31 (CB 20) but adds the variation: Mate in III exactly; all the men except the B are fidated. Unsound. 1 Rc3, Rc6. But the MSS. overlook 1 Pg7 + , Kh7 ; 2 Ktf7 + d, Kg6 ; 3 Rh6 m. The variation is sound. It is PP 103.

53 = Fn. 47 = PP 57 is CB 19.

54 = Fn. 48 = PP 58. Another setting of CB 6 (Wh. Kf3, Rb5, d7, Kta6, Bc5, Pc6 ; Bl. Ka8, Ktc8, Bd6, e5, Pg3). 1 Kg2 ; 2 R or Kt m. accordingly.

55. 1 . . , Rf8 ; 2 . . , Rf7 and 1 . . , Rf1 ; 2 Qf7, Rg8 + ; or 2 Pf7, Rf5 + , are both sufficient defences.

56. 1 Pg7 + , R × P ; 2 Ktf7 m. ; or 1 . . , Kh7 ; 2 Ktf7 or g4 m. Variation: Remove Pf5, and make Rh1 immovable. Unsound. 1 Pg7 + , Kh7 and escapes.

57. 1 . . , Rg1 + ; 2 K~, Rg2 (or R +).

58 = Fn. 55 = PP 63 is a variation of PL 1 (add Bl. Ktb5). Mate in II exactly. 1 Bb7; 2 Ktf7 m. Variation: Omit the Ktb5, = PL 1 exactly.

59 = Fn. 56 = PP 64. A variant of CB 32. Mate in II exactly. Unsound. 1 Bg7, Rh5. Or 1 Bc7, Rh5 or f5. Or 1 Pb7 + , Ka7 (not R × P + as in MS., for 2 Kt × R m.). Or 1 K~, Ra7. Or 1 Pc7, R × P. Variation: Omit Pc4. Sound. 1 Pb7 + , Ka7; 2 Ktc4 m.; or 1 . . , R × P + ; 2 Kt × R m. This is PP 65.

60 = Fn. 57 = PP 66. Wh. Kf6, Ra7, Ktc5, d6; Bl. Kd8, Kte7, f8. Mate in II. Unsound. 1 Rd7 + , Kt × R + . Or 1 R × Kt, Kth7 + . A setting of CB 1.

61 = Fn. 58 = PP 67. Wh. Kb6, Rh7, Ktd6, e5; Bl. Kd8, Ktb8, c7. Mate in II exactly. 1 R × Kt, Kt~; 2 Kt or R m. accordingly. Another variation of CB 1.

62 = Fn. 60 = PP 69. Wh. Kf1, Rg7, Qf6, Be4; Bl. Kh8, Rf7, Ktf8, g6, Bf5, g8. Mate in II exactly; Rg7 is fidated from K, Qf6 is fidated generally. Unsound. 1 Rh7 + , B × R. Or 1 R × B + , Kh7; 2 Rh8 + , Kt × R. Variation: Remove Ktg6. Sound. 1 R × B + , Kh7; 2 Rh8 m. The variation is PP 70. The position is a variation of CB 9.

63 = Fn. 61 = PP 71. A variant of PL 10 (Rg7 on h7, add Bl. Ktf3; reflect). Mate in II exactly. 1 Rd7; 2 Pb7 or Rc7 or Kt × B m. accordingly. Apparently 1 Re7 or f7 will do as well. Variation: Remove Ktc3. Unsound. 1 Ka6, Bb8. This is PP 72.

64 = Fn. 63 = PP 75. A variant of CB 4 (Kh6 on d6, Ra1 on a2; colours changed). Mate with Pb6 in II exactly; Ra2 is fidated. 1 Kc7; 2 Pb7 m. Variation: Kd6 on h6. Unsound. This is really CB 4. PP diagrams it again as PP 76.

65 = Fn. 62 = PP 73. Wh. Kg5, Ra7, Qf6; Bl. Kh8, Ktf8, Bg8. Mate in II exactly; Ra7 is fidated from K, and Q is fidated generally. Unsound. 1 Rh7 + , Kt × R + . Or 1 K~, B~. Or 1 Qg7 + , Kh7. Variation: Ra7 on e7. Sound. 1 Qg7 + ; 2 Qh8 m. This is PP 74. The position is another variant of CB 9. So also is

66 = Fn. 64 = PP 77. Wh. Ka6, Rd7, Qc6; Bl. Ka8, Ktc8, Bb8. Mate in II exactly; all the men are fidated. 1 Rd6; 2 Qb7 m. Variation (diagrammed again as PP 78): Rd7 on h7. Unsound. 1 Rc7, Bd6. Or 1 Rb7, Kta7.

67 = Fn. 59 = PP 68. A variant of CB 33 (Rf6 on e6, Bl. Qf5 for Pg4; reflect). Sound. Mate in II exactly. 1 Kb5. Variation: Remove Qc5. Unsound.

68 = Fn. 136 = PP 173. A variant of CB 49 (Bb5 on c6, Rb3, c3, on a4, b4; reflect). Mate in III exactly. 1 Bd4, Bb8; 2 Pb7 + ; 3 Kt m. Or 1 . . , R × B; 2 Ktc7 + ; 3 Ra8 m.

69 = Fn. 137 = PP 174. Wh. Ra1, Kta3, Bd6, Pb6, c6; Bl. Ka8, Rc8, h7. Mate in III exactly. 1 Ktb5 + d, Ra7; 2 Ra6, R × R; 3 Pb7 m. Or 2 . . , R × P; R × R m. Or 2 . . , Rc7; 3 Kt × R m. (Cf. CB 42.) Variation: Kta3 on a4. 1 Ktc3 + , Ra7; 2 Ktb5, R × R; 3 Pb7 m. Or 2 . . , R × P; 3 R × R m. Or 2 . . , Rc7; 3 Kt × R m. This is PP 175.

70 = Fn. 138 = PP 176. A variant of CB 67 (omit Bd5). Mate in III exactly. Unsound. 1 Rd1, Rc7; 2 Rh1, Rh2. Or 1 Ra1, Rc7; 2 Ra8 + , Rb8. Variation: Rb2, c3, on c2, a3. Now sound. 1 Rb1, Rb2 or 3 (or Rh2; 2 Rb7, &c.); 2 Rh1; 3 Ktf7 m. This is PP 177.

71 = Fn. 139 = PP 178. Wh. Ra1, Kta6, Bd6, Pb6, c6; Bl. Ka8, Re2, f3. Mate in III exactly (cf. CB 43). 1 Ktc5 + d, Ra2; 2 R × R + , Ra3; 3 R × R m. Or 1 . . , Ra3; 2 Kte6; 3 Ktc7 or R × R m. accordingly. Variation: Re2, f3, on f2, e3. Unsound. 1 Ktc5 + , Ra3; 2 Re6, Rf7, &c. This is PP 179.

72 = Fn. 140 is position of CB 110. Mate in III exactly. 1 Rf1 (or Rd1, &c.); 2 Rc1; 3 Rc8 m. Variation: Black plays and White mates in II exactly. 1 . . , Kd8 (or Kf8, &c.); 2 Rc1; 3 Rc8 m.

73 = Fn. 135 = PP 172. Wh. Rh1, Kth6, Bb6, Pf6, g6; Bl. Kh8, Ra4, b4, Be6 (a variant of CB 49). Mate in III exactly. Unsound. 1 Bd4, Bg8; 2 R on *h* file, Be6. If 1 Kt f7 + , Kg8.

104. Wh. Kd6, Rc6, e6; Bl. Kd6, is BS 62 (see CB 53), but the text adds a variation (diagrammed separately as PP 130): Add Bl. Bc4. Mate in III exactly, each Wh. piece moving once, and the Bl. B only allowed to move if it makes a capture. 1 Re2, B × R; 2 Ke6; 3 Rc8 m. This is CB 57 without the Wh. P.

114. Wh. Rd4, f6, Kte4, e6; Bl. Ke5, is BS 72 (CB 47), but adds a variation in IV exactly (= PP 189). 1 Rb4; 2 Ktd8; 3 Ktc6 +; 4 Rd6 m.

116. 'Aurei primo trahunt et uolunt mattare rubeos ad tres tractus, et uidetur quod fieri possit, trahendo primo alphinum in A (c5) dicendo scac; deinde dicendo scac de rocco in B (e2), et tercio mat de milite. Non tamen fit, quia poterit redire ad primum locum.'

117. 1 Rd8 +; 2 Ktg5 +; 3 Be5 m. Contrast with CB 74.

118 = Fn. 134 = PP 153 is the same problem as PL 75 (BS 33, CB 50), but the text is different from either BS or CB.

119 = Fn. 65 = PP 93. See PL 1 above.

120 = Fn. 68 = PP 95. See PL 23 above.

121. 1 Rh8 +; 2 Rh7 +; 3 Pf7 m.

122. 1 Ktf5 +; 2 Kte7; 3 R × R or Bf6 m. Variation: Rh1 is not fidated. Unsound. 1 Ktf5 +, Rh7; 2 Kte7, R × R.

123. 1 Pe7, Rc4. Or 1 Kth6 +, Kh8; 2 any, Bg6. Or 1 Kt elsewhere + d, Bg6. Variation: Add Wh. Pd4. Sound. 1 Pe7, Bg6; 2 R(g3)h3; 3 Rh8 m. Or 1 . . , R × P; 2 Kth6 +; 3 Ktf7 m. The variation is PP 142.

124. 1 Ra8; 2 Rh8 +; 3 R × R m.

125. 1 Ktg5 +, Rh3; 2 Pf5, Rd7; 3 R × R +, Rh7. Or 3 Pg7 +, R × P. Or 3 Ktf7 +, R × Kt. And if 2 Rh2, Rd7, &c. Variation: Rd2, c3, on c2, d3. Sound. 1 Ktg5 +, Rh3; 2 Rd1; 3 Rd8 or Pg7 or Ktf7 m. accordingly. This is PP 145.

126. 1 Ktf7 +; 2 Rh7; 3 Rh8 or P × R or Kth6 m. accordingly.

127 = Fn. 75 = PP 148. A variant of CB 42 (Re7 on a7, omit Kg1) with same solution, but adds variation: Rf8 on e8. Unsound. 1 Ktg5 +, Rh7; 2 any, R × B. This is PP 150.

128. 1 Rh1 +, Rh2; 2 Pg7 +; 3 Pf7 m. Or 1 . . , Kg8; 2 Pf7 +; 3 Pg7 or Rh8 m. Variation: Ke6 on a6. Unsound. 1 Rh1 +, Rh2; 2 Pg7 +, Kg8; 3 Pf7 +, K × P. This is PP 155. Cf. Picc. 118.

129. 1 Ktg5 +, Rh7; 2 Rh6; 3 Pg7 m. 'Si tu trahas alio modo, tu non potes lucrari.' *Lucrari* is rare in the older texts, but common in the later ones.

130. 1 Pc7, Ba6. Or 1 Kt × B +, Ra7; 2 ~, R × B. Or 1 Re3, Ba2 or Ra7. Variation: Ra1, b3, on b1, a3. Still unsound. 1 Re1, Ra7.

131 = Fn. 79 = PP 158. A variant of PL 130 (Kta5 on a6, Rb3 on a3, omit Bc4, add Wh. Be5). 'Aurei primo trahunt et uolunt matare rubeos ad tres tractus, et fit hoc modo. Tu qui habes aureos trahe primo tuum militem in A (c5), et est scac discoopertum. Et ipse cooperiet se de suo rocco, et tu trahes tuum militem in B (d7), et non poterit se deffendere quin matetur. Sed si tu traheres tuum alphinum primo in C (c7), ipse finget unum tractum de suo rocco, et postea caperet tuum alphinum et deffenderetur. Item si tu remoueres tuum regem ipse traheret suum roccum in D (a7), et deffenditur.' *Fingere unum tractum*, MF. *feindre un trait*, ME. *to feign a draught*, is the regular mediaeval term for 'to play a waiting or non-attacking move'.

132 = Fn. 80 = PP 159. Another variant of PL 130 (Kta5 on a6, Rf7 on g7, add Wh. Be5). Mate in III exactly; Ra1 is fidated. Unsound. 1 Kc5, Ra7. Or 1 B × R, B × Kt, and 2 . . , R × B. Or 1 Ktb4 +, Ra7. Variation (separately diagrammed in PP 160): Bc4 on c5. Sound. 1 Kt × B +, Ra7; 2 Ktd7, &c.

133. 1 Ktf5 +, Rh7; 2 Rg7; 3 Rh7 m. It can also be solved by 1 Ktg8 +. Variations: (1) add Wh. Kf4; (2) add Wh. Kf5. Both are unsound. 1 Ktf5 +, Rh7; 2 Rg7, R +.

134. 1 Ra7, R × R; 2 Kte7 +; 3 Rg8 m. Or 1 . . , Bh8; 2 Kt × B +; 3 Rh7 m. Or 1 . . , Bd8; 2 Kth8 +, &c. Or 1 . . , R~; 2 Ktf8 + d; 3 Rh7 m.

135. 1 Kt × B +; 2 Rd6; 3 R × R(a7) or Rd8 m. accordingly.

136 = Fn. 85 = PP 165. 'Tu qui habes aureos trahe primo tuum roccum in B (e7) uel in C (e6) et quicquid rubei faciant tu matabis ad tercium si bene ludas.' 1 Re7 is sufficient (1 . . , R × R; 2 Bd6 +; 3 Ra8 m. Or 1 . . , Rf6; 2 Rb7 +; 3 Ra8 m. Or 1 . . , Kc8; 2 Rc7 +; 3 Ra8 or Bd6 m. accordingly), but 1 Re6 seems to be met by 1 . . , Rd7.

137 = Fn. 86 = PP 166. Wh. Rd1, h1, Kth6, Bd6, f5, Pg6, f6; Bl. Kh8, Rc3,

c7, Be6. Mate in III exactly. This is similar to PL 126. 1 Ktf7 + ; 2 Rh7 ; 3 P × R, Rg7, Rh8, or Kth6 m. accordingly. Variation: Add Bl. Bd5. Unsound. 1 Ktf7 +, Kg8 ; 2 Rh7, B × Kt ; 3 P × B +, R × P. This is PP 167.

138. 1 Kth8 + ; 2 Pf7 + ; 3 P × R m.

139 = Fn. 88 = PP 169. A variant of BS 43, CB 71 (omit Rb7, Pb3, Kg5, Pg2). Mate in III exactly; all the men are fidated. Unsound. 1 Rh5 or Rc1, Rc6. Or 1 Rd1, b1, a1, R(c7) opposite R.

140. 1 Bb4 ; 2 Ktc7 + ; 3 Ra8 m.

141 = Fn. 89 = PP 170. Wh. Rg2, h1, Ktg6, Bd6, Pe6, f6 ; Bl. Kg8, Re4, f3. Mate in III exactly. 1 Rh6 (or h5), R × fP ; 2 Ktf4 + ; 3 R × R m. Or 1 . . , R × eP ; 2 Kte5 + ; 3 R × R m. Or 1 . . , Rg3 or g4 ; 2 R × R, &c.

142. 1 Ra8 + ; 2 Ktd7 + ; 3 Ra2 m.

164 = Fn. 172 = PP 214. Wh. Kh1, Ra1, Ktb4, Ba3, Pb7, c7 ; Bl. Ka8, Rg3, Ktf3. Mate with Kt in IV exactly, is a shortened version of the Dilārām mate. 1 Bc5 + d ; 2 Ra8 + ; 3 Pb7 + ; 4 Kta6 m.

165 = Fn. 142 = PP 217 is CB 118 reflected, with Wh. Q fidated.

166 = Fn. 143 = PP 218. Wh. Ke6, Rd6, Ktd4, e4, Qe7, Pc6, e5 ; Bl. Ke8, Ra8, Ktg4. Mate with Pe5 in IV exactly. Unsound. 1 Ktf6 +, Kt × Kt ; 2 P × Kt, Ra1 ; 3 Kte2, Rf1 ; or 3 Ktf3, Re1 +. Or 1 Rd8 +, R × R ; 2 Ktd6 +, R × Kt + ; 3 P × R, Ktf6. A variant of CB 114, &c.

167 = Fn. 145 = PP 220. Wh. Kh6, Ra1, Ktb4, Ba3, d5, Pb6, c6 ; Bl. Ka8, Re3, f2. Mate in IV exactly. Unsound. 1 Bc4 +, Ra3. 'Videtur istud partitum idem cum precedente, sed est penitus diversum, et provenit ista diversitas ex positione regis.' The problem referred to follows in PL, but precedes in F and PP.

168 = Fn. 144 = PP 219. In diagram of PL 167 remove Kh6 to g1 and reflect. Now sound. A new setting of CB 115, allowing an extra line of play.

170 = PP 223 is really BS 76, CB 113 (Rd4 on d1, Pf6 on g7, add Bl. Kth8, Bg3, Ph7). The extra men make no difference to the solution.

171 = Fn. 146 = PP 222 is BS 87, CB 101, but the diagram is older (add Wh. Ka1 ; Bl. Rc2, b3, Ktc3). The text differs from BS. 'Aurei primo trahunt et uolunt matare rubeos in loco ubi scribitur A (h6) uel B (f8) ad quatuor tractus et fit hoc modo. Trahe primo roccum in A et dicas ei scac, et alium in B et dicas ei scac, et firgiam in C (f6) et dicas ei scac, et ipse accipiet vnum de roccis tuis, et tu trahe alium in angulum et dicas ei scac et mat.' The use of *firgia* is rare in PL, and generally occurs only in positions added from sources other than BS, and probably French.

172. 1 Bd6 + ; 2 Ra8 + ; 3 Pb7 + ; 4 Pb6 m.

173. 'Aurei primo trahunt et uolunt aurei matare rubeos ad v tractus, et debes isto modo dare partitum: accipias quam partem tu uis. Tu qui habes aureos trahe primo alphinum in A (h6), postea in B (f4), postea dicas scac de pedone, et postea scac de rocco in angulo. Si uadat in C (g2), tu dabis scac et mat de rocco in E (g1). Si uadat in D (e2), tu dabis ei mat in F (e1). Quidquid ipse faciat, fac primos duos tractus in A, et in B de alphino, et postea facies secundum quod ipse trahet, ut per te uidere poteris.' But if Black plays 1 . . , Rb7 ; 2 . . , R × R + ; or 1 . . , Ktc6 ; 2 . . , Ktd8 or e5 + ; the mate in V is spoiled. The position in Fn. 187 (omit Qc2 ; Kf7 on c2) is upset by 1 . . , Ktc4 ; 2 . . , Kte3 +. The text is important for the light which it throws upon the method of propounding a wager-game.

174 = Fn. 188 = PP 224. Wh. Kg6, Ra8, f1, Bc8 ; Bl. Kh8. Mate with B in V exactly: is a variant of CB 135. 1 Kf7 ; 2 Kf6, Kh8 ; 3 Rg1 ; 4 Rh1 + ; 5 Be6 m. Or 2 . . , Kh6 ; 3 Rf5 ; 4 Rh5 + ; 5 Be6 m. Or 2 . . , Kg8 ; 3 Kg6 ; 4 Rh1 + ; 5 Be6 m.

175. 1 Rf3 ; 2 Bh6 ; 3 Kc6 ; 4 Rf8 ; 5 Pd6 m. Cf. Picc. 161, Luc. 111.

176. 1 Ra8 +, &c. Another setting of the Dilārām mate.

177 = Fn. 199 = PP 228. Wh. Ka1, Ra6, Qa5, b5, b6, c5, c6, e5 ; Bl., Kb8. Mate on c5 in V exactly. This is another setting of CB 133, with a different text from BS. The Queen is again named *firgia*.

178 = Fn. 200 = PP 229 is CB 230 (diagram varies slightly).

192 = Fn. 211 = PP 267. A variant setting of BS 120 (CB 151 ; Rb8 on a8, Kh8 on g8). The solution is similar.

194 = BS 112, CB 142, but with different text.

240 = PP 296. Wh. Kb3, Rh8, Ktf8, Bh6; Bl. Ka1; mate in VIII exactly, by 1 Kte6; 2 Rc8; 3 Ktd4; 4 Ra8; 5 Kc4; 6 Ra1; 7 Ra2; 8 Re2 m. This is really the same as CB 188. The CB position occurs in M 38, PF 196, Lobk. 30, and with accidental omission of R in W 174.

244. 1 Bc4+; 2 Rg1+; 3 Rc1+; 4 Rc3+; 5 Pd5+; 6 Re3+; 7 Re6+; 8 Ktg5+; 9 B × Kt m. Cf. Cott. 1, K 28, Ash. 30.

263. 1 Qb7+; 2 Ra8+; 3 Rc8+; 4 Rc6+; 5 Re6+; 6 Re4+; 7 Rc4+; 8 Rc2+; 9 Bc1+; 10 Rc4+; 11 Re4+; 12 Re6+; 13 Rc6+; 14 Rc8+; 15 Ra8 m.

264 = Fn. 263 = PP 321. Wh. Ka8, Rc8, Ktb5, c5, Qf6, Bb4, c4, Pf3, g3, g6, going to first line; Bl. Kd1, Rc1, c2, Bh1, h8; mate with B on c8 in XV; the Wh. Kts and Bl. Rs are fidated, and the Bl. Rs are debarred from making a capture. This is only a variant setting of CB 216. The following problem in PL (265) is the CB position in which the new Q leaps to give check. The present setting preserves the Muslim solution.

271. Wh. Kd6, Pc6, e6; Bl. Kd8; dot on d6. 'Aurei primo trahunt et uolunt matare regem rubeum, et est iste ludus subtilis, et rex rubeus non potest reueri clausus, ut uerbi gratia dicatur. Scac de pedone ex parte dextra. Si uadat rex rubeus uersus partem dextram, aurei *seruabunt* eum, et facient reginam de alio, et matabunt eum. Deinde aurei habent tractum ante, et uolunt trahere pedonem ex parte dextra. Si tu scias bene deffendere, non matabis. Statim ibis uersum partem sinistram, et ipse ibit cum rege ubi fit punctus. Et tu descendas cum tuo. Ipse ibit sub pedone suo. Si tu ascendas directe, matus es. Si ascendas uersus cantonem bene deffendis. Si ipse faciat reginam non ascendas, sed uadas directe uersus eam. Si ipse dat scacum, deffende directe. Si uadat cum regina noua duos tractus, uade uersus cantonem, et quicquid ipse faciat bene deffendas, si caute ludas.' Cf. CB 140, &c. The text of this problem is important for the light it throws upon the sources of the new material in PL, Fn., and PP. The italicized word *seruabunt* makes the sentence unintelligible. It is clearly due to a blunder of the scribe who, with a French text before him, misread *suiront* (L. *sequuntur*) as *s'uiront* or *seruiront*. The writer of Fn. (Fn. 271) has *warderont*, and therefore had a Latin text before him with *seruabunt*. PP 332, on the other hand, has *chil dor le suiront*, and consequently is derived neither from PL nor from Fn.

275 = Fn. 275 = PP 338. The Knight's Tour, CB 244.

277. Wh. Kb6, Rb7; Bl. Kc8. Mate in XII or less, the R only moving to give mate. Cf. CB 207.

279. CB 227 (add Wh. Qe7). Also in W 182, &c.

283 = Fn. 283 = PP 335. Wh. Ke5, Rd5, Qe6, f5; Bl. Ke7, Rh8. Black plays and draws. This is the variation of BS 184: see CB 253.

284 = BS 189 (CB 251), but the text is different.

286. Also in W 171, &c. It is the main play of CB 279.

287. Also in W 176, &c. It is CB 240.

288. Also in W 177, &c. It is CB 235.

289. 1 Kf2, Kh2; 2 Rb4; 3 Rb3, Kh2; 4 Kf1; 5 Rb2, Ph2; 6 Rb5, P × R; 7 Pa6; 8 Pa7; 9 Pa8 = Q; 10 Kf2, Pb1 = Q; 11 Kf1, Qd1; 12 Qb7, Qe2+; 13 Kf2; 14 Qc6; 15 Qd5; 16 Qe4; 17 Qf3; 18 Qg2 m. If 11 . . , Qc2; 12 Qc6, &c.

290 = Fn. 290. CB 277 (Kb8 on a8, Pc6 on c7, reflect). The PL solution is in XII. It begins 1 Pf8 = Q; 2 Ke8; 3 Kd8; 4 Ke7, and the position is that in CB after move 2.

(*b*) PROBLEMS FROM FN.

52. 1 Rb8+; 2 Rd8 m.

67 is the variation of PL 7, with the text problem of PL 7 as variation.

141. 1 Rh8+; 2 Rb5; 3 Ra8+; 4 B m.

270 = PP 347. 1 Kc2; 2 Kb1; 3 Ka1; 4 Ka2; 5 Ka3; 6 Ka4; 7 Ka5; 8 Ka6; 9 Kb6; 10 Ra2; 11 Ra7; 12 Ka6; 13 Rb7; 14 Ka7; 15 Ka8; 16 Kb8; 17 Kc8; 18 Kd8; 19 Ke8; 20 Kf7; 21 Rb8; 22 Rh8 +; 23 Rh7; 24 Rh5 m.

(*c*) Problems from PP.

The following problems appear as variations only in BS, but in PP they are diagrammed separately.

PP	BS	PP	BS	PP	BS	PP	BS	PP	BS	PP	BS	PP	BS
30	9	53	30	98	5	110	45			232	99	244	108
39	16	84	37	101	10	129	62	188	26	241	107	248	109
50	27	86	39	102	26	177	41	223	76	242	107	314	173

The following problems appear as variations only in PL but in PP they are diagrammed separately.

PP	PL	PP	PL	PP	PL	PP	PL	PP	PL	PP	PL	PP	PL
9	6	65	59	74	65	90	7	97	47	145	125	160	132
17	41	70	62	76	64	91	26	100	18	150	127	167	137
62	49	72	63	78	66	96	46	103	52	155	128	175	69
								130	104			179	71
								142	123			189	114

36. Wh. Kb5, Rd7, Qc6, Pc5 (going to c1); Bl., Ka8, Ktc8, Bb8, d5, Pb4, d6. Mate in II exactly; the R fidated from the K, the Q fidated from all. Unsound. 1 Qb7 +, Ka7; 2 Qa8 +, Bb7. Or 1 Q × B, P × P. Cf. CB 9.

92. See under PL 27 above.

94. See under PL 33 above.

100. See under CB 35.

180. 1 R × R (h3), R × R(a7); 2 Bb7; 3 R × B or Ktf7 m. acc. Or 1 . . , Rh7 or c3; 2 Ra8; 3 R × B or Ktf7 m. acc. Or 1 . . , B × Kt; 2 Ra8 +; 3 R × R or R × B m.: or 2 R × B +; 3 Ra8 or R × R m.

181. 1 Ktf5 +, Rh3; 2 R × R +; 3 Kte7 m. Or 1 . ., Kg8; 2 Re7; 3 Kt × R or Re8 or Pf7 m.

182. A variant of PP 181 (Rf3 on f4, Be5 white, add Bl. Qf5; omit Wh. Pf6). Mate in III exactly. 1 Ktf7 +, Kg8; 2 Rh7; 3 Rg7 or h8 m. Or 2 . . , Rh4; 3 Rg7 m. Or 2 . . , B × Q; 3 Rg7 or h8 or R × B m. (It can also be solved by 1 B × R, Q × P (or R × R); 2 Ktf7 +; 3 Rh8 m. Or 1 . . , Bg8; 2 Rg7; 3 Ktf7 or R × B m. acc.).

183. 1 Bc7, R × B; 2 Qg7 +; 3 Ktf7 or f5 m. acc. Or 1 . . , B × Kt; 2 Pg7 +; 3 R × B m. Or 1 . . , R +; 2 Ktf5 +; 3 R × B m. Or 1 . . , R on line 2; 2 Ktf5 +; 3 R × B or Qg7 m. acc.

184. 1 Ktf7 +; 2 Rh8 +; 3 Kth6 m.

185. 1 R × B, R × B; 2 Ktf7 +; 3 Rh8 m.

186. 1 Ktg4 +, Bh3; 2 R × B +; 3 R × R m. Or 1 . . , Bh7; 2 Pg7 +; 3 P × R m.

187. A variant of PP 186 (Bf5 on d5). Mate in III exactly. Unsound. 1 Rc3, Rh7; 2 Pg7 +, R × P +. Or 1 Ktg4 +, Rh7; 2 R(g3)h3, R × B.

215. 1 Rd1; 2 Ktf6; 3 Rd5; 4 B m.

230. 1 Qh6, B × Q; 2 Kte4; 3 Ktg5; 4 Qf6; 5 Qg7 m.

346. Wh. Kb6, Rb7, c7, Bh6; Bl. Ka8, Ba6. Mate on a8, the Wh. B being immovable and the Bl. B fidated. A variant of CB 219 &c. The MS. solution is similar.

I now turn to the second of the great European problem collections, that which goes by the name of *Civis Bononiae*. We possess a number of MSS. of the complete work, and some other MSS. either unfinished or selections from the greater work. These are all in Latin, and were copied in Italy. The complete book does not appear to have been translated, although there are some Italian MSS. which are certainly derived from this collection. The MSS. of this group are as follows:

L = MS. Lasa, originally in a private library in Rome, now in the library of Baron v. d. Lasa. This is a small quarto parchment MS., written in a hand of the second half of the 15th c., which consists of ii + 242 leaves (i, blank; ii a, a note partly in cypher; ii b, blank; 1 a, blank; 1 b, the prefatory poem; 2 a–145 b, the 288 chess problems of the collection; 146 a–153 b, blank diagrams, of which those on 146, 147, 148 a, 149 b, 150 a have been filled by a slightly later hand; 154 a–193 b, 80 problems of tables; 194 a–217 b, 48 problems of merels; 218 a–225 b, blank diagrams of merels, of which the first has been partially filled; 226 a–233 b, 16 diagrams of the 'Ship' puzzle under different conditions; 234 a–234 b, blank). This is the most accurate of all the CB MSS., and the diagrams are for the most part identical with those in BS.

R = MS. Vittorio Emanuel Lib., Rome, No. 273. A beautifully executed parchment MS. of the middle of the 15th c., of 217 quarto leaves (1–4 a, blank; 4 b, the poem; 5 a–148 b, a leaf between ff. 62 and 63 being omitted in the foliation, the 288 problems of chess; 149 a–186 b, 76 problems of tables; 187–188, blank diagrams of tables; 189 a–212 b, 48 problems of merels; 213 a, blank diagram of merels; 213 b–216 b, blank).

B = MS. Vatican, Barberini, Lat. 254, formerly in the Palazzo Barberini, Rome. A MS. similar to the last and of the same date, of 4 + 240 leaves (1–4, blank except for a few unimportant notes; 1 a, the poem; 1 b, blank; 2 a–144 b, a leaf between ff. 52 and 65 being omitted in the foliation, the 288 problems of chess; 145 a–160 b, blank chess diagrams, the first of which has been partially filled by a later hand; 161 a–198 b, 76 problems of tables; 199 a–206 b, blank diagrams of tables; 207 a–230 b, 48 problems of merels; 231 a–238 b, blank diagrams of merels; 239, blank).

F = MS. Nat. Lib., Florence, XIX. 7, 37, formerly in the Magliabechian Library. A paper quarto MS. of the second half of the 15th c., which originally consisted of 246 leaves, some of which are now missing (1 a, a title in a slightly more recent hand: 'Libro de belli partiti al giuoco de scacchi composto per vn valenthuomo Spagnolo,' of which the last five words have been erased; 1 b, 2 a, blank; 2 b, an index of the 'pulcherrima partita' in 2, 3, and 12 moves; 3, 4 a, blank; 4 b, an extract from the *Vetula*; 5 a–6 a, an index to the problems in five and more moves; 6 b–7 a, hints on the use of problems for gambling purposes; 7 b, blank; 8 a–167 b, 320 problems of chess, of which 16 on ff. 47 a–54 b are now missing; 168 a–207 b, 80 problems of tables, of which 8 on ff. 181, 188, 205, 206 are now missing; 208 a–231 b, 48 problems of merels, of which 4 on ff. 211, 212 are missing; 232 a–237 a,

238 a, 239 a, 13 chess problems; 237 b, 238 b, 239 b–241 b, 248, blank diagrams of chess; 242–245 are missing). This MS. is of considerable importance, because it was written by a chess-player, who has made numerous cross-references and notes. The writer has added a number of chess problems to the CB collection, the solutions of which throw important light upon the rules and nomenclature of chess in Italy in the 15th c.[15]

A fifth MS. of the CB work, with the title 'Tractatus partitorum scacchorum, tabularum et merelorum, scriptus anno 1454,' which was formerly in Florence (VI, B. 1), has not been seen since the middle of last century. It has been assumed that the MS. was the private property of the last Grand Duke of Tuscany, and that he took it with him when he retired to Salzburg. It began with the prefatory poem, and contained problems of chess, tables, and merels, the last following the order of R and B (see *Qst.*, 183).

Ad. = MS. Brit. Mus., Add. 9351, purchased in 1833. A composite volume which begins with an incomplete copy of the CB work, the leaves of which have been disarranged at some time. The games portion of the MS. occupies 73 leaves, but the modern foliation is somewhat capricious, omitting many blank leaves and including (ff. 45 and 46) a folded sheet of paper which is no part of the original MS. (an unnumbered leaf, blank except for a library note; 1–7, blank; an unnumbered leaf, blank; 8–25 b, 44 problems of tables, the last 10 having solutions in Italian; 5 unnumbered leaves, blank; 30–43 a 53 problems of merels; 43 b and 3 unnumbered leaves, blank; 44 a (old 2 a), the title '1466. Tractatus partitorum schachorum, tabullarum, & merelleorum,' the poem, and a note, 'Notandum est quod rubei pro albis denotantur, et nigri pro nigris habentur' (the same note followed the poem in the missing Florence MS.); 44 b, 47 a–64 a, 72 problems of chess, being CB 1–71 and another position; 64 b and an unnumbered leaf, blank diagrams of chess). The MS. is a quarto paper MS., indifferently written, with two problems on each page, the diagrams being at the foot of the page.

Leon = A quarto paper MS. of 120 pages, now in the possession of Mr. J. A. Leon, London, which formerly belonged to Sig. S. Dubois. An earlier pagination is still legible, and reveals the fact that the present arrangement of the MS. is very different from the original one. The MS. originally consisted of 186 pages (1–171, 171*, 172–185, arranged in 15 sheets of 12 pages and 2 of 4 pages. 66 pages are now missing. If the leaves are arranged in the original order, it becomes evident that the writer (of the first part of the

[15] There has been considerable controversy as to whether there is anything missing from the first sheet of the MS. The old foliation commences with f. 8. Some of the earlier leaves have a more modern foliation, thus 4 a is '1', 5 a is '3', 6 a is '4', 7 a is '5'. The second sheet of the MS. begins with f. 7, as can be easily established from the missing sheet ff. 47–54. This leaves a sheet of 6 leaves, and not of 8, for the first of the MS. Moreover, neither the index (5 a–6 a) nor the list of beautiful problems (2 b) is complete. The former omits the problems in II, III, and IV moves, and it is only necessary to make a list of these to see that the missing portion must have occupied two pages. The completion of the list of beautiful problems must have occupied one page at least. It seems evident that two leaves are missing, but this with the present leaves would make 8 instead of 6. I think, therefore, that the two present leaves 3 and 4, the last page of which contains the extract from the *Vetula* (see p. 521), which occur very awkwardly in the MS., did not originally belong to it, and that they have taken the place of the missing leaves.

16th c.) began by making a selection of 104 problems from the CB work, to which he added two other positions, the second (on p. 106, now p. 64) being a problem of the modern chess; that then he made a second selection from CB, again inserting two positions (pp. 124, 125, now pp. 102, 129) from some other source.

Gu. = A quarto paper MS., now in Mr. J. G. White's library, formerly in the Franz collection, Berlin. It consists of 40 leaves unnumbered, and contains 76 problems of chess (33 diagrams are chequered without system; in 16, h1 is black) from the CB work. On the inside cover is the note, 'Ludus scachorum repertus fuit a Xerse Philosopho pro correctione Euilmerodach fratris Nabucadonosor cum esset tyrannus qui suos magistros et sapientes occidere consueuit et hoc solatio indirecte attractus fuit ad emendationem. Inuentio huius ludi fuit anno 600 ante D. N. I. Christi incarnationem. Di Alex^ro^ Padoani', in a hand of *c.* 1550; and on f. 39 a the MS. ends with 'Explicit liber de partitis scacorum. Deo gratias. Amen. Scriptus per me Paulum Guarinum de fortliuio in milesimo quingentesimo duodecimo die quarto mensis Ianuarij, Iulio secundo pontifice maximo Imperante'.

Paulo Guarino, who wrote this MS. in 1512, was a man of mark in his day who played an important part in the affairs of Forli. He died in 1520.[16]

In addition to these Latin MSS. there are two small Italian collections which are probably translations from the CB work. These are:

Ricc. = MS. Riccardi Lib., Florence, O. III. 30, 2871. A composite paper octavo MS., containing different treatises in hands of the 15th and 16th cc. It contains ff. 1 a–31 a, 'Ordine intorno ai cambj della fiera di Piacenza'; ff. 32 and 33 are blank; ff. 34 a–57 b, 'Giuocho degli Scacchi'; ff. 58 a–65 a, 'Rime sacre'. The last two treatises are by the same writer. There is an old foliation (ff. 1–26), which shows that the problem collection was originally a separate quarto work, and that the original leaves 1 and 8 are missing. There are now 46 problems and 1 unfilled diagram. The chessboards are chequered white and green, h1 being alternately green and white.[17] The chessmen are drawn conventionally. All the positions except the last two belong to the CB collection.

Ricc. 1 = CB 1; 2 = 22; 3, 4 = 28, 29; 5 = 41; 6 = 47; 7 = 50; 8 = 52; 9 = 53 (text = 62); 10, 11 = 84, 85; 12 = 143 (text = 99); 13, 14 missing; 15 = 145; 16 = 149; 17 = 162; 18 = 171; 19 = 177; 20 = 184; 21 = 233; 22 = 239; 23 = 197; 24 = 62; 25 = 91; 26 = 99; 27 = 106; 28 = 244; 29 = 211; 30 = 249; 31 = 102; 32, 33 = 104, 105; 34–36 = 110–112; 37 = 136; 38 = 140; 39 = 268; 40 = 11; 41 = 15; 42 = 86; 43 = 101; 44 = 179; 45 = 128; 46 = 208; 47, 48 see below, p. 699.

Bonc. 3 = MS. Boncompagni Lib., Rome, no. N. 3. This composite chess volume contains 8 leaves (ff. 65–72), with 16 problems from the CB work in a hand of the 16th c.

16 An interesting sketch of Guarino's life will be found in a note to Fiske's *Chess in Iceland*, 211–13.

17 The problem on 56 a (no. 47) has an unfilled diagram; the following diagram and the unfilled one are not chequered.

Bonc. 3. I, 1 = CB 4; 2 = 52; 3 = 1; 4 = 136; 5 = 141; 6 = 207; 7 = 168; 8 = 57; 9 = 53; 10 = 172; 11 = 188; 12 = 11; 13 = 47; 14 = 50; 15, 16 = 105, 106.

The CB work is also one of the sources from which some of the later compilers, e.g. Lucena, obtained some of their material.

The MSS. L, R, B, Ad. begin with a Latin poem, which is intended to explain the purpose and contents of the MS., and conceals the writer's name. Many attempts have been made to discover this name, but the riddle has never been solved, and is, indeed, probably insoluble. I quote the verses from L:

Ubicumque fueris, ut sis gratiosus,
Ne te subdas otiis, nam uir otiosus
Siue sit ignobilis siue generosus,
Vt testatur sapiens, erit uitiosus.

Vt a te remoueas uicium prefatum,
Legas et intelligas hunc meum tractatum,
Et sic cum nobilibus cordis adoptatum
Certus sum quod poteris inuenire statum.

Statim ad scaccarii me uoluo partita
In quo multipliciter fiunt infinita,
Quorum hic sunt plurima luculenter sita,
Ne forte mens labilis quicquam sit oblita.

Ibi semel positum numquam iteratur:
Postea de tabulis certum dogma datur,
Tunc merellos doceo quibus plebs iocatur,
Et sic sub compendio liber terminatur.

Hec huius opusculi series est tota.
Quis sim scire poteris tradens tot ignota.
Versuum principiis sillabas tu nota,
Eorundem media litera remota.

Ciuis sum Bononie ista qui collegi,
Qui sub breuiloquio uaria compegi,
Disponente domino opus quod peregi
Presentari principi posset siue regi.[18]

The most interesting part of this poem of *Civis Bononiae*, the citizen of Bologna—to adopt the name which he has chosen for himself—is the concluding four verses. There is no reference to any predecessors in the task of collecting problems, and the material is described as largely unknown. There is, however, no claim to originality, and *Civis Bononiae* appears as a compiler only, not as a composer. It is interesting to note the recognition of the immense number of chess problems which can be composed, and the humble place which merels occupies in the trinity of games, 'merels at which the commonalty play'. The statement that no problem occurs a second time ignores the deliberate repetition of CB 25 as CB 283, 284, and 285, and the unintended repetition of CB 216 as CB 271, and otherwise can only be

[18] Apart from mere differences in spelling, the only variant readings of importance are: line 11, R, B, Ad., *scita*; line 12, Ad., *quicumque*; line 15 Ad., *vocatur*.

accepted in a very literal sense, for many ideas are repeated in settings that only differ very little from one another.

The clue to the author's name is given in the fifth verse: 'You may know who I am that deal with so much that is unknown. Note the syllables in the beginnings of the verses; remove the middle letters.' Unfortunately, we do not know what verses or lines we are to select, nor what meaning we are to attach to the 'middle letters'.

None of the CB MSS. are much older than 1450, and there seems no ground for supposing that the work itself is much older than the existing MSS. It probably belongs to the last century of the mediaeval game, and this is probably the explanation both of the fact that the work did not spread beyond Italy, and also of the uniform order of the material in the different MSS.[19] If this view of the date of the CB collection is well founded, it is obvious that it is possible, and indeed probable, that the *Bonus Socius* work was the main source used by *Civis Bononiae.*

The arrangement of the CB work is not so orderly as that of the *Bonus Socius* work. In the latter, the classification of the chess problems by the number of moves extends throughout: in CB it only extends as far as CB 258, the last of a group of Exercises and mates in *n* moves. CB 259 is a mate in IV, and for the rest of the collection there is no attempt at any arrangement. CB 262, 271, and 283–5 are the only problems in this part of the CB work which are contained in the *Bonus Socius* collection. CB 259–88 has all the appearance of being an appendix or after-thought to the work as originally planned, these problems having come to the compiler's knowledge after the completion of his original collection. These problems were not submitted to the same rigorous examination which had been given to the original collection, and the solutions of CB 267, 269, 272, and 278 are at fault, while all the MSS. diagram CB 271 incorrectly.

In attempting to ascertain the relationships of the various MSS. of the CB work, we are limited to the evidence obtained from a careful collation of the problem diagrams. In this way I have arrived at the following pedigree.

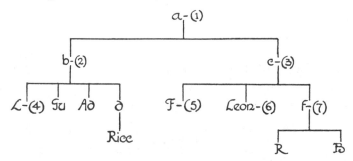

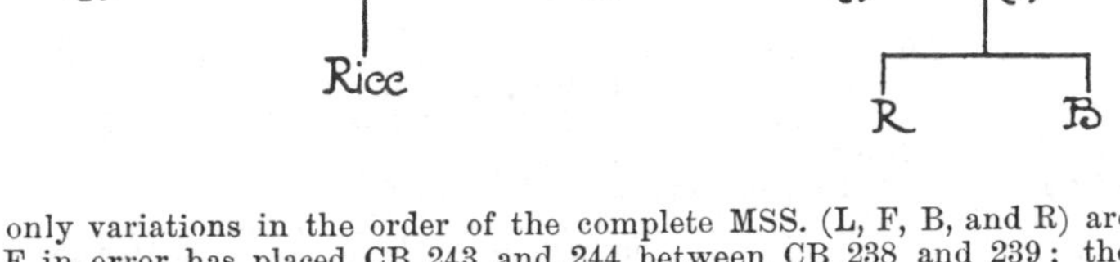

[19] The only variations in the order of the complete MSS. (L, F, B, and R) are: (*a*) the writer of F in error has placed CB 243 and 244 between CB 238 and 239; the result of turning over two leaves at once in the MS. from which he was copying; (*b*) R, B, and F place the third of the three sheets containing problems of merels in front of the other two, with the result that their order is CB 33–48, 1–32.

I add notes which direct attention to the diagrams which have supplied the evidence for the different steps of the table:

(1) Signs of an original error appear in CB 69, 169, 170, 266, 271, 280.
(2) See CB 21, 68, 69.
(3) See CB 64, 66, 104, 121, 129, 157, 158, 185, 189, 204, 221, 222, 260, 271.
(4) L is isolated by CB 2, 32, 178, 194, 271; is connected with Gu. by CB 11, 40, 49, 157, 189, 264. Ricc. is connected with this group by CB 85, 86, 104.
(5) F is isolated by CB 6, 121, 170, 188, 202, 280.
(6) The position of Leon is somewhat doubtful. CB 64, 66, 104, 157, 158 place it on this side; CB 40 connects it with the sub-group R, B; CB 83 with B; but CB 118, 124, 146 are more correct than in the other MSS. on this side.
(7) See CB 40, 61, 68, 79, 118, 121, 167, 256, 266, 285, 286. R is isolated by CB 77, 116, 170, 180; B by CB 76, 83, 85, 86, 97, 137, 140, 239, 241, 255, 270, 278. It is the least accurate of all the CB MSS.

The CB collection consists of 267 problems ending in mate (51 in II, 58 in III, 32 in IV, 18 in V, 20 in VI, 20 in VII, 10 in VIII, 6 in IX, 5 in X, 8 in XI, 7 in XII, 2 in XIII, 3 in XIV, 3 in XV, 1 in XVI, 2 in XVII, 1 in XVIII, 1 in XIX, and 19 in an unspecified number of moves), 5 unclassified problems (of which two are really games ending in 'Bare King'), 14 Exercises, and 2 self-mates (a third appears as a variation of CB 124, a mate in V). In 75 positions the loser has no pieces other than King, and in 55 mate-problems the winner's King is omitted. Many of the mates are conditional: in 31 mate is to be given by a Pawn, in 26 by a Bishop, and in 5 by other pieces, generally the Queen; in 18 the mate is to be given upon a specified square, 5 of these being mates in the 'four points', and 1 in the 'point estraunge' of the Anglo-Norman MSS.

The Muslim element in the collection is surprisingly small. I have only identified 29 positions with manṣūbāt in Muslim MSS.[20] Nine more are so similar in style to Muslim positions that I think we can accept them as assuredly Muslim also.[21] Variations on these problems will account for 44 more positions in CB.[22] Even so, the total Muslim element in the collection will only amount to 82 problems—only 28 per cent. of the whole. Often the Muslim position is simplified by the omission of non-essential pieces, so that the defence is weakened; or the position is diagrammed at a later stage, so that the solution is shortened.

The small proportion of Muslim work is in part due to the alterations in rule in Europe, and specially in Lombardy. The abandonment of the win by Bare King in the Lombard assize made the whole of the Muslim strategy of the End-game obsolete, and many of the finest of the manṣūbāt became useless

[20] Viz. CB 1 (Ar. 300), 58 (29), 73 (53), 75 (400), 96 (120), 101 (50), 117 (83), 121 (199), 133 (352), 148 (83), 152 (86), 155 (27), 161 (133), 185 (19), 188 (361), 194 (271), 195 (206), 206 (206), 216 (214), 219 (208), 236 (562), 241 (46), 243 (565), 246 (41), 255 (217), 257 (330), 271 (214), 277 (407), 281 (568).

[21] Viz. CB 9 (see Ar. 24), 11, 74, 109, 122, 142, 196, 229, 244.

[22] Viz. 34, 266, 270; 10, 12; 2, 5, 7, 8, 17, 20, 24. 27, 32, 35, 36, 37, 38, 42, 43, 44, 45, 49, 51, 54, 55, 56, 61, 65, 66, 67, 69, 70, 72, 80, 88, 93, 115, 116, 123, 130, 132, 267. The last 39 of these are based on the 'Dilārām' problem (Ar. 83), but the variations are so far removed from the Muslim spirit that it is rather unfair to the Muslim composers to reckon them as Muslim at all.

as a result. We may, perhaps, see the beginnings of a European attempt to reconstruct a science of the End-game in the simpler problems, in which the powers of a single piece, or the combined powers of a few pieces, are explored (e.g. the games with Kings and Rooks only).

Any comparison of the European problems, as contained in BS and CB, with the Muslim manṣūbāt is bound to be to the disadvantage of the former. The Muslim composer was an artist with a clear ideal and a skilful hand. The early European composer neither adopted the ideals of the Muslim masters nor substituted others of his own. His problems lack verisimilitude, and there is no pretence that they represent positions which might have been obtained in the course of actual play. The European player saw no incongruity in Pawns on the first line of the board, or in Aufins upon squares that no Aufin could reach in the course of a game. Again and again we meet with two white or two black Aufins moving on squares of the same colour. In a later MS. (Picc.) we shall meet with all four Aufins on the same diagonal.[23]

The European composer set to work to diminish rigorously the resources of the defence by the reduction of force, by the abandonment of the Muslim tradition that the winner's King should be under threat of an obvious and immediate mate, by the omission of the winner's King. This robbed the mate-drive—the commonest type of manṣūba ending in mate—of all point, and we find hardly any European problems of this class. On the other hand, the abandonment of this type of problem opened the way to the composition of problems in which the first move was no longer a check, and of 246 sound problems and variations in CB, no less than 132 (53 per cent.) commence with non-checking moves. In some of the later collections the proportion is still higher.

Obvious results of all this are the smaller number of pieces employed in a problem, and the great disproportion between the forces of the attack and defence, which I have already mentioned as one of the simplest means of discriminating between European and Muslim work. In CB the average number of pieces to a diagram is only 6·4 (or excluding the unsimplified Muslim positions, 6·1), and the attack has 2½ men to every 1 for the defence (or excluding the same problems, 3 to every 1 for the defence).

The unavoidable conclusion is that the average European composer had far less ability than the average Muslim, and the European preference for problems the solution of which only took a very few moves supports this view also. The average length of the solutions of over 300 mate-manṣūbāt in the Muslim MSS. is 8 moves, and half of them are in V–VIII moves; the average length of the mates in CB is 5 moves, and more than half are in II–IV moves. The favourite length of a Muslim mate was 5; of a European mate, 2 or 3 moves.

But even in this limited field, and with all the wider opportunities for

[23] In CB five problems show Pawns on the player's first line, 76 problems have Aufins on impossible squares, 24 of these have two Aufins of the same colour moving on squares of the same colour. The favourite arrangement in the last case is Bd5, e6 in order to command f7 and g8.

expressing his ideas upon the chessboard which the abandonment of all conventions afforded him, the mediaeval European composer was singularly clumsy in his work. His powers of construction were very limited, and when alternative solutions or awkward defences came to light, he was without the skill or the patience to remedy the defects in his work by the reconstruction of his diagram. Instead, he had recourse to the invention of special conditions which should govern the play in that particular problem, and so exclude the undesired line of play, and make good the flaws in his work. These bizarre conditions are attached to about one quarter of the problems in CB. An undesired first move is excluded by such a condition as *roccus primo tractu non movetur* (CB 16), or *miles non faciet primum tractum* (CB 20), or even by a more stringent prohibition still, *roccus punctatus est immobilis* (CB 2), or *alfinus non movetur nisi possit capere* (CB 46)—conditions which obviously may cut out awkward moves at a later stage also. Inconvenient defences by the capture of the attacking pieces, or a diversity of attacks depending upon the capture of defensive force, are prevented by the fidation of pieces entirely or in part: *omnes utriusque partis sunt affidati* (CB 10), *roccus est affidatus a rege et regina ab omnibus* (CB 9). The same device is used to strengthen the defence in variations in which there was intended to be no solution. Pieces are allowed abnormal moves—*in isto partito roccus valet alfinum et roccum et utriusque tractum facit* (CB 22); *pedo vadit sicut pedo et regina, et quando est pedo semper vadit superius* (CB 245)—or are forbidden legal moves—*quando aliquis pedonum erit facta regina non saltabit sed faciet unum tractum* (CB 241), or *si contingat aliquem pedonem fieri reginam non faciet nisi unum tractum et unum, hoc est quod non poterunt saltare ut consueverunt regine nove* (CB 232).[24] Pawns, necessary to block certain squares, are allowed to move in the reverse direction, so that they may not interfere with the intended solution. A Queen on the player's first line is declared to be a newly promoted Pawn, and allowed the privilege leap (CB 180). Stalemate is prevented by the addition of a piece which can only move when the King cannot—*alfinus niger numquam trahitur donec rex suus uel pedo possit ludere* (CB 212); *miles niger non movetur nisi quando capit vel rex suus erit clausus* (CB 232), or the stalemated player forfeits his move, and his opponent plays again. These are illustrations of the ways in which the European composer invented conditions in order to make his solution work. The crudeness of the method is patent.

Notwithstanding his weakness as a composer, the mediaeval European problemist made some important contributions to the development of his branch of chess. The simple title 'White plays and wins' of the Muslim MSS. was gradually replaced by the more exact 'White mates in x moves'. The Muslim laid no stress upon the length or method of the solution of a manṣūba. A line of play which led to a decisive result, be it mate, Bare King, or stalemate, in ten moves did just as well as one which arrived at a similar result in five moves. The European title lays stress upon the length

[24] In some cases these positions are older than the Queen's leap, and the condition is due to this fact.

of the solution, and eventually upon the shortest method of winning against the best defence. It might increase the difficulty of solution, though this possibility never really exercised any influence upon the mediaeval methods of composition, and it is only in our own day that the full logical effect of fixing the number of moves in the solution has been allowed free development. The mediaeval turned aside to lay stress upon mate in an *exact* number of moves, neither more nor less, and the typical statement of the mediaeval problem is 'White mates in *x* moves exactly (*tantum*)', or 'neither more nor less (*nec plus nec minus*)'. This condition had a great influence upon the form of composition. A mate on the move became one in II exactly, and the solver had to discover a waiting move which would allow him to postpone the mate, or another line of play. While the liberty of the attack was seriously restricted, the resources of the defence received a notable increase. A line of play which compelled a mate a move too soon, or a move which cramped the freedom of the defender's King, became valuable methods of defence.

A second European innovation was the self-mate, which may possibly (see the solution of Arch. 27 on p. 579) have developed out of the ordinary game. There is, however, very little variety in the mediaeval examples of this form of problem, and with few exceptions (CB 124 is the most notable exception) they illustrate only a single method of forcing the desired termination. In nearly every case the mated King is blocked on a corner square, and the solution occupies a considerable time. On the whole, the self-mate is more prominent in the Anglo-Norman MSS. than in BS or CB.

A third innovation was the symmetrical problem. The early composer showed a decided partiality for positions of this kind. CB 28, 41, 47, 52, 53, 59, 104, 105, 110, 128, 164, 237, 263, and 287 are examples. Muslim manṣūbāt of this character are very rare; CB 255 is almost the only example. Apparently, the European composer arranged the position at times without any underlying motive, and then tried to discover a solution. This was not always possible. It is difficult to account for CB 263 in any other way. The Florence MS. Picc. contains some more elaborate examples of symmetrical problems.

The European player was also very fond of the conditional problem, both the mate upon a specified square, and also with a specified piece. This type of problem is of Muslim origin, but the idea was developed considerably in Europe.[25] In the 16th c. the problem in which the player had to give check with a Pawn (Bishop) and mate with a second Pawn (Bishop), on successive moves, reached its greatest popularity and became the typical problem of the period. The beginning of this popularity is seen in CB 170 and 172.

But the most typical feature of the mediaeval problem of the period to which BS and CB belong is the *unsound* problem, to which there is no solution in the number of moves and under the conditions prescribed in the title. About one-third (108 out of 318 problems and variations ending in mate) of

25 I have already alluded to the prominence attached to mates of this kind in the ordinary game.

the problems in CB are of this nature. It has generally been assumed that these unsound problems arose out of the use of the problem for gambling purposes, and v. d. Linde described them as *Wettspiele*, wager-games. An occasional solution[26] suggests that a player would set up a position on the board and state the conditions of play, and would then invite his companion to undertake the attack or the defence, and to back his choice by a stake. It would be obviously an advantage for the challenger in such a case that the second player should be in doubt whether the problem were really soluble or not.

In the earlier collections, the proportion of unsound problems is low: there is only one in Alf., and one in the AN collections; but the proportion steadily rises in the later MSS., until at the end of the mediaeval period the problem without a solution was, in some circles at least, regarded as the more artistic composition.[27]

But the composer was not content with inventing unsound problems; he also manufactured unsound positions out of sound ones by making a slight change in the position of certain pieces, so slight as a rule that the alteration would easily escape notice. Of 123 problems in four moves and under in CB no less than 31 contain advice how to alter the position so as to produce a contrary result, while in the late MS. C nearly every problem is treated in this way. Occasionally we can trace the process of manufacture, and arrange the variations in a series in which the positions are alternately sound and unsound (e.g. CB 1, 34, 266, 270, or 9, 10, 12, using similar positions in other collections); but in some cases, such as the mate in IV with a Pawn, of which CB 113, 114, 118, 119, 120 are variants, or the numerous 'Dilārām' positions (close on 200 in all the European MSS.), the manufacture of variations has been carried to such an extent as to defy classification.

In some cases this doctoring of well-known problems may have been the work of the professional gamester, of whose methods we have an illuminating picture in the Latin introduction to the CB MS. F:

My master used to say that in the first *partitum* we ought to play indifferently and to lose, and that similarly we ought to lose sometimes in the course of play, because in this way men are induced to play. But I have never used this trick (*cautela*).

But in order that you may play cautiously and avoid losing, you should take care that you know the secrets of the gamester, concerning which many tricks are given.

The first is: it is certain that a good problem ought not to be what it appears, but the opposite. Therefore you should place that side of the chessmen which has the worse, but looks to have the advantage, at your edge of the board. For then, if your opponent does not know the problem, he will turn the board round and take the side which looks so much the better. However, many players do not do so, so it is not to be reckoned as a certainty.

[26] See the solution to PL 173 (p. 640). Also two problems of merels in CB (L 21, R 37: 'In isto partito tu dices illi qui tecum ludet haec uerba. Elige quos uis et primo trahe, uel ego eligam et primo traham'; and L 25, R 41: 'Cum feceris istud partitum dices illi qui tecum ludet. Elige quam partem uis et primo trahe, uel da michi electionem et ego primo traham').

[27] Thus there is a note in the solution of C 10, 'ma questo partito è più bello falso'.

Another trick is this. At the start you pretend that you do not remember the problem, and have consequently arranged the men differently from what you should have done, and this you repeat often at the start, and yet you place the men as they ought to be. In this case, if he sees a move which looks to win easily, he will think that you do not remember the problem and play accordingly. But you, recognizing that he has chosen the good side, will say, 'Before I play, I wish to see what I have done', and you will then be able to add something by which the whole problem is changed, and will urge that you ought not to play it out because you have made a great mistake because you did not set up the position correctly. And he will not be able to complain of you, because from the start he has believed that you did not know the problem. If, moreover, he again wishes to take the good side, you will again observe what I have said above, and will say that you will not play because you do not remember it, and you accordingly destroy the position and make another, or you observe some other trick.

Again, you ought to appear cautious in wagering, and to note carefully whether he takes the problem with a tremulous voice, or after a moderate amount of consideration, or whether he is ready to wager large sums, or whether he wished to take other problems which have been set up, or whether he refuses to take other positions which are to be set up, for all these things show whether he knows the problem or not.

There is also another trick which is called the *golden* one, which is worked in such a way that it compels the gamester to take the worst side. It is done thus. You know that a good problem ought not to be what it appears, but its opposite. You say that the side which appears to have the better is to lay a double stake. For unless he play carefully, in this way alone he is compelled, before you lay your wager, to say which side he wishes. For you will ask him whether he wishes you to stake double or single, and in this way you will learn which side he is choosing. Thus do some use this trick.

This certainly represents the mediaeval chess-player at his worst, and if it had been true at all generally, it is difficult to see how chess could have survived such base and fraudulent uses. But happily all the evidence goes to show that this picture can have been true of only a small minority of players, and only towards the end of the mediaeval period. It is very easy to overestimate the wager element in the problems, and indeed the whole popularity of the problem in mediaeval chess. It is not without significance that we hear nothing of this knavery, and nothing of the general use of the problem, in mediaeval literature. The burgess of Falsetown who cheats Beryn out of his property at the chessboard plays whole games of chess, and leaves the problem severely alone. Not one single passage among all the mediaeval references to chess refers to the use of problems for gambling purposes, and all the many disputes which arose in connexion with chess arose in connexion with the game, and not the problem.

The problems in the CB work now follow with shortened solutions. It would have occupied too great space to reproduce the entire text of the MS.; but I have given several solutions verbatim, not because there is any difficulty in understanding their meaning, but as specimens of the verbose style of the CB and BS texts, or because they involve expressions or statements of more general interest. I give with each diagram references to both the CB and BS collections. Where the BS reference is succeeded by a dagger, the BS position differs from that diagrammed.

CB 1 : Ar. 300.

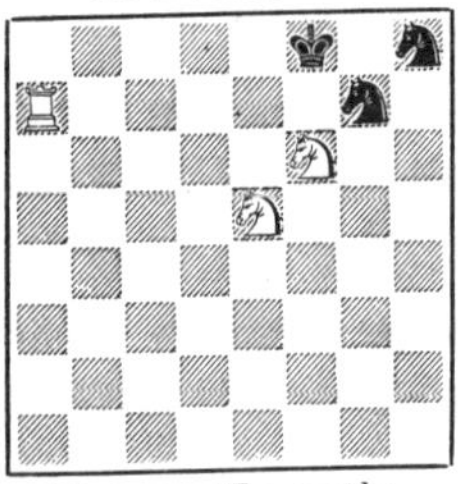

Mate in II exactly.

CB 2 : BS 3†.

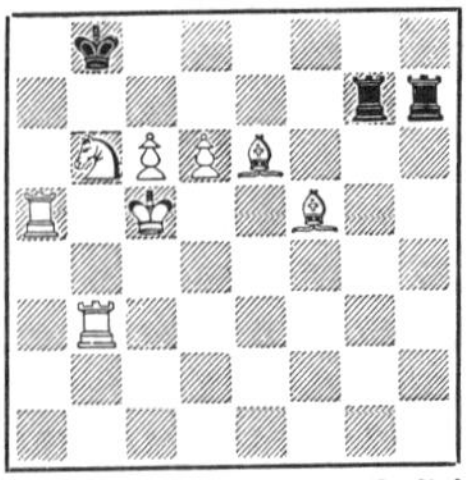

Mate in II exactly. Ra5 is immovable, Ktb6 fidated, and the Pawns may be Queens.

CB 3 : BS 6.

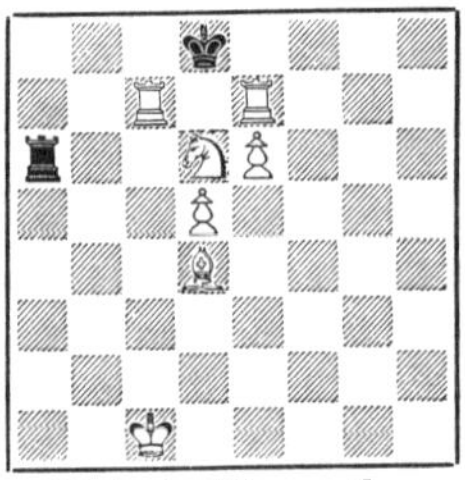

Mate in II exactly.

CB 4B : S 4.

(Bl.)
Black mates with Pawn in II exactly. Ra1 may be fidated or not. Unsound.

CB 5 : BS 5†.

Black mates with Kt or Pawn in II exactly. Unsound.

CB 6 : BS 13†.

(Bl.)

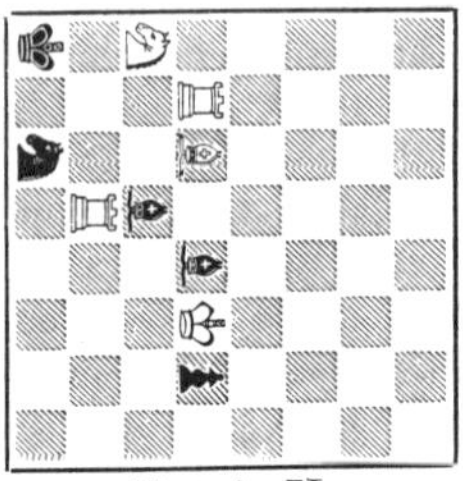

Mate in II.
Pd2 is fidated.

CB 7 : BS 12.

(Bl.)
White plays and Black mates in II exactly. Unsound.

CB 8 : BS 15.

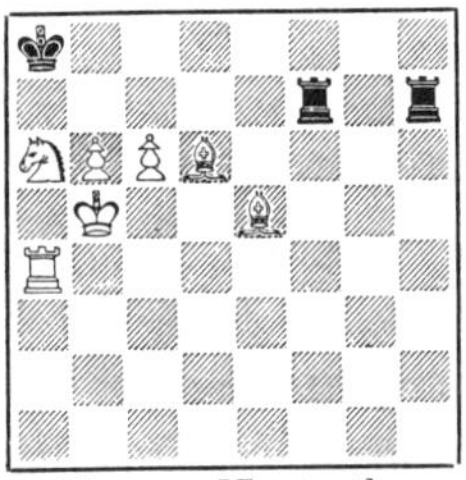

Mate in II exactly.

CB 9 : BS 14.

(Bl.)
Mate in II exactly.
Qc6 is fidated. Rd7 is fidated from King.

CB 10.

Mate with Q in II exactly. All the pieces are fidated.

CB 11 : BS 16.

Mate in II exactly.

CB 12.

(Bl.)
Mate in II exactly.
Qc6 is fidated. Rf7 is fidated from King.

CB 13 : BS 18.

Mate in II exactly.
Unsound.

CB 14 : BS 17.

(Bl.)
White plays and Black mates in II exactly. Unsound.

CB 15 : BS 20.

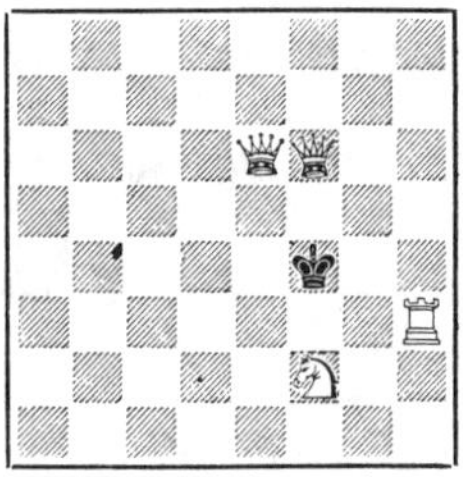

Mate in II exactly.

CB 16 : BS 21.

Mate in II exactly.
Ra7 may not play on first move.

CB 17 : BS 22†.

Mate in II exactly.

CB 18 : BS 19†.

(Bl.)
White plays and Black mates in II exactly.
Unsound.

CB 19.

Black mates in II exactly or Black wins Qb8 for nothing. Bd6 is fidated.
Unsound.

CB 20 : BS 31†.

(Bl.)
Black mates in II exactly. All the men are fidated, and Kth6 may not play on first move. Unsound.

CB 21 : BS 30.

Mate in II exactly.

CB 22 : BS 29.

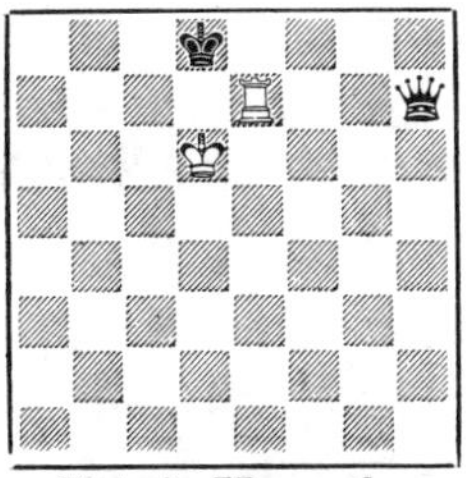

Mate in II exactly.
Re7 has also the power of a B.

CB 23 : BS 28.

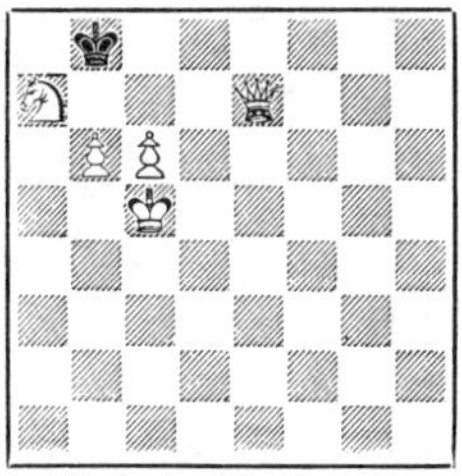

Mate in II exactly.
All the men are fidated.

CB 24 : BS 27.

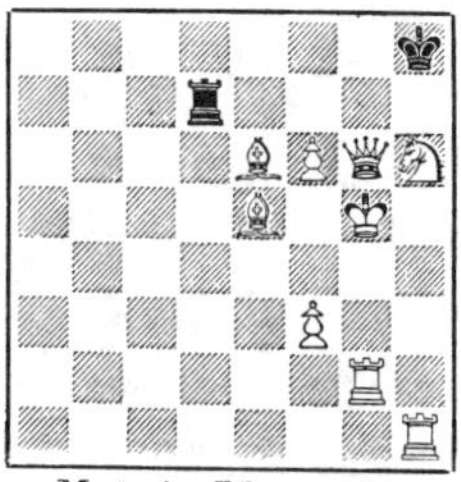

Mate in II exactly.
All the men are fidated.

CB 25: BS 26.

(Bl.)
Mate in II, III, or IV exactly.

CB 26: BS 25.

Mate in II exactly.

CB 27: BS 24.

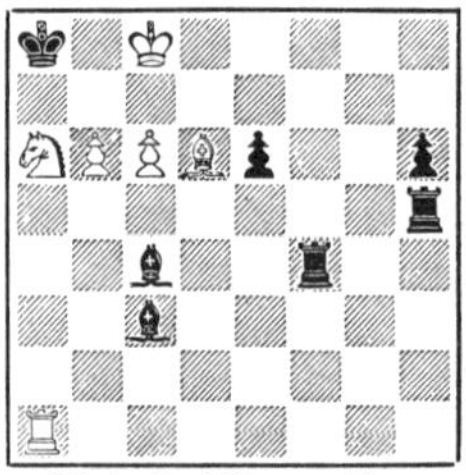

Mate in II exactly.

CB 28: BS 23.

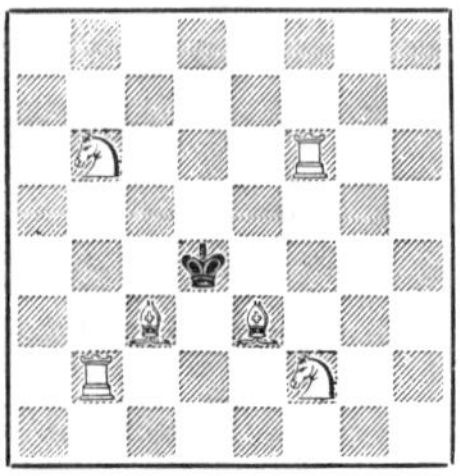

Mate in II exactly.

CB 29: BS 7.

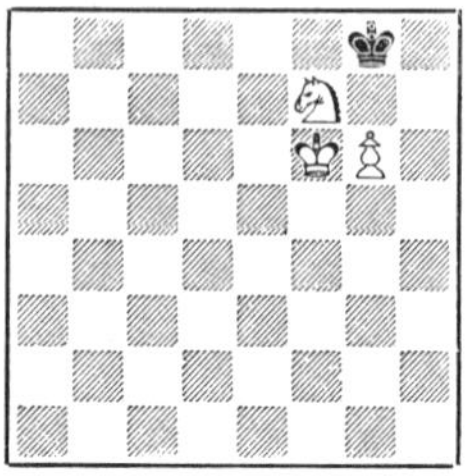

Mate in II exactly.
All the men are fidated.

CB 30: BS 8.

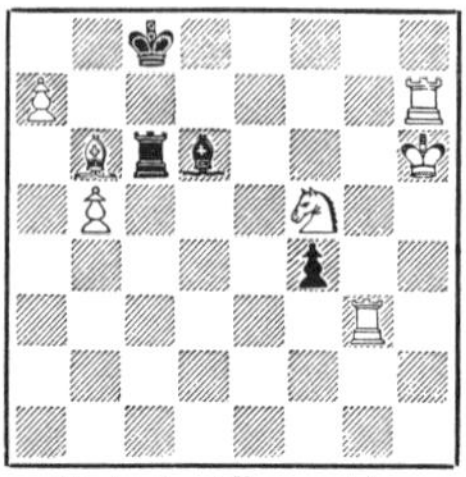

Mate in II exactly.
Ktf5 and Bb6 are fidated.

CB 31.

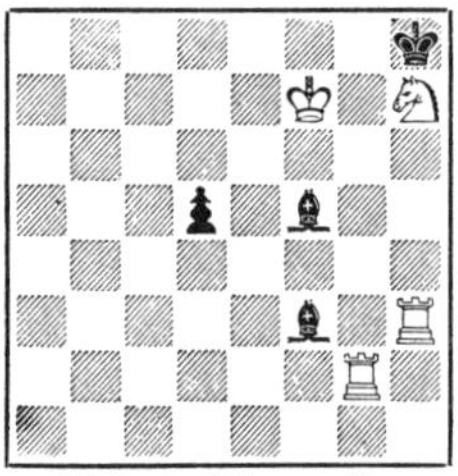

Mate in II exactly.
The Rooks are fidated.

CB 32: BS 1.

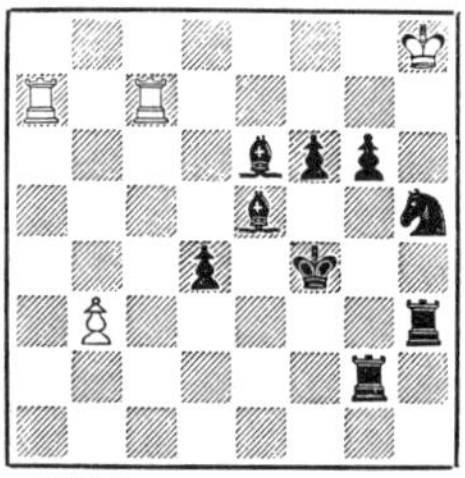

(Bl.)
Black mates in II exactly.
Unsound.

CB 33.

Mate in II exactly.
Unsound.
All the Pawns go upwards.

CB 34: BS 2.

Mate in II exactly.
Unsound.
Both Pawns go upwards.

CB 35: BS 9†.

Mate in II exactly.
The Pawns f6, g6 may be Queens.

CB 36: BS 34 var.

(Bl.)
Black mates in II exactly.
All the men are fidated.
Unsound.

CB 37.

White plays and Black mates in II exactly. All the men are fidated and the Queens are immovable. Unsound.

CB 38.

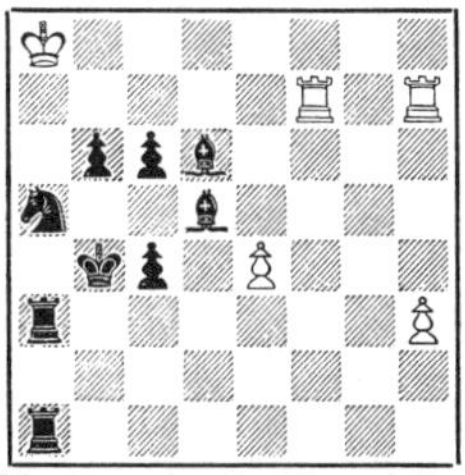

Black mates in II exactly. All the Pawns go upwards. Unsound.

CB 39.

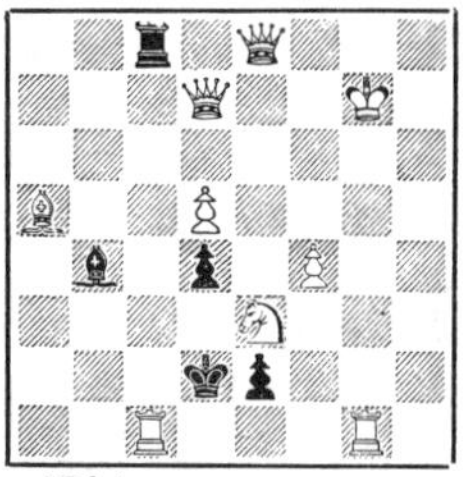

(Bl.)
Mate in II exactly.

CB 40.

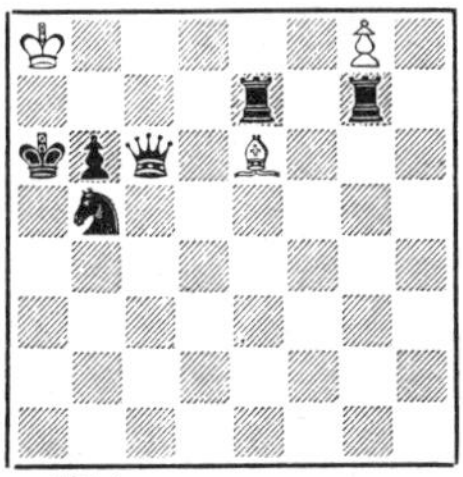

(Bl.)
Black either mates in II exactly or wins Pawn g8 for nothing. The B is fidated. Unsound.

CB 41 : BS 10.

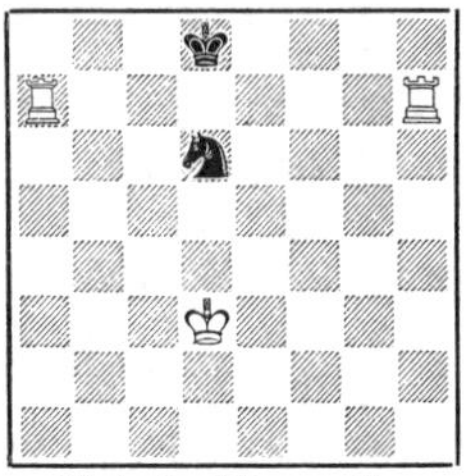

Mate in II exactly. The Kt is fidated.

CB 42.

Mate in III exactly.

CB 43 : BS 45†.

Mate in III exactly.

CB 44 : BS 73.

Black mates in III exactly. Pg2 is immovable. Unsound.

CB 45 : BS 5 var.

(Bl.)
Black mates in III exactly. Unsound.

CB 46.

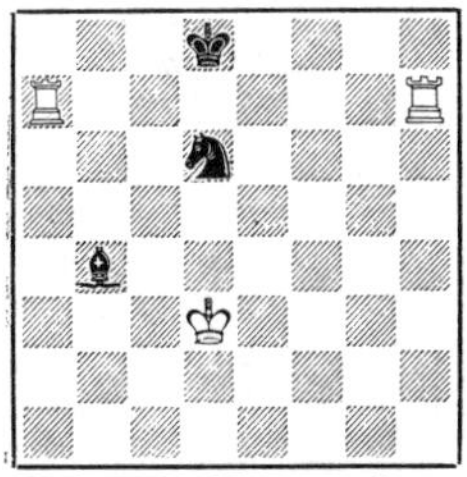

Mate in III exactly. The B can only move if it makes a capture.

CB 47 : BS 72.

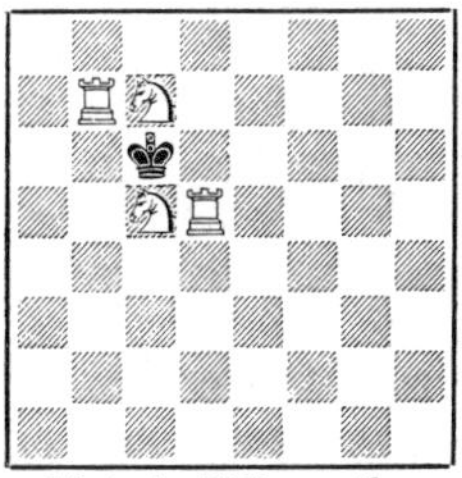

Mate in III exactly.

CB 48.

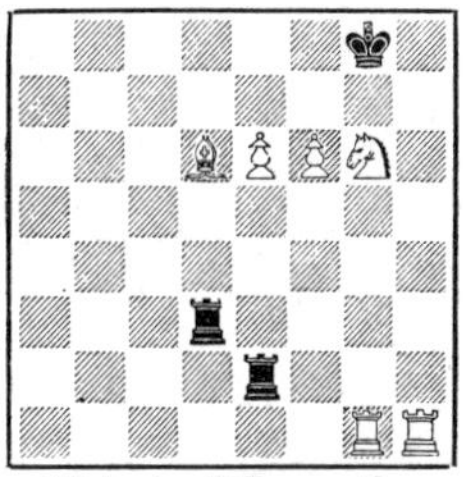

Mate in III exactly.

CB 49 : BS 32.

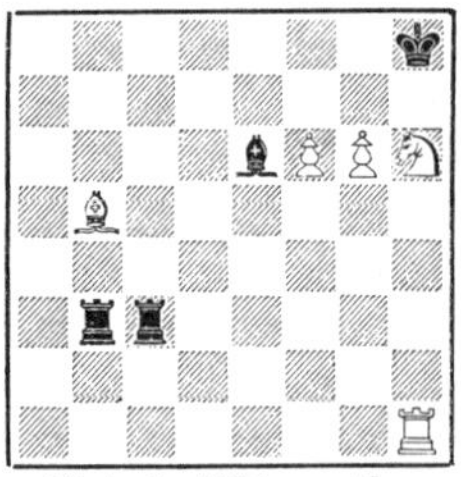

Mate in III exactly.

CB 50 : BS 33.

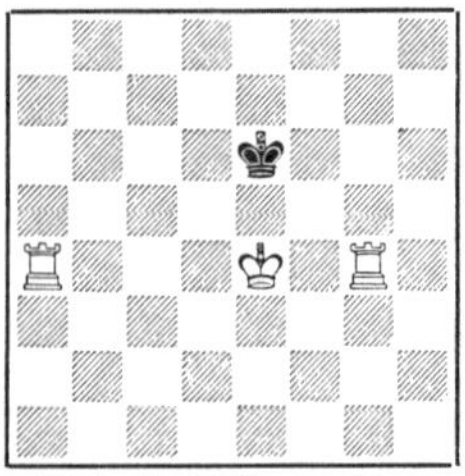

Mate in III exactly.

CB 51 : BS 34.

Mate in III exactly.
All the men are fidated.

CB 52 : BS 35.

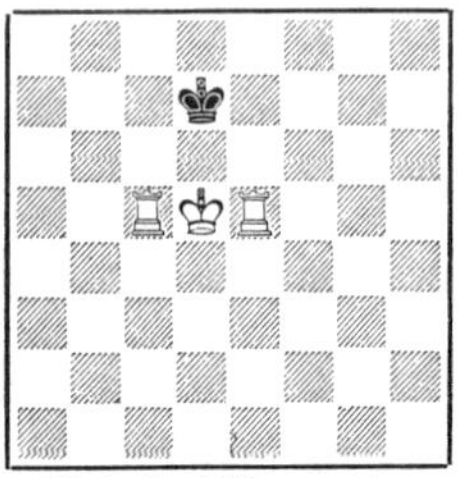

Mate in III exactly.
Each White piece moves once.

CB 53 : BS 62†.

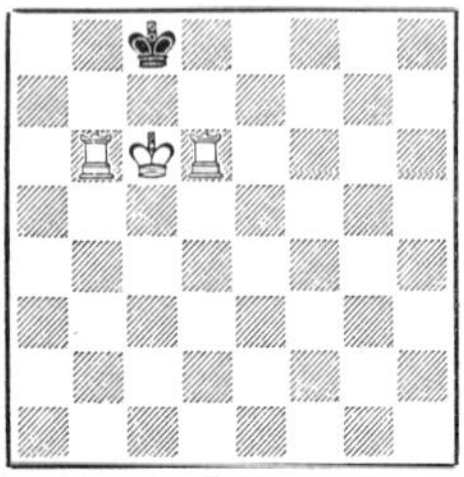

Mate in III exactly.
Each White piece moves once.

CB 54.

Mate in III exactly.

CB 55 : BS 64.

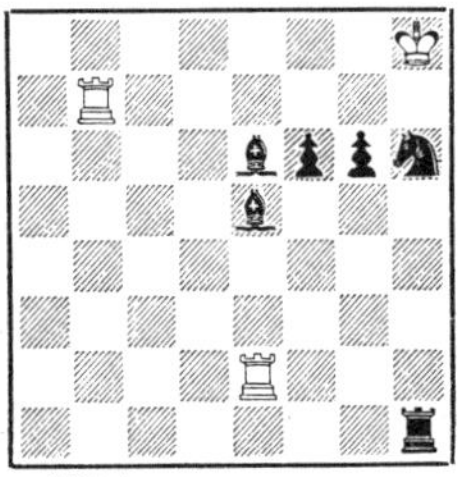

(Bl.)
Black mates in III exactly.
Unsound.

CB 56 : BS 61.

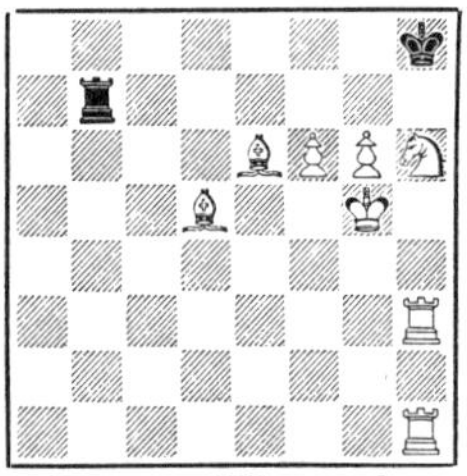

Mate in III exactly.
Rb7 is fidated.

CB 57 (corr.).

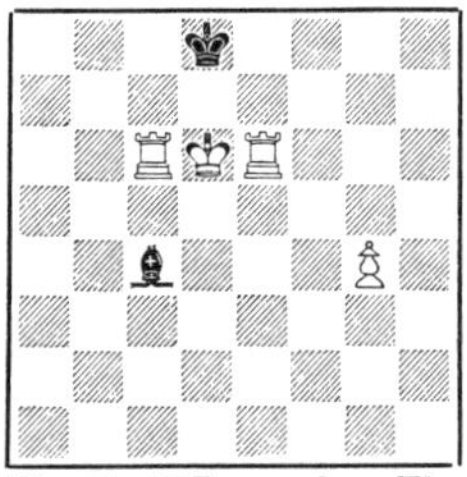

Mate in III exactly. The P is immovable; the B can only move when it captures; each White piece moves once.

CB 58 : Ar. 29.

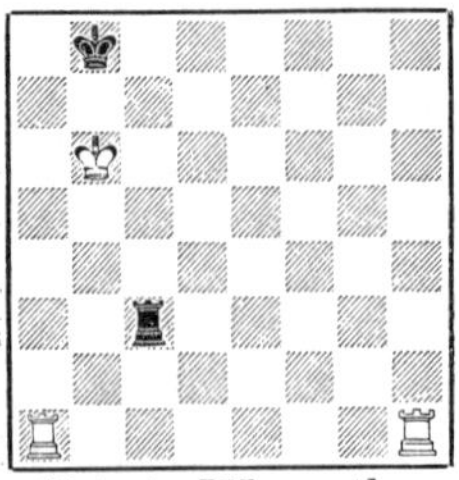

Mate in III exactly.

CB 59 : BS 71.

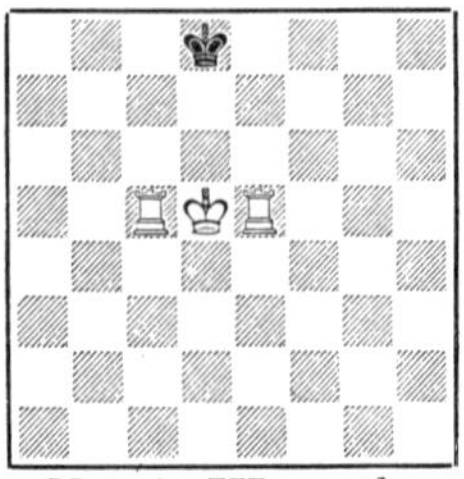

Mate in III exactly.

CB 60 : BS 37.

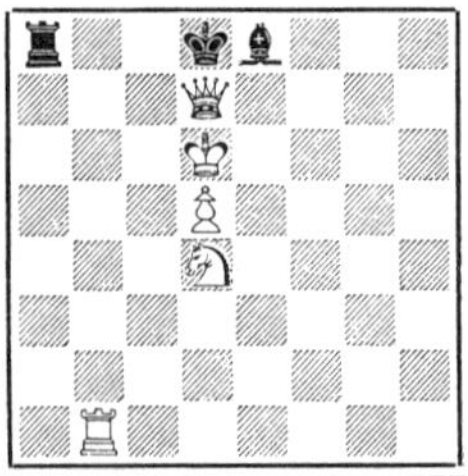

Mate [with Pawn] in III exactly. The Ktd4 is fidated.

CB 61 : BS 36.

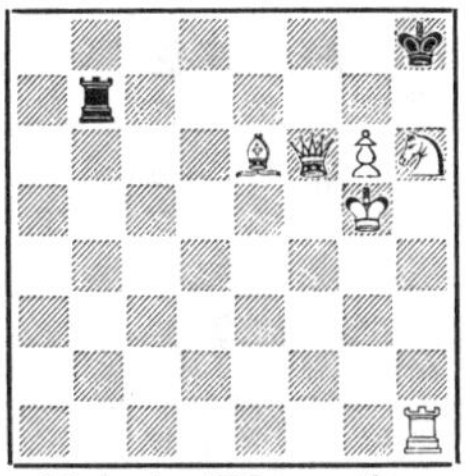

Mate in III exactly.
Rb7 and Qf6 are fidated.

CB 62 : BS 69.

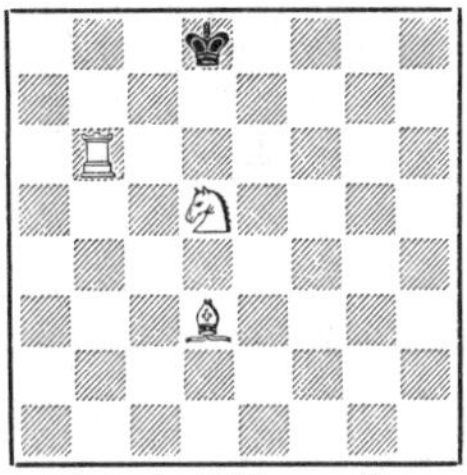

Mate in III exactly.

CB 63 : BS 70.

Mate in III exactly.

CB 64.

(Bl.)
Black mates in III exactly.
Unsound.

CB 65 : BS 38†.

Mate in III exactly.

CB 66 : BS 40.

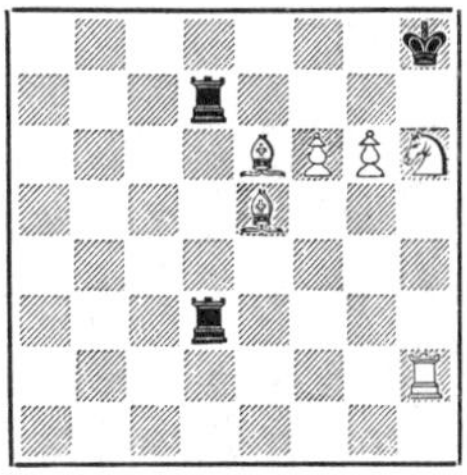

Mate in III exactly.

CB 67 : BS 41.

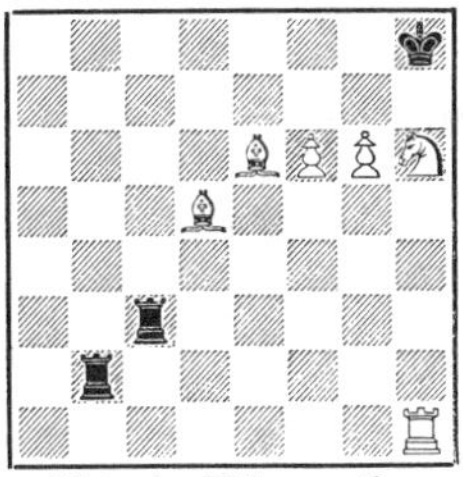

Mate in III exactly.
Unsound.

CB 68.

Mate in III exactly.

CB 69.

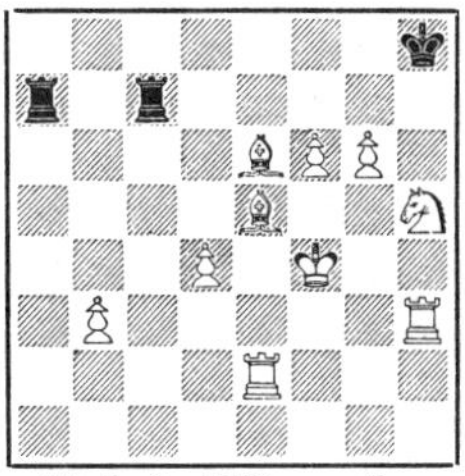

Mate in III exactly.

CB 70.

(Bl.)
Black mates in III exactly.
Pf6, g6 may also be Queens,
Kth6 may not play first
move. Unsound.

CB 71 : BS 43.

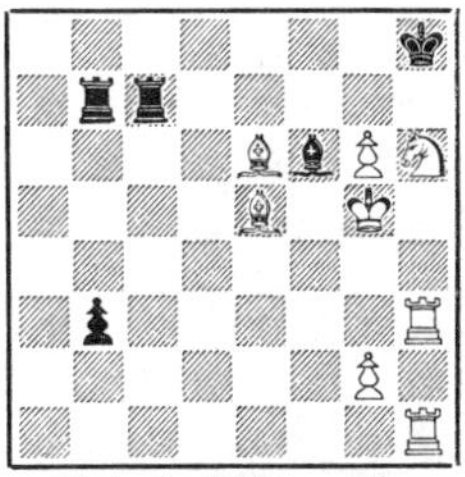

Mate in III exactly.
Unsound.

CB 72 : BS 39 var.

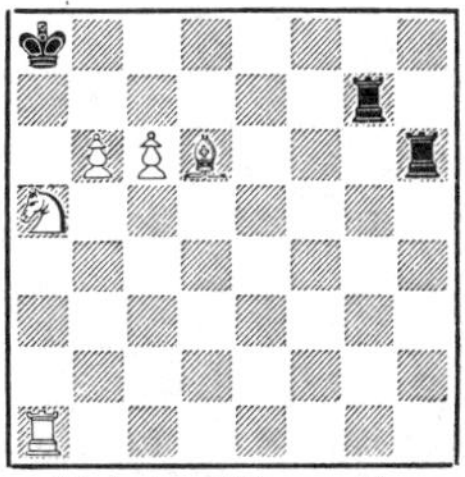

Mate in III exactly.

CB 73 : BS 42 : Ar. 53.

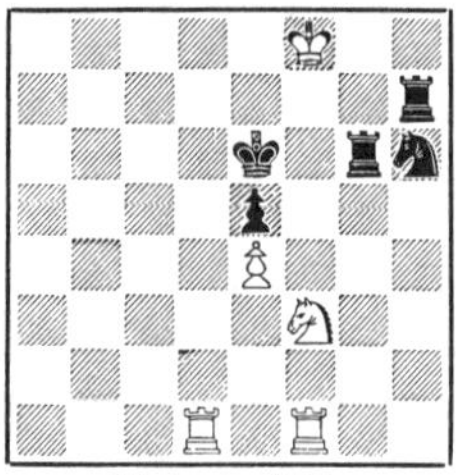

Mate in III.

CB 74 : BS 47.

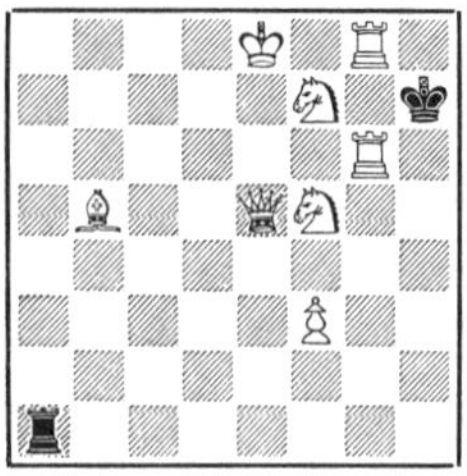

Mate with Bishop in III exactly.

CB 75 : BS 44 : Ar. 400.

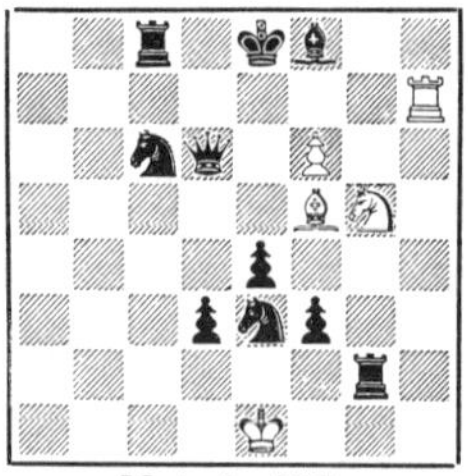

Mate in III.

CB 76 : BS 46.

(Bl.)

Black mates in III exactly. Pa7 is immovable. Unsound.

CB 77 : BS 49.

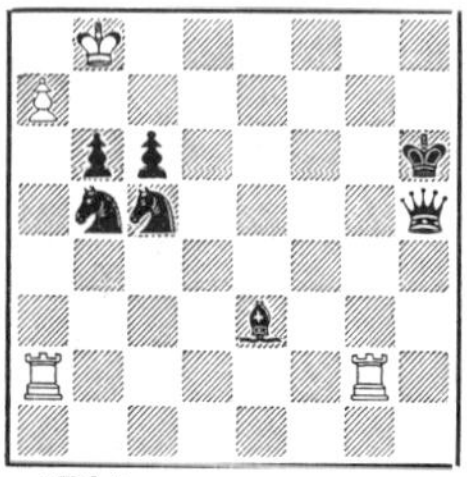

(Bl.)

Black mates in III exactly. Pa7 is immovable. Unsound.

CB 78 : BS 48.

Mate in III exactly.

CB 79 : BS 50.

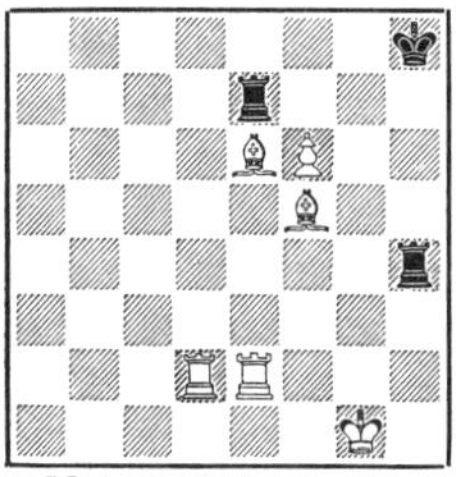

Mate in III exactly.

CB 80 : BS 51.

Mate in III exactly.

CB 81 : BS 53.

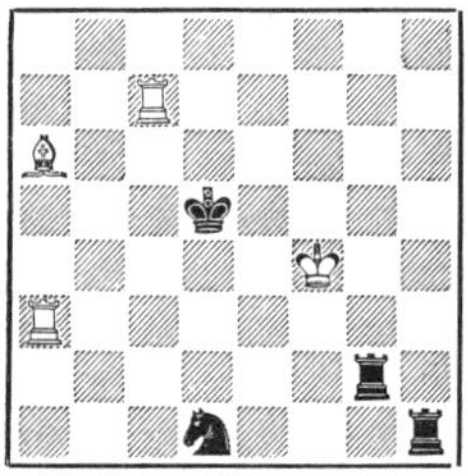

Mate in III exactly.

CB 82 : BS 52.

Mate in III exactly.

CB 83 : BS 55.

Mate in III exactly.

CB 84 : BS 54.

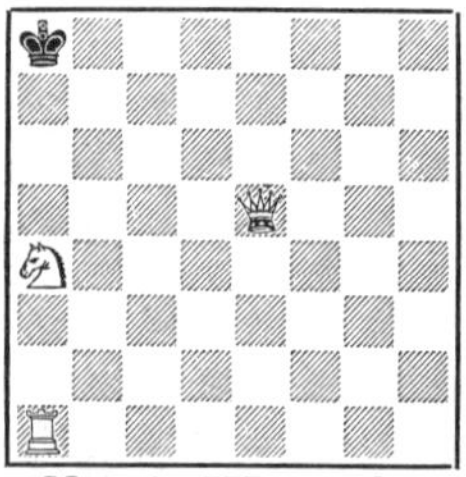

Mate in III exactly.

CB 85 : BS 56.

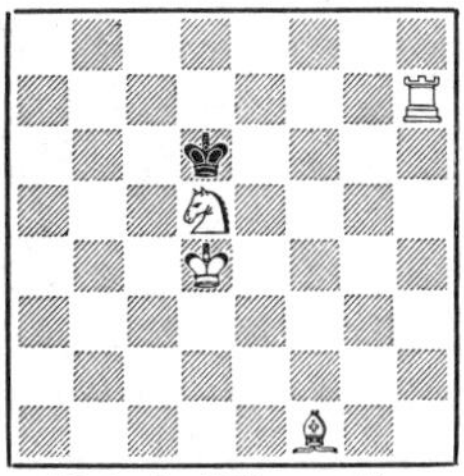

Mate in III exactly.

CB 86 : BS 57.

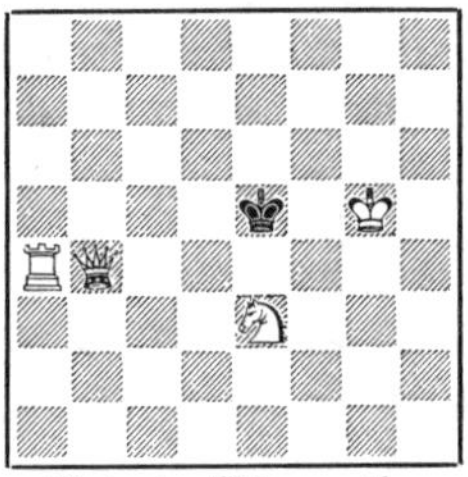

Mate in III exactly.

CB 87 : BS 58.

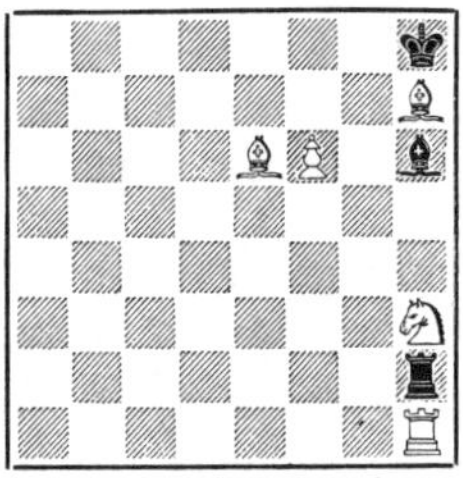

Mate in III exactly.

CB 88 : BS 59.

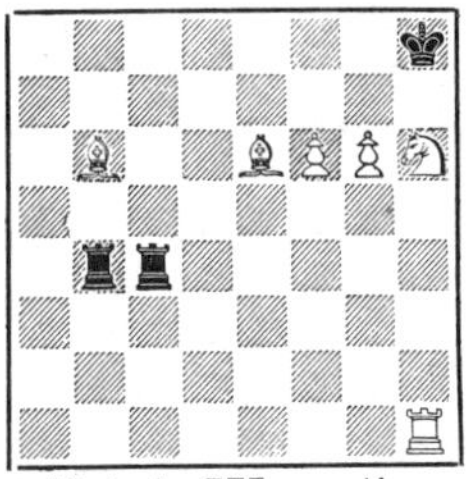

Mate in III exactly.

CB 89 : BS 60.

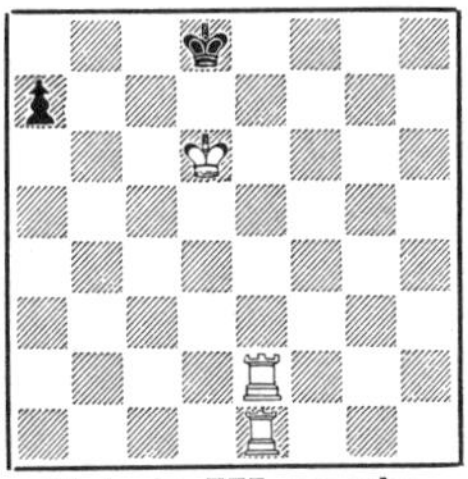

Mate in III exactly.
Each White piece moves once.

CB 90 : BS 65.

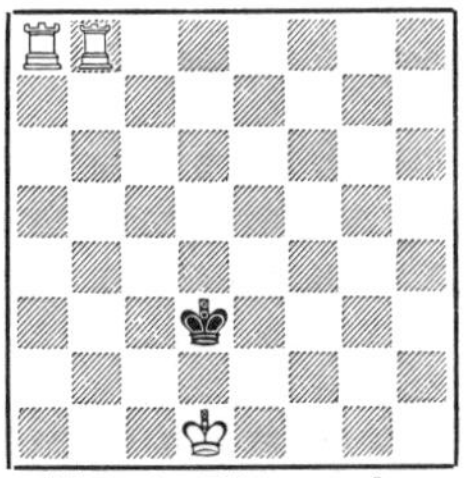

Mate in III exactly.

CB 91 : BS 63.

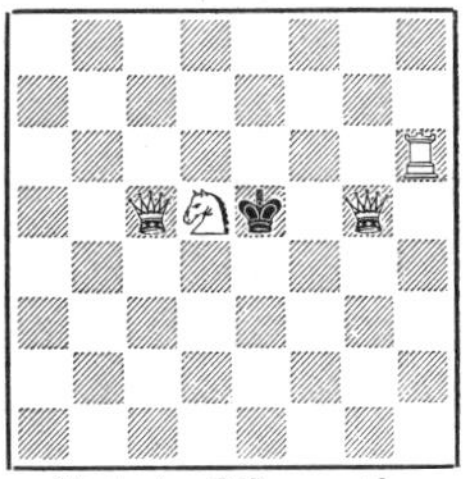

Mate in III exactly.

CB 92 : BS 66.

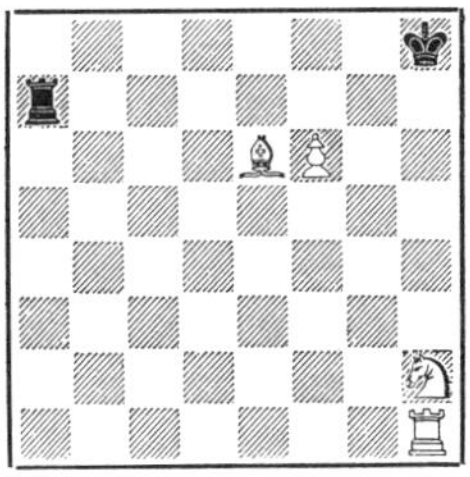

Mate in III exactly.

CB 93 : BS 67†.

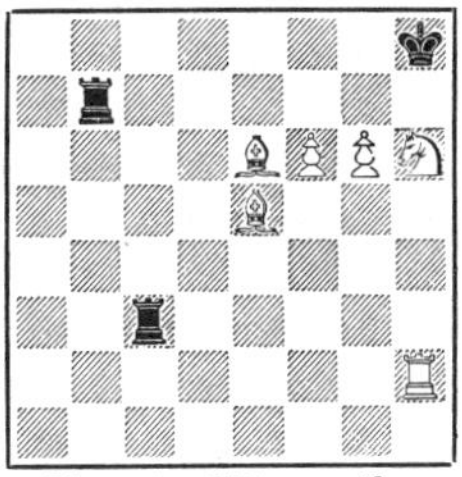

Mate in III exactly.

CB 94 : BS 68.

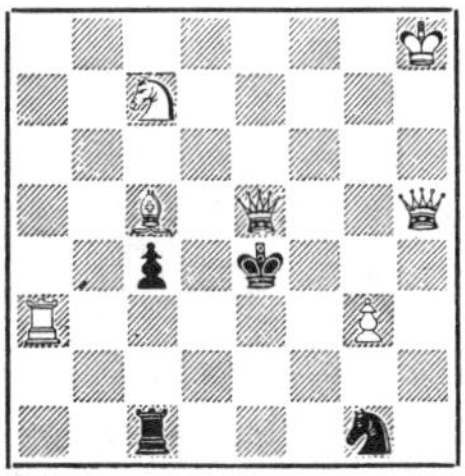

Mate with Pawn in III exactly.

CB 95 : BS 79.

Mate in IV exactly.

CB 96 : BS 83 : Ar. 120.

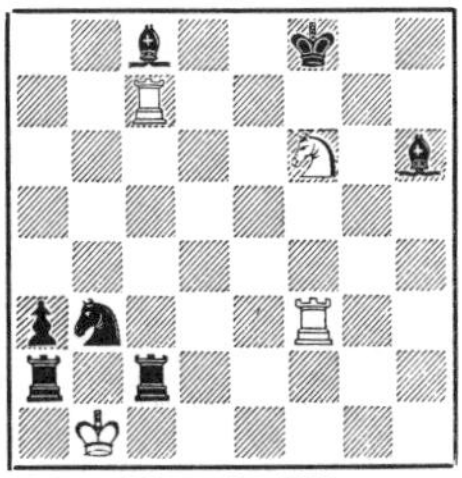

Mate in IV.

CB 97 : BS 84.

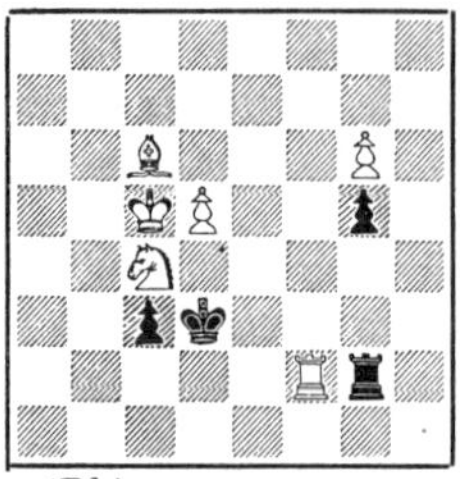

(Bl.)
Mate with Pd5 in IV exactly.

CB 98 : BS 85.

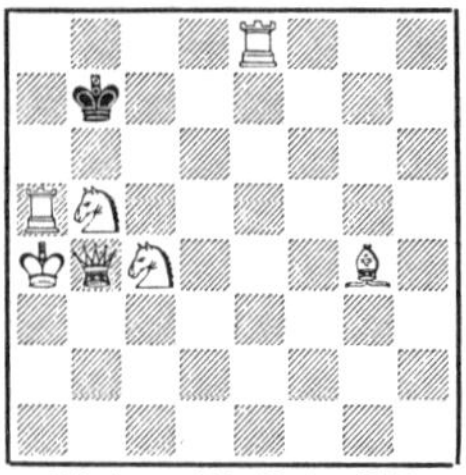

Mate with B in IV exactly.

CB 99 : BS 86.

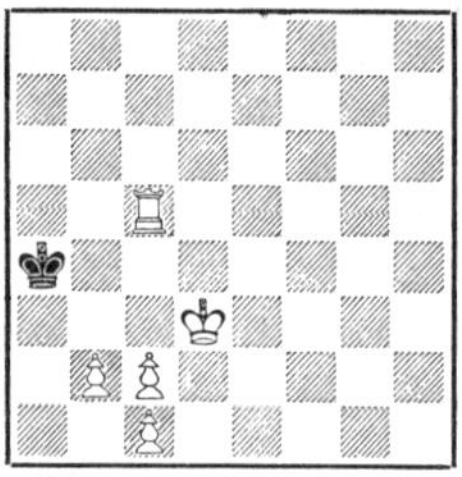

Mate in IV exactly.

CB 100 : BS 75†.

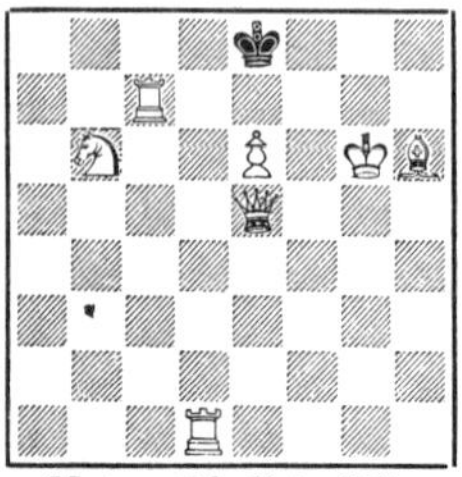

Mate with B in IV.

CB 101 : BS 87 : Ar. 50.

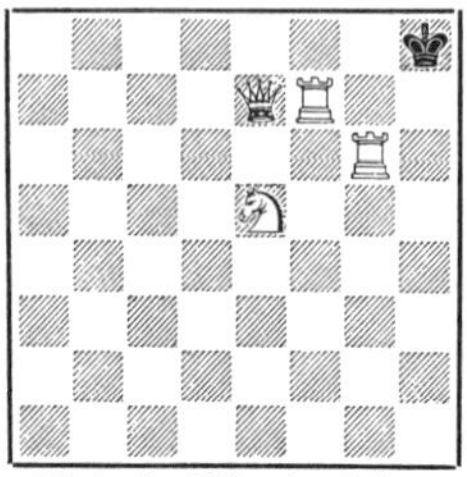

Mate in IV, checking every move.

CB 102 : BS 88.

Mate in IV.

CB 103 : BS 89.

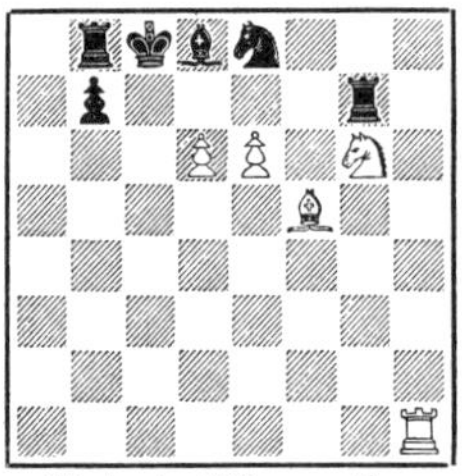

Mate in IV exactly.

CB 104 : BS 90.

Mate in IV exactly.

CB 105 : BS 91.

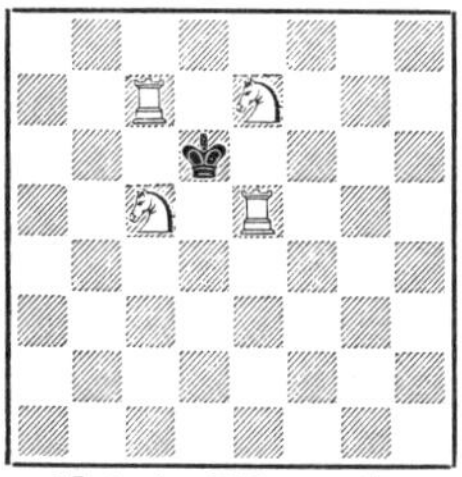

Mate in IV exactly.

CB 106 : BS 92.

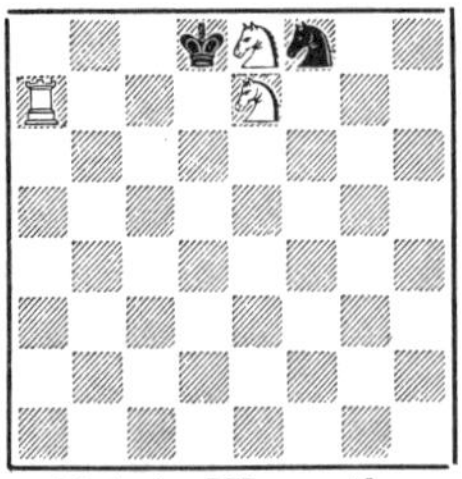

Mate in IV exactly.

CB 107 : BS 93†.

Mate in IV exactly.

CB 108 : BS 95.

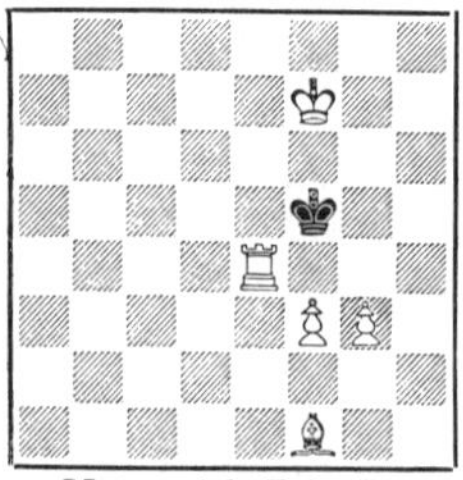

Mate with P in IV exactly.

CB 109 : BS 96.

Mate in IV exactly.

CB 110.

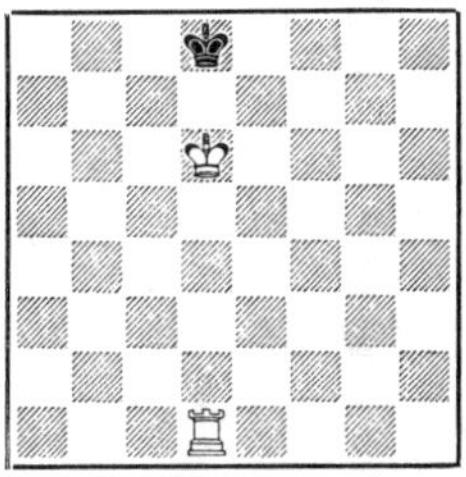

Mate in IV exactly.

CB 111.

Mate in IV exactly. The Qs are fidated, and the Bl. K must move when he can.

CB 112 : BS 74.

Mate with B on a7 in IV.

CB 113 : BS 76.

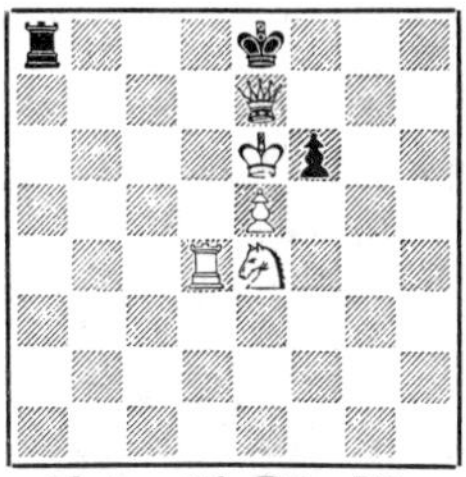

Mate with P in IV exactly.

CB 114.

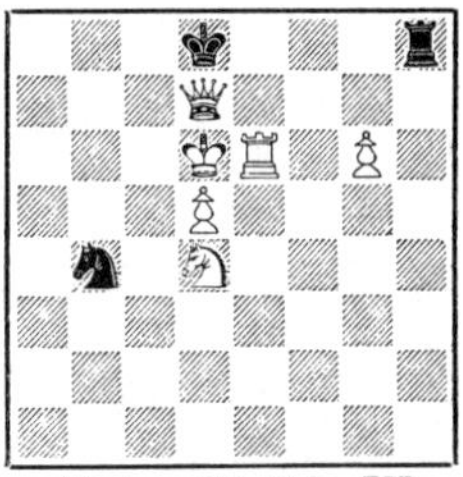

Mate with P in IV exactly. The Pg6 is immovable.

CB 115 : BS 97†.

Mate in IV or less.

CB 116 : BS 77†.

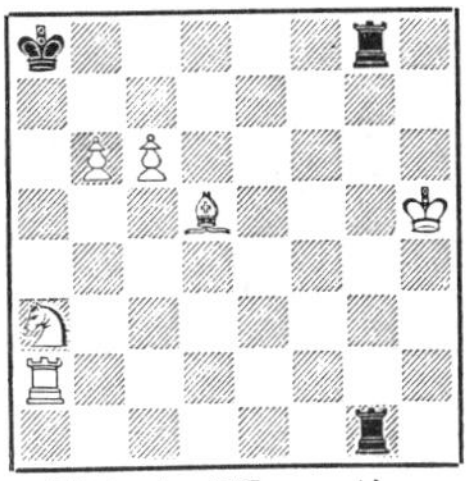

Mate in IV exactly.

CB 117 : Ar. 83.

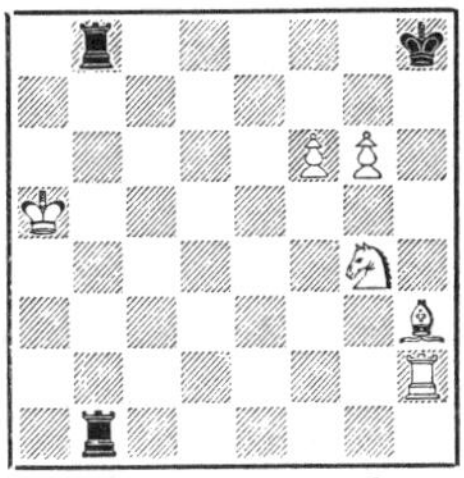

Mate in IV exactly.

CB 118 : BS 94 var.

Mate with P in IV exactly. Unsound.

CB 119 : BS 94†.

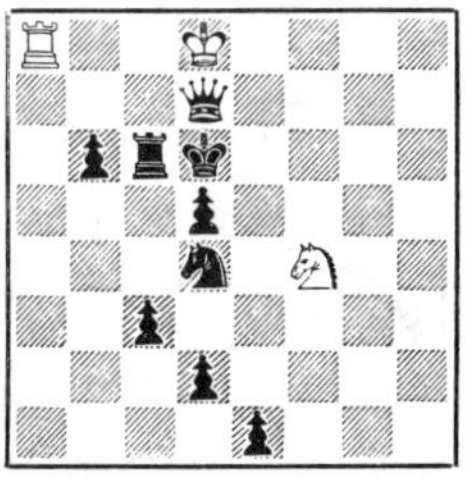

(Bl.)

Black mates with P in IV exactly. Unsound.

CB 120 : BS 78.

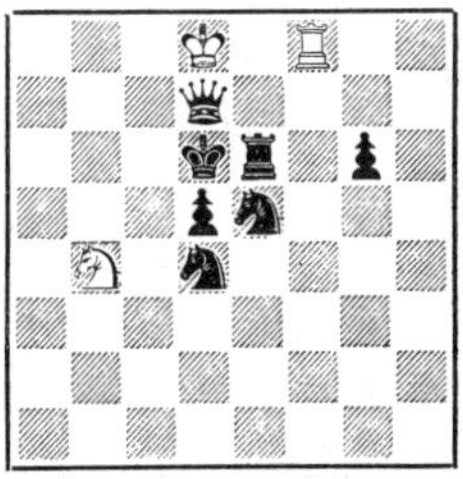

(Bl.)

Black mates with P in IV exactly. Unsound.

CB 121 : BS 80 : Ar. 199.

Mate in IV exactly.

CB 122 : BS 81.

(Bl.)
Mate in IV or less.

CB 123 : BS 82.

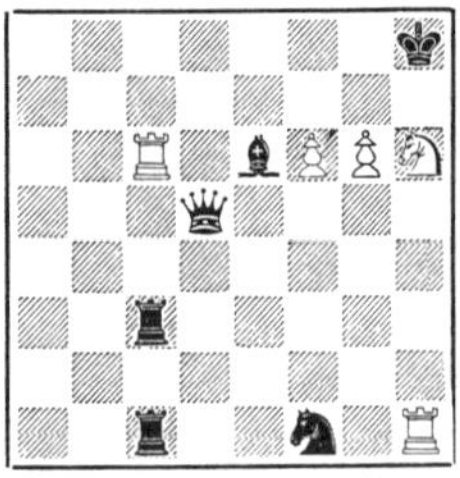

Mate in IV exactly.

CB 124 : BS 99.

Mate in V exactly, or self-mate in IV exactly.

CB 125 : BS 100.

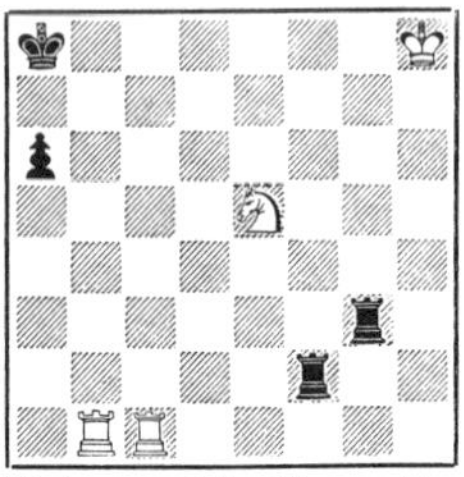

Mate on a8 in V exactly.

CB 126 : BS 101.

Mate in V exactly.

CB 127 : BS 102.

Mate with B in V exactly.

CB 128 : BS 103.

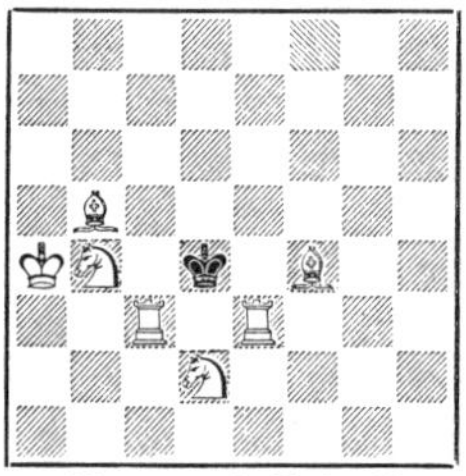

Mate with B in V exactly.

CB 129 : BS 104.

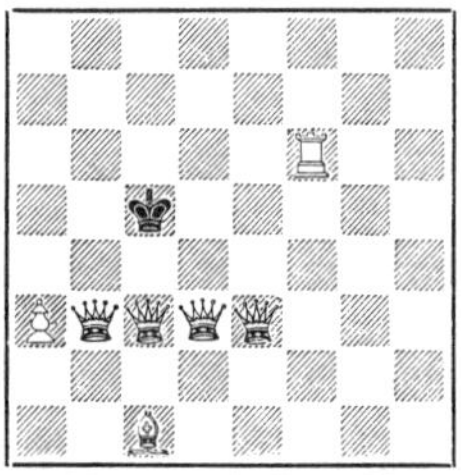

Mate with B in V exactly.

CB 130.

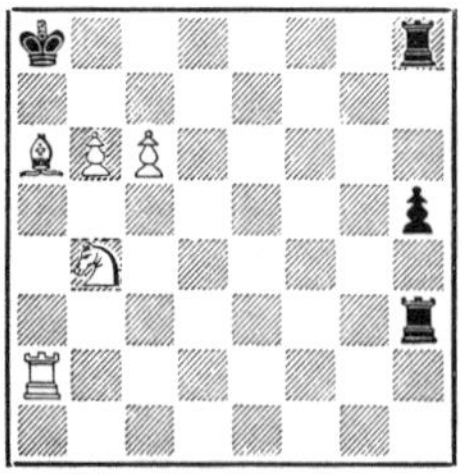

Mate in V or less.

CB 131.

Mate in V.
Ktg4 is fidated.

CB 132 : BS 98†.

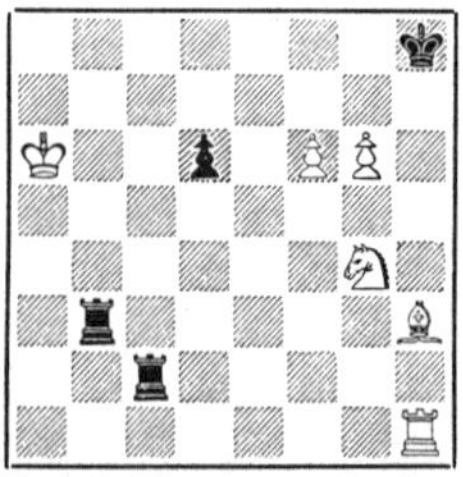

Mate in V or less, whether Pd6 goes to d8 or d1.

CB 133 : BS 105 : Ar. 352.

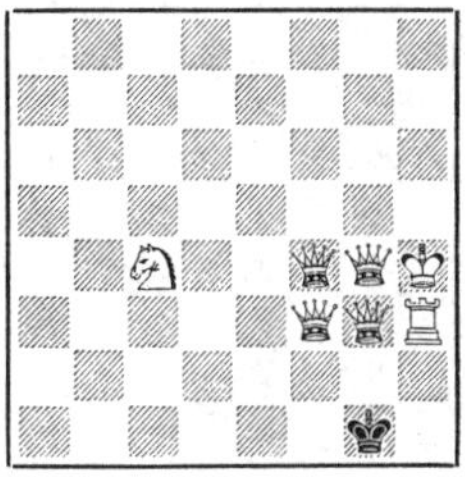

Mate on f4 in V exactly.

CB 134 : BS 106.

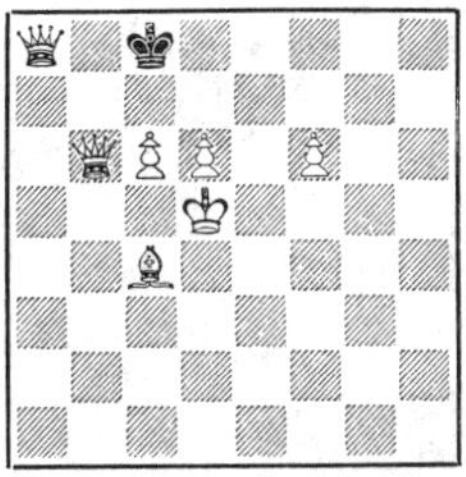

Mate with Qb6 in V exactly.

CB 135 : BS 107.

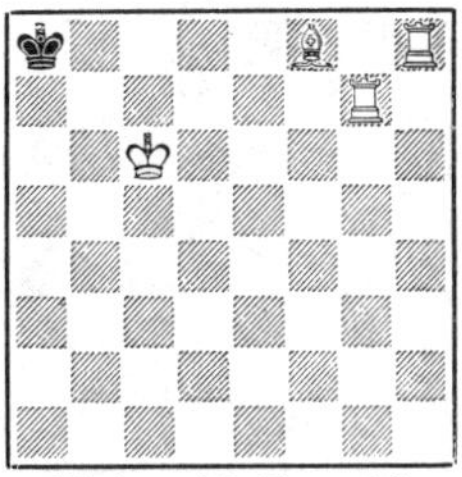

Mate with B on b8 in V exactly.

CB 136 : BS 108.

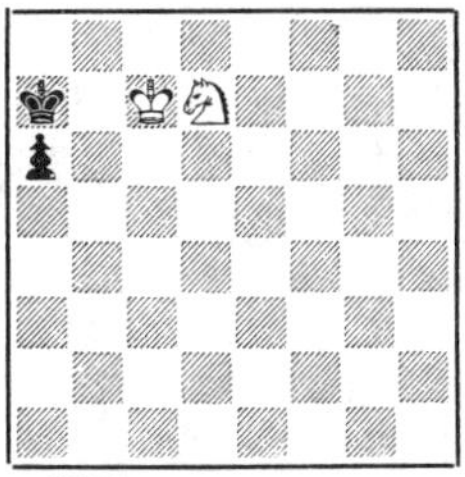

(Bl.)
Mate in V or less. Play is by alternate moves. Wh. loses if he gives stalemate. The Kt may also be on b1.

CB 137 : BS 109.

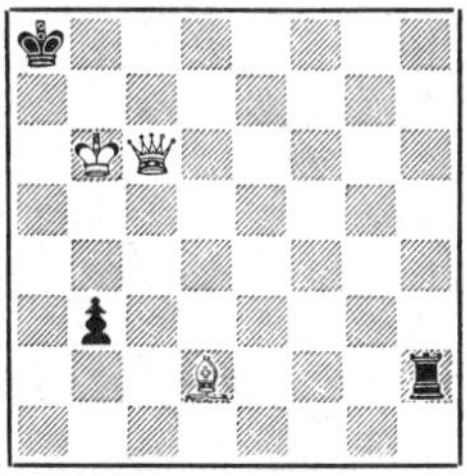

(Bl.)
Mate in V or less.

CB 138 : BS 111.

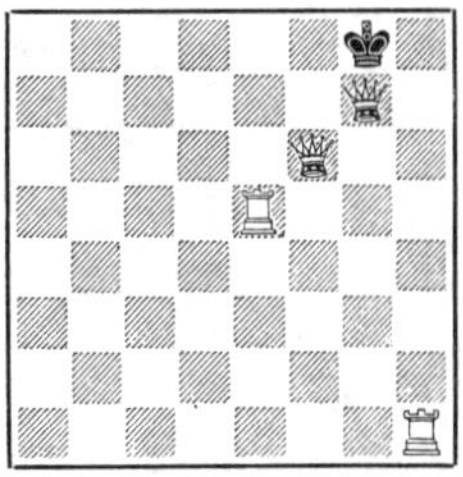

Mate on h6 in V.

CB 139 : BS 110†.

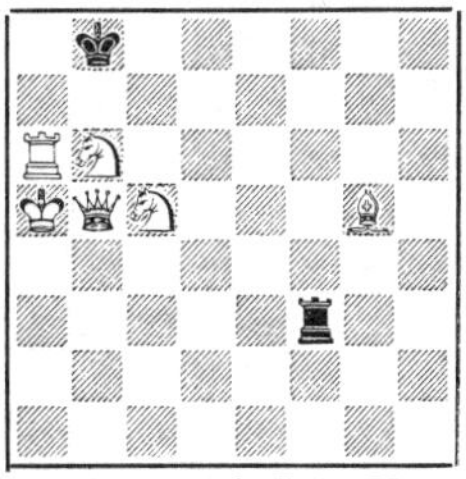

Mate with B in V exactly.

CB 140.

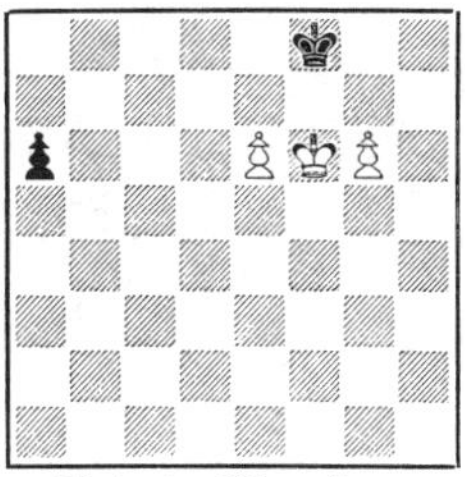

Mate in VI or less. Black must move his King when he can.

CB 141.

Mate on d5 in VI.

CB 142 : BS 112.

Mate with P in VI.

CB 143 : BS 113.

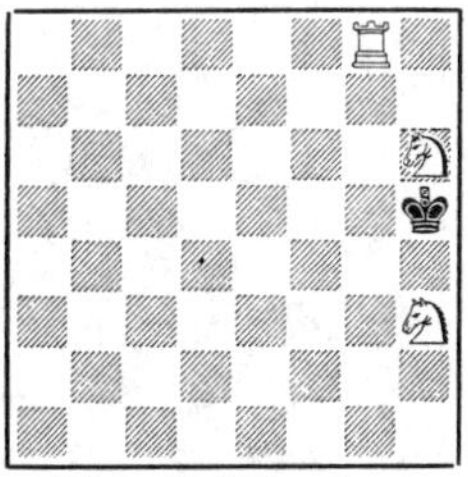

Mate in VI or less.

CB 144 : BS 114.

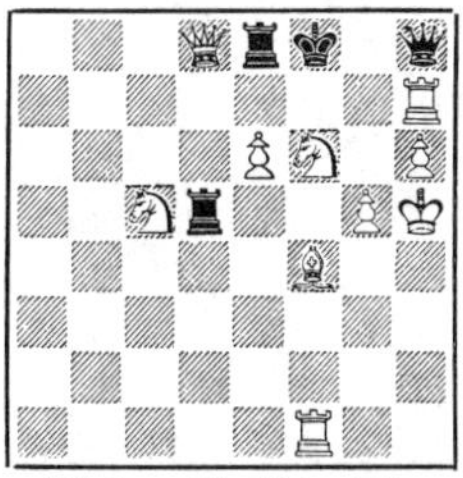

Mate with P in VI.

CB 145 : BS 115.

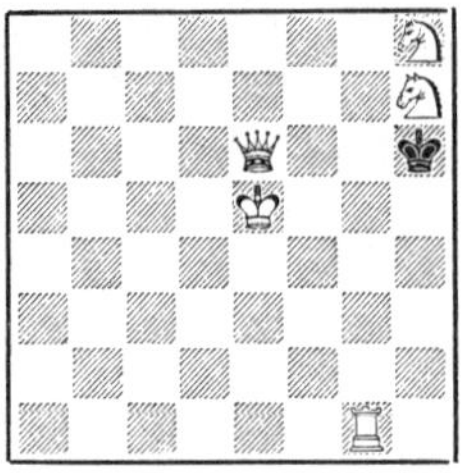

Mate on g5 in VI.

CB 146 : BS 116.

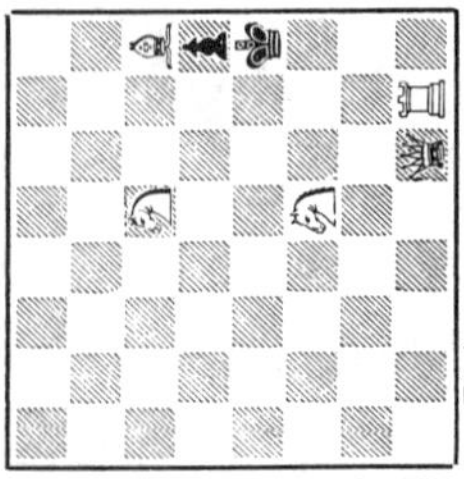

(Bl.)

Mate with Q on h8 in VI.

CB 147 : BS 117.

Mate with Pc3 in VI.

CB 148 : Ar. 83.

Mate in VI or less.

CB 149 : BS 118.

Mate on d4 in VI.

CB 150 : BS 119†.

Black mates in VI or less.
Unsound.

CB 151 : BS 120.

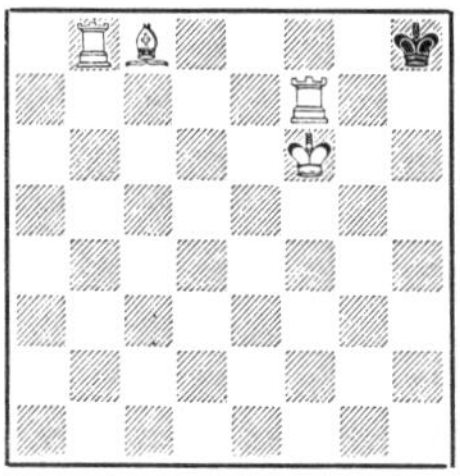

Mate with B in VI.
The Rb8 is immovable.

CB 152 : BS 121 : Ar. 86.

Mate on e3 in VI.

CB 153 : BS 122.

Mate with B in VI.

CB 154 : BS 123.

Mate on b7 in VI or less.

CB 155 : BS 124 : Ar. 27.

Black plays, and White
mates in VI or less.
Unsound.

CB 156 : BS 125.

(Bl.)

Mate in VI exactly.

CB 157 : BS 126.

Mate [on d5] in VI exactly.

CB 158 : BS 127.

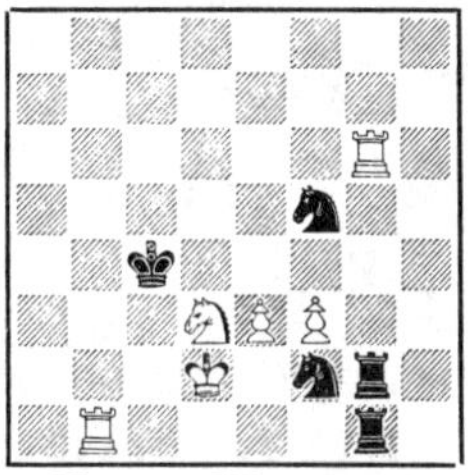

Mate in VI exactly.

CB 159 : BS 128.

Mate in VI exactly.

CB 160 : BS 129.

Mate with B in VII or less.

CB 161 : BS 131† : Ar. 133.

Black plays, and White either mates or wins the R in VII or less. Qh8 is 'new'.

CB 162 : BS 130.

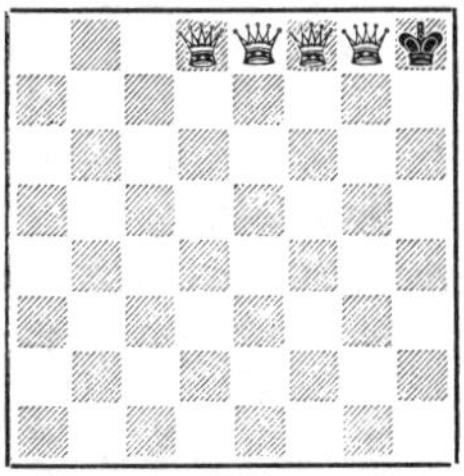

Mate in VII exactly. All the Queens are 'new'.

CB 163 : BS 132.

Mate with Pawn in VII exactly.

CB 164 : BS 133.

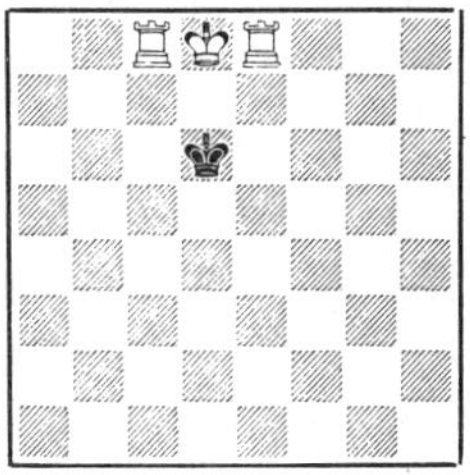

Mate in VII or less.

CB 165 : BS 134.

Mate with Pe6 in VII exactly.

CB 166 : BS 135.

Mate with Queen in VII.

CB 167 : BS 136.

Mate with Pg2 in VII exactly. Ra7 is fidated.

CB 168 : BS 137.

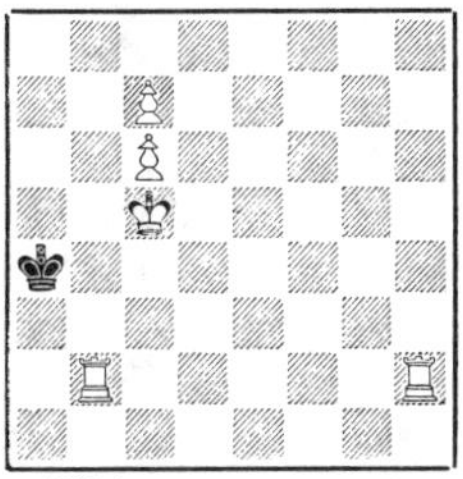

(Bl.)
Mate with Pc7 in VII exactly.

CB 169 : BS 138.

Mate with Pawn in VII exactly.

CB 170 : BS 139†.

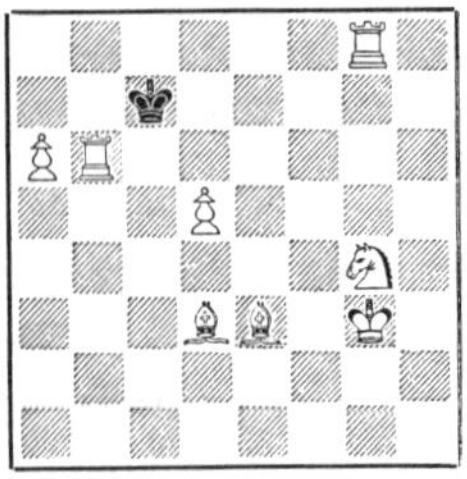

Mate with two Bs in VII exactly.

CB 171 : BS 140.

Mate in VII exactly.

CB 172 : BS 141.

Mate with the Pawns in VII exactly.

CB 173 : BS 142.

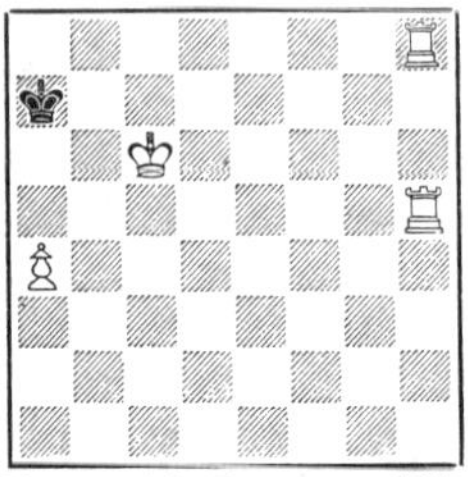

Mate with Pawn in VII exactly.

CB 174 : BS 143.

(Bl.)
Mate with B in VII exactly.

CB 175 : BS 144.

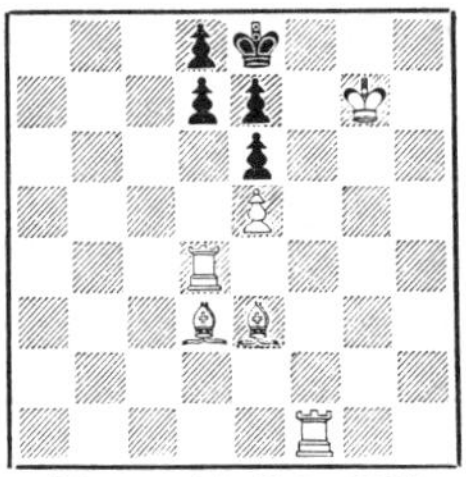

Mate with P in VII exactly.
Pd8 is immovable.

CB 176 : BS 145.

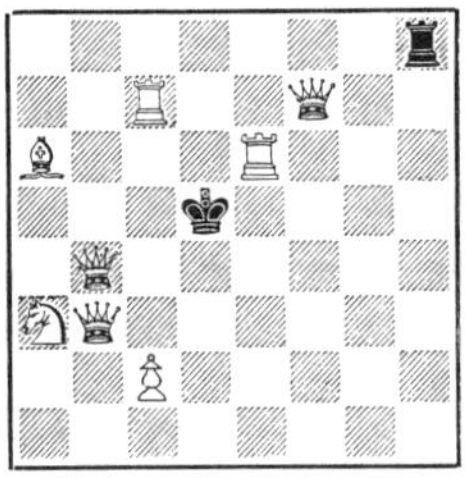

Mate with B in VII exactly.
Rh8 is fidated.

CB 177 : BS 146.

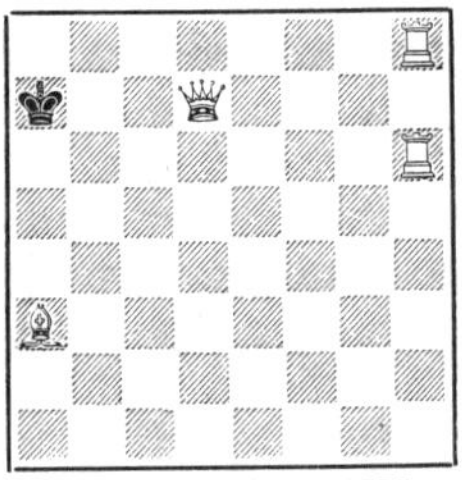

Mate with B in VII exactly.

CB 178 : BS 147.

Mate with B in VII exactly.

CB 179 : BS 149†.

Mate in VIII exactly.

CB 180 : BS 150.

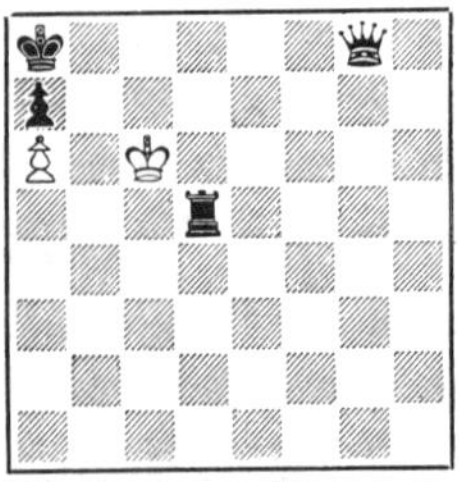

Black gives self-mate in VIII. Qg8 is 'new'.

CB 181 : BS 151.

Mate with P in VIII or less.

CB 182 : BS 152.

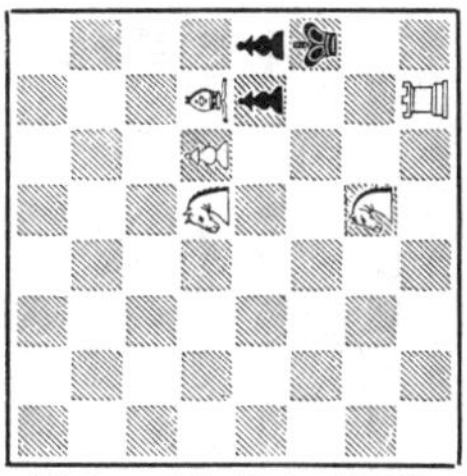

(Bl.)

Mate with B in VIII.

CB 183 : BS 153.

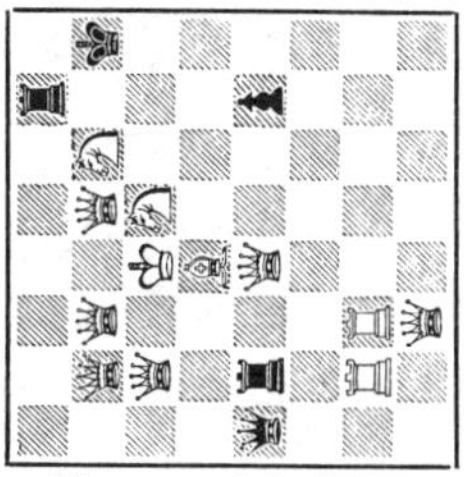

Mate on c1 in VIII exactly.

CB 184 : BS 154.

Mate with B in VIII.

CB 185 : BS 155 : Ar. 19.

Mate in VIII.

CB 186 : BS 148†.

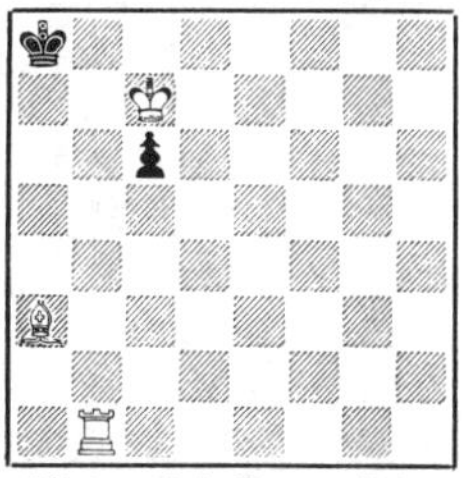

Mate with B on a7 in VIII exactly.

CB 187 : BS 156.

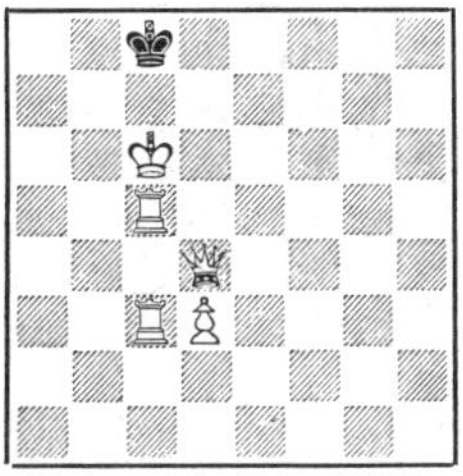

Mate with P in VIII.

CB 188 : Ar. 361.

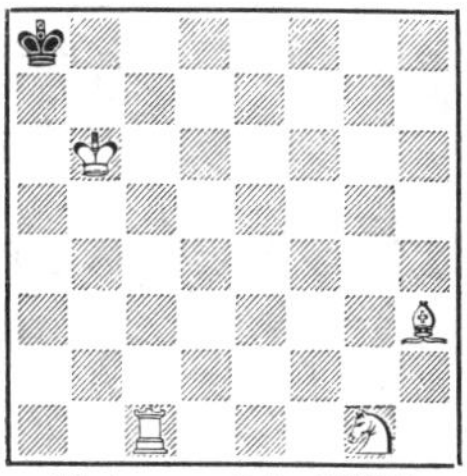

Mate on e5 in VIII exactly.

CB 189 : BS 157 var.

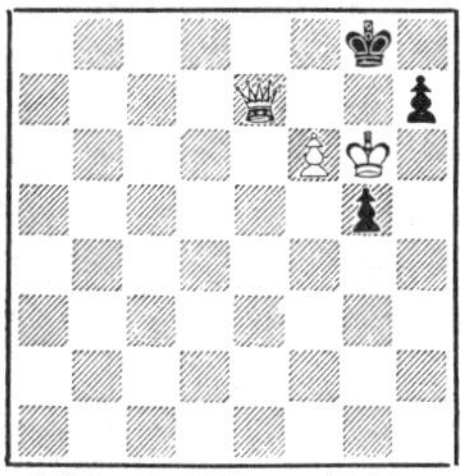

Mate in IX. All the Pawns go upwards.

CB 190 : BS 157.

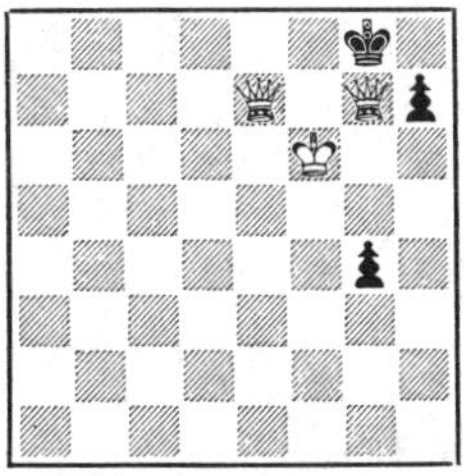

(Bl.)

Mate in IX or less.

CB 191 : BS 158.

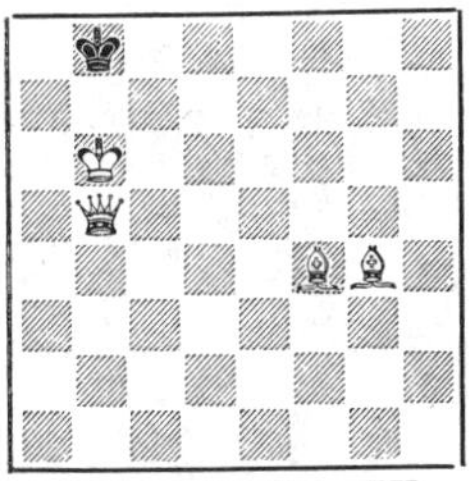

Mate with B in IX or less.

CB 192 : BS 159.

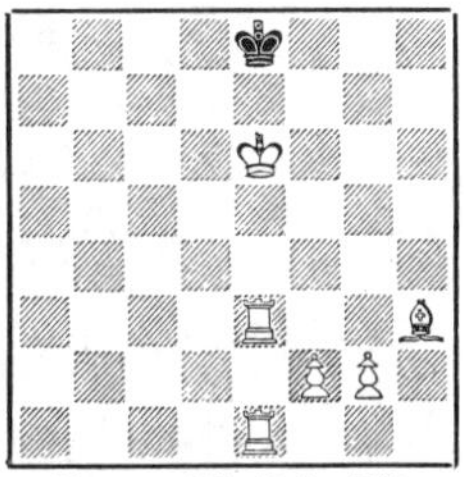

Mate with P in IX.

CB 193 : BS 160.

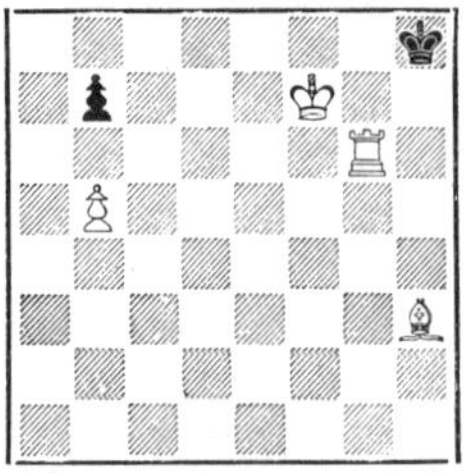

Mate with promoted P in IX exactly. The Black P is fidated.

CB 194 : BS 194 : Ar. 271.

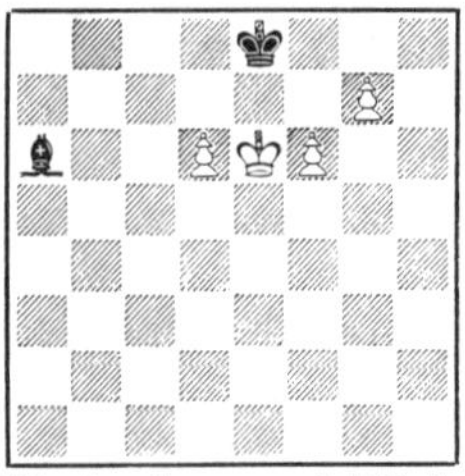

Black plays, and White mates or queens all the Pawns in IX or less.

CB 195 : Ar. 206.

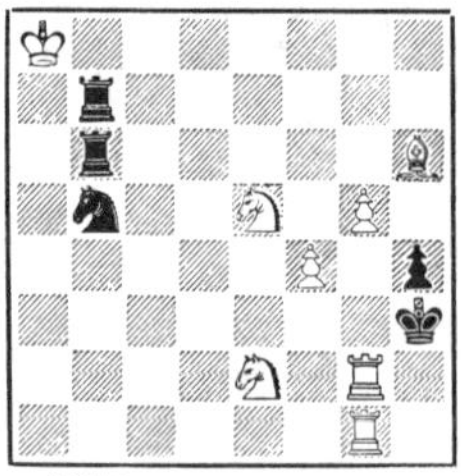

(Bl.)
Mate with B in X or less.

CB 196 : BS 161.

Mate with B in X. The Bl. R is fidated.

CB 197 : BS 162.

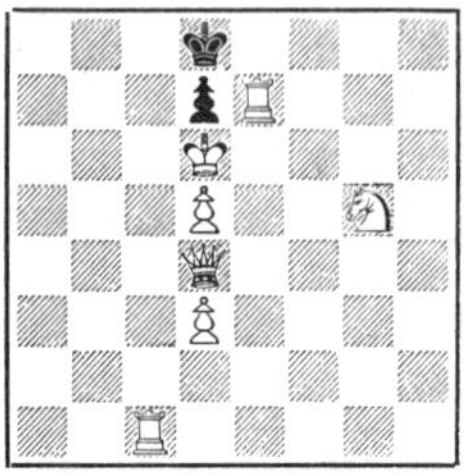

Mate with Pd3 in X exactly. The Black P is fidated.

CB 198.

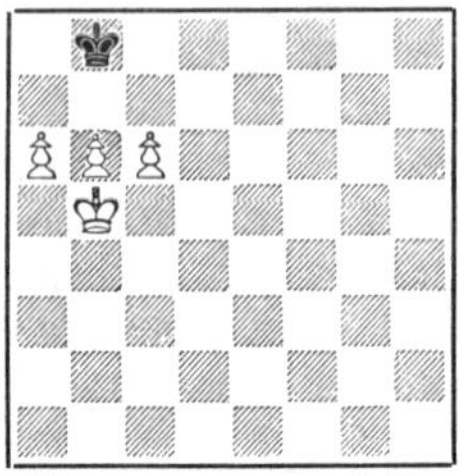

Mate, or queens all the Pawns, in X or less.

CB 199 : BS 165.

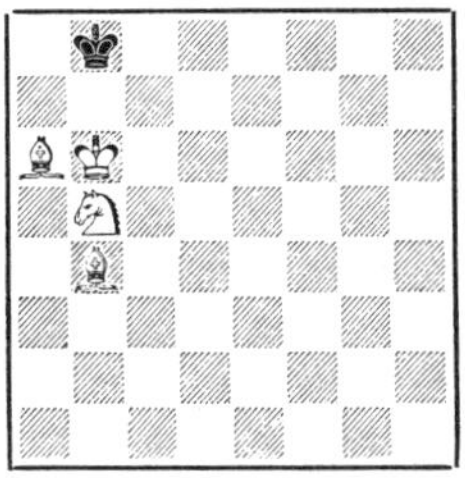

Mate with B in XI or less.

CB 200 : BS 166.

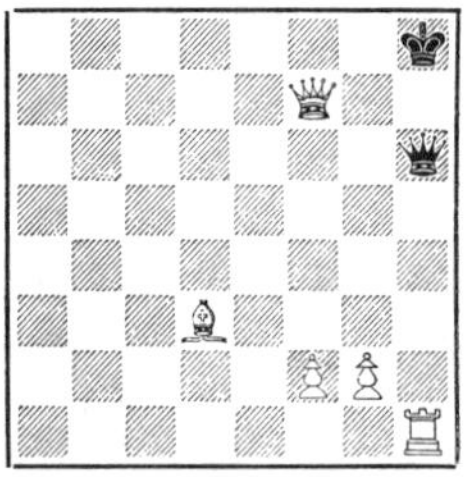

Mate with Pg3 in XI (exactly). The Black Q is fidated, and only moves when it makes a capture.

CB 201 : BS 167.

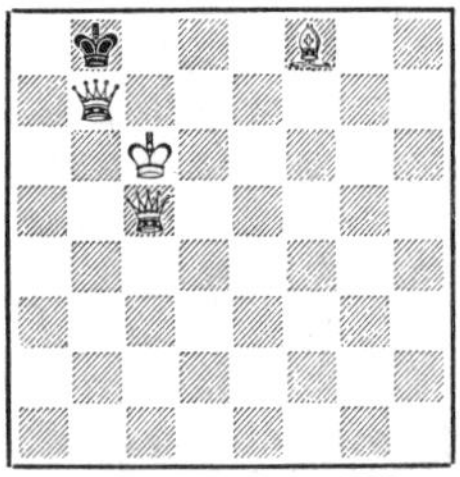

Mate with B in XI.

CB 202 : BS 168.

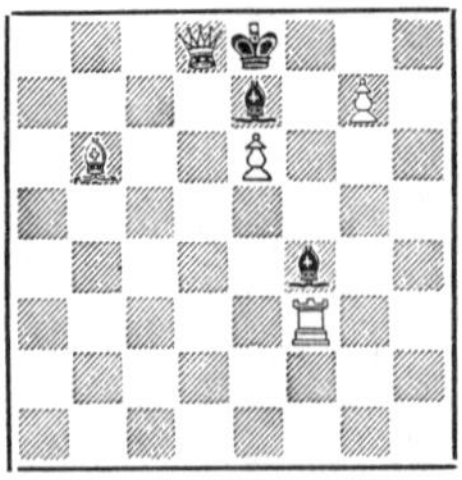

Mate in XI exactly. Both Bl. Bishops are fidated.

CB 203 : BS 169.

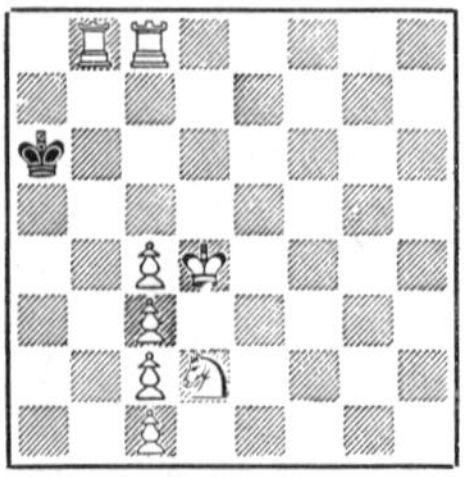

Mate (with Pc1) in XI (exactly).

CB 204 : BS 170.

Mate with Qh6 in XI.

CB 205 : BS 171.

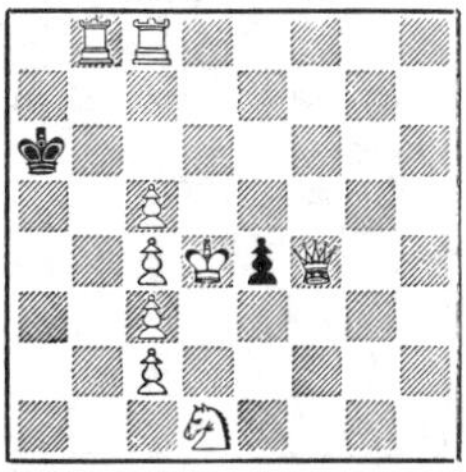

Mate on f4 in XII or less. The Bl. P is fidated.

CB 206 : BS 172 : Ar. 206.

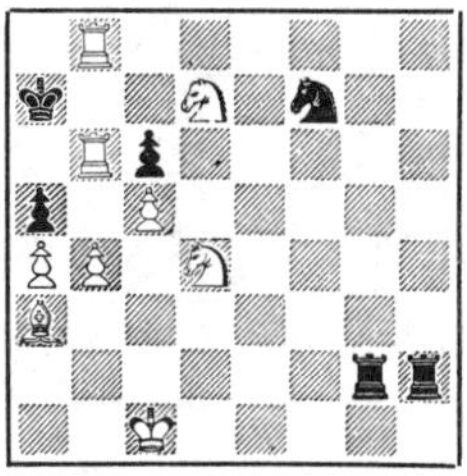

Mate with B in XII. White must give check every move.

CB 207.

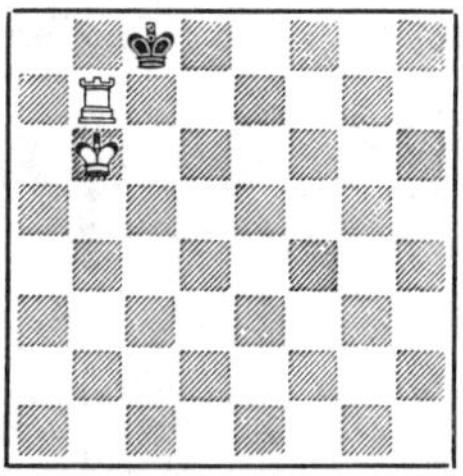

Mate in XII or less. The R may only move once, viz. when it mates.

CB 208 : BS 173.

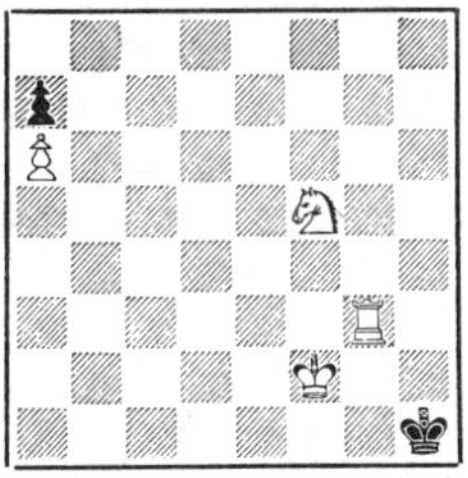

Mate with promoted Q in XII. The Black P is fidated.

CB 209.

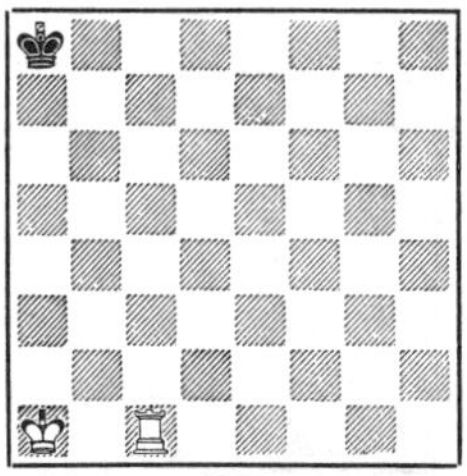

Mate in XII or less. The R may only move once, viz. when it mates.

CB 210 : BS 174.

Mate in XII or less.

CB 211 : BS 164.

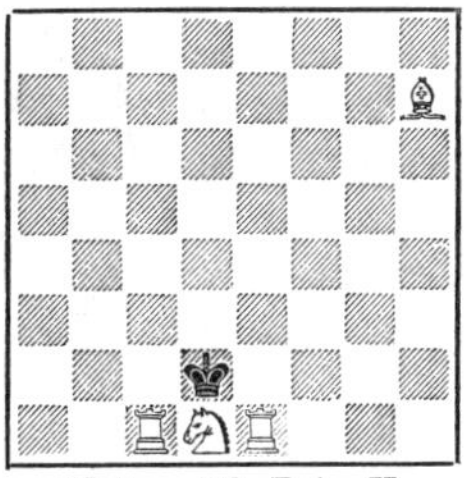

Mate with B in X.

CB 212.

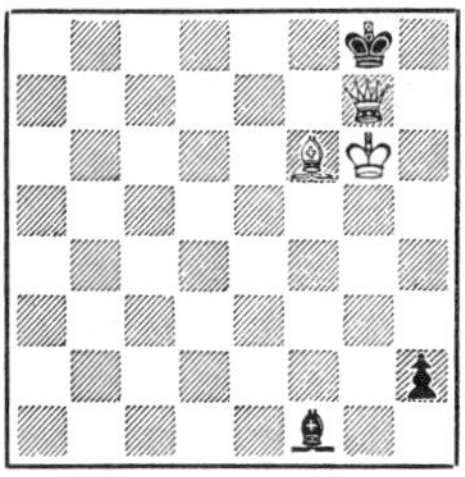

(Bl.)
Mate in XV or less. The Bl. B can only move when the K or P cannot.

CB 213 : BS 176.

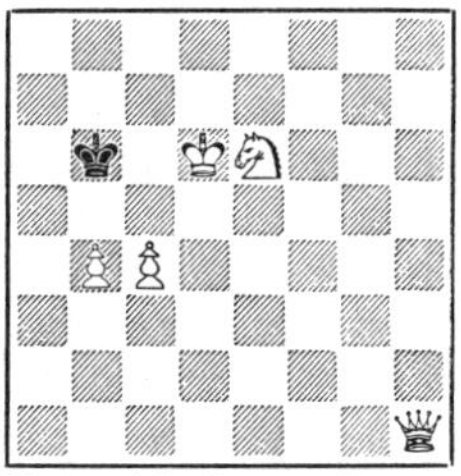

Mate with the two Pawns in XIII exactly.

CB 214.

Mate in XIV or less. The R is fidated.

CB 215 : BS 177.

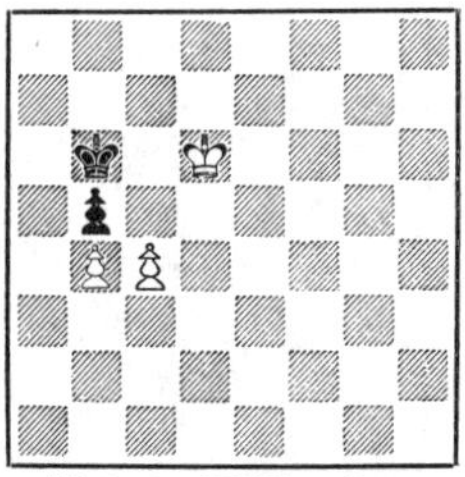

Mate in XIV or less.

CB 216 : BS 179 : Ar. 214.

(Bl.)
Mate with B on f8 in XV or less. A 'new' Q can check on its leap.

CB 217 : BS 178.

Self-mate in XV exactly (really XIII).

CB 218 : BS 191.

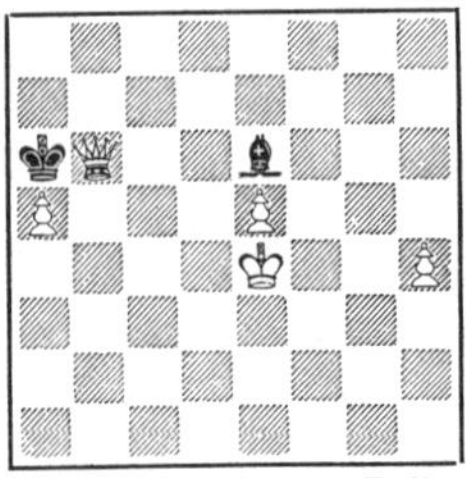

To queen Pa5 or Pe5 in XVI or less.

CB 219: BS 181†: Ar. 208.

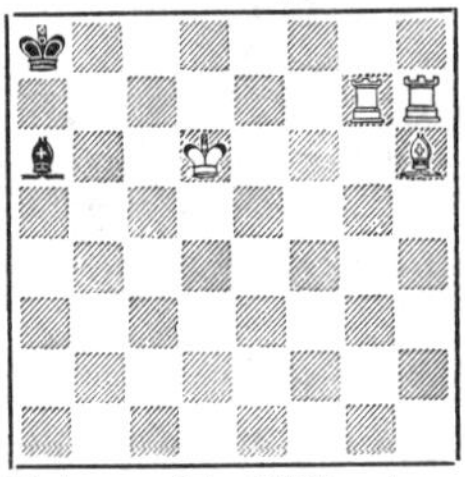

Mate on a8 in XVI or less. The Bl. B is fidated, and the Wh. B immovable.

CB 220 : BS 180.

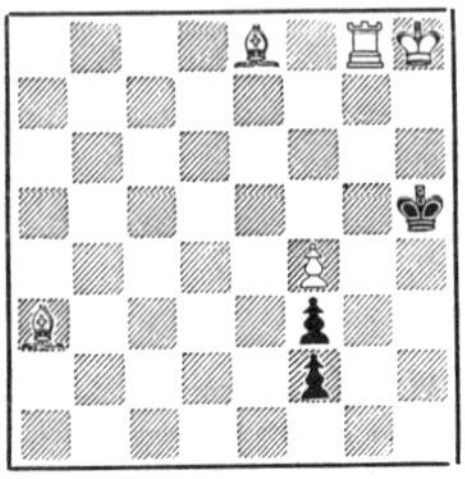

(Bl.)
Mate with P in XVII or less. The Bl. Ps are fidated.

CB 221.

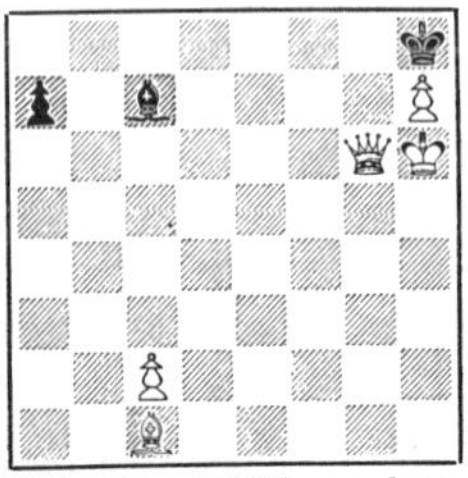

Mate in XVII or less. The Bl. B can only move when the Bl. K and P cannot.

CB 222 : BS 182.

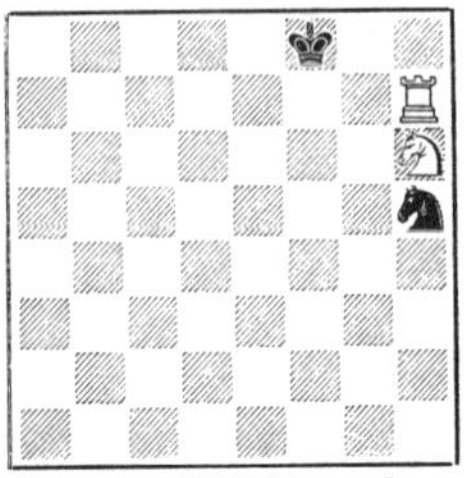

Mate in XVIII or less. The Bl. Kt can only move when the Bl. K cannot, or to make a capture.

CB 223 : BS 183.

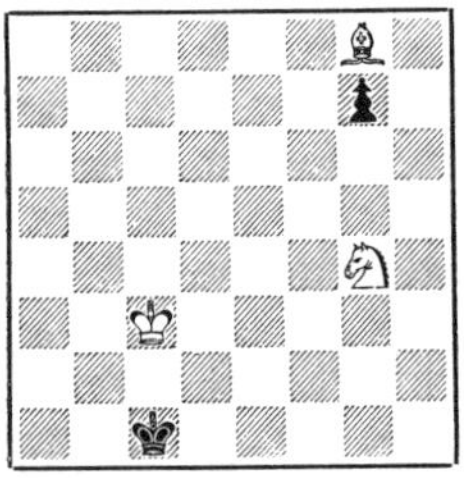

(Bl.)
Mate in XIX or less.

CB 224.

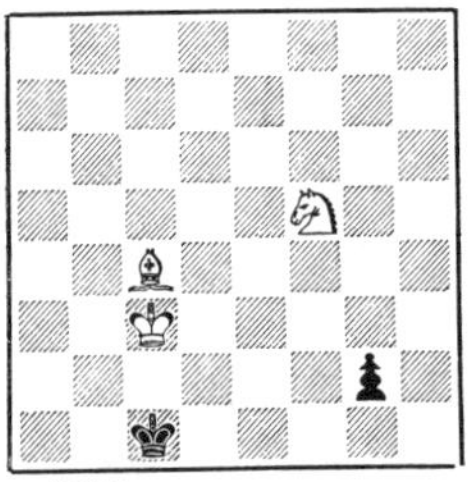

(Bl.)
Mate in *n* moves. The Bl. P can move to g3 or g4 first move. Unsound.

CB 225 : BS 188†.

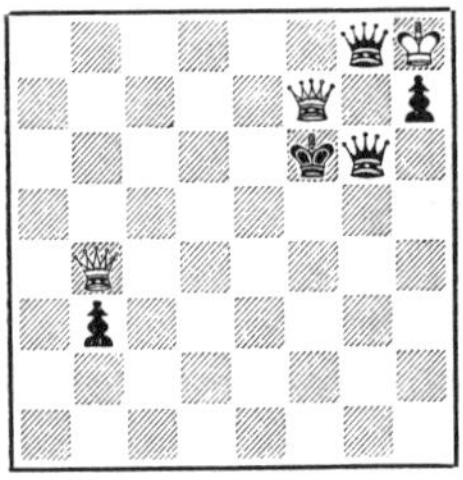

(Bl.)
Either plays. Black mates. Unsound.

CB 226.

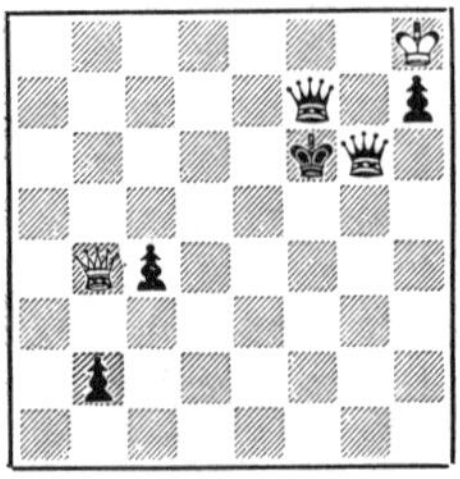

(Bl.)
Either plays, and Black mates. Unsound.

CB 227.

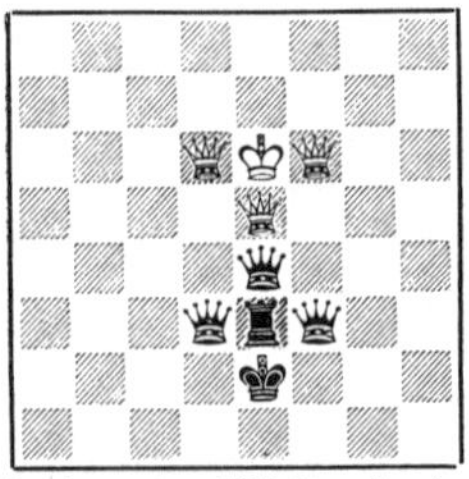

Black mates, White playing two moves first. Unsound.

CB 228.

(Bl.)
White plays and Black mates. Unsound.

CB 229: Ar. 458.

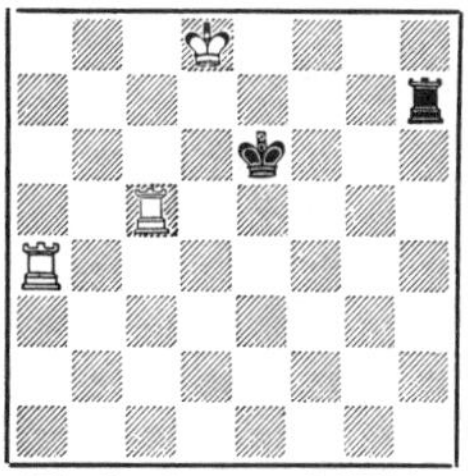

Black plays and White wins.

CB 230.

(Bl.)
Mate in V. Black only plays when checked.

CB 231.

Mate (in IV). White has four moves before Black plays.

CB 232.

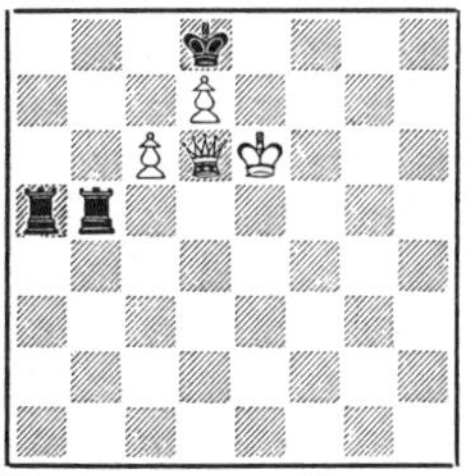

Black mates. The promoted Queens may not leap. Unsound.

CB 233.

Black captures the immovable Q. Unsound.

CB 234.

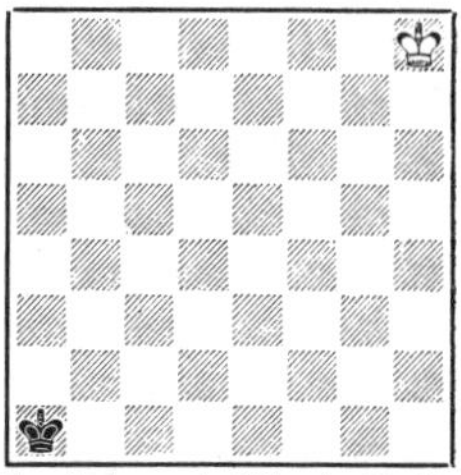

To stalemate Black. Both Kings are confined to the diagonals a1–h8 and b1–h7.

CB 235.

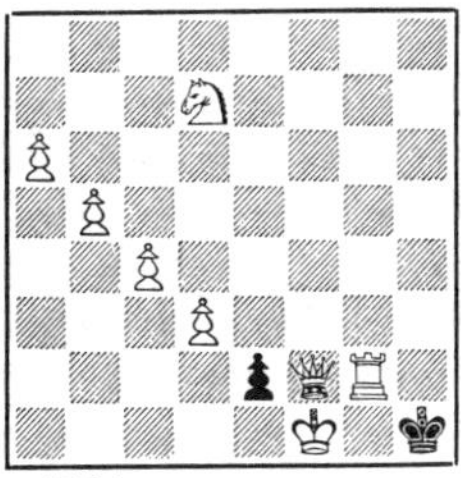

(Bl.)
Self-mate.

CB 236 : Ar. 562.

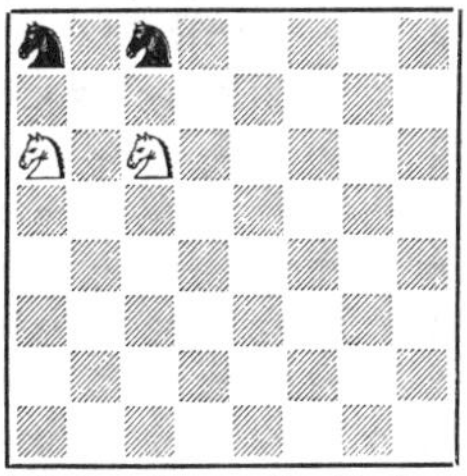

To interchange the Red and Wh. Kts in XVI moves. The Kts are confined to the square of 9 squares in the corner a8.

CB 237.

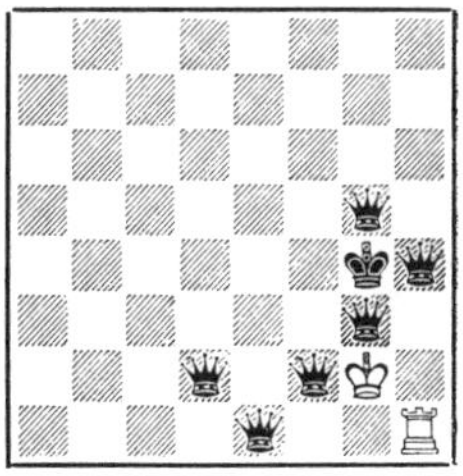

Black wins the R. Unsound.

CB 238.

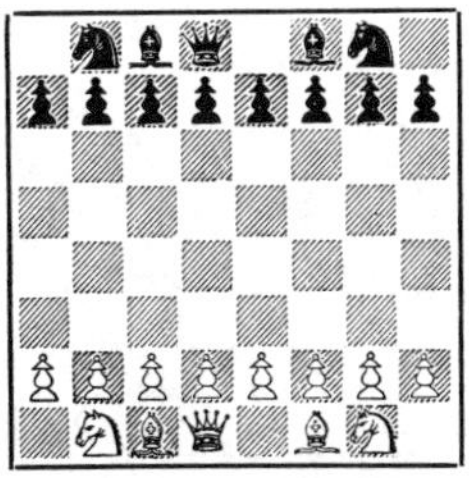

Black plays. White is to lose no man except in exchange for one of equivalent value.

CB 239.

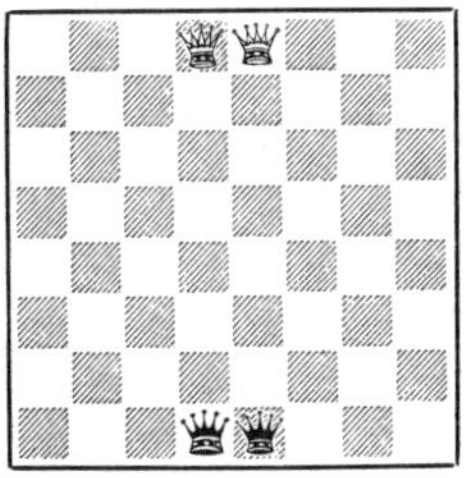

Black plays. White wins both Qs.

CB 240.

(Bl.)
Black mates. Unsound.

CB 241 : Ar. 46.

(Bl.)
Black captures the B. No new Q may leap. Unsound.

CB 242.

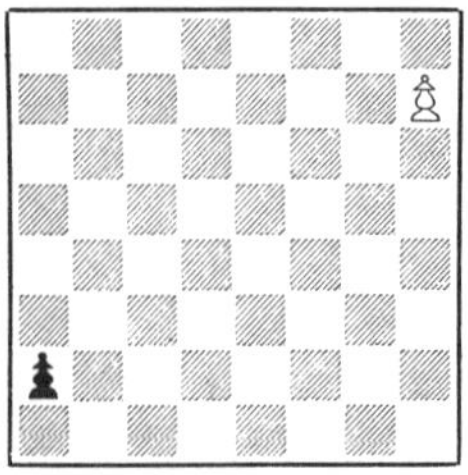

(Bl.)
Black plays. White wins the P.

CB 243 : Ar. 565.

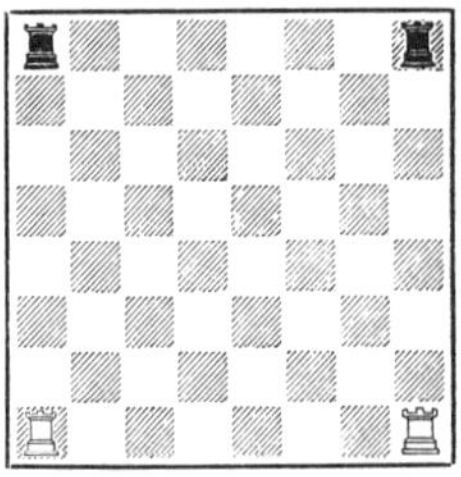

No R may cross a line commanded by an adversary's R. Black wins the White Rs. Unsound.

CB 244.

Knight's Tour on the half-board.

CB 245.

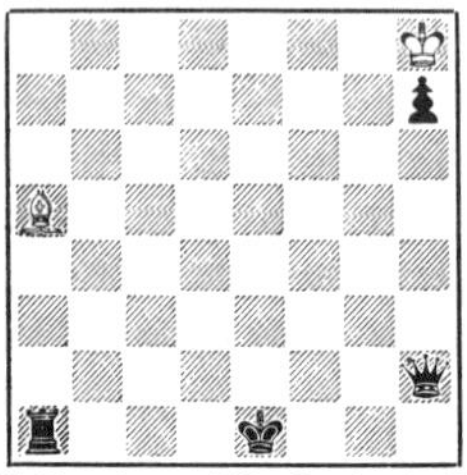

White plays, Black ejects the K from h8. The B and P are fidated from K. The P plays as a Q to line 1, and as Q or P to line 8. Unsound.

CB 246 : Ar. 41.

White plays and Black mates. Unsound.

CB 247 : BS 185.

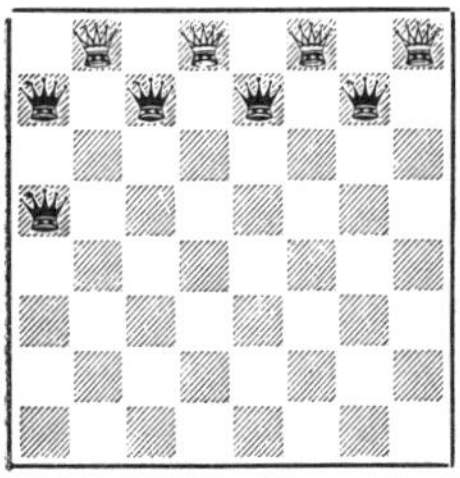

White wins.

CB 248.

White avoids mate. The B is fidated.

CB 249.

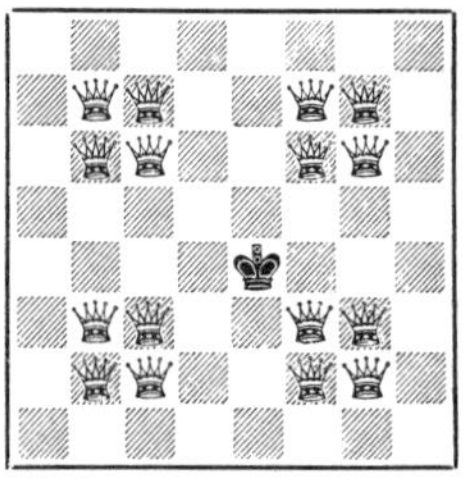

White mates the solitary K (who can play to any square) by placing 16 fidated Qs on the board.

CB 250 : BS 186†.

(Bl.)
Mate. The P is fidated, and if Bl. queens it, White loses.

CB 251 : BS 189.

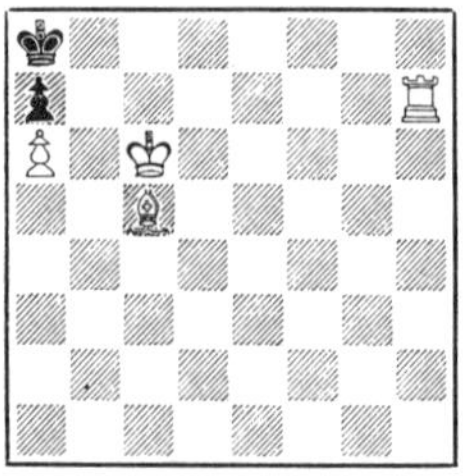

Mate on h1 with promoted P in XL or less. Pa7 is fidated.

CB 252.

Mate on h1 with promoted P. Pa6 is fidated.

CB 253: BS 184†.

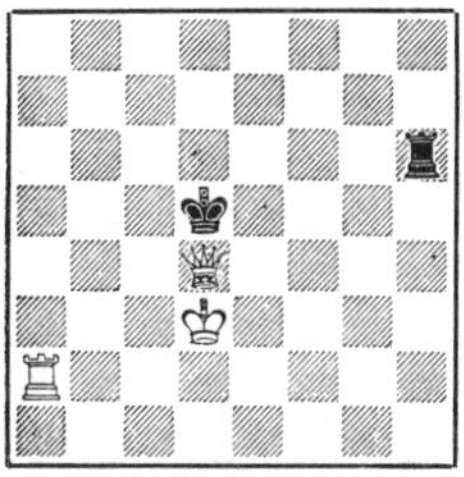

Mate in *n* moves. Unsound.

CB 254.

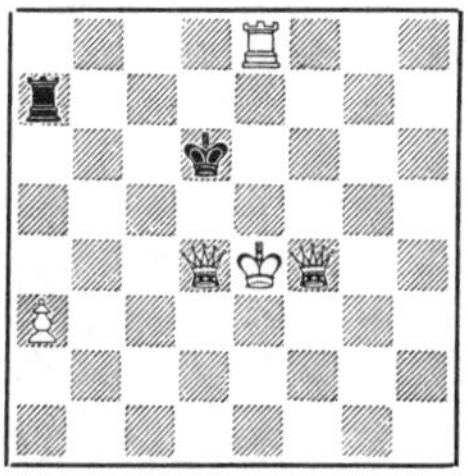

Black plays and White mates.

CB 255: BS 190: Ar. 217.

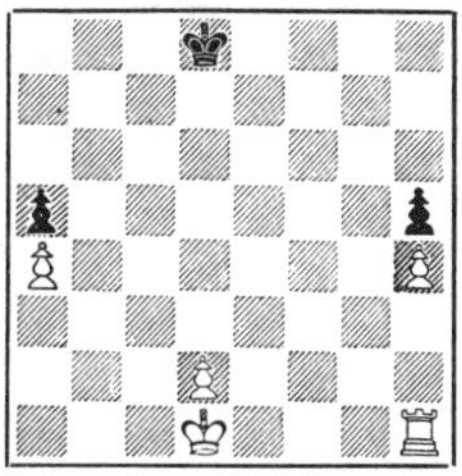

Either plays. White mates with Pa4. The Black Ps are fidated.

CB 256: BS 193†.

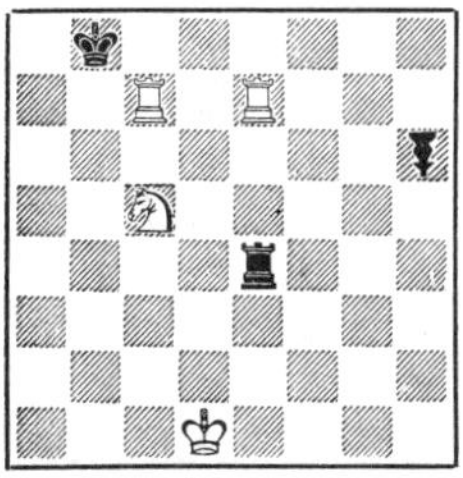

Black plays and White mates. The Bl. P can only move when K or R cannot. White loses if Bl. can play his K from a8 and b8. The Wh. K must not cross the 4th row.

CB 257: BS 192: Ar. 330.

Black plays 3 moves in succession and thereafter saves the Kt.

CB 258.

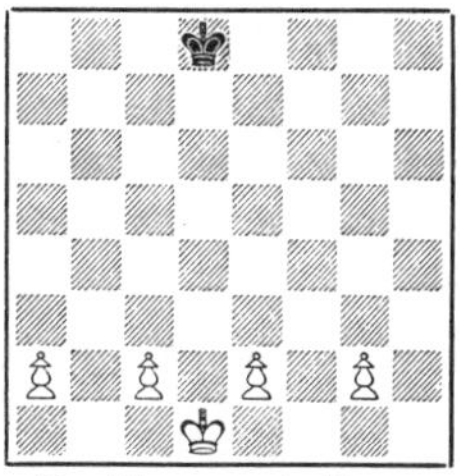

Partitum regis Francorum. White wins.

CB 259.

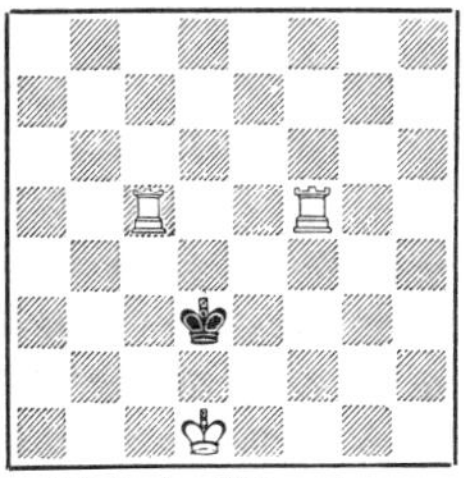

Mate in IV or less.

CB 260.

Mate in II exactly. The Bl. B is fidated. Unsound.

CB 261.

Mate in II exactly.

CB 262: BS 175.

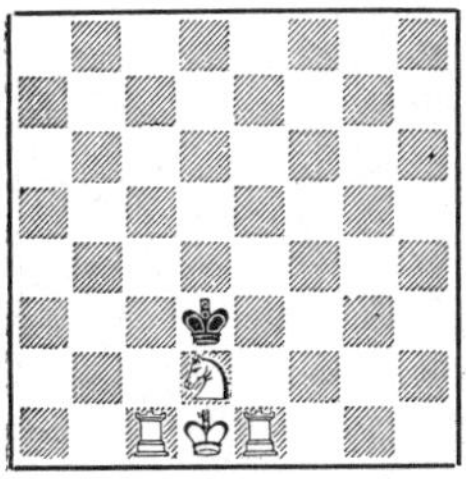

Mate in XII exactly. Neither R may leave the file on which it stands.

CB 263.

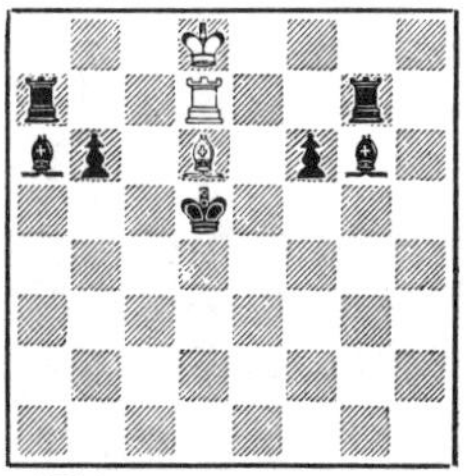

(Bl.)

Mate in II exactly. Unsound.

CB 264.

Either plays. White mates in II exactly.

CB 265.

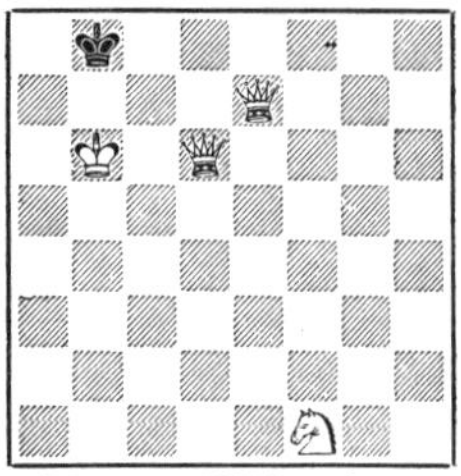

Mate in XIV or less.

CB 266.

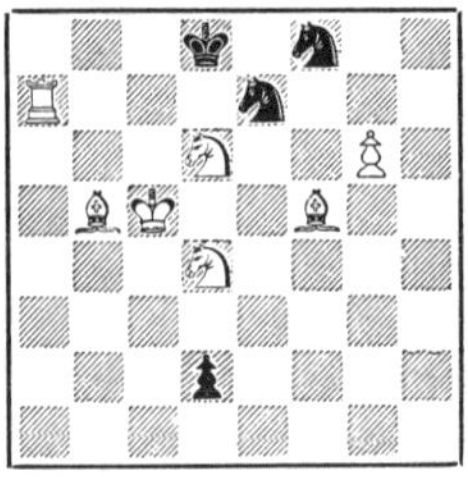

(Bl.)
Mate in II exactly.

CB 267.

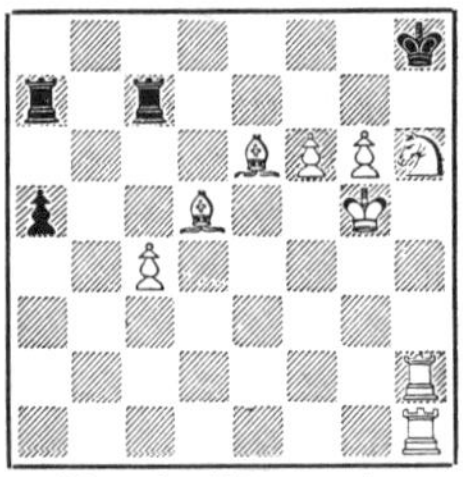

Mate in II exactly.
The Ps f6 and g6 may be Queens.

CB 268.

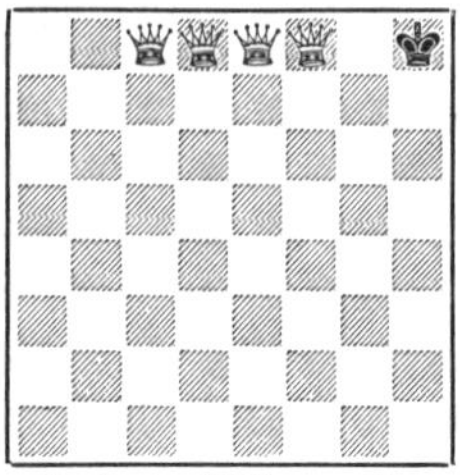

Mate in VII exactly.
All the Queens are 'new'.

CB 269.

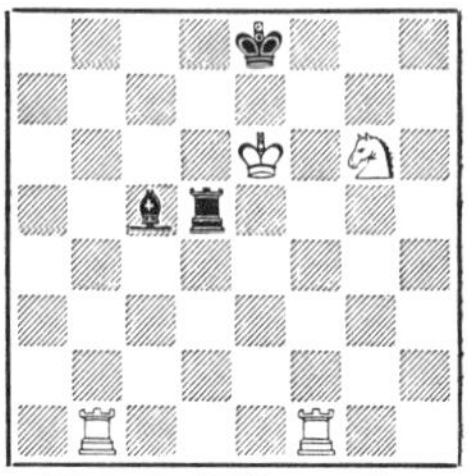

Mate in III exactly.
The Kt is fidated.

CB 270.

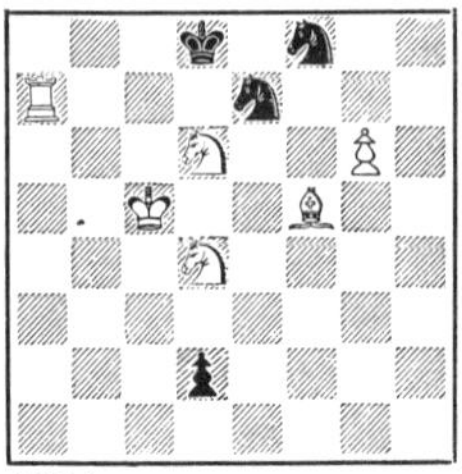

(Bl.)
Mate in III exactly.

CB 271 (corr.): Ar. 214.

Mate in XV.

CB 272.

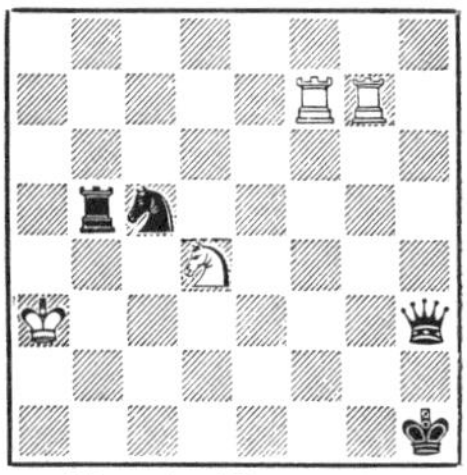

Mate in V exactly.
(Unsound.)

CB 273.

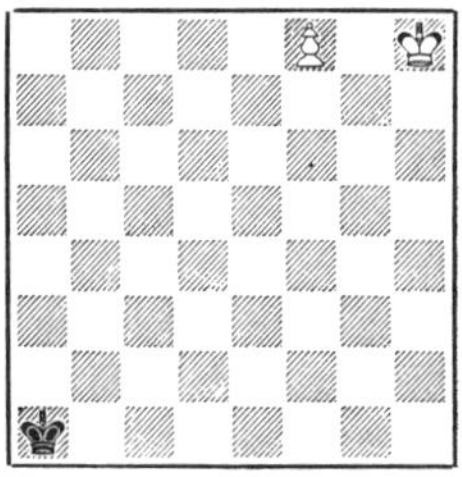

White plays and Black captures the immovable P.
Unsound.

CB 274.

Mate in II exactly.
All the Pawns go downwards.

CB 275.

Mate in II exactly.

CB 276.

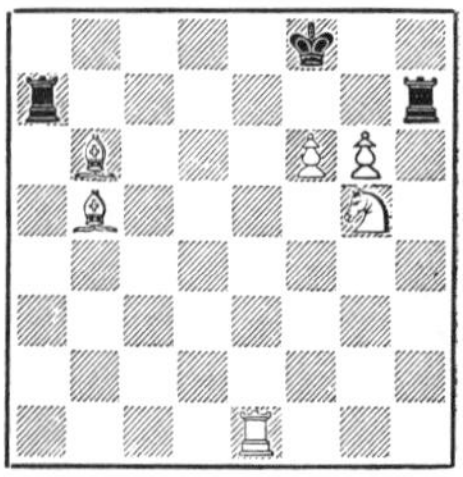

Mate in III exactly. All the men are fidated, and Wh. may not check on his first move.

CB 277 : Ar. 407.

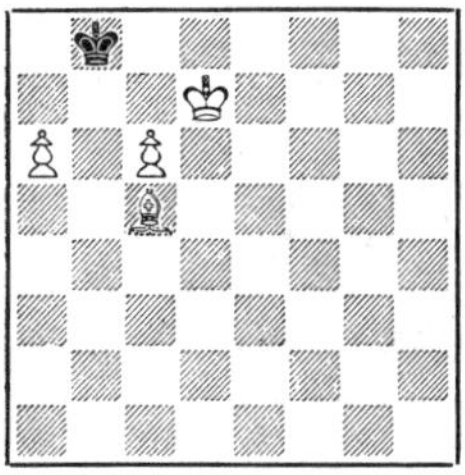

Mate in XI exactly.

CB 278.

(Bl.)
Mate in II exactly.
Said to be unsound.

CB 279.

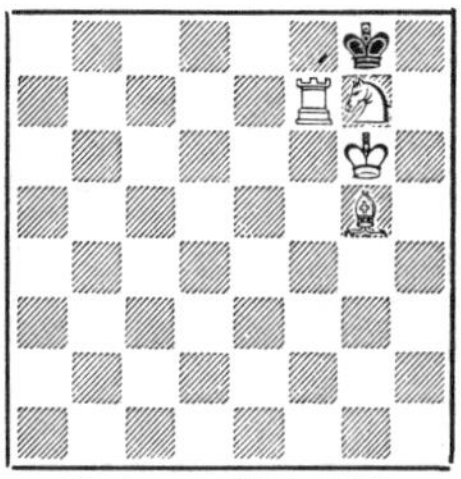

Mate on d5 in XI.

CB 280.

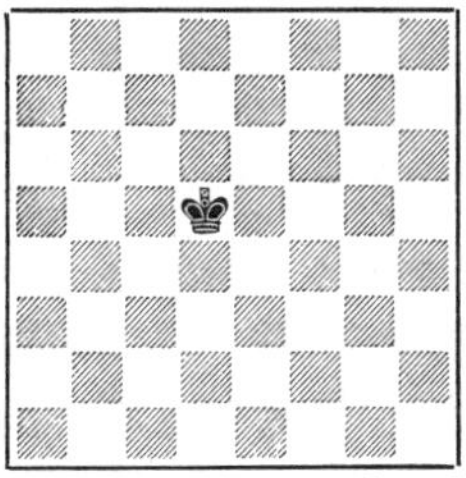

Four white Rs are placed on the board, checking each move, and mating on the 4th.

CB 281: Ar. 568.

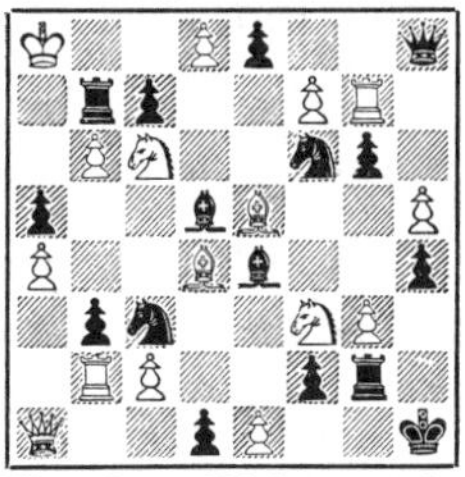

The four Bishops take all the other immovable pieces in 40 moves.

CB 282.

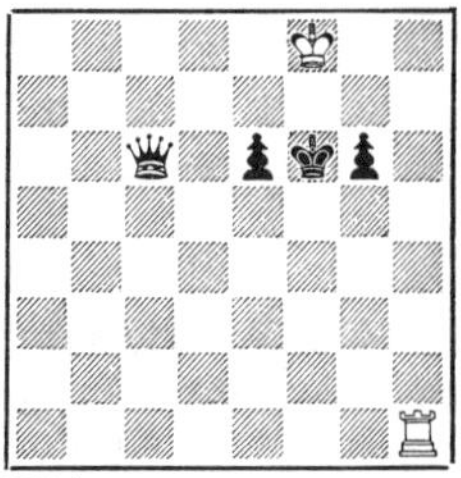

(Bl.)
Black mates. Rh1 is immovable. Unsound.

CB 283: BS 26.

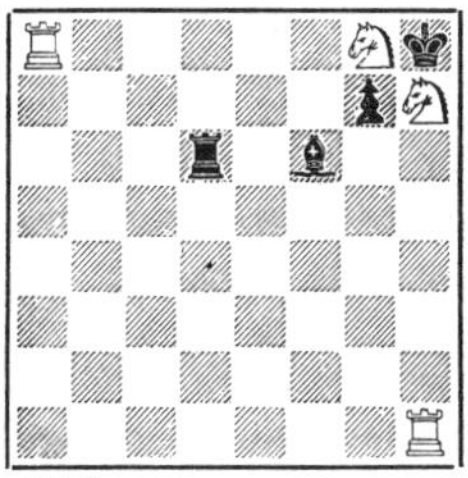

(Bl.)
Mate in II exactly.

CB 284: BS 26 var.

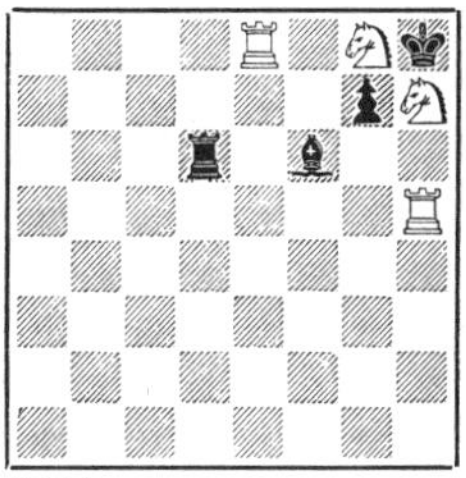

(Bl.)
Mate in III exactly.

CB 285: BS 26 var.

(Bl.)
Mate in IV exactly.

CB 286.

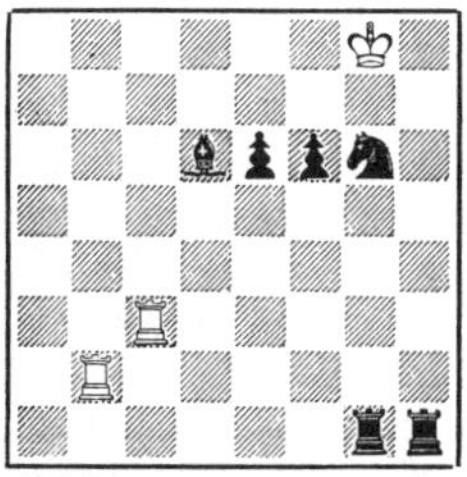

(Bl.)
Black mates in III exactly.
Unsound.

CB 287.

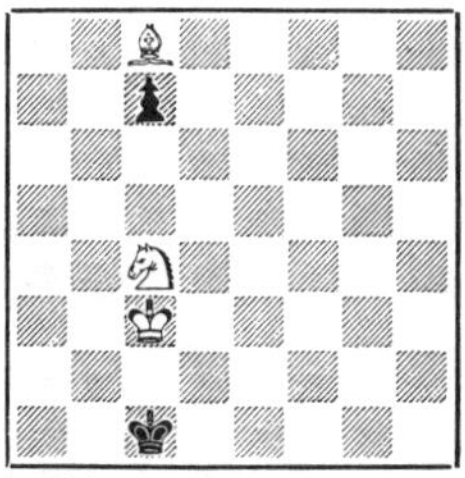

(Bl.)
White wins.

CB 288.

The Wh. Kt takes all the other pieces, finishing with Rh1 in XXV exactly.
Unsound.

SOLUTIONS TO CB.

1. 'Albi habent primum tractum et uolunt mattare nigros ad duos tractus tantum; et possunt trahendo roccum in A (f7), et est scac. Opportebit eum capere de milite et tu de tuo milite inferiori dices ei mat in puncto rubeo (g6): hoc dico si non sit rex albus. Sed si rex albus esset in B (g5), non posset fieri; quia capiendo roccum daretur ei scac, et ita non mattaretur in secundo tractu. Item si staret rex albus in C (h6), mattaretur, non dicendo scac de rocco in A, sed capiendo militem primo tractu, et secundo esset mat in A. Si autem esset pedo niger in puncto (c5) uadens ut signatum est (to c8), non fieret, quia posset eum trahere et tunc nec daretur mat de milite, nec de rocco.'

A shortened version of a Muslim problem (Ar. 300), of which the European players have made several wager positions. Cf. CB 34, 266, 270, 274 (in III), Ash. 5, Port. 5, D 25, Picc. 131, PL 60, 61, Sens 8, Ricc. 1 (all the pieces one to the left), and Gott. 4, Luc. 6, Dam. 7, WD 11, 47 (and different settings of the idea, WD 49 and 145). Alf. 65 (Bl. Kh6, Rh7, Kte6, f5; Wh. Ke8, Ktc8, d7, Rg3, g4; Bl. m. in II) shows that the idea of shortening the original m. in IV had occurred to Muslim players.

2. I give both the BS and CB texts, to show the difference between them.

BS 3 (Ra5 on a6).

'Albi primo trahunt et miles habet fiduciam, et roccus stans iuxta militem non mouetur, et pedones uadunt ut signatum est (to 8th line) uel sint regine quod idem ualet. Et uolunt albi mattare nigros ad 2um tractum, et fieri potest trahendo roccum in A (g3). Si aliud facerent albi, non mattarent nigros ad 2um tractum, quia si capiant roccum de alfino, ipse trahet alium roccum in punctum (a7). Item si trahat alfinum ante pedonem, nigri trahent suum roccum in B (h3). Semper est defensio, nisi fiat primus tractus de rocco in A.'

CB 2.

'Albi primo trahunt et mattabunt nigros in 2° tractu, et roccus punctatus (a5) est immobilis, et miles affidatus, et pedones uadunt ut signatum est (to 8th line) et sunt pedones et regine sicut placet. Uidetur quod multis modis possint mattare nigros in 2° tractu, sed non fit nisi unico modo si bene defendatur, et hoc trahendo roccum in A (g3), quia quicquid nigri faciant, recipient mat de eodem rocco uel de milite. Si autem albi caperent roccum de alfino (quod multi faciunt), nigri traherent alium roccum in B (a7) et defenderent. Uel si traherent alfinum ante pedonem uel reginam ibidem, nigri traherent suum roccum in C (h3); uel si albi trahant pedonem qui stat iuxta alfinum nigri trahunt regem. Ad omnem tractum est defensio, preterquam ad tractum rocci in A, quem tu facias.'

3. 1 Bb6 +; 2 Rd7 m. (2 Ktf7 m. is not given, nor is the alternative solution 1 Rc8 +; 2 Ktf5 m.). Variation: Kc1 on b1. The text solution fails, but the solution 1 Rc8 +; 2 Ktf5 m. *fit subtilius.*

4. No solution; 1 Pc7, Ra6; 2 Pb7 is now prevented. BS does not notice that the fidation of the Bl. R is unnecessary. Variation (not in BS): Kh6 on another row. Sound. 1 Pc7, Ra6; 2 Pb7 m.

5. (BS 5 substitutes Wh. Pd2 for Rc2, and changes colours) 1 Ktg5 + d, Bh3 +; 2 R × B +, R × R. (BS adds variation: Kf1 on g1, Rd3 fidated; m. in III exactly. Unsound. 1 Ktg5 + d, Bh7, and 2 . ., Rg3 +; or 1 Ktf4 + d, Bh3. See CB 45.)

This is the first of a very large number of positions in which the Black King is fenced in on a corner square by Pawns and Bishops, with threat of discovered check from a Rook by the removal of a Knight. The original idea of such a position is obtained from Ar. 83, the 'Dilārām problem', but all these mates in II and III exactly, are of course European work.

6. 1 Ke2, forcing Bl. to weaken his defence. A 'block' problem. CB says *fit unico modo*, overlooking the fact that 1 K × B does equally well. BS 13 prevents this by fidating Bd4 from the King, and renders the fidation of the P unnecessary by placing Kd3 on c3, Pd2 on c2—an improvement, since the position does not so openly suggest the K's move.

7. Wh. must retain the power of double interposition, hence 1 . . , R × P or Rf6 is insufficient. 1 . . , Rf7 allows 2 Ktb4 +; 3 R × R m.; and 1 . . , Rc1 or f1 is met by 2 Rh5. The MS. gives 1 fRd4; 2 R~, R × B, or 2 Ktc5 + d, Ra4 +; 3 R × R, R × R.

8. 1 Bc7, R × B; 2 Kt × R m.; or 1 . . , Rf4 or h4; 2 Ktb4 m.; or 1 . . , R elsewhere; 2 Ktc5 m. Variation (1): Ra4 on a1, a2 or a3. Unsound. 1 Bc7, R opposite R saves mate. (Variation (2) added in L in later hand: Ra4 on a1 and add Bl. Pc2. Unsound. 1 Bc7, Pc1 = Q; 2 Kt + d, Qa3 covers.)

9. 1 Q × B, Kt~; 2 Ra7 m. The fidation of the Q is unnecessary, and probably only added to preserve analogy with other versions of the position. Variations in CB only: (1) Bd5 on c5; (2) Bd5 White; (3) Bd5 removed. All sound by 1 Qb7 +; 2 Qa8 m., requiring the fidation of the Q.

Cf. CB 10, 12, Arch. 14, D 22, 23, PL 4, 6, 22, 26 (trick variation), 62, 65; and in III, PL 5, Picc. 89, L 291. The position is probably based upon a Muslim problem (? Ar. 24).

10. 1 Rd6; 2 Qb7 m. If 1 Rb1, Bd6. Cf. CB 9.

11. 1 Ra7 +; 2 Pb7 m. Cf. K 22, Port. 8, Ash. 10, C 42. (BS 16 adds variation: Kh3 on b5. Unsound. 1 Ra7 +, Kt × R +.)

12. 1 Rd7, Kt~; 2 Ra7 m.; or 1 . . , Kta7 +; 2 R × Kt m. Variations (1) add Wh. Pc5. Unsound. 1 Rd7, P × P. (If 1 K × P, Pd7.) (2) Rf7 on d7, add Wh. Pc5. Sound. 1 K × P, Kt~; 2 Ra7 m. Cf. CB 9.

13. If 1 Bd6 or h6 + d, Kt × R! If 1 P × B, R × P. If 1 Kf5 or K × B, Ktd6. If 1 Rd8 +, Kt × R +. If 1 Rg8, Ktd8 +; 2 R × Kt +, B × R. Variations: (1) in CB only, replace Bf8 by Kt. Sound. 1 Kth7 + d, B × R; 2 Bg6 m.; or 1 . . , Kt × R; 2 Kt × B m. (2) in CB and BS, add Wh. Ktb6, *quam additionem pauci sciunt* (CB). Sound. 1 K × B, Ktd6; 2 B × Kt m.; or 1 . . , Rc6 +; 2 B × R m.; or 1 . . , Pg4; 2 Bg6 m.

Cf. CB 278, Picc. 27, 39, CB 64 in III, and CB 113 &c. in IV.

14. 1 . . , Ra5 threatening; 2 . . , Ra6 +, or if 2 Pc6, R × dP +. Cf. CB 18.

15. 1 Qf7, Kf5; 2 Rf3 m. Cf. Arch. 19, Ricc. 41, Picc. 1, 38, F 292, S 37, WA 13, and WD 51.

16. 1 Bf3; 2 Kte6 or Rd7 m. BS 21, omitting Pc6 and the condition, allows other solutions by 1 Rf7, g7, e7, h7, or b7; it adds variation: Wh. K elsewhere, when 1 Kte6 +, Kt × Kt; 2 Rd7 m. is also possible. Cf. CB 274, Picc. 14, 42, 51.

17. (BS 22 raises lines 2 and 3 one each.) 1 R × Q, Rh7; 2 Rc8 m.; or 1 . . , any other; 2 Ktf7 m. The favourite keys in positions like this fail thus: 1 Bf7, Rc3 (in BS position, Ra2); and 1 Bb7, Ra5 +.

18. (BS 19 adds Kte5.) 1 . . , Ra5 threatening; 2 . . , Ra6 +; or if 2 Pc6, R × P +. Cf. CB 14.

19. 'Nigri primo trahunt et alfinus est affidatus, et dicunt nigri quod in 2º tractu aut capient reginam de dono, aut dabunt mat regi albo; et tu cogas eum dicere ante tractum quid istorum uelit facere. Si dicat quod capiet reginam de dono, non poterit quia tu caperes eum de alfino. Si dicat quod uelit albos mattare, non poterit quia cum dicet scac in A (d8), tu cooperies te de alfino affidato, et dabis ei scac, et ita in utroque casu perdet.' Cf. the similar double game, CB 40. We must understand that the undertaking to take the Queen means to take it without the loss of the capturing piece. The position is PL 53.

20. (BS 31 has Rb7 on c7.) 1 Rb3, Rf7 blocking f7 and pinning the Q. Variations (not in BS): (1) Add Bl. Pf2. Sound. 1 Rb3, Rf7; 2 Qg7 m.; or 1 Kg2; 2 Qg7 or Ktf7, according as Bl. plays, m. (2) Add. Bl. Pc2. Sound. 1 Kg2, &c., still holds.

21. 1 Rd1; 2 Rd8 m. or Ktf6 m., according as Bl. plays. Variations: (1) The Bl. Ps go to 8th line. Unsound. 1 Rd1, B × P; 2 Rd8 +, P × R = Q. Or 2 Kt + d,

Bh6. (2), not in BS; Rh3 on h4, Bl. Ps go to 8th line. Sound. 1 Q × B, Ra5; 2 Ktg5 m.

22. 1 Re6, Q~; 2 Rg8 m. Variation: Qh7 on g6 or g8. Unsound. 1 Re6, Qh7 or f7; 2 Rg8 +, Q × R. V. d. Linde (*Qst.*, 164) supposed that the modern Queen's move was developed from the union of the powers of R and B that is exemplified here. I attach no importance to this position: the problem chess of the Middle Ages must have exerted its influence (if it had any at all) against the reform, which made the bulk of the problems obsolete.

23. 1 Pb7, Kc7; 2 Pb8 = Q m. Cf. CB 29.

24. 1 Pf7, Rd4; 2 Ktg4 m. Variation: Bl. play and Wh. m. in II with same conditions. Unsound. 1 . . , Rh7, 2 Pf7, Rg7; or 2 any other, Rf7.

25. See CB 283, 284, 285, where the three varieties are separately diagrammed.

26. 1 Re6 +; 2 Bb4 m. Variations: (1) Ktf4 on c3. Unsound. 1 Re6 +, K × R; or 1 Rb6 +, B × R +; or 1 Kc4, Ba6 +; or 1 Kd3, Kc5; 2 Kte4 +, K × Kt. (2) Ktf4 on c3, Ktd5 fidated. Sound. 1 Kd3, Kc5; 2 Kte4 m. (3) not in BS. Ktf4 on c3, add Wh. Bb3. Sound. 1 Kd3, Kc5; 2 Kte4 m.

27. 1 B × R, B × Kt; 2 R × B m. If 1 . . , any other; 2 Ktc7 m.

28. 1 Rf4 +, K × B(c3); 2 Kta4 m. Or 1 . . , K × B(e3); 2 Ktd5 m.

29. 1 Pg7, Kh7; 2 Pg8 = Q m. Cf. CB 23.

30. 1 Kg6; 2 Ktd6 m.

31. 1 Rh5; 2 Rg8 m. Variation. Omit Pd5. Unsound. 1 Rh5, Bd5 +. Cf. S 9.

32. 1 Pg7 +, Kh7; or 1 B × R, Ra5; or 1 Rc2, Rc3; (or 1 Pf7, R × P +; or 1 Pd5, R +; or 1 Bg7, Ra5 or c5).

33. 1 Kt × R + d, Bf8 +; 2 R × B +, Be8. Or 1 Kt × B + d, Be8 + d; or 1 Kh7, Pg8 = Q +; (or 1 K × P, Rf7 +). Variation. Bl. may not check with a Pawn. Sound. 1 Kh7; 2 Kt(e8)c7 m.

34. I quote both texts.

BS 2.

'Albi primo trahunt, et pedones albi et nigri uadunt uno ordine ut signatum est (to 8th line), et dicunt quod mattabunt nigros ad 2um tractum. Tu defende nigros quia fieri non potest. Si ipse caperet militem nigrum de rocco tu trahe alfinum in A (d5), et si trahat regem suum inter milites nigros idem facias. Perspicias quidquid ipse faciat semper est tibi defensio. Sed aliqui faciunt istud partitum tantum de sex scaccis, sc. rege nigro et duobus militibus, et rocco albo et duobus militibus albis taliter stantibus ut hic ponuntur, et tunc mattant albi nigros ad 2um tractum. Primo dicitur scac de rocco inter album militem et regem nigrum. Capiunt eum cum milite. Tunc dicunt albi scac mat de milite inferiori.'

CB 34.

'Pedones uadunt uno ordine ut signatum est (to 8th line) et albi primo trahunt, et dicunt se uelle mattare nigros in 2o tractu, quod facere possent si rex albus staret in cruce (a5), quia tunc daretur scac de rocco in A (d7). Miles caperet eum, et de milite mat in B (c6). Sed si rex albus staret in loco ubi est scriptus, esset ei scac de milite nigro capiendo roccum. Vnde omnes tractus examina, semper invenies defensionem pro nigris si rex albus stet ibidem. Vnde si uis eum mattare, ponas in cruce regem tuum ut predixi.'

See CB 1 above.

35. BS 9 transposes text position and variation. 1 R × P; 2 Ktf7 m. or Rb8 m., according as Bl. plays. Variation: Pb2 on b3. Unsound. 1 Bf7, Ra2; or 1 Bb7, Ra5 +; or R on *h* file, Rh7. (PL 18 adds a further variation: Pb2 on b3. Kt does not move first move. Mate in III. Unsound. This is diagrammed separately in PP 100.)

36. 1 B, Q, or Pf7, Rb2; or 1 hR on *h* file or Rc1 or c3, Rf7; or 1 Kt + d, Rh7.

37. 1 . . , Rg8, and 2 . . , Rg7. Variation: Ra1 on b1. Sound. 1 . . , Rg8; 2 Rb8, any; 3 Ktg8 or f7 m.

38. 1 Rf1, Rf3; or 1 B × R, Rh5; or 1 Pb7 +, Ka7; or 1 Pc7, P × B; or 1 Bb7, Rh5 or f5; or 1 Pc5, Ra7. Variations: (1) Omit Pe4. Sound. 1 Pc7; 2 Kt m. accordingly. (2) Pc4 on d4. Sound. 1 Pb7 +; 2 Kt m. accordingly.

39. 1 Ktc4 +, Kd3; 2 Rc3 m.; or 1 . ., R × Kt; 2 gRd1 m. Variations: Wh. B for Qd7. 1 Ktc4 +, Kd3; 2 Rc3 or B m. If 1 . ., R × Kt; 2 gRd1 m.

40. 'Nigri primo trahunt, et dicunt quod capient pedonem de dono uel mattabunt albos in 2º tractu, et alfinus est affidatus. Sed tu cum albis defendas quia non fit. Et facias eum dicere ante tractum utrum predictorum uelit facere. Si dicat quod capiet pedonem de dono, non poterit quia tu capies roccum suum. Si dicat quod uelit mattare te, non poterit quia cooperies te cum alfino affidato, et est ei scac.' Cf. CB 19.

41. 1 hRg7; 2 Ra8 or g8 accordingly. (BS 10 adds variation in III exactly. 1 Ra8 or h8 +, Kt in; 2 Rb8 or g8; 3 R × Kt m.)

42. 1 Ktg5 +, Rh7; 2 Rh2, R × R; 3 Pg7 m. If 2 . ., R × P; 3 R × R m. If 2 . ., fRf7; 3 Kt × R m. If 2 . ., Rg8; 3 R × R or Ktf7 m. Variation: Re7 and f8 on f7 and e8. Sound. 1 Ktf4 + d; 2 P × R. Rg8 (if any other; 3 Ktg6 m.); 3 P × R = Q m.

43. 1 Ktf5 + d, Rh3; 2 Ktd6; 3 R × R or Ktf7 m. accordingly. If 1 . ., Rh2; 2 R × R +; 3 R × R m. Variation: Rd2 and e3 on e2 and d3. Unsound. 1 Ktf5 + d, Rh3; 2 Ktd6, R × B; or 2 Ra1, b1, c1, Ra3, b3 or c3. (BS 45 has Bl. Rs on d5, e4, sound, and e5, d4, unsound, with same solutions. The position is reflected in the MS.).

44. 1 R × R, Rf1; 2 Q × Kt, Rf7; 3 Kt × R +, Kg7; or 3 Ktf5 +, Rh7. (The BS MSS., probably in error, make Pg2 Black, which allows 1 . ., R × P +, an equally good defence. S 195 is the CB position.)

45 is the variation of BS 5 (see CB 5 above). 1 Ktg5 + d, Bh7; 2 any, Rf3 +. If 1 Ktf4 + d, Rh3; 2 Kt × R, Bd3 +. Cf. CB 54.

46. 1 Ra8, or h8, Kt in; 2 Rb8 or f8; 3 R × Kt m. This is really the BS variation to CB 41 above.

47. 1 Rh5, Kd6; 2 Kta8, Kc6; 3 Rb6 m. All the BS MSS. except BS and It. give the position as Wh. Rd4, f6, Kte4, e6; Bl. Ke5.

48. 1 Ktf8 + d, Rg3; 2 Rh7, Rf2; 3 R × R m. Variation: Rd3 and e2 on d2, e3. Unsound. (1 Ktf8 + d, Rg3; 2 Rh7, R × B !)

49. 1 Bd3, Bg8 (or R × B; 2 Ktf7 +; 3 Rh8 m.); 2 Bf5, Be6 (or R~; 3 Ktf7 m.); 3 Pg7 m. Cf. PL 68, 73.

50. 1 Rg7, Kf6; 2 aRa7; 3 Rg6 or a6 m. If 1 . ., Kd6; 2 Rc4; 3 Rc6 m.

51. 1 Pf7, Rb4; 2 Ktg4 +; 3 Pf8 = Q m. If 1 . ., Kg7; 2 Ktf5 +; 3 Rh8 m. If 1 . ., Rb2; 2 Ktf5 +; 3 Rh3 m. (Variation to BS 34 = CB 36.)

52. 1 Rc4; 2 Kc6; 3 Re8 m. Of course 1 Rc1, c2, c3 will do just as well, or White can begin with the other R. Variation (not in BS): Black play first. Unsound.

53. (BS 62, all one file to the right) 1 Re6; 2 Kb7; 3 R(b6)d6 m. Variation: Rb6 on b5. Said to be unsound (BS 62 'Sed quia istud partitum est ualde commune, pone unum roccum in punctum (c5 in BS figure), alio stante in C (e6), et non poterit mattari ad 3um tractum, quolibet faciente suum licet scientibus uideatur prima facie quod fieri possit'). BS is right, CB wrong. See Arch. 13; D 1; Picc. 84; C 88, &c.

54. 1 Ktg5 +, Rh3; 2 Ke1 or g1; 3 Pg7 or Ktf7 m. accordingly. If 1 . ., Bh3 +; 2 R × B +; 3 Pg7 or Ktf7 m. If 1 . ., Bh7; 2 B × R, &c. Variation: Rh2 on h1. Unsound. 1 Ktg5 +, Rh3; 2 K~, R × R +; and if 2 any other, Bd3 +.

55. 1 Bg7, Re1, the only move for 1 . ., R × B; 2 Ktf5 + and m. next move. and 1 . ., any other; 2 B~, and m. next move. 1 Rh3, 4, or 5, Rb6 ! abandoning powers of intervention. BS 64 ends 'Ludas istum ludum subtiliter quia subtilis est'.

56. 1 Kf5, Rb3; 2 Rc3, R × R; 3 Ktf7 m. If 1 . ., Rh7; 2 Pg7 +; 3 Ktf7 m. If 1 . ., Rf7; 2 Ktg4 +; 3 Pg7 m. If 1 . ., R on b file; 2 Pg7 +; 3 Ktg4 m.

57. 'Albi primo trahunt, et pedo est inmobilis, sed quilibet de aliis tribus facit suum tractum, et mattabunt regem nigrum in 3º tractu, et alfinus niger numquam mouetur nisi capiendo. Vnde tu cum albis trahe roccum in A (e2). Ipse capiet

eum. Trahe regem ubi erat roccus. Alfinus non potest ei dare scac quia non mouetur nisi possit capere. Vnde ipse trahet regem, et tu dabis ei mat de alio rocco.' All the MSS. except G omit the P. G 68 places a red P on g4, but does not notice that then 2 B × P + is possible, and there is no solution in III.

58. 1 Rh8 +; 2 Ra8 +; 3 R × R m. Or White may begin 1 Ra8 + &c.

59. 1 Kc6; 2 Ra5; 3 Re8 or a8 m., according as Bl. plays.

60. (CB omits the condition mate with the Pawn.) 1 Ke6, any; 2 Ktc6; 3 Pd6 m. Variation: Be8 is White. Unsound. 1 Ke6, Kc7; 2 Ktc6, R × B + (but if the condition m. with P is omitted, there is a m. in III by 2 Pd6 +; 3 Kte6 m.)

61. 1 Ktf5 +; 2 Rh6, R × R; 3 Qg7 m. (BS 36 adds variation: Rb7 alone fidated. There is now a second solution: 1 Qg7 +; 2 Ktf5 +; 3 Pg7 m.)

62. 1 Bf5, Kc8 (or e8); 2 Rb5 (or f6), Kd8; 3 Rb8 (or f8) m. accordingly.

63. 1 Rh8 +; 2 Rc1, Kd8 (or R + R; 3 Rc8 m); 3 R × R m.

64. 1 Bh6 +, Kt × R; 2 K × B, Rc8. If 1 P × B, Rc8 'quod est fere semper defensio in isto partito'. Cf. CB 13 in II.

65. 1 Ktc5 +, Ra7; 2 Pb7 +, Q × P; 3 P × Q m. BS 38 has Ra2 on a3.

66. 1 Rh1, Re7; 2 P × R, any; 3 Ktf7 m. If 1 . ., Rh7; 2 Pg7 +; 3 Ktf7 m. If 1 . ., R on 3rd line or d1 or d2, or R on 7th line except e7 and h7; 2 Rh4 or h5, &c. If 1 . ., Rh3; 2 R × R, &c. If 1 . ., R(d3)d4; 2 Ktg4 +, &c. If 1 . ., R(d3) d5 or d6 or R(d7) on d file; 2 Ktg4 or f5 +, &c.

67. Black must either be able to interpose both Rooks, or neither of them. 1 Rh4 or h5, Rd2 or e2. If 1 B(d5)~, Rb6.

68. 1 R × B, Rh7; 2 Rf8 +, Kg7; 3 Rg8 m. If 1 . ., Ra8 or b8; 2 Ktf5 +, Rh7; 3 R × R m.

69. 1 Rc2, Rh7!; 2 Ktg7, Ra8 (or R × R; 3 Rc8 m., or aR × Kt; 3 P × R m.); 3 R × R m. Variation: Re2 on g2. Other solutions are now possible: e. g. 1 Pg7 +, Kh7; 2 Pg8 = Q, Kh6; 3 Ktg7 m. If 1 . ., R × P; 2 P × R +, R × P (or Kh7; 3 Ktf6 m.); 3 Kt × R m. 'Est subtilis ludus.'

70. 1 Ra1, Rg7; 2 R × R, R × P +; or 2 P × R, K × P. If 1 R on *h* file, Rh7. (The conditions shut out 1 Ktf5 +; 2 Pg7 +; 3 P × R m., as in PL 119.) 'Ludus est subtilis.'

71. I give the texts from both collections.

BS 43.

'Albi primo trahunt et uolunt mattare nigros ad 3um tractum, et posset fieri si pedo niger staret in puncto (b4). Sed sic stando defendet. Melior tractus quem habent albi est trahere roccum in A (c1) et tunc defendunt se nigri trahendo suum roccum in punctum (b4) ad dicendum 2o scac regi albo, vnde si staret pedo in puncto non defenderetur. Sed ponamus quod sic stante pedone roccus traheretur in C (f1) uel in B (d1), uel rex albus caperet alfinum, ad istos 3 tractus unam habeas defensionem, sc. trahendo roccum tuum nigrum in crucem (h7), et postea leuiter uidebis defensionem finalem. Si uadat cum rocco albo in angulum primo tractu, tu trahas roccum tuum contra suum. Item si primitus trahat alium roccum iuxta militem, tu trahe tuum roccum in crucem. Lude subtiliter cum albis si pedo stet in puncto, trahendo roccum in A, et uidebis quod non erit defensio quae fiat in 3o tractu.'

CB 71.

'Albi primo trahunt et dicunt se uelle mattare nigros in 3o tractu tantum. Tu nigros defende quia non fit. Ipse trahet in A (c1), et tu trahas roccum tuum in punctum (b4). Si tunc trahas in B (c4), ipse trahet alfinum suum in C (h4), nisi poterit mattare in 3o. Sed si staret pedo niger in puncto (b4), mattaretur trahendo in A. Si tunc ipse in D (g7), tu dabis ei scac de rocco qui stat in A et mat de milite. Plures sunt inuasiones et defensiones. Si bene notes predicta similiter omnibus tu paruo studio poteris certificari.'

72. (BS 39 transposes text position and variation.) 1 Ktc4 + ; 2 P × R ; 3 Ktb6 m. Variation: Rh6 on d8 (BS text has also Rg7 on d7). 1 Ktc4 + ; 2 P × R, Rb8 (if any other: 3 Ktb6 m.); 3 P × R = Q m.

73. 1 Ktg5 + ; 2 Rf6 + ; 3 Rd6 m.

74. 1 Rh8 + ; 2 Rh6 + ; 3 Bd3 m.

75. 1 Re7 +, Kd8 ; 2 Rd7 + ; 3 Pf7 m. If 1 . . , Kt or Q × R ; 2 Pf7 + ; 3 Kte6 m.

76. If 1 Pe7 +, Ke8, and 2 . . , Ra6. (2 Ktg6, R × Q +.) If 1 Pf7, Rh4.

77. 1 Bg5, Ra6 ; 2 Pc7 +, K~. Variations: Ra2, f2 on a3, f1. Still unsound. Obviously the same defence is possible. (A later hand has added Wh. Bg3 and Bl. Pa5 to the diagram in R, which makes the problem sound by preventing 1 . ., Ra6.) This is Alf. 78.

78. 1 Rc8 + ; 2 Re8 + ; 3 Re6 m.

79. 1 Rd8 + ; 2 Rh2 ; 3 R m.

80. 1 Pg7 + ; 2 Ktf4 + ; 3 R × R m. (Moves 1 and 2 can be transposed.)

81. 1 Rd3 + ; 2 Bc8 + ; 3 Rd6 m.

82. 1 Pc8 = Q, Q × Q ; 2 Pg7 ; 3 B m. If 1 . ., B × R ; 2 Pg7 ; 3 B m. or Qd7 m. accordingly. If 1 . ., Qg7, Re1 or Rh4 ; 2 Kt × Q + ; 3 Re8 m.

83. 1 Ktb3 +, B × R or Bc7 or Rc6 ; 2 Kt × Kt ; 3 Kt × R or Pb7 m. accordingly. If 1 . ., Ktc6 + or Ktc4 ; 2 R × Kt + ; 3 Pb7 m.

84. 1 Ktc5 + ; 2 Qd6 ; 3 Ra8 m.

85. 1 Bd3, Ke6 ; 2 Kc5, Ke5 ; 3 Re7 m. If 1 . ., Kc6 ; 2 Ke5, Kc5 ; 3 Rc7 m.

86. 1 Qc5 ; 2 Ra7 ; 3 Re7 m.

87. 1 Ktg5, Re2 ; 2 Ktf7 + ; 3 R × B m. If 1 . ., any other ; 2 Bf5 ; 3 R or Kt m. accordingly.

88. 1 B × R ; 2 Ktf7 + ; 3 Rh8 m.

89. 1 Kc6 ; 2 Rd2 (or d1); Re8 m.

90. 1 Ra4, Ke3 (c3) ; 2 Rf8 (b7), Kd3 ; 3 Rf3 (b3) m.

91. 1 Kte7 ; 2 Rh3 ; 3 Re3 m.

92. 1 Ktg4 × ; 2 Kth6 ; 3 R × R or Ktf7 m. accordingly.

93. 1 Rh1, Re7 ; 2 P × R ; 3 Ktf7 m. (If 1 . ., Rc2 ; 2 Bc7, &c. If 1 . ., R elsewhere on c file ; 2 Ktg4 + ; 3 R × R m. If 1 . ., Rb2 ; 2 B × R, &c. If 1 . ., Rb3 ; 2 B × R or Bg3, &c. If 1 . ., Rb4 ; 2 Ktg4 +. If 1 . ., R elsewhere on *b* file ; 2 Ktf5 or g4 + ; 3 R × R m. If 1 . ., Rh3 ; 2 R × R ; 3 Ktf7 m. If 1 . ., R on 3rd row ; 2 Ktf5 + ; 3 R × R m.) BS 67 has Rh2 on h1.

94. 1 Re3 + ; 2 Be7 ; 3 Pg4 m.

95. 1 Kth6 + ; 2 Pg8 = Q + ; 3 Qg5 + ; 4 Ktf4 m.

96. 1 Kth7 + ; 2 Rf8 + ; 3 Ktf6 + ; 4 R m. accordingly.

97. 1 Ktb2 + ; 2 Ktd1 + ; 3 R × R ; 4 P × P m.

98. 1 Ra7 + ; 2 Re6 + ; 3 Rd7 + ; 4 Be2 m.

99. 1 Pc3 ; 2 Rc4 ; 3 Kc2 ; 4 Ra4 m.

100. (BS 75 moves everything one file to the left ; the CB position is probably the older.) 1 Rc8 + ; 2 Qf6 + ; 3 Re1 + ; 4 Bf4 m.

101. 1 Rh6 + ; 2 Rf8 + ; 3 Qf6 + ; 4 R m.

102. 1 Rg4 ; 2 Rc3 + ; 3 Rd3 (a3 or b3) ; 4 Rf3 m.

103. 1 Kte7 + ; 2 Rc1 +, Ktc7 (or Rc7 ; 3 R × R + ; 4 Pd7 m.) ; 3 Pd7 + ; 4 P × R m.

104. 1 Kd4 ; 2 Kd5 ; 3 Kc6 (e6), Kc8 (e8) ; 4 R m. accordingly.

105. 1 Re6 + ; 2 Ktd5 +, Kc8 ; 3 Rb6 ; 4 Rb8 m. If 2 . ., Kd8 ; 3 Re7 ; 4 Re8 m. If 2 . ., Kb8 ; 3 Ra6 ; 4 Ra8 m.

106. 1 Ktf6 ; 2 Ktc6 + ; 3 Ktd5 ; 4 Rc7 m.

107. 1 Pg7 + ; 2 Ktf7 + ; 3 Rh8 + ; 4 Rf8 m.

108. 'Albi primo trahunt et mattabunt regem nigrum ad 4um tractum de pedone eunte. Fac taliter. Primo da scac de alfino, et iterum scac de rocco in A (g4), et in B (h4), et 4° dabis mat de pedone.'

109. 1 Re7 + ; 2 Pd7 + ; 3 Kt(c4)d6 +, Kt × Kt (or R × Kt ; 4 Ktc7 m.) ; 4 P × R m.

110. 1 Rd2, Kc8 (e8); 2 Kc6 (e6), Kb8 (f8); 3 Ra2 (g2), Kc8 (e8); 4 Ra8 (g8) m.

111. 1 Qb7; 2 Qc8; 3 Qa7; 4 Qb7 m. Cf. Alf. 77.

112. 1 Rb2, Pa1 = Q; 2 Ra2+, Qa3; 3 B × Q, Ka7; 4 Bc5 m.

113. 1 Rd8+; 2 Ktd6+; 3 P × R, Pf5; 4 Pd7 m.

114. 1 Ktc6+, Kt × Kt; 2 P × Kt, Re8 or h7 (if Rf8 or g8; 3 Re8+, R × R. And if Rh6; 3 Rf6. If R elsewhere on *h* file; 3 R opposite R); 3 Re7, any; 4 Pc7 m. Variations: (1) Rh8 on f8, Re6 on f7. Unsound, for 1 Ktc6+, Kt + Kt; 2 P × Kt, R × R; 3 P × R, stalemate. (2) Rh8 on e8, Re6 on f7. Unsound, for 1 Ktc6+, Kt × Kt; 2 P × Kt, Re6+; 3 K~, R × P. Cf. BS 94 above.

115. (BS 97 places Ka6 on a5, Pa5 on a4.) I give both texts.

BS 97.

'Albi primo trahunt et mattabunt nigros ad 4um tractum uel pauciores. Trahe alfinum in A (f5) et est scac discoopertum. Si moueat regem, scac de rocco in angulo et postea scac de pedone et mat de milite. Si cooperiat se de rocco inferiori cape eum et postea trahe pedonem in B (f7), et mat de alio pedone. Si cooperiat se de rocco superiore, quod est melius, adhuc trahe pedonem in B, et mat de alio. Melius, dixi, quia si non esset pedo iuxta regem, uel roccus inferior staret in puncto (c2), nullo modo mattaretur ad 4um tractum uel minus. Istud subtile partitum est.'

CB 115.

'Albi primo trahunt et mattabunt nigros in 4o tractu uel paucioribus. Fac taliter. Trahe alfinum in A (f5). Si cooperiat se in B (h2), cape eum et da scac, suo 2o si cooperiat se, trahe pedonem in C (f7), 4o dabis ei mat. Uel si nolit cooperire se de suo rocco, cape eum de alfino, et erit mat. Si autem in principio non cooperiat se de aliquo, sed trahat regem, tunc da ei scac in angulo. Ipse capiet eum. Tunc scac de pedone et mat de milite. Si autem staret roccus punctatus in cruce (Rb2 on c2) non mattaretur in 4o tractu, quia cooperiret se de rocco superiore, et post paululum duceret regem album dicendo scac, et scac prolongaretur ludus.'

116. (BS 77 has Kta3 on a7.) 1 Ktb5+; 2 Ra8+; 3 Pb7+; 4 Pc7 m.

117. 1 Bf5+; 2 Rh8+; 3 Pg7+; 4 Kth6 m.

118. 1 Ktf6+, Kt × Kt; 2 P × Kt, Ra6; 3 any, R+. Variation: Pc6 on b6. Sound. 1 Ktf6+, Kt × Kt; 2 P × Kt, Ra6; 3 Rc6, any; 4 Pf7 m.

119. (BS 94 moves files *b–f* one to right.) 1 Rc8+, R × R; 2 Ktc6+, R × Kt; 3 P × R, Kte6 saves it. If 1 Kte6+, Kt × Kt; 2 P × Kt, Ra2; 3 Pd3, Re2; or if 3~, R × P+ saves it. (BS 94 adds Variations: (1) Omit Ps f1, e2, d3 in its setting. Unsound. 1 Ktf6+, Kt × Kt; 2 P × Kt, Ra6; 3 any, R+. (2) Omit the same three Ps and place Pc6 on b6. Now sound. 1 Ktf6+, Kt × Kt; 2 P × Kt, Ra6; 3 Rc6, any; 4 Pf7 m. These variations are really CB 118.)

120. 1 Kt(d4)c6+, Kt × Kt; 2 P × Kt, Rf7. Now 3 Kt × R is mate; 3 P × R is stalemate (*clausus es*, CB, BS); and 3 any other, allows R × Q or Rf6+, saving the mate in IV.

121. 1 R × B+; 2 Re7+, Q × R (or Kd8, 3 Rd7+; 4 Pf7 m.); 3 Pf7+; 4 Kte6 m.

122. 1 R × P+, P × R; 2 Ktd4+, Ka2 (or Ka3; 3 Ktc5 m.); 3 Bc4+, Ka3 (or K × Q; 4 Ktb3 m.); 4 Ktc5 m. Or 1 . ., Kt × R; 2 Ktd4+; 3 Bc4+; 4 Ktb3 m. If 1 . ., Ka2; 2 Ktc3+; 3 R × B m. If 1 . ., Kc2; 2 Ktd4+; 3 Ktc3 m.

123. 1 Rd6, Bc4, c8, or g4; 2 Ktf7+; 3 Rh5; 4 Rh8 or d8 m. accordingly. If 1 . ., Bg8; 2 Rd8, Rc8 (or Kth2 or Rh3; 3 R × R or Kt; 4 Ktf7 m.); 3 R × R; 4 Ktf7 or R × B m.

124. Mate in IV by 1 Ktf6+; 2 Pc4+; 3 Pe4+; 4 Rd6+; 5 Q(b7)c6 m. Self-mate in IV by 1 Ktf6+; 2 Ra5+; 3 Pe4+; 4 Rf5+, B × R 'et dant mat regi albo uelint nolint'.

125. 1 Rc8+; 2 Rc7+; 3 Ra7+; 4 Ktc6+; 5 Rb8 m.

126. 1 Ktg4 + ; 2 Kf7 ; 3 Kte5 ; 4 Ktg6 + ; 5 Bf5 m. Variation : Rh3 on h1. Unsound, for 1 Ktg4 + , Bh2 !

127. 1 Ktb4 ; 2 Ktc6 ; 3 Rh7 ; 4 Re7 + ; 5 Bd6 or h6 m.

128. 1 Re4 + ; 2 Rc4 + ; 3 Rc2 + ; 4 Ktb3 + ; 5 Bd3 m.

129. 1 Pa4 ; 2 Qf4 ; 3 Rg6 ; 4 Q(b6)c5 + ; 5 Ba3 or e3 m. Variations : (1) Pa3 a Q. (2) R immovable. Both unsound.

130. 'Albi primo trahunt et mattabunt nigros ad 5um tractum uel pauciores. Da scac discoopertum de alfino in A (c4). Si cooperiat se in B (a3), cape eum et da scac. Si non, trahe alfinum in C (e6) quam cito poteris. Si trahat roccum suum in D (c8), cape eum de alfino, et erit mat de rocco. Si trahat alibi, mattabitur semper in 5° tractu tantum. Si pedo niger non esset, defenditur.'

131. 1 Ktf6 + ; 2 Kte8 + ; 3 R(f1)g1 + ; 4 Pe6 + ; 2 P × Kt m.

132. (BS 98 has Rb3 and c2 on b2 and c3.) 1 Bf5 + , Rh2 (Kg8 is m. in IV and Rh3 is m. in V) ; 2 R × R + , Rh3 (Kg8 is m. in V) ; 3 R × R + , Kg8 ; if now the P goes to d8 (Bl. has to choose before playing), 4 Bd7, Kf8 ; 5 Rh8 m. If to d1, 4 Rb3 or c3 ; 5 R m.

133. 1 Qf5 ; 2 Qf2 ; 3 Rh1 ; 4 Rh2 ; 5 Rf2 m.

134. 1 Pc7 ; 2 Pf7 ; 3 Be6 (or a6) + ; 4 Pc8 = Q + ; 5 Q(b6)c7 m.

135. 1 Re7 ; 2 Re8 + ; 3 Ra8 + ; 4 Kb6 ; 5 Bd6 m. Variations : (1) Rg7 on b1. 1 Rb1 ; 2 Ra1 + ; 3 Ra8 + , &c. (2) Rg7 on c1, c2, c3, c4, or c5. 1 Kc7, Ka7 ; 2 Kc6, Kb8 (if Ka6 ; 3 Rc5 or b5, &c. ; and if Ka8 ; 3 R on *b* file, &c.) ; 3 Kb6, Ka8 ; 4 R on *a* file + , Kb8 ; 5 Bd6 m.

136. 'Est tractus pro tractu, et si rex niger claudatur quod non possit trahere, albi perdunt' (which is omitted in the BS 108 text). 1 Ktf6 (c3) ; 2 Ktd5, Ka7 ! ; 3 Kte7 ; 4 Ktc8 ; 5 Ktb6 m.

137. 1 Qb7 + ; 2 Bf4 ; 3 B × R ; 4 Bf4 ; 5 Bd6 m. Variation : Pb3 on b4. Unsound, for 3 . . , Pb5 and Bl. is stalemate ('et essent nigri clausi ').

138. 1 Rh8 + ; 2 Rf8 + ; 3 Rg5 + ; 4 Qh6 ; 5 Rh8 m.

139. 1 Ra8 + ; 2 Rc8 + ; 3 Ktc4 + ; 4 Rd8 + ; 5 Be7 m. Variation : Rf3 white. The same solution holds.

140. 'Albi primo trahunt, et mattabunt nigros in 6° tractu uel paucioribus, et rex niger semper mouebitur quamdiu poterit, et quum clausus erit pedo niger trahetur. Et fit taliter. Primo datur ei scac de pedone in A (e7). Si ipse uadat in B (e8), uadat rex albus ubi erat pedo, et erit mattus in 5° tractu. Sed ipse ibit in C (g8), et tu fac reginam. Si reuertatur, mattus erit in 2^{obus} tractibus. Sed ipse ibit in angulum, et tu de rege in D (f7), et in E (f8), et reginam in C, et mat de pedone.'

141. 1 Rh1 + ; 2 Kte5 ; 3 Rh8 + ; 4 Kf5 ; 5 Rh7 ; 6 Rd7 m.

142. 'De pedone eunte.' 1 Ktd4 + ; 2 Rd7 + ; 3 Rd5 + ; 4 Kte6 + ; 5 Ph3 + ; 6 Pg3 m.

143. 1 Ktg4 ; 2 Kt(g4)f2 ; 3 Ktf4 + , Kh6 ; 4 Ktg4 + ; 5 Ktf6 + ; 6 Rg6 m.

144. 1 Bd6 + ; 2 Kt(c5)d7 + ; 3 Rf7 + ; 4 Ktd7 + ; 5 P × R + ; 6 Pg6 m.

145. 1 Rh1 + ; 2 Ktf6 ; 3 Ktg6 + ; 4 Rh7 + ; 5 Qf5 + ; 6 Rh5 m.

146. 1 Re7 + ; 2 Ktd7 + ; 3 Be6 + ; 4 Re8 + ; 5 Ktf8 + ; 6 Qg7 m.

147. 1 Pb7 + ; 2 Ktc7 + ; 3 Ra8 + ; 4 Rc8 + ; 5 Qc5 + ; 6 Pc4 m.

148. 1 Bf5 + , Rh2 ; 2 R × R + , Rh3 ; 3 R × R + , Kg8 ; 4 Rh8 + ; 5 Pg7 + ; 6 Kth6 m.

149. 1 Rd8 + ; 2 Ktd5 ; 3 Ra8 + ; 4 Kd6 ; 5 Rb8 ; 6 Rb4 m.

150. (BS 119 omits Rf1, which allows several solutions in VI.) 1 R × R, Kd4 ; 2 Rf5, Ke4 ; 3 R(c1)c5, Kd3 ; 4 Rb5, K on 4th row (if on 3rd row, Bl. mates in VI) ; 5 K opposite K ; 6 R~, and 7 R m. Variation : 'Et est magisterium mattare te in 7° uel paucioribus, si excipiatur quod non debeas mattari ad aliquid latus scacarii, quia hoc leuiter fieret stantibus omnibus ut in principio.' The condition is to exclude 1 Re2 ; 2 Kd2 ; 3 Kd3 ; 4 Kd4 ; 5 Kd5 ; 6 Ke6 ; 7 Rc8 m.

151. 1 Rd7 ; 2 Rd8 + ; 3 Re8 ; 4 Re5 ; 5 Rh5 + ; 6 Be6 m.

152. 1 Rh1 + ; 2 Rh7 + ; 3 Rf7 + ; 4 Rf5 + ; 5 Rd5 + ; 6 Rd3 m. A simplified version of Ar. 86.

153. 1 Qb5 ; 2 Bf1 ; 3 Qb6 + ; 4 Ra7 + ; 5 Qc5 + ; 6 Bd3 m.

154. 1 Rc7 ; 2 Pb6 ; 3 Ktb4 ; 4 Bd6 + ; 5 Rc8 + ; 6 Rb8 m.

155. 1 . . , Ra1 ; 2 Kc2 or e2, Kte4 + ; 3 K~, R + , and can give four more checks postponing the inevitable mate to the 7th move.

156. 1 Rh7 + ; 2 Rf7 + ; 3 Ktg6 + ; 4 Re7 + ; 5 Pd5 + ; 6 P × Kt m.

157. 1 Rh1 + ; 2 Kte5 ; 3 Rh8 + ; 4 Kf5 ; 5 Rh7 ; 6 Rd7 m. We must add the condition, omitted in both CB and BS, mate on d5.

158. 1 Rb4 + ; 2 Rb5 + ; 3 Rc5 + ; 4 Rb6 + ; 5 Ra6 + ; 6 Rc1 or c3 m. accordingly.

159. 1 Rf7 ; 2 Pg4 ; 3 Pg5 ; 4 Be6 + ; 5 Rf8 + ; 6 Rg8 m.

160. 1 Qa5, Kc5 (or Kd4 ; 2 Re3, &c.) ; 2 Rf6 ; 3 Re3 ; 4 Rd3 or d6 ; 5 the other R to d6 or d3 ; 6 B + ; 7 other B m.

161. (BS 131 has Qa8 on f8, and, omitting the condition the Q is a new Q, makes the problem unsound. It adds the variation : Qf8 new, which is the CB problem.) 'Nigri primo trahunt, et dicunt albi quod mattabunt nigros uel capient roccum ad 7um tractum uel pauciores, et est regina noua, qui potest in principio facere unum tractum uel duos saltando. Vnde tu cum albis uinces, quia considerabis si ipse trahat in B (b1), et tunc facias unum tractum de regina. Si primo in A (b2), tunc saltabis more alfini, quia ipse, si erit ausus exire A et B, ne forte mattaretur uel perderet roccum, et tu uenies cum regina secundum puncta (g7, f6, e5, d4, c3). Et cum regina tua erit in uicino puncto, si ipse traheret in A, perdet. Si ubi modo stat, tu trahas regem in C (a6), et tunc necessario perdet roccum uel audiet scac mat in 7o tractu.'

162. 1 Q(g8)g6 ; 2 Q(d8)e7 ; 3 Q(e8)e6 ; 4 Q(f8)h6 ; 5 Q(e7)f6 ; 6 Q(e6)f7 + ; 7 Q(h6)g7 m.

163. 1 Bc6 + ; 2 Ktc7 + ; 3 R × R + ; 4 Ktd6 + ; 5 R × R + ; 6 Qg7 + ; 7 Ph7 m.

164. 1 Re4 ; 2 R(c8)c4 ; 3 Kc8 ; 4 Kb8 ; 5 Kb7, Kd5 ! ; 6 Kb6 ; 7 R(c4)d4 m.

165. 1 Ra8 + ; 2 Rh8 + ; 3 Pe7 + ; 4 Pd7 + ; 5 Pe8 = Q + ; 6 Rh7 + ; 7 Qf7 m.

166. 1 Re5 ; 2 Ktd3 ; 3 Ktf2 ; 4 Ktg4 ; 5 Kth6 ; 6 Ktf7 + ; 7 Qc6 m.

167. 1 Rh1 + ; 2 Rh6 ; 3 Pg7 + ; 4 Bf5 + ; 5 Rg3 + ; 6 Rg5 + ; 7 Pg3 m.

168. 1 Kb6 ; 2 R(h2)c2 ; 3 Pc5 ; 4 Pc6 ; 5 Ra2 + ; 6 Pc4 + ; 7 Pc5 m.

169. 1 Ra8 + ; 2 Kte5 ; 3 Rh8 + ; 4 Ke6 ; 5 Rg8 ; 6 Pf3 + ; 7 Pg3 m.

170. (BS 139 and all BS MSS. omit Kg3.) 1 Rc6 + ; 2 Bb5 + ; 3 Pa7 ; 4 Kth6 + ; 5 Bd3 ; 6 Bb5 + ; 7 Bc5 m.

171. 1 Rb1 ; 2 Bd6 ; 3 Ktc4 ; 4 Kta5 ; 5 Ktb7 ; 6 Ktc5 ; 7 Ra1 m.

172. 1 Rh8 + , Ka7 (b7) ; 2 Ra6 + ; 3 R(a6)a8 ; 4 Bc5 ; 5 R(h8)b8 ; 6 Pb6 (Pe6) + ; 7 Pe6 (Pb6) m.

173. 1 Rb5 ; 2 Rc8 ; 3 Pa5 ; 4 Kc5 ; 5 R(b5)b8 ; 6 Ra8 + ; 7 Pa6 m.

174. (BS 143 adds the useless condition, Wh. must check every move.) 1 Ktf3 + ; 2 Pe5 + ; 3 Rd3 + ; 4 Pc5 + ; 5 Kte6 + ; 6 Rf4 + ; 7 Bf2 m.

175. 1 Rd6 ; 2 P × P ; 3 Rf6 ; 4 Re6 + , 5 Bb5 ; 6 Bg5 ; 7 Pd7 m.

176. 1 Rc5 + ; 2 Pc3 + ; 3 Qc2 + ; 4 Rd5 + ; 5 Rd1 + ; 6 Rb1 + ; 7 Bc4 m.

177. 1 Rc6 ; 2 Rh7 ; 3 Qc8 ; 4 Qb7 ; 5 Qa6 ; 6 Rh8 + ; 7 Bc5 m.

178. 1 Bh6 + ; 2 Q × Kt + d ; 3 Rd2 + ; 4 Re2 + ; 5 Rd2 + ; 6 Re2 + ; 7 Bf4 m. The four R-moves to convert a mate in III to one in VII moves are curious. There seems no reason why one should not go on longer.

179. (BS 149 places Ka8 on b8 and gives the move to Bl. ; Wh. then mates in VIII as in CB.) 1 Ktb5 ; 2 Ktd4 ; 3 Ktc2 ; 4 Ktb4 ; 5 Kc7 ; 6 Qc6 ; 7 Qb7 + ; 8 Ktc6 m.

180. 1 Qe6 ; 2 Qf5 ; 3 Qe4 ; 4 Qd3 ; 5 Qc4 ; 6 Qb5 ; 7 Qc6 ; 8 Qb7, P × Q m.

181. 1 Ra8 + , Rc8 ; 2 R × R + , R × R ; 3 R × R + ; 4 Re8 + ; 5 Re6 + ; 6 Rg6 + ; 7 Pg4 + ; 8 P × Kt m.

182. 1 P × P + ; 2 Pf7 + ; 3 Rh8 + ; 4 Rg8 + ; 5 Rg6 + ; 6 Ktf6 + ; 7 Ktf3 + ; 8 Bf5 m.

183. 1 Rg8 + ; 2 Rc8 + ; 3 Rc6 + ; 4 Re6 + ; 5 Rg4 + ; 6 Ktd5 + ; 7 Qc3 + ; 8 Ktd3 m.

184. 1 Ra7; 2 Ktb8, Kc8; 3 Ktd7; 4 Ktb6; 5 Rd7; 6 Ktd5; 7 Ktf6+; 8 B m. If 2.., Ke8; 3 Rd7; 4 Ktc6; 5 Kte5; 6 Ktg4; 7 Ktf6+; 8 B m.

185. I give both texts. Both diagrams have A g7, B f7, C e8, D d8, E c7, F b7, G b3, H c1. CB has a dot on b5, and a cross on f3; BS, a second F on b5, and a dot on f3.

BS 155.

'Albi primo trahunt et mattabunt nigros ad 8um tractum. Fac taliter. Da ista 6 scac de militibus secundum ordinem alphabeti. Tunc de regina scac in G, et de alfino mat in H. Sed dato quod alfinus stet in puncto uel tollatur de medio, adhuc mattatur rex niger ad 8um tractum, *et debetur istud partitum scribi litteris aureis.* Da scac de milite in A, et de alio in B, de primo in C, de secundo in D, et de primo in E. Tunc trahe *subtilissimum tractum* reginam, sc. in F. Si non capiat eam mattus est. Si capiat eam, trahe regem tuum in G, et dabis mat de milite in F.'

CB 185.

'Albi primo trahunt et mattabunt nigros ad 8um tractum. Tu cum albis trahe milites alternatim usque in F, et scac de regina in G, et mat de alfino in H. Sed si alfinus stet in cruce, uel prorsus non sit adhuc, fit in 8° tractu, *et tunc est pulcherrimum partitum,* et incipitur sicut primus donec miles sit in E. Tunc trahitur regina in punctum. Si non capiat eam de pedone, mattus est de milite. Si capiat eam, trahe regem in G, et similiter est mattus de milite.'

186. (BS 148 has Rb1 on b2.) 1 Rb7; 2 Kc6; 3 Kc7; 4 Bc5; 5 Rb2; 6 Ra2+, Qa3; 7 B × Q; 8 Bc5 m.

187. 1 Rb3; 2 Rb8+; 3 Rf5; 4 R(b8)f8; 5 Qe5; 6 Pd4; 7 Qd6+; 8 Pd5 m.

188. 1 Kte2; 2 Ktf4; 3 Ktd5; 4 Ra1; 5 Ra8+; 6 Kc5; 7 Ra7; 8 Re7 m.

189. (BS 157 makes one problem of this and the following, CB 190 being the text position, and CB 189, 'sed iste ludus reputatur curialior a quibusdam si ponatur pedo albus tendens versus A (f7) et B (f8) in loco ubi stat rex albus, et rex albus in puncto rubeo (g6), et pedo niger in puncto nigro (g5) uadens ut signatum est (to g8)', the variation.) 1 Pf7+; 2 Pf8 = Q; 3 Qh8; 4 Kf7; 5 Kf8; 6 Kf7; 7 Kf8; 8 Qf6; 9 Qg7 m.

190. 1 Qh8, Pg5+ (if K × Q; 2 Kf7; 3 Kf8; 4 Qf6; 5 Q × P m.); 2 Kg6; 3 Kf7; 4 Kf8; 5 Kf7; 6 Kf8; 7 Qf6; 8 Qg7 m.

191. 1 Be6; 2 Qc6; 3 Bd6+; 4 Kb5; 5 Bf4, Ka8 (or Kb8; 6 Kb6; 7 Qb7+; 8 Bd6 m.); 6 Ka6; 7 Kb6; 8 Qb7+; 9 Bd6 m.

192. 1 Rd1; 2 Kf6; 3 Rd8+; 4 Bf5+; 5 Rd7; 6 Rh7+; 7 R(h7)h3; 8 Pg3+; 9 Pf3 m.

193. 1 Pb6; 2 Bf5+; 3 Rc6; 4 Pb7; 5 Pb8 = Q; 6 Qd6; 7 Qe7; 8 Qf6; 9 Qg7 m.

194. 1 Bc8+, Kf5; 2 Kf7, Pg8 = Q+; 3 K × Q, Kg6; 4 Kh8, Pf7; 5 B~, Pd7; 6 any, Pd8 = Q, &c. Or 4 Kf8, Pf7; 5 B~, Kf6; 6 any, Pd7; 7 any, Pd8 = Q, &c. Or 3 Kf8, Pf7; 4 Kg7, Pd7; 5 any, Pd8 = Q, &c.

195. 1 Rg3+; 2 Rh3+; 3 Pg4+; 4 Pg3+; 5 Rh1+; 6 Pf3+; 7 Pg2+; 8 Ktg4+; 9 Ktf2+; 10 Bf4 m.

196. 1 Ra8+; 2 Ra2+; 3 Re1+; 4 Rd1+; 5 Rd3+; 6 Ra4+; 7 Rd5+; 8 Ra6+; 9 Rd7+; 10 Bd6 m.

197. 1 Kte6+; 2 Qe5; 3 Qf6; 4 Re3; 5 Qe7+; 6 Ke6; 7 Pd4; 8 Pd5; 9 Pd6; 10 Pd7 m.

198. 'Albi primo trahunt, et mattabunt regem nigrum uel omnes 3 pedones fient regine ad 10um tractum uel pauciores. Da scac in A (c7). Si uadat in angulum, da scac de alio pedone, et fac eum reginam, et trahe eam in B (d6—a leap over an occupied square). Et fac aliam reginam, et trahe eam in C (c6). Tunc trahe regem in D (b6) quam cito poteris, et trahe pedonem, et dabis ei mat, uel facies reginam in 10° tractu uel paucioribus. Item si primo suo tractu uadat in E (c8), trahe regem tuum in F (c5). Tunc fac extremum pedonem reginam in angulo, et trahe

eam in G (b7), et leuiter uidebis quomodo omnes fient regine in 10° tractu uel paucioribus.'

199. 1 Ktd6; 2 Kte4; 3 Ktc5; 4 Kc6, Kb8 (or Ka7; 5 Kc7; 6 Kb6, Kb8); 5 Kd7, Ka8 (or Ka7; 6 Kc7; 7 Kb6, Kb8); 6 Kc8; 7 Kc7; 8 Kb6, Kb8. All variations have now reached the same position. 9 Kte6; 10 Ktc7+; 11 Bd6 m.

200. 1 Pg3; 2 Pf3; 3 Pg4; 4 Pf4; 5 Pg5; 6 Rh3; 7 Rh5; 8 Pg6+; 9 Rg5; 10 Bf5; 11 Pg7 m. The solution could be shortened by two moves by playing 1 Pg4; 2 Pf4. Does it date from a period anterior to the general use of the Pawn's initial double step, or did the composer think that the prolongation added to the difficulty of solution? See v. d. Lasa, 140.

201. 1 Bd6+; 2 Qc8; 3 Qb4; 4 Kb5; 5 Kc5; 6 Kc6; 7 Qb7+; 8 Bf8; 9 Qa5; 10 Qb6+; 11 Bd6 m.

202. 1 Re3; 2 Re5; 3 Rf5; 4 Rf7; 5 Pg8 = Q; 6 Qg6; 7–10 Q to c6; 11 Qd7 m.

203. (CB omits the conditions, which I add from BS 169.) 1 Rb5; 2 Pc5; 3 Pc4; 4 Pc3; 5 Pc2; 6 R(b5)b8; 7 Ra8+; 8 Pc6+; 9 Pc5+; 10 Pc4+; 11 Pc3 m.

204. 1 Pe7; 2 Pf7+; 3 Pf8 = Q; 4 Qf6; 5 Pe8 = Q; 6 Qe7; 7 Qd7; 8 Qe6; 9 Qf6; 10 Qf7+; 11 Qg7 m.

205. 1 Ra8+; 2 Pc6+; 3 Pc5+; 4 Pc4+; 5 Pc3+; 6 R(c8)b8+; 7 Kte3+; 8 Ra1+; 9 Rg1; 10 Rb2+; 11 R(b2)g2; 12 Rf1 m. Cf. CB 203.

206. 1 R(b6)b7+; 2 Pb5+; 3 Rb6+; 4 Ra6+; 5 P × P+; 6 Pb6+; 7 Ra8+; 8 Pc6+; 9 Pb7+; 10 Ktb5+; 11 Ktc7+; 12 Bc5 m.

207. The diagrams have red dots on a7, b8, c8, d8, e8, f7, g6; A h6, B g8, C f5, D f8; and cancelled pieces, Wh. Rd7, Kd6; Bl. Ke8. The solution runs: 'Albi primo trahunt, et mattabunt regem nigrum ad 12um tractum, uel pauciores, et roccus non mouetur nisi semel, et hoc quando dabit mat. Trahe regem secundum puncta. Si rex suus uadit in A, erit mat ad x (really ix) tractum. Sed ipse ibit in B, et tu in C. Si uadat in angulum, cito uidebis finem, et si uadat in D, tu in E, et quicquid faciet erit mattus ad xii uel pauciores. Et si starent ubi cancellantur rex niger defenditur, ut per te uideas. Vnde sunt duo partita.' [Leon 63 (old 105) has a different text (Wh. Kd6, Rc7; Bl. Kd8. Letters: A c6, B b7, C b8, D c8, E d8, F e8, G f7, H f6, J f5, K e6, cross h7). 'Rubei primo trahunt, et dicunt se uelle mactare nigros . . . (*sic*) tractu uel paucioribus, et fit taliter. Trahe regem in A, in B, in C, in D, in E, in F, in G, in H, et in J, et tunc si sequatur regem tuum, des sibi mact in † de rocco. Et scias quod roccus non debet se mouere nisi dando mact. Sed si rubei dicerent quod primum scacch esset mact, non esset uerum et perderent rubei. Vnde tu fallaciam intelligas, quod non est mact ad primum tractum de rocco. Quia quando dabit scac sibi discoopertum, si ipse reuertatur uersus roccum quando tu eris in J, uade in K. Postea leuiter uidebis modum mactandi. Sed si roccus rubeus staret in L (not in diagram), non mactatur, quia rex niger reuerteretur uersus roccum, et non posset mactari, prout uidebis. Si rex rubeus esset in A, fit in XI tractu, et si rex niger esset in F, fit in XII.']

208. (BS 173 omits 'in XII'.) 1 Rc3; 2 Rb3; 3 Ktg3+; 4 Ktf1+; 5 Rb6; 6 Pa7; 7 Pa8 = Q; 8 Qc6; 9 Qd5; 10 Qe4; 11 Qf3; 12 Qg2 m. BS adds Variation: Ps a6, a7, on a5, a6 respectively. White mates (in XIX) with promoted Q, and same conditions. 1 Ktd4; 2 Ktb5; 3 Rg2; 4 Rg3; 5 Rb3; 6–8 P queens; 9–13 Q to g2+; 14 Qf1; 15 Kg3; 16 Rb1; 17 Rd1; 18 Rb1; 19 Qg2m.

209. MS. solution is 1 Ka2; 2 Kb2; 3 Kc3; 4 Kb3; 5 Kc4; 6 Kb4; 7 Kc5; 8 Kb5; 9 Kc6; 10 Kb6; 11 Kc7; 12 Ra8 m. It can surely be shortened; e. g. 11 Rc8 m.

210. 1 Ktb3; 2 Ktc5; 3 Ktb7; 4 Ktd6; 5 Kb5; 6 Ka5; 7 Ka6; 8 Kb6; 9 Ktc8; 10 Kta7; 11 Ktc6; 12 R m.

211. 1 Kte3; 2 Ktc4; 3 Kte5; 4 Ktc6; 5 Kte7; 6 Ktf5; 7 Re5; 8 Kth6; 9 Ktf7+; 10 Bf5 m.

212. 1 Bh4; 2 Kf6; 3 Kf7; 4 Bf2; 5 Bd4; 6 Bf6; 7 Qf8; 8 Qe7; 9 Bd4; 10 Kg6; 11 Bf6; 12 Bh8; 13 Kf7; 14 Qf8; 15 Qg7 m.

213. 1 Ktc5; 2 Kc7; 3 Pb5; 4 Kte4; 5 Kb6; 6 Ktd6; 7 Ka6; 8 Pb6; 9 Qg2; 10 Pc5; 11 Pc6; 12 Pc7 +; 13 Pb7 m.

214. 1 Rb2; 2 Rc2; 3 Rd2; 4 Re2; 5 Ba7; 6 Ra2; 7 Rb2; 8 Rc2; 9 Rd2; 10 Re2; 11 Rf2; 12 Bc5; 13 Be3 +; 14 Rh2 m.

215. 1 Pc5 +; 2 Kd7; 3 Pc6 +; 4 Pc7; 5 Pc8 = Q, Ka6; 6 Kc7; 7 if the Bl. K is on a7, Qd7 (if on a8 or a6, 7 Qc6, &c.); 8 Qc6; 9 Q × P; 10 Qc6; 11 Pb5; 12 Qb7 +; 13 Pb6 m.

216. CB, but not BS, adds the condition 'et regine noue possunt dare scac etiam saltando', as if this were exceptional. 1 Ktf3 +; 2 Kte3 +; 3 Pb2 +; 4 Ktd2 +; 5 Pb8 = Q +; 6 Ktc2 +; 7 Qb3 +; 8 Ktc4 +; 9 Ktb4 +; 10 Rf7 +; 11 Kta6 +; 12 Ktb6 +; 13 Rd7 +; 14 Ktc7 +; 15 B m.

217. 'Albi trahunt et dicunt quod facient se mattari a nigris ad XV tractum, malis gratibus nigrorum.' 1 Ktc6; 2 Kta5; 3 Ktc4; 4 Kta3; 5 Ktc2; 6 Kta1; 7 R(c8)b8 +; 8 Ra2; 9 Rc8; 10 Rd8; 11 Rd3; 12 Ktb3; 13 Ktd4; 14 Ktf3 +; 15 Rg2, P × R m. W. Lewis, *Chess Problems* (1827), No. 63, shows that there is a mate in XIII by 9 Ktb3; 10 Rd2; 11 Rc8; 12 Re8 +; 13 Rg2, P × R m.

218. I give the solution from both collections.

BS 191.

'Albi primo trahunt, non est uis, et dicunt albi quod mattabunt nigros et fieri potest. Trahe regem tuum album in punctum (d5). Ipse fugiet cum alfino, ponendo eum in punctum nigrum (g4). Tu ibis superius uersus A (e7). Ipse trahet regem suum sub regina, et tu uade in A. Ipse trahet alfinum suum in aliud punctum nigrum (e2). Tu uadas in B (e8). Oportebit eum ascendere cum alfino, uel tu procedes cum pedone. Tunc tu descende cum rege tuo, non in A, sed indirecte uersus illam partem ubi stat alfinus, et ita capies uel fugabis alfinum, et facies reginam talem colorem, et postea leuiter mattabis eum.'

CB 218.

'Albi primo trahunt et dicunt se uelle facere reginam de pedone qui stat iuxta regem, uel de pedone qui stat iuxta alfinum ad XVI tractum uel pauciores, et fit ita. Trahe regem album uersus alfinum. Ipse descendet inferius ab alio latere pedonis, et tu uade superius. Et ipse trahet regem, et tu uadas in A (e7), et ipse trahet alfinum suum in punctum (e2) ut si trahas medium pedonem, redeat et capiat eum. Sed tu ibis in A. Ipse trahet regem, et tu ibis in B (e8), et tunc trahet ipse alfinum, et tu uadas cum rege tuo descendendo uersus alfinum. Et ibis ad eum, et fugabis uel capies eum, et facies reginam, et proinde erit ac si esset mattus.'

219. (BS 181 has Kd6 on g6, which prolongs the solution by two moves. The MS. gives no number of moves.) 1 Ra7 +; 2 R(h7)b7 +; 3 Rb5; 4 Rc7; 5 R(b5)c5; 6 Rd7; 7 Rd5 (position is now that after the 9th move in the BS solution); 8 Re5 +; 9 Rh7; 10 Rh8 +; 11 Re7; 12 Rd7; 13 Rc7; 14 Kc6; 15 Kb6; 16 Rc8 m.

220. 1 Kh7; 2 Kh6; 3 Kh5; 4 Kh4; 5 Bc5; 6 Be7; 7 Bc6; 8 Be4, Kh1!; 9 Kh3; 10 Pf3; 11 Rg4; 12 Rg3; 13 Pf2; 14 Bc5; 15 Be3; 16 Pf1 = Q; 17 Qg2 m.

221. 1 Ba3; 2 Qf5; 3 Qe4; 4 Qd5; 5 Qc4; 6 Qb3, P × Q; 7 P × P; 8–12 P queens; 13 Qd6; 14 Qe7; 15 Qf8, Be5; 16 Kg6; 17 Qg7 m. Variation: Bc7 on c8. Unsound, 'quia procuteret in E (c4), et non posset uenire regina in capturam nigri pedonis. Qui pedo si non fieret regina alterius coloris quam alia regina, non posset mattari rex niger.'

222. 1 Ke8, Ktg8; 2 Kf8, Kte7; 3 Ke8, Ktg6; 4 Kd8, Re7; 5 Kc8, Kth4; 6 Kd8, Ktf5; 7 Kc8, Kte3; 8 Kd8, Ktd5; 9 Kc8, Rh7; 10 Kd8, Ktc7; 11 Kc8, Kte6; 12 Kb8, Rc7; 13 Ka8, Ktd4; 14 Kb8, Ktb5; 15 Ka8, Kta7; 16 Kb8, Re7; 17 Ka8, Ktc6; 18 Kt~, Ra7 m. Black's moves are his best.

223. (BS 183 adds the condition 'erit tractus pro tractu'.) 1 Ktf2, Kb1; 2 Ktd3, Ka2; 3 Kb4, Ka1; 4 Ka3, Kb1; 5 Kb3, Ka1; 6 Kc2, Ka2; 7 Ktb2, Ka3; 8 Kc3, Ka2; 9 Ktc4, Ka1; 10 Kd2, Kb1; 11 Kd1, Ka1; 12 Kc1, Ka2; 13 Kc2, Ka1; 14 Kta3, Ka2; 15 Ktb1, Ka1; 16 Be6, Ka2; 17 Bc4 +, Ka1; 18 Ktd2,

Pg8 = Q; 19 Ktb3 m. Black's moves are his best. The solution in F is lengthened considerably.

224. It will take White an even number of moves to secure the position of the White men in CB 223, and Black, by means of his choice of Pg3 or g4 can permit or prevent it at pleasure. If 1 Kt or B~, Pg3 prevents it, and there is no solution.

225. Black's only chance of winning is to queen his Pawn. White prevents this by keeping his K on h8 or g7, by playing Qa3, b2, c3 according as the Bl. K plays to the *c*, *b*, or *a* line, and by following the P up and exchanging as opportunity offers.

226. 'Istud partitum ut plurimum simile est precedenti: difficilius tamen ad defendendum.' Black must queen on b8 to win. Wh. plays Qa3 if the Bl. K is on *c* file, and Qc3 if on *b* file. 'Istud partitum quia difficile est, melius uidebis per studium quam per doctrinam.'

227. 1 Qc5; 2 Q(c5)d6 ! (2 Q(c5)d4 ?, Qd5 + or Qf5 +; 3 K~, Re4 and Bl. brings R to h7 and separates the Wh. K from his Qs and wins), and play K to g7, Qs to e7, f6, g5. Now keep K and Qf6 unmoved and move Qe7 and g5 backwards and forwards. Black can do nothing.

228. 1 Be6. Then play B to c8 and K to b7, and play Ba6, c8, until it is captured. All the Bl. Qs will be of the same colour. Variation: Bl. play first and mate. Sound, for 1 Pf5 prevents the B getting to c8.

229. 1 Kd6, Rh5 ('tractus alborum est subtilis'); 2 R × R, Ra6 +; 3 K~, Ra5 +; 4 K~, R × R winning. This position occurs in Stamma.

230. 1 Ktc6; 2 Kte5; 3 Rh6; 4 Re6; 5 Ktf3 m. Variation: add Bl. Pd2. The same solution holds. Some try 1 Be6; 2 Bc4; 3 Kth6; 4 Ktf5; 5 Kth4; 6 Kt × P m., which takes one move too many.

231. 1 Ra3; 2 Rc3; 3 R × P; 4 R × B m.

232. 'Nigri primo trahunt, et dicunt se uelle mattare albos, et si contingat aliquem pedonum fieri reginam, non faciet nisi unum tractum et unum: hoc est, non poterunt saltare ut consueuerunt regine noue. Tu defende albos, quia non mattantur per uim. Ipse dabit tibi scac in A (e5). Tu capies eum de regina, et ipse alium roccum in B (c4). Tu approximabis cum rege. Ipse ibit in C (c3), et postea dabit tibi scac, et tu trahes regem tuum secundum puncta (e6, f7) et ludes etiam cum regina si expediat, et inferiorem pedonem capiet tibi per uim. De alia tu facies reginam, et erunt ambe unius coloris, ita quod si saltare posset, defenderes te leuiter. Sed modo habebit brigam, et tamen defenditur. Partitum est subtilissimum, licet quidam credant quod nichil sit quam trahunt roccum suum in punctum (a7). Sed tunc albi dant scac de pedone et mat de regina ante regem.' 1 Re5 +, Q × R; 2 Rc5, Kd6; 3 Rc3, Qd4, compelling 4 R × P, K × R looks more speedy than the text solution.

233. Since there is an odd number of squares between the Ks, White can maintain the opposition. Variation: Kg7 on h7. Now sound, for White can no longer maintain the opposition.

234. 1 Kg7, Kb2; 2 Kg6, Kc3 (if Kc2; 3 Kf5; and if Kb1; 3 Ke5. If 2 . ., Ka1; 3 Kf5, Kb1; 4 Ke4. If 3 . ., Kb2; 4 Ke5); 3 Kf6, Kd4 (or Kd3; 4 Ke5; or Kc2; 4 Kf5; or Kb1; 4 Ke5); 4 Kf5. If 1 . ., Kb1; 2 Kf6, &c.

235. 1 Qe3; 2 Qd4; 3 Qc5; 4 Qb6; 5 Rg1 +; 6 Qa7. Now drive Bl. K to f8 and obtain position Wh. Rh7, Kth6, Kb8. The game continues 1 Ka8; 2 Rf7; 3 Ktg4; 4 Kte5; 5 Ktg6; 6 Rh7; 7 Re7; 8 Kte5; 9 Ktc6 +; 10 Rb7, P × R m.

236. a8–b6, c8–a7, c6–b8, a6–c7; a7–c6, b6–c8, c7–a8, b8–a6; c6–b8, c8–a7, a8–b6, a6–c7; a7–c6, b8–a6, c7–a8, b6–c8.

237. Wh. plays simply 1 . ., Rf1; 2 . ., Rh1; or 1 . ., Rh3; 2 . ., Rh1. Variation: (1) Bl. has 7 Qs; said to be sound. It can only be so if the 7th Queen moves on squares of the other colour. (2) the 6 Qs are in the middle of the board. Unsound. Wh. simply makes for a corner of the board of the opposite colour to the squares on which the Qs move.

238. White simply copies Bl.'s moves.

239. If 1 Qd3, Qd7. If 1 Qd2, Qd6.

240. 'Nigro primo trahunt et dicunt se uelle mattare regem album. Tu illum

defende, quia non fit. Ipse trahet reginam in A (d7), et pedonem in B (e7), et regem suum in C (g5) et tu tuum in D (g7), et ipse reginam suam, et hic est tota uis si debeas ire in E (g8) uel in angulum. Et hoc semper scies per istum uersum "ipsa uel alterne rectum dant an relique dant": hoc est dicere, si regina esset in ipsa linea ubi stat rex tuus et pedo eius, uel in alternis lineis, hoc est, in tercia connumerando ipsam, uel quinta, uel septima, semper trahes regem tuum in rectum tractum, hoc est in E. Si autem regina sit in aliqua aliarum quatuor linearum, fac obliquum tractum, hoc est, in angulum. Et ipse trahet regem suum in F (h6), et ueniet regina, et claudere poterit te sed nunquam mattare, et ipsi perdent.'

241. 'Nigri trahunt primo, et dicunt se uelle capere alfinum, et quando aliquis pedonum erit facta regina, non saltabit sed faciet unum tractum et unum. Tu alfinum defende, quia non fit. Rex niger trahetur in A (f8), et rex albus in B (b8). Si rex niger in C (f7), et albus in D (b7). Si niger in E (e7) et albus in F (c7), semper faciendo cum albo rege pares tractus. Si ipse trahat pedonem dextrum, tunc facias dispares. Si trahat eum in penultima linea, tunc semper pares. Si faciat eum reginam, tunc semper dispares. Et illam regulam tenebis ubicumque regina uadat per totum tabulerium. Vnde uersus: "ipsa uel alterne dispar, sed par reliqui dant." Hoc est dicere: si regina sit in ipsa linea ubi fuit facta, uel in alternis, hoc est, in tercia, quinta et septima, semper trahas in disparem colorem a suo rege; si regina sit in aliis quatuor lineis, hoc est in linea ubi scribitur D, F, E, C, et ubi stant scripti pedones, et in sexta et in octaua, tu uade cum tuo rege albo directe contra eum, et in colore tali, et defendes alfinum. Ludus est omnium subtilissimus.'

242. If 1 Pa3, Ph6; 2–6 the Ps queen; if 7 Q leaps, Qg2 wins; and if 7 Qb7, Q leaps, wins.

243. 'Nullus nigrorum transit lineam alborum, nec e contrario, et habent tractum nigri qui est malum pro eis, quia de ratione perdunt. Roccus niger punctatus (Rh8) ibit in A (f8), et roccus albus punctatus (Rh1) in B (h7). Tunc ubicumque roccus non punctatus (Ra8) ibit uersus A (e.g. Rb8), albus non punctatus (Ra1) ibit contra eum (i.e. Rb1), donec redeat uersus angulum. Tunc trahatur in penultimam lineam ubi stat B, et ibunt rocci albi repagulando nigros, et capient eos. Sed decet quod iste ludus habeatur exercitio.' Cf. J. Kohtz' note in *Wochenschach*, 1908, p. 437.

245. 1 Bc3 +; 2 B × R, Pg6; 3 Kg7, Ph5; 4 Kh6, Pg4; 5 Kg5, Ph3; 6 Kh6!, Ph4; 7 Kh7, Pg5; 8 Bc3, Ph6; 9 Be5; 10 Kh8, &c.

246. 1 Kt × Q +, B × Kt; 2 Bd3; 3 Bb5, &c. Finally Bl. exchanges R for B and P, and Wh. plays K and Q to the corner and sacrifices Q for P.

247. 1 Q × Q(a7)!

248. 1 Be4; 2 Bc6; 3 B × R. Wh. then plays K to h1 and B to g2 or e4, and simply moves the B to and fro on g2 and e4. Variation: Remove the Bl. R and place Bc2 on b1. Still sound. Wh. plays K to h1 and B to f1, and moves Bh3 and Bf1.

249. The diagram shows the final position of the 16 Queens.

250. (BS 186 has Bc4 on a6, Kh8 on h3, and reflects. White mates under the CB conditions. Unsound.) The CB text is not very helpful and the owner of F has added a long note. His solution (omitting alternative lines of play) runs 1 Kg7, Kg2; 2 Kh6, Kh3; 3 Kg5, Kg2; 4 Kh4, Kh1; 5 Kg3, Kg1; 6 Ba6 or e6, Kf1 or h1; 7 Rf8 + or h8 +, K~; 8 Bc8 and wins. In the BS position, White has no chance of winning a move by moving the B.

251. 1 Kb5, Kb8; 2 Rh8 +, Kc7; 3 Rg8; 4 Rb8; 5 Rb7. Now obtain the position Wh. Kg3 or h3, Be3, Rf6; Bl. Kh1, and conclude by 1 Rb6, P × R; 2 Pa7 Pb5; 3 Pa8 = Q, Pb4; 4–8 Q to g2 m.

252. (This is almost identical with the variation to BS 173, see CB 208, but the solution is more tentative.) 1 Rg3; 2 Ktc3; 3 Ktb5, Kh2; 4 ~, Kh1; 5 Rg2, &c. The necessity of allowing Bl. a move at the fourth move endangers the solution. Safer seems 1 Rg4; 2 Rg3; 3 Ktc3; 4 Ktb5, Kh1; 5 Rg2, P × Kt; 6 Rg3, Pb4!; 7 Rb3, Kh2, continuing as in the BS variation, mating straightforwardly in XXIII at most.

253. 1 Ra5 +; 2 Ra6 *scacroc*, Kd5; when 3 R × R is stalemate. 'Clausus erit,

et sic albi perdunt' (not because stalemate was decisive, but because White has failed to carry out his undertaking), 'nisi habeant unam aliam reginam talis coloris.'

254. 1 Re7 +, Qe5 +; 2 Ke6, R~; 3 R opposite R, Rf8 (R × R, stalemate); 4 Rf7, R × R; 5 K × R, and Wh. plays K to b7, and queens his aP, winning.

255. White queens his dP, and plays the Q to c5; he then compels Bl. to take Ph4, and drives the K to h1, and compels the advance of the Ph5 to h2, the Wh. K being in f2. Then 1 Qb4, P × Q; 2 R to sq. on *c* file, which is commanded by the Bl. P, P advances. When the Bl. P reaches b2, Wh. plays Rc1 +, compelling the reply P × R = Q. Wh. now queens his aP, and plays it to g2, mating.

256. (BS 193 omits Ph6, and allows Wh. to stale the Bl. K and continue playing.) 1 R × R, Kta6 +; 2 Ka8, R × R; 3 Ph5, Rc7; 4 Ph4, Ktb4; 5 Kb8, Ktd5; 6 Ka8, Ktc3 (6 . . , Kte7 leads to m. in IX, *Chess Amateur*, 1912, 719); 7 Kb8, Ktb5; 8 Ka8, Kta7; 9 Kb8, Rg7; 10 Ka8, Ktc6; 11 Ph3, Ra7 m. If 1 Rd4 +, Kc2; 2 Rd6, Ktd3; 3 Rb6, Kte5 (3 Re6, Ktb4); 4 Rb7, Ktc6 +; 5 Ka8, R × R; 6 Ph5, Ra7 m.

257. 1 Ktd6; 2 Ktc4; 3 Ktb2, *scac roc*, and the Kt escapes. Some players try 1 Ktc7; 2 Kte6; 3 Ktc5 + r, Kc4!; 4 Kt × R, Bf6 +; 5 K~, Bd4; 6 K~, Kb4 and wins the Kt.

258. 'Albi primo trahunt et mattabunt regem nigrum, licet isti pedones si fierent regine, omnes essent unius coloris. Sed aliqui fient, et aliqui non fient, et poterit mattari in utroque angulo uel iuxta. Et caueas (F Sed aduertas) tibi ne rex suus uadat (F iret) retro (F adds sc. post) pedones tuos, quia tunc perderes (F omits), et non permittas pedones collaterales (F adds seu capitales) nimis fatue procedere, medii potius precedant (F adds uno puncto tantum semper), et bene mattabis eum.' F then adds: 'Hoc partitum est pulcherrimum, et multe discretionis, uulgariter nuncupatum *partitum regis francorum*.' Cf. v. d. Lasa, 126, and *Akademischer Schachklub München, Festschrift*, 1896, 41.

259. 1 Rb5, Kd4; 2 Kd2, Kc4 (e4); 3 Rg5 (a5), Kd4; 4 R m. If 1 . . , Kc4 (e4); 2 Kc2 (e2), K~; 3 R(b5)e5 or R(f5)c5; 4 Rf4 or b4 m. accordingly. Other first moves lead to m. in III.

260. If 1 K × B, Rh7. If 1 B × R, Kg7. 1 Ktf7 is m.

261. 1 Ra8 +, Bc8; 2 Kte6 (or R × B) m. If 1 . . , Kc7; 2 Kte8 (or Kt × B) m. Variation: Ra7 on b7. Unsound. 1 Rb8 +, Kc7; 2 Rc8 +, B × R.

262. 1 Kte4; 2 Ktc5; 3 Kte6; 4 Ktc7; 5 Kte8; 6 Ktg7; 7 Re6; 8 Rc5; 9 Rc6; 10 Kth5; 11 Ktf6 +; 12 Re8 m.

263. 1 R × R is m. 1 Ra8 (g8) +, Bb8 (f8) +. Variation: Black mate in III. Unsound. 1 Bc4, Bb4 + d; 2 R × R +, Kc8 and there is no mate next move.

264. White plays: 1 Kd6, Kd8; 2 Rf8 m. Black plays: 1 . . , Kd8; 2 Rc5, Ke8; 3 Rc8 m.

265. 1 Kte3, Ka8 (or Kc8; 2 Kc6; 3 Ktd5; 4 Ktc7, &c.); 2 Ktd5; 3 Ktc7; 4 Kc6; 5 Qc5; 6 Qb6; 7 Kte8; 8 Ktd6; 9 Qd8; 10 Kb5; 11 Ka6; 12 Ktc4; 13 Q(b6)c7 +; 14 Ktb6 m.

266. 1 Bc3; 2 R or Kt m. Variation: Omit Bf5. Unsound. 1 Bc3, Ktd7 +; 2 R × Kt +, K × R.

267. 'Fit unico modo.' 1 Bb7; 2 Ktf7 m. But 1 Bf7; 2 Kt~ discovering mate is also possible (v. d. Lasa).

268. Cf. CB 162. The solution is almost exactly the same.

269. 1 Rb8 +, Rd8; 2 R(f1)b1 is given, but 2 . . , B~ is a sufficient defence. 2 R on f line (or h1); 3 Rf8 (or h8) m. is necessary.

270. 1 Kb5, Kt × B; 2 P × Kt; 3 Kte6 m. If 1 . . , Pd3; 2 Kte6 +, Kt × Kt; 3 Rd7 m. Variation: Pf6 goes to f8. Unsound. 1 Kb5, Kt × B !. Cf. CB 266.

271. 1 Ktf6 +; 2 Kte6 +; 3 Pb7 +; 4 Ktd7 +; 5 Pb8 = Q +; 6 Ktc7 +; 7 Qb6 +; 8 Ktc5 +; 9 Ktb5 +; 10 Rf2 +; 11 Kta3 +; 12 Ktb3 +; 13 Rd2 +; 14 Ktc2 +; 15 Bd3 m. This is really the same as CB 216, but all the MSS. omit the Bl. Kts on e7, f7, and have thus overlooked the identity. Without them the solution, of course, does not work.

272. The MS. solution 1 Rf1 +, Kh2; 2 Rf2 +, Kh1; 3 Rh2 +, K × R;

4 Ktf3 +, Kh1; 5 Rg1 m. is foiled by 2 . . , Qg2; 3 Ktf3 +, Kh3! The position is really an unsound variation of CB 125 above.

273. 'Pedo est immobilis, et dicit rex albus quod defendet eum ne capiatur. Et rex niger approximabit eum sicut uult, quia pedo non habet aliquam custodiam. Et trahit primo rex albus, et bene defendit suum pedonem, quia ibit in disparibus punctis eiusdem coloris. Sed caueat sibi ne intret lineam punctatam (the *f* file) nisi prius intret rex niger. Et si sciat ludum defendere quum regina est angularis et inmobilis (i.e. CB 233), defendes istum, sed iste est difficilior.'

274. 1 Bf3, Kt(e7)~; 2 Ktc6 m.; or 1 . . , Kt(f8)~; 2 R or Kte6 m. accordingly. Variation: all the Pawns go in the contrary direction. 1 Pf6, and mate as in the main play.

275. 1 Kg2; 2 Bc6 or g6 m. accordingly. Variation: omit Pc5. There is now a second solution by 1 Rf8 +, K × R(d7); 2 Ktc5 m.

276. 1 Ktf7, aR~; 2 Pg7 +, Kg8; 3 Kth6 m. Bl.'s first and second moves may be transposed. Or 1 . . , Rg7 or h6; 2 Re7; 3 Re8 m.

277. 1 Pc7 +; 2 Pc8 = Q; 3 Qc6; 4 Qb7 +; 5 Be3; 6 Kc6; 7 Kd6; 8 Kc5; 9 Kc6; 10 Bc5 +; 11 Pa7 m.

278. The MS. gives 1 P × B, R × P. If 1 Kth3 + d, Kt × R. But 1 Rd8 +, Kt × R; 2 Kt × B m.; or 1 . . , B × R; 2 Ktf6 m. is possible. The problem is sound. Variation: Ktg8 on f8. Sound. 1 Kth7 + d, Kt × R; 2 Kt × B m.; or 1 . . , B × R; 2 Bg6 m. (1 Rd8 +, which is not mentioned, is equally good.)

279. 1 Kth5; 2 Ktf4; 3 Ktd3; 4 Kte5; 5 Be3; 6 Rh7 +; 7 Rh5; 8 Rh8 +; 9 Kf5; 10 Rh7; 11 Rd7 m. Variation: Kg8 on h8. Mate in X. The play is the same, but White can now save his 7th move.

280. 'In isto partito, rex est solus, et 4^or rocci ex alio latere, et dicunt dare scac in quolibet tractu, et mattare in 4° tractu uel paucioribus. Et ponamus quod rex ponatur ubi scribitur (d5). Tunc est dandus scac de rocco ubi scribitur (d2) duabus lineis mediis. Tunc ponamus quod rex uadat in A (e4), ponendus est alter roccus ex alio latere regis una linea media (g4). De aliis duobus roccis ponendis leuiter uidebis per te' (2 . . , Kf5, 3 Rf4 +, Ke6; 4 Re4 m.).

281. 'Alfini nigri et albi capiunt omnes calculos quia omnes sunt immobiles preter alfinos, et fit taliter. Albi uadunt secundum ordinem alphabeti et nigri similiter, et reuertuntur ad loca sua (e.g. B(d4)–f2–h4–f6–d8–b6–d4). Postea quilibet capit unum roccum. Postea quilibet facit duos tractus usque in angulos et capiunt reges et reginas. Vnde fertur fabulose quod isti quatuor episcopi in medio campo pepigerunt cum quatuor regibus, et tunc ponitur quod regine sint reges, quod expedirent eos de omnibus inimicis. Reges promiserunt episcopis ciuitates et castra si caperent hostes, et ceperunt alfini (qui dicuntur episcopi) omnes secundum quod predictum est, preter roccos. Tunc dicebant reges: "Ecce isti quatuor comites fortiter nos obsident." Et ceperunt singuli singulos, petentes promissa. Reges autem pacto contradixerunt, eos premiare nolentes, qui reuersi sunt, et consilio habito, quilibet fecit duos passus ita quod quilibet cepit unum regem. Et sic de episcopis reges facti sunt secundum fabulas.' (Cf. K 7.) The fable is interesting as showing that the idea that the Aufin was a Bishop was not unknown even in Italy.

282. 'Aliud partitum est supra, quod isti assimilatur, et est in xxii^o folio retrogradiendo, isto folio connumerato (i.e. CB 240). Ibi inuenies istud partitum, nisi quod non ponitur ita roccus albus non est, et ponitur hic, sed est immobilis. Vetat quod rex niger non trahitur in A (h6), vnde tracto pedone in B (e7), uadet regina, et capiet roccum, et postea respice glosam predicti partiti, et scies defendere regem album, licet rex niger possit trahi in A.'

283. 1 Rh6; 2 Ktf6 m. (There are other solutions, e.g. 1 Rh5 and 1 Kt(g8) × B +, Rd8; 2 hKt~ m.; or 1 . . , Pg8 = Q; 2 R × Q m.)

284. 1 Kte7 +, Pg8 = Q; 2 Ktg5 + d, Kg7; 3 R × Q m.

285. 1 Ktg5 +, Bh4; 2 R × B +, Rh6; 3 Ktf7 +, Kh7; 4 R × R m. This and the two preceding problems are CB 26 and its two variations, which are set out at greater length for the sake of clearness.

286. 1 Ra1, Rh2; 2 R × R, Rh3; or 2 any other, Kh7.

287. 'Albi primo trahunt et mattant nigros, quod multis uidetur impossibile; tamen fit, primo trahendo militem in A (b2), postea in B (c3), et sic ludendo per multos tractus cum rege et milite, tenendo regem nigrum in illo angulo. Et fit tractus pro tractu, ut inuenies in xxxiii° folio retrogradiendo, ubi quasi istud partitum inuenies, et cum scies illud, scies istud.' The reference is to CB 223.

288. The Kta8 can only reach h1 in an even number of moves. The problem can be solved in twenty-four moves.

It will be remembered that in my account of the *Civis Bononiae* MSS. I have mentioned that some of the MSS. give additional problems. The greatest number of these occur in F, and this additional material is of special importance, partly because it is in the same hand with the remainder of that MS., the writer of which had made a very careful study of the *Civis Bononiae* work, and partly because of the light which it throws upon the history and nomenclature of Italian chess in the 15th c. The additions to L are in a later hand than the rest of the MS. This fresh material now follows.

F 295.

(Bl.)
Black mates in XVII or less.

F 296.

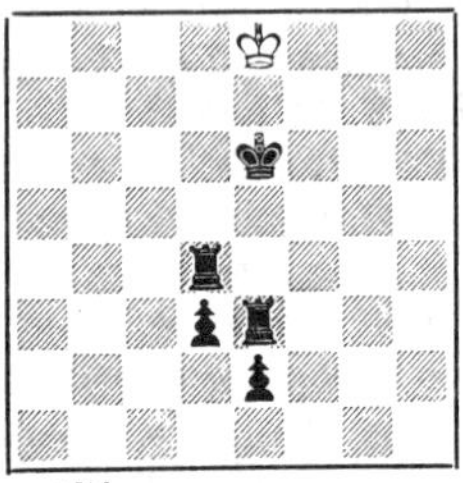

(Bl.)
White plays and Black mates with P in V exactly.

F 297.

Mate in X exactly, capturing all the Black pieces.

F 298.

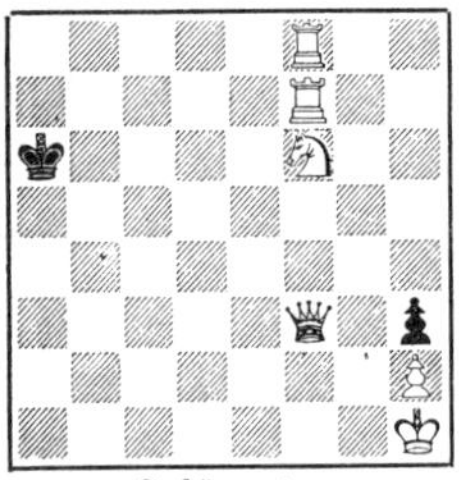

Self-mate.

F 300.

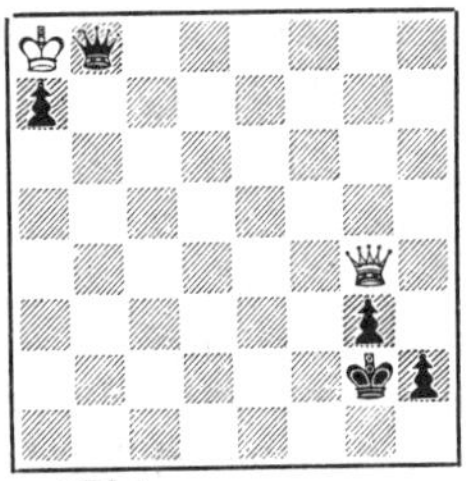

(Bl.)
Black mates.

F 301.

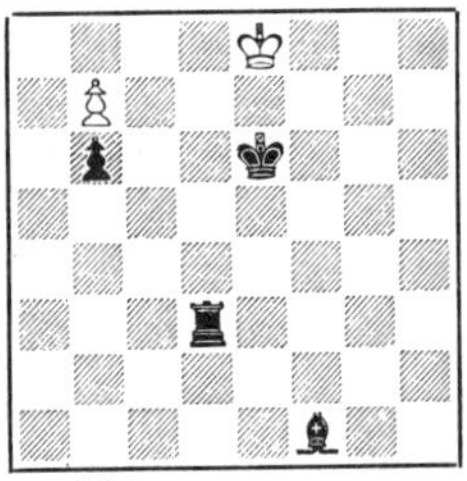

(Bl.)
Black mates with Pb6 [in XVI]. The Wh. P is fidated.

F 303.

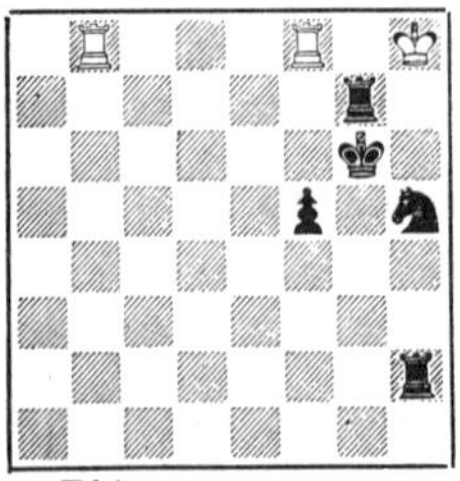

(Bl.)
Black mates in II exactly. Unsound.

F 304.

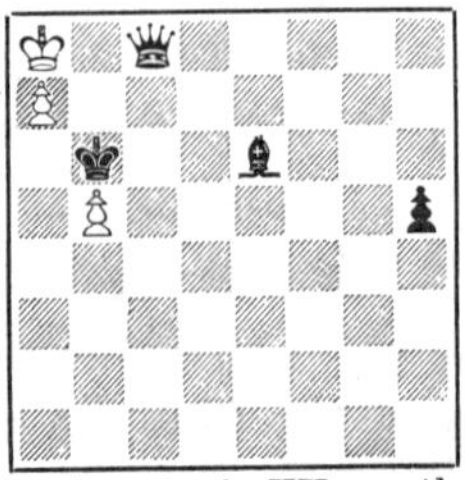

Black mates in XV exactly.

F 305.

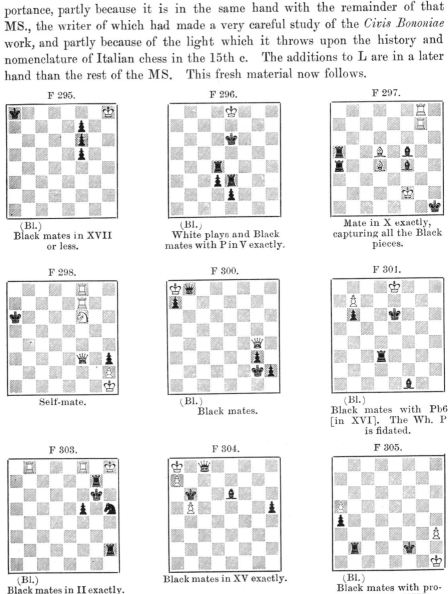

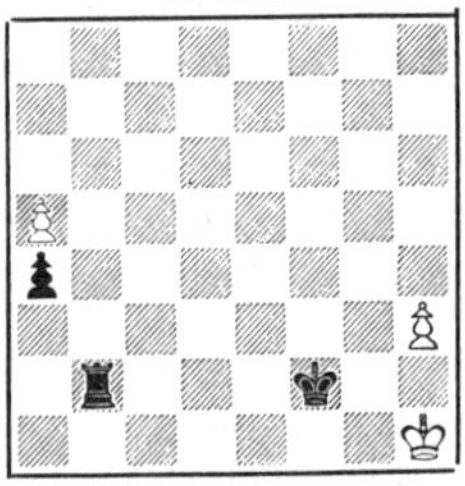

(Bl.)
Black mates with promoted P in XIII.

F 306.

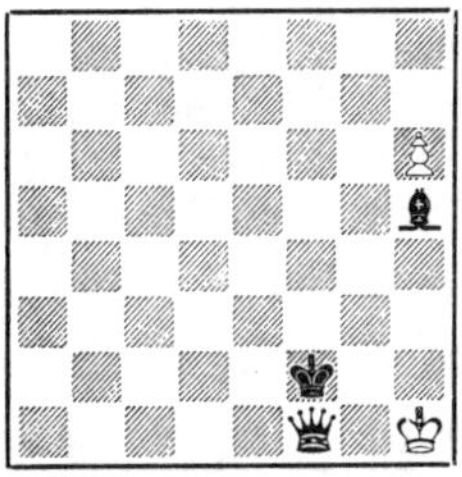

(Bl.)
Black mates in XIII or less. The Wh. K may be staled.

F 307 : Ar. 23.

(Bl.)
Black mates in IX.

F 311.

Mate in II exactly. Unsound.

F 313.

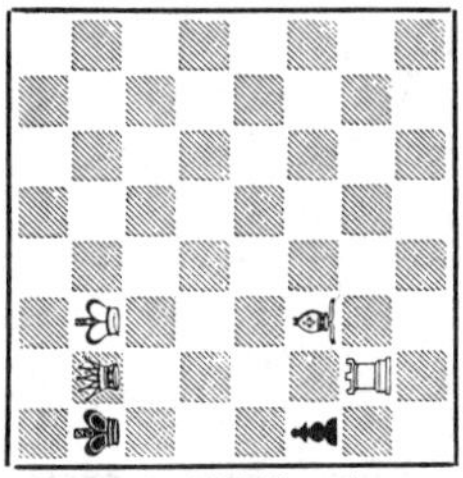

(Bl.)

Mate in XIII or less. The Bl. K may be staled.

F 314.

Mate in III exactly. Ph7 is immovable. Unsound.

F 315.

Mate with the two Bs in LXXX or less.

F 316.

(Bl.)
Mate in II exactly. Qh8 is a promoted P. Black may not give check.

F 317 (corr.).

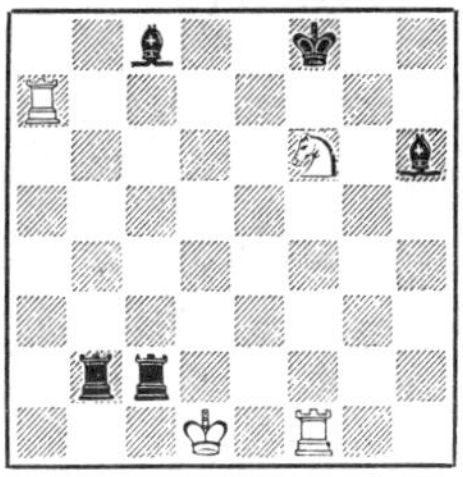

Mate in IV exactly.

F 318.

Black plays and White mates in II exactly. The Bl. R is fidated. Unsound.

F 319.

Mate in III exactly. Kg6 is immovable, but each of the other Wh. pieces is to move once.

F 320.

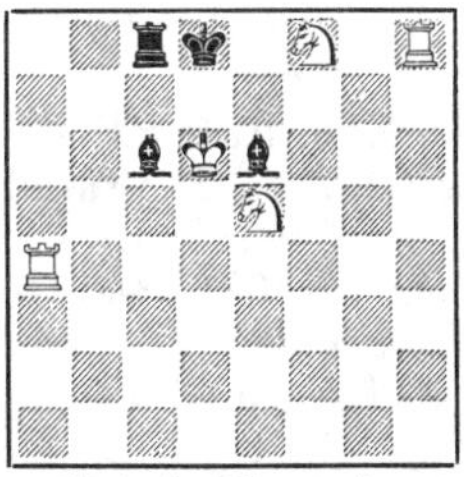

Mate in II exactly.

F 321.

Mate in II exactly. Unsound.

F 322 : Ar. 78.

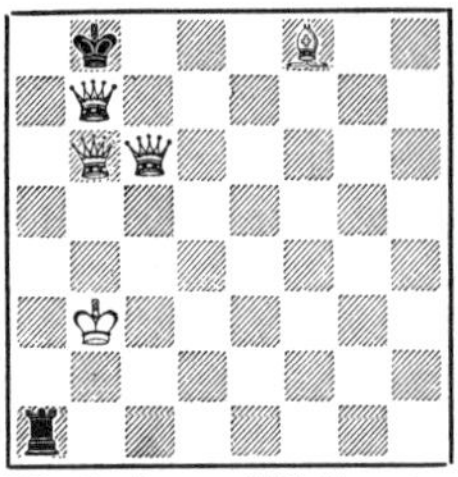

Black plays. White wins the R or mates.

F 323.

Mate with P in III exactly.

F 325.

Mate in III exactly. The Bl. R is fidated. Unsound.

F 330.

Mate in III exactly.

F 331.

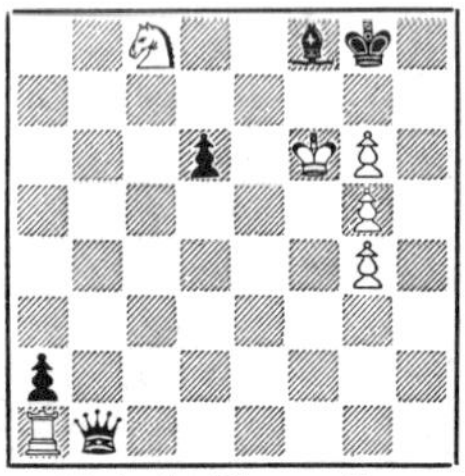

Mate in V exactly.

F 333.

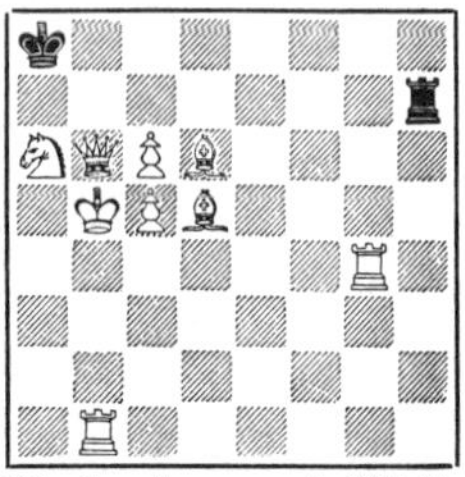

Black plays and White mates in III. The Bl. R is fidated.

SOLUTIONS

289. Wh. Kb8 ; Bl. Ka5, Pa6, b6, c6, playing to 8th row. ‘Nigri primo trahunt et dicunt se uelle mactare regem album ad centum ictus secundum rectum ludum. Et nota quod non possunt fieri pedones domine nisi hoc unico modo,’ &c. This is like CB 198. The title should be ‘Black mates or queens all the Pawns in C moves’. The text solution is 1 Pc7 + ; 2 Pb7 + ; 3 Pb8 = Q + ; 4 Qd6 ; 5 Pc8 = Q ; 6 Qd7 &c. It adds the variation (= CB 198) Kb8 on a8. 1 Ka4 ; 2 Kb4 ; 3 Ka5, Kb8 and the main position is secured.

290. Wh. Kc8, Ph2 ; Bl. Ka8, Pa7, b6, c5, playing to 8th row. Black plays and White mates. Unsound. 1 Pb7 +, Kc7 ; 2 Pb8 = Q +, Kc8 ; 3 Qc7, Ph1 = Q ; 4 Pc6 ; 5 Qb8 ; 6 Pc7 stalemate.

291. Wh. Ke6, Rd1, Ktc4, Qe7, Pe5 ; Bl. Ke8, Ra8, Ktg3. Mate in IV exactly with P. 1 Rd8 + ; 2 Ktd6 + ; 3 P × R ; 4 Pd7 m. Cf. CB 114, &c.

292. Wh. Ka1, Rg1, Kth5, Qd5, d4 ; Bl. Kf5. Mate in II exactly is CB 15.

293. Wh. Ka1, Rf1, h1, Qg5, Bc8 ; Bl. Kg8. Mate with B in VII is CB 177. These two positions are taken from a MS. in which the board is arranged at right angles to the usual position.

294. Wh. Ka8, Rg4, g8 ; Bl. Kh5, Ra1, Ktb4, Ba7, Pc6, b6, playing to 8th row. Mate in IV is really the same as CB 117. The variation, Rg4 on g2, delays the mate a move, and so makes the mate in IV unsound.

295. 1 Pf8 ‘faciendo dominam’, Kg8 ; 2 Qg7, Kf7 ; 3 Kb7, Ke8 ; 4 Kc8, Kf7 ; 5 Kd7, Kg8. The MS. continues, 6 Qh6 ; 7 Qg5 ; 8 Ke7 ; 9 Pf7 ; 10 Pf8 = Q ; 11 Kf7 ; 12 Qe7 ; 13 Kg6 ; 14 Pf6 ; 15 Qh6 (but the order of the moves depends on how Bl. plays). Now 15 . . , Kg8 ; 16 Pf7 + ; 17 Qg7 m. ; or 15 . . , Kh8 ; 16 Qg7 + ; 17 Pf7 m. ‘Hoc partitum melius habebitur per exercitium quam per doctrinam.’

296. 1 . . , Kf8 ; 2 Rd8 + ; 3 Rh3 ; 4 Rd7 ; 5 Rg7 + ; 6 Pe3 m.

297. ‘Albi primo trahunt, et obligant se uelle mactare nigros in x° ictu proprio,

hiis pactis appositis quod albi teneantur capere omnes nigros excepto rege priusquam mattetur ac etiam si nigri possunt dare unum scac albo regi uel capere unum scaccum de albis, tunc ipso facto albi perdunt.' 1 Rg1 +; 2 R(g8)g2 +; 3 Rh1 +; 4 Rg3 +; 5 R × B +; 6 Bf6 +; 7 R × B +; 8 Bf7 +; 9 R × R +; 10 R × R m.

298. 'Albi iactant se uelle facere mactari a nigris eorum malis gradibus, uel dicatur quod ludatur ad reuersum, sc. qui uincit perdat.' Drive the K to f2 by means of the Rs, and leave him no move except to f1; now 1 Ktg4 +, Kf1; 2 Qg2 +, P × Q m.

299. Wh. Ke7, Bf5, Pf6, h6; Bl. Kh8. Mate in XIV. 1 Kd7; 2 Kd8; 3 Kd7 and position is that of CB 277, mate in XI.

300. 'Nigri primo trahunt et dicunt quod mattabunt album regem. Hoc partitum est pulcherrimum et subtilissimum, et si tu cum albis uis defendere quin aliquis pedonum non fiat feminam (*gloss* aliter dominam) procures stare in linea punctorum (i. e. the *g* file) in tali modo cum regina alba, quod quando rex niger ueniet pro capiendo reginam, fac semper caute reginam esse in linea punctorum quando rex niger inuenerit se esse in aliquo punctorum in dicta linea et quando est circum circa ipse lineae fac reginam esse semper a contraria parte. Tandem nigri uincunt si bene luditur, utrique procedendo cum rege nigro in A (g7), in B (h6), in C (h5), et in D (h4). Postea pedones fiunt domine, et uincunt. Tamen hic ludus melius habetur per exercitium quam per doctrinam.' Cf. CB 225.

301. 1 Rd7; 2 Re7; 3 Rf7; 4 Kf6; 5 Kg6; 6 Rf6; 7 Bh3; 8 Kf7; 9 Bf5 +, Kh8; 10 Rc6, P × R; 11–12 bP queens; 13–16 Q via d8 to g7 m.

302. Wh. Ka6; Bl. Kc6, Ra2, b1, Ba3. Bl. mates in V with B is CB 135.

303. 1 Rh4, R × P; 2 Ktf4 +, Rh5. This is a favourite theme of the later European problemists: see 324, 326, 327, 328 below, also C 8, 19, 29, 44, 147, Sens 6, WD 3, 146, Luc. 9.

304. 1 Qb7 +; 2 Qa8, K × Q; 3 Kc7, Pb6 +; 4 Kc8, Pb7 +; 5 Kc7, Pb8 = Q +; 6 Kc8; 7 Ph4 &c. Variation Ph5 on h6, unsound. The Wh. P can queen, and get across in time to interfere. Cf. Luc. 129.

305. 'Nigri primo trahunt et dicunt uelle mattare albos ad 12^{m} vel 13^{m} ictum, et possunt de pedone vel domina.' 1 Kf1; 2 Rb4, P × R; 3–6 aP queens, P queens and Q to d1. The position is now that of PL 289 after move 10, and the mate follows in seven more moves as there.

306. 'Si albi contingerent claudi quin valeant proicere, propter hoc ludus non tabulet, nec niger amittat.' 1 Qg2 +; 2 Bf7, Ph5; 3 Bd5, Ph4; 4 Bb7, Ph3; 5 Qf1, Kh1; 6 Kg3, Kg1; 7 Qc2, Ph2; 8 Bd5, Kh1; 9 Bf3 +, Kg1; 10 Bh1, K × B; 11 Kf2, stale; 12 Q~, stale; 13 Qg2 m. Cf. CB 212.

307. 1 R × Q; 2 R × P +; 3 Kt × P +; 4 Pe4 +; 5 Ktc4 +; 6 Kte2 +; 7 Be3 +; Kh4 (h5); 8 Pg3 (Qg4) +; 9 Qg4 (Pg3) m. Bl. men are missing from c7 and d7. Cf. K 27.

308. A different setting of CB 185 (Kc3 on c4, Qc4 on c3, Be3 on e4) which gives a mate in VII (five moves of the Kts, then 6 Qb4 +; 7 Bc2 m.).

309. A variant of CB 219 (Ba6 on c8, Kd6 on b6, omit Wh. B). 'Albi primo proiciunt et iactant se uelle mattare nigros dando ei scac mat in puncto vbi nunc est infra seu in termino ictuum 50, et alfinus niger est affidatus.'

310. CB 189 with colours changed, and different text.

311. 1 Kt(g1)f3, P × R = Q; 2 Kt × Q +, R × R or Ktg4 +, Qh3. The text ends 'ubique est defensio meo credere'. Cf. CB 25.

312. CB 207 (text and variation) with diagram inverted.

313. 'Albi primo trahunt, et mactabunt nigros ad 13^{m} ictum uel in paucioribus, et intelligatur quod cum niger non poterit proicere quod fuerit clausus, propter hoc non tabuletur secundum consuetudinem recti ludi, sed pacto niger clausus expectet mat, et si ualet proicere quod proiciat.' 1 Be1, stale; 2 Bc3, Pe1; 3 Be5; 4 Bc3; 5 Qa3, stale; 6 Qb4; 7 Be5, Ka1; 8 Kc2; 9 Bc3; 10 Ba1, K × B; 11 Kb3; 12 Qc3; 13 Qb2 m. Cf. CB 212, F 306.

314. 1 Pd7 +, Kd8; 2 Ba3, Rh6. Or 1 Pc7, Ra4; 2 Kt~, R × Q +; 3 K~, R +. Cf. CB. 76.

315. Queen the Pawns, keeping the K in front of them. Post Qs in c7, f7, g6, g7, and K in b7, Be3 and d3, Bl. Ke7 or d7. Then 1 Bb5 + ; 2 Bg5 m. or conversely.

316. 1 Re3, Kt × Q ; 2 Kd5 m. (Or 1 . . , B × R ; 2 Qd7 m.) This is C 82.

317. 1 Kth7 + ; 2 Rf8 +, B × R ; 3 Ktf6 + ; 4 R m. This is really CB 96 Variation: Kd1 on e1, Rc2 on d2. Unsound, for in the above 1 . . , Ke8 ; and 3 . . , Kd8 ; 4 Rd7 + , R × R is possible.

318. 1 . . , Rh8 ; 2 Ktd8, Rh7 and can interpose.

319. 1 Ktf6 + , Rh2 ; 2 Rh7 + , R × R ; 3 R × R m.

320. 1 Re4, Ke8 ; 2 Kt × B(e6) m. Or 1 . . , B × R ; 2 Kt × B(e6) m. Or 1 . . , Bg8 ; 2 Ktf7 m. Variation: Rc8 on b8. Unsound. 1 Re4, Kc8. Cf. Arch. 16, Picc. 25, S 15, C 1, Gott. 2 (Luc. 3, Dam. 4, WD 17), Luc. 13.

321. 1 R × R(g7), Kt × B(e3) or 1 R × R(b2), Kt × B(f4).

322. 1 Rb1 +, Kc3 ; 2 R × Q, Bd6 + ; 3 K~, Bb4 shuts in R and wins it.

323. 1 Pc7 ; 2 Bc5 + ; 3 Pb7 m. Variations : I Ra1 on a2. Unsound. 1 Pc7, Rh1 ; 2 Bc5 m. II (= C 125) Kh7 on h6. Unsound. 1 Pc7, Ra4 ; 2 Bc5, Ra6. Cf. S 18, Picc. 72, 111, C 133.

324. Variant of CB 303 (Rb8 on a8, g7 on d7, h2 on h1 : colours changed). Mate in II exactly. 1 Ktf4 + ; 2 Rg7 m. Also 1 Rd8 ; 2 R × R or Kt m. accordingly.

325. 1 Ktd7, Rf7 ; 2 Kte7, Rf3. Variation: Pb2 on b3. Now sound, for 3 B discovers mate.

326. Variant of CB 303 (Rb8 on a8, f8 on e8, g7 on d7 ; colours changed). Mate in II exactly. Unsound. 1 Rd8, Kg8. Or 1 Rg7, Ra2.

327. Variant of CB 303 (Rb8 on a8, h2 on h1, Pf5 on f6 ; colours changed). Mate in II exactly. 1 Pf7 ; 2 Rh7 or Ktf6 m. accordingly.

328. Variant of CB 303 (Rb8 on a8, f8 on c8, g7 on d7, h2 on h3 ; colours changed). Mate in II exactly. 1 Rg7 ; 2 Kt m. Variations : Rh3 on h1 or h2. Unsound, as in No. 326 above.

329. Wh. Ka7, Rg1, g3, Kte2, e5, Bh6, Pf4, g5, h5, playing to 1st row ; Bl. Kh2, Rb2, b6, Pf3, h4. Mate in XII exactly with B. This is really CB 206.

330. 1 Bg7, R on line 2 or 3 ; 2 Be5 ; 3 Ktf7 m. If 1 . . , R on *h* file ; 2 R × R ; 3 Ktf7 m. Cf. CB 66, 93.

331. 1 Kte7 + ; 2 Pg7 + ; 3 Pg6 + ; 4 Kte5, Qc2 ; 5 Rh1 m. Cf. Alf. 88, D. 34, S 11, WA 7, WD 157.

(332, 334, 336–40 are all blank.)

333. A long text with many variations. I adds no conditions ; II Wh. may not play Qh5 for his first move ; III Wh. Q is immovable, and Bl. may not play Rg7 first move (why not ?) ; IV Rg1 on g2. We may group I–III together ; it will be seen that there is a solution satisfying each variation for every move of Black. 1 . . , Rh1 ; 2 Ra1, R × R ; 3 Ra4 ; 4 Kt m. acc. Or 1 . . , Rh2 or h3 ; 2 Ra1, Rb2 or b3 + ; 3 Ktb4 + ; 4 Rg8 m. Or 1 . . , Rh4 ; 2 Qa5, R × R (Rh7 ; 3 Rg8 + ; 4 Qb6 or Ktc7 m.) ; 3 Ktc7 + ; 4 Qb6 m. Also 2 Re1, R × R (Rh7 ; 3 Bf7 ; 4 Re8 or Ktc7 m.) ; 3 Re4 ; 4 Re8 or Ktc7 m. Or 1 . . , Rh5 ; 2 Qa5, Rh7 (Rh8 ; 3 Ktc7 + ; 4 Qb6 m.) ; 3 Rg8 + ; 4 Qb6 m. Also 2 Pc7 ; 3 Rg8 + ; 4 Rb8 m. Or 1 . . , Rh6 ; 2 Ra1, R × B (Rh7 ; 3 Rg7 ; 4 Rg8 or Ktc7 m.) ; 3 Ktc7 + ; 4 Ra8 m. Or 1 . . , Rh8 ; 2 Rg8 + ; 3 Bf7 ; 4 Ktc7 m. Or 1 . . , Ra7 (g7, e7, d7, f7, b7) ; 2 Ktc7 + ; 3 Rg8(a1) + ; 4 Ra1(g8) m. Or 1 . . , Rc7 ; 2 Rg8 + ; 3 Ra1 ; 4 Ktc7 m. IV is solved by 1 . . , Rh1 ; 2 Rg7, Rb1 (any other ; 3 Ra2 ; 4 Kt m.) ; 3 Ktb4 ; 4 Rg8 m. Cf. C 78.

335. Wh. Ka5, Qb5, b6, c7 ; Bl. Kb7. Mate in C, Black need not move unless he chooses or is checked. The best defence only prolongs the game to 65 moves. 1 Kb4 ; 2Kc5 ; 3 Qa4 ; 4 Kb5 ; 5–8 Q(a4)–c6 + , Kc8 ; 9 Ka6 ; 10 Qd6 ; 11 Q(b6)c7 ; 12 Kb6 ; 13 Qd5, Kd7 ; 14 Qe5 ; 15 Q(c7)d6 ; 16 Kc5 ; 17 Qe4, Ke6 ; 18 Qf4 ; 19 Q(d6)e5 ; 20 Kc6 ; 21–7 Q(e4)–d7 + , Kf5 ; 28 Kd5 ; 29 Qe6 + , Kg4 ; 30 Ke4 ; 31 Qf5 + , Kh3 ; 32 Kf3, Kh4 ; 33 Qf6 ; 34 Qg3 + , Kh5 ; 35 Kf4 ; 36 Qg5 ; 37–41 Q(g3)–f6 ; 42 Qe6, Kg6 ; 43 Qe7 ; 44 Q(g5)f6 ; 45 Qd7,

Kf7; 46 Kf5; 47–53 Q(d7)–g6+, Kg8; 54–5 K–h6; 56 Qg7; 57 Q(e7)f8; 58–9 K–f6; 60 Qh4; 61 Kg6; 62–5 Q–f7 m. Cf. K 53, which is essentially the same problem. It is worthy of note that the solution in F regularly calls the Q on b5 *regina nigra*, i. e. the Q moving on the black squares. This requires that h1 is black.

Note. Early possessors of both B and L began to add additional problems on the blank leaves that separate the chess portion of these MSS. from the tables portion which follows. In B the only addition has been erased and I cannot identify the position. In L an illiterate hand of the end of the 15th c. has added the following:

L 289. Wh. Ke5, Rb7, h8, Ktd4, d7, Bb6, g6; Bl. Ke7, Re8, Qg7, Bf7. Mate in II exactly. 1 Rc7; 2 Kt × Q or Ktf6 or Ktc6 or Ktf5 m. accordingly.

L 290. Wh. Kg7, Rc6, d4, Ktd6, e5, Qc8, Ba5, g6; Bl. Kd8, Rf4, Qb4, Be7, f5, Pc5. Mate in II exactly. Bf5 is fidated. 1 Re4; 2 Ktb7 or Kt(e5)f7 m. accordingly.

L 291. Wh. Kb5, Rf7, Qc6, Pc5; Bl. Ka8, Ktc8, Bb8, d5, Pb2, b4, d6. Mate in III exactly. Rf7 is fidated from the K, Qc6 is fidated from all, and all the Ps play to the 8th row. 1 Qb7+; 2 Rf1; 3 P × Kt or Ra1 m. accordingly.

L 292. Wh. Kd6, Ra4, h8, Kte5, f8; Bl. Kd8 (and e1), Ra8, c8, Bc6, e6. Mate in II. The MS. solution, 1 R × R; 2 Kt × B(e6) m. is foiled by 1 . . , Bg8. The problem is unsound.

L 293. Wh. Ke7, Rb8, g3, Ktf8, Qf6, f7, Bf5; Bl. Kh8, Rb6, Kte5, Pb7 going to a7. Black plays and White mates in II exactly. Unsound. No solution but 1 . . , Ra6 is intended, and is sufficient.

L 294. Wh. Kf6, Rc6, d7, Ktd6, e6, Bb5, h6; Bl. Ke8, Ra6, c7, Ktc8, h8, Bf7, f8. No text. L 295 is blank.

L 296. A variant of CB 185 var. 2 (omit Be3; Wh. Kts on h5, h6).

L 297. Wh. Kc7, Rf8, h8, Ktb8, e4, Bc5, Qf5, Pe6; Bl. Ka8, Rb1, c1, Bg4, Pb4. Mate in II exactly. Unsound. 1 R~, P × B; 2 Ktc6+, Rb8. Variation: Pb4 on b2. Now sound. 1 R~, R × B+; 2 Ktc6 m.

Ad. 64 is not contained in any other CB MSS. Wh. Kf6, Rd1, h6, Ph7; Bl. Kh8, Rh1, Kte7, Qd8, Bf2. Mate in III exactly. 1 R × Q+, Ktg8+; 2 P × Kt = Q+, R × R+; 3 Qb6 m.

Ricc. 47, without diagram, has text: 'Li bianchi traghono prima e materano li neri in sette tratti chola pedona pigniendo. Trai i rocho nell' A e l'altro nel B e dà gli ischacho; ed e' torna de l'altro, li dà ischacho nel D, ed eli andrà nel E, e tu trai il pedone chom' è usato il primo trato, e eli andià nel' efe (i. e. F), e tu trai i' rocho nel G e del chavaliere nela H, e del pedone gli dà' matto nel K.'

Ricc. 48. Wh. Kf2, Qg2, Bh5; Bl. Kh2, Ph6. Mate in XIV or less (1 Bf3; 2 Bd5; 3 Bb3; 4 Qf1; 5 Qe2; 6 Bd1; 7 Kg3; 8 Bf3; 9 Bh1; 10 Kf2; and the Q mates in two more) is a setting of F 306.

Leon contains four positions that are not taken from the CB work.

Leon 63 (105). Wh. Kd6, Rc7; Bl. Kd8, is a variant of CB 207 with the same conditions, but no number of moves. Leon has, as variations: I The first check to be mate; unsound. II Kd6 on c6; mate in XI. III Rd8 on e8; mate in XII.

Leon 64 (106) is a problem of modern chess, see p. 802, below.

Leon 102 (124). Wh. Kb6, Qc6, Bg2; Bl. Kb8, Ph8 going to a8. Mate in XIII or less, Black being obliged to play his K whenever he can. This is another setting of F 306. The solution is finished in Italian. The solution involves staling Black for a move (1 Qb7; 2–5 Be4, g6, e4, g6; 6 Qa6; 7 Be8; 8 Qb5; 9 Kc7; 10 Bc6; 11 Ba4; 12 Kb6; 13 *matto col chaluo* (B). A concluding note appears to indicate the F solution, sacrificing B on a8, and mating *dalla ferça*.

Leon 129 (125). A variant of F 304 (omit Be6; colours changed; F 304 var. is text, F 304 variation).

APPENDIX

I. The Latin Preface to the Bonus Socius Work.

(Text from MS. Florence, B. A. 6, p. 2, No. 1 (BS). collated with MS. Paris, Lat., 10286 (PL)).

Protoplausti [1] rubigine humana condicio sic cellule memoriales eclipsatur officio ut perdat quod non sepe prospicit uel iugiter meditatur. Quin ymo sicut de pertuso sacculo [2] aliunde excidit quod emittitur aliunde sic profecto quod per unam aurem ingeritur per alteram egeritur absque mora ut accedat quod legitur De Penitentia. dist. iiij. De Pertuso [3] et De Consequenti. dist. v. ne tales vers: unde et morbus. Quoniam omnium habere memoriam & penitus in nullo [4] peccare est potius [5] diuinitatis quam humanitatis ut c. De uetere iure [6] Enu. 1. ij. § Si quis autem.

Idcirco ego bonus socius sociorum [7] meorum precibus acquiescens [8] partita que uideram queque per studium de nouo [9] inueneram tam de ludis scacorum,[10] alearum, quam etiam marrelorum [11] in hoc libello redigere procuraui: ut per istorum doctrinam et exercitium de aliis que possent fieri noticia facilius habeatur. Omne enim ingenium per exercitium recipit incrementum ut ff. De Legatis, 1. legatis, § ornatricibus. Porro quoniam nil perfectum in humanis adinuentionibus [12] reperitur. ut c. De ueteri iure [6] Enu. 1. ij. § Set quia diuine. Idcirco super operis imperfectionem [13] veniam imploro deuote supplicans omnibus dominis meis socijs & amicis ad quos peruenerit presens opus ut ipsum benigne suscipiant et lima correctionis emendent que correctione nouerint indigere.[14] Actum &c.

Sequitur capitula boni socii sociorum et primo de partitis scilicet scacorum qui ad secundum tractum fiunt.

[1] Prothoplausti. [2] scaculo. [3] partuso. [4] in nullo penitus. [5] potius est. [6] uirtute. [7] ego N. de N. (*margin*, Nicolaus de Nicolai). [8] adquiescens. [9] de nouo per studium. [10] *add* &. [11] merellorum. [12] inuentionibus. [13] inspectionem. [14] PL *ends here.*

II. The Introductions to the French Translations of the Bonus Socius Work. 1. From MS. Wolfenbüttel. Extrav. 118 fl.

La Conditions humaine est tornee en tel defaut de memoire par le pechie et par la inobedience de nostre primerain pere que de legier elle pert ce que elle ne uoit souuent ou par iex ou par pensee. Quel merueille: Ce qui est mis en sac percie entre par .i. lieu et ist par lautre. Et ainsi sanz doute ce qui entre en entendement de home par une oreille sen ist par lautre. si comme il est escript ii decre. ii tistre De penitentia. Et la quatre distinction. ii chapitre qui se commence. De percusso. et ii tistre. De consecratione. en la quinte distinction. ii chapistre qui se commence Ne tales. ii uerset. Unde et morbus. Car toutes choses auoir en memoire sanz pechier ou errer en aucunes ne partient pas a home. Mes a dieu. Si comme il est ii code. en la rebriche de ueteri iure. Enucleando. en la seconde loy ou parragreffe. Si quis autem.

Et pour ce Je. N. de N. desirranz encliner aus prieres de mes compaignons Les gieus partiz tant des eschez et des tables quant des merelles. les qieux ie auoie ueuz et trouuez de nouuel par estude ay mis et ramenez en cest liure. A ce qui par la doctrine et la coustumement diceus len puisse auoir plus legiere connoissance des autres gieus qui porraient estre faiz. car par acoustumance recoit tout enging acroissement. Si com il est escript es digestes en la rebriche De legatis primo.

En la loy qui se commence. Legatis. ii parragreffe. Ornatritibus. Et toute uoies pour ce que nulle chose trouuee de home nest parfaite: si comme il apert ii code en la rebriche de ueteri iure. enucleando. en la loy seconde ii paragreffe. Sed quia diuine. Pour ce se aucune imperfections est en ceste oeure: ie en requier pardon deuotement. en priant et souppliant humblement a touz mes seignours compaignons et amis en cui mains ce present liure uendra que debonnairement le uueillent receuoir. Et se aucune chose y uoient a corrigier que il le corrigent et amendent par lime. non pas de enuie mes de debonnaire et amiable correption.

2. From MS. Paris, F. Fr. 1173, f. 2 (PP).

On dist es prouerbes anciens ke mal est science emploiie en cuer auariscieus du monstrer. car chascuns ki mix set se doit traueillier a chou ke il puist les autres enseignier. Et por chou ke ie ne vauroie iestre repris de si vilain pechiet comme dauarise. Jou nicholes de St nicholai clers a laude de chelui ki est fontaine de sapience vous. vueu enseignier et demonstrer une partie du sentement de mon cuer et especiaument sor li gieu des eskies et premiers coument par cui ne en quel lieu il fu trouves premierement. En apres de la maniere du gieu et des assises et comment il puet iestre abregies par partures. Sachiez kil fu trouves au siege de troie la grant par .i. ch'r sage et hardi et par une dame la quele estoit sa chiere amee car li ch'rs et la dame se seoient en .i. vergi et dehors les murs de la cite et regardoient comment chil de dehors requeroient chiaus de dedans et comment cil de dedans les recheuoient et se deffendoient uigueureusement et comment il prendoient et desconfisoient li vn les autres et li plus grant les plus petis, et li plus fort les plus febles et comparerent leur gieu selonc lordenement ke il (f. 2 b) auoient veu es assaus et es batailles. Et apres che ke la cites fu destruite li ch'rs et la dame repairierent en lor paiis. con apiele lombardie. et fu li gieus espandus par tout le paiis de coi vous faites et veoir le poes apertement ke lombart sont li plus sage et li plus soutil de cel gieu ki soient. Si ke por le soutillece de cel gieu le doiuent desirer a sauoir toute gentil gent et doiuent metre diligaument lor estude et especiaument amant par amors car damour damant et dame vint il premierement. Mais pour chou ke li humaine conditions est oscurchie en l'offisse de le celle memoratiue par l'empeechement de nostre premier pere si ke le pert legierement chou ke le ne voit ou pense assidueument. Jou nicholes deuant dis demourans en lombardie a le priere et a le requeste de mes compaignons ai compilet che liuret de partures ke iai escrit par men estude dou gieu des eschies et des taules et des merelles. Et por chou ke nule chose ne puet iestre parfaite je depri a mes segneurs mes amis et mes compaignons as quels chis presens liures sera parvenus sour imperfection de ceste oeure ke il le uueillent deboinairement rechevoir et corriger saucune chose iest trouuee ki ait mestier de correction.

(The two following sections of the introduction to this MS. have been quoted already, viz. in Ch. III, App. II and IV, pp. 489, 495.)

III. Introduction to MS. Florence, Bibl. Nat. XIX. 7. 37 (F).

(f. 4 b, new foliation).

Dicebat meus magister quod in primis partitis debemus de modico ludere et perdere et sic etiam in conflictu ludi debemus aliquando perdere quia ex hoc homines inducuntur ad ludendum sed hac cautela nunquam fui usus.

Vt autem caute ludas nec possis perdere est considerandum ut scias concludentis secreta circa que dantur plures cautele. prima est: Certum est quod partitum bonum non debet esse id quod apparet sed eius oppositum. Vnde tu ponas illam partem scaccorum que habet peius et uidetur habere melius a latere tuo. Nam tunc si ipse nescit partitum tam melius partitum persecutandi reuoluet scacherium. Licet hoc multi non faciunt, et ideo non est enumeranda certa.

Alia cautela est quod in principio fingas te non recordari de partito, et ideo ponas scaccos aliter quam debent esse, sepe in principio recitando et tandem pones illos ut debes. Hoc in casu si sibi uidebitur aliquis tractus occurrere de facili cogitabit te non recordari de partito, et ideo ludet. Et tu si cognoueris ipsum partem bonam eligere, dices antequam ludam uolo uidere facta mea, et poteris adicere aliquem per quod mutabis totum partitum et sudes, ceterum non deberem ludere quia quasi feci magnum errorem, non enim bene posueram partitum. (f. 5 a) Et ipse non poterit de te conqueri quia ab inicio credidit te ignorare partitum. Si autem iterum uellet capere bonam partem, iterum obseruabis supra dicta, diceres te nolle ludere quia non recordaris; et sic destrues partitum et facies aliud uel obseruabis aliquam cautelam de .7. ponendis.

Cautus eciam existas et consideres numquid uoce tremulenta partitum capiat. Item numquid modica cogitatione. Item numquid sit paratus multas pecunias ponere. Item si uoluit capere alia partita facta. Item si nollet capere partita facienda. Nam haec omnia demonstrant quod ipse scit partitum uel ignorat.

Est et alia cautela que appellatur aurea que taliter operatur quod cogit concludentem eligere partem deteriorem et fit taliter. Tu scis quod partitum bonum non debet esse id quod appareat sed eius oppositum. Dicas ergo quod pars que uidetur habere melius ponit duplum pecuniarum: nam ex hoc solo nisi caute ludat cogetur antequam ponatis pecuniam dicere quam partem uult ipse. Nam tu interrogabis numquid velit te ponere duplum uel simplum, et ex hoc habebis quam partem eligat. Et ita quidam utuntur hac cautela:

(f. 5 b is blank.)

IV. Some Notes on the Sections on Tables and Merels in the Bonus Socius and Civis Bononiae Works.

I have already in the text given particulars as to the numbers of problems of tables and merels which are included in the various MSS. of the Bonus Socius and Civis Bononiae works. As is the case in the chess section of these works, the Civis Bononiae work gives a more extensive selection of problems in these other games. Very few positions occurring in Bonus Socius are not to be found also in Civis Bononiae, but while the text of the merels section has been entirely rewritten and largely rearranged in CB, that of tables preserves both the sequence and the text of the MSS. of the French group of Bonus Socius MSS.[1] BS itself has substituted a shorter and, as it appears to me, a later selection of problems of tables for that in the MSS. of the French group.

[1] Thus PL 1–34, 36–38, 39–45 = CB 1–34, 36–38, 40–46. The French MSS. are very carelessly copied. Six positions in W (10, 12, 28, 30, 32, 33) have wrong solutions attached; M repeats no fewer than twelve problems (M 1–12 = 34–40, and PF repeats four (PF 23–26 = 27–30).

Under the name of *tables* are included a number of games on the backgammon-board, all played in practically the same way with the help of dice, and only differing in the initial arrangement, the points of re-entry and of home, and in the number of and method of using the dice. The majority of the problems are of a game called *texta* or *testa*, and in the French MSS. *le teste* or *tieste*, which required three dice. Other games named are *barail* (*sbarail, baril*, rarely in Fr. MSS. *barat*), *imperial*, *baldrac*, *bethelas*, *la buf*, *la linpole* (in M 10 only), and *minoret*. Some of these names occur in the sections on tables in Alf. and K. Minoret may simply refer to a method of using the dice, *facere minoret* (*majoret*) being the technical term for doubling the throw of the lower (higher) of two dice when only two are used (see CB 39, 74), in order to secure the effect of a third die.

At first sight, a dice-game does not appear very suitable for the composition of problems. The difficulty was surmounted by permitting the player to select his throws, or by imagining an invariable throw. Games of this kind were called *optativi* (Fr. *par souhaits*, *souhaidans*, or *a souhaidier*). There are, however, also a number of problems in which the free use of the dice is allowed; these become mathematical problems in probabilities. Thus the CB text commences:

> Ista sunt partita tabularum quae dupliciter fiunt, scilicet, optando cum lingua et proiciendo taxillos. Primo dicitur de optatiuis, id est de illis que optantur siue petuntur cum ore.

The merels problems are all of the nine men's morris, or larger merels, the board containing no diagonals. The difficulty of notation is avoided by using a variety of forms—circles, squares, triangles (shields), stars, crosses—for the merels. Some of the problems are very ingenious, and I think that they leave a more favourable impression of the ingenuity of the mediaeval composer than is the case with the problems of chess or tables.

CHAPTER VIII

THE MEDIAEVAL PROBLEM. III

Unclassified and later works.—The Munich MS.—MS. Wolfenbüttel 17, 30. Aug. 4.—Köbel's *Schachtzabel-Spiel*.—Janot's *Sensuit Jeux Partis des Eschez*.—MS. Florence XIX. 11. 87.—The Sorbonne MS.—The Casanatense MS.—Mediaeval problems in the early works of modern chess.

We have not yet exhausted the problem-material which has survived from the mediaeval period, and it is necessary to devote a third chapter to the description of a number of MSS. whose place in the development of the problem literature is less evident, or which belong to the closing years of the older game. I begin with a number of smaller collections.

Mun. = MS. Munich Lat. 19, 877 (Tegernseensis, 1877).

WA = MS. Wolfenbüttel 17, 30. Aug. 4.

Mun. is a MS. of the 15th c., written in one hand throughout, which contains a number of different treatises by Mauricius, a Doctor of the University of Paris, who lived in the 15th c. and was probably later an inmate of the Benedictine monastery of Tegernsee. Leaves 131–2, 135–8, and 140, which are separated by other treatises, contain a small collection of 26 chess problems (two to the page, except on 133 b and 135 a, the text over the diagram) with Middle-Dutch text. The chess portion has been edited by M. Rottmanner in the *Zeitschrift für deutsches Alterthum* (XXII, Berlin, 1878, 409–21). See also *Qst.*, 211–12.

WA is a quarto paper MS. with German text, which contains (*a*) a collection of 20 chess problems on 10 leaves, one a page; (*b*) a translation of Arthur Saul's *Famous Game of Chesse play* (London, 1614) on 26 leaves. The problem MS. was written *c.* 1600, and as it makes no reference to the older game being obsolete at the time, it must be one of the latest survivals of the older game. We know from Selenus that the old chess was still played at Ströbeck in 1617. The diagrams in this MS. are chequered green and white

Rook and Pawn, from MS. WA.

(h1 is white in WA 1, 3, 7, 10, 14, 16, 17, 20 only), and the pieces are represented pictorially, the King, Queen, Bishop, and Knight being drawn as king, queen, sage or judge, and gentleman, from waist upwards only showing; the Rook as a mediaeval Rook, but with the two wings shaped as horses' heads;[1] the Pawns as pillars.

The problems in Mun. will be found as follows in the CB collection:

Mun. 1 = CB *196*; 2 = CB *200*; 3 = CB *124*; 4 = CB *136*; 5 = CB *50*; 6 = CB 52; 7 = CB *185*; 8 = CB *98*; 9 = CB *197*; 10 = CB *73*; 11 = CB *83*; 12 = CB *25*; 13 = CB *75*; 14 = CB *116*; 15 = CB *97*; 16 = CB 147; 17 = CB 152; 18 = CB *158*; 19 = CB *162*; 20 = CB *163*; 21 = CB *180*; 22 = CB *179*; 23 = CB *211*; 24 = CB 279; 25 = CB *142*; 26 = CB 216.

(In Mun. 1, 4, 6, 9, 14, 16, 18, 20, and 25, the colours are the reverse of those in the corresponding positions in CB.)

The contents of WA are as follows:

WA 1 = CB *185*; 2 = CB 136; 3 = CB *152*; 4 = CB *98*; 5 = CB *83*; 6 = CB *98*; 7 = F *331*; 8 = CB *73*; 9 = CB *25*; 10 = CB *216*; 11 = CB *75*; 12 = CB *117* (Rb8 on d8, reflect: Die Schwartzen ziehent vor, vndt matten die weissen am vierten Zug. Die Alten sollen vorgehe, ein Ritter soll ein Ross erstossen, durch einer Jungfrawen willen, ein Knab der soll springen, ein Ritter soll ein Jungfraw gewinnen—a curious reminiscence of a problem legend); 13 = CB *15*; 14 = CB *158*; 15 = CB *147*; 16 = CB *124*; 17 = CB *180*; 18 = CB *141*; 19 Wh. Kb8, Rg1, g6, Bc8, Pe6; Bl. Kc6, Rb2, Ktc5, Pb5, b6. Die Schwartzen zeuch vor, den Ritter in das A (d7), den schwartzen Venden inn das B (b7), den andern in das C (b6), den schwartzen Ritter in das E (c5), mitt den Roch matte in an dem fünfften Zug. Cf. Ar. 22; 20 = CB *113*.

(In WA 2, 14, 15, the colours are the reverse of those in the corresponding positions in CB.)

These two small collections have no fewer than 13 positions in common, and the inaccuracies of the diagrams—both MSS. are very corrupt in this respect—point to a definite relationship. The collation of the diagrams and

[1] The same form of Rook occurs in the arms of the German town of Rochlitz, and (according to Randle Holme, *Academy of Armory* (Roxburghe Club, 1905), vol. ii, bk. iii, § 2,

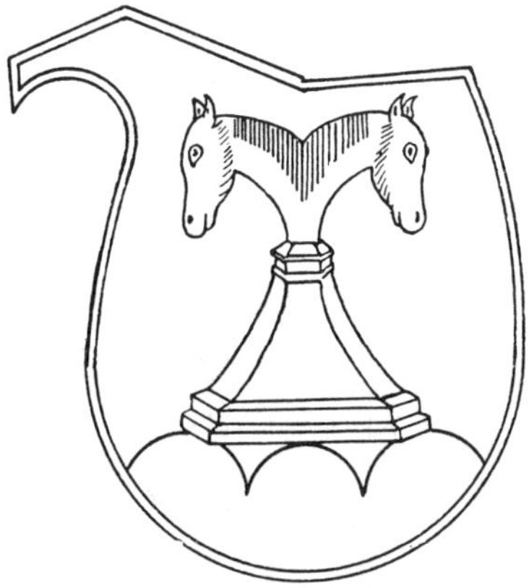

Arms of Rochlitz

(Massmann, 80.)

Rooks from Randle Holme

p. 87) in the arms of the Bavarian families of Loch and Hinderskircher. Selenus pictures the *Knight* in the same way on the title-page to his first book.

texts with the standard collections shows that neither MS. can be attached to *Bonus Socius* or to *Civis Bononiae*. Mun. has, perhaps, more resemblances to the former work, but the text varies to a far greater extent than is the case with any of the MSS. described in the preceding chapter. WA, on the other hand, contains two positions which belong to neither BS nor CB, though one of them (WA 7) occurs among the additional material which is added to the CB work in F.

Apart from the value of these MSS. as showing a still wider popularity of the problem than has as yet been shown, the most interesting feature in the two MSS. is the solution to the Dilārām position WA 12, which seems to suggest that there was a story attached to this problem.

Köbel = Jakob Köbel's *Schachtzabel Spiel*, Oppenheim, n. d., but *c.* 1520, which contains 7 problems which are also contained in Egenolff's reprint of 1536, with the title—

> Nun volgenn etlich geordente künstliche streitzüg vnd spil dardurch sich die Schachzieher üben sollen das Ritterlich spil des Schachs desto fürderlicher zu lernen vnd begreiffen,

and were finally included in Selenus (1617) as *Etliche Exempel des alten Schaches* (IV. x. 433).

The positions are not diagrammed, but are described with the help of Köbel's peculiar notation (see p. 490), and the players are described as the first player and the opponent, except in No. 3, where the first player is White, the second Black. The opponent (here Black) wins in every case—another instance of the mediaeval preference for the Black pieces. The problems follow:

Köbel 1.

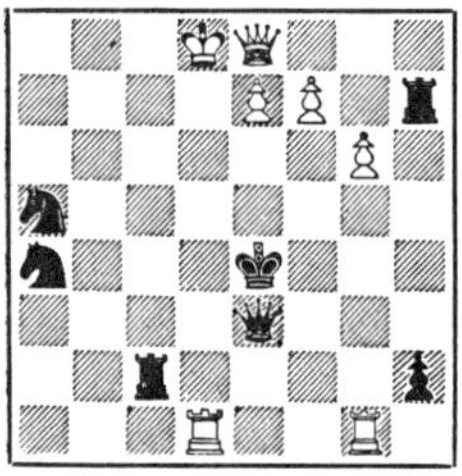

(Bl.)
Black mates in VII with Ph2.

Köbel 2.

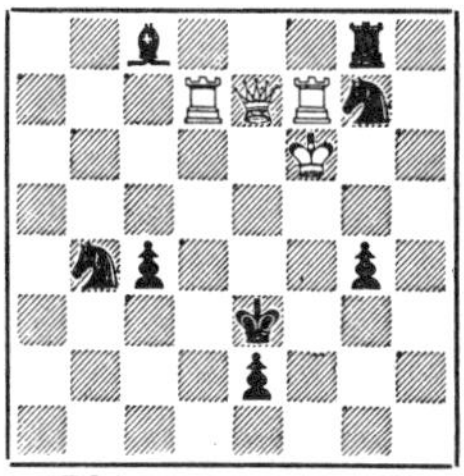

(Bl.)
Black mates in IV (really V) with Pe2.

Köbel 4.

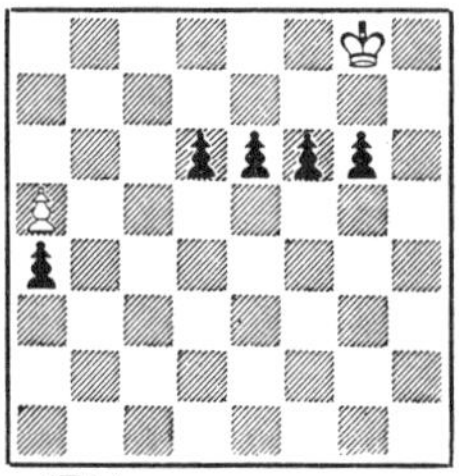

(Bl.)
Black mates in XII on f8 or h8.

Köbel 5.

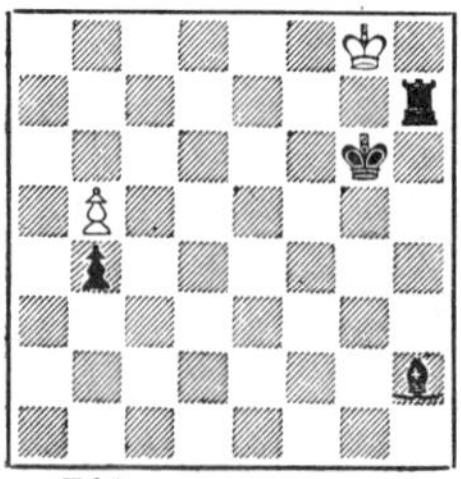

(Bl.)
Black mates in XVII with Pb4.

Köbel 6.

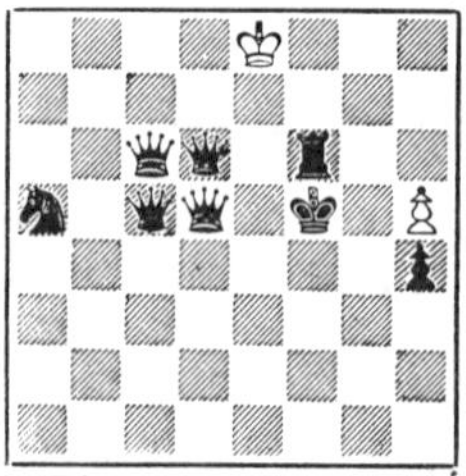

(Bl.)
Black mates in V.

Köbel 7.

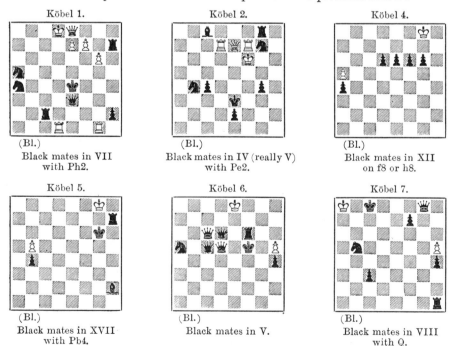

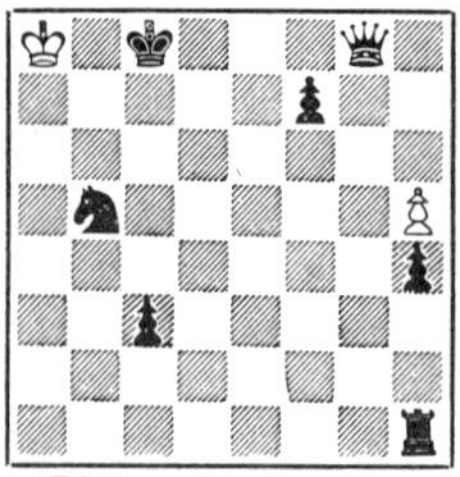

(Bl.)
Black mates in VIII with Q.

SOLUTIONS

1. 1 Ktb7 +; 2 Ktb6 +; 3 Rc6 +, Rd6; 4 Ktd8 +, 5 Ktd7 +; 6 Qf5 +; 7 Ph3 m.

2. Egenolff says, 'Der König auff *ch* (f6). sol Matt werden am fierden zug / mit dem Fenden der stat auff *gl* (e2)', and solves 1 Kte8 +; 2 Rg5 +, Rf5; 3 Ktd3 +, R × Kt +; 4 P × R vnnd sprich Matt; but another move (5Pd4 m.) is necessary, and Selenus accordingly describes the problem as mate in III with R (by 3 R × R m.), or mate in V with Pe2.

3. Wh. Ka8, Bc8; Bl. Kb6, Rg7, h7, Bh6; Black mate in XVII on a8; the Bl. B being immovable. This is a variant of CB 219. The solution begins 1 Ra7 +; 2 Kc6; 3 hRb7 +; 4 Rb3, B~; 5 Rc7 +; 6 Rd3 +; 7 cRd7, B~; 8 Kd6, B~; 9 Re3 +, and the position is now practically that of the CB solution at move 7.

4. 1 Pe7; 2 Pd7; 3 Pd8 = Q; 4 Qc7; 5 Qd6; 6 Qe5; 7 Qf4; 8 Qg5; 9 Qh6; 10 Pe8 = Q; 11 Qf7; 12 Qg7 m.

5. 1 Bf4; 2 Rg7; 3 Rf7; 4 Kf6; 5 Ke6; 6 Re7; 7 Rd7; 8 Kd6; 9 Kc6; 10 Rc7; 11 Kb6; 12 Bd6 +; 13 Rc4; 14 Ka6; 15 Pb5; 16 Pb6; 17 Pb7 m. The idea is that of CB 193, 208, 251, 252, &c.

6. 1 Q(c5)d4; 2 Q(c6)d7; 3Rf8; 4 Rf7; 5 Rd7 m. This is really CB 133. The title (Der König auff *ae* sol am fünfften zug Matt sein vnnd seind die vier Fenden vier frawen die bei ein stand) shows that Köbel used a MS. in which the diagram had 4 Ps for the Qs.

7. 1 Ktd6; 2 Ra1 +; 3 Kd7; 4 Kc7; 5 Ra5 +; 6 Rf5; 7 Pf8 = Q +; 8 Qf7 m.

Here again we have no indication as to the source used by Köbel. With the exception of Köbel 3, none of these seven positions occurs in exactly the same form anywhere else, and four of them are unique. The most interesting point about the collection is the title, which puts forward the educational value of the problem as the reason for its inclusion in Köbel's book.[2]

Sens. = *Sensuit Ieux Partis des eschez: Composez nouuellement Pour recrer tous nobles cueurs et pour euiter oysiuete a ceulx qui ont voulente: disir et affection de le scauoir et aprendre et est appelle ce Liure le ieu des princes et damoiselles. Nouellement imprime a Paris.*

A small quarto printed work of 12 unnumbered leaves (A i – C iv), of which only a single copy, now in the Vienna Library, is known.[3] It was printed by Denis Janot the younger, who was printing in Paris, 1530–40. A blank board on the title-page is chequered black and red (h1 red), and the reverse of this page has a board arranged for play, the red men on lines 1 and 2 (Kd1), the black on lines 7 and 8. Throughout, the White pieces are printed in black, the Red in red, and are represented by their names (*Roy*, *dame*, *fol*, *chl'*, *roc*, *pion*). The 21 problems are as follows:

Sens. 1 = CB *11*; 2 = CB 149; 3 = CB 162; 4 = CB *117*; 5 = CB *152*; 6 Wh. Kb6, Rd7, a2, Kta5; Red, Ka8, Rc8; In II ex. by 1 Rd8, R × R (or Rb8 +; 2 Ktb7 m.); 2 Ktc6 m. The MS. ignores the second solution by 1 Ktb3 or c4;

[2] To these examples Selenus adds (1) the problem Wh. Rc5, e5, Ktc3, e3; Bl. Kd4. Mate in IV. 1 eKtd1; 2 Ktb1; 3 Kta3; 4 cRd5 m.; (2) the so-called Fool's Mate in the modern game.

[3] The Vienna copy was in England at the close of the 18th c. In a catalogue issued by Robert Triphook of 23 Old Bond St., London, I find the entry, 'No. 350. *Sensuit Jeux Partis.* £5 5*s*. 1528. I do not know of another copy.'

2 Rb7. Cf. F 324; 7 = Picc. *20*; 8 = CB *1*; 9 = CB *47*; 10 Wh. Ke6, Ra7, h7; Bl. Ke8; In III ex. by 1 Re7 +; 2 Re8 +; &c.; 11 = PL *72*; 12 = CB *53*; 13 corr. Wh. Kd1, Ra1, h1, Ktb1, g1, Bc1, f1, Pa2, b3, c3, d2, e2, f3, g3, h2; Red, Kg5, Ra8, h8, Ktb4, c4, Bc8, f8, Qf5, 8 Ps on 7th row: In V. A shortened version of CB 185; 14 = CB 268; 15 = CB *147*; 16 = CB *217*; 17 = CB *185*; 18 = CB 244; 19 = CB *211*; 20 = CB *208*; 21 = CB 209.

The colours are reversed from CB except in Sens. 5, 19–21.

This work is an extract from a collection which was in part based upon the CB work.

I now turn to three MSS. which are in the main independent of the BS and CB works, and are in consequence of greater interest. Two of these were written in Italy, the third in France. The first is—

Picc.[4] = MS. Nat. Lib. Florence, XIX. 11, 87.

A parchment Latin MS. of the 15th c., formerly in the Magliabecchian Library, which consists of 88 24mo leaves (1–27, 27*, 28–48, 48*, 49–86; the foliation is modern), and contains 172 diagrams of chess problems on ff. 1 a – 84 b, and 3 blank diagrams on 85 and 86 a. A later hand has added the title *Regole del giuoco degli Scacchi*. The MS. has no introduction, and nothing to show its authorship or history. Only 41 problems in this MS. are to be found in the CB and BS collections, and in no case is the text to the solution identical. The compiler would seem to have first collected his diagrams, and to have added original solutions later. His solutions are briefer than those in any other MS., and are devoid of any literary style; they look more like rough notes. In order to elucidate the solutions the compiler has added symbols, such as ȯ, ♀, ⊖, Φ, ⊥, L, o-, ǂ, ⊔, Π, ♀-, ⱴ, V, to denote particular squares where the mediaeval MSS. usually employ letters.[5] Another peculiarity is the noting of the number of pieces employed above each diagram, thus to Picc. 10 is the note *Scak tresdecim*.[6] It was the compiler's intention to arrange his material by the number of moves in the solutions, but for some reason the arrangement has been abandoned in part towards the end of the MS.;[7] the majority of his positions are in II and III moves, and there are only 13 problems of VII moves and over. The Muslim element in the MS. is very small, and practically confined to the positions which the MS. has in common with CB. To a large number of problems the side-note *mentitur* is added, to show that the position is without solution. The use of this term is peculiar to this MS., BS and CB using either *non fit* or *fieri non potest*. The compiler had a decided preference for non-checking first moves, and the solutions of 43 out of 55 problems in II moves begin without a check. He was also fond of symmetrical arrangements of the pieces. He had no more feeling for possibility than any other

[4] For *Piccolo*, the name by which v. d. Lasa called this work in his letters, from the fact that the MS. has the smallest pages (10·4 cm. by 8·1) of any mediaeval problem MSS.

[5] In Picc. 1, 6, 7 the writer has used letters in the place of his symbols.

[6] In a few cases the note is wanting, and in a few more the number does not agree with the number in the diagram. The number then becomes of importance in correcting the mistake made by the writer in copying the diagram.

[7] Picc. 1–54, 131 are in II; 55–129 in III; 130, 133–43 in IV; 153–68, 172 in V; 144–6, 169, 170 in VI; 147–9 in VII, 150 in VIII, 152 in XI, 151 in XII, 132 in XXIII, 171 in *n* moves.

composer of his time. On the whole, his collection strikes me as more interesting than either BS or CB, but one does not come away from it with a high idea of the compiler's skill. In 20 problems his solution is wrong, and in 33 I have noted second solutions which had escaped his attention. Four solutions are unintelligible, possibly from errors in the diagrams.

The pieces are denoted by *R*, *f*, *al'*, *eq*^{us} (in earlier problems also *e*), *r*, *P*, and in the solutions by *rex*, *fercia*, *alphinus*, *equus*, *rocus*, *pedona*. Once (Picc. 59) the Kt appears on the diagram as *ch'r*, and once (Picc. 40) the Rook is called *rector* in a solution. Probably Picc. 59 was obtained from a French collection; the ordinary use of *equus* points to Italy as the home of the compiler.

The problems now follow:

Picc. 2.

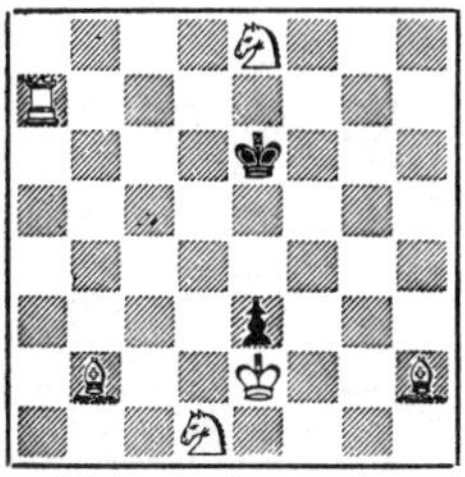

Mate in II exactly.

Picc. 3 (corr.).

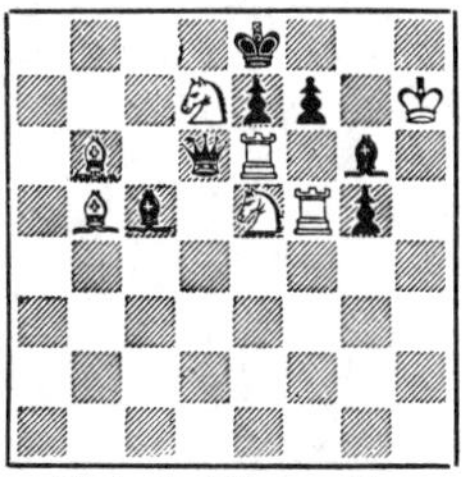

Mate in II exactly.

Picc. 6.

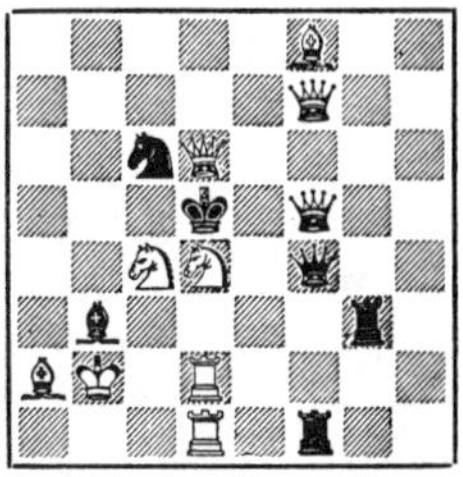

Mate in II exactly.
Unsound.

Picc. 7 (corr.).

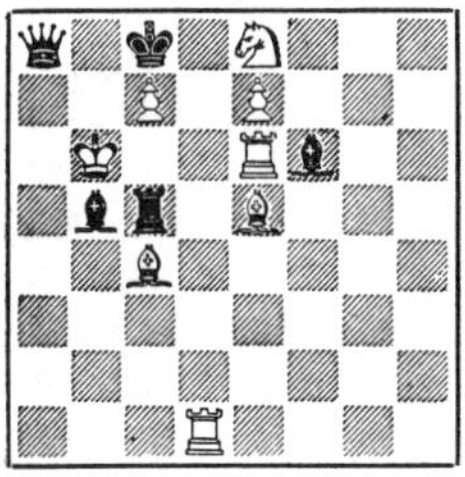

Mate in II exactly.
Rc5 is fidated.
Said to be unsound.

Picc. 8 (corr.).

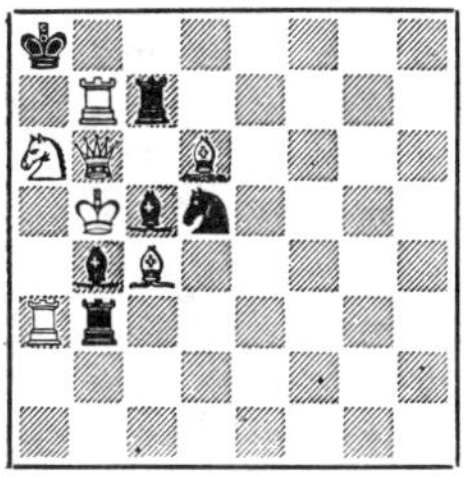

Mate in II exactly.

Picc. 9.

Mate in II exactly.

Picc. 10.

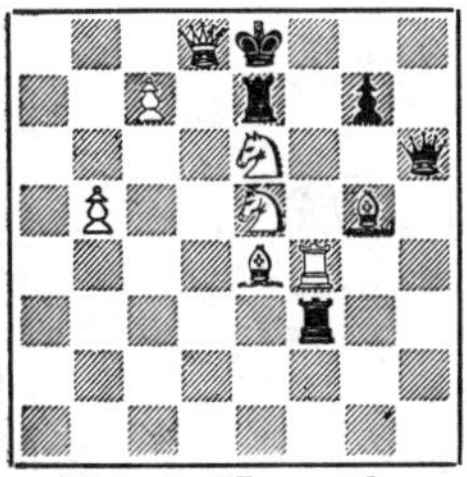

Mate in II exactly.

Picc. 11.

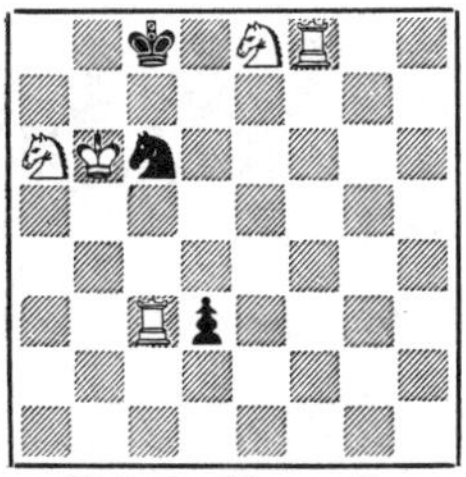

Mate in II exactly.
Unsound.

Picc. 13 = 50.

(Bl.)
Mate in II exactly.
Qc8 and Bf5 are fidated.

Picc. 15.

Mate in II exactly.
Unsound.

Picc. 17.

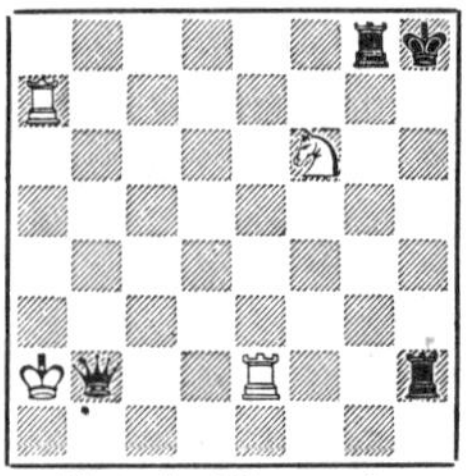

Mate in II exactly.
Re2 is fidated. Unsound.

Picc. 19 = 46.

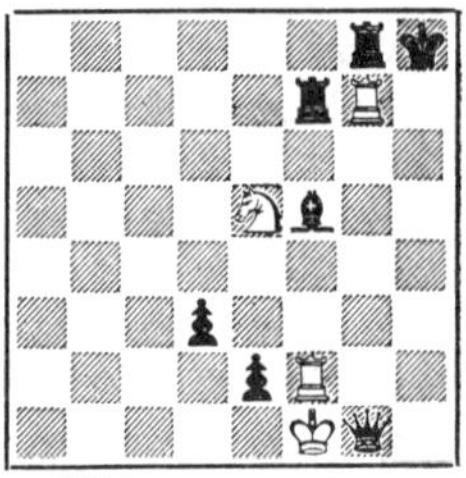

(Bl.)
Mate in II exactly.
Rg7 is fidated. Unsound.

Picc. 20 (corr.) = 23 (corr.).

(Bl.)
Mate in II exactly.

Picc. 21 (corr.) = 47.

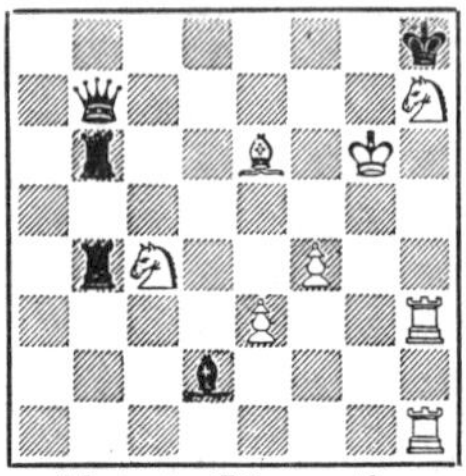

Mate in II exactly.

Picc. 26 = 48.

(Bl.)
Mate in II exactly.

Picc. 29 (corr.).

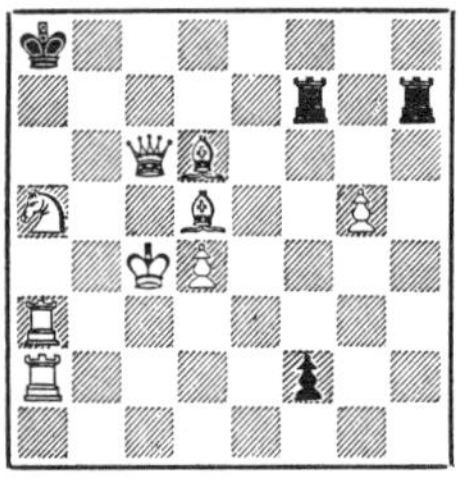

Mate in II exactly.

Picc. 30.

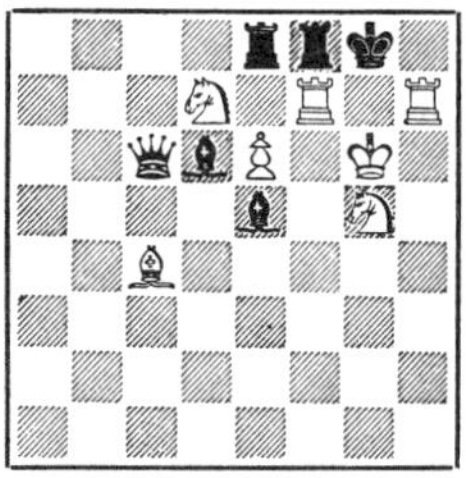

Mate in II exactly.

Picc. 33 (corr.).

Mate in II exactly.

Picc. 34 (corr.).

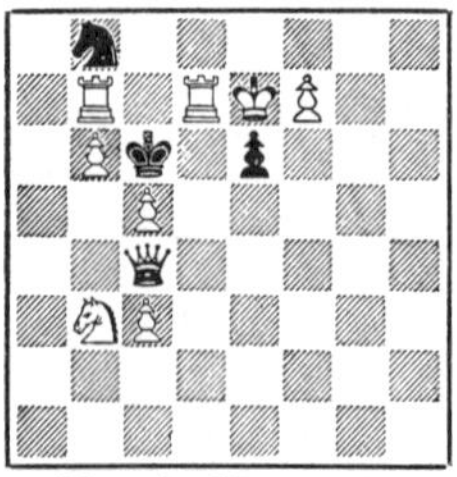

Mate in II exactly.
Unsound.

Picc. 36.

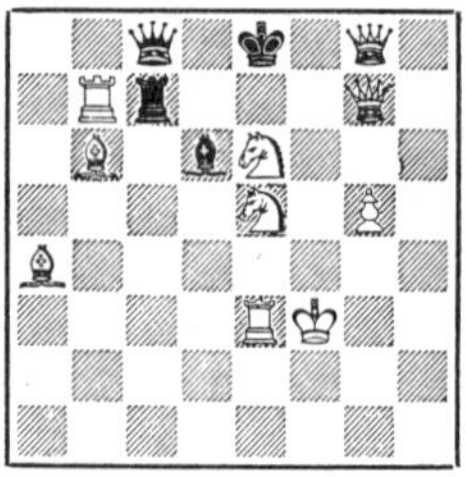

Mate in II exactly.

Picc. 41.

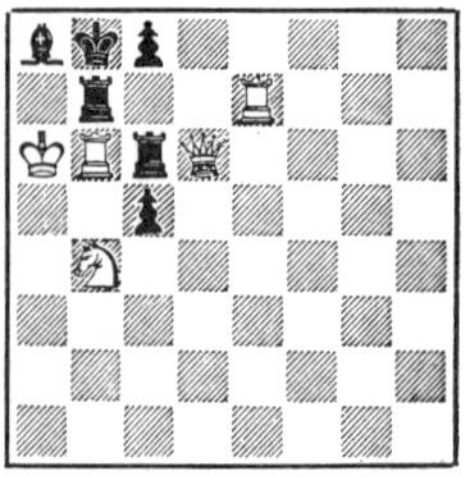

Mate in II exactly.
Kt is fidated.

Picc. 56.

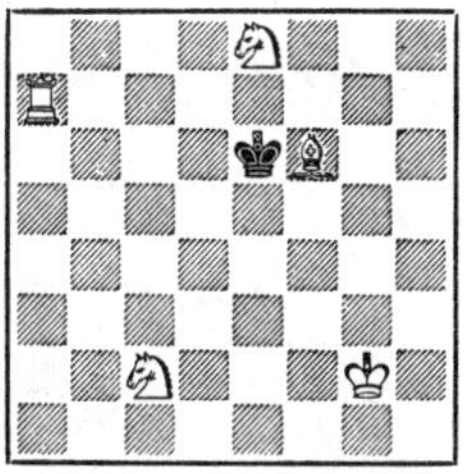

Mate in III exactly.

Picc. 57.

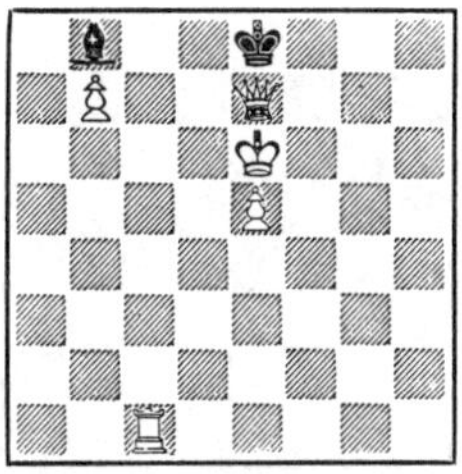

Mate in III exactly.

Picc. 59.

Mate in III exactly.

Picc. 60 (corr.).

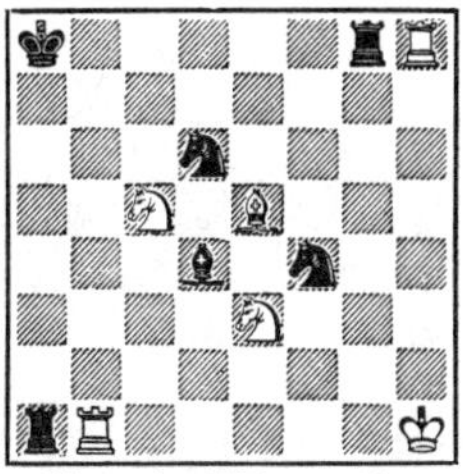

Mate in III exactly.
Unsound.

Picc. 64.

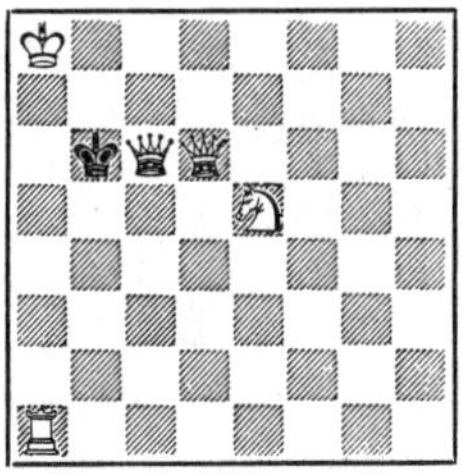

Mate in III exactly.

Picc. 65.

Mate in III exactly.

Picc. 67.

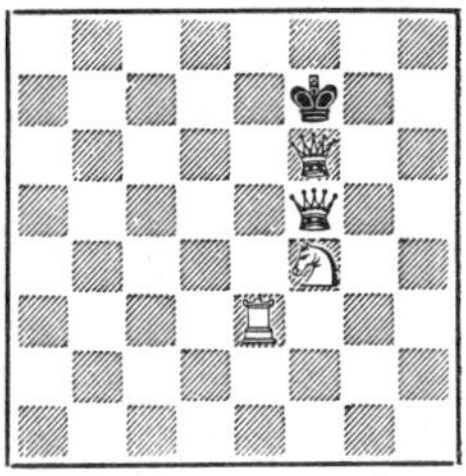

Mate in III exactly.
Unsound.

Picc. 68.

Mate in III exactly.

Picc. 72.

Mate in III exactly.

Picc. 73.

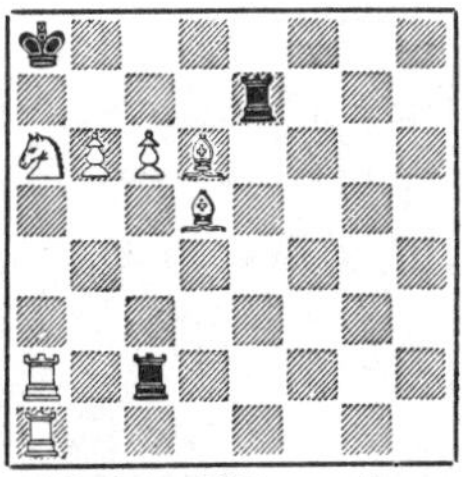

Mate in III exactly.
Unsound.

Picc. 76.

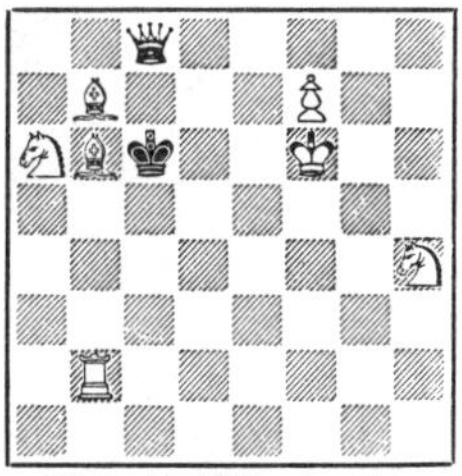

Mate in III exactly.

Picc. 78.

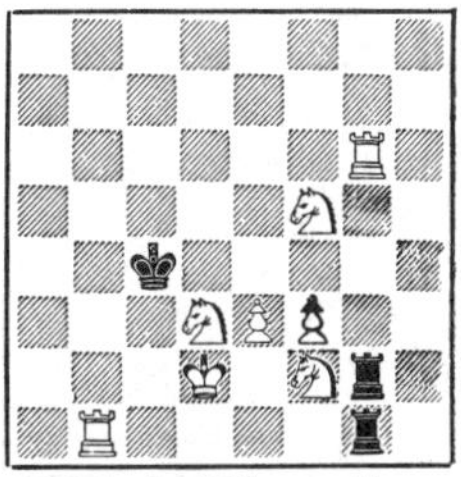

Mate in III exactly.

Picc. 80.

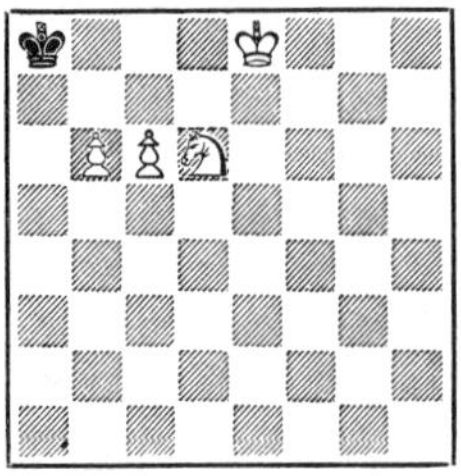

Mate in III exactly.
All the pieces are fidated.

Picc. 82.

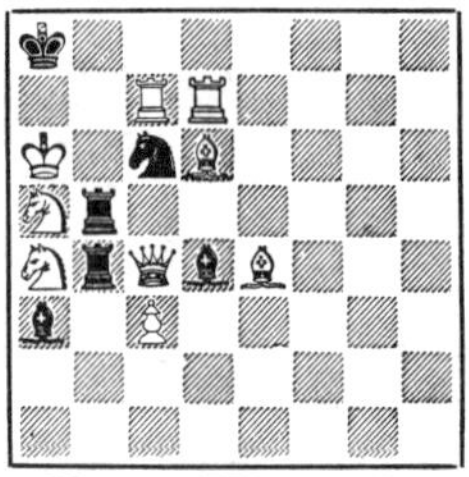

Mate in III exactly.
Unsound.

Picc. 83.

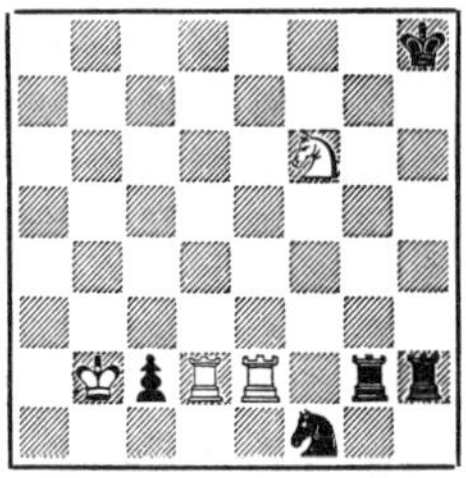

Mate in III exactly.
Re2 is fidated, and Kh8 may not move first move.

Picc. 87.

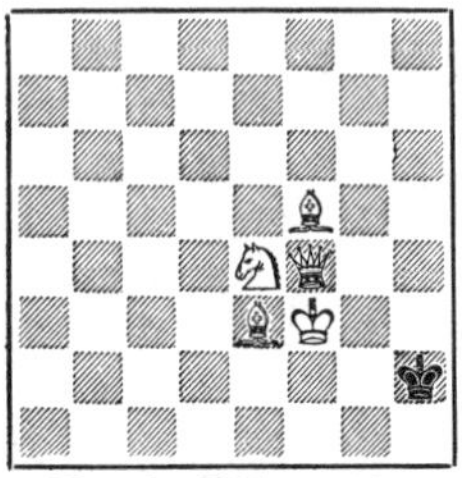

Mate in III exactly.
Unsound.

Picc. 88.

Mate in III exactly.

Picc. 90.

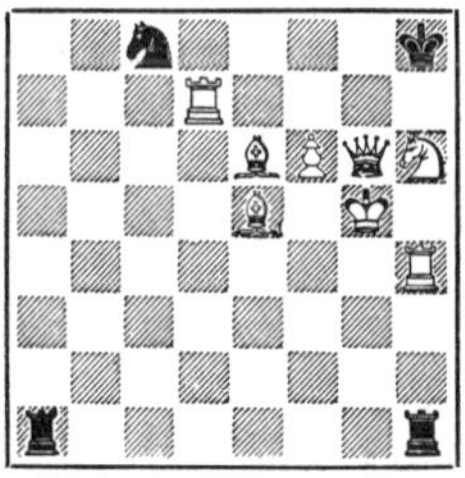

Mate in III exactly.
Unsound.

Picc. 94.

Mate in III exactly.

Picc. 95.

Mate in III exactly.
Unsound.

Picc. 96.

Mate in III exactly.

Picc. 98 (corr.).

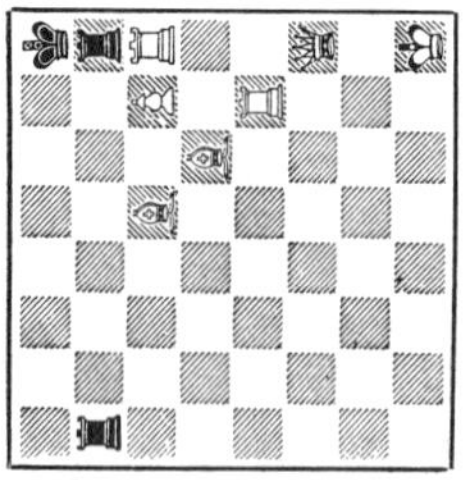

Mate in III exactly.

Picc. 100.

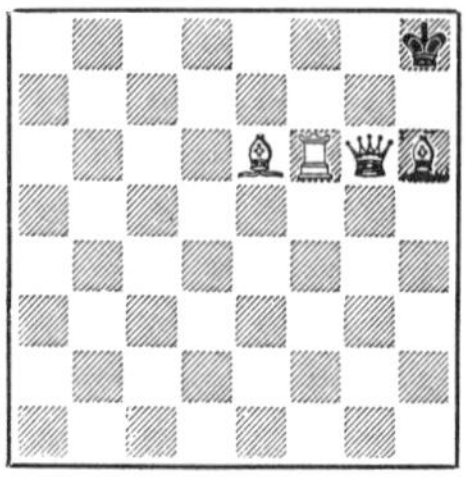

Mate in III exactly.
All the men are fidated.

Picc. 101.

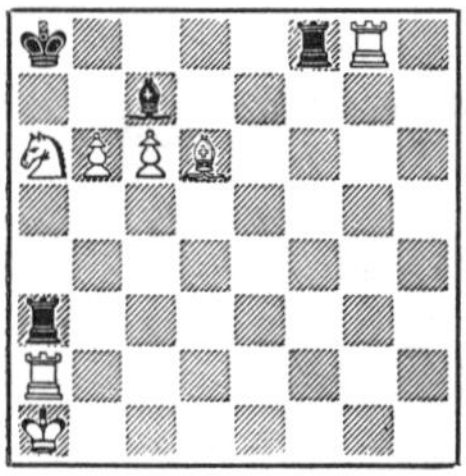

Mate in III exactly.

Picc. 102.

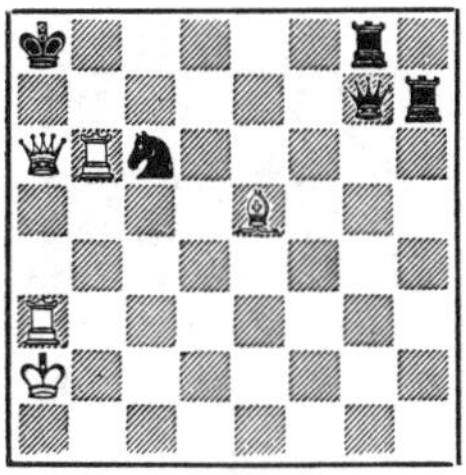

Mate in III exactly.

Picc. 103.

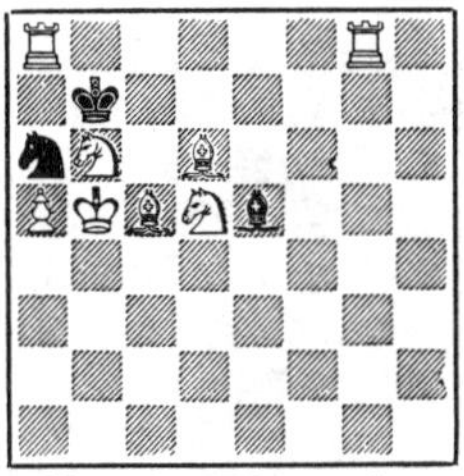

Mate in III exactly.

Picc. 104.

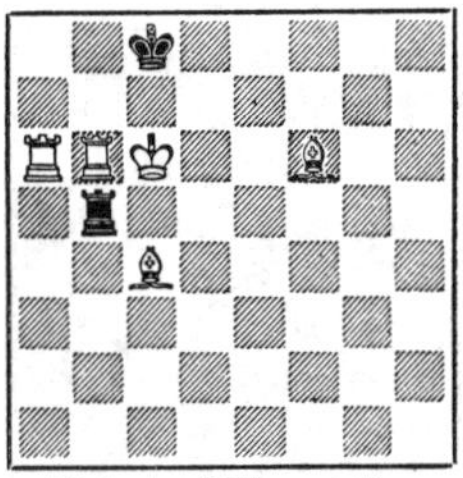

Mate in III exactly.

Picc. 106.

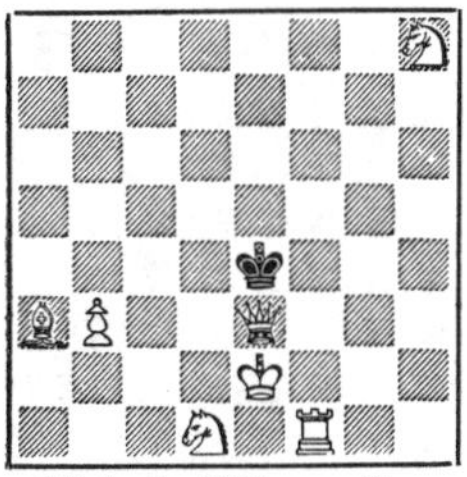

Mate in III exactly.

Picc. 107.

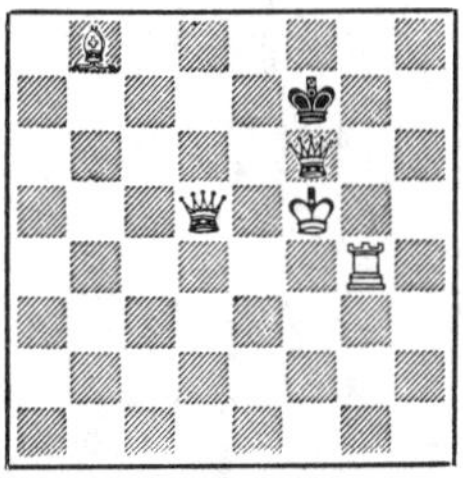

Mate in III exactly.

Picc. 109.

Mate in III exactly.
Ra7 is fidated. Unsound.

Picc. 110.

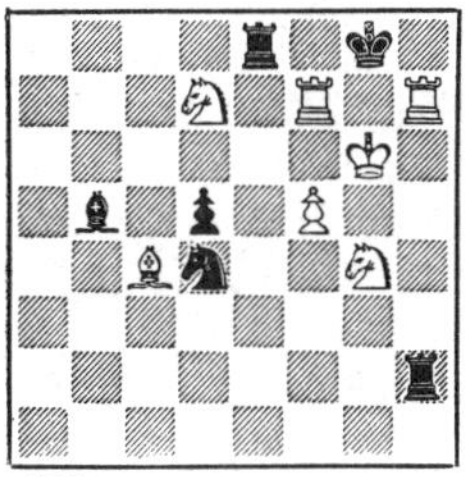

(Bl.)
Mate in III exactly.
Rh7 is immovable.

Picc. 118.

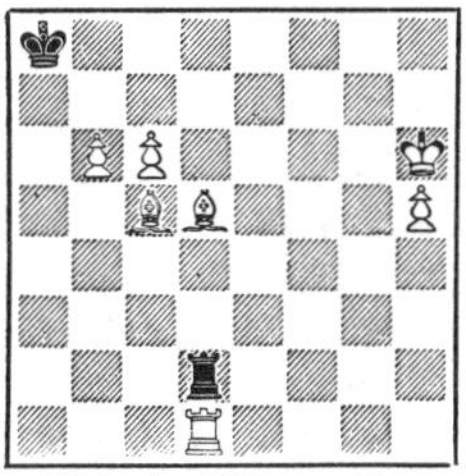

Mate in III exactly.
The Rs are fidated.

Picc. 119.

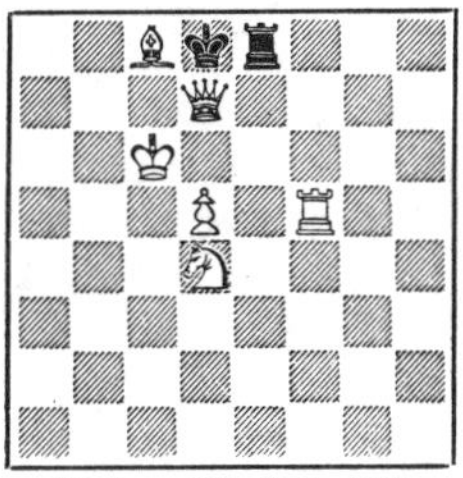

Mate with P in III exactly. The Kt is fidated.

Picc. 120.

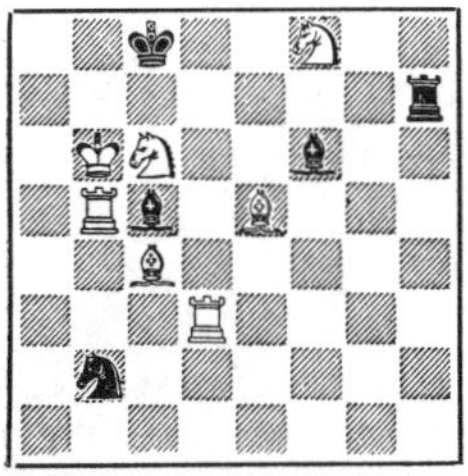

Mate in III exactly.
Wh. Bs are fidated.
Unsound.

Picc. 121.

Mate in III exactly.
Ktc4 is fidated.

Picc. 122.

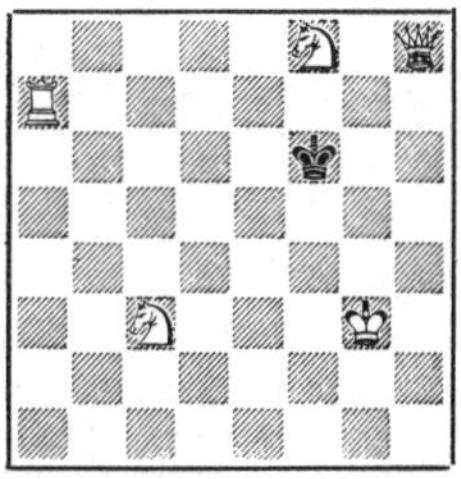

Mate in III exactly.

Picc. 123.

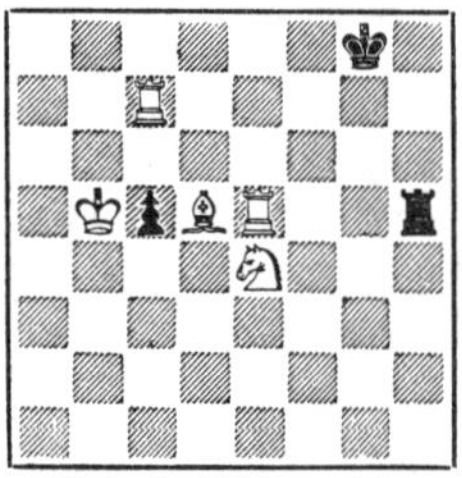

Mate in III exactly.

Picc. 124 (corr.).

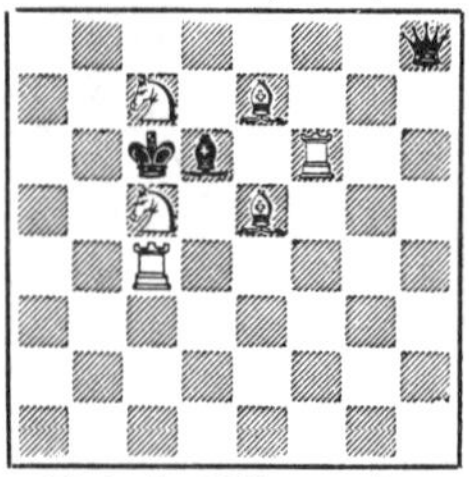

Mate in III exactly.

Picc. 125 (corr.).

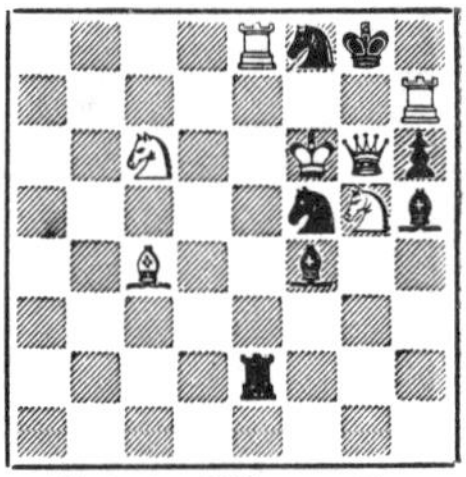

Mate in III exactly.

Picc. 126.

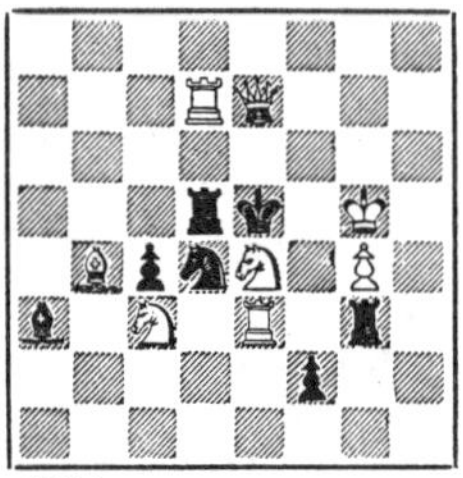

(Bl.)
Mate in III exactly.

Picc. 127.

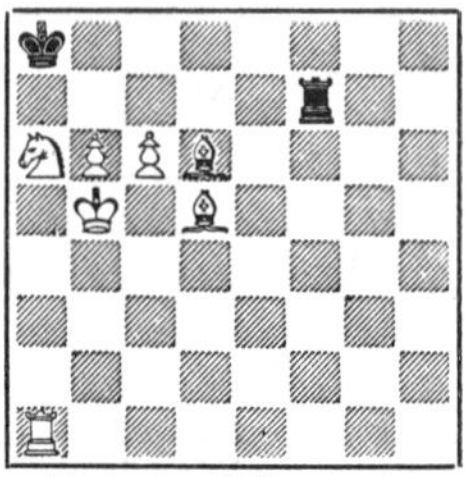

Mate in III exactly.
Rf7 is fidated. Unsound.

Picc. 129.

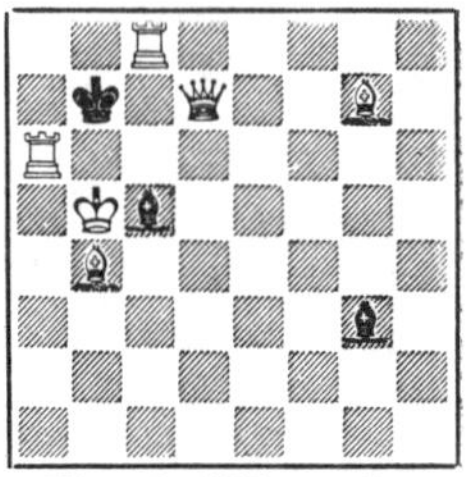

Mate in III exactly.

Picc. 134.

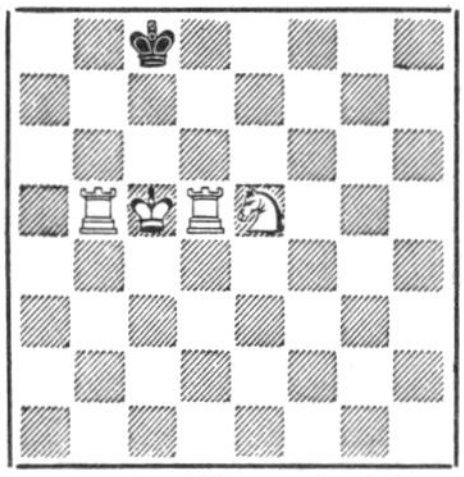

Mate in IV, each Wh. piece moving once.

Picc. 135.

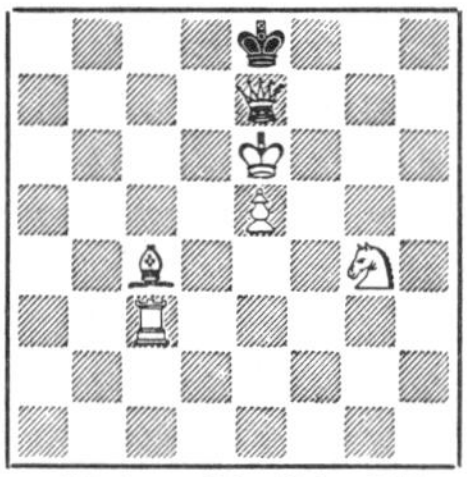

Mate with P in IV exactly.

Picc. 143.

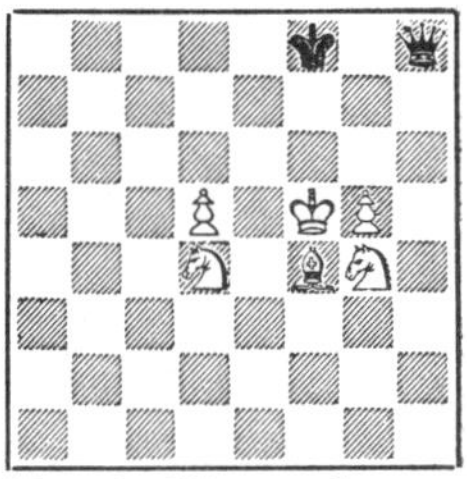

Mate in IV exactly, one P checking on 3rd move, the other mating.

Picc. 146.

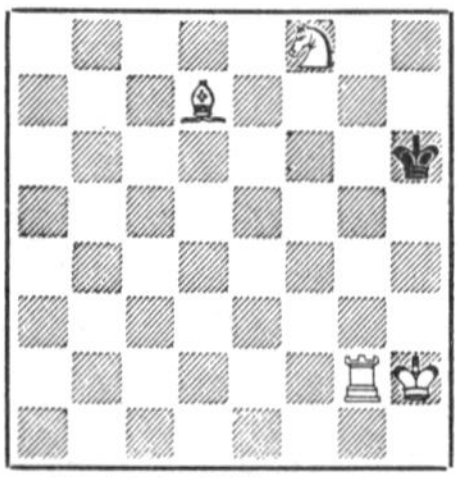

Mate in VI exactly.

Picc. 147.

Mate in VII exactly.

Picc. 148.

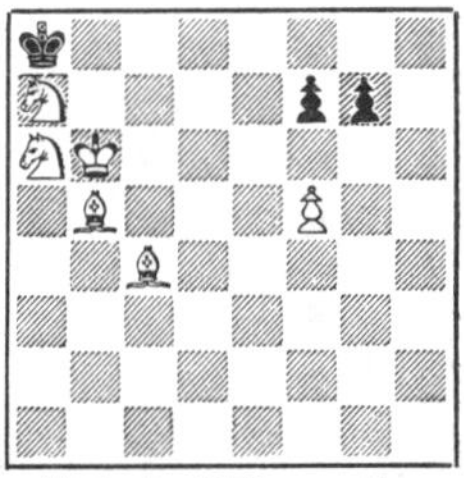

Mate in VII exactly.

Picc. 152.

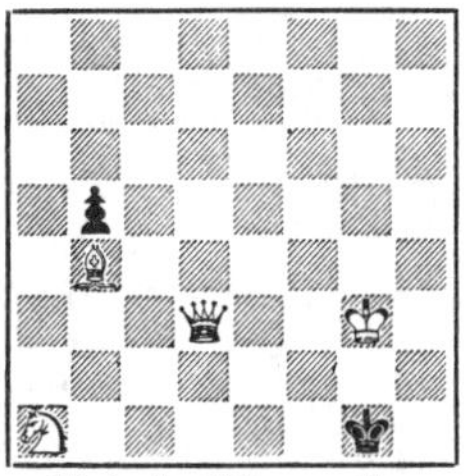

Mate in XI exactly.

Picc. 153.

Mate in V on d6. The Wh. B is immovable.

Picc. 155.

Mate in V exactly.

Picc. 156.

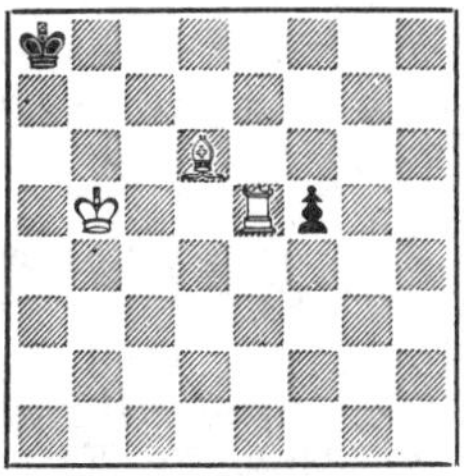

(Bl.)
Mate in V exactly.

Picc. 157.

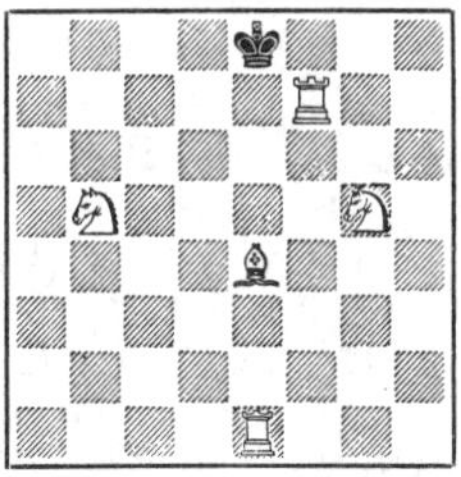

Mate in V exactly.

Picc. 159.

Mate in V exactly.

Picc. 161.

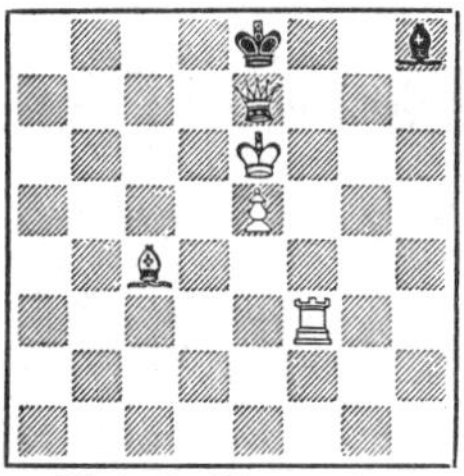

Mate in V exactly.

Picc. 165.

Mate in V exactly.

Picc. 167.

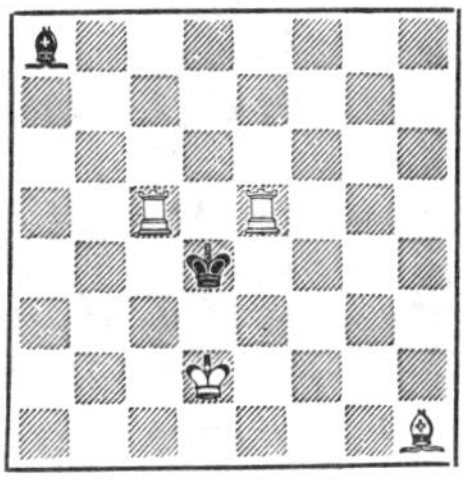

Mate in V or less.

NOTES AND SOLUTIONS

1 = CB *15*. 2. 1 Kt × P; 2 Re7 m. 3. 1 R × fP; 2 Rf8 m. Also by 1 Ktf6 + ; 2 Kt(e5)d7 m. 4. Var. of Picc. 3 (Bb5 on e4, Qd6 on c7, Bc6 on d6, omit Bg6, add Wh. Qh6, Pc6) in II ex. 1 Kt × P; 2 Bg6 m. *et aliter ludi non potest* (but 1 R × fP is adequate). 5. Wh. Ra1, h7, Ktd6, Bc6, Pb6; Bl. Kb8, Ra7, Ktb5, Bd5: in II ex. The MS. solution (1 R × R, Kt × R; 2 P × Kt m.) is unsound, for if 1 aR × R, Ktc7, if 1 hR × R (or Rc7 +), Kt × Kt, if 1 P × R +, Kt × P. There is no mate in II. 6. The MS. overlooks the mate by 1 Ktc2 +, Ktd4 (or Rd3; 2 Ktb6 m.); 2 Ktb4 m. 7. 1 Ktd6 + ; 2 Pe8 = Q m. 8. 1 Kt × B(c5) + ; 2 Rb8 m. Cf. Picc. 31. 9. 1 Rc7 + ; 2 Bc5 m. 10. 1 Q × R; 2 B m. acc. (Also by 1 Rf8 + or 1 Kt × P + .) A poor problem. 11. The MS. solution is 1 R × P, Ktd4; 2 Ktf6 m., but 1 . . , Ktd8 !

The problem is unsound. 12 = CB *23*. 13. No text or conditions. It is identical with Picc. 50. 1 Re3, Bd7 (or R × R; 2 Kt m.); 2 Ktb7 m. 14. Wh. Kc5, Ra7, Ktd4, d6, Bd5, f5; Bl. Kd8, Kte7, f8, Bh6, Pf4: *in duobus. Primo ludatur de rocco in* (b7), *enim ludi nec defendi potest.* Cf. CB 16. 15. If 1 Rf3, Rh7. If 1 Bc7, R × P +. If 1 Ktc5 +, Ra7. If 1 Pb7 +, Ka7. Var. Rf7 on g7. Now sound (C 17 is another setting) by 1 Rf3; 2 Rf8 or Ktc7 m. acc. 16. Wh. Ka3, Rc3, Qc1; Bl. Ka1, Rd2: in II ex., 1 Q × R; 2 Rc1 m. 17. If 1 Kt × R, Rg2. If 1 Rg2, Rg7. 18 = CB *2*. 19 = 46 (which the diagram is). If 1 R × R +, Kh7; 2 Rh2 +, Bh3 +. If 1 Rh2 +, Bh3 +. If 1 K × Q, Rf6. If 1 K × P, Re8. 20 = 23. 1 Ra5, P × Kt (or Kt × Q; 2 Kb5 m. Or 1 . . , Bb8; 2 Ktb6 m.); 2 Q × B m. Cf. C 25, Sens. 7, Luc. 12. 21 = 47 (which the diagram is). 1 Rd1, B × P (or R × B +; 2 Ktf6 m.); 2 Rd8 m. 22 = CB *3*. 23 = 20. 24 = 49 corr. is a var. of 20 (Wh. Kt for Qc8, Bl. P for Bb7, add Wh. Pc4), the solution of which now fails, but 1 R × P is now adequate. 25 = F 320. 26 = 48. 1 Rd8. 27 corr. Cf. CB 13 (Kts for Bs f6, f8, omit Pg5, now reflect). In II ex., 1 Kta7 +; 2 Bb6 m. 28 = 53 = CB *38*. 29. 1 Rb3, Rb7 (or Ra7; 2 Rb8 m.); 2 Kt × R m. 30. 1 Kte4, Q × Kt (or R × P +; 2 B × R m. Or 1 . . , R × R; 2 P × R m.); 2 Ktf6 m. 31. An unsound var. of 8 (Bc4 on c8, Ra3 on a4, Rb3 on c3. Kth6 is fidated) in II ex. If 1 Kt × B(b4), K × R. If 1 Be6, Kt × Q. 32 = CB *20*. 33. 1 Rf3, B(f7)~ (or B(g7)~; 2 Q × B m.); 2 R × Q m. 34. If 1 Rd6 +, K × R. If 1 Kta5 +, K × P. 35. Cf. CB 13 (Kt for Bf6, Rd4 on d3, Rc3 on c2, reflect). In II ex., 1 Rb8, Kte8 +; 2 R × Kt m. Or 1 P × Kt; 2 Bb6 or f6 or B(c8)~ m, acc. 36. 1 Ktd7, R × Kt (or Q × Kt; 2 Kt × R m. Or 1 . . , K × Kt; 2 Ktc5 m.); 2 Ktc7 m. *Nota quod ubi est fercia* * (i. e. g7) *melior esset pedona.* 37 = CB *261*. 38 = CB *15*. 39. Cf. CB 13 (add Bl. Bd8). In II ex., 1 Rg8, Rc6 + (or Kt × P; 2 R × B or B(f8)~ m.); 2 B × R m. 40. Cf. CB 17 (omit Qc2, Rh1; Pb3, on c3; add Bl. Ps on d4, f2). In II ex. Unsound. If 1 Bf7, Pf1 = Q. If 1 Bb7, Ra5 +. 41. *Notandum quod equus albus est fidatus et* (*pe*)*dona in* (c8) *descendit: omnes vero aliter ascendunt.* 1 Qc7 +; 2 Ktc6 m. Var. Omit Qd6. Now unsound. 42. Cf. CB 16 (add Wh. Pc2, d2, Bl. Kte7; omit Bf5, Pc6; Pf4 on f2 going to f8). In II ex., 1 Bf3, Ktd7 +; 2 R × Kt m. Or 1 . . , Kte6 +; 2 Kt × Kt m. Or 1 . . , Kt(f8)~; 2 Rd7 or Kte6 m. Or 1 . . , Kt(e7)~; 2 Ktc6 m. 43. Wh. Re7, g5, Bd4, e6, Pf6; Bl. Kh8, Kth6, Be4, f5, Pb3. *In duobus. Scak decem. Notandum quod pedona alba ascendit, nigra uero descendit.* No solution, and there is no mate in II. 44 corr. Wh. Kf3, Rb7, e3, Kte6, e7, Qg8, Bb5, f6, Pb6, g7; Bl. Ke8, Rc7, Qc8, Bd6, f8. In II ex., 1 Ktg6; 2 Ktc7 m. *Aliter uero ludi non potest,* but 1 Ktc6 is equally good. Cf. 36. 45. Wh. Ra7, h7, Ktd6; Bl. Kd8. *Notandum quod quocumque equo moueatur secundo luditur.* A poor problem. Contrast CB 41. 46 = 19. 47 = 21. 48 = 26. 49 = 24. 50 = 13. 51. Cf. CB 16 (add Bl. Kte7, Bh6; omit Pc6; Pf4 goes to f8). In II ex., 1 Bf3 or Rb7. Vars. I. Pf4 goes to f1. Unsound (but 1 Bf3 is adequate). II. Black plays first. Unsound, by 1 . . , Ktd7 +; 2 Ktf1. 52. Wh. Kb5, Ra2, Kta5, Pb6, c6; Bl. Ka8, Rc1, h7, Bd6. *In duobus. Scac decem.* No solution. ? Add Wh. Rg7 (position is now Picc. 112) and solve 1 Rg8 +, Bb8; 2 Ktb7 m. 53 = 28. 54. Wh. Kb5, Ra6, c8, Ktc6, e8, Qd5, Bf6; Bl. Kb7, Ra4, Kte5, Qa5, d8, e7, f7, Bc5, e3, Pf4. *In duobus. Scak xviii.* No solution. ? Add Wh. Bf5 and solve 1 Kt × Q(d8) +, K × R (or Q × Kt; 2 Ktd6 m.); 2 Ra8 m. 55. Cf. CB 44 (Rc7 on d7; add Wh. Pc7; reflect, and change colours). In III ex. Add condition Pb2 is immovable. 1 Qc5, Rg7 (or Ktb6; 2 Ra5; 3 Kt m. Or 1 . . , Kt × R; 2 Qb6; 3 Kt m. Or 1 . . , Ktb3 +; 2 B × Kt; 3 Kt m.); 2 Qb7 +; 3 Kt m. 56. *In tribus. Scak sex.* No solution. Cf. Picc. 133 in IV. 57. *In tribus. Scak septem. Primo ludatur de rege albo in* (f6). *Secundo de rocco albo in* (c8) *et tractus alphinus* (sic) *nigri ueniet in* (d6), *qui alphinus non accipiatur cum pedona, sed spingatur per unum punctum, et mactet.* 58 = CB *47*. 59. MS. solution 1 B × R; 2 Ktc7 +; 3 Bd6 m. is foiled by 1 . . , R × R +. It can be solved by 1 R × R(a3), B × B(e4); 2 Ka2; 3 Ktc7 m. Or 1 . . , B × B(d6); 2 Ktc7 +; 3 Ra8 m. Or 1 . . , Rb8 or R × R; 2 Ra4 (or a5 or Ka2); 3 Ktc7 m. The first of a series of variants which only differ in the arrangement of the four Bs. 60. No solution. It appears to be an unsound var. of Picc. 62 and 96. If 1 R × R(a1) + ; 2 R × R + , Ktc8. 61. Cf. 59 (interchange Bs g3 and e5). In III ex. 1 Ktc7 + ; 2 R × R(a3) + ; 3 R × B or R × R m. 62. Cf. 60 (Bl. B for Ktd6). In III ex. No solution. (1 R × R(a1) + ; 2 R × R + ; 3 R × B m.) 63. Cf. 59 (interchange Bs f4 and e5). In III ex. 1 R × R(a3) ; 2 Ka2 ; 3 Ktc7 or R × R m. acc. Also by 1 Ktc7 + ; 2 R × R(a3) + ; 3 R × B or R m. 64. 1 Rb1 + ; 2 Qb5 ; 3 Ktc4 m. 65. 1 Rb2 (Rb3 or Rb7 or Kb8 will do as well) ; 2 Ktc4 + ; 3 Ktc5 m. 66. Wh. Kc1, Rb1, d1, Kta5, a8, Qc4, d7, Bc5, f5 ; Bl. Kd6, Re8, Ktc8, d8. *In tribus. Scak xiii.* No solution, and as the Bl. K is in ch., the position is wrong. 67. 1 Kth5, Kg8. If 1 . . , Kf8 ; 2 Qg6 ; 3 Re8 m. 68. 1 Be3, Rh7 (or f7) ; 2 Ktc5 + ; 3 Pb7 or R × R m. Or 1 . . , R × B ; 2 Ra3 (a4 or a5) ; 3 Ktc7 m. Or 1 . . , Rh1 (or f1) ; 2 Ra2 (or a3, a4, a5) ; 3 Ktc7 m. ; or 2 Bc5 ; 3 Pb7 or Ktc7 m. 69 = CB *88*. 70. Cf. CB 67 (Rb2 on b4, reflect). In III ex. MS. says 1 Bg7 ; 2 Ktc7, *tercio patet et aliter ludi non potest.* But 1 . . , R × B is an adequate defence. But 1 Ra2, Ra3 (or Rg7 ; 2 Bc3, &c. Or 1 . . , Rf4 ; 2 B(e5)~, &c. Or 1 . . , R elsewhere ; 2 Ktb4 or c5 acc., &c.) ; 2 R × R ; 3 Ktc7 m. holds. Var. Rf3, g4, on f2, g3 ; unsound = CB 67. 71 = PL *68*. 72 = 111 corr. 1 Bc5 + , Kb8 (or Ra2 ; 2 Qc7 ; 3 R × R or Pb7 m.) ; 2 Pc7 + ; 3 Ra8 m. 73. If 1 Ra3 (a4, a5), Re6. If 1 R × R, Re6. 2 Pc7, Re3. 74. Cf. CB 56 (omit Bd5 ; add Bl. Pd2 ; reflect). In III ex. ; the Bl. R is fidated. MS. says unsound by 1 Re3, Rg5 + ; but this allows 2 Re5 ; 3 Ktc5 m. The problem is sound. 75 = CB *64*. 76. 1 Bd4 ; 2 Rb5 ; 3 Rb6 m. 77. Wh. Kf6, Rb2, Kta6, c4, Bb6, c7, Pe4, f7 ; Bl. Kc6, Ktd3, Qc8, Bb7, g3. In III ex. MS. says 1 Kta5 + ; 2 Pf8 = Q ; *reliquum patet.* But if 1 . . , Kd6 this solution fails. Contrast with 76. 78. There are three Wh. Kts. The position is clearly taken from CB 158 (in VI), but there Ktf2 and f5 are both Black. Possibly Ktf2 should be Black here also. The MS. solution (1 R × R(g1) ; 2 Ktd6) is foiled by 1 . . , R × Kt + (or if Ktf2 is black, by 1 . . , Kt × Kt +). There is a solution in III by 1 Rc6 + ; 2 Rd6 + ; 3 Rb4 m. ; or by 1 Rb4 + ; 2 Rb5 + ; 3 Ktd6 m. Var. In II ex. 1 Rb4 + ; 2 Rd6 (or Kte7 or Rd4 or Pe4) m. Also by 1 Rc6 + ; 2 Kte7 m. 79 corr. Cf. CB 71 (Pb3 on b4, Pg2 on f5 ; add Bl. Pc2 ; reflect). In III ex. Unsound. If 1 B × R (or Ktb8 + or Ktb4 +), Ba4. If 1 Rh3, Rh7 or g8 ; 2 Ktb4 (or b8) + , Ba4. If 1 K × B, Ra7. 80. 1 Ktc8 ; 2 Pb7 ; 3 Pb8 = Q m. (Also 1 Ktb5 ; 2 Pc7 + ; 3 Pb7 m. Contrast with C 59 and C 111.) 81 = CB *66* (the MS. solution is wrong). 82. If 1 Rd8 + , Rb8 ; 2 R × R + , Kt × R + ; or 2 Ra7 + , Kt × R. If 1 Rc8 + , Rb8. If 1 Ra7, Kt × R ; 2 Q × R, Bc5. If 1 Q × R, Ktb8 + ; 2 B × Kt, Bc5. If 1 R × Kt, Bc5. 83. If 1 Rd8 + , Rg8 ; 2 Rg2, Pc1 = Q + . 84 = CB *53*. 85 = CB 52. 86 = CB *70* (the condition Wh. Kt may not play first move is omitted in error). 87. MS. gives 1 Bh3 ; 2 Qg3 ; *reliquum patet* ; but if 1 . . , K × B, Bl. is now stalemate. The problem is unsound. Vars. (1) Kh2 on h1, and (2) the same thing, Black plays first, are sound. 1 . . , Kh1 ; 2 Bh3 ; 3 Qg3 ; 4 Ktf2 m. 88. 1 Rh5, Bg8 (or Ktf5 ; 2 Ktf7 + ; 3 Rh8 m.) ; 2 Qh7 ; 3 Ktf7 m. 89. Wh. Ka5, Rb5, d7, Qc6 ; Bl. Ka8, Bb8, Ktc8. In III ex. Unsound. If 1 Ka6, Bd6. The position is based on CB 9, &c. 90. If 1 R × R, R × R. If 1 Bg4, R × R (not Ktd6 as MS. gives, for then 2 Rd8 + , Kte8 ; 3 R × Kt m.). 91. Wh. Rf3, Kte5, e6, Qd8, Be4, Pb5 ; Bl. Ke8, Re7, f2, Qh6, Pg7. *In tribus. Scak xi. Primo de fercia in* (e7) : *secundo de alphino in* (c6) : *reliquum patet.* But if 1 . . , R × R there is no mate. The diagram is probably corrupt. 92 = CB *49*. 93. Wh. Ra1, Kta6, Bg6, Pb6, c6, c5 ; Bl. Ka8, Rf4, h4, Bd6. In III ex. MS. says unsound, but there is a solution by 1 Be4, Bb8 (or R × B ; 2 Ktc7 + ; 3 Ra8 m.) ; 2 Pb7 + ; 3 Kt m. Var. Bg6 on g5, said to be sound, is unsound. If 1 B~, Ra4. If 1 Ktc7 + ; 2 Ra7, Ra4. 94. 1 Kte7 + ; 2 Bc5 + ; 3 Pb7 or R × Kt m. acc. 95. If 1 Rd8, Kt × R ; 2 Ktb5 + , B × Kt + ; or 2 Bf4 + , R × B. 96. 1 R × R(a1) + ; 2 R × R + ; 3 R × Q m. 97. Cf. 59 (interchange Wh. and Bl. Bs). In III ex. 1 Ktc7 + , Kb8 (or B × Kt ; 2 R × aR + ; 3 R × B + or R m.) ; 2 B × B(d6) + ; 3 R × R(f8) m. (1 R × R(a3) is also adequate.) 98. 1 Pb7 + , 2 R × R + ; 3 Ra7 m. There are still three pieces less than the 13 stated in the MS. 99. Cf. 59 (interchange Bf4, d6). In III ex.

1 Ktc7+; 2 B×B(d6)+; 3 R×R (f8) m. (To complete the set we may add var. interchange Bd6, g3. In III ex. 1 R×R(a3), Rb8 (or ~; 2 Ktc7+; 3 Ra8 m.); 2 R×R+; 3 Ktc7 m.) 100. 1 Rf8+; 2 Rf7+; 3 Rh7 m. 101. 1 R×R(a3), Ba5 (or R×R; 2 Ktc5+; 3 R×B m.); 2 R×B; 3 Ktc7 m. Cf. 59. 102. 1 Qb7+; 2 Q×Kt+; 3 Ra8 m. Var. Omit Qg7. Unsound, for 2.., Rb7 is possible. 103. 1 aRb8+, Kt×R; 2 B×Kt; 3 Pa6 m. 104. 1 K×R; 2 Ra7+; 3 Rb8 or Be6 m. acc. 105. An unsound var. of Picc. 68 (Bg5 on g6, Rf3, h3, on f5, h5). If 1 Be4, Rd5. If 1 Rg1 or e1, Rb5. 106. 1 Ktg6; 2 Rf6; 3 Ktc3 m. 107. 1 Qe6+, Ke8 (or Kf8; 2 Bd6+; 3 Rg8 m.); 2 Rd4; 3 Rd8 m. 108 = CB *49*. 109. If 1 Kte7, Rc7; 2 Ktd7, Rc3 (c2, c1); or 2 Ra1 (b1), R×Kt. If 1 Bf4+, Rh7; 2 ~, Rh6+. Var. P for Qd6. Now sound. 1 Kte7, Rc7 (b7); 2 Pd7; 3 Ktf7 or Bf4 m. acc. If 1.., Ra5; 2 Rc1 (or b1—not Ktc4 as MS. gives); 3 Ktf7 or R m. acc. If 1.., Ra1; 2 Rb1, &c. If 1.., Ra2 (a3, a4); 2 Bf8+; &c. If 1.., Ra8; 2 Bc8, &c. 110. If 1 Be6+, P×B; 2 Ktf8, R×R. If 1 Kt×R, Kt×P; 2 R×Kt, Re6+. If 1 Ktf8, Kt×P. 111 = 72. 112. Wh. Kb5, Ra1, g7, Kta6, Pb6, c6; Bl. Ka8, Rc2, h7, Bd6. In III ex. 1 Ktc7+; 2 Rg8+; 3 R×R, Ra8 or R×B m. acc. 113 = CB *83*. 114 = CB *82*. 115 = CB 51. 116 = CB *270*. 117 = CB 45. 118. 1 Ra1+; 2 Pc7; *residuum patet*. But 1 Ra1+, Ra2; 2 Pc7, Ra6 foils it. 119. 1 Kte6+; 2 Ktd8 (not Ktc7 as in MS.); 3 Pd6 m. 120. If 1 Rd7, Rh1. If 1 Rd8+, B×R+; 2 Ka6, Bb6. Why the fidation? 121. 1 Kte7+; 2 Ktd6+; 3 Kte8 m. 122. 1 Rd7; 2 Qg7; 3 Rd5 m. 123. 1 Ktf6+, Kf8 (or Kh8; 2 K×P; 3 R m. acc.); 2 R×R; 3 Rh8 m. 124. 1 Rf1; 2 Ra1; 3 Ra6 m. 125. 1 B×R, Ktg7; 2 R×Kt(g7)+; 3 R×Kt(f8) m. Or 1.., Ktd6; 2 Rh8+; 3 R×Kt m. Or 1.., P×Kt; 2 Bg4; 3 Be6 or Kte7 m. 126. 1 Ktc5+; 2 R×R(d5)+; 3 Q m. 127. MS. intends 1 Bf3, Rf5+; 2 Bd5, R×B+; 3 Ktc5 m.; but 1.., Ra7 (2 Bd5, R×Kt) foils it. Other tries also fail. It is unsound. 128. Wh. Ra1, Kta6, Pc6, b6, e1; Bl. Ka8, Bd6. In III ex. 1 Rd1; 2 Rd7; 3 Ra7 m. 129. 1 R(a6)a8; 2 Be5; 3 Qc6 m. 130 = CB *117*. 131 = CB *1*. 132. Wh. Ka6, Rg7, h7, Pf8, f1; Bl. Ka8, Pg1, g8. In XXIII, six pieces, the Bl. being fidated. The text is partially in Italian, but is corrupt. ? Omit Pf8, g8, make *h*-file 8th row, and mate with P. This seems possible in XXIII or thereabouts. Cf. CB 208, 251, 252. 133. Position is Picc. 56. In IV ex. 1 Kte3; 2 Kf3; 3 R~; 4 Re7 m. 134. 1 Rb1; 2 Ktc4; 3 Kb6; 4 Rd8 m. 135. 1 Kf6; 2 Ba6; 3 Rc8+; 4 Pe6m. 136. Position is Picc. 100. In IV ex. All pieces fidated. 1 Qf7; 2 Rg6; 3 Rg8+ (not Rg7 as MS. gives); 4 Qg6 m. (Also by 1 Bg4; 2 Rf7; 3 Rh7 (or Be6); 4 Be6 (or Rh7) m.) 137 = *135*. 138. Wh. Kh5, Rh6, Ktc7, Qf4, f6, g4, g6; Bl. Kg8. In IV ex. Said to be unsound. 1 Q(g4)f5. But 2 Qe6; 3 Q(e6)f7+; 4 Rh8 m. is possible. The problem is sound. Cf. CB 133 in V. 139 = CB 111 (omit Ka1, Ph6, and Wh. can stale Bl. and continue playing). 140. Wh. Kb6, Rd7, e7, Bd4, e4; Bl. Ka8, Rd3, e3, Bd6, e6. In IV, checking each move. 1 Ra7+; 2 R(e7)b7+; 3 Ra8+; 4 R(a8)×B m. Cf. F 297. 141. Wh. Kc6, Rd1, Kte4, Qc7, Pc5; Bl. Kc8, Rh8. In IV ex. with P. *Notandum quod stabulatum* (i. e. when staled) *expectat mactum inuitum* = CB *113*. 142 = CB *101*. 143. 1 Kte6+; 2 Ktf6; 3 P+; 4 P m. 144 corr. = CB *101*. 145 = CB 144. 146. 1 Rg8; 2 Kg3; 3 Kf4; 4 Rg6; 5 Rg3; 6 Rh3 m. The B seems unnecessary. 147. 1 Rg7; 2 Kh7; 3 Kg6; 4 Kf6; Kd8 (b8); 5 Re7; 6 Rd1 (not Re8 as MS.); 7 Rd8 m. If 4.., Kf8; 5 Ke6; 6 Rf7; 7 Rg8 m. Other solutions exist. 148. 1 Ktc7+; 2 Ktc6+; 3 Be6+; 4 P×P (not Pf6 as in MS.); 5 Pe7; 6 Pe8 = Q; 7 Qd7 m. Or 4 Kta6 (Kt×P); 5 Ktc5; 6 Ktb7; 7 Ktd6 m. 149 = CB *162*. 150. Cf. CB 189 (Q for Pf6, Kg8 on h8; reflect). Bl. Ps ascend. In VIII ex. 1 Qb7+; 2 Qa8. The alteration saves a move of the CB solution and avoids the abnormal move of the Wh. P. 151 = CB *277* (but in XII). 152. 1 Qe2; 2 Ktc2; 3 Ktd4; 4 Kte6; 5 Ktg5; *reliqua patent*. Many continuations are possible, e. g. 6 Bd2; 7 Bf4; 8 Kf3; 9 Kth3; 10 Qf1; 11 Qg2 m. 153. 1 Ktb4+; 2 Kb6; 3 Ra8+; 4 Ktc6; 5 Rd8 m. 154 = CB *135*. 155. 1 Bc6; 2 Ba4; 3 Ktc7; 4 Ktg4+; 5 B m. 156. 1 Kb6; 2 Rh5; 3 Rh8+; 4 B×P; 5 Bd6 m. 157. 1 Rc1; 2 Rc2; 3 Ktd4; 4 Kt(d4)e6+; 5 B m. 158.

An extended version of CB 112 in V. 159. 1 Qc6+; Kc8 (or Kb8; 2 Rd1; 3 Qb6; 4 Qc7, &c.); 2 Rd1; 3 Rd8+; 4 Kc4; 5 Ra8 m. 160 = CB *135*. 161. Probably a Pawn-mate is intended. 1 Rc3 (only move given in MS.), Bf6; 2 K × B; 3 Ba6; 4 Rc8; 5 Pe6 m. 162. Wh. Kf7, Bc5, Qf6; Bl. Kh8, Rc2, Pc6. In V. *Primo de alphino in* (e3), *secundo de eodem in* (g5), *tertio de fercia in* (g7) *dando scaccum, reliqua patent.* This is probably an inaccurate attempt to give CB 137. 163 corr. Wh. Kc8, Rh8, Ba2, Pb1, c5, going to a1, a5; Bl. Ka8. In V ex. 1 Kc7+; 2 Pa1 = Q; 3 Ra8+; 4 Qc3; 5 Ra5 m. 164 = CB *133*. 165. 1 Pg7+; 2 P × Kt = Q+; 3 Rc8; 4 Qg7; 5 Rh8 m. 166 corr. Cf. 156 (Kb5 on b6, Re5 on e6). In V. 1 Re1; 2 Rh1; 3 Rh8+; 4 B × Q; 5 Bd6 m. The MS. solution is wrong. 167. 1 Rg5, Bc6; 2 R × B; 3 Rc4 m. 168. Wh. Kd6, Ra3, e3, Bf1, Pc2, d2; Bl. Kc8. In V ex. 1 Re8+; 2 Pc3; 3 Pc4; 4 Bd3; 5 Rb8 m. 169 is an extended version of CB 112 in VI. 170 = D 49. 171 = CB 239. 172 = CB *135*.

S = MS. Paris, 24274 (fonds de Sorbonne, 1426).

This is a MS. of the late 15th c. from the Richelieu Library, which contains, f. 1, the French version of Cessolis by Ferron, f. 44 a Latin collection of 197 problems of chess, and f. 148 a French treatise, *Comment les heraulx furent premièrement fondés.*

The collection of problems is in the same hand with the Ferron work, and was possibly intended to supplement the chess information of the morality by practical exercises in the movement and combination of the pieces, just as is the case in D, Arch., and Köbel. There is no attempt to arrange the problems in any way, and it is soon evident that the collection is a compilation from three distinct sources.[8] The first of these is the *Bonus Socius* work, from which no less than 59 problems have been taken with the original solutions. All of these problems (S 92, 93, 95–106, 124–46, 168–89) are taken from the first 61 problems in the *Bonus Socius* work, and they are diagrammed with much accuracy. A collation of them shows that the parent MS. belonged to neither of the French groups of the *Bonus Socius* MSS. The second source, from which 74 positions in S are derived (S 1–52, 94, 114–15, 120–3, 147–9, 155, 159, 162, 166, 190–7), was a Latin MS., which contained many positions which occur in the *Bonus Socius* and *Civis Bononiae* collections, but with a text that was different from that in either of these works. The remaining 64 problems belong to a third work of a particularly interesting character. These problems may be identified by the fact that the solutions regularly give the moves of both players, even where there is no choice of move, and by certain peculiarities of diction, e.g. the use of the word *necessario.* They are also very different in type from those of other works; they are often very puerile, but there are none of the wager-games or problems intentionally unsound, and they employ a more advanced type of move than what is usual in the *Civis Bononiae* work. They are probably among the latest of the mediaeval compositions, and composed in France by a player away from

[8] That S is a compilation also appears from the text to S 1, which must have always been the first problem of the MS., for it alone commences with a large initial in red ink. The solution refers to the adjoining problem (*partitus contiguus*) as a similar position. The problem intended is, however, not S 2 but S 191.

the main current of chess activity. From certain mistakes in S it is clear that that MS. is not the work of the composer of these problems.

One or two peculiarities of nomenclature may be mentioned. I have already made use of the fact that the MS. (in problems from the second source only) uses the name *domina* for a Queen produced by the promotion of a Pawn. In place of *regina* or *domina*, the problems of the third source occasionally use the name *fera*, which is also almost the only name used in the diagrams (in the forms *fere*, *fire*, *fiere*, *ferce*—S 44 only: *regina* occurs very rarely in diagrams). The Bishop is generally *alfinus* or *alphinus* (dat. pl. *alphinibus*, S 111), but once (S 42) *delphinus* is used. Both the non-BS sources use *pingere pedonem* for to advance a Pawn. *Cantum*, the corner, replaces the usual *angulus* in S 108.

I now proceed to give the contents of the MS., omitting the problems taken from the *Bonus Socius* work, which have been given already in the tables, summarizing the contents of the MSS. of that group.

S 36.

Mate in II exactly.

S 38.

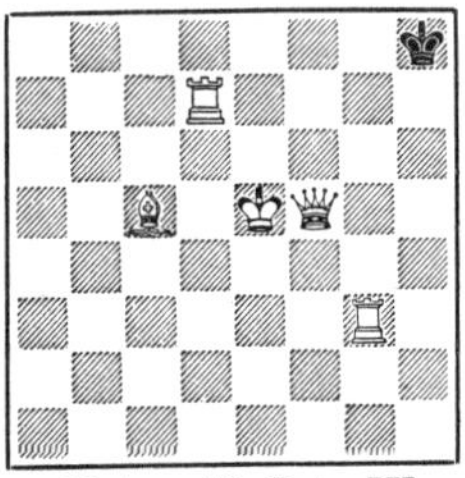

Mate with B in IV exactly.

S 39.

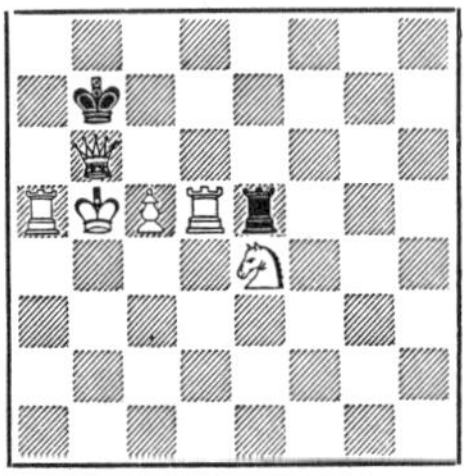

Mate in II exactly.

S 53 (corr.).

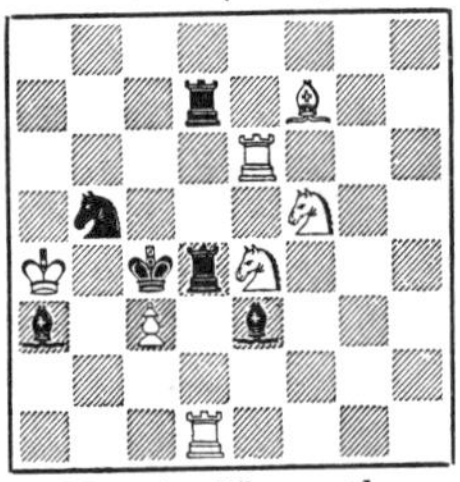

Mate in II exactly.

S 54.

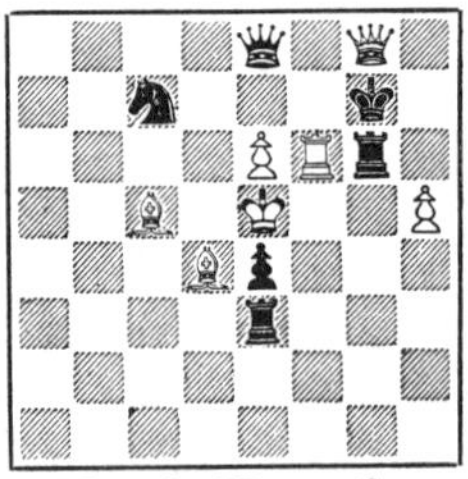

Mate in II exactly.

S 56.

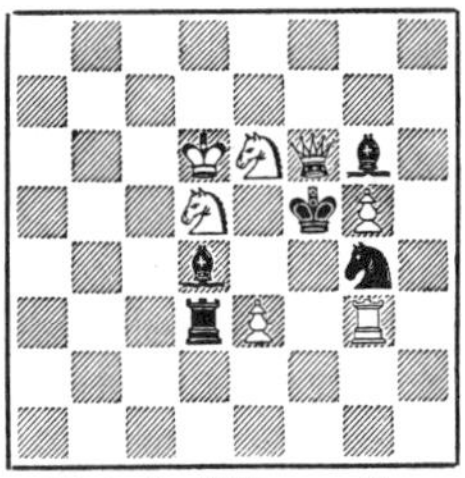

Mate in III exactly. Unsound.

S 57.

Mate in II exactly.

S 58 (corr.).

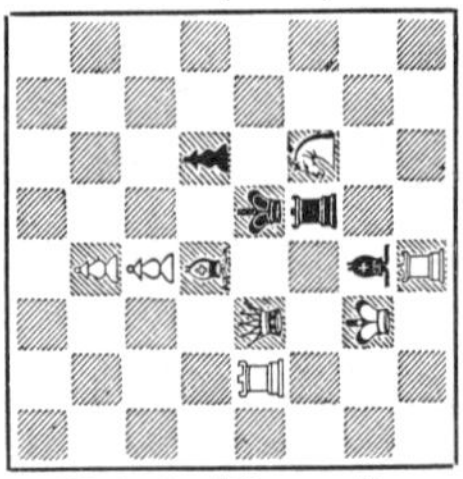

(Bl.)

Mate in II exactly.

S 59.

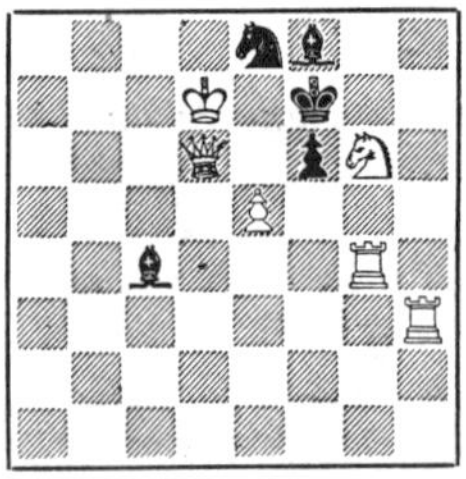

Mate in II exactly.

S 61.

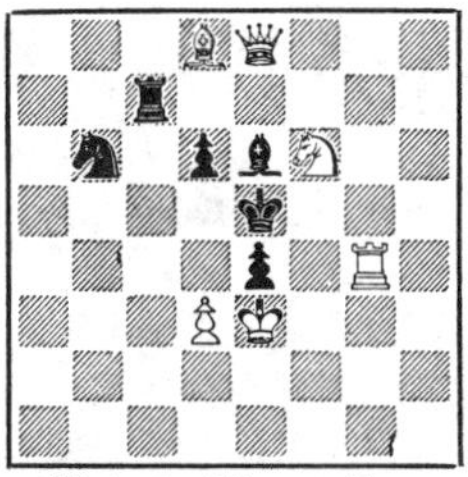

Mate in II exactly.

S 62.

Mate in II exactly.

S 63.

Mate in II exactly.

S 64.

Mate in II exactly.

S 65.

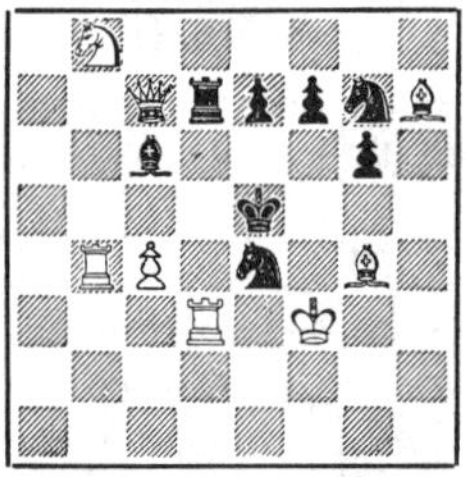

Mate in II exactly.

S 66.

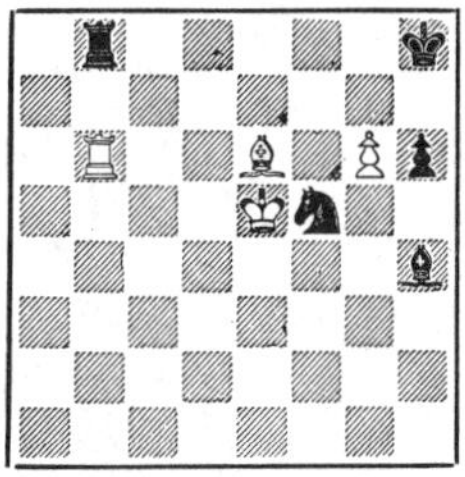

Mate in II exactly.

S 67.

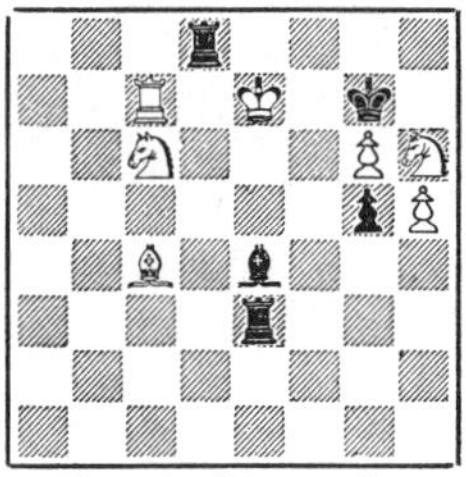

Mate in II exactly.

S 68.

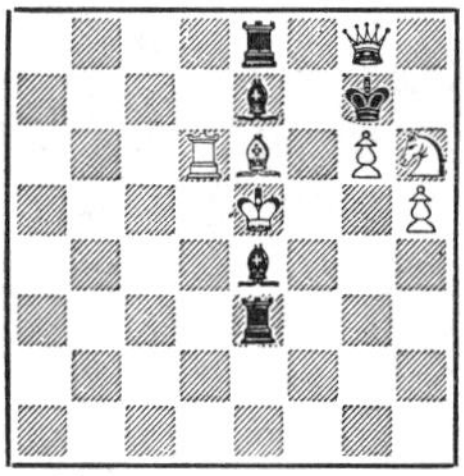

Mate in II exactly.

S 69.

Mate in II exactly.

S 70.

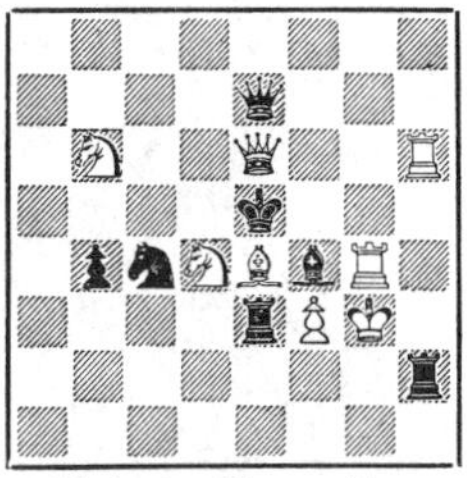

Mate in II exactly.

S 71.

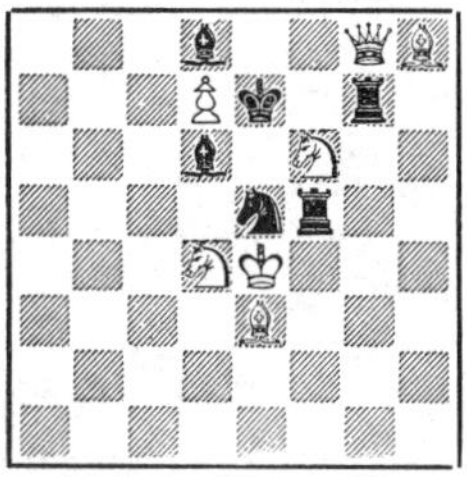

Mate in II exactly.

S 72.

Mate in II exactly.

S 73.

Mate in II exactly.

S 74.

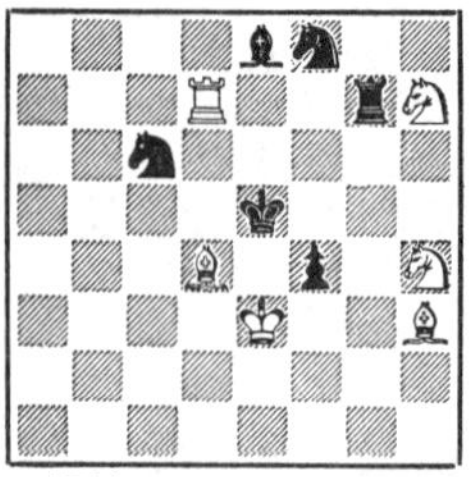

(Bl.)
Mate in II exactly.

S 75 (corr.).

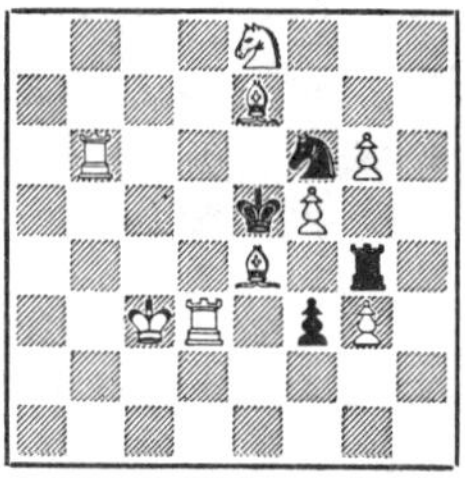

Mate in II exactly.

S 76.

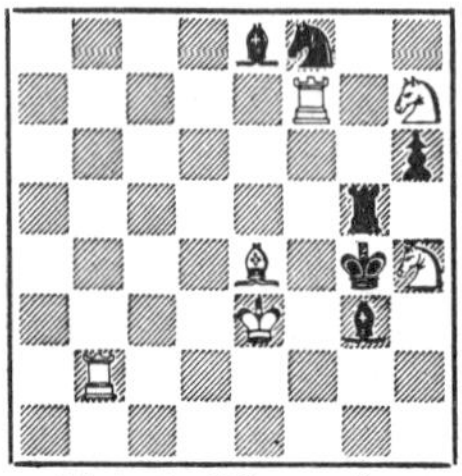

Mate in II exactly.

S 77.

Mate in II exactly.

S 78.

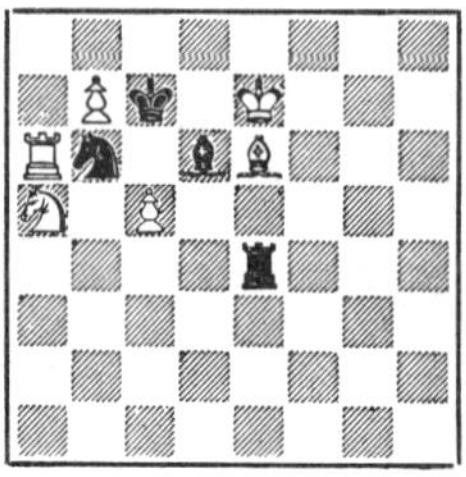

Mate in II exactly.

S 79 (corr.).

Mate in II exactly.

S 81.

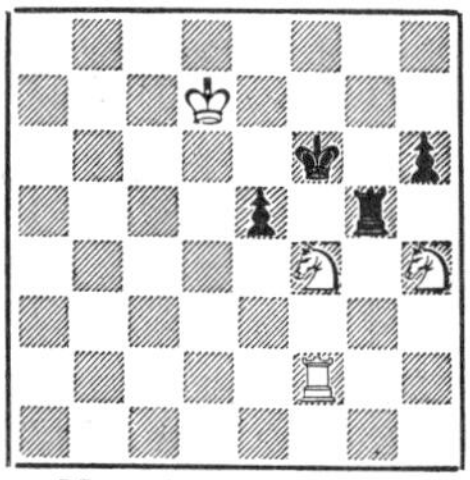

Mate in II exactly.

S 82.

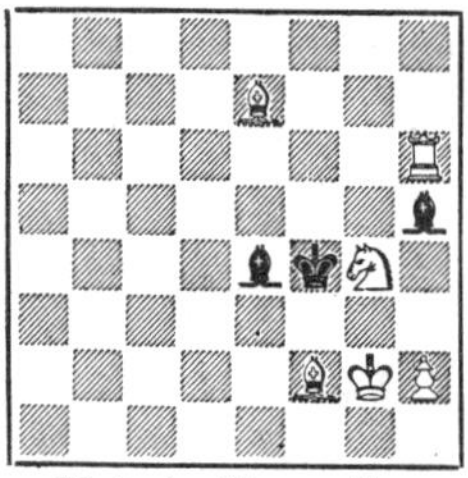

Mate in II exactly.

S 83.

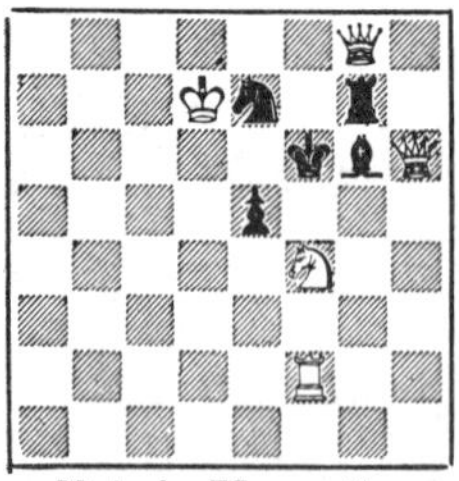

Mate in II exactly.

S 85.

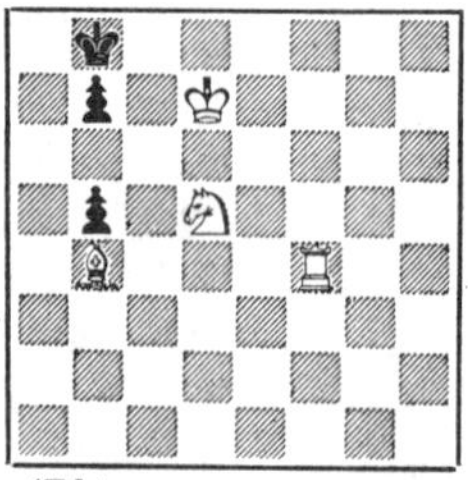

(Bl.)
Mate in II exactly.

S 86.

Mate in II exactly.

S 87.

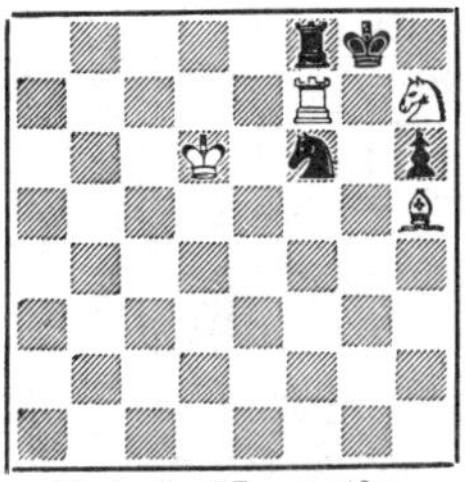

Mate in II exactly.

S 88 (corr.).

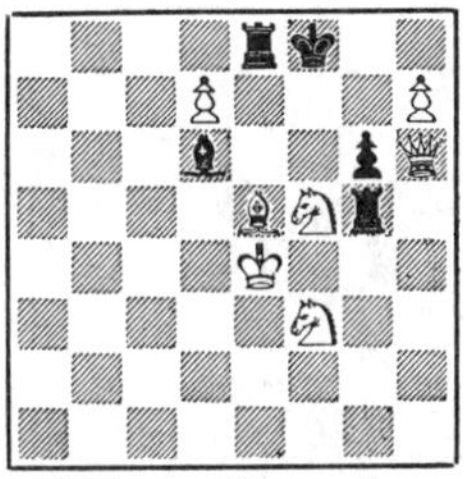

Mate in II exactly.

S 89.

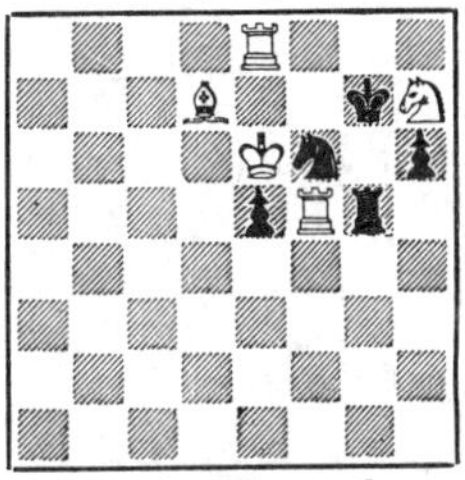

Mate in II exactly.

S 90.

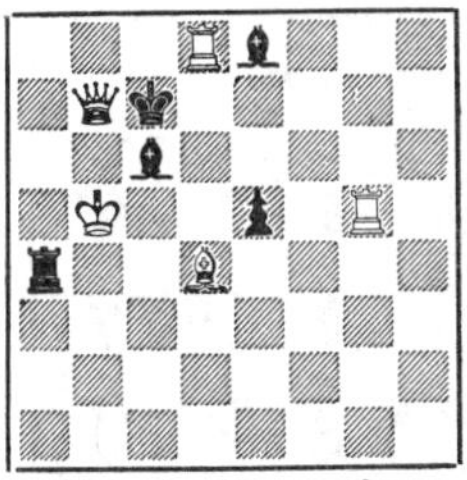

Mate in II exactly.

S 91 (corr.).

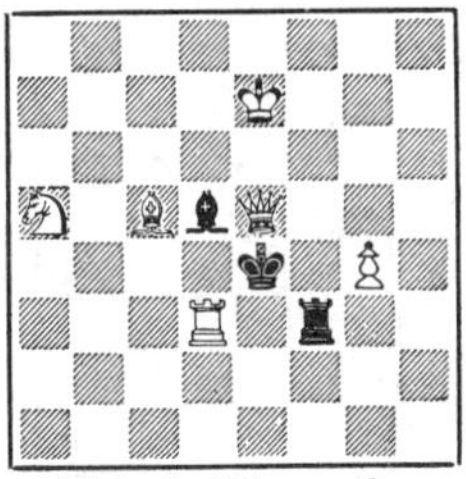

Mate in II exactly.

S 107.

Mate in II exactly with B.

S 108.

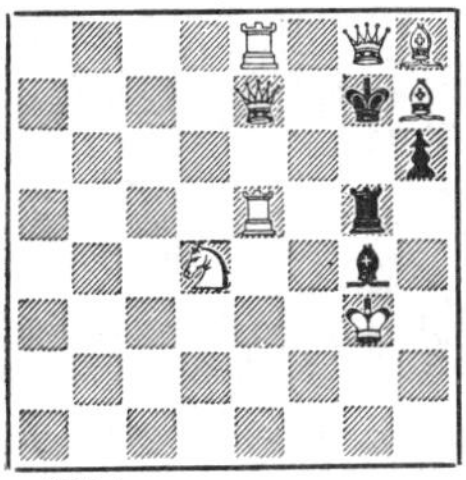

(Bl.)
Mate in II exactly.
Unsound.

S 109.

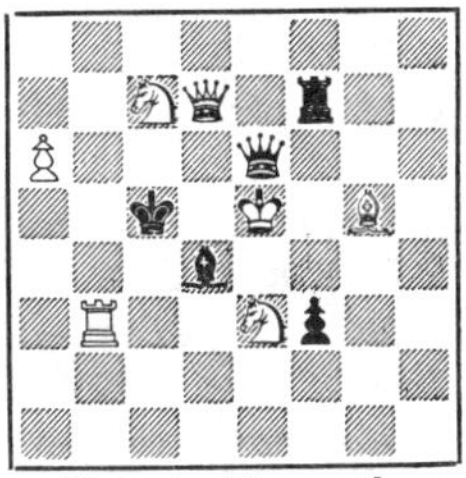

Mate in II exactly.

S 110.

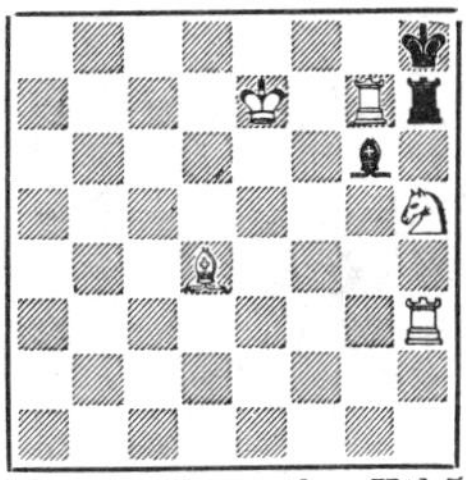

Mate in II exactly. Kth5 does not play first move.

S 112.

Mate in II exactly.

S 113.

Mate in II exactly.

S 116 (corr.).

Mate in II exactly.

S 117 (corr.).

Mate in II exactly.
Unsound.

S 118.

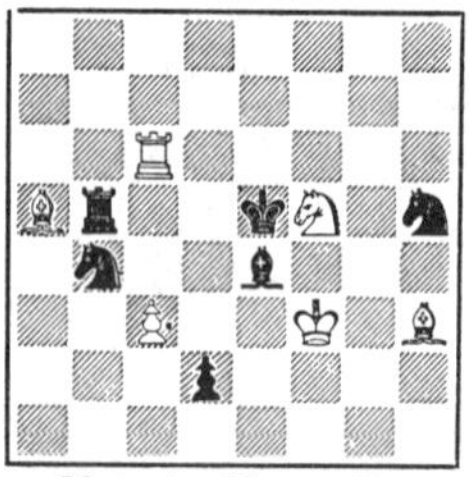

Mate in II exactly.

S 119 (corr.).

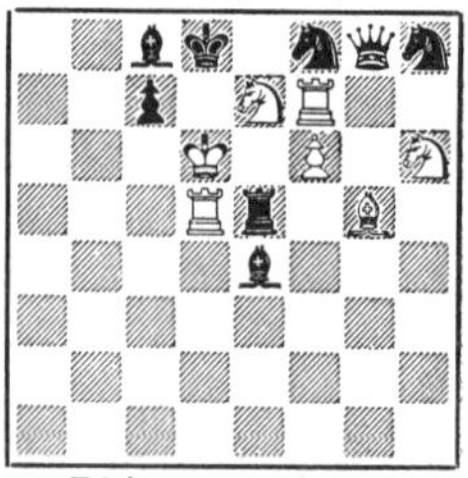

(Bl.)
Mate in II exactly.

S 151.

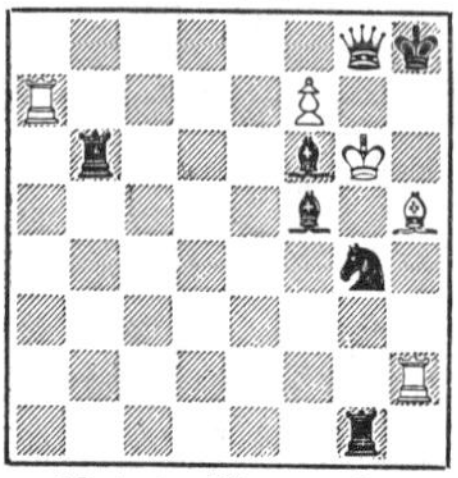

Mate in II exactly.
Black may not give check.

S 153.

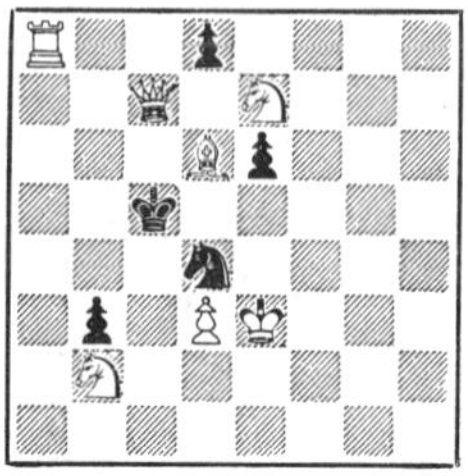

Mate in II exactly.

S 154.

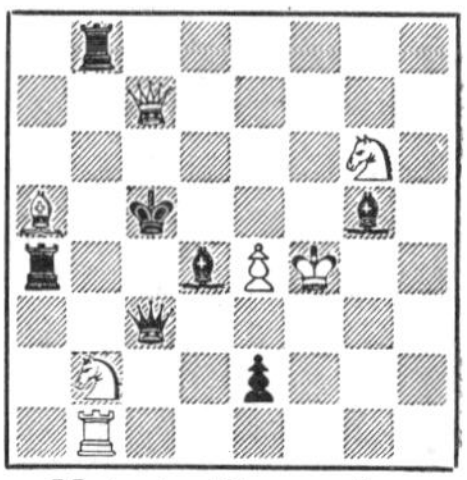

Mate in II exactly.

S 156.

Mate in II exactly.

S 158.

Mate in II exactly.

S 159.

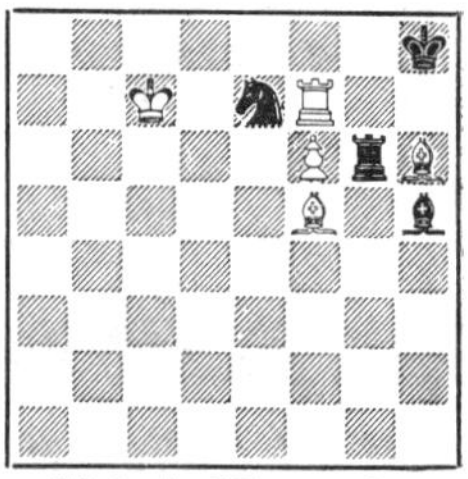

Mate in II exactly.

S 160.

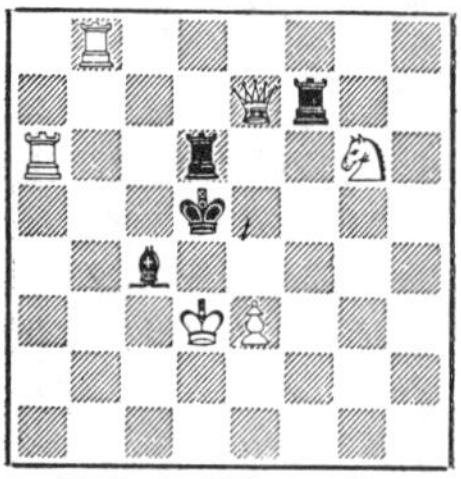

Mate in II exactly.

S 161 (corr.).

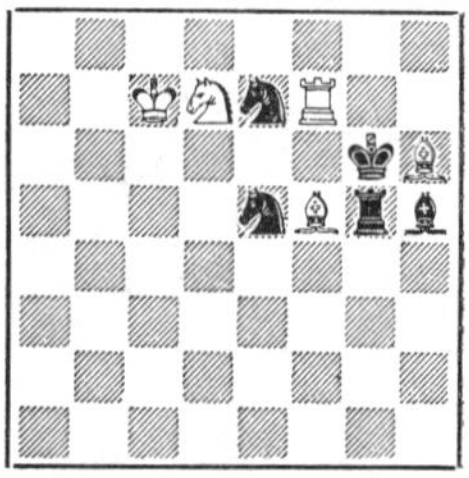

Mate in II exactly.

S 162 (corr.).

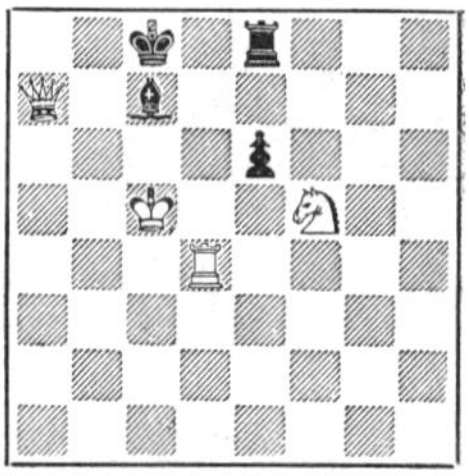

Mate in II exactly.
Ktf5 is fidated.

S 163.

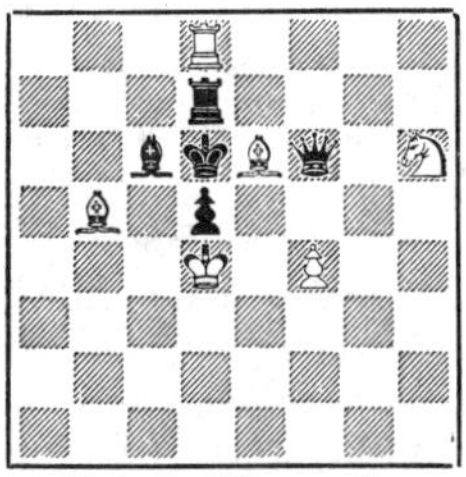

Mate in II exactly.

S 164 (corr.).

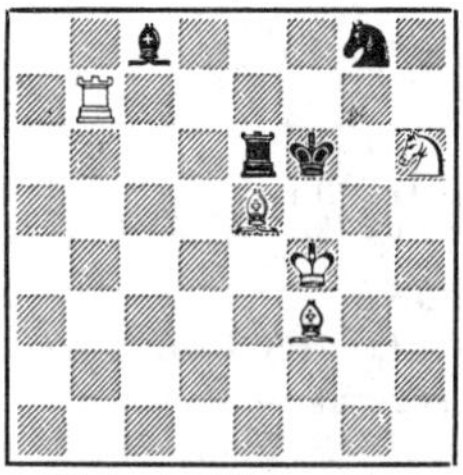

Mate in II exactly.

S 165.

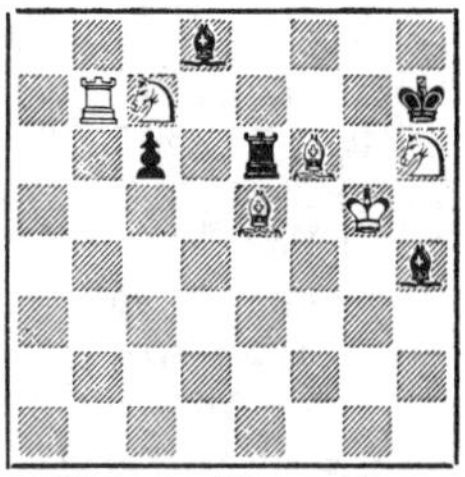

Mate in II exactly.

NOTES AND SOLUTIONS

S 1. Wh. Kf6, Re7, Ktf2, Ph6 ; Bl. Kf8, Ph7. Mate with Ph6 ; the Bl. P is fidated. Cf. CB 208. 2 = CB 84. 3 = CB 82. 4 = CB *43.* 5 = CB *194.* 6 = F *297.* 7. Wh. Kd7, Ra1, Kta5, Pb3 ; Bl. Ka8. In V ex. 1 Ktc6 + ; 2 Ra7 + ; 3 Kd6 ; 4 Kc7 ; 5 Ra5 m. 8 = CB 20. 9 = CB *31.* 10 = CB *33.* 11 = D *34.* 12 = CB 105. 13 = CB 47. 14 is a version of CB 185 in VII. 15 = F *320.* 16. Wh. Rf8, h5, Ktg8, h7, Pg6 ; Bl. Kh8, Pg7, Rf5. In II ex. Uns. If 1 Kt(g8)f6 + , P × R = Q. If 1 Rh6, Rh5. Cf. CB 283. 17 = Sens. *10.* 18. Cf. F 323 (Kh7 on h6, add Bl. Pf6, g6). In III ex. with P. *Pedones nigri qui sunt ante regem album saltant prima vice si volunt.* Uns. 1 Pc7, Pf4 or g4 ; 2 Bc5 is m. Var. Omit Pf6, g6. Uns. 1 Bc5 + , Ra4 ; 2 Pc7, Ra6 + . It is abnormal to allow Ps already on their 3rd sqs. to leap as if on their 2nd. 19 = CB *189.* 20 = CB *135.* 21 = CB *53.* 22 = PL *58.* Cf. CB 267. 23 = CB *198.* 24 = CB *162.* 25 = CB *113.* 26 = CB *112.* 27 = CB *119.* 28 = CB *120.* 29 = CB *140.* 30 = CB *230.* 31 = CB *135.* 32 = CB *117.* 33 = CB *257.* 34 = CB *42* var. 35 = CB *111* (omitting Ka1, Ph6 : *si rex niger est clausus debet spectare*). 36. 1 Qb7 + ; 2 Pa8 = Q m. 37 = CB *15.* 38. 1 Rd8 + ; 2 Rg5 ; 3 Rh8 + ; 4 B m. Var. In V ex. 1 Rd8 + ; 2 R(g3)g8 ; 3 Rd7 ; 4 Rh8 + ; 5 B m. 39. 1 Rd8, R × P + (any other ; 2 Ra7 m.) ; 2 Kt × R m. 40 corr. Wh. Ke2, Ktc6, Bb8, c8, Pa6, b6 ; Bl. Ka8. In II. ex. All the men are fidated. 1 Pa7 ; 2 Pa8 = Q m. 41 = CB 29 (only P fidated). 42 = CB *30.* 43 = CB 78. 44 = CB 75. 45 = CB 79. 46 = CB *74.* 47 = CB 76. 48 = CB 86. 49 = CB 94. 50 = CB 85. 51 = CB 186. 52 = CB *126.* 53. 1 Rc6 + ; 2 Kte3 m. 54. 1 R × R + , Kf8 (or Kh8 ; 2 Bf6 m.) ; 2 Pe7 m. 55. Wh. Ke6, Rc6, Qc7, Bf6, Pb7, f7 ; Bl. Kd8, Rf8, Bb8, Pe7. *Albi primo trahunt et mattabunt nigros ad duos tractus et fit in tribus modis, scilicet de regina in illis locis tribus vbi ludi potest scilicet ubicumque fit* A (b6, b8, d6), *et ipse necessario accipiet alphinum album cum suo pedone, et secundo tractu math de rocho in* B (c8), *uel de regina predicta in* D (c7). An absurdity, for Bl. is mate in the diagram. The text, however, precludes any emendation. 56. 1 Pe4 + , B × P ; 2 any, Kg6. If 2 . . , B × Q ; 3 Kte7 m. *ergo sit cautus ad capiendum.* 57. *Albi primo trahunt et uolunt mattare nigros in duobus tractibus. Tu accipe nigros quia fieri non potest. Si albi trahunt primo tractu pedonem in* A (e7), *capies eum cum alphino. Ipsi trahunt rocum suum in* B (b8) *dando scach. Tunc capias* (l. *cooperies*) *te de regina que stat in tractu eundo in* C (c8). *Sed si unus ex pedonibus albis esset in cruce* (a6 ; i. e. add Wh. Pa6), *tunc ipse adquiret quia daret tibi scach de sua regina in* A *predicta, et postea math de rocho similiter in* B, *quia non poteris te cooperire cum aliqua ex tuis reginis occasione sua cum pedone quia non poteris prelium saltare.* 1 Pe7 + , B × P ; 2 Rb8 + , Q(a8 or e8)c8. (If 1 Qe7 + , B × Q, &c.) Var. Add Wh. Pa6. Sound. 1 Qe7, B × Q ; 2 Rb8 m., for Q(a8) cannot pass attack of Pa6, nor Q(e8) that of Pe6. Of importance for the mediaeval rules, see p. 465. 58. 1 Qd2 + (or f2 + or f4 +) ; 2 Re4 m. 59. 1 Pe6 + ; 2 Kth8 or Kte7 (Kte5 or f4) m. acc. 60 corr. Wh. Kd2, Rb3, f4, Ktc5, e5, Bc4, e8, Pc2 ; Bl. Kd4, Ktc6, Bd5, Pd3, d6. In II ex. 1 Pc3 + ; 2 Kt × P m. 61. 1 Pd4 + ; 2 Qg6 m. (*math saltando cum regina tua*).

62. 1 R × Kt +; 2 Ktf8 or Kte5 (or R × R) m. acc. 63. 1 Ke3 +; 2 Kta6 or R × R m. acc. 64. 1 R × Q +; 2 Ph8 = Q m. 65. 1 Rb5 +; 2 Ktc7 m. 66. 1 R × R +; 2 Rg8 m. 67. 1 K × R +; 2 Rf7 or h7 m. acc. 68. 1 Ktf5 +; 2 Pg7 m. 69. 1 R × Kt +; 2 Rg8 or Ktd5 m. acc. 70. 1 Rg5 +; 2 Ktb5 m. 71. 1 Bc5 +; 2 Kte6 m. 72. 1 Pg5 +; 2 Be8 m. 73. 1 B × Kt +; 2 Ktd6 m. 74. 1 Ktf3 +; 2 Kt × Kt m. 75. 1 Re6 +; 2 Ktg7 m. 76. 1 Rf4 +; 2 Ktf6 or Kt × R m. acc. 77. 1 P × Kt +; 2 Bc2 m. 78. 1 P × Kt +; 2 Ra8 m. 79. 1 Kth5 +; 2 Rc8 m. 80. Wh. Kb7, Ra6, c1, Kta5, d1, Bc6, e6, Pc5, e5; Bl. Kb5, Rd5, Kte7, Bd4, Pa3. In II ex. MS. solves 1 Ktc3 +, Kb4 or K × P; 2 Kta2 m. In either case 2 . . , Kb5 is possible. I see no way of correcting the position. 81. 1 Kte6 +; 2 R × R m. 82. 1 Rf6 +; 2 Ph3 m. 83. 1 Kte6 +, Ktf5 + *et propter hoc forsitan credit non esse math, sed* 2 Q × R m. 84 = *82*. 85. 1 Bd6 +; 2 Ra4 m. 86. 1 P × Kt +; 2 Rf6 m. 87. 1 Kt × Kt +; 2 Rh7 m. 88. 1 Qg7 +; 2 Kt × R m. 89. 1 R × R +; 2 Bf5 m. 90. 1 Rg7 +; 2 Bb6 m. 91. 1 Rd4 +; 2 Ktc6 m. 94 = CB *117*. 107. 1 R × R +; 2 Be5 m. 108. MS. gives 1 R × R +; 2 Qg6 +, Kg7. It overlooks 1 Qf6 +; 2 Qg6 or R × R m. acc. (I assume that the Bl. P ascends, for otherwise 1 . . , P × R would be more obvious than the MS. defence.) 109. 1 Be7 +; 2 Rb5 m. 110. 1 Kf7; 2 Kt × R or Bf6 m. acc. Var. Bg6 on f8. Uns. If 1 Kf7, R × R +; 2 Kt × R +, Bh6. 111. Cf. 110 (omit Bd4, add Bl. Be5). In II ex. 1 Ktf6; 2 R m. 112. 1 P × R +; 2 Qb7 m. 113. 1 Kt × B +; 2 Ktf6 or Re7 m. acc. 114 = CB *81*. 115 = CB *83*. 116. 1 Kt × R +; 2 Kta6 or Qf7 m. acc. 117. If 1 Pc7 +; R × P. 118. 1 Bc7 +; 2 Kte7 m. 119. 1 R × Kt +, Qe8; 2 K × R m. 120 = CB *128*. 121 = CB *103*. 122 = CB 73. 123 = CB 67. 147 is an extended version of CB 136 in VI or less. 148 = BS 11 (text differs). 149. Cf. CB 259 (Kd3 on d4: in V). 150. Cf. CB 207 (Wh. Ke6, Rd7; Bl. Kb8). The R only moves to give mate. Uns. 151. 1 Bf3 +; 2 R × B m. 152. Wh. Kd8, Ktb8, g8, Bc8, f8, Pa7, b7, c7, e7, f7, h7; Bl. Kd4, Qe4. Wh. mate; the Bl. Q is fidated. Uns. Bl. plays K to a1 and Q to c2 or b3. Cf. CB 248. 153. 1 Ra5 +; 2 Pd4 m. 154. 1 Kt × R +; 2 Kte5 m. 155 = CB 175. 156. 1 Ktd2 +; 2 Pc4 m. 157. Wh. Kh5, Rb6, d4, Kte3, Pd3, h2; Bl. Kf5, Rd5, Pf3. In II ex. MS. solves 1 Rf4 +, K × R +; 2 Kt × R m. But 2 . . , Kf5 is possible. As diagrammed the Bl. K is in check. 158. 1 R × P +; 2 Bf6 or Ktf5 m. acc. 159. 1 Rh7 +; 2 Pf7 m. 160. 1 Pe4 +; 2 Q × R or R × R m. acc. 161. 1 Kt × Kt +; 2 Rh7 m. 162. 1 Ktd6 +; 2 Ktc8 m. 163. 1 R × R +; 2 Pf5 m. 164. 1 Kt × Kt +; 2 Rg7 m. 165. 1 Kt × R +; 2 Ktf8 m. 166. Wh. Kf4, Ra7, Ktf7, Bf3; Bl. Kg6, Re6, Qh6. In II ex. 1 Kth8 +; 2 Rf7 m. 167. Wh. Kg6, Rb6, h7, Ktc3, Ba6, Pf4; Bl. Ke6, Rc6, Kte3, Qf6, Pd5. In II ex. 1 Bc8 +; 2 Kte4 m. (but 2 . . , P × Kt is possible). 190 is a version of CB 217; Wh. self-mates in XI. 191. Wh. Kf6, Re7, Ktf2, Ph5; Bl. Kf8, Ph6. Wh. mates, the Bl. P is fidated. Uns.; is a var. of CB 208 and S 1. 192. Cf. F 290 (Ph2 on h7, Pc5 on c6). Black plays and White mates, with conditions (1) *non potest rex capere reginam in saltu nisi det sibi scach in saltu et non aliter* . . . (2) *si nigri non possunt trahere debent spectare math.* Unsound. 193 = CB *250*. 194 = CB 246 (*Hic est partitum omnium pulcerrimum quem oportet ludere longo exercitu et frequenti* (?) *addiscere. Quia si omnia scriberentur esset multum prolixa scriptura quare astute ludas et deffenditur ab omni insultu alborum*). 195 = CB 44. 196 = CB 115. 197. Wh. Kg5, Qh6, Bh4, Pa6, b3, e2, h7; Bl. Kf7, Qe7. Wh. mates, which is impossible unless he makes a black Q (i. e. queen on b8 or h8). This Bl. can prevent. The diagram is incorrect. The solution begins 1 Bf6, Kg7. Probably we must lower the Wh. K, Q, and B one sq. each, when 1 Bf5 (now), Kg7 has some point. Apparently the promoted Q cannot leap. The collection ends with *Et hec sufficiant* at the foot of this page. (Note: The colours are the reverse of those in the corresponding problems in CB in the cases of S 8, 47, 48, 124, 194, and 195.)

C = MS. Bibl. Casanatense, Rome, 791.

A quarto paper MS. containing a Latin treatise on the game of Rythmomachy,[9] written by an Englishman in the time of Edward IV, at the instance of George Neville, Archbishop of York (1465–76), and dedicated to Marcus, Cardinal of St. Mark, and a collection of 158 chess problems with Italian text, both of which treatises were copied in Rome in 1511 by Joannes Chachi of Terni in Umbria. The MS. consists of 118 leaves, only the chess portion being foliated (12 unnumbered leaves—1 a, the title *De ludo Arithmomachia*; 3 a–11 a, the treatise on this game, ending with the date of copying, *Anno Domini 1511 die 23 Novembr. Rome*, 12, blank diagrams for chess on *recto* and *verso*; ff. 1–79, the chess work, ending with *Ex anno 1511 die Mercurij 30 Julij, Rome*, at the foot of 79 b; followed by 26 unnumbered leaves with blank diagrams of chess, at the foot of the last, the autograph *Joannes Chachi de Ynteramna, 1511*; + 1 leaf, blank).

The chess work is divided into three sections: the first, without special title, extends from f. 1 to f. 62 a, and was evidently intended to contain sound problems of old chess only. By accident, one position of new chess (C 12) and a few unsound problems have been included. The second section begins on f. 62 b, with the title *Partiti falsi che pareno ligieri et non si possono dar*, and ends on f. 74 a, with the note *Qui finiscono li partiti che pareno boni et sono falsi.* It accordingly contains unsound problems. The third section begins on f. 74 b, with the title *De la D(onna). Partiti ala rabiosa*, and contains problems of the modern chess. The problems are not arranged by the length of the solutions.

More than half of the problems are in two or three moves exactly; no less than 58 being in three. Chachi's preference was thus for short problems; he also appears to have preferred unsound problems to sound ones. To 44 of his problems he adds notes as to how the position can be altered to produce the contrary result, and in C 10 says *Ma questo partito è piu bello falso.* His liking for the conditional mate, and specially the variety in which the player is to give check on one move with one Pawn, and to give mate on the following move with a second Pawn, only reflects the taste of the Italian players of the 16th cent.

This MS. has a special interest as dating from the transition period when the old and the modern game were co-existent; Chachi must have known both varieties of chess, for he has not added any note as to the differences between the two games, or their respective rules. Neither does he give any indication as to which game was the more popular with players or problem-lovers.

[9] Commonly called in England *the Philosopher's game*. It was played on a board of 8 × 16 squares with 24 men a side. In the MS. C these consist of 8 circular men moving to any adjacent square, 8 triangular men moving in the same 8 directions but into the second square, and 8 square men who moved still in the same 8 directions but into the third square. The triangular men consequently leaped over one, and the square men over two squares. In later accounts the moves and the initial arrangement of the men differ somewhat. The method of capture was very complicated, and depended in part upon combinations of the numbers which each counter or man bore. The game is described in the *Vetula*, and another MS. of the C text is contained in the MS. Ash. Cf. C. de Boissière (Buxerius), *Le tresexcellent et ancien ieu Pythagorique dict Rythmomachia*, Paris, 1554; W. F(ulke), *The Philosopher's Game*, London, 1563; and Selenus, pp. 443–95.

C 7.

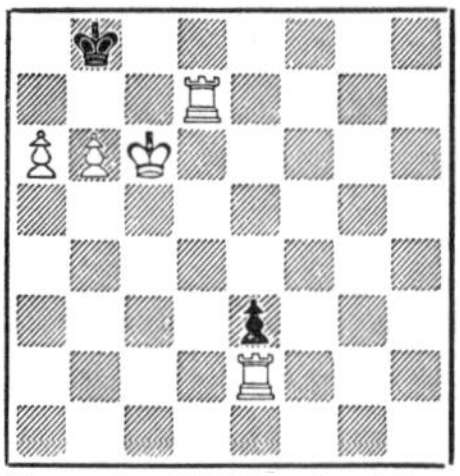

Mate in VIII, checking with one P on 7th move and mating with the other. Pe3 is fidated.

C 11.

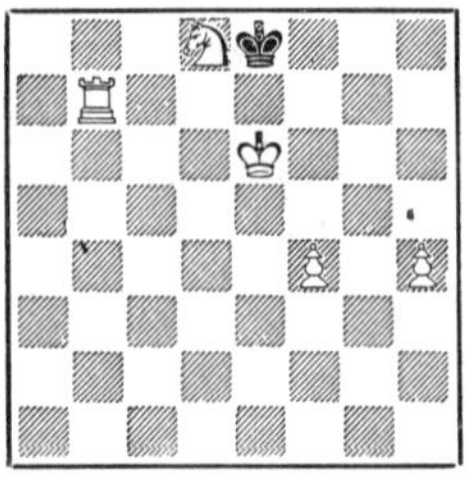

Mate in VI, checking with one P on 5th move and mating with the other.

C 22.

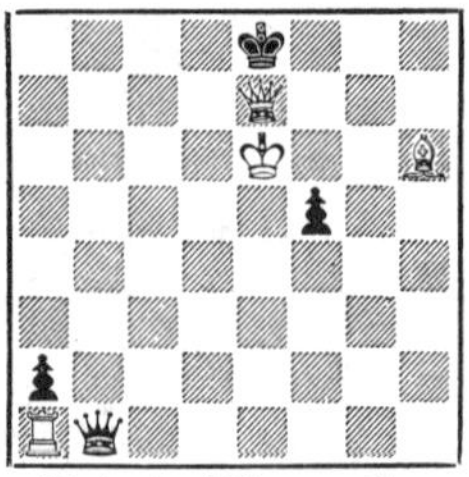

Mate in III exactly.

C 23.

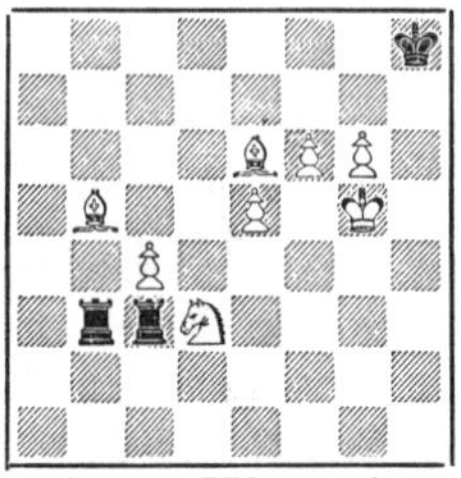

Mate in III exactly.

C 30.

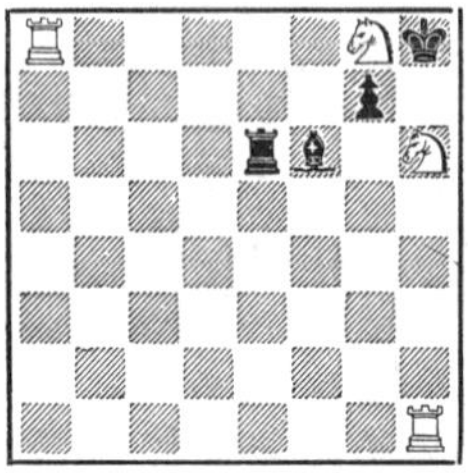

(Bl.)
Mate in IV exactly.

C 36.

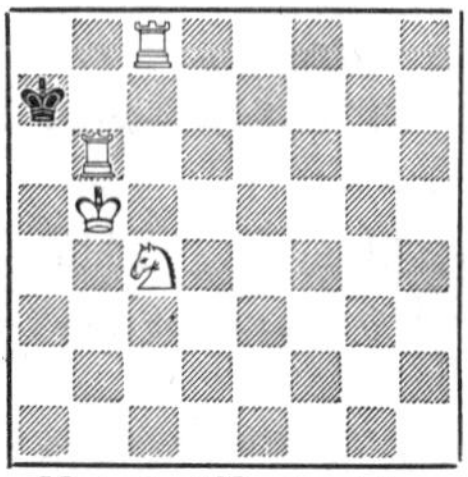

Mate in IV, checking each move.

C 45.

Mate in IX exactly.

C 48.

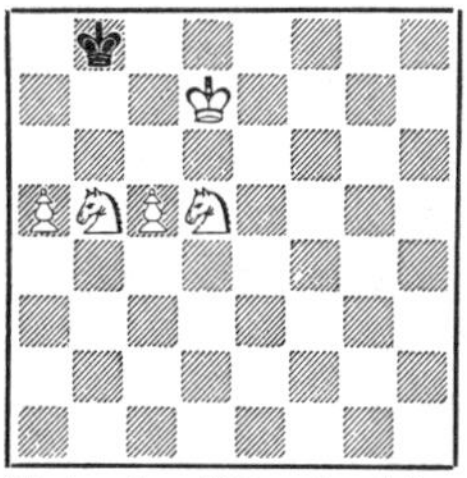

Mate in VI, checking with one P on 5th move and mating with the other.

C 49 = 101.

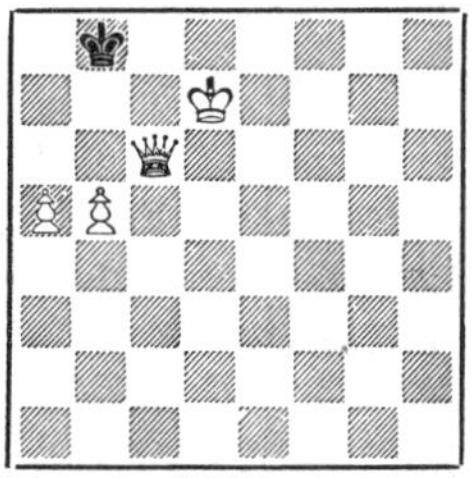

Mate in VIII, checking with one P on 7th move and mating with the other.

C 50.

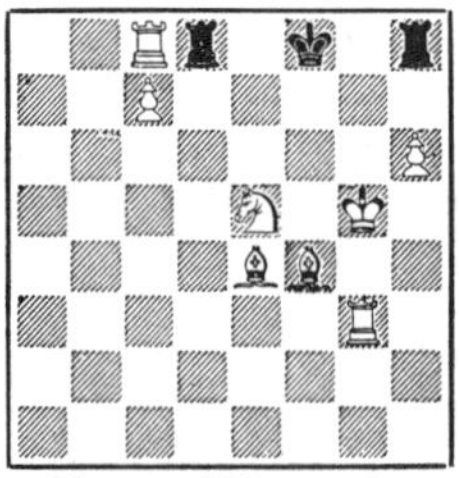

Mate in III exactly.

C 51.

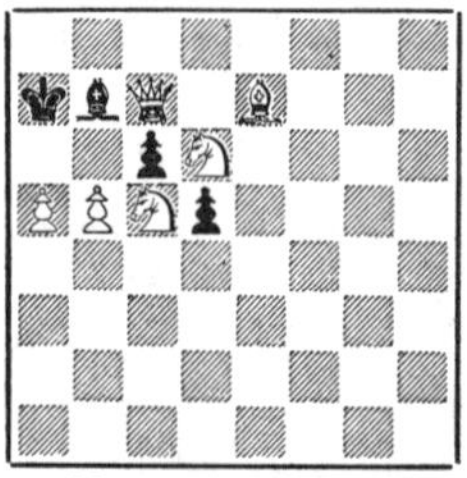

Mate with B in V exactly.

C 53.

Mate in XI, checking with one P on 10th move and mating with the other.

C 54.

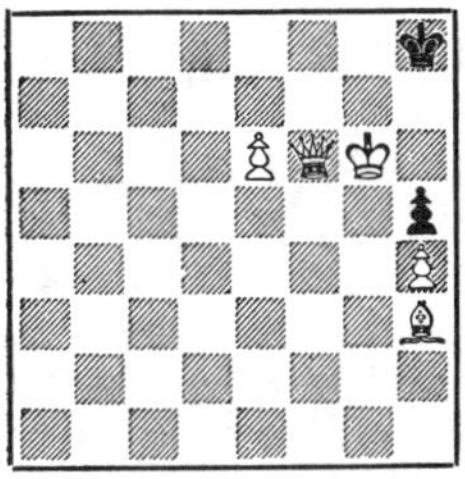

Mate with Ph4 in XI.

C 57.

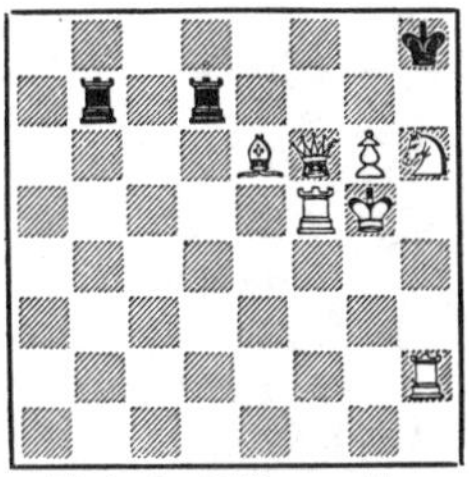

Mate in III exactly.
The Black Rs are fidated.

C 58.

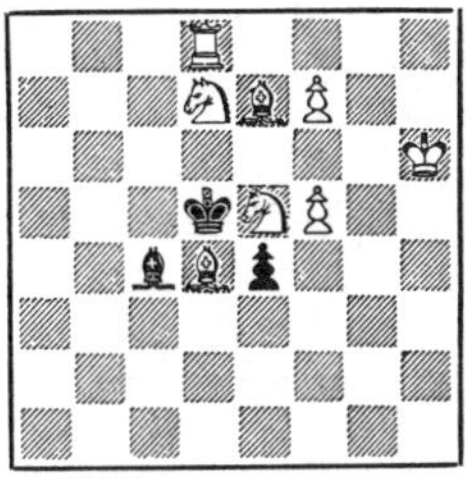

(Bl.)
Mate in III exactly.

C 60 (corr.).

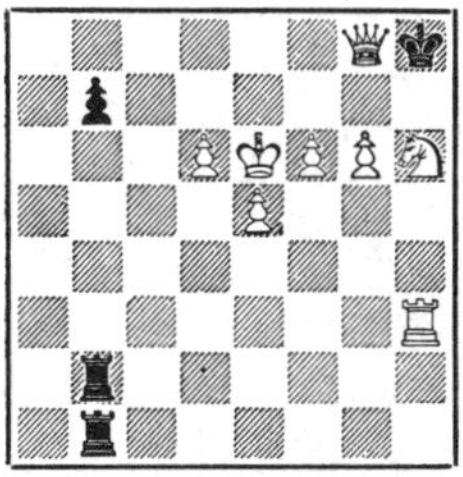

Mate in III exactly. The Bl. Rs are fidated, the Wh. R is immovable, and all the Ps play to the 8th row.

C 61.

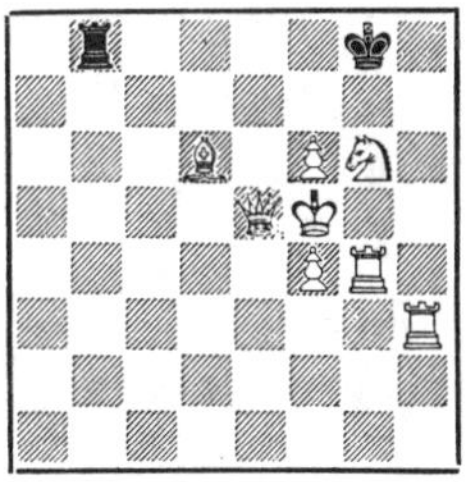

Mate in III exactly.
The Bl. R is fidated.

C 62 (corr.).

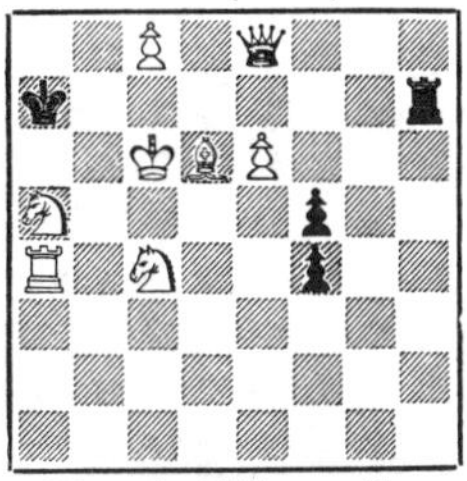

Mate in III exactly.
Rh7 is fidated, and Pc8 is immovable.

C 63 (corr.).

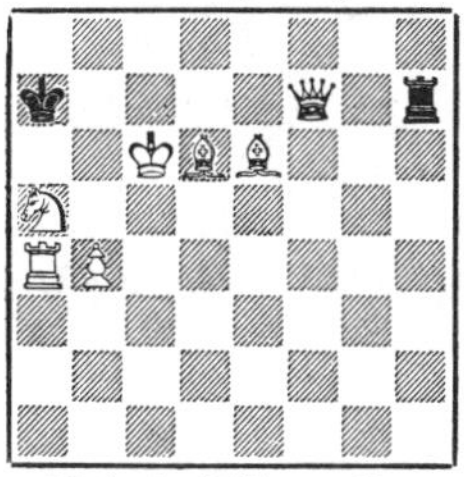

Mate in III exactly.

C 64.

(Bl.)
Mate in III exactly.

C 66.

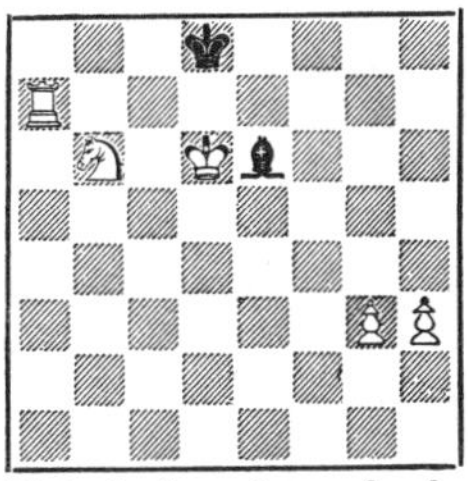

Mate in L or less, checking with one P on the penultimate move and mating with the other.

C 67 (corr.).

Mate in III exactly.

C 68.

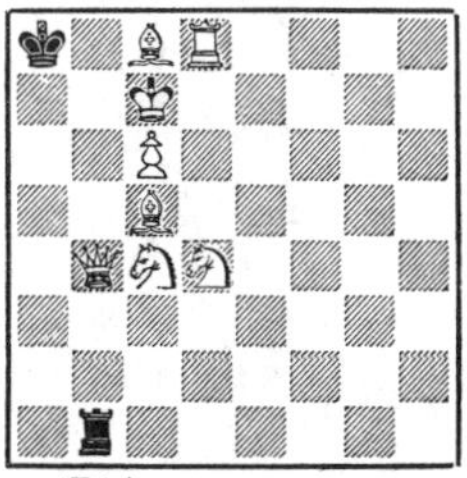

(Bl.)
Mate in III exactly.
The Bl. R is fidated.

C 70.

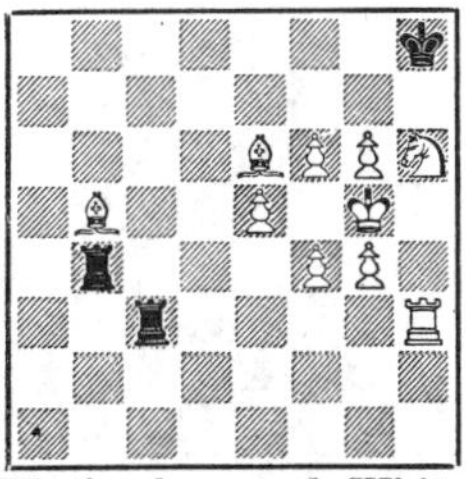

Black plays and White mates in III exactly.
The Rs are fidated.

C 71 (corr.).

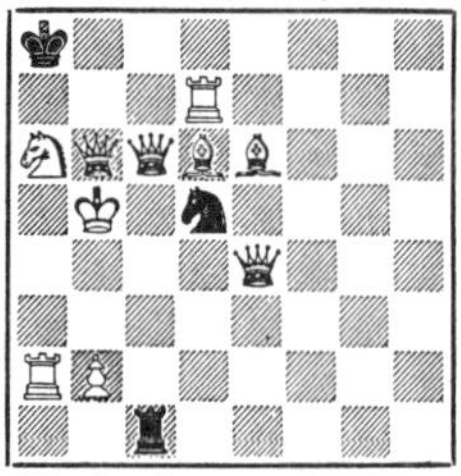

Black plays and White mates in III exactly.

C 72.

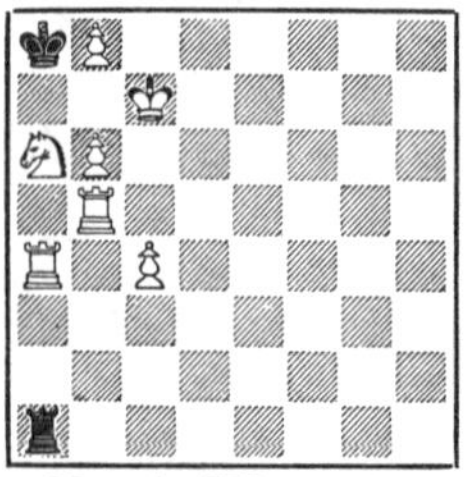

Mate in III exactly. Ra1 is fidated.

C 73 (corr.).

Mate in III exactly. The Black men are fidated and Kc6 is immovable.

C 74.

Mate in III exactly. Rb1 is fidated.

C 75.

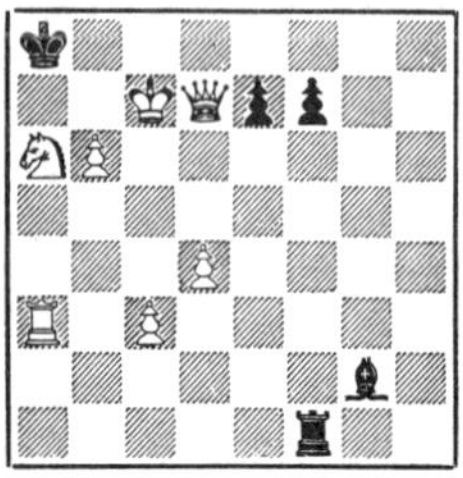

Mate in III exactly. Rf1 is fidated, and all the Ps play to the 8th row.

C 79.

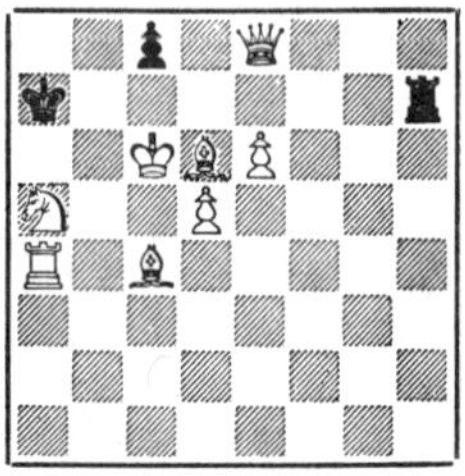

Mate in III exactly. Rh7 is fidated, and Pc8 is immovable.

C 81.

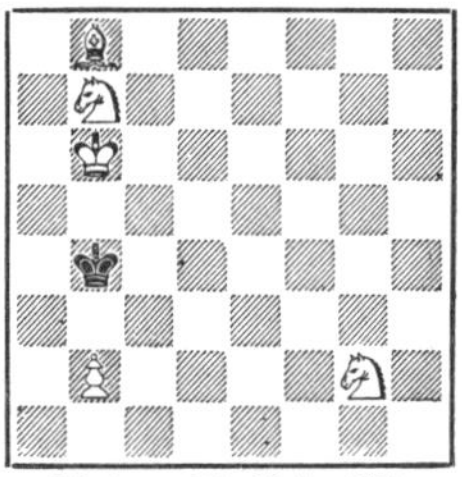

Mate with P in IV exactly.

C 83.

Mate with P in V exactly.

C 86.

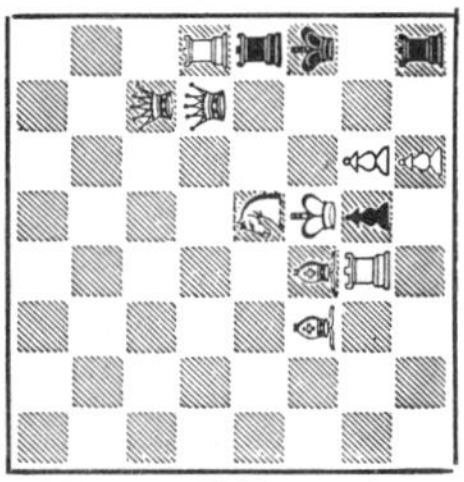

Mate in III exactly. All the Ps play to the *a* file.

C 92.

Knight's tour on the half-board.

C 99.

(Bl.)

Mate with Pa5. The Pa4 is fidated.

C 113.

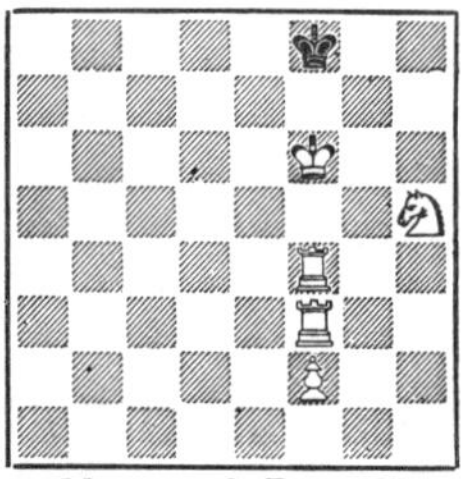

Mate with P in VI exactly.

C 114 (corr.).

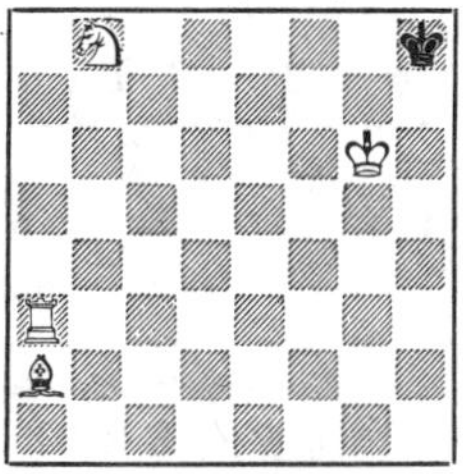

Mate with B in VII exactly.

C 115 (corr.).

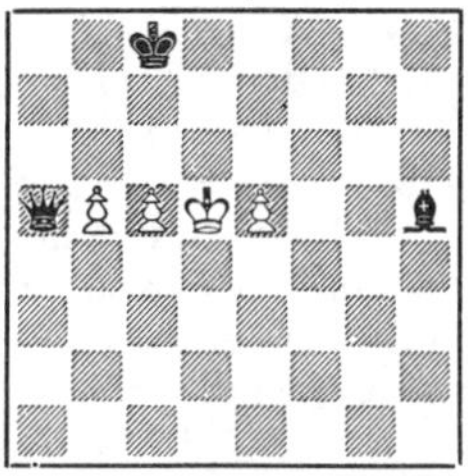

Black plays and White mates or win the B.

C 117 (corr.).

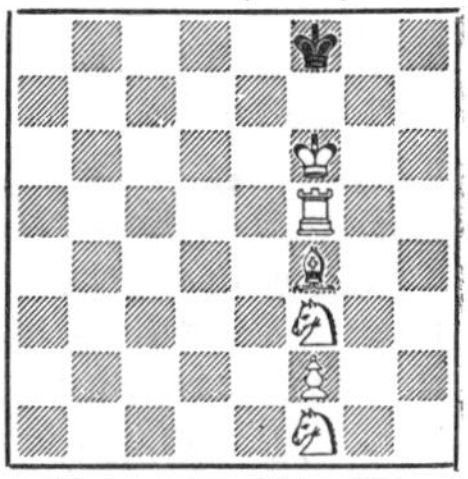

Mate with P in VI.

C 124.

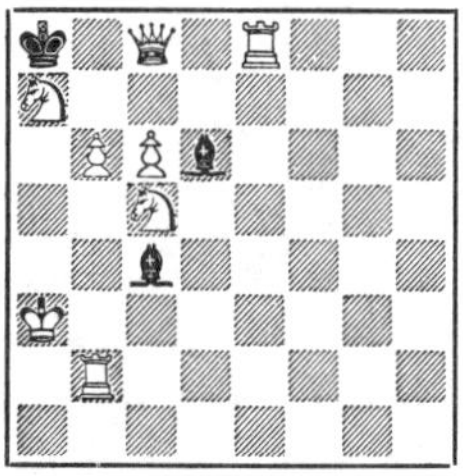

Mate in V exactly. Said to be unsound.

C 139.

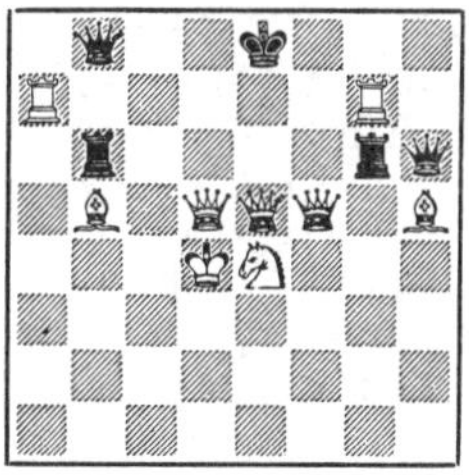

Mate in III exactly. Unsound.

C 145.

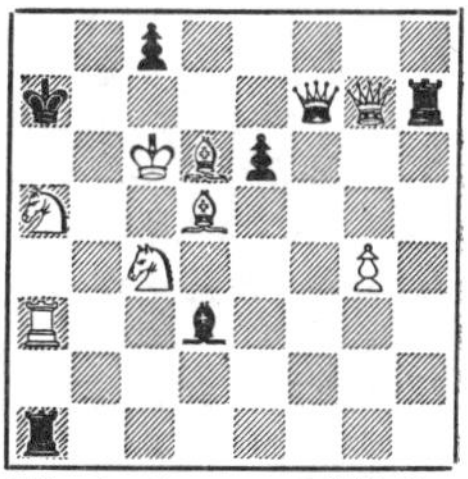

Black plays and White mates in III exactly. Rh7 is fidated. Unsound.

NOTES AND SOLUTIONS

C 1 = F 320. 2 = CB *66*. 3 is a version of CB *186* in VI ex. 4 is a version of CB *117* in V. 5 = CB 52. 6. Wh. Ra1, Kta6, Bd6, Pb6, c6; Bl. Ka8, Rf8, g7. In III ex. 1 B × R; 2 Bd6; 3 Ktc7 m.; or 2 Ktc7 +; 3 Ra8 m. acc. as Bl. plays. Cf. CB 43. Var. Rf8, g7, on f7, e8. Uns. If 1 Bb8 or f8, Ra7. 7. 1 Rc7; 2 Kc5; 3 Kc4; 4 Kd3; 5 Ra2, Ka8 !; 6 Ke2; 7 Pa7 +; 8 Pb7 m. 8 = F *303*. 9 is a version of CB *112* in V. 10 = CB *45*. 11. 1 Ktf7; 2 Rb8 +; 3 Rh8; 4 Pf5 +; 5 Pf6 +; 6 Ph5 m. 13. Wh. Kg5, Rh2, Kth6, Bd6, e6, Pf6, g6; Bl. Kh8, Rc7, Pc4. In III ex.; the bl. R is fidated. 1 B × P &c. Var. Pc4 on c3. Uns. If 1 Bc4, Rf7; 2 Be6, Pc2. 14 = CB *93*. 15. Wh. Ke1, Ra1, Ktc1, Bh2, Pe2, e3, e4, e5, e6, e7; Bl. Ke8. In VI ex. 1 Ktb3; 2 Ra8; 3 Ra7 &c. Cf. CB 133. 16 is a version of CB *6*. 17 = Picc. *15*. 18 = CB *98*. 19. Cf. F *303*. 20 = CB *117*. 21 = CB 28. 22. 1 Bf4; 2 Rg1; 3 Rg8 m. Var. Pf5 on f6. Uns. Based on D 56. 23. 1 Bd7; 2 Pg7 +; 3 Bf5 m. *Questo partito se può meter de dar mato de a(lfino) in 3 tratti.* 24 = CB *114*. 25 = Picc. *20*. 26 = CB *56*. 27 = CB 1. 28. Wh. Ke4, Rb7, Ktd8; Bl. Ka8, Kta4. *Dice lo b. che darà mato al n. ouero le leuarà lo c. Dice lo n. che iocando auanti è contento.* 1 . . , Ktc5 + r; 2 Kd5; 3 Ktc6 *et così serà asediato lo R. n. et incluso lo c. et serà forza che piglate detto c.* 29. Cf. F *303*. 30 1 Ktf4 +; 2 Kt(g8)e7 +; 3 R + B +; 4 R × R m. Cf. C 97, 98, the three positions forming a corresponding group to CB 283, 284, 285. 31 = CB *2*. 32 = C 31, but in III ex., Ktb6 being fidated. 33 is a version of CB 207 in XIII. 34. Wh. Kg5, Kth6, Rh1, Bb5, e6, Pe4, f6, g6; Bl. Kh8, Rb3, c3. In III ex. 1 Pg7 +; 2 Pg8 = Q +; 3 Ktf7 m. 35 in III is C 36 after first move. 36. 1 Rc7 +; 2 Rc8 +; 3 Ra6 +; 4 Ktd6 m. 37. Wh. Kd6, Ra6, h7; Bl. Kd8,

Ktb6. In II ex. 1 R × Kt &c. Var. Ra6 on a7. Uns. 38, 39, and 40 are variations of CB *114*. 41 = CB *24*. 42 = CB *11*. 43. Wh. Kb5, Rh7, Pb6, c6; Bl. Kb8. In V ex. with the two Ps. 1 Rd7; 2 Ka5; 3 Ka6; 4 Pb7+; 5 Pc7 m. Contrast with C 7. 44. Cf. F 303. 45. 1 Ktb8; 2 cRd8+; 3 Re1; 4 Rc1; 5 dRc8; 6 Ktd7; 7 R(c1)c6 &c. 46 = CB *162*. 47 = CB *133*. 48. 1 Pa6; 2Kte7; 3 Ktc8; 4 Ktc7+; 5 Pa7+; 6 Pc6 m. Var. Kb8 on a8. Uns. 49. 1 Kd8, Ka8!; 2 Kc8; 3 Kc7; 4 Qb7+; 5 Kc6; 6 Pa6; 7 Pb6+; 8 Pa7 m. 50. 1 Kf6, R × P+ (or Rg8; 2 Bd6+ &c., or Rh7; 2 Bd6+ &c., or Ke8; 2 Bc6 or g6+ &c., or R × R; 2 Bd6+ &c.); 2 B × R+; 3 R × R m. Var. Rd8 on e8. Uns. If 1 Kf6, R × P+. 51. 1 Ktc8+; 2 Ktb6+; 3 Qb8+; 4 Kta6+; 5 Bc5 m. 52. Cf. CB *64*. 53. 1 Ktc7; 2 Kte8; 3 Ktg7; 4 Pf5; 5 Pf4; 6 Pg5; 7 Pg4; 8 Kf8; 9 Bf6+; 10 Pg6+; 11 Pg5 m. 54. 1 Qg7+; 2 Kf6; 3 Pe7; 4 Pe8 = Q; 5 Qe6; 6 Qf5; 7 Qg4; 8 Bg5; 9 Ph5; 10 Ph6; 11 Ph7 m. 55 = D *16*. 56 = CB 37 but in III ex.: Bl. play first and all the men are fidated. 57. 1 Qe7; 2 Rf8+; 3 Rg8 m. or 2 Ktf7+; 3 Rh7 m. acc. as Bl. plays. 58. 1 Ktc5+; 2 Kg5; 3 Pf6 m. Var. Kh6 on h7. Uns. 59. Cf. Picc. *80*. 60. 1 Kf7; 2 Kf8; 3 Ktf7 m. 61. 1 Rh7; 2 Kte7; 3 R(g4)h4 m. Var. Rh3, g4, on g3, h4. Uns. If 1 Rh7, K × R; 2 Kte7, Rb3. If 1 Rg4 or g5, Rb7. 62. 1 Qf7; 2 Kta3; 3 Kt(a5)c4 m. Var. Ra4 on a3. Uns. 63. 1 Pb5, Rh4; 2 Bg4; 3 Ktc4 m. Var. Ra4 on a2. Uns. 64. 1 Be6; 2 Kc8 (if 1 . . , Pd8 = Q; 2 Qe7; 3 Kt m. 65. Cf. 64. 66. Obtain the position Wh. Kg2, Rf6, Ktf7, Pg3, h3; Bl. Kh5, Bg4. Now 1 Ph4; 2 Rh6+; 3 Ktd6; 4 Rg6+; 5 Rg5+; 6 Ktf5+; 7 Rg7+; 8 Pg4; 9 Pg5; 10 Pg6; 11 Ph5; 12 Ph6; 13 Rf7; 14 Ktg3; 15 Kte4; 16 Ktg5; 17 P+; 18 P m. 67. 1 Rf1 (not the only move), Bg7; 2 P × B+ (or R × B); 3 Ktf7 m. 1 . . , P × R, and 1 . . , Bd5 are no better. Var. Qc6 on c7, Qc7 on c8. Said to be uns. but 1 Ktc3, Be5; 2 Kt × B; 3 Ktf7 m. 68. Really uns. 1 Re8, Rg1 (or h1); 2 Kd6, Rg8 (or h8) or 2 Kta3 (or a5), R+ saves the mate. Var. Rd8 on h8, Qb4 on c3. Uns. 69 = CB *100*. 70. 1 . . , Rc7; 2 Bd7; 3 Ktf4+; 4 Pg7 m. or 3 Pg7+; 4 Kt m. acc. as Bl. plays. If 1 . . , any other; 2 Pg7+; 3 Pg8 = Q+; 4 Ktf7 m. Var. Bl. Rs on b3, c4. Uns. 71. 1 . . , Ktc7+; 2 Ka5, R × Q; 3 Rd8+; 4 Rb8 m. Or 1 . . , Ktc3+; 2 P × Kt, Rb1+; 3 Kc4; 4 Kt m. Var. Rd7 on f7. Uns. 72. 1 Kc8, R × R; 2 Ra5, R × R; 3 Ktc7 m. Var. Wh. Rs on a5, b4. Uns. 73. 1 Kta6, Rh3 (or Rh5; 2 Ktc7+; 3 Kt m.); 2 Ktb3; 3 Ktc7 m. Var. Ra3 on a2. Uns. 74. 1 Kt(c6)b4; 2 Kc8; 3 Ktc7 m. Var. Pf8 on g8. Uns. 75. 1 Kc8, Pe8 = Q; 2 Q × Q; 3 Ktc7 m. Var. Rf1 on e1. Uns. 76 = CB 49. 77 = Picc. *127*. 78. Cf. F *333*. 79. 1 Qf7, Rh4 (or R × Q; 2 Pe7; 3 Ktb7 m.); 2 Kc7; 3 Ktc6 m. Var. Pe6 on f6. Uns. 80 = CB *44* after first move. 81. 1 Kta5; 2 Kte3; 3 Ktc2+; 4 Pb3 m. 82 = F *316*. 83. 1 Rh7+; 2 Ktf6+; 3 Pe7+; 4 Rf7+; 5 Pg7 m. Var. Rh1 on g1. Uns. 84. Cf. PL *141*. 85 = CB *233*. 86. 1 Bd6+; 2 Pf6+, P × P *per forza*; 3 Rg8 m. 87 = CB *105*. 88 = CB *53*. 89 = CB *252* (in XIV). 90 = CB 236. 91 = CB *222*. 92. By slightly altering the order of the last four moves (28–31–30–29) the tour can be continued as a re-entrant tour over the whole board. 93 = CB *135*. 94 = CB *257*. 95. Cf. Picc. *135*. 96 = CB *22*. 97. Cf. C 30 (Ra8, h1, on b8, h2). In II ex. 1 Kt × B+; 2 m. acc. 98. Cf. C 30 (Ra8, h1, on e8, h5). In III ex. Really uns. 1 Kte7+, Kh7; 2 Rh8+, B × R! 99. Obtain position Wh. Kc3, Rd2, Ktc5, Be6, Pa5; Bl. Kb1, Pa4, Bl. to play, and continue 1 . . , Ka1 (c1); 2 Bc4; 3 Rd5; 4 Ktb3+; 5 Rb5 &c. 100 is a similar problem. 101 = 49. 102 = F *297*. 103, 104. To place four Rs and four Qs, all fidated, on the board, checking the Bl. K every move, and mating with the last one to be placed. Uns., for the Bl. K can occupy the square on which the last piece should play. The desired positions are Ra8, b7, g2, h1, Qd4, d5, e4, e5; or Re4, f3, g2, h1, Qb6, b7, c6, c7. 105 = CB 249. 106 = CB 239. 107 = CB *135*. 108 = CB *153*. 109 = 60. 110 = CB *212*. 111 = 59 but Bl. plays first. 112 = CB *254*. 113. 1 Rg4; 2 Rg8+; 3 Rc3; 4 Rg7; 5 Rd7+; 6 Pf3 m. 114. 1 Rh3+; 2 Rh7; 3 Rg7; 4 Rd7; 5 Rd8+; 6 Ktc6+; 7 Bc4 m. 115. 1 . . , Kd8 (Bf7+ loses the B); 2 Kd6; 3 Pe6, &c. 116 = CB *251*. 117. 1 Re5; 2 Re8+; 3 Bd6; 4 Ktg5; 5 Rh8+; 6 Pf3 m. 118. Wh. Ke6, Rb7, f6, Pa3, d3, d4, d5; Bl. Ke8. In V with Pd3. 1 Rb4; 2 Rf8+; 3 Pd6+; 4 Pd5+; 5 Pd4 m. 119. Cf. CB *113*. 120 = CB *135*. 121 = CB *47*. 122. Cf. CB *135*. 123 = CB 48. 124. The position appears to be defective for 1 Qd7+; 2 Pc7; 3 Qc6+; 4 any; 5 Qb7 m. is possible (v. d. Lasa). 125 = F *323*. 126 = CB 44. 127 = CB *250*. 128 is an uns. var. of CB *33*. 129. Cf. CB *25*. 130 = CB *76*. 131 is an uns. var. of CB *125*. 132 = CB *140*. 133. Cf. F 323. 134 is an uns. var. of CB *7*. 135 = 132. 136. Cf. CB *114*. 137. Cf. CB *8*. 138. Cf. CB *113*. 139. If 1 Kt+, Kf8. If 1 R(a7)e7 or R(g7)e7+, Kd8. 140 = 126. 141 = CB *14*. 142 is an uns. var. of CB *76*. 143. Cf. C 68 (Rd8 on h8, Rb1 on b2, Qb4 on c3; add Bl. Qb4). In III ex., Rb2 is fidated. Uns. 1 Q × Q, Re2 (or Rg2 or h2, but not R × Q as in MS., for then 2 Ba6+; 3 Ktb6 m.). 144. Cf. CB *55*. 145. 1.., Rh5; 2 Kc7, Ka6; 3 Kc6, R × B. Cf. C 62, 79. 146 = Picc. *127*. 147. Cf. F 303.

There are other works of the transitional period which include problems, both of the old and of the modern game. Of these

Per. = MS. L. 27, Bibl. Comunale di Perugia

is a paper quarto MS. of 196 leaves, of which the first 165 contain diagrams ruled for chess. Only the first 66 have been filled with chess, and only four others for other games (f. 163a 'Ludus dominarum' is draughts; 163b, 164b, 165a, are games with the draughtsmen, headed 'Ludus rebellionis') on the chessboard. Ff. 166–90 contain a transcript of the CB collection of merels problems. The chess problems and positions, usually headed 'Regula', rarely have any text other than the title which gives the conditions and the letter 'f' or 'd', according as the position is one of the old or the modern game. The MS. is written in one hand of the 16th c., a later hand has added the title 'Ludus latrunculorum'. The first 7 diagrams contain 12 Exercises (1 = CB *234*; 2 = CB 243; 3 = CB 207, 209; 4 = K 3, CB 233, 236; 5 = CB *232*, 6 = CB 273; 7 = K 6. I do not recognize the second positions on Per. 2 and 7). Eleven other positions are taken from the CB work (31 = CB 219; 46 = 254; 47 = 251; 49 = 257; 53 = 250; 55 = 253; 56 = 219; 59 = 211; 62 = 208; 64 = 212; 65 = 277), and one from the extended CB (48 = F 322). Five other positions described as old have not been identified by me. These are—

Per. 50. Wh. Ke5, Be4, Pa4, h2; Bl. Ke8, P(fidated)a4. Mate in ? X moves. 51. Wh. Kf5, Pb5; Bl. Kh5, Qa5, Pc5. Mate with Pawn in ? X moves, 'bene optime'—probably incorrectly diagrammed. 52. Wh. Ke5, Rb7, Qh5, Pe4, f3, f5; Bl. Ka8, Rc6. Mate in XV or less, 'bene optime'. 61. Wh. Ka6, Rb1, c4, Bf4, Ph4; Bl. Ka8, Ph3. Mate with Pawn in XII or less. Apparently 1 Rb8+; 2 Bd6; 3 Rg4; 4–6 P queens; 7–12 Q to b7 m. is intended, but the Bl. Pawn queens in time to interfere. 63. Wh. Kc8, Qb8, Pg3; Bl. Ka1, Bb3, P(immovable and fidated)b1. Mate with Pawn in XII or less. Solved in MS. by 1–5 P queens; 6 Qh7, &c. If the Wh. Pawn had been on g4, the solution would have run 1–4 P queens; 5 Qg6, &c.

The remaining positions are either problems or endings of the modern game, or diagrams showing the initial arrangement for certain forms of odds (10–19, 21, 22); thus Per. 10 gives White a (modern) Queen with power to move as a Knight, and Black a second Queen in the place of his two Rooks; 18 is the odds of the 'capped Pawn (g2)', and 22 is Arch. 28.

Another work of the same transitional period, which contains problems both of the old and of the modern game, is Lucena's *Repeticion de amores e arte de axedres* (*c.* 1497) (= Luc.). The 150 problems in this work are arranged by the number of moves, and are each headed *De la dama de dos, iii,* &c., or *Del viejo de dos, iii,* &c., according as they are of the new or the old game. These headings are not always correct, and probably depend upon the nature of the source from which Lucena had obtained them. One of these sources was the CB work, and the Spanish solutions in Lucena's work are close translations of the original Latin.[10]

The problems of the older game follow:

Luc. 95.

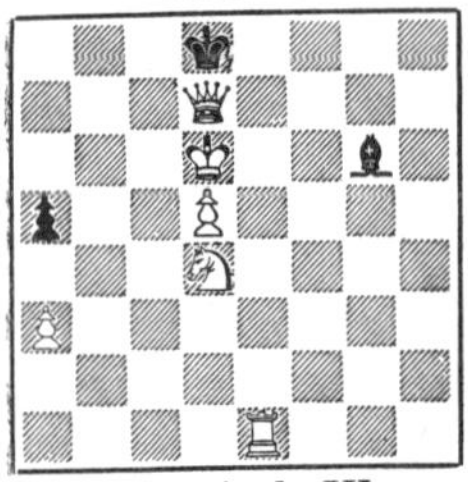

Del viejo de IV. Mate with Pd4.

Luc. 97.

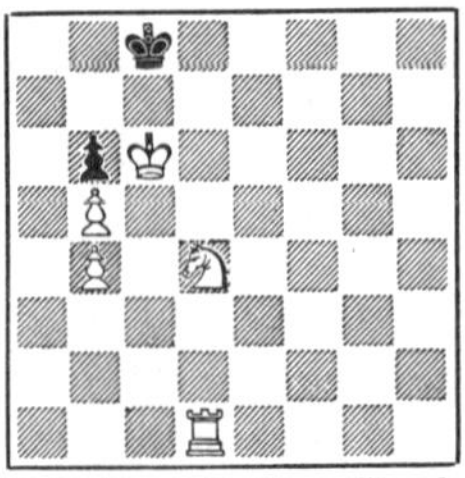

Del viejo de V. Check with one P on 4th move, and mate with the other.

Luc. 101.

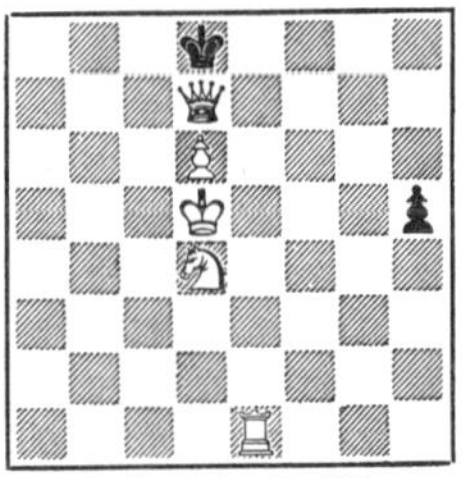

Del viejo de IV. Mate with Pd6.

NOTES AND SOLUTIONS

10 = CB *14*. 11 = CB 8. 12 = Picc. *20*. 13 = F 320. 14 = CB *2*. 15. Cf. CB *6*. 18 = CB *88*. 19 = CB 90. 20 = CB *84*. 21 = CB 86. **22 = CB 87.** 23 = CB 89. 24 = CB 65. 25 = CB *58* (add Wh. Pa3). *El blanco tiene la mano y dize que dará xaque y mate al negro en tres lances ni mas ni menos. El primero de roque en* A (h8), *y el cubresse; despues iugad del otro roque donde estaua el primero y es mate al otro lance porque nunca el iuego se dize robado si prendiendo da mate.* 26 = CB 63. 27 = CB 52. 28 = CB 42. 29 = CB 46. 30 = CB 55. 31 = CB 60. 32 (= 75 *dela dama*) = CB 50. 33 = CB *64*. 34 (= 92 *dela dama*) = CB 101. 35 = CB 107. 36 = CB 98. 37 = CB 109. 38 (= 91 *dela dama*) = CB 97. 39 = CB *117*. 40 = CB 45. 41 = CB 44. 42 = CB 49. 43 = CB 83. 44 (= 73 *dela dama*) = CB 85. 45 = CB 95. 46 = CB 96. 47 = CB *79*. 48 = CB 76. 49 = CB 77. 50 = CB 81. 51 = CB 72. 52 = CB 75. 53 = CB 71. 54 = CB *67*. 55 (= 17 *dela dama*) = CB 73. 56 = CB *66*. 57 = CB 70. 58 = CB *82*. 59 = CB 80. 60 = CB 74. 61 = CB 78. 62 = CB 108. 63 = CB 116. 64 = CB 100. 65 = CB 103. 66 = CB 54. 67 = CB 61. 78 = C *68*. 79 = CB 56. 80 = Ad. *64*. 94 = CB *120*. 95. *Y es vn juego comun que quasi todo hombre lo sabe o lo puede bien contar.* 1 Re8 +, B × R; 2 Ktc6, B × Kt; 3 P × B, Pa4; 4 Pc7 m. Var. *Empero haze le vn sotil enganno . que allega hombre el peon blanco al negro al punto* (a4) *y el que mira crebe que non se puede dar porque queda el negro ahogado en aquella manera.* But 1 Rb1; 2 Ke6, Kc7 (any other; 3 Ktc6 +; 4 P m.); 3 Ke7; 4 Pd6 m. Cf. CB 113. 96 = CB *96*. 97. 1 Ktb3; 2 Rd8 +; 3 Kta5; 4 Pb6 +; 5 Pb5 m. 101. 1 Ktc6 +; 2 Re7 +; 3 Ra7; 4 Pd7 m. 102 = CB *100*. 110 = C *83*. 111 = PL *175*. 112 = CB *135*. 113 = CB *135*. 114 = CB 134. 132 = CB 147. 139. Cf. C *114*. 144 = CB *177*. 145 = CB 53. 146 = CB 62.

[10] Luc. 10-15, 18-67, 78-80, 94-102, 109-14, 132, 139, 145-6 are headed *del viejo*. Of these 98-100, 109 are of the modern game, while 144 is really *del viejo*.

Problems without Q and B may of course be either old or new: in such cases I accept the statement of the MS. Similar problems, often taken from mediaeval MSS., occur in the other 16th c. MSS.

Finally, an Italian MS. of the first half of the 17th c.,[11] which is based upon Damiano's *Libro da imparare giocare a scacchi*, Rome, 1512, and is now in Mr. J. G. White's library (=WD), contains a chapter, *Qui prencipia li giochi de partido al'antiga*, with a selection of 27 problems of the old game. These follow:

WD 147.

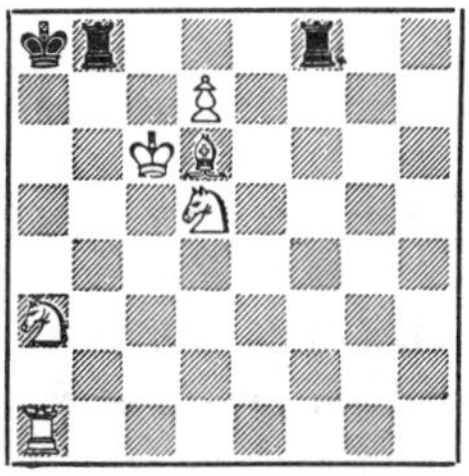

Mate in III exactly.
The Bl. Rs are fidated.
Unsound.

WD 158.

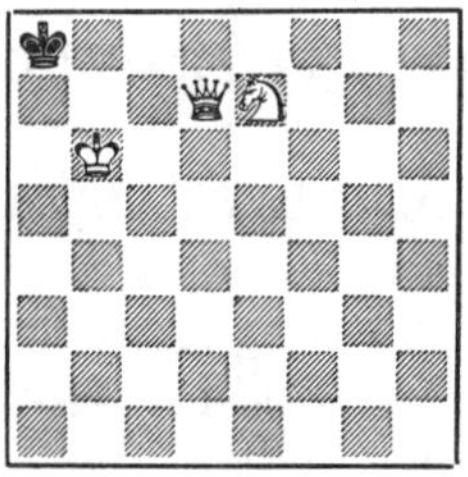

Mate in VI exactly.

WD 162.

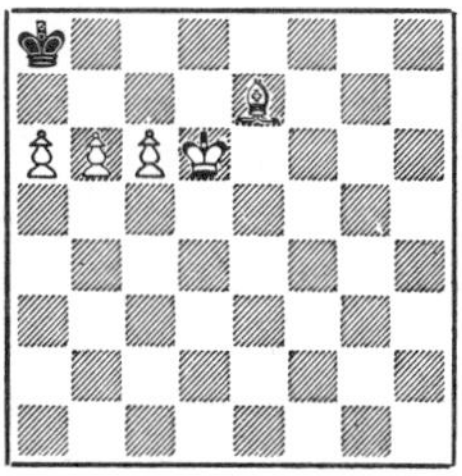

Mate with P in VII exactly.

WD 163.

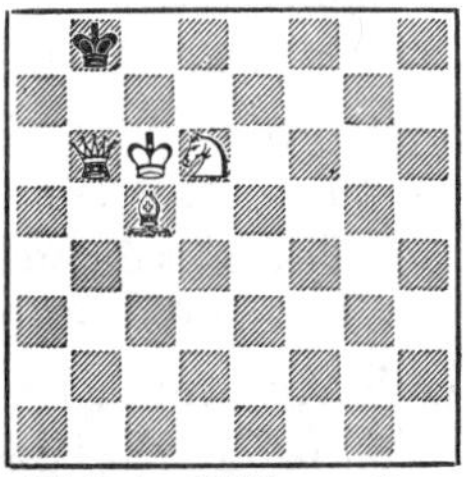

Mate in VIII exactly.

WD 164.

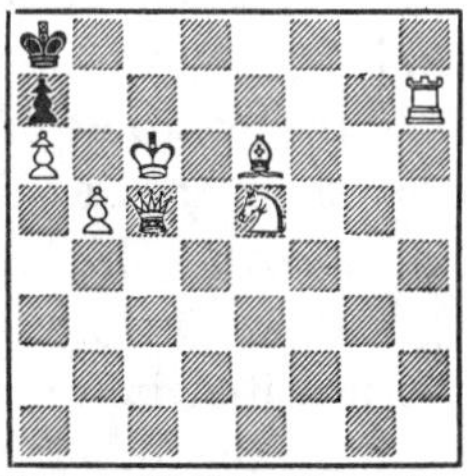

Mate with P in X exactly.
Pa7 is fidated.

WD 168 (corr.).

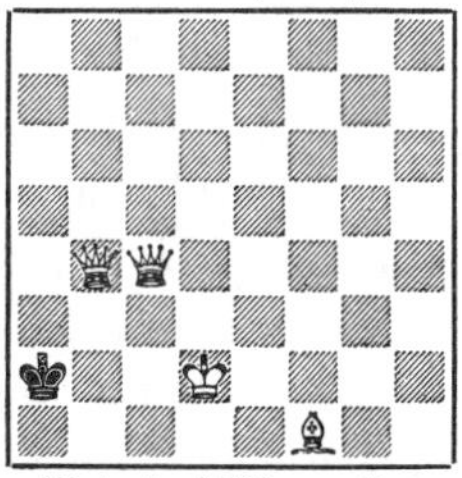

Mate in XII exactly.

NOTES AND SOLUTIONS

WD 143. Cf. CB *5*. 144. Cf. CB *33*. 145. Cf. CB *1*. 146. Cf. F 303. 147 = Dam. 20 (as here the B is 'al antica'). The MS. solves 1 Pd8 = Q, Rc8 + (or Rf7; 2 Ktb5 +; 3 Kt(d5)c7 m.); 2 Ktc7 +; 3 Kt(a3)b5 m. (which requires the Q to be 'ala rabiosa'). If 1 . . , Rf3, 'no mate' (but 2 Ktc7 +; 3 Ktb5 m.). The problem has been quoted (cf. v. d. Lasa, 178) as showing that the modern move of the B is older than that of the Q. I think the evidence too slender. 148 = CB *75*. 149. Cf. CB. *66*. 150. Cf. F 325. 151 = Luc. *101*. 152 = CB *100*. 153 = CB *112*. 154 = CB *101*. 155 = CB *117*. 156 = CB *133*. 157 = F *331*. 158. 1 Ktd5; 2 Ktb4; 3 Kc7; 4 Qc6; 5 Qb7 +; 6 Ktc6 m. 159. Cf. 158 (Qd7 on a6, Kte7 on d8). In VI ex. 1 Ktf7; 2 Ktd6; 3 Ktc8; 4 Kta7; 5 Qb7 +; 6 Ktc6 m. 160. Cf. CB *185*. 161. Cf. CB *185*. 162. 1 Kd7; 2 Pc7 +; 3 Pc8 = Q; 4 Qc6; 5 Bc5; 6 Pa7 +; 7 Pb7 m. 163. 1 Ba3; 2 Kc5; 3 Kb5; 4 Kc6; 5 Bc5; 6 Ktc4; 7 Qc7 +; 8 Ktb6 m. 164. 1 Rh4; 2 Ra4; 3 Ra5; 4 Ktd7 +; 5 Qb6; 6 Pa7; 7 Kb6; 8 Ka6; 9 Pb6; 10 Pb7 m. 165 = F *297*. 166 = CB *189*. 167. Cf. CB. *277*. 168. 1 Kc2; 2 Bd3; 3 Qb5; 4 Qc3; 5 Qd2; 6 Kc3; 7 Qc1; 8 Qb2 +; 9 Bf5; 10 Qa4; 11 Qb3 +; 12 Bd3 m. 169 = CB 128.

[11] This is the MS. which I have already used (p. 353) for the light which it throws on the Muslim chess of the early 17th c.

CHAPTER IX

CHESS IN MEDIAEVAL LITERATURE

Longer chess incidents in the *Chansons de geste*.—The magic chess of the Arthurian romances.—Chess in the *Beast romances*.—Allegories based on chess.—Other comparisons and metaphors.

I HAVE already had occasion to remark how numerous are the references to chess in the romance literature of mediaeval Europe. In most cases the references are, quite naturally, simple and incidental, and merely show the position which the game held in popular estimation, but there are still a number of passages in which the mention of chess is of greater interest, either as playing a definite part in the development of the story, or as containing in greater detail an account of play, with its technicalities and accompaniment of banter.

This literary use of chess originated in France, but with the translation of the Old French romances into the other European languages the use became more general. The German Minnesingers, in particular, made much use of chess metaphors.

Although I have already referred incidentally to many of these chess passages, it will, I think, not be without interest if I collect together some of the more considerable of them. Here, as indeed in all my use of mediaeval French literature, I am much indebted to Strohmeyer's paper, *Das Schachspiel im Altfranzösischen* (Abhandlungen Herrn Prof. Dr. Adolf Tobler ... dargebracht, Halle, 1895).

The romance in the plot of which chess plays the most striking part is that of *Garin de Montglane* (13th c.), one of the Charlemagne cycle. This poem opens with a long account of a game of chess which supplies unity to the whole romance. In this story[1] Garin arrives at the court of Charlemagne with a great reputation as a chess-player, and Charlemagne proposes to test it.

Tu seiz molt des eschais ia ta ie esproue
Joons antre nos. ij. a vn ieu afiei
Si ne te doit displaire.

Garin agrees, and Charlemagne prescribes the terms of play, confirming them by a solemn oath when Garin expresses doubts as to the honesty of his

[1] I have used the extract from a Vatican MS. printed in A. Keller's *Romvart*, Mannheim, 1844, 346 seq.

intentions. If Garin wins he is to have the realm of France and Charlemagne's Queen to wife; if he loses he is to lose his head. The chess are produced:

> Or a on leschasquier enmi la sale mis,
> Ainz plus riche eschasquier ne vint dons que soit vis
> Touz fus d'or et d'argent tresgeteiz et claufis,
> La bordeure entour fu faite d'un rubis,
> Touz bordes d'esmerades et de riche safis,
> Tus .v.c. en i ot, de son suis ie touz fis
> Que la piere en valoit .c. s. de parezis.

and the barons of France take their places around the table to watch the game. This is not described in detail, but a few moves are indicated.[2] Before long it is interrupted by an outburst of temper on the part of Charlemagne, and the whole room is in uproar. The Duke of Burgundy, however, succeeds in restoring peace, and Garin ends by checkmating the King. He declines to take advantage of the terms of the wager, and in exchange accepts the town of Montglane (Lyons), then in the hands of the Saracens. Later in the poem, Garin's younger sons repair to Charlemagne's court, and take many opportunities of reminding the king of his defeat. One of them even goes so far as to refuse to play chess with the king, because he had not carried out the terms of the wager which he had made with Garin.

In *Floire et Blanchefleur* (12th c.) the hero finds Blanchefleur a captive of the Saracens, and determines to rescue her. He learns that the porter of the prison is very covetous and a keen chess-player, and uses this knowledge to gain access to the dungeon. He induces the porter to challenge him to play at chess, and refuses to play except for a considerable wager. They play on three successive days, and Floire allows the porter to win on each occasion. The porter wins the stakes—in the English version the final game was played for £40 and a gold cup—but Floire obtains admission to the prison.

This romance was translated into most of the European languages, and was the basis of Boccaccio's *Philicopo*. In this recension the chess passage is amplified considerably;[3] as a rule, however, the translations give no details.

[2] E.g.:
> Li rois ait trait vn roc que Garins covresa . . .
> Garins trait vn aufin si prent vn chevalier . . .
> Un autre trait a fait Karles li fis Pepin,
> A vn petit poon enportait vn aufin,
> A l'autre trait apres ieta vn roc sonnin . . .
> Garins trait vn poon, se uait .j. roc porte . . .
> Eschec se dist Garins, au roc tot a outre,
> Le roc en aportei . . .
> Garins ot le roi petit san faut mate.

[3] The following extracts from Boccaccio's version contain some technicalities of chess:
'Philocopo giocando conobbe se piu saper del giuoco che 'l castellano, ristrinse adunque Philicopo il re del castellano ne la sua sedia con l'uno de suoi rocchi, & col caualiero, havendo il re a la sinistra sua l'uno de gli alfini, il castellano assediò quello di Philicopo con molti scacchi, & solamente un punto per sua salute gli rimase nel salto del suo rocco. Ma Philicopo a cui giocar conueniva, doue mouer doueua il caualliero suo secondo per dare scaccomatto al re, & conoscendo bene, mosse il suo rocco, & ne 'l punto rimaso per salute al suo re lo puose, il castellano lieto cominciò a ridere ueggendo che matto era Philicopo doue Philicopo harria lui potuto mattare, & dandogli con una pedona pingente scacco, quiui il mattò . . . Acconciossi il secondo giuoco . . Philicopo . . havendo quasi a fine recato il giuoco, & essendo per mattare il castellano, & mostrando con alcuno atto di cio auederse tauolò quel gioco . . . Incominciosi il terzo giuoco, & giocato per lungo spatio Philicopo n' hebbe il meglio, et lo castellano cio

In *Huon of Bordeaux* (written *a.* 1200) the hero arrives at King Yvorin's palace disguised as a minstrel's varlet. When asked what he can do, Huon rolls off a long list of accomplishments:

'I can mew a sparhawke / and I can chase the herte / & the wyld bore, and blowe the pryce, and serue the houndes of theyr ryghtes, and I can serue at the table before a grete prynce, and I can playe at chesse and tables as well as ony other can do / nor I neuer founde man coulde wynne of me yf I lyst.' Lord Berners, *Duke Huon of Burdeux,* E.E.T.S., 177.[4]

To test his veracity, the king makes him play with his daughter, who was a master-player, on the wager 'that yf she wynne thou shalt lese thy hede/& yf thou canst mate her . . . thou shalt haue her one nyght in thy bed/to do with her at thy pleasure, & a c. marke of money there with'. The game began, Huon only stipulating that the spectators should keep silence throughout the game.

Then ye chesse were made redy; then Huon sayd, 'lady, what game wyl ye play at?' 'frende,' quod she, 'at ye game accustomed, that is, to be mated in ye corner' / ...ther were paynims that beheld Huon / but he cared not for ony of them / but studyed on his game, ye whiche they had begon, so that Huon had lost parte of his pawnes.[5]

Some banter between the lady and Huon followed, but, luckily for him, the lady fell in love with him and lost the game. Huon was greatly elated and boasted to the king,

'Sir, now may ye se how I can play / for yf I wyll a lytell more study / wolde mate your doughter where as I lyst.'

The king was very wroth with his daughter for losing, 'when so many grete men thou hast mated,' but Huon released him from his wager for 100 marks.

In *Tristan* (12th c.), Tristram is sent to Ireland by King Mark to fetch his bride Yseult. On the journey they play chess, and in error drink from

conoscendo si comincio a cruciare & a tingersi uel uiso & a sottigliarsi se potesse il giuoco per maestria recuperare, ma quanto piu giocaua, tanto piu ne haueua il peggio. Philicopo gli levò con un alfine il caualiero & diegli scacco, il castellano per questo tratto crucciato oltre a misura a piu de la perdita de bisanti che del giuoco, die de le mani ne gli scacci, & quelli & lo scacchiero gittò a terra.'

The Flemish version by Diederic v. Assenede (*Horae Belgicae*, iii, Leipzig, 1836, lines 2687–2753) also contains a number of chess terms. In this version they play for 100, 200, and finally 300 besants and a gold cup. In the Icelandic version (*Flóres Saga ok Blankiflúr*, ed. Kölbing, Halle, 1896, 56) they play *skáktafl* for $\overset{ii}{c}$. *aura gulls*; in the Swedish version (*Flores och Blanzeflor*, Stockholm, 1844, 40) they play *skaktafuil* for *ij. hundredha öra gull.*

[4] The French poem (Paris, 1860, 7408–9) has

Si sai des tables et des eskiés asés
Qu'il n'est nus hom qui m'en péust paser.

The match of chess between Huon and Yvorin's daughter was a favourite subject for the decoration of ivory mirror cases. There are two examples in the South Kensington Museum.

[5] Or in the French (7491–7500):

Adont ont fait l'eskekier aporter,
Qui estoit d'or et d'argent painturé,
Li eskiek furent de fin or esmeré.
'Dame, dist Hues, quel ju volés juer?
Volés as trais, u vous volés as dés?'
—'Or soit as trais' dist la dame al vis cler (see p. 410 above).
Adont commencent à lor ju à penser.
Li paien ont moult Huon regardé,
Mais à son ju entent li bacelers
De se maisnie perdi l'enfes asés . .

a love philtre. The result is disastrous, and the guilty passion that arose between Tristram and Yseult in consequence is the chief motive of the whole of the latter portion of the romance.[6]

In the tale of *Beryn* (Fr. *a.* 1350, English tr. *c.* 1400), Beryn, a merchant on his first voyage, is invited on his arrival at Falsetown to play at chess. The cunning burgess allows Beryn to win easily at the first, and finally they play for the wager that the loser shall either undertake to do the winner's bidding or drink all the salt-water in the sea. Beryn loses, but by the help of one Geffrey he escapes from the dilemma. The burgess must first stop all fresh water from flowing into the sea.[7]

In several romances the hostility existing between certain of the characters is traced back to a quarrel over a game of chess. As we have already seen from *Garin de Montglane*, passions often ran high during a game, and the

[6] In Gottfried v. Strassburg's German version, *Tristan* (*c.* 1210), this incident begins (2217–25):

von aventiure ez dô geschach
daz Tristan in dem schiffe ersach
ein schâchzabel hangen
an brete und an den spangen
vil schône und wol gezieret,
ze wunsche gefeitieret;
dâ bî hienc ein gesteine
von edelen helfenbeine
ergraben meisterlîche.

There are other allusions to chess in the romance; cf. Löseth, *Le Roman en prose de Tristan*, Paris, 1891, 481. One incident, as developed by Heinrich v. Freiberg, *Tristan* (*c.* 1300), 4144 seq., contains some German chess technicalities.

Den künic und die künegin
gar minneclichen vander
sitzen bî ein ander,
do sie ein schâchzâbel zugen.
ir ougenblikke lieplich vlugen
uber das bret oft entwer
von eime hin zem andern her,
von eime her zem andern hin . . .
. . . der künic sprach
zer küniginne 'dâ schâch!'
'Dâ schâch!' sprach diu künigîn;
'hie buoz mit dem ritter mîn!'
'Abschâch!' sprach der künec sân.
Sî gedâht 'Abschâch wirt iu getân.'
. . . Nu wart vorrücket ein stein.
des huob ein kriec under in zwein.

Buoz (sb. m.) is the MLG. *but*, Eng. *boot*, compensation paid, amends made. It occurs frequently in MHG. and MLG., as also the verb *büezen*, in the sense of capture in return, and often combined with *schach* or *mat*, as *schach buoz*, *mat buoz*, a capture giving check, mate; generally, however, in a transferred sense: 'ich wil mit rehter künste iu sagen mates buoz'; *Wartburgkrieg* (*c.* 1260, ed. Simrock, p. 57). The chess-meaning is established by a passage in Stephan's *Schachbuch*, 5460–7. (See Eiserhardt, *Mittelalt. Schachterminologie der Deutschen*, 16–18.) *Abschach* (sb. m.) is the regular MHG. term for discovered check. It still survived in Lessing's time (see *Nathan*, II, i). The problem MS. WA, f. 3a, has the verb *abschachen.*

[7] *Tale of Beryn*, E.E.T.S., 1641–1823.

. . So when they had i-dyned, the cloth was vp i-take; 1731
A Chese þere was i-brouȝt forth: but tho gan sorow to wake.
The Ches was al of yvery, the meyne fressh & newe
I-pulsshid, & i-pikid, of white, asure, & blewe . . .
The meyne were i-set vp: they gon to pley(e) fast: 1746
Beryn wan the first, þe second, & þe þird;
And atte fourth(e) game, (right) in the ches a-myd,
þe Burgeyse was i-matid . . .

The burgess now proposes his wager: he 'was the best pleyer atte ches of all the wyde marchis, or many a myle aboute'.

He set the meyne efft ageyn, & toke better hede
Then he did tofore, & so he had(de) nede.
The Burgeyse toke a-visement long on euery drauȝte;
So with(in) an houre or to, Beryn he had i-cauȝte
Somwhat oppon the hipp, þat Beryn had þe wers . . .
'Draw on', seyd the Burgeyse: 'Beryn. ye have þe wers.' . .
The Burgeyse, whils þat Beryn was in hevy þouȝt,
The next drauȝt after, he toke a roke for nauȝte . . .
The Burgeyse seid: 'Comyth nere. ye shul see þis man,
How he shall be mated, with what man me list.'
He drouȝe, & seyd 'chek mate' (1777–1822).

jibes which accompanied the play made defeat more bitter. From taunts it was not a far cry to actual blows, and the chessboard and pieces were often made to serve duty as weapons of attack or defence. The quarrel might even end in the death of one of the players. That these quarrels were based upon fact is seen from legal proceedings of the period, e.g.:

16. Sept. 1394. Reg. de la loy, 1393–1401 (G.) Bans de .x. libvres. A Tournai. avoir feru Jehan Dolee d'un tavlier parmi le visage jusques a efusion de sang.

In the romance of *Foulques Fitzwarin* (written *a.* 1235),[8] the hatred which John of England exhibited against Foulque is attributed to a quarrel over a game of chess which John and Foulque had played when children in the court of King Henry II. In the scuffle John had smitten Foulque with the chessboard and drawn blood, and Foulque had thereupon knocked John down with his fists.

A more disastrous quarrel of this kind is described in *Oger de Danemarche*, one of the Charlemagne romances of the 12th c. The two lads, Bauduinet, the son of Oger, and Charlot, the son of Charlemagne, play chess at Easter. Charlot loses his temper on losing the game, and first insults and then with the chessboard kills Bauduinet. Both versions of the poem which I have seen are of chess interest.[9]

[8] *Hist. Fulke Fitzwarine*, London, 1855. Cf. Leland, *Collect.*, 1774, i. 233; &c.

[9] Both versions are quoted in *Ogier de Danemarche* (Paris, 1842). That in the text itself is quite short:

Il et Callos prisent un esquekier,
Au ju s'asisent por aus esbanier,
Sont lor esches assis sor le tablier.
Li fix au roi traist son paon premier,
Bauduinés traist son aufin arier,
Le fix au roi le volt forment coitier,
Sur l'autre aufin a trait son chevalier.
Tant traist li uns avant et l'autre arier,
Bauduinés li dist mat en l'anglier.

The longer account of this episode in the version preserved in MS. Brit. Mus. Kings, 15. VI. f (ff. 124–7) is quoted in the introduction to the Paris edition (lxiv, lxvii). It introduces much of interest to the historian of chess.

Emmy la salle fist aporter l'eschequier,
Ouvre d'or et d'argent, li eschet furent chier;
Dist à Baudouinet: 'Pensés du revenger;
De bien garder vos gens, bien les sauray chasser.'
Et dist Baudouinet: 'Sire, g'i jouay hier
Tant que tout estonné en ai le hannepier.'
— 'Vous jouerés à moy' dist Charlot au vis cler.
Lors va assir son ju et sa gent apointier.
Et Baudouinet print son jeu à commencier, ...
Charlot le fils du roy s'est as eschès assis,
Contre Baudouinet qui tant fu bien aprins.
Charlot a trait premier, li fiers et li hardis:
Il trait un paonnet qui d'or estoit macis,
Et Baudouinet trait qui bien estoit apris;
Aus quatre premiers trais a un chevalier prins:
D'un rock lui dist escheck et puis getta un ris,
Et lui dist: 'Monseignour, tost est ce jeu faillis;
Joués de vostre rois car il est mal assis.'
Et quant Charlot l'entent si en est engramis:
Il a couvert son jeu d'un aufin par advis,
Et Baudouinet trait s'a son chevalier prins;
En sus du roy le trait, plus près de lui l'a mis,
Et Charlot trait un rok, qui n'y est alentis.
'Sire, dist Baudouin, vous estes desconfis:

There are two chess incidents in *Renaud de Montaubon* (13th c.), another romance of the Charlemagne cycle, both of a sanguinary character. The first is very similar to the *Oger* incident: in the second, the chessmen serve as weapons of offence. The former is told thus in Caxton's *Foure Sons of Aymon*, E.E.T.S., 61, the English version of the romance :

The barons cam out after dyner for to plaie & sporte hemself; and berthelot the neuew of Charlemayn called reynawde for to playe with him / wherof grewe a gret myscheef / for afterwarde many a good knyghte deied therfor, & many a fayr chylde was faderless, as here after ye shall here / if ye herken well.

Now was set Berthelot & the worthi reynawde for to playe at the ches, whiche were of yvori / wherof ye borde was of golde massy / & so long they playd that debate fell bytwene them two, bi suche maner that berthelot called renaude 'hour-sone' / & toke vp his hande & smot reynawde in the vysage, so that the blood fell to the grounde / And whan reynawde sawe hymself thus shamfully outraged he was right wrothe & sore angred, & sware by god, hym shold yll betyd; therfor thenne toke reynaude ye ches borde, and smote berthelot vpon his hede so harde, that he cloued hym to the teeth / and thus berthelot fell doune deed to ye grounde afore hym.[10]

Je prenderay vo rok de tous les plus petis.'
— 'Baudouin, dist Charlot, lassiés ester tels diz :
Un homs qui tant parole est bien souvent reprins,
Et si dit à la fois chose dont il vault pis.'
— 'Sire, ce dist li enffes, par Dieu de paradis,
Mieux valent les paroles, les gabes, et les ris
Or jeu de l'eschequier, qui tant est seignouris,
Que tant le remanant, ce dient li marchis ;
Le jeu se veult gaber, s'en est tous li délis.
Sire, ce dist li enffes, li homs qui veult jouer
Au jeu de l'eschequier, qui tant fait à louer,
De gabez et de mos doit le sien jeu parer,
Et qui en a le pis, il le doit enclurer;
Car tels joue aus eschès qui ne scet point mater
Fors que de chevalier ou de son rock jouer;
Mais qui es quatre poins scet le roy aengler
Et dire eschek et mat du paonnet mener,
Je dy c'on le doit bien et prisier et loer :
Folie le me fait yci renouveller,
Car vous en savés plus que tout li baceler
Que j'aie point véu en ce palais jouer.'
Adont le fist escheck, son roy fist remuer,
Et Charlot se couvry de fierge pour garder.
Tant manèrent le jeu, si con j'oy compter
Que Baudouinet va vne fierge estorer.
Et puis de point en point le va tant admener
Qu'il fist le roy Charlot tellement aengler
Que tout droit à l'anglet il l'a fait arrester ;
D'un rock lui dist escheck, car bien le scet trouver,
Et d'un paonet va Charlot mat appeller.
Et quant Charlot le vit, en lui n'ot qu'aïrer :
Lors dist : 'Coistron bastart' . . . . .
— 'Bastart, ce dist Charlot, vous en fault-il grouller?'
Il saisi l'eschequier, s'en va l'enffant frapper,
Amont parmi le chef lui va tel cop frapper
Qui lui a fait les ex de la teste voler,
Et lui fist devant lui la cervelle espaulcer.

The author of the prose version (*Ogier le Dannoys*, Paris, 1500, quoted in Twiss, ii. 130) manages in his account of the game to reveal his ignorance of chess. Charlot begins by moving *ung petit paonnet* and taking a Knight. Baudouin replies by moving a Pawn and taking two Knights. He then says *eschac* with his King. Charlot covers his Rook and takes a Pawn. Baudouin next moves his Knight, and places it next his King. And then they quarrel.

10 Similar incidents are described in *Doon de la Roche*, in the *Bastart de Bouillon*, in *Guy of Warwick*, and in *Galyen restoré*. In the *Bastart de Bouillon*, the young Bastart plays chess with

In the second incident, Renaud has Richard Duke of Normandy prisoner, and sends his men to bring him to the gibbet. They find Richard playing chess with Renaud's young son Yvonet in the vaulted hall. He pays no attention to their request to come out and be hanged, and when the officers laid violent hands upon him he killed one with a Fers, which he was on the point of moving, a second with a Rook, and a third with an Aufin. At this the others took to flight, and Richard invited Yvonet to finish the game. In the French version, the Fers is first described as made of ivory, and later as being big and square, and the Aufin has a gilded top.[11]

A somewhat similar use of the chessboard and men will be found in Chrestien de Troyes' *Percival* (*c.* 1175), and in the German version *Parzival*, of Wolfram v. Eschenbach (1200–10), the introduction of the chess being made to emphasize the suddenness of a surprise. Gauvain is discovered in the company of a lady in her sister Vergulat's castle. No weapons are at hand, but Gauvain wields the heavy chessboard as a shield, and the lady puts the enemy to flight with the chessmen (St.).

In *Parise la Duchesse* (ed. Paris, 1860, 37), the Duchess's son Hugh, who had learnt chess as a youth and was a player of great skill, plays with four young nobles for 100 *sols de deniers* apiece. He won so easily that he offered to teach them how to play. They refused in great anger and attempted to kill him. In the unequal conflict Hugh defended himself successfully with the chessboard.

In some of these passages, e. g. *Oger*, the attempt is made to describe the course of the game in some detail. The most successful attempt of the kind is that in *Les Esches amoureux*, which I have used in connexion with the *short assize* (p. 478); the liveliest is that in Jacques de Longuyon's *Vœux du*

his cousin and mates him four times in succession, whereupon the defeated player fells him with the chessboard. In *Guy of Warwick*, Fabour is playing Sadok, the son of Soudan Triamour, and gives him a check. Upon this the young prince miscalls him, and smites him with a Rook. Fabour kills him with the board (Chess is mentioned several times in this romance. The only other reference of any length is quoted above, p. 436). In *Galyen restoré*, a quarrel over a game of chess is the cause of the hero discovering his parentage. Galyen plays with his uncle Thibert after supper, and being the better player (F. *ouurier*), he won a Rook, and said 'Uncle, you are mate.' Thibert in a fit of passion deals his nephew a blow over the head with the board, calling him 'Bastard, filz de putain'.

[11] Caxton does not show much knowledge of chess in his translation of this passage (ed. cit. 477). The *Dame* is not recognized as the chess Queen ('the duk rycharde . . . helde in his hande a lady of yvery, wherwyth he wolde have gyven a mate to yonnet'). The conclusion of the game is given briefly: 'yonnet . .. played wyth his roke that he sholde not be mated / but he myght not save the mate.' In the published text of the French poem (Stuttgart, 1862, 388–90) the most interesting lines are:

Richars . . . point tint un fierte dont il cuida joer ;
Blanche ert de fin ivoire, que n'i ot qu'amender . . .
Doncques a trait le roi por son poon garder

(Yvonet's continuation of the game), and the account of the fracas which was given to Renaud by the survivors:

Il jooit as eschez en la sale voutée ;
Tantost come le primes par l'espaule aornée,
L'un feri d'une fierte qui grans est et quarée ;
Deci qu'en la cervele li est, biax sire, entrée.
L'autre feri d'un roc par itel randonée
Que il l'abati mort sans brait et sans criée ;
Donc a pris .i. aufin qui la teste ot dorée,
Si en feri un autre, l'arme s'en est alée.

Renaud and Charlemagne are interrupted when playing chess at a later part of the romance, but the incident is without importance. See the Caxton translation (ed. cit., 151).

Paon (1312), which I quote from the Scotch version, *The Buik of the most noble and vailzeand Conqueror Alexander the Great*, Bannatyne Club, Edinburgh, 1831, 207 seq., as the most vivid picture that I know of a mediaeval game of chess with its accompanying play of wit. Unfortunately, the moves are described very inexactly. The lady, Fezonas, who gives her opponent the odds of Knight and move, undertakes to give mate in the corner with an Aufin, and every chess-player must have known that this was an impossibility in the mediaeval game.[12]

. . . Thus thir folk in great solas,
And in short time assembled was,
The ches was asked sone I hecht,
And men thame brocht wele at richt,
Sic ane chekker that neuer ar,
Was sene ane better seilden quare,
The leifis of gold war fare and fyne,
Subtyle wrocht with ane engyne,
The poyntis of emeraudes schynand schyre,
And of rubeis burnand as fyre,
The ches of sapheris war I wys,
And of topace that richest is,
Pigmeus thame maid with slicht,
Thay war full fare to se with sicht.[13]
In silken carpetis of the Grece
Auld Cassamus gart bring the ches.
Himself has set the alphyis (F. *eschés*),
And lauchand said he on this wys,
'Lordingis lat se quha will assay.'
Said Perdicas, 'Schir ȝe sall play.'
'Perfay,' said Cassamus, 'I na ken,
I am ane churle to cary men.
Betuix me and my alphis (F. *asne*) we sall
Bynd vp the oxin in the stall.
This is it that euer can I,
Bot eit and drink allanerly.
The Bauderane sall begin perfay,
And Fesonas sall him assay,
To leif thare melancoling,
For thay ar baith in lele lufing.'
The Bauderane said, 'I refuse nocht,
Na ȝit the amorous thocht.
The king of lufe will I nocht tyne,
For all is hirris here and hyne.'
Fesonas said to mak him wraith,
'To mekill, shir, drede I ȝour skaith.
Quhat I sall haue outher rouk or knicht,
To auantage bot ȝe me hecht,
That it be without wrething.
Ȝe sall be met (*mate*) without lesing
In ane nuke with ane alphing.'[14]
Said Ideas, 'Ȝe menance fast, cousing.

[12] The *Vœux du Paon*, a magnificent MS. of which is one of the treasures of the Bodleian, was also translated into Dutch, and v. d. Linde quotes in his *Het Schaakspel in Nederland*, 19, the present incident from this translation. The French text (from the Bodleian MS.) is quoted in Michel's edition of the *Chron. de Benoit*, Paris, 1838, ii, pp. 514–17.

[13] The description of the chess in the French runs:

Tels ert li eschekiers, qu'onques mieudres ne fu ;
Les listes (*a*) sont d'or fin, à trefoire fondu,
Et li point (*b*) d'esmeraudes, verdes com pré herbu,
E de rubins vermaus, aussi com d'ardant fu.
Li eschec de saphirs, le roi asseuru
E de riches topasses à toute l'or vestu.
Pigmalyun les fist, li fiex Candeolu : (*c*)
Molt sont bel à veoir, drechié e espandu.

(Variants from another MS. cited in the appendix to Ducange : (*a*) *lices*; (*b*) *Li paon*, i. e. the Pawns ; (*c*) for this and the two preceding lines are substituted :

Roy, fierce, cheualier, auffin, roc, et cornu,
Furent fet de saphir et si ot or molu,
Li autre de topace ; o toute lor vetu.

The first of these lines is probably corrupt, since *auffin* and *cornu* are different names for the same piece.)

[14] Fezonas' speech in the French runs :

'Vous aurés d'avantage ou roc ou cavalier,
Si m'aiiés en couvent que c'iert sans courecier ;
Et je vous dirai coi en l'angle tout derrier
D'un villain en courant por le roi justicier.'

The poem uses *coi* (L. *quietus*) throughout for mate. *Villain* for the Aufin is also unusual. The Dutch version has here :

Ic wil u geven groot vordeel ;
Roc of riddre, welc gi kiest ;
Mare gevalt dat gi verliest,
Dat gi u niet belgen en selt.
Ic sal uwen coninc met gewelt
Achter in den hornec driven
Met enen ouden, daer hi sal bliven.

Manance aucht to bere cumpany
To wrang winning and succudry,
But or the play all endit be,
For all ȝour fere I hope to se
ȝour great mannance full halely.'
Fesonas said hir preuelly,
'Gif ȝe be ȝelous I will him pray
That he ȝour lufe wald put away
And to allege ȝour mekill ill.'
Said Ideas, 'ȝe say ȝour will.
Quhan I lufe outher him or her,
I keip nocht of sic messinger.'
The Bauderane hard the speche all,
And luked to Ideas the small;
Quhan sho persauit sho changit hew.
Her visage that was freshe and new
Vox ridder weill than rose on rys.
Cassamus tuke ane cod (*cushion*) of prys,
And by the playeris lenit him syne.
'Be God', said that palasyne,
'Lo here ane lytstar wele at richt
That sone sa fyne hew can dicht.
Draw on, shir Bauderane, for ȝe may
Haue wele the first draucht of the play.'
'I grant wele,' said the maydin fre,
'That the first draucht the Bauderanes be,
Bot I sall haue the nixt I wis,
And mete him syne all maugre his
With ane alphine gif I may speid.'
'Damo,' said the Bauderane, 'God forbeid.'
'Mak thar ane note,' said Cassamus.
'Schir,' said the maydin, 'be Marcus,
I am sa sikker I vnderta,
That in the letter sho sekes ane stra.
I am nocht of my fallowes play,
Ideas the fare and gay,
Na ȝit her sister Idorus;
Bot quhen it lykes to Venus
And Alexander the nobill king,
I sall haue lemmen at lyking,
Quhilk sall of body douchty be
And of hand baith large and fre.'
'Fare nec (*niece*)', said Cassamus the ald,
'I trow ȝe be the halest hald.'
Thus thay playit with gammin and gle,
The knichtis of Grece and of Calde,
And spak of amouris and of droury,
Sporting thame richt merelly.
All out the ches lay
The knichtis of Grece to se the play.
The Bauderane drew ane poun but let,
That befoir the feires was set;
And the maydin hir knicht in hy
To stele the poun all preuelly.
The Bauderane drew his feiris on ane
To kepe the poun or he war tane;
And sho hir alphyne for to ga
The fers or ellis to gar hir ga
On bak and leif the poun at the last.[15]
'Dame,' said the Bauderane, 'ȝe preis me fast.'
'Schir,' said sho, 'lat ȝour siching be,
And nocht forthy sa mot I the.
Thay haue na watter for to pas.'
And he thocht and in ane study was;
And she him draue to hething ay.
'Schir Bauderane,' sho said, 'perfay,
ȝour siching thare nocht pas the se,
Weill neir ȝow may thay gaistned be.'
Quod Ideas, 'Dame, be Dyany,
ȝe can speke full hethingly.'
Quhen Fesonas hard that she was wraith,
Thare had they rekned with vther baith,
Na had the knichtis of Grece that ware,
On ather halfe standand thare,
That wele persauit thare inuy,
Engenered all of Ielusy.
Cassamus smylit with lufsum cheir,
And said, 'Wicked toung was euill to steir.'
And syne can sing quhen he had said,
For he that speche wald doun war laid.
The Bauderane ashamed was,
And changit colouris in his face,
And to his poun ane knicht drew syne.
And Fesonas with hir alphyne
Tuke his feirs[16] and said in hy,
'Dame, in ȝour word may nane affy.'
And the Bauderane richt subtelly,
Answered without melancoly,
And said sichand, 'My sweit thing,
I am tane throw behalding.'
Quhen thay had hard that ressoun all,
Abased thay war baith great and small.
Quhat he menit thay vnderstode na thing,
For thare was doubill vnderstanding.
Said Fesonas, 'ȝe speik wysly;
The draucht is mine.' 'Draw hardely.'

15 Le paon de la fierge a fait avant aler :
E la pucele a trait liement, sans muser,
Ce cevalier à diestre por le paon embler.
Li Baudrains traist sa fierge por son paon sauver
E cele son aufin, qui cuida conquester
La fierge ou le paon ou faire reculer.

16 Si traist .i. chevalier por son roc delivrer.
Fezonas del aufin va sa fierge haper.

'I say eschesk.' 'Dam, that I heir.'
'Delyueris it than.' 'Blythly, my deir.'
'Lat now quhat ȝe do thair till.'
'Madame, ȝe haist ȝow mair than skill.'
'Auyse ȝow schir or ȝe be wraith
To-day and hald to-morne baith.'
'Madame, sa lang will I nocht stand.'
With that he tuke his rouk in hand,
And wald haue drawen as thocht he than.[17]
'Amends ȝour check, schir,' said sho than,
And spak ay taryand him hethingfully:
'Schir, wraik ȝow nocht sa egarly.
ȝe lufe with lele hart and trew
Ane lady fare and bricht of hew.
Worthy and of gude hauing,
And, schir, na raith suld haue resting
Quharesa the lufe had harbry tane.'
The Bauderane than said on ane,
'Dame, ȝe say suth be all that is,
Sa and God will, I think I wis,
And with fyne hart and stedfastly,
Quhen swete vmbethinking suddanly
Me takes and partes my hart in twa,
And thyrlis sumtyme with thochtis thra,
Quha sa micht se hir fassoun all,
Hir face and hir middle small,
Portured and shapin suthfastly,
As quhylum I saw that lady
In Venus chalmer at our gaddering,
Quhen we playit at the suthfast king,
Is na man na he aucht to be,
Affrayit at hir fyne bounte.'
'Amendis ȝour chek, shir,' said that may,
'We think our lyttill on our play:
I sall haue of ȝour men, I wis,
Or ȝe of myne sen thus it is.
ȝe think our mekill on that Caldiane.'
Said Ideas, 'Dame, be Dyane,
ȝe ar our wilfull for to say
ȝour will in ernest or in play.'
'Gif I make gammin,' said Fesonas,
'That is for sporting and solas
Thir knichtis of Grece wilfully;
They wald I made thame cumpany.'
'Ye are sle, dame,' said the Bauderane,
'And sewis it weill sa God me sane
But threid or nedill all subtelly.'
Thay draw thare drauchtis sa comonly;
Quhat sall I say? they playit sa lang,
And warned ay vther amang.
The Bauderane couth nocht of the play,
Samekill as sho weill far away.
Dame Fesonas the fare and meik
Countred him into speik.
'Schir,' said that shene, 'ȝe can weill mare
Of this play than I wenit langare.
Now draw wysly, for mister. is,
ȝe salbe met sa haue I blis,
Outher in the nuke or in the score,[18]
As I haue said ȝow oft before.'
'Dam,' said the Bauderane, 'sa mot I the.
I hald me pait how euir it be,
ȝe haue ane nuke quhare of God wait,
That weill titar mycht mak me mait,
Than I and all that euer I haue,
Mycht mak me mait sa God me saue.'
Than leuch thay all with gamyn and glis,
And sho apartly aschamyt is.
Hir face woxe rede that ere was cleir.
Said Gaudifeir, 'Fare sister deir,
Foly is to mak debait,
Speik fare, or he gais his gait.'
'Schir,' said that schene, 'sa God me rede,
I na thocht euill in word or deid.'
'Dam, nane did I,' said the Bauderane,
'Bot wikked I war sa God me sane,
Gif I na durst sic ane mait abyde.'
Quhen Cassamus thame hard that tyde,
His hart was blyth for Ioy in hy;
He tuke his cod and haistaly
Kest at the chais and spilt the play,
And lauchand syne can to thame say,
'Amuffis thow nocht, and be nocht hait,
The honour is myne, ȝe baith ar met (*mate*).'[19]

In several mediaeval romances of the Arthurian cycle we meet with references to magic chessboards, upon which the chessmen play of their own

17 Maintenant son roc prent,
Com hom pensis vot traire: e celle le reprint.

18 Vous serés mas en l'angle e, s'il vous plaist, en voie. The exact meaning of *voie* (way) and *score* (line, crack, path) is not clear to me.

19 Another attempt at the description of a game occurs in *Raoul de Cambrai* (written *a.* 1270, ed. Paris, 1882, 1585–90):

As eschès goue R. de Cambrisis
Si com li om qi bien en est apris.
Il a son roc par force en roie mis,
Et d'un poon a .i. chevalier pris.
Par poi q'il n'a et maté et conquis
Son compaingnon qi ert au giu asis.

accord, or occasionally, when touched with a magic ring. All these references may be traced back to one common origin, an incident in the Celtic story of Peredur the son of Evrawc in the *Mabinogion*. This story is the principal source of Chrestien de Troyes' romance of *Percival*, and the inspiration of the whole cycle of romances.

In the Celtic story, Peredur comes to the Castle of Wonders and sees there a *gwyddbwyll* board, on which the men were playing against each other by themselves. The side which Peredur favoured lost the game, and the men on the other side set up a shout as though they had been living men. Peredur was wroth at this and threw the game into a lake, and the necessity for recovering the game was the occasion of further adventures on Peredur's part.

The exact nature of the game *gwyddbwyll*[20] is now unknown, and was probably unknown in Chrestien's day. It was certainly a *board-game*, and it was only natural that Chrestien and his successors should substitute the familiar chess for the old Celtic game (*Percival*, 22442–540). In later translations into Welsh of some of the French Arthurian romances the chess of the French version is replaced by the Celtic *tawlbwrdd* (e. g. *Y seint greal*, 1874, p. 246).

In the romance of *Lancelot* (prose, 13th c.) the hero is shown the magic chess by a lady who tells him that, however well he can play, the pieces will mate him in the angle of the board (MS. Fribourg, f. 30 a: 'si bien n'en sauroiz joer que vos n'i soiez mater en l'angle'). He essays a game, which is described with some attempt at completeness (see p. 472) in both the French and the Dutch versions.[21] In *Artur* (MS. Richel., 337, f. 218 b, G), a knight plays three games on the board and is each time mated in the angle. In a version of *Gauvain*, known through the Dutch translation *Walewein*, the

[20] The game *gwyddbwyll* is frequently mentioned in the *Mabinogion* and in other early Welsh works. None of the references give any clue as to the nature of the game, but none imply that there was any differentiation of piece other than that necessary to distinguish the one side from the other. In *Campeu Charlymaen* 'gwyddbwyll' is used to translate the F. *tables*: in *Bwn o Hamtwn*, on the other hand, *tables* is translated 'tawlbwrdd'. This latter game is mentioned repeatedly in the *Ancient Laws of Wales* (ed. 1841), and one passage (p. 436) shows that tawlbwrdd was played between two sides, one with 16 men, the other with 8 men and a King. It is, therefore, possible that this game was really identical with the Norse game hnefatafl (see p. 445). In this case the translation in *Bwn o Hamtwn* is incorrect, and as loose as translations are apt to be.

The word *gwyddbwyll* is historically identical with the Irish word *fidchell*, and this latter word occurs repeatedly in early Irish works as the name of a game. Thus it occurs in *Cormac's Glossary* (ed. W. Stokes, 1862–8), where it is said that 'in the first place the fidchell is four-cornered, its squares are right-angled, and black and white are on it, and moreover, it is different people that in turn win the game'. Other Irish references add nothing to our knowledge, with the possible exception of—(1) a passage in the *Acallamh* (Stokes and Windisch, *Irish Texts*, 4th ser., i; and O'Grady, *Silva Gadelica*), 7726–7843, which describes how Cailte and the King of Connaught played at *fidchell*. When the board was brought, three men were missing. Cailte fetched 3 gold and 3 silver men from a cairn where a game had been hidden. Each of these men was as big as a big man's fist, and he told the King that he had left 300 men, half gold and half silver, in the cairn. (2) The 15th c. *Book of Lismore* (still unedited), describing a gift of a *fidchell* to Pope Boniface in the 7th c., says that it had nine lines, and half of the pieces were men and half women. By the 15th c. the real nature of the game was certainly completely forgotten.

[21] The board in the Dutch version is said to be worth a dozen marks, and the pieces were of gold and silver.

hero comes to a castle in which a hall is arranged as a chessboard, on which chessmen the size of life move of themselves when touched with a magic ring. In the romance of *Gauvain et l'échiquier* the story turns upon a magic board of silver and ivory, which flies through the air to Arthur's court and disappears in as wonderful a way (St. 398). The magic chess is introduced also in the *Quête du Saint Graal* (ed. Bordeaux, 1841, i. 438–40).

In the English *Merlin* (E.E.T.S., 362) the construction of such a board is attributed to the magician Guynebans.

Than Guynebans hym-self made with his owne handes a Chekier of golde and Ivory half parted, ffor he was right sotill of soche crafte, as he wolde hym entirmete, and the pownes, and all the other meyne were golde and yvory fresshly entailled. Whan Guynebans hadde made redy the Cheker and the chesse, that oon myght well ther-with pleyen alle that wolden, he made soche a coniursion by his art, that alle tho that þere sette for to pleyen, ther ne sholde be noon, but that the chesse sholde hym maten, wheder he wolde or noon, in that oon of the corners of the cheker; ne neuer sholde the same cheker be mated, till the beste knyght of the worlde dide it mate, and also he moste be of soche grace, that neuer he falsed his loue, and ther-to hym be-hooveth to be kynges sones and quenes.[22]

From the *Chansons de geste* and the Arthurian romances chess passed quite naturally into the *Beast-epic*, and a contest at chess between Ysengrim the wolf and Renard the fox—in which several games are played, at first for a gold mark apiece, and after Ysengrim had won £100, for a more serious wager—forms one of the episodes in the *Roman de Renart*.[23] A parallel instance of 'beast-chess' is to be found in the Sprüche, which mention as their author *Der Spervogel* and date from the beginnings of the Minnesang

[22] 'The chessboard of Gwenddolen, when the men were placed upon it they would play of themselves. The chessboard was of gold and the men of silver', which Lady C. Guest quotes from a Welsh MS. in her *Mabinogion* (ed. 1849, i. 383), is in the original a *gwyddbwyll*. So are all the chessboards mentioned in her translation.

[23] Ed. Méon, 1826, iii. 20937–73. The game was played after dinner. The lines of most chess interest are the following:

Ysengrin fu du jeu apris,
Del paonnet a un roc pris;
Apres le roc a pris la fierce.
Tant jouerent c'ainz qu'il fust tierce
Gaaigna Ysengrins cent livres.

There are three other references to chess in Méon's edition of the *Renart* romances. (1) *Renart le nouvel*, 2521–7 (Méon, iv), mentions a splendid chessboard:

Et ens ou lever dou mengier
A fait Renart d'un eskiekier
Tout de fin or le roi present,
Et les eskies; mil mars d'argent
Vaut l'eskiekiers od les eskies, &c.

(2) *Le couronnement Renart*, 3343–9 (Méon, iv), has an interesting parallel drawn from the fact that the player at the board does not always see the best moves:

Que cil qui juent as eschés
Ne voient pas tous les bons très
Qui demeurent sour l'eschakier,
Anchois avient c'uns de derier,
D'encoste, de lés ou de lonch
Voit teil chose qui la selonch
Trairoit, qu'il gaingneroit le geu.

(A similar observation is made in Whetstone's *Promos and Cassandra*, II. ii.:

But as at Cheastes though skylful players play
Skyllesse vewers may see what they omyt.)

(3) *Renart le nouvel*, 5904–32 (Meon, iv), introduces several chess terms in an allegorical passage, see below, p. 749.

(early 13th c.). In this story a wolf plays chess with a man. The story was amplified considerably by a later poet.[24]

The Dominican, Francisco Colonna or Columna, wrote in 1467 a curious mystical work with the title *Hypnerotomachia Poliphili*, which was first printed at Venice in 1499, and was later translated into French (*Discours du Songe de Poliphile*, Paris, 1546) and English (*The Strife of Love in a Dream*, London, 1592). In this work there is an account of 'living chess', *Vno gioco de scachi in ballo a tre mensure de soni*, in which Colonna adopts a fanciful set of names for the chessmen and gives some information as to the moves:

Si il sono conteniua uno tempo, quelle uniforme octo (*adolescentule*) consumauano quel tempo in translatarse in altro quadrato. Non poteano retrocedere, si non meritamente per hauere immune salito sopra la linea, delle quadratione oue faceua residentia il Re, Ne rectamente procedere nisi per linea diagonale. Vno Secretario & uno Equite in uno tempo tre quadrati transiuano, il *Secretario* (also *Taciturnulo* — B) per linea diagonale, lo *Equite* per dui aequilateri recti & uno dalla linea deuio, & per omni lato poteano transferirse. Gli *Custodi del arce* (also *custodi della rocha*—R) molti quadri rectamente ualeano & licentemente trapassare. Dique in uno tempo poteuano discorrere tre, quatro, o cinque quadrati, seruando la mensura, & festinante il grado. Il *Re* poteua ascendere sopra quale quadrato non impedio, o uero cum praesidio occupato, anci pole prehendere, & egli interdicto il quadrato, oue altri poteno salire, & si caso egli fusse opportuno e che egli ceda cum admonitione praecedente. Ma la *Regina* per omni quadrato del suo colore oue primo fermoe la sedia. Et bene e che sempre propinqua segui dogni lato il marito suo.

Three games of chess were played, and the course of play is vaguely indicated. The third game began 1 Pd4, Pd5; 2 Pc4.

Colonna's chess pageant possesses some importance, first as the probable inspiration of Bishop Vida's Virgilian designation of the Rook, second as the pattern of the tournament of living chess in the fifth book of Rabelais' *Faicts et dictes heroiques du bon Pantagruel*, Lyons, 1564. Here again, the moves are described (see p. 465) and three games are played, but now of the modern game. The accounts of the game are far too sketchy for us to recover the play, but the first game commenced 1 Pd5 (for the Golden players who begin correspond to our Black men), Pd4.

Another account of an imaginary game of living chess is contained in Rhingieri's *Cento Giuochi liberali et d'ingegno*, Bologna, 1551, ch. xcviii (cf. v. d. Linde, ii. 329–34).

We have already seen in the Moralities how readily chess lent itself to allegorical treatment. General literature provides other examples of various

[24] *Der Spervogel* in *Des Minnesangs Frühling*, 4th ed., 1888, 27:

Ein wolf unde ein witzic man
sazten schâchzabel an:
Si wurden spilnde umbe guot.
der wolf begonde sînen muot
nâch sînem vater wenden.
do kom ein wider dar gegân:
dô gab er beidiu roch umb einen venden.

The longer version is quoted in the notes to the same edition from Lassberg's *Liedersaal*, ii. 605. It introduces no fresh matter of chess interest.

The oft-quoted story of the ape that played chess appeared first in the *Il Cortano* of Conte Baldassar Castiglione, 1518. Twiss, ii. 97–100, quotes Thomas Hoby's translation. The story is supposed to be told by one of a group of courtiers who were competing as to which could tell the tallest story.

kinds. The spiritual and natural life, war and all struggles, the course of love, all are depicted as games of chess or described by means of chess terms.

Gautier de Coincy (*c.* 1230) includes a long and elaborate allegory of the spiritual life, imagined as a game of chess between God and the Devil, in his *Miracles de la Sainte Vierge* (ed. Paris, 1857, cols. 7–10, 128 lines in all). The Devil has driven man into an angle of the board and is on the point of mating him:

Tost nous aura en l'angle traiz;
Nous serons pris et mat ce cuit.

His strongest move had been the expulsion of Adam and Eve from the Garden of Eden. At this moment God comes to the rescue, and makes a Fers which covers the check and finally mates the enemy:

Mes touz ces traiz fit il en vain,
Quar Diex une tel fyerce fist
Qui le mata et desconfit.
Quant li doux Diex vit vers la fin
Que n'avait truie nes d'aufin
Et qu'anemis par son desroi
Chevalier, Roc, fierce ne Roi,
Nes ne poon ni voulait laissier
Au jeu se daigna abaissier,
Et fist un trait soutil et gent
Par quoi rescout toute sa gent . . .
C'est fierce traist par tel sens,
Que l'anemi mate par tel sens.

The Fers that so happily turns the tables upon the Devil is the Virgin Mary, and Gautier devotes many lines to the praise of this piece:

Ceste fierce n'est pas d'ivoire;
Ainz est la fierce au roy de gloire
Qui rescout toute sa meisnée
Qu'avoit déables defrainée. . . .
Ceste fierce le mate en roie;
Ceste fierce le mate en angle;
Ceste fierce li tolt la jangle;
Ceste fierce li tolt sa proie;
Ceste fierce touzjors l'asproie;
Ceste fierce touzjors le point;
Ceste fierce de point en point
Par fine force le dechace.

The poet is so delighted with his allegory that he returns to it again and again.[25] We find the same explanation of the Fers as the Virgin Mary in other French works.[26] The idea obviously originated in the European idea that the Fers was the Queen. The last extract from Gautier de Coincy shows conclusively that the Fers had only its weak Muslim move.

In *Renart le nouvel*, 5904–32, the life of the unrepentant sinner is described under the figure of a game of chess upon *l'eskiekier de convoitise*, in which—

Diaules vous dist eskiec et mat
Dou fin de larghe consience,
Ou point d'estroite passience,
En l'angle d'orguel.[27]

[25] See cols. 62, 63, and 632, the last passage extending to 46 lines. I quote from it:

Bien mate cil par soutilz traiz,
Et bien angle le déable,
Qui de douz cuer et d'amiable
Aime la douce Mère Dieu
Et tout tins as le miex du gieu.
Mais en l'angle iert maz en la fin,
Ne jà n'ara poon n'aufin,
Roy, chevalier, fierce, ne roc,
Qui li vaille un bel œf de coc.

[26] E.g. Jean de Condé (1310–40) has (*Dits et Contes de Baudouin de Condé et son fils Jean de Condé*, Bruxelles, 1867, III. lviii, 203):

Ce fu la beneoite virge
De l'eschequier la vraie firge
Dont li dyables fu matez.

Another example occurs in the fable *De monacho in flumine periclitato*, 206–15, quoted in Michel, *Chron. de Benoît*, iii. p. 517.

[27] The passage concludes *Satan as eschiés materés*, using a rare verb.

The comparison of warfare with chess is perhaps more obvious, and has given rise to many of the transferred senses which the words 'check', 'checkmate', 'mate', possess in English.[28] Three more elaborate comparisons of this kind may be mentioned. Herbort v. Fritzlar in his *Liet von Troye* (1200–10, ed. Quellenburg, 1837) treats in this way a battle between the Greeks and the Amazons,[29] and a passage in the *Murtner Siegeslied* (vol. ii. 169) uses chess terms to describe an expedition of the Swiss Confederation against the Comte de Romont.[30] The longest and most important, however, is the account of Conradin's unsuccessful war to recover Sicily in the *Roman de la Rose*, 6674–750, which contains a very interesting reference to the two endings in French chess, mate and *have*, or Bare King, which has hitherto been completely misunderstood:

En la premeraine bataille
L'assailli por li desconfire,
Eschec et mat li alla dire
Désus son destrier auferrant
Du trait d'un paonnet errant,
Ou milieu de son eschiquier.
De Conradin parler ne quier,
Son neveu, dont l'exemple est preste,
Dont li rois Karles prist la teste
Maugré les princes d'Alemaigne;
Henri, frère le roi d'Espaigne,
Plain d'orguel et de traïson,
Fist il morer en sa prison.
Cil dui comme folz garçonnés,
Roz et fierges[31] et paonnés
Et chevaliers as gieus perdirent
Et hors de l'eschiquier saillirent.
Tel paor orent d'être pris
Au gieu qu'il orent entrepris.
Car qui la vérité regarde,
D'estre mat n'auroient-il garde,
Puisque sans roi se combatoient;
Eschec et mat riens ne doutoient.
Ne cil haver ne le pooit
Qui contre eus as éschies jouit,
Fust à pié, fust sus les arçons,
Car l'on ne have pas garçons,
Fox, chevaliers, fierges ne ros.
Car selon la verite des motz
Je nen quiers point nulluy flater
Ainsi comme il va du matter.
Puisque des eschiés me sovient
Se tu riens en sés, il convient
Que cil soit roi, que l'on fait haves,
Quant tuit si homme sunt esclaves,
Si qu'il se voit seus en la place,
Ne ni voit chose qui li place:
Ains s'enfuit par ses anemis
Qui l'ont en tel povreté mis.
L'en ne puet autrement haver,
Ce sevent tuit, large et aver.
Car ainsinc le dist Attalus
Qui des echez controva l'us,
quant il traitoit d'arismétique;
Et verra en Policratique,
Q'il s'enfléchi de la matire,
Et des nombres devoit escripre,
Où ce biau geu jolis trova
Que par demonstrance prova.
Por ce se mistrent-il en fuie,
Por la prise qui lor ennuie:
Qu'ai-je dit? por prise eschever
Mais por la mort qui plus grever
Les péust et qui pis valoit,
Car li gens malement aloit
Au mains par devers lor partie

[28] Cf. *Octouian* (written *a.* 1400), 1746: 'There was many an hethen hounde, that they chekmatyde.'

[29] Die frowen folgeten in nâch
und tâten in einen schâch
ûf und nider umb den stat.
sie wâren vil nâch worden mat (14557-60).

[30] Man treib mit ihm schafzabelspil:
der fenden hat er verloren vil,
die huot ist im zwürent zerbrochen;
sîn roch die mochten in nit verfân,
sîn ritter sach man trûrig stân:
schôch matt ist im gesprochen.

[31] Some MSS., the Paris edition of 1531, and the prose text as printed, Paris, 1521, substitute *sergens* for *fierge*. This is the blunder of a scribe who in his ignorance of chess read *ferge* as *ſerge* (cf. p. 608), and corrected his reading into *sergens* (sergeant).

Qui de Diex s'iere de departie
Et la bataille avoit emprise
Contre la foi de saincte Eglise.
Et qui eschec dit lor éust,
N'iert-il qui covrir le péust,
Car la fierche avoit esté prise
Au gieu de la première assise,
Ou li rois perdit comme fos
Ros, chevaliers, paons et fos,
Si n'ert-ele pas là présente ;
Mais la chétive, la dolente
Ne pot foïr ne soi deffendre
Puisque l'en li ot fait entendre
Que mal et mort gisoit Mainfrois
Par chief, par piés et par mains frois.
Et puisque ci bons rois oï
Qu'il s'en erent ainsinc foï
Les prist-il fuitis ambedeus,
Et puis fist sa volonté d'eus,
Et de mains autres prisonniers
De lor folie parçonniers.

The passage opens with an allusion to the fate of Manfred, King of Sicily (sl. 1266), who is said to have been mated on his dappled-grey horse in the middle of the chessboard by a Pawn errant—an expression which occurs frequently in the Latin problem MSS. to describe the mating Pawn. It then goes on to speak contemptuously of Conradin's attempt to regain his uncle's throne. The poet declares that Conradin and his cousin Henry of Castile first lost their Rooks, Queens, Pawns, and Knights, and then jumped off the board themselves to avoid capture. Apparently, the intention is to represent these two nobles as the Fools (*Aufins*). They ran no risk of mate, because they played without a King; nor of losing by *have* (Bare King), because one does not say *have* to Pawn, Bishop, Knight, Queen, or Rook. It is only the King who can be made *have*, and he only by losing all his men and remaining alone on the board. So Attalus, the inventor of the game, fixed the rule. Nor could Conradin cover a check, for he had lost his Queen in the first battle.[32]

Previous writers, following Freret, have explained *haver* as meaning 'to warn' or 'to hail', and supposed that it refers to the announcement of check. This explanation would give a very strained meaning to lines 6707–14, and there can be little doubt that *haver* is the verb connected with the chess technicality *have*, meaning 'Bare King' (see p. 467).

The chess passage in the *Roman de la Rose* was the inspiration of the well-known parallel in Chaucer's *Book of the Duchess* (written 1369), 617–741, in which the poet compares the death of Blanche, Duchess of Lancaster, to the loss of the Fers in a game played with false Fortune:

Atte ches with me she gan to pleye;
With hir false draughtes divers
She stal on me, and took my fers.
And whan I saw my fers aweye,
Alas! I couthe no lenger pleye,
But seyde, 'farwel, swete, y-wis,
And farwel al that ever ther is!'
Therwith Fortune seyde 'chek here!'
And 'mate!' in mid pointe of the chekkere
With a poune erraunt, allas!
Ful craftier to pley she was
Than Athalus, that made the game
First of the ches: so was his name.
But god wolde I had ones or twyes
Y-koud and knowe the Ieupardyes
That coude the Grek Pithagores!
I shuld have pleyd the bet at ches,
And kept my fers the bet therby;
And thogh wherto? for trewely
I hold that wish nat worth a stree!
Hit had be never the bet for me.

[32] Was the chess parallel suggested by Conradin's addiction to chess? See p. 432.

For Fortune can so many a wyle,
Ther be but fewe can her begyle,
And eek she is the las to blame;
My-self I wolde have do the same,
Before god, hadde I been as she;
She oghte the more excused be.
For this I say yet more therto,
Hadde I be god and mighte have do
My wille, whan my fers she caughte
I wolde have drawe the same draughte
For, also wis god yive me reste,
I dar wel swere she took the beste!
But through that draughte I have lorn
My blisse; Allas! that I was born!

Like Gautier de Coincy, Chaucer probably based his use of the Fers on the social ideas suggested by the other name of this piece, and on the fact that the Fers was the only piece which was associated with the female sex. The comparative weakness of the Fers gives an air of unreality to the whole argument, and it is small wonder that Chaucer should represent himself as exclaiming:

But there is (noon) a-lyve here
Wolde for a fers make(n) this wo.

Still less convincing is the use of the chess Queen in the ballade which Charles, Duke of Orleans, writing *c.* 1409, wrote on the occasion of the death of his wife. His indebtedness to the *Book of the Duchess* is very obvious.

J'ay aux eschés joué devant Amours,
Pour passer temps avecques Faulx-dangier;
Et seurement me suy gardé tousjours
Sans rien perdre, jusques au derrenier,
Que Fortune luy est venu aidier;
Et par meschief, que maudite soit-elle!
A ma dame prise soudainnement:
Par quoy suy mat, je le voy clèrement,
Si je ne fais une dame nouvelle.

En ma dame j'avoye mon secours
Plus qu'en aultre: car souvent d'encombrier
Me délivroit, quant venoit à son cours,
Et en gardes faisoit mon jeu lier.
Je n'avoye pion, ne chevalier,
Auffin, ne rocq, qui puissent ma querelle
Si bien aidier: il y pert vrayement:
Car j'ay perdu mon jeu entièrement,
Si je ne fais une dame nouvelle.

Je ne me sçay jamais garder des tours
De Fortune, qui maintes fois changier
A fait mon jeu et tourner à rebours.
Mon dommage scet bientost espier:
Elle m'assault sans point me desfier;
Par mon serement, oncques ne congneu telle,
En jeu party suy si estrangement,
Que je me rens en n'y voy sauvement
Si je ne fais une dame nouvelle.[33]

To represent death as saying checkmate to men is a natural metaphor which was quite a commonplace in Middle English. Thus Skelton (*a.* 1529), in his *Deedmans Hed*, has:

Oure days be datyd
To be checkmatyd
With drawttys of deth.[34]

[33] In Champollion-Figeac's edition of the poems of Charles of Orleans, Paris, 1842, 118.

[34] Thus Hoccleve, *How to learn to die* (c. 1412, ed. E.E.T.S.), 161: 'The ryche and poore folk eek certainly She (i. e. Death) sesith / shee sparith right noon estaat; Al þat lyf berith / with her chek is maat.' Bradshaw, *St. Werburge* (1513, ed. E.E.T.S., 58), 1470: '... it is to late Whan dethe with his darte / sayth to vs chekemate.' *Songs, carols, and other misc. poems* (ed. E.E.T.S.) p. 111: 'Then to repent yt ys to late, / When on his cheke he ys chekmate.' *Ibid.*, p. 88. *Ibid.*, p. 88: 'This day I satt full royally in a chayre / Tyll sotyll deth knokkid at my gate, / And vnavised he said to me "chekmate"!'

The comparison of the course of love to a game of chess was a favourite conceit with the troubadours of France and minnesingers of Germany. Thus Conon de Bethune (*a.* 1224) in one of his poems complains:

Before I was smitten with this love, I was able to teach others the game; even now I know well how to contrive another's game, but my own I know not how to play. I am like a man who sees clearly at chess and can teach others quite well, but when he plays himself he loses his head, and is unable to cover himself from mate.

And Rüdiger v. Hünchkover (1290–3) in his *Wittich vom Jordan* (v. d. Linde, ii. 167) says of love, 'Daz sî dan saget schâch und mat.'

The popularity of chess led to the use of many of the special chess terms in metaphorical and transferred senses. In this way, some of these terms, e.g. *check*, *checkmate*, *mate* in most European languages, *jeopardy*, *pawn* (in the phrase 'to be a pawn in the game') in English, have come into general use, and the connexion with chess is largely forgotten. In the Middle Ages this metaphorical use of chess terms was carried further. Philippe Mouskes, Bishop of Tournai, in his *Chronique* (written 1243) repeatedly uses *fierge* (fers) in the sense of a force without which it was not easy to win in war. For instance:

Dont jura li boins rois le siége
Tant qu'il leur aura pris sans fierge (19604–5).

and—

S'orent eust xii fois siege
Mais a la traisme, sans friege,
Furent mate et amati
Et leur mur a tiere flati (27045–8).

To these I may add two passages from Chrestien de Troyes. In *Perceval*:

Ains ne combati volontiers
Fors dont quant on le sorqueroit:
Dont ert ferus qui il feroit
Puis le mattoit d'eskiès de fierge (11349–52).

and in *Cliges* (Halle, 1889):

Trois joies et trois enors ot;
L'une fu del chastel qu'il prist,
L'autre de ce que li promist
Li rois Artus qu'il li donroit
Quant sa guerre finée avroit,
Le meillor reiaume de Gales,
Le jor le fist roi an ses sales:
La graindre joie fu la tierce
De ce que s'amie fu fierce
De l'eschaquier don il fu rois (2364–73).

Mouskes also uses *roc* in a metaphorical sense when telling of the death of Gui, Count de la Fol, by a missile from an engine at the siege of Avignon:

Par quoi (the missile) le jour sans roc matèrent
La rose de cevalerie (26312–3).

So also in the *Credo* of Henri de Heiz, 191–8 (quoted in Bouteiller, *La Guerre de Metz en 1324*, Paris, 1875, p. 368 seq.):

Tour prent, affin que son roc pert.[35]

[35] Cf. for the expression *sans roc mater*, 'to succeed with inferior force or without using all one's resources', the Provençal Blacasset, *Gerra mi play*, 'Al flac jelos cuj dir mat ses tot roc' (i.e. au flasque jaloux je pense dire mat sans nulle roc).

To depict the common soldiers as Pawns is an obvious metaphor. The *Guerre de Metz*, 226–7, amplifies the comparison, and when the soldiers perform better than was anticipated an allusion is made to the promotion of the Pawn to the rank of fierce:

Et pour meter cialx de Bahaigne
Sont li paon devenus fierce . . .
Poon fierce sont devenus;
Ains que la guerre prengne fin
Seront poon pour roc tenus,
Pour chevalier et pour aufin.[36]

Here the aufin is mentioned as one of the better pieces. More striking, however, is the use of this piece to designate a coward or contemptible person—a use of the term borrowed from the weakness of the chess piece and its deceptive leap. Thus Jourdain Fantosme (*c.* 1175) has:

Je n'aura Robert de Vaus si bon sabelin
Ne mangié la viande, ne bëu de tel vin
Quant verra tanz beaus escuz, tans healmes Peitavins
Ne volsist en l'eschequier devenir un aufin (586–91).

The *Hist. des ducs de Norm. et des rois d'Anglet.* (1206), 108 (G) has:

Car li rois qui a Bordiaus avoit esté, s'en revenoit arriere vers Poitau, et si li manda avoec que bien seust il que il ne voloit par iestre offins, ne onques mais dus de Bourgogne n'avoit tant esté en garnison comme il avoit si li grevoit moult.

In *La Vengeance Raguidel*, 4270–8 (St.), a knight, angered that Arthur will not grant his wish before he has stated it, exclaims:

C'est la fins; Hui devenra cis rois aufins, Se ensi m'en vois escondis.

And in the English *Morte d'Arthur* (*c.* 1440), 1343, we read:

Myche wondyre have I, þat syche an alfyne as thow dare speke syche wordez.[37]

Three other chess expressions may be noted. Check-rook, the forking of King and Rook, was perhaps the most dangerous of all attacks in the older game, and the term is often used, particularly by German poets, to denote a great misfortune. Thus Meister Otto in his *Keiser Eraclius* (beg. 13th c.) has:

Ez ist ein schädelîch schâchroch
dem herzen und dem lîbe
swer bî einem übeln wîbe
alten unde wonen muoz.[38]

[36] Pawn promotion is also used metaphorically by the Provençal poet Elies Cairel (quoted in Levy, *Provenzalisches Suppl.-Wörterbuch*, Leipzig, 1894, s. v. *fersa*):

Al marques man de cui es Monferratz
Qe · is traga enan · anz qe · l jocs sia jogatz,
E fassa oimais de son pezonet fersa.

[37] Cf. also *Vie de St. Georges* (*c.* 1180), *Les Œuvres de Simund de Freine*, Paris, 1909, 1096–1107:

Savez, George que mei semble?
Quant tuz traitres sunt ensemble,
Tant savez de lur manére
Porter poëz la banére,
Fait avez cum traitre fin;
Autretant freit un aufin.
Aufin qui est en coverte
Par eschec, a descoverte
Sovent prent roc u peonet
Par la traïson del trait.
Traï avez Apolin
Dunt vus prendrez maté fin.

[38] Cf. Audelay, *Poems* (of 1426), E.E.T.S., 23:

After chec for the roke ware fore the mate,
For ȝif the fondement be false, the worke most nede falle,
Withyn a lyty stounde.

The mate in an angle of the board similarly stands for the most decisive of all events. Strohmeyer gives a number of instances of the allegorical use of the term, from which I quote:

(1) Méon, *Nouv. Recueil*, ii. 202: 'Ainz que la mort qui tout estrangle Vous die eschec et mat en l'angle.' (2) *Fabl. misc. du R.*, no. 7218: 'Bien m'a dit li evesque eschac Et m'a rendu maté en l'angle.' (3) *Margot conv.* (Jubinal, i. 323): 'or vous puis bien dire eschac Si iestes mas en l'angle boutez.' (4) Deschamps, *Œuvres comp.*, 1878–91, v. 351–2: 'et les souris m'ont mat en l'angle.'

It was also a favourite metaphor with the Provençal poets. Thus T. d'Albertat et de Pierre, *Peire*, has 'Albert, al corn del taulier Vos dirai mat'; and Aimeri de Bellinoy, *Cossiros*, 'El corn del taulier n'er matz'.

Finally, we have in Italian, Provençal, French, and German poets a number of allusions to doubling the chessboard, or the squares of the chessboard, meaning a number transcending all calculation.[39] The allusion is, of course, to the sum of the Geometrical Progression, 1, 2, 4, 8, &c., to 2^{63}, which, measured in grains of wheat, was Sassa's reward in the Arabic legend. The calculation of this series is discussed in Leonardo Pisano's *Liber Abbaci*, written 1202, where two varieties of the series are described:

duplicatio quidem scacherii duplici modo proponitur, quorum unus est cum sequens punctum sui antecedentis duplum sit: alius cum sequens punctum omnium antecedentum punctorum duplum esse proponatur (ed. Roma, 1857, i. 309 seq.).

Another Latin work on the subject was translated into French by Robert du Herlin, 1493 (*Le compte des lxiv poins de l'escequier doublé*, MS. Paris, f. fr. 2000, ff. 51–5).

[39] E. g. (1) Dante, *Divina Commedia, Paradiso*, xxviii. 92: 'Ed eran tante che'l numero loro Piu che'l doppiar degli scacchi s'imila.' (2) P. Vidal, *Tant an ben*: 'Mil tans es doblatz sos bes Qu'el comtes de l'escaquier.' (3) Thierri de Soissons (St.): 'Quant recort sa douce chiere, . . . alors puis de deus eschequiers Doubler les poincts tous entiers De fine beauté pleniere.' (4) Guiot de Provins (St.): 'Or puex, hui est li jors, Les poins de l'eschaiquier Doubleir de ma dolor.' (5) *Roman de la Violette*, Paris, 1834, 77: 'Molt bien poroit de l'eskiekier Les poins de sa doulor doubler.' (6) Ibid., 258: 'Qui me doubleroit l'eskiekier D'estrelins, nes prendroie mie, Parsi que fausist l'escremie.' (7) Wolfram v. Eschenbach, *Willehalm* (*a.* 1220; ed. Lachmann, p. 151): 'der marcrâf sagt im rehte: Ir hers mich bevilte, der zende ûz zwispilte ame schâchzabel ieslîch velt mit cardamôm' (Eiserhardt).

CHAPTER X

CHESSBOARDS AND CHESSMEN

Mediaeval boards.—Combined boards for chess and other games.—Carved chessmen.—The 'Charlemagne chessmen'.—The Lewis chessmen.—Conventional chessmen.—The Ager and Osnabrück pieces.—The 'St. Louis chessmen'.—Chessmen in MSS. and printed books.—Chess in cookery.—Chess in heraldry.

Pictures of games of chess in progress are fairly frequent in illuminated mediaeval manuscripts, and although the details of the drawing are often incorrect or conventional we may draw some conclusions from them respecting the furniture of chess, the size and general appearance of the chessboard, and the ordinary shapes of the chessmen.

The chessboard was, as a rule, both larger and more massive than in modern times. I do not recollect a single passage in the literature of the Middle Ages which mentions boards of leather or softer material. The boards are made of wood or metal, and this explains the frequency and the effectiveness with which they were used in the romances as weapons of offence or defence. The field of play was surrounded by a broad raised edge or border, which was often elaborately decorated. Cessolis lays stress upon the raised border as emblematic of the wall of a city; in Caxton's translation (ed. Axon, 158):

as to the seconde / wherfore ye bordour of theschequyer is hyher than the table wyth in. hit is to be vnderstande y^t^ the bordour aboute representeth the walle of ye citie / whiche is right hyghe / And therfor made ye philosopher the bordour more hyghe than ye tablier.

Many of the extracts from romances in the preceding chapter refer to the magnificence of the board.[1] When not in use it was hung up on the wall by means of a ring. In the *Liber Mir. S. Fidis* (ed. Paris, 1897, IV. viii. 190) Raimund de Montpezat is delivered from prison by St. Foy, and in token of the miracle carries off a chessboard which was hanging on the wall of his dungeon, and deposits it at the Saint's shrine at Conques.[2] In *Parzival*,

[1] Thus boards of gold and silver are mentioned in *Garin de Montglane*, *Huon of Bordeaux*, and *Oger*; of gold in the *Vœux du Paon* and *Renart le nouvel*; of gold and ivory in *Merlin*. The board in *Renaud de Montaubon* is of ivory. The extracts from *Garin de Montglane* and *Tristan* speak of richly decorated borders. In addition to these I may quote from the Provençal *Chanson d'Antioch* (Levy): 'Demandet us escaxs d'evori e d'aur fi; De maravites blanc son talhat li alfi E li roc e las fersas'; from *Morolf*, 13 a: 'Schâchzabel mit golde durchslagen Besetzt mit smaragd und jâchant: Das gesteine wîz unde rôt' (Massm.); and from *Wilhelm v. Oranse*:

Do hiez bringen die künegin
Ein schachzâbel von elfenbein.
Ouch brâhte man zweier hande gestein
Von zwier varwe daz edel schein.
Hie was smareis unde saphir.
Ouch was von rîcher gezier
Das schâchzabel gemachet.
Iz wart ir brâht von arabi.—(i. 49, Massm.)

[2] 'Ubi dum astans multa corde in dubio agitaret, tandem ei menti succurrit ut quia pre nimio pondere vinculorum machinamenta ad sancte virginis basilicam vehere nequibat, saltem tabulam scachorum ibi pendentem in testimonium sue evasionis ferre debeat.'

Photograph by Hanfstaengl

INLAID BOARD FOR MERELS AND CHESS
National Museum, Munich

[*Face page* 757

Gawain uses a chessboard, which was hanging up by an iron ring, as a shield.[3]

Only a few chessboards have survived from the 16th and earlier centuries, preserved because of the unusual beauty of the decoration. One of the finest of these is a board with a deep border, inlaid with ivory, mother-of-pearl, and metal, the work of Hans Sebald Beham, 1520–40, which is now in the National Museum, Munich. Of this I give an illustration. There is an elaborate board of rock-crystal in the Cluny Museum, Paris, of German workmanship of the 14th or early 15th century. Another decorated board of the 15th century is in a Florence Museum.

While some of these boards are intended for chess only, at quite an early date it became usual to combine together boards for the favourite games of the period. The inventories quoted above, pp. 447–9, contain many examples,[4] and a considerable number of boards of this character exist still, of Italian, German, Flemish, and Dutch manufacture.[5] V. d. Linde (ii. 314 and *Qst.*, 291–4) gives lists of chessboards and pieces in the museums at Nuremburg, Cassel, and Munich. In this country, there are several specimens in the South Kensington Museum. These boards are made in two halves hinged together, so that when closed they form a box, and when opened they provide an inner surface with a raised border, and an outer surface, each of which can be used as a game-board. In the earlier examples each of the halves is a square. The inner surface is nearly always devoted to tables (backgammon), and the dividing ridge across the middle of the open board may have given rise to the ordinary English name of *a pair of tables* for the backgammon board. On one side of the outer surface the chessboard was marked, and on the other the larger (or nine men's) merels-board. At the present day combined boards of the box pattern are generally made of two oblong halves, so that when opened the two halves form a square. The inner surface is still given to backgammon, but now the whole outer surface is occupied by the chessboard. This points to a decline in popularity of the game of merels, draughts having taken its place in England. On the Continent, however, and specially in Italy and Germany, the ordinary flat chessboard still generally has the merels diagram upon the reverse side.

The most elaborate board of the box pattern which I have seen is one at

[3] Dô vant diu maget reine
ein schâchzabelgesteine,
und ein bret, wol erleit, wît:
daz brâht sî Gâwâne in den strît.
an eim îsenînem ringez hienc,
dâ mit ez Gâwân enpfienc.
ûf disen vierecken schilt
was schâchzabels vil gespilt:
der wart in sêr zerhouwen.—(viii. 419–27.)

[4] The Norsemen appear to have combined boards very early. The *Króka-Refs Saga* (see p. 444) mentions a board for chess and hnefatafl, while a fragment of a board, on the one side for the larger merels, on the other for an unknown game, was found in the Gokstad ship. It is figured in Du Chaillu's *Viking Age*, 1889, ii. 168.

[5] Apparently, Englishmen obtained their chessboards and men from abroad. In 1464 Parliament passed an Act (in Pynson, *Acts Parlt.*, 3 Edw. IV) which forbade the importation of 'cisours, rasours, shetes, cardes à juer, espinges, patins, agules pur sakkes vulgarement nommes paknedels' (in Berthelet's translation of 1543: 'cysours, rasers, Chessemen, playeng cardes, cobes, patyns, paknedels'). In the reign of Elizabeth, Stafford (*Brief concepte of Eng. pollicy*, 48 b) gives a list of articles which he thought might be made in England, among them being 'cardes, tables, and Chesses, since we will needes have such things.'

South Kensington (154, 1900), of Venetian work of the 16th century. It has chess on the outer and tables on the inner surface, while two slides constructed so as to fit inside the closed box have, the one, chess and the ordinary mediaeval board for fox and geese (our 'solitaire' board) on opposite sides, the other, the larger merels and an enlarged board for fox and geese.

More mediaeval chessmen than boards have come down to our time, but there are few complete sets. We may conveniently divide the existing pieces into two classes: chessmen which are carvings of real kings, queens, knights, &c.; and chessmen which represent the different pieces by some conventional form. Ivory (often mentioned in the chess incidents in the romances and much admired),[6] walrus-ivory, bone, rock-crystal, jasper, amber, ebony and other hard woods, are the materials generally employed.

The most important chessmen of the more elaborate type which exist to-day are the so-called Charlemagne chessmen, now in the Bibliothèque Nationale, Paris, and the Lewis chessmen, of which part are in the British Museum and part in the National Museum, Edinburgh.

The Paris chessmen are now 17 in number, but one of them, the Indian raja on his elephant, with an Arabic inscription on the base which is reproduced as the frontispiece of this work, obviously has no real connexion with the remaining pieces. These consist of two Kings, two Queens, three Chariots (Rooks), four Horsemen (Knights), four Elephants (Bishops), and one Foot-soldier (Pawn). The Kings and Queens are carved sitting within a semicircular pavilion, which in one King and one Queen is crenellated, and in the others has a less ornate top. The curtains across the front of the pavilion are held back by pages in the case of the Kings, by maidens in that of the Queens. A similar piece, representing an old man (probably an Aufin) sitting under a crenellated pavilion, is now in the same cabinet. Two Kings of similar design are in the Bargello Museum. The most noteworthy feature about the carving of the other pieces is the fact that the Rooks are represented by Chariots. This is, of course, the original meaning of the term *Rook*, but it is not easy to see how the tradition of this survived among European players, and was able to dictate the fashion of the piece.

Prior to the Revolution these chessmen were preserved in the Abbey of St. Denys, Paris, where they were seen by Jacques Doublet, the author of the *Histoire de l'Abbaye de S. Denys*, Paris, 1625. Doublet gives the popular tradition that the chessmen had been presented to the abbey by Charlemagne. Modern expert opinion, however, considers them to be of French workmanship of the 12th century at earliest.

The Lewis chessmen were discovered in 1831 in a sand-bank at the head of the Bay of Uig, on the west coast of the island of Lewis, one of the outer Hebrides. There is no circumstantial account of the discovery, but it appears that they were found in a small chamber of dry-built stone, resembling an oven, about 15 feet below the top of the sand-bank. The chessmen were

[6] Cf. the Provençal G. de St. Gregori, *Razo e dreit*, 'plus a'l cor blanc que nulhs escacx d'evori' (her body was whiter than any chessmen of ivory).

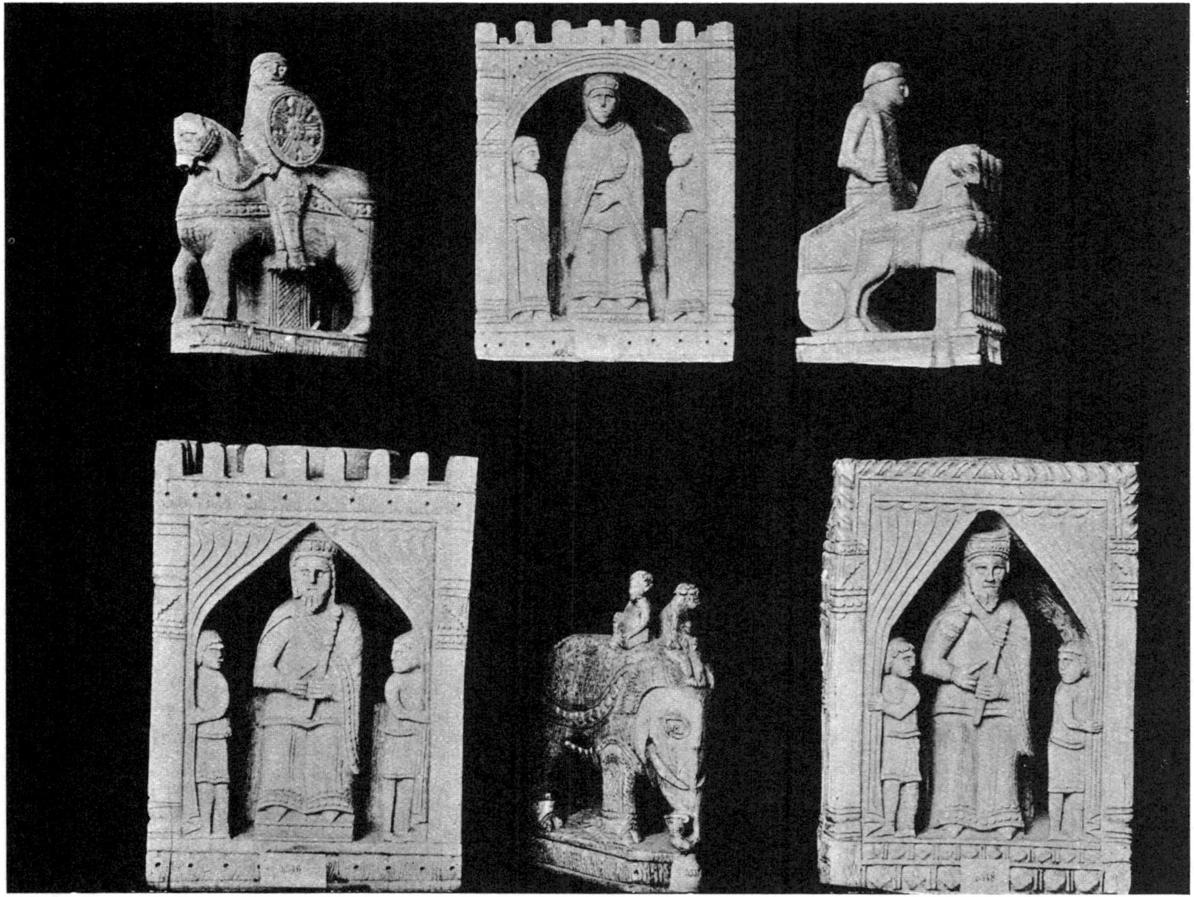

Photograph by A. Giraudon

THE CHARLEMAGNE CHESSMEN. BIBL. NAT., PARIS

Top row: Knight, Queen, Rook. Lower row: King, Aufin, King

exhibited by Mr. Roderick Ririe at a meeting of the Society of Antiquaries of Scotland, April 11, 1831, but before the members had raised the money to purchase them Mr. Kirkpatrick Sharpe stepped in and bought 10 of the pieces, while the remaining 67 chessmen, 14 tablemen, and a buckle were bought for the British Museum. On the dispersion of Mr. Sharpe's collection, the Lewis chessmen, now 11 in number, Mr. Sharpe having obtained another one from Lewis, were purchased by Lord Londesborough, and at the sale of the latter's collection in 1888 they were purchased by the Society of Antiquaries for the Scottish National Museum. All the game-pieces, as well as the buckle, are carved of walrus-ivory. The 78 chessmen comprise 8 Kings, 8 Queens, 16 Bishops, 15 Knights, 12 Rooks, and 19 Pawns, of which 2 Kings, 3 Queens, 3 Bishops, a Knight, and 2 Rooks are now at Edinburgh. The Kings and Queens are carved seated, the Kings holding a half-drawn sword across the knees, the Queens usually resting the head on the right hand. Seven of the Bishops (2 at Edinburgh) are also seated, the other 9 are standing. All are represented with the crozier. The Knights are on horseback with spear in the right hand and shield on the left arm. The Rooks are armed warriors on foot, with helmet, shield, and sword. The Pawns are of various shapes and sizes, but most have octagonal bases. Two of them bear some ornamentation. A Queen of the same type as the Lewis Queens was found in County Meath, Ireland, in the first half of the 19th century. It is now in a private museum in Dublin.[7]

The carving of the Rooks as warriors on foot undoubtedly points to Icelandic workmanship. La Peyrère, *Lettre à M. La Mothe* (1664), Paris, 1663, 56, describing the Icelandic chessmen, says:

> La difference qu'il y a de leur pièces aux notres, est, que nos Fous sont des Evesques parmy eux . . . Leur Rocs sont de petits Capitaines, que les escoliers Islandois que sont icy apelent Centurions. Ils sont representez, l'espee au costé, les joues enflés, et sonnant du cor, qu'ils tiennent des deux mains.

Sir Frederic Madden, in his *Historical Remarks* (*Archaeologia*, 1852, xxiv; also separately printed, and in *CPC.*, i), endeavoured to prove that these pieces are of Icelandic carving of the middle of the 12th century. The latest authority, Mr. O. M. Dalton (*Cat. Ivory Carvings . . . in the B. Mus.*, London, 1909), ascribes them to the 12th century, and thinks that they may be of British carving. Wilson had already claimed a Scotch origin for them. Both views depend upon the assumption that the chessmen are as old as the 13th century.

If there were any truth in the tradition which Capt. Thomas discovered to be current in Lewis, they may be the work of Icelandic carvers of the beginning of the 17th century only.[8]

[7] A rough woodcut of it was given in O'Donovan's *Leabhar na g-Ceart*, Dublin, 1847, lxii. Other Norse chessmen are depicted in Fabricius, *Danmarkshistorie*, 1861, i. 494 (a seated Bishop), in Worsaae, *Nordiske Oldsager i det kongelige Museum i Kjöbenhavn*, Kjöbenhavn, 1854, 160 (a King, Bishop, and Pawn) and in Engelhardt, *Guide illustré du Musée des Antiquités du Nord*, Copenhague, 1870, 57 (a Knight);—v. d. Linde, ii. 312.

[8] The tradition is to the effect that a shepherd employed by George Mor Mackenzie (who settled in Lewis, 1614–15) murdered a sailor, who had swum ashore from a wreck with the

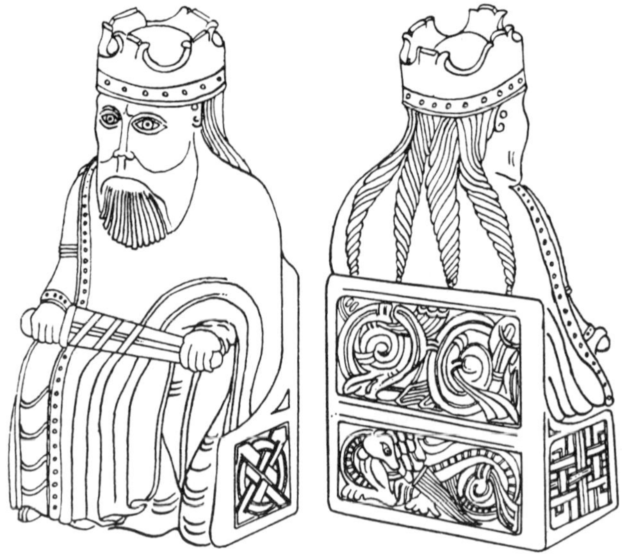

King. Lewis chessmen in British Museum.

Queens. Lewis chessmen and from Co. Meath.

Bishops, Knights, and Rooks. Lewis chessmen.

In addition to these chessmen, there is a number of other carvings in European Museums which have been assumed to be chess-pieces. In some cases the identification is very doubtful,[9] and, if chessmen, the disappearance

Chess Bishops. German early 13th century (Kunstkammer, Berlin).

of the remainder of what must have been sets of great beauty and value is somewhat inexplicable. Many of these pieces represent the men on horseback,

chessmen in a bag. The shepherd buried the bag in the sand, and never prospered afterwards. Capt. F. & W. L. Thomas, in *Proc. Soc. Antiq. Scotl.*, 1863, iv. 411. In addition to the works already mentioned, information respecting the Lewis chessmen is also contained in Wilson, *Prehist. Annals Scotl.*, ii. 341; and *Proc. Soc. Antiq. Scotl.*, 1889, xxiii. 9.

[9] Thus the 'English Castle (13th cent.)' at South Kensington (8987, 1863), which is figured in an article on 'Curious Chessmen', *Country Life*, Feb. 2 and 16, 1907, cannot be a chessman at all, since the Castle did not appear in chess until the 16th c. An ivory carving in the Ashmolean Museum, Oxford, of the early 13th c., also diagrammed in the same article, and representing two armed horsemen passing one another, is very doubtfully chess, though there is a somewhat similar piece in the Bargello Museum which is said to be of French work of the 11th (!) c. Two pieces figured in Wilson, *Prehist. Annals Scotl.*, ii. 357, 358, and described as chessmen, the one from the Clerk collection, Penicuik, the other from the Nat. Museum, Edinburgh, are probably not chessmen at all.

Twelve chessmen from the Bargello Museum are depicted in Magee, *Good Companion*, Florence, 1910, 50, 51. Several of these are wrongly named. The second is not a Rook but an Aufin, the fourth is a King, the fifth a Pawn, the seventh is possibly, and the eleventh certainly, not a chessman at all.

Photograph by A. Giraudon

THE CHARLEMAGNE CHESSMEN

Top row: ? King, Pawn, Queen. Lower row: King (back view), Aufin, King (back view)

and the horse is often surrounded by diminutive foot-soldiers, usually archers, the object being to increase the stability of the piece by adding weight to the base in compensation for the height. Of this kind are a damaged King of

Pawns. Lewis chessmen.

German workmanship (13th c.) in the British Museum, a Knight in the Kunstkammer of the Berlin Museum (German, early 14th c.), another (German, 15th c.) in the Nuremburg Museum, a Bishop in the Antiquarium, Regensburg, and another (German, 13th c.) at Nuremburg. It is interesting to note how often the Aufin was carved as a Bishop, even in lands where the normal nomenclature shows no sign of any association of the Aufin with the Church. I give illustrations of two other German Bishops of the early 13th c., one in the Berlin Museum, the other at Leipzig. At a later date the Aufin was occasionally carved as a monk, as in a 16th c. set in the Cassel Museum.

Knight (Kunstkammer, Berlin).

It was only the wealthy who could have afforded to possess the elaborate carved chessmen with which we have been dealing; the ordinary player must have been content with simpler pieces of conventional pattern. Wirnt v. Gravenberg implies this in the passage quoted on p. 484 from his *Wigalois*,

'Dice-boards and Courier made of ivory lay before the great ladies. They played with noble pieces, not with wooden ones as we now see women playing.'

But even these conventional chessmen might be made of costly materials, gold and silver, rock-crystal, or jasper, and decorated with jewels. The romance-writers generally pause a moment to indicate the magnificence of the chessmen before they describe the game.

The oldest type of conventional chessmen carved for European players would seem to have been one in which the Kings and Queens were represented by figures shaped roughly like a throne, the Aufin and Knight by

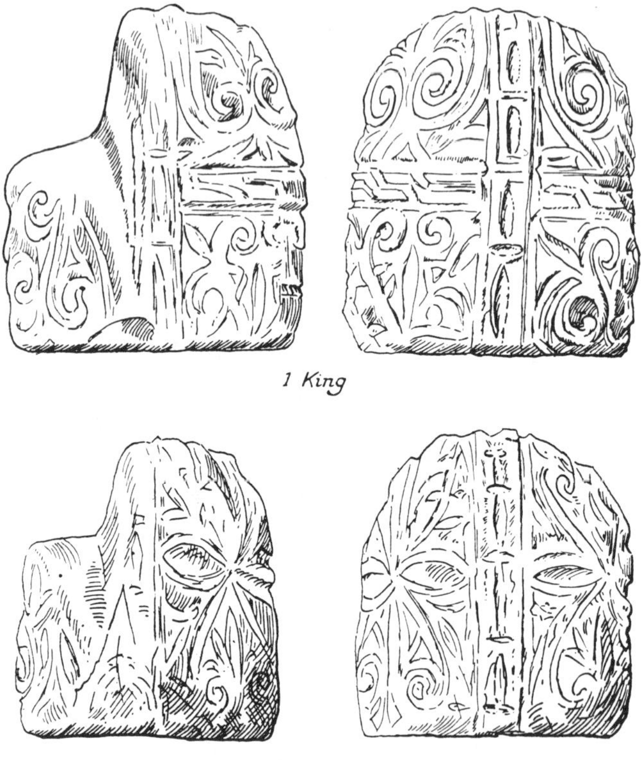

1 King

2 Queen

The Ager chessmen

cylindrical figures, the Aufin with two projecting humps—possibly to represent the elephant's tusks, the Knight with one hump to represent the horse's head, the Rook by a narrow rectangular block with a deep depression across the top, and the Pawn by a smaller thimble-shaped piece. Two incomplete sets of this type, both carved in rock-crystal, have survived, one in the treasury of the parish church of Ager, a village near Urgel in Catalonia, the other in the Dom treasury at Osnabrück.

The Ager chessmen are now fifteen in number, twenty-nine having disappeared since the visitation of the church in 1547 by Abbot Don Juan

DAMAGED GERMAN CHESS-KING. BRITISH MUSEUM

Sobrino.[10] According to tradition, the chessmen were given to the church by one of the Counts of Urgel, a family associated with other gifts of chessmen (see pp. 405–7). Ten of the pieces are covered with tracery, and apparently were originally mounted upon bases of red glass; the remaining five are quite plain, and somewhat smaller. The chased pieces are a King (base 56 mm. in diameter, height 70 mm.), a Queen (base 52 mm., height 66 mm.), two Bishops (base 45 mm., height 60 mm.), two Knights (base 45 mm., height 55 mm.), a Rook (base 46 mm. by 19 mm., height 40 mm.), and three Pawns (base 26 mm., height 35 mm.). The plain pieces are a King, a Bishop, a Knight, a Rook, and a Pawn.

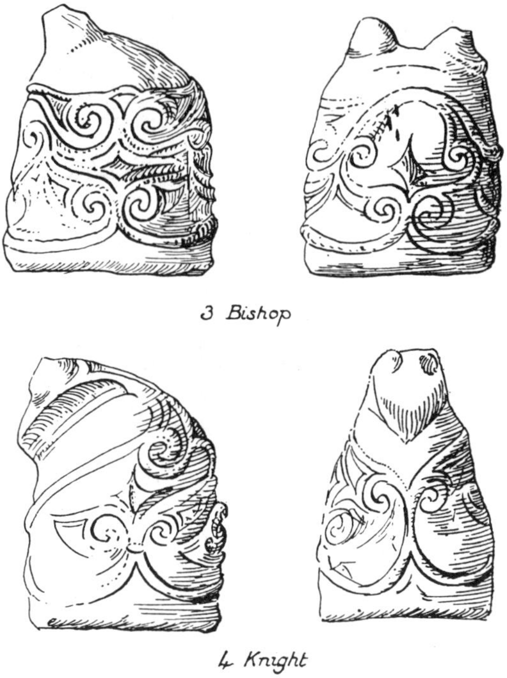

The Ager chessmen

Brunet y Bellet (*Ajedrez*, 226–32, 275), to whom we owe the knowledge of the existence of these chessmen and the drawings which I reproduce, thought that the chased men were the superior pieces and the plain ones the Pawns, each Pawn reproducing in undecorated form the shape of its master-piece. In this I think that he is assuredly wrong. There is no evidence outside the pages of the *Moralities* that the Pawns were ever differentiated in form. The presence or absence of decoration seems to me to be a simple and natural way of separating the two sides.

The Osnabrück chessmen are also fifteen in number, ten or eleven having disappeared since they were seen by M. Joly in 1646.[11] They resemble the Ager chessmen very closely, but are not in such good preservation, and I find it difficult to identify all the pieces from the photograph, which I reproduce. They are rather smaller than the Ager chessmen, the largest being only 5 cm. in height, and standing on a base of diameter 3 cm. Here again the two sides appear to be distinguished by the presence or absence of decoration, and

[10] 'Una caxa de fusta ab quaranta cuatre pessas de crestall Diuise son Squachs, creuse los dona lo compte d'Urgell,' quoted in Villanueva, *Viage literario á las iglesias de España*, ix. 141. Villanueva remarks in passing that this is not the only set of chessmen which is preserved in a Spanish church.

[11] He mentions them in his *Voyage fait à Mvnster . . . en 1646 et 1647*, Paris, 1670, 180 : 'Il y a encore 25. ou 26. eschets qu'on dit estre de luy (Charlemagne), qui sont de cristal, et ont diverses figures, les uns estans ronds, les autres quarrés, et les autres pointus, sans ressembler aux nostres d'apresant.'

there is evidence that the chased pieces were again mounted upon bases of red glass. The popular tradition which attributes these chessmen to Charlemagne is just as mistaken as the parallel tradition regarding the pieces in the Bibliothèque Nationale: recent expert opinion places these in the 12th c. at earliest.[12]

According to v. d. Linde (ii. 317) there are two similar pieces at Copenhagen, the one a Knight, the other a Bishop.

5 Pawn and Rook

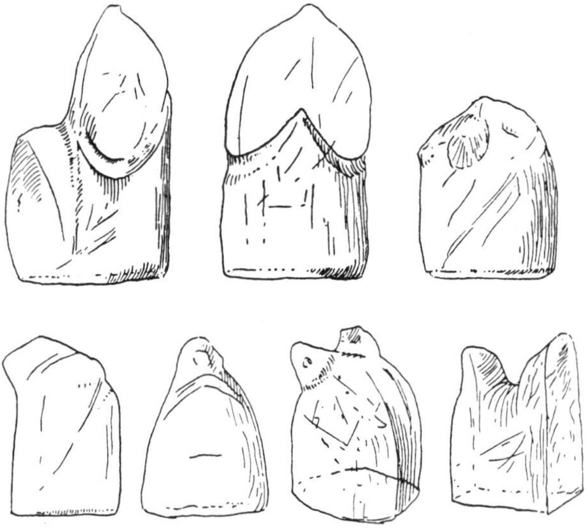

6 The plain pieces

The Ager chessmen

There are thirteen chessmen, of bone or ivory, in the Mediaeval Room at the British Museum which approximate in form to this type of piece, but the use of an easier material for carving has resulted in a more symmetrical and finished shape of piece. Four of these are Kings. Five are Bishops, of which three have oval bases and flat tops from which two points project horizontally, one being from Moorfields, London, while the other two are cylindrical in shape with two tusks projecting vertically from one side of the top. Four are Knights with oval bases and flat tops from which a single nose

[12] Cf. C. Berlage, *Mittheilung ü. d. kirchlichen Alterthümer Osnabrücks*, 1878, xi. 273; and v. d. Linde, ii. 316–17, and *Qst.*, 57.

Face page 766]

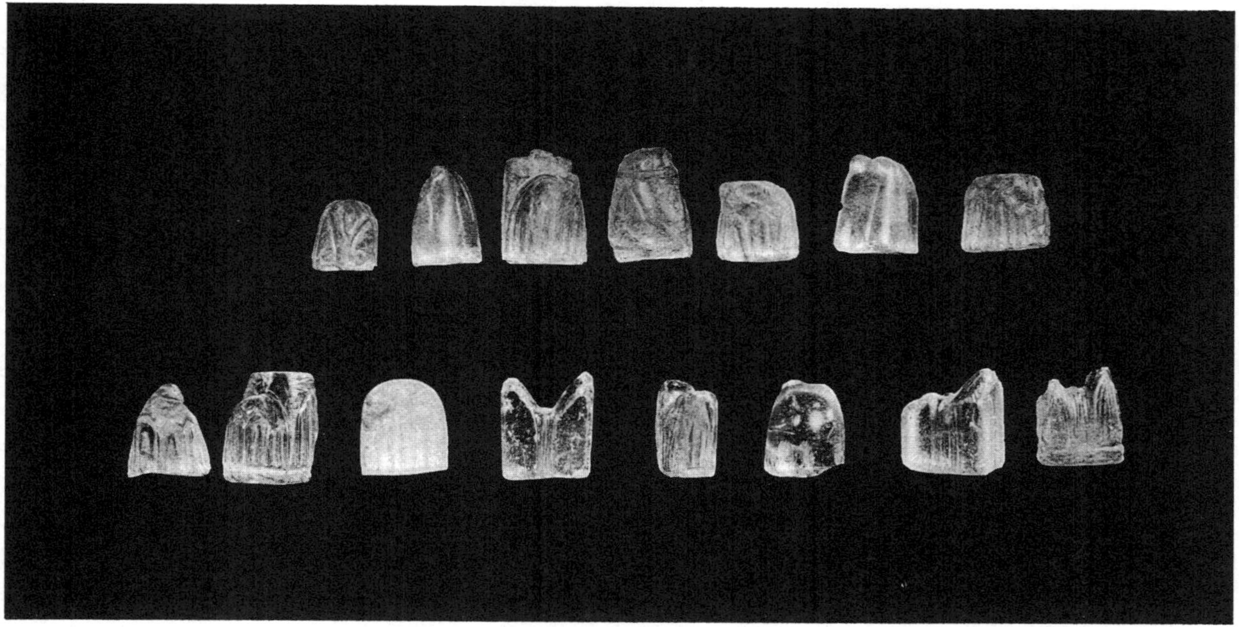

THE CHARLEMAGNE CHESSMEN. THE DOM, OSNABRÜCK

Top row: Pawn (?), Knight, King, Queen (?), Aufin, Knight, Aufin.
Lower row: Queen (?), King, Aufin, Rook, Rook (end view), Knight, Rook, Rook.

projects horizontally. One of these was found in Moorfields, and another at Helpstone, Northamptonshire.[13]

There are doubtless many similar pieces elsewhere, thus the Bargello Museum has a King of the London pattern, and also a Rook with its easily recognized divided top. We have seen that reference was made to this shape of the piece in the *Winchester Poem* and in Neckam, while I have already given illustrations of Muslim pieces of the same shape. The fact that one of

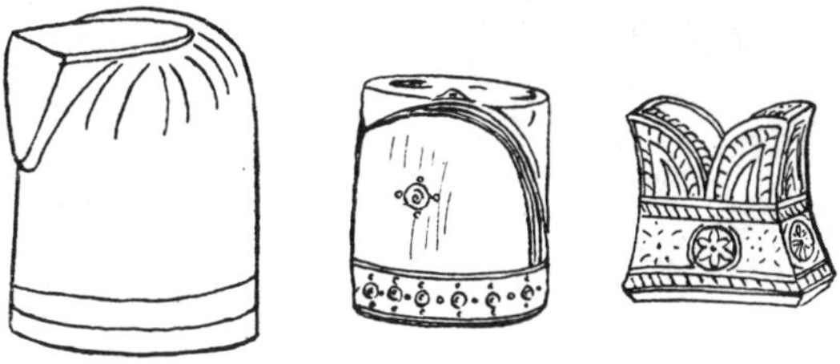

Knight. Brit. Mus. King. Brit. Mus. Rook. Bargello Mus.

Bishop from Helpstone Northants. Brit. Mus. Bishop from Beverley Brit. Mus. Bishop from Northampton Castle (Arch. Journal XXXIX, 421)

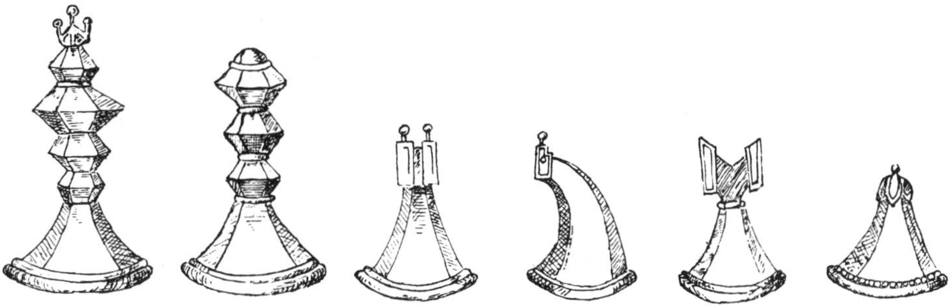

The 'St. Louis chessmen'. Cluny Museum.

the London Kings was found at Catania, Sicily, suggests that all the chessmen of this type reproduce early Muslim forms of the chessmen.

A further step in the development of the modern type of chessmen is illustrated by two interesting sets in the Cluny Museum, Paris.

[13] There are other game-pieces in the same case which are labelled as chessmen, but are certainly wrongly described, since they have all come from excavations of sites going back to early Saxon times. The pieces of jet found in the course of the excavations into the Mote Hill, Warrington (*Proc. Hist. Soc. Lanc. and Cheshire*, 1857, v. 59), the similar piece from Norfolk, and the bone piece found at Woodperry, Oxfordshire (*Arch. Journal*, iii. 121) cannot be chess, any more than the Norse pieces figured in Du Chaillu, op. cit., ii. 354. Similar pieces to these last are in the Pitt-Rivers Museum, Oxford.

The more important of these consists of thirty-one pieces, the one side cut out of clear, the other out of cloudy crystal, and all mounted with gold plate. I have already alluded to the board which belongs to this set. It was for long in the possession of the royal house of France, and was only presented to the Museum when the set was spoiled by the loss of one of the Queens during the reign of Louis XVIII. Tradition has it that this set was sent by the Old Man of the Mountain to St. Louis:[14] as a matter of fact the set is most probably of German workmanship of the late 14th or early 15th century, and never saw the East at all. In this set the Kings and Queen begin to approach the modern form of these pieces, and the only men which would present any difficulty to modern players are the Rooks, which preserve the mediaeval shape.

Mediaeval chessmen. Cluny Museum.

In the other set, the two-headed appearance of the Rook is more pronounced. This set is but little later than the 'St. Louis chessmen'.

Another set in the Cluny Museum is interesting as showing an attempt to simplify the form of the chessmen so that they could be easily turned on a lathe. This set, turned in bone and coloured white and black, is complete. The catalogue describes it as 'ancien et qui parait d'origine septentrionale'. I know of no other set which resembles this. The major pieces are partly distinguished by height, and partly by differences in the shape of the top. I am not certain about the identification; what I take to be the Bishop is somewhat like the insignificant modern French *Fou* (Bishop).

We have already seen that several of the problem MSS. depict the chessmen in such a way that we can infer what was the ordinary type of chessmen

[14] Joinville, *St. Louis*, ed. Paris, 1871, 138, mentions the chess in a list of presents which the Old Man of the Mountain sent St. Louis: 'Et il li envoia . . . jeux de tables et de eschez; et toutes ces choses estoient fleuretées de ambre, et estoit l'ambre, lié sur le cristal à beles vignetes de bon or fin.'

Brunet y Bellet (op. cit., 268–79) tries to prove that this set is the one which was presented to the Church of St. Giles, Nîmes, by the Countess Ermessind of Barcelona (p. 406).

in use at the time of the writing of the MS. The Alfonso MS. gives instructions for the fashioning of the more elaborate pieces—the King on his throne with crown and sword, the Queen as the standard-bearer (*alferez* or *mayor del Rey*), the Bishop as an elephant with howdah full of armed men, the Knight as a horseman, the Rook as a mass of horsemen crowded together, the Pawn as a foot-soldier—but goes on to say that the diagrams show the

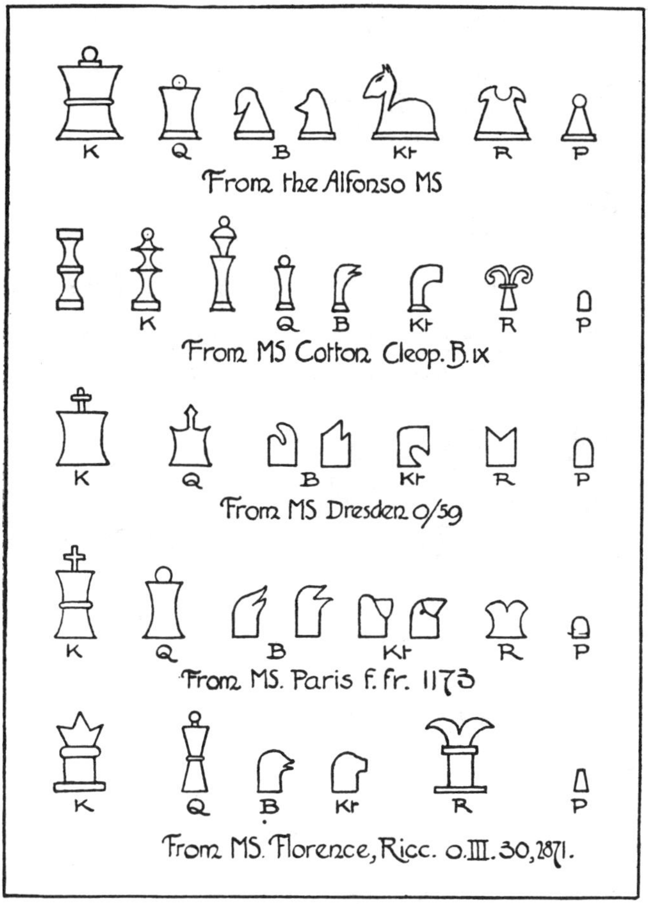

Figures of Chessmen from Problem MSS

appearance of the chessmen that were ordinarily used in Spain. I reproduce the forms of the pieces, not only from the problem MSS., but from other early printed books and pictures of games, arranging the pieces in the illustrations in the following order, starting from the left-hand side: King, Queen, Bishop, Knight, Rook, Pawn. Some sixteenth- and seventeenth-century works, e. g. Tarsia and Selenus, combine a turned base with the head and shoulders of a human figure; these, I imagine, were only exceptionally in real use. The

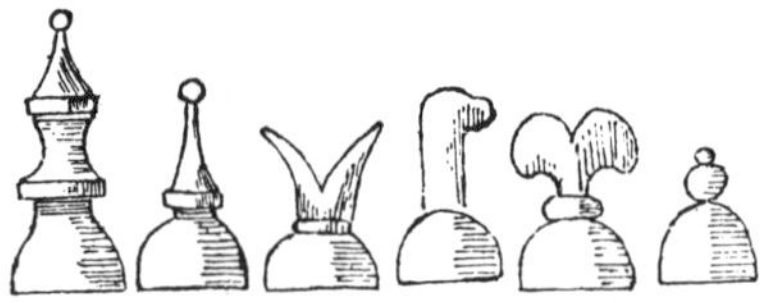

Chessmen from Caxton's *Game and Playe of the Chesse.*

Chessmen from *Volgarizzamento.*

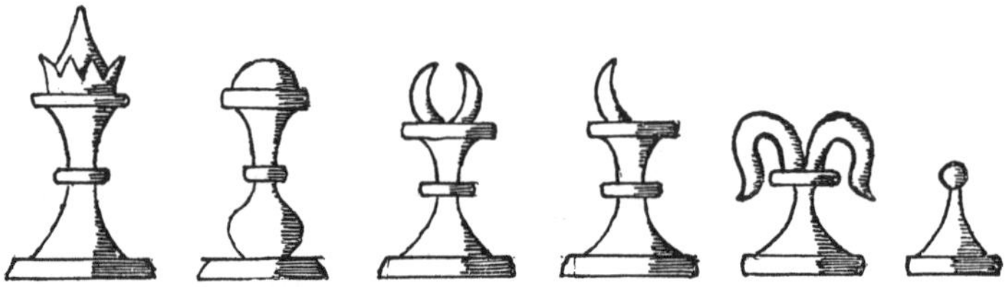

Chessmen from Publicius, *Ars oratoria.*

Chessmen from Lucena.

TYPES OF FIFTEENTH-CENTURY CHESSMEN.

Chessmen from Damiano (problems).

Chessmen from Damiano, 5th edition.

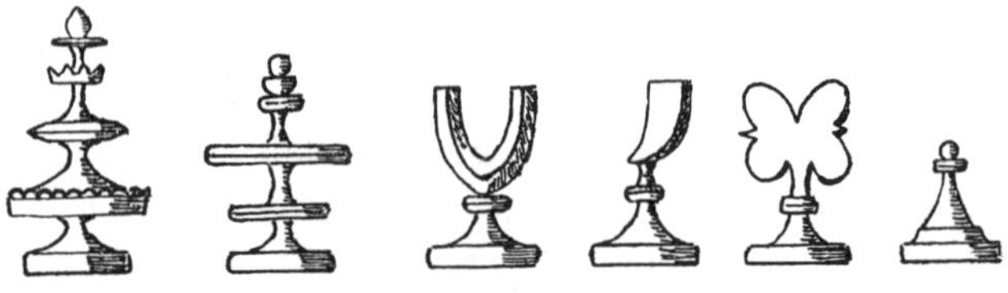

Chessmen from Egenolff (title-page).

Chessmen from Egenolff (text).

Chessmen from Köbel (after Massmann).

Chessmen from Gracco's Problems, MS. Bonc., N. 2.

Chessmen from a Damiano MS. in the possession of Mr. J. G. White.

Chessmen from Selenus, ornamentation of sub-title page.

Chessmen from Selenus, game pp. 216, 217.

Chessmen from *Studies of Chess*, 1804.

German pieces of the sixteenth century show a free treatment of the Rook, in which the two-headed shape is obscured by the additional ornamentation of form. Some German sets of this period are still more fanciful; an amber set at Cassel represents the King by a sceptre, the Queen by a flower, the Bishop by a book, &c.

The modern form of the Rook as a tower appears first in the fifth edition of Damiano, published between 1524 and 1550, and the older shape of the piece disappeared with startling rapidity. The more elaborate sets placed the tower upon the back of an elephant, as in the illustration at the head of the chapter on the Rook in Selenus.

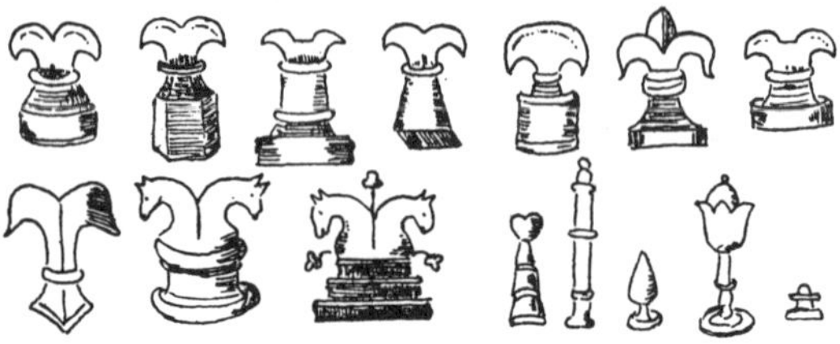

Rooks and other chess charges, from Randle Holme.

French chessmen, 18th c. *Encyclopédie méthodique*, 1792.

Rowbothum, in his translation of Gruget (Damiano), 1562, adds to his original a note on the shapes of the English pieces of his day:

> Our Englishe Cheastmen are commonly made nothing like vnto these foresayde fashions: to wit, the King is made the highest or longest: the Queene is longest nexte vnto him: the Bishoppe is made with a sharpe toppe and clouen in the middest not muche vnlyke to a bishops Myter: the knight hath his top cut asloope, as thoughe beynge dubbed knight: the Rooke is made lykest to the Kinge, and the Queene, but that he is not so long: the Paunes be made smalest & least of all, & thereby they may best be knowen.

According to Beale (1656), the Rook (here called Rooke, Rock, or Duke) is sometimes fashioned with a round head, sometimes like a castle. Randle

Holme (in his *Academy of Armory* (text of 1681–2, ed. Roxburghe Club, 1905), ii. 66) says:

The King is the first and highest of all the chessepins . . . The Queene is the next pin[15] in height to the King. . . . The Bishops are the pins with cloven heads. . . . The Knights are the pins which haue their heads cut aslant like a feather in a helmet. . . . The Rooks are the pins which haue round buttoned caps on their heads, and these signifie the countrey peasants.

It is interesting to note that this form of Knight is still manufactured in England. I give a drawing of one which I recently purchased with a cheap set.

Chessmen of fanciful shapes and forms are often made as curiosities. For actual play, most players would prefer to use the 'Staunton chessmen', the pattern of which Howard Staunton designed in 1849.

Staunton Chessmen

Occasionally in the Middle Ages dishes were prepared in the form of a chessboard with its pieces. Thus, at a Munich feast in 1476 (Westenrieder's *Beitr.* iii. 139) the eighth course was—

ain schâchzagl von mandlmilch praun und weiss; die roch und all stain waren von zucker.

One of the chief features of a banquet which Cardinal Wolsey gave to the French Ambassador at Hampton Court in 1528 was, according to Stowe (*Chronicle*, 1631, 537), a sweetmeat in the shape of a chessboard. It was intended as a delicate compliment to the French nation 'who be very expert in that play'.

A Munich MS. cookery book (Monac. germ., 997, 48a) gives instructions 'ein hübschen Schachzagl machen'.

It was inevitable that so favourite a recreation of the nobility should have left its mark upon heraldry. The division of the field into small squares of alternate colours need have nothing to do with chess, although the heraldic term *checky* or *checquey*, a derivative of the word *check*, shows that its similarity with the division of the chessboard was soon grasped by heralds. On the other hand, the use of the chessmen as heraldic charges must be derived from

[15] Pin was used in the sense of a chessman from 1680, or so, to about 1800. Thus Cowper (*Task*, vi. 271) describes a player—

At the chequer'd board . . with a hand
Trembling, as if eternity were hung
In balance on his conduct of a pin.

chess. None of the chessmen is used so frequently as the *Rook*, in its typical mediaeval form with two heads. To many writers on heraldry who only associate the Rook with its modern shape as a tower, the form of the heraldic *rook*, *roc*, or *chess-rook*, has been a great puzzle. As long ago as the middle of the seventeenth century, Menestrier tried to explain the shape as that of the reverse end of the lance,[16] and this explanation has often been repeated by later writers. To any one familiar with the shape of the Rook in mediaeval pictures of chess there can be no difficulty at all in recognizing the identical form, or a simple development of it, in a coat of arms. According to Papworth (*Alphabetical Dictionary of Coats of Arms*, London, 1874) chess-rooks appear in the arms of the following English families: Rookwood [Rockwood, Rokewood, 1364],

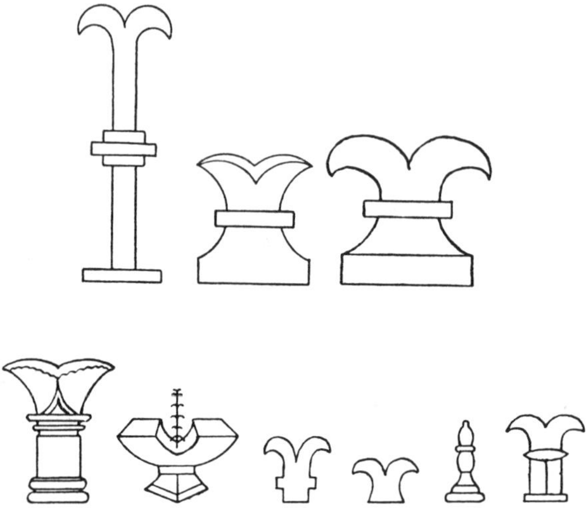

Chess-rook in heraldry.

Abelyn(e [Abyleyne, Aylin], Elloft(s, Hondisacre, Smart [Smert], Fitzsymon, Colvill, Holwell [Hollowell], Ellereck [Ellerker], Rook(e [Rock(e], Werdon, Arthur, Orm(e)sby, Hewe, Rocold. To this list Randle Holme adds Bodenham, Bunbury, Pickering, Dawkin. V. d. Linde (ii. 189 n.) says that the Rook is borne by the following German and Swiss families: Bemmel, Bitterl, Bröcker (1441), Derrer, Eckenbrecht, Fronhofen, Halbherr, Hangenohr, Heilingen (1292), Hohenbalken, Hoyten, Immerseel, Marzach (14th c.), Marokko (1473), Montfort, Neufahrer, Neustetter, Redemin, Rochlitz (1364), Rochow (1319), Stürmer, Sultzer, Thierbach (1435), Vittel, Vogt (1353, plainly due to the influence of Cessolis), Walch; and the Rook with two horses' heads by Fend, v. Möringen, Gollnhüter, Herzheimer, Hinderskircher, Loch, Ostroban, v. Trazberg, Tönzelin (1520), Vendius. Basterot (*Traité Élementaire*, Paris, 1863, 24 n.) says that the Rook is borne by the following French families: Bernard

[16] *La Science de la Noblesse* (originally published at Lyon, 1659), Paris, 1691, 49: 'Roc est le fer morné d'une lance de Tournoi, ou recourbé à la manière des extremitez des croix ancrées. On l'appelle aussi Roc d'Echiquier, parce que les Tours des Échecs, que les Espagnols nomment Roque, ont le meme forme.'

de Champigny, Besnard de Rezay, Boucherimbaud, Bouthet du Rivault, Chabert, Deifau de Pontalba, Du Cheyron du Pavillon, Guitton, Lescout d'Aux, Livron, Marchant, Le Normand, La Roche de Grane, La Roche Saint-Andre, La Roche Fontenilles, Rochette, Rochemore, Rogon, Roquelaure, Roque de la Madelaine, Roquemaure, Roquemorel, Roquette. Brunet y Bellet (op. cit., 416 seq.) gives the following Spanish families as using the Rook in their coats of arms: Rocaberti, Rocamora, Roca, Roquesens, Romeu, Bernat, Claramunt, Rocafull, Roig.

A reference to the Rook in Dante's *Purgatorio*, xxiv. 28–30,

> Vidi per fame a vuoto usar li denti
> Ubaldin della Pila e Bonifazio
> Che pasturo col rocco molte genti

has puzzled the commentators not a little. It probably refers to a crozier, the top of which was shaped like the mediaeval Rook, as already explained by Boccaccio and Benvenuto de' Rambaldi da Imola in the fourteenth century.[17]

[17] V. d. Lasa, 199–205, discusses the point at length.

CHAPTER XI

THE BEGINNINGS OF MODERN CHESS

Time and place of first appearance.—Early literature of the modern game.—*Le Jeu des Eschés de la Dame, moralisé.*—The Catalan *Schachs d'amor.*—The Göttingen MS.—Lucena.—Damiano.—Vida and Caldogno.—Egenolff.—Early problems of the modern game.

THERE is nothing in the chess records of the third quarter of the fifteenth century to suggest that the position of the game in popular favour was in any way different from what it had been at any time during the preceding century, or that chess-players were contemplating any changes in the method of play. There is no change in the character or the number of the references to chess in general literature: these still point to as wide a popularity of the *game* as ever. There are no signs of any diminution of activity on the part of the compilers of collections of *problems*: many of the existing problem MSS. were copied at this time. The moves of the chessmen had in each country been fixed for at least a hundred years, and writers use them with no sense of the possibility of an impending change. Francesco Colonna wrote his ballets of living chess for the mediaeval game in 1467, and John Sherwood uses the move of the mediaeval Bishop to illustrate the move of certain pieces in Rythmomachy in his account of that game, written between 1465 and 1476.[1]

But in this case the appearances are deceptive. The spirit of experiment was not dead: on the contrary, it was more active, more daring than ever. Suddenly, in the closing years of the century, we find a new variety of chess disputing with the older game in popularity in Italy, France, and the Peninsula. *Chess* is no longer a sufficiently distinctive name; the mediaeval game is known as *the old chess*, It. *scacchi al antica*, Sp. *axedrez del viejo*, Fr. *le viel jeu des eschés*; the new game takes on a variety of names; It. *scacchi de la donna* or *alla rabiosa*, Sp. *axedrez de la dama*, Fr. *eschés de la dame* or *de la dame enragée*, and when at length it reaches Germany in 1536, *current* or *welsches Schachspiel*.

The new game differed from the old in two points only. In everything else the old local assizes and rules remained untouched: there was no intention of substituting a uniform type of game for the national varieties of chess that existed in mediaeval Europe. The Queen and Bishop simply exchanged their mediaeval rules and privileges for the moves which they still retain—the

[1] 'Trianguli autem in tercium locum, non quidem ut Miles in scacho, trahuntur, sed uel directe dextrorsum sinistrorsum ante seu retro, uel omnino angulariter quem ad modum in ludo scaccorum Alphinus.' MS. Casanatense (C), vii a.

Queen moving at choice to any square in a diagonal, horizontal, or vertical direction, so long as the way is clear; the Bishop moving at choice to any square in a diagonal direction, so long as the way is clear. The new moves involved the abandonment of the older privileges of leaping *over* an occupied square which the Bishop always, and the Queen exceptionally, possessed; but they left the pieces with greatly enhanced powers, the Queen, originally far weaker than Rook or Knight, and only little stronger than the Bishop, becoming practically twice as strong as the Rook, the strongest piece in the older game. Incidentally, the Pawn also gained in value, for no alteration was made in its promotion rank, and the queening of a Pawn now increased the attack to a degree that was in nearly every case irresistible. It is not surprising that the new game should be widely called by a name which emphasized the predominant position of the new Queen (It. *donna*, Sp. *dama*, Fr. *dame*). It is probable, also, that the less obvious name in Italian, *scacchi alla rabiosa*, 'mad chess', arose in the same way, the term *rabiosa* being an epithet of the new Queen. It is used so in the earliest French reference.

The changes in the move of the Queen and Bishop completely altered the method of play at chess. The initial stage in the Muslim or mediaeval game, which lasted until the superior forces came into contact, practically ceased to exist; the new Queen and Bishop could exert pressure upon the opponent's forces in the first half-dozen moves, and could even, under certain circumstances, effect mate in the same period. The player no longer could reckon upon time to develop his forces in his own way; he was compelled to have regard to his opponent's play from the very first. It became necessary to examine into the validity of the different possible ways of commencing the game. Thus analysis came into being, and the game was played in a more scientific way. Moreover, the possibility of converting the comparatively weak Pawn into a Queen of immense strength made Pawn-play once more as important a feature of the game as it had been before the general abandonment of the win by Bare King. It was no longer possible to regard the Pawns as useful only to clear a road by their sacrifice for the superior pieces. Thus the whole course of the game was quickened by the introduction of more powerful forces. The reproach of 'slowness' could no longer be applied to the new game. It is probable that the German name of *Current Schachspiel* is the result of the recognition of this fact. Whether chess has actually gained as an intellectual and strategical game is doubtful. It has certainly gained in other ways, since the increase in force adds materially to the penalties of mistakes, and shortens and intensifies the struggle.

Unfortunately, no early accounts of the new chess deal with it from the historical standpoint, and we are left without definite evidence for the time and place of its first appearance, the reason for its invention, and the explanation of its rapid spread throughout Europe.

V. d. Lasa (169) places the commencement of the gradual transition to the new game in the second half of the fifteenth century, somewhere about 1475, and, following the general opinion in his day, he supposes that the new game was invented in Spain.[2] He would accordingly allow a period of 20 years for the new game to become generally known in Spain, France, and Italy. I am inclined to think that this is too long a period, and that the new game spread with far greater rapidity. I think that we should otherwise find some reference to the new game earlier than the closing decade of the century. I am not disposed to place the invention of the new moves earlier than 1485.

The earliest records of the new game occur in three MSS., two of French and one of Catalan origin, and in the printed Spanish work of Lucena. There are other early Italian MSS. which contain problems of the new game, of which one has been assigned to the end of the 15th c. It is difficult to decide between the claims of Italy, France, and Spain to have been the earliest home of the new chess; but Italy has probably the best claim. The French morality in using the name *eschés de la dame enragée* points, I think, to an Italian rather than to a Spanish parentage. Lucena makes no claim in his work for a Spanish discovery, and expressly states that he had collected the material for his book in Rome, all Italy, and France. Egenolff is too late for his evidence to be allowed much weight, but his name *welsches Schachspiel* (Italian chess) shows that the game spread to Germany from Italy. Had the game originally spread from Spain, it would have reached Germany with equal probability by way of France. I attach some weight to the fact that the main centre of chess activity in the 15th century was neither Spain nor France, but Italy.

It has often been supposed that the discovery of the new game was due to the popularity of the problem, and the disrepute which the wager-game and the methods of the professional problem-player had brought upon chess. V. d. Lasa (115) says, 'the interest in the chess problem of the old game was in the 14th and 15th c. predominant'. I do not think that this statement can be maintained in the face of the numerous references to the game (as opposed to the problem) which have been collected from the literature of the 12th–16th cc. The problem lovers were probably more active in transcribing books than numerous; their art was dependent upon the written record to a far greater extent than was the actual game itself. All the evidence points to a very wide practice in playing chess that lasted throughout the mediaeval and into the modern period.

At the same time it is true that the new game was the invention of the player, not the problemist. This is brought out with great distinctness in the early literature of the modern game. These works continue to include the problems of the older game long after the new game had become general among players. The reform meant that the greater part of the problem material that had been collected with such care became obsolete and useless. Against this the problemist fought a long but a losing battle.

It has sometimes been urged that the new game was the result of the new life which the invention of printing and the geographical discoveries of the

[2] V. d. Linde (i. 319, and *Qst.*, 241) thought the reformed game was probably invented in Southern France.

later 15th c. inaugurated. It is possible that the rapid adoption of the game may have been assisted in this way, but it must be remembered that this new life left other games—tables, merels, dice, and card games—untouched, and there seems no reason why it should have only affected chess.

However this may be, the rapidity with which the new game displaced the old game was phenomenal. We may measure this by the disappearance of the special names of the game, and the use of the simple term *chess* to denote the new game. In Italy and Spain the old game was obsolete in all places in the main stream of life by 1510. It may have lived for another generation in out-of-the-way places, or in the case of lovers of the old problems; thus Chachi of Terni was copying problems of old chess in 1511, and Guarino of Forli in 1512. The last evidence for the existence of the old game in France was the publication of a collection of old problems in 1530–40. We have no evidence at all touching the date of the introduction of the new game into England, but Roger Hartwell of London was amusing himself with the solution of the mediaeval problems in the Ashmole MS. in 1529, and this is the latest evidence for the use of the older game in England. Before 1550 the new game had been introduced and generally adopted. It is to this form of chess that Henry, Earl of Surrey (ex. 1547), refers in the following poem, *To the Ladie that scorned her louer* (first printed in *Tottel's Miscellany*, 1557):

Although I had a check,
To geue the mate is hard.
For I haue found a neck,
To kepe my men in gard.
And you that hardy ar
To geue so great assay
Vnto a man of warre
To driue his men away,
I rede you, take good hede,
And marke this foolish verse:
For I will so prouide,
That I will haue your ferse.
And when your ferse is had,
All all youre warre is donne:
Then shall your selfe be glad
To ende that you begon.
For yf by chance I winne
Your person in the feeld:
To late then come you in
Your selfe to me to yeld.
For I will vse my power
As captain full of might,
And such I will devour,
As vse to shew me spight.
And for because you gaue
Me checke in such degre,
This vantage loc I haue:
Now cheke, and garde to the.
Defend it if thou may:
Stand stiffe, in thine estate.
For sure I will assay
If I can giue the mate.

(NOTE.—The chess allusion is this: the lady has given check, and the lover covers the check—*neck* = covered check. He then sees that he can win the lady's Queen, by means of a check. The move which gives check, and at the same time attacks the Queen, is announced by the words 'check and guard'—the oldest instance of the warning that the Queen was under attack that I know. It was frequent in English, French, German, and Icelandic chess in the first half of the 19th c.)

The new game was late in reaching Germany, and it was a novelty in 1536 when Egenolff describes it. When Gustavus Selenus wrote his chess-work in 1616, the old game only survived in Germany in the village of Ströbeck. This village may quite well have been the last place on the continent of Europe where the old chess was regularly played. In Iceland it may have lasted another hundred years (p. 857). Everywhere in the full stream of life the new game displaced the older chess in a single generation.

One of the earliest, if not quite the earliest, of the works which deal with the new chess, is the belated morality *Le Jeu des Eschés de la Dame, moralisé*, which exists in a single MS. of the late 15th c., since 1846 in the British Museum (MS. Add. 15820).[3] It is a small 4to vellum MS. of sixty-one leaves, and is probably the author's holograph. There is nothing to throw any light upon its previous history, and the author's name nowhere appears. From his wide acquaintance with the works of the Early Fathers I imagine that he may have been a member of one of the religious orders. He appears to have just learnt the special features of the new game when he formed the idea of composing a morality on the *Queen's chess* for an unknown patroness of noble birth,[4] using the successive moves of a fictitious game as the occasions for much tedious moralizing upon the temptations to which a lady is liable, and upon the defences which religion can afford. The work is complete in an Introduction and fifteen chapters. I have already given the interpretation of the chessmen, and some account of the work from the point of view of the Moralities.

But apart from this, the work has a special interest of its own in the author's naïve remarks on the new game. Thus (f. 1a):

> Touttefoys l'inuention est à moy estrange à cause que il s'appelle de la dame enragée. Et croy que c'est le tiltre que aucuns ont baillé qui estoient hommes indiscretz. Il me semble que non sans cause ce que si ie puis à la prosecution du liure a mon pouoir je excuseray, non obstant si a lore donné si très grant preuilege aulx dames et aulx foulz que les rochz qui sont les très sages et prudens capitaines et les cheualiers discret ne seruent plus de rien. Car après la descouerte du pyon, la dame par la garde du fol au quatriesme cop matte le roy usques en son siège.

It is fortunate that the author was puzzled by the name of the new chess—'eschés de la dame enragée',[5] for in this way he throws light upon the origin of the Italian *alla rabiosa*.

His chess terms are *roy*, *dame* or *royne*, *fol* (rarely *delphin* or *alphin*) 'que telz sont appellés selon nostre vulgaire langaige', *chevalier*, *roch*, *pion*. The moves of his game are about as weak as can be:

	1	2	3	4	5	6	7	8	9
The Enemy.	Pe4	Qh5	Bc4	omitted	Pd3	Bg5	Ktf3	Ke2	Ke3
The Lady.	Pe5	Pg6	P × Q	Pd5	P × B	Q × B	Qc1 +	Q × cP +	Q × dP m.

[3] Cf. my article 'An Early Work of Modern Chess,' *BCM.*, 1909, 283–7. See also above, p. 558.

[4] The MS. opens: 'Pour ce que le congnoys vostre esperit si tres bon et vostre desir si actif des choses vertueuses singulièrement en tant que touche les liures, aussi que ie vous suis debteur, et presuposant que vostre très excellente et magnifique noblesse saura bien supporter ce que ie ne puis et ne scauroye payer, j'ai deliberé en mon rural et rustique langaige au moins mal que possible me sera m'en aquitter. Priant vostre begnin vouloir à la lecture du liure estre present pour mes garrulitéz excuser. C'est cause se pourra nommer et intituler Le Jeu des Eschés de la dame moralisé, pour la difference des autres liures des anciens philosophes sur le viel Jeu des eschés composés.'

[5] On f. 1 b we read in the list of the Adversary's pieces, 'la dame non surnommé enragée est ambition'. What then was the *dame enragée*?

The last move of the Lady is described thus: 'la dame .. prent le pion de fiction (i.e. QP) et donne eschec et mat de son pion qui s'appelle amour de Dieu' (i.e. KP, the Pawn which guards the Queen). The author clearly knew but little about chess.

To the end of the 15th c. has also been ascribed a quarto MS. of forty-one leaves in the possession of the Counts of Sobradiel (Real Capilla del Palau, Barcelona, MS. xiv) which contains, ff. 1–8a, 9b–13a, a Catalan poem of 576 lines (arranged in sixty-four stanzas) with the title *Hobra jntitulada scachs damor feta per don franci de Castelui e narcis vinyoles e mossen fenollar sots nom de tres planetas ço es Març venus e Mercuri per conjunccio e jnfluencia dels quals fon jnuentada.* The poem describes the successive steps in the courtship of Venus by Mars by means of a game of chess which these two divinities are supposed to play in the presence of Mercury. Francisco de Castellvi takes the part of Mars, Narciso Viñoles that of Venus, and the Abbot Fenollar that of Mercury. The chessmen have allegorical meanings, not unlike those of the pieces in *Les Eschez amoureux.*[6] The successive stanzas are allotted to the three players in the above order, Castellvi and Viñoles describing their moves in turn, and Fenollar explaining or prescribing the laws of the reformed chess, according to which the game is played. Marginal notes establish the succession of moves and the game may very well have been played over the board. The score follows; Castellvi had the Red men, Viñoles the Green:

Castellvi.	*Viñoles.*	*Castellvi.*	*Viñoles.*	*Castellvi.*	*Viñoles.*
1 Pe4	Pd5	8 Q × P	bKtd7	15 Pd5	P × P
2 P × P	Q × P	9 Ktb5	Rc8	16 Be3	Bd6
3 Ktc3	Qd8	10 Kt × aP	Ktb6	17 Rd1	Qf6
4 Bc4	Ktf6	11 Kt × R	Kt × Kt	18 R × P	Qg6
5 Ktf3	Bg5	12 Pd4	Ktd6	19 Bf4	B × B
6 Ph3	B × Kt	13 Bb5 +	Kt × B	20 Q × Kt +	Kf8
7 Q × B	Pe6	14 Q × Kt +	Ktd7	21 Qd8 mate.	

In the course of the poem, Fenollar gives a good deal of information about the rules and etiquette of the game as played in Aragon. He tells us, for example, that the Pawn can be taken in passing; that the King when moved for the first time can leap to a third square, provided he does not cross a square commanded by an opponent, but that he cannot leap out of check or take when leaping; that a player may have only one Queen on the board at a time, that a Pawn cannot advance to queen until the player has no Queen on the board, that one Queen cannot take another, and that to lose the Queen is to lose the game. He classifies mates into *mates ahogado* (stalemate), *mates robado* (Bare King), and *mates comun.* Check must be notified, the touched piece must be played, the touched opponent must be captured, the touched square occupied. The player may not make two moves in his turn of play.[7]

[6] Mars plays with K (*rey*) reason, Q (*reyna*) will, R (*roch*) desire, Kt (*cauall*) praises, B (*orfil*) thoughts, P (*peon*) favours; Venus with K honour, Q beauty, R modesty, Kt disdain, B sweet looks, P courtesies.

[7] See Paluzie y Lucena, *Manual de Ajedrez*, Barcelona, 1912, vi. 254, from whence the above account is taken. The poem exhibits some striking resemblances to Vida's *Scacchia Ludus*, described below, but on the whole I regard it as describing an earlier phase of chess than that in Vida. The limitation to Pawn-promotion is mentioned in the Alfonso MS. (see p. 459), but it can hardly have been general in Spain after 1500. This is the latest mention of it.

Two other works belonging to the closing years of the 15th century deal with chess from the point of view of the player, and contain collections of Openings (here called *rules*, L. *regula*, Sp. *regla*) as well as problems of the new game. These are a small 4to MS. in the Göttingen University Library (MS. Philos. 85,=Gott.), and the *Repeticion de Amores e Arte de Axedres con CL iuegos de partido* of the Spaniard Lucena. Neither work bears a date, but Lucena dedicated his chess work to Prince John of Spain, the son of Ferdinand and Isabella, who died Oct. 4, 1497, not long after his marriage. Lucena's book must have been printed before this date—it is thought in the earlier part of the same year. It is generally assumed that the Göttingen MS. is the older work, but this is by no means established, and in some ways the work is more advanced in character than Lucena's work. It deals exclusively with the new game, and makes no allusion to the older chess; Lucena, on the other hand, describes the differences between the two games, and includes problems of the older game; clearly he belongs to a transitional period. The analysis in the Göttingen MS. shows a greater command of, and familiarity with, the new game than Lucena exhibits in his book. Both works have a certain amount of material in common, but this does not necessarily mean that either writer had access to the other's work, for both may have been using older material. It is, however, singular that a later MS. of the 16th c. (Paris f. allem., 107; see below) repeats the Openings of the Göttingen MS. in a slightly modernized form as the work of Lucena. If this ascription is correct, we are compelled to the conclusion that the Göttingen MS. is Lucena's later, because more mature, work on chess.

The Göttingen MS. is a quarto parchment MS. of thirty-three leaves, of which ff. 1–15a are occupied by twelve Openings of games, f. 16 is blank, and ff. 17–31b contain a selection of thirty problems, one on each page with diagram and solution; these are arranged according to the length of the solutions, which run from two to ten moves. The MS. is complete.

The MS. gives no explanation of the rules of the new game, and was therefore written at a time when, and in a country where, the new game was commonly known, or at least for a player who was familiar with it. This player is nowhere named, but he is addressed as *Dominatio vestra*, *Magnifice domine*, *Serenissime Princeps,* and the pronoun *Vos* is regularly used for him in the MS.;[8] he was evidently a nobleman of high rank. That the author belonged to France seems clear from certain peculiarities of the MS.: (1) the use of *stultus* (once *estultus*) for the Bishop in the commencement of the work. From the third Regula onwards the author falls into the use of the more familiar *alphinus*. V. d. Linde and v. d. Lasa argue from the form *estultus* that the writer belonged to Southern France. This may be so, but the evidence is rather slender to be the basis of an argument. (2) The use of *R* (roy), *Da* (dame), *Fo* (fol), *Ch* (chevalier), *Ro* (roc), *P* (Pion) to denote the pieces on the problem diagrams. This is not necessarily conclusive, for the

[8] The single exception occurs in the solution to Gott. 10, where the writer falls inadvertently into the more usual *tu* of the problem MSS.

author may have copied the diagrams from a French MS. (3) The Openings use the King's leap to the third square only, either as a Rook or a Knight—a move associated with French and Spanish chess.[9]

The twelve Openings are for us the most important features of the work, and their appearance at all is a sign of the great difference which the adoption of the new moves of Queen and Bishop made in the nature of chess. Henceforward *analysis*—the investigation into the effectiveness of different methods of commencing the game—becomes the ruling motive in the literature of chess. The twelve Openings in Gott. may be divided into 4 *attacks* in which the Prince is the first player, and 8 *defences* in which he is the second player. As a rule, no attempt is made to estimate the result of any of the Openings, or to carry them to a conclusion, but it is fair to assume that the author intended to give his patron the winning play. Some of the Openings are carried well into the Mid-game, the third Rule is carried to the 24th move, the eighth to the 33rd, and the twelfth to the 25th, and it is accordingly possible to form an estimate of the author's strength as a player. For his time, he must have been a player of no mean ability. As an example of his notation, I quote the commencement of the first game; as an example of his play, the third and twelfth games.

Prima Regula. Ludet dominatio vestra pedonem regis ad quatuor punctos numerando de domo regis: et si aduersarius idem luserit, ludite equitem regis ad iii p. estulti regis: et si custodierit pedonem cum pedone stulti regis, accipite suum pedonem cum equite: et si accipit cum pedone, date ei scacum cum regina ad iiii p. rochi sui regis: et si se coperuerit cum pedone equitis, accipite pedonem sui regis et date scacum pro rocho: et si non se coperuerit et luserit ad ii p. sue habitationis, accipite eundem pedonem et dicite scacum. . . .

Regula tertia.				*Regula duodecima.*			
1 Pe4	Pe5	13 P × P	B × P	1 Pc4	Pc5	13 Pb5	Ph6
2 Ktf3	Ktc6	14 B × B(d5)	Kt × B	2 Ktc3	Pe6	14 Pa4	Kt × Kt +
3 Bc4	Bc5	15 B × B	aP × B	3 Pe4	Ktc6	15 B × Kt	Bd4 +
4 Pc3	Qe7	16 Re1	Ktf4	4 Pf4	Pd6	16 Kh1	Pe5
5 Pd3	Ph6	17 Qc2	Qd6	5 Ktf3	Bd7	17 Ra2	Kte7
6 Be3	Bb6	18 Re3	Rd8	6 Pd3	Rc8	18 Pa5	B × Kt
7 Pa3	Pd6	19 Ktc4	Qg6	7 Be2	*Kc7*	19 B × B	Pf6
8 Ph3	Be6	20 Kte1	Pb5	8 Rf1	Kb8	20 P × P	P × P
9 bKtd2	Ktf6	21 Kt × eP	Kt × Kt	9 *Kg1*	Pg6	21 Bg4	B × B
10 Rc1	Rf8	22 R × Kt	Kt × P +	10 Bd2	Bg7	22 Q × B	hRf8
11 Rf1	*Kg8*	23 Kf1	Ktf4	11 Pa3	Ktd4	23 R(a2)f2	R × R
12 *Kg1*	Pd5	24 Re3	&c.	12 Pb4	Ka8	24 R × R	Qg8
						25 Qd7	Qd8

Regula XII ends *Est ludus magnae defensionis*, but the first player obtains the better game by 26 Qe6, Rc7; 27 Bd2.

An interesting feature in these games is the use made of the King's leaps to bring the King into a position of safety. In five cases in the MS. the King leaps to K Kt sq. after the King's Rook has moved to K B sq. The

[9] The only fact known about the history of the MS. is derived from a note on the inner cover which records its presentation to the University in 1752 by Frederick Börner, M.D., of Göttingen.

result is the position arrived at in the present day by castling on the King's side, but in Gott. it takes *two* moves, generally but not necessarily consecutive. From this double move the later rule of castling has developed, indeed MS. Paris f. allem. 107, which repeats the above-quoted games as *Lucenes art iv* and *xi*, shortens the first by a move by substituting castling in one move for the two moves of the older work.

The Göttingen MS. analysis is no haphazard collection of commencements of games, but is an attempt to deal with the Openings in a systematic way. The four commencements, 1 Pe4, 1 Pd4, 1 Pf4 (Reg. XI), and 1 Pc4 (XII), were all probably suggested by the author's experience in the older game. To each of the last two he devotes a rule, to 1 Pd4 he gives two rules (IX is a *Queen's Gambit accepted*, X begins 1 Pd4, Pd5; 2 Bf4, Bf5), to 1 Pe4 eight rules, in all of which the opponent replies 1 . . , Pe5. One rule is given to the *King's Bishop's Opening* (V, 2 Bc4, Pc6), and the remainder deal with the various Openings beginning 1 Pe4, Pe5; 2 Ktf3. Four defences are tried, the so-called *Damiano Gambit* (I),[10] the *Petroff* (IV), the *Philidor* (II and VIII, the first to the advantage of the attack, the second to that of the defence), and 2 . . , Ktc6, which the author seems to have recognized as the best. He continues the game as a *Guioco Piano* (III), as a *Ruy Lopez* (VI, defended 3 . . , Bc5) and as a *Staunton* (VII).

I deal with the 30 problems in this MS. below (p. 794).

Lucena's work is a broad octavo of 124 unnumbered leaves, of which the first 73 are occupied by a poem on a love subject which has no connexion with chess, and need not detain us. The author describes himself thus:

> Lucena hijo del muy sapientissimo doctor y reuerendo prothonotario don Johan remirez de Lucena embaxador y del consejo delos reyes nuestros senores studiando enel preclarissimo studio dela muy noble cibtad de Salamanca.

and his work was probably printed in this city. It is a book of considerable rarity.[11] The exact nature of his father's occupation is disputed, but he is said to have filled an official position at Rome, and was himself an author. The son had travelled in Italy and France before he became a student at the University of Salamanca.

Lucena's *Arte de axedres* opens with a learned dedication to Prince John, in which the author makes a considerable parade of his knowledge of the names of classical writers. He then continues with twelve Rules, and a collection of 150 problems from 2 to 10 moves in length, both of the old chess (*del viejo*) and the new (*dela dama*), which are illustrated by rude woodcuts. The first Rule treats of the rules of chess, the following eleven with Openings, each of which is illustrated by a woodcut of the chessmen as arranged for

[10] I adopt the ordinary names of the Openings as used by English players of the present day; they are generally quite modern, and as a rule do not commemorate the name of the earliest authority to call attention to the Opening. It would, however, be pedantic to attempt to change the present well-established usage.

[11] Copies are known to exist in the following libraries; British Museum, Brussels, Madrid, Escorial, Siena, Rio de Janeiros; and in the private collections of Mr. J. G. White (Cleveland, U.S.A.), Mr. J. Rimington Wilson (Broomhead Hall, nr. Sheffield), Mr. A. C. White (New York), Mr. E. B. Cook (Hoboken, U.S.A.).

play. The white men are placed at the lower edge of the diagram in the third Rule only. The men on the first and second rows are inverted in these diagrams; in the problem diagrams none of the men is inverted.

In the first Rule, Lucena describes the differences between 'the game which we now play, which is called *Dela Dama*, and the old game which was formerly used', and gives the moves of the chessmen; he then goes on to give, without any attempt at arrangement, a number of definitions, rules, and pieces of advice. The most interesting part of the description of the moves is that relating to the Pawn and the King:

> The Pawns for the first move can go one square or two, but afterwards only one, and in a straight direction. They take aslant, and can *passar batalla*, i.e. if the opponent's Pawn stands facing yours, your Pawn can go on a square beyond that of contact, it being in the power of the other to allow it to pass him or to take it. Also, when it reaches the row of the opponent's King, it becomes a Queen and gives check without moving; and not only as Queen, but, if you adopt the method of play which I use, the Pawn on becoming a Queen can, for the first move which it makes, take and give check as a Queen and Knight. . . .
>
> Also the King himself can for the first move leap to the third square as he likes, provided he is not in check, even as a Knight in order to avoid the mate of the desperate (as it is called). But he cannot leap over check, nor can he leap after he has been checked even if he has not moved. He cannot leap over a row in which he could not enter because of check.

The other points in the chapter may be summarized thus. The Spanish text will be found in the appendix to this chapter.

1. The undertaking to mate with a Pawn does not involve a check with a Pawn on the penultimate move, unless this is specially stated. 2. The undertaking to mate with a particular Pawn is satisfied even if that Pawn is queened, and mates as a Queen. 3. Stalemate is a mate which does not win a double stake.[12] 4. If a player omits to announce check, the opponent can disregard it. If the first player calls attention to it before he plays again, the opponent must recall his move, and remedy the check. If he omits to do this, that check has no effect, and the opponent may even move along the line of attack of the checking piece to remedy a later check from another piece. 5. If the odds of the *transposed King* are given (Kh1, Re1), that King cannot leap, unless it is expressly stated in the conditions that he may do so. 6. The player who gives the odds of KBP cannot leap with his King, unless it is expressly arranged so. 7. The touched piece must be played, even if there is no stake, unless it would leave the King in check, when the King must be moved. If the player touches a square with the piece, he must move to that square.

8. It is advantageous always to play with men of one colour, viz. the black. If the opponent insists on having the black men, give the board a half-turn, and you will still have your King on the left of the Queen. 9. If you play at night, place the candle on your left-hand side, if by day,

[12] The win by Bare King (*robado*) is not mentioned here, but a remark at the end of Luc. 25 (see p. 734), that when *robado* and mate occur on the same move the mate counts, and not the *robado*, shows that this Ending still existed.

place your opponent facing the light. It will be the worse for your opponent if you play him when he has just eaten and drunk freely. During a game drink water, not wine. Play for a small stake, so that the thought of it may not trouble you. 10. Always break through on the Queen's wing, never on the King's wing.

Lucena concludes this chapter by stating that the Openings that follow are the best that he has seen played in Rome and all Italy, in France and Spain. It must be confessed that some of them are extraordinarily feeble. His second Rule (see below) shows him confused between the old and the new game. He overlooks a mate on the move, because he has forgotten the Bishop's new move, and ends with a mate which the new Queen can spoil by capturing the mating piece. It looks as though Lucena had written his book in a great hurry, directly he had learnt something of the new game.

Lucena's analysis consists of eleven Openings, of which the first seven (II–VIII) are devoted to the attack, and the remaining four (IX–XII) to the defence. It is less systematic than the Göttingen MS., and curiously omits all mention of the Opening 1 Pd4. On the other hand, he adds two Openings of minor importance, 1 Pe3 (X) and 1 Pb3 (XII). In the Openings beginning 1 Pe4, he just notices the *French Defence* (VII) and the *Centre Counter Gambit* (VI). He devotes two games to the *King's Bishop's Opening* (XI begins 2 Bc4, Pc6; VIII, 2 Bc4, Pd6). The other Openings included are the *Damiano Gambit* (II), the *Philidor* (IV), the *Petroff* (V), the *Giuoco Piano* (III), and the *Ruy Lopez* [IX, defended 3 . . , Kt(g1)e2]. As specimens of Lucena's analysis, I quote a variation of his second, his third, and his twelfth Rules.

La segunda regla		12 Qf3 +	Kh4	8 Ktc3	*Kg8*	2 Bb2	Pc6
1 Pe4	Pe5	13 Pg3 +	Kh3	9 Be3	B × B	3 Pg3	Pb5
2 Ktf3	Pf6	14 Qh5 +	Kg2	10 P × B	Ph6	4 Bg2	Pe6
3 Kt × P	P × Kt (*a*)	15 Pe5 m. (*d*)		11 Qd2	Qe7	5 Pd4	Pf5
4 Qh5 +	Ke7	*La tercera regla*		12 Rd1	Be6	6 Pe3	Pg6
5 Q × P +	Kf7	1 Pe4	Pe5	13 *Kc1*	aRd8	7 Pf4	Ktf6
6 Bc4 +	Pd5	2 Ktf3	Ktc6	14 Pg4	Pd5	8 Ktf3	Bg7
7 B × P +	Kg6	3 Bc4	Bc5	15 P × P	Kt × P	9 Rf1	Bb7
8 Qg3 +	Kf6 (*b*)	4 Pd3	Ktf6	16 Kt × Kt	B × Kt	10 *Kg1*	Pa5
9 Qf4 +	Kg6	5 Ph3	Pd6	17 B × Kt (*e*)		11 Ktd2	Ktd7
10 Qf7 + (*c*)	Kg5	6 Bb5	Pa6	*La dozena regla*		12 Ph4	Rf8
11 Pd3 +	Kg4	7 Ba4	Rf8	1 Pb3	Pd5	13 Ktg5	Qe7 (*f*)

NOTES.—(*a*) 3 . . , Qe7 is also given. (*b*) 8 . . , Qg5 is also analysed. (*c*) Overlooking 10 Bf7 m. (*d*) But 15 . . , Q × B is possible. (*e*) 'Y despues venios conla dama ala segunda casa del cauallo y mirad como le teneys mas subiecto que el a vos sabiendo quiar el juego.' (*f*) 'Y despues trasponeos podreys romper por el peon del arfil dela dama que si os lleuasse el peon del cauallo con la dama iugariedes el arfil sobre ella y sobre el roque & assi seguiendo el iuego lo lleuas mejor puesto que no el.'

I have already used his problems of the older game in Chapter X; those of the new game will be found below, p. 797.

Lucena's work would appear to have exerted very little influence at any time. Polerio appears to have derived some problems from it, and there is a MS. Portuguese translation by Antonio das Neues, which bears the date 1648, in a MS. in the Nat. Library, Lisbon (H 2. 54, ff. 134–61), which also contains a translation of Ruy Lopez' chess work; but otherwise, W. Lewis was the first writer to give an account of the work from the point of view of chess, in his *Letters on Chess from C. F. Vogt, translated by U. Ewell*, 1848, pp. 3–7.

Very different was the popularity of the first Italian work on the new game, which made its first appearance in the beginning of the 16th c. This was Damiano's *Qvesto libro e da imparare giocare a scachi et de li partiti*, which was printed in Rome in 1512 [13] by Stephen Guillireti and Hercules Nani, and was dedicated to Sr. Joangeorgio Caesarino Romano. This work ran through eight editions in the 16th c., was reprinted in the 17th c. (1606 problems only, 1607) by Antonio Porto, 'gentilhomo di Corte dell' Alt. Ser. Duca di Sauoia', and (1618) by Donato Rascioti, each of whom tried to pass off the work as his own; was translated into French by Claude Gruget of Paris, and published after his death in 1560, whence into English by James Rowbothum (editions of 1562 and 1569), and also into German. The last version was never printed, but it exists in MS. Nat. Lib. Paris, f. allem., 107.[14]

All that we know of Damiano himself is that he was a native of Odemira in the south of Portugal, and that he was an apothecary by profession. He subscribes himself to the dedication of the 1512 edition (the only edition which contains a dedication), 'Damiano portugese S.P.D.'

His work contains ten chapters, the contents of which are thus given in the 1512 edition:

> El primo capitulo deli nome deli scachi, e del sito dessi & dele regule uniuersale. El secundo capitulo de lo primo modo de Jocare. Et terzo capitulo del secundo modo da Jocare. El quarto capitulo del modo de iocare quando se dara una pedona. El quinto capitulo del modo de iocare quando se dara lo pedona e lo trato. El sexto capitulo come se debe iocare quando se dara lo caualo per la pedona. El septimo capitulo come se debe iocare quando se dara lo caualo francho. El octaua capitulo deli trati sutili che se dicano in uulgare Spagnolo se dicano primore. El nono capitulo deli ioci deli partiti. El ultimo capitulo del arte del iocare ala mente.

To the eighth and ninth chapters there is both an Italian and a Spanish text. The problems (72 in number) are called *jochi deli partiti ala rabiosa* in the Italian, *joegos de partidos de la dam(m)a* in the Spanish text.

The description of the moves of the pieces (Re, donna, delphino *che vole dire principe*, cauallo *che e tanto come caualiere*, rocho,[15] pedona) is accompanied by rough woodcuts of the chessmen. In the earlier editions the Bishop and

[13] The 1512 edition is said to be 'nouiter impressum'. For this reason Mr. Ross Pinsent (*BCM.*, 1906, 232) has suggested that there must have been an earlier edition. The library catalogue of Bologna University mentions (A. V. cap. 136, 16) an edition, Roma, Stefano Guillireti, 1502, but the work is unfortunately no longer in the library, so that it is impossible to say whether the date 1502 is, as seems most likely, an error of the catalogue for 1512, or not. Mr. Pinsent (*BCM.*, 1907, 98, 'Damiano and Carreras') has shown that there are many references in Carrera's work to Damiano which do not apply to any of the existing editions. The same is true of some at least of the references in Salvio, e.g. the 1634 edition, p. 14, refers to a move of Damiano's in the Ruy Lopez Opening, and this Opening is not contained in any of the editions.

[14] The bibliography of the editions of Damiano presents many difficulties. It was first worked out by v. d. Linde, i. 357. A valuable discussion on the matter, with many illustrations from the different editions, by Mr. Pinsent, will be found in the *BCM.*, 1906, 231, 285. See also Mr. J. G. White's criticism of these articles, *BCM.*, 1906, 423.

[15] The Italian MS. WD makes some additions to this chapter: of importance in this connexion is the note 'Rocco *quasi dicat forteza ouero Rocca*', and the variant 'Delfino *ouero Arfilo*'.

Rook have their mediaeval forms, but the fifth and following editions substitute new woodcuts, and the Rook is replaced by a Tower or Castle. The most important passages are those relating to the moves of the King and Pawn.

El Re . . . ha liberta de saltare tre case come lui vole a salto di cauallo o de donna anchora che non habia la via mentre che sta in casa sua che non se sia mosso del suo locho per benche in Italia se vsa saltare el re tutto el tauogliero hauendo la via & anchora mouere vna pedona & metre il re in la casa dela pedona & ha questa liberta se non ha hauuto schaco & questa vsanza non mi pare bona. perche alanticha el re non salta se non tre case la prima volta & cosi si vsa in Spagna et in Portogallo de donde vsiti li grandi giocatori.

. . . El mouimento dela pedona e la prima volta andare tre case se vole . . . vna pedona non puo passare bataglia de altra pedona quando se da scacho al re per ha coprire con essa altro modo puo passar se vole el contrario & se non puo pigliarlo in la via anchora che meglio saria non potere passar bataglia.[16]

The rules which Damiano gives in this chapter are in the main only of the nature of advice: No move should be played aimlessly; do not commit oversights (Sp. *cegera*, blindnesses); do not play fast; when you have a good move look for a better; when receiving odds exchange whenever possible except at a loss; with a winning advantage do not be tempted to disarrange your game merely to win a Pawn; use the King's leap to place it on a good square; do not move the Pawns which stand in front of your King after its leap; spread out your pieces; try and maintain KP and QP, and if possible the two BPs on their 4th squares. But it is worth noting that the rule that the board is to be placed so that the square h1 is white is definitely stated for the first time.

Damiano's analysis is shorter than that of either of his predecessors, and he declares that there are only two ways of commencing the game, 1 Pe4, which is the better, and 1 Pd4. Under the first method he includes variations of the *Petroff*, the gambit now called after him, and the *Guioco Piano*. The second method is the *Queen's Gambit accepted*. Damiano adds some examples of games at odds, the inclusion of which shows that the game had gained ground since Lucena's time. Judged by his Openings, of which I give two specimens, Damiano must have been a mediocre player; but his reputation during the three hundred years following his death rested, not on his analysis, but upon his collection of problems, of which we now know that hardly a single one was his own creation!

Altra Via.

1	Pe4	Pe5
2	Ktf3	Ktc6
3	Bc4	Bc5
4	Pc3	Ktf6
5	Pd3	Pd6
6	Rf1	Bg5
7	Qb3	Kta5
8	B × P +	Kf8
9	Qa4	Pc6
10	Pb4	K × B
11	Q × Kt	Q × Q
12	P × Q &c.	

White gives KBP.

1	Pe4	Pe5
2	Ktf3	Pf5
3	P × P	Pd5
4	Pg4	Pe4
5	Qe2	Qe7
6	Ktd4	Pc5
7	Ktb5	Pd4
8	Bg2	Pa6
9	Kta3	Ktf6
10	Pg5	Ktd5
11	B × eP	Ktf4
12	Qf3	B × P
13	Q × Kt	B × B
14	Rg1	Bd3 +
15	Kf2	Qe2 +
16	Kg3	Qe6
17	Qg4	Bd6 +
18	Kh4	Bf5
19	Qf3	Rf8
20	Q~	Qe4 +

White gives QKt.

1	Pe4	Pe5
2	Ktf3	Ktc6
3	Bc4	Bc5
4	Pc3	Bb6
5	Pd4	Pd3
6	Ph3	Ktf6
7	Bg5	Ph6
8	Bh4	Pg5
9	Kt × P	P × Kt
10	B × P	Rg8
11	Ph4, &c.	

[16] The MS. WD adds to the account of the Rook's move the rules respecting *castling* which were followed in Italy *c.* 1620: 'la prima uolta che'l se muoue puol saltar nella casa del Re:

The concluding chapter of Damiano's book gives some hints on blindfold play which are mainly concerned with notation, and are certainly of very little use to the would-be blindfold player. The latter is recommended to master a notation in which the squares are numbered from 1 to 64!

Two MSS. based upon Damiano's work are of interest. The first of these (= WD) has already been used in Chapter X as one of my authorities for the mediaeval problem. It is now in Mr. J. G. White's library. It consists of 125 leaves, not all filled, and the text (Italian) is in a hand of *c.* 1620. The MS. bears the same title as Damiano's work, and it incorporates the whole of the printed text, but the account of the moves has been brought up to date, and an account of the rules of the older game, presumably forgotten in 1620, is added. The collection of subtleties (19) and problems (129, and 25 of the older game) includes Damiano's collection, but appears to have been made independently. There is no acknowledgement of indebtedness to Damiano, and the writer probably intended his readers to believe that the book was an original work. Since the author makes a careful distinction between Turks and Moors, it has been supposed that the MS. may have been the work of Paolo Boi: this opinion has nothing to recommend it, and I reject it as quite improbable. Damiano's work was antiquated even in Boi's day, and the analysis which Boi would have written would have been very different.

The other MS. is the 16th c. German translation which I have already mentioned (Nat. Lib. Paris, f. allem. 107). This paper MS. of 90 leaves contains Damiano's Openings, Subtleties, and Problems. The games are given in a contracted form, the two sides are distinguished by the use of black and red ink, and the successive moves of each player are written on separate lines. The names of the chessmen (in the problem solutions *Kung*; *frow*; *alte*, in the verses *narr*; *ritter*, in the verses *knecht*; *roch*; and *fendel*) are replaced by astronomical symbols. The problems end regularly with a line of verse, which hits off some striking feature of the problem. Damiano's work ends on f. 61 b, but ff. 70 a–87 b contain other chess entries,[17] of which the most important is a collection of 14 Openings, each of which is attributed to *Lucene*. This collection is based upon the games in the Göttingen MS., but the analysis has been brought up to date by the substitution of castling for the older King's leap.

The new game was not long in finding its poet, and both Marcus (Antonius) Hieronymus Vida (B. at Cremona 1490, D. 1566), Bishop of Alba (1532), and Francisco Bernardino Caldogno (B. *c.* 1497), wrote Latin poems on chess. The

seruendo el Re de la sua per saluarlo, non hauendo pero il Re auuto scaco ne essendosi mosso prima perche non si potria permutare.'

[17] On f. 70 a is a half Knight's-tour, *furor militis*, which is almost identical with the tour in Gianuzio; 70 b is a key to the numerical notation of the Board; 71 a, an end-game (Wh. Kc6, Ba6, Ktb4; Bl., Ka7 or a8) without solution; 71 b, a problem (Wh. Kc6, Be3, Ktb5, Pb6; Bl., Kc8, Pe4) in III, solved by 1 Bg5; 2 Ktd6; 3 Pb7 m.; 72 b has 8 lines of verse; 73 a–84 a, Lucena's games; 84 b, *Regula* (a solution of the ending K, B, and Kt *v.* K); 85 a, *Alia Regula*. A game: 1 Pe4, Pe5; 2 Ktf3, Qf6; 3 Pc3, Bc5; 4 Pd4, Bb6; 5 Be3 (or 5 Ph3, Ph6; 6 Kt×eP, Pd6; 7 Ktf3), Pd6; 6 P×eP, P×eP; 7 Bg5, Qg6; 8 Qd8 m.; and the beginning of a solution of a Knight's tour (*furor militis*); 86 b–87 b, a poem which seems intended to assist one to remember the sequence of the 72 problems.

former poem attained a great popularity in the 16th c.: it was repeatedly printed, and translations or imitations exist in most of the European languages. The latter poem remains in a single MS. in the Bartolina Library, Vicenza.

Vida wrote his poem on chess in his youth, but he only printed it under the title of *Scacchia, Ludus* in 1527, in a volume of his collected poems, of which some copies are dedicated to Francis the dauphin of France (D. 1536), and others to Henry, son of Henry, King of England (Henry VIII's natural son Henry, Duke of Richmond, B. 1517, D. 1536). The poem had been in circulation in MS. for some time, and an unauthorized edition, the pages of which are headed *Scacchorum Liber*, had been printed without the author's name in 1525, probably in Florence. This edition, of which only a single copy in the Wolfenbüttel library is known, begins with an epistle addressed to John Taylor, Archdeacon of Buckingham and Derby, and signed Hilary Berthulph. Taylor's presence on the Continent is explained by the fact that he had been sent by Henry VIII to negotiate a peace with the Queen Mother of France after the battle of Pavia.[18] In this epistle Berthulph narrates how the poem had been sent him in Basel by his friend John Hone, and had been strongly approved (*vehementer probatum*) by every one who read it, and specially by Erasmus, with whom he used to play chess.[19] It is possible that the publication of this unauthorized edition may have led to the authorized edition of 1527.

The two texts prove, when compared, to differ to a remarkable extent. The text of the edition of 1527 has been revised throughout, and the poem is reduced as a result from 742 to 658 lines. All references to Vida's contemporaries have been removed, and the nomenclature adopted for the chessmen has been systematically changed. With this, all the internal evidence for the date of the poem has disappeared, with the exception of that contained in the concluding lines:

Omnia quae puero quondam mihi ferre solebant
Seriades, patrii canerem dum ad flumina Serii.

The text of the 1525 edition, accordingly, becomes of great importance in connexion with the history of the poem. The older text was also printed in Paris in 1529, and a MS. copy of *c.* 1540 exists in the British Museum (MS. Harl. 6518). In the opening lines Vida tells how he has written this poem, on a subject never before attempted by the poets, at the instance of (Federigo) Fregoso (B. at Genoa *c.* 1480, Cardinal 1539, D. 1541), and he expresses the hope that it may afford some relaxation to (Giuliano) de Medici in the heavy task which he and his brother (Giovanni, later Pope Leo X, a keen chess-

[18] I owe this and other bibliographical notes on the 1525 edition to v. d. Lasa, who was the first to discover the existence of the two texts. He devotes the greater part of ch. viii of the *Forschungen* to the older text of Vida's poem.

[19] Erasmus did not take his chess very seriously. The epistle describes him as standing to play, and as carrying on a conversation both of wit (*purissimi sales*) and wisdom (*colloquia maxime seria*) the whole time.

player)[20] had undertaken in repelling the French invaders of Italy. V. d. Lasa (190) has shown that the allusions to Italian events point definitely to the early summer of 1513 as the date of the poem. Vida was then aged twenty-three.

The aim of the poem is to describe in Virgilian Latin a game of chess played between Apollo and Mercury in the presence of the other Gods. This involves a description of the pieces and their moves. Vida apparently experienced some difficulty in deciding on a suitable classical nomenclature for the Bishop and Rook. In the earlier version the Bishops are represented as *sagittiferi centauri*, Centaurs with bows and arrows; in the later version the Centaurs have disappeared and the Bishop is an Archer (*sagittifer juvenis*). In the earlier version the Rooks are represented as Cyclops,[21] and their place on the board is thus described

Extremis bini, referant qui vasta Cyclopum
Corpora, considunt in sulcis agmina vtrinque
Claudentes sua quisque, altis proque arcibus astant.

In the later version the Rooks appear as warring towers borne upon the backs of elephants:

Tum geminae, velut extremis in cornibus, arces
Hinc atque hinc altis stant propugnacula muris,
Quas dorso immanes gestant in bella elephanti.

Elsewhere in the poem the name *Elephas* is used, generally, however, with an allusion to the tower it is supposed to carry on its back.

I do not think that any chess motive lies behind any of Vida's attempts to find a name for the Bishop and Rook. The mediaeval names were probably meaningless to him, and a fastidious sense refused to let him use such unclassical terms as *alfinus* and *rochus* in his poem. He simply ran over the possibilities which his classical studies suggested, and adopted those that pleased him best. He found the elephant with the tower on its back in Livy.

The extraordinary thing is that Vida's choice of names should have caught the popular fancy. All three terms—*Archer* for the Bishop, *Elephant* and *Tower* (*Castle*) for the Rook—were adopted by players in different parts of Western Europe. Even the term *Amazon*, which he used occasionally for the Queen, was tried by the writers of chess books.[22] No one remembered that *Archer* had once been used by a mediaeval poet for the Pawn, or that the Elephant was already on the chessboard as the Aufin or Bishop.

The term *Archer* first appeared in France, where Gruget introduced it in

[20] Cf. P. Jovius, Ep. Nucerinus, *De vita Leonis X*, iv. 86 'Latrunculos autem adeo subtiliter et acute vel cum exercitatissimis colludebat, ut nemo ei vel peritia vel celeritate committendi conficiendique proelii aequari posse videretur.'

[21] B. Mommeianus of Toulouse in his *Ludi Latrunculorum brevis descriptio*, Paris, 1560, an imitation of Vida's poem, uses *Cyclops* for the Bishop, *Centaurus* for the Rook.

[22] Gruget uses *Amazon* instead of *Dame* (1560) in French; Beale and Randle Holme give it as an alternative for Queen in English; Uflacker has it as an alternative for *Königin* in German.

his translation of Damiano, *Le plaisant Ieu des Eschecs,* Paris, 1560, and used it regularly throughout the book. Although Rabelais used the same name in his account of living chess in the Fifth Book of his *Pantagruel*, first printed after the author's death in 1564, it never became usual, and the older *Fou* soon regained its former position. When Rowbothum translated Gruget's book (1562) he gave *Archer* as alternative with Bishop, alleging that it was the older name. Later writers, in dealing with chess, e. g. Beale (1656) and Randle Holme (1688), continued to mention the name *Archer*, but it never was really used by English players. In Germany, on the other hand, the name *Schütze* passed into regular use, displacing the older *Alte* in the latter part of the 16th c., and continuing in use (Wielius, 1606; Selenus, 1616; Uflacker, 1799) until the existing term *Läufer* took its place in the course of the 18th c.[23]

The history of the chess term *Elephant* is very similar. It hardly touched French (Gruget has *Les Rocs sont Éléfans*) and English (Rowbothum has *The Rockes some call Elephants*), but occurs repeatedly in 17th and 18th c. German chess-books as an alternative name of the Rook (e. g. in Wielius, 1606; Selenus, 1616; *Piazza Universelle*, 1641; Uflacker, 1799), in Danish, in Swedish, and in Icelandic. A modern Icelandic *Spilabók* (Akureyri, 1858) still gives *Fill* (= elephant) as an alternative for *Hrókur*. The name is, however, no longer used by players in any part of Europe.

The third of Vida's names, *Tower* or *Castle*, has taken its place in the nomenclature of chess in every European country except England and Iceland. In England, *Castle* is used almost as widely as the older *Rook*.[24] This result has been doubtless assisted considerably by the modern shape of the piece, which lends itself more readily to manufacture than either the Archer or Elephant. Notwithstanding this, the new name was slow in making its way. *Rocco* was still the ordinary term in Italy in the middle of the 18th c., although Lolli (1763) mentions *Torre* as an alternative name.[25] In French, Pasquier uses *Tour* in his *Recherches de la France*, 1560, but *Roc* remained the ordinary term for another century, and the 1669 edition of Greco is probably the earliest chess work to use *Tour* exclusively. In England, Rowbothum has *Rooke or Tower* in his list of the pieces, but *Rooke* only in his analysis. The earliest instance of the term *Castle* which I have found occurs in a letter of William Drummond of Hawthornden (*Works*, 1655, 253), based upon Pasquier's work, which was written about 1632. In this he speaks of 'Rooks, Fortresses or Castles,' 'Rooks or Towers,' 'Towers or Castles.' Beale (1656) does not use *Castle* for the piece, but has the verb 'to castle'. In Germany Wielius and Selenus give *Thurm* as an alternative name for the Rook, but *Thurm* did not become the ordinary name of the piece

[23] Gallitalo's Dutch translation of Rabelais (Amsterdam, 1682) has *Schutter* for the Bishop.

[24] The name *Castle* is, perhaps, losing ground in England. It seems to have reached its greatest popularity in the 18th c., when Joseph Thurston wrote on chess (Poems, 1737):

Thus, tho' called *Rooks* (as vulgar wits will err)
Yet *Castles* always is their *Nom de Guerre*.

[25] Minsheu, *Guide into Tongues* (2nd ed., 1627) has 'Rooke, F. *Roc, tour,* It. *rocca, tore,* Sp. *roque*, L. *rupes*, *turris scaccaria*.'

until the end of the 18th c., and *Roch* only became obsolete in the early 19th c. The Dutch *Kasteel* (now obsolete) and *Toren*, the Swedish *Torn*, and the Danish *Taarn* all date from the 18th c., the Spanish and Portuguese *Torre* and *Castillo* belong apparently to the 19th c.

The alteration in the shape of the Rook, and the new idea that the piece was a Tower, gave an opportunity to the amateur etymologist which he was not long in seizing. The Italian name of the chessman, *rocco*, was associated with a similar, but totally distinct word, *rocca*, a rock or fortress, and the Tower was explained as the figure of a Rocca, this being assumed to be the true spelling of the name of the chessman. We find this explanation suggested in various Italian MSS. of the early 17th c., e. g. in WD and some of the Greco MSS., and still earlier in Rowbothum. The idea that *rocco* and *rocca* were in some way connected may even have been in Colonna's mind when—before the Rook had been carved as a Tower—he described the Rooks in his *Hypnerotomachia Poliphili* (written 1467) as ‘dui custodi della rocha o uero arce’.

As the means of the introduction of the *Castle* into chess, Vida's poem has had a more lasting influence on the game than its author could ever have anticipated.[26]

Caldogno's poem, *De ludo scachorum*, of 178 lines is less ambitious, and aims at giving a number of hints more or less useful to chess-players. Among these are the following:

Do not be in too great haste to use the King's leap: it is best to use it to leap to one of the two wings, by which the King is brought to a place of safety and the Rook is liberated (two moves, 1 Rf1 or d1; 2 Kg1 or c1 accordingly, are intended): some players think that the King is safer on his own square: do not bring your Queen out too early: do not exchange Knight or Bishop for two Pawns (a piece of advice repeated by Ruy Lopez; in the older game it was generally sound to exchange the Bishop for two Pawns): the sacrifice of a piece to expose the King after his leap is often good play: double your Rooks: do not obstruct the range of your Bishops: in the end-game, when your opponent has a single Bishop left, place your King on a square of the other colour to that of the Bishop: do not try to win a drawn (*tabulatus*) game: with the worse game, try for a draw. The poem ends with the lines—

Quisnam sit melior, Equus an Alphilus?
Tunc laudatur Equus si lusor sit mediocris;
Si bonus est lusor, Alphilus clarior extat:
Sic fuit a quodam responsio facta perito.

Altogether, the poem gives one a very favourable opinion of Caldogno's knowledge of chess.

Egenolff, when reprinting Köbel's edition of Mennel's *Schachzabel* (Frankfort, 1536), added a chapter on the new game which had just reached Germany. The text of this chapter will be found in the Appendix to this

[26] Vida's description of the moves and rules, and the game (a Queen's Gambit), contain nothing of material importance. The name *Scacchis*, which Vida bestowed upon the nymph who was the means of teaching chess to mankind, has not commended itself to players, and *Caïssa*, the creation of Sir William Jones (1763), has supplanted it entirely.

chapter. Its main interest lies in the use of the adjective *welsch*, i. e. Italian, to describe the new game.

I now turn to the problems of the reformed chess which are contained in the Göttingen MS., Lucena, Damiano and the MSS. based upon this work, and in the three other problem-collections of the earlier half of the sixteenth century which add some problems of the new game to their more extensive collection of problems of the older game. A few of these problems are based upon older material: in these cases I add an asterisk to the reference to the older position. In many cases the condition is that mate shall be given by one Pawn, the move following immediately upon a check from another Pawn: this condition I have, for the sake of brevity, condensed into 'mate with two Pawns.'

I begin with the positions from the Göttingen MS.:

Gott. 5.

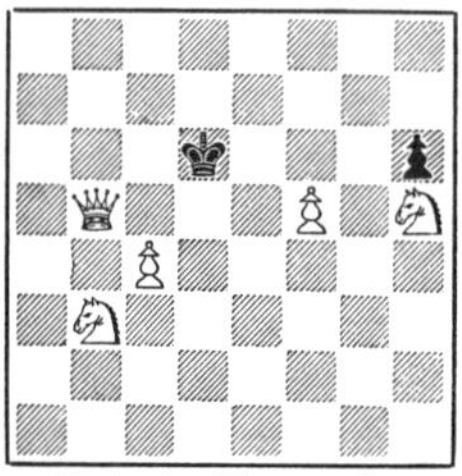

Mate in II exactly.

Gott. 7.

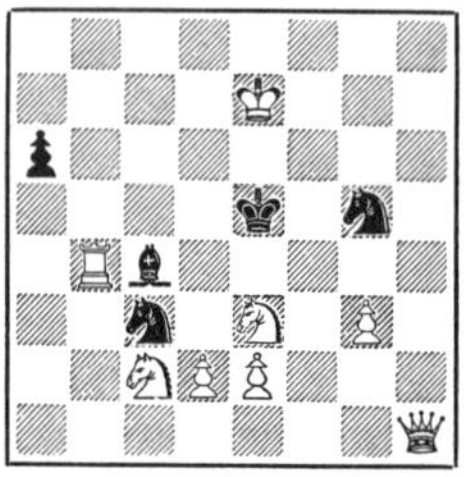

Mate with Pawn in III exactly.

Gott. 8.

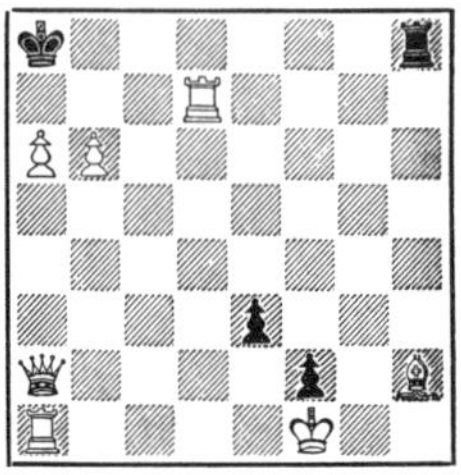

Mate with Pb6 in III exactly. The Black Ps are immovable.

Gott. 9.

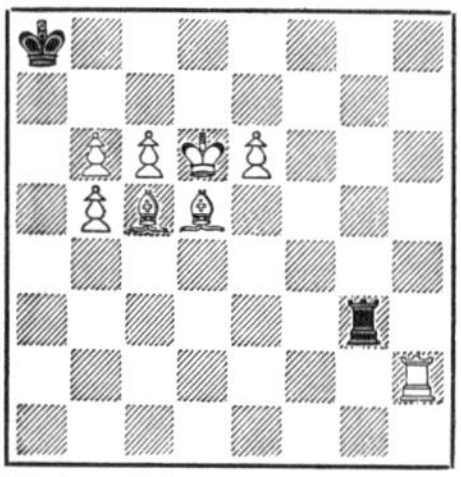

Mate with two Pawns in IV exactly. The Wh. K is immovable.

Gott. 11.

Mate with two Pawns in IV exactly.

Gott. 12.

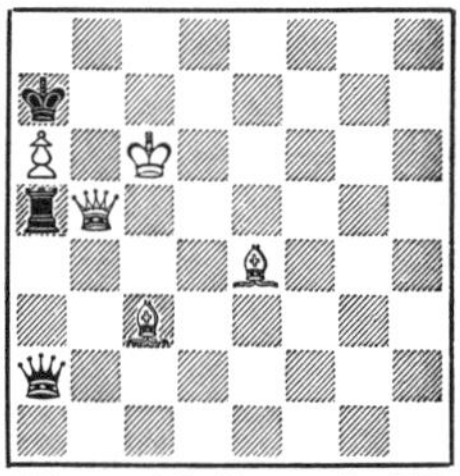

Mate with Pawn in IV exactly.

Gott. 13.

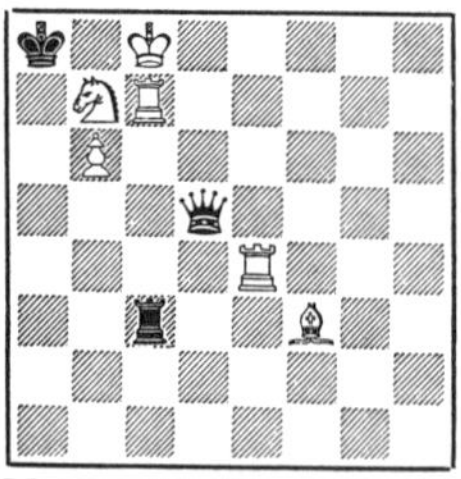

Mate with Pawn in IV exactly. All the Black pieces are fidated.

Gott. 14.

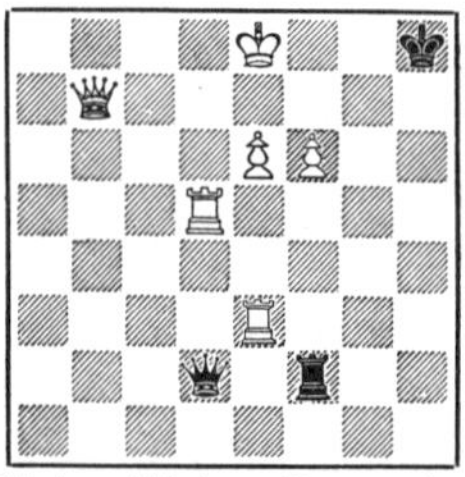

Mate with two Pawns in V exactly. The Bl. Q is fidated.

Gott. 15.

Mate with Pawn in V exactly.

Gott. 16.

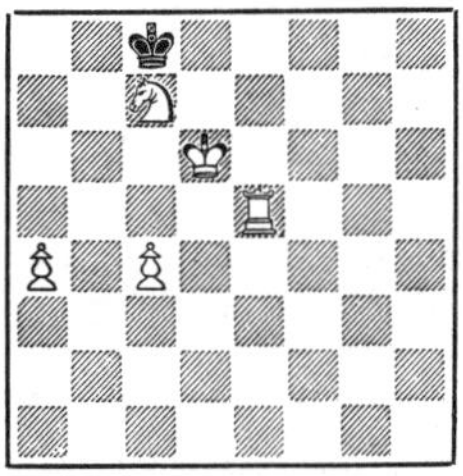

Mate with two Pawns in V exactly.

Gott. 17.

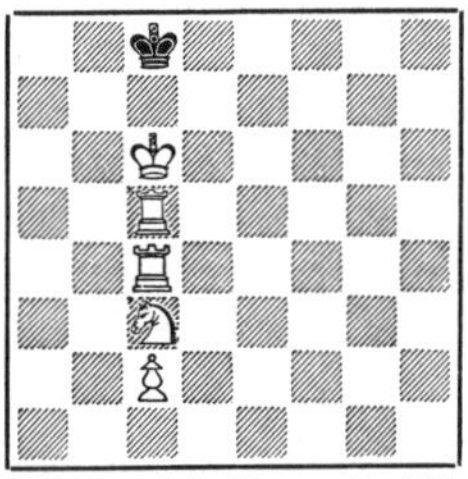

Mate with Pawn in VI exactly.

Gott. 18.

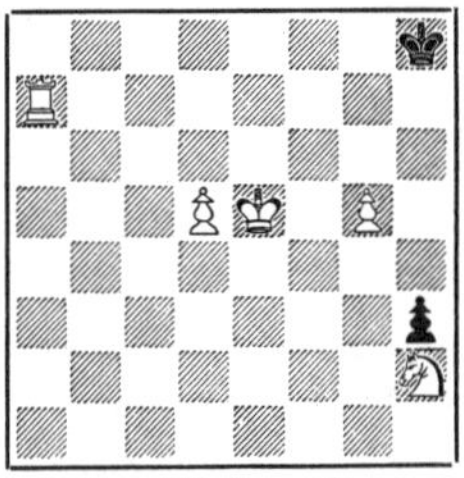

Mate with two Pawns in VI exactly.

Gott. 19.

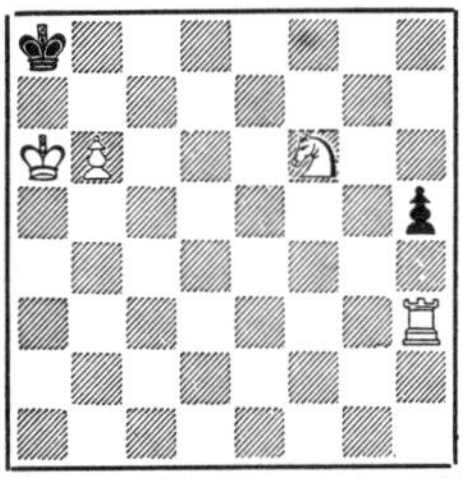

Mate with Pawn in VI exactly. The Bl. P is fidated.

Gott. 20.

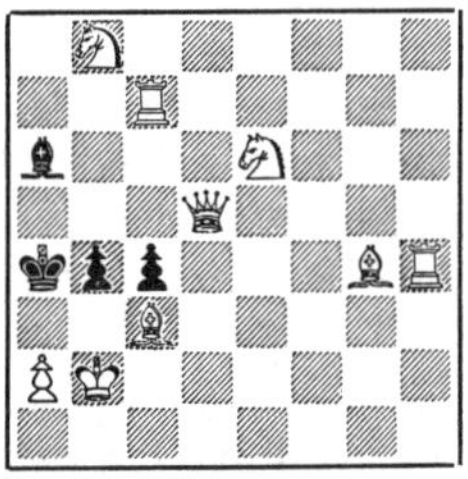

Mate with Pawn in VI exactly.

Gott. 22.

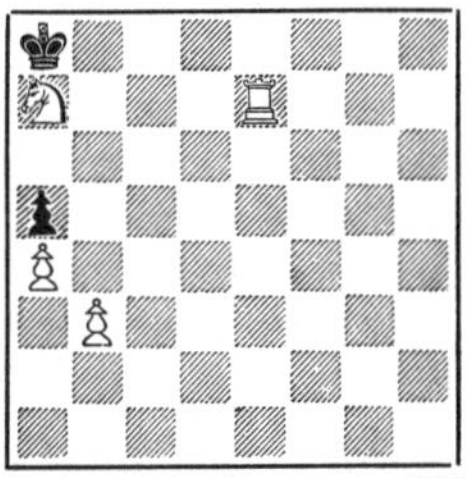

Mate with Pawn in VI or less. The Rook is immovable.

Gott. 23.

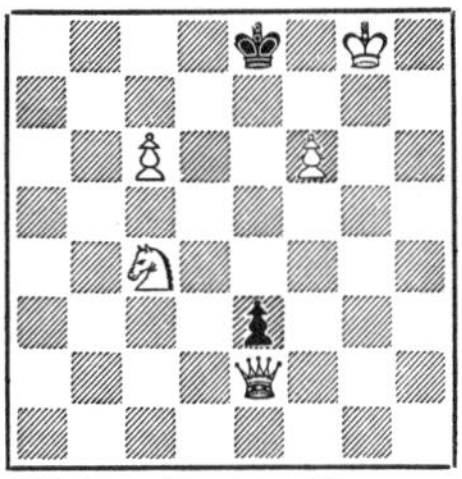

Mate with two Pawns in VI exactly.

Gott. 24.

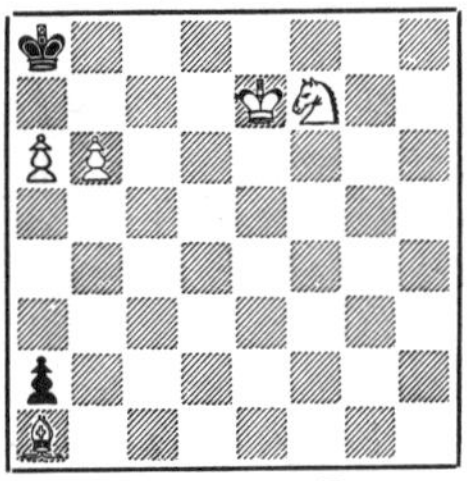

Mate with two Pawns in VII exactly.

Gott. 25.

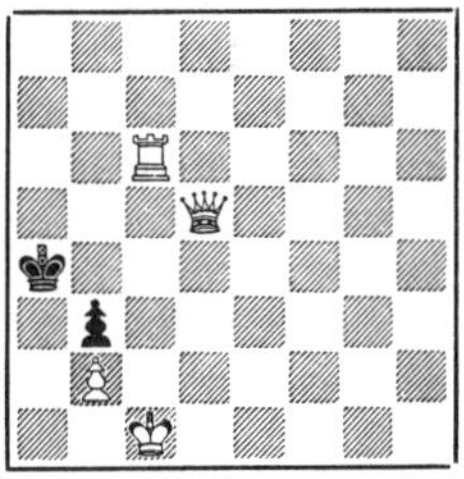

Mate with Pawn in VII exactly.

Gott. 27.

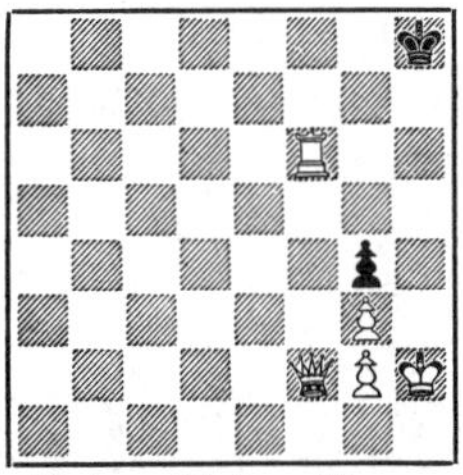

Mate with two Pawns in VIII exactly.

Gott. 28.

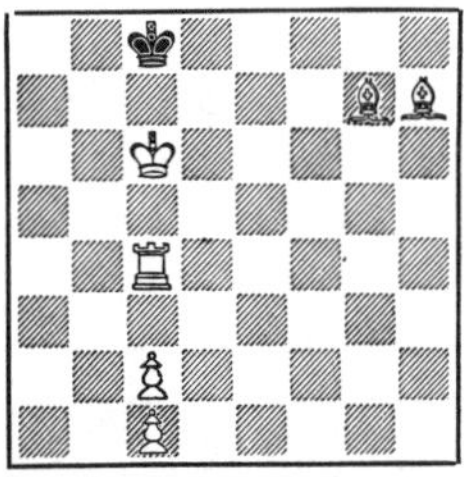

Mate with two Pawns in IX exactly.

Gott. 29.

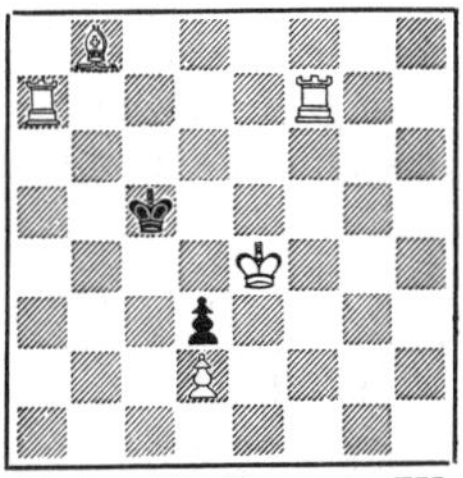

Mate with Pawn in IX exactly.

SOLUTIONS

Gott. 1. Var. of F 303* (Wh. Kb6, Ra3, b7, Kta5, Pb4, c4; Bl. Ka8, Rc8, e8, Pe2). In II ex. Uns. If 1 Pb5, Pe1 = Q. Other solutions as in F.

2. Var. of F. 320* (Wh. Kf6, Ra8, h2, Ktd8, e5, Ph7; Bl. Kf8, Rh8, Be6, g4). In II ex. 1 Re2.

3. Var. of F 303* (Wh. Kg6, Qc2, Rg7, Kth6, Pe6; Bl. Kh8, Rd8, h4). In II ex. 1 Qh2.

4. Var. of CB 1* (Wh. Kc6, Ra7, Ktd5, e6; Bl. Ke8, Ktf7, g8). In II ex., the Kts fidated, and Wh. K immovable. 1 Kt(d5)c7 +; 2 Kt(c7)e8 m.

5. 1 Qb7; 2 Qd5 m.

6. Var. of CB 47* (Wh. Rc3, e5, Ktd3, d5; Bl. Kd4, Pg6). In III ex. *Et quia omnis subtilitas dependet a pedone, si fuerit interrogatum quomodo ambulat pedo, dicetis quod si ipse dat vobis albos quod ambulat versus vos, si nigros versus illum.*

7. 1 Qh8 +; 2 Q × Kt; 3 Pd3 m.

8. 1 Pa7, Rh6; 2 Qe6, &c. Or 1 . . , R × B; 2 Ke2, &c. Or 1 . . , R on 8th line; 2 Qg8, &c.

9. 1 Rh4, Rg8 or a3 (or Kb8; 2 Rh8 +, &c.); 2 Ra4 +, &c.

10. Var. of CB 114* (Wh. Kd6, Rh1, Ktd4, Pd5, d7; Bl. Kd8, Rf8, Qg8). In IV with P. Uns. 1 Kte6 +, Q × Kt + ; 2 P × Q, Rh8.

11. 1 Qc7 +; 2 Qe4 +; 3 Pd7 +; 4 Pf6 m.

12. 1 Bd4 +; 2 Kc7 +; 3 Qb7 +; 4 P × Q m.

13. 1 Ra4 +; 2 Ktc5 +; 3 Ra7 +; 4 Pb7 m.

14. 1 Rh5 +; 2 Rg3 +; 3 Qg7 +; 4 Pf7 +; 5 P × R m.

15. 1 Qc7 +; 2 Ra8 +; 3 Ktd7 +; 4 P × Kt +; 5 Pb7 m.

16. 1 Re8 +; 2 Ra8; 3 Pc5 +; 4 Pc6 +; 5 Pa5 m.

17. 1 Rd4; 2 Rd8 +; 3 Ktb5 +; 4 Rd3; 5 Ra3 +; 6 Pc3 m.

18. 1 Ktg4; 2 Ktf6; 3 Ra8 +; 4 Rg8; 5 Pg6 +; 6 Pd6 m.

19. 1 Ktd7; 2 Rb3; 3 Rb4; 4 Rh4; 5 Rh8 +; 6 Pb7 m.

20. 1 Bd1 +; 2 Qd7 +; 3 Qd3; 4 P × P +; 5 P × P +; 6 Pc5 m.

21. Cf. Gott. 15 (omit Qe5). In VI with P. ex. 1 Ktd7 +, Ktb6 +; 2 Kc7, Pb4; 3 Rb7 + ; 4 Ra7; 5 P × Kt +; 6 Pb7 m.

22. 1 Pb4, P × P !; 2 Ktc8, Pb3; 3 Pa5, Pb2; 4 Ktb6 +; 5 Pa6; 6 Pa7 m.

23. 1 Ktb6; 2 Qh2; 3 Qd6; 4 Qc5; 5 P +; 6 P m.

24. 1 Kd7; 2 Kte5; 3 Ktc4; 4 Kta5; 5 Bd4; 6 P +; 7 P m.

25. 1 Kb1; 2 Ka1; 3 Rc1; 4 Qc5 +; 5 Rc2; 6 Ka2; 7 Pb3 m.

26. Var. of C 48* (Wh. Kc6, Ktb5, d5, Pa5, c5; Bl. Ka8). In VII ex. with two Ps. 1 Kt(d5)c7 +; 2 Ktd6; 3 Ktc8 +; 4 Kd7; 5 Pa6 +; 6 Pa7 +; 7 Pc6 m.

27. 1 Rf8 +; 2 Qf7 +; 3 Qg8; 4 Rf7; 5 Qg7 +; 6 Rf3; 7 Pg4 +; 8 Pg3 m.

28. 1 Rd4; 2 Rd8 +; 3 Ba1; 4 Rd7; 5 Bd3, Kb4; 6 Rb7 +; 7 Ra7 +; 8 Pc3 +; 9 Pc2 m.

29. 1 R(a7)b7; 2 Bh2; 3 Rf6; 4 bRb6; 5 Bg1 +; 6 Rf2; 7 Re2 +; 8 Bd4; 9 Pd3 m.

30. Var. of WD 164* (Wh. Kc5, Qd7, Re5, Pa6, b5; Bl. Ka8). In X with Pb5. Same solution, except 4 Qc7 +.

Since practically the whole of these thirty problems are repeated in the works of Lucena and Damiano, I give a table showing the common material of these three collections.

G	Luc.	D	WD	G	Luc.	D	WD	G	Luc.	D	WD	G	Luc.	D	WD	G	Luc.	D	WD
1	1	1	3	7	72	10	5	13	90	30	38	19	124	54	103	25	136	62	112
2	3	4	17	8	76	12	127	14	106	41	72	20	127	57	88	26	138	64	114
3	5	6	4	9	81	22	10	15	109	43	76	21	128	58	90	27	141	66	117
4	6	7	11	10	82	23	128	16	99	35	77	22	129	59	92	28	143	68	120
5	8	2	13	11	83	24	20	17	122	52	99	23	131	61	96	29	149	71	123
6	70	14	6	12	89	27	27	18	123	51	98	24	135	—	—	30	150	72	125

A careful comparison of the three works, Gott., Luc., and Dam., gives, however, no support to the idea that any one of these works is based upon any other. It is probable that collections of problems of the reformed game were made at an early date, and the extent of the material common to these works may be due to the fact that all used an early manuscript collection of problems.

Altogether, there are 75 positions of the modern game in Lucena's work.

Luc. 7.

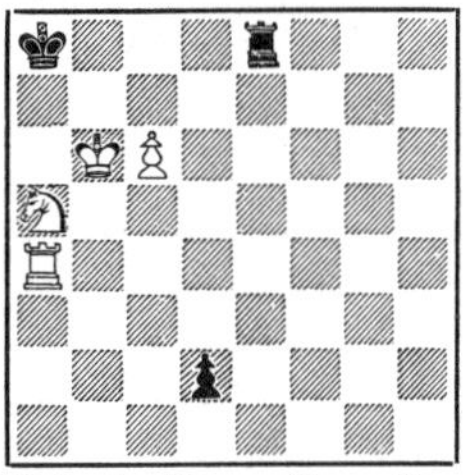

Mate in II exactly. The Black pieces are fidated.

Luc. 16.

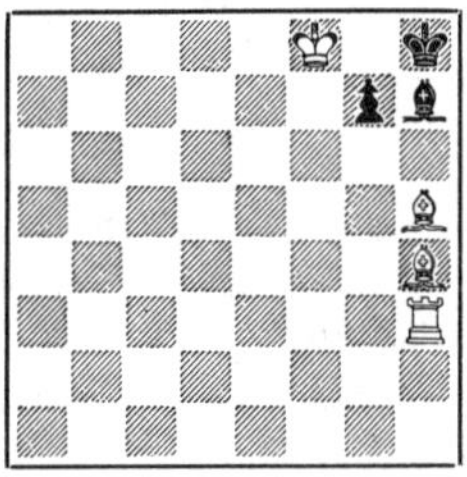

Mate in III exactly. Bh5 may not play first move.

Luc. 69.

Mate in III exactly.

Luc. 93.

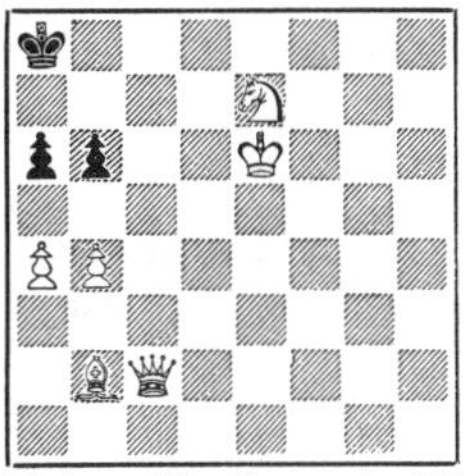

Mate with Pawn in IV exactly. The Black men are fidated.

Luc. 98 (old !).

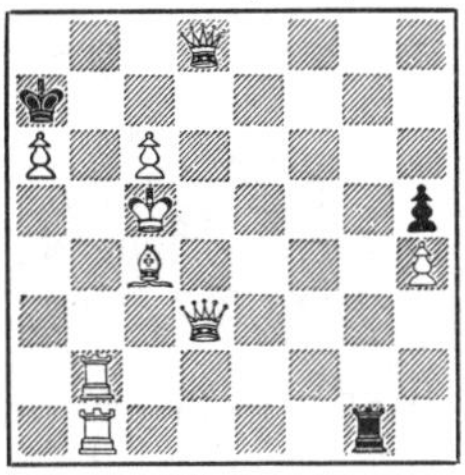

Mate with two Pawns in V exactly.

Luc. 100.

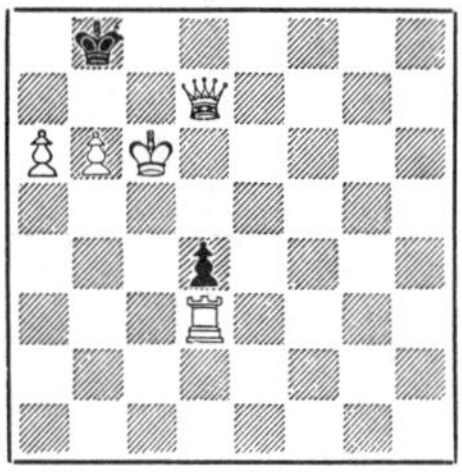

Mate with two Pawns in V exactly.

Luc. 103.

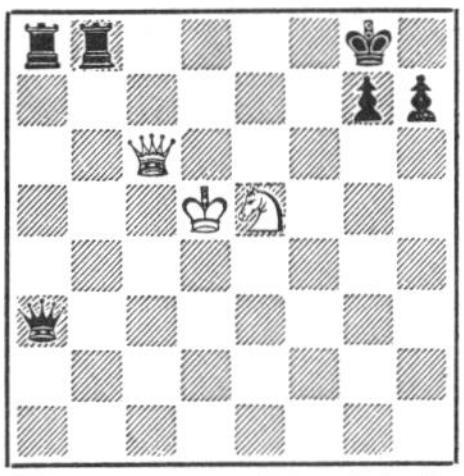

Mate in V. The Black men are fidated.

Luc. 105.

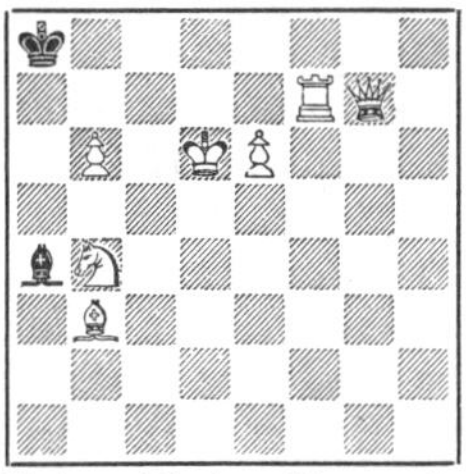

Mate with two Pawns in V exactly. Qg7 is immovable.

Luc. 108.

Mate with Pawn in V exactly. The Black men are fidated.

Luc. 117.

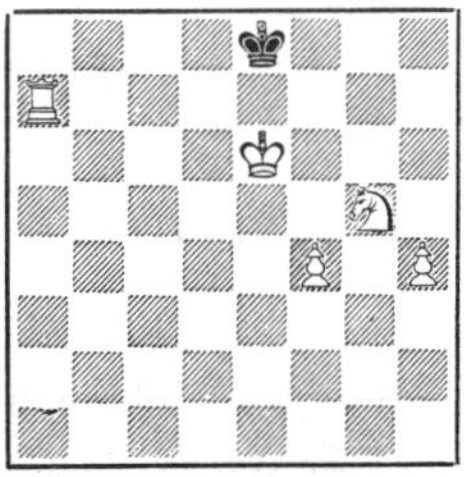

Mate with two Pawns in VI exactly.

Luc. 125.

Mate with two Pawns in VI.

Luc. 126 (corr.).

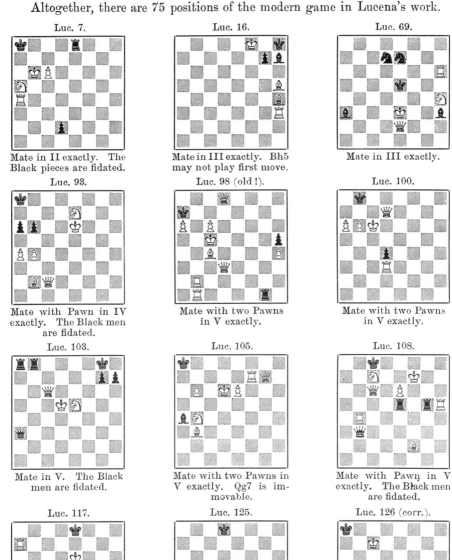

Mate with Pawn in VI exactly.

Luc. 130.

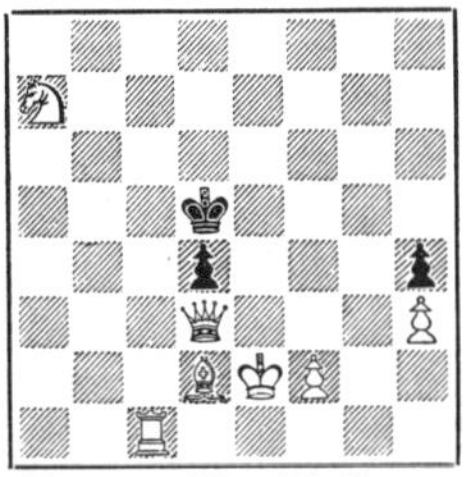

Mate on d5 with Pawn in VI exactly.

Luc. 137.

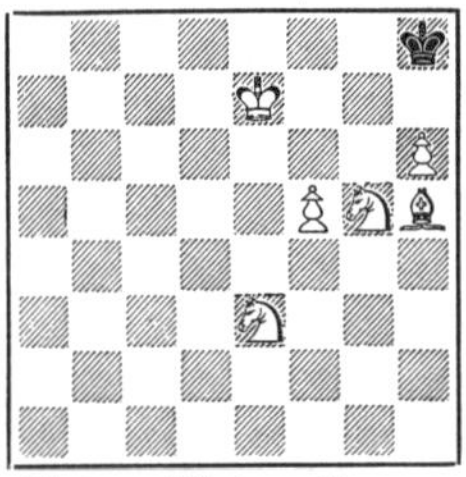

Mate with two Pawns in VI exactly.

Luc. 148.

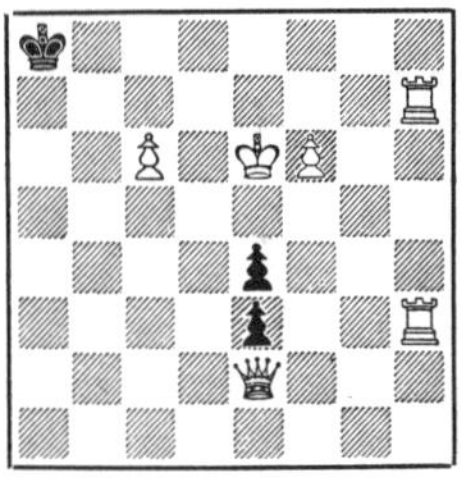

Mate with two Pawns in IX exactly.

SOLUTIONS

The remaining positions are as follows:

Luc. 4 = CB 3*. 9 = F 303*. 17 = 55. 68 Cf. Gott. *8*. 73 = 44. 74 = CB *52**. 75 = 32. 77 Cf. CB *46**. 84 = CB 106*. 86 Cf. CB 47. 87 = CB 99. 88 = CB 102. 91 = *38*. 92 = *34*. 104 Var. of *100*. 107 Cf. 100. 115 = CB *158*. 118 Cf. CB *143*. 119 = CB *154*. 120 = CB *149*. 121 Cf. *98*. 133 Cf. CB 168. 134 = CB 173. 140 Cf. C 7.

Luc. 2 (corr.). Cf. F 311 (Wh. Kb6, Ra5, c8, Kta7, b7; Bl. Ka8, Rc5). In II ex. Unsound.

7. 1 Pc7, &c.

16. 1 Bf6, P × B; 2 Bg6; 3 R × B m.

69. 1 Kd3 +, Kf4 (or Kd5; 2 Qe4 +; 3 Qc4 m.); 2 Qf3 +; 3 R or Q m. acc.

71. Wh. Kf7, Qe1, Bb8; Bl. Ka8, Pb7 going to b8. In III ex. 1 Qa5 +; 2 Ke7, Kb8; 3 Qd8 m.

85. Wh. Kf6, Bc5, Pg5; Bl. Kh8. In IV ex. with P. 1 Kf7; 2 Bf8; 3 Bg7 +; 4 Pg6 m.

93. 1 Qc8 +; 2 Be5, Pa5 (or Pb5; 3 Ktc6; 4 Pa5 m.); 3 Qb8 +; 4 Pb5 m.

98. 1 Qh7 +; 2 Rb7 +; 3 Qb6 +; 4 P +; 5 P m.

100. 1 Qd6 +; 2 Rg3; 3 Qd4; 4 P +; 5 P m.

103. 1 Qe6 +, Kh8; 2 Ktf7 +; 3 Kth6 +; 4 Qg8 +; 5 Ktf7 m. The so-called Philidor's legacy!

105. 1 Rf8 +; 2 Bd5 +; 3 Kta6 +; 4 Pb7 +; 5 Pe7 m.

108. 1 Ktd5 +; 2 Rb8 +; 3 Rh8 +; 4 Bh4 +; 5 Pe7 m.

116. Wh. Ke5, Ra7, h7, Pe6; Bl. Ke8. In VI ex. with P. 1 aRd7; 2 Kd6; 3 Kc7; 4 Kd8; 5 dRg7 +; 6 Pe7 m.

117. 1 Ktf7; 2 Ra8 +; 3 Rh8; 4 Pf5 +; 5 Pf6 +; 6 Ph5 m.

125. 1 Kte6 +; Kc8; 2 Rb6; 3 Rb8; 4 Rf8; 5 P +; 6 P m.

126. 1 Ktc3; 2 Rd8; 3 Bc5; 4 Rb7; 5 Rd6 +; 6 Pb4 m.

130. 1 Rc6; 2 Ktc8; 3 Kte7 +; 4 Be3; 5 Qf5 +; 6 P × P m.

137. 1 Bf3; 2 Be4; 3 Ktg4; 4 Kte5; 5 Kt(e5)f7 +; 6 Ph7 +; 7 Pf6 m. Var. Kh8 on g8. Uns.

142. Wh. Ke5, Ra1, f1, Pe6; Bl. Kh8, Pf2. In VIII ex. with P. 1 Ra7; 2 Rf7; 3 Kd6; 4 Kd7; 5 Rh1 +; 6 R(h1)h7; 7 R(f7)g7 +; 8 Pe7 m.

147. Wh. Kf4, Rc1, f1, Pc5, f5; Bl. Ke8. In IX ex. with 2 Ps. 1 cRd1; 2 Rg1; 3 Rg8; 4 dRd8; 5 Ke5; 6 Rc8; 7 gRf8; 8 P +; 9 P m. (The order of moves 2 to 8 depends on Black's play.)

148. 1 Qa6 +; 2 Rg3; 3 Re3; 4 Rb3 +; 5 Qa7 +; 6 Rh8 +; 7 Qb7 +; 8 Pc7 +; 9 Pf7 m.

It was Damiano's intention to confine his problems to those of the reformed game, and it was quite an accident that one position of the older game (Dam.

20 = WD 147) was included. Of his 71 other problems, all but one (Dam. 9) are found either in Lucena or in the Göttingen MS., if not in both.

Damiano prefixes to his collection of problems a small collection of happy pieces of play, the like of which might easily occur to any player. These he calls subtleties, It. *tratti sutili*, Sp. *primore*, Ger. (Paris, f. allem. 107) *list*.

Dam. S. 1.

Black plays 1 . . R × P and White wins a piece.

Dam. S. 3.

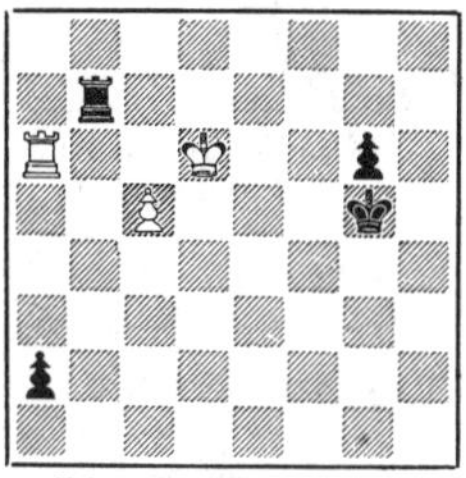

(Bl.)
Black plays.

Dam. S. 4.

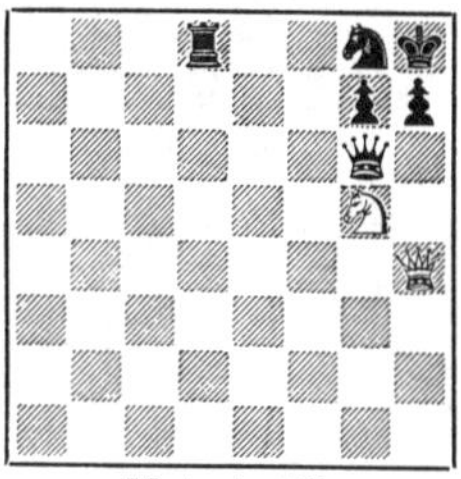

Mate in II.

Dam. S. 5.

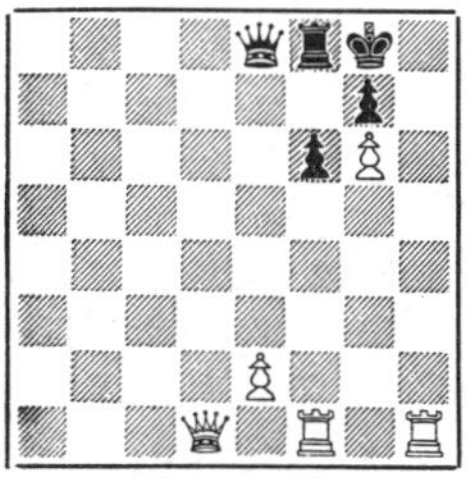

Mate in V.

Dam. S. 6.

White wins.

Dam. S. 7.

White wins a piece.

Dam. S. 8.

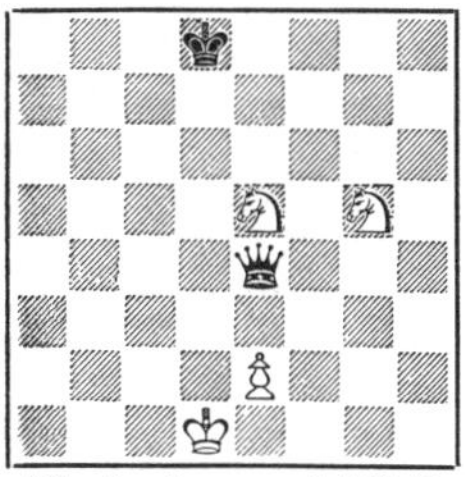

Black plays and White wins.

Dam. S. 9.

Mate in III.

Dam. S. 10.

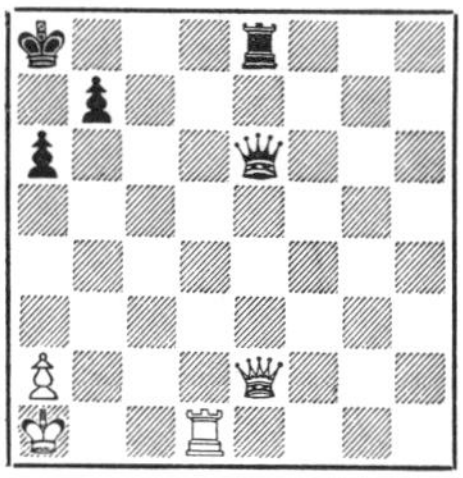

White wins the Rook.

Dam. S. 11.

Black plays and White mates in V.

Dam. S. 12.

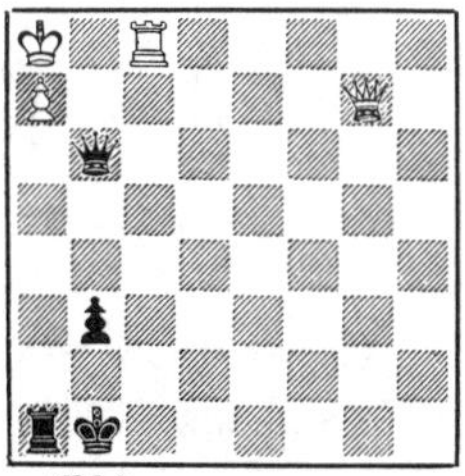

(Bl.)
Device to exchange Queens.

Dam. S. 13.

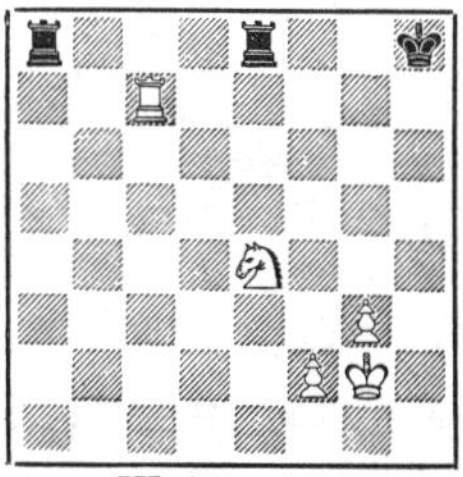

White wins.

Dam. S. 15.

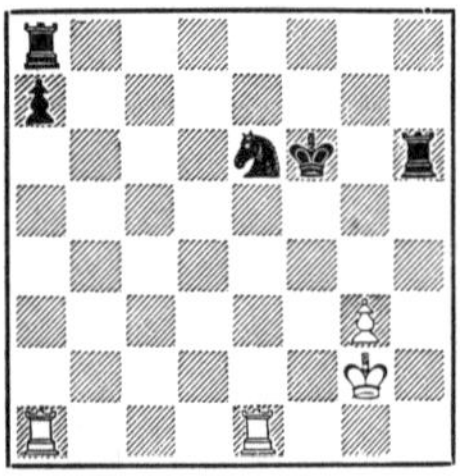

Gain of a piece.

Dam. S. 16.

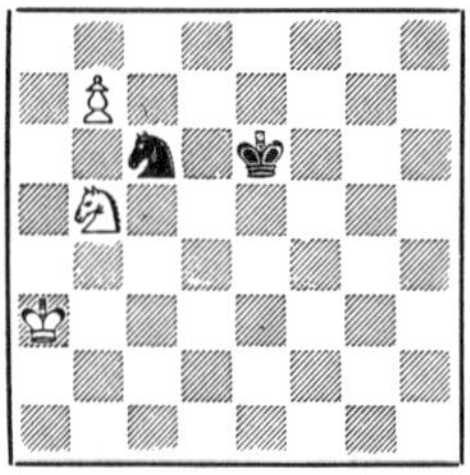

Device to queen the Pawn.

Dam. 9.

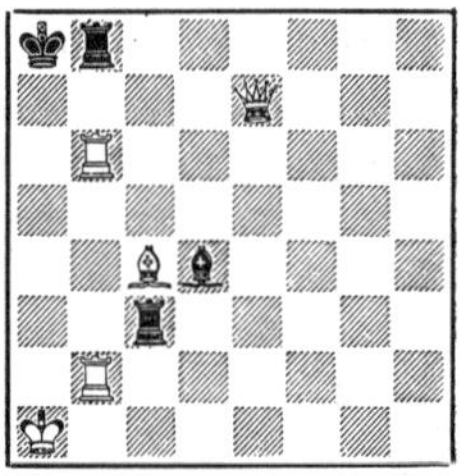

Mate in II without making a capture.

SOLUTIONS

I. Subtleties.

1. 1 . . , R × P; 2 R × B +, K × R; 3 Ktf4 + r.
2. Wh. Kd4, Pf5 (playing to f1); Bl. Kb4, Pa4. Wh. plays and wins. 1–4 P to f1 = Q, P to a8 = Q; 5 Qb1 +, Ka5; 6 Qa1 +.
3. If 1 . . , Pg7; 2 R × P, Pg8 = Q; 3 Rg2 +.
4. 1 Q × P +; 2 Ktf7 m.
5. 1 Rh8 +; 2 Rh1 +; 3 Rh8 +; 4 Qh1 +; 5 Qh7 m.
6. 1 Q × P +; 2 Ra2 +.
7. 1 Bf5 +, Bd7; 2 R × B, R × R; 3 Rd1, Rg7; 4 Ktc5 wins a piece.
8. 1 . . , Q × Kt; 2 Ktf7 + r.
9. 1 Q × R, R × Q; 2 Rd8 +; 3 R × R m.
10. 1 Rd8 +, Ka7; 2 R × R.
11. 1 . . , Ka8; 2 Ktc7 +; 3 Kta6 +; 4 Qb8; 5 Ktc7 m.
12. 1 Q × R +; 2 P × Q.
13. 1 Ktf6 and the mate cannot be saved.
14. Wh. Ka1, Qa5, Bf3; Bl. Ka8, Pa6, b7. Mate in II. 1 Q × P +; 2 Q × P m.
15. 1 R × Kt +, K × R; 2 Ra6 +; 3 R × R.
16. 1 Ktd4 +, Kt × Kt; 2 Pb8 = Q.

II. Problems.

The following positions in Damiano occur in Lucena. I add the references to the problems which also occur in MS. WD.

D	WD	L	D	WD	L	D	WD	L	D	WD	L	D	WD	L	D	WD	L
3	15	7	17	16	73	29	37	86	38	83	100	47	91	117	60	94	130
5	2	4	18	18	74	31	39	93	39	—	105	48	93	118	63	113	137
8	—	2	19	19	75	32	40	85	40	81	103	49	95	119	65	116	140
11	9	69	21	23	77	33	73	104	42	74	108	50	97	126	67	118	142
13	7	17	25	41	84	34	80	107	44	78	110	53	101	121	69	121	147
15	8	71	26	42	92	36	—	98	45	87	115	55	86	125	70	122	148
16	14	16	28	28	88	37	79	97	46	89	116	56	—	120			

Dam. 9. 1 Qa7 +; 2 Ra6 m.

Mr. White's Italian MS., based upon the work of Damiano (= WD), contains 19 subtleties and 129 problems of the reformed game. While the majority of those in Damiano are repeated, the collection is really independent, and contains a number of other positions. These now follow:

WD 21.

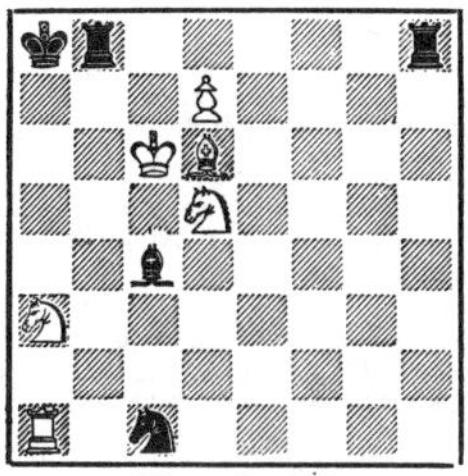

Mate in II.

WD 25.

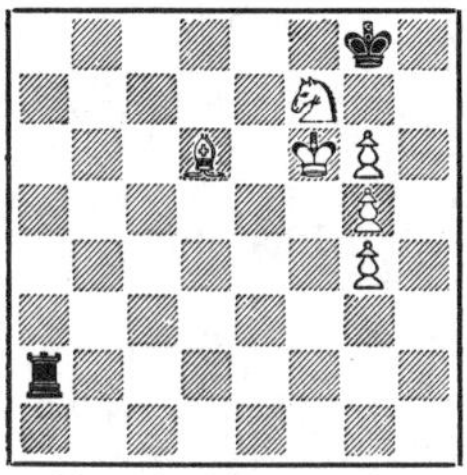

Mate in IV exactly.

WD 29.

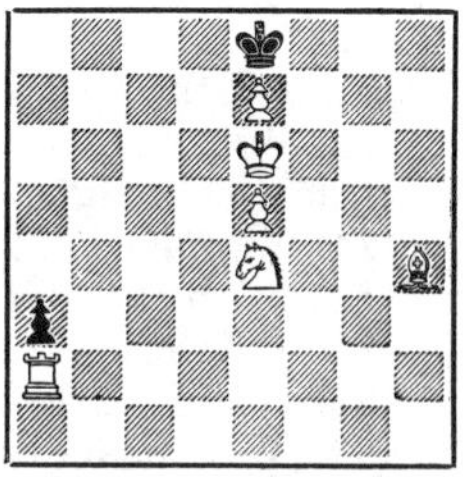

Mate in IV exactly with Pawn.

WD 34.

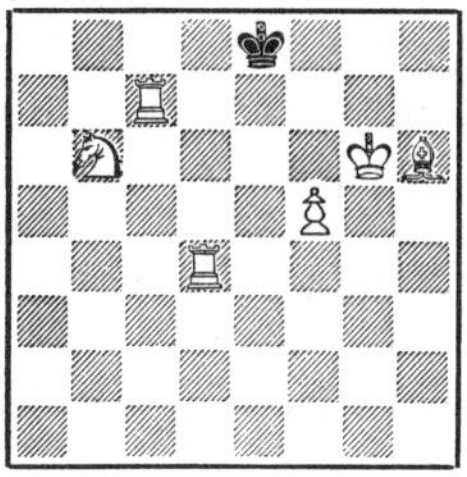

Mate in IV exactly with Bishop.

WD 54.

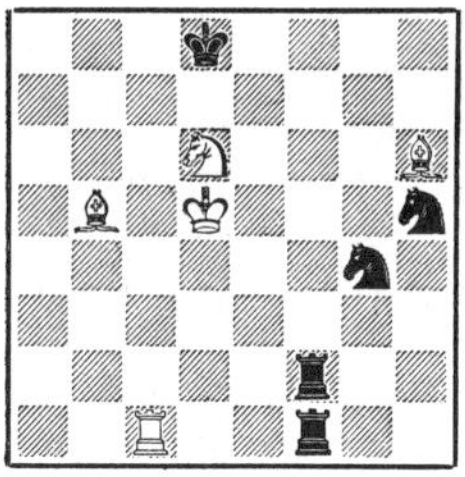

Mate in III exactly.

WD 66.

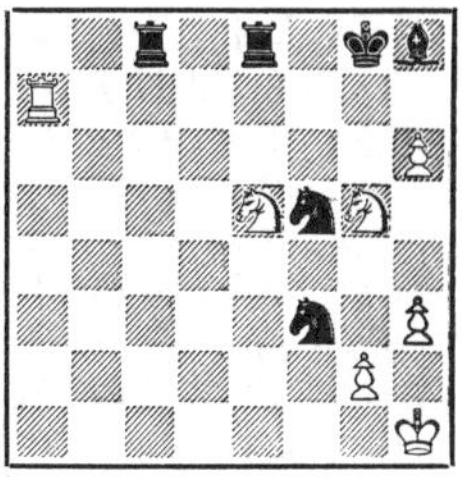

Mate in III.

WD 69.

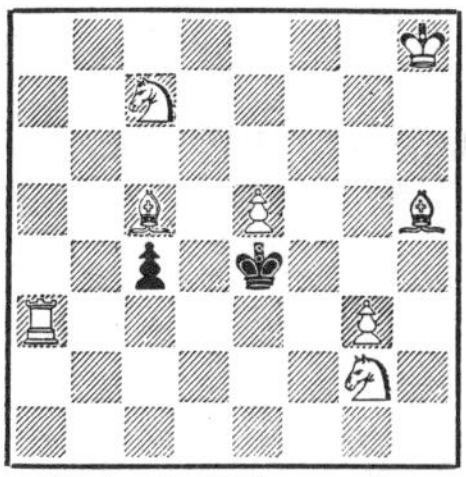

Mate in III exactly with Pawn.

WD 107.

Mate in VI exactly with Pawn.

WD 110.

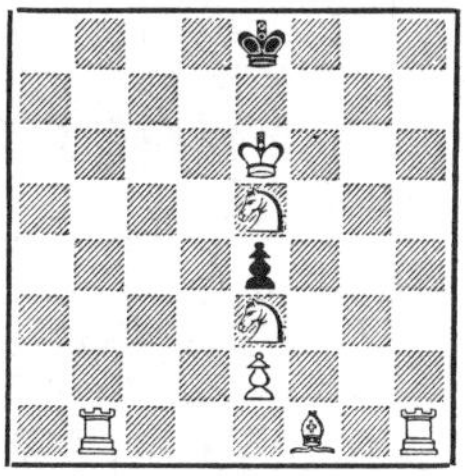

Mate in VI exactly with Pawn.

SOLUTIONS

I. Subtleties.

1. Wh. Ke1, Pe2; Bl. Ke8. Black plays.

2. Wh. Kc3, Rf3, Ph3 (going to h1); Bl. Ka4, Pa2, h2. Wh. wins, although the Bl. are fidated. Wh. drives the Bl. K to a8 and confines him there while he sacrifices the R on g3.

3 = CB *250.* 4–19 are Damiano's Subtleties 1–16.

II. Problems.

(The remaining problems in WD will be found as follows: 1 = CB *41.* 12 = Dam. 9. 26 = CB *99.* 30 = CB *116.* 31 = *25.* 32 = CB *96.* 35 = CB 108. 36 var. CB *53* in IV. 43 = CB *112.* 44 = CB *57.* 45 var. CB *5.* 47 cf. CB *1.* 48 = CB *110.* 49 var. CB *1.* 50 = CB *59.* 51 cf. CB *15.* 52 = CB *264.* 56 = CB *81.* 58 = Luc. *86.* 59 = CB *89.* 60 = Sens. 10. 61 = CB *92.* 63 = CB 65 (Luc. 24). 67 = CB *76.* 68 cf. CB *80.* 70 = Luc. 27. 71 = *1.* 75, no diagram. 82 = CB *135.* 100 = WD *158**. 102 = WD 158*. 104 var. Gott. 17.

105 var. CB 147. 108 var. CB *149**. 109 var. CB *158*. 115 = CB 164. 119 cf. CB 188*. 124 cf. F *297*. 126 = CB 207.)

21. 1 Ktb5 +; 2 dKtc7 m. Or 1 Ktc7 +; 2 aKtb5 m.

22. Wh. Ka1, Rd1, Ktc4, d3, d5, e4; Bl. Kd4. In IV ex. 1 Kt(d3)e5 +; 2 Kt(d5)e3; 3 Rg1; 4 Rg4 m.

24. Wh. Kb4, Rd1, Ktd3, d5, Bb8, Pf2; Bl. Kd4. In IV ex. 1 Kte5 +; 2 Kte3; 3 Rg1; 4 Rg4 m.

25. 1 Kth6 +; 2 Pg7 +; 3 Pg6 +; 4 Bf4 m.

29. 1 Rg2; 2 Kd6, Kf7 (or Pa1 = Q; 3 Ktf6 +; 4 Pe6 m.); 3 Kd7; 4 Pe6 m.

33. Wh. Kd6, Be7, Pa6, b6, c6; Bl. Ka8. In IV ex. with 2 Ps. 1 Kd7; 2 Bc5; 3 Pb7 +; 4 P m.

34. 1 Rc8 +; 2 Pf6 +; 3 Re4 +; 4 B m.

46. Wh. Ke1, Rb7, d7, Ktc6, Bc4, Pc5, d6; Bl. Kc8, Ra7, h2. In II ex. 1 Rb8 +; 2 Kte5 m. Cf. Fn 52.

53. Wh. Kf4, Ra7, h6, Kte6, g6; Bl. Kf6. In III ex. with Kt. 1 Kte7; 2 Ktd5 +; 3 Ktf6 m.

54. 1 Rc8 +; 2 Re8 +; 3 Re6 m.

55. Wh. Kf1, Qe1, Ra3, Kta4; Bl. Ka8, Ra8. In III ex. 1 Ktc5 +; 2 Qe5 +; 3 Ra8 m.

57. Wh. Kd6, Re7, Ktc7, e5; Bl. Kd8. In III ex. 1 Kte6 +; 2 Rc7 +; 3 Ktc6 m.

62. Wh. Ka3, Rh8, Kte8, Pa4; Bl. Ka8. In III ex. 1 Ktd6 +; 2 Pa5; 3 Ra8 m.

64. Wh. Kc5, Rh6, Ktd5, Bg5; Bl. Ke5. In III ex. 1 Kte7; 2 Rh3; 3 Re3 m. Cf. 65.

65. Wh. Ke1, Rh3, Ktd5, Pe2, e3; Bl. Ke4. In III ex. 1 Kte7; 2 Rh6; 3 Re6 m. Cf. 64.

66. 1 Rg7 +; B or Kt × R (or Kf8; 2 Rf7 +; 3 Ph7 m.); 2 Ph7 +; 3 Ktg6 m.

69. 1 Re3 +; 2 Be7; 3 Pg4 m.

84. Wh. Kc6, Rc5; Bl. Ka8. In V ex. without moving the K. 1 Rb5; 2 Rd5, Ka6 (or ~; 3 Rd8 +; 4 Rc8; 5 Ra8 m.); 3 Rd7; 4 Rd4; 5 Ra4 m.

85. Wh. Ke6, Ra7, Ktb4, Pg4; Bl. Kh8. In V ex. with P. 1 Ktd5; 2 Ktf6; 3 Ra8; 4 Rg8 +; 5 Pg5 m.

106. Wh. Kc6, Bb5, Ktc5; Bl. Ka8. In VI ex. 1 Kc7; 2 Kta6; 3 Ktb8; 4 Ba6; 5 Ba7 +; 6 Ktc6 m.

107. 1 Rd5; 2 Rd8 +; 3 Re8; 4 Re7; 5 Rg7 +; 6 Pe3 m.

110. 1 Ktg6; 2 Rh8 +; 3 Ktd5 +; 4 Rb6 +; 5 Rc8 +; 6 Pe3 m.

111. Wh. Kf6, Bh1, h2; Bl. Kh8. In VI ex. 1 Kf7; 2 Bf4; 3 Bh6; 4 Bf8; 5 Bg7 +; 6 Be4 m.

129. Wh. Kd8, Qc3, Rb1, b2, Bc4, Pa6, c6; Bl. Ka7, Re1, f1, Ba8. In VI or less with 2 Ps. 1 Qg7 +, Rf7; 2 Q × R +, Re7 (or Bb7; 3 Qf2, &c.); 3 Q × R +, Bb7; 4 Qc5 +; 5 cP × B +; 6 Pa7 m.

We have already seen that three of the MSS. of mediaeval problems also include positions composed under the rules of the new game. The *Civis Bononiae* MS. Leon contains a single position of this kind on p. 106 old (now p. 64), introduced without anything to show that it differs from the other problems in the MS. The text of the solution runs:

'Nigri dicunt se uelle mactare rubeos in IX tractus cum pedona pungente, et primo ludunt rubei ludendo pedonam quia nil aliud possunt ludere, et quia esset tabula; et ludunt pedonam quousque euaserit mulier, et cum facta fuerit mulier, nigri dabunt ei scac de rocco in A (d5). Necesse est ut rubei se cooperiant cum muliere in B (d4), et nigri dabunt scacch de muliere in C (d2). Rubei accipient cum muliere sua dando ei scacch, et ipsi se cooperient cum pedone dicendo scacch cum pedone suo regi. Et rex rubeus debet se dimouere, et ire in D (e1) . . . accipiendo cum pedone mulierem rubeam, et dicendo scacch, et alio tractu erit mact de pedone in E (g2).'

That is, 1 . . , Ph4; 2–5 P to g3, P to ḥ8=Q; 6 Rd5+; 7 Qd2+; 8 Pc2+; 9 P×Q+; 10 Pg2 m. The vocabulary of this solution is unusual, and quite different from that of the rest of the MS.

The Florence Italian *Bonus Socius*, MS. It., begins with a collection of 53 problems, the text of each of which commences with the words *a la rabiosa.* Another position without solution occurs at the conclusion of the BS text. These problems of new chess are almost entirely unique to this MS., and show a great partiality for symmetrical arrangements; see for example Nos. 8, 10, 21, 22, 25, 29, 35, 44. The problems now follow:

Leon 64 (corr.).

White plays and Black mates in IX with Pg7.

It. 1.

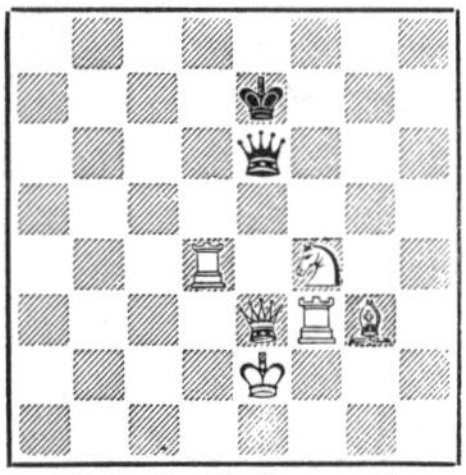

Mate in III exactly with Bishop.

It. 3 (corr.).

Mate in III exactly with Bishop.

It. 5.

Mate in II exactly.

It. 7.

Mate in II exactly.

It. 8.

Mate in II exactly.

It. 9 = 31.

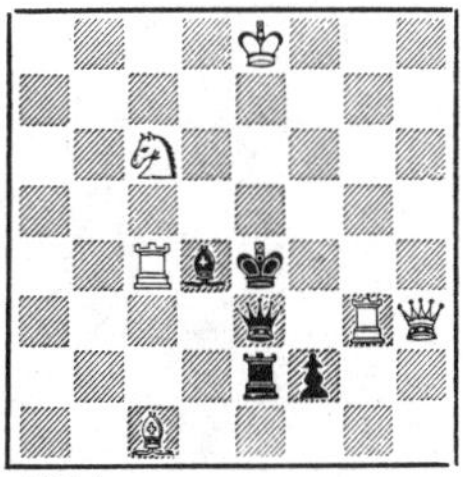

(Bl.)
Mate in II exactly.

It. 11 (corr.).

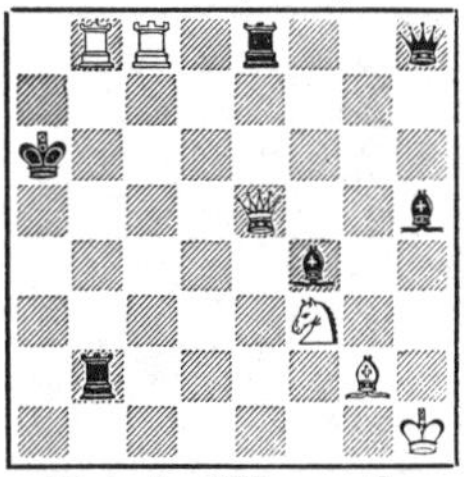

Mate in III exactly.

It. 16.

(Bl.)
Mate in II exactly.

It. 17.

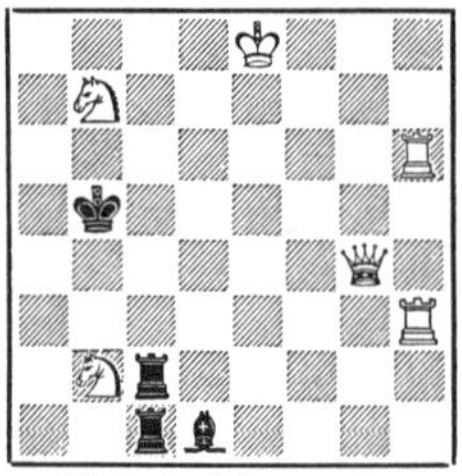

Mate in II exactly.

It. 20.

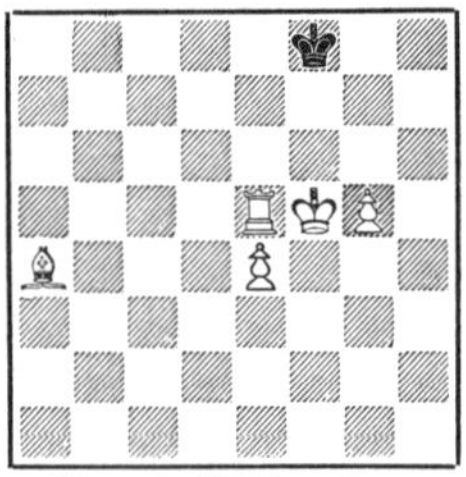

Mate in VII or less.

It. 21.

Mate in III exactly.

It. 22.

Mate in II exactly.

It. 23.

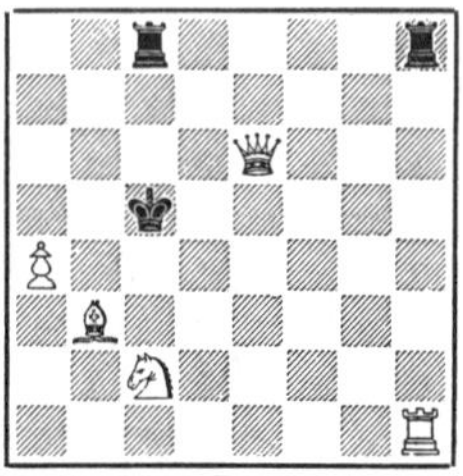

Mate in II exactly.

It. 24.

(Bl.)
Mate in III exactly
with Bishop.

It. 25 (corr.).

Mate in III exactly.

It. 26.

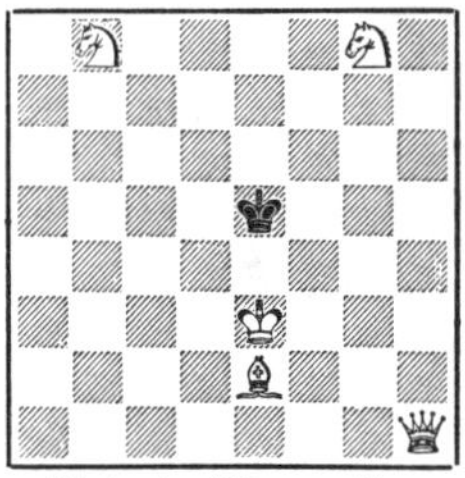

Mate in IV exactly
with two Kts.

It. 28.

Mate in II exactly.

It. 30.

Mate in II exactly.

It. 33.

Mate in III exactly.

It. 34.

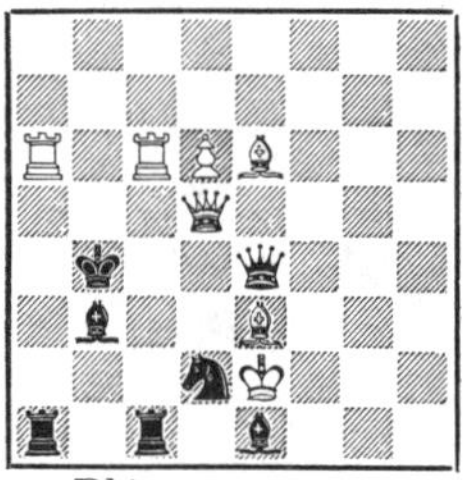

(Bl.)
Mate in II exactly.

It. 39.

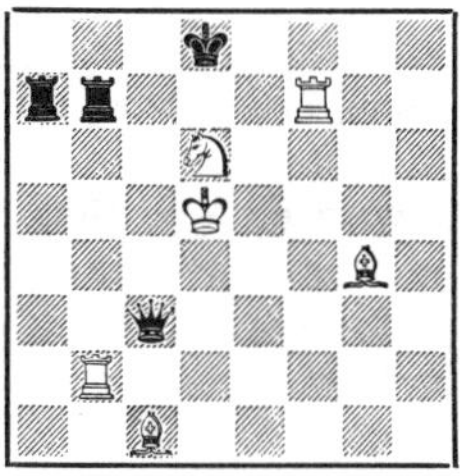

Mate in III exactly.

It. 40.

Mate in IV on c7.

It. 41.

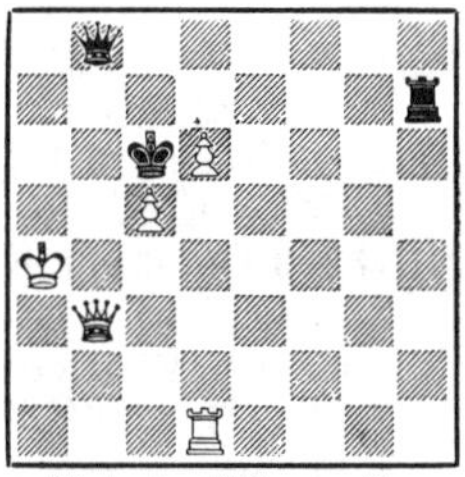

Mate in III exactly.

It. 42.

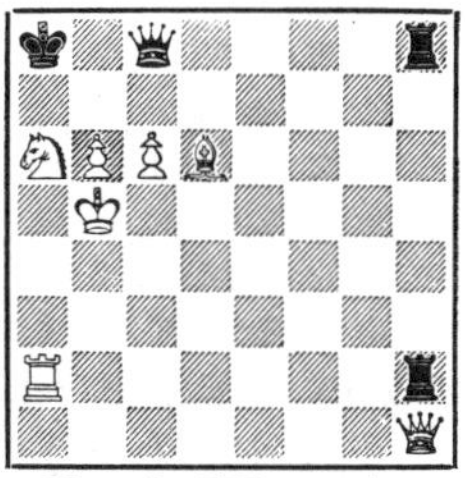

Mate in III exactly.

It. 43.

Mate in II exactly.

It. 44.

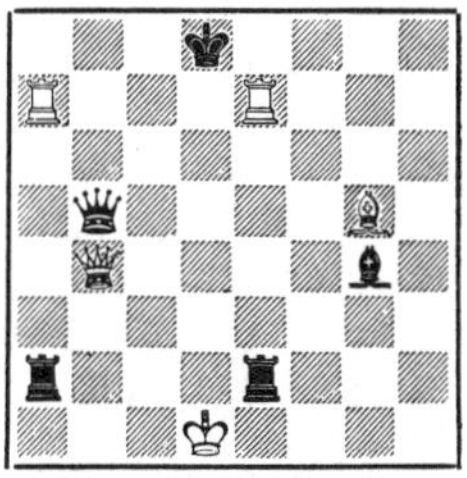

Mate in II exactly.

It. 45.

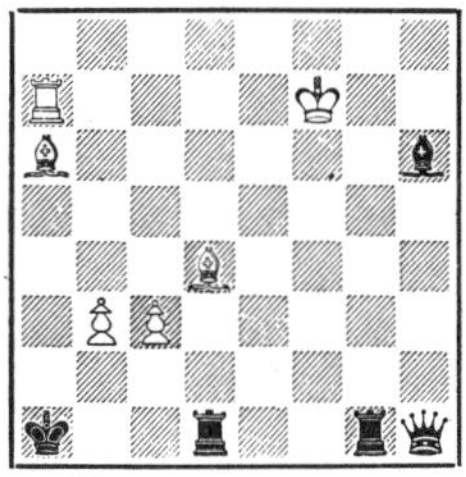

(Bl.)
Mate in IV exactly.

It. 48.

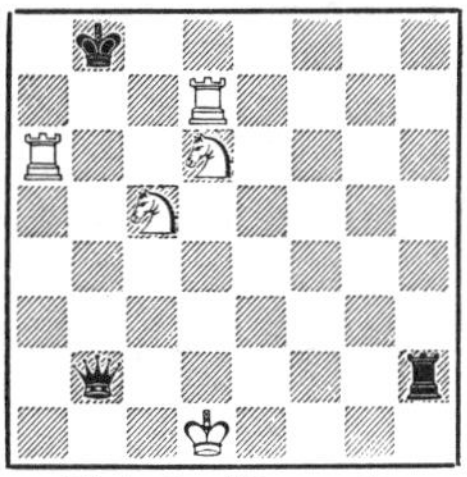

Mate in II exactly.

It. 55 (corr.).

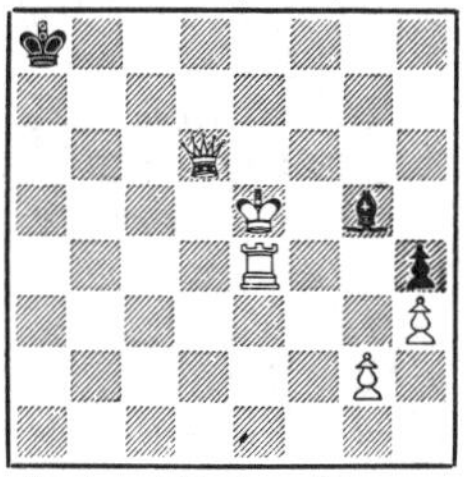

Mate with two Pawns.

It. 57.

Mate in VI with three Pawns.

It. 58.

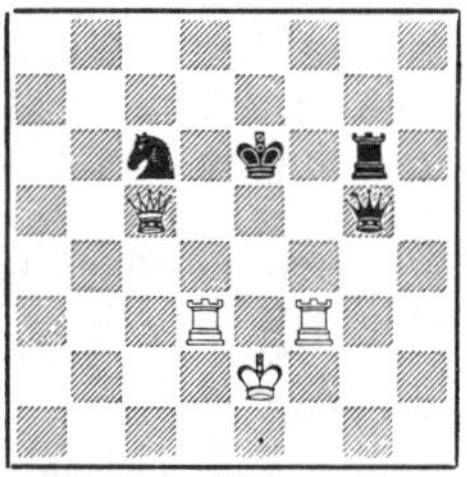

Mate in IV exactly.

It. 298.

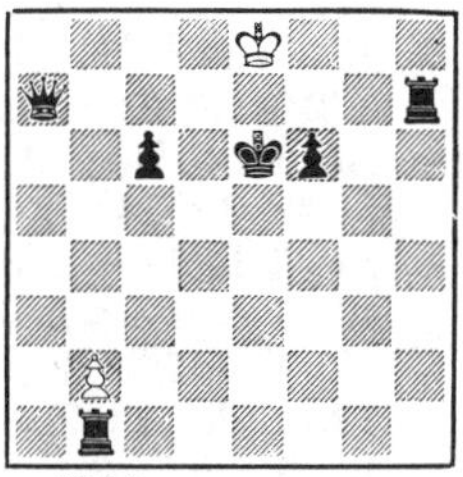

(Bl.)
Mate with two Pawns in XII.

SOLUTIONS

It. 1. 1 Kt × Q; 2 Rd8 (or f8); 3 Bh4 m.

2. Wh. Qe6, Ra6, Ktc2; Bl. Kc5. In II ex. 1 Qe4; 2 Qc6 m.

3. 1 Qd4 +; 2 Kt × P +; 3 B × Q m.

4. Wh. Ke3, Qc4, Rf8, Bh4, Kte2; Bl. Kd7. In IV ex. with Kt. 1 Bd8; 2 Rf7; 3 Qc7 +; 4 Ktf4 m.

5. 1 Qd6 +; 2 Qf6 m.

6 (corr.). Position of It. 4. In III ex. 1 Bd8; 2 Qc7 +; 3 Ktf4 m.

7. 1 Qd7 +; 2 Qd6 m.

8. 1 Qf6 +, Ke8 (or Kc7; 2 Qb6 m.); 2 Ktd6 m.

9. 1 Qe6 +, Kf4 (or Kd3; 2 Ktb4 m.); 2 Qg4 m.

10. Wh. Rb2, f6, Bd2, d6, Ktb6, f2; Bl. Kd4. In II ex. 1 either B +; 2 the other B mates accordingly.

11. 1 Bf1 +, Ka7 (or R in; 2 Qb5 +; 3 Qb6 m.); 2 Qc5 +; 3 Q × R m.

12. Cf. 11 (Rb8 on a8, Ka6 on b7, Bf4 on b6, add Wh. Ktb4). In II ex. 1 Kth4 +, R × B (or Bf3; 2 B × B m.); 2 Qd5 m.

13. Wh. Kf8, Qe3, Pe2 going to e1; Bl. Ke1. In II. 1 Qe4; 2 Pe1 = Q m.

14. Position of It. 1, omitting Bg3. In III ex. 1 Ktg6 +; 2 Kd1 (or f1); 3 Rf8 m.

15. Wh. Qd6, Kta2, b6; Bl. Kb5. In II. 1 Ktb4; 2 Qc5 m.

16. 1 R × Kt +; 2 Pg4 m.

17. 1 Qb4 +; 2 Rb6 m.

18. Cf. 11 (Rb8 on a8, Ka6 on b7, add Wh. Bf2). In II ex. 1 Kth4 +; 2 B × B m.

19. Wh. Ka1, Pe5, f5, g5, h5; Bl. Ka8, Bh6, eight Ps on seventh row. Wh. wins. 1 Pg6.

20. 1 Kg6; 2 Kh6; 3 Bd7; 4 Re8 +; 5 Pg6 +; 6 Pe5 m.

21. 1 Re6 +; 2 Qg8 +; 3 Q × Kt m.

22. 1 R × R(e6) +; 2 R(e6) × R m.

23. 1 Pa5; 2 Qb6 or d5 m. accordingly.

24. 1 Rb3 +; 2 Qb8 +; 3 Bb5 m.

25. 1 Bf6 +; 2 Bf5 +; 3 fRd4 m.

26. 1 Qc6; 2 Qh6; 3 Ktd7 +; 4 Kte7 m.

27. Wh. Ke6, Bf5, Pd6, f6; Bl. Ke8. In III ex. 1 Be4, Kf8; 2 Pd7; 3 Pd8 = Q m.

28. 1 Qd6, &c.

29. Wh. Rc1, f1, Bd8, e8; Bl. Kd6. In VI ex. with two Bs. 1 fRe1; 2 Bc7; 3 Bf7; 4 Bb6; 5 Be3 +; 6 Bg6 m.

30. 1 B × Q; 2 Re3 m. 31 = 9.

32. Wh. Kf6, Qg4, Bg1, Ktb8; Bl. Kd6. In II ex. 1 Qc8; 2 Qc6 m.

33. 1 Ktb5 +; 2 Rc6 +; 3 Re6 m. The idea is that of CB 73 (Ar. 53).

34. 1 Qb5 +; 2 cRb6 m.

35. Wh. Kc6, Ra1, h8; Bl. Ka8, Qb2, Ba6, c8. In II ex. Unsound.

36. Wh. Kg6, Qf1, Bg1, Ktb8; Bl. Kg8. In VI ex. 1 Qh3; 2 Qh8 +; 3 Qc8; 4 Kf6; 5 Qg4; 6 Qd7 m.

37. Wh. Rd1, g1, Bd6, Kte4; Bl. Ke8, Ktb3. In III ex. 1 Rg7, Kd8 (or Kt~; 2 Ktf6 +; 3 Rg8 m.); 2 Bc7 +; 3 Ktd6 or Rd8 m. accordingly.

38. Wh. Ka1, Qc8, Be8, Pb1 going to h1; Bl. Ka3, Pc1. Self-mate in III. 1 Qc5 +; 2 Qd4; 3 Qb2 +, P × Q m.

39. 1 Bg5 +; 2 Rf8 +; 3 Rc8 or e8 m. accordingly.

40. 1 Rd7 +; 2 Bh4 +; 3 Rh8 +; 4 Rc8 m.

41. 1 Qd5 +; 2 Pc6 +; 3 Qg8 m.

42. 1 Pc7 +; 2 Ktc5 +; 3 R × Q m.

43. 1 Qg7; 2 Q × B(d7) or Kt(f6) m. accordingly.

44. 1 R(e7)d7 +; 2 Rd8 m.

45. 1 Bf1 +; 2 Pc2 +; 3 Ra1 +; 4 R × R m.

46. Wh. Kd2, Qa8, Rg8, Bh1; Bl. Ke5. In II. 1 Rg6; 2 Qe4, or d5 m. accordingly.

47. = Gott. 9.

48. 1 Rd8 + ; 2 Rc8 or Kte6 m.

49. Wh. Ke5, Qa2, Kta7, c4, Pf2 ; Bl. Kd8. In III ex. 1 Kd6 ; 2 Kte5 ; 3 Qf7 or g8 m. accordingly.

55. Wh. first confines the Bl. K to a8 and only liberates by playing Q(g1)h1 and Pg3 + d. After Pg4, he confines the K to h8, and by a sacrifice on g3 makes way for his Ph3 to advance.

56. A Kt's tour on the half-board which can be completed as a re-entrant tour.

57. 1 Qb7 ; 2 Rd7 ; 3 Rd6 + ; 4 Pc5 + ; 5 Pd5 + ; 6 Pe5 m.

58. 1 Q × Kt +, Ke7 (or Ke5 ; 2 Rd5 + ; 3 R(d5)d3 + ; 4 Qd5 m.) ; 2 Qc7 +, Ke6 (or Ke8 ; 3 Rd8 + ; 4 Qf7 m.) ; 3 Qf7 + ; 4 Qd5 m.

298. (No text or solution ; I solve :) 1 Qf7 + ; 2 Rd1 + ; 3 Qd7 + ; 4 Qa7 + ; 5 Qa6 + ; 6 Rd4 ; 7 Rb4 + ; 8 Qa7 + ; 9 Rh8 + ; 10 Qb7 + ; 11 Pc7 + ; 12 Pf7 m.

The third of these MSS. with problems of the reformed chess is the work of Chachi, in the Casanatense Library, Rome—MS. C. In this MS. the third section, ff. 74 b–79 b, is devoted to problems *Dela D(onna)* ; *partiti ala rabiosa*. Another problem, C 12, has been inserted in a previous section in error, but Chachi has corrected his mistake by adding the heading *partito, ala rabiosa*.

C 12.

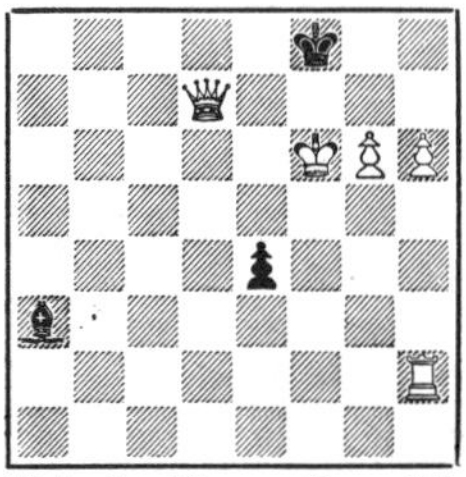

Mate in V exactly with Pawn g6. Pe4 is fidated, and Ba3 must take if it is moved.

C 151.

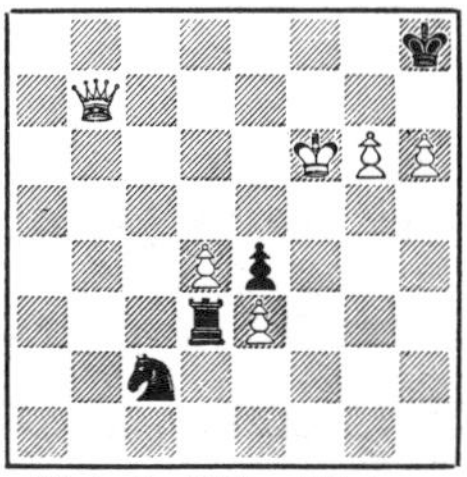

Mate in III with two Pawns.

C 152.

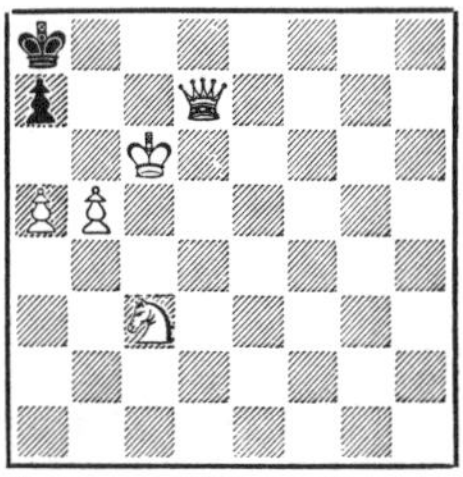

Mate in XI with two Pawns. The Bl. Pawn is fidated.

C 153 (corr.).

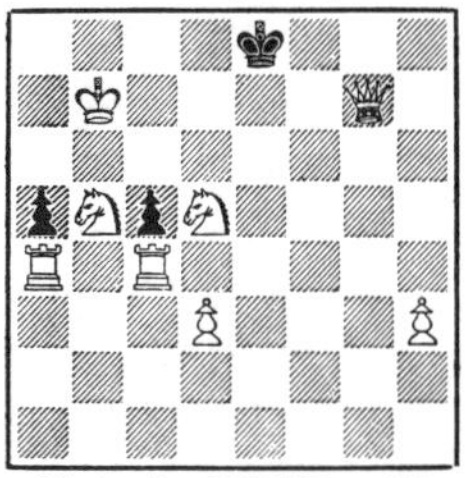

Mate (in XXIV) with two Pawns.

C 154 (corr.).

Mate in XXI with two Pawns.

C 155.

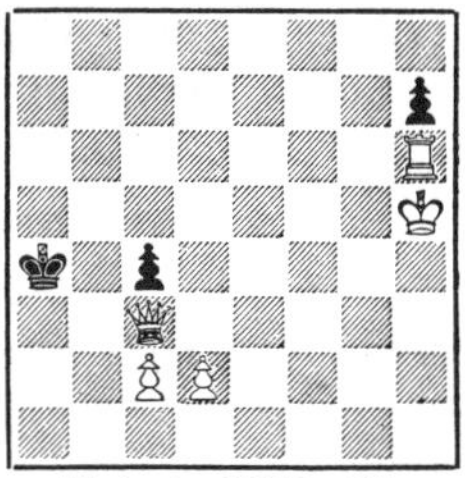

Mate in XVI with two Pawns.

C 156 (corr.).

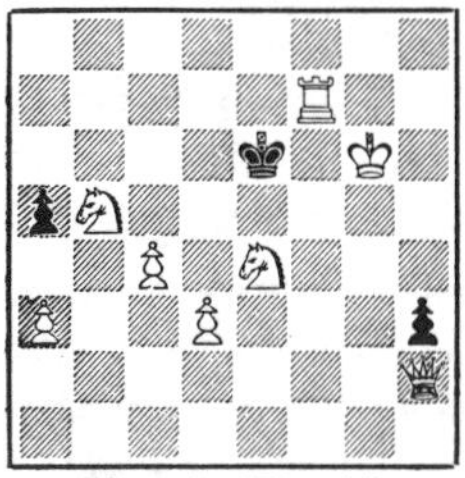

Mate in VI with two Pawns.

C 157.

Mate in III exactly.

C 158.

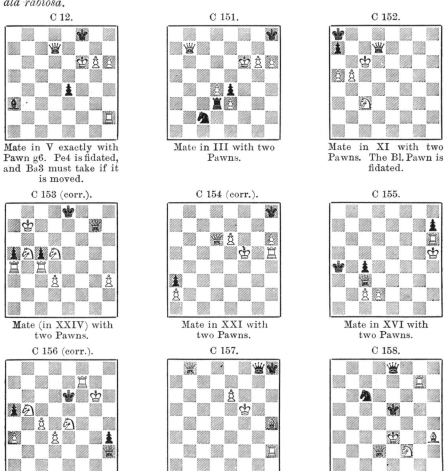

Mate in III exactly.

SOLUTIONS

C 12 = 148. 1 Ph7; 2 Rc2; 3 Rc3; 4 Rc8 +; 5 Pg7 m.

149. Wh. Kf3, Rg2, Pa3 going to a8; Bl. Kh3, Pa2, h2. Mate in XXII with promoted P on h8; Pa2 is fidated. (Secure the position—Wh. Kf8, Rc7; Bl. Kh8, Ph6; now 19 Rb7, Ph7; 20 Rb3, P × R; 21 Pa2; 22 Pa1 = Q m.)

150. Luc. *71*.

151. 1 Q × P; 2 P +; 3 P m.

152. 1 Qc7; 2 Qc8 +; 3 Qd7 +; 4 Pb6; 5 Ktb5; 6 Qc7 +; 7 Qe5; 8 Qd4; 9 Pa6; 10 P +; 11 P m.

153. (The MS. solution is very loose. I solve:) 1 Ktb6; 2 Ktd7; 3 Kte5; 4 Ktc6 +, Ke8; 5 Ra1; 6 Kc2; 7 Rc1; 8 Ktc3, Pa1 = Q; 9 Re1 +; 10 Re4 +; 11 Qh8 +; 12 P × Q; Wh. now obtains the position—Wh. Kd6, Qh8, Ktc3, d4, Pe5, h4; Bl. Kf7 or g6, Pc4; 20 Kt(c3)e2; 21 Ktg1; 22 Kt(g1)f3; 23 P +; 24 P m.

154. 1 Rh2; 2 Qe7; 3–6 K to b1; 7 Rf2; 8 Qf7 +; 9 Rb2; 10 Qf6 +, Kh7 !; 11–16 P to a8 = Q +; 17 Q(a8)f3; 18 Qh5; 19 Q(f6)e5; 20 Ph7 +; 21 Pe7 m.

155. 1 Kg5; 2 Kf5; 3 Ke5; 4 Kd5; 5 Kd4; 6 Qa3; 7 Qb3 +; 8 Qa2 +; 9 Qb1 +; 10 P × P; 11 Kc4; 12 Kc5; 13 Kd4; 14 Qa2 +; 15 Pc4 +; 16 Pc3 m.

156. 1 Kt(e4)c3; 2 Qg3; 3 Qg5; 4 Qd5 +; 5 P × Q; 6 Pd4 m.

157. 1 Qf8, Q × Q + (or Kh7; 2 Qh6 +; 3 Bf6 m.); 2 Bf6 +; 3 Rh8 m.

158. 1 Kte4, Qd8 !; 2 Qd6 +; 3 Rg5 m. Var. Ktc6 on b5; Uns., for 2 . . , Kt × Q; 3 . . , Q × R is now possible.

APPENDICES

I. EXTRACT FROM LUCENA.

(A, f. i[b]) La primera regla es a dotrinar alos que no saben nada en este juego: porque no caresca mi obra de principio. en lo qual sabiendo como juega cada pieza se conoscera la differencia que es entre el juego que agora jugamos que se dize dela dama: y el viejo que antes se vsaua: la qual declaracion aprouechara assi mesmo para entender la diuersitad delos juegos de partido que son ciento y cincuenta como rosario complido: el qual bien sabido aprouechara para saber mucho jugar de peones: los quales puestos todos arreo en la segunda barra del tablero teniendo casa blanca a man (A, f. ii) derecha assentareys los roques en las vltimas casas de cada parte en la barra primera: y cabe ellos los cauallos: luego los arfiles: despues rey blanco en casa negra: y rey negro en casa blanca: y junto con elles las damas: y assi bien entablado vuestro juego conuiene sepays como se muda y prende cada pieza. Los peones primeramente pueden el primer lance jagar a vna casa o a dos despues a vna siempre y por barra y prenden por esquina: y pueden passar batalla que quiere dezir que estando el peon del otro en contrario podeys passar vuestro peon otra casa mas adelante dela casa del encuentro quedando enla eleccion del otro dexar lo passar o prender lo. Item que allegando a la barra del rey de su contrario tiene fuerza de dama y da xaque sin trasponer: y no solo como dama pero si vuestras mercedes quisieren al juego que yo vso que por aquella vez que entra dama y el primer lance que della iugare que prenda y de xaque como dama y cauallo por lo mucho que alas mugeres se les deue: y de alli adelante por barra: o por esquina solamente al juego viejo el primer lance que iuega puede saltar tres casas por barra o por esquina: mas no puede prender: y puede saltar sobre otra pieza qualquiera que sea de aqui adelante de asa en casa y por esquina el rey assi mesmo el primer lance puede saltar a tercera casa como quisiere saluo con xaque sino fuere de cauallo por euitar el mate delos desesperados que llaman: mas que no trasponga sobre xaque no que no pueda trasponer si le han dado xaque que bien puede si no se ha mudado mas que no salta sobre la barra en la qual si quisiesse entrar no pudiesse por xaque. Los arfiles van por esquina de parte a parte saluo que al iuego vieio siempre van de tres en tres casas y tanbien por esquina; y puede saltar y tomar sobre otra pieza si quiere: los cauallos iuegan de tercera en tercera casa no iugando por esquina: ni por barra. Los roques siempre por barra y no por esquina ni como cauallos. Resta agora declarar algunas dubdas que muchas vezes entre los que poco saben comunmente acaescen: y es que si digo daros he mate de peon que se entiende con peon y no xaque de vno y mate de otro si no lo especifican. Item que si digo: yos dare mate con este peon señalando lo que si lo hazeys dama y le days mate conella vale. Itemque mate ahogado es mate no para ganar doblado como dando xaque y mate el qual me paresce buen iuego: & no se deue vsar de otra manera por que (A, f. ii[b]) os despierta y haze alcanzar muchos lanzes assi mesmo acaesce que el otro os da xaque y calla lo y vos no viendo lo jugays otra cosa que si el otro despues de hauer vos jugado antes que toca pieza dize sallid de xaque que se torne lo que jugastes & salgays de xaque en otra manera aviendo vos jugado y el tocado pieza que no salgays porque cada vez se lo harie quienquiera porque podrie hombre jugar de vn cauallo: o de otra pieza sobre vuestra dama: o sobre otra qualquiera pieza y dezir sallid de xaque: y despues lleuaros la por cuya causa no solamente no haueys de sallir de xaque pero si con otra pieza os diesse xaque podeys entrar en la mesma barra del xaque callado: saluo si conla mesma pieza no os diesse otra vez xaque. Assi mesmo aprouecha mucho vsar jugar siempre con vnos juegos special con los negros: y quando assi los tuuiessedes en vso y el otro no quisiesse jugar si no conellos boluelde el tablero: y assi es todo vna cosa porque siempre os viene el rey a man ysquierda. Si jugaredes de noche con vna sola candela hazed si pudieredes que este siempre a man ysquierda porque no turba tanto la vista y si jugaredes de dia que agays astentar al otro en derecho de la luz que es vna grande vantaja: quiere tanbien este juego tomar al otro sobre hauer comido y beuido: aunque para hauer de jugar mucho tiempo aprouecha hauer comido algo liuianamente porque no se desuanesca la cabeza el beuer sea agua y no vino en ninguna manera: y el que fuere estudiante crebame porque se que es que si quiere que le aproueche assi para el ingenio como para la memoria que juegue poco tiempo y el precio sea tan poco que perdido no le pese: porque desta manera alterarie el ingenio y turbaria la memoria. Item si vos me days el rey traspuesto se entiende que vos no podeys trasponer saluo si por pacto no lo sacassedes. Item que quien da el peon del arfil del rey no se traspone sino lo saca assi mesmo por partido. Item que aunque no se ponga jugando precio en tocando pieza ha de jugar della saluo si fuere dela encubierta que entonces ha de iugar del rey. Item que avnque tocada la pieza haya de iugar della que no por esso aunque toque casa la de assentar enella por euitar bozes. Finalmente conuiene ordenar bien vuestro juego enlo qual consiste la perfecion desta sciencia: y despues saber a cometer quando es tiempo y quando no estar quedo. y la manera del romper es siempre por la parte de la dama: y no por la parte del rey: haziendos alli fuerte hasta el tiem (A, f. iij) po dela mayor necessitad: porque alas vezes y por la mayor parte descubriendo vuestro rey podeys perder el juego: y assi teniendo vuestro rey en saluo podeys sin miedo con la otra gente darle guerra que de necessitad no puede hazer sino deffender se quedando vos señor del campo para lo quel de que suerte se ha de platicar entiendo escriuir todos los meiores iuegos que yo en Roma & por toda Italia y Francia y España he visto iugar a iugadores : y yo he podido por mi mesmo alcanzar.

II. EXTRACT FROM EGENOLFF.

(E, f. ij^{b}) *Ein ander art das Schachspil zu ziehen / so mann nennet Current oder das welsch Schachspiel.*

Das Currennt Schachspill ist vast einerlei mit dem rechtem Schachspil / allein das in etzlichen steinenn einn vnderschiedt ist der geng halber / das dieselbigenn einn besonder art vnnd gerechtigkeit habenn im Current hin vnd wider / hindersich vnd fürsich zulauffen / daher dann disem spil der zunamen gebenn wordenn / das es Current genant wirt. Nun sein der itzt angezogenen stein so in disem spil jre besondere läuff haben / nur drei / nemlich die Kunigin / . die beide Altenn / solchs verstehe zu gleich vff beiden seitten odder theilen.

Die Künigin im Current hat die gröst freiheit vnd her (E, f. iij) tigkeit das sie die zwergks vnnd breite / über eck vnnd wie sie wil / nahet odder fern (so jr doch sunst niemandt im weg steht) alles jres gefallens lauffen mag / Vnnd ist in dem so viel besser dann die Rach / das sie nit allein die leng vnd breitte / sonder auch die zwergk oder über eck (das dann die Rach nit thun dörffen) lauffen mag / vnnd was jr fürkompt rauben vnnd nemen.

Die Alten haben diese art im Current / das sie nit allein auff das drit veldt jrer farb (wie oben im andern spill bemeldet) sonder auch nechst vor jnenn / das vierdt / fünfft / sechst &c. vnnd also fürthers bisz an die spang hinan/hindersich vnd fürsich (doch alles der richt nach vnd über eck) lauffen vnd rauben / auch also wo sie stehn zu allen seittenn über eck als fern odder nahe jre art vnd gelegenheit erfordert / hinausz wischen mögenn.

Sunst so habenn die übrigenn stein alle jre alte vnnd gewönliche des gemeinen Schachspils / ordenung / vnnd wirt mit allem ziehenn / rauben / Schach vnnd Matten in aller weisz hierin gehalten wie es sunst mit dem gemeinen Schachspil gehalten wirt / Doch so bedarff es weithers vnnd fleissigers vffsehens wie dann soliche die übung am besten gibt vnd leret.

CHAPTER XII

FROM LOPEZ TO GRECO

The great chess activity of Southern Europe during the second half of the sixteenth century.—Ruy Lopez.—Leonardo and Paolo Boi.—Polerio.—Salvio and Carrera.—Greco.—The introduction of castling and other changes in the game.—The problem.

No new chess work was published for nearly fifty years after the appearance of Damiano's small book of 1512. This was certainly not due to any decline in the popularity of chess; the fact that no less than seven editions of Damiano were published in Rome before 1560 is sufficient evidence for the keenness of the chess life in that city. But this period was essentially one in which players were learning the possibilities of the new game and feeling their way towards new methods of development. By 1560 Damiano's book can have been of little use to any one but a mere beginner at chess. It is noteworthy that no Roman publisher thought it worth his while to bring out a new edition of Damiano after the middle of the century, although in less advanced parts of Italy the work was still sufficiently useful to justify a Venetian reprint in 1564. In Rome itself, the chief centre of chess in Italy,[1] the time was ripe for the appearance of a work that was more up to date, and the leading players felt themselves ready to try their skill against the players of other countries, and specially those of Spain and Portugal, those countries from which Damiano had told them that the greatest masters of the game proceeded. The opportunity was not long denied them.

But there were difficulties in the way of an even contest. Just as was the case with the mediaeval game, the rules of the new chess—now *chess* with no distinguishing epithet—varied from place to place, and the player who visited foreign lands found himself compelled to play with different rules from those to which he was accustomed. There were not only the differences handed down from the old game; each country was developing new rules and discarding old ones in the new game, and the variations were fast becoming

[1] There were good players in Sicily during this period (1520–1555). Carrera (88) mentions Arimini and Branci of Palermo, and Don Matteo li Genchi of Termine, who wrote some verses on the laws of chess which were no longer in existence when Carrera wrote in 1617.

considerable. Thus about 1560, the points of difference between the chess of Spain, France, and Italy, the only countries of which we have definite information, were somewhat as follows:

1. In Spain, the player who robbed his opponent of all his pieces, or who stalemated his opponent's King, won half his stakes—an inferior form of victory. Elsewhere, these games were only drawn.

2. In Spain and Portugal the Pawn could be taken *in passing*, in Italy it could not be so taken. If a player was in check and could remedy the check by advancing a Pawn two squares, and so passing the attack of a hostile Pawn, this move was forbidden in Italy, but permitted elsewhere, e. g. in the position—Wh. Ka3, Ra2, Pb2; Bl. Kc2, Bc5, Pa4, b5 (*Handbuch*, 1843, 10), White was mate in Italy: elsewhere, he could play 1 Pb4+, and win the game.

3. In Spain, the unmoved King, if not in check, could leap to any unoccupied third square (e. g. from e1 to c1, c2, c3, d3, e3, f3, g1, g2, g3) provided he did not cross the line of attack of a hostile piece. In France he could do the same, and in addition, if the squares between the King and a Rook were unoccupied, the player could play Kg1 (c1) and Re1 all in one move.[2] In Italy the rule was different in different places. In some places the Spanish rule was followed; in others the King was allowed a more extended leap, and could also move a Pawn one square forward to make room for the King on the same move; in others a form of castling was allowed in which the King could leap as far as the R sq. and the Rook as far as K sq.; in others, the only form of castling permitted was the modern one, K–K Kt sq. (or Q B sq.) and R–K B sq. (or Q sq.); in others again, the King could not leap at all.[3]

4. After a check had been given to the King, although the check was remedied without the King moving, the power of leaping was lost in some parts of Italy; in other parts of Italy and in Spain and Portugal the King retained the power of leaping so long as he remained unmoved.

We know nothing of the position of chess in Spain during the first half

[2] Gruget says: 'Et en France nous luy faisons faire deux pas le long de sa frontière, pourvu qu'il n'y ait plus de pièces entre luy et la Tour et mettez la Tour en la place du Roy.' Rabelais says: 'A la première desmarche, si leur filière estoyt trouvée vuide d'aultres officiers, fors les Custodes (i. e. the *Rooks*), ils les peuvent mettre en leur siège, et à costé de luy se retirer.' Pasquier, *Les Recherches de la France*, Paris, 1560, says of the King: 'sa conseruation luy permet de faire vn saut extraordinaire de sa cellule en celle de la Tour.'

[3] For this summary I rely on (1) the extract quoted from Damiano's book on p. 788; (2) the following passage from Ruy Lopez (1561, f. 16 a): 'La libertad de podar de la primera vez andar tres casas, del modo que quisiere, ò como peon, ò como cauallo, ò como Roque, ò arfil, ò dama, para andelante: ò qualquiera delos lados por su linea: ò como cauallo por qualquiera delas otras dos lineas, despues de la suya, ò esquinado como arfil por encima de pieça, ò peon suyo, ò ageno, ò como quisiere. Toda esta libertad le vino de ser Rey. La qual a ninguna otra pieça es concedida. Advierta se que en algunas partes de Italia se usa saltar el Rey del primer salto toda su linea, desde su casa hasta la postrera del Roque: y juntar el Rocque a el para hazar el salto todo de un lanze: y en otras partes no mas de tres casas desde la suia hasta la del cavallo, y por la parte dela dama, desde la suia hasta el arfil, y esto llegando qualquiera delos roques junto el mismo rey todo de vn lanze: y en otras se usa, de mas de esto, de un lanze mover un peon, qualquisieren, de la secunda linia, y meter el Rey en la casa que antes estava el peon, pero todos estos usos no son buenos, ni consonantes ala razon:' (3) the Sicilian rule as given by Carrera (1617), see below. (4) Actius, *De ludo scacchorum* (1583), Quaest. vii.

of the century. In the end of the year 1559, the accession of a new pope (Pius IV, of the family of Medici) brought a number of foreign clergy to Rome on ecclesiastical business. Among others there came a Spanish priest, Ruy Lopez, an inhabitant of Zafra, a small town in Estremadura, some forty miles to the S.W. of Badajoz, and a native of Segura, a small town to the south of Zafra, who had the reputation of being one of the first chess-players of Spain. While in Rome, Ruy Lopez employed his leisure time in playing chess with the Roman players. All that we know for certain of this visit is contained in a single sentence in the chess work which Lopez published on his return to Spain,[4] but it is pretty clear that he convinced the Roman players that they had still much to learn before they would be the equals of the master-players of Spain. It is also clear that Lopez made his acquaintance with Damiano's book at this time, and that he formed a very poor opinion of its worth.

Among the opponents whom Lopez met at this time was one who called himself 'the boy of Rome'. This player was in all probability Giovanni Leonardo di Bona, a young law student from Cutri in Calabria, who was known as 'Il Puttino' (the youth, or the small) and was destined to take very high rank among chess-players. On this occasion he played a variety of 'el gambito de Damian' (to adopt the name which Lopez gives to this weak Opening) which is not mentioned in Damiano's analysis, and the game took this form:

1 Pe4, Pe5; 2 Ktf3, Pf6; 3 Kt × P, P × Kt (apparently the Italians did not know that 3 . . , Qe7 avoided most of the difficulties of this defence, though the Spanish players had known it since the time of Lucena); 4 Qh5 +, Pg6; 5 Q × eP +, Qe7; 6 Q × R, Ktf6 (the move on which the Italians relied to keep the White Queen out of play: this had been discovered since Damiano); 7 Pd4, Kf7; 8 Bc4 +, Pd5; 9 B × P +, Kt × B, and Lopez won eventually.

Another result of this visit was that Lopez learnt a slang (originally a wrestling) term of the Italian players, and was afterwards instrumental in giving the word an international currency. This is the word *gambit*, of which Lopez tells us in his chess work (108 a):

> It is derived from the Italian *gamba*, a leg, and *gambitare* means to set traps, from which a *gambit game* means a game of traps and snares, and it is used to describe this Opening because of all the Openings which Damiano gave, this is the most brilliant and trappy.[5]

Ruy Lopez had, I think, been for some time in the habit of noting down Openings in which he was interested, and the discovery that Damiano had

[4] f. 102 b. 'Ninguna cosa de aquestas toco Damian, siendo juego quo lo hazen algunos jugadores principalmente con los no saben mucho; y aun conmigo mesmo lo jugo algunos vezes un estremado jugador que se hazia llamar el muchacho de Roma; y esto estando en Roma al principio del pontificado del papa Pio 4 en el anno de 1560.'

[5] 'Quanto a lo vltimo que en este capitulo pro metimos declarar: conuiene saber que este vocablo *gambito* deciende propriamente de la lengua Italiana: porque a cerca delos Italianos *gamba*, quiere dezir *pierma* en Espanol, y *gambitare* quiere dezir en nuestro Castellano *armar çancadilla*, y de aqui juego del gambito quiere dezir juego de lazos y çancadillas: porque en

published a book fired him with the intention of writing a book of his own. He carried out this intention with dangerous rapidity—dangerous because it resulted in a list 8 pages long of misprints and other errors—and his book was published not long after his return to Spain in the spring of 1561 (the *privilege* is dated the last day of February, 1561). The title-page runs:

Libro de la invencion liberal y arte del juego del Axedrez, muy vtil y prouechosa: assi para los que de nueuo quisieren deprender à jugarlo, como para los que lo saben jugar. Compuesta aora nueuamente por Ruylopez de Sigura clerigo, vezino dela villa Cafra. Dirigida al muy illustre señor don Garcia de Toledo, ayo y mayordomo mayor del Serenissimo Principe don Carlos nuestro señor. En Alcala en casa de Andres de Angulo. 1561. Con privilegio. Esta tassado à cinco blancas el pliego.

The volume is a quarto of 8 unnumbered and 150 numbered leaves. It is divided into four books, of which the first is divided into 27 chapters, the second into 29, the third into 24, and the fourth into 15 chapters. The first book treats of the origin and utility of chess, with many quotations from Cessolis, Reyna's Spanish translation of which had appeared as recently as 1549, and includes general advice to players and a code of laws for the game. The second book contains a miscellaneous collection of Openings, and was probably in MS. before the visit to Italy. The third book is a severe criticism of Damiano's analysis of games without odds, and the fourth book a similar criticism of his games at odds. In both books Lopez adds new Openings, and endeavours to correct what he considered to be faulty in Damiano.

The advice to players in the first book is divided into 36 paragraphs. There is very little that is really new in the first 18 of these: in the main they are taken (without acknowledgement) from Damiano. The advice to place your opponent with the sun in his eyes if you play by day, and with the candle at his right hand if you play by night, is in Lucena, and was probably a trick well known to Spanish players. The advice not to sacrifice Knight or Bishop for two Pawns, unless you can see a certain victory as a result, is in Caldogno's poem. The next group of 8 paragraphs deals with certain End-games, and brings out very clearly the differences which the Spanish

todos las juegos que Damian compuso ni ordeno otro juego de mas primor, ni de mas lazos que este dicho juego.'

The term *gambit* was thus originally applied to the Damiano Gambit, and although Lopez includes many other Openings which are now called gambits (*King's Gambit, King's Bishop's Gambit, Queen's Gambit*), he never uses the term in connexion with any of them. The names *Gambitto del Re, del Cavallo, dell Alfiero, della Donna, Pedina del Gambitto*, are first used in the *Regole* (see p. 822) and, together with *contragambitto* in the Polerio MSS.: they were generally current by 1600.

The first copies printed of Tarsia's translation of Lopez (elsewhere the form *gambito* is regularly used) have in two places on p. 133 the form *gomito* (= elbow). In the later copies this misprint is corrected to *gombito*. Later Italian books and MSS. vary between *gambitto* and *gambetto*, the latter being the spelling at the present day. Polerio has generally *-itto* (very rarely *-etto*), Gianuzio has *-etto*, the *Regole* *-itto* and *-ito*, the Boncompagni tracts *-itto*, rarely *-etto*, Salvio *-itto*, Carrera *-itto*, *-ito*, and *gomito* (from Tarsia), Greco *-etto*, *-eto* (often *ganbetto*), Piacenza *-etto* (and *sgambetto*), Ponziano and Lolli *-itto* (although Ponziani (1782, 7) says that the form in *-etto* is really more correct. He also has *Gomito di Damiano* from Tarsia), Cozio *-itto*.

The term was introduced into France and England by Greco. The *Mountstephen* Greco (1623) has, f. 78 a, 'As ye first of Joachimo's Gambetto's'.

wins by *Bare King* (*robado*) and Stalemate (*mate ahogado*) made in the game.[6] In such endings as Kt and 2 Ps *v.* Kt and 2 Ps; and R, Kt, and 2 Ps *v.* R, Kt, and 2 Ps, it was always worth the Spanish player's while to sacrifice his Knight for the two Pawns.

The concluding paragraphs are of less interest. They deal, in the main, with the exact value of certain odds, in which Lopez held opinions different from those generally held in his time.

The code of laws deals with the following points: the penalty for false moves (1) and captures (2), the touched piece must be played (3), the penalties for capturing (4) or moving (5) with a pinned piece, an unannounced check is to be ignored (6), the odds-giver has the move unless otherwise arranged (7), the meaning of 'mate with a Pawn' (8), whether the King could leap when the odds of the castled King were given (9), taking in passing (10), the Italian habit of moving King and Rook or Pawn on the same move is forbidden (11), the meaning of 'mate on a particular square' (12), of 'check and mate with a Pawn' (13), of a fidated piece (14), a fidated Pawn is no longer fidated if it be queened (15), the odds-receiver is responsible for seeing that the odds are given (16), the 50 moves rule in the Ending (17), the player may not touch other squares with the piece in his hand than the square to which he means to play it (18).

In his second book Lopez treats of the following Openings: 1 Pe4, Pe5; 2 Pc3 (i–iii); King's Bishop's Opening (iv–vii); Lopez Gambit (viii–xii); 1 Pe4, Pd5 (xxix); and the King's Gambit (declined 2 . . , Ktf6, xix–xx; 2 . . , Pd6, xxi; 2 . . , Bc5, xxvi; accepted 3 Ktf3 and continued 3 . . , Ktf6, xiii–xv, or 3 . . , Kte7, xvi; accepted 3 Bc4 and continued 3 . . , Ktf6, xvii–xviii, or 3 . . , Qh4+, xxii–xxv, or 3 . . , Pc6, xxvii, or 3 . . , Pf5, xxviii). In his third book Lopez takes Damiano's analysis as his text, and submits it to a close and hostile examination. In the course of this he attacks Damiano's statement that there are three replies to 1 Pe4, Pe5; 2 Ktf3, which defend the *e*-Pawn, and asserts that there are five—2 . . , Pf6; 2 . . , Pd6; 2 . . , Ktc6; 2 . . , Bd6; and 2 . . , Qe7,—forgetting in his turn that 2 . . , Qf6, is a sixth reply of this kind. He also attacks Damiano's opinion that the best reply is 3 . . , Ktc6, endeavouring to prove that the *Ruy Lopez game* gives White the superior game. I quote this attempt as a specimen of Lopez's analysis. He claims that 3 . . , Pd6, the *Philidor*, is the best defence, quite forgetting that this move confines the King's Bishop, which only five chapters before he had said should not be done. At the end of this book he mentions six Openings, often played by beginners, as being so bad that no player of any skill would adopt them. They are 1 Ktf3, 1 Ktc3, 1 Pc4, 1 Pf4, 1 Pg3, and 1 Pb3. Since Lopez's day all of these have taken their places among the recognized Openings.

[6] Thus R *v.* Kt was everywhere drawn unless the Kt could be separated from the K, when the Spaniard won by robado, the Italian by mate: R and B *v.* R was won by robado in Spain, by mate in Italy; R *v.* B was won by robado in Spain, but was drawn in Italy: a single Pawn could always win in Spain, either by stalemate or mate: RP and B not commanding the queening square was a draw in Italy, a win by robado or stalemate in Spain.

1 Pe4 / Pe5 2 Ktf3 / Ktc6 3 Bb5 / —

	IX	X			XI	XII	XIII	XIV
3	— / Pd6	— / Bc5						
4	B × Kt[a] / —	B × Kt / dP × B			Pc3 / Pd6	— / gKte7		— / Qe7
5		Kt × P / B × P +	— / Qd4		Pd4 / P × P[f]	Pd4 / P × P		Rf1[1] / Ktf6
6		K × B / Qd4 +[b]	Ktg4 / Q × P +	Ktd3 / Q × eP +	P × P / Bb4 +	P × P / Bb4 +	— / Bb6	*Kg1* / Kt × P
7			Kte3 / B × Kt	Qe2 / Q × Q +	Ktc3 / Bd7	Ktc3 / Pd5	Pd5 / Kt(c6)b8	Pd4 / P × P
8			fP × B[c] / Q × gP	K × Q / Bb6	Bg5 / Ktf6	P × P / Q × P[g]	Ktc3[h] / Rf8	P × P / Bb6
9			Rf1 / Bg4[a]	Pc4 / Bf5	Qd3 / Qe7		Ktg5 / Ph6	Re1 / Pd5
10				Kte1 / Ktf6	Ktd2 / B × Kt		Ktf3 / Pc6	Ktc3 / Be6
11				Pd3 / *Kg6*	P × B[d] / —		Ba4 / Pd6[k]	Kt × Kt / P × Kt
12				Be3 / hRe8				R × P / aRd8
13				Kd2 / B × B				Bg5 / Pf6
14				P × B / aRd8				Bc4 or / Qe2
15				Ktc3[e] / Ktg4				
16				Ktd1 / Kte5				

Notes.—[a] And Bl. obtains a doubled Pawn. [b] And wins Kt with better game. All this is Gott. VI. [c] Or 8 dP × P, Q × gP; 9 Rf1, Bh3. [d] With better game. [e] Or 15 Ke2, Ktg4; 16 Pe4, B × eP; 17 P × B, R × P + and mates shortly. [f] Or 5 . . , Bb6; 6 Pd5. [g] With good game. Or 8 Pe5, Bg4. [h] Or 8 Pd6, P × P; 9 Q × P, Qc7; 10 Q × Q. [k] With good game. [1] Or 5 B × Kt, dP × B, and the doubled Pawn is no disadvantage.

That Lopez deals with a wider range of Openings than any of his predecessors, and, unlike them, pays no attention to the problem, is probably the reason why v. d. Lasa and others have described him as 'the great personality with whom the theory of the Openings of the modern chess commences'. Apart from this, later writers have not allowed him any great merit as an analyst. Ponziani, generally a sound critic, says of him (1801, 37), 'This writer makes but little advance on Damiano; like the latter, he has only a few Openings, which are both inconclusive and unmethodical, so that he affords but little assistance to the student. He was an unfruitful genius, and entirely devoid of the enthusiasm so necessary for the successful conduct of the attack in this game.' This judgement, however, is certainly too severe, but the Modenese masters were hardly likely to do justice to Lopez's services to chess. Living before the great rival schools of chess which divided the players of the 18th and early 19th cc. had arisen, Lopez yet belongs essentially to that school of chess which we are accustomed to associate with the name of Philidor. In his analysis, and specially in the games in his second book, we may trace the genesis of that theory of Pawn-play which Philidor reduced to a system two centuries later. His most typical Openings are his Pawn game, 1 Pe4, Pe5 ; 2 Pc3 ; the King's Bishop's Opening, and the Philidor. He attached great importance to the retention of the liberty to advance the King's Bishop's Pawn at an early period of the game, and the discovery of the King's Gambit was probably the result of an experiment to see how early in the game that advance could safely be made: in his hands the King's Gambit is not an attacking game, and he devoted more attention to the safer Bishop's Gambit than to the Knight's Gambit. In the latter his defences have all been long obsolete. In all his analysis he refrained from playing Pd4 until he had prepared the way by Pc3, and even then he was more disposed to play Pd3 than to venture on Pd4. In all this he probably only reflects the attitude of the earlier Spanish players towards the game.

Strength in analysis does not always accompany strength in play, and whatever may be the final judgement on Lopez as an analyst, the fact remains that for nearly twenty years he was the first player in Spain. His nearest rivals were Alfonso Ceron (Zerone or Girone) of Granada, to whom the authorship of a work on chess has been attributed,[7] and Medrano. All three players were noted for their skill in blindfold play, and Lopez and Ceron, at least, played chess before Philip II of Spain (1556–98), and were liberally rewarded for their skill. Lopez was presented by the king with a golden chain for his neck, from which was suspended a Rook, and obtained preferment to a rich benefice.[8]

Philip II was not the only monarch of his time who patronized chess-players, and the royal examples were widely followed. The patronage of good players by the wealthier nobles and clergy was a great feature of the chess-life of the period, and many allusions are made to the custom in the pages of Salvio and Carrera, the two writers to whom we owe a great deal of our knowledge of the chess history of the years 1560–1630. Throughout the greater part of this period Giacomo Buoncompagno, the Duke of Sora (B. 1538, D. 1612), stands out as the Maecenas of Italian chess, and most of the great players of the period played in his palace and were liberally rewarded for doing so.[9] Thus he rewarded Ruy Lopez with a benefice of 2,000

[7] Carrera, 95 ; and *Bibl. Hisp. Nova* (1783, i. 17, and ii. 666), 'Alphonsus Ceron libello egit: *De Juego del Axedrez*, sive de Latrunculorum ludo, quem exactissime comprehenderat' (v. d. Linde, *16 Jrh.*, 53).

[8] But not the bishopric to which some writers of the 19th c., e. g. George Walker ('Ruy Lopez, the chess bishop', *Fraser's Magazine*, 1841, 168), have raised him.

[9] Giacomo Buoncompagno was the natural son of Pope Gregory XIII (Ugo Buoncompagno of Bologna) for whom Gregory accepted in 1578 the offer of the crown of Ireland. His yearly income was estimated at 120,000 crowns. The family (now Boncompagni-Ludovisi) still possess two composite MSS. of chess treatises which were collected by Giacomo and his son Francisco (see below, pp. 821-3 and 828).

crowns a year (Carrera, 64). It was to this nobleman that Giovanni Domenico Tarsia dedicated in 1584 his Italian translation of Ruy Lopez's book.[10]

The two leading Italian players of the early part of this period were Paolo Boi, surnamed 'il Siracusano', of Syracuse in Sicily (B. 1528, D. 1598), and the already-mentioned Giovanni Leonardo, surnamed 'il Puttino', of Cutri in Calabria (B. *c.* 1542, D. *c.* 1587, aged 45), both of whom excelled in blindfold play, Boi playing three games in this way at the same time. Boi was a fast player, whose play was famed for its brilliance; Leonardo a slow player, whose play was noted for its accuracy. Both Salvio and Carrera had known Boi in the last years of his life, and both give the main facts of his chess career—Carrera in simple outline, while Salvio tells the story of the lives of Leonardo and Boi, 'veramente lumi e splendori di questa professione', in the form of a romance. Much of the detail of this work, *Il Puttino*, is clearly unhistorical, and it is not easy to distinguish the basis of truth from the superstructure of fable,[11] but the facts appear to have been somewhat as follows:

1560. Leonardo, then a young student of law in Rome, played Ruy Lopez and was beaten (Lopez).

1566–72. Boi, after having defeated all his opponents at home, resolved to travel in search of opponents. His intention was to go ultimately to Spain, 'where he heard that there were very famous players who were honoured and rewarded, not only by certain nobles, but by the King (Philip II) himself, who took no small delight in the game'. He travelled throughout Italy, playing the greater players, including Leonardo, and was honoured by many princes, specially by the Duke of Urbino and Pope Pius V, who would have given him a rich benefice if he had been willing to take orders. Leonardo and he proved of equal strength in chess (Carrera).[12]

[10] *Il Giuoco degli Scacchi di Rui Lopez Spagnuolo*, nuouamente tradotto in lingua Italiana da M. Gio. Domenico Tarsia . . In Venetia, presso Cornelio Arriuabene, 1584. Two variants of this edition are known (see p. 814 n.). Tarsia's translation is the source of all later editions of Lopez, of which there were several French editions (1609, 1615, 1636, 1665, 1674), and also of Selenus's German translation (see p. 852).

[11] Salvio's motive is the glorification of Leonardo at the expense of Boi. He gives as his authorities Boi and Rosces, but has treated his material very freely. His chronology is particularly weak.

[12] Salvio, who omits all reference to Lopez's visit in 1560, speaks instead of a visit which Lopez paid to Rome in the year 1572, the first year of the papacy of Gregory XIII (Ugo Buoncompagno), when Lopez beat Leonardo, who was then a young student. He goes on to say that Leonardo retired to Naples and devoted himself exclusively to chess for two years. During these years, Boi, a young man, came from Sicily and played against Leonardo. Finally, at the end of this period, Leonardo set out for Spain in search of Lopez, intending to have his revenge at chess.

There are difficulties in the chronology of this; neither Boi nor Leonardo can be fairly described as young men in 1572, and it does not harmonize with Carrera's account of Boi's life, an account which involves no difficulties regarding dates. It would seem inconceivable that Boi could have been in Italy, and especially in Rome, in 1566–72 without meeting Leonardo. I believe that Salvio has simply transferred Lopez's visit of 1560 from the commencement of the papacy of Pius IV to that of Gregory XIII, and has in consequence crowded the events of the years 1560–72 into the two years 1572–4. The only difficulty which I see in this explanation is the statement in Carrera that Giacomo Buoncompagno gave Lopez a benefice of the yearly value of 2,000 crowns. In 1561 Buoncompagno was only 13 years of age, and it looks as if Lopez must have been in Italy again to meet this prince. Carrera may, however, be wrong in this statement, for he has everywhere made two people out of Ruy Lopez and 'il chierico di Zafra'.

In 1574–5 Leonardo, accompanied by Giulio Cesare Polerio, of Lanciano, and Tomaso Caputo, surnamed Rosces, visited Spain and defeated Ruy Lopez and Ceron, the contest taking place in the presence of Philip II. A little later Boi arrived in Madrid and in his turn defeated the same two Spanish players. Philip II rewarded both players liberally, granting Boi certain official appointments in Sicily producing an income of 500 crowns a year. He also gave Boi a letter recommending him to his brother, Don John of Austria, the text of which, dated Madrid, August 22, 1575, Carrera has happily preserved. Both players also visited Lisbon, and played with the chess-loving King Sebastian of Portugal (B. 1554, D. 1578). This monarch gave Leonardo the name of *il Cavaliero errante*.

1582–5. During the viceroyalty of the Duke d'Ossuna, Leonardo and Boi played frequently together in his palace. Leonardo held the position of Agent to the Prince of Bisignano, and was finally poisoned at this Prince's palace by a jealous rival, *c.* 1587. Boi, who had been captured by Algerian pirates when returning from Spain, but had obtained his freedom by means of his knowledge of chess, resided when in Naples in the palace of the Duke of Urbino, who allowed him 300 crowns a year. He seemed unable to settle for long in one place, and after a while he resumed his travels. For a time he was agent to a lady of the name of Squarciafico in Genoa, and we hear of him in Milan, and Venice, and as travelling in Hungary, where he played chess with the Turks while riding on horseback. Finally he returned to Sicily after nearly 20 years' absence, in 1597, but he had no settled residence, travelling from one town to another in order to play chess.

1598. Boi was invited to return to Naples. Not long after his arrival he died in his lodgings, as a result of poison. Only three days before his death he had played chess with Salvio. In this game Boi had made a five-move combination, by which he won Salvio's Queen. Salvio had, however, looked two moves further ahead, and had seen that he would win Boi's Queen and the game. 'Youth can more than age; you are in the prime of life, and I am seventy years old', was the veteran's comment. He had found chess a profitable occupation; Carrera (65) estimated his chess gains, excluding presents and the income from his appointment, at 30,000 crowns.

Salvio and Carrera give the names of many other chess-players of Southern Italy and Sicily, both of contemporaries of Paolo Boi and of the following generation, and Carrera took great trouble to ascertain the relative strengths of the players whom he names. A few may be named here as of greater importance or skill:

The Sicilian Barons, del Biscari (D. 1614) and di Siculiana (who played with Boi at the odds of the Pawn in 1597), were two liberal patrons of Sicilian players; other Sicilian players of the first rank were Clariano Rosso (D. 1604, Carrera's master), D. Salvatore Albino, surnamed 'il Beneventano', a priest of Benevento, Alonso Ortega (a Spaniard who was in Palermo in 1611 and excelled as a blindfold player), D. Girolamo (Geronimo) Cascio, a priest from Piazza, of whom more below, and D. Mariano Marano, a priest of Sortino. To Italy generally belonged il Raguseo and his opponents D. Giovanni Marignano, a professor of Ravenna, and Giovanni di Castro, Archbishop of Tarento; to Rome, Giulio Cesare Polerio, of whom anon; to Naples, Roscio (Leonardo's other travelling companion), Michele di Mauro (Salvio's master, who retired on the money he gained in chess from the Prince Gesualdo), Giovanni Domenico di Leonardis, who secured an annual pension of 200 crowns from Philip III of Spain (1598–1621) by his chess, and Dr. Alessandro Salvio.

Many of the players of this period kept note-books in which they recorded the openings of games for reference or later use. The keen chess-life of the time led to so rapid a development of the science of the Openings, that the existing text-books soon became obsolete, and it was imperative that the player who desired to excel should have more up-to-date information. Among those who are said to have written MSS. of this kind are the Spanish players Ceron, Avalos (resident in Naples in 1590 or thereabouts), and Busnardo, the Portuguese player Santa Maria (perhaps the author of the Portuguese book from which Salvio obtained some of the Openings in his work of 1634), and the Italian players Boi, Leonardo, Michele di Mauro, and Polerio. None of these players felt disposed to print his collection of Openings; the high stakes for which players played made it desirable to keep information as to new Openings private, but a wealthy patron could always obtain a copy from the players whom he included in his retinue. In this way the surviving MSS. of this class have for the most part escaped destruction. Most active of all in the multiplication of copies would seem to have been Polerio.

Giulio Cesare Polerio, surnamed 'l'Apruzzese', of Lanciano, near the Adriatic coast, first appears as the servant (*criato*) of Leonardo on his journey to Spain. After his return to Italy, he settled in Rome and became a member of the household of Giacomo Buoncompagno, Duke of Sora, who gave him a rental in Giantro of the annual value of 300 crowns. He was esteemed the first player of Rome in 1606, when D. Girolamo Cascio came from Piazza in Sicily in search of the wealth which skill in chess promised in those days. Cascio and Polerio played in the Duke's palace, and Cascio proved the victor. He became the 'favourite' of the Duke, and gained for himself an income of 250 crowns a year, and for his brother the presentation to a canonry.

We possess some six MSS. written by, or emanating from, Polerio:

(1) MS. Nat. Lib. Paris, f. it. 955: a folio note-book written in several hands, of 78 leaves, not all filled, which was in the possession of a chess-player in the retinue of the King of Spain on August 7, 1584, as appears from a loose sheet of paper now pasted in the MS. This player may have been Polerio himself, as v. d. Linde thought. At any rate, the MS. was in his possession later, for it bears the title, 'Questo libro è di Giulio Polerio Lancianese', and contains Polerio's rough draft of the dedication of the Boncompagni MS. (No. 2). The MS. is just a rough note-book in which games were entered as they came into the writer's possession. On the rectos of the leaves 9–17 is the beginning of a translation of the games in the

second book of Ruy Lopez's work. The versos of these leaves contain other Openings. The compiler seems to have had access to the MSS. kept by Santa Maria, Avalos, Busnardo, and Leonardo. He has also noted down 67 problem positions, of which 53 are derived from Lucena.

(2) MS. Boncompagni-Ludovisi, Rome, N. 3, contains ff. 333–481 (separately foliated 1–152, the last 3 leaves blank), a holograph collection of 98 Openings, 12 Subtleties, and 38 Problems, dedicated by Polerio to his patron Jacomo Buoncompagno, Duca di Sora, which he had been preparing for $3\frac{1}{2}$ years. This MS. can hardly be later than 1590.

(3) MS. J. A. Leon, London. This MS. was discovered by Mr. Leon, bound up with a copy of Tarsia's *Lopez* and Barozzi's *Rythmomachia* (Venice, 1572). It consists of 32 pages, and is in the same hand as many annotations and corrections in the Tarsia; the handwriting is believed to be that of Polerio. The MS. is unfinished, but its 46 Openings are identical with, and follow in the same order as, those of the earlier part of the preceding MS. It contains no dedication, title, or problems. (See Mr. Leon's account, 'Notes on a recently discovered Polerio MS.', *BCM.*, 1894, 317–36.)

(4) MS. Toulouse, 766: 'Ordini di giuochi degli scacchi in diuersi modi, cosi di mano, come sotto mano, cio è in offenza e difenza, con altri bellissimi partiti, sono di G. Cesare Polerio, alias l'Apruzzese, cio è giocandosi del pari.' A holograph MS. of 56 quarto leaves, containing 49 Openings and 40 Problems. It is practically identical with the following MS., but must have been written first. This puts its date *a.* 1594.

(5) MS. Nat. Lib. Paris, f. it. 948: a small quarto MS. of 56 leaves, with the same title as the Toulouse MS. on f. 3a, but with a dedication to an unnamed patron on ff. 1a–2a, which is dated Roma, 31 July, 1594, and refers to the work which he had written for the Duke of Sora a few years previously. This MS. is an improved and corrected copy of the Toulouse MS., and, like it, is in Polerio's handwriting.

(6) An Italian MS., in Florence until 1827, and later in the possession of M. Doazan of Paris, since whose death it has been lost sight of. Its contents were fortunately copied (rearranged in a tabular form) by v. d. Lasa in 1855, and several lithographed copies of the transcript were distributed by v. d. Lasa. The Doazan MS. was a quarto MS., which was divided into four books—*Giuochi piani di diversi valentissimi giuocatori*, 33 chapters; *Giuochi sotto mano di diversi*, 13 chapters; *Gambitti*, 35 chapters; *Giuochi di Giulio Cesare Polerio Lancianese*, 42 chapters; and *Partiti diversi* (problems) 6 chapters.

Many of the Openings prove on examination to be common to this MS. and Paris 955, and, from certain indications in the latter MS., I believe that it was one of the sources used by the writer of the Doazan MS. This MS., however, in addition, contains 19 games which are attributed to Giovanni Domenico d'Arminio, whom Salvio (1634) names as the leading player in the chess academy which met in Naples in 1634 in the house of Alessandro Rovito, Judge of the Gran Corte della Vicaria, and Advocate Fiscal of the province of Cosenza in Calabria. Another game is ascribed to D. Antonio Mancino, another member of the same academy, and the MS. includes other games in the Neapolitan manner; I think, therefore, that we cannot put the MS. earlier than 1630–40, and that it is the work of a Neapolitan player who had obtained access to Paris 955.

[(7) Caze (1706), in his *Livre sur les parties de gambit* (1706), includes a number of games from a MS. in the library of M. le Président de Thou, which were there attributed to il Calabrese, Domingo (i.e. Domenico), and Leon (i.e. Leonardo). This MS. must belong to a rather later date than MS. Doazan.]

A more ambitious work, in essence an Italian version of Ruy Lopez, with the addition of some Italian games of the style contained in the Polerio MSS., exists in two MSS. which, however, exhibit some small differences in their contents. These MSS. are—

(8) MS. Florence XIX. 7, 65 : a MS. of 151 leaves which has lost its first leaf. The present front leaf has the title, *L'eleganzia, sottilita, verita della virtuosissima professione dei scacchi.*

(9) MS. J. G. White, Cleveland, U.S.A. : a MS. of 171 leaves (14 unnumbered, 161 foliated, 6 unnumbered), with the Ranozzi coat of arms and the title (probably more modern) *Regole per il Giuoco de' Scacchi.* On f. 1 a of this MS. is the title of the Florence MS. In the Florence MS. chapters 48–79, and in the *Regole* chapters 48–80, do not belong to the Lopez work.[13] V. d. Linde (*16. Jrh.*, 77) identified the author of this translation of Lopez with Polerio, with whose handwriting that of the MS. has many resemblances. Although Mr. Leon (*BCM.*, 1894, 318) has pointed out that the chapters in the Tarsia which was bound up with his Polerio MS. have been renumbered to agree with the Florence MS., v. d. Lasa rejects the Polerio authorship on the ground that the MS. contains inconsistencies which a player of Polerio's ability would have certainly removed. I think that he lays too great stress upon these; a change of plan in the course of writing the work may prove an adequate explanation.

In addition to these MSS., there is a number of smaller MSS. in the two composite manuscript volumes N. 2 and N. 3 in the Boncompagni-Ludovisi Library. I also add a brief description of the remaining chess MSS. of this period which are known to me:

(10) MS. Bonc. N. 2, ff. 1–24: a poem in 36 verses of 8 lines each, and a collection of 24 problems, by Rotilio Gracco, with dedication to Jacomo Buoncompagno, Duca di Sora, written between 1572 and 1584 (as appears from the list of the Duke's titles). The poem describes in detail a game played before the Duke by Cesare (i. e. Polerio) and Don Lorenzo.[14]

[13] Fl. cap. 1–70 = Regole 1–70; Fl. 71–3 are not in Regole; Fl. 74, 75 = Regole 71, 72; Regole 73–6 are not in Fl.; Fl. 76–end = Regole 77–end. On a blank page at the end of Regole has been added in another hand a 'gambito di Giuglio Cesare', i. e. of Polerio. Neither MS. contains any problems.

[14] The poem is not without interest. Two stanzas are devoted to a description of the board and pieces. Polerio offers Lorenzo the choice of men by letting him choose between

(11) MS. Bonc. N. 2, ff. 71–121 = *Bonc. 2*: a collection of 108 problems, two to each recto, the versos blank, with solutions in the numerical notation which Polerio always employed in the solutions of problems. This MS. may very well be by Polerio.

(12) MS. Bonc. N. 3, ff. 37–62: an anonymous treatise on Openings of chess with 44 general remarks. This MS. has, so far as the contents of the earlier part go, a remarkable resemblance to some of the earlier MSS. of Greco.

(13) MS. Bonc. N. 3, ff. 73–6: 16 problems of modern chess, two columns to the page.

(14) MS. Bonc. N. 3, ff. 325–8: the rough draft of an attempt to arrange the defences to the King's Knight's Opening in an orderly way.[15]

(15) MS. British Museum, Add. 28710: a Spanish MS. of the late 16th c., contains on ff. 352 b–373 a, an incomplete treatise on certain Endings of chess, with some definitions and rules; the latter are of interest.

(16) MS. Paris, Arsenal, 2891, ff. 493–6 b: the second volume of a portfolio which belonged to Philibert de la Marche, contains a French treatise on chess, *Remarques sur le ieu des eschets,* which contains some valuable notes upon the differences between chess as played in France, Italy, and Spain.

The importance of the Italian MSS. in this list which contain Openings is, from the historical point of view, very great. They date from the time when Italian players were most active in exploring new lines of play, and we see in them the successive steps by which the new Openings took a standard form. They provide a most valuable picture of Roman chess before the Roman players yielded to the influence of the Neapolitan players and adopted their rules, which we can set against the pictures of Spanish, Neapolitan, and Sicilian chess which we possess in the works of Lopez, Salvio, and Carrera respectively. Four of the MSS. give interesting details about the origin of many of the games, which enable us to add life to the bald lists of players in the pages of Salvio and Carrera, and also preserve the names of other players of high excellence whom these writers omit to mention. But most important of all, from the standpoint of the history of the development of the theory of chess, the games are sufficient in number, and often carried sufficiently far into the middle game, for us to compare the tactics of the Italian players of 1570–1600 with those of their predecessors, and specially with those exhibited in Lopez's analysis.

To turn from the pages of Ruy Lopez to those of the Polerio games (for instance, in v. d. Linde's *16. Jrh.*) is, according to v. d. Lasa, 'to step from darkness into light, for the earlier treatment of the game, meritorious as it

his two hands, one of which contains a white Pawn, the other a red. Lorenzo chooses the white, and Polerio thus secures the right to begin. The game ran as follows: 1 Pe4, Pe5; 2 Ktf3, Ktc6; 3 Bc4, Bc5; 4 Pc3, Qe7; 5 0–0, Pd6; 6 Pd4, Bb6; 7 Bg5, Ktf6; 8 Pa4, Pa6; 9 Bd5, Ktb8; 10 bKtd2, Pc6; 11 Ba2, Bg4; 12 Qb3, Ba7; 13 Qd1, Pg6; 14 P×P, P×P; 15 B×P+, Kd8; 16 Kt×eP, Q×Kt; 17 B×Kt+, Kc8; 18 Q×B+, Ktd7; 19 B×R, Q×B; 20 Be6, Qe8; 21 Ktc4, Kc7; 22 Qf4+, Kd8; 23 Qd6, Bb8; 24 Q×Kt+, Q×Q; 25 B×Q, K×B; 26 Ktb6+, Kd6; 27 Kt×R, Ba7; 28 fRd1+, Kc5; 29 Rd4, Pa5; 30 aRd1, Pb5; 31 Pb4+, P×P; 32 P×P mate.

[15] In addition to these larger works there are still a few odd notes of Openings or Problems on odd pages in these two MSS.

was for its time, was placed very much in the shadow by the lively and brilliant combinations of the aspiring Italian school.' The first thing that strikes the reader is the great advance in the number of Openings, and in the grasp of the intention and possibilities of each line of play. To the already known Openings in the older writers these MSS. add the Queen's Gambit declined (by 2 . . , Pc6 only); the Fianchetto defences, the Caro-Kann, the Sicilian, 1 Pe4, Ktc6, and 1 Pe4, Pd6; all the known varieties of the King's Gambits excepting the Allgaier (5 Ktg5) and the Cunningham [16]; the Centre Gambit (one game beginning 1 Pe4, Pe5; 2 Pd4, P×P; 3 Bc4, Ktc6; 4 Ktf6, Bc5, transposes into a position in the Scotch Game); the Calabrese Counter Gambit, Berlin Defence, and Boden-Kieseritzky Gambit in the Bishop's Openings; the Greco Counter Gambit, the Two Knights' Defence, and the Four Knights' Game in the King's Knight's Opening.

The majority of these Openings are attacking ones, in which the aim is to develop the major pieces as rapidly as possible to the places where they can exert their greatest pressure on the opponent. The formation of a centre is a secondary, not the main, consideration. These principles of development are quite different from those which lie behind Lopez's method of play, and lead naturally to the preference for other Openings than those which he favoured. The typical Openings of these MSS. are the Giuoco Piano, and the King's Knight's Gambits. The defence often takes the form of a counter-gambit, and this term dates from this time. Thus the less lively Bishop's Gambit is met by Count Annibale Romeo of Ferrara's Contro-gambitto, 1 Pe4, Pe5; 2 Pf4, P×P; 3 Bc4, Pf5, and the dull Bishop's Opening by Leonardo's counter-attack, 1 Pe4, Pe5; 2 Bc4, Pf5. In the match at Madrid between Leonardo and Lopez two schools of play met, and youth was on the side of the player of the more open and attacking game. Little wonder is it that Lopez was defeated.[17]

[16] One variety, said to be a favourite in Spain, is given its Spanish name of *Guzpatarra* (lit. a boys' game). It began: 1 Pe4, Pe5; 2 Pf4, P×P; 3 Pd4, Qh4+; 4 Pg3, P×P; 5 Kg2. Salvio tells how Gio. Domenico d'Arminio and he had played it, Salvio winning by 2–1, with one draw (stalemate).

[17] It may be of interest to give the three games from these MSS. which were played between the leading Italian and Spanish masters:

Leonardo *v.* Lopez (*Vscita contra la Donna auanti al Rè che principiò il Calabrese contra Ruy Lopes, compilata per me G. C. P.*, MS. Bonc., f. 47): 1 Pe4, Pe5; 2 Ktf3, Ktc6; 3 Bc4, Bc5; 4 Pc3, Qe7; 5 Pb4, Bb6; 6 Pa4, Pa6; 7 Ba3, Pd6; 8 Pd3, Ktf6; 9 Qe2, Bg4; 10 bKtd2.

Leonardo *v.* Lopez (*Gioco quando se haura la mano e l'altra uole rompere per la pedona di Rè, e fu' contra il Clerico e Gio. Leonardo in Ispagna*; MS. 955, f. 16a): 1 Pe4, Pe5; 2 Ktf3, Pd6; 3 Bc4, Pf5; 4 Pd3, Be7; 5 Qe2, Pc6; 6 Ph3, Pf4; 7 Pg3, P×P; 8 P×P, *Kc7*; 9 Ktc3, Ktf6; 10 Pb4, following with Pa4 and *Kg2*, *e restera co li pezzi liberi et il gioco del nero mal posto.*

Scovara *v.* Paolo Boi (*Gioco che giocava il Siracusano con un creato dell' Archivescovo di Siviglia, primo giocator di Spagna*, Bonc. f. 84b; *Vscita che usaua Scouara gran giocator di Spagna contra il Siracusano*, MS. 955, f. 31b): 1 Pe4, Pe5; 2 Bc4, Bc5; 3 Ktf3, Ktc6; 4 Pc3, Qe7; 5 Pd4, P×P; 6 P×P, Q×P+; 7 Be3, Bb4+; 8 Ktc3, Pd5; 9 Bd3, Qe7; 10 Ph3, Ktf6; 11 *Kg1*, Rf8; 12 Pg4, *Kg8*; 13 Rh2, Bd6; 14 Rg2, *e cosi ritrouandosi il gioco in questa postura o simile secondo alcuna uolta si uariava qualche tratto per il più uenceva il Spagnuolo ancorche tenesse una pedona meno, e ueramente ogni giocatore ne restava meravigliato di un gioco cosi rotto dalla parte del Rè con una pedona meno.* Polerio examines this Opening under the Roman rules (*Gioco simile alla Italiana, rompendo con la pedona di Donna prima che si salta di Rè*, Bonc., f. 86), playing 10 0–0 (*salta in parte di Rè all' ordinario*), B×Kt; 11 P×B, Bg4; 12 Re1, Be6; 13 Qb3, Ktd8; 14 Bg5, Ktf6; 15 Kte5, 0–0; 16 Pf4, *e cosi ancorche tenga una pedona meno resta con buonissima postura di uencere il gioco forzatamente.* Under the Neapolitan rules, White could not 'leap' on move 10, because the check on move 6 deprived him of the liberty to leap at all.

That these principles of play were characteristic of Italian players generally, and not of the Roman players only, is evident from an examination of the analysis in the works of Gianutio and Salvio, which were published during this period in other parts of Italy.

Horatio Gianutio of Mantia published his *Libro nel quale si tratta della Maniera di giocar' a Scacchi*, in Turin, in 1597, dedicating it to Count Francesco Martinengo di Malpaga. This work, now of some rarity, is a quarto of 57 (51 numbered, 47 and 48 being each repeated) leaves, with a few Openings with and without odds, and 11 Problems. Its main interest for us consists in the passage dealing with the King's move :

> Il Rè ha podestà di saltare la prima volta tre case se vuole ò la à salto di Cauallo ò di Donna : & questo mentre non se sia mosso della sua prima casa, & se auertischa, che saltando il Rè dalla sua banda, il Rocco si deue mettere à casa d'Alfiero, & il Rè à casa di Cauallo, & se dalla banda della Donna, il Rè à casa d'Alfiero, et il Rocco a casa di Donna, & questo s'osserua per tutta la Spagna, et molte parti d'Italia, mà non generalmente. Il salto d'Italia si è non passar con il Rocco la casa dell'Alfieri & mettere il Rè doue meglio piace à giuocatori, & di questa maniera di saltare si serueremo in tutti li giuochi di questa nostra opereta.

And, as a matter of fact, Gianutio uses the following 'leaps'; Kg2 by itself, Kh1 and Rf1 ; Ka1 and Rc1 (very frequent) ; Kb1 and Rc1.

Gianutio only deals with six Openings, all of which are to be found in earlier writers. He devotes most space to the Two Knights' Defence, which had come into fashion among Italian players about 1585, but there is very little of importance in any of Gianutio's analysis. He was weaker than the leading Roman or Neapolitan players.

Dr. Alessandro Salvio has been mentioned already as one of the leading Neapolitan players from 1595 onwards, and considerable use has been made of the historical parts of his chess books. These are three in number :

1. *Trattato dell' Inventione et arte liberale del gioco di scacchi*, Naples, 1604 : a quarto of 8 + 186 + 2 pages, dedicated to Fulvio di Costanzo, Marchese di Corleto, which contains 31 chapters with Openings, 11 with games at odds, and 21 *giochi di partiti* or problems, some being supplied from actual play.

2. *La Scaccaide*, Naples, 1612 and 1618 (*JT.*, 2234–5) : a chess tragedy, of which no copies are known to exist. From some quotations in Carrera, it appears that the prologue gave some historical information about Italian players. Salvio himself refers to it in his work of 1634 in the table of contents of the Fourth Book (the reprint of his 1604 work), 'Cap. 4. quello ch'è descritto nella tragedia ', although the chapter itself does not mention it.

3. *Il Puttino, altramente detto, il cavaliero errante del Salvio, Sopra il gioco de' Scacchi con la sua Apologia contra il Carrera . .*, Naples, 1634, quarto, 8 + 72 pages, bound up with *Trattato dell' Invention . . . Seconda Impressione*, Naples, 1634, quarto, 16 + 64 pages.[18] The *Il Puttino* is dedicated to Pietro Giordano Ursino, the *Trattato* to Mario di Bologna, 'mio padrone'. The former work

[18] In some copies the *Trattato*, which is called *Libro Quarto* in the table of contents, is placed before *Il Puttino*.

contains the romance based on the career of Leonardo, large extracts from Cessolis, 13 chapters containing *gambitti*, 7 containing *giochi piani* (by which Salvio and his contemporaries meant all games that were not gambits), and 13 containing problems. The *Trattato* is practically a reprint of the games and problems of the 1604 edition. The section *Usanza del giocare in diuerse parti* is also brought up to date; I shall make use of this later in dealing with the development of castling.

Although Salvio followed the rules of Neapolitan chess in his analysis, and uses the so-called *free castling*, he is generally careful in other points to note that certain moves are played *alla Napolitana*, especially where this might escape a foreigner's attention. These points usually have to do with the rule that the King forfeited his right to castle after receiving a check, which often made play to give or avoid an early check advisable that would otherwise appear without purpose. Some Neapolitan players, he tells us in cap. xl of the 1604 work, would sooner lose a piece than the right to castle. Thus, 1604, viii, he plays 1 Pe4, Pd5; 2 P × P, Q × P; 3 Kte2 *alla Napolitana*, to preserve the power of castling, and 1604, xxxvi, at odds of Pawn and move, 1 Pe4, Pe6; 2 Pd4, Pd5; 3 Pe5, Pc5; 4 Pc3, P × P; 5 P × P, Qa4 +; 6 Ktc3, Ktc6; 7 Qh5 +, *giocandosi alla Napolitana*, &c., *ma non giocandosi alla Napolitana . . . non accadeua dare scacco.* More subtle is the difference in 1634, Gambitto V, 1 Pe4, Pe5; 2 Pf4, P × P; 3 Ktf3, Pg5; 4 Ph4, Pg4; 5 Kte5, Qe7; 6 Pd4, Pf5; 7 B × fP, Pd6; 8 Bg5, Ktf6; 9 Ktc3, Pc6; 10 B × Kt, Q × B; 11 Ktc4, Pb5; 12 Kt~, *se si giocarà alla Spagnola potrà perdere le Ped. del Rè nero* (Black has played first in this game) *con la ped. dell' Alf., mà se giocarassi alla Napolitana, non prenda, mà spinga la Ped. dell' Alf. di Rè un'altra casa.*

I may, perhaps, quote two other games which have some interest of their own. 1634, Gambitto xxi, begins with the note that this is another form of the gambit which had never been thought of,[19] when Sr. Mutio of Alessandro (a third-class player in the Naples Academy) saw it played between D. Geronimo Cascio and another player. Owing to Sarratt's blunder in translating this passage, this Opening has received the name of the *Muzio Gambit* (Sarratt, *Damiano, Ruy Lopez, and Salvio*, 1813, 209)! The Opening runs 1 Pe4, Pe5; 2 Pf4, P × P; 3 Ktf3, Pg5; 4 Bc4, Pg4; 5 Kh1 and Rf1, P × Kt; 6 Q × P, Qe7; 7 Q × P, Kth6; 8 Q × cP, Ktc6; 9 Ktc3, Qd6; 10 Ktd5 and must win. 1634, Gioco Piano ii, was played between Gio. Domenico de Leonardis and Salvio, and is called *Gioco Piano*. It runs 1 Pe4, Pe5; 2 Pd3, Bc5; 3 Be2, Ktf6; 4 Pf4, P × P; 5 B × P, Pc6; 6 Ktf3, Qb6; 7 Q or B guards bP, Ktg5.

[19] In this Salvio is in error, The Opening occurs, but without analysis, in both the Boncompagni and the Leon Polerio MSS. of *c.* 1590, and there is another earlier example (unfortunately faulty) in the Mountstephen Greco MS. of 1623, f. 78 a; 1–5 as in Salvio (5 Kh1 and Rf1 *al modo Italiano*); 6 Q × P, Bh6; 7 Pd4, Qf6; 8 Pe5, Qc6; 9 Qb3, Qg6; 10 B × P, B × B; 11 R × B, Kth6; 12 Ktd2, Kh8 and Rg8 (*al modo Italiano*); 13 Qf3, Ktc6; 14 Pc3, Kta5; 15 Rf6. The remainder is defective.

The variety 5 B × P + is in the Polerio MSS. from the play of Carlos Avalos, a Spaniard resident in Naples about 1590, who, after Leonardo's death, inherited the jewels which Philip II had bestowed on that master.

Although Salvio only adds this last Opening to those of the Polerio MSS., his analysis is quite independent, though on similar lines of development. Later writers, e. g. Ponziani and Lewis, have justly given high praise to his work. For his time, he was an analyst of exceptional ability.

Between the dates of Salvio's two works on the practical game, D. Pietro Carrera (B. 1571 at Militello in the valley of Noto, Sicily; D. 1647 at Messina), priest of Militello and the author of some works on the history of Sicily, published his *Il Gioco degli Scacchi*, Militello, 1617, a bulky quarto of 640 pages all told. This is a far more methodical work than either of Salvio's, and in all departments excepting the analysis is a valuable work, containing much of importance from the point of view of the historian. In his analysis he follows the Sicilian rules under which the King had no power at all of leaping. This deprives him entirely of the possibility of the brilliancy of play which is characteristic of the Roman MSS. and Salvio, but, in addition, Carrera was devoid of any analytical ability and his work is full of blunders. In his section on the Damiano Gambit he twice misses a mate on the move. His work has an archaic character, and, like the Göttingen MS., he divides the possible Openings into four (1 Pe4, 1 Pd4, 1 Pf4, and 1 Pc4). His contribution to the theory of the Openings is limited to three feeble varieties of the King's Gambit (3 Qg4, 3 Qh5 +, and 3 Ph4). His methodical tendencies are shown in the full discussion of all varieties of odds, and by the forty-one chapters which he devotes to the problem, in Sicilian called *tratto posticco*. In his last book he describes a new variety of chess of his own invention on a 10 × 8 board, with four extra pieces on each side, viz., two Pawns, a *Centauro* (b1, b8) with the moves of Rook and Knight, and a *Campione* (i1, i8) with the moves of Bishop and Knight. The game never got beyond the book stage.

In this work Carrera (422) ventures on a single occasion to criticize a move in a Queen's Gambit in Salvio's work of 1604, and in this way incurred the wrath of the Neapolitan master, already vexed because Carrera had not recognized that a blindfold player mentioned in the prologue to *La Scaccaide* was Salvio himself. Salvio devoted the Third Book of his 1634 work to a bitter attack on Carrera under the title *Apologia contra il Carrera*. The warfare did not end here, for Valentino Vespajo, a friend of Carrera (who had abandoned chess before 1634), replied to Salvio in a still more bitter pamphlet, now of great rarity,[20] *Riposta in difesa di D. Pietro Carrera contra l'Apologia di Alessandro Salvio*, Catania, 1635. Vespajo accuses Salvio of ignoring the fact that Carrera wrote under the Sicilian rules of chess, and goes on to point out inaccuracies in Salvio's historical statements, concluding with the sweeping assertion, 'Il Salvio non merita d'esser creduto in nulla' (52). One of these misstatements refers to the last great Italian player of this period, Gioachino Greco.

Greco, surnamed 'Cusentino', and more frequently 'il Calabrese', was a man

[20] Only three copies are known: in the Bibl. de l'Arsenal, Paris, and the Catania and Palermo Libraries.

of poor parentage and no education, a native of Celico near Cosenza in Calabria, the same province of the kingdom of Naples which had produced the masters Giovanni Leonardo and Michele di Mauro. He learnt his chess from the works of Ruy Lopez and Salvio (1604), and when we first meet with him he was living in Rome under the patronage of a number of wealthy prelates, Cardinal Savelli, Monsr. Corsini of Casa Minutoli Tegrimi, Monsr. Francesco Buoncompagno (a son of the Duke of Sora who inherited his father's interest in chess: he was born 1596, made Cardinal April 19, 1621, and Archbishop of Naples in 1626, and died 1641), and others. For these patrons he made extracts from a manuscript collection of games which he seems to have commenced to keep in 1619, prefixing to the copies much introductory matter relating to chess.[21] He soon left Rome in search of the fortune which was supposed to await chess-players in foreign lands, and in 1621 he was at the court of the Duke of Lorraine in Nancy, to whom he gave a splendidly executed copy of his MS., which is dated July 5, 1621. From Nancy he proceeded to Paris, where the leading players were the Duke of Nemours, M. Arnault le Carabin, and M. Chaumont de la Salle, and in a very short time he gained 5,000 crowns by his play. In 1622 he crossed to England and had the misfortune to fall in with thieves on his way to London, who robbed him of all his money. In London he played with all the leading players, and two at least of these, Sir Francis Godolphin and Nicholas Mountstephen, secured copies of his MS., the copy made for the latter containing, in addition to Greco's own games, extracts from Ruy Lopez and the 1604 Salvio,

[21] In its fullest form, this matter includes (in addition to the dedication (1), a section *Ai lettori* (2), and a sonnet (3)) sections entitled *Del gioco de scacchi* (4), dealing with the invention of chess, the moves of the pieces, check, and mate; *Leggi del Gioco* (5); *Vsanza che nel gioco si osserva in diversi parti* (6), giving the rules of different countries; *Astutie de giocatori* (7); *Regole da tenersi per imparar a giocare di memoria all' nobilissimo gioco de scacchi* (8).

The bibliography of the Greco MSS. has been unsatisfactory in the past. V. d. Linde (*16. Jrh.*, 94), ignoring the clear statement of the Boncompagni MS. N. 3 (f. 1), dates the Boncompagni MS. *post 1626*, and did not discover that the MS. is not one work but two.

To Greco's Roman period belong:

1. *Trattato del Gioco de Scacchi di Gioachino Greco Cusentino. Diuiso in Sbaratti & Partiti.* Dedication to Monsr. Corsini di Casa Minutoli Tegrimi, dated Rome, Feb. 12, 1620. Contains §§ 1, 2, 8; now in v. d. Lasa's library.

2. *Trattato del nobilissimo Gioco de Scacchi, il quale è ritratto di Guerra & di Ragion di Stato. Diuiso in Sbaratti, Partiti, & Gambetti, Giochi moderni, Con bellissimi Tratti occulti tutti diuersi. Di Gioacchino Greco Calabrese. L'Anno MDCXX.* Dedication to an unnamed Cardinal of Casa Orsina. Contains §§ 1, 2, 3, 4, 5, 6, 7, 8; now in the Corsini library, Rome (MS. Cors. 669).

3. Without title, commencing *Primo modo di giochare a scachi*, and ending with a reference to the other MS. which he gave to Monsr. Buoncompagno (No. 4) as 'libro magore', and a brief recommendation to his patron signed *gioachimo greco.* Now bound in MS. Boncompagni-Ludovisi, N. 3, ff. 77 (text begins 79)–160.

4. *Libretto di giochare a schachi conposto da giochimo greco Calabrese di la tera di celico. Gioachino Greco prattica in Casa del Cardinal Sauelli, et Monsr. Boncompagno.* Contains § 1. Bound in MS. Boncompagni-Ludovisi, N. 3, ff. 161 (text 163)–322 (text ends 320). Since Francisco Buoncompagno is described as Monsr. and not as Cardinal, this MS. was written before April, 1621.

From the similarity of its contents, we may add to these MSS.:

5. The Lorraine MS., with the same title (except for date MDCXIX) as No. 2 above. Dedication to Henry, Duke of Lorraine, dated Nansi, July 5, 1621. Contains §§ 1, 2, 3, 4, 5, 6, 7, 8. This MS. now belongs to the Grand Duke of Tuscany, and is presumably at Salzburg in Austria. Our knowledge of this MS. is derived from the copy which Sr. Fantacci made for Staunton in 1854.

6. A French translation of the last MS., made by Guillaume Polydore Ancel, Nancy, 1622, is now in the Dresden Library, MS. O. 60.

and, I think, also from an Italian MS. of the Polerio group.[22] Greco returned to Paris in 1624, and during this stay in France he regained a portion at least of his fortune, and rearranged his MS., eliminating the longer and less attractive games, and adding many brilliancies. We possess a number of MSS. (or copies of MSS.) which he made for French patrons during this second visit to Paris, 1624–6.[23] He next made his way to Madrid, where he played at the court of Philip IV, defeating all opponents.[24] Finally he was induced to accompany a Spanish nobleman to the West Indies, where he died before 1634, leaving all his fortune to the Jesuits. He never revisited Italy after 1621, and his reputation was made after that year. This explains the fact that his influence has never extended to his native country.

In his earlier MSS. there is little to show that Greco was a player of more than moderate skill. He follows older works closely; the games in the MS. which he wrote for Monsr. Corsini are little more than an extract from Ruy Lopez; and he makes no attempt to adapt his material to the rules current in Italy. None of the games from Lopez is brought up to date by the introduction of castling. In the few remaining games (derived in part

[22] To the English visit belong:

7. *The Booke of The ordinary games at Chestes. Composed by Joachino Greco an Italian, Borne in Calabria: written for Nicholas Mountstephen dwellinge at Ludgate in London: Anno Domini* 1623°. Text in Italian. MS. Bodl. Lib. Oxford, Add. A. 277. This contains games from Lopez in addition.

8. A MS. with the same title (ending *Mount-Stephen. 1623.*) and Italian text, now in Mr. J. G. White's library. This MS. adds games from Salvio.

9. A MS. with the same title (ending at the word *Calabria*), and Italian text, Brit. Mus., MS. Sloan 1937. The text is almost identical with that of No. 7.

10. A MS. with the same title as No. 9, in v. d. Lasa's library, which omits the Lopez games in No. 7.

These MSS. are—so far as the Greco games are concerned—practically identical. Nos. 7, 9, and 10 use red ink for the White moves, and black ink for the Black moves. From a less complete MS. of this group Beale obtained the games which he included in his *Royall Game of Chesse-Play: The study of Bioachimo, the famous Italian*, London, 1656.

[23] To the second French visit belong:

11. *Trattato sopra la nobilta del Gioco di Scacchi dove in esso contiene vn vero ritratto di Guerra et governo di stato diviso in sbaratti et partiti et gambetti et giochi ordinarii con tratti diversi belissimi. Composto per Gioacchino Greco Italiano Calavrese.* The date Parigi, 1624, occurs on ff. 6a and 146a. MS. Bibl. Nat. Paris, f. it., 952.

12. *Trattato del Nobilissimo et Militare Essercitio de Scacchi nel quale si contengono molti bellissimi tratti et la vera Scienza di esso gioco. Composto da Gioachino Greco Calabrese.* Contains §§ 1, 4. In Mr. J. G. White's library.

13. A MS. with the same title as No. 11, containing §§ 1, 2, 4, 5, 6, 7, 8, and on f. 163a the date Parigi, 1625. Now in v. d. Lasa's library.

14. A MS. without title, but with dedication to an unnamed Signor, and with the date, parigi 1624, on f. 3a. MS. Grenoble 2008.

15. *Il nobillissimo Gioco delli Scacchi.* MS. Orleans 481.

16. A MS. with the same title as No. 12, containing §§ 1, 4, 5, and the date 1625 on f. 22a. Bibl. Nat. Paris, f. it. 1378. A shortened text.

17. A MS. with the same title as No. 12, containing §§ 1, 2, 4, 5, 6, 7, 8, and the same text of the games as No. 16. Formerly in the possession of Mr. A. Samuda, now in Mr. J. G. White's library.

18. *Le Ieu des Eschecs de Ioachim Grec Calabrois.* A French translation of c. 1660, containing §§ 4 and 5. The date, Paris 1625, on p. 135, is taken from the Italian original. Now in Mr. J. G. White's library.

19. *Jeu deschets de Mr. Talon medicin* 1550 (read 1660), MS. Bibl. Nat. Paris, f. it. 1379, is an extract from a Greco MS. (MS. Bibl. Nat. Paris, f. fr. 14886, is a copy of the printed French edition.)

20. *Primo modo de Gioco de partito composto per Gioachimo Greco Calabrese*, MS. Nat. Lib. Lisbon, H. 1. 31, contains problems only.

[24] So Vespajo (50), correcting Salvio's statement that Marano had defeated Greco at the Spanish court. He quotes evidence to prove that Marano never played at this Court at all.

from Salvio) he uses the free castling which had become usual in Rome shortly before his time. The MSS. of his Roman period are in the main collections of Openings, not Games. In his English MSS. he begins to adapt his play to the rules of the country in which he was writing. Thus in one game (Bodl. Add. A. 277, f. 49 b) he takes a Pawn *in passing*, but in most of the games he still uses the free castling (in this MS. called *al modo Italiano*). It is only after the revision of 1624–5 that we find the normal non-Italian rules of castling (called for long in Italy *arroccamento alla Calabrista*, after Greco) adopted in his games throughout.

The Greco MSS. of the English and the second French visits are no longer collections of Openings only, but are collections of games in which the play is continued until the mate is reached or in sight. The concluding combinations are often extraordinarily brilliant and suggestive, although it must be admitted that they are often only possible as the result of weak moves on the opponent's part. A complete game appeals to a larger public than does analysis, however accurate, and it is to this novel feature of Greco's work that its instant and lasting popularity was due. The early MSS. of his games were treasured by their owners and their friends (in England the games were in the 'Delights' of King Charles I), and Francis Beale anticipated their displeasure when he published a selection of *Gambetts* from a MS., the fruit of Greco's English visit. The rearranged work of 1624–5 remained in MS. until 1669, when a French translation was published in Paris which has served as the original of all later editions, of which forty-one are known, in French, English, German, Dutch, Danish, and Italian.[25]

Greco's games are naturally based upon the favourite Italian Openings of his day, and it is hardly to be expected that he should have made any considerable addition to the large number of Openings that were then known. He is, however, our oldest authority for the Cunningham Gambit (approached in MS. Bonc. N. 3, f. 126 b, by 1 Pe4, Pe5; 2 Pf4, P×P; 3 Bc4, Be7; 4 Ktf3, Bh4+), and for 1 Pf4, Pe5; 2 P×P, Qh4+ (the Lorraine MS.). With the exception of these and a very few other games, Greco's later MSS. are made up from the traps in the Openings which were familiar to most Italian players, and from the Openings in the Polerio and other Roman MSS. These last he has continued to the mate by adding his unsound continuations and brilliant conclusions. Greco's great service to chess lies in the fact that he made this material known to a wider circle of players than Polerio and his contemporaries ever reached. In this way his MSS. became one of the most important productions in the literature of chess.

Both Salvio and Greco record with care the different local rules of chess existing in their day, and make it possible to continue the history of castling from the point at which I left it on p. 812.

[25] An excellent bibliography will be found in Prof. Hoffmann's *Games of Greco*, London, 1900, from the pen of Mr. J. A. Leon, a great authority on the early history and bibliography of the modern game.

In Rome the modern form of castling (Kg1 and Rf1; Kc1 and Rd1) had come into ordinary use by 1585. In the Roman MSS. of 1585–95 this move is described as *saltare* (vb., *salto*, n.) *in parte di Rè* (*Donna*) *come s'usa* or *all'ordinario*, or simply *saltare* (*salto*). Soon after 1600, possibly through Cascio's influence, the Roman players adopted the *free castling*, which permitted the Rook to be played to any square up to and including the K sq., and the King to be placed on any square on the other side of the Rook up to and including R sq. This form of castling is employed in all Greco's MSS. of his Roman period. The old power of leap to 'the third square' as Knight or Aufin or Rook survived alongside of the combined move, and the privilege of leaping or castling remained so long as the King was unmoved.

In Naples, Calabria, and Florence, the old leap of the King had been replaced (with the single exception that the unmoved King could leap once along the back row by himself after the Rook had moved by itself) by the free castling, with the additional limitation that a check deprived him of the power of castling at all. The usual term is *saltare* (*salto*), but Salvio (1604) also uses *arroccare*.

In Sicily and Genoa the King had no power of leaping (or castling) at all. Salvio (1634) adds that some Sicilian players were beginning to allow the King the Knight's leap for his first move.

In Milan, Turin, and Bologna, the Roman rule was followed, with the exception that the King's solitary leap was abandoned. In other parts of Italy the Roman rule was followed in its entirety.

The general tendency in Italy after Salvio's day was towards uniformity in the rules of castling, the free castling of the Roman players displacing the local variety. This took time: in Venice, players in 1665 were still playing Kh1, Re1, and Pg3 or h3 (cf. p. 812, note 3) as one move (Mortali, *Modo facile*, Venice, 1665). In 1683 Dr. Francesco Piacenza (*I Campeggiamenti degli Scacchi*, Turin) bemoans the existence of several errors and abuses in castling which he had seen committed by players: thus in Umbria players allowed the King in castling to cross over an attacked square; some Neapolitan players allowed the King to castle after he had been moved provided he had not received a check, other players allowed the King to leap as a Rook on the back row over the moved Rook as far as R sq. (see p. 38, Naples, &c.); in other parts players combined the free castling with Pg3 (or 4) or Ph3 (or 4) as a single move, and others castled in such a way that the Rook gave check or attacked a piece or Pawn. In the 18th c. the Modenese masters allowed free castling and also after a check had been received (Cozio says that this rule did not apply to Rome or Naples), provided the Rook did not as a result attack any man.[26] Cozio follows the practice of Savoy, castling as in France, but with the condition that the Rook did not attack any hostile man. All forbid the moving of a Pawn on the same move. The great

[26] That this was not forbidden in Salvio's day is seen from cap. iv of the 1604 work (the game which was described in *La Scaccaide*): 1 Pe4, Pe5; 2 Ktf3, Ktc6; 3 Bc4, Ktf6; 4 Ktg5, Pd5; 5 P×P, Kt×P; 6 Kt×P, K×Kt; 7 Qf3+, Ke6; 8 Ktc3, Kte7; 9 Kh1 and Re1 attacking the eP, &c.

reputation of the Modenese masters led to the general adoption of their rules in Italy, and free castling survived until the end of the nineteenth century in remote parts of Italy, although the influence of C. Salvioli and the chess magazine *La nuova Revista degli Scacchi* (1876–1903) had led to the adoption of all the ordinary European rules in all Italian chess clubs some twenty years earlier. The Rome Chess Club had made the change in 1877 (*BCM.*, 1895, 88).

In Spain, castling was of much later introduction. In all the Spanish games in the Roman MSS. the old leap is alone used, and the manœuvre Rf1 and Kg1 takes two moves to accomplish. Salvio says in 1604 that castling was still unknown in Spain, but in 1634 he was able to add that in some parts players had begun to play Rf1 and Kg1 or Rd1 and Kc1 as a single move.[27]

In France and England the modern form of castling was already in general use among the best players at the time of Greco's visits, and, although Greco makes no reference to it, the King's leap still survived in France, but not in England. There was in both countries a period during which players were a little uncertain as to the positions of the King and Rook after castling; in France this period came to an end before 1620, but in England it was prolonged as late as 1640, when Jo. Barbier, in republishing Arthur Saul's *Famous game of Chesse-play*,[28] found it necessary to be more explicit than Saul had been ('the standing of the King in his shifting (or changing) ought to be certaine, and not as you please to place him as some play it'), and gave the modern rule exactly.[29] The older solitary leap of the King is given in

[27] Gianutio states that castling was general in Spain in 1597, but he was probably mistaken. I do not consider him so reliable an authority as Salvio.

[28] Originally published in 1614, and based on no previous book. The work is more curious than useful, but its classification of the different mates deserves to be remembered. 'The Queenes mate, a gracious Mate. The Bishops Mate, a gentle Mate. The Knights Mate, a gallant Mate. The Rookes Mate, a forcible Mate. The Pawnes Mate, a disgracefull Mate. The Mate by discovery, the most industrious Mate of all. The Mate in a corner of the Field, Alexanders Mate. The Mate in the middest of the Field, an unfortunate Mate. The Mate on the side of the Field, a Cowards Mate. The Blind Mate (a mate which the winner does not see is mate), a shamefull Mate. The Stale, a dishonourable Mate. The Mate at two Draughts a Fooles Mate.' (Barbier, 1640, adds the *Schollars Mate*, 1 Pe4, Pe5; 2 Qh5, Ktc6: 3 Bc4, Pd6; 4 Q×P m.; 'The French calls it Le Mat du Bergier, the Shepherds Mate, as implying, if Peasants would be Chesse-players, such a Mate might a man soone give them.')

Saul regularly uses the name *Duke* in the place of *Rook*, a usage which was followed by Beale ('Rockes, Rookes or Dukes') and Randle Holme ('The Rooks . . . called also *Rocks* or *Dukes*'). There is an interesting allusion to this in the Induction to Middleton's *Game at Chess*:

> *Error*: Behold there's the full number of the game,
>   Kings and their Pawns, Queens, Bishops, Knights, and Dukes.
> *Ignorance*: Dukes? they're called Rooks by some.
> *Error*: Corruptedly;
>   *Le roc* the word, *custode de la roche*,
>   The keepers of the forts, in whom both Kings
>   Repose such confidence.

[29] The verb *castle* first occurs in Beale (1656). The earlier writers use *exchange* (Saul), *change* (Barbier, Beale), *leap* (Drummond), or *shift* (Barbier). *Leap* is used as an alternative for *castle* in Charles Jones's edition of *Hoyle's Games Improved*, 1775, and in all subsequent editions down to 1866, in Kenny's *Chess Grammar*, 1817, &c. In most other European languages a derivative of *Rook* (*rocco*, &c.) is used, e. g. Fr. roquer, roque (earlier sauter, saut); It. arroccare, arroccarsi (attorrarsi), arroccamento, arroccatura (attorramento); Sp. enrocar (vb.); Pg. rokar-se (vb.); Ger. rochiren, rochade (Allgaier has also rochen, rochgang); Du. rocheeren,

MS. Paris, Ars. 2891, f. 494 b, and in La Marinière's *Maison academique*, Paris, 1659, the original of a long succession of manuals or games, which were rarely brought up to date and were often a hundred years behind the times in their rules of chess.[30] Here, as in all the French editions of Greco's games from 1669 onwards, the leap is said to be out of fashion. Its last appearance in a work of any authority occurs in Asperling's *Traitté du Jeu Royal des Échets*, Lausanne, n. d., towards the end of the 17th c.[31]

The remaining points about which there were diversities of rule in different countries may be stated more briefly.

Taking in passing (*passar* or *non passar battaglia*). Outside Italy the player had the option of taking a Pawn in passing: in Italy a Pawn could not be taken in passing. The rule, given on p. 812, that a Pawn could not be played past the attack of a Pawn on the opponent's fifth rank to cover a check, is not mentioned in any later writer, but Asperling does not allow it in his analysis.[32]

Bare King (*robado*). The Spanish rule by which this ending was counted a half-win is mentioned by Salvio (1634), and apparently also by the Modenese writers (1760–80), as being still in existence.[3]

Stalemate. This was still reckoned as a half-win in Spain as late as 1600, but the rule became obsolete in the course of the next 150 years. In Italy and France (MS. Paris, Ars. 2891, f. 494 b, calls it *estre au marests*) stalemate was a drawn game. In England during the 17th and 18th cc. the player who gave stalemate lost the game. This rule appears first in Saul (1614), and was only abandoned as a result of Sarratt's influence in the new rules of the London Chess Club in 1808. It is given in Charles Jones's *Hoyle's Games Improved*, London, 1775, and, as the text of the chess portion of this work was still printed in 1866 with very little alteration, the rule may have been followed in out-of-the-way places almost to the end of the 19th c. V. d. Linde (*Leerboek*, 274) met an American in 1861 who still claimed that the stalemated King had won.

Pawn Promotion. In Spain and Italy in Greco's time the Pawn could only be promoted to the rank of Queen, and there was no limit to the number of Queens that a player could have at any moment. In France promotion was

rochade; Dan. rokkere, rokade; Sw. rokaden, roquera; Ic. hróka (rokkera, hrókskipta), hrókskipti; Cz. rochâda (sb.); Pol. rohuje, roszuje, rokowac; Croat. rohiráti, rohada, rošada; Russ. rokerovka; Finnish, rokeerata. Modern Gr. text-books give *μετατίθεσθαι* (but Contopoulos, *Lexicon Eng.-Gk.*, Athens, 1904, has the noun *ῥοκάρισμα*), and Hungarian books, elsanczolás.

[30] The account of the King's move is unchanged in all the French editions: it appears in the English adaptation, Seymour's *Court Gamester*, London, 1719, and in subsequent editions; and remained in the German versions until the Hamburg edition of 1760 of the *Neue Königliche L'Hombre* (in the 1791 edition the text was at last rewritten).

[31] This work (p. 11) distinguishes between the King's power to leap (*sauter*) alone, and to castle (*rocquer*). As examples of its use of the leap I quote ch. xvii: 1 Pe4, Pe5; 2 Ktf3, Pd6; 3 Bc4, Pf5; 4 Pd4, fP × P; 5 Ktg5, Pd5; 6 dP × P, P × B; 7 Q × Q +, K × Q; 8 Ktf7 +, Ke8; 9 Kt × R, Bf5; 10 *Ke3*, &c.

[32] Thus ch. i, 1 Pe4, Pe5; 2 Ktf3, Ktc6; 3 Bb5, Bd6; 4 Pc3, Ktf6; 5 Pd4, Kt × eP; 6 Qe2, Pf5; 7 P × P, Be7; 8 Ktd4, Pg6; 9 Kt × fP, P × Kt; 10 Qh5 +, Kf8; 11 Bh6 +, Kg8; 12 Bc4 m. Under the modern European rules 12 . . , Pd5 is possible.

[33] Ponziani and Lolli refer to a rule of some French players that a *blind mate* (see p. 832, n. 28) only counted as a half-win.

both limited and extended at an early date. In Estienne Pasquier's *Les Recherches de la France*, Paris, 1560, when a Pawn reaches the eighth rank—

En ce cas on les surroge au lieu des pieces d'honneur qui pour avoir este prises sont iettees hors le tablier.[34]

Greco does not mention this rule, but it is in La Marinière and his successors. The editions of Greco give the Italian rule, and we meet accordingly in the later manuals, which have combined the texts of the Greco games with that of La Marinière, with the contradiction that one part of the book limits promotion to the rank of Queen and allows the player to have as many Queens as he can make, while the other part only allows promotion to the rank of the best piece which has been lost. Philidor, who learnt his chess in the schools of Lopez and La Marinière, deplores in *L'Analyze* (1749) the custom of the French players who permitted a plurality of Queens.

This French rule was adopted by English players also. Saul apparently allows promotion to any rank without conditions:

And comming at the last in place
  Where Knights and Lords did dwell,
Their King shall give to them like grace,
  Because they serv'd him well.
Thus being Bishops Knights or Rookes
  Their King they'll better steed,
The Kings may make of them a Queene,
  If they have any need.

but later writers, e. g. Beale,[35] ruled that the promoted Pawn could only take the place of a captured piece. This rule is repeated in Lambe's *History of Chess*, London, 1764, and in all the later editions of *Hoyle*, beginning with Charles Jones's edition of 1775; the latest in which I have seen it is an edition of 1866. Unrestricted promotion was, however, certainly practised by English players from the time of Saul onwards. The writer of the *Letter to the Craftsman on the Game of Chess*, 1733, gives the rule of Pawn-promotion

[34] Pasquier alludes to two forms of odds-giving in the concluding paragraphs of this account of chess:

'Bien vous dirai-ie auoir veu vn Lyonnois oster toutes les pieces d'honneur, & ne retenir que le Roy avec ses Pions, desquels jouant deux fois contre vne, il rapportoit la victoire contre de tres-bons ioueurs. Je lui ay veu mettre vn anneau sur vn Pion, sous ceste stipulation qu'il ne pourroit Mater le Roy qu'auecques ce Pion; vne autre fois passer plus outre, & mettre encores vn anneau autour d'vn Pion de son aduersaire, a la charge qu'il le forceroit de la Mater auecques ceste piece; & en l'vn & l'autre ieu rapporter victoire de son opinion, contre vn homme qui n'estoit point mis au rang des petits ioueurs.'

The former game is included in the mediaeval MS. Arch. (see Arch. 28), and both are given in MS. Per., and are described in Carrera, the first, p. 263, the second, p. 259; whence in Staunton's *Chess Player's Companion* (London, 1849), pp. 384 and 388. J. Mendheim of Berlin (D. 1836) and the Rev. C. E. Ranken (D. 1905) were noted for their skill in playing the first game.

[35] Beale says, 'You may immediately make him a Queen, or what piece you have already lost, yea in forraigne Countries, and amongst the best players here, you may have two or three Queens at a time'. Drummond of Hawthornden (*Works*, 1655, 253) says, 'When they can win and ascend the furthest part of the Chesse-bord on the Sunney side, as the first which mount a breach, in this case they are surrogated in those void Rooms of the pieces of honour, which because they suffered themselves to be taken, were removed off the Boord.' This account of chess is simply a free translation of that given by Pasquier, and was presumably out of date when Drummond appropriated it.

in its present form, while the Chess Club at Parsloe's adopted this rule in their code which was published in the 1790 edition of Philidor's *Analysis*:

> Every Pawn which has reached the eighth or last square of the chess-board, is entitled to make a Queen, or any other Piece that shall be thought proper; and this, even when all the Pieces remain on the chess-board.

The London Club adopted the rule in their code of 1808, re-wording it, and although Pratt and W. S. Kenny—the latter as late as 1824 (*Chess Grammar,* 1817, 1818, 1823, *Chess Exercises,* 1818, 1824)—refused to recognize the rule of the chess clubs, they were powerless to prevent its general adoption.[36]

In Italy, Piacenza (1683) upholds the older rule limiting promotion to the rank of the Queen, and includes the practice of some players of promoting to any rank among the errors and abuses of the game. At a later date the practice of Italian players changed, and the Modenese masters state the rule thus: 'The Pawn is promoted at the choice of the player to the rank of any piece that has been lost.' This rule remained in force until the closing years of the 19th century.

Neither Salvio nor Greco have anything to say about the chess rules of Germany or Iceland, and I defer all discussion of the special features of these forms of chess until I deal with the earlier history of the modern games in these countries.

The fifty years which ended with the death of Greco are not without importance in the history of the chess problem, though the brilliance of the game throughout this period tends for us to throw the problem into the background. That Polerio included a selection of problems in his MSS., and that the other collections described on pp. 822–3 were made during these fifty years, shows that the taste for the problem was not entirely dormant. These collections show, however, that that taste was slowly changing its character. With the death of the mediaeval game, the bulk of the problems so laboriously collected by Bonus Socius and Civis Bononiae became obsolete. The attempt which was made, for instance by the author of *Bonc. 2*, to save the material which was valid under the reformed rules, or to adapt older problems to the new rules,[37] was in the main unsuccessful; the problems which hit the popular fancy in Italy from 1580 to 1600 were the conditional problems in which the mate is given by a Pawn after a number of checks had been given by other Pawns. All but one of Rotilio Gracco's problems are of this type, and 74 of the 108 in *Bonc. 2* are of this kind. The more Pawns took part in the checks, the better was the problem appreciated. This meant a great increase in the average length of the solution: in Gracco the solutions are in from 5 to 35 moves, and average 15 moves; in *Bonc. 2* the average length of the

[36] An English code of rules of 1862 proposed to allow a player to refuse to promote his Pawn at all on reaching the eighth rank. This absurdity has been justly condemned by the common sense of players. It has not the slightest historical justification.

[37] Such positions in *Bonc. 2* are 20 (CB 185), 21 (207), 35 (168), 44=51 (114), 52 (96), 57 (125), 61 (127), 62 (128), 64 (136), 66 (156), 68 (158), 72 (53), 73 (164), 74 (96), 75 (99), 76 (102), 78 (103), 80–82 (106–108), 83 (113), 84 (131), 85 (144), 86 (147), 87 (151), 88–90 (142–4), 91–96 (168–173), 97 (175), 98 (179), 99 (181), 100 (188), 101 (195), 103 (203), 104 (206), 105 (208), 106 (279), 107 (25). The sequences are suggestive.

solution is 8 moves. The problems of this type are very artificial, and have little value for the practical game. They tend to be monotonous, for the apparent difficulty is commonly enhanced by blocking the advance of the Pawn with which the mate is to be given by an opposing Pawn, which has to be compelled to vacate the file by a compulsory capture. The one good service which this type of problem performed was to kill the unsound or wager problem of the Middle Ages. The deliberately unsound problem disappeared during this period.

The following problems from Rotilio Gracco may serve as examples of the favourite Italian problem from 1580 to 1600.

Gracco 2.

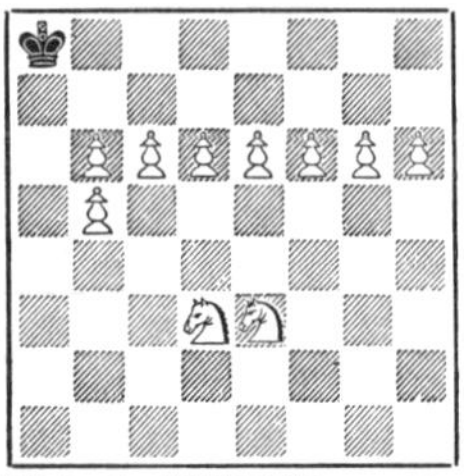

Mate in XXVIII exactly with the Pawn, after checking with all the Pawns, five separately, and three consecutively.

Gracco 11.

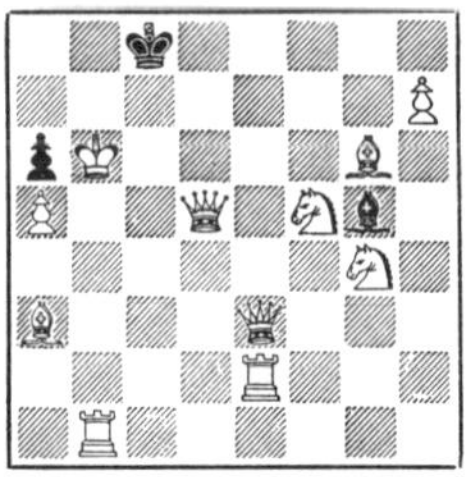

Mate in XXI exactly with the Pawn, after sacrificing all the other men.

Gracco 20.

Mate in XX exactly with the two Pawns. The Bl. Pawns are fidated.

Solutions.—2. 1 Ktd5; 2 Ktc7; 3 Ktc5; 4 Ktd7; 5 Ktd5; 6 Kte7; 7 Kte5; 8 Ktf7; 9 Ktf5; 10 Ktg7; 11 Ph7+; 12 Ktf5; 13 Kte7; 14 Pg7+; 15 Kte5; 16 Ktd7; 17 Pf7+; 18 Ktd5; 19 Ktc7; 20 Pe7+; 21 Ktc5; 22 Ktb7; 23 Pd7+; 24 Ktd5; 25 Ktc5; 26 Pc7+; 27 Pb7+; 28 Pb6 m.

11. 1 Rc2+; 2 Rc8+; 3 Qa8+; 4 Ktf6+; 5 Qd5+; 6 Q(e3)e6+; 7 Q(e6)d6+; 8 Kte7+; 9 Qd7+; 10 Bd6+; 11 Qa8+; 12 Qc8+; 13 Rb5; 14 Pa6; 15 Ph8=Q; 16 Qh5; 17 Qb5; 18 Be4+; 19 Qd5+; 20 Qb7+; 21 P×Q m.

20. 1 Bc1; 2 Bb6; 3 Bg7; 4 Rh1; 5 Qd7+; 6 Bh8; 7 Rh6; 8 Ktb4; 9 Rf6+; 10 Rf3; 11 Kta6; 12 Qb7; 13 Bg7; 14 Bh6; 15 Ktb4; 16 Ktc6+; 17 Ktd5; 18 Qc8+; 19 Pe6+; 20 Pe5 m.

This phase in the development of the problem soon lost its exaggerated character. Although Polerio reserved the superlative 'bellissimo' for problems of this type, they only form a small portion of his material, and none of the 40 problems in the Toulouse and Paris (It. 948) MSS. are in more than VII moves. Some of his 'Subtleties' were drawn from actual play, and problems of like origin form the bulk of the new material which Salvio included in his books. Many of these positions are what we should now call End-games, since only a few pieces are concerned, and the demonstration of the win or draw, and not a mate in a definite number of moves, is the exercise set the solver. The important thing is that these players in this way reasserted the Muslim convention that the problem must be possible in the sense that it might have been the termination of a real game. All succeeding problemists have observed this convention.

CHAPTER XIII

FROM GRECO TO STAMMA

Chess in Italy, 1630–1730.—In France and England, 1550–1700.—Asperling.—Cunningham.—Caze.—The Coffee-houses.—Bertin.—Stamma.—Hoyle.—Chess in Germany, 1500–1790.—In Sweden, Denmark, &c.—In Iceland.—Four-handed chess.

WITH Salvio the first great creative period in the history of the modern game came to an end. For the next hundred years we hear comparatively little of Italian chess, though it would be a mistake to think that this paucity of information meant that chess was not played as enthusiastically as ever. The game was probably just as popular with all classes of Italian society, only no player of outstanding ability arose to take the place of the earlier masters, and the inventive and literary activities of players had for the time spent themselves.[1] The small Venetian tract, *Modo facile per intendere il vago e dilettevole Giuoco degli Scacchi; composto da un' Incognito* (probably Valentino Mortali) *per li novizzi del Giuoco*, 1665, is on a far lower level than the works of Salvio, Carrera, or even Tarsia, and the more ambitious work of Dr. Francesco Piacenza, the already quoted *I Campeggiamenti degli Scacchi, o sia nuova disciplina d'attachi, difese, e partiti del giuoco degli Scacchi* . . , Turin, 1683, does not advance the science of the game in the very least. Piacenza appears from his own account[2] to have been a strong player, but he only devotes two chapters to the Openings, and in neither does he carry his analysis beyond the first three or four moves. He does not even mention the Openings beginning 1 Pe4, and confines his attention to what he calls the *sgambetto*, 1 Pd4, and the *fianchetti*, 1 Pc4 and 1 Pf4, the last being slightly inferior.[3] The value of this part of his book may be inferred from his quoting two sayings with approval, 'ante reginam noli movere pedinam' (prompted by the dread of losing the right to castle as a result of an early check from the Queen on a4 (a5)), and 'chi non s'arroca, perderà sempre'. He also expresses the opinion that it is safer to castle on the Queen's wing than on the King's.

The remainder of Piacenza's work is taken up with a discussion of various handicaps which a player may give himself by undertaking to mate with a particular piece, or on a particular square, or both combined, and by an

[1] In Spain the position was far less favourable for chess. We hear nothing of the game until the nineteenth century, and the humble position which chess fills in Spanish life at the present time would seem to point to a rapid decline in the popularity of chess after 1650.

[2] He gives the names of many players whom, to their surprise, he had beaten at different odds. The most interesting are two German players, Sr. di Casa Hox of Basel, and Sr. Rainbold of Augsburg, with whom he played when in Germany as Secretary to the Spanish ambassador. He seems to have played chess in most of the Italian towns.

[3] The modern use of the term *Fianchetto* dates from Lolli (621). Ponziani (ed. 1782, 7, 109, 110) still calls every Opening in which a wing Pawn opens, a Fianchetto, e.g. not only 1 Pe4, Pb6; but also 1 Pf4 and 1 Pc4.

account of a new chess of his own invention. This game, to which he gives the name of *arciscacchiere*, was to be played on a board of 10 × 10 squares with the ordinary chessmen (Kf1 and f8), and two extra pieces and two extra Pawns on each side. The pieces were a Centurion (placed on d1, d10), leaping to any third sq., e.g. from d1 to b3, d3, &c., and a Decurion (placed on g1, g10), with the original move of the mediaeval Queen.

There was a flourishing chess academy in Naples in the first half of the 18th c., of which Benedetto Rocco (*Giuoco degli Scacchi agli oziosi*, Naples, 1783) has preserved some particulars. The leading player was D. Scipione del Grotto (D. 1723), a priest from Salerno, who turned to chess after losing a large sum of money at cards and dice, and attained a high level of skill: in 1718 he defeated the English Admiral Byng, who visited Naples after the destruction of the Spanish fleet off Cape Passaro. Carmine Pagano of Caserta (D. *c.* 1733); Ludovico Lupinacci of Cosenza (D. 1732), who defeated a boastful French player in a match of 11 games after deliberately losing the first 5 games; D. Luigi Cigliarano, a priest from Cosenza, whose fame was said to have exceeded that of Greco; and Stefano Battiloro (D. 1754), a Piedmontese player who was unrivalled in his Pawn-play, may also be named. As usual, the keenness of the chess life resulted in renewed literary activity. M. Aurelio Severino published *La Filosofia degli Scacchi* in 1690, and is said to have had a share in the reissue of Salvio's work of 1634, with some additions,[4] in 1723, while Filippo Marinelli published in *Il Giuoco degli Scacchi fra tre*, Naples, 1722, an account of a derivative form of chess for three players, which he had invented.[5]

Chess was certainly no less popular in France and England in the second half of the 16th century than in Italy; but the general level of play was lower, because players had to depend almost entirely upon their own personal

[4] Viz. (1) *Nuova Aggiunta*, 139–46 (one game—in Lewis's *Letters on Chess from C. F. Vogt*, 44, attributed in error to Salvio—and five End-games); (2) a reprint of the *Modo facile*, 147–153, mentioned above; and (3) *Aggiunta fatta da un' altro incognito*, 153–8, who urges that an unmoved King should be allowed to castle after a check and with an attack, and that no Pawn should be queened so long as the original Queen was untaken.

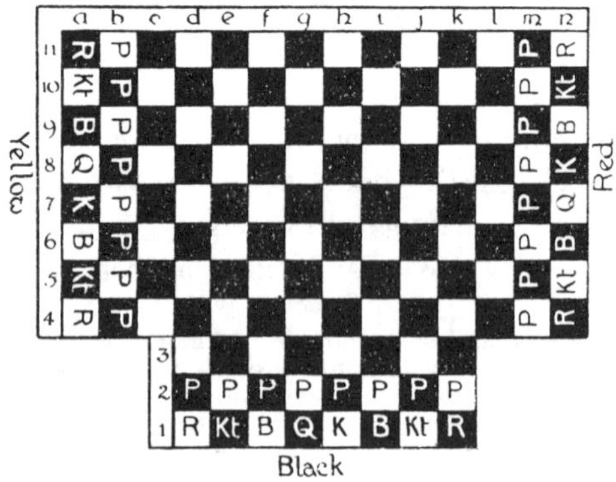

[5] The arrangement of the board is shown in the diagram. The move passes to the player's right, and all play against all. The Yellow Pawns queen on the n-file, the Red on the a-file, and the Black on the 11th row. If a Yellow or Red Pawn arrived at the Black's back row,

experience for their knowledge of chess tactics. The incomplete translations of Damiano's work can hardly have been very helpful. The game was played regularly at both Courts until the middle of the 17th century at least. In France, Catherine de' Medici (D. 1589) was a keen player, whose ambition (according to Carrera, 94) it was to meet Paolo Boi. Henri IV played chess, and Louis XIII had a 'board' of wool with spiked pieces made for use when travelling (Hyde, ii. 79). So late as 1680, Henri-Jules de Bourbon, the son of the great Condé, held a chess academy, and the Condé Museum at Chantilly contains three MS. collections of Openings which were prepared for his use. In England, Queen Elizabeth played with Roger Ascham[6] and others; and although James I used his ponderous wit to decry chess,[7] both his sons played, and the messenger who brought to Charles I the news of his approaching surrender by the Scots to the Parliament, in 1647, found him seated at the chessboard.[8] The game was very popular with the nobility and gentry in these reigns, and was cordially disliked by the Puritans. Rowbothum dedicated his translation of Gruget to Robert Dudley, Earl of Leicester, because he was a chess-player;[9] Saul dedicated his *Famous game of Chesse-play,* which is 'fit for Princes or any person of quality soever', to Lucy, Countess of Bedford; and Fr. Beale his *Royall Game of Chesse-Play* to Montague, Earl of Lindsey, while the printer heads the list of errata with the

or a Black Pawn at the Yellow or Red's back files, it became dead and could not move, but might be captured. When a player was mated (which could only be done by a single adversary, not by a combined attack), his pieces became also dead, but might be captured. Marinelli played the game in 1722, and interested Prince Eugene of Savoy in it.

6 Roger Ascham, *Works*, ed. Bennett, who adds a Life of the author, in which he says that in the beginning of the Queen's reign, Ascham acted as Latin Secretary, and 'sometimes played with her at Draughts and Chess'. Edmund Bohun, *Character of Queen Elizabeth,* mentions chess among her recreations. (Twiss, *Misc.*, 16.) Elizabeth gave Sir Charles Blount (afterwards Lord Mountjoy) 'a Queen at *Chesse* of gold richly ennameled', which he wore on his arm with a crimson ribbon, as a token of her favour after he had distinguished himself at tilting (Sir Robert Naunton, *Fragmenta Regalia,* 1641, 33).

7 'As for the Chesse, I think it ouer fond, because it is ouer-wise and Philosophicke a folly: for where all such light playes are ordained to free mens heades for a time, from the fashious thoughts on their affaires; it by the contrarie filleth and troubleth mens heades, with as many fashious toyes of the play, as before it was filled with thoughts on his affaires.' *Works* (Basilicon Doron), London, 1616. In a speech to Parliament in 1609, he compared the royal prerogative to the promotion of the Pawn in chess; Kings 'have power to exalt low things, and abase high things, and make of their subjects like men at Chess; a Pawne to take a Bishop or a Knight, and to cry up or down any of their subjects.' Lord Bacon, in his essay on *Boldness,* has 'with bold men, upon like occasion, they stand at a stay, like a stale at chess, where it is no mate, but yet the game cannot stir'; and in his *Apologie,* 'I know at Chesse a Pawn before the King is ever much plaid upon.'

8 Charles I's fondness for chess is also shown in a letter from York of Lewis Boyle, quoted in Fell Smith's *Mary Rich, Countess of Warwick,* 'The King when he is neither in the field . . . nor at the Council, passes most of his time at chess with the Marquis of Winchester. Some three days since, the King long studying how to play a Bishop, the Marquis of Winchester blurted out, "See, Sir, how troublesome these Bishops are in jest and earnestly." The King replied nothing, but looked very grim.'

Charles's elder brother, Prince Henry, 'would sometimes play at chesse' [in the printed edition of 1641, 17, printed as *obesse*—whence as a ghost-word in dictionaries], 'at biliors, and at cards' (Sir Ch. Cornwallis, *Dis. Pr. Henry,* in *Archaeologia,* xiv. 253), and his wardrobe accounts contain the entry, 'a little box with chessmen, 6*s*.' (*Archaeologia,* xi. 93).

9 In his *Epistle dedicatorie* he says, 'I knowe that bothe your Lordship with diuers other of ye noble men and gentlemen of this realme can play excellently at this game of ye Cheast, and haue as deepe knowledge therein as either French men, Italians or Spaniardes haue'.

'In Cardiff castle', says Twiss (*Misc.*, 18), 'is a picture painted on wood, with a date, 1562, representing the family of the Lord Windsor, at that period. The Father and Mother are playing at chess.'

request, 'Gentlemen, for few else will buy this book, I entreat you to correct these errors.' A MS. note in the Ashmolean copy of John Blagrave's (D. 1611) *Mathematical Jewel*, London, 1585, commemorates the author's brother, Alexander Blagrave, as 'the excellent Chess-player in England', and a note in the *Aubrey Letters*, iii. 503, preserves the name of Col. Bishop, who was reputed to be the best English player in the reign of James I.[10]

There are many allusions to chess in the Elizabethan and Stuart drama, but few show more than a superficial knowledge of chess.[11] The most considerable, perhaps, are to be found in Thomas Middleton's play, *A Game at Chess*, which was performed at the Globe Theatre in 1624, and printed shortly afterwards. In this play, which was written when all Englishmen were rejoicing in the breakdown of the negotiations for Prince Charles's Spanish marriage, the Church of Rome in general, and Gondemar, the Spanish ambassador, in particular, were satirized, and the play had to be withdrawn after the ninth performance, as a result of Gondemar's protest. Although it ran for so short a time, it had drawn crowds, and it was necessary to be at the theatre two hours before the play commenced in order to gain admission. The receipts for the nine performances amounted to £1,500, an extraordinary sum for those days. The players were summoned before the Privy Council, and, according to one account, Middleton himself was committed to prison for a time.

There are many other references to chess in the polemical literature of the time, as in *Pap with a Hatchet*, London, 1589, in the Marprelate controversy:

> If a Martin can play at Chestes as well as the nephewe his Ape, he shall knowe what it is for a Scaddle pawne, to crosse a Bishop in his owne walke. Such dydoppers must be taken up, els theile not stick to check the King.

And in Harington's *Nugae Antiquae* (Park), ii. 243, a work in which chess is mentioned several times:

> The play of chesse . . . may teach that the bishops due place is nearest the king, and though some knight can leape better over the pawnes heads, yet oft-times he leaps short, where the bishops powre, if you crosse it, reacheth the length of the whole province.[12]

All this points to a general acquaintance with the main features of chess, but to little knowledge of its finer features, and Greco's style of play must have come as a great revelation to the players who were fortunate enough to see him play. Unfortunately, however, his collection of games had the serious drawback that the games were not annotated, and neither the MSS.

[10] 'Dr. Potter, a good chess-player. Col. Bishop, his contemporary at Trinity (Oxford), accounted the best in England. I have heard Potter' [mat. Trinity, 8 July 1613, M.A. 26 June 1616, B.D. 8 July 1625, Rector of Kilmington, Somerset, 1626, till death in April 1678] 'say they two have played at Trin. Coll. (I think two days together) and neither got the mastery.'

[11] Thus in *Sir Gyles Goosecap*, iv, occurs: '*R.* 'Tis time to leave your Chests, ladies, 'tis too studious an exercise after dinner. *T.* Why is it called Chests? *H.* Therefore they leane uppon their chests that play at it. *T.* I would have it call'd the strife of wittes, for tis a game so wittie that with strife for maisterie wee hunt it eagerly.'

[12] In the *Phoenix Nest*, 1593, is a poem of twelve six-lined stanzas on *The Game of Chess*, by Nicholas Breton, which deals with the game in a very superficial manner.

nor any of the early printed editions attempted to explain the principles of play which the games illustrated. The result was that Greco's games appeared to the next few generations of players as brilliant *tours de force*, rich in suggestion for the treatment of certain positions in the Mid-game, but often dangerous as a model for the Opening, because the player could not grasp the intention of the play.

On the whole, the English player was in a worse plight than the French. The latter had at least abbreviated editions of Lopez (Paris, 1609, 1615, 1636, 1674, and Bruges, 1665), and La Marinière's Manual; the Englishman had only Saul (1614, 1618, and Barbier's editions of 1640, 1652, 1672, 1673, 1676), who denied the possibility of any theory of the game at all, and confined his analysis to the proof that the game 1 Pe4, Pe5; 2 Ktf3, Ktf6; 3 Kt × P, Kt × P; 4 Qe2, Ktf6; 5 Ktc6 +, winning the Q, was not unpreventible as some maintained.[13] Even as late as the end of the century Randle Holme (*Academy of Armory*, 1688, III, v. 263; and more fully in the MS. of 1681–2 printed by the Roxburghe Club, 1905, II, iii. 66) only deals with the barest elements of the game, and knows nothing of castling or pawn-promotion.[14]

On the other hand, the closing years of the century saw the publication by the Oxford University Press of Hyde's *Mandragorias seu Historia Shahiludii* (1694), the first really scientific contribution to the history of chess. A second volume, with the title *Historia Nerdiludii*, treated in a similar way of other Oriental games. The author, Thomas Hyde (B. 1634, D. 1702), was one of the first Oriental scholars of his age, and was successively Professor of Hebrew and of Arabic in the University, in addition to filling the position of Bodley's Librarian from 1665 until 1701. He used his vast knowledge of Arabic literature to establish the Indian origin of chess, and, although no chess-player himself, the careful use which he made of his authorities, and the copious extracts which he gives, make his work of great value even at the present time. No greater praise can be given to him than that which Nöldeke gave when he described him as 'der, nicht bloss für seine Zeit, wunderbar gelehrte, und dabei sehr verständig urtheilende Hyde' (*Pers. Studien*, II, in *Sitzungsber. d. k. Ak. d. Wissenschaften*, Vienna, 1892, cxxvi, xii).

That the standard of French chess was improving in the latter part of the 17th century is clear from the publication of the undated *Traitté du Ieu royal des Echets . . . par B. A. D. R. G. S.*, Lausanne, published by David Gentil somewhere between 1675 and 1700. A MS. note in a contemporary hand in Mr. J. G. White's copy of this work solves the riddle of the formidable array of initials, and shows that they stand for B. Asperling de Raroyne, Garde Suisse, thus confirming the tradition current at the end of the 18th century that a M. de Sperlin had published a work on chess at Lausanne

[13] He prevents this mate by 1 Pe4, Pe5; 2 Ktf3, Ktc6 or Qe7. Barbier adds the *Scholar's Mate*, and advises the player to play 1 Pe3 as the safest preparation for inflicting this mate!

[14] The 1688 text begins, 'Chess is a Royall Game, and more difficult to be understood then any other Game whatsoever, and will take vp some time in the Playing; Artists at the Game, have Played a Fortnight by times before it hath been ended.' Among the terms defined are *forke* or *dilemma*, *stale*, *blind mate*, *dead game* (= a draw), *scholar's mate*, and *remove* (= move).

about 1690.[15] Asperling must have been a strong player, and a remark on p. 7 of the *Traitté* shows that he was able to play the game blindfold. The special feature of his work is that it attempts for the first time to arrange the analysis of the Openings in an orderly manner, classifying the Openings in five groups (1) 1 Pd4, (2) irregular defences to 1 Pe4, (3) Openings beginning 1 Pe4, Pe5, in which White does not attack the King's Pawn on the second move, (4) the King's Gambits, and (5) the King's Knight's Openings.[16] His games—

> sont tirées en partie du livre Espagnol (i.e. Lopez), en partie de l'Italien de Ioachimo le Calabrois, & la plus part de mon invention.

Asperling, however, overestimates his own work; about half of his games are taken direct from Lopez or Greco, and in another quarter his alterations only relate to the concluding moves. His own contributions to the theory of the Openings are a new defence to the Queen's Gambit (1 Pd4, Pd5; 2 Pc4, P×P; 3 Pe3, *Qe6*, which Kieseritzky rediscovered in 1846, see *Sch.*, 1846, 11), some minor variations in the French Defence (1 Pe4, Pe6; 2 Pd4, Ktf6; 3 Bd3, Ktc6; 4 Ktf3, *Bb4*+ or *Pg6*), the Queen's Pawn Counter Gambit (1 Pe4, Pe5; 2 Ktf3, *Pd5*), a defence to the Ruy Lopez (1 Pe4, Pe5; 2 Ktf3, Ktc6; 3 Bb5, Bd6), and some considerable additions to the Philidor Defence, in which he strengthened the attack by 1 Pe4, Pe5; 2 Ktf3, Pd6; 3 Bc4, Pf5; 4 *Pd4*. The early Italian players never advanced the Queen's Pawn thus until the way had been prepared by a previous Pc3 (Pc6), and this move represents a new idea in the theory of the Opening. Asperling's treatment of the King's Gambit is very inferior, and shows hardly any advance on Lopez.

Apart from the recognition of the utility of an early advance of the Queen's Pawn, whether for the attack or the defence, Asperling's work belongs to the school of Lopez. It is from this player ultimately that he obtained the idea of further investigations into the two Openings, the Ruy Lopez and the Philidor, to which he devotes most attention; it is probable that these were the favourite Openings of the better French players of the period, who founded their play upon the French editions of Lopez.

Asperling draws a distinction between check and mate. Just as the term *check* by itself does not imply a mate, so the term *mate* by itself, he says, does not imply a check. In this way he explains that the *échec suffoqué*, for which he prefers the term *pat* (our stalemate) is a mate, though not a checkmate. This ending is drawn.

Asperling also gives 36 maxims which he held it is necessary that everybody who aspired to be a good player should know. These are partly borrowed

[15] Or did Asperling publish another work under his own name? Egerton's catalogue, 1798, contains the item '7713. *Du Jeu des Échets* par Sperlin, imperfect, 2*s.* 6*d.*'; Twiss (i. 83) has '*Le Jeu des Échets*, composé par M. de Sperlin, Lausanne, n.d., 12mo, pp. 120'; and George Walker (New Treatise, 1841, 286) has 'Sperlin. *Essai sur le Jeu des Échets*, composé par M. de Sperlin, Lausanne, 1698, 12mo, pp. 190.' The *Traitté* (generally known to chess-players as the *Traitté de Lausanne*) is an octavo of 112 pages.

[16] These names are the modern ones. Asperling has only a name for the Gambit.

from Lopez, partly original. The eleventh warns a player against castling too soon; the player should secure the option of castling on either wing, and keep his adversary in suspense as long as possible as to which form of castling he intends to adopt. This advice is rather feeble. The thirteenth maxim says that good players usually play Pc3 in order to prepare for Qb3 and Pd4. Other maxims warn the player against acquiring too great a fondness for his Queen. He should exchange whenever anything is to be gained by exchanging. 'Qui néglige ses avantages mérite de perdre.'

We also possess in the *Caze MS.*, described below, a collection of 17 King's Gambits played by the best Parisian players about 1680, which formed a part of a larger collection, now lost, of 200 games which Caze recorded at that time. Many of these games were played between groups of players, those on each side consulting together. The players whose games are preserved are the Abbés de Lionne and de Feuquières, MM. Jannisson, Maubisson, Lafon l'aisné, Lafon le jeune, Roussereau, Morant, maître des requêtes, de Pennautier, Auzout, and de Villette Murcey. Caze recorded no games played by M. Nicolai, premier president de la Chambre des comptes de Paris, because this player objected to his games being taken down. As late as 1850 many players disliked the recording of their games, from a fear that their chess reputations would suffer if other players had the chance of examining their combinations afterwards.

I have selected three games from this MS. for reproduction. The first was played between M. Lafon l'aisné (White) and M. Roussereau, the second between M. Lafon le jeune (White) and M. Maubisson, and the third was played between MM. Maubisson and Morant [17] (White) and MM. L'Abbé de Lionne and Auzout.

I.

White	Black
1 Pe4	Pe5
2 Pf4	P × P
3 Ktf3	Pg5
4 Ph4	Pg4
5 Kte5	Ph5
6 Bc4	Kth6
7 Pd4	Pd6
8 Ktd3	Qe7
9 Ktc3	Ktf5
10 B × P	Kt × hP
11 Qd2	Ktg6
12 0–0–0	Pc6
13 hRf1	Be6
14 Bg5	Q × B
15 Q × Q	Bh6
16 Q × B	R × Q
17 B × B	P × B
18 Rf6	Kd7
19 Ktf4	Kt × Kt
20 R × R	Resigns

II.

White	Black
1 Pe4	Pe5
2 Pf4	P × P
3 Ktf3	Pg5
4 Bc4	Pg4
5 0–0	P × Kt
6 Q × P	Qf6
7 Pc3	Ktc6
8 Pd4	Kt × P
9 Qd3	Kte6
10 Ktd2	Bd6
11 Ktf3	Kte7
12 Bd2	Pb6
13 dRe1	Be5
14 B × Kt	fP × B
15 Kt × B	Q × Kt
16 B × P	Qg7
17 B × P	Rg8
18 Qh3	Ba6
19 Rf3	Qg5
20 eRe3	Qc5
21 Bg3	Be 2
22 Bf2	B × R
23 R × B	Qd6
24 Rd3	Qf4
25 Qh5 +	Ktg6
26 Be3	Q × eP
27 Qb5	Kte4
	wins

III.

White	Black
1 Pe4	Pe5
2 Pf4	P × P
3 Bc4	Qh4 +
4 Kf1	Pg5
5 Ktf3	Qh5
6 Ph4	Bg7
7 Pd4	Ph6
8 Kf2	Qg6
9 Qd3	Pd6
10 Ktc3	Pc6
11 Pd5	Ktd7
12 Pb4	Kte5
13 Kt × Kt	B × Kt
14 Bd2	Ktf6
15 aRe1	Pg4
16 P × P	P × P
17 Pb5	Pg3 +
18 Kg1	Pc5
19 Ktd5	Kt × Kt
20 Q × Kt	Rb8
21 Ph5	Qf6
22 Ba5	Bd4 +
23 Kf1	0–0
24 Bc7	Be6
25 Pe5	B × Q
26 P × Q	B × B +
27 Re2	bRe8
28 B × P	R × R
29 B × R	Re4 mate.

17 M. Morant won the following short game with M. l'Abbé de Feuquières, who had adopted one of Ruy Lopez's defences to the Gambit: 1 Pe4, Pe5; 2 Pf4, P × P; 3 Ktf3, Kte7;

In the early eighteenth century, chess-players from all parts of Europe were attracted to the Hague by the fame of a great Scotch player, Alexander Cunningham, who was resident there from 1710 to 1730. There has been much discussion as to the identity of this player, for there were two Alexander Cunninghams living at the time, both chess-players, and both at times resident at the Hague. These were Alexander Cunningham of Block (B. 1650–60, D. 1730), the critic and opponent of Bentley,[18] and Alexander Cunningham (B. 1654, D. 1737), the author of a valuable Latin history of his times which was translated and published by Dr. William Thomson in 1787.[19] It has been generally assumed that all the references to chess which occur in Thomson's Life of Cunningham prefixed to the History, as well as those which occur elsewhere,[20] really relate to the critic, not the historian; but the solution is not so simple. The critic does not appear to have settled in the Hague before 1710, and was resident in Edinburgh from 1698 to 1709; the historian, on the other hand, must have been in the Hague, if at all, before 1707. Now Mr. J. C. White possesses a MS. volume on the King's Gambit, formerly in the Blenheim Library, which was written by a M. Caze,[21] and was given

4 Pd4, Pg5; 5 Kt×P, Ktg6; 6 Ph4, Bg7; 7 Bc4, 0–0; 8 Qh5, Ph6; 9 Q×Kt, P×Kt; 10 P×P, Re8; 11 Q×P mate.

18 The critic was probably educated in Holland and at Edinburgh, was tutor until 1693 to a son of the Duke of Queensberry, obtained through the Duke's influence the Professorship of Civil Law at the University of Edinburgh about 1698, a post which he held until 1710, when advantage was taken of the Duke's loss of influence to deprive him of it, and retired in 1710 to the Hague, where he spent the rest of his life with a handsome pension from the Duke. See *Dict. Nat. Biog.* for fuller particulars.

19 The historian was educated at Selkirk and in Holland, was tutor to James, afterwards Earl of Hyndford, 1692–5, and to the Marquess of Lorne (later the great Duke of Argyll), 1697–1700. He was in Rome in 1700, in Paris on a political mission 1700–2, and in Hanover in 1703. He was tutor to Lord Lonsdale in 1711, and British Minister in Venice 1715–20, retiring with a pension in 1720, and living in London until his death in 1737 (see *Dict. Nat. Biog.*). He was, accordingly, intimately connected with the Argyll family, and owed his career to that interest.

20 The references in Thomson's Life are collected in Twiss, i. 121–7. The first merely states that Cunningham played chess in the latter part of his life (this was probably true of both persons); the second that 'Dr. Steuart used often to play with him, at Lord Islay's, at the game of Chess, which he understood better than any man in England, in his time.' (Since Lord Islay was a Campbell, the fact relates to the historian; the opinion may be due to a confusion of the two Cunninghams); the third that 'Cunningham was domesticated with Lord Sunderland and the Duke of Argyle' (this can only be the historian); the fourth relates to the games with Lord Sunderland at the Hague (the historian); and the last says that 'Cunningham, the critic, and editor of Horace, was the best player at Chess in Europe'. Other references occur (1) in the *Life of Prof. Wodrow*, Edinb., 1828, 174, we are told that Wodrow played chess about 1700 with his old friend Cunningham of Block, 'the first player in Europe', and was told by Cunningham that he could give him Rook and Bishop, and possibly the Queen, and yet win. (2) In Leibnitz's Correspondence (ed. Dutens, vi. 271) is a letter from the mathematician to Thomas Burnet, in which we read, 'Mr. le Comte de Sunderland a gagné ici (Florence) tous nos joueurs aux échecs; ses gens prétendent qu'il est maintenant au-dessus de Mr. Cunningham et que passant dernièrement par la Hollande il lui a gagné cinq parties de suite.' In a later letter (ed. cit. vi. 278) to the same correspondent, Leibnitz expresses the hope that Cunningham would publish his views on the art of playing chess. These letters will relate to the historian.

21 Not to be confused with the earlier player of this name who played with Maurice of Nassau between 1609 and 1621. Aubrey de Marrier, *Mémoires pour servir à l'histoire de Hollande*, ed. 1680, 202 (in v. d. L., *Sch. in Nederl.*, 75), says of Prince Maurice, 'Je l'ay veu . . & souvent chez mon père . . ou bien y venant jouer aux Échecs, jeu qui faisoit son principal divertissement, car pendant la Trève, que la guerre ne l'occupait pas, il y jouoit souvent et recherchoit ceux qui le sçavoient. Il aimoit fort à cause de cela Mr. de la Caze, brave capitaine Béarnois, qui servoit dans les troupes de Hollande et qui jouoit fort bien. Ce Mr. de Caze n'avoit point de revenu plus assuré que ce qu'il gagnoit au Prince à ce jeu: ne partant point

by him to the Earl of Sunderland, with a dedicatory letter of introduction which is dated 1st Sept., 1706. This MS. contains as Game 139 the 'Gambit de Mr Cunnigham, 1 Pe4, Pe5 ; 2 Pf4, P×P ; 3 Bc4, Be7 ; 4 Ktf3, Bh4+ ; 5 Pg 3, P×P ; 6 0–0, P×P ; 7 Kh1 gagnera', and as Game 250 the same Opening with transposition of the 3rd and 4th moves, with the note 'Cette Partie est de Mr Cunnigham . . .' ; while in the letter to Lord Sunderland, Caze, when describing the contents of the MS., says that it does not contain the Gambit declined, and continues :

> Ainsi les Parties que V.G. joüa en ma presence contre Mr. de Cunnigham, & que j'escrivis pour lors, ne s'y doivent pas trouver, quoy qu'elles soient extremement belles et curieuses.

The Earl of Sunderland in question was Charles, the third and great Earl (B. 1674, succeeded 1702, D. 1722), who, according to Leibnitz (*Corr.*, vi. 271), had written a Latin work on chess. It seems clear that it was the historian who popularized the *Cunningham Gambit*, and played with Lord Sunderland, and that the critic's European reputation belongs to the period 1710–30.

Caze was of opinion that the utmost that the defence could hope to attain by accepting the King's Gambit was a drawn game (*refait*). Twenty years' experience of chess had convinced him that there were two defects in chess, one arising from the different positions of the Queens, which he proposed to remedy by placing both Queens on the left of the King (the crosswise arrangement), the other arising from the advantage of the move, which he proposed to remedy by compelling the first player to begin by 1 Pe3. In order to test his idea, he suggested to Lord Sunderland that the London players should issue a challenge to the Paris players for a match to be played a certain time after the current war had ended : two games were to be played at the same time, London having the move in the one, and Paris in the other. It is needless to say that nothing came of it ; other players were quite satisfied with chess as it was.

The most interesting point about this challenge is that it recognizes the fact that chess-players in Paris and London were beginning to collect together for play. Chess-playing had indeed become a regular feature of the coffee-houses recently established in large numbers in both capitals. In Paris there seems to have been no one café which was more frequented than any other by chess-players until the middle of the century, and chess was played in nearly every café. The best players were M. de Kermur, Sire de Légal (B. 1702, D. 1792), Philidor's teacher, and the inventor of a form of chess in which one player received 7, 8, or 9 Pawns (placed on the 3rd and 4th lines, e. g. on b3, c3, c4, d4, e4, f3, f4, g3) instead of his Queen, or 3 or 4 Pawns for his Rook ; the Marquis de Grosminy and his brother, who used to beat Légal in 1728 ; the Chevaliers de Feron and du Son, the last the

d'ordinaire de chez luy qu'il n'eût neuf à dix écus d'or, ce qui luy valoit mieux que sa Compagnie. Ils n'en jouoient qu'un à chaque partie, sans jamais doubler, mais pour ne pas rebuter le Prince, la Caze de trois à quatre fois qu'ils jouoient s'en laissoit gagner vne.'

author of a work on chess, the unpublished MS. of which afterwards belonged to the Prince of Conti; with the Chancellor d'Aguesseau and his son, the President Nicolai (see p. 843), the Duc de Mortemart, the Duc de Mirepoix, later Ambassador to England, the Abbés Chenard and Maillot, and MM. Foubert and de St. Paul, somewhat inferior in strength (Twiss, ii. 165).

In London, chess-players resorted to Slaughter's Coffee House (founded by John Slaughter, 1692, later often called Old Slaughter's, pulled down 1843–4) in St. Martin's Lane, and this was the head-quarters of English chess from 1700 to 1770.[22] Here, to a private room, came for their chess Mr. Cunningham, Lord Sunderland, Francis Earl of Godolphin (B. 1678, D. 1766), Alexander Lord Elibank (B. 1677, D. 1736), Sir Abraham Janssen (D. 1765), Dr. Black, a schoolmaster at Chiswick who obtained a Crown living through his chess (Twiss, i. 163), Dr. Cowper, Mr. Cargill, Mr. Salvador, Captain Bertin, Phillip Stamma, and Abraham de Moivre (B. 1667, D. 1750), the mathematician, who lived for nearly thirty years on the petty sums he made at Slaughter's by chess.[23]

In the *Craftsman*, No. 376, for 15 Sept., 1733, there appeared a paper with the title of *A Short Essay on the Game of Chess*, with the signature *R*. The paper was really a feeble political skit in the Tory interest, couched in the language of chess, but showing a very slight knowledge of the game.[24] It provoked a speedy reply in the Whig interest, *A Letter to the Craftsman on the Game of Chess, occasioned by his Paper on the Fifteenth of this Month*, which was dated Slaughter's Coffee House, 21 Sept., 1733. The reply, while professing to expose the blunders in the paper in the *Craftsman*, makes nearly as many of its own, even confusing Stalemate with Fool's mate, and its chief interest lies in the fact that it was the occasion of the writing of a far abler paper, *Critical Remarks upon the letter to the Craftsman* . . ., by the Rev. Lewis Rou, pastor of the Huguenot Church in New York, the dedication of which was dated 13 Dec., 1734. This MS., now unfortunately lost track of, is the oldest reference to chess in the New World.[25]

In 1735, Captain Joseph Bertin published his *Noble Game of Chess. Containing Rules and Instructions for the Use of those who have already a little Knowledge of this Game*, which was only to be procured at Slaughter's Coffee

[22] It is referred to in the concluding line of Joseph Thurston's poems on chess (*Poems*, 1737):

> Their laws, their Orders, and their Manners these,
> The rest let *Slaughter's* tell you if they please.

[23] Cf. D. W. Fiske's note in *Notes and Queries*, 9th Ser., x. 41 (19 July, 1902), separately printed (with additions) as *The Lost Manuscript of the Rev. Lewis Rou's Critical Remarks* . . , Florence, 1902.

[24] The most interesting thing in the whole paper is the concluding promise (never fulfilled) to continue with a similar account of the game of *Polish Draughts*, which is the first mention of that game that is known to me. The authorship of the *Craftsman* paper has been ascribed to Lord Bolingbroke, but Mr. Walter Sichel, the biographer of Bolingbroke, does not accept it.

[25] Cf. D. W. Fiske, *Book of the first Amer. Chess Congress*, New York, 1859, 340; and the later article named in note 23. The authorship of the Whig reply has generally been attributed to Lord John Hervey, but Prof. Fiske throws doubt upon this.

House. In this small work Bertin lays down a number of general principles to be followed in playing chess, and gives 26 games, which he divides into Gambets and the Close-game ('The close-game is, when he that plays first gives no men, unless to make a good advantage'); the former include the *Three Pawns Gambet* (Cunningham's Gambit), the Bishop's Gambit, some irregular varieties of the Knight's Gambit, and the Queen's Gambit; the latter games beginning 1 Pe4, Pe5; 2 Bc4, Bc5 or Pg6 or Pc6; 1 Pe4, Pe5; 2 Pc3; 1 Pe4, Pe6; and 1 Pd4, Pd5; 2 Pe3. We see how few are his Openings compared with those of the Italian players, and how little was really known in England of the regular forms of the King's Gambits.

In his rules, Bertin attaches great value to the retention of the move or attack, and the avoidance of any move that gives it up to the adversary. Thus, '(1) The King's Pawn, the Bishop's Pawn, and the Queen's Pawn must move before the Knights; otherwise, if the Pawns move last, the game will be much crouded by useless moves. (2) Never play your Queen till your game is tolerably well opened, that you may not lose any moves . . . (3) You must not give useless checks, for the same reason. (5) Do not Castle but when very necessary, because the move is often lost by it'. He does not lay any particular stress upon the formation of a centre of Pawns, '(12) At the beginning of a game, you may play any Pawn two moves without danger,' shows this clearly. Nor does he lay stress upon the value of the Pawn as a possible Queen. His tactics are accordingly neither of the Italian nor of the Lopez school.

Another frequenter of Slaughter's who published a work on chess was Phillip Stamma, a native of Aleppo in Syria, who was for a time interpreter of Oriental languages to the English Government.[26] Stamma had published an *Essai sur le Jeu des Échecs . . . Par le Sieur Philippe Stamma*, in Paris, in 1737, at a time when his fortunes were at a very low ebb (as appears from the dedication to Lord Harrington, 'Dans la situation où la fortune m'a reduit, la compassion Vous parlera pour moi'). This work was a collection of 100 End-games with overloaded diagrams in true Muslim style, which he claimed would be found far more useful than Greco's games to the beginner, in teaching him how to play chess. Stamma brought out a revised edition in London in 1745, under the title *The Noble Game of Chess . . . By Phillip Stamma*, in which he added a collection of 74 Openings. These he arranges under the names Knight-Close Game (our King's-Knight's Opening; all are Giuochi Piani), Bishop-Close Game (our King's-Bishop's Opening), Pawn-Close Game (1 Pe4, Pe5; 2 Pc3 or Pd4), Knight's Gambett, Bishop's Gambett, Pawn's Gambett (1 Pe4, Pe5; 2 Pf4, P×P; 3 Ph4), Three Pawns' or Cunningham's Gambett, and Queen's-Pawn's Gambett (our Queen's Gambit), the last of which he strongly recommends to players; he is the first writer to point out that the defence in this gambit must lose if the attempt is made to retain the extra Pawn. Stamma's opinions of the Openings had

[26] I think it very probable that Stamma's Whig friends at Slaughter's had secured this appointment for him.

undergone some change since the issue of his first edition, or he would never have included any King's Gambits. In 1737 he wrote:

> Pour ce qui regarde une des manières de joüer proposée par le Calabrois, qu'il appelle Gambette, personne ne voudroit joüer de la sorte, à moins qu'il ne voulût perdre, ou qu'il joüât contre quelque novice. *J'estime cette méthode tres-inutile, & sans fondement.*

In 1745 he only thinks that 'if both sides play equally well, the one who offers the Gambit has the worst of it'.

Apart from the discovery of the correct defence to Cunningham's Gambit, there is little of merit in Stamma's analysis. His advice to young players is, however, interesting from the contrast it offers to Bertin's rules.

> Open the Game, so as to make way for your Pieces to come out, that you may post them advantageously. . . . This is best done by advancing proper *Pawns*; these are the *King's*, the *Queen's*, and the *Queen's Bishop's Pawns*. . . . Castle as soon as you can conveniently. This is sometimes so necessary to be done without delay, that it may be worth while to abandon a *Pawn*, rather than lose the Opportunity. If you bring out your Pieces too soon, before you have open'd their Road, they will confine your *Pawns*, and croud your Game . . . in general it is best to bring out your Pieces under the Protection of your *Pawns*. . . .

Bertin's objection to the loss of the attack as the result of wasting time is here also, but in a milder form.

In his analysis, and in the problems and solutions (there are no diagrams), Stamma uses the algebraical notation which must have been familiar to him in the East. He designates the Pieces by the letter of their original files, thus a = QR, b = QKt, &c., and the Pawns by p, uses a cross for a check, and a star is prefixed or added to the record of the move in cases of possible obscurity to make the move clear, thus * p e 4 means the left-hand P to e4, p e 4 * the right-hand Pawn. He has no means of marking a capture, and no symbol for *castling*.[27] The importance of this reform in notation was very great. For the first time it was possible to place the move and its reply on a single line, and to introduce order and ease of reference for the unattractive record of the older works. In all the earlier printed books down to Salvio, and in the Lausanne treatise, the record of the game runs straight on as an ordinary paragraph, with nothing to separate the successive moves. In the Polerio and Greco MSS., as a rule, every move of each player occupies a single line, and in some of the MSS. of Greco's English visit the moves are numbered, each move of each player counting as a single move (e.g. 1 Pe4;

[27] Stamma uses small letters in his Openings, spacing them apart. In his problems he uses capitals, and many of his earlier imitators (the *Traité d'Amateurs* (1775), Montigny, Allgaier, and even Alexandre, 1837 and 1846) have done the same. The 'Amateurs' omit the name of the piece if it move to a square on its own file (E. 2 = Ke2) and write K. G. 1 and K. C. 1 for 0–0 and 0-0-0. The modern form of the notation, using the initial of the piece to designate it, small letters for the files, and 0-0, 0-0-0 for castling, was introduced by Moses Hirschel in his Leipzig edition of Greco and Stamma of 1784. In Hirschel's notation the square of departure is given as well as the square of arrival, thus Kt g1–f3. I use in this book a modified form of this notation, the chief differences being that I omit the square of departure (as is done in several German books), and write P × B, &c., for Pc4. I find it more convenient to know the name of the captured piece than to have its position.

2 Pe5; 3 Pf4; 4 P×P, &c.). The earlier printed Grecos, Bertin, Philidor, and indeed most chess books retaining the descriptive notation down to about 1820, give a line to each move of each player, Philidor apparently being the first to introduce the modern rule of numbering each move and its reply with the same number. Persistent attempts were made in the 18th century to get the algebraical notation adopted in England and France, but the influence of Philidor was against it, and its use to-day is practically confined to German-speaking countries. In other countries it has had the effect of compelling the adherents of the descriptive notation to discover more abbreviated forms of it than were used by the older writers.

Stamma's reputation has rested entirely upon his 100 End-games, of which many editions were printed between 1740 and 1856 in French, English, German, Dutch, and Italian. His End-games revived the dying interest in the problem, and by re-introducing to Europe the Muslim conception of the problem, which had long been forgotten, they set the fashion for the remainder of the 18th century, and made possible the whole development of the modern problem. Their reputation was certainly beyond their deserts, and Ponziani's criticism is, as usual, just: 'His problems are, to tell the truth, more perplexing than excellent, but about 18 in all are worthy of praise.'

'The problem as conceived by Stamma was a position such as might plausibly be supposed to have occurred in actual play, and in which a direct mate could be forced in a given number of moves by an ingenious and surprising process.'[28] This is, of course, the early Muslim conception of the problem (see p. 276), and Stamma's diagrams are constructed under the Muslim canons. Thus, the two sides are made equal in numbers—on the average 14·3 men go to each diagram, and of these 6·8 are White, 7·5 Black: many of the black men could be removed without injury to the solution: the White King is generally under threat of an immediate and obvious mate. Stamma lays no stress on the length of the solution; the problem is 'White to play and win'. In a third of the games, the solution is not conducted to mate, and these games may be compared with the non-mate endings of the Muslim MSS. The average length of the solutions of the remaining mate-problems is from 5 to 6 moves. None are wager-games: these had passed out of use in Europe long before Stamma's day, and were unknown in Muslim chess.

To what extent Stamma's problems are original has been disputed. V. d. Linde points out that five occur in Bertin's work, and argues that these obviously can be by neither author. It is quite possible, however, that Stamma supplied them to Bertin for the purposes of publication. Stamma himself claimed that all the positions had occurred to him in the course of actual play, but this seems incredible; moreover two or three are old favourites and can be traced back to the early Muslim masters. It has been suggested that Stamma brought his problems from the East. This is possible, but it is

[28] J. W. Allen, *BCM.*, 1903, 185, in his *Notes on the Development of the Chess Problem*, a valuable piece of pioneer work in this important field of chess.

strange that none of his problems should occur in so extensive a collection of modern Muslim problems as that of Berlin MS. Landberg, 806. On the whole, I think that we must allow Stamma a greater share in the composition of his problems than recent writers have been disposed to do.

The year 1745 not only saw the publication of Stamma's *Noble Game of Chess*, but also that of Edmond Hoyle's *Short Treatise on the Game of Piquet . . . To which are added, some Rules and Observations for playing well at Chess*, at the price of one shilling, a manual which ran through eight editions and was generally bound up with similar manuals on other games as *Hoyle's Games*. The author of this small work (B. *c.* 1679, D. 1769) was better known to his contemporaries as the originator of the scientific study of whist, but the great success of his *Short Treatise on the Game of Whist* (first published in 1742, sixteen editions in the author's lifetime) induced him to write a series of similar manuals on other games, quadrille, backgammon, piquet and chess, which have preserved his name for his successors. Hoyle's work on whist grew out of his lessons, which he gave orally, and it is probable that the lessons which he gave on chess at five shillings each led to the publication of the *Rules and Observations*. In 1761 he published his *Essay towards making the Game of Chess easy learned*, and after his death in 1808 his lectures were published as the *Game of Chess, including (37) Chess Lectures.*

The *Rules and Observations* did not profess to teach the rudiments of chess, but merely gave a number of rules which were intended to help the player to play well. These consist of 26 numbered paragraphs, with an explanation in 3 paragraphs and a supplement of 14 additional rules, the whole ending with a code of five laws of chess. Many of the rules are derived from Bertin, but Hoyle was no slavish imitator of Bertin. His fifth rule—'If your Game happens to be crowded, endeavour to free it by making Exchanges of Pieces or Pawns, and Castle your King as soon as you conveniently can'—shows this clearly. He lays greater stress than any of his predecessors on the importance of the King in the End-game, and the proper play of the Pawns.[29] He does not allow that doubled Pawns are always disadvantageous, and would rather sacrifice his Queen for a Piece and a Pawn or two than abandon the attack.

Hoyle's work has probably always circulated among less expert players, and it was not until close on 1800 that editions of the *Games* begin to show any sign of the influence of Philidor's play. Even then, the only result was the inclusion of the analysis from Philidor's work of 1749. Until the last third of the nineteenth century, editions of the *Games* followed one another without any critical revision, and continued to repeat rules which had been dropped by chess-players since soon after 1800. It is evident that the reputation of *Hoyle's Games* has never rested upon the section on chess.

[29] Hoyle begins the preface to his *Essay*, London, 1761, by saying, 'Few people in England, till within these thirty years, understood how to play the Pawns to perfection: and the lovers of Chess are principally indebted to Sir Abraham Janssen, Mr. Montgomery, and Mr. Bofan for this knowledge.'

The games in Hoyle's lectures are for the most part puerile and played in a spirit totally opposed to the rules which he gave in his chess books. He was not a chess-player, and what merit there is in his *Rules and Observations* is due to the fidelity with which he recorded the advice of better players than himself.

GERMANY, 1540–1790.

If we hear but little of German chess during the first three centuries of the modern game, it is due, not to any decline in the popularity of chess after 1500, but rather to the isolation of the German player, which prevented him from profiting from the advance made by players elsewhere. All indications point to chess having been the favourite indoor recreation of the upper and middle classes throughout the whole of this period. A few references must suffice. The game is mentioned in the letters and lives of the early reformers. John Frederick, Elector of Saxony, and Ernest, Duke of Brunswick, were playing in prison, 1547, when the news of the Elector's condemnation to death was brought (Juan Ochoa de la Salde, *Carolea Inchiridion*, Lisbon, 1585; in Twiss, *Misc.*, ii. 20). Visch and Hessels were similarly at chess when Ryhove of Ghent haled them forth to instant execution in 1578 (Motley, *Dutch Republic*, VI, i). The village of Ströbeck was already famous for its chess in 1600 (Heigius, *Quaest. jur. civ. et Saxon.*, Wittenberg, 1601, in Selenus, 425). Hyde (ii. 8) tells how the Danish, Swedish, German, and Croatian merchants played at the Fairs, and how the position of an unfinished game was written down before a notary, so that the game might be renewed at the next Fair. There are many elaborate chessboards, in German and other museums, dating from about 1600 and of German workmanship. These bear witness to the popularity of chess.

The first evidence after Egenolff for the rules of German chess is contained in the *Cartel des Schach-Spieles am Kaiserlichen Hofe*, a broadside printed in 1577, which is preserved in Selenus, 115. This document, which bears the signature *Vdt. Pythagoras. Decretum Scacharistarum Aulicorum 21 Junii, (15)77*, gives nine rules of play, which may be summarized thus:

(1) Every Pawn can move two squares at its first move; (2) the Pawn can be taken in passing; (3) so long as the King has not been checked, he can castle, each piece moving as far as it likes (Alsz lang der König kein Schach empfangen, mag Er mit dem Rochen, wechszlen, alsz weit Er mit beeden stucken wil, doch musz das feld darzwischen leer seyn); (4) after a check the King can no longer castle; (5) the Pawn becomes a Queen directly it reaches the 8th rank; (6) a player can have as many Queens as he can make; (7) bare King is not a check, but *robada*; (8) stalemate is a *tavola*; (9) both these endings are drawn.

In the light of the rules of the older game in Egenolff, and of the rules of later German writers, this Cartel can only be regarded as a pronouncement against the native German rules on the part of some body of players who had a slight knowledge of the rules of Italy and Spain.

Our next authority is the extremely rare *Schachzabel* of Lucas Wielius

(Strassburg, 1606), a translation of Vida to which the translator has added a brief account of chess. The exceptional features in his rules are—

(1) The four Pawns on the *a*, *d*, *e*, and *h* files alone can make the double step for their first move. Vida, it is true, allows this liberty to all the Pawns, but others, who play chess daily, make the above-described distinction. (2) The King moves one square only in all directions. (3) The Pawn is promoted to the rank of Queen, but only after the loss of the original Queen. Some players say that the opponent must make a move before the promotion is effective. (4) Only one man may be played in each move. (5) There are two other mates beside checkmate—Bare King and Stalemate. In each case the winner must have sufficient force left to give checkmate.

Wielius knows nothing of castling, and nothing of the later habit of opening the game with two simultaneous moves.

In 1616, Augustus, Duke of Brunswick-Lüneburg (B. 1579, D. 1666), writing under the pseudonym of 'Gustavus Selenus', published his great work on chess, *Das Schach- oder König-Spiel* (Leipzig, 1616). This work is a translation of Tarsia's Italian version of Ruy Lopez, but the Duke has made large additions of an historical character, which make his book of value. Unfortunately, he transcribed Tarsia's games into 'the intolerable notation of the first sixty-four numerals', and this deprived his work of all chance of influencing the play of his countrymen. His additions to the analysis of his original are exceedingly weak, and show the Duke to have been more industrious than gifted as a player.

Selenus naturally adopts the rules of his Italian original, but many of his notes throw light upon the points in which the practice of German players differed. Thus:

(53) The King's privilege move is confined to the mediaeval leap; he cannot capture on the leap, and the practice of some players who advance a Pawn in order to make room for the King and play the leap all in one move is forbidden. (87) It is doubtful whether all the Pawns, or only the Pawns on files *a*, *d*, *e*, and *h*, can make the double step on their first move. It is usual to allow the Pawns on files *c* and *f* the same privilege so long as no check has been received or piece been lost. (88) The Pawn is to be promoted to the rank of Queen, but only after the loss of the original Queen. If it reaches the 8th rank before promotion is possible, it remains there immune from capture until the Queen has been sacrificed. Some players restrict this fidation to the four Pawns on the Queen's wing, and leave those on the King's wing to take their chance. The best players allow promotion to the rank of Queen whether the original Queen has been lost or not. English players allow promotion to any rank. (122) A blind mate is not a lost game. If the game is reduced to King and any piece against King, checkmate cannot be given. (126) It is not necessary to warn the opponent that the Queen is attacked. (127) A bare King cannot be mated; his last piece must be left untaken. (128) Stalemate is a draw. In some places the player giving stalemate forfeits ten times his stake.

A number of smaller works, based upon Selenus, appeared in the course of the 17th and early 18th cc., but the next work of any importance is a MS. of 1728 by G. F. D. v. B., the *Kurze jedoch gründliche und accurate Anweisung und Regeln vom Schach-Spiel*, of which a summary is given in the *Qst.*, 325–8. This work restricts the double step to the four Pawns on the *a*, *d*, *e*, and *h* files, limits promotion to the rank of any lost piece (if the Pawn reaches the

8th rank before promotion is possible, it must remain there as a Pawn and liable to capture, until a piece has been sacrificed), defines castling as Re1 and Kf1 (or d1), and forbids it after a check, punishes the player who gives stalemate by the loss of the game, and declares that the mate only counts a half-win if the loser has no other piece remaining.

There is a number of smaller German treatises on chess of the eighteenth century, many the work of Jews, which reveal the gradual adoption of the French rules of play, and the relegation of the special German features to that variety of the game in which the players each began by moving two men on their first moves, of which I have given an account, pp. 389–91. But the older usages died hard. The modern rules were given in Hirsch Baruch's *Schach-Tractat*, Berlin, 1747; but Philidor (1749) deplored two customs as obtaining in Germany—the Italian rule of *passar battaglia*, and the method of playing Kg1, Rf1, and Ph3 on one and the same move. I have found no native authority for the first usage apart from the curious adoption of the Italian rules in Hamburg *c.* 1830–42, but as late as 1866 v. d. Linde met an opponent at the Hague who accompanied his move of castling with Ph3 (*16. Jrh.*, 119). We may trace the older usages still in the rules of chess which Allgaier gave in his *Anweisung* (Vienna, 1795: I use the 1823 edition). The material rules are—

(6) It is not permitted to move two men at once on the first move: just as little is it allowable to move a Pawn in castling. (10) It is only obligatory to say check to the King, and not, as some insist,[30] to the Queen or the Rooks. (13) It is permissible to deprive the hostile King of all his men, and to mate him by himself. (16) If the King is stalemated, the game is abandoned as drawn. It is a matter for agreement whether the stalemated King should lose half his stake. (17) Every Pawn which advances to the opponent's first line obtains at once the rank and power of the Queen, or of any other piece of the player's own selection which at that time was already lacking to the player. If, however, the case arises that a Pawn reaches such a square before the player has lost a single Piece, this Pawn remains standing until a Piece is removed from the board, with whose power the Pawn is immediately endued.[31]

Allgaier (Holm).

Allgaier adds a long note to this last rule, beginning, 'This rule has been accepted almost everywhere in Germany as valid, and yet cases can arise in which it cannot be brought into practice without violating the fundamental rules of chess.' He explains this by the attached position (the position of the inactive White pieces is immaterial: I follow the arrangement in Holm's *Regler for Schachspillet*, Copenhagen, 1841, 16), in which Bl. must play 1 . . , Kf7. Now follows 2 P × R and must remain a P, Pa6; 3 Kt(e4) ×

30 Some players held that the Queen could not be captured unless a warning (*Gardez*) had been given the preceding move. V. d. Linde met such a player in Berlin in 1873 (*16. Jrh.*, 119).

31 The *Kurtzer und Deutlicher Unterricht*, 1740, which claimed to be a translation of Bertin, limited promotion to the master-piece of the file upon which the Pawn 'queened', and if that piece was still untaken, the next-better piece. It adds that some players made the Pawn a Queen whether the original Queen was taken or not, but this is a matter for arrangement between the players.

P(d6)+. If Black took the Kt, the Ph8 would become a Kt at once and the Bl. K would be in check, so 3.., Kg6; 4 Kt×B+. If now Kf6; 5 Q×eP mate, for if the Q be taken, the idle Pawn becomes a Queen and checks. Allgaier realized the absurdity of this, and accordingly expressed the hope that the French rule might be generally adopted; failing this, he suggested that the player might lift any of his pieces he liked (except the Queen) from the board, and substitute it for the Pawn. In 1842, Adolf Anderssen was still arguing against the plurality of Queens in his *Aufgaben für Schachspieler.* It was owing to Karl Schorn (B. 1802, D. 1850) that Bledow and the Berliner Schachgesellschaft, and as a result all Germany, finally abandoned the restrictions to free Pawn promotion.

Sweden, Denmark, &c.

Most chess books, from Carrera and Selenus down, repeat the statement in Olaus Magnus's *Historia de gentibus septentrionalibus*, Rome, 1555, XV. xii, that Norse parents were in the habit of proving the dispositions of the suitors for their daughters by playing chess with them, and noting their conduct during the game.

Gustavus Adolphus was a chess-player, but Charles XII (D. 1718) is probably the king of Sweden whose chess is most widely known, as a result of Frederick the Great's allusion in a letter of 23 Dec., 1740, 'Je suis comme le Roi d'Échecs de Charles XII, qui marchait toujours.' Voltaire, in his *Hist. de Charles XII*, had said that Charles lost all his games because he moved his King more than any other piece.[32]

The oldest Swedish text-book of chess is C. W. v. Königstedt's *Kort Afhandling*, Stockholm, 1784. The author states that in his time most Swedish players began by moving two pieces, and informs his readers that 'great players never castle'. In his edition of 1806, he is less positive, and has substituted 'Good players seldom castle'.

The oldest Danish text-book is the *Forsög til almindelige og särdeles Grund-Regler for Konge- eller Shakspillet*, Kiöbenhavn, 1774. The game, however, had been played continuously since the Middle Ages, when Danish versions of some of the French Romances were made. La Peyrère, *Lettre à M. La Mothe*, Paris, 1663, tells how he played chess with the Countess Ulfeld in 1644, in Copenhagen, the chessmen being actual representations of kings, queens, bishops, horsemen, and elephants carrying towers on their backs.

There is apparently no chess literature in Finland. I am told that at the present day chess (*shakkipeli*) is only played by children.[32a]

[32] Cf. F. Amelung, *Karl der Zwölfte ..*, in *Balt. Schachbl.*, Heft vii, 270–6, and *C. A. Freiherr v. Grotthus, der Favorit und Schachgenosse König Karl des Zwölften in Bender*, ibid., Heft viii, 453–75. Amelung quotes the Swedish Historian Frixell (whom he considers a more reliable authority than Voltaire) to the effect that Charles used at chess to fix upon some piece of his opponent's which he chased with supreme disregard for his own men until he captured it, when he selected another victim and pursued this in the same manner.

[32a] The Finnish nomenclature is K, kuningas; Q, rouva; B, juoksuri; Kt, juoksija; R, torni; P, sotamies; check, shakkaus; checkmate, sakkimatti.

ICELAND, 1500 TO THE PRESENT DAY.

Many travellers, from the middle of the sixteenth century onwards, refer to the wide diffusion of chess in Iceland. Native references are perhaps less frequent, but the *Búalög* (*c.* 1530) states that it costs 12 alnir (perhaps equivalent to 7*s.*) to learn chess; Bishop Jón Árison, *c.* 1530, mentions chess in an eight-lined poem on games, which is quoted in *Íslenzkar Gátur*, Kaupmannahöfn, 1892, iv. 362; and Gottskálk Jónsson of Glaumbæ (D. 1593) translated the *Innocent Morality* into Icelandic (see above, p. 534).

The earliest foreign reference is probably that by Peder Clausson Friis (D. 1614) in his *Om Iisland*, finally revised just before 1600. He devotes a brief section to *Skag-tafll*:

> They (the Icelanders) have also in their country especially occupied themselves with the practice of the game of chess (*skagetafl* or *skagspill*), which they are said to play in such a masterly and perfect way that they sometimes spend some weeks' time—playing each day—on a single game, before they can bring it to an end by the victory of the one or the other combatant.[33]

Friis was followed by Dithmar Blefken, *Islandia*, Lugd. Bat., 1607, 38:

> Hyberno vero tempore ad multos dies lecto se continent, atque ludo scaccorum . . . exercent: interim famuli cibum illis praeparatum ad lectum deferunt;

by La Peyrère, *Lettre à M. La Mothe* (written 1644), Paris, 1663, 56:

> J'obmetois de vous dire une particularité de l'esprit des Islandois, qui n'est pas à mespriser. C'est qu'ils sont tous joueurs d'eschets, et qu'il n'est point de si chetif paisan en Islande, qui n'ait pas chez luy son jeu d'eschets, faits de sa main, et d'os de poisson, taillé à la pointe de son couteau;[34]

by Robert, Visct. Molesworth (D. 1725; in Denmark in 1692), *Account of Denmark*, London, 1694, 39:

> The Inhabitants (of Island and Feroe) are great Players at Chess;

and by other writers of the eighteenth century,[35] some of whom will be quoted below, because they give fuller information as to the method of play.

Ólafur Davíðsson, who wrote the article on chess in *Íslenzkar Gátur* (iv. 274–98), expresses considerable doubt as to both the extent of the diffusion of chess in the island and the excellence of the play. His own experience of North Iceland was that the game was but little played, and that many people were entirely ignorant of the rules. He thinks that the earlier travellers were misled, by finding peasants playing chess, into thinking that everybody played, and that the later works have simply copied the older statement. He points out that it is a very rare thing for any one to be named in Icelandic books as a good chess-player, although the names of good wrestlers, swimmers, and

[33] See Fiske, *Chess in Iceland*, 35, where the original text is given.

[34] La Peyrère goes on to give the differences between the French and Icelandic names and appearances of the chessmen.

[35] E.g. Horrebow (*Nat. Hist. Iceland*, 1750, London, 1758, 139), Eggert Ólafsson (*Reise igjennem Island*, Kiøbenhavn, 1772, i. 462–4), and Dr. v. Troil (*Letters on Iceland*, London, 1780, 93).

jumpers are frequently recorded.[36] Fiske, however, says that the inhabitants of the isle of Grimsey, about 60 miles north of Iceland, have long been noted for their addiction to chess.

Two references to Icelandic chessmen occur in the correspondence of the famous Danish antiquary, Olaus Worm (*Olai Wormii et ad eum doctorum virorum epistolae*, Hauniae, 1751, 356). In the first, the priest Magnús Ólafsson (D. 1636) sent, in 1627–8, a gift of a set of carved chessmen, accompanying the gift by a short Latin poem, *De skakis*, modelled upon an ancient Icelandic metrical form (see Fiske, op. cit., 33). In the second, another Icelandic priest, Stefán Ólafsson (D. *c.* 1686), sent, in 1646, a carved snuff-box, and told Worm that the carver, an artisan of Kyrkjubær, also carved bone chessmen and sold them at a moderate price (Fiske, 43).

This last correspondent was also the author of three chess lays, which he addressed to one Þorsteinn Magnússon, when he had lost a piece at chess. Prof. Fiske gives (38–40) the following English translation from the pen of Mr. Sigfús Blöndal:

I.

My malediction I utter—May Steini's men fall in heaps! May my fearful incantations bewitch him, so that peril shall beset two or three of his pieces at once! May the Old One (*gamla*—the Queen) lose her life! May the wee Pawns grow fewer and fewer on the squares, and may he be mated both with the low and high mates!

II.

Jón is the better man at chess; he has wrested from me each Rook; the quiet of my Bishop, my Knight, and my Pawns is ruthlessly broken; the Old One is moving about aimlessly, not seeing her prey when within reach; my King is overmastered and completely checkmated.

III.

She is spoiling all beautifully, that damned jade, your Queen (*fru*), whom you are now moving; she steals away from her house, clever in her coarse boastfulness, neatly picking the stupid Rook from the throng. The Knight, on hand, kept ready for combat, well guided, falls afeard despite his own wrath, and dares only attack sullenly a puny Pawn, while the cowardly Rook, fearful of the Bishop's menace, keeps to his border line and thus evades the stratagems of the enemy.[37]

There are allusions here to some of the special features of the Icelandic chess which differentiated it for long from the game of any other part of Europe. These rules relate to the conclusion of the game only, but there is evidence to show that—apart from these peculiarities, which were common to all forms of Icelandic chess—there were different ways or assizes in which the game could be played. Thus Dr. v. Troil, *Letters on Iceland*, London, 1780, 93,[38] says:

They are famous for playing at Chess, and had formerly two sorts of this game, one of which was called *júngfrúrskák* (Lady's chess), and the other *riddaraskák* (Knight's Chess). At present only the last is common.

[36] He mentions as noted chess-players, Benedikt Jónsson of Hrappsey (D. 1746) and his son Bogi (D. 1803), and the brothers Bishop Pétur and Chief-justice Jón Pétursson.
[37] The Icelandic text, and a valuable commentary, will be found in Fiske, 38–40.
[38] The work was originally published in Swedish at Upsala, 1777.

Íslenzkar Gátur (286–8) adds to these the names of other varieties of chess, e.g. *manntalsskák*, *frúrskák*, *valdskák*, *drepskák*,[39] of which only the last two are now played. An attempt is made to explain the differences between *manntalsskák*, *frúrskák*, and *riddaraskák*, but the result is not convincing. Apparently, the last players of *frúrskák* died in the earlier half of the eighteenth century,[40] and the game died with them. I am inclined to think that these names originated at a time when the reformed chess was displacing the older game in Iceland, and that they became obsolete when the older game was finally abandoned. One would naturally conclude that the *frúrskák* (*júngfrúrskák*) was identical with the *échecs de la dame*, i.e. was the modern game, and although v. Troil identifies the *riddaraskák* with the modern game, it is possible that he was wrongly informed. He wrote nearly fifty years after the disappearance of the second variety of the game.[41]

Valdskák (guard-chess) is a modern variety of the game in which no piece can be taken which is guarded by another man. Some players allow a piece that is only guarded by the King to be captured. In opposition to this variety, the ordinary chess is sometimes called *drepskák* (capturing-chess).

There is no Icelandic text-book of chess older than the brief account in the *Spilabók*, published by Jósef Grímsson at Akureyri in 1857.[42] It is therefore not surprising to find that there has been much uncertainty of rule among Icelandic players. Many of the recorded varieties of move must be explained in this way.

Íslenzkar Gátur and the *Spilabók* detail the following peculiarities of rule:

(1) Some players allow the Pawn the double step for the first time of moving.

(2) Most allow the King to move once as a Knight; some restrict the privilege to its first time of play, others allow it at any time.

(3) There is considerable irregularity as to Castling, but 'free castling' in the Italian fashion is not allowed. The following varieties are given in *Ísl. Gátur* (the *Spilabók* gives the modern castling only)—Kh1 and Re1 or Kb1 and Rd1; Kh1 and Rf1 or Ka1 and Rc1; Ka1 or h1 and Re1; Kb1 or g1 and Re1.

(4) Some limit Pawn-promotion to the rank of a piece which has been lost. Others promote to the rank of the master-piece of the file upon which the Pawn queens. If the King's Pawn queens on the King's file, it is fidated unless it is taken on the move following its arrival at the queening square. Some give it the move of the Queen and Knight, but most the King's move

[39] Chess is now called *skák*, *skáktafl*, *manntafl*, or *mannskák*. *Refskák* (fox-chess) is the game of fox and geese played on the 'solitaire' board.

[40] They are said to have been the schoolmaster Pál Vídalín (flourished 1690–7), Þorstein Sigurðsson, sheriff of Norður-Múlasýslu, and Álf Gíslason of Kaldaðarnesi in Flóa (D. 1733).

[41] Ólafur Davíðsson admits that the accounts of *frúrskák* are contradictory, and makes the same suggestion that I make in the text.

[42] A MS. account of Icelandic chess by Jónas Gam (D. c. 1734) is in the library of the High School, Copenhagen (Rostgaard Collection, 41, 8vo). Apparently the MS. is based upon one of the shortened editions of Selenus which were issued during the 17th c., but adds some information about Icelandic chess (*Ísl. Gátur*, 281).

only. Some give the same privilege to any Pawn which queens on the King's file.

(5) Most players give a warning that the opponent's Queen is attacked, saying, *Madam.*

(6) Some deprive a piece which is used to cover a check of all offensive power (see p. 509). Such a piece is called *leppur.*

(7) Some forbid a player to take his opponent's last man, unless he can give mate on the third or seventh move afterwards.

(8) Bare King (*bert*) is an inferior form of victory; stalemate (*patt*) is a drawn game.

The most extraordinary features of Icelandic chess are those relating to checkmate. Like Arthur Saul, the Icelandic player esteems different mates very differently, and it is more disgraceful to receive some than it is to receive others. Among mates to which no disgrace is attached are those in which mate is given by the Queen (*drottníngarmát,* formerly *frúarmát*), Rook (*hróksmát*), Knight (*riddarapissa, -peisa,* or *pissari*), and Bishop (*biskupsmát*). The disgraceful mates (*skammarmát,* 'shame-mate') are those which are inflicted with a Pawn (*peðmát, peðsmát,* or *peðrífur*), of which many different kinds are recognized,[43] or upon a particular square, e. g. on a corner square (*hornskítsmát* or *hornskítur*), in the centre of the board (*mát á miðju borði*), and most disgraceful of all, mate on the King's own square (*heimamát, heimaskít heimaskítsmát*), especially if the King has never moved.

Still more remarkable are the low mates (*lág mát*) and high mates (*há mát*), to which Stefan Ólafsson alludes in the poems quoted above. The game is not necessarily ended with the mate, but the victor can continue moving as long as he can give a fresh mating-position each move. In this case the first three mates are called *low mates,* and all the following mates are called *high mates.* To certain mating positions special names were given, e. g. *gleiðarmát* (*gleidarmát* or *flenniskuð*) or 'straddle-mate' (Wh. Qh1, Ra1, h8; Bl. Ka8), *gatrífur* (meaning lost), *sinn undir hvort eyra,* or 'box on each ear' (two Pawn-mates in succession). Eggert Ólafsson gives an account of this method of play in his *Reise igjennem Island,* Kiøbenhavn, 1772, i. 462–4, which describes a survey of Iceland which he made in 1752–7. To illustrate this prolongation of mate I have put together the position in the diagram. White can now play 1 Rh8, *hróksmát*; 2 Ra1, *tröfaldur hróksmát;* 3 Qh1, *gleiðarmát*; 4 Bf3, *biskupsmát*; 5 Ktc7, *riddarapissa*; 6 Pb7, *peðmát*; 7 Pb8=Q, *útkomumát.* The first three mates are the low, the remainder are high mates. According to Eggert Ólafsson, good players could give six or seven successive

Position in illustration of the low and high mates.

[43] Mate with the Pawn at the moment of promotion, *útkomumát,* with the following special forms: if inflicted by the King's Pawn, *blóðsótt* (lit. dysentery), *blóðskitur, blóðskitsmát, blóðköngsmát, lallamát,* and probably *kóngsmát, fretstertsmát, fretstertumát, freðstertsmát, fuðryttumát*; if by the Rook's Pawn, *lánga skuðarmát* or *lángskuðarmát*; if by the Queen's Pawn, *apturskvettumat.* Other technicalities are *þrátefli,* perpetual check, and *jafntefli,* drawn game.

mates, and nine is the greatest number possible. According to Mr. Blöndal, this method of play is now obsolete. The *Spilabók* and *Íslenzkar Gátur*, however, seem to imply that it is still occasionally played.

FOUR-HANDED CHESS.

Many derivative games of chess have been proposed since Marinelli invented his three-handed chess in 1722, but the only ones which have shown any signs of continued vitality are the games in which the board is enlarged and arranged to make a game for four players. The earliest allusion to any game of this kind is contained in Coxe's account of his visit to Russia in 1772, which is quoted in Twiss, i. 27:

> The Russians have also another method of playing at Chess, namely, with four persons at the same time, two against two; and for this purpose, the board is larger than usual, contains more men, and is provided with a greater number of squares. I was informed that this method was more difficult, but far more agreeable than the common game.

The game which Coxe saw was probably that which A. v. Petroff described in the *Schachzeitung*, 1850, 377. The board is a square of 16 × 16 squares, from which 64 squares have been removed (the four rectangles of 8 × 2 squares in the middle of each edge, viz. e1, f1 to l1, and e2, f2 to l2, &c.). The small square of 16 squares now left at each angle of the board becomes a citadel belonging to the player on whose right-hand side it lies, and only accessible from his camp. All the Kings are on the right of the Queens, partners sit opposite one another, the move goes round clockwise as in whist, and each player has a third Rook, Knight, and Bishop as reserve forces, which he can arrange in his citadel as he pleases (Verney, *Chess Eccentricities*, London, 1885, 71).

Slightly later in date to Coxe is the anonymous pamphlet, *Gesetze des Schachs zu Vieren*, Gotha, 1779, and Altenburg, 1792, which v. d. Linde (ii. 357) attributes to Duke Ernest II of Gotha-Altenburg. In this variety the board consists of 128 squares, two rows of eight squares each being added to each side of the ordinary chessboard. All the Kings are placed on black squares, partners sit opposite one another, and the move goes round clockwise (Verney, op. cit., 76).

A variant type upon a board of this shape, invented by Dr. Theodorich Martensen in 1814 or 1815, was still played in Lüneburg in 1848 (*Sch.*, 1848, 286; Verney, 74). In this form the partners sit side by side, and the move passes from South to East to West to North.

A third type of board made its appearance in K. E. G.'s *Unterricht im Schachspiel unter Vieren*, Dessau, 1784, which served as the basis of the earliest English work on four-handed chess, the *Rules for playing the game of Chess en quatre*, London, n.d. (an octavo pamphlet of 16 pages), and of Coch's Danish work *Skak en quatre*, Kjöbenhavn, 1816. This game was played upon a board of 160 squares, obtained from the ordinary chessboard by adding three rows of eight squares each to the four sides of the board. The partners sat opposite one another, the four Queens were all placed upon white squares, and the move went round anti-clockwise. This is true also of the game described in Albers' *Unterricht im Schachspiel*, Lüneburg, 1821 (who names this type of board 'the English', and the 128-squares board 'the Lüneburg' board), and of the form of the game now played in England (see Verney, 6).

A variant type of game on this board was invented by K. Enderlein, who founded the Berlin Vier-Schach-Verein in 1815, and published his *Anweisung zum Vierschachspiel*, Berlin, 1826. In his variety the Queens are placed to the left of the Kings, the partners sit opposite one another, and the move goes round clockwise.

A fourth type of board was adopted by the Mecklenburg-Schwerin players in 1828, a player having seen this board in use in Paris about four years previously. Two ordinary chessboards with the pieces arranged for play are placed side by side so as to make a board of 16 × 8 squares. The partners sit side by side, and the move passes in a crosswise manner (*Sch.*, 1848, 358; Verney, 81).

In most of these games it has been found necessary to introduce special rules, often restricting the ordinary moves of the chessmen; for these the reader must consult Verney's *Chess Eccentricities*.[44]

The latest derivative game of chess is *Schachraumspiel*, or Three dimensional chess (see Dr. Ferd. Maach, *Das Schachraumspiel*, 1908).

[44] For Kieseritzky's Baltic Four-handed chess, played upon a board in the shape of an eight-rayed star, see Livonus, *Das baltische Vierschach*, 1855, and *Sch.*, 1865, 330, 353. The game was invented about 1835.

CHAPTER XIV

PHILIDOR AND THE MODENESE MASTERS

Philidor, his chess career, and system of play.—Del Rio, Lolli, and Ponziani.—The Italian school of play.—The modern problem.—The Parisian Amateurs.—Deschapelles.—Sarratt and his services to English chess.—Allgaier.—The Automaton Chessplayer.

THERE is no name in the annals of chess which is more widely known than that of André (baptized François-André) Danican Philidor (B. 1726, D. 1795).[1] For more than forty years his was the leading personality in the chess circles of Paris and London, and the ease with which he maintained his supremacy over all players with whom he came in contact was the origin of the legend, only shattered by the advent of Paul Morphy, that he was the greatest player the world could ever expect to see.[2] In his own day Philidor was equally famous as chess-player and as musician. His first *motett* was performed at the Chapel Royal, Versailles (where he began life as a choir-boy), when he was only eleven years old, and when in after-life he turned from sacred to operatic music, more than twenty operas from his pen were performed with success in Paris in the reign of Louis XVI.

Philidor had already made considerable progress as a chess-player when he left the choir of the Chapel Royal in 1740. For the next three years he played regularly in the Parisian cafés, and specially with Légal, at that time the best player in France. At the start Légal gave him the odds of a Rook, but by 1743 he was no longer able to give Philidor, now 17 years of age, any odds. In the following year Philidor surprised the Parisian players by playing two opponents at one time without sight of the board, a performance which the Chevalier de Jaucourt thought worthy of being chronicled in the article on chess which he contributed to the great *Encyclopédie* of Diderot and D'Alembert, 1751–65. During this period chess brought him into contact with two noted Frenchmen, the philosophers Voltaire and Jean-Jacques Rousseau, both persistent but weak players.[3]

[1] He belonged to a family, originally from Dauphiné, which had been connected for three generations with the band of the Chapel Royal. The first of the family had succeeded a hautboy player named Filidori, and had adopted that name after Louis XIII had playfully used it in praise of his playing. The family name was really Danican.

[2] The tradition was diligently fostered by George Walker. How far he really believed in it is doubtful: there is only too good reason to believe that much of his excessive laudation of Philidor was written with the deliberate intention of belittling (and annoying) contemporary players with whom Walker was not always on good terms.

[3] There are several allusions to chess in Rousseau's *Confessions*. The best known are those in which he recounts his first games at chess, and the disastrous effect that the study of Greco's games had on his play, and his encounter with the Prince de Conti, *c.* 1760. To the dismay of the latter's entourage, he won two games from the Prince, justifying his conduct with the words, 'Monseigneur, j'honore trop V. A. S., pour ne pas la gagner toujours aux

The collapse of a musical engagement which had taken Philidor to Holland in 1745 was the immediate cause of his adopting chess as a career. He found himself stranded without resources in Rotterdam, but was able to earn a living by playing chess and Polish draughts, and the presence of the English army in Holland not only provided him with many opponents who were ready to pay handsomely for their games, but introduced him to many gentlemen whose acquaintance was of the greatest value to him afterwards. One immediate result was a visit to England in 1747, under the auspices of Sir Abraham Janssen, the strongest English player and one of the very few players to whom Philidor did not always give odds. During this visit Philidor played a match with Stamma at Slaughter's. Ten games in all were to be played, and Philidor gave the odds of the move, allowed his opponent to score all drawn games as won, and betted 5 to 4 on each game. The result was a great triumph for the young Frenchman, who only lost one game and gave up another as drawn.[4]

Philidor returned to Holland in 1748 in order to secure subscribers among his friends in the English army for a book on chess upon which he was engaged. In this he was most successful. The English Envoy-Plenipotentiary, Lord Sandwich, subscribed for ten copies, and the Duke of Cumberland for fifty. Philidor returned to London to see the *Analyze du Jeu des Échecs* through the press, with a list of 127 subscribers and 433 copies sold. I shall deal later with the success of this book. The discovery that Frederick the Great was a chess-player attracted Philidor to Berlin in 1750, but, although he was at Potsdam and played before the King, Frederick did not venture on a game himself. In Berlin Philidor gave an exhibition of blindfold play, playing three games at the same time and winning them all. After a round of visits in Germany and England, he returned to France in the autumn of 1754, after an absence of nine years.

During these years French players had at last realized the desirability of having some head-quarters. At first they chose a café which had been recently opened by a Sicilian named Procope (Gay, *Bibl. Anecd.*, 1864, 124), but when the lettered world, attracted by the possibility of seeing Voltaire and Rousseau

échecs.' A game purporting to have been played on this occasion has been often printed (Ellis, *Chess Sparks*, 1895, 2; Mason, *Social Chess*, 1900, 90), but it is a literary forgery. It made its first appearance in the *Palamède*, 1843, 41–2, in a romantic version of the meeting between Rousseau and the Prince, and was supplied by Doazan. The latter obtained it from the *Doazan MS.* (see p. 821), where it is given as by Busnardo. A more impudent forgery is the game which the Abbé Roman describes in his poem *Les Échecs*, Paris, 1807, as having been played between himself and Rousseau in 1770. The game is none other than the first of the Gambits in the French editions of Greco! See L. Grünberg, 'Rousseau Joueur d'Échecs', in the *Annales de la Société J.-J. Rousseau*, iii (and as a separate print, Geneva, 1907), and my note, 'Rousseau and Chess', *BCM.*, 1908, 329.

[4] On this visit he played at the *Duke of Rutland's Chess*, an enlarged variety on a 14 × 10 board, the invention of John, the third Duke (D. 1779). Each player had 14 Pawns on his second row (who could move 1, 2, or 3 squares for their first move) and 14 Pieces on the first row, on the following files: a, n, R; b, m, Crowned Castle (with move of K or R); c, d, l, Kt: e, f, j, k, B; g, Q; h, K: i, Concubine (with move of R or Kt). The descriptions in Sharpe's 1767 edition of Hyde, i. xxv, and in Twiss, i. 155, do not quite agree. The best players of the game were Janssen (after whose death it dropped into disuse), Stamma, Dr. Cowper, and Mr. Salvador. In less than three months Philidor was able to give any of these players the odds of the Knight at this game.

at the chessboard, began to crowd thither, the more serious chess-players removed to the Café de la Régence in the Place du Palais-Royal, which, except for a brief interruption during the First Revolution, has ever since been the centre of the Parisian chess life. Here Philidor played a match with Légal in which he proved himself at last the superior of his old master, and here for the next fifteen years he took his recreation in playing chess, while he devoted his main energies to musical composition. It was not until 1772 that he found time to revisit his old friends in London.

Philidor found Slaughter's deserted since 1770, and the Salopian Coffee-house, Charing Cross, the new head-quarters of the London players. The result of his visit was another migration, for it led to the formation of a *Chess Club*, strictly limited to 100 members at a three-guinea subscription, which made Parsloe's, St. James's Street, its home. The aim of the founders was to make it possible to secure Philidor's presence in London for the season (February to May) in each year, but all the best people crowded to join, and the club started as one of the most fashionable clubs in London. In 1776 the roll of members included Charles James Fox, the Marquess of Rockingham, Lord Mansfield, Erskine, Wedderburne, Gibbon, Elliott the defender of Gibraltar, and General Burgoyne. It was the last rally of the English nobility to claim chess as the game most typical of their order, and it was part of the irony of fate that the man for whose benefit the club was established should have done most by his literary labours to destroy this historic connexion with chess. For it was the diffusion of analysis, and the rise in the standard of play which resulted from the realization of the principles of the game, which effected the change. The chess-player had now to study if he wished to excel.

The example of the London players was followed in 1783 in Paris, and a chess club was established near the Palais-Royal under the patronage of Monsieur le Comte de Provence (later Louis XVIII), who was himself a member. The subscription was 100 francs, and each club gave special privileges to the members of the other.

The members of the London club raised a fund every year to defray Philidor's expenses, and from 1775 Philidor spent the Spring of each year in London and the rest of the year in Paris. This arrangement lasted until the Revolution, and after the Spring of 1793, Philidor never returned to Paris. In 1777 he published a second, and in 1790 a third edition of the *Analyze du Jeu des Échecs*, both editions being under the patronage of the London club. A comparison of the lists of subscribers to these editions, 283 to the second, including every member of the London and 50 members of the Paris club, and only 56 (all English) to the third, shows the great change which had come over the position of the London club. The fashionable world had moved away, and it had become the resort of chess-players only. When the season of 1790 opened, only fourteen members attended the first dinner, and although Philidor in his letter to his family described the prospects for the season as brilliant, the club felt that something must be done to increase its attractions.

They accordingly resolved that the blindfold performances which Philidor had commenced in 1782 should for the future be fortnightly instead of annually as before. These performances had created an extraordinary excitement at first, and the newspapers of 1782 are very amusing reading. The *Morning Post* of 28 May says, in its account of the performance in which Philidor played Count Brühl [5] and Mr. Bowdler at the same time, seeing neither board, and drawing the first and losing the second game:

> The celebrated Mr. Philidor, whose unrivalled excellence at the game of Chess has long been distinguished, invited the members of the Chess-club, and the amateurs in general of that arduous amusement, to be present on Saturday last at a spectacle of the most curious kind, as it was to display a very wonderful faculty of the human mind, which faculty, however, is perhaps exclusively at present his own. . . . The idea of the intellectual labour that was passing in the mind of Mr. Philidor, suggested a painful perception to the spectators, which, however, was quite unnecessary, as he seldom paused half a minute, and seemed to undergo little mental fatigue. . . . When the intrinsic difficulty of the game is considered, as well as the great skill of his adversaries, who, of course, conducted it with the most subtle complications; this exertion seems absolutely miraculous, and certainly deserves to be recorded as a proof, at once interesting and astonishing, of the power of human intelligence.

And the *World* of the same date begins its account:

> This brief article is the record of more than sport and fashion: it is a *phenomenon* in the *history of man*, and so should be hoarded among the best samples of human memory—till memory shall be no more.[6]

Fourteen performances of this character are on record in which Philidor played now two and now three simultaneous blindfold games, or (in his later years) two games blindfold and a third across the board, and the games played on seven of these occasions are in existence. His total score for nine such performances (10 wins, 4 draws, 6 losses) does not argue any surpassing ability as a blindfold player. Philidor's achievements in this method of play have been entirely eclipsed by many later players, notably by P. Morphy, Louis Paulsen, J. H. Zukertort, J. H. Blackburne, and H. N. Pillsbury. The last-named player contested twenty games on one occasion, and there seems no limit—apart from that imposed by the time the play must take—to the number of games that a player with this faculty might play at one time.[7]

In 1787 the Chess Club was joined by the Rev. George Atwood, F.R.S. (B. 1746, D. 1807), a distinguished mathematician, who held a comfortable sinecure under Government as Patent Searcher of the Customs. Atwood was

[5] John Maurice, Count Brühl (B. 1736, D. 1809), Minister of Saxony in England, was one of the strongest players of the London club. Philidor gave him the Knight for two moves. Mr. Bowdler, Lord Harrowby, Mr. Jennings, and the Hon. Henry Conway were of about equal strength. Count Brühl was a liberal friend to Philidor during the last years of his life.

[6] And yet the performances of the Jesuit Sacchieri of Turin, lecturer in Mathematics at Pavia in the first half of the eighteenth century, who played three and four games at one time blindfold, were known in England. They had been recounted in Keysler's *Travels*, i, in *The Gentleman's Magazine*, March 1746, and in Lambe's *Hist. Chess*, 1764, 54, and were repeated later in Twiss, i. 20 (quoting Keysler's *Turin*, 1749).

[7] See A. Binet, *Psychologie des grands calculateurs et joueurs d'échecs*, 1894, for a discussion of the phenomenon of blindfold chess.

not a strong player, but he made up for this by the industry with which he took down games played at the club from 1787 to 1800. He took part in Philidor's last blindfold performance, on 20 June, 1795, and it was with him that Philidor played his last game of chess nine days later. The master died on 24 August of that year.[8]

Atwood left his chess papers to his friend Joseph Wilson,[9] and after the latter's death they were offered for sale in 1833. One note-book containing the record of the games was bought by George Walker, and formed the basis of his *Selection of Games at Chess, actually played by Philidor and his Contemporaries*, London, 1835. This note-book is now in the Rimington-Wilson Library. Another MS. (probably not from Atwood's pen), containing six games played by Philidor blindfold, is now with the remainder of Prof. Allen's chess library in the Ridgemont Branch Library, Philadelphia.

It is unfortunate that all these games belong to the last period of Philidor's life, when he had passed the age of greatest strength as a player, and that all were played against opponents far weaker than himself. Both of these facts must be borne in mind in attempting any estimate of Philidor's ability as a player.

Walker's *Selection of Games* does not create a very favourable impression of the standard of play in Philidor's time. It was an age of mediocre players, among whom Philidor stood easily first, but even he made mistakes repeatedly which would have been fatal against players of average skill who were not frightened into incapacity by the reputation of the master. At its best Philidor's play falls short of that accuracy of conception and richness of combination which characterized the play of De la Bourdonnais and MacDonnell. On the other hand there is plenty of evidence of real capacity for chess, and an untouched reserve of genius which would have resulted in a far higher level of practical skill if he had ever been called upon to show it. The *Analyze du Jeu des Échecs* of his youth gives a far more favourable opinion of his talent than the games of his old age.

Philidor was only 23 years old when the *Analyze* was written. It is a notable work, revealing a singular maturity of judgement in one so young, and it had an instant success, and one far more lasting than that of any other chess-book of the kind. Two reissues were necessary in the year of its publication, and many other reprints and editions followed before Philidor introduced any changes in the book. It was only at long intervals (1777 and 1790) that he revised the work, and the revision meant little more than the addition of other Openings; and although in the edition of 1777 he modified some of the too confident assertions of the original work, the main features of the *Analyze* remained unchanged. Criticism and emendation alike were consistently ignored by Philidor: secure in his possession of the chess throne

[8] The standard work on Philidor's life is Prof. George Allen's *Life of Philidor*, Philadelphia, 1863, which contains as an appendix an acute criticism of Philidor as author and player, by v. d. Lasa. To both work and appendix I am greatly indebted.

[9] Wilson was a former owner of the copy of the Mountstephen Greco MS., which is now in Mr. J. G. White's library.

of France and England, he probably declined to admit the right of any of his contemporaries to oppose their judgement to his. Since his death the *Analyze* has been reprinted often: it formed the basis of the first Russian work on chess, and is probably still the best-known work on the subject in France, Spain, and the Spanish-speaking countries of America.

The secret of this remarkable success is the lucidity, the assurance, and the brevity of the book. No previous writer had attempted to explain the reasons for particular moves with the detail and directness which Philidor adopted. An example will illustrate this. In the first game, 1 Pe4, Pe5; 2Bc4, Bc5; 3 Pc3, Ktf6; 4 Pd4, he makes this note: 'This Pawn is play'd two Moves for two very important Reasons; the first is, to hinder your Adversary's King's Bishop to play upon your King's Bishop's Pawn; and the second, to put the Strength of your Pawns in the Middle of the Exchequer, which is of great Consequence to attain the making of a Queen'. Advice like this was what players wanted, and would remember.[10]

Then Philidor wrote with all the confidence of youth. He was not afraid to express an opinion. To players used to Stamma's Openings without a single note of advice or warning, or Bertin's unsatisfying phrase, 'and the players may finish the game', at the end of each piece of analysis, Philidor's clear and precise statements came as a revelation. Did the player wish to play the King's Knight's Opening (1 Pe4, Pe5; 2 Ktf3), Philidor was there to tell him, 'Playing the King's Knight the second Move is entirely wrong; because it not only loses the Attack, but gives it to the Adversary'; did he wonder about the strength of the popular Pawn game of the day, 1 Pe4, Pe5; 2 Pc3, Philidor again is ready to answer him, 'Playing this Pawn the second Move . . . is demonstratively ill played, because the Move is certainly lost by the Adversary's pushing the Queen's Pawn two steps; consequently the attack goeth on the other side, and very probably the Game; for when once the Move is lost, it is very difficult to regain it with good Players.' It did not matter that Philidor was wrong in both cases: the beginner feels that any guide is better than none.[11]

Moreover, all Philidor's guidance was consistent. He had evolved a theory of play, and he believed in it thoroughly. All his notes are written with the single intention of making this system clear, of exemplifying it, of pushing it home. As he says in his Preface to the 1749 edition:

> My chief intention is to recommend myself to the Public, by a Novelty no one has thought of, or perhaps ever understood well; I mean how to play the Pawns: They are the very Life of this Game; They alone form the Attack and the Defence; on their good or bad Situation depends the Gain or Loss of the Party. A Player, who, when he has play'd a Pawn well, can give no Reason for his moving it to such a Square, may be compared to a General, who with much Practice has little or no Theory.

[10] In my quotations I use the first English edition, *Chess Analysed*, London, 1750, unless I say otherwise.

[11] Both statements were modified in the 1777 edition, but the games are unaltered. Of the Knight's Opening he merely says, 'This game is not quite exact; but the first moves of the White (the second player) are very well calculated, especially when some odds are granted'; and in the Pawn game he omits the dangerous word 'demonstratively'.

And the whole of this system was unfolded in four games and ten back games or variations, all carried, if not to the actual mate, at least to a position in which the win was evident, and all skilfully composed in such a way that the principles which they were designed to teach were displayed to the best advantage. There was no opportunity for the bewilderment with which the beginner rose from the study of Greco's 94 games or Stamma's 74 Openings.

It is by these four games that the *Analyze* should be judged: if Philidor added to them six other games (four gambits, a new Observation on the Gambit called Cunningham, and a Queen's Gambit, otherwise Gambit of Aleppo) illustrating the popular Openings of the day, it was only in deference to the expectations of the public.[12] For the system they were unnecessary. Nor ought we to test every move in each game to find whether it is the absolutely best at the moment—unless Philidor has advanced an opinion as to the soundness of the opening, or the move is a critical one for the establishment of the truth of his system. It is the general plan of the whole play that is the important thing from Philidor's point of view, and the *Analyze* is even more a work on Mid-game tactics than an analysis of the Openings.

Philidor belonged essentially to the school of Lopez, which, as a result of the many French editions of Lopez's work in the 17th century, had become the school of the majority of French players. But he was not only the first player to realize and state the principles that lay behind Lopez's analysis, but also the first player to carry those principles to their logical conclusions and to embody them in a system of play. Philidor has often been ridiculed for his statement that the Pawns 'sont l'âme des Échecs', but his system went far to make them so. Everything is subordinated to the effort to conduct a Pawn to queen. The utmost liberty of action must be preserved for the Pawns. The formation of a strong centre of Pawns is advocated as the simplest initial step towards this end. Since the Bishop's Pawns will be required for the support of the centre Pawns, the Knights must not be played to c3 and f3 until after their advance.

It is obvious that the result of the rigid application of these principles must result in slow and, on the whole, uninteresting games. The natural opening to adopt is the King's Bishop's Game, because the development of this Bishop on the second move obstructs none of the Pawns. The obvious criticism on the Philidorian system is that the liberty of the stronger pieces is unduly curtailed for the benefit of the weaker Pawns. Moreover, the demonstration of the system in the *Analyze* games does not carry conviction. In every game Philidor unduly favours White (who plays the attack in the first two, and the defence in the third and fourth games) by not allowing Black to adopt the strongest moves at his disposal. It was almost obligatory on Philidor to prove that the King's Knight's Opening is bad, since the early play of the Knight runs counter to his whole system, but to

[12] In the 1777 edition Philidor added six Regular Parties, of which the first five are Bishop's Openings and the last is a Sicilian defence (without special name), and two Salvio Gambits (so named for the first time). The 'Gambit of Aleppo' (so in Lambe, *Hist. Chess*, 1764, 58) commemorates Stamma's fondness for this Opening.

dismiss it on the strength of 1 Pe4, Pe5; 2 Ktf3, Pd6; 3 Bc4, *Pf5*; 4 Pd3 ignoring the stronger move 4 Pd4, or of 3 Pd4, *Pf5*; 4 P×eP, fP×P; Pd5; 6 Pf4 ignoring both 6 *Pe6* and 4 *Ktc3*, was to invite criticism which was not long in forthcoming.

The *Analyze* of 1749 concludes with an able analysis of a special position in the Ending R and B *v.* R, although Philidor was wrong in thinking that all positions could be brought into this particular one. With this investigation the scientific and systematic investigation of the Endings really began.

It was natural that the earliest criticism of the *Analyze* should come from Italy, because the Italian players had never accepted the Lopez principles. Moreover, just at the time that Philidor was elaborating his system, a group of highly gifted players, certainly the most gifted players Italy has ever produced, were themselves occupied in elaborating the principles of play of Salvio, Greco, and the other Italian players of the sixteenth century. These were D. Domenico Lorenzo Ponziani (B. 1719, D. 1792), Professor of Civil Law in the University of Modena from 1742 to 1772, Canon of the Cathedral, 1766, and Capitular Vicar, 1785,[13] and his two friends and fellow-townsmen, the lawyer Ercole del Rio, and Giambattista Lolli, who are generally known by the name of the Modenese Masters.

Ercole del Rio was already the author of a small chess-book, *Sopra il giuoco degli Scacchi, Osservazioni pratiche d'anonimo Autore Modenese*, Modena, 1750, before the Modenese masters had obtained any knowledge of the eighteenth-century authors in France and England. This work follows the model of Salvio in containing Openings and problems or End-games, but it is far in advance of it, both in arrangement and in the accuracy and importance of the analysis. Here for the first time we meet with the Scotch Game and the Ruy Lopez defended by 3 . . , Pa6. As an introduction to the Openings del Rio's work was far superior to any work in existence in 1750, but it was admittedly written for advanced players, and even for these it was not an easy text-book, since del Rio was very sparing in notes or explanations. Accordingly Lolli formed the plan of annotating it fully, and of making it the basis for a great encyclopedic work on the game. This he did in the *Osservationi teorico-pratiche sopra il giuoco degli scacchi,* Bologna, 1763, a folio of 632 pages. By this time Philidor's book had reached Modena.

Lolli's book is divided into three parts, of which the first is the annotated text of del Rio's volume of 1750, preceded by a letter from that writer with many valuable hints for the player; the second is a similar treatise dealing with the defence, written expressly for the book by del Rio, and elaborately annotated by Lolli—a very necessary thing, for del Rio's text was even more difficult than that of the earlier work; and the third is a treatise on the Ending by Lolli himself, concluding with a carefully selected collection of 100 problems which was intended to challenge comparison with Stamma's 100 positions.

[13] See his life in *Chess Monthly*, New York, 1857, 126, whence in *Chess World*, 1866, 327, *Sch.*, 1862, 97, and *BCM.*, 1893, 295.

It is in the second part of Lolli's book (pp. 365–8) that del Rio deals with the *Analyze*. After a word of generous praise for the piece of End-game analysis, he devotes his attention to Philidor's games, with the idea of seeing to what extent they justify Philidor's principles of play, and he shows that three of the four games are faulty, since the defence in the First, and the attack in the Fourth, can be strengthened to equality of position at least, while the attack in the Third can be strengthened to superiority. His conclusion that Philidor's demonstration was really unsuccessful is a just one. Incidentally he disputes Philidor's claim that the King's Gambits 'give no Advantage to him who attacks, or to him who defends them; if both play equally well, the Game becomes most commonly a drawn Game', and quotes with approval a line from a poem by Carlo Salvio in the 1634 Salvio (Bk. II, p. 40), 'Gambitto a giocator farsi non lice'.

It was not until six years later that Ponziani published his *Il giuoco incomparabile degli scacchi . .*, *Opera d'Autore Modenese,* Modena, 1769. A second and improved edition with the same title followed in 1782, and in this later edition Ponziani lays down the principles of play of the Italian school.

Ponziani, as del Rio and Lolli had done, confines his attention to the Opening and the Ending, and leaves the Mid-game untouched. He also follows Lolli's example in dividing his Openings into games for the attack and games for the defence, an unnatural division, since the move which in the former case leads to victory, in the latter leads to defeat, and the reader finds a difficulty in estimating the real value of a line of play. Notwithstanding this, his analysis deserves very high praise, and no later work of the Italian chess with free castling took its place.[14]

The fundamental principle of the Italian school is the maintenance of the maximum amount of liberty for the Pieces. These are placed as speedily as possible in the positions in which they will exert most pressure upon the more vulnerable points of the enemy's array—at first f2 (f7). No importance is attached to the formation of a centre of Pawns, except as a means of opening a path for the major pieces, nor on the maintenance of a centre when formed; in so far as a Pawn centre restricts the activity of the Pieces, it is discouraged. The main use of the Pawns is to drive back the opponent's Pieces from their best positions in order to gain more ground for the player's own Pieces. The most natural opening to adopt is the Giuoco Piano, because in it the development of the Pieces is most direct, and the attack upon f2 (f7) is in view from the first move. The ideal is the open game.

It is clear that under this system the player is in a far better position to take advantage of a blunder of his opponent than under the Philidorian system, but it is by no means so clear that his position will be equally

[14] Ponziani discusses more Openings than Lolli, but the only new ones are the Allgaier Gambit (very briefly mentioned in the 1769 work, Venice ed. of 1801, 232), and the Ponziani counter attack in Staunton's Opening (1 Pe4, Pe5; 2 Ktf3, Ktc6; 3 Pc3, *Pf5*; in the 1782 work, 114).

favourable if the game comes to the End-game stage. It is the weakness of the Italian system that in paying attention to the effective use of the major pieces as weapons of attack, it neglects the prospective value of the Pawns. In a way it is based on an attitude towards the problem of play as one-sided as the Philidorian, but the defects of the Italian system are less obvious, and probably less serious, because the weaker and not the stronger forces suffer. That a far more interesting type of game results by adopting the principles of the Italian school has always been a strong recommendation. In the special points of difference between Philidor and the Modenese masters the verdict of posterity is entirely in favour of the latter. The Bishop's Opening is practically obsolete, the Philidor Defence is hardly played, and the soundness of the King's Knight's Opening is universally admitted.

In their attitude towards the problem the Modenese masters and their contemporary composers came under the influence of Stamma's work, and the idea that the problem should be the brilliant termination of a possible game lies behind the majority of the direct mates in the Lolli and Ponziani collections. Beyond this Stamma's influence did not extend, and the Muslim notion that equality of force was necessary to secure plausibility was not adopted. The result is that the Italian problems are not overloaded with unnecessary pieces, while the greater skill and lighter touch of the composers have produced work of greater piquancy. The sense of continuity with the past was maintained by the composition of self-mates and conditional problems (the latter to a reduced extent), and by the preservation of all that was best in Salvio and Damiano. The most important departure from the practice of Stamma lay in the title of the problem. The Italian players laid stress upon the length of the solution, and therefore on the shortest method of winning.

After the time of Ponziani the chess problem gradually ceased to have any intimate connexion with the game of chess, developing its own special literature and appealing to its own public, until it has become impossible to make the old claim that the study of the problem has any real effect upon proficiency in the game itself.[15] The real representative of the mediaeval problem in this connexion is the End-game. I do not, therefore, propose to devote any portion of the remaining chapters to the chess problem, and merely indicate here in rough outline the main lines of its later development. For a long time the cult of the problem was mainly confined to England and Germany; after 1830 the problem began to appeal to an ever-widening circle, and in the latter part of the nineteenth century one of its most important advances is associated with Bohemia.[16]

The Lolli and Ponziani collections became known in Northern Europe

[15] The change is emphasized by the change of name in English from *position* or *situation* to *problem*, which was first definitely used by William Lewis in the title of his 1827 work, *Chess Problems.* (An earlier use in the English version of Montigny's work, *Stratagems of Chess*, London, 1816, iv, 'These situations are in reality so many problems, the solution of which is required to be found', may have suggested the use of the term to Lewis.)

[16] Only a few problem-lovers have so far concerned themselves with the history of the development of their art. Allen's papers in the *BCM.*, 1903-4, have been already mentioned. Kohtz and Kockelkorn, in *Das indische Problem*, Potsdam, 1903, have done valuable work

through the wholesale appropriations which were made with quite inadequate acknowledgement by the compilers of chess-books in the early nineteenth century, the most prominent offender perhaps being Montigny, who published *Les Stratagèmes des Échecs* anonymously in Paris in 1802, a work which was translated into German, English, and Danish, with the result that the composers of the period worked on the Italian model.

The Stamma problem remained the ruling type of direct-mate problem until the time of the publication of Alexandre's great but carelessly compiled *Collection des plus beaux problèmes d'Échecs,* Paris, 1846, and the general characteristics of this phase in the development of the modern problem may be conveniently studied in that work. A new era, the problems of which are often described as belonging to the *transitional school*, dates from the publication of the Rev. Henry A. Loveday's famous 'Indian Problem' in the *Chess Player's Chronicle* for February, 1845. The next generation of composers slowly evolved the foundation principles of the existing art of problem composition. The immediate effect of the publication of the Indian problem was twofold. It resulted in a remarkable diminution in the length of the solution of later problems, and concentrated attention upon problems in five moves and under. It directed attention to the importance of the theme or idea which the problem was intended to illustrate, and during the earlier portion of the transitional period composers used their ingenuity to discover new and suitable themes which could be expressed in the form of a problem of two, three, or four moves. The comparatively small number of themes which are suitable for presentation in two or three moves, and the large number of ways in which the same theme could be presented, led to the definition of canons of taste by which the varying merits of different settings of the same idea could be estimated. In this way such features as economy of material, difficulty of solution, neatness of construction, accuracy of solution, became recognized as beauties in a problem, and a check or a capture on the key-move as a blemish or even worse.

With the exhaustion of the themes that could be expressed in the shorter problems, two courses became possible: to proceed to the still comparatively unexplored field of the problem in four moves, or to endeavour to obtain originality by the combination in a single problem of a number of themes expressible in two or three moves. The vast majority of players adopted the latter course, and the difficulty of satisfying all the recognized canons of taste by which the older type of problem had been tested in a problem that contained a combination of themes resulted in players in different countries attaching differing values to the various canons, so that four national schools of composers arose in the period 1860–80, the American,

in the history of the period, 1840–50. Cf. also 'Drei alte Meister', in the *Festschrift d. Akad. Schachklubs*, München, 1911, pp. 41–128. I have also used Mr. B. G. Laws' 'Modern Standards of Problem Composition', *BCM.*, 1896, 257, 305, 346.

Both the *Deutsches Wochenschach* and the *Wiener Schachzeitung* have in recent years contained many important articles on the history of the modern problem. At the present time Mr. Alain C. White of New York is engaged in an important attempt to deal with the history of the development of the two-move problem.

the Bohemian, the English, and the German, each definable in terms of the different values they attached to particular features of the problem. Towards the end of the 19th c. there was a marked tendency towards uniformity of ideal, and with the general recognition of the features to be aimed at, and to be avoided, the modern school of problem composition came into existence.

The obvious criticism on this school is that it attributes an exaggerated importance to its laws—really nothing more than conventions—of composition. It is due to the literary labours of the veteran problemists, J. Kohtz and C. Kockelkorn, and especially to the inspiration of their brilliant monograph, *Das indische Problem* (Potsdam, 1903), that a new school of composers has arisen in Germany which has broken loose from the restrictions which the canons of the modern school place upon the free play of originality of idea.

During the last fifty years the annual output of problems has been enormous, and even at the present time there is no sign of any diminution in the number published year by year. Many newspapers publish one or two problems in their chess column every week; every chess magazine devotes a considerable portion of its space to the problem; and beyond this there is a growing list of books which deal with the problem alone. Already this list extends to more than 500 volumes.

With the Modenese masters, and the contemporary work, *Il giuoco degli scacchi*, of Count Carlo Cozio, Turin, 1766, Italian chess ceased to play any important part in the development or literature of the game, and the centre of the chess life of Europe passed definitely to France and England.[17]

The leading players in Paris before the Revolution were Philidor, Verdoni, Léger, Carlier, and Bernard. In 1775 the last four published the *Traité théorique et pratique du jeu des échecs par une société d'amateurs* (commonly known as the *Traité des amateurs*), in which they challenged comparison with the *Analyze*. Their criticism of Philidor was sufficiently mild—'en rendant tout l'hommage qui est dû au plus grand Joueur de l'Europe, on se permettra d'observer ici que nombre de Parties qui composent son Traité sont plus instructives que correctes, & que ses assertions sur le gain ou la perte *forcés* de ces Parties sont souvent hasardées & démenties par la combinaison & l'expérience'. The Amateurs devote considerable attention to the game at odds, but the work as a whole, written in full agreement with the principles of the Philidorian school, is not one of any great importance, although it was once much admired.[18]

The Revolution put an end to the existence of the Paris club, and even interrupted play at the Café de la Régence for a time. But by 1798 Bernard and Carlier had succeeded in collecting a body of players again, and in this

[17] Details of the later chess life in Italy will be found in *Sch.*, 1847 (344), 1861 (369), 1862 (7, 33), 1867 (271, 335, 365), 1868 (37).

[18] The same criticism applies to E. Stein's *Nouvel Essai sur le Jeu des Échecs*, La Haye, 1789. Stein (B. 1748 in Alsace, D. 1812) was a Jewish player who created a great reputation in Holland by his play. He was engaged to teach chess to the sons of William V, the last Stadtholder of the Netherlands. He was able to play two games simultaneously, without sight of the board, at the same time with a game of billiards.

year Alexandre Louis Honoré Lebreton Deschapelles (B. 1780, D. 1847) came rapidly to the front rank, and made good his claim to be recognized as the leading French player. Deschapelles was a player with great natural gifts for chess,[19] and he was able to give odds to all competitors with whom he came in contact. This confirmed him in his opinion that the study of Opening analysis was waste of time—an opinion which in his case was probably true, so long as he kept to the odds of the Pawn and move, or two moves, or played at Légal's Game of the Pawns; but it led to the curious result that Cochrane, in 1821, did better against him without odds than with them. Deschapelles' leading pupil was De la Bourdonnais, whose achievements will be related in the next chapter. When De la Bourdonnais surmounted the odds of Pawn and two moves in 1821, Deschapelles withdrew from chess and played whist instead. Like other great players, the latter was very jealous of his reputation as the best player of his time, and in 1836, after the close of the De la Bourdonnais–MacDonnell match, he challenged any English player to play him at the odds of the Pawn and two moves; but, although the challenge was accepted by W. Lewis, nothing came of it.

Philidor's death was a great blow to the chess club at Parsloe's, and although Verdoni was induced to settle in England, he could hardly be expected to fill the vacant throne. With the deaths of Verdoni in 1804 and Count Brühl in 1809, the club ceased to possess any importance for English chess, and its existence was almost forgotten when the actual end came about the year 1825.

That the decline in the fortunes of this somewhat exclusive club was not due to any fall in the popularity of chess in London, or England generally, is shown by the continuous succession of new chess-books, or new editions of existing books, which were published between 1795 and 1825. If we except Sarratt's works and the introduction added to the English edition of Montigny's *Stratagèmes*, which appeared in 1817 (though this introduction borrowed its maxims for play from Hoyle without acknowledgement), most of these books owed any merit which they might possess to the fidelity with which they reproduced Philidor's Games with the original notes. Nearly all of them were out of date in many important particulars at the time of issue, and some are so carelessly put together that they are not even self-consistent in their rules of play. All teach that stalemate is a lost game for the stalemating player, and all, except the Rev. Thomas Pruen's *Introduction*, Cheltenham, 1804, restrict Pawn promotion to the rank of a piece already lost. Peter Pratt, a weak player, to whom Lewis gave the odds of the Knight in a match in 1817, and a persistent proposer of innovations in the game,[20] in his anonymously

[19] According to his own story, Deschapelles learnt chess by watching Bernard play for one evening, and the second day afterwards he reached his full strength as a player. His life is given in the *Palamède*, Nov., 1847 (and *Sch.*, 1848, 156). The *Gentleman's Mag.*, July, 1807, contained an account of a series of games played between two committees headed respectively by Deschapelles and Carlier.

[20] Thus in the *Theorie*, he wished to change the names Queen, Rook, and Pawn, to Minister, Peer, and Commoner, to call castling *closeting*, to allow the King to castle out of, and over, check, and in castling with the Queen's side to play Kb1 and Rd1. In the *Studies*, 1810,

published *Theorie of Chess*, 1799, and *Studies of Chess*, 1803,[21] and W. S. Kenny, who styled himself a teacher of chess, in his *Practical Chess Grammar*, 1817, not only give these older rules in their descriptions of the moves, but add the code of rules which had been adopted by the Parsloe players, which had abandoned all restrictions on Pawn promotion.

In the main these handbooks give maxims of play which are founded on Hoyle, and are only slightly coloured by the Philidorian theory of Pawn play.

The first player to break away from the Philidorian tradition was J. H. Sarratt, a London schoolmaster who had learnt his chess from Verdoni, and a member, or a frequent visitor, of the London Chess Club which was founded 6 April, 1807, and met at Tom's Coffee House in Cornhill. It was due to his influence that the London club in their code of rules declared stalemate to be a drawn game, and so abandoned the last special feature of the English chess. The inclusion of this code in Sarratt's books, and later in those of Lewis and George Walker, led to its general adoption in England.

Sarratt's reputation as a player was very high. His pupil Lewis wrote of him that he 'was the finest and most finished player whom I have ever seen, alike excellent in attack and defence, and capable of unravelling intricate positions with ease and accuracy'. His style of play came as a revelation to English players of his time, modelled as it was upon the principles of the Italian masters, Salvio, del Rio, and Lolli. It was not the least of his services to English chess that he introduced his generation to the work of the older masters, Damiano, Lopez, and Salvio, in a series of translations. That, as we now know to be the case, these translations were careless, inaccurate, and incomplete, did not rob them of their value at the time they were made,[22] though this discovery has had a very damaging effect on his reputation as a writer. It is unfortunate that the badness of this portion of Sarratt's literary work should have prevented his successors from recognizing the importance and real merit of his other services to chess.

In his *Treatise*, London, 1808, and *New Treatise*, London, 1821 (prepared for press and published after Sarratt's death by Lewis, who generously suppressed his own share in the work), Sarratt, who styles himself 'Professor of Chess', appears as an enthusiastic disciple of del Rio. Although in deference to the practice of his contemporaries he gives the pride of place

ii. 339, he proposes that the Pawn whose promotion is due before a piece has been lost should become a Hydra with a move doubling that of the Knight, for which he substitutes (1825, 520) a Cadet moving as a Rook but confined to the 8th rank. *The Elements of Chess*, Boston, 1805, improved on the *Theorie* by devising a Republican nomenclature, K Governor, Q General, KR and QR First and Second Colonel, KB and QB First and Second Major, K Kt and Q Kt, First and Second Captain, P Pioneer. I have read somewhere that a similar proposal was made in France during the Revolution.

[21] This latter work contains Sir William Jones's youthful poem *Caïssa*, written in imitation of Vida's poem in 1763. The heroine of this poem, the Dryad Caïssa, has become the modern player's Muse of Chess. This poem was first published in Sir William Jones's *Poems*, Oxford, 1772.

[22] *Damiano, Ruy Lopez and Salvio*, 1813; *Gianutio and Gustavus Selenus*, 1817. Sarratt's carelessness is shown by the fact that he never discovered that Selenus was a translation of the Tarsia Lopez which he had translated four years before. This series of translations was completed by Lewis's *Stamma*, 1818, *Greco*, 1819, and *Carrera*, 1822, and by Cochrane's *Treatise* (the Amateurs and del Rio), 1822.

to the Bishop's Opening in his earlier book (a practice which Lewis followed and Walker and Staunton first abandoned in England), his predilections were for the open game, the Giuoco Piano and the King's Knight's Gambits. Thus he condemns the French Defence, 'This beginning, which is frequently played by unskilful players, is very improper, as all the pieces remain confined and useless' (1808, 87), and expresses strong dislike for the less open Bishop's Gambit, 'This is a dangerous, and perhaps an exceptionable move: but there are few players who know how to oppose it properly' (1808, 171). In this work the so-called Cochrane Gambit appears for the first time. The *New Treatise* contains a first attempt to analyse the Muzio Gambit, contributed by W. Lewis. The reintroduction of this Gambit, Sarratt's favourite Opening, was, however, due neither to Sarratt nor to Verdoni, who was wont to call it 'my gambit'. We now know from the Atwood MS. that the members of the club at Parsloe's were examining it and trying it against Philidor in 1795.[23] Joseph Wilson, its introducer, had probably found it in his Mountstephen Greco MS. In the hands of these early players it was a very risky game for the attack, since they conducted the Opening in the same tame way that they played the Bishop's Opening, and the attack was soon exhausted. Sarratt was the first player to push the attack in the Italian spirit, and his success with it led to the great reputation of the Opening in the first half of the nineteenth century.

The first real sign of any advance in the standard of German chess is supplied by the appearance of Allgaier's *Neue theoretisch-praktische Anweisung zum Schachspiel*, Vienna, 1795, a work of real ability and originality which ran through seven editions before it was supplanted by the *Handbuch* in 1843. The first four editions were published during Allgaier's lifetime, and were carefully revised by him. The substitution of a tabular arrangement for the old succession of games and variations which Allgaier made in the third edition (1811) was a great improvement, though players were singularly slow in recognizing the advantages of the new idea. In my references to the *Anweisung* I use the fourth edition (1819), the last issued under Allgaier's supervision. In this edition he introduces an analysis of what he styles 'A new form of the Gambit'; to which he could find no satisfactory defence. In consequence of this, later writers have given the name of the Allgaier Gambit to this Opening.[24]

Johann Allgaier (B. 1763, D. 1823) was an officer in the Imperial, and later the Austrian, army who had acted as chess-tutor to the Emperor's sons, and after his retirement in 1816 he ranked as the best player in Vienna.[25]

[23] Cf. my paper, 'Parsloe's in January and February, 1795', in *BCM.*, 1907, 445. Other Openings played at this time were the Cotter Gambit, which we call the Allgaier; and Mortemar, which we call the Sicilian.

[24] This Opening is mentioned in *Ponziani*, 1782, 134, and was played in Milan in 1796 by an Engineer named Balzarette (*CPC.*, 1852, 308). For some time both the Kieseritzky and the Allgaier Gambits were included under the name of Allgaier, although Allgaier devotes very little attention to the former Opening.

[25] For Allgaier's life, see *Sch.*, 1866, 10, and 1872, 209; also *Neue Berliner Schachzeitung*, 1870, 193.

He had played chess in Milan, and was accordingly familiar with the Italian method of play, and this knowledge coloured his play, although in the main his inclinations were more in the direction of the Philidorian system. Thus he lays down the Philidorian rule, 'Where possible, one must not move the Knights until the Bishops' Pawns are advanced', but recognizes the possibility of exceptions in the next sentence, 'Exceptions to this rule will often be necessary owing to the position of the game (40)'. Of the King's Knight's Opening he says, 'Lolli and his followers hold this move of the Knight (2 Ktf3) to be very good. Philidor on the contrary declares that it is faulty and contrary to rule, because the Knight when moved obstructs the movement of the Bishop's Pawn. In my opinion it is not bad at all, for experience and long practice at chess have taught me that by this move one may win much with the least want of care on the opponent's part, and can lose nothing by playing with the greatest care one's self.' This is no blind adherence to the Philidorian school. A personal characteristic is the stress which Allgaier lays on the importance of securing a majority of Pawns on the King's wing.

Since Allgaier's work was unnoticed in England and France, it had less influence than it deserved. Even in Germany it was overshadowed by the greater fame of Philidor's book.

No account of the chess life of the second half of the eighteenth century would be complete which did not mention the *Automaton Chessplayer* whose public performances created immense interest between 1771 and 1836. By this name is known an ingenious machine which was constructed in Vienna in 1769 by a mechanical genius named Wolfgang Kempel or von Kempelen (B. 1734, D. 1804).

The Automaton was a life-size figure in Oriental costume, seated behind a chest about 4 ft. long, 2 ft. wide, and 3 ft. high, on which was placed a chessboard. The figure played chess with all comers, moving the pieces with its left hand. Everything was done to convey the impression that no one was concealed within the figure, and that the figure played in some mysterious way under the influence of the exhibitor; as a matter of fact the movements of the figure were directed by a player who was concealed within the chest. The ingenuity of the invention consisted in the manner in which the player was able to conceal himself in the interior while apparently the whole was shown and in the device by which he was kept informed of the moves made upon the board, which was out of his sight. The device was really quite simple: a strong magnet was fixed within the base of each chessman, and from the inner surface of the chest immediately below the board were suspended small iron balls by threads. As long as the chessman stood on a particular square, the corresponding ball was attracted against the roof of the chest, and as soon as it was lifted from its place the ball fell to the length of the thread. The general appearance of the machine will be gathered from the figure, which is reproduced from the first volume of the *Chess Player's Chronicle*, 1841.

The Automaton was first exhibited in Vienna in 1770, and at once created

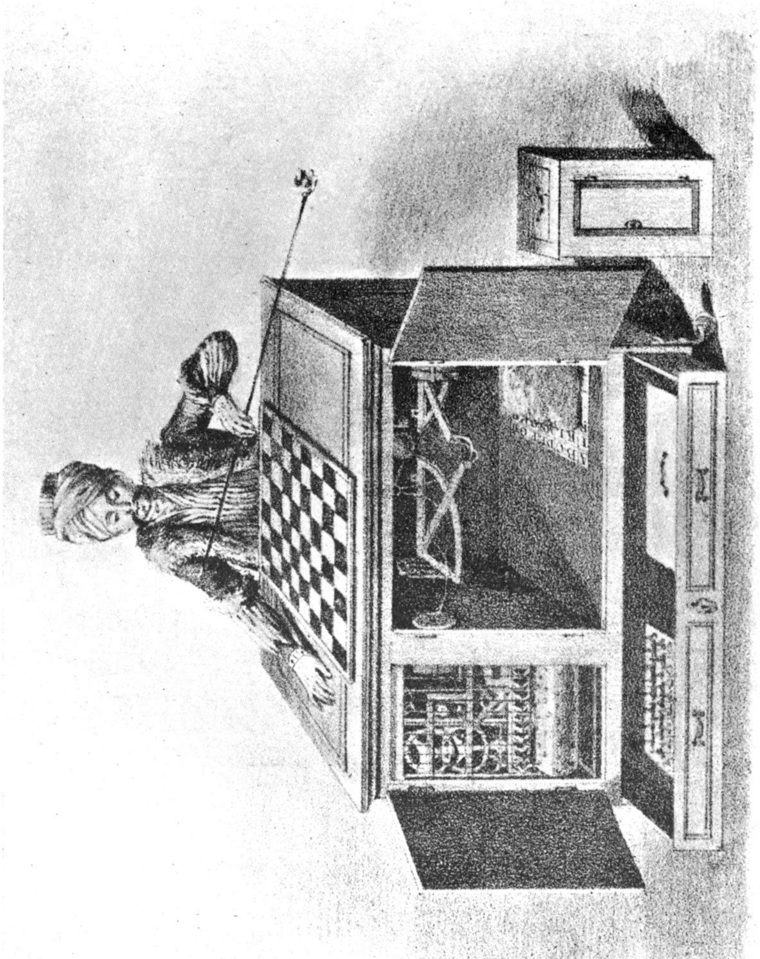

THE AUTOMATON CHESSPLAYER

a sensation, and started a long controversy as to the manner in which the machine worked. An early account in some letters of K. G. v. Windisch was reprinted as a pamphlet and published in Germany when the Automaton began its travels in 1783. In this year v. Kempelen visited Dresden, Leipzig, and Paris, and in the following year he exhibited the Automaton in London at 8 Savile Row, Burlington Gardens, visitors paying five shillings each for admission.

After v. Kempelen's death in 1804 the Automaton was bought by L. Maelzel, who toured with it in Germany from 1805 to 1808. In 1809 it was at Schönbrunn, where Napoleon was making his head-quarters during the Wagram campaign, and Napoleon played against the figure—or rather against Allgaier, who was inside it—and was beaten.[26] Not long after, Prince Eugène de Beauharnais purchased the Automaton for 30,000 francs, in order to learn the secret,[27] but in 1817 Maelzel bought it back, and resumed his exhibition tours. He was in Paris in 1818, in London from the winter of 1818 until 1820, and in Amsterdam in 1821 and 1822. Finally in 1826 he arrived in New York, and exhibited in the United States and Havana until 1836. Maelzel died in 1837, and at the sale of his effects the Automaton was bought by Mr. Ohl of Philadelphia. Ohl sold it in 1840 to Dr. John K. Mitchell, who put the machine together again. It ultimately found its way to the Chinese Museum in Philadelphia, and was destroyed by fire in 1854.

It was essential for the success of the exhibition that the Automaton should win its games, and strong players had to be engaged to direct its play. In this way Allgaier (1809), Weyle, Alexandre (1818), Boncourt (1818), Lewis (1818–9), Williams (1819), Mouret (1820)—who gave Pawn and move to all comers and only lost six games out of 300 (a selection of these was published in 1820, and is incorporated in Geo. Walker's *Chess Studies*, 1844, ch. vi), and finally sold the secret to the *Magasin Pittoresque* in 1834—and, in America, Wilhelm Schlumberger (D. 1836), the chess master of Saint-Amant, were at one time and another engaged by Maelzel to inhabit the Automaton.[28]

[26] Napoleon was a persistent but a very weak player. Three games purporting to be played by him are in existence. One of these (a Scotch Game), said to have been played in St. Helena between Napoleon and Bertrand, and first printed in Capt. Kennedy's *Reminiscences in the Life of Aug. Fitzsnob* (*Waifs and Strays*, 1862), is certainly fictitious. The second game, said to have been played with Mme. von Remusat, 29 March, 1804, and a third game (*I.L.N.*, 1844, 352), played against the Automaton in Vienna, are also of very doubtful authenticity.

[27] Frederick the Great is also said to have bought the Automaton about 1785, or at least to have paid a high price to learn its secret. Allen throws doubt upon this story.

[28] There is an extensive literature of the Automaton. I have in the main followed v. d. Linde's summary, ii. 337–52, but have consulted other accounts, Twiss, i. 12, 186, and *Misc.*, ii. 114; Tomlinson, *Amusements of Chess*, 1845; and Allen, *Hist. Autom. Chess-player in America* (*Book First Amer. Chess Congress*, 1859, 420–84).

CHAPTER XV

THE NINETEENTH CENTURY

Lewis.—De la Bourdonnais and MacDonnell.—The Berlin Pleiades.—Staunton and Saint-Amant.—The chess magazine and newspaper column.—The 1851 Tournament.—Anderssen and Morphy.—Steinitz and the Modern School.

Sarratt died in 1821, and his friend and chess pupil William Lewis (B. 1787, D. 1870) [1] was by general consent regarded as having succeeded to the throne of English chess. He had been in intimate connexion with Sarratt since 1816, had assisted him in his analytical work for the new edition of his *Treatise*, and now acted as his literary executor and saw this (1822) and the *New Treatise* (1821) through the press. In the place of Sarratt's magniloquent title of 'Professor of Chess' he used the humbler one of 'Teacher of Chess'.

Lewis's first action was to pay a visit to Paris in April, 1821, in order to try conclusions with Deschapelles, still the acknowledged champion of French chess. On this journey he was accompanied by John Cochrane (B. ? 1792, D. 1878), a young barrister who, after Lewis, was probably the strongest of the London players. There had been very little intercourse between the leading players of England and France since the death of Verdoni, and the relative strength of Sarratt and Deschapelles had never been ascertained. It was, however, generally accepted that Deschapelles was the strongest player of his time, and Sarratt appears to have acquiesced in this opinion, although there was apparently no stronger reason for it than the fact that the general standard of French chess had been higher than that of English chess in the end of the eighteenth century. The result of Lewis's visit was to show that there was very little, if any, difference in strength between Deschapelles and himself. Three games were played, in which Deschapelles gave Lewis the odds of Pawn and move, and of these Lewis won one and drew the other two. Had they played on even terms there can be no doubt that Lewis's knowledge of the Openings would have made him the more successful player.

The second French player of that period was Louis Charles Mahé de la Bourdonnais (B. 1797, D. 1840, a grandson of that Mahé de la Bourdonnais, Governor of Mauritius, who won a great victory over the English fleet off Madras in 1746), to whom Deschapelles was giving the odds of Pawn and

[1] See my life of 'William Lewis', *BCM.*, 1906, 8, 49. The life in the *Dict. Nat. Biog.* (see the correction in the Appendix) is unsatisfactory.

two moves.[2] Cochrane, who was in receipt of the same odds from Lewis,[3] played De la Bourdonnais on level terms, and Deschapelles gave Pawn and two moves to both players. The result of this triangular match was that De la Bourdonnais won both his matches and Cochrane lost both his. At the conclusion of these matches, which were played at St. Cloud, Cochrane proposed to Deschapelles that they should play without odds, but that Deschapelles should wager 2 to 1 on his play, and Cochrane won more than a third of the games which were played in this way.

It was possibly a result of this visit to Paris that the London club was anxious in 1824 to play a match with Paris by correspondence. Nothing came of this, but instead a match was arranged with the Edinburgh club, which commenced 23 April, 1824, and was not completed until the Spring of 1828.[4] According to the terms of the match three games were to be played, the first two being played at the same time, each club having the move in one of these. If a game was drawn, the side which had commenced that game was to commence the next game. The side which first won a game was to have the move in the third game. The leading players who took part in the match were, for the London club, W. Lewis, J. Cochrane (who left England while the first two games were in progress), Joseph Parkinson (an architect with whom Lewis had played some of his first games in 1813), Joseph Wood (another early opponent of Lewis's), W. Fraser (who played a match with MacDonnell in 1831 on even terms), Brand, and T. Mercier; for Edinburgh, the bailie, James Donaldson (D. 1847).[5] The result of the match was a victory for the Scotch club by 2 games to 1 with 2 draws, the London club having thrown away the second game in a winning position. Owing to the working of the conditions the Edinburgh players had the move in every game but one.

This match is interesting from the light it throws upon the progress which Sarratt's freer style of play had made in England. The Edinburgh players began with a Bishop's Opening in true Philidorian style; the London players began—probably at Cochrane's suggestion—with an Opening from del Rio, at that time little known, which showed the advantage to the attack of an open Queen's file. In two of the later games Edinburgh adopted the same Opening, and their success with it led to the name of the 'Scotch

[2] In 1815, Harry Wilson, who was playing even with Lewis in 1819, had played with De la Bourdonnais, giving him the odds of the Knight. De la Bourdonnais' life is given in *Deutsches Wochenschach*, 1912, 1–7, with portrait.

[3] Lewis was giving Cochrane the odds of the Knight in 1820, but played a match with him in 1821–2 at the odds of Pawn and two moves, which he won (W. 2, L. 1). Cochrane, a dashing player with a brilliant style, has the reputation of having invented many attacks in the Openings, all unsound. The one now known by his name, the Cochrane Gambit, is not one of these, as it is already in Sarratt's *Treatise* of 1808. He left England in 1824 to take up an appointment in India, and did not return until 1841, when he played a long series of games with Staunton, and proved himself to be still one of the strongest English players.

[4] The earliest correspondence match of which particulars are extant was one between The Hague and Breda in 1804 (v. d. Linde, *Het Schaakspel*, 137). The Amsterdam club played Rotterdam in 1824, and Antwerp in 1827–9.

[5] The remaining players were: London, Benj. Keen, Peter Pratt, Abr. Samuda, C. Tomlin, and — Willshire; Edinburgh, Capt. Aytoun, Rev. H. Liston, Sir S. Stirling, Bt., and Messrs. Buchanan, Burnett, W. Crawford, Jas. Gregory, Mackersy, Meiklejohn, More, Pender, J. Rose, Wauchope, and Wylie.

Game' being given to it. This was not the only Opening that commenced a long spell of popularity at this moment. In 1824, the first year of the London–Edinburgh match, Capt. W. D. Evans (B. 1790, D. 1872), of the mercantile marine, discovered the beautiful variation of the Giuoco Piano which is now known as the *Evans Gambit.*[6]

The leader of the new school of play was Lewis himself, and after the close of the correspondence match he gradually withdrew himself from active play and devoted his energies to the analysis of the Openings from the new point of view. In the work of spreading the knowledge of the new ideas he was ably seconded by a small circle of keen younger players who had grouped themselves about him. Two of these must be mentioned as of greater importance: Alexander MacDonnell (B. 1798, D. 1835),[7] the son of a Belfast physician and Secretary to the Committee of West India Merchants in London, to whose exploits I shall return below, and George Walker (B. 1803, D. 1879),[8] a London publisher, who devoted himself for many years to the work of establishing a chess club on a permanent basis in the West End of London, and to the maintenance of interest in chess by brightly written magazine articles and by the issue of useful text-books at popular prices.[9] As an analyst Walker was far inferior to Lewis, and his books contained little that was really new; their importance lay in the fact that they appealed to a wider public than Lewis reached, and thus did more to raise the general level of play in England.

Lewis's analytical labours resulted in the publication of the *Progressive Lessons*, the First Series (intended for beginners) in 1831, and the Second Series (for advanced players) in 1832.[10] The appearance of the Second Series in 1832 is one of the landmarks in the history of the modern game. The *Lessons* had an immediate and lasting effect upon the practical game in England, while, by the encouragement that the work gave the reader to undertake analysis for himself, it determined the direction of the studies of the Berlin players and thus had a great deal to do with the development of modern chess. All subsequent writers on the Openings have consciously or unconsciously built upon the foundations which Lewis laid in this work.

It is in the *Lessons* that we find the first analysis of the Evans Gambit, here termed the Evans Game, and of the once popular Compromised Defence

6 See *Sch.*, 1873, 1; 1874, 278; and *BCM.*, 1898, 129 and 175.

7 I follow the spelling of the name on MacDonnell's tombstone at Kensal Green. Greenwood Walker and George Walker write M'Donnell. Lewis, in his MS. note-book now in v. d. Lasa's library, wrote M'Donnel as a rule, but occasionally Macdonnel.

8 See my life of 'George Walker', *BCM.*, 1906, 189.

9 *New Variations on the Muzio Gambit*, 1831; *New Treatise*, 1832, 1833, 1841, and, with new title, *Art of Chess-Play*, 1846; *Selection of Games*, 1835; *Chess made Easy*, 1836, 1850; *Chess Studies*, 1844; *Jaenisch's Chess Preceptor*, 1847; *Chess and Chessplayers* (a reprint of his magazine articles), 1850; and an edition of Philidor in 1832. The most important of these books is the *Chess Studies* (a new edition appeared in 1893), which contains 1,020 games played between 1780 and 1844.

10 In addition to the translations named in note 22 on p. 874, and the *Lessons*, Lewis published *Oriental Chess*, 1817; *Elements*, 1822; *Chess Problems*, 1827 and 1833; *Fifty Games*, 1832; *A Selection of Games* (De la Bourdonnais-MacDonnell), 1835; *Chess for Beginners*, 1835, 1837, and 1846; *Chess Board Companion*, 1838 (nine editions); *First Series of Progressive Lessons* (a second edition), 1842; *Treatise*, 1844. A note-book in which Lewis recorded the score of many games which he played between 1813 and 1840 is now in the v. d. Lasa library.

in the Scotch Game (1 Pe4, Pe5; 2 Ktf3, Ktc6; 3 Pd4, P × P; 4 Bc4, *Bb4*+). But Lewis did not confine himself to the analysis of new or less-known Openings; he enriched existing ones with many unexpected novelties, e. g. in the Bishop's Opening he introduced the counter-attack 1 Pe4, Pe5; 2 Bc4, Bc5; 3 Pc3, *Pd5*, by which the attack is carried over to the Black, and the development of the White on the Philidorian system is prevented. That the latter was not the motive behind the new move may be gathered from Lewis's remark (*Treatise*, 1844, 24):

> It is generally advantageous for your Pawns to occupy the centre of the board, because they impede the progress of your adversary's pieces; the King's and Queen's Pawns at their fourth squares are generally well placed, but it is difficult to maintain them in that position; and if you are forced to advance one of them, their power considerably diminishes; be not, therefore, over-anxious to establish two Pawns abreast in the centre.

We may discover the reason for the move in the resulting open Queen's file; the correct estimation of the value of this was perhaps Lewis's chief contribution to the development of the theory of the game.

That Lewis, while recognizing the value of the formation of a strong centre of Pawns, did not regard it as the only tactics governing the Opening development and Mid-game play, shows that he had moved a long way from the Philidorian position. We see the same in the absence of any advice as to the postponement of the development of the Knights until after the movement of the Bishop's Pawns. In all this he approximates to the Italian School, though here again his attitude is different from that of Sarratt, who was ready to adopt free castling and all the Italian rules. Lewis really occupies an intermediate position, adopting all that is best from the two rival schools, and following now the one, now the other, as circumstances demand. The result was a great increase in the brightness of the game, and many combinations became possible which would have been impossible under the Philidorian system, in which it was difficult to give up the idea of the necessity of the formation of a centre of Pawns. The new school, which we may term the Lewis or English school, governed the practice of all English and German players down to the time of Wilhelm Steinitz. It reached its highest point in the play of Paul Morphy.

George Walker's energy led to the establishment of the Westminster Club in 1831,[11] and this club at once took the leading place in English chess. In the early part of 1834 they accepted a challenge from the Paris club (dated 29 Jan. 1834) to a correspondence match of two games, which lasted 1834–6, and were both won by the Paris players under the leadership of Pierre C. F. de Saint-Amant (B. 1800, D. 1872), a pupil of Schlumberger and De la Bourdonnais. In the game opened by Westminster, Paris played the French Defence, then known as the 'King's Pawn one', at that time the most popular Opening in France, and the modern name dates from this match.

[11] The club came to an end in 1843, and its place was taken by the St. George's Club (1843–1900).

More important in every way was a series of matches which were played in the summer and autumn of the same year, 1834, between De la Bourdonnais and MacDonnell, who, as a result of the withdrawal of Deschapelles and Lewis from play, were recognized as the strongest players of France and England respectively.[12] The exact details of the matches are not known,[13] but De la Bourdonnais won a considerable majority of the games. Lewis published a selection of 50 of the games in 1835, which was translated into German by Bledow, 1835, and Greenwood Walker published 83 in his *Games by the late Alexander M'Donnell*, 1836. It was the first match which was adequately reported, and the games were recognized as worthy of the reputation of the players. To-day they take high rank among the classics of chess. De la Bourdonnais exhibited an accuracy of conception and richness of combination in his play which is all the more admirable because his book-knowledge of the game was small, and MacDonnell's play has seldom been surpassed for daring adventure. The 50th game of the matches is a brilliant example of MacDonnell's style of play.[14] The 39th game, won by De la Bourdonnais,

[12] De la Bourdonnais was the chess pupil of Deschapelles, but the latter, after his pupil had surmounted the odds of Pawn and two moves in 1821, withdrew from play rather than give shorter odds. De la Bourdonnais was in England in 1823, and defeated most of the leading English players, including Lewis (W. 5, L. 2). In 1834, he played upwards of seventy games with Lewis, but the score is unknown (*CPC.*, 1841, 9). MacDonnell was the pupil of Lewis. Of twenty-one recorded games between May, 1828, and March, 1829, at the odds of Pawn and two moves, each won nine; only two games at the odds of Pawn and move are on record, one drawn, the other won by Lewis. MacDonnell was a slow player, with an extraordinary gift for giving odds successfully.

[13] The authorities are: (*a*) Greenwood Walker's edition; (*b*) *Report of Westminster Club*, 1834 (by Geo. Walker); (*c*) Geo. Walker's *Chess Studies*; (*d*) Geo. Walker in *CPC.*, iv. 369; (*e*) Reprint of games in *CPC.*, ii and iii (? supplied by Lewis); (*f*) *Palamède*, 1836, 26 (De la Bourdonnais); (*g*) *Palamède*, 1844, 266 (Saint-Amant says De la Bourdonnais told him that he allowed MacDonnell some games in the last match). Cf. *CPM.*, 1864, 72, 115, 161 (Geo. Walker), 161, 203, 232.

Five matches of 21, 9, 11, 11, 11 games (excluding draws) were played out, and part of a sixth. All agree as to the score of the first four matches (I, B. 16, M. 5, Drawn 4; II, 4, 5, 0; III, 6, 5, 1; IV, 8, 3, 7. According to (*d*) the other matches resulted: V, 7, 4, 1; VI, 5, 4, 0. The score of the existing games of VI is, however, 4, 5, 0.

Greenwood Walker says that he took down *all* the games as played, and gives the score of 83, and mentions one (No. 14) as omitted because it was badly played. His total score is 41, 29, 13. The other editions of the games add No. 85 (won by M.), which was first published in *CPC.*, ii. 232 (where it is not described as a game of the match). The total score is given in (*b*) as 44, 30, 14 = 88 games; in (*c*) as 46, 26, 13 (but the games themselves give 45, 27, 13) = 85 games; (*d*) 44, 28, 13 = 85 games; (*e*) 44, 28, 13 = 85 games. In (*a*) M. plays first in games 70–74; (*c*) reverses the players in 71 and 73, (*e*) in 73 only. From internal evidence (*c*) seems to be right, and if we correct the totals in (*a*) accordingly, and an obvious misprint in the result of game 82, and then add the results of games 14 and 85, the revised totals of (*a*) are 45, 27, 13, and agree with the corrected figures for (*c*). All the editions make B. play first in games 77–80, and internal evidence supports them, though it was clearly impossible that B. could have played first in four consecutive games in the ordinary course of events. Centurini (*CPM.*, 1864, 232) suggested that B. gave M. the odds of three games in the last match (to be of 15 games), and that these were assumed to be the games that should have come between 77 and 78, 78 and 79, and 79 and 80. This would make the total score 45, 30, 13 [cf. (*b*)], and agree with M.'s statement that he won eight of the last twelve games [cf. also (*g*)]. This may be the explanation, but it is also possible, since Geo. Walker only obtained the games of the last matches *en bloc*, that they have been disarranged; some may also be wrongly ascribed, thus, internal evidence suggests that M., not L., opened and won game 80. According to (*f*), B. played other than match games with M., and even attempted to give him odds. B. speaks here of a total of 100 games.

[14] The game ran: De la Bourdonnais *v.* MacDonnell; 1 Pd4, Pd5; 2 Pc4, P × P (MacDonnell always accepted the Queen's Gambit); 3 Pe4, Pe5; 4 Pd5, Pf5; 5 Ktc3, Ktf6; 6 B × P, Bc5; 7 Ktf3, Qe7; 8 Bg5, B × P +; 9 Kf1, Bb6; 10 Qe2, Pf4; 11 Rd1, Bg4; 12 Pd6, P × P; 13 Ktd5, Kt × Kt; 14 B × Q, Kte6 +; 15 Ke1, K × B; 16 Qd3, Rd8; 17 Rd2, Ktc6; 18 Pb3, Ba5;

formed the subject of Méry's poem, *Une revanche de Waterloo* (Paris, 1836), and the 54th, won by MacDonnell, that of the Rev. A. D'Arblay's rejoinder, *Caïssa rediviva* (London, 1836). These poems bear witness to the enthusiasm which the matches created.

The importance of this decade (1830–39) in the chess history of the nineteenth century is not due only to this international match and to the publication of Lewis's *Lessons*; the decade also saw the commencement of a new era, in which Central Europe, and especially Germany, began to play a prominent part in the progress of the game.

There had been a chess club in Berlin from about 1803, but it was so exclusive that it excluded the strongest Berlin player, Julius Mendheim (a leading problemist in his day, who died 1836), and of such mediocrity in chess that Deschapelles in 1807 had been able to give the odds of the Rook to the strongest players.[15] But about 1830 the younger players in Berlin founded the Berliner Schachgesellschaft, and from 1835 L. E. Bledow (B. 1795, D. 1846), a schoolmaster in the Berlin Gymnasium, collected around him a group of players who combined enthusiasm with talent for chess, and introduced them to the Lewis school of play. In 1837 this group comprised seven players—Bledow, the cousins W. Hanstein (B. 1811, D. 1850) and C. Mayet (B. 1810, D. 1868), the painters B. Horwitz (B. 1807, D. 1885) and K. Schorn (B. 1802, D. 1850), the diplomatist Baron Tassilo von Heydebrand und der Lasa (B. 1808, D. 1899), and Lieut. P. R. von Bilguer (B. 1813, D. 1840); and later generations look back to them as the Seven Stars of Berlin, or more briefly as the Pleiades.[16]

These seven players were only associated for the short period of two years, but this was long enough to give rise to projects which were only carried out later. It was Bledow's ambition to see a German chess magazine which should do for Germany what the *Palamède* (founded by De la Bourdonnais, 1836) had done for France, and the *Chess Player's Chronicle* (founded by Staunton, 1841) for England. He just lived to see the first number of the *Schachzeitung* issued, in July, 1846. It was the ambition of v. Bilguer and v. d. Lasa to see a German text-book on the game which should be the standard work on chess for German players, and although v. Bilguer did not live to see it issued, the *Handbuch des Schachspiels von P. R. v. Bilguer* was published by v. d. Lasa in 1843, and at once took its place as the best of all text-books. Since that date the *Handbuch* has passed through seven

19 Pa3, aRc8 (probably foreseen when the Q was sacrificed on move 13); 20 Rg1, Pb5; 21 B × P, B × Kt; 22 P × B, Ktd4 (a formidable move); 23 Bc4, Kt × fP +; 24 Kf2, Kt × R(d2); 25 R × P +, Kf6; 26 Rf7 +, Kg6; 27 Rb7, Kt(d7) × B; 28 P × Kt, R × P; 29 Qb1, Bb6; 30 Kf3, Rc3 (foreseen at move 20); 31 Qa2, Ktc4 +; 32 Kg4, Rg8; 33 R × B, P × R; 34 Kh4, Kf6; 35 Qe2, Rg6; 36 Qh5, Kte3 and wins. Cf. *BCM.*, Christmas No., 1893, 37.

15 This club nominally played three correspondence matches (Breslau, 1829–33; Hamburg, 1833–6; Posen, 1839–40), but in each case it had recourse to non-members to conduct the games; in the first two, Mendheim, in the third the Pleiades. The match Berlin–Magdeburg, 1833–4, was played by the Schachgesellschaft.

16 V. d. Lasa objected to the name *Pleiades* because this group of stars only shine faintly (257). The name was used by Falkbeer, *CPM.*, 1863, 58. For further details concerning the Pleiades cf. v. d. Lasa's *Berliner Schacherinnerungen,* 1859, and my own article, 'The Berlin Pleiades', *BCM.*, 1899, 407.

editions and an eighth is in process of issue at the present time, and in spite of numerous rivals it still remains the foremost work on those branches of chess of which it treats. It made the names of the Berlin seven famous in Europe, and brought them in contact with players from other parts of Germany and from farther afield also.[17] Berlin became the rallying ground of German chess, and Hanstein, Mayet, and v. d. Lasa the standard by which other German players gauged their strength.

Bledow's interest in all sides of chess was also shown in the collection of a valuable chess library, which was acquired after his death by the Royal Library of Berlin. It is possible that his example may have led v. d. Lasa to take an interest in the literature and history of the game, but it was the chapter on previous chess authors in Ponziani's *Giuoco incomparabile* which made that interest active and induced v. d. Lasa to include in the *Handbuch* a section on the history and literature of chess. Right from the very first numbers of the *Schachzeitung* v. d. Lasa began to contribute to that magazine articles on special points in the history of the game, which were distinguished by the accuracy of their information and by the moderation of their judgement. After his retirement from the Diplomatic Service in 1864 he devoted himself to the study of the history of the game and the collection of a chess library, which at his death was second only to that of Mr. J. G. White of Cleveland, Ohio, U.S.A. He was soon recognized as one of the greatest authorities on chess history, and he laid a great part of the foundations upon which Dr. Antonius v. d. Linde (B. 1834, D. 1897) built. In the closing years of his life he wrote a most valuable history of chess in Europe—that part of the subject which he had made peculiarly his own—under the modest title of 'Researches in the History and Literature of Chess' (*Zur Geschichte u. Literatur des Schachspiels, Forschungen*, Leipzig, 1897), which will long rank among the most important works on its special subject. V. d. Linde was a more voluminous writer, but he lacked the gift of orderliness, and was unable in his books to conceal his likes and dislikes. The *Geschichte u. Litteratur des Schachspiels*, Berlin, 1874, and the *Quellenstudien*, 1881, are rather mines in which the student must delve for information than works which he can read for pleasure. They also have a permanent value for the historian, and are a lasting monument to the industry and self-sacrifice of their author.

But it was not only in Germany that players began to acquire an international fame between 1830 and 1840. The Russian player A. v. Petroff (D. 1867), the Livonian L. A. B. F. Kieseritzky (B. 1805, D. 1855), the Viennese — Hampe,[18] have all given their names to Openings to the analysis of which they have made important contributions. Even in Hungary, a country of whose earlier chess we know nothing, the Pesth players,

[17] Prominent among them being C. F. v. Jaenisch (B. 1813, D. 1872), the Russian analyst of chess whose *Analyse nouvelle*, 1842–3, was almost contemporary with the *Handbuch*. He and v. d. Lasa gave one another help in their respective books. V. Jaenisch professed himself a warm supporter of the Philidorian system.

[18] Hampe was the first player to show that 1 Pe4, Pe5; 2 *Ktc3* was playable. Its popularity in Vienna during his lifetime gave this opening the name of the Vienna Opening.

J. Szen[19] and J. J. Löwenthal (B. 1810, D. 1876), were sufficiently strong to defeat the Paris club in a correspondence match in 1843. Their success in the defensive opening 1 Pe4, Pe5 ; 2 Ktf3, Ktc6 ; 3 Bc4, *Be7*, has given this opening the name of the Hungarian Defence.

The deaths of MacDonnell in 1835 and of De la Bourdonnais in 1840 were severe blows to English and French chess. In France, Saint-Amant was generally regarded as De la Bourdonnais' successor, and there is a story telling how Deschapelles in his inimitable style presented him to the chess club as 'le plus fort joueur de l'Europe' (*Palamède*, 1845, 30). In England there was an interregnum until Howard Staunton (B. 1810, D. 1874), a player who learnt his chess at the Divan and other London chess resorts, came to the front in 1840–1. By his memorable victory over Saint-Amant by 11 games to 6 (with four draws) in a match of 21 games for £100 a side, which was played in Paris in the late autumn of 1843, he made good his claim to be the first player in England and France. The games of this match are a great contrast to those of the De la Bourdonnais–MacDonnell matches, in that both players avoided the open game and played close Openings—the Sicilian, the Queen's Gambit Declined, and 1 Pc4 (often called *the English Game*, from Staunton's success with it in the match)—in which the early play is directed towards securing a favourable position for the End-game. In this they showed a tendency towards a new system of play more like that of Philidor than that of Ponziani, but taking a broader view of positional advantage than Philidor ever adopted. For this reason the games have never enjoyed the same reputation as those of the earlier match, though they are accepted as classical specimens of play. The international significance of the match had been seized by the public at once, and with the victory of Staunton England was regarded as having gained the position which France had held since the time of Philidor. It was before the days of championships, or Staunton would have been hailed as champion of the world. As a matter of fact Staunton both regarded himself and was regarded by others very much in that light. Although he played other matches in the next few years, the Saint-Amant match was really the climax of his career as a player.[20]

Like Philidor and Lewis, Staunton combined high analytic powers with skill as a player. His *Chess-Player's Handbook*, London, 1847, took rank at once as the leading English text-book on chess, and added greatly to his reputation both at home and abroad. Although it was admittedly based upon the German *Handbuch*, it contains much original analysis and exhibits throughout an independence of judgement which added greatly to the value of the work. Few chess-books have had a larger sale.[21]

[19] A deadly End-game player (Freeborough), who was in France and England in 1838, when De la Bourdonnais gave him the odds of Pawn and two moves (Szen winning 13 games out of 25) or Pawn and move (with even score). On his return journey he visited Berlin in 1839. He barely held his own either against the other French and English players, Boncourt, George Walker, and F. Slous (W. 3, D. 3, L. 4), or against the Pleiades (W. 3, D. 1, L. 4).

[20] See my life of 'Howard Staunton', *BCM.*, 1908, 465, 513.

[21] Staunton also published the *Chess-Player's Companion*, 1849, a treatise on games at odds, with a large selection of his own games; *Chess Praxis*, 1860, a supplement to the *Handbook*; and the *Chess Player's Text-Book*, 1849, a work for beginners.

To the *Handbuch*, and in a less degree to Staunton's *Handbook*, we owe the introduction of the systematic nomenclature of the Openings which exists to-day. Earlier writers had known very few Openings by special names. Ruy Lopez has only the name Gambito de Damian (Damiano Gambit), and the Italian school of the 16th c. only added the names the King's Gambit with its main subdivisions, the Knight's and Bishop's Gambits (*Regole*), and the Queen's Gambit. Salvio used the term Giuoco Piano for all games not Gambits (= Greco's Sbaratti), and its modern meaning only dates from Lolli. The Greco MSS. add the name of the Sicilian Game which, reintroduced into play in England at the end of the 18th c., was called Mortemar, until Sarratt (*Damiano*, &c., 1813, 367) reintroduced its older name. Caze (1706) added the name of the Cunningham Gambit, Philidor (1777) that of the Salvio Gambit, and Sarratt (1821) that of the Muzio Gambit, a name which had been already introduced in England as a result of his mistranslation of Salvio in his 1813 volume (209). Cochrane (1822) was apparently the first writer to speak of a Lopez Gambit. George Walker added the names of several Openings; 1831, the King's Bishop Game; 1832, Allgaier Gambit (restricted to 5 . . , Ktg5; this was called the Cotter Gambit in England *c.* 1800; Staunton appears to have first extended the name to include 5 . . , Kte5 (Walker's King's Knight's Gambit), for which the modern name of the Kieseritzky Gambit was introduced in Germany about 1846, *Sch.*, 1846, 200), Cochrane Gambit, Evans Game (so in Lewis the same year), changed before long to the Evans Gambit; 1841, Greco Counter Gambit. Bilguer used the name Two Knights' Defence in 1839. The 'Queen's Pawn two' Opening of Cochrane received its modern name of the Scotch Opening about 1840. Jaenisch (*Analyse nouvelle*, 1842–3) appears to have invented the names French Defence (called earlier in England 'King's Pawn one') and Centre Gambit. To the *Handbuch* we owe the Petroff and Philidor Defences, and the Ruy Lopez, for which German players later substituted 'The Spanish Game'. Hardly any of these names possess any historical significance; they were given at a time when the history of the Openings was quite unknown. The practical convenience of an international nomenclature, and the difficulty of persuading players to accept any change in it, have discouraged historians, v. d. Linde excepted, from attempting an historical terminology.

The great increase in the number of people interested in the chess problem, and the attention paid to the doings of the more prominent players, both of which were characteristic of the middle of the nineteenth century, resulted in a development of chess literature in two directions, the chess magazine, and the chess column in the newspaper. In both cases the interest of the public is somewhat ephemeral, and the support precarious, and few magazines or columns have ever reached a continuous life of even ten years. The earliest chess-magazine was the French *Palamède*, founded in 1836 and abandoned in 1839; a second series was started in 1842 and in its turn came to an end in 1847. The first English magazine, George Walker's *Philidorian*, existed for the one year 1838. In 1841 Staunton started the *Chess Player's Chronicle*, first as part of the *British Miscellany*, but shortly as an independent magazine, and made the inclusion of a large number of games by himself and other leading players of the day a special feature. Under Staunton's editorship the *Chronicle* was issued regularly until 1852; a new series lasted from 1853 to 1856, and a third series 1859–62. I have already mentioned the commencement of the *Schachzeitung* in 1846; this magazine has had an uninterrupted life until the present day. It was soon followed by the Dutch *Sissa*, 1847–75. Since then there have been magazines started in most countries of the civilized world. To-day the longest established magazines are in England the *British Chess Magazine*, Leeds, founded 1881; and abroad, the *Schachzeitung* (1846), the *Stratégie* (1867), *Deutsches Wochenschach* (1889), and the *Wiener Schachzeitung* (1896).

The first newspaper to contain a regular column devoted to chess was the *Liverpool Mercury*, in which Egerton Smith edited one from 9 July, 1813, to 20 Aug., 1814. The oldest existing column is that in the *Illustrated London News*, which dates from 25 June, 1842. This column was conducted by Howard Staunton from 1845 until his death in 1874. The number of the newspaper columns which have been started is very great. A list published by Mr. A. C. White in the *Norwich Mercury* in 1907 contained over 1,300 entries from all parts of the world, and yet made no pretence to completeness.[22] Most of these columns exist primarily in the interest of the problem, but a few also contain articles of permanent historical value.

With the institution of the weekly newspaper column and the monthly magazine as regular features of chess, the only thing still wanted to complete the modern organization of chess life was the Tournament, by which the leading players of different countries might be brought together for play.[23] The year 1851 is memorable as the date of the first International Tournament, which was held in London during the Great Exhibition of that year. Staunton, to whose efforts the existence of the Tournament was largely due, acted as Secretary to the influential Committee of management. Sixteen competitors entered for the main Tournament, and play was arranged on the 'knock out' principle, the losers in each round retiring and the winners proceeding to the next round. In each round the players played a small match, the best of 3 games in the first, and of 7 games in the following rounds. Adolf Anderssen, a Breslau schoolmaster (B. 1818, D. 1879), who attended as one of the representatives of the Berlin club, won the first prize, and by so doing became in popular estimation the first player of Europe.[24]

The method of play adopted in the London Tournament was open to

22 Made up thus: Great Britain and Ireland, 387; rest of Europe, 419 (Germany, 120; Austria, 73); Asia, 12; Africa, 10; America, 428 (U.S.A., 350); Australasia, 74.

23 The first player to suggest an international Tournament seems to have been Bledow. A letter to v. d. Lasa, 12 Sept., 1843, in which he suggested the holding of one in Trier (Treves), was printed in *Sch.*, 1848, 306.

24 The official account of the Tournament was written by Staunton, *Chess Tournament*, 1852, a book which is sadly disfigured by the ungenerous way in which Anderssen's victory was received.

grave objections. The chance of the draw brought some of the strongest players together in the first round, with the result that the final order was not an order of strength of play, but depended largely on the fortune of the pairing. In later Tournaments, from that of London, 1862, onwards,[25] every competitor plays against every other one, and the final order is determined by the total number of victories thus obtained.

The institution of the Tournament for the player was followed in 1854 by that of the Tourney for the problem-composer. The first of the Problem-Tourneys was conducted by the *Chess Player's Chronicle*, and entries were limited to British composers. Later Tourneys have generally been of an international character.

With the commencement of the era of magazines, tournaments, tourneys, and newspaper columns, I have reached the limit which I have prescribed for myself. I shall only add the briefest of references to the crowded chess life of the last sixty years.

With Anderssen's triumph in the 1851 Tournament the supremacy of chess passed into German hands, and Germany might claim to be the first chess country of Europe. But circumstances had changed since the time of Philidor, and a claim of this kind, probably never really tenable at any time, had become an absurdity with the general rise in the standard of chess in all countries. The sceptre of chess was henceforward an individual, not a national, possession.

That Anderssen's victory was no chance one was made clear by his success in later Tournaments. Between 1851 and 1878 he took part in twelve Tournaments and his name appeared on the prize list in every one of them, while on seven occasions he won the first prize (London 1851 and 1862, Hamburg 1869, Barmen 1869, Baden 1870, Crefeld 1871, Leipzig 1876). But after 1860 the opinion that the Tournament was not the best way of discovering the strongest player of the day became general, and the match became the recognized test.[26] It was as a result of his match with Wilhelm Steinitz, in 1866, which he lost by 6 games to 8, that Anderssen's supremacy is assumed to have come to an end. Anderssen himself seems to have troubled very little about it, and although he continued in active play for another dozen years, he never made any proposals for a second match. Even before the Steinitz match his supremacy had suffered a temporary eclipse during the meteoric career of Paul Morphy (B. 1837, D. 1884), of New Orleans, on whose visit to Europe Anderssen, like every other player who tried conclusions with the young American master, was decisively beaten. The match took place in Paris in the end of 1857, and Morphy won it by 7 games to 2, with 2 draws.

[25] The newer method of play was first tried in a small tournament which took place after the close of the Great Tournament of 1851, under the auspices of the London Chess Club.

[26] The right to compete in an open Tournament is now generally restricted to players of recognized skill, and the title of *master* is generally restricted to these players. In Germany there is a regular system by which the title of *master* is obtained; in England and most other countries it is more a matter of reputation.

In the play of Morphy and Anderssen the principles of the Lewis school reached their highest development. Both were players of rare imaginative gifts, and their play has never been paralleled for brilliancy of style, beauty of conception, and depth of design. In Morphy these qualities blazed forth from sheer natural genius; in Anderssen they were the result of long practice and study, the foundations being laid in the composition of the problem.

Wilhelm Steinitz (B. 1836, D. 1900), a Bohemian Jew who made his home first in England and later in the United States, was the first player to use the title of Champion of the World, and to realize the monetary value of the position. He successfully defended the title from 1866 until 1894, when Emanuel Lasker (B. 1868), a Prussian Jew, defeated him in a match for the championship by 10 wins to 5, with 4 draws. Mr. Lasker has retained the championship ever since.

From its history it follows that the championship is a personal possession, subject as regards the condition of tenure to no tribunal except the favour of the public. A result of this is that the acceptance of a challenge is a matter for negotiations, often long and delicate, before the exact conditions of the contest are arranged. The stake is now an essential feature, and the amount of the stake has risen enormously since Staunton and Saint-Amant or Anderssen and Steinitz played for £100 a side. Steinitz and J. H. Zukertort (B. 1842, D. 1888) once played for £400 a side, and the stakes in the Steinitz–Lasker match were actually £800 a side. There is no chance now for an unknown adventurer.

During the long championship of Steinitz a great change came over the style of play adopted by the leading players, and the attractive methods of the period 1830–60 were dropped in Tournaments and matches. This new method of play, generally known as the Modern School, is usually associated with the name of Steinitz, though he was not the sole originator and not the most successful exponent of it. The Modern School is the direct result of the modern Tournament system, which penalizes a player heavily for the loss of a game. When the result of each round depends upon a single game, the player naturally declines to risk anything by a direct attack when the failure of the attack will leave him with a compromised position. The Modern School is essentially safety play. The range of Openings is restricted to those in which the chances of surprises are fewest, the Ruy Lopez, the Queen's Gambit Declined, &c., and Gambits and the Open Game are eschewed. The tactics of the early part of the game are directed towards the establishment of a safe position which presents no weak points by which the opponent can force an entry. This has substituted strategy for the older attacking combinations, and has given rise to a new theory of Pawn-play. The Pawn is now regarded as strongest at home, and weaker the more it is advanced, because in its advance it leaves behind it 'holes' or squares which cannot be guarded by Pawns. The tactics of the Mid-game consist in making use of any small weakness in the opponent's position, or in compelling him to create small weaknesses, and the minute advantages that are gained in this way are held stubbornly until with the reduction of forces they become of sufficient value to decide the game. The Modern School is dull and unenterprising in comparison with the school which it has displaced, but 'it keeps the draw in hand', and is supposed to pay better in matches and tournaments. But when we see a player like H. N. Pillsbury (B. 1872, D. 1906), possessing the gift of imagination and the courage to adopt the older methods in a Tournament, repeatedly taking a high position among the prize-winners, we may be permitted to doubt whether the Modern School is all that it is claimed to be, or has said the last word upon the tactics of play.

INDEX

'Abdalmalik b. Marwān, caliph, 193.
Abschach, M. Ger. technicality, 739 n.
Abyssinian chess (*săntărij*): nomenclature of game, 363 n, of pieces, 221; description, 362–4.
Achmes, 165.
Actius, Thomas, 389.
al-'Adlī, 56, 169–75, 186 n, 198, 208, 212, 231; ta'bīyāt, 235–9; problems, 270–6, 306–9, 311, 314–5, 318, 323, 328, 330; calculating-board, 338; derived games, 340.
Agathias, 162.
Ager chessmen, 764–6.
Ahlwardt, 171.
al-Aḥwaṣ, 194.
Aiol, 433, 440 n, 441 n.
Alaska, chess in, 374–5.
Alea, 409.
Aleutian Islands, chess played, 374.
Alexander (Scotch romance), 743–5.
Alexandre, Roman de, 432 n.
Alexei, Tsar of Russia, 383.
Alexis Comnena, Eastern Emperor, 166.
Alfonsi, Petro, 407.
Alfonso VI, King of Castile, 203, 407.
Alfonso X, King of Castile, 568.
Alfonso MS., 181, 279, 303–4, 326, 348–51, 410, 452, 454, 457, 485–9, 568–73, 769.
Algeria, Muslim chess played, 360.
'Alī, caliph, 191.
'Alī Shaṭranjī, 171, 177, 205, 280; problems, 328–9, 332–3.
b. Aliqlīdisī, 169–70.
'Alīyāt (Muslim master-players), 197–8, 231.
Allen, Lake, 466 n.
Allgaier, J., 168, 390, 853, 875–6.
Alquerque (189 n, 194 n), 569, 581, 614–5. *See* Merels.
Alquerque de doze, 615.
Amateurs, Parisian, 872, 874 n.
Amazon (chessman) = Queen, 426 n, 791.
Amelung, F., 202 n, 383 n, 384 n, 420 n, 535, 854 n.
al-Amīn, caliph, 196.
Ammenhausen, Kunrat v., 484, 548.
al-Āmulī, 177, 280, 340–4.
Analysis: Chinese chess, 130–1; Muslim chess, 232–3, al-Lajlāj, 247–65; mediaeval European chess, 418; modern chess, 777; *Göttingen MS.*, 783–4; Lucena, 786; Damiano, 788; Ruy Lopez, 815–6; Philidor, 866–7.
Ananta, 62.
Anderssen, A., 854, 887–9.
Andreas, J., 456 n.
Anglo-French MSS. used, descriptions of, 557, 579–82.
Anglo-Norman group of Problem MSS., 579–607.
Annam, Chinese chess played, 108, 117.
Annamese chess (*chhôeu trâng*), 108, 117–8.
Ape plays chess, 748 n.
Apomazares (Abū Ma'shar), 165.
Apostolic Canons, 166, 380.
Arabic MSS. used, descriptions of, 171–6, 178–9, 182.
Arabic chess: *see* Muslim chess.
Arabic technical chess-terms, 220–7, 360.
b. 'Arabshāh, 171, 177, 204, 344–6.
Archer (chessman) = Bishop, 425 n, 791–2: = Pawn, 505.
Archinto MS., 573–9.
Ardashīr (Artakhshīr), son of Pāpak (Bābakān), 149, 153, 155, 210–1.
Armenia, Muslim chess played, 378.
Arminio, Giovanni D. d', 821, 824 n.
Arrangement of the chessmen: primitive, 46; Indian, early, 57, 69, modern, 80; Malay, 99; Burmese, 111–2; Siamese, 115; Chinese, 125; Corean, 135; Japanese, 141–2; Muslim, early, 224, modern, 357–60; Rumi chess, 362; Abyssinian, 363; Soyot, 372–3; European, 452–3.
Arras, Engebrans de, 557.
Artur, 746.
Ashmole MS., 601, 605–7, 779.
Ashta kashte, 38, 40.
Ashṭapāda, 33–7, 40, 42, 52–3, 61.
Asperling, 833, 841–2.
Assizes, 455; short assize, 476–82.
Astronomical chess, 343, 349, 569.
Astronomical explanation of nard, 152, 162, 209.
Astronomical game (China), 121–3, 133.
b. al-Athīr, 163 n, 198 n, 202.
Atranj (qaṭranj), 347.
Attalus, mythical inventor of chess, 501–2, 751.
Atwood, Rev. G., 864–5.
Audelay, 754.
Aufin: mediaeval European name of the Bishop, 424; metaphorical use of, 470, 754.
Automaton chess-player, 876–7.
Ayenbite of Inwyt, 441 n.
Aymonier, 117–8.
Azan, Moses, 416 n.

Backgammon, 38. *See* Nard, Tabla, Tables.
Backgammon-board, 757.
Bag for keeping the chessmen, 450, 451; parable of, 533, 535–6, 552, 555, 557.
Bālabhārata, 37.
Balhait, mythical Indian king, 209–12, 216.
Ballad poetry, chess mentioned in: Russian, 382; Scotch, 435.
Bambra-ka-thūl chessmen, 88–90, 223.
Bāna, 52–3.
Barcelona, Ermessind, Countess of, 406, 414.
Bare King, 45, 61, 66, 103, 222, 228, 267–70, 376, 452, 454, 460, 462, 464, 467, 469, 607, 750, 781, 785 n, 812, 814–5, 833, 851.
Bargello Museum, chessmen in, 758.
Baruch, Hirsch, 853.
Bastian, Dr. A., 109–11, 113 n.
Batak chess: *see* Malay chess.
Baysio, Guido de, 456 n.
Beale, F., 391, 772, 792, 829 n, 834, 839.
Beaumanoir, P. de: *Blonde of Oxford*, 429; *Manekine*, 435 n.
Beham, Hans Sebald, 757.
Bequests of chessmen, 404–5, 450.
Beringen, H. v., 484, 548.
Bernard, 872.
Bernard, Saint, 411.

Bertin, Capt. J., 389-91, 846-7.
al-Bērūnī, 57-60, 71, 76-7, 218.
Beryn, 739.
Bethune, Conon de, 753.
Bharhut, Stupa of, 40.
Bhavishya Purāṇa, 48-9.
Biblical characters as chess-players, 219.
Bilguer, P. R. v., 883.
Bishop (chessman) = primitive Elephant: so named in England, Iceland, &c., 424; so carved, 759, 762-3. Variety of European names for the piece, 424-6; regarded as a spy or thief, 470, 490, 501-2, 505, 507, 527; mediaeval estimation of its value, 470. Introduction of the modern move, 776.
Bishop, Col., 840.
Black chessmen preferred, 224, 473, 582, 785.
Blackburne, J. H., 864.
Blagden, C. O., 99, 103.
Blagrave, A., 840.
Blancardin, 433 n.
Bland, N., 165, 175, 177, 182-3, 185, 217, 342.
Bledow, L. E., 883.
Blindfold play, 35: Japanese, 140; Muslim, 191-2, 204-6; European, 428, 789, 817, 819, 861, 862, 864.
Blöndal, S., 856, 859.
Board-games: classified, 31; antiquity and diffusion, 29; possible origin in magical processes, 32 n, 50; American (patolli), 31 n; Byzantine, 162; Celtic, 31 n, 746; Chinese, 120; classical, 30, 161 n; early Egyptian, 29-30; European, 613-7; early Indian, 32-3; Japanese, 147; Malay, 95 n; Mongol, 370; Muslim, 199; Norse, 445; Russian, 380-1; Siamese, 114 n; early Syrian, 30.
Boat (chessman) = Rook: Bengal, 71; Java, 99; Siam, 115; Annam, 118; Russia, 386.
Boccaccio, 737.
Bodel, Jehan, 432 n.
Boeve de Haumtone, 433 n.
Bogle, G., 368.
Boi, P., 789, 818-9, 824 n, 839.
Boncompagni MSS., 645, 821, 822-3, 828 n.
Bond to abstain from games, 440, 446-7.
Bonus Socius, 618; MSS., 619; MSS. classified, 625; authorship, 627; preface, 626, 700; contents, 629.
Bourbon, Henri-Jules de, 839.
Bourdonnais, L. C. de la, 873, 878-9, 882-5.
Brahma-jāla Sutta, 34, 56.
Brāhmānābād: *see* Bambra-ka-thūl.
Branch, W. S., 616.
Brant, S., 536.
Brooke, Raja, 99-104.
Browne, Prof., 149, 202 n.
Bruhl, Count, 864, 873.
Brunet y Bellet, 40 n, 407, 546, 765.
Brunswick-Lüneburg, Augustus, Duke of: *see* Selenus.
Brussels MS., 624.
Buddhism and chess, 47, 60, 95, 108-9, 138.
Buoncompagno, Francesco, Card. Archbishop of Naples, 828.
Buoncompagno, Giacomo, Duca de Sora, 817, 820-2.
Buoz, M.Ger. technicality, 739 n.
Būrd, būrj (game-ending): Hindustani chess, 82; Parsi chess, 84, 92, 181, 281.
Burgundy, Charles the Bold, Duke of, 432, 449.
Buriat chess, 370.
Burmese chess (*sittuyin*), 108-13; nomenclature of games, 109, of pieces, 111; ancestry, 108; chessboard, 109-10; chessmen, 110-1; opening play, 111-2; rules, 112-3; connexion with Siamese chess, 108, 116.
Butrimof, I., 384.
Buzecca (Borzaga, Buchecha), 192, 428.
Buzūrjmihr, 154, 156-8, 178, 272.
Byelaef, A. P., 370.
Byzantine chess: *see* Round chess.

Café de la Régence, 862.
Caïssa, 793 n, 874 n.
Caldogno, F. B., 789, 793.
Cambodian chess: *see* Annamese chess.
Camel (chessman) = primitive Elephant (our Bishop): modern India, 60, 79; Siberia (Mongol chess), 377. In derived games, 214-5, 341, 344.
Camino, Rizardus de, 431.
Cardan, H., 417 n.
Carmina Burana, 473.
Carrera, P., 787 n, 817-9, 827.
Cartel, 851.
Casanatense MS., 727-33, 807-8.
Cascio, Girolamo, 820.
Castle (chessman) = Rook: modern India, 79; Europe, 423 n; origin of the name, 791-3; first so carved, 772. (The Fīl compared to a fortress, 222.)
Castling: nomenclature, 360, 387, 832-3; early references, 788 n, 812; history of, 830-3, 857.
Catalonian wills, 405-7, 413-4.
Caxton, W., 453 n, 540, 547, 741.
Caze, the elder, 844 n; the younger, 844-5.
Caze MS., 822, 843, 844-5.
Centaur (chessman) = Bishop, 791: = Rook, 791 n.
Cercar la liebre, 616. *See* Fox and geese.
Ceron, Alfonso, 817.
Cervantes, 536.
Cessolis, James de, 398, 453, 461-2, 497, 502, 537-49; problem appendices added to MSS. of the sermon, 573, 607, 706, 719.
Chachi, J., 727, 776, 779, 807.
Championship of chess, 888, 889.
Chariot (chessman) = Rook: India, 44, 60, 71, 79; Malay, 98; Burma, 111; China, 127; Corea, 136; Japan, 142; Persia, 160; Muslim chess, 160; Tibet, 367; Mongol chess, 367, 371, 377; traces in European chess, 160, 758. = our Bishop: modern Southern Indian chess, 60, 79.
Charlemagne chessmen (so-called), 87, 160, 403, 759, 765-6.
Charles I, King of England, 839.
Charles XII, King of Sweden, 854.
Chartier, Alain, 558.
Chatrang, M.Per. name of chess, 150, 163.
Chatrang-nāmak, 47, 150-5, 162.
Chaturājī, 68. *See* Four-handed chess.
Chaturanga: derivation and original meaning, 42-4; transferred to chess, 44; from chess to a dice race-game, 61, 62 n; name of a race-game, 39-40, 42, 61-3.
Chaucer, G., 564, 751.
Chaupur, 37-8, 50 n, 120.
Check: Indian term, 82 n; Malay, 98-9; Burmese, 113; Chinese, 128; Corean, 137; Japanese, 144; Persian and Muslim, 159;

Arabic, 225; Central and Northern Asia, 367, 369, 370, 373; Russian, 387; European, 396.
Check, discovered, 103, 225, 739 n.
Check-rook, 225, 395, 401; as surname, 401; how to avoid, 471, 555 n; in metaphor, 754.
Checkmate, 45, 225, 228, 267, 401; derivation, 159; as surname, 430; as name of the game, 385-6, 447; in metaphor, 536, 752-3.
Chequers: name of inn, 441.
Chernevski, 378.
Chess: a war-game, 25, 42-7, 221; general statement of pedigree, 26-9. Associated with nard (tables), 208, 429-35, 439 n, 447-50, 568, 581, 618. Divisions of a game, 234. Invention, 44-7; in legend, Muslim, 207-19, European, 161, 501-2, 541-2; previous theories, 48-50, 75; date of invention, 47. Name of the game, 26-7; derivatives of Skr. *chaturanga*, 42, 96-7, 109, 117, 150, 162, 167, 186, 367-8, 372, 376, 395; L. *scaci* and derivatives, 168, 399-401; other names, 61, 96, 114, 117, 121-2, 134, 138, 385, 400. Played for a stake, 192, 414, 440, 474-5, 534, 736-9, 742, 747, 889. Primitive arrangement of the board, 46; origin of powers of move, 46; of rules, 45. Use of dice in, 46-7, 409-10.
Chessboard: Indian, 40-2; Malay, 97-8; Burmese, 109-10; Siamese, 114; Chinese 125; Corean, 135; Japanese, 141-2; Muslim, 220, 354; European, 452, 756-8, 851.
Chess-clubs: St. Petersburg, 385; London, 391, 833, 835, 874; Parsloe's, 835, 863-5; 873; Paris, 863, 872; Westminster, 881; Berlin, 854, 883; Rome, 832.
Chessmakers: Russian, 383; Scotch, 420; English, 450.
Chess-matches, 862, 882, 885, 888, 889.
Chessmen: Indian, 87-91; Malay, 105-6; Burmese, 110; Siamese, 114; Chinese, 126; Corean, 135; Japanese, 141; Muslim, 223, 354, 361; Abyssinian, 363; Siberian, 371, 373, 375; Russian, 383, 387-8; European, 758-73; Staunton, 773. Carved for European market, 90-1, 134. Importation to England forbidden, 757.
Chinese chess (*siang k'i*), 121-34; pedigree, 119-20; nomenclature of game, 121, of pieces, 126; history, 123-4, confused with older game, 122; chessboard, 125; rules, 128; problems, 129; openings, 130; illustrative games, 132; derived games, 133; played in Siam, 113, in Annam, 108, 117.
Chō Yō, 139 n, 143-4, 147-8.
Circular chess: *see* Round chess.
Citadel on chessboard, 342, 344.
Citadel chess, 343.
Civis Bononiae, 618, 643; MSS., 643; MSS. classified, 647; poem, 646; contents, 648; Muslim element, 648; problems, 650-94.
Classes of players: Japan, 139; Muslim, 231.
Clef d'amors, 437.
Cluny Museum, chessmen in, 767-8.
Cnut, King of England, 404, 419, 443.
Cochrane, James, 87.
Cochrane, John, 874 n, 878.
Cochrane, Capt. J. D., 373.
Coer de Lion, 432 n.
Coffee-houses and chess, 845, 862-3.
Coincy, Gautier de, 439, 749.
Colours of chessmen: India, 90, 155; Burma, 111; China, 126; Corea, 135; Muslim, 224.
Colston, E., 109-13.
Columna, Francisco de, 748, 776, 793.
Columna, Guido de, 501.
Comnena, Anna, 166.
Companions (of Muḥammad) and chess, 191.
Comte de Poitiers, 434.
Concordant and discordant Queens (Muslim chess), 231.
Conditional problems: Muslim, 277-8; European, 651, 835, 870.
Conradin, 402, 750-1.
Constantinople MSS., description of, 171-8.
Cookery, chess in, 770.
Corean chess (*tjyang keui*), 134-7; nomenclature of game, 134, of pieces, 135; chessboard, 135; rules, 136; illustrative game, 137.
Corpus Poem, 506, 518.
Correspondence games, 845, 879, 881, 885.
Cotton MS., 580, 583-8.
Courier game, 392, 483-5.
Courtship, value of chess in, 436.
Cox, Capt. Hiram, 48, 109-13.
Cox-Forbes theory of the ancestry of chess, 48-50, 68, 75.
Coxe, 384, 859.
Cozio, C., 831, 872.
Cracow Poem, 463-4, 470-2, 508, 522-6.
Craftsman, 846; reply, 834, 846.
Cresswell, J., 74-5.
Cross-cut squares: *see* Marked squares.
Crusade, chess in First, 203, 418.
Crystal chessmen, 383, 404, 764-6, 768.
Culin, Stewart, 31 n, 37, 49-50, 135, 137, 188 n, 374.
Cunningham, Alexander, 844-5.
Cuvelhier, 432.
Cyclops (chessman) = Rook, 791: = Bishop, 791 n.

Dabshalim, mythical Indian King, 154, 210, 216.
Dame (chessman) = Queen, 426-8.
Damiani, Cardinal, 167, 408-9, 414.
Damiano, 463, 772, 787-9, 796, 799, 811, 813-6.
Daniel, Metropolitan, 381.
Dante, 755 n, 775.
Death says 'Checkmate', 536.
Decimal chess, 341, 346, 348. Cf. 33, 35.
Del Rio, Ercole, 868-9, 874.
Derived games of chess: Chinese, 133-4; Japanese, 145-7; Muslim, 215, 339-47; modern Indian, 86, 181, 347-8; Spanish, 348, 482, 569; German, 483-5; Carrera, 827; Piacenza, 838; Duke of Rutland's game, 862 n. *See also* Three- and Four-handed chess; Three-dimensional chess.
Deschapelles, 873, 878-9.
Destructorium vitiorum, 534, 561.
Deventer Poem, 505, 516.
Devil plays chess, 439, 475, 533-5, 557-8, 749, 780.
Dēwasārm, mythical Indian King, 151, 154, 216.
Dhanapāla, 62.
Diagonals of chessboard, 98, 102, 110, 349.
Dice: use in India, 36-7, 75, 90; in board-

games, 46 ; in chess, 46-7, 68-77, 340, 409-10, 454, 458 n ; in other games, 568.
Didactic European literature of chess, 496-528.
Diffusion of chess, 29.
Dilārām problem, 280, 311, 318, 357, 586, 588, 623, 706.
Dilārām's legacy, 335.
Doazan MS., 821.
Dog (chessman) = Queen, 377.
Domostroi, 381.
Doubling of squares, 51, 155, 167, 182, 213, 217-8, 755.
Dozy, 158-60.
Draughts, 33, 181, 370, 373-4, 386, 399, 615.
Drawn game, 82, 84-5, 136, 267-70, 372.
Dreams, interpretation of, 167 ; cf. 205.
Dresden MS., 466, 476, 580, 607-13.
Drummond, W., 792, 834 n.
Ducas, 167.
Duke (chessman) = Rook, 832 n.
Durgāprasāda, 82, 201 n, 362.

Eastern Empire, chess in, 161-8.
Ecclesiastical dislike of chess, 166-7, 380-1, 408-11.
Education, chess in, 393, 432-3.
Edward I, King of England, 449.
Egenolff, Chr., 389, 463, 471, 490-4, 778-9, 793, 810, 851.
Egypt, Muslim chess played, 360.
Einsiedeln Poem, 160, 411, 459, 497, 512.
Elegy, 503, 515.
Elephant (chessman) = Bishop : position on board in early Indian chess, 57, 60, 66 ; early move, 55, 59-60, 108. = Rook : in modern Indian chess, 79-80 ; in European chess, 423 n, 424, 791-2.
Elizabeth, Queen of England, 839.
Elliott, Sir H. M., 216-7.
End-game : Chinese, 132 ; Muslim decisions, 266-9 ; in European chess, 457, 868.
Enfances Vivien, 440 n.
English chess : mediaeval, 464-8 ; modern, 832-5, 839-41, 846-7, 850-1, 863-4, 873-5, 878-82, 885 ; technicalities, 532, 779.
Escaques, 349.
Eschenbach, Wolfram v., 755.
Eschez amoureux, 467, 469, 476-82, 555.
Etiquette of play : Muslim, 233.
European chess, mediaeval : ancestry, 394 ; introduction, 402-4, 418 ; early references, 405-13 ; nomenclature, 421-8 ; earliest rules, 452 ; early changes in, 453-4, 457.
European chess, modern : rise of, 776-80 ; rules *c.* 1560, 811-2 ; completion of reforms, 831-5 ; games, 780, 781, 785, 786, 788, 816, 823 n, 824 n, 826, 831 n, 833 n, 843, 882 n.
European influence in Asiatic forms of chess : India, 78, 86, 90-1 ; Malay, 99, 106-7 ; Muslim, 352-5 ; Siberia, 374-5.
Evans, Capt. W. D., 880.
Evil-Merodach, King of Babylon, 541.
Exchequer, 401, 419.
Exercises, 271, 335-8, 607, 733.
b. Ezra, Abraham, 385, 460, 509, 526.

Falkener, E., 42, 58-9, 71, 74, 77, 109 n, 113-6, 161 n.
False moves, 557, 751, 781, 815.
Fantosme, Jourdain de, 754.
Ferron, Jehan, 545.
Fers (chessman) = Queen : of feminine gender, Russia, 386 ; Europe, 395, 423, 425 ; in metaphor, 749, 752-3.
Ferumbras, 429 n.
Fianchetto, 837.
Abū'l-Fidā', 163 n.
Fidchell, 746 n.
Fierabras, 429 n.
Fihrist, 169.
Fīl (chessman) = Elephant (our Bishop) : European perversions of the name, 424-5.
Fīlūthā'ūs, J., 360.
Firdawsī, 155-7, 207, 213-5 ; his enlarged chess, 215, 341.
Firdawsī at-Tahīhal, 178.
Firzān (chessman) = Queen : derivation, 159. *See* Fers.
Fiske, Willard, 47, 443-5, 617, 846 n, 854 n, 855-6.
Fitzherbert, 536.
Flanders, Ferrand, Count of, 436.
Floire and Blanchefleur, 168 n, 737.
Florence MSS., descriptions of, 619-20, 643, 645, 708-19, 803-7, 822.
Flores Historiarum, 431.
Fool (chessman) = Bishop (France), 424.
Fool's mate, 707 n, 832 n.
Forbes, Prof. Duncan, 44 n, 48, 67, 69, 75, 77, 106 n, 112, 121 n, 163, 173, 177, 242 n, 328-9, 403, 466 n.
Forced game, 459, 473.
Fouché of Chartres, 203.
Foulques Fitzwarin, 740.
Fountaine MS., 622.
Four-handed chess : Indian dice-game, 45, 48, 49, 58, 68-77 ; modern Indian game, 74-5 ; Spanish, 348 ; Modern varieties, 859-60.
Four points, 104, 474, 741 n.
Four Seasons, Game of, 348.
Fox and geese, 371, 617, 758.
France, Marie de : *Eliduc*, 437 ; *Milun*, 432 n.
French chess : mediaeval, 464-8 ; modern, 812, 832-5, 839, 841-3, 845, 861-3, 872-3, 878-9, 885.
Freret, 120 n, 751.
Freudensprung, 392.
Friis, P. C., 855.
Fritzlar, H. v., 535, 750.
Frondes Caducae, 548.

Gaimar, 419, 432 n.
Galen, 164, 272, 331.
Gallensis : *see* Waleys.
Gambit, 813.
Gamblers and problems, 652-3.
Games, Early Buddhist list of, 34.
Garin de Montglane, 736.
Gau and Talkhand, 213-5.
Gauvain, 746-7.
Gavalata, 38-40, 42.
Geometrical Progression : *see* Doubling of squares.
Georgian chess, 355, 378.
German chess : mediaeval, 463-4 ; modern, 388-93, 851-4, 862, 875-7, 883-4, 888 ; technicalities, 739.
Gerona bequest, 404.
Gesta Romanorum, 467, 550-4, 561-3.

Ghalaṭāt al-mashhūra, 346, 357.
Ghulam Kassim, 87.
Gianutio, 825.
Gildemeister, 63, 159, 193 n, 198 n, 210 n, 215, 407.
Gillay, K. A., 82-5.
Gilmour, Rev. J., 370.
Gotha-Altenburg, Ernest II Duke of, 859.
Göttingen MS., 474, 782-4, 789, 794-7.
Govardhana, 62.
Gracco, Rotilio, 822, 835-6.
Gravenburg, Wirnt v., 484, 763.
Great (Complete, Timur's) chess, 204, 344-6; other forms, 346, 347, 348.
Greco, 465, 823, 827-30, 832, 840.
Greek chess, modern (*skaki*), 168.
Greek chess-players, mythical, 219.
Grimm, V., 358-9.
Gruget, C., 787, 791.
Guarinus, P., 645, 779.
Gueldres, Adolphus Duke of, 450.
Guerre de Metz, 754.
Gustavus Adolphus, King of Sweden, 854.
Guy of Warwick, 436, 742 n.
Gwyddbwyll, 746.

b. al-Habbārīya, 182.
Abū Ḥafṣ ash-Shaṭranjī, 195.
b. Abī Ḥajala, 175, 176, 271, 279, 324.
Ḥājjī Khalīfa, 169, 177.
al-Ḥākim, 174-6.
al-Ḥākim biamrillāh, Sultan of Egypt, 202.
Halāyudha, 55.
Hamilton, 80, 357.
b. Ḥanbal, 187-9.
Handbuch (Bilguer), 378, 390, 883-4, 886.
Abū Ḥanīfa, 187-9.
Harington, 840.
Harivaṃsa, 35, 62 n.
Hartwell, Roger, 601, 779.
Harūn ar-Rashīd, caliph, 164, 194-7.
Hashran, mythical Indian King, 208-9, 216.
Hāve, OF. technicality, 467.
Hechte, Pferrer zu dem, 548.
Heiz, Henri de, 753.
Henri IV, King of France, 839.
Henry VII, King of England, 475.
Henry VIII, King of England, 450.
Heraldry, chess in, 700 n, 773-5.
Herbert, J. A., 550-1.
Herlin, Robert du, 755.
Himly, Karl, 117, 119-29, 132, 145.
Hindustani chess, 78, 80-2.
Hippocrates, 164.
Hishām, caliph, 193.
Hnefatafl, 445.
Hoffmann, Prof. J. J., 125 n, 138.
Holland, William IV, Count of, 450.
Hollingworth, H. G., 127 n, 130.
Holme, Randle, 705 n, 772, 774, 792, 841.
Holt, H. F. W., 121, 122 n, 127 n.
Horse (chessman) = Knight in Southern Europe, 421, 426.
Horseman (chessman): *see* Knight.
Horsey, 382.
Höst, G., 356.
Hoyle, E., 391, 850.
Hoyle's Games, 833-4, 850.
Hu Ying Lin Pi T'sung, 124.
Hüan Kwai Lu, 123.
Huc and Gabet, 369.
Hünchkover, R. v., 753.
Huon of Bordeaux, 63, 410, 439, 476, 738.
Hut, Ger. technicality, 471.
Hyde bequest, 454.
Hyde, T., 67, 89, 152 n, 156 n, 162, 166, 168, 179, 186 n, 386, 401, 496, 532, 841, 851.

Icelandic chess, 443-4, 468, 759, 855-9.
I-go: *see* Wei k'i.
Impromptu chessmen: Malay, 105; Muslim, 220.
Impromptus during play: Muslim, 179, 184; European, 741 n.
Indian ancestry of Chinese games, 94.
Indian army, the 'four elements', 42-4.
Indian problem, 94, 871.
Ingold, 471, 554.
Innocent III, Pope, 631.
Innocent Morality, 452, 465, 530-4, 559-61.
Intellectual game: Southern Indian name of chess, 61.
Inventories of chess, 447-51.
Irish reference to chess, 420.
Irwin, E., 121 n, 122 n.
Íslenzkar Gátur, 855-9.
It pedes ad bellum, 506, 518.
Italian chess: mediaeval, 461-3; modern, 811-3, 817-27, 831-8, 868-72.
Italian school, 821-5, 869-70.
Ivan the Terrible, Tsar of Russia, 382.

Jacobi, 35 n, 53-5, 149.
Jaenisch, C. F., 378, 386.
James I, King of England, 839.
James I, King of Scotland, 431.
Janssen, Sir A., 862.
Japanese chess (*sho-gi*), 138-48: nomenclature of game, 138, of pieces, 142; history, 138-9; tournaments, 139; literature, 140; chessboard, 140; chessmen, 141; rules, 143-5; Openings, 144; gradation of odds, 145; illustrative game, 145; derived games, 145-7; problems, 147-8.
Jeopardy, 366.
Jeu des esches de la dame moralisé, 558, 780.
Jews and chess, 254, 428, 446-7, 853, 889; literature, 509-11, 526.
John I, King of Aragon, 431.
John, King of England, 432.
Jones, Sir William, 48, 68, 73, 874.
Judge (chessman) = Rook, 530-3. = Bishop, 543. In derived game, 348.
b. Juraij, 203.

al-Kaiwānī, 182.
Kāla, 52.
Kalhaṇa, 53, 68.
Kalīla wa Dimna, 27, 57, 154, 215.
Kalmucks, Mongol chess played, 369, 370.
Kāmandaki, 42, 44, 46.
Kanauj, Kanuj (Kānyakubja), 52, 156.
Kārnāmak, 26, 149-50.
Katanof, Prof., 370, 372.
Kempelen, W. v., 876-7.
Kenny, Charles, 835, 874.
b. Khallikān, 200, 211-2, 216.
Kholmogory, 383.
Kieseritzky, L. A. B. F., 884.
King (chessman): crosswise arrangement in Indian, 80; Malay, 99; Siamese, 115;

modern Asiatic (Muslim) chess, 224, 357-8; suggested in Europe, 845; position fixed in Europe, 453. Power to leap on first move: in Indian chess, 81-2; Malay chess, 99, 101; modern Muslim chess, 354, 358, 359; in European chess, 457, 461-4, 783-4, 788, 793, 812, 831-3, 857. Move restricted in Europe, 465-6.
King's MS., 581.
Kingdoms, Game of the three, 133.
Kingston Russel, 431.
Kirkcudbright, 420.
Klemich, O., 391.
Knight (chessman), 421-2.
Knight's tour: *see* Tour.
Knightly Orders and chess, 411.
Köbel, 453 n, 463, 470-2, 565, 706.
Ko chĭ king Yüan, 123-4.
Kohtz, J., and Kockelkorn, C., 872.
Königstedt, C. W. v., 390, 854.
Korkser chess, 391.
Kormch Books, 380.
Krukof, N., 386.
Kurtze und deutliche Unterricht, 389, 855 n.
Kurze Anweisung, 389, 852-3.

b. al-Labbān ad-Dānī, 203.
Ladies play chess: Muslim, 192; Europe, 435.
al-Lajlāj, 169, 172-4, 178, 200-1, 362; analysis, 240-65; problems, 311, 318, 331.
Lala Raja Babu, 82 n, 83, 87, 362.
Lancelot, 472, 746.
Lasa, T. von der, 47, 59, 150, 161, 402, 406, 407, 460, 477, 478 n, 496, 497, 498, 500, 505, 510, 529, 545, 619, 625, 627, 643, 708, 775, 777-8, 782, 821-3, 883-4.
Lasker, E., 889.
Latrunculorum ludus, 397 n, 400.
Lausanne Treatise, 389, 833, 841. *See* Asperling.
Lawfulness of chess discussed: Muslim, 187-90; ecclesiastical, 166-7, 380-1, 408-11; Lombard jurists, 411.
Lee MSS., 175-6.
Legal decisions: Pawn mate, 456, 785; assizes, 456.
Légal, Sire de, 845-6, 861, 863.
Leicester, Robert Dudley, Earl of, 839.
Leo X, Pope, 790-1.
Leon, J. A., 644, 802, 821, 822, 830 n.
Leonardis, Giovanni Domenico di, 820.
Leonardo, Giovanni, 813, 818-9, 824.
Levanto, Galwan de, 549.
Lewis chessmen, 758-61.
Lewis, W., 787, 827, 878-83.
Leyden, Lucas v., 484.
Libro che insegna giochar a scachi (MS. WD), 353, 735, 789, 800-2.
Limb chess, 343.
Linde, A. van der, 47, 59, 69, 74, 77, 87 n, 119 n, 121, 147, 182 n, 202 n, 242 n, 359 n, 377, 390, 391 n, 393, 402, 405 n, 460, 473, 477, 496-7, 503-4, 509, 570, 627, 629, 757, 766, 774, 782, 787, 820, 822, 833, 849, 853, 884, 886.
Liveret, MF. or Eng. technicality, 534.
Living chess, 748.
Lolli, G., 868-71, 874.
Lombard chess, 461-3, 489; players, 428, 431, 628.
London players, 846.
Long assize, 455, 464, 594.
Lopez, Diego, 96.
Lopez, Ruy, 240, 461, 787, 813-7, 822-4, 841, 852.
Lost chess books and MSS., 417, 810 n, 846.
Loubère, La, 113.
Louis XIII, King of France, 839.
Low, Capt. J., 113, 116.
Lucena, 453 n, 460, 474, 734, 778, 782, 784-6, 789, 797-800, 808-10, 821.
Lüders, H., 32, 36 n, 37 n, 38 n, 52.
Ludus scacorum, 399; parallels, 399.
Lydgate, J., 471 n, 475 n, 501.

Mabinogion, 746.
Macdonald, D. B., 187.
Macdonell, Prof. A. A., 42 n, 43, 44, 47, 52, 54, 68 n, 119 n, 156.
MacDonnell, A., 880, 882, 885.
MacGleans, 99, 103.
Madden, Sir F., 403, 466 n, 759.
Magazines, Chess, 886-7.
Magic chessboards, 745-7.
Magnus, Olaus, 854.
Mágus Saga, 468.
Mahābhāshya, 33, 38.
Mahābhārata, 35-6, 42, 43.
al-Mahdī, caliph, 194, 318.
Maḥmūd of Ghaznī, 202.
Maidens' Game, 459, 473.
Maisir, 188.
b. Makhsharī, 212.
Malay chess (*chator*, *main gajah*), 95-107; diffusion, 95; nomenclature of game, 96; of pieces, 98; chessboard, 98; rules, 99-104; Openings, 104; illustrative games, 104; chessmen, 105; pedigree, 106. *See* 66, 85.
Mālik b. Anas, 187-9, 192, 196.
Malmesbury, William of, 203, 419.
al-Ma'mūn, caliph, 197.
Mānasollāsa, 56.
Mangesa Rāmakrishna Telanga, 91-2.
Mangiolino, 428.
Manqala, 95 n, 114 n, 365.
Manṣūba, Muslim problem, 266-335; derivation of word, 266; classification of manṣūbāt, 270; MSS. discussed, 271-81; general style, 276; conditional, 277; in European MSS., 564, 568, 570, 574, 582, 607, 648-51.
Mānu, Code of, 36, 44.
Map, Walter, 436.
Marinelli, 356, 838.
Marinière, La, 833-4.
Markings on Asiatic chessboards, 32 n, 39-42, 64-5, 98, 109-10, 126, 220.
al-Marrākoshī, 203, 407.
Marsden, Dr., 96, 99.
Martin V, King of Aragon, 447, 567, 624.
Mashā'īkhī, Muslim ta'bīya, 237, 258-60.
al-Mas'ūdī, 36, 154, 164, 184, 195, 198-9, 209-10, 339.
Mate: derivation of word, 159, in European languages, 401-2, derived senses, 402. Refinements: to be given with specified piece, 651; Bishop, 278, 474; Pawn, 84, 91, 474, 794, 835, cf. 144; to be given on specified square, 144, 277, 651; angle, 144, 474, in metaphor, 755; four points, 104, 474, 482; special terms, 468, 858. Classified, 832 n, 858 (blind mate, 832 n, 833 n, 852).
Matigan-i-chatrang: *see Chatrang-nāmak*.
Maussac donation, 403-4.
al-Māwardī, 199.
b. Mazzalṭob, Solomon, 511.

Medici, Catherine de, 839.
Medinese victory, 57, 229.
Mendheim, J., 834 n, 883.
Menials play chess, 439.
Mennel, Jacob, 463, 548.
Merels, 30 n, 31 n, 50 n, 133, 189, 194, 383, 399, 449, 613-5, 757; in BS and CB collections, 702.
Merlin, 747.
Metaphors from chess: Arabic, 185; Persian, 281; European, 753-5.
Metellus, 413, 416.
Mid-game tactics, Muslim, 245.
Middleton, T., 832 n, 840.
Miniatures of games, 473, 476,
Mir. S. Fidis, Liber, 756.
Mochingoma, Japanese chess, 143-4.
Modern school, 889-90.
Mongol chess (*shatara*), 369-78; possible traces in Europe, 388-93.
Monmouth, Geoffrey of, 430.
Moralities, 529-63.
Morocco, Muslim chess played, 356.
Morolf, 756 n.
Morphy, Paul, 861, 864, 881, 888-9.
Mort Aymeri de Narbonne, 475.
Morte d'Arthur, 754.
Mortali, V., 837.
Moura, 118,
Mouskes, Philippe de, 433 n, 753.
Muhammadan: *see* Muslim.
Mujannaḥ, Muslim ta'bīya, 237, 243, 245, 247-60.
al-Muktafī, caliph, 199, 306-7.
Multiple move at commencement of game: Nīlakanṭ·ha, 66; Parsi chess, 83-4; Mongol chess, 376; Russian chess, 385; Europe, 388-93. During game (Europe): King and Queen, 462-3; King and Pawn, 463, 812, 831: *see* Castling.
Murtner Siegeslied, 750.
Muslim chess (*shaṭranj, shiṭranj*): literature, 169-85; origin, 185; introduction, 187; legality, 187-90; history, 186-206; legends, 207-19; early players, 191; master-players, 197-8, 231; nomenclature, 221; chessmen, 223; moves, 224-7; values of chessmen, 227; rules, 228; notation, 229-30; classes of players, 231; odds, 232-3; etiquette of play, 233; Opening play, 234-45; ta'bīyāt, 235-45; al-Lajlāj's analysis, 247-65; mid-game tactics, 245; End-game, 266-70; manṣūbāt, 270-335; mikhāriq, 271, 335-8; derived games, 339-51; modern game, 352-65.
Muslim legal schools and chess, 187-90.
al-Mustanṣir billāh, Sultan of Egypt, 202.
al-Mu'taḍid, caliph, 199.
al-Mu'taṣim, caliph, 197, 198, 312, 316.
al-Mutawakkil, caliph, 198.
al-Mu'tazz, caliph, 198; his son, b. al-Mu'tazz, 183, 185, 198 n.

Abū'n-Na'ām, 197, 227, 231; ta'bīya, 239; problems, 307, 309-10, 317.
Napoleon, Emperor, 877.
Nard, nardshīr, 57 n, 150, 152-4, 162, 208-10, 370, 376, 399; astronomical explanation, 162; Firdawsi's game, 157. Mod. name tawūla, 162.
Neapolitan chess: rules, 826, 831; players, 16th c., 820, 821; 18th c., 838.
Nebolsin, P., 370.
Neck, Eng. technicality, 534.
Neckam, A., 468, 478, 500-3, 511.
Nègre, Jouvenal, 431.
Neuenburg, Siboto, Count, 450.
Neves, Antonio de, 786.
Newspaper columns, 887.
Nicephorus, Eastern Emperor, 163-4, 195.
Nīlakanṭ·ha, 40, 62 n, 63-6, 80, 389, 392.
Nine castle (Chinese chess), 126, 130, 133; (Corean chess), 136.
Nine holes, 614.
Nītisāra, 42, 44.
Nöldeke, Prof., 149-54, 213-4.
Nomenclature, 26-8; Indian, 79; Burmese, 111; Siamese, 115; Annamese, 118; Chinese, 126-7; Corean, 135; Japanese, 142; Persian, 158-60; Muslim, 221-7; Abyssinian, 221; Central and N. Asiatic, 366-8; Georgian, 378; Russian, 386; European, 420-8; Mod. Greek, 168; Finnish, 854 n.
Nomocanon of Eastern Church, 167, 380.
Normandie, Hist. des ducs de, 754.
Normandy, Robert, Duke of, 431.
Notation: Muslim, 229; European, 469, 495; Köbel, 490; Stamma, 848; numerical, 470 n, 789, 823, 852.
Nūshīrwān (Khusraw I), Sāsānian Shāh of Persia, 27, 150-7.
Nyout, 39, 50.

Oblong chess, 205, 340.
Occupations of feudal noble, 428, 437-8.
Odds: transposed King, 65, 785, 815; Malay, 104; Japanese, 145; Muslim, 232-4; European, 474, 785, 788, 815, 834 n, 845, 873.
Oderbornius, P., 382.
Oefele, A. v., 95-105.
Oger de Danemarche, 476, 740.
Ohashi family, 139-40.
Ólaf's Saga, Saint, 420.
Ólafsson, E., 858.
Ólafsson, M., 856.
Ólafsson, S., 856.
Olivier, Leo, 168.
'Omar b. al-Khaṭṭāb, caliph, 187, 190, 212.
'Omar Khayyām, 183.
'Omāra al-Yamanī, 201.
Openings: Malay, 104; Chinese, 130; Japanese, 144; European, mediaeval, 472; modern, 783-4, 786, 788, 815, 823-4, 825, 826-7, 830, 837, 842, 845, 847, 868, 869, 875, 880-1, 885, 886.
Orleans, Charles, Duke of, 431, 469, 471 n, 621, 752.
Orleans, Louis, Duke of, 431.
Orseln, Werner v., 411.
Osnabrück chessmen, 765.
Otte, Meister, 754.
Owen, George, 441.

Pachīsī, 31 n, 37-8, 40, 49, 50, 72, 76.
Paciulo, L., 417 n.
Pallas, P. S., 369.
Pañchadandachattraprabandha, 63.
Paris players, 17th c., 843; 18th c., 845-6.
Parise la Duchesse, 433 n, 742.
Parker, H., 30 n, 40, 50 n, 62 n, 79 n, 82.
Parsi chess, 66, 78, 80-6, 92-4.
Parsloe's, 835, 863-5, 873.
Pasquier, E., 792, 812 n, 834.

Paston, Margery, 431.
Patolli, 31 n.
Paulsen, Louis, 864.
Pavloff, A. A., 374.
Pawn (chessman): in Cessolis, 543–4. Double step, European introduction, 457; limitations, 458–9, 462, 464, 788, 851–2, 857; in Indian chess, 66, 83; Rumi chess, 372; N. Asiatic chess, 372. Taking in passing: Malay chess, 101; European chess, 461, 462, 465, 785, 788, 812, 833, 852. Doubled Pawns forbidden (Japan), 144.
Pawn-promotion: Nīlakaṇṭ'ha, 66; Four-handed dice chess, 73; Hindustani chess, 78, 81; Parsi chess, 83, 86; Malay chess, 101–2; Burmese chess, 110, 112; Siamese chess, 111–6; Muslim chess, 226; Mongol chess, 372; Russian chess, 385; Ströbeck, 392. European chess: nomenclature, 426–7; in metaphor, 754; to Queen only, 452, 461, 462, 777, 833–5, 851; to Queen only after loss of original Queen, 458–9, 498, 781, 852; to any lost piece, 834–5, 854, 857; to any piece, 834–5; Pawn may remain dummy, 835, 852–3.
Pchela, 381.
Perédolsky, 373.
Perpetual check: Nīlakaṇṭ'ha, 66; Hindustani chess, 82; Parsi chess, 84; Chinese chess, 128.
Persian chess: under Sāsānians, 149–60; importance of early, 158; modern Muslim game, 358.
Persian MSS. used, description of, 174, 177, 181–2.
Perugia MS., 733.
Peter the Great, Tsar of Russia, 383–4.
Petteia, 161, 166.
Peyrère, La, 854–5.
Philidor, 356, 391, 853, 861–70.
Philidor's legacy, 798.
Philip II, King of Spain, 817–9.
Philip III, King of Spain, 820.
Philip IV, King of Spain, 829.
Philometer, mythical inventor of chess, 501, 541.
Philosopher's game: *see* Rythmomachy.
Piacenza, F., 354, 831, 835, 837–8.
Piccolo MS., 708.
Pillsbury, H. N., 864, 890.
Pinsent, Ross, 787 n.
Pisano, Leonardo, 218, 755.
Pistoia, C. de, 456.
Platt, C., 41, 89, 348, 388.
Pleiades, Berlin, 883–4.
Plowden, W. C., 363.
Poems on chess: Arabic, 182–5, 337; Persian, 183; European, 496–511, 781, 789–93, 822, 840.
Polerio, G. C., 819–22, 835; MSS. 820–1.
Ponziani, 816, 827, 868–71, 884.
Porter MS., 600–5.
Porto, A., 787.
Position of board fixed, 453.
Pratt, P., 391, 835, 873.
Problems: Parsi, 91–4; Malay, 105; Chinese, 129; Japanese, 140, 147–8; Muslim: *see* Manṣūba; modern Turkish, 357; Mediaeval European, 564–735; nomenclature, 366; Muslim ancestry, 564–5; Muslim element, 648; educational value, 564; brevity an excellence, 565, 649; not widely popular, 565; non-checking keys frequent, 649, 708; construction methods, 649–50; number of moves fixed, 650; mate in *n* moves exactly, 651; self-mate, 651; symmetrical problem, 651; conditional problem, 651; unsound problem, 651–2; tricks of professional gamester, 652–3; MSS., Alf., 568–73; Arch., 573–9; AN MSS., 579–607; D, 607–13; BS, 618–42; CB, 643–99; Mun. and WA, 704–6; Köbel, 706–7; Sens., 707; Picc., 708–19; S, 719–26; C, 727–33; Per., 733; Luc., 704–5; WD, 735. Modern European: early problems, 794–808; late 17th c., 835–6; Stamma, 849; Modenese masters, 870–1; later development, 871–2.
Promotion in Japanese chess, 143.
Provençal references to chess, 753–5, 758.
Proverbs, Russian, 387.
Pruen, Rev. T., 873.
Pseudo-Bertin: *see Kurtze und deutliche Unterricht.*

Qābus b. Washmgīr, 202.
Qaflān, mythical inventor of chess, 209, 313.
Qā'īm, qām, 229, 281, 376.
Qaṭranj: *see* Atranj.
Quarrels at chess, 413, 433, 436, 443, 444, 739.
Queen (chessman) in European chess, 423, 426–8. Warned when attacked: Malay chess, 103; Russian chess, 385; European chess, 388–9, 391, 779, 858. With mediaeval European leap, 457–9, 462–4, 468; and in modern Asiatic games, 353, 362. Permitted Knight's move, 355, 378, 384, 785, 857. Curious problem restriction, 465.
Queen's-Pawn Opening popular in mediaeval Europe, 472–3.
Quek, 442.
Qur'ān and chess, 187–8.

Rabelais, 465, 748, 792.
Rabrab, 197, 227, 231; ta'bīyāt, 238; problems, 306, 307, 311, 312.
Rādhakant, 48–9, 73.
ar-Rāḍī, caliph, 199–200.
Raffles, Sir T. Stamford, 100–3.
ar-Rāghib, 184 n, 194, 197.
Raghunandana: *see Tithitattva.*
Rāmāyaṇa, 33, 42, 43, 111.
Ramsey Chron., 419.
Raoal de Cambrai, 436, 745 n.
Rapidity of play, 359.
Rascioti, D., 787.
Ratnākara, 53.
Raulin, J., 535.
Rāvan, King of Lankā, 48 n.
ar-Rāzī, 169, 170, 198, 231, 246, 266, 273; problems, 306, 307, 311, 314.
Reims Poem, 519.
Renart, 747, 749.
Renaud de Montauban, 741.
Reval MS., 535.
Rhingieri, 748.
Rhys Davids, 34–5.
ar-Ristāmī, 215.
River on Chinese chessboard, 121 n, 125.
Robado, Sp. technicality, 461, 785, 814–5, 833, 851.
Robert, King of Hungary, 420.
Robert of Brunne, 430.
Robert of Gloucester, 430.
Robinson, H. C., 96–106.
Rocco, B., 838.
Rockhill, 369.

Roland, 434.
Rose, Roman de, 467, 750.
Rosen, A. E., 370.
Rook (chessman) : derivation of name, 159 ; European names, 395, 422–3, 792–3 ; early shape of piece, 89, 224, 705, 767 ; in metaphor, 704–5, 753 ; in Cessolis, 543 ; in heraldry, 705 n, 774–5 ; named Agresara (forerunner), 63.
Rou, Rev. L., 846.
Round chess (ar-rūmīya), 165, 205, 342, 347 n, 580.
Rousseau, J.-J., 861.
Rowbothum, J., 772, 787, 792, 839.
Rowland, J., 466 n.
Royal game = chess, 400.
Rozhochany, 420.
Rudraṭa, 54, 59.
Rules of modern chess : Lucena, 785 ; Damiano, 788 ; Lopez, 815.
Rūmī chess, 78, 361–2.
Ruodlieb, 411, 415, 475.
Russian chess (*shakhmaté*), 378–88 ; ancestry, 377 ; history, 380–4 ; peculiarities of rule, 384 ; nomenclature of game, 385 ; of pieces, 386 ; proverbs, 387 ; chessmen, 387.
Rythmomachy, 435 n, 601, 727, 776.

Sabelin, S., 379, 383.
Sachau, E., 57 n, 59, 158 n.
Sa'dī, 202 n.
aṣ-Ṣafadī, 186 n, 197, 201, 204, 211.
Sage (chessman) = Bishop, 424.
Sa'īd b. Jubair, 191–2.
Saif, Muslim ta'bīya, 226, 237, 240, 242, 260–1.
St. Alexius, 433 n.
Saint-Amant, P. C. F., 877, 881, 885.
St. André, G. de, 546.
St. Louis chessmen, 768.
St. Nicholas, Nicholas de, 527.
Salimbene, 456.
Salisbury, John of, 438 n, 502, 540.
Salt, H., 362.
Salvio, A., 411, 787 n, 817–9, 825–7, 869, 874.
San sai dzu e, 122, 138.
Santa Maria, 820.
as-Sarakhsī, 169, 170.
Sardārnāma, 65 n, 91, 181.
Sarratt, J. H., 391, 826, 833, 874–5.
Ṣaṣṣa (Ṣiṣṣa) b. Dāhir, mythical inventor of chess, 182, 201, 211–2, 217, 222, 362.
Saturankam, dice-game : *see* Chaturanga.
Saul, A., 391, 466, 704, 832–3, 839, 841.
Savenkof, 366–84.
Saxony, John Frederick, Elector of, 851.
Sayyāl, Muslim ta'bīya, 226, 237, 240–2, 263–5.
Scaccarium, 401.
Scaccum, scaccus, 391–9.
Scachs d'amor, 459, 781.
Schools of play (modern European chess) : Lopez, 817 ; Italian, 824, 869–70 ; Bertin, 847 ; Philidor, 867 ; Lewis, 881 ; modern, 889–90.
Schroeder, P., 171, 173–4, 178.
Science of play in Europe, mediaeval, 470.
Scott, Sir J. G. (Shway Yoe), 109, 111–3.
Sebastian, King of Portugal, 819.
Sĕjarah Malayu, 96.
Selenus, 192 n, 292, 484, 570 n, 769, 772, 779, 852.
Self-mate (problem), 651.
Sensuit Ieux Partis des eschez, 707.
ash-Shāfi'ī, 187, 190, 192, 272.
Shāh (chessman) : derivation, 159 ; in European languages, 395–9, 407.
Shāhnāma, 150, 153–9, 178, 213, 341.
Shahrām (Shihrām), mythical Indian king, 154–5, 211–6.
Shāhrukh, son of Tīmūr, 167, 204.
Shāhrukhīya, 204 n.
Shaṭranj, Arabic name of chess, pronunciation, 186 ; popular etymologies, 151, 186 n, 209 ; European derivatives, 395.
Ship, aṣ-Ṣafadī's problem of, 280, 620.
Short assize, 476–82.
Siamese chess (*makruk*), 113–7 ; nomenclature of game, 114 ; of pieces, 115 ; rules, 115 ; illustrative game, 116.
Siang k'i : *see* Astronomical game *and* Chinese chess.
Siberian chess, 369–77.
Sicilian players, 16th c., 811 n, 819.
Sīga, 39, 40.
Singha, G. R., 80–2.
Sinhasanavatrikinsika, 63.
b. Sīrīn, 165, 192.
Ṣiṣṣa : *see* Ṣaṣṣa.
Skeat, W. W., 95–9, 104–5.
Skelton, 752.
Slaughter's Coffee-house, 846, 863.
Socius, 627.
Socrates, 272, 331.
Sorbonne MS., 719–26.
Sorokin, 379.
Soyot chess, 370–3.
Spain, Chess in Muhammadan, 203.
Spanish chess, 457, 778, 781–7, 812–7, 832–3, 837 n.
Specimen games: Hindustani chess, 82 ; Parsi, 85 ; Malay, 104 : Siamese, 116 ; Chinese, 132 ; Corean, 137 ; Japanese, 145 ; modern Muslim (Egypt), 360, (Algiers), 361 ; Soyot, 372 n.
Spectators and chess, 233, 475.
Spervogel, 747.
Spilabók, 857–8.
Square of chessboard, 51, 220, 399.
Ssanang Ssetsen, 369.
Stake in chess, 374, 412, 431, 474–5, 534, 581, 737–9, 786 ; in championship, 889.
Stalemate, 57, 60, 65–6 ; Hindustani chess, 82 ; Parsi, 84 ; Malay, 103 ; Burmese, 113 ; Siamese, 116 ; Chinese, 128 ; Japanese, 144 ; Muslim, 229, 267, 319, 326 ; Mongol, 376 ; Russian, 387 ; European, 389–91, 460–1, 462, 464, 466, 609, 781, 785, 814–5, 833, 842, 851, 852, 858, 874.
Stamma, P., 220, 224 n, 230, 356–7, 391, 470, 846–50, 862.
State patronage of chess, Japan, 139.
Staunton, H., 773, 885–7.
Steinitz, W., 881, 889.
Steinschneider, 165 n.
Stephan, 548.
Stoglaf, 381.
Stories attached to problems, 311, 316. 327, 335, 582, 693, 705.
Stowe, 773.
Ströbeck, 66, 102, 390–3, 483–5, 779, 851.
Strohmeyer, 434, 736, 755.
Subandhu, 51.
Subtleties (Damiano), 789, 799, 100.
as-Su'dīya, Chess, 342, 459, 478.
b. Sukaikir, 178, 188, 190, 200, 206, 211.

aṣ-Ṣūlī, 169–73, 176, 199–201, 211, 221, 227, 231; taʿbīyāt, 235–40, 245; problems, 271–6, 306–17, 318; exercise, 337.
Sunderland, Charles, Earl of, 845.
Surrey, Henry, Earl of, 389, 799.
Sutrakrilānga, 35.
Swinton, G., 181.
Syamakiṣora, 82.
Sylvester, Protohierarch, 381.
Symes, 109, 111.
Syria, Muslim chess played, 356, 358.

aṭ-Ṭabarī, 163, 198, 202.
Taʿbīyāt, 112, 235–44.
Tabla, taula: Ar. tawūla; Rus. tablei; = nard, 153, 162, 380–3.
Tables: Chinese, 120; in European MSS., 569, 581, 702.
Tablut, 445.
Tabula, history of word, 407, 411, 413.
T'ai Ping Yü Lan, 122–4.
Takhtarītus, 151–4.
Talkhand, 213–5.
Ta-ma, 132.
Tarsia, 769, 818, 852.
Taverns, chess in, 441.
Teriace, John de, 537.
ath-Thaʿālibī, 155, 185, 198 n, 213 n.
Thomas, F. W., 42 n, 51–3.
Three-handed chess, 133–4, 838.
Three-dimensional chess, 860.
Tibetan chess (*chandaraki*), 368–9.
Tīmūr, Mongol Sultan, 167, 171, 182, 204–6, 331; Tīmūr's chess: *see* Great chess.
Tiruvengadāchārya Shastrī, 82–4, 87, 91–4.
Tithitattva, 48, 69–72.
Touch and move: Japan, 144; Europe, 475, 781, 785.
Tournaments: Japan, 139; modern Europe, 887–90.
Tourneys, Problem, 888.
Tours: Knight's, 54, 64, 335–7, 589, 609, 674, 730, 789 n; Knight-Fers, 336; Knight-Fīl, 336; Elephant, 54–5; Rook, 54.
Town statutes, 440 n.
Towns built on plan of chessboard, 33.
Trimberg, H. v., 535.
Tripoli, Muslim chess played, 356.
Tristan, 738.
Tristrem, Sir, 428, 455.
Trithem, 538.
Troil, v., 856–7.
Troyes, Chrestien de: *Cliges*, 753; *Ivain*, 467; *Percival*, 753.
Tungus, Mongol chess played, 373.
Turberville, 382.
Turkestan, Muslim and Russian chess played, 359.
Turkey, Muslim and European chess played, 359.
Turkish MSS. used, description of, 178, 181–2.
Twiss, R., 343, 355.
Tylor, E. B., 31 n, 42 n.

Ufūba, 365.
Ulysses, mythical inventor of chess, 482.
Universities and chess, 441.
Urgel, Ermengard, Count of, 405, 413.
Uryankhs, Mongol chess played, 370–3.
b. Abī Uṣaibiʿa, 170, 203.

Vaidyanātha Pāyaguṇḍa, 60, 66, 86.
Valentia, Lord, 362.
Values of chessmen: China, 127 n; Japan, 143; Muslim, 227–8; European, 228.
Vengeance Raguidel, 754.
Verdoni, 872–5.
Verney, Capt., 859–60.
Vespajo, Valentino, 827.
Vetula, 410, 507, 520, 643.
Viana, Prince of, 448.
Vida, M. A. H., Bishop of Alba, 789–93.
Vignay, Jehan de, 545.
Villani, 192 n.
Vinayaka Rajarama Tope, 79 n, 91–2.
Violette, Roman de la, 755 n.
Voeux du Paon, 472, 474, 476, 772.

Wace: *Brut*, 430; *Roman de Rou*, 434 n.
Wager games: in Alf., 570, 572, 651–2.
Wagner, J. L., 374.
Walewein, 746.
Waleys, John of (Gallensis), 530–2.
Walīd I, caliph, 193.
Walker, George, 181, 182, 865, 881.
Ward, Eng. technicality, 471.
Weber, Prof. A., 48, 55, 63, 65–6, 69.
Wei kʿi, 28 n, 114, 123, 124, 129, 137, 139 n, 140.
Welled Selasse, Ras of Tigre, 362–3.
White, A. C., 887.
White, J. G., 179, 479 n, 787 n, 841, 884. MSS.: Gu., 645; Arch., 573–9; WD, 353, 735, 789, 800, 822, 844.
Wielius, 389, 851–2.
Wigalois, 483, 763.
Wilkinson, R. J., 95 n, 98 n, 103 n.
Wilkinson, W. H., 125–30, 135–7.
Winchester Poem, 419, 499, 514.
Windisch, E., 51 n.
Wu Ti, Chinese Emperor, 120, 122, 133.
Wycliffe, 441 n.

Xerxes, mythical inventor of chess, 217, 541, 645.

b. Yaḥya, Bonsenior, 510.
Yakovlef, E. K., 370, 372.
Yakutat Indians' (Alaska) chessmen, 374.
al-Yaʿqūbī, 151, 186 n, 207, 208, 212.
Yukagiris, chess played, 373.

Zagareli, 378.
Zatrikion, Byzantine name of chess, 162–3.
b. az-Zayyāt, 198, 221; problem, 312.
Zibrt, 420 n.
Zimmermann, 98–102.
Zonares, John, 166, 167, 380.
Zukertort, J. H., 864.
Zwetre, Reinmar v., 446, 529.

OTHER TITLES IN THIS HARDBACK REPRINT PROGRAMME FROM OXBOW BOOKS (OXFORD) AND POWELLS BOOKS (CHICAGO)

www.oxbowbooks.com www.powellschicago.com

ISBN 0–19–	Author	Title
8264011	ALEXANDER Paul J.	The Patriarch Nicephorus of Constantinople
8143567	ALFÖLDI A.	The Conversion of Constantine and Pagan Rome
9241775	ALLEN T.W	Homeri Ilias (3 volumes)
6286409	ANDERSON George K.	The Literature of the Anglo-Saxons
8219601	ARNOLD Benjamin	German Knighthood
8208618	ARNOLD T.W.	The Caliphate
8142579	ASTIN A.E.	Scipio Aemilianus
8144059	BAILEY Cyril	Lucretius: De Rerum Natura (3 volumes)
814167X	BARRETT W.S.	Euripides: Hippolytos
8228813	BARTLETT & MacKAY	Medieval Frontier Societies
8219733	BARTLETT Robert	Trial by Fire and Water
8118856	BENTLEY G.E.	William Blake's Writings (2 volumes)
8111010	BETHURUM Dorothy	Homilies of Wulfstan
8142765	BOLLING G. M.	External Evidence for Interpolation in Homer
814332X	BOLTON J.D.P.	Aristeas of Proconnesus
9240132	BOYLAN Patrick	Thoth, the Hermes of Egypt
8114222	BROOKS Kenneth R.	Andreas and the Fates of the Apostles
8214715	BUCKLER Georgina	Anna Comnena
8203543	BULL Marcus	Knightly Piety & Lay Response to the First Crusade
8216785	BUTLER Alfred J.	Arab Conquest of Egypt
8148046	CAMERON Alan	Circus Factions
8143516	CAMERON Alan	Claudian
8148054	CAMERON Alan	Porphyrius the Charioteer
8148348	CAMPBELL J.B.	The Emperor and the Roman Army 31 BC to 235
826643X	CHADWICK Henry	Priscillian of Avila
826447X	CHADWICK Henry	Boethius
8222025	COLGRAVE B. & MYNORS R.A.B.	Bede's Ecclesiastical History of the English People
8131658	COOK J.M.	The Troad
8219393	COWDREY H.E.J.	The Age of Abbot Desiderius
8241895	CROMBIE A.C.	Robert Grosseteste and the Origins of Experimental Science 1100–1700
8644043	CRUM W.E.	Coptic Dictionary
8148992	DAVIES M.	Sophocles: Trachiniae
814153X	DODDS E.R.	Plato: Gorgias
825301X	DOWNER L.	Leges Henrici Primi
814346X	DRONKE Peter	Medieval Latin and the Rise of European Love-Lyric
8142749	DUNBABIN T.J.	The Western Greeks
8154372	FAULKNER R.O.	The Ancient Egyptian Pyramid Texts
8221541	FLANAGAN Marie Therese	Irish Society, Anglo-Norman Settlers, Angevin Kingship
8143109	FRAENKEL Edward	Horace
8142781	FRASER P.M.	Ptolemaic Alexandria (3 volumes)
8201540	GOLDBERG P.J.P.	Women, Work and Life Cycle in a Medieval Economy
8140215	GOTTSCHALK H.B.	Heraclides of Pontus
8266162	HANSON R.P.C.	Saint Patrick
8581351	HARRIS C.R.S	The Heart and Vascular System in Ancient Greek Medicine
8224354	HARRISS G.L.	King, Parliament and Public Finance in Medieval England to 1369
8581114	HEATH Sir Thomas	Aristarchus of Samos
8140444	HOLLIS A.S.	Callimachus: Hecale
8212968	HOLLISTER C. Warren	Anglo-Saxon Military Institutions
9244944	HOPKIN-JAMES L.J.	The Celtic Gospels
8226470	HOULDING J.A.	Fit for Service
2115480	HENRY Blanche	British Botanical and Horticultural Literature before 1800
8219523	HOUSLEY Norman	The Italian Crusades
8223129	HURNARD Naomi	The King's Pardon for Homicide – before AD 1307
9241783	HURRY Jamieson B.	Imhotep
8140401	HUTCHINSON G.O.	Hellenistic Poetry
9240140	JOACHIM H.H.	Aristotle: On Coming-to-be and Passing-away
9240094	JONES A.H.M	Cities of the Eastern Roman Provinces
8142560	JONES A.H.M.	The Greek City
8218354	JONES Michael	Ducal Brittany 1364–1399
8271484	KNOX & PELCZYNSKI	Hegel's Political Writings
8212755	LAWRENCE C.H.	St Edmund of Abingdon
8225253	LE PATOUREL John	The Norman Empire
8212720	LENNARD Reginald	Rural England 1086–1135
8212321	LEVISON W.	England and the Continent in the 8th century
8148224	LIEBESCHUETZ J.H.W.G.	Continuity and Change in Roman Religion
8143486	LINDSAY W.M.	Early Latin Verse
8141378	LOBEL Edgar & PAGE Sir Denys	Poetarum Lesbiorum Fragmenta
9240159	LOEW E.A.	The Beneventan Script
8115881	LOOMIS Roger Sherman	Arthurian Literature in the Middle Ages
8241445	LUKASIEWICZ, Jan	Aristotle's Syllogistic
8152442	MAAS P. & TRYPANIS C.A .	Sancti Romani Melodi Cantica
8113692	MANDEVILLE Bernard	The Fable of the Bees (2 volumes)
8142684	MARSDEN E.W.	Greek and Roman Artillery—Historical
8142692	MARSDEN E.W.	Greek and Roman Artillery—Technical
8148178	MATTHEWS John	Western Aristocracies and Imperial Court AD 364–425
9240205	MAVROGORDATO John	Digenes Akrites
8223447	McFARLANE K.B.	Lancastrian Kings and Lollard Knights
8226578	McFARLANE K.B.	The Nobility of Later Medieval England
814296X	MEIGGS Russell	The Athenian Empire
8148100	MEIGGS Russell	Roman Ostia
8148402	MEIGGS Russell	Trees and Timber in the Ancient Mediterranean World
8141718	MERKELBACH R. & WEST M.L.	Fragmenta Hesiodea
8143362	MILLAR F.G.B.	Cassius Dio
8142641	MILLER J. Innes	The Spice Trade of the Roman Empire

8147813	MOORHEAD John	Theoderic in Italy
8264259	MOORMAN John	A History of the Franciscan Order
8181469	MORISON Stanley	Politics and Script
8142218	MORITZ L.A.	Grain-Mills and Flour in Classical Antiquity
8274017	MURRAY H.J.R.	History of Board Games
8274033	MURRAY H.J.R.	History of Chess
9240582	MUSURILLO H.	Acts of the Pagan Martyrs & Christian Martyrs (2 volumes)
9240213	MYRES J.L.	Herodotus The Father of History
9241791	NEWMAN W.L.	The Politics of Aristotle (4 volumes)
8219512	OBOLENSKY Dimitri	Six Byzantine Portraits
8270259	O'DONNELL J.J.	Augustine: Confessions (3 volumes)
8144385	OGILVIE R.M. & RICHMOND I.A.	Tacitus: Agricola
263268X	OSLER Sir William	Bibliotheca Osleriana
8116020	OWEN A.L.	The Famous Druids
8131445	PALMER, L.R.	The Interpretation of Mycenaean Greek Texts
8143427	PFEIFFER R.	History of Classical Scholarship (volume 1)
8143648	PFEIFFER Rudolf	History of Classical Scholarship 1300–1850
8111649	PHEIFER J.D.	Old English Glosses in the Epinal-Erfurt Glossary
8142277	PICKARD-CAMBRIDGE A.W.	Dithyramb Tragedy and Comedy
8269765	PLATER & WHITE	Grammar of the Vulgate
9256497	PLATNER S.B. & ASHBY T.	A Topographical Dictionary of Ancient Rome
8213891	PLUMMER Charles	Lives of Irish Saints (2 volumes)
820695X	POWICKE Michael	Military Obligation in Medieval England
8269684	POWICKE Sir Maurice	Stephen Langton
821460X	POWICKE Sir Maurice	The Christian Life in the Middle Ages
8225369	PRAWER Joshua	Crusader Institutions
8225571	PRAWER Joshua	The History of The Jews in the Latin Kingdom of Jerusalem
8143249	RABY F.J.E.	A History of Christian Latin Poetry
8143257	RABY F.J.E.	A History of Secular Latin Poetry in the Middle Ages (2 volumes)
8214316	RASHDALL & POWICKE	The Universities of Europe in the Middle Ages (3 volumes)
8154488	REYMOND E.A.E & BARNS J.W.B.	Four Martyrdoms from the Pierpont Morgan Coptic Codices
8148380	RICKMAN Geoffrey	The Corn Supply of Ancient Rome
8141556	ROSS Sir David	Aristotle: De Anima
8141076	ROSS Sir David	Aristotle: Metaphysics (2 volumes)
8141084	ROSS Sir David	Aristotle: Parva Naturalia
8141092	ROSS Sir David	Aristotle: Physics
9244952	ROSS Sir David	Aristotle: Prior and Posterior Analytics
8142307	ROSTOVTZEFF M.	Social and Economic History of the Hellenistic World (3 volumes)
8142315	ROSTOVTZEFF M.	Social and Economic History of the Roman Empire (2 volumes)
8264178	RUNCIMAN Sir Steven	The Eastern Schism
814833X	SALMON J.B.	Wealthy Corinth
8171587	SALZMAN L.F.	Building in England Down to 1540
8218362	SAYERS Jane E.	Papal Judges Delegate in the Province of Canterbury 1198–1254
8221657	SCHEIN Sylvia	Fideles Crucis
8148135	SHERWIN WHITE A.N.	The Roman Citizenship
825153X	SHERWIN WHITE A.N.	Roman Society and Roman Law in the New Testament
9240167	SINGER Charles	Galen: On Anatomical Procedures
8113927	SISAM, Kenneth	Studies in the History of Old English_Literature
8113668	SKEAT Walter	Langland: The Vision of William Concerning Piers the Plowman (2 volumes)
8642040	SOUTER Alexander	A Glossary of Later Latin to 600 AD
8270011	SOUTER Alexander	Earliest Latin Commentaries on the Epistles of St Paul
8222254	SOUTHERN R.W.	Eadmer: Life of St. Anselm
8251408	SQUIBB G.	The High Court of Chivalry
8212011	STEVENSON & WHITELOCK	Asser's Life of King Alfred
8212011	SWEET Henry	A Second Anglo-Saxon Reader—Archaic and Dialectical
8143443	SYME Sir Ronald	Ammianus and the Historia Augusta
8148259	SYME Sir Ronald	History in Ovid
8143273	SYME Sir Ronald	Tacitus (2 volumes)
8142714	THOMPSON E.A.	The Goths in Spain
9256500	THOMPSON Sir E.Maunde	Introduction to Greek and Latin Palaeography
8200951	THOMPSON Sally	Women Religious
924023X	WALBANK F.W.	Historical Commentary on Polybius (3 volumes)
8201745	WALKER Simon	The Lancastrian Affinity 1361–1399
8161115	WELLESZ Egon	A History of Byzantine Music and Hymnography
8140185	WEST M.L.	Greek Metre
8141696	WEST M.L.	Hesiod: Theogony
8148542	WEST M.L.	The Orphic Poems
8140053	WEST M.L.	Hesiod: Works & Days
8152663	WEST M.L.	Iambi et Elegi Graeci
9240221	WHEELWRIGHT Philip	Heraclitus
822799X	WHITBY M. & M.	The History of Theophylact Simocatta
8206186	WILLIAMSON, E.W.	Letters of Osbert of Clare
8208103	WILSON F.P.	Plague in Shakespeare's London
8247672	WOODHOUSE C.M.	Gemistos Plethon
8114877	WOOLF Rosemary	The English Religious Lyric in the Middle Ages
8119224	WRIGHT Joseph	Grammar of the Gothic Language